PRAISE FOR
**THE BANTAM NEW COLLEGE
ITALIAN AND ENGLISH DICTIONARY**

". . . thorough, accurate, well-organized, clear, and up to date . . . Relevant to the student's contemporary life . . . It is bound to become a mainstay in the field."
—Albert N. Mancini, Professor of Romance Languages, The Ohio State University

"Both the method and the execution seem to me excellent . . . It would be impossible to find elsewhere as good a dictionary of this size."
—Beatrice Corrigan, Professor Emeritus, Editor, University of Toronto Press

"Apart from its accurate philological approach, its most useful grammatical apparatus, and other singular features, this concise dictionary is the first which is based primarily on *American* English usage . . . It contains numerous up-to-date colloquial and technical terms which cannot be found in any other similar dictionary."
—M. Ricciardelli, Professor of Italian and Comparative Literatures, Editor of *Forum Italicum*

Comprehensive, authoritative, and completely modern, **THE BANTAM NEW COLLEGE ITALIAN AND ENGLISH DICTIONARY** is a landmark in foreign language reference works.

THE BANTAM NEW
COLLEGE DICTIONARY SERIES

Robert C. Melzi, Author

ROBERT C. MELZI, D. in L., A.M., Ph.D., was trained in Italy, at the University of Padua, and in the United States, at the University of Pennsylvania. He has done extensive linguistic research, traveling frequently to his native country. Now Professor of Romance Languages at Widener College, he has contributed articles and reviews to many learned journals and is the author of *Castelvetro's Annotations to the Inferno,* The Hague and Paris, 1966. (Castelvetro was one of Italy's foremost philologists.) Professor Melzi is a Cavaliere in the Order of Solidarity of the Republic of Italy.

Edwin B. Williams (1891–1975), General Editor

EDWIN B. WILLIAMS, A.B., A.M., Ph.D., Doct. d'Univ., LL.D., L.H.D., was Chairman of the Department of Romance Languages, Dean of the Graduate School, and Provost of the University of Pennsylvania. He was a member of the American Philosophical Society and the Hispanic Society of America. Among his many works on the Spanish, Portuguese, and French languages are *The Williams Spanish and English Dictionary* (Scribner's, formerly Holt) and *The Bantam New College Spanish and English Dictionary*. He created and coordinated the Bantam series of original dictionaries—English, Spanish, French, Italian, Latin, and (forthcoming) German.

THE BANTAM NEW COLLEGE
ITALIAN & ENGLISH
DICTIONARY

DIZIONARIO
INGLESE ed ITALIANO

BY ROBERT C. MELZI
Widener College

THE BANTAM NEW COLLEGE
ITALIAN & ENGLISH DICTIONARY
A Bantam Book / April 1976
2nd printing .... January 1978

ISBN 0-553-11771-8

Published simultaneously in the United States and Canada

PRINTED IN THE UNITED STATES OF AMERICA

CONTENTS

PREFACE

Inasmuch as the basic function of a bilingual dictionary is to provide semantic equivalences, syntactical constructions are shown in both the source and the target languages on both sides of the Dictionary. In performing this function, a bilingual dictionary must fulfill six purposes. That is, an Italian and English dictionary must provide (1) Italian words which an English-speaking person wishes to use in speaking and writing (by means of the English-Italian part), (2) English meanings of Italian words which an English-speaking person encounters in listening and reading (by means of the Italian-English part), (3) the spelling, pronunciation, and inflection of Italian words and the gender of Italian nouns which an English-speaking person needs in order to use Italian words correctly (by means of the Italian-English part), (4) English words which an Italian-speaking person wishes to use in speaking and writing (by means of the Italian-English part), (5) Italian meanings of English words which an Italian-speaking person encounters in listening and reading (by means of the English-Italian part), and (6) the spelling, pronunciation, and inflection of English words which an Italian-speaking person needs in order to use English words correctly (by means of the English-Italian part).

It may seem logical to provide the pronunciation and inflection of English words and the pronunciation and inflection of Italian words and the gender of Italian nouns where these words appear as target words inasmuch as target words, according to (1) and (4) above, are sought for the purpose of speaking and writing. Thus the user would find not only the words he seeks but all the information he needs about them in one and the same place. But this technique is impractical because target words are not alphabetized and could, therefore, be found only by the roundabout and uncertain way of seeking them through their translations in

PREFAZIONE

Dato che la funzione principale di un dizionario bilingue è quella di fornire all'utente equivalenze semantiche, le costruzioni sintattiche sono indicate in entrambe le lingue, quella di partenza e quella di arrivo, in entrambe le parti del Dizionario. Per compiere questa funzione, un dizionario bilingue deve raggiungere sei scopi differenti. Cioè, un dizionario italiano e inglese deve fornire (1) nella parte inglese-italiano, le parole italiane che la persona anglofona vuole adoperare parlando e scrivendo l'italiano; (2) nella parte italiano-inglese, il significato in inglese delle parole italiane che tale persona oda nella lingua parlata o legga in libri o giornali; (3) nella parte italiano-inglese, l'ortografia, la pronunzia, la flessione delle parole italiane e il genere dei nomi italiani che la persona anglofona deve conoscere per servirsi correttamente della lingua italiana; (4) nella parte italiano-inglese, le parole inglesi che la persona italofona vuole adoperare parlando o scrivendo l'inglese; (5) nella parte inglese-italiano, il significato in italiano delle parole inglesi che tale persona oda nella lingua parlata o legga in libri o giornali; (6) nella parte inglese-italiano, l'ortografia, la pronunzia figurata e la flessione delle parole inglesi che la persona italofona deve conoscere per servirsi correttamente della lingua inglese.

A prima vista potrebbe sembrare logico che la pronunzia e la flessione delle parole inglesi e la pronunzia e la flessione delle parole italiane e il genere dei nomi italiani fossero indicati dove queste parole si trovano nella lingua d'arrivo, dato che le parole della lingua d'arrivo, secondo i punti (1) e (4) enunciati più sopra, sono consultate da coloro che vogliono parlare e scrivere in lingua straniera. In questa maniera l'utente troverebbe non solo le parole che cerca, ma tutte le informazioni che gli sono necessarie, nello stesso luogo. Questa tecnica, peraltro, non è pratica poiché le parole della lingua d'arrivo non si trovano in ordine

the other part of the dictionary. And this would be particularly inconvenient for persons using the dictionary for purposes (2) and (5) above. It is much more convenient to provide immediate alphabetized access to pronunciation and inflection where the words appear as source words.

alfabetico e potrebbe quindi essere trovate solo in maniera complicata nella parte opposta del dizionario. E ciò sarebbe specialmente scomodo per coloro che usano il dizionario per gli scopi (2) e (5) menzionati più sopra. È molto più semplice aggiungere la pronunzia e la flessione nella serie alfabetica in cui le parole si trovano nella loro lingua di partenza.

Since Italian is an almost perfectly phonetic language, IPA transcription of Italian words has been omitted. The only elements of pronunciation not shown by standard spelling are the values of tonic e and o (§1; pp. 3, 4) the stress of words stressed on the third syllable from the end (§3,3; p. 5), the value of intervocalic s when unvoiced, and the values of z and zz when voiced (§1; p. 4); these are shown in the entry words themselves.

Dato che l'italiano è una lingua quasi perfettamente fonetica, non si è data la trascrizione delle parole italiane nell'alfabeto dell'Associazione Fonetica Internazionale. Considerando che l'ortografia comune non mostra il vario timbro della e (§1, p. 3) e della o (§1, p. 4) quando esse sono toniche, l'accento delle parole sdrucciole (§3,3, p. 5), la pronunzia della s sorda (§1, p. 4) e la pronunzia delle z e zz sonore (§1, p. 4), si è data tale informazione nell'esponente stesso.

All words are treated in a fixed order according to the parts of speech and the functions of verbs, as follows: adjective, article, substantive, pronoun, adverb, preposition, conjunction, transitive verb, intransitive verb, reflexive verb, auxiliary verb, impersonal verb, interjection.

Ogni singola voce è trattata secondo uno schema fisso che si riferisce alle parti del discorso o alle funzioni del verbo, nel seguente ordine: aggettivo, articolo, sostantivo, pronome, avverbio, preposizione, congiunzione, verbo transitivo, verbo intransitivo, verbo riflessivo, verbo ausiliare, verbo impersonale e interiezione.

Meanings with labels come after more general meanings. Labels (printed in roman and in parentheses) refer to the preceding entry or phrase (printed in boldface).

I significati accompagnati da sigle si trovano dopo quelli di accezione più generale. Tali sigle (che sono sempre stampate in carattere romano e in parentesi) si riferiscono all'esponente precedente, stampato in grassetto, o alla frase precedente, ugualmente stampata in grassetto.

In view of the fact that the users of this Italian and English bilingual dictionary are for the most part English-speaking people, definitions and discriminations are provided in English. They are printed in italics and in parentheses and refer to the English word which they particularize:

Dato che gli utenti di questo dizionario bilingue italiano e inglese sono per lo più anglofoni, definizioni e locuzioni esplicative sono apportate in inglese. Sono stampate in corsivo e in parentesi e si riferiscono sempre alla parola inglese il cui significato cercano di spiegare:

porter ['portər] *s (doorman)* portiere *m; (man who carries luggage)* facchino; . . .
órdine *m* order; . . . series (*e.g., of years*); college (*e.g., of surgeons*); . . .

English adjectives are always translated by the Italian masculine form

Gli aggettivi inglesi sono sempre tradotti in maschile italiano, anche se il

regardless of whether the translation of the exemplary noun modified would be masculine or feminine:

nome che qualificano sia un femminile italiano:

    tough [tʌf] *adj* duro; ... ; (*luck*) cattivo; ...

In order to facilitate the finding of the meaning and use sought for, changes within a vocabulary entry in part of speech and function of verb, in irregular inflection, in the use of an initial capital, in the gender of Italian nouns, and in the pronunciation of English words are marked with parallels: ‖, instead of the usual semicolons.

Per facilitare l'uso del Dizionario, i raggruppamenti sono stati fatti secondo le parti del discorso, la funzione del verbo, la flessione irregolare, l'uso della maiuscola iniziale, il genere dei nomi italiani e la pronunzia delle parole inglesi e sono separati da sbarrette verticali: ‖, invece del punto e virgola che è stato generalmente usato.

Since vocabulary entries are not determined on the basis of etymology, homographs are included in a single entry. When the pronunciation of an English homograph changes, this is shown in the proper place after parallels:

Dato che gli esponenti in questo Dizionario non sono stati selezionati su base etimologica, tutti gli omografi sono inclusi sotto il medesimo esponente. Il cambio di pronunzia di un omografo inglese è indicato al posto adatto dopo sbarrette verticali:

    frequent [ˈfrikwənt] *adj* frequente ‖ [friˈkwɛnt]
      or [ˈfrikwənt] *tr* ...

However, when the pronunciation of an Italian homograph changes, the words are entered separately:

Però, quando la pronunzia di un omografo italiano cambia, si hanno esponenti separati:

    retina *f* small net
    rètina *f* (anat) retina
    tóc·co -ca (-chi -che) *adj* ... ‖ *m* touch; ...
    tòc·co *m* (-chi) chunk, piece; ...

Periods are omitted after labels and grammatical abbreviations and at the end of vocabulary entries.

Il punto è stato omesso dopo sigle, abbreviazioni grammaticali, ed alla fine di ogni articolo.

Proper nouns are listed in their alphabetical position in the main body of the Dictionary. Thus **Svezia** and **svedese** do not have to be looked up in two different sections of the book. And all subentries are listed in strictly alphabetical order.

Tutti i nomi propri sono posti nella loro posizione alfabetica nel corpo del Dizionario: quindi **Svezia** e **svedese** non si trovano in sezioni separate di questo libro. Per la medesima ragione di semplicità d'uso, le parole e frasi contenute sotto ogni esponente sono poste in ordine alfabetico.

The gender of Italian nouns is shown on both sides of the Dictionary, except that the gender of masculine nouns ending in -o, feminine nouns ending in -a and -ione, masculine nouns modified by an adjective ending in -o, and feminine nouns modified by an adjective

Il genere dei nomi italiani è indicato in entrambe le parti del Dizionario, eccezion fatta nella parte inglese-italiano, per le parole maschili che terminano in -o, per le parole femminili che terminano in -a e in -ione, per i nomi maschili accompagnati da un

ending in -a is not shown on the English-Italian side.

aggettivo che termina in -o e per i nomi femminili accompagnati da un aggettivo che termina in -a.

The feminine form of an Italian adjective used as a noun (or an Italian feminine noun having identical spelling with the feminine form of an adjective) which falls alphabetically in a separate position from the adjective is treated in that position and is listed again as a cross reference under the adjective:

Quando un nome femminile italiano ha la medesima grafia della forma femminile di un aggettivo o quando tale forma femminile di aggettivo è usata come nome, lo si trova elencato nella sua posizione alfabetica come nome e poi di nuovo come rinvio interno sotto l'aggettivo:

nòta *f* mark, score, . . .
nò•to -ta *adj* . . . ǁ *m* . . . ǁ *f* see **nota**

The centered period is used in vocabulary entries of inflected words to mark off, according to standard orthographic principles in the two languages, the final syllable that has to be detached before the syllable showing the inflection is added:

Qualora l'esponente italiano o inglese sia un vocabolo a flessione, un punto leggermente elevato sopra il rigo è stato usato per separare, secondo le regole ortografiche di ciascuna delle due lingue, la sillaba finale che dev'essere rimossa prima che la nuova desinenza di flessione possa essere attaccata al corpo dell'esponente, per es.:

vèc•chio -chia (-chi -chie) *adj* . . .
put•ty ['pʌti] *s* (-ties) . . . ǁ *v* (*pret & pp* -tied) . . .
hap•py ['hæpi] *adj* (-pier; -piest) . . .

If the entry word cannot be divided by a centered period the full form is given in parentheses:

Se l'esponente non può essere scisso a mezzo del suddetto punto, la forma completa è indicata in parentesi:

mouse [maʊs] *s* (**mice** [maɪs]) . . .
mouth [maʊθ] *s* (**mouths** [maʊðz]) . . .
die [daɪ] *s* (**dice** [daɪs]) . . . ǁ *s* (**dies**) . . . ǁ *v* (*pret & pp* died; *ger* dying) *intr* . . .

Many Italian verbs which take an indirect object have, as their equivalent, English verbs which take a direct object. This is shown on both sides of this Dictionary by the insertion of (with *dat*) after the Italian verb, e.g.,

Molti verbi italiani che reggono un oggetto indiretto hanno come equivalenti inglesi verbi che reggono un oggetto diretto. Questa equivalenza è indicata in entrambe le parti del Dizionario con l'aggiunta di (with *dat*) dopo il verbo italiano, per es.:

ubbidire §176 *intr* . . . ; (with *dat*) to obey
obey [o'be] *tr* ubbidire (with *dat*)

On the Italian-English side inflection is shown by: a) numbers that refer to the grammatical tables of articles, pronouns, etc., and to the tables of model verbs; they are placed before the abbreviation indicating the part of speech:

Nella parte italiano-inglese la flessione si indica: a) con numeri che si riferiscono alle tavole grammaticali degli articoli, dei pronomi, ecc., e alle tavole dei verbi modello; questi numeri sono posti innanzi all'abbreviazione indicante la parte del discorso:

mì•o -a §6 *adj & pron poss*
lui §5 *pron pers*
congiùngere §183 *tr & ref*

b) the first person singular of the present indicative of verbs in which the stress falls on either an **e** or an **o** not stressed in the infinitive or on the third syllable from the end, whatever the vowel may be:

b) con la prima persona singolare del presente dell'indicativo dei verbi non sdruccioli all'infinito in cui l'accento tonico cade o su una **e** o su una **o**, o su qualsiasi vocale di una parola sdrucciola:

> ritornare (ritórno) *tr* . . .
> visitare (visito) *tr* . . .

---

c) the feminine endings of all adjectives which end in **-o**:

c) con la desinenza femminile di tutti gli aggettivi che terminano in **-o** nel maschile:

> laborió•so -sa [s] *adj* . . .

---

d) the plural endings of nouns and adjectives which are formed irregularly:

d) con la desinenza plurale dei nomi e aggettivi che si formano in maniera irregolare:

> bràc•cio *m* (-cia *fpl*) . . . ‖ *m* (-ci) . . .
> cit•tà *f* (-tà) . . .
> dià•rio -ria (-ri -rie) *adj* . . . ‖ *m* . . . ‖ *f* . . .
> fotogram•ma *m* (-mi) . . .
> fràn•gia *f* (-ge) . . .
> laburi•sta (-sti -ste) *adj* . . . ‖ *mf* . . .
> la•go *m* (-ghi) . . .
> òr•co *m* (-chi) . . .
> òtti•co -ca (-ci -che) *adj* . . . ‖ *m* . . . ‖ *f* . . .

---

e) the full plural forms of all nouns that cannot be divided by a center period or whose plural cannot be shown by such division:

e) con la completa forma plurale di quei nomi che non possono essere scissi col suddetto punto o che hanno mutamenti interni:

> re *m* (re) . . .
> caporeparto *m* (capireparto) . . .

I wish to express my gratitude to many persons who helped me in the production of this book and particularly to Dr. Edwin B. Williams who, ever since graduate school, has been a constant inspiration and who has established the principles upon which this book was compiled, to my wife and children, who patiently aided and abetted me through ten years of research and compilation, to Richard J. Wiezell, Sebastiano DiBlasi, Walter D. Glanze, and to Giacomo De Voto, Miro Dogliotti, and Michele Ricciardelli.

Labels and abbreviations

Sigle ed abbreviazioni

abbr abbreviation—abbreviazione
(acronym) word formed from the initial letters or syllables of a series of words—parola costituita dalle lettere o sillabe iniziali di una serie di parole
adj adjective—aggettivo
adv adverb—avverbio
(aer) aeronautics—aeronautica
(agr) agriculture—agricoltura
(alg) algebra—algebra
(anat) anatomy—anatomia
(archaic) arcaico
(archeol) archeology—archeologia
(archit) architecture—architettura
(arith) arithmetic—aritmetica
art article—articolo
(astr) astronomy—astronomia
(astrol) astrology—astrologia
(aut) automobile—automobile
aux auxiliary verb—verbo ausiliare
(bact) bacteriology—batteriologia
(baseball) baseball
(basketball) pallacanestro
(bb) bookbinding—legatoria
(Bib) Biblical—biblico
(billiards) biliardo
(biochem) biochemistry—biochimica
(biol) biology—biologia
(bot) botany—botanica
(bowling) bowling
(boxing) pugilato
(bridge) bridge
(Brit) British—britannico
(cards) carte da gioco
(carp) carpentry—falegnameria
(checkers) gioco della dama
(chem) chemistry—chimica
(chess) scacchi
(coll) colloquial—familiare
(com) commercial—commerciale
comb form elemento di parola composta
comp comparative—comparativo
cond conditional—condizionale
conj conjunction—congiunzione
(cricket) cricket
(culin) cooking—cucina
dat dative—dativo
def definite—determinativo, definito
dem demonstrative—dimostrativo
(dentistry) medicina dentaria
(dial) dialectal—dialettale
(dipl) diplomacy—diplomazia

(disparaging) sprezzante
(eccl) ecclesiastical—ecclesiastico
(econ) economics—economia
(educ) education—istruzione
e.g., or *e.g.*, per esempio
(elec) electricity—elettricità
(electron) electronics—elettronica
(ent) entomology—entomologia
(equit) horseback riding—equitazione
f feminine noun—nome femminile
(fa) fine arts—belle arti
fem feminine—femminile
(fencing) scherma
(fig) figurative—figurato
(fin) financial—finanziario
(football) football americano
fpl feminine noun plural—nome femminile plurale
fut future—futuro
(geog) geography—geografia
(geol) geology—geologia
(geom) geometry—geometria
ger gerund—gerundio
(golf) golf
(gram) grammar—grammatica
(herald) heraldry—araldica
(hist) history—storia
(hort) horticulture—orticoltura
(hunt) hunting—caccia
(ichth) ichthyology—ittiologia
i.e., cioè
imperf imperfect—imperfetto
impers impersonal verb—verbo impersonale
impv imperative—imperativo
ind indicative—indicativo
indef indefinite—indefinito, indeterminativo
inf infinitive—infinito
(ins) insurance—assicurazione
interj interjection—interiezione
interr interrogative—interrogativo
intr intransitive verb—verbo intransitivo
invar invariable—invariabile
(Italian cards) carte italiane
(jewelry) gioielleria
(joc) jocular—faceto
(journ) journalism—giornalismo
(law) diritto, legge
(letterword) word in the form of an abbreviation which is pronounced by sounding the names of its letters in

succession and which functions as a part of speech—parola in forma di abbreviazione che si ottiene pronunziando consecutivamente la denominazione di ciascuna lettera e che funziona come parte del discorso

(lexicography) lessicografia
(ling) linguistics—linguistica
(lit) literary—letterario
(log) logic—logica
m masculine noun—nome maschile
(mach) machinery—macchinario
masc masculine—maschile
(math) mathematics—matematica
(mech) mechanics—meccanica
(med) medicine—medicina
(metallurgy) metallurgia
(meteor) meteorology—meteorologia
mf masculine or feminine noun according to sex—nome maschile o nome femminile secondo il sesso
m & f see below between (mythol) and (naut)
(mil) military—militare
(min) mining—lavorazione delle miniere
(mov) moving pictures—cinematografo
mpl masculine noun plural—nome maschile plurale
(mus) music—musica
(mythol) mythology—mitologia
m & f masculine and feminine noun without regard to sex—nome maschile e femminile senza distinzione di sesso
(naut) nautical—nautico
(nav) naval—navale
neut neuter—neutro
num number—numero
(obs) obsolete—in disuso
(obstet) obstetrics—ostetricia
(opt) optics—ottica
(orn) ornithology—ornitologia
(painting) pittura
(pathol) pathology—patologia
(pej) pejorative—peggiorativo
perf perfect—perfetto, passato
pers personal—personale; person—persona
(pharm) pharmacy—farmacia
(philately) filatelia
(philol) philology—filologia
(philos) philosophy—filosofia
(phonet) phonetics—fonetica
(phot) photography—fotografia
(phys) physics—fisica
(physiol) physiology—fisiologia
pl plural—plurale
(poet) poetical—poetico
(poker) poker
(pol) politics—politica
pp past participle—participio passato
poss possessive—possessivo
pref prefix—prefisso
prep preposition—preposizione

prep phrase prepositional phrase—frase preposizionale
pres present—presente
pret preterit—passato remoto
pron pronoun—pronome
(pros) prosody—prosodia
(psychoanal) psychoanalysis—psicanalisi
(psychol) psychology—psicologia
(psychopath) psychopathology—psicopatologia
qlco or *qlco* qualcosa—something
qlcu or *qlcu* qualcuno—someone
(racing) corse
(rad) radio—radio
ref reflexive verb—verbo riflessivo o pronominale
rel relative—relativo
(rel) religion—religione
(rhet) rhetoric—retorica
(rok) rocketry—studio dei razzi
(rowing) canottaggio
(rr) railroad—ferrovia
(rugby) rugby
s substantive—sostantivo
(scornful) sprezzante
(Scot) Scottish—scozzese
(sculp) sculpture—scultura
(sew) sewing—cucito
sg singular—singolare
(slang) gergo
s.o. or *s.o.* someone—qualcuno
(soccer) calcio
spl substantive plural—sostantivo plurale
(sports) sport
ssg substantive singular—sostantivo singolare
s.th or *s.th* something—qualcosa
subj subjunctive—congiuntivo
suf suffix—suffisso
super superlative—superlativo
(surg) surgery—chirurgia
(surv) surveying—agrimensura, topografia
(taur) bullfighting—tauromachia
(telg) telegraphy—telegrafia
(telp) telephone—telefonia
(telv) television—televisione
(tennis) tennis
(tex) textile—tessile
(theat) theater—teatro
(theol) theology—teologia
tr transitive verb—verbo transitivo
(trademark) marchio di fabbrica
(typ) printing—tipografia
(U.S.A.) S.U.A.
v verb—verbo
var variant—variante
(vet) veterinary medicine—medicina veterinaria
(vulg) vulgar—volgare, ordinario
(wrestling) lotta
(zool) zoology—zoologia

PART ONE

Italian-English

Italian Spelling and Pronunciation

§1. The Italian Alphabet. 1. The twenty-one letters of the Italian alphabet are listed below with their names and their sounds in terms of approximate equivalent English sounds. Their gender is masculine or feminine.

LETTER	NAME	APPROXIMATE SOUND
a	a	Like *a* in English *father*, e.g., **facile, padre.**
b	bi	Like *b* in English *boat*, e.g., **bello, abate.**
c	ci	When followed by e or i, like *ch* in English *cherry*, e.g., **cento, cinque;** if the i is unstressed and followed by another vowel, its sound is not heard, e.g., **ciarla, cieco.** When followed by a, o, u, or a consonant, like *c* in English *cook*, e.g., **casa, come, cura, credere.** The digraph **ch**, which is used before e and i, has likewise the sound of *c* in English *cook*, e.g., **chiesa, perché.**
d	di	Like *d* in English *dance*, e.g., **dare, madre.**
e	e	Has two sounds. One like *a* in English *make*, shown on stressed syllables in this DICTIONARY by the acute accent, e.g., **séra, trénta;** and one like *e* in English *met*, shown on stressed syllables in this DICTIONARY by the grave accent, e.g., **fèrro, fèsta.**
f	effe	Like *f* in English *fool*, e.g., **farina, efelide.**
g	gi	When followed by e or i, like *g* in English *general*, e.g., **gelato, ginnasta;** if the i is unstressed and followed by another vowel, its sound is not heard, e.g., **giallo, giorno.** When followed by a, o, u, or a consonant, like *g* in English *go*, e.g., **gamba, goccia, gusto, grado.** The digraph **gh**, which is used before e and i, has likewise the sound of *g* in English *go*, e.g., **gherone, ghisa.** When the combination **gli** (a) is a form of the definite article or the personal pronoun, (b) is final in a word, or (c) is intervocalic, it has the sound of Castilian *ll*, which is somewhat like *lli* in English *million*, e.g., (a) **gli uomini, gli ho parlato ieri,** (b) **battagli,** (c) **figlio, migliore.** When it is (a) initial (except in the word **gli,** above), (b) preceded by a consonant, or (c) followed by a consonant, it is pronounced like *gli* in English *negligence*, e.g., (a) **glioma,** (b) **ganglio,** (c) **negligenza.** The combination **gl** followed by a, e, o, or u is pronounced like *gl* in English *globe*, e.g., **glabro, gleba, globo, gluteo, inglese, poliglotto.** The digraph **gn** has the sound of Castilian *ñ*, which is somewhat like *ni* in English *onion*, e.g., **signore, gnocco.**
h	acca	Always silent, e.g., **ah, hanno.** See **ch** under **c** above and **gh** under **g** above.
i	i	Like *i* in English *machine*, e.g., **piccolo, sigla.** When unstressed and followed by another vowel, like *y* in English *yes*, e.g., **piatto, piede, fiore, fiume.** For i in **ci**, see **c** above, in **gi**, see **g** above, and in **sci**, see **s** below.

3

LETTER	NAME	APPROXIMATE SOUND
l	elle	Like *l* in English *lamb*, e.g., **labbro, lacrima.**
m	emme	Like *m* in English *money*, e.g., **mano, come.**
n	enne	Like *n* in English *net*, e.g., **nome, cane.**
o	o	Has two sounds. One like *o* in English *note*, shown on stressed syllables in this DICTIONARY by the acute accent, e.g., **dópo, sóle**; and one like *ou* in English *ought*, shown on stressed syllables in this DICTIONARY by the grave accent, e.g., **còsa, dònna.**
p	pi	Like *p* in English *pot*, e.g., **passo, carpa.**
q	cu	This letter is always followed by the letter **u** and the combination has the sound of *qu* in English *quart*, e.g., **quanto, questo.**
r	erre	Like *r* in English *rubber*, with a slight trill, e.g., **roba, carta.**
s	esse	Has two sounds. When initial and followed by a vowel, when preceded by a consonant and followed by a vowel, and when followed by c [k] f, p, q, or t, like *s* in English *see*, e.g., **sale, falso, scappare, spazio, stoffa**; and when standing between two vowels and when followed by b, d, g [g], l, m, n, r or v, like *z* in English *zero*, e.g., **paese, sbaglio, svenire**. However, s standing between two vowels in some words and initial s followed by b, d, g [g], l, m, n, r, or v in some foreign borrowings are pronounced like *s* in *see*, e.g., **casa*, tesa, smoking, slam**. In this DICTIONARY this is indicated by the insertion of [s] immediately after the entry word. However, when initial s stands between two vowels in a compound, its pronunciation remains that of initial s, e.g., **autoservizio** and this is not indicated. The digraph sc, when followed by e or i has the sound of *sh* in English *shall*, e.g., **scelta, scimmia**; if the i is unstressed and followed by another vowel, its sound is not heard, e.g., **sciame, sciopero**. The trigraph sch has the sound of *sc* in English *scope*, e.g., **scherzo, schiavo.**
t	ti	Like *t* in English *table*, e.g., **terra, pasto.**
u	u	Like *u* in English *rule*, e.g., **luna, mulo**. When followed by a vowel, like *w* in English *was*, e.g., **quanto, guerra, nuovo.**
v	vu	Like *v* in English *vain*, e.g., **vita, uva.**
z	zeta	Has two sounds. One like *ts* in English *nuts*, e.g., **grazia, zucchero**; and one like *dz* in English *adze*, e.g., **zero, mezzo**. In this DICTIONARY the sound of *dz* in *adze* is indicated by the insertion of [dz] immediately after the entry word. If the sound is long, [ddzz] is inserted

* Intervocalic s is generally voiced in the north of Italy.

2. The following five letters are found in borrowings from other languages.

LETTER	NAME	EXAMPLES
j	i lunga	**jazz, jingo**
k	cappa	**kiosco, kodak**
w	doppia vu	**water-polo, whisky**
x	ics	**xenofobo, xilofono**
y	ipsilon	**yacht, yoghurt**

3. Consonants written double are longer than consonants written single, that is, it takes a longer time to pronounce them, e.g., **camino** *chimney* and **cam-**

mino *road*, **capello** *hair* and **cappello** *hat*. Special attention is called to the following double consonants: **cc** followed by **e** or **i** has the sound of *ch ch* in English *beach chair*, that is, a lengthened *ch* (not the sound of *ks*), *e.g.*, **accento; cch** has the sound of *kk* in English *bookkeeper*, *e.g.*, **becchino; cq** has the sound of *kk* in English *bookkeeper*, e.g., **acqua; gg** followed by **e** or **i** has the sound of *ge j* in English *carriage joiner*, e.g., **peggio; ggh** has the sound of *g g* in English *tag game*, e.g., **agghindare.**

§2. Division of Syllables. In the application of the following rules for the syllabic division of words, the digraphs **ch, gh, gl, gn,** and **sc** count as single consonants.

(a) When a single consonant stands between two vowels it belongs to the following syllable, e.g., **ca·sa, fu·mo, ami·che, la·ghi, fi·glio, biso·gno, la·sciare.**

(b) When a consonant group consisting of two consonants of which the second is **l** or **r** stands between two vowels, the group belongs to the following syllable, e.g., **nu·cleo, so·brio, qua·dro.**

(c) When a consonant group consisting of two or more consonants of which the first or the second is **s** stands between two vowels, that part of the group beginning with **s** belongs to the following syllable, e.g., **ta·sca, bo·schi, fine·stra, super·sti·zione, sub·strato.**

(d) When a consonant group consisting of two or three consonants of which the first is **l, m, n,** or **r** stands between two vowels, the **l, m, n,** or **r** belongs to the preceding syllable, the other consonant or consonants to the following syllable, e.g., **al·bero, am·pio, prin·cipe, mor·te, in·flazione, com·pleto.**

(e) When a double consonant stands between two vowels or between a vowel and **l** or **r**, the first belongs to the preceding syllable, the second to the following syllable, e.g., **bab·bo, caval·lo, an·no, car·ro, mez·zo, sup·plica, lab·bro, quat·tro.**

§3. Stress and Accent Marks. 1. Whenever stress is shown as part of regular spelling, it is shown on **a, i,** and **u** by the grave accent mark, e.g., **libertà, giovedì, gioventù**, on close **e** and **o** by the acute accent mark, e.g., **perché**, and on open **e** and **o** by the grave accent mark, e.g., **caffè, parlò**. This occurs (a) in words ending in a stressed vowel, as in the above examples, (b) in stressed monosyllables in which the vocalic element is a diphthong of which the first letter is unstressed **i** or **u**, e.g., **già, più, può**, and (c) on the stressed monosyllable of any pair of monosyllables of which one is stressed and the other unstressed, in order to distinguish one from the other, e.g., **dà** *he gives* and **da** *from*, **è** *is* and **e** *and*, **sé** *himself* and **se** *if*, **sì** *yes* and **si** *himself*.

2. Whenever stress is not shown as part of regular spelling, it is often difficult to determine where it falls.

(a) In words of two syllables, the stress falls on the syllable next to the last, e.g., **ca'sa, mu'ro, ter'ra.** If the syllable next to the last contains a diphthong, that is, a combination of a strong vowel (**a, e,** or **o**) and a weak vowel (**i** or **u**), the strong vowel is stressed, regardless of which vowel comes first, e.g., **da'ino, ero'ico, ne'utro, fia'to, dua'le, sie'pe, fio're, buo'no.**

(b) In words of more than two syllables, the stress may fall on the syllable next to the last, e.g., **anda'ta, canzo'ne, pasto're** or on a preceding syllable, e.g., **fis'sile, gon'dola, man'doria.** In these positions also the stressed syllable may contain a diphthong, e.g., **inca'uto, idra'ulico, fio'cina.**

(c) If a weak vowel in juxtaposition with a strong vowel is stressed, the two vowels constitute two separate syllables, e.g., **abba·i'no, ero·i'na, pa·u'ra, miri'ade, vi'a.**

(d) Two strong vowels in juxtaposition constitute two separate syllables, e.g., **pa·e'se, aure'ola, ide'a, oce'ano.**

(e) Two weak vowels in juxtaposition generally constitute a diphthong in which the first vowel is stressed in some words, e.g., **flu'ido** and the second vowel in others, e.g., **piu'ma.**

(f) If a word ends in a diphthong, the diphthong is stressed, e.g., **marina'i, parla'i, ero'i.**

3. In this DICTIONARY, stress is understood or shown on all words that do not bear an accent mark as part of regular spelling according to the following principles. In the application of these principles, individual vowels and not diphthongs are counted as units. In some words in which it is not necessary to show stress, an accent mark is used to show the quality of the stressed vowels **e** and **o**.

As in regular Italian spelling, stress is shown on **a, i,** and **u** by the grave accent mark, on close **e** and **o** by the acute accent mark, and on open **e** and **o** by the grave accent mark.

(a) It is understood that in words of more than one syllable in which no accent mark is shown, the stress falls on the vowel next to the last, e.g., **casa,** fiato, duale, abbaino, paura. In such words as sièpe, fióre, buòno, paése, fluènte, eròe, nói, pòi, the accent mark is used to show the quality of the vowel.

(b) An accent mark is placed on the stressed vowel if the word is stressed on the third vowel from the end, e.g., mùsica, sìmbolo, dàino, incàuto, marinàio, contìnuo, infànzia. If this vowel is e or o, the acute or grave accent mark must correspond to the quality of the vowel, e.g., fiòcina, rómpere, nèutro, eròico, assèdio, filatóio.

(c) Contrary to the above-mentioned principle of counting vowels, an accent mark is placed on the strong vowel of a final diphthong, e.g., marinài, assài.

(d) Contrary to the above-mentioned principle of counting vowels, an accent mark is placed on the i of final ia, ie, ii, and io, e.g., farmacìa, scìa, farmacìe, mormorìi, gorgoglìo, fìo.

(e) An accent mark is placed on some borrowings ending in a consonant, e.g., hàrem, revòlver.

(f) The loss of the last vowel or last syllable of a word does not alter the position of the stress of the word, e.g., la maggior parte, in alcun modo, fan bene.

§4. The Definite Article and Combinations with Prepositions.

		MASC	MASC	MASC	FEM	FEM
		BEFORE CONSONANT	BEFORE S IMPURE OR Z[1]	BEFORE VOWEL	BEFORE CONSONANT	BEFORE VOWEL
	SG	il	lo	l'	la	l'
	PL	i	gli	gli[2]	le	le[3]
WITH a	SG	al	allo	all'	alla	all'
	PL	ai	agli	agli[2]	alle	alle[3]
WITH di	SG	del	dello	dell'	della	dell'
	PL	dei	degli	degli[2]	delle	delle[3]
WITH con	SG	col	collo	coll'	colla	coll'
	PL	coi	cogli	cogli[2]	colle	colle[3]
WITH da	SG	dal	dallo	dall'	dalla	dall'
	PL	dai	dagli	dagli[2]	dalle	dalle[3]
WITH in	SG	nel	nello	nell'	nella	nell'
	PL	nei	negli	negli[2]	nelle	nelle[3]
WITH su	SG	sul	sullo	sull'	sulla	sull'
	PL	sui	sugli	sugli[2]	sulle	sulle[3]

[1] Other letters and groups of letters, which occur in a few words, are gn, pn, ps, sc, x, and i before a vowel, sometimes spelled j or y.

[2] These forms may drop the i before words beginning with i, e.g., gl'inglesi.

[3] The e of these forms is not elided, e.g., le erbe.

7

§5. Personal and Reflexive Pronouns.

PERSONS	SUBJECT	PERSONAL DIRECT OBJECT	PERSONAL INDIRECT OBJECT	REFLEX. & RECIPROCAL DIRECT & INDIRECT OBJECT	PERSONAL PREPOSITIONAL OBJECT	REFLEX. & RECIPROCAL PREPOSITIONAL OBJECT
SG						
1	io *I*	mi *me*	mi *to me*	mi *myself; to myself*	me *me*	me *myself*
2	tu *you*	ti *you*	ti *to you*	ti *yourself; to yourself*	te *you*	te *yourself*
3 MASC	egli, lui *he*	lo *him or it*	gli *to him*	si *himself; to himself*	lui *him*	sè *himself*
3 FEM	lei, essa *she*	la *her or it*	le *to her*	si *herself; to herself*	lei, essa *her*	sè *herself*
2 FORMAL	Lei *you*	La *you*	Le *to you*	si *yourself; to yourself*	Lei *you*	sè *yourself*
PL						
1	noi *we*	ci *us*	ci *to us*	ci *ourselves; to ourselves; each other; to each other*	noi *us*	noi *ourselves; each other*
2	voi *you*	vi *you*	vi *to you*	vi *yourself; yourselves; to yourself; to yourselves; each other; to each other*	voi *you*	voi *yourself; yourselves; each other*
3 MASC	loro, essi *they*	li *them*	loro *to them*	si *themselves; to themselves; each other; to each other*	loro, essi *them*	sè *themselves; each other*
3 FEM	loro, esse *they*	le *them*	loro *to them*	si *themselves; to themselves; each other; to each other*	loro, esse *them*	sè *themselves; each other*
2 FORMAL	Loro *you*	Li } Le } *you*	Loro *to you*	si *yourselves; to yourselves; each other; to each other*	Loro *you*	sè *yourselves; each other*

ci and vi both mean also *here, there, to it, in it, to them, in them, about it.*

ne means *of, from,* or *with him, her, it, them; some, any; from here, from there, thence, about it.*

meco *with me,* teco *with you,* and seco *with him, with himself; with her, with herself; with you, with yourself, with yourselves; with them, with themselves; with each other* may be used instead of con me, con te, and con sè respectively.

8

COMBINATION OF DIRECT AND INDIRECT OBJECT

PERSONS		
1 SG & 3 SG	me lo me la }	him, her, it to me
1 SG & 3 PL	me li me le }	them to me
2 SG & 3 SG	te lo te la }	him, her, it to you
2 SG & 3 PL	te li te le }	them to you
3 SG & 3 SG	glielo gliela }	him, her, it to him him, her, it to her
3 SG & 3 PL	glieli gliele }	them to him them to her
2 SG FORMAL & 3 SG	Glielo Gliela }	him, her, it to you
2 SG FORMAL & 3 PL	Glieli Gliele }	them to you

PERSONS		
1 PL & 3 SG	ce lo ce la }	him, her, it to us
1 PL & 3 PL	ce li ce le }	them to us
2 PL & 3 SG	ve lo ve la }	him, her, it to you
2 PL & 3 PL	ve li ve le }	them to you
3 SG & 3 PL	lo la }	VERB loro him, her, it to them
3 PL & 3 PL	li le }	VERB loro them to them
3 SG & 2 PL FORMAL	lo la }	VERB Loro him, her, it to you
3 PL & 2 PL FORMAL	li le }	VERB Loro them to you

The form si (third singular and plural reflexive and reciprocal indirect object) changes to se before one of the direct objects lo, la, li, and le, e.g., se lo mette he puts it on; se n'è andato he went away.

In combinations, ne occupies the same position as lo, la, li, and le, e.g., me ne, and forms one word with gli, namely, gliene.

9

86 Possessive Adjectives and Pronouns

PERSON, NUMBER & SEX OF POSSESSOR	GENDER & NUMBER OF POSSESSIVE ADJECTIVE OR PRONOUN ACCORDING TO THE GENDER & NUMBER OF THE PERSON OR THING POSSESSED				MEANING OF ADJECTIVE	MEANING OF PRONOUN
	MSG	MPL	FSG	FPL		
SG						
1	il mio	i miei	la mia	le mie	*my*	*mine*
2	il tuo	i tuoi	la tua	le tue	*your*	*yours*
3 MASC	il suo	i suoi	la sua	le sue	*his*	*his*
3 FEM	il suo	i suoi	la sua	le sue	*her*	*hers*
3 NEUT	il suo	i suoi	la sua	le sue	*its*	*its*
2 FORMAL	il Suo	i Suoi	la Sua	le Sue	*your*	*yours*
PL						
1	il nostro	i nostri	la nostra	le nostre	*our*	*ours*
2	il vostro	i vostri	la vostra	le vostre	*your*	*yours*
3	il loro	i loro	la loro	le loro	*their*	*theirs*
2 FORMAL	il Loro	i Loro	la Loro	le Loro	*your*	*yours*

The definite article, shown here, is not generally used (a) in direct address, e.g., mio caro amico *my dear friend*, (b) after the verb essere, e.g., la casa è nostra *the house is ours*, and (c) when a singular form modifies the name of a relative, e.g., sua sorella *his sister*.

With forms of the indefinite article, the possessive adjective, whether standing before or after the noun, is translated by *of* plus the possessive pronoun, e.g., un amico mio *a friend of mine*; una sua zia *an aunt of his* (or *of hers*).

The forms of the possessive pronouns also have the force of nouns, e.g., il mio *my property, my belongings*; i suoi *his people, relatives, followers, troops, retinue*, etc.; la mia *my letter*; la sua *his opinion*.

87. The Demonstrative Adjective.

	MASC BEFORE CONSONANT	MASC BEFORE s IMPURE OR z (see note 1, p. 7)	MASC BEFORE VOWEL	FEM BEFORE CONSONANT	FEM BEFORE VOWEL
SG PL	quel *that* quei *those*	quello quegli	quell' quegli	quella quelle	quell' quelle
SG PL	questo *this* questi *these*	questo questi	questo or quest' questi	questa queste	questa or quest' queste

11

§8. The Demonstrative Pronoun.

	MASC	FEM	MASC
SG	quello *that one*	quella	quegli *that one;*
PL	quelli *those*	quelle	*the former*
SG	questo *this one*	questa	questi *this one;*
PL	questi *these*	queste	*the latter*

The demonstrative pronoun **quello** is often followed by **che, di,** or **da** and the masculine singular form may be shortened to **quel** before these words.

SG	colui *that one*	colei
PL	coloro *those*	coloro
SG	costui *this one*	costei
PL	costoro *these*	costoro

code·sto -sta -sti -ste and **cote·sto -sta -sti -ste** are demonstrative adjectives and demonstrative pronouns and mean *that (of yours)*.

89. Indefinite Article and Numeral Adjective.

MASC BEFORE CONSONANT	MASC BEFORE s IMPURE OR z (see note 1, p. 7)	MASC BEFORE VOWEL	FEM BEFORE CONSONANT	FEM BEFORE VOWEL
un *a, an; one*	uno	un	una	un'

§10. Indefinite Pronoun uno.

MASC	FEM
uno *one*	una

§11. Correlative Indefinite Pronoun.

	MASC	FEM
SG	l'uno . . . l'altro *one . . . the other*	l'una . . . l'altra
PL	gli uni . . . gli altri *some . . . the others*	le une . . . le altre

§12. Reciprocal Indefinite Pronoun.

	MASC	FEM
SG	l'un l'altro *each other, one another*	l'una l'altra
PL	gli uni gli altri	le une le altre

Table of Regular Endings of Italian Verbs

The stem to which the endings of the gerund, past participle, present participle, imperative, present indicative, present subjunctive, imperfect indicative, preterit indicative, and imperfect subjunctive are attached is obtained by dropping the ending of the infinitive, viz., **-are**, **-ere**, **-ire**.

The stem to which the endings of the future indicative and present conditional are attached is obtained by dropping the -e of the ending of the infinitive of all conjugations and changing the a of the ending of the infinitive of the first conjugation to e.

The letters before the names of some of the tenses of this table correspond to the designation of the tenses shown on the following page.

Letters printed in italics have a written accent that is not part of the regular spelling.

TENSE	FIRST CONJUGATION	SECOND CONJUGATION	THIRD CONJUGATION
inf	-are	-ére (or -ere)	-ire
ger	-ando	-èndo	-èndo
pp	-ato	-uto	-ito
pres part	-ante	-ènte	-ènte
(a) *impv*	-a -ate	-i -éte	-i -ite
(b) *pres ind*	-o -i -a -iamo -ate -ano	-o -i -e -iamo -éte -ono	-o -i -e -iamo -ite -ono
(c) *pres subj*	-i -i -i -iamo -iate -ino	-a -a -a -iamo -iate -ano	-a -a -a -iamo -iate -ano
(d) *imperf ind*	-avo -avi -ava -avamo -avate -*à*vano	-*é*vo -*é*vi -*é*va -evamo -evate -*é*vano	-ivo -ivi -iva -ivamo -ivate -*ì*vano
(e) *pret ind*	-*à*i -asti -ò -ammo -aste -*à*rono	-*é*i -ésti -è -*é*mmo -éste -*é*rono	-*ì*i -isti -*ì* -immo -iste -*ì*rono
imperf subj	-assi -assi -asse -*à*ssimo -aste -*à*ssero	-*é*ssi -*é*ssi -*é*sse -*é*ssimo -*é*ste -*é*ssero	-issi -issi -isse -*ì*ssimo -iste -issero
(f) *fut ind*	-er-ò -er-*à*i -er-à -er-*é*mo -er-éte -er-anno	-ò -*à*i -à -*é*mo -éte -anno	-ò -*à*i -à -*é*mo -éte -anno

TENSE	FIRST CONJUGATION	SECOND CONJUGATION	THIRD CONJUGATION
pres cond	-er-èi	-èi	-èi
	-er-ésti	-ésti	-ésti
	-er-èbbe	-èbbe	-èbbe
	-er-émmo	-émmo	-émmo
	-er-éste	-éste	-éste
	-er-èbbero	-èbbero	-èbbero

MODEL VERBS
ORDER OF TENSES

(a) imperative
(b) present indicative
(c) present subjunctive

(d) imperfect indicative
(e) preterit indicative
(f) future indicative

In addition to the infinitive, gerund, and past participle, which are shown in line one of these tables, all simple tenses are shown if they contain at least one irregular form, except (1) the present conditional, which is always formed on the stem of the future indicative, (2) the imperfect subjunctive, which is always formed on the stem of the *2nd sg* of the preterit indicative, and (3) the present participle, which is generally formed by changing the final -do of the gerund to -te (exceptions being shown in parentheses after the gerund).

Letters printed in italics have a written accent that is not part of the regular spelling.

§100 ACCÈDERE—accedèndo—acceduto
    (e) accedètti *or* accedéi *or* accèssi; accedésti; accedètte *or* accedé *or* accèsse; accedémmo; accedéste; accedèttero *or* accedérono *or* accèssero

§101 ACCÈNDERE—accendèndo—accéso
    (e) accési, accendésti, accése, accendémmo, accendéste, accésero

§102 ADDURRE—adducèndo—addótto
    (b) adduco, adduci, adduce, adduciamo, adducéte, add*ù*cono
    (c) adduca, adduca, adduca, adduciamo, adduciate, add*ù*cano
    (d) adducévo, adducévi, adducéva, adducevamo, adducevate, adducévano
    (e) addussi, adducésti, addusse, adducémmo, adducéste, add*ù*ssero

§103 AFFÌGGERE—affiggèndo—affisso
    (e) affissi, affiggésti, affisse, affiggémmo, affiggéste, aff*ì*ssero

17

§104 AFFLÌGGERE—affliggèndo—afflitto
(e) afflissi, affliggésti, afflisse, affliggémmo, affliggéste, afflìssero

§105 ALLÙDERE—alludèndo—alluso
(e) allusi, alludésti, alluse, alludémmo, alludéste, allùsero

§106 ANDARE—andando—andato
(a) va or va' or vai, andate
(b) vò or vado, vai, va, andiamo, andate, vanno
(c) vada, vada, vada, andiamo, andiate, vàdano
(f) andrò, andràì, andrà, andrémo, andréte, andranno

§107 ANNÈTTERE—annettèndo—annèsso or annéttere, annetténdo, annésso
(e) annettéi or annèssi or annéssi; annettésti; annetté or annèsse or annésse; annettémmo; annettéste; annettérono or annèssero or annéssero

§108 APPARIRE—apparèndo—apparso
(a) apparisci or appari; apparite
(b) apparisco or appàio; apparisci or appari; apparisce or appare; appariamo; apparite; apparìscono or appàiono
(c) apparisca or appàia; apparisca or appàia; apparisca or appàia; appariamo; appariate; apparìscano or appàiano
(e) apparvi or apparìi or apparsi; apparisti; apparve or apparì or apparse; apparimmo; appariste; appàrvero or apparìrono or appàrsero

§109 APPÈNDERE—appendèndo—appéso
(e) appési, appendésti, appése, appendémmo, appendéste, appésero

§110 APRIRE—aprèndo—apèrto
(e) aprìi or apèrsi; apristi; aprì or apèrse; aprimmo; apriste; aprìrono or apèrsero

§111 ÀRDERE—ardèndo—arso
(e) arsi, ardésti, arse, ardémmo, ardéste, àrsero

§112 ASPÈRGERE—aspergèndo—aspèrso
(e) aspèrsi, aspergésti, aspèrse, aspergémmo, aspergéste, aspèrsero

§113 ASSÌDERE—assidèndo—assiso
(e) assisi, assidésti, assise, assidémmo, assidéste, assìsero

§114 ASSÌSTERE—assistèndo—assistito
(e) assistéi or assistètti; assistésti; assisté or assistètte; assistémmo; assistéste; assistérono or assistèttero

18

§115 ASSÒLVERE—assolvèndo—assòlto *or* assoluto

(e) assolvéi *or* assolvètti *or* assòlsi; assolvésti; assolvé *or*
assolvètte *or* assòlse; assolvémmo; assolvéste; assolvérono *or* assolvèttero *or* assòlsero

§116 ASSÙMERE—assumèndo—assunto

(e) assunsi, assumésti, assunse, assumémmo, assuméste,
assùnsero

§117 ASSÙRGERE—assurgèndo—assurto

(e) assursi, assurgésti, assurse, assurgémmo, assurgéste,
assùrsero

§118 AVÈRE—avèndo—avuto

(a) abbi, abbiate
(b) ho, hai, ha, abbiamo, avete, hanno
(c) *a*bbia, *a*bbia, *a*bbia, abbiamo, abbiate, *a*bbiano
(e) *è*bbi, avésti, *è*bbe, avémmo, avéste, *è*bbero
(f) avrò, avr*a*i, avrà, avrémo, avréte, avranno

§119 AVVIARE—avviando—avviato

(b) avvìo, avvìi, avvìa, avviamo, avviate, avvìano
(c) avvìi, avvìi, avvìi, avviamo, avviate, avvìino

§120 BÉRE—bevèndo—bevuto

(a) bévi, bevéte
(b) bévo, bévi, béve, beviamo, bevéte, bévono
(c) béva, béva, béva, beviamo, beviate, bévano
(d) bevévo, bevévi, bevéva, bevevamo, bevevate, bevévano
(e) bévvi *or* bevéi *or* bevètti; bevésti, bévve *or* bevé *or*
bevètte; bevémmo; bevéste; bévvero *or* bevérono *or*
bevèttero
(f) berrò, berr*a*i, berrà, berrémo, berréte, berranno

§121 CADÉRE—cadèndo—caduto

(e) caddi, cadésti, cadde, cadémmo, cadéste, c*a*ddero
(f) cadrò, cadr*a*i, cadrà, cadrémo, cadréte, cadranno

§122 CECARE—cecando—cecato

(a) cièca *or* cèca; cecate
(b) cièco *or* cèco; cièchi *or* cèchi; cièca *or* cèca; cechiamo;
cecate; ciècano *or* cècano
(c) cièchi *or* cèchi; cièchi *or* cèchi; cièchi *or* cèchi;
cechiamo; cechiate; cièchino *or* cèchino
(f) cecherò, cecher*a*i, cecherà, cecherémo, cecheréte,
cecheranno

§123 CÈDERE—cedèndo—ceduto

(e) cedéi *or* cedètti; cedésti; cedé *or* cedètte; cedémmo;
cedéste; cedérono *or* cedèttero

19

§124 **CHIÈDERE**—chiedèndo—chièsto
(e) chièsi, chiedésti, chièse, chiedémmo, chiedéste, chièsero

§125 **CHIÙDERE**—chiudèndo—chiuso
(e) chiusi, chiudésti, chiuse, chiudémmo, chiudéste, chiùsero

§126 **CÌNGERE**—cingèndo—cinto
(e) cinsi, cingésti, cinse, cingémmo, cingéste, cìnsero

§127 **CÒGLIERE**—coglièndo—còlto
(a) cògli, cogliéte
(b) còlgo, còglie, cogliamo, cogliéte, còlgono
(c) còlga, còlga, còlga, cogliamo, cogliate, còlgano
(e) còlsi, cogliésti, còlse, cogliémmo, cogliéste, còlsero

§128 **COMINCIARE**—cominciando—cominciato
(b) comìncio, cominci, comìncia, cominciamo, comìnciate, comìnciano
(c) cominci, cominci, cominci, cominciamo, comìnciate, comìncino
(f) comincerò, comincerài, comincerà, comincerémo, comincerete, comìnceranno

§129 **COMPÈTERE**—competèndo—*pp* missing

§130 **CÒMPIERE**—compièndo—compiuto
(a) cómpi, compite
(b) cómpio, cómpi, cómpie, compiamo, compite, cómpiono
(c) cómpia, cómpia, cómpia, compiamo, compiate, cómpiano
(d) compivo, compivi, compiva, compivamo, compivate, compìvano
(e) compiéi *or* compìi; compiésti *or* compisti; compié *or* compì; compiémmo *or* compimmo; compiéste *or* compiste; compiérono *or* compìrono

§131 **COMPRÌMERE**—comprimèndo—comprèsso
(e) comprèssi, comprimésti, comprèsse, comprimémmo, compriméste, comprèssero

§132 **CONCÈDERE**—concedèndo—concèsso
(e) concedéi *or* concèssi *or* concedètti; concedésti; concedé *or* concèsse *or* concedètte; concedémmo; concedéste; concedérono *or* concèssero *or* concedèttero

§133 **CONCÈRNERE**—concernèndo—*pp* missing
(e) concernéi *or* concernètti; concernésti; concerné *or* concernètte; concernémmo; concernéste; concernérono *or* concernèttero

20

§134 CONÓSCERE—conoscèndo—conosciuto
    (e) conóbbi, conoscésti, conóbbe, conoscémmo, conoscéste, conóbbero

§135 CONQUÌDERE—conquidèndo—conquiso
    (e) conquisi, conquidésti, conquise, conquidémmo, conquidéste, conquìsero

§136 CONSÙMERE—*ger* missing—consunto
    (a) missing
    (b) missing
    (c) missing
    (d) missing
    (e) consunsi, consunse, consùnsero
    (f) missing

§137 CONVÈRGERE—convergèndo—convèrso
    (e) convèrsi *or* convergéi; convergésti; convèrse *or* convergé; convergémmo; convergéste; convèrsero *or* convergérono

§138 CONVERTIRE—convertèndo—convertito
    (e) convertìi *or* convèrsi; convertisti; convertì or convèrse; convertimmo; convertiste; convertìrono *or* convèrsero

§139 CÓRRERE—corrèndo—córso
    (e) córsi, corrésti, córse, corrémmo, corréste, córsero

§140 COSTRUIRE—costruèndo—costruito
    (a) costruisci, costruite
    (b) costruisco, costruisci, costruisce, costruiamo, costruìte, costruìscono
    (c) costruisca, costruisca, costruisca, costruiamo, costruiate, costruìscano
    (e) costruìi *or* costrussi; costruisti; costruì *or* costrusse; costruimmo; costruiste; costruìrono *or* costrùssero

§141 CRÉDERE—credèndo—creduto
    (e) credéi *or* credètti; credésti; credé *or* credètte; credémmo; credéste; credérono *or* credèttero

§142 CRÉSCERE—crescèndo—cresciuto
    (e) crébbi, crescésti, crébbe, crescémmo, crescéste, crébbero

§143 CUCIRE—cucèndo—cucito
    (b) cùcio, cuci, cuce, cuciamo, cucite, cùciono
    (c) cùcia, cùcia, cùcia, cuciamo, cuciate, cùciano

§144a CUÒCERE—cuocèndo *or* cocèndo (cocènte)—còtto *or* cociuto

(a) cuòci, cocéte
(b) cuòcio, cuòci, cuòce, cociàmo, cocéte, cuòciono
(c) cuòcia, cuòcia, cuòcia, cociamo, cociate, cuòciano
(d) cocévo, cocévi, cocéva, cocevamo, cocevate, cocévano
(e) còssi, cocésti, còsse, cocémmo, cocéste, còssero
(f) cocerò, coceràí, cocerà, cocerémo, coceréte, coceranno

§144b DARE—dando—dato
(a) dà or dàí or da'; date
(b) dò or dò; dài; dà; diamo; date; danno
(c) dìa, dìa, dìa, diamo, diate, dìano
(e) dièdi or dètti; désti; diède or dètte or diè; démmo; déste; dièdero or dèttero
(f) darò, daràí, darà, darémo, daréte, daranno

§145 DECÌDERE—decidèndo—deciso
(e) decisi, decidésti, decise, decidémmo, decidéste, decìsero

§146 DELÌNQUERE—delinquèndo—pp missing
(a) missing
(c) missing
(e) missing

§147 DEVÒLVERE—devolvèndo—devoluto
(e) devolvéi or devolvètti; devolvésti; devolvé or devolvètte; devolvémmo; devolvéste; devolvérono or devolvèttero

§148 DIFÈNDERE—difendèndo—diféso
(e) difési, difendésti, difése, difendémmo, difendéste, difésero

§149 DILÌGERE—diligèndo—dilètto
(a) missing
(b) missing
(c) missing
(d) missing
(e) dilèssi, diligésti, dilèsse, diligémmo, diligéste, dilèssero
(f) missing

§150 DIPÈNDERE—dipendèndo—dipéso
(e) dipési, dipendésti, dipése, dipendémmo, dipendéste, dipésero

§151 DIRE—dicèndo—détto
(a) di' or dì; dite
(b) dico, dici, dice, diciamo, dite, dìcono
(c) dica, dica, dica, diciamo, diciate, dìcano
(d) dicévo, dicévi, dicéva, dicevamo, dicevate, dicévano
(e) dissi, dicésti, disse, dicémmo, dicéste, dìssero
(f) dirò, diràí, dirà, dirémo, diréte, diranno

§152 DIRÌGERE—dirigèndo—dirètto
   (e) diréssi, dirigésti, dirésse, dirigémmo, dirigéste, diréssero

§153 DISCÈRNERE—discernèndo—*pp* missing
   (e) discernéi; discernésti; discerné *or* discernètte; discernémmo; discernéste; discernérono *or* discernèttero

§154 DISCÙTERE—discutèndo—discusso
   (e) discussi, discutésti, discusse, discutémmo, discutéste, discùssero

§155 DISSÒLVERE—dissolvèndo—dissòlto
   (e) dissòlsi *or* dissolvéi *or* dissolvètti; dissolvésti; dissòlse *or* dissolvé *or* dissolvètte; dissolvémmo; dissolvéste; dissòlsero *or* dissolvérono *or* dissolvèttero

§156 DISTÌNGUERE—distinguèndo—distinto
   (e) distinsi, distinguésti, distinse, distinguémmo, distinguéste, distìnsero

§157 DIVÈRGERE—divergèndo—*pp* missing
   (e) obsolete

§158 DIVÌDERE—dividèndo—diviso
   (e) divisi, dividésti, divise, dividémmo, dividéste, divìsero

§159 DOLÉRE—dolèndo—doluto
   (a) duòli, doléte
   (b) dòlgo, duòli, duòle, doliamo, doléte, dòlgono
   (c) dòlga, dòlga, dòlga, doliamo, doliate, dòlgano
   (e) dòlsi, dolésti, dòlse, dolémmo, doléste, dòlsero
   (f) dorrò, dorrài, dorrà, dorrémo, dorréte, dorranno

§160 DOVÉRE—dovèndo—dovuto
   (b) dèbbo *or* dèvo; dèvi; dève; dobbiamo; dovéte; dèbbono *or* dèvono
   (c) dèva *or* dèbba; dèva *or* dèbba; dèva *or* dèbba; dobbiamo; dobbiate; dèvano *or* dèbbano
   (e) dovéi *or* dovètti; dovésti; dové *or* dovètte; dovémmo; dovéste; dovérono *or* dovèttero

§161 ELÌDERE—elidèndo—eliso
   (e) elisi, elidésti, elise, elidémmo, elidéste, elìsero

§162 EMÈRGERE—emergèndo—emèrso
   (e) emèrsi, emergésti, emèrse, emergémmo, emergéste, emèrsero

§163 ÉMPIERE & EMPIRE—empièndo—empito *or* empiuto
   (a) émpi, empite

(b) émpio, émpi, émpie, empiamo, empite, émpiono
(c) émpia, émpia, émpia, empiamo, empiate, émpiano
(d) empivo, empivi, empiva, empivamo, empivate, empìvanŏ
(e) empiéi or empìi; empiésti; or empisti; empié or empì; empiémmo or empimmo; empiéste or empiste; empiérono or empìrono
(f) empirò, empirài, empirà, empirémo, empiréte, empiranno

§164 ÈRGERE—ergèndo—èrto
(e) èrsi, ergésti, èrse, ergémmo, ergéste, èrsero

§165 ESÌGERE—esigèndo—esatto
(e) esigéi or esigètti; esigésti; esigé or esigètte; esigémmo; esigéste; esigérono or esigèttero

§166 ESÌMERE—esimèndo—*pp* missing
(e) esiméi or esimètti; esimésti; esimé or esìmètte; esimémmo; esiméste; esimérono or esimèttero

§167 ESPÀNDERE—espandèndo—espanso
(e) espandéi or espandètti or espansi; espandésti; espandé or espandètte or espanse; espandémmo; espandéste; espandérono or espandèttero or espànsero

§168 ESPÈLLERE—espellèndo—espulso
(e) espulsi, espellésti, espulse, espellémmo, espelléste, espùlsero

§169 ESPLÒDERE—esplodèndo—esplòso
(e) esplòsi, esplodésti, esplòse, esplodémmo, esplodéste, esplòsero

§170 ÈSSERE—essèndo—stato
(a) sii, siate
(b) sóno, sèi, è, siamo, siète, sóno
(c) sìa, sìa, sìa, siamo, siate, sìano
(d) èro, èri, èra, eravamo, eravate, èrano
(e) fui, fósti, fu, fummo, fóste, fùrono
(f) sarò, saràì, sarà, sarémo, saréte, saranno

§171 ESTÒLLERE—estollèndo—*pp* missing
(e) missing

§172 EVÀDERE—evadèndo—evaso
(e) evasi, evadésti, evase, evadémmo, evadéste, evàsero

§173 FARE—facèndo—fatto
(a) fa or fàì or fa'; fate

(b) fàccio or fò; fài; fa; facciamo; fate; fanno
(c) fàccia, fàccia, fàccia, facciamo, facciate; fàcciano
(d) facévo, facévi, facéva, facevamo, facevate, facévano
(e) féci, facésti, féce, facémmo, facéste, fécero
(f) farò, faràí, farà, farémo, faréte, faranno

§174 **FÈNDERE**—fendèndo—fenduto or fésso
    (e) fendéí or fendètti; fendésti; fendé or fendètte; fendémmo; fendéste; fendérono or fendèttero

§175 **FÈRVERE**—fervèndo—*pp* missing
    (e) fervéí or fervètti; fervésti; fervé or fervètte; fervémmo; fervéste; fervérono or fervèttero

§176 **FINIRE**—finèndo—finito
    (a) finisci, finite
    (b) finisco, finisci, finisce, finiamo, finite, finìscono
    (c) finisca, finisca, finisca, finiamo, finiate, finìscano

§177 **FLÈTTERE**—flettèndo—flèsso
    (e) flettéí or flèssi; flettésti; flettê or flèsse; flettémmo; flettéste; flettérono or flèssero

§178 **FÓNDERE**—fondèndo—fuso
    (e) fusi, fondésti, fuse, fondémmo, fondéste, fùsero

§179 **FRÀNGERE**—frangèndo—franto
    (e) fransi, frangésti, franse, frangémmo, frangéste, frànsero

§180 **FRÌGGERE**—friggèndo—fritto
    (e) frissi, friggésti, frisse, friggémmo, friggéste, frìssero

§181 **GIACÉRE**—giacèndo—giaciuto
    (b) giàccio; giaci; giace; giacciamo or giaciamo; giacete; giàcciono
    (c) giàccia, giàccia, giàccia, giacciamo, giacciate, giàcciano
    (e) giàcqui, giacésti, giàcque, giacémmo, giacéste, giàcquero

§182 **GIOCARE**—giocando—giocato
    (a) giuòca or giòca; giocate
    (b) giuòco or giòco; giuòchi or giòchi; giuòca or giòca; giochiamo; giocate; giuòcano or giòcano
    (c) giuòchi or giòchi; giuòchi or giòchi; giuòchi or giòchi; giochiamo; giochiate; giuòchino or giòchino
    (f) giocherò, giocheràí, giocherà, giocherémo, giocheréte, giocheranno

§183 **GIÙNGERE**—giungèndo—giunto
    (e) giunsi, giungésti, giunse, giungémmo, giungéste, giùnsero

§184 GODÉRE—godèndo—goduto
- (e) godéi or godètti; godésti; godé or godètte; godémmo; godéste; godérono or godèttero
- (f) godrò, godràì, godrà, godrémo, godréte, godranno

§185 IMBÉVERE—imbevèndo—imbevuto
- (e) imbévvi, imbevésti, imbévve, imbevémmo, imbevéste, imbévvero

§186 INCÓMBERE—incombèndo—*pp* missing
- (e) incombéi or incombètti; incombésti; incombé or incombètte; incombémmo; incombéste; incombérono or incombèttero

§187 INDÙLGERE—indulgèndo—indulto
- (e) indulsi, indulgésti, indulse, indulgémmo, indulgéste, indùlsero

§188a INFERIRE—inferèndo—inferito or infèrto
- (a) inferisci, inferite
- (b) inferisco, inferisci, inferisce, ìnferiamo, inferite, inferìscono
- (c) inferisca, inferisca, inferisca, inferiamo, inferiate, inferìscano
- (e) inferìi or infèrsi; inferisti; inferì or infèrse; inferimmo; inferiste; inferìrono or infèrsero

§188b INSTARE—instando—*pp* missing

§189 INTRÌDERE—intridèndo—intriso
- (e) intrisi, intridésti, intrise, intridémmo, intridéste, intrìsero

§190 INTRÙDERE—intrudèndo—intruso
- (e) intrusi, intrudésti, intruse, intrudémmo, intrudéste, intrùsero

§191 IRE—*ger* missing—ito
- (a) *sg* missing, ite
- (b) missing
- (c) missing
- (d) ivo, ivi, iva, ivamo, ivate, ìvano
- (e) *1st sg* missing, isti, *3rd sg* missing, *1st pl* missing, iste, ìrono

§192 LÈDERE—ledèndo—léso or lèso
- (e) lési, ledésti, lése, ledémmo, ledéste, lésero

§193 LÈGGERE—leggèndo—lètto
- (e) lèssi, leggésti, lèsse, leggémmo, leggéste, lèssero

§194 LIQUEFARE—liquefacèndo—liquefatto
  (a) liquefà, liquefate
  (b) liquefò or liquefàccio; liquefài; liquefà liquefacciamo;
     liquefate; liquefanno
  (c) liquefàccia, liquefàccia, liquefàccia, liquefacciàmo,
     liquefacciate, liquefàcciano
  (d) liquefacévo, liquefacévi, liquefacéva, liquefacevamo,
     liquefacevate, liquefacévano
  (e) liqueféci, liquefacésti, liqueféce, liquefacémmo, lique-
     facéste, liquefécero
  (f) liquefarò, liquefaràì, liquefarà, liquefarémo, liquefaréte,
     liquefaranno

§195 MALEDIRE—maledicèndo—maledétto
  (a) maledici, maledite
  (b) maledico, maledici, maledice, malediciamo, maledite,
     maledìcono
  (c) maledica, maledica, maledica, malediciamo, malediciate,
     maledìcano
  (d) maledicévo *or* maledivo; maledicévi *or* maledivi;
     maledicéva *or* malediva; maledicevamo *or* male-
     divamo; maledicevate *or* maledivate; maledicévano
     or maledìvano
  (e) maledìi *or* maledissi; maledisti *or* maledicésti; maledì
     or maledisse; maledimmo *or* maledicémmo; male-
     diste *or* maledicéste; maledìrono *or* maledìssero
  (f) maledirò, malediràì, maledirà, maledirémo, malediréte,
     malediranno

§196 MALVOLÉRE—*ger* missing—malvoluto
  (a) missing
  (b) missing
  (c) missing
  (d) missing
  (e) missing
  (f) missing

§197 MANCARE—mancando—mancato
  (b) manco, manchi, manca, manchiamo, mancate, màncano
  (c) manchi, manchi, manchi, manchiamo, manchiate,
     mànchino
  (f) mancherò, mancheràì, mancherà, mancherémo, manche-
     réte, mancheranno

§198 MÉTTERE—mettèndo—mésso
  (e) misi, mettésti, mise, mettémmo, mettéste, mìsero

§199 MÌNGERE—mingèndo—minto
  (e) minsi, mingésti, minse, mingémmo, mingéste, mìnsero

§200 MÒRDERE—mordèndo—mòrso
(e) mòrsi, mordésti, mòrse, mordémmo, mordéste, mòrsero

§201 MORIRE—morèndo—mòrto
(a) muòri, morite
(b) muòio, muòri, muòre, moriamo, morite, muòiono
(c) muòia. muòia, muòia, moriamo, moriate, muòiano
(f) morrò or morirò; morràì or moriràì; morrà or morirà; morrémo or morirémo; morréte or moriréte; morranno or moriranno

§202 MUÒVERE—muovèndo or movèndo (movènte)—mòsso
(a) muòvi, movéte
(b) muòvo, muòvi, muòve, moviamo, movéte, muòvono
(c) muòva, muòva, muòva, moviamo, moviate, muòvano
(d) movévo, movévi, movéva, movevamo, movevate, movévano
(e) mòssi, movésti, mòsse, movémmo, movéste, mòssero
(f) moverò, moveràì, moverà, moverémo, moveréte, moveranno

§203 NÀSCERE—nascèndo—nato
(e) nàcqui, nascésti, nàcque, nascémmo, nascéste, nàcquero

§204 NASCÓNDERE—nascondèndo—nascósto
(e) nascósi, nascondésti, nascóse, nascondémmo, nascondéste, nascósero

§205 NEGLÌGERE—negligèndo—neglètto
(a) missing
(b) missing
(c) missing
(e) neglèssi, negligésti, neglèsse, negligémmo, negligéste, neglèssero

§206 NUÒCERE—nuocèndo—nociuto
(a) nuòci, nocéte
(b) nuòccio or nòccio; nuòci; nuòce; nociamo; nocéte; nuòcciono or nòcciòno
(c) nòccia, nòccia, nòccia, nociamo, nociate, nòcciano
(d) nocévo, nocévi, nocéva, nocevamo, nocevate, nocévano
(e) nòcqui, nocésti, nòcque, nocémmo, nocéste, nòcquero
(f) nocerò, noceràì, nocerà, nocerémo, noceréte, noceranno

§207 OFFRIRE—offrèndo (offerènte)—offèrto
(e) offrìi or offèrsi; offristi; offrì or offérse; offrimmo; offriste; offrìrono or offèrsero

§208 OTTÙNDERE—ottundèndo—ottuso
(e) ottusi, ottundésti, ottuse, ottundémmo, ottundéste, ottùsero

§209 PAGARE—pagando—pagato
 (b) pago, paghi, paga, paghiamo, pagate, pàgano
 (c) paghi, paghi, paghi, paghiamo, paghiate, pàghino
 (f) pagherò, pagheràì, pagherà, pagherémo, pagheréte, pagheranno

§210 PARÉRE—parèndo (parvènte)—parso
 (a) missing
 (b) pàio; pari; pare; pariamo or paiamo; paréte; pàiono
 (c) pàìa; pàìa; pàìa; pariamo or paiamo; pariate or paiate; pàiano
 (e) parvi, parésti, parve, parémmo, paréste, pàrvero
 (f) parrò, parràì, parrà, parrémo, parréte, parranno

§211 PÀSCERE—pascèndo—pasciuto
 (a) pascéi or pascètti; pascésti; pascé or pascètte; pascémmo; pascéste; pascérono or pascèttero

§212 PÈRDERE—perdèndo—pèrso or perduto
 (c) perdéi or pèrsi or perdètti; perdésti; perdé, or pèrse or perdètte; perdémmo; perdéste; perdérono or pèrsero or perdèttero

§213 PERSUADÉRE—persuadèndo—persuaso
 (e) persuasi, persuadésti, persuase, persuadémmo, persuadéste, persuàsero

§214 PIACÉRE—piacèndo—piaciuto
 (b) piàccio, piaci, piace, piacciamo, piacéte, piàcciono
 (c) piàccia, piàccia, piàccia, piacciamo, piacciate, piàcciano
 (e) piàcqui, piacésti, piàcque, piacémmo, piacéste, piàcquero

§215 PIÀNGERE—piangèndo—pianto
 (e) piansi, piangésti, pianse, piangémmo, piangéste, piànsero

§216 PIÒVERE—piovèndo—piovuto
 (e) piòvvi, piovésti, piòvve, piovémmo, piovéste, piòvvero

§217 PÒRGERE—porgèndo—pòrto
 (e) pòrsi, porgésti, pòrse, porgémmo, porgéste, pòrsero

§218 PÓRRE—ponèndo—pósto
 (a) póni, ponéte
 (b) póngo, póni, póne, poniamo, ponéte, póngono
 (c) pónga, pónga, pónga, poniamo, poniate, póngano
 (d) ponévo, ponévi, ponéva, ponevamo, ponevate, ponévano
 (e) pósi, ponésti, póse, ponémmo, ponéste, pósero

§219 POTÉRE—potèndo (potènte or possènte)—potuto
 (a) missing
 (b) pòsso, puòi, può, possiamo, potéte, pòssono

29

(c) pòssa, pòssa, pòssa, possiamo, possiate, pòssano
(e) potéi *or* potètti; potésti, poté *or* potètte; potémmo; potéste; potérono *or* potèttero
(f) potrò, potrài, potrà, potrémo, potréte, potranno

§220 PRÈNDERE—prendèndo—préso
(e) prési, prendésti, prése, prendémmo, prendéste, présero

§221 PROVVEDÉRE—provvedèndo—provveduto *or* provvisto
(e) provvidi, provvedésti, provvide, provvedémmo, provvedéste, provvìdero

§222 PRÙDERE—prudèndo—*pp* missing
(e) *1st sg* missing; *2nd sg* missing; prudé *or* prudètte; *1st pl* missing; *2nd pl* missing; prudérono *or* prudèttero

§223 RÀDERE—radèndo—raso
(e) rasi, radésti, rase, radémmo, radéste, ràsero

§224 REDÌGERE—redigèndo—redatto
(e) redassi, redigésti, redasse, redigémmo, redigéste, redàssero

§225 REDÌMERE—redimèndo—redènto
(e) redènsi, redimésti, redènse, redimémmo, rediméste, redènsero

§226 RÈGGERE—reggèndo—rètto
(e) rèssi, reggésti, rèsse, reggémmo, reggéste, rèssero

§227 RÈNDERE—rendèndo—réso
(e) rési *or* rendéi *or* rendètti; rendésti; rése *or* rendé *or* rendètte; rendémmo; rendéste; résero *or* rendérono *or* rendèttero

§228 RETROCÈDERE—retrocedèndo—retrocèsso *or* retroceduto
(e) retrocèssi *or* retrocedéi *or* retrocedètti; retrocedésti; retrocèsse *or* retrocedé *or* retrocedètte; retrocedémmo; retrocedéste; retrocèssero *or* retrocedérono *or* retrocedèttero

§229 RIAVÉRE—riavèndo—riavuto
(a) riabbi, riabbiate
(b) riò, riài, rià, riabbiamo, riavéte, rìanno
(c) riàbbia, riàbbia, riàbbia, riabbiamo, riabbiate, riàbbiano
(e) rièbbi, riavésti, rièbbe, riavémmo, riavéste, rièbbero
(f) riavrò, riavrài, riavrà, riavrémo, riavréte, riavranno

§230 RIDARE—ridando—ridato
(a) ridài *or* ridà; ridate
(b) ridò, ridài, ridà, ridiamo, ridate, ridanno
(c) ridìa, ridìa, ridìa, ridiamo, ridiate, ridìano

(e) ridièdi *or* ridètti; ridésti; ridiède *or* ridètte; ridémmo; ridéste; ridièdero *or* ridèttero

(f) ridarò, ridarài, ridarà, ridarémo, ridaréte, ridaranno

§231 RÌDERE—ridèndo—riso

(e) risi, ridésti, rise, ridémmo, ridéste, rìsero

§232 RIFLÈTTERE—riflettèndo—riflèsso *or* riflettuto

§233 RIFÙLGERE—rifulgèndo—rifulso

(e) rifulsi, rifulgésti, rifulse rifulgémmo, rifúlgéste, rifúlsero

§234 RILÙCERE—rilucèndo—*pp* missing

§235 RIMANÉRE—rimanèndo—rimasto

(b) rimango, rimani, rimane, rimaniamo, rimanéte, rimàngono

(c) rimanga, rimanga, rimanga, rimaniamo, rimaniate, rimàngano

(e) rimasi, rimanésti, rimase, rimanémmo, rimanéste, rimàsero

(f) rimarrò, rimarrài, rimarrà, rimarrémo, rimarréte, rimarranno

§236 RINCORARE—rincorando—rincorato

(a) rincuòra, rincorate

(b) rincuòro, rincuòri, rincuòra, rincoriamo, rincorate, rincuòrano

(c) rincuòri, rincuòri, rincuòri, rincoriamo, rincoriate, rincuòrino

§237 RISOLARE—risolando—risolato

(a) risuòla, risolate

(b) risuòlo, risuòli, risuòla, risoliamo, risolate, risuòlano

(c) risuòli, risuòli, risuòli, risoliamo, risoliate, risuòlino

§238 RISPÓNDERE—rispondèndo—rispósto

(e) rispósi, rispondésti, rispóse, rispondémmo, rispondéste, rispósero

§239 RÓDERE—rodèndo—róso

(e) rósi, rodésti, róse, rodémmo, rodéste, rósero

§240 RÓMPERE—rompèndo—rótto

(e) ruppi, rompésti, ruppe, rompémmo, rompéste, rùppero

§241 ROTARE—rotando—rotato

(a) ruòta, rotate

(b) ruòto, ruòti, ruòta, rotiamo, rotate, ruòtano

(c) ruòti, ruòti, ruòti, rotiamo, rotiate, ruòtino

§242 SALIRE—salèndo—salito
  (b) salgo, sali, sale, saliamo, salite, sàlgono
  (c) salga, salga, salga, saliamo, saliate, sàlgano

§243 SAPÉRE—sapèndo (sapiènte)—saputo
  (a) sappi, sappiate
  (b) sò, sai, sa, sappiamo, sapéte, sanno
  (c) sàppia, sàppia, sàppia, sappiamo, sappiate, sàppiano
  (e) sèppi, sapésti, sèppe, sapémmo, sapéste, sèppero
  (f) saprò, sapràì, saprà, saprémo, sapréte, sapranno

§244 SCÉGLIERE—sceglièndo—scélto
  (a) scégli, scegliéte
  (b) scélgo, scégli, scéglie, scegliamo, scegliéte, scélgono
  (c) scélga, scélga, scélga, scegliamo, scegliate, scélgano
  (e) scélsi, scegliésti, scélse, scegliémmo, scegliéste, scélsero

§245 SCÉNDERE—scendèndo—scéso
  (e) scési, scendésti, scése, scendémmo, scendéste, scésero

§246 SCÈRNERE—scernèndo—*pp* missing
  (e) scernéi *or* scernètti; scernésti; scerné *or* scernètte; scernémmo; scernéste; scernérono *or* scernèttero

§247 SCÌNDERE—scindèndo—scisso
  (e) scissi, scindésti, scisse, scindémmo, scindéste, scìssero

§248 SCOIARE—scoiando—scoiato
  (a) scuòia, scoiate
  (b) scuòio, scuòi, scuòia, scoiamo, scoiate, scuòiano
  (c) scuòi, scuòi, scuòi, scoiamo, scoiate, scuòino

§249 SCÒRGERE—scorgèndo—scòrto
  (e) scòrsi, scorgésti, scòrse, scorgémmo, scorgéste, scòrsero

§250 SCRÌVERE—scrivèndo—scritto
  (e) scrissi, scrivésti, scrisse, scrivémmo, scrivéste, scrìssero

§251 SCUÒTERE—scotèndo—scòsso
  (a) scuòti, scotéte
  (b) scuòto, scuòti, scuòte, scotiamo, scotéte, scuòtono
  (c) scuòta, scuòta, scuòta, scotiamo, scotiate, scuòtano
  (d) scotévo, scotévi, scotéva, scotevamo, scotevate, scotévano
  (e) scòssi, scotésti, scòsse, scotémmo, scotéste, scòssero

§252 SEDÉRE—sedèndo—seduto
  (a) sièdi, sedéte
  (b) sièdo *or* sèggo; sièdi; sième; sediamo; sedéte; sièdono *or* sèggono
  (c) sièda *or* sègga; sièda *or* sègga; sièda *or* sègga; sediamo; sediate; sièdano *or* sèggano
  (e) sedéi *or* sedètti; sedésti; sedé *or* sedètte; sedémmo; sedéste; sedérono *or* sedèttero

§253 SEPPELLIRE—seppellèndo—sepólto *or* seppellito
- (a) seppellisci, seppellite
- (b) seppellisco, seppellisci, seppellisce, seppelliamo, seppel- lite, seppellìscono
- (c) seppellisca, seppellisca, seppellisca, seppelliamo, seppel- liate, seppellìscano

§254 SODDISFARE—soddisfacèndo—soddisfatto
- (a) soddisfa *or* soddisfài *or* soddisfa'
- (b) soddisfàccio *or* soddisfò *or* soddisfo; soddisfài *or* soddisfi; soddisfà *or* soddisfa; soddisfacciamo; sod- disfate; soddisfanno *or* soddìsfano
- (c) soddisfàccia *or* soddisfi; soddisfàccia *or* soddisfi; soddi- sfàccia *or* soddisfi; soddisfacciamo; soddisfacciate; soddisfàcciano *or* soddìsfino
- (d) soddisfacévo, soddisfacévi, soddisfacéva, soddisface- vamo, soddisfacevate, soddisfacévano
- (e) soddisféci, soddisfacésti, soddisféce, soddisfacémmo, soddisfacéste, soddisfécero
- (f) soddisfarò, soddisfaràì, soddisfarà, soddisfarémo, soddi- sfaréte, soddisfaranno

§255 SOLÉRE—solèndo—sòlito
- (a) missing
- (b) sòglio, suòli, suòle, sogliamo, soléte, sògliono
- (c) sòglia, sòglia, sòglia, sogliamo, sogliate, sògliano
- (e) missing
- (f) missing

§256 SÒLVERE—solvèndo—soluto
- (e) solvéi *or* solvètti; solvésti; solvé *or* solvètte; solvémmo; solvéste; solvérono *or* solvèttero

§257 SONARE—sonando—sonato
- (a) suòna, sonate
- (b) suòno, suòni, suòna, soniamo, sonate, suònano
- (c) suòni, suòni, suòni, soniamo, soniate, suònino

§258 SÓRGERE—sorgèndo—sórto
- (e) sórsi, sorgésti, sórse, sorgémmo, sorgéste, sórsero

§259 SOSPÈNDERE—sospendèndo—sospéso
- (e) sospési, sospendésti, sospése, sospendémmo, sospendéste, sospésero

§260 SPÀNDERE—spandèndo—spanto
- (e) spandéi *or* spandètti *or* spansi; spandésti; spandé *or* spandètte *or* spanse; spandémmo; spandéste; spandé- rono *or* spandèttero *or* spànsero

§261 SPÀRGERE—spargèndo—sparso
- (e) sparsi, spargésti, sparse, spargémmo, spargéste, spàrsero

33

§262 SPÈGNERE—spegnèndo—spènto
 (b) spéngo *or* spèngo; spégni *or* spègni; spégne *or* spègne;
    spegniamo; spegnéte; spéngono *or* spèngono
 (c) spénga *or* spènga; spénga *or* spènga; spénga *or* spènga;
    spegniamo; spegniate; spéngano *or* spèngano
 (e) spènsi, spegnésti, spènse, spegnémmo, spegnéste, spèn-
    sero

§263 STARE—stando—stato
 (a) sta *or* stai *or* sta'; state
 (b) stò, stài, sta, stiamo, state, stanno
 (c) stìa, stìa, stìa, stiamo, stiate, stìano
 (e) stètti, stésti, stètte, stémmo, stéste, stèttero
 (f) starò, starài, starà, starémo, staréte, staranno

§264 STRÌDERE—stridèndo—*pp* missing
 (e) stridéi *or* stridètti; stridésti; stridé *or* stridètte; stri-
    démmo; stridéste; stridérono *or* stridèttero

§265 STRÌNGERE—stringèndo—strétto
 (e) strinsi, stringésti, strinse, stringémmo, stringéste, strìn-
    sero

§266 STRÙGGERE—struggèndo—strutto
 (e) strussi, struggésti, strusse, struggémmo, struggéste,
    strùssero

§267 SVÈLLERE—svellèndo—svèlto
 (b) svèllo *or* svèlgo; svèlli; svèlle; svelliamo; svelléte;
    svèllono *or* svèlgono
 (c) svèlla *or* svèlga; svèlla *or* svèlga; svèlla *or* svèlga;
    svelliamo; svelliate; svèllano *or* svèlgano
 (e) svèlsi, svellésti, svèlse, svellémmo, svelléste, svèlsero

§268 TACÉRE—tacèndo—taciuto
 (b) tàccio, taci, tace, taciamo, tacéte, tàcciono
 (c) tàccia, tàccia, tàccia, taciamo, taciate, tàcciano
 (e) tàcqui, tacésti, tàcque, tacémmo, tacéste, tàcquero

§269 TÀNGERE—tangèndo—pp missing
 (a) missing
 (b) *1st sg* missing; *2nd sg* missing; tange; *1st pl* missing;
    2nd pl missing; tàngono
 (c) *1st sg* missing; *2nd sg* missing; tanga; *1st pl* missing;
    2nd pl missing; tàngano
 (d) *1st sg* missing; *2nd sg* missing; tangéva; *1st pl* missing;
    2nd pl missing; tangévano
 (e) missing
 (f) *1st sg* missing; *2nd sg* missing; tangerà; *1st pl* missing;
    2nd pl missing; tangeranno

§270 **TÈNDERE**—tendèndo—téso
  (e) tési, tendésti, tése, tendémmo, tendéste, tésero

§271 **TENÉRE**—tenèndo—tenuto
  (a) tièni, tenéte
  (b) tèngo, tièni, tiène, teniamo, tenéte, tèngono
  (c) tènga, tènga, tènga, teniamo, teniate, tèngano
  (e) ténni, tenésti, ténne, tenémmo, tenéste, ténnero
  (f) terrò, terrài, terrà, terrémo, terréte, terranno

§272 **TÒRCERE**—torcèndo—tòrto
  (e) tòrsi, torcésti, tòrse, torcémmo, torcéste, tòrsero

§273 **TRARRE**—traèndo—tratto
  (a) trài, traéte
  (b) traggo, trài, trae, traiamo, traéte, tràggono
  (c) tragga, tragga, tragga, traiamo, traiate, tràggano
  (d) traévo, traévi, traéva, traevamo, traevate, traévano
  (e) trassi, traésti, trasse, traémmo, traéste, tràssero

§274 **UCCÌDERE**—uccidèndo—ucciso
  (e) uccisi, uccidésti, uccise, uccidémmo, uccidéste, uccìsero

§275 **UDIRE**—udèndo *or* udièndo—udito
  (a) òdi, udite
  (b) òdo, òdi, òde, udiamo, udite, òdono
  (c) òda, òda, òda, udiamo, udiate, òdano
  (f) udirò *or* udrò; udirài *or* udrài; udirà *or* udrà; udirémo *or* udrémo; udiréte *or* udréte; udiranno *or* udranno

§276 **ÙRGERE**—urgèndo—*pp* missing
  (a) missing
  (e) missing

§277 **USCIRE**—uscèndo—uscito
  (a) èsci, uscite
  (b) èsco, èsci, èsce, usciamo, uscite, èscono
  (c) èsca, èsca, èsca, usciamo, usciate, èscano

§278 **VALÉRE**—valèndo—valso
  (b) valgo, vali, vale, valiamo, valéte, vàlgono
  (c) valga, valga, valga, valiamo, valiate, vàlgano
  (e) valsi, valésti, valse, valémmo, valéste, vàlsero
  (f) varrò, varrài, varrà, varrémo, varréte, varranno

§279 **VEDÉRE**—vedèndo—veduto *or* visto
  (e) vidi, vedésti, vide, vedémmo, vedéste, vìdero
  (f) vedrò, vedrài, vedrà, vedrémo, vedréte, vedranno

§280 **VEGLIARE**—vegliando—vegliato
  (b) véglio, végli, véglia, vegliamo, vegliate, végliano
  (c) végli, végli, végli, vegliamo, vegliate, véglino

§281 VÉNDERE—vendèndo—venduto
    (e) vendéi *or* vendètti; vendésti; vendé *or* vendètte; ven-
    démmo; vendéste; vendérono *or* vendèttero

§282 VENIRE—venèndo (veniènte)—venuto
    (a) vièni, venite
    (b) vèngo, vièni, viène, veniamo, venite, vèngono
    (c) vènga, vènga, vènga, veniamo, veniate, vèngano
    (e) vénni, venisti, vénne, venimmo, veniste, vénnero
    (f) verrò, verrài, verrà, verrémo, verréte, verranno

§283 VÈRTERE—vertèndo—*pp* missing

§284 VÌGERE—vigèndo—*pp* missing
    (a) missing
    (b) *1st sg* missing; *2nd sg* missing; vige; *1st pl* missing;
        2d pl missing; vìgono
    (c) *1st sg* missing; *2d sg* missing; viga; *1st pl* missing;
        2d pl missing; vìgano
    (d) *1st sg* missing; *2d sg* missing; vigéva; *1st pl* missing;
        2d pl missing; vigévano
    (e) missing

§285 VÌNCERE—vincèndo—vinto
    (e) vinsi, vincésti, vinse, vincémmo, vincéste, vìnsero

§286 VÌVERE—vivèndo—vissuto
    (e) vissi, vivésti, visse, vivémmo, vivéste, vìssero
    (f) vivrò, vivrài, vivrà, vivrémo, vivréte, vivranno

§287 VIZIARE—viziando—viziato
    (b) vìzio, vizi, vìzia, viziamo, viziate, vìziano
    (c) vizi, vizi, vizi, viziamo, viziate, vìzino

§288 VOLÉRE—volèndo—voluto
    (a) vògli, vogliate
    (b) vòglio, vuòi, vuòle, vogliamo, volète, vògliono
    (c) vòglia, vòglia, vòglia, vogliamo, vogliate, vògliano
    (e) vòlli, volésti, vòlle, volémmo, voléste, vòllero
    (f) vorrò, vorrài, vorrà, vorrémo, vorréte, vorranno

§289 VÒLGERE—volgèndo—vòlto
    (e) vòlsi, volgésti, vòlse, volgémmo, volgéste, vòlsero

§290 VOLTEGGIARE—volteggiando—volteggiato
    (b) voltéggio, voltéggi, voltéggia, volteggiamo, volteggiate,
        voltéggiano
    (c) voltéggi, voltéggi, voltéggi, volteggiamo, volteggiate,
        voltéggino
    (f) volteggerò, volteggerài, volteggerà, volteggerémo, vol-
        teggeréte, volteggeranno

A, a [α] *m* & *f* first letter of the Italian alphabet

a *prep* (**ad** in front of a vowel) to, e.g., **diede il libro a Giovanni** he gave the book to John; in, e.g., **a Milano** in Milan; at, e.g., **a casa** at home; within, e.g., **a tre miglia da qui** within three miles from here; on, e.g., **portare una catena al collo** to wear a chain on one's neck; e.g., **al sabato** on Saturdays; for, e.g., **a vita** for life; by, e.g., **fatto a mano** made by hand; with, e.g., **una gonna a pieghe** a skirt with pleats; as, e.g., **eleggere a presidente** to elect as chairman; into, e.g., **fu gettato a mare** he was thrown into the sea; of, e.g., **un quarto alle due** fifteen minutes of two

àba·co *m* (**-chi**) (archit) abacus

abate *m* abbot

abbacchiare §287 *tr* to knock down (*e.g., olives*); to sell too cheap ‖ *ref* to lose courage; to be dejected

abbacchia·to -ta *adj* (coll) dejected

abbàc·chio *m* (**-chi**) baby lamb (*slaughtered*)

abbacinare (**abbàcino**) *tr* to dazzle; to deceive

abbadéssa *f* var of badessa

abbagliante *adj* dazzling ‖ *m* (aut) bright light, high beam

abbagliare §280 *tr* to dazzle; to deceive; to blind (*with the lights of a car*)

abbà·glio *m* (**-gli**) error; **prendere abbaglio** to make a mistake

abbaiaménto *m* bark (*of dog*)

abbaiare §287 *intr* to bark; to yelp

abbaino *m* dormer window; skylight; attic

abbambinare *tr* to walk (*a heavy piece of furniture*)

abbandonare (**abbandóno**) *tr* to abandon; to give up; to let go (*e.g., the reins*); to let fall; (sports) to withdraw from ‖ *ref* to yield; to lose courage

abbandóno *m* abandon, abandonment; desertion; neglect; relaxation; renunciation (*of a right*); cession (*of property*); withdrawal (*from a fight*)

abbarbicare §197 (**abbàrbico**) *intr* & *ref* to cling; to hold on

abbassalin·gua *m* (**-gua**) tongue depressor

abbassaménto *m* lowering; reduction; drop, fall

abbassare *tr* to lower; to dim (*lights*); to turn (*the radio*) lower; **abbassare le armi** to surrender; **abbassare la cresta** to yield ‖ *ref* to lower oneself; to drop

abbas·so *m* (**-so**) angry shout (*of a crowd*) ‖ *adv* down, below; downstairs ‖ *interj* down with!

abbastanza *adj invar* enough ‖ *adv* enough; rather, fairly

abbàttere *tr* to demolish; to fell; to shoot down; to refute (*an argument*); to depress ‖ *ref* to be depressed, be downcast

abbattiménto *m* demolition; felling; shooting down; chill; (fig) depression; **abbattimento alla base** (econ) basic exemption (*from taxes*)

abbattu·to -ta *adj* dejected, downcast ‖ *f* clearing (*of trees*)

abbazìa *f* abbey; abbacy

abbecedà·rio *m* (**-ri**) speller, primer

abbelliménto *m* embellishment, ornamentation

abbellire §176 *tr* to embellish, adorn; to landscape

abbeverare (**abbévero**) *tr* to water (*animals*) ‖ *ref* to quench one's thirst

abbevera·tóio *m* (**-tói**) watering trough

abbic·cì *m* (**-cì**) alphabet; speller; primer; ABC's, rudiments

abbiènte *adj* well-to-do ‖ *m*—**gli abbienti** the haves; **gli abbienti e nullatenenti** the haves and the have-nots

abbiettézza or **abiettézza** *f* abjectness, baseness

abbièt·to -ta or **abièt·to -ta** *adj* abject, base, low

abbiezióne or **abiezióne** *f* wretchedness, baseness

abbigliaménto *m* attire, wear

abbigliare §280 *tr* & *ref* to dress; to dress up

abbinaménto *m* coupling; merger

abbinare *tr* to couple; to join, merge

abbindolare (**abbìndolo**) *tr* to dupe, deceive

abbiosciare §128 *ref* to fall down; to lose heart, be downcast

abbisognare (**abbiságno**) *intr* to be in need

abboccaménto *m* interview, conversation

abboccare §197 (**abbócco**) *tr* to swallow (*the hook*); to fit (*pipes*) ‖ *intr* to bite (*said of fish*); to fall; to fit (*said of pipes*) ‖ *ref* to confer

abbocca·to -ta *adj* palatable; slightly sweet (*wine*)

abbonacciare §128 *ref* to calm down, abate (*said of weather*)

abbonaménto *m* subscription; **abbonamento postale** mailing permit

abbonare (**abbòno**) *tr* to take out a subscription for (*s.o.*) ‖ *ref* to subscribe ‖ §257 *tr* to remit (*a debt*); to forgive

abbona·to -ta *mf* subscriber; commuter

abbondante *adj* abundant, plentiful; heavy (*rain*)

abbondanza *f* abundance, plenty

abbondare (**abbóndo**) *intr* (ESSERE & AVERE) to abound; to exceed; **abbondare di** or **in** to abound in

abbonire §176 *tr* to calm; to placate ‖ *ref* to calm down

abbordàbile *adj* accessible, approachable; negotiable (*curve*)

abbordàg·gio *m* (-gi) boarding (*of an enemy ship*); andare all'abbordaggio di to board

abbordare (**abbórdo**) *tr* to board (*an enemy ship*); to negotiate (*a curve*); to face (*a problem*); (fig) to button-hole

abborracciare §128 *tr* to botch, bungle

abborracciatura *f* botch, bungle

abbottonare (**abbottóno**) *tr* to button || *ref* (coll) to keep to oneself

abbottonatura *f* buttoning; row of buttons

abbozzare (**abbòzzo**) *tr* to sketch; to hew (*e.g., a statue*); (naut) to tie up || *intr* (coll) to take it

abbòzzo *m* sketch, draft

abbracciabò·sco *m* (-schi) (bot) woodbine

abbracciare *m* embrace, embracing || §128 *tr* to embrace, hug; to seize (*an opportunity*); to become converted to (*e.g., Christianity*); to enter (*a profession*); to span, encompass || *ref* to cling; to embrace one another

abbràc·cio *m* (-ci) embrace, hug

abbrancare §197 *tr* to grab; to herd || *ref* to cling; to join a herd

abbreviaménto *m* abbreviation, shortening

abbreviare §287 (**abbrèvio**) *tr* to abbreviate, shorten, abridge

abbreviatura *f* shortening, abridgment

abbreviazióne *f* abbreviation

abbrivo or **abbrivio** *m* headway (*of a ship*); prendere l'abbrivio to gather momentum

abbronzante [dz] *adj* suntanning || *m* suntan lotion

abbronzare [dz] (**abbrónzo**) *tr & ref* to bronze; to tan

abbronza·to -ta [dz] *adj* tanned, suntanned

abbronzatura [dz] *f* tan, suntan

abbruciacchiare §287 *tr* to singe

abbrunare *tr* to brown; to hang crepe on || *ref* to wear mourning

abbrunire §176 *tr* to turn brown; to tan; to burnish

abbrustolire §176 *tr* to toast; to singe || *ref* to tan; to become sunburned

abbrutiménto *m* degradation, brutishness

abbrutire §176 *tr* to degrade; to brutalize || *intr & ref* to become brutalized

abbuiare §287 *tr* to darken; to hush up, hide || *ref* to grow dark; to become gloomy || *impers*—abbuia it's growing dark

abbuòno *m* allowance, discount; handicap (*in racing*)

abburattaménto *m* sifting

abburattare *tr* to sift, bolt

abdicare §197 (**àbdico**) *tr & intr* to abdicate; abdicare a to give up, renounce; to abdicate (*e.g., the throne*)

abdicazióne *f* abdication

aberrare (**abèrro**) *intr* to deviate

aberrazióne *f* aberration

abéte *m* fir

abetina *f* forest of fir trees

abiàti·co *m* (-ci) (coll) grandson

abièt·to -ta *adj* abject, base, low

abigeato *m* (law) cattle rustling

àbile *adj* able, clever, capable; (mil) fit

abili·tà *f* (tà) ability, skill

abilitare (**abìlito**) *tr* to certify (*e.g., a teacher*); to qualify, license

abilita·to -ta *adj* certified (*teacher*)

abilitazióne *f* qualification; certification (*of teachers*)

abissale *adj* abysmal

Abissinia, l' *f* Abyssinia

abissi·no -na *adj & mf* Abyssinian

abisso *m* abyss; fountain (*of knowledge*); slough (*of degradation*)

abitàbile *adj* inhabitable

abitàcolo *m* (aer) cockpit; (aut) cab, interior; (naut) compass bowl; **abitacolo eiettabile** (aer) ejection capsule

abitante *mf* inhabitant; resident

abitare (**àbito**) *tr* to inhabit; to occupy || *intr* to dwell, live, reside

abitati·vo -va *adj* living, e.g., **condizioni abitative** living conditions

abita·to -ta *adj* inhabited, populated || *m* built-up area

abita·tóre -trice *mf* dweller

abitazióne *f* dwelling; housing

àbito *m* suit (*for men*); dress (*for women*); garb, attire; habit; **abiti** clothes; **abito da ballo** evening gown; **abito da cerimonia** formal dress; **abito da inverno** winter suit; winter clothes; **levarsi l'abito** to doff the cassock; **prender l'abito** to enter the Church

abituale *adj* habitual

abituare (**abituo**) *tr* to accustom || *ref* to grow accustomed

abitudinà·rio -ria *adj* (-ri -rie) set in his ways

abitùdine *f* habit, custom

abituro *m* (poet) shanty, hut

abiura *f* abjuration

abiurare *tr* to abjure

ablati·vo -va *adj & m* ablative

ablazióne *f* (med) removal; (geol) erosion

abluzióne *f* ablution

abnegare §209 (**abnégo & abnègo**) *tr* to renounce, abnegate

abnegazióne *f* abnegation, self-denial

abnòrme *adj* abnormal

abolire §176 *tr* to abolish

abolizióne *f* abolition

abominàbile *adj* abominable

abominare (**abòmino**) *tr* to abominate, detest

abominazióne *f* abomination

abominévole *adj* abominable

aborìge·no -na *adj* aboriginal || *m* aborigine; **aborigeni** aborigines

aborrire §176 & (**abòrro**) *tr* to abhor, loathe || *intr*—aborrire da to shun, shrink from

abortire §176 *intr* to abort

abòrto *m* abortion, miscarriage; **aborto di natura** monstrosity

abrasióne *f* abrasion; erosion

abrasi·vo -va *adj & m* abrasive

abrogare §209 (**àbrogo**) *tr* to abrogate

abrogazióne *f* abrogation

abruzzése *adj* of the Abruzzi ‖ *mf* person of the Abruzzi ‖ *m* dialect of the Abruzzi

àbside *f* (archit) apse

abusare *intr*—abusare **di** to go to excesses in (*e.g., smoking*); to take advantage of; to impose on

abusi‧vo -va *adj* illegal, abusive; unwarranted

abuso *m* abuse, excess

acà‧cia *f* (-cie) acacia

acanto *m* acanthus

àcaro *m* (ent) acarus, mite, tick; acaro **della scabbia** itch mite

ac‧ca *m* & *f* (-ca or -che) h (*letter*); **non valere un'acca** (coll) to not be worth a fig

accadèmia *f* academy

accadèmi‧co -ca (-ci -che) *adj* academic ‖ *mf* academician

accadére §121 *intr* (ESSERE) to happen, occur

accadu‧to -ta *adj* happened, occurred ‖ *m* fact, event; what has taken place

accagliare §280 *tr*, *intr* (ESSERE) & *ref* to curdle, coagulate

accalappia‧ni *m* (-ni) dogcatcher

accalappiare §287 *tr* to catch (*a dog*); to snare; (fig) to fool

accalcare §197 *tr* to crowd ‖ *ref* to throng

accaldare *ref* to get hot; to become flushed

accalda‧to -ta *adj* hot; perspired

accalorare (accalóro) *tr* to excite ‖ *ref* to get excited

accalora‧to -ta *adj* excited, animated

accampaménto *m* encampment, camp; camping

accampare *tr* to encamp; to advance, lay (*a claim*) ‖ *ref* to camp, encamp

accaniménto *m* animosity, bitterness; obstinacy, stubbornness

accanire §176 *ref* to persist; to work doggedly; **accanirsi contro** to harass

accani‧to -ta *adj* obstinate, persistent; furious; fierce, ruthless, bitter (*fight*)

accanto *adv* near, nearby; accanto **a** near

accantonaménto *m* tabling (*e.g., of a discussion*); reserve (*of money*); (mil) billeting; (sports) camping

accantonare (accantóno) *tr* to set aside (*money*); (mil) to billet

accaparraménto *m* cornering (*of market*)

accaparrare *tr* to corner (*merchandise*); to hoard; to put a down payment on (*e.g., a house*); (coll) to gain (*somebody's affection*)

accaparra‧tóre -trice *mf* monopolizer; hoarder

accapigliare §280 *ref* to pull each other's hair; to scuffle; to come to blows

accapo or **a capo** *m* paragraph

accappa‧tóio *m* (-tói) bathrobe

accapponare (accappóno) *tr* to castrate (*a rooster*); *ref* to wrinkle; **mi si accappona la pelle** I get gooseflesh

accarezzare (accarézzo) *tr* to caress, fondle; to pet; to nurture (*e.g., a*

hope); **accarezzare le spalle di** to strike; to club

accartocciare §128 (accartòccio) *tr* to wrap up in a cone ‖ *ref* to curl up

accartoccia‧to -ta *adj* curled up

accasare [s] *tr* & *ref* to marry

accasciaménto *m* dejection

accasciare §128 *tr* to weaken, enfeeble; to depress ‖ *ref* to weaken; to lose heart

accasermare [s] (**accasèrmo**) *tr* to quarter, billet

accatastare *tr* to register (*real estate*); to pile, heap up

accattabri‧ghe *mf* (-ghe) quarrelsome person, scrapper

accattare *tr* to beg for; to borrow (*e.g., ideas*) ‖ *intr* to beg

accattonàg‧gio *m* (-gi) begging, mendicancy

accattó‧ne -na *mf* mendicant, beggar

accavalcare §197 *tr* to straddle; to go over

accavalciare §128 *tr* to bestride

accavallare *tr* to superimpose; to cross (*one's legs*) ‖ *ref* to pour forward, run high (*said of waves*)

accecaménto *m* blinding

accecare §122 *tr* to blind; to countersink ‖ *intr* (ESSERE) to become blind ‖ *ref* to blind oneself

acceca‧tóio *m* (-tói) countersink

accèdere §100 *intr* (ESSERE) to enter, approach; to accede

acceleraménto *m* acceleration

accelerare (accèlero) *tr* & *intr* to accelerate

accelera‧to -ta *adj* accelerated; intensive (*course*); local (*train*) ‖ *m* local train

acceleratóre *m* accelerator

accelerazióne *f* acceleration

accèndere §101 *tr* to kindle; to turn on (*e.g., the light*); to light (*e.g., a match, a cigar*) ‖ *ref* to catch fire; to become lit; **accendersi in viso** to become flushed

accendisìgaro *m* lighter

accendi‧tóio *m* (-tói) candle lighter

accenditóre *m* lighter

accennare (accénno) *tr* to nod; to point at; to sketch ‖ *intr* to refer; to hint

accénno *m* nod; sign; allusion

accensióne *f* lighting, kindling; (aut) ignition; (law) contraction (*of a debt*); **accensione improvvisa** spontaneous combustion

accentare (accènto) *tr* to accent

accènto *m* accent; stress; (poet) accent (*word*); **accento tonico** stress accent

accentraménto *m* centralization

accentrare (accèntro) *tr* to concentrate, centralize

accentuare (accèntuo) *tr* to accentuate ‖ *ref* to become aggravated

accentuazióne *f* accentuation

accerchiaménto *m* encirclement

accerchiare §287 (accérchio) *tr* to encircle, surround

accertàbile *adj* verifiable

accertaménto *m* ascertainment, verification; determination (*e.g., of taxes*)

accertare (accèrto) tr to assure; to ascertain, verify; to determine (the tax due) || ref to make sure

accé·so -sa [s] adj lit; turned on; on (e.g., radio); excited, aroused; bright (color)

accessìbile adj accessible; moderate (price)

accessióne f accession

accèsso m access, approach; admittance, entry; fit (of anger, of coughing)

accessò·rio -ria (-ri -rie) adj accessory || m accessory; (mach) accessory, attachment

accétta f hatchet, axe, cleaver; **tagliato con l'accetta** rough-hewn

accettàbile adj acceptable

accéttare (accètto) tr to accept

accettazióne f acceptance; receiving room; (econ) acceptance

accèt·to -ta adj agreeable; welcome; **male accetto** unwelcome

accezióne f meaning, acceptation

acchiappafarfal·le m (-le) butterfly net

acchiappamó·sche m (-sche) fly catcher

acchiappare tr to grab, seize; (coll) to catch in the act

acchito m (billiards) break; **di primo acchito** at first

acciaccare §197 tr to crush; to trample upon; (coll) to lay low (e.g., by illness)

acciac·co m (-chi) illness, infirmity, ailment

acciaiare §287 tr to convert into steel; to strengthen with steel

acciaieria f steel mill, steelworks

ac·ciàio m (-ciài) steel; **acciaio inossidàbile** stainless steel

acciaiòlo m whetstone

acciambellare (acciambèllo) tr to shape in the form of a doughnut || ref to curl up

acciarino m flintlock; linchpin; (nav) war nose (of a torpedo)

accidèmpoli interj (slang) darn it!

accidentale adj accidental

accidenta·to -ta adj paralyzed; uneven, rough (road); broken (ground)

accidènte m accident; crack-up; (coll) paralytic stroke; (coll) hoot, fig; (coll) pest, menace (child); (mus) accidental; **accidènti!** (coll) darn!, damn!; **correre come un accidente** to run like the devil; **mandare un accidente a** to wish ill luck to; **per accidente** perchance

accìdia f sloth

accidió·so -sa [s] adj slothful

acciglliare §280 ref to frown, knit one's brow

accìngere §126 ref—**accingersi a** to get ready to

-àccio -àccia suf adj & mf (-acci -acce) no good, e.g., **gentaccia** no good people; good-for-nothing, e.g., **ragazzaccio** good-for-nothing boy

acciò or **acciocché** conj (poet) so that

acciottolare (acciòttolo) tr to pave with cobblestones

acciottola·to -ta adj cobblestone || m cobblestone pavement

acciottolì·o m (-i) clatter (e.g., of dishes)

accipicchia interj (coll) darn it!

acciuffare tr to seize, grab, pinch (a thief)

acciu·ga f (-ghe) anchovy

acclamare tr to acclaim || intr to voice one's approval

acclamazióne f acclamation

acclimatare (acclìmato) tr & ref to acclimate

acclimatazióne f acclimatation

acclive adj (poet) steep

acclivi·tà f (-tà) acclivity

acclùdere §105 tr to enclose

acclu·so -sa adj enclosed

accoccare §197 (accòcco & accócco) tr (poet) to nock (the arrow)

accoccolare (accòccolo) ref to squat down

accodare (accódo) tr to line up || ref to line up, queue

accogliènte adj cozy, hospitable, inviting

accogliènza f reception, welcome

accògliere §127 tr to receive; to welcome; to grant (a request) || ref (poet) to gather

accoglitrice f receptionist

accòlito m acolyte, altar boy; follower

accollare (accòllo) tr to overload (a cart); **accollare qlco a qlcu** to charge s.o. with s.th || intr to go up to the neck (said of a dress) || ref to assume, take upon oneself

accolla·to -ta adj high-necked (dress); high-cut (shoes) || f accolade

accollatura f neck, neckhole

accòlta f (poet) gathering

accoltellare (accoltèllo) tr to knife

accomandante m limited partner

accomandatà·rio m (-ri) (law) general partner

accomàndita f (law) limited partnership

accomiatare tr to dismiss || ref to take leave

accomodaménto m arrangement; compromise; settlement

accomodante adj accommodating, obliging

accomodare (accòmodo) tr to arrange; to fix; to settle || intr to be convenient || ref to adapt oneself; to agree; to sit down; **si accomodi** have a seat, make yourself comfortable

accomodatura f arrangement; repair

accompagnaménto m retinue; cortege; (mus) accompaniment; (law) writ of mandamus; (mil) softening-up (by gunfire)

accompagnare tr to accompany; to escort; to follow; to match || ref—**accompagnarsi a** or **con** to join

accompagna·tóre -trice mf escort; guide; (mus) accompanist

accomunare tr to mingle, mix; to unite, associate; to share

acconciaménto m arrangement

acconciare §128 (accóncio) tr to prepare for use; to arrange; to set (e.g., the hair) || ref to adorn oneself; to dress one's hair; to adapt oneself

acconcia·tóre -trice mf hairdresser

acconciatura *f* hairdo; headdress

accòn·cio -cia *adj* (-ci -ce) proper, fitting

accondiscendènte *adj* acquiescing, acquiescent

accondiscendènza *f* acquiescence

accondiscéndere §245 *intr* to acquiesce, consent; to yield

accònsentire (acconsènto) *intr* to consent, acquiesce

acconsenziènte *adj* consenting, acquiescing

accontentare (accontènto) *tr* to satisfy, please || *ref* to be satisfied, be pleased

accónto *m* installment

accoppare (accòppo) *tr* (coll) to kill; (coll) to beat to death || *ref* (coll) to get killed

accoppiaménto *m* pairing; mating; (mach) parallel operation

accoppiare §287 (accòppio) *tr* to couple, pair, cross (*è.g., animals*) || *ref* to mate, copulate

accoppiata *f* daily double (*in races*)

accoraménto *m* sadness, sorrow

accorare (accòro) *tr* to stab to death; to sadden || *ref* to sadden, grieve

accora·to -ta *adj* saddened, grieving

accorciare §128 (accórcio) *tr & ref* to shorten; to shrink

accorciatura *f* shortening; shrinking

accordare (accòrdo) *tr* to harmonize (*colors*); to reconcile (*people*); to tune up; to grant; (gram) to make agree || *ref* to agree; to match

accorda·to -ta *adj* tuned up || *m* (econ) credit limit

accorda·tóre -trice *mf* (mus) tuner

accordatura *f* tuning

accòrdo *m* agreement, accordance; (law) mutual consent; (mus) harmony; **d'accordo** O.K., agreed; **d'accordo con** in accord with; **di comune accordo** with one accord; **essere d'accordo** to agree; **mettersi d'accordo** to come to an agreement

accòrgere §249 *ref* to perceive, notice; **accorgersi di** to become aware of, realize; **senza accorgersi** inadvertently

accorgimento *m* smartness; device, trick

accórrere §139 *intr* (ESSERE) to run up, rush up

accortézza *f* alertness; shrewdness, perspicacity

accòr·to -ta *adj* alert; shrewd, perspicacious

accosciare §128 (accòscio) *ref* to squat

accostàbile *adj* approachable

accostaménto *m* approach; combination (*e.g., of colors*)

accostare (accòsto) *tr* to approach; to bring near; to leave (*a door*) ajar || *intr* to be near; to cling, adhere; (naut) to come alongside; (naut) to maneuver alongside a pier; (naut) to change direction, haul || *ref* to approach, come near; to cling (*e.g., to a faith*)

accosta·to -ta *adj* ajar

accò·sto -sta *adj* (coll) near || *m* approach; help || **accosto** *adv* near; **accosto a** near, close to

accovacciare §128 *ref* to crouch

accovonare (accovóno) *tr* to sheave

accozzàglia *f* hodgepodge; motley crowd

accozzare (accòzzo) *tr* to jumble up; to collect, gather (*people*) together || *ref* to collect, congregate

accòzzo *m* jumble, medley

accreditàbile *adj* chargeable (*e.g., account*); creditable

accreditaménto *m* crediting

accreditare (accrédito) *tr* to credit, believe; to accredit (*an ambassador*); to credit (*one's account*)

accredita·to -ta *adj* confirmed (*news*); accredited

accréscere §142 *tr & ref* to increase

accresciménto *m* increase

accucciare §128 *ref* to curl up (*said of dogs*)

accudire §176 *tr* (coll) to attend (*a sick person*) || *intr*—**accudire a** to take care of

acculturazióne *f* acculturation

accumulare (accùmulo) *tr, intr & ref* to accumulate; to gather

accumulatóre *m* storage battery

accumulazióne *f* accumulation

accuratézza *f* care, carefulness

accura·to -ta *adj* careful, painstaking

accusa *f* accusation, charge; **pubblica accusa** (law) public prosecutor

accusare *tr* to accuse, charge; to betray; to acknowledge (*receipt*); (cards) to declare, bid

accusati·vo -va *adj & m* accusative

accusa·to -ta *adj* accused || *mf* defendant

accusató·re -trice *mf* accuser; **pubblico accusatore** (law) public prosecutor, district attorney

accusatò·rio -ria *adj* (-ri -rie) accusatory, accusing

acèfa·lo -la *adj* headless; without the first page (*said of a manuscript*)

acèr·bo -ba *adj* unripe, green, sour

àcero *m* maple tree, sugar maple

acèrri·mo -ma *adj* bitter, fierce

acetato *m* acetate

acèti·co -ca *adj* (-ci -che) acetic

acetificare §197 (acetìfico) *tr* to acetify

acetilène *m* acetylene

acéto *m* vinegar; **aceto aromatico** aromatic spirits; **sotto aceto** pickled

acetóne *m* acetone

acetósa [s] *f* (bot) sorrel

acetosèlla [s] *f* wood sorrel

acetó·so -sa [s] *adj* vinegarish || *f* see **acetosa**

Acherónte *m* Acheron

Achille *m* Achilles

acidificare §197 (acidìfico) *tr* to acidify

acidi·tà *f* (-tà) acidity; **acidità di stomaco** heartburn

àci·do -da *adj* acid, sour || *m* acid; **sapere d'acido** to taste sour

acidu·lo -la *adj* acidulous

àcino *m* berry (*of grapes*); bead (*of rosary*)

acme *f* acme; crisis

acne *f* acne

acònito *m* (bot) monkshood

àcqua *f* water; rain; purity (*e.g., of a diamond*); acqua a catinelle pouring rain; acqua alta high water; acqua corrente running water; acqua dolce fresh water; drinking water; acqua in boccal mum's the word!; acqua morta stagnant water; acqua ossigenata hydrogen peroxide; acqua potabile drinking water; acqua salata salt water; acqua viva spring; all'acqua di rose very mild; avere l'acqua alla gola to be in dire straits; della più bell'acqua of the first water; fare acqua to leak (*said of a boat*); fare un buco nell'acqua to waste one's efforts; portare acqua al mare to carry coals to Newcastle; prendere l'acqua to get wet; sott'acqua (fig) underhand; tirare l'acqua al proprio mulino to be grist to one's mill; versare acqua in un cesto to waste one's efforts

acquafòrte *f* (acquefòrti) etching

acquaforti·sta *mf* (-sti -ste) etcher

ac·quàio -quàia (-quài -quàie) *adj* watering (*trough*) || *m* sink

acquaiò·lo -la *adj* water || *m* water carrier; (sports) water boy

acquamarina *f* (acquemarine) aquamarine

acquaplano *m* aquaplane

acquaràgia *f* turpentine

acquarèllo *m* var of acquerello

acquà·rio *m* (-ri) aquarium || Acquario *m* (astr) Aquarius

acquartierare (acquartièro) *tr* (mil) to quarter || *ref* to be quartered

acquasanta *f* holy water

acquasantièra *f* (eccl) stoup

acquàti·co -ca *adj* (-ci -che) aquatic, water

acquattare *ref* to crouch, squat

acquavite *f* brandy; liquor, rum

acquazzóne *m* downpour, heavy shower

acquedótto *m* aqueduct

àcque·o -a *adj* aqueous, watery

acquerelli·sta *mf* (-sti -ste) watercolorist

acquerèllo *m* watercolor; watered-down wine

acquerùgiola *f* fine drizzle

acquiescènte *adj* acquiescent

acquietare (acquièto) *tr* to pacify, placate || *ref* to quiet down

acquirènte *mf* buyer, purchaser; il miglior acquirente the highest bidder

acquisire §176 *tr* to acquire

acquisi·tóre -trice *mf* salesperson, agent || *m* salesman || *f* saleswoman

acquistare *tr* to purchase, buy; to acquire; to gain (*e.g., ground*) || *intr* to improve

acquisto *m* buy, purchase; acquisition

acquitrino *m* marsh

acquitrinó·so -sa [s] *adj* marshy

acquolina *f*—far venire l'acquolina in bocca a to make one's mouth water

acquó·so -sa [s] *adj* watery

acre *adj* sour; pungent; acrid; bitter (*words*)

acrèdine *f* acrimony, sourness

acrimònia *f* acrimony

acro *m* acre

acròba·ta *mf* (-ti -te) acrobat

acrobàti·co -ca (-ci -che) *adj* acrobatic || *f* acrobatics

acrobatismo *m* acrobatics

acrobazìa *f* acrobatics; stunt, feat

acrocòro *m* plateau

acrònimo *m* acronym

acròpo·li *f* (-li) acropolis

acròsti·co *m* (-ci) acrostic

acuire §176 *tr* to sharpen, whet

acuità *f* acuity

acùle·o *m* (-i) quill; prickle, thorn; stinger (*of an insect*)

acume *m* acumen

acuminare (acùmino) *tr* to sharpen, whet

acumina·to -ta *adj* pointed, sharp

acùsti·co -ca (-ci -che) *adj* acoustic(al) || *f* acoustics

acutézza *f* acuteness, sharpness

acutizzare [ddzz] *tr* & *ref* to sharpen

acu·to -ta *adj* acute, sharp || *m* high note

ad *prep* var of a before words beginning with a vowel

adagiare §290 *tr* to lay down gently; to lower gently || *ref* to lie down; to stretch out

adà·gio *m* (-gi) adage; (mus) adagio || *adv* slowly; gently; (mus) adagio

Adamo *m* Adam

adattàbile *adj* adaptable

adattaménto *m* adaptation; adaptability

adattare *tr* to adapt, fit || *ref* to adapt oneself; to become adapted; adattarsi a to go with; to match; to be becoming to

adat·to -ta *adj* suitable, adequate

addebitaménto *m* debiting

addebitare (addèbito) *tr* to debit; addebitare una spesa a qlcu to debit s.o. with an expense

addèbito *m* charge; (com) debit; elevare l'addebito di qlco a qlcu (law) to charge s.o. with s.th

addènda *mpl* addenda

addèndo *m* (math) addend

addensare (addènso) *tr* to thicken || *ref* to thicken; to gather, throng

addentare (addènto) *tr* to bite || *ref* (mach) to mesh

addentatura *f* bite; (carp) tongue (*of tongue and groove*)

addentella·to -ta *adj* toothed, notched || *m* chance, occasion; (archit) toothing

addentrare (addéntro) *tr* to penetrate || *ref* to penetrate; to proceed

addéntro *adv* inside; addentro in into; inside of

addestraménto *m* training

addestrare (addèstro) *tr* & *ref* to train

addestra·tóre -trice *mf* trainer

addèt·to -ta *adj* assigned; attached; pertaining || *m* attaché; addetto stampa press secretary

addì *adv* the (+ *a certain date*), e.g., addì 27 gennaio the 27th of January

addiàc·cio *m* (-ci) sheepfold; bivouac

addiètro *m* (naut) stern; per l'addietro in the past || *adv* behind; ago; dare

addietro to back up; **lasciarsi addietro** to delay; **tempo addietro** some time ago; **tirarsi addietro** to back away

addi·o m (-i) farewell; **dare l'addio to** say good-bye; **dare l'estremo addio** to pay one's last respects; **fare gli addii** to say good-bye || *interj* farewell!, good-bye!

addire §151 *tr* (poet) to consecrate || *ref* to be suitable, be becoming; **addirsi a** to be becoming to

addirittura *adv* directly; even, without hesitation; absolutely, positively

addirizzare *tr* to straighten up; **addirizzare le gambe ai cani** to try the impossible

additare *tr* to point out

additi·vo -va *adj & m* additive

addivenire §282 *intr* (ESSERE)—**addivenire a** to come to, reach (*e.g., an agreement*)

addizionale *adj* additional || *f* supplementary tax

addizionare (addizióno) *tr & intr* to add

addizionatrice *f* adding machine

addizióne *f* addition

addobbaménto m adornment, decoration

addobbare (addòbbo) *tr* to adorn, bedeck, decorate

addobba·tóre -trice *mf* decorator

addòbbo m adornment, decoration; hangings (*in a church*)

addocilire §176 *tr* to soften up

addolcire §176 *tr* to sweeten; to calm down || *ref* to mellow, soften

addolorare· (addolóro) *tr & ref* to grieve; **addolorarsi per** to grieve over, lament

addolora·to -ta *adj* sorrowful || **l'Addolorata** *f* (eccl) Our Lady of Sorrows

addòme m abdomen

addomesticàbile *adj* tamable

addomesticaménto m taming

addomesticare §197 **(addomèstico)** *tr* to tame; to accustom || *ref* to become accustomed

addomestica·to -ta *adj* tame, domesticated

addominale *adj* abdominal

addormentare (addorménto) *tr* to put to sleep; to numb || *ref* to fall asleep; to be asleep (*said of a limb*)

addormenta·to -ta *adj* asleep; numbed

addossare (addòsso) *tr* to put on; **addossare qlco a qlco** to lean s.th against s.th; **addossare qlco a qlcu** to put s.th on s.o.; (fig) to entrust s.o. with s.th || *ref* to take upon oneself; to crowd together; **addossarsi a** to lean against; to crowd

addossa·to -ta *adj* leaning

addòsso *adv* on; on oneself, on one's back; about oneself; **addosso a** on, upon; against; **avere la sfortuna addosso** to be always unlucky; **dare addosso a qlcu** to assail s.o.; **levarsi d'addosso** to get rid of; **levarsi i panni d'addosso** to take the shirt off one's back

addót·to -ta *adj* adduced, alleged

addottorare (addottóro) *tr* to confer the doctor's degree on || *ref* to receive the doctor's degree

addurre §102 *tr* to adduce; to allege; (poet) to bring

Ade m Hades

adeguare (adéguo) *tr* to equalize; to bring in line || *ref* to conform, adapt oneself

adeguazióne *f* equalization

adémpiere· §163 *tr* to fulfill, accomplish || *ref* to come true

adempiménto m fulfillment, discharge (*of one's duty*)

adempire §176 *tr* to fulfill, accomplish || *ref* to come true

adenòide *adj* adenoid || **adenoidi** *fpl* adenoids

adèpto m follower; initiate

aderènte *adj* adherent || *mf* adherent, supporter

aderènza *f* adherence; (mach) friction; (pathol) adhesion; **aderenze** connections

aderire §176 *intr* to adhere; to stick; **aderire a** to grant (*e.g., a request*); to concur with; to subscribe to

adescare §197 **(adésco)** *tr*· to lure, bait, entice; (mach) to prime (*a pump*)

adesióne *f* adhesion; support; (phys) adherence

adesi·vo -va *adj & m* adhesive

adèsso *adv* now, just now; **da adesso in poi** from now on; **per adesso** for the time being

adiacènte *adj* adjacent

adiacènza *f* adjacency; **adiacenze** vicinity

adianto m (bot) maidenhair

adibire §176 *tr* to assign; to use

adipe m fat

adipó·so -sa [s] *adj* adipose

adirare *ref* to get angry

adira·to -ta *adj* angry, mad

adire §176 *tr* to apply to (*the court*); to enter into possession of (*an inheritance*)

adocchiare §287 **(adòcchio)** *tr* to eye; to ogle; to spot

adolescènte *adj & mf* adolescent

adolescènza *f* adolescence

adombrare (adómbro) *tr* to shade; to hide, veil || *ref* to shy (*said of a horse*); (fig) to take umbrage

Adóne m Adonis

adontare (adónto) *tr* (obs) to offend || *ref* to take offense

adoperare (adòpero & adópero) *tr* to use, employ || *ref* to exert oneself; to do one's best

adoràbile *adj* adorable

adorare (adóro) *tr* to adore; to worship || *intr* (archaic) to pray

adora·tóre -trice *mf* worshiper || m (joc) admirer, suitor

adorazióne *f* adoration, worship

adornare (adórno) *tr* to adorn || *ref* to bedeck oneself

adór·no -na *adj* adorned, bedecked; (poet) fine, beautiful

adottante *mf* (law) adopter

adottare (adòtto) *tr* to adopt

adotti·vo -va *adj* adoptive; foster (*child*)

adozióne *f* adoption

Adriàti·co -ca *adj* (**-ci -che**) Adriatic ‖ **Adriatico** *m* Adriatic

adulare (àdulo) *tr* to flatter; to fawn on

adula·tóre -trice *mf* flatterer

adulatò·rio -ria *adj* (**-rì -rie**) flattering; fawning

adulazióne *f* adulation; fawning

adulterante *adj* & *m* adulterant

adulteri·no -na *adj* bastard; adulterated

adultè·rio *m* (**-ri**) adultery

adùlte·ro -ra *adj* adulterous ‖ *m* adulterer ‖ *f* adulteress

adul·to -ta *adj* & *mf* adult

adunanza *f* assembly

adunare *tr* & *ref* to assemble, gather

adunata *f* reunion, meeting; (mil) muster

adun·co -ca *adj* (**-chi -che**) hooked, crooked

adunghiare §287 *tr* (poet) to claw

adu·sto -sta *adj* skinny; (poet) burnt

aerare (àero) *tr* to air, ventilate

aerazióne *f* aeration; airing

aère·o -a *adj* aerial; air; overhead; high, lofty; airy, fanciful ‖ *m* airplane; (rad & telv) aerial

aerobrigata *f* (mil) wing

aerocistèrna *f* (aer) tanker

aerodinàmi·co -ca (**-ci -che**) *adj* aerodynamic(al); streamlined ‖ *f* aerodynamics

aeròdromo *m* airfield, airdrome

aerofaro *m* airport beacon

aerofotogram·ma *m* (**-mi**) aerial photograph

aerogiro *m* helicopter

aerògrafo *m* spray gun (*for painting*)

aerolìnea *f* airline; **aerolinea principale** trunkline

aeròlito *m* aerolite, meteorite

aeromarìtti·mo -ma *adj* air-sea

aeròmetro *m* aerometer

aeromòbile *m* aircraft; **aeromobile senza pilota** drone, pilotless aircraft

aeromodellismo *m* model-airplane building

aeromodelli·sta *mf* (**-sti -ste**) model-airplane builder

aeromodèllo *m* model airplane

aeromotóre *m* windmill; aircraft motor

aeronàu·ta *m* (**-ti**) aeronaut

aeronàuti·co -ca (**-ci -che**) *adj* aeronautic(al) ‖ *f* aeronautics

aeronave *f* airship, aircraft

aeroplano *m* airplane

aeropòrto *m* airport, airfield

aeroportuale *adj* airport

aerorazzo [ddzz] *m* rocket spaceship

aeroriméssa *f* hangar

aerosbar·co *m* (**-chi**) landing of airborne troops

aeroservi·zio [s] *m* (**-zi**) air service

aerosilurante [s] *f* torpedo plane

aerosiluro [s] *m* aerial torpedo

aerosòl [s] *m* aerosol

aerosostenta·to -ta [s] *adj* airborne

aerospaziale *adj* aerospace

aerospà·zio *m* (**-zi**) aerospace

aerostàti·co -ca (**-ci -che**) *adj* aerostatic(al) ‖ *f* aerostatics

aeròstato *m* aerostat

aerostazióne *f* air terminal

aerotas·sì *m* (**-sì**) taxiplane

aerotrasportare (aerotraspòrto) *tr* to airlift

aerotrasporta·to -ta *adj* airlifted; airborne

aerovìa *f* (aer) beam (*course indicated by a radio beam*); (aer) air lane

afa *f* sultriness; **fare afa a** (coll) to be a pain in the neck to

afèresi *f* apheresis

affàbile *adj* affable, agreeable

affaccendare (affaccèndo) *tr* to busy ‖ *ref* to busy oneself, bustle

affaccenda·to -ta *adj* busy, bustling; occupied with busywork

affacciare §128 *tr* to show or display at the window; to bring forward (*e.g., an objection*); to raise (*a doubt*) ‖ *ref* to show oneself (*at the door or window*); to present itself (*said of a doubt*)

affaccia·to -ta *adj* facing

affagottare (affagòtto) *tr* to bundle ‖ *ref* to bundle up; to dress sloppily

affamare *tr* to starve

affama·to -ta *adj* starved, ravenous ‖ *mf* starveling; hungry person; wretch

affannare *tr* to worry, to afflict ‖ *intr* to pant; to be out of breath ‖ *ref* to worry; to bustle around

affanna·to -ta *adj* panting; out of breath; worried

affanno *m* shortness of breath; grief, sorrow

affannó·so -sa [s] *adj* panting; wearisome

affardellare (affardèllo) *tr* to bundle together; (mil) to pack

affare *m* affair, matter; business; condition, quality; deal; **affari business**; **affari esteri** foreign affairs; **un buon affare** a good deal; a bargain

affarismo *m* sharp business practice

affari·sta *mf* (**-sti -ste**) unscrupulous operator

affaristi·co -ca *adj* (**-ci -che**) sharp

affascinante *adj* fascinating, charming

affascinare (affàscino) *tr* to fascinate, charm; to seduce; to spellbind ‖ (affàscino) *tr* to bundle, to sheave

affascina·tóre -trice *adj* fascinating, charming ‖ *mf* charmer, spellbinder

affastellare (affastèllo) *tr* to fagot (*twigs*): to sheave, bundle (*e.g., hay*); to pile, heap (*wood, crops, etc*); (fig) to jumble up

affaticare §197 *tr* to fatigue, tire, weary ‖ *ref* to get tired; to weary; to toil

affatica·to -ta *adj* weary, tired

affatto *adv* quite, entirely; **niente affatto** not at all; **non . . . affatto** not at all

affatturare *tr* to bewitch; to adulterate (*e.g., food*)

affermare (affèrmo) *tr* to affirm, assert ‖ *intr* to nod assent ‖ *ref* to take hold (*said, e.g., of a new product*)

affermati·vo -va *adj* & *f* affirmative

affermazióne *f* affirmation; assertion,

statement; success (*e.g., of a new product*); (sports) victory

afferrare (**affèrro**) *tr* to grab, grasp; to catch, nab || *ref* to cling

affettare (**affètto**) *tr* to slice; to cut up || (**affètto**) *tr* to affect

affetta·to -ta *adj* affected || *m* cold cuts

affettatrice *f* slicing machine

affettazióne *f* affectation

affetti·vo -va *adj* emotional

affèt·to -ta *adj* afflicted, burdened || *m* affection, love; feeling

affettuosi·tà [s] *f* (**-tà**) love, affection

affettuó·so -sa [s] *adj* affectionate, loving, tender

affezionare (**affezióno**) *tr* to inspire affection in || *ref*—**affezionarsi a** to become fond of

affeziona·to -ta *adj* affectionate, loving; **Suo affezionatissimo** best regards; **tuo affezionatissimo** love, as ever

affezióne *f* affection

affiancare §197 *tr* to place next; to favor, help; (mil) to flank

affiataménto *m* harmony; teamwork

affiatare *tr* to harmonize

affibbiare §287 *tr* to buckle, fasten; to deliver (*a blow*); to play (*a trick*); to slap (*a fine*)

affidaménto *m* consignment, delivery; trust, confidence; **dare affidamento** to be trustworthy; **fare affidamento su** to rely upon

affidare *tr* to entrust; to commit (*to memory*); **affidare qlco a qlcu** to entrust s.o with s.th || *ref* to trust; **affidarsi a** to trust in

affievoliménto *m* weakening

affievolire §176 *tr* to weaken || *ref* to grow weaker

affiggere §103 *tr* to post; to fix (*one's eyes or glance*) || *ref* to gaze, stare

affigliare §280 *tr & ref* var of **affiliare**

affilacoltèl·li *m* (**-li**) steel (*for sharpening knives*)

affilara·sóio *m* (**-sói**) strop

affilare *tr* to sharpen, hone, whet; to make thin || *ref* to become thin

affila·to -ta *adj* sharp, sharpened; thin || *f* sharpening

affila·tóio *m* (**-tói**) sharpener

affilatrice *f* grindstone

affiliare §287 *tr* to affiliate || *ref* to become affiliated; **affiliarsi a** to become a member of

affilia·to -ta *adj* affiliated || *mf* affiliate; foster child; member of a secret society

affiliazióne *f* affiliation

affinare *tr* to sharpen; to refine, purify; to improve (*e.g., one's style*) || *ref* to improve

affinché *conj* so that, in order that; **affinché non** lest

affine *adj* akin, related; similar || *mf* in-law || *m* kinsman || *f* kinswoman || *adv*—**affine di** in order to

affini·tà *f* (**-tà**) affinity

affiochire §176 *tr* to make hoarse; to weaken || *ref* to become hoarse; to grow dim (*said of a candle*)

affioraménto *m* surfacing; (min) outcrop

affiorare (**affióro**) *intr* to surface, emerge; to appear, to show

affissare *tr* (poet) to fix || *ref* to concentrate; (poet) to gaze

affissióne *f* posting, bill posting

affis·so -sa *adj* fixed; posted || *m* bill, poster; door or window; (gram) affix

affittacàme·re *m* (**-re**) landlord || *f* landlady

affittanza *f* rent

affittare *tr* to rent || *ref*—**si affitta for** rent

affitto *m* rent, rental; **dare in affitto** to rent (*to grant by lease*); **prendere in affitto** to rent (*to take by lease*)

affittuà·rio -ria *mf* (**-ri -rie**) renter; tenant

affliggènte *adj* tormenting, distressing

affliggere §104 *tr* to afflict, distress || *ref* to grieve

afflit·to -ta *adj* afflicted, grieving || *mf* afflicted person, wretch

afflizióne *f* affliction, distress

afflosciare §128 (**afflòscio**) *tr* to cause to sag; to weaken || *ref* to droop; to sag; to be deflated; to faint

affloscire §176 *tr & ref* var of **afflosciare**

affluènte *adj & m* confluent

affluènza *f* confluence; abundance; crowd

affluire §176 *intr* (ESSERE) to flow (*said of river*); to flock (*said of people*); to pour in (*said of earnings*)

afflusso *m* flow

affogaménto *m* drowning

affogare §209 (**affógo**) *tr* to drown; to smother || *intr* (ESSERE) to drown

affoga·to -ta *adj* drowned; poached (*egg*)

affollaménto *m* crowd, throng

affollare (**affòllo & affòllo**) *tr* to crowd; to overcome || *ref* to crowd

affolla·to -ta *adj* crowded

affondaménto *m* sinking

affondami·ne *m* (**-ne**) mine layer

affondare (**affóndo**) *tr* to sink; to stick || *ref* to sink

affondata *f* (aer) nosedive

affóndo *m* (fencing) lunge || *adv* deeply

afforestare (**afforèsto**) *tr* to reforest

affossare (**affòsso**) *tr* to ditch; (fig) to table (*e.g., a proposal*); to hollow out || *ref* to become sunken or hollow (*said, e.g., of cheeks*)

affossatóre *m* ditchdigger; gravedigger

affrancare §197 *tr* to set free; to free; to redeem (*a property*); to stamp || *ref* to free oneself; to take heart

affrancatrice *f* postage meter

affrancatura *f* stamp, stamping

affràngere §179 *tr* to weary; (obs) to break down (*the spirit*)

affran·to -ta *adj* weary; broken down, broken-hearted

affratellaménto *m* fraternization

affratellare (**affratèllo**) *tr* to bind in brotherly love || *ref* to fraternize

affrescare §197 (**affrésco**) *tr* to fresco; to paint in fresco

affré·sco *m* (-schi) fresco
affrettare (affrétto) *tr & ref* to hurry, hasten
affretta· to -ta *adj* hurried
affrontare (affrónto) *tr* to face, confront ‖ *ref* to meet in combat; to come to blows
affronta·to -ta *adj*—**affrontati** (herald) combattant
affrónto *m* affront, offense
affumicare §197 (affùmico) *tr* to smoke; to blacken; to smoke out; to smoke (*meat or fish*)
affumica·to -ta *adj* smoked; dark (*glasses*)
affusolare [s] (affùsolo) *tr & ref* to taper
affusola·to -ta [s] *adj* tapered; slender
affusto *m* gun carriage
afga·no -na *adj & mf* Afghan
àfo·no -na *adj* voiceless
afori·sma *m* (-smi) aphorism
afó·so -sa [s] *adj* sultry
Africa, l' *f* Africa
africa·no -na *adj & mf* African
afrodisìa·co -ca *adj & m* (-ci -che) aphrodisiac
afta *m* mouth ulcer; **afta epizootica** (vet) foot-and-mouth disease
àgata *f* agate ‖ **Agata** *f* Agatha
agènda *f* notebook; agenda
agènte *adj* active ‖ *m* agent; broker; merchant; officer; **agente delle tasse** tax collector; **agente di cambio** stockbroker; money changer; **agente di commercio** broker, commission merchant; **agente di custodia** jailer; **agente di polizia** police officer, policeman; **agente di spionaggio** informer; **agente provocatore** agent provocateur
agenzia *f* agency; office, branch; **agenzia immobiliare** real-estate office
agevolare (agévolo) *tr* to facilitate, help
agevolazióne *f* facility; **agevolazione di pagamento** easy terms
agévole *adj* easy
agevolézza *f* facility
aggallare *intr* to come to the surface
agganciaménto *m* docking (*in space*); (rr) coupling
agganciare §128 *tr* to hook; (rr) to couple; (mil) to engage (*the enemy*)
aggàn·cio *m* (-ci) docking (*in space*); (rr) coupling
aggég·gio *m* (-gi) gadget
aggettivale *adj* adjectival
aggettivo *m* adjective
agghiacciaménto *m* freezing
agghiacciante *adj* hair-raising, frightful
agghiacciare §128 *tr* to freeze ‖ *ref* to freeze; to be horrified
agghiaccia·to -ta *adj* frozen, icy
agghindare *tr & ref* to preen, primp
àg·gio *m* (-gi) agio; **fare aggio to be at** a premium
aggiogare §209 (aggiógo) *tr* to yoke
aggiornaménto *m* adjournment (*e.g., of a meeting*); bringing up to date
aggiornare (aggiórno) *tr* to bring up to date; to adjourn ‖ *ref* to keep up with the times
aggiraménto *m* surrounding, outflanking
aggirare *tr* to surround, outflank; to swindle ‖ *ref* to roam, wander; **aggirarsi su** to approximate; to be almost
aggiudicare §197 (aggiùdico) *tr* to adjudicate, award ‖ *ref* to win
aggiudicazióne *f* adjudication, award
aggiùngere §183 *tr* to add; to join, connect ‖ *ref* to be added; to join
aggiunta *f* addition
aggiuntare *tr* to attach, join
aggiun·to -ta *adj & m* associate, assistant, deputy ‖ *f* see **aggiunta**
aggiustàbile *adj* repairable
aggiustaménto *m* settlement; adjustment; (mil) correction (*of fire*)
aggiustare *tr* to fix, repair; to adjust; (mil) to correct (*cannon fire*); **aggiustare per le feste** (coll) to fix; (coll) to give a good beating to ‖ *ref* (archaic) to come closer; (coll) to manage; (coll) to come to an agreement
aggiusta·tóre -trice *mf* repairer, fixer ‖ *m* repairman
aggiustatura *f* fixing, repairing, repair
agglomerare (agglòmero) *tr & ref* to pile up; to crowd together
agglomerato *m* built-up area; **agglomerato urbano** urban center
agglutinare (agglùtino) *tr & ref* to agglutinate
agglutinazióne *f* agglutination
aggobbire §176 *tr* to bend, bend over ‖ *intr* (ESSERE) *& ref* to hunch over
aggomitolare (aggomìtolo) *tr* to coil ‖ *ref* to curl up
aggradare *intr* (with *dat*) (poet) to please; **come Le aggrada** as you please
aggradire §176 *tr* to appreciate ‖ *intr* (poet) (with *dat*) to please
aggraffare *tr* to hook; to grab; to join (*metal sheets*) with a double seam; to stitch, staple
aggraffatrice *f* folding machine; (mach) can sealer
aggranchire §176 *tr* to benumb; to deaden, stupefy ‖ *intr* to become numb
aggrappare *tr* to grab; to clamp ‖ *ref* to cling
aggravaménto *m* aggravation
aggravante *adj* (law) aggravating (*circumstances*)
aggravare *tr* to aggravate; to overload (*e.g., one's stomach*) ‖ *ref* to get worse
aggrà·vio *m* (-vi) burden (*e.g., of taxes*); **fare aggravio a qlcu di qlco** to impute s.th to s.o.
aggraziare §287 *tr* to embellish; to render graceful ‖ *ref* to win, gain; to ingratiate oneself
aggrazia·to -ta *adj* graceful; polite
aggredire §176 *tr* to assail, attack, assault
aggregare §209 (aggrègo) *tr & ref* to join, unite
aggrega·to -ta *adj* adjunct ‖ *m* aggregation
aggressióne *f* aggression

aggressi·vo -va *adj* aggressive || *m* (mil) poison gas

aggressóre *m* aggressor

aggricciare §128 *tr* to wrinkle; (slang) to knit (*e.g., the brow*) || *ref* (poet) to shiver

aggrinzare *tr & ref* to wrinkle

aggrinzire §176 *tr & ref* var of aggrinzare

aggrondare (aggróndo) *tr* to knit (*the brow*)

aggrottare (aggròtto) *tr* to knit (*the brow*)

aggrovigliare §280 *tr* to tangle, entangle || *ref* to become entangled

aggrumare *tr & ref* to clot; to coagulate

aggruppare *tr* to group

agguagliare §280 *tr* to level; to equalize; to compare

agguantare *tr* to grab; to nab; (coll) to hit; agguantare per il collo to grab by the neck || *ref*—agguantarsi a to get hold of

agguato *m* ambush; cadere in un agguato to fall into a trap; stare in agguato to wait in ambush

agguerrire §176 *tr* to train for war; to inure to war; to inure

aghétto *m* shoestring; (mil) lanyard

agiatézza *f* comfort, wealth; vivere nell'agiatezza to live in comfort

agia·to -ta *adj* well-to-do, comfortable

àgile *adj* agile, nimble; prompt

agili·tà *f* (-tà) agility, nimbleness; promptness

à·gio *m* (-gi) comfort; opportunity; ease; agi conveniences, comforts; a Suo agio at your convenience; aver agio to have time; stare a proprio agio to feel at ease; to be comfortable; vivere negli agi to live comfortably

agiografia *f* hagiography

agiògrafo *m* hagiographer

agire §176 *intr* to act; to work; (theat) to act, perform

agitare (àgito) *tr* to agitate, shake; to stir; to stir up; to discuss (*e.g., a problem*) || *ref* to toss; to shake; to stir; to get excited

agita·to -ta *adj* rough, choppy (*sea*); troubled, upset || *mf* violently insane person

agita·tóre -trice *mf* agitator || *m* shaker

agitazióne *f* agitation

agli §4

agliàce·o -a *adj* garlicky

à·glio *m* (-gli) garlic

agnellino *m* little lamb, lambkin

agnèllo *m* lamb

agnizióne *f* recognition

agnòsti·co -ca *adj & mf* (-ci -che) agnostic

a·go *m* (-ghi) needle; pointer (*of scales*); stem (*of valve*)

agognare (agógno) *tr* to covet

agóne *m* contest; arena

agonìa *f* agony, death struggle; anguish

agonisti·co -ca *adj* (-ci -che) competitive, aggressive (*spirit*); athletic (*competition*) || *f* athletics

agonizzare [ddzz] *intr* to agonize, be in agony; (fig) to die out

agopuntura *f* acupuncture

ago·ràio *m* (-rài) needle case

agosta·no -na *adj* August, e.g., pomeriggio agostano August afternoon

agostinia·no -na *adj & m* Augustinian

agósto *m* August

agrà·rio -ria (-ri -rie) *adj & m* agrarian || *m* landlord || *f* agriculture

agrèste *adj* country

agrico·lo -la *adj* agricultural

agricoltóre *m* farmer; agriculturist

agricoltura *f* agriculture

agrifò·glio *m* (-gli) holly

agrimensóre *m* surveyor

agrimensura *f* surveying

a·gro -gra *adj* sour, bitter || *m* citrus juice; sourness, bitterness; surrounding country

agrodólce *adj* sweet and sour; (fig) acidulous (*tone*)

agronomìa *f* agronomy

agrònomo *m* agronomist

agrume *m* citrus (*tree and fruit*); agrumi citrus fruit

aguchiare §287 *intr* to knit or sew idly

agùglia *f* spire; top; (ichth) gar; (poet) eagle; (obs) needle

aguzzare *tr* to sharpen; to whet (*the appetite*)

aguzzino [ddzz] *m* slave driver; jailer

aguz·zo -za *adj* sharp, pointed

ah *interj* ah!, aha!; ha!

ahi *interj* ouch!

ahimè *interj* alas!

àia *f* yard, barnyard; threshing floor; governess || L'Aia *f* the Hague

Aiace *m* Ajax

àiola *f* lawn; flower bed

àire *m* push; short run (*preparing for a jump*); dare l'aire a to start off; prendere l'aire to take off

airóne *m* heron

aitante *adj* robust, stalwart

aiuòla *f* (poet) var of aiola

aiutante *adj* helping || *mf* assistant || *m* (mil) adjutant; aiutante di campo aide-de-camp; aiutante di sanità orderly

aiutare *tr* to help || *ref* to strive; to help oneself; to help one another

aiutato *m* first assistant (*e.g., of a surgeon*)

aiuto *m* aid, help; assistant; first assistant (*of a surgeon*)

aizzare (aìzzo) *tr* to incite, to incite to riot; to sic (*a dog*)

al §4

a·la *f* (-li & -le) wing; sail, vane (*of windmill*); blade (*e.g., of fan*); brim (*of hat*); (football) end; ala a freccia backswept wing; ala di popolo throng; fare ala a to line up along

alabarda *f* halberd

alabardière *m* halberdier

alabastri·no -na *adj* alabaster; white as alabaster

alabastro *m* alabaster

àlacre *adj* eager, lively

alacrità *f* alacrity

alàg·gio *m* (-gi) hauling, towing
alamaro *m* braid, gimp
alambic·co *m* (-chi) still
alano *m* Great Dane
alare *adj* wing (*e.g., span*) || *m* andiron || *tr* to haul
Alasca, l' *f* Alaska
ala·to -ta *adj* winged, sublime
alba *f* dawn, daybreak
albagìa *f* haughtiness
albanése [s] *adj & mf* Albanian
Albanìa, l' *f* Albania
àlbatro *m* (orn) albatross
albeggiamento *m* dawning
albeggiare §290 (albéggio) *intr* (ESSERE) to dawn; (poet) to sparkle (*said, e.g., of ice*) || *impers* (ESSERE)—albeggia the day dawns
alberare (àlbero) *tr* to plant (*trees*); to reforest; to hoist (*a mast*); to mast (*a ship*)
albera·to -ta *adj* tree-lined; (naut) masted
alberèllo *m* small tree; apothecary's jar
albergare §209 (albèrgo) *tr* to lodge; to put up at a hotel; (fig) to harbor || *intr* to lodge; to put up
alberga·tóre -trice *mf* hotelkeeper
alberghiè·ro -ra *adj* hotel
albèr·go *m* (-ghi) hotel; refuge; hospitality; albergo diurno day hostel; albergo per la gioventù youth hostel
àlbero *m* tree; poplar; (mach) shaft; (naut) mast; albero a camme (aut) camshaft; albero a gomito (aut) crankshaft; albero di distribuzione (aut) camshaft; albero di Natale Christmas tree; albero di trasmissione (aut) transmission; albero genealogico family tree
albicòc·ca *f* (-che) apricot
albicòc·co *m* (-chi) apricot tree
al·bo -ba *adj* (poet) white || *m* album; bulletin board; (law) roll; comic book; albo d'onore honor roll || *f* see alba
albóre *m* (poet) whiteness; (poet) dawn
album *m* (album) album, scrapbook
albume *m* albumen
albumina *f* albumin
àlca·li *m* (-li) alkali
alcali·no -na *adj* alkaline
alce *m* moose; elk
alchimìa *f* alchemy
alchimi·sta *m* (-sti) alchemist
alcióne *m* halcyon
alciò·nio -nia *adj* (-ni -nie) halcyon
àlco·le *m* alcohol
alcolici·tà *f* (-tà) alcoholic content
alcòli·co -ca *adj* (-ci -che) alcoholic || *m* alcoholic beverage
alcolismo *m* alcoholism
alcolizzare [ddzz] *tr* to intoxicate || *ref* to become intoxicated
alcolizza·to -ta [ddzz] *adj* intoxicated || *mf* alcoholic
alcool *m* (alcool) var of alcole
alcoolici·tà *f* (-tà) var of alcolicità
alcòoli·co -ca (-ci -che) *adj & m* var of alcolico
alcoolismo *m* var of alcolismo
alcoolizzare [ddzz] *tr* var of alcolizzare

alcoolizza·to -ta [ddzz] *adj & mf* var of alcolizzato
alcòva *f* bedroom; bed; alcove
alcunché *pron* something, anything
alcu·no -na *adj & pron* some; alcuni -ne some; quite a few, several, a good many
aldilà *m* life beyond, afterlife
àlea *f* chance, hazard; correre l'alea to try one's luck
aleggiare §290 (aléggio) *intr* to flutter; to flap the wings; to hover
aleróne *m* var of alettone
alesàg·gio *m* (-gi) (mach) bore
alesare (alèso) *tr* (mach) to bore
alesatóre *m* reamer
alesatrice *s* boring machine
Alessandria d'Egitto *f* Alexandria
alessandri·no -na *adj & mf* Alexandrian || *m* Alexandrine (*verse*)
Alessandro *m* Alexander; Alessandro Magno Alexander the Great
alétta *f* small wing; fin (*of fish*); (aer) tab; aletta di compensazione trim tab; aletta parasole (aut) sun visor
alettóne *m* (aer) aileron, flap
Aleuti·no -na *adj*—Isole Aleutine Aleutian Islands
al·fa *m* (-fa) alpha || *f* esparto
alfabèti·co -ca *adj* (-ci -che) alphabetical
alfabetizzazióne [ddzz] *f* teaching to read; learning to read
alfabèto *m* alphabet; code (*e.g., Morse*)
alfière *m* flagbearer, standardbearer; (chess) bishop
alfine *adv* finally, at last
al·ga *f* (-ghe) alga; alga marina seaweed
àlgebra *f* algebra
algèbri·co -ca *adj* (-ci -che) algebraic
Algèri *f* Algiers
Algerìa, l' *f* Algeria
algeri·no -na *adj & mf* Algerian
aliante *m* (aer) glider
alianti·sta *m* (-sti -ste) glider pilot
àli·bi *m* (-bi) alibi
alice *f* anchovy
alienàbile *adj* alienable
alienare (alièno) *tr* to alienate; to transfer, convey || *ref*—alienarsi dalla ragione to go out of one's mind
aliena·to -ta *adj* alienated || *mf* insane person; dispossessed person
alienazióne *f* alienation
alieni·sta *mf* (-sti -ste) alienist
alièno -na *adj* disinclined; (poet) foreign, alien
alimentare *adj* alimentary || alimentari *mpl* food, foodstuff || *v* (alimento) *tr* to feed; to fuel
alimentari·sta *m* (-sti) food merchant; food-industry worker
alimenta·tóre -trice *mf* stoker || *m* (mach) stoker, feeder
alimentazióne *f* nourishment; feeding; (mil) loading; alimentazione artificiale intravenous feeding
aliménto *m* food, nourishment; feed; alimenti alimony (*maintenance*)
alimònia *f* alimony
alìnea *f* (law) paragraph, section

aliquota *f* share; parcel, quota

aliscafo *m* hydrofoil

alisè·o **-a** *adj* trade (*wind*) || *m* trade wind

alitare (**àlito**) *intr* to breathe; to blow gently; **non alitare** to not breathe a word

àlito *m* breath; (fig) breeze

alìvo·lo **-la** *adj* (poet) winged; (fig) swift

alla §4

allacciaménto *m* binding; connection, linking

allacciare §128 *tr* to bind, tie; to connect; to buckle; (fig) to deceive

allacciatura *f* lacing; buckling

allagare §209 *tr* to flood, overflow

allampana·to **-ta** *adj* tall and lean, lanky

allargare §209 *tr* to broaden, widen; **allargare la mano** to be lenient; to be liberal; **allargare il freno** to give free rein || *ref* to widen, spread out; **mi si allarga il cuore** I feel relieved

allargatura *f* widening

allarmante *adj* alarming

allarmare *tr* to alarm || *ref* to worry, become alarmed

allarme *m* alarm; **allarme aereo** air-raid warning; **cessato allarme** all clear; **falso allarme** false alarm; **stare in allarme** to be alarmed

allascare §197 *tr* (naut) to ease, slacken (*a rope*)

allato *adv* (poet) near; **allato a** near; beside; in comparison with

allattaménto *m* nursing, feeding; **allattamento artificiale** bottle feeding

allattare *tr* to nurse (*at the breast*); to feed (*with a bottle*)

alle §4

alleanza *f* alliance

alleare (**allèo**) *tr* to ally || *ref* to become allied; to be connected

allea·to **-ta** *adj* allied || *mf* ally

allegare §209 (**allégo**) *tr* to enclose; to adduce; to allege; **allegare i denti** to set the teeth on edge || *intr* (hort) to ripen

allega·to **-ta** *adj* enclosed || *m* enclosure

alleggeriménto *m* lightening, easing

alleggerire §176 *tr* to lighten; to alleviate || *ref* to put on lighter clothes; **alleggerirsi di** (naut) to jettison

allegoria *f* allegory

allegòri·co **-ca** *adj* (**-ci -che**) allegorical

allegraménte *adv* cheerfully, merrily; thoughtlessly

allegrézza *f* joy, cheerfulness

allegria *f* cheer, gaiety; **stare in allegria** to be merry || *interj* good cheer!

allé·gro **-gra** *adj* cheerful, merry, gay || *m* (mus) allegro

allelùia *m* hallelujah

allenaménto *m* training

allenare (**allèno**) *tr* & *ref* to train

allena·tóre **-trice** *adj* training || *mf* trainer, coach

allentare (**allènto**) *tr* to loosen, slacken; to mitigate; (coll) to deliver (*a blow*); **essere allentato** to have a hernia || *ref* to slow up; to loosen up; to diminish

allergìa *f* allergy

allèrgi·co **-ca** *adj* (**-ci -che**) allergic

allérta *f* alert || *adv* alert, on the alert

allessare (**allésso**) *tr* to boil

allés·so **-sa** *adj* boiled || *m* boiled meat, boiled beef

allestire §176 *tr* to prepare, make ready; to rig (*e.g., a ship*); to produce (*e.g., a play*)

allettaménto *m* allure, fascination

allettante *adj* alluring, enticing

allettare (**allètto**) *tr* to allure, entice; to confine to bed; to bend (*plants*) to the ground || *ref* to be confined to bed

allevaménto *m* raising; breeding; flock

allevare (**allèvo**) *tr* to raise, breed; to rear

alleva·tóre **-trice** *mf* raiser, breeder

alleviare §287 (**allèvio**) *tr* to alleviate, lighten

allibire §176 *intr* (ESSERE) to turn pale; to be astonished, be dismayed

allibraménto *m* registration, entry; booking (*of bets*)

allibrare *tr* to register, enter; to book (*a bet*) on a horse

allibratóre *m* bookmaker (*at races*)

allietare (**allièto**) *tr* to cheer, enliven

alliè·vo **-va** *mf* pupil, student; follower, disciple || *m* trainee; **allievo ufficiale** cadet

alligatóre *m* alligator

allignare *intr* to take root; to do well, prosper

allineaménto *m* alignment; falling in line

allineare (**allineo**) *tr* to align; (typ) to justify || *ref* to align oneself, be aligned

allinea·to **-ta** *adj* aligned; **non allineato** nonaligned, uncommitted

allitterazióne *f* alliteration

allo §4

allòc·co *m* (**-chi**) horned owl; (fig) dolt, nincompoop

allocu·tóre **-trice** *mf* (poet) speaker

allocuzióne *f* (poet) speech, address

allòdola *f* lark, skylark

allogare §209 (**allògo**) *tr* to place; to let, lease; to find employment for; to invest (*money*); to marry off (*a daughter*)

allòge·no **-na** *adj* minority || *mf* member of an ethnic minority

alloggiaménto *m* (mil) lodging, quarters; (carp, mach) housing

alloggiare §290 (**allòggio**) *tr* to lodge, put up || *intr* to lodge, stay

allòg·gio *m* (**-gi**) lodging, living quarters; accommodations

allontanaménto *m* removal; estrangement

allontanare *tr* to remove; to send away; to exonerate; to dismiss; to alienate || *ref* to go away; to withdraw; to become estranged

allóra *adj* then || *adv* then; at that time; in that case; **da allora** ever since; **da allora in poi** from that time on; **fino allora** until then; **per allora** at that time

allorché *conj* when

allòro *m* laurel; **riposare sugli allori** to rest on one's laurels

allorquando *conj* (poet) when

àlluce *m* big toe

allucinante *adj* hallucinating; dazzling; deceptive

allucinare (**allùcino**) *tr* to hallucinate; to dazzle; to deceive

allucinazióne *f* hallucination

allùdere §105 *intr* to allude

allume *m* alum

alluminare (**allùmino**) *tr* to illuminate (*a manuscript*); (poet) to light

allumìnio *m* aluminum

allunàg·gio *m* (**-gi**) lunar landing; **allunaggio morbido** soft lunar landing

allunare *intr* to land on the moon

allunga *f* (mach) adapter

allungàbile *adj* extensible; extension (*table*)

allungaménto *m* lengthening

allungare §209 *tr* to lengthen; to stretch out (*e.g., the hand*); to dilute (*e.g., wine*); (coll) to deliver (*e.g., a slap*); (sports) to pass (*the ball*); **allungare il collo** to crane the neck; **allungare il passo** to walk faster || *ref* to grow longer; to stretch; to grow taller

allun·go *m* (**-ghi**) (sports) sprint; (sports) forward pass

allusióne *f* allusion

alluvióne *m* flood

almanaccare §197 *tr* to dream of || *intr* to dream, muse

almanac·co *m* (**-chi**) almanac

almèno *adv* at least; if only

aino *m* (bot) alder

àloe *m* & *f* aloe

alògeno *m* halogen

alogenuro *m* halide

alóne *m* halo

alòsa *f* (ichth) shad

alpacca *f* German silver

alpe *f* high mountain, alp || **le Alpi** the Alps

alpèstre *adj* mountainous; (fig) uncouth

alpigia·no **-na** *adj* mountain, mountainous; (fig) uncouth || *mf* mountaineer

alpinismo *m* mountain climbing

alpini·sta *mf* (**-sti** **-ste**) mountain climber

alpinìsti·co **-ca** *adj* (**-ci** **-che**) mountain-climbing

alpi·no **-na** *adj* alpine; Alpine || *m* alpine soldier

alquan·to **-ta** *adj* & *pron* some; **alquanti** **-te** some; quite a few, several, a good many || **alquanto** *adv* somewhat, rather

Alsàzia, l' *f* Alsace

alsazia·no **-na** *adj* & *mf* Alsacian

alt *m* (alt) halt, stop || *interj* halt!, stop!

altaléna *f* seesaw; swing; (fig) ups and downs; **altalena a bìlico** seesaw; **altalena sospesa** swing

altalenare (**altaléno**) *intr* to seesaw; to swing

altana *f* roof terrace

altare *m* altar

altarino *m* small altar; **svelare gli alta-**

rini (joc) to expose the skeleton in the closet

altèa *f* marsh mallow

alterare (**àltero**) *tr* to alter; to falsify; to adulterate; to anger || *ref* to alter; to become adulterated; to get angry

altera·to **-ta** *adj* altered; adulterated; feverish; angry

alterazióne *f* change, alteration; adulteration; slight fever

altercare §197 (**altèrco**) *intr* to dispute, quarrel

altèr·co *m* (**-chi**) altercation; **venire a un alterco** to get into a quarrel

alterìgia *f* haughtiness

alternare (**altèrno**) *tr* & *ref* to alternate

alternati·vo **-va** *adj* alternating || *f* alternative; choice

alterna·to **-ta** *adj* alternate; alternating (*current*)

alternatóre *m* (elec) alternator

altèr·no **-na** *adj* alternate

altè·ro **-ra** *adj* proud, haughty

altézza *f* height; width (*of cloth*); depth (*of water*); pitch (*of sound*); (astr, geom) altitude; (fig) loftiness, nobility; (naut) latitude; (typ) size; **essere all'altezza di** to be up to, be equal to; (naut) to be off || **Altezza** *f* Highness

altezzó·so **-sa** [s] *adj* haughty

altic·cio **-cia** *adj* (**-ci** **-ce**) tipsy

altìmetro *m* altimeter

altipiano *m* var of **altopiano**

altisonante [s] *adj* high-sounding

altìssi·mo **-ma** *adj* very high, highest || **l'Altìssimo** *m* the Most High

altitùdine *f* altitude

al·to **-ta** *adj* high; tall; wide (*cloth*); deep (*water*); upper; full (*day*); late (*e.g., Easter*); deep (*sleep*); early (*Middle Ages*); loud (*voice*); lofty (*peak*) || *m* top; upper part; high quarters; **alti e bassi** ups and downs; **fare alto e basso** to be the undisputed boss; **guardare qlcu dall'alto in basso** to look down one's nose at s.o.; **in alto** up || **alto** *adv* up

altofórno *m* (altifórni) blast furnace

altoloca·to **-ta** *adj* high-placed, high-ranking

altoparlante *m* loudspeaker

altopiano *m* (altipiani) plateau

altrettan·to **-ta** *adj* & *pron* as much; the same; **altrettanti** **-te** as many || **altrettanto** *adv* as much; the same

altri *indef pron invar* someone; someone else; **non altri che** no one else but

altrièri *m* & *adv* day before yesterday

altriménti *adv* otherwise

al·tro **-tra** *adj* other; next (*world*); **altro ieri** day before yesterday; **chi altro?** who else?; **domani l'altro** the day after tomorrow; **fra l'altro** among other things; **ieri l'altro** the day before yesterday; **l'altro anno** last year; **l'altro giorno** the other day; **noi altri** we; **qualcun altro** somebody else; anybody else; **quest'altro** (**giorno, mese, anno**) next (day, month, year) || *pron* other; anything else; **altro che!** why yes! || **l'altro §11** correlative indef pron || **l'altro §12** reciprocal pron

altrónde adv (poet) somewhere else; **d'altronde** besides; on the other hand

altróve adv elsewhere, somewhere else

altrui adj invar somebody else's, other people's || pron invar somebody else || **m—l'altrui** what belongs to someone else

altrui·sta (-sti -ste) adj altruistic || mf altruist

altura f height; (naut) high seas

alun·no -na mf pupil, student

alveare m beehive

àlveo m bed (of a river)

alvèolo m alveolus; socket (of tooth); cell (of honeycomb)

alzabandiè·ra m (-ra) raising of the flag

alzacristal·li m (-li) (aut) crank (to raise a window)

alzàia f tow line; towpath

alzare tr to lift, raise; to cut (cards); to shrug (one's shoulders); to set (sail); **alzare al cielo** to praise to the sky; **alzare i tacchi** to show a clean pair of heels; **alzare la cresta** to get cocky || ref to rise; to get up; **alzarsi in piedi** to stand up

alzata f raising, lifting; shrugging (of shoulders); standing up; riser (of step); three-tier candy tray; **alzata di scudi** rebellion; **alzata di testa** whim, caprice

alzavàlvo·le m (-le) (aut) valve lifter

alzo m gunsight

amàbile adj amiable; sweetish (wine)

amabili·tà f (-tà) amiability, kindness

ama·ca f (-che) hammock

amàlga·ma m (-mi) amalgam

amalgamare (amàlgamo) tr to amalgamate || ref to amalgamate; to blend

amalgamazióne f amalgamation

amante adj loving, fond || m lover || f mistress

amanuènse m amanuensis, scribe

amare tr to love; to like || ref to love one another

amareggiare §290 (amaréggio) tr to make bitter; to sadden || ref to become bitter; to sadden

amarèna f sour cherry

amarétto m macaroon

amarézza f bitterness

ama·ro -ra adj bitter || m bitters; bitterness

amarógno·lo -la adj bitterish

amarra f (naut) hawser

amarrare tr & intr var of **ammarrare**

ama·tóre -trice mf lover; amateur

amatò·rio -ria adj (-ri -rie) amatory, of love

amàzzone [ddzz] f horsewoman; female jockey; (obs) riding habit; **cavalcare all'amazzone** to ride sidesaddle || **Amazzone** f (myth) Amazon

ambage f winding path; **ambagi** circumlocutions; **senz'ambagi** without beating about the bush

ambascerìa f embassy

ambà·scia f (-sce) shortness of breath; grief, sorrow

ambasciata f embassy; ambassadorship; errand, mission

ambasciatóre m ambassador

ambasciatrice f ambassadress

ambedùe adj invar—**ambedue i** or **le** both || pron invar both

ambiare §287 intr to amble, pace (said of a horse)

ambiatura f pacing (said of a horse)

ambidè·stro -stra adj ambidextrous

ambidùe adj & pron invar var of **ambedue**

ambientare (ambiènto) tr to accustom; to place (a story in a certain period) || ref to get accustomed to one's surroundings; to orient oneself

ambienta·tóre -trice mf interior decorator; (theat) decorator

ambiènte adj room, e.g., **temperatura ambiente** room temperature || m environment; habitat; milieu; room; **trovarsi fuori del proprio ambiente** to be out of one's element

ambigui·tà f (-tà) ambiguity

ambi·guo -gua adj ambiguous

àm·bio m (-bi) amble, pacing

ambire §176 tr to be eager for || intr to be ambitious; **ambire a** to be ambitious for

àmbito m range, circle; (mus) range; **nell'ambito di** within

ambizióne f ambition

ambizió·so -sa [s] adj ambitious || mf ambitious person

ambo or **am·bi -be** adj pl—**ambo i, ambo le, ambi i, ambe le** both

ambosèssi adj invar of both sexes, e.g., **giovani ambosessi** young people of both sexes

ambra f amber; **ambra grigia** ambergris

ambròsia f ambrosia; (bot) ragweed

ambulante adj itinerant; circulating; ambulant || m mail car

ambulanza f ambulance

ambulare (àmbulo) intr (coll) to ambulate

ambulatò·rio -ria (-ri -rie) adj ambulatory || m clinic, first-aid department

Amburgo m Hamburg

amèba f amoeba

a·men m (-men) amen || interj amen!

ameni·tà f (-tà) f amenity; pleasantry

amèno -na adj pleasant, agreeable; amusing (fellow)

Amèrica, l' f America; **l'America del Nord** North America; **l'America del Sud** South America

americana f bicycle race between pairs

americanismo m Americanism

americanizzare [ddzz] tr to Americanize || ref to become Americanized

america·no -na adj & mf American || m vermouth with bitters || f see **americana**

ametista f amethyst

amianto m asbestos

amicale adj (poet) friendly

amichévole adj friendly; (sports) noncompetitive

amicìzia f friendship; **stringere amicizia con** to make friends with ami·co -ca (-ci -che) adj friendly || mf friend; beloved || m boy friend; lover, paramour; amico del cuore bosom friend || f girl friend; mistress

amidàce·o -a adj starchy

amidatura f starching

àmido m starch

Amlèto m Hamlet

ammaccare §197 tr to crush; to pound; to bruise; to dent

ammaccatura f bruise; dent

ammaestraménto m instruction, teaching; training

ammaestrare (ammaèstro & ammaéstro) tr to teach, to educate; to train (animals)

ammainare (ammàino) tr to lower (e.g., a flag)

ammalare intr (ESSERE) to fall ill || ref to fall ill; ammalarsi di to come down with

ammala·to -ta adj ill, sick || mf patient

ammaliare §287 tr to cast a spell on; to charm, enchant, fascinate; to bewitch

ammalia·tóre -trice adj charming, enchanting || mf charmer || m enchanter, sorcerer || f enchantress, sorceress

amman·co m (-chi) shortage

ammanettare (ammanétto) tr to handcuff

ammaniglia·to -ta adj shackled; (fig) closely bound, closely tied

ammannare tr to sheave (grain)

ammannire §176 tr to prepare (a dish); to dish up (a meal)

ammansare tr & ref var of ammansire

ammansa·tóre -trice mf (poet) tamer

ammansire §176 tr to tame; to calm || ref to become tamed; to calm down

ammantare tr to mantle, clothe; to cover; to hide (the truth)

ammanto m mantle, cloak; (fig) authority

ammaràg·gio m (-gi) landing on water; splashdown (of a space vehicle)

ammaraménto m var of ammaraggio

ammarare intr (aer) to land on water; (rok) to splash down

ammarrare tr (naut) to moor

ammassare tr to amass || ref to crowd, throng

ammasso m heap, pile; cluster (of stars); government stockpile

ammattiménto m worry, nuisance

ammattire §176 intr (ESSERE) to go crazy; fare ammattire to drive crazy

ammattonare (ammattóno) tr to floor with bricks

ammattona·to -ta adj floored with bricks || m brick floor; bricklaying

ammazzare tr to kill || ref to kill oneself; to get killed

ammazzasèt·te m (-te) braggart

ammazza·tóio m (-tói) slaughterhouse

ammènda f fine; satisfaction (for injury); fare ammenda to make amends

ammendaménto m emendation: improvement (of land)

ammendare (ammèndo) tr to emendate; to improve (land)

ammennìcolo m excuse; trifle; ammennicoli extras

ammés·so -sa adj admitted; ammesso che supposing that; ammesso e non concesso for the sake of argument

amméttere §198 tr to admit; to accept, suppose

ammezzare [ddzz] (ammèzzo) tr to leave half-finished (a piece of work); to fill halfway; to empty halfway

ammezzato [ddzz] m mezzanine

ammiccare §197 intr to wink; to cock one's eye

amministrare tr to administer, manage

amministra·tóre -trice mf administrator, manager; amministratore delegato chairman of the board

amministrazióne f administration, management: ordinaria amministrazione run-of-the-mill business

ammiràbile adj admirable

ammiràglia f (nav) flagship

ammiragliato m admiralty

ammirà·glio m (-gli) admiral; ammiraglio d'armata admiral; ammiraglio di divisione rear admiral; ammiraglio di squadra vice admiral; grande ammiraglio admiral of the fleet

ammirare tr to admire || intr to wonder

ammirati·vo -va adj admiring; exclamation (mark)

ammira·tóre -trice mf admirer || m suitor

ammirazióne f admiration

ammirévole adj admirable

ammissibile adj admissible; permissible

ammissióne f admission; (mach) intake; ammissione comune consensus

ammobiliaménto m furnishing; furniture

ammobiliare §287 tr to furnish

ammodernare (ammodèrno) tr to modernize

ammòdo adj invar well-mannered, polite || adv properly

ammogliare §280 (ammóglio) tr to marry, give in marriage || ref to marry, get married

ammoglia·to adj married || m married man

ammollare (ammòllo) tr to soften; to soak; to slacken (e.g., a hawser); to deliver (a slap) || ref to get soaked

ammollire §176 tr to soften; to weaken || ref to soften; to mellow

ammonìaca f ammonia

ammoniménto m warning

ammonire §176 tr to admonish, reprimand

ammoni·tóre -trice adj warning

ammonizióne f admonition, warning

ammontare m amount, total || v (ammónto) tr to pile up || intr (ESSERE) to amount

ammonticchiare §287 tr to pile up, heap up

ammorbare (ammòrbo) tr to infect, contaminate

ammorbidènte m softener

ammorbidire §176 tr to soften; to mitigate || ref to soften

ammortaménto m amortization; payment, redemption (of a loan)

ammortare (ammòrto) *tr* to amortize

ammortire §176 *tr* to deaden; to weaken, soften

ammortizzaménto [ddzz] *m* amortization, amortizement

ammortizzare [ddzz] *tr* to amortize; (aut) to absorb (*shocks*)

ammortizzatóre [ddzz] *m* (aut) shock absorber

ammosciare §128 (ammóscio) *tr, intr & ref* var of **ammoscire**

ammoscia·to -ta *adj* (coll) downcast

ammoscire §176 *tr* to make sag; to make flabby || *intr & ref* to sag; to become flabby; to droop

ammucchiare §287 *tr* to heap up, pile up || *ref* to crowd together

ammuffire §176 *intr* (ESSERE) to become moldy

ammusare *tr & intr* to nuzzle

ammutinaménto *m* mutiny, riot

ammutinare (ammùtino & ammutino) *tr* to incite to riot || *ref* to mutiny

ammutinato *m* mutineer

ammutolire §176 *intr* (ESSERE) to become silent; to be dumfounded

amnesìa *f* amnesia

amnistìa *f* amnesty

amnistiare §287 or §119 *tr* to amnesty

amo *m* hook; **abboccare all'amo** to bite, to swallow the hook

amorale *adj* immoral; amoral

amorali·tà *f* (-tà) immorality; amorality

amóre *m* love; eagerness; **amor proprio** amour-propre, self-esteem; **con amore** with pleasure; **d'amore e d'accordo** in perfect agreement; **fare all'amore** to make love; **fare l'amore** to flirt; **per amor del cielo** for heaven's sake; **per amore di** for the sake of; **un amore di bambino** a charming child; **un amore di cappello** a darling hat

amoreggiare §290 (amoréggio) *intr* to flirt; to play around

amorévole *adj* loving; kindly

amòr·fo -fa *adj* amorphous; safety (*match*)

amorino *m* cupid; cute child; love seat; (bot) mignonette

amoró·so -sa [s] *adj* loving; kindly; amorous; love (*e.g., life*) || *mf* lover || *m* fiancé || *f* fiancée

amovibile *adj* removable

amperàg·gio *m* (-gi) amperage

ampère *m* ampere

amperòmetro *m* ammeter

amperóra *m* ampere-hour

ampiézza *f* width, breadth; trajectory (*of a missile*); amplitude; **ampiezza di vedute** open-mindedness

àm·pio -pia *adj* (-pî -pie) ample; wide; roomy

amplèsso *m* (poet) embrace

ampliaménto *m* amplification, extension

ampliare §287 *tr* to enlarge, widen || *ref* to widen

amplificare §197 (amplìfico) *tr* to amplify; to widen; to exaggerate

amplifica·tóre *m* (rad & telv) amplifier

amplificazióne *f* amplification

amplitùdine *f* amplitude

ampólla *f* cruet; (eccl) ampulla

ampollièra *f* cruet stand

ampollosi·tà [s] *f* (-tà) grandiloquence, turgidity

ampolló·so -sa [s] *adj* grandiloquent, turgid

amputare (àmputo) *tr* to amputate

amputazióne *f* amputation

amulèto *m* amulet, charm

anabbagliante *m* (aut) low beam; **anabbaglianti** (aut) dimmers

anacàr·dio *m* (-di) cashew

ànace *m* var of **anice**

anacorè·ta *m* (-ti) anchorite, hermit

anacronismo *m* anachronism

anacronìsti·co -ca *adj* (-ci -che) anachronistic(al)

anàgrafe *m* bureau of vital statistics; registry of births, deaths, and marriages

anagram·ma *m* (-mi) anagram

analcòli·co -ca (-ci -che) *adj* nonalcoholic; soft (*drink*) || *m* soft drink

analfabè·ta *mf* (-ti -te) illiterate

analfabèti·co -ca *adj* (-ci -che) unalphabetized, unalphabetic

analfabetismo *m* illiteracy

analgèsi·co -ca *adj & m* (-ci -che) analgesic

anàli·si *f* (-si) analysis; breakdown; **analisi grammaticale** parsing; **analisi dell'urina** urinalysis

anali·sta *mf* (-sti -ste) analyst; **analista finanziario** financial analyst; **analista tempi e metodi** efficiency expert, efficiency engineer

analìti·co -ca *adj* (-ci -che) analytic(al)

analizzare [ddzz] *tr* to analyze; to assay (*ores*); (telv) to scan

analogìa *f* analogy

anàlo·go -ga *adj* (-ghi -ghe) analogous; similar

anamnè·si *f* (-si) (med) case history

ananasso *m* pineapple

anarchìa *f* anarchy

anàrchi·co -ca (-ci -che) *adj* anarchical || *m* anarchist

anatè·ma or **anàte·ma** *m* (-mi) anathema

anatomìa *f* anatomy

anatòmi·co -ca *adj* (-ci -che) anatomic(al)

ànatra *f* duck; drake

anatròccolo *m* duckling

an·ca *f* (-che) hip; (coll) thigh (*e.g., of a chicken*); **dare d'anche** to run away; **menare anca** to walk

ancèlla *f* maidservant

ancestrale *adj* ancestral

anche *adv* also, too; even; (poet) yet; **anche a** + *inf* even if + *ind*

anchilosare (anchilòso) *tr* to paralyze || *ref* to become paralyzed

anchilòsto·ma *m* (-mi) hookworm

àn·cia *f* (-ce) (mus) reed

ancillare *adj* servant

ancóra *adv* still, yet; again; more e.g., **ancóra cinque minuti** five minutes more

àncora *f* anchor; keeper (*of magnet*); armature (*of buzzer or electric bell*); **ancora di salvezza** last hope; **gettar l'ancora** to cast anchor; **salpare** or **levar l'ancora** to weigh anchor

ancoràg·gio *m* (-gi) anchorage, berth

ancorare (àncoro) *tr* to anchor; to tie (e.g., *a currency to gold*) || *ref* to anchor; to hold fast

ancorché *conj* although

andalu·so -sa *adj & mf* Andalusian

andaménto *m* course, progress

andante *adj* ordinary, common; continuous

andare *m* going; gait; **a lungo andare** in the long run || §106 *intr* (ESSERE) to go; to spread (*said of news*); to be (e.g., *proud*); to work (*said of machinery*); (with *dat*) to fit, e.g., **quel vestito non gli va** that suit does not fit him; (with *dat*) to please, e.g. **quel vestito non le va** that dress does not please her; **andare a cavallo** to go horseback riding; **andare a finire** to wind up; **andare a male** to spoil; **andare a picco** to sink; **andare d'accordo** to agree; **andare in cerca di** to seek; **andare in macchina** to be in press; **andare in onda** (rad & telv) to go on the air; **andare per i vent'anni** to be bordering on twenty years; **andare pazzo per** to be crazy about; **andare soldato** to be drafted; **andare via** to go away; **come va?** how are things?; **mi va il vino dolce** I like sweet wine; **ne va della vita** life is at stake; **va da sé** it goes without saying || *ref*—**andarsene** to go away, leave

anda·to -ta *adj* gone, past; finished; (coll) spoiled (e.g., *meat*) || *f* going; journey, trip; **a lunga andata** in the long run; **andata e ritorno** round trip; **dare l'andata a** to give the go-ahead to

andatura *f* gait; pace; **fare l'andatura** to set the pace

andazzo *m* bad practice, bad habit; fad

Ande, le the Andes

andicappare *tr* to handicap

andi·no -na *adj* Andean

andirivie·ni *m* (-ni) coming and going; maze; ado

àndito *m* corridor, hallway

andróne *m* hall, lobby

aneddòti·co -ca *adj* (-ci -che) anecdotal

anèddoto *m* anecdote

anelante *adj* panting

anelare (anèlo) *tr* to long for || *intr* to yearn; (poet) to pant

anèlito *m* last breath; yearning; (poet) panting; **mandare l'ultimo anelito** to breathe one's last

anellino *m* ringlet

anèllo *m* ring; link (*of a chain*); traffic circle; segment (*of a worm*); (sports) track; **ad anello** ring-shaped; **anello di congiunzione** (fig) link; **anello di fidanzamento** engagement ring || **anella** *fpl* (poet) ringlets; (archaic) rings

anemia *f* anemia

anèmi·co -ca *adj* (-ci -che) anemic

anestesìa *f* anesthesia

anestesi·sta *mf* (-sti -ste) anesthetist

anestèti·co -ca *adj & m* (-ci -che) anesthetic

anestetizzare [ddzz] *tr* to anesthetize

aneuri·sma *m* (-smi) aneurysm

anfì·bio -bia (-bi -bie) *adj* amphibian; (fig) ambiguous || *m* amphibian

anfiteatro *m* amphitheater

anfitrióne *m* (lit) generous host

anfratto *m* ravine; narrow, winding, rugged spot

anfrattuosi·tà [s] *f* (-tà) rough broken ground; winding, rough spot

anfrattuó·so -sa [s] *adj* winding, rough, craggy

angariare §287 *tr* to pester, oppress

angèli·co -ca *adj* (-ci -che) angelic(al)

àngelo *m* angel; **angelo custode** guardian angel

angherìa *f* vexation; outrage; imposition

angina *f* quinsy; **angina pectoris** angina pectoris

angipòrto *m* blind alley; narrow lane

anglica·no -na *adj & mf* Anglican

anglicismo *m* Anglicism

anglicizzare [ddzz] *tr* to Anglicize || *ref* to become Anglicized

anglòfo·no -na *adj* English-speaking || *m* English-speaking person

anglosàssone *adj & mf* Anglo-Saxon

angolare *adj* angular; corner (*stone*) || *m* angle iron || *v* (àngolo) *tr* to take an angle shot of; (sports) to kick (*the ball*) into the corner of the goal

angolazióne *f* (mov) angle shot

angolièra *f* corner shelving; corner cupboard

àngolo *m* angle; corner

angoló·so -sa [s] *adj* angular

àngora *f* Angora cat; Angora goat

angó·scia *f* (-sce) anxiety, distress, anguish

angosciare §128 (angòscio) *tr* to distress

angoscia·to -ta *adj* tormented, distressed

angoscció·so -sa [s] *adj* agonizing

anguilla *f* eel

anguillé·sco -sca *adj* (-schi -sche) as slippery as an eel

angùria *f* watermelon

angùstia *f* narrowness; scarcity; **stare in angustia** to be worried

angustiare §287 *tr* to distress, grieve || *ref* to worry

angu·sto -sta *adj* narrow

ànice *m* anise

anicino *m* anise cookie

anidride *f* anhydride

àni·dro -dra *adj* anhydrous

anilina *f* aniline

ànima *f* soul; life (e.g., *of the party*); core; kernel; bore (*of gun*); mold (*of button*); mind; enthusiasm; pith (*of fruit*); sounding post (*of violin*); web (*of rail*); **anima dannata** evil counselor; **anima mia!** darling!; **anima nera** villain; **anima viva** living soul; **buon'anima** late, e.g., **mio padre, buon'anima** my late father; **dannare l'anima** to lose patience; **la buon'anima di** the late; **rompere l'anima a** to annoy

animale *adj* animal; (poet) of the soul; (poet) animate || *m* animal; (fig) boor, lout animalé·sco -sca *adj* (-schi -sche) animal, bestial

animare (ànimo) *tr* to animate, to enliven; to promote || *ref* to become lively or heated

anima·to -ta *adj* animated (*cartoon*); animated, lively; animal

anima·tóre -trice *adj* animating || *m* moving spirit; (mov) animator

animazióne *f* animation

animèlla *f* sweetbread

ànimo *m* mind; heart, affection; courage; aprire l'animo to open one's heart; avere in animo di to have a mind to; mal animo ill will; mettersi l'animo in pace to resign oneself; perdersi d'animo to lose heart; serbare nell'animo to keep in mind

animosi·tà [s] *f* (-tà) animosity, ill will

animó·so -sa [s] *adj* bold; spirited (*animal*); hostile

anióne *m* anion

anisétta *f* anisette

ànitra *f* var of anatra

anitròccolo *m* var of anatroccolo

annacquare (annàcquo) *tr* to water; to water down

annaffiare §287 *tr* to sprinkle; to water (*wine*)

annaffia·tóio *m* (-tói) sprinkling can

annaffia·tóre -trice *adj* watering, sprinkling

annali *mpl* annals *spl*

annaspare *tr* to reel || *intr* to gesticulate; to grope; to flounder

annata *f* year; year's activity; year's rent; year's issues (*of a magazine*)

annebbiare §287 (annébbio) *tr* to befog; to dim || *ref* to become foggy; to become dim

annegaménto *m* drowning

annegare §209 (annégo) *tr & intr* (ESSERE) to drown

annerimento *m* blackening

annerire §176 *tr* to blacken || *ref* to turn black

annessióne *f* annexation

annès·so -sa *adj* united, attached || *m* annex; con tutti gli annessi e connessi everything included

annèttere §107 *tr* to annex; to attach, enclose; to unite; to ascribe (*importance*)

annichilante *adj* annihilating; devastating (*e.g., reply*)

annichilare (annichilo) *tr* to annihilate || *ref* to destroy oneself; (fig) to humble oneself

annichilire §176 *tr & ref* var of annichilare

annidare *tr* to nest; (fig) to nourish, cherish || *ref* to nest; to hide; (fig) to settle

annientamento *m* annihilation

annientare (anniènto) *tr* to annihilate; to knock down, demolish; (fig) to crush || *ref* to humble oneself

anniversà·rio -ria *adj & m* (-ri -rie) anniversary

anno *m* year; anno bisestile leap year; anno luce light-year; anno nuovo New Year; anno scolastico school year; avere . . . anni to be . . . years old; l'anno che viene next year; l'anno corrente this year; quest'altr'anno next year; un anno dopo l'altro year in, year out

annobilire §176 *tr* to ennoble

annodare (annòdo) *tr* to knot, tie; (fig) to tie up || *ref* to get entangled

annoiare §287 (annòio) *tr* to bore || *ref* to become bored

annòna *f* food; food-control agency

annonà·rio -ria *adj* (-ri -rie) food; rationing (*card*)

annó·so -sa [s] *adj* old, aged

annotare (annòto) *tr* to jot down; to chalk up; to annotate; to comment

annotazióne *f* note; notation, annotation

annottare (annòtta) *impers* (ESSERE) & *ref* to grow dark, e.g., si annotta it's growing dark; è annottato it grew dark

annoverare (annòvero) *tr* to count, number

annuale *adj* annual || *m* anniversary

annuà·rio *m* (-ri) annual, yearbook

annuire §176 *intr* to nod assent; to consent

annullaménto *m* nullification, annulment

annullare *tr* to annul, nullify, cancel; to call off || *ref* to cancel one another

annunciare §128 *tr* var of annunziare

Annunciazióne *f* Annunciation

annunziare §287 *tr* to announce; (fig) to forecast, foreshadow

annunzia·tóre -trice *mf* announcer, newscaster

annùn·zio *m* (-zi) announcement, notice; annunzio economico classified ad; annunzio pubblicitario advertisement; annunzio pubblicitario radiofonico (rad) commercial

ànnu·o -a *adj* yearly, annual

annusare [s] *tr* to smell; to snuff (*tobacco*)

annuvolaménto *m* cloudiness

annuvolare (annùvolo) *tr* to cloud, becloud || *ref* to become cloudy; to turn somber

anòdi·no -na *adj* pain-relieving; ineffective; weak, colorless (*person*)

ànodo *m* anode

anomalìa *f* anomaly

anòma·lo -la *adj* anomalous

anonimìa *f* anonymity

anòni·mo -ma *adj* anonymous || *m* anonymous author; serbare l'anonimo to preserve one's anonymity

anormale *adj* abnormal || *m* queer fellow

anormali·tà *f* (-tà) abnormality

ansa *f* handle (*of vase*); pretext; bend (*of a river*)

ansante *adj* panting

ansare *intr* to pant

ànsia *f* anxiety; essere in ansia to be worried

ansie·tà *f* (-tà) anxiety

ansimare (ànsimo) *intr* to pant

ansió·so -sa [s] *adj* anxious

antagonismo *m* antagonism

antagoni•sta (-sti -ste) *adj* antagonistic || *mf* antagonist, opponent
antagonìsti•co -ca *adj* (-ci -che) antagonistic
antàrti•co -ca *adj* (-ci -che) antarctic || Antàrtico *m* Antarctic
antecedènte *adj* preceding || *m* antecedent
antecedènza *f* antecedence
antecessóre *m* predecessor
antefatto *m* background, antecedents
anteguèr•ra (-ra) *adj* prewar || *m* prewar period
anteluca•no -na *adj* (poet) predawn
antenato *m* ancestor
antènna *f* lance; (naut) yard; (rad & telv) aèrial, antenna; (zool) antenna
antepórre §218 *tr* to prefer; to place before
anteprima *f* (mov & theat) preview
anterióre *adj* fore, front; previous; earlier
antesignano [s] *m* forerunner
anti- *pref adj* anti-, e.g., **anticomunìstico** anticommunist; un-, e.g., **antieconomico** uneconomical || *pref mf* anti-, e.g., **anticomunista** anticommunist
antiabbagliante *adj* antiglare || *m* low beam
antiàci•do -da *adj & m* antacid
antiaère•o -a *adj* antiaircraft || *f* antiaircraft defense
antibattèri•co -ca (-ci -che) *adj* antibacterial || *m* bactericide
antibiòti•co -ca *adj & m* (-ci -che) antibiotic
anticà•glia *f* (-glie) antique, curio; rubbish, junk
anticàmera *f* waiting room, anteroom; **fare anticamera** to cool one's heels
anticarro *adj invar* antitank
antichi•tà *f* (-tà) antiquity; **antichità** *fpl* antiques
anticipare (**anticipo**) *tr* to advance; to speed up; to pay in advance; to leak (*news*); to expect, anticipate || *intr* to be early
anticipa•to -ta *adj* in advance (*e.g., payment*)
anticipazióne *f* advance; collateral loan; expectation, anticipation
anticipo *m* advance; loan (*on accounts receivable*); **in anticipo** in advance
anti•co -ca *adj* (-chi -che) antique, ancient, old; **all'antica** in the old-fashioned manner; **gli antichi** the ancients; the forefathers; **in antico** in olden times
anticoncezionale *adj & f* contraceptive
anticonformi•sta *mf* (-sti -ste) nonconformist
anticonformìsti•co -ca *adj* (-ci -che) unconventional
anticongelante *adj & m* antifreeze
anticongiunturale *adj* crisis, emergency
anticòrpo *m* antibody
anticristo *m* Antichrist
antidatare *tr* to predate
antiderapante *adj* nonskid
antidetonante *adj* antiknock || *m* antiknock compound

antidiluvia•no -na *adj* antediluvian
antìdoto *m* antidote
antievanescènza *f* (rad) antifading device
antifecondati•vo -va *adj & m* contraceptive
antìfona *f* antiphon; **capire l'antifona** (fig) to get the message
antifurto *adj invar* antitheft || *m* antitheft device
antigàs *adj invar* gas (*e.g., mask*)
antigièni•co -ca *adj* (-ci -che) unsanitary
antìlope *f* antelope
antimeridia•no -na *adj* antemeridian, A.M.
antimìssile *adj invar* antimissile
antimònio *m* antimony
antincèndio *adj invar* fire-fighting; fire, e.g., **scala antincendio** fire escape
antinéb•bia *adj invar* fog || *m* (-bia) fog light
antinéve *adj invar* snow, e.g., **catena antineve** snow chain
antiorà•rio -ria *adj* (-ri -rie) counterclockwise
antipatìa *f* antipathy, dislike
antipàti•co -ca *adj* (-ci -che) antipathetic; disagreeable; uncongenial
antipièga *adj invar* crease-resistant, wrinkle-proof
antìpodi *mpl* antipodes
antipòlio *adj invar* polio (*e.g., vaccine*)
antipòrta *f* stormdoor; corridor
antiquà•rio -ria (-ri -rie) *adj* antiquarian || *m* antiquary, antiquarian
antiqua•to -ta *adj* obsolete; antiquated
antireligió•so -sa [s] *adj* antireligious, irreligious
antirùggine *adj invar* antirust
antirumóre *adj invar* antinoise
antisala [s] *f* anteroom, waiting room
antisassi [s] *adj invar* protecting against falling stones
antischiavi•sta *adj & mf* (-sti -ste) abolitionist
antisemi•ta [s] (-ti -te) *adj* anti-Semitic || *mf* anti-Semite
antisemìti•co -ca [s] *adj* (-ci -che) anti-Semitic
antisemitìsmo [s] *m* anti-Semitism
antisètti•co -ca [s] *adj & m* (-ci -che) antiseptic
antisociale [s] *adj* antisocial
antisóle [s] *adj invar* sun (*glasses*); suntan (*lotion*)
antisommergìbile [s] *adj* antisubmarine
antistatale [s] *adj* antigovernment
antitàrmi•co -ca *adj* (-ci -che) mothproof
antitèmpo *adv* early, prematurely
antìte•si *f* (-si) antithesis
antitèti•co -ca *adj* (-ci -che) antithetic(al)
antitossìna *f* antitoxin
antiuòmo *adj invar* (mil) antipersonnel
antivigìlia *f*—**l'antivigilia di** two days before
antologìa *f* anthology
antònimo *m* antonym
antrace *m* anthrax
antracite *f* anthracite

antro *m* cave; den, hovel
antròpi‧co ‧**ca** *adj* (**-ci -che**) human
antropofagìa *f* cannibalism
antropòfa‧go ‧**ga** (**-gi -ghe**) *adj* cannibalistic || *m* cannibal
antropòide *adj* anthropoid
antropologìa *f* anthropology
antropomòrfi‧co ‧**ca** *adj* (**-ci -che**) anthropomorphic
antropomòr‧fo ‧**fa** *adj* see **scimmia**
anulare *adj* ring-shaped, annular || *m* ring finger
Anvèrsa *f* Antwerp
anzi *adv* on the contrary, rather; **anzi che no** rather || *prep* (poet) before
anziani‧tà *f* (**-tà**) seniority
anzia‧no ‧**na** *adj* old, elderly; senior || *m* senior
anziché *conj* rather than
anzidét‧to ‧**ta** *adj* aforesaid
anzitutto *adv* above all, first of all
apatìa *f* apathy
apàti‧co ‧**ca** *adj* (**-ci -che**) apathetic
ape *f* bee; **ape operaia** worker; **ape regina** queen bee
aperitivo *m* apéritif
apèr‧to ‧**ta** *adj* open; frank, candid || *m* open space; **all'aperto** in the open
apertura *f* opening; aperture; approach; **ad apertura di libro** at sight; **apertura alare** (*of a bird*) wingspread; (aer) wingspan
apià‧rio *m* (**-ri**) apiary
àpice *m* apex, top; climax
apicol‧tóre ‧**trice** *mf* beekeeper, apiarist
apicoltura *f* beekeeping, apiculture
Apocalisse *f* Apocalypse, Revelation
apocalìtti‧co ‧**ca** *adj* (**-ci -che**) apocalyptic(al)
apòcri‧fo ‧**fa** *adj* apocryphal
apofonìa *f* ablaut
apogèo *m* apogee
apòlide *adj* stateless || *m* man without a country
apolìti‧co ‧**ca** *adj* (**-ci -che**) nonpolitical, nonpartisan
apologè‧ta *m* (**-ti**) apologist
apologèti‧co ‧**ca** *adj* (**-ci -che**) apologetic
apologìa *f* apology
apòlo‧go *m* (**-ghi**) apologue
apoplessìa *f* apoplexy
apoplètti‧co ‧**ca** *adj* & *m* (**-ci -che**) apoplectic
apostasìa *f* apostasy
apòsta‧ta *mf* (**-ti -te**) apostate
apostolato *m* apostolate
apostòli‧co ‧**ca** *adj* (**-ci -che**) apostolic(al)
apòstolo *m* apostle
apostrofare (**apòstrofo**) *tr* to write with an apostrophe; to apostrophize
apòstrofe *f* apostrophe (*to a person*)
apòstrofo *m* (gram) apostrophe
apoteò‧si *f* (**-si**) apotheosis
appagare §209 *tr* to satisfy, gratify || *ref*—**appagarsi di** to be content with
appaiare §287 *tr* to pair, couple; to match || *ref* to match (*said, e.g., of colors*)
appallottolare (**appallòttolo**) *tr* to

crumple into a ball || *ref* to become lumpy
appaltare *tr* to contract for
appalta‧tóre ‧**trice** *mf* contractor
appalto *m* contract; state monopoly; **appalto di sali e tabacchi** tobacco shop
appannàg‧gio *m* (**-gi**) appanage; (fig) prerogative
appannare *tr* to tarnish; to befog, becloud || *ref* to become clouded (*said, e.g., of one's eyesight*)
apparato *m* decoration; display; appliance; leadership (*of political party*); (rad, telv) set
apparecchiare §287 (**apparécchio**) *tr* to prepare; to set (*the table*) || *ref* to get ready
apparecchiatura *f* sizing (*of paper; of a wall*); preparation (*of a canvas*); apparatus
apparéc‧chio *m* (**-chi**) apparatus; sizing; preparation; gadget; (rad, telv) set; airplane; **apparecchio da caccia** fighter plane; **apparecchio telefonico** telephone
apparentare (**apparènto**) *tr* to tie, unite (*through marriage*) || *ref* to become related; to become intimate; (pol) to form a coalition
apparènte *adj* apparent, seeming
apparènza *f* appearance; **in apparenza** seemingly
apparigliare §280 *tr* to pair, team (*horses*)
apparire §108 *intr* (ESSERE) to appear, seem; to look
appariscènte *adj* showy, flashy, gaudy
apparizióne *f* apparition; appearance
appartaménto *m* apartment
appartare *tr* to set aside || *ref* to withdraw, retire
apparta‧to ‧**ta** *adj* secluded, solitary
appartenènza *f* belonging, membership; **appartenenze** accessories; annexes
appartenére §271 *intr* (ESSERE & AVERE) to belong; to pertain || *impers* (ESSERE & AVERE)—**appartiene a it** behooves, it is up to
appassionaménto *m* excitement, interest, enthusiasm
appassionare (**appassióno**) *tr* to move; to interest; to excite || *ref* to be deeply interested
appassiona‧to ‧**ta** *adj* impassioned; deep, ardent || *m* fan, amateur
appassire §176 *intr* (ESSERE) to wilt, wither; to decay; to dry up (*said, e.g., of grapes*)
appellare (**appèllo**) *tr* (law) to appeal; (poet) to call || *ref* to appeal; **appellarsi da** or **contro** (law) to appeal
appèllo *m* call, roll call; **fare appello a** to summon (*e.g., one's strength*); **fare l'appello** to call the roll; **mancare all'appello** to be absent
appéna *adv* hardly, scarcely; only; just || *conj* as soon as; **non appena as** soon as, no sooner
appèndere §109 *tr* to hang
appendice *f* appendix; feuilleton
appendicectomìa *f* appendectomy

appendicite *f* appendicitis

Appennino, l' *m* the Appennines

appesantire [s] §176 *tr* to make heavy; to burden, overwhelm || *ref* to get heavy; to get fat

appestare (appèsto) *tr* to infect; to stink up

appesta•to -ta *adj* plague-ridden || *m* plague victim

appetire §176 *tr* to crave, long for || *intr* (ESSERE & AVERE) to be appetizing

appetito *m* appetite

appetito•so -sa [s] *adj* appetizing, tempting

appetto *adv* opposite; appetto a opposite; in comparison with

appezzamento *m* plot, parcel (*of land*)

appianare *tr* to smooth, level; to settle (*a dispute*); to get around (*a difficulty*)

appiana•tóio *m* (-tói) road grader

appiattare *tr* & *ref* to hide

appiattimento *m* leveling; equalization

appiattire §176 *tr* & *ref* to flatten, to level

appiccare §197 *tr* to hang; appiccare il fuoco a to set on fire; appiccare una lite to pick a fight

appicciare §128 *tr* (coll) to string together; (coll) to kindle, light

appicciicare §197 (appiccico) *tr* to stick, glue; appicciicare uno schiaffo a to slap || *ref* to stick, adhere

appiccicatic•cio -cia *adj* (-ci -ce) sticky

appic•co *m* (-chi) grip; steep wall (*of mountain*); (fig) pretext

appiè *adv*—appiè di at the foot of; at the bottom of

appiedare (appièdo) *tr* to order (*a cavalryman*) off a horse; to order (*e.g., troops*) off a vehicle; to force out of a car (*said, e.g., of motor trouble*)

appièno *adv* (poet) fully

appigionare (appigióno) *tr* to rent || *ref*—appigionasi for rent

appigiónasi [s] *m* for-rent sign

appigliare §280 *ref* to cling, adhere; appigliarsi a un pretesto to seize a pretext

appi•glio *m* (-gli) grip; (fig) pretext

appiombo *m* perpendicular || *adv* plumb, perpendicularly

appioppare (appiòppo) *tr* to plant with poplar trees; to tie (*a vine*) to a poplar tree; (coll) to deliver (*a blow*); (coll) to pass off (*e.g., inferior goods*)

appisolare (appìsolo) *ref* to snooze, doze

applaudire §176 & (appláudo) *tr* to applaud || *intr* to applaud, clap the hands; (with *dat*) to applaud

appláuso *m* applause; applausi applause

applicàbile *adj* applicable

applicare §197 (àpplico) *tr* to apply; to attach; to give (*e.g., a slap*); to put into effect (*a law*); to assign || *ref* to apply oneself

applica•to -ta *adj* applied; appliqué || *m* clerk

applicazióne *f* application; appliqué

applique *m* (elec) wall fixture

appoggiaca•po *m* (-po) headrest; tidy (*on back of chair*)

appoggiagómi•ti *m* (-ti) elbowrest

appoggiama•no *m* (-no) mahlstick

appoggiare §290 (appòggio) *tr* to lean; to rest; to prop, support; to raise (*the tone of voice*); to give (*a slap*); to second (*a motion*); (fig) to back, support || *intr* to lean; to rest || *ref*—appoggiarsi a or su to lean on

appoggia•tóio *m* (-tói) support, rest; banister

appoggiatura *f* (mus) grace note

appòg•gio *m* (-gi) support, prop; backer; backing, support; grip; (mach) bearing

appollaiare §287 *ref* to roost

appórre §218 *tr* to affix, append

apportare (appòrto) *tr* to cause; to presage; (poet) to carry

appòrto *m* carrying; contribution; (law) share

appositamente *adv* expressly, on purpose

appòsi•to -ta *adj* proper, fitting

apposizióne *f* apposition

appòsta *adj invar* suitable || *adv* on purpose, expressly, intentionally

appostamento *m* ambush

appostare (appòsto) *tr* to ambush || *ref* to lie in ambush

apprèndere §220 *tr* to learn || *ref* (poet) to take hold

apprendi•sta *mf* (-sti -ste) apprentice

apprendistato *m* apprenticeship

apprensióne *f* apprehension, fear

apprensi•vo -va *adj* apprehensive

appressare (apprèsso) *tr* (poet) to approach || *ref* to come near

appresso *adj invar* next, following || *adv* near; later on; appresso a near; after

apprestare (apprèsto) *tr* to prepare; to supply, provide (*e.g., help*) || *ref* to prepare, get ready

apprettare (apprètto) *tr* to dress (*leather*); to size (*cloth*)

apprètto *m* tan (*for leather*); sizing (*for cloth*)

apprezzàbile *adj* appreciable

apprezzamento *m* appreciation; estimation

apprezzare (apprèzzo) *tr* to appreciate

apprezza•to -ta *adj* esteemed

appròc•cio *m* (-ci) approach; approcci advances

approdare (appròdo) *intr* (ESSERE & AVERE) to land; (with *dat*) (poet) to benefit; approdare a to come to

appròdo *m* landing

approfittare *intr*—approfittare di to capitalize on || *ref*—approfittarsi di to take advantage of

approfondire §176 *tr* to make deep; to study thoroughly || *ref*—approfondirsi in to go deep into

approntare (apprónto) *tr* to prepare, make ready

appropriare §287 (appròprio) *tr* to adapt; to bestow || *ref*—appropriarsi a to befit; appropriarsi di to appropriate; to embezzle

appropria·to -ta *adj* appropriate
appropriazióne *f* appropriation; **appropriazione indebita** fraudulent conversion, embezzlement
approssimare (appròssimo) *tr* to bring near || *ref* to approach, come near
approssimati·vo -va *adj* approximate
approssimazióne *f* approximation
approvàbile *adj* laudable
approvare (appròvo) *tr* to approve, countenance; to subscribe to (*an opinion*); to pass (*a student; a law*); to confirm
approvazióne *f* approval; confirmation; passage (*of a law*)
approvvigionaménto *m* supply
approvvigionare (approvvigióno) *tr* to supply || *ref* to be supplied
appuntaménto *m* appointment; date; **appuntamento amoroso** assignation
appuntare *tr* to sharpen; to fasten, pin; to stick (*a pin*) in; to point; to jot down, take note of; to prick up (*one's ears*); (fig) to reproach || *ref* to be turned; to aim
appunta·to -ta *adj* sharpened || *m* corporal (*of Italian police*)
appuntellare (appuntèllo) *tr* to shore up, prop up
appuntellatura *f* shoring up, propping up
appuntino *adv* precisely, meticulously
appuntire §176 *tr* to sharpen
appunti·to -ta *adj* sharp, pointed
appunto *m* note; blame, charge; **muovere un appunto a** to blame; **per l'appunto** just, precisely || *adv* exactly, precisely
appurare *tr* to ascertain
appuzzare *tr* to befoul, pollute
apribottì·glie *m* (-glie) bottle opener
apri·co -ca *adj* (-chi -che) (poet) sunny, bright
aprile *m* April
apripi·sta *m* (-sta) blade (*of bulldozer*); bulldozer
aprire §110 *tr* to open; to turn on; to dig (*e.g., a grave*) || *ref* to open; to clear up (*said of the weather*); **aprirsi con** to open one's heart to; **aprirsi il varco tra** to press through
apriscàto·le *m* (-le) can opener
aquà·rio *m* (-ri) aquarium || **Aquario** *m* (astr) Aquarius
aquàti·co -ca *adj* (-ci -che) aquatic
àquila *f* eagle; genius
aquili·no -na *adj* aquiline
aquilóne *m* north wind; kite
aquilòtto *m* eaglet; cadet (*in Italian Air Force Academy*)
Aquinate, l' *m* Saint Thomas Aquinas
ara *f* (poet) altar; are (*100 square meters*)
arabé·sca *f* (-sche) (mus) arabesque
arabesca·to -ta *adj* arabesque
arabé·sco -sca (-schi -sche) *adj* arabesque || *m* arabesque; doodle || *f* see **arabesca**
Aràbia, l' *f* Arabia
aràbi·co -ca *adj* (-ci -che) Arabic
aràbile *adj* tillable

àra·bo -ba *adj* Arabic, Arabian || *mf* Arab (*person*) || *m* Arabic (*language*)
aràchide *f* peanut (*vine*)
aragonése [s] *adj* & *mf* Aragonese
aragósta *f* (*Palinurus vulgaris*) lobster
aràldi·co -ca *adj* (-ci -che) heraldic || *f* heraldry
araldo *m* herald
arancéto *m* orange grove
aràn·cia *f* (-ce) orange
aranciata *f* orangeade
aràn·cio *adj invar* orange (*in color*) || *m* (-ci) orange tree
arancióne *adj* & *m* orange (*color*)
arare *tr* to plow; (naut) to drag (*the anchor*)
aratro *m* plow
arazzo *m* tapestry, arras
arbitràg·gio *m* (-gi) (sports) umpiring; (com) arbitrage
arbitrale *adj* judge's, umpire's
arbitrare (àrbitro) *tr* to umpire, referee || *intr* to arbitrate || *ref*—**arbitrarsi di** to take the liberty to
arbitrà·rio -ria *adj* (-ri -rie) arbitrary; wanton
arbitrato *m* arbitration
arbi·trio *m* (-tri) will; abuse, violation; **libero arbitrio** free will
àrbitro *m* arbiter; judge, referee, umpire
arboscèllo *m* small tree
arbusto *m* shrub, bush
ar·ca *f* (-che) sarcophagus; ark; chest; **arca di Noè** Noah's Ark; **arca di scienza** (fig) fountain of knowledge
àrcade *adj* & *m* Arcadian
Arcàdia *f* Arcadia, Arcady
arcài·co -ca *adj* (-ci -che) archaic
arcaismo *m* archaism
arcàngelo *m* archangel
arca·no -na *adj* mysterious, arcane || *m* mystery
arcata *f* arch; arcade
archeologia *f* archaeology
archeològi·co -ca *adj* (-ci -che) archaeological
archeòlo·go -ga *mf* (-gi -ghe) archaeologist
archètipo *m* archetype
archétto *m* (archit) small arch; (elec) trolley pole; (mus) bow
archi- *pref adj* archi-, e.g., **architettonico** architectonic || *pref m & f* archi-, e.g., **architettura** architecture
archibù·gio *m* (-gi) harquebus
Archimède *m* Archimedes
architettare (architétto) *tr* to plan (*a building*); (fig) to contrive, plot
architétto *m* architect
architettòni·co -ca *adj* (-ci -che) architectural
architettura *f* architecture
architetturale *adj* architectural
architrave *m* architrave; doorhead, lintel
archiviare §287 *tr* to file; to lay aside, shelve; (law) to throw out
archi·vio *m* (-vi) archives; record office; chancery, public records
archivi·sta *mf* (-sti -ste) archivist, file clerk

arci- *pref adj* archi-, e.g., **arcivescovile** archiepiscopal || *pref m & f* arch-, e.g., **arciprete** archpriest

arcicontèn•to -ta *adj* (coll) very glad

arcidiàcono *m* archdeacon

arcidu•ca *m* (-chi) archduke

arciduchéssa *f* archduchess

arcière *m* archer, bowman

arci•gno -gna *adj* gruff, surly

arcióne *m* saddlebow; **montare in arcioni** to mount, to mount a horse

arcipèla•go *m* (-ghi) archipelago

arciprète *m* archpriest; dean

arcivescovado *m* archbishopric

arcivéscovo *m* archbishop

ar•co *m* (-chi) bow; (archit) arch; (geom, elec) arc; **arco rampante** flying buttress

arcobaléno *m* rainbow

arco-làio *m* (-lài) reel; **girare come un arcolaio** to spin like a top

arcuare (àrcuo) *tr* to arch; to bend; to camber

arcua•to -ta *adj* bent, curved; bow (*e.g., legs*); **avere le gambe arcuate** to be bowlegged

ardènte *adj* burning; hot; ardent, impassioned

àrdere §111 *tr* to burn || *intr* to burn; to be in full swing (*said, e.g., of a war*)

ardèsia *f* slate

ardiménto *m* boldness, daring

ardire *m* boldness; presumption, impudence || §176 *intr*—**ardire** + *inf* or **ardire di** + *inf* to dare to + *inf*

arditézza *f* daring; temerity

ardi•to -ta *adj* daring; rash || *m* (hist) shock trooper

ardóre *m* intense heat; ardor

àr•duo -dua *adj* arduous

àrea *f* area, surface; group, camp; **area arretrata** backward area

àrem *m* (àrem) harem

arèna *f* arena; **scendere nell'arena** to throw one's hat in the ring

aréna *f* sand

arenare (aréno) *intr* (ESSERE) & *ref* to run aground

arenària *f* sandstone

arén•go *m* (-ghi) (hist) town meeting

arenile *m* sandy beach

arenó•so -sa [s] *adj* sandy

areòmetro *m* hydrometer

aeronàuti•co -ca *adj & f* (-ci -che) var of aeronautica

areoplano *m* var of aeroplano

areopòrto *m* var of aeroporto

areòstato *m* var of aerostato

àrgano *m* winch; (naut) capstan

argentare (argènto) *tr* to silver; to silver-plate; to back (*a mirror*) with foil

argenta•to -ta *adj* silver; silvery; silver-plated

argentatura *f* silver plating; silver plate; foil (*of mirror*)

argènte•o -a *adj* silver, silvery

argenterìa *f* silverware

argentière *m* silversmith; jeweler

argenti•no -na *adj* silver, silvery; Argentine || *mf* Argentine || *f* high-necked sweater || **l'Argentina** *f* Argentina

argènto *m* silver; (archaic) money; **argenti** silverware; **argento vivo** quicksilver

argentóne *m* German silver

argilla *f* clay

argilló•so -sa [s] *adj* clayey

arginare (àrgino) *tr* to dam, dike; to hold back, check

àrgine *m* embankment, dam; (fig) defense

ar•go *m* (-ghi) (chem) argon; (orn) grouse || **Argo** *m* Argus

argomentare (argoménto) *tr & intr* to argue

argomentazióne *f* argumentation, discussion

argoménto *m* argument; pretext; subject; **fuori dell'argomento** beside the point

argonàu•ta *m* (-ti) Argonaut

arguire §176 *tr* to deduce, infer; (archaic) to denote

argutézza *f* wit; witty remark

argu•to -ta *adj* keen, acute; witty

argùzia *f* keenness; wit

ària *f* air; climate; look; mien; aria, tune; poem; **all'aria aperta** in the open air; **a mezz'aria** in midair; halfway; **andare all'aria** to fail; **aria condizionata** air conditioning; **avere l'aria di** to seem to; to look like; **dare aria a** to air; **in aria** in the air; **tira un'aria pericolosa** a mean wind is blowing

aria•no -na *adj & mf* Aryan

aridi•tà *f* (-tà) dryness, aridity; dearth

àri•do -da *adj* arid, dry, barren; (fig) dry

arieggiare §290 (arièggio) *tr* to air; to imitate || *ref*—**arieggiarsi a** to give oneself the airs of

arïète *m* ram; (mil) battering ram || **Ariete** *m* (astr) Aries

arïétta *s* breeze; (mus) short aria

arin•ga *f* (-ghe) herring; **aringa affumicata** kippered herring, kipper

arin•go *m* (-ghi) assembly; field; joust; **scendere nell'aringo** to throw one's hat in the ring

arió•so -sa [s] *adj* airy, breezy; (fig) of wide scope

àrista *f* loin of pork

arista *f* (bot) awn

aristocràti•co -ca (-ci -che) *adj* aristocratic || *mf* aristocrat

aristocrazìa *f* aristocracy

Aristòtele *m* Aristotle

aristotèli•co -ca *adj & m* (-ci -che) Aristotelian

aritmèti•co -ca (-ci -che) *adj* arithmetical || *m* arithmetician || *f* arithmetic

arlecchino *adj invar* harlequin; fiesta (*e.g., dishes*) || **Arlecchino** *m* Harlequin

ar•ma *f* (-mi) arm, weapon; (fig) army; (mil) corps, service; **alle prime armi** at the beginning; **arma bianca** steel blade; **arma da taglio** cutting weapon; **arma delle trasmissioni** signal corps

armacòllo *m*—**ad armacollo** slung across the shoulders (*said of a rifle*)

armà•dio *m* (-di) cabinet; closet; **armadio a muro** built-in closet; **armadio**

d'angolo corner cupboard; **armadio farmaceutico** medicine cabinet; **armadio guardaroba** armoire

armaiòlo *m* gunsmith

armamentà·rio *m* (**-ri**) outfit, set (*of tools*)

armaménto *m* armament; crew; gun crew; crew (*of rowboat*); outfit, equipment

armare *tr* to arm; to dub (*s.o. a knight*); to outfit, commission (*a ship*); to cock (*a gun*); to brace, shore up (*a building*); (rr) to furnish with track || *ref* to arm oneself; to outfit oneself

arma·to -ta *adj* armed; reinforced (*concrete*) || *m* soldier || *f* army; navy; fleet; (nav) task force

arma·tóre -trice *adj* outfitting || *m* shipowner; (min) carpenter; (rr) trackwalker

armatura *f* armor; scaffold; framework, support; reinforcement (*for concrete*); (elec) plate (*of condenser*)

armeggiare §290 (**arméggio**) *intr* to fumble, fool around; to scheme; (archaic) to handle arms; (archaic) to joust

armeggí·o *m* (**-i**) fooling around; scheming, intriguing

armè·no -na *adj & mf* Armenian

arménto *m* herd

armería *f* armory

armière *m* (aer) gunner

armíge·ro -ra *adj* warlike, bellicose || *m* warrior; bodyguard

armistiziale *adj* armistice

armistí·zio *m* (**-zi**) *m* armistice

armonía *f* harmony; **in armonia con** according to

armòni·co -ca (**-ci -che**) *adj* harmonic; resonant; harmonious || *f* harmonica; **armonica a bocca** mouth organ

armonió·so -sa [s] *adj* harmonious

armonizzare [ddzz] *tr & intr* to harmonize

arnése [s] *m* tool, implement; garb, dress; (coll) gadget; **bene in arnese** well-heeled; **male in arnese** down at the heels

àrnia *f* beehive

arò·ma *m* (**-mi**) aroma, odor; zest

aromàti·co -ca *adj* (**-ci -che**) aromatic

aromatizzare [ddzz] *tr* to flavor; to spice

arpa *f* harp

arpeggiare §290 (**arpéggio**) *intr* to play arpeggios; to play a harp; to strum

arpég·gio *m* (**-gi**) arpeggio

arpía *f* Harpy; (coll) harpy

arpionare (**arpióno**) *tr* to harpoon

arpióne *m* hinge (*of door*); hook; harpoon; spike (*for mountain climbing*)

arpionismo *m* ratchet

arpi·sta *mf* (**-sti -ste**) harpist

arrabattare *ref* to exert oneself, to strive, to endeavor

arrabbiare §287 *intr* (ESSERE) to go mad (*said of dogs*) || *ref* to become angry (*said of people*)

arrabbia·to -ta *adj* mad (*dog*); angry; obstinate; confirmed

arrabbiatura *f* rage; **prendersi un'arrabbiatura** to burn up (*with rage*)

arraffare *tr* to snatch

arrampicare §197 (**arràmpico**) *ref* to climb, climb up

arrampicata *f* climbing

arrampica·tóre -trice *mf* climber; mountain climber; **arrampicatore sociale** social climber

arrancare §197 *intr* to hobble, limp; to struggle, work hard; to row hard

arrangiaménto *m* agreement; (mus) arrangement

arrangiare §290 *tr* to arrange; to fix; (coll) to steal || *ref* to manage, get along

arrecare §197 (**arrèco**) *tr* to cause; to carry, deliver

arredaménto *m* furnishing; furnishings; equipment

arredare (**arrèdo**) *tr* to furnish; to equip

arreda·tóre -trice *mf* interior decorator; upholsterer; (mov) property man

arrèdo *m* furnishings, furniture; piece of furniture; **arredi sacri** church supplies

arrembàg·gio *m* (**-gi**) boarding (*of a ship*)

arrenare (**arréno**) *tr* to sand

arrèndere §227 *tr* (archaic) to surrender || *ref* to surrender; **arrendersi a discrezione** to surrender unconditionally

arrendévole *adj* yielding, compliant, flexible

arrendevolézza *f* suppleness; compliance

arrestare (**arrèsto**) *tr* to stop; to arrest || *ref* to stop, stay

arrèsto *m* arrest; stop; pause; (mach) stop, catch; **arresti** (mil) house arrest; **in stato d'arresto** under arrest

arretrare (**arrètro**) *tr* to withdraw || *intr* (ESSERE & AVERE) & *ref* to withdraw

arretra·to -ta *adj* withdrawn; backward; back (*issue*); overdue || **arretrati** *mpl* arrears

arricchiménto *m* enrichment

arricchire §176 *tr* to enrich || *intr* (ESSERE) & *ref* to get rich

arricchi·to -ta *mf* nouveau riche

arricciacapél·li *m* (**-li**) curler

arricciare §128 *tr* to curl; to wrinkle; to screw up (*one's nose*); **arricciare il pelo** to bristle (*said of a person*); to bristle up (*said of an animal*) || *ref* to curl up

arriccia·to -ta *adj* curled up || *m* first coat (*of cement*)

arricciatura *f* curling (*of hair*); pleating (*of a skirt*); kink (*in a rope*)

arrìdere §231 *tr* (poet) to grant || *intr* to smile

arrìn·ga *f* (**-ghe**) harangue; (law) lawyer's plea

arringare §209 *tr* to harangue; (law) to plead

arrischiare §287 *tr* to endanger; to risk || *ref* to dare, venture

arrischia·to -ta *adj* risky; daring

arrivare *tr* to reach || *intr* (ESSERE) to arrive; to happen; to get along, be successful; **arrivare a** to reach; to succeed in

arriva·to -ta *adj* arrived; successful; **ben arrivato** welcome

arrivedér·ci *m* (**-ci**) good-bye || *interj* good-bye!, so long!

arrivedéria *interj* good-bye!

arrivismo *m* social climbing, ruthless ambition

arrivi·sta *mf* (**-sti -ste**) social climber

arrivo *m* arrival; (sports) goal line; (sports) finishing line

arroccare §197 (**arròcco**) *tr* to put (*e.g.*, flax) on the distaff || §197 (**arròcco**) *tr* to shelter; (chess) to castle || *ref* to seek shelter; (chess) to castle

arròc·co *m* (**-chi**) castling

arrochire §176 *tr* to make hoarse || *intr* (ESSERE) to become hoarse

arrogante *adj* arrogant, insolent

arroganza *f* arrogance, insolence

arrogare §209 (**arrògo**) *tr*—**arrogare a sé** to arrogate to oneself || *ref* to arrogate to oneself

arrolare §237 *tr* var of **arruolare**

arrossare (**arròsso**) *tr* to redden

arrossire §176 *intr* (ESSERE) to blush; to change color

arrostire §176 *tr* to roast; to toast; **arrostire allo spiedo** to barbecue on the spit || *intr* (ESSERE) & *ref* to roast

arrò·sto *m* (**-sto** & **-sti**) roast

arrotare (**arròto**) *tr* to grind, hone; to smooth; to strike, run over; to grit (*one's teeth*) || *ref* to grind (*to work hard*); to sideswipe

arrotatrice *f* floor sander

arrotatura *f* sharpening

arrotino *m* grinder

arrotolare (**arròtolo**) *tr* to roll

arrotondaménto *m* rounding; rounding out; increase (*in salary*)

arrotondare (**arrotóndo**) *tr* to make round; to round out; to supplement (*a salary*) || *ref* to round out, become plump

arrovellare (**arrovèllo**) *tr* to vex || *ref* to become angry; to strive, endeavor; **arrovellarsi il cervello** to rack one's brains

arroventare (**arrovènto**) *tr* to make red-hot || *ref* to become red-hot

arroventire §176 *tr* & *ref* var of **arroventare**

arruffapòpo·li *m* (**-li**) rabble-rouser

arruffare *tr* to tangle; to muss, rumple; to confuse

arruf·fìo *m* (**-fìi**) tangle; confusion, mess

arruffó·ne -na *mf* blunderer; swindler

arrugginire §176 *tr*, *intr* (ESSERE) & *ref* to rust

arruolaménto *m* enlistment; draft

arruolare (**arruòlo**) *tr* to recruit; to draft || *ref* to enlist

arruvidire §176 *tr* to make rough, roughen || *intr* (ESSERE) to become rough

arsenale *m* arsenal; navy yard

arsèni·co -ca (**-ci -che**) *adj* arsenic, arsenical || *m* arsenic

ar·so -sa *adj* burnt; dry, parched; **arso di** consumed with

arsura *f* sultriness; dryness

arte *f* art; ability; guile; **ad arte** on purpose; **arti e mestieri** arts and crafts

artefare §173 *tr* to adulterate

artefat·to -ta *adj* adulterated; artificial

artéfice *m* craftsman; creator

artèria *f* artery

arterioscleròsi *m* arteriosclerosis

arterió·so -sa [s] *adj* arterial

artesia·no -na *adj* artesian

àrti·co -ca *adj* (**-ci -che**) arctic || **Artico** *m* Arctic

articolare *adj* articular || *v* (**artìcolo**) *tr* & *ref* to articulate

articola·to -ta *adj* articulated; articulate; (gram) combined; jagged (*coastline*)

articolazióne *f* articulation

articoli·sta *mf* (**-sti -ste**) columnist; feature writer

artìcolo *m* article; item; paragraph; **articolo di fondo** editorial; **articolo di spalla** comment

artificiale *adj* artificial

artificière *m* pyrotechnist; (mil) demolition expert

artifi·cio *m* (**-ci**) artifice; sophistication, affectation; **artificio d'illuminazione** (mil) flare

artificiosi·tà [s] *f* (**-tà**) artfulness, craftiness; artificiality

artifició·so -sa [s] *adj* artful, crafty; artificial, affected

artigianato *m* craftsmanship

artigia·no -na *adj* of craftsmen || *m* craftsman

artigliare §280 *tr* (poet) to claw

artiglière *m* artilleryman

artiglierìa *f* artillery; **artiglieria a cavallo** mounted artillery

arti·glio *m* (**-gli**) claw; **cadere negli artigli di** to fall into the clutches of

arti·sta *mf* (**-sti -ste**) artist; actor

artìsti·co -ca *adj* (**-ci -che**) artistic

ar·to -ta *adj* (poet) narrow || *m* limb

artrite *f* arthritis

artrìti·co -ca *adj* & *mf* (**-ci -che**) arthritic

arturia·no -na *adj* Arthurian

arzigogolare [dz] (**arzigògolo**) *intr* to muse; to cavil

arzigògolo [dz] *m* fantasy; cavil

arzil·lo -la [dz] *adj* lively, sprightly; (coll) sparkling (*wine*)

arzin·ga *f* (**-ghe**) tong (*of a blacksmith*)

asbèsto *m* asbestos

ascèlla *f* armpit

ascendènte *adj* ascendant || *m* upper hand, ascendancy; **ascendenti** forefathers

ascendènza *f* ancestry, lineage

ascéndere §245 *tr* to climb || *intr* (ESSERE & AVERE) to ascend, climb

ascensionale *adj* rising; lifting

ascensióne *f* ascent, climb || **Ascensione** *f* Ascension, Ascension Day

ascensóre *m* elevator

ascésa [s] *f* ascent

ascèsso *m* abscess

ascè·ta *mf* (**-ti -te**) ascetic

ascèti·co -ca *adj* (**-ci -che**) ascetic

ascetismo *m* asceticism

à·scia *f* (**-sce**) adze

asciugacapél·li *m* (**-li**) hair drier

asciugamano *m*' towel; **asciugamano spugna** Turkish towel

asciugante *adj* drying; blotting; soaking ‖ *m* dryer

asciugare §209 *tr* to dry, dry up; to wipe; to drain (*e.g., a glass of wine*) ‖ *ref* to dry oneself; to dry, dry up

asciuga·tóio *m* (**-tói**) towel; bath towel

asciugatrice *f* dryer

asciut·to **-ta** *adj* dry; skinny; blunt (*in speech*) ‖ *m* dry land; dry climate; **all'asciutto** pennyless

ascoltare (**ascólto**) *tr* to listen to ‖ *intr* to listen

ascolta·tóre **-trice** *mf* listener

ascólto *m* listening; **stare in ascolto** to listen

ascòrbi·co **-ca** *adj* (**-ci -che**) ascorbic

ascrit·to **-ta** *adj* ascribed; belonging ‖ *m* member

ascrìvere §250 *tr* to inscribe, register; to ascribe, attribute

ascultare *tr* to sound (*s.o.'s chest*)

asèpsi [s] *f* asepsis

asètti·co **-ca** [s] *adj* (**-ci -che**) aseptic

asfaltare *tr* to tar, pave

asfalto *m* asphalt

asfissìa *f* asphyxia

asfissiante *adj* asphyxiating; poison (*gas*); boring

asfissiare §287 *tr* to asphyxiate; to bore ‖ *intr* (ESSERE) to be asphyxiated

asfodèlo *m* asphodel

Àsia, l' *f* Asia; **l'Asia Minore** Asia Minor

asiàti·co **-ca** *adj* & *mf* (**-ci -che**) Asian, Asiatic

asilo *m* shelter; asylum; home; **asilo di mendicità** poorhouse; **asilo infantile** kindergarten; **asilo per i vecchi** old-age home, nursing home

asimmetrìa [s] *f* asymmetry

asimmètri·co **-ca** [s] *adj* (**-ci -che**) asymmetric(al)

asinàggine [s] *f* stupidity, asininity

asi·nàio [s] *m* (**-nài**) donkey driver

asinata [s] *f* stupidity, folly

asinerìa [s] *f* asininity

asiné·sco **-sca** [s] *adj* (**-schi -sche**) asinine

asini·no **-na** [s] *adj* asinine

àsino [s] *m* ass, donkey; **fare l'asino a** (*a slang*) to play up to; **qui casca l'asino** here is the rub

asma *f* asthma

asmàti·co **-ca** *adj* & *mf* (**-ci -che**) asthmatic

àsola *f* buttonhole; buttonhole hem

aspàra·go *m* (**-gi**) asparagus; piece of asparagus; **asparagi asparagus** (*as food*)

aspèrgere §112 *tr* to sprinkle

aspersióne *f* aspersing, sprinkling

aspettare (**aspètto**) *tr* to wait for, await; to expect; **aspettare al varco** to be on the lookout for ‖ *intr* to wait; **fare aspettare** to keep waiting ‖ *ref* to expect

aspettativa *f* expectancy, expectation; leave of absence without pay

aspètto *m* waiting; aspect, look; **al primo aspetto** at first sight

àspide *m* asp

aspirante *adj* suction (*pump*) ‖ *m* aspirant; applicant, candidate; suitor; upperclassman (*in naval academy*)

aspirapólve·re *m* (**-re**) vacuum cleaner

aspirare *tr* to inhale, breathe in; to suck (*e.g., air*); (phonet) to aspirate ‖ *intr* to aspire

aspiratóre *m* exhaust fan

aspirazióne *f* aspiration; (aut) intake

aspirina *f* aspirin

aspo *m* reel

asportàbile *adj* removable

asportare (**aspòrto**) *tr* to remove, take away

asportazióne *f* removal

asprézza *f* sourness; roughness, harshness

a·spro **-spra** *adj* sour; rough, harsh

assaggiare §290 *tr* to taste; to sample, test; **assaggiare il terreno** (fig) to see how the land lies

assaggia·tóre **-trice** *mf* taster

assàg·gio *m* (**-gi**) taste, sample; tasting; test, trial

assài *adj invar* a lot of ‖ *m* much ‖ *adv* enough; fairly; very

assale *m* axle

assalire §242 *tr* to attack, assail; (fig) to seize

assali·tóre **-trice** *mf* assailant

assaltare *tr* to assault; **assaltare a mano armata** to stick up

assalto *m* assault, attack; (law) battery; **cogliere d'assalto** to catch unawares; **prendere d'assalto** to assault

assaporare (**assapóro**) *tr* to taste; to relish, enjoy

assassinare *tr* to assassinate; (fig) to murder

assassì·nio *m* (**-ni**) assassination, murder

assassi·no **-na** *adj* murderous ‖ *mf* assassin, murderer

asse *m* axle; shaft, spindle; (geom, phys) axis; **asse ereditario** estate; **asse stradale** median strip ‖ *f* plank; **asse da stiro** ironing board

assecondare (**assecóndo**) *tr* to help; to second; to uphold

assediante *adj* besieging ‖ *m* besieger

assediare §287 (**assèdio**) *tr* to lay siege to, besiege

assè·dio *m* (**-di**) siege; **assedio economico** economic sanctions; **cingere d'assedio** to besiege

assegnaménto *m* awarding; allowance; faith, reliance; **fare assegnamento su** to rely upon

assegnare (**asségno**) *tr* to assign; to prescribe; to distribute; to award

assegnatà·rio **-ria** *mf* (**-ri -rie**) assignee

assegnazióne *f* assignment; awarding

asségno *m* allowance; check; **assegni fringe benefits; assegni familiari** family allowance; **assegno a copertura garantita** certified check; **assegno a vuoto** worthless check; **assegno di studio** (educ) stipend; **assegno turistico** traveler's check; **assegno vademecum** certified check; **contro assegno** C.O.D.

assemblàg·gio *m* (**-gi**) (mach) assembling, assembly

assemblèa *f* assembly

assembraménto *m* gathering

assembrare (**assémbro**) *tr & ref* to gather

assennatézza *f* good judgment, discretion

assenna·to -ta *adj* sensible, prudent

assènso *m* approval, consent

assentare (**assènto**) *ref* to be absent, to absent oneself

assènte *adj* absent || *mf* absentee

assenteìsmo *m* absenteeism

assentire (**assènto**) *tr* (poet) to grant || *intr* to assent, acquiesce; **assentire con un cenno** to nod assent

assènza *f* absence

assenziènte *adj* consenting, approving

assèn·zio *m* (**-zi**) absinthe; (bot) wormwood

asserire §176 *tr* to affirm, assert

asserragliare §280 *tr* to barricade || *ref* to barricade oneself

assèrto *m* (poet) assertion

asser·tóre -trice *mf* advocate, supporter

asservimento *m* enslavement

asservire §176 *tr* to enslave; to subjugate

asserzióne *f* assertion

assessóre *m* councilman; alderman

assestaménto *m* arrangement; settling (*of a building*)

assestare (**assèsto**) *tr* to arrange; to adapt, regulate; to deliver, deal (*a blow*) || *ref* to become organized; to settle (*said of a building*)

assesta·to -ta *adj* sensible, prudent

assetare (**asséto**) *tr* to make thirsty; (fig) to inflame

asseta·to -ta *adj* thirsty; parched; eager || *mf* thirsty person

assettare (**assètto**) *tr* to tidy, straighten up || *ref* to straighten oneself up

assetta·to -ta *adj* tidy

assètto *m* arrangement; order; (naut) trim; **assetto longitudinale** (aer) pitch, attitude; **in assetto di guerra** ready for war; **male in assetto** in poor shape

asseverare (**assèvero**) *tr* to asseverate, assert

assicèlla *f* roofing board, lath; batten

assicuràbile *adj* insurable

assicurare *tr* to assure; to insure; to protect; to fasten; to deliver (*e.g., a thief*) || *ref* to make sure; to take out insurance

assicura·to -ta *adj & mf* insured || *f* insured letter

assicura·tóre -trice *mf* insurer

assicurazióne *f* assurance; insurance; **assicurazione contro gli infortuni sul lavoro** workman's compensation insurance; **assicurazione contro i danni** casualty insurance; **assicurazione incendio** fire insurance; **assicurazione infortuni** accident insurance; **assicurazione per la vecchiaia** old age insurance; **assicurazione sociale** social security; **assicurazione sulla vita** life insurance

assideraménto *m* freezing; frostbite

assiderare (**assidero**) *ref* to freeze; to become frostbitten

assìdere §113 *ref* (poet) to take one's seat (*e.g., on the throne*)

assì·duo -dua *adj* assiduous, diligent

assième *m* ensemble || *adv* together; **assieme a** together with

assiepare (**assièpo**) *tr & ref* to crowd

assillante *adj* disturbing, troublesome

assillare *tr* to beset, trouble

assillo *m* gadfly; (fig) stimulus, goad

assimilare (**assìmilo**) *tr* to assimilate; to compare

assimilazióne *f* assimilation

assiòlo *m* horned owl

assiò·ma *m* (**-mi**) axiom

assiomàti·co -ca *adj* (**-ci -che**) axiomatic

assì·ro -ra *adj & mf* Assyrian

assisa *f* (poet) uniform, livery; (geol) layer; (archaic) duty, tax; **assise** criminal court; assembly, session; (hist) assises

assistènte *mf* assistant; **assistente sanitario** practical nurse; **assistente sociale** social worker || *m*—**assistente al lavoro** foreman || *f*—**assistente di volo** (aer) hostess

assistènza *f* assistance, help; intervention; **assistenza pubblica** relief

assistenziale *adj* welfare, charity

assistere §114 *tr* to assist, help || *intr*—**assistere a** to attend, be present at

assito *m* flooring, boarding

assiuòlo *m* var of **assiolo**

asso *m* ace; **asso del volante** speed king; **piantare in asso** to walk out on

associare §128 (**assòcio**) *tr* to associate; **associare alle carceri** to take to prison || *ref* to associate; to become a member; to subscribe; to participate

associa·to -ta *adj* associate || *mf* associate, partner

associazióne *f* association; union; subscription; membership

assodare (**assòdo**) *tr* to solidify; to strengthen; to ascertain || *ref* to solidify; to strengthen

assoggettare (**assoggètto**) *tr* to subject, subdue || *ref* to submit

assola·to -ta *adj* sunny, exposed to the sun

assolcare §197 (**assólco**) *tr* to furrow

assoldare (**assòldo**) *tr* to hire, recruit

assólo *m* (mus) solo

assolutìsmo *m* absolutism

assolutìsti·co -ca *adj* (**-ci -che**) absolutist, despotic

assolu·to -ta *adj & m* absolute

assoluzióne *f* absolution

assòlvere §115 *tr* to absolve; to fulfill

assomigliare §280 *tr* to compare; to make similar, make equal || *intr* (ESSERE & AVERE) (with *dat*) to resemble, to look like; to be like || *ref* to resemble each other, look alike; **assomigliarsi a** to resemble

assommare (**assómmo**) *tr* to add; to be the epitome of; (archaic) to complete || *intr* (ESSERE) to amount

assonna·to -ta *adj* sleepy

assopire §176 *tr* to lull to sleep; to

soothe || *ref* to drowse, to nod; to calm down

assorbènte *adj* absorbent || *m* sanitary napkin

assorbiménto *m* absorption

assorbire §176 & (assòrbo) *tr* to absorb

assorbi·to -ta *adj* absorbed; **assorbito da** consumed with

assordare (assórdo) *tr* to deafen || *ref* to become deaf; to dim; to lessen

assortiménto *m* assortment; **avere in assortimento** (com) to carry, stock

assortire §176 *tr* to assort, sort out; to stock

assorti·to -ta *adj* assorted; **bene assortito** well matched

assòr·to -ta *adj* engrossed, absorbed

assottigliare §280 *tr* to thin; to sharpen; to reduce || *ref* to grow thinner

assuefare §173 *tr* to accustom || *ref* to become accustomed

assuefazióne *f* habit, custom

assùmere §116 *tr* to assume; to hire; to raise, elevate; (law) to accept in evidence

Assunta *f* Assumption

assunto *m* thesis, argument; (poet) task

assun·tóre -trice *mf* contractor

assunzióne *f* assumption; hiring; (law) examination || **Assunzione** *f* Assumption

assurdi·tà *f* (-tà) absurdity

assur·do -da *adj* absurd || *m* absurdity

assùrgere §117 *intr* (ESSERE) (poet) to rise

asta *f* staff; rod; arm (*e.g., of scale*); lance; leg (*of compass*); stroke (*in handwriting*); shaft (*of arrow*); auction; (naut) boom; (naut) mast; (elec) trolley pole; **a mezz'asta** half-mast; **vendere all'asta** to auction, auction off

astante *mf* bystander || *m* physician on duty (*in a hospital*)

astanterìa *f* receiving ward

astato *m* (chem) astatine

astè·mio -mia *adj* abstemious, temperate || *mf* teetotaler

astenére §271 *ref* to abstain

astensióne *f* abstension

astenuto *m* person who abstains from voting; abstention (*vote withheld*)

astèrgere §164 (*pp* astèrso) *tr* to wipe

asteri·sco *m* (-schi) asterisk

asticcióla *f* penholder; rib (*of umbrella*); temple (*of eyeglasses*)

àstice *m* (*Hommarus vulgaris*) lobster

asticèlla *f* (sports) bar

astinènte *adj* abstinent

astinènza *f* abstinence

à·stio *m* (-sti) grudge, rancor

astió·so -sa [s] *adj* full of malice, spiteful

astóre *m* goshawk

astràgalo *m* astragalus, anklebone

astrakàn *m* Persian lamb

astrarre §273 *tr* to abstract || *intr*—**astrarre da** to leave aside, overlook

astrat·to -ta *adj* abstract || *m* abstract

astrazióne *f* abstraction

astringènte *adj* & *m* astringent

-astro -astra *suf adj* -ish, e.g., **verdastro**

greenish || *suf mf* -aster, e.g., **poetastro** poetaster

astro *m* star, heavenly body; (bot) aster; (fig) star

astrologìa *f* astrology

astrològi·co -ca *adj* (-ci -che) astrological

astròlo·go *m* (-gi or -ghi) astrologer

astronàu·ta *mf* (-ti -te) astronaut

astronàuti·co -ca (-ci -che) *adj* astronautic(al) || *f* astronautics

astronave *f* spaceship, spacecraft

astronomìa *f* astronomy

astrònomo *m* astronomer

astronòmi·co -ca *adj* (-ci -che) astronomic(al)

astruserìa *f* abstruseness

astrusi·tà *f* (-tà) abstruseness

astru·so -sa *adj* abstruse

astùc·cio *m* (-ci) case, box

astu·to -ta *adj* astute, crafty

astùzia *f* astuteness, craftiness

àta·vo -va *mf* ancestor

ateìsmo *m* atheism

atei·sta *mf* (-sti -ste) atheist

Atène *f* Athens

atenèo *m* athenaeum; university

ateniése [s] *adj* & *mf* Athenian

àte·o -a *adj* atheistic || *mf* atheist

atlante *m* atlas || **Atlante** *m* Atlas

atlànti·co -ca *adj* (-ci -che) Atlantic || **Atlantico** *m* Atlantic

atlè·ta *mf* (-ti -te) athlete

atletéssa *f* female athlete

atlèti·co -ca (-ci -che) *adj* athletic || *f* athletics; **atletica leggera** track and field

atmosfèra *f* atmosphere

atmosfèri·co -ca *adj* (-ci -che) atmospheric

atòllo *m* atoll

atòmi·co -ca *adj* (-ci -che) atomic; (coll) stunning

atomizzare [ddzz] *tr* to atomize

atomizzatóre [ddzz] *m* atomizer

àtomo *m* atom

atòni·co -ca *adj* (-ci -che) (pathol) weak

àto·no -na *adj* (gram) atonic

atout *m* (atouts) trump

à·trio *m* (-tri) entrance hall, lobby

atróce *adj* atrocious

atroci·tà *f* (-tà) atrocity

atrofìa *f* atrophy

atròfi·co -ca *adj* (-ci -che) atrophied

atrofizzare [ddzz] *tr* & *ref* to atrophy

attaccabottó·ni *mf* (-ni) bore, pest, buttonholer

attaccabri·ghe *mf* (-ghe) (coll) quarrelsome person, scrapper

attaccaménto *m* attachment, affection

attaccapan·ni *m* (-ni) coathanger

attaccare §197 *tr* to attach; to bind, unite; to sew on; to stick; to hitch (*a horse*); to hang; to attack; to strike up (*a conversation*); to begin; to communicate (*a disease*); **attaccare un bottone a** (fig) to buttonhole || *intr* to stick; to gain a foothold, take root; to begin || *ref* to stick; to

cling; to spread (*said of a disease*);
(fig) to become attached

attaccàtic·cio -cia *adj* (-ci -ce) sticky

attacchino *m* billposter

attac·co *m* (-chi) attachment; onslaught;
fastening; beginning; seizure (*e.g., of
epilepsy*); spell (*e.g., of coughing*);
(elec) plug; (rad) jack; (sports) forward line; **attacco cardìaco** heart
attack

attagliare §280 *ref*—**attagliarsi a** to fit,
become

attanagliare §280 *tr* to grip; to seize; to
hold (*e.g., with tongs*)

attardare *ref* to tarry, delay

attecchire §176 *intr* to take root; to
take hold

atteggiaménto *m* attitude

atteggiare §290 (attéggio) *tr* to compose (*e.g., one's face*); to place ‖ *ref*
to pose; to strike an attitude

attempà·to -ta *adj* elderly

attendaménto *m* camping; jamboree (*of
Boy Scouts*)

attendare (attèndo) *ref* to encamp; to
pitch one's tent

attendènte *m* (mil) orderly

attèndere §270 *tr* to await; (archaic) to
keep; **attendere l'ora propizia** to bide
one's time ‖ *intr*—**attendere a** to attend to

attendìbile *adj* reliable

attendismo *m* wait-and-see attitude

attendì·sta (-sti -ste) *adj* wait-and-see ‖
mf fence-sitter

attenére §271 *tr* (poet) to keep (*a
promise*) ‖ *intr*—**attenere** (with *dat*)
to concern, e.g., **ciò non gli attiene**
this does not concern him ‖ *ref*—
attenersi a to conform to

attentare (attènto) *intr*—**attentare a** to
attempt (*s.o.'s life*) ‖ *ref* to make an
attempt, dare

attentato *m* attempt

attenta·tóre -trice *mf* would-be murderer; attacker

attèn·ti *m* (-ti) attention ‖ *interj* (mil)
attention!

attèn·to -ta *adj* attentive; careful

attenuare (attènuo) *tr* to extenuate,
play down; to attenuate; to mitigate

attenzióne *f* attention; **fare attenzione**
to take care; **prestare attenzione** to
pay attention

atterràg·gio *m* (-gi) landing; **atterraggio
di fortuna** emergency landing; **atterraggio senza carrello** crash-landing

atterraménto *m* landing; pinning, pin
(*in wrestling*); (boxing) knocking
down; **atterramento frenato** (aer) arrested landing

atterrare (attèrro) *tr* to fell; to knock
down; to pin (*in wrestling*); (fig) to
humiliate ‖ *intr* to land; **atterrare
scassando** or **atterrare senza carrello**
to crash-land

atterrire §176 *tr* to frighten, terrify ‖
ref to become frightened

atté·so -sa [s] *adj* awaited, expected;
atteso che considering that ‖ *f* waiting; expectation; **in attesa (di)** waiting (for)

attestare (attèsto) *tr* to certify, attest;
to prove; to join; (mil) to deploy ‖
ref (mil) to take a stand

attestato *m* certificate

attestazióne *f* testimony; affidavit; at-
testation, proof

àtti·co -ca (-ci -che) *adj & mf* Attic ‖
m attic

attì·guo -gua *adj* adjacent, contiguous

attillare *tr & ref* to preen

attillà·to -ta *adj* tight, close-fitting; tidy,
all dressed up

àttimo *m* moment, split second; **di attimo in attimo** any moment

attinènte *adj* related, pertinent

attinènza *f* relation; **attinenze** appurte-
nances; annexes

attìngere §126 *tr* to draw (*water*); to
get; (poet) to attain (*e.g., glory*)

attingi·tóio *m* (-tói) ladle

attirare *tr* to draw, attract

attitùdine *f* aptitude; attitude

attivare *tr* to activate; to expedite

attivazióne *f* activation; reassessment

attivi·tà *f* (-tà) activity; **attività** *fpl*
assets

attì·vo -va *adj* active; profit-making ‖
m assets

attizzare *tr* to stir, poke (*a fire*); (fig)
to stir up

attizza·tóio *m* (-tói) poker

àt·to -ta *adj* apt, fit ‖ *m* act, action;
gesture; (law) instrument; **all'atto
pratico** in reality; **atti** proceedings
(*of a learned society*); **atti notarili**
legal proceedings; **atto di nascita**
birth certificate; **fare atto di presenza**
to put in a brief formal appearance;
atto di vendita bill of sale; **nell'atto**
o **sull'atto** in the act

attòni·to -ta *adj* astonished

attorcigliare §280 *tr* to twist ‖ *ref* to
wind; to coil up

attóre *m* actor; (law) plaintiff; **attore
giovane** (theat) juvenile; **primo attore**
(theat) lead

attorniare §287 (attórnio) *tr* to surround; (fig) to dupe

attórno *adv* around; **andare attorno** to
walk around; **attorno a** around, near;
darsi d'attorno to busy oneself; **levarsi qlcu d'attorno** to get rid of s.o.

attortigliare §280 *tr* to twist ‖ *ref* to
wind; to coil up

attraccare §197 *tr & intr* to moor, dock

attràc·co *m* (-chi) mooring, docking

attraènte *adj* attractive

attrarre §273 *tr* to attract, draw

attrattì·vo -va *adj* attractive; alluring ‖
f attraction, charm

attraversaménto *m* crossing; **attraver-
samento pedonale** pedestrian crossing

attraversare (attravèrso) *tr* to cross; to
go through; to thwart; **attraversare
il passo a** to stand in the way of

attravèrso *adv* across; crosswise; **andare attraverso** to go down the wrong
way (*said of food or drink*); (fig) to
go wrong; **attraverso a** through, across
‖ *prep* through, across

attrazióne *f* attraction

attrezzare (attrézzo) *tr* to outfit, equip

attrezzatura *f* outfit; gear, equipment; **attrezzatura di una nave** rigging; **attrezzature** facilities

attrezzi·sta (-sti -ste) *mf* gymnast || *m* toolmaker; (theat) property man

attrézzo *m* tool, utensil; **attrezzi** gymnastic equipment

attribuire §176 *tr* to award; to attribute; **attribuire qlco a qlcu** to credit s.o. with s.th || *ref* to ascribe to oneself, claim for oneself

attributo *m* attribute

attribuzióne *f* attribution

attrice *f* actress; (law) **plaintiff; prima attrice** (theat) lead

attristare *tr* (poet) to sadden || *ref* to become sad

attri·to -ta *adj* worn, worn-out || *m* attrition; disagreement

attruppare *tr* to band, group || *ref* to mill about, throng

attuàbile *adj* feasible

attuale *adj* present; present-day, current

attuali·tà *f* (-tà) timeliness; reality; **attualità** *fpl* current events; **di viva attualità** newsworthy; timely; **in the news**

attualizzare [ddzz] *tr* to bring up to date || *ref* to become a reality

attuare (**àttuo**) *tr* to carry out, make come true || *ref* to come true

attuà·rio -ria (-ri -rie) *adj* (hist) transport (*e.g., ship*) || *m* actuary

attuazióne *f* realization

attuíre §176 *tr* to mitigate; to deaden (*a sound, a blow*) || *ref* to diminish (*said of a sound*)

audace *adj* audacious

audàcia *f* audacity

audiofrequènza *f* audio frequency

audiovisi·vo -va *adj* audio-visual

auditi·vo -va *adj* var of **uditivo**

auditóre *m* var of **uditore**

auditò·rio *m* (-ri) auditorium

audizióne *f* program; audition; (law) hearing

àuge *f* acme; **essere in auge** to enjoy a great reputation; to be in vogue; to be on top of the world

augurale *adj* well-wishing; salutatory

augurare (**àuguro**) *tr* to wish; to bid (*good day*) || *intr* to augur || *ref* to hope; to expect

àugure *m* augur

augù·rio *m* (-ri) wish; augury, omen

augustè·o -a *adj* Augustan

augu·sto -sta *adj* august, venerable

àula *f* hall; classroom; (poet) chamber (*of a palace*)

àuli·co -ca *adj* (-ci -che) courtly; noble, elevated

aumentare (**auménto**) *tr* to augment, increase || *intr* (ESSERE) to increase, rise

auménto *m* increase

àura *f* (poet) breeze; (poet) breath

àure·o -a *adj* golden, gold

aurèola *f* halo

auricolare *adj* ear; first-hand || *m* (telp) receiver; (rad) earphone

auròra *f* dawn; (fig) aurora

ausiliare *adj* auxiliary || *m* collaborator, helper

ausilià·rio -ria (-ri -rie) *adj* auxiliary; (mil) supply || *m* helper; (mil) reserve officer || *f* female member of the armed forces

ausì·lio *m* (-li) (poet) help

auspicare §197 (**àuspico**) *tr* to wish, augur

àuspice *m* sponsor; (hist) augur

auspì·cio *m* (-ci) sponsorship; (hist, poet) augury, omen; **sotto gli auspici di** under the auspices of

austeri·tà *f* (-tà) austerity

austè·ro -ra *adj* austere

australe *adj* austral, southern

Austràlia, l' *f* Australia

australia·no -na *adj & mf* Australian

Austria, l' *f* Austria

austrì·a·co -ca *adj & mf* (-ci -che) Austrian

autarchìa *f* autarky; autonomy (*of an administration*)

autàrchi·co -ca *adj* (-ci -che) autonomous, independent

autèntic·a *f* (-che) authentication of a signature or a document

autenticare §197 (**autèntico**) *tr* to authenticate

autentici·tà *f* (-tà) authenticity

autènti·co -ca (-ci -che) *adj* authentic, genuine || *f* see **autentica**

autière *m* (mil) driver

auti·sta *mf* (-sti -ste) (aut) driver

au·to *f* (-to) auto

autoabbronzante [dz] *adj* tanning || *m* tanning lotion

autoaffondaménto *m* scuttling

autoambulanza *f* ambulance

autobiografìa *f* autobiography

autobiogràfi·co -ca *adj* (-ci -che) autobiographical

autoblinda·to -ta *adj* armored

autoblin·do *m* (-do) armored car

autobótte *f* tank truck

àuto·bus *m* (-bus) bus

autocarro *m* truck, motor truck

autocèntro *m* (mil) motor pool

autocistèrna *f* tank truck

autocivètta *f* unmarked police car

autocolónna *f* row of cars

autocombustióne *f* spontaneous combustion

autocontròllo *m* self-control

autocorrièra *f* intercity bus, highway bus

autocrazìa *f* autocracy

autocriti·ca *f* (-che) self-criticism

autòcto·no -na *adj* autochthonous, independent

autodecisióne *m* free will

autodeterminazióne *f* self-determination

autodidat·ta *mf* (-ti -te) self-taught person

autodidàtti·co -ca *adj* (-ci -che) self-instructional

autodifésa [s] *f* self-defense

autodisciplina *f* self-discipline

autòdromo *m* automobile race track

autoemotè·ca *f* (-che) bloodmobile

autofilettante *adj* self-threading

autofurgóne *m* van; **autofurgone cellu-**

lare police van; **autofurgone funebre** hearse

autogiro *m* autogyro

autogovèrno *m* self-government

autògra·fo -fa *adj* autographic(al) || *m* autograph

auto·grù *f* (-grù) tow truck

autolesioni·sta *mf* (-sti -ste) person who wounds himself to avoid the draft or collect insurance

autoletti·ga *f* (-ghe) ambulance

autolibro *m* bookmobile

autolìnea *f* bus line

autò·ma *m* (-mi) automaton, robot

automàti·co -ca (-ci -che) *adj* automatic || *m* snap

automatizzare [ddzz] *tr* to automate

automazióne *f* automation

automèzzo [ddzz] *m* motor vehicle

automòbile *f* automobile, car; **automobile da corsa** racing car; **automobile di serie** stock car; **automobile fuori serie** custom-made car

automobilismo *m* motoring

automobili·sta *mf* (-sti -ste) motorist

automobilìsti·co -ca *adj* (-ci -che) car, automobile

automo·tóre -trice *adj* self-propelled || *f* (rr) automotive rail car

autonolég·gio *m* (-gi) car rental agency

autonomìa *f* autonomy; (aer, naut) cruising radius

autonomi·sta *adj* (-sti -ste) autonomous

autòno·mo -ma *adj* autonomous, independent

autoparchég·gio *m* (-gi) parking; parking lot

autopar·co *m* (-chi) parking; parking lot

autopiano *m* player piano

autopilò·ta *m* (-ti) (aer) automatic pilot

autopómpa *f* fire engine

autopsìa *f* autopsy

autorà·dio *f* (-dio) car radio

autóre *m* author; perpetrator; creator, maker

autoreattóre *m* ramjet engine

autorespiratóre *m* aqualung

autorévole *adj* authoritative

autoriméssa *f* garage

autori·tà *f* (-tà) authority

autorità·rio -ria *adj* (-ri -rie) authoritarian

autoritratto *m* self-portrait

autorizzare [ddzz] *tr* to authorize

autorizzazióne [ddzz] *f* authorization

autoscala *f* hook and ladder; ladder (of hook and ladder)

autoscuòla *f* driving school

autoservì·zio *m* (-zi) bus service, bus line; self-service

autosilo *m* parking garage

autostazióne *f* bus station

autostèllo *m* roadside motel

auto·stòp *m* (-stòp) hitchhiking; **fare l'autostop** to hitchhike

autostoppi·sta *mf* (-sti -ste) hitchhiker

autostrada *f* highway, turnpike

autosufficiènte *adj* self-sufficient

autote·làio *m* (-lài) (aut) frame

autotrasportare (**autotraspòrto**) *tr* to truck

autotrasportatóre *m* trucker

autotreni·sta *m* (-sti) truck driver, teamster

autotrèno *m* tractor trailer

autoveìcolo *m* motor vehicle

autovettura *f* car, automobile

autrice *f* authoress

autunnale *adj* autumnal, fall

autunno *m* autumn, fall

avallare *tr* to endorse (*a promissory note*); to guarantee

avallo *m* endorsement (*of a promissory note*)

avambràc·cio *m* (-ci) forearm

avampósto *m* outpost

avancàrica *f—***ad avancarica** muzzle-loading

avanguàrdia *f* vanguard; avant-garde

avanguardismo *m* avant-garde

avanguardi·sta *m* (-sti) avant-gardist; (hist) member of Fascist youth organization

avannòtto *m* small fry (*young freshwater fish*)

avanti *adj* preceding || *m* forward || *adv* forward, ahead; **andare avanti** to proceed, to go ahead; **andare avanti negli anni** to be up in years; **avanti a** in front of; **avanti che** rather than; **avanti di** before; **essere avanti** to be advanced (*in work or study*); **in avanti** ahead || *prep*—**avanti Cristo** before Christ; **avanti giorno** before daybreak || *interj* come in!

avantièri *adv* day before yesterday

avantrèno *m* (aut) front-axle assembly; (mil) limber

avanzaménto *m* advancement

avanzare *tr* to advance; to overcome; to be creditor for, e.g., **avanza cento dollari da suo fratello** he is his brother's creditor for one hundred dollars; to save || *intr* (mil) to advance || *intr* (ESSERE) to advance; to stick out; to be abundant; to be left over, e.g., **avanzano due polpette** two meatballs are left over; **avanzare negli anni** to grow older || *ref* to advance, come forward

avanza·to -ta *adj* advanced; progressive || *f* (mil) advance

avanzo *m* remainder; **avanzi** remains

avarìa *f* damage, breakdown; (naut) average

avariare §287 *tr* to damage, spoil || *intr* to spoil

avaria·to -ta *adj* damaged, spoiled

avarìzia *f* avarice, greed

ava·ro -ra *adj* avaricious, stingy || *mf* miser

avellana *f* filbert

avellano *m* filbert tree

avèllo *m* (poet) tomb

avéna *f* oats

avére *m* belongings, property; assets, credit; amount due || §118 *tr* to have; to hold; to wear; to receive, get; to stand (*a chance*); to be, e.g., **avere . . . anni** to be . . . years old; **avere caldo** to be hot; to be warm; **avere fame** to be hungry; **avere freddo** to be cold; **avere fretta** to be in a hurry;

avere **paura** to be afraid; avere **ragione** to be right; avere **sete** to be thirsty; avere **sonno** to be sleepy; avere **torto** to be wrong; avere **vergogna** to be ashamed; avere **voglia di** to be anxious to; avere **qlco** da + *inf* to have s.th to + *inf*, e.g., **ho molto lavoro da fare** I have a lot of work to do; **averla con** to be angry at; **non avere niente a che fare con** to have nothing to do with || *impers*—**v'ha** there is || *aux* to have, e.g., **ha letto il giornale** he has read the newspaper; avere **da** + *inf* to have to + *inf*, e.g., **avevo da lavorare** I had to work; **to be to** + *inf*, e.g., **ha da venire alle cinque** he is to arrive at five o'clock

avià•rio -ria (-ri -rie) *adj* bird || *m* aviary

avia•tóre -trice *mf* aviator || *f* aviatrix

aviazióne *f* aviation

avicoltóre *m* bird raiser; poultry farmer

avidi•tà *f* (-tà) avidity, greediness

àvi•do -da *adj* avid, greedy

avière *m* airman

aviogètto *m* jet plane

aviolinea *f* airline

aviopista *f* (aer) airstrip

avioriméssa *f* (aer) hangar

aviotrasporta•to -ta *adj* airborne

avi•to -ta *adj* ancestral

a•vo -va *mf* grandparent; ancestor || *m* grandfather || *f* grandmother

avocare §197 (àvoco) *tr* to demand (*jurisdiction*); to expropriate

avò•rio *m* (-rì) ivory

avul•so -sa *adj* (poet) torn, uprooted; (poet) separated

avvalére §278 *ref*—**avvalersi di** to avail oneself of

avvallaménto *m* sinking, settling

avvallare *tr* (poet) to lower (*e.g., one's eyes*) || *ref* to sink; (lit) to humiliate oneself

avvalorare (avvalóro) *tr* to strengthen, confirm || *ref* to gain strength

avvampare *tr* (poet) to inflame || *intr* (ESSERE) to burn

avvantaggiare §290 *tr* to be profitable to; to benefit || *ref* to profit; **avvantaggiarsi su** to overcome; to beat

avvedére §279 *ref*—**avvedersi di** to notice, become aware of

avvedutézza *f* discernment; shrewdness

avvedu•to -ta *adj* prudent; shrewd; **fare qlcu avveduto di** to inform s.o. of

avvelenaménto *m* poisoning

avvelenare (avveléno) *tr* to poison || *ref* to take poison; to be poisoned

avveniménto *m* happening, event

avvenire *adj invar* future, to come || *m* future; **in avvenire** in the future || §282 *intr* (ESSERE) to happen, occur; **avvenga quel che vuole** come what may

avventare (avvènto) *tr* to hurl; to deliver (*a blow*); to venture (*an opinion*) || *ref* to throw oneself

avventatézza *f* thoughtlessness, heedlessness

avventa•to -ta *adj* thoughtless, heedless; **all'avventata** heedlessly

avventi•zio -zia *adj* (-zì -zie) outside, exterior; temporary, occasional

avvènto *m* advent; elevation, rise

avven•tóre -tóra *mf* customer, consumer

avventura *f* adventure

avventuriè•ro -ra *adj* adventurous || *m* adventurer || *f* adventuress

avventuró•so -sa [s] *adj* adventurous, adventuresome

avverare (avvéro) *tr* to make true || *ref* to come true

avvèr•bio *m* (-bi) adverb

avversà•rio -ria (-ri -rie) *adj* opposing, contrary || *mf* adversary, opponent

avversióne *f* aversion

avversi•tà *f* (-tà) adversity

avvèr•so -sa *adj* adverse; (obs) opposite || **avverso** *prep* (law) against

avvertènza *f* prudence, caution; advice; avvertenze instructions, directions

avvertiménto *m* caution, warning; advice

avvertire (avvèrto) *tr* to caution, warn; to notice

avvezzare (avvézzo) *tr* to accustom; to inure; to train; **avvezzar male** to spoil || *ref* to get accustomed

avvéz•zo -za *adj* accustomed

avviaménto *m* starting; introduction; trade school; good shape (*of a business*); (mach) starting; (typ) adjustment (*of printing press*)

avviare §119 *tr* to start, set in motion; to introduce; to initiate; to begin || *ref* to set out

avvia•to -ta *adj* going, thriving (*concern*)

avvicendaménto *m* alteration, rotation (*of crops*)

avvicendare (avvicènde) *tr & ref* to alternate

avvicinaménto *m* approach; rapprochement

avvicinare *tr* to bring near or closer; to approach, go or come near to || *ref* to approach, come near; **avvicinarsi a** to come closer, approach

avvilimento *m* discouragment, dejection

avvilire §176 *tr* to degrade; to deject || *ref* to become dejected, become discouraged

avviluppare *tr* to entangle, snarl; to wrap

avvinazza•to -ta *adj & mf* drunk

avvincènte *adj* fascinating

avvincere §285 *tr* to fascinate, charm; (poet) to twine

avvinghiare §287 *tr* to claw; to clasp, clutch || *ref* to grip one another

avvì•o *m* (-i) beginning

avviságlia *f* skirmish; **prime avvisaglie** onset; first signs

avvisare *tr* to inform, advise; (archaic) to observe, notice

avvisa•tóre -trice *mf* announcer, messenger || *m* alarm; (theat) callboy; **avvisatore acustico** (aut) horn; **avvisatore d'incendio** fire alarm

avviso *m* advise; notice, poster; opinion; **avviso di chiamata alle armi** notice of induction; **sull'avviso** on one's guard

avvistare *tr* to sight

avvitaménto *m* (aer) tailspin

avvitare *tr* to screw; to fasten ‖ *ref* (aer) to go into a tailspin

avviticchiare §287 *tr* to entwine ‖ *ref* to cling

avvivare *tr* to revive; to stir up

avvizzire §176 *tr* & *intr* (ESSERE) to wither

avvocatéssa *f* woman lawyer

avvocato *m* lawyer, attorney

avvocatura *f* law, legal profession

avvòlgere §289 *tr* to wind; to wrap up; to spread over, surround ‖ *ref* to wind around; to wrap oneself up

avvolgiménto *m* winding; wrapping; (elec) coil; (mil) envelopment

avvol·tóio *m* (-tói) vulture

avvoltolare (avvòltolo) *tr* to roll up ‖ *ref* to roll around, wallow

aziènda [dz] *f* business, firm

azionare (azióno) *tr* to start; to drive, propel

azionà·rio -ria *adj* (-ri -rie) (com) stock

azióne *f* action, act; (law) suit; (com) share (*of stock*); **azione legale** prosecution; **azione privilegiata** preferred stock

azioni·sta *mf* (-sti -ste) stockholder, shareholder

azòto [dz] *m* nitrogen

azoturo [dz] *m* nitride

aztè·co -ca *adj* & *mf* (-chi -che) Aztec

azzannare *tr* to seize with the fangs

azzardare [ddzz] *tr* to risk; to advance ‖ *ref* to dare

azzarda·to -ta [ddzz] *adj* daring

azzardo [ddzz] *m* chance, hazard

azzardó·so -sa [ddzz] [s] *adj* hazardous, risky

azzeccagarbu·gli *m* (-gli) shyster

azzeccare §197 (azzécco) *tr* to hit; to deliver; to pass off (*counterfeit money*); **azzeccarla** (coll) to hit the mark

azzimare [ddzz] (àzzimo) *tr* & *ref* to spruce up

àzzi·mo -ma [ddzz] *adj* unleavened (*bread*)

azzittare & **azzittire** §176 *tr* to hush ‖ *ref* to keep quiet

azzoppare (azzòppo) *tr* to cripple ‖ *ref* to become lame or crippled

Azzòrre [ddzz] *fpl* Azores

azzuffare *ref* to come to blows; to scuffle

azzur·ro -ra [ddzz] *adj* blue ‖ *m* blue; Italian athlete (*in international competition*)

azzurrógno·lo -la [ddzz] *adj* bluish

B

B, b [bi] *m* & *f* second letter of the Italian alphabet

ba·bàu *m* (-bàu) bogey, bugbear

babbè·o -a *adj* foolish ‖ *mf* fool

babbo *m* (coll) daddy, father

babbù·cia *f* (-ce) babouche; bedroom slipper

babbuino *m* baboon

babèle *f* babel ‖ **Babele** *f* Babel

babilònia *f* confusion ‖ **Babilònia** *f* Babylon

babórdo *m* (naut) port

bacare §197 *ref* to become worm-eaten

baca·to -ta *adj* worm-eaten; rotten

bac·ca *f* (-che) berry

bacca·là *m* (-là) dried codfish; (coll) skinny person; (coll) lummox

baccalaureato *m* baccalaureate, bachelor's degree

baccanale *m* bacchanal

baccano *m* noise, hubbub; **fare baccano** to carry on

baccante *f* bacchant

baccellière *m* (hist) bachelor

baccèllo *m* pod

baccellóne *m* simpleton, fool

bacchétta *f* rod, wand, baton; **bacchetta magica** magic wand; **bacchette del tamburo** drumsticks

bacchétto *m* stick; handle (*of a whip*)

bacchettó·ne -na *mf* bigot

bàcchi·co -ca *adj* (-ci -che) Bacchic

Bacco *m* Baccus

bachè·ca *f* (-che) showcase

bachelite *f* bakelite

bacheròzzo *m* worm; earthworm; (coll) cockroach

bachicoltura *f* silkworm raising

baciama·no *m* (-ni) kissing of the hand

baciapi·le *mf* (-le) bigot

baciare §128 *tr* to kiss; **baciare la polvere** to bite the dust ‖ *ref* to kiss one another

bacia·to -ta *adj* kissed; rhymed (*couplet*)

bacile *m* basin

bacillo *m* bacillus

bacinèlla *f* small basin; (phot) tray

bacino *m* basin; reservoir; cove; (anat) pelvis; **bacino carbonifero** coal field; **bacino di carenaggio** drydock; **bacino fluviale** river basin

bà·cio *m* (-ci) kiss; **a bacio** with a northern exposure

baciucchiare §287 *tr* to keep on kissing ‖ *ref* to pet

ba·co *m* (-chi) worm; **baco da seta** silkworm

bacuc·co -ca *adj* (-chi -che)—**vecchio bacucco** dotard

bada *f*—**tenere a bada** to stave off; to delay

badare *tr* to tend, take care of ‖ *intr* to attend; to take care; to pay attention; **badare a** to mind; to watch over; to attend to; **badare alla salute** to take care of one's health

badéssa f abbess

badìa f abbey

badilata f shovelful

badile m shovel

baffo m whiskers; whisker; **baffi** mustache; whiskers; **baffo di gatto** (rad) cat's whiskers; **leccarsi i baffi** to lick one's chops; **sotto i baffi** up one's sleeve

baga·gliàio m (**-gliài**) (rr) baggage car; (rr) baggage room; (aut) baggage rack

bagaglièra f baggage room

bagaglière m baggage master

bagà·glio m (**-gli**) baggage, luggage; (of knowledge) fund

bagagli·sta m (**-sti**) porter (in a hotel)

bagarinàg·gio m (**-gi**) profiteering; (theat) scalping

bagarino m profiteer; scalper

bagà·scia f (**-sce**) harlot, prostitute

bagattèlla f trifle, bauble

baggiano m nitwit, simpleton

bà·glio m (**-gli**) (naut) beam

baglióre m shine, gleam

bagnante mf bather, swimmer; vacationer at the seashore

bagnare tr to bathe; to wet; to soak; to water, sprinkle; to moisten; (fig) to celebrate || ref to bathe; to wet one another

bagnaròla f (coll) bathtub

bagnasciu·ga f (**-ghe**) (naut) waterline

bagnino m lifeguard

bagno m bath; bathroom; bathtub; **bagno di luce** diathermy; **bagno di schiuma** bubble bath; **bagno di sole** sun bath; **bagno di vapore** steam bath; **bagno turco** Turkish bath; **essere in un bagno di sudore** to be soaked with perspiration; **fare il bagno** to take a bath

bagnomaria m (**bagnimarìa**) double boiler; bain-marie; **a bagnomaria** in a double boiler

bagórdo m carousal, revelry; **far bagordi** to carouse, revel

bàio bàia (**bài bàie**) adj & m bay || f bay; jest; trifle; **dare la baia a** to make fun of, tease

baionétta f bayonet; **baionetta in canna** with fixed bayonet

bàita f mountain hut

balaustrata f balustrade

balaùstro m baluster

balbettaménto m stammering

balbettare (**balbétto**) tr to stammer; to speak poorly (a foreign language) || intr to stammer; to babble (said of a baby)

balbettì·o m (**-i**) babble (of a baby); stammering

balbùzie f stammering

balbuzièxnte adj stammering || mf stammerer

Balcani, i the Balkans

balcàni·co -ca adj (**-ci -che**) Balkan

balconata f balcony; (theat) upper gallery

balcóne m balcony

baldacchino m canopy, baldachin

baldanza f boldness; aplomb, assurance

baldanzó·so -sa [s] adj bold; self-assured

bal·do -da adj bold; self-assured

baldòria f carousal, revelry; **fare baldoria** to carouse, revel

baldrac·ca f (**-che**) harlot, prostitute

baléna f whale

balenare (**baléno**) intr to stagger || intr (ESSERE) to flash, e.g., **gli balena un pensiero** a thought flashes through his mind || impers (ESSERE)—**balena**, it is lightning

balenièra f whaler, whaleboat

baléno m flash; flash of lightning; **in un baleno** in a flash

balenòttera f rorqual

balèstra f crossbow; (aut) spring, leaf spring

balestrière m crossbowman

bàlia f wet nurse; **balia asciutta** dry nurse; **prendere a balia** to wet-nurse

balìa f power; **in balìa di** at the mercy of

balìsti·co -ca (**-ci -che**) adj ballistic || f ballistics

balla f bale; (vulg) lie

ballàbile adj dance || m dance tune

ballare tr to dance || intr to dance; to shake; to be loose; to wobble (said, e.g., of a chair)

ballata f ballad; (mus) hallade

balla·tóio m (**-tói**) gallery; perch (in birdcage)

balleri·no -na adj dancing || m ballet dancer; dancer; dancing partner || f dancing girl; ballerina; chorus girl; ballet slipper; (orn) wagtail

ballétto m ballet; chorus

ballo m dance; chorus; ball; stake; **ballo di San Vito** Saint Vitus's dance; **ballo in maschera** masked ball; **in ballo** at stake; in question; **tirare in ballo** to drag in

ballonzolare (**ballónzolo**) intr to hop around

ballottàg·gio m (**-gi**) runoff

ballottare (**ballòtto**) tr to ballot (e.g., a candidate)

balneare adj bathing; water, watering

baloccare §197 (**balòcco**) tr to amuse with toys || ref to play; to trifle, to fool around

balòc·co m (**-chi**) toy; hobby

balordàggine f silliness

balór·do -da adj silly, foolish

balsàmi·co -ca adj (**-ci -che**) balmy; antiseptic

balsamina f balsam

bàlsamo m balm, balsam

bàlti·co -ca adj (**-ci -che**) Baltic

baluardo m bastion, bulwark

baluginare (**balùgino**) intr (ESSERE) to flicker; to flash (through one's mind)

balza f crag, cliff; flounce (on dress); fringe (on curtains, bedspreads, etc.)

balza·no -na adj white-footed (horse); odd, funny || f flounce; fringe; white mark (on horse's foot)

balzare tr to throw (a rider; said of a horse) || intr (ESSERE) to jump, leap;

to bounce; **balzare in mente a** to suddenly dawn on

balzellare (balzèllo) *intr* to hop

balzèllo *m* hop; tribute; tax; toll; **stare a balzello** to lie in wait

balzellóni *adv*—**a balzelloni** leaping, skipping

balzo *m* leap; bounce; **pigliare la palla al balzo** to take time by the forelock

bambàgia *f* cotton wool

bambinàggine *f* childishness

bambinàia *f* nursemaid; **bambinaia ad ore** baby sitter

bambiné·sco -sca *adj* (**-schi -sche**) childish

bambi·no -na *adj* childish || *mf* child

bambòc·cio *m* (**-ci**) fat baby; doll; rag doll

bàmbola *f* doll; **bambola di pezza** rag-doll

bam·bù *m* (**-bù**) bamboo

banale *adj* banal, commonplace

banali·tà *f* (**-tà**) banality, commonplaceness, triviality

banana *f* banana; hair with curls shaped as rolls

bananièra *f* banana boat

banano *m* banana plant

ban·ca *f* (**-che**) bank; embankment

bancàbile *adj* negotiable

bancarèlla *f* cart, pushcart; stall

bancà·rio -ria (**-ri -rie**) *adj* bank, banking || *m* bank clerk

bancarótta *f* bankruptcy; **fare bancarotta** to go bankrupt

banchettare (banchétto) *intr* to feast, banquet

banchétto *m* banquet

banchière *m* banker

banchìna *f* garden bench; bicycle path; sidewalk; shoulder (*of highway*); dock, pier; (rr) platform; (mil) banquette

ban·co *m* (**-chi**) bench; seat; bank; witness stand; school (*of fish*); **banco di coralli** coral reef; **banco di ghiaccio** ice pack; **banco di nebbia** fog bank; **banco di prova** (mach) bench; **banco di sabbia** sandbar; **banco d'ostriche** oyster bed; **banco lotto** lottery office

bancogiro *m* (com) transfer of funds

bancóne *m* counter; bench

banconòta *f* banknote

banda *f* band; **andare alla banda** (naut) to list; **da ogni banda** from every side; **mettere da banda** to put aside

bandèlla *f* hinge (*of door or window*); hinged leaf (*of table*)

banderuòla *f* bandcrole; weather vane

bandièra *f* flag; banner; **battere la bandiera** (*e.g.*, **italiana**) to fly the (*e.g. Italian*) flag; **mutar bandiera** to change sides

bandierare (bandièro) *tr* (aer) to feather

bandire §176 *tr* to announce (*e.g.*, *a competitive examination*); to banish

bandìsti·co -ca *adj* (**-ci -che**) (mus) band

bandi·to -ta *adj* announced; open (*house*) || *m* bandit || *f* preserve (*for hunting or fishing*)

bandi·tóre -trice *mf* town crier; auctioneer; barker

bando *m* announcement; banishment; **bandi matrimoniali** (eccl) banns; **mandare in bando** to exile, banish

bandolièra *f* bandoleer; **a bandoliera** slung across the shoulders

bàndolo *m* end of a skein; **perdere il bandolo** to lose the thread (*e.g.*, *of a story*)

bara *f* bier, coffin

barac·ca *f* (**-che**) hut, cabin; (fig) household; **fare baracca** to carouse around

baracca·to -ta *adj* lodged in a hut or a cabin; slum (*e.g.*, *section*) || *m* dweller in a hut or a cabin; slum dweller

baraccóne *m* big circus tent

baraónda *f* hubbub; mess

barare *intr* to cheat (*e.g.*, *at cards*)

bàratro *m* abyss, chasm

barattare *tr* to barter; **barattare le carte in mano a uno** to distort someone's words; **barattar parole** to chat, talk || *intr* to barter

barattière *m* grafter

baratto *m* barter

baràttolo *m* can, canister, jar

barba *f* beard; whiskers; barb, vane (*of feather*); (naut) line; **barba a punta** imperial, goatee; **fare la barba (a)** to shave; **farla in barba a qlcu** to act in spite of s.o.; to dupe s.o.; **mettere barbe** to take root; **radersi la barba** to shave

barbabiètola *f* beet; sugar beet

barbafòrte *m* horseradish

barbagian·ni *m* (**-ni**) owl; (fig) jackass

barbà·glio *m* (**-gli**) glitter, dazzle

barbaré·sco -sca (**-schi -sche**) *adj* Barbary || *m* inhabitant of the Barbary States

barbàri·co -ca *adj* (**-ci -che**) barbaric

barbà·rie *f* (**-rie**) barbarism, barbarity

barbarismo *m* barbarism

bàrba·ro -ra *adj* barbarous, barbaric || *m* barbarian

barbazzale *m* curb (*of bit*)

Barberìa, la Barbary States

barbétta *f* fetlock (*tuft of hair on horse*); goatee; (mil) barbette; (naut) painter

barbière *m* barber

barbierìa *f* barbershop

barbì·glio *m* (**-gli**) barb (*of arrow*)

barbi·no -na *adj* shoddy; botched; stingy

bàr·bio *m* (**-bi**) (ichth) barbel

barbiturato *m* barbiturate

barbitùri·co -ca (**-ci -che**) *adj* barbituric || *m* barbiturate

barbo *m* var of **barbio**

barbò·gio -gia *adj* (**-gi -gie**) senile

barbóne *m* long beard, thick beard; poodle; (coll) bum, hobo

barbó·so -sa [*s*] *adj* boring

barbugliare §280 *tr* to stutter (*e.g.*, *a word*) || *intr* to stutter; to bubble, gurgle

barbu·to -ta *adj* bearded

bar·ca *f* (**-che**) boat; heap; (fig) family

affairs; **barca a motore** motorboat; **barca da pesca** fishing boat; **barca a remi** rowboat

barcàc·cia *f* (**-ce**) (theat) stage box

barcaiòlo *m* boatman

barcamenare (**barcaméno**) *ref* to manage, get along

barcarizzo *m* (naut) gangway

barcaròla *f* barcarole

barcata *f* boatful

barchéssa *f* tool shed

barchétta *f* small boat; (naut) log chip

barcollare (**barcòllo**) *intr* to totter, stagger

barcollóni *adv* staggering, tottering

barcóne *m* barge

bardare *tr* to harness ‖ *ref* to get dressed

bardatura *f* harnessing; harness

bardo *m* bard

bardòsso *m* —**a bardosso** (archaic) bareback

barèlla *f* stretcher

barellare (**barèllo**) *tr* to carry on a stretcher ‖ *intr* to totter, stagger

barenatura *f* (mach) boring

bargèllo *m* (hist) chief of police; (hist) police headquarters

bargi·gllo *m* (**-gli**) wattle

baricèntro *m* center of gravity; (fig) essence, gist

barile *m* barrel, cask

barilòtto *m* keg

bàrio *m* barium

bari·sta *mf* (**-sti -ste**) bartender, barkeeper ‖ *m* barman ‖ *f* barmaid

baritonale *adj* baritone

barìto·no -na *adj* barytone ‖ *m* baritone

barlume *m* glimmer, gleam

baro *m* cheat, cardsharp

baròc·co -ca *adj* & *m* (**-chi -che**) baroque

baròmetro *m* barometer

baróne *m* baron

baronéssa *f* baroness

barra *f* bar; link; rod; sandbar; **andare alla barra** to plead a case; **barra del timone** (naut) tiller; **barra di torsione** (aut) torsion bar; **barra spaziatrice** space bar (*of typewriter*)

barrare *tr* to cross, draw lines across (*a check*)

barrétta *f* bar (*e.g., of chocolate*)

barricare §197 (**bàrrico**) *tr* to barricade ‖ *ref* to barricade oneself

barricata *f* barricade

barrièra *f* barrier; bar; **barriera corallina** barrier reef

barrire §176 *intr* to trumpet (*said of elephant*)

barrito *m* trumpeting, cry of an elephant

barroc·ciàio *m* (**-ciài**) cart driver

barròc·cio *m* (**-ci**) cart

baruffa *f* fight, quarrel

barzellétta [dz] *f* joke

basale *adj* basal

basalto *m* basalt

basaménto *m* foundation (*of building*); baseboard; base (*of column*)

basare *tr* to base ‖ *ref*—**basarsi su** to be based on; to rest on

ba·sco -sca *adj* & *mf* (**-schi -sche**) Basque

basculla *f* balance, scale

base *f* base, foundation; (fig) basis; **a base di** composed of, made of; **base navale** naval base, naval station; **in base a** according to

basétta *f* sideburns

bàsi·co -ca *adj* (**-ci -che**) (chem) basic

basilare *adj* basic, fundamental

Basilèa *f* Basel

basìli·ca *f* (**-che**) basilica

basìli·co *m* (**-ci**) basil

basilissa *f* (fig) queen bee

bàsolo *m* large paving stone

bassacórte *f* barnyard

bassézza *f* baseness

bas·so -sa *adj* low; shallow; late (*e.g., date*); (fig) base, vile; **basso di statura** short ‖ *m* bottom; hovel (*in Naples*); (mus) basso ‖ **basso adv** low; down; **a basso, da basso or in basso** downstairs

bassofóndo *m* (**bassifóndi**) (naut) shallows, shallow water; **bassifondi** underworld, slums

bassopiano *m* lowland

bassorilièvo *m* bas-relief

bassòt·to -ta *adj* stocky ‖ *m* basset hound

bassotuba *m* bass horn

bassura *f* lowland; (fig) baseness

basta *f* hem; basting (*with long stitches*) ‖ *interj* enough!

bastante *adj* sufficient, adequate; comfortable (*income*)

bastar·do -da *adj* bastard; irregular ‖ *m* bastard

bastare *intr* to suffice, be enough; **basta!** enough!; **basta che** + *subj* as long as + *ind*; **bastare a sé stesso** to be self-sufficient; **non basta che** + *subj* not only + *ind*

bastévole *adj* sufficient

bastiménto *m* ship; shipload

bastióne *m* bastion; (fig) defense, rampart

basto *m* packsaddle; (fig) burden

bastonare (**bastóno**) *tr* to club, cudgel; **bastonare di santa ragione** to give a good thrashing to

bastonata *f* clubbing, cudgeling; **darsi bastonate da orbi** to thrash one another soundly

bastoncino *m* small stick; roll; (anat) rod

bastóne *m* stick, cane; pole; club; baton; staff; French bread; **bastone a leva** crowbar; **bastone animato** sword cane; **bastone da golf** club; **bastone da montagna** alpenstock; **bastone da passeggio** walking stick; **bastone da sci** ski pole; **bastoni** suit in Neapolitan cards corresponding to clubs; **mettere il bastone tra le ruote** to throw a monkey wrench into the machinery

batàc·chio *m* (**-chi**) clapper (*of bell*); cudgel

batata *f* sweet potato

batisfèra *f* bathysphere

batista *f* batiste, cambric

batòsta *f* blow; (fig) blow

bàtrace *or* batrace *m* batrachian

battà·glia *f* (-glie) battle; campaign

battagliare §280 *intr* to fight

battagliè·ro -ra *adj* fighting, warlike

battà·glio *m* (-gli) clapper (*of bell*); knocker

battaglióne *m* battalion

battèllo *m* boat; battello di salvataggio lifeboat; battello pneumatico rubber raft

battènte *m* leaf (*e.g., of door*); knocker; tapper (*of alarm clock*)

bàttere *m*—in un batter d'occhio in the twinkling of an eye || *tr* to beat; to hit; to strike; to strike (*the hour; said of a clock*); to click (*teeth, heels*); to clap (*hands*); to stamp (*one's foot*); to mint (*coins*); to fly (*a flag*); to beat (*time*); to scour (*the countryside*); to flap (*the wings*); (sports) to bat; (sports) to kick (*a penalty*); battere a macchina to type; battere il naso in to chance upon; battere la fiacca to goof off; battere la grancassa per to ballyhoo; bàttere la strada to be a streetwalker; senza batter ciglio without batting an eye || *intr* (ESSERE) to beat down (*said, e.g., of rain*); to beat (*said of the heart*); to chatter (*said of teeth*); to knock (*at the door*); battere in ritirata to beat a retreat; battere in testa (aut) to knock

batteria *f* battery; set (*of utensils*); (sports) heat

batterici·da (-di -de) *adj* bactericidal || *m* bactericide

battèri·co -ca *adj* (-ci -che) bacterial

battè·rio *m* (-ri) bacterium

batteriologìa *f* bacteriology

batteriòlo·go -ga *mf* (-gi -ghe) bacteriologist

batteri·sta *mf* (-sti -ste) jazz drummer

battesimale *adj* baptismal

battèsimo *m* baptism; tenere a battesimo to christen

battezzare (battèzzo) [ddzz] *tr* to christen || *ref* to receive baptism; to assume the name of

battibaléno *m*—in un battibaleno in the twinkling of an eye

battibéc·co *m* (-chi) squabble

batticuòre *m* palpitation; (fig) trepidation

battilò·ro *m* (-ro) goldsmith; silversmith

battimano *m* applause

battimuro *m*—giocare a battimuro to pitch pennies (against a wall)

battipalo *m* pile driver

battipan·ni *m* (-ni) clothes beater

battira·me *m* (-me) coppersmith

battiscó·pa *m* (-pa) washboard, baseboard

batti·sta *adj & mf* (-sti -ste) Baptist

battistèro *m* baptistry

battistra·da *m* (-da) outrider; (sports) leader; (aut) tread

battitappéto *m* carpet sweeper

bàttito *m* beating; palpitation; ticking; wink; pitter-patter (*of rain*)

batti·tóio *m* (-tói) leaf (*e.g., of door*); casement; cotton beater

battitóre *m* (hunt) beater; (baseball) batter

battitrice *f* threshing machine

battitura *f* thrashing, whipping; threshing (*e.g., of wheat*)

battu·to -ta *adj* beaten; hammered || *m* pavement || *f* beat; stroke, keystroke; meter (*in poetry*); witticism, quip; (hunt) battue; (mus) bar; (tennis) service; (theat) line; (theat) cue; battuta d'aspetto (mus) pause; dare la battuta to give the cue

batùffolo *m* wad; (fig) bundle

baule *m* trunk; baule armadio wardrobe trunk; fare i bauli to be on one's way; fare il baule to pack one's trunk

baulétto *m* small trunk; handbag; jewel case

bava *f* slobber; foam, froth; burr (*on metal edge*); avere la bava alla bocca to be frothing at the mouth; bava di vento breath of air, soft breeze

bavaglino *m* bib

bavà·glio *m* (-gli) gag

bavarése [*s*] *adj & mf* Bavarian || *f* Bavarian cream; chocolate cream

bàvero *m* collar

bavièra *f* beaver (*of helmet*) || la Baviera Bavaria

bavó·so -sa [*s*] *adj* slobbering, slobbery

bazza *f* [ddzz] protruding chin; windfall

bazzana [ddzz] *f* sheepskin

bazzècola [ddzz] *f* trifle, bauble

bazzicare §197 (bàzzico) *tr* to frequent

bazzòt·to -ta [ddzz] *adj* soft-boiled; uncertain (*weather*)

beare (bèo) *tr* to delight || *ref* to be delighted, be enraptured

beatificare §197 (beatìfico) *tr* to beatify

beatitùdine *f* beatitude, bliss

bea·to -ta *adj* blissful, happy; blessed || *mf* blessed

be·bè *m* (-bè) baby

beccàc·cia *f* (-ce) woodcock

beccaccino *m* snipe

beccafi·co *m* (-chi) figpecker, beccafico

bec·càio *m* (-cài) butcher

beccamòr·ti *m* (-ti) gravedigger

beccare §197 (bécco) *tr* to peck; to pick; (coll) to catch || *ref* to peck one another; to quarrel

beccata *f* peck

beccheggiare §290 (becchéggio) *intr* (naut) to pitch

becchég·gio *m* (-gi) (naut) pitching

beccherìa *f* butcher shop

becchìme *m* food for poultry

becchino *m* gravedigger

béc·co *m* (-chi) beak, bill; tip, point; nozzle (*e.g., of teapot*); billy goat; (vulg) cuckold; bagnarsi il becco (joc) to wet one's whistle; mettere il becco in (coll) (joc) to stick one's nose into; non avere il becco di un quattrino to not have a red cent

beccùc·cio *m* (-ci) small bill; lip, spout

beccuzzare *tr* to peck || *ref* to bill (*said of doves*)

béce·ro -ra *adj* (coll) boorish || *m* (coll) boor

bedui·no -na *adj & m* Bedouin

befana *f* (coll) Epiphany; old hag

bèffa *f* jest, mockery; **farsi beffa di** to make fun of

beffar·do -da *adj* mocking

beffare (**bèffo**) *tr* to mock, deride || *ref* —**beffarsi di** to make fun of

beffeggiare §290 (**befféggio**) *tr* to scoff at, deride

bè·ga *f* (**-ghe**) quarrel; trouble

beghina *f* Beguine; bigoted woman

begònia *f* begonia

bèl *adj* apocopated form of **bello**, used only before masculine singular nouns beginning with a consonant except impure **s, z, gn, ps,** and **x**, e.g., **bel ragazzo**

belare (**bèlo**) *tr* to croon || *intr* to bleat, baa; to moan

belato *m* bleat, baa

bèl·ga *adj & mf* (**-gi -ghe**) Belgian

Bèlgio, il Belgium

bèll' *adj* apocopated form of **bello**, used only before singular nouns of both genders beginning with a vowel, e.g., **bell'amico; bell'epoca**

bèlla *adj fem* of **bello** || *f* belle; girlfriend; final draft; (sports) final game; (sports) rubber match; **alla bell'e meglio** the best one could; **bella di notte** (bot) four-o'clock

belladònna *f* belladonna

bellétto *m* rouge, makeup

bellézza *f* beauty; **che bellezza!** how lovely!; **la bellezza di** as much as

bellici·sta *adj* (**-sti -ste**) bellicose

bèlli·co -ca *adj* (**-ci -che**) war, warlike

bellicó·so -sa [s] *adj* bellicose

belligerante *adj & m* belligerent

belligeranza *f* belligerence

bellimbusto *m* fop, dandy, beau

bèl·lo -la (declined like **quello** §7) *adj* beautiful; lovely; handsome; good-looking; pleasing; fine; quite a, e.g., **una bella cifra** quite a sum; fair; pretty; **bell'e fatto** ready-made; taken care of; **farla bella** to start trouble; (coll) to do it, e.g., **l'hai fatta bella** you've done it; **farsi bello** to dress up; **farsi bello di** to appropriate || *m* beauty; beautiful; climax; fine weather; beau; **il bello è** the funny thing is; **sul più bello** just then; **sul più bello che** just when || *f* see **bella** || **bello** *adv*—**bel bello** slowly

bellospìrito *m* (**begli spiriti**) wit, bel-esprit

bellui·no -na *adj* wild, fierce

bellumóre *m* (**begli umori**) jolly fellow

bel·tà *f* (**-tà**) beauty (*woman*); (lit) beauty

bélva *f* wild beast

belvedére *adj* (rr) observation (*car*) || *m* belvedere; (naut) topgallant

Belzebù *m* Beelzebub

bemòlle *m* (mus) flat

benama·to -ta *adj* beloved

benarriva·to -ta *adj* welcome

benché *conj* although, albeit

bènda *f* bandage; band; blindfold; **benda gessata** cast, surgical dressing

bendàg·gio *m* (**-gi**) bandage

bendare (**bèndo**) *tr* to bandage; **bendare gli occhi a** to blindfold

bendispó·sto -sta *adj* well-disposed

bène *adj* well; well-born || *m* goal, aim; good; love; sake; **bene dell'anima** profound affection; **beni** (econ) assets, goods; **beni di consumo** consumer goods; **beni immobili** real estate; **beni mobili** personal property, chattels; **beni rifugio** hedge (*e.g., against inflation*); **è un bene** it is a blessing; **fare del bene** to do good; **per il Suo bene** for your sake; **voler bene a** to love, like; to care for || *adv* well; all right; properly; **ben bene** quite carefully; **star bene** to be well; **va bene** O.K., all right

benedetti·no -na *adj & m* Benedictine

benedét·to -ta *adj* blessed; holy

benedire §195 *tr* to bless; to praise; **andare a farsi benedire** (coll) to go to wrack and ruin; **mandare a farsi benedire** (coll) to get rid of, dump

benedizióne *f* benediction; boon

beneduca·to -ta *adj* well-behaved

benefattóre *m* benefactor

benefattrice *f* benefactress

beneficare §197 (**benèfico**) *tr* to benefit, help

beneficènza *f* welfare; charity, beneficence

beneficiale *adj* beneficial

beneficiare §128 *intr* to benefit

beneficià·rio -ria *adj & mf* (**-ri -rie**) beneficiary

beneficiata *f* benefit performance; streak of good luck; streak of bad luck

benefì·cio *m* (**-ci**) benefice; profit; favor; benefit

benèfi·co -ca *adj* (**-ci -che**) beneficial; beneficent

benemerènte *adj* deserving, well-deserving

benemèri·to -ta *adj* worthy, deserving || *m*—**benemerito della patria** national hero || *f*—**la Benemerita** the Carabinieri

beneplàcito *m* approval, consent; **a beneplacito di** at the pleasure of

benèssere *m* well-being, comfort; prosperity

benestante *adj* well-to-do || *mf* well-to-do person

benestare *m* approval; prosperity; **dare il benestare a** to approve

benevolènte *adj* benevolent

benevolènza *f* benevolence

benèvo·lo -la *adj* well-meaning; benevolent

benfat·to -ta *adj* well-done; well-favored; shapely

benga·la *m* (**-li & -la**) fireworks

benga·li *adj & m* (**-li**) Bengalese

beniami·no -na *mf* favorite child; favorite

benigni·tà *f* (**-tà**) benignity; graciousness; mildness (*of climate*)

beni-gno -gna *adj* benign; gracious; mild (*climate*)

benintenziona-to -ta *adj* well-meaning

benintéso [s] *adv* of course, naturally

bènna *f* bucket, scoop (*e.g., of dredge*)

benna-to -ta *adj* (lit) well-born

benpensante *m* sensible person; conformist

benportante *adj* well-preserved

benservito *m* testimonial, recommendation; **dare il benservito a** to dismiss, fire

bensì *adv* indeed || *conj* but

bentorna-to -ta *adj & m* welcome || *interj* welcome back!

benvenu-to -ta *adj & m* welcome; **dare il benvenuto a** to welcome

benvi-sto -sta *adj* well-thought-of

benvolére *tr*—**farsi benvolere da qlcu** to enter the good graces of s.o.; **prendere a benvolere qlcu** to be well-disposed toward s.o.

benvolu-to -ta *adj* liked, loved

benzina *f* gasoline, gas; benzine; **far benzina** (coll) to get gas

benzi-nàio *m* (-nài) gasoline dealer; gas-station attendant

benzòlo *m* benzene

beóne *m* drunkard, toper

bequadro *m* (mus) natural

berciare §128 (**bèrcio**) *intr* (coll) to yell

bére *m* drink, drinking || §120 *tr* to drink; (fig) to swallow; **bere come una spugna** to drink like a fish; **darla a bere** to make believe

bergamòt-to -ta *adj* bergamot || *m* bergamot orange || *f* bergamot pear

berìllio *m* beryllium

berlina *f* pillory; berlin, coach; (aut) sedan; **mettere alla berlina** to pillory

berlinése [s] *adj* Berlin || *mf* Berliner

Berlino *m* Berlin

bermuda *mpl* Bermuda shorts || **le Bermude** Bermuda

bernòccolo *m* bump, protuberance; (fig) knack

berrétta *f* biretta

berrétto *m* cap; **berretto a sonagli** cap and bells; **berretto da notte** nightcap; **berretto gogliardico** student cap

bersagliare §280 *tr* to harass, pursue; to bomb, bombard

bersà-glio *m* (-gli) target; butt (*of a joke*); target (*of criticism*)

bèrta *f* pile driver; **dar la berta a** to ridicule

bertùc-cia *f* (-ce) Barbary ape; **fare la bertuccia di** to ape

bestémmia *f* blasphemy

bestemmiare §287 (**bestémmio**) *tr* to blaspheme, curse

bestemmia-tóre -trice *adj* blasphemous || *mf* blasphemer

béstia *f* beast, animal; **andare in bestia** to fly into a rage; **bestia da soma** beast of burden; **bestia nera** pet aversion, bête noire; **bestie grosse** cattle

bestiale *adj* beastly, bestial

bestiali-tà *f* (-tà) beastliness; blunder

bestiame *m* livestock; **bestiame da cortile** barnyard animals; **bestiame grosso** cattle

bestino *m* gamy odor; stench of perspiration

bestiòla *f* tiny animal; pet

bestsèl-ler *m* (-ler) best seller

Betlèmme *f* Bethlehem

betonièra *f* cement mixer

béttola *f* tavern

bettolière *m* tavern keeper

bettònica *f* betony; **conosciuto più della bettonica** very well-known

betulla *f* birch

bèuta *f* flask

bevanda *f* drink, beverage

beverà-g-gio *m* (-gi) beverage, potion

bevìbile *adj* drinkable

bevi-tóre -trice *mf* drinker

bevuta *f* drink, drinking

bezzicare §197 (**bézzico**) *tr* to peck; to vex || *ref* to fight one another

biacca *f* white lead

biada *f* feed; **biade** harvest

bianca-stro -stra *adj* whitish

biancheria *f* laundry; linen; underwear; **biancheria da letto** bed linen; **biancheria da tavola** table linen; **biancheria di bucato** freshly laundered clothes; **biancheria intima** underclothes

bianchézza *f* whiteness

bianchire §176 *tr* to blanch; to bleach; to polish

bian-co -ca (-chi -che) *adj* white; clean; **bianco come un cencio lavato** as white as a ghost || *m* white; **dare il bianco a** to whitewash; **in bianco** blank (*paper*); **mangiare in bianco** to eat a bland or non-spicy diet; **ricamare in bianco** to embroider

biancóre *m* whiteness

biancospino *m* hawthorn

biasciare §197 (**biàscico**) *tr* to chew with difficulty; to peck at (*one's food*); to mumble

biasimare (**biàsimo**) *tr* to blame

biasimévole *adj* blamable, censurable

biàsimo *m* blame, censure; **dare una nota di biasimo a** to censure

biauricolare *adj* binaural

Bibbia *f* Bible

bibe-rón *m* (-rón) nursing bottle

bibita *f* soft drink

bìbli-co -ca *adj* (-ci -che) Biblical

bìblio-bus *m* (-bus) bookmobile

bibliòfi-lo -la *mf* bibliophile

bibliografìa *f* bibliography

bibliotè-ca *f* (-che) library; bookshelf, stack; collection (*of books*); **biblioteca ambulante** walking encyclopedia

bibliotecà-rio -ria *mf* (-ri -rie) librarian

bìbu-lo -la *adj* absorbent (*e.g., paper*)

bì-ca *f* (-che) pile of sheaves

bicarbonato *m* bicarbonate; **bicarbonato di soda** bicarbonate of soda, baking soda

bicchierata *f* glassful; wine party

bicchière *m* glass

bicchierino *m* small glass, liquor glass; **bicchierino da rosolio** whiskey glass, jigger

biciclétta *f* bicycle

bicilìndri-co -ca *adj* (-ci -che) two-cylinder

bicìpite *adj* two-headed || *m* biceps
bicòc•ca *f* (-che) castle built on a hill; shanty, hut
bicolóre *adj* two-color
bicòrno *m* two-cornered hat
bidèllo *m* school janitor, caretaker
bidènte *m* two-pronged pitchfork
bidimensionale *adj* two-dimensional
bidóne *m* can (*for milk*); drum (*for gasoline or oil*); jalopy; (slang) fraud
bidon•ville *f* (-ville) shantytown
biè•co -ca *adj* (-chi -che) awry; sullen; cross; fierce; **guardar bieco** to look askance (at)
bièlla *f* connecting rod
biennale *adj* biennial || *f* biennial show
biènne *adj* biennial
bièn•nio *m* (-ni) biennium
biètola *f* Swiss chard
biétta *f* wedge, chock; (naut) batten
bifase *adj* diphase
biffa *f* (surv) rod
biffare *tr* to cross out; (surv) to level
bìfi•do -da *adj* bifurcate
bifocale *adj* bifocal
bifól•co *m* (-chi) ox driver; clodhopper, boor
biforcaménto *m* bifurcation
biforcare §197 (bifórco) *tr* to bifurcate
biforcazióne *f* bifurcation, branching off; fork (*of a road*)
biforcu•to -ta *adj* forked; cloven (*e.g., hoof*)
bifrónte *adj* two-faced
bi•ga *f* (-ghe) chariot
bigamìa *f* bigamy
bìga•mo -ma *adj* bigamous || *mf* bigamist
bighellonare (bighellóno) *intr* to idle, dawdle, dally
bighellò•ne -na *mf* idler, dawdler
bigino *m* (slang) pony (*used to cheat*)
bì•gio -gia *adj* (-gi -gie) gray, grayish; (fig) undecided
bigiotterìa *f* costume jewelry; costume jewelry store
bigliardo *m* billiards
bigliet•tàio *m* (-tài) ticket agent; (rr) conductor
biglietterìa *f* ticket office; (theat) box office
bigliétto *m* note; card; ticket; **biglietto d'abbonamento** commutation ticket; season ticket; **biglietto d'andata e ritorno** round-trip ticket; **biglietto di banca** banknote; **biglietto di lotteria** lottery ticket, chance; **biglietto d'invito** invitation; **biglietto di visita** calling card; business card; **biglietto di Stato** banknote; **mezzo biglietto** half fare
bigné *m* (bigné) puff, creampuff
bigodino *m* curler; roller
bigón•cia *f* (-ce) vat; bucket; **a bigonce** abundantly
bigón•cio *m* (-ci) vat; tub; (theat) ticket box (*for stubs*)
bigottismo *m* bigotry
bigòt•to -ta *adj* bigoted || *mf* bigot
bilàn•cia *f* (-ce) balance, scale; **bilancia commerciale** balance of trade; **bilan-**

cia dei pagamenti balance of payments || **Bilancia** *f* (astr) Libra
bilanciare §128 *tr & ref* to balance
bilancière *m* balance; balance wheel; rope-walker's balancing rod
bilàn•cio *m* (-ci) balance; **bilancio consuntivo** balance sheet; **bilancio preventivo** budget; **fare il bilancio** to balance; to strike a balance
bile *f* bile; **rodersi dalla bile** to burn with anger
bìlia *f* billiard ball; marble; (billiards) pocket
biliardino *m* pocket billiards; pinball machine
biliardo *m* billiards
biliare *adj* bile; gall (*stone*)
bili•co *m* (-chi) balance, equipoise; **in bilico** in balance; **tenere in bilico** to balance
bilingue *adj* bilingual
bilióne *m* billion; trillion (Brit)
bilió•so -sa [s] *adj* bilious
bim•bo -ba *mf* child
bimensile *adj* bimonthly
bimèstre *m* period of two months
bimotóre *adj* twin-engine || *m* twin-engine plane
binà•rio -ria (-ri -rie) *adj* binary || *m* (rr) track; **binario morto** (rr) siding; **uscire dai binari** (rr) to run off the track; (fig) to go astray
bina•to -ta *adj* binary; twin (*e.g., guns*)
binda *f* (aut) jack
binòcolo *m* binoculars; **binocolo da teatro** opera glasses
binò•mio -mia (-mi -mie) *adj* binomial || *m* binomial; couple, pair
biòccolo *m* wad (*of cotton*); flake (*of snow*); flock (*of wool*)
biochìmi•co -ca (-ci -che) *adj* biochemical || *m* biochemist || *f* biochemistry
biodegradàbile *adj* biodegradable
biofisica *f* biophysics
biografia *f* biography
biogràfi•co -ca *adj* (-ci -che) biographic(al)
biògra•fo -fa *mf* biographer
biologìa *f* biology
biòlo•go *m* (-gi) biologist
biondeggiare §290 (biondéggio) *intr* to be or become blond; to ripen (*said of grain*)
bión•do -da *adj* blond, fair || *m* blond; blondness || *f* blonde
biopsìa *f* biopsy
biòssido *m* dioxide
bipartìti•co -ca *adj* (-ci -che) two-party, bipartisan
biparti•to -ta *adj* bipartite || *m* two-party government
bipede *adj & m* biped
bipènne *f* double-bitted ax
biplano *m* biplane
bipósto *adj invar* having seats for two || *m* two-seater
birba *f* rascal, rogue
birbante *m* scoundrel, rascal; (joc) madcap, wild young fellow
birbanterìa *f* knavery; trick
birbonata *f* trick

birbó·ne -na *adj* wicked ‖ *mf* rascal, rogue, scoundrel

bireattóre *m* twin jet

birichinata *f* prank

birichi·no -na *adj* prankish; spirited ‖ *mf* rogue; urchin

birillo *m* pin; **birilli** ninepins; tenpins

Birmània, la Burma

birra *f* beer; **birra chiara** light beer; **birra scura** dark beer

bir·ràio *m* (**-rài**) brewer; beer distributor

birrerìa *f* brewery; tavern; beer saloon

bis *adj invar*—**treno bis** (rr) second section ‖ *m* (**bis**) encore ‖ *interj* encore!

bisàc·cia *f* (**-ce**) knapsack; saddlebag; bag (*of mendicant friar*)

Bisànzio *m* Byzantium

bisa·vo -va *mf* great-grandparent; ancestor ‖ *m* great-grandfather ‖ *f* great-grandmother

bisbèti·co -ca (**-ci -che**) *adj* shrewish; crotchety; cantankerous ‖ *f* (fig) shrew

bisbigliare §280 *tr & intr* to whisper

bisbì·glio *m* (**-gli**) whisper

bisbòccia *f*—**fare bisboccia** to revel

bisboccióne *m* reveler

bis·ca *f* (**-che**) gambling house

Biscàglia *f* Biscay, e.g., **Baia di Biscàglia** Bay of Biscay; **la Biscaglia** Biscay

biscaglina *f* (naut) Jacob's ladder

biscazziere *m* gaming-house operator; habitué of a gaming house; marker (*at billiards*)

bischero *m* (mus) peg

bì·scia *f* (**-sce**) snake; **biscia d'acqua** water snake

biscottare (**biscòtto**) *tr* to toast

biscotterìa *f* cookie factory; cookie store

biscottièra *f* cookie jar

biscottifì·cio *m* (**-ci**) cookie factory

biscòt·to -ta *adj* twice-baked ‖ *m* cookie

biscròma *f* (mus) demisemiquaver

bisdòsso *m*—**a bisdosso** bareback

bisecare [s] §197 (**bìseco**) *tr* to bisect

bisènso [s] *m* double meaning

bisessuale [s] *adj* bisexual

bisestile *adj* leap (*year*)

bisettimanale [s] *adj* biweekly

bisettrice [s] *f* bisector

bisezióne [s] *f* bisection

bisìlla·bo -ba [s] *adj* disyllabic

bislàc·co -ca *adj* (**-chi -che**) queer, extravagant

bislun·go -ga *adj* (**-ghi -ghe**) oblong

bismuto *m* bismuth

bisnòn·no -na *mf* great-grandparent; **bisnonni** ancestors ‖ *m* great-grandfather ‖ *f* great-grandmother

bisógna *f* (lit) task, job

bisognare (**bisógna**) *intr* (with *dat*) to need, e.g., **gli bisognavano tre litri di benzina** he needed three liters of gasoline ‖ *impers*—**bisogna** + *inf* it is necessary to, e.g., **bisogna partire** it is necessary to leave; **bisogna che** + *subj* must, to have to, e.g., **bisogna che me ne vada** I must go,

I have to go; **bisognando** if need be; **non bisogna** one should not; **più che non bisogna** more than necessary

bisognévole *adj* needy

bisógno *m* need; want, lack; **aver bisogno di** to need; **c'è bisogno di** there is need of; **se ci fosse bisogno** if need be

bisognó·so -sa *adj* needy ‖ **i bisognosi** the needy

bisolfato [s] *m* bisulfate

bisolfito [s] *m* bisulfite

bisolfuro [s] *m* bisulfide

bisónte *m* bison

bistec·ca *f* (**-che**) beefsteak, steak; **bistecca al sangue** rare steak

bisticciare §128 *intr & ref* to quarrel, bicker

bistìc·cio *m* (**-ci**) quarrel, bickering; play on words, pun

bistrattare *tr* to mistreat

bistu·ri *m* (**-ri**) bistouri, surgical knife

bisul·co -ca [s] *adj* (**-chi -che**) cloven

bisun·to -ta *adj* greasy

bitagliènte *adj* double-edged

bitòrzolo *m* wart (*on humans, plants, or animals*); pimple (*on human face*)

bitta *f* (naut) bollard

bitume *m* bitumen, asphalt

bituminó·so -sa [s] *adj* bituminous

bivaccare §197 *intr* to bivouac; to spend the night

bivac·co *m* (**-chi**) bivouac

bì·vio *m* (**-vi**) fork (*of road*); **essere al bivio** (fig) to be at the crossroads

bizantì·no -na [dz] *adj* Byzantine

bizza [ddzz] *f* tantrum; **fare le bizze** to go into a tantrum

bizzarrìa [ddzz] *f* extravagance, oddity

bizzar·ro -ra [ddzz] *adj* bizarre, odd; skittish (*e.g., horse*)

bizzèffe [ddzz] *adv*— **a bizzeffe** plenty, in abundance

bizzó·so -sa [ddzz] *adj* irritable

blandire §176 *tr* to blandish, coax; to soothe, mitigate

blandìzie *fpl* blandishment

blan·do -da *adj* bland

blasfemare (**blasfèmo**) *tr & intr* to blaspheme

blasfè·mo -ma *adj* blasphemous

blasona·to -ta *adj* emblazoned

blasóne *m* coat of arms, blazon

blaterare (**blàtero**) *intr* to babble

blatta *f* water bug, cockroach

blenoraggìa *f* gonorrhea

blè·so -sa *adj* lisping

blindàg·gio *m* (**-gi**) armor

blindare *tr* to armor

bloccare §197 (**blòcco**) *tr* to block; to blockade; to stop; to jam; to close up; to freeze (*e.g., prices*); (sports) to block ‖ *intr*—**bloccare su** to vote as a block for ‖ *ref* to stop

blòc·co *m* (**-chi**) block; blockade; notebook, pad; freezing (*e.g., of wages*); **in blocco** in bulk

bloc-notes *m* (**-notes**) notebook

blu *adj invar & m* blue

blua·stro -stra *adj* bluish

bluffare *intr* to bluff

blusa *f* blouse; smock

bò·a *m* (-a) boa ‖ *f* buoy
boà·rio -ria *adj* (-ri -rie) cattle
boa·ro -ra *adj* ox ‖ *m* stable boy
boato *m* roar; boato sonico sonic boom
bobina *f* spool (*of thread*); coil (*of wire*); reel (*of movie film*; *of magnetic tape*); roll (*of film*); cylinder, bobbin; (elec) coil; bobina d'accensione spark coil
bóc·ca *f* (-che) mouth; nozzle; muzzle (*of gun*); pit (*of the stomach*); opening; straits; pass; a bocca aperta agape; bocca da fuoco cannon; di buona bocca easily pleased; in bocca al lupo! good luck!; per bocca orally; rimanere a bocca asciutta to be foiled; to be left high and dry; tieni la bocca chiusa! shut up!
boccacce·sco -sca *adj* (-schi -sche) written by or in the style of Boccaccio; bawdy, licentious
boccàc·cia *f* (-ce) ugly mouth; grimace; fare le boccacce to make faces
boccà·glio *m* (-gli) nozzle (*of hose or pipe*); mouthpiece (*of megaphone*)
boccale *adj* oral ‖ *m* jug, tankard
boccapòrto *m* hatch; port; mouth (*of oven or furnace*); chiudere i boccaporti to batten the hatches
boccascè·na *m* (-na) proscenium, front (*of stage*)
boccata *f* mouthful; andare a prendere una boccata d'aria to go out for a breath of fresh air
boccétta *f* small bottle, vial; small billiard ball
boccheggiante *adj* gasping; moribund
boccheggiare §290 (bocchéggio) *intr* to gasp
bocchétta *f* nozzle (*of sprinkling can*); mouthpiece (*of wind instrument*); opening (*of drainage or ventilation system*); bocchetta stradale manhole
bocchino *m* cigarette holder; mouthpiece (*of cigarette or of musical instrument*)
bòc·cia *f* (-ce) decanter; ball (*for bowling*); bocce bowls
bocciare §128 (bòccio) *tr* to score (*at bowling*); to reject (*a proposal*); to flunk (*a student*)
bocciatura *f* failure
boccino *m* jack (*at bowls*)
bocciòlo *m* bud
bóccola *f* buckle; earring; (mach) bushing
bocconcino *m* morsel; (culin) stew
boccóne *m* mouthful; piece; morsel; buttar giù un boccone amaro to swallow a bitter pill; levarsi il boccone di bocca to take the bread out of one's mouth (to help someone); mangiare un boccone to have a bite ‖ bocconi *adv* flat on one's face
boè·mo -ma *adj* & *mf* Bohemian
boè·ro -ra *adj* & *m* Boer
bofonchiare §287 (bofónchio) *intr* to snort, grumble
bò·ia *m* (-ia) hangman, executioner
boiata *f* (slang) infamy; (slang) trash
boicottàg·gio *m* (-gi) boycott
boicottare (boicòtto) *tr* to boycott

bòl·gia *f* (-ge) pit (*in hell*)
bólide *m* (astr) bolide, fireball; (aut) racer; (joc) lummox; andare come un bolide to go like a flash
bolina *f* (naut) bowline; di bolina (naut) close-hauled
bolivia·no -na *adj* & *mf* Bolivian
bólla *f* bubble; blister; ticket; bolla di consegna receipt; bolla di spedizione delivery ticket; bolla di sapone soap bubble; bolla papale papal bull
bollare (bóllo) *tr* to stamp; to brand
bolla·to -ta *adj* stamped; sealed
bollatura *f* stamp; brand; postage
bollènte *adj* boiling, scalding hot
bollétta *f* ticket; receipt; bill; essere in bolletta (coll) to be broke
bollettà·rio *m* (-ri) receipt book
bollettino *m* bulletin; receipt; bollettino dei prezzi correnti price list; bollettino di versamento (com) deposit ticket; bollettino meteorologico weather forecast
bollire (bóllo) *tr* & *intr* to boil
bolli·to -ta *adj* boiled ‖ *m* boiled beef
bollitura *f* boiling
bóllo *m* mark, cancellation; revenue stamp; postmark; seal; bollo a freddo seal (*embossed*); bollo postale cancellation, postmark
bollóre *m* boiling; sultriness; (fig) passion, excitement; alzare il bollore to begin to boil
bollo·so -sa [s] *adj* blistery
bolscevi·co -ca *adj* & *mf* (-chi -che) Bolshevik
bolscevismo *m* Bolshevism
ból·so -sa *adj* broken-winded (*horse*); asthmatic
bòma *f* (naut) boom
bómba *f* bomb; bubble gum; fireworks; (aer) double loop; (journ) scandal; bomba a idrogeno hydrogen bomb; bomba a mano hand grenade; bomba antisommergibile depth charge; bomba a orologeria time bomb; bomba atomica atom bomb; bomba H (acca) H bomb; tornare a bomba (fig) to get back to the point
bombàggio *m* swelling (*of a spoiled can of food*)
bombardaménto *m* bombing, bombardment
bombardare *tr* to bomb, bombard; to besiege (*with questions*)
bombardière *m* (aer) bomber; (mil) artilleryman
bombétta *f* derby (*hat*)
bómbola *f* bottle, cylinder; bombola d'ossigeno oxygen tank
bombonièra *f* candy box
bomprèsso *m* (naut) bowsprit
bonàc·cia *f* (-ce) calm; calm sea; (fig) normalcy; (com) stagnation
bonacció·ne -na *adj* good-hearted, good-natured
bonarie·tà *f* (-tà) kindheartedness, good nature
bonà·rio -ria *adj* (-ri -rie) kindhearted, good-natured
boncinèllo *m* hasp
bonìfi·ca *f* (-che) reclamation; re-

claimed land; improvement (e.g., of morals); clearing of mines; (metallurgy) hardening and tempering

bonificare §197 (bonìfico) tr to reclaim; to discount, make a reduction of; to clear of mines

bonìfi·co m (-ci) discount

bonòmìa f good nature; simple-heartedness

bon·tà f (-tà) goodness; kindness; **avere la bontà di** to be kind enough to; **bontà mia (sua, etc.)** through my (his, her, etc.) kindness; **per mia (sua, etc.) bontà** through my (his, her, etc.) efforts

bòra f northeast wind

borace m borax

borbogliare §280 (borbóglio) intr to gurgle; to rumble

borbòni·co -ca (-ci -che) adj Bourbon || m Bourbonist

borbottare (borbòtto) tr to mutter || intr to mutter; to gurgle; to rumble (said, e.g., of thunder)

borbottì·o m (-ì) mutter; gurgle; rumble

bòrchia f upholsterer's nail; boss, stud

bordare (bórdo) tr to border, hem

bordata f (naut) tack; (nav) broadside

bordatura f border, hem

bordeggiare §290 (bordéggio) intr (naut) to tack

bordèllo m brothel

borde·rò m (-rò) list; note; (theat) box office, receipts

bórdo m side (of ship); border, hem; edge, rim; (naut) tack; (naut) board; **a bordo** on board; **a bordo di** on board; on, in; **bordo d'entrata** (aer) leading edge; **bordo d'uscita** (aer) trailing edge; **d'alto bordo** (naut) big, sea-going; (fig) high-toned; **virare di bordo** (naut) to change course

bordóne m staff; bass stop (of organ); drone (of insect); **tener bordone a** (mus) to accompany; (fig) to hold the bag for

bordura f hem, edge; rim

boreale adj northern, boreal

borgata f hamlet, village

borghése [s] adj middle-class || mf bourgeois, person of the middle class; civilian; **in borghese** in civilian clothes; in plainclothes

borghesìa f bourgeosie, middle class; **alta borghesìa** upper middle class

bór·go m (-ghi) borough; small town; suburb

borgógna m Burgundy (wine) || **la Borgogna** Burgundy

borgognóne m iceberg

borgomastro m burgomaster

bòria f haughtiness, vainglory

bòri·co -ca adj (-ci -che) boric

borió·so -sa [s] adj haughty, puffed-up; blustery

bòro m boron

borotal·co m (-chi) talcum powder

bórra f flock (for pillows); (fig) rubbish, filler

borràc·cia f (-ce) canteen (e.g., for carrying water)

bórro m gully

bórsa f bag; pouch; bourse, exchange; (sports) purse; **borsa da viaggio** traveling bag; **borsa dell'acqua** hot-water bag; **borsa della spesa** shopping bag; **borsa di ghiaccio** ice bag; **borsa di studio** scholarship; **borsa merci** commodity exchange; **borsa nera** black market; **borsa valori** stock exchange; **essere di borsa larga** to be generous; **o la borsa o la vita!** your money or your life!; **pagare di borsa propria** to pay out of one's own pocket

borsaiòlo m pickpocket

borsanéra f black market

borsaneri·sta mf (-sti -ste) black marketeer

borseggiare §290 (borséggio) tr to pick the pocket of; to rob

borseggia·tóre -trice mf pickpocket

borség·gio m (-gi) theft

borsellino m purse

borsétta f handbag, pocketbook

borsétto m man's purse

borsi·sta mf (-sti -ste) recipient of a scholarship; stockbroker

borsìsti·co -ca adj (-ci -che) stock-exchange

borsite f bursitis

boscàglia f thicket, underbrush

boscaiòlo m woodcutter

boscheréc·cio -cia adj (-ci -ce) wood, woodland; rustic; pastoral

boschétto m coppice, copse

boschì·vo -va adj wooded, wood

bò·sco m (-schi) woods, forest; **bosco ceduo** or **da taglio** tree farm

boscó·so -sa [s] adj wooded, woody

bòsforo m (lit) straits || **Bosforo** m Bosphorus

bòsso m boxwood

bòssolo m box; cartridge case

botàni·co -ca (-ci -che) adj botanic(al) || m botanist || f botany

bòtola f trap door

bòtolo m small snarling dog

bòtta f hit; bump; rumble (e.g., of an explosion); thrust, lunging (in fencing); (fig) disaster; **botta dritta** (fencing) lunge; **botta e risposta** give-and-take; **botte da orbi** severe beating

bot·tàio m (-tài) cooper

bótte f barrel, cask, casket

botté·ga f (-ghe) store, shop; **chiudere bottega** to close up shop

botte·gàio -gàia (-gài -gàie) adj store, shop || mf storekeeper, shopkeeper

botteghino m box office; lottery agency

bottìglia f bottle; **bottiglia Molotov** Molotov cocktail

bottiglierìa f wine store, liquor store

bottino m booty, spoil; capture; cesspool; sewage

bòtto m hit, bump; explosion; noise; toll (of bell); **di botto** all of a sudden

bottoncino m small button; cuff button; **bottoncino di rosa** rosebud

bottóne m button; stud; bud; **attaccare un bottone a** (fig) to buttonhole; **botton d'oro** (bot) buttercup; **bottone automatico** snap; **bottone della**

luce (elec) pushbutton; **bottoni gemelli** cuff links; **bottoni gustativi** taste buds

bottonièra f row of buttons; buttonhole; (elec) panel (*with buttons*)

bova·ro -ra adj & m var of **boaro**

bovile m ox stable

bovi·no -na adj cattle, cow; bovine ‖ m bovine

box m (**box**) locker (*e.g., in a station*); box stall (*for a horse*); pit (*in auto racing*); garage (*on the ground floor of a split-level*); play pen

boxare (**bòxo**) *intr* to box

boxe f boxing

bòzza f stud, boss; bump (*caused by blow*); rough copy, draft; **bozze** (typ) galleys, galley proof

bozzèllo m (mach) block and tackle

bozzétto m sketch

bòzzolo m cocoon; lump (*of flour*)

bra·ca f (**-che**) safety belt; (naut) sling; **brache** (archaic) breeches; (joc) trousers

braccare §197 *tr* to stalk; to hunt out

braccétto—a braccetto arm in arm

bracciale m armlet, armband; arm rest

braccialétto m bracelet

bracciante m laborer

bracciata f armful; stroke (*in swimming*); **bracciata a rana** breaststroke; **bracciata sul dorso** backstroke

bràc·cio m (**-cia** fpl) arm (*of body*); unit of length (*about 60 centimeters*); **a braccia aperte** with open arms; **avere le braccia legate** to have one's hands tied; **braccia** laborers; **braccio destro** right-hand man; **braccio di ferro** Indian wrestling; **fare a braccio di ferro** to play at Indian wrestling; **sentirsi cascare le braccia** to lose courage ‖ m (**-ci**) arm (*e.g., of sea, chair, lamp, etc.*); beam (*of balance*); **braccio diretto** cutoff (*of river*)

bracciòlo m arm; arm rest; banister

brac·co m (**-chi**) hound, beagle

bracconàg·gio m (**-gi**) poaching

bracconière m poacher

brace f embers; (coll) charcoal; **farsi di brace** to blush

brachétta f flap (*of trousers*); (bb) joint; **brachette** shorts

brachière m truss (*for hernia*)

bracière m brazier

braciòla f chop, cutlet

bra·do -da adj wild, untamed

bra·go -ghi (lit) mud, slime

brama f ardent desire; covetousness; longing

bramare *tr* to desire intensely; to covet; to long for

bramino m Brahmin

bramire §176 *intr* to roar; to bell (*said of a deer*)

bramito m bell (*of deer*)

bramosìa [s] f covetousness; greed

bramó·so -sa [s] adj (lit) covetous, greedy

bran·ca f (**-che**) branch (*of tree*); flight (*of stairs*); **branche** (poet) clutches

brànchia f gill

brancicare §197 (**bràncico**) *tr* to finger, handle ‖ *intr* to grope

bran·co m (**-chi**) flock, herd; (pej) crowd

brancolare (**bràncolo**) *intr* to grope

branda f cot

brandèllo m tatter, shred

brandire §176 *tr* to brandish

brando m (lit) sword

brano m shred, bit; excerpt; **cadere a brani** to fall apart; **fare a brani** to tear apart

brasare *tr* to braze (*to solder with brass*); (culin) to braise

brasile m brazil (*nut*) ‖ **Il Brasile** Brazil

brasilia·no -na adj & mf Brazilian

bravàc·cio m (**-ci**) braggart, swaggerer

bravare *tr* to challenge; to threaten ‖ *intr* to brag

bravata f swagger, bluster; boast; stunt

bra·vo -va adj good, able; honest; goodhearted; brave; **alla brava** rapidly; **bravo ragazzo** good boy; **fare il bravo** to boast, be a braggart ‖ m mercenary soldier; bravo, hired assassin ‖ **bravo!** *interj* well done!, bravo!

bravura f ability; bravery; bravura

brèc·cia f (**-ce**) breach, gap; crushed stone

brefotrò·fio m (**-fi**) foundling hospital

Bretagna, la Brittany

bretèlla f suspenders; strap, shoulder strap

brètone adj Breton; Arthurian

brève adj brief, short; **in breve** in a nutshell; **per farla breve** in short ‖ m (eccl) brief ‖ adv (lit) in short

brevettare (**brevétto**) *tr* to patent

brevétto m patent; (aer) license; (obs) commission

brevià·rio m (**-ri**) compendium; handbook, vade mecum; (eccl) breviary

brevi·tà f (**-tà**) brevity

brézza [ddzz] f breeze

brezzare (**brézzo**) [ddzz] *tr* to winnow ‖ *intr* to blow gently

bricchétta f briquet

bric·co m (**-chi**) kettle, pot

briconata f rascality

bricó·ne -na m/f rascal

bricconerìa f rascality

briciola f crumb; **ridurre in briciole** to crumb, crumble

briciolo m bit, fragment; (fig) least bit; **andare in briciloli** to crumble; **mandare in briciloli** to crumble

bri·ga f (**-ghe**) worry, trouble; **attaccar briga** to pick a fight; **darsi la briga di** to worry about; **trovarsi in una briga** to be in trouble

brigadière m noncommissioned officer (*in carabinieri*); (hist) brigadier

brigantàg·gio m (**-gi**) brigandage

brigante m brigand

brigantino m (naut) brig, brigantine; **brigantino goletta** (naut) brigantine

brigare §209 *tr* to plot; to scheme to get ‖ *intr* to plot, scheme

brigata f company; (mil) brigade

brì·glia f (**-glie**) bridle; harness (*for holding baby*); (naut) bobstay; **a briglia sciolta** at full speed; **tirare le briglie a** to bridle

brillante adj brilliant ‖ m cut diamond

brillare *tr* to husk, hull (*rice*); to explode (*e.g., a mine*) ‖ *intr* to shine, sparkle; **far brillare** to explode, blow up

brillì·o *m* (*-i*) shine, sparkle

bril·lo -la *adj* tipsy

brina *f* frost

brinare *tr* to frost; to turn (*e.g., hair*) gray ‖ *impers* (ESSERE)—**è brinato** there was frost; **brina** there is frost

brinata *f* frost

brindare *intr* to toast; **brindare alla salute** di to toast

brìndisi *m* (*-si*) toast; pledge; **fare un brindisi a** to toast

brì·o *m* (*-i*) sprightliness, liveliness, verve, spirit

briò·scia *f* (*-sce*) brioche

briò·so -sa [s] *adj* sprightly, lively

briscola *f* briscola (*game*); trump (*card*)

britànni·co -ca *adj* (*-ci -che*) British, Britannic

britan·no -na *adj* British ‖ *mf* Briton

brìvido *m* shake, shiver; thrill; **brìvido di freddo** chill, shiver

brizzola·to -ta *adj* grizzled

bròc·ca *f* (*-che*) pitcher; pitcherful; shoot, bud; hobnail

broccatèllo *m* brocatel

broccato *m* brocade

bròc·co *m* (*-chi*) twig; shoot; center pin (*of shield or target*); (coll) nag; **dar nel brocco** to hit the bull's eye

bròccolo *m* (bot) broccoli; **broccoli broccoli** (*as food*)

bròda *f* slop, thin or tasteless soup; mud

brodàglia *f* slop

brodétto *m* fish soup

bròdo *m* broth; **andar in brodo di giuggiole** (fig) to swoon with joy; **brodo in dadi** cube bouillon; **brodo ristretto** consommé

brodó·so -sa [s] *adj* thin, watery (*soup*)

brogliàc·cio *m* (*-ci*) (com) daybook, first draft; (naut) first draft of logbook

brò·glio *m* (*-gli*) plot, intrigue; maneuver; **broglio elettorale** political maneuver

bròlo *m* (archaic) garden; (lit) garland

bromìdri·co -ca *adj* (*-ci -che*) hydrobromic

bròmo *m* bromine

bromuro *m* bromide

bronchìte *f* bronchitis

brón·cio *m* (*-ci*) pout, pouting; **fare il broncio** to sulk; **tenere il broncio a** to harbor a grudge against

brón·co *m* (*-chi*) bronchial tube; thorny branch; ramification (*of antlers*)

brontolare (bróntolo) *tr* to grumble (*to express with a grumble*); to grumble at ‖ *intr* to grumble, mutter; to rumble; to gurgle (*said of water*)

brontolì·o *m* (*-i*) grumble, mutter, rumble; gurgle

brontoló·ne -na *mf* grumbler; curmudgeon

bronzare [dz] (brónzo) *tr* to bronze

brónze·o -a [dz] *adj* bronze; tanned

bronzina [dz] *f* little bell; (mach) bearing; (mach) bushing

brónzo [dz] *m* bronze

brossura *f* brochure; **in brossura** paperback

brucare §197 *tr* to browse, graze

bruciacchiare §287 *tr* to singe

bruciante *adj* burning

bruciapélo *m*—**a bruciapelo** point-blank

bruciare §128 *tr* to burn; to burn down; to singe; to scorch; to cauterize (*a wound*); (sports) to overcome with a burst of speed; **bruciare le tappe** to go straight ahead; to press on ‖ *intr* (ESSERE) to burn; to smart, sting ‖ *ref* to burn (*e.g., one's fingers*); to get burnt; to blow (*one's brains*) out; to burn out (*said of an electric light or fuse*); **bruciarsi i vascelli alle spalle** to burn one's bridges behind one

bruciatìc·cio *m* (*-ci*) burnt material; **sapere di bruciaticcio** to taste burnt

brucia·to -ta *adj* burnt; burnt out ‖ *m* burnt taste or smell ‖ *f* roast chestnut

bruciatóre *m* burner; heater; **bruciatore a gas** gas burner; **bruciatore a nafta** oil burner

bruciatorì·sta *m* (*-sti*) oil burner mechanic

bruciatura *f* burn

bruciòre *m* burning; burn; inflammation; **bruciore agli occhi** eye inflammation; **bruciore di stomaco** heartburn

bru·co *m* (*-chi*) caterpillar; worm

brùffolo *m* (coll) small boil

brughièra *f* waste land; heath

brulicare §197 (brùlico) *intr* to crawl; to swarm (*e.g., with bees*); to teem (*with people*)

brulichì·o *m* (*-i*) crawling; swarming; teeming

brul·lo -la *adj* barren, bare

bruma *f* shipworm; (lit) fog; (lit) winter

bruna·stro -stra *adj* brownish

brunìre §176 *tr* to burnish

bru·no -na *adj* brown; dark (*bread; complexion*) ‖ *m* brown; dark; brunet; **vestire a bruno** to dress in black ‖ *f* brunette

bru·sca *f* (*-sche*) horse brush; **con le brusche** curtly

bruschézza *f* brusqueness

bruschino *m* scrub brush

bru·sco -sca (*-schi -sche*) *adj* sour; curt; gruff; sharp (*weather*); dangerous; sudden ‖ *m* twig ‖ *f* see **brusca**

brùscolo *m* speck, mote; **fare di un bruscolo una trave** to make a mountain out of a molehill

brusì·o *m* (*-i*) buzz, buzzing; (fig) whispering (*gossip*)

brutale *adj* brutal

brutali·tà *f* (*-tà*) brutality

brutalizzare [ddzz] *tr* to brutalize

bru·to -ta *adj* & *m* brute

brutta *f* rough copy

bruttare *tr* (lit) to soil

bruttézza *f* ugliness; (fig) lowliness

brut·to -ta *adj* ugly, homely; foul (*weather*); bad (*news*); **alle brutte** at the worst; **con le brutte** harshly; **farla brutta a** to play a mean trick on;

guardare **brutto** to look irritated; **vedersela brutta** to foresee trouble ‖ *m* worst; bad weather ‖ *f* see **brutta**

bruttura *f* ugliness

bùbbola *f* lie; trifle

bùbbolo *m* jingle bell (*on horse*)

bubbòni·co -ca *adj* (-ci -che) bubonic

bu·ca *f* (-che) hole; pit; hollow; **buca cieca** trap (*for hunting*); **buca del biliardo** pocket; **buca delle lettere** mailbox; **buca del suggeritore** prompter's box; **buca sepolcrale** grave

bucané·ve *m* (-ve) snowdrop

bucanière *m* buccaneer

bucare §197 *tr* to pierce; to prick; to puncture (*a tire*)

bucato *m* wash; laundry; **di bucato** freshly laundered; **fare il bucato in famiglia** (fig) to not air one's family affairs, to not wash one's dirty linen in public

bucatura *f* piercing; puncturing; puncture; **bucatura di una gomma** flat tire

bùc·cia *f* (-ce) rind, peel; skin (*of a person; of fruit and vegetables*); tender bark; **fare le bucce a** (coll) to thwart, frustrate

bucherellare (bucherèllo) *tr* to riddle

bu·co *m* (-chi) hole; **fare un buco nell'acqua** to fail miserably

bucòli·co -ca *adj* (-ci -che) bucolic, pastoral

Budda *m* Buddha

buddismo *m* Buddhism

buddi·sta *mf* (-sti -ste) Buddhist

budèl·lo *m* (-la *fpl*) bowel; **budella** bowels; guts ‖ *m* (-li) casing (*for salami*); pipe; blind alley

budino *m* pudding

bùe *m* (buòi) ox (*for draft*); steer (*for meat*); **bue muschiato** musk ox

bùfalo *m* buffalo

bufèra *f* storm; **bufera di neve** snowstorm; **bufera di pioggia** rainstorm; **bufera di vento** windstorm

buffa *f* cowl; gust of wind; (archaic) trick, jest

buffare *tr* to huff (*at checkers*) ‖ *intr* to joke; (archaic) to blow

buffetteria *f* (mil) accouterments

buffétto *m* tap, slight blow

buf·fo -fa *adj* funny, comical ‖ *m* gust of wind; comic ‖ *f* see **buffa**

buffonata *f* buffoonery; antics

buffóne *m* buffoon, clown; (hist) jester; **buffone di corte** court jester

buffoneria *f* buffoonery

buffoné·sco -sca *adj* (-schi -sche) clownish

bugia *f* lie; candlestick; **bugia ufficiosa** white lie

bugiar·do -da *adj* lying, false ‖ *mf* liar

bugigàttolo *m* cubbyhole

bugna *f* ashlar; (naut) clew

bugnato *m* ashlar; (archit) boss

bù·io -ia (*pl* -i -ie) *adj* dark ‖ *m* darkness; **buio pesto** pitch dark

bulbo *m* bulb

bùlga·ro -ra *adj & mf* Bulgarian ‖ *m* Russian leather

bulinare *tr* to engrave

bulino *m* burin

bullétta *f* tack

bullonare (bullóno) *tr* to bolt

bullóne *m* bolt

buon *adj* apocopated form of **buono**, used before masculine singular nouns except those beginning with impure s, z, gn, ps, and x

buon' *adj* apocopated form of **buona** used before feminine singular nouns beginning with a vowel, e.g., **buon'ora**

buonagràzia *f* (buonegràzie) courtesy, good manners; **con Sua buonagrazia** with your permission

buonamano *f* (buonemani) tip, gratuity

buonànima *f* departed; **la buonanima di** the late lamented

buonavò·glia *m* (-glia) intern (*in a hospital*); (coll) lazybones ‖ *f* good will

buoncostume *m* morals

buòngu·stàio *m* (-stài) gourmet; connoisseur

buò·no -na *adj* good; kind; high (*society*); cheap (*price*); **alla buona** plainly; without ceremony; **buono a nulla** good-for-nothing; **con le buone** kindly, gently; **che Dio la mandi buona** a may God be kind with; **essere in buona con** to be on good terms with ‖ *m* good person; bond; ticket; **buono a nulla** ne'er-do-well; **buono del tesoro** government bond; **buono di consegna** delivery order; **buono premio** trading stamp

buonsènso *m* common sense

buontempó·ne -na *adj* jolly ‖ *m* playboy ‖ *f* fun-loving girl; playgirl

buonumóre *m* good humor, good cheer

buonuscita *f* indemnity, bonus; severance pay

burattare *tr* to sift

buratti·nàio *m* (-nài) puppeteer; puppet maker

burattinata *f* clowning

burattino *m* puppet

buratto *m* sifter, sifting machine

burbanza *f* haughtiness, arrogance

burbanzó·so -sa [s] *adj* haughty, arrogant

bùrbe·ro -ra *adj* gruff, surly

bùr·chio *m* (-chi) (naut) lighter

burgun·do -da *adj & mf* Burgundian

burla *f* joke, jest; prank; **mettere in burla** to ridicule; **fuori di burla** joking aside

burlare *tr* to ridicule ‖ *intr* to be joking ‖ *ref*—**burlarsi di** to make fun of

burlé·sco -sca (-schi -sche) *adj* funny; mocking; burlesque; jocose ‖ *m* burlesque; mock-heroic

burlétta *f* joke, jest; **mettere in burletta** to ridicule

burló·ne -na *mf* joker, jester

buròcrate *m* bureaucrat

burocràti·co -ca *adj* (-ci -che) bureaucratic; clerical (*error*)

burocrazia *f* bureaucracy; red tape

burra·sca *f* (-sche) storm

burrascó·so -sa [s] *adj* stormy

burrièra *f* butter dish

burrifi·cio *m* (-ci) butter factory, dairy

burro *m* butter

burróne *m* canyon, ravine

burró·so -sa [s] *adj* buttery

buscare §197 *tr* to get; to catch ‖ *intr* to be damaged ‖ *ref*—**buscarsi un malanno** to catch a cold

busécchia *f* casing (*for sausage*)

busillis *m*—**qui sta il busillis** here's the rub, that's the trouble

bussa *f* hit, blow; **venire alle busse** to come to blows

bussare *intr* to knock; **bussare a quattrini** (fig) to hit somebody for a loan

bussata *f* knock (*at the door*)

bussa-tòio *m* (-tòi) knocker

bùssola *f* sedan chair; door; revolving door; swinging door; ballot box; (mach) bushing; (aer & naut) compass; **perdere la bussola** to lose one's bearings

bussolòtto *m* dice box

busta *f* envelope; briefcase; **busta a finestrella** window envelope; **busta primo giorno** first-day cover; **in busta a parte** under separate cover

bustapa-ga *f* (-ga) pay envelope

bustarèlla *f* bribery; kickback

bustina *f* powder, dose; small envelope; (mil) cap, fatigue cap

busto *m* chest, trunk; bust; corset

butirró-so -sa [s] *adj* buttery

buttafuò-ri *m* (-ri) bouncer (*in a night club*); (theat) callboy; (naut) outrigger

buttare *tr* to throw; to waste (*e.g., time*); to give off (*e.g., smoke*); **buttar giù** to demolish; to swallow; (fig) to discredit; to jot down; **buttar via** to throw away; to cast aside ‖ *intr* to secrete, ooze ‖ *ref* to throw oneself; to let oneself fall; **buttarsi giù** (fig) to become downcast

butterare (**bùttero**) *tr* to pock, pit

bùttero *m* pockmark; cowboy

buzzo [ddzz] *m* (vulg) belly; **di buzzo buono** with energy; willingly

C

C, c [t/i] *m & f* third letter of the Italian alphabet

càbala *f* cabala; cabal, intrigue

cabina *f* cabin, stateroom; car, cage (*of elevator*); cockpit (*of airplane*); booth (*of telephone*); cab (*of locomotive*)

cablàg-gio *m* (-gi) (elec) cable (*in auto or radio*)

cablare *tr* to cable

cablografare (**cablògrafo**) *tr* to cable

cablogram-ma *m* (-mi) cablegram, cable

cabotàg-gio *m* (-gi) coasting trade, coastal traffic

cabrare *intr* to zoom

cabrata *f* zoom

cacào *m* cocoa

cacasènno *m* (slang) wiseacre

cacatò-a *m* (-a) cockatoo

càc-cia *m* (-cia) pursuit plane, fighter; (nav) destroyer ‖ *f* chase, hunt; pursuit; **caccia alle streghe** witch hunt

cacciagióne *f* small game; venison; kill (*e.g., of game birds*)

cacciapiè-tre *m* (-tre) (rr) cowcatcher

cacciare §128 *tr* to hunt; to chase; to rout; to send out; to stick, thrust; to utter (*e.g., a cry*); **caccia fuori** to pull out; **cacciar via** to chase away ‖ *ref* to hide; to intrude; to get; to wind up; to thrust oneself; **cacciarsi negli affari di** to butt into the affairs of

cacciasommergìbi-li *m* (-li) subchaser, submarine chaser

cacciata *f* hunting party; expulsion

cacciatóra *f* hunting jacket; **alla cacciatora** (culin) stewed with herbs

cacciatóre *m* hunter; (aer) fighter pilot; **cacciatore di frodo** poacher; **cacciatore di teste** headhunter

cacciatorpediniè-re *m* (-re) destroyer

cacciatrice *f* huntress

cacciavi-te *m* (-te) screwdriver

càccola *f* gum (*on edge of eyelid*); (slang) snot

caccoló-so -sa [s] *adj* gummy (*eyelid*); (slang) snotty

ca-chi (-chi) *adj* khaki ‖ *m* Japanese persimmon; khaki

cacic-co *m* (-chi) Indian chief; boss (*in Latin America*)

cà-cio *m* (-ci) cheese; **come il cacio sui maccheroni** (coll) at the right moment

cacofóni-co -ca *adj* (-ci -che) cacophonous

cac-tus *m* (-tus) cactus

cadau-no -na *adj* each ‖ *pron* each one

cadàvere *m* corpse, cadaver

cadavèri-co -ca *adj* (-ci -che) cadaverous

cadènte *adj* falling (*star*); rickety (*house*); run-down, decrepit (*person*)

cadènza *f* cadence, rhythm; accent (*peculiar to a region*)

cadére §121 *intr* (ESSERE) to fall; to sink; to slough (*said, e.g., of crust*); to fail; (gram) to end; **cadere a proposito** to come in handy; to come at the right moment; **cadere dalle nuvole** to be dumfounded

cadétto *m* cadet

càdmio *m* cadmium

caducità *f* transiency, brevity

cadu-co -ca *adj* (-ci -che) fleeting; deciduous

cadu-no -na *adj & pron* var of **cadauno**

cadu-to -ta *adj* fallen; lost, gone astray; **i caduti** the fallen, the dead ‖ *f* fall; crash (*of stock market*); slump (*of prices*)

caf-fè *m* (-fè) coffee; café

caffeina *f* caffeine

caffetteria *f* cafeteria

caffettièra *f* coffeepot

cafó·ne -na *adj* loud, gaudy ‖ *m* boor, lout

cagionare (cagióno) *tr* to cause, produce

cagióne *f* cause, reason; **a cagione di** because of

cagionévole *adj* sickly, delicate

cagliare §280 *tr, intr* (ESSERE) **& ref** to curdle, curd

cagliata *f* curd

cà·glio *m* (-gli) rennet

cagna *f* bitch

cagnara *f* barking (*of dogs*); uproar, confusion

cagné·sco -sca (-schi -sche) *adj* dog-like, doggish ‖ *m*—**guardare in cagnesco** to look askance at; **stare in cagnesco con** to be angry with

Caino *m* Cain

Càiro, il Cairo

caia *f* cove; (naut) hold

calabrése [s] *adj & mf* Calabrian

calabróne *m* hornet

calafatare *tr* (naut) to caulk

cala·màio *m* (-mài) inkwell

calamaro *m* squid

calamita *f* magnet; (*mineral*) loadstone; (fig) magnet, attraction

calami·tà *f* (-tà) calamity, disaster

calamitare *tr* to magnetize

calamitó·so -sa [s] *adj* calamitous

càlamo *m* reed, quill

calandra *f* calender; (aut) grille

calandrare *tr* to calender

calante *adj* waning (*moon*)

calàp·pio *m* (-pi) snare; noose

calapran·zi *m* (-zi) dumbwaiter

calare *tr* to lower; to strike (*sails*) ‖ *intr* (ESSERE) to fall, sag (*said, e.g., of prices*); to grow shorter (*said of days*); to come down; to shrink (*said, e.g., of meat*); to lose weight; to set (*said, e.g., of the sun*); to wane (*said of the moon*); (mus) to drop in pitch ‖ *ref* to let oneself down; to dive

calata *f* lowering; descent; invasion; fall; wharf; (coll) intonation; **calata del sole** sunset

cal·ca *f* (-che) crowd, throng

calca·gno *m* (-gni) heel ‖ *m* (-gna *fpl*) (fig) heel; **alle calcagna di** at the heels of

calcare *m* limestone ‖ §197 *tr* to trample; to trace (*on paper*); to tread (*the boards*); to emphasize; **calcare la mano** to exaggerate; **calcare le orme di** to follow in the footsteps of

calce *m*—**in calce** at the foot of the page; **in calce a** at the foot of ‖ *f* lime; **calce viva** quicklime

calcedònio *m* chalcedony

calcestruzzo *m* concrete

calciare §128 *tr & intr* to kick

calciatóre *m* soccer player; football player

calcificare §197 (**calcìfico**) *tr & ref* to calcify

calcificazióne *f* calcification

calcina *f* mortar; lime

calcinàc·cio *m* (-ci) flake of plaster; **calcinacci** ruins, rubble

calci·nàio *m* (-nài) lime pit

calcinare *tr* to calcine; to lime (*e.g., a field*)

càl·cio *m* (-ci) kick; soccer; calcium; (*e.g., of rifle*) butt; **calcio d'inizio** (sports) kickoff

calciocianamide *m* calcium cyanamide

cal·co *m* (-chi) tracing; cast; imprint

calcografia *f* copper engraving

calcolare (**càlcolo**) *tr* to calculate; to estimate, reckon; to compute; to consider

calcola·tóre -trice *adj* calculating ‖ *m* calculator; computer; schemer ‖ *f* calculating machine, adding machine

càlcolo *m* calculation; estimate; planning; calculus; (pathol) calculus, stone; **calcolo biliare** gallstone; **calcolo errato** miscalculation; **fare calcolo su** to count upon

calcolò·si *f* (-si) (pathol) stones

calcomanìa *f* decalcomania

caldàia *f* boiler

cal·dàio *m* (-dài) cauldron, boiler

caldalléssa *f* boiled chestnut

caldana *f* flush

caldano *m* brazier

caldarròsta *f* roast chestnut

caldeggiare §290 (**caldéggio**) *tr* to favor, support; to recommend

calde·ràio *m* (-rài) coppersmith; boiler-maker

calderóne *m* cauldron

cal·do -da *adj* warm; hot; rich (*voice*); **caldo, caldo** quite recent ‖ *m* heat; warmth; **aver caldo** to be warm (*said of people*); to be hot (*said of people*); **fa caldo** it is warm; it is hot; **non mi fa nè caldo nè freddo** it leaves me cold, it does not move me

calefazióne *f* heating

caleidoscò·pio *m* (-pi) kaleidoscope

calendà·rio *m* (-ri) calendar

calènde *fpl*—**calende greche** Greek calends

calendimàggio *m* May Day

calèsse *m* buggy, gig

calére *impers*—**non mi cale** (lit) I don't care

calettare (**calétto**) *tr* to dovetail, mortise ‖ *intr* to fit

calibrare (**càlibro**) *tr* to gauge, calibrate

càlibro *m* caliber; (mach) calipers; (fig) quality, importance

càlice *m* wine cup; (bot) calyx; (eccl) chalice

cali·cò *m* (-cò) calico

califfo *m* caliph

calìgine *f* fog, mist; (fig) darkness

caliginó·so -sa [s] *adj* foggy, misty; (fig) dark, gloomy

calla *f*—**calla dei fioristi** calla lily

calle *f* lane, alley

callifu·go *m* (-ghi) corn remedy

calligrafia *f* penmanship; handwriting

calli·sta *mf* (-sti -ste) chiropodist

callo *m* corn; callus; **fare il callo a** to get used to; **pestare i calli a qlcu** to step on s.o.'s feet

callosi·tà [s] *f* (-tà) callosity; callus

calló·so -sa [s] *adj* corny; callous; hard

calma *f* calm, tranquillity

calmante *adj* sedative, calming, soothing || *m* sedative

calmare *tr* to calm, soothe, appease || *ref* to calm down; to subside, abate

calmierare (calmièro) *tr* to fix the price of

calmière *m* ceiling price; price control

cal·mo -ma *adj* calm, quiet, still || *f* see **calma**

calo *m* decrease; shrinkage

calomelano *m* calomel

calóre *m* heat; warmth; fervor, ardor; (pathol) rash, inflammation; (vet) rut, mating season

caloria *f* calorie

calòri·co -ca *adj* (-ci -che) caloric

calorifero *m* heater, radiator

caloró·so -sa [s] *adj* warm; hot; cordial; heated

calò·scia *f* (-sce) var of **galoscia**

calòtta *f* skullcap; case (*e.g., of watch*); (aut) hubcap; (mach) cap; **calotta cranica** skull

calpestare (calpésto) *tr* to trample

calpestì·o *m* (-i) trampling

calùgine *f* down (*of bird*)

calùnnia *f* calumny, slander

calunniare §287 *tr* to calumniate, slander

calunnia·tóre -trice *mf* slanderer

calunnió·so -sa [s] *adj* slanderous

Calvàrio *m* (Bib) Calvary

calvizie *f* baldness

cal·vo -va *adj* bald

calza *f* sock; stocking; wick; **calza da donna** stocking; **calze** hose, hosiery; **fare la calza** to knit

calzamàglia *f* tights

calzare *m* footwear || *tr* to wear, put on (*shoes, gloves, or socks*) || *intr* to fit (*said of any garment*); to suit

calzascar·pe *m* (-pe) shoehorn

calza·tóio *m* (-tói) shoehorn

calzatura *f* footwear; **calzature** footwear

calzaturière *m* shoe manufacturer

calzaturiè·ro -ra *adj* shoe (*e.g., industry*) || *m* shoe worker

calzaturifì·cio *m* (-ci) shoe factory

calzeròtto *m* woolen sock

calzet·tàio *m* (-tài) hosier

calzettóne *m* knee-high woolen sock (*for mountain boots*)

calzifì·cio *m* (-ci) hosiery mill

calzino *m* sock; **calzini corti** socks; half hose; **calzini lunghi** knee-high socks

calzo·làio *m* (-lài) shoemaker; cobbler

calzoleria *f* shoemaker's shop; shoe store

calzoncini *mpl* shorts

calzóne *m* trouser leg; **calzoni** trousers; pants; slacks; **calzoni a zampe d'elefante** bell-bottom trousers, flares

camaleònte *m* chameleon

camarilla *f* cabal, clique

cambiadì·schi *m* (-schi) record changer

cambiale *f* promissory note, IOU

cambiaménto *m* change, modification

cambiare §287 *tr* to change, exchange; to shift (*gears*) || *intr* to change, switch || *ref* to change (*clothing*); **cambiarsi in** to turn into

cambiavalu·te *m* (-te) moneychanger

càm·bio *m* (-bi) change; switch; rate of exchange; (mil) relief; **cambio a cloche** shift lever, stick; **cambio di velocità** gearshift; **in cambio di** in exchange for, in place of

cam·brì *m* (-brì) cambric

cambusa *f* (naut) galley

cambusière *m* steward

càmera *f* room; bedroom; chamber; **camera ardente** funeral parlor; **Camera dei comuni** House of Commons; **Camera dei deputati** House of Representatives; **camera d'aria** inner tube; **camera di sicurezza** detention cell; vault (*of bank*)

camera·ta *m* (-ti) friend, comrade || *f* dormitory; barracks; roomful (*of students or soldiers*)

cameratismo *m* comradeship

camerièra *f* waitress; maid, chambermaid

camerière *m* waiter; steward; valet

camerino *m* small room; toilet, lavatory; (nav) noncommissioned officer's quarters; (theat) dressing room

càmice *m* gown (*of physician*); smock (*of painter*); (eccl) alb

camiceria *f* shirt store; shirt factory

camicétta *f* blouse

camìcia *f* shirt; casing, jacket (*e.g., of boiler*); lining (*e.g., of furnace*); vest (*of sailor*); folder; **camicia da giorno** chemise; **camicia da notte** nightgown; **camicia di forza** strait jacket; **camicia di maglia** coat of mail; **camicia nera** black shirt (*Fascist*); **camicia rossa** red shirt (*Garibaldine*); **dare la camicia** to give the shirt off one's back; **essere nato con la camicia** to be born with a silver spoon in one's mouth; **perdere la camicia** to lose one's shirt

cami·ciàio -ciàia *mf* (-ciài -ciàie) shirtmaker, haberdasher

camiciòla *f* sport shirt; undershirt; T-shirt; (obs) vest

camiciòtto *m* smock (*of mechanic*); jumper; sport shirt

caminétto *m* small fireplace; fireplace

camino *m* fireplace; chimney, smokestack; shaft (*in mountain*); mouth (*of volcano*); (naut) funnel

cà·mion *m* (-mion) truck

camionale *f* highway

camioncino *m* small truck; panel truck, pickup truck

camionétta *f* small truck; van (*e.g., of police*)

camioni·sta *m* (-sti) truckdriver, teamster

camma *f* (mach) cam; (mach) wiper

cammellière *m* camel driver

cammèllo *m* camel

cammèo *m* cameo

camminaménto *m* (mil) communication trench

camminare *intr* to walk; to go, run

camminata *f* walk; gait; (obs) hall with fireplace

cammina·tóre -trice *mf* walker; runner

cammino *m* road, way, route; path (*e.g., of the moon*); course; journey; **cammin facendo** on the way; **cammino battuto** beaten path; **cammino coperto** (mil) covered way; **mettersi in cammino** to set out, start out

camomilla *f* camomile

camòrra *f* underworld

camò·scio *m* (**-sci**) chamois

campagna *f* country; countryside; country property; season (*for harvesting*); campaign; **andare in campagna** to go on vacation (in the country)

campagnò·lo -la *adj* country, rural ǁ *mf* peasant

campale *adj* field (*artillery*); pitched, decisive (*battle*)

campana *f* bell; bell glass, bell jar; lamp shade; (archit) bell; **a campana** bell-bottomed; **campana a martello** alarm bell, tocsin; **campana di vetro** bell glass; **campana pneumatica** caisson

campanàc·cio *m* (**-ci**) cowbell

campanaro *m* bell ringer; (archaic) bell founder

campanèlla *f* small bell; door knocker; curtain ring; (bot) bluebell

campanèllo *m* bell; small bell; doorbell, chimes; **campanello d'allarme** alarm bell

campanile *m* steeple, belfry; native city or town

campanilismo *m* parochialism

campano *m* cowbell

campare *tr* to keep alive; to save; to bring out the details of ǁ *intr* (ESSERE) to live; to survive; **si campa** one ekes out a living

campa·to -ta *adj*—**campato in aria** without any foundation ǁ *f* span

campeggiare §290 (**campéggio**) *intr* to camp, encamp; to stand out

campeggia·tóre -trice *mf* camper

campég·gio *m* (**-gi**) camping, outing; campground; (bot) logwood

campeggi·sta *mf* (**-sti -ste**) camper

campèstre *adj* field, country; (sports) cross-country

campidò·glio *m* (**-gli**) capitol ǁ **Campidoglio** *m* Capitoline (*hill*); Capitol (*temple*)

campionare (**campióno**) *tr* to sample

campionà·rio -ria (**-ri -rie**) *adj* of samples; trade (*exposition*) ǁ *m* sample book, catalogue, pattern book

campionato *m* championship, title

campióne *m* champion; sample; specimen; standard; **campione senza valore** uninsured parcel, sample post

campionéssa *f* championess

campionissimo *m* world champion, ace

campo *m* field; camp; ground; tennis court; golf course; center (*e.g., for refugees*); **campo addestramento** training camp; **campo d'aviazione** airfield, airport; **campo di battaglia** battlefield; **campo petrolifero** oil field; **lasciare il campo** to retreat; **mettere in campo** to bring up, adduce; **piantare il campo** to pitch camp

camposanto *m* cemetery, churchyard

camuffare *tr* to disguise, mask; to camouflage ǁ *ref* to disguise oneself

camu·so -sa *adj* snub-nosed

Canadà, il Canada

canadése [s] *adj* & *mf* Canadian

canàglia *f* scoundrel; rabble

canagliata *f* knavery, mean trick

canale *m* canal; irrigation ditch; network (*of communications*); pipe, drain; (anat) duct, tract; (rad, telv) channel; (theat) aisle; **Canale della Manica** English Channel; **Canale di Panama** Panama Canal; **Canale di Suez** Suez Canal

canalizzare [ddzz] *tr* to channel; to install pipes in; (elec) to wire

canalizzazióne [ddzz] *f* channeling; piping; ductwork; (elec) wiring

canalóne *m* ravine

cànapa *f* hemp

cana·pè *m* (**-pè**) sofa, couch; (culin) canapé

cànapo *m* rope, cable

Canàrie, le the Canaries

canarino *m* canary

cancàn *m* noise, racket

cancellare (**cancèllo**) *tr* to cancel, erase; to obliterate; to write off (*a debt*); to scratch (*a horse*) ǁ *ref* to vanish, fade

cancellata *f* railing

cancellatura *f* erasure

cancellazióne *f* cancellation; erasure (*of a tape*)

cancelleria *f* chancellery; stationery

cancellière *m* chancellor; court clerk; registrar, recorder

cancèllo *m* gate, railing, grating

canceró·so -sa [s] *adj* cancerous ǁ *mf* cancer victim

cànchero *m* trouble; troublesome person; (coll) cancer

cancrèna *f* gangrene; **andare in cancrena** to become gangrenous

cancrenó·so -sa [s] *adj* gangrenous

cancro *m* cancer; (bot) canker ǁ **Cancro** *m* (astr) Cancer

candeggiante *adj* bleaching ǁ *m* bleaching agent, bleach

candeggiare §290 (**candéggio**) *tr* to bleach

candeggina *f* bleach

candég·gio *m* (**-gi**) bleaching

candéla *f* candle; candlestick; candlepower; (aut) spark plug; **studiare a lume di candela** to burn the midnight oil; **tenere la candela a** to favor the love affair of

candelabro *m* candelabrum

candelière *m* candlestick

candelòra *f* Candlemas

candelòtto *m* big wax candle; **candelotto lacrimogeno** tear-gas canister

candida·to -ta *mf* candidate

candidatura *f* candidature, candidacy

càndi·do -da *adj* white; candid

candire §176 *tr* to candy

candi·to -ta *adj* candied ǁ *m* candied fruit

candóre *m* whiteness; candor

cane *m* dog; hound; hammer, cock (*of gun*); ham actor; **cane barbone**

poodle; **cane bastardo** mongrel; **cane da ferma** setter; **cane da guardia** watchdog; **cane da presa** retriever; **cane da punta** pointer; **cane grosso** big shot; **cane guida per ciechi** seeing eye dog; **cane sciolto** (pol) lone wolf; **come un cane** all alone; **come un cane in chiesa** as an unwelcome guest; **da cani** poorly; **menare il can per l'aia** to beat around the bush; **non c'è un cane** there is nobody there; **raddrizzare le gambe ai cani** to perform an impossible task

canèstro m basket

cànfora f camphor

cangiante adj changeable (color); changing, iridescent

canguro m kangaroo

canìcola f dog days

canile m doghouse, kennel

canino adj canine || m canine tooth

canìzie f gray hair; head of gray hair; old age

canna f cane, reed; rod (for fishing or measuring); pipe (of organ); barrel (of gun); **canna da zucchero** sugar cane; **canna di caduta** disposal chute; **canna fumaria** chimney; **canna della gola** (coll) windpipe

cannèlla f small tube; tap (of barrel); cinnamon

cannèllo m pipe, tube; stick (e.g., of licorice); (chem) pipette; **cannello ossiacetilenico** acetylene torch; **cannello ossidrico** oxyhydrogen blowpipe

cannellóni mpl cannelloni

cannéto m cane field

cannìbale m cannibal

cannìc•cio m (-ci) wicker frame; shade made out of rushes

cannocchiale m spyglass; **cannocchiale astronomico** telescope

cannonata f cannonade, cannon shot; (slang) hit

cannoncino m small gun; **cannoncino antiaereo** antiaircraft gun

cannóne m gun, cannon; pipe, stovepipe; box pleat; shin (of cattle); **è un cannone** (coll) he's the tops

cannoneggiare §290 **(cannonéggio)** tr to cannonade, shell

cannonièra f gunboat

cannonière m gunner, artilleryman; kicker (in soccer)

cannùc•cia f (-ce) reed; thin tube; stem (e.g., of pipe); straw (for drinking); (chem) pipette

canòa f canoe; launch

canòcchia f mantis shrimp

cànone m canon; rule; rent; fee, charge (for use of radio)

canonicato m canonry

canòni•co -ca (-ci -che) adj canonical, canon (law) || m canon; priest || f parsonage, rectory

canonizzare [ddzz] tr to canonize

canò•ro -ra adj song (bird); melodious

canottàg•gio m (-gi) boating, rowing

canottièra f undershirt, T-shirt; skimmer, boater

canottière m oarsman

canòtto m skiff, scull, shell

canovàc•cio m (-ci) dishcloth; embroidery cloth; plot (of novel or play)

cantàbile adj singable; songlike; cantabile || m song

cantamban•co m (-chi) jongleur, wandering minstrel; mountebank

cantante adj singing, song || mf singer

cantare m song; chant; laisse, epic strophe || tr to sing; to chant || intr to sing; to chant; (coll) to squeal

cantàride f Spanish fly

càntaro m urn

cantastò•rie m (-rie) minstrel

canta•tóre -trice adj singing || mf singer

cantau•tóre -trice mf singer composer

canterano m chest of drawers

canterellare (**canterèllo**) tr & intr to sing in a low voice, hum

canteri•no -na adj singing, warbling; decoy (bird) || mf songster, singer

càntero m urinal

canticchiare §287 tr & intr to hum

cànti•co m (-ci) canticle

cantière m shipyard, dockyard; navy yard; undertaking, work in progress; **avere in cantière** to have in hand, be working at; **cantiere edile** building site; builder's yard

cantilèna f singsong; **la stessa cantilena** the same old tune

cantimban•co m (-chi) var of **cantambanco**

cantina f cellar; wine cellar; wine shop, canteen

cantinière m cellarman; butler; wineshop keeper; sommelier

canto m song, singing; chant; canto; crow (of rooster); chirping (of grasshopper); corner, edge; (mus) voice part; **canto del cigno** swan song; **dal canto mio** for my part; **d'altro canto** on the other hand; **da un canto** on the one hand

cantonata f corner (of street); **prendere una cantonata** to make a blunder

cantóne m corner (of room or building); canton

cantonièra f corner cupboard; (rr) section worker's house

cantonière m road laborer; (rr) section hand

cantóre m choir singer; cantor; (poet) singer

cantùc•cio m (-ci) nook, niche

canutézza f hoariness

canutiglia f gold thread

canu•to -ta adj gray-haired; white-haired; (poet) white

canzonare (**canzóno**) tr to mock, ridicule

canzonatò•rio -ria adj (-ri -rie) mocking

canzonatura f mockery, gibe

canzóne f song; canzone

canzonétta f canzonet; popular song

canzonetti•sta mf (-sti -ste) singer (e.g., in a nightclub) || m songster || f songstress

canzonière m songbook; collection of poems; song writer

caolino m kaolin

caos *m* chaos

caòti·co -ca *adj* (**-ci -che**) caotic

capace *adj* capacious; capable, intelligent; legally qualified; **capace di** with a capacity of (*e.g., fifty people*); **essere capace di** to be able to; **fare capace di** to convince of

capaci·tà *f* (**-tà**) capacity; capability

capacitare (**capàcito**) *tr* to persuade || *ref* to become convinced

capanna *f* hut, cabin; thatched cottage; bathhouse

capannèllo *m* group, crowd

capanno *m* hunting box; cabana, bath-house

capannóne *m* large shed; hangar

caparbiàggine *f* var of **caparbietà**

caparbie·tà *f* (**-tà**) obstinacy, stubborness

capàr·bio -bia *adj* (**-bi -bie**) stubborn, hard-headed

caparra *f* down payment, deposit; performance bond

capatina *f* short visit

capeggiare §290 (**capéggio**) *tr* to lead

capeggia·tóre -trice *mf* leader

capellini *mpl* small vermicelli

capéllo *m* hair; **averne fin sopra i capelli** to have one's fill; **capelli** hair; **capelli a spazzola** crew cut; **c'è mancato un capello che** + *subj* he came close to + *ger*; **far rizzare i capelli a qlcu** to make s.o.'s hair stand on end

capellóne *m* hippie, beatnik

capellu·to -ta *adj* hairy; long-haired

capelvènere *m* maidenhair

capèstro *m* halter; gallows

capezzale *m* bolster; (fig) bedside

capézzolo *m* nipple, teat; udder

capidò·glio *m* (**-gli**) var of **capodoglio**

capiènza *f* capacity (*e.g., of bus*)

capigliatura *f* head of hair

capillare *adj* capillary; (fig) far-reaching

capinéra *f* (orn) blackcap

capintè·sta *m* (**-sta**) boss; (sports) head, leader

capire §176 *tr* to understand; **capire a volo** to grasp immediately || *intr*— **non capire dalla contentezza** to be bursting with joy || *ref* to understand each other; to agree

capitale *adj* capital; mortal (*sin*) || *m* capital; principal; **capitale sociale** capital stock || *f* capital (*of country*)

capitalismo *m* capitalism

capitali·sta *mf* (**-sti -ste**) capitalist

capitalisti·co -ca *adj* (**-ci -che**) capitalistic

capitalizzare [ddzz] *tr* to capitalize; to compound (*interest*)

capitana *f* flagship

capitanare *tr* to lead, captain

capitanería *f* (hist) captaincy; **capitaneria di porto** harbor-master's office; coast guard office; port authority's office

capitano *m* captain; skipper, master (*of ship*); commander (*in air force*); **capitano di corvetta** or **capitano di fregata** (nav) lieutenant commander;

capitano di gran cabotaggio master; **capitano di lungo corso** master; **capitano di porto** harbor master; **capitano di vascello** (nav) commander

capitare (**càpito**) *intr* (ESSERE) to arrive; to happen, occur; to happen to get, e.g., **capitò a casa mia alle tre** he happened to get to my house at three; **capitare bene** to be lucky; **dove capita** at random

capitazióne *f* poll tax

capitèllo *m* (archit) capital; (bb) head-band

capitolare *adj & m* capitular || *v* (**capitolo**) *intr* to capitulate, surrender

capitolato *m* (com) specifications

capitolazióne *f* capitulation

capitolo *m* chapter; article, paragraph (*of contract*)

capitombolare (**capitómbolo**) *intr* to tumble

capitómbolo *m* tumble; **fare un capitombolo** (fig) to collapse

capitóne *m* big eel

capitozzare (**capitòzzo**) *tr* to poll (*a tree*)

capo *m* head; chief; boss, leader; top; (geog) cape; (nav) chief petty officer; **a capo scoperto** bareheaded; **capo d'accusa** (law) charge; **capo del governo** prime minister; **capo dello stato** president, chief of state; **capo di vestiario** garment; **capo scarico** scatterbrain; **col capo nel sacco** (fig) heedlessly; **da capo** all over (again); **fare capo a** to flow into; **in capo a** at the end of (*e.g., one month*); **in capo al mondo** at the end of the world; **per sommi capi** briefly; **rompersi il capo** to rack one's brain; **scoprirsi il capo** to take one's hat off; **senza capo né coda** without rhyme or reason; **venire a capo di** to come to the end of

capobanda *m* (**capibanda**) bandmaster; ringleader

capocamerière *m* headwaiter

capocannonière *m* (**capicannonièri**) petty gunnery officer; (soccer) leader in number of goals

capòcchia *f* head (*e.g., of a match*)

capòc·cia *m* (**-ci & -cia**) head of household; foreman, boss (*e.g., of roadworkers or farmers*)

capocòmi·co *m* (**-ci**) head of dramatic company

capocòr·da *m* (**capicòrda**) (elec) binding post, terminal

capocrònaca *m* (**capicrònaca**) leading article

capocronista *m* (**capicronisti**) city editor

capocuòco *m* (**capocuòchi & capicuòchi**) chef

capodanno *m* (**capodanni & capi d'anno**) New Year's Day

capodò·glio *m* (**-gli**) sperm whale

capofàbbrica *m* (**capifàbbrica**) foreman, superintendent

capofabbricato *m* (**capifabbricato**) air-raid warden

capofamìglia *m* (capifamìglia) head of the family

capofila *m* (capifila) head of a line || *f* (capofila) head of a line

capofitto *adj invar*—a capofitto headlong

capogiro *m* vertigo, dizziness; da capogiro dizzying, e.g., prezzi da capogiro dizzying prices

capolavó·ro *m* (-ri) masterpiece

capolèttera *m* (capilèttera) letterhead; (typ) first large bold letter of a paragraph

capolinea *m* (capilìnea) terminal, terminus

capolino *m*—fare capolino to peep

capolista *m* (capilista) first (*of a list*); (sports) leader || *f* (capolista) first (*of a list*)

capoluò·go *m* (-ghi) capital (*of province*); county seat

capomacchini·sta *m* (-sti) chief engineer

capomastro *m* (capomastri & capimastri) foreman; building contractor

capomùsica *m* (capimùsica) bandmaster

capoofficina *m* (capiofficina) superintendent (*of shop*)

capopàgina *m* (capipàgina) heading (*of newspaper*)

capopèzzo *m* (capipèzzo) gunnery sergeant

capopòpolo *m* (capipòpolo) demagogue

caporale *m* corporal

caporeparto *m* (capireparto) department manager, floor walker; shop foreman

caporióne *m* ringleader

caposaldo *m* (capisaldi) (fig) main point, basis; (mil) stronghold; (surv) datum

caposezióne *m* (capisezióne) department head

caposquadra *m* (capisquadra) group leader; (sports) team captain

capostazióne *m* (capistazióne) station master

capostìpite *m* founder (*of family*); prototype, archetype

capotamènto *m* var of cappottamento

capotare (capòto) *intr* var of cappottare

capotasto *m* nut (*of violin*)

capotàvola *m* (capitàvola) head of the table, honored guest

capòte *f* (aut) top

capotrèno *m* (capitrèno & capotrèni) (rr) conductor

capottamènto *m* var of cappottamento

capottare (capòtto) *intr* var of cappottare

capoufficio *m* (capiufficio) office manager

capovèrso *m* paragraph; (typ) indentation

capovòlgere §289 *tr* to overturn; (fig) to upset || *ref* to overturn; (fig) to be or become reversed

capovolgimènto *m* upset; (fig) reversal

capovòlta *f* overturn; turn (*in swimming*)

cappa *f* cape, cloak; mantle; letter K; shroud (*of clouds*); (naut) trysail;

cappa del cielo vault of heaven; navigare alla cappa (naut) to lay to

cappèlla *f* chapel; cappella mortuaria undertaker's parlor || Cappella Sistina Sistine Chapel

cappel·làio *m* (-lài) hatter, hat maker or dealer

cappellano *m* chaplain

cappellata *f* hatful

cappelleria *f* hat store

cappellièra *f* hatbox

cappèllo *m* hat; bonnet; cap (*of mushroom*); head (*of nail*); cowl (*of chimney*); preamble (*of newspaper article*); cappello a cencio slouch hat; cappello a cilindro top hat; cappello a cono dunce cap; cappello a due punte cocked hat; cappello a tre punte three-cornered hat; cappello del lume lampshade; cappello di feltro felt hat; cappello di paglia straw hat; cappello floscio fedora; fare di cappello to take one's hat off; prendere cappello to take offense

cappellóne *adj invar* Western (*movie*) || *m* big hat; (coll) recruit; (mov) Western character

càppero *m* (bot) caper; capperi! (coll) wow!

càp·pio *m* (-pi) bow; noose; loop

capponàia *f* chicken coop

cappóne *m* capon

cappòtta *f* cape; navy coat; hood (*of car*)

cappottamènto *m* upset, rolling over

cappottare (cappòtto) *intr* to upset, roll over

cappottatura *f* (aer) cowl

cappòtto *m* overcoat; lurch (*at the close of game*); (cards) slam; cappotto da mezza stagione lightweight coat

cappuccino *m* espresso with cream; Capuchin (*friar*)

Cappuccétto *m*—Cappuccetto Rosso Little Red Ridinghood

cappùc·cio *m* (-ci) hood, cowl; cabbage; cap (*of fountain pen*)

capra *f* goat; nanny goat; tripod

ca·pràio -pràia *mf* (-prài -pràie) goatherd

caprét·to -ta *mf* kid

capriata *f* truss (*to support roof*)

capríc·cio *m* (-ci) whim, fancy, caprice; tantrum; flirting; (mus) capriccio

capricció·so -sa [*s*] *adj* whimsical, capricious; naughty; fanciful, bizarre

Capricòrno *m* (astr) Capricorn

caprifò·glio *m* (-gli) honeysuckle

caprimul·go *m* (-gi) (orn) goatsucker

capri·no -na *adj* goatlike, goatish || *m* smell of goat

capriòla *f* female roe deer; caper, somersault; fare capriole to cut capers, to caper

capriòlo *m* roe deer; roebuck

capro *m* he-goat, billy goat; capro espiatorio scapegoat

capróne *m* he-goat, billy goat

càpsula *f* capsule; percussion cap; cap (*of bottle*); (rok) capsule

captare *tr* to captivate; to catch, intercept; to harness (*a waterfall*); (rad, telv) to pick up (*a signal*)

captazióne *f* undue influence (*to secure an inheritance*)

capzió·so -sa [s] *adj* insidious, treacherous

carabàttola *f* (coll) trifle

carabina *f* carbine

carabinière *m* carabineer; Italian military policeman, carabiniere; (*hist*) cavalryman

caracollare (caracòllo) *intr* to caracole, caper; (coll) to trot along

caracòllo *m* caracole, caper

caraffa *f* carafe, decanter

caràmbola *f* carom

carambolare (caràmbolo) *intr* to carom

caramèlla *f* piece of hard candy; taffy; (coll) monocle; **caramelle** hard candy

caramellare (caramèllo) *tr* to caramel; to candy

caramèllo *m* caramel (*burnt sugar*)

caramènte *adv* affectionately

carati·sta *m* (-sti) shareholder (*in ship or business*)

carato *m* carat; share (*of ship*)

caràttere *m* character; type; handwriting; characteristic; disposition; **carattere corsivo** (typ) italic; **carattere maiuscolo** capital; **carattere minuscolo** small letter, lower case; **carattere neretto** or **grassetto** (typ) boldface

caratteri·sta *m* (-sti) character actor || *f* (-ste) character actress

caratteristi·co -ca (-ci -che) *adj & f* characteristic

caratterizzare [ddzz] *tr* to characterize

caratura *f* share (*in business or ship*)

cara·vàn *m* (-vàn) trailer, mobile home

caravanserrà·glio *m* (-gli) caravansary

caravèlla *f* caravel; carpenter's glue

carbo·nàio -nàia (-nài -nàie) *adj* coal || *m* coal man, coal dealer || *f* charcoal pit; coalbin, bunker; coal yard

carbonato *m* carbonate

carbón·chio *m* (-chi) (agr) smut (*on wheat*); (jewelry) carbuncle

carboncino *m* charcoal (*pencil and drawing*)

carbóne *m* coal; charcoal; carbon (*of arc light or primary battery*); **carbone bianco** hydroelectric power; **carbone dolce** charcoal; **carbone fossile** coal; **fare carbone** to coal

carbòni·co -ca *adj* (-ci -che) carbonic

carbonièra *f* coal yard; (naut) collier; (rr) tender

carbonile *m* (naut) bunker

carbònio *m* (chem) carbon

carbonizzare [ddzz] *tr* to carbonize; to char

carbùncolo *m* boil, carbuncle; (archaic) ruby

carburante *m* fuel

carburatóre *m* carburetor

carburazióne *f* (aut) mixture

carburo *m* carbide

carcassa *f* carcass; framework; (aut) jalopy; (fig) wreck

carcerare (càrcero) *tr* to jail

carcerà·rio -ria *adj* (-ri -rie) jail, prison

carcera·to -ta *adj* imprisoned || *mf* prisoner

càrce·re *m* (-ri *fpl*) jail, prison

carcerière *m* jailer, prison guard

carciòfo *m* artichoke

cardàni·co -ca *adj* (-ci -che) universal (*e.g., joint*)

cardano *m* universal joint

cardatrice *f* carding machine

cardellino *m* goldfinch

cardìa·co -ca (-ci -che) *adj* heart, cardiac || *m* heart patient

cardinale *adj* cardinal || *m* (eccl, orn) cardinal

cardinali·zio -zia *adj* (-zi -zie) cardinal, cardinal's

càrdine *m* hinge; (fig) pivot, mainstay (*e.g., of theory*)

càr·dio *m* (-dî) cockle (*mollusk*)

cardiochirurgia *f* heart surgery

cardiogram·ma *m* (-mi) cardiogram

cardiòlo·go *m* (-gi) cardiologist

cardiòpalmo *m* tachycardia

cardiopatìa *f* heart disease

cardo *m* (bot) thistle; (bot) cardoon

carèna *f* ship's bottom; (aer) outer cover (*of airship*); (bot) rib

carenàg·gio *m* (-gi) careening a ship; careen

carenare (carèno) *tr* to careen (*a ship*)

carenatura *f* streamlining; **carenatura di fusoliera** (aer) turtleback

carènza *f* lack, want

carestìa *f* famine; scarcity (*e.g., of manpower*)

carézza *f* caress; **fare una carezza a** to caress

carezzare (carézzo) *tr* to caress

carezzévole *adj* caressing, fondling; sweet, suave; blandishing

cariare §287 *tr* to cause (*a tooth*) to decay; to corrode || *ref* to decay; to rot

cariàtide *f* caryatid

caria·to -ta *adj* decayed

càri·ca *f* (-che) office, appointment; charge; (fig) insistence

caricaménto *m* loading

caricare §197 (càrico) *tr* to load; to burden; to wind (*a watch*); to fill (*a pipe*); to charge (*a battery*); to deepen (*a color*); **caricare la mano to** exceed; **caricare le dosi** to exaggerate || *ref* to burden oneself

carica·to -ta *adj* exaggerated, affected

carica·tóre -trice *adj* loading || *m* clip, magazine (*for rifle*); loader (*of gun*); cassette (*of tape recorder*); charger (*of battery*); longshoreman; (phot) cartridge, cassette

caricatura *f* caricature, cartoon; **mettere in caricatura** to ridicule

caricaturi·sta *mf* (-sti -ste) cartoonist, caricaturist

càrice *m* (bot) sedge

càri·co -ca (-chi -che) *adj* loaded; burdened; vivid (*color*); strong (*tea*); charged (*battery*) || *m* loading; load, burden; charge; cargo || *f* see **carica**

càrie *f* caries, decay

cari·no -na *adj* nice, pretty, cute; **questa è carina!** this is funny!

cari·tà f (-tà) charity; alms; (poet) love; **per carità** please

caritatévole adj charitable

caritati·vo -va adj (obs) charitable

carlin·ga f (-ghe) fuselage

Carlo m Charles

Carlomagno m Charlemagne

carlóna f—**alla carlona** carelessly, haphazardly

carlòtta f charlotte ‖ **Carlotta** Charlotte

carme m poem, lyric poem

carmì·nio m (-ni) carmine

carnagióne f complexion

car·nàio m (-nài) carnage; slaughter house; mass of humanity

carnale adj carnal, sensual; full (e.g., brother, cousin)

carname m carrion

carne f flesh; meat; **bene in carne** plump; **carne da macello** cannon fodder; **carne suina** pork; **carne viva** open wound; **essere solo carne ed ossa** to be nothing but skin and bones; **in carne ed ossa** in person, in the flesh; **troppa carne al fuoco** too many irons in the fire

carnéfice m executioner

carneficina f slaughter, carnage

càrne·o -a adj fleshy, meaty; flesh-colored

carnet m (**carnet**) notebook; checkbook; backlog

carnevale m carnival

carnièra f hunting jacket; gamebag

carnière m gamebag

carnìvo·ro -ra adj carnivorous ‖ mpl carnivores; Carnivora

carnò·so -sa [s] adj fleshy

ca·ro -ra adj dear (beloved; high in price) ‖ **caro** adv dear ‖ m high price; beloved; **i miei cari** my parents; my relatives; my friends

carógna f carcass; cad, rotter; **carogne** carrion

carosèllo m tournament; carousel, merry-go-round

caròta f carrot; (fig) lie

caròtide f carotid artery

carovana f caravan; group, crowd; union of longshoremen; apprenticeship; (naut, nav) convoy; **far carovana** to join a tour; **fare la carovana** to be an apprentice

carovanniè·ro -ra adj caravan ‖ f desert trail

carovì·ta m (-ta) high cost of living; cost-of-living increase

carovìve·ri m (-ri) high cost of living; cost-of-living increase

carpa f (ichth) carp

carpentière m carpenter

carpire §176 tr to snatch, seize; to extract, worm (a secret)

carpóni adv on all fours; **avanzare carponi** to crawl

carradóre m cart maker, wheelwright

car·ràio -ràia (-rài -ràie) adj passable for vehicles ‖ f cart road

carrarèc·cia f (-ce) country road; rut

carreggiata f paved road; track (of vehicles); (fig) right path

carrellare (**carrèllo**) intr (mov, telv) to dolly

carrellata f (mov) dolly shot, tracking shot

carrèlio m car (for narrow-gauge track); carriage (of typewriter); cart (for shopping); (aer) landing gear; (mach, rr) truck; (mov, telv) dolly; **carrello d'atterraggio** (aer) undercarriage, landing gear; **carrello elevatore** fork-lift truck

carrétta f cart; tramp steamer

carrettata f cartful; **a carrettate** abundantly

carrettière m cart driver, drayman; teamster

carrétto m small cart; **carretto a mano** pushcart

carriàg·gio m (-gi) wagon; **carriaggi** (mil) baggage train

carrièra f career; **di gran carriera** at top speed

carrieri·sta mf (-sti -ste) unscrupulous go-getter

carriòla f wheelbarrow

carro m wagon; cart; wagonload; cartload; carload; (rr) car; (astr) Plough; (poet) chariot; **carri armati** (mil) armor; **carro allegorico** float (in a pageant); **carro armato** (mil) tank; **carro attrezzi** (aut) tow truck, wrecker; **carro bestiame** (rr) cattle car; **carro botte** or **carro cisterna** (aut) tank truck; (rr) tank car; **carro di Tespi** traveling show; **carro funebre** hearse; **carro gru** (rr) wrecking crane; **carro marsupio** (rr) double decker (used to transport automobiles); **carro merci** (rr) freight car; **Gran Carro** (astr) Big Dipper; **mettere il carro innanzi ai buoi** to put the cart before the horse; **Piccolo Carro** (astr) Little Dipper ‖ m (**carra** fpl) carload; wagonload; cartload

carròzza f wagon carriage; **carrozza letti** (rr) sleeping car; **carrozza ristorante** (rr) dining car; **carrozza salone** (rr) club car; **con la carrozza di S. Francesco** on shank's mare; **signori, in carrozza!** (rr) all aboard!

carrozzàbile adj open to vehicular traffic ‖ f road open to vehicular traffic

carrozzèlla f small wagon; baby carriage; wheelchair; hackney

carrozzino m baby carriage; sidecar

carrozzóne m wagon; hearse; caravan (e.g., of gypsies); (rr) car

carruba f carob

carrubo m carob tree

carrùcola f pulley

carta f paper; document (e.g., of identification); **alla carta** à la carte; **carta assorbente** blotter; **carta astronomica** astronomical map; **carta bianca** blanche; carte blanche; **carta bollata** stamped paper (for official documents); **carta carbone** carbon paper; **carta catramata** tar paper; **carta da disegno** drawing paper; **carta da gioco** playing card; **carta da giornale** newsprint; **carta da imballaggio** or **da impacco** wrapping paper; **carta da lettera** or **da lettere** writing paper; **carta geografica** map, chart; **carta igienica** toilet paper; **carta oleata** wax paper; **carta torna-**

sole litmus paper; **carta velina** India paper; tissue paper; **carta vetrata** sandpaper; **carte** papers, writings; **carte francesi** cards in the four suits spades, hearts, diamonds, and clubs; **carte napoletane** cards in the four suits gold coins, cups, swords, and clubs; **fare le carte** to shuffle the cards; **fare le carte a qlcu** to tell s.o.'s fortune with cards

cartacarbóne *f* (**cartecarbóne**) carbon paper

cartàc·cia *f* (**-ce**) waste paper

cartàc·o -a *adj* (**-i -e**) paper

Cartàgine *f* Carthage

car·tàio *m* (**-tài**) papermaker; paper dealer; (cards) dealer

cartamonéta *f* paper money

cartapècora *f* parchment

cartapésta *f* papier-mâché

cartà·rio -ria *adj* (**-ri -rie**) paper

cartastràccia *f* (**cartestracce**) wrapping paper; wastepaper

cartég·gio *m* (**-gi**) correspondence; (aer, naut) reckoning

cartèlla *f* lottery ticket; card (*e.g., of bingo*); page of manuscript; Manila folder; schoolbag; briefcase; binding (*of book*); **cartella clinica** clinical chart; **cartella di rendita** government bond; **cartella esattoriale** tax bill; **cartella fondiaria** bond certificate

cartellino *m* label; nameplate (*on door*); file; (sports) contract; **cartellino di presenza** timecard; **cartellino signaletico** criminal record

cartèllo *m* poster; sign (*on store*); (com) cartel, trust; **cartello di sfida** challenge; **cartello stradale** traffic sign

cartellóne *m* show bill, theater poster; bill (*for advertising*); **tenere il cartellone** to find public favor, make a hit, be the rage

car·ter *m* (**-ter**) chain guard (*of bicycle*); (aut) crankcase

cartièra *f* papermill

cartilàgine *f* cartilage, gristle

cartina *f* dose; cigarette paper; small map

cartòc·cio *m* (**-ci**) paper cone; charge (*of gun*); cornhusk; (archit) scroll

cartògrafo *m* cartographer

carto·làio *m* (**-lài**) stationer

cartoleria *f* stationery store

cartolina *f* card, post card; **cartolina precetto** induction notice

cartomante *mf* fortuneteller

cartoncino *m* light cardboard, calling card; **cartoncino natalizio** Christmas card

cartóne *m* cardboard, carton; **cartone animato** (mov) animated cartoon

cartùc·cia *f* (**-ce**) cartridge; shot, shell; **mezza cartuccia** (fig) half pint

cartuccièra *f* cartridge belt

casa [s] *f* house; dwelling; home; household; **andare a casa** to go home; **casa base** (baseball) home base; **casa colonica** farm house; **casa da gioco** gambling house; **casa del diavolo** faraway place; **casa di bambole** playhouse, doll's house; **casa di correzione** reform school; **casa di cura** sanatorium, private clinic; **casa di riposo** convalescent home, nursing home; **casa di spedizione** shipping agency; **casa di tolleranza** bawdyhouse; **casa madre** home office, headquarters; **esser di casa** to be intimate; **fuori casa** (sports) away; **in casa** (sports) home; **metter su casa** to set up housekeeping; **sentirsi a casa** to feel at home; **stare a casa** to stay at home; **star di casa** to dwell, live

casac·ca *f* (**-che**) coat; **voltar casacca** to be a turncoat

casàccio *m*—**a casaccio** at random; heedlessly

casalin·go -ga (**-ghi -ghe**) [s] *adj* home, domestic; stay-at-home; homey; home-made || **casalinghi** *mpl* household articles || *f* housewife

casamatta [s] *f* casemate, bunker

casaménto [s] *m* apartment house, tenement; tenants

casata [s] *f* house, lineage

casato [s] *m* birth, family; (obs) family name

cascame *m* waste; remnants (*e.g., of silk*)

cascante *adj* flabby, loose; (poet) languid, dull

cascare §197 *intr* (ESSERE) to fall, droop; to fit (*said of clothes*); **cascare dalla noia** to be bored to death; **cascare dal sonno** to be overwhelmed with sleep; **cascare diritto** to escape unscathed; **non casca il mondo** the world is not coming to an end

cascata *f* fall, waterfall; necklace (*e.g., of pearls*); **a cascata** flood of, e.g., **telefonate a cascata** flood of telephone calls || **le Cascate del Niagara** Niagara Falls

cascina *f* farm house; dairy barn

ca·sco *m* (**-schi**) helmet, crash helmet; electric hairdrier; cluster (*e.g., of bananas*)

caseggiato [s] *m* built-up zone; block, row of houses; apartment house

caseifi·cio *m* (**-ci**) dairy, creamery, cheese factory

casèlla [s] *f* pigeonhole; square (*of paper*); **casella postale** post-office box

casellante [s] *mf* gatekeeper || *m* (rr) trackwalker

casellà·rio [s] *m* (**-ri**) filing cabinet; row of post-office boxes; **casellario giudiziale** criminal file

casèllo [s] *m* tollgate (*on turnpike*); (rr) trackwalker's house

casèrma *f* barracks; fire station

casino [s] *m* country house; clubhouse; (slang) whorehouse; (slang) noise, racket

casìsti·ca *f* (**-che**) case study; (eccl) casuistry

caso *m* case; chance; fate; vicissitude; opportunity; **a caso** inadvertently; **al caso** eventually; **caso fortuito** (law) act of God; **caso mai** assuming that, in the event that; **è il caso** it is the moment; **far caso a qlco** to notice s.th; **in ogni caso** in any event; **mettere il caso che** suppose; **mi fa caso** I am surprised; **non fare caso a** to make nothing of, pay no attention to; per caso perchance

casolare [s] *m* hut, hovel; isolated farmhouse

casòtto [s] *m* cabana, bathhouse; sentry box

Càspio *adj* Caspian

càspita *interj* you don't say!

cassa *f* box; chest; case; stock (*of rifle*); cash; cash register; desk (*e.g., in hotel*); check-out (*in a supermarket*); **a pronta cassa** by cash; **cassa acustica** loudspeaker; **cassa di risparmio** savings bank; **cassa malattia** health insurance; **cassa rurale** farmers' credit cooperative; **in cassa** in hand (*said of money*)

cassafórma *f* (**casseforme**) (archit) form (*for cement*)

cassafòrte *f* (**cassefòrti**) safe

cassapanca *f* (**cassapanche & casse-panche**) wooden chest

cassare *tr* to erase, cancel; to cross off; (law) to annull

cassata *f* Neapolitan ice cream with soft core; Sicilian cake

cassazióne *f* annulment, abolition; cancellation

casserétto *m* (naut) poop

càssero *m* (naut) quarterdeck; **cassero di poppa** (naut) cockpit

casseruòla *f* saucepan

cassétta *f* small box; coach box; (theat) box office; **cassetta dei ferri** workbox; **cassetta delle lettere** mail box; **cassetta di cottura** dish warmer; **cassetta di sicurezza** safe-deposit box; **cassetta per ugnature** miter box

cassettièra *f* chest of drawers

cassétto *m* drawer; **cassetto di distribuzione** (mach) slide valve

cassettóne *m* chest of drawers; (archit) coffer, caisson

cassiè•re -ra *mf* cashier; teller

cassóne *m* large case, large box; chest; caisson (*for underwater construction*); body (*of truck*); (mil) caisson

cassonétto *m* cornice

cast *m* cast (*of actors*)

casta *f* caste

castagna *f* chestnut; **castagna d'India** horse chestnut

castagnéto *m* chestnut grove

castagno *m* chestnut tree; chestnut (*lumber*); **castagno d'India** horse chestnut tree

casta•no -na *adj* chestnut (*color*)

castellana *f* chatelaine

castellano *m* lord of the castle, squire

castellétto *m* scaffold; (min) gallows, headframe

castèl•lo *m* castle; works (*e.g., of watch*); scaffold; jungle gym; hydraulic boom, bucket lift (*on truck*); (naut) forecastle; **castello di menzogne** pack of lies; **castello in aria** castle in Spain || *m* (**-la** *fpl*) (archaic) castle

castigare §209 *tr* to punish; (poet) to correct, castigate

castigatézza *f* purity (*e.g., of style*)

castiga•to -ta *adj* decent, modest; pure (*language*)

Castiglia, la Castile

castiglia•no -na *adj & mf* Castilian

casti•go *m* (**-ghi**) punishment; (fig) scourge; **mettere in castigo** (coll) to punish

casti•tà *f* (**-tà**) chastity; (fig) purity

ca•sto -sta *adj* chaste; pure, elegant (*language or style*)

castóne *m* setting (*of stone*)

castòro *m* beaver

castrare *tr* to castrate; to spay; (fig) to expurgate

castra•to -ta *adj* castrated; spayed; (fig) effeminate || *m* mutton (of castrated sheep); eunuch

castróne *m* wether (*sheep*); gelding (*horse*); (fig) nincompoop

castronerìa *f* (vulg) stupidity

casuale *adj* fortuitous, casual; sundry (*e.g., expenses*)

casuali•tà *f* (**-tà**) chance, accident

casùpola [s] *f* hut, hovel

cataclì•sma *m* (**-smi**) cataclysm

catacómba *f* catacomb

catafal•co *m* (**-chi**) catafalque

catafàscio *adv*—a catafascio topsy-turvy

catalès•si *f* (**-si**) catalepsy

catàl•si *f* (**-si**) catalysis

catalizza•tóre -trice [ddzz] *adj* catalytic || *m* catalyst

catalogare §209 (**catàlogo**) *tr* to catalogue

catàlo•go *m* (**-ghi**) catalogue

catapècchia *f* hovel

catapla•sma *m* (**-smi**) poultice, plaster; (fig) bore

catapulta *f* catapult

catapultare *tr* to catapult

cataratta *f* cataract; sluice (*of canal*)

catarro *m* catarrh

catar•si *f* (**-si**) catharsis

catàrti•co -ca *adj* (**-ci -che**) cathartic

catasta *f* pile, heap

catastale *adj* land (*office*)

catasto *m* real-estate register; land office

catàstrofe *f* catastrophe; wreck

catastròfi•co -ca *adj* (**-ci -che**) catastrophic

catechismo *m* catechism

catechizzare [ddzz] *tr* to catechize

categorìa *f* category; weight (*in boxing*); (sports) class

categòri•co -ca *adj* (**-ci -che**) categorical; classified (*telephone directory*)

caténa *f* chain; range (*of mountains*); (archit) tie beam; **catene da neve** tire chains; **mordere la catena** to champ the bit

catenàc•cio *m* (**-ci**) bolt; (fig) jalopy; (journ) giant-size headline

catenèlla *f* chain

cateratta *f* var of **cataratta**

catèrva *f* great quantity, large number

catetère *m* catheter

cateterizzare [ddzz] *tr* to catheterize

catinèlla *f* water basin; **piovere a catinelle** (coll) to rain cats and dogs

catino *m* basin

càtodo *m* cathode

Catóne *m* Cato; **Catone il Maggiore** Cato the Elder

catòr•cio *m* (**-ci**) (coll) piece of junk

catramare *tr* to tar

catramatrice *f* asphalt-paving machine

catrame *m* tar, coal tar

càttedra *f* desk (*of teacher*); chair, professorship

cattedrale *adj* & *f* cathedral

cattedràti·co -ca (*-ci -che*) *adj* pedantic || *m* professor

catte·gù *m* (*-gù*) catgut

cattivare *tr* to captivate

cattivèria *f* wickedness; piece of wickedness

cattivi·tà *f* (*-tà*) captivity

catti·vo -va *adj* bad; wicked; vicious (*animal*); worthless; poor (*reputation; condition*); nasty; naughty; (*archaic*) cowardly || *mf* wicked person || *m* bad taste; **sapere di cattivo** to taste bad

cattolicità *f* catholicity

cattòli·co -ca (*-ci -che*) *adj* catholic || *adj* & *mf* Catholic

cattura *f* capture, seizure; arrest

catturare *tr* to capture, seize; to arrest

caucàsi·co -ca *adj* & *mf* (*-ci -che*) Caucasian

caucciù *m* (**caucciù**) rubber

càusa *f* cause, motive; fault; lawsuit, action; **a causa di** on account of; **causa civile** civil suit; **causa penale** criminal suit; **fare causa** to take legal action; **intentare causa a** to bring suit against

causale *adj* causal || *f* cause

causare (**càuso**) *tr* to cause

causìdi·co *m* (*-ci*) amicus curiae; (*joc*) pettifogger

càusti·co -ca *adj* (*-ci -che*) caustic

cautèla *f* caution; precaution, care

cautelare *adj* guaranteeing, protecting || *v* (**cautèlo**) *tr* to guarantee, protect || *ref* to take precautions

cauterizzare [ddzz] *tr* to cauterize

càu·to -ta *adj* cautious, prudent; cagey

cauzióne *f* security, bail; **dare cauzione** to give bail

cava *f* quarry; cave; (*fig*) mine

cavadènti *m* (*-ti*) (coll) tooth puller, poor dentist

cavagno *m* (coll) basket

cavalcare §197 *tr* to ride; to cross over (*e.g., a river*) || *intr* to ride; **cavalcare a bisdosso** to ride bareback; **cavalcare all'amazzone** to ride sidesaddle

cavalcata *f* ride; cavalcade

cavalcatura *f* mount

cavalca·vìa *m* (*-vìa*) bridge (*between two buildings*); overpass

cavalcióni *adj*—**a cavalcióni** (**di**) astride

cavalierato *m* knighthood

cavalière *m* rider (*on horseback*); knight; cavalier; chevalier; **a cavaliere** astride; **cavaliere d'industria** adventurer; **cavaliere errante** knight errant; **essere a cavaliere di** to overlook (*e.g., a valley*); to stretch over (*e.g., two centuries*)

cavalla *f* mare

cavalleggièro *m* cavalryman

cavalleré·sco -sca *adj* (*-schi -sche*) chivalrous, knightly

cavallería *f* cavalry; chivalry, knighthood; (fig) chivalry

cavallerizza *f* manège, riding school; horsemanship; horsewoman

cavallerizzo *m* horseman; riding master

cavallétta *f* grasshopper

cavallétto *m* tripod; easel; trestle (*of ski lift*); scaffold (*e.g., of stonemason*); sawhorse, sawbuck

cavalli·no -na *adj* horse, horse-like || *m* foal, colt || *f* foal, filly; **correre la cavallina** to be on the loose; to sow one's wild oats

cavallo *m* horse; knight (*in chess*); crotch (*of pants*); **a cavallo** on horseback; **a cavallo di** astride; **andare col cavallo di San Francesco** to ride shank's mare; **cavallo a dondolo** hobbyhorse; **cavallo di battaglia** battle horse; (fig) specialty, forte; **cavallo da corsa** race horse; **cavallo da tiro** draft horse; **cavallo di Frisia** cheval-de-frise; **cavallo di ritorno** confirmed news; **cavallo vapore** metric horsepower; **essere a cavallo** (fig) to have turned the corner

cavallóne *m* big horse; billow

cavallùc·cio *m* (*-ci*) little horse; **a cavalluccio** on one's shoulders; **cavalluccio marino** (ichth) sea horse

cavare *tr* to dig; to extract (*e.g., a tooth*); to pull out (*e.g., money*); to draw; **cavare il cuore a qlcu** to move s.o. to compassion; **cavare una spina dal cuore a qlcu** to ease s.o.'s mind || *ref* to take off (*e.g., one's hat*); **cavarsela** to overcome an obstacle; to get out of trouble; **cavarsi la camicia di dosso** to give the shirt off one's back; **cavarsi la fame** to eat one's fill; **cavarsi la voglia** to satisfy one's wishes

cavastiva·li *m* (*-li*) bootjack

cavatap·pi *m* (*-pi*) corkscrew

cavaturàccio·li *m* (*-li*) corkscrew

cavèrna *f* cave, cavern

cavernó·so -sa [s] *adj* cavernous; deep (*voice*)

cavèzza *f* halter; (fig) check

càvia *f* guinea pig; **cavia umana** (fig) guinea pig

caviale *m* caviar

cavìc·chio *m* (*-chi*) peg

cavì·glia *f* (*-glie*) ankle; bolt; pin, dowel, peg

caviglièra *f* ankle support

cavillare *intr* to cavil, quibble

cavillo *m* quibble

cavilló·so -sa [s] *adj* quibbling, captious

cavi·tà *f* (*-tà*) cavity

ca·vo -va *adj* hollow || *m* hollow; cable; trough (*between two waves*); (naut) hawser; **cavo di rimorchio** towline; **cavo telefonico** telephone cable || *f* see cava

cavolfióre *m* cauliflower

càvolo *m* cabbage; **cavolo di Bruxelles** Brussels sprouts (*food*); (bot) Brussels sprout; **non capire un cavolo** (vulg) to not understand a blessed thing

cazzòtto *m* (vulg) punch, sock

cazzuòla *f* trowel

ce §5
cecare §122 *tr* to blind
cèc·ca *f* (-che) magpie; fare cecca to misfire
cecchino *m* sniper
céce *m* chickpea
ceci·tà *f* (-tà) blindness
cè·co -ca *adj & mf* (-chi -che) Czech
Cecoslovàcchia, la Czechoslovakia
cecoslovac·co -ca *adj & mf* (-chi -che) Czechoslovak
cèdere §123 *tr* to cede; to give up; to sell at cost; cedere il passo to let s.o. through; cedere la strada to yield the right of way; non cederla to be second to none ‖ *intr* to give in, yield; to give way, succumb; to sag
cedévole *adj* yielding; soft; pliable
cedìglia *f* cedilla
cedimento *m* cave-in; (fig) yielding
cèdola *f* slip; coupon
cedri·no -na *adj* citron; citron-like; cedar, cedar-like
cédro *m* (*Citrus medica*) citron; (*Cedrus*) cedar; cedro del Libano cedar of Lebanon
CEE *m* (letterword) (Comunità Economica Europea) EEC (*European Economic Community - Common Market*)
cefalèa *f* slight headache; headache
cèfalo *m* (ichth) mullet
cèffo *m* snout; (pej) face; brutto ceffo ugly mug
ceffóne *m* slap in the face
celare (cèlo) *tr* to hide, conceal
cela·to -ta *adj* hidden ‖ *f* sallet
celebèrri·mo -ma *adj* very famous, renowned
celebrare (cèlebro) *tr & intr* to celebrate
celebrazióne *f* celebration
cèlebre *adj* famous, renowned, celebrated
celebri·tà *f* (-tà) celebrity
cèlere *adj* swift, rapid; express (*train*); short, quick; prompt ‖ Celere *f* special police
celeri·tà *f* (-tà) swiftness, rapidity; speed (*e.g., of a machine gun*)
celèste *adj* heavenly, celestial; blue, sky-blue ‖ *m* blue, sky blue; celesti heavenly spirits; (mythol) gods
celestiale *adj* celestial, heavenly
cèlia *f* jest; mettere in celia to deride; per celia in jest
celiare §287 (cèlio) *intr* to jest, joke
celibatà·rio -ria (-ri -rie) *adj* single ‖ *m* old bachelor
celibato *m* celibacy; bachelorhood
cèlibe *adj* single, unmarried ‖ *m* bachelor
cèlla *f* cell; cella frigorifera walk-in refrigerator; cella campanaria belfry
cèllofan *or* cellofàn *m* cellophane
cèllula *f* cell; cellula fotoelettrica photoelectric cell
cellulare *adj* cellular; ventilated (*fabric*); solitary (*confinement*)
cellulòide *f* celluloid
celluló·so -sa [s] *adj* cell-like, cellular ‖ *f* cellulose
cèl·ta *mf* (-ti -te) Celt

cèlti·co -ca *adj* (-ci -che) Celtic; venereal (*disease*)
cementare (cemènto) *tr* to cement
cemènto *m* cement, concrete; cemento armato reinforced concrete
céna *f* supper; Ultima Cena Last Supper
cenàcolo *m* cenacle
cenare (céno) *intr* to sup, have supper
cenciaiò·lo -la *mf* ragpicker
cén·cio *m* (-ci) rag, duster (*for cleaning*)
cenció·so -sa [s] *adj* tattered, ragged
cénere *adj* ashen ‖ *f* ash; cinder; andare in cenere to go up in smoke; ceneri ashes (*of a person*); ridurre in cenere to burn to ashes ‖ le Ceneri Ash Wednesday
cenerèntola *f* (fig) Cinderella ‖ Cenerèntola *f* Cinderella (*of the fable*)
cén·gia *f* (-ge) ledge (*of a mountain*)
cénno *m* sign; wave (*with hand*); nod; wag; wink; gesture; hint; notice; ai cenni di at the orders of; fare cenno a *or* di to mention; fare cenno di no to shake one's head; fare cenno di sì to nod assent
cenò·bio *m* (-bi) monastery
cenobi·ta *m* (-ti) monk, cenobite
censiménto *m* census
censire §176 *tr* to take the census of
cènso *m* wealth, income; census (*in ancient Rome*)
censóre *m* censor; faultfinder; (educ) proctor
censuà·rio -ria (-ri -rie) *adj* income; tax (*register*) ‖ *m* taxpayer
censura *f* censure; censorship; fault-finding
censurare *tr* to censure; to criticize, find fault with
centàuro *m* centaur
centellinare *tr* to sip; to take a nip of
centellino *m* sip, nip
centenà·rio -ria (-ri -rie) *adj & mf* centenary, centennial ‖ *m* centenary, centennial (*anniversary*)
centèsi·mo -ma *adj* hundredth ‖ *m* hundredth; centime; cent; penny
centigrado *m* centigrade
centigrammo *m* centigram
centimetro *m* centimeter; tape measure
cèntina *f* (archit) centering; (aer) rib
centi·nàio *m* hundred; un centinaio di about a hundred ‖ *m* (-nàia *fpl*)—a centinaia by the hundreds
cènto *adj*, *m & pron* a hundred, one hundred; per cento per cent
centomila *adj*, *m & pron* a hundred thousand, one hundred thousand
centóne *m* cento
centopiè·di *m* (-di) centipede
centrale *adj* central ‖ *f* headquarters, home office; powerhouse, generating station; telephone exchange; centrale di conversione (elec) transformer station; centrale telefonica central
centralini·sta *mf* (-sti -ste) telephone operator
centralino *m* telephone exchange
centralizzare [ddzz] *tr* to centralize
centrare (cèntro) *tr* to center; to hit the center of

centrattac·co *m* (-chi) (sports) center forward

centrifu·go -ga *adj* (-ghi -ghe) centrifugal || *f* centrifuge

centrino *m* centerpiece

centrìpe·to -ta *adj* centripetal

centri·sta *mf* (-sti -ste) (pol) centrist

cèntro *m* center; **al centro** downtown; **far centro** to hit the mark

centrocampo *m* (soccer) midfield

centuplicare §197 (**centùplico**) *tr* to multiply a hundredfold

cèntu·plo -pla *adj & m* hundredfold

céppo *m* trunk, stump; log; block (*for beheading*); brake shoe; stock (*of anchor*); **ceppi** stocks, fetters || **il Ceppo** (coll) Christmas

céra *f* wax; face, aspect, air, look; **di cera** waxen; pale; **cera da scarpe** shoe polish; **avere buona cera** to look well; **fare buona cera a** to welcome

ceralac·ca *f* (-che) sealing wax

ceràmi·co -ca (-ci -che) *adj* ceramic || *f* ceramics

cerare (**céro**) *tr* to wax

Cèrbero *m* Cerberus

cerbiatto *m* fawn

cerbottana *f* blowgun, peashooter

cer·ca *f* (-che) search, quest; **in cerca di** in search of

cercare §197 (**cérco**) *tr* to seek, look for; to desire, yearn for; **cercare il pelo nell'uovo** to be a faultfinder, to nitpick || *intr* to try

cerca·tóre -trice *adj* seeking || *mf* seeker; mendicant || *m* prospector

cérchia *f* coterie; compass, limits (*of a wall*); circle (*of friends*)

cerchiare §287 (**cérchio**) *tr* to hoop (*a barrel*); to circle, encircle

cér·chio *m* (-chi) circle; hoop; loop; **fare il cerchio della morte** (aer) to loop the loop; **in cerchio** in a circle || *m* (-chia *fpl*) (archaic) circle

cerchióne *m* rim; tire (*of metal*)

cereale *adj & m* cereal

cerebrale *adj* cerebral

cère·o -a *adj* waxen; wax-colored, pale

cerfò·glio *m* (-gli) chervil

cerimònia *f* ceremony; **fare cerimonie** to stand on ceremony; to make a fuss

cerimoniale *adj & m* ceremonial

cerimonière *m* master of ceremonies (*at court*)

cerimonió·so -sa [s] *adj* ceremonious

cerino *m* wax match; taper

cernéc·chio *m* (-chi) tuft (*of hair*)

cernièra *f* hinge; clasp (*of handbag*); **a cerniera** hinged; **cerniera lampo** zipper

cèrnita *f* sorting, selection, grading

céro *m* church candle; **offrire un cero** to light a candle

ceróne *m* make-up (*of actor*)

ceròtto *m* adhesive tape; (fig) bore; **cerotto per i calli** corn plaster

certame *m* (poet) combat; competition, contest (*of poets*)

certézza *f* certitude, assurance, conviction, certainty

certificare §197 (**certìfico**) *tr* to certify, certificate

certificato *m* certificate

cèr·to -ta *adj* such, some; convinced; certain; real, positive || *m* certainty; **di certo** or **per certo** for certain || **certi** *pron* some || **certo** *adv* undoubtedly

certósa *f* Carthusian monastery, charterhouse

certosi·no *m* Carthusian monk; chartreuse (*liquor*); **da certosino** with great patience

certu·no -na *adj* (obs) some || **certuni** *pron* some

cerùle·o -a *adj* cerulean

cerume *m* ear wax

cervellétto *m* cerebellum

cervelli·no -na *adj & mf* scatterbrain

cervèllo *m* (**cervèlli & cervèlla** *fpl*) brain; head; mind; **dare al cervello** to go to one's head

cervellòtì·co -ca *adj* (-ci -che) queer, extravagant

cervice *f* (anat) cervix; (poet) nape of the neck

cerviè·ro -ra *adj* lynx-like; || *m* lynx

cervi·no -na *adj* deer-like || **Cervino** *m* Matterhorn

cèrvo *m* deer; (ent) stag beetle; **cervo volante** kite

Cèsare *m* Caesar

cesàre·o -a *adj* Caesarean; (poet) courtly

cesellare (**cesèllo**) *tr* to chase, chisel; to carve, engrave; to polish (*e.g., a poem*)

cesella·tóre -trice *mf* chaser, engraver, chiseler

cesellatura *f* chasing, engraving; polished writing

cesèllo *m* burin, graver

cesóia *f* shears, metal shears; **cesoie** shears (*for gardening*)

cesoiatrice *f* shearing machine

cèspite *m* source (*of income*); (poet) tuft

céspo *m* tuft

cespù·glio *m* (-gli) bush, shrub, thicket

cèssa *f*—**senza cessa** without letup

cessare (**cèsso**) *tr* to stop, interrupt || *intr* to cease, stop; **cessare di** + *inf* to stop + *ger*

cessazióne *f* cessation, discontinuance; **cessazione d'esercizio** going out of business

cessionà·rio *m* (-ri) assignee

cèsso *m* (vulg) privy, outhouse

césta *f* basket, hamper

cestinare *tr* to throw into the wastebasket; to reject (*a book, article, etc.*)

césto *m* basket; tuft; head (*e.g., of lettuce*)

cesura *f* caesura

cetàceo *m* cetacean

cèto *m* class; **ceto medio** middle class

cétra *f* lyre; cither; inspiration

cetriolino *m* gherkin

cetriòlo *m* cucumber; (fig) dolt

che *adj* what; which; what a, e.g., **che bella giornata!** what a beautiful day! || *pron interr* what || *pron rel* who; whom; that; which; (coll) in which || *m*—**essere un gran che** to be a big shot, to be somebody || *adv* how, e.g., **che bello!** how nice!; **non . . . che** only, e.g., **non venne che Luigi** only Luigi came; no one but, e.g., **non restò che mio cugino** no one but my cousin stayed || *conj* that; (*after comparatives*) than, as

ché *adv* (coll) why || *conj* (coll) because; (coll) so that

checché *pron* (lit) whatever, no matter what

checchessìa *pron* (lit) anything, everything

chèla *f* claw

che·pì *m* (**-pì**) kepi

cherubino *m* cherub

chetare (**chéto**) *tr* to quiet; to placate || *ref* to quiet down, become quiet

chetichèlla *f*—**alla chetichella** surreptitiously, stealthily

ché·to -ta *adj* quiet, still

chi *pron interr* who; whom || *pron rel* who; whom; **chi . . . chi** some . . . some

chiàcchiera *f* chatter, idle talk; gossip; glibness; **fare quattro chiacchiere** to have a chat

chiacchierare (**chiàcchiero**) *intr* to chat; to gossip

chiacchierata *f* talk, chat; **fare una chiacchierata** to visit

chiacchieri·no -na *adj* talkative, loquacious

chiacchieri·o -o *m* (**-i**) chattering, jabbering (*of a crowd*)

chiacchieró·ne -na *adj* talkative, loquacious || *mf* chatterbox

chiama *f* roll call; **fare la chiama** to call the roll; **mancare alla chiama** to be absent at the roll call

chiamare *tr* to call; to hail (*a cab*); to invoke, call upon; **chiamare al telefono** to call up; **esser chiamato a** to have the vocation for || *ref* to be named; **si chiama Giovanni** his name is John

chiamata *f* call; (law) designation (*of an heir*); (telp) ring; (theat) curtain call; (typ) catchword

chiappa *f* (vulg) buttock; (slang) catch (*e.g., of fish*)

chiarét·to -ta *adj & m* claret

chiarézza *f* clarity, clearness

chiarificare §197 (**chiarìfico**) *tr* to clarify

chiarificazióne *f* clarification

chiariménto *m* explanation

chiarire §176 *tr* to clear up, explain; to unravel || *intr* (ESSERE) to clear, become clear || *ref* to make oneself clear; to assure oneself

chia·ro -ra *adj* clear; bright; light (*color*); honest; clear-cut; plain (*language*); illustrious, famous || *m* light; bright color; brightness; **chiaro di luna** moonlight; **con questi chiari di luna** in these troubled times; **mettere in chiaro** to clarify, explain || **chiaro** *adv* plainly; **chiaro e tondo** bluntly, frankly

chiaróre *m* light, glimmer

chiaroveggènte *adj & mf* clairvoyant

chiaroveggènza *f* clairvoyance

chiassata *f* uproar, disturbance, racket; noisy scene

chiasso *m* uproar; alley; **fare chiasso** to cause a sensation

chiassó·so -sa [s] *adj* noisy; gaudy

chiatta *f* barge; pontoon

chiavarda *f* bolt

chiave *f* key; wrench; (archit) keystone; (mus) clef; **avere le chiavi di** to own; **chiave a rollino** adjustable wrench; **chiave a tubo** socket wrench; **chiave di volta** keystone; **chiave inglese** monkey wrench; **fuori chiave** off key; **sotto chiave** under lock and key

chiavétta *f* key; cock; cotter pin

chiàvi·ca *f* (**-che**) sewer

chiavistèllo *m* bolt

chiazza *f* spot, blotch

chiazzare *tr* to spot, blotch; to mottle

chiazza·to -ta *adj* spotted, mottled

chic·ca *f* (**-che**) sweet, candy

chìcchera *f* cup

chicchessìa *pron indef* anyone, anybody

chicchirichì *m* cock-a-doodle-doo

chic·co *m* (**-chi**) grain, seed; bead (*of rosary*); bean (*of coffee*); **chicco di grandine** hailstone; **chicco d'uva** grape

chièdere §124 *tr* to ask; to ask for; to beg (*pardon*); to require; to sue (*for damages or peace*); **chiedere a qlcu di** + *inf* to ask s.o. to + *inf*; **chiedere in prestito** to borrow; **chiedere qlco a qlcu** to ask s.o. for s.th || *ref* to wonder

chiéri·ca *f* (**-che**) tonsure; priesthood

chiéri·co *m* (**-ci**) clergyman; altar boy; (archaic) clerk

chièsa *f* church

chiesuòla *f* small church; clique, set (*e.g., of artists*); (naut) binnacle

chì·glia *f* (**-glie**) keel; **chiglia mobile** (naut) centerboard

chilo *m* kilo, kilogram; **fare il chilo** to take a siesta

chilociclo *m* kilocycle

chilogrammo *m* kilogram

chilohèrtz *m* kilohertz

chilometràg·gio *m* (**-gi**) distance in kilometers

chilomètri·co -ca *adj* (**-ci -che**) kilometric; interminable (*e.g., speech*)

chilòmetro *m* kilometer

chilo·watt *m* (**-watt**) kilowatt

chimèra *f* chimera; daydream, utopia

chimèri·co -ca *adj* (**-ci -che**) chimerical

chìmi·co -ca (**-ci -che**) *adj* chemical || *m* chemist || *f* chemistry

chimòno *m* kimono

china *f* slope, decline; India ink; cinchona

chinare *tr* to bend; to lower (*one's eyes*); **chinare il capo** to nod assent; **chinare la fronte** to yield, give in || *ref* to bend, stoop

china·to -ta *adj* bent, lowered; bitter; with quinine, e.g., **vino chinato** wine with quinine

chincàglie *fpl* notions, knickknacks, sundries

chincaglière *m* notions or knicknack dealer

chincaglierìa *f* knicknack; **chincaglierie** knicknacks, notions

chinina *f* quinine (*alkaloid*)

chinino *m* quinine (*salt of the alkaloid*)

chi·no -na *adj* bent, lowered || *f* see **china**

chiòc·cia *f* (-ce) brooding hen

chiocciare §128 (chiòccio) *intr* to cluck; to sit, brood; to crouch

chiocciata *f* brood

chiòc·cio -cia (-ci -ce) *adj* hoarse || *f* see **chioccia**

chiòcciola *f* snail; (anat) cochlea; (mach) nut

chioccolì·o *m* (-i) cackle (*of hen*); gurgle (*of water*)

chiodare (chiòdo) *tr* to nail

chioda·to -ta *adj* nailed shut; hobnailed

chiòdo *m* nail; spike; obsession; craze; (coll) debt; **chiodi** climbing irons; **chiodo a espansione** expansion bolt; **chiodo da cavallo** horseshoe nail; **chiodo di garofano** clove; **chiodo ribattino** rivet

chiòma *f* hair; mane; foliage; (astr) coma

chioma·to -ta *adj* hairy, long-haired; leafy

chiòsa *f* gloss

chiosare (chiòso) *tr* to gloss, comment on

chiò·sco *m* (-schi) kiosk, stand, newsstand; pavilion, bandstand

chiòstra *f* circular range (*of mountains*); (poet) enclosure; (poet) set (*of teeth*); (poet) zone, region

chiòstro *m* cloister

chiòt·to -ta *adj* quiet, still; **chiotto chiotto** still as a mouse

chiromante *mf* palmist

chiromanzìa *f* palmistry

chiropràtica *f* chiropractice

chirurgìa *f* surgery

chirùrgi·co -ca *adj* (-ci -che) surgical

chirur·go *m* (-ghi & -gi) surgeon

chissà *adv* maybe

chitarra *f* guitar; **chitarra hawaiana** ukulele

chitarri·sta *mf* (-sti -ste) guitar player

chiùdere §125 *tr* to shut, close; to lock; to turn off; to fasten; to block (*a road*); to fence in; to nail shut (*a box*); to strike (*a balance*); to conclude, wind up; **chiudere a chiave** to lock; **chiudere bottega** to go out of business; **chiudere il becco** (slang) to shut up || *intr* to shut, close; to lock || *ref* to shut, close; to lock; to withdraw; to cloud over

chiùnque *pron indef invar* anybody, anyone || *pron rel invar* whoever, whomever; anyone who, anyone whom

chiurlo *m* (orn) curlew

chiusa [s] *f* fence; lock (*of canal*); end, conclusion (*e.g., of letter*)

chiusino [s] *m* manhole

chiu·so -sa [s] *adj* shut, closed, locked; stuffy (*air*); high-bodiced (*dress*);

close (*vowel*) || *m* enclosure, corral; close || *f* see **chiusa**

chiusura [s] *f* closing, end; fastener; lock; **chiusura lampo** zipper, slide fastener

ci §5

ciabatta *f* slipper; old shoe

ciabat·tàio *m* (-tài) cobbler

ciabattare *intr* to shuffle along

ciabattino *m* cobbler, shoemaker

ciàc *f* (mov) clappers

cialda *f* wafer; thin waffle

cialdóne *m* cone (*for ice cream*)

ciaitró·ne -na *mf* rogue, scoundrel; slovenly person

ciambèlla *f* doughnut; **ciambella di salvataggio** life saver

ciambellano *m* chamberlain

ciampicare §197 (ciàmpico) *intr* to stumble along

ciana *f* (slang) fishwife

cianamide *f* cyanamide

ciàn·cia *f* (-ce) chatter, prattle, idle gossip

cianciare §128 (ciàncio) *intr* to chatter, prattle

cianciafrùscola *f* trifle, bagatelle

cianfrusà·glia *f* (-glie) trifle, trinket; rubbish, trash, junk

cianìdri·co -ca *adj* (-ci -che) hydrocyanic

cianògeno *m* cyanogen

cianuro *m* cyanide

ciao *interj* (coll) hi!, hello!; (coll) goodbye!, so long!

ciarla *f* chatter, prattle, idle talk; gossip

ciarlare *intr* to chatter, prattle

ciarlatanata *f* charlatanism, quackery

ciarlatanerìa *f* charlatanism

ciarlatané·sco -sca *adj* (-schi -sche) charlatan

ciarlatano *m* charlatan, quack

ciarliè·ro -ra *adj* talkative, garrulous

ciarpame *m* rubbish, junk

ciaschedu·no -na *adj indef* each || *pron indef* each one, everyone

ciascu·no -na *adj indef* each || *pron indef* each one, everyone

cibare *tr* & *ref* to feed

cibà·rio -ria (-ri -rie) *adj* alimentary || **cibarie** *fpl* foodstuffs, victuals

cibo *m* food; meal; (fig) dish

cicala *f* cicada; grasshopper; locust; (fig) chatterbox; (naut) anchor ring

cicalare *intr* to prattle, babble; to chatter

cicaléc·cio *m* (-ci) prattle, babble; chatter

cicatrice *f* scar

cicatrizzare [ddzz] *tr* to heal (*a wound*) || *intr* (ESSERE) & *ref* to heal, scar

cicatrizzazióne [ddzz] *f* closing, healing (*of a wound*)

cic·ca *f* (-che) butt (*of cigar or cigarette*); (slang) chewing gum

ciccare §197 *intr* to chew tobacco; (coll) to boil with anger

cicchettare (cicchétto) *tr* (slang) to prime (*a carburetor*); (slang) to dress down, reprimand || *intr* to tipple

cicchétto *m* nip (*of liquor*); (slang) dressing down

cìc·cia *f* (-ce) (joc) flesh; (joc) fat
cicció·ne -na *mf* fatty
ciceróne *m* guide ‖ **Cicerone** *m* Cicero
ciclàbile *adj* open to bicycles; bicycle, e.g., **pista ciclabile** bicycle trail
cìcli·co -ca *adj* (-ci -che) cyclic(al)
ciclì·sta *mf* (-sti -ste) cyclist, bicyclist
ciclo *m* cycle; (coll) bicycle; **ciclo operativo** (econ) turnover
ciclomotóre *m* motorbike
ciclomotorì·sta *mf* (-sti -ste) driver of motorbike
ciclóne *m* cyclone
ciclòpe *m* cyclops
ciclòpi·co -ca *adj* (-ci -che) cyclopean, gigantic
ciclopista *f* bicycle trail
ciclostilare (*tr*) to mimeograph
ciclostile *or* ciclostilo *m* mimeograph
ciclotróne *m* cyclotron
cicógna *f* stork
cicòria *f* chicory; endive
cicuta *f* hemlock
ciè·co -ca (-chi -che) *adj* blind; **alla cieca** blindly ‖ *mf* blind person ‖ *m* blind man; **i ciechi** the blind
cièlo *m* sky; heaven; weather, climate; roof (*e.g., of wagon*); **a ciel sereno** in the open air; **cielo a pecorelle** mackerel or fleecy sky; **dal cielo** from above; **non stare né in cielo né in terra** to be utterly absurd; **per amor del cielo** for heaven's sake; **portare al cielo** to praise to the skies; **santo cielo!** good heavens!; **volesse il cielo che . . .** I would that . . . !
cifra *f* number, figure; Arabic numeral; sum, total; digit; initial, monogram; cipher, code; **cifra d'affari** amount of business, turnover; **cifra tonda** round number
cifrare *tr* to cipher, code; to embroider (*a monogram*)
cifrà·rio *m* (-ri) code, cipher
cì·glio *m* (-glia *fpl*) eyelash; eyebrow; **a ciglio asciutto** with dry eyes; **ciglia** (zool) cilia; **senza batter ciglio** without batting an eye ‖ *m* (-gli) (fig) edge, brow
ciglióne *m* bank, embankment
cigno *m* swan; cob
cigolante *adj* creaky, squeaky
cigolare (cigolo) *intr* to squeak, creak
cigolì·o *m* (-i) squeak, creak
Cile, il Chile
cilécca *f*—fare cilecca to misfire
cileccare §197 (cilécco) *intr* to goof, blunder; to fail
cilè·no -na *adj* & *mf* Chilean
cilè·stro -stra *adj* (poet) azure, blue
cilì·cio *m* (-ci) sackcloth
ciliè·gia *f* (-gie & -ge) cherry
ciliè·gio *m* (-gi) cherry tree
cilindrare *tr* to calender (*e.g., paper*); to roll (*a road*)
cilindrata *f* (aut) cylinder capacity, piston displacement
cilìndri·co -ca *adj* (-ci -che) cylindric(al)
cilindro *m* cylinder; top hat; roll, roller
cima *f* top, summit; tip (*e.g., of a pole*); peak (*of mountain*); edge, end; rope, cable; head (*e.g., of let-*

tuce); (coll) genius; **da cima a fondo** from top to bottom
cimare *tr* to cut the tip off; to shear; (agr) to prune
cimasa *f* (archit) coping
cìmbalo *m* gong; (obs) cymbal; **in cimbali** tipsy; in a tizzy
cimè·lio *m* (-li) relic, souvenir, memento
cimentare (cimènto) *tr* to risk (*e.g., one's life*); to provoke; (archaic) to assay ‖ *ref* to expose oneself; to venture
ciménto *m* risk, danger; (archaic) assay
cìmice *f* bug; bedbug; (coll) thumbtack
cimièro *m* crest; (poet) helmet
ciminièra *f* chimney (*of factory*); smokestack (*of locomotive*); funnel (*of steamship*)
cimitèro *m* cemetery, graveyard; (fig) ghosttown
cimósa [s] *or* cimóssa *f* selvage; blackboard eraser
cimurro *m* distemper; (joc) cold
Cina, la China
cinabro *m* cinnabar; crimson; red ink
cin·cia *f* (-ce) titmouse
cinciallégra *f* great titmouse
cincilla *f* chinchilla
cincischiare §287 *tr* to shred; to wrinkle, crease; to waste (*time*); to mumble (*words*) ‖ *intr* to wrinkle, crease
cine *m* (coll) cinema
cineamatóre *m* amateur movie maker
cine·asta *m* (-sti) motion-picture producer; movie fan; movie actor ‖ *f* movie actress
cinecàmera *f* movie camera
cinedilettante *mf* amateur movie maker
cinegiornale *m* newsreel
cinelàndia *f* movieland
cine·ma *m* (-ma) movies; movie house
cinematografare (cinematògrafo) *tr* to film, shoot
cinematografia *f* cinema, motion pictures, movie industry
cinematogràfi·co -ca *adj* (-ci -che) movie, motion-picture; movie-like
cinematògrafo *m* motion picture; movie theater; (fig) hubbub; (fig) funny sight
cineparchég·gio *m* (-gi) drive-in movie
cinepar·co *m* (-chi) drive-in movie
cineprésa [s] *f* movie camera
cinère·o -a *adj* ashen
cinescò·pio *m* (-pi) kinescope, TV tube
cinése [s] *adj* & *mf* Chinese
cineteatro *m* movie house; **cineteatro all'aperto** outdoor movie
cinetè·ca *f* (-che) film library
cinèti·co -ca (-ci -che) *adj* kinetic ‖ *f* kinetics
cingallégra *f* var of cinciallegra
cìngere §126 *tr* to surround; to gird (*e.g., the head*); to gird on (*e.g., the sword*); **cìngere cavaliere** to dub a knight; **cìngere d'assedio** to besiege
cinghia *f* belt, strap; **tirare la cinghia** to tighten one's belt
cinghiale *m* wild boar
cinghiata *f* lash
cingola·to -ta *adj* track-driven, caterpillar

cìngolo *m* endless metal belt, track; girdle, belt (*of a priest*)

cinguettare (**cinguétto**) *intr* to chirp, twitter; to babble

cinguettì·o *m* (**-i**) chirp, twitter; (fig) babble

cìni·co -ca (**-ci -che**) *adj* cynical ‖ *m* cynic

cinìglia *f* chenille

cinìsmo *m* cynicism

cinòfilo *m* dog lover

cinquanta *adj*, *m* & *pron* fifty

cinquantenà·rio -ria (**-ri -rie**) *adj* fifty-year-old; occurring every fifty years ‖ *m* fiftieth anniversary

cinquantènne *adj* fifty-year-old ‖ *mf* fifty-year-old person

cinquantèn·nio *m* (**-ni**) period of fifty years, half century

cinquantèsi·mo -ma *adj*, *m* & *pron* fiftieth

cinquantina *f* about fifty; **sulla cinquantina** about fifty years old

cinque *adj* & *pron* five; **le cinque** five o'clock ‖ *m* five; fifth (*in dates*)

cinquecenté·sco -sca *adj* (**-schi -sche**) sixteenth-century

cinquecènto *adj*, *m* & *pron* five hundred ‖ *f* small car ‖ **il Cinquecento** the sixteenth century

cinquina *f* set of five; five numbers (*drawn at Italian lotto*); (mil) pay

cinta *f* fence, wall; circuit, enclosure; circumference (*of a city*)

cintare *tr* to surround; to fence in; to hold (*in wrestling*)

cin·to -ta *adj* surrounded, girded ‖ *m* belt; girdle; **cinto erniario** truss ‖ *f* see **cinta**

cìntola *f* waist; belt; **con le mani alla cintola** idling, loafing

cintura *f* belt; waist; waistband; lock (*in wrestling*); **cintura di salvataggio** life preserver; **cintura di sicurezza** safety belt

cinturare *tr* to surround

cinturino *m* strap (*of watch or shoes*); hem (*e.g., of cuffs*)

cinturóne *m* belt; Sam Browne belt

ciò *pron* this; that; **a ciò** for that purpose; **a ciò che** so that; **ciò nondimeno** or **ciò nonostante** though, nevertheless; **con tutto ciò** in spite of everything; **per ciò** therefore

ciòc·ca *f* (**-che**) lock (*of hair*); cluster (*e.g., of cherries*)

ciòc·co *m* (**-chi**) log; **dormire come un ciocco** to sleep like a log

cioccolare *adj invar* chocolate ‖ *f* chocolate (*beverage*)

cioccolatino *m* chocolate candy

cioccolato *m* chocolate; **cioccolato al latte** milk chocolate

cioè *adv* that is to say, namely; to wit; rather

ciondolare (**cióndolo**) *tr* to dangle ‖ *intr* to dawdle; to stroll, saunter

ciòndolo *m* pendant, charm

ciondolóne *m* idler ‖ *adv* dangling

ciòtola *f* bowl

ciòttolo *m* pebble, small stone; cobblestone

ciottoló·so -sa [*s*] *adj* pebbly

cip *m* (**cip**) chip (*in gambling*)

cipì·glio *m* (**-gli**) frown

cipólla *f* onion; bulb (*e.g., of a lamp*); nozzle (*of sprinkling can*)

cippo *m* column; bench mark

ciprèsso *m* cypress

cipria *f* face powder; **cipria compatta** compact

ciprió·ta *adj* & *mf* (**-ti -te**) Cypriot

Cipro *m* Cyprus

circa *adv* about, nearly ‖ *prep* concerning, regarding, as to

cir·co *m* (**-chi**) circus; **circo equestre** circus; **circo glaciale** cirque; **circo lunare** walled plain

circolante *adj* circulating; lending (*library*) ‖ *m* available cash (*of a corporation*)

circolare *adj* circular; cashier's (*check*) ‖ *f* circular (*letter*); (rr) beltline ‖ *v* (**cìrcolo**) *intr* to circulate

circolazióne *f* circulation; traffic; currency; **circolazione sanguigna** bloodstream; circulation of blood

cìrcolo *m* circle; circulation (*of blood*); reception (*e.g., at court*); club, set, group

circoncìdere §145 *tr* to circumcise

circoncisióne *f* circumcision

circonci·so -sa *adj* circumcised

circondare (**circóndo**) *tr* to surround, encircle; to overwhelm (*e.g., with kindness*) ‖ *ref* to surround oneself; to be surrounded

circondà·rio *m* (**-ri**) district; surrounding territory

circonduzióne *f* rotation (*e.g., of the body in calisthenics*)

circonferènza *f* circumference

circonflès·so -sa *adj* circumflex

circonlocuzióne *f* circumlocution

circonvallazióne *f* city-line road; (rr) beltline

circonvenire §282 *tr* to circumvent; to outwit

circonvenzióne *f* circumvention

circonvici·no -na *adj* neighboring, nearby

circoscrit·to -ta *adj* circumscribed

circoscrivere §250 *tr* to circumscribe

circoscrizióne *f* district; circuit

circospèt·to -ta *adj* circumspect, cautious

circospezióne *f* circumspection

circostante *adj* neighboring, surrounding, nearby ‖ **circostanti** *mpl* neighbors; bystanders, onlookers

circostanza *f* circumstance

circostanziale *adj* circumstantial

circostanziare §287 *tr* to describe in detail; to circumstanciate

circostanzia·to -ta *adj* detailed, circumstantial

circuire §176 *tr* to circumvent

circùito *m* circuit; race (*of automobiles or bicycles*); **circuito stampato** (rad, telv) printed circuit

circumnavigare §209 (**circumnàvigo**) *tr* to circumnavigate

circumnavigazióne *f* circumnavigation

cirìlli·co -ca *adj* (**-ci -che**) Cyrillic

Ciro *m* Cyrus
cirro *m* cirrus
cirrò·si *f* (**-si**) cirrhosis
cispa *f* gum (*on edge of eyelids*)
cisposità [s] *f* gum; gumminess
cispó·so -sa [s] *adj* gummy
ciste *f* cyst
cistèrna *f* cistern; tank
cisti *f* cyst
cistifèllea *f* gall bladder
citante *mf* (law) plaintiff
citare *tr* to cite, quote; to mention; (law) to summon, subpoena
citazióne *f* citation, quotation; mention; (law) summons, subpoena; (mil) commendation
citillo *m* (zool) gopher
citòfono *m* intercom
citostàti·co -ca *adj* (**-ci -che**) (biochem) cancer-inhibiting
citrato *m* citrate
cìtri·co -ca *adj* (**-ci -che**) citric
citrul·lo -la *adj* simple, foolish ‖ *mf* simpleton, fool
cit·tà *f* (**-tà**) city, town ‖ **Città del Capo** Cape Town; **Città del Messico** Mexico City; **Città del Vaticano** Vatican City; **città fungo** boom town
cittadèlla *f* citadel
cittadinanza *f* citizenship
cittadi·no -na *adj* city, town, civic ‖ *mf* citizen; city dweller, urbanite ‖ *m* townsman
ciù·co *m* (**-chi**) (coll) donkey, ass
ciuffo *m* lock, forelock; tuft; (bot) tassel
ciuffolòtto *m* (orn) bullfinch
ciurlare *intr*—**ciurlare nel manico** to play fast and loose
ciurma *f* crew, gang, mob
ciurmare *tr* (archaic) to charm; (archaic) to trick, inveigle
ciurmatóre *m* swindler, charlatan
civètta *f* barn owl, little owl; unmarked police car; ship used as decoy; (fig) coquette, flirt
civettare (**civétto**) *intr* to flirt
civetteria *f* coquettishness, coquetry
civettuò·lo la *adj* coquettish; attractive
cìvi·co -ca *adj* (**-ci -che**) civic; town, city
civile *adj* civil; civilian ‖ *mf* civilian
civili·sta *mf* (**-sti -ste**) attorney, solicitor
civilizzare [ddzz] *tr* to civilize ‖ *ref* to become civilized
civilizzazióne [ddzz] *f* civilizing (*e.g., of barbarians*); civilization
civil·tà *f* (**-tà**) civilization; civility
civismo *m* good citizenship
clac·son *m* (**-son**) horn (*of a car*)
claire *f* (**claire**) grating (*in front of a store window*)
clamóre *m* clamor, uproar
clamoró·so -sa [s] *adj* noisy; clamorous
clan *m* (**clan**) clan; clique
clandesti·no -na *adj* clandestine
clangóre *m* clangor, clang
clarinetti·sta *mf* (**-sti -ste**) clarinet player
clarinétto *m* clarinet
clarino *m* clarion
classe *f* class

classicheggiante *adj* classicistic
classicismo *m* classicism
classici·sta *mf* (**-sti -ste**) classicist
classici·tà *f* (**-tà**) classical spirit; classical antiquity
clàssi·co -ca (**-ci -che**) *adj* classic(al) ‖ *m* classic
classifi·ca *f* (**-che**) rank, rating (*in competitive testing*); classification; (sports) rating
classificare §197 (**classifico**) *tr* to classify; to rate, rank ‖ *ref* to score
classificazióne *f* classification
claudicante *adj* lame, limping
claudicare §197 (**clàudico**) *intr* to limp
clauné·sco -sca *adj* (**-schi -sche**) clownish
clàusola *f* provision, proviso; clause; close, conclusion (*e.g., of a speech*); **clausola rossa** instructions for payment (*in bank-credit documents*); **clausola verde** shipping instructions (*in bank-credit documents*)
clausura *f* (eccl) seclusion; (fig) secluded place
clava *f* club, bludgeon
clavicémbalo *m* harpsicord
clavìcola *f* clavicle, collarbone
clemàtide *f* clematis
clemènte *adj* clement, indulgent; mild (*climate*)
clemènza *f* clemency; mildness
cleptòmane *adj & mf* kleptomaniac
clericale *adj* clerical ‖ *m* clericalist
clericalismo *m* clericalism
clèro *m* clergy
clessidra *f* water clock; sandglass
clicchetti·o *m* (**-i**) clicking, click-clack (*e.g., of a typewriter*)
cli·ché *m* (**-ché**) cliché; stereotype (*plate*)
cliènte *m* client, customer, patron
clientèla *f* clientele, customers; practice (*of a professional man*)
cli·ma *m* (**-mi**) climate
climatèri·co -ca *adj* (**-ci -che**) climacteric; crucial
climatè·rio *m* (**-ri**) climacteric; crucial period
climàti·co -ca *adj* (**-ci -che**) climatic
climatizzazióne [ddzz] *f* air conditioning
clìni·co -ca (**-ci -che**) *adj* clinic ‖ *m* clinician; highly skilled physician ‖ *f* clinic; private hospital
cli·sma *m* (**-smi**) enema
clistère *m* enema; **clistere a pera** fountain syringe
cloa·ca *f* (**-che**) sewer
cloche *f* (**cloche**) woman's wide-brimmed hat; (aer) stick; (aut) floor gearshift
clorare (**clòro**) *tr* to chlorinate
clorato *m* chlorate
cloridri·co -ca *adj* (**-ci -che**) hydrochloric
clòro *m* chlorine
clorofilla *f* chlorophyll
clorofòr·mio *m* (**-mi**) chloroform
cloroformizzare [ddzz] *tr* to chloroform
cloruro *m* chloride

coabitare (coàbito) *intr* to live together; to cohabit

coabitazióne *f* sharing (*of an apartment*)

coaccusa·to -ta *adj* jointly accused ‖ *m* codefendant

coacèrvo *m* accumulation (*e.g., of interest*)

coadiutóre *m* coadjutor

coadiuvante *adj* helping ‖ *m* helper

coadiuvare (coàdiuvo) *tr* to assist, advise

coagulare (coàgulo) *tr & ref* to coagulate, clot

coagulazióne *f* coagulation, clotting

coàgulo *m* clot

coalescènza *f* coalescence

coalizióne *f* coalition

coalizzare [ddzz] *tr & ref* to unite, rally

coartare *tr* to coerce, force

coartazióne *f* coercion, forcing

coatti·vo -va *adj* forceful, compelling

coat·to -la *adj* coercive

coautóre *m* coauthor

coazióne *f* coercion

cobalto *m* cobalt

cocaina *f* cocaine

cocainòmane *mf* cocaine addict

coc·ca *f* (-che) notch (*of arrow*); corner, edge (*e.g., of a handkerchief*); three-mast galley

coccarda *f* cockade

cocchière *m* coachman, cab driver

còc·chio *m* (-chi) coach; chariot

cocchiume *m* bung

còc·cia *f* (-ce) sword guard; (coll) head, noggin

còccige *m* coccyx

coccinèlla *f* ladybug

cocciniglia *f* cochineal

còc·cio *m* (-ci) earthenware; broken piece of pottery

cocciutàggine *m* stubbornness

cocciu·to -ta *adj* stubborn

còc·co *m* (-chi) coconut (*tree and nut*); (bact) coccus; (coll) egg; (coll) darling, favorite

cocco·dè *m* (-dè) cackle

coccodrillo *m* crocodile

còccola *f* berry (*of cypress*); darling girl

coccolare (còccolo) *tr* to fondle, cuddle ‖ *ref* to nestle, cuddle up; to bask

còcco·lo -la *adj* (coll) nice, darling ‖ *m* darling boy ‖ *f* see **coccola**

coccolóne or **coccolóni** *adv* squatting

cocènte *adj* burning

cocktail *m* (cocktail) cocktail; cocktail party

còclea *f* dredge; (anat) cochlea

cocómero *m* watermelon; (coll) simpleton

cocorita *f* parakeet

cocuzza *f* (coll) pumpkin; (coll) head, noggin

cocùzzolo *m* crown (*of hat*); peak (*of mountain*)

códa *f* tail; train (*of skirt*); pigtail (*of hair*); **coda di paglia** (coll) uneasy conscience; **con la coda dell'occhio** out of the corner of the eye; **con la coda tra le gambe** with its tail between its legs; (fig) crestfallen; **di**

coda last; **fare la coda** to stand in line; **in coda** in a row; at the tail end

codardia *f* (lit) cowardice

codar·do -da *adj* cowardly ‖ *mf* coward

codazzo *m* (pej) trail (*of people*)

codeina *f* codein

codé·sto -sta §7 *adj* ‖ §8 *pron*

còdice *m* code; codex; **codice della strada** traffic laws; **codice di avviamento postale** zip code

codicillo *m* codicil

codificare §197 (codìfico) *tr* to codify

codi·no -na *adj* reactionary; conformist ‖ *m* pigtail (*of a man*); (fig) reactionary; conformist ‖ *f* small tail

códolo *m* tang, shank (*e.g., of knife*); handle (*of spoon or knife*); head (*of violin*)

coeducazióne *f* coeducation

coefficiènte *m* coefficient

coerciti·vo -va *adj* coercive

coercizióne *f* coercion

coerède *mf* coheir

coerènte *adj* coherent; consistent

coerènza *f* coherence; consistency

coesióne *f* cohesion

coesistènza *f* coexistence

coesìstere §114 *intr* to coexist

coesi·vo -va *adj* cohesive

coetàne·o -a *adj & m* contemporary

coè·vo -va *adj* contemporaneous, coeval

cofanétto *m* small chest, small coffer

còfano *m* chest, coffer; box, case (*for ammunition*); (aut) hood

còffa *f* masthead, crow's-nest

cofirmatà·rio -ria *adj & mf* (-ri -rie) cosigner

cogitabón·do -da *adj* (poet & joc) thoughtful, meditative

cogitare (cògito) *tr & intr* (poet & joc) to cogitate

cógli §4

cògliere §127 *tr* to gather; to hit (*the target*); to pluck (*flowers*); to grab, seize; (fig) to guess; **cogliere in flagrante** to catch in the act; **cogliere la palla al balzo** to seize time by the forelock; **cogliere nel giusto** to hit the nail on the head; **cogliere qlcu alla sprovvista** to catch s.o. napping; **cogliere sul fatto** to catch in the act

coglióne *m* (vulg) testicle; (vulg) simpleton, fool

coglioneria *f* (vulg) great stupidity

cognata *f* sister-in-law

cognato *m* brother-in-law

cògni·to -ta *adj* (poet & law) well-known

cognizióne *f* cognition, knowledge

cognóme *m* surname, family name

coguaro *m* cougar

cói §4

coibènte *adj* nonconducting ‖ *m* nonconductor

coincidènza *f* coincidence; harmony, identity; transfer (*from one streetcar or bus to another*); (rr) connection

coincìdere §145 *intr* to coincide

coinquilino *m* fellow tenant

cointeressare (cointerèsso) *tr* to give a share (*of profit*) to

cointeressa·to -ta *adj* jointly interested || *mf* party having a joint interest
cointeressènza *f* interest, share
coinvòlgere §289 *tr* to involve
còito *m* coitus, intercourse
cól §4
colà *adv* over there
colabròdo *m* colander, strainer
colàg·gio *m* (-gi) loss, leak
colapa·sta *m* (-sta) colander
colare (cólo) *tr* to filter, strain; to sift (*wheat*); to cast (*metals*); **colare a picco** to sink || *intr* to leak, drip; to flow (*said of blood*); **colare a picco** to sink
colata *f* casting (*of metal*); stream of lava; slide (*of snow or rocks*)
colatíc·cio *m* (-ci) drip, dripping
cola·tóio *m* (-tói) colander, strainer
colazióne *f* breakfast; lunch; **colazione al sacco** picnic; **prima colazione** breakfast; **seconda colazione** lunch
colbac·co *m* (-chi) busby
colèi §8 *pron dem*
colèn·do -da *adj* (archaic) honorable
colè·ra *m* (-ra) cholera
colesterina *f* cholesterol
coli·brì *m* (-brì) hummingbird
còli·co -ca *adj* & *f* (-ci -che) colic
colino *m* strainer
cólla §4
còlla *f* glue; paste; **colla di pesce** isinglass
collaborare (collàboro) *intr* to collaborate; to contribute (*to newspaper or magazine*)
collaboratóre *m* collaborator; contributor (*to newspaper or magazine*)
collaborazióne *f* collaboration
collaborazioni·sta *mf* (-sti -ste) collaborationist
collana *f* necklace; series, collection (*of literary works*)
collante *adj* & *m* adhesive
collare *m* collar || *v* (còllo) *tr* to lift or lower (*with a rope*)
collasso *m* collapse
collaterale *adj* & *m* collateral
collaudare (collàudo) *tr* to test; to approve; to pass
collauda·tóre -trice *mf* tester
collàudo *m* test
collazionare (collazióno) *tr* to collate
cólle §4
còlle *m* hill; low peak; mountain pass
collè·ga *mf* (-ghi -ghe) colleague, associate
collegaménto *m* connection, telephone connection; contact; (mil) liaison
collegare §209 (collégo) *tr* to join, connect || *intr* to agree, be in harmony || *ref* to become allied; to make contact, make connection (*e.g., by phone*)
collegiale *adj* collegiate || *mf* boarding-school student
collegiata *f* collegiate church
collè·gio *m* (-gi) college (*e.g., of surgeons*); boarding school, academy
còllera *f* anger, wrath; **montare in collera** to become angry
collèri·co -ca *adj* (-ci -che) hot-tempered, choleric

collètta *f* collection; collect (*in church*)
collettivismo *m* collectivism
collettivi·tà *f* (-tà) collectivity, community
colletti·vo -va *adj* collective || *m* party worker (*of leftist party*)
collétto *m* collar; flank (*of a tooth*)
collet·tóre -trice *adj* connecting; collecting (*pipe*) || *m* collector; tax collector; manifold; (elec) commutator (*of D.C. device*); (elec) collector (*of A.C. device*); **collettore d'ammissione** intake manifold; **collettore di scarico** exhaust manifold
collettoria *f* tax office; small post office
collezionare (collezióno) *tr* to collect (*e.g., stamps*)
collezióne *f* collection; collection, series (*of literary works*)
collezioni·sta *mf* (-sti -ste) collector
collìdere §135 *intr* to collide
collimare *tr* to point (*a telescope*) || *intr* to coincide, match; to dovetail
collina *f* hill; **in collina** in the hill country
collinó·so -sa [s] *adj* hilly
colli·rio *m* (-ri) eyewash
collisióne *f* collision; (fig) conflict; **entrare in collisione** to collide
cóllo §4
còllo *m* neck; piece (*of baggage*); package, parcel; **al collo** in a sling; (fig) downhill; **collo del piede** instep; **collo d'oca** crankshaft; **in collo** in one's arms (*said of a baby*)
collocaménto *m* placement, employment; **collocamento a riposo** retirement; **collocamento in aspettativa** leave of absence without pay; **collocamento in malattia** sick leave
collocare §197 (còlloco) *tr* to place; to find employment for; to sell; **collocare a riposo** to retire; **collocare in aspettativa** to give a leave of absence without pay; **collocare in malattia** to grant sick leave to
collocazióne *f* location (*of a book in a library*); catalogue card
colloidale *adj* colloidal
collòide *m* colloid
colloquiale *adj* colloquial
collò·quio *m* (-qui) talk, conference; colloquy; colloquium, symposium
colló·so -sa [s] *adj* gluey, sticky
collotòrto *m* (collitòrti) bigot, hypocrite
collòttola *f* nape or scruff of the neck
collùdere §105 *intr* to be in collusion
collusióne *f* collusion
collutó·rio *m* (-ri) mouthwash
colluttare *intr* to scuffle, fight
colluttazióne *f* scuffle, fight
cólma *f* high-water level (*during high tide*)
colmare (cólmo) *tr* to fill, fill up; to fill in (*with dirt*); to overwhelm; **colmare una lacuna** to bridge a gap
colmata *f* silting; reclaimed land; sand bank
cól·mo -ma *adj* full, filled up || *m* top, peak, summit; (archit) ridgepole; (fig) acme; **al colmo di** at the height

of; **è il colmo** that's the limit || *f* see **colma**

colofóne *m* colophon

colofònia *f* rosin

colombàia *f* dovecot

colombèlla *f* ingenue; **a colombella** vertically

colóm·bo -ba *mf* pigeon, dove || **Colombo** *m* Columbus

colònia *f* colony; cologne; settlement; summer camp; **colonia penale** penal colony; penitentiary || **Colonia** *f* Cologne

coloniale *adj* colonial || *m* colonial; colonist; **coloniali** imported foods

colòni·co -ca *adj* (**-ci -che**) farm (*e.g.*, *house*)

colonizzare [ddzz] *tr* to colonize; to settle

colonizzazióne [ddzz] *f* colonization

colonna *f* column; row; **colonna sonora** sound track; **Colonne d'Ercole** Pillars of Hercules

colonnato *m* colonnade

colonnèllo *m* colonel

colonnétta *f* small column; gasoline pump

colò·no -na *mf* sharecropper; colonist; settler; (*poet*) farmer

coloránte *adj* coloring || *m* dye; stain

colorare (colóro) *tr* & *ref* to color; to stain

colora·to -ta *adj* colored; stained (*glass*)

colorazióne *f* coloring

colóre *m* color; paint; suit (*of cards*); flush (*at poker*); shade; character (*of a deal*); **di colore** colored (*man*); **farne di tutti i colori** to be up to all kinds of deviltry; **farsi di tutti i colori** to change countenance

colorifi·cio *m* (**-ci**) paint factory; dye factory

colorire §176 *tr* to color

colori·to -ta *adj* colored, flushed; expressive || *m* color, complexion; (*fig*) expression

coloritura *f* coloring; characteristic; political complexion

colóro §8

colossale *adj* colossal

Colossèo *m* Coliseum

colòsso *m* colossus

cólpa *f* fault; sin; guilt; (*law*) injury; **avere la colpa** to be guilty; to be wrong; **essere in colpa** to be guilty

colpévole *adj* guilty || *mf* guilty person; culprit

colpevoli·sta *mf* (**-sti -ste**) person who prejudges s.o. guilty

colpire §176 *tr* to hit, strike; to harm; to impress; **colpire nel segno** to hit the mark

cólpo *m* hit, blow; strike; tip, rap; knock; shot; round (*of gun*); cut, slash (*of knife*); thrust (*e.g.*, *of spear*); lash (*of animal's tail*); toot (*of car's horn*); **andare a colpo sicuro** to know where to hit; **colpo apoplettico** stroke; **colpo da maestro** master stroke; **colpo d'aria** draft; **colpo d'ariete** water hammer; **colpo di fortuna** stroke of luck; **colpo di fulmine** love at first sight; **colpo di**

grazia coup de grâce; **colpo di mano** surprise attack; **colpo di scena** dramatic turn of events; **colpo di sole** sunstroke; **colpo di spugna** wiping the slate clean; **colpo di stato** coup d'état; **colpo di telefono** telephone call; **colpo di testa** sudden decision, inconsiderate action; **colpo di vento** gust of wind; **colpo d'occhio** view; glance, look; **di colpo** at once; **fallire il colpo** to miss the mark; **fare colpo** to make a hit; **sul colpo** then and there; **tutto in un colpo** all at once

cólpo·so -sa [s] *adj* unpremeditated; involuntary (*e.g.*, *manslaughter*)

coltèlla *f* butcher knife; (*elec*) knife switch

coltellàc·cio *m* (**-ci**) hunting knife; butcher knife; (*naut*) studding sail

coltellata *f* stab, gash, slash; **fare a coltellate** to fight with knives

coltelleria *f* cutlery

coltelli·nàio *m* (**-nài**) cutler

coltèllo *m* knife; **a coltello** edgewise (*said of bricks*); **avere il coltello per il manico** to have the upper hand; **coltello a serramanico** switchblade knife; pocketknife

coltivare *tr* to cultivate

coltiva·to -ta *adj* cultivated

coltivatóre *m* farmer

coltivazióne *f* cultivation

cól·to -ta *adj* cultivated; learned (*word*) || *m* garden; (*archaic*) worship

cóltre *f* blanket; comforter; (fig) pall; **coltri** bedclothes

coltróne *m* quilt

coltura *f* cultivation; crop; culture (*e.g.*, *of silkworms*, *bacteria*)

colubrina *f* culverin

colùi §8 *pron dem*

comandaménto *m* commandment

comandante *m* commanding officer; commandant; (nav) captain; **comandante del porto** harbor master; **comandante in seconda** (naut) first mate

comandare *tr* to command, order; to direct (*employees*); to register (*a letter*); (mach) to regulate; (mach) to control; (poet) to overlook, command the view of (*e.g.*, *a valley*); **comandare a bacchetta** to command in a dictatorial manner || *intr* to command; **comandi!** (mil) at your orders!

comando *m* command, order

comare *f* godmother; (coll) friend, neighbor; (coll) gossip

combaciare §128 *tr* (archaic) to gather || *intr* to fit closely together; to tally, dovetail; to coincide

combattènte *adj* fighting || *m* combatant

combàttere *tr* & *intr* to combat || *ref* to fight one another

combattiménto *m* combat; fight; battle; **fuori combattimento** knockout, K.O.; **fuori combattimento tecnico** technical knockout, T.K.O.; **mettere fuori combattimento** to knock out; (fig) to weaken

combatti·vo -va *adj* pugnacious, combative

combattu·to -ta *adj* heated (*discussion*); overcome (*by doubt*); torn (*between two opposing feelings*)

combinare *tr* to combine; to match (*e.g., colors*); to organize || *intr* to agree; **combinare a** to succeed in || *ref* to agree; to chance, happen; to combine

combinazióne *f* combination; chance; coverall (*for mechanics or flyers*)

combrìccola *f* gang

combustìbile *adj* combustible || *m* fuel, combustible

combustióne *f* combustion; (poet) upheaval

combutta *f* gang, band; **essere in combutta** to be in cahoots

cóme *m* manner, way; **il come e il perchè** the why and the wherefore || *adv* as; like; as for; how; **come mai?** why?; **e come!** and how!; **ma come?** what?, how is it? || *conj* as; as soon as; while; how; because; since; **come se** as if

comecchè *conj* (lit) although; (poet) wherever

comedóne *m* blackhead

cométa *f* comet

comici·tà *f* (-tà) comicalness

còmi·co -ca (-ci -che) *adj* comic(al) || *m* comic; author of comedies; comic actor

comignolo *m* chimney pot; ridge (*of roof*)

cominciare §128 *tr* & *intr* to begin, start, commence

comitato *m* committee

comitiva *f* group, party; (poet) retinue

comì·zio *m* (-zi) (pol) meeting, rally; (hist) comitia

còm·ma *m* (-mi) paragraph, article (*of law or decree*)

commèdia *f* comedy; play, drama; (fig) farce; **commedia di carattere** comedy of character; **commedia d'intreccio** comedy of intrigue; **far la commedia** to pretend, feign; **finire in commedia** to end ludicrously; **finire la commedia** to stop faking

commediante *mf* actor; comedian (*amusing person*); (fig) hypocrite

commediògra·fo -fa *mf* playwright, comedian

commemorare (**commèmoro**) *tr* to commemorate

commemorati·vo -va *adj* commemorative, memorial

commemorazióne *f* commemoration

commènda *f* commandership (*of an order*); (eccl) commendam

commendàbile *adj* commendable

commendare (**commèndo**) *tr* (lit) to commend, praise; (obs) to entrust

commendati·zio -zia (-zi -zie) *adj* introductory || *f* letter of introduction; recommendation

commendatóre *m* commander (*of an order*)

commendévole *adj* commendable

commensale *mf* guest; table companion

commensurare (**commènsuro** & **commensuro**) *tr* to compare; to proportion, prorate

commentare (**comménto**) *tr* to comment, comment on

commentà·rio *m* (-ri) commentary; diary, journal

commenta·tóre -trice *mf* commentator

comménto *m* comment; fare **commenti** to criticize; **non far commenti!** don't waste your time talking!

commerciàbile *adj* marketable

commerciale *adj* commercial; common, ordinary

commerciali·sta *mf* (-sti -ste) business-administration major; attorney specializing in commercial law

commerciante *mf* merchant, dealer

commerciare §128 (**commèrcio**) *tr* to deal in; to buy and sell || *intr* to deal

commèr·cio *m* (-ci) commerce, trade; illegal traffic; (poet) intercourse; **commercio all'ingrosso** wholesale (trade); **commercio al minuto** retail (trade); **fuori commercio** not for sale; **in commercio** for sale

commés·so -sa *adj* committed || *mf* clerk (*in a store*) || *m* salesman; clerk (*in a court*); janitor (*in a school*); **commesso viaggiatore** traveling salesman || *f* saleslady; order (*of merchandise*)

commestìbile *adj* edible || **commestibili** *mpl* staples, groceries; foodstuffs

comméttere §198 *tr* to join, connect; to commit; to charge, commission; to peg; (poet) to entrust || *intr* to join, fit

commettitura *f* joint, seam

commiato *m* leave; **dare commiato a** to dismiss; **prender commiato** to take one's leave

commilitóne *m* comrade, comrade in arms

comminare *tr* (law) to determine, fix (*a penalty*)

comminatò·rio -ria *adj* threatening

commiserare (**commisero**) *tr* to pity, feel sorry for

commiserazióne *f* commiseration

commissariale *adj* commissioner's, e.g., **funzioni commissariali** commissioner's functions; commissar's functions

commissariato *m* commissary; inspector's office

commissà·rio *m* (-ri) commissary; inspector; commissioner; **commissario del popolo** commissar; **commissario di bordo** purser; **commissario di pubblica sicurezza** police inspector; **commissario tecnico** (sports) soccer commissioner

commissionare (**commissióno**) *tr* to commission, order

commissionà·rio -ria (-ri -rie) *adj* commission || *m* commission merchant

commissióne *f* commission, agency; order (*of merchandise*); committee; errand; commitment (*of an act*)

commisurare *tr* to proportion (*e.g., crime to punishment*)

committènte *mf* buyer, customer

commodòro *m* commodore

commòs·so -sa *adj* moved; moving

commovènte *adj* moving, touching

commozióne *f* commotion; emotion; **commozione cerebrale** (pathol) concussion

commuòvere §202 *tr* to move; to touch; to stir || *ref* to be moved; to be touched

commutare *tr* to commute; to switch || *ref* to turn

commuta·tóre -trice *adj* commutative || *m* (elec) change-over switch; (elec) commutator (*switch*); (telp) plugboard || *f* converter

commutatori·sta *mf* (-sti -ste) (telp) operator

commutazióne *f* commutation; (telp) selection; (elec) switchover

co·mò *m* (-mò) chest; chest of drawers

còmoda *f* commode

comodare (**còmodo**) *tr* to lend || *intr* (with *dat*) to please, e.g., **non le comoda** it doesn't please her

comodino *m* night table; (theat) bit player; **fare il comodino a** (coll) to follow sheepishly

comodi·tà *f* (-tà) comfort; convenience; opportunity

còmo·do -da *adj* comfortable; convenient; easy; loose-fitting; calm || *m* convenience; ease; advantage; comfort; opportunity; **a Suo comodo at your convenience; comodo di cassa** credit (*at the bank*); **con comodo** without hurrying; **fare comodo** to come in handy; (with *dat*) to please, -e.g., **non gli fa comodo** it doesn't please him; **fare il proprio comodo** to think only of oneself; **stia comodo!** make yourself at home! || *f* see **comoda**

compaesa·no -na *mf* fellow citizen || *m* fellow countryman || *f* fellow countrywoman

compàgine *f* strict union; connection; assemblage; (fig) cohesion

compagna *f* companion, mate; (archaic) company

compagnìa *f* company; **Compagnia di Gesù** Society of Jesus; **compagnia stabile** (theat) stock company

compa·gno -gna *adj* like, similar || *m* fellow; companion, comrade; mate; partner; **compagno d'armi** comrade in arms; **compagno di viaggio** fellow traveler || *f* see **compagna**

companàti·co *m* (-ci) food to eat with bread

comparàbile *adj* comparable

comparati·vo -va *adj* & *m* comparative

compara·to -ta *adj* comparative

comparazióne *f* comparison

compare *m* godfather; best man (*at wedding*); fellow; confederate

comparire §108 *intr* to appear; to be known; to cut a figure

comparizióne *f* appearance (*in court*)

comparsa *f* appearance; (theat) extra, supernumerary; (law) petition, brief; **far comparsa** to cut a figure

compartecipare (**compartécipo**) *intr* to share

compartecipazióne *f* sharing; **compartecipazione agli utili** profit sharing

compartécipe *adj* sharing

compartimónto *m* circle, clique; district; (naut, rr) compartment

compartire §176 & (**comparto**) *tr* to divide up, distribute

compassa·to -ta *adj* measured; stiff, formal; reserved; self-controlled

compassionare (**compassióno**) *tr* to pity

compassióne *f* compassion, pity

compassionévole *adj* compassionate; pitiful

compasso *m* compass; **compasso a grossezza** calipers

compatibile *adj* excusable; compatible

compatimónto *m* compassion; condescension

compatire §176 *tr* to pity; to forgive, overlook; to bear with; **farsi compatire** to become an object of ridicule || *intr* to pity

compatriò·ta *mf* (-ti -te) compatriot

compattézza *f* compactness

compat·to -ta *adj* compact, tight

compendiare §287 (**compèndio**) *tr* to epitomize, summarize

compèn·dio *m* (-di) compendium, summary; **fare un compendio di** to abstract

compendió·so -sa [s] *adj* compendious, brief, succinct

compenetràbile *adj* penetrable

compenetrabilità *f* penetrability

compenetrare (**compènetro**) *tr* to penetrate; to permeate; to pervade || *ref* to be overcome; **compenetrarsi di** to be conscious of

compensare (**compènso**) *tr* to compensate, pay; to balance, offset; to clear (*checks*)

compensa·to -ta *adj* compensated; laminated || *m* laminate; plywood

compensazióne *f* compensation; offset; (com) clearing (*of checks*)

compènso *m* reward; retribution, pay; **in compenso** on the other hand

cómpera *f* var of **compra**

comperare (**cómpero**) *tr* & *intr* var of **comprare**

competènte *adj* competent

competènza *f* competence; jurisdiction; **competenze honoraria**

compètere §129 *intr* to compete; to concern; to have jurisdiction

competiti·vo -va *adj* competitive

competi·tóre -trice *mf* competitor, contender

competizióne *f* competition, contest

compiacènte *adj* complaisant, obliging

compiacènza *f* complaisance, kindness; pleasure

compiacére §214 *tr* to gratify || *intr* (with *dat*) to please, e.g., **non posso compiacere a tutti** I cannot please everybody || *ref* to be pleased; **compiacersi con** to congratulate; **compiacersi di** to be kind enough to

compiacimónto *m* pleasure; congratulation; approval

compiaciu·to -ta *adj* pleased, satisfied

compiàngere §215 *tr* to pity || *ref* to feel sorry

compian·to -ta *adj* lamented (*departed person*) || *m* sympathy; (poet) sorrow; (poet) lament

compiegare §209 (compiègo) *tr* to enclose (*in a letter*)

cómpiere §130 *tr* to complete, finish; to fulfill, accomplish; **compiere . . . anni** to be . . . years old; **compiere gli anni** to have a birthday || *ref* to happen; to come true

compilare *tr* to compile

compila·tóre -trice *mf* compiler

compilazióne *f* compilation

compiménto *m* fulfillment, accomplishment

compire §176 *tr* to complete, finish; to fulfill, accomplish; **per compir l'opera** as if it weren't enough || *ref* to happen; to come true

compitare (cómpito) *tr* to syllabify; to read poorly; to spell, spell letter by letter

compitazióne *f* spelling letter by letter

compitézza *f* courtesy, politeness

cómpito *m* task; exercise; homework

compi·to -ta *adj* courteous, polite; (poet) adequate

compiu·to -ta *adj* accomplished

compleanno *m* birthday; **buon compleanno** happy birthday

complementare *adj* complementary; additional (*tax*) || *f* graduated income tax

compleménto *m* complement; (mil, nav) reserve

complessióne *f* build, physique

complessi·tà *f* (**-tà**) complexity

complessi·vo -va *adj* total, aggregate

complès·so -sa *adj* complex, complicated; compound (*fracture*) || *m* whole; complex; **in complesso** in general

completare (complèto) *tr* to complete, carry through; to supplement, round off

complè·to -ta *adj* complete, full; overall, thoroughgoing; **al completo** full (*e.g., bus*) || *m* set (*of matching items*); suit of clothes; **completo femminile** lady's tailor-made suit; **completo maschile** suit

complicare §197 (còmplico) *tr* to complicate || *ref* to become complicated

complica·to -ta *adj* complicated, complex

complicazióne *f* complication

cómplice *mf* accomplice, accessory

complici·tà *f* (**-tà**) complicity

complimentare (compliménto) *tr* to compliment || *ref*—**complimentarsi con** to congratulate

compliménto *m* compliment; congratulation; favor; **complimenti** regards; **complimenti!** congratulations!; **fare complimenti** to stand on ceremony; **senza complimenti** without ceremony; without any further ado

complimentó·so -sa [s] *adj* ceremonious; complimentary

complottare (complòtto) *intr* to plot

complòtto *m* plot, machination

complù·vio *m* (**-vi**) valley (*of roof*)

componènte *adj* component || *mf* member || *m* component (*component part*) || *f* component (*force*)

componìbile *adj* sectional (*e.g., bookcase*)

componiménto *m* composition, settlement (*of a dispute*)

compórre §218 *tr* to compose; to arrange; to settle (*a quarrel*); to lay out (*a corpse*); (typ) to set

comportaménto *m* behavior

comportare (compòrto) *tr* to allow, tolerate; to entail || *ref* to behave; to handle (*said, e.g., of a motor*); **comportarsi male** to misbehave

compòrto *m* (com) delay

compòsi·to -ta *adj* composite || **composite** *fpl* (bot) Compositae

composi·tóio *m* (**-tói**) (typ) composing stick

composi·tóre -trice *mf* compositor, typesetter; composer || *f* typesetting machine

composizióne *f* composition; settlement

compósta *f* compote; **composta di frutta** stewed fruit

compostézza *f* neatness, tidiness; good behavior; orderliness

compostièra *f* compote, compotier

compó·sto -sta *adj* compound; neat, tidy; well-behaved || *m* compound || *f* see **composta**

cómpra *f* purchase; shopping; **compre** shopping

comprare (cómpro) *tr* to buy, purchase; to buy off || *intr* to buy, shop; to trade

compra·tóre -trice *mf* buyer, purchaser

compravéndere §281 *tr* to make a deal in, to transfer (*e.g., a house*)

compravéndita *f* transaction; transfer (*e.g., of real estate*)

comprèndere §220 *tr* to comprehend, include, comprise; to overwhelm; to understand; to forgive

comprendò·nio *m* (**-ni**) (joc) understanding

comprensìbile *adj* understandable, comprehensible

comprensióne *f* comprehension, understanding

comprensi·vo -va *adj* comprehensive; understanding

comprensò·rio *m* (**-ri**) land to be reclaimed; area, zone, e.g., **comprensorio turistico** tourist area

comprè·so -sa [s] *adj* comprised, included; understood; deeply touched; immersed

comprèssa *f* compress

compressióne *f* compression

comprès·so -sa *adj* compressed; (fig) repressed; (aut) supercharged || *f* see **compressa**

compressóre *m* compressor; **compressore stradale** road roller

comprimà·rio *m* (**-ri**) (med) associate chief of staff; (theat) second lead

comprìmere §131 *tr* to compress; to repress, restrain; to tamp

compromés·so -sa *adj* jeopardized, in danger || *m* compromise; referral (*to arbitration*)

compromettènte *adj* compromising

comprométtere §198 *tr* to compromise; to endanger; to involve, commit; (law) to refer (*to arbitration*)

compróprie·tà *f* (-tà) joint ownership

comproprietà·rio -ria *mf* (-ri -rie) joint owner

compròva *f* confirmation

comprovare (compròvo) *tr* to confirm; to circumstantiate

compulsare *tr* to consult, peruse; to summon (*to appear in court*)

compulsi·vo -va *adj* compulsive

compun·to -ta *adj* contrite, repentant

compunzióne *f* compunction

computàbile *adj* computable

computare (còmputo) *tr* to compute

computi·sta *mf* (-sti -ste) bookkeeper

computisterìa *f* bookkeeping

còmputo *m* computation, reckoning

comunale *adj* municipal, town (*e.g., hall*); community-owned; (poet) common

comunanza *f* community; in comunanza in common

comune *adj* common || *m* normalcy; commune, municipality, town; town hall; (hist) guild; (nav) common seaman; in comune in common || *f* commune (*in communist countries*); (theat) main stage entrance; andare per la comune to follow the crowd; per la comune commonly

comunèlla *f* cabal, clique; passkey (*in a hotel*); (law) mutual insurance (*of cattlemen*); fare comunella con to consort with

comunicàbile *adj* communicable

comunicante *adj* communicant; communicating || *m* priest who gives communion

comunicare §197 (comùnico) *tr* to communicate; to administer communion to || *intr* to communicate || *ref* to spread; to receive communion, to commune

comunicati·vo -va *adj* communicable, spreading; communicative

comunicato *m* communiqué; comunicato commerciale advertisement, ad; comunicato stampa press release

comunicazióne *f* communication; statement; (telp) connection; comunicazioni communications

comunióne *f* community; (law) community property || Comunione *f* Communion

comunismo *m* communism

comuni·sta (-sti -ste) *adj* communist || *mf* communist; (law) joint tenant

comunìsti·co -ca *adj* (-ci -che) communistic

comuni·tà *f* (-tà) community

comunità·rio -ria *adj* (-ri -rie) community, e.g., interessi comunitari community interests

comùnque *adv* however, nevertheless || *conj* however, no matter how

cón §4 *prep* with; by (*e.g., boat*); con + art + inf by + ger, e.g., col leggere by reading

conato *m* effort, attempt

cón·ca *f* (-che) washbowl, washbasin; copper water jug; valley, hollow; (poet) shell; conca idraulica drydock

concatenaménto *m* (poet) concatenation

concatenare (concaténo) *tr* to link || *ref* to unfold, ensue

concatenazióne *f* concatenation

concàusa *f* joint cause; (law) aggravation

cònca·vo -va *adj* concave; hollow || *m* hollow

concèdere §132 *tr* to grant, concede; to stretch (*a point*) || *ref* to let oneself go, give oneself over

concènto *m* harmony; (fig) agreement

concentraménto *m* concentration

concentrare (concèntro) *tr* to concentrate; to center || *ref* to concentrate, focus; to center

concentra·to -ta *adj* concentrated; condensed (*e.g., milk*) || *m* purée (*e.g., of tomatoes*)

concentrazióne *f* concentration; (chem) condensation

concèntri·co -ca *adj* (-ci -che) concentric

concepìbile *adj* conceivable

concepiménto *m* conception; (fig) formulation

concepire §176 *tr* to conceive; (fig) to nurture

concerìa *f* tannery

concèrnere §133 *tr* to concern

concertare (concèrto) *tr* to scheme, concert; (mus) to orchestrate, arrange || *ref* to agree

concerta·to -ta *adj* agreed upon; (mus) with accompaniment || *m* ensemble (*of orchestra, soloists, and chorus*)

concerta·tóre -trice *mf* arranger || *m* plotter, schemer

concertazióne *f* (mus) arrangement

concerti·sta *mf* (-sti -ste) concert performer, soloist

concèrto *m* concert; concerto; (fig) choir

concessionà·rio *m* (-ri) sole agent, concessionaire; dealer; lessee (*of business establishment*)

concessióne *f* concession; dealership; admission

concessi·vo -va *adj* concessive

concès·so -sa *adj* granted, admitting

concètto *m* concept; opinion

concettó·so -sa [s] *adj* concise; full of ideas; full of conceits

concettuale *adj* conceptual

concezióne *f* conception; formulation

conchìglia *f* shell, conch; (sports) jock guard, protective cup

conchiùdere §125 *tr*, *intr* & *ref* var of concludere

cón·cia *f* (-ce) tanning

conciapèl·li *m* (-li) tanner

conciare §128 (cóncio) *tr* to tan; to cure (*e.g., tobacco*); to arrange; to straighten up; to reduce; to cut (*a precious stone*); **conciare per le feste** (coll) to give a good beating to || *ref* to get messed up, get dirty

conciatét·ti *m* (**-ti**) roofer

conciató·re -trice *mf* tanner

conciliàbile *adj* reconcilable

conciliàbolo *m* conventicle, secret meeting

conciliante *adj* conciliatory

conciliare *adj* council || *m* member of an ecclesiastical council || §287 *tr* to conciliate, reconcile; to settle (*a fine*); to promote (*e.g., sleep*); to obtain (*a favor*) || *ref* to become reconciled

concilia·tóre -trice *adj* conciliatory || *mf* conciliator, peacemaker || *m* justice of the peace

conciliazióne *f* conciliation || **la Conciliazione** the Concordat (*of 1929 between Italy and the Vatican*)

conci·lio *m* (**-li**) council; church council

concimàia *f* manure pit

concimare *tr* to manure

concimazióne *f* spreading of manure; chemical fertilization

concime *m* manure; fertilizer

cón·cio -cia (**-ci -ce**) *adj* tanned || *m* ashlar; dung, manure; (archaic) agreement; **concio di scoria** cinder block || *f* see **concia**

conciofossecosaché *conj* (archaic) since

concionare (**concióno**) *intr* (archaic) to harangue

concióne *f* (archaic) harangue; (archaic) assembly

conciossiacosaché *conj* (archaic) since

concisióne *f* concision, brevity

conci·so -sa *adj* concise, brief

concistòro *m* consistory; (fig) assembly

concitare (**còncito**) *tr* to excite, stir up

concita·to -ta *adj* excited; (poet) decisive

concitazióne *f* impetus; excitement

concittadi·no -na *mf* fellow citizen

conclave *m* conclave

conclùdere §105 *tr* to conclude || *intr* to conclude; to be convincing || *ref* to conclude, end; **concludersi con** to end with; to result in

conclusionale *adj* (law) summary

conclusióne *f* conclusion; **conclusioni** (law) summation

conclusi·vo -va *adj* conclusive

conclu·so -sa *adj* concluded; terminated; (poet) closed

concomitante *adj* concomitant

concordanza *f* concordance, agreement; (gram) concord; **concordanze** concordance (*e.g., to the Bible*)

concordare (**concòrdo**) *tr* to agree on; to make agree || *intr* & *ref* to come to an agreement

concordato *m* agreement; concordat; settlement (*with creditors*)

concòrde *adj* in agreement

concòrdia *f* concord, harmony

concorrènte *adj* competitive || *m* (com) competitor; (sports) contestant

concorrènza *f* competition

concorrenziale *adj* competitive (*e.g., price*)

concórrere §139 *intr* to converge; to concur; to compete

concórso *m* attendance; concurrence; combination (*of circumstances*); competition; competitive examination; contest; **concorso di bellezza** beauty contest; **concorso di pubblico** turnout; **fuori concorso** not entering the competition; in a class by itself

concretare (**concrèto**) *tr* to realize (*e.g., a dream*); to conclude, accomplish || *ref* to come true

concretézza *f* concreteness, consistency

concrè·to -ta *adj* concrete, real; practical || *m* practical matter; **in concreto** really, in reality

concubina *f* concubine

concubinàg·gio *m* (**-gi**) concubinage

concubinato *m* var of **concubinaggio**

conculcare §197 *tr* (lit) to trample under foot; (lit) to violate

concupire §176 *tr* (poet) to lust for

concupiscènza *f* concupiscence, lust

concussióne *f* extortion, shakedown; **concussione cerebrale** (pathol) concussion

condanna *f* conviction; sentence; (fig) blame, condemnation

condannare *tr* to condemn; to find guilty, convict; to sentence; to damn (*to eternal punishment*); to declare incurable; to wall up

condanna·to -ta *adj* condemned || *m* convict

condensare (**condènso**) *tr* & *ref* to condense

condensa·to -ta *adj* condensed (*e.g., milk*)

condensatóre *m* condenser

condensazióne *f* condensation

condiménto *m* condiment, seasoning

condire §176 *tr* to season

condiret·tóre -trice *mf* associate manager

condiscendènte *adj* condescending

condiscendènza *f* condescension

condiscéndere §245 *intr* to condescend

condiscépo·lo -la *mf* schoolmate, school companion

condividere §158 *tr* to share

condizionale *adj* & *m* conditional || *f* (law) suspended sentence

condizionare (**condizióno**) *tr* to condition; to treat (*to prevent spoilage*)

condizionatóre *m* air conditioner

condizióne *f* condition; term (*of sale*); **a condizione che** provided that; **condizioni** condition, shape (*e.g., of a shipment*); **essere in condizione di** to be in a position to

condoglianza *f* condolence; **fare le condoglianze a** to extend one's sympathy to

condolére §159 *ref* to condole

condomì·nio *m* (**-ni**) condominium

condòmi·no -na *mf* joint owner (*of real estate*)

condonare (**condóno**) *tr* to condone; to remit

condóno *m* pardon, parole

condót·to -ta *adj* country (*doctor*) || *m* duct, canal; conduit || *f* behavior, conduct; district (*of country doctor*); transportation; pipeline; (theat) baggage; **condotta forzata** fiume

conducènte *m* driver; bus driver; motorman

condù·plex *mf* (**-plex**) (telp) party-line user

condurre §102 *tr* to lead; to drive (*a car*); to round up (*cattle*); to pipe (*e.g., gas*); to conduct; to trace (*a line*); to take; to bring; to manage; **condurre a termine** to bring to fruition, realize ‖ *intr* to lead ‖ *ref* to behave; to betake oneself, go; **condursi a** (poet) to be reduced to (*e.g., poverty*)

conduttivi·tà *f* (**-tà**) conductivity

condutti·vo -va *adj* conductive

condut·tóre -trice *adj* guiding, leading ‖ *m* operator (*of a bus*); driver (*of a car*); (rr) engineer; (rr) ticket collector; (phys) conductor

conduttura *f* conduit, pipeline

conduzióne *f* conduction; leasing

conestàbile *m* constable (*keeper of a castle*)

confabulare (**confàbulo**) *intr* to confabulate, commune; to connive, scheme

confacènte *adj* suitable, appropriate; helpful

confare §173 *ref*—**confarsi a** to agree with, e.g., **le uova non gli si confanno** eggs do not agree with him

confederare (**confèdero**) *tr & ref* to confederate

confedera·to· -ta *adj & m* confederate

confederazióne *f* confederation

conferènza *f* conference; lecture; **conferenza illustrata** chalk talk; **conferenza stampa** press conference

conferenziè·re -ra *mf* speaker, lecturer

conferimènto *m* conferring, bestowal

conferire §176 *tr* to confer, bestow; to add; to contribute ‖ *intr* to confer; to contribute; **conferire alla salute** to be healthful

confèrma *f* confirmation; **a conferma di** (com) in reply to, confirming

confermare (**confèrmo**) *tr* to confirm; to verify; to retain (*in office*) ‖ *ref* to become more sure of oneself; to prove to be; to remain (*in the conclusion of a letter*)

confessare (**confèsso**) *tr & ref* to confess

confessionale *adj* confessional; church; church-related, parochial (*e.g., school*) ‖ *m* confessional

confessióne *f* confession

confès·so -sa *adj* acknowledged, self-admitted; **confesso e comunicato** having made one's confession and taken communion

confessóre *m* confessor

confettièra *f* candy store, confectioner's shop

confettièra *f* candy box

confettière *f* candy maker; candy dealer, confectioner

confètto *m* sugar-covered nut, sweetmeat; losenge, drop

confettura *f* candy; preserves, jam; **confetture** confectionery

confezionare (**confezióno**) *tr* to make; to tailor (*a suit*)

confezióne *f* preparation, manufacturing; packaging; **confezioni** ready-made clothes

confezioni·sta *mf* (**-sti -ste**) ready-made clothier

conficcare §197 *tr* to drive (*a nail*); to thrust (*a knife*) ‖ *ref* to become embedded

confidare *tr* to trust (*a secret*) ‖ *intr* to trust ‖ *ref* to confide

confidènte *adj* confident ‖ *mf* confident; informer

confidènza *f* confidence; secret; familiarity

confidenziale *adj* confidential; friendly

confìggere §104 *tr* to plunge, thrust

configurazióne *f* configuration

confinante *adj* bordering ‖ *mf* neighbor

confinare *tr* to exile; to confine ‖ *intr* to border

confinà·rio -ria *adj* (**-ri -rie**) border (*e.g., zone*)

Confindùstria *f* (acronym) **Confederazione Nazionale degli Industriali** National Confederation of Industrialists

confine *m* border, boundary line; boundary mark, landmark

confino *m* exile (*in a different town*)

confi·sca *f* (**-sche**) confiscation

confiscare §197 *tr* to confiscate

confìt·to· -ta *adj* nailed; bound; tied; **confitto in croce** nailed to the cross

conflagrazióne *f* conflagration

conflitto *m* conflict

conflittualità *f* confrontation; belligerent attitude

confluènte *m* confluent

confluènza *f* confluence

confluire §176 *intr* to flow together, join; to converge

confóndere §178 *tr* to confuse; to overwhelm (*with kindness*); to humiliate; **confondere con** to mistake for ‖ *ref* to mix; to become confused

conformare (**confórmo**) *tr* to shape; to conform ‖ *ref* to conform

conformazióne *f* conformation

confórme *adj* faithful, exact; in agreement; true (*copy*)

conformeménte *adv* in conformity

conformi·sta *mf* (**-sti -ste**) conformist

conformi·tà *f* (**-tà**) conformity; **in conformità di** in conformity with, in accord with

confortante *adj* comforting

confortare (**confòrto**) *tr* to comfort

confortévole *adj* comforting, consoling; comfortable

confòrto *m* comfort, solace; convenience; corroboration; **conforti religiosi** last rites

confratèllo *m* brother, confrere

confratèrnita *f* brotherhood

confricare §197 *tr* to rub

confrontare (**confrónto**) *tr* to compare, confront; to consult ‖ *intr* to correspond confrónto *m* comparison; (law) cross examination; **a confronto di** or **in confronto a** in comparison with; with regard to .

confusaménte *adv* vaguely, hazily

confusionale *adj* confusing; confused

confusionà·rio -ria (-ri -rie) *adj* blundering; scatterbrain || *mf* blunderer; scatterbrain

confusióne *f* confusion, disorder; noise; error; embarrassment; shambles

confu·so -sa *adj* confused, mixed; vague, hazy; **in confuso** indistinctly

confutare (cònfuto) *tr* to confute

confutazióne *f* confutation

congedare (congèdo) *tr* to dismiss; to let (*a tenant*) go; (mil) to discharge || *ref* to take leave

congeda·to -ta *adj* discharged || *m* discharged soldier

congèdo *m* dismissal; leave; permission to leave; (mil) discharge; envoy, envoi; **congedo per motivi di salute** sick leave; **dare il congedo a** to discharge; **prender congedo** to take leave

congegnare (congégno) *tr* to assemble (*machinery*); to contrive, cook up

congégno *m* contrivance, gadget; mechanism; design (*of a play*)

congelaménto *m* freezing; frostbite

congelare (congèlo) *tr* & *ref* to freeze, congeal

congela·tóre -trice *adj* freezing || *m* freezer; freezer unit; freezing compartment (*of a refrigerator*)

congènere *adj* similar, alike

congeniale *adj* congenial

congèni·to -ta *adj* congenital

congèrie *f* congeries

congestionare (congestióno) *tr* to congest

congestióne *f* congestion

congettura *f* conjecture

congetturare *tr* to conjecture

congiùngere §183 *tr* & *ref* to unite, join

congiuntiva *f* (anat) conjunctiva

congiuntivìte *f* (pathol) conjunctivitis

congiunti·vo -va *adj* conjunctive; subjunctive || *m* subjunctive || *f* see congiuntiva

congiun·to -ta *adj* joined; joint || *m* relative

congiuntura *f* juncture; joint; circumstance, situation; **bassa congiuntura** (econ) unfavorable circumstance; (econ) crisis

congiunzióne *f* conjunction

congiura *f* conspiracy, plot

congiurare *intr* to conspire, plot

congiura·to -ta *adj* & *m* conspirator

conglobare (conglòbo) *tr* to lump together

conglomerare (conglòmero) *tr* & *ref* to pile up, conglomerate

conglomera·to -ta *adj* & *m* conglomerate

congratulare (congràtulo) *intr* to rejoice || *ref*—**congratularsi con** to congratulate

congratulazióne *f* congratulation

congrèga *f* gang; cabal; religious brotherhood

congregare §209 (congrègo) *tr* & *ref* to congregate

congregazióne *f* congregation

congressi·sta *mf* (-sti -ste) delegate || *m* congressman || *f* congresswoman

congrèsso *m* congress, assembly; conference; convention

congruènte *adj* congruous

congruènza *f* congruence

còn·gruo -grua *adj* congruous; congruent

conguagliare §280 *tr* to adjust; to make up (*what is owed*)

conguà·glio *m* (-gli) balance; adjustment (*of wages*)

coniare §287 (cònio) *tr* to mint, coin

coniatura *f* mintage, coinage

còni·co -ca (-ci -che) *adj* conic(al) || *f* conic section

conìfera *f* conifer

coniglièra *f* warren, rabbit hutch

conì·glio *m* (-gli) rabbit

cò·nio *m* (-ni) die (*to mint coins*); mintage; wedge; **dello stesso conio** (fig) of the same feather; **di nuovo conio** newly-minted; new-fangled

coniugale *adj* conjugal

coniugare §209 (còniugo) *tr* to conjugate || *ref* to marry, get married

coniuga·to -ta *adj* coupled, paired || *mf* spouse, consort

coniugazióne *f* conjugation

còniuge *mf* spouse; **coniugi** *mpl* husband and wife

connaturale *adj* inborn, innate

connatura·to -ta *adj* deep-seated, deep-rooted; congenital

connazionale *mf* fellow countryman

connessióne *f* connection

connés·so -sa & connès·so -sa *adj* connected, tied

connéttere & connèttere §107 *tr* to connect, link || *ref* to refer

connetti·vo -va *adj* connective

connivènte *adj* conniving

connivènza *f* connivance

connotare (connòto) *tr* to connote

connotato *m* personal characteristic

connù·bio *m* (-bi) wedding, union

còno *m* cone

conòcchia *f* distaff

conoscènte *mf* acquaintance

conoscènza *f* knowledge; acquaintance; understanding; consciousness; **conoscenza di causa** full knowledge; **essere a conoscenza di** to be acquainted with; **prendere conoscenza di** to take cognizance of

conóscere §134 *tr* to know; to recognize; **conoscere i propri polli** to know one's onions; **conoscere per filo e per segno** to know thoroughly; **conoscere ragioni** to listen to reason; **darsi a conoscere** to make oneself known; to reveal oneself || *intr* to reason || *ref* to acknowledge oneself to be; to know one another

conoscìbile *adj* knowable

conosci·tóre -trice *mf* connoisseur, expert

conosciu·to -ta *adj* known, well-known; proven

conquìdere §135 *tr* (poet) to conquer

conquista *f* conquest

conquistare *tr* to conquer, win

conquista•tóre -trice *adj* conquering || *m* conqueror; lady killer

consacrare *tr* to consecrate || *ref* to dedicate oneself

consacrazióne *f* consecration

consanguineità *f* consanguinity

consanguìne•o -a *adj* consanguineous; fratello consanguineo half brother on the father's side || *m* kin

consapévole *adj* aware, conscious

consapevolézza *f* awareness, consciousness

còn•scio -scia *adj* (-sci -sce) conscious

consecuti•vo -va *adj* consecutive

conségna *f* delivery; (mil) order; (mil) confinement (*to barracks*); in consegna (com) on consignment

consegnare (conségno) *tr* to deliver; to entrust; (mil) to confine (*to barracks*)

consegnatà•rio *m* (-ri) consignee

conseguènte *adj* consequent; consistent; conseguente a resulting from; consistent with

conseguènza *f* consequence; consistency; in conseguenza di as a result of

conseguìbile *adj* attainable

conseguimento *m* attainment

conseguire (conséguo) *tr* to attain; to obtain || *intr* to ensue, result

consènso *m* consent, approval; consensus

consensuale *adj* mutual-consent (*e.g., agreement*)

consentiménto *m* consent

consentire (consènto) *tr* to allow, permit || *intr* to agree, consent; to yield; to admit

consenziènte *adj* consenting

consèr•to -ta *adj* intertwined; folded (*arms*); di conserto in agreement

consèrva *f* preserve; purée (*e.g., of tomatoes*); tank (*for water*); sauce (*e.g., of cranberries*); conserve alimentari canned goods; di conserva together, in a group; far conserva di to preserve

conservare (consèrvo) *tr* to conserve; to keep; to cure (*e.g., meat*); to cherish (*a memory*) || *ref* to keep; to remain; to keep in good health

conservati•vo -va *adj* preserving; conservative || *m* conservative

conserva•tóre -trice *adj* preserving; conservative || *mf* keeper, curator; conservative

conservatoría *f* registrar's office (*in a court house*)

conservatò•rio *m* (-ri) conservatory; girl's boarding school (*run by nuns*)

conservatorismo *m* conservatism

conservazióne *f* conservation; preservation; self-preservation; canning

consèsso *m* assembly

consideràbile *adj* considerable; large, important

considerare (considero) *tr* to consider; to rate; (law) to provide for

considera•to -ta *adj* considered; considerato che considering that, since;

tutto considerato all in all, considering

considerazióne *f* consideration

considerévole *adj* considerable

consigliare *adj* council, councilmanic || §280 *tr* to advise, counsel || *ref* to consult

consigliè•re -ra *mf* counselor, advisor || *m* chancellor (*of embassy*); councilman; consigliere delegato chairman of the board

consì•glio *m* (-gli) advice, counsel; will (*of God*); decision, idea; council; consiglio d'amministrazione (com) board of directors; consiglio dei ministri cabinet; consiglio municipale city council; l'eterno consiglio the will of God; venire a più miti consigli to become more reasonable

consimile *adj* similar

consistènte *adj* consistent, solid; trustworthy

consistènza *f* consistency, resistance; foundation, grounds

consìstere §114 *intr* to consist; consistere in to consist of

consociare §128 (consòcio) *tr* to syndicate, unite

consociu•to -ta *adj* syndicated, united

consociazióne *f* syndicate, association, group

consò•cio -cia *mf* (-ci -cie) fellow shareholder; associate, partner

consolare *adj* consular || *v* (consòlo) *tr* to console, cheer, comfort || *ref* to rejoice; to take comfort

consolato *m* consulate

consola•tóre -trice *adj* comforting || *mf* comforter

consolazióne *f* consolation

cònsole *m* consul

consò•le *f* (-le) console

consòlida *f*—consolida maggiore comfrey; consolida reale field larkspur

consolidaménto *m* consolidation

consolidare (consòlido) *tr* to consolidate || *ref* to consolidate; to harden

consolida•to -ta *adj* consolidated; joint (*e.g., balance sheet*); hardened || *m* funded public debt; government bonds

consonante *adj & f* consonant

consonànti•co -ca *adj* (-ci -che) consonant

consonanza *f* consonance; agreement; (mus) harmony

cònso•no -na *adj* consonant

consorèlla *f* sister (*e.g., company*) || *f* sister of charity; sister branch; sister firm

consòrte *adj* (poet) equally fortunate; (poet) united || *mf* consort, mate, spouse

consorteria *f* political clique

consòr•zio *m* (-zi) syndicate, consortium; (poet) society

constare (cònsto) *intr* to consist || *impers* to be known; to be proved; to understand, e.g., gli consta che Lei ha torto he understands that you are wrong

constatare (constato & cònstato) *tr* to verify, ascertain, establish

constatazióne *f* ascertainment, verification

consuè•to -ta *adj* usual, customary; **consueto a** accustomed to, used to || *m* manner, custom; **di consueto** generally

consuetudinà•rio -ria *adj* (**-ri -rie**) customary; common (*law*)

consuetùdine *f* custom; common law; (poet) familiarity

consulènte *adj* advising, consulting || *mf* adviser, expert

consulènza *f* expert advice

consulta *f* council

consultare *tr* to consult || *ref* to take counsel; to counsel with one another; **consultarsi con** to take counsel with

consultazióne *f* consultation; reference; **consultazione popolare** referendum

consulti•vo -va *adj* advisory

consulto *m* consultation (*of physicians*); legal conference

consul•tóre -trice *mf* adviser, expert || *m* councilman

consultò•rio *m* (**-ri**) clinic, dispensary

consumare *tr* to consume; to perform, to consummate || *ref* to be consumed, to waste away

consuma•to -ta *adj* consummate, accomplished; consummated (*marriage*); consumed, worn out

consuma•tóre -trice *adj* consuming || *mf* consumer; customer (*of a restaurant*)

consumazióne *f* consummation (*e.g., of a crime*); consumption (*of food*); food or drink

consumismo *m* consumerism

consumo *m* consumption; wear

consunti•vo -va *adj* end-of-year (*e.g., report*); (econ) consumption || *m* balance sheet

consun•to -ta *adj* worn-out

consunzióne *f* consumption

contàbile *adj* bookkeeping || *mf* accountant; bookkeeper, clerk; **esperto contabile** certified public accountant

contabili•tà *f* (**-tà**) accounting, bookkeeping; accounts

contachìlome•tri *m* (**-tri**) odometer; (coll) speedometer

contadiné•sco -sca *adj* (**-schi -sche**) farm, farmer; rustic

contadì•no -na *adj* rustic || *mf* peasant, farmer

contado *m* country, countryside

contagiare §290 *tr* to infect

contà•gio *m* (**-gi**) contagion

contagió•so -sa [s] *adj* contagious

contagi•rì *m* (**-ri**) tachometer

contagóc•ce *m* (**-ce**) dropper, eyedropper

contaminare (**contàmino**) *tr* to contaminate; to pollute

contaminazióne *f* contamination; pollution

contante *adj & m* cash; **in contanti** cash

contare (**cónto**) *tr* to count; to limit; to regard, value; to propose; **contarle grosse** (coll) to tell tall tales || *intr* to count; **contare su** to count on

contasecón•di *m* (**-di**) watch with second hand

conta•to -ta *adj* limited; numbered (*e.g., days*)

conta•tóre -trice *adj* counting || *mf* counter || *m* meter; **contatore dell'acqua** water meter; **contatore della luce** electric meter

contattare *tr* to contact

contatto *m* contact

cónte *m* count

contèa *f* county

conteggiare §290 (**contéggio**) *tr* to charge (*e.g., a bill*) || *intr* to count

contég•gio *m* (**-gi**) reckoning, calculation; (sports) count; **conteggio alla rovescia** countdown

contégno *m* behavior; reserve, reserved attitude; air

contegnó•so -sa [s] *adj* reserved, dignified

contemperare (**contèmpero**) *tr* to adapt; to mitigate, moderate

contemplare (**contèmplo**) *tr* to contemplate

contemplati•vo -va *adj* contemplative

contemplazióne *f* contemplation

contèmpo *m*—**nel contempo** meanwhile

contemporaneaménte *adv* at the same time

contemporàne•o -a *adj* contemporaneous || *mf* contemporary

contendènte *adj* fighting || *m* contender, fighter; (law) contestant

contèndere §270 *tr* to contest, oppose || *intr* to contend, fight || *ref* to fight

contenére §271 *tr* to contain || *ref* to restrain oneself; to behave

conteniménto *m* containment

contenitóre *m* container

contentare (**contènto**) *tr* to satisfy, content || *ref* to be satisfied

contentézza *f* gladness, contentedness, contentment

contentino *m* gratuity, makeweight, gift to a customer

contèn•to -ta *adj* contented, glad, happy; satisfied || *m* (poet) happiness, contentedness

contenuto *m* content; contents

contenzióne *f* contention

contenzióso [s] *m* legal matter; legal department (*of a corporation*)

conterìe *fpl* beads, sequins

conterrà•neo -nea *adj* from the same country || *m* fellow countryman || *f* fellow countrywoman

conté•so -sa [s] *adj* coveted || *f* contest; dispute; **venire a contesa** to dispute

contéssa *f* countess

contestare (**contèsto**) *tr* to serve (*e.g., a summons*); to deny; to challenge, contest; **contestare qlco a qlcu** to charge s.o. with s.th

contestazióne *f* notification, summons; dispute, confrontation; challenge

contè•sto -sta *adj* (poet) intertwined || *m* context

contì•guo -gua *adj* contiguous

continentale *adj* continental

continènte *adj & m* continent

continènza *f* continence

contingentaménto *m* import quota

contingentare (**contingènto**) *tr* to assign a quota to (*imports*)

contingènte *adj* possible, contingent; (obs) due || *m* contingent; import quota; **contingente di leva** draft quota

contingènza *f* contingency

continuare (contìnuo) *tr* to continue || *intr* to last, continue; **continuare a +** *inf* to keep on + *ger*

continuazióne *f* continuation

continui·tà *f* (-tà) continuity

conti·nuo -nua *adj* continuous; direct (*current*); **di continuo** continuously

cón·to -ta *adj* (archaic) well-known; (poet) gentle; (poet) narrated || *m* figuring; account; bill, invoice; check (*in a restaurant*); opinion; worth, value; **a conti fatti** everything considered; **chiedere conto di** to call to account; **conto all'indietro** countdown; **di conto** valuable; **estratto conto** (com) statement; **fare conto di +** *inf* to intend to + *inf*; **fare conto su** to count on; **fare di conto** to count; **fare i conti senza l'oste** to reckon without one's host; **il conto non torna** the sums do not jibe; **in conto** on account; **in conto di** in one's position as; **per conto di** in the name of; **per conto mio** as far as I am concerned; **render conto di** to give an account of; **rendersi conto di** to realize, be aware of; **tener conto di** to reckon with; **tener di conto** to treat with care; **torna conto** it is worthwhile

contòrcere §272 *tr* to twist || *ref* to writhe

contorciménto *m* contortion, writhing

contornare (contórno) *tr* to surround

contórno *m* outline; contour; circle (*of people*); side dish (*of vegetables*)

contorsióne *f* contorsion; gyration (*e.g., of a dancer*); squirm

contòr·to -ta *adj* twisted (*e.g., face*)

contrabbandare *tr* to smuggle

contrabbandiè·re -ra *adj* smuggling || *mf* smuggler; bootlegger

contrabbando *m* contraband; smuggling; **di contrabbando** by smuggling; (fig) without paying

contrabbasso *m* contrabass, bass viol

contraccambiare §287 *tr* to reciprocate, return || *intr* to reciprocate

contraccàm·bio *m* (-bi) exchange; **in contraccambio di** in exchange for, in return for

contraccólpo *m* shock, rebound; recoil (*of a rifle*); backlash (*of a machine*)

contrada *f* road; (poet) region

contraddire §151 (*impv sg* **contraddici**) *tr* to contradict || *ref* to contradict oneself; to contradict one another

contraddistinguere §156 *tr* to earmark || *ref* to stand out

contraddittò·rio -ria (-ri -rie) *adj* contradictory; incoherent || *m* open discussion, debate

contraddizióne *f* contradiction

contraènte *adj* contracting; acting || *mf* contractor (*person who makes a contract*); (law) party

contraère·o -a *adj* antiaircraft

contraffare §173 *tr* to counterfeit; to fake, sham || *intr* (archaic) to disobey || *ref* to camouflage oneself, disguise oneself

contraffat·to -ta *adj* counterfeit; adulterated; apocryphal

contraffat·tóre -trice *mf* counterfeiter; falsifier

contraffazióne *f* forgery; fake; imitation; piracy (*of book*); mockery (*of justice*)

contrafförte *m* spur (*of mountain*); crossbar (*to secure door*); (archit) buttress

contraggènio *m*—**a contraggenio** against one's will

contral·to (-to) *adj* alto || *m* contralto (*voice*) || *f* contralto (*singer*)

contrammirà·glio *m* (-gli) rear admiral

contrappasso *m* retributive justice

contrappesare [s] (**contrappéso**) *tr* to counterweight, counterbalance

contrappéso [s] *m* counterweight, counterpoise

contrappórre §218 *tr* to oppose; to compare || *ref*—**contrapporsi a** to oppose

contrappò·sto -sta *adj* opposing || *m* opposite, antithesis

contrappunto *m* counterpoint

contrare (cóntro) *tr* (boxing) to counter; (bridge) to double

contrariare §287 *tr* to oppose, counter; to thwart; to contradict; to bother, vex

contrarie·tà *f* (-tà) contrariety, vexation; setback

contrà·rio -ria (-ri -rie) *adj* contrary, opposite || *m* opposite; **al contrario** on the contrary; **al contrario di** unlike; **avere qlco in contrario** to have some objection, object

contrarre §273 *tr & ref* to contract

contrassegnare (contrasségno) *tr* to earmark, mark

contrasségno *m* earmark; proof

contrastare *tr* to oppose; to obstruct; to prevent || *intr* to contrast; to disagree; (poet) to quarrel || *ref* to contend

contrasto *m* contrast; fight, dispute; (telv) contrast knob

contrattàbile *adj* negotiable

contrattaccare §197 *tr* to counterattack

contrattac·co *m* (-chi) counterattack

contrattare *tr* to contract for, negotiate a deal for || *intr* to bargain

contrattèmpo *m* mishap

contrat·to -ta *adj* contracted || *m* contract

contrattuale *adj* contractual

contravveléno *m* antidote

contravvenire §282 *intr* (with *dat*) to contravene; **contravvenire a** to infringe upon

contravvenzióne *f* violation; ticket, fine; **in contravvenzione** in the wrong; **intimare una contravvenzione a** to give a ticket to

contrazióne *f* contraction

contribuènte *mf* taxpayer

contribuire §176 *intr* to contribute

contributo *m* contribution

contribu·tóre -trice *mf* contributor

contribuzióne *f* contribution
contristare *tr & ref* to sadden
contri·to -ta *adj* contrite
contrizióne *f* contrition
cóntro *m* con, contrary opinion || *adv* —contro di against, versus; dar contro a to oppose; di contro opposite, facing; per contro on the other hand || *prep* against, versus; at; contro pagamento upon payment; contro vento into the wind; contro voglia unwillingly
controbàttere *tr* (mil) to counterattack; (fig) to contest
controbilanciare §128 *tr* to counterpoise, counterbalance
controcanto *m* (mus) counterpoint
controcarro *adj invar* antitank
controchìglia *f* keelson
controcorrènte *f* countercurrent; undertow; (fig) undercurrent || *adv* upstream
controdado *m* lock nut
controffensiva *f* counteroffensive
controfigura *f* (mov) stand-in; (mov) stuntman
controfilo *m*—a controfilo against the grain
controfinèstra *f* storm window
controfirma *f* countersign
controfirmare *tr* to countersign
controfòdera *f* inner facing (*of a suit, between lining and cloth*)
controfuò·co *m* (-chi) backfire (*to check the advance of a forest fire*)
controindicare §197 (controìndico) *tr* to contraindicate
controllare (contròllo) *tr* to control, check || *ref* to control oneself
contròllo *m* control, check; restraint; (rad, telv) knob
controllóre *m* (com) comptroller; (rr) ticket collector, conductor
controluce *f* picture taken against the light || *adv* against the light
contromano *adv* against traffic
contromar·ca *f* (-che) check, stub (*e.g., of ticket*)
contromàr·cia *f* (-ce) countermarch; (aut) reverse, reverse gear
contromezzana [ddzz] *f* (naut) topsail
contronòta *f* countermanding note
contropalo *m* strut
controparte *f* (law) opponent
contropedale *m* foot brake (*of a bicycle*)
contropélo *m* close shave (*in the opposite direction of hair's growth*) || *adv* against the grain; the wrong way (*said of the hair*); against the nap; accarezzare contropelo to stroke the wrong way
contropiède *m* counterattack; cogliere in contropiede to catch off balance
contropòrta *f* storm door
controproducènte *adj* counterproductive, self-defeating
controproposta *f* counterproposition
contropròva *f* proof; second balloting
contrórdine *m* countermand
controrèplica *f* retort; (law) rejoinder
controriforma *f* Counter Reformation
controrivoluzióne *f* counterrevolution
controsènso *m* nonsense; mistranslation
controspallina *f* (mil) epaulet
controspionàg·gio *m* (-gi) counterespionage
controvalóre *m* equivalent
controvènto *m* (archit) strut; (archit) crossbrace || *adv* windward
controvèrsia *f* controversy
controvèr·so -sa *adj* controversial, moot
controvòglia *adv* unwillingly
contumace *adj* (archaic) contumacious; (law) absent from court; (law) guilty of nonappearance
contumàcia *f* quarantine; (archaic) contumacy; (law) nonappearance; in contumacia (law) in absentia
contumèlia *f* contumely
contundènte *adj* blunt
conturbante *adj* disturbing, upsetting
conturbare *tr* to disturb, upset || *ref* to become perturbed
contusióne *f* bruise, contusion
contu·so -sa *adj* bruised
contuttoché *conj* although
contuttociò *conj* although
convalescènte *adj* convalescent
convalescènza *f* convalescence
convalescenzià·rio *m* (-ri) convalescent home
convàlida *f* validation; confirmation
convalidare (convàlido) *tr* to validate; to confirm; to strengthen (*e.g., a suspicion*)
convégno *m* meeting, convention
conveniènte *adj* convenient; adequate; useful; profitable (*business*); cheap, reasonable
conveniènza *f* convenience; suitability, fitness; propriety; profit; convenienze conventions
convenire §282 *tr* to fix (*e.g., a price*); (law) to summon || *intr* (ESSERE) to convene; to agree; to fit, be appropriate; (poet) to flow together || *ref* to be proper; (with *dat*) to behoove, befit, e.g., gli si conviene it behooves him || *impers*—conviene it is necessary
convènto *m* convent; monastery
convenu·to -ta *adj* agreed upon || *m* agreement; (law) defendant; convenuti conventioners, delegates
convenzionale *adj* conventional
convenzióne *f* convention
convergènte *adj* converging, convergent
convergènza *f* convergence
convèrgere §137 *intr* to converge
convèrsa *f* lay sister; flashing (*on a roof*)
conversare (convèrso) *intr* to converse
conversazióne *f* conversation
conversióne *f* conversion; change of heart; (mil) wheeling
convèrso *m* lay brother
convertibile *adj* convertible || *m* (aer) fighter-bomber || *f* (aut) convertible
convertibili·tà *f* (-tà) convertibility
convertire §138 *tr* to convert, change; to translate || *ref* to convert, change; (poet) to address oneself

converti·to -ta *adj* converted || *mf* convert

convertitóre *m* converter

convès·so -sa *adj* convex

convincènte *adj* convincing

convìncere §285 *tr* to convince; to convict || *ref* to become convinced

convinciménto *m* conviction

convìn·to -ta *adj* convinced, confirmed; convicted

convinzióne *f* conviction

convìta·to -ta *adj* invited || *mf* guest (*at a banquet*)

convìto *m* banquet

convitto *m* boarding school

convit·tóre -trice *mf* boarding-school student

convivènte *adj* living together

convivènza *f* living together; **convivenza illecita** cohabitation; **convivenza umana** human society

convìvere §286 *intr* to live together; to cohabit

conviviale *adj* convivial

convì·vio *m* (**-vi**) banquet

convocare §197 (**còvoco**) *tr* to summon, convoke; to convene

convocazióne *f* convocation

convogliare §280 (**convòglio**) *tr* to convoy, escort; to convey, carry

convò·glio *m* (**-gli**) convoy; cortege; (**rr**) train

convolare (**convólo**) *intr*—**convolare a nozze** to get married

convòlvolo *m* (bot) morning-glory

convulsióne *f* convulsion

convul·so -sa *adj* convulsive; convulsed; choppy (*style*)

coonestare (**coonèsto**) *tr* to justify, palliate

cooperare (**coòpero**) *intr* to cooperate

cooperati·vo -va *adj* & *f* cooperative

coopera·tóre -trice *adj* coadjutant, cooperating || *m* coadjutor

cooperazióne *f* cooperation

coordinaménto *m* coordination

coordinare (**coórdino**) *tr* to coordinate; to collect (*ideas*)

coordinatì·vo -va *adj* (gram) coordinate

coordina·to -ta *adj* & *f* coordinate

coordinazióne *f* coordination

coòrte *f* cohort

copèr·chio *m* (**-chi**) lid, cover; top (*of box*)

copertina *f* small blanket, child's blanket; cover (*of book*)

copèr·to -ta *adj* covered; protected; cloudy; obscure || *m* cover; shelter; **al coperto** under cover; indoors; secure || *f* blanket, cover; seat cover; case, sheath; (naut) deck; **coperta da viaggio** steamer rug, lap robe; **far coperta a** to cover up for

copertóne *m* canvas; casing, shoe (*of tire*); **copertone cinturato** belted tire

copertura *f* covering; cover; coverage; whitewash; (boxing) defensive stance; (archit) roof

còpia *f* copy; (poet) abundance; (archaic) opportunity; **brutta copia** first draft; **copia a carbone** carbon copy; **copia dattiloscritta** typescript; **per**

copia conforme certified copy (*formula appearing on a document*)

copialètte·re *m* (**-re**) letter file; copying press

copiare §287 (**còpio**) *tr* to copy

copiati·vo -va *adj* indelible; copying

copiatura *f* copying; copy; plagiarism

copiglia *f* cotterpin

copilò·ta *mf* (**-ti -te**) copilot

copióne *m* (theat) script

copiosi·tà [s] *f* (**-tà**) copiousness

copió·so -sa [s] *adj* copious

copi·sta *mf* (**-sti -ste**) scribe; copyist

copisterìa *f* copying office; public typing office

còppa *f* cup, goblet; bowl; pan (*of balance*); trophy; (aut) crankcase; (aut) housing; **coppe** suit of Neapolitan cards corresponding to hearts

coppàia *f* chuck (*of lathe*)

còppia *f* couple; pair; **a coppie** two by two; **far coppia fissa** to go steady

coppière *m* cupbearer

coppiglia *f* var of **copiglia**

còppo *m* earthenware jar (*for oil*); roof tile

copribu·sto *m* (**-sto**) bodice

copricapo *m* headgear

copricaté·na *m* (**-na**) chain guard (*on bicycle or motorcycle*)

coprifuò·co *m* (**-chi**) curfew

coprinu·ca *m* (**-ca**) havelock

coprire §110 *tr* to cover; to occupy (*a position*); to coat (*e.g., a wall*); to drown (*a noise*) || *ref* to cover oneself; (econ) to hedge

copriteiè·ra *m* (**-ra**) cozy

coprivan·de *m* (**-de**) dish cover

cò·pto -pta *adj* Coptic || *mf* Copt

còpula *f* copulation; (gram) copula

coque *f* see **uovo**

corà·ggio *m* (**-gi**) courage; effrontery; (obs) heart; **fare coraggio a** to hearten, encourage; **prendere il coraggio a quattro mani** to screw up one's courage

coraggió·so -sa [s] *adj* courageous

corale *adj* choral; (archaic) cordial; (fig) unanimous || *m* chorale

coralli·no -na *adj* coral

corallo *m* coral

corame *m* engraved leather

coramèlla *f* razor strop

Corano *m* Koran

corata *f* haslet

coratèlla *f* giblets

corazza *f* breastplate, cuirass; shoulder pad (*in football*); armor plate; carapace, shell

corazzare *tr* to armor || *ref* to armor, protect oneself

corazza·to -ta *adj* armor-plated, armored; plated; protected || *f* battleship, dreadnought

corazzière *m* cuirassier; mounted carabineer

còrba *f* basket

corbellerìa *f* (coll) blunder

corbèllo *m* basket; basketful

corbézzolo *m* (bot) arbutus; **corbezzoli!** gosh!

còrda *f* rope; tightrope; string (*of an*

instrument); chord; woof; cord; plumbline; **dare la corda a** to wind (*a clock*); **essere con la corda al collo** to have a rope around one's neck; **mostrare la corda** to be thread-bare; **tagliare la corda** to take off, leave; **tenere sulla corda** to keep in suspense

cordame *m* cordage

cordata *f* group of climbers tied together

cordellina *f* (mil) braided cord, braid; (mil) lanyard

cordiale *adj & m* cordial

cordiali•tà *f* (-tà) cordiality

cordièra *f* (mus) tailpiece

cordò•glio *m* (-gli) sorrow, grief

cordonata *f* gradient

cordóne *m* cordon; (anat, elec) cord; curbstone; **cordone litorale** sandbar; **cordone sanitario** sanitary cordon

corèa *f* St. Vitus's dance || **Corea** *f* Korea

corea•no -na *adj & mf* Korean

coréggia *f* leather strap

coreografìa *f* choreography

coreògrafo *m* choreographer

coriàce•o -a *adj* tough, leathery

coriàndolo *m* (bot) coriander; **coriandoli** confetti

coricare §197 (còrico) *tr* to put to bed || *ref* to lie down, go to bed

corindóne *m* corundum

corìn•zio -zia *adj & mf* (-zi -zie) Corinthian

cori•sta *mf* (-sti -ste) choir singer, choirmaster || *m* chorus man; (mus) tuning fork; (mus) pitch pipe

coriza [dz] or **corizza** [ddzz] *f* coryza

cormorano *m* cormorant

cornàcchia *f* rook, crow

cornamusa *f* bagpipe

cornata *f* butt; hook, goring (*by bull*)

còrne•o -a *adj* horn, horn-like || *f* cornea

cornétta *f* (mus) cornet; (mus) cornet player; (telp) receiver; (hist) pennon (*of cavalry*)

cornétto *m* little horn; amulet (*in shape of horn*); crescent (*bread*); ear trumpet

cornice *f* cornice; frame; (typ) box; (archit) pediment

cornicióne *m* (archit) ledge; (archit) cornice

cornificare §197 (cornìfico) *tr* (joc) to cuckold

cornìola *f* carnelian

còrniola *f* (bot) dogberry

còrniolo *m* (bot) dogwood

còrno *m* horn; wing (*of army*); edge, end; (mus) horn; **corno da caccia** hunting horn; **corno da scarpe** shoe horn; **corno dell'abbondanza** horn of plenty; **corno dogale** (hist) Doge's hat; **corno inglese** (mus) English horn; **non capire un corno** to not understand a blessed thing; **non valere un corno** to not be worth a fig; **un corno!** (slang) heck no! || *m* (còrna *fpl*) horn (*of animal*); **alzare le corna** to raise one's head; to become rambunctious; **dire corna di** to speak evil of; **fare le corna** to make horns, to touch wood (*to ward off the evil eye*); **mettere le corna a** to cuckold (*one's husband*); to be unfaithful to (*one's wife*); **portare le corna** to be cuckolded; **rompersi le corna** to get the worst of it

cornu•to -ta *adj* horny; horn-shaped; (vulg) cuckolded

còro *m* choir; chorus; chancel

corollà•rio *m* (-rì) corollary

coróna *f* crown; coronet; wreath, garland; range (*of mountains*); collection (*e.g., of sonnets*); stem (*of watch*); felloe (*of wheel*); (astr) corona; (rel) string (*of beads*); (mus) pause; **fare corona a** to surround

coronaménto *m* crowning; (archit) capstone; (naut) taffrail

coronare (coróno) *tr* to crown; to top, surmount

coronà•rio -ria *adj* (-ri -rie) coronary; (hist) rewarded with a garland

corpétto *m* baby's shirt; waistcoat, vest

corpino *m* bodice; vest

còrpo *m* body; substance; staff (*of teachers*); (mil) corps; (typ) em quad; **a corpo a corpo** hand-to-hand (*fight*); (sports) in a clinch; **a corpo morto** heavily; doggedly; **andare di corpo** to have a bowel movement; **avere in corpo** (fig) to have inside; **corpo del reato** corpus delicti; **corpo di Bacco!** good Heavens!; **corpo di ballo** ballet; **corpo di commissariato** (mil) supply corps; **corpo di guardia** guard, guardhouse; **corpo semplice** (chem) simple substance; **prendere corpo** to materialize

corporale *adj* bodily, body || *m* (eccl) corporal, Communion cloth

corporativismo *m* corporatism (*e.g., of Fascist Italy*)

corporati•vo -va *adj* corporative, corporate

corpora•to -ta *adj* corporate

corporatura *f* size, build

corporazióne *f* corporation

corpòre•o -a *adj* corporeal

corpó•so -sa [s] *adj* heavy-bodied

corpulèn•to -ta *adj* corpulent

corpùscolo *m* particle; (phys) corpuscle

Corpus Dòmini *m* (eccl) Corpus Christi

corredare (corrèdo) *tr* to provide, furnish; to annotate, accompany

corredino *m* layette

corrèdo *m* trousseau; outfit, garb; actor's kit; furniture; equipment; apparatus (*e.g., footnotes*)

corrèggere §226 *tr* to correct; to straighten (*e.g., a road*); to rewrite, revise (*news*); to touch up the flavor of || *ref* to reform

corrég•gia *f* (-ge) leather strap

corregionale *adj* fellow || *mf* person of the same section of the country

correità *f* complicity

correlare (corrèlo) *tr* to correlate

correlati•vo -va *adj* correlative

correla•tóre -trice *mf* second reader (*of a doctoral dissertation*)

correlazióne *f* correlation; (gram) sequence

corrènte *adj* current; running; fluent; recurring; run-of-the-mill || *m*—**essere al corrente di** to be acquainted with; to be abreast of; **mettere al corrente di** to acquaint with || *f* current; draft (*of air*); stream (*of water*); mass (*of lava*); (elec) current; (fig) tide; **contro corrente** upstream; **corrente alternata** (elec) alternating current; **corrente continua** (elec) direct current; **corrente di rete** (elec) house current

córrere §139 *tr* to travel; to run (*a risk; a race*); **correre la cavallina** to sow one's wild oats || *intr* (ESSERE & AVERE) to run; to speed; to race; to flow; to fly (*said of time*); to elapse; to be (*e.g., the year 1820*); to be current (*said of coins*); to spread (*said of gossip*); to mature (*said of interest*); to intervene (*said of distance*); to have dealings; **ci corre!** there is quite a difference!; **ci corre poco che cadesse** he narrowly escaped falling; **correre a gambe levate** to run at breakneck speed; **corre l'uso** it is the fashion; **corrono parole grosse** they are having words; **non corre buon sangue fra loro** there is bad blood between them

corresponsàbile *adj* jointly responsible

corresponsióne *f* payment; (fig) gratitude

correttézza *f* correctness

corretti·vo -va *adj* corrective || *m* flavoring

corrèt·to -ta *adj* correct; flavored; spiked

corret·tóre -trice *mf* corrector; **correttore di bozze** proofreader

correzionale *adj* correctional

correzióne *f* correction

còrri còrri *m* rush

corri·dóio *m* (-**dói**) corridor; hallway; (tennis) alley; (theat) aisle

corridóre *adj* running || *m* racer; runner (*in baseball*)

corrièra *f* mail coach; bus

corrière *m* courier; mail; carrier (*of merchandise*)

corrispetti·vo -va *adj* equivalent, proportionate || *m* requital, compensation

corrispondènte *adj* corresponding, equivalent || *mf* correspondent

corrispondènza *f* correspondence

corrispóndere §238 *tr* to pay, compensate || *intr* to correspond

corri·vo -va *adj* rash; indulgent

corroborante *adj* corroborating || *m* tonic

corroborare (**corròboro**) *tr* to corroborate; to invigorate

corroborazióne *f* corroboration

corródere §239 *tr* to corrode; to erode

corrómpere §240 *tr* to spoil; to corrupt; to suborn || *ref* to putrefy, rot

corrosióne *f* corrosion

corrosi·vo -va *adj* & *m* corrosive

corró·so -sa *adj* corroded; eroded

corrót·to -ta *adj* corrupted, corrupt; putrefied, rotten || *m* (archaic) lament

corrucciare §128 *tr* to anger, vex || *ref* to get angry

corrùc·cio *m* (-**ci**) anger, vexation

corrugaménto *m* wrinkling; (geol) fold

corrugare §209 *tr* to wrinkle, knit (*one's brow*) || *ref* to frown

corruscare §197 *intr* (poet) to shine

corruttèla *f* corruption

corruttìbile *adj* corruptible

corrut·tóre -trice *adj* corrupting, depraving || *m* seducer; briber

corruzióne *f* corruption; putrefaction, decomposition

córsa *f* race; run; trip; fare; (mach) stroke; (hist) privateering; **a tutta corsa** at full speed; **corsa al galoppo** flat race; **corsa al trotto** harness racing; **corsa semplice** one-way ticket; **corse** horse racing; **da corsa** race, for racing, e.g., **cavallo da corsa** race horse; **di corsa** running, in a hurry; **fare una corsa** to run an errand; **prendere la corsa** to begin to run

corsalétto *m* corselet

corsa·ro -ra *adj* privateering || *m* privateer, corsair, pirate

corsétto *m* corset

corsìa *f* aisle; ward (*in hospital*); runner (*of carpet*); lane (*of highway*); **corsia d'accesso** entrance lane; **corsia d'uscita** exit lane

Còrsica, la Corsica

corsivi·sta *mf* (-**sti -ste**) (journ) political writer

corsi·vo -va *adj* cursive; (poet) running; (poet) current || *m* cursive handwriting; (typ) italics

córso *m* course; navigation (*by sea*); path (*of stars*); parade; large street; boulevard; tender (*of currency*); current rate, current price (*of stock at the exchange*); **corso d'acqua** watercourse; **fuori corso** (coin) no longer in circulation; **in corso** in circulation; in progress; **in corso di** in the course of; **in corso di stampa** in press

còr·so -sa *adj* & *mf* Corsican

cor·sóio -sóia (-**sói -sóie**) *adj* running (*knot*); (mach) on rollers || *m* slide (*of slide rule*); (mach) slide

córte *f* court; **corte bandita** open house; **Corte d'appello** appellate court; **Corte di cassazione** Supreme Court; **fare la corte a** to pay court to, woo

cortéc·cia *f* (-**ce**) bark; crust (*of bread*); (fig) appearance; (anat) cortex

corteggiaménto *m* courtship

corteggiatóre *m* wooer, suitor

cortég·gio *m* (-**gi**) retinue; cortege

cortèo *m* procession; parade; funeral train; wedding party

cortése *adj* courteous, polite; (lit) liberal; (poet & hist) courtly

cortesìa *f* courtesy, politeness; (lit) liberality; (poet & hist) courtliness; **per cortesia** please

còrtice *f* cortex

cortigia·no -na *adj* flattering; courtly || *mf* courtier; flatterer || *f* courtesan

cortìle *m* courtyard; barnyard

cortina f curtain; **cortina di ferro** iron curtain; **cortina di fumo** smoke screen; **oltre cortina** behind the iron curtain

cortisóne m cortisone

cór·to -ta adj short; close (*haircut*); **alle corte** in short; **essere a corto di** to be short of; **per farla corta** in short

cortocircùito m short circuit

cortometràg·gio m (-gi) (mov) short

cor·vè f (-vè) tiresome task, drudgery; **corvè di cucina** kitchen police

corvétta f corvette

corvi·no -na adj raven-black

còrvo m raven; crow

còsa [s] f thing; **belle cose!** or **buone cose!** regards!; **che cosa** what; **cosa da nulla** a mere trifle, nothing at all; **cos'ha?** what's the matter with you (him, her)?; **cosa pubblica** commonweal; **cosa strana** no wonder; **cose** belongings; **per la qual cosa** wherefore; **per prima cosa** first of all; **sopra ogni cosa** above all; **tante belle cose!** best regards!; **una cosa** something; **una cosa nuova** a piece of news

cosac·co -ca (-chi -che) adj Cossack's ‖ mf Cossack

cò·scia f (-sce) thigh; haunch; leg (*of gun*); (archit) abutment; **coscia di montone** leg of lamb

cosciènte adj conscious; sensible; aware

cosciènza f conscience; consciousness; conscientiousness; awareness

coscienzió·so -sa [s] adj conscientious

cosciòtto m leg; leg of lamb

coscrìt·to -ta adj conscript ‖ m conscript, recruit, draftee

coscrìvere §250 tr to conscript

coscrizióne f conscription, draft

così [s] adj invar—**un così . . .** or **un . . . così** such a ‖ adv thus; like this; so; **così . . . come** as . . . as; **così così** so so; **e così via** and so on, and so forth; **per così dire** so to speak

cosicché [s] conj so that

cosiddét·to -ta [s] adj so-called

cosiffat·to -ta [s] adj such, similar

cosìno [s] m (coll) little fellow

cosmèti·co -ca adj & m (-ci -che) cosmetic

còsmi·co -ca adj (-ci -che) cosmic; outer (*space*)

còsmo m cosmos; outer space

cosmòdromo m space center

cosmologìa f cosmology

cosmonàu·ta mf (-ti -te) cosmonaut, astronaut

cosmopòli·ta adj & mf (-ti -te) cosmopolitan

còso [s] m (coll) thing, what-d'you-call-it

cospàrgere §261 tr to spread; to sprinkle

cospèrgere §112 tr (poet) to wet, sprinkle

cospètto m presence; **al cospetto di** in the presence of

cospì·cuo -cua adj distinguished, outstanding; huge, immense; (poet) conspicuous

cospirare intr to conspire, plot

cospira·tóre -trice mf conspirator

cospirazióne f conspiracy, plot

còsta f side; rib; coast, seashore; slope; welt (*along seam*); wale (*in fabric*); (naut) frame

costà adv there; over there

costaggiù adv down there

costante adj & f constant

Costantinòpoli f Constantinople

costanza f constancy ‖ **Costanza** f Constance

costare (còsto) intr (ESSERE) to cost; to be expensive; **costare caro** to cost dear; **costare un occhio della testa** to cost a fortune

costarica·no -na or **costaricènse** adj & mf Costa Rican

costassù adv up there

costata f rib roast; side

costeggiare §290 (costéggio) tr to sail along; to run along; to border on ‖ intr to coast

costèi §8 pron dem

costellare (costèllo) tr to stud, star

costellazióne f constellation

costernare (costèrno) tr to dismay, cause consternation to

costernazióne f consternation

costì adv there

costiè·ro -ra adj coast, coastal; offshore ‖ f coastline; gentle slope

costipare tr to constipate; to heap, pile ‖ ref to become constipated

costipazióne f constipation

costituènte adj constituent; constituting ‖ m member of constituent assembly; (chem) constituent

costituire §176 tr to constitute; to form ‖ ref to form; to become; to appoint oneself; to give oneself up (*to justice*); **costituirsi in giudizio** (law) to sue (*in civil court*); **costituirsi parte civile** (law) to appear as a plaintiff (*in civil court*)

costituto m (law) pact, agreement; (naut) master's declaration (*to health authorities*)

costituzionale adj constitutional

costituzióne f constitution; charter; composition; (law) appearance; surrender (*to justice*)

còsto m cost; **a costo di** at the price of; **ad ogni costo** at any cost; **a nessun costo** by no means; **a tutti i costi** at any cost, in any event; **costo della vita** cost of living; **sotto costo** below cost

còstola f rib; spine (*of book*); back (*of knife*); **avere qlcu alle costole** to have s.o. at one's heels; **rompere le costole a** (fig) to break the bones of; **stare alle costole di** to be at the back of

costolétta f chop, cutlet

costolóne m (archit) groin

costóro §8 pron dem

costó·so -sa [s] adj costly

costrìngere §265 tr to force, constrain; (poet) to compress

costrittì·vo -va adj constrictive

costrizióne f constriction

costruire §140 tr to construct, build

costrut·to **-ta** *adj* constructed || *m* profit; sense; (gram) construction; **dov'è il costrutto?** what's the point?

costruttóre *m* builder

costruzióne *f* construction; building

costùi §8 *pron dem*

costumanza *f* custom

costumare *intr* (+ *inf*) to be in the habit of (+ *ger*) || *intr* (ESSERE) to be the custom; to be in use

costumatézza *f* good manners

costuma·to **-ta** *adj* polite, well-bred

costume *m* custom, manner; costume, dress; bathing suit

costumi·sta *mf* (**-sti -ste**) (theat) costumer

costura *f* seam

cotale *adj & pron* such || *adv* (archaic) thus

cotan·to **-ta** *adj & pron* (poet) so much || **cotanto** *adv* (poet) such a long time

còte *f* flint

coténna *f* pigskin; rind; (coll) hide, skin

coté·sto **-sta** §7 *adj dem* || §8 *pron dem*

cóti·ca *f* (**-che**) (coll) hide, skin (*of porker*)

cotógna *f* quince (*fruit*)

cotognata *f* quince jam

cotógno *m* quince (*tree*)

cotolétta *f* chop, cutlet

cotóne *m* cotton; thread; **cotone fulminante** guncotton; **cotone idrofilo** absorbent cotton; **cotone silicato** mineral wool

cotonière *m* cotton manufacturer

cotonniè·ro **-ra** *adj* cotton || *mf* cotton worker

cotonifi·cio *m adj* (**-ci**) cotton mill

cotonó·so **-sa** [s] *adj* cotton; cottony

còtta *f* cooking; baking; drying (*of bricks*); (sports) exhaustion; (coll) drunkenness; (joc) infatuation, love; (eccl) surplice; **cotta d'armi** coat of mail

cottimi·sta *mf* (**-sti -ste**) pieceworker

còttimo *m* piecework

còt·to **-ta** *adj* cooked; baked; burnt; suntanned; (joc) half-baked; (joc) in love; (sports) exhausted || *m* brick || *f see* **cotta**

cottura *f* cooking; **a punto di cottura** (culin) done just right

coutènte *mf* (law) joint user; (telp) party-line user

cóva *f* brooding; nest

covare (**cóvo**) *tr* to brood, to hatch; to harbor or nurse (*an enmity*); to nurture (*a disease*); **covare con gli occhi** to look fondly at; **covare le lenzuola** to loll around || *intr* to smolder (*said of fire or passion*)

covata *f* brood, covey

covile *m* doghouse; den

cóvo *m* shelter; den, lair; **farsi il covo** (fig) to gather a nestegg; **uscire dal covo** to stick one's nose out of the house

covóne *m* sheaf; cock (*of hay*)

còzza *f* cockle

cozzare (**còzzo**) *tr* to hit; to butt (*one's head*) || *intr* to butt; (fig) to clash;

cozzare contro to bump into || *ref* to hit one another; to fight

còzzo *m* butt; clash, conflict

crac *m* crash

crampo *m* cramp

cràni·co **-ca** *adj* (**-ci -che**) cranial

crà·nio *m* (**-ni**) cranium, skull

cràpula *f* excess (*in eating and drinking*)

cras·so **-sa** *adj* crass, gross; large (*intestine*)

cratère *m* crater; bomb crater

cràuti *mpl* sauerkraut

cravatta *f* tie, necktie; **cravatta a farfalla** bow tie; **fare cravatte** to be a usurer

creanza *f* politeness; **buona creanza** good manners

creare (**crèo**) *tr* to create; to name, elect

creati·vo **-va** *adj* creative

crea·to **-ta** *adj* created || *m* creation, universe

crea·tóre **-trice** *adj* creative || *mf* creator

creatura *f* creature; baby; **povera creatura!** poor thing!

creazióne *f* creation; (poet) election

credènte *adj* believing || *mf* believer

credènza *f* credence, faith, belief; sideboard, buffet; (coll) credit

credenziale *f* letter of credit; **credenziali** credentials

credenzière *m* butler

crédere §141 *tr* to believe; to think; **lo credo bene!** I should say so! || *intr* to believe; to trust; **credere a** to believe in; **credere in Dio** to believe in God || *ref* to believe oneself to be

credìbile *adj* credible

credibilità *f* credibility

crédito *m* credit

credi·tóre **-trice** *mf* creditor

crèdo *m* credo, creed

credulità *f* credulity

crèdu·lo **-la** *adj* credulous

crèma *f* cream; custard; **crema da scarpe** shoe polish; **crema di bellezza** beauty cream; **crema di pomodoro** cream of tomato soup; **crema evanescente** vanishing cream; **crema per barba** shaving cream

cremaglièra *f* rack; cogway, cograil

cremare (**crèmo**) *tr* to cremate

crema·tóio *m* (**-tói**) crematory

cremató·rio *m* (**-ri**) crematory

cremazióne *f* cremation

cremerìa *f* creamery

crèmisi *adj & m* crimson

Cremlino *m* Kremlin

cremlinologìa *f* Kremlinology

cremortàrtaro *m* cream of tartar

cremó·so **-sa** [s] *adj* creamy

crèn *m* horseradish

creolina *f* creolin

crè·olo **-la** *adj & mf* Creole

creosòto *m* creosote

crèpa *f* crack, crevice; rift

crepàc·cio *m* (**-ci**) crevasse; fissure

crepacuòre *m* heartbreak

crepapància *m*—**mangiare a crepapancia** to burst from eating too much

crepapèlle *m*—**ridere a crepapelle** to split one's sides laughing

crepare (**crèpo**) *intr* to burst; to crack; to chip; (slang) to croak; **crepare dalla sete** to die of thirst; **crepare dalle risa** to die laughing; **crepare d'invidia** to be green with envy

crepitare (**crèpito**) *intr* to crackle (*said of fire or weapons*); to rustle (*said of leaves*)

crepiti·o *m* (**-ìi**) crackle; rustle; pitter-patter (*of rain*)

crepuscolare *adj* twilight; (fig) dim

crepùscolo *m* twilight

crescènte *adj* rising, growing; crescent (*moon*) ‖ *m* (astr & heral) crescent

crescènza *f* growth

créscere §142 *tr* to grow, raise; to increase ‖ *intr* (ESSERE) to grow; to increase; to rise (*said, e.g., of prices*); to wax (*said of the moon*); **farsi crescere** to grow (*a beard*)

crescióne *m* watercress

créscita *f* growth; outgrowth; rise (*of water*)

crèsima *f* confirmation

cresimare (**crèsimo**) *tr* to confirm

Crèso *m* (mythol) Croesus

cré·spo -spa *adj* crispy, kinky; (archaic) wrinkled ‖ *m* crepe ‖ *f* wrinkle; ruffle

crésta *f* comb (*of chicken*); crest; **abbassare la cresta** to come down a peg or two; **alzare la cresta** to become insolent

crestàia *f* (coll) milliner

créta *f* clay

cretése [s] *adj* & *mf* Cretan

cretineria *f* idiocy

creti·no -na *adj* & *mf* idiot, cretin

cribro *m* (poet) sieve

cric·ca *f* (**-che**) clique, gang; group; crevice

cric·co *m* (**-chi**) (aut) jack

cricéto *m* hamster

cri cri *m* chirping (*of crickets*)

criminale *adj* criminal; (law) penal ‖ *mf* criminal

criminali·sta *mf* (**-sti -ste**) penal lawyer, criminal lawyer

criminalità *f* criminality

crìmine *m* crime

criminologia *f* criminology

criminòlo·go *m* (**-gi**) criminologist

criminó·so -sa [s] *adj* criminal

crinale *adj* (poet) hair ‖ *m* ridge (*of mountains*)

crine *m* horsehair; (poet) hair; (poet) sunbeam

crinièra *f* mane

crinolina *f* crinoline

cripta *f* crypt

criptocomuni·sta *mf* (**-sti -ste**) fellow traveler

crisàlide *f* chrysalis

crisantèmo *m* chrysanthemum

cri·si *f* (**-si**) crisis; shortage (*of houses*); attack (*e.g., of fever*); outburst (*of tears*); (econ) slump; **crisi ancillare** or **domestica** servant problem; **in crisi** in difficulties

cristalleria *f* glassware; crystal service; glassware shop; glassworks

cristallièra *f* china closet

cristalli·no -na *adj* crystalline ‖ *m* crystalline lens

cristallizzare [ddzz] *tr* & *ref* to crystallize

cristallo *m* crystal; glass; pane (*of glass*); windshield; **cristallo di rocca** rock crystal; **cristallo di sicurezza** (aut) safety glass

cristianaménte *adv* in a Christian manner, like a Christian; (coll) decently; **morire cristianamente** to die in the faith

cristianésimo *m* Christianity

cristianità *f* Christendom

cristia·no -na *adj* & *mf* Christian

Cristo *m* Christ; **avanti Cristo** before Christ (B.C.); **dopo Cristo** after Christ (A.D.); **un povero cristo** (slang) a poor guy

critè·rio *m* (**-ri**) criterion; judgment

crìti·ca *f* (**-che**) criticism; critique; slur

criticare §197 (**crìtico**) *tr* to criticize, censure; to find fault with

crìti·co -ca (**-ci -che**) *adj* critical ‖ *mf* critic; (coll) faultfinder ‖ *f* see **critica**

crittografia *f* cryptography

crittogram·ma *m* (**-mi**) cryptogram

crivellare (**crivèllo**) *tr* to riddle

crivèllo *m* sieve, riddle

croa·to -ta *adj* & *mf* Croatian

Croàzia, la Croatia

croccante *adj* crisp, crunchy ‖ *m* almond brittle, peanut brittle

crocchétta *f* croquette

cròcchia *f* chignon, topknot

crocchiare §287 (**cròcchio**) *intr* to crackle; to sound cracked or broken; to cluck (*said of a hen*); to crack (*said of joints*)

cròc·chio *m* (**-chi**) group (*of people*); **far crocchio** to gather around

cróce *f* cross; x (*mark made by illiterate person*); tail (*of coin*); (fig) trial; **Croce del Sud** Southern Cross; **croce di Malta** Maltese cross; **Croce Rossa** Red Cross; **croce uncinata** swastika; **fare una croce sopra** to forget about; **gettare la croce addosso** (fig) to put the blame on; **mettere in croce** to crucify

crocefisso *m* crucifix

crocerossìna *f* Red Cross worker

croceségno *m* cross, x (*mark made instead of signature*)

crocétta *f* (naut) crosstree

croce·vìa *m* (**-vìa**) crossroads, intersection

crocia·to -ta *adj* crossed; crusading; see **parola** ‖ *m* crusader ‖ *f* crusade

crocièra *f* cruise; (archit) cross (*vault*); (mach) cross (*of universal joint*)

crocière *m* (orn) crossbill

crocifiggere §104 *tr* to crucify

crocifissióne *f* crucifixion

crocifis·so -sa *adj* crucified ‖ *m* crucifix

crò·co *m* (**-chi**) crocus

crogiolare (**crògiolo**) *tr* to cook on a low fire; to simmer; to temper (*glass*) ‖ *ref* to bask; to snuggle (*e.g., in bed*)

crògiolo *m* cooking on a low fire; simmering; tempering (*of glass*)

crogiòlo *m* crucible; (fig) melting pot

crollare (**cròllo**) *tr* to shake (*e.g., one's head*) ‖ *intr* (ESSERE) to fall down, collapse ‖ *ref* to shake

cròllo *m* shake; fall, collapse

cròma *f* (mus) quaver

cromare (**cròmo**) *tr* to plate with chromium

croma·to -ta *adj* chromium-plated; chrome ‖ *m* chrome yellow

cromatura *f* chromium plating

cròmo *m* chrome, chromium

cromosfèra *f* chromosphere

cromosò·ma [s] *m* (**-mi**) chromosome

cròna·ca *f* (**-che**) chronicle; report, news; **cronaca bianca** news of the day; **cronaca giudiziaria** court news; **cronaca mondana** social column; **cronaca nera** police and accident report; **cronaca rosa** wedding column; stork news

cròni·co -ca (**-ci -che**) *adj* chronic ‖ *mf* incurable

croni·sta *mf* (**-sti -ste**) reporter; chronicler

cronistòria *f* chronicle

cronologìa *f* chronology

cronològi·co -ca *adj* (**-ci -che**) chronologic(al)

cronometrare (**cronòmetro**) *tr* to time

cronomètri·co -ca *adj* (**-ci -che**) chronometric(al); split-second

cronometri·sta *m* (**-sti**) (sports) timekeeper

cronòmetro *m* stopwatch; chronometer

crosciare §128 (**cròscio**) *tr* (archaic) to heave, throw ‖ *intr* to rustle (*said of dry leaves*); to pitter-patter (*said of rain*)

cròsta *f* crust; bark (*of tree*); scab; slough; shell (*of crustacean*); poor painting

crostàceo *m* crustacean

crostata *f* pie

crostino *m* toast

crostó·so -sa [s] *adj* crusty

croupier *m* (croupier) croupier

crucciare §128 *tr* to worry, vex; to chagrin ‖ *ref* to worry; to become angry

cruccia·to -ta *adj* afflicted; worried; angry; chagrined

crùc·cio *m* (**-ci**) sorrow; (obs) anger; **darsi cruccio** to fret

cruciale *adj* crucial

crucivèr·ba *m* (**-ba**) crossword puzzle

crudèle *adj* cruel

crudel·tà *f* (**-tà**) cruelty

crudézza *f* crudity; harshness

cru·do -da *adj* raw; rare (*meat*); (poet) cruel

cruèn·to -ta *adj* (lit) bloody

crumiro *m* scab (*in strikes*)

cruna *f* eye (*of a needle*)

cru·sca *f* (**-sche**) bran; (coll) freckles

cruscante *adj* Della-Cruscan; affected ‖ *m* member of the Accademia della Crusca

cruschèllo *m* middlings

cruscòtto *m* (aut) dashboard; (aer) instrument panel

cuba·no -na *adj* & *mf* Cuban

cubatura *f* volume

cùbi·co -ca *adj* (**-ci -che**) cubic; cube (*root*)

cubitale *adj* very large (*handwriting or type*)

cùbito *m* cubit; (poet) elbow

cubo *m* cube

cuccagna *f* plenty; windfall; Cockaigne

cuccétta *f* berth

cucchiàia *f* large spoon; ladle; trowel; bucket (*of power shovel*); **cucchiaia bucata** skimmer

cucchiaiàta *f* spoonful; tablespoonful

cucchiaino *m* teaspoon; teaspoonful; spoon (*lure*)

cuc·chiàio *m* (**-chiài**) spoon; spoonful; tablespoon; **cucchiaio da minestra** soupspoon

cucchiaióne *m* ladle

cùc·cia *f* (**-ce**) dog's bed; **a cuccia!** lie down!

cucciare §128 *intr* (ESSERE) & *ref* to lie down (*said of a dog*)

cucciolata *f* litter (*e.g., of puppies*)

cùcciolo *m* puppy; cub; (fig) greenhorn

cuc·co *m* (**-chi**) cuckoo; simpleton; darling (*child*)

cuccuru·cù *m* (**-cù**) cock-a-doodle-doo

cucina *f* kitchen; cuisine; kitchen range; **cucina componibile** kitchen with sectional cabinets; **cucina economica** kitchen range; **fare da cucina** to prepare a meal

cucinare *tr* to cook; (fig) to fix

cucinétta *f* kitchenette

cuciniè·re -ra *mf* cook

cucire §143 *tr* to sew; to stitch ‖ *ref*— **cucirsi la bocca** to keep one's mouth shut

cucirino *m* sewing thread

cuci·tóre -trice *adj* sewing ‖ *mf* sewing machine operator ‖ *f* seamstress; sewing machine (*for bookbinding*); **cucitrice a grappe** stapler

cuci·to -ta *adj* sewn ‖ *m* sewing; needlework

cucitura *f* seam; sewing; stitches

cu·cù *m* (**-cù**) cuckoo

cuculo or **cùculo** *m* cuckoo

cùffia *f* bonnet (*for baby*); coif; (rad) headset; (telp) headpiece; (theat) prompter's box

cugi·no -na *mf* cousin

cui *pron invar* whose; to which; whom; which; of whom; of which; **per cui** (coll) therefore

culatta *f* breech (*of a gun*)

culinà·rio -ria (**-ri -rie**) *adj* culinary ‖ *f* gastronomy

culla *f* cradle

cullare *tr* to rock (*a baby*); (fig) to delude ‖ *ref* to have delusions

culminante *adj* highest; culminating

culminare (**cùlmino**) *intr* to culminate

cùlmine *m* top, summit

culo *m* (vulg) behind; (slang) bottom (*of glass or bottle*): **culi di bicchiere** (coll) fake diamonds

cul·to -ta *adj* cultivated; learned (*e.g., word*) ‖ *m* cult, worship

cul·tóre -trice *mf* devotee

cultura *f* culture; **cultura fisica** physical culture

culturale *adj* cultural

cumino *m* (bot) caraway seed; (bot) cumin

cumulati·vo -va *adj* cumulative

cùmulo *m* heap, pile; concurrence (*of penal sentences*); cumulus

cuna *f* cradle

cùneo *m* wedge; chock; (archit) voussoir

cunétta *f* ditch; gutter

cunìcolo *m* small tunnel; burrow

cuòcere §144a *tr* to cook; to bake (*bricks*); to burn, dry up; (fig) to stew ‖ *intr* to cook; to burn; to dry up; (with *dat*) to grieve, to pain

cuò·co -ca *mf* (**-chi -che**) cook

cuòio *m* (**cuòi**) leather; **avere il cuoio duro** to have a tough hide; **cuoio capelluto** scalp ‖ *m* (**cuoia** *fpl*) (archaic) leather; **tirare le cuoia** (slang) to croak, to kick the bucket

cuòre *m* heart; **avere il cuore da coniglio** to be chicken-hearted; **avere il cuore da leone** to be lion-hearted; **cuori** (cards) hearts; **di cuore** gladly; heartily; **fare cuore a** to encourage; **stare a cuore** to be important

cupidìgia *f* cupidity, greed, covetousness

Cupido *m* Cupid

cùpi·do -da *adj* greedy, covetous

cu·po -pa *adj* dark; deep (*color, voice*); sad, gloomy

cùpola *f* dome, cupola; crown (*of hat*)

cura *f* care; interest; cure; ministry; (poet) anxiety; **a cura di** edited by (*e.g., text*)

curare *tr* to take care of; to heed ‖ *intr* to see to it ‖ *ref* to take care of oneself; to care; to deign; **curarsi di** to care for

curatèla *f* (law) guardianship

curati·vo -va *adj* curative

cura·to -ta *adj* cured; healed ‖ *m* curate

cura·tóre -trice *mf* curator; trustee; editor (*of critical edition*); receiver (*in bankruptcy*)

curculióne *m* (ent) weevil

cur·do -da *adj* & *mf* Kurd

cùria *f* curia; bar

curiale *adj* curia; legal

curiale·sco -sca *adj* (**-schi -sche**) hairsplitting, legalistic

curiosare [s] (**curióso**) *intr* to pry around, snoop; to browse around

curiosi·tà [s] *f* (**-tà**) curiosity; whim; curio

curió·so -sa [s] *adj* curious; bizarre, quaint

curro *m* roller

cursóre *m* process server; court messenger; slide (*of slide ruler*)

curva *f* curve, bend; sweep; **curva di livello** contour line

curvare *tr* to curve, bend; **curvare la fronte** to bow down, yield ‖ *intr* to curve (*said of a road*); to take a curve, negotiate a curve ‖ *ref* to curve, bend; to bow; to become bent; to warp

curvatura *f* curving, bending; warp; stoop, curvature; camber

cur·vo -va *adj* bent, curved ‖ *f* see **curva**

cuscinétto *m* small pillow; pad (*for ink*); buffer (*zone*); (mach) bearing; **cuscinetto a rulli** roller bearing; **cuscinetto a sfere** ball bearing

cuscino *m* pillow; cushion

cùspide *f* point (*e.g., of arrow*); (archit) steeple

custòde *adj* guardian (*angel*) ‖ *m* custodian; janitor; warden; guard; (coll) policeman, cop

custòdia *f* safekeeping, custody; case (*e.g., of violin*); trust; (mach) housing

custodire §176 *tr* to keep; to protect, guard; to be in charge of (*prisoners*); to take care of; to cherish (*a memory*)

cutàne·o -a *adj* cutaneous

cute *f* (anat) skin

cuticagna *f* (joc) nape of the neck

cuticola *f* epidermis; cuticle; dentine

cutireazióne *f* skin test (*for allergic reactions*)

cutréttola *f* (orn) wagtail

D

D, d [di] *m* & *f* fourth letter of the Italian alphabet

da *prep* from; to; at; on; through; between; since; with; by, e.g., **è stato arrestato dalla polizia** he was arrested by the police; worth, e.g., **un libro da mille lire** a book worth a thousand lire; worthy of, e.g., **azione da gentiluomo** action worthy of a gentleman; at the house, office, shop, etc., of, e.g., **dal pittore** at the house of the painter; **da Giovanni** at John's; **dall'avvocato** at the lawyer's office; **d'altro lato** on the other hand; **d'ora in poi** from now on

dabbasso *adv* downstairs; down below

dabbenàggine *f* simplicity, foolishness

dabbène *adj invar* honest, upright, e.g., **un uomo dabbene** an honest man; simple, foolish, e.g., **un dabben uomo** a Simple Simon

daccanto *adv* near, nearby

daccapo *adv* again, all over again; **andar daccapo** to begin a new paragraph; **daccapo a piedi** from top to bottom

dacché *conj* since

dado *m* cube; pedestal (*of column*); (mach) nut; (mach) die (*to cut threads*); **dadi** dice; **giocare ai dadi** to shoot craps; **il dado è tratto** the die is cast

daffare *m* things to do; bustle; **darsi daffare** to bustle, bustle about

da·ga *f* (**-ghe**) dagger

dagli §4 ‖ *interj*—**dagli al ladro!** stop thief!; **e dagli!** cut it out!

dài §4

dài·no -na *mf* fallow deer ‖ *m* fallow deer; buckskin

dal §4

dàlia *f* dahlia

dalla §4

dallato *adv* aside; sideways

dalle §4

dalli *interj*—**dalli al ladro!** stop thief!; **e dalli!** cut it out!

dallo §4

dàlma·ta *adj & mf* (**-ti -te**) Dalmatian

Dalmàzia, la Dalmatia

daltòni·co -ca *adj* (**-ci -che**) color-blind

daltonismo *m* color blindness

dama *f* lady; dancing partner; checkers; **andare a dama** (checkers) to be crowned; **dama di compagnia** companion; **dama di corte** lady-in-waiting

damare *tr* (checkers) to crown

damascare §197 *tr* to damask

damaschinare *tr* to damascene

dama·sco *m* (**-schi**) damask ‖ **Damasco** *f* Damascus

damerino *m* fop, dandy

damigèlla *f* (lit) damsel; (orn) demoiselle; **damigella d'onore** bridesmaid

damigiana *f* demijohn

danaro *m* var of **denaro**

danaró·so -sa [s] *adj* wealthy, rich

dande *fpl* leading strings

danése [s] *adj* Danish ‖ *mf* Dane ‖ *m* Danish (*language*); Great Dane

Danimarca, la Denmark

dannare *tr* to damn; to bedevil ‖ *ref* to be damned; to fret

danna·to -ta *adj* damned; wicked; terrible (*e.g., fear*) ‖ *m* damned soul

dannazione *f* damnation

danneggiare §290 (**dannéggio**) *tr* to damage; to injure, impair

danneggia·to -ta *adj* damaged; injured, impaired ‖ *mf* victim

danno *m* damage; injury; (ins) loss; **chiedere i danni** to ask for indemnification; **far danni a** to damage; **rifare i danni a** to indemnify; **tuo danno** so much the worse for you

dannó·so -sa [s] *adj* damaging, harmful

dante *m*—**pelle di dante** buckskin

danté·sco -sca *adj* (**-schi -sche**) Dantean, Dantesque

danti·sta *mf* (**-sti -ste**) Dante scholar

Danùbio *m* Danube

danza *f* dance; dancing

danzare *tr & intr* to dance

danza·tóre -trice *mf* dancer

dappertutto *adv* everywhere

dappiè *adv*—**dappiè di** at the foot of

dappiù *adv*—**dappiù di** more than

dappòco *adj invar* worthless

dappòi *adv* (obs) afterwards, after

dapprèsso *adv* near, nearby, close

dapprima *adv* first, in the first place

dapprincìpio *adv* first, in the beginning; over again

dardeggiare §290 (**dardéggio**) *tr* to hurl darts at; to beat down on; to look daggers at ‖ *intr* to hurl darts; to beat down

dardo *m* dart, arrow; tip (*of blowtorch*)

da·re *m* (**-re**) (com) debit; **dare e avere** debit and credit ‖ §144b *tr* to give; to set (*fire*); to hand over; to lay down (*one's life*); to render (*e.g., unto Caesar*); to give away (*a bride*); to take (*an examination*); to tender (*one's resignation*); to say (*good night*); to shed (*tears*); **dare acqua a** to water; **dare alla luce** to give birth to; to bring out (*e.g., a book*); **dare aria a** to air; **dare . . . anni a qlcu** to think that s.o. is . . . years old; **dare a ridire** to give rise to complaint; **dare da intendere** to lead to believe; **dare fastidio a** to bother, annoy; **dare fondo a** to use up; **dare gli otto giorni a** to dismiss, fire; **dare il benvenuto a** to welcome; **dare il vla a** to start (*e.g., a race*); **dare la colpa a** to declare guilty; to put the blame on; **dare la mano a** to shake hands with; **dare l'assalto a** to assault; **dare luogo a** to give rise to; **dare noia a** to bother; **dare per certo a** to assure; **dare ragione a** to agree with; **dare torto a** to disagree with; **dare via** to give away ‖ *intr* to burst; to begin; to beat down (*said of the sun*); **dare a** to verge on; to face, overlook; **dare addosso a** to attack, persecute; **dare ai** or **sui nervi di** to irritate, irk; **dare alla testa a** to go to one's head, e.g., **il vino gli dà alla testa** wine goes to his head; **dare contro a** to disagree with; **dare del ladro a** to call (s.o.) a thief; **dare del Lei a** to address formally; **dare del tu a** to address familiarly; **dare di volta il cervello a** to go raving mad, e.g., **gli ha dato di volta il cervello** he went raving mad; **dare giù** to abate; **dare in** to hit; **dare in affitto** to rent, lease; **dare nell'occhio** to attract attention; to hit the eye; **dare nel segno** to hit the target ‖ *ref* to put on, e.g., **darsi la cipria** to put powder on; **darsela a gambe** to take to one's heels; **darsela per intesa** to become convinced; to take for granted; **darsele** to strike one another; **darsi a** to give oneself over to; **darsi delle arie** to put on airs; **darsi il vanto di** to boast of; **darsi un bacio** to kiss one another; **darsi la mano** to shake hands; **darsi la morte** to commit suicide; **darsi pace** to resign oneself; **darsi pensiero** to worry; **darsi per malato** to declare oneself ill; to fall ill; **darsi per vinto** to give in, submit; **può darsi** it's possible, maybe; **si dà il caso** it happens

dàrsena *f* dock; basin

data *f* date; deal (*of cards*); **a . . . data** (com) . . . days hence, on or before . . . days; **di fresca data** new (*e.g., friend*); **di vecchia data** old (*e.g., friend*)

datare *tr* to date ‖ *intr*—**a datare da** beginning with

datà·rio *m* (**-ri**) date stamp

dati·vo -va *adj & m* dative

da·to -ta *adj* inclined, bent; addicted; given; appointed (*date*); **dato e non concesso** assumed for the sake of argument; **dato che** since || *m* **datum** || *f* see **data**

da·tóre -trice *mf* giver, donor; **datore di lavoro** employer; **datore di sangue** blood donor; **datori di lavoro** management

dàttero *m* date; (zool) date shell

dattilografare (dattilògrafo) *tr* to typewrite, type

dattilografía *f* typewriting

dattilògra·fo -fa *mf* typist

dattiloscopía *f* examination of fingerprints

dattiloscrit·to -ta *adj* typewritten || *m* typescript

dattórno *adv* near, nearby; **darsi dattorno** to strive; **stare dattorno a** to cling to; **togliersi dattorno qlcu** to get rid of s.o.

davanti *adj invar* fore, front || **davan·ti** *m* (**-ti**) front, face || *adv* ahead, in front; **davanti a** in front of; **levarsi davanti a qlcu** to get out of someone's way; **passare davanti a** to pass, outstrip

davanzale *m* window sill

davanzo *adv* more than enough

davvéro *adv* indeed; **dire davvero** to speak in earnest

daziare §287 *tr* to levy a duty on

dà·zio *m* (**-zi**) duty, custom; custom office

dèa *f* goddess

debellare (debèllo) *tr* (lit) to crush

debilitare (debìlito) *tr* to debilitate

debilitazióne *f* debilitation

débi·to -ta *adj* due || *m* debit; debt; **debito pubblico** national debt

debi·tóre -trice *mf* debtor

débole *adj* weak; faint; gentle (*sex*); **debole di mente** feeble-minded || *m* weakness, weak point; weakness, foible; weakling

debolézza *f* weakness, debility

debordare (debórdo) *intr* (ESSERE & AVERE) to overflow

debòscia *f* debauchery

deboscia·to -ta *adj* debauched || *mf* debauchee

debuttare *adj* beginning || *mf* beginner || *f* debutante

debuttare *intr* to come out, make one's debut; (theat) to perform for the first time; (theat) to open

debutto *m* debut; (theat) opening night, opening

dècade *f* ten; period of ten days; (mil) ten days' pay

decadènte *adj & m* decadent

decadènza *f* decadence; lapse (*of insurance policy*); (law) forfeiture

decadére §121 *intr* (ESSERE) to decline; to lose one's standing; (ins) to lapse; **decadere da** (law) to forfeit

decadiménto *m* decadence; (law) forfeiture

decadu·to -ta *adj* fallen upon hard times

decaffeinizzare [ddzz] *tr* to decaffeinate

decalcificatóre *m* water softener

decalcomanìa *f* decalcomania

decàlo·go *m* (**-ghi**) decalogue

decampare *intr* to decamp; **decampare da** to abandon (*a plan*)

decano *m* dean

decantare *tr* to praise, extol; to decant; (lit) to purify || *intr* to undergo decantation

decapàggio *m* (metallurgy) pickling

decapitare (decàpito) *tr* to behead, decapitate

decapitazióne *f* beheading

decappottàbile *adj & f* (aut) convertible

decèdere §123 *intr* (ESSERE) to die; to decease

decelerare (decèlero) *tr & intr* to decelerate

decennale *adj & m* decennial

decènne *adj & mf* ten-year-old

decèn·nio *m* (**-ni**) decade

decènte *adj* decent; proper

decentralizzare [ddzz] *tr* to decentralize

decentrare (decèntro) *tr* to decentralize

decènza *f* decency; propriety

decèsso *m* decease, demise

decìdere §145 *tr* to decide; to persuade || *intr & ref* to decide; **deciditi!** make up your mind!

decifràbile *adj* decipherable

decifrare *tr* to decipher, decode; (fig) to puzzle out (*e.g., somebody's intentions*); (mus) to sight-read

dècima *f* tithe

decimale *adj & m* decimal

decimare (dècimo) *tr* to decimate

decìmetro *m* decimeter; **doppio decimetro** ruler

dèci·mo -ma *adj, m & pron* tenth || *f* see **decima**

decisionale *adj* decision-making

decisióne *f* decision

decisi·vo -va *adj* decisive, conclusive

deci·so -sa *adj* determined, resolute; appointed (*time*)

declamare *tr* to declaim || *intr* to declaim; to inveigh

declamazióne *f* declamation

declaratò·rio -ria *adj* (**-ri -rie**) declarative

declinare *tr* to decline; to declare, show; (gram) to decline; (lit) to bend || *intr* to set (*said, e.g., of a star*); to slope; to diminish

declinazióne *f* declination; (gram) declension

declino *m* decline

declì·vio *m* (**-vi**) declivity, slope

decollàg·gio *m* (**-gi**) take-off; lift-off

decollare (decòllo) *tr* to decapitate || *intr* (aer) to take off; (lit) to bend || *intr* to set (*said, e.g., of a star*); to slope; to diminish

decòllo *m* take-off; lift-off

decolorante *adj* bleaching || *m* bleach

decompórre §218 *tr, intr & ref* to decompose

decomposizióne *f* decomposition

decompressióne *f* decompression

decongelare (decongèlo) *tr* to thaw; (com) to unfreeze

decontaminare (decontàmino) *tr* to decontaminate

decorare (decòro) *tr* to decorate

decorati·vo -va *adj* decorative

decora·tóre -trice *mf* decorator

decorazióne *f* decoration
decòro *m* decorum, propriety; decor; dignity; decoration
decoró·so -sa [s] *adj* fitting, decorous, proper; dignified
decorrènza *f* beginning, effective date; lapse
decórrere §139 *intr* (ESSERE) to elapse; to begin; (lit) to run; **a decorrere da** effective, beginning with
decór·so -sa *adj* past || *m* period, span; course; development; **nel decorso di** in the course of
decòt·to -ta *adj* (com) insolvent || *m* decoction
decozióne *f* (com) insolvency
decrèpi·to -ta *adj* decrepit
decréscere §142 *intr* (ESSERE) to decrease
decretare (decréto) *tr* to decree
decréto *m* decree; **decreto legge** decree law
decùbito *m* recumbency
decuplicare §197 (decùplico) *tr* to multiply tenfold
dècu·plo -pla *adj* tenfold || *m* tenfold part
decurtare *tr* to diminish, decrease
decurtazióne *f* decrease
dèda·lo -la *adj* (lit) ingenious || *m* maze, labyrinth
dèdi·ca *f* (-che) dedication; inscription (*in a book*)
dedicare §197 (dèdico) *tr* to dedicate; to inscribe (*a book*) || *ref* to devote oneself
dèdi·to -ta *adj* devoted; addicted
dedizióne *f* devotion; (obs) surrender
dedurre §102 *tr* to deduce; to deduct; to derive; (hist) to found (*a colony*)
deduzióne *f* deduction
defalcàbile *adj* deductible
defalcare §197 *tr* to deduct, withhold
defal·co *m* (-chi) deduction, withholding
defecare §197 (defèco) *tr* (chem) to purify || *intr* to defecate
defenestrare (defenèstro) *tr* to throw out of the window; (fig) to fire; (pol) to unseat
defenestrazióne *f* defenestration; (fig) firing, dismissal
deferènte *adj* deferential; (anat) deferent
deferènza *f* deference
deferire §176 *tr* to submit; (law) to commit; **deferire il giuramento a qlcu** to put s.o. under oath || *intr* to defer
defezionare (defezióno) *intr* to desert, defect
defezióne *f* defection
deficiènte *adj* deficient, lacking || *mf* idiot
deficiènza *f* deficiency; idiocy
dèfi·cit *m* (-cit) deficit
deficità·rio -ria *adj* (-ri -rie) lacking; deficit (*e.g., budget*)
defilare *tr* to defilade || *ref* to protect oneself
denfinìbile *adj* definable
definire §176 *tr* to define; to settle (*an argument*)

definiti·vo -va *adj* definitive; **in definitiva** after all
defini·to -ta *adj* definite
definizióne *f* definition; settlement (*of an argument*)
deflagrare *intr* to burst into flame; (fig) to burst out
deflazionare (deflazióno) *tr* (com) to deflate
deflazióne *f* deflation
deflèttere §177 *intr* to deflect
deflettóre *m* (aut) vent window; (mach) baffle
deflorare (deflòro) *tr* to deflower
defluire §176 *intr* (ESSERE) to flow down; (fig) to pour out
deflusso *m* flow; outflow, outpour; ebbtide
deformare (defórmo) *tr* to deform; to cripple; to alter (*a word*)
defórme *adj* deformed, crippled
deformi·tà *f* (-tà) deformity
defraudare (defràudo) *tr* to defraud, bilk
defun·to -ta *adj* dead; deceased; defunct; late || *mf* dead person, deceased || *m* deceased; **i defunti** the deceased
degenerare (degènero) *intr* (ESSERE & AVERE) to degenerate; to worsen
degenera·to -ta *adj* degenerate, perverted || *mf* degenerate, pervert
degenerazióne *f* degeneracy, degeneration
degènere *adj* degenerate
degènte *adj* bedridden; hospitalized || *mf* patient; inpatient
degènza *f* confinement; hospitalization
dégli §4
deglutire §176 *tr* to swallow
degnare (dégno) *tr* to honor || *ref* to deign, condescend
degnazióne *f* condescension
dé·gno -gna *adj* worthy; **degno di nota** noteworthy
degradante *adj* degrading
degradare *tr* to degrade; to downgrade; (mil) to break || *ref* to become degraded
degradazióne *f* degradation
degustare *tr* to taste
degustazióne *f* tasting
dèh *interj* oh!
déi §4
deiezióne *f* excrement; (geol) detritus
deificare §197 (deìfico) *tr* to deify
dei·tà *f* (-tà) deity
dèl §4
dela·tóre -trice *mf* informer
delazióne *f* informing; (law) administration of an oath
dèle·ga *f* (-ghe) proxy, power of attorney
delegare §209 (dèlego) *tr* to delegate
delega·to -ta *adj* delegated || *m* delegate; (eccl) legate
delegazióne *f* delegation
deletè·rio -ria *adj* (-ri -rie) deleterious
delfino *m* dolphin; (hist) dauphin
delibare *tr* to relish; to touch on; to ratify (*a foreign decree*)

delibazióne *f* ratification (*of a foreign decree*)

deliberare (delìbero) *tr* to deliberate; to decide; to award (*at auction*) || *intr* to deliberate

delibera·to -ta *adj* deliberate; resolved

deliberazióne *f* deliberation; decision

delicatézza *f* delicacy; gentleness; tactfulness; luxury

delica·to -ta *adj* delicate; gentle; tactful

delimitare (delìmito) *tr* to delimit

delineare (delìneo) *tr* to outline, sketch || *ref* to take shape; to appear

delinquènte *m* criminal

delinquènza *f* delinquency; delinquenza minorile juvenile delinquency

delìnquere §146 *intr* to commit a crime

delì·quio *m* (-qui) fainting spell, swoon; cadere in deliquio to faint

delirare *intr* to be delirious; to rave; (lit) to stray

delì·rio *m* (-ri) delirium; frenzy; andare in delirio to go wild; cadere in delirio to become delirious

delitto *m* crime

delittuó·so -sa [s] *adj* criminal

delìzia *f* delight; (hort) Delicious (*variety of apple*)

deliziare §287 *tr & ref* to delight

delizió·so -sa [s] *adj* delicious; delightful

délla §4

délle §4

déllo §4

dèl·ta *m* (-ta) delta

delucidare (delùcido) *tr* to elucidate; to remove the sheen from

delucidazióne *f* elucidation; removal of sheen

delùdere §105 *tr* to disappoint; to deceive; to foil

delusióne *f* disappointment; deception

delu·so -sa *adj* disappointed; deceived

demagnetizzare [ddzz] *tr* to demagnetize

demagogìa *f* demagogy

demagò·go *m* (-ghi) demagogue

demandare *tr* (law) to commit

demà·nio *m* (-ni) state land, state property

demarcare §197 *tr* to demarcate

demarcazióne *f* demarcation

demènte *adj* demented, crazy; idiotic || *mf* insane person; idiot

demènza *f* insanity, madness; idiocy

demèrito *m* demerit

demilitarizzare [ddzz] *tr* to demilitarize

democrà·ti·co -ca (-ci -che) *adj* democratic || *mf* democrat

democrazìa *f* democracy || Democrazia Cristiana Christian Democratic Party

democristia·no -na *adj* Christian Democratic || *mf* Christian Democrat

demogrà·fi·co -ca *adj* (-ci -che) demographic

demolire §176 *tr* to demolish

demoli·tóre -trice *adj* wrecking; destructive || *mf* wrecker

demolizióne *f* demolition

dèmone *m* demon

demonìa·co -ca *adj* (-ci -che) fiendish; demoniacal

demò·nio *m* (-ni) demon; avere il demonio addosso to be full of the devil

demoralizzare [ddzz] *tr* to demoralize || *ref* to become demoralized

demoralizza·to -ta [ddzz] *adj* demoralized, dejected

denaro *m* money; denier (*of nylon thread*); avere il denaro contato to be short of money; denari suit of Neapolitan cards corresponding to diamonds

denatura·to -ta *adj* denatured

denegare §209 (dènego or denégo) *tr* to deny

denigrare *tr* to denigrate; to backbite

denominare (denòmino) *tr* to call, designate

denomina·tóre -trice *adj* designating || *m* denominator

denominazióne *f* denomination; designation

denotare (denòto) *tr* to denote

densi·tà *f* (-tà) density

dèn·so -sa *adj* dense, thick

dentale *adj & f* dental

dentare (dènto) *tr* to notch, scallop || *intr* to teethe

dentaruòlo *m* teething ring

denta·to -ta *adj* toothed

dentatura *f* set of teeth; teeth (*of gear*)

dènte *m* tooth; peak (*of mountain*); pang (*of jealousy*); fluke (*of anchor*); prong (*of fork*); battere i denti to shiver; dente canino canine tooth; dente del giudizio wisdom tooth; dente di latte baby tooth; dente di leone (bot) dandelion; mettere i denti to teethe

dentellare (dentèllo) *tr* to notch, scallop; to perforate (*stamps*)

dentellatura *f* notch; perforation (*of postage stamps*); (archit) denticulation

dentèllo *m* notch, scallop; lace; (archit) dentil

dentièra *f* denture, plate; cog

dentifrì·cio -cia (-ci -cie) *adj* tooth || *m* dentifrice

denti·sta *mf* (-sti -ste) dentist

dentizióne *f* teething

déntro *adv* inside, in; dentro di inside of; within; essere dentro (coll) to be behind bars; in dentro inward || *prep* inside of

denuclearizzare [ddzz] *tr* to denuclearize

denudare *tr* to denude; to strip; (lit) to unveil

denunciare §128 *tr* var of denunziare

denùnzia *f* denunciation; announcement; report

denunziare §287 *tr* to denounce; to accuse; to announce; to report

denutri·to -ta *adj* undernourished

denutrizióne *f* undernourishment

deodorante *adj & m* deodorant

deodorare (deodóro) *tr* to deodorize

depauperare (depàupero) *tr* to impoverish

depennare (depénno) *tr* to strike out, expunge

deperìbile *adj* perishable

deperiménto *m* deterioration; decline

deperire §176 *intr* (ESSERE) to deteriorate; to perish; to decay

depilatò·rio -ria *adj & m* (**-ri -rie**) depilatory

deplorare (**deplòro**) *tr* to deplore; to reproach

deplorévole *adj* deplorable; reproachable

depolarizzare [ddzz] *tr* to depolarize

depórre §218 *tr* to lay; to lay down (*crown, arms*); to depose (*e.g., a king*); to take off (*clothes*); to give up (*hope*); to renounce; **deporre l'abito talare** to doff the cassock

deportare (**depòrto**) *tr* to deport

deporta·to -ta *adj* deported || *mf* deportee

deportazióne *f* deportation

depositare (**depòsito**) *tr* to deposit; to register, check || *intr* to settle (*said, e.g., of sand*)

depos**ità·rio -ria** (**-ri -rie**) *adj* deposit || *mf* depositary

depòsito *m* deposit; checking (*e.g., of a suitcase*); registration; heap (*e.g., of refuse*); warehouse; morgue; receiving ward; (mil) depot; **deposito bagagli** baggage room

deposizióne *f* deposition; Descent from the Cross

deprava·to -ta *adj* depraved

depravazióne *f* depravation

deprecare §197 (**deprèco**) *tr* to deprecate

depredare (**deprèdo**) *tr* to plunder

depredazióne *f* depredation

depressióne *f* depression

deprès·so -sa *adj* depressed

deprezzaménto *m* depreciation

deprezzare (**deprèzzo**) *tr* to depreciate; to underestimate || *intr* (ESSERE) to depreciate

deprimènte *adj* depressing

deprìmere §131 *tr* to humble, discourage; to depress

depurare *tr* to purify

deputare (**dèputo**) *tr* to deputize, delegate

deputa·to -ta *mf* deputy, delegate; representative

deputazióne *f* deputation, delegation

deragliaménto *m* derailment

deragliare §280 *intr* to be derailed, to run off the track

derapàg·gio *m* (**-gi**) skidding

derapare *intr* to skid

derelit·to -ta *adj & mf* derelict

derelizióne *f* dereliction

dereta·no -na *adj & m* posterior

deridere §231 *tr* to deride, mock

derisióne *f* derision, ridicule

derisò·rio -ria *adj* (**-ri -rie**) derisory, derisive

deriva *f* (aer) vertical stabilizer; (aer, naut) leeway; (naut) drift; **alla deriva** adrift

derivare *tr* to derive; to branch off (*e.g., a canal*) || *intr* (ESSERE) to be derived, arise; to drift

deriva·to -ta *adj* derivative || *m* derivative (*word*) || *f* (math) derivative

derivazióne *f* derivation; (elec) shunt; (telp) extension

dermatòlo·go *m* (**-gi**) dermatologist

dermòide *f* imitation leather

dèro·ga *f* (**-ghe**) exception; **in deroga a** deviating from

derogare §209 (**dèrogo**) *intr* to transgress; **derogare a** to deviate from

derrata *f* foodstuff; **derrate** foodstuff, produce

derubare *tr* to rob

dèr·vis *m* (**-vis**) or **dervì·scio** *m* (**-sci**) dervish

desalazióne [s] *f* desalinization

desalificare [s] §197 (**desalìfico**) *tr* to desalt

dé·sco *m* (**-schi**) dinner table; meal

descritti·vo -va *adj* descriptive

descrìvere §250 *tr* to describe

descrizióne *f* description

desegregazióne [s] *f* desegregation

desensibilizzare [s] [ddzz] *tr* to desensitize

desèrti·co -ca *adj* (**-ci -che**) desert, wild

desèr·to -ta *adj* deserted; **andare deserto** to be unattended || *m* desert

desideràbile [s] *adj* desirable

desiderare (**desìdero**) [s] *tr* to desire; **farsi desiderare** to make oneself scarce; to be dilatory

desidè·rio [s] *m* (**-rî**) desire; craving; lust; **lasciar desiderio di sé** to be greatly missed

desideró·so -sa [s] *adj* desirous

designare [s] *tr* to designate

designazióne [s] *f* designation

desinare *m* dinner || *intr* to dine

desinènza *f* (gram) ending

desì·o *m* (**-î**) (lit) desire

desìstere [s] §114 *intr* to desist

desolante *adj* distressing

desolare (**dèsolo**) *tr* to distress; (lit) to devastate

desola·to -ta *adj* desolate; distressed

desolazióne *f* desolation; distress

dèspo·ta *m* (**-ti**) despot

despòti·co -ca *adj* (**-ci -che**) var of dispotico

despotismo *m* var of dispotismo

des·sèrt *m* (**-sèrt**) dessert

destare (**dèsto**) *tr* to awaken; to stir up || *ref* to wake up

destinare *tr* to destine; to assign; to address

destinatà·rio -ria *mf* (**-ri -rie**) consignee; addressee

destinazióne *f* destination; assignment

destino *m* destiny; (com) destination

destituire §114 *tr* to demote; to dismiss; to deprive

destituzióne *f* demotion; dismissal

dé·sto -sta *adj* awake; (fig) wide-awake

dèstra *f* right, right hand

destreggiare §290 (**destréggio**) *intr* to maneuver || *ref* to manage shrewdly

destrézza *f* skill, dexterity

destrière or **destrièro** *m* (lit) steed

dè·stro -stra *adj* right; skillful || *f* see **destra**

destròr·so -sa *adj* clockwise; right-hand; (bot) dextrorse

destròsio *m* dextrose

desùmere [s] §116 *tr* to obtain; to infer
detecti·ve *m* (-ve) detective
detèc·tor *m* (-tor) (rad) detector
detenére §271 *tr* to hold; to detain
deten·tóre -trice *mf* holder; receiver (*of stolen goods*)
detenu·to -ta *mf* prisoner
detenzióne *f* illegal possession; detention
detergènte *adj & m* detergent
detèrgere §164 (*pp* detèrso) *tr* to cleanse; to wipe
deterioràbile *adj* perishable
deteriorare (deterióro) *tr* to spoil || *intr* (ESSERE) & *ref* to deteriorate, spoil
determinare (detèrmino) *tr* to determine; to fix; to decide; to cause || *ref* to decide; to happen
determinatézza *f* determination; precision
determinati·vo -va *adj* (gram) definite
determina·to -ta *adj* given; resolved, determined
determinazióne *f* determination
deterrènte *adj & m* deterrent
detersi·vo -va *adj* cleansing || *m* cleanser; detergent
detestàbile *adj* detestable
detestare (detèsto) *tr* to detest
detettóre *m* detector; **detettore di bugie** lie detector
detonare (detòno) *intr* to explode, detonate
detonatóre *m* blasting cap, detonator
detonazióne *f* detonation; report
detrarre §273 *tr* to take away; (lit) to detract
detrat·tóre -trice *mf* detractor
detrazióne *f* detraction; deduction
detriménto *m* detriment
detrito *m* debris; detritus; (fig) outcast, outlaw
detronizzare [ddzz] *tr* to dethrone
détta *f*—**a detta di** according to
dettagliante *m* retailer
dettagliare §280 *tr* to tell in detail; to itemize; to retail || *intr*—**pregasi dettagliare** please send detailed information
dettà·glio *m* (-gli) detail; retail
dettame *m* (lit) law, norm
dettare (dètto) *tr* to dictate; (lit) to compose, write; **dettar legge** to impose one's will
dettato *m* dictation; (lit) style
dettatura *f* dictation
dét·to -ta *adj* called, named; **detto (e) fatto** no sooner said than done || *m* saying || *f* see detta
deturpare *tr* to disfigure, mar
deturpazióne *f* disfigurement, disfiguration
devalutazióne *f* devaluation
devastare *tr* to devastate, lay waste; (fig) to disfigure
devasta·tóre -trice *adj* devastating || *m* devastator
devastazióne *f* devastation
deviaménto *m* switching; derailment; (fig) straying
deviare §119 *tr* to turn aside; to lead astray; (rr) to switch; (rr) to derail

|| *intr* to deviate; to wander; to go astray; (rr) to run off the track
deviatóre *m* (rr) switchman; (elec) two-way switch
deviazióne *f* deviation; detour; curvature (*of the spine*); (phys) declination; (phys) deflection; (rr) switching
deviazionismo *m* deviationism
deviazioni·sta *mf* (-sti -ste) deviationist
devoluzióne *f* transfer
devòlvere §147 *tr* to transfer || *intr & ref* (lit) to roll down
devò·to -ta *adj* devoted; devout, pious || *m* devout person; worshiper
devozióne *f* devotion
di §4 *prep* of; in, e.g., **la più bella della famiglia** the prettiest one in the family; (*with definite article*) some, e.g., **mi occorrono dei fiammiferi** I need some matches; than, e.g., **più veloce del baleno** faster than lightning; from, e.g., **è di Milano** he is from Milan; off, e.g., **smontare di sella** to get off the saddle; about, e.g., **discutere di politica** to talk about politics; with, e.g., **ornare di fiori** to adorn with flowers; made of, e.g., **una casa di mattoni** a house made of bricks; by, e.g., **di notte** by night; for, e.g., **amor di patria** love for one's country; worth, e.g., **casa di dieci milioni** house worth ten million; in the amount of, e.g., **multa di mille lire** fine in the amount of one thousand lire; son of, e.g., **Carlo Giovannini di Filippo** Carlo Giovannini son of Philip; daughter of, e.g., **Anna Ponti di Antonio** Anna Ponti daughter of Anthony; **di corsa** running; **di gran lunga** greatly; by far; **di . . . in** from . . . to; **di là da** beyond; **di nascosto** stealthily; **di qua da** on this side of; **di quando in quando** from time to time; **di tre metri** three meters long or wide or high
dì *m* (dì) day; **a dì** (e.g., **ventisei**) this (e.g., twenty-sixth) day; **conciare per il dì delle feste** (coll) to beat up
diabète *m* diabetes
diabèti·co -ca *adj & mf* (-ci -che) diabetic
diabòli·co -ca *adj* (-ci -che) diabolic(al)
diàcono *m* deacon
diadè·ma *m* (-mi) diadem (*of king*); tiara (*of lady*)
diàfa·no -na *adj* diaphanous
diafonìa *f* (telp) cross talk
diafram·ma *m* (-mi) diaphragm; (fig) partition
diàgno·si *f* (-si) diagnosis
diagnosticare §197 (diagnòstico) *tr* to diagnose
diagonale *adj & f* diagonal
diagram·ma *m* (-mi) diagram; chart
diagrammare *tr* to diagram
dialettale *adj* dialectal
dialètti·co -ca (-ci -che) *adj* dialectic(al) || *m* dialectician || *f* dialectic; (philos) dialectics
dialètto *m* dialect
dialettòfo·no -na *adj* dialect-speaking || *m* dialect-speaking person

dialogare §209 (**diàlogo**) *intr* to carry on a dialogue

dialoga·to -ta *adj* written in the form of a dialogue || *m* dialogue

diàlo·go *m* (-ghi) dialogue

diamante *m* diamond; **diamante tagliavetro** glass cutter

diametrale *adj* diametric(al)

diàmetro *m* diameter

diàmine *interj* good heavens!; the devil!; sure!

diana *f* (mil) reveille || **Diana** *f* Diana

dianzi *adv* (lit) a short while ago

diàpa·son *m* (-son) (mus) pitch; (mus) tuning fork

diapositiva *f* (phot) slide, transparency

dià·rio -ria (-ri -rie) *adj* daily || *m* diary; journal; **diario scolastico** homework book || *f* per diem

diarrèa *f* diarrhea

diascò·pio *m* (-pi) slide projector

diàspro *m* jasper

diàstole *f* diastole

diatermìa *f* diathermy

diatriba *f* diatribe

diavolàc·cio *m* (-ci) devil; **buon diavolaccio** good fellow

diavolerìa *f* deviltry; devilment; evil plot

diavolè·rio *m* (-ri) hubbub, uproar

diavoléto *m* hubbub, uproar

diavolétto *m* little devil, imp

diàvolo *m* devil; **avere il diavolo in corpo** to be nervous; **avere un diavolo per capello** to be in a horrible mood; **buon diavolo** good fellow; **essere come il diavolo e l'acqua santa** to be at opposite poles; **fare il diavolo a quattro** to make a racket; to try very hard

dibàttere *tr* to debate || *ref* to struggle; to writhe

dibattiménto *m* debate; (law) pleading, trial

dibàttito *m* debate

dicastèro *m* department, ministry

dicèmbre *m* December

dicerìa *f* rumor, gossip

dichiarare *tr* to declare, state; to find (*guilty*); to proclaim; to nominate, name || *ref* to declare oneself to be; to declare one's love; to plead (*e.g., guilty*)

dichiarazióne *f* declaration; avowal (*of love*); return (*of income tax*); **dichiarazioni** representations

diciannòve *adj & pron* nineteen; **le diciannove** seven P.M. || *m* nineteen; nineteenth (*in dates*)

diciannovèsi·mo -ma *adj, m & pron* nineteenth

diciassètte *adj & pron* seventeen; **le diciassette** five P.M. || *m* seventeen; seventeenth (*in dates*)

diciassettèsi·mo -ma *adj, m & pron* seventeenth

diciottèsi·mo -ma *adj, m & pron* eighteenth

diciòtto *adj & pron* eighteen; **le diciotto** six P.M. || *m* eighteen; eighteenth (*in dates*)

dici·tóre -trice *mf* reciter

dicitura *f* caption, legend; (lit) wording, language

dicotomìa *f* dichotomy

didascalìa *f* note, notice; caption; legend (*e.g., on coin*); (mov) subtitle

didascàli·co -ca *adj* (-ci -che) didactic

didàtti·co -ca (-ci -che) *adj* didactic; elementary school (*director, principal*) || *f* didactics

didéntro *m* (coll) inside

didiètro *m* behind; back (*of house*) || *adv* behind

dièci *adj & pron* ten; **le dieci** ten o'clock || *m* ten; tenth (*in dates*)

diecimila *adj, m & pron* ten thousand

diecina *f* about ten

dière·si *f* (-si) dieresis

diè·sis *m* (-sis) (mus) sharp

dièta *f* diet; **dieta idrica** fluid diet

dietèti·co -ca (-ci -che) *adj* dietetic || *f* dietetics

dieti·sta *mf* (-sti -ste) dietitian

diètro *adj invar* back, rear || *m* back, rear || *adv* back, behind; **dal di dietro** from behind; **di dietro** hind (*legs*); back (*side*); behind, back (*e.g., of cupboard*) || *prep* behind; beyond; after; upon; **dietro a** behind; beyond; after; according to; **dietro consegna** on delivery; **dietro domanda** upon application; **dietro versamento** upon payment; **essere dietro a** to be in the process of

dietrofrónt *m* (mil) about face

difatti *adv* indeed

difèndere §148 *tr* to defend, protect || *ref* to protect oneself; (coll) to get along

difensi·vo -va *adj & f* defensive

difen·sóre -sóra or **difenditrice** *adj* defense || *mf* defender

difésa [s] *f* defense; bulwark; protection; **legittima difesa** self-defense; **pigliare le difese di** to defend, back up; **venire in difesa di** to go to the defense of

difettare (**difétto**) *intr* to be lacking; to be defective; **difettare di** to lack

difetti·vo -va *adj* defective

difètto *m* lack; blemish; fault; defect; **essere in difetto** to be at fault; **far difetto a** to lack, e.g., **gli fa difetto il denaro** he lacks money

difettó·so -sa [s] *adj* defective

diffamare *tr* to defame, slander

diffama·tóre -trice *mf* defamer, slanderer

diffamazióne *f* defamation, slander

differènte *adj* different

differènza *f* difference; spread; variance; **a differenza di** unlike; **c'è una bella differenza** it's a horse of another color

differenziale *adj & m* differential

differenziare §287 (**differènzio**) *tr* to differentiate

differiménto *m* deferment

differire §176 *tr* to postpone, defer || *intr* to be different; to differ

difficile *adj* hard, difficult; awkward (*situation*); hard-to-please; unlikely

|| *mf* hard-to-please person || *m—* **fare il difficile** to be hard to please; **qui sta il difficile!** here's the trouble!

difficol·tà *f* (-tà) difficulty; defect; obstacle; objection

difficoltó·so -sa [*s*] *adj* difficult, troublesome; fastidious

diffida *f* notice; warning

diffidare *tr* to give notice to; to warn || *intr* to mistrust

diffidènte *adj* distrustful

diffidènza *f* mistrust

diffóndere §178 *tr* to spread; to circulate; to broadcast || *ref* to spread; to dwell at length

diffórme *adj* unlike; (obs) deformed

diffrazióne *f* diffraction

diffusióne *f* spreading; circulation (*of a newspaper*); diffusion; (rad) broadcast

diffu·so -sa *adj* diffuse; widespread

diffusóre *m* diffuser (*to soften light*); baffle (*of loudspeaker*); (mach) choke

difilato *adv* forthwith, right away

difrónte *adj invar* in front

difterite *f* diphtheria

di·ga *f* (-ghe) dike; dam

digerènte *adj* alimentary (*canal*), digestive (*tube*)

digeríbile *adj* digestible

digerire §176 *tr* to digest; to tolerate, stand

digestióne *f* digestion

digesti·vo -va *adj* digestive

digèsto *m* digest

digitale *adj* digital || *f* (bot) digitalis

digitalina *f* (pharm) digitalin

digiunare *intr* to fast

digiu·no -na *adj* without food; deprived; **digiuno di cognizioni** ignorant; **tenere digiuno** to keep in ignorance || *m* fast; **a digiuno** on an empty stomach; **fare digiuno** to fast

digni·tà *f* (-tà) dignity; **dignità** *fpl* dignitaries

dignità·rio *m* (-ri) dignitary

dignitó·so -sa [*s*] *adj* dignified

digradare *tr* to shade (*colors*) || *intr* to slope; to fade

digredire §176 *intr* to digress

digressióne *f* digression

digrignare *tr* to show (*one's or its teeth*); to grit (*one's teeth*)

digrossare (**digròsso**) *tr* to rough-hew; to whittle down; (fig) to refine || *ref* to become refined

diguazzare *tr* to beat (*a liquid*) || *intr* to wallow; to splash

dilagare §209 *intr* to flood, to overflow; to spread abroad

dilaniare §287 *tr* to tear to pieces || *ref* to slander one another

dilapidare (**dilàpido**) *tr* to squander

dilatare *tr* to expand; to dilate || *ref* to expand; to spread

dilatazióne *f* expansion; dilation

dilatò·rio -ria *adj* (-ri -rie) delaying; dilatory

dilavare *tr* to wash away, erode

dilava·tó -ta *adj* dull, flat; wan

dilazionare (**dilazióno**) *tr* to delay, put off; (com) to extend

dilazióne *f* delay; (com) extension

dileggiare §290 (**diléggio**) *tr* to mock

dilég·gio *m* (-gi) mockery, scoffing; **mettere in dileggio** to scoff at

dileguare (**diléguo**) *tr* to scatter || *intr* (ESSERE) to disappear, vanish; to melt

dilèm·ma *m* (-mi) dilemma

dilettante *mf* amateur; dilettante

dilettanté·sco -sca *adj* (-schi -sche) amateurish

dilettare (**dilètto**) *tr* to delight || *ref* to delight; **dilettarsi a** + *inf* to delight in + *ger*; **dilettarsi di** to pursue as a hobby, e.g., **si diletta di pittura** he pursues painting as a hobby

dilettévole *adj* delectable, delightful

dilèt·to -ta *adj* beloved || *m* loved one; pleasure; hobby

diligènte *adj* diligent

diligènza *f* diligence; stagecoach

dilucidare (**dilùcido**) *tr* to elucidate

diluire §176 *tr* to dilute

dilungare §209 *tr* (archaic) to stretch || *ref* to expatiate; to be ahead by several lengths (*said of a race horse*)

dilungo *m—a* **un dilungo** more or less

diluviare §287 *tr* to devour || *intr* (ESSERE & AVERE) to rain (*said, e.g., of bullets*) || *impers* (ESSERE)—**diluvia** it is pouring

dilù·vio *m* (-vi) deluge, flood; **diluvio universale** Flood

dimagrante *adj* reducing

dimagrare *tr* to thin down || *intr* (ESSERE) to become thin; to lose weight; to become exhausted (*said of land*); (fig) to become meager

dimagrire §176 *intr* (ESSERE) to become thin; to lose weight, reduce

dimanda *f* var of **domanda**

dimane *adv* (coll) tomorrow

dimani *m & adv* var of **domani**

dimenare (**diméno**) *tr* to wag (*the tail*); to beat (*eggs*); to wave (*one's arms*); to stir up (*a question*) || *ref* to toss; to busy oneself

dimensióne *f* dimension; (fig) nature

dimenticanza *f* oversight, neglect; **andare in dimenticanza** to be forgotten

dimenticare §197 (**diméntico**) *tr* to forget; to forgive || *ref* to forget; **dimenticarsi di** to forget; to neglect

dimenticatóio *m—***mettere nel dimenticatoio** (coll) to forget

diménti·co -ca *adj* (-chi -che) forgetful; neglectful

dimés·so -sa *adj* humble, modest (*demeanor*); low (*voice*); shabby (*clothes*)

dimestichézza *f* familiarity

diméttere §198 *tr* to dismiss; to release || *ref* to resign

dimezzare [*ddzz*] (**dimèzzo**) *tr* to halve

diminuire §176 *tr* to lessen, reduce; to lower (*prices*) || *intr* (ESSERE) to diminish

diminuti·vo -va *adj & m* diminutive

diminuzióne *f* diminution

dimissionare (**dimissióno**) *tr* to dismiss, discharge || *ref* to resign

dimissionà·rio -ria *adj* (-ri -rie) resigning, outgoing

dimissióne *f* resignation; **dare le dimis-sioni** to resign.

dimól•to **-ta** *adj & m* (coll) much || **dimolto** *adv* (coll) much

dimòra *f* stay; residence; (lit) delay; **mettere a dimora** to install; to plant (*trees*); **senza dimora** (lit) without delay; **senza fissa dimora** vagrant

dimorare (**dimòro**) *intr* to stay; to reside; (lit) to delay

dimostràbile *adj* demonstrable

dimostrante *m* demonstrator

dimostrare (**dimóstro**) *tr* to demonstrate; to register (*e.g., anger*); **dimostrare trent'anni** to look thirty || *intr* to demonstrate || *ref* to prove oneself to be

dimostrati•vo **-va** *adj* demonstrative; (mil) diverting

dimostra•tóre **-trice** *mf* demonstrator

dimostrazióne *f* demonstration

dinàmi•co **-ca** (**•ci •che**) *adj* dynamic || *f* dynamics

dinamismo *m* dynamism

dinamite *f* dynamite

dìna•mo *f* (**-mo**) generator, dynamo

dinanzi *adj invar* front, e.g., **la porta dinanzi** the front door; preceding, e.g., **il mese dinanzi** the preceding month || *adv* ahead; beforehand; (lit) before; **dinanzi a** before, in front of

dina•sta *m* (**-sti**) dynast

dinastìa *f* dynasty

dinàsti•co **-ca** *adj* (**-ci •che**) dynastic

dìndo *m* (coll) turkey

dindòn *m* ding-dong || *interj* ding-dong!

diniè•go *m* (**-ghi**) denial

dinoccola•to **-ta** *adj* gangling; clumsy (*gait*)

dinosàuro [s] *m* dinosaur

dintórno *m*—**dintorni** surroundings, neighborhood || *adv* around; **dintorno a** around

dì•o **-a** *adj* (**-i -e**) (poet) godly || *m* (**dèi**) god; **gli dei** the gods || **Dìo** *m* God; **che Dio la manda** cats and dogs (*said of rain*); **come Dio volle** at long last; **come Dio vuole** botched (*piece of work*); **Dio ci scampi!** God forbid!; **Dio santo!** good heavens!; **grazie a Dio** God willing; thank God; **voglia Dio** God grant

diòce•si *f* (**-si**) diocese

diodo *m* (electron) diode

diomedèa *f* (orn) albatross

diottrìa *f* (opt) diopter

dipanare *tr* to unravel, unwind

dipartiménto *m* department

dipartire §176 *tr* (archaic) to divide || *intr* (**diparto**) (ESSERE) *& ref* (lit) to depart

dipartita *f* (lit) departure; (lit) demise

dipendènte *adj* dependent || *mf* employee

dipendènza *f* dependence; employment; annex; (com) branch; **in dipendenza di** as a consequence of

dipèndere §150 *intr* (ESSERE) to depend; **dipendere da** to depend on

dipingere §126 *tr* to paint; **dipingere a olio** to paint in oils; **dipingere a tempera** to distemper || *ref* to paint one-

self; to put make-up on; to appear, e.g., **gli si dipinse in volto la paura** fear appeared on his face

dipin•to **-ta** *adj* painted || *m* painting, picture

diplò•ma *m* (**-mi**) diploma, certificate

diplomare (**diplòmo**) *tr* to grant a degree to; to graduate || *ref* to receive a degree; to graduate

diplomàti•co **-ca** (**-ci -che**) *adj* diplomatic; true, faithful (*copy*) || *m* diplomat || *f* diplomatics

diploma•to **-ta** *adj* graduated || *mf* graduate || *m* alumnus || *f* alumna

diplomazìa *f* diplomacy

dipòi *adv* after, thereafter

diportare (**dipòrto**) *ref* (lit) to behave; (obs) to have a good time

dipòrto *m* recreation; (obs) sport; **andare a diporto** to go on an outing; to go for a walk

diprèsso *adv*—**a un dipresso** about, approximately

diradare *tr* to thin out (*vegetation*); to disperse; to space out (*one's visits*) || *intr* (ESSERE) *& ref* to diminish; to disperse

diramare *tr* to prune; to circulate (*notices*); to issue (*a communiqué*) || *ref* to branch out; to spread

diramazióne *f* branch; ramification; issuance

dire *m* talk; **per sentito dire** by hearsay; **stando al dire** according to his words || §151 *tr & intr* to say; to tell; to call (*e.g., s.o. a genius*); to talk; **detto (e) fatto** no sooner said than done; **dica pure!** go ahead!; speak up!; **dire bene di** to speak well of; **dire di no** to say no; **dire di sì** to say yes; **direi quasi** I dare say; **dire la sua** to have one's say; **dire male di** to speak ill of; **dirla grossa** to make a blunder; to tell a tall tale; **dirlo chiaro e tondo** to speak bluntly; **dirne un sacco e una sporta a** to pour insults upon; **è tutto dire** that's all; **non c'è che dire** it's a fact; **non fo per dire** I do not want to boast; **per così dire** so to speak; **per meglio dire** rather; **trovarci a dire** to find fault with; **trovare da dire con** to have words with; **voler ben dire** to be sure; **voler dire** to mean || *ref*—**dirsela con** to connive with; **si dice** it is said

dirètro *m & adv* (archaic) behind, back

direttìssima *f* (rr) high-speed line; **per direttissima** straight up (*in mountain climbing*)

direttìssimo *m* express train

diretti•vo **-va** *adj* managerial || *m* board of directors || *f* directive; direction; guideline

dirèt•to **-ta** *adj* direct; **diretto a** addressed to; directed at; bound for || *m* through train

diret•tóre **-trice** *mf* manager; principal || *m* director; **direttore di macchina** (naut, nav) chief engineer; **direttore di tiro** (nav) gunnery officer; **direttore di un giornale** editor; **direttore d'or-**

chestra orchestra leader; **direttore responsabile** publisher; **direttore tecnico** (sports) manager ‖ *f* see **direttrice**

direttò·rio -ria (**-ri -rie**) *adj* directorial ‖ *m* directory

direttrice *adj fem* directing; guiding; front (*wheels*) ‖ *f* directress; line of action

direzionale *adj* directional; managerial

direzióne *f* direction; management; run (*of events*)

dirigènte *adj* leading; managerial ‖ *m* employer; boss; leader; executive

dirìgere §152 *tr* to direct; to turn; to lead ‖ *ref* to address oneself; **dirigersi verso** to head for

dirigìbile *adj* & *m* dirigible

dirimpètto *adj invar* & *adv* opposite; **dirimpetto a** opposite to; in comparison with

dirìt·to -ta *adj* straight; right; unswerving; (coll) smart ‖ *m* law; obverse, face (*of coin*); fee, dues; (fin) right; **a buon diritto** rightly so; **di diritto** by law; **diritti d'autore** copyright; **diritti di segreteria** registration fee; **diritti doganali** customs duty; **diritti speciali di prelievo** (econ) special drawing rights; **diritto canonico** canon law; **diritto consuetudinario** common law; **diritto internazionale** international law; **in diritto** according to law ‖ *f* right, right hand ‖ **diritto** *adv* straight; **tirare diritto** to go straight ahead

dirittura *f* direction; uprightness; (sports) straightaway, home stretch

dirizzóne *m* blunder

diroccare §197 (**diròcco**) *tr* to knock down ‖ *intr* (ESSERE) (archaic) to fall down

dirocca·to -ta *adj* dilapidated, rickety

dirompènte *adj* fragmentation (*bomb*)

dirottaménto *m* hijacking; skyjacking (*of an airplane*)

dirottare (**dirótto**) *tr* to detour (*traffic*); to hijack (*e.g., a ship*); to skyjack (*an airplane*) ‖ *intr* to change course

dirottatóre *m* hijacker; skyjacker (*of a plane*)

dirót·to -ta *adj* copious, heavy (*rain, tears*); (lit) craggy; **a dirotto** cats and dogs (*said of rain*)

dirozzare [ddzz] (**dirózzo**) *tr* to roughhew; to refine ‖ *ref* to become polished

dirugginire §176 *tr* to take the rust off; to limber up; to gnash (*one's teeth*); to clear (*one's mind*)

dirupa·to -ta *adj* rocky, craggy

dirupo *m* rock; crag, cliff

disabbigliare §280 *tr* & *ref* to undress, disrobe

disabita·to -ta *adj* uninhabited

disabituare (**disabìtuo**) *tr* to disaccustom ‖ *ref* to become unaccustomed

disaccenta·to -ta *adj* unaccented

disaccòrdo *m* disagreement

disadat·to -ta *adj* unfit

disadór·no -na *adj* unadorned, bare

disaffezionare (**disaffezióno**) *tr* to alien-ate the affection of; to estrange ‖ *ref* to become estranged

disaffezióne *f* dislike

disagévole *adj* troublesome, uncomfortable

disagiare §290 *tr* to trouble, inconvenience

disagia·to -ta *adj* uncomfortable; needy

disà·gio *m* (**-gi**) discomfort; need

disalberare (**disàlbero**) *tr* to dismast

disambienta·to -ta *adj* bewildered, strange

disàmina *f* examination, scrutiny

disaminare (**disàmino**) *tr* to scrutinize; to weigh

disamorare (**disamóro**) *tr* to alienate the affection of; to estrange ‖ *ref* to become estranged

disancorare (**disàncoro**) *intr* to weigh anchor; to leave port ‖ *ref* to weigh anchor; (fig) to free oneself

disanimare (**disànimo**) *tr* to dishearten

disappetènza *f* loss of appetite

disapprovare (**disappròvo**) *tr* to disapprove

disapprovazióne *f* disapproval

disappunto *m* disappointment

disarcionare (**disarcióno**) *tr* to unsaddle, unhorse; to kick out

disarmare *tr* to disarm; to dismantle (*a scaffold*); to ship (*oars*); (naut) to unrig ‖ *ref* to disarm; (fig) to give up

disarma·to -ta *adj* unarmed, defenseless

disarmo *m* disarmament; dismantling; unrigging

disarmonìa *f* discord; contrast

disarmòni·co -ca *adj* (**-ci -che**) discordant

disarticolare (**disartìcolo**) *tr* to limber up; to disjoint ‖ *ref* to become dislocated

disassociare §128 (**disassòcio**) *tr* to disassociate

disastra·to -ta *adj* damaged ‖ *mf* victim

disastro *m* disaster, calamity; wreck

disastró·so -sa [s] *adj* disastrous

disattèn·to -ta *adj* inattentive; careless

disattenzióne *f* inattention; carelessness

disattivare *tr* to deactivate (*e.g., a mine*)

disavanzo *m* (com) deficit

disavvedu·to -ta *adj* heedless

disavventura *f* misfortune

disavvertènza *f* inadvertence

disavvezzare (**disavvézzo**) *tr* to break (*s.o.*) of a habit ‖ *ref*—**disavvezzarsi da** to give up or lose the habit of

disavvéz·zo -za *adj* unaccustomed

disbórso *m* disbursement, outlay

disboscare §197 (**disbòsco**) *tr* to deforest

disbrigare §209 *tr* to dispatch ‖ *ref* to extricate oneself

disbri·go *m* (**-ghi**) prompt execution, dispatch

discacciare §128 *tr* (lit) to chase away

discanto *m* (mus) harmonizing

discàpito *m* damage; **tornare a discapito di** to be detrimental to

discàri·ca *f* (**-che**) discharge (*e.g., of pollutants*); dumping (*of refuse*); unloading (*of a ship*)

discàri•co m (-chi) exculpation; **a discarico di** in defense of

discatóre m hockey player; discus thrower

discendènte adj descending; sloping; down (train) || mf descendant

discendènza f descent; pedigree

discéndere §245 tr to go down || intr (ESSERE & AVERE) to descend, go down; to slope; to fall (said, e.g., of thermometer); to get off; **discendere in picchiata** (aer) to nose-dive

discènte mf student, pupil

discépo•lo -la mf disciple

discèrnere §153 tr to discern

discernìbile adj discernible

discerniménto m discernment

discésa [s] f descent; slope; drop

discettare (discètto) tr (lit) to discuss

dischiodare (dischiòdo) tr to take the nails out of

dischiùdere §125 tr to open; to reveal

discin•to -ta adj scantily dressed; untidy; in disarray

disciògliere §127 tr to dissolve, melt; (lit) to untie || ref to dissolve, melt

disciplina f discipline; whip, scourge

disciplinare adj disciplinary || m regulation || tr to discipline

disciplina•to -ta adj obedient

di•sco m (-schi) disk; (phonograph) record; bob (of pendulum); (ice hockey) puck; (sports) discus; (rr) signal; (pharm) tablet; **disco combinatore** (telp) dial; **disco microsolco** microgroove record; **disco volante** flying saucer

discòfilo m record lover

discòide m (pharm) tablet, pill

dìsco•lo -la adj undisciplined, wild || m rogue, rascal

discolorare (discolóro) tr to discolor || ref to pale

discolorazióne f discoloration; paleness

discólpa f defense

discolpare (discólpo) tr to defend

disconnèttere §107 tr to disconnect

disconóscere §134 tr to ignore, to disregard; to be ungrateful for

discontinuare (discontìnuo) tr to perform sporadically || intr to lose continuity

disconti•nuo -nua adj uneven

disconvenire §282 intr (ESSERE) (lit) to disagree || impers (ESSERE) (lit) to be improper

discoprire §110 (discòpro) tr to discover

discordante adj discordant

discordare (discòrdo) intr (ESSERE) to disagree, differ

discòrde adj discordant; opposing

discòrdia f discord, dissension

discórrere §139 intr to talk, chat; (coll) to keep company; **discorrere del più e del meno** to make small talk; **e via discorrendo** and so forth

discórso m discourse; conversation; speech; **pochi discorsi!** (coll) cut it out!

discostare (discòsto) tr to remove || ref to withdraw; to differ

discò•sto -sta adj distant || **discosto** adv far

discotè•ca f (-che) record library; discotheque

discreditare (discrédito) tr to discredit

discrédito m discredit

discrepanza f discrepancy

discretaménte adv rather; fairly well

discré•to -ta adj discreet; fairly large; fair

discrezióne f discretion

discriminante adj discriminatory; extenuating || m (math) discriminant

discriminare (discrìmino) tr to discriminate; to extenuate

discriminazióne f discrimination

discussióne f discussion; argument

discus•so -sa adj controversial

discùtere §154 tr to discuss || intr to discuss; to argue

discutìbile adj moot, debatable

disdegnare (disdégno) tr to disdain, scorn || ref (obs) to be angry

disdégno m disdain, scorn

disdegnó•so -sa [s] adj disdainful

disdétta f ill luck; (law) notice

disdicévole adj unbecoming, unseemly

disdire §151 tr to retract; to belie; to cancel; to countermand; to terminate the contract of || ref to retract; **disdire a** to be unbecoming to

disdòro m shame; **tornare a disdoro di** to bring shame on

disegnare [s] (diségno) tr to draw; to sketch; to design; (obs) to elect

disegna•tóre -trice [s] mf cartoonist; designer || m draftsman

diségno [s] m drawing; sketch; outline; plan; design; **disegno animato** (mov) cartoon; **disegno di legge** (law) bill

disellare [s] (disèllo) tr var of **dissellare**

diserbante adj weed-killing || m weed-killer

diseredare (disèredo) tr to disinherit

disereda•to -ta adj disinherited || **i diseredati** the underprivileged

disertare (disèrto) tr to desert; (lit) to lay waste || intr to desert

disertóre m deserter

diserzióne f desertion

disfaciménto m disintegration

disfare §173 tr to undo; to defeat; to melt; to unknit; to break up (housekeeping); **disfare il letto** to remove the bedclothes || ref to spoil (said, e.g., of meat); **disfarsi di** to get rid of

disfatta f defeat

disfattismo m defeatism

disfatti•sta mf (-sti -ste) defeatist

disfat•to -ta adj undone; defeated; melted; broken up; ravaged || f see **disfatta**

disfida f (lit) challenge

disfunzióne f malfunction

disgelare (disgèlo) tr & intr to thaw

disgèlo m thaw

disgiùngere §183 tr & ref to separate

disgiunti•vo -va adj disjunctive

disgràzia f disfavor; bad luck, misfortune; accident; **per disgrazia** unfortunately

disgrazia‧to -ta *adj* unlucky; wretched
disgregaménto *m* disintegration
disgregare §209 (disgrègo) *tr & ref* to disintegrate
disgregazióne *f* disintegration
disguido *m* miscarriage, missending (*of a letter*)
disgustare *tr* to disgust, sicken ‖ *ref* to become disgusted, sicken; to have a falling-out, to part company
disgusto *m* disgust, repugnance
disgustó‧so -sa [s] *adj* disgusting
disidratare *tr* to dehydrate
disìlla‧bo -ba *adj* disyllabic ‖ *m* disyllable
disillùdere §105 *tr* to delude, deceive ‖ *ref* to become disillusioned
disillusióne *f* disillusion
disimboscare §197 (disimbòsco) *tr* to put back in circulation
disimparare *tr* to unlearn, forget
disimpegnare (disimpégno) *tr* to release; to free, to open; to loosen; to redeem (*a pledge*); to clear; to perform ‖ *ref* to succeed
disimpégno *m* release; redemption; performance; disengagement; **di disimpegno** for every day (*e.g., a suit*); main (*e.g., hallway*)
disimpiè‧go *m* (-ghi) unemployment; (mil) withdrawal
disincagliare §280 *tr* to set afloat; (fig) to disentangle
disincantare *tr* disenchant
disinfestare (disinfèsto) *tr* to exterminate
disinfestazióne *f* extermination
disinfettante *adj & m* disinfectant
disinfettare (disinfètto) *tr* to disinfect
disingannare *tr* to disillusion ‖ *ref* to become disillusioned
disinganno *m* disillusion
disinnescare §197 (disinnésco) *tr* to defuse
disinnestare (disinnèsto) *tr* to disconnect; to throw out, disengage
disinserire §176 *tr* (elec) to disconnect; (aut) to disengage
disintasare [s] *tr* to unclog
disintegrare (disìntegro) *tr & ref* to disintegrate
disintegrazióne *f* disintegration
disinteressare (disinterèsso) *tr* to make (*s.o.*) lose interest ‖ *ref* to lose interest; to take no interest
disinteressa‧to -ta *adj* selfless, unselfish
disinterèsse *m* disinterest; unselfishness
disintossicare §197 (disintòssico) *tr* to free of poison; (fig) to clean the air in ‖ *ref* to shake the drug habit
disinvòl‧to -ta *adj* free and easy; fresh, forward
disinvoltura *f* naturalness, ease of manners, offhandedness; freshness; impudence
disì‧o *m* (-i) (poet) desire
disìstima *f* scorn, low regard, disesteem
disìstimare *tr* to scorn, hold in low regard
dislivèllo *m* difference of level; disparity
dislocaménto *m* transfer of troops; (naut) displacement

dislocare §197 (dislòco) *tr* to transfer (*troops*); to post (*sentries*); (naut) to displace
dislocazióne *f* (mil) transfer; (geog, naut, psychol) displacement
dismisura *f* excess; **a dismisura** excessively
disobbedire §176 *intr* var of **disubbidire**
disobbligare §209 (disòbbligo) *tr* to free from an obligation ‖ *ref* to repay a favor
disoccupa‧to -ta *adj* unemployed, jobless; idle; unoccupied ‖ *m* unemployed person; **i disoccupati** the jobless
disoccupazióne *f* unemployment
disone‧stà *f* (-stà) dishonesty; shamelessness
disonè‧sto -sta *adj* dishonest; shameless; immoral
disonorante *adj* disgraceful
disonorare (disonóro) *tr* to dishonor, disgrace; to seduce
disonóre *m* dishonor, shame
disonorévole *adj* dishonorable; shameful
disoppilare (disòppilo) *tr* to clear of obstructions
disópra *adj invar* upper ‖ *m* (disópra) upper part, top; **prendere il disopra** to have the upper hand ‖ *adv* above; **al disopra di** above
disordinare (disórdino) *tr* to cancel, countermand; to confuse; to mess up ‖ *intr* to indulge ‖ *ref* to become disorganized
disordina‧to -ta *adj* confused; messy; untidy; intemperate
disórdine *m* confusion; mess; disarray; disorder; intemperance
disorganizzare [ddzz] *tr* to disorganize; to disrupt
disorganizzazióne [ddzz] *f* disorganization, disorder; disruption
disorientaménto *m* disorientation; confusion, bewilderment
disorientare (disoriènto) *tr* to cause (*s.o.*) to lose his way; to confuse; to disorient ‖ *ref* to be bewildered; to lose one's bearings
disorienta‧to -ta *adj* disoriented; confused, bewildered; lost, astray
disormeggiare §290 (disorméggio) *tr* to unmoor
disossare (disòsso) *tr* to bone ‖ *ref* (lit) to lose weight
disótto [s] *adj invar* below ‖ *m* (disótto) lower part, bottom ‖ *adv* below; **al disotto di** below, underneath
disotturare *tr* to unclog
dispàc‧cio *m* (-ci) dispatch; urgent letter; **dispaccio telegrafico** telegram
dispara‧to -ta *adj* disparate
disparére *m* disagreement
dispari *adj invar* odd, uneven
dispari‧tà *f* (-tà) disparity
dispàrte *adv*—in **disparte** apart, aside; **starsene in disparte** to keep aloof
dispèn‧dio *m* (-di) expenditure; waste
dispendió‧so -sa [s] *adj* expensive; wasteful

dispènsa *f* cupboard; pantry; distribution; number (*of magazine*); installment (*of book*); dispensation; (naut) storeroom; (coll) store

dispensare (dispènso) *tr* to exempt, free; to distribute ‖ *ref*—**dispensarsi da** to get out of

dispensà·rio *m* (**-ri**) dispensary

dispensa·tóre -trice *mf* dispenser

dispensiè·re -ra *mf* dispenser ‖ *m* steward

dispepsìa *f* dyspepsia

dispèpti·co -ca *adj* & *mf* (**-ci -che**) dyspeptic

disperare (dispèro) *intr* to despair; **fare disperare** to drive crazy ‖ *ref* to despair

dispera·to -ta *adj* hopeless ‖ *m* poor wretch; **come un disperato** desperately ‖ *f*—**alla disperata** with all one's might

disperazióne *f* desperation, despair

dispèrdere §212 *tr* to scatter; to waste ‖ *ref* to disperse; (fig) to waste one's energies

dispersióne *f* dispersion; loss; (elec) leakage

dispersività *f* tendency toward disorganization

dispersi·vo -va *adj* dispersive; disorganized

dispèr·so -sa *adj* scattered; lost; dispersed; missing in action

dispersóre *m* (elec) leakage conductor

dispètto *m* spite; (lit) haughtiness; **a dispetto di** in spite of; **far dispetto a** to provoke

dispettó·so -sa [s] *adj* pestiferous; spiteful, resentful

dispiacènte *adj* sorry; distressing

dispiacére *m* sorrow, displeasure ‖ §214 *intr* (ESSERE) to be displeasing; to be sorry, e.g., **mi dispiace** I am sorry; (with *dat*) to displease; (with *dat*) to dislike, e.g., **le mie parole gli dispiacciono** he dislikes my words; **Le dispiace?** would you please?; **se non Le dispiace** if you don't mind

dispiegare §209 (**dispiègo**) *tr* to manifest; (lit) to unfurl ‖ *ref* to spread out; to flow out

displù·vio *m* (**-vi**) divide, watershed; ridge (*of roof*)

disponìbile *adj* available; open-minded

disponibili·tà *f* (**-tà**) availability; inactive status; **disponibilità** *fpl* available funds

dispórre §218 *tr* to dispose; to prepare ‖ *intr* to provide; to dispose; **disporre di** to have (*available*) ‖ *ref* to get ready

dispositivo *m* gadget; device; (mil) deployment

disposizióne *f* arrangement; inclination, disposition; disposal; instruction; (law) provision

dispó·sto -sta *adj* arranged; disposed; provided; willing; **ben disposto** disposed ‖ *m* (law) proviso

dispòti·co -ca *adj* (**-ci -che**) despotic

dispotismo *m* despotism

dispregiati·vo -va *adj* disparaging; (gram) pejorative

disprè·gio *m* (**-gi**) contempt; disrepute

disprezzàbile *adj* contemptible; negligible

disprezzare (disprèzzo) *tr* to despise

disprèzzo *m* contempt, scorn

dìsputa *f* dispute; debate

disputàbile *adj* debatable

disputare (dìsputo) *tr* to contest; to discuss; to vie for (*victory*) ‖ *intr* to dispute, debate; to vie ‖ *ref* to vie for

disqualificare §197 (**disqualìfico**) *tr* to disqualify

disquisizióne *f* disquisition

dissacrare *tr* to desecrate

dissacrazióne *f* desecration

dissaldare *tr* to unsolder

dissanguare (dissànguo) *tr* to bleed ‖ *ref* to bleed; to ruin oneself

dissangua·to -ta *adj* bled white; **morire dissanguato** to bleed to death

dissapóre *m* disagreement

disseccare §197 (**dissécco**) *tr* to dry ‖ *ref* to dry up

disselcinare §128 (**dissélcino**) *tr* to remove the cobblestones from

dissellare (dissèllo) *tr* to unsaddle

disseminare (dissémino) *tr* to disseminate; to scatter

dissensióne *f* dissension

dissènso *m* dissent; disagreement

dissenterìa *f* dysentery

dissentire (dissènto) *intr* to dissent

dissenziènte *adj* dissenting ‖ *mf* dissenter

disseppellire §176 *tr* to exhume

dissertare (dissèrto) *intr* to discourse

dissertazióne *f* dissertation

disservì·zio *m* (**-zi**) poor service

dissestare (dissèsto) *tr* to unsettle; to disarrange

dissesta·to -ta *adj* financially embarrassed; mentally deranged

dissèsto *m* financial embarrassment; mental derangement

dissetante *adj* thirst-quenching

dissetare (disséto) *tr* to quench the thirst of ‖ *ref* to quench one's thirst

dissezióne *f* dissection

dissidènte *adj* & *m* dissident

dissidènza *f* dissent

dissì·dio *m* (**-di**) dissent; disagreement

dissigillare *tr* to unseal ‖ *ref* (lit) to melt

dissìmile *adj* unlike

dissimulare (dissìmulo) *tr* to dissimulate, disguise ‖ *intr* to dissimulate

dissimulazióne *f* dissimulation

dissipare (dissìpo) *tr* to dissipate; to squander; to clear up (*a doubt*) ‖ *ref* to dissipate

dissipa·to -ta *adj* & *mf* profligate

dissipa·tóre -trice *mf* squanderer

dissipazióne *f* dissipation

dissociare §128 (**dissòcio**) *tr* to dissociate, disassociate ‖ *ref* to dissociate or disassociate oneself

dissociazióne *f* dissociation

dissodare (dissòdo) *tr* to cultivate

dissolutézza *f* profligacy

dissolu·to -ta *adj* & *mf* profligate

dissoluzióne *f* dissolution

dissolvènza *f* (mov) fade-out; **dissolvenza incrociata** (mov) lap dissolve

dissòlvere §155 *tr* to dissolve; to clear up (*a doubt*); (obs) to untie ‖ *ref* to dissolve

dissomiglianza *f* dissimilarity

dissonanza *f* dissonance

dissotterrare (dissottèrro) *tr* to exhume; to unearth

dissuadére §213 *tr* to dissuade

dissuè·to -ta *adj* (lit) unaccustomed

dissuggellare (dissuggèllo) *tr* to unseal

distaccaménto *m* (mil) detachment

distaccare §197 *tr* to detach; to remove; to transfer; to outdistance ‖ *ref* to stand out; to withdraw, become separated

distacca·to -ta *adj* detached; branch (*office*)

distac·co *m* (**-chi**) detachment; separation; (sports) spread (*in points*)

distante *adj* distant; aloof; different ‖ *adv* far away

distanza *f* distance; **mantenere le distanze** to keep one's distance; **tenere a distanza** to keep at arm's length

distanziare §287 *tr* to outdistance

distare *intr* to be distant

distèndere §270 *tr* to stretch; to spread; to unfurl; to relax; to knock down; to write ‖ *ref* to stretch; to spread out; to relax

distensióne *f* relaxation; relaxation of tension

disté·so -sa [s] *adj* stretched out; full (*voice*); lank (*hair*) ‖ *m*—**per disteso** in full ‖ *f* expanse; row; **a distesa** with full voice; at full peal

distillare *tr* to distill; to exude; to pour; to trickle ‖ *intr* (ESSERE) to trickle ‖ *ref*—**distillarsi il cervello** to rack one's brain

distilla·to -ta *adj* distilled ‖ *m* distillate

distilla·tóre -trice *mf* distiller ‖ *m* still

distilleria *f* distillery

distinguíbile *adj* distinguishable

distinguere §156 *tr* to distinguish; to make out; to tell (*one thing from another*); to divide

distinta *f* note, list; **distinta di versamento** deposit slip

distintaménte *adj* distinctly; sincerely yours

distinti·vo -va *adj* distinctive ‖ *m* emblem, insignia, badge

distin·to -ta *adj* distinct; distinguished; sincere (*greetings*); reserved (*seat*); **Distinto Signor . . .** (*on an envelope*) Mr. . . . ‖ *f* see **distinta**

distinzióne *f* distinction

distògliere §127 *tr* to dissuade; to deter; to distract; to turn (*one's eyes*) away

distòrcere §272 *tr* to distort; to twist ‖ *ref* to become distorted; to sprain (*e.g., one's ankle*)

distorsióne *f* distortion; sprain; **distorsione acustica** wow

distrarre §273 *tr* to distract; to divert;

to amuse; to pull (*a muscle*) ‖ *ref* to become distracted; to relax

distrat·to -ta *adj* absent-minded

distrazióne *f* absent-mindedness; distraction; diversion (*of money*); pull (*of muscle*)

distrét·to -ta *adj* (obs) close; (obs) hard-pressed ‖ *m* district; precinct (*e.g., of police*); circuit (*of court*); ward (*in city*); **distretto militare** draft board; **distretto postale** postal zone ‖ *f* stricture; necessity

distrettuale *adj* district

distribuire §176 *tr* to distribute; to pass out; to allot; to deploy (*troops*); (theat) to cast (*roles*); (mov) to release; (mil) to issue (*e.g., clothing*)

distribu·tóre -trice *adj* distributing, dispensing ‖ *mf* distributor, dispenser ‖ *m* distributor; **distributore automatico** vending machine; **distributore di benzina** gasoline pump

distribuzióne *f* distribution; issue; delivery; (aut) timing gears; (mov) release; (fig) dispensation

districare §197 *tr* to unravel ‖ *ref* to extricate oneself

distrofia *f* dystrophy

distrùggere §266 *tr* to destroy; to ruin

distrutti·vo -va *adj* destructive

distruzióne *f* destruction

disturbare *tr* to disturb, bother; **disturbo?** may I come in? ‖ *ref* to bother; to go out of one's way

disturba·tóre -trice *mf* disturber; **disturbatore della quiete pubblica** disturber of the peace

disturbo *m* trouble, bother; disturbance; (rad) interference; **disturbi atmosferici** static, atmospherics; **togliere il disturbo** a to take leave of

disubbidiènte *adj* disobedient

disubbidiènza *f* disobedience

disubbidire §176 *intr* to disobey; (with *dat*) to disobey

disuguaglianza *f* inequality; disparity

disuguale *adj* uneven; unequal

disuma·no -na *adj* inhumane; unbearable

disunióne *f* disunion

disunire §176 *tr* to disunite

disusa·to -ta *adj* obsolete, out of use

disuso *m* disuse; **in disuso** obsolete

disùtile *adj* useless; burdensome ‖ *m* worthless fellow; (com) loss

disvì·o *m* (**-i**) miscarriage, missending (*of a letter*)

ditale *m* thimble; fingerstall

ditata *f* poke with a finger; finger mark; dab (*with a finger*)

dito *m* (**dita** *fpl*) finger; toe; **avere le dita d'oro** to have a magic touch; **dita della mano** fingers; **dita del piede** toes; **legarsela al dito** to never forget ‖ *m* (**diti**) finger, e.g., **dito indice** index finger; **dito anulare** ring finger; **dito medio** middle finger; **dito mignolo** little finger; **dito pollice** thumb

ditta *f* firm, house; office

dittàfono *m* intercom; dictaphone

dittatóre *m* dictator

dittatura *f* dictatorship
dittongare §209 (**dittòngo**) *tr* to diphthongize
dittòn·go *m* (**-ghi**) diphthong
diurèti·co **-ca** *adj & m* (**-ci -che**) diuretic
diur·no **-na** *adj* daily; daytime || *f* (theat) matinée
diutur·no **-na** *adj* long-lasting
diva *f* díva; (mov) star; (lit) goddess
divagare §209 *tr* to amuse; to distract || *intr* to digress || *ref* to relax
divagazióne *f* distraction; digression; relaxation
divampare *intr* (ESSERE & AVERE) to blaze, flare
divano *m* divan; couch, sofa
divaricare §197 (**divàrico**) *tr* to spread (*one's legs*); to open up (*an incision*)
divà·rio *m* (**-ri**) difference
divèllere §267 *tr* to eradicate, uproot
diveni·re *m* (**-re**) (philos) becoming || §282 *intr* (ESSERE) (lit) to become; (archaic) to come
diventare (**divènto**) *intr* (ESSERE) to become; **diventare di tutti i colori** to blush; to be embarrassed; **diventare grande** to grow up; **diventare matto** to go mad; **diventare pallido** to turn pale; **diventare piccolo** to grow smaller; **diventare rosso** to blush
divèr·bio *m* (**-bi**) argument; **venire a diverbio** to have an altercation
divergènza *f* divergency
divèrgere §157 *intr* to diverge
diversificare §197 (**diversifico**) *tr* to diversify || *ref* to be diversified; to differ
diversióne *f* diversion
diversi·tà *f* (**-tà**) diversity
diversi·vo **-va** *adj* diverting || *m* diversion
diver·so **-sa** *adj* different; **diver·si -se** several, e.g., **diverse ragazze** several girls || **diver·si -se** *pron* several
divertènte *adj* diverting, amusing
divertimento *m* amusement, pastime; fun; (mus) divertimento
divertire (**divèrto**) *tr* to amuse, entertain; (lit) to turn aside || *ref* to have fun, enjoy oneself; (lit) to go away
diverti·to **-ta** *adj* amused; amusing
divétta *f* starlet
divezzare (**divézzo**) *tr* to wean || *ref*— **divezzarsi da** to get out of the habit of
dividèndo *m* dividend
dividere §158 *tr* to divide; to partition; to split; to share in (*e.g., s.o.'s grief*) || *ref* to be divided; to become separated; **dividersi fra** to divide one's time between
divièto *m* prohibition; **divieto d'affissione** post no bills; **divieto di parcheggio** no parking; **divieto di sosta** no stopping; **divieto di svolta** no turns; **divieto di transito** no thoroughfare
divinare *tr* (lit) to divine
divina·tóre **-trice** *adj* divining || *m* diviner

divinazióne *f* divination
divincolare (**divìncolo**) *tr & ref* to wriggle
divini·tà *f* (**-tà**) divinity
divinizzare [ddzz] *tr* to deify
divi·no **-na** *adj* divine
divisa *f* uniform; motto; part (*in hair*); **divise** foreign exchange
divisare *tr* (lit) to intend
divisìbile *adj* divisible
divisióne *f* division; partition; (sports) league
divisionismo *m* (painting) divisionism; (pol) separatism
divismo *m* (mov) star system; (mov) adulation of stars
divisóre *m* (math) divisor
divisò·rio **-ria** (**-ri -rie**) *adj* dividing || *m* partition; (math) divisor
di·vo **-va** *adj* (lit) divine || *m* (theat, mov) star; (lit) god || *f* see **dìva**
divolgare §209 (**divólgo**) *tr & ref* var of **divulgare**
divorare (**divóro**) *tr* to devour; to gulp down; to consume; **divorare la via** to burn up the road
divora·tóre **-trice** *adj* consuming || *mf* consumer (*e.g., of food, books*)
divorziare §287 (**divòrzio**) *intr* to become divorced; **divorziare da** to divorce
divorzia·to **-ta** *adj* divorced || *m* divorcé || *f* divorcée
divòr·zio *m* (**-zi**) divorce
divulgare §209 *tr* to divulge; to publicize; to popularize || *ref* to spread; to become popular
divulga·tóre **-trice** *adj* popularizing || *mf* popularizer; **divulgatore di calunnie** scandalmonger; **divulgatore di notizie** telltale
divulgazióne *f* publicizing; popularization
divulsióne *f* (surg) dilation
dizionà·rio *m* (**-ri**) dictionary; **dizionario geografico** gazetteer
dizióne *f* diction; reading (*of poetry*)
do [do] *m* (do) (mus) do; (mus) C
dóc·cia *f* (**-ce**) shower; gutter (*on roof*); spout; (fig) dash of cold water; **fare la doccia** to take a shower
docciare §128 (**dóccio**) *tr, intr* (ESSERE) *& ref* to shower
doccióne *m* trough, gutter; gargoyle
docènte *adj* teaching || *m* teacher; **libero docente** certified university teacher
docènza *f* teaching post; **libera docenza** lectureship
dòcile *adj* docile; tame; amenable (*person*); workable (*material*)
documentare (**documénto**) *tr* to document || *ref* to gather information
documentà·rio **-ria** *adj & m* (**-ri -rie**) documentary
documénto *m* document; paper; **documenti di bordo** ship's papers
dodecafonìa *f* twelve-tone system
dodecasilla·bo **-ba** *adj* twelve-syllable, dodecasyllable
dodicèsi·mo **-ma** *adj, m & pron* twelfth
dódici *adj & pron* twelve; **le dódici**

twelve o'clock ‖ *m* twelve; twelfth (*in dates*)

dó·ga *f* (-ghe) stave

dogale *adj* (hist) of the doge

dogana *f* duty; customs; custom house

doganière *m* customs officer

dòge *m* (hist) doge

dò·glia *f* (-glie) (lit) pain, pang; **doglie** labor pains

dò·glio *m* (-gli) barrel; (lit) large jar

doglió·so -sa [*s*] *adj* (lit) sorrowful

dòg·ma *m* (-mi) dogma

dogmàti·co -ca (-ci -che) *adj* dogmatic ‖ *mf* dogmatist

dogmatismo *m* dogmatism

dólce *adj* sweet; soft; gentle; fresh (*water*); mild (*climate*); delicate (*feet*); **dolce far niente** sweet idleness ‖ *m* sweet; sweet dish; **dolci** candy

dolceama·ro -ra *adj* bittersweet

dolcézza *f* sweetness; mildness; gentleness

dolcia·stro -stra *adj* sweetish

dolcière *m* candy maker; pastry baker

dolcificare §197 (dolcìfico) *tr* to sweeten

dolciume *m* sweet; **dolciumi** candy

dolènte *adj* aching; sorrowful; sorry

dolére §159 *intr* (ESSERE & AVERE) to ache, e.g., **gli dolgono i denti** his teeth ache ‖ *ref* to grieve ‖ *impers* (ESSERE) to be sorry, e.g., **mi duole che Lei non possa venire** I am sorry that you won't be able to come

dolicònice *m* bobolink

dòllaro *m* dollar

dòlo *m* fraud, malice, guile

dolomite *f* dolomite ‖ **Dolomiti** *fpl* Dolomites

dolorante *adj* aching

dolorare (dolóro) *intr* (lit) to ache

dolóre *m* ache; sorrow; contrition

doloró·so -sa [*s*] *adj* painful; sorrowful

doló·so -sa [*s*] *adj* intentional, fraudulent; (law) felonious

domàbile *adj* tamable

domanda *f* question; application; appeal; (econ) demand; **domanda suggestiva** (com) leading question; **fare una domanda** to ask a question

domandare *tr* to ask; to ask for; **domandare la parola** to ask for the floor ‖ *intr* to inquire ‖ *ref* to wonder; (lit) to be called

doma·ni *m* (-ni) tomorrow ‖ *adv* tomorrow; **a domani** until tomorrow; **domani a otto** a week from tomorrow; **domani l'altro** the day after tomorrow

domare (dómo) *tr* to tame; to extinguish; to quell

doma·tóre -trice *mf* tamer

domattina *adv* tomorrow morning

doméni·ca *f* (-che) Sunday

domenicale *adj* Sunday (*e.g., rest*)

domenica·no -na *adj* & *m* Dominican (*e.g., order*)

domesticare §197 (domèstico) *tr* to domesticate

domèsti·co -ca (-ci -che) *adj* family; household; familiar; domestic ‖ *mf* domestic, servant ‖ *f* maid; **alla domestica** family style; **domestica a mezzo servizio** part-time domestic

domiciliare *adj* house ‖ §287 *tr* (com) to draw ‖ *ref* to dwell; to settle

domicì·to -ta *adj* residing

domicì·lio *m* (-li) domicile, residence; principal office; **domicilio coatto** imprisonment; **franco domicilio** free delivery

dominare (dòmino) *tr* to dominate, rule; to master; to overlook ‖ *intr* to prevail; to reign ‖ *ref* to control oneself

domina·tóre -trice *mf* ruler

dominazióne *f* domination; rule

domineddìo *m invar* (coll) the Lord God

dominica·no -na *adj* & *mf* Dominican (*e.g., Republic*)

domì·nio *m* (-ni) dominion; domain

dòmi·no *m* (-no) domino (*cloak*); dominoes (*game*)

dòn *m* (used only before singular Christian name) don (*Spanish title*); Don (*priest*); uncle (*familiar title of elderly man*)

donare (dóno) *tr* to donate; to give as a present ‖ *intr*—**donare a** to be becoming to

dona·tóre -trice *mf* donor; **donatore di sangue** blood donor

donazióne *f* gift, donation

donchisciotté·sco -sca *adj* (-schi -sche) quixotic

dónde *adv* wherefrom, whence

dondolare (dóndolo) *tr* to swing, rock ‖ *ref* to swing, rock; to loaf around

dondolì·o *m* (-i) swinging, rocking

dóndolo *m*—**a dondolo** rocking (*chair, horse*); **andare a dondolo** to loaf around

dondoló·ne -na *mf* idler, loafer

dongiovan·ni *m* (-ni) Don Juan

dònna *f* woman; ladyship; (lit) lady; (coll) Mrs.; (coll) maid; (cards) queen; **da donna** woman's, e.g., **scarpe da donna** woman's shoes; **donna cannone** fat lady (*of circus*); **donna di casa** housewife; **Nostra Donna** Our Lady

donnaiòlo *m* ladies' man, philanderer

donné·sco -sca *adj* (-schi -sche) womanly, feminine

dònnola *f* weasel

dóno *m* gift; **in dono** as a gift

donzèlla [*dz*] *f* (lit) damsel

donzèllo [*dz*] *m* (coll) doorman; (lit) page

dópo *adv* afterwards, later; **dopo che** after; **dopo di** after ‖ *prep* after; **dopo + *pp*** after having + *pp*

dopobar·ba *adj invar* after-shaving ‖ *m* (-ba) after-shaving lotion

dopodomani *m* & *adv* the day after tomorrow

dopoguèr·ra *m* (-ra) postwar era

dopolavóro *m* government office designed to organize workers' leisure time

dopopranzo *m* afternoon ‖ *adv* in the afternoon

doppiàg·gio *m* (-gi) (mov) dubbing

doppiare §287 (**dóppio**) *tr* to double; (mov) to dub

doppière *m* candelabrum

doppiétta *f* double-barreled shotgun; (aut) double shift

doppiézza *f* duplicity

dóp·pio -pia (**-pi -pie**) *adj* double; coupled; double-dealing || *adv* twice, twofold || *m* double; twice as much; (tennis) doubles; (theat) understudy

doppióne *m* duplicate; (philol) doublet

doppiopèt·to *adj invar* double-breasted || *m* (**-to**) double-breasted suit

dorare (**dòro**) *tr* to gild; (culin) to brown; **dorare la pillola** to sugar-coat the pill

dora·to -ta *adj* gilt, golden

doratura *f* gilding

dormicchiare §287 *intr* to doze

dormiente *adj* sleeping || *mf* sleeper

dormiglió·ne -na *mf* sleepyhead

dormire (**dòrmo**) *tr & intr* to sleep; **dormire a occhi aperti** to be overcome with sleep; **dormire della grossa** to sleep profoundly; **dormire tra due guanciali** to be safe and secure

dormita *f* long sleep; **fare una bella dormita** to have a long sleep

dormitò·rio *m* (**-ri**) dormitory

dormivé·glia *m* (**-glia**) drowsiness

dorsale *adj* dorsal; back (*bone*) || *m* head (*of bed*); back (*of chair*) || *f* (geog) ridge

dòrso *m* back; (sports) backstroke

dosàg·gio *m* (**-gi**) dosage

dosare (**dòso**) *tr* to dose

dosatura *f* dosage

dòse *f* dose

dòsso *m* back; (lit) summit; **levarsi di dosso** to take off; **mettersi in dosso** to put on

dotare (**dòto**) *tr* to provide with a dowry; to endow; to bless

dotazióne *f* dowry; endowment; supply

dòte *f* dowry; gift; endowment

dòt·to -ta *adj* learned, erudite || *m* scholar; (anat) duct

dottorale *adj* doctoral

dottó·re -réssa *mf* doctor

dottrina *f* doctrine; Christian doctrine

dóve *m* where; **per ogni dove** everywhere || *adv* where; **da dove** or **di dove** from where; which way; **fin dove** up to what point; **per dove** which way || *conj* where; whereas

dovére *m* duty, obligation; homework; **a dovere** properly; **doveri** regards; **farsi un dovere di** to feel duty-bound to; **mettere qlcu a dovere** to put s.o. in his place; **più del dovere** more than one should; **sentirsi in dovere di** to feel duty-bound to || §160 *tr & intr* to owe || *aux* (ESSERE & AVERE) must, e.g., **deve farlo** you must do it; to have to, e.g., **dovei partire** I had to leave; ought to, e.g., **dovrebbe lucidare la macchina** he ought to polish the car; should, e.g., **dovresti immaginarti** you should imagine; to be to, e.g., **il treno doveva arrivare alle sei** the train was to arrive at six; to be supposed to, e.g., **deve aver fatto un lungo viaggio** he is supposed to have taken a long journey

doveró·so -sa [s] *adj* proper, right

dovizia *f* (lit) abundance, wealth

dovunque *adv* wherever, anywhere; everywhere

dovu·to -ta *adj & m* due

dozzina [ddzz] *f* dozen; room and board; **da** or **di dozzina** common, ordinary; **tenere a dozzina** to board

dozzinale [ddzz] *adj* common, ordinary

dozzinante [ddzz] *mf* boarder

dra·ga *f* (**-ghe**) dredge

dragàg·gio *m* (**-gi**) dredging

dragami·ne *m* (**-ne**) minesweeper

dragare §209 *tr* to dredge

dràglia *f* (naut) stay

dra·go *m* (**-ghi**) dragon; **drago volante** kite

dragóna *f* sword strap

dragoncèllo *m* (bot) tarragon

dragóne *m* dragon; dragoon

dram·ma *m* (**-mi**) drama, play; **dramma musicale** (hist) melodrama || *f* drachma; dram

drammàti·co -ca (**-ci -che**) *adj* dramatic || *f* drama, dramatic art

drammatizzare [ddzz] *tr* to dramatize

drammatur·go *m* (**-ghi**) playwright, dramatist

drappég·gio *m* (**-gi**) drape; pleats

drappeggiare §290 (**drappéggio**) *tr* to drape || *ref* to be draped

drappèlla *f* pennon (*on bugler's trumpet*)

drappèllo *m* squad, platoon

drapperìa *f* dry goods; dry-goods store

drappo *m* cloth, silk cloth; (billiards) green cloth, baize

dràsti·co -ca *adj* (**-ci -che**) drastic

drenàg·gio *m* (**-gi**) drainage

drenare (**drèno**) *tr* to drain

dressàg·gio *m* (**-gi**) *m* training (*of animals*)

dribblare *tr & intr* (sports) to dribble

drit·to -ta *adj* straight; (lit) correct; **dritto come un fuso** straight as a ramrod || *m* (fig) old fox || *f* right; (naut) starboard

drizza *f* (naut) halyard

drizzare *tr* to straighten; to address; to erect; to cock (*the head*); to direct (*a blow*); **drizzare le gambe ai cani** to do the impossible; **drizzare le orecchie** to prick up one's ears || *intr* (naut) to hoist the halyard || *ref* to stand erect

dro·ga *f* (**-ghe**) drug; spice; seasoning

drogare §209 (**drògo**) *tr* to drug; to spice, season

drogherìa *f* grocery (store)

droghière *m* grocer

dromedà·rio *m* (**-ri**) dromedary

dru·do -da *adj* (archaic) faithful; (lit) strong || *m* (obs) vassal; (lit) lover

drùi·da *m* (**-di**) druid

drupa *f* (bot) drupe, stone fruit

duale *adj & m* dual

dualismo *m* dualism

duali·tà *f* duality

dùb·bio -bia (**-bi -bie**) *adj* doubtful || *m* doubt; misgiving; **mettere in dub-**

bio to question; to risk; **senza dubbio** no doubt

dubbió·so -sa [s] *adj* dubious; doubtful; (*lit*) dangerous

dubitare (**dùbito**) *intr* to doubt; to suspect; **dubitare di** to mistrust; to doubt; **non dubitare!** don't worry!

du·ca *m* (**-chi**) duke; (*lit*) leader

ducato *m* duchy; ducat

duce *m* leader; duce

duchéssa *f* duchess

duchessina *f* young duchess

duchino *m* young duke

due *adj* & *pron* two; **le due** two o'clock || *m* two; second (*in dates*) || *f*—**fra le due** between two alternatives

duecenté·sco -sca *adj* (**-schi -sche**) thirteenth-century

duecentèsi·mo -ma *adj, m* & *pron* two hundredth

duecènto *adj, m* & *pron* two hundred || **il Duecento** the thirteenth century

duellante *adj* dueling || *m* duelist

duellare (**duèllo**) *intr* to duel

duèllo *m* duel; contest; debate; **sfidare a duello** to challenge to a duel

duemila *adj, m* & *pron* two thousand || **Duemila** *m* twenty-first century

duepèz·zi *m* (**-zi**) two-piece bathing suit

duétto *m* (mus) duet

dulcamara *f* (bot) bittersweet

dulcina *f* artificial sweetening

duna *f* dune

dunque *m*—**venire al dunque** to come

to the point || *adv* then || *conj* therefore, hence || *interj* well!

duodèno *m* (anat) duodenum

duòlo *m* (lit) grief

duòmo *m* cathedral; dome (*e.g., of a boiler*)

du·plex *m* (**-plex**) (telp) party line

duplicare §197 (**dùplico**) *tr* to duplicate

duplica·to -ta *adj* & *m* duplicate

duplicatóre *m* duplicator

dùplice *adj* twofold, double || *f* (racing) daily double

duplici·tà *f* (**-tà**) duplicity

duràbile *adj* durable, lasting

duràci·no -na *adj* clingstone || *f* clingstone peach

duralluminio *m* duralumin

durare *tr* to endure, bear || *intr* to last; **durare a** + *inf* to keep on + *ger*; **durare in carica** to remain in office

durata *f* duration; lasting quality; **di lunga durata** long-lasting

durante *prep* during; throughout

duratu·ro -ra *adj* enduring, lasting

durévole *adj* lasting, durable

durézza *f* hardness; toughness; rigidity

du·ro -ra *adj* hard; hard-boiled (*egg*); durum (*wheat*); tough (*skin*); harsh; (phonet) voiceless || *m* hard part; hard floor; hard soil; **il duro sta che . . .** the trouble is that . . . ; **tener duro** to hold out

duróne *m* callousness, callosity

dùttile *adj* ductile; tractable

E

E, e [e] *m* & *f* fifth letter of the Italian alphabet

e *conj* and

ebani·sta *m* (**-sti**) cabinetmaker

ebanisterìa *f* cabinetmaking; cabinetmaker's shop

ebanite *f* ebonite, vulcanite

èbano *m* ebony

ebbène *interj* well!

ebbrézza *f* intoxication, drunkenness

èb·bro -bra *adj* intoxicated || *mf* drunk

ebdomadà·rio -ria *adj* & *m* (**-ri -rie**) weekly

èbete *adj* stupid, dull, dumb

ebollizióne *f* boil, boiling

ebrài·co -ca (**-ci -che**) *adj* Hebrew, Hebraic || *m* Hebrew (*language*)

ebrè·o -a *adj* & *mf* Hebrew || *m* Hebrew (*language*); Jew; **ebreo errante** Wandering Jew

è·bro -bra *adj* & *mf* var of **ebbro**

ebùrne·o -a *adj* (lit) ivory

ecatòmbe *f* hecatomb, slaughter

eccedènte *adj* exceeding || *m* excess

eccedènza *f* excess, surplus

eccèdere §123 *tr* to exceed || *intr* to go too far

eccellènte *adj* excellent

eccellènza *f* excellence || **Eccellenza** *f* Excellency

eccèllere §162 *intr* (ESSERE) to excel

eccèl·so -sa *adj* unexcelled; very high || **—l'Eccelso** *m* the Most High

eccentrici·tà *f* (**-tà**) eccentricity

eccèntri·co -ca (**-ci -che**) *adj* eccentric; suburban || *mf* vaudeville performer || *m* (mach) eccentric

eccepìbile *adj* objectionable

eccepire §176 *tr* (law) to take exception to || *intr* (law) to object

eccessi·vo -va *adj* excessive; overweening (*opinion*)

eccèsso *m* excess; **all'eccesso** excessively; **andare agli eccessi** to go to extremes; **dare in eccessi** to fly into a rage; **eccesso di peso** excess weight

eccètera *adv* and so forth, et cetera

eccètto *prep* except, but; **eccetto che** except that; unless

eccettuare (**eccèttuo**) *tr* to except

eccettua·to -ta *adj* excepted || **eccettuato** *prep* except

eccezionale *adj* exceptional

eccezióne *f* exception; objection; **ad eccezione di** with the exception of; **d'eccezione** extraordinary; **sollevare un'eccezione** (law) to take exception

ecchimò·si *f* (**-si**) bruise

eccì·dio *m* (**-di**) massacre

eccitàbile *adj* excitable

eccitaménto *m* instigation; excitement

eccitante *adj* stimulating ‖ *m* stimulant

eccitare (**èccito**) *tr* to excite ‖ *ref* to become excited or aroused; (sports) to warm up

eccitazióne *f* excitement; (elec) excitation

ecclesiàsti·co -ca (**-ci -che**) *adj* ecclesiastical ‖ *m* clergyman

ècco *tr invar* here is (are), there is (are); **ecco che** here, e.g., **ecco che viene** here he comes; **eccoci** here we are; **ecco fatto** that's it; **eccola** here she is; here it is; **eccomi** here I am; **eccone** here are some ‖ *intr invar* here I am; here it is; **quand'ecco** suddenly ‖ *interj* look!

eccóme *interj* and how!, indeed!

echeggiare §290 (**echéggio**) *intr* (ESSERE & AVERE) to echo

eclètti·co -ca *adj* & *mf* (**-ci -che**) eclectic

eclissare *tr* to eclipse ‖ *ref* to be eclipsed; (coll) to vanish, sneak away

eclis·si *f* (**-si**) eclipse

eclìtti·ca *f* (**-che**) ecliptic

èclo·ga *f* (**-ghe**) var of egloga

è·co *m* & *f* (**-chi** *mpl*) echo; **far eco a** to echo

ecogoniòmetro *m* sonar

ecologìa *f* ecology

economato *m* comptroller's or administrator's office

economìa *f* administration; management; economy; economics; **economìa aziendale** business management; **economia di mercato** free enterprise; **economia domestica** home economics; **economia politica** political economy; economics; **economie** savings; **fare economia** to save

econòmi·co -ca *adj* (**-ci -che**) economic(al); cheap

economi·sta *mf* (**-sti -ste**) economist

economizzare [ddzz] *tr* & *intr* to economize, save

ecòno·mo -ma *adj* thrifty ‖ *m* comptroller; administrator

ecosistè·ma [s] *m* (**-mi**) ecosystem

ecumèni·co -ca *adj* (**-ci -che**) ecumenical

eczè·ma [dz] *m* (**-mi**) eczema

édera *f* ivy

edìcola *f* shrine; newsstand

edificante *adj* edifying

edificare §197 (**edìfico**) *tr* to build; to edify ‖ *intr* to build

edifica·tóre -trice *adj* building ‖ *mf* builder

edificazióne *f* building; edification

edifì·cio *m* (**-ci**) building, edifice; pack (e.g., of lies); structure

edile *adj* building, construction ‖ *m* builder, construction worker

edili·zio -zia (**-zî -zie**) *adj* building, construction ‖ *f* building trade

edìpi·co -ca *adj* (**-ci -che**) Oedipus (e.g., complex)

Edipo *m* Oedipus

èdi·to -ta *adj* published

edi·tóre -trice *adj* publishing ‖ *mf* publisher; editor (e.g., of a text)

editorìa *f* publishing; publishers

editoriale *adj* editorial; publishing ‖ *m* editorial

editoriali·sta *mf* (**-sti -ste**) editorial writer

editto *m* edict

edizióne *f* edition; performance; (fig) vintage

edonismo *m* hedonism

edoni·sta *mf* (**-sti -ste**) hedonist

edòt·to -ta *adj* (lit) informed, acquainted; **rendere qlcu edotto su qlco** (lit) to inform s.o. of s.th

edredóne *m* eider, eider duck

educanda *f* boarding-school girl; convent-school girl

educandato *m* (convent) boarding school for girls

educare §197 (**èduco**) *tr* to educate; to rear, bring up; to train; to accustom, inure; (lit) to grow

educatì·vo -va *adj* educational

educa·to -ta *adj* educated; polite, well-bred

educa·tóre -trice *mf* educator

educazióne *f* education; breeding, manners; **educazione civica** civics

edule *adj* edible

efèbo *m* (coll) sissy

efèlide *f* freckle

effeminatézza *f* effeminacy

effemina·to -ta *adj* effeminate; frivolous

efferatézza *f* savagery

effervescènte *adj* effervescent

effervescènza *f* effervescence

effettivaménte *adv* really

effettì·vo -va *adj* real, true; effective; full (e.g., member); regular (e.g., army officer) ‖ *m* effective; total amount; (mil) manpower

effètto *m* effect, result; (com) promissory note; (billiards) English; (sports) spin; **a questo effetto** for this purpose; **effetti** effects, belongings; **effetto di luce** play of light; **effetto ottico** optical illusion; **fare effetto** to make a sensation; **fare l'effetto di** to give the impression of; **in effetto** in fact; **mandare a effetto** to carry out; **porre in effetto** to put into effect

effettuàbile *adj* feasible

effettuare (**effèttuo**) *tr* to bring about; to contrive; to actuate; **effettuare** (**una corsa, un servizio**) to run, e.g., **l'autobus effettua una corsa ogni mezz'ora** the bus runs every half hour

efficace *adj* effective; forceful (writer)

efficà·cia *f* (**-cie**) effectiveness, efficacy; (law) validity

efficiènte *adj* efficient

efficiènza *f* efficiency; **in piena efficienza** in full working order; **in top condition**

effigiare §290 *tr* to portray, represent

effì·gie *f* (**-gie** or **-gi**) effigy; image

effìme·ro -ra *adj* ephemeral

efflusso *m* flow, outflow

efflù·vio *m* (**-vi**) effluvium; emanation (e.g., of light)

effrazióne *f* (law) burglary

effusióne *f* effusion; outflow; shedding (of blood); effusiveness

egemonìa *f* hegemony

egè•o -a *adj* Aegean

ègida *f* aegis

Egitto, l' *m* Egypt

egizia•no -na *adj* & *mf* Egyptian

eglantina *f* sweetbrier

eglefino *m* haddock

égli §5 *pron pers* he

èglo•ga *f* (-ghe) eclogue

egocèntri•co -ca *adj* & *mf* (-ci -che) egocentric

egoismo *m* egoism, selfishness

egoi•sta (-sti -ste) *adj* selfish || *mf* egoist

egoìsti•co -ca *adj* (-ci -che) egoistic(al)

egotismo *m* egotism

egoti•sta (-sti -ste) *adj* egotistic || *mf* egotist

egrè•gio -gia *adj* (-gi -gie) (lit) outstanding; **Egregio Signore** Mr. (*before a man's name in an address on a letter*); Dear Sir

eguaglianza *f* equality

eguale *adj* var of **uguale**

egualità•rio -ria *adj* & *m* (-ri -rie) equalitarian

éhi *interj* hey!

éi *pron* (lit) he; (archaic) they

eiaculazióne *f* ejaculation

eiettàbile *adj* ejection (*seat*)

eiezióne *f* ejection

él *pron* (archaic) he

elaborare (elàboro) *tr* to elaborate; to digest; to secrete

elabora•to -ta *adj* elaborate || *m* written exercise

elaboratóre *m* computer

elaborazióne *f* elaboration; data processing

elargire §176 *tr* to donate

elargizióne *f* donation

elastici•tà *f* (-tà) elasticity; agility; (com) oscillation; (com) range

elàsti•co -ca (-ci -che) *adj* elastic || *m* rubber band; bedspring

élce *m* & *f* holm oak

elefante *m* elephant; **elefante marino** sea elephant

elefantéssa *f* female elephant

elegante *adj* elegant, fashionable

elegantó•ne -na *mf* fashion plate || *m* dandy, dude

eleganza *f* elegance, stylishness

elèggere §193 *tr* to elect

eleggìbile *adj* eligible

elegia *f* elegy

elegia•co -ca *adj* elegiac

elementare *adj* elementary || **elementari** *fpl* elementary schools

eleménto *m* element; rudiment; member; cell (*of battery*); **elementi personnel**, e.g., **elementi femminili** female personnel

elemòsina *f* alms; (eccl) collection; **chiedere l'elemosina** to beg; **vivere d'elemosina** to live on charity

elemosinare (elemòsino) *intr* to beg

Èlena *f* Helen

elencare §197 (elènco) *tr* to list; to enumerate

elèn•co *m* (-chi) list; **elenco telefonico** telephone directory

eletti•vo -va *adj* elective

elèt•to -ta *adj* elect; distinguished

(*audience*); precious (*metal*); chosen (*people*) || *mf* elect

elettorato *m* electorate, constituency

elet•tóre -trice *mf* voter; elector

elettràuto *m* automobile electrician; automotive electric shop

elettrici•sta *mf* (-sti -ste) electrician

elettrici•tà *f* (-tà) electricity

elèttri•co -ca (-ci -che) *adj* electrical || *m* electrical worker

elettrificàre §197 (elettrìfico) *tr* to electrify

elettrizzare [ddzz] *tr* to electrify (*e.g., a person*) || *ref* to become electrified

ellètro *m* amber

elettrocalamita *f* electromagnet

elettrocardiògrafo *m* electrocardiograph

elettrocardiogram•ma *m* (-mi) electrocardiogram

elettrodinàmi•co -ca (-ci -che) *adj* electrodynamic || *f* electrodynamics

elèttrodo *m* electrode

elettrodomèsti•co -ca (-ci -che) *adj* electric household || *m* electric household appliance

elettroesecuzióne *f* electrocution

elettròge•no -na *adj* generating (*unit*)

elettròli•si *f* (-si) electrolysis

elettrolìti•co -ca *adj* (-ci -che) electrolytic

elettròlito *m* electrolyte

elèttromagnèti•co -ca *adj* (-ci -che) electromagnetic

elettromo•tóre -trice *adj* electromotive || *m* electric motor || *f* electric train; electric railcar

elettróne *m* electron

elettróni•co -ca *adj* (-ci -che) electronic || *f* electronics

elettropómpa *f* electric pump

elettrosquasso *m* electroshock

elettrostàti•co -ca (-ci -che) *adj* electrostatic || *f* electrostatics

elettrotècni•co -ca (-ci -che) *adj* electrotechnical || *m* electrician; electrical engineer || *f* electrical engineering

elettrotrèno *m* electric train

elevaménto *m* elevation

elevare (èlevo & elèvo) *tr* to lift, elevate; (math) to raise || *ref* to rise

elevatézza *f* loftiness, dignity

eleva•to -ta *adj* high, lofty

eleva•tóre -trice *adj* elevating || *m* elevator

elevazióne *f* elevation; (sports) jump; (math) raising

elezióne *f* election; choice

èlfo *m* elf

èli•ca *f* (-che) propeller; (geom) helix

elicoidale *adj* helicoidal

elicòttero *m* helicopter

elìdere §161 *tr* to annul; to elide || *ref* to neutralize one another

eliminare (elìmino) *tr* to eliminate

eliminatò•rio -ria (-ri -rie) *adj* eliminating || *f* (sports) heat

eliminazióne *f* elimination; extermination

èlio- *comb form adj* helio-, e.g., **eliocentrico** heliocentric || *comb form*

m & f helio-, e.g., **elioterapìa** helio-therapy
èlio *m* helium
eliocèntri·co -ca *adj* (**-ci -che**) helio-centric
eliògrafo *m* heliograph
elioteràpi·co -ca *adj* (**-ci -che**) sunshine (*treatment*); sunbathing (*establishment*)
eliotrò·pio *m* (**-pi**) heliotrope; blood-stone
elipòrto *m* heliport
elisabettia·no -na *adj* Elizabethan
elì·sio -sia *adj* (**-si -sie**) Elysian
elisióne *f* elision
eli·sir *m* (**-sir**) elixir
èlitra *f* elytron, shard
élla *pron* (lit) she || **Ella** *pron* (lit) you
ellèboro *m* hellebore
ellèni·co -ca *adj* (**-ci -che**) Hellenic
ellisse *f* ellipse
ellis·si *f* (**-si**) (gram) ellipsis
ellìtti·co -ca *adj* (**-ci -che**) elliptical
-èllo -èlla *suf adj* little, e.g., **poverello** poor little
elmétto *m* helmet; tin hat
élmo *m* helmet
elogiare §290 (**elògio**) *tr* to praise
elò·gio *m* (**-gi**) praise, encomium; write-up; **elogio funebre** eulogy
eloquènte *adj* eloquent
eloquènza *f* eloquence
elò·quio *m* (**-qui**) (lit) speech, diction
élsa *f* hilt
elucidare (**elùcido**) *tr* to elucidate
elùdere §105 *tr* to elude, evade
elusi·vo -va *adj* elusive
elvèti·co -ca *adj & mf* (**-ci -che**) Helvetian
elzevì·ro -ra [dz] *adj* Elzevir || *m* Elzevir book; (journ) literary article
emacia·to -ta *adj* emaciated, lean
emanare *tr* to send forth; to issue || *intr* (ESSERE) to emanate; to come forth
emanazióne *f* emanation; issuance
emancipare (**emàncipo**) *tr* to emancipate || *ref* to become emancipated
emancipazióne *f* emancipation
emarginare (**emàrgino**) *tr* to note in the margin; (fig) to put aside, neglect
emarginato *m* marginal note
emàti·co -ca *adj* (**-ci -che**) blood, hematic
ematite *f* hematite
embar·go *m* (**-ghi**) embargo
emblè·ma *m* (**-mi**) emblem
emblemàti·co -ca *adj* (**-ci -che**) emblematic
embolìa *f* embolism
èmbrice *m* flat roof tile; shingle
embriologìa *f* embryology
embriònale *adj* embryonic
embrióne *m* embryo
emendaménto *m* emendation (*of a text*); amendment (*to a law*)
emendare (**emèndo**) *tr* to correct; to emend; to amend (*a law*) || *ref* to reform
emergènza *f* emergence; emergency
emèrgere §162 *intr* (ESSERE) to emerge;

to surface (*said of a submarine*); to loom; to stand out
emèri·to -ta *adj* emeritus (*professor*); famous
emerotè·ca *f* (**-che**) periodical library
emersióne *f* emersion; surfacing
emèr·so -sa *adj* emergent
emèti·co -ca *adj & m* (**-ci -che**) emetic
eméttere §198 *tr* to emit, send forth; to utter (*a statement*); (com) to issue
emiciclo *m* hemicycle; floor (*of legislative body*)
emicrània *f* migraine, headache
emigrante *adj & mf* emigrant
emigrare *intr* (ESSERE & AVERE) to emigrate
emigra·to -ta *adj & mf* emigrant
emigrazióne *f* emigration; migration (*e.g., of birds*)
eminènte *adj* eminent
eminènza *f* eminence; (eccl) Eminence
emisfèro *m* hemisphere
emissà·rio *m* (**-ri**) emissary; outlet (*river or lake*); drain
emissióne *f* emission; issuance; (rad) broadcast
emisti·chio *m* (**-chi**) hemistich
emittènte *adj* emitting; issuing; (rad) broadcasting || *f* (rad) transmitting set; broadcasting station
emofilìa *f* hemophilia
emoglobìna *f* hemoglobin
emolliènte *adj & m* emollient
emoluménto *m* fee, emolument
emorragìa *f* hemorrhage
emorròidi *fpl* hemorrhoids, piles
emostàti·co -ca (**-ci -che**) *adj* hemostatic || *m* hemostat
emotè·ca *f* (**-che**) blood bank
emotivi·tà *f* (**-tà**) emotionalism
emoti·vo -va *adj* emotional || *mf* emotional person
emottisi *f* (pathol) hemoptysis
emozionante *adj* emotional, moving
emozionare (**emozióno**) *tr* to move, stir; to thrill
emozióne *f* emotion
empiastro *m* var of **impiastro**
émpiere §163 *tr & ref* var of **empire**
empie·tà *f* (**-tà**) impiety; cruelty
ém·pio -pia *adj* (**-pi -pie**) impious; pitiless, wicked
empire §163 *tr* to fill; (lit) to fulfill; **empire qlcu di insulti** to heap insults on s.o. || *ref* to get full
empire·o -a *adj* heavenly, sublime || *m* empyrean
empìri·co -ca (**-ci -che**) *adj* empirical || *mf* empiricist
empirismo *m* empiricism
empiri·sta *mf* (**-sti -ste**) empiricist
émpito *m* (lit) rush; fury
empò·rio *m* (**-ri**) emporium, mart
emulare (**èmulo**) *tr* to emulate
emulazióne *f* emulation, rivalry; (law) evil intent
èmu·lo -la *adj* emulous || *mf* emulator
emulsionare (**emulsióno**) *tr* to emulsify
emulsióne *f* emulsion
encefalite *f* encephalitis
encìcli·ca *f* (**-che**) encyclical
enciclopedìa *f* encyclopedia

enciclopèdi•co -ca *adj* (**-ci -che**) encyclopedic

enclave *f* enclave

enclìti•co -ca *adj & f* (**-ci -che**) enclitic

encomiàbile *adj* praiseworthy

encomiare §287 (**encòmio**) *tr* to praise

encò•mio *m* (**-mi**) encomium, praise

endecasìlla•bo -ba *adj* hendecasyllabic || *m* hendecasyllable

endemìa *f* endemic

endèmi•co -ca *adj* (**-ci -che**) endemic

èndice *m* nest egg; (obs) souvenir

endocàr•dio *m* (**-di**) (anat) endocardium

endocarpo *m* (bot) endocarp

endòcri•no -na *adj* endocrine

endourba•no -na *adj* inner-city

endovenó•so -sa [s] *adj* intravenous

energèti•co -ca (**-ci -che**) *adj* energy (*e.g., crisis*); (med) tonic || *m* (med) tonic

energìa *f* energy, power

enèrgi•co -ca *adj* (**-ci -che**) energetic

energùme•no -na *mf* wild or mad person

ènfa•si *f* (**-si**) emphasis; forcefulness

enfàti•co -ca *adj* (**-ci -che**) emphatic

enfiare §287 (**énfio**) *tr & ref* to swell

enfisè•ma *m* (**-mi**) emphysema

enfitèu•si *f* (**-si**) lease (*of land*)

enìg•ma *m* (**-mi**) enigma, riddle, puzzle

enigmàti•co -ca *adj* (**-ci -che**) enigmatic, puzzling

-ènne *suf adj* -year-old, e.g., **ragazzo diciassettenne** seventeen-year-old boy || *suf mf* -year-old person, e.g., **diciassettenne** seventeen-year-old person

ennèsi•mo -ma *adj* nth

-èn•nio *suf m* (**-ni**) period of . . . years, e.g., **ventennio** period of twenty years

enòlo•go -ga *mf* (**-gi -ghe**) oenologist

enórme *adj* enormous

enormemènte *adv* enormously

enormi•tà *f* (**-tà**) enormity; outrage; absurdity

Enrico *m* Henry

ènte *m* being; entity; corporation; agency, body

enterocli•sma *m* (**-smi**) enema

enti•tà *f* (**-tà**) entity; value, importance

entomologìa *f* entomology

entram•bi -be *adj*—**entrambi i** both || *pron* both

entrante *adj* next (*e.g., week*)

entrare (**éntro**) *intr* (ESSERE) to enter; to go (*said of numbers*); to get (*into one's head*); **entrarci** to make it, e.g., **con questi soldi non c'entro** I can't make it with this money; **entrarci come i cavoli a merenda** to be completely out of line; **entrare a** to begin to; **entrare in** to enter (*e.g., a room*); to fit in; to go in (*said of a number*); to get into (*one's head*); **entrare in amore** to be in heat (*said of animals*); **entrare in ballo** to come into play; **entrare in carica** to take up one's duties; **entrare in collera** to get angry; **entrare in collisione** to collide; **entrare in contatto** to establish contact; **entrare in gioco** to come into play; **entrare in guerra** to go to war; **entrare in società** to make one's debut; **entrare nella parte di** (theat)

to play the role of; **entrare in vigore** to become effective; **Lei non c'entra** this is none of your business; **questo non c'entra** this is beside the point

entrata *f* entry; entrance; **entrata di favore** (theat) complimentary ticket; **entrate** income

entratura *f* entry, entrance; assumption (*of a position*); familiarity

éntro *adv* inside || *prep* within; **entro di** within, inside of

entrobórdo *m* inboard motorboat

entrotèrra *f* inland, hinterland

entusiasmare *tr* to carry away, enthuse || *ref* to be carried away, to become enthused

entusiasmo *m* enthusiasm

entusia•sta (**-sti -ste**) *adj* enthusiastic || *mf* enthusiast, devotee

entusiàsti•co -ca *adj* (**-ci -che**) enthusiastic

enucleare (**enùcleo**) *tr* to elucidate; (surg) to remove

enumerare (**enùmero**) *tr* to enumerate

enumerazióne *f* enumeration

enunciare §128 *tr* to enunciate, state

enunciatì•vo -va *adj* (gram) declarative

enunciazióne *f* enunciation, statement

enzi•ma [dz] *m* (**-mi**) enzyme

èpa *f* (lit) belly, paunch

epàti•co -ca *adj* (**-ci -che**) hepatic, liver

epatite *f* (pathol) hepatitis

epènte•si *f* (**-si**) epenthesis

eperlano *m* (ichth) smelt

èpi•co -ca *adj & f* (**-ci -che**) epic

epicurè•o -a *adj & m* epicurean

epidemìa *f* epidemic

epidèmi•co -ca *adj* (**-ci -che**) epidemic (al)

epidèrmi•co -ca *adj* (**-ci -che**) epidermal; (fig) superficial, skin-deep

epidèrmide *f* epidermis

Epifanìa *f* Epiphany

epiglòttide *f* (anat) epiglottis

epìgono *m* follower; descendant

epìgrafe *f* epigraph

epigram•ma *m* (**-mi**) epigram

epigrammàti•co -ca *adj* (**-ci -che**) epigrammatic

epilessìa *f* (pathol) epilepsy

epilètti•co -ca *adj & m* (**-ci -che**) epileptic

epìlo•go *m* (**-ghi**) epilogue; conclusion

episcopale *adj* episcopal

episcopalia•no -na *adj & mf* Episcopalian

episcopato *m* episcopate, bishopric

episòdi•co -ca *adj* (**-ci -che**) episodic

episò•dio *m* (**-di**) episode

epìstola *f* epistle

epistolà•rio *m* (**-ri**) letters, correspondence

epitàf•fio *m* (**-fi**) epitaph

epitè•lio *m* (**-li**) epithelium

epiteto *m* epithet; insult

epitomare (**epìtomo**) *tr* to epitomize

epitome *f* epitome

èpo•ca *f* (**-che**) epoch; period; moment; **fare epoca** to be epoch-making

epopèa *f* epic

eppure *conj* yet, and yet

epsomite *f* Epsom salt**

epurare *tr* to cleanse; to purge

epurazióne *f* purification; purge

equànime *adj* calm, composed; impartial

equanimità *f* equanimity; impartiality

equatóre *m* equator

equatoriale *adj* & *m* equatorial

equazióne *f* equation

equèstre *adj* equestrian

equilàte·ro -ra *adj* equilateral

equilibrare *tr* to balance; (aer) **to trim** || *ref* to balance one another

equilibra·to -ta *adj* level-headed

equilibra·tóre -trice *adj* stabilizing || *m* (aer) horizontal stabilizer

equilì·brio *m* (-**bri**) equilibrium, balance; (fig) proportion; **equilibrio politico** balance of power

equilibrì·sta *mf* (-**sti** -**ste**) acrobat, equilibrist

equi·no -na *adj* & *m* equine

equinoziale *adj* equinoctial

equinò·zio *m* (-**zi**) equinox

equipaggiaménto *m* equipment, outfit

equipaggiare §290 *tr* to equip, outfit; (naut) to fit out; (naut) to man

equipàg·gio *m* (-**gi**) equipage; (naut) crew, complement; (sports) team; (rowing) crew

equiparare *tr* to equalize (*e.g., salaries*)

équipe *f* team

equipollènte *adj* equivalent

equi·tà *f* (-**tà**) equity, fair-mindedness

equitazióne *f* horsemanship

equivalènte *adj* & *m* equivalent

equivalére §278 *intr* (ESSERE & AVERE) —**equivalere a** to be equivalent to || *ref* to be equal

equivocare §197 (**equìvoco**) *intr*—**equivocare su** to mistake, misunderstand

equìvo·co -ca (-**ci** -**che**) *adj* equivocal; ambiguous || *m* misunderstanding

è·quo -qua *adj* equitable, fair

èra *f* era, age; **era spaziale** space age

erà·rio *m* (-**ri**) treasury

èrba *f* grass; **erba limoncina** lemon verbena; **erba medica** alfalfa; **erbe** vegetables; **erbe aromatiche** herbs; **far l'erba** to cut the grass; **in erba** (fig) budding; **metter a erba** to put to pasture

erbàc·cia *f* (-**ce**) weed

erbaggi *mpl* vegetables

erbaió·lo -la *mf* fresh vegetable retailer

erbici·da *m* (-**di**) weed-killer

erbivéndo·lo -la *mf* fresh fruit and vegetable retailer

erbìvo·ro -ra *adj* herbivorous

erborì·sta *mf* (-**sti** -**ste**) herbalist

erbó·so -sa [s] *adj* grassy

Èrcole *m* Hercules

ercù·le·o -a *adj* Herculean

erède *m* heir || *f* heiress

eredi·tà *f* (-**tà**) inheritance; heredity

ereditare (**erèdito**) *tr* to inherit

eredità·rio -ria *adj* (-**ri** -**rie**) hereditary; crown (*prince*)

ereditièra *f* heiress

eremì·ta *m* (-**ti**) hermit

eremitàg·gio *m* (-**gi**) hermitage

èremo *m* hermitage

eresìa *f* heresy

eresiar·ca *m* (-**chi**) heretic

erèti·co -ca (-**ci** -**che**) *adj* heretical || *mf* heretic

erèt·to -ta *adj* erect, straight

erezióne *f* erection

ergastola·no -na *mf* lifer

ergàstolo *m* life imprisonment; prison for persons sentenced to life imprisonment

èrgere §164 *tr* (lit) to erect; (lit) to lift || *ref* to rise (*said, e.g., of a mountain*)

èrgo *m* *invar*—**venire all'ergo** to come to a conclusion || *adv* thus, hence

èri·ca *f* (-**che**) heather

erìgere §152 *tr* to erect, build || *ref* to rise; **erigersi a** to set oneself up as

eritrè·o -a *adj* & *mf* Eritrean

ermafrodì·to -ta *adj* & *m* hermafrodite

ermellìno *m* ermine

ermèti·co -ca *adj* (-**ci** -**che**) airtight; watertight; hermetic

èrnia *f* hernia; **ernia del disco** (pathol) herniated disk

eródere §239 *tr* to erode

eròe *m* hero

erogare §209 (**èrogo**) *tr* to distribute; to bestow

erogazióne *f* distribution; bestowal

erò·i·co -ca *adj* (-**ci** -**che**) heroic

eroicò·mi·co -ca *adj* (-**ci** -**che**) mockheroic

eroìna *f* heroine; (pharm) heroin

eroìsmo *m* heroism

erómpere §240 *intr* to erupt, burst out

erosióne *f* erosion

erò·ti·co -ca *adj* (-**ci** -**che**) erotic

erotìsmo *m* eroticism

èrpete *m* (pathol) herpes, shingles

erpicare §197 (**érpico**) *tr* to harrow

érpice *m* harrow

errabón·do -da *adj* (lit) wandering

errante *adj* errant; wandering

errare (**èrro**) *intr* to wander; **to err;** (lit) to stray

erra·to -ta *adj* mistaken, wrong

erròne·o -a *adj* erroneous

erróre *m* error, mistake; fault; (lit) wandering; **errore di lingua** slip of the tongue; **errore di scrittura** slip of the pen; **errore di stampa** misprint; **errore giudiziario** miscarriage of justice; **salvo errore od omissione** barring error or omission

ér·to -ta *adj* arduous, steep; erect || *f* arduous ascent; **all'erta** on the alert

erudìre §176 *tr* to educate, instruct

erudì·to -ta *adj* erudite, learned || *m* scholar, savant

erudizióne *f* erudition, learning

eruttare *tr* to belch forth (*e.g., lava*); to utter (*obscenities*) || *intr* to belch

eruttì·vo -va *adj* eruptive

eruzióne *f* eruption

esacerbare (**esacèrbo**) *tr* to embitter; to exacerbate || *ref* to become embittered

esagerare (**esàgero**) *tr* & *intr* to exaggerate

esagera·to -ta *adj* exaggerated, excessive || *mf* exaggerator

esagerazióne *f* exaggeration

esagitare (esàgito) *tr* to perturb

esàgono *m* hexagon

esalare *tr* to exhale; **esalare l'ultimo respiro** to breathe one's last ‖ *intr* to spread (*said of odors*)

esalazióne *f* exhalation; fume, vapor

esaltare *tr* to exalt; to excite ‖ *ref* to glorify oneself; to become excited

esalta·to -ta *adj* frenzied, excited ‖ *mf* hothead

esame *m* examination; checkup, test; **dare gli esami** to take an examination; **esame attitudinale** aptitude test; **esame del sangue** blood test; **esame di riparazione** make-up test; **fare gli esami** to prepare a test (*for a student*); **prendere in esame** to take in consideration

esàmetro *m* hexameter

esaminan·do -da *mf* candidate; examinee

esaminare (esàmino) *tr* to examine; to test

esamina·tóre -trice *mf* examiner

esàngue *adj* bloodless; (fig) pale

esànime *adj* lifeless

esasperante *adj* exasperating

esasperare (esàspero) *tr* to exasperate ‖ *ref* to become exasperated

esasperazióne *f* exasperation

esattézza *f* exactness; punctuality

esat·to -ta *adj* exact; punctual

esattóre *m* tax collector; bill collector

esattorìa *f* tax collector's office; bill collector's office

esaudire §176 *tr* to grant

esauriènte *adj* exhaustive; convincing

esauriménto *m* depletion (*e.g., of merchandise*); (pathol) exhaustion; (naut) drainage

esaurire §176 *tr* to exhaust; to play out (*e.g., a hooked fish*); to use up ‖ *ref* to be exhausted; to be depleted; to be sold out

esauri·to -ta *adj* exhausted; depleted; sold out; out of print

esau·sto -sta *adj* exhausted; empty

esautorare (esàutoro) *tr* to deprive of authority; to discredit (*a theory*)

esazióne *f* exaction; collection

é·sca *f* (**-sche**) bait; punk (*for lighting fireworks*); tinder (*for lighting powder*): **dare esca a** to foment

escandescènza *f*—**dare in escandescenze** to fly off the handle

escava·tóre -trice *mf* excavator, digger ‖ *m* excavator; **escavatore a vapore** steam shovel ‖ *f* (mach) excavator

escavazióne *f* excavation

eschimése [s] *adj* & *mf* Eskimo

esclamare *tr* & *intr* to exclaim

esclamati·vo -va *adj* exclamatory; exclamation (*mark*)

esclùdere §105 *tr* to exclude; to keep or shut out

esclusióne *f* exclusion; **a esclusione di** with the exception of

esclusiva *f* sole right, monopoly; (journ) scoop

esclusivi·sta (-sti -ste) *adj* clannish; bigoted ‖ *mf* bigot; (com) sole agent

esclusi·vo -va *adj* exclusive; intolerant, bigoted ‖ *f* see **esclusiva**

esclu·so -sa *adj* excluded, excepted

escogitare (escògito) *tr* to think up, invent; to think out

escoriare §287 (escòrio) *tr* & *ref* to skin

escoriazióne *f* abrasion

escreménto *m* excrement

escrescènza *f* excrescence

escrè·to -ta *adj* excreted ‖ *m* excreta

escursióne *f* excursion; (mach) sweep; (mil) transfer; **escursione termica** (meteor) temperature range

escursioni·sta *mf* (**-sti -ste**) excursionist, sightseer

escussióne *f* (law) examination, cross-examination

esecrare (esècro) *tr* to execrate

esecrazióne *f* execration

esecuti·vo -va *adj* & *m* executive

esecu·tóre -trice *mf* (mus) performer ‖ *m* executor; **esecutore di giustizia** executioner ‖ *f* executrix

esecuzióne *f* accomplishment, completion; performance; execution; **esecuzione capitale** capital punishment

esegè·si *f* (**-si**) exegesis

eseguire (eséguo) & §176 *tr* to execute, carry out; to perform

esèm·pio *m* (**-pi**) example; **a mo' d'esempio** as an illustration; **dare il buon esempio** to set a good example; **per esempio** for instance

esemplare *adj* exemplary ‖ *m* copy; specimen ‖ *v* (esèmplo) *tr* (lit) to copy

esemplificare §197 (esemplìfico) *tr* to exemplify

esentare (esènto) *tr* to exempt

esènte *adj* exempt, free

esenzióne *f* exemption

esèquie *fpl* obsequies, funeral rites

esercènte *adj* practicing ‖ *mf* dealer, merchant

esercire §176 *tr* to practice; to run (*a store*)

esercitare (esèrcito) *tr* to exercise; to tax (*e.g., s.o.'s patience*); to practice, ply (*a trade*); to wield (*e.g., power*) ‖ *ref* to practice

esercitazióne *f* exercise, training; **esercitazioni militari** drilling

esèrcito *m* army; (fig) flock; **Esercito della Salvezza** Salvation Army

eserci·zio *m* (**-zi**) exercise; practice; training; homework; occupation; drill; **d'esercizio** (com) administrative (*expenses*); **esercizio finanziario** fiscal year; **esercizio provvisorio** (law) emergency appropriation; **esercizio pubblico** establishment open to the public; **esercizio spirituale** (eccl) retreat

esibire §176 *tr* to exhibit ‖ *ref* to show oneself, appear; **esibirsi di** to offer to

esibizióne *f* exhibition

esigènte *adj* demanding, exigent

esigènza *f* demand, requirement, exigency

esìgere §165 *tr* to demand; to require; to exact; to collect

esigìbile *adj* due; collectable

esigui·tà *f* (**-tà**) meagerness, scantiness

esì·guo -gua *adj* meager, scanty

esilarante *adj* exhilarating; laughing (*gas*)

esilarare (esìlaro) *tr* to amuse ‖ *ref* to be amused

èsile *adj* slender, thin; weak

esiliare §287 *tr* to exile ‖ *ref* to go into exile; to withdraw

esilia·to -ta *adj* exiled ‖ *m* exile (*person*)

esì·lio *m* (-lii) exile, banishment

esìmere §166 *tr* to exempt ‖ *ref*—esìmersi da to avoid (*an obligation*)

esì·mio -mia *adj* (-mi -mie) distinguished, eminent

-èsi·mo -ma *suf adj & pron* -eth, e.g., ventesimo twentieth; -th, e.g., diciannovesimo nineteenth

esistènte *adj* existent; extant

esistènza *f* existence

esistenzialismo *m* existentialism

esìstere §114 *intr* (ESSERE) to exist

esitante *adj* hesitant

esitare (èsito) *tr* to retail ‖ *intr* to hesitate; (med) to resolve itself

esitazióne *f* hesitation; haw (*in speech*)

èsito *m* result, outcome; sale; outlet; (philol) late form; dare esito a (com) to reply

esiziale *adj* ruinous, fatal

èsodo *m* exodus, flight

esòfa·go *m* (-gi) esophagus

esonerare (esònero) *tr* to exempt, release

esònero *m* exemption, release

Esòpo *m* Aesop

esorbitante *adj* exorbitant

esorbitare (esòrbito) *intr*—esorbitare da to go beyond

esorcismo *m* exorcism

esorcizzare [ddzz] *tr* to exorcise

esordiènte *adj* beginning, budding ‖ *mf* beginner ‖ *f* debutante

esòr·dio *m* (-di) beginning

esordire §176 *intr* to make a start; (theat) to debut; (theat) to open

esortare (esòrto) *tr* to exhort

esortazióne *f* exhortation

esò·so -sa *adj* greedy, avaricious; hateful; exorbitant (*price*)

esòti·co -ca *adj* (-ci -che) exotic

esotismo *m* exoticism; borrowing (*from a foreign language*)

espàndere §167 *tr* to expand ‖ *ref* to spread out; to confide

espansióne *f* expansion; effusiveness

espansionismo *m* expansionism

espansivi·tà *f* (-tà) effusiveness

espansi·vo -va *adj* expansive; effusive

espan·so -sa *adj* flared; expanded, dilated

espatriare §287 *intr* to emigrate

espà·trio *m* (-tri) emigration

espediènte *m* expedient, makeshift; ruse; vivere di espedienti to live by one's wits

espedire §176 *tr* to expedite ‖ *ref*—espedirsi di to get rid of

espèllere §168 *tr* to expel, eject

esperiènza *f* experience; experiment

esperiménto *m* experiment; test

espèr·to -ta *adj* & *m* expert

espettorare (espèttoro) *tr & intr* to expectorate

espiare §119 *tr* to expiate; to placate (*the gods*); espiare una pena to serve a sentence

espiató·rio -ria *adj* (-ri -rie) expiatory

espiazióne *f* expiation

espirare *tr & intr* to breath out, to exhale

espirazióne *f* exhaling

espletare (esplèto) *tr* to dispatch, complete

esplicare §197 (èsplico) *tr* to carry out; (lit) to explain

esplicati·vo -va *adj* explanatory

esplìci·to -ta *adj* explicit

esplòdere §169 *tr* to shoot; to fire (*a shot*) ‖ *intr* (ESSERE & AVERE) to explode; to burst forth

esploditóre *m* blasting machine

esplorare (esplòro) *tr* to explore; to search, probe; (telv) to scan

esplora·tóre -trice *mf* explorer ‖ *m* (nav) gunboat; giovane esploratore boy scout

esplorazióne *f* exploration; (telv) scanning

esplosióne *f* explosion, blast; (fig) outburst

esplosi·vo -va *adj & m* explosive

esponènte *adj* (typ) superior ‖ *m* spokesman; dictionary entry; catchword (*of dictionary*); (math) exponent; (naut) net weight

espórre §218 *tr* to expose, show; to expound; to abandon (*a baby*); to lay out (*a corpse*); to lay open (*to danger*) ‖ *intr* to show, exhibit ‖ *ref* to expose oneself

esportare (espòrto) *tr* to export

esporta·tóre -trice *mf* exporter

esportazióne *f* export, exportation

esposimetro *m* exposure meter

esposi·tóre -trice *mf* commentator; exhibitor

esposizióne *f* exposition; abandonment (*of a baby*); exhibit, fair; line (*of credit*); exposure (*of a house*); (phot) exposure

espó·sto -sta *adj* exposed; aforementioned ‖ *m* petition, brief; foundling

espressióne *f* expression; feeling

espressi·vo -va *adj* expressive

esprès·so -sa *adj* manifest; express; prepared on the spot ‖ *m* espresso; messenger; special-delivery letter; special-delivery stamp

esprimere §131 *tr* to express; to convey (*an opinion*); (lit) to squeeze ‖ *ref* to express oneself

espropriare §287 (espròprio) *tr* to expropriate ‖ *ref* to deprive onself; espropriarsi di to divest oneself of

espròprio *m* (-pri) expropriation

espugnare *tr* to take by storm

espulsióne *f* expulsion; (mach) ejection

espulsóre *m* ejector

espurgare §209 *tr* to expurgate

èssa §5 *pron pers* she; it

ésse §5 *pron pers* they

essènza *f* essence

essenziale *adj* essential ‖ *m* main point

èssere *m* being; existence; condition; (coll) character; in essere in good shape ‖ §170 *intr* (ESSERE) to be;

c'è there is; ci sono there are; ci sono! I get it!; come sarebbe a dire? what do you mean?; come se nulla fosse as if nothing had happened; esserci to have arrived, to be there; essere di to belong to; essere per to be about to; può essere maybe; sarà maybe; sia . . . sia both . . . and; whether . . . or || *aux* (ESSERE) (to form passive) to be, e.g., fu investito da un tassametro he was run over by a taxi; (to form the compound tenses of certain intransitive verbs and all reflexive verbs) to have, e.g., sono arrivati they have arrived; mi sono appena alzato I have just got up || *impers* (ESSERE) to be, e.g., è giusto it is fair

éssi §5 *pron pers* they

essiccare §197 *tr* to dry || *ref* to dry up

essicca·tóio *m* (-tói) drier

essiccazióne *f* drying

èsso §5 *pron pers* he; it; chi per esso his representative

essudare *intr* to exude

èst *m* east

èsta·si *f* (-si) ecstasy; andare in estasi to become enraptured

estasiare §287 *tr* to enrapture, delight || *ref* to become enraptured

estate *f* summer

estàti·co -ca *adj* (-ci -che) ecstatic, enraptured

estemporàne·o -a *adj* extemporaneous

estèndere §270 *tr* to extend; to broaden (e.g., one's knowledge); to draw up (a document) || *ref* to extend

estensibile *adj* applicable; inviare saluti estensibili a to send greetings to be extended to (e.g., another person)

estensióne *f* extension; extent; expanse (e.g., of water); (mus) compass, range

estensi·vo -va *adj* extensive

estèn·so -sa *adj*—per esteso fully

estensóre *adj* extensible || *m* compiler (e.g., of a dictionary); (sports) exerciser, chest expander

estenuante *adj* exhausting

estenuare (estènuo) *tr* to exhaust || *ref* to become exhausted

esterióre *adj* exterior || *m* outside appearance

esteriori·tà *f* (-tà) appearance

esternare (estèrno) *tr* to reveal, manifest || *ref* to confide

estèr·no -na *adj* external; outside; day (student) || *m* exterior, outside; (baseball) outfielder; all'esterno outside; in esterno (mov) on location

èste·ro -ra *adj* foreign || *m* foreign countries; all'estero abroad

esterrefat·to -ta *adj* terrified

esté·so -sa [s] *adj* extended, wide; per esteso in full

estè·ta *mf* (-ti -te) aesthete

estèti·co -ca (-ci -che) *adj* aesthetic || *f* aesthetics

esteti·sta *mf* (-sti -ste) beautician

estima·tóre -trice *mf* appraiser; admirer

èstimo *m* appraisal; assessment

estìnguere §156 *tr* to extinguish; to quench (thirst); to pay off (a debt) || *ref* to die out

estinguìbile *adj* extinguishable; payable

estìn·to -ta *adj* extinguished; extinct || *m* deceased, dead person

estintóre *m* fire extinguisher

estirpare *tr* to uproot; to eradicate; to pull (a tooth)

estirpa·tóre -trice *mf* eradicator || *m* (agr) weeder

estivare *tr & intr* to summer

esti·vo -va *adj* summer; summery

estòllere §171 *tr* to extol

èstone *adj & mf* Estonian

estòrcere §272 *tr* to extort; estorcere qlco a qlcu to extort s.th from s.o.

estorsióne *f* extortion

estradare *tr* (law) to extradite

estradizióne *f* extradition

estràne·o -a *adj* extraneous, foreign; aloof || *mf* outsider

estrapolare (estràpolo) *tr* to extrapolate

estrarre §273 *tr* to extract, draw; to pull (a tooth)

estrat·to -ta *adj* extracted || *m* extract; abstract; certified copy; (typ) offprint; estratto conto bank statement; estratto dell'atto di nascita copy of one's birth certificate

estrazióne *f* extraction; drawing (of lottery)

estrèma *f* (sports) wing, end

estremi·sta *adj & mf* (-sti -ste) extremist

estremi·tà *f* (-tà) end; tip, top; extremity; le estremità the extremities

estrè·mo -ma *adj* extreme; esalare l'estremo respiro to breath one's last || *m* extremity; end, extreme; essere agli estremi to be near the end; estremi essentials || *f see* estrema

estrìnse·co -ca *adj* (-ci -che) extrinsic

èstro *m* horsefly; whim, fancy; inspiration; estro venereo heat (of female animal)

estromèttere §198 *tr* to oust, expel

estró·so -sa [s] *adj* fanciful, whimsical; inspired

estrovèr·so -sa or estroverti·to -ta *adj & mf* extrovert

estrùdere §190 *tr* to extrude

estuà·rio *m* (-ri) estuary

esuberante *adj* exuberant; buoyant

esuberanza *f* exuberance; buoyancy; a esuberanza abundantly

esulare (èsulo) *intr* (ESSERE & AVERE) to go into exile; esulare da to be alien to

esulcerare (esùlcero) *tr* to ulcerate on the surface; (fig) to exacerbate

esulcerazióne *f* superficial ulceration; (fig) exasperation, exacerbation

èsule *mf* exile (person)

esultante *adj* exultant, jubilant

esultare *intr* to exult

esumare *tr* to exhume; to revive (e.g., a custom)

esumazióne *f* exhumation; revival

e·tà *f* (-tà) age; che età ha? how old is he (or she)?; ha la sua età he (or she) is no longer a youngster; l'età di mezzo Middle Ages; maggiore età majority; mezza età middle age; minore età minority

etamine *f* cheesecloth

ètere *m* ether

etère•o -a *adj* ethereal
eternare (etèrno) *tr* to immortalize || *ref* to become immortal
eterni•tà *f* (-tà) eternity
etèr•no -na *adj* eternal, everlasting || *m* eternity; **in eterno** forever
eterodòs•so -sa *adj* heterodox
eterogène•o -a *adj* heterogeneous
èti•ca *f* (-che) ethics
etichétta *f* label; card (*e.g., of a library*); etiquette; **etichetta gommata** sticker
etichettare (etichétto) *tr* to label
èti•co -ca (-ci -che) *adj* ethical; consumptive || *m* consumptive || *f* see **etica**
etile *m* ethyl
etilène *m* ethylene
etìli•co -ca *adj* (-ci -che) ethyl
ètimo *m* etymon
etimologia *f* etymology
etìope *adj & mf* Ethiopian
Etiòpia, l' *f* Ethiopia
etiòpi•co -ca *adj* (-ci -che) Ethiopian
etisìa *f* tuberculosis
ètni•co -ca *adj* (-ci -che) ethnic(al)
etnografìa *f* ethnography
etnologìa *f* ethnology
etru•sco -sca *adj & mf* (-schi -sche) Etruscan
ettàgono *m* heptagon
èttaro *m* hectare
ètte *m* (coll) particle, jot, whit, tittle
ètto or ettogrammo *m* hectogram
-étto -étta *suf adj* rather, e.g., **piccoletto** rather small; -ish, e.g., **rotondetto** roundish
ettòlitro *m* hectoliter
eucalipto *m* eucalyptus
eucaristìa *f* Eucharist
eufemismo *m* euphemism
eufonìa *f* euphony
eufòni•co -ca *adj* (-ci -che) euphonic
euforìa *f* euphoria
eufòri•co -ca *adj* (-ci -che) euphoric
eufuismo *m* euphuism
eugenèti•co -ca (-ci -che) *adj* eugenic || *f* eugenics
eunu•co *m* (-chi) eunuch
europè•o -a *adj & mf* European
Euròpa, l' *f* Europe
eurovisióne *f* European television chain
eutanasìa *f* euthanasia
Eva *f* Eve
evacuaménto *m* evacuation
evacuare (evàcuo) *tr* to evacuate || *intr* to evacuate; to have a bowel movement
evacuazióne *f* evacuation; bowel movement

evàdere §172 *tr* to evade; to complete (*a deal*); to answer (*a letter*); to execute (*orders*) || *intr* (ESSERE) to flee, escape
evanescènza *f* evanescence; (rad) fading
evanescènte *adj* evanescent; vanishing
evangèli•co -ca *adj* (-ci -che) evangelic (al)
evangeli•sta *m* (-sti) evangelist
evangelizzare [ddzz] *tr* to evangelize; to campaign for; to subject to political propaganda
evaporare (evapóro) *tr & intr* to evaporate
evaporatóre *m* evaporator; humidifier
evaporazióne *f* evaporation
evasióne *f* evasion, escape; (com) reply; **dare evasione a** to complete (*an administrative matter*)
evasì•vo -va *adj* evasive
eva•so -sa *adj* escaped || *m* escapee
evasóre *m* tax dodger
eveniènza *f* eventuality, contingency; **nell'evenienza che** in the event (that); **per ogni evenienza** just in case
evènto *m* event; **eventi correnti** current events; **fausto or lieto evento** happy event
eventuale *adj* contingent
eventuali•tà *f* (-tà) eventuality
eversì•vo -va *adj* upsetting; destructive
evidènte *adj* evident; clear
evidènza *f* evidence; clearness; **mettersi in evidenza** to make oneself conspicuous; **tenere in evidenza** (com) to keep active
evirare *tr* to emasculate
evitare (èvito) *tr* to avoid, shun; **evitare qlco a qlcu** to spare s.o. s.th, to save s.o. from s.th
èvo *m* age, era; **evo antico** ancient times; **evo moderno** modern times; **medio evo** Middle Ages
evocare §197 (èvoco) *tr* to evoke
evoluire §176 *intr* (aer, nav) to maneuver
evolu•to -ta *adj* developed; progressive; modern
evoluzióne *f* evolution
evòlvere §115 *tr* to develop || *ref* to evolve
evvi•va *m* (-va) cheer || *interj* long live!, hurrah for!
èx *adj invar* ex-, e.g., **la sua ex moglie** his ex-wife; ex, e.g., **ex dividendo** ex dividend
ex li•bris *m* (-bris) bookplate
extraconiugale *adj* extramarital
extraeuropè•o -a *adj* non-European
ex vó•to *m* (-to) votive offering
eziologìa *f* etiology

F

F, f ['ɛffe] *m & f* sixth letter of the Italian alphabet
fa *m* (fa) (mus) F, fa
fabbisógno *m invar* need; requirement
fàbbri•ca *f* (-che) building, construction; factory, plant

fabbricante *mf* builder, manufacturer
fabbricare §197 (fàbbrico) *tr* to manufacture; to fabricate
fabbrica•to -ta *adj* built || *m* building
fabbricazióne *f* building; erection; manufacturing; fabrication (*invention*)

fabbro m blacksmith; locksmith; (fig) master; **fabbro ferraio** blacksmith

faccènda f business, matter; **faccende domestiche** household chores

faccendiè•re -ra mf operator, schemer

faccétta f small face; face, facet

facchinàg•gio m (-gi) porterage; (fig) drudgery

facchino m porter; **lavorare come un facchino** to work like a slave

fàc•cia f (-ce) face; countenance; **avere la faccia di** to have the gall to; **di faccia a** opposite; **faccia da galeotto** (coll) gallows bird; **faccia tosta** cheek, gall; **in faccia a** in front of

facciale adj facial

facciata f façade; page; (fig) surface appearance

face f (lit) torch

facè•to -ta adj facetious

facèzia f pleasantry, banter; **scambiar facezie** to banter with each other

fachiro m fakir

fàcile adj easy; inclined; loose (morals); glib (tongue); **è facile** it is probable || m something easy

facili•tà f (-tà) facility, ease; inclination; **facilità di pagamento** easy payments, easy terms; **facilità di parola** glibness

facilitare (facìlito) tr to facilitate; to grant (credit); to give (easy terms)

facilitazióne f facilitation; easy terms; cut rate

facinoró•so -sa [s] adj criminal || m hoodlum, thug

facoltà f (-tà) faculty; power; school (of a university); **facoltà** fpl means, wealth

facoltati•vo -va adj optional

facoltó•so -sa [s] adj wealthy, affluent

facóndia f loquacity, gift of gab

facón•do -da adj loquacious

facsìmi•le m (-le) facsimile

faènza f faïence || **Faenza** f Faenza

fàg•gio m (-gi) (bot) beech

fagia•no -na mf pheasant

fagiolino m string bean

fagiòlo m bean; (coll) sophomore; **andare a fagiolo a** (coll) to fit perfectly; **fagiolo bianco** lima bean

fà•glia f (-glie) (geol) fault

fagòtto m bundle; (mus) bassoon; **far fagotto** (coll) to pack up

fàida f vengeance, vendetta

faìna f stone marten

falange f phalanx

fal•bo -ba adj tawny

falcata f step, stride; bucking

falce f scythe; crescent (of moon); **falce messoria** sickle

falcétto m sickle

falciare §128 tr to mow

falcia•tóre -trice mf mower || f mowing machine

falcidiare §287 tr to reduce; to cut down

fal•co m (-chi) hawk; **falco pescatore** osprey

falcóne m falcon

falconerìa f falconry

falconière m falconer

falda f band, strip; flake (of snow); gable (of roof); brim (of hat); foot (of mountain); slab (of stone); waist plate (of armor); hem (of suit); flounce (of dress); layer (of rock); flap, coattail; **falda della camicia** shirttail; **falde** straps (to hold a baby); **mettersi in falde** to wear tails

falegname m carpenter; cabinetmaker

falegnamerìa f carpentry; cabinetmaking; carpenter shop; woodworker shop

falèna f moth

falla f hole, leak; (archaic) fault

fallace adj fallacious, deceptive

fallà•cia f (-cie) fallacy

fallare intr & ref (lit) to be mistaken

fallìbile adj fallible

fallimentare adj bankrupt; ruinous

falliménto m bankruptcy; (fig) collapse, failure

fallire §176 tr to miss (the target) || intr (ESSERE) to go bankrupt; to fail || intr (AVERE) (lit) to be mistaken

falli•to -ta adj & mf bankrupt

fallo m error, fault; sin; flaw; phallus; (sports) penalty; (sports) foul; **cadere in fallo** to make the wrong move; to be mistaken; **cogliere in fallo** to catch in the act; **far fallo a** to fail, e.g., **gli faccio fallo** I fail him; **senza fallo** without fail

fa•lò m (-lò) bonfire

falpa•là f (-là) flounce, furbelow

falsare tr to falsify, alter; (lit) to forge

falsari•ga f (-ghe) guideline (for writing); model, pattern; **seguire la falsariga di** to follow in the footsteps of

falsà•rio m (-ri) forger; counterfeiter

falsétto m falsetto

falsificare §197 (falsìfico) to falsify; to forge, fake

falsificazióne f falsification; forgery; misrepresentation

falsi•tà f (-tà) falsehood; falsity

fal•so -sa adj false; wrong (step); assumed (name); bogus, counterfeit, fake (money); phony || m falsehood; perjury; forgery; **commettere un falso** to perjure oneself; to commit forgery; **giurare il falso** to bear false witness; to perjure oneself

fama f fame; reputation; **cattiva fama** notoriety

fame f hunger; dearth; **aver fame** to be hungry; **avere una fame da lupo** to be as hungry as a wolf, to be as hungry as a bear; **morire di fame** to starve to death; to be ravenous

famèli•co -ca adj (-ci -che) starving, famished

famigera•to -ta adj notorious

famìglia f family; community; **di famiglia** intimate; **in famiglia** at home

famì•glio m (-gli) beadle, usher; hired man

familiare adj family; familiar, intimate; homelike || m member of the family

familiari•tà f (-tà) familiarity; **avere familiarità con** to be familiar with

familiarizzare [ddzz] *tr* to familiarize

famó·so -sa [s] *adj* famous, illustrious

fanale *m* lamp, lantern; (rr) headlight; **fanale di coda** taillight

fanalino *m* small light; (aut) parking light; (aut) tail light

fanàti·co -ca (-ci -che) *adj* fanatic, fanatical || *mf* fanatic

fanatismo *m* fanaticism

fanatizzare [ddzz] *tr* to make a fanatic of

fanciulla *f* girl; spinster; bride

fanciullè·sco -sca *adj* (**-schi -sche**) childish; children's

fanciullézza *f* childhood; (fig) infancy

fanciulo·lo -la *adj* childish; childlike || *mf* child || *m* boy || *f* see **fanciulla**

fandònia *f* fib, tale, yarn

fanèllo *m* (orn) linnet; (orn) finch

fanfara *f* military band; fanfare

fanfaróne *m* braggart

fangàtura *f* mud bath

fanghìglia *f* mud, slush

fan·go *m* (**-ghi**) mud; **fare i fanghi** to take mud baths

fangó·so -sa [s] *adj* muddy

fannullo·ne -na *mf* idler, loafer

fanóne *m* whalebone

fantaccino *m* infantryman, foot soldier

fantascientìfi·co -ca *adj* (**-ci -che**) science-fiction

fantasciènza *f* science fiction

fantasìa *f* fantasy, fancy, whim; (mus) fantasia; **di fantasia** fancy

fantasió·so -sa [s] *adj* fanciful; imaginative

fanta·sma *m* (**-smi**) ghost, spirit; phantom; **fantasma poetico** poetic fancy

fantasticare §197 (**fantàstico**) *tr* to imagine, dream up || *intr* to daydream

fantasticherìa *f* imagination, daydreaming

fantàsti·co -ca *adj* (**-ci -che**) fantastic || **fantàstico** *interj* unbelievable!

fante *m* infantryman, foot soldier; (cards) jack; (obs) youth

fanterìa *f* infantry

fanté·sca *f* (**-sche**) (joc, lit) housemaid

fantino *m* jockey

fantòc·cio *m* (**-ci**) puppet

fantomàti·co -ca *adj* (**-ci -che**) ghostly; mysterious

farabutto *m* scoundrel, heel

faraóna *f* guinea fowl

faraóne *m* Pharaoh; (cards) faro

farcire §176 *tr* to stuff

fardèllo *m* bundle; burden; **far fardello** to pack one's bags

fare *m* doing; break (*of day*); way (*of acting*); **sul far della sera** at nightfall || §173 *tr* to do; to make; to work; to take (*e.g., a walk, a step*); to give (*a sigh*); to deal (*cards*); to suffer (*hunger*); to lead (*a good or bad life*); to render (*service*); to log (*e.g., 15 m.p.h.*); to be, e.g., **tre volte tre fa nove** three times three is nine; to build (*e.g., a house*); to put together (*a collection*); to prepare (*dinner*); to say, utter (*a word*); to have (*a dream*); to give (*fruit*); to pay (*atten-*

tion); to play (*a role*); to stir up (*pity*); to mention (*a name*); **fare il** (or **la**) to be a (*e.g., carpenter*); **fare + *inf*** to have + *inf*, e.g., **gli ho fatto . . .** I had him . . . ; to make + *inf*, e.g., **il medico mi fece . . .** the doctor made me . . .; to have + *pp*, e.g., **farò fare . . .** I shall have . . . done; **fare acqua** to leak, to take in water; to get a supply of water; (coll) to urinate; **fare a metà** to divide in half; **fare a pugni** to come to blows; **fare a tempo** to be on time; **fare benzina** to buy gasoline; **fare caldo** a to keep warm, e.g., **questa coperta gli fa caldo** this blanket keeps him warm; **fare carbone** to coal; **fare . . . che** to have been . . . since, e.g., **fanno tre mesi che siamo in questa città** it has been three months since we have been in this city; **fare che + *subj*** to see to it that + *ind*, e.g., **faccia che comincino a lavorare subito** see to it that they begin to work at once; **fare colpo** to make an impression; **fare corona** a to crown; **fare cuore** a to encourage; **fare del male** a to harm; **fare di + *inf*** to see to it that + *ind*; **fare di tutto** to do one's best; **fare festa** a to cheer; **fare fiasco** to fail; **fare finta di** to pretend to; **fare fronte** a to face, meet; **fare fuoco su** to fire upon; **fare il gioco di** to play into the hands of; **fare il pappagallo** to parrot, ape; **fare il pieno** to fill up (*with gasoline*); **fare la bocca** a to get used to; **fare la calza** to knit; **fare la coda** to queue up, line up; **fare la festa** a to kill; **fare la guardia** to stand guard; **fare la mano** a to get used to; **fare le cose in famiglia** to wash one's dirty linen at home; **fare le cose in grande stile** to splurge; **fare legna** to gather firewood; **fare l'occhio** to become accustomed; **fare mente** to pay attention; **fare onore** a to do honor to; **fare paura** a to frighten; **fare sangue** to bleed; **fare sapere** a qlcu to let s.o. know; **fare scalo** (aer, naut) to make a call; **fare sì che** to act in such a way that; to see to it that; **fare silenzio** to keep silent; **fare specie** a to amaze, e.g., **il tuo comportamento gli fa specie** your behavior amazes him; **fare tesoro di** to prize; **fare una bella figura** to look good; to make a fine appearance; **fare una mala figura** to look bad; to make a bad showing; **fare una malattia** (coll) to get sick; **fare vela** to set sail; **fare venire** to send for; **fare vigilia** to fast; **farla corta** to cut it short; **farla franca** to get off scot-free; **farla grossa** to commit a blunder; **farla in barba** a to outwit; **farne di cotte e di crude**, **farne di tutti i colori**, or **farne più di Carlo in Francia** to engage in all sorts of mischief; to paint the town red; **non fare che + *ind*** to do nothing but + *inf* || *intr*—**averla a che fare con** to have words with; to have to deal with; **fare a coltellate** to have a fight with knives; **fare a girotondo** to play ring-around-the-rosy; **fare al caso di** to fit; to suit; **fare a meno di** to do without; **fare da** to serve as, e.g., **fare da cuscino** to serve as a pillow; **fare da cena** to fix dinner; **fare di cappello** to take one's hat off; **fare presto** to hurry; **fare per** to be just the thing for; **fare tardi** to be late || *ref* to become; to cut (*e.g., one's hair*); to move, e.g., **farsi in là** to move farther; **farsi avanti** to come forward; **farsi beffe di** to make fun of; **farsi bello** to bedeck oneself; to dress up; **farsi bello di** to boast about; to appropriate; **farsi gioco di** to make fun of; **farsi le labbra** to put lipstick on; **farsi strada** to make one's way; **farsi una ragione di** to rationalize, explain to oneself; **farsi un baffo** to not give a hoot; **si fa giorno** it is getting light; **si fa tardi** it is getting late || *impers*—**che tempo fa?** what's the weather like?; **fa** ago, e.g., **alcune settimane fa** a few weeks ago; **fa estate** it is like summer; **fa fino** it is smart; **fa freddo** it is cold; **fa luna** there is moonlight, the moon is out; **fa nebbia** it is foggy; **fa notte** it is nighttime; it is dark; it is getting dark; **fa sole** it is sunny, the sun is out; **fa tipo** or **fa tono!** that's classy!; **non fa nulla** it doesn't matter, never mind

farètra *f* quiver
farfalla *f* butterfly; bow tie; (mach) butterfly valve; (coll) promissory note
farfallóne *m* large butterfly; blunder; Don Juan
farfugliare §280 *intr* to mumble, mutter
farina *f* flour; **farina d'avena** oatmeal; **farina di legno** sawdust; **farina di ossa** bone meal; **farina gialla** yellow corn meal
farinàce·o -a *adj* farinaceous || **farinacei** *mpl* flour-yielding cereals
farinata *f* porridge
faringe *f* pharynx
faringite *f* pharingitis
farinó·so -sa [s] *adj* floury; powdery (*snow*); crumbly, friable
farisèo *m* Pharisee; (fig) pharisee
farmacèuti·co -ca *adj* (*-ci -che*) pharmaceutical, drug
farmacia *f* pharmacy; drugstore; medicine cabinet; **farmacia di guardia** or **di turno** drugstore open all night and Sunday
farmaci·sta *mf* (*-sti -ste*) pharmacist, druggist
fàrma·co *m* (*-ci* or *-chi*) remedy, medicine
farneticare §197 (**farnètico**) *intr* to rave
farnèti·co -ca (*-chi -che*) *adj* raving || *m* delirium; craze
faro *m* lighthouse, beacon; (aut) headlight; **faro retromarcia** (aut) back-up light
farràgine *f* hodgepodge
farraginó·so -sa [s] *adj* confused, mixed

farsa *f* farce; burlesque
farsè·sco -sca *adj* (*-schi -sche*) farcical, ludicrous
farsétto *m* sweater; (hist) doublet
fascétta *f* girdle; band; wrapper; clamp; **fascetta editoriale** advertising band (*of book*)
fà·scia *f* (*-sce*) band; belt; bandage; newspaper wrapper; **fascia del cappello** hatband; **fascia di garza** gauze bandage; **fascia elastica** abdominal supporter; (aut) piston ring; **fasce del neonato** swaddling clothes; **in fasce** newborn; **sotto fascia** in a wrapper
fasciame *m* (naut) planking; (naut) plating
fasciare §128 to bind; to bandage; to wrap; to surround
fasciatura *f* bandaging, dressing
fascicolo *m* number, issue; pamphlet; file, dossier; (bb) fasciculus
fascina *f* fagot
fascina·tóre -trice *mf* charmer
fàscino *m* fascination, charm
fà·scio *m* (*-sci*) bundle; sheaf; bunch (*of flowers*); pencil or beam (*of rays*); fascist party
fascismo *m* fascism
fasci·sta *adj & mf* (*-sti -ste*) fascist
fase *f* phase, stage; (aut) cycle; (astr, elec, mach) phase
fastèllo *m* bundle, fagot
fasti *mpl* records, annals; notable events; (hist) Roman calendar
fasti·dio *m* (*-di*) annoyance; (coll) loathing, nausea; **avere in fastidio** to loathe; **dar fastidio a** to annoy; **fastidi** troubles, worries
fastidió·so -sa [s] *adj* annoying, irksome; irritable; (obs) disgusting
fasti·gio *m* (*-gi*) top, summit
fa·sto -sta *adj* (lit) propitious || *m invar* pomp, display || *mpl* see **fasti**
fastó·so -sa [s] *adj* pompous, ostentatious
fata *f* fairy; **buona fata** fairy godmother; **Fata Morgana** Fata Morgana (*mirage; Morgan le Fay*)
fatale *adj* fatal; inevitable; irresistible (*woman*)
fatalismo *m* fatalism
fatali·sta *mf* (*-sti -ste*) fatalist
fatali·tà *f* (*-tà*) fatality, fate
fatalóna *f* vamp
fata·to -ta *adj* fairy, enchanted; (lit) predestined
fati·ca *f* (*-che*) fatigue, weariness; labor; **a fatica** with difficulty; **da fatica** draft (*e.g., horse*); of burden (*beast*); **durar fatica a** + *inf* to have trouble in + *ger*
faticare §197 *intr* to toil; **faticare a** to be hardly able to
faticó·so -sa [s] *adj* burdensome, heavy; (lit) weary
fatìdi·co -ca *adj* (*-ci -che*) fatal
fato *m* fate, destiny
fatta *f* kind, sort; **essere sulla fatta di** to be on the trail of
fattàc·cio *m* (*-ci*) (coll) crime
fattézze *fpl* features

fattìbile *adj* feasible, possible
fattispècie *f*—**nella fattispecie** in this particular case
fat·to -ta *adj* made, e.g., **fatto a mano** handmade; broad (*daylight*); deep (*night*); ready-made (*e.g., suit*); **ben fatto** well-done; shapely; **esser fatto per** to be cut out for; **fatto di** made of; **venir fatto a** to happen, chance, e.g., **gli venne fatto d'incontrarmi** he happened to meet me ‖ *m* fact; act, deed; feat; action; business, affair; **badare ai fatti propri** to mind one's own business; **cogliere sul fatto** to catch in the act; **dire a qlcu il fatto suo** to give s.o. a piece of one's mind; **fatto compiuto** fait accompli; **fatto d'arme** feat of arms; **fatto si è** the fact remains that; **in fatto di** concerning; as of; **sapere il fatto proprio** to know one's business; **venire al fatto** to come to the point ‖ *f* see **fatta**
fat·tóre -tóra or -toréssa *mf* farm manager ‖ *m* maker; factor; steward ‖ *f* stewardess; manager's wife
fattoria *f* farm; stewardship
fattorino *m* delivery boy, messenger boy; conductor (*of streetcar*)
fattrice *f* (zool) dam
fattucchiè·re -ra *mf* magician ‖ *m* sorcerer ‖ *f* sorceress, witch
fattura *f* preparation; workmanship; bill, invoice; (coll) witchcraft; (lit) creature
fatturare *tr* to adulterate; to invoice, bill
fattura·to -ta *adj* adulterated ‖ *m* (com) turnover
fatturi·sta *mf* (-sti -ste) billing clerk
fà·tuo -tua *adj* fatuous
fàuci *fpl* jaws; (fig) mouth
fàuna *f* fauna
fàuno *m* faun
fàu·sto -sta *adj* propitious, lucky
fau·tóre -trice *mf* supporter, promoter
fava *f* broad bean; **pigliare due piccioni con una fava** to catch two birds with one stone
favèlla *f* speech; (lit) tongue
favilla *f* spark; **far** or **mandare faville** to sparkle
favo *m* honeycomb
fàvola *f* fable; tale; **favola del paese** talk of the town
favoló·so -sa [s] *adj* fabulous; mythical
favóre *m* favor; help; cover (*e.g., of night*); **a favore di** for the benefit of; **di favore** special (*price*); complimentary (*ticket*); **favore politico** patronage; **per favore** please; **per favore di** courtesy of
favoreggiaménto *m* abetting, support
favoreggiare §290 (**favoréggio**) *tr* to abet, support
favoreggia·tóre -trice *mf* abettor, supporter, backer
favorévole *adj* favorable; propitious
favorire §176 *tr* to favor; to accept; to oblige, accommodate; **favorire qlcu di qlco** to oblige s.o. with s.th.; **favorisca** + *inf* please + *inf*, be kind

enough to + *inf*; **favorisca alla cassa** please pay the cashier; **favorisca uscire!** please leave!; **tanto per favorire?** won't you please join us (*at a meal*)?; please help yourself!
favorita *f* royal mistress
favoritismo *m* favoritism
favori·to -ta *adj* & *mf* favorite ‖ *m* protegé; **favoriti** sideburns ‖ *f* see **favorita**
faziόne *f* faction; **essere di fazione** to be on guard duty
fazió·so -sa [s] *adj* factious ‖ *m* partisan
fazzolétto *m* handkerchief; **fazzoletto da collo** neckerchief
fé *f* var of **fede**
feb·bràio *m* (-brài) February
fèbbre *f* fever; fever blister; **febbre da cavallo** (coll) very high fever; **febbre da fieno** hay fever; **febbre dell'oro** gold fever
febbricitante *adj* feverish
febbrile *adj* feverish
Fèbo *m* Phoebus
féc·cia *f* (-ce) dregs; (fig) dregs (*of society*); **fino alla feccia** to the bitter end
fèci *fpl* feces
fècola *f* starch
fecondare (**fecóndo**) *tr* to fecundate
fecondazióne *f* fecundation; **fecondazione artificiale** artificial insemination
fecondi·tà *f* (-tà) fecundity
fecón·do -da *adj* fecund, prolific
féde *f* faith; certificate; wedding ring; faithfulness; **far fede** to bear witness; **in fede di che** in testimony whereof; **in fede mia!** upon my word! **prestar fede a** to put one's faith in; **tener fede alla parola data** to keep one's word
fedecommésso *m* fideicommissum; trusteeship
fedéle *adj* faithful, devoted ‖ *mf* faithful person; **i fedeli** the faithful
fedel·tà *f* (-tà) faithfulness, allegiance; fidelity; **ad alta fedeltà** hi-fi
fèdera *f* pillowcase
federale *adj* federal
federali·sta *mf* (-sti -ste) federalist
federati·vo -va *adj* federative
federa·to -ta *adj* federate, federated
federazióne *f* federation; (sports) league
Federico *m* Frederick
fedifra·go -ga *adj* (-ghi -ghe) unfaithful, treacherous
fedina *f* police record; **avere la fedina sporca** to have a bad record; **fedine** sideburns
fégato *m* liver; courage; **fegato d'oca** pâté de foie gras; **rodersi il fegato** to be consumed with rage
félce *f* fern
feldspato *m* feldspar
felice *adj* happy; blissful; glad; felicitous
felici·tà *f* (-tà) happiness; bliss
felicitare (**felícito**) *tr* to make happy; **che Dio vi feliciti!** God bless you! ‖

ref to rejoice; **felicitarsi con qlcu per qlco** to congratulate s.o. for or on s.th

felicitazióne *f* congratulation

feli·no -na *adj* & *m* feline

fellóne *m* (lit) traitor

félpa *f* plush

felpa·to -ta *adj* covered with plush; soft (*e.g., step*)

féltro *m* felt; felt hat

felu·ca *f* (-che) two-cornered hat; (naut) felucca

fémmina *adj* & *f* female

femminile *adj* feminine, female || *m* feminine gender

femminili·tà *f* (-tà) femininity, womanliness

femminismo *m* feminism

fèmore *m* femur; thighbone

fendènte *m* slash with a sword

fèndere §174 *tr* to split, cleave; to plow (*water*); to rend (*air*); to make one's way through (*a crowd*) || *ref* to split; to come apart

fenditura *f* split, breach, fissure

fenice *f* phoenix

fenì·cio -cia (-ci -cie) *adj* & *mf* Phoenician || **la Fenicia** Phoenicia

fèni·co -ca *adj* (-ci -che) carbolic

fenicòttero *m* flamingo

fenòlo *m* phenol

fenomenale *adj* phenomenal

fenòmeno *m* phenomenon; freak, monster; **essere un fenomeno** to be unbelievable

ferace *adj* (lit) fertile

ferale *adj* (lit) mortal, deadly

fèretro *m* bier, coffin

feriale *adj* working (*day*); weekday

fèrie *fpl* vacation; **ferie retribuite** vacation with pay

ferire §176 *tr* to wound; to strike; **senza colpo ferire** without striking a blow || *ref* to wound oneself

feri·to -ta *adj* wounded, injured || *m* wounded person; injured person; **i feriti** the wounded; the injured || *f* wound, injury

feritóia *f* loophole; embrasure

feri·tóre -trice *mf* assailant

férma *f* setting (*of setter or pointer*); (mil) service; (mil) enlistment

fermacarro *m* (rr) buffer

fermacar·te *m* (-te) paperweight; large paper clip

fermacravat·ta *m* (-ta) tiepin

fermà·glio *m* (-gli) clasp; buckle; clip; brooch

fermare (**férmo**) *tr* to stop; to pay (*attention*); to fasten; to close, shut; to detain (*in police station*); to set (*game*); to reserve (*seats*) || *ref* to stop; to stay

fermata *f* stop; **fermata a richiesta** or **facoltativa** stop on signal

fermentare (**ferménto**) *tr* & *intr* to ferment

fermentazióne *f* fermentation

ferménto *m* ferment

fermézza *f* firmness; steadfastness

fér·mo -ma *adj* firm; stopped; quiet (*water*); (fig) steadfast; **fermo in**

posta general delivery; **fermo restando che** seeing that; **stare fermo** to be quiet || *m* stop; detention; **mettere il fermo a** to stop (*a check*)

fermopòsta *m* general delivery || *adv* care of general delivery

feróce *adj* fierce; wild

ferò·cia *f* (-cie) ferocity, ferociousness, fierceness

feròdo *m* (aut) brake lining

ferragósto *m* Assumption; mid-August holiday

ferrame *m* ironware

ferramén·to *m* (-ti) iron or metal bracket; iron or metal trimming || *m* (-ta *fpl*)—**ferramenta** hardware

ferrare (**fèrro**) *tr* to shoe (*a horse*); to hoop (*a barrel*)

ferra·to -ta *adj* iron; ironclad; shod (*horse*); spiked (*shoe*); well-versed || *f* pressing, ironing; mark or burn (*caused by ironing*); (coll) iron grate

ferravèc·chio *m* (-chi) scrap-iron dealer, junkman

fèrre·o -a *adj* iron; ironclad

ferrièra *f* ironworks; (obs) iron mine

fèrro *m* iron; tool; anchor; sword; **ai ferri** on the grill, broiled (*e.g., steak*); **essere sotto i ferri del chirurgo** to go under the knife; **ferri** shackles; **ferri del mestiere** tools of the trade; **ferro battuto** wrought iron; **ferro da arricciare** curling iron; **ferro da calza** knitting needle; **ferro da cavallo** horseshoe; **ferro da stiro** iron, flatiron; **ferro fuso** cast iron; **ferro grezzo** pig iron; **mettere a ferro e fuoco** to put to fire and sword; **venire ai ferri corti** to get into close quarters

ferromodellismo *m* hobby of model railroads

ferrotranvièri *mpl* transport workers

ferrovìa *f* railroad; **ferrovia a dentiera** rack railway; **ferrovia sopraelevata** elevated railroad

ferrovià·rio -ria *adj* (-ri -rie) railroad

ferrovière *m* railroader

fèrtile *adj* fertile

fertilizzante [ddzz] *adj* fertilizing || *m* fertilizer

fertilizzare [ddzz] *tr* to fertilize

fervènte *adj* fervent

fèrvere §175 *intr* to be fervent; to rage (*said, e.g., of a battle*); to go full blast

fèrvi·do -da *adj* fervent

fervóre *m* fervor; (fig) heat

fervorino *m* lecture, sermon

fesserìa *f* (slang) stupidity, nonsense; (slang) trifle

fés·so -sa *adj* cracked; cleft; (slang) dumb || *m* (lit) cranny; **fare fesso qlcu** (slang) to play s.o. for a sucker

fessura *f* crack; cranny

fèsta *f* feast; holiday; birthday; saint's day; **a festa** festively; **buone feste!** happy holiday!; **conciare per le feste** to drub the daylights out of; **fare festa a** to welcome; **fare le feste** to spend the holidays; **far festa** to celebrate; to take the day off; **far la festa**

a to do in, kill; **festa del ceppo** Christmas; **festa da ballo** or **danzante** dancing party; **festa della mamma** Mother's Day; **festa del papà** Father's Day; **festa di precetto** (eccl) day of obligation; **festa nazionale** national holiday; **mezza festa** half holiday

festante *adj* cheerful

festeggiaménto *m* celebration

festeggiare §290 (**festéggio**) *tr* to celebrate, fete; to cheer

festi·no -na *adj* (lit) rapid || *m* party

festivi·tà *f* (-**tà**) festivity

festi·vo -va *adj* festive, holiday

festóne *m* festoon

festó·so -sa [s] *adj* cheerful, merry

festu·ca *f* (-**che**) straw; (fig) mote

fetènte *adj* stinking; stink (*bomb*) || *mf* (fig) stinker, louse

fetic·cio *m* (-**ci**) fetish

feticismo *m* fetishism

fèti·do -da *adj* stinking, fetid

fèto *m* fetus

fetóre *m* stench

fétta *f* slice; **tagliare a fette** to slice

fettina *f* thin slice; twist (*of lemon*); **fettina di vitello** veal cutlet

fettùc·cia *f* (-**ce**) tape, ribbon

fettuccine *fpl* noodles

feudale *adj* feudal

feudalismo *m* feudalism

feudatà·rio -ria (-**ri** -**rie**) *adj* feudatory || *m* feudal vassal

fèudo *m* fief

fiaba *f* fairy tale; tale, yarn

fiacca *f* tiredness; sluggishness; **batter la fiacca** to loaf, to goof off

fiaccare §197 *tr* to weaken; to weary; to break || *ref* to weaken; to break (*e.g., one's neck*)

fiacche·ràio *m* (-**rài**) (coll) hackman, cabman

fiacchézza *f* weakness; sluggishness

fiac·co -ca *adj* (-**chi** -**che**) weak; sluggish; slack || *f* see **fiacca**

fiàccola *f* torch; **fiaccola della discordia** firebrand

fiaccolata *f* torchlight procession

fiala *f* vial, phial

fiamma *f* flame; blaze; (mil) insignia; (nav) pennant; **alla fiamma** (culin) flaming; **dare alle fiamme** to set on fire; **diventare di fiamma** to blush; **in fiamme** afire

fiammante *adj* blazing; **nuovo fiammante** brand-new

fiammata *f* blaze; flare-up

fiammeggiante *adj.* flaming, blazing; (archit) flamboyant

fiammeggiare §290 (**fiamméggio**) *tr* to singe || *intr* to flame, blaze

fiammìfero *m* match

fiammin·go -ga (-**ghi** -**ghe**) *adj* Flemish; Dutch (*e.g., master*) || *mf* Fleming || *m* Flemish (*language*); (orn) flamingo

fiancata *f* blow with one's hip; dig, sarcastic remark; side, flank; (nav) broadside

fiancheggiare §290 (**fianchéggio**) *tr* to flank; to border (*a road*); to support

fiancheggia·tóre -trice *mf* supporter, backer

fian·co *m* (-**chi**) flank, side; hip; **di fianco** sideways; **fianco a fianco** side by side; **fianco destr'!** (mil) right face!; **fianco destro** (naut) starboard; **fianco sinistr'!** (mil) left face!; **fianco sinistro** (naut) port; **prestare il fianco a** to leave oneself wide open to; **tenersi i fianchi dal ridere** to split one's sides laughing

Fiandre, le *fpl* Flanders

fia·sca *f* (-**sche**) flask

fiaschetteria *f* tavern, wine shop

fia·sco *m* (-**schi**) straw-covered wine bottle; flask; fiasco

fiata *f* (archaic) time

fiatare *intr* to breathe; **senza fiatare** without breathing a word

fiato *m* breath; (archaic) stench; **avere il fiato grosso** to be out of breath; **bere d'un fiato** to gulp down; **col fiato sospeso** holding one's breath; **dare fiato a** to blow, sound (*a trumpet*); **d'un fiato** or **in un fiato** without interruption; in one gulp; **fiati** (mus) winds; **senza fiato** out of breath

fiatóne *m*—**avere il fiatone** to be out of breath

fibbia *f* clasp, buckle

fibra *f* fiber

fibró·so -sa [s] *adj* fibrous

ficcana·so [s] *mf* (-**si** *mpl* -**so** *fpl*) (coll) busybody, meddler; nosy person

ficcare §197 *tr* to stick; to drive (*e.g., a nail*); to push; **ficcare gli occhi addosso a** to gaze at, stare at; **ficcare il naso negli affari degli altri** to poke one's nose in other people's business || *ref* to hide; to butt in; to get involved

fi·co *m* (-**chi**) fig; fig tree

ficodìndia *m* (*pl* **fichidindia**) prickly pear

fidanzaménto *m* engagement, betrothal

fidanzare *tr* to betroth || *ref* to become engaged

fidanza·to -ta *adj* engaged || *m* fiancé || *f* fiancée

fidare *tr* to entrust || *intr* to trust || *ref* to have confidence; **fidarsi a** (coll) to dare to; **fidarsi di** to trust, rely on

fida·to -ta *adj* trustworthy, reliable

fi·do -da *adj* (lit) faithful, trusted || *m* loyal follower; credit; **far fido** to extend credit

fidùcia *f* faith, confidence; (com) credit; **di fiducia** trustworthy

fiducià·rio -ria (-**ri** -**rie**) *adj* fiduciary || *mf* fiduciary, trustee

fiducio·so -sa [s] *adj* confident, hopeful

fièle *m* invar gall, bile; acrimony

fienile *m* hayloft

fièno *m* hay

fierìsti·co -ca *adj* (-**ci** -**che**) of a fair, e.g., **attività fieristica** activity of a fair

fiè·ro -ra *adj* fierce; dignified; proud || *f* fair; exhibit; wild beast fièvole *adj* feeble, weak

fifa *f* (coll) scare; **avere la fifa** (coll) to be chicken; **avere una fifa blu** (coll) to be scared stiff

fifó·ne -na *mf* (coll) scaredy-cat

fìggere §104 *tr* (lit) to drive, thrust || *ref*—**fìggersi in capo** to get into one's head

figlia *f* daughter; (com) stub; **figlia consanguinea** stepdaughter on the father's side

figliare §280 *tr & intr* to whelp (*said of animals*)

figlia·stro -stra *mf* stepchild || *m* stepson || *f* stepdaughter

figliata *f* litter (*e.g., of pigs*)

fì·glio -glia *mf* child, offspring || *m* son; **figli** children; **figlio consanguineo** stepson on the father's side || *f* see **figlia**

figliòc·cio -cia (-ci -ce) *mf* godchild || *m* godson || *f* goddaughter

figliolanza *f* children, offspring

figliò·lo -la *mf* child || *m* son, boy || *f* daughter, girl

figura *f* figure; illustration; figurehead; face card; **far bella figura** to make a good showing; **far cattiva figura** to make a poor showing; **far figura** to look good; **figura retorica** figure of speech

figurante *m/f* (theat) extra, super

figurare *tr* to feign; to represent || *intr* to figure; to appear; to make a good showing || *ref* to imagine; **si figuri!** imagine!

figurati·vo -va *adj* (fa) figurative

figura·to -ta *adj* figurative (*speech*); transcribed (*pronunciation*); illustrated (*book*)

figurina *f* figurine; card, picture (*of a series of athletes or entertainment celebrities*)

figurini·sta *mf* (-sti -ste) dress designer; costume designer

figurino *m* fashion plate; fashion magazine

figuro *m* scoundrel; gangster

figuróne *m*—**fare un figurone** to make a very good showing

fila *f* row; file, line; series; **di fila** in a row; **fare la fila** to wait in line; **file ranks**

filàc·cia *f* (-ce) lint

filacció·so -sa [s] or **filacció·so -sa** [s] *adj* thready, stringy

filaménto *m* filament

filamentó·so -sa [s] *adj* thready, stringy; thread-like

filanda *f* spinning mill; silk spinning mill

filante *adj* spinning; shooting (*star*); thready; flowing (*e.g., line*)

filantropia *f* philanthropy

filantròpi·co -ca *adj* (-ci -che) philanthropic

filàntro·po -pa *mf* philanthropist

filare *m* row, line || *tr* to spin; to drip; ooze; to rest on (*one's oars*); to make (*e.g., ten knots*); (naut) to pay out; (mus) to hold (*a note*); **filare l'amore** to be in love || *intr* to spin (*said of a spider*); to rope, thread (*said of wine*

or *syrup*); to make sense; to drip; **fare filare dritto qlcu** to keep s.o. in line; **filare a** to do (*e.g., twenty miles an hour*); **filare all'inglese** to take French leave; **fila via!** (coll) get out!

filarmòni·co -ca (-ci -che) *adj* philharmonic || *f* philharmonic society

filastròc·ca *f* (-che) rigmarole; nursery rhyme

filatelìa *f* philately

filatèli·co -ca (-ci -che) *adj* philatelic(al) || *mf* philatelist

fila·to -ta *adj* spun; well-constructed (*speech*) || *m* yarn

fila·tóio *m* (-tói) spinning wheel

filatura *f* spinning; spinning mill

filettare (filétto) *tr* to fillet; (mach) to thread

filettatura *f* stripe (*on a cap*); (mach) thread

filétto *m* fillet; stripe; snaffle (*on a horse's bit*); fine stroke (*in handwriting*); (mach) thread; (typ) ornamental line, headband; (typ) rule

filiale *adj* filial || *f* branch office

filiazióne *f* filiation

filibustière *m* filibuster, buccaneer; adventurer

filièra *f* (mach) drawplate; (mach) die (*to cut threads*)

filigrana *f* filigree; watermark (*in paper*)

filippi·no -na *adj* Philippine || *m* Filipino || **le Filippine** the Philippines

Filippo *m* Philip

filistè·o -a *adj & m* philistine; Philistine

Fillide *f* Phyllis

film *m* (film) film; movie, motion picture; **film parlato** or **sonoro** talking picture

filmare *tr* to film

filmina *f* filmstrip

filmìsti·co -ca *adj* (-ci -che) movie, motion-picture

filmotè·ca *f* (-che) film library

fi·lo *m* (-li) thread; wire; yarn; blade (*of grass*); breath (*of air*); string (*of pearls*); edge (*of razor*); **dare del filo da torcere** to cause trouble; **essere ridotto a un filo** to be only skin and bones; **fil di voce** thin voice; **filo a piombo** plumb line; **filo d'acqua** thin stream; **filo della schiena** or **delle reni** spine; **filo spinato** barbed wire; **passare a fil di spada** to put to the sword; **per filo e per segno** in detail; from beginning to end; **senza fili** wireless; **stare a filo** to stand upright; **tenere i fili** (fig) to pull wires; **tenere in filo** to keep in line; **un filo di** a bit of || *m* (-la *fpl*) string (*e.g., of cooked cheese*); (archaic) file, row

filo·bus *m* (-bus) trolley bus

filodiffusióne *f* wired wireless; cable TV

filodrammàti·co -ca *adj & mf* (-ci -che) (theat) amateur

filogovernati·vo -va *adj* on the government side

filologìa *f* philology

filòlo·go -ga (-gi -ghe) *adj* philologic(al) || *m* philologist

filóne *m* vein (*of ore*); ripple (*of a cur-*

rent); stream; loaf (*of bread*); (lit) mainstream; **filone d'oro** gold lode
filó·so -sa [s] *adj* stringy
filosofìa *f* philosophy
filosòfi·co -ca *adj* (**-ci -che**) philosophic(al)
filòso·fo -fa *mf* philosopher
filovìa *f* trolley bus line
filtrare *tr* to filter; to percolate (*coffee*) || *intr* to filter, permeate
filtrazióne *f* filtering, filtration
filtro *m* filter; philter
filugèllo *m* silkworm
filza *f* string (*of pearls*); series (*of errors*); row; dossier, file; basting (*of dress*)
finale *adj* final, last; consumer (*goods*) || *m* end, ending; (mus) finale; (sports) finish || *f* end, ending; (sports) finals
finali·sta *mf* (**-sti -ste**) finalist
finali·tà *f* (**-tà**) end, purpose
finanche *adv* even
finanza *f* finance
finanziaménto *m* financing
finanziare §287 *tr* to finance
finanzià·rio -ria (**-ri -rie**) *adj* finance, financial || *f* (com) holding company
finànzia·tóre -trice *mf* financial backer
finanzièra *f* frock coat; **alla finanziera** with giblet gravy
finanzière *m* financier; (coll) customs officer
fin·ca *f* (**-che**) column, row (*of ledger*)
finché *conj* until, as long as; **finché non** until
fine *adj* fine, thin; choice, nice || *m* end, purpose; conclusion; (lit) limit, border; **a fin di bene** to good purpose, for the best; **secondo fine** ulterior motive || *f* end, conclusion; **condurre a fine** to bring to fruition; **fine di settimana** weekend; **in fin dei conti** after all; **senza fine** endless
fine-settima·na *m or f* (**-na**) weekend
finèstra *f* window; (lit) gash, wound; **finestra a ganghèri** casement window; **finestra a ghigliottina** sash window; **finestra panoramica** picture window; **finestre** (lit) eyes
finestrino *m* (aut, rr) window
finézza *f* thinness; delicacy; finesse; kindness
fingere §126 *tr* to feign, pretend; (lit) to invent || *intr* to feign, pretend || *ref* to pretend to be
finiménto *m* finishing touch; **finimenti** harness
finimóndo *m* fracas, uproar
finire §176 *tr* to end; to put an end to; **finiscila!** cut it out! || *intr* (ESSERE) to end, to be over; to abut; to wind up; **finire con** + *inf* to wind up + *ger*; **finire di** + *inf* to finish + *ger*, e.g., **ho finito di farmi la barba** I have finished shaving
fini·to -ta *adj* finished; accomplished; finite; exhausted; **aver finito** to be through; **falla finita!** cut it out!; **farla finita con** to be through with; **farla finita con la vita** to end one's life
finitura *f* finish, finishing touch

finlandése [s] *adj* Finnish || *mf* Finlander, Finn || *m* Finnish (*language*)
Finlàndia, la Finland
finni·co -ca *adj* & *mf* (**-ci -che**) Finnic
fi·no -na *adj* fine, thin; refined; pure; sheer; **fare fino** (coll) to be refined || *adv* even; **fin a quando?** till when?; **fin da domani** beginning tomorrow; **fin da ora** beginning right now; **fin dove?** how far?; **fin in cima** up to the top; **fino a** until; down to; up to; as far as; **fin qui** up to now; up to this point
finòc·chio *m* (**-chi**) fennel; (vulg) fairy, queer
finóra *adv* up to now, heretofore
finta *f* pretense; fly (*of trousers*); (sports) feint; **far finta di** + *inf* to pretend to + *inf*, to feign + *ger*
fintantoché *conj* until
fin·to -ta *adj* false (*teeth*); fake; fictitious; sham (*battle*) || *mf* hypocrite || *f* see **finta**
finzióne *f* pretense; fiction; figment
fio *m*—**pagare il fio** to pay the piper; **pagare il fio di** to pay the penalty for
fioccare §197 (**fiòcco**) *intr* (ESSERE) to fall (*said of snow*); to flow (*said, e.g., of complaints*) || *impers* (ESSERE) —**fiocca** it is snowing
fiòc·co *m* (**-chi**) bow, knot; flake (*of snow*); flock, tuft (*of wool*); (naut) jib; **coi fiocchi** excellent; made to perfection; **fiocco pallone** (naut) spinnaker
fioccó·so -sa [s] *adj* flaky
fiòcina *f* harpoon
fiò·co -ca *adj* (**-chi -che**) feeble, faint
fiónda *f* sling; slingshot
fio·ràio -ràia (**-rài -ràie**) *mf* florist || *f* flower girl
fiorami *mpl*—**a fiorami** with flower design
fiordaliso *m* fleur-de-lis; (bot) iris; (lit) lily
fiòrdo *m* fjord
fióre *m* flower; prime (*of life*); best, pick; bloom; **a fior d'acqua** on the surface; skimming the water; **a fior di labbra** in a low tone, sottovoce; **a fior di pelle** skin-deep, superficial; **fior di** (coll) a lot of; **fiore di latte** cream; **fiori** (cards) clubs; **primo fiore** down (*soft hairy growth*)
fiorènte *adj* flourishing, thriving
fiorenti·no -na *adj* & *mf* Florentine
fiorettare (**fiorétto**) *tr* (fig) to overembellish
fiorétto *m* little flower; choice, pick; overembellishment; choice passage (*from life of saint*); foil; button of foil
fioricoltóre *m* var of **floricoltore**
fioricoltura *f* var of **floricoltura**
fiorino *m* florin
fiorire §176 *tr* to cause to flower; to adorn with flowers || *intr* (ESSERE) to flower, bloom; to flourish; to break out (*said of skin eruption*); to get moldy
fiori·sta *mf* (**-sti -ste**) florist
fiori·to -ta *adj* flowering; flowery;

mottled; moldy; studded (*e.g., with errors*)

fioritura *f* flowering; flourish; mold; (pathol) eruption

fiorrancino *m* (orn) kinglet, firecrest

fiorràn·cio *m* (-ci) marigold

fiòtto *m* gush, surge; (obs) wave

Firènze *f* Florence

firma *f* signature; power of attorney; good reputation; (mil) enlisted man; **buona firma** famous writer; **farci la firma** (coll) to accept quite willingly; **firma di favore** guarantor's signature

firmaiòlo *m* (mil) enlisted man

firmaménto *m* firmament

firmare *tr* to sign

firmatà·rio -ria (-ri -rie) *adj* signatory || *mf* signer, signatory

fisarmòni·ca *f* (-che) accordion

fiscale *adj* fiscal, tax

fischiare §287 *tr* to whistle; to boo || *intr* to whistle; to ring (*said of ears*); to blow (*said, e.g., of a factory whistle*)

fischiettare (fischiétto) *tr & intr* to whistle

fischiétto *m* whistle (*instrument*)

fi·schio *m* (-schi) whistle; hiss, boo; blow (*of whistle*); ringing (*in the ears*)

fi·sciù *m* (-sciù) kerchief, fichu

fisco *m invar* treasury; internal revenue service

fìsi·co -ca (-ci -che) *adj* physical; bodily || *m* physicist; physique; (obs) physician || *f* physics

fìsima *f* whim, fancy, caprice

fisiologìa *f* physiology

fisiològi·co -ca *adj* (-ci -che) physiological

fisionomìa or **fisonomìa** *f* physiognomy; countenance, face; appearance

fisionomi·sta *mf* (-sti -ste) person good at faces; physiognomist

fi·so -sa *adj* (lit) fixed

fissàg·gio *m* (-gi) (phot) fixing

fissare *tr* to fix; to fasten; to gaze at; to reserve; to hire; **fissare lo sguardo** to gaze || *ref* to gaze, stare; to become obsessed; to settle down

fissati·vo -va *adj* fixing

fissa·to -ta *adj* fixed; (coll) cracked || *mf* (coll) crackpot

fissa·tóre -trice *adj* (phot) fixing || *m* fixer; **fissatore per capelli** hair spray; hair dressing

fissazióne *f* fixation; fixed idea

fissile *adj* fissionable

fissionàbile *adj* fissionable

fissióne *f* fission

fis·so -sa *adj* fixed; regular || *m* pay

fistola *f* (pathol) fistula; (lit) pipe

fitta *f* pang, stitch; crowd; great amount; (coll) blow; (obs) quagmire

fittàvolo *m* tenant farmer

fittì·zio -zia *adj* (-zi -zie) fictitious

fit·to -ta *adj* fixed, dug in; thick, dense; pitch (*dark*) || *m* thick; rent; tenancy || *f* see **fitta**

fittóne *m* (bot) taproot

fiuma·no -na *adj* river; from Fiume || *m* person from Fiume || *f* flood, stream

fiumara *f* torrent

fiume *m* river; **a fiumi** like a river

fiutare *tr* to snuff, sniff; to smell

fiutata *f* snuff, sniff

fiuto *m* sense of smell; snuff; flair

flàcci·do -da *adj* flabby

flacóne *m* flacon

flagellare (flagèllo) *tr* to scourge, lash, flagellate

flagèllo *m* whip, scourge; pest, plague; (coll) mess

flagrante *adj* flagrant; **in flagrante** (**delitto**) in the act

flan *m* (flan) pudding; (typ) mat

flanèlla *f* flannel

flàn·gia *f* (-ge) flange

flato *m* gas, flatus

flatulènza *f* flatulence

flautino *m* flageolet

flauti·sta *mf* (-sti -ste) flutist

flàuto *m* flute; **flauto diritto** or **dolce** (mus) recorder

fla·vo -va *adj* (lit) blond, golden

flèbile *adj* mournful

flebite *f* phlebitis

flèmma *f* apathy; coolness; phlegm

flemmàti·co -ca *adj* (-ci -che) phlegmatic(al)

flessibile *adj* flexible, pliable

flessióne *f* bending; (com) fall, drop; (gram) inflection

flessuó·so -sa [s] *adj* lithe, willowy; winding; flowing (*style*)

flèttere §177 *tr* to flex; (gram) to inflect

flirtare *intr* to flirt

flòra *f* flora

floreale *adj* floral

floricoltóre *m* floriculturist

floricoltura *f* floriculture

flòri·do -da *adj* florid; flourishing

flò·scio -scia *adj* (-sci -sce) flabby; soft (*hat*)

flòtta *f* fleet

flottante *adj* floating || *m* (com) floating stock

flottare (flòtto) *tr & intr* to float

flottìglia *f* flottilla

fluènte *adj* flowing

fluidità *f* fluidity

flùi·do -da *adj & m* fluid; fluent (*style*)

fluire §176 *intr* (ESSERE) to flow; to pour

fluitazióne *f* log driving

fluorescènte *adj* fluorescent

fluorescènza *f* fluorescence

fluorìdri·co -ca *adj* (-ci -che) hydrofluoric

fluorite *f* fluor, fluorite

fluorizzazióne [ddzz] *f* fluoridation

fluòro *m* fluorine

fluoruro *m* fluoride

flusso *m* flow; flood (*of tide*); high tide; (pathol) flow (*e.g., of blood*); (phys) flux

flutto *m* (lit) wave

fluttuare (flùttuo) *intr* to fluctuate; to bob, toss; to waver; to surge, stream

fluviale *adj* fluvial, river

fobìa *f* phobia

fò·ca *f* (-che) seal; sealskin

focàc·cia *f* (-ce) flat, rounded loaf; cake

focaccina *f* bun

fo·càia *adj fem* (-càie) flint

focale *adj* focal

fóce *f* mouth (*of river*)

focèna *f* porpoise

fochi·sta *m* (-sti) fireman, stoker; fire-works manufacturer

foco·làio *m* (-lài) (pathol) focus; (fig) hotbed

focolare *m* hearth; firebox; fireside, home

focó·so -sa [s] *adj* fiery, high-spirited

fòdera *f* lining (*of suit*); cover, case

foderare (fòdero) *tr* to line; to cover

fòdero *m* sheath, scabbard; raft

fó·ga *f* (-ghe) ardor, impetus

fòg·gia *f* (-ge) fashion, shape; a foggia di shaped like

foggiare §290 (fòggio) *tr* to shape, fashion

fòglia *f* leaf; petal; foil (*of gold*); mangiare la foglia (fig) to get wise, catch on

fogliame *m* foliage

fò·glio *m* (-gli) sheet; bill, banknote; folio; newspaper; permit; foglio d'avviso notice; foglio di congedo (mil) discharge; foglio d'iscrizione application; foglio di via (mil) travel orders; foglio modello blank form; foglio rosa (aut) permit; foglio volante flier, handbill

fógna *f* sewer, drain

fognatura *f* sewerage

fòla *f* tale, fable

fola·ga *f* (-ghe) (zool) coot

folata *f* gust; (lit) flight (*of birds*)

folclóre *m* folklore

folgorante *adj* striking; flashing; meteoric (*career*)

folgorare (fólgoro) *tr* to strike (with lightning) || *intr* to flash by || *impers* —folgora it is thundering

fólgore *m* (lit) thunderbolt || *f* flash of lightning; thunderbolt

fólla *f* crowd; (fig) flock

follare (fóllo) *tr* to full

fòlle *adj* mad, crazy; (aut) neutral; (mach) loose (*pulley*)

folleggiare §290 (folléggio) *intr* to act foolishly; to frolic

follemènte *adv* desperately, madly

follétto *m* elf; little imp

follìa *f* madness, lunacy; folly; alla follia madly; far follìe per to be crazy about

follìcolo *m* follicle

fól·to -ta *adj* thick; beetle (*brow*); deep (*night*) || *m* depth (*e.g., of the night*); thick (*e.g., of the battle*)

fomentare (foménto) *tr* to foment

fòmite *m* (lit) instigation; impetus

fónda *f* anchorage; lowland; saddlebag; alla fonda at anchor

fónda·co *m* (-chi) (hist) warehouse

fondale *m* depth (*of river, sea*); (theat) backdrop

fondamentale *adj* fundamental, basic

fondamén·to *m* (-ti) ground, foundation; basis; fare fondamento su to count on; fondamenti elements; senza fondamento baseless; without getting anywhere || *m* (-ta *fpl*)—fondamenta foundations (*of a building*)

fondare (fóndo) *tr* to found; to build; to charter || *ref*—fondarsi su to rely on; to be based upon

fondatézza *f* basis, ground, foundation

fonda·to -ta *adj* well-founded

fonda·tóre -trice *mf* founder

fondazióne *f* foundation

fondèllo *m* bottom, base

fondènte *m* flux

fóndere §178 *tr* to smelt; to melt; to blow (*a fuse*); to cast (*a statue*); to blend (*colors*) || *intr* to melt; to blend || *ref* to melt; to blend; to burn out

fonderìa *f* foundry

fondià·rio -ria (-ri -rie) *adj* real-estate, land || *f* real-estate tax

fondìna *f* holster; (coll) soup dish

fondi·sta *mf* (-sti -ste) editorialist; (sports) long-distance runner

fóndita *f* (typ) font

fonditóre *m* smelter, founder

fón·do -da *adj* deep || *m* bottom; fund; innermost nature; seat; end; background; land, property; a doppio fondo with a false bottom; a fondo thoroughly; a fondo perduto as an outright grant; dar fondo (naut) to cast anchor; dar fondo a to exhaust; di fondo (journ) editorial; (sports) long-distance; fondi funds; lees; fondi di bottega remnants; fondi di caffè coffee grounds; fondo comune d'investimento mutual fund; fondo d'ammortamento sinking fund; fondo di beneficenza community chest; fondo tinta foundation (*in make-up*); in fondo in the end; at the bottom; after all

fonè·ma *m* (-mi) phoneme

fonèti·co -ca (-ci -che) *adj* phonetic || *f* phonetics

fonògeno *m* pickup (*of record player*)

fonògrafo *m* phonograph, Gramophone

fonogram·ma *m* (-mi) telegram delivered by telephone

fonologìa *f* phonology

fonorivelatóre *m* pickup (*of record player*)

fonovalìgia *f* portable phonograph

fontana *f* fountain; spring; source

fónte *m* (lit) stone; spring; source; fonte battesimale font || *f* spring; fountain; source; da fonte autorevole on good authority

foraggiare §290 *tr* to subsidize || *intr* to forage

foràg·gio *m* (-gi) forage, provender, fodder

foràne·o -a *adj* rural; outer; (naut) outer (*dock*)

forare (fóro) *tr* to pierce; to bore; to puncture || *intr* to have a flat tire || *ref* to be punctured

foratura *f* puncture

fòrbice *f*—a forbice (sports) scissors (*e.g., kick*); forbici scissors; clippers; forbici per le unghie nail clippers

forbire §176 *tr* to wipe; to polish; to shine

fór·ca *f* (-che) fork; pitchfork; gallows; mountain pass; fare la forca a qlcu (slang) to betray s.o.; (slang) to do s.o. dirt; fatto a forca V-shaped

forcèlla *f* fork (*of bicycle or motor-cycle*); mountain pass; fork-shaped pole; hairpin; cradle (*of handset*); (coll) wishbone (*of chicken*)

forchétta *f* fork; (coll) wishbone (*of chicken*); **alla forchetta** (culin) cold (*e.g., lunch*)

forchettata *f* forkful; blow with a fork

forchettóne *m* carving fork

forcina *f* hairpin

fòrcipe *m* forceps

forcóne *m* pitchfork

forellino *m* pinhole

forèsta *f* forest

forestale *adj* forest, park

foresterìa *f* guest quarters (*in college or monastery*)

forestierismo *m* borrowing (*from another language*)

forestiè•ro -ra *adj* foreign || *mf* foreigner; stranger; outsider

forfettà•rio -ria *adj* (*-ri -rie*) job, e.g., **contratto forfettario** job contract; all-inclusive, e.g., **combinazione forfettaria** all-inclusive price agreement

fórfora *f* dandruff

fòr•gia *f* (*-ge*) forge; smithy

forgiare §290 (**fòrgio**) *tr* to forge

foriè•ro -ra *adj* forerunning || *mf* forerunner, harbinger

fórma *f* shape; form; mold (*e.g., for cakes*); wheel (*of cheese*); (typ) form; **forma da cappelli** hat block; **forma da scarpe** shoe tree; shoe last (*used by shoemaker*); **forme** shape, body; good manners; **salvare le forme** to save face

formaggièra *f* dish for grated cheese

formàg•gio *m* (*-gi*) cheese

formaldèide *f* formaldehyde

formale *adj* formal; prim

formalismo *m* formality

formali•tà *f* (*-tà*) formality

formalizzare [ddzz] *tr* to scandalize || *ref* to be shocked

formare (**fórmo**) *tr & ref* to form

forma•to -ta *adj* formed || *m* format

formazióne *f* formation

fòrmica *f* (trademark) Formica

formi•ca *f* (*-che*) ant

formi•càio *m* (*-cài*) anthill; (fig) swarm

formichière *m* anteater

formicolare (**formìcolo**) *intr* to swarm; to crawl || *intr* (ESSERE) to creep (*said, e.g., of a leg*)

formicolì•o *m* (*-ì*) swarm; creeping sensation, numbness

formidàbile *adj* formidable

formó•so -sa [s] *adj* shapely, buxom

fòrmula *f* formula; (aut) category, class; **formula dubitativa** (law) lack of evidence; **formula piena** (law) acquittal

formulare (**fòrmulo**) *tr* to formulate

formulà•rio *m* (*-ri*) formulary; form

fornace *f* furnace, kiln

for•nàio -nàia *mf* (*-nài -nàie*) baker

fornèllo *m* stove, range; (*of boiler*) firebox; bowl (*of pipe*); (min) shaft; **fornello a gas** gas range; **fornello a spirito** kerosene stove; chafing dish

fornire §176 *tr* to furnish, supply

forni•tóre -trice *mf* supplier, purveyor

fornitura *f* supply; order; delivery

fórno *m* oven; furnace; kiln; bakery; (theat) empty house; **al forno** or **in forno** baked; **alto forno** blast furnace; **forno crematorio** crematorium; **far forno** (theat) to play before an empty house

fóro *m* hole

fòro *m* forum; (law) bar

forosétta [s] *f* (lit) peasant girl

fórse *m* doubt; **mettere in forse** to endanger; to put in doubt || *adv* perhaps, maybe

forsenna•to -ta *adj* mad, insane || *mf* lunatic

fòrte *adj* strong; firm; bad (*cold*); fat, hefty; fast (*color*); offensive (*joke*); hard (*smoker*); main (*dish*); (lit) thick || *m* strong person; fortress; bulk, main body; forte; (lit) thick; **sapere di forte** to have a strong flavor; **farsi forte** to bear up; **farsi forte di** to appropriate, use; to be cocksure of || *adv* hard, strong; much; loud; openly; a lot; fast; swiftly

fortézza *f* fortress; strength; fortitude

fortificare §197 (**fortìfico**) *tr* to fortify || *ref* to be strengthened; to dig in

fortificazióne *f* fortification

fortino *m* blockhouse, redoubt

fortùi•to -ta *adj* fortuitous

fortuna *f* fortune; luck; good luck; fate, destiny; (lit) storm; **avere fortuna** to be lucky; to be a hit; **buona fortuna!** good luck!; **di fortuna** makeshift, emergency; **non aver la fortuna di** to not be fortunate enough to; **per fortuna** luckily

fortunale *m* storm, tempest

fortuna•to -ta *adj* fortunate, lucky

fortunó•so -sa [s] *adj* eventful

forùncolo *m* boil; pimple

forviare §119 *tr* to mislead, lead astray || *intr* to go astray

fòrza *f* strength; force; power; police; (phys) force; **a forza di** by dint of; **a tutta forza** at full speed; **bassa forza** (mil) enlisted personnel; **di forza** by force; **di prima forza** first-rate; **far forza a** to encourage; to force; **fare forza a sé stesso** to restrain oneself; **forza!** courage!; **forza di corpo** (typ) height-to-paper; **forza maggiore** force majeure, act of God; **forza muscolare** brawn; **forza pubblica** police; **forza viva** kinetic energy; **per forza** of course; under duress

forzare (**fòrzo**) *tr* to force; to strain; to rape; to tamper with (*a lock*); **forzare il passo** to hasten one's step; **forzare la consegna** (mil) to violate orders

forza•to -ta *adj* forced; force (*e.g., feed*) || *m* convict

forzière *m* chest, coffer

forzó•so -sa [s] *adj* compulsory; imposed by law

forzu•to -ta *adj* husky, robust

foschìa *f* smog; mist; haze

fó·sco -sca *adj* (-schi -sche) dark; gloomy; misty

fosfato *m* phosphate

fosforeggiare §290 (fosforéggio) *intr* to phosphoresce; to glow

fosforescènte *adj* phosphorescent

fòsforo *m* phosphorus

fòssa *f* grave; hollow; hole, ditch; moat; pit; den (*of lions*); fossa biologica sewage-treatment plant; fossa di riparazione (aut) pit; fossa settica septic tank

fossato *m* ditch; moat

fossétta *f* dimple

fòssile *adj* & *m* fossil

fossilizzare [ddzz] *tr* to fossilize || *ref* to become fossilized

fòsso *m* ditch; moat

fò·to *f* (-to) photo

fotocòpia *f* photocopy

fotocopiare §287 (fotocòpio) *tr* to photocopy

fotoelèttri·co -ca (-ci -che) *adj* photo-electric || *f* (mil) searchlight

fotogèni·co -ca *adj* (-ci -che) photo-genic

fotogiornale *m* pictorial magazine

fotografare (fotògrafo) *tr* to photo-graph

fotografìa *f* photography; photograph

fotogràfi·co -ca *adj* (-ci -che) photo-graphic

fotògrafo *m* photographer

fotogram·ma *m* (-mi) (phot) frame

fotoincisióne *f* photoengraving

fotolampo *m* flashlight

fotòmetro *m* exposure meter

fotomontàg·gio *m* (-gi) photomontage

fototubo *m* phototube

fra *m invar* brother, e.g., fra Cristoforo Brother Christopher || *prep* among; between; in, within

frac *m* (frac) swallow-tailed coat

fracassare *tr* to crash, smash || *ref* to crash

fracasso *m* crash; uproar; (coll) slew

fràdi·cio -cia (-ci -cie) *adj* rotten; soaked || *m* rotten part; decay; wet ground

fràgile *adj* fragile; brittle; frail

fragilità *f* fragility, frailty

fràgola *f* strawberry

fragóre *m* din; peal; roar

fragoró·so -sa [s] *adj* noisy

fragrante *adj* fragrant

fraintèndere §270 *tr* to misunderstand

frammassóne *m* Freemason

frammassonerìa *f* Freemasonry

frammentare (framménto) *tr* to frag-ment

frammentà·rio -ria *adj* (-ri -rie) frag-mentary

framménto *m* fragment

framméttere §198 *tr* to interpose || *ref* to meddle; frammettersi in to intrude in, to butt into

frammèzzo [ddzz] *adv* in the middle || *prep* in the midst of

frammischiare §287 *tr* to mix || *ref* to concern oneself

frana *f* landslide; (fig) collapse

franare *intr* to slide; to collapse

francesca·no -na *adj* & *mf* Franciscan

francé·sco -sca (-schi -sche) *adj* (ar-chaic) French || Francesco *m* Francis || Francesca *f* Frances

francése *adj* French || *m* French (*lan-guage*); Frenchman (*person*); i fran-cesi the French || *f* Frenchwoman

francesismo *m* gallicism

francesizzare [ddzz] *tr* to Frenchify

franchézza *f* frankness

franchì·gia *f* (-gie) franchise; exemp-tion; deductible insurance; (naut) shore leave; franchigia postale frank-ing privilege

Frància, la France

fran·co -ca (-chi -che) *adj* free; frank; Frankish; farla franca to get off scot free; franco di porto prepaid, post-paid; franco domicilio home delivery, free delivery || *m* franc || Franco *m* Frank

francobóllo *m* postage stamp, stamp

frangènte *m* breaker, surf; essere nei frangenti to be in bad straits

fràngere §179 *tr* to crush; (lit) to break || *ref* to break, comb (*said of waves*)

frangétta *f* bangs

fràn·gia *f* (-ge) fringe; embellishment; shoreline; bangs; frangia di corallo coral reef

frangibile *adj* breakable

frangiflut·ti *m* (-ti) breakwater

frangi·vènto *m* (-vènto) windbreak

frangizòl·le *m* (-le) disc harrow

Frankfur·ter *m* (-ter) hot dog

fran·tóio *m* (-tói) crusher; frantoio a mascelle jawbreaker

frantumare *tr* to crush; to break to pieces || *ref* to be crushed; to go to pieces

frantume *m* fragment; andare in fran-tumi to go to pieces

frappé *m* (frappé) shake; frappé; frappé alla menta mint julep; frappé di latte milk shake

frappórre §218 *tr* to interpose || *ref* to interfere; to intervene

frasà·rio *m* (-ri) language, speech

fra·sca *f* (-sche) branch; bush; orna-ment; whim; frivolous woman, flirt

frase *f* sentence; (mus) phrase; frase fatta cliché; frase idiomatica idiom; frasi words; frasi di commiserazione condolences

fraseggiare §290 (fraséggio) *intr* to use phrasing; to use big words; (mus) to phrase

fraseologìa *f* phraseology

fràssino *m* ash tree

frastagliare §280 *tr* to cut out (*e.g., paper*)

frastaglia·to -ta *adj* indented, jagged; ornamented

frastornare (frastórno) *tr* to disturb; (lit) to prevent

frastuòno *m* din, roar

frate *m* friar, monk, brother

fratellanza *f* brotherhood

fratellastro *m* stepbrother; half brother

fratèllo *m* brother; fratelli brothers and sisters; fratello consanguineo half brother on the father's side; fratello

di latte foster brother; **fratello ge- mello** twin
fraterni•tà *f* (**-tà**) fraternity
fraternizzare [ddzz] *intr* to fraternize
fratèr•no -na *adj* fraternal, brotherly
fratrici•da (**-di -de**) *adj* fratricidal ‖ *mf* fratricide
fratrici•dio *m* (**-di**) fratricide
fratta *f* brushwood; (coll) hedge
frattàglie *fpl* giblets, chitterlings, offal
frattanto *adv* meantime, meanwhile
frattèmpo *m*—**nel frattempo** meanwhile
frattura *f* fracture; break; breach
fratturare *tr* & *ref* to fracture, break
fraudolènto *adj* fraudulent
frazionare (**frazióno**) *tr* to fractionate; to break up
frazionà•rio -ria *adj* (**-ri -rie**) fractional
frazióne *f* fraction; hamlet; (eccl) breaking of the host
fréc•cia *f* (**-ce**) arrow, bolt; steeple, spire; clock (*on hosiery*); (archit) rise; (fig) aspersion; **freccia consen- siva** arrow (*on traffic light*); **freccia direzionale** (aut) turn signal
frecciata *f* arrow shot; taunt, gibe; **dare una frecciata a** to hit for a loan
freddare (**fréddo**) *tr* to chill; to kill
freddézza *f* chill; cold, coldness; cool- ness, cold shoulder; sang-froid
fréd•do -da *adj* cold; cool, chilly; frigid ‖ *m* cold, cold weather; chill; **a freddo** cold; cooly; **avere freddo** to be cold (*said of people*); **fare freddo** to be cold (*said of weather*); **freddo cane** biting cold; **sentire freddo** to feel cold; **sudare freddo** to be in a cold sweat
freddoló•so -sa [*s*] *adj* chilly (*person*)
freddura *f* joke, pun; cold weather
fredduri•sta *mf* (**-sti -ste**) punster
fregagióne *f* rubbing, rubdown, mas- sage
fregare §209 (**frégo**) *tr* to rub; to strike (*a match*); (slang) to steal; (slang) to cheat, dupe; (vulg) to make love with ‖ *ref* to rub (*e.g., one's hands*); **fregarsene di** (vulg) to not give a hoot about
fregata *f* rubbing; (nav) frigate; (orn) frigate bird; (slang) cheating
fregatura *f* (slang) cheating; (slang) hitch, halt
fregiare §290 (**frégio**) *tr* to decorate; to fret
fré•gio m (**-gi**) decoration; insignia (*on cap of officer*); (archit) frieze
fré•go m (**-ghi**) line, stroke
frégola *f* rut, heat; (slang) mania, craze
fremènte *adj* throbbing; thrilling
frèmere §123 *tr* (lit) to beg insistently ‖ *intr* to throb; to be thrilled; to shake, tremble, rustle; to shudder (*with horror*); (fig)—to boil; (fig) to fret
frèmito *m* throb; thrill; shudder; roar; quiver
frenare (**fréno**) *tr* to brake, stop; to bridle (*a horse*); to curb (*passions*); to restrain (*e.g., laughter*); **frenare la corsa** to slow down ‖ *intr* to put the brakes on ‖ *ref* to control oneself

frenatóre *m* (**rr**) brakeman
frenesìa *f* frenzy; (fig) craze, fever; (lit) thought
frenèti•co -ca *adj* (**-ci -che**) frenzied; frantic; crazy, enthusiastic
fréno *m* bit, bridle; brake; (fig) check; (mach) lock; **freno ad aria compressa** air brake; **mordere il freno** to champ the bit; **senza freno** wild, unbridled; **tenere a freno** to keep in check
frenologìa *f* phrenology
frequentare (**frequènto**) *tr* to frequent; to attend ‖ *intr* to associate
frequenta•tóre -trice *mf* patron, cus- tomer; frequenter, habitué
frequènte *adj* frequent; rapid (*pulse*); (lit) crowded
frequènza *f* frequency; attendance; **fre- quenza ultraelevata** ultrahigh fre- quency
frèsa *f* milling cutter; burr (*of dentist's drill*)
fresatrice *f* milling machine
fresatura *f* (mach) milling
freschézza *f* freshness; coolness
fré•sco -sca (**-schi -sche**) *adj* fresh; cool; **fresco di malattìa** just recov- ered; **fresco di stampa** fresh off the press; **fresco di studi** fresh out of school; **star fresco** to be in a fix; to be all wrong ‖ *m* cool weather; tropi- cal fabric; **di fresco** recently; **fare fresco** to be cool (*said of weather*); **mettere al fresco** (coll) to put in the clink; **per il fresco** in cool weather
frescó•ne -na *mf* (slang) dumbell
frescura *f* coolness, freshness
frétta *f* hurry, haste; **avere fretta** to be in a hurry; **in fretta** in a hurry; **in fretta e furia** in a rush
frettazzo *m* plasterer's wooden trowel; steel brush
frettoló•so -sa [*s*] *adj* hurried, hasty
freudismo *m* Freudianism
friàbile *adj* friable, crumbly
friabilità *f* friableness
fricassèa *f* fricassee
friggere §180 *tr* to fry; **mandare qlcu a farsi friggere** to tell s.o. to go to the devil ‖ *intr* to fry; to sizzle; to fret
friggitorìa *f* fried-food shop
frigidézza *f* frigidity
frigidi•tà *f* (**-tà**) coldness; frigidity
frigi•do -da *adj* cold; frigid
fri•gio -gia *adj* (**-gi -gie**) Phrygian
frignare *intr* to whimper
frigorìfe•ro -ra *adj* refrigerating ‖ *m* refrigerator; (journ) morgue
fringuèl•lo -la *mf* chaffinch, finch
frinire §176 *intr* to chirp
frisata *f* gunnel
frittata *f* omelet; **fare la frittata** (coll) to make a mess of it
frittèlla *f* fritter; pancake; (coll) grease spot
frit•to -ta *adj* fried; cooked, ruined ‖ *m* fry, fried platter
frittura *f* frying; fry, fried platter
frivolézza *f* frivolity
frìvo•lo -la *adj* frivolous; flighty
frizionare (**frizióno**) *tr* to massage

frizióne *f* friction; massage; (aut) clutch

frizzante [ddzz] *adj* crisp, brisk (*weather*); sparkling (*wine*)

frizzare [ddzz] *intr* to tingle; to sparkle, fizz (*said of wine*); (fig) to sting

frizzo [ddzz] *m* jest, witticism; gibe, dig

frodare (**fròdo**) *tr* to cheat, swindle

fròde *f* fraud; **frode fiscale** tax evasion or fraud

fròdo *m invar* customs evasion; **di frodo** smuggled

fró·gia *f* (**-ge** or **-gie**) nostril (*of horse*)

fròl·lo -la *adj* high (*meat*); soft, tender; (fig) weak

frónda *f* branch, bough; political opposition; **fronde** foliage; ornaments

frondó·so -sa [s] *adj* leafy

frontale *adj* front; frontal

frónte *m* (mil, pol) front; **far fronte a** to face; to face up to; to meet (*expenses*); **tenere fronte a** to face, resist || *f* forehead, brow; countenance; title page; headline; (fig) face; **a fronte** opposite, facing; **a fronte di** (com) in reference to; **dietro front!** (mil) about face!; **di fronte a** in the face of; facing; **di fronte a tutti** in plain view; **fronte destr'!** (mil) right face!; **mettere a fronte** to compare; **tenere a fronte** to have in front of one's eyes

fronteggiare §290 (**frontéggio**) *tr* to face, front || *ref* to face one another

frontespì·zio *m* (**-zi**) title page

frontièra *f* border, frontier

frontóne *m* (archit) pediment; (archit) gable

frónzolo *m* bauble, gewgaw; **fronzoli** finery, frippery

fròtta *f* crowd; swarm; flock

fròttola *f* fib; popular poem; **frottole** humbug

frugale *adj* frugal (*meal; life*); temperate (*in eating or drinking*)

frugare §209 *tr* to rummage through; to search (*a person*) || *intr* to rummage, poke around

frùgo·lo -la *mf* restless child, imp

fruire §176 *tr* to enjoy || *intr*—**fruire di** to enjoy

fruitóre *m* user

frullare *tr* to beat, whip || *intr* to flutter; to spin; **frullare per il capo a** to get into the head of, e.g., **cosa gli è frullato per il capo?** what got into his head?

frulla·to -ta *adj* whipped || *m* shake (*drink*)

frullatóre *m* electric beater

frullino *m* egg beater

fruménto *m* wheat

frumentóne *m* corn

frusciare §128 *intr* to rustle

frusci·o *m* (**-i**) rustle, rustling

frusta *f* whip; egg beater

frustare *tr* to whip, lash; (fig) to censure; (coll) to wear out (*clothes*)

frustata *f* lash; (fig) censure

frustino *m* whip, crop

fru·sto -sta *adj* worn out, threadbare || *f* see **frusta**

frustrare *tr* to frustrate, baffle; to discomfit

frut·ta *f* (**-ta** & **-te**) fruit; **essere alle frutta** to be at the end of the meal, to be having one's dessert

fruttare *tr* & *intr* to yield

fruttéto *m* orchard

frutticoltóre *m* fruit grower

fruttièra *f* fruit dish

fruttìfe·ro -ra *adj* fruit-bearing; fruitful, profitable; (lit) fecund

fruttificare §197 (**fruttìfico**) *intr* to fructify; to yield

fruttivéndo·lo -la *mf* fruit dealer

frutto *m* fruit; **frutti di mare** shellfish; **mettere a frutto** to make yield

fruttuó·so -sa [s] *adj* fruitful, profitable

fu *adj invar* late (*deceased*); son of the late . . . ; daughter of the late . . .

fucilare *tr* to shoot

fucilata *f* rifle shot

fucilazióne *f* execution by a firing squad

fucile *m* rifle, gun; **fucile ad aria compressa** air gun; **fucile da caccia** shotgun; **un buon fucile** a good shot

fucileria *f* fusillade

fucilière *m* rifleman

fucina *f* forge, smithy

fu·co *m* (**-chi**) (bot) rockweed; (zool) drone

fùcsia *f* fuchsia

fu·ga *f* (**-ghe**) flight; leak; row (*e.g., of rooms*); spurt (*in bicycle race*); (mus) fugue; **di fuga** hastily; **prendere la fuga** to take flight; **volgere in fuga** to put to flight; to take flight

fugace *adj* passing, fleeting

fugare §209 *tr* (lit) to avoid; (lit) to put to flight; (lit) to dispel

fuggènte *adj* passing, fleeting

fuggévole *adj* fleeting

fuggia·sco -sca (**-schi -sche**) *adj* fleeing, fugitive || *mf* fugitive; refugee

fuggi fug·gi *m* (**-gi**) stampede

fuggire *tr* to flee; to avoid || *intr* (ESSERE) to flee, run away; (sports) to take the lead; **fuggire a** to flee from

fuggiti·vo -va *adj* & *mf* fugitive

fulcro *m* fulcrum; (fig) pivot

fulgènte *adj* (lit) resplendent

fùlgi·do -da *adj* resplendent

fulgóre *m* resplendency, radiance

fulìggine *f* soot

fulligginó·so -sa [s] *adj* sooty

fulmicotóne *m* guncotton

fulminante *adj* crushing (*illness*); withering (*look*); explosive || *m* exploding cap; (coll) match

fulminare (**fùlmino**) *tr* to strike by lightning; to strike down; to confound, dumfound || *ref* (elec) to burn out, to blow out || *impers* (ESSERE)— **fulmina** it is lightning

fùlmine *m* lightning, thunderbolt; **fulmine a ciel sereno** bolt out of the blue

fulmìne·o -a *adj* swift, instant

ful·vo -va *adj* tawny

fumaiòlo *m* chimney; smokestack; (naut) funnel

fumante adj smoking; steaming; dusty

fumare tr to smoke; (lit) to exhale || intr to smoke; to steam; to fume; **fumare come un turco** to smoke like a chimney

fumata f smoking; smoke signal; **fare una fumata** to have a smoke

fuma·tóre -trice mf smoker

fumetti·sta mf (-sti -ste) cartoonist

fumétto m cartoon; **fumetti** comics

fumigare §209 (fùmigo) tr (obs) to fumigate || intr to steam, smoke

fumigazióne f fumigation

fumi·sta m (-sti) heater man; joker, hoaxer

fumisterìa f fondness for practical jokes; bamboozling

fumo m smoke; vapor, steam; smoking; (coll) hot air; **andare in fumo** to go up in smoke; **fumi** vapors, fumes; **mandare in fumo** to squander; to thwart; **sapere di fumo** to taste smoky; **vedere qlcu come il fumo negli occhi** to not be able to stand s.o.; **vender fumo** to peddle influence

fumòge·no -na adj smoke, e.g., **cortina fumogena** smoke curtain

fumó·so -sa [s] adj smoky; obscure

funambolismo m tightrope walking; (fig) acrobatics

funàmbo·lo -la mf tightrope walker; (fig) acrobat

fune f rope, cable; **fune portante** suspension cable

fùnebre adj funeral; funereal; gloomy

funerale adj & m funeral

funerà·rio -ria adj (-ri -rie) funeral

funère·o -a adj funereal; funeral

funestare (funèsto) tr to afflict

funè·sto -sta adj baleful; mournful

fungàia f mushroom farm; mushroom bed; flock, swarm

fùngere §183 intr—**fungere da** to act as

fun·go m (-ghi) mushroom; fungus; **fungo atomico** mushroom cloud; **venir su come i funghi** to mushroom

fungó·so -sa [s] adj fungous

funicolare adj cable, cable-driven || f funicular railway

funivìa f cableway

funzionale adj functional

funzionalità f functionalism

funzionaménto m working order; functioning

funzionare (funzióno) intr to work; to function; **funzionare da** to act as

funzionà·rio -ria mf (-ri -rie) functionary, official; public official

funzióne f function; office; duty; (eccl) service; **facente funzione** acting; **mettere in funzione** to make (s.th) work

fuò·co m (-chi) fire; burner (of gas range); focus; (fig) home; (lit) thunderbolt; **al fuoco!** fire! (warning); **andare per il fuoco** (culin) to boil over; **cuocere a fuoco lento** (culin) to simmer; **dar fuoco a** to set fire to; **di fuoco** fiery; blushing; **far fuoco** to fire; **fuochi artificiali** fireworks; **fuoco di fila** enfilade; **fuoco!** (mil) fire!; **fuoco di paglia** (fig) flash in the pan; **fuoco di segnalazione** flare; **fuoco fatuo** will-o'-the-wisp; **fuoco**

incrociato cross fire; **fuoco nutrito** drumfire; **mettere a fuoco** to focus; **mettere una mano sul fuoco** to be absolutely sure, to swear by it

fuorché prep except; **fuorché di** except to

fuòri adv outside, out; aside; e.g., **lasciar fuori** to leave aside; **andar di fuori** (culin) to boil over; **dar fuori** to do away with; to squander; **di fuori** outside; **far fuori** to publish; **fuori di** out of; outside of; beyond (a doubt); off (the road); beside (oneself); **fuori d'uso** out of style; obsolete; **il di fuori** the outside; **in fuori** protruding; forward; **mettere fuori** to throw out; to spread; to exhibit || prep beyond; out of; outside; **fuori commercio** not for sale; **fuori concorso** in a class by itself (himself, etc.); **fuori luogo** untimely, out of place; **fuori (di) mano** far away; solitary; **fuori testo** inserted, tipped in

fuoribór·do m (-do) outboard; outboard motor

fuoricombattimén·to (-to) adj knocked out || m knockout

fuorigió·co m (-co) (sports) offside

fuorilég·ge mf (-ge) outlaw

fuorisè·rie (-rie) adj custom-built || m & f custom model || f custom-built car

fuoristra·da m (-da) land rover

fuoriusci·to -ta adj exiled || mf political exile || f leak; flow; protrusion

fuorvia·to -ta adj mislead, misguided

furberìa f slyness, cunning

fur·bo -ba adj sly, cunning || mf knave; **furbo di tre cotte** slicker

furènte adj furious

furerìa f (mil) company headquarters

furétto m ferret

furfante m sharper, scoundrel

furfanterìa f rascality

furgoncino m small delivery van

furgóne m truck; patrol wagon; hearse; **furgone cellulare** prison van

furgoni·sta mf (-sti -ste) truck driver, teamster

fùria f fury; strength, violence; hurry; **a furia di** by dint of; **con furia** in a hurry; **far furia a** to urge; **montare in furia** to go berserk; to fly off the handle

furibón·do -da adj furious, wild

furière m soldier attached to company headquarters

furió·so -sa [s] adj furious; fierce; mad

furóre m furor, frenzy; violence; longing; **far furore** to be a hit, to be all the rage

furoreggiare §290 (furoréggio) intr to be a hit, to be all the rage

furti·vo -va adj stealthy; furtive; stolen (e.g., goods)

furto m theft; stolen goods; **di furto** stealthily; **furto con scasso** burglary

fusa [s] fpl—**fare le fusa** to purr

fuscèllo m twig

fusciac·ca f (-che) sash (around the waist)

fusèllo [s] *m* spindle; axle, shaft
fusìbile *adj* fusible ‖ *m* (elec) fuse
fusióne *f* fusion; melting; merger; blending (*of colors*)
fu•so -sa *adj* melted; molten
fuso [s] *m* spindle; shank (*of anchor*); shaft (*of column*); (aut) axle; **fuso orario** time zone
fusolièra *f* (aer) fuselage
fustagno *m* fustian
fustàia *f* adult forest, full-grown forest
fustèlla *f* (perforating) punch; (pharm) price stub

fustigare §209 (**fùstigo**) *tr* to whip
fusto *m* trunk (*of tree*); stalk; stem (*of key*); beam (*of balance*); butt (*of gun*); trunk, body; frame (*of armchair*); tank (*for holding liquids*); drum (*metal receptacle*); holding stick (*of umbrella*); shaft (*of column*); **d'alto fusto** full-grown (*tree*)
fùtile *adj* futile, trifling
futilità *f* futility
futurismo *m* futurism
futuri•sta *mf* (**-sti -ste**) futurist
futu•ro -ra *adj* & *m* future

G

G, g [dʒi] *m* & *f* seventh letter of the Italian alphabet
gabardi•ne *f* (**-ne**) gabardine; gabardine raincoat or topcoat
gabbamón•do *m* (**-do**) cheat, sharper
gabbanèlla *f* gown (*of physician or patient*); robe
gabbano *m* cloak; frock; **mutare gabbano** to be a turncoat
gabbare *tr* to dupe, cheat ‖ *ref*—**gabbarsi di** to make fun of
gàbbia *f* cage; ox muzzle; dock (*in courtroom*); (mach) housing; (naut) top; (naut) topsail; **gabbia d'imballaggio** crate; **gabbia toracica** rib cage
gabbiano *m* sea gull
gabbo *m*—**farsi gabbo di** to make fun of; **prendere a gabbo** to make light of
gabèlla *f* (obs) customs, duty
gabellare (**gabèllo**) *tr* to palm off; to swallow (*e.g., a tall story*); (obs) to tax
gabinétto *m* office (*of doctor, dentist, lawyer*); cabinet; chamber (*of judge*); toilet; closet; laboratory; **gabinetto da bagno** bathroom; **gabinetto di decenza** toilet, bathroom
ga•gà *m* (**gà**) fop, dandy; lounge lizard
gaggia *f* acacia
gagliardétto *m* pennon; pennant
gagliardìa *f* (lit) vigor; (lit) prowess
gagliar•do -da *adj* vigorous; stalwart; hearty (*e.g., voice*)
gagliòf•fo -fa *adj* loutish; rascal ‖ *mf* lout; rascal
gaiézza *f* gaiety, vivacity
gàio gàia *adj* (**gài gàie**) gay, vivacious
gala *m* & *f* gala; gala affair; **di gala** formal; **mettersi in gala** to dress up ‖ *f* frill; bow tie (*for formal attire*); (naut) bunting
galalite *f* casein plastic, galalith
galante *adj* gallant, courtly; amorous; pretty, graceful
galanteria *f* gallantry, courtliness
galantuò•mo *m* (**-mini**) honest man; (coll) my good fellow
galàssia *f* galaxy
galatèo *m* good manners
galèna *f* (min) galena
galeóne *m* galleon
galeòt•to -ta *adj* (archaic) intermediary

(*in love affairs*) ‖ *m* galley slave; convict; (archaic) procurer
galèra *f* galley; forced labor
gali•lèo -lèa (**-lèi -lèe**) *adj* & *m* Galilean
galla *f* (bot) gall; (pathol) blister; **a galla** afloat; **tenersi a galla** (fig) to keep alive; to manage; **venire a galla** to come to the surface
galleggiante *adj* floating ‖ *m* float
galleggiare §290 (**galléggio**) *intr* to float
galleria *f* tunnel; gallery; balcony; mall, arcade; wind tunnel
Galles, il Wales
gallése [s] *adj* Welsh ‖ *m* Welshman; Welsh (*language*) ‖ *f* Welsh woman
gallétta *f* cracker; hardtack; (naut) ball on top of flagpole
gallétto *m* cockerel; (fig) gallant; (fig) whippersnapper; (mach) wing nut; **fare il galletto** to swagger
gàlli•co -ca *adj* & *m* (**-ci -che**) Gallic
gallina *f* hen; **gallina faraona** guinea fowl
gal•lo -la *adj* Gallic; (sports) Bantam (*weight*) ‖ *m* rooster, cock; weathercock; Gaul; Gallic (*language*); **fare il gallo** to strut; **gallo cedrone** wood grouse; **gallo d'India** turkey
gallòc•cia *f* (**-ce**) (naut) cleat
gallóne *m* braid; stripe; chevron; gallon
galoppare (**galòppo**) *intr* to gallop; (fig) to rush around
galoppata *f* gallop
galoppa•tóio *m* (**-tói**) bridle path
galoppino *m* errand boy; **galoppino elettorale** ward heeler
galòppo *m* gallop; **andare al piccolo galoppo** to canter; **di gran galoppo** at full speed; **piccolo galoppo** canter
galò•scia *f* (**-sce**) overshoe, rubber
galvanizzare [ddzz] *tr* to electroplate; (fig) to galvanize
galvanoplàsti•ca *f* (**-che**) electroplating
gamba *f* leg; stem; (aer) shock strut; **a gambe all'aria** upside down; **a gambe levate** at top speed; upside down; **darsela a gambe** to take to one's heels; **essere in gamba** to be in good shape; to be on the ball; **essere male in gamba** to be in bad shape; **gamba di legno** peg leg; **gambe a ciambella** bowlegs; **le gambe mi fanno giacomo** my knees shake;

prèndere qlcu sotto gamba to make light of s.o.; **raddrizzare le gambe ai cani** to try the impossible

gambale *m* legging, gaiter; boot last; leg (*of boot*)

gamberétto *m* shrimp

gàmbero *m* (*Astacus, Cambarus*) crawfish

gambétto *m* stumble; trip; (chess) gambit

gambo *m* stem

gamèlla *f* (mil) mess kit, mess tin

gamma *f* gamut; range; **gamma d'onda** (rad) wave band

ganà·scia *f* (-sce) jaw; (aut) brake shoe; **mangiare a quattro ganasce** to eat like a horse

gàn·cio *m* (-ci) hook; clasp; hanger

gan·ga *f* (-ghe) gang; (min) gangue

gànghero *m* hinge; clasp; **uscire dai gangheri** to fly off the handle

gàn·glio *m* (-gli) ganglion

ganzo [dz] *m* (slang) lover; (coll) slicker

gara *f* competition, match; **fare a gara** to compete; **gara d'appalto** competitive bidding

garagi·sta *m* (-sti) garage man

garante *adj* responsible || *m* guarantor; **farsi garante per** to vouch for

garantire §176 *tr* to guarantee; to secure (*a mortgage*)

garanti·to -ta *adj* guaranteed, warranted; downright, absolute (*liar*)

garanzìa *f* guarantee, warranty; insurance, assurance

garbare *tr* (naut) to shape (*a hull*) || *intr* (ESSERE) (with *dat*) to like, e.g., **non gli garbano le Sue parole** he does not like your words

garbatézza *f* politeness, courtesy

garba·to -ta *adj* polite, courteous

garbo *m* politeness, good manners; gesture; act; shape (*of a hull*); good cut (*of clothes*); elegance (*in painting or writing*); **a garbo** correctly

garbù·glio *m* (-gli) tangle, confusion; mess

gardènia *f* gardenia

gareggiare §290 (garéggio) *intr* to compete, vie

garétta *f* var of **garitta**

garétto *m* var of **garretto**

garganèlla *f—***bere a garganella** to gulp down

gargarismo *m* gargling; gargle

gargarizzare [ddzz] *intr & ref* to gargle

gargaròzzo *m* throat, gullet

garitta *f* railroad-crossing box; (mil) sentry box; (rr) brakeman's box

garòfano *m* carnation, pink

garrése [s] *m* withers

garrétto *m* ankle (*of man*); hock (*of horse*)

garrire §176 *intr* to chirp, twitter; to flap; (archaic) to quarrel

garrito *m* chirp, twitter

garròtta *f* garrote

gàrru·lo -la *adj* garrulous

garza [dz] *f* gauze

garzonato [dz] *m* apprenticeship

garzó·ne -na [dz] *mf* helper || *m* helper, boy; apprentice; (archaic) bachelor; **garzone di stalla** stableboy

gas *m* (gas) gas; gasoline; **gas asfissiante** poison gas; **gas delle miniere** firedamp; **gas esilarante** laughing gas; **gas illuminante** illuminating gas; **gas lacrimogeno** tear gas

gasdótto *m* gas pipeline

gasificare §197 (gasìfico) *tr* var of **gassificare**

gasòlio *m* Diesel oil

gasòmetro *m* var of **gassometro**

gassificare §197 (gassìfico) *tr* to gasify

gassi·sta *m* (-sti) gasworker; gas fitter; gas-meter reader

gassòmetro *m* gasholder; gas tank

gassó·so -sa [s] *adj* gaseous, gassy || *f* soda, pop

gastronomìa *f* gastronomy

gatta *f* she-cat, tabby; **comprare la gatta nel sacco** to buy a pig in a poke; **gatta ci cova** something is rotten in Denmark; **pigliare una gatta da pelare** to take on a heavy burden, to get a tiger by the tail

gattabùia *f* (coll) clink, lockup

gattamòrta *f* (gattemòrte) hypocrite

gattino *m* kitten; (bot) catkin

gat·to -ta *mf* cat || *m* tomcat; tamper, pile driver; **gatto a nove code** cat-o'-nine-tails; **gatto soriano** tortoiseshell cat; **quattro gatti** a handful of people || *f* see **gatta**

gattóni *adv* on all fours

gattopardo *m* (zool) serval; **gattopardo americano** ocelot

gattù·cio *m* (-ci) compass saw; (ichth) small dotted dogfish

gaudènte *adj* jovial || *m* bon vivant

gàu·dio *m* (-di) joy, happiness

gavazzare *intr* (lit) to revel

gavétta *f* mess kit, mess gear; **venire dalla gavetta** to come up through the ranks

gavitèllo *m* buoy

gazza [ddzz] *f* magpie

gazzarra [ddzz] *f* racket, uproar

gazzèlla [ddzz] *f* gazelle

gazzétta [ddzz] *f* newspaper; gazette; newsmonger, gossip; **Gazzetta Ufficiale** Official Gazette (*in Italy*); Congressional Record (*U.S.A.*)

gazzettino [ddzz] *m* small newspaper; column, e.g., **gazzettino rosa** social column; newsmonger, gossip

gazzósa [ddzz] *f* var of **gassosa**

gèl *m* gel

gelare (gèlo) *tr* to freeze; to nip || *intr* (ESSERE) & *ref* to freeze || *impers* (ESSERE & AVERE)—**gela** it is freezing

gelata *f* frost

gela·tàio -tàia *mf* (-tài -tàie) ice-cream dealer

gelaterìa *f* ice-cream parlor

gelatièra *f* ice-cream freezer

gelatière *m* ice-cream dealer

gelatina *f* gelatin; jelly; **gelatina di frutta** fruit jelly; gum drop

gelatinizzare [ddzz] *tr & ref* to gelatinize; to jell

gela·to -ta *adj* frozen || *m* ice cream;

gelato da passeggio ice cream on a stick, popsicle

gèli·do -da adj icy, ice-cold

gèlo m frost; ice; cold; diventare di gelo to remain dumfounded; farsi di gelo to be cold or aloof; sentirsi il gelo addosso to get a chill

gelóne m chilblain

gelosìa [s] f jealousy; great care; shutter

geló·so -sa [s] adj jealous; solicitous

gèlso m mulberry

gelsomino m jasmine

gemebón·do -da adj (lit) moaning

gemellàggio m sisterhood (of two cities)

gemèl·lo -la adj twin; sister (ship) || mf twin || gemelli mpl cufflinks || Gemelli mpl (astr) Gemini

gèmere §123 tr (lit) to lament || intr (ESSERE & AVERE) to moan, groan; to suffer; to squeak (said of a wheel); to ooze; to coo (said of a dove)

gèmito m moan; howl (of wind)

gèmma f gem; (bot) bud

gemma·to -ta adj gemmate; jeweled

gendarme m gendarme, policeman

genealogìa f genealogy

generalato m generalship

generale adj general || m general; generale d'armata (mil) general; generale di brigata brigadier general; generale di corpo d'armata lieutenant general; generale di divisione major general || f (mil) assembly; stare sulle generali to speak in vague generalities

generali·tà f (-tà) generality; majority; generalità fpl personal data

generalizzare [ddzz] tr to generalize; to bring into general use || intr to generalize, deal in generalities

generare (gènero) tr to beget; to generate || ref to occur

genera·tóre -trice adj generating || m generator || f generatrix

generazióne f generation

gènere m genus; kind, type; genre; (gram) gender; del genere similar, alike; farne di ogni genere to commit all sorts of mischief; genere umano mankind; generi alimentari foodstuffs; generi diversi sundries, assorted articles; in genere generally

genèri·co -ca (-ci -che) adj generic; vague; all-round; general (e.g., practitioner) || mf (theat) actor playing bit parts || m vagueness, imprecision

gènero m son-in-law

generosi·tà [s] f (-tà) generosity

generó·so -sa [s] adj generous; rich (wine)

gène·si f (-si) genesis || il Genesi Genesis

genèti·co -ca (-ci -che) adj genetic(al) || f genetics

genetlìa·co -ca (-ci -che) adj birth || m birthday

gengiva f (anat) gum

genìa f set, gang; (lit) breed

geniale adj clever; genial; inspired, genius-like

geniali·tà f (-tà) cleverness, ingeniousness; genius; (lit) geniality

genière m (mil) engineer

gè·nio m (-ni) genius; (mil) corps of engineers; andare a genio (with dat) to like, e.g., la musica moderna non gli va a genio he does not like modern music; fare qlco di genio to do s.th willingly

genitale adj genital || genitali mpl genitals

geniti·vo -va adj & m genitive

geni·tóre -trice mf parent

gen·nàio m (-nài) January

genocìdio m genocide

Gènova f Genoa

genovése [s] adj & mf Genoese

gènte adj (archaic) gentle || f people; nation; family; (nav) crew; gente d'arme soldiers; gente di mal affare riffraff; gente di mare sailors

gentildònna f gentlewoman

gentile adj gentle; nice; genteel || Gentili mpl heathen

gentilézza f gentleness; kindness; per gentilezza kindly, please

gentili·zio -zia adj (-zi -zie) of noble family; (lit) ancestral

gentiluò·mo m (-mini) gentleman, nobleman

genuì·no -na adj genuine

genziana f gentian

geofìsi·co -ca (-ci -che) adj geophysical || f geophysics

geografìa f geography

geogràfi·co -ca adj (-ci -che) geographic(al)

geògra·fo -fa mf geographer

geologìa f geology

geòlo·go -ga mf (-gi -ghe) geologist

geòme·tra m (-tri) geometrician; land surveyor

geometrìa f geometry

gerà·nio m (-ni) geranium

gerar·ca m (-chi) leader

gerarchìa f hierarchy

geràrchi·co -ca adj (-ci -che) hierarchical; per via gerarchica through proper channels

Geremìa f Jeremiah

geremìade f jeremiad

gerènte m manager, director; gerente responsabile (journ) managing editor

gèr·go m (-ghi) jargon

geriatrìa f geriatrics

Gèrico f Jericho

gèrla f pannier (carried on the back)

Germània, la Germany

germàni·co -ca adj (-ci -che) Germanic

germànio m germanium

germanizzare [ddzz] tr to Germanize

germa·no -na adj german, e.g., fratello germano brother-german; Germanic || m (lit) brother-german; germano nero (orn) coot; germano reale (orn) mallard

gèrme m germ; (lit) offspring

germici·da (-di) adj germicidal || m germicide

germinare (gèrmino) *intr* (ESSERE & AVERE) to germinate

germogliare §280 (germóglio) *tr* to put forth || *intr* (ESSERE & AVERE) to bud, sprout

germó·glio *m* (-gli) bud, sprout

geroglìfi·co -ca *adj* & *m* (-ci -che) hieroglyphic

Geròlamo *m* Jerome

gerontocò·mio *m* (-mi) or gerotrò·fio *m* (-fi) old people's home, nursing home

gerùn·dio *m* (-di) gerund

Gerusalèmme *f* Jerusalem

gessare (gèsso) *tr* to plaster; to lime (*a field*)

gèsso *m* gypsum; plaster; chalk; (sculp) plaster cast

gessó·so -sa [s] *adj* plastery, chalky, chalklike

gèsta *f* (archaic) army; gesta *fpl* deeds, exploits

gestante *f* pregnant woman

gestazióne *f* gestation

gesticolare (gestìcolo) *intr* to gesticulate

gestióne *f* management, operation; data processing

gestire §176 *tr* to manage, operate || *intr* to gesticulate; (theat) to make gestures

gèsto *m* gesture; attitude; act, deed

ge·stóre -strice *mf* manager, operator; gestore di stazione (rr) station agent

gestualità *f* bodily movements (*e.g., of an actor*)

Gesù *m* Jesus; Gesù Cristo Jesus Christ

gesui·ta *m* (-ti) Jesuit

gesuìti·co -ca *adj* (-ci -che) Jesuitic(al)

gettare (gètto) *tr* to throw; to cast; to pour; to lay (*e.g., a floor*); to send forth; to yield; to broadcast (*seed*); to risk (*one's life*); gettare la colpa addosso a qlcu to lay the blame on s.o.; gettare le armi to lay down one's arms; gettar giù to fell, knock down; gettar sangue to bleed || *ref* to throw oneself; to plunge; to flow, empty (*said of a river*)

gettata *f* pour, pouring; jetty; shoot, sprout; cast; range (*of a gun*); gettata cardiaca (med) rate of flow of blood

gèttito *m* yield; waste; far gettito di to waste

gètto *m* throw; gush; shoot, sprout; cast; precast concrete slab; (aer) jet; a getto (aer) jet; a getto continuo continuously; di getto spontaneously; far getto di to waste; primo getto first draft

gettonare (gettóno) *tr* (coll) to call up from a pay station; (coll) to make the selection of (*a record in a juke-box*)

gettóne *m* counter, token; attendance fee; (cards) chip

gettopropulsióne *f* jet propulsion

ghepardo *m* cheetah

ghép·pio *m* (-pi) kestrel

gheri·glio *m* (-gli) kernel, meat (*of nut*)

gherlino *m* (naut) warp, line

ghermìnèlla *f* trick, sleight of hand; trickery

ghermire §176 *tr* to claw; to seize

gheróne *m* gusset

ghétta *f* gaiter; ghette spats

ghétto *m* ghetto

ghiacciàia *f* icebox, cooler

ghiac·ciàio *m* (-ciài) glacier; ghiacciaio continentale polar cap

ghiacciare §128 *tr* to freeze || *intr* (ESSERE) to freeze || *impers* (ESSERE) —ghiaccia it is freezing

ghiaccia·to -ta *adj* iced; ice-cold; frozen || *f* flavored crushed ice

ghiàc·cio -cia (-ci -ce) *adj* icy, ice-cold || *m* ice; ghiaccio secco dry ice

ghiaccìo·lo -la *adj* crumbly, breakable || *m* icicle; popsicle

ghiàia *f* gravel, crushed stone

ghianda *f* fringe (*on a curtain*); (bot) acorn; ghiande mast (*for swine*)

ghiandàia *f* (orn) jay

ghiàndola *f* gland

ghibelli·no -na *adj* & *m* Ghibelline

ghièra *f* ferrule; ring

ghigliottina *f* guillotine; a ghigliottina sash (*window*)

ghigliottinare *tr* to guillotine

ghigna *f* (coll) grimace

ghignare *intr* to grimace; to sneer

ghigno *m* sneer, smirk; grin

ghinèa *f* guinea

ghìngheri *m invar*—in ghingheri dressed up

ghiót·to -ta *adj* fond; gluttonous; eager; dainty (*food*) || *f* (culin) dripping pan

ghiottó·ne -na *mf* glutton; (zool) glutton, wolverine

ghiottonerìa *f* gluttony; tidbit; (fig) rarity

ghiòzzo [dzz] *m* dolt; (ichth) gudgeon

ghirba *f* jar; (coll) skin, life

ghiribizzo [dzz] *m* (coll) whim, caprice

ghirigòro *m* doodle, curlicue

ghirlanda *f* garland, wreath

ghiro *m* dormouse; dormire come un ghiro to sleep like a log

ghisa *f* cast iron

già *adv* already; once upon a time; formerly || *interj* indeed!

giac·ca *f* (-che) jacket, coat; giacca a due petti double-breasted coat; giacca a vento windbreaker

giacché *conj* since

giacènte *adj* lying; idle (*capital*); unclaimed (*letter*); in abeyance

giacènza *f* lying; stay, abeyance; giacenze di capitali idle capital; giacenze di magazzino unsold stock of merchandise

giacére §181 *intr* (ESSERE) to lie; to be in abeyance; (lit) to be prostrate

giaci·glio *m* (-gli) pallet, cot

giacimento *m* field, bed; giacimento petrolifero oil field

giacinto *m* hyacinth

Giàcomo *m* James

giaculatòria *f* ejaculation (*prayer*); litany (*monotonous account*); curse

giada *f* jade

giaggiòlo *m* (bot) iris

giaguaro *m* jaguar

giaiétto *m* jet (*black coal*)

gialappa *f* (pharm) jalap

gialla·stro -stra *adj* yellowish

gial·lo -la *adj* yellow; detective (*book or picture*); white (*with fear*) ‖ *m* yellow; detective story, whodunit; suspense movie; giallo dell'uovo egg yolk

giamaica·no -na *adj & mf* Jamaican

giàmbi·co -ca *adj* (-ci -che) iambic

giambo *m* iamb

giammài *adv* never

giansenismo *m* Jansenism

Giappóne, il Japan

giapponése [s] *adj & mf* Japanese

giara *f* crock, jar

giardinàg·gio *m* (-gi) gardening

giardinétta *f* station wagon

giardiniè·re -ra *mf* gardener ‖ *f* jardiniere; mixed pickles; mixed salad; wagonette; station wagon

giardino *m* garden; giardino d'infanzia kindergarten; giardino pensile roof garden; giardino zoologico zoological garden

giarrettièra *f* garter

Giasóne *m* Jason

giavanése [s] *adj & mf* Javanese

giavellòtto *m* javelin

gibbó·so -sa *adj* gibbous, humped; humpbacked; rough (*ground*)

gibèrna *f* cartridge box; cartridge belt

gi·bus *m* (-bus) opera hat

gi·ga *f* (-ghe) gigue, jig

gigante *adj & m* giant

gigante·sco -sca *adj* (-schi -sche) gigantic

gigantéssa *f* giantess

gigióne *m* ham actor

gi·glio *m* (-gli) Madonna lily; fleur-de-lys

gilda *f* guild

gi·lè *f* (-lè) vest, waistcoat

gimnòto *m* electric eel

ginecologia *f* gynecology

ginecòlo·go -ga *mf* (-gi -ghe) gynecologist

gine·pràio *m* (-prài) juniper thicket; (fig) mess

ginépro *m* juniper

ginèstra *f* (bot) Spanish broom

Ginèvra *f* Geneva

ginevri·no -na *adj & mf* Genevan

gingillare *ref* to trifle; to idle

gingillo *m* trifle, bauble

ginnà·sio *m* (-si) secondary school; gymnasium

ginna·sta *mf* (-sti -ste) gymnast

ginnàsti·co -ca (-ci -che) *adj* gymnastic ‖ *f* gymnastics; ginnastica a corpo libero or ginnastica da camera calisthenics

ginni·co -ca *adj* (-ci -che) gymnastic

ginocchiata *f* blow with the knee; blow on the knee

ginocchièra *f* kneepad; elastic bandage (*for knee*); kneepiece (*of armor*)

ginòc·chio *m* (-chi) knee; avere il ginocchio valgo to be bowlegged; avere il ginocchio varo to be knock-kneed; in ginocchio on one's knees ‖ *m* (-chia *fpl*) knee; fino alle ginocchia knee-deep; gettarsi alle ginocchia di to go down on one's knees to; mettere qlcu in ginocchio to bring s.o. to his knees

ginocchióni *adv* on one's knees

giocare §182 *tr* to play; to stake, bet, risk, gamble; to make a fool of ‖ *intr* to play; to gamble; to circulate (*said of air*); (fig) to play a role; giocare a to play; to wager; giocare a mosca cieca to play blindman's buff; giocare con to risk; giocare d'armi to fence; giocare d'azzardo to gamble; giocare di to use (*e.g., one's wits*); giocare di gomiti to elbow one's way; giocare di mano to steal; giocare sulle parole to play on words; to pun ‖ *ref* to risk (*e.g., one's life*); to gamble away

giocata *f* wager, stake; game, play

gioca·tóre -trìce *mf* player; gambler; speculator

giocàttolo *m* toy, plaything

giocherellare (giocherèllo) *intr* to play, trifle

giochétto *m* children's game; child's play; dirty trick

giò·co *m* (-chi) game; gambling; play; wager, stake; set; joke; (cards) hand; entrare in gioco to come into play; fare gioco a to come in handy to; fare il doppio gioco to be guilty of duplicity; fare il gioco di to play into the hands of; giochi di equilibrio balancing act; gioco da ragazzi child's play; gioco d'azzardo gambling; game of chance; gioco dei bussolotti (fig) jugglery; gioco di destrezza game of skill; gioco di parole play on words, pun; gioco di prestigio sleight of hand; gioco di società parlor game; metter in gioco to risk; to stake; per gioco for fun; prendersi gioco di to make fun of

giocofòrza *m*—è giocofòrza + *inf* it is necessary + *inf*

giocolière *m* juggler

giocón·do -da *adj* merry, joyful

giocó·so -sa [s] *adj* jocose, jolly

giogàia *f* dewlap; chain of mountains

gió·go *m* (-ghi) yoke; beam (*of balance*); rounded peak; pass

giòia *f* joy, happiness; darling; jewel; darsi alla pazza gioia to have a wild time

gioielleria *f* jewelry; jewelry store

gioiellière *m* jeweler

gioièllo *m* jewel

gioió·so -sa [s] *adj* joyful

gioire §176 (*pres part* missing) *intr* to rejoice

Giòna *m* Jonas

Giordània, la Jordan (*country*)

giorda·no -na *adj & mf* Jordanian ‖ Giordano *m* Jordan (*river*)

Giórgio *m* George

giorna·làio -làia *mf* (-lài -làie) newsdealer

giornale *m* newspaper; magazine; (com) journal; giornale di bordo log, logbook; giornale murale poster; giornale radio newscast

giornaliè·ro -ra *adj* daily || *mf* day laborer

giornalismo *m* journalism

giornali·sta *mf* (-sti -ste) journalist; giornalista pubblicista free-lance writer || *m* newspaperman || *f* newspaperwoman

giornalménte *adv* daily

giornata *f* day; day's work; birthday; pay, salary; battle; day's march; giornata campale pitched battle; giornata della mamma Mother's Day; giornata lavorativa workday; vivere alla giornata to live from hand to mouth

giórno *m* day; a giorni within the next few days; a giorni . . . a giorni some days . . . others; a giorno open, openwork (*needlework*); full (*light*); ai giorni nostri nowadays; al giorno d'oggi nowadays; buon giorno good day; good morning; good-bye; dare gli otto giorni a to dismiss, fire; di ogni giorno everyday (*e.g., clothes*); essere a giorno to be up to date; giorno dei morti All Souls' Day; giorno di lavoro workday; giorno di paga payday; giorno fatto broad daylight; giorno feriale weekday; giorno festivo holiday; mettere a giorno to bring up to date; otto giorni oggi one week from today; passare un brutto giorno to have a bad time; un giorno o l'altro one of these days

giòstra *f* joust; merry-go-round

giostrare (giòstro) *intr* to joust; to get along, manage; to idle, loiter

Giosuè *m* Joshua

Giottè·sco -sca *adj* (-schi -sche) of the school of Giotto

giovaménto *m* benefit, advantage

gió·vane *adj* young; youthful; fresh (*e.g., cheese*); Younger, e.g., Plinio il Giovane Pliny the Younger || *m* young man; boy, apprentice; i giovani the young || *f* young woman

giovanile *adj* youthful

Giovanni *m* John; Giovanni Battista John the Baptist

giovanòtta *f* young woman

giovanòtto *m* young man; (coll) bachelor

giovare (gióvo) *tr* (lit) to help || *intr* (with *dat*) to help, to be of use to || *ref* to avail oneself || *impers* (ESSERE) —non giova it's no use

Giòve *m* Jupiter

giove·dì *m* (-dì) Thursday; giovedì santo Maundy Thursday

giovèn·ca *f* (-che) heifer

gioventù *f* youth

giovévole *adj* helpful, beneficial

gioviale *adj* jovial

giovinézza *f* youth

gip *f* (gip) jeep

gippóne *m* large jeep, panel truck

giràbile *adj* endorsable

giradi·schi *m* (-schi) record player

giradito *m* (pathol) felon

giraffa *f* giraffe; (mov, telv) boom, crane

girafilièra *f* diestock

giramà·schio *m* (-schi) tap wrench

giraménto *m*—giramento di testa vertigo, dizziness

giramón·do *m* (-do) globetrotter

giràndola *f* girandole; pinwheel; (fig) weathercock

girandolare (giràndolo) *intr* to stroll, saunter

girante *mf* endorser || *f* blade (*e.g., of fan*)

girare *tr* to turn; to tour; to go around, travel over; to switch (*the conversation*); to film, shoot; to transfer (*a phone call*); to endorse; (mil) to surround || *intr* to turn; to circulate; to spin (*said of one's head*) || *ref* to turn; to toss and turn

girarròsto *m* turnspit; girarrosto a motore rotisserie

girasóle *m* sunflower

girata *f* turn; walk, ramble; (com) endorsement; (cards) deal; (coll) tongue-lashing

giratà·rio -ria *mf* (-ri -rie) endorsee

giravòlta *f* turn, pirouette; bend; sudden change of mind

girellare (girèllo) *intr* to stroll, wander around

girèllo *m* rump; go-cart, walker

girévole *adj* revolving

girino *m* tadpole; bicycle rider competing on the Tour of Italy

giro *m* periphery; turn, revolution; ride; size (*of hat*); edge (*of glass*); round (*of a doctor*); (sports) tour; (sports) lap; (com) transfer; (cards) hand; (theat) tour; a giro di posta by return mail; andare in giro to poke along; giro collo neckline; giro d'affari volume of business, turnover; giro di parole circumlocution; fare il giro di to tour; mettere in giro to spread (*news, gossip*); nel giro di within (*a period*); prendere in giro to poke fun at

girobùssola *f* gyrocompass

girondolare (giróndolo) *intr* var of girandolare

giróne *m* (sports) conference; (sports) division; (sports) league; (archaic) circle

gironzolare [dz] (girónzolo) *intr* to stroll, saunter

giropilò·ta *m* (-ti) gyropilot

giroscò·pio *m* (-pi) gyroscope

girotóndo *m* ring-around-a-rosy

giròtta *f* weather vane

girovagare §209 (giròvago) *intr* to roam, wander

giròva·go -ga (-ghi -ghe) *adj* wandering; strolling (*player*) || *m* vagrant, hobo

gita *f* trip, excursion, outing

gita·no -na *adj* & *mf* Gypsy

gitante *mf* excursionist, vacationist

gittata *f* range (*of gun*)

giù *adv* down; andar giù to go down; to deteriorate; to get worse; buttar giù to throw down; (culin) to start to cook, e.g., buttar giù gli spaghetti to start to cook the spaghetti; (fig) to jot down; da . . . in giù for the past . . . ; dar giù to look worse (*said of a sick person*); **esser giù** to be downcast; **giù dì lì** thereabouts; **in giù** down; downstream; **mandar giù** to swallow; **non andar giù** to not be able to stomach or swallow, e.g., **non gli vanno giù i bugiardi** he cannot stomach liars; **venire giù** to come down; to crumble; to collapse

giubba *f* coat, jacket; mane

giubbétto *m* small coat; bodice; jerkin

giubbòtto *m* jacket (*e.g., of a motorcyclist*); **giubbotto salvagente** (aer, naut) life jacket

giubilare (giùbilo) *tr* to retire, to pension ‖ *intr* to rejoice

giubilèo *m* jubilee

giùbilo *m* jubilation, exultation

giuda *m* Judas ‖ **Giuda** *m* Judas

giudài·co -ca *adj* (**-ci -che**) Judaic

giudaismo *m* Judaism

giudè·o -a *adj* Judean; Jewish ‖ *mf* Judean; Jew

giudicare §197 (giùdico) *tr* to judge; to find (*e.g., s.o. innocent*); to try (*a case*) ‖ *intr* to judge, deem

giudicato *m* (hist) Sardinian region; **passare in giudicato** (law) to become final

giùdice *m* judge; magistrate, justice; **giudice conciliatore** justice of the peace; **giudice popolare** member of the jury

giudizià·rio -ria *adj* (**-ri -rie**) judicial, judiciary

giudì·zio *m* (**-zi**) judgment; wisdom; trial; sentence; **giudizio di Dio** (hist) ordeal; **giudizio finale** Last Judgment; **metter giudizio** to mend one's ways

giudizió·so -sa [s] *adj* judicious, wise

giùggiola *f* jujube; (joc) trifle; **andare in brodo di giuggiole** to swoon, become ecstatic

giugno *m* June

giugulare *adj* jugular ‖ *v* (**giùgolo**) *tr* to cut the throat of

giulèbbe *m* julep

giuliana *f* (culin) julienne ‖ **Giuliana** Juliana

giuli·vo -va *adj* gay

giullare *m* jongleur; (pej) mountebank

giumén·to -ta *mf* beast of burden ‖ *f* female saddle horse

giun·ca *f* (**-che**) (naut) junk

giunchìglia *f* (bot) jonquil

giun·co *m* (**-chi**) (bot) rush

giùngere §183 *tr* to join (*e.g., one's hands*) ‖ *intr* (ESSERE) to arrive; **giungere a** or **in** to arrive at, reach; **giungere a** + *inf* to succeed in + *ger;* **mi giunge nuovo** it's news to me

giungla *f* jungle

Giunóne *f* Juno

giunòni·co -ca *adj* (**-ci -che**) Junoesque

giunta *f* addition; makeweight; strip (*of cloth*); junta; committee; **di prima giunta** at the very beginning; **per giunta** in addition

giuntare *tr* to join

giuntatrice *f* (mov) splicer

giunto *m* (mach) joint, coupling;

giunto a sfere ball-and-socket joint; **giunto cardanico** universal joint

giuntura or **giunzióne** *f* joint; juncture, seam

giuò·co *m* (**-chi**) var of **gioco**

giuraménto *m* oath; **deferire il giuramento a** to put under oath

giurare *tr* to swear, pledge ‖ *intr* to swear

giura·to -ta *adj* sworn ‖ *m* juror

giurìa *f* committee; jury

giurìdi·co -ca *adj* (**-ci -che**) juridical

giurisdizióne *f* jurisdiction

giurisprudènza *f* jurisprudence

giurì·sta *mf* (**-sti -ste**) jurist

Giusèppe *m* Joseph

Giuseppina *f* Josephine

giusta *prep* according to; in accordance with

giustappórre §218 *tr* to juxtapose

giustézza *f* correctness, justness; (typ) measure

giustificàbile *adj* justifiable

giustificare §197 (giustìfico) *tr* to justify ‖ *ref* to excuse oneself

giustificazióne *f* justification

giustizia *f* justice; **far giustizia a** to execute; **farsi giustizia da sé** to take the law into one's own hands; **render giustizia a** to do justice to

giustiziare §287 *tr* to execute

giustizière *m* executioner; (obs) judge

giu·sto -sta *adj* just; opportune ‖ *m* just man; just price; rights, due ‖ *giusto adv* just, justly

già·bro -bra *adj* smooth (*face*)

glaciale *adj* glacial; (fig) icy

gladiatóre *m* gladiator

gladiòlo *m* gladiolus

glàndola *f* var of **ghiandola**

glassa *f* glaze, icing

glassare *tr* to glaze, ice

glèba *f* clod, lump of earth

gli §4 art ‖ **§5 pers pron**

glicerina *f* glycerin

glìcine *m* wistaria

gliéla; gliéle; gliéli; gliélo; gliéne §5

globale *adj* total, aggregate

glòbo *m* globe; **globo oculare** eyeball

globulare *adj* globular, global

glòbulo *m* globule; (physiol) corpuscle

gloglottare (gloglòtto) *intr* to gobble; to gurgle

gloglotti·o *m* (**-i**) gobble, gobbling; gurgle

glòria *f* glory

gloriare §287 (glòrio) *tr* (lit) to exalt ‖ *ref* to boast; to glory

glorificare §197 (glorìfico) *tr* to glorify

glorió·so -sa [s] *adj* glorious; proud

glòssa *f* gloss

glossà·rio *m* (**-ri**) glossary

glòttide *f* glottis

glottòlo·go -ga *mf* (**-gi -ghe**) linguist

glucòsio *m* glucose

glùtine *m* gluten

gnòc·co *m* (**-chi**) potato dumpling

gnòmo *m* gnome

gnòrri *m invar*—**fare lo gnorri** to feign ignorance

gòb·bo -ba *adj* hunchbacked ‖ *mf*

hunchback || f hump; hunch; hump (of gibbous moon); hook (of nose)

góc·cia f (-ce) drop; bead; **avere la goccia al naso** to have a runny nose; **goccia d'acqua** raindrop

góc·cio m (-ci) drop, swallow

gócciola f drop; bead

gocciolare (gócciolo) tr & intr to drip

gocciola·tóio m (-tói) dripstone

gocciolì·o m (-i) drip, trickle

godére §184 tr to enjoy || intr to take pleasure; to revel; to profit || ref to enjoy; **godersela** to have a good time

godìbile adj enjoyable

godiménto m enjoyment, pleasure

goffàggine f clumsiness

gòf·fo -fa adj awkward; ill-fitting

gógna f pillory; **mettere alla gogna** to pillory

góla f throat; neck; gluttony; gorge (of mountain); mouth (of cannon); flue (of chimney); (archit) ogee; **far gola a** to tempt; **mentire per la gola** to lie shamelessly; **tornare a gola** to repeat (said of food)

golétta f neck (of shirt); (naut) schooner

gòlf m (gòlf) sweater, cardigan; (sports) golf

gólfo m gulf; **golfo mistico** orchestra pit || **Golfo Persico** Persian Gulf

Gòlgota, il Golgotha

goliardo m goliard; university student

golosi·tà [s] f (-tà) gluttony; tidbit

golo·so -sa [s] adj gluttonous; appetizing

gómena f hawser

gomitata f blow with the elbow; nudge

gómito m elbow; bend; **alzare il gomito** to crook the elbow; **dare di gomito a** to nudge

gomìtolo m skein, clew

gómma f gum; rubber; eraser; tire; **bucare una gomma** to have a flat tire; **gomma arabica** gum arabic; **gomma a terra** flat tire; **gomma da masticare** chewing gum; **gomma lacca** shellac

gommapiuma f foam rubber

gomma·to -ta adj gummed; with tires

gommatura f gumming; (aut) tires

gommi·sta m (-sti) tire dealer; tire repairman

gommó·so -sa [s] adj gummy

góndola f gondola; (aer) pod

gonfalóne m gonfalon

gonfiare §287 (gónfio) tr to inflate, blow up; to bloat; to swell; to exaggerate; to puff up || intr (ESSERE) to swell || ref to swell; to puff up; to bulge, balloon

gonfiatura f inflation; exaggeration

gonfiézza f swelling; grandiloquence

gón·fio -fia (-fi -fie) adj inflated, swollen; conceited || m swelling, bulge

gonfióre m swelling

gongolare (góngolo) intr to rejoice; to be elated

goniòmetro m goniometer; protractor

gònna f skirt; **gonna pantaloni** culottes

gonnèlla f skirt; (fig) petticoat

gonnellino m kilt; ballerina skirt

gón·zo -za [dz] mf simpleton, fool

gòra f millpond; marsh; (coll) spot

górbia f tip (of umbrella)

gorgheggiare §290 (gorghéggio) tr & intr to warble; to trill

gorghég·gio m (-gi) warbling; trill

gór·go m (-ghi) whirlpool; (lit) river

gorgogliare §280 (gorgóglio) intr to gurgle

gorgó·glio m (-gli) gurgle

gorgoglì·o m (-i) gurgling

goril·la m (-la) gorilla

gòta f cheek; (lit) side

gòti·co -ca adj & m (-ci -che) Gothic

Gòto m Goth

gótta f (pathol) gout

gottazza f (naut) scoop

gottó·so -sa [s] adj gouty

governale m fin (of bomb); (obs) rudder

governante adj governing || m ruler || f governess; housekeeper

governare (govèrno) tr to rule, govern; to steer (a ship); to tend (animals); to wash and dry (dishes); to run (e.g., a bank) || intr to steer

governati·vo -va adj government

govèrno m government; tending (e.g., of animals); running (of household); cleaning (of house); blending (of wine); (archaic) steering

gózzo m crop, craw (of bird); (pathol) goiter

gozzovigliare §280 intr to go on a spree

gracchiare §287 intr to caw

gràc·chio m (-chi) caw; (orn) chough

gracidare (gràcido) intr to croak; to honk (said, e.g., of a goose)

gràcile adj weak, frail; thin, delicate

gradasso m swaggerer, braggadocio

grada·to -ta adj graded; gradual

gradazióne f gradation; alcoholic proof; **gradazione vocalica** (phonet) ablaut

gradévole adj pleasant

gradiménto m pleasure; acceptance (of a product); liking

gradinata f steps; tier (of seats)

gradino m step; (fig) stepping stone

gradire §176 tr to like; to welcome

gradì·to -ta adj agreeable; welcome (guest); kind (letter)

grado m degree; rank; (nav) rating; (archaic) step; **a buon grado o a mal grado** willy-nilly; **a grado a grado** little by little; **a Suo grado** according to your wishes; **di buon grado** willingly; **di secondo grado** secondary (school); **essere in grado di** to be in a position to; **saper grado a** (lit) to be grateful to

graduale adj & m gradual

graduare (gràduo) tr to graduate

gradua·to -ta adj graduated || m noncommissioned officer

graduatòria f ranking; rank

graffa f clamp; brace, bracket

graffiare §287 tr to scratch; (coll) to swipe

graffiétto m tiny scratch; marking gage

gràf·fio m (-fi) scratch

grafìa f writing, spelling; (gram) graph

gràfi•co -ca (-ci -che) *adj* graphic ‖ *m* graph, diagram; designer (*for printing industry*); member of printers' union ‖ *f* graphic arts

grafite *f* graphite

grafologìa *f* graphology

gragnòla *f* hail

gramàglia *f* crepe; widow's weeds; **in gramaglie** in mourning

gramigna *f* couch grass; weed

grammàti•co -ca (-ci -che) *adj* grammatical ‖ *m* grammarian ‖ *f* grammar

grammo *m* gram

grammofòni•co -ca *adj* (**-ci -che**) phonograph, recording

grammòfono *m* phonograph, record player

gra•mo -ma *adj* poor, sad; wretched, miserable; frail, sickly

gran *adj* apocopated form of **grande**, used before singular and plural nouns beginning with a consonant sound other than *gn, pn, ps*, impure *s, x,* and *z*

gra•na *m* (**-na**) Parmesan cheese ‖ *f* (**-ne**) cochineal; grain (*of wood, metal, etc*); (slang) dough; (coll) trouble

granàglie *fpl* grain, cereals

gra•nàio *m* (**-nài**) granary, barn

granata *adj invar* & *m* garnet (*color*) ‖ *f* pomegranate (*fruit*); garnet; broom; grenade

granatière *m* grenadier

granatina *f* grenadine

Gran Bretagna, la Great Britain

grancassa *f* bass drum

grancèvola *f* spider crab

gràn•chio *m* (**-chi**) crab; claw (*of hammer*); (coll) cramp; **prendere un granchio** to make a blunder

grandangolare *adj* wide-angle

grande *adj* big, large; great; tall; high (*mass; voice*); long (*time*); capital (*letter*); full (*speed*); grown-up ‖ *m* grownup; grandeur; grandee; **fare il grande** to show off; **i grandi** the great; **in grande** on a large scale; lavishly

grandézza *f* size; enormity; greatness; quantity; **in grandezza naturale** life-size; **grandezze** ostentatiousness

grandezzó•so -sa [s] *adj* ostentatious

grandiloquènza *f* grandiloquence

grandinare (**gràndino**) *tr* (obs) to hail ‖ *intr* to hail ‖ *impers* (ESSERE & AVERE)—**grandina** it is hailing

grandinata *f* hailstorm

gràndine *f* hail

grandiosi•tà [s] *f* (**-tà**) grandeur, magnificence

grandió•so -sa [s] *adj* grandiose, grand

grandu•ca *m* (**-chi**) grand duke

granduchéssa *f* grand duchess

granèllo *m* grain, seed; speck

grànfia *f* clutch

granìco•lo -la *adj* grain, wheat

granire §176 *tr* to grain; to stipple; (mus) to make (*the notes*) clear-cut ‖ *intr* to teethe

granita *f* sherbet, water ice

granito *m* granite

granitura *f* knurl, milled edge

grano *m* wheat; grain of wheat; grain; speck; **grano duro** durum wheat; **grano saraceno** buckwheat; **grano turco** corn

granturco *m* corn

granulare *adj* granular ‖ *v* (**grànulo**) *tr* to granulate

granulatóre *m* crusher

grànulo *m* granule, pellet, bud

granuló•so -sa [s] *adj* granular; lumpy; gritty; friable, crumbly

grappa *f* eau de vie; clamp, brace

grappétta *f* staple; crampon

grappino *m* (naut) grapnel

gràppolo *m* bunch, cluster

grassàg•gio *m* (**-gi**) (aut) lubrication

grassatóre *m* highwayman

grassazióne *f* holdup

grassétto *m* boldface

grassézza *f* fatness; richness

gras•so -sa *adj* fat; rich; greasy; risqué ‖ *m* fat, suet; grease; shortening

grassòc•cio -cia *adj* (**-ci -ce**) pudgy, plump

grata *f* grate, grating

gratèlla *f* strainer; sieve; broiler

gratìc•cia *f* (**-ce**) (theat) gridiron

gratìc•cio *m* (**-ci**) lattice, trellis

graticola *f* gridiron; grating; graticule

gratìfi•ca *f* (**-che**) bonus

gratificare §197 (**gratìfico**) *tr* to give a bonus to; (fig) to pelt (*with insults*)

gratificazióne *f* bonus

gratis *adv* gratis, free, for nothing

gratitùdine *f* gratitude

gra•to -ta *adj* grateful, appreciative ‖ *f* see **grata**

grattacapo *m* trouble, worry

grattacièlo *m* skyscraper

grattare *tr* to scratch; to scrape; to grate; (slang) to snitch ‖ *intr* to scratch; to grate

grattùgia *f* grater

grattugiare §290 *tr* to grate

gratùi•to -ta *adj* gratuitous, free

gravame *m* burden; tax; (law) appeal; **fare gravame a qlcu di qlco** to impute s.th to s.o.

gravare *tr* to burden, oppress; (obs) to seize ‖ *intr* (ESSERE & AVERE) to weigh; to lie; to be sorry, e.g., **gli grava d'avermi disturbato** he is sorry to have bothered me ‖ *ref*—**gravarsi di** to take upon oneself

grave *adj* heavy; burdensome; grave, serious ‖ *m* (phys) body; **stare sul grave** to put on airs

graveolènte *adj* stinking

gravézza *f* heaviness; burden; oppression; (obs) taxation

gravidanza *f* pregnancy

gràvi•do -da *adj* pregnant; fraught

gravi•tà *f* (**-tà**) gravity

gravitare (**gràvito**) *intr* to gravitate; to weigh, lie

gravitazióne *f* gravitation

gravó•so -sa [s] *adj* heavy; hard, burdensome; oppressive

gràzia *f* grace; pardon, mercy; delicacy; kindness; **di grazia!** please!;

essere nelle grazie di qlcu to be in s.o.'s good graces; fare grazia di qlco a qlcu to spare s.o. s.th; grazia di Dio abundance, bounty; grazie! thank you!; grazie tante! thanks a lot!; in grazia di thanks to; male grazie bad manners; per grazie as a favor; render grazia a to thank; saper grazia a to be thankful to

graziare §287 tr to pardon; graziare qlcu di qlco to grant s.th to s.o.

grazió·so -sa [s] adj graceful, pretty; gracious; (lit) free, gratuitous

Grècia, la Greece

grè·co -ca (-ci -che) adj & mf Greek || f fret, fretwork; bullion (on Italian general's hat); tunic

gregà·rio -ria (-ri -rie) adj gregarious || m private; follower

grég·ge m (-gi or -ge fpl) flock, herd

grég·gio -gia (-gi -ge) adj coarse; raw, unrefined || m crude oil

gregoria·no -na adj Gregorian

grembiale m var of grembiule

grembiule m apron; frock; smock

grembiulino m pinafore

grèmbo m lap; womb; bosom

gremire §176 tr to crowd || ref to become crowded

gremi·to -ta adj overcrowded

gréppia f manger, crib

gréto m dry gravel bed of a river

grettézza f stinginess; narrow-mindedness

grét·to -ta adj stingy; narrow-minded

grève adj heavy; uncouth; (lit) grievous

gréz·zo -za [ddzz] adj raw, crude; coarse

gridare tr to cry out; to cry for (help); (coll) to scold || intr to cry out, shout

grido m cry (of animal) || m (grida fpl) cry; scream; shout; yell; fame; di grido famous; grido di guerra war cry; ultimo grido latest fashion

grifa·gno -gna adj rapacious, fierce

griffa f hobnail; (mov, phot) sprocket

grifo m snout (of pig); (pej) snoot; (lit) griffin

grifóne m vulture; (mythol) griffin

grigia·stro -stra adj grayish

grì·gio -gia adj & m (-gi -gie) grey

grigiovérde adj invar olive-drab || m olive-drab uniform

grìglia f gridiron, broiler; grate, grille; (elec) grid (of vacuum tube)

grillare tr to grill, broil || intr to sizzle; to bubble (said of fermenting wine); to have a sudden whim

grillétto m trigger

grillo m cricket; whim, fancy

grimaldèllo m picklock

grìnfia f claw, clutch; grinfie clutches

grinta f grim or forbidding face

grinza f wrinkle; crease; non fare una grinza to be perfect

grinzó·so -sa [s] adj wrinkled; creased

grippare intr & ref to bind, jam

grisèlla f (naut) ratline

gri·sou m (-sou) firedamp

grissino m breadstick

Groenlàndia, la Greenland

grómma f incrustation, deposit

grónda f eaves; slope (of ground)

grondàia f gutter (of roof)

grondare (gróndo) tr to drip || intr (ESSERE) to ooze (said, e.g., of perspiration); to drip; grondare di sangue to stream with blood

groppa f back (of animal); top (of mountain); restare sulla groppa a to be stuck with, e.g., gli sono restati sulla groppa cento esemplari he is stuck with one hundred copies

groppata f bucking (of horse)

gróppo m knot, tangle; lump (in throat); squall

groppóne m back, rump

gròssa f gross; dormire della grossa to sleep like a log

grossézza f bigness; thickness; density; swelling (of river); (fig) coarseness; grossezza d'udito hardness of hearing

grossi·sta mf (-sti -ste) wholesaler

gròs·so -sa adj big, large; thick; heavy (seas); swollen (river); hard (breathing); offensive (words); coarse (e.g., salt); pregnant; deep (voice); (coll) important; alla grossa approximately; di grosso a lot, very much; dirla grossa to talk nonsense; farla grossa to make a blunder; grosso d'udito hard of hearing; in grosso wholesale; spararle grosse to tell tall tales || m bulk; main body (e.g., of an army) || f see grossa

grossola·no -na adj coarse; boorish, uncouth; big (blunder)

gròtta f grotto; (coll) inn

grotté·sco -sca (-schi -sche) adj & m grotesque || f (hist) grotesque painting

grovièra f Gruyère cheese

grovì·glio m (-gli) tangle, snarl

gru f (gru) (orn, mach) crane

grùc·cia f (-ce) crutch; clothes hanger; (obs) wooden leg

grufolare (grùfolo) intr to nuzzle || ref to wallow (in mud)

grugnire §176 tr & intr to grunt

grugnito m grunt

grugno m snout; (pej) snoot; fare il grugno to sulk

grui·sta m (-sti) crane operator

grullerìa f foolishness

grul·lo -la adj silly, simple

gruma f deposit, incrustation

grumo m lump; clot

grùmolo m heart (e.g., of lettuce); small lump

grumó·so -sa [s] adj lumpy; incrusted, scaly

gruppo m group; main body (e.g., of runners); club; gruppo elettrogeno generating unit; gruppo motore (aut) power plant

grùzzolo m hoard, pile; farsi il gruzzolo to feather one's nest

guadagnare tr to earn; to win; to gain; to pick up (speed); to reach (port) || intr to win; to look better || ref to win; to win over; guadagnarsi il pane or la vita to earn one's living

guadagno m earnings; profit; a basso

guadagno (rad, telv) low-gain; **ad alto guadagno** (rad, telv) high-gain
guadare *tr* to wade, ford
guado *m* ford; (bot) woad; **passare a guado** to ford
guài *interj* woe!
guaina *f* case; scabbard, sheath; corset; (aut) seat cover
guàio *m* (**guài**) trouble ‖ *interj* see **guài**
guaire §176 *intr* to yelp; to whine
guaito *m* yelp, whine
gualcire §176 *tr* to crumple
gualdrappa *f* saddlecloth
Gualtièro *m* Walter
guàn·cia *f* (**-ce**) cheek; moldboard; cheek side (*of gunstock*)
guanciale *m* pillow; **dormire tra due guanciali** to sleep safe and sound
guan·tàio -tàia *mf* (**-tài -tàie**) glove maker; glove merchant
guantería *f* glove factory
guantièra *f* glove case; tray
guanto *m* glove; **gettare il guanto** to fling down the gauntlet; **raccogliere il guanto** to take up the gauntlet; **trattare con i guanti gialli** to handle with kid gloves
guantóne *m* big glove; **guantoni da pugilato** boxing gloves
guardabarriè·re *m* (**-re**) (rr) gatekeeper, crossing watchman
guardabò·schi *m* (**-schi**) forester
guardacàc·cia *m* (**-cia**) gamekeeper
guardacò·ste *m* (**-ste**) coast guard; coast-guard cutter
guardafi·li *m* (**-li**) (elec) lineman
guardali·nee *m* (**-nee**) (rr) trackwalker; (sports) linesman
guardama·no *m* (**-no**) guard (*of sabre or rifle*); work glove; (naut) handrail
guardaportó·ne *m* (**-ne**) doorman
guardare *tr* to look at; to protect, watch; to pay attention to; to face, overlook; (obs) to keep to (*one's bed*); (obs) to keep (*a holiday*); **guardare a vista** to keep under close watch; **guardare dall'alto in basso** to look down one's nose at; **guardare di sotto in su** to leer at ‖ *intr* to look; to pay attention; **Dio guardi!** God forbid!; **guardare a** to face (*said, e.g., of a room*); **guardare di non + inf** to be careful not to + **inf**; **guardare in faccia** to face (*e.g., danger*); **stare a guardare** to keep on the sidelines ‖ *ref* to look at one another; to look at oneself; **guardarsi da** to keep from; to guard against
guardarò·ba *m* (**-ba**) wardrobe; linen closet; checkroom, cloakroom
guardarobiè·re -ra *mf* checkroom attendant ‖ *f* hatcheck girl
guardasigil·li *m* (**-li**) minister of justice (*in Italy*); (Brit) Lord Privy Seal; (U.S.A.) attorney general; (hist) keeper of the seals
guardaspal·le *m* (**-le**) bodyguard
guardata *f* quick look, glance
guarda·vìa *m* (**-vìa**) guardrail; median strip
guàrdia *f* watch; guard; top water level; flyleaf; **di guardia** on duty;

fare la guardia a to watch; **guardia campestre** forester; **guardia carceraria** prison guard; **guardia del corpo** guard, body guard; **guardia di finanza** customs officer; **guardia d'onore** honor guard; **guardia forestale** forester; park guard; **guardia giurata** private policeman; **guardia medica** emergency clinic; **guardia municipale** police officer; **guardia notturna** night watch; **mettere qlcu in guardia** to warn s.o.; **montare la guardia** to be on guard duty, keep guard; **stare in guardia** to be on one's guard
guardiamari·na *m* (**-na**) (nav) ensign
guardiano *m* keeper; warden; watchdog; (eccl) superior; **guardiano notturno** night watchman
guardina *f* lockup; **in guardina** in jail
guardinfante *m* bustle (*worn under the back of a woman's skirt*)
guardin·go -ga *adj* (**-ghi -ghe**) wary
guàrdolo *m* welt (*in shoe*)
guardóne *m* peeping tom
guarenti·gia *f* (**-gie**) guarantee
guaribile *adj* curable
guarigióne *f* cure, recovery
guarire §176 *tr* to cure; to heal ‖ *intr* (ESSERE) to recover; to heal
guaritóre *m* healer; quack
guarnigióne *f* (mil) garrison
guarnire §176 *tr* to equip; to rig; to trim; (naut) to rig; (culin) to garnish ‖ *intr* to add beauty
guarnizióne *f* decoration; trimming; lining; (culin) garniture; (mach) gasket; (mach) washer
Guascógna, la Gascony
guascó·ne -na *adj & mf* Gascon
guastafè·ste *mf* (**-ste**) kill-joy
guastare *tr* to ruin, spoil; to undo; to wreck, (obs) to lay waste; **guastare le uova nel paniere a** to spoil the plans of ‖ *ref* to spoil; to worsen (*said, e.g., of the weather*); (mach) to break down; **guastarsi con qlcu** to quarrel with s.o.; **guastarsi il sangue** to blow one's top
guastatóre *m* commando
gua·sto -sta *adj* ruined, spoiled; wrecked ‖ *m* breakdown; corruption; discord
guatare *tr* (lit) to look askance or with fear at
Guayana, la Guyana
guazza *f* dew
guazzabù·glio *m* (**-gli**) muddle, mess
guazzare *tr* to make (*an animal*) wade in a river ‖ *intr* to wallow
guazzétto *m* stew, ragout
guazzo *m* puddle, pool; gouache
guèl·fo -fa *adj & mf* Guelph
guèr·cio -cia (**-ci -ce**) *adj* cross-eyed; one-eyed; almost blind ‖ *mf* cross-eyed person; one-eyed person
guèrra *f* war; warfare; **guerra a coltello** internecine feud; **guerra di Troia** Trojan war; **guerra fredda** cold war; **guerra lampo** blitzkrieg; **guerra mondiale** world war

guerrafon·dàio -dàia (-dài -dàie) *adj* warmongering || *mf* warmonger

guerreggiare §290 (guerréggio) *tr* to fight, war against || *intr* to fight || *ref* to make war on one another

guerré·sco -sca *adj* (**-schi -sche**) warlike

guerriè·ro -ra *adj* war, warlike || *mf* fighter || *m* warrior

guerrìglia *f* guerrilla

guerriglièro *m* guerrilla (*soldier*)

gufo *m* misanthrope; (*orn*) horned owl

gùglia *f* spire; peak

gugliata *f* needleful

Guglièlmo *m* William

guida *f* guide; guidance; driving; runner (*rug*); guidebook; manual (*of instruction*); (aut) steering; **guida a destra** right-hand drive; **guide** reins (*of horse*); (mach) slide

guidaiòlo *m* leader (*among animals*)

guidare *tr* to guide, lead; to steer; to drive || *intr* to drive || *ref* to restrain oneself

guida·tóre -trice *mf* driver

guiderdóne *m* (lit) premium, prize

guidóne *m* pennant, pennon

guidoslitta *f* bobsled

guidovìa *f* ski lift

Guinèa, la Guinea

guinzà·glio *m* (**-gli**) leash; (fig) fetter, shackle

guisa *f* way, manner; **in guisa che** so that; **in guisa di** under the guise of

guit·to -ta *adj* miserly, niggardly || *m* strolling player

guizzare *intr* to dart; to wriggle; to flash (*said of lightning*); (naut) to yaw || *intr* (ESSERE) to slip away

guizzo *m* dart; wriggle; flash

gù·scio *m* (**-sci**) shell; pod (*of pea*); tick (*of mattress*); **guscio di noce** nutshell; **guscio d'uovo** eggshell

gustare *tr* to taste; to relish || *intr* (ESSERE & AVERE) to please; to like, e.g., **gli gustano le gite in barca** he likes boat rides

gusto *m* taste; pleasure, fun; whim; style; **di cattivo gusto** tasteless; **di gusto** gladly, with gusto; **prendere gusto per** to take a liking for; **prendersi il gusto di** to relish; **provar gusto** to have fun

gustó·so -sa [s] *adj* tasty

guttapèrca *f* gutta-percha

gutturale *adj* & *f* guttural

H

H, h [ˈɑkkɑ] *m* & *f* eighth letter of the Italian alphabet

handicappare *tr* var of **andicappare**

hangar *m* (**hangar**) hangar

havaia·no -na *adj* & *mf* Hawaiian

henné *m* henna

hertz *m* hertz

hertzia·no -na *adj* Hertzian

hi-fi *f* (coll) hi-fi

hockei·sta *mf* (**-sti -ste**) hockey player

hollywoodia·no -na *adj* Hollywood, Hollywood-like

hurrà *interj* hurrah!

I

I, i, [i] *m* & *f* ninth letter of the Italian alphabet

i §4 *def art* the

iarda *f* yard

iato *m* hiatus

iattanza *f* boasting, bragging

iattura *f* misfortune, calamity

ibèri·co -ca *adj* (**-ci -che**) Iberian

ibernare (ibèrno) *intr* to hibernate

ibi·sco *m* (**-schi**) hibiscus

ibridare (ìbrido) *tr* & *intr* to hybridize

ìbri·do -da *adj* & *m* hybrid

icàsti·co -ca *adj* (**-ci -che**) figurative; realistic

-ìccio -ìccia *suf adj* -ish, e.g., **gialliccio** yellowish

iconocla·sta *mf* (**-sti -ste**) iconoclast

iconografìa *f* iconography

iconoscò·pio *m* (**-pi**) iconoscope

iddì·o *m* (**-i**) god || **Iddio** *m* God

idèa *f* idea; goal, purpose; bit, touch; **avere idea di** to have a mind to; **dare l'idea di** to seem; **farsi un'idea di** to

grasp the notion of; **idea fissa** fixed idea; **neanche per idea** not in the least

ideale *adj* & *m* ideal

idealismo *m* idealism

ideali·sta *mf* (**-sti -ste**) idealist

idealisti·co -ca *adj* (**-ci -che**) idealistic

idealizzare [ddzz] *tr* to idealize

ideare (idèo) *tr* to conceive

idea·tóre -trice *mf* inventor

idem *adv* ditto

idènti·co -ca *adj* (**-ci -che**) identical

identificare §197 (identìfico) *tr* to identify || *ref* to resemble each other; **identificarsi con** to identify with

identificazióne *f* identification

identi·tà *f* (**-tà**) identity

ideologìa *f* ideology

idi *mpl* & *fpl* ides

idillìa·co -ca *adj* (**-ci -che**) idyllic

idìl·lio *m* (**-li**) idyll; romance

idiò·ma *m* (**-mi**) language, idiom

idiomàti·co -ca *adj* (**-ci -che**) idiomatic

idiosincrasìa *f* aversion; (med) idio-syncrasy
idiò·ta (-**ti** -**te**) *adj* idiotic ‖ *mf* idiot
idiotismo *m* idiom; idiocy
idiozìa *f* idiocy
idolatrare *tr & intr* to idolize
idolatrìa *f* idolatry
ìdolo *m* idol
idonei·tà *f* (-**tà**) fitness, aptitude; quali-fication
idòne·o -**a** *adj* fit; qualified; opportune
idra *f* hydra
idrante *m* hydrant, fireplug
idratante *adj* moisturizing
idratare *tr & ref* to hydrate
idrato *m* hydrate
idràuli·co -**ca** (-**ci** -**che**) *adj* hydraulic ‖ *m* plumber ‖ *f* hydraulics
ìdri·co -**ca** *adj* (-**ci** -**che**) water, e.g., **forza idrica** water power
idrocarburo *m* hydrocarbon
idroelèttri·co -**ca** *adj* (-**ci** -**che**) hydro-electric
idròfi·lo -**la** *adj* absorbent
idrofobìa *f* hydrophobia, rabies
idròfo·bo -**ba** *adj* hydrophobic, rabid
idròfu·go -**ga** *adj* (-**ghi** -**ghe**) waterproof
idrogenare (**idrògeno**) *tr* to hydrogenate
idrògeno *m* hydrogen
idròpi·co -**ca** (-**ci** -**che**) *adj* dropsical ‖ *mf* patient suffering from dropsy
idropisìa *f* dropsy
idroplano *m* hydroplane (*boat*)
idropòrto *m* seaplane airport
idrorepellènte *adj* water-repellent
idroscalo *m* seaplane airport
idro·scì *m* (-**scì**) water ski
idroscivolante *m* (naut) hydroplane
idrosilurante *m* torpedo plane
idròssido *m* hydroxide
idroterapìa *f* hydrotherapy
idrovìa *f* inland waterway
idrovolante *m* seaplane, hydroplane
idròvo·ro -**ra** *adj* suction (*pump*) ‖ *f* suction pump
ièna *f* hyena
ièri *m & adv* yesterday; **ieri l'altro** the day before yesterday; **ieri notte** last night; **ieri sera** last evening, last night, yesterday evening
ietta·tóre -**trice** *mf* hoodoo
iettatura *f* evil eye; bad luck, jinx
igiène *f* hygiene; sanitation
igièni·co -**ca** *adj* (-**ci** -**che**) hygienic, sanitary
igname *m* yam
igna·ro -**ra** *adj* unaware; inexperienced
igna·vo -**va** *adj* (lit) slothful
ignizióne *f* ignition
ignòbile *adj* (lit) ignoble
ignomìnia *f* ignominy; outrage
ignominió·so -**sa** [s] *adj* ignominious
ignorante *adj* ignorant; illiterate ‖ *mf* ignoramus
ignoranza *f* ignorance
ignorare (**ignòro**) *tr* to not know; to ignore
ignò·to -**ta** *adj & m* unknown
ignu·do -**da** *adj* (lit) naked ‖ *m* (lit) naked person
il §4 *def art* the
ilare *adj* cheerful

ilari·tà *f* (-**tà**) cheerfulness; laughter
ìlice *f* (lit) ilex, holm oak
ìlio *m* (anat) ilium
illanguidire §176 *tr* to weaken ‖ *intr* (ESSERE) to get weak
illazióne *f* inference
illéci·to -**ta** *adj* illicit, unlawful ‖ *m* unlawful act
illegale *adj* illegal
illeggiadrire §176 *tr* to embellish
illeggìbile *adj* illegible
illegìtti·mo -**ma** *adj* illegitimate
illé·so -**sa** *adj* unhurt, unharmed
illettera·to -**ta** *adj & mf* illiterate
illiba·to -**ta** *adj* spotless, pure
illimita·to -**ta** *adj* unlimited
illìri·co -**ca** *adj* (-**ci** -**che**) Illyrian
illògi·co -**ca** *adj* (-**ci** -**che**) illogical
illùdere §105 *tr* to delude
illuminare (**illùmino**) *tr* to illuminate; to brighten; to enlighten ‖ *ref* to grow bright
illumina·to -**ta** *adj* illuminated; en-lightened; educated
illuminazióne *f* illumination; enlighten-ment
illuminismo *m* Age of Enlightenment
illusióne *f* illusion; delusion; **farsi illu-sioni** to indulge in wishful thinking
illusionismo *m* sleight of hand; magic
illusioni·sta *mf* (-**sti** -**ste**) magician
illu·so -**sa** *adj* deluded ‖ *mf* deluded person
illusò·rio -**ria** *adj* (-**ri** -**rie**) illusory, illusive
illustrare *tr* to illustrate; to explain, elucidate ‖ *ref* to become famous
illustra·to -**ta** *adj* illustrated, pictorial
illustra·tóre -**trice** *mf* illustrator
illustrazióne *f* illustration; illustrious person
illustre *adj* illustrious, famous
illustrìssi·mo -**ma** *adj* distinguished; honorable; **Illustrissimo Signore** Dear Sir; Mr. (*addressing a letter*)
imbacuccare §197 *tr & ref* to muffle up; to wrap up
imbaldanzire §176 *tr* to embolden ‖ *intr* (ESSERE) & *ref* to grow bold
imballàg·gio *m* (-**gi**) wrapping, packag-ing
imballare *tr* to wrap up, package; to bale; to race (*the motor*); **imballarsi in una gabbia** to crate ‖ *ref* to race (*said of a motor*)
imballa·tóre -**trice** *mf* packer
imballo *m* packing; packaging, wrap-ping; racing (*of motor*)
imbalsamare (**imbàlsamo**) *tr* to em-balm; to stuff (*animals*)
imbambola·to -**ta** *adj* gazing, staring; stunned, dumfounded; sleepy-eyed; sluggish
imbandierare (**imbandièro**) *tr* to bedeck with flags
imbandire §176 *tr* to prepare (*food, a meal, a table*) lavishly
imbarazzante *adj* embarrassing, awk-ward
imbarazzare *tr* to embarrass; to en-cumber, hamper; to upset (*the stomach*)

imbarazza·to -ta *adj* embarrassed, perplexed; upset (*stomach*); ill-at-ease

imbarazzo *m* embarrassment; annoyance; **imbarazzo di stomaco** upset stomach

imbarbarire §176 *tr & ref* to make barbarous; to corrupt (*a language*)

imbarcadèro *m* landing pier

imbarcare §197 *tr* to ship; to load, embark; to ship (*water*) ‖ *ref* to sail; to embark; to curve (*said of furniture*)

imbarca·tóio *m* (-**tói**) landing pier

imbarcazione *f* boat; **imbarcazione di salvataggio** lifeboat

imbar·co *m* (-**chi**) embarkation; port of embarkation

imbardare *intr & ref* (aer) to yaw; (aut) to swerve, lurch

imbardata *f* (aer) yaw; (aut) swerve, lurch

imbarilare *tr* to barrel

imbastardire §176 *tr* to corrupt ‖ *ref* to become corrupt

imbastire §176 *tr* (sew) to baste; (fig) to sketch out

imbastitura *f* (sew) basting

imbàttere *ref*—**imbattersi bene** to be lucky; **imbattersi in** to come across; **imbattersi male** to have bad luck

imbattìbile *adj* unbeatable

imbavagliare §280 *tr* to gag

imbeccare §197 (imbécco) *tr* to feed (*a fledgling*); (fig) to prompt

imbeccata *f* beakful; (fig) prompting

imbecillàggine *f* imbecility

imbecille *adj & mf* imbecile

imbecilli·tà *f* (-**tà**) imbecility

imbèlle *adj* unwarlike; cowardly

imbellettare (imbellétto) *tr* to apply rouge, to apply make-up on ‖ *ref* to put on make-up

imbellire §176 *tr* to embellish

imbèrbe *adj* beardless; callow

imbestialire §176 *tr* to enrage ‖ *intr* (ESSERE) & *ref* to become enraged

imbévere §185 *tr* to soak; to soak up; to imbue ‖ *ref* to become soaked; to become imbued

imbiancare §197 *tr* to whiten; to bleach; to whitewash ‖ *intr* (ESSERE) & *ref* to turn white (*said, e.g., of hair*); to clear up (*said of weather*)

imbiancatura *f* bleaching (*of laundry*); whitening; whitewashing

imbianchiménto *m* bleaching

imbianchino *m* whitewasher; house painter; (pej) dauber

imbianchire §176 *tr* to whiten; to bleach ‖ *ref* to turn white

imbiondire §176 *tr* to bleach (*hair*) ‖ *intr* to become blond; to ripen (*said of wheat*)

imbizzarrire [ddzz] *intr* (ESSERE) & *ref* to become skittish (*said of a horse*); to become infuriated

imbizzire [ddzz] §176 *intr* (ESSERE) to get angry

imboccare §197 (imbócco) *tr* to feed by mouth; to put (*an instrument*) in one's mouth; to take, enter (*a road*); to prompt ‖ *intr* (ESSERE) to flow; to open (*said of a road*); (mach) to fit

imboccatura *f* entrance (*of street*); inlet; opening, top (*e.g., of bottle*); bit (*of bridle*); (mus) mouthpiece; **avere l'imboccatura a** to be experienced in

imbóc·co *m* (-**chi**) entrance; inlet; opening

imbonimènto *m* claptrap

imbonire §176 *tr* to lure, entice (*s.o. to buy or enter*)

imbonitóre *m* barker

imborghesire §176 *tr* to render middle-class ‖ *intr* (ESSERE) to become middle-class

imboscare §197 (imbòsco) *tr* to hide; to hide (*s.o.*) underground ‖ *ref* to shirk; to be a slacker

imbosca·to -ta *adj* (mil) shirking, draft-dodging ‖ *m* (mil) slacker; (mil) goldbrick ‖ *f* ambush; **tendere un'imboscata** to set an ambush

imboscatóre *m* accomplice of a draft dodger; hoarder (*of scarce items*)

imboschire §176 *tr* to forest

imbottare (imbótto) *tr* to barrel

imbottigliare §280 *tr* to bottle; to bottle up ‖ *ref* to get bottled up (*said of traffic*)

imbottire §176 *tr* to pad, fill; to stuff; to pad (*a speech*)

imbottita *f* bedspread, quilt

imbottitura *f* padding

imbra·ca *f* (-**che**) breeching strap (*of harness*); safety belt; (naut) sling

imbracare §197 *tr* to sling

imbracciare §128 *tr* to fasten (*shield*); to level (*gun*)

imbrancare §197 *tr & ref* to herd

imbrattacar·te *mf* (-**te**) scribbler

imbrattamu·ri *mf* (-**ri**) dauber

imbrattare *tr* to soil, dirty; to smudge, smear

imbrattaté·le *mf* (-**le**) dauber

imbratto *m* dirt; smudge, smear; daub; scribble; swill

imbrigliare §280 *tr* to bridle

imbroccare §197 (imbròcco) *tr* to hit (*the target*); to guess right

imbrodare (imbròdo) *tr* to soil

imbrogliare §280 (imbròglio) *tr* to cheat; to mix up; to tangle; to confuse; **imbrogliare le vele** (naut) to take in the reef ‖ *ref* to get tangled up; to get confused; to turn bad (*said of weather*)

imbrò·glio *m* (-**gli**) cheat; tangle; (naut) reef; **cacciarsi in un imbroglio** to get involved in a mess

imbroglió·ne -na *mf* swindler

imbronciare §128 (imbróncio) *intr* (ESSERE) & *ref* to pout, sulk ‖ *ref* to lower (*said of the weather*)

imbroncia·to -ta *adj* sulky, surly; cloudy, overcast

imbrunire *m*—**sull'imbrunire** at nightfall ‖ §176 *intr* (ESSERE) to turn brown ‖ *impers* (ESSERE)—**imbrunisce** it is growing dark

imbruttire §176 *tr* to mar; to make ugly ‖ *intr* (ESSERE) & *ref* to grow ugly

imbucare §197 *tr* to mail; to put in a hole ‖ *ref* to hide

imburrare *tr* to butter
imbuto *m* funnel
imène *m* (anat) hymen, maidenhead
imitare (ìmito) *tr* to imitate
imita·tóre -trice *mf* imitator; (theat) mimic
imitazióne *f* imitation
immacola·to -ta *adj* immaculate
immagazzinare [ddzz] *tr* to store, store up
immaginare (immàgino) *tr* to imagine; to guess; to invent || *ref*—si immagini! of course!; not at all!
immaginà·rio -ria *adj* (-ri -rie) imaginary
immaginativa *f* imagination
immaginazióne *f* imagination
immàgine *f* image; picture
immaginó·so -sa [s] *adj* imaginative
immalinconire §176 *tr* to sadden || *intr* (ESSERE) & *ref* to become melancholy
immancàbile *adj* unfailing; certain
immane *adj* monstrous; gigantic
immangiàbile *adj* uneatable, inedible
immantinènte *adv* (lit) immediately
immarcescibile *adj* incorruptible
immateriale *adj* immaterial
immatricolare (immatricolo) *tr* to matriculate
immatricolazióne *f* matriculation
immatu·ro -ra *adj* immature; premature
immedesimare (immedésimo) *tr* to identify; to blend || *ref* to identify oneself
immediataménte *adv* immediately
immediatézza *f* immediacy
immedia·to -ta *adj* immediate
immemoràbile *adj* immemorial
immèmore *adj* forgetful
immèn·so -sa *adj* immense, huge
immèrgere §162 *tr* to immerse; to plunge || *ref* to plunge; to become absorbed
immerita·to -ta *adj* undeserved
immeritévole *adj* undeserving
immersióne *f* immersion; submersion (*of a submarine*); (naut) draft
immèttere §198 *tr* to let in; immettere qlcu nel possesso di (law) to grant s.o. possession of
immigrante *adj* & *mf* immigrant
immigrare *intr* (ESSERE) to immigrate
immigrazióne *f* immigration; (biol) migration
imminènte *adj* imminent
imminènza *f* imminence
immischiare §287 *tr* to involve || *ref* to meddle; to become involved
immiserire §176 *tr* to impoverish || *intr* (ESSERE) & *ref* to become impoverished; to become debased
immissà·rio *m* (-ri) tributary
immissióne *f* letting in, introduction; intake; insertion (*in lunar orbit*)
immòbile *adj* motionless, immobile; real (*property*) || immobili *mpl* real estate
immobiliare *adj* real, e.g., proprietà immobiliare real estate; real-estate, e.g., imposta immobiliare real-estate tax
immobilizzare [ddzz] *tr* to immobilize; to pin down; to tie up (*capital*)

immodè·sto -sta *adj* indecent; immodest
immolare (immòlo) *tr* to immolate
immondézza *f* filth; impurity
immondez·zàio *m* (-zài) rubbish heap, dump; garbage can
immondìzia *f* trash; garbage; filth
immón·do -da *adj* filthy, dirty; unclean
immorale *adj* immoral
immorali·tà *f* (-tà) immorality
immortalare *tr* to immortalize
immortale *adj* immortal
immortalità *f* immortality
immò·to -ta *adj* (lit) motionless
immune *adj* immune
immunizzare [ddzz] *tr* to immunize
immutàbile *adj* immutable
immuta·to -ta *adj* unchanged
i·mo -ma *adj* (lit) bottom, lowest || *m* (lit) bottom; (lit) depth
impaccare §197 *tr* to pack, wrap up
impacchettare (impacchétto) *tr* to pack, bundle
impacciare §128 *tr* to hamper; to embarrass || *ref* to meddle
impaccia·to -ta *adj* hampered; clumsy
impàc·cio *m* (-ci) embarrassment; hindrance; trouble; essere d'impaccio to be in the way
impac·co *m* (-chi) wrapping; (med) compress
impadronire §176 *ref*—impadronirsi di to seize; to take possession of; to master (*a language*)
impagàbile *adj* invaluable, priceless
impaginare (impàgino) *tr* (typ) to make up (*in pages*), paginate
impaginato *m* (typ) page proof
impagliare §280 *tr* to cane (*a chair*); to stuff (*an animal; a doll*); to pack in straw
impalare *tr* to impale; to tie to a pole or stake || *ref* to stiffen up
impala·to -ta *adj* stiff, rigid
impalcatura *f* scaffold; frame, framework
impallidire §176 *intr* to turn pale; to blanch; to grow dim (*said of a star*); (fig) to wane
impalmare *tr* (lit) to wed
impalpàbile *adj* impalpable
impaludare *tr* to make swampy or marshy || *intr* to become marshy
impanare *tr* to bread; to thread (*a screw*) || *intr* to screw in
impaniare §287 *tr* to trap, ensnare || *ref* to fall into the trap
impantanare *tr* to turn into a swamp || *ref* to get stuck, to sink (*in vice*)
impaperare (impàpero) *ref* to fluff, make a slip
impappinare *tr* to confuse || *ref* to blunder; to stammer
imparare *tr* to learn; imparare a memoria to learn by heart || *intr* imparare a to learn to, to learn how to
impareggiàbile *adj* peerless, unmatched
imparentare (imparènto) *tr* to bring into the family || *ref*—imparentarsi con to marry into
ìmpari *adj* odd, uneven
imparrucca·to -ta *adj* bewigged
impartire §176 *tr* to impart
imparziale *adj* impartial

impasse *f* blind alley; deadlock; (cards) finesse

impassibile *adj* impassible, impassive

impastare *tr* to knead; to mix; to smear with paste

impasta·to -ta *adj* kneaded; smeared; **impastato di** tainted with; overwhelmed with (*sleep*)

impasto *m* paste; pastiche

impastoiare §287 (**impastóio**) *tr* to fetter, hamstring

impataccare §197 *tr* to besmear, soil

impattare *tr* to even up;¡ to tie (*a game*); **impattarla con** to tie (*a person*)

impatto *m* impact

impaurire §176 *tr* to scare ‖ *ref* to get scared

impàvi·do -da *adj* fearless

impaziènte *adj* impatient

impazientire §176 *intr* (ESSERE) & *ref* to get impatient

impaziènza *f* impatience

impazzare *intr* (ESSERE) to be wild with excitement; to go mad; (culin) to curdle

impazzata *f*—**all'impazzata** at top speed; berserk

impazzire §176 *intr* (ESSERE) to go crazy; **fare impazzire** to drive crazy

impeccàbile *adj* impeccable

impeciare §128 (**impécio**) *tr* to tar

impedènza *f* impedance

impediménto *m* hindrance, obstacle, impediment

impedire §176 *tr* to impede, hinder; to obstruct ‖ *intr* to prevent; **impedire** (with *dat*) **di** + *inf* or **che** + *subj* to prevent from + *ger*

impegnare (**impégno**) *tr* to pawn; to reserve (*a room*); to engage (*the enemy*); to keep occupied; to pledge ‖ *ref* to obligate oneself; to go all out; to become entangled

impegnati·vo -va *adj* demanding (*activity*); binding ·(*promise*)

impegna·to -ta *adj* pawned; pledged; occupied; committed

impégno *m* commitment; obligation; task; zeal; **senza impegno** without promising

impegolare (**impégolo**) *tr* to tar ‖ *ref* to become entangled

impelagare §209 (**impèlago**) *ref* to bog down; to become entangled

impellicciare §128 *tr* to fur; to veneer

impenetràbile *adj* impenetrable

impenitènte *adj* impenitent; confirmed

impennàg·gio *m* (-gi) (aer) empennage

impennare (**impénno**) *tr* to feather; (fig) to give wings to ‖ *ref* to rear (*said of a horse*); to take umbrage; (aer) to zoom

impennata *f* rearing ·(*of horse*); (aer) zoom

impensàbile *adj* unthinkable

impensa·to -ta *adj* unexpected

impensierire §176 *tr* & *ref* to worry

imperante *adj* prevailing

imperare (**impèro**) *intr* to rule, reign; to prevail; **imperare su** to rule over

imperati·vo -va *adj* & *m* imperative

imperatóre *m* emperor

imperatrice *f* empress

impercettibile *adj* imperceptible

imperdonàbile *adj* unforgivable

imperfèt·to -ta *adj* & *m* imperfect

imperfezióne *f* imperfection

imperiale *adj* imperial ‖ *m* upper deck (of *bus or coach*); **imperiali** imperial troops

imperiali·sta *adj* & *mf* (-sti -ste) ·imperialist

impè·rio *m* (-ri) empire; rule

imperió·so -sa [s] *adj* imperious; imperative

imperi·to -ta *adj* (lit) inexperienced

imperitu·ro -ra *adj* immortal; everlasting, imperishable

imperizia *f* inexperience

imperlare (**impèrlo**) *tr* to bead; to cover with beads (of *perspiration*)

impermalire §176 *tr* to provoke ‖ *ref*) to become provoked

impermeàbile *adj* waterproof ‖ *m* raincoat

imperniare §287 (**impèrnio**) *tr* to pivot; (fig) to base

impèro *adj invar* Empire ‖ *m* empire; control, sway

imperscrutàbile *adj* inscrutable

impersonale *adj* impersonal

impersonare (**impersóno**) *tr* to impersonate ‖ *ref*—**impersonarsi in** to be the embodiment of; (theat) to impersonate

impertèrri·to -ta *adj* undaunted

impertinènte *adj* impertinent, pert

impertinènza *f* impertinence

imperturbàbile *adj* imperturbable

imperturba·to -ta *adj* unperturbed

imperversare (**impervèrso**) *intr* to storm, rage; to be the rage

impèr·vio -via *adj* (-vi -vie) impassable

impeto *m* impetus; onslaught; violence; outburst; **d'impeto** rashly

impetrare (**impètro**) *tr* to beg for; to obtain by entreaty ‖ *intr* (ESSERE) (lit) to turn to stone

impetti·to -ta *adj* puffed up with pride

impetuó·so -sa [s] *adj* impetuous

impiallacciare §128 *tr* to veneer

impiallacciatura *f* veneer, veneering

impiantare *tr* to install (*a machine*); to set up (*a business*); to open (*an account*)

impiantito *m* floor, flooring

impianto *m* installation; plant; system

impiastrare *tr* to plaster; to dirty

impiastricciare §128 *tr* to plaster; to daub; to soil

impiastro *m* (med) plaster; (fig) bore

impiccagióne *f* hanging

impiccare §197 *tr* to hang

impicciare §128 *tr* to hinder; to bother ‖ *ref* to meddle, butt in; **impicciarsi degli affari propri** to mind one's own business

impìc·cio *m* (-ci) hindrance; trouble; **essere d'impiccio** to be in the way

impicció·ne -na *mf* meddler

impiccolire §176 *tr* to reduce in size ‖ *ref* to shrink in size

impiegare §209 (**impiègo**) *tr* to employ;

to use; to devote (*one's energies*); to spend (*time*); to invest (*capital*); to take (*time*) ‖ *ref* to have a job

impiegatì·zio -zia *adj* (-zì -zie) employee, white-collar

impiega·to -ta *mf* employee; clerk

impiè·go *m* (-ghi) employment; use; job; place of business; investment

impietosire [s] §176 *tr* to move to pity ‖ *ref* to be moved to pity

impietrire §176 *tr*, *intr* (ESSERE) & *ref* to turn to stone

impigliare §280 *tr* to entangle ‖ *ref* to become entangled

impigrire §176 *tr* to make lazy ‖ *intr* (ESSERE) & *ref* to get lazy

impinguare (impìnguo) *tr* & *ref* to fatten

impinzare *tr* to stuff ‖ *ref* to stuff oneself; impinzarsi il cervello to stuff one's brain (*with knowledge*)

impiombare (impiómbo) *tr* to lead; to plumb, seal with lead; to fill (*a tooth*); (naut) to splice (*a cable*)

impiombatura *f* seal; filling (*of tooth*); — (naut) splicing

impipare *ref*—impiparsi di (slang) to not give a hoot about

implacàbile *adj* implacable

implicare §197 (ìmplico) *tr* to implicate; to imply

implìci·to -ta *adj* implicit, implied

implorare (implòro) *tr* to implore

implume *adj* unfledged, featherless

impolìti·co -ca *adj* (-ci -che) unpolitical; impolitic, injudicious

impollinare (impòllino) *tr* to pollinate

impoltronire §176 *tr* to make lazy ‖ *ref* to get lazy

impolverare (impólvero) *tr* to cover with dust ‖ *ref* to get covered with dust

impomatare *tr* to pomade; to smear with pomade

imponderàbile *adj* imponderable; weightless

imponderabilità *f* imponderability; weightlessness

imponènte *adj* imposing; stately

imponìbile *adj* taxable ‖ *m* taxable income

impopolare *adj* unpopular

impopolarità *f* unpopularity

impòrre §218 *tr* to place, put; to impose; to order; to compel; to give (*a name*) ‖ *intr* (ESSERE) to be imposing; (with *dat*) to order, command ‖ *ref* to command respect; to win favor; to be necessary

importante *adj* important; sizable ‖ *m* important thing

importanza *f* importance; size; darsi importanza to assume an air of importance

importare (impòrto) *tr* to import; to imply; to involve ‖ *intr* (ESSERE) to be of consequence ‖ *impers* (ESSERE) —importa it matters; non importa never mind

importa·tóre -trice *mf* importer

importazióne *f* importation; import

impòrto *m* amount

importunare *tr* to bother, importune

importu·no -na *adj* importunate, bothersome ‖ *mf* bore

imposizióne *f* imposition; giving (*of a name*); order, command; taxation

impossessare (impossèsso) *ref*—impossessarsi di to seize; to master (*a language*)

impossìbile *adj* & *m* impossible

impossibili·tà *f* (-tà) impossibility

impossibilitare (impossibilito) *tr* to make impossible; to make unable or incapable

impossibilita·to -ta *adj* unable

impòsta *f* tax; shutter; (archit) impost; imposta complementare surtax; imposta sul valore aggiunto value-added tax

impostare (impòsto) *tr* to start, begin; to state (*a problem*); to mail; to lay (*a stone*); to open (*an account*); to attune (*one's voice*); to lay the keel of (*a ship*) ‖ *ref* to take one's position, get ready

impostazióne *f* beginning, starting; laying; mail, mailing; (com) posting

impo·stóre -stóra *mf* impostor

impostura *f* imposture

impotènte *adj* weak; impotent

impotènza *f* impotence

impoverimènto *m* impoverishment

impoverire §176 *tr* to impoverish ‖ *intr* (ESSERE) & *ref* to become impoverished

impraticàbile *adj* impracticable; impassable

impratichire §176 *tr* to train, familiarize ‖ *ref* to become familiar (*e.g., with a task*)

imprecare §197 (imprèco) *tr* to wish (*e.g., s.o.'s death*) ‖ *intr* to curse

imprecazióne *f* imprecation, curse

imprecisàbile *adj* undefinable

imprecisióne *f* inexactness, inaccuracy

impreci·so -sa *adj* vague, inexact

impregnare (imprégno) *tr* to impregnate

impremedita·to -ta *adj* unpremeditated

imprendìbile *adj* impregnable

imprendi·tóre -trice *mf* contractor ‖ *m*—imprenditore di pompe funebri undertaker

imprenditoriale *adj* managerial

imprepara·to -ta *adj* unprepared

impreparazióne *f* unpreparedness

imprésa [s] *f* enterprise; undertaking; achievement; firm, concern; (theat) management; impresa (di) pompe funebri undertaking establishment

impresà·rio [s] *m* (-rì) manager; (theat) impresario

imprescindìbile *adj* essential, indispensable; unavoidable

impresentàbile *adj* unpresentable

impressionàbile *adj* impressionable

impressionante *adj* striking, impressive; frightening

impressionare (impressióno) *tr* to impress; (phot) to expose ‖ *ref* to become frightened; (phot) to be exposed

impressióne *f* impression

imprestare (imprèsto) *tr* (coll) to lend

imprèstito *m* (philol) borrowing
imprevedìbile *adj* unforeseeable
imprevedu·to -ta *adj* unforeseen
imprevidènte *adj* improvident
imprevi·sto -sta *adj* unforeseen, unexpected || imprevisti *mpl* unforeseen events
imprigionare (imprigióno) *tr* to imprison
imprìmere §131 *tr* to impress; to imprint; to impart (*e.g., motion*)
improbàbile *adj* improbable, unlikely
ìmpro·bo -ba *adj* dishonest; laborious
improdutti·vo -va *adj* unproductive
imprónta *f* print, imprint; mark; impronta digitale fingerprint
improntare (imprónto) *tr* to impress, imprint; to mark
improntitùdine *f* audacity, impudence
impronunziàbile *adj* unpronounceable
impropè·rio *m* (-ri) insult
improprie·tà *f* (-tà) impropriety; error
imprò·prio -pria *adj* (-pri -prie) improper, inappropriate; (math) improper
improrogàbile *adj* unextendible
improvvi·do -da *adj* improvident
improvvisare *tr* to improvise || *ref* to suddenly decide to become
improvvisa·to -ta *adj* improvised; impromptu || *f* surprise; surprise party
improvvisazióne *f* improvisation
improvvi·so -sa *adj* sudden || *m* (mus) impromptu; all'improvviso or d'improvviso suddenly
imprudènte *adj* imprudent; rash
imprudènza *f* imprudence; rashness
impudènte *adj* shameless; brazen; impudent
impudènza *f* shamelessness; impudence
impudicìzia *f* immodesty
impudì·co -ca *adj* (-chi -che) immodest, indecent
impugnare *tr* to grip, seize; to take up (*arms*); to impugn, contest
impugnatura *f* handle; grip, hold; hilt, haft
impulsi·vo -va *adj* impulsive
impulso *m* impulse; dare impulso a to promote, foment
impuneménte *adv* with impunity
impunità *f* impunity
impuni·to -ta *adj* unpunished
impuntare *intr* to stumble, trip; to stutter || *ref* to stutter; to balk; to be stubborn; impuntarsi a or di + *inf* to stubbornly insist on + *ger*
impuntigliare §280 *ref* to persist, insist
impuntire §176 *tr* to tuft (*e.g., a pillow*)
impuntura *f* backstitch
impuri·tà *f* (-tà) impurity; unchastity
impu·ro -ra *adj* impure; unchaste
imputàbile *adj* attributable
imputare (ìmputo) *tr* to impute; to charge, accuse; (com) to post
imputa·to -ta *mf* accused, defendant
imputazióne *f* imputation; charge, accusation; (com) posting
imputridire §176 *tr & intr* (ESSERE) to rot
in *prep* in; at; into; to; on; upon; through; during; married to, e.g.,

Maria Roberti in Bianchi Marie Roberti married to Bianchi; as, e.g., in premio as a prize; by, e.g., in automobile by car; of, e.g., studente in legge student of law; essere in quattro to be four; in alto up; in breve soon; in a word; in giù down; in là there; in qua here; in realtà really; in seguito a because of
-ina *suf fem* about, e.g., cinquantina about fifty
inabbordàbile *adj* unapproachable
inàbile *adj* unfit; ineligible; awkward
inabili·tà *f* (-tà) unfitness; awkwardness; inability
inabilitare (inabìlito) *tr* to incapacitate; to render unfit; to disqualify
inabilitazióne *f* disqualification
inabissare *tr* to plunge || *ref* to sink
inabitàbile *adj* uninhabitable
inabita·to -ta *adj* uninhabited
inaccessìbile *adj* inaccessible; unfathomable
inaccettàbile *adj* unacceptable
inacerbire §176 *tr* to exacerbate || *ref* to grow bitter
inacidire §176 *tr & ref* to sour
inadattàbile *adj* unadaptable; maladjusted
inadat·to -ta *adj* inadequate
inadegua·to -ta *adj* inadequate
inadempiènte *adj* not fulfilling; inadempiente agli obblighi di leva draft-dodging
inafferràbile *adj* that cannot be caught or captured; incomprehensible; elusive
inalare *tr* to inhale
inalatóre *m* inhaler
inalberare (inàlbero) *tr* to hoist || *ref* to rear; to fly into a rage
inalteràbile *adj* unalterable
inamidare (inàmido) *tr* to starch
inamida·to -ta *adj* starched; pompous, starchy
inammissìbile *adj* inadmissible
inamovìbile *adj* irremovable
inamovibili·tà *f* (-tà) irremovability; tenure
inane *adj* inane; futile
inanella·to -ta *adj* curly; beringed
inanima·to -ta *adj* inanimate; lifeless
inanizióne *f* starvation
inappagàbile *adj* unquenchable
inappaga·to -ta *adj* unsatisfied
inappellàbile *adj* definitive, final
inappetènza *f* lack of appetite
inapprezzàbile *adj* inappreciable, imperceptible; inestimable
inappuntàbile *adj* faultless, impeccable
inarcare §197 *tr* to arch; to raise (*one's eyebrows*)
inargentare (inargènto) *tr* to silver
inaridire §176 *tr* to dry; to parch || *ref* to dry up
inarrestàbile *adj* irresistible
inarrivàbile *adj* unattainable; inimitable
inarticola·to -ta *adj* indistinct, inarticulate
inascolta·to -ta *adj* unheeded
inaspetta·to -ta *adj* unexpected
inasprimento *m* exacerbation

inasprire §176 *tr* to aggravate || *ref* to sour; to become embittered; to become sharper; to become fierce or furious

inastare *tr* to hoist (*flag*); to fix (*bayonets*)

inattaccàbile *adj* unattackable; unassailable; **inattacabile da** resistant to

inattendìbile *adj* unreliable

inatté·so -sa [s] *adj* unexpected

inaudi·to -ta *adj* unheard-of

inaugurale *adj* inaugural; maiden (*voyage*)

inaugurare (**inàuguro**) *tr* to inaugurate; to usher in (*the New Year*); to open (*e.g., an exhibit*); to unveil (*a statue*); to sport for the first time

inaugurazióne *f* inauguration

inauspica·to -ta *adj* (lit) inauspicious

inavvedu·to -ta *adj* careless, rash

inavvertènza *f* inadvertence, oversight

inavverti·to -ta *adj* unnoticed; inadvertent, thoughtless

inazióne *f* inaction

incagliare §280 *tr* to hamper; to run aground || *intr* (ESSERE) & *ref* to run aground; (fig) to get stuck

incà·glio *m* (-**gli**) running aground; hindrance, obstacle

incalcinare *tr* to whitewash; to lime (*a field*)

incalcolàbile *adj* incalculable

incallire §176 *tr* to make callous || *intr* (ESSERE) to become callous; to become inured

incalli·to -ta *adj* callous; inveterate

incalzante *adj* pressing

incalzare *tr* to press, pursue || *intr* to be imminent; to be pressing || *ref* to follow one another in rapid succession

incamerare (**incàmero**) *tr* to confiscate

incamminare *tr* to launch; to guide, direct || *ref* to set out; to be on one's way

incanagli·to -ta *adj* vile, despicable

incanalare *tr* to channel || *ref* to flow

incancrenire §176 *tr* to affect with gangrene || *ref* to become gangrenous; (fig) to become callous

incandescènte *adj* incandescent; (fig) red-hot

incandescènza *f* incandescence

incannare *tr* to reel, wind

incantare *tr* to bewitch; to auction off || *ref* to become enraptured; to be spellbound; to jam, get stuck (*said of machinery*)

incanta·tóre -trice *adj* enchanting || *m* enchanter || *f* enchantress

incantésimo *m* enchantment, spell

incantévole *adj* enchanting, charming

incanto *m* enchantment; bewitchery; auction; **d'incanto** marvelously well

incanutire §176 *tr*, *intr* (ESSERE) & *ref* to turn gray-headed, to turn gray (*said of a person*)

incanuti·to -ta *adj* hoary

incapace *adj* incapable; (law) incompetent || *mf* oaf; (law) incompetent

incapaci·tà *f* (-**tà**) incapacity; (law) incompetence

incaparbire §176 *intr* (ESSERE) & *ref* to be obstinate; to be determined

incaponire §176 *ref* to get stubborn; to be determined

incappare *intr* (ESSERE) to stumble

incappottare (**incappòtto**) *tr* to cover with a coat || *ref* to wrap oneself in a coat

incappucciare §128 *tr* to cover with a hood

incapricciare §128 *ref*—**incapricciarsi di** to take a fancy to; to become infatuated with

incapsulare (**incàpsulo**) *tr* to encapsulate; to cap

incarcerare (**incàrcero**) *tr* to jail, incarcerate; (fig) to confine

incaricare §197 (**incàrico**) *tr* to charge || *ref*—**incaricarsi di** to take charge of; to take care of

incarica·to -ta *adj* in charge; visiting (*professor*) || *mf* deputy; **incaricato d'affari** chargé d'affaires

incàri·co *m* (-**chi**) task; appointment, position; **per incarico di** on behalf of

incarnare *tr* to incarnate, embody

incarna·to -ta *adj* incarnate || *m* pink complexion

incarnazióne *f* incarnation

incarnire §176 *intr* (ESSERE) & *ref* to grow in (*said of a toenail*)

incarni·to -ta *adj* ingrown (*toenail*)

incartaménto *m* file, dossier

incartapecori·to -ta *adj* shriveled up

incartare *tr* to wrap up (*in paper*)

incasellare [s] (**incasèllo**) *tr* to file; to sort out

incasellatóre [s] *m* post-office file clerk

incassare *tr* to box up; to put (*a watch*) in a case; to mortise (*a lock*); to channel (*a river*); to cash (*a check*); (fig) to take (*e.g., blows*) || *intr* to fit; to take it

incasso *m* receipts

incastellatura *f* scaffolding

incastonare (**incastóno**) *tr* to set, mount (*a gem*); **incastonare citazioni in un discorso** to stud a speech with quotations

incastrare *tr* to insert; to mortise; (fig) to corner || *intr* to fit || *ref* to fit; to become imbedded; to telescope (*said, e.g., of a train in a collision*)

incastro *m* joint; insertion; (carp) tenon; (carp) mortise

incatenare (**incaténo**) *tr* to chain, put in chains; to tie down, restrain

incatramare *tr* to tar

incàu·to -ta *adj* unwary, careless

incavallatura *f* truss (*to support roof*)

incavare *tr* to hollow out; to groove

incava·to -ta *adj* hollow

incavatura *f* hollow

incavicchiare §287 *tr* to peg

incavigliare §280 *tr* to peg

incavo *m* hollow; cavity; **incavo dell'ascella** armpit

incazzottare (**incazzòtto**) *tr* (naut) to furl

incèdere *m* stately walk || §123 *intr* to walk stately

incendiare §287 (incèndio) *tr* to set on fire; (fig) to inflame || *ref* to catch fire

incendià·rio -ria *adj & mf* (-ri -rie) incendiary

incèn·dio *m* (-di) fire; incendio doloso arson

incenerire §176 *tr* to reduce to ashes; to wither (*e.g., with a look*) || *ref* to turn to ashes

inceneritóre *m* incinerator

incensare (incènso) *tr* (eccl) to incense; (fig) to flatter

incensa·tóre -trice *mf* incense burner; (fig) flatterer

incensière *m* incense burner

incènso *m* incense

incensura·to -ta *adj* uncensured; (law) having no previous record

incentivo *m* incentive

inceppare (incèppo) *tr* to hinder; to shackle || *ref* to jam (*said of firearm*)

incerare (incèro) *tr* to wax

incerata *f* oilcloth; (naut) raincoat

incernierare (incernièro) *tr* to hinge

incertézza *f* uncertainty, incertitude

incèr·to -ta *adj* uncertain; irresolute || *m* uncertainty; incerti extras; incerti del mestiere cares of office, occupational annoyances, occupational hazards

incespicare §197 (incéspico) *intr* to stumble

incessàbile *adj* (lit) ceaseless

incessante *adj* unceasing, incessant

incèsto *m* incest

incestuó·so -sa [s] *adj* incestuous

incètta *f* cornering (*of market*)

incettare (incètto) *tr* to corner (*market*)

incetta·tóre -trice *mf* monopolizer

inchiavardare *tr* to key, bolt

inchièsta *f* probe, inquest; (journ) inquiry

inchinare *tr* to bend; to bow (*the head*) || *intr* (lit) to go down (*said of stars*) || *ref* to bow; to yield

inchi·no -na *adj* bent; bowing || *m* bow; curtsy

inchiodare (inchiòdo) *tr* to nail; to spike; to rivet; to tie, bind; to stop (*a car*) suddenly; to transfix || *ref* to freeze (*said, e.g., of brakes*); (fig) to be tied down; (fig) to go into debt

inchiostrare (inchiòstro) *tr* (typ) to ink

inchiòstro *m* ink; inchiostro di china India ink, Chinese ink

inciampare *intr* to trip, stumble

inciampo *m* stumbling block, obstacle; essere d'inciampo a to be in the way of

incidentale *adj* incidental

incidènte *adj* incidental || *m* incident; accident; argument, question

incidènza *f* incidence

incìdere §145 *tr* to engrave; to cut; to record (*a record, a tape; a song*); incìdere all'acqua forte to etch || *intr*—incidere su to weigh heavily on (*expenses, a budget*); to leave a mark on

incinerazióne *f* incineration; cremation

incinta *adj fem* pregnant

incipiènte *adj* incipient

incipriare §287 *tr* to powder || *ref* to powder oneself

incirca *adv* about; all'incirca more or less

incisióne *f* engraving; cutting (*of a record*); recording (*of a tape; of a song*); incision; incisione all'acquaforte etching

incisi·vo -va *adj* incisive; sharp (*photograph*) || *m* incisor

inciso *m* (gram) parenthetical clause; (mus) theme; per inciso incidentally

incisóre *m* engraver, etcher

incitare *tr* to incite, provoke

incivile *adj* uncivilized; uncouth

incivilire §176 *tr* to civilize || *ref* to become civilized

inclemènte *adj* inclement, harsh

inclemènza *f* inclemency, harshness

inclinare *tr* to tilt; to bow, bend; to incline || *intr* (fig) to lean || *ref* to bend

inclinazióne *f* inclination; slope; inclinazione laterale (aer) bank; inclinazione magnetica magnetic dip

incline *adj* inclined

incli·to -ta *adj* famous; noble

inclùdere §105 *tr* to enclose, include

inclusi·vo -va *adj* including; inclusivo di including

inclu·so -sa *adj* enclosed; included; inclusive || *f* enclosed letter

incoerènte *adj* incoherent

incògliere §127 *tr* (lit) to catch in the act || *intr*—incogliere a to happen to

incògni·to -ta *adj* unknown || *m* incognito; unknown; in incognito incognito || *f* (math) unknown quantity; (fig) puzzle

incollare (incòllo) *tr* to glue, paste; to size (*paper*) || *intr* to stick || *ref* to stick; to take on one's shoulders

incollatura *f* neck (*of horse*); glueing, sticking

incollerire §176 *intr & ref* to get angry

incolloca·to -ta *adj* unemployed

incolonnare (incolónno) *tr* to set up in columns

incolonnatóre *m* tabulator

incolóre *adj* colorless

incolpàbile *adj* blamable; (lit) guiltless

incolpare (incólpo) *tr*—incolpare di to charge with

incól·to -ta *adj* uncultivated; unkempt

incòlume *adj* unharmed, unhurt

incolumità *f* safety, security

incombènte *adj* (*danger*) impending; (*duty*) incumbent

incombènza *f* task, charge, incumbency

incómbere §186 *intr* (ESSERE) to be impending; to be incumbent

incombustibile *adj* incombustible

incominciare §128 *tr & intr* (ESSERE) to begin

incommensuràbile *adj* immeasurable; (math) incommensurable

incomodare (incòmodo) *tr* to bother, disturb || *ref* to bother; non s'incomodi! don't bother!

incòmo·do -da *adj* bothersome, inconvenient || *m* inconvenience; ailment;

levare l'incomodo a to get out of the way of

incomparàbile *adj* incomparable

incompatìbile *adj* incompatible; unforgivable

incompetènte *adj & mf* incompetent

incompiu·to -ta *adj* unfinished

incomplè·to -ta *adj* incomplete

incompó·sto -sta *adj* untidy; unkempt; unbecoming (*behavior*)

incomprensìbile *adj* incomprehensible

incomprensióne *f* lack of understanding

incompré·so -sa [s] *adj* misunderstood

incomprimìbile *adj* irrepressible; incompressible

inconcepìbile *adj* inconceivable

inconciliàbile *adj* irreconcilable

inconcludènte *adj* inconclusive; insignificant

inconcus·so -sa *adj* (lit) unshaken

incondiziona·to -ta *adj* unconditional

inconfessàbile *adj* unspeakable, vile

inconfessa·to -ta *adj* unavowed

inconfondìbile *adj* unmistakable

inconfutàbile *adj* irrefutable

incongruènte *adj* inconsistent

incòn·gruo -grua *adj* incongruous

inconoscìbile *adj* unknowable

inconsapèvole *adj* unaware, unconscious

incòn·scio -scia *adj & m* (**-sci -sce**) unconscious

inconseguènte *adj* inconsistent, inconsequential

inconsidera·to -ta *adj* inconsiderate

inconsistènte *adj* flimsy; inconsistent

inconsistènza *f* flimsiness; inconsistency

inconsolàbile *adj* inconsolable

inconsuè·to -ta *adj* unusual

inconsul·to -ta *adj* ill-advised, rash

incontamina·to -ta *adj* uncontaminated

incontenìbile *adj* irrepressible

incontentàbile *adj* insatiable; hard to please; exacting

incontinènza *f* incontinence

incontrare (**incóntro**) *tr* to meet; to encounter, meet with || *intr* (ESSERE) to catch on (*said, e.g., of fashions*) || *ref* to meet; to agree || *impers* (ESSERE) to happen

incontrastàbile *adj* indisputable

incontrasta·to -ta *adj* undisputed

incóntro *m* meeting; encounter; success; meet; game, fight, match; occasion, opportunity; **all'incontro** on the other hand; opposite; **andare incontro a** to go towards; to go to meet; to face; to meet (*expenses*); to accommodate; **farsi incontro a** to advance toward

incontrollàbile *adj* uncontrollable

incontrolla·to -ta *adj* unchecked

incontrovertìbile *adj* incontrovertible

inconveniènte *adj* inconvenient || *m* inconvenience, disadvantage

incoraggiante *adj* encouraging

incoraggiare §290 *tr* to encourage

incorare §257 (**incuòro**) *tr* to hearten

incordare (**incòrdo**) *tr* to string (*e.g., a racket*); to tie up (*with a cord*) || *ref* to stiffen (*said of a muscle*)

incornare (**incòrno**) *tr* (taur) to gore

incorniciare §128 *tr* to frame; (journ) tó border; (slang) to cuckold

incoronare (**incoróno**) *tr* to crown

incoronazióne *f* coronation

incorporàbile *adj* absorbable; adaptable

incorporare (**incòrporo**) *tr* to incorporate; to absorb || *ref* to incorporate

incorpòre·o -a *adj* incorporeal

incorreggìbile *adj* incorrigible

incórrere §139 *intr* (ESSERE)—**incorrere in** to incur

incorrót·to -ta *adj* uncorrupt

incosciènte *adj* unconscious; unaware; irresponsible || *mf* irresponsible person

incosciènza *f* unconsciousness; irresponsibility; madness

incredìbile *adj* incredible, unbelievable

incrèdu·lo -la *adj* incredulous || *mf* disbeliever; doubter

incrementare (**increménto**) *tr* to increase, boost

increménto *m* increase, increment, boost

incresció·so -sa [s] *adj* disagreeable, unpleasant

increspare (**incréspo**) *tr* to ripple; tó wrinkle; to knit (*the brow*); to pleat || *ref* to ripple

incretinire §176 *tr* to make stupid; (fig) to deafen || *intr* (ESSERE) to become stupid; to lose one's mind

incriminare (**incrìmino**) *tr* to incriminate

incrinare *tr* to flaw; to ruin

incrinatura *f* crack, flaw

incrociare §128 (**incrócio**) *tr* to cross || *intr* (naut) to cruise || *ref* to cross one another; to interbreed

incrociatóre *m* (nav) cruiser

incró·cio *m* (**-ci**) crossing; cross; crossroads; crossbreed

incrollàbile *adj* unshakable

incrostare (**incròsto**) *tr* to incrust; to inlay (*e.g., with mosaic*) || *ref* to become incrusted

incrostazióne *f* incrustation

incrudelire §176 *tr* to enrage || *intr* to commit cruelties || *intr* (ESSERE) to become cruel; **incrudelire su** to commit cruelties upon

incruèn·to -ta *adj* bloodless

incubare (**ìncubo & ìncubo**) *tr* to incubate

incubatrice *f* incubator; brooder

incubazióne *f* incubation; **in incubazione** brewing (*said of an infectious disease*)

ìncubo *m* nightmare

incùdine *f* anvil; **essere tra l'incudine e il martello** to be between the devil and the deep blue sea

inculcare §197 *tr* to inculcate

incunàbolo *m* incunabulum

incuneare (**incùneo**) *tr & ref* to wedge

incuràbile *adj & mf* incurable

incurante *adj* careless, indifferent

incùria *f* malpractice; neglect

incuriosire [s] §176 *tr* to intrigue || *ref* to be intrigued

incursióne *f* incursion; **incursione aerea** air raid

incurvare *tr* to bend; (lit) to lower ‖ *intr* (ESSERE) & *ref* to bend; to warp

incurvatura *f* bend, curve

incustodì•to -ta *adj* unguarded, unwatched

incùtere §154 *tr* to inspire; **incutere terrore a** to strike with terror

indaco *adj* & *m* indigo

indaffara•to -ta *adj* busy

indagare §209 *tr* & *intr* to investigate; **indagare su** to investigate

indaga•tóre -trice *adj* probing, searching ‖ *mf* investigator

indàgine *f* investigation, inquiry

indarno *adv* (lit) in vain

indebitare (**indébito**) *tr* to burden with debts ‖ *ref* to run into debt

indebita•to -ta *adj* indebted

indébi•to -ta *adj* undue; unjust; fraudulent (*conversion*) ‖ *m* what one does not owe; excess payment

indebolimènto *m* weakening

indebolire §176 *tr*, *intr* (ESSERE) & *ref* to weaken

indecènte *adj* indecent

indecènza *f* indecency; outrage

indecifràbile *adj* indecipherable

indecisióne *f* indecision

indecì•so -sa *adj* uncertain; undecided; indecisive

indecoró•so -sa [s] *adj* indecorous, unseemly

indefès•so -sa *adj* indefatigable

indefinìbile *adj* indefinable

indefinì•to -ta *adj* indefinite; undefined

indegni•tà *f* (-tà) indignity

indé•gno -gna *adj* unworthy; disgraceful

indelèbile *adj* indelible

indelica•to -ta *adj* indelicate

indemagliàbile *adj* runproof

indemonia•to -ta *adj* possessed by the devil; restless

indènne *adj* undamaged, unscathed; **tener indenne** to guarantee against harm or damage

indenni•tà *f* (-tà) indemnity; indemnification; **indennità di carica** special emolument; bonus; **indennità di carovita** cost-of-living allowance; **indennità di preavviso** severance pay; **indennità di trasferta** per diem

indennizzare [ddzz] *tr* to indemnify

indennizzo [ddzz] *m* indemnification; indemnity

inderogàbile *adj* inescapable

indescrivìbile *adj* indescribable

indesideràbile *adj* undesirable

indesidera•to -ta *adj* unwished-for; undesirable

indeterminati•vo -va *adj* indefinite

indetermina•to -ta *adj* indeterminate; (gram) indefinite

indi *adv* (lit) then; (lit) thence; **da indi innanzi** (lit) from that moment on

India, l' *f* India; **le Indie Occidentali** the West Indies; **le Indie Orientali** the East Indies

india•no -na *adj* & *mf* Indian; **fare l'indiano** to feign ignorance ‖ *f* printed calico

indiavola•to -ta *adj* devilish, fierce; impish (*child*)

indicare §197 (**ìndico**) *tr* to indicate; to show

indicati•vo -va *adj* & *m* indicative

indica•to -ta *adj* appropriate, fitting; recommended, advisable

indica•tóre -trice *adj* indicating, pointing ‖ *m* indicator; **indicatore di direzione** (aut) turn signal; **indicatore di livello** gauge; **indicatore di pressione** pressure gauge; **indicatore di velocità** (aut) speedometer; **indicatore stradale** road sign; **indicatore telefonico** telephone directory

indicazióne *f* indication; direction; **indicazioni per l'uso** instructions

indice *m* index finger; pointer, gauge; indicator; sign, indication; index; (typ) fist; **indice delle materie** table of contents ‖ **Indice** *m* Index; **mettere all'Indice** to put on the Index; to ban, index

indicìbile *adj* inexpressible, unspeakable

indietreggiare §290 (**indietréggio**) *intr* (ESSERE & AVERE) to withdraw

indiètro *adv* back; behind; **all'indietro** backwards; **dare indietro** to return, give back; **domandare indietro** to ask back; **essere indietro** to be slow (*said of a watch*); to be behind; to be backward, be slow; **tirarsi indietro** to withdraw; to step back

indifendìbile *adj* indefensible

indifé•so -sa [s] *adj* defenseless

indifferènte *adj* indifferent; **essere indifferente a** to be the same to; **lasciare indifferente** to leave cold

indifferènza *f* indifference

indìge•no -na *adj* indigenous ‖ *m* native

indigènte *adj* indigent, poor

indigestìbile *adj* indigestible

indigestióne *f* indigestion

indigè•sto -sta *adj* indigestible; (fig) dull, boring

indignare *tr* to anger, shock ‖ *ref* to be aroused, be indignant

indigna•to -ta *adj* indignant, outraged

indignazióne *f* indignation

indigni•tà *f* (-tà) indignity

indimenticàbile *adj* unforgettable

indipendènte *adj* & *m* independent

indipendènza *f* independence

indire §151 *tr* to announce publicly; (lit) to declare (*war*)

indirèt•to -ta *adj* indirect

indirizzare *tr* to direct; to address

indirizzà•rio *m* (-ri) mailing list

indirizzo *m* address; direction

indiscernìbile *adj* indiscernible

indisciplina *f* lack of discipline

indisciplina•to -ta *adj* undisciplined

indiscré•to -ta *adj* indiscreet; tactless

indiscrezióne *f* indiscretion; gossip; news leak

indiscus•so -sa *adj* unquestioned

indiscutìbile *adj* indisputable

indispensàbile *adj* indispensable ‖ *m* essential

indispettire §176 *tr* to annoy ‖ *ref* to get annoyed

indisponènte *adj* vexing, irritating

indispórre §218 *tr* to indispose; to disgust

indisposizióne *f* indisposition

indispó·sto -sta *adj* indisposed

indissolùbile *adj* indissoluble

indistìn·to -ta *adj* indistinct

indistruttìbile *adj* indestructible

indisturba·to -ta *adj* undisturbed

indìvia *f* endive

individuàbile *adj* distinguishable

individuale *adj* individual

individuali·tà *f* (-**tà**) individuality

individuare (**indivìduo**) *tr* to individuate; to outline; to single out

indivìduo *m* individual; fellow

indivisìbile *adj* indivisible

indivì·so -sa *adj* undivided

indiziare §287 *tr* to cast suspicion on

indizià·rio -ria *adj* (-**ri** -**rie**) circumstancial

indì·zio *m* (-**zi**) clue; token; symptom

indòcile *adj* indocile, unteachable

Indocina, l' *f* Indochina

indocinése [s] *adj* & *mf* Indochinese

indoeuropè·o -a *adj* & *m* Indo-European

indolcire §176 *tr* to sweeten ‖ *ref* to become sweet

indole *f* temper, disposition; nature

indolènte *adj* indolent

indolenziménto *m* soreness, stiffness; numbness

indolenzire §176 *tr* to make sore or stiff; to benumb ‖ *ref* to become sore or stiff

indolenzì·to -ta *adj* sore, stiff; numb

indolóre *adj* painless

indomàbile *adj* indomitable

indoma·ni *m* (-**ni**) morrow, next day; **l'indomani dì . . .** the day after . . .

indoma·to -ta *adj* (lit) indomitable, untamed

indòmi·to -ta *adj* (lit) indomitable, untamed

Indonèsia l' *f* Indonesia

indonesia·no -na *adj* & *mf* Indonesian

indorare (**indòro**) *tr* to gild; (culin) to brown; (fig) to sugar-coat

indoratura *f* gilding

indossare (**indòsso**) *tr* to wear; to put on

indossatrice *f* mannequin, model

indòsso *adv* on, on one's back; **avere indosso** to have on, wear

Indostàn, l' *m* Hindustan

indosta·no -na *adj* & *mf* Hindustani

indòtto *m* (elec) armature (*of motor*)

indottrinare *tr* to indoctrinate

indovinare *tr* to guess; **indovinarla** to guess right; **non indovinarne una** to never hit the mark

indovina·to -ta *adj* felicitous

indovinèllo *m* puzzle, riddle

indovi·no -na *mf* soothsayer, fortune-teller

indù *adj invar* & *mf* Hindu

indùb·bio -bia *adj* (-**bi** -**bie**) undoubted, undisputed

indubita·to -ta *adj* undeniable

indugiare §290 *tr* to delay ‖ *intr* to linger; to hesitate ‖ *ref* to linger

indù·gio *m* (-**gi**) delay; **rompere gli indugi** to come to a decision; **senza ulteriore indugio** without further delay

indulgènte *adj* indulgent

indulgènza *f* indulgence

indùlgere §187 *tr* to grant; to forgive ‖ *intr* to be indulgent; **indulgere a** to indulge; to yield to

indulto *m* (law) pardon

induménto *m* garment; **indumenti intimi** undergarments, unmentionables

indurire §176 *tr* to harden ‖ *intr* (ESSERE) to harden; to get stiff

indurre §102 *tr* to induce

indùstria *f* industry; **grande industria** heavy industry

industriale *adj* industrial ‖ *m* industrialist

industrializzare [ddzz] *tr* to industrialize

industriare §287 *ref* to try, try hard; **industriarsi a** or **per** + *inf* to try to + *inf*, to do one's best to + *inf*

industrió·so -sa [s] *adj* industrious

indut·tóre -trice *adj* inducing, provoking ‖ *m* (elec) field (*of motor*)

induzióne *f* induction

inebetire §176 *tr* to dull; to stun ‖ *intr* (ESSERE) & *ref* to become dull; to be stunned

inebriare §287 (**inèbrio**) *tr* to intoxicate ‖ *ref* to get drunk

inebriante *adj* intoxicating

ineccepìbile *adj* unexceptionable

inèdia *f* starvation, inanition; boredom

inèdi·to -ta *adj* unpublished; new, novel

ineduca·to -ta *adj* uneducated; ill-mannered

ineffàbile *adj* ineffable

inefficace *adj* ineffectual, ineffective

inefficàcia *f* inefficacy

inefficiènte *adj* inefficient

ineguale *adj* unequal; uneven

inelegante *adj* inelegant; shabby

ineleggìbile *adj* ineligible

ineluttàbile *adj* inevitable, inescapable

inenarràbile *adj* unspeakable

inerènte *adj* inherent

inèrme *adj* unarmed, defenseless

inerpicare §197 (**inèrpico**) *ref* to clamber

inèrte *adj* inert

inèrzia *f* inertia; inactivity

inesattézza *f* inaccuracy

inesat·to -ta *adj* inaccurate, inexact; uncollected

inesaudì·to -ta *adj* unanswered

inesaurìbile *adj* inexhaustible

inescusàbile *adj* inexcusable

inesigìbile *adj* uncollectable

inesistènte *adj* inexistent

inesoràbile *adj* inexorable

inesperiènza *f* inexperience

inespèr·to -ta *adj* inexperienced; unskilled

inesplicàbile *adj* inexplicable

inesplica·to -ta *adj* unexplained

inesplora·to -ta *adj* unexplored

inesplò·so -sa *adj* unexploded

inespressì·vo -va *adj* inexpressive

inesprimìbile *adj* inexpressible

inespugnàbile *adj* impregnable; incorruptible

inespugna·to -ta *adj* unconquered

inestimàbile *adj* priceless, invaluable

inestinguìbile *adj* inextinguishable

inestirpàbile *adj* ineradicable

inestricàbile *adj* inextricable

inèt·to -ta *adj* inept

ineva·so -sa *adj* unfinished (*business*); unanswered (*mail*)

inevitàbile *adj* unavoidable, inevitable

inèzia *f* trifle, bagatelle

infagottare (infagòtto) *tr* & *ref* to bundle up

infallìbile *adj* infallible

infamante *adj* shameful, disgraceful

infamare *tr* to disgrace; to slander

infame *adj* infamous; villainous; (coll) horrible || *mf* villain

infàmia *f* infamy; (coll) botch, bungle

infangare §209 *tr* to splash with mud; (fig) to stain, spot

infante *adj* & *mf* infant, baby || *m* infante || *f* infanta

infantile *adj* infantile, childish

infànzia *f* infancy, childhood

infarcire §176 *tr* to cram; (culin) to stuff

infarinare *tr* to sprinkle with flour; to powder; (fig) to cram || *ref* to be covered with flour

infarinatura *f* sprinkling with flour; (fig) smattering

infastidire §176 *tr* to annoy || *ref* to be annoyed, lose one's patience

infaticàbile *adj* indefatigable, tireless

infatti *adv* indeed; really

infatuare (infàtuo) *tr* to infatuate || *ref* to become infatuated

infatua·to -ta *adj* infatuated

infàu·sto -sta *adj* unlucky, fatal

infecón·do -da *adj* barren

infedéle *adj* unfaithful; inaccurate || *mf* infidel

infedel·tà *f* (-tà) unfaithfulness; inaccuracy; infidelity

infelice *adj* unhappy, unfortunate; unfavorable || *mf* wretch

infelici·tà *f* (-tà) unhappiness

inferióre *adj* inferior; lower; **inferiore a** a lower than; less than; smaller than

inferiorità *f* inferiority

inferire §188a *tr* to inflict; to infer; (naut) to bend (*a sail*)

infermare (infèrmo) *tr* (lit) to weaken || *intr* (ESSERE) to get sick

infermerìa *f* infirmary

infermiè·re -ra *adj* nursing || *m* male nurse || *f* nurse; **infermiera diplomata** trained nurse

infermieristi·co -ca *adj* (-ci -che) nursing

infermi·tà *f* (-tà) infirmity

infér·mo -ma *adj* infirm; sick || *m* patient

infernale *adj* infernal

infèr·no -na *adj* (lit) lower (*region*) || *m* hell; inferno

inferocire §176 *tr* to infuriate || *intr*—**inferocire su** to be pitiless to || *intr* (ESSERE) to become infuriated

inferriata *f* grating, grill

infervorare (infèrvoro & infervóro) *tr* to excite, stir up || *ref* to get excited; to become absorbed

infestare (infèsto) *tr* to infest

infettare (infètto) *tr* to infect

infetti·vo -va *adj* infectious

infèt·to -ta *adj* infected; corrupted

infezióne *f* infection

infiacchire §176 *tr* to weaken || *intr* (ESSERE) & *ref* to grow weak

infiammàbile *adj* inflammable

infiammare *tr* to inflame; to ignite || *ref* to catch fire, ignite

infiamma·to -ta *adj* burning; aflame; inflamed, excited

infiammazióne *f* inflammation

infi·do -da *adj* untrustworthy

infierire §176 *intr* to become cruel; to be merciless to; to rage (*said, e.g., of a disease*)

infievolire §176 *tr* to weaken

infiggere §103 *tr* to thrust, stick, sink || *ref*—**infiggersi in** to creep in; to work in

infilare *tr* to thread (*a needle*); to insert (*a key*); to transfix (*with a sword*); to put on (*e.g., a coat*); to pull on (*one's pants*); to slip on (*a dress*); to slip (*e.g., one's arm into a sleeve*); to string (*beads*); to hit (*the target*); to take (*a road*); to enter through (*a door*); **infilare l'uscio** to slip away; **infilarle tutte** to succeed all the time; **non infilarne mai una** to never succeed || *ref* to slip; to sink; to slide (*e.g., through a crowd*)

infilata *f* row; string (*e.g., of insults*); (mil) enfilade; **d'infilata** lengthwise

infiltrare *ref* to infiltrate; to seep; (fig) to creep

infilzare *tr* to pierce; to string; (sew) to baste

infilzata *f* string (*of pearls, of lies, etc.*)

infi·mo -ma *adj* lowest, bottom

infine *adv* finally

infingar·do -da *adj* lazy, slothful

infini·tà *f* (-tà) infinity

infinitèsi·mo -ma *adj* & *m* infinitesimal

infiniti·vo -va *adj* (gram) infinitive

infini·to -ta *adj* infinite || *m* infinite; infinity; (gram) infinitive; (math) infinity; **all'infinito** ad infinitum

infino *adv* (lit)—**infino a** until; as far as; **infino a che** as long as

infinocchiare §287 (infinòcchio) *tr* (coll) to fool, bamboozle

infioccare §197 (infiòcco) *tr* to adorn with tassels

infiorare (infióro) *tr* to adorn with flowers; (fig) to sprinkle; (fig) to embellish || *ref* to be covered with flowers

infiorescènza *f* inflorescence

infirmare *tr* to weaken; to invalidate

infischiare §287 *ref*—**infischiarsi di** to not care a hoot about

infisso *m* frame (*e.g., of door*); fixture

infittire §176 *tr*, *intr* (ESSERE) & *ref* to thicken

inflazionare (inflazióno) *tr* to inflate

inflazióne *f* inflation

inflessìbile *adj* inflexible

inflessióne *f* inflection
inflèttere §177 *tr* (lit) to inflect
infliggere §104 *tr* to inflict
influènte *adj* influential
influènza *f* influence; (pathol) influenza
influenzare (influènzo) *tr* to influence, sway
influire §176 *intr* to have an influence; influire su to influence || *intr* (ESSERE) —influire in to flow into
influsso *m* influence; (lit) plague
infocare §182 *tr* to make glow with heat || *ref* to catch fire; to get excited
infoca·to -ta *adj* red-hot; sultry
infognare (infógno) *ref* (coll) to sink (e.g., in vice); (coll) to get stuck (e.g., in debt)
infoltire §176 *tr* & *intr* (ESSERE) to thicken
infónda·to -ta *adj* unfounded, groundless
infóndere §178 *tr* to infuse, instill
inforcare §197 (infórco) *tr* to pitch (hay); to bestride; to mount (a horse or bicycle); to put on (one's eyeglasses)
inforcatura *f* pitching with a fork; crotch
informare (infórmo) *tr* to inform; (fig) to mold || *ref* to conform; to inquire; informarsi da to seek or get information from; informarsi di or su to inquire about; to find out about
informati·vo -va *adj* informative, informational
informa·tóre -trice *adj* underlying || *mf* informer; (journ) reporter || *m* informant (of a foreign language)
informazióne *f* piece of information; chiedere informazioni sul conto di to inquire about; informazioni information
infórme *adj* shapeless
informicolire §176 *ref* to tingle; informicolirsi a to go to sleep, e.g., gli si è informicolita la gamba his leg went to sleep
infornare (infórno) *tr* to put in the oven; to bake
infornata *f* batch (of bread); (coll) flock
infortunare *ref* to get hurt
infortuna·to -ta *adj* injured || *mf* casualty, victim
infortù·nio *m* (-ni) accident, mishap; infortunio sul lavoro job-connected injury
infossare (infòsso) *tr* to bury || *ref* to cave in, settle; to become sunken (said of eyes or cheeks)
infracidare (infràcido) *tr* var of infradiciare
infracidire §176 *intr* to rot
infradiciare §128 (infràdicio) *tr* to drench || *ref* to get drenched; to rot (said of fruit)
inframmettènza *f* interference, meddling
inframméttere §198 *tr* to interpose || *ref* to meddle, interfere
inframmezzare [ddzz] (inframmèzzo) *tr* to intersperse

infràngere §179 *tr* & *ref* to break
infrangibile *adj* unbreakable
infran·to -ta *adj* broken, shattered
infaròs·so -sa *adj* & *m* infrared
infrascrit·to -ta *adj* mentioned below
infrastruttura *f* underpinning; infrastructure; (rr) roadbed
infrazióne *f* infraction, breach
infreddatura *f* mild cold
infreddolire §176 *ref* to feel cold, to be chilled
infrenàbile *adj* irrepressible
infrequènte *adj* infrequent
infrollire §176 *tr* to make (meat) high || *intr* (ESSERE) & *ref* to get high (said of meat); (fig) to soften
infruttuó·so -sa [s] *adj* unprofitable
infuòri *adv* out; all'infuori outward; all'infuori di except
infuriare §287 *tr* to infuriate, enrage || *intr* to get blustery; to rage || *intr* (ESSERE) to lose one's temper
infusióne *f* infusion; sprinkling (of holy water)
infuso *m* infusion
ingabbiare §287 *tr* to cage; to jail; to corner; to build the framework of
ingabbiatura *f* frame, framework
ingaggiare §290 *tr* to hire; to engage || *ref* to sign up; to get tangled up
ingàg·gio *m* (-gi) engagement; (sports) bonus (for signing up)
ingagliardire §176 *tr* to strengthen || *ref* to become strong
ingannare *tr* to deceive; to cheat; to elude; to beguile || *ref* to be mistaken
inganna·tóre -trice *adj* deceptive || *mf* impostor
ingannévole *adj* deceitful; deceptive
inganno *m* deception; illusion
ingarbugliare §280 *tr* to entangle; to jumble || *ref* to get mixed up; to become embroiled
ingegnare (ingégno) *ref* to manage; to scheme
ingegnère *m* engineer
ingegneria *f* engineering; ingegneria civile civil engineering; ingegneria meccanica mechanical engineering
ingégno *m* brain, intelligence; talent; genius; expediency; (lit) machinery
ingegnosità [s] *f* ingeniousness
ingegnó·so -sa [s] *adj* ingenious; euphuistic
ingelosire [s] §176 *tr* to make jealous || *intr* (ESSERE) & *ref* to become jealous
ingemmare (ingèmmo) *tr* to adorn or stud with gems
ingenerare (ingènero) *tr* to engender
ingèni·to -ta *adj* inborn
ingènte *adj* huge, vast
ingentilire §176 *tr* to refine
ingenui·tà *f* (-tà) ingenuousness; ingenuous act
ingè·nuo -nua *adj* ingenuous, artless || *m* (theat) artless character || *f* (theat) ingénue
ingerènza *f* interference
ingerire §176 *tr* to ingest, swallow || *ref* to meddle

ingessare (ingèsso) *tr* to put in a plaster cast; to plaster up

ingessatura *f* (surg) plaster cast

inghiaiare §287 *tr* to gravel, cover with gravel

Inghilterra, l' *f* England; **la Nuova Inghilterra** New England

inghiottire (inghiótto) & §176 *tr* to swallow; to swallow up; to pocket (*one's pride*)

inghirlandare *tr* to bedeck with garlands; (lit) to encircle

ingiallire §176 *tr* & *intr* (ESSERE) to turn yellow

ingigantire §176 *tr* to exaggerate || *intr* (ESSERE) to grow larger, increase

inginocchiare §287 (inginòcchio) *ref* to kneel down

inginocchia•tóio *m* (-tói) prie-dieu

ingioiellare (ingioièllo) *tr* to bejewel; (fig) to stud

ingiù *adv* down; **all'ingiù** downwards

ingiùngere §183 *tr* to order, command || (*with dat*) to order, command, e.g., **il giudice ingiunse all'imputato di rispondere** the judge ordered the accused to answer

ingiunzióne *f* order; (law) injunction

ingiùria *f* insult, abuse; damage, wear

ingiuriare §287 *tr* to insult

ingiurió•so -sa [s] *adj* insulting

ingiustificàbile *adj* unjustifiable

ingiustifica•to -ta *adj* unjustified

ingiustìzia *f* injustice

ingiu•sto -sta *adj* unjust, unfair || *m* unjust person

inglése [s] *adj* English; **all'inglese** in the English fashion; **andarsene all'inglese** to take French leave || *m* Englishman; English (*language*) || *f* Englishwoman

ingoiare §287 (ingóio) *tr* to swallow; to gulp down; **ingoiare un rospo** (fig) to swallow one's pride

ingolfare (ingólfo) *tr* (aut) to flood || *ref* to form a gulf; to get involved; (aut) to flood

ingollare (ingóllo) *tr* to swallow, gulp down

ingolosire [s] §176 *tr* to make the mouth of (*s.o.*) water || *intr* (ESSERE) & *ref* to have a craving

ingombrante *adj* cumbersome

ingombrare (ingómbro) *tr* to clutter

ingóm•bro -bra *adj* encumbered, cluttered || *m* encumbrance; **essere d'ingombro** to be in the way

ingommare (ingómmo) *tr* to glue

ingordìgia *f* greed

ingór•do -da *adj* greedy, covetous

ingorgare §209 (ingórgo) *ref* to get clogged up

ingór•go *m* (-ghi) blocking, congestion; **ingorgo stradale** traffic jam

ingovernàbile *adj* uncontrollable

ingozzare (ingózzo) *tr* to gobble, gulp down; to swallow; to cram (*e.g., a goose for fattening*)

ingranàg•gio *m* (-gi) gear, gearwheel; (fig) meshes; **ingranaggio di distribuzione** (aut) timing gear; **ingranaggio elicoidale** worm gear

ingranare *tr* to engage (*a gear*); **ingranare la marcia** to throw into gear || *intr* to be in gear; to succeed

ingrandiménto *m* enlargement; increase

ingrandire §176 *tr* to enlarge; to increase; || *intr* (ESSERE) & *ref* to increase, get larger

ingrassare *tr* to fatten; to lubricate || *intr* (ESSERE) & *ref* to get fat; to get rich

ingrassa•tóre -trice *mf* greaser, lubricator || *f* grease gun; lubricating machine

ingratitùdine *f* ingratitude

ingra•to -ta *adj* ungrateful; thankless || *mf* ingrate

ingraziare §287 *ref* to ingratiate oneself with

ingrediènte *m* ingredient

ingrèsso *m* entrance; admittance, entry; **ingressi** hallway furniture; **primo ingresso** debut

ingrossaménto *m* enlargement; swelling

ingrossare (ingròsso) *tr* to enlarge; to swell; to make bigger; to dull (*the mind*); to raise (*one's voice*) || *intr* (ESSERE) & *ref* to swell; to thicken; to become fat; to become pregnant; to become important

ingròsso *m*—**all'ingrosso** wholesale; approximately, more or less

ingrullire §176 *tr* to drive crazy || *intr* (ESSERE) & *ref* to become silly; **fare ingrullire** to drive crazy

inguadàbile *adj* not fordable

inguainare (inguaìno) *tr* to sheathe

ingualcibile *adj* wrinkle-free, wrinkle-proof

inguanta•to -ta *adj* with gloves on; **con le mani inguantate** with gloves on

inguarìbile *adj* incurable

ìnguine *f* (anat) groin

ingurgitare (ingùrgito) *tr* to swallow, gulp down

inibire §176 *tr* to inhibit

inibi•tóre -trice *adj* inhibiting || *m* inhibitor

inidòne•o -a *adj* unfit, unqualified

iniettare (iniètto) *tr* to inject || *ref* to become bloodshot; **iniettarsi di sangue** to become bloodshot

iniezióne *f* injection

inimicare §197 *tr* to make an enemy of; to alienate || *ref*—**inimicarsi con** to fall out with

inimicìzia *f* enmity

inimitàbile *adj* inimitable, matchless

ininterrót•to -ta *adj* uninterrupted

iniqui•tà *f* (-tà) injustice; iniquity

inì•quo -qua *adj* unjust; wicked

iniziale *adj* & *f* initial

iniziare §287 *tr* to initiate || *ref* to begin

iniziativa *f* initiative; sponsorship; **iniziativa privata** private enterprise

inizia•tóre -trice *adj* initiating || *mf* initiator, promoter

iniziazióne *f* initiation

inì•zio *m* (-zi) beginning, start

innaffiare §287 *tr* var of **annaffiare**

innaffia•tóio *m* (-tói) var of **annaffiatoio**

innalzaménto *m* elevation

innalzare *tr* to raise; to elevate; **innalzare al cielo** to praise to the sky || *ref* to rise; to tower

innamorare (**innamóro**) *tr* to charm, fascinate; to inspire with love || *ref* to fall in love

innamora·to -ta *adj* in love, enamored; fond || *mf* sweetheart || *m* boyfriend || *f* girl friend

innanzi *adj invar* previous, prior (*e.g.*, day) || *adv* ahead, before; **innanzi a** in front of; **innanzi di** + *inf* before + *ger*; **mettere innanzi** to prefer; to place before; to advance (*an excuse*); **per l'innanzi** before, in the past; **tirare innanzi** to get along || *prep* before; above; **innanzi tempo** ahead of time; **innanzi tutto** above all

innà·rio *m* (**-ri**) hymnal

inna·to -ta *adj* inborn, innate

innegàbile *adj* undeniable

inneggiare §290 (**innéggio**) *intr*—**inneggiare a** to sing the praises of

innervosire [s] §176 *tr* to make nervous

innescare §197 (**innésco**) *tr* to bait (*a hook*); to prime (*a bomb*)

inné·sco *m* (**-schi**) primer; detonator

innestare (**innèsto**) *tr* (hort & surg) to graft; (surg) to implant; (med) to inoculate (*a vaccine*); (mach) to engage; (elec) to plug in (*e.g.*, *a plug*); **innestare la marcia** (aut) to throw into gear || *ref* to be grafted; **innestarsi in** to merge with; **innestarsi su** to connect with

innèsto *m* (hort & surg) graft; (surg) implant; (med) inoculation; (mach) engagement; (mach) coupling; (elec) plug

inno *m* hymn; **inno nazionale** national anthem

innocènte *adj* innocent || *m* innocent; **innocenti** foundlings

innocènza *f* innocence

innò·cuo -cua *adj* innocuous, harmless

innominàbile *adj* unmentionable

innomina·to -ta *adj* unnamed

innovare (**innòvo**) *tr* to innovate

innovazióne *f* innovation

innumerévole *adj* countless, innumerable

-ino -ina *suf adj* little, e.g., **poverino** poor little; hailing from, e.g., **fiorentino** hailing from Florence, Florentine || *suf f* see **-ina**

inoccupa·to -ta *adj* unoccupied || *m* person looking for his first job

inoculare (**inòculo**) *tr* to inoculate

inoculazióne *f* inoculation

inodó·ro -ra *adj* odorless

inoffensì·vo -va *adj* inoffensive

inoltrare (**inóltro**) *tr* (com) to forward (*e.g.*, *a request*) || *ref* to advance

inóltre *adv* besides, in addition

inóltro *m* (com) forwarding

inondare (**inóndo**) *tr* to inundate, flood; to swamp

inondazióne *f* flood, inundation

inoperosità [s] *f* idleness

inoperó·so -sa [s] *adj* idle

inopina·to -ta *adj* (lit) unexpected

inopportu·no -na *adj* inopportune, untimely

inoppugnàbile *adj* incontestable; indisputable

inorgàni·co -ca *adj* (**-ci -che**) inorganic

inorgoglire §176 *tr* to make proud || *intr* (ESSERE) & *ref* to grow proud

inorridire §176 *tr* to horrify || *intr* (ESSERE) to be horrified

inospitale *adj* inhospitable

inosservante *adj* unobservant

inosserva·to -ta *adj* unnoticed; unperceived

inossidàbile *adj* stainless

inquadrare *tr* to frame; to arrange

inquadratura *f* framing; (mov, phot) frame

inqualificàbile *adj* unspeakable

inquietante *adj* disquieting

inquietare (**inquièto**) *tr* to worry || *ref* to worry; to get angry

inquiè·to -ta *adj* worried; restless; angry; (lit) stormy

inquietùdine *f* worry; restlessness; preoccupation

inquili·no -na *mf* tenant

inquinaménto *m* pollution

inquinare *tr* to pollute

inquirènte *adj* investigating

inquisi·tóre -trice *adj* inquiring || *m* inquisitor

inquisizióne *f* inquisition

insabbiare §287 *tr* to cover with sand; to pigeonhole; to shelve || *ref* to get covered with sand; to bury oneself in sand; to get stuck

insaccare §197 *tr* to bag; to stuff (*e.g.*, salami); (mil) to hem in; (fig) to bundle up; (coll) to gulp down || *ref* to be packed in; to crumple up; to disappear behind a thick bank of clouds (said, *e.g.*, *of the sun*)

insaccato *m* participant in a sack race; **insaccati** cold cuts, lunch meat

insalata *f* salad; (fig) mess

insalatièra *f* salad bowl

insalubre *adj* unhealthy

insaluta·to -ta *adj* unsaluted; **andarsene insalutato ospite** to take French leave

insanàbile *adj* incurable; implacable

insanguinare (**insànguino**) *tr* to bloody; to cover with blood; to bathe in blood

insa·no -na *adj* insane

insaponare (**insapóno**) *tr* to soap; to lather; (fig) to soft-soap

insaporire §176 *tr* to flavor || *intr* (ESSERE) to become tasty

insaputa *f*—**all'insaputa di** without the knowledge of, unbeknown to

insaziàbile *adj* insatiable

insazia·to -ta *adj* insatiate, unsatisfied

inscatolare (**inscàtolo**) *tr* to can

inscenare (**inscèno**) *tr* to stage

inscindìbile *adj* inseparable

inscrìvere §250 *tr* (geom) to inscribe

inscrutàbile *adj* inscrutable

inscurire §176 *tr*, *intr* (ESSERE) & *ref* to darken

insecchire §176 *tr* to dry || *intr* (ESSERE) & *ref* to dry up

insediaménto *m* installation (*into an office*); assumption (*of an office*)

insediare §287 (insèdio) *tr* to install || *ref* to be installed; to take one's seat; to settle

inségna *f* badge, insignia, emblem; ensign, flag; coat of arms; motto; sign (*e.g., on a restaurant*); traffic sign

insegnaménto *m* education, instruction

insegnante *adj* teaching || *mf* teacher

insegnare (inségno) *tr* to teach; to show || *intr* to teach

inseguiménto *m* pursuit

inseguire (inséguo) *tr* to pursbe, chase; to chase after

insellare (insèllo) *tr* to saddle; to put on (*e.g., one's glasses*); to bend

insellatura *f* saddling; bending

insenatura *f* inlet, cove

insensatézza *f* nonsense, folly

insensa·to -ta *adj* nonsensical, foolish || *mf* scatterbrain

insensìbile *adj* insensible; unresponsive; insensitive

inseparàbile *adj* inseparable || *m* (orn) lovebird

insepól·to -ta *adj* unburied

inserire §176 *tr* to insert; to plug in || *ref* to slip in; to butt in

inseri·tóre -trice *adj* (elec) connecting || *m* (elec) connector, plug || *f* sorter (*of punch cards*)

insèrto *m* file, folder; insert; spliced film

inservìbile *adj* useless, worthless

inserviènte *m* attendant, porter; (eccl) server

inserzionare (inserzióno) *intr* to advertise

inserzióne *f* insertion; advertisement

inserzioni·sta (-sti -ste) *adj* advertising || *mf* advertiser

insettìci·da *adj & m* (-di -de) insecticide

insettìfu·go m (-ghi) insect repellent

insètto *m* insect; **insetti** vermin

insìdia *f* trap, ambush; **insìdie** lure

insidiare §287 *tr* to ensnare; to try to trap; to try to seduce; to attempt (*someone's life*)

insidió·so -sa [s] *adj* insidious

insième *m* whole, entirety; harmony; ensemble; set; **d'insieme** general, comprehensive; **nell'insieme** as a whole || *adv* together

insigne *adj* famous; notable; arrant (*knave*)

insignificante *adj* insignificant; petty

insignire §176 *tr* to decorate; **insignire qlcu di un titolo** to bestow a title upon s.o.

insignorire §176 *tr* (lit) to invest with a fief || *intr* (ESSERE) to enrich oneself || *ref* to enrich oneself; **insignorirsi di** to seize; to take possession of

insilare *tr* to silo, ensile

insilato *m* ensilage

insincè·ro -ra *adj* insincere

insindacàbile *adj* final, indisputable

insino *adv* (lit)—**insino a** until; as far as; **insino a che** as long as

insinuante *adj* insinuating

insinuare (insìnuo) *tr* to stick, thrust;

to insinuate; (law) to register || *ref* to creep, filter; to ingratiate oneself; **insinuarsi in** to worm one's way into

insinuazióne *f* insinuation, hint

insìpi·do -da *adj* insipid, vapid

insistènte *adj* insistent

insistere §114 *intr* to insist

insi·to -ta *adj* inborn, inherent

insociévole *adj* unsociable

insoddisfat·to -ta *adj* dissatisfied

insofferènte *adj* intolerant

insoffrìbile *adj* unbearable, insufferable

insolazióne *f* sunning; sun bath; sunstroke; sunny exposure

insolènte *adj* insolent

insolentire §176 *tr* to insult, abuse || *intr* to be insolent

insolènza *f* insolence; insult

insòli·to -ta *adj* unusual

insolùbile *adj* insoluble

insolu·to -ta *adj* unsolved; not dissolved; unpaid

insolvènza *f* insolvency

insolvìbile *adj* insolvent; bad (*debt*)

insómma *adv* in conclusion || *interj* well!

insommergìbile *adj* unsinkable

insondàbile *adj* unfathomable

insònne *adj* sleepless

insònnia *f* insomnia

insonnoli·to -ta *adj* sleepy, drowsy

insonorizzazióne [ddzz] *f* soundproofing

insopportàbile *adj* unbearable

insorgènte *adj* appearing || *mf* insurgent

insorgènza *f* appearance (*of illness*)

insórgere §258 *intr* (ESSERE) to rise up, revolt; to appear

insormontàbile *adj* unsurmountable, insurmountable

insór·to -ta *adj & m* insurgent

insospettàbile *adj* above suspicion; unexpected

insospetta·to -ta *adj* not suspect; unexpected

insospettire §176 *tr* to make suspicious || *intr* (ESSERE) & *ref* to become suspicious

insostenìbile *adj* indefensible; unbearable

insostituìbile *adj* irreplaceable

insozzare (insózzo) *tr* to soil, sully

inspera·to -ta *adj* unexpected; unhoped-for

inspiegàbile *adj* unexplainable

inspirare *tr* to inhale, breathe in

inspirazióne *f* inhalation

instàbile *adj* unstable

installare *tr* to install; to set up, settle; to induct (*in an office*) || *ref* to settle

installatóre *m* plumber; erector

installazióne *f* installation; plumbing

instancàbile *adj* untiring

instante *adj* insistent; impending || *m* petitioner

instare (*pp* missing) *intr* to insist; to threaten, be imminent

instaurare (instàuro) *tr* to establish

instaurazióne *f* establishment

instigare §209 *tr* var of **istigare**

instillare *tr* var of **istillare**

instituire §176 *tr* var of **istituire**

instruire §176 *tr* var of **istruire**
instrumento *m* var of **istrumento**
instupidire §176 *tr* var of **istupidire**
insù *adv* up; **all'insù** up
insubordina·to -ta *adj* insubordinate
insuccèsso *m* failure
insudiciare §128 (**insùdicio**) *tr* to soil, dirty; to sully || *ref* to get dirty
insufficiènte *adj* insufficient; failing (*in school*)
insufficiènza *f* insufficiency; failure (*in school*)
insulare *adj* insular
insulina *f* insulin
insulsàggine *f* silliness, nonsense
insul·so -sa *adj* insipid; simple, silly
insultante *adj* insulting
insultare *tr* to insult || *intr* (with *dat*) to insult
insulto *m* insult; (pathol) attack
insuperàbile *adj* insuperable; unparalleled
insupera·to -ta *adj* unsurpassed
insuperbire §176 *tr, intr* (ESSERE) & *ref* to swell with pride
insurrezióne *f* insurrection
insussistènte *adj* nonexistent, unfounded
intabarrare *tr* to wrap up
intaccare §197 *tr* to notch; to corrode; to scratch; to attack (*said of a disease*); to damage (*e.g., a reputation*); to cut into (*capital*) || *intr* to stutter
intaccatura *f* notch; (carp) mortise
intagliare §280 *tr* to carve; to engrave
intà·glio *m* (**-gli**) carving; intaglio
intanare *ref* to hide
intangibile *adj* intangible; inviolable
intanto *adv* meanwhile; (coll) yet; (coll) finally; **intanto che** while; **per intanto** at present; in the meantime
intarsiare §287 *tr* to inlay; (fig) to stud
intarsia·to -ta *adj* inlaid
intàr·sio *m* (**-si**) inlay; inlaid work
intasare [s] *tr* to clog; to tie up (*traffic*); to stop up || *ref* to be clogged up; to be tied up; to be stopped up (*said of nose*)
intascare §197 *tr* to pocket
intat·to -ta *adj* intact, untouched
intavolare (**intàvolo**) *tr* to start (*a conversation*); to broach (*a subject*); to launch (*negotiations*)
intavolato *m* boarding, planking
integèrri·mo -ma *adj* of the utmost honesty
integrale *adj* integral; whole; whole-wheat (*bread*); built-in || *m* integral
integralismo *m* policy of the complete absorption of the body politic by an ideology
integrante *adj* constituent, integral
integrare (**ìntegro**) *tr* to integrate || *ref* to complement each other
integrazióne *f* integration
integrità *f* integrity
ìnte·gro -gra *adj* whole, complete; honest, upright; intact
intelaiatura *f* frame; framework
intellètto *m* intellect, mind; understanding
intellettuale *adj* & *mf* intellectual

intellettuali·tà *f* (**-tà**) intellectuality; intelligentsia
intellettualòide *mf* highbrow
intelligènte *adj* intelligent; clever
intelligènza *f* intelligence; understanding; **essere d'intelligenza con** to be in collusion with
intellighènzia *f* intelligentsia
intelligibile *adj* intelligible
intemera·to -ta *adj* pure, spotless || *f* reprimand, scolding; long, boring speech
intemperante *adj* intemperate
intemperanza *f* intemperance
intempèrie *fpl* inclement weather
intempesti·vo -va *adj* untimely
intendènte *m* district director; **intendente di finanza** director of customs office; **intendente militare** commissary, quartermaster
intendènza *f* office of the district director; intendance; **intendenza militare** quartermaster corps
intèndere §270 *tr* to understand; to hear; to intend; to turn (*e.g., one's eyes*); to mean; **dare ad intendere a** to lead (*s.o.*) to believe (*s.th*); far **intendere** to give to understand; **farsi intendere** to force obedience; to make oneself understood; **intender dire che** to hear that; **intendere a rovescio** to misunderstand; **intendere a volo** to catch on quickly (to); **intendere ragione** to listen to reason; **lasciare intendere** to give to understand || *intr* to aim (*toward a goal*) || *ref* to come to an agreement; **intendersela con** to be in collusion with; to have an affair with; **intendersi di** to be a good judge of; to be an expert in
intendiménto *m* understanding, comprehension; aim, goal
intendi·tóre -trice *mf* connoisseur, expert; **a buon intenditore poche parole** a word to the wise is sufficient
intenerire §176 *tr* to soften; (fig) to move || *ref* to soften; (fig) to be moved
intensificare §197 (**intensìfico**) *tr* & *ref* to intensify
intensi·tà *f* (**-tà**) intensity
intensi·vo -va *adj* intensive
intèn·so -sa *adj* intense
intentare (**intènto**) *tr* (law) to bring (*action*)
intenta·to -ta *adj* unattempted
intèn·to -ta *adj* intent || *m* intent, goal; **coll'intento di** with the purpose of
intenzionale *adj* intentional
intenziona·to -ta *adj*—**bene intenzionato** well-meaning; **essere intenzionato di** to intend to
intenzióne *f* intention; purpose; **con intenzione** on purpose
intepidire §176 *tr* & *ref* var of **intiepidire**
interbase *f* (baseball) shortstop
intercalare *m* refrain; pet word or phrase || *tr* to intercalate; to inset
intercalazióne *f* intercalation; inset
intercapèdine *f* air space
intercèdere §123 *tr* to seek, get (*a par-*

don for s.o.) || *intr* to intercede || *intr* (ESSERE)—**intercedere tra** to intervene or elapse between; to extend between; to exist between

intercettare (intercètto) *tr* to intercept; to tap (*a phone*)

intercetta·tóre -trice *mf* interceptor

intercettóre *m* (aer) interceptor

intercomunale *adj* long-distance (*call*)

intercórrere §139 *intr* (ESSERE) to elapse; to happen; to be, to stand

interdét·to -ta *adj* dumfounded; forbidden || *m* interdict; (coll) dumbell

interdire §151 *tr* to prohibit; (eccl) to interdict; (law) to disqualify

interessaménto *m* interest, concern

interessante *adj* interesting; **in stato interessante** in the family way

interessare (interèsso) *tr* to interest; to concern || *intr* to be of interest || *ref*—**interessarsi a** to take an interest in; **interessarsi di** to concern oneself with

interessa·to -ta *adj* interested; selfish || *m* interested party

interèsse *m* interest; self-interest

interessènza *f* (com) share, interest

interferènza *f* interference

interferire §176 *intr* to interfere

interfogliare §280 **(interfòglio)** *tr* to interleave

interiezióne *f* interjection

interinato *m* temporary office or tenure

interi·no -na *adj* acting || *m* temporary appointee

interióra *fpl* entrails

interióre *adj* interior || **interiori** *mpl* entrails

interlìnea *f* interlining; (typ) leading

interlineare *adj* interlinear || *v* **(interlìneo)** *tr* (typ) to lead

interlocu·tóre -trice *mf* participant (*in a discussion*); person speaking

interloquire §176 *intr* to take part in a discussion; to chime in

interlù·dio *m* (-di) interlude

intermedià·rio -ria (-ri -rie) *adj* & *mf* intermediary || *m* middleman

intermè·dio -dia (-di -die) *adj* intermediate || *mf* supervisor

intermèzzo [ddzz] *m* intermezzo; entr'acte; interval

interminàbile *adj* interminable, endless

intermissióne *f* intermission

intermittènte *adj* intermittent

internaménto *m* internment

internare (intèrno) *tr* to intern; to confine; to commit (*an insane person*) || *ref* to go deep (*into a problem*)

interna·to -ta *adj* interned || *m* internee; inmate; boarder; boarding school

internazionale *adj* international

internazionalizzare [ddzz] *tr* to internationalize

interni·sta *mf* (-sti -ste) internist

intèr·no -na *adj* inside, internal; inland; interior; boarding (*student*) || *m* inside; interior; (med) intern; lining (*of coat*); **all'interno** inside; **interni** (mov) indoor shots || **gli Interni** the Italian Ministry of Internal Affairs

intè·ro -ra *adj* entire, whole; full (*price*); (lit) upright, honest || *m* whole; **per intero** completely

interpellare (interpèllo) *tr* to interpellate; to question; to consult

interpetrare (intèrpetro) *tr* var of interpretare

interplanetà·rio -ria *adj* (-ri -rie) interplanetary

interpolare (intèrpolo) *tr* to interpolate

interpolazióne *f* interpolation

interpónte *m* (naut) between-deck

interpórre §218 *tr* to interpose || *ref* to intervene

interpretare (intèrpreto) *tr* to interpret

interpretazióne *f* interpretation

intèrprete *mf* interpreter

interpunzióne *f* punctuation

interrare (intèrro) *tr* to bury, inter; to fill in (*e.g., a marsh*) || *ref* to become silted

interra·to -ta *adj* underground; **piano interrato** basement

interrogare §209 **(intèrrogo)** *tr* to question; to interrogate

interrogati·vo -va *adj* interrogative || *m* why; question

interrogatò·rio -ria (-ri -rie) *adj* questioning || *m* (law) interrogatory; **interrogatorio di terzo grado** third degree

interrogazióne *f* interrogation; quiz, examination; **interrogazione retorica** rhetorical question

interrómpere §240 *tr* to interrupt

interruttóre *m* (elec) switch; **interruttore di linea** (elec) controller

interruzióne *f* interruption

interscàm·bio *m* (-bi) interchange

interscolàsti·co -ca *adj* (-ci -che) interscholastic; intercollegiate

intersecare §197 **(intèrseco)** *tr* & *ref* to intersect

intersezióne *f* intersection

interstellare *adj* interstellar

interstì·zio *m* (-zi) interstice

interurba·no -na *adj* interurban, intercity; (telp) long-distance || *f* (telp) long-distance call

intervallo *m* interval; pause; (educ) recess; (theat) intermission

intervenire §282 *intr* (ESSERE) to intervene; (surg) to operate; **intervenire a** to take part in

interventi·sta *mf* (-sti -ste) interventionist

intervènto *m* intervention; attendance; (surg) operation

intervenzióne *f* intervention

intervista *f* interview; **fare un'intervista a** to interview

intervistare *tr* to interview

intè·so -sa *adj* understood; intended; designed; **bene inteso** of course; **non darsene per inteso** to not pay attention; **rimanere inteso** to agree || *f* understanding, agreement; entente

intèssere (intèsso) *tr* to interweave; to wreathe (*a garland*)

intestardire §176 *ref* to get obstinate; to be determined

intestare (intèsto) *tr* to caption; to label; (typ) to head (*a page*); intestare qlco a qlcu to register s.th in the name of s.o.; intestare una fattura a to issue a bill in the name of ‖ *ref* to become obstinate; to take it into one's head

intesta·to -ta *adj* headed; registered (*stock*); obstinate; (law) intestate

intestazióne *f* heading; registration (*of stock*)

intestinale *adj* intestinal

intesti·no -na *adj* & *m* intestine; intestino crasso large intestine; intestino tenue small intestine

intiepidire §176 *tr* & *ref* to warm up; to cool off

intiè·ro -ra *adj* & *m* var of intero

intimare (ìntimo & intimo) *tr* to intimate; to order, command; to declare (*war*); to impose (*a fine*); (law) to enjoin

intimazióne *f* intimation; order; (law) injunction

intimidazióne *f* intimidation

intimidire §176 *tr* to intimidate; to threaten ‖ *ref* to become bashful

intimi·tà *f* (-tà) intimacy; privacy

inti·mo -ma *adj* intimate; inmost; biancheria intima underwear, lingerie ‖ *m* intimate friend; depth (*of one's heart*)

intimorire §176 *tr* to frighten

intingere §126 *tr* to dip ‖ *intr—*intingere in to dip in ‖ *ref—*intingersi in un affare to have a finger in the pie

intingolo *m* sauce, gravy; fancy dish

intirizzire [ddzz] §176 *tr* to benumb ‖ *intr* (ESSERE) & *ref* to become numb or stiff; to become stiff and frostbitten

intirizzi·to -ta [ddzz] *adj* numb

intisichire §176 *tr* to make tubercular; (fig) to weaken ‖ *intr* (ESSERE) to become tubercular; to wither

intitolare (intìtolo) *tr* to title; to dedicate ‖ *ref* to be named; to assume the title of

intoccàbile *adj* & *m* untouchable

intolleràbile *adj* intolerable

intollerante *adj* intolerant

intonacare §197 (intònaco) *tr* to plaster; to whitewash; to cover (*e.g., with tar*) ‖ *ref—*intonacarsi la faccia (joc) to put on one's warpaint

intòna·co *m* (-chi) plaster; roughcast

intonare (intòno) *tr* to intone; to harmonize; (mus) to tune ‖ *ref* to harmonize, go

intonazióne *f* intonation; harmony

intòn·so -sa *adj* uncut; (lit) unsheared

intontire §176 *tr* to stun ‖ *intr* (ESSERE) & *ref* to become stunned

intoppare (intòppo) *tr* to stumble upon ‖ *intr* (ESSERE) & *ref* to stumble

intòppo *m* obstacle, hindrance

intorbidare (intórbido) *tr* to cloud; to muddy; to obfuscate; to upset (*friendship*); to stir up (*passions*) ‖ *ref* to become cloudy or muddy; to become obfuscated

intorbidire §176 *tr* & *ref* to cloud; to muddy

intormentire §176 *tr* to benumb ‖ *intr* (ESSERE) to become numb

intórno *adv* around, about; all'intorno all around; intorno a around; about; levarsi qlcu d'intorno to get rid of s.o.

intorpidire §176 *tr* to benumb ‖ *ref* to become numb

intossicare §197 (intòssico) *tr* to poison, intoxicate

intossicazióne *f* poisoning, intoxication

intraducibile *adj* untranslatable; inexpressible

intraferro *m* spark gap; air gap

intralciare §128 *tr* to hamper; to intertwine ‖ *ref* to become hampered

intràl·cio *m* (-ci) hindrance; essere d'intralcio to be in the way; intralcio del traffico traffic congestion

intralicciatura *f* lattice truss (*of high-tension tower*)

intrallazzare *intr* to deal in the black market

intrallazza·tóre -trice *mf* black marketeer

intrallazzo *m* black-market dealing; kickback

intramezzare [ddzz] (intramèzzo) *tr* to alternate

intramontàbile *adj* undying, immortal

intransigènte *adj* & *mf* intransigent, die-hard

intransitàbile *adj* impassable

intransiti·vo -va *adj* intransitive

intrappolare (intràppolo) *tr* to entrap

intraprendènte *adj* enterprising

intraprendènza *f* enterprise, initiative

intraprèndere §220 *tr* to undertake

intrattàbile *adj* unmanageable, intractable

intrattenére §271 *tr* to entertain ‖ *ref* to linger; intrattenersi su to dwell upon

intrattenimento *m* entertainment

intravedére §279 *tr* to glimpse, catch a glimpse of; to foresee

intravenó·so -sa [s] *adj* intravenous

intrecciare §128 (intréccio) *tr* to braid; to twine; to cross (*one's fingers*); (fig) to weave; to begin (*a dance*) ‖ *ref* to become embroiled; to become intertwined; to crisscross

intréc·cio *m* (-ci) knitting; intertwining; plot (*of novel*); (theat) intrigue

intrepidézza *f* intrepidness, intrepidity

intrèpi·do -da *adj* intrepid

intricare §197 *tr* (lit) to entangle

intrica·to -ta *adj* tangled; intricate

intri·co *m* (-chi) tangle, jumble

intrìdere §189 *tr* to soak; to knead

intrigante *adj* intriguing ‖ *mf* schemer

intrigare §209 *tr* to tangle ‖ *intr* to intrigue ‖ *ref* (coll) to meddle

intri·go *m* (-ghi) intrigue; trouble

intrìnse·co -ca (-ci -che) *adj* intrinsic; intimate ‖ *m* intimate nature, core

intri·so -sa *adj* soaked ‖ *m* mash

intristire §176 *intr* (ESSERE) to wither; to waste away

introdót·to -ta *adj* introduced; well-known; knowledgeable, expert

introdurre §102 *tr* to introduce; to insert; to open (*a speech*); to show in || *ref* to slip in

introdutti·vo -va *adj* introductory

introduzióne *f* introduction

introitare (intròito) *tr* to collect, take in

intròito *m* receipts, collection; (eccl) introit

introméttere §198 *tr* to insert; to introduce; to involve || *ref* to meddle; to pry

intromissióne *f* meddling; intrusion; intervention

intronare (intròno) *tr* to deafen; to stun

intronizzare [ddzz] *tr* to enthrone

introspetti·vo -va *adj* introspective

introspezióne *f* introspection

introvàbile *adj* unobtainable; inaccessible

introvèr·so -sa *adj & mf* introvert

intrúdere §190 *tr* (lit) to slip in || *ref* to intrude; to trespass

intrufolare (intrùfolo) *tr* (coll) to slip (*e.g., one's hand into somebody's pocket*) || *ref* to slip in, intrude

intrù·glio *m* (-gli) concoction, brew; hodgepodge; imbroglio; mess

intrusióne *f* intrusion

intru·so -sa *adj* intrusive || *mf* intruder

intuire §176 *tr* to know by intuition; to guess; to sense

intuiti·vo -va *adj* intuitive; obvious

intùito *m* intuition; insight

intuizióne *f* intuition

inturgidire §176 *intr* (ESSERE) & *ref* to swell

inuma·no -na *adj* inhuman; inhumane

inumare *tr* to bury, inhume

inumazióne *f* burial, inhumation

inumidire §176 *tr* to moisten || *ref* to get wet

inurbaménto *m* migration to the city

inurba·no -na *adj* uncouth, unmannerly

inurbare *ref* to move into the city; to become citified

inusa·to -ta *adj* unused; unusual

inusita·to -ta *adj* unusual; out-of-the-way

inùtile *adj* useless; worthless

inutilizzàbile [ddzz] *adj* unusable

inutilizzare [ddzz] *tr* to waste (*e.g., time*)

inutilizza·to -ta [ddzz] *adj* unused

inutilménte *adv* needlessly, to no purpose || *interj* no use!

invadènte *adj* meddlesome, intrusive

invàdere §172 *tr* to invade; to encroach on; to spread over; to overcome

invaghire §176 *tr* to charm || *ref* to fall in love

invalére §278 *intr* (ESSERE) to become established; to prevail

invalicàbile *adj* impassable, unsurmountable

invalidàbile *adj* voidable

invalidaménto *m* invalidity; invalidation

invalidare (invàlido) *tr* to void, invalidate; to negate (*e.g., evidence*)

invalidi·tà *f* (-tà) invalidity; invalidation; sickness, disability

invàli·do -da *adj* void, invalid; sick, disabled || *m* disabled person; invalid

inval·so -sa *adj* prevailing

invano *adv* in vain, vainly

invariàbile *adj* invariable

invaria·to -ta *adj* unchanging; unchanged

invasare *tr* to pot (*a plant*); to fill up (*a reservoir*); to possess, obsess

invasa·to -ta *adj* possessed, obsessed

invasióne *f* invasion

inva·so -sa *adj* invaded || *m* potting (*of plant*); capacity (*of reservoir*)

inva·sóre -ditrice *adj* invading || *m* invader

invecchiaménto *m* aging

invecchiare §287 **(invècchio)** *tr & intr* (ESSERE) to age

invéce *adv* on the contrary, instead; **invece di** instead of

inveire §176 *intr* to inveigh, rail

invelenire §176 *tr* to envenom; to embitter || *intr* (ESSERE) & *ref* to grow bitter

invendìbile *adj* unsalable

invendica·to -ta *adj* unavenged

invendu·to -ta *adj* unsold

inventare (invènto) *tr* to invent

inventariare §287 *tr* to inventory

inventà·rio *m* (-ri) inventory

inventi·vo -va *adj* inventive || *f* inventiveness

inven·tóre -trice *adj* inventive || *mf* inventor

invenzióne *f* invention; (lit) find

inverdire §176 *intr* (ESSERE) to turn green

inverecóndia *f* immodesty

inverecón·do -da *adj* immodest

invernale *adj* winter; wintry

inverniciare §128 *tr* to paint; to varnish

invèrno *m* winter

invéro *adv* (lit) truly, indeed

inverosimiglianza [s] *f* unlikelihood

inverosìmile [s] *adj* unlikely

inversióne *f* inversion

invèr·so -sa *adj* inverse, opposite; (coll) cross || *m* inverse

inversóre *m* inverter; **inversore di spinta** (aer) thrust reverser

invertebra·to -ta *adj* & *m* invertebrate

invertire §176 & **(invèrto)** *tr* to invert; to reverse

inverti·to -ta *adj* inverted || *m* invert

investigare §209 **(invèstigo)** *tr* to investigate

investiga·tóre -trice *adj* investigating || *mf* investigator; detective

investigazióne *f* investigation

investiménto *m* investment; collision

investire (invèsto) *tr* to invest; to collide with; **investire di insulti** to cover with insults || *ref*—**investirsi di** to become conscious of (*e.g., one's authority*); (theat) to become identified with (*a character*)

investi·tóre -trice *mf* investor

investitura *f* investiture

invetera·to -ta *adj* inveterate, confirmed

invetria·to -ta *adj* glazed || *f* window; window pane
invettiva *f* invective
inviare §119 *tr* to send
invia·to -ta *mf* envoy; correspondent
invìdia *f* envy
invidiàbile *adj* enviable
invidiare §287 *tr* to envy; to begrudge; **non aver niente da invidiare a** to be just as good as
invidió·so -sa [s] *adj* envious
invigorire §176 *tr* to strengthen, invigorate || *intr* (ESSERE) & *ref* to grow stronger
invilire §176 *tr* to dishearten; to vilify; to lower (*prices*) || *intr* (ESSERE) & *ref* to lose heart; to lose one's reputation
inviluppare *tr* to envelop; to wrap up
invincìbile *adj* invincible
invì·o *m* (-i) dispatch; shipment; remittance; envoy (*of a poem*)
inviolàbile *adj* inviolable
inviperire §176 *ref* to become enraged
invischiare §287 *tr* to smear with birdlime; to ensnare || *ref* to become ensnared
invisìbile *adj* invisible
invì·so -sa *adj* disliked, hated
invitante *adj* attractive, inviting
invitare *tr* to invite; to summon; (*cards*) to bid; (*cards*) to open; (*mach*) to screw (*e.g., a light bulb*) in; to screw (*e.g., a lid*) on
invita·to -ta *adj* invited || *m* guest
invìto *m* invitation; inducement; bottom of stairway; (*cards*) opening
invìt·to -ta *adj* unvanquished
invocare §197 (**invòco**) *tr* to invoke
invocazióne *f* invocation
invogliare §280 (**invòglio**) *tr* to induce, entice || *ref* to yearn, long
involare (**invólo**) *tr* to steal; to abduct || *intr* (ESSERE) (aer) to take off || *ref* to disappear; to fly away
invòlgere §289 *tr* to wrap, envelop; to involve || *ref* to become entangled
invòlo *m* (aer) take-off
involontà·rio -ria *adj* (-ri -rie) involuntary
invòlto *m* bundle; wrapper
invòlucro *m* wrapping; shell (*of boiler*); (aer) envelope
involu·to -ta *adj* (fig) involved; (lit) enveloped
invòlvere §147 (*pret* missing; *pp* also **invòlto**) *tr* (lit) to envelop
invulneràbile *adj* invulnerable
inzaccherare (**inzàcchero**) *tr* to bespatter
inzeppare (**inzéppo**) *tr* to cram, stuff
inzuccherare (**inzùcchero**) *tr* to sweeten
inzuppare *tr* to soak || *ref* to get drenched
ìo *m* ego; self || §5 *pron pers*
iòdio *m* iodine
iodìdri·co -ca *adj* (-ci -che) hydriodic
ioduro *m* iodide
iògurt *m* yogurt
iò·le *f* (-le) (naut) yawl; (sports) shell
ióne *m* ion
iòni·co -ca *adj* & *m* (-ci -che) Ionic

ionizzare [ddzz] *tr* to ionize
iòsa [s] *f*—**a iosa** in abundance
iperacidità *f* hyperacidity
ipèrbole *f* (geom) hyperbola; (rhet) hyperbole
iperbòli·co -ca *adj* (-ci -che) hyperbolic(al)
ipereccita·to -ta *adj* overexcited
ipermercato *m* shopping center
ipersensìbile *adj* hypersensitive; supersensitive
ipersostentatóre *m* landing flap
ipertensióne *f* hypertension
ipnò·si *f* (-si) hypnosis
ipnòti·co -ca *adj* & *m* (-ci -che) hypnotic
ipnotismo *m* hypnotism
ipnotizzare [ddzz] *tr* to hypnotize
ipnotizza·tóre -trice [ddzz] *adj* hypnotizing || *m* hypnotizer
ipocondrìa·co -ca *adj* & *mf* (-ci -che) hypoohondriac
ipocrisìa *f* hypocrisy
ipòcri·ta (-ti -te) *adj* hypocritical || *mf* hypocrite
ipodèrmi·co -ca *adj* (-ci -che) hypodermic
iposolfito [s] *m* hyposulfite
ipotè·ca *f* (-che) mortgage
ipotecare §197 (**ipotèco**) *tr* to mortgage
ipotecà·rio -ria *adj* (-ri -rie) mortgage
ipotenusa *f* hypotenuse
ipòte·si *f* (-si) hypothesis; **nella miglior delle ipotesi** at best; **nell'ipotesi che** in the event; **per ipotesi** by supposition
ipotèti·co -ca *adj* (-ci -che) hypothetic(al)
ipotizzare [ddzz] *tr* to hypothesize
ìppi·co -ca (-ci -che) *adj* horse, horse-racing || *f* horse racing
ippocampo *m* sea horse
ippocastano *m* horse chestnut tree
ippòdromo *m* race track
ippoglòsso *m* (ichth) halibut
ippopòtamo *m* hippopotamus
iprite *f* mustard gas
ira *f* wrath, anger, ire
irachè·no -na *adj* & *mf* Iraqi
iracóndia *f* wrath, anger
iracón·do -da *adj* wrathful
irania·no -na *adj* & *mf* Iranian
irascìbile *adj* irascible
ira·to -ta *adj* irate, angry
ire §191 *intr* (ESSERE) (lit) to go
irida·to -ta *adj* rainbow-hued || *m* world bicycle champion
ìride *f* rainbow; (anat, bot) iris
Irlanda, l' *f* Ireland
irlandése [s] *adj* Irish || *m* Irishman; Irish (*language*) || *f* Irishwoman
ironìa *f* irony
iròni·co -ca *adj* (-ci -che) ironic(al)
iró·so -sa [s] *adj* angry, wrathful
irradiare §287 *tr* to illuminate; to irradiate, radiate; to brighten; (rad) to broadcast || *intr* to radiate || *ref* to radiate; to spread
irraggiare §290 *tr* to illuminate; to irradiate, radiate, beam; to brighten; (rad) to broadcast || *intr* to radiate || *ref* to radiate; to spread

irraggiungìbile adj unattainable
irragionévole adj unreasonable
irrancidire §176 intr (ESSERE) & ref to get rancid
irrazionale adj irrational
irreale adj unreal
irreconciliàbile adj irreconcilable
irrecuperàbile adj irretrievable, irrecoverable
irredentismo m irredentism
irredenti•sta mf (-sti -ste) irredentist
irredèn•to -ta adj not yet redeemed
irredimìbile adj irredeemable
irrefrenàbile adj unrestrainable
irrefutàbile adj irrefutable
irregimentare (**irregiménto**) tr to regiment
irregolare adj irregular
irregolari•tà f (-tà) irregularity
irreligió•so -sa [s] adj irreligious
irremovìbile adj irremovable; obstinate
irreparàbile adj irreparable; unavoidable
irreperìbile adj not to be found; unaccounted for (e.g., soldier)
irreprensìbile adj irreproachable
irreprimìbile adj irrepressible
irrequiè•to -ta adj restless, restive
irresistìbile [s] adj irresistible
irresolùbile [s] adj unbreakable (bond; contract); insoluble; unsolvable
irresolu•to -ta [s] adj irresolute
irrespiràbile adj unbreathable
irresponsàbile adj irresponsible
irrestringìbile adj unshrinkable
irretire §176 tr to ensnare, entrap
irrevocàbile adj irrevocable
irriconoscìbile adj unrecognizable
irriducìbile adj irreducible; stubborn
irriflessi•vo -va adj thoughtless, rash
irrigare §209 tr to irrigate
irrigazióne f irrigation
irrigidire §176 tr to chill || intr & ref to stiffen, harden; to get cool
irri•guo -gua adj well-watered; irrigating
irrilevante adj irrelevant
irrilevanza f irrelevance
irrimediàbile adj irremediable
irripetìbile adj unrepeatable
irrisióne f (lit) derision, mockery
irrisò•rio -ria adj (-ri -rie) mocking; paltry
irritàbile adj peevish; irritable
irritante adj irritating || m irritant
irritare (**irrito**) tr to irritate; to anger; to chafe || ref to become irritated
irritazióne f irritation
irriverènte adj irreverent
irrobustire §176 tr & ref to strengthen
irrómpere §240 (pp missing) intr to burst
irrorare (**irròro**) tr to sprinkle; to bathe, wet; to spray
irroratrice f sprayer; **irroratrice a zaino** portable sprayer
irruènte adj (lit) impetuous, rash
irruzióne f foray, raid; irruption
irsu•to -ta adj hairy, bristling
ir•to -ta -ta adj prickly; shaggy (hair); **irto di** bristling with
iscrivere §250 tr to inscribe; to register || ref to register; to sign up

iscrizióne f inscription; registration
Islam, l' m Islam
Islanda, l' f Iceland
islandése [s] adj Icelandic || mf Icelander || m Icelandic (language)
isola f island; block; **isola spartitraffico** traffic island
isolaménto m isolation; (elec) insulation
isola•no -na adj island || mf islander
isolante adj insulating || m (elec) insulation
isolare (**ìsolo**) tr to isolate; (elec) to insulate || ref to keep apart
isola•to -ta adj isolated; (elec) insulated || m city block; (sports) independent
isolatóre m (elec) insulator
isolazionismo m isolationism
isolazioni•sta mf (-sti -ste) isolationist
isolétta f isle
isòscele adj isosceles
isòto•po -pa adj isotopic || m isotope
ispani•sta mf (-sti -ste) Hispanist
ispa•no -na adj Hispanic
ispanoamerica•no -na adj & mf Spanish-American
ispessire §176 tr & ref to thicken
ispettorato m inspectorship
ispet•tóre -trice mf inspector; **ispettore di produzione** (mov) production manager
ispezionare (**ispezióno**) tr to inspect
ispezióne f inspection
ispi•do -da adj bristly
ispirare tr to inspire || ref to be inspired
ispirazióne f inspiration
Israèle m Israel
israelia•no -na adj & mf Israeli
israeli•ta adj & mf (-ti -te) Israelite
issare tr to hoist
issòpo m hyssop
istallare tr & ref var of installare
istantàne•o -a adj instantaneous || f snapshot
istante m instant, moment; petitioner
istanza f petition; request, application; (law) instance; **in ultima istanza** as a final decision
istèri•co -ca (-ci -che) adj hysteric(al) || mf hysteric
isterilire §176 tr to make barren || ref to become barren
isterismo m hysteria, hysterics
istigare §209 tr to instigate, prompt
istiga•tóre -trice mf instigator
istillare tr to instill, implant; **istillare il collirio negli occhi** to put drops in the eyes
istinti•vo -va adj instinctive
istinto m instinct
istituire §176 tr to institute, found; (lit) to decide
istituto m institute; institution; bank; **istituto di bellezza** beauty parlor
istitu•tóre -trice mf founder; teacher, instructor || m tutor || f governess; nurse
istituzionalizzare [ddzz] tr to institutionalize
istituzióne f institution
istmo m isthmus
istologìa f histology

ìstoriare §287 (istòrio) *tr* to adorn with historical figures

istradare *tr* to direct || *ref* to wend one's way

ìstrice *m & f* (European) porcupine

istrióne *m* ham actor; buffoon

istrióni·co -ca *adj* (**-ci -che**) histrionic

istrionismo *m* histrionics

istruire §176 *tr* to instruct; to train; (law) to draw up, prepare (*a case*) || *ref* to learn

istruì·to -ta *adj* learned, educated

istruménto *m* (law) instrument

istrutti·vo -va *adj* instructive

istrut·tóre -trice *mf* instructor; (sports) coach

istruttò·rio -ria (-ri -rie) *adj* investigating, preliminary || *f* (law) preliminary investigation

istruzióne *f* instruction; (law) prelimi-

nary investigation; **istruzioni** instructions; directions

istupidire §176 *tr* to make dull; to stupefy

Itàlia, l' *f* Italy

italia·no -na *adj & mf* Italian

itàli·co -ca *adj* (**-ci -che**) italic; Italic; (lit) Italian || *m* italics

italòfo·no -na *adj* Italian-speaking || *m* Italian-speaking person

itinerante *adj* itinerant

itinerà·rio *m* (**-ri**) itinerary

ittèri·co -ca *adj* (**-ci -che**) jaundiced

itterìzia *f* jaundice

ittiologìa *f* ichthiology

Iugoslàvia, la Yugoslavia

iugosla·vo -va *adj & mf* Yugoslav

iugulare *adj & tr* var of **giugulare**

iuta *f* jute

ivi *adv* (lit) there

L, l ['elle] *m & f* tenth letter of the Italian alphabet

la §4 *def art* the || *m* (mus) la, A; **dare il la** to set the tone || **§5** *pers pron*

là *adv* there; **al dì là da venire** to come, future; **al dì là (di)** beyond; **andare di là** to go in the next room; **andare troppo in là** to go too far; **farsi in là** to move aside; **in là con gli anni** advanced in years; **l'al di là** the life beyond; **più in là** further; **più in là di** beyond; **va' là!** come on!

làb·bro *m* (**-bri**) edge (*of wound*); (lit) lip || *m* (**-bra** *fpl*) lip; **labbro leporino** harelip

labiale *adj & f* labial

làbile *adj* (coll) weak; (lit) fleeting

labiolettura *f* lip reading

labirinto *m* labyrinth, maze

laboratò·rio *m* (**-ri**) laboratory; workshop; **laboratorio linguistico** language laboratory

laborió·so -sa [s] *adj* hard-working, laborious; labored (*e.g., digestion*)

laburi·sta (-sti -ste) *adj* Labour || *mf* Labourite

lac·ca *f* (**-che**) lacquer

laccare §197 *tr* to lacquer; to japan; to polish (*nails*)

lac·chè *m* (**-chè**) lackey

lac·cio *m* (**-ci**) lasso; snare; noose; string; (fig) bond; **laccio delle scarpe** shoelace; **laccio emostatico** tourniquet

lacciòlo *m* snare

lacerare (làcero) *tr* to lacerate; to tear || *ref* to tear

làce·ro -ra *adj* torn; tattered

lacèrto *m* (lit) shred of flesh; (lit) biceps

lacòni·co -ca *adj* (**-ci -che**) laconic

làcrima *f* tear; drop

lacrimare (làcrimo) *tr* (lit) to weep

over || *intr* to water (*said of the eyes*); (lit) to weep

lacrima·to -ta *adj* (lit) lamented

lacrimévole *adj* pitiful

lacrimóge·no -na *adj* var of **tear** (*e.g., gas*)

lacrimó·so -sa [s] *adj* teary, watery (*eyes*); tearful; lachrymose

lacuna *f* gap, lacuna; blank (*in one's mind*); **colmare una lacuna** to bridge a gap

lacustre *adj* lake

laddóve *conj* while, whereas

ladré·sco -sca *adj* (**-schi -sche**) thievish

la·dro -dra *adj* thieving; foul (*weather*); bewitching (*eyes*) || *mf* thief; **ladro di strada** highwayman || *f* inside pocket (*of suit*)

ladróne *m* thief; highwayman; **ladrone di mare** pirate

ladrùncolo *m* petty thief, pilferer

laggiù *adv* down there

lagnanza *f* complaint

lagnare *ref* to complain; to moan

lagno *m* complaint, lament

la·go *m* (**-ghi**) lake; pool (*of blood*)

làgrima *f* var of **lacrima**

laguna *f* lagoon

lai *m* (lai) lay; **lai** *mpl* (lit) lamentations

laicato *m* laity

lài·co -ca (-ci -che) *adj* lay || *m* layman

lài·do -da *adj* foul; obscene

la·ma *m* (**-ma**) llama; lama || *f* (**-me**) blade (*of knife*); marsh; (lit) lowland

lambiccare §197 *tr* to distill || *ref* to strive; **lambiccarsi il cervello** to rack one's brains

lambìc·co *m* (**-chi**) still

lambire §176 *tr* to lap; to graze, to touch lightly

lamèlla *f* thin sheet

lamentare (laménto) *tr* to bemoan, lament || *ref* to moan; to complain

lamentazióne *f* lamentation

lamentévole *adj* plaintive; lamentable
laménto *m* complaint, lament; moan
lamentó·so -sa [s] *adj* plaintive, doleful
lamétta *f* razor blade
lamièra *f* plate; armor plate
lamierino *m* sheet metal, lamina
làmina *f* sheet, lamina
laminare (làmino) *tr* to laminate; to roll (*steel*)
lamina·tóio *m* (**-tói**) rolling mill
làmpada *f* lamp, light; **lampada al neon** neon lamp; **lampada a petrolio** oil lamp; **lampada a stelo** pole lamp; **lampada di sicurezza** (min) safety lamp; **lampada fluorescente** fluorescent lamp; **lampada lampo** (phot) flash bulb
lampadà·rio *m* (**-ri**) chandelier
lampadina *f* bulb; **lampadina tascabile** flashlight
lampante *adj* shiny; clear; lamp (*oil*)
lampeggiare §290 (**lampéggio**) *tr* (lit) to flash (*a smile*) || *intr* to flash; (aut) to blink; (coll) to flash the turn signals || *impers* (ESSERE & AVERE)— **lampeggia** it lightens, it is lightning
lampeggiatóre *m* (aut) turn signal; (phot) flashlight
lampio·nàio *m* (**-nài**) lamplighter
lampióne *m* street lamp
lampíride *f* glowworm
lampo *m* lightning; flash of lightning; (fig) flash
lampóne *m* raspberry
lana *f* wool; **buona lana** (coll) rogue, rascal; **lana d'acciaio** steel wool; **lana di vetro** fiberglass, glass wool
lancétta *f* lancet; hand (*of watch*); pointer (*of instrument*)
làn·cia *f* (**-ce**) lance, spear; nozzle (*of fire hose*); launch; **lancia di salvataggio** lifeboat
lanciabóm·be *m* (**-be**) trench mortar
lanciafiam·me *m* (**-me**) flamethrower
lanciamissi·li (**-li**) *adj* missile-launching || *m* missile launcher
lanciaraz·zi [ddzz] *m* (**-zi**) rocket launcher
lanciare §128 *tr* to throw, hurl; to drop (*from an airplane*); to launch (*e.g., an advertising campaign*) || *ref* to hurl oneself; (rok) to blast off; **lanciarsi col paracadute** to parachute, bail out
lanciasilu·ri *m* (**-ri**) torpedo tube
lancia·to -ta *adj* hurled, flung; flying, e.g., **partenza lanciata** flying start
lancia·tóre -trice *mf* hurler, thrower; (baseball) pitcher
lancière *m* lancer
lancinante *adj* piercing
làn·cio *m* (**-ci**) throw; publicity campaign; (aer) drop; (aer) release (*of bombs*); (baseball) pitch; (rok) launch; **lancio del peso** shot put
landa *f* moor; wasteland
lanerie *fpl* woolens
languidézza *f* languidness, languor
làngui·do -da *adj* languid; sad (*eyes*)
languire (lànguo) & §176 *intr* to languish
languóre *m* languor; languishing; weakness; tenderness

laniè·ro -ra *adj* wool (*industry*)
lanifi·cio *m* (**-ci**) woolen mill
lanó·so -sa [s] *adj* woolly; kinky (*hair*); bushy (*face*)
lantèrna *f* lantern
lanùgine *f* down
lanzichenéc·co *m* (**-chi**) landsknecht
laónde *conj* (lit) wherefore
laotia·no -na *adj* & *mf* Laotian
lapalissia·no -na *adj* self-evident
lapidare (làpido) *tr* to stone (to death); (fig) to pick to pieces
làpide *f* stone tablet; tombstone
lapillo *m* lapillus
là·pis *m* (**-pis**) pencil
lappare *intr* to lap
làppola *f* (bot) burdock; (bot) bur
lappóne *adj* Lappish || *mf* Lapp || *m* Lapp (*language*)
Lappónia, la Lapland
lardellare (lardèllo) *tr* to lard; to stuff with bacon
lardo *m* lard; **nuotare nel lardo** to live on easy street
largheggiare §290 (**larghéggio**) *intr* to be liberal; to be lavish
larghézza *f* width; liberality; abundance; **larghezza di vedute** broadmindedness
largire §176 *tr* (lit) to bestow liberally
largizióne *f* bestowal; donation
lar·go -ga (**-ghi -ghe**) *adj* broad, wide; ample; liberal; abundant; (phonet) open; **prenderla larga** to keep away || *m* width; open sea; square; (mus) largo; **al largo di** (naut) off; **fare largo a** to open the way to; **farsi largo** to elbow one's way; **prendere il largo** to run away; (naut) to put to sea; **tenersi al largo** to keep at a distance || *f*—**alla larga!** keep away! || *largo adv*—**girare largo** to keep away
làrice *m* larch
laringe *f* larynx
laringite *f* laryngitis
laringoia·tra *mf* (**-tri -tre**) laryngologist
laringoscò·pio *m* (**-pi**) laryngoscope
larva *f* (ent) larva; (lit) ghost; (lit) skeleton; (lit) sham
lasagne *fpl* lasagne
lasciapassa·re *m* (**-re**) safe-conduct; permit
lasciare §128 *tr* to leave; to let; to let go of; **lasciar cadere** to drop; **lasciarci le penne** (coll) to die; (coll) to be skinned alive; **lasciar correre** to let go; **lasciar detto** to leave word; **lasciar fare** to leave alone; **lasciare in pace** to leave alone; **lasciare libero** to let go; **lasciare scritto** to leave in writing || *ref* to abandon oneself; to abandon one another
làscito *m* (law) bequest
lascívia *f* lasciviousness
lascí·vo -va *adj* lascivious
lassatí·vo -va *adj* mildly laxative || *m* mild laxative
lassismo *m* laxity
las·so -sa *adj* lax || *m* lasso; **lasso di tempo** period of time
lassù *adv* up there, up above
lastra *f* slab; paving stone; (phot)

plate; exposed X-ray film; **farsi le lastre** (coll) to be X-rayed
lastricare §197 (**làstrico**) *tr* to pave
lastricato *m* paving, pavement
làstri·co *m* (**-ci** or **-chi**) pavement; roadway; **ridursi sul lastrico** to fall into abject poverty
lastróne *m* slab; plate glass
latènte *adj* latent
laterale *adj* lateral ‖ *m* (soccer) halfback
laterì·zio **-zia** (**-zi** **-zie**) *adj* brick ‖ **laterizi** *mpl* bricks, tiles
làtice *m* latex
latifondi·sta *mf* (**-sti** **-ste**) rich landowner
latifóndo *m* large landed estate
lati·no **-na** *adj* Latin; lateen (*sail*) ‖ *m* Latin
latitante *adj* hiding ‖ *mf* fugitive
latitanza *f* flight from justice
latitùdine *f* latitude
la·to **-ta** *adj* wide; broad (*meaning*) ‖ *m* side; **d'altro lato** on the other hand
la·tóre **·trice** *mf* bearer
latrare *intr* to bark
latrato *m* bark
latrina *f* toilet, lavatory, washroom
latta *f* tin; can
lattàia *f* milkmaid
lat·tàio *m* (**-tài**) milkman, dairyman
lattante *adj & m* suckling
latte *m* milk; **latte detergente** cleansing cream; **latte di gallina** flip; (bot) star-of-Bethlehem; **latte in polvere** powdered milk; **latte magro** or **scremato** skim milk
lattemièle *m* whipped cream
làtte·o **-a** *adj* milky
latterìa *f* dairy; creamery
làttice *m* var of latice
latticèllo *m* buttermilk
latticì·nio *m* (**-ni**) dairy product
lattiginó·so **-sa** [s] *adj* milky
lattonière *m* tinsmith
lattu·ga *f* (**-ghe**) lettuce; head of lettuce; frill
làudano *m* paregoric, laudanum
laudati·vo **-va** *adj* laudatory
làurea *f* wreath; doctorate; doctoral examination
laurean·do **-da** *mf* candidate for the doctorate
laureare (**làureo**) *tr* to confer the doctorate on; to award (*s.o.*) the title of; (lit) to wreathe ‖ *ref* to receive the doctorate; (sports) to get the tile of
laurea·to **-ta** *adj* laureate ‖ *m* alumnus, graduate
làuro *m* laurel
làu·to **-ta** *adj* sumptuous, rich
lava *f* lava
lavabianche·rìa *f* (**-rìa**) washing machine
lavàbile *adj* washable
lavabo *m* washstand; lavatory
lavacristallo *m* windshield washer
lavacro *m* washing; font; purification; **santo lavacro** baptism
lavàg·gio *m* (**-gi**) washing; **lavaggio a secco** dry cleaning; **lavaggio del cervello** brainwashing

lavagna *f* slate; blackboard; **lavagna di panno** felt board; **lavagna luminosa** overhead projector
lavama·no *m* (**-no**) washstand
lavanda *f* washing; pumping (*of stomach*); lavender
lavandàia *f* laundrywoman; **lavandaia stiratrice** laundress (*woman who washes and irons*)
lavan·dàio *m* (**-dài**) laundryman; **lavandaio stiratore** launderer
lavanderìa *f* laundry; **lavanderia a gettone** laundromat; **lavanderia a secco** dry-cleaning establishment
lavandino *m* sink
lavapiat·ti *mf* (**-ti**) dishwasher (*person*)
lavare *tr* to wash; to cleanse; **lavare a secco** to dry-clean; **lavare il capo a** to scold ‖ *ref* to wash oneself; **lavarsi le mani** to wash one's hands
lavastovi·glie *mf* (**-glie**) dishwasher ‖ *m & f* dishwasher (*machine*)
lavata *f* washing; **lavata di capo** scolding
lavati·vo *m* (coll) enema; (coll) bore; (coll) goldbricker
lava·tóio *m* (**-tói**) laundry room; washtub
lava·tóre **-trice** *mf* washer ‖ *m* washerman; (mach) purifier ‖ *f* washerwoman; washing machine
lavatura *f* washing; **lavatura a secco** dry cleaning; **lavatura di piatti** dishwater; washing of dishes; (fig) watery soup
lavèllo *m* wash basin; sink
lavoràbile *adj* workable
lavorante *mf* helper, apprentice
lavorare (**lavóro**) *tr* to work; to till ‖ *intr* to work; to perform; to be busy; to trade; **lavorare ai ferri** to knit; **lavorare di fantasia** to daydream; **lavorare di ganasce** to eat voraciously; **lavorare di gomiti** to elbow one's way; **lavorare di mano** to pilfer; **lavorare di traforo** to work with a jig saw
lavorati·vo **-va** *adj* working; workable
lavora·to **-ta** *adj* wrought; tilled
lavora·tóre **-trice** *mf* worker ‖ *m* workman; workingman ‖ *f* workingwoman
lavorazióne *f* working; manufacturing; tilling
lavori·o *m* (**-i**) bustle; steady work; scheming
lavóro *m* work; labor; steady work; homework; piece of work; (coll) trouble; **a lavori ultimati** when the work is finished; **lavori forzati** hard labor; **lavori in economia** time and material contract work; **lavori teatrali** theatrical productions; **lavoro a cottimo** piecework; **lavoro a maglia** knitting; **lavoro di cucito** needlework; **mettere al lavoro** to press into service
lazzarétto [ddzz] *m* lazaretto
lazzaróne [ddzz] *m* cad; (coll) goldbricker
le §4 *def art* the ‖ §5 *pers pron*
leale *adj* loyal; sincere
leali·sta *mf* (**-sti** **-ste**) loyalist
leal·tà *f* (**-tà**) loyalty; sincerity

lébbra f leprosy
lebbró·so -sa [s] adj leprous || mf leper
lécca-léc·ca m (-ca) (coll) lollypop
leccapiat·ti m (-ti) glutton; sponger
leccapiè·di mf (-di) bootlicker
leccarda f dripping pan
leccare §197 (lécco) tr to lick; to fawn on; (fig) to polish || ref to make oneself up
lecca·to -ta adj affected; polished || f licking
léc·cio m (-ci) holm oak
leccornia f dainty morsel, delicacy
léci·to -ta adj licit, permissible; **mi sia lecito** may I || m right
lèdere §192 tr to damage, injure
lé·ga f (-ghe) league; alloy; **di bassa lega** poor, in poor taste; **fare lega** to unite
legale adj legal; lawyer's; official || m lawyer
legali·tà f (-tà) legality, lawfulness
legalità·rio -ria adj (-ri -rie) (pol) observing the rule of law
legalizzare [ddzz] tr to legalize; to authenticate
legame m bond; connection; relationship
legaménto m tie, bond; ligament; (phonet) liaison
legare §209 (légo) tr to tie; to bind; to unite; to set (a stone); to bequeath; to alloy; (bb) to bind || intr to bond; to mix (said of metals); to go together || ref to unite; **legarsela al dito** to never forget
legatà·rio -ria mf (-ri -rie) legatee
lega·to -ta adj muscle-bound || m legate; bequest; (mus) legato
lega·tóre -trice mf bookbinder
legatoria f bookbindery
legatura f typing; binding; ligature; bookbinding; (mus) tie
legazióne f legation
légge f law; act; **dettar legge** to lay down the law; **è fuori della legge** he is an outlaw; **legge stralcio** emergency law
leggènda f legend; story, tall tale; (journ) caption
leggendà·rio -ria adj (-ri -rie) legendary
lèggere §193 tr, intr & ref to read
leggerézza f lightness; nimbleness; thoughtlessness; fickleness
leggè·ro -ra adj light; nimble; thoughtless; slight; fickle; **alla leggera** lightly || **leggero** adv lightly
leggia·dro -dra adj graceful, lovely
leggìbile adj legible, readable
leggì·o m (-i) lectern; music stand
legiferare (legifero) intr to legislate
legionà·rio -ria adj & m (-ri -rie) legionary
legióne f legion
legislati·vo -va adj legislative
legisla·tóre -trice mf legislator
legislatura f legislature
legittimare (legittimo) tr to legitimize
legittimi·tà f (-tà) legitimacy
legitti·mo -ma adj legitimate; pure; just, right || f (law) legitim
lé·gna f (-gna & -gné) firewood; (fig) fuel

legnàia f woodpile; woodshed
legname m timber, lumber
legnata f clubbing, thrashing
légno m wood; stick; ship; coach; timber; **legno compensato** plywood; **legno dolce** softwood; **legno forte** hardwood
legnòlo m ply (e.g., of a cable)
legnó·so -sa [s] adj wooden; tough (meat); dry (style)
legu-lèio m (-lèi) pettifogger
legume m legume; **legumi** vegetables; legumes
leguminósa [s] f leguminous plant; **leguminose** legumes
lèi §5 pron pers; **dare del Lei a** to address formally
lémbo m edge, border; patch (of land)
lèm·ma m (-mi) entry (in a dictionary)
lèmme lèmme adv (coll) slowly
léna f energy; enthusiasm; (lit) breath
lèndine m nit
lène adj (lit) light, soft, gentle; (phonet) voiced
lenire §176 tr to soothe, assuage
lenóne m panderer, procurer
lenóna f procuress
lènte f lens; bob, pendulum bob; **lente d'ingrandimento** magnifying glass; **lenti** glasses
lentézza f slowness
lenticchia f lentil
lentìggine f freckle
lentigginó·so -sa [s] adj freckly
lèn·to -ta adj slow; slack; (lit) loose (hair); (lit) loose-fitting (garment) || **lento** adv slowly
lènza f fishline
lenzuò·lo m (-li) sheet; (fig) blanket; **lenzuolo a due piazze** double sheet; **lenzuolo funebre** winding sheet, shroud || m (-la fpl) sheet; **lenzuola** pair of sheets (in a bed)
leoncino m lion cub
leóne m lion; **leone d'America** cougar; **leone marino** sea lion || **Leone** m (astr) Leo
leonéssa f lioness
leopardo m leopard
lepidézza f wit; witticism
lèpi·do -da adj witty, facetious
lepisma f (ent) silverfish
lèpre adj invar rendezvous, e.g., **razzo lepre** rendezvous rocket || f hare
lepròtto m leveret, young hare
lèr·cio -cia adj (-ci -ce) filthy
lerciume m filth, dirt
lèsbi·co -ca (-ci -che) adj & mf Lesbian || f Lesbian (female homosexual)
lésina f awl; stinginess; miser
lesinare (lésino & lèsino) tr to begrudge || intr to be miserly
lesionare (lesióno) tr to damage; to crack open
lesióne f damage; injury; lesion
lé·so -sa adj damaged; injured
lessare (lésso) tr to boil
lessicale adj lexical
lèssi·co m (-ci) lexicon
lessicografia f lexicography
lessicogràfi·co -ca adj (-ci -che) lexicographic(al)
lessicògrafo m lexicographer

lessicologìa _f_ lexicology

lés·so -sa _adj_ boiled ‖ _m_ boiled meat; soup meat

lè·sto -sta _adj_ swift; nimble; quick; **alla lesta** hastily; **lesto di lingua** ready-tongued; **lesto di mano** light-fingered

lestofante _m_ swindler

letale _adj_ lethal, deadly

leta·màio _m_ (**-mài**) dunghill

letame _m_ manure, dung

letàrgi·co -ca _adj_ (**-ci -che**) lethargic

letar·go _m_ (**-ghi**) lethargy; hibernation

letìzia _f_ happiness, joy

lèttera _f_ letter; **alla lettera** literally; **lettera morta** unheeded, e.g., **le sue parole rimasero lettera morta** his words remained unheeded; **lettere letterature; lettere credenziali** credentials; **scrivere in tutte lettere** to spell out

letterale _adj_ literal

letterà·rio -ria _adj_ (**-ri -rie**) literary; learned (_word_)

letterà·to -ta _adj_ literary; literate ‖ _m_ man of letters; (coll) literate, learned person

letteratura _f_ literature

lettièra _f_ litter; bedding

letti·ga _f_ (**-ghe**) sedan chair; stretcher

lètto _m_ bed; bedding; **di primo letto** born of the first marriage; **letti gemelli** twin beds; **letto a castello** bunk bed; **letto a due piazze** double bed; **letto a scomparsa** Murphy bed; **letto a una piazza** single bed; **letto bastardo** oversize bed; **letto caldo** hot-bed; **letto di morte** deathbed; **letto operatorio** operating table

lèttone or **lettóne** _adj_ Lettish ‖ _mf_ Lett ‖ _m_ Lett, Lettish (_language_)

Lettónia, La Latvia

let·tóre -trice _mf_ reader; lecturer; meter reader ‖ _m_ reader (_e.g., for microfilm_); **lettore perforatore** reader (_of punch cards_)

lettura _f_ reading; lecture; **lettura del pensiero** mind reading

letturi·sta _m_ (**-sti**) meter reader

leucemìa _f_ leukemia

leucorrèa _f_ leucorrhea

lèva _f_ lever; (mil) draft; (mil) class; **essere di leva** to be of draft age; **fare leva su** to use (_s.o.'s emotions_)

levachio·di _m_ (**-di**) claw hammer

levante _adj_ rising ‖ _m_ east; Levant

levanti·no -na _adj & mf_ Levantine

levare (**lèvo**) _tr_ to lift, raise; to weigh (_anchor_); to pull (_a tooth_); to break (_camp_); to collect (_mail_); to remove, take away; to subtract; **levare alle stelle** to praise to the sky; **levare il disturbo** to take leave of ‖ _ref_ to arise; to get up; to take off; to satisfy (_e.g., one's hunger_); to rise (_said of wind_); **levarsi dai piedi** to get out of the way; **levarsi dai piedi** or **di mezzo qlcu** to get rid of s.o.

levata _f_ rise; reveille; collection (_of mail_); withdrawal (_of merchandise from warehouse_); **levata di scudi** uprising

levatàc·cia _f_ (**-ce**) getting up at an im-

possible hour; **ho dovuto fare una levataccia** I had to get up way too early

leva·tóio -tóia _adj_ (**-tói -tóie**)—**ponte levatoio** drawbridge

levatrice _f_ midwife

levatura _f_ intellectual breadth

leviatano _m_ leviathan

levigare §209 (**lèvigo**) _tr_ to polish

levigatrice _f_ sander; buffer

levi·tà _f_ (**-tà**) (lit) levity

levitazióne _f_ levitation

levrière _m_ greyhound

lezióne _f_ lesson; lecture; reading

lezió·so -sa [s] _adj_ affected, mincing

lézzo [ddzz] _m_ stench; filth

li _def art masc plur_ (obs) the; **li tre novembre** the third of November (_in official documents_) ‖ §5 _pers pron_

lì _adv_ there; **di lì** that way; **di lì a un anno** a year hence; **essere lì lì per** to be about to; **fin lì** up to that point; **giù di lì** more or less; **lì per lì** on the spot

libanése [s] _adj & mf_ Lebanese

Lìbano, il Lebanon

libare _tr_ to toast; to taste ‖ _intr_ to toast

libazióne _f_ libation

libbra _f_ pound

libéc·cio _m_ (**-ci**) southwest wind

libèllo _m_ libel; (law) brief

libèllula _f_ dragonfly

liberale _adj & m_ liberal

liberali·tà _f_ (**-tà**) liberality

liberare (**lìbero**) _tr_ to free; to pay in full for; to open into (_said, e.g., of a hall opening into a room_); to clear, empty (_a room_) ‖ _ref_—**liberarsi da** or **di** to get rid of

libera·tóre -trice _adj_ liberating ‖ _mf_ liberator

liberismo _m_ free trade

lìbe·ro -ra _adj_ free; vacant; without a revenue stamp (_document_); open (_syllable; heart_); outspoken

liber·tà _f_ (**-tà**) freedom; release (_e.g., from mortgage_); **libertà provvisoria** bail, parole; **libertà vigilata** probation; **mettersi in libertà** to put comfortable house clothes on; **rimettere in libertà** to set free

liberti·no -na _adj & mf_ libertine

Lìbia, la Libya

lìbi·co -ca _adj & mf_ (**-ci -che**) Libyan

libìdine _f_ lust; greed

libidinó·so -sa [s] _adj_ lustful

libido _f_ libido

li·bràio _m_ (**-brài**) bookseller

librare _ref_ to balance; to soar; (aer) to glide

libratóre _m_ (aer) glider

librerìa _f_ bookstore; library (_room_); bookshelf; book collection

libré·sco -sca _adj_ (**-schi -sche**) bookish

librétto _m_ booklet; card; (mus) libretto; **libretto di banca** passbook; **libretto degli assegni** checkbook; **libretto di circolazione** car registration; **libretto ferroviario** railroad pass; **libretto di risparmio** passbook (_of savings bank_)

libro _m_ book; ledger; register (_e.g., of births_); **a libro** folding; **libro di**

bordo log; **libro in brossura** paperback; **libro mastro** ledger; **libro paga (com)** payroll

liceale *adj* high-school ‖ *mf* high-school student

licènza *f* permit; license; diploma; (mil) leave; **con licenza parlando!** excuse my language!; **dar licenza a** to dismiss; **prender licenza da** to take leave of

licenziaménto *m* dismissal; **licenziamento in tronco** firing on the spot

licenziare §287 (**licènzio**) *tr* to dismiss; to O.K. (*a book to be published*); to graduate ‖ *ref* to take leave; to give notice, resign; to graduate

licenzió•so -sa [s] *adj* licentious

licèo *m* high school; lycée

lichène *m* lichen

licitazióne *f* auction; (bridge) bidding

lido *m* shore; sand bar

liè•to -ta *adj* glad; blessed (*event*)

liève *adj* light; slight

lievitare (**lièvito**) *tr* to leaven ‖ *intr* (ESSERE & AVERE) to rise; to ferment

lièvito *m* yeast; leaven; **lievito in polvere** baking powder

li•gio -gia *adj* (**-gi -gie**) devoted

lignàg•gio *m* (**-gi**) ancestry, lineage

ligustro *m* privet

lil•la (**-la**) *adj* *invar* & *m* lilac

lilliputia•no -na *adj* & *mf* Lilliputian

lima *f* file; **lima per le unghie** nail file

limacció•so -sa [s] *adj* miry, muddy

limare *tr* to file; to polish (*e.g., a speech*); to gnaw, plague

limatura *f* filing; filings

limbo *m* (lit) edge; (fig) limbo ‖ **Limbo** *m* (theol) Limbo

limétta *f* nail file; (bot) lime

limitare *m* threshold ‖ *v* (**límito**) *tr* to limit; to bound

limitazióne *f* limitation

límite *m* limit; boundary; check; (soccer) penalty line; **limite di carico** maximum weight; **limite di età** retirement age; **limite di velocità** speed limit; **senza limiti** limitless

limitro•fo -fa *adj* neighboring (*country*)

limo *m* mud, mire

limonare (**limóno**) *intr* (coll) to spoon

limonata *f* lemonade; (med) citrate of magnesia

limóne *m* lemon tree; lemon

limó•so -sa [s] *adj* slimy

limpi•do -da *adj* limpid, clear

lince *f* lynx, wildcat

linciàg•gio *m* (**-gi**) lynching

linciare §128 *tr* to lynch

lin•do -da *adj* neat; clean

linea *f* line; degree (*of temperature*); **conservare la linea** to keep one's figure; **in linea** abreast; (telp) connected; **in linea d'aria** as the crow flies; **linea del fuoco** firing line; **linea del cambiamento di data** international date line; **linea di circonvallazione** (rr) beltline; **linea di condotta** policy; **linea di partenza** starting line; **linea laterale** (sports) side line

lineaménti *mpl* lineaments; elements

lineare *adj* linear ‖ *v* (**líneo**) *tr* to delineate

lineétta *f* dash; hyphen

linfa *f* (anat) lymph; (bot) sap; **dar linfa** (bot) to bleed

lingòtto *m* (metallurgy) pig, ingot; **lingotto d'oro** bullion

lingua *f* tongue; language; strip (*of land*); **essere di due lingue** to speak with a forked tongue; **in lingua** in the correct language; **lingua di gatto** ladyfinger; **lingua lunga** backbiter; **lingua sciolta** glib tongue; **mala lingua** wicked tongue

linguacciu•to -ta *adj* talkative; sharptongued

linguàg•gio *m* (**-gi**) language

linguèlla *f* (philately) gummed strip

linguétta *f* tongue (*of shoe*); (mach) pin; (mus) reed

linguísti•co -ca (**-ci -che**) *adj* linguistic ‖ *f* linguistics

linifí•cio *m* (**-ci**) flax-spinning mill

linimènto *m* liniment

lino *m* flax; linen

linósa [s] *f* flaxseed, linseed

linotipi•sta *mf* (**-sti -ste**) linotypist

liocòrno *m* unicorn

liofilizzare [ddzz] *tr* to freeze-dry

liquefare §194 *tr* & *ref* to liquefy

liquefazióne *f* liquefaction

liquidare (**líquido**) *tr* to liquidate; to close out; to dismiss; to settle

liquidazióne *f* liquidation; clearance; **liquidazione del danno** (ins) adjustment

liquidità *f* liquidity

líqui•do -da *adj* liquid; (com) due ‖ *m* liquid; cash ‖ *f* liquid

liqui•gàs *m* (**-gàs**) liquid gas

liquirízia *f* licorice

liquóre *m* liqueur; (pharm) liquor

liquorí•sta *mf* (**-sti -ste**) liqueur manufacturer or dealer

lira *f* lira; pound; (mus) lyre ‖ **Lira** *f* (astr) Lyra

lìri•co -ca (**-ci -che**) *adj* lyric; (mus) operatic ‖ *m* lyric poet ‖ *f* lyric; lyric poetry; opera

lirismo *m* lyricism

Lisbóna *f* Lisbon

li•sca *f* (**-sche**) fishbone; lisp

lisciare §128 *tr* to smooth; **lisciare il pelo a** to butter up, flatter; to beat up ‖ *ref* to preen

li•scio -scia *adj* (**-sci -sce**) smooth; straight (*drink*); black (*coffee*); **passarla liscia** to get away scot-free

liscívia *f* lye; bleach

lisciviatrice *f* washing machine

li•so -sa *adj* worn-out, threadbare

lista *f* list; strip, band; stripe; **lista delle spese** shopping list; **lista delle vivande** bill of fare; **lista elettorale** slate (*of candidates*)

listare *tr* to border; to stripe

listèllo *m* lath; (archit) listel

listino *m* price list; market quotation

litanía *f* litany

lite *f* quarrel; lawsuit

litigante *adj* quarreling ‖ *mf* quarreler; (law) litigant

litigare §209 (lìtigo) *tr*—**lltigare qlco a qlcu** to fight with s.o. for s.th || *intr* to quarrel; to litigate || *ref*— **litigarsi qlco** to strive for s.th
liti·gio *m* (-gi) quarrel, litigation
litigió·so -sa [s] *adj* quarrelsome
litio *m* lithium
litografia *f* lithography
litògrafo *m* lithographer
litorale *adj* littoral || *m* seashore, coastline
litro *m* liter
Lituània, la Lithuania
litua·no -na *adj* & *mf* Lithuanian || *m* Lithuanian (*language*)
liturgia *f* liturgy
litùrgi·co -ca *adj* (-ci -che) liturgical
liu·tàio *m* (-tài) lute maker
liuto *m* lute
livèlla *f* level; **livella a bolla d'aria** spirit level
livellaménto *m* leveling; equalization
livellare (livèllo) *tr* to level; to equalize; to survey || *intr* (ESSERE) & *ref* to become level
livella·tóre -trice *adj* leveling || *mf* surveyor || *f* bulldozer
livellazióne *f* leveling
livèllo *m* level; **livello delle acque** sea level
lìvi·do -da *adj* livid, black-and-blue || *m* bruise
lividóre *m* bruise
livóre *m* grudge; hatred
Livórno *f* Leghorn
livrèa *f* livery
lizza *f* tilting ground; **entrare in lizza** to enter the lists
lo §4 *def art* the || §5 *pers pron*
lòb·bia *m* & *f* (-bia *mpl* & *fpl*) homburg
lòbo *m* lobe
locale *adj* local || *m* room; place (*of business*); (naut) compartment; **locale notturno** night spot
locali·tà *f* (-tà) locality, spot
localizzare [ddzz] *tr* to localize; to locate || *ref* to become localized
localizzazióne [ddzz] *f* localization; **localizzazione dei guasti** troubleshooting
locanda *f* inn
locandiè·re -ra *mf* innkeeper
locandina *f* playbill; flyer; small poster
locare §197 (lòco) *tr* to rent, lease
locatà·rio -ria *mf* (-ri -rie) lessee, renter
loca·tóre -trice *mf* lessor
locazióne *f* rent; lease; **dare in locazione** to rent
locomotiva *f* locomotive, engine
locomo·tóre -trice *adj* locomotive || *m* & *f* (rr) electric locomotive
locomotori·sta *m* (-sti) (rr) engineer
locomozióne *f* locomotion; transportation
lòculo *m* burial niche
locusta *f* locust
locuzióne *f* locution, expression; phrase; idiom
lodàbile *adj* praiseworthy
lodare (lòdo) *tr* to praise || *ref* to praise oneself, brag; **lodarsi di** (poet) to be pleased with

lodatì·vo -va *adj* laudatory
lòde *f* praise; **con la lode** cum laude; **con lode** plus (*on a report card*)
lodévole *adj* praiseworthy, commendable
lòdo *m* arbitration
logaritmo *m* logarithm
lòg·gia *f* (-ge) lodge; (archit) loggia
loggióne *m* (theat) upper gallery
lògi·co -ca (-ci -che) *adj* logical; **esser logico** to think logically || *m* logician || *f* logic
logìsti·co -ca (-ci -che) *adj* logistic || *f* logistics
lò·glio *m* (-gli) cockle
logoraménto *m* wear; attrition
logorare (lógoro) *tr* to wear out; to fray || *ref* to wear away; to become threadbare
logorì·o *m* (-ì) wear and tear
lógo·ro -ra *adj* worn out; threadbare
lòlla *f* chaff
lombàggine *f* lumbago
lombar·do -da *adj* & *mf* Lombard
lombata *f* loin, sirloin
lómbo *m* loin; hip; (lit) ancestry
lombrì·co *m* (-chi) earthworm
londinése [s] *adj* London || *mf* Londoner
Londra *f* London
longànime *adj* patient, forbearing
longanimi·tà *f* (-tà) patience, forbearance
longevità *f* longevity
longè·vo -va *adj* long-lived
longherina *f* beam, girder
longheróne *m* (aer) longeron; (aer) spar; (aut) main frame member
longitùdine *f* longitude
longobar·do -da *adj* & *mf* Lombard
lontananza *f* distance
lonta·no -na *adj* distant, remote; vague; indirect || *m* (lit) far-away place || *f*—**alla lontana** from a distance; vaguely; distant (*e.g., relative*) || **lontano** *adv* far; **da lontano** from afar; **lontano da** away from; far from; **rifarsi da lontano** to start from the very beginning
lóntra *f* otter
lónza *f* pork loin; (poet) leopard
lòppa *f* chaff; skin (*of plant*); slag, dross
loquace *adj* loquacious; (fig) eloquent
loquèla *f* (lit) tongue; (lit) style
lordare (lórdo) *tr* to soil, dirty
lór·do -da *adj* soiled, dirty; gross (*weight*)
lordume *m* dirt, filth
lordura *f* dirt, filth; soil
lóro §5 *pron pers* || §6 *adj poss* & *pron*
losan·ga *f* (-ghe) rhombus; (herald) lozenge
ló·sco -sca *adj* (-schi -sche) squint-eyed; cross-eyed; (fig) shady
lóto *m* mud
lòto *m* lotus
lòtta *f* fight; struggle; wrestling; **essere in lotta** to be at war; **lotta libera** catch-as-catch-can
lottare (lòtto) *intr* to fight; to quarrel; to struggle; to wrestle

lotta·tóre -trice *mf* fighter; wrestler
lotteria *f* lottery
lottizzare [ddzz] *tr* to divide into lots
lòtto *m* lotto; parcel, lot
lozióne *f* lotion
lùbri·co -ca *adj* (**-ci -che**) lewd; (*lit*) slippery
lubrificante *adj & m* lubricant
lubrificare §197 (**lubrìfico**) *tr* to lubricate
lucchétto *m* padlock
luccicare §197 (**lùccico**) *intr* to sparkle; to shine
luccichi·o *m* (**-i**) glittering; shining; sparkle
luccicóne *m* big tear
lùc·cio *m* (**-ci**) pike
lùcciola *f* firefly; usherette (*in movie*); **prendere lucciole per lanterne** to make a blunder; to be seeing things
luce *f* light; sunlight; opening; glass (*of mirror*); leaf (*e.g., of door*); (*archit*) span; (*coll*) electricity; **alla luce del sole** in plain view; **fare luce** to shed light; **luce degli occhi** eyesight; **luce del giorno** daylight; **luce della luna** moonlight; **luce di arresto** (*aut*) stoplight; **luce di incrocio** (*aut*) dimmer, low beam; **luce di posizione** (*aut*) parking light; **luce di profondità** (*aut*) high beam; **luci** (*poet*) eyes; **luci della ribalta** (*fig*) stage, boards; **mettere alla luce** to give birth to; **mettere in luce** to reveal; to publish; **venire alla luce** to be born; to come to light
lucènte *adj* shiny, shining
lucentézza *f* brightness; sheen
lucèrna *f* lamp; light; **lucerne** (*lit*) eyes || **Lucerna** *f* Lucerne
lucernà·rio *m* (**-ri**) skylight
lucèrtola *f* lizard
lucherino *m* (*orn*) siskin
Lucìa *f* Lucy
lucidare (**lùcido**) *tr* to shine, polish; to trace (*a figure*)
lucida·tóre -trice *mf* polisher (*person*) || *f* (*mach*) floor polisher
lucidatura *f* polish; tracing (*on paper*)
lucidi·tà *f* (**-tà**) polish; lucidity
lùci·do -da *adj* bright; lucid || *m* shine; tracing; **lucido per le scarpe** shoe polish
lucìfe·ro -ra *adj* (*poet*) light-bringing || **Lucìfero** *m* Lucifer, morning star
lucignolo *m* wick
lucrare *tr* to win, acquire
lucro *m* gain, earnings, lucre; **lucro cessante** (*law*) loss of earnings
lucró·so -sa [s] *adj* lucrative
ludì·brio *m* (**-bri**) mockery; laughing-stock
lù·glio *m* (**-gli**) July
lùgubre *adj* gloomy, dismal
lui §5 *pron pers*
luìgi *m* louis || **Luìgi** *m* Louis
luma·ca *f* (**-che**) snail
lume *m* light; lamp; **lume degli occhi** eyesight; **lume delle stelle** starlight; **lumi** eyesight; **lumi di luna** hard times; **perdere il lume degli occhi**

to lose one's self-control; **reggere il lume a** to close one's eyes to; **studiare al lume di candela** to burn the midnight oil
lumeggiare §290 (**luméggio**) *tr* to illuminate, to shed light on
lumicino *m* faint light; **essere al lumicino** to be on one's last legs
luminare *m* star; luminary
luminària *f* illumination
lumino *m* night light; votive light; rush light
lumInó·so -sa [s] *adj* luminous; bright (*idea*)
luna *f* moon; **andare a lune** to be fickle; **avere la luna di traverso** to be in a bad mood; **luna calante** waning moon; **luna crescente** crescent moon; **luna di miele** honeymoon
lunare *adj* lunar, moon
lunària *f* (*min*) moonstone; (*bot*) honesty
lunà·rio *m* (**-ri**) almanac; **sbarcare il lunario** to live from hand to mouth
lunàti·co -ca *adj* (**-ci -che**) moody; whimsical
lune·dì *m* (**-dì**) Monday
lunétta *f* lunette; fanlight
lunga *f*—**alla lunga** in the long run; **alla più lunga** at the latest; **andare per le lunghe** to last a long time, drag on; **di gran lunga** by far; **farla lunga** to dillydally
lungàggine *f* delay, procrastination
lunghézza *f* length; **lunghezza d'onda** wave length; **prendere la lunghezza di** to measure
lungi *adv* (*lit*) far
lungimirante *adj* (*fig*) far-sighted
lun·go -ga (**-ghi -ghe**) *adj* long; sharp (*tongue*); nimble (*fingers*); tall; thin (*soup*); (*coll*) slow; **a lungo** for a long time; at length; **a lungo andare** in the long run; **lungo disteso** sprawling || *m* length; **in lungo e in largo** far and wide; **per il lungo** lengthwise || *f* see **lunga** || **lungo** *prep* along; during
lungofiume *m* river road
lungola·go *m* (**-ghi**) lakeshore road
lungomare *m* seashore road
lungometrà·gio *m* (**-gi**) full-length movie, feature film
lunòtto *m* (*aut*) rear window
luò·go *m* (**-ghi**) place; passage; site; (*geom*) locus; **aver luogo** to take place; **aver luogo in** to be laid in (*e.g., a certain place*); **dar luogo a** to give rise to; **del luogo** local; **far luogo** to make room; **fuori luogo** inopportune(ly); **in alto luogo** high-placed; **in luogo di** instead of; **luogo comune** commonplace; **luogo di decenza** toilet; **luogo di nascita** birthplace; **luogo di pena** penitentiary; **non luogo a procedere** (*law*) no ground for prosecution; (*law*) **nolle prosequi**; **sul luogo** on the spot; **on the premises**
luogotenènte *m* lieutenant
lupa *f* she-wolf
lupanare *m* (*lit*) brothel

lupé•sco -sca *adj* (-schi -sche) wolfish
lupétto *m* young wolf; cub (*in Boy Scouts*)
lupinèlla *f* sainfoin
lupi•no -na *adj* wolfish
lu•po -pa *mf* wolf; lupo cerviero lynx; lupo di mare seadog; lupo mannaro werewolf || *f* see lupa
lùppolo *m* hops
lùri•do -da *adj* filthy, dirty
lusco *m*—tra il lusco e il brusco at twilight
lusin•ga *f* (-ghe) flattery; illusion
lusingare §209 *tr* to flatter || *ref* to be flattered; to hope
lusinghiè•ro -ra *adj* flattering; promising
lussare *tr* to dislocate
lussazióne *f* dislocation

lusso *m* luxury; di lusso de luxe; lusso di abundance of
lussuó•so -sa [s] *adj* luxurious, sumptuous
lussureggiante *adj* luxuriant
lussùria *f* lust
lussurió•so -sa [s] *adj* lustful, lecherous
lustrare *tr* to polish, shine; to lick (*s.o.'s boots*) || *intr* to shine, be shiny
lustrascar•pe *m* (-pe) bootblack
lustrino *m* sequin; tinsel
lu•stro -stra *adj* shiny, polished || *m* shine, polish; period of five years; dare il lustro a to shine, polish
lutto *m* mourning; bereavement; a lutto black-edged (*e.g., stationery*); lutto stretto deep mourning
luttuó•so -sa [s] *adj* mournful

M

M, m ['emme] *m & f* eleventh letter of the Italian alphabet
ma *m* but; ma e se ifs and buts || *conj* but; yet || *interj* who knows?; too bad!
màca•bro -bra *adj* macabre
maca•co *m* (-chi) macaque; (fig) dumbbell
macadàm *m* macadam
macadamizzare [ddzz] *tr* to macadamize
mac•ca *f* (-che) abundance; a macca (coll) abundantly; (coll) without paying
maccarèllo *m* mackerel
maccheróni *mpl* macaroni
màcchia *f* spot, stain; brushwood; thicket; (fig) blot; alla macchia clandestinely; (painting) done in pointillism; darsi alla macchia to join the underground; to escape the law; macchia solare sunspot; senza macchia spotless
macchiare §287 *tr* to stain, soil || *ref* to become stained; macchiarsi d'infamia to soil one's reputation
macchiétta *f* caricature; comedian; fare la macchietta di to impersonate, to parody
macchiettare (macchiétto) *tr* to speckle
macchietti•sta *mf* (-sti -ste) cartoonist; comedian; impersonator
màcchina *f* machine; engine; car, automobile; machination; andare in macchina to go to press; fatto a macchina machine-made; macchina da presa (mov) camera; macchina da proiezione projector; macchina fotografica camera; macchina per or da cucire sewing machine; macchina per or da scrivere typewriter; scrivere a macchina to typewrite
macchinale *adj* mechanical
macchinare (màcchino) *tr* to plot
macchinà•rio *m* (-ri) machinery
macchinazióne *f* machination

macchinétta *f* gadget; macchinetta del caffè coffee maker
macchini•sta *m* (-sti) engineer; (theat) stagehand
macchinó•so -sa [s] *adj* heavy, ponderous; complicated
macedònia *f* fruit salad, fruit cup
macel•làio *m* (-lài) butcher
macellare (macèllo) *tr* to butcher
macelleria *f* butcher shop
macèllo *m* slaughterhouse; butchering; carnage; disaster
macerare (màcero) *tr* to soak; to mortify (*the flesh*) || *ref* to waste away
macèria *f* low wall; macerie ruins
màce•ro -ra *adj* emaciated; skinny || *m* soaking vat (*for papermaking*)
machiavèlli•co -ca *adj* (-ci -che) Machiavellian
macigno *m* boulder
macilèn•to -ta *adj* emaciated, pale, wan
màcina *f* millstone; (coll) grind
macinacaf•fè *m* (-fè) coffee grinder
macinapé•pe *m* (-pe) pepper mill
macinare (màcino) *tr* to grind, mill; to burn up (*e.g., the road*)
macina•to -ta *adj* ground || *m* grindings; ground meat || *f* grinding
macinino *m* grinder; (coll) jalopy
mà•cis *m & f* (-cis) mace (*spice*)
maciste *m* strong man (*in circus*)
maciullare *tr* to brake (*flax or hemp*); to crush
macrocòsmo *m* macrocosm
màdia *f* bread bin; kneading trough
màdi•do -da *adj* wet, perspiring
madònna *f* lady || Madonna *f* Madonna
madornale *adj* huge; gross (*error*)
madre *f* mother; stub; mold; madre nubile unwed mother
madreggiare §290 (madréggio) *intr* to take after one's mother
madrelingua *f* mother tongue
madrepàtria *f* mother country
madrepèrla *f* mother-of-pearl
madresélva *f* (coll) honeysuckle

madrevite *f* (mach) nut; die; **madrevite ad alette** wing nut

madrigna *f* stepmother

madrina *f* godmother; **madrina di guerra** war mother

mae·stà *f* (-stà) majesty; **lesa maestà** lese majesty

maestó·so -sa [s] *adj* majestic, stately

maèstra *f* teacher; (fig) master; **maestra giardiniera** kindergarten teacher

maestrale *m* northwest wind (*in Mediterranean*)

maestranze *fpl* workmen

maestria *f* skill, mastery

maè·stro -stra *adj* masterly; main ‖ *m* teacher; master; instructor; northwester (*in Mediterranean*); **maestro di cappella** choirmaster ‖ *f* see **maestra**

mafió·so -sa [s] *adj* Mafia ‖ *mf* member of the Mafia; gaudy dresser

ma·ga *f* (-ghe) sorceress

magagna *f* fault, weak spot

magagna·to -ta *adj* spoiled (*fruit*)

magari *adv* even, maybe ‖ *conj* even if ‖ *interj* would that . . . !

magazzinàg·gio [ddzz] *m* (-gi) storage

magazziniè·re -ra [ddzz] *mf* stockroom attendant ‖ *m* warehouseman

magazzino [ddzz] *m* warehouse; store; inventory; (phot, journ) magazine; **grandi magazzini** department store

maggése [s] *adj* May ‖ *m* (agr) fallow

màg·gio *m* (-gi) May; May Day

maggiolino *m* cockchafer

maggiorana *f* sweet marjoram

maggioranza *f* majority

maggiorare (maggióro) *tr* to increase

maggiorazióne *f* increase, appreciation

maggiordòmo *m* butler; majordomo

maggióre *adj* bigger, greater; major; main; higher (*bidder*); older, elder; (mil) master (*e.g., sergeant*); biggest, greatest; highest; oldest, eldest; andare per la maggiore to be all the rage; **maggiore età** majority ‖ *m* (mil) major; oldest one; **maggiori** ancestors

maggiorènne *adj* of age ‖ *mf* grownup, adult

maggiorènte *mf* notable

maggiori·tà *f* (-tà) (mil) C.O.'s office

maggiorità·rio -ria *adj* (-ri -rie) majority

magia *f* magic

màgi·co -ca *adj* (-ci -che) magic

Magi *mpl* Magi, Wise Men

magióne *f* (lit) home, dwelling

magistèro *m* education, teaching; mastery; (chem) precipitation

magistrale *adj* teacher's; masterly ‖ *f* teacher's college

magistrato *m* magistrate

magistratura *f* judiciary

màglia *f* knitting; stitch; link; undershirt; sports shirt; (hist) mail; (fig) web; **lavorare a maglia** to knit

maglieria *f* knitting mill; yarn shop; knitwear store

magliétta *f* polo shirt, T-shirt; buckle (*to secure rifle strap*); picture hook; buttonhole

maglifi·cio *m* (-ci) knitwear factory

mà·glio *m* (-gli) sledge hammer; mallet; drop hammer

maglióne *m* heavy sweater, jersey

magnàni·mo -ma *adj* magnanimous

magnano *m* (coll) locksmith

magnate *m* (lit) magnate, tycoon

magnèsio *m* magnesium

magnète *m* magnet; magneto

magnèti·co -ca *adj* (-ci -che) magnetic

magnetismo *m* magnetism

magnetite *f* loadstone

magnetizzare [ddzz] *tr* to magnetize

magnetòfono *m* tape recorder

magnificare §197 (magnìfico) *tr* to extol, praise; to magnify (*to exaggerate*)

magnificènza *f* magnificence

magnìfi·co -ca *adj* (-ci -che) magnificent; munificent; wonderful, splendid

ma·gno -gna *adj* (lit) great; the Great, e.g., **Alessandro Magno** Alexander the Great

magnòlia *f* magnolia

ma·go *m* (-ghi) magician; wizard

magóne *m* (coll) gizzard; (coll) grief; **avere il magone** (coll) to be in the dumps

magra *f* low water; (fig) dearth, want

magrézza *f* leanness; scarcity

ma·gro -gra *adj* lean, thin; meager ‖ *m* lean meat; **meatless day** ‖ *f* see **magra**

mài *adv* never; ever; **non . . . mai** never, not ever; **come mai?** how come?

maia·le -la *mf* pig; hog ‖ *m* pork ‖ *f* sow

maialé·sco -sca *adj* (-schi -sche) piggish

maiòli·ca *f* (-che) majolica

maionése [s] *f* mayonnaise

mà·is *m* (-is) corn, maize

maiuscolétto *m* (typ) small capital

maiùsco·lo -la *adj* capital ‖ *m*—**scrivere in maiuscolo** to capitalize ‖ *f* capital letter

Malacca, la Malay Peninsula

malaccèt·to -ta *adj* unwelcome

malaccòr·to -ta *adj* imprudent; awkward

malacreanza *f* (malecreanze) instance of bad manners; **malecreanze** bad manners

malaféde *f* (malefédi) bad faith

malaffare *m*—**donna di malaffare** prostitute; **gente di malaffare** underworld

malagévole *adj* rough (*road*); hard (*work*)

malagràzia *f* (malegràzie) rudeness, uncouthness

malalìngua *f* (malelìngue) slanderer, backbiter

malanda·to -ta *adj* run-down; shabby

malandri·no -na *adj* dishonest; bewitching (*eyes*) ‖ *m* highwayman

malànimo *m* ill will; **di malanimo** reluctantly

malanno *m* misfortune; illness; (joc) menace

malaparata *f* (coll) danger, dangerous situation

malapéna *f*—**a malapena** hardly

malària *f* malaria

malatìc·cio -cia *adj* (-ci -ce) sickly

mala·to -ta *adj* sick, ill; essere malato agli occhi to have sore eyes; fare il malato to play sick || *mf* patient; i malati the sick

malattìa *f* sickness; illness; disease; malattie del lavoro occupational diseases

malaugura·to -ta *adj* unfortunate; ill-omened

malaugù·rio *m* (-ri) ill omen

malavìta *f* underworld

malavòglia *f* (malevòglie) unwillingness; di malavoglia reluctantly

malcapita·to -ta *adj* unlucky || *m* unlucky person

malcàu·to -ta *adj* rash, heedless

malcón·cio -cia *adj* (-ci -ce) battered

malcontèn·to -ta *adj* dissatisfied, malcontent || *mf* malcontent || *m* dissatisfaction

malcostume *m* immorality; bad practice

malcrea·to -ta *adj* ill-bred

maldè·stro -stra *adj* clumsy, awkward

maldicènte *adj* gossipy, slanderous || *mf* gossip, slanderer, backbiter

maldicènza *f* gossip, slander

male *m* evil; ill; trouble; andare a male to go to pot; aversela a male to take offense; di male in peggio from bad to worse, worse and worse; fare del male to do ill; fare male to be in error; fare male a to hurt; farsi male to get hurt; to hurt oneself; far venire il mal di mare a to make seasick; (fig) to nauseate; Lei fa male you should not; mal d'aereo airsickness; mal di capo headache; mal di cuore heart disease; mal di denti toothache; mal di gola sore throat; mal di mare sea-sickness; mal di montagna mountain sickness; mal di pancia bellyache; mal di schiena backache; mandare a male to spoil; mettere male to sow discord; prendere a male to take amiss; voler male a to bear a grudge against || *adv* badly, poorly; male educato ill-bred; meno male! fortunately!; restar male to be disappointed; sentirsi male to feel sick; stare male to be ill; star male a to not fit, e.g., questo vestito gli sta male this suit does not fit him; veder male qlco to disapprove of s.th; veder male qlcu to dislike s.o.

maledettaménte *adv* (coll) damned

maledét·to -ta *adj* cursed, damned

maledire §195 *tr* to curse

maledizióne *f* malediction, curse || *interj* damn it!, confound it!

maleduca·to -ta *adj* ill-bred || *mf* boor

malefatta *f* var of malafatta

malefì·cio *m* (-ci) curse, spell; witchcraft; witchery

malèfi·co -ca *adj* (-ci -che) maleficent

maleolènte *adj* (lit) malodorous

malèrba *f* weed, weeds

malése *adj & mf* Malay

Malésia, la Malaysia

malèssere *m* malaise; uneasiness; worry

malevolènza *f* malevolence; malice

malèvo·lo -la *adj* malevolent; malicious

malfama·to -ta *adj* ill-famed; notorious

malfat·to -ta *adj* botched; misshapen || *m* misdeed

malfat·tóre -trice *mf* malefactor

malfér·mo -ma *adj* wobbly, unsteady

malfì·do -da *adj* untrustworthy

malgarbo *m* bad manners, rudeness

malgovèrno *m* misrule; mismanagement; neglect

malgrado *prep* in spite of; mio malgrado in spite of me || *conj* although

malìa *f* spell, charm

maliar·do -da *adj* enchanting, charming || *mf* magician || *f* enchantress, witch

malignare *intr* to gossip

maligni·tà *f* (-tà) maliciousness; malevolence; malignancy

mali·gno -gna *adj* malicious, evil; unhealthy; malignant || il Maligno the Evil One

malinconìa *f* melancholy; melancholia

malincòni·co -ca *adj* (-ci -che) melancholy, wistful

malincuóre *m*—a malincuore unwillingly, against one's will

malintenziona·to -ta *adj* evil-minded || *mf* evildoer

malinté·so -sa [s] *adj* misunderstood; misapplied || *m* misunderstanding

malió·so -sa [s] *adj* malicious; cunning; mischievous; bewitching

malìzia *f* malice; trick; mischief

malizió·so -sa [s] *adj* malicious; clever, artful; mischievous

malleàbile *adj* malleable; manageable

malleva·dóre -drice *mf* guarantor

malleverìa *f* surety

mallo *m* hull, husk

mallòppo *m* bundle; (aer) trail cable; (coll) lump (*in one's throat*); (slang) swag, booty

malmenare (malméno) *tr* to manhandle

malmés·so -sa *adj* shabby, seedy; tasteless

malna·to -ta *adj* uncouth; unfortunate; harmful

malnutri·to -ta *adj* undernourished

malnutrizióne *f* malnutrition

ma·lo -la *adj* (lit) bad

malòc·chio *m* (-chi) evil eye

malóra *f* ruin; mandare in malora to ruin; va in malora! go to the devil!

malóre *m* malaise; fainting spell

malpràti·co -ca *adj* (-ci -che) inexperienced

malsa·no -na *adj* unhealthy; unsound

malsicu·ro -ra *adj* unsafe; insecure

malta *f* mortar; plaster; (obs) mud

maltèmpo *m* bad weather

malto *m* malt

maltòlto *m* ill-gotten gains

maltrattaménto *m* mistreatment

maltrattare *tr* to mistreat, maltreat

malumóre *m* bad humor; di malumore in a bad mood

malva *f* mallow

malvà·gio -gia (-gi -gie) *adj* wicked || *mf* wicked person || il Malvagio the Evil One

malversare (**malvèrso**) *tr* to embezzle; to misappropriate

malversazióne *f* embezzlement; misappropriation

malvestì·to -ta *adj* shabby, seedy

malvi·sto -sta *adj* disliked; unpopular

malvivènte *mf* criminal; (lit) profligate

malvolentièri *adv* unwillingly

malvolére *m* malevolence; indolence || §196 *tr* to dislike

mamma *f* mother, mom; (lit) breast; **mamma mia** dear me!

mammaluc·co *m* (**-chi**) simpleton

mammèlla *f* breast; udder

mammìfe·ro -ra *adj* mammalian || *m* mammal

màmmola *f* violet; (fig) shrinking violet

mam·mùt *m* (**-mut**) mammoth

manata *f* slap; handful; **dare una manata a** to slap

man·ca *f* (**-che**) left hand, left

mancante *adj* missing, lacking; unaccounted for

mancanza *f* lack; absence; defect; mistake; **in mancanza di** for lack of

mancare §197 *tr* to miss || *intr* (AVERE) to be at fault; **mancare a** to break (*e.g., one's word*); **mancare di** to be wanting; to lack; **mancare di parola** to break one's word || *intr* (ESSERE) to fail (*said, e.g., of electric power*); to be lacking, e.g., **manca il sale nell'arrosto** salt is lacking in the roast; to be missing; to be absent, e.g., **mancano tre soci** three members are absent; to be, e.g., **mancano dieci minuti alle quattro** it is ten minutes to four; (with *dat*) to lack, e.g., **gli mancano le forze** he lacks the strength; to miss, e.g., **mi manca la sua compagnia** I miss his company; **mancare a** to be absent from (*e.g., the roll call*); to be . . . from, e.g., **mancano dieci chilometri all'arrivo** we are ten kilometers from the journey's end; **mancare ai vivi** (lit) to pass away; **sentirsi mancare** to feel faint || *impers*—**mancare poco che + *subj*** to narrowly miss + *ger*, e.g., **ci mancò poco che fosse investito da un'automobile** he narrowly missed being hit by a car; **non ci mancherebbe altro!** that would be the last straw!, I should say not!

manca·to -ta *adj* unsuccessful; missed (*opportunity*); abortive (*attempt*), e.g., **omicidio mancato** abortive attempt to murder; manqué, e.g., **un poeta mancato** a poet manqué

manchévole *adj* faulty

manchevolézza *f* fault, shortcoming

màn·cia *f* (**-ce**) tip, gratuity; **mancia competente** reward

manciata *f* handful

manci·no -na *adj* left-handed; underhanded || *mf* left-handed person || *f* left hand, left; (mach) floating crane

man·co -ca *adj* (**-chi -che**) left; (lit) sinister, ill-omened; (lit) lacking || *m* (lit) lack; **senza manco** (coll) without fail || **manco** *adv*—**manco male!**

(coll) at least!; **manco per idea!** (coll) not at all! || *f* see **manca**

mandaménto *m* jurisdiction

mandante *m* (law) principal

mandare *tr* to send; to condemn (*to death*); to commit (*to memory*); to send forth (*e.g., smoke, buds*); to operate (*a machine*); **che Dio ce la mandi buona!** may God help us!; **mandare ad effetto** to carry out; **mandare all'altro mondo** to dispatch, kill; **mandare a monte** to ruin; **mandare a picco** to sink; **mandare a quel paese** to send to the devil; **mandare a spasso** to fire, dismiss; to get rid of; **mandar giù** to swallow; **mandare in malora** to ruin; **mandare in pezzi** to break to pieces; **mandare per le lunghe** to delay || *intr*—**mandare a chiamare** to send for; **mandare a dire** to send word

mandarino *m* mandarin; (*Citrus nobilis*) tangerine; (*Citrus reticulata*) mandarin orange

mandata *f* sending; delivery (*of merchandise*); group; gang (*e.g., of thieves*); turn (*of key*); **chiudere a doppia mandata** to double-lock

mandatà·rio *m* (**-ri**) mandatary, trustee

mandato *m* mandate; order; **mandato di cattura** arrest warrant; **mandato di comparizione** subpoena; **mandato di perquisizione** search warrant

mandìbola *f* jaw

mandolino *m* mandolin

màndorla *f* almond; kernel (*of fruit*)

mandorla·to -ta *adj* almond || *m* nougat

màndorlo *m* almond tree

mandràgola *f* mandrake

màndria *f* herd

mandriano *m* herdsman

mandrillo *m* mandrill

mandrino *m* (mach) mandrel; (mach) driftpin

mandritta *f*—**a mandritta** to the right

mane *f*—**da mane a sera** from morning till night

maneggévole *adj* usable; manageable; accessible to small craft (*sea*)

maneggiare §290 (**manéggio**) *tr* to work (*e.g., clay*); to handle; to wield (*a sword*); to knead (*dough*); to manage; (equit) to train

manég·gio *m* (**-gi**) handling; intrigue; horsemanship; management; riding school; manège

mané·sco -sca *adj* (**-schi -sche**) ready-fisted; hand (*e.g., weapons*)

manétta *f* throttle (*on a motorcycle*); **manette** handcuffs, manacles

manfòrte *f*—**dar manforte a** to help

manganèllo *m* bludgeon, cudgel

manganése [s] *m* manganese

màngano *m* calender; mangle

mangeréc·cio -cia *adj* (**-ci -ce**) edible

mangeria *f* graft, peculation

mangiàbile *adj* edible

mangiana·stri *m* (**-stri**) tape recorder

mangia-pane *m* (**-pane**) idler

mangia-prèti *m* (**-prèti**) priest hater

mangiare *m* eating; food || *v* §290 *tr*

to eat; to bite, gnaw; to erode; to embezzle, graft; (cards, chess) to take; **mangiar la foglia** to get wise || *intr* to eat; **mangiare alle spalle di qlcu** to eat at the expense of s.o. || *ref* to eat up; **mangiarsi il fegato** to be green with envy; **mangiarsi la parola** to break one's promise; **mangiarsi le unghie** to bite one's nails; **mangiarsi una promessa** to break one's promise
mangiasòldi *adj invar* money-eating, e.g., **macchina mangiasoldi** money-eating contraption
mangiata *f* (coll) fill, hearty meal, bellyful
mangiatóia *f* manger, crib
mangia·tóre -trice *mf* eater
mangime *m* fodder; feed; poultry feed
mangimìsti·co -ca *adj* (-**ci** -**che**) feed, e.g., **attrezzature mangimistiche** feed machinery
mangió·ne -na *mf* great eater, glutton
mangiucchiare §287 (**mangiùcchio**) *tr* to nibble
mangusta *f* mongoose
mania *f* mania, craze; complex; whim; **mania di grandezza** delusions of grandeur
mania·co -ca (-**ci** -**che**) *adj* maniacal; enthusiastic || *m* maniac; fan, enthusiast
màni·ca *f* (-**che**) sleeve; hose; (coll) crowd, bunch; **essere di manica larga** to be broad-minded; **essere nelle maniche di qlcu** to be in the favor of s.o.; **è un altro paio di maniche** this is a horse of another color; **in maniche di camicia** in shirt sleeves; **manica a vento** air sleeve, windsock; **manica per l'acqua** hose || **la Manica** the English Channel
manicarétto *m* dainty, delicacy
manichino *m* mannequin; cuff; (obs) handcuff; **fare il manichino** to model
màni·co *m* (-**chi** & -**ci**) handle; stock (*of rifle*); shaft (*of golf club*); stem (*of spoon*); (mus) neck; **manico di scopa** broomstick
manicò·mio *m* (-**mi**) insane asylum, madhouse
manicòtto *m* muff; (mach) collar; (mach) nipple; (mach) sleeve
manicu·re *mf* (-**re**) manicure, manicurist (*person*) || *f* (-**re**) manicure (*treatment*)
manicuri·sta *mf* (-**sti** -**ste**) manicurist
manièra *f* manner, fashion, way; **belle maniere** good manners; **di maniera** (lit, painting) Manneristic; **di maniera che** so that; **in nessuna maniera** by no means; **maniere bad manners**
maniera·to -ta *adj* mannered, affected; genteel
maniè·ro -ra *adj* tame, gentle || *m* manor house, mansion || *f* see **maniera**
manieró·so -sa [s] *adj* genteel; mannered
manifattura *f* manufacture; factory; product; ready-made wear
manifestare (**manifèsto**) *tr* to manifest

|| *intr* to demonstrate || *ref* to turn out to be
manifestazióne *f* manifestation; demonstration
manifestino *m* leaflet, handbill
manifè·sto -sta *adj* manifest, clear || *m* poster, placard; manifest; (pol) manifesto; **manifesto di carico** (naut) manifest
maniglia *f* handle; knob; (naut) link (*of chain*)
manigóldo *m* criminal; scoundrel
manipolare (**manìpolo**) *tr* to concoct; to adulterate; (telg) to transmit
manipola·tóre -trice *mf* schemer || *m* telegraph key
manìpolo *m* sheaf; (eccl; hist) maniple; (fig) handful
maniscal·co *m* (-**chi**) blacksmith
manna *f* manna; godsend
mannàia *f* axe; knife (*of guillotine*)
mano *f* hand; way (*in traffic*); coat (*of paint*); (lit) handful; (fig) finger; fingertip; **alla mano** plain, affable; **a mani nude** barehanded; **a mano** by hand; **a mano a mano** little by little; **a mano armata** armed (*e.g.*, *robbery*); at gunpoint; **aver contro mano** to buck traffic; **a quattro mani** four-handed; **avere le mani bucate** to be a spendthrift; **avere le mani in pasta** to have one's fingers in the pie; **avere le mani lunghe** to be light-fingered; **battere le mani** to clap; **con le mani in mano** idle; **dare la mano a** to shake hands with; **dare man forte a** to help; **dare una mano** to pitch in; **dare una mano a** to lend a hand to; **di lunga mano** beforehand; **essere colto con le mani nel sacco** to be caught red-handed; **essere svelto di mano** to be light-fingered; **far man bassa (su)** to plunder; **fuori mano** out of the way; **mani di burro** butterfingers; **mani in alto!** hands up!; **man mano (che)** as; **mettere mano a** to begin; **mettere le mani sul fuoco** to guarantee; to swear; **per mano di** at the hands of; **prendere la mano** to balk; to get out of hand; **tenere la mano a** to abet; **venire alle mani** to come to blows
manodòpera *f* labor, manpower; **manodopera qualificata** skilled labor
manòmetro *m* manometer
manométtere §198 *tr* to tamper with
manomissióne *f* tampering
manomòrta *f* (law) mortmain
manòpola *f* mitten; handgrip; strap (*to hold on to*); (rad, telv) knob; (hist) gauntlet
manoscrit·to -ta *adj* & *m* manuscript
manoscrìvere §250 *intr* to write in one's own handwriting
manovale *m* laborer, helper; hod carrier
manovèlla *f* handle, crank; lever
manòvra *f* maneuver; (rr) shifting; **fare manovra** to maneuver; (rr) to shift
manovrare (**manòvro**) *tr* to maneuver; to handle, drive; (rr) to shift || *intr* to maneuver; (rr) to shunt, shift; (fig) to plot

manovratóre *m* motorman; driver; (rr) brakeman; (rr) flagman

manrovè•scio *m* (-sci) backhanded slap

mansalva *f*—**rubare a mansalva** to help oneself freely (*e.g.*, *to the till*)

mansarda *f* mansard

mansióne *f* duty, function

mansuè•to -ta *adj* tame; meek

mansuetùdine *f* tameness; meekness

mantèlla *f* coat; (mil) cape

mantellina *f* (mil) cape

mantèllo *m* woman's coat; coat (*of animal*); (fig) cloak; (mil) cape; (mach) casing

mantenére §271 *tr* to keep; to maintain; to hold (*e.g.*, *a position*) || *ref* to stay alive; to last; to remain, stay, continue

mantenimento *m* keeping; maintenance

mantenu•to -ta *adj* kept || *m* gigolo || *f* kept woman

màntice *m* bellows; folding top (*of carriage*); (aut) convertible top

manto *m* mantle; coat; cloak

Màntova *f* Mantua

mantovana *f* valance

manuale *adj & m* manual

manualizzare [ddzz] *tr* to make (*e.g.*, *a machine*) hand-operated; to include in a manual; to prepare a manual of

manù•brio *m* (-bri) handlebar; handle; dumbbell

manufat•to -ta *adj* manufactured || *m* manufactured product; manufacture

manutèngolo *m* accomplice

manutenzióne *f* maintenance, upkeep

manza [dz] *f* heifer

manzo [dz] *m* steer; beef

maometta•no -na *adj & mf* Mahometan, Mohammedan

maomettismo *m* Mahometanism, Mohammedanism

Maométto *m* Mahomet

maóna *f* barge

mappa *f* map; bit (*of key*)

mappamóndo *m* globe; map òf the world

marachèlla *f* mischief

maramèo *m*—**fare marameo** to thumb one's nose

mara•sma *m* (-smi) utter confusion; (pathol) decrepitude, feebleness

maratóna *f* marathon

maratonè•ta *m* (-ti) Marathon runner

mar•ca *f* (-che) mark, label; make, brand; token; ticket; (hist, geog) march; **di marca** of quality; **marca da bollo** revenue stamp; **marca di fabbrica** trademark

marcare §197 *tr* to mark; to label; to brand; to keep the score of; to score (*e.g.*, *a goal*); to accentuate

marcatèm•po *m* (-po) timekeeper

marca•to -ta *adj* marked, pronounced

marchésa *f* marchioness, marquise

marchése *m* marquess, marquis

marchia•no -na *adj* gross (*error*)

marchiare §287 *tr* to brand

màr•chio *m* (-chi) brand; initials; characteristic; trademark

màr•cia *f* (-ce) march; operation; pus; (aut) gear, speed; (mil) hike; (sports)

walk; **far marcia indietro** to back up; (naut) to back water; **marcia indietro** (aut) reverse; **marcia nuziale** wedding march

marciapiède *m* sidewalk; (rr) platform

marciare §128 *intr* to march; (mil) to advance; (sports) to walk; (coll) to function; **far marciare qlcu** to keep s.o. in line

màr•cio -cia (-ci -ce) *adj* rotten; infected; corrupt || *m* rotten part; decayed part; corruption || *f* see **marcia**

marcire §176 *intr* (ESSERE) to rot

marciume *m* rot; pus; decay

mar•co *m* (-chi) mark

marconigram•ma *m* (-mi) radiogram

marconi•sta *mf* (-sti -ste) radio operator

mare *m* sea; bunch, heap; **al mare** at the seashore; **alto mare** high sea; **fa mare** the sea is rough; **gettare a mare** to throw overboard; **mare grosso** rough sea; **mare territoriale** territorial waters; **promettere mari e monti** to promise the moon; **tenere il mare** to be seaworthy

marèa *f* tide; sea (*e.g.*, *of mud*); **alta marea** high tide; **bassa marea** low tide; **marea di quadratura** neap tide; **marea di sizigia** spring tide

mareggiata *f* coastal storm

maremòto *m* seaquake

mareògrafo *m* tide-level gauge

maresciallo *m* marshall; warrant officer

marétta *f* choppy sea; instability

margarina *f* margarine

margherita *f* daisy; **margherite** beads

marginale *adj* marginal

marginatóre *m* margin stop (*of typewriter*); (typ) try square

màrgine *m* margin; edge; **margine a scaletta** thumb index

marijuana *f* marijuana, marihuana

marina *f* seashore; seascape; navy; **marina mercantile** merchant marine

mari•nàio *m* (-nài) seaman, sailor

marinara *f* middy blouse

marinare *tr* to marinate; **marinare la scuola** to cut school, play truant

marinarè•sco -sca *adj* (-schi -sche) sailor, seamanlike

marina•ro -ra *adj* sea, sailor; seamanlike; nautical || *m* (coll) sailor || *f* see **marinara**

mari•no -na *adj* marine, nautical || *f* see **marina**

mariòlo *m* rascal

marionétta *f* puppet, marionette

maritale *adj* marital

maritare *tr* to marry || *ref* to get married

marito *m* husband

maritti•mo -ma *adj* maritime, sea || *m* merchant seaman

marmàglia *f* riffraff, rabble

marmellata *f* jam, preserves; **marmellata di arancia** orange marmalade

marmi•sta *m* (-sti) marble worker; marble cutter

marmitta *f* pot, kettle; (aut) muffler

marmittóne *m* (coll) sad sack

marmo *m* marble

marmòc•chio *m* (-chi) brat

marmòre·o -a *adj* marble
marmorizzare [ddzz] *tr* to marble
marmòtta *f* marmot; woodchuck; (fig) sluggard; (rr) switch signal
marmottina *f* salesman's sample case
marna *f* marl
marnare *tr* to marl
marocchi·no -na *adj* & *mf* Moroccan || *m* morocco leather
Maròcco, il Morocco
maróso [s] *m* billow, surge
marra *f* hoe; fluke (*of anchor*)
marrano *m* Marrano; (fig) scoundrel; (lit) traitor
marronata *f* (coll) blunder, boner
marróne *adj invar* maroon, tan || *m* chestnut; (coll) blunder
Marsìglia *f* Marseille
marsigliése [s] *adj* Marseilles || *m* native or inhabitant of Marseilles || *f* Marseillaise
marsina *f* swallow-tailed coat
Marte *m* Mars
marte·dì *m* (-dì) Tuesday; **martedì grasso** Shrove Tuesday
martellare (martèllo) *tr* to hammer; to pester (*with questions*) || *intr* to throb; (fig) to insist
martellata *f* hammer blow
martellétto *m* hammer (*of piano or bell*); lever (*of typewriter*)
martèllo *m* hammer; **martello dell'uscio** knocker; **martello perforatore** jack-hammer
martinétto *m* jack; **martinetto a vite** screw jack
martingala *f* half belt (*sewn in back of sports jacket*); martingale (*of harness*)
martinic·ca *f* (-che) wagon brake
martìn pescatóre *m* kingfisher
màrtire *m* martyr
martì·rio *m* (-ri) martyrdom
martirizzare [ddzz] *tr* to martyrize
màrtora *f* marten
martoriare §287 (martòrio) *tr* to torment
marxi·sta *adj* & *mf* (-sti -ste) Marxist
marzapane *m* marzipan
marziale *adj* martial
marzia·no -na *adj* & *mf* Martian
marzo *m* March
mas *m* (mas) torpedo boat
mascalzóne *m* cad, rascal
mascèlla *f* jaw; jawbone
màschera *mf* usher || *f* mask; masque; **maschera antigas** gas mask; **maschera di bellezza** beauty pack; **maschera respiratoria** oxygen mask; **maschera subacquea** diving helmet
mascheraménto *m* camouflage
mascherare (màschero) *tr*, *intr* & *ref* to mask; to camouflage
mascherata *f* masquerade
mascherina *f* little mask, loup; tip (*of shoe*); (aut) grille; (phot) mask
maschiare §287 *tr* (mach) to tap
maschiétta *f* tomboy; **alla maschietta** bobbed (*hair*); **tagliare i capelli alla maschietta** to bob the hair
maschiétto *m* baby boy; pintle
maschile *adj* masculine; manly; men's;

male (*sex*); boys' (*school*) || *m* masculine
mà·schio -schia *adj* manly, virile; male || *m* male; keep, donjon; tenon; (mach) tap; (carp) tongue
mascolinizzare [ddzz] *tr* to make masculine or mannish || *ref* to act like a man
mascoli·no -na *adj* masculine; mannish (*woman*)
masnada *f* mob, gang; (obs) group
masnadière *m* highwayman
massa *f* mass; body (*of water*); (elec) ground; **mettere a massa** (elec) to ground; **in massa** in a body; **massa ereditaria** (law) estate
massacrante *adj* killing, fatiguing
massacrare *tr* to massacre; to ruin; to wear out, fatigue
massacro *m* massacre
massaggiare §290 *tr* to massage
massaggiatóre *m* masseur
massaggiatrice *f* masseuse
massàg·gio *m* (-gi) massage
massàia *f* housewife
massèllo *m* block (*of stone*); (metallurgy) pig, ingot
masseria *f* farm
masserizie *fpl* household goods
massicciata *f* roadbed; (rr) ballast
massic·cio -cia (-ci -ce) *adj* massive; bulky; heavy; (fig) gross || *m* massif
màssi·mo -ma *adj* maximum; top || *m* maximum; limit; **al massimo** at the most || *f* maxim; maximum temperature
massi·vo -va *adj* massive
masso *m* rock, boulder
Massóne *m* Mason
Massoneria *f* Masonry
mastèllo *m* washtub
masticare §197 (màstico) *tr* to chew, masticate; to mumble (*words*); to speak (*a language*) poorly; **masticare amaro** to grumble
masticazióne *f* mastication
màstice *m* mastic; glue; putty
mastino *m* mastiff
mastodòn·ti·co -ca (-ci -che) *adj* mammoth
ma·stro -stra *adj* master || *m* ledger; master, e.g., **mastro meccanico** master mechanic
masturbare *tr* & *ref* to masturbate
matassa *f* skein; trouble
matemàti·co -ca (-ci -che) *adj* mathematical || *m* mathematician || *f* mathematics
materassino *m* (sports) mat; **materassino pneumatico** air mattress
materasso *m* mattress; (boxing) sparring partner
matèria *f* matter; substance; subject; (coll) pus; **dare materia a** to give ground for; **materia grigia** gray matter; **materie coloranti** dyestuffs; **materie prime** raw materials
materiale *adj* material; rough, bulky || *m* material; equipment, supplies; (fig) makings, stuff; **materiale ferroviario** (rr) rolling stock; **materiale stabile** (rr) permanent way

materni·tà *f* (-**tà**) maternity; maternity hospital; maternity ward

matèr·no -**na** *adj* maternal; mother (*tongue, country*)

matita *f* pencil; **matita per gli occhi** eye-shadow pencil; **matita per le labbra** lipstick; cosmetic pencil

matrice *f* matrix; stub

matrici·da *mf* (-**di** -**de**) matricide

matrici·dio *m* (-**di**) matricide

matricola *f* register, roll; registration (*number*); registry; beginner, novice; freshman (*in university*); **far la matricola a** to haze

matricola·to -**ta** *adj* notorious, arrant

matrigna *f* stepmother

matrimoniale *adj* matrimonial; double (*bed*); married (*life*)

matrimonialménte *adv* as husband and wife

matrimò·nio *m* (-**ni**) matrimony, marriage; wedding

matròna *f* matron

matronale *adj* matronly

matta *f* joker, wild card

mattacchió·ne -**na** *mf* jester, prankster

mattana *f* tantrum; fit of laughter

matta·tóio *m* (-**tói**) slaughterhouse

matterèllo *m* rolling pin

mattina *f* morning; **di prima mattina** early in the morning; **la mattina** in the morning

mattinale *adj* morning || *m* morning report

mattinata *f* morning; (*theat*) matinée

mattiniè·ro -**ra** *adj* early-rising

mattino *m* morning; **di buon mattino** early in the morning

mat·to -**ta** *adj* crazy; whimsical; dull; false (*jewelry*); wild (*desire*); **andare matto per** to be crazy about; **da matti** unbelievable; **fare il matto** to cut a caper; **matto da legare** raving mad || *f* see **matta**

mattòide *adj* & *mf* madcap

mattonare (**mattóno**) *tr* to pave with bricks

mattonato *m* brick floor; **restare sul mattonato** to be utterly destitute

mattóne *m* brick; (*fig*) bore

mattonèlla *f* tile; cushion (*of billiard table*)

mattuti·no -**na** *adj* morning || *m* matins

maturan·do -**da** *mf* lycée student who has to take the baccalaureate examination

maturare *tr* to ripen; to ponder; to pass (*a lycée pupil*) || *intr* (ESSERE) to ripen, mature; to fall due

maturazióne *f* ripening

maturi·tà *f* (-**tà**) maturity; ripening; lycée final

matu·ro -**ra** *adj* ripe; mature; due

Matusalèmme *m* Methuselah

mausolèo *m* mausoleum

mazza *f* club; mallet; sledge hammer; cane; mace; golf club; (baseball) bat

mazzacavallo *m* well sweep

mazzapic·chio *m* (-**chi**) mallet; sledge

mazzata *f* heavy blow, wallop (*with club*)

mazzeran·ga *f* (-**ghe**) (mach) tamper

mazzière *m* macer; (cards) dealer

mazzo *m* bunch; bouquet; deck (*of cards*); **fare il mazzo** to shuffle the cards

mazzuòla *f* sledge hammer

mazzuòlo *m* sledge; mallet; wedge (*of golf club*); drumstick (*for bass drum*)

me §5 *pron pers*

meandro *m* meander; labyrinth

MEC *m* (letterword) (**Mercato Europeo Comune**) European Economic Community, Common Market

Mècca, la Mecca; (fig) the Mecca

meccàni·co -**ca** (-**ci** -**che**) *adj* mechanical || *m* mechanic || *f* mechanics; process (*e.g., of digestion*); machinery

meccanismo *m* machinery; mechanism; movement (*of watch*)

meccanizzare [ddzz] *tr* to mechanize || *ref* to become mechanized

mecenate *m* patron (*of the arts*)

méco §5 *prep phrase* (lit) with me

medàglia *f* medal

medaglióne *m* medallion; locket; biographical sketch

medési·mo -**ma** *adj* & *pron* same; -self, e.g., **egli medesimo** he himself; very e.g., **la verità medesima** the very truth

mèdia *f* average; secondary school; middle school; (math) mean; **media oraria** average speed || **mèdia** *mpl* media (*of communication*)

mediana *f* median; (soccer) middle line

mediàni·co -**ca** *adj* (-**ci** -**che**) medium

media·no -**na** *adj* median || *m* (sports) halfback || *f* see **mediana**

mediante *prep* by means of

mediare §287 (**mèdio**) *tr* & *intr* (ESSERE) to mediate

media·to -**ta** *adj* indirect

media·tóre -**trice** *adj* mediating || *mf* mediator; broker; commission merchant

mediazióne *f* mediation; brokerage; broker's fee, commission

medicaménto *m* medicine

medicamentó·so -**sa** [s] *adj* medicinal

medicare §197 (**mèdico**) *tr* to medicate; to treat

medicastro *m* quack

medicazióne *f* medication; dressing

medichéssa *f* (pej) lady doctor

medicina *f* medicine

medicinale *adj* medicinal || *m* medicine

mèdi·co -**ca** (-**ci** -**che**) *adj* medical || *m* doctor, physician; healer; **fare il medico** to practice medicine; **medico chirurgo** surgeon; **medico condotto** board-of-health doctor; country doctor; **medico curante** family physician

medievale *adj* medieval

medievali·sta *mf* (-**sti** -**ste**) medievalist

mè·dio -**dia** (-**di** -**die**) *adj* average; median; middle; secondary (*school*); medium || *m* middle finger || *f* see **media**

mediòcre *adj* mediocre

mediocri·tà *f* (-**tà**) mediocrity

medioèvo *m* Middle Ages

medioleggèro *m* welterweight

mediomàssimo *m* light heavyweight
meditabón·do -da *adj* meditative
meditare (**mèdito**) *tr* & *intr* to meditate
medita·to -ta *adj* considered
meditazióne *f* meditation
mediterrà·neo -nea *adj* inland (*sea*) ||
Mediterraneo *adj* & *m* Mediterranean
mè·dium *mf* (**-dium**) medium
medusa *f* jellyfish
mefistofèli·co -ca *adj* (**-ci -che**) Mephistophelian
mefiti·co -ca *adj* (**-ci -che**) mephitic
megaciclo *m* megacycle
megàfono *m* megaphone
megalomanìa *f* megalomania
megalòpo·li *f* (**-li**) megalopolis
mega-òhm *m* (**-òhm**) megohm
megèra *f* hag, termagant, vixen
mèglio *adj invar* better; (coll) best ||
|| *m*—**il meglio** the best; **nel meglio di**
(coll) in the middle of || *f*—**avere la
meglio** to get the upper hand; **avere
la meglio di** to get the better of
|| *adv* better; best; rather; **stare
meglio** to feel better; to be becoming; to fit better; **stare meglio a** to
be becoming to; to fit; **tanto meglio!**
so much the better!
méla *f* apple; nozzle (*of sprinkling
can*); **mela cotogna** quince (*fruit*);
mela renetta pippin
melagrana *f* pomegranate
melanzana [dz] *f* eggplant
melassa *f* molasses, treacle
mela·to -ta *adj* honey, honeyed
melèn·so -sa *adj* dull, silly
melissa *f* (bot) balm
mellìflu·o -a *adj* mellifluous
mélma *f* mud, slime
melmó·so -sa [s] *adj* muddy, slimy
mélo *m* apple tree
melodìa *f* melody
melòdi·co -ca *adj* (**-ci -che**) melodic
melodió·so -sa [s] *adj* melodious
melodram·ma *m* (**-mi**) melodrama;
lyric opera; (fig) melodrama
melodrammàti·co -ca *adj* (**-ci -che**)
melodramatic
melograno *m* pomegranate tree
melóne *m* melon; cantaloupe; **melone
d'acqua** watermelon
membrana *f* membrane; parchment;
diaphragm (*of telephone*); (zool) web
membratura *f* frame
mèm·bro *m* (**-bri**, *considered individually*) limb; member; penis || *m*
(**-bra** *fpl*, *considered collectively*)
limb (*of human body*)
membru·to -ta *adj* burly, husky
memoràbile *adj* memorable
memoràn·dum *m* (**-dum**) memorandum;
agenda, calendar; note; note paper
mèmore *adj* (lit) mindful, grateful
memòria *f* memory; souvenir; memoir;
dissertation; (law) brief
memoriale *m* memoir; memorial
memorizzare [dzz] *tr* to memorize
ména *f* intrigue
mena·bò *m* (**-bò**) (typ) layout, dummy
menadito *m*—**a menadito** at one's
fingertips; perfectly
menare (**méno**) *tr* to lead; to bring

(*luck*); to wag (*the tail*); to deliver
(*a blow*); (coll) to hit; **menare a
effetto** to carry out; **menare buono di**
to approve of; **menare il can per l'aia**
to beat around the bush; **menare per
le lunghe** to delay; **menare vanto to**
boast
ménda *f* (lit) fault, flaw
mendace *adj* lying, false, mendacious
mendà·cio *m* (**-ci**) (law) falsehood
mendicante *adj* & *m* mendicant
mendicare §197 (**méndico**) *tr* & *intr* to
beg
mendici·tà *f* (**-tà**) indigence, poverty
mendi·co -ca *adj* & *mf* (**-chi -che**)
mendicant
menefreghìsmo *m* I-don't-care attitude
menestrèllo *m* minstrel
méno *adj invar* less || *m* less; least;
minus (*sign*); **i meno** the few; **per lo
meno** at least || *adv* less; least;
minus; **a meno che** unless; **da meno**
inferior; **fare a meno di** to do without; to spare; **meno . . . di** less . . .
than; **meno male** fortunately; **meno
. . . meno** the less . . . the less; **non
poter fare a meno di** + *inf* to not be
able to help + *ger*, e.g., **la conferenza non poteva fare a meno di
essere un successo** the conference
could not help being a success;
quanto meno at least; **senza meno**
without fail; **venir meno** to swoon,
pass out; to fail; to lose, e.g., **gli
venne meno il cuore** he lost his
courage; **venir meno di** to break
(*one's word*) || *prep* except; less,
minus; of, e.g., **le sette meno dieci**
ten minutes of seven
menomare (**mènomo**) *tr* to lessen, diminish; (fig) to hurt, damage
mèno·mo -ma *adj* least
menopàusa *f* menopause
mènsa *f* (prepared) table; mess, mess
hall; (eccl) altar; communion table;
(poet) mass; (poet) altar; **mensa
aziendale** company cafeteria
mensile *adj* monthly || *m* monthly salary or allowance
mensili·tà *f* (**-tà**) monthly installment
mènsola *f* bracket; corner shelf; neck
(*of harp*); mantel (*of chimney*); console
ménta *f* mint
mentale *adj* mental; (anat) chin
mentali·tà *f* (**-tà**) mentality, mind
ménte *f* mind; **a mente di** according to;
avere in mente to mean; to intend;
di mente mental; **mente direttiva**
mastermind; **scappare di mente a**
qlcu to escape s.o.'s mind, e.g., **gli è
scappato di mente** it escaped his
mind; **uscire di mente** to go out of
one's mind; **venire in mente a qlcu**
to remember, e.g., **non gli è venuto
in mente di spedire la lettera** he did
not remember to mail the letter
mentecat·to -ta *adj* & *mf* lunatic
mentìna *f* mint; **mentina digestiva**
after-dinner mint
mentire §176 & (**mènto**) *intr* to lie;

mentire per la gola to lie through one's teeth

menti·to -ta *adj* false; disguised

menti·tóre -trice *adj* lying || *mf* liar

ménto *m* chin

mentòlo *m* menthol

méntre *m*—**in quel mentre** at that very moment; **nel mentre che** at the time when || *conj* while; whereas

me·nù *m* (**-nù**) menu

menzionare (**menzióno**) *tr* to mention

menzióne *f* mention

menzógna *f* lie

menzognè·ro -ra *adj* false, deceptive; lying, untruthful

meraviglia *f* marvel, wonder; **a meraviglia** wonderfully; **destare le meraviglie di** to amaze; **dire meraviglie di** to praise to the skies; **fare meraviglia** (with *dat*) to amaze; **far meraviglie** to work wonders

meravigliare §280 (**meraviglio**) *tr* to amaze; to astonish || *ref* to be astonished

meraviglió·so -sa [s] *adj* marvelous, wonderful || *m* (lit) supernatural

mercan·te -téssa *mf* merchant, dealer

mercanteggiare §290 (**mercantéggio**) *tr* to sell || *intr* to deal; to haggle

mercantile *adj* mercantile; merchant (*marine*) || *m* cargo boat, freighter

mercanzìa *f* merchandise; (coll) junk

mercato *m* market; trafficking; **a buon mercato** cheap; **far mercato di** to traffic in; **sopra mercato** besides; into the bargain

mèrce *f* merchandise, goods; commodity

mercé *f* favor, grace; mercy; **alla mercé di** at the mercy of; **mercé a** thanks to; **mercé sua** thanks to him (her, etc.)

mercéde *f* pay; (lit) reward

mercenà·rio -ria *adj* & *m* (**-ri -rie**) mercenary

merceria *f* notions store; **mercerie** notions

mercerizzare [ddzz] *tr* to mercerize

mèr·ci *adj invar* freight (*train, car, etc.*) || *m* (**-ci**) freight train

mer·ciàio -ciàia *mf* (**-ciài -ciàie**) notions store owner

merciaiòlo *m* small businessman; **merciaiolo ambulante** peddler

mercole·dì *m* (**-dì**) Wednesday

mercuriale *f* market report; price ceiling

mercùrio *m* mercury || **Mercurio** *m* Mercury

merènda *f* afternoon snack, bite

meretrice *f* harlot

meridia·no -na *adj* & *m* meridian || *f* sundial

meridionale *adj* meridional, southern || *mf* southerner

meridióne *m* south; South

merig·gio *m* (**-gi**) noon

merin·ga *f* (**-ghe**) meringue

meritare (**mèrito**) *tr* to deserve; to win || *intr* (eccl) to merit; **bene meritare di** to deserve the gratitude of || *impers*—**merita** it is worth while to

meritévole *adj* deserving, worthy

mèrito *m* merit; **in merito a** concerning; **per merito di** thanks to; **render merito a** to reward

meritò·rio -ria *adj* (**-ri -rie**) meritorious

merlan·go *m* (**-ghi**) whiting

merlatura *f* battlement

merlétto *m* lace, needlepoint

mèrlo *m* blackbird; merlon; (fig) simpleton

merluzzo *m* cod

mè·ro -ra *adj* bare, mere; (poet) pure

merovìngi·co -ca (**-ci -che**) *adj* Merovingian || *f* Merovingian script

mesata [s] *f* month's wages

méscere (*pp* **mesciuto**) *tr* to pour (*e.g., wine*); (poet) to mix

meschini·tà *f* (**-tà**) pettiness; narrowmindedness; meanness, stinginess

meschi·no -na *adj* petty; narrowminded; wretched; puny || *mf* wretch

méscita *f* pouring; counter; bar

mescolanza *f* mixture, blend

mescolare (**méscolo**) *tr* to mix, blend; to shuffle (*cards*); to stir (*e.g., coffee*) || *ref* to mix, blend; to mingle; to consort; **mescolarsi in** to mind (*somebody else's business*)

mescolatrice *f* mixer, blender

mése [s] *m* month; month's pay

mesétto [s] *m* short month

mesóne *m* (phys) meson

méssa *f* (eccl & mus) Mass; **messa a fuoco** (phot) focusing; **messa a punto** adjustment; clear statement, outline of a problem; (aut) tune-up; **messa a terra** (elec) grounding; **messa cantata** high mass; **messa in marcia** or **in moto** (mach) starting; **messa in orbita** (rok) orbiting; **messa in piega** waving (*of hair*); **messa in scena** staging; **messa in vendita** putting up for sale

messaggerìe *fpl* delivery service

messaggè·ro -ra *mf* messenger; postal clerk

messàg·gio *m* (**-gi**) message

messale *m* missal

mèsse *f* harvest; crop

Messìa *m* Messiah

messiàni·co -ca *adj* (**-ci -che**) Messianic

messica·no -na *adj* & *mf* Mexican

Mèssico, il Mexico

messinscèna *f* staging; faking

mésso *m* clerk; (poet) messenger

mestare (**mésto**) *tr* to stir || *intr* to intrigue

mesta·tóre -trice *mf* ringleader; schemer

mèstica *f* (painting) filler

mesticare §197 (**mèstico**) *tr* to prime (*a canvas*); to mix (*colors*)

mestierante *mf* potboiler (*person*); tradesman, craftsman

mestière *m* trade, craft; (archaic) task; **di mestiere** by trade; habitual; **essere del mestiere** to be up in one's line

mestièri *m*—**essere di** or **far mestieri** to be necessary

mestizia *f* sadness

mè·sto -sta *adj* sad

méstola *f* ladle; trowel

méstolo *m* kitchen spoon; **avere il mestolo in mano** to be the boss

mèstruo *m* menses, menstruation

mèta f goal, aim; (rugby) goal line

méta f heap, stack (*e.g., of hay*)

me·tà f (-tà) half; ·middle; halfway; better half; **a metà** halfway, in the middle; **aver qlco a metà con qlcu** to go half and half with s.o.

metabolismo m metabolism

metafisi·co -ca (-ci -che) adj metaphysical || m metaphysician || f metaphysics

metafonèsi f umlaut, metaphony

metafonìa f umlaut, metaphony

metàfora f metaphor

metafòri·co -ca adj (-ci -che) metaphoric(al)

metàlli·co -ca adj (-ci -che) metallic

metallizzare [ddzz] tr to cover with metal

metallo m metal; timbre (*of voice*); (poet) metal object; **il vile metallo** filthy lucre

metallòide m nonmetal

metallurgìa f metallurgy

metallùrgi·co -ca (ci -che) adj metallurgic(al) || m metalworker

metalmeccàni·co -ca (-ci -che) adj metallurgic(al) and mechanical || m metalworker

metamòrfo·si f (-si) metamorphosis

metanizzare [ddzz] tr to provide with methane

metano m methane

metanodótto m natural gas pipeline

metàte·si f (-si) metathesis

metèora f meteor; atmospheric phenomenon

meteorite m & f meteorite

meteorologìa f meteorology

meteorològi·co -ca adj (-ci -che) meteorologic(al); weather (*forecast*)

meteoròlo·go -ga mf (-gi -ghe) meteorologist

metic·cio -cia adj & mf (-ci -ce) half-breed

meticoló·so -sa [s] adj meticulous

metìli·co -ca adj (-ci -che) methyl

metòdi·co -ca (-ci -che) adj methodical; subject (*e.g., index*) || mf methodical person || f methodology

metodi·sta adj & mf (-sti -ste) Methodist

mètodo m method

metràg·gio m (-gi) length in meters; **corto metraggio** short; **lungo metraggio** full-length movie, feature film

metratura f length in meters

mètri·co -ca (-ci -che) adj metric(al) || f metrics, prosody

mètro m meter; (fig) yardstick; (lit) words

métro m (coll) subway

metrònomo m (mus) metronome

metronòt·te m (-te) night watchman

metròpo·li f (-li) metropolis

metropolita·no -na adj metropolitan || m policeman, traffic cop || f subway

metrovìa f subway

méttere §198 tr to put, place; to set (*e.g., foot*); to run (*e.g., a nail into a board*); to cause (*fear; fever*); to employ; to admit; to put forth; to give out; (coll) to charge; (coll) to install; (aut) to engage (*a gear*); **metterci**

to take (*e.g., an hour*); **mettere a confronto** to compare; **mettere a freno** to check; **mettere a fuoco** (phot) to focus; **mettere al bando** to banish; **mettere all'asta** to auction off; **mettere al mondo** to give birth to; **mettere a nudo** to lay bare; **mettere fuori** to pull out; to give out (*news*); to throw (*s.o.*) out; **mettere giù** to lower; **mettere in onda** to broadcast; **mettere in pericolo** to endanger; **mettere la pulce nell'orecchio** a to put a bug in the ear of; **mettere qlcu alla porta** to show s.o. the door; **mettere su** to set up; (coll) to put (*e.g., a coat*) on; **mettere su qlcu contro qlcu** to excite s.o. against s.o. || intr to sprout; to lead (*said, e.g., of a road*) || ref to put on, to don; to place oneself, put oneself; to take shape; **mettersi** a to begin to; **mettersi al bello** to clear up (*said of weather*); **mettersi a letto** to go to bed; **mettersi a sedere** to sit down; **mettersi con** to start to work with; **mettersi in ferie** to take one's vacation; **mettersi in malattia** to fall ill; **mettersi in mare** to put to sea; **mettersi in maschera** to wear a masked costume; **mettersi in salvo** to get out of danger; to save oneself; **mettersi in viaggio** to set out on a journey; **mettersi in vista** to make oneself conspicuous || impers—**mette conto** it is worth while

mettima·le mf (-le) troublemaker

mezzadrìa [ddzz] f sharecropping

mezza·dro -dra [ddzz] mf sharecropper

mezzaluna [ddzz] f (**mezzelune**) half-moon; crescent (*symbol of Turkey and Islam*); curved chopping knife; lunette (*of fortification*)

mezzana [ddzz] f procuress; (naut) mizzen

mezzanave [ddzz] f—**a mezzanave** amidships

mezzanino [ddzz] m mezzanine

mezza·no -na [ddzz] adj median; medium; middle || m procurer || f see **mezzana**

mezzanòtte [ddzz] f (**mezzenòtti**) midnight

mezzatinta [ddzz] f (**mezzetinte**) half-tone

méz·zo -za adj overripe, rotten

mèz·zo -za [ddzz] adj half; middle || m half; middle; medium; means; vehicle; **a mezzo (di)** by (*e.g., messenger*); **andar di mezzo** to suffer the consequences; to be the loser; **entrare di mezzo** to interpose oneself; **esserci di mezzo** to be present; to be at stake; **giusto mezzo** happy medium; **in mezzo a** among; in the lap of, e.g., **in mezzo alle delicatezze** in the lap of luxury; **in quel mezzo** meanwhile; **levar di mezzo** to get rid of; **mezzi** means; facilities; **mezzi di comunicazione di massa** mass media; **per mezzo di** by means of

mezzobusto [ddzz] m (**mezzibusti**) (sculp) bust; **a mezzobusto** half-length (*e.g., portrait*)

mezzo·dì [ddzz] *m* (**-dì**) noon; south; South

mezzogiórno [ddzz] *m* noon; south; South

mezzùc·cio [ddzz] *m* (**-ci**) expedient

mi §5 *pron*

miagolare (**miàgolo**) *intr* to meow

miagolì·o *m* (**-i**) meow, mew

mi·ca *f* (**-che**) mica; (obs) crumb ‖ *adv*—**mica male** (coll) not too bad!; **non . . . mica** not . . . ever; not at all

mìc·cia *f* (**-ce**) fuse

michelàc·cio *m* (**-ci**) (coll) lazy bum

micidiale *adj* deadly; (fig) unbearable

mì·cio -cia *mf* (**-ci -cie**) (coll) pussy cat

micrò·bio *m* (**-bi**) microbe

microbiologìa *f* microbiology

microbo *m* microbe

microfà·rad *m* (**-rad**) microfarad

microferrovìa *f* model railroad

micro·film *m* (**-film**) microfilm

microfilmare *tr* to microfilm

micròfono *m* microphone

microlettóre *m* microfilm reader

micromotóre *m* small motor; motorcycle

microónda *f* microwave

microschèda *f* microcard

microscòpi·co -ca *adj* (**-ci -che**) microscopic(al)

microscò·pio *m* (**-pi**) microscope

microsól·co *adj invar* microgroove ‖ *m* (**-chi**) microgroove; microgroove, long-playing record

microtelèfono *m* French telephone, handset

midólla *f* crumb; (coll) marrow

midól·lo *m* (**-la** *fpl*) marrow; (bot & fig) pith; **midollo spinale** (anat) spinal cord

mièle *m* honey

miètere (**mièto**) *tr* to reap; (lit) to kill

mietitrebbiatrice *f* combine

mieti·tóre -trice *mf* reaper, harvester

mietitura *f* harvesting

mi·gliàio *m* (**-gliàia** *fpl*) thousand

mì·glio *m* (**-glia** *fpl*) mile; milestone; **miglio marino** nautical mile; **miglio terrestre** mile ‖ *m* (**-gli**) millet

miglioraménto *m* improvement

migliorare (**migliór**o) *tr*, *intr* (ESSERE & AVERE) & *ref* to improve

miglióre *adj* better; best

migliorìa *f* improvement (*e.g., of real estate*)

mignatta *f* leech

mìgnolo *adj masc* little (*finger or toe*) ‖ *m* little finger; little toe

migrare *intr* to migrate

migra·tóre -trice *adj* & *m* migrant

migrazióne *f* migration

Milano *f* Milan

miliardà·rio -ria *adj* & *mf* (**-ri -rie**) billionaire

miliardo *m* billion

milionà·rio -ria *adj* & *mf* (**-ri -rie**) millionaire

milióne *m* million

milionèsi·mo -ma *adj* & *m* millionth

militante *adj* & *m* militant

militare *adj* military ‖ *m* soldier ‖ *v* (**mìlito**) *intr* to be a member; to militate; to be in the armed forces; **militare in** to be a member of (*e.g., a party*)

militaré·sco -sca *adj* (**-schi -sche**) military, soldierly

militarismo *m* militarism

militari·sta -sti -ste) *adj* militaristic ‖ *mf* militarist

militarizzare [ddzz] *tr* to militarize; to fortify

milite *m* militiaman; soldier; **milite del fuoco** fireman; **Milite Ignoto** Unknown Soldier

militesènte *adj* exempt from military service ‖ *m* man exempt from military service

milizia *f* militia; (mil) service; struggle; **milizie celesti** heavenly host

miliziano *m* militiaman

millantare *tr* to boast of ‖ *ref* to brag, boast

millanta·tóre -trice *mf* braggart

millanterìa *f* bragging

mille *adj*, *m* & *pron* (**mila**) thousand, a thousand, one thousand ‖ **il Mille** the eleventh century; the year one thousand

millecènto *m* eleven hundred ‖ *f* car with a 1100 cc. motor

millefò·glie *m* (**-glie**) puff-paste cake

millenà·rio -ria (**-ri -rie**) *adj* millennial ‖ *m* millennium

millèn·nio *m* (**-ni**) millennium

millepiè·di *m* (**-di**) millipede

millèsi·mo -ma *adj* & *m* thousandth

milliam·père *m* (**-père**) milliampere

milligrammo *m* milligram

millimetra·to -ta *adj* divided into squares of one millimeter square

millìmetro *m* millimeter

milli·vòlt *m* (**-vòlt**) millivolt

milza *f* spleen

mimare *tr* & *intr* to mime

mimetizzare [ddzz] *tr* (mil) to camouflage

mimetizzazióne [ddzz] *f* (mil) camouflage

mìmi·co -ca (**-ci -che**) *adj* mimic; sign (*language*) ‖ *f* mimicry; (theat) gestures; (theat) miming

mi·mo -ma *mf* mime ‖ *m* (orn) mockingbird

mina *f* lead (*of pencil*); (mil) mine; **mina anticarro** antitank mine; **mina antiuomo** antipersonnel mine

minaccévole *adj* (lit) threatening

minàc·cia *f* (**-ce**) threat, menace

minacciare §128 *tr* to threaten, menace

minacció·so -sa [s] *adj* threatening

minare *tr* to mine; to undermine

minaréto *m* minaret

minatóre *m* miner

minatò·rio -ria *adj* (**-ri -rie**) threatening

minchionare (**minchióno**) *tr* (slang) to make a sucker of

minchióne *m* (slang) sucker

minerale *adj* mineral ‖ *m* mineral; ore

mineralogìa *f* mineralogy

minerà·rio -ria *adj* (**-ri -rie**) mining

minèr·vo -va *m* (**-va**) safety match

minèstra *f* vegetable soup

minestróne *m* minestrone; hodgepodge

mìngere §199 *intr* to urinate

mingherlì·no -na *adj* frail, thin

miniare §287 *tr* to paint in miniature; to illuminate

miniatura *f* miniature

miniaturizzare [ddzz] *tr* to miniaturize

miniaturizzazióne [ddzz] *f* miniaturization

minièra *f* mine

mini·gòlf *m* (**-gòlf**) miniature golf

minigònna *f* miniskirt

mìnima *f* lowest temperature; (mus) minim

minimizzare [ddzz] *tr* to minimize

mìni·mo -ma *adj* smallest, least; minimum ‖ *m* minimum; **al minimo** at the least; **girare al minimo** or **tenere il minimo** (aut) to idle ‖ *f* see **minima**

mìnio *m* red lead; rouge

ministeriale *adj* ministerial

ministèro *m* ministry; cabinet; department; **pubblico ministero** public prosecutor

ministra *f* (joc) wife of minister; (joc) female minister; (poet) minister

ministro *m* minister; secretary; administrator; **ministro degli Esteri** foreign minister; (U.S.A.) Secretary of State

minoranza *f* minority

minorare (**minóro**) *tr* to lessen; to disable

minora·to -ta *adj* disabled ‖ *mf* disabled person

minorazióne *f* reduction; disability

minóre *adj* smaller, lesser; minor; smallest, least; younger; youngest ‖ *m* minor

minorènne *adj* underage ‖ *mf* minor

minorìle *adj* juvenile (*e.g.*, *court*)

minori·tà *f* (**-tà**) minority

minuétto *m* minuet

minù·gia *f* (**-gia & -gie**) (mus) catgut

minùsco·lo -la *adj* small (*letter*); diminutive ‖ *m & f* small letter

minuta *f* first draft, rough copy

minutàglia *f* trifles; small fry

minutante *m* secretary; retailer

minuteria *f* trinkets, notions

minu·to -ta *adj* minute; small (*change*); common (*people*) ‖ *m* minute; **al minuto** retail; **di minuto in minuto** at any moment; **minuto secondo** second; **nel minuto** in detail; **per minuto** minutely ‖ *f* see **minuta**

minùzia *f* trifle; minuzie minutiae

minuzió·so -sa [s] *adj* meticulous

minùzzolo *m* scrap, crumb; small boy

mìo mia §6 *adj & pron poss* (**mièi mie**)

mìope *adj* nearsighted ‖ *mf* nearsighted person

miopìa *f* nearsightedness

mira *f* aim; sight; target, goal; **prendere di mira** to aim at; to torment

miràbile *adj* admirable ‖ *m* wonder

mirabìlia *fpl* wonders; **far mirabilia** to perform wonders; **dir mirabilia di** to speak highly of

mirabolante *adj* amazing, astonishing

miracola·to -ta *adj* miraculously cured ‖ *mf* miraculously cured person

miràcolo *m* miracle; wonder; **dir mira-**

coli di to praise to the skies; **per miracolo** by mere chance

miracoló·so -sa [s] *adj* miraculous; wonderful

miràg·gio *m* (**-gi**) mirage

mirare *tr* (lit) to look at; (lit) to aim at ‖ *intr* to aim; **mirare a** to aim at; **mirare a + inf** to aim to + inf; **to intend to + inf**

mirìade *f* myriad

mirino *m* sight (*of gun*); (phot) finder

mirra *f* myrrh

mirtìllo *m* blueberry; whortleberry, huckleberry

mìrto *m* myrtle

misantropìa *f* misanthropy

misàntro·po -pa *adj* misanthropic ‖ *mf* misanthrope

miscèla *f* mixture, blend

miscelare (**miscèlo**) *tr* to mix, blend

miscellàne·o -a *adj* miscellaneous ‖ *f* miscellany

mischia *f* fight; (sports) scrimmage

mischiare §287 *tr* to mix, blend; to shuffle (*cards*) ‖ *ref* to mix

misconóscere §134 *tr* to not appreciate, undervalue

miscredènte *adj* misbelieving ‖ *mf* misbeliever

miscù·glio *m* (**-gli**) mixture, blend

miseràbile *adj* pitiful, miserable; poor, wretched

miseran·do -da *adj* pitiable

miserère *m* Miserere; **essere al miserere** to be in one's last hours

miserévole *adj* pitiful; pitiable

misèria *f* destitution, misery; wretchedness; lack, want; trifle; **piangere miseria** to cry poverty

misericòrdia *f* mercy

misericordió·so -sa [s] *adj* merciful

mìse·ro -ra *adj* unhappy, wretched; poor; meager; mean; too small, too short

misfatto *m* misdeed, misdoing

misirìz·zi [s] *m* (**-zi**) tumbler (*toy*); (fig) chameleon

misògi·no -na *adj* misogynous ‖ *m* misogynist

missile *adj & m* missile; **missile antimissile** antimissile missile; **missile intercontinentale** I.C.B.M.; **missile teleguidato** guided missile

missilìsti·co -ca *adj* (**-ci -che**) missile

missionà·rio -ria *adj & m* (**-ri -rie**) missionary

missióne *f* mission

missiva *f* missive

misterió·so -sa [s] *adj* mysterious

mistèro *m* mystery

mìstica *f* mysticism; mystical literature

misticismo *m* mysticism

mìsti·co -ca *adj & mf* (**-ci -che**) mystic ‖ *f* see **mistica**

mistificare §197 (**mistìfico**) *tr* to hoax

mistificazióne *f* hoax

mì·sto -sta *adj* mixed ‖ *m* mixture; mixed train

mistura *f* mixture

misura *f* measure; size; bounds; fitting; **a misura che** in proportion as; **di**

misura (sports) with a narrow margin; su misura made-to-order

misuràbile *adj* measurable

misurare *tr* to measure; to deliver (*e.g., a slap*); to budget (*expenses*); to try on (*clothes*); to weigh (*the outcome*) || *intr* to measure || *ref* to compete; to limit oneself; misurarsi con to try conclusions with

misura·to -ta *adj* moderate; scanty

misurino *m* measuring spoon or cup

mite *adj* mild; tame; low (*price*)

mìti·co -ca *adj* (-ci -che) mythical

mitigare §209 (mìtigo) *tr* to mitigate; to assuage, allay || *ref* to abate

mìtilo *m* mussel

mito *m* myth

mitologìa *f* mythology

mitològi·co -ca *adj* (-ci -che) mythologic(al)

mitòmane *mf* compulsive liar

mi·tra *m* (-tra) submachine gun || *f* miter

mitràglia *f* grapeshot; scrap iron; (coll) machine gun

mitragliare §280 (mitràglio) *tr* to machine-gun

mitragliatrice *f* machine gun

mitraglièra *f* heavy machine gun

mitraglière *m* machine gunner

mittènte *mf* sender; shipper

mo' *m*—apocopated form of modo by way of; a mo' d'esempio as an illustration

mòbile *adj* movable; personal (*property*); (fig) fickle; (rr) rolling (*stock*) || *m* piece of furniture; cabinet; (phys) body; mobili furniture

mobìlia *f* furniture

mobiliare *adj* (fin) security; (law) movable || §287 (mobìlio) *tr* to furnish

mobilière *m* furniture maker; furniture dealer

mobilità *f* mobility

mobilitare (mobìlito) *tr & intr* to mobilize

mobilitazióne *f* mobilization

mò·ca *m* (-ca) mocha; caffè moca Mocha coffee

mocassino *m* mocassin

mocciare §197 (móccico) *intr* (slang) to snivel; (slang) to run (*said of the nose*); (slang) to whimper

moccicó·so -sa [s] *adj* (slang) snotty

móc·cio *m* (-ci) snot, snivel

mocció·so -sa [s] *adj* snotty || *m* brat

mòccolo *m* end of candle, snuff; (joc) snot; (slang) curse word; reggere il moccolo a qlcu to be a third party to a couple's necking

mòda *f* fashion, vogue; andar di moda to be fashionable; to be all the rage; fuori moda outdated

modali·tà *f* (-tà) modality; method

modanatura *f* molding

mòdano *m* mold

modèlla *f* model

modellare (modèllo) *tr* to model; to mold || *ref* to pattern oneself

modella·tóre -trice *mf* pattern maker; molder

modellino *m* (archit) model, maquette

modèllo *adj invar* model || *m* model; fashion; style; pattern

moderare (mòdero) *tr* to moderate, control

moderatézza *f* moderation

modera·to -ta *adj* moderate; (mus) moderato || *m* middle-of-the-roader

modera·tóre -trice *adj* moderating || *m* moderator

modernizzare [ddzz] *tr & ref* to modernize

modèr·no -na *adj & m* modern

modèstia *f* modesty; scantiness, meagerness

modè·sto -sta *adj* modest; humble

mòdi·co -ca *adj* (-ci -che) reasonable

modìfi·ca *f* (-che) modification; alteration

modificare §197 (modìfico) *tr* to modify; to change; to alter

modiglióne *m* (archit) modillion

modista *f* milliner

modisterìa *f* millinery; millinery shop

mòdo *m* manner, mode, way; custom; idiom; (gram) mood; (mus) mode; · ad ogni modo anyhow; nevertheless; ad un modo equally; a modo proper; properly; a suo modo in his own way; bei modi good manners; di modo che so that; in malo modo poorly; in modo da so as to; in nessun modo by no means; in ogni modo anyhow; in qualche modo somehow; modo di dire idiom; turn of phrase; modo di fare behavior; modo di vedere opinion; per modo di dire so to speak

modulare (mòdulo) *tr* to modulate

modulazióne *f* modulation; modulazione d'ampiezza amplitude modulation;· modulazione di frequenza frequency modulation

mòdulo *m* module; blank, form

moffétta *f* skunk

mògano *m* mahogany

mòg·gio *m* (-gi) bushel

mò·gio -gia *adj* (-gi -gie) downcast, crestfallen

mó·glie *f* (-gli) wife

moìne *fpl* blandishments

mòla *f* grindstone; (coll) millstone

molare *adj* grinding; molar || *m* molar || *v* (mòlo) *tr* to grind

molassa *f* molasse, sandstone

molatóre *m* grinder (*person*); sander (*person*)

molatrice *f* grinder (*machine*); sander (*machine*); molatrice di pavimenti floor sander

mòle *f* size; pile; bulk, mass; huge structure

molècola *f* molecule

molestare (molèsto) *tr* to bother, annoy

molèstia *f* bother, trouble, annoyance

molè·sto -sta *adj* bothersome, troublesome

molibdèno *m* molybdenum

molinétto *m* (naut) winch

mòlla *f* spring; (fig) mainspring; molla a balestra leaf spring; molle tongs; molle del letto bedspring; prendere qlco con le molle to keep at a reasonable distance from s.th

mollare (mòllo) *tr* to let go; to slacken; to drop *(anchor)*; (coll) to soak ‖ *intr* to give up; (coll) to soak; **molla!** (coll) cut it out!

mòlle *adj* wet, soaked; soft; mild; easy *(life)*; weak *(character)*; flexible ‖ *m* softness; soft ground; **tenere a molle** to soak

mollécca *f* soft-shell crab

molleggiaménto *m* suspension; springiness

molleggiare §290 (mollèggio) *tr* to provide with springs, to make elastic; (aut) to provide with suspension ‖ *intr* to be springy, to have bounce ‖ *ref* to bounce along

mollég∙gio *m* (-gi) springs; (aut) suspension; springiness

mollétta *f* hairpin; clothespin; **mollette** sugar tongs

mollettièra *f* puttee

mollettóne *m* swansdown

mollézza *f* softness

molli∙ca *f* (-che) crumb *(soft inner portion of bread)*; **molliche** crumbs

mollifìcare §197 (mollìfico) *tr* & *ref* to mollify; to soften

mòl∙lo -la *adj* soft ‖ *m*—**mettere a mollo** to soak ‖ *f* see **molla**

mollu∙sco *m* (-schi) mollusk

mòlo *m* pier, wharf

moltéplice *adj* multiple, manifold

moltilaterale *adj* multilateral, many-sided

moltipli∙ca *f* (-che) front sprocket *(of bicycle)*

moltiplicare §197 (moltìplico) *tr* & *ref* to multiply

moltitùdine *f* multitude, crowd

mól∙to -ta *adj* much, a lot of; very, e.g., **ho molta sete** I am very thirsty ‖ *pron* much; a lot; **a dir molto** mostly; **ci corre molto** there is a great difference ‖ **mol∙ti -te** *adj* & *pron* many ‖ **molto** *adv* very; quite; much; a lot; widely; long; **fra non molto** before long; **non . . . molto** (coll) not . . . at all

momentàne∙o -a *adj* momentary

moménto *m* moment; opportune time; (slang) trifle; (phys) momentum; **dal momento che** since; **per il momento** for the time being; **sul momento** this very moment

mòna∙ca *f* (-che) nun

monacale *adj* monachal, conventual

monacato *m* monkhood

monachésimo *m* monachism, monasticism

monachina *f* little nun; **monachine** sparks

mòna∙co *m* (-ci) monk; (archit) king post ‖ **Monaco** *m* Monaco ‖ *f* Munich

monar∙ca *m* (-chi) monarch

monarchìa *f* monarchy

monàrchi∙co -ca *adj* (-ci -che) monarchical; monarchist(ic) *(advocating a monarch)* ‖ *mf* monarchist

monastèro *m* monastery

monàsti∙co -ca *adj* (-ci -che) monastic(al)

moncherino *m* stump *(without hand)*

món∙co -ca *adj* (-chi -che) one-handed; one-armed; incomplete ‖ *mf* cripple

moncóne *m* stump

mondana *f* prostitute

mondani∙tà *f* (-tà) worldliness

monda∙no -na *adj* mundane; worldly; society; fashionable ‖ *m* playboy ‖ *f* see **mondana**

mondare (móndo) *tr* to peel, pare; to thresh; to weed; to prune; (fig) to cleanse

mondari∙so *mf* (-so) rice weeder

mondez∙zàio *m* (-zài) dump

mondiale *adj* world, world-wide; (coll) stupendous

mondiglia *f* chaff; trash; refuse

mondina *f* rice weeder

món∙do da *adj* clean-peeled; (lit) pure ‖ *m* world; hopscotch; (coll) heap, bunch; **bel mondo** smart set; **cascasse il mondo!** (coll) come what may!; **da che mondo è mondo** since the world began; **essere nel mondo della luna** to be absent-minded; **mandare all'altro mondo** (coll) to send packing; **mettere al mondo** to give birth to; **mondo della luna** world of fancy; **un mondo a lot; venire al mondo** to be born ‖ **Mondo** *m*—**Terzo Mondo** Third World

monega∙sco -sca *adj* & *mf* (-schi -sche) Monacan

monellerìa *f* prank

monèl∙lo -la *mf* urchin, brat ‖ *f* romp

monéta *f* money; coin; piece of money; purse *(in horse races)*; change; **batter moneta** to mint money; **moneta sonante** cash

monetà∙rio -ria (-ri -rie) *adj* monetary ‖ *m*—**falso monetario** counterfeiter

monetizzare [ddzz] *tr* to express in money; to transform into cash

mòngo∙lo -la *adj* & *mf* Mongolian

monile *m* necklace; jewel

mònito *m* admonition, warning

monitóre *m* monitor

mònna *f* (obs) lady; (coll) monkey

monoàlbero *adj invar* (aut) single-camshaft, valve-in-head *(distribution)*

monoaurale *adj* monaural

monoblòc∙co -co (-co) *adj* single-block ‖ *m* (aut) cylinder block

monocilìndri∙co -ca *adj* (-ci -che) (mach) single-cylinder

monòco∙lo -la *adj* one-eyed ‖ *m* monocle

monocolóre *adj invar* one-color; one-party

monofa∙se *adj* (-si & -se) single-phase

monogamìa *f* monogamy

monòga∙mo -ma *adj* monogamous ‖ *m* monogamist

monografìa *f* monograph

monogram∙ma *m* (-mi) monogram

monolìti∙co -ca *adj* (-ci -che) monolithic

monolito *m* monolith

monòlo∙go *m* (-ghi) monologue

monomanìa *f* monomania

monò·mio *m* (-mi) monomial

monopàttino *m* scooter

monopèt·to (-to) *adj* single-breasted ‖ *m* single-breasted suit

monoplano *m* (aer) monoplane

monopò·lio *m* (-li) monopoly

monopolizzare [ddzz] *tr* to monopolize

monopósto *adj invar* one-man ‖ *m* single-seater

monorotàia *adj invar* single-track ‖ *f* monorail

monoscò·pio *m* (-pi) (telv) test pattern

monosìlla·bo -ba *adj* monosyllabic ‖ *m* monosyllable

monòssido *m* monoxide

monoteìsti·co -ca *adj* (-ci -che) monotheistic

monotipìa *f* monotype

monotipo *m* monotype

monotonìa *f* monotony

monòto·no -na *adj* monotonous

monsignóre *m* monsignor

monsóne *m* monsoon

mónta *f* horseback riding; stud; jockey

montacàri·chi *m* (-chi) freight elevator

montàg·gio *m* (-gi) (mach) assembly; (mov) editing; (mov) montage

montagna *f* mountain; **montagna di ghiaccio** iceberg; **montagne russe** roller coaster

montagnó·so -sa [s] *adj* mountainous

montana·ro -ra *adj* mountain ‖ *mf* mountaineer

monta·no -na *adj* mountain

montante *adj* rising ‖ *m* riser, upright; (football) goal post; (aer) strut; (boxing) uppercut; (com) aggregate amount

montare (mónto) *tr* to mount; to go up (*the stairs*); to set (*jewels*); to frame (*a painting*); to whip (*e.g., eggs*); to excite; to exaggerate (*news*); to decorate (*a house*); to cover (*said of a male animal*); (mach) to assemble; (mov) to edit; **montare la testa a** to excite; to give a swell head to ‖ *intr* (ESSERE) to jump; to climb; to go up; to rise; to swell; **montare alla testa a** to go to the head of; **montare in collera** to get angry ‖ *impers*—**non monta** it doesn't matter, never mind

monta·tóre -trice *mf* (mach) assembler; (mov) editor

montatura *f* assembly; frame (*of glasses*); appliqué; setting (*of gem*); (journ) ballyhoo; (mov) editing; **montatura pubblicitaria** publicity stunt

montavivan·de *m* (-de) dumbwaiter

mónte *m* mountain; bank; mount (*in palmistry*); (cards) discard; **a monte** uphill; upstream; **andare a monte** to fail; **mandare a monte** to cause to fail; **monte di pietà** pawnbroker's; **monte di premi** pot (*in a lottery*)

montenegri·no -na *adj* & *mf* Montenegrin

montessoria·no -na *adj* Montessori

montóne *m* ram; mutton; rounded stone

montuó·so -sa [s] *adj* mountainous

montura *f* uniform

monumentale *adj* monumental

monuménto *m* monument

moquètte *f* (**moquètte**) wall-to-wall carpeting

mòra *f* mulberry; blackberry; brunette; Moorish woman; arrears; penalty (*for arrears*); (archaic) heap of stones

morale *adj* moral ‖ *m* morale; **giù di morale** downcast; **su di morale** in high spirits ‖ *f* morals, ethics; moral (*of a fable*)

moraleggiare §290 (**moraléggio**) *intr* to moralize

moralismo *m* moralism

morali·tà *f* (-tà) morality; morals

moralizzare [ddzz] *tr* & *intr* to moralize

moratòria *f* moratorium

morbidézza *f* softness

mòrbi·do -da *adj* soft; sleek; pliable ‖ *m* soft ground

morbillo *m* measles

mòrbo *m* disease; plague

morbó·so -sa [s] *adj* morbid

mòrchia *f* sediment; dregs of oil

mordace *adj* biting, mordacious

mordènte *adj* biting; (chem) mordant; (mach) interlocking ‖ *s* strength; (chem) mordant

mòrdere §200 *tr* to bite; to grab; to corrode; **mordere il freno** to champ the bit

mordicchiare §287 (**mordìcchio**) *tr* to nibble

morèl·lo -la *adj* blackish; black (*horse*) ‖ *m* black horse

morènte *adj* dying ‖ *mf* dying person

moré·sco -sca (-schi -sche) *adj* Moresque, Moorish ‖ *f* Moorish dance

morét·to -ta *adj* brunet ‖ *m* Negro boy; dark-skinned boy; chocolate-covered ice-cream bar ‖ *f* Negro girl; dark-skinned girl; mask; (orn) scaup duck

morfè·ma *m* (-mi) morpheme

morfina *f* morphine

morfinòmane *mf* morphine addict

morfologìa *f* morphology

morìa *f* pestilence; high mortality

moribón·do -da *adj* moribund

morigera·to -ta *adj* temperate, moderate

morire §201 *intr* (ESSERE) to die; to die out; to end (*said of a street*); **morire di noia** to be bored to death

moritu·ro -ra *adj* about to die, doomed

mormóne *mf* Mormon

mormorare (mórmoro) *tr* to murmur; to whisper ‖ *intr* to murmur; to whisper; to babble (*said of a brook*); to rustle; to gossip

mormorì·o *m* (-i) whisper; murmur

mò·ro -ra *adj* Moorish; dark-skinned; dark-brown ‖ *m* Moor ‖ *m* mulberry tree ‖ *f* see **mora**

morosi·tà [s] *f* (-tà) delinquency (*in paying one's bills*)

moró·so -sa [s] *adj* delinquent (*in paying one's bills*) ‖ *m* (coll) boyfriend; **i morosi** (coll) the lovers ‖ *f* (coll) girl friend

mòrsa *f* vise; (archit) toothing

morsétto *m* clamp; (elec) binding post

morsicare §197 (**mòrsico**) *tr* to bite
morsicatura *f* bite
morsicchiare §287 (**morsìcchio**) *tr* to nibble
mòrso *m* bite; bit
mor·tàio *m* (**-tài**) mortar
mortale *adj* mortal; deadly || *m* mortal
mortali·tà *f* (**-tà**) mortality
mortarétto *m* firecracker
mòrte *f* death; end; **averla a morte con** to harbor hatred for; **morte civile** (*law*) attainder, loss of civil rights
mortèlla *f* myrtle
mortificare §197 (**mortìfico**) *tr* to mortify || *ref* to feel ashamed
mòr·to -ta *adj* dead; still (*life*); **morto di fame** dying of hunger; **morto di paura** scared to death || *mf* dead person, deceased || *m* hidden treasure; (*cards*) dummy, widow; **fare il morto** to float on one's back; to play possum; **morto di fame** ne'er-do-well, good-for-nothing; **suonare a morto** to toll
mortò·rio *m* (**-ri**) funeral
mortuà·rio -ria *adj* (**-ri -rie**) mortuary
mosài·co -ca (**-ci -che**) *adj* Mosaic || *m* mosaic
mó·sca *f* (**-sche**) fly; imperial (*beard*); **mosca bianca** one in a million; **mosca cieca** blindman's buff; **fare venire la mosca al naso a** to make angry || **Mosca** *f* Moscow
moscaiòla *f* fly netting; flytrap
moscardino *m* dandy; (*zool*) dormouse
moscatèl·lo -la *adj* muscat || *m* muscatel
moscato *m* muscat grape; muscat wine
moscerino *m* gnat
moschèa *f* mosque
moschettière *m* musketeer; Italian National soccer player
moschétto *m* musket
moschettóne *m* snap hook
moschici·da *adj* (**-di -de**) fly-killing
mó·scio -scia *adj* (**-sci -sce**) flabby, soft
moscóne *m* big fly; pesky suitor
moscovi·ta *adj* & *mf* (**-ti -te**) Muscovite
Mosè *m* Moses
mòssa *f* gesture; movement; move; fake; post; **fare la mossa** to sprout (*said of plants*); **mossa di corpo** bowel movement; **prendere le mosse** to begin; **stare sulle mosse** to be about to begin; to be eager to take off (*said of a horse*)
mossière *m* starter (*in a race*)
mòs·so -sa *adj* moved; in motion; plowed; rough (*sea*); blurred (*picture*); wavy (*hair; ground*) || *f* see **mossa**
mostarda *f* mustard; candied fruit
mósto *m* must
móstra *f* show; pretense, simulation; exhibit; display window; lapel; face (*of watch*); sample; (*mil*) insignia; (*obs*) military parade; **far mostra di sé** to show off; **mettersi in mostra** to show off
mostrare (**móstro**) *tr* to show; to put on; **mostrare a dito** to point to;

mostrare la corda to be threadbare || *ref* to show up; to show oneself
mostreggiatura *f* lapel; cuff
mostrina *f* (mil) insignia
móstro *m* monster
mostruó·so -sa [s] *adj* monstruous
mòta *f* mud, mire
mo·tèl *m* (**-tèl**) motel
motivare *tr* to cause; to justify
motivazióne *f* justification, reason
motivo *m* motive, reason; motif; theme; (coll) tune; **a motivo di** because of; **motivo per cui** wherefore
mò·to *m* (**-ti**) motion; movement; emotion; riot; **mettere in moto** to start || *f* (**-to**) (coll) motorcycle
motobar·ca *f* (**-che**) motorboat
motocannonièra *f* gunboat
motocarro *m* three-wheeler (*truck*)
motocarrozzétta *f* three-wheeler (*vehicle with sidecar*)
motociclétta *f* motorcycle
motocicli·sta *mf* (**-sti -ste**) motorcyclist
motocorazza·to -ta *adj* armored, panzer
motofalciatrice *f* power mower
motofurgóne *m* delivery truck
motolàn·cia *f* (**-ce**) motorboat, speedboat
motonàuti·co -ca (**-ci -che**) *adj* motorboat || *f* motorboating
motonave *f* motor ship
motopescheréc·cio *m* (**-ci**) motor fishing boat
mo·tóre -trice *adj* motive (*power*); (mach) drive || *m* motor; engine; car; **a motore** motorized, motor; **motore rotativo** (aut) rotary engine; **primo motore** prime mover || *f* see **motrice**
motorétta *f* motor scooter
motorino *m* small motor; motor bicycle; **motorino d'avviamento** (aut) starter
motori·sta *m* (**-sti**) mechanic
motoristi·co -ca *adj* (**-ci -che**) motor
motorizzare [ddzz] *tr* to motorize
motoscafo *m* motorboat; **motoscafo da corsa** speedboat
motosé·ga *f* (**-ghe**) chain saw
motosilurante *f* torpedo boat
motoveìcolo *m* motor vehicle
motovelièro *m* motor sailer
motrice *f* (rr) engine, motor; (aut) tractor; **motrice a vapore** steam engine
motteggiare §290 (**mottéggio**) *tr* to mock, jeer at || *intr* to jest
mottég·gio *m* (**-gi**) mockery, jest
mòtto *m* witticism; motto; (lit) word
movènte *m* stimulus, motive
movènza *f* bearing, carriage; flow (*of a sentence*); cadence
movìbile *adj* movable
movimenta·to -ta *adj* lively; eventful
moviménto *m* motion, movement; traffic; **movimento di cassa** cash turnover
moviòla *f* (mov) viewer and splicer
mozióne *f* motion; (lit) movement
mozzare (**mózzo**) *tr* to lop off; to sever; **mozzare la testa a** to cut off the head of

mozzicóne *m* stump; butt (*e.g., of cigar*)

móz·zo -za *adj* cut off; truncated; cropped (*ears*); docked (*tail*); hard (*breathing*) ‖ *m* cabin boy; mozzo di stalla stable boy

mòzzo [ddzz] *m* hub

muc·ca *f* (-che) milch cow

mùc·chio *m* (-chi) pile, heap; bunch

mucillàgine *f* mucilage

mu·co *m* (-chi) mucus, phlegm

mucó·so -sa [s] *adj* mucous ‖ *f* mucous membrane

muda *f* molt

muffa *f* mold; mildew; fare la muffa to be musty

muffire §176 *intr* (ESSERE) to be musty

mùffola *f* mitten; muffle (*of furnace*)

muflóne *m* mouflon

mugghiare §287 (mùgghio) *intr* to bellow; to roar

mùggine *m* (ichth) mullet

muggire §176 & (muggo) *intr* to moo, low; to roar; to howl

muggito *m* bellow; moo, low; roar

mughétto *m* lily of the valley

mu·gnàio -gnàia *mf* (-gnài -gnàie) miller

mugolare (mùgolo) *intr* to yelp; to moan

mugolì·o *m* (-ì) yelp; moan

mugò·lio *m* (-li) pine tar

mugugnare *intr* (coll) to mumble; (coll) to grumble

mugugno *m* (coll) grumble

mulattière *m* mule driver, muleteer

mulattiè·ro -ra *adj* mule ‖ *f* mule track

mulat·to -ta *adj* & *mf* mulatto

muliebre *adj* womanly, feminine

mulinare *tr* to twirl; to scheme ‖ *intr* to whirl; to muse; to buzz (*in the mind*)

mulinèllo *m* twirl; whirlpool; whirlwind; fishing reel; whirligig; fare mulinello con to twirl

mulino *m* mill; mulino ad acqua water mill; mulino a vento windmill

mu·lo -la *mf* mule; (slang) bastard

multa *f* penalty, fine

multare *tr* to fine

multilaterale *adj* multilateral, many-sided

mùlti·plo -pla *adj* & *m* multiple

mùmmia *f* mummy

mummificare §197 (mummìfico) *tr* to mummify

mùngere §183 *tr* to milk

mungi·tóre -trice *mf* milker ‖ *f* milking machine; milk maid

mungitura *f* milking

municipale *adj* municipal, city

municipalizzazióne [ddzz] *f* municipalization; city management

munici·pio *m* (-pi) municipality; city council; city hall

munificènza *f* munificence

munìfi·co -ca *adj* (-ci -che) munificent

munire §176 *tr* to fortify; to provide; munire di to equip with ‖ *ref* to provide oneself

munizióne *f* (obs) fortification; munizioni ammunition; building supplies

muòvere §202 *tr* to move; to wag; to

propel, run; to lift (*one's finger*); to take (*a step*); to pose (*a question*); to stir up (*laughter*); to institute (*a lawsuit*); muovere accusa a to reproach ‖ *intr* (ESSERE) to begin; to move, start ‖ *ref* to move; to travel; to stir; to set out; to be moved; muoviti! hurry up!

mura *fpl* see muro

muràglia *f* wall; (fig) obstacle; muraglia cinese Chinese Wall

muraglióne *m* high wall, rampart

murale *adj* & *m* mural

murare *tr* to wall; to wall in ‖ *intr* to build a wall; murare a secco to build a dry wall ‖ *ref* to close oneself in

murata *f* (naut) bulwark

muratóre *m* bricklayer, mason

muratura *f* bricklaying, stonework

muriàti·co -ca *adj* (-ci -che) muriatic

mu·ro *m* (-ri) wall; muro del pianto Wailing Wall; muro del suono sound barrier ‖ *m* (-ra *fpl*)—mura walls (*of a city*)

musa *f* muse

muschia·to -ta *adj* musk (*e.g., ox*)

mù·schio *m* (-schi) musk; (coll) moss

mu·sco *m* (-schi) moss

mùscolo *m* muscle; (fig) sinew; (coll) mussel

muscoló·so -sa [s] *adj* muscular

muscó·so -sa [s] *adj* (lit) mossy

musèo *m* museum

museruòla *f* muzzle

musétta *f* nose bag

mùsi·ca *f* (-che) music; band; cambiare musica to change one's tune

musicale *adj* musical

musicante *adj* music-playing (*angels*) ‖ *mf* band player; second-rate musician

musicare §197 (mùsico) *tr* to set to music

musicassétta *f* cassette, tape cartridge

music-hall *m* (-hall) *m* vaudeville, burlesque

musici·sta *mf* (-sti -ste) musician

musicologìa *f* musicology

musicòlo·go *m* (-gi) musicologist

muso *m* muzzle, snout; (coll) mug; (fig) nose; avere il muso lungo to make a long face; mettere il muso to pout

musó·ne -na *mf* pouter, sulker

mussare *tr* to publish with great fanfare (*a piece of news*) ‖ *intr* to foam (*said of wine*)

mùssola or mussolina *f* muslin

mussolinia·no -na *adj* of Mussolini

mùssolo *m* mussel

mustàc·chio *m* (-chi) shroud (*of bowsprit*); mustacchi moustache

musulma·no -na [s] *adj* & *mf* Moslem

muta *f* change; shift; molt; set (*of sails*); pack (*of hounds*); (mil) watch

mutàbile *adj* changeable

mutande *fpl* shorts, briefs, drawers

mutandine *fpl* panties; mutandine da bagno trunks

mutare *tr, intr* (ESSERE) & *ref* to change

mutazióne *f* mutation; (biol) mutation, sport

mutévole *adj* changeable; fickle

mutilare (mùtilo) *tr* to mutilate, maim
mutila·to -ta *adj* mutilated || *mf* cripple; amputee; **mutilato di guerra** disabled veteran
mutismo *m* silence, willful silence; (*pathol*) dumbness
mu·to -ta *adj* mute; dumb; silent (*movie*); unexpressed || *mf* mute || *f* see **muta**
mùtria *f* sulking attitude; proud demeanor

mùtua *f* mutual benefit society; medical insurance; **mettersi in mutua** to go on sick leave
mutuali·tà *f* (**-tà**) mutuality; mutual benefit institutions
mutuare (mùtuo) *tr* to borrow; to lend
mutua·to -ta *mf* person insured by mutual benefit society; person insured by medical insurance
mù·tuo -tua *adj* mutual; borrowing || *m* loan || *f* see **mutua**

N

N, n [ˈɛnne] *m & f* twelfth letter of the Italian alphabet
nababbo *m* nabob
Nabucodònosor *m* Nebuchadnezzar
nàcchera *f* castanet
nafta *f* crude oil; naphta; Diesel oil
naftalina *f* naphthalene
nàia *f* cobra; (slang) army discipline; (slang) military service
nàiade *f* naiad
nàilon *m* nylon
nanna *f* sleep (*of child*); **fare la nanna** to sleep (*said of child*)
na·no -na *adj & mf* dwarf
nàpalm *m* napalm
napoleòne *m* napoleon (*gold coin*) || **Napoleone** *m* Napoleon
napoleòni·co -ca *adj* (**-ci -che**) Napoleonic
napoleta·no -na *adj & mf* Neapolitan || *f* espresso coffee machine
Nàpoli *f* Naples
nappa *f* tassel; tuft; kid (*leather*)
narciso *m* narcissus
narcòti·co -ca *adj & m* (**-ci -che**) narcotic
narcotizzare [ddzz] *tr* to drug, dope; to anesthetize
narghi·lè *m* (**-lè**) hookah
narice *f* nostril
narrare *tr* to narrate, tell, recount
narrati·vo -va *adj* narrative; fictional || *f* narrative; fiction
narra·tóre -trice *mf* narrator, storyteller
narrazióne *f* narration; tale, story; narrative
nasale [s] *adj & f* nasal
nascènte *adj* nascent; budding; rising (*sun*); dawning (*day*)
nàscere *m* beginning, origin || §203 *intr* (ESSERE) to be born; to bud; to shoot; to dawn; to rise; to spring up; **nascere con la camicia** to be born with a silver spoon in one's mouth
nàscita *f* birth; birthday; origin
nascitu·ro -ra *adj* unborn, future || *mf* unborn child
nascóndere §204 *tr* to hide; **nascondere a** to hide from || *ref* to hide; to lurk
nascondì·glio *m* (**-gli**) hiding place; hideout; cache
nascondino *m* hide-and-seek; **giocare a nascondino** to play hide-and-seek
nascó·sto -sta *adj* hidden, concealed; secret; **di nascosto** secretly

nasèllo [s] *m* catch (*of latch*); (ichth) hake
naslèra [s] *f* nose ring
naso [s] *m* nose; (fig) face; **aver buon naso** to have a keen sense of smell; **ficcare il naso negli affari degli altri** to pry into the affairs of others; **menare per il naso** to lead by the nose; **naso aduneo** hooknose; **restare con un palmo di naso** to be duped
nassa *f* pot (*for fishing*); **nassa per aragoste** lobster pot
nastrino *m* ribbon; badge
nastro *m* ribbon; band; tape; streamer; tape measure; **nastro del cappello** hatband; **nastro isolante** friction tape; **nastro per capelli** hair ribbon
nastùr·zio *m* (**-zi**) nasturtium
natale *adj* native, natal || **natali** *mpl* birth; birthday; **dare i natali a** to be the birthplace of || **Natale** *m* Christmas
natali·tà *f* (**-tà**) birth rate
natalì·zio -zia (**-zi -zie**) *adj* natal; Christmas || *m* birthday
natante *adj* swimming; floating || *m* craft
natatóia *f* fin
natató·rio -ria *adj* (**-ri -rie**) swimming
nàti·ca *f* (**-che**) buttock
nati·o -a *adj* (**-i -e**) (poet) native
nativi·tà *f* (**-tà**) birth, nativity || **Natività** *f* Nativity
nati·vo -va *adj* native; natural, inborn || *mf* native
N.A.T.O. *f* (acronym) (North Atlantic Treaty Organization)—**la N.A.T.O.** NATO
na·to -ta *adj* born; **nata** née; **nato e sputato** the spit and image of; **nato morto** stillborn || *mf* child
natura *f* nature; **natura morta** still life; **in natura** in kind
naturale *adj* natural || *m* nature, disposition; **al naturale** life-size
naturalézza *f* naturalness; spontaneity
naturalismo *m* naturalism
naturali·sta *mf* (**-sti -ste**) naturalist
naturali·tà *f* (**-tà**) naturalization
naturalizzare [ddzz] *tr* to naturalize || *ref* to become naturalized
naturalizzazióne [ddzz] *f* naturalization
naturalménte *adv* naturally; of course
naufragare §209 (nàufrago) *intr* (ESSERE

& AVERE) to be shipwrecked; to sink, to fail

naufrà·gio m (-gi) shipwreck; failure

nàufra·go -ga (-ghi -ghe) adj shipwrecked ‖ mf shipwrecked person; (fig) outcast

nàusea f nausea; disgust; **avere la nausea** to be sick at one's stomach

nauseabón·do -da adj sickening, nauseating; (fig) unsavory

nauseante adj sickening, nauseous

nauseare (nàuseo) tr to nauseate, sicken

nausea·to -ta adj sickened, disgusted

nàuti·co -ca (-ci -che) adj nautical ‖ f sailing, navigation

navale adj naval, navy, sea

navata f nave; **navata centrale** nave; **navata laterale** aisle

nave f ship, vessel, boat; craft; **nave ammiraglia** flagship; **nave a motore** motorboat; **nave appoggio** tender; **nave a vela** sailboat; **nave da carico** freighter; **nave da guerra** warship; **nave petroliera** tanker; **nave portaerei** aircraft carrier; **nave rompighiaccio** icebreaker; **nave traghetto** ferryboat

navétta f shuttle; **fare la navetta to** shuttle

navicèlla f nacelle, cabin (of airship); car (of balloon)

navigàbile adj navigable

navigabili·tà f (-tà) navigability; seaworthiness

navigante adj sailing ‖ m sailor

navigare §209 (nàvigo) tr & intr to navigate, to sail

naviga·to -ta adj seawise; wordly-wise

navigazióne f navigation

navì·glio m (-gli) ship, craft, boat; fleet; navy; canal; **naviglio mercantile** merchant marine

nazionale adj national ‖ f national team

nazionalismo m nationalism

nazionali·sta mf (-sti -ste) nationalist

nazionalìsti·co -ca adj (-ci -che) nationalistic

nazionali·tà f (-tà) nationality

nazionalizzare [ddzz] tr to nationalize

nazionalizzazióne [ddzz] f nationalization

nazióne f nation

nazi·sta adj & mf (-sti -ste) Nazi

nazzarè·no -na [ddzz] adj & mf Nazarene ‖ **il Nazzareno** the Nazarene

ne §5 pron & adv

né conj neither, nor; **né . . . né** neither . . . nor

neanche adv not even; nor; not . . . either

nébbia f fog, haze, mist; **fa nebbia** it is foggy; **nebbia artificiale** smoke screen

nebbióne m thick fog, pea soup

nebbió·so -sa [s] adj foggy, hazy, misty

nebulare adj nebular

nebulizzare [ddzz] tr to atomize

nebulizzatóre [ddzz] m atomizer

nebulósa [s] f nebula

nebulosi·tà [s] f (-tà) fogginess, haziness, mistiness

nebuló·so -sa [s] adj foggy, hazy, misty ‖ f see **nebulosa**

néces·saire m (-saire) vanity case; sewing kit

necessariaménte adv necessarily

necessà·rio -ria (-ri -rie) adj necessary, needed; essential ‖ m necessity; **necessities** (of life)

necessi·tà f (-tà) necessity; need, want; **di necessità** necessarily

necessitare (necèssito) tr to require; to force ‖ intr to be in want; to be necessary; **necessitare di** to need

necrologìa f necrology, obituary

necrològi·co -ca adj (-ci -che) obituary

necromanzìa f necromancy

necròsi f necrosis, gangrene

nefan·do -da adj heinous, nefarious

nefa·sto -sta adj ill-fated; ominous

nefrite f nephritis

negare §209 (négo & nègo) tr to deny, negate; to refuse

negati·vo -va adj & f negative

nega·to -ta adj unfit, unsuited

negazióne f negation, denial; (gram) negative

neghittó·so -sa [s] adj lazy, slothful

neglèt·to -ta adj neglected; untidy

négli §4

negligènte adj negligent, careless

negligènza f negligence, carelessness; dereliction (of duty)

neglìgere §205 tr to neglect

negoziàbile adj negotiable

negoziante mf merchant, shopkeeper; dealer; **negoziante all'ingrosso** wholesaler; **negoziante al minuto** retailer; shopkeeper, storekeeper

negoziare §287 (negòzio) tr to negotiate, transact ‖ intr to negotiate, deal

negoziati mpl negotiations

negozia·tóre -trice mf negotiator

negò·zio m (-zi) business; transaction; store, shop; **negozio di cancelleria** stationery store

negrière m slave trader; slave driver

negriè·ro -ra adj slave ‖ m slave trader; slave driver

né·gro -gra adj & mf Negro

negromante m sorcerer

néi §4

nél §4

nélla §4

nélle §4

néllo §4

némbo m rain cloud; cloud (e.g., of dust)

Nembròd m Nimrod

nèmesi f invar nemesis ‖ **Nemesi** f Nemesis

nemi·co -ca (-ci -che) adj inimical, hostile, unfriendly; enemy; (fig) adverse ‖ mf enemy, foe; **Il Nemico** the Evil One

nemméno adv not even; nor; not . . . either

nènia f funeral dirge; lamentation

nenùfaro m water lily

nèo m mole (on the skin); flaw, blemish; neon; beauty spot

neoclassicheggiante adj in the direction of the neoclassical

neòfi·ta *mf* (**-ti -te**) neophyte
neolati·no -na *adj* Neo-Latin, Romance
neologismo *m* neologism
neomicina *f* neomycin
nèon *m* neon
neona·to -ta *adj* newborn || *mf* infant, baby; newborn child
neozelandése [dz][s] *adj* New Zealand || *mf* New Zealander
nepènte *f* nepenthe
Nepóte *m* Nepos
neppure *adv* not even; nor; not . . . either
nequizia *f* iniquity, wickedness
nera·stro -stra *adj* blackish
nerbata *f* heavy blow
nèrbo *m* whip; sinew; bulk; strength (*of an opposing force*)
nerboru·to -ta *adj* muscular, sinewy
nereggiare §290 (**neréggio**) *intr* to look black; to be blackish
nerétto *m* (*typ*) boldface
né·ro -ra *adj* black; dark; gloomy; dark-red (*wine*) || *mf* black; Negro || *m* black
nerofumo *m* lampblack
Neróne *m* Nero
nervatura *f* ribbing
nervi·no -na *adj* nerve (*gas*); nervine (*medicine*)
nèrvo *m* nerve; sinew; **avere i nervi** to be in a bad mood
nervosismo [s] *m* nervousness, irritability
nervó·so -sa [s] *adj* nervous, irritable; sinewy, vigorous (*style*) || *m* bad mood; **avere il nervoso** to be in a bad mood
nèsci *m*—**fare il nesci** to feign ignorance
nèspola *f* medlar; **nespole** (coll) blows
nèspolo *m* medlar tree
nèsso *m* connection, link; **avere ·nesso** to cohere
nessu·no -na *adj* no, not any || **nessuno** *pron* nobody, no one; none; not anybody; not anyone; **nessuno dei due** neither one
nettapén·ne *m* (**-ne**) penwiper
nettare (**nétto**) *tr* to clean, to cleanse
nèttare *m* nectar
nettézza *f* cleanness, cleanliness; neatness; **nettezza urbana** department of sanitation; garbage collection
nét·to -ta *adj* clean; clear; sharp; net || **netto** *adv* clearly, distinctly
nettùnio *m* neptunium
Nettuno *m* Neptune
netturbino *m* street cleaner
neurologia *f* neurology
neurò·si *f* (**-si**) neurosis
neuròti·co -ca *adj* (**-ci -che**) neurotic
neutrale *adj* & *mf* neutral
neutrali·sta *adj* & *mf* (**-sti -ste**) neutralist
neutrali·tà *f* (**-tà**) neutrality
neutralizzare [ddzz] *tr* to neutralize
nèu·tro -tra *adj* neuter; neutral
neutróne *m* neutron
ne·vàio *m* (**-vài**) snowfield; snowdrift
néve *f* snow; **neve carbonica** dry ice
nevicare §197 (**névica**) *impers* (ESSERE) —**nevica** it is snowing

nevicata *f* snowfall
nevischio *m* sleet
nevó·so -sa [s] *adj* snowy
nevralgia *f* neuralgia
nevrastèni·co -ca *adj* & *mf* (**-ci -che**) neurasthenic
nevvéro (i.e., **n'è vero** for **non è vero**) see **non**
niacina *f* niacin
nìb·bio *m* (**-bi**) (orn) kite
nicchia *f* niche; nook, recess
nicchiare §287 (**nicchio**) *intr* to waver
nïc·chio *m* (**-chi**) shell; nook
nichel *m* nickel
nichelare (**nìchelo**) *tr* to nickel, to nickel-plate
nichelatura *f* nickel-plating
nichelino *m* nickel (*coin*)
nichèlio *m* var of **nichel**
Nicòla *m* Nicholas
nicotina *f* nicotine
nidiata *f* nestful; brood
nidificare §197 (**nidìfico**) *intr* to build a nest, to nest
nido *m* nest; home; nursery; den (*of thieves*)
niènte *m* nothing; nothingness; **dal niente** from scratch; **di niente** you're welcome || *pron* nothing; not . . . anything; **quasi niente** next to nothing
nientediméno *adv* no less, nothing less
Nilo *m* Nile
ninfa *f* nymph
ninfèa *f* white water lily
ninnananna *f* lullaby, cradlesong
ninnolo *m* toy; trinket
nipóte *mf* grandchild || *m* grandson; nephew; **nipoti** descendants || *f* granddaughter; niece
nippòni·co -ca *adj* (**-ci -che**) Nipponese
nirvana, il nirvana
niti·do -da *adj* clear, distinct
nitóre *m* brightness; elegance
nitrato *m* nitrate
nitrire §176 *intr* to neigh
nitrito *m* neigh; (chem) nitrite
nitro *m* niter; **nitro del Cile** Chile saltpeter
nitroglicerina *f* nitroglycerin
nitruro *m* nitride
niu·no -na *adj* (poet) var of **nessuno**
nìve·o -a *adj* snow-white
Nizza *f* Nice
no *adv* no; not; **come no?** why not; certainly; **dire di no** to say no; **no?** is it not so?; **non dir di no** to consent; **proprio no** certainly not
nòbile *adj* noble; second (*floor*) || *m* nobleman || *f* noblewoman
nobiliare *adj* noble, of nobility
nobilitare (**nobìlito**) *tr* to ennoble
nobil·tà *f* (**-tà**) nobility
nòc·ca *f* (**-che**) knuckle
nocchière *m* or **nocchièro** *m* petty officer; (poet) pilot, helmsman
nocchieru·to -ta *adj* knotty
nòc·chio *m* (**-chi**) knot (*in wood*)
nocciòla *adj invar* hazel (*in color*) || *f* hazelnut; filbert
nocciolina *f* little nut; **nocciolina americana** peanut; roasted peanut
nòcciolo *m* stone, pit, kernel; **il noc-**

ciolo della questione the crux of the matter

nocciòlo *m* hazel (*tree*); filbert (*tree*)

nóce *m* walnut tree || *f* walnut (*fruit*); **noce del collo** Adam's apple; **noce di cocco** coconut; **noce di vitello** filet of veal; **noce moscata** nutmeg

nocévole *adj* harmful

noci·vo -va *adj* harmful, detrimental

nòdo *m* knot; crux, gist (*of a question*); junction; lump (*in one's throat*); (naut) knot; (phys) node; **lì è il nodo** there's the rub; **nodo d'amore** true-love knot; **nodo ferroviario** rail center, junction; **nodo scorsoio** noose; **nodo stradale** highway center, cross-roads

nodó·so -sa [s] *adj* knotty

Noè *m* Noah

noi §5 *pron pers* we; us; **noi altri** we, e.g., **noi altri italiani** we Italians

nòia *f* boredom; bother, trouble; bug (*in a motor*); **venire a noia** (with *dat*) to weary; **dar noia** (with *dat*) to bother

noiàl·tri -tre *pron* we; us; **noialtri italiani** we Italians

noió·so -sa [s] *adj* boring, annoying

noleggiare §290 (**noléggio**) *tr* to rent; to hire, to charter || *ref*—**si noleggia, si noleggiano** for rent

noleggiatóre *m* hirer; lessor (*e.g., of a car*)

nolég·gio *m* (**-gi**) rent, lease; car rental; chartering; freightage

nolènte *adj* unwilling

nòlo *m* rent, hire; **a nolo** for hire

nòmade *adj* nomad, nomadic || *mf* nomad

nóme *m* name; fame; reputation; (gram) noun; **a nome di** on behalf of; **in nome di** in the name of; **nome commerciale** firm name; **nome depositato** registered name; **nome di battesimo** Christian name; **nome e cognome** full name

noméa *f* name, reputation; notoriety

nomìgnolo *m* nickname; **affibbiare un nomignolo a** to nickname

nòmina *f* appointment; **di prima nomina** newly appointed

nominale *adj* nominal; noun

nominare (**nòmino**) *tr* to name, call; to mention; to elect; to appoint

nominati·vo -va *adj* nominative; with names in alphabetical order; (fin) registered || *m* nominative; name; model number

non *adv* no, not; none, e.g., **non troppo presto** none too soon; **non appena** as soon as; **non c'è di che** you are welcome; **non . . . che** but, only; **non è vero?** is it not so?, isn't it so? La traduzione in inglese di questa domanda dipende generalmente dalla proposizione che la precede. Se la proposizione è affermativa, l'interrogazione sarà negativa, p.es. **Lei mi scriverà, non è vero?** You will write me. Won't you? Se la proposizione è negativa, l'interrogazione sarà positiva, p.es. **Lei non beve birra, non è**

vero? You do not drink beer. Do you? Se il soggetto della proposizione è un nome sostantivo, sarà rappresentato nell'interrogazione da un pronome personale, p.es. **Giovanni ha finito, non è vero?** John has finished. Hasn't he?

nonagenà·rio -ria *adj & mf* (**-ri -rie**) nonagenarian

nonagèsi·mo -ma *adj, pron & m* ninetieth

nonconformi·sta *mf* (**-sti -ste**) nonconformist

noncurante *adj* careless, indifferent

noncuranza *f* carelessness, indifference

nondiméno *conj* yet, nevertheless

nòn·no -na *mf* grandparent || *m* grandfather || *f* grandmother

nonnulla *m invar* nothing, trifle

nò·no -na *adj, m & pron* ninth

nonostante *prep* in spite of, notwithstanding; **nonostante che** although, even though

nonpertanto *adv* nevertheless, still, yet

non plus ultra *m* ne plus ultra, acme

nonsènso *m* nonsense

non so ché *adj invar* indefinable || *m invar* something indefinable

nontiscordardi·mé *m* (**-mé**) forget-me-not

nòrd *m* north

nòrdi·co -ca (**-ci -che**) *adj* Nordic; northern, north || *mf* northerner

nòrma *f* rule, regulation; **a norma di legge** according to law; **per Sua norma** for your guidance

normale *adj* normal; normative; perpendicular || *f* perpendicular line

normali·tà *f* (**-tà**) normality, normalcy

normalizzare [ddzz] *tr* to normalize, to standardize

Normandìa, la Normandy

norman·no -na *adj & mf* Norman || *m* Norseman

normati·vo -va *adj* normative || *f* normativeness

normògrafo *m* stencil

norvegése [s] *adj & mf* Norwegian

Norvègia, la Norway

nosocò·mio *m* (**-mi**) hospital

nossignóra (*i.e., no signora*) *adv* no, Madam

nossignóre (*i.e., no signore*) *adv* no, Sir

nostalgìa *f* nostalgia, longing; homesickness

nostàlgi·co -ca (**-ci -che**) *adj* nostalgic; homesick || *m* worshiper of the good old days (*esp. of Fascism*)

nostra·no -na *adj* domestic, national; home-grown; regional

nò·stro -stra §6 *adj & pron poss*

nostròmo *m* boatswain

nòta *f* mark; score; memorandum; list; bill, invoice; report (*on a subordinate*); (mus) note; **note caratteristiche** personal folder, efficiency report (*of an employee*); **prender nota di** to take down

notàbile *adj* notable, noteworthy || *m* notable

no·tàio *m* (**-tài**) notary (public); lawyer

notare (nòto) *tr* to mark, check; to note, to jot down; to observe; to bring out; **farsi notare** to attract attention, make oneself conspicuous; **nota bene** note well, take notice

notariale or **notarile** *adj* notarial

notazióne *f* notation; annotation; observation

nò·tes *m* (-tes) notebook

notévole *adj* noteworthy, remarkable

notìfi·ca *f* (-che) notification, notice; service (*e.g.*, *of a summons*)

notificare §197 (**notìfico**) *tr* to report; to serve (*a summons*); to declare . . (*e.g.*, *one's income*)

notificazióne *f* notification, notice; service (*e.g.*, *of a summons*)

notìzia *f* knowledge; report; piece of news; **aver notìzie di** to hear from; **notìzie** news; **una notìzia** a news item

notizià·rio *m* (-ri) news report, news bulletin; (rad) newscast; **notiziario sportivo** sports page; (rad, telv) sports news

nò·to -ta *adj* known, well-known ‖ *m* south wind; (coll) swimming ‖ *f* see **nota**

notorie·tà *f* (-tà) general knowledge; affidavit; notoriety

notò·rio -ria *adj* (-ri -rie) well-known

nottàmbu·lo -la *adj* nighttime; night-wandering ‖ *mf* nightwalker; night owl

nottata *f* night; **far nottata bianca** to spend a sleepless night

nòtte *f* night; **buona notte** good night; **di notte** at night, by night, in the nighttime; **la notte di lunedì** Sunday night; Monday night; **lunedì notte** Monday night; **notte bianca** sleepless night; **notte di San Silvestro** New Year's Eve; watch night

nottetèmpo *adv*—**di nottetempo** at night, in the nighttime

nòttola *f* wooden latch; (zool) bat

nottolino *m* small wooden latch; ratchet, catch

nottur·no -na *adj* nocturnal, night ‖ *m* nocturne

novanta *adj*, *m & pron* ninety

novantènne *adj* ninety-year-old ‖ *mf* ninety-year-old person

novantèsi·mo -ma *adj*, *m & pron* ninetieth

novantina *f* about ninety; **sulla novantina** about ninety years old

nòve *adj & pron* nine; **le nove** nine o'clock ‖ *m* nine; ninth (*in dates*)

novecentismo *m* twentieth-century arts and letters

novecenti·sta (-sti -ste) *adj* twentieth-century ‖ *mf* artist of the twentieth century

novecènto *adj*, *m & pron* nine hundred ‖ **il Novecento** the twentieth century

novèlla *f* short story; (poet) news

novellie·re -ra *mf* storyteller; short-story writer

novelli·no -na *adj* early, tender; inexperienced, green

novellìstica *f* storytelling; fiction

novèl·lo -la *adj* fresh, young, tender; new ‖ *f* see **novella**

novèmbre *m* November

novenà·rio -ria *adj* (-ri -rie) nine-syllable

noverare (nòvero) *tr* to count; to enumerate; (poet) to remember

nòvero *m* number; class

novilù·nio *m* (-ni) new moon

novìssi·mo -ma *adj* (lit) last, newest

novi·tà *f* (-tà) newness, originality; novelty, innovation; latest idea; late news

noviziato *m* novitiate; apprenticeship

novi·zio -zia (-zi -zie) *mf* novice; apprentice ‖ *f* novice (*in a convent*)

novocaina *f* novocaine

nozióne *f* notion, conception

nòzze *fpl* wedding, marriage; **nozze d'argento** silver wedding; **nozze d'oro** golden wedding

nube *f* cloud

nubifrà·gio *m* (-gi) cloudburst

nùbile *adj* unmarried, single (*woman*); marriageable ‖ *f* unmarried girl

nu·ca *f* (-che) nape of the neck, scruff

nucleare *adj* nuclear

nùcleo *m* nucleus; group; (elec) core

nudismo *m* nudism

nudi·sta *adj & mf* (-sti -ste) nudist

nudi·tà *f* (-tà) nudity, nakedness

nu·do -da *adj* naked, bare; barren; simple; **mettere a nudo** to lay bare; **nudo e crudo** stark-naked; destitute ‖ *m* nude

nùgolo *m* cloud; throng, swarm

nulla *pron* nothing ‖ *m invar* nothing; nothingness

nulla òsta *m* permission; visa

nullatenènte *adj* poor ‖ *mf* have-not

nullificare §197 (**nullìfico**) *tr* to nullify

nulli·tà *f* (-tà) nothingness; nonentity; invalidity (*of a document*)

nul·lo -la *adj* void, worthless ‖ **nullo** *pron* (poet) none, no one ‖ **nulla** *m & pron* see **nulla**

nume *m* divinity, deity

numerare (nùmero) *tr* to number

numeratóre *m* numerator; numbering machine

numèri·co -ca *adj* (-ci -che) numerical

nùmero *m* number; lottery ticket; size (*of shoes*); **numero dìspari** odd number; **numero legale** quorum; **numero pari** even number

numeró·so -sa [s] *adj* numerous, large; harmonious

nùn·zio *m* (-zi) nuncio; (poet) news

nuòcere §206 *intr* to be harmful; (with *dat*) to harm

nuòra *f* daughter-in-law

nuotare (nuòto) *intr* to swim; to float; to wallow (*in wealth*)

nuotata *f* swim, dip, plunge

nuota·tóre -trice *mf* swimmer

nuòto *m* swimming; **gettarsi a nuoto** to jump into the water; **traversare a nuoto** to swim across

nuòva *f* news; late news

Nuòva York f New York

Nuòva Zelànda, la [dz] New Zealand

nuòvo -va adj new; **di nuovo** again; **nuovo di zecca** brand-new; **nuovo fiammante** brand-new; **nuovo venuto** new arrival ‖ *m*—**il nuovo** the new ‖ *f* see **nuova**

nùtria f coypu

nutrice f wet nurse; (lit) provider

nutriènte adj nourishing

nutriménto m nourishment

nutrire §176 & (**nutro**) tr to nourish;

to nurture; to harbor (e.g., hatred) ‖ ref—**nutrirsi di** to feed on or upon

nutrìti·vo -va adj nutritious, nutritive

nutrì·to -ta adj well-fed; strong; rich (food); brisk, heavy (gunfire)

nutrizióne f nutrition; food

nùvo·lo -la adj cloudy ‖ *m* cloudy weather; (lit) cloud; (fig) swarm ‖ *f* cloud

nuvoló·so -sa [s] adj cloudy

nuziàle adj wedding, nuptial

nuzialità f marriage rate

O

O, o [o] m & f thirteenth letter of the Italian alphabet·

o conj or; now; **o . . . o** either . . . or; whether . . . or ‖ interj oh!

òa·si f (-si) oasis

obbediènte adj var of **ubbidiente**

obbediènza f obedience

obbedire §176 tr & intr var of **ubbidire**

obbiettare (**obbiètto**) tr & intr var of **obiettare**

obbligare §209 (**òbbligo**) tr to oblige; to compel, to force ‖ ref to obligate oneself

obbligatìssi·mo -ma adj much obliged

obbligatò·rio -ria adj (-ri -rie) compulsory, obligatory

obbligazióne f obligation; burden; (com) debenture, bond

obbligazioni·sta mf (-sti -ste) bondholder

òbbli·go m (-ghi) obligation; duty; **d'obbligo** obligatory, mandatory; **fare d'obbligo a qlcu** + inf to be necessary for s.o. to + inf, e.g., **gli fa d'obbligo lavorare** it is necessary for him to work

obbrò·brio m (-bri) opprobrium, disgrace; **obbrobri** insults

obbrobrió·so -sa [s] adj opprobrious, disgraceful

obelì·sco m (-schi) obelisk

obera·to -ta adj overburdened

obesità f obesity

obè·so -sa adj obese, stout

òbice m howitzer

obiettare (**obiètto**) tr & intr to argue; to object

obietti·vo -va adj & m objective

obiettóre m objector; **obiettore di coscienza** conscientious objector

obiezióne f objection

obitò·rio m (-ri) morgue

obiare (**òbio**) tr to willingly pay (a fine)

obla·tóre -trice mf donor

oblazióne f donation; (eccl) oblation; (law) payment of a fine

obliare §119 tr (lit) to forget

oblì·o m (-i) (lit) oblivion

oblì·quo -qua adj oblique

obliterare (**oblìtero**) tr to obliterate, cancel

o·blò m (-blò) (naut) porthole; **oblò di accesso** door (of space capsule)

oblun·go -ga adj (-ghi -ghe) oblong

òbo·e m (-e) oboe

oboi·sta mf (-sti -ste) oboist

òbolo m mite

ò·ca f (-che) goose; gander

ocarina f ocarina, sweet potato

occasionale adj chance; immediate (cause)

occasionare (**occasióno**) tr to occasion

occasióne f occasion; opportunity; ground, pretext; bargain; **all'occasione** on occasion; **d'occasione** second-hand; occasional (verses)

occhiàia f eye socket; **occhiaie** rings under the eyes

occhia·làio m (-lài) optician

occhiale adj eye, ocular ‖ **occhiali** mpl glasses; goggles; **occhiali antisole** sunglasses; **occhiali a stringinaso** nose glasses

occhialétto m lorgnon; monocle

occhiata f glance

occhieggiare §290 (**occhiéggio**) tr to eye ‖ intr to peep

occhièllo m buttonhole; boutonniere; eyelet; half title; subhead

occhièra f eyecup

òc·chio m (-chi) eye; speck of grease (in soup); handle (of scissors); ring (of stirrup); (typ) face; (fig) bit; **a occhio e croce** at a rough guess; **a quattr'occhi** in private; **battere gli occhi** to blink; **cavarsi gli occhi** to strain one's eyes; **dar nell'occhio** to attract attention; **di buon occhio** favorably; **fare l'occhio a** to get used to; **fare tanto d'occhi** to be amazed, to open one's eyes wide; **lasciare gli occhi su** to covet; **non chiudere un occhio** not to sleep a wink; **occhio!** watch out!; **occhio della testa** outrageous price; **occhio di bue** (naut) porthole; **occhio di cubia** (naut) hawsehole; **occhio di pavone** (zool) peacock butterfly; **occhio di triglia** sheep's eyes; **occhio pesto** black eye; **occhio pollino** corn (on toes); **tenere d'occhio** to keep an eye on

occhiolino m small eye; **far l'occhiolino** to wink

occidentale adj western, occidental

occidènte adj (poet) setting (sun) ‖ m west, occident

occìpite *m* occipital bone

occlusióne *f* occlusion

occlusi•vo -va *adj* & *f* occlusive

occlu•so -sa *adj* occluded

occorrènte *adj* necessary || *m* necessary; (lit) occurrence

occorrènza *f* necessity; all'occorrenza if need be

occórrere §139 *intr* (ESSERE) to happen; (with *dat*) to need, e.g., gli occorre dell'olio he needs oil || *impers* (ESSERE)—occorre it is necessary

occultaménto *m* concealment

occultare *tr* & *ref* to hide

occul•to -ta *adj* occult; (lit) hidden

occupante *adj* occupying || *m* occupant

occupare (òccupo) *tr* to occupy; to employ || *ref* to take employment; occuparsi di to busy oneself with, to mind; to attend to

occupa•to -ta *adj* occupied; busy

occupazionale *adj* occupational

occupazióne *f* occupation

oceàni•co -ca *adj* (-ci -che) oceanic

ocèano *m* ocean

òcra *f* ocher

oculare *adj* ocular; see testimone || *m* eyepiece

oculatézza *f* circumspection, prudence

ocula•to -ta *adj* circumspect, prudent

oculi•sta *mf* (-sti -ste) oculist

od *conj* or

odali•sca *f* (-sche) odalisque

òde *f* ode

odepòri•co -ca (-ci -che) *adj* (lit) travel || *m* (lit) travelogue

odiare §287 (òdio) *tr* to hate

odièr•no -na *adj* today's, current

ò•dio *m* (-di) hatred; avere in odio to hate; essere in odio a to be hated by

odió•so -sa [s] *adj* hateful, odious

odissèa *f* odyssey || Odissea *f* Odyssey

Odissèo *m* Odysseus

odontoia•tra *mf* (-tri -tre) doctor of dental surgery, dentist

odontoiatrìa *f* odontology, dentistry

odorare (odóro) *tr* & *intr* to smell

odora•to -ta *adj* (poet) fragrant || *m* smell

odóre *m* smell, odor, scent; cattivo odore bad odor; odori herbs, spice

odoró•so -sa [s] *adj* odorous, fragrant

offèndere §148 *tr* & *intr* to offend || *ref* to take offense

offensi•vo -va *adj* & *f* offensive

offensóre *m* offender

offerènte *mf* bidder; miglior offerente highest bidder

offèrta *f* offer; offering, donation; (at an auction) bid; (com) supply

offésa [s] *f* offense; wrongdoing; ravage (of time); da offesa (mil) offensive; recarsi a offesa qlco to regard s.th as offensive

officìna *f* shop, workshop; officina meccanica machine shop

offició•so -sa [s] *adj* helpful, obliging

offrìre §207 *tr* to offer; to sponsor (a radio or TV program); to dedicate (a book); to bid (at an auction); (com) to tender || *ref* to offer oneself, to volunteer

offuscare §197 *tr* to darken, obscure; to obfuscate; to dim (mind; eyes) || *ref* to grow dark; to grow dim

oftàlmi•co -ca *adj* (-ci -che) opthalmic

oftalmòlo•go -ga *mf* (-gi -ghe) ophthalmologist

oggettività *f* objectivity

oggetti•vo -va *adj* & *m* objective

oggètto *m* object; subject, argument; article; oggetti preziosi valuables

òggi *m* today; dall'oggi al domani suddenly; overnight || *adv* today; d'oggi in poi henceforth; oggi a otto a week hence; oggi come oggi at present; oggi è un anno one year ago

oggidì *m invar* & *adv* nowadays

oggigiórno *m invar* & *adv* nowadays

ogiva *f* ogive, pointed arch; nose cone

ógni *adj indef invar* each; every, e.g., ogni due giorni every two days; ogni cosa everything; ogni tanto every now and then; per ogni dove (lit) everywhere

ogniqualvòlta *conj* whenever

Ognissan•ti *m* (-ti) All Saints' Day

ognitèmpo *adj invar* all-weather

-ógno•lo -la *suf adj* -ish, e.g., giallognolo yellowish

ognóra *adv* (lit) always

ognu•no -na *adj* (obs) each || *pron* each one, everyone

oh *interj* oh!

òhi *interj* ouch!

ohibò *interj* fie!

ohimè *interj* alas!

ohm *m* (ohm) ohm

olanda *f* Dutch linen || l'Olanda *f* Holland

olandése [s] *adj* Dutch || *m* Dutch (language); Dutchman; Dutch cheese || *f* Dutch woman

oleandro *m* oleander

oleà•rio -ria *adj* (-ri -rie) oil

olea•to -ta *adj* oiled

oleifì•cio *m* (-ci) oil mill

oleodótto *m* pipeline

oleó•so -sa [s] *adj* oily

olezzare [ddzz] (olézzo) *intr* (lit) to smell sweet

olézzo [ddzz] *m* perfume, fragrance

olfatto *m* smell

oliare §287 (òlio) *tr* to oil

oliatóre *m* oiler, oil can

olìbano *m* frankincense

olièra *f* cruet

oligarchìa *f* oligarchy

olimpìade *f* Olympiad

olìmpi•co -ca *adj* (-ci -che) Olympic; Olympian

olimpiòni•co -ca *adj* (-ci -che) Olympic || *mf* Olympic athlete

ò•lio *m* (-li) oil; ad olio oil, e.g., quadro ad olio oil painting; olio di fegato di merluzzo cod-liver oil; olio di lino linseed oil; olio di ricino castor oil; olio solare sun-tan lotion

oliva *f* olive

oliva•stro -stra *adj* livid; swarthy || *m* wild olive (tree)

olivéto *m* olive grove

Olivièro *m* Oliver

olivo *m* olive tree

ólmo *m* elm tree

olocàu·sto -sta *adj* (lit) burnt; (lit) sacrificed || *m* holocaust; sacrifice

ològra·fo -fa *adj* holographic

olóna *f* sailcloth, canvas

oltracciò *adv* besides

oltraggiare §290 *tr* to outrage; to insult

oltràg·gio *m* (-gi) outrage; offense; ravages (*of time*); **oltraggio al pudore** offense to public morals; **oltraggio al tribunale** contempt of court

oltraggió·so -sa [s] *adj* outrageous

oltranza *f*—**a oltranza** to the bitter end

oltranzi·sta *mf* (-sti -ste) (pol) extremist

óltre *adv* beyond; ahead; further; **oltre a** apart from; in addition to; **troppo oltre** too far || *prep* beyond; past; more than

oltrecortina *adj invar* beyond-the-iron-curtain || *m* country beyond the iron curtain

oltremare *m invar* country overseas || *adv* overseas

oltremisura *adv* (lit) beyond measure

oltremòdo *adv* (lit) exceedingly

oltrepassare *tr* to overstep; to cross (*a river*); to be beyond (. . . *years old*); (sports) to overtake

oltretómba *m*—**l'oltretomba** the life beyond

omàg·gio *m* (-gi) homage; compliment; **in omaggio** complimentary; **rendere omaggio a** to pay tribute to

òmaro *m* Norway lobster

ombeli·co *m* (-chi) navel

ómbra *f* shade; shadow; umbrage; form, mass; **nemmeno per ombra** not in the least

ombreggiare §290 (**ombréggio**) *tr* to shade

ombrèlla *f* shade (*of trees*); (bot) umbel; (coll) umbrella

ombrel·làio *m* (-lài) umbrella maker

ombrellino *m* parasol

ombrèllo *m* umbrella

ombrellóne *m* beach umbrella

ombró·so -sa [s] *adj* shady; touchy; skittish (*horse*)

omelette *f* (**omelette**) omelet

omelìa *f* homily

omeopàti·co -ca (-ci -che) *adj* homeopathic || *m* homeopathist

omèri·co -ca *adj* (-ci -che) Homeric

òmero *m* (anat) humerus; (lit) shoulder

omertà *f* code of silence of underworld

ométtere §198 *tr* to omit

ométto *m* little man; (coll) clothes hanger; (billiards) pin; (archit) king post

omici·da (-di -de) *adj* homicidal, murderous || *mf* homicide, murderer

omicì·dio *m* (-di) homicide, murder; **omicidio colposo** (law) manslaughter; **omicidio doloso** (law) first-degree murder

ominó·so -sa [s] *adj* (lit) ominous

omissióne *f* omission

òmni·bus *m* (-bus) omnibus; way train

omnisciènte *adj* all-knowing, omniscient

omogène·o -a *adj* homogeneous

omologare §209 (**omòlogo**) *tr* to con-

firm, ratify; to probate (*a will*); (sports) to validate

omòni·mo -ma *adj* of the same name || *m* namesake; homonym

omosessuale [s] *adj & mf* homosexual

ón·cia *f* (-ce) ounce; **oncia a oncia** little by little

ónda *f* wave; **a onde** wavy; wavily; **essere in onda** (rad, telv) to be on the air; **farsi le onde** to have one's hair waved; **mettere in onda** (rad, telv) to put on the air; **onda crespa** whitecap; **onda portante** (rad, telv) carrier wave

ondata *f* wave, billow; gust (*e.g., of smoke*); rush (*of blood*); wave (*of cold weather*)

ondatra *f* muskrat

ónde *pron* from which; of which || *adv* whereof; hence; (poet) wherefrom || *prep* **onde** + *inf* in order to || *conj* **onde** + *subj* so that

ondeggiante *adj* waving, swaying

ondeggiare §290 (**ondéggio**) *intr* to wave, sway; to waver

ondina *f* mermaid; (mythol) undine; (mythol) mermaid

ondó·so -sa [s] *adj* wavy

ondulare (**óndulo & òndulo**) *tr* to wave; to corrugate (*e.g., metal*) || *intr* to sway

ondula·to -ta *adj* wavy (*hair*); corrugated (*e.g., metal*); bumpy (*road*)

ondulazióne *f* undulation; **ondulazione permanente** permanent wave

-óne -óna *suf mf* big, e.g., **librone** big book; **dormigliona** big sleeper || **-óne** *suf m* (applies to both sexes) big, e.g., **donnone** *m* big woman

ònere *m* (lit) onus, burden

oneró·so -sa [s] *adj* onerous, burdensome

onestà *f* honesty; (poet) modesty

onè·sto -sta *adj* honest; fair; (poet) modest || *m* moderate amount; honest gain; honest person

ònice *m* onyx

onnipossènte & onnipotènte *adj* almighty, omnipotent

onnisciènte *adj* omniscient

onniveggènte *adj* all-seeing

onnìvo·ro -ra *adj* omnivorous

onomàsti·co -ca (-ci -che) *adj* onomastic || *m* name day || *f* study of proper names

onomatopèi·co -ca *adj* (-ci -che) onomatopeic

onoràbile *adj* honorable

onoranza *f* honor; **onoranze** homage; **onoranze funebri** obsequies

onorare (**onóro**) *tr* to honor || *ref* to deem it an honor

onorà·rio -ria (-ri -rie) *adj* honorary || *m* fee, honorarium

onora·to -ta *adj* honored; honest; honorable

onóre *m* honor; **d'onore** honest, e.g., **uomo d'onore** honest man; **estremi onori** last rites; **fare gli onori di casa** to receive guests; **fare onore a** to honor; **onore al merito** credit where credit is due; **onor del mento** (lit) beard

onorévole *adj* honorable ‖ *m* honorable member (*of parliament*)

onorificènza *f* dignity; decoration

onorifi•co -ca *adj* (**-ci -che**) honorific; honorary (*e.g., title*)

ónta *f* dishonor, shame; **a onta di** in spite of; **avere onta** to be ashamed; **fare onta a** to bring shame upon; **in onta a** against

ontano *m* alder

O.N.U. (acronym) *f* (**Organizzazione delle Nazioni Unite**) United Nations, U.N.

onu•sto -sta *adj* (poet) laden

opa•co -ca *adj* (**-chi -che**) opaque

opale *m* opal

opali•no -na *adj* opaline ‖ *f* shiny cardboard; luster (*fabric*)

òpera *f* work; organization, foundation; day's work; (mus) opera; **mettere in opera** to install; to start work on; to make ready; to begin using; **opera di consultazione** reference work; **opera morta** (naut) upper works; **opera viva** (naut) quickwork; **per opera di** thanks to

ope•ràio -ràia (**-rài -ràie**) *adj* workman's, worker's; working ‖ *m* workman, worker; **operaio a cottimo** pieceworker; **operaio a giornata** day laborer; **operaio specializzato** craftsman, skilled workman ‖ *f* workwoman

operante *adj* actively engaged; operative

operare (**òpero**) *tr* to operate; to work (*a miracle*); (surg) to operate on ‖ *intr* to operate; to be actively engaged ‖ *ref* to be operated on; to occur, take place

operati•vo -va *adj* operative; operations, e.g., **ricerca operativa** operations research

opera•to -ta *adj* operated; embossed ‖ *m* behavior; patient operated on

opera•tóre -trice *mf* operator ‖ *m* (mov) cameraman

operatò•rio -ria *adj* (**-ri -rie**) surgical (*operation*); operating (*room*); (math) operational

operazióne *f* operation; transaction

operétta *f* short work; (mus) operetta

operisti•co -ca *adj* (**-ci -che**) operatic

operosi•tà [s] *f* (**-tà**) industry

operó•so -sa [s] *adj* industrious; active

opi•mo -ma *adj* (lit) fat; rich, fertile

opinare *intr* to opine, deem

opinióne *f* opinion

opòs•sum *m* (**-sum**) opossum

oppia•to -ta *adj* opiate (*mixed with opium*); dulled by drugs ‖ *m* opiate (*medicine containing opium*)

òppio *m* opium

oppiòmane *adj* opium-eating; opium-smoking ‖ *mf* opium addict

oppórre §218 *tr* to oppose; to offer, put up (*resistance*) ‖ *ref* to be opposite; **opporsi a** to oppose, to be against

opportuni•sta *mf* (**-sti -ste**) opportunist

opportuni•tà *f* (**-tà**) opportunity; opportuneness

opportu•no -na *adj* opportune

opposi•tóre -trice *mf* opponent

opposizióne *f* opposition; (law) appeal; **fare opposizione a** to object to

oppó•sto -sta *adj* opposite; contrary ‖ *m* opposite; **all'opposto** on the contrary

oppressióne *f* oppression

oppressi•vo -va *adj* oppressive

opprès•so -sa *adj* oppressed; overcome, overwhelmed ‖ **oppressi** *mpl* oppressed people

oppressóre *m* oppressor

opprimènte *adj* oppressive

opprìmere §131 *tr* to oppress; to overcome, overwhelm; to weigh down

oppugnare *tr* to refute, controvert

oppure *adv* otherwise ‖ *conj* or else; or rather

optare (**òpto**) *intr* to choose; (com) to exercise an option

optometri•sta *mf* (**-sti -ste**) optometrist

opulèn•to -ta *adj* opulent

opùscolo *m* booklet, brochure, pamphlet; **opuscolo d'informazioni** instruction manual

opzióne *f* option

ór *adv* now; **or ora** right now; **or sono** ago

óra *f* hour; time; period (*in school*); **alla buon'ora!** finally!; **a ore** by the hour; **a tarda ora** late; **che ora è?** or **che ore sono?** what time is it?; **da un'ora all'altra** from one moment to the next; **dell'ultima ora** up-to-date (*news*); **di buon'ora** early; early in the morning; **di ora in ora** at any moment; **d'ora in avanti** from this moment on; **d'ora in poi** from now on; **far l'ora** to kill time; **fin ora** until now; **non vedere l'ora di** + *inf* to be hardly able to wait until + *ind*; **ora di cena** suppertime; **ora di punta** rush hour, peak hour; **ora legale** daylight-saving time; **ore piccole** late hours; **un'ora di orologio** one full hour ‖ *adv* now

oràcolo *m* oracle

òra•fo -fa *adj* goldsmith's ‖ *m* goldsmith

orale *adj* & *m* oral

oralménte *adv* orally; by word of mouth

oramài *adv* now; already

oran•go *m* (**-ghi**) orangutan

orà•rio -ria (**-ri -rie**) *adj* hourly; per hour; clockwise ‖ *m* timetable; schedule; roster; **essere in orario** to be on time; **orario di lavoro** working hours; **orario d'ufficio** office hours

ora•tóre -trice *mf* orator

oratò•rio -ria (**-ri -rie**) *adj* oratorical ‖ *m* (eccl) oratory; (mus) oratorio ‖ *f* oratory, public speaking

orazióne *f* oration; prayer; **orazione domenicale** Lord's Prayer

orbare (**òrbo**) *tr* (lit) to bereave; (lit) to deprive

òrbe *f* (lit) orb; (lit) world

orbène *adv* well

òrbita *f* orbit; (fig) sphere
orbitare (òrbito) *intr* to orbit
orbitazióne *f* orbiting
òr·bo -ba *adj* bereaved; deprived; blind ‖ *m* blind man
òrca *f* killer whale
òrcadi *fpl* Orkney Islands
orchèstra *f* orchestra; band; orchestra pit
orchestrale *adj* orchestral ‖ *mf* orchestra player, orchestra performer
orchestrare (orchèstro) *tr* to orchestrate; (fig) to organize
orchestrina *f* dance band; dance-band music
orchidèa *f* orchid
ór·cio *m* (**-ci**) jar, jug, crock
orciòlo *m*—a orciolo puckered up (*lips*)
òr·co *m* (**-chi**) ogre
òrda *f* horde
ordàlia *f* (hist) ordeal
ordigno *m* gadget, contrivance; tool; **ordigno esplosivo** infernal machine
ordinale *adj* & *m* ordinal
ordinaménto *m* disposition; regulation
ordinanza *f* ordinance; (mil) orderly; **d'ordinanza** regulation (*e.g., uniform*); **in ordinanza** (mil) in formation
ordinare (órdino) *tr* to order; to straighten up; to range; to regulate; to ordain; to trim
ordinà·rio -ria (**-ri -rie**) *adj* ordinary; plain; inferior; workday (*suit*) ‖ *m* ordinary; full professor; **d'ordinario** ordinarily, usually
ordina·to -ta *adj* orderly, tidy; ordained ‖ *f* ordinate; straightening up; (aer) frame; (naut) bulkhead
ordinazióne *f* order; ordination
órdine *m* order; row; tier; series (*e.g., of years*); college (*e.g., of surgeons*); nature (*of things*); (law) warrant, writ; **in ordine a** concerning; **ordine del giorno** order of the day; **ordine d'idee** train of thought
ordire §176 *tr* to warp (*cloth*); to hatch (*a plot*)
ordi·to -ta *adj* plotted ‖ *m* warp (*of fabric*)
orécchia *f* ear; dog-ear; **con le orecchie tese** all ears
orecchiale *m* earphone (*of sonar equipment*)
orecchiétta *f* (anat) auricle
orecchino *m* earring
oréc·chio *m* (**-chi**) ear; hearing; dog-ear; moldboard; **fare orecchio da mercante** to turn a deaf ear ‖ *m* (**orécchia** *fpl*) (archaic) ear
orecchióne *m* long-eared bat; (mil) trunnion; **orecchioni** (pathol) mumps
oréfice *m* goldsmith; jeweler
oreficería *f* goldsmith shop; jewelry shop
orfanézza *f* orphanage (*condition*)
òrfa·no -na *adj* orphaned ‖ *mf* orphan
orfanotrò·fio *m* (**-fi**) orphanage (*institution*)
Orfèo *m* Orpheus
organdi *m* organdy
organétto *m* hand organ; mouth organ; **organetto di Barberia** hand organ

orgàni·co -ca (**-ci -che**) *adj* organic ‖ *m* personnel, staff ‖ *f* (mil) organization
organigram·ma *m* (**-mi**) organization chart
organino *m* hand organ, barrel organ
organismo *m* organism
organi·sta *mf* (**-sti -ste**) organist
organizzare [ddzz] *tr* to organize
organizza·tóre -trice [ddzz] *mf* organizer
organizzazióne [ddzz] *f* organization; **Organizzazione delle Nazioni Unite** United Nations
òrgano *m* organ; part (*of a machine*); **organo di stampa** mouthpiece
orgasmo *m* orgasm; agitation, excitement
òr·gia *f* (**-ge**) orgy
orgó·glio *m* (**-gli**) pride
orgoglió·so -sa [s] *adj* proud
orientale *adj* & *mf* oriental; Oriental
orientaménto *m* orientation; bearing; trend; trim (*of sail*); **orientamento scolastico e professionale** aptitude test; vocational guidance
orientare (oriènto) *tr* to orient; to guide; to trim (*a sail*) ‖ *ref* to find one's bearings
oriènte *m* orient; **grand'oriente** grand lodge ‖ **Oriente** *m* Orient, East; **Estremo Oriente** Far East; **Medio Oriente** Middle East; **Vicino Oriente** Near East
orifi·zio *m* (**-zi**) orifice, opening
origano *m* wild marjoram
originale *adj* original; odd ‖ *mf* queer character, odd person ‖ *m* original; copy (*for printer*)
originare (origino) *tr* to originate ‖ *intr* (ESSERE) & *ref* to originate
originà·rio -ria *adj* (**-ri -rie**) originating; native; original
orìgine *f* origin; source; extraction
origliare §280 *intr* to eavesdrop
origlière *m* (lit) pillow
orina *f* var of **urina**
orinale *m* chamber pot, urinal
orinare *tr* & *intr* to urinate
orina·tóio *m* (**-tói**) urinal, comfort station
oriòlo *m* (orn) oriole
oriun·do -da *adj* native ‖ *m* (sports) native son
orizzontale [ddzz] *adj* horizontal ‖ **orizzontali** *fpl* horizontal words (*in crossword puzzle*)
orizzontare [ddzz] (**orizzónto**) *tr* to orient ‖ *ref* to get one's bearings
orizzónte [ddzz] *m* horizon
Orlando *m* Roland
orlare (órlo) *tr* to hem, border; **orlare a zigzag** to pink
órlo *m* edge; brim; hem, border; (fig) brink; **orlo a giorno** hemstitch
órma *f* footprint; **orme** remains, vestiges; **calcare le orme di** to follow the footsteps of
ormeggiare §290 (**orméggio**) *tr* & *ref* (naut) to moor
ormég·gio *m* (**-gi**) mooring; **mollare gli ormeggi** (naut) to cast off
ormóne *m* hormone

ornamentale *adj* ornàmental

ornaménto *m* ornament

ornare (órno) *tr* to adorn

orna·to -ta *adj* adorned; ornate || *m* ornament; ornamental design

ornitòlo·go -ga *mf* (*-gi -ghe*) ornithologist

òro *m* gold; (fig) money; **d'oro** gold, golden; **ori** gold objects; jewels; suit of Neapolitan cards corresponding to diamonds; **oro zecchino** pure gold; **per tutto l'oro del mondo** for all the world

orologerìa *f* watchmaking; clockmaking; watchmaker's shop

orolo·giàio *m* (*-giài*) watchmaker; clockmaker

orolò·gio *m* (*-gi*) watch; clock; **orologio a pendolo** clock; **orologio a polvere** sandglass; **orologio a scatto** digital clock; **orologio da polso** wristwatch; **orologio della morte** deathwatch; **orologio solare** sundial

oròscopo *m* hóroscope

orpèllo *m* Dutch gold; (fig) tinsel

orrèndo *m* horrible

orrìbile *adj* horrible

òrri·do -da *adj* horrid || *m* horridness, gorge, ravine

orripilante *adj* bloodcurdling, hairraising

orróre *m* horror; awe; **aver in** or **per orrore** to loath; **fare orrore a** to horrify

órsa *f* she-bear || **Orsa** *f*—**Orsa maggiore** Great Bear; **Orsa minore** Little Bear

orsacchiòtto *m* bear cub; Teddy bear

ór·so -sa *mf* bear; **orso bianco** polar bear; **orso grigio** grizzly bear || *f* see **orsa**

orsù *interj* come on!

ortàg·gio *m* (*-gi*) vegetable

ortàglia *f* vegetable garden; vegetable

ortènsia *f* hydrangea

orti·ca *f* (*-che*) nettle; hives

orticària *f* hives, nettle rash

orticoltóre *m* truck gardener; horticulturist

òrto *m* garden, vegetable garden; (lit) sunrise; **orto botanico** botanical garden; **orto di guerra** Victory garden

ortodòs·so -sa *adj* orthodox || *m* Greek Catholic

ortografìa *f* orthography; spelling

ortola·no -na *adj* garden || *m* truck farmer, gardener

ortopèdi·co -ca (*-ci -che*) *adj* orthopedic || *m* orthopedist

òrza *f* bowline; windward; **andare all'orza** to sail close to the wind

orzaiòlo [dz] *m* (pathol) sty

orzare (òrzo) *intr* to sail close to the wind; to luff

orzata [dz] *f* orgeat

orzata *f* (naut) luff

òrzo [dz] *m* barley

osannare *intr* to cry or sing hosanna; **osannare a** to acclaim, applaud

osare (òso) *intr* to dare

osceni·tà *f* obscenity

oscè·no -na *adj* obscene; (coll) horrible

oscillante *adj* oscillating

oscillare *intr* to oscillate; to swing; to wobble; to waver, hesitate

oscillazióne *f* oscillation; fluctuation

oscuraménto *m* darkening, dimming; blackout

oscurare *tr* to darken; to blot out; to dim || *ref* to get dark; **oscurarsi in volto** to frown

oscuri·tà *f* (*-tà*) obscurity; darkness; ignorance

oscu·ro -ra *adj* obscure, dark; opaque (*style*) || *m* obscurity, darkness; essere all'oscuro di to be in the dark about

osmòsi *f* osmosis

ospedale *m* hospital

ospedalière *m* hospital worker

ospedaliè·ro -ra *adj* hospital || *m* hospitaler

ospedalizzare [ddzz] *tr* to hospitalize

ospitale *adj* hospitable || *m* hospital

ospitali·tà *f* (*-tà*) hospitality

ospitare (òspito) *tr* to lodge, shelter, accommodate; to entertain; (sports) to play (*an opposing team*) at home

òspite *mf* host; guest; **andarsene insalutato ospite** to take French leave; **ospiti** company (*guests at home*)

ospi·zio *m* (*-zi*) hospice; hostel; (lit) hospitality; ospizio dei vecchi nursing home; ospizio di mendicità poorhouse

ossatura *f* frame, framework; skeleton

òsse·o -a *adj* bony

ossequènte *adj* (lit) respectful; (lit) reverent

ossequiare §287 (**ossèquio**) *tr* to pay one's respects to; to honor

ossè·quio *m* (*-qui*) respect; reverence; **i miei ossequi** my best regards; **in ossequio a** in conformity with; **porgere i propri ossequi a** to pay one's respects to

ossequió·so -so [s] *adj* obsequious; respectful

osservante *adj & m* observant

osservanza *f* observance; deference

osservare (ossèrvo) *tr* to observe

osserva·tóre -trice *adj* observing, observant || *mf* observer

osservatò·rio *m* (*-ri*) observatory

osservazióne *f* observation; rebuke

ossessionare (ossessióno) *tr* to obsess; to harass, bedevil

ossessióne *f* obsession

ossès·so -sa *adj* possessed || *mf* person possessed

ossìa *conj* or; to wit

ossidante *adj* oxidizing || *m* oxidizer

ossidare (òssido) *tr & ref* to oxidize

òssido *m* oxide; **ossido di carbone** carbon monoxide

ossidulo *m* protoxide; **ossidulo di azoto** nitrous oxide

ossificare §197 (**ossìfico**) *tr & ref* to ossify

ossigenare (ossìgeno) *tr* to oxygenate; to bleach (*the hair*); to infuse strength into || *ref* to bleach (*the hair*)

ossìgeno *m* oxygen; (fig) transfusion, shot in the arm

ossìto·no -na *adj & m* oxytone

òs·so m (-si) bone (of animal); stone (of fruit); **osso di balena** whalebone; **osso di seppia** cuttlebone; **osso duro da rodere** hard nut to crack; **osso sacro** sacrum; **rimetterci l'osso del collo** to be thoroughly ruined; **rompersi l'osso del collo** to break one's neck ‖ m (-sa fpl) bone (of a person); **avere le ossa rotte** to be dead-tired

ossu·to -ta adj bony; scrawny

ostacolare (**ostàcolo**) tr to hinder; to obstruct; **ostacolare l'azione** (sports) to interfere

ostàcolo m obstacle; obstruction; (golf) hazard; (sports) hurdle

ostàg·gio m (-gi) hostage

ostare (**òsto**) intr (lit) to be in the way; (with dat) to hinder; **nulla osta** no objection, permission granted

òste ostéssa mf innkeeper ‖ **oste** m & f (lit) army in the field ‖ m (poet) enemy

ostèllo m hostel; (poet) abode

ostentare (**ostènto**) tr to show, display; to affect, feign

ostenta·to -ta adj affected, ostentatious

ostentazióne f show, ostentation

osteopatìa f osteopathy

osterìa f tavern, inn, taproom

ostéssa f see **oste**

ostètri·ca f (-che) midwife

ostetrìcia f obstetrics

ostètri·co -ca (-ci -che) adj obstetrical ‖ m obstetrician ‖ f see **ostetrica**

òstia f wafer; Host; sacrificial victim

òsti·co -ca adj (-ci -che) hard; (lit) repugnant, distasteful

ostile adj hostile

ostili·tà f (-tà) hostility

ostinare ref to be stubborn; to persist

ostina·to -ta adj obstinate; persistent

ostinazióne f obstinacy

ostracismo m ostracism; **dare l'ostracismo a** to ostracize

ostracizzare [ddzz] tr (poet) to ostracize

òstri·ca f (-che) oyster; **ostrica perlifera** pearl oyster

ostri·càio m (-cài) oyster bed; oyster-man

ostruire §176 tr to obstruct; to stop up

ostruzióne f obstruction

Otèllo m Othello

otorinolaringoia·tra mf (-tri -tre) ear, nose, and throat specialist, otorhinolaryngologist

ótre f wineskin; **otre di vento** windbag (person)

ottàni·co -ca adj (-ci -che) octane

ottano m octane

ottanta adj, m & pron eighty

ottantènne adj eighty-year-old ‖ mf eighty-year-old person

ottantèsi·mo -ma adj, m & pron eightieth

ottantina f about eighty; **essere sull'ottantina** to be about eighty years old

ottava f octave

Ottaviano m Octavian

ottavìno m (mus) piccolo; (com) commission of ⅛ of 1%

otta·vo -va adj & pron eighth ‖ m eighth; octavo ‖ f see **ottava**

ottemperare (**ottèmpero**) intr (with dat) to obey; **ottemperare a** to comply with

ottenebrare (**ottènebro**) tr to becloud

ottenére §271 tr to obtain, get

ottétto m octet

òtti·co -ca (-ci -che) adj optic(al) ‖ m optician ‖ f optics

ottimismo m optimism

ottimi·sta mf (-sti -ste) optimist

ottimìsti·co -ca adj (-ci -che) optimistic

òtti·mo -ma adj very good, excellent ‖ m best; highest rating

òtto adj & pron eight; **le otto** eight o'clock ‖ m eight; eighth (in dates); (sports) racing shell with eight oarsmen; **otto giorni** a week; **otto volante** roller coaster

ottóbre m October

ottocenté·sco -sca adj (-schi -sche) nineteenth-century ‖ **l'Ottocento** the nineteenth century

ottocènto adj, m & pron eight hundred ‖ **l'Ottocento** the nineteenth century

ottoma·no -na adj & m Ottoman ‖ m ottoman (fabric) ‖ f ottoman (sofa)

ottomila adj, m & pron eight thousand

ottoname m brassware

ottonare (**ottóno**) tr to coat with brass

ottóne m brass; **ottoni** (mus) brasses ‖ **Ottone** m Otto

ottuagenà·rio -ria adj & mf (-ri -rie) octogenarian

ottùndere §208 tr (fig) to deaden; (lit) to blunt

otturare tr to fill; to plug; to stop; to obstruct, stop up (e.g., a channel) ‖ ref to clog up

otturatóre m breechblock; (phot, mov) shutter; (mach) cutoff (of cylinder)

otturazióne f filling (of tooth)

ottu·so -sa adj obtuse; blunt

ovàia f ovary

ovale adj oval ‖ m oval; oval face

ovatta f wadding; absorbent cotton

ovattare tr to pad, wad; to muffle

ovazióne f ovation

óve adv (lit) where ‖ conj (lit) if; (poet) while

òvest m west

Ovìdio m Ovid

ovile m sheepcote, fold

ovi·no -na adj ovine ‖ **ovini** mpl sheep

òvo m var of **uovo**

ovoidale adj egg-shaped

òvulo m pill shaped like an egg; (biol) ovum; (bot) ovule

ovùnque adv (lit) wherever; (lit) everywhere

ovvéro conj or; to wit

ovvìa interj come on!

ovviare §119 intr—(with dat) to obviate

òv·vio -via adj (-vi -vie) obvious

oziare §287 (**òzio**) intr to idle, loiter

ò·zio m (-zi) idleness; leisure

oziosi·tà [s] f (-tà) idleness

ozió·so -sa [s] adj idle; useless, vain

ozòno [dz] m ozone

P, p [pi] *m* & *f* fourteenth letter of the Italian alphabet

pacare §197 *tr* (poet) to placate

pacatézza *f* tranquillity, serenity

paca·to -ta *adj* serene, tranquil

pac·ca *f* (-che) slap

pacchétto *m* parcel, package; book (*of matches*); pack (*of cigarettes*)

pàcchia *f* (coll) hearty meal; (coll) godsend, windfall

pacchia·no -na *adj* boorish, uncouth || *mf* boor

pacciamantura *f* mulching

pacciame *m* mulch

pac·co *m* (-chi) package; **pacchi postali** parcel post (*service*); **pacco dono** gift package; **pacco postale** parcel by mail

paccottiglia *f* shoddy goods, junk; trinkets

pace *f* peace; **lasciare in pace** to leave alone; **mettersi il cuore in pace** to resign oneself

pachidèr·ma *m* (-mi) pachyderm

pachista·no -na *adj* & *mf* Pakistani

paciè·re -ra *mf* peacemaker

pacificare §197 (**pacìfico**) *tr* to pacify; to appease; to mediate || *ref* to make one's peace

pacifica·tóre -trice *adj* pacifying || *mf* peacemaker

pacificazióne *f* pacification; appeasement

pacìfi·co -ca (-ci -che) *adj* peaceful, pacific; **è pacifico che** it goes without saying that || *m* peaceable person || **Pacìfico** *adj* & *m* Pacific

pacifismo *m* pacifism

pacifi·sta *mf* (-sti -ste) pacifist

pacioccó·ne -na *mf* chubby, easygoing person

padèlla *f* frying pan; bedpan; **cadere dalla padella nella brace** to jump from the frying pan into the fire

padiglióne *m* pavilion; hunting lodge; roof (*of car*); ward (*of a hospital*); (naut) rigging, tackle; **padiglione auricolare** (anat) auricle of the ear

Pàdova *f* Padua

padre *m* father; sire; **padre di famiglia** provider; (law) head of household; **Padre Eterno** Heavenly Father

padreggiare §290 (**padréggio**) *intr* to resemble one's father

padrino *m* godfather; second (*in duel*)

padrona *f* owner, boss, mistress; **padrona di casa** lady of the house

padronale *adj* proprietary; private (*e.g., car*)

padronanza *f* command; **padronanza di sé stesso** self-control

padróne *m* owner, boss, master; essere **padrone di** + *inf* to have the right to + *inf*; **padrone di casa** landlord; **padrone di sé** cool and collected

padroneggiare §290 (**padronéggio**) *tr* to master, control

paesàg·gio *m* (-gi) landscape

paesaggi·sta *mf* (-sti -ste) landscapist

paesa·no -na *adj* country || *mf* villager || *m* countryman || *f* countrywoman; **alla paesana** according to local tradition

paése *m* country; village; **i Paesi Bassi** the Netherlands; (hist) the Low Countries; **mandare a quel paese** to send to blazes

paesi·sta *mf* (-sti -ste) landscapist

paffu·to -ta *adj* chubby, plump

pa·ga *f* (-ghe) salary; wages; repayment; **mala paga** poor pay (*person*)

pagàbile *adj* payable

pagàia *f* paddle

pagaménto *m* payment; **pagamento alla consegna** c.o.d.

paganésimo *m* paganism

paga·no -na *adj* & *mf* pagan, heathen

pagare §209 *tr* to pay; to pay for; **far pagare** to charge; **pagare di egual moneta** to repay in kind; **pagare il fio per** to pay (the penalty) for; **pagare in natura** to pay in kind; **pagare salato** to pay dearly; **pagare un occhio della testa** to pay through the nose || *intr* to pay

paga·tóre -trice *mf* payer

pagèlla *f* report card

pàg·gio *m* (-gi) page (*boy attendant*)

paghe·rò *m* (-rò) promissory note, I.O.U.

pàgina *f* page (*e.g., of book*)

paginatura *f* pagination

pàglia *f* straw; thatch (*for roof*); **paglia di ferro** steel wool; **paglia di legno** excelsior

pagliaccé·sco -sca *adj* (-schi -sche) clownish

pagliaccétto *m* rompers

pagliacciata *f* buffoonery, antics

pagliàc·cio *m* (-ci) clown, buffoon; **fare il pagliaccio** to clown

pa·gliàio *m* (-gliài) heap of straw; haystack

paglieric·cio *m* (-ci) straw mattress

paglieri·no -na *adj* straw-colored

pagliétta *f* skimmer, boater; steel wool; (coll) pettifogger

pagnòtta *f* loaf of bread; (coll) bread

pa·go -ga *adj* (-ghi -ghe) satisfied || *f* see **paga**

paguro *m* (zool) hermit crab

pà·io *m* (-ia *fpl*) pair, couple; **è un altro paio di maniche** this is a horse of another color; **fare il paio** to match perfectly

paiòlo *m* caldron, kettle; (mil) platform

Pakistan, il Pakistan

pala *f* shovel; blade (*e.g., of turbine*); paddle (*of waterwheel*); peel (*of baker*); **pala d'altare** altarpiece

paladi·no -na *mf* champion || *m* paladin; **farsi paladino di** to champion

palafitta *f* pile dwelling; piles (*to support a structure*)

palafrenière *m* groom

palafréno *m* palfrey

palan·ca *f* (-che) beam, board; (naut)

gangplank; copper coin; **palanche** (coll) money

palanchino *m* palanquin; (naut) pulley

palandrana *f* (joc) long, full coat

palata *f* shovelful; stroke (*of oar*); **a palate** by the bucketful

palatale *adj & f* palatal

palati·no -na *adj* palatine; (anat) palatal

palato *m* palate

palazzina *f* villa

palazzo *m* palace; large office or government building; mansion; **palazzo dello sport** sports arena; **palazzo di città** city hall; **palazzo di giustizia** courthouse

palchetti·sta (-sti -ste) *mf* (theat) box-holder || *m* person who lays floors

palchétto *m* shelf; (theat) small box; (journ) box

pal·co *m* **(-chi)** flooring; scaffold; stand, platform; (theat) box; (theat) stage

palcoscèni·co *m* **(-ci)** (theat) stage

palesare (paléso) *tr* to reveal, manifest || *ref* to show oneself

palése *adj* plain, manifest; **fare palese** to manifest, reveal

palèstra *f* gymnasium; palestra

palétta *f* small shovel, scoop; blade (*of turbine*)

palettata *f* shovelful

palétto *m* stake; bolt (*of door*)

palificazióne *f* pile work (*in the ground for foundation*); line of telephone poles

pà·lio *m* **(-lii)** embroidered cloth (*given as prize*); **metter in palio** to offer as a prize; **palio di Siena** colorful horse-race at Siena

palissandro *m* Brazilian rosewood

palizzata *f* palisade; picket fence

palla *f* ball; bullet; sphere; **dar palla nera a** to blackball; **palla da cannone** cannon ball; **palla di neve** snowball; **prendere la palla al balzo** to seize the opportunity

pallabase *f* baseball

pallacanè·stro *f* **(-stro)** basketball

pallamuro *m* handball

pallanuòto *f* water polo

pallavó·lo *f* **(-lo)** volleyball

palleggiare §290 **(palléggio)** *tr* to toss (*e.g., a javelin*); to shift from one hand to another || *intr* (tennis) to knock a few balls; (soccer) to dribble || *ref*—**palleggiarsi la responsabilità** to shift the responsibility

pallég·gio *m* **(-gi)** (tennis) knocking back and forth; (soccer) dribbling

palliati·vo -va *adj & m* palliative

pallidézza *f* paleness

pàlli·do -da *adj* pale; faint

pallina *f* marble; small ball; **pallina antitarmica** mothball

pallino *m* little ball; (bowling) jack; bullet; **a pallini** polka-dot; **avere il pallino di** to be crazy about; **pallini buckshot**; polka dots

palloncino *m* child's balloon; Chinese lantern

pallóne *m* (soccer) ball; (aer) balloon;

pallone di sbarramento barrage balloon; **pallone gonfiato** (fig) stuffed shirt; **pallone sonda** trial balloon

pallonétto *m* (tennis) lob

pallóre *m* pallor, paleness

pallòttola *f* pellet; ball; bullet

pallottolière *m* abacus

pallovale *f* rugby

palma *f* palm; **tenere in palma di mano** to hold in the highest esteem

palmare *adj* evident, plain

palménto *m* millstone; **mangiare a quattro palmenti** (coll) to stuff oneself eating

palméto *m* palm grove

palmipede *adj* palmate, web-footed

palmi·zio *m* **(-zi)** palm

palmo *m* span; palm (*of hand*); foot (*measure*); **a palmo a palmo** little by little; **restare con un palmo di naso** to be disappointed

palo *m* pole (*of wood or metal*); beam; pile; (soccer, football) goal post; **fare il palo** to be on the lookout (*said of thieves*); **palo indicatore** signpost; **saltare di palo in frasca** to digress

palombaro *m* diver

palómbo *m* dogfish

palpàbile *adj* palpable

palpare *tr* to touch; to palpate

pàlpebra *f* eyelid; **battere le palpebre** to blink

palpeggiare §290 **(palpéggio)** *tr* to finger, touch repeatedly

palpitante *adj* throbbing; burning (*question*); fluttering (*e.g., with love*)

palpitare (pàlpito) *intr* to palpitate, pulsate; (fig) to pine

palpitazióne *f* palpitation

pàlpito *m* heartbeat; (fig) throb

pal·tò *m* **(-tò)** overcoat

paltoncino *m* child's winter coat; lady's topcoat

paludaménto *m* (joc) array, attire

palude *f* marsh, bog

paludó·so -sa **[s]** *adj* marshy

palustre *adj* marshy

pàmpino *m* grape leaf

panacèa *f* panacea, cure-all

pàna·ma *m* **(-ma)** Panama hat

panamé·gno -gna *adj & mf* Panamenian

panamènse *adj & mf* Panamenian

panare *tr* (culin) to bread

pan·ca *f* **(-che)** bench; **scaldare le panche** (coll) to loaf around; (coll) to waste one's time at school

pancétta *f* potbelly; bacon

panchétto *m* footstool

panchina *f* bench

pàn·cia *f* **(-ce)** belly; **a pancia all'aria** on one's back; **mangiare a crepa pancia** to stuff oneself like a pig; **mettere su pancia** to grow a potbelly; **salvar la pancia per i fichi** to not take any chances; **tenersi la pancia dalle risate** to split one's side laughing

panciata *f* belly flop

pancièra *f* bellypiece; body girth

panciòlle *m*—**in panciolle** frittering one's time away

panciòtto *m* waistcoat; vest; **panciotto a maglia** cardigan
panciu·to -ta *adj* potbellied
pàncre·as *m* (-as) pancreas
pandemò·nio *m* (-ni) pandemonium
pane *m* bread; thread (*of screw*); cake (*e.g., of butter*); loaf (*of sugar*); (metallurgy) pig; **a pane di zucchero** conic(al); **dire pane al pane e vino al vino** to call a spade a spade; **essere come pane e cacio** to be hand and glove; **essere pane per i propri denti** to be a match for s.o.; **guadagnarsi il pane** to earn one's living; **pane a cassetta** sandwich bread; **pane azzimo** unleavened bread, matzoth; **pan di Spagna** angel food cake, sponge cake; **pane integrale** graham bread; **render pan per focaccia** to give tit for tat
panegìri·co *m* (-ci) panegyric
panetterìa *f* bakery
panettière *m* baker
panétto *m* pat (*e.g., of butter*)
pànfilo *m* yacht
panfrutto *m* plum cake
pangrattato *m* bread crumbs
pània *f* birdlime; **cadere nella pania** to fall into the trap
pàni·co -ca (-ci -che) *adj* panicky ‖ *m* panic
pani·co *m* (-chi) (bot) Italian millet
panièra *f* basket; basketful
panière *m* basket; basketful
panificazióne *f* breadmaking
panifì·cio *m* (-ci) bakery
panino *m* roll, bun; **panino imbottito** sandwich
panna *f* cream, heavy cream; **essere in panna** (naut) to lie to; (aut) to have a breakdown; **mettere in panna** (naut) to heave to; **panna montata** whipped cream
panne *f* (aut) breakdown; **essere in panne** (aut) to have a breakdown
pannèllo *m* linen cloth; pane; panel (*of machine*); (archit; elec) panel
pannìcolo *m* (anat) membrane, tissue
panno *m* cloth; woolen cloth; film, membrane; **bianco come un panno** as white as a ghost; **mettersi nei panni di** to put oneself in the boots of; **non stare più nei propri panni** to be beside oneself with joy; **panni** clothes; **panno verde** baize
pannòcchia *f* ear (*of corn*)
pannolino *m* linen cloth; diaper; sanitary napkin
panòplia *f* panoply
panora·ma *m* (-mi) panorama
panoràmi·co -ca *adj* (-ci -che) panoramic ‖ *f* panoramic view; (mov) panoramic scene
pantaloncini *mpl* trunks
pantalóni *mpl* trousers; **pantaloni da donna** slacks
pantano *m* bog, quagmire
panteismo *m* pantheism
pànteon *m* pantheon
pantèra *f* panther; (slang) police car
pantòfola *f* slipper
pantomima *f* pantomine, mimicry

panzana *f* (lit) fib, lie
Pàolo *m* Paul
paonaz·zo -za *adj* & *m* purple
pa·pa *m* (-pi) pope; **ad ogni morte di papa** once in a blue moon; **morto un papa se ne fa un altro** nobody is indispensable
pa·pà *m* (-pà) daddy, papa
papàbile *adj* likely to be elected ‖ *mf* front runner ‖ *m* cardinal likely to be elected to the papacy
papale *adj* papal (*e.g., benediction*); Papal (*States*)
papali·no -na *adj* papal ‖ *m* advocate of papal temporal power ‖ *f* skullcap
paparazzo *m* freelance photographer
papato *m* papacy
papàvero *m* poppy; **alto papavero** (fig) big shot
pàpera *f* young goose; slip of the tongue; spoonerism; **fare una papera** to make a boner
pàpero *m* gander
papiro *m* papyrus
pappa *f* bread soup, farina, pap; **pappa molla** (fig) jellyfish
pappafì·co *m* (-chi) (naut) topgallant; (slang) goatee
pappagallo *m* parrot; bedpan; (slang) masher
pappagòr·gia *f* (-ge) double chin, jowl
pappare *tr* (coll) to gulp; (fig) to gobble up fraudulently
pappata·ci *m* (-ci) gnat
pappina *f* light pap; poultice
pàpri·ca *f* (-che) paprika
para *f* crepe rubber
paràbola *f* parable; (geom) parabola
parabórdo *m* (naut) fender
parabréz·za [ddzz] *m* (-za) windshield
paracadutare *tr* to parachute, airdrop ‖ *ref* to parachute
paracadu·te *m* (-te) parachute
paracadutismo *m* parachute jumping; (sports) sky diving
paracaduti·sta *mf* (-sti -ste) parachutist; skydiver ‖ *m* paratrooper
paracarro *m* spur stone
paracól·pi *m* (-pi) doorstop
paràcqua *m* (paràcqua) umbrella
paradèn·ti *m* (-ti) (sports) mouthpiece
paradisìa·co -ca *adj* (-ci -che) heavenly
paradiso *m* paradise
paradossale *adj* paradoxical
paradòsso *m* paradox
parafa *f* initials
parafan·go *m* (-ghi) fender, mudguard
parafare *tr* to initial
paraffina *f* paraffin
parafiam·ma *m* (-ma) fire-proof partition
parafrasare (paràfraso) *tr* to paraphrase
paràfra·si *f* (-si) paraphrase
parafùlmine *m* lightning rod
parafuò·co *m* (-co) screen, fender (*in front of fireplace*)
paràg·gio *m* (-gi) lineage; **paraggi** neighborhood, vicinity
paragonàbile *adj* comparable
paragonare (paràgono) *tr* to compare
paragóne *m* comparison; **a paragone di**

in comparison with; **mettere a para-gone** to compare; **senza paragone** beyond compare

paragrafare (**paràgrafo**) *tr* to paragraph

paràgrafo *m* paragraph

paraguaia·no -na *adj & mf* Paraguayan

paràli·si *f* (**-si**) paralysis

paralìti·co -ca *adj & mf* (**-ci -che**) paralytic

paralizzare [ddzz] *tr* to paralyze

parallè·lo -la *adj & m* parallel || *f* (geom) parallel line; **parallele** (sports) parallel bars

paralume *m* lamp shade

paramano *m* cuff, wristband; (archit) facing brick

paraménto *s* facing (*of a wall*); (eccl) vestment

parami·ne *m* (**-ne**) (nav) paravane

paramó·sche *m* (**-sche**) fly net

paran·co *m* (**-chi**) tackle

paranin·fo -fa *mf* matchmaker

paranòi·co -ca *adj & mf* (**-ci -che**) paranoiac

paraòc·chi *m* (**-chi**) blinker (*on horse*)

parapètto *m* parapet

parapì·glia *m* (**-glia**) hubbub

parapiòg·gia *m* (**-gia**) umbrella

parare *tr* to adorn; to hang; to protect; to parry (*a thrust*); to offer; to drive (*e.g., cattle*) || *intr*—**dove va a parare?** what are you driving at? || *ref* to protect oneself; (eccl) to don the vestments; **pararsi dinanzi a** to loom up in front of

parasóle *m* parasol; (aut) sun visor

paraspal·le *m* (**-le**) (sports) shoulder pad

parassi·ta (**-ti -te**) *adj* parasitic || *m* parasite

parassità·rio -ria *adj* (**-ri -rie**) parasitic(al)

parassìti·co -ca *adj* (**-ci -che**) parasitic(al)

parastatale *adj* government-controlled || *mf* employee of government-controlled agency

parastin·chi *m* (**-chi**) (sports) shin guard

parata *f* fence, bar; (fencing) parry; (soccer) catch; (mil) parade; **mala parata** dangerous situation

paratìa *f* bulkhead

parato *m* hangings; **parati** hangings; (naut) bilgeways

paratóia *f* sluice gate

paraur·ti *m* (**-ti**) (aut) bumper; (rr) buffer

paravènto *m* screen

Par·ca *f* (**-che**) Fate

parcare §197 *tr & intr* to park

parcèlla *f* bill, fee, honorarium; parcel, lot (*of land*)

parcheggiare §290 (**parchéggio**) *tr & intr* to park

parchég·gio *m* (**-gi**) parking; parking lot

parchìmetro *m* parking meter

par·co -ca (**-chi -che**) *adj* frugal; parsimonious || *m* park; parking; parking lot; **parco dei divertimenti** amusement park

paréc·chio -chia (**-chi -chie**) *adj indef* a good deal of, a lot of; **parecchi** several || *pron* a good deal, a lot; **parecchi** several || **parecchio** *adv* a lot; rather

pareggiare §290 (**paréggio**) *tr* to level; to equal; to match; to balance; to recognize || *intr* (sports) to tie

pareggia·to -ta *adj* accredited (*school*)

parég·gio *m* (**-gi**) leveling; matching; (sports) tie; **pareggio del bilancio** balancing of the budget

parentado *m* kinsfolk, kindred; relationship; **concludere il parentado di** to arrange for the wedding of

parènte *mf* relative; (lit) parent; **parenti** kin

parentèla *f* relationship; relations

parènte·si *f* (**-si**) parenthesis; break, interval; **fra parentesi** parenthetically; in parentheses; **parentesi quadra** bracket

parére *m* opinion, mind; advice; **a mio parere** in my opinion || §210 *intr* (ESSERE) to seem; **che Le pare?** what is your opinion?; **ma Le pare!** not at all!; **mi pare che** + *subj* it seems to me that + *ind*; I guess that + *ind*; **non Le pare?** don't you think so?; **non mi pare vero** I can't believe it

paréte *f* wall; **tra le pareti domestiche** within the four walls of the home

pargolét·to -ta *adj* (poet) infantile || *mf* (poet) child

pàrgo·lo -la *adj* (poet) infantile || *mf* (poet) child

pari *adj invar* equal, even; **camminare di pari passo** to walk at the same rate; **essere pari** to be quits; **essere pari al proprio compito** to be equal to the task; **fare un salto a piè pari** to jump with feet together; **pari pari** verbatim; **rimanere pari con** (sports) to be tied with; **saltare a piè pari** to skip (*e.g., a page*); to dodge (*a difficulty*); **trattare da pari a pari** to treat as an equal || *m* peer; **al pari di** as, like; **del pari** also; **in pari** even, leveled; **senza pari** matchless, peerless || *f*—**stare alla pari con** to be an even match for

parìa *f* peerage

pà·ria *m* (**-ria**) pariah

parificare §197 (**parìfico**) *tr* to level; to match; to accredit (*a school*); to balance

Parigi *f* Paris

parigi·no -na *adj & mf* Parisian || *f* slow-burning stove; Parisian woman; (rr) switching spur

parìglia *f* pair, couple; team (*of horses*); (cards) two of a kind; **rendere la pariglia** to give tit for tat

pariménti *adv* likewise

pari·tà *f* (**-tà**) parity

paritèti·co -ca *adj* (**-ci -che**) joint (*e.g., committee*)

parlamentare *adj* parliamentary || *mf* member of parliament || *m* (mil) envoy || *v* (**parlaménto**) *intr* to parley

parlaménto *m* parliament

parlante *adj* talking; life-like || *mf* speaker

parlantina *f* glibness

parlare *m* talk, speech; dialect ‖ *tr* to speak (*a language*) ‖ *intr* to speak, talk; to discuss; **chi parla?** (telp) hello!; **far parlare di sé** to be talked about; **parlare chiaro** to speak bluntly; **parlare del più e del meno** to make small talk; **parlare tra sé e sé** to talk to oneself ‖ *ref* to talk to one another

parla·to -ta *adj* spoken; current (*speech*); talking (*movie*) ‖ *m* talkie; (mov) sound track; (theat) dialogue ‖ *f* speech, talk; dialect

parla·tóre -trice *mf* speaker

parlatò·rio *m* (**-ri**) visting room (*e.g., in jail*)

parlottare (**parlòtto**) *intr* to whisper in secret

parmigia·no -na *adj & mf* Parmesan ‖ *m* Parmesan cheese

parnaso *m* Parnassus (*poetry, poets*) ‖ **il Parnaso** Mount Parnassus

paro *m*—**in un par d'ore** in a couple of hours ‖ *adv*—**andare a paro** to keep abreast; **mettere a paro** to compare

parodia *f* parody; **fare la parodia di** to parody

parodiare §287 (**paròdio**) *tr* to parody

paròla *f* word; speech; **avere parole con** to have words with; **buttare la mezza parola** to make an allusion; **dare la parola a** to give the floor to; **di poche parole** of few words; **domandare la parola a** to ask for the floor; **essere di parola** to keep one's word; **essere in parola con** to have dealings with; **mangiarsi la parola** to break one's word; **mangiarsi le parole** to slur one's words; **non far parola** to not breathe a word; **parola crociata** crossword puzzle; **parola d'ordine** password; **parola macedonia** acronym **parola sdrucciola** proparoxytone; **parole** lyrics; **parole di circostanza** occasional words; **prendere la parola** to take the floor; **rivolgere la parola a** to address; **venire a parole** to begin to quarrel

parolàc·cia *f* (**-ce**) dirty word; swearword

paro·làio -làia (**-lài -làie**) *adj* wordy, verbose ‖ *mf* windbag

parolière *m* lyricist

parossismo *m* paroxysm; climax

parossìto·no -na *adj* paroxytone

parotite *f* (pathol) parotitis; **parotite epidemica** (pathol) mumps

parrici·da *mf* (**-di -de**) patricide

parrocchétto *m* parakeet; (naut) foretopsail; (naut) fore-topmast

parrocchia *f* parish

parrocchia·no -na *mf* parishioner

pàrro·co *m* (**-ci**) rector, parson

parruc·ca *f* (**-che**) wig; (fig) old fogey

parsimònia *f* parsimony

parsimonió·so -sa [s] *adj* parsimonious

partàc·cia *f*—**fare una partaccia** to break one's word; **fare una partaccia a** to make a scene in front of; to rebuke loudly

parte *f* part; share; section; side; party; partiality; (theat) role; **a parte** separately; (theat) aside; **d'altra parte** on the other hand; **da parte** aside; **da parte mia** as for me; **fare le parti** to divide in shares; **gran parte di** a great deal of; **in parte** partially; **la maggior parte di** most of; **parte civile** (law) plaintiff; **parte . . . parte** some . . . some; **part . . . part;** **prendere in mala parte** to take amiss

partecipante *adj* participating ‖ *mf* participant; (sports) contestant

partecipare (**partécipo**) *tr* to announce; (lit) to share in ‖ *intr*—**partecipare a** to share in; to participate in; **partecipare di** to partake of (*e.g., the nature of an animal*)

partecipazióne *f* announcement; card; announcement (*of a wedding*); share in a business); participation (*in some action*)

partécipe *adj* sharing, partaking

parteggiare §290 (**partéggio**) *intr* to side; **parteggiare per** to side with

Partenóne *m* Parthenon

partènte *adj* departing ‖ *mf* person departing, traveler; (sports) starter

partenza *f* departure; sailing; (sports) start; **di partenza** or **in partenza** about to leave; **partenza lanciata** (sports) running start

particèlla *f* particle

partici·pio *m* (**-pi**) participle

particolare *adj* particular; private; **in particolare** especially ‖ *m* detail

particolareggiare §290 (**particolaréggio**) *tr* to detail

particolarismo *m* regionalism, particularism

particolarìsti·co -ca *adj* (**-ci -che**) particularistic; individualistic

particolari·tà *f* (**-tà**) peculiarity; detail

partigianerìa *f* partisanship, factionalism

partigia·no -na *adj & mf* partisan

partire §176 *tr* (lit) to divide ‖ *v* (**parto**) *intr* to depart; (fig) to arise; **a partire da** beginning with; **far partire** to start (*e.g., a car*) ‖ *ref* to depart, leave

parti·to -ta *adj* parted ‖ *m* match (*in marriage*); (pol) party; **ridotto a mal partito** in bad shape; **mettere la testa a partito** to reform; **partito preso** parti pris; **prendere partito** to take sides; to make up one's mind; **trarre il miglior partito da** to make the best of ‖ *f* panel (*e.g., of door*); lot (*of goods*); game; match; party; round (*of golf*); (com) entry; **partita di caccia** hunting party; **partita doppia** (com) double entry; **partita semplice** (com) single entry

partitura *f* (mus) score

partizióne *f* partition, division

parto *m* birth, childbirth

partorire §176 *tr* to bear, bring forth

parvènza *f* (lit) appearance

parziale *adj* partial, one-sided

parziali·tà *f* (**-tà**) partiality

pàscere §211 *tr, intr & ref* to pasture, graze

pa·scià *m* (**-scià**) pasha

pasciu·to -ta *adj* well-fed

pascolare (pàscolo) *tr* & *intr* to pasture
pàscolo *m* pasture
Pasqua *f* Easter; contento come una Pasqua as happy as a lark; Pasqua fiorita Palm Sunday
pasquale *adj* paschal (*e.g., lamb*)
passàbile *adj* passable, tolerable
passàg•gio *m* (-gi) passage; transfer; crossing; traffic; passageway; ride; promotion; (sports) pass; aprirsi il passaggio to make one's way; di passaggio in passing; transient (*visitor*); essere di passaggio to be passing by; passaggio a livello railroad crossing; passaggio zebrato zebra crossing; vietato il passaggio no thoroughfare
passamano *m* passing from hand to hand; ribbon; (coll) railing, handrail
passante *adj* passing (*shot*) || *mf* passerby || *m* strap
passapòrto *m* passport
passare *tr* to cross; to pass; to undergo (*a medical examination*); to move; to hand; to pay; to send (*word*); to pierce; to spend (*time*); to strain; to go over; to let have (*e.g., a slap*); to overstep (*the bounds*); passare in rassegna to pass in review; passare per le armi to execute; passare un brutto quarto d'ora to have a bad ten minutes; passare un guaio to have a hard time; passarla a qlcu (coll) to forgive s.o.; passarla liscia (coll) to get off unscathed; passarsela bene (coll) to have a good time || *intr* (ESSERE) to pass; to go; to filter (*said of air, light*); to move; to spoil (*said of food*); to be overcooked; to be promoted; to become; to enter; (lit) to be over; fare passare qlcu to let s.o. come in; passare a nozze to get married; passare a seconde nozze to remarry; passare avanti a to overcome; passare di mente a to forget, *e.g.*, gli è passata di mente la riunione he forgot the meeting; passare di moda to go out of style; passare in giudicato (law) to be no longer appealable; passare per to pass so; passare per il rotto della cuffia to barely make it; passare sopra qlco to overlook s.th; passi! come in!; passo! (rad) over!; passo (cards) pass
passata *f* purée; dare una passata a to glance at; dare una passata di straccio a to rub lightly with a rag; to give a lick and a promise to; di passata hurriedly
passatèmpo *m* pastime; hobby
passati•sta *mf* (-sti -ste) traditionalist
passa•to -ta *adj* past; last; overcooked; essere passato (coll) to be no longer in one's prime; passato di moda out of fashion || *m* past; purée; passato prossimo present perfect; passato remoto preterit || *f* see passata
passatóia *f* runner (*rug*)
passa•tóio *m* (-tói) stepping stone
passeggè•ro -ra *adj* passing || *mf* passenger; passeggero clandestino stowaway

passeggiare §290 (passéggio) *tr* to walk (*e.g., a horse*) || *intr* to walk, promenade
passeggiata *f* promenade; walk; drive, ride; drive, road; fare una passeggiata to take a walk; to take a ride
passeggiatrice *f* streetwalker
passég•gio *m* (-gi) walk; promenade; andare a passeggio to take a walk
passerèlla *f* gangway; catwalk; footbridge
pàsse•ro -ra *mf* sparrow || *f*—passera di mare (ichth) flounder
passibile *adj*—passibile di subject to, liable to
passiflòra *f* passionflower
passino *m* colander, strainer
passione *f* passion
passivi•tà *f* (-tà) passivity; (com) deficit
passi•vo -va *adj* passive || *m* (com) liabilities; (com) debit side; (gram) passive
pas•so -sa *adj*—see uva || *m* step; passage; pass (*in mountain*); pace; footstep; pitch (*of screw, helix, etc.*); (aut) wheelbase; (phot) tread; (phot) size (*of roll*); a grandi passi with great strides; andare al passo to march in step; to walk (*said of a horse*); a passi di gigante by leaps and bounds; a passo di corsa running; a passo d'uomo walking, at a walk; aprire il passo to open the way; di buon passo at a good clip; di pari passo at the same rate; fare quattro passi to take a stroll; passo doppio paso doble; passo d'uomo manhole; step; passo falso misstep; (fig) stumble; sbarrare il passo to block the way; seguire i passi di to walk in the footsteps of || *interj* (cards) pass!; over!
pasta *f* paste; dough; di pasta grossa uncouth, coarse; pasta alimentare pasta, macaroni products; pasta all'uovo egg noodles; pasta asciutta pasta with sauce and cheese; pasta dentifricia toothpaste; una pasta d'uomo a good-natured man
pastasciutta *f* pasta with sauce and cheese
pasteggiare §290 (pastéggio) *intr* to dine
pastèllo *adj invar* & *m* pastel || *m* crayon
pastétta *f* batter; (coll) trickery
pastic•ca *f* (-che) lozenge, tablet; pasticche per la tosse cough drops
pasticceria *f* pastrymaking; pastry; pastry shop
pasticciare §128 (pasticcio) *tr* & *intr* to bungle; to scribble
pasticciè•re -ra *mf* pastry cook; confectioner
pasticcino *m* cookie; patty
pastic•cio *m* (-ci) pie (*of meat, macaroni, etc*); bungle; mess; cacciarsi nei pasticci to wind up in the soup
pasticció•ne -na *mf* bungler
pastifi•cio *m* (-ci) spaghetti and macaroni factory
pastiglia *f* lozenge, tablet; pastiglia per la tosse cough drop

pastina·ca *f* (-che) parsnip
pa·sto -sta *adj* (archaic) fed || *m* meal; **pasto a prezzo fisso** table d'hôte || *f* see **pasta**
pastóia *f* hobble; (fig) shackle
pastóne *m* mash
pastóra *f* shepherdess
pastorale *adj* pastoral
pastóre *m* shepherd; pastor
pastori·zio -zia (-zi -zie) *adj* shepherd || *f* sheep raising
pastorizzare [ddzz] *tr* to pasteurize
pastó·so -sa [s] *adj* pasty; mellow
pastrano *m* overcoat
pastura *f* pasture; hay; fodder
patac·ca *f* (-che) large, worthless coin; fake; (coll) medal; (coll) spot
patata *f* potato
patatràc *m* (**patatràc**) crash
patèlla *f* kneecap; (zool) limpet
patè·ma *m* (-mi) affliction; **patema d'animo** anxiety
patenta·to -tn *adj* licensed; (coll) well-known
patènte *adj* patent || *f* license; driver's license; **patente sanitaria** (naut) bill of health
patentino *m* (aut) permit
pateréc·cio *m* (-ci) whitlow
paternale *adj* (obs) paternal || *f* reprimand
paterni·tà *f* (-tà) paternity; authorship
patèr·no -na *adj* paternal; fatherly
paternòstro *m* Lord's Prayer; **è vero come il paternostro** it is the gospel truth
patèti·co -ca (-ci -che) *adj* pathetic; mawkish || *m* pathos; mawkishness
pathos *m* pathos
patibile *adj* endurable
patibolare *adj* gallows
patibolo *m* executioner's instrument; scaffold
patimento *m* suffering
pàtina *f* patina; coating (*on paper*); varnish; fur (*on tongue*)
patinare (**pàtino**) *tr* to gloss, glaze (*e.g., paper*)
patire §176 *tr* to suffer; (gram) to be the recipient of (*an action*) || *intr* to suffer
pati·to -ta *adj* suffering, sickly || *mf* fan || *m* boyfriend || *f* girlfriend
patòge·no -na *adj* pathogenic
patologia *f* pathology
patològi·co -ca *adj* (-ci -che) pathologic(al)
patos *m* var of **pathos**
patrasso *m*—**andare a patrasso** to die; to go to ruin; **mandare a patrasso** to kill; to ruin
pàtria *f* fatherland, native land
patriar·ca *m* (-chi) patriarch
patriarcale *adj* patriarchal
patrigno *m* stepfather
patrimoniale *adj* patrimonial; property (*tax*); capital (*e.g., transaction*)
patrimò·nio *m* (-ni) patrimony; estate; fortune; (fig) heritage
pà·trio -tria (-tri -trie) *adj* paternal; of one's country (*e.g., love*) || *f* see **patria**

patriò·ta *mf* (-ti -te) patriot; (coll) fellow citizen
patriòtti·co -ca *adj* (-ci -che) patriotic
patriottismo *m* patriotism
patrì·zio -zia (-zi -zie) *adj & m* patrician || **Patrizio** *m* Patrick
patrocinante *adj* pleading (*lawyer*)
patrocinare *tr* to favor, sponsor; to plead
patrocina·tóre -trice *mf* defender; pleader
patroci·nio *m* (-ni) support; sponsorship; (law) defense; **patrocinio gratuito** public defense
patronato *m* patronage; charitable institution, foundation; **patronato scolastico** state aid fund
patronéssa *f* sponsor; trustee (*of charitable institution*)
patròno *m* patron saint; patron; sponsor; trustee (*of charitable institution*); (law) counsel
patta *f* flap (*of garment*); bill (*of anchor*); (coll) potholder; **essere or far patta** to be even, tie
patteggiamento *m* negotiation
patteggiare §290 (**pattéggio**) *tr & intr* to negotiate
pattinàggio *m* skating
pattinare (**pàttino**) *intr* to skate; to skid (*said of a car*)
pattina·tóio *m* (-tói) skating rink
pattina·tóre -trice *mf* skater
pàttino *m* skate; guide block (*of an elevator*); (aer) skid, runner; **pattino a rotelle** roller skate
pattino *m* racing shell with outrigger floats
patto *m* pact; **a nessun patto** by no means; **a patto che** provided (that); **patto sociale** social contract; **venire a patti** to come to terms
pattuglia *f* patrol
pattugliare §280 *tr & intr* to patrol
pattuire §176 *tr & intr* to negotiate
pattui·to -ta *adj* agreed || *m* agreement
pattume *m* litter, garbage
pattumièra *f* dustpan; trash bin
patùrnie *fpl*—**avere le paturnie** (coll) to be in the dumps
paura *f* fear; **aver paura di** to be afraid of; **da far paura** frightful; **dar or metter paura a** to frighten; **per paura che** for fear that; lest
pauró·so -sa [s] *adj* fearful
pàusa *f* pause
pausare (**pàuso**) *tr* (lit) to interrupt || *intr* (lit) to pause
paventare (**pavènto**) *tr & intr* to fear
pavesare (**pavéso**) *tr* to deck with flags; to dress (*a ship*)
pavése [s] *adj*—see **zuppa** || *m* pavis (*shield*); (naut) bunting
pàvi·do -da *adj* cowardly, timid
pavimentare (**pavimento**) *tr* to pave
pavimentazióne *f* paving, pavement
pavimén·to *m* floor; bottom (*of sea*); paving (*of street*)
pavoncèlla *f* lapwing
pavó·ne -na or -néssa *mf* peacock
pavoneggiare §290 (**pavonéggio**) *ref* to swagger, strut
pazientare (**paziènto**) *intr* to be patient

paziènte *adj & mf* patient

paziènza *f* patience; **fare scappare la pazienza a** to drive mad; **pazienza!** too bad!

pazzé·sco -sca *adj* (-schi -sche) crazy, wild

pazzìa *f* madness, insanity; folly; **fare pazzie** to act like a fool

paz·zo -za *adj* crazy, insane; **andar pazzo per** to be crazy about ‖ *mf* crazy person

pèc·ca *f* (-che) imperfection

peccaminó·so -sa [s] *adj* sinful

peccare §197 (pècco) *intr* to sin; to be lacking; to be at fault

peccato *m* sin; **che peccato!** what a pity!; **è un peccato** it's a shame

pecca·tóre -trice *mf* sinner

pécchia *f* bee

pecchióne *m* drone

péce *f* pitch; **pece greca** rosin

pechinése [s] *adj & mf* Pekingese

Pechino *f* Peking

pècora *f* sheep

peco·ràio *m* (-rài) shepherd

pecorèlla *f* small sheep, lamb

pecori·no -na *adj* sheep; sheepish ‖ *m* sheep-milk cheese ‖ *f* sheep manure

peculato *m* embezzlement, peculation

peculiare *adj* peculiar

peculiari·tà *f* (-tà) peculiarity

pecù·lio *m* (-li) nest egg, savings; (obs) cattle

pecùnia *m* (lit) money

pecunià·rio -ria *adj* (-ri -rie) pecuniary

pedàg·gio *m* (-gi) toll

pedagogìa *f* pedagogy, pedagogics

pedagògi·co -ca *adj* (-ci -che) pedagogic(al)

pedagò·go -ga *m* (-ghi -ghe) pedagogue

pedalare *intr* to pedal

pedale *m* trunk (*of tree*); pedal; treadle (*e.g., of sewing machine*)

pedalièra *f* pedals, pedal keyboard; (aer) rudder bar

pedalino *m* (coll) sock, short stocking

pedana *f* footrest; platform; bedside rug; hem (*of skirt*); (aut) running board; (sports) springboard

pedante *adj* pedantic ‖ *m* pedant

pedanterìa *f* pedantry

pedante·sco -sca *adj* (-schi -sche) pedantic

pedata *f* kick; footprint; tread (*of step*)

pedèstre *adj* pedestrian

pedia·tra *mf* (-tri -tre) pediatrician

pediatrìa *f* pediatrics

pedicu·re *mf* (-re) pedicure

pedicu·ro -ra *mf* var of **pedicure**

pediiù·vio *m* (-vi) foot bath

pedina *f* (checkers) checker, man; (chess) pawn

pedinare *tr* to shadow, follow about

pedisse·quo -qua *adj* servile

pedivèlla *f* pedal crank

pedóne *m* (pedestrian); (chess) pawn

pedule *m* stocking foot ‖ *fpl* climbing shoes, sneakers

pedùncolo *m* (anat, bot, zool) peduncle

pegamòide *f* imitation leather

pèggio *adj invar* worse; **il peggio** worst, e.g., **il peggio ragazzo** the worst boy; ‖ *m* worst; **andare per il peggio** to be getting worse ‖ *f* worst; **alla peggio** if worst comes to worst; **averne la peggio** to get the worst of it ‖ *adv* worse; worst; at worst; **peggio** + *pp* less + *pp*; least + *pp*; **tanto peggio** so much the worse

peggioraménto *m* deterioration, worsening

peggiorare (peggióro) *tr & intr* to worsen

peggió·re (-ri) *adj* worse; worst ‖ *m* worst

pégli §4

pégno *m* pledge, pawn

pégola *f* pitch; (coll) bad luck

péi §4

pél §4

pèla·go *m* (-ghi) (poet) open sea; (coll) mess; **pelago di guai** sea of trouble

pelame *m* hair, coat

pelandróne *m* (coll) shirker, do-nothing

pelapata·te *m* (-te) potato peeler

pelare (pélo) *tr* to fleece; to pluck; to pare, peel; to clear (*land*); (fig) to strip; to scald, burn ‖ *ref* (coll) to shed; to become bald

pela·to -ta *adj* peeled; hairless, bald; barren ‖ *m* (coll) baldy; **pelati** peeled tomatoes ‖ *f* fleecing, plucking; (joc) baldness, bald spot

pélla §4

pellàc·cia *f* (-ce) tough hide

pellame *m* skins, hides

pèlle *f* skin, hide; **a fior di pelle** slightly, superficially; **essere nella pelle di** to be in the boots of; **fare la pelle a** to bump off; **non stare più nella pelle** to be beside oneself with joy; **pelle di dante** buckskin; **pelle d'oca** goose skin, goose flesh; **pelle d'uovo** mull; **pelle pelle** skin-deep, superficial

pélle §4

pellegrinàg·gio *m* (-gi) pilgrimage

pellegrinare *intr* (lit) to go on a pilgrimage

pellegri·no -na *adj* wandering; (lit) foreign; (lit) strange, quixotic ‖ *mf* pilgrim, traveler

pelleróssa *mf* (pellirosse) redskin

pelletterìa *f* leather goods; leather goods store

pellicano *m* pelican

pelliccerìa *f* furrier's store; furrier's trade, fur industry

pellìc·cia *f* (-ce) fur

pellic·ciàio -ciàia *mf* (-ciài -ciàie) furrier

pelliccióne *m* fur jacket

pellìcola *f* film; **pellicola in rotolo** roll film; **pellicola piana** film pack; **pellicola sonora** sound film; **pellicola vergine** unexposed film

pellirós·sa *mf* (-se) var of **pellerossa**

pélo *m* hair (*of beard*); pile (*of carpet*); fur; **avere pelo sul cuore** not to be easily moved; **cercare il pelo nell'uovo** to split hairs; **di primo pelo** green, inexperienced; **non avere peli sulla lingua** to not mince one's words; **pelo dell'acqua** water surface; **per un pelo** by a hair's breadth

peloponnesìa·co -ca *adj* (-ci -che) Peloponnesian

peló·so -sa [s] *adj* hairy; self-serving (*e.g., charity*)

péltro *m* pewter

pelùria *f* down, soft hair

péna *f* penalty; concern; compassion; pain, suffering; grief; **a mala pena** barely; **essere in pena per** to worry about; **fare pena** to arouse compassion; **pena infamante** degrading punishment; loss of civil rights; **sotto pena di** under penalty of; **valere la pena** to be worthwhile

penale *adj* penal || *f* penalty

penali·sta *mf* (-sti -ste) criminal lawyer

penali·tà *f* (-tà) penalty

penalizzare [ddzz] *tr* (sports) to penalize

penare (péno) *intr* to suffer; to find it difficult

pencolare (pèncolo) *intr* to totter; to waver

pendà·glio *m* (-gli) pendant; **pendaglio da forca** gallows bird

pendènte *adj* leaning; hanging; pending || *m* pendant

pendènza *f* inclination, pitch; controversy; balance; **in pendenza** pending

pèndere §123 *intr* to hang; to lean; to slope; to pitch

pendice *f* slope, declivity

pen·dìo *m* (-dìi) slant; slope

pèndola *f* clock

pendolare *adj* pendulum-like; commuting; transient (*tourist*) || *mf* commuter || *v* (pèndolo) *intr* to sway back and forth; to waver; (nav) to cruise back and forth

pèndolo *m* pendulum; clock

pèndu·lo -la *adj* (lit) hanging

penetrante *adj* penetrating, piercing

penetrare (pènetro) *tr* to penetrate, pierce || *intr* to penetrate || *ref*— **penetrarsi di** to be convinced of; to become aware of

penicillina *f* penicillin

peninsulare *adj* peninsular

penìsola *f* peninsula

penitènte *adj & mf* penitent

penitènza *f* penitence; punishment

penitenzià·rio -ria *adj & mf* (-ri -rie) penitentiary

pénna *f* feather; pen; peen (*of hammer*); (mus) plectrum; **penna a sfera** ball-point pen; **penna d'oca** quill; **penna stilografica** fountain pen

pennàc·chio *m* (-chi) panache; plume, tuft; cloud (*of smoke*)

pennaiòlo *m* hack writer

pennarèllo *m* felt-tip pen

pennellare (pennèllo) *intr* to brush; (med) to pencil

pennellata *f* brush stroke

pennèllo *m* brush; (naut) signal flag; (naut) kedge; **pennello per la barba** shaving brush; **stare a pennello** to fit to a T

pennino *m* pen; penpoint, nib

pennóne *m* flagpole; (naut) yard; (mil) pennant

pennu·to -ta *adj* feathered || **pennuti** *mpl* birds

penómbra *f* penumbra; semidarkness; faint light; **vivere in penombra** to live in obscurity

penó·so -sa [s] *adj* painful

pensàbile *adj* thinkable

pensante *adj* thinking

pensare (pènso) *tr* to think; to think of || *intr* to think; to worry; **dar da pensare a** to cause worry to, *e.g.*, **suo figlio gli dà da pensare** his son causes him worry; **pensa ai fatti tuoi** (coll) mind your own business; **pensa alla salute** (coll) don't worry!; **pensare a** to think of; **pensare di** to plan, intend to

pensata *f* bright idea, brainstorm

pensa·tóre -trice *mf* thinker

pensièro *m* thought; **dare pensiero a** to cause worry to; **darsi pensiero per** to worry about; **essere sopra pensiero** to be absorbed in thought

pensieró·so -sa [s] *adj* thoughtful, pensive

pènsile *adj* hanging, overhead

pensilina *f* marquee

pensionaménto *m* retirement

pensionante *mf* boarder, paying guest

pensionare (pensióno) *tr* to pension

pensiona·to -ta *adj* pensioned || *mf* pensioner || *m* boarding school

pensióne *f* pension; boarding house; **in pensione** retired; **tenere a pensione** to board (*a lodger*); **vivere a pensione** to board (*said of a lodger*)

pensó·so -sa [s] *adj* thoughtful, pensive

pentàgono *m* pentagon

pentagram·ma *m* (-mi) (mus) staff, stave

pentàmetro *m* pentameter

Pentecòste, la Pentecost, Whitsunday

pentiménto *m* repentance; correction (*e.g., in a manuscript*); change of heart

pentire (pènto) *ref* to repent; to change one's mind; **pentirsi di** to repent

penti·to -ta *adj* repentant, repenting; **pentito e contrito** in sackcloth and ashes

péntola *f* pot, kettle; potful; **pentola a pressione** pressure cooker

penùlti·mo -ma *adj* next to the last || *f* penult

penùria *f* shortage, scarcity

penzolare (pènzolo) [dz] *intr* to dangle, hang down

penzolóni [dz] *adv* dangling

peònia *f* peony

pepaiòla *f* pepper shaker; pepper mill

pepare (pépo) *tr* to pepper

pepa·to -ta *adj* peppered; peppery

pépe *m* pepper; **pepe della Giamaica** allspice; **pepe di Caienna** red pepper, cayenne pepper

peperóne *m* (bot) pepper

pepita *f* nugget

per *prep* by; through; throughout; for; because of; to, in order to; in favor of; considering; **essere per** to be about to; **per + adj** or **adv + che + subj** however **+ adj** or **adv + ind**, e.g., **per intelligente che sia** however intelligent he is; **per caso** perchance; **per che cosa?** what for?; **per l'appunto** exactly, just; **per lungo** lengthwise; **per me** as for me; **per ora** now; **per parte mia** as for me; **per poco** hardly, scarcely, **per quanto** + *adj* or *adv* + *subj* however + *adj* or *adv* + *pres ind*, e.g., **per quanto disperatamente provi** however desperately he attempts; **per tempo** early; **per traverso** diagonally; **per via che** (coll) because; **stare per** to be about to

péra *f* pear (*fruit*); bulb, light bulb; (joc) head

peraltro *adv* besides, moreover

peranco *adv* yet

perbacco *interj* by Jove!

perbène *adj invar* nice, well brought up

percalle *m* percale

percènto *m* percent; percentage

percentuale *adj* percentage || *f* percent; commission, bonus

percepìbile *adj* collectable

percepire §176 *tr* to perceive; to receive (*a salary*)

percettìbile *adj* perceptible

percetti•vo -va *adj* perceptive

percezióne *f* perception

perché *m* why, reason; **il perché e il percome** the why and the wherefore || *pron rel* for which || *adv* why || *conj* because; so that

perciò *conj* therefore, accordingly

percóme *m & conj* wherefore

percorrènza *f* stretch, distance

percórrere §139 *tr* to cross; to cover, go through

percórso *m* crossing, distance

percòssa *f* hit, blow; contusion

percuòtere §251 *tr* to hit, beat; (fig) to shake || *intr* to strike

percussióne *f* percussion

percussóre *m* firing pin

perdènte *adj* losing || *mf* loser

pèrdere §212 *tr* to lose; to waste; to miss (*e.g., a train*); to ruin; to leak || *intr* to lose; to leak; to be inferior || *ref* to get lost; to waste one's time; **perdersi d'animo** to lose heart; **perdersi in un bicchier d'acqua** to become discouraged for nothing

perdifiato *m*—**a perdifiato** at the top of one's lungs

perdigiór•no *mf* (-**no**) idler

perdinci *interj* good Heavens!

pèrdita *f* loss; leak; **a perdita d'occhio** as far as the eye can see; **perdite** (mil) casualties

perditèm•po *mf* (-**po**) idler || *m* waste of time

perdizióne *f* perdition

perdonàbile *adj* pardonable

perdonare (**perdóno**) *tr* to forgive; to spare; **perdonare a qlcu qlco** or **perdonare qlco di qlco** to forgive s.o. for s.th || *intr* (with *dat*) to pardon

perdóno *m* forgiveness, pardon

perdurare *intr* (ESSERE & AVERE) to last; to persevere

perdu•to -ta *adj* lost; **andar perduto** to be desperately in love; to get lost

peregrinare *intr* to wander

peregrinazióne *f* wandering

peregri•no -na *adj* far-fetched, outlandish

perènne *adj* everlasting; perennial

perentò•rio -ria *adj* (-**ri** -**rie**) peremptory

perequare (**perèquo**) *tr* to equalize

perequazióne *f* equalization

perfèt•to -ta *adj & m* perfect

perfezionaménto *m* improvement; (educ) specialization

perfezionare (**perfezióno**) *tr* to improve, polish up; to perfect || *ref* to improve; (educ) to specialize

perfezióne *f* perfection; **a** or **alla perfezione** to perfection

perfidia *f* perfidy

pèrfi•do -da *adj* perfidious, treacherous; (coll) foul, nasty

perfini•re *m* (-**re**) punch line

perfino *adv* even

perforante *adj* piercing, perforating

perforare (**perfóro**) *tr* to pierce; to perforate; to punch; to bore

perfora•tóre -trice *mf* key-punch operator || *m* drill || *f* punch; drill; pneumatic drill, rock drill

perforazióne *f* perforation

pergamèna *f* parchment, vellum

pèrgamo *m* (lit) pulpit

pèrgola *f* bower, pergola

pergolato *m* arbor, pergola; grape arbor

pericolante *adj* tottering, unsafe

pericolo *m* danger; **non c'è pericolo** don't worry

pericoló•so -sa [s] *adj* dangerous

periferìa *f* periphery; suburbs

perifèri•co -ca *adj* (-**ci** -**che**) peripheral

perifra•si *f* (-**si**) periphrasis

perìmetro *m* perimeter

periodare *m* writing style || *v* (**perìodo**) *intr* to turn a phrase

periòdi•co -ca (-**ci** -**che**) *adj* periodic(al) || *m* periodical

perìodo *m* period; age; (gram) sentence; (phys) cycle; **il periodo delle feste** holiday time

peripezìa *f* vicissitude

pèriplo *m* circumnavigation

perire §176 *intr* (ESSERE) to perish

periscò•pio *m* (-**pi**) periscope

peritale *adj* expert

peritare (**pèrito**) *ref* (lit) to hesitate

peri•to -ta *adj* expert, skilled || *mf* expert; **perito agrario** land surveyor; **perito calligrafo** handwriting expert; **perito chimico** chemist; **perito industriale** industrial engineer

peritonèo *m* peritoneum

perizia *f* skill; survey; appraisal

periziare §287 (**perizio**) *tr* to estimate, appraise

pèrla *f* pearl; (med) capsule

perlàce•o -a *adj* pearly

perla•to -ta *adj* pearly, smooth

perlìfe•ro -ra *adj* pearl-producing

perlina *f* bead

perloméno *adv* at least

perlopiù *adv* mostly, generally

perlustrare *tr* to patrol

perlustrazióne *f* patrol, patrolling

permaló·so -sa [s] *adj* touchy, grouchy
permanènte *adj* permanent || *f* permanent wave
permanènza *f* permanence; stay; continuance (*in office*); duration (*of a disease*); **in permanenza** permanent (*employee*); **buona permanenza!** may your stay be happy!
permanére §235 (*pp* **permaso**) *intr* (ESSERE) to remain, stay
permeàbile *adj* permeable
permeare (pèrmeo) *tr* to permeate
permés·so -sa *adj* permitted, allowed; **è permesso?** may I come in? || *m* permit; (mil) pass, leave
perméttere §198 *tr* to permit, allow, let; **permette?** do you mind? || *ref* to take the liberty; to afford
permissìbile *adj* permissible
pèrmuta *f* barter; exchange
permutàbile *adj* tradable, exchangeable
permutare (pèrmuto) *tr* to barter; (math) to permute
pernàcchia *f* (vulg) raspberry
pernice *f* partridge
perniciò·so -sa [s] *adj* pernicious || *f* pernicious malaria
pèr·nio *m* (-ni) var of **perno**
pèrno *m* pivot; pin; kingbolt; swivel; heart (*of the matter*); kernel (*of the story*); support (*of the family*); (mach) journal; **fare perno** to pivot
pernottare (pernòtto) *intr* to spend the night, stay overnight
péro *m* pear tree
però *conj* but, yet; however, nevertheless; **e però** (lit) therefore
peróne *m* fibula
peronòspora *f* downy mildew
perorare (pèroro) *tr* & *intr* to perorate; (law) to plead
perorazióne *f* peroration; (law) pleading
peròssido *m* peroxide; **perossido d'idrogeno** hydrogen peroxide
perpendicolare *adj* & *f* perpendicular
perpendìcolo *m* plumb line; **a perpendicolo** perpendicularly
perpetrare (pèrpetro & perpètro) *tr* (lit) to perpetrate
perpètua *f* priest's housekeeper
perpetuare (perpètuo) *tr* to perpetuate
perpè·tuo -tua *adj* perpetual, life || *f* see **perpetua**
perplessi·tà *f* (-tà) perplexity
perplès·so -sa *adj* perplexed; (lit) ambiguous
perquisire §176 *tr* to search
perquisizióne *f* search
persecu·tóre -trice *mf* persecutor, oppressor
persecuzióne *f* persecution
perseguire (perséguo) *tr* to pursue; to persecute; to pester
perseguitare (perséguito) *tr* to persecute; to pursue; to pester
perseveranza *f* perseverance
perseverare (persèvero) *intr* to persevere
persia·no -na *adj* Persian || *m* Persian; Persian lamb || *f* slatted shutter; **persiana avvolgìbile** Venetian blind

pèrsi·co -ca (-ci -che) *adj* Persian || *m* (ichth) perch; (obs) peach || *f* (coll) peach
persino *adv* var of **perfino**
persistènte *adj* persistent
persistènza *f* persistence
persìstere §114 *intr* to persist
pèr·so -sa *adj* lost, wasted; (archaic) reddish-brown; **a tempo perso in** one's spare time
persóna *f* person; **per persona** apiece; **per capita; persona di servizio** servant; **persone** people
personàg·gio *m* (-gi) personage; character
personale *adj* personal || *m* figure, body; personnel, staff; crew || *f* oneman show
personali·tà *f* (-tà) personality; personage
personificare §197 **(personìfico)** *tr* to personify
perspicace *adj* perspicacious; farsighted
perspicàcia *f* perspicacity
perspì·cuo -cua *adj* perspicuous
persuadére §213 *tr* to persuade || *ref* to become convinced
persuasióne *f* persuasion
persuasi·vo -va *adj* persuasive; pleasing || *f* persuasiveness
persuა·so -sa *adj* convinced; resigned
pertanto *conj* therefore; **non pertanto** nevertheless
pèrti·ca *f* (-che) perch; pole
pertinace *adj* pertinacious, persistent
pertinà·cia *f* (-cie) pertinacity, obstinacy
pertinènte *adj* pertinent, relevant
pertinènza *f* pertinence; competence
pertósse *f* whooping cough
pertù·gio *m* (-gi) hole
perturbare *tr* to perturb || *ref* to be perturbed
perturbazióne *f* perturbation; disturbance
Perù, il Peru; **valere un Perù** to be worth a king's ransom
peruvia·no -na *adj* & *mf* Peruvian
pervàdere §172 *tr* (lit) to pervade
pervenire §282 *intr* (ESSERE) to arrive; to come; **pervenire a** to reach
perversióne *f* perversion
perversi·tà *f* (-tà) perversity
pervèr·so -sa *adj* perverse; wicked
pervertiménto *m* perversion
pervertire (pervèrto) *tr* to pervert || *ref* to become perverted
perverti·to -ta *adj* perverted || *mf* pervert
pervicace *adj* (lit) obstinate
pervìn·ca *f* (-che) periwinkle
pésa [s] *f* weighing; scale
pesage *m* (pesage) weigh-in; place for weighing in jockeys
pesalètte·re [s] *m* (-re) postal scale
pesante [s] *adj* heavy
pesantézza [s] *f* heaviness; weight
pesare (péso) [s] *tr* to weigh || *intr* to weigh; **pesare a qlcu** to weigh upon s.o.
pesa·tóre -trice [s] *mf* scale or weigh-

bridge operator; **pesatore pubblico** inspector for the department of weights and measures

pesatura [s] *f* weighing

pé·sca *f* (-sche) fishing; catch (*of fish*) **pesca alla traina** trawling; **pesca d'altura** deep-sea fishing; **pesca di beneficenza** benefit lottery

pè·sca *f* (-sche) peach

pescàg·gio *m* (-gi) (naut) draft

pescàia *f* dam, weir

pescare §197 (pésco) *tr* to fish; to draw (*a card*); to dig up (*a piece of news*); to dive for (*pearls*); **pescare con la lenza** to angle for (*fish*) || *intr* to fish; (naut) to displace; **pescare con la lenza** to angle; **pescare di frodo** to poach; **pescare nel torbido** to fish in troubled waters

pesca·tóre -trice *mf* fisher; **pescatore di canna** angler; **pescatore di frodo** poacher

pésce *m* fish; (typ) omission; (coll) biceps; **a pesce** headlong; **non sapere che pesci pigliare** to not know which way to turn; **pesce d'aprile** April fool; **pesce gatto** catfish; **pesce martello** hammerhead || **Pesci** *mpl* (astr) Pisces

pescecane *m* (pescecani & pescicani) shark; (fig) war profiteer

pescheréc·cio -cia (-ci -ce) *adj* fishing || *m* fishing boat

pescheria *f* fish market

peschièra *f* fishpond; fishpound (*net*)

pescivéndo·lo -la *mf* fishmonger, fish dealer || *f* fishwife, fishwoman

pè·sco *m* (-schi) peach tree

pesi·sta [s] *m* (-sti) (sports) weight lifter

péso -sa [s] *adj* (coll) heavy || *m* weight; burden; bob (*of clock*); (racing) weigh-in; (sports) shot; **di peso** bodily; **peso lordo** gross weight; **peso massimo** (sports) heavyweight; **peso specifico** specific gravity; **rubare sul peso** to give short weight; **usare due pesi e due misure** to have a double standard || *f see* pesa

pessimismo *m* pessimism

pessimi·sta *mf* (-sti -ste) pessimist

pessimìsti·co -ca *adj* (-ci -che) pessimistic

pèssi·mo -ma *adj* very bad, very poor

pésta *f* track, footprint; **lasciar nelle peste** to leave in the lurch; **seguir le peste di** to follow in the footsteps of

pestàggio *m* beating, clubbing

pestare (pésto) *tr* to pound; to trample; to step on; **pestare le orme di** to follow in the footsteps of; **pestare i piedi** to stamp the feet; **pestare sodo** to beat up

pèste *f* plague, pest

pestèllo *m* pestle

pestife·ro -ra *adj* pestiferous

pestilènza *f* pestilence; stench

pestilenziale *adj* pestilential; pernicious

pé·sto -sta *adj* crushed; thick (*darkness*) || *m* Genoese sauce || *f see* pesta

pètalo *m* petal

petardo *m* petard, firecracker

petènte *mf* petitioner

petizióne *f* petition; **petizione di principio** begging the question

péto *m* wind, gas

Petrarca *m* Petrarch

petrarché·sco -sca *adj* (-schi -sche) Petrarchan

petrolièra *f* (naut) tanker

petrolière *adj* incendiary || *m* petroleum-industry worker; incendiary; oilman (*producer*)

petrolìfe·ro -ra *adj* oil-yielding

petrò·lio *m* (-li) petroleum; coal oil, kerosene

petró·so -sa [s] *adj* (lit) stony

pettegolare (pettégolo) *intr* to gossip

pettegolézzo [ddzz] *m* gossip, rumor

pettégo·lo -la *adj* gossipy || *mf* gossip

pettinare (pèttino) *tr* to comb; to card; (coll) to scold

pettinatóre *m* carder

pettinatrice *f* hairdresser; carding machine

pettinatura *f* coiffure, hairstyling

pèttine *m* comb; (zool) scallop; **a pettine perpendicular** (*parking*)

pettino *m* dickey; bib (*of an apron*); plastron

pettirósso *m* robin redbreast

pètto *m* breast, chest; bust; bosom; **a un petto** single-breasted; **avere al petto** to feed at the breast; **a due petti** or **a doppio petto** double-breasted; **stare a petto** to be equal

pettorale *adj* pectoral || *m* pectoral; breast collar (*of horse*)

pettorina *f var of* pettino

pettoru·to -ta *adj* strutting, haughty

petulante *adj* importunate; impertinent

petulanza *f* importunity; impertinence

petùnia *f* petunia

pèzza *f* piece (*of cloth*); diaper; patch (*in suit or tire*); bolt (*of paper or cloth*); **pezza d'appoggio** supporting document, voucher; **trattare come una pezza da piedi** to wipe one's boots on

pezza·to -ta *adj* spotted, dappled

pezzatura *f* dapple (*on a horse*); size (*e.g., of a loaf of bread*)

pezzènte *mf* beggar

pezzétto *m* little bit; scrap, snip

pèzzo *m* piece; cut (*of meat*); coin; (journ) article; **andare** or **cadere a pezzi** to fall apart; **a pezzi e bocconi** by fits and starts; **fare a pezzi** to break to pieces; to blow to bits; **pezzo di ricambio** spare part; **pezzo d'uomo** hunk of a man; **pezzo duro** brick ice cream; **pezzo forte** forte; **pezzo fuso** cast, casting; **un bel pezzo** a good while; **un pezzo grosso** a big shot

pezzuòla *f* small piece of cloth; (coll) handkerchief

phy·lum *m* (-lum) phylum

piacènte *adj* attractive, pleasant

piacére *m* pleasure; **a piacere** at will; **a Suo piacere** as you please; **fare piacere a** to do a favor for; to please; **per piacere** please; **piacere!**

pleased to meet you! || §214 *intr* (ESSERE) to please; to be pleasing; (with *dat*) to please; e.g., **come piace a Dio** as it pleases God; to like, e.g., **gli piace il ballo** he likes dancing

piacévole *adj* pleasant, pleasing

piacevolézza *f* pleasantness; off-color joke

pia·ga *f* (-ghe) sore; ulcer; wound; plague; (joc) bore; **piaga di decubito** bedsore

piagare §209 *tr* to make sore, injure

piàg·gia *f* (-ge) (archaic) declivity; (lit) clime, country

piaggiare §290 *tr* (lit) to flatter, blandish || *intr* (archaic) to coast

piagnistèo *m* whining

piagnó·ne -na *mf* (coll) weeper, crybaby

piagnucolare (**piagnùcolo**) *intr* to whimper, whine

piagnucoló·ne -na *mf* whimperer, crybaby

piagnucoló·so -sa [*s*] *adj* whimpering, whining

pialla *f* (carp) plane

piallàc·eio *m* (-ci) veneer

piallare *tr* (carp) to plane

piallatrice *f* (carp) planer

piallatura *f* (carp) planing

piana *f* plain; wide table

pianale *m* plain; platform; (rr) flatcar, platform car

pianeggiante *adj* plane, level

pianèlla *f* mule (*slipper*); tile

pianeròttolo *m* landing (*of stairs*); ledge

pianè·ta *m* (-ti) planet; horoscope || *f* (eccl) chasuble

piàngere §215 *tr* to shed (*tears*); to mourn, lament; **piangere miseria** to cry poverty || *intr* to cry, weep

piangimisè·ria *mf* (-ria) poverty-crying penny pincher

piangiucchiare §287 *intr* to whimper

pianificare §197 (**pianìfico**) *tr* to level; (econ) to plan

pianifica·tóre -trice *mf* planner

pianino *m* (coll) barrel organ

piani·sta *mf* (-sti -ste) pianist

pia·no -na *adj* plane; plain, flat || *m* plain; plane; floor; plateau; plan; map; (mus) piano; **di primo piano** first-class; **in piano** horizontal; **piano di coda** (aer) tail assembly; **piano di studio** curriculum; **piano regolatore** building plan; **piano terra** ground floor; **primo piano** (phot) close-up; (theat) foreground || *f* see **piana** || *piano adv* slowly; softly

pianofòrte *m* piano; **pianoforte a coda** grand piano

pianòla *f* player piano

pianòro *m* plateau

pianotèr·ra *m* (-ra) ground floor

pianta *f* plant; sole (*of foot*); plan, map; floor plan; **di sana pianta** wholly; **in pianta stabile** permanent (*employee*); **pianta rampicante** (bot) climber

piantagióne *f* plantation

piantana *f* scaffolding

piantare *tr* to plant; to set up (*e.g., a gun emplacement*); to pitch (*a tent*); **piantala!** (slang) cut it out!; **piantare baracca e burattini** (coll) to clear out; **piantar chiodi** (coll) to go into debt; **piantare gli occhi addosso a** to stare at; **piantare in asso** to leave in the lurch || *ref* to place oneself; to abandon one another

pianta·to -ta *adj* planted; stuck; driven; **bien piantato** well-built (*person*)

pianta·tóre -trice *mf* planter

pianterréno *m* ground floor

piantito *m* (coll) floor

pianto *m* weeping, tears; sadness; (bot) sap; (coll) sight, mess

piantonare (**piantóno**) *tr* to watch, guard

piantóne *m* watchman; (mil) orderly; (mil) sentry; (bot) cutting, shoot; **piantone di guida** (aut) steering wheel column

pianura *f* plain

piastra *f* plate; piaster (*coin*)

piastrèlla *f* tile; small flat stone; bounce (*of an airplane on landing*)

piastrellaménto *m* bump, bounce (*of motorboat or airplane*)

piastrelli·sta *m* (-sti) tiler, tile layer

piastrina *f* or **piastrino** *m* small plate; (mil) dog tag; (biol) platelet

piatire §176 *intr* (lit) to argue; (coll) to beg insistently

piattafórma *f* platform; roadbed (*of highway*); (rr) turntable; (pol) plank; **piattaforma di lancio** launching pad

piattèllo *m* small dish; bobèche; clay pigeon

piattina *f* electric cord; metal band; (min) wagon

piattino *m* saucer

piat·to -ta *adj* flat || *m* dish, plate; pan (*of scale*); pot (*in gambling*); course (*of meal*); cover (*of book*); flat (*e.g., of blade*); **piatti** (mus) cymbals; **piatto del grammofono** turntable; **piatto del giorno** plat du jour; **piatto di lenticchie** (*Bib & fig*) mess of pottage; **piatto fondo** soup dish; **piatto forte** pièce de résistance

piàttola *f* (zool) crab louse; (coll) cockroach; (vulg) bore

piazza *f* square; plaza; crowd; market; fortress; **andare in piazza** (coll) to become bald; **da piazza** common, ordinary; **di piazza** for hire (*e.g., cab*); **fare la piazza** (com) to canvass for customers; **far piazza pulita di** to get rid of; to clean out; **mettere in piazza** to noise abroad; **piazza d'armi** parade ground; **scendere in piazza** to take to the streets

piazzafórte *f* (**piazzefòrti**) stronghold, fortress

piazzale *m* large square, esplanade, plaza

piazzaménto *m* placement; (sports) position (*of a team*)

piazzare *tr* to place; to sell || *ref* to place; to show (*said of a racing horse*)

piazza·to -ta *adj* placed; arrived (*at a high position*) ‖ *f* row, brawl

piazzi·sta *m* (**-sti**) salesman; traveling salesman

piazzòla *f* court, place; rest area (*off a highway*); (mil) emplacement; **piazzola di partenza** (golf) tee

pi·ca *f* (**-che**) (orn) magpie

picaré·sco -sca *adj* (**-schi -sche**) picaresque

pic·ca *f* (**-che**) pike; pique; **per picca** out of spite; **picche** (cards) spades; **rispondere picche** (fig) to answer no

piccante *adj* piquant, racy

piccare §197 *tr* (obs) to prick ‖ *ref* to become angry; **piccarsi di** to pride oneself on

pic·chè *f* (**-chè**) piqué

picchettaménto *m* picketing

picchettare (**picchétto**) *tr* to stake out; to picket

picchétto *m* stake; picket; (mil) detail

picchiare §287 *tr* to hit, strike ‖ *intr* to knock; to strike; to tap (*said, e.g., of rain*); (aer) to nose-dive; **picchiare in testa** (aut) to knock ‖ *ref* to hit one another

picchiata *f* hit, blow; (aer) nose dive

picchia·tóre -trice *mf* hitter ‖ *m* (boxing) puncher

picchierellare (**picchierèllo**) *tr & intr* to tap

picchiettare (**picchiétto**) *tr* to tap; to scrape; to speckle ‖ *intr* to tap

picchiet·tìo *m* (**-tìi**) patter (*e.g., of rain*)

pic·chio *m* (**-chi**) knock; (orn) woodpecker; **di picchio** all of a sudden

picchiòtto *m* knocker (*on door*)

piccinerìa *f* pettiness

picci·no -na *adj* little, tiny; petty ‖ *mf* child; baby

picciòlo *m* stem (*e.g., of cherry*); leafstalk, petiole

piccionàia *f* dovecote; loft; attic; (theat) upper gallery

piccióne -na *mf* pigeon; **pigliare due piccioni con una fava** to hit two birds with one stone

pic·co *m* (**-chi**) peak; (naut) gaff; **andare a picco** to sink; to go to ruin; **a picco** vertically; **picco di carico** (naut) derrick

piccolézza *f* smallness; trifle

pìcco·lo -la *adj* small; low (*speed*); short (*distance*); young; petty; **da piccolo** when young; **in piccolo** on a small scale; **nel mio piccolo** with my modest abilities ‖ *mf* child

piccóne *m* pick

piccòzza *f* mattock (*for mountain climbing*)

pidocchierìa *f* stinginess; meanness

pidòc·chio *m* (**-chi**) louse; **pidocchio rifatto** (slang) parvenu

pidocchió·so -sa [s] *adj* lousy; stingy

piè *m* (**piè**) (lit) foot; **ad ogni piè sospinto** on every occasion; **saltare a piè pari** to skip with the feet together; (fig) to skip over

piède *m* foot; leg (*of table*); stalk (*of salad*); bottom (*of column*); trunk (*of tree*); footing; **alzarsi in piedi** to stand up; **a piede libero** free; **a piedi**

on foot; **a piedi nudi** barefooted; **con i piedi di piombo** cautiously; **essere in piedi** to be up and around; **fare con i piedi** to botch; **mettere un piede in fallo** to stumble; **piede di porco** crowbar; **prendere piede** to take hold; **puntare i piedi** to balk; **su due piedi** offhand; **tenere il piede in due staffe** to carry water on both shoulders

piedestallo or **piedistallo** *m* pedestal

piedritto *m* buttress

piè·ga *f* (**-ghe**) bend; crease; pleat; crimp; wrinkle; (fig) turn; **prendere una cattiva piega** to take a turn for the worse

piegare §209 (**piègo**) *tr* to bend; to wave (*hair*); to fold; to pleat; to bow (*head*) ‖ *intr* to turn ‖ *ref* to bow; to bend; to buckle; to yield

piega·tóre -trice *mf* folder ‖ *f* folding machine

piegatura *f* fold, crease

pieghettare (**pieghétto**) *tr* to pleat

pieghévole *adj* folding; pliant; (fig) versatile ‖ *m* folder

pieghevolézza *f* flexibility

piè·go *m* (**-ghi**) folder; bundle of papers

pièna *f* flood; rise (*of river*); crowd; (fig) overflow; **in piena** overflowing

pienézza *f* plenitude, fullness

piè·no -na *adj* full; solid; broad (*daylight*); full (*honors*); **a pieno** or **in pieno** to the full; **colpire nel pieno** to hit the bull's eye; **pieno di** alive with; **pieno di sé** conceited; **pieno zeppo** replete, chock-full ‖ *m* fullness; height (*e.g., of winter*); **fare il pieno** (aut) to fill up ‖ *f* see **piena**

pie·tà *f* (**-tà**) mercy; pity; (lit) piety

pietanza *f* main course

pietó·so -sa [s] *adj* pitiful, piteous; merciful

piètra *f* stone; rock; **pietra angolare** cornerstone; **pietra da affilare** whetstone; **pietra da sarto** French chalk; **pietra dello scandalo** source of scandal; **pietra di paragone** touchstone; **pietra focaia** flint; **pietra miliare** milestone; **pietra tombale** tombstone; **posare la prima pietra** to lay the cornerstone

pietrificare §197 (**pietrìfico**) *tr & ref* to petrify

pietrina *f* flint (*for lighter*)

pietri·sco *m* (**-schi**) rubble; (rr) ballast

Piètro *m* Peter

pietró·so -sa [s] *adj* (lit) stony

pievano *m* parish priest

pìffero *m* pipe, fife

pìgia *m*—**pigia pigia** crowd, throng

pigia·ma *m* (**-ma & -mi**) pajamas

pigiare §290 *tr* to squeeze, press ‖ *intr* to insist ‖ *ref* to squeeze

pigia·tóre -trice *mf* presser (*of grapes*) ‖ *f* wine press

pigiatura *f* pressing, squeezing

pigionante *mf* tenant

pigióne *f* rent, rental; **dare a pigione** to rent; to grant the possession of; **prendere a pigione** to rent; to hold for payment

pigliamó·sche *m* (-sche) flypaper; fly-trap; (orn) flycatcher

pigliare §280 *tr* to take, catch; to mistake; **che Le piglia?** what's the matter with you? || *ref*—**pigliarsela (con)** to get angry (at)

pi·glio *m* (-gli) hold; countenance; **dar di piglio a** to grab

pigménto *m* pigment

pigmè·o -a *adj & mf* pygmy; Pygmy

pigna *f* strainer (*at the end of a suction pipe*); bunch (*of grapes*); (bot) pine cone

pignatta *f* pot

pignò·lo -la *adj* finicky, fussy || *m* pine nut

pignóne *m* pinion; embankment

pignoraménto *m* (law) seizure

pignorare (pìgnoro) *tr* (law) to seize

pigolare (pìgolo) *intr* to peep (*said, e.g., of young birds*)

pigolì·o·m (-i) peep (*e.g., of a young bird*)

pigrìzia *f* laziness

pi·gro -gra *adj* lazy; (lit) sluggish

pila *f* pier; buttress (*of bridge*); heap; sink; font; (elec) cell; (elec) battery; **pila atomica** atomic pile

pilastro *m* pier, pillar

pillàcchera *f* mud splash; (fig) fault

pillola *f* pill; (slang) bullet; **addolcire la pillola** to sugar-coat the pill

pilóne *m* pier; pylon

pilò·ta (-ti -te) *adj* pilot || *mf* pilot; (aut) driver

pilotàg·gio *m* (-gi) piloting; steering

pilotare (pilòto) *tr* to pilot; to drive

pilotina *f* (naut) pilot boat

piluccare §197 *tr* to pluck (*e.g., grapes one by one*); to nibble, pick at; to scrounge; (lit) to consume

piménto *m* allspice

pinacotè·ca *f* (-che) picture gallery

pinéta *f* pine grove

pingue *adj* fat; rich

pinguèdine *f* fatness, corpulence

pinguino *m* penguin

pinna *f* fin (*of fish*); flipper; (zool) pen shell (*mussel*)

pinnàcolo *m* pinnacle

pino *m* pine tree; **pino marittimo** pinaster; **pino silvestre** Scotch fir

pinòlo *m* pine nut

pinta *f* pint

pinza *f* claw (*of lobster*); **pinza emostatica** hemostat; **pinza tagliafili** wire cutter; **pinze clippers**; pliers; pincers

pinzatrice *f* stapler

pinzétte *fpl* tweezers, pliers

pinzòche·ro -ra *mf* bigot

pì·o -a *adj* (-i -e) pious; charitable || **Pio** *m* Pius

piòg·gia *f* (-ge) rain

piòlo *m* peg; rung (*of ladder*); picket, stake

piombàggine *f* graphite

piombare (piómbo) *tr* to lead; to seal; to knock down; to fill (*a tooth*) || *intr* to fall; to swoop down

piombatura *f* leading; filling (*of tooth*)

piombino *m* weight; seal; plumb; plumb bob

piómbo *m* lead; **a piombo** perpendicularly; **di piombo** suddenly

pionerìsti·co -ca *adj* (-ci -che) pioneering

pionière *m* pioneer

piòppo *m* poplar; **pioppo tremolo** aspen

piorrèa *f* pyorrhea

piotare (piòto) *tr* to sod

piova·no -na *adj* rain (*water*)

piova·sco *m* (-schi) rain squall

piovènte *m* pitch, slope

piòvere §216 *intr* (ESSERE) to rain; to pour; to flock (*said of people*); **piovere addosso a** to rain down on; **piovere su** to flow down over || *impers* (ESSERE & AVERE)—**piove** it is raining; it is leaking (*from rain*); **piove a catinelle** or **a dirotto** it is raining cats and dogs

piovigginare (piovìggina) *impers* (ESSERE & AVERE)—**pioviggina** it is drizzling

piovigginó·so -sa [s] *adj* drizzling, drizzly

piovór·no -na *adj* (lit) var of **piovoso**

piovosi·tà [s] *f* (-tà) raininess; rainfall

piovó·so -sa [s] *adj* rainy

piòvra *f* octopus; (fig) leech

pipa *f* pipe; **non valere una pipa di tabacco** to not be worth a tinker's dam

pipare *intr* to smoke a pipe

pipata *f* pipe, pipeful

pipistrèllo *m* (zool) bat

pipita *f* hangnail; (vet) pip

pira *f* (lit) pyre

piràmide *f* pyramid

pira·ta *adj invar* pirate || *m* (-ti) pirate; **pirata dell'aria** skyjacker; **pirata della strada** hit-and-run driver

pirateggiare §290 (**piratéggio**) *intr* to pirate

pirateria *f* piracy; **pirateria letteraria** piracy of literary works

Pirenèi *mpl* Pyrenees

pìri·co -ca *adj* (-ci -che) fireworks; **polvere pirica** gunpowder

pirite *f* pyrite

piroétta *f* pirouette

pirò·ga *f* (-ghe) pirogue

pirolisi *f* (chem) cracking

piróne *m* (mus) tuning pin

piròscafo *m* steamship; **piroscafo da carico** (naut) freighter; **piroscafo da passeggeri** passenger ship

piroscissióne *f* (chem) cracking

pirotècni·co -ca (-ci -che) *adj* pyrotecnic || *m* pyrotecnist || *f* fireworks, pyrotechnics

pisciare §128 *intr* (vulg) to urinate

piscia·tóio *m* (-tói) (vulg) street urinal

piscina *f* swimming pool

pisèllo [s] *m* pea; **pisello odoroso** sweet pea

pisolare (pìsolo) *intr* (coll) to doze

pìsolo *m* (coll) nap; **schiacciare un pisolo** (coll) to take a nap

pisside *f* (eccl) pyx; (bot) pyxidium

pista *f* track; ring (*of circus*); race track, speedway (*for car races*); ski run; (aer) runway; **pista ciclabile** bicycle trail; **pista da ballo** dance floor; **seguire una pista** to follow a clue

pistàc·chio *m* (**-chi**) pistachio

pistillo *m* (bot) pistil

pistòla *f* pistol

pistolettata *f* pistol shot

pistolòtto *m* lecture, talking-to; theatrical peroration

pistóne *m* piston; plunger

pitagòri·co -ca *adj & m* (**-ci -che**) Pythagorean

pitale *m* (coll) chamber pot

pitoccare §197 (**pitòcco**) *intr* to beg

pitòc·co *m* (**-chi**) beggar; miser

pitóne *m* python

pittima *f* plaster; (fig) bore

pit·tóre -trice *mf* painter

pittoré·sco -sca *adj* (**-schi -sche**) picturesque

pittòri·co -ca *adj* (**-ci -che**) pictorial

pittura *f* painting; picture; (coll) paint

pitturare *tr* to paint; to varnish || *ref* to put on make-up

più *adj invar* more; several || *m* (**più**) plus; most; **credersi da più** to believe oneself superior; **dal più al meno** about, more or less; **i più** most, the majority; **parlare del più e del meno** (coll) to make small talk || *adv* more; again; **a più non posso** to the very utmost; **in più** besides; **mai più** never again; **non poterne più** to be exhausted; **per di più** besides; **per lo più** for the most part; **più o meno** more or less; **tanto più** moreover; **tutt'al più** mostly

piuma *f* feather, plume; **piume** (fig) bed

piumàc·cio *m* (**-ci**) feather pillow

piumàg·gio *m* (**-gi**) plumage

piumino *m* down; comforter; puff, powder puff; feather duster

piuttòsto *adv* rather; somewhat

piva *f* bagpipe; **tornare con le pive nel sacco** to return bitterly disappointed

pivèllo *m* greenhorn; whippersnapper

pivière *m* (orn) plover

pizza *f* pizza; (mov) canister; (coll) bore

pizzaiò·lo -la *mf* owner of pizzeria || *m* pizza baker || *f*—**alla pizzaiola** prepared with tomato and garlic sauce

pizzardóne *m* (coll) cop, officer

pizzicàgno·lo -la *mf* grocer; sausage dealer

pizzicare §197 (**pìzzico**) *tr* to pinch; to pluck; to bite, burn; (mus) to pick, twang

pizzicherìa *f* delicatessen, grocery

pìzzi·co *m* (**-chi**) pinch

pizzicóre *m* itch

pizzicòtto *m* pinch; **dar pizzicotti a** to pinch

pizzo *m* peak (*of mountain*); goatee; lace

placare §197 *tr* to placate || *ref* to calm down

plac·ca *f* (**-che**) plate; plaque; tag, badge; (elec, rad) plate; (pathol) blotch, spot

placcare §197 *tr* to plate; (sports) to tackle

plàci·do -da *adj* placid

plafond *m* (**plafond**) ceiling; (aer) ceiling; (com) top credit

pla·ga *f* (**-ghe**) (lit) clime, region

plagiare §290 *tr* to plagiarize

plagià·rio -ria (**-ri -rie**) *adj* plagiaristic || *mf* plagiarist

plà·gio *m* (**-gi**) plagiarism

planare *intr* (aer) to glide

planata *f* (aer) gliding

plàn·cia *f* (**-ce**) (naut) gangplank; (naut) bridge

planetà·rio -ria (**-ri -rie**) *adj* planetary || *m* planetarium; (aut) planetary gear

plantare *m* arch support

pla·sma *m* (**-smi**) plasma

plasmare *tr* to mold, shape

plàsti·ca *f* (**-che**) plastic art; plastics; plastic surgery; plastic

plasticare §197 (**plàstico**) *tr* to mold, shape; to cover with plastic

plàsti·co -ca (**-ci -che**) *adj* plastic || *m* relief map; maquette; plastic bomb || *f* see plastica

plastilina *f* modeling clay

plastron *m* (plastron) ascot

plàtano *m* plane tree; **platano americano** buttonwood tree

platèa *f* audience; (theat) orchestra; (archit) foundation

plateale *adj* obscene; plebeian

plàtina *f* (typ) platen

platinare (**plàtino**) *tr* to platinize; **to bleach** (*hair*)

plàtino *m* platinum

Platóne *m* Plato

plaudènte *adj* enthusiastic

plàudere (**plàudo**) & **plaudire** (**plàudo**) *intr* to applaud; (with *dat*) to applaud, e.g., **plaudere alla generosità** to applaud the generosity

plausibile *adj* plausible

plàuso *m* (lit) applause, praise

plebàglia *f* rabble

plèbe *f* populace; (lit) crowd

plebè·o -a *adj & mf* plebeian

plebiscito *m* plebiscite

plenà·rio -ria *adj* (**-ri -rie**) plenary

plenilù·nio *m* (**-ni**) full moon

plenipotenzià·rio -ria *adj & m* (**-ri -rie**) plenipotentiary

plètora *f* plethora

plèttro *m* (mus) pick, plectrum

pleurite *f* (pathol) pleurisy

plì·co *m* (**-chi**) sealed document; bundle of papers; **in plico a parte** or **in plico separato** under separate cover

plotóne *m* platoon; **plotone d'esecuzione** firing squad

plùmbe·o -a *adj* lead, leaden

plurale *adj & m* plural; **al plurale** in the plural

plurilìngue *adj* multilingual

plurimotóre *adj* multimotored || *m* multimotor

pluristàdio *adj invar* (rok) multistage

plusvalènza *f* unearned increment

plusvalóre *m;* surplus value (*in Marxist economics*)

Plutarco *m* Plutarch

plutocrazìa *f* plutocracy

Plutóne *m* Pluto

plutònio *m* plutonium
pluviale *adj* rain || *m* waterspout
pneumàti·co -ca (*-ci -che*) *adj* pneumatic, air || *m* tire; **pneumatico da neve** snow tire
po' *m* see **poco**
pochézza *f* lack, scarcity
pò·co -ca (*-chi -che*) *adj* little; short (*distance*); poor (*health; memory*); (*with collective nouns*) few, e.g., **poca gente** few people; (*with plural nouns*) a few, e.g., **fra pochi mesi** in a few months; (*with plural nouns having singular meaning in English*) little, e.g., **pochi quattrini** little money || *m invar* little; short distance; short time; **a ogni poco** often; **da poco** a little while ago; of no account; **da un bel po'** quite a while; quite a while ago; **fra poco** in a little while; **manca poco a** it won't be long till; **manca poco che** (*e.g., il ragazzo*) **non** + *subj* (e.g., the boy) almost + *ind*; **per poco non** almost; **poco di buono** good-for-nothing; **poco fa** a little while ago; **saper di poco** to taste flat; **un poco di** or **un po' di** a little || *f*—**poca di buono** hussy || *poco adv* little; **poco bene** poorly; **poco dopo** shortly after; **poco male** not too poorly
podagra *f* gout
podére *m* farm, country property
poderó·so -sa [s] *adj* powerful
pode·stà *m* (*-stà*) (hist) mayor; (hist) podesta
podia·tra *mf* (*-tri -tre*) chiropodist
pò·dio *m* (*-di*) podium; platform; (archit) base
podismo *m* foot racing
podi·sta *mf* (*-sti -ste*) foot racer
poè·ma *m* (*-mi*) long poem
poesìa *f* poetry; poem
poè·ta *m* (*-ti*) poet
poetéssa *f* poetess
poèti·co -ca (*-ci -che*) *adj* poetic(al) || *f* poetics
pòg·gia *f* (*-ge*) leeward
poggiare §290 (**pòggio**) *tr* to lean || *intr* to be based; (mil) to move; (naut) to sail before the wind; (archaic) to rise
poggiatè·sta *m* (*-sta*) headrest; (aut) head restrainer
pòg·gio *m* (*-gi*) hillock, knoll
poggiòlo *m* balcony
pòi *m* future || *adv* then; later; **a poi** until later; **poi dopo** later on
poiana *f* buzzard
poiché *conj* since, as; (lit) after
pòker *m* poker (*game*); four of a kind; **poker di re** four kings
polac·co -ca (*-chi -che*) *adj* Polish || *mf* Pole || *f* (mus) polonaise
polare *adj* pole, polar
polarizzare [ddzz] *tr* to polarize
pòl·ca *f* (*-che*) polka
polèmi·co -ca (*-ci -che*) *adj* polemical || *f* polemics
polemizzare [ddzz] *intr* to engage in polemics
polèna *f* (naut) figurehead
polènta *f* corn mush

polentina *f* poultice
poliambulanza *f* clinic, emergency ward
policlìni·co m (*-ci*) polyclinic
polifonìa *f* polyphony
polìga·mo -ma *adj* polygamous || *m* polygamist
poliglòt·ta *adj* & *mf* (*-ti -te*) polyglot
poliglòt·to -ta *adj* & *mf* polyglot
polìgono *m* polygon; **poligono di tiro** shooting range
polìgrafo *m* author skilled in many subjects; multigraph
polinesia·no -na *adj* & *mf* Polynesian
polinò·mio *m* (*-mi*) polynomial
pòlio *f* (coll) polio
poliomielite *f* poliomielitis, infantile paralysis
pòlipo *m* (pathol, zool) polyp
polisìlla·bo -ba *adj* polysyllabic || *m* polysyllable
poli·sta *m* (*-sti*) polo player
politea·ma *m* (*-mi*) theater
politècni·co -ca (*-ci -che*) *adj* polytechnic || *m* polytechnic institute
politei·sta (*-sti -ste*) *adj* polytheistic || *mf* polytheist
politeìsti·co -ca *adj* (*-ci -che*) polytheistic
politézza *f* smoothness
polìti·ca *f* (*-che*) politics; policy
politicante *mf* petty politician
polìti·co -ca (*-ci -che*) *adj* political || *m* politician || *f* see **politica**
polìtti·co m (*-ci*) polyptych
polizìa *f* police; **polizia sanitaria** health department; **polizia stradale** highway patrol; **polizia tributaria** income-tax investigation department
polizié·sco -sca *adj* (*-schi -sche*) police (*car*); detective (*story*)
poliziòtto *adj masc* police (*dog*) || *m* policeman; detective; **poliziotto in borghese** plain-clothes man
pòlizza *f* policy; ticket (*e.g., of pawnbroker*); **polizza di carico** bill of lading
pólla *f* spring (*of water*)
pol·làio *m* (*-lài*) chicken coop
pollaiò·lo -la *mf* chicken dealer
pollame *m* poultry
pollastra *f* pullet; (coll) chick
pollerìa *f* poultry shop
pòllice *m* thumb; big toe; inch
pollicoltura *f* poultry raising
pòlline *m* pollen
pollivéndo·lo -la *mf* poultry dealer
póllo *m* chicken; (fig) sucker; **conoscere i propri polli** (fig) to know one's onions; **pollo d'India** turkey
pollóne *m* (bot) shoot; (fig) offspring
polmóne *m* lung; **a pieni polmoni** at the top of one lungs; **polmone d'acciaio** iron lung
polmonìte *f* pneumonia
pòlo *m* pole; polo shirt; (sports) polo
Polònia, la Poland
pólpa *f* meat; pulp; flesh (*of fruit*); (fig) gist; **in polpe** (hist) in knee breeches
polpàc·cio *m* (*-ci*) calf (*of leg*); cut of meat; ball of thumb

polpastrèllo *m* finger tip
polpétta *f* meat ball; meat patty, cutlet
polpettóne *m* meat loaf; (fig) hash
pólpo *m* (zool) octopus
polpó·so -sa [s] *adj* pulpy, fleshy
polpu·to -ta *adj* meaty
polsino *m* cuff
pólso *m* pulse; wrist; cuff, wristband; strong hand, energy; **di polso** energetic
poltiglia *f* mash; slush
poltrire §176 *intr* to idle; to loll in bed
poltróna *f* armchair; (theat) orchestra seat; **poltrona a orecchioni** wing chair; **poltrona a sdraio** chaise longue; **poltrona letto** day bed
poltroncina *f* parquet-circle seat
poltró·ne -na *mf* lazybones, sluggard || *f* see **poltrona**
poltronería *f* laziness
poltronìssima *f* (theat) first-row seat
pólvere *f* dust; powder; **in polvere** powdered; **polvere da sparo** gunpowder; **polvere di stelle** stardust; **polvere nera** or **pirica** gunpowder; **polveri** gunpowder
polverièra *f* powder magazine; (fig) tinderbox, trouble spot
polverifi·cio *m* (-ci) powder works
polverina *f* (pharm) powder
polverino *m* pounce, sand
polverizzare [ddzz] *tr* to crush, powder; to atomize; to pulverize
polverizza·to -ta [ddzz] *adj* powdered (*sugar*)
polverizzatóre [ddzz] *m* atomizer
polveróne *m* dust cloud
polveró·so -sa [s] *adj* dusty; powdery (*snow*)
pomata *f* ointment; pomade
pomella·to -ta *adj* dapple-grey
pomèllo *m* cheek; cheekbone; pommel, knob
pomeridia·no -na *adj* afternoon, P.M.
pomerig·gio *m* (-gi) afternoon
pomiciare §128 (pómicio) *tr* to pumice || *intr* (slang) to spoon
pomicióne *m* (slang) spooner
pomidòro *m* var of **pomodoro**
pómo *m* apple; knob; pommel (*of saddle*); **pomo della discordia** apple of discord; **pomo di Adamo** Adam's apple; **pomo di terra** potato
pomodòro *m* tomato; **pomodoro di mare** (zool) sea anemone
pómolo *m* (coll) knob, handle
pómpa *f* pump; pomp; state; **in pompa magna** all dressed up; **pompa aspirante** suction pump; **pompa premente** force pump; see **imprenditore** and **impresa**
pompare (pómpo) *tr* to pump; to pump up
pompèlmo *m* grapefruit
pompière *m* fireman
pompó·so -sa [s] *adj* pompous
pòn·ce *m* (-ci) punch
ponderare (pòndero) *tr* to weigh, ponder; to weight || *intr* to think it over
pondera·to -ta *adj* considerate, careful
ponderó·so -sa [s] *adj* ponderous

ponènte *m* west; west wind; West; West Wind
pónte *m* bridge; metal scaffolding; (aut) axle; (naut) deck; **fare il ponte** to take the day off between two holidays; **fare ponti d'oro a** to offer a good way out to; **ponte aereo** airlift; **ponte delle segnalazioni** (rr) gantry; **ponte di chiatte** pontoon bridge; **ponte di comando** (naut) bridge; **ponte di volo** flight deck; **ponte levatoio** drawbridge; **ponte radio** radio communication; **ponte sospeso** suspension bridge
pontéfice *m* pontiff; (hist) pontifex
pontéggio *m* scaffolding
ponticèllo *m* small bridge; nosepiece (*of eyeglasses*); (mus) bridge
pontière *m* (mil) engineer
pontificale *adj* pontifical || *m* pontifical mass
pontifi·cio -cia *adj* (-ci -cie) papal
pontile *m* pier
pontóne *m* pontoon, barge
ponzare (pónzo) *tr* (coll) to strain to accomplish || *intr* (coll) to rack one's brains
popeli·ne *f* (-ne) broadcloth
popola·no -na *adj* popular || *mf* commoner
popolare *adj* popular || *v* (pòpolo) *tr* to people, populate || *ref* to be inhabited
popolarità *f* popularity
popola·to -ta *adj* peopled; crowded
popolazióne *f* population
pòpolo *m* people; crowd; **popolo grasso** (hist) rich bourgeoisie; **popolo minuto** (hist) artisans, common people
popoló·so -sa [s] *adj* populous
popóne *m* (coll) melon
póppa *f* breast; (naut) stern; (lit) ship; **a poppa** astern, aft
poppante *adj & mf* suckling
poppare (póppo) *tr* to suckle
poppa·tóio *m* (-tói) nursing bottle
poppavìa *f*—**a poppavia** astern, aft
pòr·ca *f* (-che) ridge (*between furrows*); sow
porcaccio·ne -na *m* cad, rake || *f* slut
por·càio *m* (-cài) swineherd; pigsty
porcellana *f* porcelain, china; (bot) purslane
porcellino *m* piggy; **porcellino d'India** guinea pig
porchería *f* dirt; (coll) dirty trick; (coll) botch
porchétta *f* roast suckling pig
porcile *m* pigsty
porci·no -na *adj* pig || *m* (bot) boletus
pòr·co -ca *mf* (-ci -che) pig, hog, swine; pork; **porco mondo!** (slang) heck! || *f* see **porca**
porcospino *m* porcupine
pòrfido *m* porphyry
pòrgere §217 *tr* to hand, offer; to relate; **porgere l'orecchio** to lend an ear || *intr* to declaim || *ref* to appear, show up
pornografìa *f* pornography
pòro *m* pore
poró·so -sa [s] *adj* porous
pórpora *f* purple

porpora·to -ta *adj* purple || *m* purple; cardinal

porpori·no -na *adj* purple

pórre §218 *tr* to put; to repose (*trust*); to set (*a limit; one's foot*); to lay (*a stone*); to pose (*a question*); to pay (*attention*); to suppose; to advance (*the candidacy*); **porre gli occhi addosso a** to lay one's eyes on; **porre in dubbio** to cast doubt on; **porre mano a** to set to work at; **porre termine a** to put an end to; **posto che** since, provided || *ref* to place oneself; **porsi in cammino** to set out or forth; **porsi in salvo** to reach safety

pòrro *m* wart; (bot) leek

pòrta *f* door; gate; (cricket) wicket; (sports) goal; **di porta in porta** door-to-door; **fuori porta** outside the city limits; **mettere alla porta** to dismiss, fire; **porta di servizio** delivery entrance; **porta scorrevole** sliding door; **porta stagna** (naut; theat) safety door

portabagà·gli *m* (-gli) porter; baggage rack

portabandiè·ra *m* (-ra) standard-bearer

portàbile *adj* portable

portàbi·ti *m* (-ti) coat hanger

portabotti·glie *m* (-glie) bottle rack

portacar·te *adj invar & m* (-te) folder

portacati·no *adj invar* washstand-supporting || *m* (-no) washstand

portacéne·re *m* (-re) ashtray

portachia·vi *m* (-vi) key ring

portaci·pria *m* (-pria) compact

portadi·schi *m* (-schi) record cabinet, record rack; turntable

portadól·ci *m* (-ci) candy dish

portaère·i *f* (-i) aircraft carrier

portaferi·ti *m* (-ti) (mil) stretcher bearer

portafinèstra *f* (portefinèstre) French window

portafió·ri *m* (-ri) flower vase

portafò·gli *m* (-gli) or **portafò·glio** *m* (-gli) billfold, wallet; pocketbook; portfolio

portafortu·na *m* (-na) charm, amulet

portafrut·ta *m* (-ta) fruit dish

portafusìbi·li *m* (-li) fuse box

portagiò·ie *m* (-ie) jewel box

portaimmondì·zie *m* (-zie) trash can, garbage can

portainsé·gna *m* (-gna) standard-bearer

portalàmpa·da *m* (-da) (elec) socket

portale *m* portal

portalètte·re (-re) *mf* letter carrier || *m* postman, mailman

portamaz·ze *m* (-ze) caddie

portaménto *m* posture; gait; (fig) behavior

portami·na *m* (-na) mechanical pencil

portamissi·li (-li) *adj invar* missile-carrying || *m* missile carrier

portamoné·te *m* (-te) purse

portamùsi·ca *m* (-ca) music stand

portante *adj* carrying; (archit) weight-bearing; (aer) lifting; (rad) carrier || *m* amble

portantina *f* sedan chair; stretcher

portantino *m* bearer (*of sedan chair*); stretcher bearer

portanza *f* (archit) capacity; (aer) lift

portaombrèl·li *m* (-li) umbrella stand

portaórdi·ni *m* (-ni) (mil) messenger

portapac·chi *m* (-chi) parcel delivery man; basket (*on bicycle*)

portapén·ne *m* (-ne) penholder

portapiat·ti *m* (-ti) dish rack

portaposa·te [s] *m* (-te) silverware chest

portapran·zi [dz] *m* (-zi) dinner pail

portaraz·zi (-zi) [ddzz] *adj invar* missile-carrying || *m* missile carrier

portare (pòrto) *tr* to carry; to bring; to take; to carry along; to lead; to herald; to praise; to wear; to drive (*car*); to run (*a candidate*); to adduce; to nurture (*hatred*); (aut) to hold (*e.g., five people*); **portare a conoscenza di** to let know; **portare avanti** to carry forward; **portare in alto** to lift; **portare via** to steal; to take away || *intr* to carry (*said of a gun*) || *ref* to move; to behave; to be (*a candidate*)

portaritrat·ti *m* (-ti) picture frame

portasapó·ne *m* (-ne) soap dish

portasigarét·te *m* (-te) cigarette case

portasìga·ri *m* (-ri) cigar case; humidor

portaspil·li *m* (-li) pincushion

portata *f* course (*of a meal*); capacity; flow (*of river*); compass (*of voice*); range (*of voice or gun*); importance; (naut) burden; (naut) tonnage; **a portata di mano** within reach; **a portata di voce** within call, within earshot

portatèsse·re *m* (-re) card case

portàtile *adj* portable

porta·to -ta *adj* worn; **portato a** leaning toward || *m* result, effect || *f* see **portata**

porta·tóre -trice *mf* bearer

portatovagliòlo *m* napkin ring

portauò·vo *m* (-vo) eggcup

portavó·ce *m* (-ce) megaphone; (fig) mouthpiece

porte-enfant *m* (porte-enfant) baby bunting

portèllo *m* wicket; leaf (*of cabinet door*); (naut) porthole

portènto *m* portent

portica·to -ta *adj* arcaded || *m* arcade

pòrti·co *m* (-ci) portico, arcade, colonnade; shed

portiè·re -ra *mf* concierge || *m* janitor, doorman; (sports) goalkeeper || *f* portiere (*in church door*); (aut) door

porti·nàio -nàia (-nài -nàie) *adj* door, door-keeping || *mf* doorkeeper, concierge

portineria *f* janitor's quarters

pòrto *m* port, harbor; transportation charge; port wine; goal; **condurre a buon porto** to carry to fruition; **franco di porto** prepaid, postpaid; **porto a carico del mittente** postage prepaid; **porto assegnato** charges to be paid by addressee; **porto d'armi** permit to carry arms; **porto franco** free port

Portogallo, il Portugal

portoghése [s] *adj & mf* Portuguese;

fare il portoghese (theat) to crash the gate
portóne *m* portal
portorica•no -na *adj & mf* Puerto Rican
Portorico *m* Puerto Rico
portuale *adj* port, harbor || *m* dock worker, longshoreman
porzióne *f* portion
pòsa [s] *f* laying (*e.g., of cornerstone*); posing (*for portrait*); posture, affectation, pose; dregs; (phot) exposure; (lit) rest; **senza posa** relentless; relentlessly
posami•ne (-ne) [s] *adj invar* minelaying || *f* minelayer
posare [s] (**pòso**) *tr* to lay, put down || *intr* to lie; to settle; to pose; **posare a** to pose as || *ref* to settle; to alight; (lit) to rest
posata [s] *f* cover, place (*at table*); table utensil (*knife, fork or spoon*); **posate** knife, fork and spoon
posateria [s] *f* service (*of knives, forks, and spoons*)
posa•to -ta [s] *adj* sedate, quiet; placed || *f* see **posata**
posa•tóre -trice [s] *mf* poseur || *m* layer, installer (*of cables or pipes*)
pòscia *adv* then, afterwards; **poscia che** after
poscritto *m* postscript
posdatare *tr* var of **postdatare**
posdomani *adv* (lit) day after tomorrow
positivaménte *adv* for sure
positi•vo -va *adj* positive || *f* (phot) positive, print
posizióne *f* position; status; (fig) stand
pospórre §218 *tr* to put off, postpone; to put last; **posporre qlco a qlco** to put or place s.th after s.th
pòssa *f* (lit) strength, vigor
possanza *f* (lit) power
possedére §252 *tr* to possess; to own; to master (*a language*); **essere posseduto da** to be enthralled with; to be possessed by
possediménto *m* possession, property
posseditrice *f* owner, possessor
possènte *adj* (lit) powerful
possessióne *f* possession
possessi•vo -va *adj* possessive
possèsso *m* possession
possessóre *m* owner, possessor
possìbile *adj* possible || *m*—**fare il possibile** to do one's best
possibili•sta (-sti -ste) *adj* pragmatically flexible || *mf* pragmatically flexible person, possibilist
possibili•tà *f* (-tà) possibility; opportunity; **possibilità** *fpl* means
possidènte *mf* proprietor, owner; **possidente terriero** landowner
pòsta *f* post; mail; post office; box (*in stable*); ambush; bet; **a giro di posta** by return mail; **a posta** on purpose; **darsi la posta** to set up an appointment; **fare la posta a** to have under surveillance; **fermo in posta** general delivery; **levare la posta** to pick up the mail; **posta aerea** air mail; **posta dei lettori** (journ) letters to the editor; **poste** postal department

pósta *f* (archaic) planting; (archaic) footprint
postagi•ro *m* (-ro & -ri) postal transfer of funds
postale *adj* postal, mail || *m* mail; mail train (boat, bus, or plane)
postare (**pòsto**) *tr* (mil) to post || *ref* (mil) to take a position
postazióne *f* (mil) emplacement
postbèlli•co -ca *adj* (-ci -che) postwar
postbruciatóre *m* (aer) afterburner
postdatare *tr* to postdate
posteggiare §290 (**postéggio**) *tr & intr* to park
posteggia•tóre -trice *mf* parking-lot attendant; customer (*in a parking lot*); (coll) outdoor merchant; **posteggiatore abusivo** parking violator
postég•gio *m* (-gi) parking lot; stand (*in outdoor market*); **posteggio di tassi** cabstand
posterióre *adj* back; subsequent, later
posteri•tà *f* (-tà) posterity
pòste•ro -ra *adj* later, subsequent || **posteri** *mpl* posterity, descendants
postic•cio -cia (-ci -ce) *adj* artificial; false (*e.g., tooth*); temporary || *m* wiglet, ponytail || *f* row of trees
posticipare (**posticipo**) *tr* to postpone
posticipa•to -ta *adj* deferred
postièrla *f* postern
postiglióne *m* postilion
postilla *f* marginal note
postillare *tr* to annotate
posti•no -na *mf* letter carrier || *m* mailman, postman
pósto *m* place; room; seat; job, position; spot; (mil) post; **a posto in** order; orderly; **al posto di** instead of; **essere a posto** to have a good job; **mettere a posto** to find a good job for; (coll) to keep quiet; **quel posto** (coll) seat of the pants; (coll) toilet; **posto a sedere** seat; **posto di blocco** road block; (rr) signal tower; **posto di guardia** (mil) guardhouse; **posto di medicazione** or **di pronto soccorso** first-aid station; **posto in piedi** standing room; **posto letto** bed (*e.g., in hospital*); **posto telefonico pubblico** public telephone, pay station; **rimettere a posto** to fix, repair; **saper stare al proprio posto** to know one's place; **sul posto** on the spot
postrè•mo -ma *adj* (lit) last
postrìbolo *m* (lit) brothel
postulante *adj* petitioning || *mf* petitioner, applicant; (eccl) postulant
postulare (**pòstulo**) *tr* to postulate
pòstu•mo -ma *adj* posthumous || **postumi** *mpl* sequel; (pathol) sequelae
potàbile *adj* drinkable
potare (**póto**) *tr* to trim, prune
potassa *f* potash
potàssio *m* potassium
potatura *f* pruning, polling
potentato *m* (lit) potentate
potènte *adj* powerful; influential || **i potenti** the powers that be
potènza *f* power, might; (math) power; **all'ennesima potenza** (math) to the nth power; (fig) to the nth degree; **in potenza** potential; potentially

potenziale adj & m potential
potére m ability; authority, power; **in potere di** in the hands of; **potere d'acquisto** purchasing power; **potere esecutivo** executive; **potere giudiziario** judiciary; **quarto potere** fourth estate ‖ §219 intr to be powerful; **non ne posso più** I am at the end of my rope; **si può?** may I come in? ‖ aux (ESSERE & AVERE) to be able; **non posso fare a meno di** + inf I can't help + ger; **non potere fare a meno di** to not be able to do without; **posso**, etc. I can; I may, etc.; **potrei**, etc. I could; I might, etc.
pote·stà f (-stà) power, authority
poveràc·cio -cia mf (-ci -ce) poor guy, poor soul
pòve·ro -ra adj poor; needy, wretched; lean (gasoline mixture); **povero in canna** as poor as a church mouse ‖ mf pauper; beggar; poor devil ‖ **i poveri** the poor
pover·tà f (-tà) poverty; paucity, scantiness
poveruòmo m (used only in sg) poor devil
pozióne f potion, brew
pózza f pool, puddle
pozzànghera f puddle
pozzétto m small well; manhole; forecastle (in small boat)
pózzo m well; shaft; **pozzo artesiano** artesian well; **pozzo delle catene** (naut) chain locker; **pozzo di scienza** fountain of knowledge; **pozzo di ventilazione** (min) air shaft; **pozzo nero** cesspool; **pozzo petrolifero** oil well; **pozzo trivellato** deep well; **un pozzo di** (fig) a barrel of
Praga f Prague
prammàti·co -ca (-ci -che) adj pragmatic ‖ f social custom; **di prammatica** obligatory, de rigueur
pranzare [dz] intr to dine
pranzo [dz] m dinner; **dopo pranzo** afternoon
pras·si f (-si) practice, praxis
pratería f prairie
pràti·ca f (-che) practice; knowledge; matter; file, dossier; business; experience; (naut) pratique; **aver pratica con** to be familiar with (people); **aver pratica di** to be familiar with (things); **far pratica** to be an apprentice; **fare le pratiche** to make an application; **in pratica** practically; **insabbiare una pratica** to pigeonhole a matter
praticàbile adj practicable; passable ‖ m (theat) raised platform
praticante adj practicing ‖ mf apprentice; novice; churchgoer
praticare §197 (pràtico) tr to practice; to frequent; to be familiar with; to make (e.g., a hole); to grant (a discount) ‖ intr to practice; **praticare in** to frequent
pratici·tà f (-tà) utility; practicality
pràti·co -ca (-ci -che) adj practical; experienced ‖ f see **pratica**
pratic ó·ne -na mf (pej) old hand
prato m meadow

pratolina f daisy
pra·vo -va adj (lit) wicked
preaccennare (preaccénno) tr to mention in advance
preaccenna·to -ta adj aforementioned
preallarme m early warning
Prealpi fpl foothills of the Alps
preàmbolo m preamble
preannunziare §287 (preannùnzio) tr to foretell, forebode
preannùn·zio m (-zi) advance information; foreboding
preautunnale adj pre-fall
preavvertire (preavvèrto) tr to forewarn
preavvisare tr to give advance notice to; to forewarn
preavviso m forewarning; notification of dismissal
prebèlli·co -ca adj (-ci -che) prewar
prebènda f prebend; (fig) easy money, sinecure
precà·rio -ria adj (-ri -rie) precarious
precauzióne f precaution
precedènte adj preceding ‖ m precedent; **precedenti** background; **precedenti penali** previous offenses, record
precedènza f precedence; (aut) right of way; (fig) priority
precèdere §123 tr & intr to precede
precettare (precètto) tr (mil) to call back from furlough
precètto m precept; (eccl) obligation
precettóre m tutor
precipitare (precìpito) tr to precipitate; to hasten; (chem) to precipitate ‖ intr (ESSERE) to fall; to fail; to rush (said of events); (chem) to precipitate ‖ ref to rush
precipitó·so -sa [s] adj hasty, headlong
precipì·zio m (-zi) precipice, cliff; ruin; **a precipizio** headlong
preci·puo -pua adj chief, principal, primary
precisare tr to say exactly, specify, clarify; to fix (a date)
precisazióne f clarification
precisióne f precision
preci·so -sa adj precise, exact; punctilious; identical, same; sharp, e.g., **alle sette precise** at seven o'clock sharp
precla·ro -ra adj (lit) illustrious
preclùdere §105 tr to preclude
precòce adj precocious, premature
preconcèt·to -ta adj preconceived ‖ m preconception; prejudice, bias
preconizzare [ddzz] tr to foretell, forecast; (eccl) to preconize
precórrere §139 tr (lit) to precede ‖ intr (lit) to occur before
precursóre m precursor
prèda f booty, prize; prey
predace adj (lit) preying, predatory
predare (prèdo) tr to pillage; to prey upon
preda·tóre -trice adj predacious, rapacious ‖ mf plunderer
predecessóre m predecessor
predèlla f dais; altar step; platform
predellino m footboard
predestinare (predestino & predèstino) tr to predestine

predét•to -ta adj aforementioned
prediale adj field, rural || f land tax
prèdi•ca f (-che) sermon
predicare §197 (prèdico) tr & intr to preach
predicato m predicate; essere in predicato di + inf to be rumored to + inf; essere predicato per to be considered for
predica•tóre -trice mf preacher
predicazióne f preaching; sermon
predicòzzo m (coll) lecture, scolding
predilèt•to -ta adj & m favorite
predilezióne f predilection
prediligere §149 (pres part missing) tr to prefer; to like best
predire §151 tr to foretell
predispórre §218 tr to predispose, prearrange || ref to prepare oneself
predisposizióne f predisposition
predizióne f prediction
predominare (predòmino) tr to overcome || intr to predominate; to prevail
predomi•nio m (-ni) predominance
predóne m marauder; predone del mare pirate
preesistere §114 intr (ESSERE) to preexist
prefabbricare §197 (prefàbbrico) tr to prefabricate
prefazióne f preface
preferènza f preference; a preferenza rather; usar preferenze a to favor
preferibile adj preferable
preferire §176 tr to prefer
preferi•to -ta adj preferred, favored || mf favorite; pet
prefètto m prefect
prefettura f prefecture
prèfi•ca f (-che) professional mourner, paid mourner; (coll) crybaby
prefiggere §103 tr to set, fix; (gram) to prefix || ref to plan
prefis•so -sa adj appointed; prefixed || m (gram) prefix; (telp) area code
prefissòide m prefixed combining form
pregare §209 (prègo) tr to beg, pray; to ask, request; farsi pregare to take a lot of asking; La prego please; prego! please!; beg your pardon!; you are welcome!
pregévole adj valuable
preghièra f entreaty; prayer
pregiare §290 (prègio) tr (lit) to praise, esteem || ref to be honored, to have the pleasure
pregia•to -ta adj precious; esteemed; la Sua pregiata (lettera) your favor, your kind letter; pregiatissimo Signore (com) dear Sir; pregiato Signore (com) dear Sir
prè•gio m (-gi) value, worth; esteem; avere in pregio to value
pregiudicare §197 (pregiùdico) tr to damage, harm, jeopardize
pregiudica•to -ta adj prejudged; prejudiced; compromised; bound to fail || m previous offender
pregiudiziale adj (law) pretrial; (pol) essential || f (law) pretrial
pregiudiziévole adj prejudicial, detrimental

pregiudì•zio m (-zi) prejudice, bias; harm, damage
pregnante adj pregnant
prè•gno -gna adj pregnant; saturated
prè•go m (-ghi) (lit) prayer || interj please!; beg your pardon!; you are welcome!
pregustare tr to foretaste, anticipate with pleasure
preistòri•co -ca adj (-ci -che) prehistoric(al)
prelato m prelate
prelazióne f (law) preemption; (obs) privilege
prelevaménto m (com) withdrawal
prelevare (prelèvo) tr to withdraw (money); to capture
prelìba•to -ta adj excellent, delicious
prelièvo m withdrawal; (med) specimen
preliminare adj preliminary || preliminari mpl preliminary negotiations
prelùdere §105 intr to make an introductory statement; (with dat) to precede, usher in
prelù•dio m (-di) prelude; (of an opera) overture
prematu•ro -ra adj premature
premeditare (premèdito) tr to premeditate
premeditazióne f premeditation; con premeditazione (law) with malice prepense
prèmere §123 tr to press; to push; to squeeze || intr (ESSERE & AVERE) to press; to be urgent; premere a to matter to, e.g., gli preme it matters to him; premere su to press, put pressure on
premèssa f premise; introduction (to a book)
preméttere §198 tr to state at the onset; to place at the beginning
premiare §287 (prèmio) tr to award a prize to, reward
premiazióne f awarding of prizes
preminènte adj prominent, preeminent
prè•mio m (-mi) prize; premium; bonus; award
prèmito m straining (to defecate)
premolare adj & m premolar
premonire §176 tr (lit) to foretell
premonizióne f premonition
premorire §201 intr (ESSERE) (with dat) to predecease
premunire §176 tr to fortify || ref—premunirsi contro to provide against; premunirsi di to provide oneself with
premura f haste; attention, care; aver premura (di) to be in a hurry (to); di premura hastily; far premura (with dat) to urge
premuró•so -sa [s] adj attentive, careful
prèndere §220 tr to take; to catch; to lift; to pick up; to fetch; to get; to receive; prendere a calci to kick; prendere a pugni to punch; prendere a servizio to employ, hire; prendere commiato to take leave; prendere con le buone to treat with kid gloves; prendere in castagna to catch in the act; prendere il sole to sun oneself; prendere la fuga to take flight;

prendere la mano to run away (*said of a horse*); **prendere le mosse** to begin (*said, e.g., of a story*); **prendere lucciole per lanterne** to commit a gross error; **prender paura** to get scared; **prendere per** to take for; **prendere per il naso** to lead by the nose; **prendere quota** (aer) to gain altitude; **prendere sonno** to fall asleep; **prendere un granchio** to make a blunder ‖ *intr* to take root; to set (*said of cement*); to catch (*said of fire*); to turn (*left or right*); **prendere a + inf** to begin to + *inf* ‖ *ref* to grab one another; to get along together; **prendersela con** to become angry with; to lay the blame on; **prendersi a** to take hold of

prendi-tóre -trice *mf* receiver; payee (*of a note*); margin buyer ‖ *m* (baseball) catcher

prenóme *m* first name, given name

prenotare (prenòto) *tr* to reserve, book ‖ *ref* to register

prenotazióne *f* reservation, booking

preoccupante *adj* worrisome

preoccupare (preòccupo) *tr* to preoccupy; **preoccupare la mente di** to win the favor of ‖ *ref* to worry

preoccupazióne *f* preoccupation, worry

preordinare (preórdino) *tr* to foreordain; to prearrange

preparare *tr* to prepare; to prime; to steep, brew ‖ *ref* to be prepared; to brew (*said, e.g., of a storm*)

peparatì-vo -va *adj* preparatory ‖ **preparativi** *mpl* preparations

prepara-to -ta *adj* prepared; well-equipped ‖ *m* patent medicine; (med) preparation; **preparato anatomico** dissection, anatomical specimen

preparatò-rio -ria *adj* (-ri -rie) preparatory

preparazióne *f* preparation

preponderante *adj* preponderant, prevailing

preponderanza *f* preponderance

prepórre §218 *tr* to prefix; to place before; to prefer; **preporre (qlcu) a** to place (*s.o.*) at the head of

preposizióne *f* preposition

prepósto *m* chief; (eccl) provost

prepotènte *adj* arrogant, overbearing; urgent (*desire*) ‖ *m* bully

prepotènza *f* arrogance; outrage; **di prepotenza** by force

prerogatíva *f* prerogative

présa [s] *f* hold, grip; handle; potholder; capture; pinch (*e.g., of salt*); setting (*of cement*); intake; (cards) trick; (elec) jack; (mov) take; **a pronta presa** quick-setting (*cement*); **dar presa a** to give rise to; **essere alle prese** to come to grips; **far presa** to stick (*said of glue*); to set (*said of cement*); to take root; **far presa su** to impress; **mettere alle prese** to pit (*e.g., animals*); **presa d'acqua** spigot, faucet; **presa d'aria** outlet (*of air hose*); air shaft; **presa di corrente** (elec) wall socket, outlet, receptacle; **presa di terra** (elec) ground; **presa**

in giro kidding, joke; **venire alle prese** to come to grips

presà-gio *m* (-gi) forecast; portent

presagire §176 *tr* to forecast; to portend

presalà-rio [s] *m* (-ri) (educ) stipend

prèsbite *adj* far-sighted ‖ *mf* far-sighted person

presbiteria-no -na *adj* & *mf* Presbyterian

prescégliere §244 *tr* to choose, select

prescìndere §247 (*pret* **prescindéi** & **prescissi**) *intr*—**a prescindere da** except for; **prescindere da** to leave out

prescolàsti-co -ca *adj* (-ci -che) preschool

prescrit-to -ta *adj* prescribed

prescrìvere §250 *tr* to prescribe ‖ *intr* (ESSERE) (law) to prescribe, to lapse

prescrizióne *f* prescription; (law) extinctive proscription

presegnale [s] *m* warning sign

presentàbile *adj* presentable

presentare (presènto) *tr* to present; to introduce; **presentare la candidatura di** to nominate; **presentat'arm!** present arms! ‖ *ref* to show up, appear; to come, arise (*said, e.g., of an opportunity*)

presenta-tóre -trice *mf* presenter; (rad, telv) announcer ‖ *m* master of ceremonies

presentazióne *f* presentation; introduction

presènte *adj* present; **avere presente** to have in mind; **fare presente qlco a qlcu** to bring s.th to s.o.'s attention; **tenere presente** to keep in mind ‖ *m* present; bystander, onlooker; **al presente** at present; **di presente** immediately ‖ *interj* here!

presentiménto [s] *m* presentiment, foreboding

presentire [s] (**presènto**) *tr* to have a presentiment of

presènza *f* presence; attendance; **di presenza** in person; **presenza di spirito** presence of mind

presenziare §287 (**presènzio**) *tr* to attend; to witness ‖ *intr*—**presenziare a** to be present at; to witness

presè-pio *m* (-pi) Nativity, crèche

preservare [s] (**presèrvo**) *tr* to preserve, protect

preservatì-vo -va [s] *adj* & *m* prophylactic

prèside [s] *m* principal (*of secondary school*); **preside di facoltà** dean

presidènte [s] *m* president; chairman; **presidente del Consiglio** premier

presidentéssa [s] *f* president; chairwoman

presidènza [s] *f* presidency; chairmanship

presì-dio [s] *m* (-di) garrison; (fig) defense, help; **presidi medical aids**

presièdere §141 (**presièdo**) *tr* to preside over ‖ *intr* to preside; **presiedere a** to preside over

prèssa *f* crowd; haste; (mach) press; **far pressa** (poet) to urge

pressacar-te *m* (-te) paperweight

pressaforàg-gio *m* (-gio) baler, hay baler

pressante *adj* pressing, urgent
pressappòco *adv* more or less
pressare (prèsso) *tr* to press; to urge
pressióne *f* pressure; **far pressione su** to put pressure on; **pressione sanguigna** blood pressure; **sotto pressione** under steam
prèsso *m*—**nei pressi di** in the neighborhood of || *adv* near, nearby; **a un di presso** approximately; **da presso** close; **press'a poco** more or less || *prep* near; about; at; according to; at the house of; at the office of; care of; with, e.g., **godere fama presso to** enjoy popularity with
pressoché *adv* almost, about, nearly
pressurizzare [ddzz] *tr* to pressurize
prestabilire §176 *tr* to preestablish
prestabíli·to -ta *adj* appointed
prestanó·me *m* (-me) straw man, figurehead
prestante *adj* strong, vigorous; comely
prestanza *f* vigor; (lit) comeliness
prestare (prèsto) *tr* to lend; to loan; to give (*ear; help*); to pay (*attention*); to render (*obedience*); to take (*oath*); to keep (*faith*); **prestar man forte to** give aid; **prestar servizio** to work || *ref* to lend oneself; to be suitable; to be willing; to volunteer
presta·tóre -trice *mf* lender; **prestatore d'opera** worker; **prestatori d'opera** labor
prestazióne *f* service; performance
prestigia·tóre -trice *mf* magician, juggler
prestì·gio *m* (-gi) prestige; spell, influence; ledgerdemain
prestigió·so -sa [s] *adj* captivating, spellbinding; illusory
prèstito *m* loan; (philol) borrowing; **dare a prestito** to lend; **prendere a prestito** to borrow
prè·sto -sta *adj* (archaic) quick || *m* (mus) presto || *adv* soon; fast; quick, quickly; early; **al più presto** at the earliest possible time; **ben presto** soon; **far presto** to hurry; **più presto che può** as soon as you can; **presto detto** easy to say
presùmere §116 *tr & intr* to presume
presunti·vo -va *adj* presumptive; budgeted, estimated (*expenditure*)
presun·to -ta *adj* alleged, supposed; estimated (*expenditure*)
presuntuó·so -sa [s] *adj* presumptuous; bumptious
presunzióne *f* presumption; conceit
presuppórre [s] §218 *tr* to presuppose
presuppósto [s] *m* assumption
prète *m* priest; minister; wooden frame (*to hold bed warmer*)
pretendènte *m* suitor; pretender
pretèndere §270 *tr* to demand, claim; **pretenderla a** to pretend to be || *intr*—**pretendere a** to be a suitor for; to claim (*e.g., a throne*)
pretensióne *f* demand; pretention; pretense
pretensió·so -sa [s] or pretenzió·so -sa [s] *adj* pretentious
preterintenzionale *adj* (law) unintentional; (law) justifiable

pretèri·to -ta *adj & m* preterit
preté·so -sa [s] *adj* alleged, ostensible; assumed (*name*) || *f* pretense; pretension
pretèsto *m* pretext, excuse; **sotto il pretesto di** under pretense of
pretòni·co -ca *adj* (-ci -che) pretonic
pretóre *m* judge, magistrate (*of lower court*)
prèt·to -ta *adj* pure, genuine
pretura *f* lower court
prevalènte *adj* prevalent, prevailing
prevalènza *f* prevalence; **essere in prevalenza** to be in the majority; **in prevalenza** for the most part
prevalére §278 *intr* (ESSERE & AVERE) to prevail || *ref* to take advantage
prevaricare §197 (prevàrico) *intr* to transgress; to graft
prevarica·tóre -trice *mf* grafter
prevedére §279 *tr* to foresee; to provide for (*said of a statute*)
prevedíbile *adj* foreseeable
prevenire §282 *tr* to precede; to anticipate; to forewarn; to prejudice
preventivi·sta *mf* (-sti -ste) estimator
preventi·vo -va *adj* preventive; prior; estimated (*budget*) || *m* estimate
prevenu·to -ta *adj* forewarned; biased, prejudiced || *m* defendant
prevenzióne *f* prevention; prejudice, bias
previdènte *adj* provident, prudent
previdènza *f* providence; foresight; **previdenza sociale** social security
previdenziale *adj* social (*e.g., responsibility*); social-security (*e.g., contribution*)
prè·vio -via *adj* (-vi -vie) with previous, e.g., **previo accordo** with previous agreement
previsióne *f* foresightedness; **in previsione di** anticipating; **previsioni del tempo** weather forecast
previ·sto -sta *adj* foreseen, expected || *m* expected time; estimated amount
prezió·so -sa [s] *adj* precious, valuable; affected; **fare il prezioso** (coll) to play hard to get || **preziosi** *mpl* valuables, jewels
prezzare (prèzzo) *tr* to care about; to price
prezzémolo *m* parsley
prèzzo *m* price; cost; **mettere a prezzo** (fig) to sell; **prezzo di favore** special price; **prezzo d'ingresso** admission; **tenere in gran prezzo** to value highly, to esteem highly; **ultimo prezzo** rock-bottom price
prezzolare (prèzzolo) *tr* to hire (*e.g., a gunman*); to bribe
prigióne *f* prison, jail; (naut) brig
prigionía *f* imprisonment; bondage
prigioniè·ro -ra *adj* imprisoned || *mf* prisoner || *m* stud bolt
prillare *intr* to spin, whirl
prima *f* first grade (*in school*); (rr) first class; (theat) first night; (aut) first (gear); **alla prima** or **sulle prime** at the outset || *adv* before; first; prior; ahead; **di prima** previous; **prima che** before; **prima di** ahead of; before;

prima o poi sooner or later; quanto prima as soon as possible

primàrio -ria (-ri -rie) adj primary || m (elec) primary; (med) chief of staff

primati•sta mf (-sti -ste) (sports) record holder

primato m primacy; (sports) record

primavèra f spring; springtime; (bot) primrose

primaverile adj spring; spring-like

primeggiare §290 (priméggio) intr to excel

primiè•ro -ra adj (lit) prior; (lit) pristine || f (cards) meld

primiti•vo -va adj & m primitive

primizia f first fruits; scoop, beat

pri•mo -ma adj first; early (dawn); prime (cost); raw (material); sulle prime at first || m first; minute; primo arrivato first comer || f see prima

primogèni•to -ta adj first-born; (fig) beloved || mf first-born child

primòrdi mpl beginning, origin

primordiale adj primordial, primeval

primula f primrose || Primula f—la Primula Rossa the Scarlet Pimpernel

principale adj principal, main || m (coll) boss, chief

principalménte adv chiefly, mainly

principato m principality

principe adj princeps || m prince; il principe di Galles the Prince of Wales; principe ereditario crown prince

principé•sco -sca adj (-schi -sche) princely

principéssa f princess

principiante adj beginning || mf beginner

principiare §287 tr & intr (ESSERE & AVERE) to begin; a principiare da beginning with

princi•pio m (-pi) beginning; principle; in principio at the beginning, at first

princisbécco m pinchbeck; restare or rimanere di princisbecco to be dumfounded

prióre m prior

priori•tà f (-tà) priority

priorità•rio -ria adj (-ri -rie) priority, e.g., progetto prioritario priority project

pri•sma m (-smi) prism

privare tr to deprive; to remove

privativa f government monopoly; salt and tobacco store; patent

priva•to -ta adj private || m private individual

privazione f privation, loss

privilegiare §290 (privilègio) tr to privilege; (fig) to endow

privilegia•to -ta adj privileged; preferred (stock) || m privileged person

privilè•gio m (-gi) privilege

pri•vo -va adj deprived; privo di lacking

prò m (pro) profit, advantage; a che pro? what's the use?; buon pro! good appetite!; far pro to be good for the health; il pro e il contro the pros and the cons || prep pro, in favor of

probàbile adj probable

probabili•tà f (-tà) probability; chance; odds

probante adj proving; evidential

probatò•rio -ria adj (-ri -rie) probative, evidential

problè•ma m (-mi) problem

prò•bo -ba adj (lit) honest

procàc•cia mf (-cia) messenger; mail carrier

procacciare §128 tr to get, procure || ref to eke out (a living); to get into (trouble)

procace adj buxom, sexy; saucy, petulant

procèdere §123 (procèdo) intr to proceed, take action || intr (ESSERE) to proceed, go ahead

procediménto m procedure; behavior

procedura f procedure

procèlla f (lit) storm, tempest

procellària f (orn) petrel

processare (procèsso) tr to try, prosecute

processióne f procession

procèsso m process; trial; processo verbale minutes

processuale adj trial

procinto m—in procinto di on the point of

procióne m raccoon

procla•ma m (-mi) proclamation

proclamare tr to proclaim

proclamazióne f proclamation

proclìti•co -ca adj & f (-ci -che) proclitic

proclive adj inclined, disposed

proclivi•tà f (-tà) proclivity

procrastinare (procràstino) tr to procrastinate, put off || intr to procrastinate

procreare (procrèo) tr to procreate

procura f agency; power of attorney; Procura della Repubblica attorney general's office; district attorney's office

procurare tr to procure, to get; to cause; procurare che to see to it that; procurare di to try to || ref to get, acquire

procura•tóre -trice mf proxy; agent; attorney-at-law; (sports) manager; Procuratore della Repubblica district attorney

pròda f shore, bank; (archaic) prow

pròde adj brave || m brave person, hero

prodézza f prowess; accomplishment

prodiè•ro -ra adj prow, e.g., cannone prodiero prow gun; preceding (in a row of ships)

prodigare §209 (pròdigo) tr to squander, lavish || ref to do one's best

prodi•gio m (-gi) prodigy; wonder

prodigió•so -sa [s] adj prodigious; wonderful

pròdi•go -ga adj (-ghi -ghe) lavish, prodigal; prodigo di profuse in

prodità•rio -ria adj (-ri -rie) traitorous

prodótto m product; result; prodotti in scatola canned goods; prodotti (ortofrutticoli) produce

produrre §102 tr to produce; to turn out; to yield; to breed; to cause; (lit) to prolong; (law) to exhibit || *ref* (theat) to perform, appear

produtti•vo -va *adj* productive

produttivìsti•co -ca *adj* (**-ci -che**) productivity, e.g., **fine produttivìstico** productivity policy

produt•tóre -trice *adj* producing || *mf* producer; agent; manufacturer's representative || *m* salesman || *f* saleswoman

produzióne *f* production; output; **produzione in massa** or **in serie** mass production

proè•mio *m* (**-mi**) preamble, proem

profanare *tr* to profane, desecrate

profanazióne *f* profanation, desecration

profa•no -na *adj* profane; lay, uninformed || *m* layman; **il profano** the profane

proferire §176 *tr* (lit) to utter; (lit) to proffer

professare (professo) *tr* to profess; to practice (*e.g., law*) || *intr* to practice || *ref* to profess oneself to be

professionale *adj* professional; occupational (*disease*); trade (*school*)

professióne *f* profession; **fare il ladro di professione** to be a confirmed thief; **fare qlco di professione** to pursue the trade of s.th, e.g., **fa il falegname di professione** he pursues the trade of carpenter

professioni•sta *mf* (**-sti -ste**) professional

professorale *adj* professorial; pedantic

profes•sóre -soréssa *mf* professor; teacher; **professore d'orchestra** orchestra member

profè•ta *m* (**-ti**) prophet

profetéssa *f* prophetess

profèti•co -ca *adj* (**-ci -che**) prophetic

profetizzare [ddzz] *tr* to prophesy

profezìa *f* prophecy

profferire §176 (*pp* **profferto**; *pret* **profferì** & **proffèrsi**) *tr* to offer; (lit) to utter

profi•cuo -cua *adj* profitable

profilare *tr* to outline; to sketch; to hem; (mach) to shape || *ref* to be outlined; to loom

profilas•si *f* (**-si**) prophylaxis

profila•to -ta *adj* outlined; hemmed; (mach) shaped || *m* structural piece

profilàtti•co -ca *adj* (**-ci -che**) prophylactic

profilatura *f* hemming; (mach) shaping

profilo *m* profile; sketch; outline

profittare *intr* to profit, benefit

profitta•tóre -trice *mf* profiteer

profittévole *adj* (lit) profitable

profitto *m* profit; progress; **profitti e perdite** profit and loss

proflù•vio *m* (**-vi**) overflow; (pathol) discharge

profondare (profóndo) *tr* & *intr* to sink

profóndere §178 *tr* to squander, lavish || *ref* to be profuse

profondi•tà *f* (**-tà**) depth

profón•do -da *adj* deep; profound; searching (*e.g., investigation*) || *m* bottom; depth; subconscious

pro fórma *adj invar* pro forma; perfunctory || *m* (coll) formality

pròfu•go -ga (**-ghi -ghe**) *adj* fugitive || *mf* refugee

profumare *tr* to perfume || *intr* to smell

profumataménte *adv* lavishly

profuma•to -ta *adj* perfumed, fragrant

profumerìa *f* perfumery; perfume shop

profumo *m* perfume; bouquet (*of wine*)

profusióne *f* profusion; **a profusione** in profusion

profu•so -sa *adj* profuse

progè•nie *f* (**-nie**) progeny, offspring; (pej) breed

progeni•tóre -trice *mf* ancestor

progettare (progètto) *tr* to plan; to design

progetti•sta *mf* (**-sti -ste**) planner; designer; wild dreamer

progètto *m* project; plan; draft (*of law*); **far progetti** to plan; **progetto di scala reale** (cards) possible straight flush

prògno•si *f* (**-si**) prognosis

program•ma *m* (**-mi**) program; plan; curriculum; cycle (*of washing machine*); (mov) feature; (theat) playbill; **programma politico** platform

programmare *tr* to program; to plan

programma•tóre -trice *mf* programmer

programmazióne *f* programming

progredire §176 *intr* (ESSERE & AVERE) to progress, advance

progredì•to -ta *adj* advanced

progressióne *f* progression

progressi•sta *adj* & *mf* (**-sti -ste**) progressive

progressi•vo -va *adj* progressive

progrèsso *m* progress; progression, advance; **fare progressi** to progress

proibire §176 *tr* to prohibit; to prevent

proibì•to -ta *adj* forbidden; **è proibito entrare** no admission; **è proibito fumare** no smoking

proibizióne *f* prohibition

proibizionismo *m* prohibition

proiettare (proiètto) *tr* to project; to cast (*a shadow*) || *intr* to project || *ref* to be projected, project

proièttile *m* projectile, missile

proiettóre *m* projector, projection machine; searchlight; (aut) headlight; **proiettore acustico** sonar projector

proiezióne *f* projection; **proiezione rallentata** slow motion

pròle *f invar* offspring, progeny

proletariato *m* proletariat

proletà•rio -ria *adj* & *mf* (**-ri -rie**) proletarian

proliferare (prolìfero) *intr* to proliferate

prolificare §197 (**prolìfico**) *intr* to proliferate

prolìfi•co -ca *adj* (**-ci -che**) prolific

prolis•so -sa *adj* prolix, long-winded; long (*e.g., beard*)

pròlo•go *m* (**-ghi**) prologue; preface

prolun•ga *f* (**-ghe**) extension

prolungaménto *m* prolongation, extension

prolungare §209 *tr* to prolong, extend || *ref* to extend; to speak at great length

prolunga•to -ta *adj* extended, protracted

prolusióne *f* inaugural lecture

promemò·ria or **pro memò·ria** m (-ria) reminder

promés·so -sa adj promised || mf betrothed || f promise; promising individual

promettènte adj promising

prométtere §198 tr to promise; to threaten (e.g., a storm) || intr to promise; **promettere bene** to be very promising || ref—**promettersi a Dio** to make a vow to God; **promettersi in matrimonio** to become engaged

prominènte adj prominent

promì·scuo -scua adj promiscuous; coeducational; mixed (marriage; races); (gram) epicene

promontò·rio m (-ri) promontory, cliff

promo·tóre -trice adj promoting || mf promoter

promozióne f promotion

promulgare §209 tr to promulgate

promuòvere §202 tr to promote; to pass (a student); to initiate (legal suit); to induce (e.g., perspiration)

pronipóte mf great-grandchild || m great-grandson; grandnephew; **pronipoti** descendants || f great-granddaughter; grandniece

prò·no -na adj (lit) prone

pronóme m pronoun

pronominale adj (gram) pronominal; (gram) reflexive (verb)

pronosticare §197 (pronòstico) tr to prognosticate, forecast

pronòsti·co m (-ci) prognostication, forecast; sign, omen

prontézza f readiness; quickness, promptness

prón·to -ta adj ready; first (aid); quick; prompt; ready (cash) || **pronto** interj (telp) hello!

prontuà·rio m (-ri) handbook

pronùn·cia f (-cie) or **pronunzia** f pronunciaton; (law) judgment

pronunziare §287 tr to pronounce; to utter; to pass (sentence); to make (a speech) || ref to pass judgment

pronunzia·to -ta adj pronounced, marked; prominent (nose, chin, beard) || m (law) sentence

propaganda f propaganda; advertisement; advertising

propagandi·sta mf (-sti -ste) propagandist; advertiser; agent; detail man

propagandìsti·co -ca adj (-ci -che) advertising

propagare §209 tr to propagate; to spread || ref to spread

propàggine f offspring; (geog) spur, counterfoot; (hort) layer

propalare tr (lit) to spread, divulge

propellènte adj & m propellent

propèllere §168 tr to propel

propèndere §123 (pp propènso) intr to incline, tend

propensióne f propensity, inclination

propèn·so -sa adj inclined, bent

propinare tr to administer (e.g., poison); **propinare qlco a qlcu** to put s.th over on s.o.

propìn·quo -qua adj (lit) near; (lit) related

propiziare §287 tr to propitiate, appease

propi·zio -zia adj (-zi -zie) propitious, favorable

proponiménto m intention, plan

propórre §218 tr to propose, present; to propound; **proporre come candidato** to nominate || ref—**proporsi di** to propose to, resolve to

proporzionare (proporzióno) tr to proportion, prorate

proporzióne f proportion

propòsito m purpose; **a proposito** opportune; opportunely; proper; by the way; **a proposito di** on the subject of; **di proposito** deliberately; **fuor di proposito** out of place; **parlare a proposito** to speak to the point

proposizióne f proposition; (gram) clause; **proposizione subordinata** dependent clause

propòsta f proposal; **proposta di legge** bill

propriaménte adv exactly; properly

proprie·tà f (-tà) propriety; ownership; property; **la proprietà** property owners; **proprietà immobiliare** real estate; **proprietà letteraria** copyright; **sulla proprietà** on the premises

proprietà·rio -ria mf (-ri -rie) owner, proprietor

prò·prio -pria (-pri -prie) adj peculiar, characteristic; proper (e.g., name); own, e.g., **il mio proprio libro** my own book || m one's own; **i propri** one's folks; **lavorare in proprio** to work for oneself || **proprio** adv just, really, exactly; **non . . . proprio** not . . . at all; **proprio adesso** just, just now

propugnare tr to advocate; (lit) to fight for

propugna·tóre -trice mf (lit) advocate

propulsare tr to propel; (lit) to repulse

propulsióne f propulsion

propulsóre m propeller, motor

pròra f prow, bow

proravia f—**a proravia** (naut) fore

pròro·ga f (-ghe) delay, extension

prorogare §209 (pròrogo) tr to extend; to put off, delay

prorómpere §240 intr to overflow; to burst (into tears)

prosa f prose

prosài·co -ca adj (-ci -che) prose; prosaic

prosàpia f (lit) ancestry

prosa·tóre -trice mf prose writer

proscè·nio m (-ni) forestage

prosciògliere §127 tr to free; to exonerate

prosciugare §209 tr to drain, reclaim || ref to dry up

prosciutto m ham; **prosciutto cotto** boiled ham; **prosciutto crudo** prosciutto

proscrìvere §250 tr to proscribe, outlaw

prosecuzióne [s] f prosecution, pursuit

proseguiménto [s] m prosecution, pursuit

proseguire [s] (proséguo) tr to follow, pursue || intr (ESSERE & AVERE) to continue

prosèlito *m* proselyte

prosodìa *f* prosody

prosopopèa *f* conceit

prosperare (pròspero) *intr* to prosper, thrive

prosperi·tà *f* (-tà) prosperity || *interj* gesundheit!

pròspe·ro -ra *adj* prosperous, thriving; flourishing; successful || *m* (coll) match

prosperó·so -sa [s] *adj* flourishing; healthy; buxom

prospettare (prospètto) *tr* to face, overlook; to outline || *intr*—**prospettare su** to face || *ref* to look; to appear; to loom up

prospetti·vo -va *adj* prospective || *f* perspective; prospect; view

prospètto *m* prospect, view; front (*of building*); diagram; outline; prospectus

prospettóre *m* prospector

prospiciènte *adj* facing

prossimaménte *adv* shortly

prossimi·tà *f* -tà proximity, nearness; **in prossimità di** near

pròssi·mo -ma *adj* near, close; next; immediate (*cause*) || *m* neighbor, fellow man

pròstata *f* prostate

prosternare (prostèrno) *ref* to prostrate oneself

prostituire §176 *tr* to prostitute

prostituta *f* prostitute

prostituzióne *f* prostitution

prostrare (pròstro) *ref* to prostrate oneself

prostrazióne *f* prostration

protagoni·sta *mf* (-sti -ste) protagonist

protèggere §193 *tr* to protect; to help, defend; to favor, promote

proteìna *f* protein

protèndere §270 *tr & ref* to stretch

pròte·si *f* (-si) (philol) prothesis; (surg) prosthesis

protèsta *f* protest, protestation

protestante *adj & mf* protestant; Protestant

protestare (protèsto) *tr* to protest; to reject (*faulty merchandise*) || *intr & ref* to protest

protestatà·rio -ria (-ri -rie) *adj* protesting || *m* protester

protèsto *m* (com) protest

protèt·to -ta *adj* protected || *m* protegé || *f* protegée

protettorato *m* protectorate

protet·tóre -trice *adj* patron || *mf* protector, guardian || *m* patron || *f* patroness

protezióne *f* protection; patronage

pròto *m* (typ) foreman

protocòllo *adj invar* commercial (*size*) || *m* protocol; **mettere a protocollo** to register, record

protopla·sma *m* (-smi) protoplasm

protòtipo *m* prototype; (fig) epitome

protozòi [dz] *mpl* protozoa

protrarre §273 *tr* to protract, extend || *ref* to continue

protrùdere §190 *intr* to protrude (*said, e.g., of a broken bone*)

protuberante *adj* protruding, bulging

pròva *f* test, examination; proof; try, attempt; probationary period (*of employment*); trial; token (*e.g., of friendship*); (sports) competition, event; (theat) rehearsal; **a prova di bomba** bombproof; foolproof; **a tutta prova** thoroughly tested; **in prova** on approval; **mettere a dura prova** to test (*e.g., one's patience*); **mettere alla prova** to test (*e.g., one's ability*); **mettere in prova** to fit (*a suit*); **prova del fuoco** trial by fire; **prova dell'acido** acid test; **prova generale** dress rehearsal; **prova indiziaria** circumstantial evidence

provare (pròvo) *tr* to test; to try; to try on; to try out; to taste; to prove; to feel (*e.g., anger*); (theat) to rehearse || *intr* to try || *ref* to compete

proveniènza *f* origin

provenire §282 *intr* (ESSERE) to stem, originate

provènto *m* income, proceeds

provenzale *adj & mf* Provençal

provèr·bio *m* (-bi) proverb; byword

provétta *f* test tube

provèt·to -ta *adj* (lit) masterful

provìn·cia *f* (-ce) province; **in provincia** outside of the big cities

provinciale *adj* provincial || *mf* small-town person || *f* provincial highway, state highway

provino *m* gauge; (mov) screen test

provocare §197 **(pròvoco)** *tr* to provoke; to bring about, cause; to arouse; to entice

provoca·tóre -trice *adj* provoking || *mf* provoker

provocatò·rio -ria *adj* (-ri -rie) provoking, provocative

provocazióne *f* provocation; challenge

provvedére §221 *tr* to prepare; to supply; **provvedere che** to see to it that || *intr* to take the necessary steps; **provvedere a** to provide for; **provvedere a** + *inf* to provide for + *ger*; **provvedere nei confronti di** to take steps against

provvediménto *m* measure, step

provvedi·tóre -trice *mf* provider || *m* superintendent; **provveditore agli studi** superintendent of schools

provvedu·to -ta *adj* supplied; careful

provvidènza *f* providence; windfall; **provvidenze** provisions, help

provvidenziale *adj* providential

pròvvi·do -da *adj* (lit) provident

provvigióne *f* (com) commission

provvisò·rio -ria *adj* (-ri -rie) provisional, temporary

provvi·sto -sta *adj* supplied || *f* supply, provision; **fare le provviste** to shop

prozìa *f* grandaunt

prozì·o *m* (-i) granduncle

prua *f* bow, prow

prudente *adj* prudent, cautious

prudènza *f* prudence, discretion

prùdere §222 *intr* to itch; **sentirsi prudere le mani** to feel like giving s.o. a beating

prugna *f* plum; **prugna secca** prune

prugno *m* plum tree
prùgnola *f* sloe
prùgnolo *m* sloe, blackthorn
pruno *m* thorn
prurito *m* itch
pseudònimo *m* pseudonym; alias; pen name
psicanàlisi *f* psychoanalysis
psicanali·sta *mf* (-sti -ste) psychoanalyst
psicanalizzare [ddzz] *tr* to psychoanalyze
psiche *f* psyche; cheval glass
psichìa·tra *mf* (-tri -tre) psychiatrist
psichiatrìa *f* psychiatry
psichi·co -ca *adj* (-ci -che) psychic
psicologìa *f* psychology
psicològi·co -ca *adj* (-ci -che) psychological
psicòlo·go -ga *mf* (-gi -ghe) psychologist
psicopàti·co -ca (-ci -che) *adj* psychopathic || *mf* psychopath
psicò·si *f* (-si) psychosis
psicosomàti·co -ca *adj* (-ci -che) psychosomatic
psicotèoni·co -ca (-ci -che) *adj* psychotechnical || *m* industrial psychologist || *f* industrial psychology
psicòti·co -ca *adj* (-ci -che) psychotic
pubblicare §197 (pùbblico) *tr* to publish
pubblicazióne *f* publication; **pubblicazioni di matrimonio** marriage banns
pubblicismo *m* communications; advertising
pubblici·sta *mf* (-sti -ste) free-lance newspaper writer; publicist
pubblicìsti·co -ca (-ci -che) *adj* advertising; political-science || *f* newspaper business
pubblicità *f* publicity; advertising
pubblicità·rio -ria (-rî -rie) *adj* advertising || *m* advertising agent
publicizzare [ddzz] *tr* to publicize
publicizzazióne [ddzz] *f* publicizing
pùbbli·co -ca *adj & m* (-ci -che) public; **mettere in pubblico** to publish
pubertà *f* puberty
pudibón·do -da *adj* (lit) modest, bashful; (lit) prudish
pudicìzia *f* modesty; prudery
pudi·co -ca *adj* (-chi -che) modest, chaste; bashful; (lit) reserved
pudóre *m* modesty; decency; shame
puericoltóre *m* pediatrician
puerile *adj* puerile, childish
puerili·tà *f* (-tà) puerility, childishness
puèrpera *f* lying-in patient
pugilato *m* boxing
pugilatóre *m* boxer, prize fighter
pùgile *m* boxer, prize fighter
pugili·sta *m* (-sti) boxer, prize fighter
pù·glia *f* (-glie) stake (in gambling)
pugnace *adj* (lit) pugnacious
pugnalare *tr* to stab
pugnalata *f* stab
pugnale *m* dagger
pugno *m* fist; fistful; punch; **avere in pugno** to have in one's grasp; **di proprio pugno** in one's own hand; **fare a pugni** to fight; to clash

pula *f* chaff
pulce *f* flea; **mettere una pulce nell'orecchio di** to put a bug in the ear of; **pulce tropicale** jigger, chigger
pulcèlla *f* maid, maiden
pulcinèlla *f*—**pulcinella di mare** (orn) Atlantic puffin || **Pulcinel·la** *m* (-la) buffoon; Punch, Punchinello
pulcino *m* chick
pulédra *f* filly
pulédro *m* colt, foal
pulég·gia *f* (-ge) pulley
pulire §176 *tr* to clean; to shine (shoes); to wipe; to polish
puliscipiè·di *m* (-di) doormat
puli·to -ta *adj* clean; polished; clear (conscience) || *f*—**dare una pulita a** to give a lick and a promise to
pulitura *f* cleaning; **pulitura a secco** dry cleaning
pulizìa *f* cleaning; cleanliness; **fare le pulizie** to clean house
pullulare (pùllulo) *intr* to swarm
pùlpito *m* pulpit
pulsante *m* knob; push button
pulsare *intr* to throb; to pulsate
pulvìscolo *m* fine dust; haze
pulzèlla *f* var of pulcella
pu·ma *m* (-ma) cougar
pungènte *adj* pungent; bitter (cold)
pùngere §183 *tr* to sting; (fig) to goad
pungiglióne *m* stinger (of bee); (fig) sting; (obs) goad
pungitópo *m* (bot) butcher's broom
pungolare (pùngolo) *tr* to goad, prod
punire §176 *tr* to punish
punizióne *f* punishment; penalty
punta *f* point, tip; prong; brad; bit, trifle; needle (of phonograph); avant-garde; point (of dog); (lit) wound; (fig) peak; (mach) broach; **averne fino alla punta dei capelli** to be sick and tired; **fare la punta a** to sharpen; **in punta di penna** elegantly; **prendere di punta** to treat roughly; to face up to; **punta delle dita** fingertip; **punta di piedi** tiptoe
puntale *m* tip, ferrule
puntaménto *m* aiming
puntare *tr* to aim; to aim at; to point; to thrust; to dot; to bet; to stare at; to fix (one's eyes); **puntare i piedi** to stiffen up; (fig) to balk || *intr* to aim; to point; to pin; to bet; **puntare su** to count on; **puntare verso** to march on; to sail toward
puntaspil·li *m* (-li) pincushion
puntata *f* jab (with weapon); excursion; bet; issue, number (of magazine); installment (of story); (mil) incursion
punteggiare §290 (puntéggio) *tr* to dot; (gram) to punctuate
punteggiatura *f* dotting; punctuation
puntég·gio *m* (-gi) score
puntellare (puntèllo) *tr* to prop, brace; to support
puntèllo *m* prop, brace; support
punterìa *f* aiming; aiming gear; (aut) tappet
punteruòlo *m* punch; awl
puntì·glio *m* (-gli) obstinacy, stubbornness; punctilio

puntigliό·so -sa [s] *adj* punctilious, scrupulous; obstinate, stubborn

puntina *f* brad; needle; thumbtack

puntino *m* small dot; G-string; a **puntino** to a T

punto *m* point; period; dot; place, spot; extent; stitch; **dare dei punti a** to be superior to; **di punto in bianco** all of a sudden; **di tutto punto** thoroughly; **due punti** colon; **essere a buon punto** to be well advanced; **essere sul punto di + inf** to be about to + *inf*; **fare il punto** (fig; naut) to take one's bearings; **in punto** on the dot; **in punto franco** in bond; **in un punto** together; **mettere a punto** to get in working order; (aut) to tune up; **mettere i punti sulle i** to dot one's i's; **punto assistenza** service agency; **punto di partenza** starting point; **punto di vista** viewpoint; **punto esclamativo** exclamation point; **punto e virgola** semicolon; **punto fermo** full stop; **punto interrogativo** question mark; **punto morto** (mach) dead center; **punto stimato** (naut) dead reckoning; **qui sta il punto!** here's the rub!; **vincere ai punti** (boxing) to win by points, win by decision ‖ *adv*—**né punto né poco** not at all; **non . . . punto** not at all

puntóne *m* rafter

puntuale *adj* punctual, prompt

puntuali·tà *f* (**-tà**) punctuality, promptness

puntura *f* sting; stitch (*sharp pain*); (coll) injection; **puntura lombare** spinal anesthesia

punzecchiare §287 (**punzécchio**) *tr* to keep on stinging; to tease, torment

punzecchiatura *f* sting, bite

punzonare (**punzóno**) *tr* to mark or stamp with a punch

punzonatrice *f* punch press

punzóne *m* punch; nailset

pupa *f* doll; (zool) pupa

pupazzetti·sta *mf* (**-sti -ste**) cartoonist

pupazzétto *m* caricature; cartoon; **pupazzetto di carta** paper doll

pupazzo *m* puppet; **pupazzo di stoffa** rag doll

pupil·lo -la *mf* pupil; ward, protégé ‖ *f* pupil (*of eye*); protégée

pupo *m* (coll) baby

purché *conj* provided, providing

pure *adv* too, also; indeed; (lit) only; **pur di** only in order to; **quando pure** even if; **se pure** even if ‖ *conj* though, although; but, yet

pu·rè *m* (**-rè**) purée; **purè di patate** mashed potatoes

purézza *f* purity

pur·ga *f* (**-ghe**) laxative; purification; purge

purgante *adj* purging ‖ *m* laxative

purgare §209 *tr* to purge; to purify; to expurgate ‖ *ref* to take a laxative

purgati·vo -va *adj* laxative

purgatò·rio *m* (**-ri**) purgatory

purificare §197 (**purìfico**) *tr* to purify

purismo *m* purism

purità *f* purity

purita·no -na *adj & m* puritan; Puritan

pu·ro -ra *adj* pure; clear; simple, mere

purosàn·gue *adj invar & m* (**-gue**) thoroughbred

purpùre·o -a *adj* (lit) purple

purtròppo *adv* unfortunately

purulèn·to -ta *adj* purulent

pus *m* pus

pusillànime *adj* pusillanimous

pùstola *f* pustule; pimple

puta caso *adv* possibly, maybe

putifè·rio *m* (**-ri**) hubbub

putrefare §173 *intr* (ESSERE) & *ref* to putrefy, rot

putrefazióne *f* putrefaction

putrèlla *f* I beam

pùtri·do -da *adj* putrid ‖ *m* corruption

putta *f* (coll) girl; (lit) prostitute

puttana *f* (vulg) whore

put·to -ta *adj* (archaic) meretricious ‖ *m* figure of a child ‖ *f* see **putta**

puzza *f* var of **puzzo**

puzzare *intr* to stink, smell

puzzo *m* stench, smell, bad odor

pùzzola *f* polecat, skunk

puzzolènte *adj* stinking, smelly

puzzonata *f* (coll) contemptible action; (coll) botch, bungle

puzzóne *m* (coll) skunk (*person*)

Q

Q, q [ku] *m & f* fifteenth letter of the Italian alphabet

qua *adv* here; **da un (giorno, mese, anno) in qua** for the past (day, month, year); **di qua da** on this side of; **in qua** on this side; here

quàcche·ro -ra or **quàcque·ro -ra** *adj & mf* Quaker; **alla quacquera** in a plain fashion

quadèrno *m* copybook; **quaderno di cassa** cash book

quadràngo·lo -la *adj* quadrangular ‖ *m* quadrangle

quadrante *m* quadrant; dial; face (*of watch*); **quadrante solare** sundial

quadrare *tr* to square ‖ *intr* (ESSERE & AVERE) to square; **quadrare a** to be satisfactory to; **quadrare con** to fit

quadra·to -ta *adj* square; sound (*mind*) ‖ *m* square; diaper; (boxing) ring; (nav) wardroom

quadratura *f* squaring; concreteness; (astr) quadrature

quadrèl·lo *m* (**-li**) square ruler; square tile ‖ *m* (**-la** *fpl*) (lit) bolt, arrow

quadreria *f* picture gallery; collection

quadretta·to -ta *adj* checkered

quadrétto *m* small painting; checker, small square; (fig) picture

quadriennale *adj* four-year ‖ *f* quadrennial

quadrifò·glio *m* (-gli) four-leaf clover; **a quadrifoglio** cloverleaf

quadrì·glio *m* (-gli) (cards) quadrille

quadrimensionale *adj* four-dimensional

quadrimestrale *adj* four-month

quadrimèstre *m* four-month period; four-month payment

quadrimotóre *adj* four-motor ‖ *m* four-motor plane

quadrireattóre *m* four-motor jet

quà·dro -dra *adj* square; (fig) solid ‖ *m* picture; painting; sight; square; table, summary; panel, switchboard; (theat) scene; **quadri** bulletin board; (mil) cadres; (cards) diamonds

quadrìmane *adj* quadrumanous ‖ *m* monkey; ape

quadruplicare §197 (quadrùplico) *tr* & *ref* to quadruple

quadrùplice *adj* quadruple; **in quadruplice copia** in four copies

quàdru·plo -pla *adj* & *m* quadruple

quaggiù *adv* down here

quàglia *f* quail

quagliare §280 *tr, intr* (ESSERE) & *ref* var of **cagliare**

qualche *adj invar* some, e.g., **qualche giorno** some day; some, e.g., **qualche elefante è bianco** some elephants are white; any, e.g., **ha qualche libro da vendere?** do you have any books to sell?; a few, e.g., **qualche giorno** a few days

qualchedu·no -na *pron indef* var of **qualcuno**

qualcòsa [s] *m* (fig) something; (fig) somebody ‖ *pron indef* something; anything; **qualcosa di buono** something good

qualcu·no -na *pron indef* some; any; somebody; anybody ‖ *m* somebody

quale *adj* which, what; what a, e.g., **quale onore!** what an honor!; as, e.g., **il pane, quale vedi, è fresco** the bread, as you can see, is fresh; **quale che sia** regardless of ‖ *pron* which; what; (archaic) who; **il quale** who, whom; **per la quale** o.k.; well-bred; commendable; terrific; **quale . . . quale** some . . . some ‖ *prep* as, e.g., **quale ministro** as a minister

qualìfi·ca *f* (-che) rating; position; quality, qualification

qualificare §197 (qualìfico) *tr* to qualify; to classify; to rate, give a rating to ‖ *ref* to introduce oneself; to qualify

qualifica·to -ta *adj* aggravated (*assault*); qualified (*personnel*); specialized (*worker*)

quali·tà *f* (-tà) quality; capacity

qualóra *conj* if; (lit) whenever

qualsìasi [s] *adj invar* any; whatever; ordinary

qualunque *adj invar* any; whatever; common, ordinary; **in qualunque modo** anyway, anyhow; **qualunque altro** anybody else; **qualunque cosa** anything; no matter what

qualvòlta *conj* (lit) whenever

quando *m* when ‖ *adv* when; **di quando in quando** from time to time; **quando . . . quando** sometimes . . . sometimes ‖ *conj* when; whenever; while; **da quando** since

quantìsti·co -ca *adj* (-ci -che) quantum

quanti·tà *f* (-tà) quantity; number

quantitativo *m* quantity

quan·to -ta *adj* how much; as much; how great; how great a; what a; **quan·ti -te** how many; as many ‖ *m* quantum ‖ *pron* how much; as much; how great; how long; that which; what; whatever; **a quanto si dice** according to what is rumored; **da quanto** from what; for how long; **fra quanto** how soon; **per quanto io ne sappia** as far as I know; **quanto più** (or **meno**) . . . **tanto più** (or **meno**) the more (or the less) . . . the more (or the less); **quan·ti -te** how many; all those; as many as; **quanti ne abbiamo?** what's the date? ‖ **quanto** *adv* how much; as much as; **in quanto** as; **in quanto che** inasmuch as; **per quanto** although; no matter; nevertheless; **quanto a** as to, as for; **quanto mai** as never before; **quanto meno** at least; **quanto prima** as soon as possible

quantunque *conj* although, though

quaranta *adj, m* & *pron* forty; **gli anni quaranta** the forties; **i quaranta** the forties (*in age*)

quarantèna *f* quarantine

quarantènne *adj* forty-year-old ‖ *mf* forty-year-old person

quarantèsi·mo -ma *adj, m* & *pron* fortieth

quarantina *f* about forty; **essere sulla quarantina** to be about forty years old

quarantòtto *adj* forty-eight ‖ *m* forty-eight; (coll) hubbub, uproar

quarésima *f* Lent

quartabuòno *m* triangle (*in drafting*); **tagliare a quartabuono** to miter

quartétto *m* quartet; **quartetto d'archi** string quartet

quartière *m* quarter, district; (mil) quarters; (coll) apartment; **quartier generale** headquarters; **senza quartiere** (*fight*) without quarter

quar·to -ta *adj* & *pron* fourth ‖ *m* fourth; quarter; quarter of a kilo; quarter of a liter; (naut) watch; **l'una e un quarto** a quarter after one; **l'una meno un quarto** a quarter to one

quarzo *m* quartz

quasi *adv* almost, nearly; **quasi che** as if; **quasi mai** hardly ever; **senza quasi** without any ifs and buts

quassù *adv* up here

quat·to -ta *adj* crouching; squatting; **quatto quatto** stealthy, silent; **starsene quatto quatto** to not make a sound

quattordicènne *adj* fourteen-year-old ‖ *mf* fourteen-year-old person

quattordicèsi·mo -ma *adj, m* & *pron* fourteenth

quattórdici *adj* & *pron* fourteen; **le**

quattórdici two P.M. || *m* fourteen; fourteenth (*in dates*)

quattrino *m* penny; (fig) bit; **quattrini** money

quattro *adj* four; a few, e.g., **quattro gatti** a few people; **a quattro mani** (mus) for four hands || *pron* four; **dirne quattro a** to upbraid; **farsi in quattro** to go all out; **in quattro e quattr'otto** in a few minutes; **le quattro** four o'clock || *m* four; fourth (*in dates*); racing shell with four oarsmen

quattrocènto *adj, m & pron* four hundred || **il Quattrocento** the fifteenth century

quattromila *adj, m & pron* four thousand

quégli §7 *adj* || §8 *pron*

quéi §7 *adj*

quél §7 *adj* || §8 *pron*

quéll' §7 *adj*

quél·lo -la §7 *adj* || §8 *pron*—**per quello che so io as** far as I know

quèr·cia *f* (-ce) oak tree

querci·no -na *adj* oaken .

querèla *f* complaint

querelante *adj* complaining || *mf* plaintiff

querelare (**querèlo**) *tr* to sue || *ref* (law) to sue; (lit) to complain

querela·to -ta *adj* accused || *mf* defendant

quèru·lo -la *adj* (lit) plaintive

quesito *m* question; problem; (lit) request

quésti §7 *pron*

questionare (**questióno**) *intr* to quarrel

questionà·rio *m* (-ri) questionnaire

questióne *f* question; (coll) quarrel; **questione di gabinetto** call for a vote of confidence; **venire a questione** to quarrel

qué·sto -sta §7 *adj* || §8 *pron*—**e con questo?** so what?; **per questo** therefore; **questa** this matter; **questo · · · quello** the former . . . the latter

questóre *m* police commissioner; sergeant at arms (*of congress*)

quèstua *f* begging; collection of alms; **andare alla questua** to go begging; **vietata la questua** no begging

questura *f* police department; police headquarters

questurino *m* (coll) policeman

què·to -ta *adj* var of **quieto**

qui *adv* here; **di qui** hence, from here; this way; **di qui a un anno** one year hence; **di qui in avanti** from now on; **qui vicino** nearby

quiescènza *f* quiescence; retirement

quietanza *f* receipt

quietanzare *tr* to receipt

quietare (**quièto**) *tr* to quiet, calm; to satisfy (*e.g., thirst*) || *ref* to quiet down

quiète *f* quiet, calmness

quiè·to -ta *adj* quiet, calm; still; **stia quieto!** don't worry! || *m* quiet life

quindi *adv* then; therefore; (archaic) thence, from there

quindicènne *adj* fifteen-year-old || *mf* fifteen-year-old person

quindicèsi·mo -ma *adj, m & pron* fifteenth

quindici *adj & pron* fifteen; **le quindici** three P.M. || *m* fifteen; fifteenth (*in dates*)

quindicina *f* about fifteen; two weeks, fortnight; semimonthly pay

quindicinale *adj* fortnightly

quinquennale *adj* five-year

quinta *f* (theat) wing; (mus) fifth; **dietro le quinte** behind the scenes

quintale *m* quintal (*100 kilos*)

quintèrno *m* signature of five sheets; (bb) quire

quintessènza *f* quintessence

quintétto *m* quintet

quin·to -ta *adj, m & pron* fifth || *f* see **quinta**

quisquilia *f* trifle

quivi *adv* (lit) over there; (lit) then

quòrum *m* quorum

quòta *f* quota; share; altitude; elevation; level (*of stock market*); market average; odds (*in betting*); subscription (*to club*); **quota zero** (fig) point of departure

quotare (**quòto**) *tr* to quote (*a price*); to value, esteem || *ref* to sign up for, e.g., **si quotò duemila lire** he signed up for two thousand lire

quotazióne *f* quotation

quotidia·no -na *adj & m* daily

quoziènte *m* quotient; (sports) percentage; **quoziente d'intelligenza** I.Q.

R

R, r ['erre] *m & f* sixteenth letter of the Italian alphabet

rabàrbaro *m* rhubarb

rabberciare §128 (**rabbèrcio**) *tr* (coll) to patch up

ràbbia *f* rage, anger; rabies

rabbino *m* rabbi

rabbió·so -sa [s] *adj* furious; rabid

rabbonire §176 *tr* to pacify || *ref* to calm down

rabbrividire §176 *intr* (ESSERE) to shiver, shudder

rabbuffare *tr* to rebuke; to dishevel

rabbuffo *m* rebuke; **fare un rabbuffo a** to rebuke

rabbuiare §287 *ref* to darken, turn dark

rabdomante *m* dowser, diviner

rabé·sco *m* (-schi) arabesque; scrawl, scribble

ràbi·do -da *adj* rabid

raccapezzare (**raccapézzo**) *tr* to put together; to gather (*news*); to find (*one's way*); to make out (*what is* *meant*) || *ref*—non raccapezzarsi to not be able to get one's bearings

raccapricciante *adj* bloodcurdling

raccapric·cio *m* (-ci) horror

raccartocciare §128 (raccartòccio) *tr* & *ref* to shrivel

raccattare *tr* to pick up; to gather

racchétta *f* racket; **racchetta da neve** snowshoe; **racchetta da sci** ski pole

ràc·chio -chia *adj* (-chi -chie) (coll) ugly, homely

racchiùdere §125 *tr* to contain, hold

raccògliere §127 *tr* to pick up; to gather; to collect (*e.g.*, *stamps*); to take up (*the gauntlet*); to receive; to reap; to furl (*sail*); to draw in (*a net*); to fold (*the wings*); to shelter (*e.g.*, *foundlings*); **raccogliere i passi** to stop walking || *ref* to gather; to concentrate

raccoglimento *m* concentration; meditation

raccogli·tóre -trice *mf* collector, compiler || *m* folder

raccòl·to -ta *adj* crouched; collected; engrossed; snug, intimate || *m* harvest || *f* harvest; collection; **chiamare a raccolta** to rally

raccomandàbile *adj* recommendable; **poco raccomandabile** unreliable

raccomandare *tr* to recommend; to secure (*e.g.*, *a boat*); to register (*mail*); to exhort || *ref* to recommend oneself; to entreat; **mi raccomando** please; **raccomandarsi a** to beg, implore; **raccomandarsi alle gambe** to take to one's heels

raccomandà·to -ta *adj* recommended; registered || *m* protégé || *f* protégée; registered letter

raccomandazióne *f* recommendation; registration (*of mail*); exhortation

raccomodare (raccòmodo) *tr* to fix; to mend

racconciare §128 (raccóncio) *tr* to fix; to mend || *ref* to clear up (*said of the weather*); to tidy oneself up

raccontare (raccónto) *tr* to tell; **raccontarla bene** to be good at telling lies

raccónto *m* tale; story; narrative

raccorciaménto *m* shortening

raccorciare §128 (raccòrcio) *tr* to shorten

raccordare (raccòrdo) *tr* to link, connect

raccòrdo *m* link, connection; **raccordo a circolazione rotatoria** traffic circle; **raccordo anulare** (rr) belt line; **raccordo ferroviario** junction; spur; siding; **raccordo stradale** connecting road

raccostare (raccòsto) *tr* & *ref* to draw near

raccozzare (raccòzzo) *tr* to scrape together

ràchide *m* & *f* backbone; midrib (*of leaf*); shaft (*of feather*)

rachìti·co -ca *adj* (-ci -che) stunted; weak; (pathol) rickety

rachitismo *m* rickets

racimolare (racìmolo) *tr* to glean; to scrape together

rada *f* roadstead; cove

ràdar *m* radar

addobbare (raddòbbo) *tr* (naut) to refit

raddolcire §176 *tr* & *ref* to sweeten; to mellow

raddoppiare §287 (raddóppio) *tr, intr* (ESSERE) & *ref* to double, redouble

raddrizzare *tr* to straighten; (elec) to rectify || *ref* to straighten up

raddrizzatóre *m* (elec) rectifier

ràdere §223 *tr* to shave; to raze; to graze, skim || *ref* to shave

radézza *f* rarity, rareness; thinness; sparsity (*of vegetation*); space, distance (*e.g.*, *between trees*)

radiante *adj* radiating

radiare §287 *tr* to strike off; to expel; to condemn (*a ship*); **radiare dall'albo degli avvocati** to disbar

radiatóre *m* radiator

radiazióne *f* radiation; expulsion

ràdi·ca -ca *f* (-che) brier; (coll) root

radicale *adj* & *mf* radical || *m* & *f* (philol) radical, root || *m* (chem, math) radical

radicare §197 (ràdico) *tr* & *intr* to root

radice *f* root; base or foot (*e.g.*, *of a mountain or tower*); **mettere radice** to take root; **svellere dalle radici** to pull up by the roots; to eradicate

rà·dio *adj invar* radio || *m* (-di) (anat) radius; (chem) radium || *f* (-dio) radio; **radio fante** (mil) grapevine

radioabbonato *m* (rad) subscriber (*to radio broadcasting*)

radioama·tóre -trice *mf* radio fan; radio ham

radioannunciatóre *m* radio announcer

radioascolta·tóre -trice *mf* radio listener

radioatti·vo -va *adj* radioactive

radiobùssola *f* radio compass

radiocanale *m* radio channel

radiocomanda·to -ta *adj* radio-controlled

radiocròna·ca *f* (-che) newscast

radiocroni·sta *mf* (-sti -ste) newscaster

radiodiffóndere §178 *tr* to broadcast

radiodiffusióne *f* broadcasting

radiofaro *m* radio beacon

radiofòni·co -ca *adj* (-ci -che) radio

radiofonògrafo *m* radiophonograph

radiofò·to *f* (-to) radiophoto

radiofrequènza *f* radiofrequency

radiologìa *f* radiology

radiomontatóre *m* radio assembler

radioónda *f* radio wave; **radioonde** airwaves

radioricevènte *adj* radio || *f* radio set; radio station

radioriparatóre *m* radio repairman

radiosegnale *m* radio signal

radiosentièro *m* range of a radio beacon

radió·so -sa [s] *adj* radiant

radiosorgènte *f* quasar

radiostazióne *f* radio station

radiostélla *f* quasar

radiotas·sì *m* (-sì) radio-dispatched taxi

radiotelescò·pio *m* (-pi) radiotelescope

radiotrasméttere §198 *tr* & *intr* to broadcast, radio

radiotrasmissióne *f* broadcast

radiotrasmittènte *adj* broadcasting ‖ *f* broadcasting station

ra·do -da *adj* rare; thin; sheer; sparse, scattered; **di rado** seldom, rarely

radunare *tr & ref* to assemble, gather

radunata *f* gathering; (mil) assembly; **radunata sediziosa** unlawful assembly

raduno *m* assembly, gathering

radura *f* clearing, glade

ràfano *m* (bot) radish

raffazzonare (raffazzóno) *tr* to mend, patch up

raffazzonatura *f* patchwork, hodge-podge

rafférma *f* confirmation; stay (*in office*); return to office; (mil) reenlistment

raffermare (rafférmo) *tr* to reaffirm; to secure; (coll) to reconfirm; to re-appoint, reelect; to return (*e.g., a mayor*) to office ‖ *intr* (ESSERE) & *ref* to reenlist; (coll) to harden

raffér·mo -ma *adj* stale (*bread*) ‖ *f see* **rafferma**

ràffi·ca *f* (-che) gust; blast; burst (*e.g., of machine gun*); **a raffiche** gusty

raffigurare *tr* to represent; to symbolize

raffinare *tr* to refine; to polish ‖ *intr* (ESSERE) to become refined

raffinatézza *f* refinement, polish

raffinatura *f* refinement (*of oil*)

raffinazióne *f* refining

raffineria *f* refinery

ràf·fio·m (-fi) hook; grappling iron

rafforzare (rafforzo) *tr* to strengthen

raffreddaménto *m* cooling

raffreddare (raffréddo) *tr* to make cold; to cool; **raffreddare gli spiriti di qlcu** to dampen s.o.'s enthusiasm ‖ *intr* (ESSERE) & *ref* to get cold; to cool

raffreddóre *m* cold

raffrontare (raffrónto) *tr* to compare; (law) to bring face to face

raffrónto *m* comparison; confrontation

ràfia *f* raffia

raganèlla *f* rattle; (zool) tree frog

ragazza *f* girl; spinster; (coll) girl friend; **ragazza copertina** cover girl; **ragazza squillo** call girl

ragazzata *f* boyish prank

ragaz·zo -za *mf* youth, young person ‖ *m* boy; (coll) boyfriend ‖ *f see* **ragazza**

raggelare (raggèlo) *intr* (ESSERE) to freeze

raggiante *adj* radiant; beaming

raggiare §290 *tr & intr* to radiate

raggièra *f* rayed halo; **a raggiera** radially

ràg·gio *m* (-gi) ray; beam; spoke; (geom) radius; **raggio d'azione** radius, range of action; **raggio di sole** sunbeam

raggiornare (raggiórno) *tr* (coll) to bring up to date ‖ *intr* (ESSERE) to dawn ‖ *impers* (ESSERE)—**raggiorna** it is dawning

raggirare *tr* to trick, swindle ‖ *ref* to roam, wander; **raggirarsi su** to turn on (*e.g., a certain subject*)

raggiro *m* trickery, swindle

raggiungere §183 *tr* to reach; to catch up with, rejoin

raggiungìbile *adj* attainable

raggomitolare (raggomìtolo) *tr* to roll up ‖ *ref* to curl up; to cuddle

raggranellare (raggranèllo) *tr* to gather; to scrape together

raggrinzire §176 *tr & ref* to crease, wrinkle

raggrumare *tr & ref* to clot, coagulate

raggruppaménto *m* grouping; group

raggruppare *tr & ref* to group, assemble

ragguagliare §280 *tr* to compare; to balance; to inform in detail; to level

ragguà·glio *m* (-gli) comparison; detailed report

ragguardévole *adj* considerable, notable

ragionaménto *m* reasoning; discussion

ragionare (ragióno) *intr* to reason; to discuss ‖ *impers ref*—**si ragiona** it is rumored

ragióne *f* reason; account; rate; justice; (math) ratio; **a maggior ragione** with all the more reason; **a ragione** within reason; **aver ragione** to be right; **aver ragione di** to get the best of; **dar ragione a qlcu** to admit that s.o. is right; **di santa ragione** hard, a great deal; **farsi ragione** to be resigned; **in ragione di** at the rate of; **ragion per cui** and therefore; **ragione sociale** (com) trade name; **rendere di pubblica ragione** to publicize

ragioneria *f* accounting; bookkeeping

ragionévole *adj* reasonable

ragioniè·re -ra *mf* accountant; book-keeper

ragliare §280 *tr* to bray

rà·glio *m* (-gli) bray

ragnatéla *f* spider web

ragno *m* spider

ra·gù *m* (-gù) meat gravy; stew

ràion *m* rayon

rallegraménto *m* congratulation, act of congratulating; **rallegramenti** congratulations

rallegrare (rallégro) *tr* to cheer up; to rejoice, gladden ‖ *ref* to cheer up; to rejoice; **rallegrarsi con** to congratulate

rallentare (rallènto) *tr, intr & ref* to slow down; to lessen

rallentatóre *m* slow-motion projector; **al rallentatore** slow-motion

ra·màio m (-mài) tinker, coppersmith

ramaiòlo *m* ladle

ramanzina [dz] *f* reprimand

ramare *tr* to copperplate; (agr) to spray with copper sulfate

ramarro *m* green lizard

ramazza *f* broom; (mil) cleaning detail; (mil) soldier on cleaning detail

rame *m* copper; etching

ramerino *m* (coll) rosemary

ramificare §197 (ramìfico) *intr & ref* to branch; to branch off; to branch out, ramify

ramìn·go -ga *adj* (-ghi -ghe) wandering

ramino *m* copper pot; rummy (*card game*)

rammagliare §280 *tr* to reknit; to mend a run in (*a stocking*)

rammaricare §197 (rammàrico) *tr* to afflict ‖ *ref* to be sorry, regret; **rammaricarsi di** to be sorry for rammàri·co *m* (-chi) regret

rammendare (rammèndo) *tr* to darn

rammèndo *m* darn

rammentare (rammènto) *tr* to remember; to remind ‖ *ref*—rammentarsi di to remember

rammenta·tóre -trice *mf* prompter

rammollire §176 *tr & ref* to soften

rammolli·to -ta *adj* soft; soft-headed ‖ *m* dodo, jellyfish

ramo *m* branch; bough; point (*of antler*); ramo di pazzia streak of madness

ramoscèllo *m* twig; ramoscello d'olivo olive branch

rampa *f* ramp; flight (*of stairs*); launching platform

rampicante *adj* climbing ‖ *m* (ichth) perch; (orn) climber

rampino *m* hook; tine, prong; pretext

rampógna *f* (lit) reprimand

rampòllo *m* spring (*of water*); scion; shoot (*of a plant*); (joc) offspring

rampóne *m* harpoon; crampon

rana *f* frog

rànci·do -da *adj* rancid

ràn·cio -cia (-ci -ce) *adj* (poet) orange ‖ *m* (mil) mess

rancóre *m* rancor; grudge; serbar rancore to bear malice

randa *f* (naut) spanker; (obs) edge

randà·gio -gia *adj* (-gi -gie) wandering; stray

randellare (randèllo) *tr* to cudgel; to bludgeon; to blackjack

randèllo *m* cudgel; bludgeon

ran·go *m* (-ghi) rank; station

rannicchiare §287 *tr* to cause to curl up ‖ *ref* to crouch; to cower; to cuddle up

ranno *m* lye; buttar via il ranno e il sapone to waste one's time and effort

rannuvolare (rannùvolo) *tr & ref* to cloud; to darken

ranòcchia *f* frog

ranòc·chio *m* (-chi) frog

rantolare (ràntolo) *intr* to wheeze

ràntolo *m* wheezing; death rattle

ranùncolo *m* buttercup

rapa *f* turnip; valere una rapa to be not worth a fig

rapace *adj* rapacious ‖ rapaci *mpl* birds of prey

rapare *tr* to shave (*s.o.'s head*) ‖ *ref* to shave one's head; to have one's head shaved

rapidi·tà *f* (-tà) rapidity, swiftness

ràpi·do -da *adj* rapid, swift ‖ *m* (rr) express ‖ rapide *fpl* rapids

rapiménto *m* rape, abduction; rapture

rapina *f* pillage, plunder; misappropriation; prey; (lit) fury; rapina a mano armata armed robbery

rapinare *tr* to rob, plunder; to hold up; rapinare qlco a qlcu to rob s.o. of s.th

rapina·tóre -trice *mf* robber, plunderer

rapire §176 *tr* to rape, abduct; to kidnap; to enrapture

rapi·tóre -trice *mf* kidnaper

rappacificare §197 (rappacìfico) *tr* to reconcile ‖ *ref* to become reconciled

rappezzare (rappèzzo) *tr* to patch; to piece; rappezzarla to get out of trouble

rappèzzo *m* patch; patchwork

rapportare (rappòrto) *tr* to report; to transfer (*a design*) ‖ *ref* to refer

rapporta·tóre -trice *mf* reporter ‖ *m* protractor

rappòrto *m* report; relation; relationship; (math) ratio; chiamare a rapporto to summon; chiedere di mettersi a rapporto to ask for a hearing; fare rapporto to report; in rapporto a concerning; mettersi a rapporto to report; sotto ogni rapporto in every respect

rapprèndere §220 *tr & ref* to coagulate

rappresàglia [s] *f* reprisal; retaliation

rappresentante *adj* representing; representative ‖ *mf* representative; agent; rappresentante di commercio agent

rappresentanza *f* delegation; proxy; agency; representation

rappresentare (rappresènto) *tr* to represent; to play; to portray

rappresentati·vo -va *adj* representative

rappresentazióne *f* representation; description; (theat) performance; rappresentazione teatrale diurna matinée; sacra rappresentazione (theat) mystery, miracle play

rapsodìa *f* rhapsody

raraménte *adv* seldom, rarely

rarefare §173 *tr* to rarefy ‖ *ref* to become rarefied

rari·tà *f* (-tà) rarity

ra·ro -ra *adj* rare; di raro seldom

rasare [s] *tr* to shave; to mow; to trim; to smooth ‖ *ref* to shave

raschiare §287 (ràschio) *tr* to scrape; to scratch ‖ *intr* to clear one's throat

raschiétto *m* scraper; erasing knife; footscraper

rà·schio *m* (-schi) clearing one's throat; hoarseness; frog in the throat

rasentare (rasènto) *tr* to graze; to scrape; to border on; to come close to

rasènte *adv* close; rasente a close to ‖ *prep* close to

ra·so -sa [s] *adj* shaved; trimmed; brimful; disreputable (*clothes*); flush ‖ *m* satin ‖ *adv*—raso terra down-to-earth; volare raso terra to skim the ground; to hedgehop

ra·sóio [s] *m* (-sói) razor; rasoio a mano libera straight razor; rasoio di sicurezza safety razor

raspa *f* rasp

raspare *tr* to rasp; to irritate; to stamp, paw; (coll) to steal ‖ *intr* to rasp; to scratch (*said of a chicken*); to scrawl

raspo *m* grape stalk; scraper; (vet) mange

rassègna *f* review; exposition

rassegnare (rasségno) *tr* to resign; rassegnare le dimissioni to resign ‖ *ref* to resign oneself; to submit

rassegnazióne *f* resignation

rasserenare (rasseréno) *tr & ref* to brighten; to cheer up

rassettare (rassètto) *tr & ref* to tidy up

rassicurare *tr* to reassure ‖ *ref* to be reassured

rassodare (rassòdo) *tr* to harden; to strengthen ‖ *intr* (ESSERE) & *ref* to harden

rassomigliare §280 (rassomìglio) *tr* to compare ‖ *intr* (ESSERE) (with *dat*) to resemble ‖ *ref* to resemble each other

rastrellaménto *m* roundup; mop-up operation

rastrellare (rastrèllo) *tr* to rake; to round up; to mop up; to drag (*e.g.*, *the bottom*)

rastrellièra *f* rack; crib

rastrèllo *m* rake

rastremare (rastrèmo) *tr* to taper

rata *f* installment; quota; a rate on time; by installments

rateale *adj* installment

rateizzare [ddzz] *tr* to prorate; to divide (*a payment*) into installments

ratifi·ca *f* (-che) ratification

ratificare §197 (ratìfico) *tr* to ratify

rat·to -fa *adj* (lit) swift ‖ *m* rat; (lit) rape ‖ ratto *adv* (lit) swiftly

rattoppare (rattòppo) *tr* to patch, patch up

rattrappire §176 *tr* to cramp; to make numb, benumb ‖ *ref* to become cramped; to become numb

rattristare *tr* & *ref* to sadden

raucèdine *f* hoarseness

ràu·co -ca *adj* (-chi -che) hoarse, raucous

ravanèllo *m* radish

ravizzóne *m* (bot) rape

ravvedére §279 (*fut* ravvedrò & ravvederò; *pp* ravveduto) *ref* to repent; to mend one's ways

ravvedu·to -ta *adj* repentant; reformed

ravviare §119 *tr* to arrange, adjust; to poke (*fire*) ‖ *ref* to tidy up; (lit) to reform

ravvicinaménto *m* approach; reconciliation; rapprochement

ravvicinare *tr* to bring up; to reconcile ‖ *ref* to approach; to become reconciled; ravvicinarsi a to approach

ravviluppare *tr* to wrap up; to wind up; to bamboozle ‖ *ref* to become tangled

ravvisare *tr* to recognize

ravvivare *tr* to revive; to enliven; to brighten; to stir (*fire*) ‖ *ref* to revive

ravvòlgere §289 *tr* to wrap up

razioci·nio *m* (-ni) reasoning; reason; common sense

razionale *adj* rational

razionalizzare [ddzz] *tr* (com, math) to rationalize

razionaménto *m* rationing

razionare (razióno) *tr* to ration

razióne *f* ration; portion

razza *f* race; breed; kind; di razza purebred; far razza to reproduce; passare a razza to go to stud

razza [ddzz] *f* (ichth) ray; razza cornuta manta ray

razzìa *f* raid; foray; insect powder

razziale *adj* racial

razziare §119 *tr* & *intr* to foray

razzismo *m* racism

razzi·sta *mf* (-sti -ste) racist

razzo [ddzz] *m* rocket; (coll) spoke; (mil) flare

razzolare (ràzzolo) *intr* to scratch (*said of chickens*); (coll) to rummage

re [e] *m* (re) king

re [ɛ] *m* (re) (mus) re

reagènte *m* reagent

reagire §176 *intr* to react

reale *adj* real, actual; royal, regal

realismo *m* realism; royalism

reali·sta *mf* (-sti -ste) realist; royalist

realisti·co -ca *adj* (-ci -che) realistic

realizzare [ddzz] *tr* to carry out; to realize; to build ‖ *ref* to come true

realizzazióne [ddzz] *f* realization; realizzazione scenica production

realizzo [ddzz] *m* conversion into cash; profit taking; forced sale

realménte *adv* really, indeed

real·tà *f* (-tà) reality; actuality; realtà romanzesca truth stranger than fiction

reato *m* crime

reatti·vo -va *adj* reactive

reattóre *m* reactor; jet plane; jet engine

reazionà·rio -ria (-ri -rie) *adj* & *mf* reactionary

reazióne *f* reaction; (mach) backlash; a reazione jet-propelled

réb·bio *m* (-bi) prong

recalcitrante *adj* balky, restive; essere recalcitrante a to be opposed to, to resist

recalcitrare (recàlcitro) *intr* to be balky; to kick; (with *dat*) to buck, resist

recapitare (recàpito) *tr* to deliver

recàpito *m* address; delivery; far recapito in to be domiciled in; recapiti (com) notes

recare §197 (rèco) *tr* to bring; to cause; recare ad effetto to carry out; recare qlco alla memoria di qlcu to remind s.o. of s.th; recare qlco a lode di qlcu to praise s.o. for s.th ‖ *ref* to go, betake oneself

recèdere §123 *intr* (ESSERE & AVERE) to recede

recensióne *f* book review; collation

recensire §176 *tr* to review; to collate

recensóre *m* reviewer

recènte *adj* recent; di recente recently

recessióne *f* recession

recèsso *m* recess; subsiding (*of fever*); ebb tide

recìdere §145 *tr* to cut off; to chop off

recidiva *f* relapse; second offense

recingere §126 *tr* to enclose, pen in

recinto *m* enclosure; pen, yard; compound; playpen; paddock; recinto delle grida floor of the exchange

recipiènte *m* container

reciprocità *f* reciprocity

recipro·co -ca *adj* (-ci -che) reciprocal

reci·so -sa *adj* cut off; abrupt

rècita *f* show, performance

recitare (rècito) *tr* to recite; to portray, play; recitare la commedia to put on an act ‖ *intr* to perform, play; recitare a soggetto (theat) to improvise

recitazióne *f* recitation; diction; acting

reclamare *tr* to claim, demand || *intr* to complain

récla•me *f* (-me) advertising; advertisement; **fare réclame a** to advertise; to boost

reclami•sta *mf* (-sti -ste) advertising agent; show-off || *m* advertising man

reclamìsti•co -ca *adj* (-ci -che) advertising

reclamo *m* complaint; **fare reclamo** to complain

reclinare *tr* to bow || *intr* to recline

reclusióne *f* seclusion; imprisonment

reclu•so -sa *adj* recluse || *mf* recluse; prisoner

reclusò•rio *m* (-ri) penitentiary

rècluta *f* recruit; rookie

reclutaménto *m* recruitment

reclutare (**rècluto**) *tr* to recruit

recòndi•to -ta *adj* concealed; inmost; recondite

recriminare (**recrìmino**) *intr* to recriminate

recuperare (**recùpero**) *tr* see **ricuperare**

redarguire §176 *tr* to berate

redat•tóre -trice *mf* compiler; newspaper editor; **redattore capo** managing editor; **redattore pubblicitario** copywriter; **redattore responsabile** publisher; **redattore viaggiante** correspondent

redazionale *adj* editorial, editor's (*e.g., policy*)

redazióne *f* writing; draft; version; (journ) city room

redazza *f* mop; (naut) swab

redditi•zio -zia *adj* (-zi -zie) lucrative

rèddito *m* income, revenue; yield; **reddito nazionale** gross national product

redèn•to -ta *adj* redeemed, set free

reden•tóre -trice *mf* redeemer || **Redentore** *m*—**il Redentore** the Redeemer

redenzióne *f* redemption

redìgere §224 *tr* to compile; to write up, compose

redìmere §225 *tr* to redeem; to ransom; to save

rèdine *f* rein

redivi•vo -va *adj* come back to life

rèduce *adj* back (*from war*) || *mf* veteran

réfe *m* thread

referèn•dum *m* (-dum) referendum; **referendum postale** mail questionnaire

referènza *f* reference

referenziare (**referènzio**) *tr* to give references to; to write references for || *intr* to have good references

referenzia•to -ta *adj* with good references, e.g., **impiegato referenziato** employee with good references

refèrto *m* report (*of a physician*)

refettò•rio *m* (-ri) refectory

refezióne *f* lunch, light meal; **refezione scolastica** school lunch

refrattà•rio -ria *adj* (-ri -rie) refractory

refrigerante *adj* cooling || *m* refrigerator; (chem) condenser

refrigerare (**refrìgero**) *tr* to refrigerate; to cool || *ref* to cool off

refrigè•rio *m* (-ri) relief, comfort

refurtiva *f* stolen goods

refuso *m* misprint

regalare *tr* to present; to deliver (*a slap*); to throw away (*money*); **è regalato** it's a steal

regale *adj* regal; royal; imposing

regalìa *f* gratuity; bonus

regalità *f* regality, royalty

regalo *m* present, gift

regata *f* regatta

reggènte *adj & m* regent

reggènza *f* regency

règgere §226 *tr* to hold, hold up; to stand, withstand; to guide; (gram) to govern; **reggere il sacco a** to connive with; **reggere l'animo di** + *inf* to bear or stand + *ger*, e.g., **non gli regge l'animo di vederla piangere** he cannot stand seeing her cry || *intr* to hold; to be valid; to last, hold out (*said of weather*); **reggere** (with *dat*) to withstand (*e.g., the cold*); **reggere al paragone** to bear comparison || *ref* to stand up; to hold; to be ruled; **reggersi a** to hold on to; to be governed as (*e.g., a republic*); **reggersi a galla** to float

règ•gia *f* (-ge) royal palace

reggical•ze *m* (-ze) girdle

reggilibro *m* book end

reggimentale *adj* regimental

reggiménto *m* regiment

reggipètto *m* brassiere

reggisé•no *m* (-ni & -no) brassiere

regìa *f* monopoly; (mov) direction; (theat) production

regici•da *mf* (-di -de) regicide

regici•dio *m* (-di) regicide

regime *m* regime; diet; flow (*e.g., of river*); government; authoritarian government; (mach) rate; **regime secco** total abstinence

regina *f* queen; **regina claudia** greengage; **regina madre** queen mother

reginétta *f* young queen; queen (*of a beauty contest*)

rè•gio -gia *adj* (-gi -gie) royal || **i regi** the king's soldiers

regióne *f* region

regi•sta *mf* (-sti -ste) coordinator; (theat) producer; (mov) director

registrare *tr* to register, record; to enter; to tally, log; to adjust; to tune up (*a musical instrument*) || *ref* to register

registra•tóre -trice *mf* registrar || *m* recorder; **registratore di cassa** cash register

registrazióne *f* registration; record, entry; adjustment; (aut) tune-up; (telv) videotaping; (telv) video-taping studio; (telv) video-taped program

registro *m* register; registration; classbook; regulator (*of watch*); stop (*of organ*); **cambiar registro** to change one's tune; **dar registro a** to regulate (*a watch*)

regnante *adj* reigning; prevailing || **i regnanti** the rulers

regnare (**régno**) *intr* to reign, rule; to prevail; to take hold (*said of a root*)

régno *m* kingdom; reign

règola *f* rule; regulation; moderation; **a regola d'arte** to a T; **di regola** as a rule; **in regola** in good order; **mettere in regola** to put in order; **regole** menstruation; **secondo le regole** by the book

regolamentare *adj* regulation || *v* (**regolaménto**) *tr* to regulate

regolaménto *m* regulation; settlement; **regolamento edilizio** building code

regolare *adj* regular; steady (*employment*); stock (*material*) || *v* (**règolo**) *tr* to regulate; to adjust; to set (*a watch*); to focus (*a lens*); to settle (*an account*) || *ref* to behave; to control oneself

regolari·tà *f* (-**tà**) regularity

regolarizzare [ddzz] *tr* to regularize

regolatézza *f* regularity; moderation

regola·to -**ta** *adj* regular, orderly

regola·tóre -**trice** *adj* regulating; see **piano** || *m* ruler; regulator (*of watch*); (mach) governor; **regolatore dell'aria** register; **regolatore di volume** (rad, telv) volume control

regolazióne *f* regulation

regolìzia *f* (coll) licorice

règolo *m* ruler; slat; (orn, hist) kinglet; **regolo calcolatore** slide rule

regredire §176 (*pres participle* **regrediènte**; *pp* **regredito** & **regrèsso**) *intr* (ESSERE & AVERE) to retrogress

regrèsso *m* regression; abatement (*of fever*); (com) recourse

reièt·to -**ta** *adj* rejected || *mf* outcast

reimbarcare §197 *tr* & *ref* to reship; to transship

reimbar·co *m* (-**chi**) reshipment; transshipment

reincarnare *tr* to reincarnate || *ref* to become reincarnated

reincarnazióne *f* reincarnation

reinserimènto *m* integration

reintegrare (**reintegro**) *tr* to restore; to reinstate; to indemnify

reità *f* guilt

reiterare (**reitero**) *tr* to reiterate

relativi·tà *f* (-**tà**) relativity

relati·vo -**va** *adj* relative

rela·tóre -**trice** *adj* reporting || *mf* relator (*of proceedings*); presenter (*of a bill*); dissertation supervisor

relazióne *f* relation; relationship; report; **relazione amorosa** affair; **relazioni** relations; connections

re·lè *m* (-**lè**) (elec) relay

relegare §209 (**rèlego**) *tr* to banish; to store away

religióne *f* religion

religió·so -**sa** [s] *adj* religious || *m* clergyman || *f* nun

relìquia *f* relic

relìt·to -**ta** *adj* residual || *m* shipwreck; air crash; derelict; shoal, bar

remare (**rèmo** & **rémo**) *intr* to row

rema·tóre -**trice** *mf* rower || *m* oarsman

reminiscènza *f* reminiscence

remissióne *f* submissiveness; remission

remissi·vo -**va** *adj* submissive

rèmo *m* oar; **remo alla battana** paddle

rèmora *f* hindrance; (lit) delay

remò·to -**ta** *adj* remote; **passato remoto** (gram) preterit

réna *f* sand

Renània, la the Rhineland

Renata *f* Renée

rèndere §227 *tr* to return, give back; to give (*thanks*); to render (*justice*); to yield; to translate; to make (*known*); **render conto di** to give an account of; **rendere di pubblica ragione** to publicize; **rendere l'anima a Dio** to give up the ghost; **rendere pan per focaccia** to give tit for tat || *intr* to pay, yield || *ref* to make oneself; to betake oneself; to become; (lit) to surrender; **rendersi conto di** to realize

rendicónto *m* account; report; **rendiconti** proceedings

rendiménto *m* rendering; yield; output; (mech) efficiency

rèndita *f* private income; yield; Italian Government bond

rène *m* kidney

renèlla *f* (pathol) gravel

renétta *f* pippin

réni *fpl* loins; **spezzare le reni a** to break the back of

renitènte *adj* opposed || *m*—**renitente alla leva** draft dodger

rènna *f* reindeer; reindeer skin

Rèno *m* Rhine

rè·o -**a** *adj* guilty; (lit) wicked || *m* guilty person; accused

reòstato *m* (elec) rheostat

reparto *m* department; (mil) unit; **reparto d'assalto** shock troops

repèllere §168 *tr* to repel

repentàglio *m* jeopardy; **mettere a repentaglio** to jeopardize

repènte *adj*—**di repente** suddenly

repenti·no -**na** *adj* sudden

reperìbile *adj* available

reperimènto *m* finding

reperire §176 *tr* to find

repèrto *m* (archeol) find; (law) evidence; (law) exhibit; (med) report

repertò·rio *m* (-**ri**) repertory; catalogue

rèpli·ca *f* (-**che**) repetition; replica; (law) rebuttal; (theat) repeat performance; **in replica** in reply

replicare §197 (**rèplico**) *tr* to repeat; to reply, answer; (theat) to repeat (*a performance*)

reportàg·gio *m* (-**gi**) news coverage; reporting

repòr·ter *m* (-**ter**) reporter

repressióne *f* repression; constraint

repressi·vo -**va** *adj* repressive; controlling, checking (*e.g., a disease*)

reprìmere §131 *tr* to repress; to hold back (*tears*) || *ref* to restrain oneself

rèpro·bo -**ba** *adj* & *m* reprobate

repùbbli·ca *f* (-**che**) republic

repubblica·no -**na** *adj* & *mf* republican

repulisti *m*—**fare repulisti** (coll) to make a clean sweep

repulsióne *f* repulsion

repulsi·vo -**va** *adj* var of **ripulsivo**

reputare (**rèputo**) *tr* to think, esteem, repute

reputazióne *f* reputation

rèquie *m* & *f* (eccl) requiem || *f* rest, respite

Rèquiem *m* & *f* Requiem

requisire §176 *tr* to requisition, commandeer

requisito *m* requisite, requirement

requisitòria *f* scolding, reproach; (law) summation

requisizióne *f* requisition

résa [s] *f* surrender; rendering (*of an account*); delivery (*of merchandise*); return (*e.g., of newspapers*); yield; **resa a discrezione** unconditional surrender

rescìndere §247 *tr* to rescind

resezióne [s] *f* (surg) resection

residènte [s] *adj & mf* resident

residènza [s] *f* residence

residenziale [s] *adj* residential

residua•to -ta [s] *adj* residual

resì•duo -dua [s] *adj* residual ‖ *m* residue; remainder; balance

rèsina *f* resin

resipiscènza [s] *f* (lit) repentance

resistènte [s] *adj* resistant; strong; fast (*color*) ‖ *mf* member of the Resistance

resistènza [s] *f* resistance ‖ **Resistenza** *f* Resistance

resìstere [s] §114 *intr* to resist; (with *dat*) to withstand; (with *dat*) to endure; (with *dat*) to resist

rèso [s] *m* rhesus

resocónto [s] *m* report, relation

respingènte *m* (rr) bumper, buffer

respìngere §126 *tr* to drive back, beat off; to reject; to fail (*a student*); to vote down

respìn•to -ta *adj* rejected ‖ *mf* failure (*pupil*)

respirare *tr & intr* to breathe, respire

respiratò•rio -ria *adj* (•ri •rie) respiratory

respirazióne *f* breathing

respiro *m* breath; breathing; respite

responsàbile *adj* responsible; **responsabile di** responsible for

responsabili•tà *f* (•tà) responsibility

respònso *m* decision (*of an oracle*); report (*of a physician*); return (*of an election*); (lit) response

rèssa *f* crowd; **far ressa** to crowd

rèsta *f* string (*of garlic or onions*); awn (*e.g., of wheat*); (coll) fishbone; (*for a lance*) (hist) rest

restante *adj* remaining ‖ *m* remainder

restare (**rèsto**) *intr* (ESSERE) to remain; to stay; to be located; (lit) to stop; **non restare a…che** to have no alternative but to, e.g., **non gli resta che andarsene** he has no alternative but to go; **non restare a qlcu qlco da +** *inf* to not have s.th + to + *inf*, e.g., **non gli resta molto da finire** he does not have much to finish; **resta a vedere** it remains to be seen; **restare qlco a qlcu** to have s.th left, e.g., **gli restano tre dollari** he has three dollars left; **restare sul colpo** to die on the spot; **resti comodo** please don't get up!

restaurare (**restàuro**) *tr* to restore, renovate

restaurazióne *f* restoration

restàuro *m* restoration (*of a building*)

restì•o -a (•i •e) *adj* balky, restive ‖ *m* balkiness

restituire §176 *tr* to give back, return; (lit) to restore ‖ *ref* (lit) to return

restituzióne *f* restitution, return

rèsto *m* remainder; change; balance; **del resto** besides, after all; **resti** remains

restrìngere §265 (*pp* **ristrétto**) *tr* to narrow down; to shrink; to take in (*a suit*); to limit (*expenses*); to tighten (*a knot*); to bind (*the bowels*); to restrict ‖ *ref* to contract; to narrow

restrizióne *f* restriction

retàg•gio *m* (•gi) (lit) heritage

retata *f* haul; (fig) roundup

réte *f* net; network; (soccer) goal; **rete a strascico** trawl; **rete da pesca** fishing net; **rete del letto** bedspring; **rete metallica** wire mesh; window screen; **rete per i capelli** hair net; **rete viaria** highway network

reticèlla *f* small net; hair net; mantle (*of gas jet*)

reticènte *adj* secretive, dissembling; evasive, noncommittal

reticènza *f* secretiveness; evasiveness

reticolato *m* grid (*on map*); wire entanglement

reticolo *m* grid

retina *f* small net

rètina *f* (anat) retina

retino *m* small net; (typ) screen

retòri•co -ca (•ci -che) *adj* rhetorical ‖ *m* rhetorician ‖ *f* rhetoric

retràttile *adj* retractile

retribuire §176 *tr* to remunerate

retributi•vo -va *adj* retributive; salary (*e.g., conditions*)

retrì•vo -va *adj* backward

rètro *m* back; verso; back of store ‖ *adv* (lit) behind; **retro a** (lit) behind

retroatti•vo -va *adj* retroactive

retrobottè•ga *m & f* (•ga *mpl* -ghe *fpl*) back of store

retrocàmera *f* back room

retrocàrica *f*—**a retrocarica** breechloading

retrocèdere §228 *tr* to demote; (com) to return; (com) to give a discount to ‖ *intr* (ESSERE & AVERE) to retreat

retrocessióne *f* demotion; (sports) assignment to a lower division

retrodatare *tr* to antedate, predate

retrògra•do -da *adj* backward; retrograde

retroguàrdia *f* rearguard

retromàr•cia *f* (-ce) (aut) reverse

retrorazzo [ddzz] *m* retrorocket

retrosapóre *m* aftertaste

retroscè•na *m* (-na) intrigue, maneuver ‖ *f* backstage

retrospetti•vo -va *adj* retrospective

retrotèr•ra *m* (-ra) hinterland; (fig) background

retrotrèno *m* rear end (*of vehicle*); (aut) rear assembly

retroversióne *f* retroversion; retranslation

retrovìe *fpl* zone behind the front

retrovisi•vo -va *adj* rear-view, e.g., **specchietto retrovisivo** rear-view mirror

retrovisóre *m* rear-view mirror

rètta *f* board and lodging; straight line; **dar retta a** to pay attention to

rettangolare *adj* rectangular

rettàngolo *m* rectangle

rettìfi·ca *f* (-che) straightening; rectification; (mach) grinding; (mach) reboring

rettificare §197 (**rettìfico**) *tr* to straighten; to rectify; (mach) to grind; (mach) to rebore

rettifica·tóre -trice *adj* rectifying || *mf* rectifier (*person*) || *m* rectifier (*apparatus*)

rettifilo *m* straightaway

rèttile *m* reptile

rettili·neo -nea *adj* rectilinear || *m* straightaway || *f* straight line

rettitùdine *f* straightness; uprightness, rectitude

rèt·to -ta *adj* straight; correct; upright; (geom) right || *m* right; recto; (anat) rectum || *f* see **retta**

rettóre *m* rector; president (*of university*)

reumàti·co -ca *adj* (-ci -che) rheumatic

reumatismo *m* rheumatism

reverèn·do -da *adj* & *m* reverend

reverènte *adj* var of **riverente**

reverènza *f* var of **riverenza**

revisióne *f* revision; (mach) overhaul

revisionismo *m* revisionism

revisóre *m* inspector; **revisore dei conti** auditor; **revisore di bozze** proof-reader

reviviscènza *f* rebirth

rèvo·ca *f* (-che) revocation; recall; repeal

revocare §197 (**rèvoco**) *tr* to revoke; to recall; to repeal

revòl·ver *m* (-ver) revolver

revolverata *f* gun shot

revulsióne *f* (med) revulsion

ri- *pref* re-, e.g., **rivivere** to relive; again, e.g., **rifare** to do again; back, e.g., **riandare** to go back

riabbonare (**riabbòno**) *tr* to renew the subscription of || *ref* to renew one's subscription

riabbracciare §128 (**riabbràccio**) *tr* to embrace again; to greet again

riabilitare (**riabìlito**) *tr* to rehabilitate || *ref* to reestablish one's good name

riaccèndere §101 *tr* to rekindle || *ref* to become rekindled

riaccompagnare *tr* to take home

riaccostare (**riaccòsto**) *tr* to bring near; to bring together || *ref* to draw near

riacquistare *tr* to buy back; to recover

riaddormentare (**riaddormènto**) *tr* to put back to sleep || *ref* to go back to sleep

riaffacciare §128 (**riaffàccio**) *tr* to present again || *ref* to reappear

riaffermare (**riaffèrmo**) *tr* to reaffirm

riaggravare *tr* to make worse || *ref* to get worse again

rialesare (**rialèso**) *tr* to rebore

riallacciare §128 (**riallàccio**) *tr* to tie again || *ref* to be tied or connected

rialto *m* knoll, height; **fare rialto** (coll) to eat better than usual

rialzare *tr* to lift, raise; to increase || *ref* to rise

rialzi·sta *mf* (-sti -ste) bull (*in stock market*)

rialzo *m* rise; raise; knoll, height; **giocare al rialzo** to bull the market

riammobiliare §287 *tr* to refurnish

rianimare (**riànimo**) *tr* to revive; to encourage || *ref* to revive; to recover one's spirits, to rally

riapertura *f* reopening

riapparire §108 *intr* (ESSERE) to reappear

riapparizióne *f* reappearance

riaprire §110 *tr* & *ref* to reopen

riarmare *tr* to rearm; to reinforce; to refit || *intr* & *ref* to rearm

riarmo *m* rearmament

riar·so -sa *adj* dry, parched

riassaporare (**riassapóro**) *tr* to relish again

riassettare (**riassètto**) *tr* to tidy up

riassicurare *tr* to reinsure; to fasten again; to reassure

riassorbire §176 & (**riassòrbo**) *tr* to reabsorb

riassùmere §116 *tr* to hire again; to summarize, sum up

riassunto *m* précis, abstract; résumé

riassunzióne *f* rehiring; resumption

riattaccare §197 *tr* to attach again; (coll) to begin again; (telp) to hang up

riattare *tr* to repair, fix

riattivare *tr* to reactivate

riavére §229 *tr* to get again; to recover; to get back || *ref* to recover

riavvicinaménto *m* var of **ravvicinamento**

riavvicinare *tr* & *ref* var of **ravvicinare**

ribadire §176 *tr* to clinch (*a nail*); to rivet; to drive home (*an idea*); to back up (*a statement*)

ribaldo *m* scoundrel, rogue

ribalta *f* lid with hinge; trap door; (theat) footlights; (theat) forestage; (fig) limelight; **a ribalta** hinged

ribaltàbile *adj* collapsable (*e.g., seat*) || *m* dump-truck lift; dump truck

ribaltare *tr* & *ref* to upset, turn over

ribassare *tr* & *intr* (ESSERE) to lower

ribassi·sta *mf* (-sti -ste) bear (*in stock market*)

ribasso *m* fall, decline; discount, rebate; **giocare al ribasso** to be a bear

ribàttere *tr* to clinch (*a nail*); to return (*a ball*); to iron smooth; to belabor (*a point*) || *intr* to answer back

ribattezzare [ddzz] (**ribattézzo**) *tr* to rebaptize

ribattino *m* rivet

ribellare (**ribèllo**) *tr* to rouse to rebellion || *ref* to rebel; **ribellarsi a** to rebel against

ribèlle *adj* rebellious || *mf* rebel

ribellióne *f* rebellion

ri·bes *m* (-bes) currant; gooseberry

ribobinazióne *f* rewind (*of a tape*)

riboccare §197 (**ribócco**) *intr* (ESSERE & AVERE) to overflow

ribollire (**ribóllo**) *tr* to boil again ||

intr to boil over; to simmer; to ferment

ribrézzo [ddzz] *m* repugnance, disgust

ributtare *tr* to return (*a ball*); to throw up; to reject; to push back || *intr* to sprout; (with *dat*) to disgust, nauseate

ricacciare §128 *tr* to drive back || *intr* to sprout || *ref* to sneak away, disappear

ricadére §121 *intr* (ESSERE) to fall back; to fall down; to relapse; **ricadere su** to devolve upon

ricaduta *f* relapse

ricalcare §197 *tr* to transfer (*a design*); to imitate; **ricalcare le orme di** follow in the footsteps of

rical·co *m* (**-chi**) copy, copying; **a ricalco** multiple-copy

ricamare *tr* to embroider

ricambiare §287 *tr* to return; to repay || *ref* to change clothes

ricàm·bio *m* (**-bi**) exchange; spare part; refill; metabolism; **di ricambio** spare (*part*)

ricamo *m* embroidery; needlework; **ricami** (*fig*) embellishments

ricapitolare (**ricapitolo**) *tr* to recapitulate

ricaricare §197 (**ricàrico**) *tr* to reload; to wind (*a watch*); to charge (*a battery*)

ricattare *tr* to blackmail

ricatta·tóre ·trice *mf* blackmailer

ricatto *m* blackmail

ricavare *tr* to draw, extract; to obtain, derive

ricavato *m* proceeds; (fig) fruit, yield

ricavo *m* proceeds

ricchézza *f* wealth; **ricchezza mobile** income from personal property; **ricchezze** riches

ric·cio ·cia (**-ci ·ce**) *adj* curly || *m* curl; shaving; burr; scroll (*of violin*); crook (*of crozier*); (zool) hedgehog; **riccio di mare** (zool) sea urchin

ricciolo *m* curl

ricciolu·to ·ta *adj* curly

ricciu·to ·ta *adj* curly

ric·co ·ca *adj* (**-chi ·che**) rich || **i ricchi** the rich

ricér·ca *f* (**-che**) search; research; **ricerca operativa** operations research

ricercare §197 (**ricérco**) *tr* to search for again; to seek; to investigate; (poet) to pluck (*a musical instrument*)

ricercatézza *f* affectation; sophistication

ricerca·to ·ta *adj* sought after, wanted; affected; sophisticated

ricetrasmettitóre *m* two-way radio

ricétta *f* prescription; recipe

ricettàcolo *m* receptacle; depository

ricettare (**ricètto**) *tr* to receive (*stolen goods*); to prescribe

ricettà·rio *m* (**-ri**) recipe book; prescription pad

ricetta·tóre ·trice *mf* fence, receiver of stolen goods

ricetti·vo ·va *adj* receptive

ricètto *m* (poet) refuge

ricévere §141 *tr* to receive; to get; to contain; to withstand

ricevimento *m* reception; receipt

ricevi·tóre ·trice *mf* addressee || *m* receiver; collector; registrar of deeds; **ricevitore postale** postmaster

ricevitoria *f* collection office; **ricevitoria postale** post office

ricevuta *f* receipt; **accusare ricevuta di** to acknowledge receipt of

ricezióne *f* (rad, telv) reception; **accusare ricezione** to acknowledge receipt

richiamare *tr* to call back; to recall; to call (*e.g.,* attention); to quote; to chide || *ref* to refer

richiamato *m* soldier recalled to active duty

richiamo *m* call; recall; admonition; cross reference; advertisement

richièdere §124 *tr* to ask again; to demand; to require; to apply for || *ref* to be required

richiè·sto ·sta *adj*—**essere richiesto** to be in demand || *f* request; demand; petition, application

richiùdere §125 *tr & ref* to shut again

riciclare *tr* to recycle (*e.g., in the chemical industry*)

ricino *m* castor-oil plant

ricognitóre *m* scout; reconnaissance plane; (law) recognition

ricognizióne *f* recognition; (mil) reconnaissance

ricollegare §209 (**ricollégo**) *tr* to connect || *ref* to be connected; to refer

ricolmare (**ricólmo**) *tr* to fill to the brim; to overwhelm

ricominciare §128 *tr & intr* (ESSERE) to begin again, resume

ricomparire §108 *intr* (ESSERE) to reappear

ricomparsa *f* reappearance

ricompènsa *f* compensation, recompense; reward; (mil) award

ricompensare (**ricompènso**) *tr* to compensate, recompense; to reward

ricomperare (**ricómpero**) *tr* var of **ricomprare**

ricompórre §218 *tr* to recompose; to plan again || *ref* to regain one's composure

ricomprare (**ricómpro**) *tr* to buy again; to buy back

riconcentrare (**riconcèntro**) *tr* to concentrate again; to gather (*one's thoughts*) || *ref* to be withdrawn

riconciliare §287 (**riconcìlio**) *tr* to reconcile || *ref* to become reconciled

ricondurre §102 *tr* to bring back; to take back || *ref* to go back

riconfermare (**riconférmo**) *tr* to reconfirm

riconfortare (**riconfòrto**) *tr* to comfort

ricongiùngere §183 *tr & ref* to reunite

riconoscènte *adj* grateful

riconoscènza *f* gratitude

riconóscere §134 *tr* to recognize; (mil) to reconnoiter

riconoscimento *m* recognition; **in riconoscimento di** in recognition of

riconquistare *tr* to reconquer

riconsegnare (**riconségno**) *tr* to give back, to return

riconsiderare (riconsìdero) *tr* to reconsider

ricontare (ricónto) *tr* to recount, count again

riconversióne *f* reconversion

riconvertire §138 *tr* to reconvert; to recycle

ricopèr·to -ta *adj* covered; coated

ricopertura *f* covering; seat cover

ricopiare §287 **(ricòpio)** *tr* to make a fair copy of; to recopy; to copy

ricoprire §110 *tr* to cover; to coat; to hide ‖ *ref* to become covered

ricordanza *f* (poet) memory

ricordare (ricòrdo) *tr* to remember; to remind; to mention ‖ *ref* to remember; **ricordarsi di** to remember

ricòrdo *m* memory; souvenir; **ricordo marmoreo** marble statue

ricorrènte *adj* recurrent, recurring

ricorrènza *f* recurrence; anniversary

ricórrere §139 *intr* (ESSERE & AVERE) to run again; to run back; to resort; to recur; (law) to appeal; **ricorrere a** to have recourse to

ricórso *m* recurrence; recourse; appeal

ricostituènte *adj* invigorating ‖ *m* tonic

ricostituire §176 *tr* to reconstitute, to reform; to reinvigorate

ricostruire §140 *tr* to rebuild; to reconstruct

ricostruzióne *f* rebuilding; reconstruction

ricòtta *f* Italian cottage cheese; **di ricotta** weak

ricoverare (ricóvero) *tr* to shelter ‖ *ref* to take shelter

ricóvero *m* shelter; nursing home; (med) admission; **ricovero antiaereo** air-raid shelter

ricreare (ricrèo) *tr* to recreate; to refresh ‖ *ref* to relax

ricreati·vo -va *adj* refreshing; recreational

ricreatò·rio -ria (-ri -rie) *adj* recreation, recreational ‖ *m* recreation room; playground

ricreazióne *f* recreation; recess

ricrédere §141 *intr*—**far ricredere qlcu** to make s.o. change his mind ‖ *ref* to change one's mind

ricréscere §142 *intr* (ESSERE) to grow again; to swell

ricucire §143 *tr* to sew up

ricuòcere §144a *tr* to cook again; to anneal

ricuperare (ricùpero) *tr* to recover; (naut) to salvage; (sports) to make up for *(rained-out game)*

ricùpero *m* recovery; salvage; rally; making up *(for lost time or postponed game)*

ricur·vo -va *adj* bent; bent over

ricusare *tr* to refuse

ridacchiare §287 *intr* to titter, giggle

ridancia·no -na *adj* prone to laughter; amusing

ridare §230 *(1st sg pres ind* **ridò***) tr* to give back; to give again; **ridare fuori** to vomit ‖ *intr* (coll) to reappear, e.g., **gli ha ridato il foruncolo** his boil has reappeared ‖ *intr*

(ESSERE)—**ridare giù** to have a relapse

ridda *f* round; confusion; throng

ridènte *adj* laughing; bright, pleasant

ridere §231 *tr* (poet) to laugh at ‖ *intr* to laugh; (poet) to shine; **far ridere i polli** to be utterly ridiculous; **ridere sotto i baffi** to laugh up one's sleeve ‖ *ref*—**ridersi di** to laugh at

ridestare (ridésto) *tr & ref* to reawaken

ridicolizzare [ddzz] *tr* to ridicule; to twit

ridìco·lo -la *adj* ridiculous ‖ *m* ridicule; ridiculousness

ridipìngere §126 *tr* to paint again

ridire §151 *tr* to tell again; to repeat; to tell *(to express)*; **avere** or **trovare a** or **da ridire (su)** to find fault (with)

ridistribuzióne *f* redistribution

ridivenire §282 or **ridiventare (ridivènto)** *intr* (ESSERE) to become again

ridonare (ridóno) *tr* to give back

ridondante *adj* redundant

ridondare (ridóndo) *intr* (ESSERE & AVERE) (fig) to overflow; **ridondare a** or **in** to redound to

ridòsso *m* back; shelter; **a ridosso** sheltered; as a shelter; behind, close behind

ridót·to -ta *adj* reduced; **mal ridotto** down at the heel ‖ *m* lounge; (theat) foyer ‖ *f* (mil) redoubt

ridurre §102 *tr* to reduce; to adapt; to translate; to lead; to curtail; (mus) to arrange ‖ *ref* to be reduced; to retire

riduttóre *m* (mach) reduction gear

riduzióne *f* reduction; (mus) arrangement

riecheggiare §290 **(riechéggio)** *tr & intr* to echo

riedificare §197 **(riedìfico)** *tr* to rebuild

rieducare §197 **(rièduco)** *tr* to reeducate

rielèggere §193 *tr* to reelect

rielezióne *f* reelection

riemèrgere §162 *intr* to resurface

riempiménto *m* fill

riempire §163 *tr* to fill; to stuff

riempiti·vo -va *adj* expletive ‖ *m* expletive; fill-in

rientrante *adj* hollow *(cheeks)*; (mil) reentrant

rientranza *f* recess

rientrare (rièntro) *intr* (ESSERE) to reenter; to come back; to recede; (coll) to shrink; **rientrare in** to recover *(one's expenses)*; **rientrare in sé** to come to one's senses

rièntro *m* reentry

riepilogare §209 **(riepìlogo)** *tr* to sum up, recapitulate

riepìlo·go *m* **(-ghi)** recapitulation

riesame *m* reexamination

riesaminare (riesàmino) *tr* to reexamine

riesumare *tr* to exhume; (fig) to dig up; (fig) to bring back

rievocare §197 **(rièvoco)** *tr* to recall

rifaciménto *m* adaptation; recasting

rifare §173 *(3d sg* **rifà***) tr* to do again, redo; to remake; to imitate; to indemnify; to prepare again; to repeat;

to make (*a bed*) ‖ *ref* to recover; to become again; to recoup one's losses; to begin; **rifarsi con** to get even with; **rifarsi da** to begin with

rifasciare §128 *tr* to rebind

riferiménto *m* reference

riferire §176 *tr* to wound again; to refer; to relate ‖ *ref*—**riferirsi a** to refer to; to concern

riffa *f* raffle; lottery; (coll) violence; **di riffa o di raffa** by hook or crook

rifilare *tr* to trim; (coll) to reel off (*a list of names*); (coll) to deal (*a blow*); (coll) to palm off

rifinire §176 *tr* to give the finishing touch to; to wear out ‖ *intr* to stop ‖ *ref* to wear oneself out

rifiorire §176 *tr* (lit) to revive ‖ *intr* to bloom again ‖ *intr* (ESSERE) to flourish; to grow better; to reappear

rifischiare §287 *tr* to whistle again; (coll) to report ‖ *intr* to talk, gossip

rifiutare *tr* to refuse; (lit) to reject ‖ *intr* (cards) to renege, renounce ‖ *ref* to refuse, deny

rifiuto *m* refusal; refuse, rubbish; rejection; rebuff, spurn; (fig) wreck; (cards) renege; **di rifiuto** waste, e.g., **materiale di rifiuto** waste material

riflessióne *f* reflexion

riflessi·vo -**va** *adj* thoughtful; (gram) reflexive

riflès·so -**sa** *adj* reflex, e.g., **azione riflessa** reflex action ‖ *m* reflection; (physiol) reflex; **di riflesso** vicarious

riflèttere §177 (*pp* **riflettuto** & **riflèsso**) *tr* & *intr* to reflect ‖ *ref* to be reflected

riflettóre *m* searchlight; reflector

rifluire §176 *intr* (ESSERE & AVERE) to flow; to flow back

riflusso *m* flow; ebb, ebb tide

rifocillare *tr* to refresh (*with food*) ‖ *ref* to take refreshment

rifóndere §178 *tr* to melt again; to recast; to refund; to reedit

rifórma *f* reform; (mil) rejection ‖ **Riforma** *f*—**la Riforma** the Reformation

riformare (**rifórmo**) *tr* to reform; to amend; (mil) to reject

riformati·vo -**va** *adj* reformatory

riforma·tóre -**trice** *adj* reforming ‖ *mf* reformer

riformatò·rio *m* (-**ri**) reform school, reformatory

riforniménto *m* supply; refueling; **fare rifornimento di** to fill up with; **rifornimenti** supplies

rifornire §176 *tr* to supply; to restock; **rifornire di benzina** to refuel

rifràngere §179 *tr* to crush ‖ *ref* to break (*said of waves*) ‖ §179 (*pp* **rifratto**) *tr* to refract ‖ *ref* to be refracted

rifrat·tóre -**trice** *adj* refracting ‖ *m* refractor

rifrazióne *f* refraction

rifriggere §180 *tr* to fry again; to rehash ‖ *intr* to fry too long or in too much oil

rifrit·to -**ta** *adj* fried again; (fig) hack-

neyed ‖ *m* taste of stale fat; (fig) rehash

rifuggire *tr* to avoid ‖ *intr*—**rifuggire da** to abhor ‖ *intr* (ESSERE) to take refuge

rifugiare §290 *ref* to take refuge, take shelter

rifugiato *m* refugee

rifù·gio *m* (-**gi**) refuge; **rifugio alpino** mountain hut; **rifugio antiaereo** air-raid shelter; **rifugio antiatomico** fallout shelter

rifùlgere §233 *intr* (ESSERE & AVERE) to shine

rifusióne *f* recast; refund, reimbursement

ri·ga *f* (-**ghe**) line; row; rank; ruler; part (*in hair*); stripe; (fig) quality

rigàglie *fpl* giblets

rigàgnolo *m* rivulet; gutter (*at the side of a road*)

rigare §209 *tr* to rule, line; to stripe; to mark; to rifle (*gun*) ‖ *intr*—**rigare diritto** to toe the line

rigatino *m* gingham

rigattière *m* second-hand dealer

rigatura *f* ruling; rifling (*of gun*)

rigenerare (**rigenero**) *tr* to regenerate; to reclaim; to recycle ‖ *ref* to become regenerate

rigeneratóre *m*—**rigeneratore per i capelli** hair restorer

rigettare (**rigètto**) *tr* to throw back; to reject; to recast; (slang) to throw up ‖ *intr* to sprout

rigètto *m* rejection

righèllo *m* ruler

rigidi·tà *f* (-**tà**) rigidity; rigor; stiffness; **rigidità cadaverica** rigor mortis

rìgi·do -**da** *adj* rigid, stiff; severe

rigirare *tr* to keep turning; to dupe; to invest; to encircle ‖ *intr* to ramble ‖ *ref* to turn around; to tumble

ri·go *m* (-**ghi**) line; **rigo musicale** (mus) staff

rigò·glio *m* (-**gli**) luxuriance; bloom; gurgling

rigonfiare §287 (**rigónfio**) *tr* to inflate ‖ *intr* (ESSERE) & *ref* to swell up

rigóre *m* rigor; severity; precision; **a rigor di termini** strictly speaking; **di rigore** de rigueur; (sports) penalty (*e.g., kick*)

rigorismo *m* rigorism, strictness, severity

rigori·sta *mf* (-**sti** -**ste**) rigorist ‖ *m* (soccer) kicker of penalty goal

rigoró·so -**sa** [s] *adj* rigorous, strict

rigovernare (**rigovèrno**) *tr* to clean, wash (*dishes*); to groom, tend (*animals*)

riguadagnare *tr* to regain

riguardare *tr* to look again; to look back; to examine; to consider; to take care of; to concern ‖ *intr*—**riguardare a** to look out for; to face (*said of a window*) ‖ *ref* to take care of oneself; **riguardarsi da** to keep away from

riguardo *m* care; esteem; regard; **a questo riguardo** in this regard; **ri-**

guardo a as far as . . . is concerned; senza riguardo a irrespective of

riguardó·so -sa [s] *adj* considerate

rigurgitare (rigùrgito) *tr & intr* to regurgitate

rilanciare §128 *tr* to toss back; to re-establish (*e.g., fashions*); (poker) to raise

rilasciare §128 *tr* to free, let go; to relax; to grant || *ref* to relax

rilà·scio m (-sci) release; delivery; granting, issue (*of a document*)

rilassante *adj* relaxing

rilassare *tr & ref* to relax

rilassatézza *f* laxity

rilegare §209 **(rilégo)** *tr* to tie again; to bind, rebind (*a book*); to set (*a stone*)

rilega·tóre -trice *mf* binder

rilegatura *f* binding

rilèggere §193 *tr* to reread

rilènto m—**a rilento** slowly

rilevaménto m survey; (naut) bearing

rilevare (rilièvo) *tr* to lift again; to observe; to draw; to bring out; to survey; to take over; to pick up; (mil) to relieve || *intr* to be delineated; to be of import || *ref* to rise again; to recover

rilevatà·rio m (-ri) successor; (law) assignee

rilièvo m relief; survey; remark; assumption (*of debts*); taking over (*of business*); **mettere in rilievo** to bring out; to set off

rilò·ga f (-ghe) traverse rod

rilucènte *adj* shiny, shining

rilùcere §234 *intr* to shine

riluttante *adj* reluctant

riluttanza *f* reluctance

rima *f* rhyme; slit; crevice; **rispondere per le rime** to answer in kind, to retort

rimandare *tr* to send back; to refer; to dismiss; to put off, postpone; to refer; **rimandare a ottobre** to condition (*a student*)

rimando m delay; reference; footnote; repartee; postponement; (sports) return

rimaneggiare §290 **(rimanéggio)** *tr* to rearrange; to reshuffle; to shake up (*personnel*); to rewrite (*news*)

rimanènte *adj* remaining || *m* remainder; remnant; **i rimanenti** the rest

rimanènza *f* remainder

rimanére §235 *intr* (ESSERE) to remain, stay; to be in agreement; to have left, e.g., **mi sono rimasti solo tre dollari** I only have three dollars left; to be located; (poet) to stop; **rimanerci** (coll) to be killed; (coll) to be duped; **rimanere da** to depend on, e.g., **questo rimane da Lei** this depends on you

rimangiare §290 *tr* to eat again || *ref*—**rimangiarsi la parola** to go back on one's word

rimarcare §197 *tr* to mark again; to point out

rimar·co m (-chi) remark, notice

rimare *tr & intr* to rhyme

rimarginare (rimàrgino) *tr, intr & ref* to heal

rimaritare *tr & ref* to marry again

rimasù·glio m (-gli) leftover

rima·tóre -trice *mf* poet; rhymster

rimbalzare *intr* (ESSERE & AVERE) to bounce back, rebound

rimbalzo m rebound

rimbambire §176 *intr* (ESSERE) & *ref* to become feeble-minded (*from old age*)

rimbambì·to -ta *adj* feeble-minded || *mf* dotard

rimbeccare §197 **(rimbécco)** *tr* to peck; to retort

rimbecilli·to -ta *adj* feeble-minded

rimboccare §197 **(rimbócco)** *tr* to tuck up; to tuck in; to fill to the brim

rimbombare (rimbómbo) *intr* (ESSERE & AVERE) to thunder, boom

rimbómbo m thunder, boom

rimborsare (rimbórso) *tr* to reimburse, pay back

rimbórso m repayment

rimboscare §197 **(rimbòsco)** *tr* to reforest || *ref* to take to the woods

rimboschiménto m reforestation

rimboschire §176 *tr* to reforest || *intr* (ESSERE) to become wooded

rimbrottare (rimbròtto) *tr* to scold

rimbròtto m scolding

rimediare §287 **(rimèdio)** *tr* (coll) to scrape together; (coll) to patch up || *intr* (with *dat*) to remedy; to make up (*lost time*)

rimè·dio m (-di) remedy

rimembranza *f* remembrance

rimeritare (rimèrito) *tr* to reward

rimescolare (riméscolo) *tr* to stir; to shuffle (*cards*)

riméssa *f* remittance; shipment; harvest; store; loss; sprout; carriage house; garage; (sports) return; (sports) putting in play; **rimessa del tram** carbarn

rimestare (rimésto) *tr* to stir

rimèttere §198 *tr* to remit; to put back; to set back; to sprout; to postpone, defer; to ship; to vomit; to recover; to deliver; to straighten up; (sports) to return; **rimetterci** to lose; **rimettere a nuovo** to renovate; **rimettere in ordine** to tidy up; **rimettere in piedi** to rebuild, restore || *intr* (coll) to sprout; (coll) to grow; (lit) to abate || *ref* to recover; to quiet down; to defer; to be clearing (*said of weather*); **rimettersi a** to go back to (*e.g., bed*); **rimettersi a + inf** to start + *ger* + again; **rimettersi in cammino** to start off again

rimirare *tr* to stare at

rimmel m mascara

rimodellare (rimodèllo) *tr* to remodel

rimodernare (rimodèrno) *tr* to modernize; to remodel; to bring up to date || *ref* to become modern

rimóⁿto *tr* reassembly; return (*of migratory birds*); revamping (*of shoes*); (mil) remount

rimontare (rimónto) *tr* to rewind; to go up (*a stream*); to vamp (*shoes*); to renovate; to regain; to reassemble (*a machine*); (mil) to remount || *intr* (ESSERE & AVERE) to climb again; to go back (*in time*)

rimorchiare §287 (**rimòrchio**) *tr* to tow; to drag along

rimorchiatóre *m* tugboat; tow car

rimòr•chio *m* (**-chi**) tow; trailer; **prendere a rimorchio** to take in tow

rimòrdere §200 *tr* to bite again; to prick (*said, e.g., of conscience*)

rimòrso *m* remorse

rimostranza *f* remonstrance

rimostrare (**rimóstro**) *tr* to show again || *intr* to remonstrate; **rimostrare a** to remonstrate with

rimozióne *f* removal; demotion

rimpannucciare §128 *tr* to outfit better || *ref* to be better dressed; to be better off

rimpastare *tr* to knead again; to re-shuffle, remake

rimpasto *m* reshuffling, rearrangement

rimpatriare §287 *tr* to repatriate || *intr* to be repatriated

rimpà•trio *m* (**-tri**) repatriation

rimpètto *adv* opposite; **di rimpetto a** opposite to; in comparison with

rimpiàngere §215 *tr* to regret; to mourn

rimpianto *m* regret

rimpiattare *tr* & *ref* to hide; **giocare a rimpiattarsi** to play hide-and-seek

rimpiattino *m* hide-and-seek

rimpiazzare *tr* to replace

rimpiazzo *m* replacement, substitute

rimpiccolire §176 *tr* to make smaller || *intr* (ESSERE) to get smaller

rimpinzare *tr* to stuff, cram

rimproverare (**rimpròvero**) *tr* to chide, reproach; **rimproverare qlcu di qlco** or **rimproverare qlco a qlcu** to reproach s.o. for s.th

rimpròvero *m* reproach, rebuke

rimuginare (**rimùgino**) *tr* & *intr* to rummage; to stir; to ruminate

rimunerare (**rimùnero**) *tr* to reward || *intr* to pay

rimunerati••vo -va *adj* remunerative; rewarding

rimunerazióne *f* remuneration

rimuòvere §202 *tr* to remove; to demote; to move

rinàscere §203 *intr* (ESSERE) to be born again; to grow again; to revive; **far rinascere** to revive

rinascimento *m* rebirth || **Rinascimento** *m* Renaissance

rinàscita *f* rebirth

rincagna•to -ta *adj* snub (*nose*)

rincalzare *tr* to hill (*plants*); to underpin; to tuck in

rincalzo *m* reinforcement; support

rincantucciare §128 *tr* & *ref* to hide in a corner

rincarare *tr* to raise the price of; to raise; **rincarare la dose** to add insult to injury || *intr* (ESSERE) to rise, go up (*said of prices*)

rincasare [s] *intr* (ESSERE) to return home

rinchiùdere §125 *tr* to enclose, shut in

rinchiu•so -sa [s] *adj* shut in; musty || *m*—**saper di rinchiuso** to smell musty

rincitrullire §176 *intr* (ESSERE) to grow stupid

rincóntro *m*—**a rincontro** opposite

rincorare §236 *tr* to encourage || *ref* to take heart

rincórrere §139 *tr* to pursue, chase

rincórsa *f*—**prendere la rincorsa** to take off (*for a jump*); to get a running start

rincréscere §142 *intr* (ESSERE) (with *dat*) to displease; to be sorry, e.g., **gli rincresce** he is sorry; to mind, **Le rincresce? do you mind?**

rincrescimento *m* regret

rincrudire §176 *tr* to sharpen; to embitter || *intr* (ESSERE) to become bitter; to get worse

rinculare *intr* (ESSERE & AVERE) to back up; to recoil

rinculo *m* recoil

rinfacciare §128 *tr* to throw in one's face

rinfarcire §176 *tr* to stuff

rinfiancare §197 *tr* to support

rinfocolare (**rinfòcolo**) *tr* to rekindle; to revive

rinfoderare (**rinfòdero**) *tr* sheathe

rinforzare (**rinfòrzo**) *tr* to reinforce; strengthen || *intr* (ESSERE) & *ref* to become stronger

rinfòrzo *m* reinforcement

rinfrancare §197 *tr* to reassure || *ref* to buck up

rinfrescante *adj* refreshing || *m* mild laxative

rinfrescare §197 (**rinfrésco**) *tr* to refresh; to restore; to renew || *intr* (ESSERE & AVERE) to cool off (*said of the weather*) || *ref* to have some refreshments; to cool off

rinfré•sco *m* (**-schi**) refreshment

rinfusa *f*—**alla rinfusa** at random; pell-mell; in bulk

ringalluzzire §176 *tr* & *ref* to perk up

ringhiare §287 *intr* to growl, to snarl

ringhièra *f* railing

rìn•ghio *m* (**-ghi**) growl, snarl

ringiovanimento *m* rejuvenation

ringiovanire §176 *tr* to rejuvenate || *intr* (ESSERE) to grow or look younger

ringraziamento *m* thanks

ringraziare §287 *tr* to thank; to dismiss

ringuainare (**ringuaìno**) *tr* to sheathe

rinnegare §209 (**rinnègo** & **rinnégo**) *tr* to forswear; to repudiate

rinnega•to -ta *adj* & *m* renegade

rinnovamento *m* renewal; reawakening

rinnovare (**rinnòvo**) *tr* to renew; to renovate; to restore; to replace || *ref* to occur again; to renew

rinnovellare (**rinnovèllo**) *tr* to repeat; (poet) to renew || *intr* (ESSERE) & *ref* to change; to renew

rinnòvo *m* renewal

rinocerónte *m* rhinoceros

rinomanza *f* renown

rinoma•to -ta *adj* renowned, famous

rinsaldare *tr* to starch; (fig) to strengthen || *ref* to become confirmed (*in one's opinion*)

rinsanguare (rinsànguo) *tr* to give new strength to || *ref* to regain strength; to recover

rinsavire §176 *intr* (ESSERE) to return to reason

rintanare *ref* to burrow; to hide

rintóc·co *m* (-chi) toll (*of bell*)

rintontire §176 *tr* to stun, to daze

rintracciare §128 *tr* to track down

rintronare (rintròno) *tr* to deafen; to make rumble || *intr* (ESSERE & AVERE) to thunder; to rumble

rintuzzare *tr* to dull, blunt; to repel; to repress

rinùn·cia *f* (-ce) or **rinùnzia** *f* renunciation

rinunziare §287 *tr* to renounce || *intr* (with *dat*) to give up, renounce, e.g., **rinunziò al trono** he renounced the throne

rinvangare §209 *tr & intr* var of **rivangare**

rinvenire §282 *tr* to find || *intr* (ESSERE) to come to; **far rinvenire** to bring to, revive

rinviare §119 *tr* to send back; to postpone; to refer; to adjourn; to remit (*to a lower court*)

rinvigorire §176 *tr* to strengthen || *intr* (ESSERE) & *ref* to regain strength

rinvì·o *m* (-i) return; postponement; adjournment; reference; (law) continuance

rì·o *m* (-i) (lit) sin; (lit) brook; (coll) canal

rioccupare (rioccupo) *tr* to reoccupy

rioccupazióne *f* reoccupation

rionale *adj* neighborhood

rióne *m* district; neighborhood

riordinare (riórdino) *tr* to rearrange; to reorganize; to order again

riorganizzare [ddzz] *tr* to reorganize

riottó·so -sa [s] *adj* (lit) quarrelsome; (lit) unruly, rebellious

ripa *f* (lit) bank (*of river*); (lit) escarpment

ripagare §209 *tr* to repay; to pay again

riparare *tr* to protect; to mend, fix, repair; to make up (*an exam*) || *intr* —**riparare a** to make up for || *intr* (ESSERE) & *ref* to take refuge; to betake oneself

riparazióne *f* repair; reparation; redress; (educ) make-up

riparlare *intr* to speak again; **ne riparleremo!** you will see!

riparo *m* repair; shelter

ripartire §176 *tr* to divide; to distribute; to share || (**riparto**) *intr* (ESSERE) to leave again; to start again || §176 *ref* to split up

ripartizióne *f* division; distribution

riparto *m* division; distribution; allotment

ripassare *tr* to cross again; to brush up, review; to repass; to sift again; to check; to read over; (mach) to overhaul || *intr* (ESSERE) to go by; to come by

ripassata *f* checkup; review; (coll) rebuke

ripassa·tóre -trice *mf* checker

ripasso *m* return (*of birds*); (coll) review

ripensare (ripènso) *intr* to keep thinking; **ripensare a** to think of again; to think over again

ripentire (ripènto) *ref* to repent; **ripentirsi di** to repent

ripercórrere §139 *tr* to retrace

ripercuòtere §251 *tr* to reflect; to strike again || *ref* to reverberate

ripescare §197 (ripésco) *tr* to fish again; (fig) to dig up

ripètere *tr & intr* to repeat || *ref* to be repeated

ripeti·tóre -trice *mf* repeater; coach; tutor || *m* (rad, telv) rebroadcasting station; (rad) relay

ripetizióne *f* repetition; review; tutoring; **a ripetizione** repeating (*firearm*)

ripiano *m* terrace; ledge; shelf; landing; (com) balancing

ripic·co *m* (-chi) pique; spite

ripi·do -da *adj* steep

ripiegaménto *m* bend; (mil) withdrawal, retreat

ripiegare §209 (ripiègo) *tr* to fold, fold over || *intr* to do better; (mil) to fall back || *ref* to bend over; to withdraw into oneself

ripiè·go *m* (-ghi) expedient

ripiè·no -na *adj* full; stuffed || *m* stuffing; (culin) filling

ripigliare §280 *tr* to reacquire; to catch again; to begin again || *intr* to recover || *ref* to renew a quarrel

ripiombare (ripiómbo) *tr* to make plumb; (fig) to plunge back || *intr* (ESSERE) (fig) to plunge back

ripopolare (ripòpolo) *tr* to repopulate; to restock (*e.g., a pond*)

ripórre §218 *tr* to put back; to place (*one's hope*); to repose (*one's trust*) || *ref* to back down; **riporsi a** + *inf* to start + *ger* again

riportare (ripòrto) *tr* to bring back; to report; to get; to transfer (*a design*); (com) to carry forward; (hunt) to retrieve; (math) to carry || *ref* to go back

ripòrto *m* filler; retrieving; (com) balance carried forward; (math) number carried

riposante [s] *adj* restful

riposare [s] (ripòso) *tr, intr & ref* to rest

ripòso [s] *m* rest; repose; Requiem; retirement; **buon riposo!** sleep well!; **mettere a riposo** to retire; **riposo!** (mil) at ease

riposti·glio *m* (-gli) closet

ripó·sto -sta *adj* innermost || *m* (coll) pantry

riprèndere §220 *tr* to take back; to take up again; to get back; to take in (*a garment*); to catch (*s.th thrown in the air*); to take up (*arms*); to get; to reconquer; to start again, resume; to reprehend; to recover; (mov, telv) to shoot; **riprendere moglie** to remarry || *intr* to start again; to recover, improve; to pick up (*said of a* *motor*) ‖ *ref* to recover; to catch oneself up

riprésa [s] *f* resumption; (aut) pickup; (theat) revival; (mov) shooting, take; (boxing) round; (soccer) second half; (mus, pros) refrain; **a più riprese** several times

ripresentare (ripresènto) *tr* to present again

ripristinare (ripristino) *tr* to restore; to reestablish

ripristino *m* revival, restoration

riprodurre §103 *tr* to reproduce; to express ‖ *ref* to reproduce; to occur

riprodut·tóre -trice *adj* reproducing ‖ *mf* reproducer ‖ *m* reproducer (*e.g., of sound*)

riproduzióne *f* reproduction; playback (*e.g., of tape*)

ripromèttere §198 *tr* to promise again ‖ *ref* to hope; to propose; to hope for

ripròva *f* new proof; confirmation

riprovare (ripròvo) *tr* to try again; to try on again; to feel, experience again; to flunk; to censure ‖ *ref* to try again

riprovazióne *f* disapproval

ripudiare §287 *tr* to repudiate

ripugnante *adj* repugnant, repulsive

ripugnanza *f* repugnance; aversion

ripugnare *intr* (with *dat*) to disgust, revolt, be repugnant to

ripulire §176 *tr* to clean again; to tidy up; to clean up; to polish ‖ *ref* to be dressed up; to become polished

ripulita *f*—**dare una ripulita a** to give a lick and a promise to; **fare una ripulita** (fig) to clean house

ripulsi·vo -va *adj* repulsive

riquadrare *tr* to square; to decorate (*a room*) ‖ *intr* to measure; to square

riquadro *m* square

risac·ca [s] *f* (**-che**) undertow; backwash

risàia [s] *f* rice field

risalire [s] §242 *tr* to go up again; to stem (*the tide*); **risalire la corrente** to go upstream ‖ *intr* (ESSERE) to climb again; to reascend; (com) to appreciate; to date back

risaltare [s] *tr* to jump again ‖ *intr* (ESSERE & AVERE) to rebound ‖ *intr* to stand out; **far risaltare** to emphasize

risalto [s] *m* emphasis; prominence; relief; foil

risanare [s] *tr* to heal; to reclaim (*land*); to redevelop (*urban areas*); to reorganize ‖ *intr* (ESSERE) to heal; to improve

risapére [s] §243 *tr* to find out

risapu·to -ta [s] *adj* well-known

risarciménto [s] *m* indemnification, redress

risarcire [s] §176 *tr* to indemnify; to compensate

risata [s] *f* outburst of laughter

risatina [s] *f* chuckle

riscaldaménto *m* heating; inflammation

riscaldare *tr* to heat; to warm up; to inflame ‖ *ref* to warm up; to go in heat; to perspire; to get excited

riscaldo *m* inflammation; prickly heat; padding (*for clothes*)

riscattare *tr* to ransom; to redeem ‖ *intr* (ESSERE) to click again (*said, e.g., of a ratchet*)

riscatto *m* ransom; redemption

rischiarare *tr, intr* (ESSERE) & *ref* to clear, clear up

rischiare §287 *tr* to risk ‖ *intr* to run a risk

ri·schio *m* (**-schi**) risk

rischió·so -sa [s] *adj* risky

risciacquare (risciàcquo) *tr* to rinse

risciacquatura *f* rinse; swill

risciàcquo *m* rinsing (*of mouth*); mouthwash

riscónto *m* (com) discount

riscontrare (riscóntro) *tr* to compare, collate; to check; to reply to ‖ *intr* to reply; to tally ‖ *ref* to tally

riscóntro *m* comparison; check, control; draft; correspondence; reply; **far riscontro** to correspond; **far riscontro con** to correspond to; **far riscontro di** to check; **mettere a riscontro** to compare; **riscóntri** drafts (*of air*); parts (*that fit together*)

riscoprire §110 *tr* to rediscover

riscòssa *f* insurrection; recovery, reconquest; (mil) counterattack

riscossióne *f* collection

riscrivere §250 *tr* to rewrite; to write back

riscuòtere §251 *tr* to shake; to wake up; to collect; to get; to redeem ‖ *ref* to wake up; to come to one's senses

riseccare [s] §197 (risécco) *tr, intr* (ESSERE) & *ref* to dry up

risecchire [s] §176 *intr* (ESSERE) & *ref* to dry up

risentiménto [s] *m* resentment, pique

risentire [s] (risènto) *tr* to hear again; to feel ‖ *intr*—**risentire di** to feel the effects of ‖ *ref* to take offense; to wake up; to come to one's senses; (telp) to talk again; **a risentirci!** (telp) until we talk again!; **risentirsi con** to resent (*a person*); **risentirsi di** to feel the effects of; **risentirsi per** to resent (*an act*)

risenti·to -ta [s] *adj* heard again; resentful; strong; swift; incisive

riserbare [s] (risèrbo) *tr* var of **riservare**

risèrbo [s] *m* var of **risèrvo**

risèrva [s] *f* preservation; exclusive rights; preserve; reserve; supply; backlog; reservation; circumspection; vintage

riservare [s] (risèrvo) *tr* to reserve

riservatézza [s] *f* reservedness

riserva·to -ta [s] *adj* reserved; private; classified

riservista [s] *m* (**-sti**) reservist

risèrvo [s] *m* discretion

risguardo *m* end paper

risièdere [s] *intr* to reside

risma *f* ream; (fig) type

riso [s] *m* rice ‖ *m* (risa *fpl*) laugh; laughter; jest; cheer; (lit) smile

risolare [s] §257 *tr* to resole

risolino [s] *m* smile; giggle

risollevare [s] **(risollèvo)** *tr* to raise again; to lift ‖ *ref* to rise

risolutézza [s] *f* resoluteness

risolu·to -ta [s] *adj* resolved, determined

risoluzióne [s] *f* resolution; resolve; dissolution

risòlvere [s] §256 *(pret ind* **risolvéi** or **risolvètti** or **risòlsi;** *pp* **risòlto)** *tr* to resolve; to solve; to dissolve; to persuade ‖ *ref* to dissolve; to resolve

risolvìbile [s] *adj* solvable

risonante [s] *adj* resounding

risonanza [s] *f* resonance; (fig) sensation

risonare [s] §257 *tr* to ring again; (lit) to repeat ‖ *intr* (ESSERE & AVERE) to resonate; to resound; to ring again; to echo

risórgere [s] §258 *intr* (ESSERE) to rise again; to revive, to come back to life; to recover

risorgiménto [s] *m* renaissance; resurgence ‖ **Risorgimento** *m* Risorgimento

risórsa [s] *f* resource

risór·to -ta [s] *adj* arisen; reborn

risòtto [s] *m* risotto, rice cooked with broth

risparmiare §287 *tr* to save; to spare

rispàr·mio *m* **(-mi)** saving; sparing; savings; **risparmi** savings; **senza risparmio** lavishly

rispecchiare §287 **(rispècchio)** *tr* to reflect

rispedire §176 *tr* to send back; to forward; to reship

rispedizióne *f* reshipment

rispettàbile *adj* respectable

rispettare (rispètto) *tr* to respect; **farsi rispettare** to command respect; **rispettare sé stesso** to have self-respect

rispetti·vo -va *adj* respective

rispètto *m* respect; observance; restriction (*e.g., in building*); comparison; regard; **con rispetto parlando** excuse the word; **di rispetto** (naut) spare (*e.g., parts*); **rispetti** regards; **rispetto di sé medesimo** self-respect; **rispetto umano** fear of what people will say

rispettó·so -sa [s] *adj* respectful; respectable *(distance)*

risplendènte *adj* resplendent

risplèndere §281 *intr* (ESSERE & AVERE) to shine

rispóndere §238 *tr* to answer; **risponder picche** (coll) to say no ‖ *intr* to answer; **rispondere a** to answer (*e.g., a letter*); **rispondere con un cenno del capo** to nod assent; **rispondere di** to be responsible for; **rispondere in** to face, overlook

risposare (rispòso) *tr & ref* to marry again, remarry

rispósta *f* answer, reply, response

rissa *f* scuffle, brawl

rissó·so -sa [s] *adj* quarrelsome

ristabilire §176 *tr* to reestablish ‖ *ref* to recover

ristagnare *tr* to tin; to solder ‖ *intr* to stagnate

ristampa *f* reprint

ristampare *tr* to reprint

ristorante *m* restaurant

ristorare (ristòro) *tr & ref* to refresh

ristora·tóre -trice *adj* refreshing ‖ *m* restaurant

ristòro *m* refreshment; compensation

ristrettézza *f* narrowness; scarcity; **ristrettezza d'idee** narrow-mindedness

ristrét·to -ta *adj* narrow; limited; in straitened circumstances; concentrated, condensed (*e.g., broth*)

ristrutturazióne *f* restructuring

risù·chio [s] *m* **(-chi)** whirlpool

risultante [s] *adj* resulting ‖ *m & f* resultant; (phys) resultant

risultare [s] *intr* (ESSERE) to result; to prove to be, turn out to be; to appear

risultato [s] *m* result

risurrezióne [s] *f* resurrection

risuscitare [s] **(risùscito)** *tr* to resurrect; to revive ‖ *intr* to be resurrected; to be revived

risvegliare §280 **(risvéglio)** *tr & ref* to awaken; to reawaken

risvé·glio *m* **(-gli)** awakening, reawakening

risvòlto *m* cuff; lapel; inside flap (of book); minor aspect (of a question)

ritagliare §280 *tr* to cut again; to clip; to trim

rità·glio *m* **(-gli)** clipping (of paper); scrap (of meat); cutting (of fabric); bit (of time); **al ritaglio** retail

ritappezzare (ritappézzo) *tr* to repaper

ritardare *tr* to delay; to slow down, retard; ‖ *intr* to tarry; to be late; to be slow (said of a watch)

ritardatà·rio -ria *mf* **(-ri -rie)** latecomer; (com) delinquent

ritardo *m* delay; retard; lateness; **essere in ritardo** to be late

ritégno *m* reservation; discretion; **senza ritegno** shamelessly

ritemprare (ritèmpro) *tr* to temper again; to invigorate ‖ *ref* to harden

ritenére §271 *tr* to retain; to hold; to withhold; to believe, think ‖ *ref* to restrain oneself; to consider oneself; to be considered

ritentare (ritènto) *tr* to try again; (law) to retry

ritirare *tr* to withdraw; to pay (a note); to throw back; to shoot again; to accept delivery of; to take back (a promise) ‖ *intr* to shrink ‖ *ref* to shrink; to withdraw; to fall back, retreat; to retire

ritirata *f* toilet; (mil) retreat

ritiro *m* withdrawal; retreat; retirement; shrinkage; (metallurgy) shrinking

ritma·to -ta *adj* measured (step)

ritmi·co -ca *adj* **(-ci -che)** rhythmic(al)

ritmo *m* rhythm; **a ritmo serrato** at a quick pace

rito *m* rite; (fig) ritual, ceremony; **di rito** customary

ritoccare §197 **(ritócco)** *tr* to retouch; to brush up

ritóc·co *m* **(-chi)** retouch; improvement; change

ritòrcere §272 *tr* to twist, twine; to wring; to retort

ritornare (ritórno) *tr* to return, give back ‖ *intr* (ESSERE) to return, go back, come back; **ritornare in sé** to come back to one's senses

ritornèllo *m* refrain; chorus (*of song*)

ritórno *m* return; reoccurrence; **di ritorno** reoccurring; **essere di ritorno** to be back; **far ritorno** to. return; **ritorno di fiamma** backfire

ritòr·to -ta *adj* twisted ‖ *m* twist

ritrarre §273 *tr* to retract; to draw; to portray ‖ *intr*—**ritrarre da** to look like ‖ *ref* to retreat; to portray oneself

ritrasméttere §198 *tr* (rad, telv) to retransmit, rebroadcast

ritrattare *tr* to treat again; to retract; (coll) to portray ‖ *ref* to recant

ritrattazióne *f* retraction

ritratti·sta *mf* (-sti -ste) portrait painter

ritratto *m* portrait, picture; photograph; **ritratto parlante** spit and image

ritri·to -ta *adj* (fig) stale, trite

ritrósa [s] *f* (coll) cowlick

ritrosìa [s] *f* coyness, shyness

ritró·so -sa [s] *adj* coy, shy; **a ritroso** backwards ‖ *f* see **ritrosa**

ritrovare (ritròvo) *tr* to discover; to find; to regain; to meet again ‖ *ref* to meet again; to find oneself; to find one's bearings; **non ritrovarcisi** to be out of sorts

ritrovato *m* discovery, find

ritròvo *m* meeting; nightspot; **ritrovo estivo** summer resort; **ritrovo notturno** night club

rit·to -ta *adj* upright; straight; right ‖ *m* face (*of medal*); prop; (sports) post ‖ *f* (lit) right hand

rituale *adj* & *m* ritual

riunióne *f* reunion; meeting; assembly; **riunione alla sommità** summit conference

riunire §176 *tr* to assemble; to reunite; to reconcile ‖ *ref* to gather together; to meet; to be reunited; to rally

riuscire §277 *intr* (ESSERE) to go out again; to turn out, turn out to be; to lead (*said, e.g., of a door*); to succeed; **riuscire a** + *inf* to succeed in + *ger* ‖ *impers*—**riesce** (with *dat*) **di** + *inf* to succeed in + *ger*, e.g., **non gli è riuscito di farsi ricevere** he did not succeed in being received

riuscita *f* success; result; outlet

riva *f* shore; bank; (naut) board

rivale *adj* & *mf* rival

rivaleggiare §290 **(rivaléggio)** *intr* to compete; **rivaleggiare con** to rival

rivalére §278 *ref*—**rivalersi di** to use; **rivalersi su qlcu** to resort to s.o. for compensation; to fall back on s.o., to have recourse to s.o.

rivali·tà *f* (-tà) rivalry

rivalsa *f* compensation; revenge; (com) recourse

rivalutare (rivàluto & rivaluto) *tr* to revalue

rivalutazióne *f* reassessment

rivangare §209 *tr* to rake up; to mull over ‖ *intr* to reminisce

rivedére §279 *tr* to see again; to review; to check; to reread; to revise; to read (*proof*) ‖ *ref* to see one another; **a rivederci! rivederci!** good-bye!, au revoir!

rivedìbile *adj* deferred (*for draft*)

rivelare (rivélo) *tr* to reveal; to detect; (phot) to develop

rivela·tóre -trice *adj* revealing ‖ *m* (phot) developer; (rad) detector; **rivelatore di mine** mine detector

rivelazióne *f* revelation

rivéndere §281 *tr* to resell; (fig) to surpass

rivendicare §197 **(rivéndico)** *tr* to demand; to claim

rivendicazióne *f* demand; claim

rivéndita *f* resale; shop; **rivendita sali e tabacchi** cigar store

rivendi·tóre -trice *mf* seller, dealer, retailer

rivendùgliolo *m* peddler; huckster

rivèrbero *m* reverberation; reflection; glare; echo

riverènte *adj* reverent

riverènza *f* reverence; curtsy, bow

riverire §176 *tr* to revere; to pay one's respects to

riversare (rivèrso) *tr* to pour again; to transfer ‖ *ref* to overflow

rivèr·so -sa *adj* on one's back

rivestiménto *m* coating; covering; lining

rivestire (rivèsto) *tr* to dress again; to coat; to line; to cover; to wear; to have (*importance*); to hold (*a rank*) ‖ *ref* to get dressed again; to wear; to be covered

rivièra *f* coast ‖ **Riviera** *f* Riviera

riviera·sco -sca *adj* (-schi -sche) coastal; riverside

rivìncere §285 *tr* to win back

rivìncita *f* revenge; return match; **prendersi la rivincita** to get even

rivista *f* review; parade; magazine, journal; revue; proofreading

rivìvere §286 *tr* to relive ‖ *intr* (ESSERE) to live again; to revive

rivo *m* (lit) rivulet, brook

rivolare (rivólo) *intr* (ESSERE & AVERE) to fly again

rivolére §288 *tr* to want back

rivòlgere §289 *tr* to turn again; to revolve; to overturn; to train (*a weapon*); to address; to deter ‖ *ref* to turn; to turn around; **rivolgersi a** to apply to

rivolgiménto *m* turn; revolution; upheaval

rivòlta *f* revolt; cuff

rivoltante *adj* revolting

rivoltare (rivòlto) *tr* to overturn; to turn inside out; to toss (*salad*); to upset ‖ *ref* to turn around; to revolt; to toss

rivoltèlla *f* revolver; spray gun

rivoltellata *f* revolver shot

rivoltó·so -sa [s] *adj* rebellious ‖ *m* rioter; rebel

rivoluzionare (rivoluzióno) *tr* to revolutionize

rivoluzionà·rio -ria *adj & mf* (-ri -rie) revolutionary

rivoluzióne *f* revolution

rizza *f* (naut) rigging

rizzare *tr* to raise; to hoist; to pay (*attention*); to build; (naut) to lash ‖ *ref* to rise; to bristle (*said of hair*); to rear up (*said of a horse*)

ròba *f* things, stuff; property

robinia *f* locust tree

robivèc·chi m (-chi) junk dealer

robu·sto -sta *adj* robust; burly

róc·ca *f* (-che) distaff

ròc·ca *f* (-che) fortress

roccafòrte *f* (roccheforti) stronghold

rocchétto *m* spool; reel; coil; roll (*of film*); pinion, rear sprocket wheel; (eccl) rochet; **rocchetto d'accensione** ignition coil; **rocchetto d'induzione** induction coil

ròc·cia *f* (-ce) rock; crag; cliff

rocciò·so -sa [s] *adj* rocky

rò·co -ca *adj* (-chi -che) hoarse; (poet) faint

rodàg·gio m (-gi) breaking in, running in; adjustment period (*to a new situation*); **in rodaggio** (aut) being run in

Ròdano *m* Rhone

rodare (ròdo) *tr* to break in; (aut) to run in

ródere §239 *tr* to gnaw; to bite; to corrode ‖ *ref* to worry, to fret

Ròdi *f* Rhodes

rodi·o m (-i) gnawing

rodi·tóre -trice *adj* gnawing ‖ *mf* rodent

rodomónte *m* braggart

rogare §209 (rògo) *tr* to draw up (*a contract*); (law) to request

** rògito** *m* (law) instrument, deed

rógna *f* mange; itch

rognóne *m* (culin) kidney

rognó·so -sa [s] *adj* scabby, mangy

rò·go m (-ghi) pyre; stake

rollì·o m (-i) roll (*of ship*)

Ròma *f* Rome

romané·sco -sca *adj* (-schi -sche) Roman (*dialect*)

Romanìa, la Rumania

romàni·co -ca *adj & m* (-ci -che) Romanesque

roma·no -na *adj & mf* Roman; **pagare alla romana** to go Dutch

romanticismo *m* romanticism

romànti·co -ca (-ci -che) *adj* romantic ‖ *mf* romanticist

romanza *f* romance; ballad

romanzare *tr* to fictionalize

romanzé·sco -sca *adj* (-schi -sche) romantic; of chivalry; novelistic

romanzière *m* novelist

roman·zo -za *adj* Romance (*language*) ‖ *m* novel; story; romance; fiction; **romanzi** fiction; **romanzo a fumetti** comic strip; comic book; **romanzo d'appendice** serial story, feuilleton; **romanzo giallo** whodunit; **romanzo rosa** love story

rombare (rómbo) *intr* to thunder

rómbo *m* thunder, roar

romè·no -na *adj & mf* Rumanian

romi·to -ta *adj* (lit) lonely ‖ *m* (coll) hermit

rómpere §240 *tr* to break; to bust; **rompere la testa a** to annoy, pester ‖ *intr* to overflow; to be wrecked; to break; **rompere in pianto** to burst out crying ‖ *ref* to fly to pieces; **rompersi la testa** to rack one's brains

rompicapo *m* annoyance; puzzle; jig-saw puzzle

rompicòllo *m* madcap; **a rompicollo** headlong, rashly; at breakneck speed

rompighiàc·cio m (-cio) icebreaker; ice pick

rompiscàto·le m (-le) bore, pest

roncì·glio m (-gli) (poet) hook

róncola *f* pruning hook

rónda *f* patrol; beat (*of policeman*)

rondèlla *f* (mach) washer

róndine *f* swallow

rondóne *m* European swift

ronfare (rónfo) *intr* (coll) to snore; (coll) to purr

ronzare [dz] **(rónzo)** *intr* to buzz; to hum

ronzino [dz] *m* jade, nag

ronzì·o [dz] *m* (-i) buzzing; humming

ròsa *adj invar & m* pink ‖ *f* rose; group; rosette; **rosa dei venti** compass card; **rosa del Giappone** (bot) camelia; **rosa delle Alpi** (bot) rhodo-dendron; **rosa di tiro** (mil) dispersion

ro·sàio m (-sài) rosebush

rosà·rio m (-ri) rosary; **recitare il ro-sario** to count one's beads

rosa·to -ta *adj* rosy

ròse·o -a *adj* rosy

roséto *m* rose garden

rosétta *f* rosette; hard roll; (mach) washer

rosicanti [s] *mpl* rodents

rosicchiare [s] §287 *tr* to gnaw; to pick (*a bone*); to bite (*one's fingernails*)

rosmarino *m* (bot) rosemary

rosolare (ròsolo) *tr* (culin) to brown

rosolìa *f* German measles

rosóne *m* (archit) rosette; (archit) rose window

ròspo *m* toad; ugly person; unsociable person; **ingoiare un rospo** to swallow a bitter pill

rossa·stro -stra *adj* reddish

rossétto *m* rouge; **rossetto per le labbra** lipstick

rós·so -sa *adj* red; red-headed; Red; **diventare rosso** to blush ‖ *mf* red-head; Red (*Communist*) ‖ *m* red

rossóre *m* redness; blush

rosticcerìa *f* grill; rotisserie

rotàbile *adj* open to vehicular traffic (*road*); (rr) rolling (*stock*) ‖ *f* road open to vehicular traffic

rotàia *f* rail; rut; **uscire dalle rotaie** to jump the track; (fig) to go astray

rotare §257 *tr & intr* to rotate; to circle

rotativa *f* (typ) rotary press

rotazióne *f* rotation

roteare (ròteo) *tr* to roll (*the eyes*); to flourish (*a sword*) ‖ *intr* to circle

rotèlla *f* small wheel; caster; roller; kneecap; disk (*of ski pole*); **gli**

manca una rotella he has a screw loose

rotocàl·co m (-chi) rotogravure

rotolare (ròtolo) tr & intr (ESSERE) to roll || ref to turn over; to wallow

ròtolo m roll; bolt; coil; **a rotoli** to rack and ruin

rotolóne m tumble; **a rotoloni** falling down; to rack and ruin

rotón·do -da adj round; rotund || f rotunda; terrace

rótta f break; rout; (aer, naut) course; **a rotta di collo** at breakneck speed; **mettere in rotta** to rout

rottame m fragment; wreck; **rottami** scraps, debris; wreckage; **rottami di ferro** scrap iron

rót·to -ta adj broken; shattered; inured || m break, tear; **e rotti** odd, e.g., **duecento e rotti** two hundred odd; **per il rotto della cuffia** hardly; just about || f see rotta

rottura f break; breakage; rupture; breakdown (of relations); crack

ròtula f kneecap

rovèllo m (lit) anger

rovènte adj red-hot

róvere m & f oak tree || m oak (lumber)

rovè·scia f (-sce) cuff; **alla rovescia** inside out; upside down; the wrong way

rovesciaménto m upset; overturn

rovesciare §128 (rovèscio) tr to overturn; to upset; to throw back (one's head); to spill (liquid); to pour; to hurl (insults); to turn inside out || intr to throw up || ref to spill; to pour; to upset

rovè·scio -scia (-sci -sce) adj reverse; inverse; inside out; upside down; backwards || m reverse; wrong side; downpour; upset; (com) crash; (tennis) backhand; **a rovescio** upside down; backwards || f see rovescia

rovéto m bramble; brier patch

rovina f ruin; blight; **andare in rovina** to go to ruin; **mandare in rovina** to ruin; **rovine** ruins

rovinare tr to ruin || intr (ESSERE) to collapse || ref to go to ruin

rovinì·o m (-i) clatter; crash

rovinó·so -sa [s] adj ruinous

rovistare tr to rummage through

róvo m bramble

ròzza [ddzz] f nag

róz·zo -za [ddzz] adj rough; coarse

ruba—**andare a ruba** to sell like hotcakes; **mettere a ruba** to plunder

rubacchiare §287 tr to pilfer

rubacuò·ri (-ri) adj ravishing || m ladykiller || f vamp

rubare tr to steal; **rubare a man salva** to pillage, loot || intr to steal; **rubare sul peso** to give short measure

ruberìa f thieving, stealing

rubicón·do -da adj rubicund

rubinétto m faucet; cock

rubino m ruby; jewel (of watch)

rubiz·zo -za adj well-preserved (person)

rubri·ca f (-che) title, heading; directory; (journ) section

rude adj (lit) rough; (lit) rude

rùdere m ruin

rudimentale adj rudimentary

rudiménto m rudiment

ruffia·no -na mf go-between || m pimp, panderer || f bawd, procuress

ru·ga f (-ghe) wrinkle; (bot) rocket

rùggine f rust; ill-will; (bot) blight

rugginó·so -sa [s] adj rusty

ruggire §176 tr & intr to roar

ruggito m roar

rugiada f dew

rugó·so -sa [s] adj wrinkled, wrinkly

rullàg·gio m (-gi) (aer) taxiing

rullare tr to roll || intr to roll; to taxi

rullì·o m (-ì) roll; rub-a-dub

rullo m roll; platen (of typewriter); pin (in tenpins); **rullo compressore** road roller

rumè·no -na adj & mf var of romeno

ruminare (rùmino) tr & intr to ruminate

rumóre m noise; rumor; ado; **far molto rumore** to create a stir

rumoreggiare §290 (rumoréggio) intr to rumble

rumoró·so -sa [s] adj noisy; rumbling; controversial

ruolino m roster

ruòlo m roll; role; list; **di ruolo** regular, full-time; **fuori ruolo** temporary, part-time

ruòta f wheel; paddle wheel; revolving server (in convent); **a quattro ruote** four-wheel; **dar la ruota a** to sharpen; **esser l'ultima ruota del carro** to be the fifth wheel to a wagon; **far la ruota** to spread its tail, strut (said, e.g., of a peacock); to turn cartwheels (said, e.g., of an acrobat); **ruota dentata** cog, cogwheel; **ruota idraulica** water wheel; **seguire a ruota** to follow closely

rupe f cliff

rurale adj rural, farm, farmer

ruscèllo m brook

ruspa f road grader

ruspante m barnyard chicken

russare intr to snore

Rùssia, la Russia

rus·so -sa adj & mf Russian

rustica·no -na adj rustic, boorish

rùsti·co -ca (-ci -che) adj rustic; coarse || m tool shed; cottage; (lit) peasant

rutilante adj (lit) shiny

ruttare tr (lit) to belch || intr (vulg) to belch

rutto m (vulg) belch

ruttóre m (elec) contact breaker

ruvidézza f or **ruvidi·tà** f (-tà) coarseness; roughness

rùvi·do -da adj coarse; rough

ruzzare [ddzz] intr to romp

ruzzolare (rùzzolo) tr to roll || intr (ESSERE) to tumble down; to roll

ruzzolóne m tumble; **a ruzzoloni** tumbling down

S

S, s ['ɛsse] *m & f* seventeenth letter of the Italian alphabet

s- *pref* dis-, e.g., **sleale** disloyal; e.g., **sconto** discount; un-, e.g., **scatenare** to unchain, unleash

sàbato *m* Saturday; (*of Jews*) Sabbath; **sabato inglese** Saturday afternoon off

sabbàti·co -ca *adj* (**-ci -che**) sabbatical

sàbbia *f* sand; **sabbia mobile** quicksand

sabbiatura *f* sand bath; sandblast

sabbièra *f* (rr) sandbox

sabbió·so -sa [s] *adj* sandy

sabotàg·gio *m* (**-gi**) sabotage

sabotare (**sabòto**) *tr* to sabotage

sac·ca *f* (**-che**) bag; satchel; (mil) pocket; **sacca d'aria** (aer) air pocket; **sacca da viaggio** traveling bag; duffel bag

saccarina *f* saccharine

saccènte *mf* wiseacre, know-it-all

saccheggiare §290 (**sacchéggio**) *tr* to pillage, plunder

sacchég·gio *m* (**-gi**) pillage, plunder

sacchétto *m* little bag, pouch

sac·co *m* (**-chi**) bag; sack; sackcloth; pouch; (boxing) punching bag; (fig) heap, lot; **fare sacco** to sag; **mettere a sacco** to sack; **mettere nel sacco** to outwit; **sacco alpino** knapsack; **sacco a pelo** or **a piuma** sleeping bag; **sacco postale** mailbag

saccòc·cia *f* (**-ce**) (coll) pocket

sacerdòte *m* priest; (fig) devotee

sacerdotéssa *f* priestess

sacerdòzio *m* priesthood; ministry

sacramentale *adj* sacramental; (joc) habitual, ritual

sacraménto *m* sacrament

sacrà·rio *m* (**-ri**) memorial; sanctuary, shrine

sacrestia *f* var of **sagrestia**

sacrificare §197 (**sacrifico**) *tr* to sacrifice; to waste; to force || *ref* to sacrifice oneself

sacrifì·cio *m* (**-ci**) sacrifice

sacrilè·gio *m* (**-gi**) sacrilege

sacrìle·go -ga *adj* (**-ghi -ghe**) sacrilegious

sacri·sta *m* (**-sti**) sexton

sacristia *f* var of **sagrestia**

sa·cro -cra *adj* sacred

sacrosan·to -ta *adj* sacrosanct; sacred (*truth*)

sàdi·co -ca (**-ci -che**) *adj* sadistic || *mf* sadist

sadismo *m* sadism

saétta *f* stroke of lightning; hand (*of watch*); (mach) bit; (lit) arrow

saettare (**saétto**) *tr* to shoot; **saettare sguardi a** to look daggers at

saettóne *m* (archit) strut

sagace *adj* sagacious, shrewd

sagà·cia *f* (**-cie**) sagacity

saggézza *f* wisdom

saggiare §290 *tr* to assay; to test; (dial) to taste

saggia·tóre -trice *mf* assayer || *m* assay balance

saggina *f* sorghum

sàg·gio -gia (**-gi -ge**) *adj* wise || *m* sage; assay; sample; proof; theme; test; rate (*of interest*); display; **di saggio** examination (*copy*)

saggi·sta *mf* (**-sti -ste**) essayist

sagittària *f* (bot) arrowhead

sagittà·rio *m* (**-ri**) (obs) archer || Sagittario *m* Sagittarius

sàgola *f* (naut) halyard

sàgoma *f* outline; target; model, pattern; (joc) character

sagomare (**sàgomo**) *tr* to outline; to mold; to shape

sagomato *m* billboard

sagra *f* anniversary consecration (*of church*); festival

sagrato *m* elevated square in front of a church; churchyard; (coll) curse

sagrestano *m* sexton, sacristan

sagrestia *f* sacristy, vestry

sàia *f* serge

sàio *m* (**sài**) habit (*of monk or nun*); doublet; frock coat

sala *f* axletree; hall, room; (bot) cattail, reed mace; **sala da ballo** dance hall; **sala da pranzo** dining room; **sala d'aspetto** waiting room; anteroom; **sala operatoria** operating room

salac·ca *f* (**-che**) (coll) sardine; (coll) shad

salace *adj* salacious; pungent

salamandra *f* salamander

salame *m* salami

salamelèc·co *m* (**-chi**) salaam

salamòia *f* brine

salare *tr* to salt; (coll) to cut (*school*)

salaria·to -ta *adj* wage-earning || *m* wage earner

salà·rio *m* (**-ri**) pay, wages

salassare *tr* to bleed

salasso *m* bloodletting

sala·to -ta *adj* salted; salty; dear, expensive; (fig) sharp || *m* salt pork; cold cuts || *f* salting

salda *f* starch solution (*used in laundering*)

saldacón·ti *m* (**-ti**) bookkeeping department; credit department; ledger; bookkeeping machine

saldare *tr* to solder; to set (*a bone*); to weld; to pay, settle || *ref* to knit (*said of a bone*); (lit) to heal

saldatóre *m* solderer; welder; soldering iron

saldatura *f* soldering; setting (*of bones*); joint; continuity; **saldatura autogena** welding

saldézza *f* firmness

sal·do -da *adj* firm; valid (*reason*); flawless || *m* balance; clearance sale; job lot; payment; **saldi** remnants || *f* see **salda**

saldobrasatura *f* soldering

sale *m* salt; wit; (lit) sea; **restare di sale** to be dumbfounded; **sale inglese** Epsom salts; **sali aromatici** smelling salts; **sali da bagno** bath salts

salgèmma *f* rock salt

sàlice *m* willow tree; salice piangente weeping willow

salicilato *m* salicylate

saliènte *adj* projecting; (fig) salient ‖ *m* projection

salièra *f* saltcellar, salt shaker

salini·tà *f* (-tà) salinity

sali·no -na *adj* saline; salty ‖ *f* salt bed

salire §242 *tr* to climb ‖ *intr* (ESSERE) to climb; to go up; to rise; salire in or su to get on (*e.g.*, *a train*)

saliscén·di *m* (-di) latch; saliscendi *mpl* ups and downs

salita *f* climbing; ascent, rise; slope; in salita uphill

saliva *f* saliva

salma *f* corpse, body

salma·stro -stra *adj* briny; saltish ‖ *m*—sapere di salmastro to smell or taste salty

salmerie *fpl* wagon train; (mil) supplies

salmì *m*—in salmì (culin) in a stew

salmo *m* psalm

salmodiare §287 (salmòdio) *intr* to chant, sing hymns, intone

salmóne *m* salmon

salnitro *m* saltpeter

Salomóne *m* Solomon

salóne *m* hall; salon, drawing room; (naut) saloon; salone da barbiere barber shop; salone dell'automobile auto show

salòtto *m* drawing room; living room, parlor; reception room

salpare *tr* to weigh (anchor) ‖ *intr* (ESSERE) to weigh anchor

salsa *f* sauce

salsapariglia *f* sarsaparilla

salsèdine *f* saltiness

salsìc·cia *f* (-ce) sausage

salsièra *f* gravy boat

sal·so -sa *adj* salty; saline ‖ *m* saltiness ‖ *f* see salsa

saltabeccare §197 (saltabécco) *intr* to hop

saltaleóne *m* coil spring

saltare *tr* to jump; to skip; to sauté; (sports) to vault; to hurdle; far saltare to kick out; to blow up (*e.g.*, *a mine*); saltare la sbarra (coll) to go A.W.O.L. ‖ *intr* (ESSERE & AVERE) to jump; to pop off, e.g., mi è saltato un bottone one of my buttons has popped off; to blow out (*said of a fuse*); saltare agli occhi to be self-evident; saltare a piè pari to skip with both feet; saltar fuori to pop out (*said of the eyes*); to appear suddenly; saltare in mente a to come to the mind of; saltare il ticchio a (qlcu) di to feel like + *ger*, e.g., gli è saltato il ticchio di cantare he felt like singing; saltare la mosca al naso a (qlcu) to blow one's top, e.g., le è saltata la mosca al naso she blew her top; saltare per aria to blow up; saltare su to start (*to make a sudden jerk*); saltare su a + *inf* to begin suddenly to + *inf*

salta·tóre -trice *mf* jumper, hurdler

saltellare (saltèllo) *intr* to skip, hop

saltellóni *adv*—a saltelloni skipping, hopping

saltimban·co *m* (-chi) acrobat, tumbler; mountebank

salto *m* jump; leap; fall; skip; (*of animals*) mating; (fig) step; a salti skipping, jumping; al salto sauté; fare quattro salti to dance; fare un salto to hop, hurry; salto a pesce jackknife (*dive*); salto coll'asta pole vaulting; salto in altezza high jump; salto in lunghezza broad jump; salto mortale somersault; salto nel vuoto leap in the dark

saltuà·rio -ria *adj* (-ri -rie) desultory, occasional

salubre *adj* salubrious, healthy, healthful

salume *m* pork product

salumeria *f* pork butcher shop

salumiè·re -ra *mf* pork butcher

salutare *adj* healthful ‖ *tr* to greet; to salute; (lit) to proclaim

salute *f* health; salvation; safety ‖ *interj* good luck!; to your health!; gesundheit!

saluto *m* salute; greeting; salutation; distinti saluti sincerely yours

salva *f* salvo; outburst; a salve with blank cartridges, with blanks

salvacondótto *m* safe-conduct

salvada·nàio *m* (-nài) piggy bank

salvagèn·te *m* (-te & -ti) life preserver; fender (*of trolley car*) ‖ *m* (-te) safety island

salvaguardare *tr* to safeguard

salvaguàrdia *f* safeguard

salvaménto *m* safety

salvamotóre *m* circuit breaker; fuse box

salvapun·te *m* (-te) pencil cap; tap (*on sole of shoe*)

salvare *tr* to save; to spare (*a life*); to rescue ‖ *ref* to save oneself; to be rescued; si salvi chi può! every man for himself!

salvatàg·gio *m* (-gi) rescue

salvatóre *m* savior, rescuer ‖ il Salvatore the Saviour

salvazióne *f* salvation

salve *interj* hello!, hail!

salvézza *f* salvation; safety

sàlvia *f* (bot) sage

salviétta *f* napkin; paper napkin; paper towel

sal·vo -va *adj* safe; saved; secure ‖ *m*—mettere in salvo to put in a safe place; mettersi in salvo to reach safety ‖ *f* see salva ‖ salvo *prep* except; salvo che unless; salvo il vero unless I am mistaken

samarita·no -na *adj* & *mf* Samaritan

sambu·co *m* (-chi) elder tree

san *adj* apocopated and unstressed form of santo

sanàbile *adj* curable

sanare *tr* to heal; to remedy; to reclaim (*land*); to normalize

sanatò·rio *m* (-ri) sanatorium

sancire §176 *tr* to ratify, sanction; to establish

sàndalo *m* sandal; sandalwood; flat-bottom boat

sandolino *m* canoe, skiff, kayak
sangue *m* blood; **agitarsi il sangue** to fret; **all'ultimo sangue** (*duel*) to the death; **al sangue rare** (*meat*); **a sangue freddo** in cold blood; cold-blooded; **cavar sangue da una rapa** to draw blood from a stone; **farsi cattivo sangue** to get angry; **il sangue non è acqua** blood is thicker than water; **puro sangue** thoroughbred; **sangue dal naso** nosebleed; **sangue freddo** calmness, composure
sangui·gno -**gna** *adj* blood (*circulation*); bloody; sanguine, ruddy || *m* (lit) color of blood
sanguinante *adj* bloody, bleeding
sanguinare (**sànguino**) *intr* to bleed; to be rare (*said of meat*)
sanguinà·rio -**ria** *adj* (-**ri** -**rie**) sanguinary
sanguinó·so -**sa** [s] *adj* bloody; bleeding; (fig) stinging
sanguisu·ga [s] *f* (-**ghe**) leech
sani·tà *f* (-**tà**) health; healthfulness; soundness (*of body*); sanity; health department
sanità·rio -**ria** (-**ri** -**rie**) *adj* health; sanitary || *mi* physician
sa·no -**na** *adj* healthy; sound; **sano e salvo** safe and sound
sant' *adj* apocopated form of **santo** and **santa**
santa *f* saint
santabàrbara *f* (**santebàrbare**) (nav) powder magazine
santarellina *f* goody-goody girl
santificare §197 (**santífico**) *tr* to sanctify
santíssi·mo -**ma** *adj* most holy || *m* Eucharist
santi·tà *f* (-**tà**) sanctity, holiness; sainthood, saintliness
san·to -**ta** *adj* saintly, holy; sacred; blessed, livelong, e.g., **tutto il santo giorno** all the livelong day || *m* saint; name day; (fig) someone || *f* see **santa**
santorég·gia *f* (-**ge**) (bot) savory
santuà·rio *m* (-**ri**) sanctuary
sanzionare (**sanzióno**) *tr* to sanction; to ratify
sanzióne *f* sanction
sapére *m* knowledge; **sapere fare** savoir-faire || §243 *tr* to know; to find out; to know how to; **far sapere** to let know; **saperla lunga** to know a thing or two; **un certo non so che** a certain something, something vague || *intr*— **sapere di** to know; to taste; to smell; to smack of; **mi sa che** I think that; **non voler più saperne di** to not want to have anything to do with; **sapere male** (with *dat*) to feel sorry, e.g., **gli sa male he feels sorry** || *ref*—**che io mi sappia** as far as I know
sàpido -**da** *adj* savory; witty
sapiènte *adj* wise; talented; trained (*dog*) || *m* wise man
sapientó·ne -**na** *mf* wiseacre, know-it-all
sapiènza *f* wisdom; knowledge
saponària *f* (bot) soapwort

saponata *f* soapsuds; lather; (fig) soft soap
sapóne *m* soap; **sapone da toletta** toilet soap; **sapone per la barba** shaving soap
saponétta *f* cake of soap
saponière *m* soap maker
saponifi·cio *m* (-**ci**) soap factory
saponó·so -**sa** [s] *adj* soapy
sapóre *m* taste; savor; flavor
saporire §176 *tr* to savor
saporitaménte *adv* heartily; soundly
sapori·to -**ta** *adj* tasty; flavorful; salty; expensive
saporó·so -**sa** [s] *adj* savory; witty
saputèl·lo -**la** *adj* cocksure || *m* smart aleck
sarac·co *m* (-**chi**) hand saw
saracè·no -**na** *adj* Saracen, Saracenic || *m* Saracen; quintain
saraciné·sca *f* (-**sche**) metal shutter (*of store*); sluice gate; (hist) portculis
sarcasmo *m* sarcasm
sarcàsti·co -**ca** *adj* (-**ci** -**che**) sarcastic
sarchiare §287 *tr* to weed
sarchia·tóre -**trice** *mf* weeder || *f* (agr) cultivator
sarchièllo *m* weeding hoe
sàr·chio *m* (-**chi**) hoe
sarcòfa·go *m* (-**gi** & -**ghi**) sarcophagus
sarcràuti *mpl* sauerkraut
Sardégna, la Sardinia
sardèlla *f* pilchard; sardine
sardina *f* pilchard; sardine
sar·do -**da** *adj* & *mf* Sardinian
sardòni·co -**ca** *adj* (-**ci** -**che**) sardonic
sarménto *m* vine shoot, running stem
sarta *f* dressmaker
sàrtie *fpl* (naut) shrouds
sarto *m* tailor
sartorìa *f* dressmaker's shop; tailor shop; dressmaking; tailoring
sassaiòla *f* shower of stones
sassata *f* blow with a stone
sasso *m* stone, rock; pebble; (poet) tombstone; **di sasso** stony; **restare di sasso** to be taken aback; **tirare sassi in colombaia** to cut one's nose to spite one's face
sassòfono *m* saxophone
sàssone *adj* & *mf* Saxon
sassó·so -**sa** [s] *adj* stony
Sàtana *m* Satan
satanasso *m* Satan; devil
satèllite *m* satellite
sa·tin *m* (-**tin**) sateen
satinare *tr* to gloss
sàtira *f* satire
satireggiare §290 (**satiréggio**) *tr* to satirize, lampoon || *intr* to compose satires
satíri·co -**ca** *adj* (-**ci** -**che**) satiric(al) || *m* satirist
sàtiro *m* satyr
satól·lo -**la** *adj* sated, full
saturare *tr* (**sàturo**) *tr* to saturate; to steep; (fig) to fill; (com) to glut (*a market*)
saturni·no -**na** *adj* Saturnian; saturnine
Saturno *m* (astr) Saturn
sàtu·ro -**ra** *adj* saturated; (fig) full; (lit) sated

sàu•ro -ra *adj & m* sorrel (*horse*)

Savèrio *m* Xavier

sà•vio -via (-vi -vie) *adj* wise ‖ *m* wise man, sage

savoiar•do -da *adj & mf* Savoyard ‖ *m* ladyfinger

saxòfono *m* saxophone

saziare §287 *tr* to satisfy; to cloy, satiate

sazietà *f* satiety, surfeit; **mangiare a sazietà** to eat one's fill

sà•zio -zia *adj* (**-zi -zie**) sated; full; satisfied

sbaciucchiare §287 (**sbaciùcchio**) *tr* to kiss again and again ‖ *ref* to neck

sbadatàggine *f* carelessness; oversight

sbada•to -ta *adj* careless; heedless

sbadigliare §280 *intr* to yawn

sbadì•glio *m* (**-gli**) yawn

sbafa•tóre -trice *mf* sponger

sbafo *m*—**a sbafo** sponging; **mangiare a sbafo** to sponge

sbagliare §280 *tr* to miss; to mistake; **sbagliarla** to be sadly mistaken ‖ *intr & ref* to be mistaken; to make a mistake

sbaglia•to -ta *adj* wrong; mistaken

sbà•glio *m* (**-gli**) error, mistake

sbalestrare (**sbalèstro**) *tr* to fling with the crossbow; to send (*an employee*) far away ‖ *intr* to speak amiss; to ramble; to blunder

sbalestra•to -ta *adj* unbalanced; ill-at-ease

sballare *tr* to unpack; **sballarle grosse** to tell tall tales ‖ *intr* to overbid

sballa•to -ta *adj* unpacked; absurd, wild

sballottare (**sballòtto**) *tr* to toss

sbalordire §176 *tr* to stun; to amaze; to bewilder ‖ *intr* to lose consciousness; to be dumfounded

sbalorditi•vo -va *adj* amazing

sbalzare *tr* to upset; to send far away; to overthrow; to emboss ‖ *intr* (ESSERE) to bounce

sbalzo *m* leap, jump; climb; emboss-ment, relief; **a sbalzi** by leaps and bounds; **di sbalzo** all of a sudden

sbancare §197 *tr* to clear (*ground*) of rocks; to ruin; (*cards*) to break (*the bank*)

sbandaménto *m* skid; swerve; disband-ment; breaking up; (naut) list

sbandare *tr* to disband; (naut) to cause to list ‖ *intr* to list; to skid; to swerve; to deviate ‖ *ref* to disband; to break up

sbanda•to -ta *adj* disbanded; stray; alienated ‖ *mf* alienated person ‖ *m* straggler ‖ *f* listing (*of ship*); skid-ding (*of vehicle*); **prendere una sbandata per** to get a crush on

sbandierare (**sbandièro**) *tr* to wave (*a flag*); to display

sbaragliare §280 *tr* to rout; to crush

sbarà•glio *m*—**mettere allo sbaraglio** to endanger

sbarazzare *tr* to clear out; to free ‖ *ref* —**sbarazzarsi di** to get rid of

sbarazzi•no -na *adj* mischievous ‖ *mf* scamp; **alla sbarazzina** cocked, at an angle (*said of a hat*)

sbarbare *tr* to shave; to uproot ‖ *ref* to shave

sbarbatèllo *m* greenhorn, fledgling

sbarcare §197 *tr* to unload; to dis-charge; to disembark; to pass; to strew (*fodder*); **sbarcare il lunario** to make ends meet ‖ *intr* (ESSERE) to come ashore, land

sbarca•tóio *m* (**-tói**) landing pier

sbar•co *m* (**-chi**) unloading; landing

sbarra *f* bar; (typ) dash

sbarraménto *m* barrage; obstacle

sbarrare *tr* to bar; to block (*the way*); to open (*one's eyes*) wide, e.g., **sbarrò gli occhi** he opened his eyes wide

sbarrétta *f* bar; **sbarrette verticali** (typ) parallels

sbatacchiare §287 *tr* to slam; to flap ‖ *intr* to slam

sbatàc•chio *m* (**-chi**) shore, prop

sbàttere *tr* to flap; to fling; to slam; to beat; to toss; to send away; to make pale; **sbatter fuori** to throw out ‖ *intr* to flap; to slam

sbattighiàc•cio *m* (**-cio**) cocktail shaker

sbattitóre *m* electric mixer

sbattiluò•va *m* (**-va**) egg beater

sbattu•to -tu *adj* haggard, downcast

sbavare *tr* to slobber over; (mach) to trim ‖ *intr* to drivel, slobber; to run (*said of colors*)

sbavatura *f* drivel; run (*of colors*); burr (*of metal*); deckle edge; verbosity

sbeccare §197 (**sbécco**) *tr & ref* to chip

sbeffeggiare §290 (**sbefféggio**) *tr* to make fun of

sbellicare §197 *ref*—**sbellicarsi dalle risa** to burst with laughter

sbèrla *f* (coll) slap

sberlèffo *m* scar; grimace; **fare gli sberleffi a** to make faces at

sbevazzare *intr* to guzzle

sbevucchiare §287 *intr* to tipple

sbiadire §176 *tr & intr* (ESSERE) to fade

sbiadi•to -ta *adj* faded; dull

sbiancare §197 *tr* to whiten ‖ *ref* to become white; to pale

sbianchire §176 *tr* (culin) to blanch

sbiè•co -ca (-chi -che) *adj* oblique; **di sbieco** on the bias; **guardare di sbieco** to look askance at ‖ *m* cloth cut diagonally

sbigottire §176 *tr* to terrify, dismay ‖ *intr* (ESSERE) & *ref* to be dismayed

sbilanciare §128 *tr* to unbalance; to up-set ‖ *intr* to lose one's balance ‖ *ref* to commit oneself

sbilàn•cio *m* (**-ci**) disequilibrium; (com) deficit

sbilèn•co -ca *adj* (**-chi -che**) twisted, crooked

sbirciare §128 *tr* to leer at, ogle; to eye closely

sbìr•ro -ra *adj* (coll) smart ‖ *m* (pej) cop

sbizzarrire [ddzz] §176 *tr* to cure the whims of ‖ *ref* to indulge one's whims

sbloccare §197 (**sblòcco**) *tr* to unblock; to raise the blockade of; to free

sbòbba *f* slop, dishwater

sboccare §197 (**sbócco**) *tr* to break the

mouth of (*a bottle*); to remove a few drops from (*a bottle*) ‖ *intr* (ESSERE) to flow; to open (*said of a street*); **sboccare in** to turn out to be

sbocca·to -ta *adj* foulmouthed; foul (*language*); chipped at the mouth (*said of a bottle*)

sbocciare §128 (**sbòccio**) *intr* (ESSERE) to bud, burgeon, bloom

sbóc·co *m* (**-chi**) outlet; **avere uno sbocco di sangue** to spit blood

sbocconcellare (**sbocconcèllo**) *tr* to nibble at; to chip, nick

sbollentare (**sbollènto**) *tr* to blanch

sbollire §176 *intr* to stop boiling; to calm down

sbolognare (**sbológno**) *tr* (coll) to palm off; (coll) to get rid of

sbórnia *f* (coll) drunk, jag; **smaltire la sbornia** to sober up

sborsare (**sbórso**) *tr* to pay out, disburse

sbórso *m* disbursement, outlay

sbottare (**sbòtto**) *intr*—**sbottare a** + *inf* to burst out + *ger*

sbottonare (**sbottóno**) *tr* to unbutton ‖ *ref* (fig) to unbosom oneself

sbozzare (**sbòzzo**) *tr* to rough-hew; to sketch, outline

sbraca·to -ta *adj* without pants; slovenly; vulgar

sbracciare §128 *intr* to gesticulate ‖ *ref* to roll up one's sleeves; to wear sleeveless clothes; to gesticulate; to do one's best

sbraccia·to -ta *adj* bare-armed

sbraitare (**sbràito**) *intr* to scream

sbraitó·ne -na *mf* bigmouth

sbranare *tr* to tear to pieces

sbrano *m* tear, rent

sbrattare *tr* to clean; to clear

sbreccare §197 (**sbrécco**) *tr* to chip, nick

sbrecciare §128 (**sbréccio**) *tr* to open a gap in

sbréndolo *m* tatter, rag

sbriciolare (**sbrìciolo**) *tr* to crumb ‖ *ref* to crumble

sbrigare §209 *tr* to transact; to take care of ‖ *ref* to hasten, hurry; **sbrigarsela** to get out of trouble; **sbrigarsi di** to get rid of; **sbrigati!** make it snappy!, hurry up!

sbrigativ·o -va *adj* quick, brisk; businesslike

sbrigliare §280 *tr* to unbridle; to reduce (*a hernia*); to lance (*an infected wound*) ‖ *ref* to cut loose

sbrinare *tr* to defrost

sbrindella·to -ta *adj* tattered

sbrodolare (**sbròdolo**) *tr* to soil; (fig) to drag out ‖ *ref* to slobber

sbrogliare §280 (**sbròglio**) *tr* to untangle; to clean up ‖ *ref* to extricate oneself; **sbrogliarsela** to get out of a tight spot

sbronzare (**sbrónzo**) *ref* (coll) to get drunk

sbruffare *tr* to squirt out of the mouth; to spatter; to bribe ‖ *intr* to tell tall tales

sbruffo *m* sprinkle, squirt; bribe

sbruffó·ne -na *mf* braggart

sbucare §197 *intr* (ESSERE) to pop out, come out

sbucciare §128 *tr* to peel; to skin ‖ *ref* to slough (*said of snakes*); **sbucciarsela** (coll) to goldbrick

sbucciatura *f* slight abrasion

sbudellare (**sbudèllo**) *tr* to disembowel ‖ *ref*—**sbudellarsi dalle risa** to burst with laughter, split one's sides laughing

sbuffare *tr* & *intr* to puff

sbuffo *m* puff; gust (*of wind*); **a sbuffo** puffed (*sleeve*)

sbullonare (**sbullóno**) *tr* to unbolt

sc- *pref* dis-, e.g., **sconto** discount; es-, e.g., **scalare** to escalate; ex-, e.g., **scusare** to excuse

scàbbia *f* scabies

sca·bro -bra *adj* rough; stony; tight (*style*)

scabró·so -sa [s] *adj* scabrous

scacchièra *f* checkerboard; chessboard

scacchière *m* (mil) sector; (obs) checkerboard; exchequer

scacciaca·ni *m* & *f* (-ni) toy gun; gun shooting only blanks

scacciamó·sche *m* (-sche) fly swatter

scacciapensiè·ri *m* (-ri) jew's-harp

scacciare §128 *tr* to chase away, drive away; to expel -

scaccino *m* sexton, sacristan

scac·co *m* (-chi) chessman; checker; check; square; **a scacchi** checkered; **dare scacco matto a** to checkmate; **in scacco** or **sotto scacco** in check; **scacchi** chess; **scacco matto** checkmate

scàccoli *mpl* cement piles

scaccomatto *m* checkmate

scadènte *adj* inferior, poor, shoddy

scadènza *f* term, maturity; obligation; **a breve scadenza** short-term; **a lunga scadenza** long-term

scadére §121 *intr* (ESSERE) to decay, to decline; to fall due; to expire; (naut) to drift

scafandro *m* diving suit; **scafandro astronautico** space suit

scaffale *m* bookcase; shelf

scafo *m* hull

scagionare (**scagióno**) *tr* to exonerate, exculpate

scàglia *f* scale (*of fish*); chip; plate (*of medieval armor*); flake (*of soap*); tile (*of slate roof*)

scagliare §280 *tr* to hurl, fling, throw; to scale (*fish*) ‖ *ref* to dash, to rush; to flake

scaglionare (**scaglióno**) *tr* to echelon; to stagger (*e.g., payments*)

scaglióne *m* terrace (*of mountain*); echelon; scale; **a scaglioni** graded (*e.g., income tax*)

scala *f* stairs; ladder; scale; (cards) straight; (rad) dial; **a scala** scaled, graded; **fare le scale** to climb the stairs; **scala a chiocciola** spiral stairway; **scala a gradini** or **a libretto** stepladder; **scala mobile** escalator; (econ) sliding scale; **scala porta** aerial ladder; **scala reale** (poker) straight flush; **su larga scala** large-scale; **su scala nazionale** on a national scale

scalandróne *m* (naut) gangway

scalare *adj* graded, scaled; gradual || *m* (com) running balance || *tr* to climb, ascend; to scale, grade; to reduce

scalata *f* climb, ascent; **dar la scalata a** to climb; to climb up to

scalcagna•to -ta *adj* down-at-the-heel

scalcare §197 *tr* to slice, carve

scalciare §128 *intr* to kick

scalcina•to -ta *adj* (*wall or plaster*) that is peeling off; worn-out; down-at-the-heels

scalda-acqua *m* (**-acqua**) hot-water heater

scaldaba•gno *m* (**-gno**) hot-water heater; **scaldabagno a gas** gas heater

scaldalèt•to *m* (**-ti & -to**) bedwarmer

scaldare *tr* to warm, warm up; to heat, heat up || *intr* (mach) to become hot || *ref* to warm up; to heat up; **scaldarsi la testa** to get excited

scaldavivan•de *m* (**-de**) hot plate

scaldino *m* hand warmer

scalèa *f* flight of stairs, stairway

scalèo *m* stepladder

scalétta *f* small ladder; small stairs; (mov) rough draft

scalfire §176 *tr* to graze, scratch; to cut (*e.g., glass*)

scalfittura *f* graze, scratch

scalinata *f* stairway, perron

scalino *m* step (*of a stair*); (fig) ladder

scalmana *f* chill; flush; **prendere una scalmana per** to take a fancy to

scalmanare *ref* to hustle, bustle; to fuss

scalmana•to -ta *adj* panting; hotheaded

scalmo *m* (naut) oarlock

scalo *m* pier, dock; (naut) ways; (naut) port of call; **fare scalo** (naut) to call, stop; (aer) to land; **scalo di alaggio** (naut) slip; **scalo merci** (rr) freight yard; **senza scalo** (aer, naut) nonstop

scalógna *f* (coll) bad luck

scalógno *m* (bot) scallion

scalòppa *f* veal chop

scaloppina *f* veal cutlet, scallop

scalpellare (scalpèllo) *tr* to chisel

scalpellino *m* stone cutter

scalpèllo *m* chisel; (surg) scalpel; **scalpello a taglio obliquo** skew chisel

scalpicciare §128 *tr & intr* to shuffle

scalpitare (scàlpito) *intr* to paw the ground

scalpóre *m* scene; **fare scalpore** to raise a fuss

scaltrézza *f* shrewdness, cunning

scaltrire §176 *tr* to polish, refine; to sharpen the wits of || *ref* to catch on; to improve

scal•tro -tra *adj* shrewd, smart

scalzare *tr* to take the shoes or stockings off of; to undermine || *ref* to take off one's shoes or stockings

scal•zo -za *adj* barefoot

scambiare §287 *tr* to exchange; to mistake || *ref* to exchange (*presents*)

scambiévole *adj* mutual

scàm•bio *m* (**-bi**) exchange; (rr) switch;

libero scambio free trade; **scambio di persona** mistaken identity

scamicia•to -ta *adj* in shirt sleeves; extremist || *m* extremist; tunic, waist

scamoscia•to -ta *adj* chamois, suede

scampagnata *f* excursion, outing

scampanare *intr* to peal, chime; to flare (*said of a garment*)

scampanellare (scampanèllo) *intr* to ring loud and clear

scampanì•o *m* (**-ì**) toll, peal

scampare *tr* to save, rescue; **scamparla bella** to have a narrow escape || *intr* (ESSERE)—**scampare a** to escape from; to take refuge in

scampo *m* escape; safety; (zool) Norway lobster; **non c'è scampo** there is no way out

scàmpolo *m* remnant; **scampoli di tempo** free moments

scanalare *tr* to channel, groove, rabbet || *intr* to overflow

scanalatura *f* channel, groove, rabbet

scandagliare §280 *tr* to sound

scandà•glio *m* (**-gli**) sounding lead; **fare uno scandaglio** to make a sounding or survey

scandalismo *m* scandalmongering, yellow journalism

scandalizzare [ddzz] *tr* to scandalize, shock || *ref* to be scandalized

scàndalo *m* scandal

scandaló•so -sa [s] *adj* scandalous

scandina•vo -va *adj & mf* Scandinavian

scandire §176 *tr* to scan; to syllabize; (telv) to scan

scàndola *f* wood shingle

scannare *tr* to slaughter, butcher

scanna•tóio *m* (**-tói**) slaughterhouse; gyp joint

scanno *m* bench; seat; sand bar

scansafati•che *mf* (**-che**) loafer

scansare *tr* to move; to avoid || *ref* to get out of the way

scansìa *f* shelf; bookcase

scansióne *f* scansion; (telv) scanning

scanso *m*—**a scanso di** in order to avoid

scantinare *intr* to make a blunder; (mus) to be out of tune

scantinato *m* basement

scantonare (scantóno) *tr* to round (*a corner*) || *intr* to duck around the corner

scanzona•to -ta *adj* flippant; unconventional

scapaccióne *m* clout; **dare uno scapaccione a** to clout, slap

scapa•to -ta *adj* scatterbrained || *m* scatterbrain

scapestra•to -ta *adj & m* libertine

scapigliare §280 *tr* to dishevel || *ref* to be disheveled

scapiglia•to -ta *adj* disheveled; libertine; unconventional; free and easy

scapitare (scàpito) *intr* to lose

scàpito *m* damage; loss; **a scapito di** to the detriment of

scàpola *f* shoulder blade

scapolare *m* scapular || *v* (**scàpolo**) *tr* (coll) to escape, avoid || *intr*—**scapolare da** to get out of (*danger*)

scàpo·lo -la *adj* unmarried ‖ *m* bachelor. ‖ *f* see **scapola**

scappaménto *m* escapement (*of watch, of piano*); (aut) exhaust

scappare *tr*—**scapparla bella** to have a narrow escape ‖ *intr* (ESSERE) to flee; to abscond; to run; to get away; to escape; to stick out; to burst out (*said, e.g., of sun*); **far scappare la pazienza a qlcu** to make s.o. lose his patience, to tax s.o.'s patience; **scappare a gambe levate** to run away, beat it; **scappare da** to burst out, e.g., **gli è scappato da ridere** he burst out laughing; **scappar detto di** to blurt out that, e.g., **gli scappò detto di non poterne più** he blurted out that he could not hold out; **scappare di mente** to escape one's mind; **scappar fuori con** to come out with

scappata *f* excursion; sally; escapade; bolt (*of horse*); **fare una scappata** to take a run; **scappata spiritosa** witticism

scappatóia *f* subterfuge; loophole

scappellare (scappèllo) *ref* to tip one's hat

scappellòtto *m* smack, slap (on the head); **entrare a scappellotto** (coll) to squeeze in; **passare a scappellotto** (coll) to squeeze through with influence

scapricciare §128 *tr* to satisfy the whims of

scarabèo *m* beetle; scarab (*stone*); **scarabeo sacro** scarab; **scarabeo stercorario** dung beetle

scarabocchiare §287 (**scarabòcchio**) *tr* to scribble; to blot (*with ink*)

scarabòc·chio *m* (**-chi**) ink blot; scribble; scrawl

scarafàg·gio *m* (**-gi**) cockroach

scaramanzìa *f* exorcism; **per scaramanzia** to ward off the evil eye, for good luck

scaramazza *adj fem* irregular (*pearl*)

scaramùc·cia *f* (**-ce**) skirmish

scaraventare (scaravènto) *tr* to hurl, chuck; to transfer suddenly

scarcerare (scàrcero) *tr* to release from jail

scardinare (scàrdino) *tr* to unhinge

scàri·ca *f* (**-che**) discharge; volley; evacuation; (elec) discharge; (fig) shower

scaricabarili *m*—**giocare a scaricabarili** (fig) to pass the buck

scaricare §197 (**scàrico**) *tr* to unload; to discharge; to hurl (*insults*); to wreak (*anger*); to free (*from responsibility*) ‖ *ref* to unburden oneself; to flow (*said of a river*); to discharge; to run down (*said of a battery or a watch*)

scaricatóre *m* longshoreman; (elec) lightning arrester

scàri·co -ca (**-chi -che**) *adj* empty, unloaded; discharged; clear (*sky*); free; run-down (*e.g., clock*) ‖ *m* unloading; discharge; exhaust; waste, refuse; **a mio (tuo, etc.) scarico** in my (your, etc.) defense ‖ *f* see **scarica**

scarlattina *f* scarlet fever

scarlat·to -ta *adj* & *m* scarlet

scarmigliare §280 *tr* to dishevel

scarnificare §197 (**scarnìfico**) or **scarnire** §176 *tr* to bone, take the flesh off; to make thin; to wear down to the bone

scarni·to -ta or **scar·no -na** *adj* boned; meager; skinny

scaròla *f* escarole, endive

scarpa *f* shoe; wedge, skid; scarp; **fare le scarpe a** to undercut; **scarpe al sole** violent death; **scarpe da sci** ski boots

scarpata *f* escarp, escarpment; slope (*of embankment*); blow with a shoe; **scarpata continentale** continental slope

scarpétta *f* small shoe; low shoe; **scarpette chiodate** spikes; **scarpette da ginnastica** gym shoes

scarpinare *intr* to trudge

scarpóne *m* heavy boot; clodhopper

scarròc·cio *m* (**-ci**) (aer, naut) leeway

scarrozzare (scarròzzo) *tr* to take for a ride ‖ *intr* to go for a ride; to go for a walk

scarrozzata *f* ride, drive

scarseggiare §290 (**scarséggio**) *intr* (ESSERE) to be scarce, be in short supply; **scarseggiare di** to be short of

scarsèlla *f* pocket; (obs) purse

scarsézza *f* or **scarsi·tà** *f* (**-tà**) scarcity, dearth, lack

scar·so -sa *adj* short; scarce; scanty, scant; weak (*wind*); **scarso a** short of

scartabellare (scartabèllo) *tr* to leaf through (*a book*)

scartafàc·cio *m* (**-ci**) note pad, notebook; poorly-bound copybook

scartaménto *m* (rr) gauge; **a scartamento ridotto** narrow-gauge; small-size; small-scale

scartare *tr* to unpack, unwrap; to discard (*cards*); to remove; to scrap (*e.g., a machine*); (mil) to reject ‖ *intr* to swerve; to side-step

scartata *f* unwrapping; side step; swerving; (fig) scolding

scartina *f* discard

scarto *m* discard; reject; swerve; (mil) rejected soldier; (sports) difference; **di scarto** inferior

scartocciare §128 (**scartòccio**) *tr* to unwrap; to unfold; to husk (*corn*)

scartòffie *fpl* old papers, trash

scassare *tr* to uncrate; to plow up; (coll) to ruin, bust ‖ *ref* (coll) to break down

scassinare *tr* to pick (*a lock*); to burglarize; to break open

scassina·tóre -trice *mf* burglar; **scassinatore di casseforti** safe-cracker

scasso *m* plowing, tilling; burglary

scatenare (scaténo) *tr* to unchain; to trigger; to excite, stir up ‖ *ref* to break loose

scàtola *f* box; can; **a scatola chiusa** sight unseen; **in scatola** canned; **rompere le scatole a** (vulg) to bug, pester; **scatola armonica** music box; **scatola a sorpresa** jack-in-the-box;

scatola cranica cranium, skull; **scatola del cambio** (aut) transmission, gear box

scatolame *m* boxes; canned food

scatolifi·cio *m* (**-ci**) box factory

scattare *tr* to take (*a picture*) ǁ *intr* (ESSERE & AVERE) to jump, spring; to go off (*said of a trap*); to go up (*said of the cost of living*); to go into action, begin

scatto *m* click (*of camera, gun*); outburst; sprint; automatic increase (*in salary*); shutter release; **a scatti** in jerks; **di scatto** suddenly

scaturire §176 *intr* (ESSERE) to spring; to pour, gush; to stem

scavalcare §197 *tr* to jump over; to pass over; to unsaddle; to skip (*a stitch*) ǁ *intr* (ESSERE) to dismount ǁ *ref* (coll) to rush

scavallare *intr* to caper, cavort

scavare *tr* to dig; to dig up, unearth

scava·tóre -trice *adj* excavating ǁ *m* digger ǁ *f* digger, excavator

scavezzacòllo *m* scamp; daredevil; **a scavezzacollo** headlong, at breakneck speed

scavezzare (**scavézzo**) *tr* to lop; to burst; to break; to take the halter off (*a horse*)

scavo *m* digging, excavation

scazzottare (**scazzòtto**) *tr* to beat up

scégliere §244 *tr* to choose; to pick out

sceic·co *m* (**-chi**) sheik

scelleratàggine *f* or **scelleratézza** *f* wickedness, villainy

scellera·to -ta *adj* wicked ǁ *m* villain

scellino *m* shilling

scél·to -ta *adj* choice; selected; (mil) first-class ǁ *f* choice; pick; selection; **di prima scelta** choice

scemare (**scémo**) *tr* to diminish, reduce; to lower the level of ǁ *intr* (ESSERE) & *ref* to lessen, diminish

scemènza *f* foolishness, stupidity

scé·mo -ma *adj* silly, foolish ǁ *mf* simpleton, fool

scempiàggine *f* silliness, foolishness

scém·pio -pia (**-pi -pie**) *adj* simple; single; (lit) wicked ǁ *m* ruination; (lit) slaughter; **fare scempio di** to ruin; (lit) to slaughter

scèna *f* scene; stage; acting; scenery; **esser di scena** (theat) to be on; **mettere in scena** (theat) to stage; **scene di prossima programmazione** (mov) coming attractions

scenà·rio *m* (**-ri**) scenery; scenario, setting

scenari·sta *mf* (**-sti -ste**) scenarist; script writer

scenata *f* scene (*outbreak of anger*)

scéndere §245 *tr* to descend, go down; to bring down ǁ *intr* (ESSERE) to descend, go down; to get off; to come (*to an agreement*); to step (*into the ring*); to put up (*at a hotel*); to check in (*at a hotel*)

scendilèt·to *m* (**-to**) scatter rug; bathrobe

sceneggiare §290 (**scenéggio**) *tr* to write a scenario for; to adapt for the stage

sceneggia·tóre -trice *mf* scenarist

sceneggiatura *f* (mov) screenplay; (rad, telv) continuity

scenètta *f* (theat) sketch

scenògrafo *m* scene designer

scenotècni·ca *f* (**-che**) stagecraft

sceriffo *m* sheriff

scèrnere §246 *tr* to discern; to distinguish; to select

scervellare (**scervèllo**) *ref* to rack one's brains

scervella·to -ta *adj* scatterbrained

scésa [s] *f* discent; slope

scespiria·no -na *adj* Shakesperean

scetticismo *m* skepticism

scètti·co -ca (**-ci -che**) *adj* skeptic(al) ǁ *m* skeptic

scèttro *m* scepter

sceverare (**scévero**) *tr* (lit) to distinguish

scé·vro -vra *adj* (lit) free, exempt

schèda *f* card; slip, form; **scheda elettorale** ballot; **scheda perforata** punch card

schedare (**schèdo**) *tr* to file

schedà·rio *m* (**-ri**) card index, card catalogue; file cabinet

schég·gia *f* (**-ge**) splinter; chip

scheggiare §290 (**schéggio**) *tr* & *ref* to splinter

schelètri·co -ca *adj* (**-ci -che**) skeleton, skeletal; succint

schèletro *m* skeleton

schè·ma *m* (**-mi**) diagram; draft; model; scheme; **schema di montaggio** (electron) hookup

schérma *f* fencing

schermàglia *f* argument

schermare (**schérmo**) *tr* to screen; (elec) to shield

schermire §176 *tr* to protect; (obs) to fence with ǁ *ref*—**schermirsi da** to ward off, parry; to protect oneself from

schermi·tóre -trice *mf* fencer

schérmo *m* screen; protection; (elec) shield; **farsi schermo di** to use as protection; **farsi schermo delle mani** to ward off a blow with one's hands

schernire §176 *tr* to deride

schérno *m* derision, ridicule, mockery

scherzare (**schérzo**) *tr* (coll) to mock ǁ *intr* to play; to joke, trifle

schérzo *m* play; joke, jest; freak (*of nature*); child's play; trick; **neppure per scherzo** under no circumstances; **per scherzo** in jest; **stare allo scherzo** to take a joke

scherzó·so -sa [s] *adj* joking; playful

schiacciaménto *m* crushing; flattening

schiaccianó·ci *m* (**-ci**) nutcracker

schiacciante *adj* crushing

schiacciapata·te *m* (**-te**) ricer

schiacciare §128 *tr* to crush; to take (*a nap*); to squelch (*a rumor*); to subdue (*the details of a painting*); to mash (*potatoes*); to tread on, step on (*s.o.'s foot*); to flatten; to run (*s.o.*) over; to make (*s.o.'s figure*) look squatty; to crack (*nuts*); to flunk; (tennis) to smash

schiacciata *f* hot cake; (tennis) smash

schiaffare tr (coll) to fling, clap
schiaffeggiare §290 (**schiafféggio**) tr to slap; to buffet
schiaffo m slap, box
schiamazzare intr to squawk, cackle; to honk; to make a racket
schiamazzo m squawking, cackle; honk; hubbub
schiantare tr to crush, burst || intr (ESSERE) (coll) to burst; (coll) to croak || ref to break, crack, split
schianto m break, crack; crash; bang; knockout (extraordinary, attractive person or thing); **di schianto** all of a sudden; **schianto al cuore** heartache
schiappa f splinter; (coll) good-for-nothing
schiarimento m elucidation
schiarire §176 tr to make clearer; to make (the hair) light; to clear; to explain; to elucidate || intr (ESSERE) to become light || ref to clear (one's throat); to fade || impers (ESSERE) —**schiarisce** it is getting light
schiarita f clearing (of weather); improvement (in relations)
schiatta f race, stock
schiattare intr (ESSERE) to burst
schiavi·sta (-sti -ste) adj slave (e.g., state) || mf antiabolitionist
schiavi·tù f (-tù) slavery; bondage
schia·vo -va adj enslaved || mf slave
schiccherare (**schicchero**) tr to scribble; to soil; to sketch; to dash off; to blurt out; (coll) to clean out
schidionare (**schidióno**) tr to put on the spit
schidióne m spit
schièna f back; divide; crown (of road); **giocare di schiena** to buck
schienale m back (of chair; cut of meat)
schièra f crowd; flock; herd; (mil) rank
schieramento m alignment
schierare (**schièro**) tr to line up || ref to line up; **schierarsi dalla parte di** to side with
schièt·to -ta adj pure; frank, honest
schifare tr to loathe; to disgust || ref— **schifarsi di** to feel disgusted with
schifa·to -ta adj disgusted
schifiltó·so -sa [s] adj fastidious; squeamish
schifo m disgust, loathing; skiff; shell; **fare schifo a** to disgust; to make sick
schifó·so -sa [s] adj disgusting, sickening; (slang) tremendous
schioccare §197 (**schiocco**) tr to snap (the fingers); to click (the tongue); to smack (the lips); to crack (a whip) || intr to crack
schiòc·co m (-chi) crack, snap; click; smack
schiodare (**schiòdo**) tr to take the nails out of
schioppettata f gunshot; earshot
schiòppo m gun, shotgun; **a un tiro di schioppo** within earshot
schiùdere §125 tr & ref to open
schiuma f foam, froth; lather; head (of beer); dregs, scum; meerschaum;

avere la schiuma alla bocca to froth at the mouth
schiumaiòla f skimmer
schiumare tr to scum; to skim || intr to foam, froth; to lather
schiumó·so -sa [s] adj foamy
schivare tr to avoid; to avert || ref to shy
schi·vo -va adj averse; bashful, shy
schizzare tr to spray; to sprinkle; to ooze (venom); to sketch; **schizzare fuoco dagli occhi** to have fire in one's eyes || intr (ESSERE) to gush; to squirt; to dart; **gli occhi gli schizzano dall'orbita** his eyes are popping out of his head
schizzétto m sprayer; syringe; water pistol
schizzinó·so -sa [s] adj finicky, fastidious
schizzo m spray; splash; sketch; survey (e.g., of literature)
sci m (sci) ski
scìa f wake; track; trail; **scia di condensazione** contrail
sciàbola f saber
sciabordare (**sciabórdo**) tr to shake, agitate || intr to break (said of waves)
sciacallo m jackal
sciacquadi·ta m (-ta) finger bowl
sciacquare (**sciàcquo**) tr to rinse
sciacquatura f rinse
sciacquì·o m (-i) splash, dash
sciàcquo m rinsing (of the mouth); mouthwash
sciagura f calamity, misfortune
sciagura·to -ta adj unfortunate; wretched
scialacquare (**scialàcquo**) tr to squander
scialare tr to squander || intr to be well off; to live it up
scial·bo -ba adj pale, faded; wan
scialle m shawl; **scialle da viaggio** traveling blanket
scialo m squandering; opulence; **a scialo** lavishly
scialuppa f launch; lifeboat
sciamanna·to -ta adj slovenly
sciamannó·ne -na mf slovenly person || f slattern
sciamare intr (ESSERE & AVERE) to swarm
sciame m swarm; flock
sciampagna f champagne
scianca·to -ta adj cripple, lame; wobbly (table)
sciangài m pick-up-sticks || **Sciangài** f Shanghai
sciarada f charade
sciare §119 intr to ski; to back water
sciarpa f scarf; sash (e.g., of an officer or of a mayor)
scias·sì m (-sì) chassis
sciàtica f (pathol) sciatica
scia·tóre -**trice** mf skier
sciatterìa f or **sciattézza** f slovenliness
sciat·to -ta adj slovenly, sloppy
scìbile m knowledge
sciènte adj conscious; knowing
scientìfi·co -ca adj (-ci -che) scientific
sciènza f science; knowledge

scienzia·to -ta *mf* scientist

scilinguágnolo *m* frenum (*of tongue*); avere lo scilinguagnolo sciolto to have a loose tongue

Scilla *f* Scylla; fra Scilla e Cariddi between Scylla and Charibdis

scimitarra *f* scimitar

scimmia *f* monkey; (coll) drunk; fare la scimmia a to ape; scimmia antropomorfa anthropoid ape

scimmié·sco -sca *adj* (-schi -sche) monkeyish; apish

scimmiottare (scimmiòtto) *tr* to ape

scimpan·zé *m* (-zé) chimpanzee

scimuni·to -ta *adj* idiotic || *mf* idiot

scindere §247 *tr* (lit) to split; to separate

scintilla *f* spark; sparkle; (fig) scintilla; scintilla elettrica jump spark

scintillare *intr* to spark; to sparkle

scintìlli·o *m* (-i) sparkle, brilliance

scioccare §197 *tr* to shock

sciocchézza *f* silliness; trifle

sciòc·co -ca (-chi -che) *adj* silly, foolish || *mf* fool, blockhead

sciògliere §127 *tr* to loosen; to release; to unfasten, untie; to solve; to disperse; to dissolve; to limber; to fulfill (*a promise*); to unfurl (*sails*) || *ref* to loosen up; to get loose; to dissolve; to melt (*into tears*)

scioglilìn·gua *m*(-gue) tongue twister

sciogliménto *m* melting; dissolution; fulfillment; denouement

sciolìna *f* ski wax

scioltézza *f* nimbleness, agility; freedom (*of movement*); ease

sciòl·to -ta *adj* loose; glib; free; blank (*verse*)

scioperante *adj* striking || *mf* striker

scioperare (sciòpero) *intr* to strike

sciopera·to -ta *adj* loafing; lazy || *m* loafer

sciòpero *m* strike; walkout; sciopero a singhiozzo slowdown strike; sciopero bianco sit-down strike; sciopero della fame hunger strike; sciopero di solidarietà sympathy strike; sciopero pignolo slowdown

sciorinare *tr* to display; to tell (*lies*); to air (*laundry*)

sciovìa *f* ski lift

sciovinismo *m* chauvinism, jingoism

scipì·to -ta *adj* insipid

scippo *m* snatching (*e.g., of a bag*)

sciròc·co *m* (-chi) sirocco; southeast

sciròppo *m* syrup

sci·sma *m* (-smi) schism

scismàti·co -ca *adj* (-ci -che) schismatic

scissióne *f* split; (biol, phys) fission

scis·so -sa *adj* split, rent

scisto *m* schist

sciupare *tr* to spoil; to wear out; to waste; to rumple || *ref* to wear; to run down (*said of health*); to get rumpled

sciupa·to -ta *adj* ruined; worn out; wasted; run down

sciupì·o *m* (-i) waste

sciupó·ne -na *mf* waster, squanderer

sciu·scià *m* (-sciá) bootblack; urchin

scivola *f* chute

scivolare (scìvolo) *intr* (ESSERE & AVERE) to slide, glide; to steal; scivolare d'ala (aer) to sideslip

scivolata *f* slide, glide; scivolata d'ala (aer) sideslip

scìvolo *m* chute; (aer) slip (*for seaplanes*)

scivolóne *m* slip, slide

scivólo·so -sa [s] *adj* slippery

scoccare §197 (scòcco) *tr* to shoot (*an arrow*); to give (*a buss*); to strike (*the hour*) || *intr* (ESSERE) to dart; to spring; to strike (*said of a clock*); to shoot

scocciare §128 (scòccio) *tr* (coll) to break; (coll) to bother; (naut) to unhook || *ref* to be bored

scoccia·tóre -trìce *mf* (coll) nuisance

scocciatùra *f* (coll) bother, annoyance

scòc·co *m* (-chi) darting; stroke (*e.g., of three*); (naut) hook; scocco di baci bussing, kissing

scodèlla *f* bowl; soup plate

scodellare (scodèllo) *tr* to dish out

scodellino *m* small bowl; (mil) pan (*of musket lock*)

scodinzolare (scodìnzolo) *intr* to wag its tail; to waddle (*said of a woman*)

scoglièra *f* reef (*of rocks*); scogliera corallina coral reef

scò·glio *m* (-gli) rock; reef; cliff; stumbling block

scoiare §248 *tr* to skin

scoiàttolo *m* squirrel

scolabrò·do *m* (-do) colander, strainer

scolafrit·to *m* (-to) strainer

scolapa·sta *m* (-sta) (coll) colander

scolare (scólo) *tr* to drain; (fig) to polish off || *intr* (ESSERE) to drip || *ref* to melt

scolaré·sco -sca (-schi -sche) *adj* school || *f* schoolchildren; student body

scola·ro -ra *mf* pupil; student

scolàsti·co -ca (-ci -che) *adj* school; scholastic || *m* scholastic, schoolman || *f* scholasticism

scola·tóio *m* (-tói) drain; strainer

scolatura *f* drip, drippings; dregs

scollaccia·to -ta *adj* low-necked; wearing a low-cut dress; dirty, obscene

scollare (scòllo) *tr* to cut off at the neck; to unglue || *ref* to wear a low-necked dress; to come unglued

scollatura *f* neckline; ungluing; scollatura a barchetta low neck; scollatura a punta V neck

scòllo *m* neck, neckline

scólo *m* drain; drainage; (slang) clap

scolopèndra *f* centipede

scolorare (scolóro) *tr*, *intr* (ESSERE), & *ref* to fade, discolor; to pale

scolorire §176 *tr*, *intr* (ESSERE), & *ref* to fade, discolor

scolpare (scólpo) *tr* to excuse

scolpire §176 *tr* to sculpture; to engrave; to emphasize

scólta *f* (lit) sentry; fare la scolta to stand guard

scombaciare §128 *tr* to pull apart, separate

scombinare *tr* to disarrange; to upset

scómbro *m* mackerel

scombù·glio m (-gli) (coll) disorder

scombussolare (scombùssolo) tr to up-set

scomméssa f bet, wager

scomméttere §198 tr to bet; to separate

scommetti·tóre -trice mf bettor

scomodare (scòmodo) tr to trouble, disturb || ref to take the trouble

scomodi·tà f (-tà) trouble, inconvenience

scòmo·do -da adj awkward, unwieldy; uncomfortable || m inconvenience

scompaginare (scompàgino) tr to up-set; (typ) to pi

scompagna·to -ta adj odd

scomparire §108 intr (ESSERE) to dis-appear; to make a bad showing

scompar·so -sa adj disappeared; extinct || mf deceased || f disappearance; death

scompartiménto m compartment; par-tition

scompènso m lack of compensation; imbalance

scompigliare §280 tr to disarray; to trouble, upset

scompì·glio m (-gli) disarray; upset

scompisciare §128 tr (vulg) to piss on || ref (vulg) to wet oneself; scom-pisciarsi dalle risa (coll) to split one's sides laughing

scomplè·to -ta adj incomplete

scompórre §218 tr to decompose, dis-integrate; to rumple; to dishevel; to upset; to dismantle, take apart; (typ) to pi || ref to lose one's composure

scompó·sto -sta adj unseemly

scomùni·ca f (-che) excommunication

scomunicare §197 (scomùnico) tr to ex-communicate; (joc) to ostracize

sconcertare (sconcèrto) tr to upset; to disconcert || ref to become discon-certed

sconcézza f obscenity, indecency

scón·cio -cia (-ci -ce) adj dirty, filthy, obscene || m obscenity; shame

sconclusiona·to -ta adj inconsequen-tial; incoherent; rambling

sconcordanza f disagreement; (gram) lack of agreement

scondi·to -ta adj unseasoned

sconfessare (sconfèsso) tr to disavow; to retract

sconfessióne f disavowal

sconfiggere §104 tr to defeat, rout; to pull (a nail); to unfasten

sconfinare intr to cross the border; sconfinare da to stray from

sconfina·to -ta adj boundless, unlimited

sconfitta f defeat, rout

sconfortante adj discouraging

sconfortare (sconfòrto) tr to discour-age; to distress || ref to become dis-couraged

sconfòrto m depression; distress

scongelare (scongèlo) tr to thaw

scongiurare tr to conjure; to implore

scongiuro m conjuration; entreaty

sconnès·so -sa adj disconnected; inco-herent

sconnèttere §107 tr to disconnect; to take apart || intr to be incoherent

sconoscènte adj unappreciative

sconosciu·to -ta adj unknown || mf stranger

sconquassare tr to smash, shatter

sconquassa·to -ta adj broken-down; upset

sconquasso m destruction; confusion; smash-up

sconsacrare tr to desecrate

sconsideratézza f thoughtlessness

sconsidera·to -ta adj inconsiderate

sconsigliare §280 tr to dissuade, dis-courage

sconsiglia·to -ta adj thoughtless

sconsola·to -ta adj disconsolate

scontare (scónto) tr to expiate; to dis-count; to serve (time in jail)

scontentare (scontènto) tr to dissatisfy

scontèn·to -ta adj & m discontent

scónto m discount; part payment; (fig) partial remission

scontrare (scóntro) tr to meet; (naut) to turn (the wheel) sharply || ref to clash; to collide; to come to blows

scontrino m check, ticket

scóntro m collision; battle, encounter; clash; ward (of key)

scontró·so -sa [s] adj peevish, cross

sconveniènte adj unfavorable; un-seemly, unbecoming; indecent

sconvenire §282 intr (ESSERE) to be un-seemly or unbecoming

sconvòlgere §289 tr to upset; to dis-concert

sconvolgiménto m upsetting; sconvolgi-mento di stomaco stomach upset; sconvolgimento tellurico upheaval

sconvòl·to -ta adj upset; disconcerted; distracted

scópa f broom; scopa per lavaggio mop

scopare (scópo) tr to sweep

scopata f sweep

scoperchiare §287 (scopèrchio) tr to uncover; to take the lid off

scopèr·to -ta adj uncovered; open; bare; exposed; unpaid || m open ground; open air; overdraft; (econ) short sale; (com) balance; allo scoperto in the open; overdrawn (check); short (sale) || f discovery; alla scoperta openly

scòpo m purpose, goal, aim

scoppiare §287 (scòppio) tr to uncouple || intr (ESSERE) to burst; to blow; to explode; to break (said, e.g., of news); (fig) to die (e.g., of over-eating); scoppiare a to burst out (laughing or crying)

scoppiettare (scoppiétto) intr to crackle

scoppietti·o m (-i) crackle

scòp·pio m (-pi) burst; explosion; out-break; outburst; blowout (of tire); a scoppio internal-combustion (en-gine); scoppio di tuono clap of thunder

scòppola f drop (of plane in air pocket); (coll) rabbit punch

scopriménto m uncovering; unveiling

scoprire §110 tr to uncover; to unveil; to discover; to expose || ref to take off one's clothes; to take one's hat off; to reveal oneself

scopri·tóre -trice *mf* discoverer
scoraggiaménto *m* discouragement
scoraggiante *adj* discouraging
scoraggiare §290 *tr* to discourage, dishearten ‖ *ref* to be or become discouraged
scoraménto *m* (lit) discouragement
scorbuto *m* scurvy
scorciare §128 (**scórcio**) *tr* to shorten; to foreshorten ‖ *intr* (ESSERE) to shorten, grow shorter; to look foreshortened ‖ *ref* to shorten, grow shorter
scorciatóla *f* shortcut, cutoff
scór·cio *m* (**-ci**) foreshortening; end, close (*of a period*); **di scorcio** foreshortened
scordare (**scòrdo**) *tr* to forget; to put out of tune ‖ *ref* to forget; to get out of tune
scoróg·gia *f* (**-ge**) (vulg) fart
scoreggiare §290 (**scoréggio**) *intr* (vulg) to fart
scòrgere §249 *tr* to perceive, to discern
scòria *f* slag, dross; (fig) scum, dregs; **scorie atomiche** atomic waste
scorna·to -ta *adj* humiliated, ridiculed; hornless
scòrno *m* humiliation, ridicule
scorpacciata *f* bellyful; **fare una scorpacciata di** to stuff oneself with
scorpióne *m* scorpion ‖ **Scorpione** *m* (astrol) Scorpio
scorrazzare *tr* to wander over ‖ *intr* to run around; to move about; (fig) to ramble; (mil) to raid
scórrere §139 *tr* to raid; to glance over ‖ *intr* (ESSERE) to flow; to run; to glide
scorrerìa *f* raid, foray, incursion
scorrettézza *f* imprecision; impropriety
scorrèt·to -ta *adj* incorrect; improper
scorrévole *adj* sliding; flowing, fluent ‖ *m* slide (*of slide rule*)
scorribanda *f* raid, foray, incursion
scór·so -sa *adj* past, last ‖ *m* error, slip ‖ *f* glance; short stay
scor·sóio -sóia *adj* (**-sói -sóie**) slip (*knot*)
scòrta *f* escort; provision, stock; **di scorta** spare (*tire*); **fare di scorta a** to escort; **scorta d'onore** (mil) honor guard; **scorte** (com) stockpile; (com) supplies; **scorte morte** agricultural supplies; **scorte vive** livestock
scortare (**scòrto**) *tr* to escort; to foreshorten
scortecciare §128 (**scortéccio**) *tr* to strip the bark from; to peel off; to scrape ‖ *ref* to peel off
scortése *adj* discourteous, impolite
scortesìa *f* discourtesy, impoliteness
scorticare §197 (**scórtico**) *tr* to skin; to be overdemanding with (*students*); to fleece ‖ *ref* to skin (*e.g., one's arm*)
scòrza *f* bark; skin, hide; (fig) appearance; **scorza di limone** lemon peel
scoscendiménto *m* landslide; cliff
scoscé·so -sa [s] *adj* sloping, steep
scòssa *f* shake; jerk; **scossa di pioggia**

downpour; **scossa di terremoto** earth tremor; **scossa elettrica** electric shock; **scossa tellurica** earthquake
scossóne *m* jolt, jerk
scostaménto *m* removal; separation
scostare (**scòsto**) *tr* to move away; to try to avoid ‖ *intr* (ESSERE) to stand away ‖ *ref* to step aside; to stray
scostuma·to -ta *adj* dissolute, debauched
scotennare (**scoténno**) *tr* to scalp; to skin (*an animal*)
scòtta *f* whey; (naut) sheet
scottante *adj* burning (*question*); outrageous (*offense*)
scottare (**scòtto**) *tr* to burn; to scald; to sear; to boil (*eggs*); (fig) to sting ‖ *intr* to burn; to be hot (*said of stolen goods*) ‖ *ref* to get burnt
scottatura *f* burn; (fig) blow, jolt
scòt·to -ta *adj* overcooked, overdone ‖ *m*—**pagare lo scotto** to foot the bill; **pagare lo scotto di** to expiate ‖ *f* see **scotta**
scoutismo *m* scouting
scovare (**scóvo**) *tr* to rouse (*game*); to find, discover
scovolino *m* pipe cleaner; (mil) small swab
scóvolo *m* (mil) swab
scòzia *f* (archit) scotia ‖ **la Scozia** Scotland
scozzése [s] *adj* Scotch, Scottish ‖ *m* Scotch, Scottish (*language*); Scotchman ‖ *f* Scotchwoman
scozzonare (**scozzóno**) *tr* to break in (*a horse*); to train
scranna *f* (hist) seat
screanza·to -ta *adj* ill-mannered, rude
screditare (**scrédito**) *tr* to discredit
scremare (**scrèmo**) *tr* to cream
scrematrice *f* cream separator
screpolare (**scrèpolo**) *tr*, *intr* (ESSERE), & *ref* to crack; to chap
screpolatura *f* crack; chap (*of skin*)
screziare §287 (**scrèzio**) *tr* to mottle, variegate
scrè·zio *m* (**-zi**) tiff
scri·ba *m* (**-bi**) scribe (*Jewish scholar*)
scribacchiare §287 *tr* to scribble, scrawl
scribacchino *m* scribbler; hack
scricchiolare (**scricchiolo**) *intr* to crack, creak
scricchiolì·o *m* (**-i**) crack, creak
scricciolo *m* wren
scrigno *m* jewel box
scriminatura *f* part (*in hair*)
scrit·to -ta *adj* written ‖ *m* writing ‖ *f* sign; inscription; contract; **scritta luminosa** electric sign
scrit·tóio *m* (**-tói**) writing desk
scrit·tóre -trice *mf* writer
scrittura *f* handwriting; penmanship; writing; contract; entry; (theat) booking; **Sacra Scrittura** Holy Scripture; **scrittura privata** contract; **scrittura pubblica** deed, indenture; **scrittura a macchina** typing
scritturale *adj* scriptural ‖ *m* clerk; copyist; fundamentalist
scritturare *tr* (theat) to book, engage
scrivanìa *f* desk

scrivano m clerk, copyist, typist
scrivere §250 tr & intr to write; **scrivere a macchina** to type
scroccare §197 (scròcco) tr to sponge (a meal); to manage to get (a prize) || intr to sponge
scrocca•tóre -trice mf sponger
scròc•co m (-chi) sponging; creaking; **a scrocco** sponging; spring (lock); switchblade (knife)
scroccó•ne -na mf sponger
scròfa f sow; slut
scrollare (scròllo) tr to shake; to shrug (one's shoulders) || ref to get into action; to pull oneself together
scrollata f shake; **scrollata di spalle** shrug
scrosciare §128 (scròscio) intr (ESSERE & AVERE) to pelt down; (fig) to thunder
scrò•scio m (-sci) thunder, roar; **scroscio di pioggia** downpour; **scroscio di tuono** thunderclap
scrostare (scròsto) tr to pick (a scab); to scrape; to peel off || ref to peel off
scrosta•to -ta adj peeling; scaly
scròto m scrotum
scrùpolo m scruple; scrupulousness
scrupoló•so -sa [s] adj scrupulous
scrutare tr to scan, scrutinize
scruta•tóre -trice adj inquisitive || mf teller (of votes)
scrutina•tóre -trice mf teller (of votes)
scruti•nio m (-ni) poll, vote; evaluation (of an examination); count (of votes); **scrutinio segreto** secret ballot
scucire §143 tr to unstitch; (coll) to cough up || ref to come unstitched
scucitura f unstitching; rip
scuderìa f stable
scudétto m badge; escutcheon; (sports) badge of victory
scudièro m esquire
scudisciare §128 tr to whip
scudi•scio m (-sci) whip
scudo m shield; escutcheon; **far scudo a** to shield
scùffia f (coll) load (intoxication); **fare scuffia** to capsize; **prendersi una scuffia per** to fall for, to fall in love with
scugnizzo m Neapolitan urchin
sculacciare §128 tr to spank
sculacciata f spank, spanking
sculaccióne m spank, spanking
sculettare (sculétto) intr to waddle
scul•tóre -trice mf sculptor || f sculptress
scultura f sculpture
scuòla f school; **scuola allievi ufficiali** military academy; officers' candidate school; **scuola dell'obbligo** mandatory education; **scuola di danza** dancing school; **scuola di dressaggio** obedience school (for dogs); **scuola di guerra** war college; **scuola di guida** driving school; **scuola di perfezionamento per laureati** postgraduate school; **scuola di taglio** sewing school; **scuola materna** kindergarten; **scuola mista** coeducational school

scuòla•bus m (-bus) school bus
scuòtere §251 tr to shake; to shake up; **scuotere di dosso** to shake off
scure f ax; cleaver
scurire §176 tr, intr (ESSERE), & ref to darken
scu•ro -ra adj dark || m darkness; dark; shutter; **essere allo scuro** to be in the dark
scurrile adj scurrilous
scusa f excuse; apology; pretext; **chiedere scusa** to apologize
scusare tr to excuse; to pardon; to apologize for; **scusi!** pardon me! || ref to apologize; to beg off
sdaziare §287 tr to clear through customs
sdebitare (sdébito) tr to free from debt || ref to become free of debt; **sdebitarsi con** to repay a favor to
sdegnare (sdégno) tr to scorn; to arouse, enrage || ref to get mad
sdégno m indignation, anger; (lit) scorn
sdegnó•so -sa [s] adj indignant; haughty
sdenta•to -ta adj toothless
sdilinquire §176 tr to weaken || intr (ESSERE) & ref to swoon; to become mawkish
sdoganare tr to clear through customs
sdolcina•to -ta adj mawkish
sdolcinatura f mush, slobber
sdoppiare §287 (sdóppio) tr & ref to split
sdoppiaménto m splitting
sdottoreggiare §290 (sdottoréggio) intr to pontificate
sdràia f chaise longue; deck chair
sdraiare §287 tr to lay down || ref to stretch out (e.g., on the ground)
sdràio m (sdrài) stretching out; **mettersi a sdraio** to lie down
sdrucciolare (sdrùcciolo) intr (ESSERE & AVERE) to slip, slide
sdrucciolévole adj slippery
sdrùccio•lo -la adj proparoxytone || m slip; slope; proparoxytone
sdruccio16ni adv slipping, sliding
sdrucire (sdrùcio) & §176 tr to tear, rend, rip
sdrucitura f tear, rend, rip
se m (se) if || §5 pron || conj if; whether; **se mai** in the event; **se no** otherwise; **se non tu** (lui, lei, etc.) nobody else but you (him, her, etc.), e.g., **non puoi essere stato se non tu** it could not have been anyone else but you; **se non altro** at least; **se non che** but; **se pure** even if
sé §5 pron himself; herself; itself; yourself; themselves; yourselves; oneself; **di per sé stesso** by itself; **fuori di sé** beside oneself; **rientrare in sé** to come back to one's senses; **uscire di sé** to be beside oneself
sebbène conj although, though
sèbo m sebum, tallow
séc•ca f (-che) sand bank, shoal; drought; **dare in secca** to run aground; **in secca** hard up
seccante adj drying; annoying
seccare §197 (sécco) tr to dry; to bore;

to bother, annoy || *intr* (ESSERE) to dry up || *ref* to dry up; to be annoyed

secca·tóio *m* (-**tói**) drying room; squeegee (*to remove water from wet decks*)

secca·tóre -trice *mf* bore, pest

seccatura *f* drying; trouble, nuisance

sécchia *f* bucket, pail; **piovere a secchie** to rain cats and dogs

secchièllo *m* little bucket

séc·chio *m* (-**chi**) bucket, pail; bucketful; **secchio dell'immondezza** trash can

séc·co -ca (-**chi -che**) *adj* dry; lanky; sharp || *m* dryness; dry land; drought; **a secco** dry (*cleaning*); **dare in secco** to run aground; **in secco** hard up; **lavare a secco** to dry-clean || *f* see **secca**

secenté·sco -sca *adj* (-**schi -sche**) seventeenth-century

secontési·mo -ma *adj, m & pron* six hundredth

secèrnere §153 (*pp* **secrèto**) *tr* to secrete

secessióne *f* secession

séco §5 *prep phrase* (lit) with oneself; along, e.g., **portare seco** to bring along

secolare *adj* secular; century-old; worldly || *m* layman

sècolo *m* century; age; world

secónda *f* second; second-year class; **a seconda con the wind; a seconda di** according to; **in seconda** (aut) in second; (mil) second in command

secondare (**secóndo**) *tr* to second

secondà·rio -ria *adj* (-**ri -rie**) secondary

secondino *m* prison guard, turnkey

secón·do -da *adj* second; (lit) favorable || *m* second; second course; (nav) executive officer || *f* see **seconda** || *pron* second || **secondo** *prep* according to; **secondo me** (**te, etc.**) in my (your, etc.) opinion

secondogèni·to -ta *adj* second-born

secrezióne *f* secretion

sèdano *m* celery

sedare (**sèdo**) *tr* to calm, placate

sedati·vo -va *adj & m* sedative.

sède *f* seat; branch; residence; period; (gram) syllable; (rr) right of way; **in separata sede** in private; (law) **with change of venue; Santa Sede** Holy See; **sede centrale** main office, home office

sedentà·rio -ria *adj* (-**ri -rie**) sedentary || *m* sedentary person

sedère *m* sitting; rear, backside || *v* §252 *intr* (ESSERE) to sit, to be seated; to be in session; to be located || *ref* to sit down

sèdia *f* chair; seat; see; **sedia a braccioli** armchair; **sedia a dondolo** rocking chair; **sedia a pozzetto** bucket seat; **sedia a sdraio** deck chair; **sedia da posta** (hist) mail coach; **sedia di vimini** wicker chair; **sedia elettrica** electric chair; **sedia girevole** swivel chair

sedicènne *adj* sixteen-year-old || *mf* sixteen-year-old person

sedicènte *adj* so-called, self-styled

sedicèsi·mo -ma *adj, m & pron* sixteenth

sédici *adj & pron* sixteen; **le sedici** four P.M. || *m* sixteen; sixteenth (*in dates*)

sedile *m* seat; bench; bottom (*of chair*); (aut) bucket seat

sediménto *m* sediment

sediòlo *m* sulky

sedizióne *f* sedition

sedizió·so -sa [s] *adj* seditious

seducènte *adj* seductive; alluring

sedurre §102 *tr* to seduce; to allure; to lead astray; to charm, captivate

seduta *f* sitting; session, meeting; **seduta fiume** (pol) uninterrupted session; **seduta stante** on the spot

sedut·tóre -trice *adj* seductive; alluring; charming || *mf* seducer

seduzióne *f* seduction; allurement; charm

sefardi·ta (-**ti -te**) *adj* Sephardic || *mf* Sephardi

sé·ga *f* (-**ghe**) saw; **a sega** serrated; **sega a nastro** band saw; **sega circolare** buzz saw; **sega da carpentiere** lumberman's saw; **sega intelaiata a lama** bucksaw; **sega meccanica** power saw

ségala *f* rye

segali·gno -gna *adj* rye; lean, wiry

segare §209 (**ségo**) *tr* to saw; to cut

segatrice *f* power saw; **segatrice a disco** circular saw; **segatrice a nastro** band saw

segatura *f* cutting; sawdust

seggétta *f* commode

ség·gio *m* (-**gi**) seat (*e.g., in congress*); **seggio elettorale** voting commission

sèggiola *f* chair; **seggiola a sdraio** deck chair

seggiolino *m* child's chair; stool; bucket seat; **seggiolino eiettabile** (aer) ejection seat

seggiolóne *m* highchair; easy chair

seggiovia *f* chair lift

segheria *f* sawmill

seghetta·to -ta *adj* serrated

seghétto *m* hacksaw; **seghetto da traforo** coping saw

segménto *m* segment; **segmento elastico** (aut) piston ring

segnaccènto *m* accent mark

segnàcolo *m* (lit) symbol, sign

segnalare *tr* to signal; to point out || *ref* to distinguish oneself

segnalazióne *f* signaling; sign, signal; nomination; recommendation; **dare la segnalazione a** to notify; **fare segnalazioni** to signal; **segnalazioni stradali** road signs

segnale *m* sign; signal; bookmark; **segnale di allarme** (mil) alarm; **segnale di occupato** (telp) busy signal; **segnale di via libera** (telp) dial tone; **segnale orario** (rad, telv) time signal; **segnali stradali** road signs

segnalèti·co -ca *adj* (-**ci -che**) identification (*mark*) || *f* road signs

segnalibro *m* bookmark

segnaline·e *m* (-**e**) lineman

segnapósto *m* place card

segnapun·ti *m* (-**ti**) scorekeeper

segnare (ségno) *tr* to mark; to under-score, underline; to jot down; to say (*e.g., five o'clock, said of a watch*); to brand; (sports) to score; **segnare a dito** to point to || *ref* to cross one-self

segnatas·se *m* (-se) postage-due stamp

segnatura *f* signing; signature; library number; (eccl) chancery; (sports) final score; (typ) signature

segnavèn·to *m* (-to) weather vane

ségno *m* mark; bookmark; symbol; sign; signal; boundary; (mus) signa-ture; **a segno che** so that; **a tal segno** to such a point; **essere fatto segno di** to be the target of; **in segno di** as a token of; **mettere a segno** to check, control; **segno della Croce** sign of the Cross; **segno di croce** cross (*mark*); **segno d'interpunzione**, or **di punteggiatura**, or **grafico** punctuation mark; **segno di riconoscimento** identifica-tion mark

ségo *m* tallow, suet

segregare §209 (sègrego) *tr* to segre-gate; to secrete || *ref* to withdraw

segregazióne *f* segregation; **segrega-zione cellulare** solitary confinement

segregazioni·sta *mf* (-sti -ste) segrega-tionist

segretariato *m* secretariat

segretà·rio -ria *mf* secretary; clerk

segreterìa *f* secretary's office; secretary-ship

segretézza *f* secrecy

segré·to -ta *adj* secret; secretive || *m* secret; secrecy; **segreto d'alcova** boudoir secret; **segreto di Pulcinella** open secret

seguace *mf* follower

seguènte *adj* following, next

segù·gio *m* (-gi) bloodhound; (fig) pri-vate eye

seguire (séguo) *tr* to follow; to attend || *intr* (ESSERE) to continue; to follow, ensue; (with *dat*) to follow

seguitare (séguito) *intr*—**seguitare a** + *inf* to keep on + *ger*, e.g., **seguitare a parlare** to keep on talking; **seguiti!** go ahead!

séguito *m* following; retinue; follow-ers; sequence; sequel; pursuit; **di seguito** in succession; **far seguito a** to refer to; **in seguito** thereafter; **in seguito a** as a consequence of

sèi *adj* & *pron* six; **le sei** six o'clock || *m* six; sixth (*in dates*)

seicènto *adj, m* & *pron* six hundred || *f* car with a motor displacing 600 cubic centimeters || **il Seicento** the seventeenth century

seimila *adj, m,* & *pron* six thousand

sélce *f* silica; flint; (lit) stone; **selci** paving blocks

selciare §128 (sélcio) *tr* to pave

selcia·to -ta *adj* paved || *m* paving

seletti·vo -va *adj* selective

selezionare (selezióno) *tr* to select, sort out

selezióne *f* selection; choice

sèlla *f* saddle

sel·làio *m* (-lài) saddler

sellare (sèllo) *tr* to saddle

sellerìa *f* saddler's shop; saddlery; (aut) upholstery

sélva *f* woods, forest

selvaggina *f* game

selvàg·gio -gia (-gi -ge) *adj* savage; vicious (*horse*) || *m* savage; unsocia-ble person

selvàti·co -ca *adj* (-ci -che) wild

selvicoltura *f* forestry

sèlz *m* (sèlz) seltzer, club soda

semàforo *m* traffic light; semaphore

semànti·co -ca (-ci -che) *adj* semantic || *f* semantics

sembiante *m* (lit) look; **fare sembianti di** to pretend

sembianza *f* look; (lit) similarity

sembrare (sémbro) *intr* (ESSERE) to seem, look, appear || *impers*—**sembra** it seems

séme *m* seed; stone (*of fruit*); (cards) suit

seménta *f* sowing season; (lit) seed

seménte *f* seed

semènza *f* seed; brads (*used in uphol-stery*)

semenzà·io *m* (-zài) hotbed, seedbed

semestrale *adj* semiannual, semiyearly

semèstre *m* semester; half year

sèmi- *pref adj* semi-, e.g., **semicircolare** semicircular; half-, e.g., **semichiuso** half-closed || *pref mf* semi-, e.g., **semicerchio** semicircle; half, e.g., **semitono** half tone; demi-, e.g., **semidio** demigod

semiapèr·to -ta *adj* half-open; ajar

semiasse *m* (mach) axle (*on each side of differential*)

semicér·chio *m* (-chi) semicircle

semichiu·so -sa [s] *adj* half-closed

semicingola·to -ta *adj* & *m* half-track

semicircolo *m* semicircle

semiconduttóre *m* semiconductor

semiconvit·tóre -trice *mf* day student

semicù·pio *m* (-pi) sitz bath

semi-dìo *m* (-dèi) demigod

semidòt·to -ta *adj* semilearned

semifinale *f* semifinal

sémina *f* sowing; sowing season

seminare (sémino) *tr* to sow, seed; to plant; (coll) to leave behind

seminà·rio *m* (-ri) seminary; seminar

seminari·sta *m* (-sti) seminarian

semina·to -ta *adj* sown, seeded || *m* sown land; **uscire dal seminato** to digress

semina·tóre -trice *mf* sower || *f* (mach) seeder, seeding machine

seminterrato *m* basement

seminu·do -da *adj* half-naked

semioscurità *f* partial darkness

semirigi·do -da *adj* semirigid; inelastic

semirimòr·chio *m* (-chi) semitrailer

semisè·rio -ria [s] *adj* (-ri -rie) serio-comic

semisfèra *f* (geom) hemisphere

semi·ta (-ti -te) *adj* Semitic || *mf* Semite

semitòno *m* (mus) semitone, half tone

semmài *conj* if ever; in the event that

sémola *f* bran; (coll) freckles

semolino *m* semolina

semovènte *adj* self-propelled

sempitèr·no -na *adj* (lit) everlasting
sémplice *adj* simple; single; plain; mere; (mil) private; (nav) ordinary || *m* medicinal herb; **semplici** simple folk
sempliciò·ne -na *adj* simple || *mf* simpleton
semplici·tà *f* (-tà) simplicity
semplificare §197 (**semplìfico**) *tr* to simplify || *ref* to become easier or simpler
sèmpre *adv* always; ever; yet; **da sempre** from time immemorial; **di sempre** same, same old; **e poi sempre** ever and ever; **ma sempre** but only; **per sempre** forever; **sempre che** provided; **sempre meglio** better and better; **sempre meno** less and less; **sempre però** but only; **sempre vostro** very truly yours
semprevérde *adj, m & f* evergreen
sènape *f* mustard
senapismo *m* mustard plaster
senato *m* senate
sena·tóre -trice *mf* senator
senése [s] *adj & mf* Sienese
sonile *adj* old; of old age
senilismo *m* (pathol) senility
senilità *f* old age
senióre *adj & m* elder, senior
Sènna *f* Seine
sénno *m* wisdom; **far senno** to come back to one's senses; **senno di poi** hindsight; **uscir di senno** to go out of one's mind
séno *m* chest; breast, bosom; cove; (anat) sinus; (math) sine; (fig) heart; **in seno a** within
senonché or **se non che** *conj* but
sensale *m* broker; commission merchant
sensa·to -ta *adj* sensible, reasonable; sane
sensazionale *adj* sensational
sensazióne *f* sensation
sensìbile *adj* sensible; perceptible; appreciable; sensitive; responsive (*e.g., to affection*) || *m* world of the senses
sensibili·tà *f* (-tà) sensitivity; sensibility
sensibilizzare [ddzz] *tr* to sensitize
sensiti·vo -va *adj* sensitive || *m* medium
sènso *m* sense; feeling; meaning; aspect; tone, fashion; direction; **ai sensi di legge** according to law; **a senso** free (*translation*); **doppio senso** double entendre; **in senso contrario** in the opposite direction; **perdere i sensi** to lose consciousness; **riprendere i sensi** to come to; **sensi carnal** appetite, flesh; **senso unico** one-way; **senso vietato** no entry, one-way
sensò·rio -ria *adj* (-ri -rie) sensory
sensuale *adj* sensual, carnal; sensuous
sensualità *f* sensuality
sentènza *f* sentence; maxim
sentenziare §287 (**sentènzio**) *tr* to pass sentence upon, sentence || *intr* to pontificate
sentenziò·so -sa [s] *adj* sententious
sentièro *m* path, pathway
sentimentale *adj* sentimental; mawkish
sentimentalismo *m* sentimentalism
sentiménto *m* feeling; sentiment; sense;

uscire di sentimento (coll) to go out of one's mind
sentina *f* bilge; sink (*of vice*)
sentinèlla *f* sentry, sentinel
sentire *m* feeling || *v* (**sènto**) *tr* to feel; to hear; to listen to; to consult (*a doctor*); to smell; to taste **farsi sentire** to make oneself heard || *intr* to feel; to listen; to smell; to taste; **non sentirci di quell'orecchio** to turn a deaf ear; **sentirci bene** to have keen hearing || *ref* to feel; **non sentirsela di** to not have the courage to; **sentirsela** to feel up to it
senti·to -ta *adj* heartfelt
sentóre *m* inkling, feeling; sign; (lit) smell
sènza *prep* without; beyond (*e.g., comparison*); **senza + inf** without + *ger*; **senza che + subj** without + *ger*; **senza di + pron** without + *pron*, e.g., **senza di lui** without him; **senz'altro** without any doubt, of course
senza·dìo *m* (-dìo)—**i senzadio** the godless
senzapà·tria *m* (-tria) man without a country; renegade
senzatét·to *m* (-to) homeless person; **i senzatetto** the homeless
separare *tr & ref* to separate
separazióne *f* separation
sepolcrale *adj* sepulchral
sepolcréto *m* cemetery
sepólcro *m* sepulcher, grave
sepoltura *f* burial; grave
seppellire §253 *tr* to bury
séppia *adj invar* sepia || *f* cuttlefish
seppure *conj* even if
sè·psi *f* (-psi) sepsis
sequèla *f* series
sequènza *f* sequence
sequestrare (**sequèstro**) *tr* to seize, confiscate; to kidnap; to confine; to quarantine; (law) to attach, sequester
sequèstro *m* seizure; attachment; **sequestro di persona** unlawful detention
séra *f* evening; night; **da mezza sera** cocktail (*dress*); dark (*suit*); **da sera** evening (*gown*); formal (*attire*)
serac·co *m* (-chi) serac
serafino *m* seraph
serale *adj* evening; night
seralménte *adv* in the evening; every evening
serata *f* evening; soiree, evening party; **serata d'addio** (theat) farewell performance; **di beneficenza** benefit performance
serbare (**sèrbo**) *tr* to keep; to save (*e.g., a place*); to bear (*a grudge*) || *ref* to keep oneself; to stay
serba·tóio *m* (-tói) tank; reservoir; cartridge clip
sèr·bo -ba *adj & mf* Serbian || *m*—**in serbo** in store
serbocroa·to -ta *adj & mf* Serbo-Croatian
serenata *f* serenade
serenìssi·mo -ma *adj* Serene (*Highness*)
sereni·tà *f* (-tà) serenity

seré·no -na *adj* serene; clear, fair (*weather*)

sergènte *m* sergeant; carpenter's clamp; sergente maggiore first sergeant

sèri·co -ca *adj* (-ci -che) silk

sè·rie *f* (-rie) series; (sports) division; fuori serie (aut) custom-built; in serie (aut) standard; (elec) in series

serietà *f* seriousness; gravity

serigrafìa *f* silkscreen process

sè·rio -ria (-ri -rie) *adj* serious; stern; poco serio unreliable (*man*); loose (*woman*) || *m* seriousness; sul serio in earnest; really, e.g., bello sul serio really beautiful

sermonare (sermóno) *tr & intr* (lit) to sermonize

sermóne *m* sermon

sermoneggiare §290 (sermonéggio) *intr* to preach; to lecture

seròti·no -na *adj* late; (lit) evening

sèrpa *f* coach box

sèrpe *f* snake, serpent; a serpe coiled, in a coil; nutrirsi or scaldarsi la serpe in seno to nourish a viper in one's bosom

serpeggiare §290 (serpéggio) *intr* to zig-zag; to wind; to creep, spread

serpènte *m* snake, serpent; serpente a sonagli rattlesnake

serpenti·no -na *adj* serpentine || *m* serpentine; coil (*of pipe*) || *f* zigzag, turn (*of winding road*); coil (*of pipe*)

sérqua *f* dozen; lot, large number

sèrra *f* dike, levee; hothouse; sierra; un serra serra a milling crowd

serrafi·la *m* (-le) rear-guard soldier || *f* rear ship (*of convoy*)

serrafilo *m* electrician's pliers; (elec) binding post

serrà·glio *m* (-gli) menagerie; seraglio

serramànico *m*—a serramanico clasp (*knife*); switchblade (*knife*)

serrame *m* lock

serramento *m* closing, bolting || serramén·ti & -ta *fpl* closing devices, doors, windows, and shutters

serranda *f* shutter (*of store*)

serrare (sèrro) *tr* to shut, close; to pursue (*the enemy*); to increase (*tempo*); to furl (*sails*); to lock; to clench (*one's teeth, one's fists*); to shake (*hands*) || *intr* to shut; to be tight || *ref* to be wrenched, e.g., gli si serrò il cuore his heart was wrenched; serrarsi addosso a to press (*the enemy*)

serrata *f* lockout

serrate *m*—serrate finale (sports) finish

serra·to -ta *adj* shut (*e.g., door*); con-cise (*style*); tight (*game*); rapid (*gal-lop*); closed (*ranks*); thick (*crowd*) || *f* see serrata

serratura *f* lock

sèrto *m* (poet) crown, wreath

sèrva *f* (pej) maidservant, maid

servènte *adj* (*gentleman*) in waiting || *m* gunner; (obs) servant

servìbile *adj* usable

serviènte *m* (eccl) server

servi·gio *m* (-gi) service; favor

servile *adj* servile; menial; modal (*auxiliary*)

servire (sèrvo) *tr* to serve; to wait on; in che posso servirLa? what can I do for you?; may I help you?; per servirLa at your service || *intr* to serve || *intr* (ESSERE & AVERE) to serve; to answer the purpose; to last; (with *dat*) (coll) to need, e.g., gli serve il martello he needs the hammer; non servire a nulla to be of no use; servire da to act as || *ref* to help oneself; servirsi da to patronize, deal with; servirsi di to avail oneself of, use

servitóre *m* servant; tea wagon; servitor suo umilissimo your humble servant

servi·tù *f* (-tù) servitude; captivity; servants, help; servitù di passaggio (law) easement

serviziévole *adj* obliging, accommodating

servi·zio *m* (-zi) service; favor; turn; a mezzo servizio part-time (*domestic help*); di servizio delivery (*entrance*); for hire (*car*); domestic (*help*); fuori servizio out of commission; in servizio in commission; servizi kitchen and bath; facilities; servizi pubblici public services; public works; servizio attivo active duty; servizio permanente effettivo service in the regular army

sèr·vo -va *adj* (lit) enslaved || *m* slave; servant; servo della gleba serf || *f* see serva

servoassistì·to -ta *adj* servocontrolled

servofréno *m* (aut) power brake

servomotóre *m* servomotor

servostèrzo *m* (aut) power steering

sèsamo *m* sesame; apriti sesamo! open sesame!

sessanta *adj, m & pron* sixty

sessantènne *adj* sixty-year-old || *mf* sixty-year-old person

sessantèsi·mo -ma *adj, m & pron* six-tieth

sessantina *f* about sixty

sessióne *f* session

sèsso *m* sex; il sesso debole the fair sex

sessuale *adj* sexual

sestante *m* sextant

sestétto *m* sextet

sestière *m* district, section

sè·sto -sta *adj & pron* sixth || *m* sixth; curve (*of an arch*); fuori sesto out of sorts; mettere in sesto to arrange; to set in order; sesto acuto (archit) ogive

sèt *m* (sèt) set; set all'aperto (mov) location

séta *f* silk; seta artificiale rayon

setacciare §128 *tr* to sift, sieve

setàc·cio *m* (-ci) sieve

setàce·o -a *adj* silky

séte *f* thirst; aver sete to be thirsty; to lust after; sete di thirst for

seterìa *f* silk mill; seterie silk goods

setifì·cio *m* (-ci) silk mill

sétola *f* bristle; (joc) stubble

sètta *f* sect

settanta *adj, m & pron* seventy

settantènne *adj* seventy-year-old || *mf* seventy-year-old person

settantèsi·mo -ma *adj, m & pron* seventieth

settantina *f* about seventy

settà·rio -ria *adj* & *mf* (-ri -rie) sectarian

sètte *adj* & *pron* seven; le sette seven o'clock || *m* seven; seventh (*in dates*); V-shaped tear (*in clothing*)

settecentèsi·mo -ma *adj, m* & *pron* seven hundredth

settecènto *adj, m* & *pron* seven hundred || il Settecento the eighteenth century

settèmbre *m* September

settennale *adj* seven-year (*e.g., plan*)

settènne *adj* seven-year-old || *mf* seven-year-old child

settentrionale *adj* northern || *mf* northerner

settentrióne *m* north; (astr) Little Bear

setticemia *f* septicemia

sètti·co -ca *adj* (-ci -che) septic

settimana *f* week; week's wages; settimana corta five-day week

settimanale *adj* & *m* weekly

settìmi·no -na *adj* premature (*baby*) || *m* (mus) septet

sètti·mo -ma *adj, m* & *pron* seventh

sètto *m* septum

settóre *m* sector; section, branch; dissector, anatomist; coroner's pathologist

sevè·ro -ra *adj* severe, stern

seviziare §287 *tr* to torture

sevìzie *fpl* cruelty

sezionale *adj* sectional

sezionare (sezióno) *tr* to cut up; to divide up; to dissect

sezióne *f* section; dissection; chapter (*of club*); department (*of agency*); (geom) cross section

sfaccenda·to -ta *adj* loafing || *mf* loafer

sfaccettare (sfaccétto) *tr* to facet

sfacchinare *intr* (coll) to toil, drudge

sfacchinata *f* (coll) drudgery, grind

sfacciatàggine *f* brazenness, impudence

sfaccia·to -ta *adj* brazen, impudent; loud, gaudy; fare lo sfacciato to be fresh

sfacèlo *m* breakdown, collapse

sfà·glio *m* (-gli) swerve (*e.g., of horse*); (cards) discard

sfaldare *tr* to exfoliate; to cut into slices || *ref* to flake, scale; (fig) to collapse, crumble

sfamare *tr* to feed (*the hungry; the family*) || *ref* to get enough to eat

sfare §173 *tr* to undo || *ref* to spoil (*said, e.g., of meat*)

sfarzo *m* pomp, display; luxury

sfarzó·so -sa [s] *adj* sumptuous, luxurious

sfasare *tr* to throw out of phase; (coll) to depress || *intr* (ESSERE) (aut) to misfire; (elec) to be out of phase

sfasciare §128 *tr* to remove the bandage from; to unswathe; to smash, shatter || *ref* to go to pieces; to lose one's figure

sfatare *tr* to discredit; to unmask

sfatica·to -ta *adj* lazy || *mf* loafer

sfat·to -ta *adj* overdone; overripe; undone (*bed*); ravaged (*by age*)

sfavillare *intr* to spark, sparkle

sfavóre *m* disfavor

sfavorévole *adj* unfavorable

sfebbra·to -ta *adj* free of fever

sfegata·to -ta *adj* (coll) rabid, fanatical

sfèra *f* sphere; (coll) hand (*of clock*); a sfera ball-point (*pen*); a sfere ball (*bearing*); sfera di cuoio (sports) pigskin

sfèri·co -ca *adj* (-ci -che) spherical

sferrare (sfèrro) *tr* to unshoe (*a horse*); to unchain; to draw (*a weapon from a wound*); to deliver (*a blow*) || *ref* to hurl oneself

sfèrza *f* whip, scourge

sferzare (sfèrzo) *tr* to whip, scourge

sfiancare §197 *tr* to break open; to tire out; to fit (*clothes*) too tight || *ref* to burst open; to get worn out

sfiatare *intr* to leak (*said, e.g., of a tire*) || *intr* (ESSERE) to leak (*said of air or gas*) || *ref* to waste one's breath

sfiata·tóio *m* (-tói) vent

sfibbiare §287 *tr* to unbuckle, unfasten; to untie (*a knot*)

sfibrante *adj* exhausting

sfibrare *tr* to grind (*wood*) into fibers; to shred (*rags*) into fibers; to weaken, wear out

sfida *f* challenge

sfidare *tr* to challenge, dare; to brave, defy; to endure (*the challenge of time*); sfidare che to bet that

sfidù·cia *f* (-cie) mistrust; (pol) no confidence

sfiducia·to -ta *adj* downcast, depressed

sfigurare *tr* to disfigure || *intr* to make a bad impression; to lose face

sfilacciare §128 *tr* & *ref* to ravel, fray

sfilare *tr* to unstring; to take off (*one's shoes*); to count (*beads*); to unthread; to dull (*a blade*); to ravel || *intr* (ESSERE) to march, parade; to follow one another || *ref* to become unthreaded; to become frayed; to run (*said of knitted work*); to break one's back

sfilata *f* parade; row; sfilata di moda fashion show

sfilza *f* row, sequence

sfinge *f* sphinx

sfiniménto *m* exhaustion

sfinire §176 *tr* to exhaust, wear out || *ref* to be worn out

sfintère *m* sphincter

sfiorare (sfióro) *tr* to graze; to barely touch (*a subject*); to skim; (lit) to barely reach

sfioratóre *m* spillway

sfiorire §176 *intr* (ESSERE) to wither, fade

sfit·to -ta *adj* not rented

sfocare §197 (sfòco) *tr* to put out of focus; to blur

sfociare §128 (sfócio) *tr* to dredge (*the mouth of a river*) || *intr* (ESSERE) to flow; sfociare in (fig) to lead to

sfoderare (sfòdero) *tr* to unsheathe; to show off, sport, display; to take the cover or lining off || *intr* to be drawn out

sfogare §209 (sfógo) *tr* to vent, give vent to || *intr* (ESSERE) to flow; to pour out; sfogare in to turn into || *ref*—sfogarsi a + *inf* to have one's fill of + *ger;* **sfogarsi con** to unburden oneself to; **sfogarsi su qlcu** to take it out on s.o.

sfoga·tóio *m* (-tói) vent

sfoggiare §290 (**sfòggio**) *tr* to display, sport; to show off

sfòg·gio *m* (-gi) display, ostentation

sfòglia *f* foil; skin (*of onion*); layer of puff paste; (ichth) sole

sfogliare §280 (**sfòglio**) *tr* to pluck (*a flower*); to defoliate (*a tree*); to leaf through (*a book*); to deal (*cards*); to husk (*corn*); to press (*dough*) into layers ‖ *ref* to shed its leaves; to flake

sfogliata *f* defoliation; puff paste; **dare una sfogliata a** to glance through

sfó·go *m* (-ghi) exhaust; outlet; vent; (coll) eruption (*of skin*)

sfolgorare (**sfólgoro**) *intr* (ESSERE & AVERE) to shine, blaze

sfolgorì·o *m* (-i) glittering, blazing

sfollagèn·te *m* (-te) billy

sfollaménto *m* evacuation; layoff

sfollare (**sfòllo**) *tr* to clear; to cut the staff of ‖ *intr* (ESSERE & AVERE) to disperse, evacuate; to cut down the staff

sfolla·to -ta *adj* driven from home ‖ *mf* evacuee

sfoltire §176 *tr* to thin out

sfondare (**sfóndo**) *tr* to stave in; to break through; to be heavy on (*the stomach*) ‖ *intr* to give ‖ *ref* to break open

sfóndo *m* background

sfondóne *m* (coll) blunder, error

sforbiciare §128 (**sfòrbicio**) *tr* to clip, shear

sforbiciata *f* clipping; (sports) scissors; (sports) scissors kick

sformare (**sfórmo**) *tr* to pull out of shape; to take out of the mold ‖ *intr* to get mad

sforma·to -ta *adj* out of shape ‖ *m* pudding

sfornare (**sfórno**) *tr* to take out of the oven

sfornire §176 *tr* to deprive; to strip

sfortuna *f* bad luck, misfortune

sfortuna·to -ta *adj* unsuccessful; unlucky, unfortunate

sforzare (**sfòrzo**) *tr* to strain; to force ‖ *ref* to strive, endeavor

sforza·to -ta *adj* forced, unnatural

sfòrzo *m* effort; strain; stretch (*of imagination*); **senza sforzo** effortlessly

sfóttere *tr* (vulg) to make fun of

sfracassare *tr* to smash, crash

sfracellare (**sfracèllo**) *tr & ref* to shatter, smash

sfrangiare §290 *tr* to ravel

sfrattare *tr* to evict; to deport ‖ *intr* to be evicted

sfratto *m* eviction; notice of eviction

sfrecciare §128 (**sfréccio**) *intr* (ESSERE & AVERE) to speed by

sfregaménto *m* rubbing

sfregare §209 (**sfrégo**) *tr* to rub; to scrape; to strike (*a match*)

sfregiare §290 (**sfrégio & sfrègio**) *tr* to disfigure, slash

sfregia·to -ta *adj* disfigured, slashed ‖ *m* scarface

sfré·gio or **sfrè·gio** *m* (-gi) slash, scar, gash; insult

sfrenare (**sfréno & sfrèno**) *tr* to take the brake off; to give free rein to ‖ *ref* to kick over the traces

sfriggere §180 *intr* to sizzle

sfrigolì·o *m* (-i) sizzle

sfrondare (**sfróndo**) *tr* to defoliate; to lop off; to trim down ‖ *ref* to lose leaves

sfrontatézza *f* effrontery, impudence

sfronta·to -ta *adj* brazen, impudent

sfrusciare §128 *intr* to rustle

sfruttare *tr* to exploit; to exhaust (*e.g., a mine*); to take advantage of

sfrutta·tóre -trice *mf* exploiter, developer (*e.g., of an invention*)

sfuggènte *adj* fleeting; receding (*forehead*); shifty (*glance*)

sfuggire *tr* to avoid, flee ‖ *intr* (ESSERE) to flee, escape, get away; (with *dat*) to escape, e.g., **nulla gli sfugge** nothing escapes him; to break, e.g., **sfuggì a una promessa** he broke a promise; **lasciarsi sfuggire** to let slip

sfuggita *f*—**di sfuggita** hastily; incidentally; **dare una sfuggita** to run down (*e.g., to the post office*)

sfumare *tr* to shade down; to tone down; to trim (*hair*) ‖ *intr* (ESSERE) to vanish; to shade

sfumatura *f* nuance, shade; razor clipping

sfumino *m* stump (*in drawing*)

sfuriare §287 *tr* to vent (*one's anger*) ‖ *intr* to rave

sfuriata *f* outburst of anger; gust (*of wind*); **fare una sfuriata a** to give a scolding to

sgabèllo *m* stool, footstool

sgabuzzino *m* cubbyhole

sgambettare (**sgambétto**) *tr* to trip ‖ *intr* to toddle; to kick (*said of a baby*); to scamper

sgambétto *m* trip, stumble; **dare lo sgambetto a** to trip

sganasciare §128 *tr* to dislocate the jaw of; to break the jaw of; to tear apart ‖ *intr* to steal right and left ‖ *ref* to break one's jaw; **sganasciarsi dalle risa** to split one's sides laughing

sganciare §128 *tr* to unhook; to lay out money); to drop (*bombs*) ‖ *intr* to drop bombs; (coll) to go away ‖ *ref* to get unhooked; (mil) to disengage oneself; **sganciarsi da** to get rid of

sgangherare (**sgànghero**) *tr* to unhinge; to burst ‖ *ref*—**sgangherarsi dalle risa** to split one's sides laughing

sganghera·to -ta *adj* unhinged; broken down; rickety; coarse (*laughter*)

sgarbatéz·za *f* rudeness; incivility; clumsiness

sgarba·to -ta *adj* rude; clumsy

sgarberìa *f* var of **sgarbatezza**

sgarbo *m*—**fare uno sgarbo a** to be rude to

sgargiante *adj* loud, flashy, showy

sgarrare *intr* to go wrong

sgattaiolare (**sgattàiolo**) *intr* (ESSERE) to slip away; to wriggle out

sgelare (sgèlo) *tr* & *intr* to thaw, melt
sgèlo *m* thaw
sghém·bo -ba *adj* crooked; a sghembo
askew || sghembo *adv* askew; side-
ways
sghèrro *m* hired assassin; gendarme
sghiacciare §128 *tr* to thaw
sghignazzare *intr* to guffaw
sghignazzata *f* guffaw
sghimbè·scio -scia *adj*—a or di sghim-
bescio askew, crooked
sghiribizzo [ddzz] *m* whim, fancy
sgobbare (sgòbbo) *intr* to drudge, plod,
plug
sgobbó·ne -na *mf* plugger, plodder,
drudge
sgocciolare (sgócciolo) *tr* to let drip ||
intr to drip (*said of container*) || *intr*
(ESSERE) to drip (*said of liquid*)
sgocciola·tóio *m* (-tói) dish rack; drip
pan
sgocciolatura *f* dripping; drippings
sgócciolo *m* last drop; essere agli sgoc-
cioli to be coming to an end
sgolare (sgólo) *ref* to shout oneself
hoarse
sgomberare (sgómbero) *tr* & *intr* var
of sgombrare
sgómbero *m* moving
sgombrané·ve *m* (-ve) snowplow (*truck*)
sgombrare (sgómbro) *tr* to clear; to
vacate || *intr* to move, vacate
sgóm·bro -bra *adj* clear || *m* moving;
(ichth) mackerel
sgomentare (sgoménto) *tr* to frighten;
to dismay
sgomén·to -ta *adj* dismayed || *m* dis-
may; rimanere di sgomento to be
dismayed
sgominare (sgòmino) *tr* to rout
sgomma·to -ta *adj* unglued; without
tires; with poor tires
sgonfiare §287 (sgónfio) *tr* to deflate;
to damn with faint praise (*e.g., a
play*); (coll) to bore || *intr* (ESSERE)
to boast; to balloon || *ref* to go down
(*said of swelling*); to go flat (*said of
a tire*); (fig) to collapse
sgón·fio -fia *adj* deflated, flat
sgonfiòtto *m* jelly doughnut; puff (*in
clothing*)
sgórbia *f* (carp) gouge
sgorbiare §287 (sgòrbio) *tr* to scribble;
(carp) to gouge
sgòr·bio *m* (-bi) ink spot; scribble,
scrawl
sgorgare §209 (sgórgo) *tr* to unclog ||
intr (ESSERE) to gush
sgottare (sgótto) *tr* to bail out (*a boat*)
sgozzare (sgózzo) *tr* to slaughter; to
slit the throat of; (fig) to bleed,
fleece
sgradévole *adj* disagreeable, unpleasant
sgradire §176 *tr* to refuse || *intr* to be
displeasing
sgradi·to -ta *adj* unpleasant; unwelcome
sgraffignare *tr* to snitch, snatch
sgrammatica·to -ta *adj* ungrammatical
sgranare *tr* to shell (*e.g., peas*); to count
(*one's beads*); to seed (*grapes*); to
open (*one's eyes*) wide; (mach) to
disengage || *ref* to crumble; to scratch
oneself

sgranchire §176 *tr* to stretch (*e.g., one's
legs*)
sgranocchiare §287 (sgranòcchio) *tr* to
crunch, munch
sgrassare *tr* to remove the grease from;
to skim (*broth*); to scour (*wool*)
sgravare *tr* to relieve, lighten || *ref* to
be relieved; to give birth
sgrà·vio *m* (-vi) lightening, lessening; a
sgravio di coscienza to ease one's
conscience
sgrazia·to -ta *adj* gawky, clumsy
sgretolare (sgrétolo) *tr* & *ref* to crumble
sgretola·to -ta *adj* crumbling, falling
down
sgridare *tr* to scold, chide
sgridata *f* scolding, reprimand
sgrondare (sgróndo) *tr* to cause to drip
|| *intr* to drip, trickle
sgroppare (sgròppo) *tr* to wear (*a
horse*) out || *intr* to buck (*said of a
horse*)
sgroppare (sgróppo) *tr* to untie
sgrossare (sgròsso) *tr* to rough-hew;
(fig) to refine
sgrovigliare §280 *tr* to untangle
sguaiatàggine *f* uncouthness
sguaia·to -ta *adj* crude, vulgar; un-
couth || *mf* vulgar person; uncouth
person
sguainare *tr* to unsheathe; to show
(*one's nails*)
sgualcire §176 *tr* to crumple || *ref* to
become crumpled
sgualdrina *f* trollop, strumpet
sguardo *m* glance, look; eyes
sguarnire §176 *tr* to untrim; (mil) to
strip, dismantle
sguàtte·ro -ra *mf* dishwasher, scullion
|| *f* kitchenmaid, scullery maid
sguazzare *tr* to waste, squander || *intr*
to splash; to wallow; to be lost (*in
shoes too big or clothes too loose*)
sguinzagliare §280 *tr* to unleash, let
loose
sgusciare §128 *tr* to shell, hull || *intr*
(ESSERE) to slip; sgusciare di soppiatto to slip away
shòp·ping *m* (-ping) shopping; shopping
bag; fare lo shopping to go shopping
shràpnel *m* (shràpnel) shrapnel
si *m* (-si) (mus) si || §5 *pron*
sì *m* (sì) yes; yea; stare tra il sì e il no
to not be able to make up one's
mind; un . . . sì e l'altro no every
other (*e.g., day*)
sìa *conj* see essere
siamése [s] *adj* & *mf* Siamese
siberia·no -na *adj* & *mf* Siberian
sibilante *adj* & *f* sibilant
sibilare (sìbilo) *intr* to hiss
sibilla *f* sibyl
sìbilo *m* hiss, hissing
sicà·rio *m* (-ri) hired assassin
sicché *conj* so that
siccità *f* drought
siccóme *adv* as || *conj* since; as; how
Sicilia, la Sicily
sicilia·no -na *adj* & *mf* Sicilian
sicomòro *m* sycamore
sicumèra *f* cocksureness, overconfi-
dence
sicura *f* safety lock (*on gun*)

sicurézza *f* security; assurance; safety; certainty; reliability; **di sicurezza** safety; **sicurezza sociale** social security

sicu·ro -ra *adj* sure; safe; steady; **di sicuro** certainly ‖ *m* safety; **camminare sul sicuro** to take no chances ‖ **sicuro** *adv* certainly ‖ *f* see **sicura**

sicur·tà *f* (**-tà**) insurance

siderale *adj* sidereal

sidère·o -a *adj* sidereal

siderùrgi·co -ca (**-ci -che**) *adj* iron-and-steel ‖ *m* iron-and-steel worker

sidro *m* cider, hard cider

sièpe *f* hedge; (fig) wall

sièro *m* serum

sièsta *f* siesta; **fare la siesta** to take a nap, take a siesta

siffat·to -ta *adj* such

sifìlide *f* syphilis

sifóne *m* siphon; siphon bottle; trap

siga·ràio -ràia (**-rài -ràie**) *mf* cigar maker ‖ *m* (ent) grape hopper; ‖ *f* cigarette girl

sigarétta *f* cigarette

sìgaro *m* cigar

sigillare *tr* to seal

sigillo *m* seal; **avere il sigillo alle labbra** to have one's lips sealed; **sigillo sacramentale** seal of confession

sigla *f* acronym; initials; abbreviation; letterword; **sigla musicale** theme song

siglare *tr* to initial

significare §197 (**signìfico**) *tr* to mean; to signify; **significare qlco a qlcu** to inform s.o. of s.th

significati·vo -va *adj* significant; meaningful

significato *m* meaning; **senza significato** meaningless

signóra *f* Madam, Mrs.; lady; mistress, owner; wife ‖ **Nostra Signora** Our Lady

signóre *m* sir, Mr.; gentleman; rich man; lord, master, owner; man; **il signore desidera?** what is your pleasure?; **per signori** stag ‖ **Signore** *m* Lord

signoreggiare §290 (**signoréggio**) *tr* to rule over; to master; to tower over; to overshadow ‖ *intr* to be the master

signorìa *f* seigniory; rule; **La Signoria Vostra** your Honor; **Sua Signoria** his Lordship; your Lordship

signorìle *adj* seigniorial; gentlemanly; ladylike; elegant, refined

signorìna *f* miss; Miss; young lady; spinster

signorìno *m* master, young gentleman

signornò *adv* no, Sir

signoró·ne *-na mf* (coll) rich person

signoròtto *m* lordling

signorsì *adv* yes, Sir

silenziatóre *m* silencer (*of firearm*); (aut) muffler

silèn·zio *m* (**-zi**) silence; (mil) taps; **fare silenzio** to be silent; **ridurre al silenzio** (mil) to silence

silenzió·so -sa [s] *adj* silent; noiseless

sìlfide *f* sylphid

silfo *m* sylph

silhouèt·te *f* (**-te**) silhouette

sìlice *f* silica

silìcio *m* silicon

silicóne *m* silicone

siliquastro *m* redbud

sìllaba *f* syllable

sillabare (**sìllabo**) *tr* to syllabify; to spell

sillabà·rio *m* (**-ri**) reader, primer

sìllabo *m* syllabus

silo *m* silo

silòfono *m* xylophone

siluétta *f* silhouette

silurante *adj* torpedoing, torpedo ‖ *f* destroyer; torpedo boat

silurare *tr* to torpedo; (fig) to fire, dismiss; (fig) to undermine

siluro *m* torpedo

silva·no -na *adj* sylvan

silvèstre *adj* (lit) sylvan; (lit) wild; (lit) hard, arduous

simboleggiare §290 (**simboléggio**) *tr* to symbolize

simbòli·co -ca *adj* (**-ci -che**) symbolic

simbolismo *m* symbolism

sìmbolo *m* symbol

similari·tà *f* (**-tà**) similarity

sìmile *adj* similar; such ‖ *m* like; **i propri simili** fellow men

similòro *m* tombac

simmetrìa *f* symmetry

simmètri·co -ca *adj* (**-ci -che**) symmetrical

simonìa *f* simony

simpamina *f* benzedrine

simpatèti·co -ca *adj* (**-ci -che**) sympathetic

simpatìa *f* like, liking; **cattivarsi la simpatia di** to make oneself well liked by

simpàti·co -ca (**-ci -che**) *adj* nice, pleasant, congenial ‖ *m* (anat) sympathetic system

simpatizzante [ddzz] *adj* sympathizing ‖ *mf* sympathizer

simpatizzare [ddzz] *intr* to sympathize; to become friends

simpò·sio *m* (**-si**) symposium

simulare (**sìmulo**) *tr* to simulate

simula·tóre -trice *mf* faker, impostor ‖ *m* simulator

simultàne·o -a *adj* simultaneous

sin- *pref adj* syn-, e.g., **sìnonimo** synonymous ‖ *pref m & f* syn-, e.g., **sinònimo** synonym

sin *adv*—**sin da** ever since

sinagò·ga *f* (**-ghe**) synagogue

sincerare (**sincèro**) *tr* (lit) to convince ‖ *ref*—**sincerarsi di** to ascertain

sincè·ro -ra *adj* sincere; pure

sinché *conj* until

sìncope *f* fainting spell; (phonet) syncope; (mus) syncopation

sincronismo *m* syncronism; **sincronismo orizzontale** (telv) horizontal hold; **sincronismo verticale** (telv) vertical hold

sincronizzare [ddzz] *tr* to syncronize

sìncro·no -na *adj* syncronous

sindacale *adj* mayoral; union

sindacalismo *m* trade unionism

sindacali·sta *mf* (**-sti -ste**) union member; union leader

sindacare §197 (**sìndaco**) *tr* to criticize; to scrutinize

sindaca·to -ta *adj* controlled, scrutinized || *m* control; labor union; syndicate; **sindacato giallo** company union

sìnda·co *m* (**-ci**) mayor; controller; auditor

sinecura *f* sinecure

sinfonìa *f* symphony; (*of an opera*) overture; (coll) racket (*noise*)

sinfòni·co -ca *adj* (**-ci -che**) symphonic

singhiozzare (**singhiòzzo**) *intr* to sob; to hiccup; to jerk

singhiòzzo *m* sob; hiccups; **a singhiozzo** in jerks; by fits and spurts

singolare *adj* singular || *m* singular; (tennis) singles

sìngo·lo -la *adj* single || *m* individual; shell for one oarsman; (rr) roomette; (telp) private line; (tennis) singles

singulto *m* hiccups; sob

sinistra *f* left hand; left

sinistrare *tr* to ruin; to damage

sinistra·to -ta *adj* injured, damaged, ruined || *mf* victim (*of bombing or flood*)

sinistrismo *m* leftism

sinistri·sta *adj* (**-sti -ste**) leftish, leftist

sini·stro -stra *adj* left; sinister || *m* accident; (boxing) left || *f* see **sinistra**

sinistròlde *adj* & *mf* leftist

sino *adv* var of **fino**

sinologìa *f* Sinology

sinòni·mo -ma *adj* synonymous || *m* synonym

sinò·psi *f* (**-psi**) (mov) synopsis

sinóra *adv* var of **finora**

sinòs·si *f* (**-si**) synopsis

sinòtti·co -ca *adj* (**-ci -che**) synoptic(al)

sintas·si *f* (**-si**) syntax

sinte·si *f* (**-si**) synthesis

sintèti·co -ca *adj* (**-ci -che**) synthetic(al); concise

sintetizzare [ddzz] *tr* to synthesize

sintogram·ma *m* (**-mi**) (rad) dial

sìntomo *m* symptom

sintonìa *f* harmony; (rad) tuning

sintonizzare [ddzz] *tr* (rad) to tune

sintonizzatóre [ddzz] *m* (rad) tuner

sinuó·so -sa [s] *adj* sinuous, winding

sionismo *m* Zionism

sipà·rio *m* (**-ri**) curtain; **sipario di ferro** iron curtain

sirèna *f* siren; mermaid; **sirena da nebbia** foghorn

Sìria, la Syria

siria·no -na *adj* & *mf* Syrian

sirìn·ga *f* (**-ghe**) panpipe; syringe; catheter; grease gun; (orn) syrinx

siringare §209 *tr* to catheterize

siròcchia *f* (obs) sister

si·sma *m* (**-smi**) earthquake

sismògrafo *m* seismograph

sismologìa *f* seismology

sissignóre *adv* yes, Sir!

sistè·ma *m* (**-mi**) system

sistemare (**sistèmo**) *tr* to arrange; to put in order; to systematize; to settle; to find a job for; to find a husband for; (coll) to fix || *ref* to settle; to get married

sistemazióne *f* arrangement; settlement; job, position

sìstole *f* systole

sitibón·do -da *adj* (lit) thirsty

si·to -ta *adj* (lit) located || *m* (lit) site, spot, location; (mil) sight; (coll) musty odor

situare (**sìtuo**) *tr* to locate, place, situate

situazióne *f* situation; condition

slabbrare *tr* to chip; to open (*a wound*) || *intr* to overflow || *ref* to become chipped; to reopen (*said of a cut*)

slacciare §128 *tr* to untie; to unfasten; to unbutton || *ref* to get undone; to get unbuttoned

sladinare *tr* (sports) to train; (mach) to run in, break in

slanciare §128 *tr* to hurl, throw || *ref* to hurl oneself; to rise (*said, e.g., of a tower*)

slancia·to -ta *adj* slender; soaring

slàn·cio *m* (**-ci**) leap; outburst (*of feeling*); momentum; **di slancio** with a rush; **prendere lo slancio** to get a running start

slargare §209 *tr* to widen; to warm (*the heart*) || *ref* to widen, spread out

slattare *tr* to wean

slava·to -ta *adj* pale, washed out

sla·vo -va *adj* Slav, Slavic || *mf* Slav || *m* Slavic (*language*)

sleale *adj* disloyal; unfair (*competition*)

slealtà *f* (**-tà**) disloyalty

slegare §209 (**slégo**) *tr* to untie

slega·to -ta *adj* untied; disconnected

slip *m* (slip) briefs; tank suit, bathing suit (*for men*)

slitta *f* sled, sleigh; (mach) carriage

slittaménto *m* skid; slide

slittare *intr* to sled; to skid; to slide

slogare §209 (**slògo**) *tr* to dislocate || *ref* to become dislocated; to dislocate (*e.g., an arm*)

slogatura *f* dislocation

sloggiare §290 (**slòggio**) *tr* to dislodge; to evict || *intr* to vacate

slòg·gio *m* (**-gi**) moving; eviction

slovac·co -ca *adj* & *mf* (**-chi -che**) Slovak

smacchiare §287 *tr* to clean; to deforest

smacchiatóre -trice *mf* cleaner || *m* cleaning fluid; spot remover

smac·co *m* (**-chi**) letdown; slap in the face

smagliante *adj* dazzling, shining

smagliare §280 *tr* to break the links of; to undo the meshes of; to remove (*a fish*) from the net || *intr* to shine, dazzle || *ref* to run (*said, e.g., of knitted fabric*); to free itself from the net

smagliatura *f* run (*in stockings*); (fig) break

smagrire §176 *tr* to impoverish || *intr* (ESSERE) & *ref* to become thin or lean

smaliziare §287 *tr* to make wiser || *ref* to get wiser

smaltare *tr* to enamel; to glaze

smaltire §176 *tr* to digest; to sleep off (*a drunk*); to swallow (*an offense*);

to sell off; to get rid of; to drain off (*water*)

smalti·tóio *m* (-tói) drain, sewer

smalto *m* enamel; **smalto per le unghie** nail polish

smancerìe *fpl* affectation; mawkishness

smanceró·so -sa [s] *adj* prissy

smangiare §290 *tr* to erode, eat away ‖ *ref* to be consumed (*e.g., by hatred*)

smània *f* frenzy; craze, yearning; **dare in smanie** to be in a frenzy

smaniare §287 *intr* to be delirious; to yearn, crave

smanió·so -sa [s] *adj* eager; disturbing

smantellare (smantèllo) *tr* to dismantle; to demolish; to disable (*a ship*)

smargias·so -sa *mf* braggart, boaster

smarriménto *m* loss; bewilderment; discouragement

smarrire §176 *tr* to lose ‖ *ref* to get lost; to get discouraged

smascellare (smascèllo) *ref*—**smascellarsi dalle risa** to split one's sides laughing

smascherare (smàschero) *tr* & *ref* to unmask

smazzata *f* (cards) deal; (cards) hand

smembraménto *m* dismemberment

smembrare (smèmbro) *tr* to dismember

smemorataggine *f* forgetfulness

smemora·to -ta *adj* absent-minded; forgetful ‖ *mf* absent-minded or forgetful person

smentire §176 *tr* to belie; to refute; to retract; to be untrue to ‖ *ref* to not be consistent, to contradict oneself

smentita *f* denial; retraction

smeraldo *m* emerald

smerciare §128 (smèrcio) *tr* to sell, sell out

smèr·cio *m* (-ci) sale

smèr·go *m* (-ghi) (zool) merganser

smerigliare §280 *tr* to grind, polish; to sand

smeriglia·to -ta *adj* polished; sand (*paper*); emery (*cloth*); frosted (*glass*)

smeri·glio *m* (-gli) emery; (orn) merlin; (ichth) porbeagle

smerlare (smèrlo) *tr* to scallop

smèrlo *m* scallop (*along the edge of a garment*)

smés·so -sa *adj* hand-me-down, castoff

sméttere §198 *tr* to stop; to stop wearing; to break up (*housekeeping*); **smetterla** to cut it out ‖ *intr*—**smettere di** + *inf* to stop + *ger*

smezzare [ddzz] (smèzzo) *tr* to halve

smidollare (smidóllo) *tr* to remove the marrow from; (fig) to emasculate

smilitarizzare [ddzz] *tr* to demilitarize

smil·zo -za *adj* slender; poor, worthless

sminare *tr* to remove mines from

sminuire §176 *tr* to belittle

sminuzzare *tr* to crumble; to mince; to expatiate on ‖ *ref* to crumble

smistaménto *m* sorting (*of mail*); (rr) shunting, shifting

smistare *tr* to sort; (rr) to shift; (soccer) to pass; (rad) to unscramble

smisura·to -ta *adj* immense, huge

smitizzante [ddzz] *adj* debunking, demythologizing

smitizzare [ddzz] *tr* to debunk; to demythologize

smobiliare §287 *tr* to remove the furniture from

smobilitare (smobilíto) *tr* to demobilize

smobilitazióne *f* demobilization

smoccolare (smòccolo & smóccolo) *tr* to snuff (*a candle*) ‖ *intr* (slang) to swear, curse

smoda·to -ta *adj* excessive, immoderate

smòg *m* smog

smóking *m* (smóking) dinner jacket, tuxedo

smontàbile *adj* dismountable

smontàg·gio *m* (-gi) disassembling, dismantling

smontare (smónto) *tr* to take apart; to dismantle; to cause (*e.g., whipped cream*) to fall; to take (*a precious stone*) out of its setting; to dishearten; to dissuade; to drop (*s.o.*) off; **smontare la guardia** to come off guard duty ‖ *intr* (ESSERE) to dismount; to get off or out (*of a conveyance*); to fade; to drop (*said, e.g., of beaten eggs*) ‖ *ref* to become downcast

smòrfia *f* grimace; mawkishness; **fare le smorfie a** to make faces at

smorfió·so -sa [s] *adj* mawkish, prissy

smòr·to, -ta *adj* pale, wan; faded

smorzare (smòrzo) *tr* to attenuate; to lessen; to tone down; to turn off (*light*); (phys) to dampen

smorzatóre *m* (mus) damper

smòs·so -sa *adj* moved; loose

smottaménto *m* mud slide

smozzicare §197 (smózzico) *tr* to crumble; to mince; to clip, mince (*one's words*)

smun·to -ta *adj* emaciated, pale, wan

smuòvere §202 *tr* to budge; to till; (fig) to move ‖ *ref* to budge; to move away; **smuoviti!** get going!

smussare *tr* to blunt; to bevel; (fig) to soften

snaturalizzare [ddzz] *tr* to denaturalize; to denationalize

snaturare *tr* to change the nature of; to distort, misrepresent

snatura·to -ta *adj* distorted; monstrous, unnatural

snebbiare §287 (snébbio) *tr* to drive the fog from; to clear (*e.g., one's mind*)

snellézza *f* slenderness; nimbleness

snellire §176 *tr* & *ref* to slenderize

snèl·lo -la *adj* slender; nimble; lively

snervante *adj* enervating

snervare (snèrvo) *tr* to enervate, prostrate ‖ *ref* to become enervated

snidare *tr* to drive out, flush

snòb *adj invar* snobbish ‖ *mf* (snòb) snob

snobbare (snòbbo) *tr* to snub, slight

snobismo *m* snobbishness, snobbery

snobìsti·co -ca *adj* (-ci -che) snobbish

snocciolare (snòcciolo) *tr* to spill (*a secret*); to peel off (*sums of money*); to pit, stone (*fruit*)

snodare (snòdo) *tr* to untie; to limber up; to exercise; to loosen up (*e.g.,* *s.o.'s tongue*) ‖ *ref* to become loose; to wind (*said, e.g., of a road*)

snòdo *m* (mach) joint; **a snodo** flexible

soave *adj* sweet, gentle

sobbalzare *intr* to jerk, jolt

sobbalzo *m* jerk, jolt; **di sobbalzo** with a jolt

sobbarcare §197 *tr* to overburden ‖ *ref* —**sobbarcarsi a** to take it upon oneself to

sobbór·go *m* (-ghi) suburb

sobillare *tr* to instigate, stir up

sobilla·tóre -trice *mf* instigator

sobrietà *f* sobriety, temperance

sò·brio -bria *adj* sober, temperate; plain

socchiùdere §125 *tr* to half-shut; to leave ajar

socchiu·so -sa [s] *adj* ajar

soccómbere §186 *intr* to succumb

soccórrere §139 *tr* to help ‖ *intr* (lit) to occur

soccórso *m* help, succor; **mancato soccorso** failure to render assistance; hit-and-run driving

sociale *adj* social; company (*e.g., outing*)

socialismo *m* socialism

sociali·sta (-sti -ste) *adj* socialistic ‖ *mf* socialist

sociali·tà *f* (-tà) gregariousness; social responsibility

socie·tà *f* (-tà) society; company; **in società** in partnership; **società anonima** corporation; **società a responsabilità limitata** limited company; **Società delle Nazioni** League of Nations; **società finanziaria** holding company; **società in accomandita** limited partnership; **società per azioni** corporation

sociévole *adj* sociable; gregarious

sò·cio *m* (-ci) member; cardholder; partner; shareholder; **socio fondatore** charter member; **socio sostenitore** patron, sustaining member

sociologìa *f* sociology

sociòlo·go -ga *mf* (-gi -ghe) sociologist

sòda *f* soda

sodalì·zio *m* (-zi) society; brotherhood, fraternity; friendship

soddisfacènte *adj* satisfying, satisfactory

soddisfare §173 (*2d sg pres ind* soddisfài *or* soddisfì; *3d pl pres* soddisfanno *or* soddìsfano; *1st, 2d & 3d sg pres subj* soddisfaccia *or* soddisfì; *3d pl pres subj* soddisfàcciano *or* soddìsfino) *tr* to satisfy ‖ *intr* (with *dat*) to satisfy ‖ *ref* to be satisfied

soddisfat·to -ta *adj* satisfied

soddisfazióne *f* satisfaction

sòdi·co -ca *adj* (-ci -che) sodium

sòdio *m* sodium

sò·do -da *adj* hard; hard-boiled; stubborn; solid; **prenderle sode** to get a good thrashing ‖ *m* hard ground; untilled soil; solid foundation; **venire al sodo** to come to the point; **mettere in sodo** to ascertain ‖ *f* see **soda** ‖ **sodo** *adv* hard

sodomìa *f* sodomy

so·fà *m* (-fà) couch, sofa; **sofà a letto** sofa bed

sofferènte *adj* sickly, ailing; (lit) long-suffering

sofferènza *f* suffering, pain; bad debt; **in sofferenza** overdue

soffermare (soffèrmo) *tr*—**soffermare il passo** to come to a stop ‖ *ref* to linger, pause

soffiare §287 (sóffio) *tr* to blow; to whisper; (checkers) to huff; (coll) to steal ‖ *intr* to blow; to bellow; (slang) to squeal (*about somebody's offense*); **sofflare sul fuoco** to stir up trouble ‖ *ref* to blow (*one's nose*)

soffia·to -ta *adj* blown ‖ *m* soufflé ‖ *f* (slang) squealing, **darsi una soffiata di naso** to blow one's nose

soffiatóre *m* glass blower

sòffice *adj* soft

soffierìa *f* glass factory; blower

soffiétto *m* bellows; hood (*of carriage*); (journ) puff, ballyhoo

sóf·fio *m* (-fi) blow; breath; **in un soffio** in a jiffy; **soffio al cuore** heart murmur

soffióne *m* blowpipe; fumarole; (bot) dandelion; (coll) spy

soffitta *f* attic, garret

soffìtto *m* ceiling

soffocaménto *m* choking

soffocante *adj* stifling; oppressive

soffocare §197 (sòffoco) *tr* to choke; to stifle; to suffocate; to smother; to repress

sòffo·co *m* (-chi) sultriness

soffóndere §178 *tr* (lit) to suffuse

soffregare §209 (soffrégo) *tr* to rub lightly

soffrìggere §180 *tr* to fry lightly ‖ *intr* to mutter

soffrire §207 *tr* to suffer; to endure; **non poter soffrire** to not be able to stand ‖ *intr* to suffer; to ail; **soffrire di** to be troubled with

soffritto *m* fried onions and bacon

sofistica·to -ta *adj* adulterated; sophisticated, studied

sofisti·co -ca *adj* (-ci -che) sophistic; faultfinding ‖ *f* sophistry

soggetti·sta *mf* (-sti -ste) scriptwriter

soggetti·vo -va *adj* subjective

soggèt·to -ta *adj* subject ‖ *m* subject; (coll) character; (law) person; **cattivo soggetto** hoodlum; **recitare a soggetto** to improvise

soggezióne *f* subjection; awe, embarrassment; **mettere a soggezione** to awe

sogghignare *intr* to sneer

soggiacére §181 *intr* (ESSERE & AVERE) to be subject; to succumb

soggiogare §209 (soggiógo) *tr* to subjugate, subdue

soggiornare (soggiórno) *intr* to sojourn, stay

soggiórno *m* sojourn, stay; living room; sitting room (*in hotel*)

soggiùngere §183 *tr* to add

soggólo *m* wimple (*of nun*); throatlatch (*on horse*); (mil) chin strap

sòglia *f* doorsill; threshhold

sògliola *f* sole

sognare (sógno) *tr* to dream of ‖ *intr*

to dream; **sognare ad occhi aperti** to daydream

sogna·tó·re -trice *adj* dreaming || *mf* dreamer

sógno *m* dream; **nemmeno per sogno** (coll) by no means

sòia *f* (bot) soy

sòl *m* (sòl) (mus) sol

so·làio *m* (-lài) attic, loft; (agr) crib

solare *adj* solar; bright; clear || *v* §257 *tr* to sole

solàr·rio *m* (-rî) solarium

solatí·o -a (-i -e) *adj* sunny || *m—a* **solatio** with a southern exposure

solcare §197 (sólco) *tr* to furrow; to plow (*the waves*)

sól·co *m* (-chi) furrow; rut; groove (*of phonograph record*); (fig) path; (naut) wake

solcòmetro *m* (naut) log

soldaté·sco -sca (-schi -sche) *adj* soldier || *f* soldiery; soldiers; undisciplined troops

soldatino *m* toy soldier

soldato *m* soldier; **andare soldato** to enlist; **soldato di ventura** soldier of fortune; **soldato scelto** private first class; **soldato semplice** private

sòldo *m* soldo (*Italian coin*); coin; money; (mil) pay; (fig) penny; **a soldo a soldo** a penny at a time; **al soldo di** in the pay of; **tirare al soldo** to be a tightwad

sóle *m* sun; sunshine; (fig) day, daytime; **sole artificiale** sun lamp; **sole a scacchi** (joc) hoosegow, calaboose

soleggia·to -ta *adj* sunny

solènne *adj* solemn; (joc) first-class

solenni·tà *f* (-tà) solemnity

solennizzare [ddzz] *tr* to solemnize

solére §255 *intr* (ESSERE) + *inf* to be accustomed to + *inf*, e.g., **suole arrivare alle sette** he is accustomed to arrive at seven || *impers* (ESSERE) —**suole** + *inf* it generally + *3d sg ind*, e.g., **suole nevicare** it generally snows

solèrte *adj* (lit) diligent, industrious

solèrzia *f* (lit) diligence

solét·to -ta *adj* (lit) alone, lonely || *f* sole; inner sole; (archit) slab, cement slab

sòlfa *f* (mus) solfeggio; **la solita solfa** the same old story

solfanèllo *m* var of **zofanello**

solfara *f* sulfur mine

solfato *m* sulfate

solfeggiare §290 (solféggio) *tr* to sol-fa

solfìe·ro -ra *adj* sulfur

solfito *m* sulfite

sólfo *m* var of **zòlfo**

solfòri·co -ca *adj* (-ci -che) sulfuric

solforó·so -sa [s] *adj* sulfurous

solfuro *m* sulfide

solidale *adj* solidary; (law) joint; (law) jointly responsible; (mach) built-in; **solidale con** integral with

solidarie·tà *f* (-tà) solidarity; (law) joint liability

solidarizzare [ddzz] *intr* to make common cause, become united

solidificare §197 (solidìfico) *tr* to solidify; to settle

solidi·tà *f* (-tà) solidity; (fig) soundness

sòli·do -da *adj* solid; (law) joint || *m* solid; **in solido** jointly

solilò·quio *m* (-qui) soliloquy

solin·go -ga *adj* (-ghi -ghe) (lit) lonely; (lit) solitary (*enjoying solitude*)

solino *m* detachable collar; **solino duro** stiff collar

soli·sta *mf* (-sti -ste) soloist

solità·rio -ria (-ri -rie) *adj* solitary, lonely || *m* solitaire; solitary

sòli·to -ta *adj* usual, customary; **esser solito** to be accustomed to || *m* habit, custom; **come il solito** as usual; **di solito** usually

solitùdine *f* solitude, loneliness

sollazzare *tr* to amuse || *ref* to have a good time, amuse oneself

sollazzo *m* (lit) amusement; **essere il sollazzo di** to be the laughingstock of

sollecitare (sollécito) *tr* to solicit; to urge; to induce; (mach) to stress || *intr* & *ref* to hasten

sollecitazióne *f* solicitation; urging; (mach) stress

solléci·to -ta *adj* quick, prompt; diligent; solicitous, anxious || *m* (com) solicitation, urging

sollecitùdine *f* solicitude; promptness; diligence; **cortese sollecitudine** (com) prompt attention

solleóne *m* dog days

solleticare §197 (sollético) *tr* to tickle; (fig) to flatter

solléti·co *m* (-chi) tickling; stimulation; **fare il solletico a** to tickle

sollevaménto *m* lifting; **sollevamento di pesi** weight lifting

sollevare (sollèvo) *tr* to lift; to relieve; to pick up; to raise (*e.g., a question*); to excite; to elevate || *ref* to rise; to lift oneself; to pick up (*said of courage or health*)

sollevazióne *f* uprising

sollièvo *m* relief

sollùchero *m—andare in solluchero** to become ecstatic; **mandare in solluchero** to thrill

só·lo -la *adj* lone, lonely, alone; only; single; **fare da solo** to operate all by oneself; **solo soletto** all by myself (yourself, himself, etc.); within oneself; **un solo** only one || *m* (mus) solo || **solo** *adv* only || **solo** *conj* only; **solo che** provided that

solstí·zio *m* (-zi) solstice

soltanto *adv* only

solùbile *adj* soluble

soluzióne *f* solution; installment; **soluzione di comodo** compromise; **soluzione provvisoria** stopgap

solvènte *adj* & *m* solvent

solvènza *f* solvency

solvìbile *adj* collectable; solvent

sòma *f* burden, load

Somàlia, la Somaliland

sòma·lo -la *adj* & *mf* Somali

soma·ro -ra *mf* donkey, ass

someggia·to -ta *adj* carried by pack animal; carried on mule back

somigliante *adj* similar; **essere somigliante a** to look like || *m* same thing

somiglianza *f* similarity, resemblance

somigliare §280 *tr* to resemble; (lit) to compare || *intr* (ESSERE & AVERE) (with *dat*) to resemble; to seem to be || *ref* to resemble each other

sómma *f* addition; sum; summary

sommare (sómmo) *tr* to add; to consider; *tutto sommato* all in all || *intr* to amount

sommà•rio -ria (-ri -rie) *adj* summary || *m* summary; abstract; (journ) subheading

sommèrgere §162 *tr* to submerge; (fig) to plunge; (fig) to flood (*with insults*) || *ref* to submerge

sommergìbile *adj* & *m* submarine

sommés•so -sa *adj* submissive; subdued (*voice*)

somministrare *tr* to administer; to provide; to deliver (*a blow*); to adduce (*proof*)

somministrazióne *f* administration; provision

sommi•tà *f* (**-tà**) summit

sóm•mo -ma *adj* highest; supreme || *m* top; peak, summit || *f* see somma

sommòssa *f* insurrection, riot

sommoviménto *m* tremor (*of earth*); arousal (*of passions*); riot

sommozzatóre *m* skin diver; (nav) frogman

sommuòvere §202 *tr* (lit) to agitate; (lit) to stir up, excite

sonaglièra *f* collar with bells

sonà•glio *m* (**-gli**) bell; rattle; raindrop; pitter-patter (*of the rain*)

sonante *adj* ringing, sounding; ready (*cash*)

sonare §257 *tr* to sound; to play; to strike (*the hour*); to ring (*a bell*); (coll) to dupe, cheat; (coll) to give a sound thrashing to; **sonare le campane a distesa** to ring a full peal || *intr* (ESSERE & AVERE) to play; to ring (*said of a bell*); to sound; (lit) to spread (*said of reputation*)

sona•to -ta *adj* played; past, e.g., *le tre sonate* past three o'clock; *cinquant'anni sonati* past fifty years of age || *f* ring (*of bell*); (mus) sonata; (coll) thrashing; (coll) cheating

sona•tóre -trice *mf* (mus) player

sónda *f* sound; probe; drill

sondàg•gio *m* (**-gi**) sounding; probe; drilling; **sondaggio d'opinioni** opinion survey, public opinion poll

sondare (sóndo) *tr* to sound; to probe; to drill; to survey (*public opinion*)

soneria *f* alarm (*of clock*)

sonétto *m* sonnet

sonnacchió•so -sa [s] *adj* sleepy, drowsy

sonnàmbu•lo -la *mf* sleepwalker

sonnecchiare §287 (sonnécchio) *intr* to drowse, take a nap; to nap, nod

sonnellino *m* nap

sonnìfe•ro -ra *adj* soporific; narcotic || *m* sleeping medicine; narcotic

sónno *m* sleep; (lit) dream; **aver sonno** to be sleepy; **far venir sonno a** to bore; **prender sonno** to fall asleep

sonnolèn•to -ta *adj* sleepy; lazy

sonnolènza *f* drowsiness; laziness

sonori•tà *f* (**-tà**) sonority; acoustics

sonorizzare [ddzz] *tr* to voice; (mov) to dub || *ref* to voice

sonò•ro -ra *adj* sound (*wave*); sonorous; (phonet) sonant, voiced

sontuó•so -sa [s] *adj* sumptuous

sopèr•chio -chia *adj* & *m* (**-chi -chie**) var of soverchio

sopire §176 *tr* to appease, calm

sopóre *m* drowsiness

soporìfe•ro -ra *adj* soporific

soppanno *m* interlining; lining (*of shoes*)

sopperire §176 *intr*—**sopperire a** to provide for; to make up for

soppesare [s] (soppéso) *tr* to heft; (fig) to weigh

soppiantare *tr* to supplant by scheming; to kick out; to replace; to trick

soppiatto *m*—**di soppiatto** stealthily

sopportàbile *adj* bearable, tolerable

sopportare (soppòrto) *tr* to bear, support; to suffer, endure

sopportazióne *f* forbearance, endurance

soppressióne *f* suppression, abolition

sopprìmere §131 *tr* to suppress, do away with

sópra *adj invar* upper; above, preceding || *m* upper, upper part; **al di sopra** above; **al di sopra di** above, over; beyond; **di sopra** upper || *adv* above; up; on top || *prep* on; upon; on top of; over; beyond; above; versus; **sopra pensiero** absorbed in thought

sopràbito *m* overcoat, topcoat

sopraccàri•co -ca (-chi -che) *adj* overburdened || *m* overload; overweight; (naut) supercargo

sopraccenna•to -ta *adj* above-mentioned

sopraccì•glio *m* (**-gli** & **-glia** *fpl*) brow, eyebrow; window frame

sopraccita•to -ta *adj* above-mentioned

sopraccopèrta *f* bedspread; book jacket, dust jacket || *adv* (naut) on deck

sopraddét•to -ta *adj* above-mentioned

sopraffare §173 *tr* to overcome, overpower

sopraffazióne *f* overpowering; abuse

sopraffinèstra *f* transom window

sopraffì•no -na *adj* first-class; superfine

sopraggitto *m* (sew) overcasting

sopraggiùngere §183 *intr* (ESSERE) to arrive; to happen

sopraintèndere §270 *tr* var of soprintendere

sopralluò•go *m* (**-ghi**) inspection, investigation on the spot

sopralzo *m* var of soprelevazione

soprammercato *m*—**per soprammercato** in addition, to boot

soprammòbile *m* knickknack

soprannaturale *adj* & *m* supernatural

soprannóme *m* nickname

soprannominare (soprannòmino) *tr* to nickname

soprannùmero *adj invar* in excess; overtime || *m*—**in soprannumero** extra; in excess

sopra•no -na *adj* upper; (lit) supreme

|| sopra·no *mf* (-ni -ne) soprano (*person*) || *m* soprano (*voice*)
soprappensièro *adj invar & adv* immersed in thought
soprappéso [s] *m*—per soprappeso besides, into the bargain
soprap·più *m* (-più) plus, extra; in soprappiù besides, into the bargain
soprapprèzzo *m* extra charge, surcharge
soprascarpa *f* overshoe
soprascrit·to -ta *adj* written above || *f* address
soprassalto *m* start, jump; di soprassalto with a start
soprassedére §252 *intr* to wait; (with *dat*) to postpone
soprassòldo *m* extra pay; (mil) warzone indemnity
soprastare §263 *intr* (ESSERE) to be the boss
soprattac·co *m* (-chi) rubber heel
soprattassa *f* surtax; surcharge
soprattutto *adv* above all, especially
sopravanzare *tr* to overcome || *intr* (ESSERE) to be left over
sopravanzo *m* surplus
sopravvalutare *tr* to overrate
sopravvenire §282 *tr* (lit) to overrun || *intr* (ESSERE) to arrive; to happen, occur; (with *dat*) to befall
sopravvènto *m* windward; avere il sopravvento to have the upper hand || *adv* windward
sopravvissu·to -ta *adj* surviving || *mf* survivor
sopravvivènza *f* survival
sopravvivere §286 *intr* (ESSERE) to survive; (with *dat*) to survive, to outlive
soprelevare (soprelèvo) *tr* to elevate (*e.g., a railroad*); to increase the height of (*building*)
soprelevazióne *f* elevation; addition of one or more floors
soprintendènte *m* superintendent
soprintendènza *f* superintendency
soprintèndere §270 *tr* to oversee
sopròsso *m* (coll) bony outgrowth
sopruso *m* abuse of power
soqquadro *m*—a soqquadro upside down, topsy-turvy
sòrba *f* sorb apple; (coll) hit, blow
sorbettièra *f* ice-cream freezer
sorbétto *m* ice cream; sherbet
sorbire §176 *tr* to sip; (fig) to swallow, endure
sòrbo *m* sorb; service tree
sór·cio *m* (-ci) mouse
sòrdi·do -da *adj* sordid; dirty
sordina *f* (mus) sordino, mute; (mus) soft pedal; in sordina quietly; stealthily; mettere in sordina (mus) to muffle
sór·do -da *adj* deaf; dull (*pain*); deep-seated (*hatred*); hollow (*sound*); (phonet) surd, voiceless; sordo come una campana stone-deaf || *mf* deaf person
sordomu·to -ta *adj* deaf and dumb || *mf* deafmute
sorèlla *f* sister
sorellastra *f* stepsister

sorgènte *adj* rising || *f* spring; well (*of oil*); (fig) source; sorgente del fiume riverhead
sórgere §258 *intr* (ESSERE) to rise; to arise; to spring forth; sorgere su un'ancora (naut) to lie at anchor
sorgi·vo -va *adj* spring (*water*)
sór·go *m* (-ghi) sorghum
sormontare (sormónto) *tr* to surmount; to overcome || *intr* to fit
sornió·ne -na *adj* cunning, sly || *m* sneak
sorpassare *tr* to get ahead of; to surpass; to overstep; to go above
sorpasso *m* (aut) passing
sorprendènte *adj* surprising, astonishing
sorprèndere §220 *tr* to surprise; to catch; sorprendere la buona fede di to take advantage of || *ref* to be surprised
sorprésa [s] *f* surprise; surprise investigation; di sorpresa suddenly; unprepared; by surprise
sorrèggere §226 *tr* to sustain, support; to bolster
sorridere §231 *tr* (lit) to say with a smile || *intr* to smile; sorridere a to appeal to, e.g., le sorride l'idea di questa gita the idea of this trip appeals to her; to smile upon, e.g., gli sorrideva la vita life was smiling upon him
sorriso [s] *m* smile
sorsata *f* gulp, draught
sorseggiare §290 (sorséggio) *tr* to sip
sórso *m* sip; a sorso a sorso sipping
sòrta *f* kind, sort
sòrte *f* luck, lot, fate; chance; kind; (com) principal; per sorte of each kind; by chance; tirare a sorte to cast lots
sorteggiare §290 (sortéggio) *tr* to choose by lot; to raffle; sorteggiare un premio to draw a prize
sortég·gio *m* (-gi) drawing
sortilè·gio *m* (-gi) sortilege; sorcery, magic
sortire §176 *tr* (lit) to get by lot; (lit) to have (*results*); (lit) to allot || (sòrto) *intr* (ESSERE) to come out (*said, e.g., of a newspaper*); (coll) to be drawn (*by lot*); (coll) to go out; (mil) to make a sally
sortita *f* witticism; (mil) sally, sortie; (theat) appearance
sorvegliante *adj* watchful || *mf* overseer, caretaker; guardian || *m* watchman; foreman
sorveglianza *f* surveillance; supervision
sorvegliare §280 (sorvéglio) *tr* to oversee, watch over; to check, control
sorvolare (sorvólo) *tr* to fly over; to overfly; (fig) to avoid, skip
sorvólo *m* overflight
sò·sia *m* (-sia) double, counterpart
sospèndere §259 *tr* to hang; to suspend; (chem) to prepare a suspension of; (law) to stay
sospensióne *f* suspension; suspense; (law) stay; sospensione cardanica gimbals

sospensò•rio *m* (-ri) jockstrap, supporter

sospé•so -sa [s] *adj* suspended; suspension (*bridge*); in sospeso in suspense; in abeyance || *m* employee who has been disciplined by suspension; (com) pending item

sospettare (sospètto) *tr* to suspect || *intr*—sospettare di to suspect; to fear

sospèt•to -ta *adj* suspected; suspicious || *m* dash; suspicion

sospettó•so -sa [s] *adj* suspicious

sospingere §126 *tr* (fig) to drive; (lit) to push

sospirare *tr* to long for, crave; fare sospirare to keep waiting || *intr* to sigh

sospiro *m* sigh; longing; (lit) breath; a sospiri little by little

sossópra *adv* upside down

sòsta *f* stop; reprieve; (rr) demurrage

sostanti•vo -va *adj & m* substantive

sostanza *f* substance; sostanza grigia gray matter

sostanziale *adj* substantial

sostanzió•so -sa [s] *adj* substantial

sostare (sòsto) *intr* to stop, pause

sostégno *m* prop; (fig) support

sostenére §271 *tr* to support; to sustain; to take (*an examination*); to defend (*a thesis*); to prop up; to stand (*alcohol*); to play (*a role*) || *ref* to support oneself; to hold up (*said, e.g., of a theory*); to take nourishment

sosteni•tóre -trice *mf* backer, supporter

sostentaménto *m* sustenance, support

sostentare (sostènto) *tr* to support, keep || *ref* to feed, eat

sostenu•to -ta *adj* reserved, austere; rising (*prices*); bullish (*market*); starchy (*manner*)

sostituibile *adj* replaceable

sostituire §176 *tr* to replace, substitute for, take the place of; sostituire (*qlco* or *qlcu*) a to substitute (*s.th.* or *s.o.*) for

sostitu•to -ta *adj* acting; associate, assistant || *m* replacement, substitute

sostituzióne *f* replacement, substitution

sostrato *m* substratum

sottàbito *m* slip

sottacére §268 *tr* (lit) to withhold

sottacéto *adj invar* pickled || sottaceti *mpl* pickles

sott'àcqua *adv* underwater

sotta•no -na *adj* lower (*town*) || *f* skirt; petticoat; (eccl) cassock; gettare la sottana alle ortiche to doff the cassock

sottécchi *adv*—di sottécchi stealthily, secretly; guardare di sottécchi to peep, look furtively (at)

sottentrare (sottèntro) *intr* (ESSERE) (with *dat*) to replace

sotterfù•gio *m* (-gi) subterfuge

sottèrra *adv* underground

sotterràne•o -a *adj* subterranean, underground; secret, clandestine || *m* cave, vault; dungeon; underground passage || *f* (rr) subway, underground

sotterrare (sottèrro) *tr* to bury

sottigliézza *f* thinness; subtlety

sottile *adj* thin; subtle; (naut) lightweight || *m*—guardare troppo per il sottile to split hairs

sottilizzare [ddzz] *intr* to quibble

sottintèndere §270 *tr* to understand || *ref* to be understood, be implied

sottinté•so -sa [s] *adj* understood, implied || *m* innuendo

sótto *adj invar* lower || *m* lower part || *adv* under; underneath; al di sotto below; al di sotto di under, below; di sotto lower; underneath; downstairs; di sotto a under, below; farsi sotto to sneak up; metter sotto to run over (*with a vehicle*); sotto a under; sotto di under || *prep* under; beneath; below; just before; prendere sotto gamba to underestimate; sotto braccio arm in arm; sotto carico (naut) being loaded; sotto i baffi up one's sleeve; sotto le armi in the service; sotto mano within reach; sotto voce under one's breath, sotto-voce

sottoascèl•la *m* (-la) underarm pad

sottobanco *adv* under the counter

sottobicchière *m* coaster

sottobò•sco *m* (-schi) underbrush, thicket

sottobràccio *adv* arm in arm

sottòcchio *adv* under one's eyes

sottoccupa•to -ta *adj* underemployed

sottochiave *adv* under lock and key

sottocó•da *m* (-da) crupper

sottocommissióne *f* subcommittee

sottocopèrta *adv* (naut) below decks

sottocòp•pa *m* (-pa) mat; coaster; (aut) oil pan

sottocòsto *adj invar & adv* below cost

sottocutàne•o -a *adj* subcutaneous

sottofà•scia *m* (-scia) wrapper; spedire sottofascia to mail (*a newspaper*) in a wrapper || *f* (-sce) wrapper (*for cigars*)

sottogamba *adv* lightly; prendere sottogamba to underestimate

sottogó•la *m & f* (-la) chin strap; throatlatch (*of harness*)

sottolineare (sottolíneo) *tr* to underline, underscore; to emphasize

sott'òlio *adv* in oil

sottomano *m* writing pad || *adv* underhand; within reach

sottomari•no -na *adj & m* submarine

sottomés•so -sa *adj* conquered; subdued; submissive

sottométtere §198 *tr* to subdue, crush; to defer, postpone; to present (*a bill*); to subject || *ref* to submit, yield

sottomissióne *f* submission

sottopan•cia *m* (-cia) bellyband, girth

sottopassàg•gio *m* (-gi) underpass; lower level (*of highway*)

sottopiatto *m* saucer

sottopórre §218 *tr* to subject; to submit || *ref* to submit; sottoporsi a to submit to; to undergo (*e.g., an operation*)

sottopó•sto -sta *adj* subject; exposed || *m* subordinate

sottoprèzzo *adj invar* cut-rate || *adv* at a cut rate

sottoprodótto *m* by-product

sottórdine *m* suborder; **in sottórdine** secondary

sottoscà·la *m* (**-la**) space under the stairs; closet under the stairs

sottoscrit·to -ta *adj & mf* undersigned

sottoscrit·tóre -trice *mf* subscriber

sottoscrìvere §250 *tr* to subscribe; to sign, undersign; to underwrite || *intr* to subscribe

sottoscrizióne *f* subscription

sottosegretà·rio *m* (**-ri**) undersecretary

sottosópra *adj invar* upset; **mettere sottosopra** to upset; to turn upside down || *m* confusion, disorder || *adv* upside down

sottostante *adj* lower; subordinate || *m* subordinate

sottostare §263 *intr* (ESSERE) to be located below; to be subject; to yield, submit; (with *dat*) to undergo (*e.g., an examination*)

sottosuòlo *m* subsoil; cellar

sottosvilùppa·to -ta *adj* underdeveloped

sottotenènte *m* second lieutenant; **sottotenente di vascello** (nav) lieutenant j.g.

sottotèr·ra *m* (**-ra**) basement || *adv* underground

sottotétto *m* attic, garret

sottotìtolo *m* subtitle; (mov) caption

sottovalutare *tr* to underrate

sottovènto *m & adv* leeward

sottovèste *f* slip (*undergarment*)

sottovóce *adv* sotto voce, under one's breath

sottrarre §273 *tr* to subtract; **sottrarre a** to take away from, steal from || *ref*—**sottrarsi a** to avoid; to escape from

sottrazióne *f* subtraction

sottufficiale *m* noncommissioned officer

sovènte *adv* often

soverchiante *adj* overwhelming

soverchiare §287 (sovèrchio) *tr* to overwhelm; to excel; to bully; (lit) to overflow || *intr* to be in excess

soverchia·tóre -trice *adj* overbearing || *mf* overbearing person, oppressor

sovèr·chio -chia (**-chi -chie**) *adj* excessive; overbearing || *m* overbearing action

sovè·scio *m* (**-sci**) plowing under (*of green manure*)

soviètti·co -ca (**-ci -che**) *adj* Soviet || *mf* Soviet citizen

sovrabbondante *adj* superabundant

sovrabbondare (sovrabbóndo) *intr* (ESSERE & AVERE) to be superabundant; to go to excesses

sovraccaricare §197 (sovraccàrico) *tr* to overload

sovraccàri·co -ca (**-chi -che**) *adj* overburdened || *m* overload; overweight

sovraespó·sto -sta *adj* overexposed

sovraggiùngere §183 *intr* (ESSERE) var of sopraggiungere

sovralimentazióne *f* (aut) supercharging

sovrani·tà *f* (**-tà**) sovereignty

sovra·no -na *adj & mf* sovereign

sovrappopolare (sovrappòpolo) *tr* to overpopulate

sovrappórre §218 *tr* to overlay; to superimpose; **sovrapporre qlco a** to lay s.th on || *ref* to be superimposed; to be added; **sovrapporsi a** to put oneself above

sovrapproduzióne *f* overproduction

sovrastampa *f* overprint

sovrastante *adj* overlooking, overhanging; impending

sovrastare *tr* to tower over; to hang over; to surpass; to excel || *intr* (ESSERE & AVERE)—**sovrastare a** to tower over; to overlook; to hang over; to surpass; to excel

sovratensióne *f* (elec) surge

sovreccitare (sovrèccito) *tr* to overexcite

sovrespórre §218 *tr* to overexpose

sovrimpòsta *f* surtax

sovrimpressióne *f* double exposure

sovruma·no -na *adj* superhuman

sovvenire §282 *tr* (lit) to help || *intr* (with *dat*) (lit) to help || *impers* (ESSERE)—**sovviene** (with *dat*) **di** remember, *e.g.*, **gli sovviene spesso dei suoi cari** he often remembers his dear ones || *ref*—**sovvenirsi di** to remember

sovvenzionare (sovvenzióno) *tr* to subsidize, grant a subvention to

sovvenzióne *f* subsidy, subvention

sovversi·vo -va *adj & m* subversive

sovvertire (sovvèrto) *tr* to subvert

sóz·zo -za *adj* dirty, filthy, foul

sozzura *f* dirt, filth

spaccalé·gna *m* (**-gna**) woodcutter

spaccamón·ti *m* (**-ti**) braggart

spaccaòs·sa *m* (**-sa**) butcher's cleaver

spaccare §197 *tr* to break, burst; to crack; to unpack; to chop; to split || *ref* to crack; to break; to split

spacca·to -ta *adj* broken; split; (coll) identical; (coll) true || *f* (sports, theat) splits

spaccatura *f* break; crack; cleavage; split

spacchétto *m* vent (*in jacket*)

spacciare §128 *tr* to sell out; to palm off; to spread (*reports*); to expedite; to abandon (*as hopeless*); (slang) to push (*e.g., dope*) || *ref*—**spacciarsi per** to pretend to be, pass oneself off as

spaccia·to -ta *adj* (coll) cooked, done for; (coll) hopeless

spaccia·tóre -trice *mf* passer (*of bad currency or stolen goods*); **spacciatore di notizie false** gossipmonger

spàc·cio *m* (**-ci**) sale; passing (*of counterfeit money*); spreading (*of false news*); post exchange; tobacco shop

spac·co *m* (**-chi**) break; split; tear; crack; vent (*in jacket*)

spacconata *f* brag, braggadocio

spaccó·ne -na *mf* braggart, braggadocio

spada *f* sword; **a spada tratta** doggedly; **spade** suit of Neapolitan cards corresponding to spades

spadaccino *m* swordsman; swashbuckler

spadóne *m* two-handed sword

spadroneggiare §290 (**spadronéggio**) *intr* to be domineering or bossy

spaesa·to -ta *adj* out-of-place

spaghétto *m* (coll) fear, jitters; **avere lo spaghetto** (coll) to be scared stiff; **spaghetti** spaghetti

Spagna, la Spain

spagnòla *f* Spanish woman; Spanish influenza

spagnolétta *f* espagnolette; spool; (coll) cigarette; (coll) peanut

spagnò·lo -la *adj* Spanish || *m* Spaniard (*individual*); Spanish (*language*); **gli spagnoli** the Spanish || *f* see **spagnola**

spa·go *m* (-ghi) string, twine; (coll) fear, jitters

spaiare §287 *tr* to break a pair of

spaia·to -ta *adj* unmatched

spalancare §197 *tr* to open wide || *ref* to open up; to gape

spalare *tr* to shovel; to feather (*oar*)

spalla *f* shoulder; back; abutment (*of bridge*); (theat) stooge, straight man; **alle spalle di qlcu** behind s.o.'s back; **a spalla** on one's back; **fare spalla a** to help; **lavorare di spalle** to elbow one's way; (fig) to worm one's way up; **vivere alle spalle di** to sponge on

spalliàrm *interj* (mil) shoulder arms!

spallata *f* push with the shoulder; shrug of the shoulders

spalleggiare §290 (**spalléggio**) *tr* to back, support; (mil) to carry on one's back

spallétta *f* parapet, retaining wall; jamb

spallièra *f* back (*of chair*); head (*of bed*); foot (*of bed*); espalier

spallina *f* epaulet; shoulder strap

spallùccia *f*—**fare spallucce** to shrug one's shoulders

spalmare *tr* to spread; to smear

spalto *m* glacis; **spalti** seats (*of a stadium*)

spanare *tr* to strip the thread of || *ref* to be stripped (*said, e.g., of the thread of a nut*)

spanciare §128 *tr* to disembowel, gut || *intr* to belly-flop; to bulge (*said of a wall*) || *ref*—**spanciarsi dalle risa** to split one's sides laughing

spanciata *f* belly flop; bellyful; **fare una spanciata** to stuff oneself

spàndere §260 *tr* to spread; to spill; to shed (*tears*); to squander || *ref* to spread

spanna *f* span

spannare *tr* to skim (*milk*)

spannocchiare §287 (**spannòcchio**) *tr* to husk (*corn*)

spappolare (**spàppolo**) *tr* to crush, squash || *ref* to become mushy

sparadrappo *m* adhesive tape; (obs) plaster, poultice

sparagnare *tr* (coll) to save

sparare *tr* to gut, disembowel; to shoot; to let go with (*a kick*); to remove

the hangings from; **spararne delle grosse** to tell tall tales

sparato *m* shirt front, dickey

sparatòria *f* shooting

sparecchiare §287 (**sparécchio**) *tr* to clear (*the table*); to clear away (*one's tools*); to eat up

sparég·gio *m* (-gi) disparity; deficit; (sports) play-off

spàrgere §261 *tr* to spread; to shed; to spill || *ref* to spread

spargiménto *m* spreading; **spargimento di sangue** bloodshed

spargisa·le [s] *m* (-le) salt shaker

sparigliare §280 *tr* to break a pair of; to break (*a set*)

spariglia·to -ta *adj* unmatched

sparire §176 *intr* (ESSERE) to disappear

sparlare *intr* to backbite; **sparlare di** to backbite, slander

sparo *m* shot

sparpagliare §280 *tr* & *intr* to scatter

spar·so -sa *adj* scattered; dotted; speckled; hanging loosely (*e.g., hair*)

sparta·no -na *adj* & *mf* Spartan

spartiàc·que *m* (-que) watershed

spartiné·ve *m* (-ve) snowplow

spartire §176 *tr* to divide, share; to separate; **non aver nulla da spartire con** to have nothing to do with

spartito *m* (mus) score; (mus) arrangement

spartitràffi·co *m* (-co) median strip

spar·to -ta *adj* (lit) spread || *m* esparto grass

sparu·to -ta *adj* lean, wan; meager

sparvière *m* sparrow hawk; mortarboard

spasimante *m* (joc) lover, wooer

spasimare (**spàsimo**) *intr* to writhe; **spasimare per** to long for; to be madly in love with

spàsimo *m* pang; severe pain; longing

spasmo *m* spasm

spasmòdi·co -ca *adj* (-ci -che) spasmodic

spassare *tr* to amuse || *ref*—**spassarsela** to have a good time

spassiona·to -ta *adj* dispassionate, unbiased

spasso *m* fun, amusement; walk; (coll) funny guy; **andare a spasso** to go out for a walk; **essere a spasso** to be out of a job; **mandare a spasso** to fire, dismiss; to get rid of; **per spasso** for fun; **portare a spasso** to lead by the nose; **prendersi spasso di** to make fun of

spassó·so -sa [s] *adj* amusing, droll

spàsti·co -ca *adj* & *mf* spastic

spato *m* spar

spatofluòre *m* fluorspar

spàtola *f* spatula; putty knife; slapstick (*of harlequin*)

spauràc·chio *m* (chi) scarecrow; bugaboo, bugbear

spaurare *tr* & *ref* (lit) var of **spaurire**

spaurire §176 *tr* to frighten || *ref* to be scared

spaval·do -da *adj* bold, swaggering

spaventapàs·seri *m* (-ri) scarecrow

spaventare (spavènto) *tr* to scare, frighten || *ref* to be scared

spaventévole *adj* frightening, dreadful

spavènto *m* fright, fear

spavento·so -sa [s] *adj* frightful, fearful

spaziale *adj* space

spaziare §287 *tr* (typ) to space || *intr* to soar; to range, rove (*said, e.g., of eye*)

spazia·tóre -trice *adj* spacing || *f* space bar (*of typewriter*)

spaziatura *f* spacing

spazientire §176 *tr* to make (*s.o.*) lose his patience || *intr* (ESSERE) & *ref* to lose patience

spà·zio *m* (-zi) space; (fig) room; **spazio aereo** air space; **spazio cosmico** outer space

spazió·so -sa [s] *adj* spacious, roomy; wide

spazzacamino *m* chimney sweep

spazzami·ne *m* (-ne) mine sweeper

spazzané·ve *m* (-vè) snowplow

spazzare *tr* to sweep; to plow (*snow*); to clean up

spazzata *f*—**dare una spazzata a** to give a lick and a promise to

spazzatrice *f* street sweeper

spazzatura *f* sweeping; sweepings; rubbish, trash

spazzatu·ràio *m* (-rài) or **spazzino** *m* street cleaner; trashman, garbage collector, trash collector

spàzzola *f* brush; **capelli a spazzola** crew cut

spazzolare (spàzzolo) *tr* to brush

spazzolino *m* little brush; (elec) brush; **spazzolino da denti** toothbrush; **spazzolino per le unghie** nailbrush

spazzolóne *m* push broom

specchiare §287 (spècchio) *tr* (lit) to reflect || *ref* to look at oneself (*in a mirror*); to be reflected; **specchiarsi in qlcu** to model oneself on s.o.

specchièra *f* mirror; dressing table; full-length mirror

specchiétto *m* mirror; synopsis; **specchietto retrovisivo** (aut) rear-view mirror

spèc·chio *m* (-chi) mirror; synopsis; shore (*of lake or river*); panel (*of door or window*); sheet (*of water*); (sports) goal line; (sports) board; **specchio di poppa** (naut) transom; **specchio ustorio** burning glass

speciale *adj* special

speciali·sta *mf* (-sti -ste) specialist

speciali·tà *f* (-tà) specialty; (mil) special services; **specialità farmaceutica** patent or proprietary medicine

specializzare [ddzz] *tr* & *ref* to specialize

spè·cie *f* (-cie) species; kind, sort; appearance, semblance; **fare specie** (with *dat*) (coll) to be surprised, e.g., **gli fa specie** he is surprised; **in specie** especially; **sotto specie di** under pretext of

specifi·ca *f* (-che) itemized list; specification

specificare §197 (specìfico) *tr* to specify; to itemize

specìfi·co -ca (-ci -che) *adj* & *m* specific || *f* see **specifica**

specillo *m* (med) probe

speció·so -sa [s] *adj* specious

spè·co *m* (-chi) (lit) cave

spècola *f* observatory

spècolo *m* (med, surg) speculum

speculare (spèculo) *tr* to observe; to meditate on || *intr* to speculate

specula·tóre -trice *adj* speculating || *mf* speculator; **speculatore al rialzo** bull; **speculatore al ribasso** bear

speda·to -ta *adj* footworn

spedire §176 *tr* to expedite; to prepare; to ship, send, forward; (law) to deliver

spedi·to -ta *adj* rapid; free, easy

spedi·tóre -trice *mf* shipper, sender; shipping clerk

spedizióne *f* shipment, shipping; sending, forwarding; expedition; (naut) papers; **di spedizione** expeditionary

spedizionière *m* shipper, forwarder, forwarding agent

spègnere §262 *tr* to extinguish, put out; to turn off; to slake (*lime*); to kill; to mix (*flour*) with water or milk; to quench; to obliterate (*a memory*) || *ref* to burn out; to go out (*said of a light*); to fade, die away; to die

spegni·tóio *m* (-tói) snuffer

spegnitura *f* (theat) blackout

spelacchiare §287 *tr* to strip of hair || *ref* to shed hair or fur

spelacchia·to -ta *adj* mangy; (pej) baldy

spelare (spélo) *tr* to strip of hair; to pluck (*e.g., a chicken*); (fig) to fleece || *ref* to shed hair or fur; to get bald

spellare (spèllo) *tr* to skin; (fig) to skin, fleece

spelón·ca *f* (-che) cave; hovel, den

spème *f* (poet) hope

spendacció·ne -na *mf* spendthrift

spèndere §220 *tr* to spend

spenderéc·cio -cia *adj* (-ci -ce) spendthrift, prodigal

spennacchiare §287 *tr* to pluck; (fig) to fleece || *ref* to lose its feathers

spennare (spénno) *tr* & *ref* var of **spennacchiare**

spennellare (spennèllo) *tr* to dab

spensieratézza *f* thoughtlessness

spensiera·to -ta *adj* thoughtless, careless; carefree, happy-go-lucky

spèn·to -ta *adj* extinguished; turned off; slaked (*lime*); dull (*color*); low (*tone*)

spenzolare [dz] (spènzolo) *tr* & *intr* to hang || *ref*—**spenzolarsi da** to hang out of

speranza *f* hope; prospect, expectation

speranzó·so -sa [s] *adj* hopeful

sperare (spèro) *tr* to candle (*eggs*); to hope for; to expect || *intr* to hope; to trust

spèrdere §212 *tr* (lit) to scatter; (lit) to lose (*one's way*) || *ref* to lose one's way, get lost

sperdu·to -ta *adj* lost, astray; godforsaken (*place*)

sperequazióne *f* disproportion; inequality; unjust distribution

spergiurare *tr & intr* to swear falsely; **giurare e spergiurare** to swear over and over again

spergiu·ro -ra *adj* perjured ‖ *mf* perjurer ‖ *m* perjury

spericola·to -ta *adj* reckless, daring

sperimentale *adj* experimental

sperimentare (speriménto) *tr* to test, try out; to experience

sperimenta·to -ta *adj* experienced

spèr·ma *m* (-**mi**) sperm

speronare (speróno) *tr* (naut) to ram

speróne *m* spur; abutment; (nav) ram

sperperare (spèrpero) *tr* to squander

spèrpero *m* squandering

spèr·so -sa *adj* lost, stray

spertica·to -ta *adj* too long; too tall; exaggerated, excessive

spésa [**s**] *f* expense; shopping; buy, purchase; **fare la spesa** to shop; **fare le spese di** to be the butt of; **lavorare per le spese** to work for one's keep; **pagare le spese** to bear the charges; **spese** expenses; room and board; **spese di manutenzione** upkeep; **spese minute** petty expenses; **spese processuali** (law) costs

spesare [**s**] (**spéso**) *tr* to support

spesa·to -ta [**s**] *adj* with all expenses paid

spès·so -sa *adj* thick; many (*times*) ‖ **spesso** *adv* often; **spesso spesso** again and again

spessóre *m* thickness

spettàbile *adj* esteemed; **Spettabile Ditta** (com) Gentlemen

spettàcolo *m* spectacle, show; sight; **dar spettacolo di sé** to make a show of oneself; **spettacolo all'aperto** outdoor performance

spettacoló·so -sa [**s**] *adj* spectacular; (coll) exceptional; (coll) sensational

spettanza *f* concern; pay

spettare (spètto) *intr* (ESSERE)—**spettare a** to belong to ‖ *impers* (ESSERE) —**spetta a** it behooves, it is up to

spetta·tóre -trice *mf* spectator, bystander; **spettatori** public, audience

spettegolare (spettégolo) *intr* to gossip

spettinare (spèttino) *tr* to muss the hair of

spettrale *adj* ghost-like; spectral

spèttro *m* specter, ghost; spectrum

speziale *m* dealer in spices; (coll) pharmacist

spèzie *fpl* spices

spezieria *f* grocery; (coll) drug store, pharmacy; **spezierie** spices

spezzare (spèzzo) *tr* to break; to smash; to interrupt ‖ *ref* to break

spezzatino *m* stew; **spezzatini** change

spezza·to -ta *adj* broken; fragmentary; interrupted ‖ *m* stew; (theat) set piece; **spezzati** change

spezzettare (spezzétto) *tr* to mince

spezzóne *m* small aerial bomb; fragmentation bomb; fragment

spìa *f* spy; indication; peephole; (aut) gauge; (aut) pilot light; **fare la spia** to be an informer

spiacccicare §197 (**spiàccico**) *tr* to squash, crush ‖ *ref* to be squashed

spiacènte *adj* sorry; (lit) disliked

spiacére §214 *intr* (ESSERE) (with *dat*) to dislike, e.g., **queste parole gli spiacciono** he dislikes these words; to mind, e.g., **se non Le spiace** if you don't mind ‖ *ref*—**spiacersi di** to be sorry for ‖ *impers* (ESSERE) (with *dat*)—**gli spiace** he is sorry

spiacévole *adj* unpleasant

spiàg·gia *f* (-**ge**) beach, shore

spianare *tr* to grade (*land*); to roll (*dough*); to pave (*the way*); to iron (*pleats*); to raze, demolish; to level (*a gun*); **spianare la fronte** to smooth one's brow ‖ *intr* (ESSERE) to be level

spianata *f* esplanade; **dare una spianata a** to level

spianatóia *f* board (*for rolling dough*)

spiana·tóio *m* (-**tói**) rolling pin

spianatrice *f* grader

spiano *m* leveling; esplanade; **a tutto spiano** at full blast; continuously

spiantare *tr* to uproot; to raze, level; to ruin (*financially*) ‖ *ref* to ruin oneself

spianta·to -ta *adj* ruined ‖ *m* pauper

spiare §119 *tr* to spy on; to keep an eye on

spiattellare (spiattèllo) *tr* to blurt out

spiazzo *m* square; plain; clearing

spiccare §197 *tr* to detach; to pick; to enunciate; to begin; to draw up (*a commercial paper*); to issue (*a warrant*); **spiccare il volo** (aer) to take off ‖ *intr* to stand out ‖ *ref* to separate (*said, e.g., of the stone of a peach*)

spicca·to -ta *adj* clear, distinct; typical; outstanding

spìc·chio *m* (-**chi**) section (*of fruit*); clove (*of garlic*); slice (*e.g., of apple*); arm (*of cross*)

spicciare §128 *tr* to clear up; to wait on; to dispatch (*business*) ‖ *intr* (ESSERE) to flow forth, gush out ‖ *ref* to hurry up, make haste

spicciati·vo -va *adj* expeditious, quick; straightforward; gruff

spiccicare §197 (**spìccico**) *tr* to unglue; to enunciate; to utter ‖ *ref* to come unglued; **spiccicarsi di** to get rid of

spìc·cio -cia (-**ci -ce**) *adj* expeditious, quick; unhampered; small (*change*) ‖ **spicci** *mpl* change

spicciolata *adj fem*—**alla spicciolata** little by little; a few at a time

spìccio·lo -la *adj* small (change); (coll) plain ‖ **spiccioli** *mpl* small change

spìc·co -ca (-**chi -che**) *adj* freestone (*e.g., peach*) ‖ *m*—**fare spicco** to stand out

spidocchiare §287 (**spidòcchio**) *tr* to delouse

spièdo *m* spit; **allo spiedo** barbecued

spiegàbile *adj* explainable

spiegaménto *m* (mil) array; (mil) deployment

spiegare §209 (**spiègo**) *tr* to unfold; to let go (*with one's voice*); to unfurl; to spread (*wings*); to deploy (*troops*); to explain; to show, demonstrate; **spiegare il volo** (aer) to take off ‖ *ref* to become unfurled or unfolded;

to make oneself understood; to come to an understanding; to realize

spiega•to -ta *adj* open; full (*voice*)

spiegazióne *f* explanation

spiegazzare *tr* to crumple, rumple

spieta•to -ta *adj* pitiless, ruthless

spifferare (**spiffero**) *tr* (coll) to blurt out || *intr* to blow in (*said of wind*)

spiffero *m* (coll) draft

spi•ga *f* (**ghe**) panicle (*of oats*); (bot) ear, spike; **a spiga** herringbone

spiga•to -ta *adj* herringbone

spighétta *f* braid; (bot) spikelet

spigionare (**spigióno**) *ref* to be or become vacant

spiglia•to -ta *adj* easy, free and easy

spi•go *m* (**-ghi**) lavender

spigolare (**spigolo**) *tr* to glean

spigola•tóre -trice *mf* gleaner

spigolo *m* corner; edge; (archit) arris

spilla *f* brooch, pin; **spilla da cravatta** tiepin; **spilla di sicurezza** safety pin

spillare *tr* to draw off, tap; to wheedle, worm (*money*) || *intr* to leak (*said of container*) || *intr* (ESSERE) to leak (*said of liquid*)

spillàti•co *m* (**-ci**) (law) pin money (*for one's wife*)

spillo *m* pin; gimlet; trifle; **a spillo** spikelike; **spillo da balia** or **di sicurezza** safety pin

spillóne *m* hatpin; bodkin

spilluzzicare §197 (**spilluzzico**) *tr* to pick at, nibble; to scrape together

spilorcería *f* stinginess

spilòr•cio -cia (**-ci -ce**) *adj* stingy || *mf* miser, tightwad

spilungó•ne -na *mf* lanky person

spina *f* thorn; quill, spine (*of porcupine*); bone (*of fish*); (fig) preoccupation, worry; **alla spina** (*beer*) on tap; **a spina di pesce** herringbone (*fabric*); **con una spina nel cuore** sick at heart; **essere sulle spine** to be on pins and needles; **spina della botte** tap; bunghole; **spina dorsale** spinal column; (fig) backbone; **spina elettrica** plug

spinà•cio *m* (**-ci**) spinach (*plant*); **spinaci** spinach (*as food*)

spinapésce *m—a* **spinapesce** herringbone

spina•to -ta *adj* barbed (*wire*); herringbone (*fabric*)

spìngere §126 *tr* to push, press; to prod, goad || *ref* to push; to reach

spi•no -na *adj* thorny || *m* thorn || *f* see **spina**

spinóne *m* griffon

spinó•so -sa [s] *adj* thorny

spinòtto *m* wrist pin

spinta *f* push; pressure; poke, prod; stress

spinterògeno *m* (aut) distributor unit; ignition system

spin•to -ta *adj* pushed; bent, inclined; (coll) risqué; (coll) far-out, offbeat || *f* see **spinta**

spintóne *m* (coll) push, shove

spionag•gio *m* (**-gi**) espionage, spying

spioncino *m* peephole

spió•ne -na *mf* spy, stool pigeon

spiovènte *adj* drooping; sloping; falling || *m* slope; drainage area (*of a mountain*)

spiòvere §216 *intr* to fall, to hang down (*said, e.g., of hair*); to flow down || *impers* (ESSERE)—**è spiovuto** it stopped raining

spira *f* turn (*of a coil*); coil (*of serpent*); **a spire** spiral

spirà•glio *m* (**-gli**) small opening; gleam (*of light or hope*)

spirale *adj* spiral || *f* spiral; hairspring; wreath (*of smoke*); **spirale di fumo** smoke ring

spirare *tr* to send forth; (lit) to inspire, infuse; (lit) to show (*kindness*) || *intr* to blow; to emanate; to die; to expire

spirita•to -ta *adj* possessed; wild, mad

spiríti•co -ca *adj* (**-ci -che**) spiritual; spiritualistic

spiritismo *m* spiritualism

spirito *m* spirit; wit; mind; spirits, alcohol; sprite; **bello spirito** wit (*person*); **fare dello spirito** to be witty; to crack jokes; **l'ultimo spirito** (lit) one's last breath; **spirito di corpo** esprit de corps; **spirito di parte** partisanship; **spirito sportivo** sportsmanship

spiritosàggine [s] *f* witticism

spiritó•so -sa [s] *adj* witty; alcoholic

spirituale *adj* spiritual

spizzi•co *m* (**-chi**)—**a spizzico** or **a spizzichi** little by little; **a little at a time**

splendènte *adj* resplendent, shining

splèndere §281 *intr* (ESSERE & AVERE) to shine

splèndi•do -da *adj* splendid; gorgeous; bright || *m*—**fare lo splendido** to be a big spender

splendóre *m* splendor; brightness; beauty

splène *m* (anat) spleen

spòcchia *f* haughtiness

spodestare (**spodèsto**) *tr* to dispossess; to dethrone; to oust

spoetizzare [ddzz] *tr* to disillusion

spòglia *f* slough (*of snake*); skin (*of onion*); husk (*of corn*); (lit) body; (lit) outer garment; **sotto mentite spoglie** under false pretense; **spoglie** spoils

spogliare §280 (**spòglio**) *tr* to undress, strip; to strip of armor; to defraud, deprive; to free; to check, examine; to husk (*corn*); to go through (*e.g., correspondence*) || *ref* to undress; to slough (*said, e.g., of a snake*); **spogliarsi di** to get rid of; to divest oneself of; to shake (*a habit*)

spogliarelli•sta *f* (**-ste**) stripteaser

spogliarèllo *m* striptease

spoglia-tóio *m* (**-tói**) dressing room; locker room

spò•glio -glia (**-gli -glie**) *adj* stripped, bare; free || *m* cast-off clothing; sorting; scrutiny; counting (*of votes*); **di spoglio** second-hand (*material*) || *f* see **spoglia**

spòla *f* bobbin; shuttle; **fare la spola** to shuttle

spolétta *f* bobbin, spool; (mil) fuse

spolmonare (spolmóno) *ref* (coll) to talk, sing, or shout oneself hoarse

spolpare (spólpo) *tr* to gnaw (*a bone*); to eat up (*fruit*); (fig) to fleece

spolverare (spólvero) *tr* to dust off, whisk; to powder, dust; to pounce

spolveratura *f* dusting; powdering; sprinkling, smattering (*of knowledge*); **dare una spolveratura a** to brush up on

spolverina *f* (coll) duster

spolverino *m* duster, smock; powder-sugar duster; pounce; (coll) whisk broom

spolverizzaménto [ddzz] *m* sprinkling (*with powder*)

spolverizzare [ddzz] *tr* to dust, powder, pounce

spólvero *m* dusting; powdering; pounce; smattering, sprinkling (*of knowledge*); display

spónda *f* bank (*of river*); side; cushion (*of billiard table*)

sponsale *adj* (lit) wedding || **sponsali** *mpl* (lit) wedding

spontàne·o -a *adj* spontaneous; artless

spopolare (spòpolo) *tr* to depopulate || *intr* to be a hit; to become depopulated or deserted

spoppare (spóppo) *tr* to wean

sporàdi·co -ca *adj* (-ci -che) sporadic

sporcacció·ne -na *adj* filthy || *mf* filthy person; (fig) dirty mouth

sporcare §197 (spòrco) *tr* to dirty; to soil || *ref* to get dirty; to soil oneself; **sporcarsi la fedina** (coll) to get a black mark on one's record

sporcizia *f* dirt, filth

spòr·co -ca (-chi -che) *adj* dirty, filthy; foul; **farla sporca** to pull a dirty trick || *m* dirt, filth

sporgènte *adj* leaning; protruding; beetle (*brow*)

sporgènza *f* prominence, projection

spòrgere §217 *tr* to stick out; to stretch out; to lodge (*a complaint*) || *intr* (ESSERE) to project, jut out || *ref* to lean out

spòrt *m* (spòrt) sport; game; **per sport** for fun, for pleasure

spòrta *f* shopping bag; bagful; basket; basketful; shopping; **a sporta** wide-brimmed (*hat*)

sportèllo *m* door; panel; window (*in bank, station, etc.*); wicket; branch (*of a bank*); (theat) box office

sportivi·tà *f* (-tà) sportsmanship

sporti·vo -va *adj* sporting; sportsman-like; athletic || *m* sportsman

spòr·to -ta *adj* projecting; jutting out || *m* projection; removable shutter (*on store door or window*) || *f* see **sporta**

spòsa *f* bride; wife; **andare in sposa a** to get married to; **sposa promessa** fiancée

sposali·zio -zia (-zi -zie) *adj* (lit) nuptial || *m* wedding

sposare (spòso) *tr* to marry; to unite; to embrace (*a cause*); to fit perfectly; to give in marriage || *ref* to get married, marry

spòso *m* bridegroom; **sposi** newlyweds

spossare (spòsso) *tr* to exhaust || *ref* to become worn out

spossatézza *f* exhaustion

spostaménto *m* shift; movement; displacement; change

spostare (spòsto) *tr* to move; to change, shift; to upset || *ref* to move; to shift; to get out of place; to be upset

spòsta·to -ta *adj* ill-adjusted, out of place || *mf* misfit

spran·ga *f* (-ghe) bar, crossbar

sprangare §209 *tr* to bar, bolt

sprazzo *m* spray; flash; burst

sprecare §197 (sprèco) *tr* to waste; to miss (*an opportunity*) || *ref* to waste one's efforts

sprè·co *m* (-chi) waste; squandering

sprecó·ne -na *adj & mf* spendthrift

spregévole *adj* contemptible, despicable

spregiare §290 (sprègio) *tr* to despise

sprè·gio *m* (-gi) contempt, scorn

spregiudica·to -ta *adj* open-minded, unbiased || *m* open-minded person

sprèmere §123 *tr* to squeeze, press; **spremere le lacrime a** to move to tears || *ref*—**spremersi il cervello** to rack one's brain

spremifrut·ta *m* (-ta) squeezer

spremilimó·ni *m* (-ni) lemon squeezer

spremuta *f* squeezing; **spremuta d'arancia** orange juice

spretare (sprèto) *ref* to doff the cassock

sprezzante *adj* contemptuous, haughty

sprezzare (sprèzzo) *tr* (lit) to despise

sprèzzo *m* disdain, contempt

sprigionare (sprigióno) *tr* to exhale, emit; to free from prison || *ref* to free oneself; to escape, come forth, issue (*said, e.g., of steam*)

sprimacciare §128 *tr* to beat, fluff (*e.g., a pillow*)

sprizzare *tr* to spout; to sparkle with (*joy, health*) || *intr* (ESSERE) to spurt; to fly (*said of sparks*); to sparkle

sprizzo *m* sprinkle; spurt; spark

sprofondare (sprofóndo) *tr* to send to the bottom; to destroy, ruin; to sink || *intr* (ESSERE) to sink; to founder; to cave in; to be sunk (*e.g., in meditation*)

sprolò·quio *m* (-qui) long rigmarole

spronare (spróno) *tr* to spur, goad

spróne *m* spur; prodding; example; guimpe; buttress; abutment (*of bridge*); **a sprone battuto** at full speed; at once; **dar di sprone a** to spur on; **sprone di cavaliere** (bot) rocket larkspur

sproporziona·to -ta *adj* out of proportion, disproportionate

sproporzióne *f* disproportion

sproposita·to -ta *adj* out of proportion; excessive; gross (*error*)

spropòsito *m* blunder, gross error; excessive amount; **a sproposito** out of place; inopportunely

sprovvedu·to -ta *adj* deprived; brainless, witless

sprovvi·sto -sta *adj* deprived; devoid, lacking; **alla sprovvista** suddenly; unawares, off guard

spruzzabianche·rìa m (-rìa) sprinkler (*to sprinkle clothes*)

spruzzare tr to sprinkle, spray; to powder (*sugar*)

spruzzatóre m sprayer; (aut) nozzle (*of carburetor*)

spruzzo m spray; splash (*of mud*)

spudora·to -ta adj shameless; impudent

spugna f sponge; **dare un colpo di spugna** to wipe the slate clean; **gettare la spugna** to throw in the towel

spugnare tr to sponge; to swab

spugnatura f sponge bath

spugnó·so -sa [s] adj spongy

spulciare §128 tr to pick the fleas off; to scrutinize, examine minutely

spuma f foam, froth

spumante adj sparkling || m sparkling wine; champagne

spumare intr to froth

spumeggiante adj sparkling; vaporous; foamy

spumeggiare §290 (**spuméggio**) intr to foam

spumóne m spumoni

spumó·so -sa [s] adj foamy, frothy

spunta f check; check list; check mark

spuntare tr to blunt; to unpin; to overcome; to clip, trim; to check off; **spuntarla** to come out on top; to overcome || intr (ESSERE) to appear; to sprout; to rise; to well up (*said of tears*); to pop out; to break through || ref to become blunt; to die down

spuntino m bite, snack; **fare uno spuntino** to have a bite

spunto m sourness (*of wine*); (theat) cue; (sports) sprint; (fig) starting point, origin

spuntóne m spike; pike; crag

spurgare §209 tr to purge, clear; to clean up || ref to expectorate

spur·go m (-ghi) discharge; reject (*e.g., book*)

spù·rio -ria adj (-ri -rie) spurious

sputacchiare §287 tr to spit upon || intr to sputter

sputacchièra f spittoon, cuspidor

sputare tr to spit; to cough up; (fig) to spew (*venom*); **sputare sangue** to spit blood; (fig) to sweat blood || intr to spit

sputasentènze mf (-ze) wiseacre

sputo m spit, sputum; spitting

squadernare (**squadèrno**) tr to leaf through; **squadernare qlco a qlcu** to put s.th under the nose of s.o. || ref to come apart (*said of a book*)

squadra f square (*for measuring right angles*); squad, group; (mil) squadron; (sports) team; **a squadra** at right angles; **fuori squadra** out of kilter; **squadra di pompieri** fire company; **squadra mobile** flying squad

squadrare tr to square; (fig) to examine, study

squadriglia f (aer, nav) squadron

squadróne m squadron (*of cavalry*)

squagliare §280 tr to melt || ref to melt; **squagliarsela** to take French leave

squalìfi·ca f (-che) disqualification

squalificare §197 (**squalìfico**) tr to disqualify || ref to disqualify oneself; to prove to be unqualified

squàlli·do -da adj wretched, dreary, gloomy; faint (*smile*); (lit) emaciated

squallóre m wretchedness, dreariness, gloominess

squalo m shark

squama f scurf (*shed by the skin*); (bot, pathol, zool) scale

squamare tr & ref to scale

squamó·so -sa [s] adj scaly

squarciagóla adv—**a squarciagola** at the top of one's voice

squarciare §128 tr to rend, tear apart; to dispel (*a doubt*) || ref to become torn; to open

squàr·cio m (-ci) tear, rip; passage (*of book*)

squartare tr to quarter

squartatura f quartering

squassare tr to shake violently; to wreck

squattrina·to -ta adj penniless || m pauper

squilibra·to -ta adj unbalanced, deranged || mf mad or insane person

squili·brio m (-bri) lack of balance; **squilibrio mentale** insanity; unbalanced mental condition

squillante adj ringing, shrill; sharp

squillare intr to ring; to ring out; to blare

squillo m ring; peal; blare, blast (*of horn*); || f call girl

squinternare (**squintèrno**) tr to tear (*a book*) to pieces; (fig) to upset

squisi·to -ta adj exquisite

squittire §176 intr to squeak; to squeal

sradicare §197 (**sràdico**) tr to uproot; to eradicate; to pull (*a tooth*)

sragionare (**sragióno**) intr to talk nonsense

sregola·to -ta adj intemperate; dissolute

srotolare (**sròtolo**) tr to unroll

stàb·bio m (-bi) pen; manure, dung

stabbiòlo m pigpen

stàbile adj stable; real (*estate*); permanent; stock (*company*) || m building

stabiliménto m plant, factory; establishment; settlement, colony; conclusion (*of a deal*)

stabilire §176 tr to establish; to decide || ref to settle

stabili·tà f (-tà) stability, steadiness

stabilito m (law) agreement of sale (*drawn up by a broker*)

stabilizzare [ddzz] tr & ref to stabilize

stabilizza·tóre -trice [ddzz] mf stabilizing person || m (aer) stabilizer; (elec) voltage stabilizer

staccare §197 tr to detach; to unhitch; to outdistance; to draw (*a check*); to tear off; to take (*one's eyes*) away; to begin; to enunciate (*words*) || intr to stand out; (coll) to stop working || ref to come off; **staccarsi da** to come off (*e.g., the wall*); to leave (*one's home; the shore*); (aer) to take off from

stacciare §128 tr to sift, sieve

stàc•cio *m* (**-ci**) sieve

staccionata *f* fence; hurdle; stockade

stac•co *m* (**-chi**) tearing off; cut of cloth (*for a suit*); interval; **fare stacco** to stand out

stadèra *f* steelyard; **stadera a ponte** weighbridge

stàdia *f* leveling rod

stà•dio *m* (**-di**) stadium; stage

staffa *f* stirrup; heel (*of sock*); gaiter strap; clamp; (*mach*) bracket; **perdere le staffe** to lose one's nerve

staffétta *f* courier, messenger; pilot (*car*); **a staffetta** relay

staffière *m* groom, footman; servant

staffilare *tr* to whip, belt, lash

staffilata *f* lash

staffile *m* stirrup strap; whip

stàg•gio *m* (**-gi**) stay, upright

stagionale *adj* seasonal ‖ *mf* seasonal worker

stagionare (**stagióno**) *tr* to season, cure

stagiona•to -ta *adj* seasoned, ripe

stagióne *f* season; **da mezza stagione** spring-and-fall (*coat*); **di fine stagione** year-end (*sale*)

stagliare §280 *tr* to hack ‖ *ref* to stand out

staglia•to -ta *adj* sheer (*cliff*)

sta•gnàio *m* (**-gnài**) tinsmith; plumber

stagnante *adj* stagnant

stagnare *tr* to tin; to solder; to stanch ‖ *intr* to stagnate

stagnaro *m* var of **stagnaio**

stagnina *f* tin can

stagnino *m* (coll) var of **stagnaio**

sta•gno -gna *adj* watertight; airtight ‖ *m* tin; pond, pool

stagnòla *f* tin foil; tin can

stàio *m* (**stài**) bushel (*container*); **a staio** (coll) top (*hat*) ‖ *m* (**stàia** *fpl*) bushel (*measure*); **a staia** in abundance

stalla *f* stable

stallìa *f* (com) lay day

stallière *m* stableman, stableboy

stallo *m* seat; stall; (chess) stalemate

stallóne *m* stallion

stamane, stamani or **stamattina** *adv* this morning

stambéc•co *m* (**-chi**) ibex

stambèr•ga *f* (**-ghe**) hovel

stambù•gio *m* (**-gi**) hole, hovel

stamburare *tr* to puff up, to boast about ‖ *intr* to drum

stame *m* (bot) stamen; thread, yarn

stamigna *f* cheesecloth

stampa *f* printing; print; (fig) print; (fig) mold; **stampe** printed matter

stampàg•gio *m* (**-gi**) (mach) stamping

stampare *tr* to stamp; to print; to impress; to publish ‖ *ref* (fig) to be ingraved

stampatèllo *m*—**in stampatello** in block letters; **scrivere in stampatello** to print (*with pen or pencil*)

stampa•to -ta *adj* printed; impressed ‖ *m* printed form; **stampati** printed matter

stampa•tóre -trice *mf* printer

stampèlla *f* crutch

stamperìa *f* print shop

stampìglia *f* rubber stamp; billboard; overprint

stampigliare §280 *tr* to stamp; to overprint

stampinare *tr* to stencil

stampino *m* stencil

stampo *m* mold; stencil; stamp, kind; decoy

stanare *tr* to flush (*game*); (fig) to dig up

stancare §197 *tr* to tire, fatigue; to bore ‖ *ref* to tire, weary

stanchézza *f* tiredness, weariness

stan•co -ca *adj* (**-chi -che**) tired; tired out; (lit) left (*hand*)

standardizzare [ddzz] *tr* to standardize

stan•ga *f* (**-ghe**) bar; shaft (*of cart*); beam (*of plow*)

stangata *f* blow

stanghétta *f* small bar; bolt (*of lock*); temple (*of spectacles*); (mus) bar

stanòtte *adv* tonight; last night

stante *adj* being; standing; **a sé stante** by itself, independent ‖ *prep* because of; **stante che** since

stan•tìo -tìa *adj* (**-tìi; -tìe**) stale; musty

stantuffo *m* piston; plunger

stanza *f* room; stanza; **essere di stanza** (mil) to be stationed; **stanza da bagno** bath room; **stanza di compensazione** clearing house; **stanza di soggiorno** living room

stanziare §287 *tr* to allocate; to appropriate; to budget ‖ *ref* to settle

stanzino *m* small room; closet

stappare *tr* to uncork

stare §263 *intr* (ESSERE) to stay; to stand; to live; to be; to be located; to linger; to last; to stick (*e.g., to a rule*); (poker) to stand pat; **come sta?** how are you?; **lasciar stare** to leave alone; **lasciar stare che** to leave aside that; **non stare in sé dalla gioia** to be beside oneself with joy; **sta bene!** O.K.!; **starci** to fit, e.g., **ci stanno trecento persone** three hundred people fit there; **starci di** to be in favor of, e.g., **io ci starei d'andare al cine** I would be in favor of going to the movies; **stare + ger** to be + *ger*, e.g., **stava leggendo** he was reading; **stare a** to be up to; to stand on (*ceremony*); to base oneself on; to take (*a joke*); to cost, e.g., **a quanto sta il prosciutto?** how much does the ham cost?; **stare a + inf** to keep + *ger*, e.g., **stai sempre a sognare** you always keep dreaming; to take + *inf*, e.g., **stette poco a decidere** he took little time to decide; **stare a cuore** (with *dat*) to deem important, e.g., **gli sta a cuore il lavoro** he deems his work important; **stare a pancia all'aria** to not do a stroke of work; **stare al proprio posto** to keep one's place; **stare a segno** to behave properly; **stare a vedere** to be possible, e.g., **sta a vedere che non viene?** could it be possible that he won't come?; **stare bene** to be well; to be well-off; (with *dat*) to fit, to become, e.g., **questo vestito gli sta**

bene this suit fits him well, this suit becomes him; to serve right, e.g., **gli sta bene!** it serves him right!; **stare comodo** to be at ease; to remain seated; **stare con** (fig) to be on the side of; **starsene** to stay apart, e.g., **se ne sta solo soletto** he stays apart or all alone; **stare fermo** to be quiet; to not move; **stare in forse** to doubt; to be doubtful; **stare sulle proprie** to stand aloof; **stare su** to stand erect; **stare su tardi** to stay up late; **stia comodo!** remain seated!

starna f gray partridge

starnazzare *intr* to flap its wings; to flutter; to cackle

starnutare *intr* to sneeze

starnuto m sneeze

stasare [s] *tr* to unplug, unblock

staséra [s] *adv* tonight, this evening

sta·si f (-si) (com) stagnation; (pathol) stasis

statale *adj* government; state || *mf* government employee

stàti·co -ca (-ci -che) static || f statics

stati·no -na *adj* (coll) migratory || m itemized list; (educ) registration form

stati·sta m (-sti) statesman

statisti·co -ca (-ci -che) *adj* statistical || m statistician || f statistics; **fare una statistica (di)** to survey; **statistiche statistics** (*data*)

stati·vo -va *adj* nonmigratory; permanent || m stand (*of microscope*)

stato m state; condition; plight; frame (*of mind*); status; estate (*social class*); **di stato** public (*e.g., school*); **essere in stato di arresto** to be under arrest; **stati extracts from vital statistics; Stati Pontifici Papal States; Stati Uniti United States; stato civile** marital status; vital statistics; **stato confessionale** state under ecclesiastical rule; **stato cuscinetto** buffer state; **stato di preallarme** state of emergency; **stato di previsione** preliminary budget; **stato interessante** pregnancy; **stato maggiore** (mil) general staff

statoreattóre m ramjet engine

stàtua f statue

statuà·rio -ria (-ri -rie) *adj* statuary; statuesque || m sculptor

statunitènse *adj* & *mf* American (*U.S.A.*)

statura f stature; height

statuto m statute

stavòlta *adv* (coll) this time

stazionaménto m parking; **stazionamento vietato** no parking

stazionare (stazióno) *intr* to park

stazionà·rio -ria *adj* (-ri -rie) stationary

stazióne f station; bearing; posture; **stazione balneare** shore resort; **stazione climatica** health resort, spa; **stazione di rifornimento** service station; **stazione di tassametri** cab stand; **stazione estiva** summer resort; **stazione generatrice** power plant; **stazione orbitale** orbiting station; **stazione sanitaria** clinic

stazza f tonnage; (naut) displacement

stazzare *tr* (naut) to gauge; (naut) to displace

stazzonare (stazzóno) *tr* to crumple

steatite f French chalk

stéc·ca f (-che) small stick; slat (*of shutter*); rib (*of umbrella*); bone (*of whale*); carton (*of cigarettes*); rail (*of fence*); letter opener; chisel (*of sculptor*); (billiards) cue; (billiards) miscue; (surg) splint; **fare una stecca** (billiards) to miscue; (mus) to sing or play a sour note

steccadèn·ti m (-ti) (coll) toothpick

steccare §197 (stécco) *tr* to fence; to put in a splint || *intr* to play or sing a sour note; (billiards) to miscue

steccato m fence; (racing) inside track

stecchétto m small stick; **tenere a stecchetto** to keep on a strict diet; to keep short of money

stecchino m toothpick

stecchi·to -ta *adj* stiff; lean, lank; dry (*twig*); dumfounded

stéc·co m (-chi) stick, twig

stecconata f stockade; fence

stélla f star; rowel (*of spur*); speck of fat (*in soup*); (fig) sky; **a stella** star-shaped; stellar; **montare alle stelle** to be sky-high (*said, e.g., of prices*); **portare alle stelle** to praise to the skies; **stella alpina** edelweiss; **stella cadente** shooting star; **stella di mare** starfish; **stella filante** shooting star; confetti; **stella polare** polestar, lodestar

stellare *adj* stellar; (mach) radial || v (stéllo) *tr* to spangle with stars; to stud

stella·to -ta *adj* starry; star-spangled; star-shaped; studded

stellétta f (mil) star; (typ) asterisk; **guadagnarsi le stellette** (mil) to earn a promotion; **portare le stellette** (mil) to be in the service

stellina f starlet

stelloncino m (journ) short paragraph

stèlo m stem, stalk

stèm·ma m (-mi) coat of arms; genealogy (*of a manuscript*)

stemperare (stèmpero) *tr* to dilute; to blunt; to untemper; (lit) to waste || *ref* to melt; to become dull or blunt

stendardo m banner, standard

stèndere §270 *tr* to stretch; to hang up (*laundry*); to spread; to draw up (*a document*); (mil) to deploy; **stendere a terra** to knock down || *ref* to stretch out

stendibianche·rìa m (-rìa) clothes rack, clotheshorse

stenodattilògra·fo -fa *mf* shorthand typist

stenografare (stenògrafo) *tr* to take down in shorthand

stenografia f shorthand, stenography

stenogràfi·co -ca *adj* (-ci -che) stenographic, shorthand

stenògra·fo -fa *mf* stenographer

stenòsi f (pathol) stricture

stenotipìa f stenotypy

stentare (stènto) *tr* to eke out (*a living*)

‖ *intr* to barely make ends meet; **stentare a** to hardly be able to; to find it hard to

stenta·to -ta *adj* hard; stunted; strained (*smile*)

stènto *m* privation; hardship; **a stento** hardly; with difficulty; **senza stento** without any trouble

stèr·co *m* (**-chi**) dung

stereofòni·co -ca *adj* (**-ci -che**) stereo, stereophonic

stereoscòpi·co -ca *adj* (**-ci -che**) stereoscopic

stereoscò·pio *m* (**-pi**) stereoscope

stereotipa·to -ta *adj* stereotyped

sterilizzare [ddzz] *tr* to sterilize

sterlina *f* pound sterling

sterminare (**stèrmino**) *tr* to exterminate

stermina·to -ta *adj* immense, boundless

stermì·nio *m* (**-ni**) extermination; (coll) large amount, lots

stèrno *m* breastbone

sterpàglia *f* brushwood; undergrowth

stèrpo *m* dry twig; bramble

sterrare (**stèrro**) *tr* to excavate

sterratóre *m* digger

sterzare (**stèrzo**) *tr* to diminish by one third; to thin out (*woodland*); (aut) to steer ‖ *intr* to swerve

sterzata *f* swerve

stèrzo *m* handle bar; (aut) steering gear; (aut) steering wheel

stésa [s] *f* coat (*of paint*); string (*of clothes on line*)

stés·so -sa *adj* same, e.g., **lo stesso mese** the same month; very, e.g., **tuo fratello stesso** your very brother; **essere alle stesse** to be just the same; **io stesso** I myself; **lui stesso** he himself, etc.; **per sé stesso** by himself; **by itself** ‖ *pron* same; same thing; **fa lo stesso** it's all the same, it makes no difference

stesura [s] *f* drawing up (*of a contract*); **prima stesura** first draft

stetoscò·pio *m* (**-pi**) stethoscope

stìa *f* chicken coop

Stige *m* Styx

stì·gio -gia *adj* (**-gi -gie**) Stygian

stigmate *fpl* stigmata

stilare *tr* to draft properly

stile *m* style

stilè *adj invar* stylish

stilétto *m* dagger, stiletto

stilizzare [ddzz] *tr* to stylize

stilla *f* (lit) drop, droplet

stillare *tr* to exude; to distill ‖ *intr* (ESSERE) to ooze, drip, exude ‖ *ref*—**stillarsi il cervello** to rack one's brains

stillici·dio *m* (**-di**) dripping; repetition

stilo *m* stylus; arm (*of steelyard*); dagger; gnomon (*of sundial*); (poet) style ‖ *f* (coll) fountain pen

stilogràfi·ca *f* (**-che**) fountain pen

stima *f* appraisal; esteem; (naut) dead reckoning; **a stima d'occhio** more or less

stimare *tr* to estimate; to deem; to esteem ‖ *ref* (coll) to think a lot of oneself

stima·tóre -trice *mf* appraiser; admirer

stìmmate *fpl* var of **stigmate**

stimolante *adj & m* stimulant

stimolare (**stìmolo**) *tr* to stimulate

stìmolo *m* influence; stimulus

stin·co *m* (**-chi**) shinbone; shin; **stinco di santo** saintly person, saint; **rompere gli stinchi a** to annoy

stìngere §126 *tr, intr* (ESSERE) & *ref* to fade

stipa *f* kindling wood, brushwood

stipare *tr & ref* to crowd, jam

stipendiare §287 (**stipèndio**) *tr* to employ, hire; to pay a salary to

stipendia·to -ta *adj* salaried ‖ *mf* salaried person

stipèn·dio *m* (**-di**) pay, salary

stipétto *m* (naut) closet, cabinet

stìpite *m* jamb; stock, family; (bot) trunk (*of palm tree*)

stìpo *m* cabinet

stipulare (**stìpulo**) *tr* to draw up (*a contract*); to stipulate

stiracchiare §287 *tr* to stretch; to eke out (*a living*); to twist (*a meaning*); to haggle over ‖ *intr* to haggle; to economize ‖ *ref* to stretch out

stirare *tr* to stretch; to iron, press ‖ *intr* to iron ‖ *ref* to stretch out

stira·tóre -trice *mf* ironer, presser

stiratura *f* ironing; stretching

stirerìa *f* ironing shop

stiro *m*—**ferro da stiro** see **ferro**

stirpe *f* family; birth, origin

stitichézza *f* constipation

stìti·co -ca *adj* (**-ci -che**) constipated; (fig) tight

stiva *f* (naut) hold; (lit) beam (*of plow*)

stivàg·gio *m* (**-gi**) stowage

stivale *m* boot; **dei miei stivali** good-for-nothing; **lustrare gli stivali a qlcu** to lick s.o.'s boots

stivalétto *m* high shoe

stivalóne *m* boot; **stivaloni da equitazione** riding boots; **stivaloni da palude** hip boots

stivare *tr* to stow

stivatóre *m* stevedore

stizza *f* anger; irritation

stizzire §176 *tr* to anger, vex ‖ *ref* to get angry

stizzó·so -sa [s] *adj* peevish, irritable

stoccafisso *m* stockfish

stoccata *f* thrust (*with dagger or rapier*); dig, sarcastic remark; touch (*for money*)

stòc·co *m* (**-chi**) dagger; rapier; stalk (*of corn*)

Stoccólma *f* Stockholm

stòffa *f* cloth, material; (fig) stuff, makings

stoicismo *m* stoicism

stòi·co -ca *adj* (**-ci -che**) stoic, stoical ‖ *m* stoic; Stoic

stoino *m* doormat

stòla *f* stole

stòli·do -da *adj* foolish, silly

stoltézza *f* foolishness, silliness

stól·to -ta *adj* silly ‖ *mf* fool

stomacare §197 (**stòmaco**) *tr* to disgust; to nauseate

stomachévole *adj* disgusting, sickening

stòma·co *m* (-ci or -chi) stomach; maw (*of animal*); dare di stomaco to vomit

stonare (stòno) *tr* to sing or play out of tune; to upset || *intr* to sing or play out of tune; to be out of place; to not harmonize

stona·to -ta *adj* out-of-tune; upset; clashing (*color*)

stonatura *f* jarring sound; clash (*of colors*); lack of harmony

stóppa *f* tow; oakum; di stoppa flaxen; weak, trembling; stoppa incatramata oakum

stoppàc·cio *m* (-ci) wad

stóppie *fpl* stubble

stoppino *m* wick

stoppó·so -sa [s] *adj* stubby; stringy

stórcere §272 *tr* to twist; to twitch; to wrench (*one's ankle*); to roll (*one's eyes*) || *ref* to twist; to writhe; to bend

stordiménto *m* bewilderment; dizziness

stordire §176 *tr* to bewilder; to daze || *intr* to be bewildered || *ref* to dull one's senses

storditàggine *f* carelessness; mistake, blunder

stordi·to -ta *adj* careless; bewildered; amazed; dizzy || *mf* scatterbrain

stòria *f* history; story, tale; fact; fare storie to stand on ceremony; un'altra storia a horse of another color

stòri·co -ca (-ci -che) *adj* historical || *m* historian

storièlla *f* tale, short story; joke

storiografìa *f* historiography

storióne *m* sturgeon

stormire §176 *intr* to rustle

stórmo *m* swarm, flock; (aer) group

stornare (stórno) *tr* to ward off; to dissuade; to divert (*funds*); to write off (*as noncollectable*)

stornèllo *m* Italian folksong; (orn) starling

stór·no -na *adj* dapple-gray || *m* (com) transfer; (orn) starling

storpiare §287 (stòrpio) *tr* to cripple; to clip (*one's words*)

stòr·pio -pia (-pi -pie) *adj* crippled || *m* cripple

stòr·to -ta *adj* twisted; crooked; crippled || *f* twist; dislocation; retort

stoviglie *fpl* dishes; lavare le stoviglie to wash the dishes

stra- *pref adj* extra-, e.g., straordinario extraordinary; over-, e.g., stracarico overloaded

stràbi·co -ca *adj* (-ci -che) crosseyed

strabiliante *adj* astonishing, amazing

strabiliare §287 *tr* to amaze || *intr* & *ref* to be amazed

strabismo *m* strabismus, squint

straboccare §197 (strabócco) *intr* to overflow

strabocchévole *adj* overflowing

strabuzzare [ddzz] *tr* (coll) to roll (*one's eyes*)

stracàri·co -ca *adj* (-chi -che) overloaded, overburdened

stracca *f*—pigliare una stracca to be dead tired

straccale *m* breeching (*of harness*); straccali (coll) suspenders

straccare §197 *tr* (coll) to tire

stracciaiò·lo -la *mf* ragpicker

stracciare §128 *tr* to tear, rend; to comb (*natural silk*)

stràc·cio -cia (-ci -ce) *adj* torn, in rags; waste (*paper*) || *m* rag, tatter; tear, rend; combed silk

stracció·ne -na *mf* tatterdemalion

straccivéndo·lo -la *mf* ragpicker; rag dealer

strac·co -ca *adj* (-chi -che) tired; worn-out; alla stracca lazily || *f* see stracca

stracòt·to -ta *adj* overcooked, overdone || *m* stew

stracuòcere §144a *tr* to overcook, overdo

strada *f* roadway; street; da strada vulgar, common; divorare la strada to burn up the road; essere in mezzo a una strada to be in a bad way; fare strada a to pave the way for; farsi strada to make one's way; prender la strada to set forth; strada carrozzabile carriage road; strada dell'orto easy way out; strada ferrata railroad; strada maestra main road; tagliare la strada a to stand in the way of; (aut) to cut in front of

stradale *adj* road; street; traffic (*e.g., accident*); highway (*police*) || *m* avenue || *f* highway patrol

stradà·rio *m* (-ri) street directory

strafalcióne *m* blunder, gross error

strafare §173 *tr* to overdo; to overcook

strafóro *m* drilled hole; di straforo stealthily

strafottènte *adj* unconcerned, nonchalant; arrogant, impudent

strafottènza *f* nonchalance, unconcern; arrogance, impudence

strage *f* butchery, massacre, carnage; (coll) multitude, lot

stragrande *adj* enormous, huge

stralciare §128 *tr* to prune, trim (*grapevines*); to eliminate, remove; (com) to liquidate

stràl·cio *adj invar* interim; emergency (*e.g., law*); liquidating || *m* (-ci) excerpt; clearance sale; a stralcio at a bargain

strale *m* (lit) arrow

strallo *m* (naut) stay

stralunare *tr* to roll (*one's eyes*)

straluna·to -ta *adj* upset; wild-eyed

stramazzare *tr* to fell || *intr* (ESSERE) to fall down

stramazzo *m* sluice; (coll) straw mattress

stramberìa *f* eccentricity

stram·bo -ba *adj* odd, queer, eccentric; crooked (*legs*); squint (*eyes*)

strame *m* litter; fodder

strampala·to -ta *adj* strange; preposterous, absurd

stranézza *f* strangeness; oddity

strangolare (stràngolo) *tr* to strangle; (naut) to furl

strangola·tóre -trice *mf* strangler

straniare §287 *tr* (lit) to draw away || *ref* to become estranged

straniè·ro -ra adj foreign, alien; (lit) strange || mf foreigner, alien

stra·no -na adj strange, odd; (lit) estranged

straordinà·rio -ria (-ri -rie) adj extraordinary; extra || mf temporary employee || m overtime

strapagare §209 tr to overpay; to pay too much for

strapazzare tr to rebuke, upbraid; to mishandle; to bungle || ref to overwork oneself

strapazza·to -ta adj crumpled; bungled; scrambled (eggs); overworked || f upbraiding, rebuke; fatigue

strapazzo m misuse; fatigue; excess; da strapazzo working (clothes); hackneyed, second-rate

strapèrdere §212 tr & intr to lose hopelessly || intr to be wiped out

straplè·no -na adj chock-full

strapiombare (strapiómbo) intr to overhang, jut out

strapiómbo m overhang; a strapiombo sheer (cliff)

strapotènte adj overpowerful

strappare tr to pull; to tear, rend; to wring (s.o.'s heart); strappare le lacrime a qlcu to move s.o. to tears; strappare qlco a qlcu to pry s.th out of s.o.; to snatch s.th from s.o. || ref to tear (e.g., one's hair)

strappata f pull, tug, snatch

strappo m pull; tear, rip; infraction, breach; pulling away (on a bicycle); patch (of sky); a strappi in jerks; strappo muscolare pulled muscle; sprain

strapuntino m folding seat, jump seat; bucket seat; (naut) mattress

straric·co -ca adj (-chi -che) (coll) immensely rich

straripare intr (ESSERE & AVERE) to overflow

strascicare §197 (stràscico) tr to drag; to shuffle; strascicare le parole to drawl

strascichi·o m (-i) shuffle (of feet)

stràsci·co m (-chi) train (of skirt); trail; sequel, aftermath; a strascico dragging

strascinare (stràscino) tr to drag || ref to drag oneself, drag

strascinì·o m (-i) shuffle

stràscino m dragnet, trawl

stratagèm·ma m (-mi) stratagem

strategìa f strategy

stratè·gico -ca adj (-ci -che) strategic

stratè·go m (-ghi) strategist; general, commander

stratificare §197 (stratìfico) tr to stratify

strato m layer; coat, coating; stratum; (meteor) stratus

stratosfèra f stratosphere

strattóne m jerk, tug

stravagante adj extravagant; whimsical, capricious || mf eccentric

stravèc·chio -chia adj (-chi -chie) aged (cheese, wine, etc.); very old

stravincere §285 tr to overpower

straviziare §287 intr to be intemperate

stravi·zio m (-zi) intemperance, excess

stravòlgere §289 tr to roll (the eyes); to distort; to derange

straziante adj heartbreaking; excruciating (pain); horrible

straziare §287 tr to torture; to dismay; to mangle; to murder (a language)

strazia·to -ta adj torn, stricken

strà·zio m (-zi) suffering, pain; torture; shame; boredom; fare strazio di to squander

stré·ga f (-ghe) witch; sorceress

stregare §209 (strégo) tr to bewitch

stregóne m sorcerer; witch doctor

stregonerìa f witchcraft; sorcery

strègua f standard, criterion; alla stregua di on the basis of

strema·to -ta adj exhausted

strènna f Christmas gift, New Year's gift; special New Year's issue

strè·nuo -nua adj strenuous

strepitare (strèpito) intr to make a noise; to shout, make a racket

strèpito m noise, racket; fare strepito to make a hit

strepitó·so -sa [s] adj loud, noisy; resounding (success)

streptomicìna f streptomycin

stressa·to -ta adj under stress

strétta f grasp, clench; tightening (of brakes); hold; press, crush; pang; mountain pass; mettere alle strette to drive into a corner; stretta dei conti rendering of accounts; stretta di mano handshake; stretta finale climax

strettézza f narrowness; strettezze straits, hardship

strét·to -ta adj narrow; tight; bare (necessities); pure (e.g., dialect); strict; clenched (fist); heavy (heart); minimum (price); (phonet) close || m straits, narrows || f see stretta || **stretto** adv tightly

strettóia f narrow stretch; hardship; bandage

strìa f stripe, streak

striare §119 tr to stripe, streak

stricnìna f strychnine

stridènte adj jarring; clashing (colors); strident (sound)

stridere §264 tr to grit (one's teeth) || intr to shriek; to squeak; to creak; to clash (said of colors); to croak (said of raven); to hoot (said of owl); to howl (said of wind) || ref (coll) to be resigned

strido m (-di & -da fpl) shriek; squeak

stridóre m shriek; creak, squeak; gnashing (of teeth)

stridu·lo -la adj shrill

strigare §209 tr to disentangle || ref to extricate oneself

strìglia f currycomb

strigliare §280 tr to curry; to upbraid || ref to groom oneself

strillare tr to shout; (coll) to scold; (coll) to hawk (newspapers) || intr to scream

strillo m shriek; shout, scream

strilló·ne -na mf loud-mouthed person || m newsdealer; newsboy, paperboy

striminzi·to -ta *adj* shrunken; tight; stunted; skinny

strimpellare (strimpèllo) *tr* to thrum; to thrum on

strinare *tr* to singe; to burn (*with a flatiron*)

strin·ga *f* (-**ghe**) lace; shoelace

stringa·to -ta *adj* terse, concise

stringere §265 *tr* to tighten; to grip; to shake, clasp (*a hand*); to drive into a corner; to squeeze; to embrace; to close (*an alliance, a deal*); to wring (*one's heart*); to clench (*the fist*); (lit) to gird (*a sword*); (mus) to accelerate; **stringere d'assedio** to besiege; **stringere i freni** to put the brakes on || *intr* to be tight; **il tempo stringe** time is running short; **stringi, stringi** at the very end, in conclusion || *ref* to squeeze close together; to shrink; to coagulate; to draw close; **stringersi a** to snuggle up to; **stringersi addosso a** to attack; **stringersi nelle spalle** to shrug one's shoulders

stringina·so [s] *m* (-**so**) pince-nez

strì·scia *f* (-**sce**) strip, band; trail; stripe; line; **a strisce** striped; **striscia d'atterramento** airstrip; **striscia di cuoio** strop

strisciante *adj* crawling; (fig) fawning

strisciare §128 *tr* to shuffle (*feet*); to graze; **strisciare una riverenza** to curtsy || *intr* to creep, crawl; to graze by || *ref* to fawn; **strisciarsi a** to rub one's back against

strisciata or **strisciatura** *f* sliding; trail

strì·scio *m* (-**sci**) rubbing; shuffling; **ballare di striscio** to shuffle; **da** or **di striscio** superficial (*wound*)

striscióne *m* festoon; festooned sign; flatterer; **striscione d'arrivo** landing (*in gymnastics*); **striscione del traguardo** (sports) tape

striscióni *adv* crawling

stritolare (strìtolo) *tr* to crush, smash

strizzalimó·ni *m*(-**ni**) lemon squeezer

strizzare *tr* to squeeze, press; to wink (*the eye*); **strizzare l'occhio** to wink

strizza·tóio *m* (-**tói**) wringer

strò·fa or **strò·fe** *f* (-**fe**) strophe

strofinàc·cio *m* (-**ci**) dust cloth

strofinare *tr* to rub; to polish || *ref* to rub oneself; to fawn

strofinata *f*—**dare una strofinata a** to give a lick and a promise to

strofinì·o *m* (-**i**) rubbing; wiping

stròla·ga *f* (-**ghe**) (orn) loon

strombatura *f* embrasure

strombazzare *tr* to glorify; **strombazzare i propri meriti** to toot one's own horn || *intr* to blast away on the trumpet

strombazza·tóre -trice *mf* show-off

strombettare (strombétto) *tr* to trumpet, toot

stroncare §197 (strónco) *tr* to break off; to break down; to eliminate; (fig) to criticize severely

stroncatura *f* devastating criticism

strònzio *m* strontium

strónzo *m* (vulg) turd

stropicciare §128 *tr* to rub (*hands*); to

drag, shuffle (*feet*); (coll) to crumple || *ref*—**stropicciarsene** (coll) to not give a hoot

stropicci·o *m* (-**i**) rubbing; shuffling

stròzza *f* (coll) gullet, throat

strozzare (stròzzo) *tr* to strangle; to stop up; to fleece, swindle || *ref* to choke; to narrow

strozza·to -ta *adj* choked; choking; strangulated (*hernia*)

strozzatura *f* narrowing

strozzinàg·gio *m* (-**gi**) usury

strozzino *m* usurer, loan shark

struggere §266 *tr* to melt; to consume || *ref* to melt; to pine away; to be upset; **struggersi di** to be consumed by

struggiménto *m* melting; longing; torment

strumentale *adj* instrument (*flying*); capital (*goods*); instructional (*language, in multi-lingual regions*); (gram, mus) instrumental

strumentali·sta *mf* (-**sti -ste**) instrumentalist

strumentalizzare [ddzz] *tr* to use, take advantage of

strumentare (struménto) *tr* to orchestrate

struménto *m* instrument; tool, implement; **strumento a corda** stringed instrument; **strumento a fiato** wind instrument; **strumento di bordo** (aer) flight recorder

strusciare §128 *tr* to rub; to shuffle (*feet*); to crumple; to wear out || *ref*—**strusciarsi a** to fawn on

strutto *m* lard, shortening

struttura *f* structure

strutturare *tr* to organize, structure

struzzo *m* ostrich

stuccare §197 *tr* to putty; to stucco; to surfeit || *ref* to grow weary

stucchévole *adj* sickening

stuc·co -ca (-**chi -che**) *adj* bored; **stucco e ristucco** sick and tired || *m* putty; stucco; plaster of Paris; **rimanere di stucco** to be taken aback

studèn·te -téssa *mf* student

studenté·sco -sca (-**schi -sche**) *adj* student; student-like || *f* student body

studiare §287 *tr* to study; **studiarle tutte** to consider every angle || *intr* to study; to try || *ref* to try; to gaze at oneself

studia·to -ta *adj* affected, studied

stù·dio *m* (-**di**) study; school district; office (*of professional man*); studio; (hist) university; (lit) wish; (mus) étude; **a studio** on purpose; **essere allo studio** to be under consideration

studió·so -sa [s] *adj* studious || *m* scholar

stufa *f* stove, heater; hothouse

stufare *tr* to warm up, heat up; to stew; (coll) to bore

stufato *m* stew

stu·fo -fa *adj* (coll) bored, sick and tired || *f* see **stufa**

stuòia *f* mat; matting

stuòlo *m* throng, crowd; flock; (lit) army

stupefacènte *adj* amazing; habit-forming || *m* dope

stupefare §173 *tr* to amaze, astonish

stupefazióne *f* amazement, astonishment; stupefaction

stupèn·do -da *adj* stupendous

stupidàggine *f* stupidity; silliness; child's play, cinch

stùpi·do -da *adj* stupid; silly; (lit) amazed

stupire §176 *tr* to amaze || *ref* to be amazed

stupóre *m* amazement

stuprare *tr* to rape

stura *f* tapping; uncorking; **dar la stura a** to begin (*a speech*)

sturabottì·glie *m* (**-glie**) bottle opener

sturalavandì·ni *m* (**-ni**) plunger (*to open up clogged sink*)

sturare *tr* to uncork; to take the wax out of (*ears*); to open up (*clogged line*)

stuzzicadèn·ti *m* (**-ti**) toothpick

stuzzicare §197 (**stùzzico**) *tr* to pick (*e.g., one's teeth*); to bother; to excite, arouse; to tease; to sharpen (*appetite*)

su *adv* up; on top; upstairs; **da . . . in su** from . . . on, e.g., **dal mese scorso in su** from last month on; **di su** from upstairs; **in su up**; **metter su** to put on the fire; to instigate; **metter su bottega** to set up shop; **metter su casa** to set up housekeeping; **più su** higher; further up; **su!** come on!; let's go!; **su di** on; **su e giù** back and forth; up and down; **su per giù** more or less; **tirarsi su** to lift oneself up; to sit up; to get better, recover; **tirar su** to pick up; to grow, raise; **venir su** to grow; to come up || §4 *prep* on, upon; up; towards; over, above; onto; against; at, e.g., **sul far del giorno** at daybreak; on top of; out of, e.g., **due volte su tre** two times out of three; **mettere su superbia** to become proud; **stare sulle sue** to be reserved; **sul serio** in earnest; **su misura** made to order

suaccenna·to -ta *adj* above-mentioned

sub *m* (**sub**) (coll) skindiver

subàcque·o -a *adj* submarine

subaffittare *tr* to sublet

subaffitto *m* subletting, sublet; **prendere in subaffitto** to sublet

subaltèr·no -na *adj* & *m* subaltern; subordinate

subastare *tr* to auction off

sùbbia *f* stonecutter's chisel

subbù·glio *m* (**-gli**) turmoil, hubbub

subcosciènte *adj* & *m* subconscious

sùbdo·lo -la *adj* treacherous, deceitful

subentrare (**subéntro**) *intr* (ESSERE) (with *dat*) to succeed, follow

subire §176 *tr* to suffer; to undergo

subissare *tr* to ruin; to sink; to overwhelm || *intr* (ESSERE) to sink; to go to rack and ruin

subisso *m* ruin; (coll) lots, plenty

subitàne·o -a *adj* sudden

sùbi·to -ta *adj* (lit) sudden || *m*—**d'un subito** all of a sudden || **subito** *adv* rapidly; immediately; right away; **subito al principio** at the very beginning; **subito dopo** right after; **subito prima** right before || *interj* right away!

sublima·to -ta *adj* sublimated || *m* **sublimato corrosivo** corrosive sublimate

sublime *adj* & *m* sublime

subodorare (**subodóro**) *tr* to suspect; to get wind of

subordinare (**subórdino**) *tr* to subordinate

subordina·to -ta *adj* & *m* subordinate || *f* subordinate clause

subornare (**suborno**) *tr* to bribe

substrato *m* substratum

suburba·no -na *adj* suburban

subùr·bio *m* (**-bi**) suburb

succedàne·o -a *adj* & *m* substitute

succèdere §132 (*pp* **succeduto** or **successo**) *intr* (ESSERE) (with *dat*) to succede, to follow || *ref* to follow one another, follow one after the other || (*pret* **succèssi**; *pp* **succèsso**) *intr* (ESSERE) to happen, to come to pass; (with *dat*) to happen to, to come over, e.g., **che gli è successo?** what happened to him?

successióne *f* succession; **in successione** in succession; in a row

successi·vo -va *adj* successive; **next**

succèsso *m* success; outcome

successóre *m* successor

successò·rio -ria *adj* (**-ri -rie**) inheritance (*tax*)

succhiare §287 *tr* to suck

succhièllo *m* gimlet

succhiétto *m* pacifier

sùc·chio *m* (**-chi**) suck, sucking; (bot) sap; (coll) gimlet

succiaca·pre *m* (**-pre**) goatsucker, whippoorwill

succin·to -ta *adj* scanty (*clothing*); succinct, concise

suc·co *m* (**-chi**) juice; (fig) gist

succó·so -sa [s] *adj* juicy; pithy

succursale *f* branch, branch office

sud *m* south

sudafrica·no -na *adj* & *mf* South African

sudamerica·no -na *adj* & *mf* South American

sudàmina *f* prickly heat

sudare *tr* to sweat; to ooze; **sudare il pane** to earn one's living by the sweat of one's brow; **sudare sette camicie** to toil very hard || *intr* to perspire, sweat; to reek

sudà·rio *m* (**-ri**) shroud

suda·to -ta *adj* wet with perspiration; hard-earned || *f* sweat, sweating

suddét·to -ta *adj* aforesaid, above

sùddi·to -ta *adj* & *mf* subject

suddivìdere §158 *tr* to subdivide

sud-èst *m* southeast

sudicerìa *f* filth, filthiness; smut

sùdi·cio -cia (**-ci -cie**) *adj* dirty, filthy || *m* dirt, filth

sudiciume *m* dirt, filth

sudi·sta *mf* (**-sti -ste**) Southerner

sudóre *m* sweat, perspiration

sud-òvest *m* southwest

sufficiènte *adj* sufficient, adequate; self-sufficient ‖ *m* sufficient

sufficiènza *f* sufficiency; self-sufficiency; (educ) minimum passing grade

suffisso *m* suffix

suffragare §209 *tr* to support; to pray for

suffragétta *f* suffragette

suffrà·gio *m* (-gi) suffrage

suffumicare §197 (**suffùmico**) *tr* to fumigate

suffumi·gio *m* (-gi) treatment by inhalation; fumigation

suggellare (**suggèllo**) *tr* to seal

suggèllo *m* seal

suggeriménto *m* suggestion

suggerire §176 *tr* to suggest; to prompt

suggeri·tóre -**trice** *mf* prompter ‖ *m* (baseball) coach

suggestionàbile *adj* suggestible

suggestionare (**suggestióno**) *tr* to influence by suggestion ‖ *ref*—**suggestionarsi a** + *inf* to talk oneself into + *ger*

suggestióne *f* suggestion; fascination

suggesti·vo -**va** *adj* suggestive; fascinating; (law) leading (*question*)

sùghero *m* cork

sugli §4

sugna *f* fat; lard

su·go *m* (-ghi) juice; gravy; gist, pith; **non c'è sugo** it's no fun; there's nothing to it; **senza sugo** pointless, dull

sugó·so -**sa** [*s*] *adj* juicy

sui §4

suici·da (-**di** -**de**) *adj* suicidal ‖ *mf* suicide (*person*)

suicidare *ref* to commit suicide

suici·dio *m* (-di) suicide (*act*)

sui·no -**na** *adj* swinish; see **carne** ‖ *m* swine

sul §4

sulfamìdi·co -**ca** (-**ci** -**che**) *adj* sulfa ‖ *m* sulfa drug

sulla §4

sulle §4

sulli §4

sullo §4

sulloda·to -**ta** *adj* above-mentioned

sultano *m* sultan

summentova·to -**ta**, **summenziona·to** -**ta**, **sunnomina·to** -**ta** *adj* above-mentioned

sunteggiare §290 (**suntéggio**) *tr* to summarize

sunto *m* résumé, summary

suo sua §6 *adj* & *pron poss* (**suòi sue**)

suòcera *f* mother-in-law

suòcero *m* father-in-law; **i suoceri** the in-laws

suòla *f* sole (*of shoe*); share (*of plow*); (naut) sliding ways; (rr) flange (*of rail*)

suòlo *m* ground; soil; floor ‖ *m* (**suola** *fpl*) (coll) layer; (coll) sole (*of shoe*)

suonare (**suòno**) *tr* & *intr* var of **sonare**

suòno *m* sound; (fig) ring; **a suon di bastonate** with a sound thrashing; **a suon di fischi** with loud boos; **suono armonico** (mus) overtone

suòno·stère·o *m* (-o) stereo tape player

suòra *f* nun, sister

super- *pref adj* & *mf* super-, e.g., **supersonico** supersonic; over-, e.g., **superallenamento** overtraining

superaffollaménto *m* overcrowding

superare (**sùpero**) *tr* to surpass; to cross; to overcome; to pass; to exceed; (cards) to trump

supera·to -**ta** *adj* out-of-date, passé

supèrbia *f* pride, haughtiness; **montare in superbia** to get a swelled head

superbió·so -**sa** [*s*] *adj* proud, haughty

supèr·bo -**ba** *adj* proud, haughty; superb; spirited ‖ **i superbi** the haughty ones

supercarburante *m* high-octane gas

supercolòsso *m* supercolossal film

superdònna *f*—**si dà arie di superdonna** she thinks she's hot stuff

supereterodina *f* superheterodyne

superficiale *adj* superficial; surface; cursory, perfunctory ‖ *m* superficial fellow

superfi·cie *f* (-**ci** & **cie**) surface; area; **superficie portante** airfoil

supèr·fluo -**flua** *adj* superfluous ‖ *m* surplus

super-io *m* (-**io**) superego

superióra *f* (eccl) mother superior

superióre *adj* superior; upper; higher; above; **superiore a** higher than; more than; larger than ‖ *m* superior

superlati·vo -**va** *adj* & *m* superlative

superlavóro *m* overwork

supermercato *m* supermarket

supersòni·co -**ca** *adj* (-**ci** -**che**) supersonic

supèrstite *adj* surviving; remaining ‖ *mf* survivor

superstizióne *f* superstition

superstizió·so -**sa** [*s*] *adj* superstitious

superstrada *f* superhighway

superuòmo *m* superman

supervisióne *f* supervision

supervisóre *m* supervisor; (mov) director

supi·no -**na** *adj* supine; on one's back

suppellèttile *f* furnishings; equipment; fixtures; fund (*of knowledge*)

supplementare *adj* supplementary

suppleménto *m* supplement; (mil) reinforcement

supplènte *adj* & *mf* substitute

supplènza *f* substitute assignment

suppleti·vo -**va** *adj* additional; (gram) suppletive

sùppli·ca *f* (-**che**) supplication; plea; petition

supplicante *mf* supplicant

supplicare §197 (**sùpplico**) *tr* to beseech; to plead with; to appeal to

supplichévole *adj* beseeching, imploring

supplire §176 *tr* to replace ‖ *intr* (with *dat*) to supplement, make up for

suppliziare §287 *tr* to torture; to execute

suppli·zio *m* (-**zi**) torture, torment; **estremo supplizio** capital punishment

suppórre §218 *tr* to suppose

suppòrto *m* support, prop

suppositò·rio *m* (-**ri**) suppository

supposizióne *f* supposition; presumption

suppó•sto -sta *adj* alleged || *m* supposition || *f* suppository

suppurare *intr* (ESSERE & AVERE) to suppurate

supremazìa *f* supremacy

suprè•mo -ma *adj* supreme

surclassare *tr* to outclass

surgelare (surgèlo) *tr* to quick-freeze

surreali•sta *mf* (-sti -ste) surrealist

surrenale *adj* adrenal (*gland*)

surrène *m* (anat) adrenal gland

surriscaldare *tr* to overheat

surrogare §209 (surrògo) *tr* to replace

surroga•to -ta *adj* replaceable || *m* makeshift, substitute, ersatz

suscettìbile *adj* susceptible; touchy

suscitare (sùscito) *tr* to rouse; to give rise to; to provoke

susina *f* plum

susino *m* plum tree

susseguènte *adj* subsequent, following

susseguire (sussèguo) *intr* (ESSERE) (with *dat*) to follow || *ref* to follow one after the other

sussidiare §287 *tr* to subsidize

sussidià•rio -ria (-rî -rie) *adj* subsidiary; (nav) auxiliary || *m* supplementary text book; subsidiary

sussì•dio *m* (-dî) subsidy; assistance, relief; sussidi audiovisivi audio-visual aids; sussidi didattici teaching aids; sussidio di disoccupazione unemployment compensation

sussiè•go *m* (-ghi) stiffness, haughtiness

sussistènza *f* substance; subsistence; (mil) quartermaster corps

sussìstere §114 *intr* (ESSERE & AVERE) to subsist; to be, exist

sussultare *intr* to start, jump; to quake

sussulto *m* start, jump; sussulto di terremoto earth tremor

sussurrare *tr* to whisper; to murmur, mutter || *intr* to whisper; to rustle || *ref*—si sussurra it is rumored

sussurra-•tóre -trice *mf* whisperer; grumbler

sussurrì•o *m* (-î) whispering; murmur; rustle

sussurro *m* whisper; murmur

susta *f* temple (*of spectacles*); (coll) spring

suvvìa *interj* come!, come on!

svagare §209 *tr* to entertain; to distract || *ref* to have a good time; to relax

svaga•to -ta *adj* absent-minded; inattentive

sva•go *m* (-ghi) entertainment, diversion; avocation, hobby

svaligiare §290 *tr* to ransack; to rob; to pirate

svaligia•tóre -trice *mf* thief, robber

svalutare (svàluto & svaluto) *tr* to devaluate; to depreciate; to belittle || *ref* to depreciate

svalutazióne *f* depreciation

svanire §176 *intr* (ESSERE) to evaporate; to vanish

svani•to -ta *adj* faded, evaporated; vanished; enfeebled

svantàg•gio *m* (-gi) disadvantage

svantaggió•so -sa [s] *adj* disadvantageous

svaporare (svapóro) *intr* (ESSERE) to evaporate; to vanish

svaria•to -ta *adj* varied; svaria•ti -te several

svarióne *m* blunder, gross error

svasare *tr* to transplant from a pot; to make (*e.g., a gown*) flare

svasa•to -ta *adj* bell-mouthed, flaring

svecchiare §287 (svècchio) *tr* to renew; to rejuvenate; to modernize

svedése [s] *adj* Swedish; safety (*match*) || *mf* Swede || *m* Swedish

svéglia *f* awakening; reveille; alarm clock; dare la svéglia a to wake up

svegliare §280 *tr* & *ref* to wake up

svegliarino *m* alarm clock; (coll) rebuke

své•glio -glia *adj* (-gli -glie) awake; alert || *f* see svéglia

svelare (svélo) *tr* to reveal; to unveil || *ref* to reveal oneself; svelarsi per to reveal oneself to be

svèllere §267 *tr* (lit) to eradicate

sveltézza *f* quickness; slenderness

sveltire §176 *tr* to make shrewd; to quicken, accelerate || *ref* to become smart

svèl•to -ta *adj* quick; slender; brisk; quick-witted; alla svelta quickly; svelto di lingua loose-tongued; svelto di mano light-fingered || svelto *interj* quick!

svenare (svéno) *tr* to bleed to death; (fig) to bleed || *ref* to bleed to death; (fig) to bleed oneself white

svéndere §281 *tr* to sell below cost; to undersell

svéndita *f* clearance sale

svenévole *adj* maudlin, mawkish

svenevolézza *f* maudlinness, mawkishness

sveniménto *m* faint, swoon

svenire §282 *intr* (ESSERE) to faint

sventagliare §280 *tr* to fan; to flash, display

sventagliata *f* blow with a fan; volley

sventare (svènto) *tr* to foil, thwart; (naut) to spill (*a sail*)

sventa•to -ta *adj* careless, thoughtless

svèntola *f* fan (*to kindle fire*); (coll) box, slap; a sventola (*ears*) that stick out

sventolare (svèntolo) *tr* to wave; to fan; to winnow || *intr* to flutter || *ref* to fan oneself

sventolì•o *m* (-î) fluttering, flutter

sventraménto *m* demolition; disembowelment; hernia

sventrare (svèntro) *tr* to demolish; to disembowel; to draw (*a fowl*)

sventura *f* misfortune, mishap; bad luck

sventura•to -ta *adj* unfortunate, unlucky

sverginare (svérgino) *tr* to deflower

svergognare (svergógno) *tr* to put to shame; to unmask

svergogna•to -ta *adj* shameless

svergolare (svérgolo) *tr & ref* to warp; (mach) to twist

svernare (svèrno) *intr* to winter

svèrza [dz] *f* big splinter

sverzino [dz] *m* lash, whipcord

svestire (svèsto) *tr* to undress; to hull (*rice*); (fig) to strip ‖ *ref* to undress; **svestirsi di** to shed (*e.g., leaves*)

svettare (svétto) *tr* to pollard, top ‖ *intr* to stand out; to sway (*said of a tree*)

Svè·vo -va *adj & m* Swabian

Svèzia, la Sweden

svezzamento *m* weaning

svezzare (svézzo) *tr* to wean; **svezzare da** to break (*s.o.*) of (*e.g., a habit*)

sviare §119 *tr* to turn aside; to lead astray ‖ *intr & ref* to go astray; to straggle; (rr) to run off the track

svignare *intr* (ESSERE) to slip away ‖ *ref*—**svignarsela** to sneak away

svilire §176 *tr* to devaluate

svillaneggiare §290 (svillanéggio) *tr* to insult, abuse

sviluppare *tr* to develop; to cause; (lit) to uncoil ‖ *intr* (ESSERE & AVERE) *& ref* to develop; to break out (*said of fire*)

sviluppo *m* development; puberty

svincolare (svìncolo) *tr* to free; to clear (*at customs*)

svincolo *m*—**svincolo autostradale**

interchange; **svincolo doganale** customs clearance

svirilizzare [ddzz] *tr* (fig) to emasculate

svisare *tr* to alter, distort

sviscerare (svìscero) *tr* to eviscerate; to examine thoroughly ‖ *ref*—**sviscerarsi per** to be crazy about; to bow and scrape to

sviscera·to -ta *adj* ardent, passionate; obsequious

svista *f* slip, error, oversight

svitare *tr* to unscrew

svizze·ro -ra *adj & mf* Swiss ‖ **la Svizzera** Switzerland

svocia·to -ta *adj* hoarse

svogliatézza *f* laziness; listlessness

svoglia·to -ta *adj* lazy; listless

svolazzare *intr* to flutter, flit

svolazzo *m* flutter; short flight; curlicue, flourish

svòlgere §289 *tr* to unwrap; to unfold; to unwind; to develop; to pursue (*an activity*); to dissuade ‖ *ref* to unwind; to free oneself; to develop; to take place; to unfold

svolgimento *m* development; composition

svòlta *f* turn; curve; turning point

svoltare (svòlto) *tr* to unwrap ‖ *intr* to turn

svotare §257 or **svuotare** (svuòto) *tr* to empty

T

T, t [ti] *m & f* eighteenth letter of the Italian alphabet

tabac·càio -càia *mf* (-cài -càie) tobacconist

tabaccare §197 *intr* to take snuff

tabaccheria *f* cigar store

tabacchièra *f* snuffbox

tabac·co *m* (-chi) tobacco; **tabacco da fiuto** snuff

tabarro *m* winter coat; cloak

tabèlla *f* tablet; list; schedule; (coll) clapper, noisemaker; **tabella di marcia** timetable

tabellare *adj* (typ) on wooden blocks; scheduled

tabellóne *m* board; bulletin board; (basketball) backboard

tabernàcolo *m* tabernacle

ta·bù *adj invar & m* (-bù) taboo

tàbula *f*—**far tabula rasa di** to make a clean sweep of

tabulare (tàbulo) *tr* to tabulate

tabulatóre *m* tabulator

tabulatrice *f* printer (*of computer*)

tac·ca *f* (-che) notch; size; kind; tally; blemish; (typ) nick; **di mezza tacca** middle-sized; mediocre; **tacca di mira** rear sight (*of firearm*)

tacca·gno -gna *adj* stingy, closefisted ‖ *mf* miser

taccheggia·tóre -trice *mf* shoplifter ‖ *f* prostitute, streetwalker

taccheggiatura *f* or **tacchég·gio** *m* (-gi) shoplifting

tacchétto *m* high heel; cleat (*on soccer or football shoe*)

tacchina *f* turkey hen

tacchino *m* turkey

tàc·cia *f* (-ce) notoriety

tacciare §128 *tr*—**tacciare di** to accuse of, charge with

tac·co *m* (-chi) heel; block; (typ) underlay; **battere i tacchi** to take to one's heels

taccóne *m* (coll) patch; (coll) hobnail; **battere il taccone** to take to one's heels

taccuino *m* pocketbook; notebook

tacére *m* silence; **mettere a tacere** to silence ‖ §268 *tr* to conceal, withhold; to imply, understand ‖ *intr* to keep quiet; to stop playing; to quiet down; to be silent; **far tacere** to silence; **taci!** (coll) shut up!

tachìmetro *m* tachometer; (aut) speedometer

tacitare (tàcito) *tr* to silence, satisfy (*a creditor*); to pay off

tàci·to -ta *adj* silent; tacit

tacitur·no -na *adj* taciturn

tafano *m* horsefly, gadfly

tafferù·glio *m* (-gli) scuffle

taffe·tà *m* (-tà) taffeta; **taffetà adesivo**

or **inglese** adhesive plaster, court plaster

tàglia f ransom, reward; size; build; tally; (mach) tackle

tagliabór·se m (-se) pickpocket

tagliabò·schi m (-schi) woodcutter, woodsman

tagliacar·te m (-te) letter opener, paper knife

tagli·àcque m (-àcque) cutwater (of bridge)

tagliaèrba adj invar grass-cutting

tagliafèr·ro m (-ro) cold chisel

taglialé·gna m (-gna) woodcutter

tagliama·re m (-re) cutwater (of ship)

tagliando m coupon

tagliapiè·tre m (-tre) stonecutter

tagliare §280 tr to cut; to cut down; to cut off; to pick (a pocket); to cross (finish line); to tailor (a suit); to blend (wine); to turn off (e.g., water); **tagliare a fette** to slice; **tagliare in due** to split; **tagliare i panni addosso a qlcu** to slander s.o.; **tagliare i ponti con** to sever relations with; **tagliare i viveri a** to cut off supplies from; **tagliare la corda** to run away; **tagliare la strada a** to stand in the way of; (aut) to cut in front of; **tagliare le gambe a** to make wobbly (said of wine) || intr to cut; to bite (said of cold); **tagliare per una scorciatoia** to take a shortcut || ref to cut oneself; to tear (said of material)

tagliasiga·ri m (-ri) cigar cutter

tagliata f cut; clearing; (mil) abatis; **tagliata ai capelli** haircut

tagliatèlle fpl noodles

taglia·to -ta adj cut; fashioned; **essere tagliato per** to be cut out for; **tagliato all'antica** old-fashioned; **tagliato con l'accetta** rough-hewn || f see **tagliata**

taglia·tóre -trice mf cutter

tagliènte adj cutting || m edge

taglière m carving board

taglierina f paper cutter

tà·glio m (-gli) cut; cutting; dressmaking; cutting edge; sharpness; blending (of wines); size; denomination (of paper money); crossing (of t); (bb) fore edge; **a due tagli** double-edged; **a tagli** by the slice; **dare un taglio a** to chop; **di taglio** edgewise; **rifare il taglio a** to sharpen; **taglio cesareo** Caesarean section; **taglio d'abito** suiting; **taglio dei capelli** haircut; **venire in taglio** to come in handy

tagliòla f trap

tagliuzzare tr to shred, cut into shreds

tailandése [s] adj & mf Thai

Tailàndia, la Thailand

tailleur m (tailleur) woman's tailored costume

talal·tro -tra pron indef another, some other

tàlamo m (lit) nuptial bed

talare adj ankle-length || f soutane, cassock

talché conj so that

talco m talcum; talcum powder

tale adj such; such a; that; **il tale** such and such a; **un tale** such a; a certain; **un tal quale** such a; a certain || pron so-and-so; **il tal dei tali** so-and-so; Mr. so-and-so; **il tale** that fellow; that guy; **quel tale** that fellow, that guy; **tale e quale** like; **tali e quali** exactly, word for word; **un tale** someone, a certain person

talèa f (hort) cutting

talènto m talent; inclination; **a proprio talento** gladly, willingly; **di mal talento** grudgingly; **andare a talento a** to suit, e.g., **non gli va a talento nulla** nothing suits him

talismano m talisman

tallire §176 intr (ESSERE & AVERE) to sprout

tallonare (tallóno) tr (sports) to be at the heels of

talloncino m coupon, stub

tallóne m heel; coupon, stub; tang (of knife); **tallone d'Achille** Achilles heel

talménte adv so, so much

talóra adv sometimes

talpa f mole

talu·no -na pron indef some; someone, somebody || **talu·ni -ne** adj & pron indef some

talvòlta adv sometimes

tamarindo m tamarind

tamburaggiare §290 (tamburéggio) intr to drum; to beat down (said, e.g., of hail)

tamburèllo m tambour (for embroidering); (mus) tambourine

tamburino m drummer

tamburo m drum; barrel (of watch; of windlass); **a tamburo battente** on the spot

tamerice f tamarisk

Tamigi m Thames

tampòco adv—**né tampoco** (archaic) nor . . . either

tamponaménto m stopping, plugging; rear-end collision

tamponare (tampóno) tr to tampon, plug; to collide with; to hit from the rear; (surg) to tampon

tampóne m plug, tampon; pad; (mus) drumstick; (rr) buffer; (surg) tampon; **tampone di vapore** vapor lock

tana f burrow; den; hole; hovel; base (in children games)

tanàglie fpl var of **tenaglie**

tan·ca f (-che) can, jerry can; tank

tanfo m musty or stuffy smell

tangènte adj tangent || f tangent; (com) commission

tàngere §269 tr (lit) to touch

Tàngeri f Tangier

tànghero m boor, lout

tangìbile adj tangible

tàni·ca f (-che) var of **tanca**

tantino m—un tantino a little, e.g., **è un tantino arrabbiato** he is a little angry; a little bit, e.g., **un tantino di dolce** a little bit of cake

tan·to -ta adj & pron indef such, such a; so much; as much; **a dir tanto** or **a far tanto** at the most; **ai tanti**

(*del mese*) on such and such a day (*of the month*); **a tanto** to such a point; to such a level; **e tanto** odd, e.g., **mille dollari e tanto** a thousand odd dollars; **è tanto** it has been a long time, e.g., **è tanto che lo conosco** it has been a long time since I made his acquaintance; **fra tanto** meanwhile; **senza tanto chiasso** without any noise; **tan·ti -te** many; so many; as many; a lot, e.g., **grazie tante!** thanks a lot! **tanti . . . che** so many . . . that; **tanti . . . quanti** as many . . . as; **tanto di guadagnato** so much the better ‖ **tanto** *adv* so much; so; only, e.g., **tanto per passare il tempo** only to pass the time; anyhow; anyway; **nè tanto nè quanto** at all; **tant'è** it's the same; **tanto che** so much that, e.g., **mi ha annoiato tanto che l'ho mandato via** he bothered me so much that I dismissed him; **tanto . . . che** both . . . and, e.g., **tanto Maria che Roberto** both Mary and Robert; so much . . . that; **tanto fa** or **vale** it's all the same; **tanto meglio** so much the better; **tanto meno** so much the less; **tanto per cambiare** as usual; **tanto più . . . quanto più** the more . . . the more; **tanto . . . quanto** as . . . as ‖ *s—* **ascoltare con tanto d'orecchie** to be all ears; **di tanto in tanto** from time to time

tapi·no -na *adj* (lit) wretched ‖ *mf* (lit) wretch

tappa *f* stopping place; stop; stage, leg; (sports) lap; **bruciare le tappe** to press on, keep going; **fare tappa** to stop

tappabu·chi *mf* (-chi) makeshift, pinch hitter, substitute

tappare *tr* to cork, plug; to shut up tight ‖ *ref* to shut oneself in; to plug (*e.g., one's ears*)

tapparèlla *f* (coll) inside rolling shutter

tappéto *m* rug, carpet; (sports) canvas, mat; **mettere al tappeto** (boxing) to knock out; **tappeto erboso** lawn, green; **tappeto verde** gambling table

tappezzare (**tappèzzo**) *tr* to paper (*a wall*); to upholster

tappezzerìa *f* wallpaper; upholstery; upholsterer's shop; tapestry; wallflower

tappezzière *m* paperhanger; upholsterer

tappo *m* cork, stopper; cap; plug; **tappo a corona** bottle cap; **tappo a vite** screw cap

tara *f* tare

taràntola *f* tarantula

tarare *tr* to tare; to set, adjust

tara·to -ta *adj* net (*weight*); calibrated (*instrument*); sickly, weak

tarchia·to -ta *adj* stocky, sturdy

tardare *tr* to delay ‖ *intr* to delay; to be late

tardi *adv* late; **al più tardi** at the latest; **a più tardi!** so long!; **fare tardi** to be late; **più tardi** later; later on; **sul tardi** in the late afternoon

tardi·vo -va *adj* late; retarded, slow; belated

tar·do -da *adj* slow; late; **di età tarda** of advanced years; **tardo d'ingegno** slow-witted

tardó·ne -na *adj* slow-moving ‖ *mf* slowpoke ‖ *f* old dame, middle-aged vamp

tar·ga *f* (-ghe) plate; nameplate; shield; (aut) license plate; (sports) trophy

targare §209 *tr* (aut) to register

targatura *f* (aut) registration

targhétta *f* nameplate

tariffa *f* tariff; rate; rates

tariffà·rio -ria (-ri -rie) *adj* tariff; rate ‖ *m* price list; rate book

tarlare *tr* to eat (*said of woodworms or moths*) ‖ *intr* (ESSERE) & *ref* to become worm-eaten; to become moth-eaten

tarlo *m* woodworm; moth; bookworm; (fig) gnawing

tarma *f* moth; clothes moth

tarmare *tr* to eat (*said of moths*) ‖ *intr* (ESSERE) & *ref* to become moth-eaten

tarmici·da (**-di -de**) *adj* moth-repelling ‖ *m* moth repellent

taròc·co *m* (-chi) tarot; tarok

tarpare *tr* to clip; **tarpare le ali a** to clip the wings of

tartagliare §280 *tr* & *intr* to stutter, stammer

tàrta·ro -ra *adj* Tartar ‖ *m* tartar; Tartar ‖ **Tartaro** *m* Tartarus

tartaru·ga *f* (-ghe) turtle, tortoise; tortoise shell

tartassare *tr* to ill-treat; to harass

tartina *f* slice of bread and butter; canapé

tartufo *m* truffle; (fig) tartuffe, hypocrite

ta·sca *f* (-sche) pocket; briefcase; **aver le tasche piene di** to be sick and tired of; **da tasca** pocket; **rompere le tasche a** (vulg) to bother, annoy; **tasca in petto** inside pocket

tascàbile *adj* pocket; vest-pocket

tascapane *m* knapsack, rucksack

tascata *f* pocketful

taschino *m* vest pocket, small pocket

tassa *f* tax; (coll) duty, fee; **tassa complementare** surtax; **tassa di circolazione** road-use tax; **tassa di registro** registration fee; **tassa scolastica** tuition

tassàbile *adj* taxable

tassàmetro *m* taximeter; **tassametro di parcheggio** parking meter

tassare *tr* to tax; to assess ‖ *ref* to pledge money

tassati·vo -va *adj* positive; specific; peremptory

tassazióne *f* taxation; tax

tassèllo *m* dowel; inlay; plug; patch; reinforcement

tas·sì *m* (-sì) taxi, taxicab

tassi·sta *m* (-sti) taxi driver

tasso *m* stake (anvil); yew tree; (com) rate (*e.g., of interest*); (zool) badger; **tasso valutario fluttuante** (econ) fluctuation of currency rate

tastare *tr* to touch; to feel; to probe; **tastare il terreno** (fig) to see how the land lies

tastièra *f* keyboard; manual (*of organ*)

tasto *m* touch, feeling, feel; plug (*e.g.*, *in watermellon*); key (*of piano or typewriter*); sample (*in drilling*); **tasto bianco** white key, natural; **toccare un tasto falso** to strike a sour note

tastóni *adv*—**a tastoni** gropingly

tàtti·co -ca (-ci -che) *adj* tactical; **tactful** || *m* tactician || *f* tactics; prudence; tactfulness

tatto *m* touch; tact

tatuàg·gio *m* (**-gi**) tattoo

tatuare (tàtuo) *tr* to tattoo

taumatur·go *m* (**-gi & -ghi**) wonder-worker

tauri·no -na *adj* taurine, bull-like; bull

tavèrna *f* tavern, inn

tavernière *m* tavernkeeper

tàvola *f* board, plank; slab; table; tablet; bookplate; list; **tavola a ribalta** drop-leaf table; **tavola armonica** (mus) sound board; **tavola calda** cafeteria, snack bar; **tavola da stirare** ironing board; **tavola di salvezza** (fig) last recourse, lifesaver; **tavola imbandita** open house; **tavola nera** blackboard; **tavola operatoria** operating table; **tavola pitagorica** multiplication table; **tavola reale** backgammon; **tavole di fondazione** charter (*of a charitable institution*)

tavolàc·cio *m* (**-ci**) wooden board (*on which soldiers on guard and prisoners used to sleep*)

tavolare (tàvolo) *tr* to board up

tavolata *f* tableful

tavolato *m* planking; plateau

tavolétta *f* small table; tablet; bar (*e.g.*, *of chocolate*)

tavolière *m* chessboard table; card table; plateau, tableland

tavolino *m* small table; desk

tàvolo *m* table; desk; **tavolo di gioco** gambling table; **tavolo d'ufficio** office desk

tavolòzza *f* palette

tazza *f* cup; bowl

tazzina *f* demitasse

tazzóna *f* mug

te §5 *pron pers*

tè *m* (**tè**) tea; **tè danzante** tea dance, thé dansant

tèa *adj fem*—**rosa tea** tea rose

teatrale *adj* theatrical

teatro *m* theater; performance; drama; stage; (fig) scene; **che teatro!** what fun!; **teatro dell'opera** or **teatro lirico** opera house; **teatro di posa** (mov) studio; **teatro di prosa** legitimate theater

teatróne *m* large theater; (coll) excellent box office

Tèbe *f* Thebes

tè·ca *f* (**-che**) case; (eccl) reliquàry

tecnicismo *m* technicality

tècni·co -ca (-ci -che) *adj* technical || *m* technician; engineer || *f* technique; technics

téco §5 *prep phrase* (lit) with you

tedé·sco -sca *adj & mf* (**-schi -sche**) German

tediare §287 **(tèdio)** *tr* to bore || *ref* to get bored

tè·dio *m* (**-di**) dullness, tedium, boredom; **recare tedio a** to annoy, bother

tedió·so -sa [s] *adj* dull, tedious

tegame *m* pan; **al tegame** fried (*e.g.*, *eggs*)

tegamino *m* small pan; **uova al tegamino** fried eggs

téglia *f* pan; baking pan

tégola *f* tile; (fig) blow

tégolo *m* tile

teièra *f* teapot, teakettle

tèk *m* teak

téla *f* linen; cloth; material; canvas, oil painting; (fig) plot, trap; (lit) weft; (theat) curtain; **far tela** (coll) to beat it; **tela batista** batiste; **tela cerata** oilcloth; **tela da imballaggio** burlap; **tela di ragno** cobweb; **tela di sacco** sackcloth; **tela greggia** gunny, burlap; **tela smeriglio** emery cloth

te·làio *m* (**-lài**) loom; frame; embroidery frame; sash; stretcher (*for oil painting*); (aut) chassis; **telaio di finestra** window sash

teleama·tóre -trice *mf* TV viewer

telear·ma *f* (**-mi**) guided missile

telecabina *f* cable car

telecàmera *f* TV camera

telecomanda·to -ta *adj* remote-control

telecomando *m* remote control

telecommentatore *m* TV newscaster

telecròna·ca *f* (**-che**) TV broadcast; **telecronaca diretta** live broadcast

telecroni·sta *mf* (**-sti -ste**) TV news announcer, TV newscaster

telediffusióne *f* TV broadcasting

teledram·ma *m* (**-mi**) teleplay

telefèri·ca *f* (**-che**) cableway, telpherage

telefonare (telèfono) *tr & intr* to telephone || *ref* to call one another

telefonata *f* telephone call

telefòni·co -ca *adj* (**-ci -che**) telephone

telefoni·sta *mf* (**-sti -ste**) telephone operator, central; telephone installer

telèfono *m* telephone; **telefono a gettone** pay telephone (*operated by tokens*); **telefono a moneta** pay telephone; **telefono interno** intercommunication system, intercom

telegèni·co -ca *adj* (**-ci -che**) telegenic, videogenic

telegiornale *m* TV newscast

telegrafare (telègrafo) *tr & intr* to telegraph

telegràfi·co -ca *adj* (**-ci -che**) telegraphic

telegrafi·sta *mf* (**-sti -ste**) telegrapher; telegraph installer

telègrafo *m* telegraph; **telegrafo di macchina** (naut) engine-room telegraph; **telegrafo ottico** heliograph; wigwag; **telegrafo senza fili** wireless

telegram·ma *m* (**-mi**) telegram

teleguida *f* remote control

teleguidare *tr* to control from a distance, to operate by remote control

Telèmaco *m* Telemachus

telèmetro *m* telemeter; range finder

teleobbiettivo *m* (phot) telephoto lens

telepatìa *f* telepathy

teleproiètto *m* guided missile

telericévere §141 *tr* to receive by TV; to teleview

teleschérmo *m* television screen

telescò·pio *m* (-pi) telescope
telescrivènte *f* teletypewriter; ticker
telescriventi·sta *mf* (-sti -ste) teletype operator
teleselezióne *f* (telp) direct distance dialing
telespetta·tóre -trice *mf* televiewer
teletrasméttere §198 *tr* to televise, telecast
teletrasmissióne *f* telecast
televisióne *f* television, TV
televisi·vo -va *adj* television, TV
televisóre *m* television set
tellina *f* sunset shell or clam
télo *m* piece of cloth; yardage, length of material; (mil) side (*of tent*)
tèlo *m* (lit) dart, arrow
telóne *m* canvas; (theat) curtain
tè·ma *m* (-mi) theme; (gram) stem
téma *f* (lit) fear; per tema di (lit) for fear of
temerarie·tà *f* (-tà) recklessness, rashness
temerà·rio -ria *adj* (-ri -rie) reckless, rash; ill-founded
temére (témo & tèmo) *tr* to fear; to respect ‖ *intr* to fear; temere di to be afraid to
temeri·tà *f* (-tà) temerity
temibile *adj* frightening
tèmpera *f* tempera, distemper
temperala·pis *m* (-pis) or temperamati·te *m* (-te) pencil sharpener
temperaménto *m* middle course, compromise; temper, temperament
temperante *adj* temperate, moderate
temperanza *f* temperance
temperare (tèmpero) *tr* to mitigate; to temper; to sharpen (*a pencil*)
tempera·to -ta *adj* temperate; tempered (*metal*); watered (*wine*)
temperatura *f* temperature; temperatura ambiente room temperature
temperino *m* penknife, pocketknife
tempèsta *f* tempest, storm; tempesta in un bicchier d'acqua tempest in a teapot
tempestare (tempèsto) *tr* to pound; to pepper, pelt; to pester ‖ *intr* to storm
tempesta·to -ta *adj* studded, spangled
tempesti·vo -va *adj* timely
tempestó·so -sa [s] *adj* stormy, tempestuous
tèmpia *f* temple (*side of forehead*); tempie (lit) head
tempiale *m* temple (*in loom; of spectacles*)
tempière *m* Templar
tèm·pio *m* (-pi & -pli) temple (*edifice*)
tempi·sta *mf* (-sti -ste) person or athlete showing good timing; (mus) rhythmist
tèmpo *m* time; weather; age; period, stage; cycle (*of internal-combustion engine*); (gram) tense; (mus) tempo, (mus) movement; (sports) period; (theat, mov) part; ad un tempo at the same time; al tempo che Berta filava long ago; a suo tempo in due time; long ago; a tempo debito in due time; a tempo e luogo at the opportune time; a tempo perso in one's spare time; aver fatto il proprio tempo to be outdated; c'è sempre tempo we are still in time; col tempo in time; dare tempo al tempo to allow time to heal things; darsi del bel tempo to have a good time; da tempo for a long time; del tempo di from the time of; è scaduto il tempo utile the time is up; è tanto tempo it's been a long time; fa bel tempo the weather is fine; il Tempo Father Time; lasciare il tempo che trova to have no effect; molto tempo dopo long afterward; nel tempo che while; per tempo early; prima del tempo formerly; quanto tempo how long; sentire il tempo to feel the weather in one's bones; senza por tempo in mezzo without any delay; tempi che corrono present times; tempo fa some time ago; tempo legale legal time limit; tempo libero leisure time; tempo supplementare (sports) overtime; tempo un . . . within (*e.g., one month*); un tempo long ago
temporale *adj* temporal ‖ *m* storm
temporàne·o -a *adj* temporary, provisional
temporeggiare §290 (temporéggio) *intr* to temporize
tèmpra *f* (metallurgy) tempering, temper; (mus) timbre; (fig) fiber, timber
temprare (tèmpro) *tr* to temper (*metal*); to harden, inure ‖ *ref* to become hardened or inured
tenace *adj* tenacious; tough
tenàcia *f* tenacity
tenaci·tà *f* (-tà) strength, resistance; tenacity
tenàglie *fpl* nippers, pincers, pliers; tongs; a tenaglie (mil) pincers (*e.g., action*)
tènda *f* curtain; awning; tent
tendènza *f* tendency; trend
tendenzió·so -sa [s] *adj* tendentious
tèn·der *m* (-der) (rr) tender
tèndere §270 *tr* to stretch; to tighten; to draw (*a bow*); to cast (*nets*); to lay (*snares*); to reach out (*one's hand*); to prick up (*one's ears*); to draw (*s.o.'s attention*); to set (*sail*) ‖ *intr* to aim; to lean; to tend; to tend to be
tendina *f* curtain, blind
tèndine *m* (anat) tendon
tendiscar·pe *m* (-pe) shoetree
tenditóre *m* turnbuckle; tenditore della racchetta (tennis) press
tendóne *m* big curtain; canvas; tent (*of circus*); (theat) curtain
tendòpo·li *f* (-li) tent city
tènebre *fpl* darkness
tenebró·so -sa [s] *adj* dark, gloomy
tenènte *m* lieutenant; (mil) first lieutenant; (nav) lieutenant junior grade; tenente colonnello (mil) lieutenant colonel; tenente di vascello (nav) lieutenant senior grade
tenére §271 *tr* to hold; to have; to keep; to stand (*e.g., rough sea*); to wear; to make (*a speech*); to follow

(*a course*); **tenere a battesimo** to stand for, sponsor; **tenere al corrente** to keep informed; **tenere a memoria** to remember; **tenere da conto** to hold in high esteem; to take good care of (*s.th*); **tenere d'occhio** to keep an eye on; **tenere la destra** to keep to the right; **tenere la strada** (aut) to hug the road; **tenere la testa a partito** to mend one's ways; **tenere le distanze** to keep aloof; **tenere mano a** to connive with; **tenere presente** to bear in mind; **tenere qlco a conto** to take good care of s.th || *intr* to hold; to take root; **tenerci che** to be anxious for, e.g., **ci tengo che vinca le elezioni** I am anxious for him to win the elections; **tenere a destra** to keep to the right; **tenere alle apparenze** to stand on ceremony; to keep up appearances; **tenere da** to hail from; to take after; **tenere dietro a** to follow; to keep abreast of; **tenere duro** to hold fast; **tenere per** (sports) to be a fan of || *ref* to hold; to hold on; to keep; to keep (*e.g., ready*); to regard oneself; **tenersi a** to adhere to (*e.g., a treaty*); to hold on to; to stick to; to follow; **tenersi a galla** to stay afloat; **tenersi al largo** (naut) to keep to the open sea; **tenersi al vento** (naut) to sail to leeward; (fig) to follow a safe course; **tenersi in piedi** to stand up; **tenersi per mano** to hold hands; **tenersi sulle proprie** to keep aloof

tenerézza *f* tenderness; fondness, endearment

tène•ro -ra *adj* tender || *m* tender portion

tènia *f* tapeworm

teni•tóre -trice *mf* keeper

tènnis *m* tennis; **tennis da tavolo** table tennis, ping-pong

tenni•sta *mf* (**-sti -ste**) tennis player

tennìsti•co -ca *adj* (**-ci -che**) tennis

tenóne *m* tenon

tenóre *m* character, tone; tenor; alcoholic content; manner (*of living*); **tenore di vita** way of life; standard of living

tensióne *f* tension; **alta tensione** high tension; **tensione sanguigna** blood pressure

tentàcolo *m* tentacle

tentare (**tènto**) *tr* to try, attempt; to assay; to tempt; (lit) to touch

tentativo *m* attempt; **tentativo di furto** attempted robbery

tenta•tóre -trice *adj* tempting || *m* tempter || *f* temptress

tentazióne *f* temptation

tentennare (**tenténno**) *tr* to shake; to rock || *intr* to shake; to wobble; to hesitate; to stagger

tentóne or **tentóni** *adv* blindly; gropingly; at random

tènue *adj* small (*intestine*); (lit) tenuous, thin

tenu•to -ta *adj* bound, obliged || *f* capacity, volume; estate, farm; uniform; outfit; (sports) endurance,

resistance; **a tenuta d'acqua** watertight; **a tenuta d'aria** airtight; **tenuta dei libri** bookkeeping; **tenuta di gala** (mil, nav) full-dress uniform; **tenuta di servizio** (mil) fatigues; **tenuta di strada** (aut) roadability

tenzóne *f* combat; poetic contest

teologia *f* theology

teòlo•go *m* (**-gi**) theologian

teorè•ma *m* (**-mi**) theorem

teorèti•co -ca *adj* (**-ci -che**) theoretic(al)

teoria *f* theory; (lit) series, row

teòri•co -ca (**-ci -che**) *adj* theoretical || *m* theoretician

tèpi•do -da *adj* var of tiepido

tepóre *m* warmth

tèppa *f* underworld, rabble

teppi•sta *m* (**-sti**) hoodlum, hooligan

terapèuti•co -ca (**-ci -che**) *adj* therapeutic || *f* therapeutics

terapia *f* therapy; **terapia convulsivante** or **terapia d'urto** shock therapy

Terèsa *f* Theresa

tèrgere §162 *tr* (lit) to wipe

tergicristallo *m* windshield wiper

tergiversare (**tergivèrso**) *intr* to stall; to beat around the bush

tèr•go *m* (**-ghi**) back (*of a coin*); **a tergo** on the reverse side || *m* (**-ga** *fpl*) (lit) back; **volgere le terga** (lit) to turn one's back

termale *adj* thermal (*e.g., waters*)

tèrme *fpl* spa, hot spring

tèrmi•co -ca *adj* (**-ci -che**) thermal; heat, heating

terminale *adj* & *m* terminal

terminare (**tèrmino**) *tr* to border; to end, terminate || *intr* (ESSERE) to end, terminate

terminazióne *f* termination; completion; (gram) ending

tèrmine *m* border; marker; term; deadline; end; goal; boundary, bounds; (fig) point; **a termini di legge** according to law; **avere termine** to end; **in altri termini** in other words; **mezzo termine** half measure; **porre termine a** to put an end to; **portare a termine** to put through

terminologia *f* terminology

termistóre *m* (elec) thermistor

tèrmite *f* termite

termoconvettóre *m* baseboard radiator

termocòppia *f* thermocouple

termodinàmi•co -ca (**-ci -che**) *adj* thermodynamic || *f* thermodynamics

termòforo *m* heating pad

termòmetro *m* thermometer

termonucleare *adj* thermonuclear

tèr•mos *m* (**-mos**) thermos bottle

termosifóne *m* radiator; hot-water heating system; steam heating system

termòstato *m* thermostat

termovisièra *f* electric defroster

tèrno *m* tern (*in lotto*); **vincere un terno al lotto** to hit the jackpot

tèrra *f* earth; land; ground; world; city, town; dirt, soil; clay; **essere a terra** to be downcast; to be broke; to be flat (*said of a tire*); **rimanere a terra** to miss the boat; **sotto terra** underground; **terra bruciata** scorched earth; **terra di nessuno** no man's land; **terra di Siena** sienna; **terra ferma** terra firma; mainland; **terra** skimming the ground; (naut) close to the shore; (fig) mediocre, second-rate

terracòtta *f* (**terrecòtte**) terra cotta; earthenware

terraférma *f* mainland (*as distinguished from adjacent islands*); terra firma (*dry land, not air or water*)

terràglia *f* crockery; **terraglie** earthenware

terranò•va *m* (**-va**) Newfoundland (*dog*) || **Terranova** *f* Newfoundland

terrapièno *m* embankment

terrazza *f* terrace; **a terrazza** terraced

terrazza•no -na *mf* villager

terrazzo *m* balcony; terrace; ledge, shelf; terrazzo

terremota•to -ta *adj* hit by an earthquake || *mf* earthquake victim

terremòto *m* earthquake

terré•no -na *adj* terrestrial, earthly; ground-floor; first-floor || *m* ground floor; first floor; ground; soil; land, plot of ground; combat zone, terrain; **preparare il terreno** to work the soil; (fig) to pave the way; **scendere sul terreno** to fight a duel; **tastare il terreno** to feel one's way; **terreno di gioco** (sports) field

tèrre•o -a *adj* wan, sallow

terrèstre *adj* terrestrial; ground, land || *m* earthling

terribile *adj* terrible; awesome, awful

terrìc•cio *m* (**-ci**) soil; top soil

terriè•ro -ra *adj* land; landed

terrificare §197 (**terrìfico**) *tr* to terrify

terrìna *f* tureen

territò•rio *m* (**-ri**) territory

terróre *m* terror

terrorismo *m* terrorism

terrori•sta *mf* (**-sti -ste**) terrorist

terrorizzare [ddzz] *tr* to terrorize

terró•so -sa [s] *adj* dirty (*e.g., spinach*); dirty-earth (*color*); (chem) rare-earth (*metal*)

tèr•so -sa *adj* clear

tèrza *f* third grade; (aut) third; (eccl) tierce; (rr) third class

terzaforzì•sta (**-sti -ste**) *adj* of the third force || *m* partisan of the third force

terzaròlo *m* (naut) reef

terzétto *m* trio

terzià•rio -ria *adj* (**-ri -rie**) tertiary

terzina *f* tercet

terzino *m* (soccer) back

tèr•zo -za *adj & pron* third || *m* third; third party || *f* see **terza**

terzùlti•mo -ma *adj* third from the end

tésa [s] *f* brim (*of hat*); snare, net

tesare [s] (**téso**) *tr* to pull taut

tè•schio *m* (**-schi**) skull

tè•si *f* (**-si**) thesis; dissertation

té•so -sa [s] *adj* taut, tight; strained; outstretched (*hand*); **con le orecchie tese** all ears || *f* see **tesa**

tesorerìa *f* treasury; liquid assets

tesorière *m* treasurer

tesòro *m* treasure; treasury; thesaurus; bank vault; **far tesoro di** to treasure, prize; **tesoro mio!** my darling!

Tèspi *m* Thespis

tèssera *f* card; domino (*piece*); tessera (*of mosaic*)

tessera•to -ta *adj* card-carrying; rationed || *mf* card-carrying member; holder of ration card

tèssere *tr* to weave; to spin

tèssile *adj* textile || *m* textile; **tessili** textile workers

tessilsac•co *m* (**-chi**) garment bag

tessi•tóre -trice *mf* weaver

tessitura *f* weaving; spinning mill; (mus) range; (fig) plot

tessuto *m* cloth, fabric; tissue

tèsta *f* head; mind; bulb (*of garlic*); spindle (*of wheel*); warhead (*of torpedo*); row (*of bricks*); **a testa** apiece; per capita; **a testa a testa** neck and neck; **fare di testa propria** to act on one's own; **fare la testa grossa a** to stun; to annoy; **levarsi di testa** to forget about; **mettersi in testa di** to get it into one's head to; **non avere testa di** + *inf* to not feel like + *ger*; **non sapere dove battere la testa** to not know which way to turn; **per una corta testa** by a neck; **rompersi la testa** to rack one's brains; **tenere testa a** to face up to; **testa coda** (aut) spin; **testa di ponte** (mil) bridgehead; **testa di sbarco** beachhead; **testa e croce** head or tails

testaménto *m* will, testament || **Antico** or **Vecchio Testamento** Old Testament; **Nuovo Testamento** New Testament

testardàggine *f* stubborness

testar•do -da *adj* stubborn

testata *f* headboard (*of bed*); top; end (*e.g., of beam*); heading (*of newspaper*); butt with the head; nose (*of rocket*)

tèste *m* witness

testé *adv* (lit) a short time ago; (lit) presently, in a little while

testìcolo *m* testicle

testièra *f* headboard; crown (*of harness*); battering ram

testimòne *m* witness; **testimone di nozze** best man; **testimone di veduta** or **testimone oculare** eyewitness

testimonianza *f* testimony

testimoniare §287 (**testimònio**) *tr* to attest; to depose, testify; **testimoniare il falso** to bear false witness || *intr* to bear witness

testimò•nio *m* (**-ni**) (coll) witness

testina *f* small head; whimsical person; boiled head of veal; head (*e.g., of tape recorder*)

tèsto *m* text; pie dish; (coll) flower vase; **fare testo** to serve as a model

testó•ne -na *mf* dolt; stubborn person

testuale *adj* textual; word-for-word

testùggine *f* turtle; tortoise

tètano *m* tetanus

tè•tro -tra *adj* (lit) gloomy, dark

tétta *f* (coll) teat

tettarèlla *f* nipple

tétto *m* roof; ceiling price; home; **senza tetto** homeless; **tetto a capanna** gable roof; **tetto a padiglione** hip roof; **tetto a una falda** lean-to roof; **tetto di paglia** thatched roof

tettóia _f_ shed; pillared roof

tettóia-garage _f_ (**tettóie-garage**) carport

tettùc·cio _m_ (**-ci**) (aut) roof; (aut) top; **tettuccio a bulbo** dome; **tettuccio rigido** (aut) convertible top

ti §5 _pron_

tìbia _f_ tibia, shinbone

tic _m_ (**tic**) twitch; habit

ficchettì·o _m_ (**-i**) click (_of typewriter_); patter (_of rain_); tick (_of clock_)

fìc·chio _m_ (**-chi**) whim; tic; viciousness (_of animal_); blemish

tièpi·do -da _adj_ tepid, lukewarm

tifo _m_ typhus; **fare il tifo per** to root for; to be a fan of

tifoidèa _f_ typhoid fever

tifóne _m_ typhoon

tifó·so -sa [s] _adj_ rooting ‖ _mf_ fan, rooter

ti·glio _m_ (**-gli**) linden, lime; bast; fiber

tiglió·so -sa [s] _adj_ tough, fibrous

tigna _f_ ringworm; (coll) tightwad

tignòla _f_ clothes moth

tigra·to -ta _adj_ striped; tabby

tigre _f_ tiger

timballo _m_ pie, meat pie; timbale; (lit) drum

timbrare _tr_ to stamp; to cancel (_stamps_)

timbro _m_ stamp; character (_of a writer_); (mus) timbre; **timbro di gomma** rubber stamp; **timbro postale** postmark

timidézza _f_ shyness, bashfulness; timidity

tìmi·do -da _adj_ shy, bashful; timid ‖ _mf_ shy person

timo _m_ (anat) thymus; (bot) thyme

timóne _m_ rudder, helm; shaft, pole (_of cart_); **timone di direzione** (aer) rudder; **timone di profondità** (aer) elevator; (nav) diving plane (_of submarine_)

timonièra _f_ (naut) pilot house

timonière _m_ helmsman, steersman; coxswain

timonniè·ro -ra _adj_ rudder; tail (_feather_) ‖ _f_ see **timoniera**

timora·to -ta _adj_ conscientious; **timorato di Dio** God-fearing

timóre _m_ fear; awe; **avere timore di** to fear

timoró·so -sa [s] _adj_ timorous

tìmpano _m_ (archit) tympanum; (anat) eardrum; (mus) kettledrum; **rompere i timpani a** to deafen

tin·ca _f_ (**-che**) (ichth) tench

tinèllo _m_ pantry; breakfast room

tìngere §126 _tr_ to dye; to dirty, soil; to color ‖ _ref_ to dye (_e.g., one's hair_); to put on make-up; to become colored

tino _m_ tub, vat

tinòzza _f_ tub, washtub

tinta _f_ paint; color; dye; shade; stain; **calcare le tinte** to exaggerate; **mezza tinta** halftone, shade; **vedere qlco a fosche tinte** to take a dim view of s.th; **vedere qlco a tinte rosee** to see s.th through rose-colored glasses

tintarèlla _f_ (coll) suntan

tinteggiare §290 (**tintéggio**) _tr_ to calci-

mine; to whitewash; to tint; to paint (_e.g., a house_)

tintinnare _intr_ (ESSERE & AVERE) to jingle; to clink

tintinnì·o _m_ (**-i**) jingling; clink

tìn·to -ta _adj_ dyed; tinged; soiled; (lit) dark ‖ _f_ see **tinta**

tintó·re -ra _mf_ dyer; dry cleaner

tintorìa _f_ dyeworks; dry cleaning establishment; dyeing

tintura _f_ dyeing; dyestuff; tincture; smattering; **tintura di iodio** iodine

tipi·co -ca _adj_ (**-ci -che**) typical

tipificare §197 (**tipìfico**) _tr_ to standardize

tipizzare [ddzz] _tr_ to standardize

tipo _adj invar_ typical, e.g., **famiglia tipo** typical family ‖ _m_ type; standard, model; fellow, guy; phylum (_in taxonomy_); **bel tipo** (coll) character, card; **coi tipi di** printed in the shop of; **sul tipo di** similar to; **vero tipo** prototype, epitome

tipografìa _f_ typography; print shop

tipogràfi·co -ca _adj_ (**-ci -che**) typographical

tipògrafo _m_ typographer; owner of print shop, printer

tipòmetro _m_ (typ) line gauge

tiptologìa _f_ table rapping (_during séance_); tapping in code (_among jailbirds_)

tiraba·ci _m_ (**-ci**) (coll) spitcurl

tiràg·gio _m_ (**-gi**) draft; **a tiraggio forzato** forced-draft

tiralìne·e _m_ (**-e**) ruling pen

tirannìa _f_ tyranny

tirànni·co -ca _adj_ (**-ci -che**) tyrannical

tiran·no -na _adj_ tyrannical ‖ _mf_ tyrant

tirante _m_ brace; rod; strap; trace (_of harness_); **tirante degli stivali** bootstrap

tirapiè·di _m_ (**-di**) hangman's assistant; underling

tirapu·gni _m_ (**-gni**) brass knuckles

tirare _tr_ to pull; to draw; to tug; to suck; to haul in (_nets_); to deserve (_a slap_); to pluck; to throw; to give (_blows_); to utter (_oaths_); to shoot (_arrows, bullets_); to stretch; to tighten (_one's belt_); to print; to make (_an addition_); (sports) to force (_the pace_); **tirare a lucido** to polish; **tirare a sé** to attract; **tirare a sorte** to draw lots for; **tirare fuori** to draw out; to pull out; to get out; **tirare giù** to lower; to jot down; (coll) to gulp down; **tirare gli orecchi a** to punish by yanking the ears of; **tirare il collo a** to wring the neck of; **tirare in ballo** to bring up (_a subject_); **tirare l'acqua al proprio mulino** to look out for number one; **tirare l'anima coi denti** to be at the end of one's rope; **tirare l'aria** to draw (_said of a chimney_); **tirare le cuoia** (slang) to kick the bucket; **tirare per i capelli** to drag by the hair; to drag in; to push, coerce; **tirare per le lunghe** to stretch out; **tirare su** to lift; to raise (_children_); to pull up ‖ _intr_ to be too tight (_said of clothes_); to shoot; to blow (_said of wind_); to draw (*said, e.g., of chimney*); **tirare a** to tend toward, lean toward; **tirare a** + *inf* to try to + *inf*; **tirare a campare** (coll) to goldbrick; **tirare avanti** to go ahead; to manage to get along; **tirare di boxe** to box; **tirare diritto** to go straight ahead; **tirare di scherma** to fence; **tirare in lungo** to delay, linger; to dillydally; **tirare innanzi** to keep on going; to go ahead; **tirare sul prezzo** to haggle; **tirare via** to hurry along || *ref—* **tirarsi addosso** (coll) to bring upon oneself; **tirarsi dietro** to drag along; **tirarsi fuori da** to get out of (*e.g., trouble*); **tirarsi gente in casa** to keep open house; **tirarsi indietro** to move back; **tirarsi in là** to move aside; **tirarsi su** to get up; to recover; to roll up (*one's sleeves*); **tirarsi un colpo di rivoltella** to shoot oneself

tirastiva·li *m* (-**li**) bootjack

tirata *f* pull; stretch; tirade

tirati·ra *m* (-**ra**) (coll) yen; **fare a tira-tira per** (coll) to scramble for

tira·to -**ta** *adj* taut; forced (*smile*); drawn (*face*); tight, closefisted; **tirato con** short of || *f* see **tirata**

tira·tóre -**trice** *mf* shot; **tiratore scelto** sharpshooter; **franco tiratore** sniper

tiratura *f* printing

tirchieria *f* stinginess

tìr·chio -**chia** (-**chi** -**chie**) *adj* stingy, closefisted || *mf* miser

tirèlla *f* trace (*of harness*)

tirétto *m* (coll) drawer

tiritèra *f* rigmarole

tiro *m* pull; pair, brace (*e.g., of oxen*); throw; fire, shot; trick; **a tiro** within reach; **a un tiro di schioppo** within gunshot; **da tiro** draft; **fuori del tiro dell'orecchio** out of earshot; **tiro alla fune** tug of war; **tiro al piattello** trapshooting; **tiro a quattro** four-in-hand; **tiro a segno** rifle range; shooting gallery

tiroci·nio *m* (-**ni**) apprenticeship; internship; **tirocinio didattico** practice teaching

tiròide *f* thyroid

tirolése [s] *adj & mf* Tyrolean

tirrèni·co -**ca** *adj* (-**ci** -**che**) Tyrrhenian

Tirrèno *m* Tyrrhenian Sea

tisana *f* tea, infusion

tisi *f* consumption, tuberculosis

tisi·co -**ca** (-**ci** -**che**) *adj* consumptive; stunted || *mf* consumptive

titàni·co -**ca** *adj* (-**ci** -**che**) titanic

titànio *m* titanium

titillare *tr* to tickle

titolare *adj* titular; regular, full-time || *m* owner, boss; incumbent || *v* (**tìtolo**) *tr* to name, call

tìtolo *m* title; heading; name; caption; entry (*in dictionary*); grade; fineness (*of gold*); (chem) titer; (educ) credit; **avere titolo a** to have a right to; **a titolo di as**, by way of; **fitoli di testa** (mov) credits; **titolo al portatore** security payable to bearer; **titolo azionario** share; **titolo corrente** subtitle; **titolo di credito** instrument of credit; certificate; deed; conveyance; **titolo di studio** degree, diploma; credits; **titolo di trasporto** travel document

titubare (**tìtubo**) *intr* to hesitate; to waver

tiziané·sco -**sca** *adj* (-**schi** -**sche**) titian; Titian

ti·zio *m* (-**zi**) fellow, guy

tizzo or **tizzóne** *m* brand, firebrand

to' *interj* here!; well!

tobò·ga *m* (-**ga**) toboggan

toccafèrro *m* tag (*game*)

toccamano *m* handshake (*to close a deal*); bribe, under-the-table tip

toccante *adj* touching, moving

toccare §197 (**tócco**) *tr* to touch; to reach; to concern; to push (*a button*); to play (*an instrument*); to feel; to hit (*the target*); to border on (*e.g., the age of forty*); **toccare con mano** to make sure of; **toccare il cielo col dito** to be in seventh heaven; **toccare nel vivo** to touch to the quick; **toccare terra** to land; **toccarne molte** to get a good thrashing; **toccato! touché!** || *intr* (ESSERE) to be touching; **toccare a** to be up to, e.g., **tocca a lui** it's up to him; to have to, e.g., **le tocca partire domani** she has to leave tomorrow; to deserve, e.g., **gli è toccato il premio** he deserved the prize || *ref* to meet, e.g., **gli estremi si toccano** extremes meet

toccasa·na [s] *m* (-**na**) cure-all, panacea

tocca·to -**ta** *adj* touché; touched in the head, nutty; **già toccato** abovementioned || *f* (mus) toccata

tóc·co -**ca** (-**chi** -**che**) *adj* touched, nutty; spoiled (*fruit*) || *m* touch; knock; one o'clock (*P.M.*); (coll) stroke

tòc·co *m* (-**chi**) chunk, piece; mortarboard; toque; **un bel tocco di ragazza** a buxom lass

tò·ga *f* (-**ghe**) gown, academic gown; (hist) toga

tògliere §127 *tr* to remove, take away; to take; to cut (*telephone connection*); to deduct; to take off; to preclude, prevent; **togliere a** to take away from; **togliere al cielo** (lit) to praise to the skies; **togliere di mezzo** to remove; to do away with; **togliere la parola a** to take the floor from; **togliere l'onore a** to dishonor; **togliere una spina dal cuore a** to relieve the heart and mind of || *intr—* **tolga Dio!** God forbid! || *ref* to take off (*e.g., one's coat*); to have (*e.g., a tooth*) pulled; to satisfy (*a whim*); **togliersi di mezzo** to get out of the way; **togliersi la vita** to take one's life; **togliersi qlcu dai piedi** to get rid of s.o.

tòlda *f* (naut) deck

tolemài·co -**ca** *adj* (-**ci** -**che**) Ptolemaic

tolétta *f* dressing table; dressing room; toilet, washroom; dress, gown; **fare toletta** or **farsi la toletta** to make one's toilet

tolleràbile *adj* tolerable

tollerante *adj* tolerant; liberal
tolleranza *f* tolerance; leeway
tollerare (**tòllero**) *tr* to tolerate; to bear, stand
tòl•to **-ta** *adj* taken; except, leaving out, e.g., **tolta sua figlia** leaving his daughter out ‖ *m*—**il mal tolto** ill-gotten goods
to•màio *m* (**-mài** & **-màia** *fpl*) or **to•màia** *f* (**-màie**) upper (*of shoe*)
tómba *f* tomb, grave
tombale *adj* grave (*e.g., stone*)
tombino *m* sewer inlet
tómbola *f* bingo; (coll) tumble
tombolare (**tómbolo**) *tr* (coll) to tumble down (*the steps*) ‖ *intr* (ESSERE) to fall headlong; (coll) to go to rack and ruin; (aer) to tumble
tómbolo *m* fall, tumble; bolster; lace pillow; (coll) fatso; **fare un tombolo** to go to rack and ruin; to lose one's position
Tommaso *m* Thomas
tòmo *m* volume; (coll) character
tòna•ca *f* (**-che**) (eccl) frock; (eccl) soutane; **gettare la tonaca alle ortiche** to doff the cassock
tonare §257 *intr* to peal; to thunder ‖ *impers* (ESSERE & AVERE)—**tuona** it is thundering
tondeggiante *adj* round; rounded; chubby; curvaceous
tondino *m* coaster; iron rod (*for reinforced concrete*); (archit) molding (*at top or bottom of column*); (archit) astragal
tón•do **-da** *adj* round; (typ) roman ‖ *m* round; circle; plate, dish; (typ) roman; **in tondo** around
tónfo *m* splash; thump
tòni•co **-ca** (**-ci -che**) *adj* tonic ‖ *m* tonic (*medicine*) ‖ *f* (mus) tonic
tonificare §197 (**tonìfico**) *tr* to invigorate
tonnara *f* tuna nets
tonnellàg•gio *m* (**-gi**) tonnage
tonnellata *f* ton; **tonnellata di stazza** displacement ton
tónno *m* tuna
tòno *m* tone; tune; hue; style; (mus) pitch; (mus) key; **darsi tono** to put on airs; **di tono** stylish; **fuori di tono** out of tune
tonsilla *f* tonsil
tonsura *f* tonsure
tón•to **-ta** *adj* (coll) dumb, stupid
topàia *f* rat's nest; hovel
topà•zio *m* (**-zi**) topaz
tòpi•co **-ca** (**-ci -che**) *adj* topical ‖ *f* topic; (coll) blunder
tòpo *m* mouse; rat; **topo campagnolo** field mouse; **topo d'acqua** water rat; **topo d'albergo** hotel thief; **topo d'auto** car thief; **topo di biblioteca** bookworm
topografia *f* topography
topolino *m* little mouse ‖ **Topolino** *m* Mickey Mouse
toporagno *m* shrew
tòppa *f* patch; keyhole
tòppo *m* stump; headstock (*of lathe*)
torace *m* thorax

tórba *f* peat
tórbi•do **-da** *adj* cloudy; murky ‖ *m* trouble; **pescare nel torbido** to fish in troubled waters; **torbidi** disorder
torbièra *f* peatbog
tòrcere §272 *tr* to twist; to wring; to bend, curve; to curl (*the lips*); to lead astray ‖ *intr* (ESSERE) to bend, curve ‖ *ref* to writhe; to bend over; **torcersi dalle risa** to split with laughter
torchiare §287 (**tòrchio**) *tr* to press
tòr•chio *m* (**-chi**) press; printing press
tòr•cia *f* (**-ce**) torch
torcicòllo *m* stiff neck; (orn) wryneck
torcinaso [s] *m* (vet) twitch
tórdo *m* thrush; simpleton
torèllo *m* young bull; (naut) garboard
torèro *m* bullfighter
tórlo *m* yolk
tórma *f* crowd, throng; herd
torménta *f* blizzard
tormentare (**torménto**) *tr* to torture, torment; to pester, nag ‖ *ref* to worry
torménto *m* torture, torment; pang; bore, pest, annoyance
tornacónto *m* interest, advantage
tornante *m* curve
tornare (**tórno**) *tr* (lit) to restore; (obs) to turn ‖ *intr* (ESSERE) to return; to go back; (coll) to jibe, agree, square; **tornare a** to be profitable to; **tornare a** + *inf* verb + again, e.g., **tornare a essere** to become again; **tornare a fare** to do again; **tornare a bomba** to return to the point; **tornare a galla** to come back to the surface; **tornare a gola** to repeat (*said of food*); **tornare a onore a qicu** to do credit to s.o.; **tornare a pennello** to fit to a T; **tornare in sé** to come to; **tornare opportuno** or **utile a** to suit, e.g., **non gli tornó opportuno vendere la casa** it did not suit him to sell the house; **tornare utile** to come in handy; **tornare sulle proprie decisioni** to change one's mind
tornasóle *m* litmus
tornèllo *m* turnstile
tornèo *m* tournament, tourney
tór•nio *m* (**-ni**) lathe
tornire §176 *tr* to turn, turn up (*on a lathe*); to polish
tornitore *m* lathe operator
tórno *m* turn; period (*of time*); **levarsi di torno** to get rid of; **torno torno** all around
tòro *m* bull; (archit, geom) torus; (lit) marital bed ‖‖ **Toro** *m* (astrol) Taurus
torpèdine *f* torpedo
torpedinièra *f* destroyer escort; torpedo-boat destroyer
torpè•do *f* (**-do**) (aut) touring car
torpedóne *m* bus, motor coach
tòrpi•do **-da** *adj* torpid, sluggish; numb
torpóre *m* torpor, sluggishness; numbness
tórre *f* tower; (chess) castle; (nav) turret; **torre campanaria** bell tower; **torre d'avorio** ivory tower; **torre di**

lancio (rok) gantry; **torre pendente** leaning tower

torrefare §173 *tr* to roast (*coffee*)

torreggiante *adj* towering

torreggiare §290 (**torréggio**) *intr* to tower

torrènte *m* torrent

torrenziale *adj* torrential

torrétta *f* turret; (nav) conning tower (*of submarine*); (archit) bartizan

tòrri·do -da *adj* torrid

torrióne *m* donjon; (nav) conning tower (*of battleship*)

torróne *m* nougat

torsióne *f* torsion

tórso *m* stalk; core (*of fruit*); torso, trunk; **a torso nudo** bare-chested

tórsolo *m* core; stalk; stem; **non vale un torsolo** it's not worth a fig

tórta *f* pie; cake, tart; **torta di mele** apple pie

tòrta *f* twist

tortièra *f* baking pan

tòr·to -ta *adj* twisted; crooked; gloomy (*face*) || *m* wrong; **a torto** unjustly; **avere torto** to be wrong; **avere torto marcio** to be dead wrong; **dar torto a** to lay the blame on; **fare torto a** to wrong, e.g., **fece torto al proprio fratello** he wronged his own brother; **to bring discredit upon** || *f* see **tòrta** || **torto** *adv* askance

tórtora *f* turtledove

tortuó·so -ṣa [s] *adj* winding; ambiguous; (fig) devious

tortura *f* torture

torturare *tr* to torture; to pester || *ref* to torment oneself; **torturarsi il cervello** to rack one's brain

tosare (tóso) *tr* to clip, crop; to shear; (fig) to fleece

tosa·tóre -trice *mf* clipper, shearer || *f* clippers; lawn mower

tosatura *f* sheepshearing; clip (*of wool*)

tosca·no -na *adj* & *mf* Tuscan || *m* stogy || **Toscana, la** Tuscany

tósse *f* cough; **tosse asinina** or **canina** whooping cough

tòssi·co -ca (**-ci -che**) toxic || *m* (archaic) poison

tossicòmane *mf* drug addict

tossicomanìa *f* drug addiction

tossina *f* toxin

tossire (tósso) & §176 *intr* to cough

tostapa·ne *m* (**-ne**) toaster

tostare (tòsto) *tr* to toast; to roast (*e.g., coffee*)

tò·sto -sta *adj* (lit) prompt; (lit) impudent; (lit) brazen (*face*) || **tosto** *adv* (lit) soon; **ben tosto** (lit) very soon; **tosto che** (lit) as soon as

tòt *adj pl invar* so many, that many || *pron invar* so much, that much

totale *adj* & *m* total

totalità·rio -ria *adj* (**-ri -rie**) total, complete; totalitarian

totalizzare [ddzz] *tr* to add up; to make (*so many points*)

totalizzatóre [ddzz] *m* pari-mutuel; betting window; (mach) totalizator

tòtano *m* squid; (orn) tattler

totocàlcio *m* soccer pool

tovàglia *f* tablecloth

tovagliòlo *m* napkin

tòz·zo -za *adj* stubby, stocky || *m* piece (*of fresh bread*); crust (*of bread*)

tra *prep* among; between

trabàccolo *m* small fishing boat

traballare *intr* to shake; to totter; to wobble; to stagger; to toddle

trabìccolo *m* frame for bedwarmer; jalopy; hulk

traboccante *adj* overflowing

traboccare §197 (**trabócco**) *tr* to knock down || *intr* to overflow (*said of container*) || *intr* (ESSERE) to overflow (*said of liquid*) || *intr* (ESSERE & AVERE) to tip (*said of scales*); **far traboccare** to make (*the scales*) tip

trabocchétto *m* pitfall; trapdoor

trabóc·co *m* (**-chi**)—**trabocco di sangue** internal hemorrhage

tracagnòt·to -ta *adj* stubby, stocky || *mf* stocky person

tracannare *tr* to gulp down

tracchég·gio *m* (**-gi**) delay; (fencing) feint

tràc·cia *f* (**-ce**) track; trace, clue; trail; outline, plan; (lit) line, row; **buona traccia** right track; **fare la traccia a** to open the way for; **in** or **sotto traccia** concealed (*e.g., wiring*); **tracce** tinge; (chem) traces

tracciante *adj* tracer (*bullet*)

tracciare §128 *tr* to trace; to pave (*the way*); to outline; (lit) to track

tracciato *m* tracing, drawing; outline; map; layout

trachèa *f* trachea, windpipe

tracòlla *f* baldric; shoulder strap; **a tracolla** slung across the shoulders

tracòllo *m* collapse, debacle

tracotanza *f* arrogance

tradiménto *m* treason; treachery; **a tradimento** unawares, unexpectedly; treacherously

tradire §176 *tr* to betray; to fail (*a person; said of memory*) || *ref* to give oneself away

tradi·tóre -trice *adj* charming, seductive; treacherous; deceitful, faithless || *mf* traitor; betrayer || *f* traitress

tradizionale *adj* traditional

tradizióne *f* tradition

tradótta *f* military train

tradurre §102 *tr* to translate

tradut·tóre -trice *mf* translator

traduzióne *f* translation

traènte *mf* (com) drawer

trafela·to -ta *adj* breathless, out of breath

traférro *m* (elec) air gap; (elec) spark gap

trafficante *m* dealer, trader; trafficker

trafficare §197 (**tràffico**) *tr* to sell; to traffic in || *intr* to trade, deal; to hustle

tràffi·co *m* (**-ci**) traffic

trafficó·ne -na *mf* hustler

trafìggere §104 *tr* to pierce, stab, transfix; to wound

trafila *f* routine; red tape; (mach) drawplate

trafilare *tr* to wiredraw

trafilétto *m* (journ) short feature, special item; (journ) notice

trafitta *f* stab wound; shooting pain

trafittura *f* stab; shooting pain

traforare (**trafòro** & **trafóro**) *tr* to bore; to pierce; to carve (*wood*); to pink (*leather*); to embroider with open work

trafóro *m* boring; tunnel; open work

trafugare §209 *tr* to purloin; to sneak off with

tragèdia *f* tragedy; **far tragedie** (coll) to make a fuss

traghettare (**traghétto**) *tr* to ferry

traghétto *m* ferry; **traghetto spaziale** space shuttle

tràgi•co -**ca** (-**ci** -**che**) *adj* tragic || *m* tragedian; **il tragico** (fig) the tragic

tragitto *m* journey; (obs) ferry

traguardo *m* sight; aim; goal; finish line; (phot) viewfinder; (sports) tape

traiettòria *f* trajectory; path

tràina *f* towline; **pescare alla traina** to troll

trainare (**tràino**) *tr* to drag, tug, pull

tràino *m* drag; load; trailer

tralasciare §128 *tr* to interrupt; to omit; **non tralasciare di** to not fail to

tràl•cio *m* (-**ci**) stem (*of vine*)

tralic•cio *m* (-**ci**) ticking, bedtick; trellis; tower (*of high-tension line*)

tralice *m*—**in tralice** askance

tralignare *intr* (ESSERE & AVERE) to degenerate

tram *m* (tram) streetcar

trama *f* woof, weft; plot (*of play*); texture (*of cloth*)

tramà•glio *m* (-**gli**) trammel net

tramandare *tr* to hand down

tramare *tr* & *intr* to weave; to plot

trambusto *m* bustle

tramesti•o *m* (-**ii**) bustle, confusion

tramèzza [ddzz] *f* partition

tramezzare (**tramèzzo**) [ddzz] *tr* to interpose; to partition

tramezzino [ddzz] *m* small partition; sandwich; sandwich man

tramèzzo [ddzz] *m* partition; side dish; (sew) insertion || *adv* in between; **tramezzo a** among

tràmite *m* intermediary; (lit) pass; **per tramite di** through || *prep* (coll) by; by means of

tramòg•gia *f* (-**ge**) hopper

tramontana *f* north wind; **perdere la tramontana** to lose one's bearings

tramontare (**tramónto**) *intr* (ESSERE) to set (*said, e.g., of sun*); to end

tramónto *m* setting; sunset; decline

tramortire §176 *tr* to stun || *intr* (ESSERE) to faint, swoon

trampolière *m* wading bird; (orn) stilt

tràmpoli *mpl* stilts

trampolino *m* diving board; springboard; ski jump; (fig) springboard

tramutare *tr* to transfer; to transform

tràn•cia *f* (-**ce**) slice; (mach) shears

franèllo *m* trap, snare

tranguiare §290 *tr* to swallow; to gulp down

tranne *prep* except, save; **tranne che** unless

tranquillante *m* tranquilizer

tranquillare *tr* & *ref* (lit) to tranquilize; to calm down

tranquilli•tà *f* (-**tà**) tranquillity

tranquillizzare [ddzz] *tr* to tranquilize; to reassure || *ref* to become reassured

tranquil•lo -**la** *adj* tranquil, calm; clear (*conscience*)

transatlànti•co -**ca** *adj* & *m* (-**ci** -**che**) transatlantic

transazióne *f* compromise

transènna *f* bar, barrier

transètto *m* (archit) transept

trànsfu•ga *m* (-**ghi**) (lit) deserter

transigere §165 *tr* to settle || *intr* to compromise

transistóre *m* transistor

transitàbile *adj* passable

transitare (**trànsito**) *intr* to move; to walk

transiti•vo -**va** *adj* transitive

trànsito *m* passage; traffic; (lit) passing; **di transito** transient

transitó•rio -**ria** *adj* (-**ri** -**rie**) temporary; transitory; transitional

transizióne *f* transition

transoceàni•co -**ca** *adj* (-**ci** -**che**) transoceanic

transòni•co -**ca** *adj* (-**ci** -**che**) transonic

transunto *m* abstract, summary (*of a document*)

trantràn *m* routine

tran•vài *m* (-**vài**) (coll) streetcar

tranvìa *f* streetcar line

tranviâ•rio -**ria** *adj* (-**ri** -**rie**) streetcar

tranvière *m* streetcar conductor; motorman

trapanare (**tràpano**) *tr* to drill; (surg) to trephine

tràpano *m* drill; (surg) trephine; **trapano a vite** automatic drill

trapassare *tr* to pierce; (fig) to grieve; (poet) to cross; (lit) to pass, spend || *intr* (ESSERE) to go through; to pass (*said of an inheritance*); (lit) to pass away; **trapassare da, per** or **al di là di** to come through (*said, e.g., of a nail, light*)

trapassato *m* (lit) deceased; **trapassato prossimo** past perfect

trapasso *m* crossing; transfer; transition; (lit) passing, death

trapelare (**trapélo**) *intr* (ESSERE) to ooze; to trickle out; to leak through; (fig) to leak out

trapè•zio *m* (-**zi**) trapeze; (geom) trapezoid

trapezòide *adj* trapezoidal || *m* trapezoid

trapiantare *tr* to transplant || *ref* to transfer

trapianto *m* transplantation; transplant; **trapianto cardiaco** heart transplant

tràppola *f* trap; (coll) gadget; (fig) lie; **trappola esplosiva** booby trap

trapunta *f* quilt

trapuntare *tr* to quilt; to embroider

trapun•to -**ta** *adj* quilted; embroidered; studded || *m* embroidery || *f* see **trapunta**

trarre §273 *tr* to pull; to drag; to draw; to bring; to deduct; to lead; to unsheathe (*a sword*); to heave (*a sigh*); to spin (*silk, wool*, etc.); **il dado è tratto** the die is cast; **trarre dalla prigione** to free from prison; **trarre d'impaccio** to get (*s.o.*) out of trouble; **trarre fuori** to extract; **trarre in inganno** to deceive; **trarre in rovina** to ruin; **trarre per mano** to lead by the hand ‖ *intr* to kick (*said of a mule*); (*lit*) to run; (*lit*) to blow (*said of the wind*) ‖ *ref* to take off (*e.g., one's hat*); **trarsi d'impaccio** to get out of trouble; **trarsi indietro** to pull back; **trarsi in disparte** to move aside

trasalire [s] §176 *intr* (ESSERE & AVERE) to start, jump

trasanda·to -ta *adj* untidy, slovenly

trasbordare (trasbórdo) *tr* to transfer, transship

trasbórdo *m* transfer, transshipment

trascéndere §245 *tr* to transcend ‖ *intr* (ESSERE) to go to excesses

trascinare *tr* to drag; to stir; to enthrall; to lead astray; **trascinare la vita** to barely make ends meet ‖ *ref* to drag oneself; to drag on

trascolorare (trascolóro) *tr* to discolor; to change the color of ‖ *intr* (ESSERE) & *ref* to discolor; to change color

trascórrere §139 *tr* to pass (*time*); to skim through (*e.g., a book*); (*lit*) to go through ‖ *intr* to go to excesses ‖ *intr* (ESSERE) to elapse, pass

trascórso *m* slip (*e.g., of pen*); peccadillo

trascrivere §250 *tr* to transcribe

trascrizióne *f* transcription; registration (*e.g., of a deed*)

trascuràbile *adj* negligible

trascurare *tr* to neglect; to fail; to disregard ‖ *ref* to not take care of oneself

trascuratézza *f* negligence, neglect; carelessness; slovenliness

trascura·to -ta *adj* neglected; careless; slovenly

trasecolare (trasècolo) [s] *intr* (ESSERE & AVERE) to marvel, be astonished

trasferìbile *adj* transferable

trasferiménto *m* transfer; conveyance

trasferire §176 *tr* to transfer; to assign, convey ‖ *ref* to move

trasfèrta *f* business trip; traveling expenses, per diem

trasfigurare *tr* to transfigure; to distort (*the truth*) ‖ *ref* to be transfigured; to change countenance

trasfocatóre *m* (phot) zoom lens

trasfóndere §178 *tr* to transfuse; (fig) to instill

trasformàbile *adj* transformable; (aut) convertible

trasformare (trasfórmo) *tr* to transform; to alter ‖ *ref* to transform oneself; to be converted

trasformati·vo -va *adj* (gram) transformational

trasformatóre *m* transformer

trasformazióne *f* transformation

trasformi·sta *mf* (-sti -ste) quick-change artist

trasfusióne *f* transfusion

trasgredire §176 *tr* & *intr* to transgress

trasgressióne *f* transgression

trasgressóre *m* transgressor

trasla·to -ta *adj* figurative; metaphorical; (lit) transferred ‖ *m* figure of speech; metaphor

traslitterare (traslìttero) *tr* to transliterate

traslocare §197 (traslòco) *tr* to transfer; to move ‖ *intr* & *ref* to move

traslò·co m (-chi) moving

traslùci·do -da *adj* translucent

trasméttere §198 *tr* to transmit; (rad) to broadcast

trasmetti·tóre -trice *mf* transmitter ‖ *m* (naut) engine-room telegraph; (telg) sender

trasmigrare *intr* (ESSERE & AVERE) to transmigrate ‖ *intr* (ESSERE) to pass, pass on

trasmissióne *f* transmission; conveyance; broadcast; telecast; **trasmissione del pensiero** thought transference

trasmittènte *adj* transmitting; broadcasting ‖ *f* broadcasting station

trasmutare *tr* to transmute; to change

trasogna·to -ta [s] *adj* dreamy; daydreaming; dazed

trasparènte *adj* transparent ‖ *m* transparency

trasparènza *f* transparence; **in trasparenza** against the light

trasparire §108 *intr* (ESSERE) to appear; to shine; to show through; to show, be revealed (*said of feelings*); **far trasparire** to reveal

traspirare *intr* to perspire ‖ *intr* (ESSERE) to show, be revealed

traspirazióne *f* perspiration

traspórre §218 *tr* to transpose

trasportare (traspòrto) *tr* to transport; to carry away; to transfer; to translate; to postpone; (mus) to transpose; **lasciarsi trasportare** to be carried away ‖ *ref* to move; (fig) to go back

trasporta·tóre -trice *mf* carrier ‖ *m* (mach) conveyor belt; (phot) sprocket

traspòrto *m* transportation; transport; transfer; eagerness; moving; (mus) transposition; **trasporto funebre** funeral procession

trasposi·tóre -trice *mf* (mus) transposer

trassa·to -ta *adj* paying ‖ *m* drawee

trastullare *tr* to amuse; to entice ‖ *ref* to have a good time; to loiter

trastullo *m* play, game; fun; plaything

trasudare [s] *tr* to ooze; (fig) to exude ‖ *intr* to ooze (*said of a wall*) ‖ *intr* (ESSERE) to drip (*said of perspiration*)

trasversale *adj* transverse, cross ‖ *f* crossroad

trasvèr·so -sa *adj* transverse ‖ *m* transverse beam

trasvolare (trasvólo) *tr* to fly over, cross by air ‖ *intr*—**trasvolare su** to skip over

trasvolata *f* non-stop flight

tratta *f* tug, pull; (rr) stretch; (com)

draft; (lit) crowd; **fratta dei neri** slave trade; **fratta delle bianche** white slavery

trattàbile *adj* negotiable; friendly, sociable

trattaménto *m* treatment; working conditions; food, spread; reception, welcome; **trattamento di favore** special treatment; **trattamento di quiescenza** retirement benefits

trattare *tr* to treat; to deal with; to transact; to wield; to play (*an instrument*); to work (*e.g., iron*); to deal in; **trattare qlcu da bugiardo** to call s.o. a liar; **trattare da cane** to treat like a dog ‖ *intr* to bargain; **trattare di** to deal with; to take care of; to treat, handle ‖ *ref* to take good care of oneself ‖ *impers* (ESSERE) **si tratta di** it's question of

trattà·rio -ria *mf* (**-ri -rie**) drawee

trattativa *f* negotiation

trattato *m* treatise; treaty

trattazione *f* treatment

tratteggiare §290 (**trattéggio**) *tr* to sketch; to outline; to hatch

trattég·gio *m* (**-gi**) hatching

trattenére §271 *tr* to keep; to entertain; to withhold; to hold back; to detain ‖ *ref* to stop; to refrain; to remain

tratteniménto *m* entertainment, party; delay

trattenuta *f* withholding; checkoff

trattino *m* dash; hyphen

trat·to -ta *adj* drawn, extracted ‖ *m* stretch; span; passage; tract; gesture; throw (*of dice*); stroke (*of pen*); bearing; section; (chess) move; **a larghi tratti** in broad outline; **a tratti** from time to time; **a un tratto** all of a sudden; at the same time; **dare un tratto alla bilancia** to tip the scales; **tratti** features; **tratti del volto** features; **tratto di corda** strappado; **tratto di unione** hyphen; **tutto d'un tratto** all of a sudden; **un bel tratto** quite a while

trat·tóre -trice *mf* innkeeper; restaurateur ‖ *m* tractor; **trattore a cingoli** caterpillar tractor ‖ *f* tractor (*vehicle*)

trattoria *f* inn, restaurant

tratturo *m* cow path

traumatizzare [ddzz] *tr* to traumatize

travagliare §280 *tr* to torment; to molest ‖ *intr & ref* to toil, labor

travà·glio *m* (**-gli**) suffering; toil; trave (*to inhibit horse being shod*); **travaglio di parto** labor pains; **travaglio di stomaco** upset stomach

travasare *tr* to pour off; to decant; to transfer ‖ *ref* to spill

travaso *m* pouring off; transfer; **travaso di bile** gall bladder attack; **travaso di sangue** hemorrhage

travatura *f* roof timbers; **travatura maestra** ridgepole

trave *f* beam; joist; **fare una trave d'un fuscello** to make a mountain out of a molehill

travedére §279 *tr* to glimpse ‖ *intr* to be mistaken

travéggole *fpl*—**avere le traveggole** to see things; to see one thing for another

travèrsa *f* crossbar; crossroad; crosspiece; rung; bar (*of goalpost*); dam; rail (*of fence*); transom; slat (*to hold bedspring*); rubber pad; (rr) tie

traversare (**travèrso**) *tr* to cross

traversata *f* passage, crossing

traversìa *f* strong wind; **traversie** misfortunes

traversina *f* (rr) tie

travèr·so -sa *adj* cross; devious ‖ *m* width; crossbar; (naut) beam; (naut) side; **a traverso** (naut) on the beam; **capire a traverso** to misunderstand; **di traverso** askance; crosswise; the wrong way ‖ *f see* **travèrsa**

traversóne *m* large crossbar; westerly gale; side blow with saber

travestiménto *m* disguise; travesty

travestire (**travèsto**) *tr* to disguise; to travesty, parody ‖ *ref* to disguise oneself

traviare §119 *tr* to lead astray ‖ *intr & ref* to go astray

travicèllo *m* joist

travisare *tr* to distort

travolgènte *adj* impetuous; fascinating; sweeping

travòlgere §289 *tr* to overwhelm; to overturn; to sweep away

trazióne *f* traction

tre [e] *adj & pron* three; **le tre** three o'clock ‖ *m* three; third (*in dates*)

trébbia *f* thresher; threshing

trebbiare §287 (**trébbio**) *tr & intr* to thresh

trebbiatrice *f* thresher, threshing machine

trebbiatura *f* threshing

tréc·cia *f* (**-ce**) plait; braid; **treccia a ciambella** bun, knot

trecentèsi·mo -ma *adj, m & pron* three hundredth

trecènto *adj, m & pron* three hundred ‖ **il Trecento** the fourteenth century

tredicèsi·mo -ma *adj, m & pron* thirteenth ‖ *f* Xmas bonus

trédici *adj & pron* thirteen; **le tredici** one P.M. ‖ *m* thirteen; thirteenth (*in dates*)

trégua *f* truce; respite; **tregua atomica** nuclear test ban; **senza tregua** without letup

tremare (**trèmo**) *intr* to shake, tremble; to quiver; **far tremare** to shake

tremarèlla *f*—**avere la tremarella** (coll) to shake in one's boots

tremebón·do -da *adj* (lit) shaky

tremèn·do -da *adj* tremendous

trementina *f* turpentine

tremila *adj, m & pron* three thousand

trèmito *m* trembling; quivering

tremolare (**trèmolo**) *intr* to shake; to quiver; to flicker

trèmo·lo -la *adj* tremulous ‖ *m* (bot) aspen; (mus) tremolo

trèno *m* train; quarter (*of animal*); set (*of tires*); threnody, lamentation; **treno accelerato** local; **treno di lusso** Pullman train; **treno direttissimo** express; **treno di vita** mode of life; mode of living; **treno merci** freight train; **treno stradale** tractor-trailer

trenodìa *f* threnody

trénta *adj & pron* thirty ‖ *m* thirty; thirtieth (*in dates*)

trentèsi·mo -ma *adj, m & pron* thirtieth

trentìna *f* about thirty

Trènto *f* Trent

trepidare (trèpido) *intr* to fear; to worry

trepidazióne *f* fear, trepidation

treppiède *m* tripod; trivet

tré·sca *f* (**-sche**) intrigue; liaison

tréspolo *m* stool; pedestal; stand, perch; (coll) jalopy

triàngolo *m* triangle; **triangolo rettangolo** right triangle

tribolare (tribolo) *tr* to torment, afflict ‖ *intr* to suffer

tribolazióne *f* tribulation, ordeal

tribórdo *m* (naut) starboard

fri·bù *f* (**-bù**) tribe

tribuna *f* rostrum, platform; (sports) grandstand; **tribuna stampa** press box

tribunale *m* court, tribunal; courthouse; **tribunale dei minorenni** juvenile court; **tribunale di prima istanza** court of first instance

tributare *tr* to bestow

tributà·rio -ria (-ri -rie) *adj* tributary; tax ‖ *m* tributary

tributo *m* tribute; tax

trichè·co *m* (**-chi**) walrus

triciclo *m* tricycle

tricolóre *adj & m* tricolor

tricòrno *m* cocked hat, tricorn

tricromìa *f* three-color printing; three-color print

tridènte *m* trident

trifase *adj* three-phase

trifocale *adj* trifocal

trifò·glio *m* (**-gli**) clover; three-leaf clover

trìfola *f* (coll) truffle

trìglia *f* red mullet

trigonometrìa *f* trigonometry

trilióne *m* trillion

trillare *intr* to trill; to vibrate

trillo *m* trill; ringing

trilogìa *f* trilogy

trimestrale *adj* quarterly

trimèstre *m* quarter; quarterly dues; quarterly payment; (educ) quarter, trimester

trimotóre *m* three-engine plane

trìna *f* lace

trìn·ca *f* (**-che**) (naut) gammoning; **di trinca** clearly, cleanly; **nuovo di trinca** brand-new

trincare §197 *tr* (coll) to gulp down, swill

trincèa *f* trench

trincerare (trincèro) *tr* to dig trenches in ‖ *ref* to entrench oneself

trincétto *m* shoemaker's blade

trinchétto *m* (naut) foremast; (naut) foresail

trinciante *adj* cutting ‖ *m* carving knife

trinciapóllo *m* meat shears

trinciare §128 *tr* to carve; to shred; to advance (*rash opinions*); to cut up

trinciato *m* smoking tobacco

trinciatrice *f* shredder; slicer

Trinità *f* Trinity

trionfale *adj* triumphal

trionfante *adj* triumphant

trionfare (triónfo) *intr* to triumph

triónfo *m* triumph; center piece; tidbit dish with three or four tiers; trump (*in game of tarot*)

triparti·to -ta *adj* tripartite

triplicare §197 (**trìplico**) *tr & ref* to triple

trìplice *adj* threefold

tri·plo -pla *adj & m* triple

tripode *m* tripod

trippa *f* tripe; (coll) belly

tripudiare §287 *intr* to exult

tripù·dio *m* (**-di**) exultation

tris *m* (tris) (poker) three of a kind

trisàvola *f* great-great-grandmother

trisàvolo *m* great-great-grandfather; **trisavoli** great-great-grandparents

trisma *m* lockjaw

triste *adj* sad; gloomy, bleak

tristézza *f* sadness

tri·sto -sta *adj* wicked; wretched; poor (*figure*); (lit) sad

tritacar·ne *m* (**-ne**) meat grinder

tritaghiàc·cio *m* (**-cio**) ice crusher

tritare *tr* to chop; to grind; to mince, hash; to pound

tri·to -ta *adj* minced, hashed; worn, trite

tritòlo *m* T.N.T.

tritóne *m* (zool) newt; (fig) merman ‖ **Tritone** *m* Triton

tritti·co *m* (**-ci**) triptych; export document in triplicate; trilogy

trittòn·go *m* (**-ghi**) triphthong

triturare *tr* to mince, hash

trivèlla *f* auger, drill; post-hole digger

trivellare (trivèllo) *tr* to drill, bore

triviale *adj* vulgar

triviali·tà *f* (**-tà**) vulgarity

tri·vio *m* (**-vi**) crossroads; trivium; **da trivio** vulgar

trofèo *m* trophy; (mil) insignia (*on headpiece*)

trògolo *m* trough

tròia *f* sow; slut ‖ **Troia** *f* Troy

troia·no -na *adj & m* Trojan

trómba *f* trumpet; bugle, clarion; trunk (*of elephant*); leg (*of boot*); (anat) tube; (aut, rad) horn; **con le trombe nel sacco** crestfallen, dejected; **tromba d'aria** whirlwind; tornado; **tromba marina** waterspout; **tromba delle scale** stairwell

trombétta *f* trumpet

trombettière *m* (mil) trumpeter

trombetti·sta *m* (**-sti**) trumpet player

trombóne *m* trombone; blunderbuss

trombò·si *f* (**-si**) thrombosis

troncare §197 (**trónco**) *tr* to chop; to cut off; to clip (*words*); to break, sever; to block (*s.o.'s progress*); to apocopate

tronchése [s] *m* wire cutter

trón·co -ca (**-chi -che**) *adj* truncate; oxytone; apocopated; exhausted, dead-tired; incomplete; **in tronco** in the middle; (*dismissal*) on the spot ‖ *m* trunk; stub (*of receipt book*);

section (*of highway*); log; strain (*of a family*); (rr) branch; **tronco di cono** truncated cone; **tronco maggiore** (naut) lower mast

troncóne *m* stump

troneggiare §290 (**tronéggio**) *intr* to tower; to hold forth; **troneggiare su** to lord it over

trón·fio -fia *adj* (**-fi -fie**) haughty; bombastic

tròno *m* throne

tropicale *adj* tropical

tròpi·co *m* (**-ci**) tropic

troposfèra *f* troposphere

tròp·po -pa *adj & pron* too much; **trop·pi -pe** too many ‖ *m* too much; **questo è troppo!** enough is enough! ‖ **troppo** *adv* too; too much; **essere di troppo** to be in the way

tròta *f* trout

trottare (**tròtto**) *intr* to trot

trotterellare (**trotterèllo**) *intr* to trot along; to toddle

tròtto *m* trot; **piccolo trotto** jog trot

tròttola *f* top

trovare (**tròvo**) *tr* to find; to visit; **trovare a** or **da ridire** (**su**) to find fault (with); **trovi?** don't you think so? ‖ *ref* to find oneself; to meet; to be; to be located; to happen, e.g., **mi trovai a passare di fronte a casa sua** I happened to pass in front of his house

trovarò·be *m* (**-be**) (theat) property man ‖ *f* (theat) dresser

trovata *f* find; trick, gimmick

trovatèl·lo -la *mf* foundling, waif

trovatóre *m* troubadour

trovière *m* trouvère

truccare §197 *tr* to make up; to falsify; (aut) to soup up ‖ *ref* to put on make-up

truccatura *f* make-up; trick, gimmick

truc·co *m* (**-chi**) make-up; trick, gimmick

truce *adj* fierce, cruel; menacing

trucidare (**trùcido**) *tr* to massacre

trùciolo *m* chip, shaving

truculènto *adj* truculent

truffa *f* cheat, fraud, swindle; **truffa all'americana** confidence game

truffare *tr* to cheat, swindle

truffa·tóre -trice *mf* cheat, swindler

truismo *m* truism

truògolo *m* var of **trogolo**

truppa *f* troop; soldiers; **di truppa** (mil) enlisted (*man or woman*); **in truppa** in a flock

tu §5 *pron pers;* **a tu per tu** face to face; **dare del tu a** to address in the familiar form

tuba *f* tuba; (hist) horn, trumpet; (joc) top hat, stovepipe; (anat) tube

tubare *intr* to coo

tubatura *f* piping, tubing; pipe, tube; pipeline

tubazióne *f* tubes, pipes

tubèrcolo *m* tubercle

tubercolosà·rio [s] *m* (**-ri**) tuberculosis sanitarium

tubercolò·si *f* (**-si**)|tuberculosis

tubercoló·so -sa [s] *adj* tuberculous ‖ *mf* T.B. patient

tùbero *m* tuber

tubétto *m* tube (*for pills or toothpaste*); spool

tubino *m* small tube; derby (hat)

tubo *m* tube; pipe; (anat) canal, duct; **a tubo** tubular; **tubo di scarico** exhaust pipe; **tubo di troppopieno** overflow; **tubo di ventilazione** air shaft

tubolare *adj* tubular ‖ *m* tire (*for racing bicycle*)

tuffare *tr* to dip; to plunge ‖ *ref* to plunge; to dive

tuffa·tóre -trice *mf* diver ‖ *m* dive bomber

tuffétto *m* (orn) dabchick, grebe

tuffo *m* dive; plunge; throb; **a tuffo** (aer) diving; **scendere a tuffo** (aer) to dive; **tuffo ad angelo** (sports) swan dive; **tuffo d'acqua** downpour

tufo *m* tufa

tu·ga *f* (**-ghe**) (naut) deckhouse

tugù·rio *m* (**-ri**) hovel

tulipano *m* tulip

tumefare §173 *tr & ref* to swell

tumefazióne *f* swelling

tùmi·do -da *adj* tumid

tumóre *m* tumor

tùmulo *m* tomb; tumulus

tumulto *m* tumult, riot; commotion

tumultuó·so -sa [s] *adj* tumultuous

tungstèno *m* tungsten

tùni·ca *f* (**-che**) tunic

Tùnisi *f* Tunis

Tunisia, la Tunisia

tunisi·no -na *adj & mf* Tunisian

tuo tua §6 *adj & pron poss* (**tuòi tue**)

tuòno *m* thunder

tuòrlo *m* yolk

turàcciolo *m* cork, stopper

turare *tr* to plug, stop; to cork

turba *f* crowd; mob; (pathol) upset

turbaménto *m* commotion, perturbation; disturbance, breach (*of law and order*)

turbante *m* turban

turbare *tr* to muddy; to disturb; to upset ‖ *ref* to become cloudy; to become upset

turba·to -ta *adj* upset; disturbed; distracted

tùrbi·do -da *adj* turbid

turbina *f* turbine

turbinare (**tùrbino**) *tr* to separate in a centrifuge ‖ *intr* to whirl

tùrbine *m* whirlwind; swarm; tumult

turbinó·so -sa [s] *adj* whirling; tumultuous

turboèli·ca *m* (**-ca**) turboprop

turbogètto *m* turbojet

turbolèn·to -ta *adj* turbulent

turbolènza *f* turbulence

turbomotrice *f* (rr) turbine engine

turboreattóre *m* turbojet

turcasso *m* quiver

turchése [s] *m* turquoise

Turchia, la Turkey

turchinétto *m* bluing

turchi·no -na *adj* dark-blue ‖ *m* dark blue

tur·co -ca (**-chi -che**) *adj* Turkish; **sedere alla turca** to sit cross-legged ‖ *mf* Turk ‖ *m* Turkish (*language*); **bestemmiare come un turco** to swear like a trooper; **fumare come un turco** to smoke like a steam engine

tùrgi·do -da *adj* turgid

turibolo *m* thurible, censer

turismo *m* tourism

turi·sta *mf* (**-sti -ste**) tourist

turìsti·co -ca *adj* (**-ci -che**) tourist; travel (*e.g.,* bureau); traveler's (*check*)

turlupinare *tr* to hoodwink, swindle

turlupinatura *f* swindle, confidence game

turno *m* turn; shift; **a turno** in turn; **di turno** on duty; **fare a turno** to take turns

turpe *adj* base, abject; (lit) ugly

turpilò·quio *m* (**-qui**) foul language

turpitùdine *f* turpitude

tuta *f* overalls; **tuta antigravità** anti-G suit; **tuta da bambini** jumpers; **tuta spaziale** spacesuit

tutèla *f* guardianship; defense, protection

tutelare *adj* tutelary || *v* (**tutèlo**) *tr* to protect, defend

tùtolo *m* corncob

tu·tóre -trice *mf* guardian; protector

tuttavìa *adv* yet, nevertheless; (lit) always, continuously

tut·to -ta *adj* whole; all; full; **con tutto** in spite of, e.g., **con tutto quello che ho fatto per lui** in spite of all I have done for him; **del tutto** fully, completely; **è tutt'uno** it's all the same; **tutt'altro** completely different; on the contrary; **tutt'altro che** anything but; **tutti** every, e.g., **tutti gli scolari** every pupil; **tutti e due** both || *m* everything; whole; **con tutto che** although; **fare di tutto** to do everything possible; **in tutto** altogether || *pron* **tut·ti -te** all, everybody (*of a group*); **tutti** everybody || **tutto** *adv* quite; **tutt'a un tratto** all of a sudden; **tutto al contrario** quite the opposite

tuttofa·re *adj invar* of all trades; of all work || *m* (**-re**) factotum, jack-of-all-trades || *f* (**-re**) maid of all work

tuttóra *adv* yet, still

tzìga·no -na *adj & mf* var of **zigano**

U

U, u [u] *m & f* nineteenth letter of the Italian alphabet

ubbìa *f* prejudice, bias; complex; whim

ubbidiènte *adj* obedient

ubbidire §176 *tr* to obey || *intr* to obey; to respond (*said of a car*); (with *dat*) to obey, e.g., **gli ubbedì** he obeyed him

ubertó·so -sa [s] *adj* fruitful; fertile

ubicazióne *f* location

ubiquità *f* ubiquity; **non ho il dono dell'ubiquità** I can't be everywhere at the same time

ubì·quo -qua *adj* ubiquitous

ubriacare §197 *tr* to make drunk, intoxicate || *ref* to get drunk

ubriacatura or **ubriachézza** *f* drunkenness, intoxication

ubria·co -ca (**-chi -che**) *adj* drunk; **ubriaco fradicio** dead drunk || *mf* drunkard

ubriacó·ne -na *mf* drunkard

uccellare (**uccèllo**) *tr* to take in, cajole || *intr* to snare; to fowl; to hunt birds

uccèllo *m* bird; **uccello di bosco** fugitive; **uccello di galera** gallows bird; **uccello di passo** bird of passage

uccella·tóre -trice *mf* live-bird catcher

uccellièra *f* aviary; large birdcage

uccìdere §274 *tr* to kill || *ref* to kill oneself; to get killed; to kill one another

-ùccio -ùccia (**-ucci -ucce**) *suf adj* not very, e.g., **calduccio** not very hot; rather, e.g., **magruccio** rather thin; poor little, e.g., **caruccio** poor little darling || *suf m & f* small e.g., **cappelluccio** small hat

uccisióne *f* killing; murder

ucci·so -sa *adj* killed || *mf* victim

ucci·sóre -ditrice *mf* killer

ucraì·no -na *adj & mf* Ukrainian || **l'Ucraìna** *f* the Ukraine

udìbile *adj* audible

udiènza *f* audience; hearing; **l'udienza è aperta!** the court is now in session!

udire §275 *tr* to hear; to listen to

udito *m* hearing

uditòfono *m* hearing aid

udi·tóre -trice *adj* hearing || *mf* (educ) auditor || *m* magistrate

udìto·rio -ria (**-ri -rie**) *adj* auditory || *m* audience

ufficiale *adj* official || *m* official; officer; **primo ufficiale** (naut) first officer, mate; **ufficiale di giornata** (mil) officer of the day; **ufficiale di rotta** (aer, naut) navigator; **ufficiale giudiziario** clerk of the court; process server, bailiff; **ufficiale medico** (mil) medical officer

ufficiare §128 *tr* to officiate

uffi·cio *m* (**-ci**) duty; office; bureau; department (*of agency*); **d'ufficio** ex-officio; public, e.g., **avvocato d'ufficio** public defender; **ufficio di collocamento** placement bureau; **ufficio di compensazione** clearing house; **ufficio d'igiene** board of health

uffició·so -sa [s] *adj* unofficial; kindly; white (*lie*)

uffì·zio *m* (**-zi**) (eccl) office

ufo *m*—a ufo gratis, without paying

ugèllo *m* nozzle

ùg·gia *f* (**-ge**) darkness; gloom; dislike; **avere in uggia** to dislike

uggiolare (**ùggiolo**) *intr* to whine (*said of a dog*)

uggió·so -sa [s] *adj* gloomy; boring

ugnare *tr* to bevel; to miter

ugnatura *f* bevel; miter

ùgola *f* uvula; bagnarsi l'ugola (coll) to wet one's whistle

ugonòtto *m* Huguenot

uguaglianza *f* equality

uguagliare §280 *tr* to equal; to make equal; to equalize; to level; to compare || *ref* to compare oneself; to be equal; to be compared

uguale *adj* equal; same; even; level; per me è uguale it's the same to me || *m* equal; (math) equal sign

ùlcera *f* ulcer; sore

ulcerare (ùlcero) *tr & ref* to ulcerate

uliva *f* var of oliva

ulteriòre *adj* further, subsequent, ulterior

ùltima *f* latest news; last straw

ultimare (ùltimo) *tr* to complete, finish

ultimato *m* ultimatum

ultimìssima *f* latest edition (*of newspaper*); ultimissime late news

ùlti·mo -ma *adj* last; final; latest; latter; farthest; ultimate; least; top (*floor*); all'ultimo, dall'ultimo, nell'ultimo or sull'ultimo lately; finally, at the end || *f* see ultima

ultimogèni·to -ta *adj* last-born || *mf* last-born child

ultra- *pref adj* and *m & f* ultra-, e.g., ultraelevato ultrahigh; super-, e.g., ultrasonico supersonic (*speed*)

ultracór·to -ta *adj* ultrashort

ultraròs·so -sa *adj & m* infrared

ultraterré·no -na *adj* ultramundane; unearthly

ultraviolét·to -ta *adj & m* ultraviolet

ululare (ùlulo) *intr* to howl

ululato *m* howl

umanésimo *m* humanism

umani·sta *mf* (-sti -ste) humanist

umani·tà *f* (-tà) humanity; umanità *fpl* humanities

umanità·rio -ria *adj & mf* (-ri -rie) humanitarian

uma·no -na *adj* human; humane || *m* human nature; umani human beings

um·bro -bra *adj & m* Umbrian

umettare (umétto) *tr* to moisten, dampen

umidìc·cio -cia *adj* (-ci -ce) dampish

umidi·tà *f* (-tà) humidity, dampness

ùmi·do -da *adj* humid, damp || *m* humidity, dampness; in umido stewed (*e.g., meat*)

ùmile *adj* humble || gli umili *mpl* the meek

umiliare §287 *tr* to humiliate, humble || *ref* to humble oneself

umiliazióne *f* humiliation

umiltà *f* humility

umóre *m* humor, mood, temper; whim; (bot) sap; un bell'umore (coll) quite a character

umorismo *m* humor

umori·sta *mf* (-sti -ste) humorist

umorìsti·co -ca *adj* (-ci -che) humorous; amusing, comic, funny

un (apocopated form of uno) §9 *indef art* a, an || §9 *numeral adj* one || §12 *reciprocal indef pron*—l'un l'altro each other, one another

unànime *adj* unanimous

unanimità *f* unanimity

unàni·mo -ma *adj* unanimous

uncinare *tr* to hook, grapple

uncinétto *m* small hook; crochet hook

uncino *m* hook; grapnel; clasp; pothook; (fig) pretext; a uncino hooked

undicèsi·mo -ma *adj, m & pron* eleventh

ùndici *adj & pron* eleven; le undici eleven o'clock || *m* eleven; eleventh (*in dates*); (soccer) squad

ùngere §183 *tr* to grease; to oil; to smear; to anoint; to flatter || *ref* to smear oneself

Ungheria, l' *f* Hungary

ungh   ; fingernail; claw; hoof; fluke (*of anchor*); (fig) hairbreadth; avere le unghie lunghe to be lightfingered; unghia del piede toenail; unghie (fig) clutches

unghiata *f* nail scratch

unguènto *m* unguent, ointment

ùni·co -ca *adj* (-ci -che) only, sole; unique; single (*copy*); complete (*text*) || *f*—l'unica the only solution

unicòrno *m* unicorn

unificare §197 (unìfico) *tr* to unify; to standardize

unificazióne *f* unification; standardization

uniformare (unifórmo) *tr* to make uniform, standardize || *ref*—uniformarsi a to conform to; to comply with

unifórme *adj* uniform; standard || *f* uniform; alta uniforme (mil) full dress

unilaterale *adj* unilateral

unióne *f* union; agreement; unione libera free love

unire §176 *tr & ref* to unite

unisono [s] *m* unison; all'unisono in unison

uni·tà *f* (-tà) unity; unit; unità di misura unit of measurement

unità·rio -ria *adj* (-ri -rie) unit (*e.g., price*); united || *m* Unitarian

uni·to -ta *adj* united; joined; compact; plain (*color*); consolidated

universale *adj* universal; last (*judgment*)

universi·tà *f* (-tà) university

università·rio -ria *adj* (-ri -rie) university; college || *mf* university or college student; university or college professor

univer·so -sa *adj* universal || *m* universe

unno *m* Hun

u·no -na §9 *indef art* a, an || §9 *numeral adj* one || *m* one || §10 *pron indef* one; le una, la una, or l'una one o'clock; l'uno e l'altro both; l'uno o l'altro either, either one; per uno in single file; uno per uno one by one; each other || §11 *correlative pron* one

un·to -ta *adj* greasy || *m* grease, fat; flattery; anointed one

untuosità [s] *f* greasiness; unction, unctuousness

untuó·so -sa [s] *adj* greasy; unctuous

unzióne *f* unction

uò·mo *m* (**-mini**) man; **come un sol uomo** to a man; **uomo d'affari** businessman; **uomo del giorno** man of the hour; **uomo della strada** man of the street; **uomo di chiesa** churchman; **uomo di fatica** laborer; **uomo di fiducia** trusted man; **uomo di mare** seaman; **uomo di paglia** straw man; **uomo di parola** man of his word; **uomo in mare!** man overboard!; **uomo meccanico** automaton; **uomo morto** (rr) deadman brake; **uomo nuovo** nouveau riche; **uomo rana** frogman

uòpo *m*—**all'uopo** if need be; **essere d'uopo** (lit) to be necessary

uòse [s] *fpl* leggings

uò·vo *m* (**-va** *fpl*) egg; **meglio un uovo oggi che una gallina domani** a bird in a hand is worth two in the bush; **rompere le uova nel paniere a qlcu** to spoil s.o.'s plans; **uovo affogato** poached egg; **uovo alla coque** soft-boiled egg; **uovo all'occhio di bue** fried egg; **uovo da tè** tea ball; **uovo strapazzato** scrambled egg

uragano *m* hurricane; storm (*of applause*); **uragano di neve** blizzard

Urali *mpl* Ural Mountains

uranife·ro -ra *adj* uranium-bearing

urànio *m* uranium

urbanésimo *m* urbanization, migration toward the cities

urbanìsti·co -ca (**-ci -che**) *adj* city-planning ‖ *f* city planning

urbani·tà *f* (**-tà**) urbanity, civility; city population

urbanizzare [ddzz] *tr* to urbanize

urba·no -na *adj* urban; urbane

urètra *f* urethra

urgènte *adj* urgent, pressing

urgènza *f* urgency; d'urgenza urgent; emergency (*e.g., operation*); **fare urgenza a** to urge

ùrgere §276 *tr* to urge, press ‖ *intr* to be urgent

urina *f* urine

urinà·rio -ria *adj* (**-ri -rie**) urinary

urlare *tr* to shout; to shout down ‖ *intr* to howl; to shout, yell

urla·tóre -trice *adj* screaming ‖ *mf* screamer; loud singer

ur·lo *m* howl ‖ *m* (**-la** *fpl*) yell, scream

urna *f* urn; ballot box; (poet) grave; **urne** polls

-uro *suf* *m* (chem) **-ide**, e.g., **cloruro** chloride

urologìa *f* urology

urrà *interj* hurrah!

ursóne *m* Canada porcupine

urtare *tr* to hit; to bump; to annoy ‖ *intr*—**urtare contro** to hit, strike against; **urtare in** to hit; to stumble into ‖ *ref* to get annoyed; to clash; to bump into one another

urto *m* hit; bump; collision; onslaught; clash, disagreement; **urto di nervi** huff

Uruguai, l' *m* Uruguay

uruguaia·no -na *adj* & *mf* Uruguayan

usanza *f* usage, custom; habit, practice

usare *tr* to use, employ; to wear out;

(lit) to frequent; **usare** + *inf* to be accustomed to + *ger* ‖ *intr* to be fashionable; **usare di** to use, employ ‖ *ref* to become accustomed; **si usa** + *inf* it is customary to + *inf*

usa·to -ta *adj* used, second-hand; worn; worn-out; (lit) usual ‖ *m* usage, custom; norm; second-hand goods

usbèr·go *m* (**-ghi**) hauberk; (fig) shield, protection

uscènte *adj* ending, terminating; retiring

uscière *m* receptionist; office boy, errand boy; (coll) court clerk; (coll) bailiff; (coll) tipstaff

ù·scio *m* (**-sci**) door; **infilar l'uscio** to take French leave; **metter tra l'uscio e il muro** (fig) to corner

uscire §277 *intr* (ESSERE) to go out, leave; to come out; to flow out; to escape; to turn out, ensue; **essere uscito** to be out; **uscire da** to leave; to run off (*the track*); **uscire dai gangheri** to get mad; **uscire dal comune** to be out of the ordinary; **uscire dal segno** to go too far; **uscire dal seminato** to go astray; **uscire di mente a** to escape one's mind, e.g., **gli è uscito di mente** it escaped his mind; **uscire di sentimento** to pass out; **uscire di vita** to die; **uscire in** to lead into; **uscire per il rotto della cuffia** to barely make it

uscita *f* exit; outlay; quip, sally; gate (*e.g., in an airport*); (gram) ending; **all'uscita** on the way out; **buona uscita** severance pay; bonus; **libera uscita** day off (*of servant*); (mil) pass; **uscita di sicurezza** emergency exit

usignòlo *m* nightingale

u·so -sa *adj* (lit) accustomed ‖ *m* practice; usage; use; wear; faculty; power (*e.g., of hearing*); (lit) intimate relations; **all'uso di** in the fashion of; **avere per uso di** to be wont to; **come d'uso** as usual; **farci l'uso** to get used to it; **fuori d'uso** worn-out, out of commission; **uso esterno!** (pharm) not to be taken internally!

ustionare (ustióno) *tr* to burn, scorch

ustióne *f* burn

usuale *adj* usual; ordinary, common

usufruire §176 *intr*—**usufruire di** to have the use of; to enjoy

usura *f* usury; (mach) wear and tear; **ad usura** abundantly

usu·ràio -ràia (**-rài -ràie**) *adj* usurious ‖ *mf* usurer, loanshark

usurpare *tr* to usurp

utensile *adj* tool, e.g., **macchina utensile** machine tool ‖ *m* utensil; tool

utènte *m* user; customer, consumer

ùtero *m* uterus, womb

ùtile *adj* useful; usable; workable; legal, prescribed (*e.g., time*); **essere utile a** to help; **venire utile** to come in handy ‖ *m* usefulness; profit, gain

utili·tà *f* (**-tà**) utility, usefulness; profit, gain

utilitària *f* economy car, compact

utilizzare [ddzz] *tr* to utilize

utopìa *f* utopia
utopì-sta *mf* (-sti -ste) utopian
utopìsti-co -ca *adj* (-ci -che) utopian
uva *f* grapes; **un grano di uva passa** a raisin; **uva passa** raisins

uxorici-da *m* (-di) uxoricide ‖ *f* (-de) murderer of one's husband
uxorìci-dio *m* (-di) uxoricide; murder of one's husband
ùzzolo [ddzz] *m* whim, fancy, caprice

V

V, v [vu] *m* & *f* twentieth letter of the Italian alphabet
V. *abbr* (vostro) your
vacante *adj* vacant
vacanza *f* vacancy; vacation; **fare vacanza** to be on vacation; **vacanze** vacation
vacanzière *m* vacationer
vac-ca *f* (-che) cow
vac-càio *m* (-cài) cowboy; stable boy
vaccherìa *f* dairy farm
vacchétta *f* cowhide
vaccina *f* cow manure; cow
vaccinare *tr* to vaccinate
vaccinazióne *f* vaccination
vaccì-no -na *adj* cow; bovine ‖ *m* vaccine ‖ *f* see **vaccina**
vacillante *adj* vacillating
vacillare *intr* to totter; to vacillate; to shake; to flicker; to fail, e.g., **la memoria gli vacilla** his memory is failing; **far vacillare** to rock
vacui-tà *f* (-tà) vacuity
và-cuo -cua *adj* empty ‖ *m* vacuum
vademe-cum *m* (-cum) almanac, ready-reference handbook
vagabondàg-gio *m* (-gi) vagrancy; wandering; rambling
vagabondare (vagabóndo) *intr* to wander, rove
vagabón-do -da *adj* wandering; vagabond ‖ *mf* vagrant, bum, tramp; rover
vagare §209 *intr* to wander, ramble, rove
vagheggiare §290 (vaghéggio) *tr* to gaze fondly at; to cherish
vagire §176 *intr* to cry, whimper
vagito *m* cry, whimper
và-glia *m* (-glia) money order ‖ *f—di vaglia* worthy, capable
vagliare §280 *tr* to sift, bolt
và-glio *m* (-gli) sieve; **mettere al vaglio** to scrutinize
va-go -ga (-ghi -ghe) *adj* vague; vacant (*stare*); (lit) beautiful; (lit) roving; (poet) desirous ‖ *m* vagueness; (lit) rover; (anat) vagus
vagonata *f* carload
vagóne *m* (rr) car; **vagone frigorifero** (rr) refrigerator car; **vagone letto** (rr) sleeping car, sleeper; **vagone ristorante** (rr) dining car; **vagone volante** (aer) flying boxcar
vàio vàia (vài vàie) *adj* dark-grey ‖ *m* dark grey; (heral) vair; (zool) Siberian squirrel
vaiòlo *m* smallpox
valan-ga *f* (-ghe) avalanche
valènte *adj* capable, skillful; clever
valentìa *f* skill; cleverness

valentino *m* Valentine (*sweetheart*)
valènza *f* (chem) valence
valére §278 *tr* to win, get (*e.g., an honor for s.o.*); **che vale?** what's the use?; **valere la pena** to be worthwhile; **valere un Perù** to be worth a king's ransom ‖ *intr* (ESSERE & AVERE) to be worth; to be of avail; to be valid; to mean; to be the equivalent; **far valere** to enforce; **farsi valere** to assert oneself; **tanto vale** it's all the same; **vale a dire** that is to say; **valere meglio** to be better ‖ *ref—valersi di* to avail oneself of; to play on; to employ
valévole *adj* valid, good
valicare §197 (vàlico) *tr* to cross, pass
vàli-co *m* (-chi) mountain pass; passage; opening (*in a hedge*)
validi-tà *f* (-tà) validity
vàli-do -da *adj* valid; able, able-bodied; strong
valigerìa *f* luggage; luggage store
valigétta *f* valise; **valigetta diplomatica** attaché case
vali-gia *f* (-ge) suitcase; traveling bag; **fare le valige** to pack one's bags; **valigia diplomatica** diplomatic pouch; attaché case; **valigia per abiti** suit carrier
vallata *f* valley
valle *f* valley; **a valle** downhill; downstream
vallétta *f* (telv) assistant
vallétto *m* valet; page; (telv) assistant
vallò-ne -na *adj* & *mf* Walloon ‖ *m* narrow valley
valóre *m* value; valor, bravery; force; (fig) jewel; (math) variable; **mettere in valore** to raise the value of; **valore di mercato** market value; **valore facciale** face value; **valore locativo** rental value; **valori valuables; securities; valori mobiliari** securities
valorizzare [ddzz] *tr* to enhance the value of
valoró-so -sa [s] *adj* brave, valiant
valuta *f* currency; (com) effective date; (com) value (*of promissory note*)
valutare *tr* to estimate, appraise; to value, prize; to count, reckon; to take into consideration
valutazióne *f* estimation, appraisal; evaluation
valva *f* (bot, zool) valve
vàlvola *f* (anat, mach) valve; (elec) fuse; (rad, telv) tube, valve; **valvola a galleggiante** ball cock; **valvola di sicurezza** safety valve; **valvola in testa** overhead valve
vàl-zer *m* (-zer) waltz

vamp f (vamp) vamp
vampa f flame; blaze; flash; flush
vampata f burst (of heat); blast (of hot air); flash, flush
vampiro m vampire
vanàdio m vanadium
vanaglòria f vainglory, boastfulness
vanagliorió·so -sa [s] adj vainglorious
vandalismo m vandalism
vànda·lo -la adj & m vandal || **Vandalo** m Vandal
vaneggiare §290 (vanéggio) intr to rave; to be delirious; (lit) to open, yawn
vanè·sio -sia adj (-si -sie) vain
van·ga f (-ghe) spade
vangare §209 tr to spade up; to dig with a spade
vangèlo m gospel || **Vangelo** m Gospel
vanghétto m spud
vaniglia f vanilla
vanilò·quio m (-qui) empty talk
vani·tà f (-tà) vanity
vanitó·so -sa [s] adj vain, conceited
va·no -na adj vain; (lit) empty, hollow; **in vano** in vain || m empty space; room
vantàg·gio m (-gi) advantage; profit; odds, handicap; discount; (coll) extra; (typ) galley; **a vantaggio di** on behalf of
vantaggió·so -sa [s] adj advantageous
vantare tr to boast of; to set up (a claim) || ref to boast; **vantarsi di** to brag about, vaunt
vanteria f brag, boast, vaunt
vanto m brag, boast; **aver vanto su** (lit) to overcome
vànvera f—**a vanvera** at random
vapóre m vapor; steam; locomotive; steamship; **a tutto vapore** at full speed
vaporétto m small river boat; vaporetto (in Venice)
vaporizzare [ddzz] tr to vaporize; to spray || intr (ESSERE) & ref to evaporate
vaporizzatóre [ddzz] m vaporizer; sprayer
vaporó·so -sa [s] adj vaporous
varaménto m assemblage (of prefab pieces)
varano m monitor lizard
varare tr to launch; to pass (a law); (coll) to back, promote (a candidate)
varcare §197 tr to cross || intr (poet) to pass (said of time)
var·co m (-chi) opening; mountain pass; breach; **attendere al varco** to lie in wait for; **cogliere al varco** to catch unawares; **fare varco in** to breach
varechina f (laundry) bleach
variàbile adj & f variable
variante f variant; detour; (aut) model
variare §287 tr & intr (ESSERE & AVERE) to vary
variazióne f variation
varicèlla f chicken pox
varicó·so -sa [s] adj varicose
variega·to -ta adj variegated
varie·tà m (-tà) (theat) vaudeville || f variety

và·rio -ria (-ri -rie) adj varied; various; variable; different; **va·ri -rie** several || m variety || **varie** fpl miscellanies || **va·ri -rie** pron indef several
variopin·to -ta adj multicolored
varo m (naut) launch
vas m (vas) subchaser
va·sàio m (-sài) potter
va·sca f (-sche) tub; basin; pool; **vasca da bagno** bathtub; **vasca dei pesci** aquarium; **vasca navale** (naut) basin
vascèllo m vessel, ship
vaselina or **vasellina** f vaseline
vasellame m dishes; set of dishes; **vasellame da cucina** kitchen ware; **vasellame d'argento** silverware; **vasellame di porcellana** chinaware
vasèllo m (lit) vessel
vasi·stas [s] m (-stas) transom
vaso m vase; vessel; jar, pot; nave (of church); hall (of building); (naut) shipway; (poet) cup; **vasi vinari** wine containers; **vaso da fiori** flowerpot; **vaso da notte** chamber pot; **vaso d'elezione** (eccl) chosen vessel (viz., Saint Paul)
vassallo m vassal; (obs) helper
vas·sóio m (-sói) tray; mortarboard
vasti·tà f (-tà) vastness
va·sto -sta adj spacious; vast; (fig) deep
vate m (lit) prophet, poet
vatica·no -na adj Vatican || **Vaticano** m Vatican
vaticinare (vaticino & vaticino) tr to prophesy
vatici·nio m (-ni) prophecy
ve §5 pron
V.E. abbr (Vostra Eccellenza) Your Excellency
vècchia f old woman
vecchiàia f old age
vecchièzza f old age
vèc·chio -chia (-chi -chie) adj old; elder; **vecchio come il cucco** as old as the hills || m old man; **vecchi** old people; **vecchio del mestiere** old hand || f see **vecchia**
véc·cia f (-ce) vetch
véce f stead, e.g., **in vece mia** in my stead; (lit) vicissitude; **fare le veci di** to act for or as
vedére m seeing; looks; view, opinion || §279 tr to see; to review; to look over; **chi s'è visto s'è visto!** good-by and good luck!; **dare a vedere** to make believe; **stare a vedere** to watch; observe; **non poter vedere** to not be able to stand; **non vedere l'ora di** to be hardly able to wait for; **vedere male qlcu** to be ill-disposed toward s.o. || intr—**stare a vedere** to wait and see; **vederci bene** to see (e.g., in the dark); **vederci chiaro** to look into it; **vedere di** to try to || ref to see oneself; to see each other; **vedersela brutta** to anticipate trouble
vedétta f lookout; (nav) vedette
védova f widow
vedovanza f widowhood
vedovile adj widow's; widower's || m dower

védo·vo -va *adj* widowed ‖ *m* widower ‖ *f* see **vedova**

veduta *f* view; (lit) eyesight; **di corte vedute** narrowminded; **di larghe vedute** broadminded

veemènte *adj* vehement; violent; impassioned

veemènza *f* vehemence; violence

vegetale *adj* vegetable ‖ *m* plant, vegetable

vegetare (vègeto) *intr* to vegetate

vegetaria·no -na *adj & mf* vegetarian

vegetazióne *f* vegetation

vège·to -ta *adj* vigorous, spry

veggènte *adj* (obs) seeing ‖ *mf* fortuneteller ‖ *m* seer, prophet; **i veggenti** people having eyesight ‖ *f* seeress, prophetess

véglia *f* vigil, watch; wakefulness; evening party, soirée; party, crowd; **a veglia** unbelievable (*tale*); **veglia danzante** dance; **veglia funebre** wake

vegliardo *m* old man

vegliare (véglio) *tr* to keep watch over ‖ *intr* to stay awake; to keep watch; to stay up

veglióne *m* masked ball

veicolo *m* vehicle; carrier (*of disease*)

véla *f* sail; sailing; **alzare le vele** to set sail; **ammainare le vele** to take in sail; **a vela** under sail; **far vela** to set sail; **vela aurica** lugsail; **vela bermudiana** or **Marconi** jib; **vela maestra** mainsail

ve·làio *m* (**-lài**) sailmaker

velare *adj & f* (phonet) velar ‖ *v* (**vélo**) *tr* to veil; to cover; to muffle (*sound*); to attenuate, reduce (*a shock*); to dim, cloud; to conceal; (phot) to fog ‖ *ref* to cover oneself with a veil; to take the veil; to get dim, e.g., **gli si è velata la vista** his eyesight got dim

velà·rio *m* (**-ri**) (hist) velarium; (theat) curtain

vela·to -ta *adj* veiled; sheer (*hosiery*)

velatura *f* coating; (aer) airfoil; (naut) sails

veleggiare §290 (veléggio) *tr* (lit) to sail over (*the sea*) ‖ *intr* to sail; (aer) to glide

veleggiatóre *m* sailboat; (aer) glider

veléno *m* poison; (fig) venom

velenó·so -sa [s] *adj* poisonous; (fig) venomous

velétta *f* veil; (naut) topgallant

vèli·co -ca *adj* (**-ci -che**) sail, sailing

velièro *m* sailing ship

veli·no -na *adj* thin (*paper*) ‖ *f* carbon copy; onionskin; slant (*given to a news item*)

velìvo·lo -la *adj* (lit) gliding; (lit) sailing ‖ *m* (lit) airplane, aircraft

vellei·tà *f* (**-tà**) wild ambition, dream

vellicare §197 (vèllico) *tr* to tickle

vèllo *m* (lit) fleece; **vello d'oro** Golden Fleece

velló·so -sa [s] *adj* hairy

velluta·to -ta *adj* velvety

vellutino *m* thin velvet; velvet ribbon; **vellutino di cotone** velveteen

vellu·to -ta *adj* (lit) hairy ‖ *m* velvet; **velluto a coste** corduroy

vélo *m* veil; coating; film; skin (*e.g., of onion*); (anat, bot) velum; (fig) body; **fare velo a** to becloud; to fog

velóce *adj* speedy, quick, fast; fleeting

velocipedastro *m* poor or reckless bicycle rider

veloci·sta *mf* (**-sti -ste**) (sports) sprinter

veloci·tà *f* (**-tà**) velocity; speed; (aut) speed; **a grande velocità** by express; **a piccola velocità** by freight; **velocità di crociera** cruising speed; **velocità di fuga** (rok) escape velocity

velòdromo *m* bicycle ring or track

véna *f* vein; grain (*in wood or stone*); mood; streak (*of madness*); **di vena** willingly; **essere in vena di** to be in the mood to

venale *adj* venal

venare (véno) *tr* to vein

vena·to -ta *adj* veined; streaked; suffused; **venato di sangue** bloodshot

venatura *f* veining; (fig) streak

vendémmia *f* vintage

vendemmiare §287 (vendémmio) *tr* to harvest (*grapes*) ‖ *intr* to gather grapes; (fig) to make a killing

vendemmia·tó·re -trice *mf* vintager

véndere §281 *tr* to sell; **da vendere** plenty, more than enough; **vendere allo scoperto** (fin) to sell short; **vendere fumo** to peddle influence ‖ *intr* to sell; **vendere allo scoperto** (fin) to sell short ‖ *ref* to sell; **si vende** for sale

vendétta *f* vengeance; revenge; **gridare vendetta** to cry out for retribution

vendicare §197 (véndico) *tr* to avenge ‖ *ref* to get revenge

vendicati·vo -va *adj* vengeful, vindictive

vendica·tóre -trice *adj* avenging ‖ *mf* avenger

vendifu·mo *mf* (**-mo**) influence peddler

véndita *f* sale; shop; **in vendita** for sale; **vendita allo scoperto** (fin) short sale; **vendita per corrispondenza** catalogue sale

vendi·tóre -trice *mf* seller; clerk (*in store*) ‖ *m* salesman; **venditore ambulante** peddler; **venditore di fumo** influence peddler ‖ *f* saleslady

venefi·cio *m* (**-ci**) poisoning

venèfi·co -ca (**-ci -che**) *adj* poisonous; unhealthy ‖ *m* (lit) poisonmaker

veneràbile or **venerando** *adj* venerable

venerare (vènero) *tr* to venerate, revere; to worship

venerazióne *f* veneration; worship

vener·dì *m* (**-dì**) Friday ‖ **Venerdì Santo** Good Friday

Vènere *m* (astr) Venus ‖ *f* (mythol & fig) Venus

venè·reo -rea *adj* (**-rei -ree**) venereal

Venèzia *f* Venice; Venetia (*province*)

venezia·no -na *adj & mf* Venetian ‖ *f* Venetian blind

venezola·no -na *adj & mf* Venezuelan

vènia *f* (lit) forgiveness, pardon

venire §282 *intr* (ESSERE) to come; to turn out (*well or badly*); to turn out to be; **che viene** next, e.g., **il mese che viene** next month; **come viene** as it is; **far venire** to send for; to give, cause; **un va e vieni** a backward-and-forward motion; **venire +** *ger* to keep + *ger*; **venire +** *pp* to be + *pp*, e.g., **il portone viene aperto alle tre** the gate is opened at three; **venire a capo di** to solve; **venire ai ferri corti** to come into open conflict; **venire al dunque** or **al fatto** to come to the point; **venire alle corte** to get down to brass tacks; **venire alle mani** or **alle prese** to come to blows; **venire a parole** to have words; **venire a patti con** to come to terms with; **venire a proposito** to come in handy; **venire incontro a** to go to meet; **venire in possesso di** to come into possession of (*s.th*); to come into the hands of (*s.o.*); **venire meno** to faint; **venir meno a** to fail to keep (*one's word*); **venir su** to grow, come up; **venire via** to give way || *ref*—**venirsene** to stroll along || *impers* (with *dat*)—**viene da** feel the urge to, e.g., **gli venne da starnutire** he felt the urge to sneeze; **gli è venuto da ridere** he felt the urge to laugh; **viene detto** blurt out, e.g., **gli è venuto detto che non gli piaceva quel tipo** he blurted out that he did not like that fellow; **viene fatto di +** *inf* succeed in + *ger*, e.g., **le venne fatto di convincerli** she succeeded in convincing them; **happen to +** *inf*, e.g., **gli venne fatto di incontrarmi per istrada** he happened to meet me on the way

ventà·glio *m* (**-gli**) fan; (fig) spread; **a ventaglio** fanlike; **diramarsi a ventaglio** to fan out

ventaròla *f* weather vane

ventata *f* gust of wind; (fig) wave

ventènne *adj* twenty-year-old || *mf* twenty-year-old person

ventèsi·mo -ma *adj*, *m* & *pron* twentieth

vénti *adj* & *pron* twenty; **le venti** eight P.M. || *m* twenty; twentieth (*in dates*)

ventidue *adj* & *pron* twenty-two **le ventidue** ten P.M. || *m* twenty-two; twenty-second (*in dates*)

ventilare (**vèntilo**) *tr* to air, ventilate; to winnow (*grain*); to discuss minutely; to air (*a subject*); to broach (*a subject*); to unfurl (*a flag*) || *ref* to fan oneself

ventilatóre *m* fan, ventilator; vent; (min) ventilation shaft; (naut) funnel

ventilazióne *f* ventilation; winnowing

ventina *f* score; **una ventina (di)** twenty, about twenty

ventino *m* twenty-cent coin

ventiquattro *adj* & *pron* twenty-four; **le ventiquattro** twelve P.M. || *m* twenty-four; twenty-fourth (*in dates*)

ventiquattró·re *f* (**-re**) overnight bag; twenty-four-hour race; **ventiquattrore** *fpl* period of twenty-four hours

ventitré *adj* & *pron* twenty-three; **le ventitré** eleven P.M.; **portare il cappello alle ventitré** to wear one's hat cocked || *m* twenty-three; twenty-third (*in dates*)

vènto *m* wind; air; guy wire; **presentarsi al vento** to sail into the wind; **farsi vento** to fan oneself; **a vento** windproof; wind-propelled; **col vento in prora** downwind; **col vento in poppa** upwind; favorably, famously

vèntola *f* fireside fan; lampshade; candle sconce; blade (*of fan*)

ventó·so -sa [s] *adj* windy || *f* cupping glass; suction cup; (zool) sucker

vèntre *m* belly; **a ventre a terra** on one's belly; on one's face; at full speed (*said of a horse*)

ventricolo *m* ventricle

ventrièra *f* abdominal band or belt

ventrilòquia *f* ventriloquism

ventrìlo·quo -qua *mf* ventriloquist

ventuno *adj* & *pron* twenty-one; **le ventuno** nine P.M. || *m* twenty-one; twenty-first (*in dates*); (cards) blackjack

ventu·ro -ra *adj* next || *f* (lit) luck, fortune; (lit) good fortune; **alla ventura** at random, at a venture; **di ventura** of fortune, e.g., **soldato di ventura** soldier of fortune

venustà *f* (lit) pulchritude

venu·to -ta *mf*—**nuovo venuto** newcomer; **primo venuto** firstcomer || *f* coming, arrival

véra *f* curbstone (*of well*); (coll) wedding ring

verace *adj* true; truthful, veracious

veraci·tà *f* (**-tà**) veracity, truthfulness

veranda *f* veranda; porch

verbale *adj* verbal || *m* minutes; ticket (*given by a policeman*); **mettere a verbale** to enter into the record

verbèna *f* verbena

vèrbo *m* verb; (lit) word. || **Verbo** *m* (theol) Word

verbosità [s] *f* verbiage, verbosity

verbó·so -sa [s] *adj* windy, longwinded, verbose

verda·stro -stra *adj* greenish

vérde *adj* green; young, youthful || *m* green; al verde (coll) broke, penniless; **nel verde degli anni** in the prime of life

verdeggiante *adj* verdant

verderame *m* blue vitriol; verdigris

verdét·to -ta *adj* greenish || *m* verdict

verdógno·lo -la *adj* greenish; sallow (*face*)

verdura *f* vegetables

verecóndia *f* modesty, bashfulness

verecón·do -da *adj* modest, bashful

vér·ga *f* (**-ghe**) switch; rod; ingot, bar; pole; penis; (eccl) staff, crosier; (naut) yard; **tremare a verga a verga** to shake like a leaf

vergare §209 (**vérgo**) *tr* to switch; to rule (*paper*); to stripe; to write

vergati·no -na *adj* thin (*paper*) || *m* striped cloth

verga·to -ta *adj* striped; watermarked with stripes || *m* (obs) serge

verginale *adj* maidenly, virginal

vérgine *adj* & *f* virgin || **Vergine** *f* (eccl) Virgin; (astr) Virgo

verginità *f* virginity, maidenhood

vergógna *f* shame; **aver vergogna** to be.

ashamed; **vergogne** privates || *interj* for shame!

vergognare (**vergógno**) *ref* to be ashamed; to feel cheap; **vergognati!** shame on you!

vergognó·so -sa [s] *adj* ashamed; bashful; shameful

veridici·tà *f* (**-tà**) veracity

verìdi·co -ca *adj* (**-ci -che**) veracious

verìfi·ca *f* (**-che**) verification; control; **verifica fiscale** auditing (*of tax return*)

verificare §197 (**verìfico**) *tr* to verify; to control, check; to audit || *ref* to come true; to happen

verifica·tóre -trice *mf* checker, inspector

verismo *m* verism (*as developed in Italy*)

veri·sta *adj* & *mf* (**-sti -ste**) verist

veri·tà *f* (**-tà**) truth; **in verità** truthfully, verily

veritiè·ro -ra *adj* truthful

vèrme *m* worm; (mach) thread; **verme solitario** tapeworm

vermì·glio -glia (**-gli -glie**) *adj* vermilion; ruby (*lips*) || *m* vermilion

vèr·mut *m* (**-mut**) vermouth

vernàcolo *m* vernacular

vernice *f* varnish; paint; polish; patina; (painting) private viewing; (fig) veneer; **scarpe di vernice** patent-leather shoes; **vernice a olio** oil paint; **vernice a spruzzo** spray paint; **vernice da scarpe** shoe polish

verniciare §128 *tr* to varnish; to paint

vé·ro -ra *adj* true; real; right; pure; **non è vero?** isn't that so? La traduzione precedente è generalmente rimpiazzata da molte altre frasi. Se la prima espressione è negativa, la domanda equivalente a **non è vero?** sarà affermativa, per esempio, **Lei non lavora, non è vero?** You are not working, are you? Se la prima espressione è affermativa, la domanda sarà negativa, per esempio, **Lei lavora, non è vero?** You are working, are you not? or aren't you? Se la prima espressione contiene un ausiliare, la domanda conterrà l'ausiliare stesso senza infinito o senza participio passato, per esempio, **Arriveranno domani, non è vero?** They will arrive tomorrow, won't they? **Ha finito il compito, non è vero?** He has finished his homework, hasn't he? Se la prima espressione non contiene né un ausiliare, né una delle forme del verbo "to be" in funzione di copula, la domanda conterrà l'ausiliare "do" o "did" senza l'infinito del verbo, per esempio, **Lei è vissuto a Milano, non è vero?** You lived in Milano, did you not? **Lei non va mai al parco, non è vero?** You never go to the park, do you?; **non mi par vero** it seems unbelievable || *m* truth; actuality; **a dire il vero** to tell the truth, as a matter of fact; **dal vero** from nature; **salvo il vero** if I am not mistaken || *f* see **vera**

veróne *m* (lit) balcony

verosimiglianza *f* verisimilitude; probability, likelihood

verosìmile *adj* verisimilar; probable, likely

verricèllo *m* winch, windlass

vèrro *m* boar

verru·ca *f* (**-che**) wart

versaménto *m* spilling; payment; deposit

versante *m* depositor; slope, side

versare (**vèrso**) *tr* to pour; to spill; to shed; to pay; to deposit || *intr* to overflow; **versare in gravi condizioni** to be in a bad way || *ref* to spill; to pour (*said of people*); to empty (*said of a river*)

versàtile *adj* versatile; fickle

versa·to -ta *adj* versed; gifted; fully subscribed to (*e.g., stock of a corporation*)

verseggia·tóre -trice *mf* verse writer

versétto *m* verse (*of Bible*)

versificare §197 (**versìfico**) *tr* & *intr* to versify

versificazióne *f* versification

versióne *f* version; translation

vèrso *adj invar—***pollice verso** (hist) thumbs down || *m* verse; local accent; voice, cry; reverse (*of coin*); verso (*of page*); line (*of poetry*); singsong; gesture; direction, way, manner; respect; **andare a verso** (with *dat*) to suit, e.g., **le sue maniere non gli vanno a verso** her manners do not suit him; **a verso** properly; **contro verso** against the grain; **fare un verso** to make faces; **per un verso** on one hand; **rifare il verso** (with *dat*) to mimick; **senza verso** without rhyme or reason; **verso sciolto** blank verse || *prep* toward; near, around; about; for, toward; upon, in return for; as compared with; **verso di** toward

vèrtebra *f* vertebra

vertebrale *adj* vertebral; spinal

vertebra·to -ta *adj* & *m* vertebrate

vertènza *f* quarrel, dispute; **vertenza sindacale** labor dispute

vèrtere §283 *intr—***vertere su** to deal with, to turn on

verticale *adj* & *f* vertical

vèrtice *m* top, summit; vertex; summit conference

vertìgine *f* vertigo, dizziness; **avere le vertigini** to feel dizzy

vertiginó·so -sa [s] *adj* dizzy; breathtaking

vérza [dz] *f* cabbage

verzière [dz] *m* (lit) fruit, vegetable, and flower garden; (coll) produce market

verzura [dz] *f* verdure

vescì·ca *f* (**-che**) bladder; blister; **vescica di vento** (fig) windbag; **vescica gonfiata** swellhead; **vescica natatoria** air bladder

vescichétta *f* blister; vescicle; **vescichetta biliare** gall bladder

vescìcola *f* blister

vescovado *m* bishopric

véscovo *m* bishop

vè·spa *f* wasp, yellowjacket ‖ *f* (-spe & -spa) motor scooter

ve·spàio *m* (-spài) wasp's nest; (fig) hornet's nest

vespasiano *m* public urinal

Vèspero *m* Vesper

vesperti·no -na *adj* (lit) evening

vèspro *m* (eccl) vespers; (lit) vespertide

vessare (vèsso) *tr* (lit) to oppress

vessatò·rio -ria *adj* (-ri -rie) vexatious

vessazióne *f* oppression

vessillo *m* flag

vestàglia *f* negligee, dressing gown; vestaglia da bagno bathrobe

vèste *f* dress; cover; (lit) body; in veste di in the quality of; as; in the guise of; veste da camera negligee, dressing gown; bathrobe; veste talare (eccl) long vestment; vesti clothes

vestià·rio *m* (-ri) wardrobe

vestíbolo *m* vestibule, lobby

vestí·gio *m* (-gi & -gia *fpl*) vestige, trace; (lit) footprint

vestíre (vèsto) *tr* to dress; to don; to wear; to clothe; to cover, bedeck ‖ *intr* to dress; to fit ‖ *ref* to get dressed; to dress; to dress oneself; to buy one's own clothes

vestí·to -ta *adj* dressed; covered ‖ *m* dress; suit; clothing; vestiti clothes; vestito da donna dress; vestito da festa Sunday best; vestito da sera evening clothes, formal suit; evening gown; vestito da uomo suit

Vesùvio, il Vesuvius

vetera·no -na *adj* & *mf* veteran

veterinà·rio -ria (-ri -rie) *adj* veterinary ‖ *m* veterinarian ‖ *f* veterinary medicine

vèto *m* veto; porre il veto a to veto

ve·tràio *m* (-tràl) glass manufacturer; glass dealer; glass blower

vetra·to -ta *adj* glass, glass-enclosed; sand (*paper*) ‖ *m* glare ice, glaze ‖ *f* glass door; glass window; glass enclosure; vetrata a colori or vetrata istoriata stained-glass window

vetrería *f* glassworks; vetrerie glassware

vetria·to -ta *adj* glassy; glass-covered

vetrificare §197 (vetrífico) *tr* to vitrify ‖ *ref* to become vitrified

vetrina *f* show window; showcase, glass cabinet; mettersi in vetrina to show off; vetrine (coll) eyeglasses

vetrini·sta *mf* (-sti -ste) window dresser

vetri·no -na *adj* glass-like; brittle, fragile ‖ *m* slide (*of microscope*) ‖ *f* see vetrina

vetriòlo *m* vitriol

vétro *m* glass; glassware; window pane; piece of glass; vetro aderente contact lens; vetro infrangibile (aut) safety glass; vetro smerigliato ground glass, frosted glass

vetrorèsina *f* fiberglass

vetró·so -sa [s] *adj* vitreous, glassy

vétta *f* peak; top, tip; limb (*of tree*); (naut) end (*of hawser*); tremare come una vetta to shake like a leaf

vet·tóre -trice *adj* leading, guiding; spreading, carrying ‖ *m* carrier; (math, phys) vector

vettovagliare §280 *tr* to supply with food

vettovàglie *fpl* victuals, food; supplies

vettura *f* forwarding; coach; car; freight; in vettura! (rr) all aboard!; prendere in vettura to hire (*a conveyance*); vettura belvedere (rr) observation car; vettura da turismo (aut) pleasure car; vettura di piazza hack, hackney; vettura letto (rr) sleeping car; vettura ristorante (rr) diner

vetturétta *f* economy car, compact

vetturino *m* hackman, cab driver

vetu·sto -sta *adj* old, ancient

vezzeggiare §290 (vezzéggio) *tr* to coddle ‖ *intr* (lit) to strut

vezzeggiatí·vo -va *adj* endearing ‖ *m* endearing expression; diminutive

vézzo *m* habit; caress; necklace; bad habit; vezzi fondling, petting; mawkish behavior; charms

vezzó·so -sa [s] *adj* graceful, charming; affected, mincing

vi §5

via *m* (via) starting signal; dare il via a to give the go-ahead to ‖ *f* street; road, way; route; career; dare la via a to open the way to; in via confidenziale in confidence; in via eccezionale as an exception; per via di via, through; (coll) because of; per via gerarchica through administrative channels; per via orale orally; per via rettale rectally; prendere la via to be on one's way; venire a vie di fatto to come to blows; Via Crucis Way of the Cross; via d'acqua waterway; via di scampo (fig) way out; via d'uscita way out; Via Lattea Milky Way; vie di fatto assault and battery; vie legali legal steps ‖ *adv* away; (math) times, by; e così via and so on; e via dicendo and so on; tirar via to hurry along; via via che as ‖ *prep* via, by way of

viadótto *m* viaduct

viaggiare §290 *intr* to travel; (com) to deal

viaggia·tóre -trice *adj* traveling; homing (*pigeon*) ‖ *mf* traveler ‖ *m* traveling salesman

viàg·gio *m* (-gi) travel; journey, trip; buon viaggio! bon voyage!; viaggio d'andata e ritorno round trip; viaggio di prova (naut) trial run, shakedown cruise

viale *m* boulevard

viandante *mf* (lit) wayfarer

vià·rio -ria *adj* (-ri -rie) road, highway

viàti·co *m* (-ci) viaticum

viavài *m* coming and going; hustle and bustle

vibrante *adj* vibrant; wiry; (phonet) vibrant ‖ *f* (phonet) trill, vibrant

vibrare *tr* to jar; to deliver (*a blow*); to vibrate; (lit) to hurl ‖ *intr* to vibrate

vibra·to -ta *adj* vibrant; resolute, vigorous ‖ *m* vibrating sound

vibrazióne *f* vibration

vicariato *m* vicarage

vicà·rio *m* (-ri) vicar

vice- *pref adj* vice-, e.g., **vicereale** viceroyal || *pref m & f* vice-, e.g., **viceammiraglio** vice-admiral; assistant, e.g., **vicegovernatore** assistant governor; deputy, e.g., **vicesindaco** deputy mayor

vicediret·tóre -trice *mf* assistant manager

vicènda *f* vicissitude; rotation (*of crops*); **a vicenda** in turn

vicendévole *adj* mutual, reciprocal

vicepresidènte [s] *mf* vice president

vice·ré *m* (-ré) viceroy

vicevèrsa *adv* vice versa; (coll) instead, on the contrary

vichin·go -ga *adj & mf* (-ghi -ghe) Viking

vicinanza *f* nearness; **in vicinanza di** in the neighborhood of; **vicinanze** vicinity, neighborhood

vicinato *m* neighborhood

vici·no -na *adj* near; neighboring; next; close (*relative*) || *mf* neighbor || **vicino** *adv* nearby, near; **da vicino** closely; at close quarters; **vicino a** near; next to, close to

vicissitúdine *f* vicissitude

vi·co m (-chi) alley, lane; village; (lit) region

vìcolo *m* alley, court, place; **vicolo cieco** blind alley, dead end

videocassétta *f* video cassette

vidimare (vìdimo) *tr* to validate, visa; to sign

vidimazióne *f* validation, visa; signature

viennése [s] *adj & mf* Viennese

vieptiù *adv* (lit) more and more

vietare (vièto) *tr* to forbid, prohibit

vieta·to -ta *adj* forbidden; **senso vietato** one way; **sosta vietata** no parking; no stopping; **vietato fumare** no smoking

Vietnam, il Vietnam

vietnami·ta *adj & mf* (-ti -te) Vietnamese

viè·to -ta *adj* (lit) old-fashioned; (coll) musty-smelling, rancid

vigènte *adj* current, in force

vigere §284 *intr* to be in force

vigèsi·mo -ma *adj* twentieth

vigilante *adj* watchful, vigilant || *m* watchman

vigilanza *f* vigilance; surveillance

vigilare (vìgilo) *tr* to watch; to watch over; to police || *intr* to watch; **vigilare che** to see to it that

vigila·tóre -trice *mf* inspector || *f* camp counselor; **vigilatrice sanitaria** child health inspector

vigile *adj* (lit) watchful || *m* watch; **vigile del fuoco** fireman; **vigile urbano** policeman

vigilia *f* fast; vigil; **la vigilia di** on the eve of, the night before

vigliaccheria *f* cowardice

vigliac·co -ca (-chi -che) *adj* cowardly || *m* coward

vigna *f* vineyard

vignaiòlo *m* vine dresser

vignéto *m* vineyard

vignétta *f* vignette; **vignetta umoristica** cartoon

vignetti·sta *mf* (-sti -ste) cartoonist

vigógna *f* vicuña

vigóre *m* vigor; **in vigore** in force

vigorìa *f* vigor

vigoró·so -sa [s] *adj* vigorous

vile *adj* cowardly; vile, low, cheap; base (*metal*)

vilificare §197 (**vilìfico**) *tr* to vilify

vilipèndere §148 *tr* to despise; to show scorn for

villa *f* villa; country house; one-family detached house; (lit) country

villàg·gio m (-gi) village; **villaggio del fanciullo** boys' town

villanata *f* boorishness

villania *f* boorishness, rudeness; insult

villa·no -na *adj* rude, churlish || *mf* boor, churl; (lit) peasant

villanzó·ne -na *m* boor, uncouth person

villeggiante *mf* vacationist

villeggiare §290 (**villéggio**) *intr* to vacation

villeggiatura *f* vacation, summer vacation

villétta *f* or **villino** *m* bungalow

villó·so -sa [s] *adj* hairy

vil·tà *f* (-tà) baseness; cowardice

viluppo *m* tangle, twist

vìmine *m* withe, wicker, osier

vinàcce *fpl* pressed grapes

vi·nàio m (-nài) wine merchant

vincènte *adj* winning || *mf* winner

vincere §285 *tr* to overcome; to win; to convince; to check; to defeat; **vincere per un pelo** to nose out; **vincerla** to come out on top || *ref* to control oneself

vincetòssi·co m (-ci) swallowwort, tame poison

vincipèr·di m (-di) giveaway

vincita *f* gain; winnings

vinci·tóre -trice *adj* conquering, victorious || *mf* winner; conqueror; victor

vincolare *adj* binding; bound || *v* (**vìncolo**) *tr* to tie; to bind, obligate; to restrict the use of (*real-estate property*)

vìncolo *m* tie, bond; (law) entail; (law) restriction (*in a real-estate deed*)

vinìco·lo -la *adj* wine, wine-producing

vinile *m* vinyl

vino *m* wine; **vin caldo** mulled wine; **vino da pasto** table wine; **vino di marca** vintage wine; **vino di mele** cider

vin·to -ta *adj* vanquished, overcome, defeated; victorious (*battle*); **averla vinta su** to overcome; **darla vinta a qlcu** to let s.o. get away with murder; **darsi per vinto** to give in, yield || *m* vanquished person; **i vinti** the vanquished

viò·la *adj invar* violet || *m* (-la) violet (*color*) || *f* violet; (mus) viola; **viola del pensiero** pansy; **viola mammola** sweet violet

violacciòc·ca *f* (-che) (bot) wallflower

violà·ceo -cea *adj* violet

violare (vìolo) *tr* to violate; to run (*a blockade*)

violazióne *f* violation; **violazione di**

domicilio housebreaking, burglary; **violazione di proprietà** trespass

violentare (violènto) *tr* to violate, force; to do violence to; to rape

violèn·to -ta *adj* violent ‖ *m* violent person

violènza *f* violence; **violenza carnale** rape

violét·to -ta *adj & m* violet ‖ *f* (bot) violet

violini·sta *mf* (-sti -ste) violinist

violino *m* violin; **primo violino** concertmaster

violoncelli·sta *mf* (-sti -ste) violoncellist

violoncèllo *m* violoncello, cello

viòttolo *m* path

vìpera *f* viper, adder

viràg·gio *m* (-gi) turn; (aer) banking; (naut) tacking; (phot) toning

virare *tr* to veer; to turn (*a winch*); (aer) to bank; (phot) to tone ‖ *intr* to veer, steer; **virare di bordo** (naut) to put about; (naut) to tack

virata *f* turn, veer; (aer) banking; (naut) tacking

virginale *adj* var of **verginale**

virgi·nia *m* (-nia) Virginia tobacco ‖ *f* (-nia) Virginia cigarette

vìrgola *f* comma; (*used in Italian to set off the decimal fraction from the integer*) decimal point; **doppia vìrgola** quotation mark

virgolétta *f* quotation mark

virgulto *m* (lit) shoot; (lit) shrub

virile *adj* virile

virilità *f* virility

viròla *f* (mach) male piece

virologia *f* virology

vir·tù *f* (-tù) virtue; (lit) valor

virtuale *adj* virtual

virtualménte *adv* virtually, to all intents and purposes

virtuosismo [s] *m* virtuosity; showing off

virtuosità [s] *f* virtuosity

virtuó·so -sa [s] *adj* virtuous ‖ *mf* virtuoso

virulèn·to -ta *adj* virulent

virulènza *f* virulence

vi·rus *m* (-rus) virus

vìsce·re *m* (-ri) internal organ; **vìsceri** entrails, viscera ‖ **vìscere** *fpl* entrails, viscera; (fig) heart, feeling; (fig) bowels (*of the earth*)

vì·schio *m* (-schi) mistletoe; birdlime; (fig) trap

vischió·so -sa [s] *adj* sticky, viscous; (com) steady

vìsci·do -da *adj* viscid; clammy; (fig) unctuous

vìsciola *f* sour cherry

vìsciolo *m* sour cherry tree

viscónte *m* viscount

viscontéssa *f* viscountess

viscó·so -sa [s] *adj* viscous, sticky ‖ *f* viscose

visétto *m* small face; baby face

visìbile *adj* visible; obvious

visibì·lio *m* (-li) (coll) crowd; (coll) bunch; **andare in visibilio** to become ecstatic; **mandare in visibilio** to throw into ecstasy, enrapture

visibilità *f* visibility

visièra *f* visor; fencing mask; eyeshade; **visiera termica** (aut) electric defroster

visigò·to -ta *adj* Visigothic ‖ *mf* Visigoth

visionà·rio -ria *adj & mf* (-ri -rie) visionary

visióne *f* vision; sight; (mov, telv) showing; **in visione gratuita** for free examination; **mandare qlco a qlcu in visione** to send s.th to s.o. for his (or her) opinion; **prendere visione di** to examine; to peruse

visir *m* (-sir) vizier

vìsita *f* visit; visitation; **fare una visita** to pay a visit; **marcare visita** (mil) to report sick; **visita doganale** customs inspection

visitare (vìsito) *tr* to visit; to inspect

visita·tóre -trice *mf* visitor ‖ *f* social worker

visitazióne *f* visitation

visì·vo -va *adj* visual

viso *m* face; **far buon viso a cattivo gioco** to grin and bear it

visóne *m* mink

visóre *m* (phot) viewer; (phot) viewfinder

vi·spo -spa *adj* brisk, lively

vissu·to -ta *adj* wordly-wise

vista *f* sight, eyesight; view; vista; glance; (poet) window; **a vista** exposed, visible; **a vista d'occhio** as far as the eye can see; **essere in vista** to be expected; to be imminent; to be in the limelight; **far vista di** to pretend to; **in vista di** in view of; **mettere in vista** to show off; **vista a volo d'uccello** bird's-eye view; **vista corta** poor eyesight

vistare *tr* to validate, visa

vi·sto -sta *adj*—**visto che** seeing that, inasmuch as ‖ *m* visa; approval ‖ *f* see **vista**

vistó·so -sa [s] *adj* showy, flashy; (fig) considerable

visuale *adj* visual ‖ *f* view; line of sight

visualizzare [ddzz] *tr* to visualize

vita *f* life; livelihood; living; waist; **avere breve vita** to be short-lived; **fare la vita** to be a prostitute; **vita natural durante** for life; during one's lifetime

vitaiòlo *m* man about town; playboy, bon vivant

vitale *adj* vital

vitalità *f* vitality

vitalì·zio -zia (-zi -zie) *adj* life, lifetime ‖ *m* life annuity

vitamina *f* vitamin

vite *f* (bot) grapevine; (mach) screw; **a vite** threaded; (aer) in a tailspin; **vite autofilettante** self-tapping screw; **vite del Canadà** woodbine, Virginia creeper; **vite per legno** wood screw; **vite per metallo** machine screw; **vite perpetua** (mach) endless screw, worm gear; **vite prigioniera** stud bolt

vitèllo *m* calf; veal

vitìc·cio *m* (-ci) tendril

vìtre·o -a *adj* vitreous; glassy (*eyes*)

vìttima *f* victim

vitto *m* food; diet; **vitto e alloggio** room and board

vittòria *f* victory; **cantar vittoria** to crow; **to crow too soon**

vittorió·so -sa [s] *adj* victorious

vituperare (**vitùpero**) *tr* to vituperate

vituperévole *adj* contemptible, shameful

vitupè·rio *m* (**-ri**) shame, infamy; insult; (lit) blame

viuzza *f* narrow street, lane

viva *interj* long live!

vivacchiare §287 *intr* (coll) to get along ‖ *ref*—**si vivacchia** (coll) so, so

vivace *adj* lively, brisk; brilliant; vivacious

vivacità *f* liveliness, briskness; brilliancy, brightness; vivacity

vivaddìo *interj* yes, of course!; by Jove!

vivagno *m* selvage; edge

vi·vàio *m* (**-vài**) fishpond; fish tank; tree nursery; (fig) seedbed

vivanda *f* food

vivandiè·re -ra *mf* (mil) sutler

vìvere *m* life; living; cost of living; **viveri** food, provisions; allowance ‖ §286 *tr* to live; **vivere un brutto momento** to spend an uncomfortable moment ‖ *intr* (ESSERE) to live; **vive** (typ) stet; **vivere alla giornata** to live from hand to mouth

vivézza *f* liveliness

vìvi·do -da *adj* vivid, lively

vivificare §197 (**vivìfico**) *tr* to vivify

vivisezionare (**vivisezióno**) *tr* to vivisect; to scrutinize

vivisezióne *f* vivisection

vì·vo -va *adj* alive; living; live, vivacious; lively; vivid; high (*flame*); bright (*light*), raw (*flesh*); sharp, acute (*pain*); hearty (*thanks*); outright (*expense*); gross (*weight*); brute (*strength*); modern (*language*); kinetic (*energy*); running (*water*) ‖ *m* living being; heart (*of a question*); **al vivo** lively; lifelike; **i vivi e i morti** the quick and the dead; **toccare nel vivo** to sting to the quick ‖ **viva** *interj* see **viva**

viziare §287 *tr* to spoil; to ruin; (law) to vitiate ‖ *ref* to become spoiled

vizià·to -ta *adj* spoiled; ruined; stale (*air*)

vì·zio *m* (**-zi**) vice; defect; flaw; (law) vitiation

vizió·so -sa [s] *adj* vicious; defective ‖ *mf* profligate

vìz·zo -za *adj* withered

vocabolà·rio *m* (**-ri**) dictionary; vocabulary

vocàbolo *m* word

vocale *adj* vocal; (lit) sonorous ‖ *f* vowel

vocalizzare [ddzz] *tr* & *ref* to vocalize

vocatìvo *m* vocative

vocazióne *f* vocation

vóce *f* voice; noise, roar; word; rumor; entry; tone; **ad alta voce** aloud; **a bassa voce** in a low voice; **a viva voce** by word of mouth; **a voce** orally; **dare una voce a** (coll) to call; **dare sulla voce a** to rebuke; to con-

tradict; **fare la voce grossa** to raise one's voice; **non avere voce in capitolo** to have no say; **schiarirsi la voce** to clear one's throat; **senza voce** hoarse; **sotto voce** in a low tone; **voce bianca** child's voice (*in singing*)

vociare *m* bawl ‖ §128 (**vócio**) *intr* to bawl

vociferare (**vocìfero**) *intr* to vociferate, shout ‖ *ref*—**si vocifera** it is rumored

vó·ga *f* (**-ghe**) fashion, vogue; energy, enthusiasm; rowing

vogare §209 (**vógo**) *tr* & *intr* to row

voga·tóre -trice *mf* rower ‖ *m* oarsman; rowing machine

vòglia *f* wish; whim, fancy; willingness; birthmark; **aver voglia di** to feel like, have a notion to; **di buona voglia** willingly; **di mala voglia** unwillingly

voglió·so -sa [s] *adj* fanciful; (lit) desirous

vói §5 *pron pers* you; **voi altri** you, e.g., **voi altri americani** you Americans

voiàl·tri -tre *pron pl* you, e.g., **voialtri americani** you Americans

volano *m* shuttlecock; (mach) flywheel

volante *adj* flying; loose (*sheet*); free (*agent*) ‖ *m* steering wheel; (mach) hand wheel; shuttlecock

volantino *m* leaflet; fringe; (mach) hand wheel

volare (**vólo**) *tr* (soccer) to overthrow ‖ *intr* (ESSERE & AVERE) to fly

volata *f* flight; sprint; run; mouth (*of gun*); (tennis) volley; **di volata in a** hurry

volàtile *adj* volatile; flying (*animal*) ‖ **volatili** *mpl* birds

volatilizzare [ddzz] *tr* & *intr* (ESSERE) to volatilize

volènte *adj*—**Dio volente** God willing; **volente o nolente** willy-nilly

volentièri *adv* gladly, willingly

volére *m* will, wish; **al volere di** at the bidding of ‖ §288 *tr* to will; to want, desire; (lit) to believe, affirm; **l'hai voluto tu** it's your fault; **non vuol dire!** never mind!; **qui ti voglio** here's the rub, that's the trouble; **senza volere** without meaning to; **voglia Dio!** may God grant!; **voler bene** (with *dat*) to like; **volerci** to take, e.g., **ci vorranno due anni per finire questo palazzo** it will take two years to complete this building; **ce ne vogliono ancora tre** it takes three more of them; **voler dire** to mean; to try, e.g., **vuole piovere** it is trying to rain; **volere che** + *subj* to want + *inf*, e.g., **vuole che vengano** he wants them to come; **volere piuttosto** to prefer; **volere è potere** where there is a will there is a way; **voler male** (with *dat*) to dislike; **volerne a** to bear a grudge against; **vorrei I** should like, I'd like; **vuoi . . . vuoi** either . . . or

volgare *adj* vernacular, popular, common; vulgar ‖ *m* vernacular

volgari·tà *f* (**-tà**) vulgarity

volgarizzare [ddzz] *tr* to popularize

vòlgere §289 *tr* to turn; (lit) to translate ‖ *intr* to turn; (lit) to go by; volgere a to turn toward; to draw near, to approach; volgere in fuga to take to flight ‖ *ref* to turn; to devote oneself

vól·go *m* (-ghi) (lit) crowd, mob

volièra *f* aviary

voliti·vo -va *adj* volitional; strongminded, strong-willed

vólo *m* flight; fall; al volo on the spot; on the wing; a volo d'uccello as the crow flies; bird's-eye (*e.g.*, *view*); di volo at top speed, immediately; in volo aloft, in the air; prendere il volo to take flight; volo a vela or volo planato gliding; volo strumentale instrument flying; volo veleggiato gliding

volon·tà *f* (-tà) will; di spontanea volontà of one's own volition; pieno di buona volontà eager to please; ultime volontà last will and testament

volontariato *m* volunteer work; apprenticeship without pay; (mil) volunteer service

volontà·rio -ria (-ri -rie) *adj* voluntary ‖ *m* volunteer

volonteró·so -sa [s] *adj* willing, well-disposed

volpacchiòtto *m* fox cub; (fig) sly fox

vólpe *f* fox; (agr) smut; volpe argentata silver fox

volpi·no -na *adj* fox; fox-colored; foxy ‖ *m* Pomeranian

volpó·ne -na *mf* sly fox

vòlt *m* (vòlt) (elec) volt

vòl·ta *m* (-ta) (elec) volt ‖ *f* turn; time; vault; roof (*of mouth*); alla volta di toward; a volta di corriere by return mail; a volte sometimes; c'era una volta once upon a time there was; certe volte sometimes; dare di volta il cervello a to go crazy, e.g., gli ha dato di volta il cervello he went crazy; dar la volta to turn sour (*said of wine*); due volte twice; molte volte often; per una volta tanto only once; poche volte seldom; tante volte often; tutto in una volta at one swoop, at one stroke; in one gulp, in one swallow; una volta once; una volta che (coll) inasmuch as; una volta per sempre once and for all; una volta tanto for once; volta a crociera cross vault; volta per volta little by little; volte (math) times, e.g., cinque volte cinque five times five

voltafàc·cia *m* (-cia) volte-face; fare voltafaccia to wheel around (*said of a horse*)

voltagabba·na *mf* (-na) turncoat

voltàg·gio *m* (-gi) voltage

voltài·co -ca *adj* (-ci -che) voltaic

voltare (vòlto) *tr*, *intr* & *ref* to turn

voltastòma·co *m* (-chi) (coll) nausea; fare venire il voltastomaco a qlcu (coll) to turn s.o.'s stomach

voltata *f* turn; curve

volteggiare §290 (voltéggio) *tr* to put (*a horse*) through its paces ‖ *intr* to hover; to flit, flutter; (sports) to vault (*e.g.*, *on horseback or trapeze*)

voltég·gio *m* (-gi) (sports) vaulting

vòltmetro *m* voltmeter

vólto *m* (lit) face

voltura *f* (com, law) transfer

volùbile *adj* fickle

volubilità *f* fickleness

volume *m* volume; bulk; mass

voluminó·so -sa [s] *adj* voluminous, bulky

volu·to -ta *adj* desired; intentional ‖ *f* (archit) volute, scroll

volut·tà *f* (-tà) pleasure, enjoyment; voluptuousness

voluttuà·rio -ria *adj* (-ri -rie) luxury (*goods*)

voluttuó·so -sa [s] *adj* voluptuous, sensuous

vòmere *m* plowshare; trail spade (*of gun*)

vòmi·co -ca *adj* (-ci -che) emetic

vomitare (vòmito) *tr* & *intr* to vomit

vomitati·vo -va *adj* & *m* emetic

vòmito *m* vomit

vóngola *f* clam

vorace *adj* voracious

voraci·tà *f* (-tà) voracity

voràgine *f* chasm, gulf, abyss

vòrtice *m* vortex, whirlpool; whirlwind

vorticó·so -sa [s] *adj* whirling, swirling

vò·stro -stra §6 *adj* & *pron poss*

votare (vóto) *tr* to devote; to vote ‖ *intr* to vote ‖ *ref* to devote oneself

votazióne *f* vote, voting, poll; (educ) grades

voti·vo -va *adj* votive

vóto *m* vow; wish; votive offering; vote, ballot; grade, mark; a pieni voti with highest honors; fare un voto to make a vow; pronunciare i voti to take vows; voto di fiducia vote of confidence; voto preferenziale write-in vote; preferential ballot

vudù *m* voodoo

vudui·sta *mf* (-sti -ste) voodoo (*person*)

vulcàni·co -ca *adj* (-ci -che) volcanic

vulcanizzare [ddzz] *tr* to vulcanize

vulcano *m* volcano

vulga·to -ta *adj* disseminated ‖ Vulgata *f* Vulgate

vulneràbile *adj* vulnerable

vuotare (vuòto) *tr* to empty; vuotare il sacco to speak one's mind, unburden oneself ‖ *ref* to empty

vuò·to -ta *adj* empty; devoid ‖ *m* vacuum; emptiness; empty space; empty seat; empty feeling; empty (*e.g.*, *container*); a vuoto in vain; wide of the mark; (check) without sufficient funds; andare a vuoto to fail; (mach) to idle; cadere nel vuoto to fall on deaf ears; mandare a vuoto to thwart; sotto vuoto in a vacuum; vuoto d'aria (aer) air pocket; vuoto di cassa deficit; vuoto di potere power vacuum

W

W, w ['doppjo 'vu] *m & f*
wà•fer *m* (-fer) wafer
water-clòset *m* (-clòset) flush toilet
watt *m* (watt) watt

watt•óra *m* (-óra) watt-hour
wèstern *m* (wèstern) (mov) western
whisky *m* (whisky) whiskey
wìgwam *m* (wìgwam) wigwam

X

X, x [ɪks] *m & f*
xèno *m* xenon
xenòfo•bo -ba *mf* xenophobe

xè•res *m* (-res) sherry
xerografìa *f* xerography
xerófito *m* xerophyte

Y

Y, y ['ɪpsɪlon] *m & f*
yacht *m* (yachts) yacht
yak *m* (yak) yak

yànkee *m* (yànkees) Yankee
yìddish *adj invar & m* Yiddish

Z

Z, z ['dzɛta] *m & f* twenty-first letter
  of the Italian alphabet
zabaióne [dz] *m* eggnog
zàcchera *f* splash of mud
zaffare *tr* to plug; to bung
zaffata *f* unpleasant whiff, stench; gust
zafferano [dz] *m* saffron
zaffìro [dz] *m* sapphire
zaffo *m* plug; bung; tampon
zàgara [dz] *f* orange blossom
zàino [dz] *m* knapsack; (mil) pack
zampa *f* paw; (culin) leg; **a quattro
  zampe** on all fours; **zampa di gallina**
  crow's-foot; illegible scrawl; **zampa
  di porco** crowbar
zampare *intr* to paw; to stamp
zampettare (zampétto) *intr* to toddle;
  to scamper
zampillare *intr* (ESSERE & AVERE) to
  spurt, gush, spring
zampillo *m* spurt, gush, spring
zampino *m* little paw; **metterci lo zampino** to put one's finger in the pie
zampiróne *m* slow-burning mosquito
  repellent; foul-smelling cigarette
zampógna *f* bagpipe
zampognare (zampógno) *intr* to pipe,
  play the bagpipe
zampóne *m* Modena salami (*stuffed
  forepaw of a hog*)
zanèlla *f* gully
zàngola *f* butter churn
zanna *f* tusk; fang; **mostrare le zanne**
  to show one's teeth
zanzara [dz] [dz] *f* mosquito
zanzarièra [dz] [dz] *f* mosquito net;
  window screen
zappa *f* hoe; **darsi la zappa sui piedi**

  to cut one's nose off to spite one's
  face
zappare *tr* to hoe
zappatóre *m* hoer, digger; (mil) sapper
zar *m* (zar) czar
zàttera *f* raft; **zattera di salvataggio** life
  raft
zatterière *m* log driver
zavòrra [dz] *f* ballast; (fig) deadwood
zavorrare [dz] (zavòrro) *tr* to ballast
zàzzera *f* mop (*of hair*)
zèbra [dz] *f* zebra; **zebre zebra** crossing
zebra•to -ta [dz] *adj* zebra-striped
ze•bù [dz] *m* (-bù) zebu
zéc•ca *f* (-che) mint; (ent) tick; **nuovo
  di zecca** brand-new
zecchino *m* sequin, gold coin
zèfiro [dz] *m* zephyr
zelante [dz] *adj* zealous; studious ‖ *mf*
  zealot; eager beaver
zèlo [dz] *m* zeal; **zelo pubblico** public
  spirit
zènit [dz] *m* zenith
zénzero [dz] [dz] *m* ginger
zép•po -pa *adj* crammed, jammed ‖ *f*
  wedge; (fig) padding
zerbino [dz] *m* doormat; dandy
zerbinòtto [dz] *m* dandy, sporty fellow
zèro [dz] *m* zero
zìa *f* aunt
zibaldóne [dz] *m* notebook; collection
  of thoughts; (pej) hodgepodge
zibellino [dz] *m* sable
zibétto [dz] *m* civet cat; civet (*substance used in perfumery*)
zibibbo [dz] *m* raisin
zìga•no -na *adj & mf* gypsy
zìgomo [dz] *m* cheekbone

zigrinare [dz] *tr* to grain (*leather*); to mill, knurl (*metal*)

zigrina·to -ta [dz] *adj* shagreened, grained (*leather*); knurled

zigzàg [dz] [dz] *m* (**zigzàg**) zigzag; **andare a zigzag** to zigzag

zigzagare §209 [dz] [dz] *intr* to zigzag

zimarra [dz] *f* cassock; (obs) overcoat

zimbèllo *m* decoy (*bird*); laughingstock

zincare §197 *tr* to zinc

zinco *m* zinc

zingaré·sco -sca (-schi -sche) *adj* & *mf* gypsy

zìnga·ro -ra *mf* gypsy

zìnnia [dz] *f* zinnia

zìo *m* uncle; **zio d'America** rich uncle

zìpolo *m* peg, bung

zircóne [dz] *m* zircon

zircònio [dz] *m* zirconium

zirlare *intr* to warble; to squeak (*said of mouse*)

zitèlla *f* old maid

zittire §176 *tr* & *intr* to hoot, hiss

zit·to -ta *adj* silent; **far stare zitto** to hush up; **stare zitto** to keep quiet || *m* whisper || **zitto** *interj* quiet!; hush!; shut up!

zizzània [dz] [ddzz] *f* (bot) darnel; **seminar zizzania** to sow discord

zòccolo *m* clog, sabot; clump, clod; clodhopper; base (*of column*); pedestal; wide baseboard; (zool) hoof

zodìaco [dz] *m* zodiac

zolfanèllo *m* sulfur match

zolfara *f* var of **solfara**

zólfo *m* sulfur

zòlla *f* clod, clump; turf; lump, cube (*of sugar*)

zollétta *f* lump, cube (*of sugar*)

zòna [dz] *f* zone; area; girdle; band, stripe; ticker tape; (pathol) shingles; (telg) tape; **zona glaciale** frigid zone; **zona tropicale** tropics, tropical zone

zónzo [dz] [dz] *m*—**andare a zonzo** to stroll, loiter along

zoòfito [dz] *m* zoophite

zoologìa [dz] *f* zoology

zoològi·co -ca [dz] *adj* (-ci -che) zoological

zoòlo·go -ga [dz] *mf* (-gi -ghe) zoologist

zootecnìa [dz] *f* animal husbandry

zootècni·co -ca [dz] (-ci -che) *adj* livestock || *m* livestock specialist

zoppicante *adj* limping; halting; shaky

zoppicare §197 (zòppico) *intr* to limp; to be shaky (*in one's studies*); to wobble

zoppicatura *f* limp; wobble

zòp·po -pa *adj* crippled; lame; wobbly || *mf* cripple; lame person

zòti·co -ca [dz] (-ci -che) *adj* uncouth, boorish || *m* churl, boor

zuc·ca *f* (-che) pumpkin; (joc) pate; (coll) empty head

zuccata *f* bump with the head

zuccherare (zùcchero) *tr* to sweeten, sugar

zuccherièra *f* sugar bowl

zuccherifì·cio *m* (-ci) sugar refinery

zuccheri·no -na *adj* sugary || *m* candy; sugar plum; sugar-coated pill

zùcchero *m* sugar; **zucchero filato** cotton candy; **zucchero in polvere** powdered sugar

zuccheró·so -sa [s] *adj* sugary

zucchétto *m* scull cap; zucchetto

zucchi·no -na *m* & *f* zucchini

zuccó·ne -na *mf* dunce, dumbbell

zuffa *f* brawl, fight

zufolare (zùfolo) *tr* & *intr* to whistle

zùfolo *m* (mus) whistle, pipe

zu·lù (-lù) [dz] *adj* & *mf* Zulu

zumare [dz] *tr* & *intr* (mov, telv) to zoom

zumata [dz] *f* (mov, telv) zoom

zuppa *f* soup; (fig) mess; **zuppa inglese** cake with brandy and whipped cream; **zuppa pavese** consommé with toast and eggs

zuppièra *f* tureen

zup·po -pa *adj* drenched, soaked || *f* see **zuppa**

Zurigo *f* Zurich

zuzzurulló·ne -na [dz] [ddzz] *mf* overgrown child, just a big kid

PART TWO

Inglese-Italiano

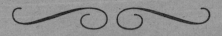

La pronunzia dell'inglese

I simboli seguenti rappresentano approssimativamente tutti i suoni della lingua inglese.

VOCALI

SIMBOLO	SUONO	ESEMPIO
[æ]	Più chiuso della a in caso.	hat [hæt]
[ɑ]	Come la a in basso.	father ['fɑðər] proper ['prɑpər]
[ɛ]	Come la e in sella.	met [met]
[e]	Più chiuso della e in ché. Specialmente in posizione finale, si pronunzia come se fosse seguita da [ɪ].	fate [fet] they [ðe]
[ə]	Come la seconda e nella parola francese gouvernement.	heaven ['hevən] pardon ['pɑrdən]
[i]	Come la i in nido.	she [ʃi] machine [məˈʃin]
[ɪ]	Come la i in ritto.	fit [fɪt] beer [bɪr]
[o]	Più chiuso della o in sole. Specialmente in posizione finale, si pronunzia come se fosse seguito da [ʊ].	nose [noz] road [rod] row [ro]
[ɔ]	Meno chiuso della o in torre.	bought [bɔt] law [lɔ]
[ʌ]	Piuttosto simile alla eu nella parola francese peur	cup [kʌp] come [kʌm] mother ['mʌðər]
[ʊ]	Meno chiuso della u in insulto.	pull [pʊl] book [bʊk] wolf [wʊlf]
[u]	Come la u in acuto.	rude [rud] move [muv] tomb [tum]

DITTONGHI

SIMBOLO	SUONO	ESEMPIO
[aɪ]	Come ai in laico.	night [naɪt] eye [aɪ]
[aʊ]	Come au in causa.	found [faʊnd] cow [kaʊ]
[ɔɪ]	Come oi in poi.	voice [vɔis] oil [ɔɪl]

SIMBOLO	SUONO	ESEMPIO
[b]	Come la **b** in **bambino**. Suono bilabiale occlusivo sonoro.	**bed** [bɛd] **robber** [ˈrɑbər]
[d]	Come la **d** in **caldo**. Suono dentale occlusivo sonoro.	**dead** [dɛd] **add** [æd]
[dʒ]	Come la **g** in **gente**. Suono palatale affricato sonoro.	**gem** [dʒɛm] **jail** [dʒel]
[ð]	Come la **d** nella pronuncia castigliana di **nada**. Suono interdentale fricativo sonoro.	**this** [ðɪs] **father** [ˈfɑðər]
[f]	Come la **f** in **fare**. Suono labiodentale fricativo sordo.	**face** [fes] **phone** [fon]
[g]	Come la **g** in **gatto**. Suono velare occlusivo sonoro.	**go** [go] **get** [gɛt]
[h]	Come la **c** aspirata nella pronuncia toscana di **casa**.	**hot** [hɔt] **alcohol** [ˈælkə͵hɔl]
[j]	Come la **i** in **ieri** o la **y** in **yo-yo**. Semiconsonante di suono palatale sonoro.	**yes** [jɛs] **unit** [ˈjunɪt]
[k]	Come la **c** in **casa** ma accompagnato da un'aspirazione. Suono velare occlusivo sordo.	**cat** [kæt] **chord** [kɔrd] **kill** [kɪl]
[l]	Come la **l** in **latino**. Suono alveolare fricativo laterale sonoro.	**late** [let] **allow** [əˈlɑu]
[m]	Come la **m** in **madre**. Suono bilabiale nasale sonoro.	**more** [mor] **command** [kəˈmænd]
[n]	Come la **n** in **notte**. Suono alveolare nasale sonoro.	**nest** [nɛst] **manner** [ˈmænər]
[ŋ]	Come la **n** in **manca**. Suono velare nasale sonoro.	**king** [kɪŋ] **conquer** [ˈkɑŋkər]
[p]	Come la **p** in **patto** ma accompagnato da un'aspirazione. Suono bilabiale occlusivo sordo.	**pen** [pɛn] **cap** [kæp]
[r]	La **r** più comune in molte parti dell'Inghilterra e nella maggior parte degli Stati Uniti e del Canadà è un suono semivocalico articolato con la punta della lingua elevata verso la volta del palato. Questa consonante è debolissima in posizione intervocalica o alla fine di una sillaba, e può appena percepirsi. L'articolazione di questa consonante ha la tendenza di influenzare il suono delle vocali contigue. La **r**, preceduta dai suoni [ʌ] o [ə], dà il proprio colorito a questi suoni e sparisce completamente come suono consonantico.	**run** [rʌn] **far** [fɑr] **art** [ɑrt] **carry** [ˈkæri] **burn** [bʌrn] **learn** [lʌrn] **weather** [ˈwɛðər]
[s]	Come la **s** in **sette**. Suono alveolare fricativo sordo.	**send** [sɛnd] **cellar** [ˈsɛlər]
[ʃ]	Come **sc** in **lasciare**. Suono palatale fricativo sordo.	**shall** [ʃæl] **machine** [məˈʃin]
[t]	Come la **t** in **tavolo** ma accompagnato da un'aspirazione. Suono dentale occlusivo sordo.	**ten** [tɛn] **dropped** [drɑpt]
[tʃ]	Come **c** in **cibo**. Suono palatale affricato sordo.	**child** [tʃaɪld] **much** [mʌtʃ] **nature** [ˈnetʃər]
[θ]	Come la **z** castigliana in **zapato**. Suono interdentale fricativo sordo.	**think** [θɪŋk] **truth** [truθ]
[v]	Come la **v** in **vento**. Suono labiodentale fricativo sonoro.	**vest** [vɛst] **over** [ˈovər] **of** [ʌv]

4

SIMBOLO	SUONO	ESEMPIO
[w]	Come la **u** in **quadro**. Suono labiovelare fricativo sonoro.	**work** [wʌrk] **tweed** [twid] **queen** [kwin]
[z]	Come la **s** in **asilo**. Suono alveolare fricativo sonoro.	**zeal** [zil] **busy** ['bɪzi] **his** [hɪz]
[ʒ]	Come la seconda **g** nella parola francese **garage**. Suono palatale fricativo sonoro.	**azure** ['eʒər] **measure** ['meʒər]

ACCENTO

L'accento tonico principale, indicato col segno grafico ˈ, e l'accento secondario, indicato col segno grafico ˌ, precedono la sillaba sulla quale cadono, per es., **fascinate** ['fæsɪ ˌnet].

La pronunzia delle parole composte

Nella parte inglese-italiano di questo Dizionario la pronunzia figurata di tutte le parole inglesi semplici è indicata in parentesi quadre che seguono immediatamente l'esponente, secondo un nuovo adattamento dell'alfabeto fonetico internazionale.

Vi sono tre generi di parole composte in inglese: (1) le parole in cui gli elementi componenti si sono uniti per formare una parola solida, come per es., **steamboat** vapore; (2) la parole in cui gli elementi componenti sono uniti da un trattino, come per es., **high-grade**ʹ di qualità superiore; (3) le parole in cui gli elementi componenti rimangono graficamente indipendenti gli uni da gli altri, per es., **post card** cartolina postale. La pronunzia delle parole inglesi composte non è indicata in questo Dizionario qualora gli elementi componenti appaiano come esponenti indipendenti nella loro normale posizione alfabetica e mostrano quindi la loro pronunzia figurata. Solo gli accenti principali e secondari di tali parole sono indicati, come per es., **steam**ʹ**boat**ʹ, **high**ʹ-**grade**ʹ, **post**ʹ **card**ʹ. Se i due membri di una parola composta inglese solida non sono separati da un accento grafico, si usa un punto leggermente elevato sopra il rigo per indicarne la divisione, come per es., **la**ʹ**dy·like**ʹ.

Nei nomi in cui l'accento secondario cade sul membro **-man** o **-men**, le vocali di tali membri si pronunziano come nelle parole semplici **man** e **men**, come per es., **mailman** ['mel ˌmæn] e **mailmen** ['mel ˌmen]. Nei nomi in cui tali membri componenti non sono accentati, le loro vocali si pronunziano come se fossero un'**e** muta francese, come per es., **policeman** [pə'lismən] e **policemen** [pə'lismən]. In questo Dizionario la trascrizione fonetica di tali nomi non è stata indicata qualora il primo membro componente appaia come esponente con la sua pronunzia in alfabeto fonetico internazionale. Gli accenti sono ciò nondimeno indicati:

mailʹ**man**ʹ *s* (-men**ʹ**)
policeʹ**man** *s* (-men)

La pronunzia dei participi passati

La pronunzia di una parola la cui desinenza è **-ed** (o **-d** dopo una **e** muta) non è indicata nel presente Dizionario, purché la pronunzia della parola stessa senza tale suffisso appaia con il suo esponente nella sua posizione alfabetica. In tale caso la pronunzia segue le regole indicate qui sotto. Si osservi che il raddoppiamento della vocale finale dopo una semplice vocale tonica non muta la pronunzia del suffisso **-ed**, per es.: **batted** ['bætɪd], **dropped** [drɑpt], **robbed** [rɑbd].

La desinenza **-ed** (o **-d** dopo una **e** muta) del preterito, del participio passato e di certi aggettivi ha tre pronunzie differenti, che dipendono dal suono in cui il tema termina:
1) Se il tema termina in suono consonantico sonoro (che non sia [d]), cioè [b], [g], [l], [m], [n], [ŋ], [r], [v], [z], [ð], [ʒ] o [dʒ] o in un suono vocalico, l'**-ed** è pronunziato [d]:

SUONO IN CUI TERMINA IL TEMA	INFINITO	PRETERITO E PARTICIPIO PASSATO
[b]	**ebb** [ɛb] **rob** [rɑb] **robe** [rob]	**ebbed** [ɛbd] **robbed** [rɑbd] **robed** [robd]

5

SUONO IN CUI TERMINA IL TEMA	INFINITO	PRETERITO E PARTICIPIO PASSATO
[g]	egg [ɛg] sag [sæg]	egged [ɛgd] sagged [sægd]
[l]	mail [mel] scale [skel]	mailed [meld] scaled [skeld]
[m]	storm [stɔrm] bomb [bɑm] name [nem]	stormed [stɔrmd] bombed [bɑmd] named [nemd]
[n]	tan [tæn] sign [saɪn] mine [maɪn]	tanned [tænd] signed [saɪnd] mined [maɪnd]
[ŋ]	hang [hæŋ]	hanged [hæŋd]
[r]	fear [fɪr] care [kɛr]	feared [fɪrd] cared [kɛrd]
[v]	rev [rɛv] save [sev]	revved [rɛvd] saved [sevd]
[z]	buzz [bʌz] fuze [fjuz]	buzzed [bʌzd] fuzed [fjuzd]
[ð]	smooth [smuð] bathe [beð]	smoothed [smuðd] bathed [beðd]
[ʒ]	massage [mə'sɑʒ]	massaged [mə'sɑʒd]
[dʒ]	page [pedʒ]	paged [pedʒd]
suono vocalico	key [ki] sigh [saɪ] paw [pɔ]	keyed [kid] sighed [saɪd] pawed [pɔd]

2) Se il tema termina in un suono consonantico sordo (che non sia [t]), cioè [f], [k], [p], [s], [θ], [ʃ] o [tʃ], l'-ed si pronunzia [t]:

SUONO IN CUI TERMINA IL TEMA	INFINITO	PRETERITO E PARTICIPIO PASSATO
[f]	loaf [lof] knife [naɪf]	loafed [loft] knifed [naɪft]
[k]	back [bæk] bake [bek]	backed [bækt] baked [bekt]
[p]	cap [kæp] wipe [waɪp]	capped [kæpt] wiped [waɪpt]
[s]	hiss [hɪs] mix [mɪks]	hissed [hɪst] mixed [mɪkst]
[θ]	lath [læθ]	lathed [læθt]
[ʃ]	mash [mæʃ]	mashed [mæʃt]
[tʃ]	match [mætʃ]	matched [mætʃt]

3) Se il tema termina in un suono dentale, cioè [t] o [d], l'-ed si pronunzia [ɪd] o [əd]:

SUONO IN CUI TERMINA IL TEMA	INFINITO	PRETERITO E PARTICIPIO PASSATO
[t]	wait [wet] mate [met]	waited ['wetɪd] mated ['metɪd]
[d]	mend [mɛnd] wade [wed]	mended ['mɛndɪd] waded ['wedɪd]

L'-ed di alcuni aggettivi aggiunto ad un tema che termina in suono consonantico (oltre a quelli che terminano in [d] o [t]), è ciò nonostante talvolta pronunziato [ɪd] e tale fenomeno è idicato con la piena pronunzia della parola in simboli dell'alfabeto fonetico internazionale, per es., blessed ['blɛsɪd], crabbed ['kræbɪd].

A, a [e] *s* prima lettera dell'alfabeto inglese

a [e] *art indef* un, uno, una, un'

aback [ə'bæk] *adv* all'indietro; **taken aback** colto alla sprovvista, sconcertato

aba·cus ['æbəkəs] *s* (-**cuses** or -**ci** [,saɪ]) pallottoliere *m;* (archit) abaco

abaft [ə'bæft] or [ə'bɑft] *adv* a poppa ‖ *prep* dietro a

abandon [ə'bændən] *s* disinvoltura ‖ *tr* abbandonare

abase [ə'bes] *tr* umiliare, degradare

abash [ə'bæʃ] *tr* imbarazzare; sconcertare

abate [ə'bet] *tr* ridurre; omettere; (law) terminare ‖ *intr* diminuire, calmarsi

aba·tis ['æbətɪs] or [ə'bætɪs] *s* (-**tis** or -**tises**) (mil) tagliata

abattoir ['æbə,twɑr] *s* macello

abba·cy ['æbəsi] *s* (-**cies**) abbazia

abbess ['æbɪs] *s* badessa

abbey ['æbi] *s* badia, abbazia

abbot ['æbət] *s* abate *m*

abbreviate [ə'brivi,et] *tr* abbreviare, raccorciare

abbreviation [ə,brivi'eʃən] *s* (*abbreviated form*) abbreviazione; (*shortening*) abbreviamento

A B C [,e,bi'si] *s* (letterword) abbiccì *m;* **A B C's** abbecedario

abdicate ['æbdɪ,ket] *tr* abdicare a ‖ *intr* abdicare

abdomen ['æbdəmən] or [æb'domən] *s* addome *m*

abduct [æb'dʌkt] *tr* rapire

abed [ə'bed] *adv* a letto

abet [ə'bet] *v* (*pret & pp* **abetted;** *ger* **abetting**) *tr* favoreggiare

abeyance [ə'be·əns] *s* sospensione; **in abeyance** in sospeso

ab·hor [æb'hɔr] *v* (*pret & pp* -**horred;** *ger* -**horring**) *tr* aborrire

abhorrent [æb'hɑrənt] or [æb'hɔrənt] *adj* detestabile

abide [ə'baɪd] *v* (*pret & pp* **abode** or **abided**) *tr* aspettare; tollerare ‖ *intr* —**to abide by** attenersi a; rimanere fedele a

abili·ty [ə'bɪlɪti] *s* (-**ties**) abilità *f,* bravura

abject ['æbdʒekt] or [æb'dʒekt] *adj* abietto, turpe

abjure [æb'dʒur] *tr* abiurare

ablative ['æblətɪv] *adj & s* ablativo

ablaut ['æblaut] *s* apofonia

ablaze [ə'blez] *adj* in fiamme; risplendente

able ['ebəl] *adj* abile, esperto; **to be able to** + *inf* potere + *inf*

able-bodied ['ebəl'bɑdid] *adj* sano; forte

abloom [ə'blum] *adj & adv* in fiore

abnormal [æb'nɔrməl] *adj* anormale

aboard [ə'bord] *adv* a bordo; **all aboard!** (rr) signori, in vettura!; **to go aboard** imbarcarsi; **to take aboard** imbarcare ‖ *prep* a bordo di; (*a bus, train, etc.*) in, su

abode [ə'bod] *s* abitazione, dimora

abolish [ə'bɑlɪʃ] *tr* abolire

A-bomb ['e,bɑm] *s* bomba atomica

abominable [ə'bɑmənəbəl] *adj* abominevole

abomination [ə,bɑmɪ'neʃən] *s* abominazione

aborigenes [,æbə'rɪdʒɪ,niz] *spl* aborigeni *mpl*

abort [ə'bɔrt] *tr* terminare prematuramente; provocare un aborto in ‖ *intr* abortire

abortion [ə'bɔrʃən] *s* aborto

abound [ə'baund] *intr* abbondare; **to abound in** or **with** abbondare di

about [ə'baut] *adv* circa, press'a poco; qua intorno; qua e là; in direzione opposta; (coll) quasi; **to be about to** star sul punto di ‖ *prep* intorno a; circa a; addosso a; tutt'intorno a; riguardo a

about'-face' *interj* (mil) dietro front!

about'-face' or **about'-face'** *s* voltafaccia; (mil) dietro front *m* ‖ **about'-face'** *intr* fare dietro front

above [ə'bʌv] *adj* soprammenzionato; superiore ‖ *s*—**from above** dal cielo; dall'alto ‖ *adv* in alto; su; più sopra ‖ *prep* sopra, sopra a; più di; al di là di, oltre; **above all** soprattutto

above-mentioned [ə'bʌv'menʃənd] *adj* summenzionato, sunnominato

abrasive [ə'bresɪv] or [ə'brezɪv] *adj & s* abrasivo

abreast [ə'brest] *adj & adv* in fila, in linea; **to keep abreast of** tenersi alla pari con; essere al corrente di

abridge [ə'brɪdʒ] *tr* compendiare; ridurre

abroad [ə'brɔd] *adv* all'estero; all'aria aperta; **to be abroad** (*said of news*) circolare

abrupt [ə'brʌpt] *adj* brusco, improvviso; (*very steep*) scosceso

abscess ['æbses] *s* ascesso

abscond [æb'skɑnd] *intr* scappare; **to abscond with** svignarsela con

absence ['æbsəns] *s* assenza; **in the absence of** in mancanza di

absent ['æbsənt] *adj* assente ‖ [æb,sent] *tr*—**to absent oneself** assentarsi

absentee [,æbsən'ti] *s* assente *mf*

absent-minded ['æbsənt'maɪndɪd] *adj* distratto, assente

absinth ['æbsɪnθ] *s* assenzio

absolute ['æbsə,lut] *adj & s* assoluto

absolutely ['æbsə,lutli] *adv* assolutamente, certamente ‖ [,æbsə'lutli] *interj* certamente!

absolve [æb'sɑlv] *tr* assolvere

absorb [æb'sɔrb] *tr* assorbire; **to be or become absorbed** essere assorto

absorbent [æb'sɔrbənt] *adj* assorbente; (*cotton*) idrofilo ‖ *s* sostanza assorbente

absorbing [æb'sɔrbɪŋ] *adj* interessantissimo

abstain [æb'sten] *intr* astenersi

abstemious [æb'stimɪ·əs] *adj* astemio

abstention [æb'stenʃən] *s* astensione; astenuto (*vote withheld*)

abstinent ['æbstɪnənt] *adj* astinente

abstract ['æbstrækt] *adj* astratto ‖ *s* compendio, sommario ‖ *tr* compendiare ‖ [æb'strækt] *tr* astrarre; (*to steal*) sottrarre

abstruse [æb'strus] *adj* astruso

absurd [æb'sʌrd] or [æb'zʌrd] *adj* assurdo

absurdi·ty [æb'sʌrdɪti] or [æb'zʌrdɪti] *s* (**-ties**) assurdità *f*

abundant [ə'bʌndənt] *adj* abbondante

abuse [ə'bjus] *s* (*misuse*) abuso; maltrattamento; insulto ‖ [ə'bjuz] *tr* (*to misuse, take unfair advantage of*) abusare di; maltrattare; insultare

abusive [ə'bjusɪv] *adj* abusivo; insultante

abut [ə'bʌt] *v* (*pret & pp* **abutted; ger abutting**) *intr*—**to abut on** confinare con

abutment [ə'bʌtmənt] *s* rinfianco; (*at either end of bridge*) spalla; (*of buttresses of bridge*) sprone *m*

abysmal [ə'bɪzməl] *adj* abissale; (*e.g., ignorance*) spropositato

abyss [ə'bɪs] *s* abisso

academic [,ækə'dɛmɪk] *adj* accademico

ac'ademic cos'tume *s* toga accademica

academician [ə,kædə'mɪʃən] *s* accademico

ac'adem'ic year' *s* anno scolastico

acade·my [ə'kædəmi] *s* (**-mies**) accademia

accede [æk'sid] *intr* accedere; **to accede to** salire a; accedere a

accelerate [æk'sɛlə,ret] *tr & intr* accelerare

accelerator [æk'sɛlə,rɛtər] *s* acceleratore *m*

accent ['æksɛnt] *s* accento ‖ ['æksɛnt] or [æk'sɛnt] *tr* accentare; (*to accentuate*) accentuare

ac'cent mark' *s* segnaccento, accento grafico

accentuate [æk'sɛntʃu,et] *tr* accentuare

accept [æk'sɛpt] *tr* accettare

acceptable [æk'sɛptəbəl] *adj* accettabile

acceptance [æk'sɛptəns] *s* accettazione

access ['æksɛs] *s* accesso

accessible [æk'sɛsɪbəl] *adj* accessibile; (*person*) abbordabile

accession [æk'sɛʃən] *s* accessione, acquisto; (*e.g., to the throne*) adito

accesso·ry [æk'sɛsəri] *adj* accessorio ‖ *s* (**-ries**) accessorio; (*to a crime*) complice *m*

accident ['æksɪdənt] *s* accidente *m*; **by accident** accidentalmente, per caso

accidental [,æksɪ'dɛntəl] *adj* accidentale ‖ *s* (mus) accidente *m*

acclaim [ə'klem] *s* acclamazione, applauso ‖ *tr & intr* acclamare, applaudire

acclimate ['æklɪ,met] *tr* acclimatare ‖ *intr* acclimatarsi

accolade [,ækə'led] *s* accollata; (fig) elogio

accommodate [ə'kamə,det] *tr* (*to adjust, make fit*) accomodare; (*to pro-*

vide with a loan) venire incontro a; (*to supply with lodging*) alloggiare; (*to oblige*) favorire; (*to have room for*) aver posto per

accommodating [ə'kamə,detɪŋ] *adj* servizievole, compiacente

accommodation [ə,kamə'deʃən] *s* (*favor*) favore *m*; (*loan*) prestito; (*adaptation*) adattamento; (*reconciliation*) conciliazione; (*compromise*) accomodamento; **accommodations** (*traveling space*) posto; (*in a hotel*) alloggio

accommoda'tion train' *s* treno accelerato

accompaniment [ə'kʌmpənɪmənt] *s* accompagnamento

accompanist [ə'kʌmpənɪst] *s* accompagnatore *m*

accompa·ny [ə'kʌmpəni] *v* (*pret & pp* **-nied**) *tr* accompagnare

accomplice [ə'kamplɪs] *s* complice *mf*

accomplish [ə'kamplɪʃ] *tr* compiere

accomplished [ə'kamplɪʃt] *adj* (*completed*) compiuto, terminato; (*skilled*) finito, compiuto

accomplishment [ə'kamplɪʃmənt] *s* (*completion*) esecuzione, realizzazione; (*something accomplished*) opera; (*acquired ability*) talento; (*military achievement*) prodezza; (*social skill*) compitezza

accord [ə'kɔrd] *s* accordo; **in accord with** in conformità con; **of one's own accord** spontaneamente; **with one accord** di comune accordo ‖ *tr* concedere ‖ *intr* accordarsi

accordance [ə'kɔrdəns] *s* accordo; **in accordance with** in conformità con

according [ə'kɔrdɪŋ] *adv*—**according as** a seconda che; **according to** secondo, a seconda di

accordingly [ə'kɔrdɪŋli] *adv* per conseguenza, perciò; in conformità

accordion [ə'kɔrdɪ·ən] *s* fisarmonica

accost [ə'kɔst] or [ə'kast] *tr* accostare, abbordare

accouchement [ə'kuʃmənt] *s* parto

account [ə'kaʊnt] *s* (*explanation*) versione; (*report*) resoconto; conto; (*statement*) estratto conto; **by all accounts** secondo la voce comune; **of account** d'importanza; **of no account** senza importanza; **on account** in acconto; **on account of** a causa di; per l'amor di; **on all accounts** in ogni modo; **on no account** in nessuna maniera; **to call to account** chiedere conto di; **to give a good account of oneself** comportarsi bene; **to take account of** prendere in considerazione; **to turn to account** trarre profitto da ‖ *intr*—**to account for** render conto di; essere responsabile per

accountable [ə'kaʊntəbəl] *adj* responsabile; (*explainable*) spiegabile

accountant [ə'kaʊntənt] *s* contabile *mf*, ragioniere *m*

accounting [ə'kaʊntɪŋ] *s* contabilità *f*, ragioneria

accouterments [ə'kutərmənts] *spl* (mil)

buffetterie *fpl; (trappings)* ornamenti *mpl*

accredit [əˈkredɪt] *tr* accreditare; **to accredit s.o. with s.th** ascrivere qlco a credito di qlcu

accrue [əˈkru] *intr* accumularsi; *(said of interest)* maturare

acculturation [əˌkʌltʃəˈreʃən] *s* acculturazione

accumulate [əˈkjumjəˌlet] *tr* accumulare || *intr* accumularsi

accuracy [ˈækjərəsi] *s* esattezza, precisione; fedeltà *f*

accurate [ˈækjərɪt] *adj* esatto, preciso; fedele

accursed [əˈkʌrsɪd] or [əˈkʌrst] *adj* maledetto

accusation [ˌækjəˈzeʃən] *s* accusa

accusative [əˈkjuzətɪv] *adj & s* accusativo

accuse [əˈkjuz] *tr* accusare

accustom [əˈkʌstəm] *tr* abituare

ace [es] *s* asso; **to be within an ace of** essere quasi sul punto di

ace′ in the hole′ *s* asso nella manica

acetate [ˈæsɪˌtet] *s* acetato

ace′tic ac′id [əˈsitɪk] *s* acido acetico

aceti·fy [əˈsetɪˌfaɪ] *v (pret & pp* -fied*) tr* acetificare || *intr* acetificarsi

acetone [ˈæsɪˌton] *s* acetone *m*

acetylene [əˈsetɪˌlin] *s* acetilene *m*

acet′ylene torch′ *s* cannello ossiacetilenico

ache [ek] *s* dolore *m* || *intr* dolere, e.g., **my tooth aches** mi duole il dente

Acheron [ˈækəˌrɑn] *s* Acheronte *m*

achieve [əˈtʃiv] *tr* compiere, conseguire

achievement [əˈtʃivmənt] *s* compimento; successo; *(exploit)* impresa, prodezza

Achil′les heel′ [əˈkɪliz] *s* tallone *m* d'Achille

acid [ˈæsɪd] *adj & s* acido

acidi·fy [əˈsɪdɪˌfaɪ] *v (pret & pp* -fied*) tr & intr* acidificare

acidity [əˈsɪdɪti] *s* acidità *f*

acid′ test′ *s* prova del fuoco

ack-ack [ˈækˈæk] *s* (slang) cannone antiaereo

acknowledge [ækˈnɑlɪdʒ] *tr* riconoscere; *(receipt of a letter)* accusare; *(a claim)* ammettere; mostrare la gratitudine per; (law) certificare

acknowledgment [ækˈnɑlɪdʒmənt] *s* riconoscimento; *(of receipt of a letter)* accusa, cenno

acme [ˈækmi] *s* acme *f*

acolyte [ˈækəˌlaɪt] *s* accolito

acorn [ˈekɔrn] or [ˈekərn] *s* ghianda

acoustic [əˈkustɪk] *adj* acustico || **acoustics** *s* acustica

acquaint [əˈkwent] *tr* mettere al corrente; **to be acquainted with** conoscere; essere al corrente di; **to become acquainted** *(with each other)* conoscersi

acquaintance [əˈkwentəns] *s* conoscenza; *(person)* conoscente *mf*, conoscenza

acquiesce [ˌækwɪˈes] *intr* acconsentire, accondiscendere

acquiescence [ˌækwɪˈesəns] *s* accondiscendenza

acquire [əˈkwaɪr] *tr* acquistare

acquisition [ˌækwɪˈzɪʃən] *s* acquisto

acquit [əˈkwɪt] *v (pret & pp* acquitted; *ger* acquitting*) tr (to pay)* ripagare; *(to declare not guilty)* assoivere; **to acquit oneself** condursi

acquittal [əˈkwɪtəl] *s* assoluzione

acre [ˈekər] *s* acro

acrid [ˈækrɪd] *adj* acrido, pungente

acrobat [ˈækrəˌbæt] *s* acrobata *mf*

acrobatic [ˌækrəˈbætɪk] *adj* acrobatico || **acrobatics** *ssg (e.g., of a stunt pilot)* acrobazie *fpl;* acrobatics *spl (gymnastics)* acrobatica

acronym [ˈækrənɪm] *s* acronimo, parola macedonia

acropolis [əˈkrɑpəlɪs] *s* acropoli *f*

across [əˈkrɔs] or [əˈkrɑs] *adv* dall'altra parte; **to get an idea across to** farsi capire da || *prep* attraverso; *(on the other side of)* al di là di, dall'altra parte di; **to come across** *(a person)* imbattersi in; **to go across** attraversare

across′-the-board′ *adj* generale

act [ækt] *s* atto; legge *f;* rappresentazione; **in the act** in flagrante || *tr (a drama)* rappresentare; *(a role)* recitare || *intr (on the stage)* recitare; *(to behave)* comportarsi; *(to perform special duties; to reach a decision)* agire; *(to have an effect)* reagire; **to act as** fungere da; **to act for** rimpiazzare; **to act on** eseguire; **to act up** (coll) fare il matto; non funzionare bene *(said, e.g., of a motor)*; **to act up to** (coll) fare festa a

acting [ˈæktɪŋ] *adj* facente funzione, interino || *s* recita

action [ˈækʃən] *s* azione; *(moving parts)* meccanismo; **to take action** iniziare azione; (law) intentare causa

activate [ˈæktɪˌvet] *tr* attivare

active [ˈæktɪv] *adj & s* attivo

activi·ty [ækˈtɪvɪti] *s (-ties)* attività *f*

act′ of God′ *s* forza maggiore

actor [ˈæktər] *s* attore *m*

actress [ˈæktrɪs] *s* attrice *f*

actual [ˈæktʃ/ʊ-əl] *adj* reale

actually [ˈæktʃ/ʊ-əli] *adv* realmente, in realtà

actuar·y [ˈæktʃ/ʊˌeri] *s (-ies)* attuario

actuate [ˈæktʃ/ʊˌet] *tr* attuare, mettere in azione; *(to motivate)* stimolare

acuity [əˈkju-ɪti] *s* acuità *f*

acumen [əˈkjumən] *s* acume *m*

acupuncture [ˈækjʊˌpʌŋktʃər] *s* agopuntura

acute [əˈkjut] *adj* acuto

ad [æd] *s* (coll) inserzione pubblicitaria

Adam [ˈædəm] *s* Adamo; **not to know from Adam** non conoscere affatto

adamant [ˈædəmənt] *adj* saldo, inflessibile

Ad′am′s ap′ple *s* pomo d'Adamo

adapt [əˈdæpt] *tr* adattare

adaptation [ˌædæpˈteʃən] *s* adattamento; *(e.g., of a play)* rifacimento

add [æd] *tr* aggiungere; *(numbers)*

sommare || *intr* aggiungere; far di conto; **to add up to** ammontare a; (coll) voler dire

adder ['ædər] *s* vipera

addict ['ædɪkt] *s* (*to drugs*) tossicomane *mf*; (*to a sport*) tifoso || [ə'dɪkt] *tr* abituare; rendere propenso alla tossicomania; **to addict oneself to** darsi a, abbandonarsi a

addiction [ə'dɪkʃən] *s* dedizione; (*to drugs*) tossicomania; (*to sports*) tifo

add'ing machine' *s* calcolatrice *f*

addition [ə'dɪʃən] *s* addizione; (*building*) annessi *mpl*; **in addition** inoltre, per di più; **in addition to** oltre a

additive ['ædɪtɪv] *adj & s* additivo

address [ə'dres] *or* ['ædres] *s* (*speech*) discorso; (*place and destination of mail*) indirizzo; (*skill*) destrezza; (*formal request*) petizione; **to deliver an address** pronunciare un discorso || [ə'dres] *tr* indirizzare; (*to speak to*) rivolgere la parola a

addressee [,ædre'si] *s* destinatario

address'ing machine' *s* macchina per indirizzi

adduce [ə'djus] *or* [ə'dus] *tr* addurre

adenoids ['ædə,nɔɪds] *spl* vegetazioni *fpl* adenoidi, adenoidi *fpl*

adept [ə'dept] *adj & s* esperto

adequate ['ædɪkwɪt] *adj* sufficiente; (*suitable*) conveniente

adhere [æd'hɪr] *intr* aderire

adherence [æd'hɪrəns] *s* aderenza

adherent [æd'hɪrənt] *adj & s* aderente *m*

adhesion [æd'hiʒən] *s* adesione; (pathol) aderenza

adhesive [æd'hisɪv] *or* [æd'hizɪv] *adj & s* adesivo

adhe'sive tape' *s* tela adesiva, cerotto

adieu [ə'dju] *or* [ə'du] *s* (**adieus** *or* **adieux**) addio || *interj* addio!

adjacent [ə'dʒesənt] *adj* adiacente

adjective ['ædʒɪktɪv] *adj* aggettivale, accessorio, secondario || *s* aggettivo

adjoin [ə'dʒɔɪn] *tr* confinare con || *intr* essere confinanti

adjoining [ə'dʒɔɪnɪŋ] *adj* confinante; vicino, attiguo

adjourn [ə'dʒʌrn] *tr* aggiornare, rinviare || *intr* rinviarsi

adjournment [ə'dʒʌrnmənt] *s* aggiornamento, rinvio

adjust [ə'dʒʌst] *tr* accomodare; regolare; (ins) liquidare || *intr* abituarsi

adjustable [ə'dʒʌstəbəl] *adj* regolabile

adjustment [ə'dʒʌstmənt] *s* aggiustamento; accomodamento; (ins) liquidazione del danno

adjutant ['ædʒətənt] *s* aiutante *mf*

ad-lib [,æd'lɪb] *v* (*pret & pp* **-libbed**; *ger* **-libbing**) *tr & intr* improvvisare

administer [æd'mɪnɪstər] *tr* amministrare; (*medicine*) somministrare; (*an oath*) dare || *intr*—**to administer to** ministrare, prestare aiuto a

administrator [æd'mɪnɪs,tretər] *s* amministratore *m*

admirable ['ædmɪrəbəl] *adj* ammirabile, ammirevole

admiral ['ædmɪrəl] *s* ammiraglio

admiral·ty ['ædmɪrəlti] *s* (**-ties**) ammiragliato

admire [æd'maɪr] *tr* ammirare

admirer [æd'maɪrər] *s* ammiratore *m*

admissible [æd'mɪsɪbəl] *adj* ammissibile

admission [æd'mɪʃən] *s* ammissione; confessione; (*entrance fee*) prezzo d'ingresso; **to gain admission** arrivare a entrare

ad·mit [æd'mɪt] *v* (*pret & pp* **-mitted**; *ger* **-mitting**) *tr* ammettere; confessare—|| *intr* dare l'ingresso; **to admit of** permettere, ammettere; consentire

admittance [æd'mɪtəns] *s* ammissione; permesso di entrare; **no admittance** divieto d'ingresso

admonish [æd'manɪʃ] *tr* ammonire

ado [ə'du] *s* confusione, trambusto; **much ado about nothing** molto rumore per nulla; **to make a big ado** fare cerimonie

adobe [ə'dobi] *s* mattone crudo

adolescence [,ædə'lesəns] *s* adolescenza

adolescent [,ædə'lesənt] *adj & s* adolescente *mf*

adopt [ə'dapt] *tr* adottare

adoption [ə'dapʃən] *s* adozione

adorable [ə'dorəbəl] *adj* adorabile

adore [ə'dor] *tr* adorare

adorn [ə'dorn] *tr* adornare

adornment [ə'dornmənt] *s* ornamento

adre'nal gland' [æd'rinəl] *s* glandola surrenale

Adriatic [,edri'ætɪk] *or* [,ædri'ætɪk] *adj* adriatico || *adj & s* Adriatico

adrift [ə'drɪft] *adj & adv* alla deriva

adroit [ə'drɔɪt] *adj* destro

adult [ə'dʌlt] *or* ['ædʌlt] *adj & s* adulto

adulterate [ə'dʌltə,ret] *tr* adulterare

adulterer [ə'dʌltərər] *s* adultero

adulteress [ə'dʌltərɪs] *s* adultera

adulter·y [ə'dʌltəri] *s* (**-ies**) adulterio

advance [æd'væns] *or* [æd'vɑns] *adj* avanzato || *s* avanzata; (*increase in price*) aumento; (*of money*) anticipo; **advances** approcci *mpl*; **in advance** in anticipo || *tr* avanzare; aumentare; (*to make earlier*) anticipare; (*money*) anticipare; (*a clock*) mettere avanti || *intr* avanzare; (said, e.g., of prices) aumentare

advanced [æd'vænst] *or* [æd'vɑnst] *adj* avanzato, progredito

advanced' stand'ing *s* trasferimento di voti scolastici

advancement [æd'vænsmənt] *or* [æd'vɑnsmənt] *s* progresso; promozione; (mil) avanzata

advance' public'ity *s* pubblicità *f* di lancio

advantage [æd'væntɪdʒ] *or* [æd'vɑntɪdʒ] *s* vantaggio; **to advantage** in maniera favorevole; **to take advantage of** approfittarsi di; abusare di || *tr* avantaggiare

advantageous [,ædvæn'tedʒəs] *adj* vantaggioso

advent ['ædvɛnt] *s* avvento

adventure [æd'ventʃər] s avventura ǁ *tr* avventurare ǁ *intr* avventurarsi

adventurer [æd'ventʃərər] s avventuriero

adventuresome [æd'ventʃərsəm] *adj* avventuroso

adventuress [æd'ventʃərɪs] s avventuriera

adventurous [æd'ventʃərəs] *adj* avventuroso

adverb ['ædvʌrb] s avverbio

adversar·y ['ædvər‚serɪ] s (-ies) avversario

adverse [æd'vʌrs] or ['ædvʌrs] *adj* avverso, contrario

adversi·ty [æd'vʌrsɪtɪ] s (-ties) avversità *f*

advertise ['ædvər‚taɪz] or [‚ædvər'taɪz] *tr* propagandare; reclamizzare ǁ *intr* fare la pubblicità; inserire un annunzio; inserzionare

advertisement [‚ædvər'taɪzmənt] or [æd'vʌrtɪsmənt] s annuncio pubblicitario, inserzione

advertiser ['ædvər‚taɪzer] or [‚ædvər'taɪzər] s inserzionista *mf*

advertising ['ædvər‚taɪzɪŋ] s pubblicità *f*, pubblicismo

ad'vertising a'gent s pubblicista *mf*

ad'vertising campaign' s campagna pubblicitaria

ad'vertising man' s agente *m* di pubblicità, reclamista *m*

advice [æd'vaɪs] s consiglio; **a piece of advice** un consiglio

advisable [æd'vaɪzəbəl] *adj* consigliabile

advise [æd'vaɪz] *tr* consigliare; informare ǁ *intr*—**to advise with** chiedere il consiglio di; avere una conferenza con

advisement [æd'vaɪzmənt] s considerazione; **to take under advisement** prendere in considerazione

adviser [æd'vaɪzər] s consigliere *m*

advisory [æd'vaɪzərɪ] *adj* consultivo

advocate ['ædvə‚ket] s difensore *m*; (*lawyer*) avvocato ǁ *tr* sostenere, propugnare

adze [ædz] s ascia

Aege'an Sea' [ɪ'dʒiən] s mare Egeo

aegis ['idʒɪs] s egida

Aeneid [i'ni·ɪd] s Eneide *f*

aerate ['eret] or ['e·ə‚ret] *tr* aerare

aerial ['erɪ·əl] or [e'ɪrɪ·əl] *adj* aereo ǁ ['erɪ·əl] s (rad & telv) antenna

aer'ial pho'tograph s aerofotogramma *m*

aerodrome ['ɛrə‚drom] s aerodromo

aerodynamic [‚erodaɪ'næmɪk] *adj* aerodinamico ǁ **aerodynamics** *ssg* aerodinamica

aeronaut ['ɛrə‚nɔt] s aeronauta *m*

aeronautic [‚ɛrə'nɔtɪk] *adj* aeronautico ǁ **aeronautics** *ssg* aeronautica

aerosol ['ɛrə‚sɔl] s aerosol *m*

aerospace ['ero‚spes] *adj* aerospaziale ǁ s aerospazio

Aesop ['isɑp] s Esopo

aesthete ['esθit] s esteta *mf*

aesthetic [ɛs'θetɪk] *adj* estetico ǁ **aesthetics** *ssg* estetica

afar [ə'fɑr] *adv* lontano; **from afar** da lontano

affable ['æfəbəl] *adj* affabile

affair [ə'fɛr] s affare *m*; (*romance*) relazione amorosa

affect [ə'fɛkt] *tr* influenzare; (*to touch the heart of*) commuovere; (*to pretend to have*) affettare

affectation [‚æfɛk'teʃən] s affettazione

affected [ə'fɛktɪd] *adj* affettato

affection [ə'fɛkʃən] s affezione

affectionate [ə'fɛkʃənɪt] *adj* affettuoso, affezionato

affidavit [‚æfɪ'devɪt] s affidavit *m*, dichiarazione sotto giuramento

affiliate [ə'fɪlɪ‚et] *adj & s* affiliato ǁ *tr* affiliare ǁ *intr* affiliarsi

affini·ty [ə'fɪnɪtɪ] s (-ties) affinità *f*

affirm [ə'fʌrm] *tr* affermare; confermare

affirmative [ə'fʌrmətɪv] *adj* affermativo ǁ s affermativa

affix ['æfɪks] s affisso ǁ [ə'fɪks] *tr* affiggere; (*a signature*) apporre; (*e.g., blame*) attribuire

afflict [ə'flɪkt] *tr* affliggere

affliction [ə'flɪkʃən] s afflizione

affluence ['æflu·əns] s opulenza, abbondanza

affluent ['æflu·ənt] *adj* opulento, abbondante; ricco ǁ s affluente *m*

afford [ə'ford] *tr* permettersi il lusso di; (*to furnish*) provvedere; (*to give*) dare

affray [ə'fre] s rissa

affront [ə'frʌnt] s affronto ǁ *tr* fare un affronto a

afghan ['æfgən] or ['æfgæn] s coperta di lana all'uncinetto ǁ **Afghan** *adj & s* afgano

afield [ə'fild] *adv* sul campo; **far afield** lontano

afire [ə'faɪr] *adj* ardente; in fuoco, in fiamme

aflame [ə'flem] *adj* in fiamme

afloat [ə'flot] *adj & adv* a galla; a bordo; (*drifting*) alla deriva; (*said of a rumor*) in circolazione

afoot [ə'fut] *adj & adv* a piedi; in movimento, in moto

aforementioned [ə'for‚menʃənd] or **aforesaid** [ə'for‚sed] *adj* suddetto

afoul [ə'faul] *adj & adv* in collisione; **to run afoul of** finire nelle mani di, impigliarsi con

afraid [ə'fred] *adj* impaurito, spaventato; **to be afraid (of)** aver paura (di)

African ['æfrɪkən] *adj & s* africano

aft [æft] or [ɑft] *adv* a poppa; indietro

after ['æftər] or ['ɑftər] *adj* seguente; di poppa ǁ *adv* dopo; (*behind*) dietro ǁ *prep* dopo; dopo di; (*in the manner of*) secondo; **to run after** corrers dietro a ǁ *conj* dopo che

afterburner ['æftər‚bʌrnər] or ['ɑftər‚bʌrnər] s (aer) postbruciatore *m*

af'ter-din'ner *adj* dopo la cena

aftereffect ['æftərɪ‚fɛkt] or ['ɑftərɪ‚fɛkt] s conseguenza

af'ter-hours' *adj* dopo le ore di ufficio

af'ter-life' s aldilà *m*; vita susseguente

aftermath ['æftər‚mæθ] or ['aftər-‚mæθ] *s* conseguenze *fpl;* gravi conseguenze *fpl*

af'ter•noon' *adj* pomeridiano ‖ *s* pomeriggio

after-shaving ['æftər ‚ʃevɪŋ] or ['aftər-‚ʃevɪŋ] *adj* dopobarba

af'ter•taste' *s* retrosapore *m*

af'ter•thought' *s* pensiero tardivo

afterward ['æftərwərd] or ['aftərwərd] *adv* dopo; **long afterward** molto tempo dopo

af'ter•while' *adv* fra un po'

again [ə'gɛn] *adv* di nuovo; ancora; un'altra volta; **again and again** ripetutamente; **as much again** due volte tanto, altrettanto; **to** + *inf* + **again** tornare a + *inf*, e.g., **to cook again** tornare a cuocere

against [ə'gɛnst] *prep* contro; (*opposite*) in faccia a; **to be against** opporsi a; **to go against the grain** ripugnare

agape [ə'gep] *adj* & *adv* a bocca aperta

age [edʒ] *s* età *f;* (*old age*) vecchiaia; (*full term of life*) vita; (*historical or geological period*) evo; generazione; **of age** maggiorenne; **to come of age** diventare maggiorenne; **under age** minorenne ‖ *tr* & *intr* invecchiare

aged [edʒd] *adj* dell'età di ‖ ['edʒɪd] *adj* vecchio, invecchiato

ageless ['edʒlɪs] *adj* eternamente giovane, che non invecchia mai

agen•cy ['edʒənsi] *s* (**-cies**) azione; agenzia; mediazione; (*of government*) ente *m*

agenda [ə'dʒɛndə] *s* agenda, ordine *m* del giorno

agent ['edʒənt] *s* agente *m;* (coll) commesso viaggiatore, agente *m* di commercio; (rr) gestore *m*

Age' of Enlight'enment *s* illuminismo

agglomeration [ə‚glamə'reʃən] *s* agglomerazione

aggrandizement [ə'grændɪzmənt] *s* aumento, innalzamento

aggravate ['ægrə‚vet] *tr* aggravare; (coll) irritare, esasperare

aggregate ['ægrɪ ‚get] *adj* & *s* aggregato, totale *m;* **in the aggregate** nel complesso ‖ *tr* aggregare; ammontare a

aggression [ə'grɛʃən] *s* aggressione

aggressive [ə'grɛsɪv] *adj* aggressivo, attivo

aggressor [ə'grɛsər] *s* aggressore *m*

aggrieve [ə'griv] *tr* affliggere

aghast [ə'gæst] or [ə'gast] *adj* atterrito

agile ['ædʒɪl] *adj* agile

agitate ['ædʒɪ ‚tet] *tr* agitare ‖ *intr* agitarsi

agitator ['ædʒɪ ‚tetər] *s* agitatore *m*

aglow [ə'glo] *adj* splendente

agnostic [æg'nastɪk] *adj* & *s* agnostico

ago [ə'go] *adv* fa, e.g., **a year ago** un anno fa; **long ago** molto tempo fa

agog [ə'gag] *adj* & *adv* ansioso; **to set agog** riempire di ansietà

agonize ['ægə ‚naɪz] *intr* soffrire straziantemente; (*to struggle*) dibattersi

ago•ny ['ægəni] *s* (**-nies**) agonia

agrarian [ə'grɛrɪ•ən] *adj* agrario ‖ *s* membro del partito agrario

agree [ə'gri] *intr* aderire, andar d'accordo; (*to consent*) acconsentire; (gram) concordare; **to agree with** confarsi a, e.g., **eggs do not agree with him** le uova non gli si confanno

agreeable [ə'gri•əbəl] *adj* gentile; gradevole; (*willing to agree*) consenziente

agreement [ə'grimənt] *s* accordo; **in agreement** d'accordo

agriculture ['ægrɪ ‚kʌltʃər] *s* agricoltura

agriculturist [‚ægrɪ'kʌltʃərɪst] *s* (*farmer*) agricoltore *m;* perito in agricoltura, agronomo

agronomy [ə'granəmi] *s* agronomia

aground [ə'graund] *adv* alla riva; **to run aground** andare or dare in secca

ague ['egju] *s* (*chill*) brivido; febbre *f*

ahead [ə'hɛd] *adv* davanti, avanti; **to get ahead** (coll) andare avanti, aver successo; **to get ahead of** sorpassare; **to go ahead** avanzare; continuare

ahoy [ə'hɔɪ] *interj*—**ship ahoy!** ehi della barca!

aid [ed] *s* aiuto; assistente *m;* (mil) aiutante *m* di campo ‖ *tr* aiutare; **to aid and abet** essere complice di

aide [ed] *s* assistente *m*

aide-de-camp ['eddə'kæmp] *s* (**aides-de-camp**) aiutante *m* di campo

ail [el] *tr* affliggere; **what ails you?** che ha? ‖ *intr* soffrire, essere malato

aileron ['elə ‚ran] *s* alerone *m*

ailing ['elɪŋ] *adj* ammalato

ailment ['elmənt] *s* malattia, indisposizione; (*chronic*) acciacco

aim [em] *s* mira; intento ‖ *tr* (*a gun*) puntare; (*words*) dirigere ‖ *intr* mirare; **to aim to** cercare di, aver l'intenzione di

air [ɛr] *adj* (e.g., *pocket*) d'aria; (e.g., *show*) aeronautico ‖ *s* aria; **by air** per via aerea; **in the open air** all'aria aperta; **to be in the air** circolare; **to be on the air** (rad, telv) essere in onda; **to go on the air** (rad, telv) andare in onda; **to put on airs** darsi delle arie; **to take the air** andar fuori; **up in the air** incerto; (slang) arrabbiato ‖ *tr* aerare, ventilare

airborne ['ɛr ‚barn] or ['ɛr ‚born] *adj* aerosostentato; aerotrasportato

air' brake' *s* freno ad aria compressa

air' cas'tle *s* castello in aria

air'-condi'tion *tr* climatizzare

air' condi'tioner *s* condizionatore *m*

air' condi'tioning *s* aria condizionata, climatizzazione

air-'cool' *tr* raffreddare con aria

air' corps' *s* aviazione, arma aeronautica

air'craft' *s* (**-craft**) aeromobile *m*

air'craft car'rier *s* portaerei *f*

airdrome ['ɛr ‚drom] *s* aerodromo

air'drop' *tr* paracadutare

air'field' *s* campo d'aviazione

air'foil' *s* superficie *f* portante, velatura

air' force' *s* forza aerea

air' gap' *s* (elec) intraferro

airing ['erɪŋ] *s* aerazione; passeggiata all'aria aperta; pubblica discussione
air' jack'et *s* (aer, naut) giubbotto salvagente
air' lane' *s* aerovia
air'lift' *s* ponte aereo, aerotrasporto || *tr* aerotrasportare
air'line' *s* linea aerea; tubo dell'aria
air' mail' *s* posta aerea
air'-mail' *adj* per via aerea || *s* lettera per posta aerea || *adv* per posta aerea || *tr* spedire per posta aerea
air'-mail let'ter *s* lettera per posta aerea
air'-mail stamp' *s* francobollo posta aerea
air'man *s* (-men) aviatore *m*, aviere *m*
air' mat'tress *s* materassino pneumatico
air'plane' *s* aeroplano, aereo
air'plane car'rier *s* portaerei *f*
air' pock'et *s* vuoto d'aria
air' pollu'tion *s* contaminazione atmosferica, inquinamento atmosferico
air' port' *s* aeroporto
air' pump' *s* pompa pneumatica
air' raid' *s* incursione aerea
air'-raid shel'ter *s* rifugio antiaereo
air'-raid warn'ing *s* allerta
air' ri'fle *s* fucile *m* ad aria compressa
air' serv'ice *s* aeroservizio
air' shaft' *s* tubo di ventilazione
air'ship' *s* aeronave *f*
airsickness ['er ,sɪknɪs] *s* male *m* d'aria
air' sleeve' *s* manica a vento
airspace ['er ,spes] *s* aerospazio
air'strip' *s* aviopista
air' ter'minal *s* aerostazione
air'tight' *adj* impermeabile all'aria, ermetico
air'waves' *spl* onde *fpl*, radioonde *fpl*
air'way' *s* aerovia; **airways** (rad) onda, onde *fpl*
air•y ['eri] *adj* (-ier; -iest) arioso; leggero; aereo
aisle [aɪl] *s* (*between rows of seats*) corsia; (*of a church*) navata laterale; (theat) canale *m*
ajar [ə'dʒɑr] *adj* socchiuso; in disaccordo
akimbo [ə'kɪmbo] *adj & adv*—**with arms akimbo** con le mani sui fianchi
akin [ə'kɪn] *adj* affine; congiunto
alabaster ['ælə ,bæstər] or ['ælə- ,bɑstər] *s* alabastro
à la carte [,ɑlə'kɑrt] *adv* alla carta
à la mode [,ɑlə'mod] or [,ælə'mod] *adv* alla moda; servito con gelato
alarm [ə'lɑrm] *s* allarme *m* || *tr* allarmare
alarm' clock' *s* sveglia
alas [ə'læs] or [ə'lɑs] *interj* ahimé!; povero me!
Albanian [æl'benɪ·ən] *adj & s* albanese *mf*
albatross ['ælbə ,trɔs] or ['ælbə ,trɑs] *s* albatro, diomedea
album ['ælbəm] *s* album *m*
albumen [æl'bjumən] *s* albume *m*
alchemy ['ælkəmi] *s* alchimia
alcohol ['ælkə ,hɔl] or ['ælkə ,hɑl] *s* alcole *m*
alcoholic [,ælkə'hɔlɪk] or [,ælkə'hɑ- lɪk] *adj* alcolico || *s* alcolizzato

alcove ['ælkov] *s* (*recess*) alcova; (*in a garden*) chiosco, padiglione *m*; cameretta attigua
alder ['ɔldər] *s* ontano, alno
al'der·man *s* (-men) assessore *m* municipale, consigliere *m* municipale
ale [el] *s* birra amara
alembic [ə'lɛmbɪk] *s* alambicco
alert [ə'lʌrt] *adj* attento; vispo || *s* allerta; **to be on the alert** stare allerta || *tr* dare l'allerta a
Aleu'tian Is'lands [ə'luʃən] *spl* Isole Aleutine
Alexander [,ælɪg'zændər] or [,ælɪg- 'zɑndər] *s* Alessandro
Alexan'der the Great' *s* Alessandro Magno
Alexandrine [,ælɪg'zændrɪn] *adj & s* alessandrino
alfalfa [æl'fælfə] *s* (bot) erba medica
algae ['ældʒi] *spl* alghe *fpl*
algebra ['ældʒɪbrə] *s* algebra
algebraic [,ældʒɪ'bre·ɪk] *adj* algebrico
Algeria [æl'dʒɪrɪ·ə] *s* l'Algeria
Algerian [æl'dʒɪrɪ·ən] *adj & s* algerino
Algiers [æl'dʒɪrz] *s* Algeri *f*
alias ['olɪ·əs] *s* pseudonimo || *adv* alias
ali•bi ['ælɪ ,baɪ] *s* (-bis) alibi *m*
alien ['eljən] or ['elɪ·ən] *adj* straniero; (*strange*) strano || *s* straniero; (*outsider*) estraneo
alienate ['eljə ,net] or ['elɪ·ə ,net] *tr* alienare
alight [ə'laɪt] *v* (*pret & pp* **alighted** or **alit** [ə'lɪt]) *intr* scendere; **to alight on** or **upon** posarsi su
align [ə'laɪn] *tr* allineare || *intr* allinearsi
alike [ə'laɪk] *adj* uguali; **to look alike** assomigliarsi || *adv* nello stesso modo
alimen'tary canal' [,ælɪ'mɛntəri] *s* tubo digestivo
alimony ['ælɪ ,moni] *s* alimonia
alive [ə'laɪv] *adj* vivo, in vita; (*lively*) vivace; **alive to** conscio di; **alive with** brulicante di, pieno zeppo di; **look alive!** fa presto!
alka·li ['ælkə ,laɪ] *s* (-lis or -lies) alcali *m*
alkaline ['ælkə ,laɪn] or ['ælkəlɪn] *adj* alcalino
all [ɔl] *adj indef* tutto, tutto il, ogni || *s* tutto || *pron* tutto; tutti; **all of** tutti || *adv* completamente; **all but** quasi; **all in** (slang) stanco morto; **in all** tutto considerato; **all the better** tanto meglio; **all the worse** tanto peggio; **far all that** per quello che, e.g., **for all that I know** per quello che io ne sappia; **in all** tutto contato; **it's all right!** va bene!; **not at all** niente affatto; prego
allay [ə'le] *tr* calmare, mitigare
all' clear' *s* fine *f* dell'allarme, cessato allarme
allegation [,ælɪ'geʃən] *s* asserzione, affermazione
allege [ə'lɛdʒ] *tr* asserire, affermare; addurre
allegiance [ə'lidʒəns] *s* fedeltà *f*, lealtà *f*

allegoric(al) [ˌælɪˈgɑrɪk(əl)] or [ˌælɪˈgɔrɪk(əl)] *adj* allegorico

allego·ry [ˈælɪˌgori] *s* (**-ries**) allegoria

aller·gy [ˈælərdʒi] *s* (**-gies**) allergia

alleviate [əˈliviˌet] *tr* alleviare

alley [ˈæli] *s* vicolo, calle *f*; (*for bowling*) pista; (*tennis*) corridoio

All' Fools' Day' *s* primo d'aprile

all' fours' spl—on all fours a quattro gambe

alliance [əˈlaɪəns] *s* alleanza

alligator [ˈælɪˌgetər] *s* alligatore *m*

alliteration [əˌlɪtəˈreʃən] *s* allitterazione

all-knowing [ˈɔlˈnoˑɪŋ] *adj* onnisciente

allocate [ˈæləˌket] *tr* assegnare; (*funds*) stanziare; (*to fix the place of*) allogare

allot [əˈlɑt] *v* (*pret & pp* **allotted**; *ger* **allotting**) *tr* distribuire, assegnare

all'-out' *adj* completo; (*ruthless*) acerrimo

allow [əˈlaʊ] *tr* permettere; ammettere; concedere ‖ *intr* **to allow for** prendere in considerazione

allowance [əˈlaʊəns] *s* (*limited share*) assegno; concessione; (*reduction in price*) sconto; tolleranza; **to make allowance for** prendere in considerazione

alloy [ˈælɔɪ] or [əˈlɔɪ] *s* lega; impurezza ‖ [əˈlɔɪ] *tr* far lega di, legare; adulterare

all-powerful [ˈɔlˈpaʊˌərfəl] *adj* onnipotente

all' right' *adj* esatto; bene; in buona salute; (*slang*) dabbene

All' Saints'' Day' *s* Ognissanti *m*

All' Souls'' Day' *s* giorno dei morti

all'spice' *s* pimento, pepe *m* della Giamaica

all'-star game' *s* partita sportiva in cui tutti i giocatori sono scelti fra i migliori

allude [əˈlud] *intr* alludere

allure [əˈlʊr] *s* fascino, incanto ‖ *tr* affascinare, incantare

alluring [əˈlʊrɪŋ] *adj* affascinante, seducente

allusion [əˈluʒən] *s* allusione

al·ly [ˈælaɪ] or [əˈlaɪ] *s* (**-lies**) alleato ‖ [əˈlaɪ] *v* (*pret & pp* **-lied**) *tr* alleare; associare; **to become allied** allearsi; imparentarsi ‖ *intr* allearsi

almanac [ˈɔlməˌnæk] *s* almanacco

almighty [ɔlˈmaɪti] *adj* onnipotente

almond [ˈɑmənd] or [ˈæmənd] *s* (*nut*) mandorla; (*tree*) mandorlo

al'mond brittle' *s* croccante *m*

almost [ˈɔlmost] or [ɔlˈmost] *adv* quasi

alms [ɑmz] *s* elemosina

aloe [ˈælo] *s* aloe *m*

aloft [əˈlɔft] or [əˈlɑft] *adv* in alto, sopra; (aer) in volo; (naut) nell'alberatura

alone [əˈlon] *adj* solo; **let alone** senza menzionare; **to leave alone** non disturbare ‖ *adv* solo, solamente

along [əˈlɔŋ] or [əˈlɑŋ] *adv* (*lengthwise*) per il lungo; (*onward*) avanti; **all along** tutto il tempo; **along with**

con; **to get along** andar d'accordo; andarsene; avanzare; aver successo; **to take along** prendere con sè ‖ *prep* lungo

along'side' *adv* a lato; **alongside of** a lato di ‖ *prep* a lato di, vicino a

aloof [əˈluf] *adj* riservato, freddo; **to keep or stand aloof from** tenersi a distanza da ‖ *adv* lontano; da solo

aloud [əˈlaʊd] *adv* ad alta voce

alphabet [ˈælfəˌbet] *s* alfabeto

alpine [ˈælpaɪn] *adj* alpino

Alps [ælps] *spl* Alpi *fpl*

already [ɔlˈredi] *adv* già

Alsace [ælˈses] or [ˈælsæs] *s* l'Alsazia

Alsatian [ælˈseʃən] *adj & s* alsaziano

also [ˈɔlso] *adv* anche

altar [ˈɔltər] *s* altare *m*

al'tar boy' *s* accolito, chierico

al'tar-piece' *s* pala d'altare

alter [ˈɔltər] *tr* alterare; (*a male animal*) castrare ‖ *intr* diventare differente, cambiare

alteration [ˌɔltəˈreʃən] *s* alterazione, modifica

alternate [ˈɔltərnɪt] or [ˈæltərnɪt] *s* sostituto, supplente *mf* ‖ [ˈɔltərˌnet] or [ˈæltərˌnet] *tr* alternare ‖ *intr* alternarsi, avvicendarsi

al'ternating cur'rent *s* corrente alternata

alternator [ˈɔltərˌnetər] or [æltərˌnetər] *s* alternatore *m*

although [ɔlˈðo] *conj* benchè, per quanto, malgrado

altimeter [ælˈtɪmɪtər] or [ˈæltəˌmitər] *s* altimetro

altitude [ˈæltɪˌtjud] or [ˈæltɪˌtud] *s* altitudine *f*

al·to [ˈælto] *s* (**-tos**) contralto

altogether [ˌɔltəˈgeðər] *adv* completamente, affatto, tutt'insieme

altruist [ˈæltruˌɪst] *s* altruista *mf*

altruistic [ˌæltruˈɪstɪk] *adj* altruistico

alum [ˈæləm] *s* allume *m*

aluminum [əˈlumɪnəm] *s* alluminio

alum·na [əˈlʌmnə] *s* (**-nae** [ni]) diplomata, laureata

alum·nus [əˈlʌmnəs] *s* (**-ni** [nai]) diplomato, laureato

alveo·lus [ælˈviˑələs] *s* (**-li** [ˌlaɪ]) alveolo

always [ˈɔlwɪz] or [ˈɔlwez] *adv* sempre

amalgam [əˈmælgəm] *s* amalgama *m*

amalgamate [əˈmælgəˌmet] *tr* amalgamare ‖ *intr* amalgamarsi

amass [əˈmæs] *tr* ammassare

amateur [ˈæmətˌər] *adj* da dilettante ‖ *s* amatore *m*, dilettante *mf*

amaze [əˈmez] *tr* stupire, meravigliare

amazing [əˈmezɪŋ] *adj* straordinario

Amazon [ˈæməˌzɑn] or [ˈæməzən] *s* rio delle Amazzoni; (myth) Amazzone *f*

ambassador [æmˈbæsədər] *s* ambasciatore *m*

ambassadress [æmˈbæsədrɪs] *s* ambasciatrice *f*

amber [ˈæmbər] *s* ambra

ambigu·ity [ˌæmbɪˈgjuˑɪti] *s* (**-ties**) ambiguità *f*

ambiguous [æmˈbɪgjuˑəs] *adj* ambiguo

ambition [æm'bɪʃən] s ambizione
ambitious [æm'bɪʃəs] adj ambizioso
amble ['æmbəl] s ambio || intr ambiare
ambulance ['æmbjələns] s ambulanza
ambush ['æmbʊʃ] s imboscata; **to lie in ambush** tendere un'imboscata || tr appostare || intr appostarsi
amelioration [ə‚miljə'reʃən] s miglioramento
amen ['e'mɛn] or ['ɑ'mɛn] s amen m || interj amen!
amenable [ə'minəbəl] or [ə'mɛnəbəl] adj docile, aperto; (accountable) responsabile
amend [ə'mɛnd] tr emendare || **amends** spl ammenda, contravvenzione; **to make amends for** fare ammenda per
amendment [ə'mɛndmənt] s emendamento
ameni·ty [ə'minɪti] or [ə'mɛnɪti] s (-ties) amenità f
American [ə'mɛrɪkən] adj & s americano
Americanize [ə'mɛrɪkə‚naɪz] tr americanizzare
amethyst ['æmɪθɪst] s ametista
amiable ['emɪ‚əbəl] adj amabile
amicable ['æmɪkəbəl] adj amichevole
amid [ə'mɪd] prep in mezzo a, fra, tra
amidship [ə'mɪd‚ɪp] adv a mezzanave
amiss [ə'mɪs] adj erroneo, sbagliato || adv erroneamente; **to take amiss** offendersi, prendere in mala parte
ami·ty ['æmɪti] s (-ties) amicizia
ammeter ['æm‚mitər] s amperometro
ammonia [ə'monɪ‚ə] s ammoniaca; acqua ammoniacale
ammunition [‚æmjə'nɪʃən] s munizione, munizioni fpl
amnes·ty ['æmnɪsti] s (-ties) amnistia || v (pret & pp -tied) tr amnistiare
amoeba [ə'mibə] s ameba
among [ə'mʌŋ] prep fra, tra, in mezzo a
amorous ['æmərəs] adj amoroso; erotico
amortize ['æmər‚taɪz] tr ammortare
amount [ə'maunt] s ammontare m || intr—**to amount to** ammontare a
ampere ['æmpɪr] s ampere m
am'pere-hour' s amperora m
amphibious [æm'fɪbɪ·əs] adj anfibio
amphitheater ['æmfɪ‚θɪ·ətər] s anfiteatro
ample ['æmpəl] adj ampio
amplifier ['æmplɪ‚faɪ·ər] s amplificatore m
ampli·fy ['æmplɪ‚faɪ] v (pret & pp -fied) tr amplificare
amplitude ['æmplɪ‚tjud] or ['æmplɪ‚tud] s ampiezza
am'plitude modula'tion s modulazione d'ampiezza
amputate ['æmpjə‚tet] tr amputare
amputee [‚æmpjə'ti] s chi ha subito l'amputazione di un arto
amuck [ə'mʌk] adv freneticamente; **to run amuck** dare in un accesso di pazzia; attaccare alla cieca
amulet ['æmjəlɪt] s amuleto
amuse [ə'mjuz] tr divertire

amusement [ə'mjuzmənt] s divertimento
amuse'ment park' s parco dei divertimenti, luna park m
amusing [ə'mjuzɪŋ] adj divertente
an [æn] or [ən] art indef var of **a**, used before words beginning with vowel or mute **h**
anachronism [ə'nækrə‚nɪzəm] s anacronismo
anaemia [ə'nimɪ·ə] s var of **anemia**
anaesthesia [‚ænɪs'θɪʒə] s anestesia
anaesthetic [‚ænɪs'θɛtɪk] adj & s anestetico
anaesthetize [æ'nɛsθɪ‚taɪz] tr anestetizzare
analogous [ə'næləgəs] adj analogo
analo·gy [ə'nælədʒi] s (-gies) analogia
analy·sis [ə'nælɪsɪs] s (-ses [‚siz]) analisi f
analyst ['ænəlɪst] s analista mf
analytic(al) [‚ænə'lɪtɪk(əl)] adj analitico
analyze ['ænə‚laɪz] tr analizzare
anarchist ['ænərkɪst] s anarchico
anarchy ['ænərki] s anarchia
anathema [ə'næθɪmə] s anatema m
anatomic(al) [‚ænə'tɑmɪk(əl)] adj anatomico
anato·my [ə'nætəmi] s (-mies) anatomia
ancestor ['ænsɛstər] s antenato
ances·try ['ænsɛstri] s (-tries) lignaggio, prosapia
anchor ['æŋkər] s ancora; **to cast anchor** gettare l'ancora; **to ride at anchor** stare all'ancora; **to weigh anchor** salpare l'ancora, salpare || tr ancorare || intr ancorarsi, stare all'ancora
ancho·vy ['æntʃovi] s (-vies) acciuga
ancient ['enʃənt] adj antico || s vecchio, anziano; **the ancients** gli antichi
ancillary ['ænsɪ‚lɛri] adj dipendente; ausiliario, ausiliare
and [ænd] or [ənd] conj e, ed; **and so on**, **and so forth** e così via
Andean [æn'di·ən] or ['ændɪ·ən] adj andino || s abitante mf della regione andina
Andes ['ændiz] spl Ande fpl
andiron ['ænd‚aɪ·ərn] s alare m
anecdote ['ænɪk‚dot] s aneddoto
anemia [ə'nimɪ·ə] s anemia
anemic [ə'nimɪk] adj anemico
an'eroid barom'eter ['ænə‚rɔɪd] s barometro aneroide
anesthesia [‚ænɪs'θɪʒə] s anestesia
anesthetic [‚ænɪs'θɛtɪk] adj & s anestetico
anesthetize [æ'nɛsθɪ‚taɪz] tr anestetizzare
aneurysm ['ænjə‚rɪzəm] s aneurisma m
anew [ə'nju] or [ə'nu] adv di nuovo, nuovamente
angel ['endʒəl] s angelo; (financial backer) (coll) finanziatore m
angelic(al) [æn'dʒɛlɪk(əl)] adj angelico
anger ['æŋgər] s ira, collera || tr adirare || intr adirarsi, incollerirsi
angle ['æŋgəl] s angolo; punto di vista

|| *intr* intrigare; **to angle for** darsi da fare per

an'gle i'ron *s* cantonale *m*, angolare *m*

angler ['æŋglər] *s* pescatore *m* alla lenza; (fig) intrigante *m*

Anglo-Saxon ['æŋglo'sæksən] *adj & s* anglosassone *mf*

an·gry ['æŋgri] *adj* (-grier; -griest) arrabbiato; (pathol) infiammato; **to become angry at** incollerirsi per; **to become angry with** adirarsi con

anguish ['æŋgwiʃ] *s* angoscia, pena

angular ['æŋgjələr] *adj* angolare

anhydrous [æn'haɪdrəs] *adj* anidro

aniline ['ænɪlɪn] or ['ænɪ͵laɪn] *s* anilina

animal ['ænɪməl] *adj & s* animale *m*

an'imated cartoon' ['ænɪ͵metɪd] *s* cartone animato

animation [͵ænɪ'meʃən] *s* animazione

animosi·ty [͵ænɪ'mɑsɪti] *s* (-ties) animosità *f*

animus ['ænɪməs] *s* odio, malanimo

anion ['æn͵aɪ·ɑn] *s* anione *m*

anise ['ænɪs] *s* anice *f*

anisette [͵ænɪ'zet] *s* anisetta

ankle ['æŋkəl] *s* caviglia

an'kle·bone' *s* malleolo

an'kle support' *s* cavigliera

anklet ['æŋklɪt] *s* calzino corto; bracciale *m* da caviglia

annals ['ænəlz] *spl* annali *mpl*

annex ['æneks] *s* annesso, dipendenza || [ə'neks] *tr* annettere, appropriarsi di

annihilate [ə'naɪ·ɪ͵let] *tr* annientare

anniversa·ry [͵ænɪ'vʌrsəri] *adj* anniversario || *s* (-ries) anniversario

annotate ['ænə͵tet] *tr* annotare

announce [ə'naʊns] *tr* annunciare

announcement [ə'naʊnsmənt] *s* annuncio, partecipazione

announcer [ə'naʊnsər] *s* annunziatore *m*

annoy [ə'nɔɪ] *tr* annoiare, seccare

annoyance [ə'nɔɪ·əns] *s* fastidio, seccatura

annoying [ə'nɔɪ·ɪŋ] *adj* noioso

annual ['ænju·əl] *adj* annuale || *s* annuario; pianta annuale

annui·ty [ə'nju·ɪti] or [ə'nu·ɪti] *s* (-ties) annualità *f*; (*for life*) vitalizio

an·nul [ə'nʌl] *v* (*pret & pp* -nulled; *ger* -nulling) *tr* annullare, cassare

annunciation [ə͵nʌnsɪ'eʃən] *s* annunzio || **Annunciation** *s* Annunciazione

anode ['ænod] *s* anodo

anoint [ə'nɔɪnt] *tr* ungere

anomalous [ə'nɑmələs] *adj* anomalo

anoma·ly [ə'nɑməli] *s* (-lies) anomalia

anonymi·ty [͵ænə'nɪmɪti] *s* (-ties) anonimia; **to preserve one's anonymity** serbare l'anonimo

anonymous [ə'nɑnɪməs] *adj* anonimo

another [ə'nʌðər] *adj & pron indef* un altro

answer ['ænsər] or ['ɑnsər] *s* risposta; (*to a problem*) soluzione || *tr* rispondere a; **this will answer your purpose** questo fa per Lei; **to answer back** (slang) dare una rispostaccia a; **to answer the door** andare a rispondere

|| *intr* rispondere; corrispondere; essere responsabile; **to answer back** (slang) dare una rispostaccia

ant [ænt] *s* formica

antagonism [æn'tægə͵nɪzəm] *s* antagonismo

antagonize [æn'tægə͵naɪz] *tr* opporsi a; creare antagonismo in

antarctic [ænt'ɑrktɪk] *adj* antartico || **the Antarctic** la regione antartica

anteater ['ænt͵itər] *s* formichiere *m*

antecedent [͵æntɪ'sidənt] *adj & s* antecedente *m*; **antecedents** antenati *mpl*

antechamber ['æntɪ͵tʃembər] *s* anticamera

antedate ['æntɪ͵det] *tr* antidatare; (*to happen before*) antecedere

antelope ['æntɪ͵lop] *s* antilope *f*

anten·na [æn'tɛnə] *s* (-nae [ni]) (*of insect*) antenna || *s* (-nas) (rad, telv) antenna

antepenult [͵æntɪ'pinʌlt] *s* terzultima sillaba

anteroom ['æntɪ͵rum] or ['æntɪ͵rʊm] *s* anticamera, sala d'aspetto

anthem ['ænθəm] *s* inno

anthill *s* formicaio

antholo·gy [æn'θɑlədʒi] *s* (-gies) antologia

anthracite ['ænθrə͵saɪt] *s* antracite *f*

anthrax ['ænθræks] *s* antrace *m*

anthropoid ['ænθrə͵pɔɪd] *adj* antropoide, antropomorfo

anthropology [͵ænθrə'pɑlədʒi] *s* antropologia

antiaircraft [͵æntɪ'er͵kræft] or [͵æntɪ'er͵krɑft] *adj* antiaereo

antibiotic [͵æntɪbaɪ'ɑtɪk] *adj & s* antibiotico

antibod·y ['æntɪ͵bɑdi] *s* (-ies) anticorpo

anticipate [æn'tɪsɪ͵pet] *tr* anticipare, prevedere; ripromettersi

anticipation [æn͵tɪsɪ'peʃən] *s* anticipazione, previsione

antics ['æntɪks] *spl* pagliacciate *fpl*, buffonate *fpl*

antidote ['æntɪ͵dot] *s* antidoto

antifreeze ['æntɪ͵friz] *s* anticongelante *m*

antiglare [͵æntɪ'gler] *adj* antiabbagliante

anti-G' suit' *s* tuta antigravità

antiknock [͵æntɪ'nɑk] *adj* antidetonante

antimissile [͵æntɪ'mɪsɪl] *adj* antimissile

antimony ['æntɪ͵moni] *s* antimonio

antinoise [͵æntɪ'nɔɪz] *adj* antirumore

antipa·thy [æn'tɪpəθi] *s* (-thies) antipatia

antipersonnel [͵æntɪ͵pʌrsə'nel] *adj* (*e.g., mine*) antiuomo

antiquarian [͵æntɪ'kwerɪ·ən] *adj & s* antiquario

antiquar·y ['æntɪ͵kweri] *s* (-ies) antiquario

antiquated ['æntɪ͵kwetɪd] *adj* antiquato

antique [æn'tik] *adj* antico, vecchio; antiquato || *s* oggetto d'epoca, antichità *f*

antique' deal'er s antiquario

antique' store' s negozio d'antiquariato

antiqui·ty [æn'tɪkwɪti] s (-ties) antichità f

anti-Semitic [ˌæntɪsɪ'mɪtɪk] adj antisemita

antiseptic [ˌæntɪ'sɛptɪk] adj & s antisettico

antislavery [ˌæntɪ'slevəri] adj antischiavista

antitank [ˌæntɪ'tæŋk] adj anticarro

antitheft [ˌæntɪ'θɛft] adj antifurto

antithe·sis [æn'tɪθɪsɪs] s (-ses [ˌsiz]) antitesi f

antitoxin [ˌæntɪ'taksɪn] s antitossina

antitrust [ˌæntɪ'trʌst] adj antitrust

antler ['æntlər] s corno di cervo

antonym ['æntənɪm] s antonimo

Antwerp ['æntwɛrp] s Anversa

anvil ['ænvɪl] s incudine m

anxie·ty [æŋ'zaɪəti] s (-ties) ansietà f; (psychol) angoscia

anxious ['æŋk/əs] adj ansioso; **anxious about** sollecito di; **anxious for** desideroso di

any ['ɛni] adj indef ogni, qualunque, qualsiasi; qualche, e.g., **do you know any boy who could help me?** conosce qualche ragazzo che possa aiutarmi?; di + art, e.g., **do you want any cheese?** vuole del formaggio?; not . . . any non . . . nessuno, e.g., **he does not read any newspaper** non legge nessun giornale ‖ adv un po', e.g., **do you want any?** ne vuole un po'?; not . . . any longer non . . . più; not . . . any more non . . . più ‖ pron ne, e.g., **do you want any?** ne vuole?

an'y·bod'y pron indef chiunque; (in interrogative sentences) qualcuno; not . . . anybody non . . . nessuno

an'y·how' adv in qualunque modo, comunque; in ogni caso; (haphazardly) alla rinfusa

an'y·one' pron indef chiunque; (in interrogative sentences) qualcuno; not . . . anyone non . . . nessuno

an'y·thing' s qualunque cosa ‖ pron indef qualcosa; qualunque cosa; tutto quanto; checchessia; **anything at all** qualunque cosa; not . . . anything non . . . niente; not . . . anything at all non . . . niente affatto, non . . . nulla; not . . . anything else non . . . nient'altro

an'y·way' adv in qualunque modo, comunque; in ogni caso; (haphazardly) alla rinfusa

an'y·where' adv dovunque, in qualsiasi luogo; not . . . anywhere non . . . in nessun luogo

apace [ə'pes] adv presto, rapidamente

apart [ə'pɑrt] adv a parte, a pezzi; separatamente; **apart from** a parte da; oltre a; **to come apart** andare a pezzi, cadere a pezzi; **to set apart** mettere in disparte; **to take apart** smontare; **to tear apart** fare a pezzi; **to tell apart** distinguere

apartment [ə'pɑrtmənt] s appartamento; (single room) stanza

apart'ment house' s casa d'appartamenti

apathetic [ˌæpə'θɛtɪk] adj apatico

apathy ['æpəθi] s apatia

ape [ep] s scimmia antropomorfa; scimmia ‖ tr imitare, scimmiottare

Apennines ['æpəˌnaɪnz] spl Appennini mpl

aperture ['æpərt/ər] s apertura

apex ['epɛks] s (apexes or apices ['æpɪˌsiz]) apice m

apheresis [ə'fɛrɪsɪs] s aferesi f

aphorism ['æfəˌrɪzəm] s aforisma m

aphrodisiac [ˌæfrə'dɪziˌæk] adj & s afrodisiaco

apiar·y ['epiˌɛri] s (-ies) apiario

apiece [ə'pis] adv a testa, per persona; ciascuno

apish ['epɪ/] adj scimmiesco; da scimmia

aplomb [ə'plɑm] s disinvoltura, baldanza

apocalypse [ə'pɑkəˌlɪps] s apocalisse f

apogee ['æpəˌdʒi] s apogeo

apologetic [əˌpɑlə'dʒɛtɪk] adj pieno di scuse

apologize [ə'pɑlə,dʒaɪz] intr chiedere scusa, scusarsi

apolo·gy [ə'pɑlədʒi] s (-gies) scusa; (makeshift) surrogato

apoplectic [ˌæpə'plɛktɪk] adj & s apoplettico

apoplexy ['æpəˌplɛksi] s apoplessia

apostle [ə'pɑsəl] s apostolo

apostrophe [ə'pɑstrəfi] s (mark) apostrofo; (rhet) apostrofe f

apothecar·y [ə'pɑθɪ,kɛri] s (-ies) farmacista mf

appall [ə'pɔl] tr sgomentare, sbigottire

appalling [ə'pɔlɪŋ] adj sconcertante

appara·tus [ˌæpə'retəs] or [ˌæpə'rætəs] s (-tus or -tuses) apparato

apparel [ə'pærəl] s confezioni fpl, vestiario

apparent [ə'pærənt] or [ə'pɛrənt] adj apparente; chiaramente visibile

apparition [ˌæpə'rɪ/ən] s apparizione

appeal [ə'pil] s appello; (attraction) attrattiva, fascino ‖ tr (a sentence) appellare contro ‖ intr dare nell'occhio; **to appeal from** (law) appellarsi contro; **to appeal to** supplicare, pregare; piacere a, e.g., **his idea appeals to me** la sua idea mi piace

appear [ə'pɪr] intr apparire; (to seem) sembrare; (said of a book) uscire; (before the public) presentarsi; (law) comparire

appearance [ə'pɪrəns] s apparizione; (of a book) pubblicazione; (outward look) apparenza; (law) comparizione; **to keep up appearances** salvare le apparenze

appease [ə'piz] tr pacificare, placare; (a desire) soddisfare

appeasement [ə'pizmənt] s pacificazione, tranquillizzazione

appel'late court' [ə'pɛlɪt] s corte f d'appello

appellation [ˌæpə'le/ən] s denominazione, nome m

append [ə'pɛnd] tr allegare, aggiungere

appendage [ə'pɛndɪdʒ] s appendice f

appendicitis [ə,pɛndɪ'saɪtɪs] s appendicite f

appen·dix [ə'pɛndɪks] s (-dixes or -dices [dɪ,siz]) appendice f

appertain [,æpər'ten] intr spettare, riferirsi

appetite ['æpɪ,taɪt] s appetito

appetizer ['æpɪ,taɪzər] s (drink) aperitivo; (food) stimulante m dell'appetito

appetizing ['æpɪ,taɪzɪŋ] adj appetitoso

applaud tr applaudire, applaudire (with dat) || intr applaudire

applause [ə'plɔz] s applauso, applausi mpl

apple ['æpəl] s mela, pomo; (tree) melo, pomo

ap'plejack' s acquavite f di mele

ap'ple of dis'cord s pomo della discordia

ap'ple of one's eye' s pupilla degli occhi di qlcu, beniamino di qlcu

ap'ple pie' s torta di mele

ap'ple pol'isher s leccapiedi mf

ap'ple-sauce' s marmellata di mele; (slang) scemenza

appliance [ə'plaɪ·əns] s apparecchio, apparato; (complicated instrument) congegno; (for domestic chores) utensile m; (act of applying) applicazione

applicant ['æplɪkənt] s postulante mf, aspirante m, candidato

application [,æplɪ'ke/ən] s applicazione; uso; richiesta, domanda

ap·ply [ə'plaɪ] v (pret & pp -plied) tr applicare; (the brakes) mettere; (e.g., a nickname) affibbiare || intr (said of a rule) essere applicabile; fare richiesta; **to apply for** sollecitare

appoint [ə'pɔɪnt] tr nominare; assegnare; (to furnish) ammobiliare

appointee [,æpɔɪn'ti] s persona nominata a una carica

appointive [ə'pɔɪntɪv] adj a nomina

appointment [ə'pɔɪntmənt] s nomina; (position) ufficio; (agreement to meet) appuntamento; **appointments** mobilia, arredamento; **by appointment** previo appuntamento

apportion [ə'por/ən] tr spartire, dividere proporzionatamente

appraisal [ə'prezəl] s stima, valutazione; (of real estate) estimo

appraise [ə'prez] tr stimare, valutare

appreciable [ə'pri/ɪ·əbəl] adj apprezzabile, notevole

appreciate [ə'pri/ɪ,et] tr apprezzare, valutare; (to be grateful for) gradire; (to be aware of) rendersi conto di; (to raise in value) valorizzare || intr aumentare di valore

appreciation [ə,pri/ɪ'e/ən] s apprezzamento, valutazione; (grateful recognition) gradimento, riconoscenza; valorizzazione

appreciative [ə'pri/ɪ,etɪv] adj grato, riconoscente

apprehend [,æprɪ'hɛnd] tr (to fear) temere; (to understand) comprendere; (to arrest) arrestare

apprehension [,æprɪ'hɛn/ən] s timore m, apprensione; comprensione; arresto

apprehensive [,æprɪ'hɛnsɪv] adj apprensivo

apprentice [ə'prɛntɪs] s apprendista mf, novizio || tr mettere in apprendistato; accettare in apprendistato

apprenticeship [ə'prɛntɪs,/ɪp] s apprendistato, carovana

apprise or **apprize** [ə'praɪz] tr avvertire, avvisare; stimare, valutare

approach [ə'prot/] s (a coming near) avvicinamento; (of night) avvicinarsi m, far m; approssimazione; (access) via d'accesso; (to a problem) impostazione; **approaches** approcci mpl || tr avvicinarsi a, avvicinare; fare approcci con || intr avvicinarsi, approssimarsi

approbation [,æprə'be/ən] s approvazione

appropriate [ə'proprɪ·ɪt] adj appropriato, acconcio || [ə'propri,et] (to take) appropriarsi di; (to set aside for some specific use) stanziare

approval [ə'pruvəl] s approvazione; consenso; **on approval** in prova

approve [ə'pruv] tr & intr approvare

approximate [ə'prɑksɪmɪt] adj approssimato, approssimativo || [ə'prɑksɪ,met] tr approssimarsi a || intr approssimarsi

apricot ['eprɪ,kɑt] or ['æprɪ,kɑt] adj color albicocca || s (fruit) albicocca; (tree) albicocco

April ['eprɪl] s aprile m

A'pril fool' s pesce m d'aprile

A'pril Fools'' Day' s primo d'aprile

apron ['eprən] s grembiale m, grembiule m; **tied to the apron strings of** attaccato alle sottane di

apropos [,æprə'po] adj opportuno || adv—**apropos of** a proposito di

apse [æps] s abside f

apt [æpt] adj atto, appropriato; (quick) pronto; **to be apt to** essere propenso a, portato a

aptitude ['æptɪ,tjud] or ['æptɪ,tud] s attitudine f

ap'titude test' s esame m attitudinale

Apulia [ə'pjulɪ·ə] s la Puglia

aqualung ['ækwə,lʌŋ] s autorespiratore m

aquamarine [,ækwəmə'rin] s acquamarina

aquaplane ['ækwə,plen] s acquaplano || intr andare in acquaplano

aquari·um [ə'kwɛrɪ·əm] s (-ums or -a [ə]) acquario, vasca dei pesci

Aquarius [ə'kwɛrɪ·əs] s (astr) Acquario

aquatic [ə'kwætɪk] or [ə'kwɑtɪk] adj acquatico || s animale acquatico; pianta acquatica; **aquatics** sport acquatici

aqueduct ['ækwə,dʌkt] s acquedotto

aqueous ['ekwɪ·əs] or ['ækwɪ·əs] adj acquoso

aq'uiline nose' ['ækwɪ,laɪn] s naso aquilino

Arab ['ærəb] adj & s arabo

Arabic ['ærəbɪk] adj & s arabo

arbiter ['ɑrbɪtər] s arbitro
arbitrary ['ɑrbɪ‚treri] adj arbitrario
arbitrate ['ɑrbɪ‚tret] tr arbitrare ‖ intr fare l'arbitro
arbitration [‚ɑrbɪ'treʃən] s arbitrato
arbitrator ['ɑrbɪ‚tretər] s arbitro
arbor ['ɑrbər] s pergola, pergolato; (mach) albero, asse m
arbore‧tum [‚ɑrbə'ritəm] s (-tums or -ta [tə]) arboreto
arbutus [ɑr'bjutəs] s (Arbutus unedo) corbezzolo
arc [ɑrk] s arco; (elec) arco voltaico ‖ intr (elec) formare un arco
arcade [ɑr'ked] s arcata, portico
arch [ɑrtʃ] adj malizioso ‖ s arco; (anat) arco del piede ‖ tr attraversare; arcuare ‖ intr inarcarsi
archaeology [‚ɑrkɪ'ɑlədʒi] s archeologia
archaic [ɑr'ke‧ɪk] adj arcaico
archaism ['ɑrke‚ɪzəm] or ['ɑrkɪ‚ɪzəm] s arcaismo
archangel ['ɑrk‚endʒəl] s arcangelo
archbishop ['ɑrtʃ'bɪʃəp] s arcivescovo
archduke ['ɑrtʃ'djuk] or ['ɑrtʃ'duk] s arciduca m
arche‧my ['ɑrtʃ'ɛnɪmi] s (-mies) nemico giurato
archer ['ɑrtʃər] s arciere m
archery ['ɑrtʃəri] s tiro con l'arco
archetype ['ɑrkɪ‚taɪp] s archetipo, prototipo
archipela‧go [‚ɑrkɪ'pɛləgo] s (-gos or -goes) arcipelago
architect ['ɑrkɪ‚tekt] s architetto
architectural [‚ɑrkɪ'tektʃərəl] adj architetturale, architettonico
architecture ['ɑrkɪ‚tektʃər] s architettura
archives ['ɑrkaɪvz] spl archivio
arch'way' s arcata
arc' lamp' s lampada ad arco
arctic ['ɑrktɪk] adj artico ‖ the Arctic la regione artica
arc' weld'ing s saldatura ad arco
ardent ['ɑrdənt] adj ardente
ardor ['ɑrdər] s ardore m
arduous ['ɑrdʒʊ‧əs] or ['ɑrdjʊ‧əs] adj arduo
area ['ɛrɪ‧ə] s area
ar'ea code' s prefisso
Argentina [‚ɑrdʒən'tinə] s l'Argentina
Argentine ['ɑrdʒən‚tin] or ['ɑrdʒən‚taɪn] adj & s argentino ‖ the Argentine l'Argentina
Argonaut ['ɑrgə‚nɔt] s argonauta m
argue ['ɑrgju] tr dibattere; (to indicate) indicare, provare; to argue out of dissuadere da; to argue s.o. into s.th persuadere qlcu di qlco ‖ intr argomentare, discutere
argument ['ɑrgjəmənt] s discussione, argomentazione; (theme) argomento
argumentative [‚ɑrgjə'mɛntətɪv] adj litigioso
aria ['ɑrɪ‧ə] or ['ɛrɪ‧ə] s aria
arid ['ærɪd] adj arido
aridity [ə'rɪdɪti] s aridità f
Aries ['ɛriz] or ['ɛri‚iz] s (astr) Ariete m

aright [ə'raɪt] adv correttamente; to set aright rettificare
arise [ə'raɪz] v (pret arose [ə'roz]; pp arisen [ə'rɪzən]) intr alzarsi; (to originate) provenire, trarre origine; (to occur) succedere, avvenire; (to be raised, as objections) avanzarsi
aristocra‧cy [‚ærɪs'tɑkrəsi] s (-cies) aristocrazia
aristocrat [ə'rɪstə‚kræt] s aristocratico
aristocratic [ə‚rɪstə'krætɪk] adj aristocratico
Aristotelian [‚ærɪstə'tilɪ‧ən] adj & s aristotelico
Aristotle ['ærɪ‚stɑtəl] s Aristotele m
arithmetic [ə'rɪθmətɪk] s aritmetica
arithmetical [‚ærɪθ'metɪkəl] adj aritmetico
arithmetician [‚ærɪθmə'trɪʃən] or [ə‚rɪθmə'trɪʃən] s aritmetico
ark [ɑrk] s arca
ark' of the cov'enant s arca dell'alleanza
arm [ɑrm] s braccio; (e.g., of a bear) zampa; (of a chair) bracciolo; (weapon) arma; arm in arm a braccetto; to be up in arms essere in armi; essere indignato; to lay down one's arms deporre le armi; to rise up in arms levarsi in armi; with open arms a braccia aperte ‖ tr armare ‖ intr armarsi
armament ['ɑrməmənt] s armamento
armature ['ɑrmə‚tʃər] s (of an animal) corazza; (of motor or dynamo) indotto; (of a buzzer or electric bell) ancora
arm'chair' s poltrona
Armenian [ɑr'minɪ‧ən] adj & s armeno
armful ['ɑrm‚fʊl] s bracciata
arm'hole' s giro manica
armistice ['ɑrmɪstɪs] s armistizio
armlet ['ɑrmlɪt] s bracciale m
armor ['ɑrmər] s armatura, corazza ‖ tr corazzare, blindare
ar'mored car' s carro armato
ar'mor plate' s lamiera di corazza
armor‧y ['ɑrməri] s (-ies) armeria; arsenale m
arm'pit' s ascella
arm'rest' s bracciolo
ar‧my ['ɑrmi] adj dell'esercito, militare ‖ s (-mies) esercito; (two or more army corps) armata
ar'my corps' s corpo d'armata
aromatic [‚ærə'mætɪk] adj aromatico
around [ə'raʊnd] adv intorno; all'intorno; dappertutto; to turn around voltarsi ‖ prep intorno a; (coll) vicino a; (approximately) (coll) circa
arouse [ə'raʊz] tr eccitare, incitare; svegliare
arpeg‧gio [ɑr'pedʒo] s (-gios) arpeggio
arraign [ə'ren] tr citare, portare in giudizio; accusare
arrange [ə'rendʒ] tr disporre, sistemare; (a dispute) comporre, accomodare; (mus) ridurre, arrangiare
arrangement [ə'rendʒmənt] s disposizione, sistemazione; composizione, accomodamento; (mus) riduzione,

arrangiamento; **arrangements** preparazione, preparativi *mpl*

array [ə'reɪ] *s* ordine *m*; *(clothes)* abbigliamento; (mil) spiegamento, schiera. || *tr* disporre; abbigliare, adornare; (mil) spiegare, schierare

arrears [ə'rɪɪz] *spl* arretrati *mpl*; **in arrears** in arretrato

arrest [ə'rest] *s* arresto; **under arrest** in arresto || *tr* arrestare; *(the attention)* attrarre

arresting [ə'restɪŋ] *adj* interessante, che fa colpo

arrival [ə'raɪvəl] *s* arrivo; persona arrivata

arrive [ə'raɪv] *intr* arrivare

arrogance ['ærəgəns] *s* arroganza

arrogant ['ærəgənt] *adj* arrogante

arrogate ['ærə‚get] *tr (to take without right)* arrogare per sé, arrogarsi; *(to claim for another)* attribuire ingiustamente

arrow ['æro] *s* freccia, saetta

ar'row-head' *s* punta di freccia; (bot) sagittaria

arsenal ['ɑrsənəl] *s* arsenale *m*

arsenic ['ɑrsɪnɪk] *s* arsenico

arson ['ɑrsən] *s* incendio doloso

art [ɑrt] *s* arte *f*

arter‐y ['ɑrtəri] *s* (‐ies) arteria

artful ['ɑrtfəl] *adj* artificioso; *(clever)* destro; *(crafty)* astuto

arthritic [ɑr'θrɪtɪk] *adj & s* artritico

arthritis [ɑr'θraɪtɪs] *s* artrite *f*

artichoke ['ɑrtɪ‚t∫ok] *s* carciofo

article ['ɑrtɪkəl] *s* articolo

articulate [ɑr'tɪkjəlɪt] *adj* articolato; facile di parola || [ɑr'tɪkjə‚let] *tr* articolare || *intr* pronunziare in modo articolato

articulation [ɑr‚tɪkjə'le∫ən] *s* articolazione

artifact ['ɑrtɪ‚fækt] *s* manufatto

artifice ['ɑrtɪfɪs] *s* artificio

artificial [‚ɑrtɪ'fɪ∫əl] *adj* artificiale

artillery [ɑr'tɪləri] *s* artiglieria

artil'lery‐man *s* (‐men) artigliere *m*, cannoniere *m*

artisan ['ɑrtɪzən] *s* artigiano

artist ['ɑrtɪst] *s* artista *mf*

artistic [ɑr'tɪstɪk] *adj* artistico

artistry ['ɑrtɪstri] *s* abilità artistica

artless ['ɑrtlɪs] *adj* ingenuo, naturale; ignorante; *(clumsy)* grossolano

arts' and crafts' *spl* arti *fpl* e mestieri *mpl*

art‐y ['ɑrti] *adj* (‐ier; ‐iest) (coll) interessato nell'arte con ostentazione

Aryan ['ɛrɪ‐ən] or ['ɑrjən] *adj & s* ariano

as [æz] or [əz] *pron rel* che; **the same as** lo stesso che || *adv* come; per esempio; **as . . . as** così . . . come; **as far as** fino a; **as far as I know** per quanto mi consta; **as for** in quanto a, per quanto concerne; **as is** (slang) com'è, nelle condizioni in cui si trova; **as long as** tanto che, mentre che; **as per secondo**; **as soon as** appena, non appena, non appena che; **as to** per quanto concerne; **as well** pure, anche; **as yet** ancora || *prep* come; da; **as a rule** come regola ||

conj come; mentre; dato che; per quanto; **as if** come se; **as it were** per così dire; **as though** come se

asbestos [æs'bestəs] *s* asbesto, amianto

ascend [ə'send] *tr* ascendere, scalare || *intr* ascendere, salire

ascension [ə'sen/ən] *s* ascensione, scalata || **Ascension** *s* Ascensione

ascent [ə'sent] *s* scalata; salita; *(slope)* erta

ascertain [‚æsər'ten] *tr* sincerarsi di, verificare

ascertainable [‚æsər'tenəbəl] *adj* verificabile

ascetic [ə'setɪk] *adj* ascetico || *s* asceta *m*

ascor'bic ac'id [ə'skɔrbɪk] *s* acido ascorbico

ascribe [ə'skraɪb] *tr* attribuire, imputare

aseptic [ə'septɪk] or [e'septɪk] *adj* asettico

ash [æ/] *s* cenere *f*; (bot) frassino

ashamed [ə'/emd] *adj* vergognoso; **to be or feel ashamed** vergognarsi

ash'can' *s* pattumiera; (coll) bomba antisommergibile

ashen ['æ/ən] *adj* cinereo

ashlar ['æ/lər] *s* bugna, bugnato

ashore [ə'/or] *adv* a terra; **to come ashore** andare a terra, sbarcare; **to run ashore** arenarsi

ash'tray' *s* portacenere *m*

Ash' Wednes'day *s* le Ceneri

Asia ['eʒə] or ['e/ə] *s* l'Asia *f*

A'sia Mi'nor *s* l'Asia *f* Minore

Asian ['eʒən] or ['e/ən] or **Asiatic** [‚eʒɪ'ætɪk] or [‚e/ɪ'ætɪk] *adj & s* asiatico

aside [ə'saɪd] *s* parola detta a parte; (theat) a parte *m* || *adv* da parte; a parte; **aside from** (coll) eccetto; separato da; **to step aside** farsi da un lato

askance [ə'skæns] *adv* di traverso, di sbieco; (fig) con sospetto

asleep [ə'slip] *adj* addormentato; **to fall asleep** addormentarsi

asp [æsp] *s* aspide *m*

asparagus [ə'spærəgəs] *s* asparago; *(as food)* asparagi *mpl*

aspect ['æspekt] *s* aspetto; *(direction anything faces)* esposizione

aspen ['æspən] *s* pioppo tremolo, tremolo

aspersion [ə'spʌrʒən] or [ə'spʌr/ən] *s* diffamazione, calunnia; (eccl) aspersione

asphalt ['æsfɔlt] or ['æsfælt] *s* asfalto || *tr* asfaltare

asphyxiate [æs'frksɪ ˌet] *tr* asfissiare

aspirant [ə'spaɪrənt] or ['æspɪrənt] *s* aspirante *mf*

aspire [ə'spaɪr] *intr* aspirare

aspirin ['æspɪrɪn] *s* aspirina

ass [æs] *s* asino

assail [ə'sel] *tr* assalire, assaltare

assassin [ə'sæsɪn] *s* assassino

assassinate [ə'sæsɪ ˌnet] *tr* assassinare

assassination [əˌsæsɪ'neʃən] *s* assassinio

assault [ə'sɔlt] *s* assalto ‖ *tr* assaltare

assault' and bat'tery *s* vie *fpl* di fatto

assay [ə'se] or ['æse] *s* saggio, esame *m* ‖ [ə'se] *tr* saggiare

assemblage [ə'semblɪdʒ] *s* assemblea; (mach) montaggio

assemble [ə'sembəl] *tr* riunire; (mach) montare, mettere insieme ‖ *intr* assembrarsi, riunirsi

assembler [ə'semblər] *s* montatore *m*

assem·bly [ə'semblɪ] *s* (-blies) assemblea, riunione; (mach) montaggio

assem'bly hall' *s* sala di riunioni

assem'bly line' *s* catena di montaggio

assem'bly·man *s* (-men) membro dell'assemblea legislativa

assent [ə'sent] *s* assenso ‖ *intr* assentire

assert [ə'sʌrt] *tr* asserire; **to assert oneself** far valere i propri diritti

assertion [ə'sʌrʃən] *s* asserzione

assess [ə'ses] *tr* stimare, valutare; (*for taxation or fine*) tassare

assessment [ə'sesmənt] *s* valutazione; tassazione

assessor [ə'sesər] *s* agente *m* delle tasse

asset ['æsət] *s* vantaggio; persona di valore; **assets** (com) attivo; (law) beni *mpl*

assiduous [ə'sɪdʒu·əs] or [ə'sɪdju·əs] *adj* assiduo

assign [ə'saɪn] *s* cessionario ‖ *tr* assegnare; (*e.g., a date*) fissare; (*a right*) trasferire

assignation [ˌæsɪg'neʃən] *s* assegnazione; trasferimento; (*date*) appuntamento amoroso

assignment [ə'saɪnmənt] *s* assegnamento; (*of rights*) trasferimento; (*schoolwork*) compito

assimilate [ə'sɪmɪ ˌlet] *tr* assimilare ‖ *intr* essere assimilato; assimilarsi

assist [ə'sɪst] *s* aiuto ‖ *tr* aiutare, assistere

assistance [ə'sɪstəns] *s* assistenza, aiuto

assistant [ə'sɪstənt] *adj* & *s* assistente *m*

associate [ə'soʃɪ·ɪt] or [ə'soʃɪ ˌet] *adj* associato *s* associato; membro limitato ‖ [ə'soʃɪ ˌet] *tr* associare ‖ *intr* associarsi

association [əˌsoʃɪ'eʃən] *s* associazione

assort [ə'sɔrt] *tr* assortire ‖ *intr* associarsi

assortment [ə'sɔrtmənt] *s* assortimento

assuage [ə'swedʒ] *tr* alleviare

assume [ə'sum] or [ə'sjum] *tr* assumere; (*to appropriate*) usurpare; (*to pretend*) fingere; (*to suppose*) supporre

assumed [ə'sumd] or [ə'sjumd] *adj* supposto, immaginario

assumption [ə'sʌmpʃən] *s* (*arrogance*) aria, arroganza; (*thing taken for granted*) supposizione; (*of an undertaking*) assunzione

assurance [ə'ʃurəns] *s* assicurazione, certezza; baldanza, fiducia in sè; (*too much boldness*) sicumera

assure [ə'ʃur] *tr* assicurare

assuredly [ə'ʃurɪdlɪ] *adv* sicuramente

astatine ['æstə ˌtin] *s* astato

asterisk ['æstə ˌrɪsk] *s* asterisco, stelloncino

astern [ə'stʌrn] *adv* a poppa, a poppavia

asthma ['æzmə] or ['æsmə] *s* asma

astonish [ə'stanɪʃ] *tr* meravigliare, stupefare

astonishing [ə'stanɪʃɪŋ] *adj* stupefacente, sorprendente

astound [ə'staund] *tr* stupefare, sbalordire

astounding [ə'staundɪŋ] *adj* stupefacente

astraddle [ə'strædəl] *adv* a cavaliere, a cavalcioni

astray [ə'stre] *adv* sulla cattiva via; **to go astray** traviarsi; **to lead astray** traviare

astride [ə'straɪd] *adj* & *adv* a cavaliere; (*said of a person*) a cavalcioni ‖ *prep* a cavaliere di; a cavalcioni di

astrology [ə'stralədʒɪ] *s* astrologia

astronaut ['æstrə ˌnɔt] *s* astronauta *mf*

astronautic [ˌæstrə'nɔtɪk] *adj* astronautico ‖ **astronautics** *ssg* astronautica

astronomer [ə'stranəmər] *s* astronomo

astronomic(al) [ˌæstrə'namɪk(əl)] *adj* astronomico

astronomy [ə'stranəmɪ] *s* astronomia

astute [ə'stjut] or [ə'stut] *adj* astuto

asunder [ə'sʌndər] *adv* a pezzi; **to tear asunder** separare, fare a pezzi

asylum [ə'saɪləm] *s* asilo

asymmetry [ə'sɪmɪtrɪ] *s* asimmetria

at [æt] or [ət] *prep* a; in; a casa di, e.g., **at John's** a casa di Giovanni; da, e.g., **at Mary's** da Maria; di, e.g., **to be surprised at** essere sorpreso di; **to laugh at** ridersi di

atheist ['eθɪ·ɪst] *s* ateista *mf*

Athenian [ə'θinɪ·ən] *adj* & *s* ateniese *mf*

Athens ['æθɪnz] *s* Atene *f*

athirst [ə'θʌrst] *adj* assetato

athlete ['æθlit] *s* atleta *mf*

athletic [æθ'letɪk] *adj* atletico ‖ **athletics** *ssg* & *spl* atletica

Atlantic [æt'læntɪk] *adj* atlantico ‖ *adj* & *s* Atlantico

atlas ['ætləs] *s* atlante *m* ‖ **Atlas** *s* Atlante *m*

atmosphere ['ætməs ˌfɪr] *s* atmosfera

atmospheric [ˌætməs'ferɪk] *adj* atmosferico ‖ **atmospherics** *spl* disturbi atmosferici

atom ['ætəm] *s* atomo

at'om bomb' *s* bomba atomica

atomic [ə'tamɪk] *adj* atomico

atom'ic age' *s* era atomica

atom'ic sub'marine *s* sommergibile *m* nucleare

atomize ['ætə ˌmaɪz] *tr* atomizzare

atomizer ['ætə ,maɪzər] *s* nebulizzatore *m*

at'om smash'er *s* acceleratore *m* di particelle

atone [ə'ton] *intr*—**to atone for** espiare

atonement [ə'tonmənt] *s* riparazione; espiazione

atop [ə'tap] *adv* in cima || *prep* in cima a

atrocious [ə'troʃəs] *adj* atroce

atroci·ty [ə'trasɪti] *s* (**-ties**) atrocità *f*

atro·phy ['ætrəfɪ] *s* atrofia || *v* (*pret & pp* **-phied**) *tr* atrofizzare || *intr* atrofizzarsi

attach [ə'tæt/] *tr* attaccare; (*to affix*) apporre; (*to attribute*) attribuire; (*law*) sequestrare; **to be attached to** essere legato a; fare parte di || *intr*—**to attach to** essere pertinente a

attaché [,ætə'/e] or [ə'tæ/e] *s* attaché *m*, addetto

attaché' case' *s* valigetta diplomatica

attachment [ə'tæt/mənt] *s* attacco, unione; affezione; (mach) accessorio; (law) sequestro

attack [ə'tæk] *s* attacco || *tr & intr* attaccare

attain [ə'ten] *tr* raggiungere || *intr*—**to attain to** raggiungere, conseguire

attainder [ə'tendər] *s* morte *f* civile

attainment [ə'tenmənt] *s* raggiungimento, realizzazione; (*accomplishment*) dote *f*

attempt [ə'tempt] *s* tentativo; (*attack*) attentato || *tr* tentare; (*s.o.'s life*) attentare a

attend [ə'tɛnd] *tr* (*to be present at*) presenziare, presenziare a, assistere a; (*to accompany*) accompagnare; (*to take care of; to pay attention to*) assistere || *intr*—**to attend to** occuparsi di, attendere a

attendance [ə'tendəns] *s* (*attending*) presenza; (*company present*) concorso; **to dance attendance** essere al servizio completo

attendant [ə'tendənt] *adj* assistente; (*accompanying*) concomitante || *s* (*servant*) inserviente *mf*; presente *m*

attention [ə'tɛn/ən] *s* attenzione; (mil) attenti *m*; **attentions** attenzioni *fpl*; **to call s.o.'s attention to s.th** fare presente qlco a qlcu; **to stand at attention** stare sull'attenti || *interj* attenti!

attentive [ə'tɛntɪv] *adj* attento, premuroso

attenuate [ə'tenju ,et] *tr* attenuare

attest [ə'tɛst] *tr* attestare || *intr*—**to attest to** attestare, testimoniare

attic ['ætɪk] *s* attico, solaio || **Attic** *adj & s* attico

attire [ə'taɪr] *s* vestiti *mpl*, vestiario || *tr* vestire

attitude ['ætɪ ,tjud] or ['ætɪ ,tud] *s* atteggiamento, attitudine *f*; **to strike an attitude** atteggiarsi

attorney [ə'tʌrnɪ] *s* avvocato; (*proxy*) procuratore *m*

attor'ney gen'eral *s* (**attor'neys gen'eral** or **attor'ney gen'erals**) procuratore *m* generale || **Attorney General** *s* (U.S.A.) ministro di grazia e giustizia

attract [ə'trækt] *tr* attrarre; (*attention*) chiamare

attraction [ə'træk/ən] *s* attrazione

attractive [ə'træktɪv] *adj* attrattivo

attribute ['ætrɪ ,bjut] *s* attributo || [ə'trɪbjut] *tr* attribuire

attrition [ə'trɪ/ən] *s* attrito; diminuzione di numero

auburn ['ɔbərn] *adj & s* biondo fulvo, rosso tizianesco

auction ['ɔk/ən] *s* asta, incanto || *tr* vendere all'asta

auctioneer [,ɔk/ə'nɪr] *s* banditore *m* || *tr & intr* vendere all'asta

audacious [ɔ'de/əs] *adj* audace

audaci·ty [ɔ'dæsɪti] *s* (**-ties**) audacia

audience ['ɔdɪ·əns] *s* (*hearing*) udienza; uditorio, pubblico

au'dio fre'quency ['ɔdɪ ,o] *s* audiofrequenza

au'dio-vis'ual aids' *spl* sussidi audiovisivi

audit ['ɔdɪt] *s* verifica or esame *m* dei conti || *tr* esaminare i conti di; (*a class*) assistere a, come uditore || *intr* assistere a una classe come uditore

audition [ɔ'dɪ/ən] *s* audizione || *tr* dare un'audizione a

auditor ['ɔdɪtər] *s* revisore *m* dei conti; (educ) uditore *m*

auditorium [,ɔdɪ'torɪ·əm] *s* auditorio

auger ['ɔgər] *s* succhiello, trivella

aught [ɔt] *s* zero; **for aught I know** per quanto ne so || *adv* affatto

augment [ɔg'mɛnt] *tr & intr* aumentare

augur ['ɔgər] *s* augure *m* || *tr & intr* vaticinare

augu·ry ['ɔgərɪ] *s* (**-ries**) augurio

august [ɔ'gʌst] *adj* augusto || **August** ['ɔgəst] *s* agosto

aunt [ænt] or [ant] *s* zia

aurora [ə'rorə] *s* aurora

auspice ['ɔspɪs] *s* auspicio; **under the auspices of** sotto gli auspici di

austere [ɔs'tɪr] *adj* austero

Australia [ɔ'streljə] *s* l'Australia *f*

Australian [ɔ'streljən] *adj & s* australiano

Austria ['ɔstrɪ·ə] *s* l'Austria *f*

Austrian ['ɔstrɪ·ən] *adj & s* austriaco

authentic [ɔ'θɛntɪk] *adj* autentico

authenticate [ɔ'θɛntɪ ,ket] *tr* autenticare

author ['ɔθər] *s* autore *m*

authoress ['ɔθərɪs] *s* autrice *f*

authoritarian [ə ,θɔrɪ'tɛrɪ·ən] or [ə- ,θɔrɪ'tɛrɪ·ən] *adj* autoritario || *s* persona autoritaria

authoritative [ə'θɔrɪ ,tetɪv] or [ə'θɔrɪ- ,tetɪv] *adj* autorevole; autoritario

authori·ty [ə'θɔrɪti] or [ə'θɔrɪti] *s* (**-ties**) autorità *f*; **on good authority** da buona fonte, da fonte autorevole

authorize ['ɔθə ,raɪz] *tr* autorizzare

authorship ['ɔθər ,/ɪp] *s* paternità letteraria

au·to ['ɔto] *s* (**-tos**) (coll) auto *f*

autobiogra·phy [,ɔtobaɪ'ɑgrəfɪ] or [,ɔtobɪ'ɑgrəfɪ] *s* (**-phies**) autobiografia

autobus [ˈɔto ˌbʌs] s autobus m
autocratic(al) [ˌɔtəˈkrætɪk(əl)] adj autocratico
autograph [ˈɔtə ˌgræf] or [ˈɔtə ˌgrɑf] adj & s autografo ‖ tr porre l'autografo su, firmare con firma autografa
automat [ˈɔtə ˌmæt] s ristorante m self-service a distribuzione automatica
automate [ˈɔtə ˌmet] tr automatizzare
automatic [ˌɔtəˈmætɪk] adj automatico ‖ s pistola automatica
automat'ic transmis'sion s trasmissione automatica
automation [ˌɔtəˈmeʃən] s automazione
automa‧ton [ɔˈtɑmə ˌtɑn] s (-tons or -ta [tə]) automa m
automobile [ˌɔtəmoˈbil] or [ˌɔtəˈmo-bil] adj & s automobile f
automobile' show' s salone m dell'automobile
automotive [ˌɔtəˈmotɪv] adj (self-propelled) automotore; automobilistico
autonomous [ɔˈtɑnəməs] adj autonomo
autonomy [ɔˈtɑnəmi] s autonomia
autop‧sy [ˈɔtɑpsi] s (-sies) autopsia
au'to trans'port rig' s autotreno per trasporto di automobili
autumn [ˈɔtəm] s autunno
autumnal [ɔˈtʌmnəl] adj autunnale
auxilia‧ry [ɔgˈzɪljəri] adj & s (-ries) ausiliare m
avail [əˈvel] s utilità f; **of no avail** che non serve a nulla ‖ tr servire (with dat); **to avail oneself of** servirsi di; approfittare di ‖ intr servire
available [əˈveləbəl] adj disponibile; **to make available to** mettere alla disposizione di
avalanche [ˈævə ˌlæntʃ] or [ˈævə ˌlɑntʃ] s valanga
avant-garde [əvɑ̃ˈgɑrd] adj d'avanguardia
avant-gardism [əˈvɑ̃ˈgɑrdɪzəm] s avanguardismo
avarice [ˈævərɪs] s avarizia
avaricious [ˌævəˈrɪʃəs] adj avaro
avenge [əˈvendʒ] tr vendicare; **to avenge oneself on** vendicarsi di
avenue [ˈævə ˌnju] or [ˈævənu] s viale m, corso
aver [əˈvʌr] v (pret & pp **averred**) ger **averring**) tr asserire, affermare
average [ˈævərɪdʒ] adj medio ‖ s media; (naut) avaria; (e.g., of goals) (sports) quoziente m; **on the average** di media ‖ tr fare la media di; fare . . . di media, e.g., **he averages one hundred dollars a week** fa cento dollari di media alla settimana
averse [əˈvʌrs] adj avverso
aversion [əˈvʌrʒən] s avversione
avert [əˈvʌrt] tr (to ward off) evitare; (to turn away) distogliere
aviar‧y [ˈevɪ ˌɛri] s (-ies) aviario, voliera
aviation [ˌevɪˈeʃən] s aviazione
aviator [ˈevɪ ˌetər] s aviatore m
avid [ˈævɪd] adj avido
avidity [əˈvɪdɪti] s avidità f

avocation [ˌævəˈkeʃən] s svago, passatempo
avoid [əˈvɔɪd] tr evitare
avoidable [əˈvɔɪdəbəl] adj evitabile
avow [əˈvaʊ] tr confessare, ammettere
avowal [əˈvaʊ‧əl] s confessione, ammissione
await [əˈwet] tr aspettare, attendere
awake [əˈwek] adj sveglio ‖ v (pret & pp **awoke** [əˈwok] or **awaked**) tr svegliare ‖ intr svegliarsi
awaken [əˈwekən] tr svegliare ‖ intr svegliarsi
awakening [əˈwekənɪŋ] s risveglio
award [əˈwɔrd] s (prize) premio; (decision by judge) sentenza ‖ tr aggiudicare
aware [əˈwɛr] adj conscio, consapevole; **to become aware of** rendersi conto di
awareness [əˈwɛrnɪs] s coscienza
awash [əˈwɑʃ] or [əˈwɔʃ] adj & adv a fior d'acqua
away [əˈwe] adj distante, assente ‖ adv lontano; via; continuamente; **away back** (coll) molto tempo fa; **away from** lontano da; **to do away with** disfarsi di, sopprimere; **to get away** scappare, sfuggire; **to go away** andarsene; **to run away** fuggire; **to send away** mandar via; **to take away** portar via
awe [ɔ] s estremo rispetto; sacro timore ‖ tr infondere rispetto a; infondere un sacro timore a
aweigh [əˈwe] adj (anchor) levato
awesome [ˈɔsəm] adj grandioso, imponente
awestruck [ˈɔ ˌstrʌk] adj pieno di sacro timore
awful [ˈɔfəl] adj terribile; imponente ‖ adv (coll) terribilmente
awfully [ˈɔfəli] adv tremendamente, terribilmente; (coll) molto
awhile [əˈhwaɪl] adv un po', un po' di tempo
awkward [ˈɔkwərd] adj (clumsy) goffo, maldestro; (unwieldly) scomodo; (embarrassing) imbarazzante
awl [ɔl] s punteruolo
awning [ˈɔnɪŋ] s tenda; (in front of a store) tendone m
A.W.O.L. [ˈewol] (acronym) or [ˈe-ˈdʌbəl ˌjuˈoˈɛl] (letterword) adj (mil) assente al contrappello
awry [əˈraɪ] adv—**to go awry** andare a capovescio; **to look awry** guardare di sbieco
ax or **axe** [æks] s scure f; **to have an axe to grind** (coll) avere un interesse speciale
axiom [ˈæksɪ‧əm] s assioma m
axiomatic [ˌæksɪ‧əˈmætɪk] adj assiomatico
axis [ˈæksɪs] s (axes [ˈæksiz]) asse m
axle [ˈæksəl] s assale m, asse m
ax'le‧tree' s assale m
ay [aɪ] s & adv sì m
Azores [əˈzorz] or [ˈezorz] spl Azzorre fpl
azure [ˈæʒər] or [ˈeʒər] adj & s azzurro, blu m

B

B, b [biː] *s* seconda lettera dell'alfabeto inglese

baa [bɑː] *s* belato || *intr* belare

babble ['bæbəl] *s* (*murmuring sound*) mormorio; (*senseless prattle*) balbettio || *tr* (*e.g., a secret*) divulgare || *intr* mormorare; balbettare; (*to talk idly*) parlare a vanvera

babe [beb] *s* bebè *m*, bambino; persona inesperta; (slang) ragazza

baboon [bæ'bun] *s* babbuino

ba·by ['bebi] *s* (**-bies**) bebè *m*, neonato; bambino; (*the youngest child*) piccolo || *v* (*pret & pp* **-bied**) *tr* coccolare, ninnare

ba'by car'riage *s* carrozzella

ba'by grand' *s* piano a mezza coda

babyhood ['bebi,hud] *s* infanzia

babyish ['bebi·ɪʃ] *adj* infantile

Babylon ['bæbɪlən] *or* ['bæbɪ,lɑn] *s* Babilonia

ba'by sit'ter *s* bambinaia ad ore

ba'by teeth' *spl* denti *mpl* di latte

baccalaureate [,bækə'lɔrɪ·ɪt] *s* baccalaureato; servizio religioso prima del baccalaureato

bacchanal ['bækənəl] *adj* bacchico || *s* baccanale *m*; (*person*) ubriacone *m*, bisboccione *m*

bachelor ['bætʃələr] *s* (*unmarried man*) scapolo, celibe *m*; (*holder of bachelor's degree*) diplomato; (*apprentice knight*) baccelliere *m*

bachelorhood ['bætʃələr,hud] *s* celibato

bacil·lus [bə'sɪləs] *s* (**-li** [laɪ]) bacillo

back [bæk] *adj* di dietro, posteriore; arretrato; contrario || *s* dorso, schiena; parte *f* posteriore, didietro; (*of a sheet or coin*) tergo; (*of a knife*) costola; (*of a room*) fondo; (*of a book*) fine *f*; (*of a chair*) schienale *m*; **behind one's back** dietro le spalle di uno; **to turn one's back on** volgere la schiena a || *adv* dietro; indietro; **a few weeks back** alcune settimane fa; **as far back as** sino da; **back of** dietro, dietro a; **to go back on one's word** mancare di parola; **to go back to** ritornare a; **to pay back** ripagare; **to send back** restituire || *tr* appoggiare; far indietreggiare || *intr* indietreggiare; rinculare; **to back down** rinunciarci; **to back off** or **out** ritirarsi; **to back up** (*said of a car*) fare marcia indietro

back'ache' *s* mal *m* di schiena

back'bite' *v* (*pret* **-bit**; *pp* **-bitten** or **-bit**) *tr* sparlare di || *intr* sparlare

back'bit'er *s* maldicente *mf*

back'board' *s* (basketball) tabellone *m*

back'bone' *s* spina dorsale; (*of a book*) costola, dorso; (fig) fermezza

back'break'ing *adj* sfiancante

back'door' *adj* segreto, clandestino

back' door' *s* porta di dietro; (fig) mezzo clandestino

back'drop' *s* (theat) fondale *m*

backer ['bækər] *s* sostenitore *m*, difensore *m*; (com) finanziatore *m*

back'fire' *s* (*for firefighting*) controfuoco; (aut) ritorno di fiamma || *intr* (aut) avere un ritorno di fiamma; (fig) raggiungere l'effetto opposto

back'ground' *s* fondo, sfondo; precedenti *mpl*; origine *f*

back'ground mu'sic *s* musica di fondo

backhand ['bæk,hænd] *adj* obliquo || *s* scrittura inclinata a sinistra; (tennis) rovescio

back'hand'ed *adj* obliquo; sarcastico; insincero

backing ['bækɪŋ] *s* appoggio; sostegno; (bb) dorso

back'ing light' *s* (aut) faro retromarcia; (theat) luce *f* per il fondale

back'lash' *s* reazione; contraccolpo; (mach) gioco

back'log' *s* ceppo; (fig) riserva

back' num'ber *s* numero arretrato; (coll) persona all'antica

back' pay' *s* paga arretrata, arretrati *mpl*

back' scratch'er *s* manina per grattare la schiena; (coll) leccapiedi *m*

back' seat' *s* (aut) sedile *m* posteriore; (fig) posizione secondaria

back'side' *s* dorso; didietro

back'slide' *v* (*pret & pp* **-slid** [,slɪd]) *intr* ricadere

back'spac'er *s* tasto ritorno

back'spin' *s* effetto

back'stage' *adj* dietro alle quinte || *s* retroscena *m* || *adv* a retroscena, dietro alle quinte

back'stairs' *adj* indiretto, segreto

back' stairs' *spl* scala di servizio

back'stitch' *s* impuntura || *tr & intr* impunturare

back'stroke' *s* (swimming) bracciata sul dorso

back'swept wing' *s* ala a freccia

back' talk' *s* risposta impertinente

back'track' *intr* ritornare sulle proprie tracce; (fig) fare macchina indietro

back'up light' *s* (aut) faro retromarcia

backward ['bækwərd] *adj* ritroso; poco progredito, retrogrado || *adv* a ritroso, all'indietro; verso il passato; alla rovescia; **backward and forward** (coll) completamente, perfettamente; **to go backward and forward** andare avanti e indietro

back'wash' *s* risacca

back'wa'ter *s* gora, ristagno; (fig) eremo

back'woods' *spl* zona boscosa lontana dai centri popolati

back'yard' *s* cortile *m* posteriore

bacon ['bekən] *s* pancetta

bacteria [bæk'tɪrɪ·ə] *spl* batteri *mpl*

bacterial [bæk'tɪrɪ·əl] *adj* batterico

bacteriologist [bæk,tɪrɪ'ɑləʤɪst] *s* batteriologo

bacteriology [bæk,tɪrɪ'ɑləʤi] *s* batteriologia

bad [bæd] *adj* (**worse** [wʌrs]; **worst** [wʌrst]) cattivo; (*coin*) falso; (*weather*) brutto; (*debt*) insolvibile; severo || *s* male *m*; **from bad to**

worse da male in peggio || adv male;
to be too bad essere peccato; to feel
bad esser spiacente; sentirsi male; to
look bad aver brutta cera

bad' breath' s fiato cattivo

bad' egg' s (slang) cattivo soggetto

badge [bædʒ] s divisa; decorazione;
simbolo, placca

badger ['bædʒər] s tasso || tr molestare

badly ['bædli] adv male; gravemente;
molto

bad'ly off' adj in cattive condizioni

badminton ['bædmintən] s badminton m

baffle ['bæfəl] s (mach) deflettore m;
(rad) schermo acustico || tr frustrare,
confondere

baffling ['bæfliŋ] adj sconcertante

bag [bæg] s sacco; borsetta; (of a
marsupial) borsa; (hunt) presa; bag
and baggage con armi e bagagli; to
be in the bag (slang) averlo nel sacco;
to be left holding the bag (coll) es-
sere piantato in asso || v (pret & pp
bagged; ger bagging) tr insaccare;
(hunt) pigliare || intr (to hang
loosely) far pieghe

baggage ['bægidʒ] s bagaglio

bag'gage car' s bagagliaio

bug'gage check' s scontrino del bagaglio

bag'gage room' s deposito bagagli

bag·gy ['bægi] adj (-gier; -giest) come
un sacco

bag'pipe' s cornamusa, zampogna

bag'pip'er s zampognaro

bail [bel] s cauzione; libertà provvisoria sotto cauzione; (bucket) sassola
|| tr liberare sotto cauzione; to bail
out (a boat) sgottare || intr—to bail
out (aer) gettarsi col paracadute

bailiwick ['beliwik] s (fig) sfera di
competenza

bait [bet] s esca; (fig) allettamento || tr
adescare; (fig) allettare

baize [bez] s panno verde

bake [bek] tr cuocere al forno || intr
cuocersi al forno; abbrustolirsi

bakelite ['beka ,lait] s bachelite f

baker ['bekər] s fornaio, panettiere m

bak'er's doz'en s tredici per ogni dozzina

baker·y ['bekəri] s (-ies) panetteria

bak'ing pan' s tortiera

bak'ing pow'der s lievito in polvere

bak'ing so'da s bicarbonato di soda

balance ['bæləns] s (scales) bilancia;
equilibrio; armonia; (of watch) bilanciere m; (remainder; amount due)
resto; (of budget) pareggio; in the
balance in bilico; to lose one's balance perdere l'equilibrio; to strike a
balance fare il bilancio || tr bilan-
ciare, pesare; (com) bilanciare, pa-
reggiare || intr bilanciarsi

bal'ance of pay'ments s bilancia dei
pagamenti

bal'ance of pow'er s equilibrio politico

bal'ance of trade' s bilancia commerciale

bal'ance sheet' s bilancio

balco·ny ['bælkəni] s (-nies) balcone
m; (theat) galleria

bald [bɔld] adj calvo; (bare) nudo;
(unadorned) semplice

bald' ea'gle s aquila col capo bianco
dell'America del Nord

baldness ['bɔldnis] s calvizie f

baldric ['bɔldrik] s tracolla

bale [bel] s balla; collo || tr imballare

baleful ['belfəl] adj minaccioso, funesto

balk [bɔk] tr ostacolare || intr inte-
starsi, impuntarsi

Balkan ['bɔlkən] adj balcanico || the
Balkans i Balcani

balk·y ['bɔki] adj (-ier; -iest) caparbio,
ostinato

ball [bɔl] s palla; pallone m; sfera; (of
the thumb) polpastrello; (of wool)
gomitolo; (projectile) palla, pallottola; (dance) ballo; on the ball
(slang) capace, efficiente; (slang) in
gamba; to play ball giocare alla
palla; to play ball with essere in
cooperazione con || tr—to ball up
(slang) confondere

ballad ['bæləd] s ballata

ball' and chain' s palla di piombo;
(fig) impedimento; (slang) moglie f

ball'-and-sock'et joint' ['bɔlən'sakit] s
giunto a sfere

ballast ['bæləst] s zavorra; (rr) pie-
trisco || tr zavorrare

ball' bear'ing s cuscinetto a sfere

ballet ['bæle] s balletto

ballistic [bə'listik] adj balistico || bal-
listics ssg balistica

balloon [bə'lun] s pallone m; (for children) palloncino; (in comic strip)
fumetto

ballot ['bælət] s scheda elettorale; voto
|| intr votare, ballottare

bal'lot box' s bussola, urna

ball'play'er s giocatore m di palla, giocatore m di baseball

ball'-point pen' s penna a sfera

ball'room' s salone m da ballo

ballyhoo ['bæli ,hu] s chiasso; monta-
tura || tr far chiasso a favore di

balm [bam] s balsamo

balm·y ['bami] adj (-ier; -iest) bal-
samico; salubre; (slang) pazzo

balsam ['bɔlsəm] s balsamo; (plant)
balsamina

Baltic ['bɔltik] adj baltico

baluster ['bæləstər] s balaustro

balustrade [,bæləs'tred] s balaustrata

bamboo [bæm'bu] s bambù m

bamboozle [bæm'buzəl] tr ingannare,
raggirare

bamboozler [bæm'buzlər] s raggira-
tore m

ban [bæn] s bando; (of marriage) pubblicazione matrimoniale; (eccl) inter-
detto, scomunica || v (pret & pp
banned; ger banning) tr proibire

banal ['benəl] or [bə'næl] adj banale

banana [bə'nænə] s banana, (tree)
banano

band [bænd] s banda, striscia; (of thin
cloth) benda; (of metal, rubber) fascia, nastro; (of hat) nastro; (mus)
banda, fanfara; to beat the band
fortemente; abbondantemente || tr
unire || intr—to band together unirsi

bandage ['bændɪdʒ] *s* benda, bendaggio || *tr* fasciare

bandanna [bæn'dænə] *s* fazzolettone colorato

band'box' *s* cappelliera

bandit ['bændɪt] *s* bandito

band'mas'ter *s* capomusica *m*

bandoleer [,bændə'lɪr] *s* bandoliera

band' saw' *s* sega a nastro

band'stand' *s* chiosco della banda

band'wag'on *s* carrozzone *m* da circo; **to jump on the bandwagon** prendere le parti del vincitore

baneful ['benfəl] *adj* nocivo; funesto

bang [bæŋ] *s* rumore *m*, scoppio; (coll) energia; (*pleasure*) (slang) piacere *m*, eccitazione; **bangs** frangetta || *adv* tutto d'un colpo || *tr* sbattere || *intr* rimbombare || *interj* bum!

bang'-up' *adj* (slang) eccellente, di prim'ordine

banish ['bænɪʃ] *tr* sbandire, mettere al bando

banishment ['bænɪʃmənt] *s* bando, esilio

banister ['bænɪstər] *s* balaustra; **banisters** balaustrata

bank [bæŋk] *s* (*of fish; of fog*) banco; (*of a river*) sponda; (*for coins*) salvadanaio; (*financial institution*) banca, banco; (*of earth, snow*) mucchio, banco; (*of clouds*) cumulo; (aer) inclinazione laterale; (billiards) sponda || *tr* (*a fire*) coprire di cenere; (*to pile up*) ammonticchiare; (*a curve*) sopraelevare; (*money*) depositare || *intr* depositare denaro; (aer) inclinarsi lateralmente; **to bank on** (coll) contare su (di)

bank'book' *s* libretto bancario, libretto di deposito

banker ['bæŋkər] *s* banchiere *m*

banking ['bæŋkɪŋ] *adj* bancario || *s* attività bancaria; professione di banchiere

bank' note' *s* biglietto di banca

bank'roll' *s* rotolo di carta moneta; soldi *mpl* || *tr* (slang) finanziare

bankrupt ['bæŋkrʌpt] *adj* & *s* fallito; **to go bankrupt** andare in fallimento || *tr* dichiarare in fallimento; far fallire

bankrupt·cy ['bæŋkrʌptsi] *s* (-cies) fallimento

banner ['bænər] *adj* importante || *s* bandiera, stendardo; (journ) titolo in grassetto

banns [bænz] *spl* bandi *mpl* matrimoniali

banquet ['bæŋqwɪt] *s* banchetto || *tr* dar un banchetto a || *intr* banchettare

bantam ['bæntəm] *adj* piccolo || *s* pollo nano

ban'tam-weight' *s* peso gallo, bantam *m*

banter ['bæntər] *s* scherzo, facezia || *intr* scherzare, celiare

baptism ['bæptɪzəm] *s* battesimo

baptismal [bæp'tɪzməl] *adj* battesimale; (*certificate*) di battesimo

Baptist ['bæptɪst] *adj* & *s* battista *mf*

baptister·y ['bæptɪstəri] *s* (-ies) battistero

baptize [bæp'taɪz] *or* ['bæptaɪz] *tr* battezzare

bar [bɑr] *s* barra; sbarra; (*of soap*) saponetta; (*of chocolate*) tavoletta; (*of sand*) banco; (*obstacle*) barriera; bar *m*; (*of public opinion*) tribunale *m*; (*legal profession*) avvocatura; (*of door or window*) spranga; (*of lead*) (typ) lingotto; (mus) battuta; **behind bars** in guardina; **to be admitted to the bar** diventare avvocato; **to tend bar** fare il barista || *prep* eccetto, salvo; **bar none** senza eccezione || *v* (*pret* & *pp* **barred;** *ger* **barring**) *tr* sbarrare; sprangare; bloccare; escludere

bar' associa'tion *s* associazione dell'ordine degli avvocati

barb [bɑrb] *s* (*of arrow*) barbiglio

barbarian [bɑr'berɪ-ən] *s* barbaro

barbaric [bɑr'bærɪk] *adj* barbaro

barbarism ['bɑrbə,rɪzəm] *s* barbarismo

barbari·ty [bɑr'bærɪti] *s* (-ties) barbarie *f*

barbarous ['bɑrbərəs] *adj* barbaro, crudele

Bar'bary ape' ['bɑrbəri] *s* bertuccia

barbecue ['bɑrbɪ,kju] *s* arrosto allo spiedo || *tr* arrostire allo spiedo

barbed [bɑrbd] *adj* irto di punte; mordace, pungente

barbed' wire' *s* filo spinato

barber ['bɑrbər] *s* barbiere *m*; (*who cuts and styles hair*) parrucchiere *m*

bar'ber-shop' *s* barberia, negozio di barbiere; negozio di parrucchiere

barbiturate [bɑr'bɪtʃə,ret] *s* barbiturato, barbiturico

bard [bɑrd] *s* bardo, poeta *m*

bare [ber] *adj* nudo; (*head*) a capo scoperto; (*unconcealed*) palese; (*empty*) vuoto; (*wire*) senza isolante; (*unadorned*) semplice; **to lay bare** mettere a nudo || *tr* denudare, scoprire

bare'back' *adj* & *adv* senza sella

barefaced ['ber,fest] *adj* impudente, sfacciato, spudorato

bare'foot' *adj* scalzo

barehanded ['ber,hændɪd] *adj* & *adv* a mani nude

bareheaded ['ber,hedɪd] *adj* a capo scoperto

barelegged ['ber,legɪd] *adj* a gambe nude

barely ['berli] *adv* appena, soltanto

bargain ['bɑrgɪn] *s* affare *m*, buon affare *m*; contrattazione; **at a bargain** a buon prezzo; **into the bargain** in soprappiù || *tr*—**to bargain away** vendere a buonissimo prezzo || *intr* contrattare, mercanteggiare; **to bargain for** aspettarsi

bar'gain sale' *s* vendita sottoprezzo

barge [bɑrdʒ] *s* barcone *m*, chiatta || *intr*—**to barge in** entrare senza chiedere permesso

baritone ['bærɪ,ton] *adj* di baritono || *s* baritono *m*

barium ['berɪ-əm] *s* bario

bark [bɑrk] *s* corteccia, scorza; (*of dog*) abbaiamento, latrato || *tr* (*e.g.,* *insults*) lanciare ‖ *intr* abbaiare, latrare

bar'keep'er *s* barista *mf*

barker ['bɑrkər] *s* banditore *m*, imbonitore *m*

barley ['bɑrli] *s* orzo

bar' mag'net *s* calamita a forma di barra allungata

bar'maid' *s* barista *f*

bar'man *s* (**-men**) barista *m*

barn [bɑrn] *s* granaio; (*for hay*) fienile *m*; (*for livestock*) stalla

barnacle ['bɑrnəkəl] *s* cirripede *m*

barn' owl' *s* civetta

barn'yard' *s* bassacorte *f*, aia

barn'yard fowl' *s* animale *m* da cortile ‖ *spl* animali *mpl* da cortile

barometer [bə'rɑmɪtər] *s* barometro

baron ['bærən] *s* barone *m*; (*industrialist*) cavaliere *m* d'industria

baroness ['bærenɪs] *s* baronessa

baroque [bə'rok] *adj & s* barocco

bar'rack-room' *adj* da caserma ‖ *s* camerata

barracks ['bærəks] *spl* caserma; camerata

barrage [bə'rɑʒ] *s* (mil) fuoco di sbarramento

barrel ['bærəl] *s* barile *m*, botte *f*; (*of gun*) canna; (mach) cilindro

bar'rel or'gan *s* organetto di Barberia

barren ['bærən] *adj* sterile; (*without vegetation*) brullo

barricade [,bærɪ'ked] *s* barricata ‖ *tr* barricare

barrier ['bærɪ-ər] *s* barriera

bar'rier reef' *s* barriera corallina

barring ['bɑrɪŋ] *prep* eccetto, salvo

barrister ['bærɪstər] *s* (Brit) avvocato

bar'room' *s* bar *m*, cantina, mescita

bar'tend'er *s* barista *mf*, barman *m*

barter ['bɑrtər] *s* baratto ‖ *tr & intr* barattare, permutare

basalt [bə'sɔlt] *s* basalto

base [bes] *adj* basale; basso; servile; (*morally low*) turpe; (*metal*) vile, non prezioso ‖ *s* base *f*; (*in children's games*) tana; (*of a word*) radice *f* basale ‖ *tr* basare

base'ball' *s* baseball *m*, pallabase *f*

base'board' *s* basamento; (*of wall*) zoccolo

Basel ['bɑzəl] *s* Basilea

baseless ['beslɪs] *adj* infondato

basement ['besmənt] *s* scantinato, piano interrato

bashful ['bæʃfəl] *adj* timido

basic ['besɪk] *adj* fondamentale; (chem) basico

ba'sic commod'ities *spl* articoli *mpl* di prima necessità

basilica [bə'sɪlɪkə] *s* basilica

basin ['besɪn] *s* catino; vasca; (*of balance*) piatto; (*of river*) bacino; (*of harbor*) darsena

ba·sis ['besɪs] *s* (**-ses** [siz]) base *f*

bask [bæsk] or [bɑsk] *intr* crogiolarsi

basket ['bæskɪt] or ['bɑskɪt] *s* cesta; (sports) cesto

bas'ket-ball' *s* pallacanestro *f*

Basque [bæsk] *adj & s* basco

bas-relief [,bɑrɪ'lif] or [,bærɪ'lif] *s* bassorilievo

bass [bes] *adj & s* (mus) basso ‖ [bæs] *s* (ichth) pesce persico

bass' drum' *s* grancassa

bass' horn' *s* bassotuba *m*

bassinet ['bæsə,net] or [,bæsə'net] *s* culla a forma di cesto; carrozzina a forma di cesto

bas·so ['bæso] or ['bɑso] *s* (**-sos** or **-si** [si]) basso

bassoon [bə'sun] *s* fagotto

bass' vi'ol ['vaɪ·əl] *s* contrabbasso

bastard ['bæstərd] *adj & s* bastardo

baste [best] *tr* (*to sew*) imbastire; (*meat*) inumidire con acqua o grasso

bastion ['bæstʃən] or ['bæstɪ·ən] *s* bastione *m*

bat [bæt] *s* mazza; (*in cricket*) maglio; (coll) colpo; (zool) pipistrello ‖ *v* (*pret & pp* **batted**; *ger* **batting**) *tr* colpire con la mazza; **without batting an eye** (coll) senza batter ciglio

batch [bætʃ] *s* (*of bread*) infornata; gruppo, numero

bath [bæθ] or [bɑθ] *s* bagno; **to take a bath** fare il bagno

bathe [beð] *tr* bagnare, lavare ‖ *intr* bagnarsi, fare il bagno

bather ['beðər] *s* bagnante *mf*

bath'house' *s* (*individual*) cabina; spogliatoio

bath'ing beau'ty *s* bellezza in costume da bagno

bath'ing cap' *s* cuffia da bagno

bath'ing resort' *s* stazione balneare

bath'ing suit' *s* costume *m* da bagno

bath'ing trunks' *spl* mutandine *fpl* da bagno

bath'robe' *s* accappatoio

bath'room' *s* stanza da bagno

bath' salts' *spl* sali *mpl* da bagno

bath'tub' *s* bagno, vasca da bagno

baton [bæ'tɑn] or ['bætən] *s* bastone *m*; (mus) bacchetta

battalion [bə'tæljən] *s* battaglione *m*

batten ['bætən] *tr* assicella; (naut) traversa; (naut) bietta ‖ *tr*—**to batten down the hatches** chiudere ermeticamente i boccaporti

batter ['bætər] *s* pasta, farina pastosa; (baseball) battitore *m* ‖ *tr* battere, tempestare di colpi; (*to wear out*) logorare

bat'tering ram' *s* ariete *m*

batter·y ['bætəri] *s* (**-ies**) (*primary cell*) pila; (*secondary cell*) accumulatore *m*; (*group of batteries*) batteria; (law) assalto; (mil & mus) batteria

battle ['bætəl] *s* battaglia; **to do battle** dar battaglia ‖ *tr* combattere contro ‖ *intr* combattere

bat'tle cry' *s* grido di guerra

battledore ['bætəl,dor] *s* racchetta; **battledore and shuttlecock** gioco del volano

bat'tle-field' *s* campo di battaglia

bat'tle-front' *s* fronte *m* di combattimento

battlement ['bætəlmənt] *s* merlatura

bat'tle roy'al *s* baruffa generale, zuffa generale

bat'tle-ship' *s* corazzata

battue [bæ'tu] or [bæ'tju] *s* (hunt) battuta

bat·ty [ˈbæti] *adj* (-tier; -tiest) (slang) pazzo, eccentrico

bauble [ˈbɔbəl] *s* bazzecola, gingillo

Bavaria [bəˈvɛrɪ·ə] *s* la Baviera

Bavarian [bəˈvɛrɪ·ən] *adj* & *s* bavarese *mf*

bawd [bɔd] *s* ruffiano; ruffiana

bawd·y [ˈbɔdi] *adj* (-ier; -iest) indecente, osceno

bawd'y·house' *s* casa di malaffare

bawl [bɔl] *s* grido; (coll) pianto || *tr*—to bawl out (slang) fare una ramanzina a || *intr* strillare; (coll) piangere

bay [be] *adj* baio || *s* baia; vano, alcova; (recess in wall) apertura nel muro; finestra sporgente; (of dog) latrato; cavallo baio; (bot) lauro; at bay in una posizione disperata || *intr* latrare

bayonet [ˈbe·ənɪt] *s* baionetta || *tr* dare baionettate a || *intr* dare baionettate

bay' win'dow *s* finestra sporgente; (slang) pancia

bazooka [bəˈzukə] *s* bazooka *m*

be [bi] *v* (pres am [æm], is [ɪz], are [ɑr]; pret was [wɑz] or [wʌz], were [wʌr]; pp been [bɪn]) *intr* essere; fare, e.g., to be a mason fare il muratore; fare, e.g., 3 times 3 is 9 tre volte tre fa nove; be as it may be comunque sia; here is or here are ecco; there are ci sono; there is c'è; to be futuro, e.g., my wife to be la mia futura sposa; to be ashamed aver vergogna; to be cold aver freddo; to be hot aver caldo; to be hungry aver fame; to be in stare a casa; to be in a hurry aver fretta; to be in with (coll) essere amico intimo di; to be off andarsene; to be out essere fuori; to be out of (coll) non aver più; to be right aver ragione; to be sleepy aver sonno; to be thirsty avere sete; to be up essere alzato; to be up to essere all'altezza di; toccare, e.g., it's up to you tocca a Lei; to be warm avere caldo; to be wrong avere torto; sbagliarsi; to be . . . years old avere . . . anni || *aux* stare, e.g., to be waiting stare aspettando; essere, e.g., the murder has been committed l'omicidio è stato commesso; dovere, e.g., he is to clean the stables tomorrow domani deve pulire la stalla || *impers* essere, e.g., it is necessary è necessario; fare, e.g., it is cold fa freddo; it is hot fa caldo

beach [bitʃ] *s* spiaggia || *tr* (a boat) arenare || *intr* arenarsi

beach'comb'er *intr* raccogliere relitti sulla spiaggia

beach'comb'er *s* girellone *m* di spiaggia

beach'head' *s* testa di sbarco

beach' robe' *s* accappatoio

beach' shoe' *s* sandalo da spiaggia

beach' umbrel'la *s* ombrellone *m* da spiaggia

beacon [ˈbikən] *s* faro || *tr* rischiarare; fare da guida a || *intr* brillare

bead [bid] *s* perlina; grano, chicco; (drop) goccia; beads (in a necklace or rosary) conterie *fpl*; to count one's beads recitare il rosario

beagle [ˈbigəl] *s* segugio, bracco

beak [bik] *s* becco; promontorio

beam [bim] *s* trave *f*; (of balance) braccio; (of light) raggio; (ship's breadth) larghezza; (smile) sorriso; (radio signal) fascio direttore; (course indicated by radio beam) aerovia; (naut) traverso || *tr* (a radio signal) dirigere; (e.g., light) irraggiare || *intr* raggiare

bean [bin] *s* fagiolo; (of coffee) chicco; (slang) testa

beaner·y [ˈbinəri] *s* (-ies) (slang) gargotta, taverna di secondo ordine

bean'pole' *s* puntello per i fagioli; (coll) palo del telegrafo

bear [ber] *s* orso; (astr) orsa; (com) ribassista *m*, giocatore *m* al ribasso || *v* (pret bore [bor]; pp borne [born]) *tr* (to carry) portare; (to give birth to) partorire; (to sustain) sostenere; (to withstand) sopportare; (a grudge) serbare; (in mind) tenere; (interest) produrre; (to pay) pagare; to bear the date aver la data; to bear out confermare; to bear witness testimoniare || *intr* (to be productive) fruttificare; (to move) dirigersi; (to be oppressive) fare pressione; to bear down on fare pressione su; avvicinarsi a; to bear up resistere; to bear with tollerare

bearable [ˈberəbəl] *adj* tollerabile

beard [bɪrd] *s* barba; (e.g., in wheat) arista

bearded [ˈbɪrdɪd] *adj* barbuto

beardless [ˈbɪrdlɪs] *adj* imberbe

bearer [ˈberər] *s* portatore *m*

bearing [ˈberɪŋ] *s* portamento; relazione, importanza; (mach) bronzina, cuscinetto; bearings orientamento; to lose one's bearings perdere la bussola; perdere l'orientamento

bearish [ˈberɪʃ] *adj* (like a bear) orsino; (e.g., prices) in ribasso; (market) al ribasso; (speculator) ribassista

bear'skin' *s* pelle *f* dell'orso; (mil) colbacco

beast [bist] *s* bestia

beast·ly [ˈbistli] *adj* (-lier; -liest) bestiale || *adv* (coll) malissimo

beast' of bur'den *s* bestia da soma

beast' of prey' *s* animale *m* da rapina

beat [bit] *s* (of heart) battito; (of policeman) ronda; (stroke) colpo; (habitual route) cammino battuto; (mus) tempo; (phys) battimento || *v* (pret beat; pp beat or beaten) *tr* battere; percuotere; (eggs) frullare; (to whip) frustare; (coll) confondere; beat it! (slang) vattene!; to beat a retreat battere in ritirata; to beat back respingere; to beat down sopprimere; to beat off respingere; to beat up (eggs) frullare; (people) dargliene a || *intr* battere; pulsare; to beat around the bush (coll) menare il can per l'aia

beat'en path' [ˈbitən] *s* cammino battuto

beater [ˈbitər] *s* frullino

beati·fy [bɪˈætɪ.faɪ] *v* (pret & pp -fied) *tr* beatificare

beating ['bitɪŋ] s battitura; (*whipping*) frustatura; (*throbbing*) pulsazione, battito; (*defeat*) sconfitta

beau [bo] s (**beaus** or **beaux** [boz]) (*dandy*) bellimbusto; (*girl's sweetheart*) spasimante m

beautician [bju'tɪʃən] s estetista mf

beautiful ['bjutɪfəl] adj bello

beauti-fy ['bjutɪ,faɪ] v (pret & pp -fied) tr abbellire

beau-ty ['bjutɪ] s (-ties) bellezza

beau'ty con'test s concorso di bellezza

beau'ty par'lor s istituto di bellezza

beau'ty sleep' s primo sonno

beau'ty spot' s neo; posto pittoresco

beaver ['bivər] s castoro; pelle f di castoro; cappello a cilindro

because [bɪ'kɔz] conj perchè; **because of** a causa di

beck [bek] s gesto; **at the beck and call of** agli ordini di

beckon ['bekən] s gesto || tr fare gesto a || intr fare gesto

becloud [bɪ'klaud] tr annebbiare; oscurare

be·come [bɪ'kʌm] v (pret **-came**; pp **-come**) tr convenire a; stare bene a, e.g., **this hat becomes you** questo cappello Le sta bene || intr diventare; farsi; convertirsi, e.g., **water became wine** l'acqua si convertì in vino; succedere, e.g., **what became of my coat?** che è successo del mio paastrano?; essere, e.g., **what will become of me?** che sarà di me?; **to become accustomed** abituarsi; **to become angry** entrare in collera; **to become crazy** impazzire; **to become ill** ammalarsi

becoming [bɪ'kʌmɪŋ] adj conveniente; appropriato; acconcio; **this is very becoming to you** questo Le sta molto bene

bed [bed] s letto; (*layer*) strato; giacimento; **to go to bed** andare a letto; **to take to one's bed** mettersi a letto

bed' and board' s vitto e alloggio; pensione completa

bed'bug' s cimice f

bed'clothes' spl lenzuola fpl e coperte fpl, biancheria da letto

bed'cov'er s coperta da letto

bedding ['bedɪŋ] s lenzuola fpl e coperte fpl; (*litter*) lettiera; (*foundation*) fondamenta fpl

bedeck [bɪ'dek] tr ornare, adornare

bedev·il [bɪ'devɪl] v (pret & pp **-iled** or **-illed**; ger **-iling** or **-illing**) tr tormentare diabolicamente; confondere

bed'fast' adj confinato a letto

bed'fel'low s compagno di letto; compagno di stanza; compagno

bedlam ['bedləm] s manicomio; pandemonio

bed' lin'en s biancheria da letto

bed'pan' s padella

bedridden ['bed,rɪdən] adj degente a letto

bed'room' s stanza da letto, camera da letto

bed'room slip'per s babbuccia, pantofola

bed'side' s capezzale m

bed'side man'ner s maniera di fare coi pazienti

bed'sore' s piaga da decubito

bed'spread' s coperta da letto

bed'spring' s rete f del letto; molla del letto

bed'stead' s fusto del letto

bed'tick' s traliccio

bed'time' s ora di coricarsi

bed'warm'er s scaldaletto

bee [bi] s ape f

beech [bitʃ] s faggio

beech'nut' s faggiola

beef [bif] s bue m, manzo; carne f di manzo; (coll) forza; (slang) lamentela || tr—**to beef up** (coll) rinforzare || intr (slang) lamentarsi

beef' cat'tle s manzi mpl da carne

beef'steak' s bistecca

beef' stew' s stufato di manzo

bee'hive' s alveare m

bee'keep'er s apicoltore m

bee'line' s—**to make a beeline for** (coll) andare direttamente verso

beer [bɪr] s birra

beer' saloon' s birreria

beeswax ['biz,wæks] s cera d'api

beet [bit] s barbabietola

beetle ['bitəl] adj sporgente, folto || s scarafaggio

bee'tle-browed' adj dalle sopracciglia folte

beet' su'gar s zucchero di barbabietola

be·fall [bɪ'fɔl] v (pret **-fell** ['fɛl]; pp **-fallen** ['fɔlən]) tr succedere a || intr succedere

befitting [bɪ'fɪtɪŋ] adj appropriato

before [bɪ'for] adv prima, prima d'ora || prep (*in time*) prima di; (*in place*) dinnanzi a, davanti a; **before Christ** avanti Cristo || conj prima che

before'hand' adv in anticipo; precedentemente

befriend [bɪ'frend] tr diventare amico di, proteggere, favorire; aiutare

befuddle [bɪ'fʌdəl] tr confondere

beg [beg] v (pret & pp **begged**; ger **begging**) tr chiedere; implorare; (*alms*) mendicare; **I beg your pardon** Le chiedo scusa; **to beg s.o. for s.th** chiedere qlco a qlcu || intr chiedere la carità; **to beg for** sollecitare; **to beg off** scusarsi; **to go begging** rimanere invenduto

be·get [bɪ'get] v (pret **-got** ['gɑt]; pp **-gotten** or **-got**; ger **-getting**) tr generare

beggar ['begər] s accattone m, mendicante m

be·gin [bɪ'gɪn] v (pret **-gan** ['gæn]; pp **-gun** ['gʌn]; ger **-ginning**) tr & intr cominciare, iniziare; **beginning with** a partire da; **to begin with** per cominciare

beginner [bɪ'gɪnər] s principiante mf

beginning [bɪ'gɪnɪŋ] s inizio, origine f, principio, esordio

begrudge [bɪ'grʌdʒ] tr invidiare; concedere con riluttanza

beguile [bɪ'gaɪl] tr ingannare; sedurre; (*to delight*) divertire

behalf [bɪ'hæf] or [bɪ'hɑf] s—**on behalf of** nell'interesse di; a nome di

behave [bɪ'hev] *intr* comportarsi; comportarsi bene

behavior [bɪ'hevjər] *s* comportamento, condotta; funzionamento

behead [bɪ'hed] *tr* decapitare

behest [bɪ'hest] *s* ordine *m*, comando

behind [bɪ'haɪnd] *s* didietro; (slang) sedere *m* ‖ *adv* dietro; (*in arrears*) in arretrato; **from behind** dal didietro ‖ *prep* dietro a, dietro di; **behind time** in ritardo

be·hold [bɪ'hold] *v* (*pret & pp* **-held** ['held]) *tr* contemplare; ammirare ‖ *interj* guarda!

behoove [bɪ'huv] *impers*—**it behooves him to** gli conviene di

being ['bi·ɪŋ] *adj* esistente; **for the time being** per ora ‖ *s* essere *m*, ente *m*

belabor [bɪ'lebər] *tr* attaccare; (fig) ribattere, confutare; (fig) insistere su

belated [bɪ'letɪd] *adj* tardivo

belch [beltʃ] *s* rutto ‖ *tr* eruttare, vomitare ‖ *intr* ruttare

beleaguer [bɪ'ligər] *tr* assediare

bel·fry ['belfrɪ] *s* (*-fries*) (*tower*) campanile *m*; (*site of bell*) cella campanaria; (slang) testa

Belgian ['beldʒən] *adj & s* belga *mf*

Belgium ['beldʒəm] *s* il Belgio

be·lie [bɪ'laɪ] *v* (*pret & pp* **-lied** ['laɪd]; *ger* **-lying** ['laɪ·ɪŋ]) *tr* (*to misrepresent*) tradire; (*to prove false*) smentire

belief [bɪ'lif] *s* fede *f*, credenza

believable [bɪ'livəbəl] *adj* credibile

believe [bɪ'liv] *tr* credere ‖ *intr* credere, aver fede; **to believe in** credere in

believer [bɪ'livər] *s* credente *mf*

belittle [bɪ'lɪtəl] *tr* menomare

bell [bel] *s* campana; (*for a door*) campanello; (*sound*) rintocco; (*on cattle*) campanaccio; (*of deer*) bramito ‖ *intr* bramire

belladonna [,belə'danə] *s* belladonna

bell′-bot′tom *adj* a campana

bell′boy′ *s* cameriere *m*, ragazzo

belle [bel] *s* bella

belles-lettres [,bel'letrə] *spl* belle lettere

bell′ glass′ *s* campana di vetro

bell′hop′ *s* cameriere *m*, ragazzo

bellicose ['belɪ,kos] *adj* bellicoso

belligerent [bə'lɪdʒərənt] *adj & s* belligerante *m*

bellow ['belo] *s* muggito; **bellows** mantice *m*; (*of camera*) soffietto ‖ *tr* gridare ‖ *intr* muggire

bell′ ring′er ['rɪŋər] *s* campanaro

bellwether ['bel,weðər] *s* pecora guida

bel·ly ['belɪ] *s* (*-lies*) ventre *m*, pancia ‖ *v* (*pret & pp* **-lied**) *intr* far pancia

bel′ly·ache′ *s* (coll) mal *m* di pancia ‖ *intr* (slang) lamentarsi

bel′ly·but′ton *s* (coll) ombelico

bel′ly dance′ *s* (coll) danza del ventre

bel′ly flop′ *s* panciata

bellyful ['belɪ,ful] *s*—**to have a bellyful** (slang) averne fino agli occhi

bel′ly·land′ *intr* (aer) atterrare sul ventre

belong [bɪ'lɔŋ] or [bɪ'laŋ] *intr* appartenere; stare bene, e.g., **this chair belongs in this room** questa sedia sta bene in questa stanza

belongings [bɪ'lɔŋɪŋz] or [bɪ'laŋɪŋz] *spl* effetti *mpl* personali

beloved [bɪ'lʌvɪd] or [bɪ'lʌvd] *adj & s* diletto, amato

below [bɪ'lo] *adv* sotto; più sotto; sotto zero, e.g., **ten below** dieci gradi sotto zero ‖ *prep* sotto, sotto di

belt [belt] *s* cintura, cinghia; (mach) nastro; (mil) cinturone *m*; (geog) fascia, zona; **to tighten one's belt** far cintura ‖ *tr* cingere; (slang) staffilare

belt′ed tire′ *s* copertone cinturato

belt′ line′ *s* linea di circonvallazione

beltway ['belt,we] *s* raccordo anulare

bemoan [bɪ'mon] *tr* lamentare; compiangere

bench [bentʃ] *s* banco, panca; tribunale *m*; (mach) banco di prova; **to be on the bench** (law) essere giudice

bend [bend] *s* curva; (*e.g., of pipe*) gomito, angolo ‖ *v* (*pret & pp* **bent** [bent]) *tr* curvare; piegare; far piegare ‖ *intr* deviare; piegare, piegarsi; **to bend over** inchinarsi

beneath [bɪ'niθ] *adv* sotto; più sotto ‖ *prep* sotto, sotto di

benediction [,benɪ'dɪkʃən] *s* benedizione

benefactor ['benɪ,fæktər] or [,benɪ-'fæktər] *s* benefattore *m*

benefactress ['benɪ,fæktrɪs] or [,benɪ-'fæktrɪs] *s* benefattrice *f*

beneficence [bɪ'nefɪsəns] *s* beneficenza

beneficent [bɪ'nefɪsənt] *adj* caritatevole; benefico

beneficial [,benɪ'fɪʃəl] *adj* benefico

beneficiar·y [,benɪ'fɪʃɪ,erɪ] *s* (*-ies*) beneficiario

benefit ['benɪfɪt] *s* beneficio; festa di beneficenza; **for the benefit of** a beneficio di ‖ *tr & intr* beneficiare

benevolence [bɪ'nevələns] *s* benevolenza; carità *f*

benevolent [bɪ'nevələnt] *adj* benevolo; (*institution*) benefico

benign [bɪ'naɪn] *adj* benigno

bent [bent] *adj* curvo; **bent on** deciso a ‖ *s* curva; tendenza, propensità *f*

Benzedrine ['benzɪ ,drin] (trademark) *s* benzedrina

benzene ['benzin] *s* benzolo

benzine [ben'zin] *s* benzina

bequeath [bɪ'kwiθ] or [bɪ'kwið] *tr* legare, lasciare in eredità

bequest [bɪ'kwest] *s* legato, lascito

berate [bɪ'ret] *tr* redarguire

be·reave [bɪ'riv] *v* (*pret & pp* **-reaved** or **-reft** ['reft]) *tr* spogliare

bereavement [bɪ'rivmənt] *s* lutto, perdita

beret [bə're] or ['bere] *s* berretto

Berlin [bər'lɪn] *adj* berlinese ‖ *s* Berlino

Berliner [bər'lɪnər] *s* berlinese *mf*

Bermuda [bər'mjudə] *s* le Bermude

ber·ry ['berɪ] *s* (*-ries*) (*dry seed*) chicco; (*fruit*) bacca

berserk [bʌr'sʌrk] *adj* infuriato || *adv* —to go berserk impazzire

berth [bʌrθ] *s* (*for a ship*) posto di ormeggio; (*bed*) cuccetta; (coll) posto

beryllium [bə'rɪlɪ-əm] *s* berillio

be-seech [bɪ'sit∫] *v* (*pret & pp* -sought ['sɔt] or -seeched) *tr* supplicare

be-set [bɪ'sɛt] *v* (*pret & pp* -set; *ger* -setting) *tr* assediare, circondare; (*e.g., with problems*) assillare

beside [bɪ'saɪd] *adv* oltre, inoltre || *prep* vicino a; in confronto di; oltre a; beside oneself fuori di sé; beside the point fuori del seminato

besides [bɪ'saɪdz] *adv* inoltre; d'altronde || *prep* oltre a

besiege [bɪ'sidʒ] *tr* assediare; (*with questions*) bombardare

besmear [bɪ'smɪr] *tr* imbrattare, sgorbiare; sporcare

besmirch [bɪ'smʌrt∫] *tr* insudiciare

bespatter [bɪ'spætər] *tr* inzaccherare

be-speak [bɪ'spik] *v* (-spoke ['spok]; -spoken) *tr* chiedere anticipatamente a; (*to show*) dimostrare

best [bɛst] *adj super* (il) migliore; ottimo || *s* meglio; at best nella miglior delle ipotesi; to do one's best fare del proprio meglio; to get the best of avere la meglio di; to make the best of adattarsi a || *adv super* meglio; had best, e.g., I had best dovrei || *tr* battere, riuscire superiore a

bestial ['bɛstjəl] or ['bɛst∫əl] *adj* bestiale

be-stir [bɪ'stʌr] *v* (*pret & pp* -stirred; *ger* -stirring) *tr* eccitare; to bestir oneself darsi da fare

best' man' *s* testimone *m* di nozze

bestow [bɪ'sto] *tr* accordare; conferire

best' sell'er *s* best-seller *m*

bet [bɛt] *s* scommessa || *v* (*pret & pp* bet or betted; *ger* betting) *tr & intr* scommettere; I bet ci scommetto; you bet (coll) evidentemente

be-take [bɪ'tek] *v* (*pret* -took ['tuk]; *pp* -taken) *tr*—to betake oneself andare, dirigersi

be-think [bɪ'θɪŋk] *v* (*pret & pp* -thought ['θɔt]) *tr* to bethink oneself pensare; ricordarsi

Bethlehem ['bɛθlɪ-əm] or ['bɛθlɪ,hɛm] *s* Betlemme *f*

betide [bɪ'taɪd] *tr* accadere a || *intr* accadere

betoken [bɪ'tokən] *tr* indicare, presagire

betray [bɪ'tre] *tr* tradire, ingannare; (*to reveal*) rivelare

betroth [bɪ'troð] or [bɪ'trɔθ] *tr* promettere in matrimonio a

betrothal [bɪ'troðəl] or [bɪ'trɔθəl] *s* fidanzamento

betrothed [bɪ'troð] or [bɪ'trɔθt] *adj* fidanzato || *s* promesso sposo, fidanzato

better ['bɛtər] *adj comp* migliore; to grow better migliorare || *s*—betters superiori *mpl*; ottimati *mpl*; to get the better of avere la meglio di || *adv* meglio; had better dovere, e.g., I had better dovrei; to be better off stare meglio; to think better of riconsiderare; you ought to know better dovrebbe vergognarsi || *tr* sorpassare; migliorare; to better oneself migliorare la propria situazione

bet'ter half' *s* metà *f*

betterment ['bɛtərmənt] *s* miglioramento

bettor ['bɛtər] *s* scommettitore *m*

between [bɪ'twin] *adv* in mezzo; in between in mezzo, fra i piedi || *prep* fra, tra

between'-decks' *s* interponte *m*

bev-el ['bɛvəl] *s* (*instrument*) falsa squadra; (*sloping part*) augnatura || *v* (*pret & pp* -eled or -elled; *ger* -eling or -elling) *tr* augnare

beverage ['bɛvərɪdʒ] *s* bevanda

bev-y ['bɛvi] *s* (-ies) (*of women*) gruppo; (*of birds*) stormo

bewail [bɪ'wel] *tr* lamentare

beware [bɪ'wer] *tr* fare attenzione a, guardarsi da || *intr* fare attenzione, guardarsi

bewilder [bɪ'wɪldər] *tr* lasciar perplesso, confondere, disorientare

bewilderment [bɪ'wɪldərmənt] *s* perplessità *f*, disorientamento

bewitch [bɪ'wɪt∫] *tr* stregare

beyond [bɪ'jɑnd] *s*—the beyond l'aldilà *m* || *adv* più lontano || *prep* al di là di; oltre a; più tardi di; beyond a doubt fuori dubbio; beyond repair irreparabile

bias ['baɪ-əs] *s* linea diagonale; pregiudizio; on the bias diagonalmente || *tr* prevenire

bib [bɪb] *s* bavaglino

Bible ['baɪbəl] *s* Bibbia

Biblical ['bɪblɪkəl] *adj* biblico

bibliogra-phy [,bɪblɪ'ɑgrəfi] *s* (-phies) bibliografia

bibliophile ['bɪblɪ-ə,faɪl] *s* bibliofilo

bicarbonate [baɪ'kɑrbə,net] *s* bicarbonato

biceps ['baɪsɛps] *s* bicipite *m*

bicker ['bɪkər] *s* bisticcio, disputa || *intr* bisticciare, disputare

bicycle ['baɪsɪkəl] *s* bicicletta

bid [bɪd] *s* offerta; (cards) dichiarazione; (coll) invito || *v* (*pret* bade [bæd] or bid; *pp* bidden ['bɪdən] or bid; *ger* bidding) *tr & intr* offrire; comandare; (cards) dichiarare

bidder ['bɪdər] *s* offerente *mf*; (cards) dichiarante *mf*; the highest bidder il miglior offerente

bidding ['bɪdɪŋ] *s* ordine *m*; offerte *fpl*; (cards) dichiarazione

bide [baɪd] *tr*—to bide one's time attendere l'ora propizia

biennial [baɪ'ɛnɪ-əl] *adj* biennale

bier [bɪr] *s* catafalco

bifocal [baɪ'fokəl] *adj* bifocale || **bifocals** *spl* occhiali *mpl* bifocali

big [bɪg] *adj* (bigger; biggest) grande; (coll) importante; (coll) stravagante; big with child incinta || *adv*—to talk big (coll) parlare con iattanza

bigamist ['bɪgəmɪst] *s* bigamo

bigamous ['bɪgəməs] *adj* bigamo

big-bellied ['bɪg ˌbelid] *adj* panciuto
Big' Dip'per *s* Gran Carro
big' game' *s* caccia grossa
big-hearted ['bɪg ˌhɑrtɪd] *adj* magnanimo, generoso
big' mouth' *s* (slang) sbraitone *m*
bigot ['bɪgət] *s* bigotto, bacchettone *m*
bigoted ['bɪgətɪd] *adj* (*in religion*) bigotto; intransigente
bigot•ry ['bɪgətri] *s* (-ries) bigottismo; intransigenza
big' shot' *s* (slang) pezzo grosso, (un) qualcuno
big' slam' *s* (bridge) grande slam *m*
big'-time op'erator *s* (slang) grosso trafficante
big' toe' *s* alluce *m*
big' wheel' *s* (slang) pezzo grosso
bike [baɪk] *s* (coll) bicicletta
bile [baɪl] *s* bile *f*
bilge [bɪldʒ] *s* sentina; (*of barrel*) ventre *m*
bilge'ways' *spl* parati *mpl*
bilingual [baɪ'lɪŋgwəl] *adj* bilingue
bilious ['bɪljəs] *adj* bilioso
bilk [bɪlk] *tr* defraudare
bill [bɪl] *s* (*of bird*) becco; (*statement of charges*) conto; (*e.g., for electricity*) bolletta; (*menu*) lista; (*money*) biglietto; (*proposed law*) disegno di legge; (*handbill*) annunzio; (*law*) atto; (*theat*) cartellone *m*; **to fill the bill** (coll) riempire i requisiti; **to foot the bill** (coll) pagare lo scotto || *tr* fare una lista di; mettere in conto a || *intr* (*said of doves*) beccuzzarsi; (*said of lovers*) baciucchiarsi
bill'board' *s* cartellone *m*; (rad, telv) titolo di testa
billet ['bɪlɪt] *s* (mil) alloggiamento; (mil) ordine *m* d'alloggiamento || *tr* (mil) alloggiare, accasermare
bill'fold' *s* portafoglio
bill'head' *s* intestazione di fattura
billiards ['bɪljərdz] *s* bigliardo
bil'ling clerk' *s* fatturista *mf*
billion ['bɪljən] *s* (U.S.A.) miliardo; (Brit) bilione *m*
bill' of exchange' *s* tratta
bill' of fare' *s* menu *m*, lista delle vivande
bill' of lad'ing ['ledɪŋ] *s* polizza di carico
bill' of rights' *s* dichiarazione dei diritti
bill' of sale' *s* atto di vendita
billow ['bɪlo] *s* ondata, cavallone *m*
bill'post'er *s* attacchino
bil•ly ['bɪli] *s* (-lies) manganello
bil'ly goat' *s* capro, caprone *m*
bimonthly [baɪ'mʌnθli] *adj* (*occurring every two months*) bimestrale; (*occurring twice a month*) bimensile
bin [bɪn] *s* cassone *m*; (*for bread*) madia; (*e.g., for coal*) deposito
binaural [baɪ'nɔrəl] *adj* biauricolare
bind [baɪnd] *v* (*pret* & *pp* **bound** [baund]) *tr* legare; allacciare; (*to bandage*) fasciare; (*to constipate*) costipare; (*a book*) rilegare; (*to oblige*) obbligare; (mach) grippare
binder ['baɪndər] *s* rilegatore *m*; (*cover*) cartella

binder•y ['baɪndəri] *s* (-ies) rilegatoria
binding ['baɪndɪŋ] *adj* obbligatorio || *s* (*of book*) rilegatura; legatura; fasciatura
bind'ing post' *s* (elec) capocorda; (*e.g., of battery*) (elec) serrafilo
binge [bɪndʒ] *s*—**to go on a binge** (coll) far baldoria
bingo ['bɪngo] *s* tombola
binnacle ['bɪnəkəl] *s* abitacolo
binoculars [bɪ'nɑkjələrz] or [baɪ'nɑkjələrz] *spl* binocolo
biochemical [ˌbaɪ·ə'kemɪkəl] *adj* biochimico
biochemist [ˌbaɪ·ə'kemɪst] *s* biochimico
biochemistry [ˌbaɪ·ə'kemɪstri] *s* biochimica
biodegradable [ˌbaɪ·odɪ'gredəbəl] *adj* biodegradabile
biographer [baɪ'ɑgrəfər] *s* biografo
biographic(al) [ˌbaɪ·ə'græfɪk(əl)] *adj* biografico
biogra•phy [baɪ'ɑgrəfi] *s* (-phies) biografia
biologist [baɪ'ɑlədʒɪst] *s* biologo
biology [baɪ'ɑlədʒi] *s* biologia
biophysics [ˌbaɪ·ə'fɪzɪks] *s* biofisica
biop•sy ['baɪ ˌɑpsi] *s* (-sies) biopsia
bipartisan [baɪ'pɑrtɪzən] *adj* (*system*) bipartitico; (*government*) bipartito
biped ['baɪpəd] *adj* & *s* bipede *m*
birch [bʌrtʃ] *s* betulla || *tr* scudisciare
bird [bʌrd] *s* uccello; **a bird in the hand is worth two in the bush** un uovo oggi vale meglio di una gallina domani; **birds of a feather** gente *f* della stessa risma; **to kill two birds with one stone** pigliare due piccioni con una fava
bird' cage' *s* gabbia
bird' call' *s* richiamo
birdie ['bʌrdi] *s* uccellino; (golf) giocata di un colpo sotto la media
bird'lime' *s* pania
bird' of pas'sage *s* uccello di passo
bird' of prey' *s* uccello da preda
bird'seed' *s* becchime *m*
bird's'-eye view' *s* vista a volo d'uccello
bird' shot' *s* pallini *mpl* da caccia
birth [bʌrθ] *s* nascita; **to give birth to** dare i natali a; mettere alla luce
birth' certif'icate *s* certificato di nascita
birth' control' *s* limitazione delle nascite
birth'day' *s* natalizio, compleanno; (*of an event*) anniversario
birth'mark' *s* voglia
birth'place' *s* patria; (*e.g., city*) luogo di nascita; **to be the birthplace of** dare i natali a
birth' rate' *s* natalità *f*
birth'right' *s* diritto acquisito sin dalla nascita
biscuit ['bɪskɪt] *s* panino soffice; (Brit) biscotto
bisect [baɪ'sekt] *tr* bisecare || *intr* (*said of roads*) incrociarsi
bisection [baɪ'sek/ən] *s* bisezione
bishop ['bɪ/əp] *s* vescovo; (chess) alfiere *m*
bishopric ['bɪ/əprɪk] *s* vescovado

bismuth ['bɪzməθ] *s* bismuto
bison ['baɪsən] or ['baɪzən] *s* bisonte *m*
bisulfate [baɪ'sʌlfet] *s* bisolfato
bisulfite [baɪ'sʌlfaɪt] *s* bisolfito
bit [bɪt] *s* (*of bridle*) morso; (*of key*) mappa; (*tool*) punta, trivella; (*small piece*) bricciolo; **a bit un po'**; (coll) un momento; **a good bit** una buona quantità; **bit by bit** poco a poco; **to blow to bits** fare a pezzi; **to champ the bit** mordere il freno; **two bits** (slang) quarto di dollaro, cinque soldi
bitch [bɪtʃ] *s* cagna; (vulg) donnaccia || *intr* (slang) lamentarsi
bite [baɪt] *s* morso; (*mouthful*) boccone *m*; **to take a bite** fare uno spuntino; mangiare un boccone || *v* (*pret* **bit** [bɪt]; *pp* **bit** or **bitten** ['bɪtən]) *tr* mordere, addentare; pungere; (*the dust*) baciare || *intr* mordere; (*said of insects*) pungere; (*said of fish*) abboccare
biting ['baɪtɪŋ] *adj* mordace; pungente
bitter ['bɪtər] *adj* amaro; (*e.g., fight*) accanito; (*cold*) pungente || *s* amaro; **bitters** amaro
bit'ter end' *s*—**to the bitter end** fino alla fine; fino alla morte
bit'ter-en'der *s* (coll) intransigente *mf*
bitterness ['bɪtərnɪs] *s* amarezza
bit'ter-sweet' *adj* dolceamaro; (fig) agrodolce || *s* dulcamara
bitumen [bɪ'tjumən] or [bɪ'tumən] *s* bitume *m*
bivou·ac ['bɪvu‚æk] or ['bɪvwæk] *s* bivacco || *v* (*pret & pp* **-acked**; *ger* **-acking**) *intr* bivaccare
biweekly [baɪ'wiklɪ] *adj* bisettimanale; quindicinale || *adv* ogni due settimane
biyearly [baɪ'jɪrlɪ] *adj* semestrale || *adv* semestralmente
bizarre [bɪ'zɑr] *adj* bizzarro
blab [blæb] *s* chiacchierone *m* || *v* (*pret & pp* **blabbed**; *ger* **blabbing**) *tr* rivelare || *intr* chiacchierare
black [blæk] *adj* nero; (*without light*) buio || *s* nero; **to wear black** vestire a lutto, vestire di nero || *intr*—**to black out** perdere i sensi
black'-and-blue' *adj* livido e pesto
black'-and-white' *adj* in bianco e nero
black'ball' *s* palla nera, voto contrario || *tr* dare la palla nera a
black'ber'ry *s* (-ries) mora
black'bird' *s* merlo
black'board' *s* lavagna, tavola nera
black'cap' *s* capinera
black'damp' *s* putizza
Black' Death' *s* peste bubbonica
blacken ['blækən] *tr* annerire; (*shoes*) lucidare; (*reputation*) sporcare
black' eye' *s* occhio pesto; (fig) cattiva reputazione
blackguard ['blægɑrd] *s* canaglia
black'head' *s* comedone *m*
blackish ['blækɪʃ] *adj* nerastro
black'jack' *s* randello; (cards) ventuno || *tr* randellare
black' mag'ic *s* magia nera

black'mail' *s* ricatto || *tr* ricattare
blackmailer ['blæk‚melər] *s* ricattatore *m*
Black' Mari'a [mə'raɪ-ə] *s* (coll) furgone *m* cellulare
black' mar'ket *s* borsa nera
black' marketeer' [‚mɑrkɪ'tɪr] *s* borsanerista *mf*
blackness ['blæknɪs] *s* nerezza
black'out' *s* oscuramento; (theat) spegnitura; (pathol) svenimento passeggero
black' sheep' *s* (fig) pecora nera
black'smith' *s* fabbro
black' tie' *s* cravatta da smoking; smoking *m*
bladder ['blædər] *s* vescica
blade [bled] *s* (*of a leaf*) pagina; (*of grass*) stelo, filo; (*of oar*) pala; (*of turbine*) paletta; (*of fan*) ventola; (*of knife*) lama; (coll) caposcarico
blame [blem] *s* colpa; **to be to blame for** aver la colpa di; **to put the blame on s.o. for s.th** attribuire a qlcu la colpa di glco; **you are to blame** è colpa Sua || *tr* biasimare, incolpare
blameless ['blemlɪs] *adj* innocente, senza colpa
blanch [blæntʃ] or [blɑntʃ] *tr* bianchire || *intr* impallidire
bland [blænd] *adj* blando; (*weather*) mite
blandish ['blændɪʃ] *tr* blandire
blank [blæŋk] *adj* (*not written on*) in bianco; (*e.g., stare*) vuoto; (*utter*) completo || *s* (*printed form*) modulo; (*cartridge*) cartuccia a salve; (*of the mind*) lacuna; **to draw a blank** (coll) non avere alcun successo || *tr*—**to blank out** cancellare
blank' check' *s* assegno in bianco; (fig) carta bianca
blanket ['blæŋkɪt] *adj* generale, combinato || *s* coperta; (*of snow*) cappa || *tr* coprire con una coperta; oscurare
blank' verse' *s* verso sciolto
blare [bler] *s* squillo || *tr* proclamare; fare echeggiare || *intr* squillare; echeggiare
blaspheme [blæs'fim] *tr & intr* bestemmiare
blasphemous ['blæsfɪməs] *adj* bestemmiatore
blasphe·my ['blæsfɪmɪ] *s* (-mies) bestemmia
blast [blæst] or [blɑst] *s* (*of air*) raffica; (*of a horn*) squillo; (*blight*) rovina; scoppio, esplosione; **at full blast** a piena velocità || *tr* rovinare; fare scoppiare, far saltare || *intr* —**to blast off** (rok) lanciarsi
blast' fur'nace *s* altoforno
blast'off' *s* lancio di missile or di nave spaziale
blatant ['bletənt] *adj* (*noisy*) rumoroso; (*obtrusive*) palmare; (*flashy*) chiassoso
blaze [blez] *s* fiammata; splendore *m*; (*on a horse's head*) stella; **in a blaze** in fiamme || *tr* proclamare; **to blaze a**

trail marcare il cammino || *intr* divampare

bleach [blitʃ] *s* candeggio, candeggina || *tr* imbiancare, candeggiare

bleachers ['blitʃərz] *spl* posti *mpl* allo scoperto o di gradinata

bleak [blik] *adj* nudo, deserto; (*cold*) freddo; (*gloomy*) triste

blear·y ['blɪri] *adj* (-**ier; iest**) (*sight*) cisposo; confuso; offuscato

bleat [blit] *s* belato || *intr* belare

bleed [blid] *v* (*pret & pp* **bled** [bled]) *tr* (*to draw blood from*) salassare; (*a tree*) estrare linfa da; (coll) sfruttare || *intr* sanguinare; (*said of a tree*) dar linfa; **to bleed to death** morire dissanguato

blemish ['blɛmɪʃ] *s* difetto; macchia || *tr* danneggiare; macchiare

blend [blend] *s* mescolanza, miscuglio; (*of gasoline*) miscela || *v* (*pret & pp* **blended** or **blent** [blent]) *tr* mescolare, miscelare || *intr* mescolarsi, miscelarsi; armonizzare; fondersi

bless [bles] *tr* benedire; (*to endow*) dotare; (*to make happy*) allietare

blessed ['blɛsɪd] *adj* benedetto; beato; fortunato; dotato

bless'ed event' *s* lieto evento

blessing ['blɛsɪŋ] *s* benedizione

blight [blaɪt] *s* (*insect; disease*) piaga; rovina; (*fungus*) ruggine *f* || *tr* rovinare, guastare

blimp [blɪmp] *s* piccolo dirigibile

blind [blaɪnd] *adj* cieco; (slang) ubriaco || *s* persiana; tendina; (*decoy*) mascheratura; preteso || *adv* alla cieca || *tr* accecare

blind' al'ley *s* vicolo cieco

blinder ['blaɪndər] *s* paraocchi *m*

blind' fly'ing *s* (aer) volo senza visibilità

blind'fold' *adj* bendato, cogli occhi bendati || *s* benda || *tr* bendare gli occhi a

blindly ['blaɪndli] *adv* alla cieca

blind' man' *s* cieco

blind'man's buff' *s* mosca cieca

blindness ['blaɪndnɪs] *s* cecità *f*

blind' spot' *s* (anat) punto cieco; (rad) zona di silenzio; (fig) debole *m*

blink [blɪŋk] *s* batter *m* di ciglio; (*glimpse*) occhiata; (*glimmer*) barlume *m;* **on the blink** (slang) fuori servizio || *tr*—**to blink one's eyes** batter il ciglio || *intr* occhieggiare; (*to wink*) ammiccare; (*to flash on and off*) lampeggiare; **to blink at** ignorare; far finta di non vedere

blinker ['blɪŋkər] *s* (*at a crossing*) luce *f* intermittente; (*on a horse*) paraocchi *m*

blip [blɪp] *s* guizzo sullo schermo radar

bliss [blɪs] *s* beatitudine *f*, felicità *f*

blissful ['blɪsfəl] *adj* beato, felice

blister ['blɪstər] *s* vescica, bolla || *tr* coprire di vesciche; (fig) bollare || *intr* coprirsi di vesciche

blithe [blaɪð] *adj* gaio, giocondo

blitzkrieg ['blɪts‚krig] *s* guerra lampo

blizzard ['blɪzərd] *s* tormenta, ventoneve *m*

bloat [blot] *tr* gonfiare || *intr* gonfiarsi

blob [blɑb] *s* (*lump*) zolla; (*of liquid*) macchia

block [blɑk] *s* (*e.g., of wood*) blocco; (*for chopping*) ceppo; (*pulley*) puleggia; ostacolo; (*of houses*) isolato; (typ) cliché *m* || *tr* bloccare; (*a hat*) mettere in forma; **to block up** tappare

blockade [blɑ'ked] *s* blocco; **to run a blockade** forzare il blocco || *tr* bloccare

block' and tack'le *s* bozzello

block'bust'er *s* (coll) superbomba

block'head' *s* imbecille *mf*

block' let'ter *s* carattere *m* stampatello

block' sig'nal *s* (rr) segnale di blocco

blond [blɑnd] *adj & s* biondo

blonde [blɑnd] *s* bionda

blood [blʌd] *s* sangue *m;* **in cold blood** a sangue freddo; **to draw blood** ferire, fare sanguinare

blood' bank' *s* emoteca

bloodcurdling ['blʌd‚kʌrdlɪŋ] *adj* orripilante

blood' do'nor *s* donatore *m* di sangue

blood'hound' *s* segugio

bloodless ['blʌdlɪs] *adj* esangue; (*e.g., revolution*) senza effusione di sangue

blood'mobile' [mo‚bil] *s* autoemoteca

blood' poi'soning *s* avvelenamento del sangue

blood' pres'sure *s* pressione sanguigna

blood' rela'tion *s* consanguineo

blood'shed' *s* spargimento di sangue, carneficina

blood'shot' *adj* iniettato di sangue

blood'stained' *adj* macchiato di sangue

blood'stream' *s* circolazione sanguigna

blood'suck'er *s* sanguisuga

blood' test' *s* esame *m* del sangue

blood'thirst'y *adj* assetato di sangue

blood' transfu'sion *s* trasfusione di sangue

blood' type' *s* gruppo sanguigno

blood' ves'sel *s* vaso sanguigno

blood·y ['blʌdi] *adj* (-**ier; -iest**) sanguinoso; (*bloodthirsty*) avido di sangue || *v* (*pret & pp* -**ied**) *tr* macchiare di sangue

bloom [blum] *s* fiore *m;* (*state of having open buds*) sboccio; (*youthful glow*) incarnato || *intr* fiorire; sbocciare

bloomers ['blumərz] *spl* pantaloni *mpl* femminili larghi fermati sotto il ginocchio

blossom ['blɑsəm] *s* fiore *m;* sboccio || *intr* sbocciare

blot [blɑt] *s* macchia || *v* (*pret & pp* **blotted;** *ger* **blotting**) *tr* macchiare; (*with blotting paper*) asciugare; **to blot out** cancellare; oscurare || *intr* macchiarsi; (*to be absorbent*) essere assorbente; (*said of a pen*) fare macchie

blotch [blɑtʃ] *s* chiazza, macchia || *tr* chiazzare

blotter ['blɑtər] *s* carta asciugante, carta assorbente; (*book*) registro

blouse [blaʊs] *s* biusa

blow [blo] *s* colpo; (*blast*) folata; (*of*

horn) squillo; (*sudden reverse*) batosta; **at one blow** d'un sol colpo; **to come to blows** venire alle mani; **without striking a blow** senza colpo ferire ‖ *v* (*pret* **blew** [blu]; *pp* **blown**) *tr* soffiare, soffiare su; (*an instrument*) suonare; (*one's nose*) soffiarsi; **to blow in** sfondare; **to blow one's brains out** bruciarsi le cervella; **to blow open** aprire completamente; **to blow out** (*e.g., a candle*) spegnere; (*a fuse*) fondere; **to blow up** (*e.g., a mine*) far brillare; (*phot*) ingrandire ‖ *intr* soffiare; (*to pant*) ansimare; (*with an instrument*) suonare; (*to puff*) sbuffare; (*slang*) andarsene; **to blow hot and cold** cambiare d'opinione ogni cinque minuti; **to blow in** (coll) arrivare inaspettatamente; **to blow out** (said, e.g., of a candle) spegnersi; (*said of a fuse*) saltare, fondersi; (*said of a tire*) scoppiare; **to blow over** passare; **to blow up** saltar per aria; (*said of a storm*) scoppiare; (coll) perdere la pazienza, scoppiare d'ira

blow'out' *s* scoppio di un pneumatico
blow'pipe' *s* (*tube*) soffione *m*; (*peashooter*) cerbottana
blow'torch' *s* saldatrice *f* a benzina
blubber ['blʌbər] *s* grasso di balena ‖ *intr* piangere, lamentarsi
bludgeon ['blʌdʒən] *s* randello ‖ *tr* randellare
blue [blu] *adj* blu, azzurro; (*gloomy*) triste; (*e.g., laws*) puritanico ‖ *s* blu *m*, azzurro; **out of the blue** inaspettatamente; **the blues** la malinconia; (mus) blues *m*; **to have the blues** essere giù di morale ‖ *tr* tingere di azzurro; (*a metal*) brunire
blue'ber'ry *s* (-ries) mirtillo
blue'bird' *s* uccello azzurro
blue' blood' *s* sangue *m* blu
blue' cheese' *s* gorgonzola americano
blue' chip' *s* (fin) azione di prim'ordine
blue' jay' *s* ghiandaia azzurra
blue' moon' *s*—**once in a blue moon** ad ogni morte di papa
blue'-pen'cil *v* (*pret & pp* -ciled or -cilled; *ger* -ciling or -cilling) *tr* correggere col lapis blu
blue'print' *s* riproduzione cianografica; (*plan*) piano ‖ *tr* riprodurre in cianografia; preparare dettagliatamente
blue'stock'ing *s* saccente *f*, sapientona
blue' streak' *s*—**like a blue streak** (coll) come un razzo
bluff [blʌf] *adj* scosceso; brusco, burbero ‖ *s* promontorio scosceso; bluff *m*; bluffatore *m* ‖ *intr* bluffare
bluing ['bluɪŋ] *s* turchinetto
bluish ['bluɪʃ] *adj* bluastro
blunder ['blʌndər] *s* errore *m* madornale ‖ *intr* pigliare un granchio
blunt [blʌnt] *adj* ottuso; (*plain-spoken*) franco ‖ *tr* rendere ottuso
bluntness ['blʌntnɪs] *s* ottusità *f*; franchezza
blur [blʌr] *s* macchia; offuscamento; confusione ‖ *v* (*pret & pp* **blurred**;

ger **blurring**) *tr* macchiare; (*the view*) offuscare
blurb [blʌrb] *s* annuncio pubblicitario
blurt [blʌrt] *tr*—**to blurt out** prorompere a dire, lasciarsi sfuggire
blush [blʌʃ] *s* rossore *m*; (*pinkish natural tinge*) incarnato ‖ *intr* arrossire; **to blush at** vergognarsi di
bluster ['blʌstər] *s* frastuono; (fig) boria ‖ *intr* (*said of the wind*) infuriare; fare il bravaccio
blustery ['blʌstəri] *adj* tempestuoso; violento; (*swaggering*) borioso
boar [bor] *s* verro; (*wild hog*) porco selvatico, cinghiale *m*
board [bord] *s* asse *m*; (*notice*) cartello; (*pasteboard*) cartone *m*; (*table*) tavola; (*meals*) vitto; (*group of administrators*) consiglio; (naut) bordo; **above board** franco; **in boards** rilegato; **on board** a bordo; (rr) in vettura; **to go by the board** andare in rovina; **to tread the boards** fare l'attore ‖ *tr* chiudere con assi; (*to provide with meals*) dare pensione a, tenere a dozzina; (*a ship*) salire a bordo di; (*a train*) salire su; (naut) abbordare ‖ *intr* essere a pensione
board' and lodg'ing *s* pensione completa
boarder ['bordər] *s* pensionante *mf*
board'ing house' *s* pensione di famiglia
board'ing school' *s* collegio di pensionanti
board' of direc'tors *s* consiglio d'amministrazione
board' of health' *s* ufficio d'igiene
board' of trade' *s* camera di commercio
board'walk' *s* passeggiata a mare
boast [bost] *s* millanteria, vanteria ‖ *intr* vantarsi
boastful ['bostfəl] *adj* millantatore
boat [bot] *s* nave *f*, battello; (*small ship*) barca, imbarcazione; (*dish*) salsiera; **in the same boat** nella stessa situazione
boat' hook' *s* alighiero
boat'house' *s* capannone *m* per i canotti
boating ['botɪŋ] *s* escursione in barca
boat'man *s* (-men) barcaiolo
boat' race' *s* regata
boatswain ['bosən] or ['bot,swen] *s* nostromo
bob [bab] *s* (*plumb*) piombino; (*short haircut*) taglio alla bebè; coda mozza (di cavallo); (*jerky motion*) strattone *m*; (*on pendulum of clock*) lente *f*; (*on fishing line*) sughero ‖ *v* (*pret & pp* **bobbed**; *ger* **bobbing**) *tr* tagliare alla bebè; far muovere a scatti ‖ *intr* muoversi a scatti; fare mossa; **to bob up** apparire
bobbin ['babɪn] *s* bobina
bob'by pin' ['babi] *s* forcina
bob'by-socks' *spl* (coll) calzini *mpl* da ragazza
bobbysoxer ['babi ,saksər] *s* (coll) ragazzina
bobolink ['babə ,lɪŋk] *s* dolicònice *m*
bob'sled' *s* guidoslitta
bode [bod] *tr & intr* presagire
bodice ['badɪs] *s* giubbetto, copribusto

bodily ['bɑdɪli] *adj* fisico, corporeo ‖ *adv* fisicamente, corporeamente; di persona; in massa

bodkin ['bɑdkɪn] *s* punteruolo; (*for lady's hair*) spillone *m*

bod•y ['bɑdi] *s* (**-ies**) corpo; (*corpse*) cadavere *m*; (*of water*) massa; (*of people*) gruppo; (*of a liquid*) sostanza; (*of truck*) cassone *m*; (*of car*) carrozzeria; (*of tree*) tronco; (coll) persona; **in a body** in massa

bod'y-guard' *s* (*of a high official*) guardia del corpo; (*e.g., of a movie star*) guardaspalle *m*

bod'y suit' *s* calzamaglia

bog [bɑg] *s* pantano, palude *m* ‖ (*pret & pp* **bogged**; *ger* **bogging**) *intr*—**to bog down** impelagarsi

bogey-man ['bogi‚mæn] *s* (**-men** [mɛn]) babau *m*

bogus ['bogəs] *adj* (coll) falso, finto

Bohemian [bo'himɪ-ən] *adj* boemo; da bohémien ‖ *s* boemo; (fig) bohémien *m*

boil [bɔɪl] *s* bollore *m*, ebollizione; (pathol) foruncolo; **to come to a boil** cominciare a bollire ‖ *tr* bollire; **to boil down** condensare ‖ *intr* bollire; **to boil away** evaporare completamente; **to boil down** condensarsi; **to boil over** andare per il fuoco

boiled' ham' *s* prosciutto cotto

boiler ['bɔɪlər] *s* caldaia; (*for cooking*) caldaio

boil'er•mak'er *s* calderaio

boiling ['bɔɪlɪŋ] *adj* bollente ‖ *s* bollore *m*, ebollizione

boisterous ['bɔɪstərəs] *adj* (*storm*) violento; (*loud*) rumoroso

bold [bold] *adj* (*daring*) coraggioso; (*impudent*) sfacciato; (*steep*) scosceso; (*clear, sharp*) netto

bold'face' *s* (typ) neretto, grassetto

boldness ['boldnɪs] *s* coraggio, audacia; sfacciataggine *f*, impudenza

boll' wee'vil [bol] *s* antonomo del cotone

bologna [bə'lonə] or [bə'lonjə] *s* mortadella

Bolshevik ['bʌlʃəvɪk] or ['bolʃəvɪk] *adj & mf* bolscevico

bolster ['bolstər] *s* cuscino; cuscinetto; (*support*) sostegno ‖ *tr* sorreggere; **to bolster up** sostenere

bolt [bolt] *s* (*arrow*) freccia; (*of lightning*) fulmine *m*; (*sliding bar*) chiavistello; (*threaded rod*) bullone *m*; (*of paper or cloth*) pezza, rotolo ‖ *adv*—**bolt upright** dritto come un fuso ‖ *tr* (*to swallow hurriedly*) ingollare; (*to fasten, e.g., a door*) sprangare; (*to fasten, e.g., two metal parts*) bullonare; (*e.g., a political party*) abbandonare ‖ *intr* (*said of people*) spiccare un salto; (*said of a horse*) prendere la mano; precipitarsi

bolt' from the blue' *s* fulmine *m* a ciel sereno

bomb [bam] *s* bomba; (*e.g., for spraying*) bombola ‖ *tr* bombardare

bombard [bam'bɑrd] *tr* bombardare; (*with questions*) bersagliare

bombardment [bam'bɑrdmənt] *s* bombardamento

bombast ['bambæst] *s* ampollosità *f*

bombastic [bam'bæstɪk] *adj* ampolloso

bomb' cra'ter *s* cratere *m*

bomber ['bamər] *s* bombardiere *m*

bomb'proof' *adj* a prova di bomba

bomb'shell' *s* bomba; (fig) colpo di bomba, colpo di sorpresa

bomb' shel'ter *s* rifugio antiaereo

bomb'sight' *s* traguardo aereo

bona fide ['bonə‚faɪdə] *adj* sincero ‖ *adv* in buona fede

bonanza [bə'nænzə] *s* (min) ricca vena; (coll) fortuna

bond [band] *s* legame *m*, vincolo; (*contractual obligation*) obbligazione; (*interest-bearing certificate*) buono, obbligazione; (*surety*) cauzione; **bonds** catene *fpl*; **in bond** sotto cauzione; (*said of goods*) in punto franco ‖ *tr* unire, connettere

bondage ['bandɪdʒ] *s* schiavitù *f*

bond'ed ware'house *s* deposito in punto franco

bond'hold'er *s* obbligazionista *mf*

bonds'man *s* (**-men**) garante *m*

bone [bon] *s* osso; (*of fish*) spina; (*of whale*) stecca; **bones** ossa *fpl*; **to have a bone to pick with** avere un conto da regolare con; **to make no bones about** (coll) ammettere; (coll) parlare esplicitamente ‖ *tr* disossare; cavare le spine a ‖ *intr*—**to bone up on** (coll) ripassare

bone'head' *s* (coll) testa dura

boneless ['bonlɪs] *adj* senz'osso; (*fish*) senza spine

boner ['bonər] *s* (slang) errore *m* madornale

bonfire ['ban‚faɪr] *s* falò *m*

bonnet ['banɪt] *s* cappello da donna; (*of child*) berrettino

bonus ['bonəs] *s* gratifica; indennità *f*; (*to an outgoing employee*) buonuscita

bon•y ['boni] *adj* (**-ier; -iest**) (*having bones*) osseo; (*emaciated*) scarno; (*fish*) spinoso

boo [bu] *s* fischio, urlaccio ‖ *tr & intr* fischiare, disapprovare

boo•by ['bubi] *s* (**-bies**) stupido

boo'by hatch' *s* (naut) portello; (slang) manicomio; (slang) prigione *f*

boo'by prize' *s* premio dato al peggior giocatore

boo'by trap' *s* (mil) trappola esplosiva; (fig) tranello

boogie-woogie ['bugi'wugi] *s* bughi-bughi *m*

book [bʊk] *s* libro; (*e.g., of matches*) pacchetto; (mus) libretto; (fig) regole *fpl*; **the Book** la Bibbia; **to be in one's book** essere nelle grazie di; **to bring s.o. to book** fare una ramanzina a ‖ *tr* registrare; (*e.g., on a horse*) allibrare; (*e.g., a room*) prenotare; (*an actor*) scritturare

book'bind'er *s* rilegatore *m*

book'bind'er•y *s* (**-ies**) rilegatoria

book'bind'ing *s* rilegatura

book'case' *s* scaffale *m*

book' end' *s* reggilibri *m*

bookie ['bʊki] s (coll) allibratore m
booking ['bʊkɪŋ] s (of a trip) prenotazione; (of an actor) scrittura
book'ing clerk' s impiegato alla biglietteria
bookish ['bʊkɪʃ] adj studioso; libresco
book'keep'er s contabile mf
booklet ['bʊklɪt] s libretto; (pamphlet) opuscolo
book'keep'ing s contabilità f
book'mak'er s (one who accepts bets) allibratore m
book'mark' s segnalibro
bookmobile ['bʊkmo‚bil] s bibliobus m
book'plate' s ex libris m
book' review' s rassegna, recensione
book'sell'er s libraio
book'shelf' s (-shelves) scaffale m
book'stand' s (rack) scansia; (stall) edicola
book'store' s libreria
book'worm' s (zool) tarlo dei libri; (fig) topo da biblioteca
boom [bum] s (of crane) braccio; (barrier) barriera galleggiante; (noise) bum m; (fin) boom m; (naut) boma; (mov, telv) giraffa || intr rimbombare; essere in condizioni floride
boomerang ['bumə‚ræŋ] s bumerang m
boom' town' s città f fungo
boon [bun] s fortuna, benedizione
boon' compan'ion s compagnone m
boor [bʊr] s bifolco, zotico
boorish ['bʊrɪʃ] adj grossolano
boost [bust] s aumento; (coll) spinta || tr spingere in su; sostenere; (prices) alzare; parlare a favore di
booster ['bustər] s (backer) sostenitore m; propulsore m a razzo; (rok) propulsore m del primo stadio; (med) seconda iniezione
boot [but] s stivale m; (kick) calcio; (patch) (aut) pezza; the boot is on the other foot la situazione è rovesciata; to be in the boots of essere nella pelle di; to boot per di più; to get the boot (coll) essere messo sulla strada; to lick the boots of leccare i piedi a; to wipe one's boots on trattare come una pezza da piedi || tr dare un calcio a; to boot out (slang) buttar fuori
boot'black' s lustrascarpe m
booth [buθ] s (stall) banco da mercato; (for telephoning, voting) cabina
boot'jack' s tirastivali m
boot'leg' adj di contrabbando || s liquore m di contrabbando || v (pret & pp -legged; ger -legging) tr vendere di contrabbando || intr vendere alcol di contrabbando
bootlegger ['but‚legər] s contrabbandiere m di liquori
boot'lick'er s [‚lɪkər] s (coll) leccapiedi mf
boot'strap' s tirante m degli stivali
boo·ty ['buti] s (-ties) bottino
booze [buz] s (coll) bevanda alcolica || intr (coll) ubriacarsi
borax ['boræks] s borace m
border ['bordər] adj confinario, con-

finante || s bordo, margine m; (between two countries) confine m || tr bordare; confinare con || intr confinare
bor'der clash' s incidente m ai confini
bor'der·line' adj incerto || s frontiera
bore [bor] s (drill hole) buco, foro; (hollow part of gun) anima; (caliber) calibro; (dull person) seccatore m; (annoyance) seccatura; (mach) alesaggio || tr bucare, forare; seccare; (mach) alesare
boredom ['bordəm] s noia, tedio
boring ['borɪŋ] adj noioso || s trivellazione
born [born] adj nato, partorito; to be born nascere; to be born again rinascere; to be born with a silver spoon in one's mouth nascere con la camicia
borough ['bʌro] s borgata, comune m
borrow ['baro] or ['bɔro] tr chiedere a or in prestito; prendere a or in prestito; ricevere a or in prestito; (to adopt) adottare; to borrow trouble preoccuparsi per nulla
borrower ['baro‚ər] or ['bɔro‚ər] s chi riceve a prestito; (law) comodatario, prestatario
borrowing ['baro‚ɪŋ] or ['bɔro‚ɪŋ] s prestito; prestito linguistico, forestierismo
bosom ['bʊzəm] s petto, seno; (e.g., of the family) grembo, seno; (of shirt) pettorina
bos'om friend' s amico del cuore
Bosporus ['baspərəs] s Bosforo
boss [bɔs] or [bas] s (coll) padrone m; (coll) direttore m; (coll) capintesta m; (coll) principale m; (archit) bugna, bozza || tr fare da padrone a || intr fare da padrone
boss·y ['bɔsi] or ['basi] adj (-ier; -iest) autoritario
botanical [bə'tænɪkəl] adj botanico
botanist ['batənɪst] s botanico
botany ['batəni] s botanica
botch [batʃ] s abborracciatura || tr abborracciare
both [boθ] adj entrambi i, tutti e due i || pron entrambi, tutti e due || conj del pari, al medesimo tempo; both . . . and tanto . . . quanto
bother ['baðər] s (worry) noia, seccatura; (person) seccatore m || tr dar noia a, seccare || intr preoccuparsi; to bother about or with occuparsi di; to bother to + inf molestarsi di + inf
bothersome ['baðərsəm] adj incomodo
bottle ['batəl] s bottiglia, fiasco || tr imbottigliare; to bottle up imbottigliare
bot'tle cap' s tappo a corona
bot'tle-neck' s collo di bottiglia; (of traffic) congestione, imbottigliamento
bot'tle o'pener ['opənər] s apribottiglie m
bottom ['batəm] adj basso; (price, dollar) ultimo; infimo || s fondo; (of chair) sedile m; base f; (of bottle) culo; (of ship) scafo; at bottom in realtà; to begin at the bottom comin-

ciare dalla gavetta; **to get at the bottom of** andare a fondo di; **to go to the bottom** andare a picco

bottomless ['batəmlis] *adj* senza fondo

boudoir [bu'dwar] *s* gabinetto di toletta (da signora)

bough [bau] *s* ramo

bouillon ['bujɑn] *s* brodo schietto

boulder ['boldər] *s* masso, roccia

boulevard ['bulə‚vard] *s* corso

bounce [bauns] *s* balzo; salto; elasticità *f;* (*of boat or plane*) piastrellamento; (fig) spirito; **to get the bounce** (slang) essere licenziato ‖ *tr* far balzare; (slang) buttar fuori ‖ *intr* rimbalzare; saltare; (aer, naut) piastrellare

bouncer ['baunsər] *s* (*in night club*) (slang) buttafuori *m*

bouncing ['baunsɪŋ] *adj* forte, vigoroso; grande, rumoroso

bound [baund] *adj* legato; collegato; obbligato; (bb) rilegato; (coll) risoluto; **bound for** destinato a, diretto per; **bound up in or with** in strette relazioni con; assorto in ‖ *s* salto; rimbalzo; limite *m*; **bounds** zona limitrofa; **out of bounds** fuori limiti; **al di là delle convenienze** ‖ *tr* delimitare

bounda·ry ['baundəri] *s* (**-ries**) confine *m*, limite *m*

bound'ary stone' *s* pietra di confine

boundless ['baundlis] *adj* illimitato, sconfinato

bountiful ['bauntɪfəl] *adj* generoso; abbondante

boun·ty ['baunti] *s* (**-ties**) dono generoso; generosità *f*, abbondanza; (*reward*) premio

bouquet [bu'ke] or [bo'ke] *s* mazzo, mazzolino; profumo, aroma *m*

bourgeois ['burʒwɑ] *adj & s* borghese *mf*

bourgeoisie [‚burʒwɑ'zi] *s* borghesia

bout [baut] *s* lotta, contesa; (*of illness*) attacco

bow [bau] *s* inchino, riverenza; (naut) prua; **to take a bow** ricevere gli applausi ‖ *tr* chinare, piegare ‖ *intr* inchinarsi; sottomettersi; **to bow and scrape** fare riverenze ‖ [bo] *s* (*weapon*) arco; (*knot*) nodo; (mus) archetto; (*stroke of bow*) (mus) arcata ‖ *tr & intr* (mus) suonare con l'archetto

bowdlerize ['baudlə‚raɪz] *tr* espurgare

bowel ['bau·əl] *s* budello; **bowels** viscere *fpl*

bow'el move'ment *s* evacuazione; **to have a bowel movement** andar di corpo

bower ['bau·ər] *s* pergolato

bowery ['bau·əri] *adj* frondoso

bowknot ['bo‚nat] *s* nodo scorsoio

bowl [bol] *s* (*dish*) ciotola; (*cup*) tazza; (*of pipe*) fornello; (*basin*) catino; (*amphitheater*) arena; (*ball*) boccia; (*delivery of ball*) bocciata; **bowls** bocce *fpl* ‖ *tr* bocciare; **to bowl down or over** abbattere ‖ *intr* giocare alle bocce

bowlegged ['bo‚lɛgd] or ['bo‚lɛgɪd] *adj* con le gambe storte

bowler ['bolər] *s* giocatore *m* di bocce

bowling ['bolɪŋ] *s* bocce *fpl*; bowling *m*, birilli *mpl*

bowl'ing al'ley *s* pista per il bowling; bowling *m*

bowl'ing green' *s* campo di bocce erboso

bowshot ['bo‚ʃat] *s* tiro d'arco

bowsprit ['bausprit] or ['bosprit] *s* (naut) bompresso

bow' tie' [bo] *s* cravatta a farfalla

bowwow ['bau‚wau] *interj* bau bau!

box [baks] *s* scatola; cassa; (*for jury*) banco; (*for sentry*) garitta; (*on coach*) cassetta; (*in stable*) posta; (*slap*) ceffone *m*; (*with fist*) pugno; (bot) bosso; (theat) palco, barcaccia; (baseball) posto del battitore; (typ) riquadratura ‖ *tr* mettere in scatola; (*to slap*) schiaffeggiare; (*to hit with fist*) fare a pugilato con; **to box in or up** rinchiudere ‖ *intr* fare a pugni, combattere

box'car' *s* vagone *m* merci coperto

boxer ['baksər] *s* pugile *m*

box'hold'er *s* palchettista *mf*

boxing ['baksɪŋ] *s* pugilato

box'ing gloves' *spl* guantoni *mpl* da pugilato

box' of'fice *s* sportello, biglietteria; (theat) incasso; (theat) successo

box'-of'fice hit' *s* grande successo

box' pleat' *s* (*of skirt*) cannone *m*

box' seat' *s* posto in palco

box'wood' *s* bosso

boy [bɔɪ] *s* ragazzo, giovane *m* ‖ *interj* accidempoli!

boycott ['bɔɪkɑt] *s* boicottaggio ‖ *tr* boicottare

boy'friend' *s* innamorato, amico

boyhood ['bɔɪhud] *s* fanciullezza

boyish ['bɔɪ·ɪʃ] *adj* giovanile

boy' scout' *s* giovane esploratore *m*

bra [brɑ] *s* (coll) reggiseno

brace [bres] *s* (*couple*) paio; (*device for maintaining tension*) tirante *m;* (*prop*) sostegno; (*tool*) trapano; (typ) graffa; **braces** (Brit) bretelle *fpl* ‖ *tr* legare; serrare; puntellare; sostenere; invigorare; **to brace oneself** pigliare animo ‖ *intr*—**to brace up** (coll) pigliare animo

brace' and bit' *s* menarola, trapano

bracelet ['breslɪt] *s* braccialetto

bracer ['bresər] *s* (coll) bicchierino

bracket ['brækɪt] *s* mensola; (*for lamp*) braccio; angolo; classifica; (typ) parentesi quadra ‖ *tr* sostenere con mensola; mettere tra parentesi quadra; classificare

brackish ['brækɪʃ] *adj* salmastro

brad [bræd] *s* chiodino, punta

brag [bræg] *s* vanto ‖ *v* (*pret & pp* **bragged;** *ger* **bragging**) *intr* vantare

braggart ['brægərt] *s* millantatore *m*

Brah·man ['brɑmən] *s* (**-mans**) bramino

braid [bred] *s* treccia; (*strip of cloth*) spighetta; (mil) cordellina ‖ *tr* intrecciare; decorare con spighette

brain [bren] *s* cervello; **brains** cervello, intelligenza; **to rack one's brains** rompersi la testa || *tr* far saltare le cervella di
brain'child' *s* (coll) parto dell'ingegno, idea geniale
brain' drain' *s* (coll) fuga di cervelli
brainless ['brenlɪs] *adj* senza testa
brain' pow'er *s* intelligenza
brain'storm' *s* (coll) ispirazione
brain' trust' *s* consiglio d'esperti
brain'wash'ing *s* lavaggio del cervello
brain' wave' *s* onda encefalica; (coll) idea geniale
brain'work' *s* lavoro intellettuale
brain·y ['breni] *adj* (-ier; -iest) intelligente
braise [brez] *tr* (culin) brasare
brake [brek] *s* freno; (*thicket*) macchia || *tr & intr* frenare
brake' drum' *s* tamburo del freno
brake' lin'ing *s* ferodo
brake'man *s* (-men) frenatore *m*
brake' shoe' *s* ganascia
bramble ['bræmbəl] *s* rovo
bran [bræn] *s* crusca
branch [bræntʃ] *s* (*of tree*) branca, ramo; (*of river*) braccio; (*of a family*) ramo; (*of business*) filiale *f*; (rr) diramazione || *intr* biforcarsi; **to branch off** or **out** ramificarsi, diramarsi
branch' line' *s* ferrovia di diramazione
branch' of'fice *s* succursale *f*
brand [brænd] *s* (*burning stick*) tizzone *m*; (*mark*; *stigma*) marchio; (*label*; *make*) marca || *tr* (*to mark with a brand*) marchiare; (*to put a stigma on*) bollare; **to brand as** tacciare di
brandied ['brændid] *adj* conservato in acquavite
brand'ing i'ron *s* ferro da marchio
brandish ['brændɪʃ] *tr* brandire
brand'-new' *adj* nuovo fiammante
bran·dy ['brændi] *s* (-dies) cognac *m*, acquavite *f*
brash [bræʃ] *adj* (*too hasty*) avventato; (*insolent*) impudente || *s* frammenti *mpl*; attacco (di malattia), indigestione
brass [bræs] or [brɑs] *s* ottone *m*; (coll) faccia tosta; (slang) alti ufficiali; **brasses** (mus) ottoni *mpl*
brass' band' *s* fanfara
brassiere [brə'zir] *s* reggiseno
brass' knuck'les *spl* tirapugni *m*
brass' tack' *s* chiodino or borchia d'ottone; **to get down to brass tacks** (coll) venire al sodo
brass·y ['bræsi] or ['brɑsi] *adj* (-ier; -iest) fatto d'ottone; sfacciato, impudente
brat [bræt] *s* marmocchio, monello
brava·do [brə'vɑdo] *s* (-does or -dos) bravata
brave [brev] *adj* coraggioso || *s* persona coraggiosa; guerriero indiano || *tr* (*to defy*) sfidare; (*to meet with courage*) affrontare
bravery ['brevəri] *s* coraggio
bra·vo ['brɑvo] *s* (-vos) bravo; applauso || *interj* bravo!

brawl [brɔl] *s* zuffa, rissa || *intr* azzuffarsi, rissare
brawn [brɔn] *s* forza muscolare
brawn·y ['brɔni] *adj* (-ier; -iest) muscoloso
bray [bre] *s* raglio || *intr* ragliare
braze [brez] *s* brasatura || *tr* brasare
brazen ['brezən] *adj* d'ottone; (*shameless*) sfrontato; (*sound*) penetrante || *tr*—**to brazen out** or **through** affrontare sfacciatamente
brazier ['brefər] *s* caldano, braciere *m*; (*workman*) ottonaio
Brazil [brə'zɪl] *s* il Brasile
Brazilian [brə'zɪljən] *adj & s* brasiliano
Brazil' nut' *s* noce *f* del Brasile
breach [britʃ] *s* (*gap*) breccia; (*failure to observe a law*) infrazione || *tr* fare breccia su, fare varco in
breach' of faith' *s* abuso di confidenza
breach' of prom'ise *s* rottura di promessa di matrimonio
breach' of the peace' *s* violazione dell'ordine pubblico
bread [bred] *s* pane *m*; **to break bread with** sedersi a tavola con || *tr* impannare
bread' and but'ter *s* pane *m* e burro; (coll) pane quotidiano
bread' crumbs' *spl* pangrattato
breaded ['bredid] *adj* impannato
bread' knife' *s* coltello da pane
bread' line' *s* coda del pane
bread' stick' *s* grissino
breadth [bredθ] *s* (*width*) larghezza; (*scope*) ampiezza
bread'win'ner *s* sostegno della famiglia
break [brek] *s* interruzione; intervallo; omissione; (*breaking*) rottura; (*of bones*) frattura; (*of day*) fare *m*, spuntare *m*; (*sudden change*) mutamento; (*from jail*) evasione; (*luck*) (coll) fortuna; **to give s.o. a break** dare a qlcu l'opportunità || *v* (*pret* **broke** [brok]; *pp* **broken**) *tr* (*to smash*) rompere, spezzare; (*to tame*) domare; (*to demote*) destituire; (*a record*) superare; (*to violate*) violare; (*to make bankrupt*) mandare al fallimento; (*to interrupt*) interrompere; (*to reduce the effects of*) attutire; (*to disclose*) rivelare; (*to bring to an end by force*) battere; (*a banknote*) cambiare; (*one's word*) mancare (with *dat*); (*a law*) rompere; **to break asunder** separare; **to break down** analizzare; **to break in** forzare; **to break open** forzare, scassinare; **to break up** dissolvere || *intr* (*to divide*) rompersi; (*to burst*) scoppiare; (*said of voice of youngster*) cambiare; (*said of voice*) indebolirsi; (*said of a crowd*) disperdersi; (*said of weather*) rischiararsi; (*said of prices*) ribassare; (*to come into being*) scoppiare; (boxing) separarsi; **to break asunder** separarsi; **to break away** scappare; **to break down** abbattersi; (aut) essere or rimanere in panna; **to break even** fare patta; **to break in** irrompere; interrompere; **to break into** forzare; **to break into a run** inco-

minciare a correre; **to break loose** liberarsi; (said of a storm) scatenarsi; **to break off** interrompere; **to break out** (said of the skin) avere un'eruzione; (said, e.g., of war) scoppiare; **to break through** aprirsi il varco; **to break up** disperdersi; **to break with** rompere le relazioni con

breakable [ˈbrekəbəl] adj fragile

breakage [ˈbrekɪdʒ] s rottura

break'down' s (in negotiations) rottura; (aut) panna; (chem) analisi f; (pathol) colasso

breaker [ˈbrekər] s (wave) frangente m

breakfast [ˈbrɛkfəst] s prima colazione || intr fare prima colazione

break'neck' adj pericoloso; **at breakneck speed** a rotta di collo, a rompicollo

break' of day' s alba

break'through' s (mil) penetrazione; (fig) scoperta sensazionale

break'up' s dispersione; dissoluzione; (of a friendship) rottura

break'wa'ter s diga, frangiflutti m

breast [brest] s petto; (of female) seno; (source of emotions) animo; **to make a clean breast of** fare una piena confessione di

breast'bone' s sterno

breast' drill' s trapano da petto

breast'feed' v (pret & pp -fed [fed]) tr allattare

breast'pin' s spilla

breast'stroke' s bracciata a rana

breath [brɛθ] s respiro, respirazione; (odor) alito; (breeze) soffio; (whisper) sussurro; (fig) vita; **out of breath** ansimante; **short of breath** corto di respiro; **to gasp for breath** respirare affannosamente; **under one's breath** sottovoce

breathe [brið] tr respirare; (to whisper) sussurrare; **to breathe one's last** esalare l'ultimo sospiro; **to not breathe a word** non dire una parola || intr respirare; **to breathe in** inspirare; **to breathe out** espirare

breath'ing spell' s attimo di respiro

breathless [ˈbrɛθlɪs] adj senza fiato, ansimante; soffocante

breath'tak'ing s emozionante, commovente

breech [britʃ] s (buttocks) natiche fpl; (rear part) parte f posteriore; (of gun) culatta; **breeches** [ˈbrɪtʃɪz] pantaloni mpl al ginocchio; pantaloni mpl da cavallo; **to wear the breeches** (coll) portare le brache

breed [brid] s razza; tipo; (stock) origine f || v (pret & pp bred [brɛd]) tr produrre; (to raise) allevare

breeder [ˈbridər] s allevatore m; riproduttore m

breeding [ˈbridɪŋ] s (e.g., of livestock) allevamento; educazione

breeze [briz] s brezza

breez•y [ˈbrizi] adj (-ier; -iest) ventilato; (brisk) vivace, brioso

brethren [ˈbrɛðrɪn] spl fratelli mpl

brevi•ty [ˈbrɛvɪti] s (-ties) brevità f

brew [bru] s pozione; bevanda || tr (beer) fabbricare; (to steep) preparare; (to plot) complottare || intr (said of beer) fermentare; (said of a storm) prepararsi

brewer [ˈbruər] s birraio

brew'er's yeast' s lievito di birra

brewer•y [ˈbruəri] s (-ies) birreria, fabbrica di birra

bribe [braɪb] s subornazione, bustarella || tr subornare, dare la bustarella a

briber•y [ˈbraɪbəri] s (-ies) subornazione, corruzione

bric-a-brac [ˈbrɪkə ˌbræk] s bric-a-brac m, cianfrusaglia, cianfrusaglie fpl

brick [brɪk] s mattone m || tr mattonare

brick'bat' s pezzo di mattone; (coll) insulto

brick'kiln' s fornace f per mattoni

bricklayer [ˈbrɪk ˌleər] s muratore m

brick'yard' s deposito di mattoni

bridal [ˈbraɪdəl] adj nuziale, da sposa

brid'al wreath' s serto nuziale

bride [braɪd] s sposa

bride'groom' s sposo

bridesmaid [ˈbraɪdz ˌmed] s damigella d'onore

bridge [brɪdʒ] s ponte m; (of violin) ponticello; (on a ship) ponte m di comando || tr gettare un ponte su; congiungere; **to bridge a gap** colmare una lacuna

bridge'head' s testa di ponte

bridle [ˈbraɪdəl] s briglia || tr mettere la briglia a; (fig) frenare || intr drizzare il capo, insuperbirsi

bri'dle path' s strada cavalcabile

brief [brif] adj breve || s sommario; (law) esposto; (eccl) breve m; **briefs** slip m || tr dare istruzioni a, mettere al corrente

brief' case' s cartella, borsa d'avvocato

brier [ˈbraɪər] s radica; pipa di radica

brig [brɪg] s (naut) brigantino; (naut) prigione

brigade [brɪˈged] s brigata

brigadier [ˌbrɪgəˈdɪr] s (coll) brigadier generale m, generale m di brigata

brigand [ˈbrɪgənd] s brigante m

brigantine [ˈbrɪgən ˌtin] or [ˈbrɪgən ˌtaɪn] s (naut) brigantino goletta

bright [braɪt] adj (shining) lucido; (light) brillante; (lively) vivo; intelligente; famoso; (idea) luminoso

brighten [ˈbraɪtən] tr illuminare; ravvivare || intr illuminarsi; ravvivarsi; rischiararsi

bright' lights' spl luci fpl abbaglianti; (aut) fari mpl abbaglianti

brilliance [ˈbrɪljəns] or **brilliancy** [ˈbrɪljənsi] s splendore m, scintillio

brilliant [ˈbrɪljənt] adj brillante

brim [brɪm] s (e.g., of cup) orlo, bordo; (of hat) ala, tesa || v (pret & pp brimmed; ger brimming) intr essere pieno sino all'orlo

brim'stone' s zolfo

brine [braɪn] s salamoia; acqua di mare

bring [brɪŋ] v (pret & pp brought

[brɔt]) *tr* far venire; provocare; (*to carry along*) portare con sè; **to bring about** causare; **to bring around** persuadere; **to bring back** restituire; **to bring down** far abbassare; (fig) umiliare; **to bring forth** dare alla luce; **to bring forward** (*an excuse*) addurre; (math) riportare; **to bring in** introdurre; far entrare; **to bring off** compiere; **to bring on** causare; **to bring oneself to** rassegnarsi a; **to bring out** (*to expose*) rivelare; (*to offer to the public*) presentare al pubblico; (*a book*) far uscire; **to bring to** far rinvenire; (*a ship*) fermare; **to bring together** riunire; **to bring up** (*children*) allevare, tirar su; (*to introduce*) allegare; (*to cough up*) rigettare

bringing-up ['brɪŋɪŋʌp] *s* educazione
brink [brɪŋk] *s* orlo
briquet [brɪ'kɛt] *s* bricchetta
brisk [brɪsk] *adj* (*quick*) svelto; (*sharp*) acuto; (*invigorating*) frizzante; (*gunfire*) nutrito
bristle ['brɪsəl] *s* setola || *intr* (*to be stiff*) irrigidirsi; (*said of hair*) rizzarsi; (*with anger*) adirarsi
bris·tly ['brɪslɪ] *adj* (-**tler**; -**tliest**) irto di setole
British ['brɪtɪʃ] *adj* britannico || **the British** i britannici, gl'inglesi
Britisher ['brɪtɪʃər] *s* britannico
Briton ['brɪtən] *s* britannico
Brittany ['brɪtənɪ] *s* la Bretagna
brittle ['brɪtəl] *adj* fragile, friabile; (*crisp*) croccante
broach [brotʃ] *s* (*pin*) spilla; (*spit*) spiedo; (mach) alesatore *m* || *tr* perforare; (*a subject*) intavolare
broad [brɔd] *adj* largo; tollerante, liberale; (*daylight*) pieno; (*story*) grossolano; (*extensive*) lato; (*accent*) pronunciato
broad'cast' *s* disseminazione; (rad) radiodiffusione || *v* (*pret & pp* -**cast**) *tr* disseminare, diffondere || (*pret & pp* -**cast** or -**casted**) *tr* radiodiffondere
broad'casting sta'tion *s* stazione radiotrasmittente
broad'cloth' *s* (*wool*) panno di lana; (*cotton*) popeline *f*
broaden ['brɔdən] *tr* allargare, estendere || *intr* allargarsi, estendersi
broad' jump' *s* salto in lunghezza
broadloom ['brɔd,lum] *adj* tessuto su telaio largo
broad-minded ['brɔd'maɪndɪd] *adj* di ampie vedute, liberale
broad-shouldered ['brɔd'ʃoldəred] *adj* largo di spalle
broad'side' *s* (nav) bordo; (nav) bordata; (*verbal criticism*) (coll) sfuriata; (*written criticism*) (coll) attacco violento
broad'sword' *s* spada da taglio
brocade [bro'ked] *s* broccato
broccoli ['brakəlɪ] *s* broccolo; (*as food*) broccoli *mpl*
brochure [bro'ʃur] *s* opuscolo, libriccino

brogue [brog] *s* accento irlandese; scarpa forte e comoda
broil [brɔɪl] *s* cottura alla graticola; carne *f* cotta alla graticola; (*quarrel*) rissa, zuffa || *tr* cucinare alla graticola; bruciare || *intr* cucinare alla graticola; (*to quarrel*) rissare, azzuffarsi
broiler ['brɔɪlər] *s* graticola, gratella; (*chicken*) pollo da cucinare alla gratella or allo spiedo
broke [brok] *adj* (coll) al verde
broken ['brokən] *adj* rotto; fratturato; (*e.g., English*) parlato male; (*tamed*) domato
bro'ken-down' *adj* avvilito; rovinato
broken-hearted ['brokən'hartɪd] *adj* affranto
broker ['brokər] *s* sensale *m*; (*on the stock exchange*) agente *m* di cambio
brokerage ['brokərɪdʒ] *s* mediazione
bromide ['bromaɪd] *s* bromuro; (coll) banalità *f*
bromine ['bromin] *s* bromo
bronchitis [braŋ'kaɪtɪs] *s* bronchite *f*
bron·co ['braŋko] *s* (-**cos**) puledro brado
broncobuster ['braŋko,bʌstər] *s* domatore *m* di puledri bradi
bronze [branz] *adj* bronzeo || *s* bronzo || *tr* bronzare || *intr* abbronzarsi
brooch [brotʃ] or [brutʃ] *s* spilla
brood [brud] *s* covata, nidiata || *tr* covare || *intr* chiocciare; meditare; **to brood on** or **over** meditare con tristezza (su)
brook [bruk] *s* ruscello || *tr*—**to brook no** non sopportare
broom [brum] or [brum] *s* scopa; (*shrub*) saggina
broom'corn' *s* sorgo
broom'stick' *s* manico di scopa
broth [brɔθ] or [braθ] *s* brodo
brothel ['braθəl] or ['braðəl] *s* postribolo, bordello
brother ['brʌðər] *s* fratello
brotherhood ['brʌðər,hud] *s* fratellanza; (*association*) confraternita
broth'er-in-law' *s* (**brothers-in-law**) cognato
brotherly ['brʌðərlɪ] *adj* fraterno || *adv* fraternamente
brow [brau] *s* ciglio; (*forehead*) fronte *f*; **to knit one's brow** aggrottare la fronte
brow'beat' *v* (*pret* -**beat**; *pp* -**beaten**) *tr* intimidire, intimorire
brown [braun] *adj* bruno; (*tanned*) abbronzato || *s* color bruno || *tr* colorare di bruno; abbronzare; (*metal*) brunire; (culin) dorare || *intr* colorarsi di bruno; abbronzarsi; brunirsi; (culin) dorarsi
brownish ['braunɪʃ] *adj* brunastro
brown' stud'y *s*—**in a brown study** assorto in fantasticherie
brown' sug'ar *s* zucchero greggio
browse [brauz] *intr* (*said of cattle*) brucare; sfogliare; **to browse around** curiosare
bruise [bruz] *s* ammaccatura, contu-

sione || *tr* ammaccare || *intr* ammaccarsi

brunet [bru'nɛt] *adj* bruno

brunette [bru'nɛt] *adj & s* bruna

brunt [brʌnt] *s* forza; scontro; peso

brush [brʌʃ] *s* pennello; spazzola; (*stroke*) pennellata; (*light touch*) tocco; (*brushwood*) macchia; (*brief encounter*) scaramuccia; (elec) spazzola || *tr* spazzolare; pennellare; **to brush aside** rigettare; **to brush up** ritoccare || *intr*—**to brush by** passar vicino; **to brush up on** ripassare

brush'-off' *s* (slang) scortesia; **to give the brush-off to** (slang) snobbare

brush'wood' *s* macchia, fratta

brusque [brʌsk] *adj* brusco

brusqueness ['brʌsknɪs] *s* bruschezza

Brussels ['brʌsəlz] *s* Bruxelles *f*

Brus'sels sprouts' *spl* cavolini *mpl*

brutal ['brutəl] *adj* brutale

brutali·ty [bru'tælɪti] *s* (-ties) brutalità *f*

brute [brut] *adj & s* bruto

brutish ['brutɪʃ] *adj* bruto

bubble ['bʌbəl] *s* bolla; (fig) chimera || *intr* bollire; (**to make a bubbling sound**) barbugliare; **to bubble over** traboccare

bub'ble bath' *s* bagno di schiuma

buccaneer [,bʌkə'nɪr] *s* bucaniere *m*

buck [bʌk] *s* (*deer*) cervo; (*goat*) caprone *m*; (*sawhorse*) cavalletto; (*rabbit*) coniglio maschio; (*bucking*) groppata; (*dandy*) damerino; (slang) dollaro; **to pass the buck** (coll) giocare a scaricabarile || *tr* resistere accanitamente || *intr* (*said of a horse*) fare salti da caprone; **to buck for** (slang) cercare di ottenere; **to buck up** (coll) rianimarsi, prender animo

bucket ['bʌkɪt] *s* secchio; bigoncia; (*e.g., of dredge*) benna; **to kick the bucket** (slang) tirare le cuoia

buck'et seat' *s* sedile *m*, strapuntino

buckle ['bʌkəl] *s* (*clasp*) fibbia, boccola; piega || *tr* affibbiare || *intr* piegarsi, curvarsi; **to buckle down to** (coll) mettersi di buzzo buono a

buck' pri'vate *s* (slang) soldato semplice

buckram ['bʌkrəm] *s* tela da fusto

buck'saw' *s* cavalletto

buck'shot' *s* pallini *mpl* da caccia

buck'tooth' *s* (-teeth) dente *m* in fuori, dente *m* sporgente

buck'wheat' *s* grano saraceno

bud [bʌd] *s* bocciolo, gemma; **to nip in the bud** troncare sul nascere || *v* (*pret & pp* **budded**; *ger* **budding**) *intr* sbocciare; nascere

Buddhism ['budɪzəm] *s* buddismo

bud·dy ['bʌdi] *s* (-dies) (coll) amico, compare *m*

budge [bʌdʒ] *tr* smuovere || *intr* muoversi

budget ['bʌdʒɪt] *s* bilancio || *tr* stanziare, preventivare; (*to schedule*) anticipare; (*time*) calcolare in anticipo

budgetary ['bʌdʒɪ,tɛri] *adj* preventivo, di bilancio

buff [bʌf] *adj* bruno giallastro; di pelle || *s* (*leather*) pelle gialla; dilet-

tante *m*; (mil) giacca di pelle gialla; (coll) pelle nuda || *tr* lucidare; (*to reduce the force of*) ammortizzare

buffa·lo ['bʌfə,lo] *s* (-loes or -los) bufalo || *tr* (coll) intimidire

buffer ['bʌfər] *s* ammortizzatore *m*; cuscinetto; (*worker*) lucidatore *m*; (mach) lucidatrice *f*; (rr) respingente *m*

buff'er state' *s* stato cuscinetto

buffet [bu'fe] *s* (*piece of furniture*) credenza; (*counter*) buffet *m* || ['bʌfɪt] *s* pugno; schiaffo || *tr* dar pugni a; schiaffeggiare; lottare con; (*to push about*) sballottare

buffet' car' [bu'fe] *s* vagone *m* ristorante

buffoon [bə'fun] *s* buffone *m*

buffoner·y [bə'funəri] *s* (-ies) buffoneria

bug [bʌg] *s* insetto; (coll) germe *m*; (*in motor*) (slang) noia; (slang) pazzo; **to put a bug in the ear of** mettere una pulce nell'orecchio di || *v* (*pret & pp* **bugged**; *ger* **bugging**) *tr* (slang) installare un sistema d'ascolto nel telefono di; (*to annoy*) (slang) seccare || *intr*—**to bug out** (slang) andarsene

bug'bear' *s* spauracchio

bug·gy ['bʌgi] *adj* (-gier; -giest) pieno di cimici; (slang) pazzo || *s* (-gies) carrozzino

bug'house' *adj* (slang) pazzo || *s* (slang) manicomio

bugle ['bjugəl] *s* tromba, cornetta

bugler ['bjuglər] *s* trombettiere *m*

build [bɪld] *s* corporatura, taglia || *v* (*pret & pp* **built** [bɪlt]) *tr* costruire, edificare; fondare, basare; **to build up** sviluppare

builder ['bɪldər] *s* costruttore *m*; costruttore *m* edile

building ['bɪldɪŋ] *s* edificio, stabile *m*; costruzione; edilizia

build'ing and loan' associa'tion *s* società *f* di credito fondiario

build'ing lot' *s* (coll) terreno da costruzioni

build'ing trades' *spl* edilizia

build'-up' *s* concentrazione; sviluppo; processo di preparazione; propaganda favorevole

built'-in' *adj* (*in a wall*) murato; (*in a cabinet*) incassato, incorporato

built'-in clos'et *s* armadio a muro

built'-up' *adj* armato; popolato

bulb [bʌlb] *s* bulbo; (*lamp*) lampadina; (*of a lamp*) globo, cipolla

Bulgarian [bʌl'gɛri·ən] *adj & s* bulgaro

bulge [bʌldʒ] *s* protuberanza, sporgenza || *intr* sporgere, gonfiarsi

bulk [bʌlk] *s* volume *m*, massa; **in bulk** in blocco; sciolto || *intr* avere importanza; aumentare d'importanza

bulk'head' *s* diga; (naut) paratia

bulk·y ['bʌlki] *adj* (-ier; -iest) voluminoso

bull [bul] *s* toro; (*in the stockmarket*) rialzista *mf*; (slang) scemenza; (eccl) bulla || *tr*—**to bull the market** giocare al rialzo

bull'dog' *s* molosso

bulldoze ['bʊl‚doz] *tr* intimidire; (*land*) livellare

bulldozer ['bʊl‚dozər] *s* livellatrice *f*, apripista *m*

bullet ['bʊlɪt] *s* palla, pallottola

bulletin ['bʊlətɪn] *s* bollettino; (*of a school*) albo; (journ) comunicato

bul'letin board' *s* tabellone *m*

bul'let-proof' *adj* blindato

bull'fight' *s* corrida

bull'fight'er *s* torero

bull'finch' *s* (orn) ciuffolotto

bull'frog' *s* rana americana

bull-headed ['bʊl‚hɛdɪd] *adj* testardo

bullion ['bʊljən] *s* lingotti *mpl* d'oro or d'argento; frangia d'oro; (*on an Italian general's hat*) greca

bullish ['bʊlɪʃ] *adj* ostinato; (*market*) al rialzo; (*speculator*) rialzista

bullock ['bʊlək] *s* manzo

bull'ring' *s* arena

bull's-eye ['bʊlz‚aɪ] *s* centro, tiro in pieno sul bersaglio; **to hit the bull's-eye** fare centro

bul-ly ['bʊli] *adj* (coll) eccellente || *s* (-lies) bravaccio || *v* (*pret* & *pp* -lied) *tr* intimidire

bulrush ['bʊl‚rʌʃ] *s* giunco; (Bibl) papiro

bulwark ['bʊlwərk] *s* baluardo; protezione || *tr* proteggere

bum [bʌm] *adj* (slang) pessimo || *s* (slang) vagabondo; **on the bum** (slang) rotto, fuori servizio || *v* (*pret* & *pp* bummed; *ger* bumming) *tr* (slang) scroccare || *intr* (slang) oziare; (slang) vivere d'elemosina; (slang) fare lo scroccatore

bumble ['bʌmbəl] *tr* abborracciare || *intr* abborracciare; (*to stagger*) barcollare; (*to stumble*) balbettare; (*said of a bee*) ronzare

bum'blebee' *s* calabrone *m*

bump [bʌmp] *s* botta, botto; (*collision*) colpo, urto; (*swelling*) bernoccolo || *tr* urtare; **to bump off** (slang) uccidere || *intr* urtare, cozzare; **to bump into** incontrarsi con; cozzare contro

bumper ['bʌmpər] *adj* (coll) abbondante || *s* bicchiere pieno fino all'orlo; (aut) paraurti *m*; (rr) respingente *m*

bumpkin ['bʌmpkɪn] *s* beota *m*

bumptious ['bʌmp/əs] *adj* vanitoso, presuntuoso

bump-y ['bʌmpi] *adj* (-ier; -iest) (*road*) irregolare, ondulato; (*air*) agitato

bun [bʌn] *s* panino; (*of hair*) crocchia, treccia a ciambella

bunch [bʌntʃ] *s* (*of grapes*) grappolo; (*of keys*) mazzo; (*of grass*) ciuffo; (*of people*) gruppo; (*of twigs*) fastello; (*of animals*) branco || *tr* (*things*) ammonticchiare; (*people*) raggruppare || *intr* raggrupparsi

bundle ['bʌndəl] *s* fascio, fastello; (*package*) pacco; (*large package*) collo; (*bunch*) mucchio || *tr* affastellare; impacchettare; ammucchiare; **to bundle off** or **out** cacciare precipitosamente; **to bundle up** infagottare || *intr*—**to bundle up** infagottarsi

bung [bʌŋ] *s* spina, cannella

bungalow ['bʌŋgə‚lo] *s* casetta, villino, bungalow *m*

bung'hole' *s* spina, foro della botte

bungle ['bʌŋgəl] *s* abborracciatura || *tr* abborracciare || *intr* lavorare alla carlona

bungler ['bʌŋglər] *s* abborraccione *m*

bungling ['bʌŋglɪŋ] *adj* goffo; mal fatto || *s* abborracciatura

bunion ['bʌnjən] *s* gonfiore *m* dell'alluce

bunk [bʌŋk] *s* letto a castello; (nav) cuccetta; (slang) sciocchezza || *intr* dormire in cuccetta

bunk' bed' *s* letto a castello

bunker ['bʌŋkər] *s* (*bin*) carbonile *m*; (mil) casamatta; (golf) ostacolo

bun-ny ['bʌni] *s* (-nies) coniglietto

bunting ['bʌntɪŋ] *s* ornamento di bandiere; (nav) gala; (orn) zigolo

buoy [bɔɪ] *or* ['bu-i] *s* boa; (*life preserver*) salvagente *m* || *tr*—**to buoy up** tenere a galla; (fig) rincuorare

buoyancy ['bɔɪ-ənsi] *or* ['bujənsi] *s* galleggiabilità *f*; (*cheerfulness*) allegria, esuberanza

buoyant ['bɔɪ-ənt] *or* ['bujənt] *adj* galleggiante; allegro, esuberante

bur [bʌr] *s* riccio, aculeo

burble ['bʌrbəl] *s* gorgoglio || *intr* gorgogliare

burden ['bʌrdən] *s* carico, peso, fardello; (*of a speech*) tema *m*; (chorus) ritornello; (naut) portata || *tr* caricare

bur'den of proof' *s* onere *m* della prova

burdensome ['bʌrdənsəm] *adj* oneroso

burdock ['bʌrdɑk] *s* lappa, lappola

bureau ['bjʊro] *s* comò *m*; (*agency*) ufficio, servizio

bureaucra-cy [bju'rɑkrəsi] *s* (-cies) burocrazia

bureaucrat ['bjʊrə‚kræt] *s* burocrate *m*

burglar ['bʌrglər] *s* scassinatore *m*

bur'glar alarm' *s* campanello antifurto

burglarize ['bʌrglə‚raɪz] *tr* scassinare

bur'glar-proof' *adj* a prova di furto

burgla-ry ['bʌrgləri] *s* (-ries) furto con scasso, scassinatura

Burgundy ['bʌrgəndi] *s* la Borgogna; (*wine*) borgogna *m*

burial ['bɛrɪ-əl] *s* sepoltura

bur'ial ground' *s* cimitero

burin ['bjʊrɪn] *s* burino, cesello

burlap ['bʌrlæp] *s* tela di iuta

burlesque [bʌr'lɛsk] *adj* burlesco || *s* farsa, burlesque *m* || *tr* parodiare

burlesque' show' *s* spettacolo di varietà, music-hall *m*

bur-ly ['bʌrli] *adj* (-lier; -liest) membruto, robusto

Burma ['bʌrmə] *s* la Birmania

burn [bʌrn] *s* bruciatura, scottatura || *v* (*pret* & *pp* burned *or* burnt [bʌrnt]) *tr* bruciare; (*to set on fire*) dar fuoco a; (*bricks*) cuocere; **to burn down** radere al suolo; **to burn up** consumare; (*the road*) divorare; (coll) fare arrabbiare || *intr* bruciare, bruciarsi; (*said of lights*) essere acceso, e.g., **the lights were burning** la luce era accesa; **to burn out** (*said of an electric bulb or a fuse*) bruciarsi;

to burn to (fig) agognare di; **to burn up** (coll) essere arrabiato; **to burn with** (e.g., envy) ardere di

burner ['bʌrnər] s (of gas fixture or lamp) becco; (of furnace) bruciatore m

burning ['bʌrnɪŋ] adj bruciante, scottante || s incendio; (ceramic) cottura finale

burn'ing ques'tion s questione di attualità palpitante

burnish ['bʌrnɪʃ] s lucidatura || tr brunire

burnt' al'mond [bʌrnt] s mandorla tostata

burp [bʌrp] s (coll) rutto || intr (coll) ruttare

burr [bʌr] s riccio, aculeo; (rough edge) bava; (dentist's drill) fresa

burrow ['bʌro] s tana, buca || intr imbucarsi, rintanarsi

bursar ['bʌrsər] s tesoriere universitario

burst [bʌrst] s esplosione; (e.g., of machine gun) raffica; (break) crepa; (of passion) accesso; (of speed) slancio || tr far scoppiare || intr scoppiare, esplodere; **to burst into** (e.g., a room) irrompere in; (e.g., angry words) esplodere in; **to burst out crying** scoppiare in lacrime; **to burst with laughter** scoppiare dalle risa

bur·y ['beri] v (pret & pp -ied) tr sotterrare; **to be buried in thought** essere immerso nel pensiero; **to bury the hatchet** fare la pace

bus [bʌs] s (buses or busses) bus m, autobus m || v (pret & pp bused or bussed; ger busing or bussing) tr trasportare con autobus

bus'boy' s secondo cameriere

bus·by ['bʌzbi] s (-bies) colbacco

bus' driv'er s conducente mf di autobus

bush [bʊʃ] s cespuglio, arbusto; **to beat around the bush** menare il can per l'aia

bushed [bʊʃt] adj (coll) stanco morto

bushel ['bʊʃəl] s staio

bushing ['bʊʃɪŋ] s (mach) bronzina

bush·y ['bʊʃi] adj (-ier; -iest) ricco di arbusti; (face) barbuto

business ['bɪznɪs] adj commerciale || s occupazione; commercio; affare m, negozio; faccenda; impiego; **it is not your business** non è affare Suo; **to know one's business** sapere il fatto proprio; **to make it one's business to** proporsi di; **to mean business** (coll) farla sul serio; **to mind one's own business** impicciarsi degli affari propri

businesslike ['bɪznɪs‚laɪk] adj metodico; serio; efficace

busi'ness-man' s (-men') commerciante m, uomo d'affari

busi'ness suit' s abito da passeggio

busi'ness-wom'an s (wom'en) commerciante f

bus'man s (-men) guidatore m d'autobus

buss [bʌs] s (coll) bacione sonoro || tr (coll) baciare sonoramente

bus' stop' s fermata degli autobus

bust [bʌst] s busto; petto; (slang) fallimento; (slang) pugno || tr (slang) rompere; (slang) far fallire; (slang) colpire, dare pugni a; (mil) degradare

buster ['bʌstər] s (coll) ragazzo; (coll) rompitore m

bustle ['bʌsəl] s (on a dress) guardinfante m; attività f || intr affrettarsi

bus·y ['bɪzi] adj (-ier; -iest) occupato || v (pret & pp -ied) tr occupare, tenere occupato; **to busy oneself with** occuparsi di

bus'y·bod'y s (-ies) ficcanaso

bus'y sig'nal s (telp) segnale m d'occupato

but [bʌt] s ma m || adv solo, solamente; **but for** se non . . . per || prep eccetto, ad eccezione di, meno, se non; **all but** quasi || conj ma; che non, e.g., **I never go out in the rain but I catch a cold** non esco mai con la pioggia che non mi pigli un raffreddore

butcher ['bʊtʃər] s macellaio || tr macellare; massacrare

butch'er knife' s coltello da cucina, coltella

butch'er shop' s macelleria

butch·er·y ['bʊtʃəri] s (-ies) macello; carneficina

butler ['bʌtlər] s cantiniere m, credenziere m

butt [bʌt] s (butting) cornata; (of rifle or gun) calcio; (of cigar) mozzicone m; (target) bersaglio; (end) estremità f; (of ridicule) zimbello; (cask) botte f || tr dare cornate a; cozzare contro || intr—**to butt into** (slang) intromettersi in

butter ['bʌtər] s burro || tr imburrare; **to butter up** (coll) adulare

but'ter·cup' s (bot) bottone m d'oro, ranuncolo

but'ter dish' s piattino per il burro, burriera

but'ter·fat' s grasso nel latte

but'ter·fly' s (-flies) farfalla

but'ter knife' s coltello per il burro

but'ter·milk' s latticello

but'ter sauce' s burro fuso

but'ter·scotch' s caramella al burro

buttocks ['bʌtəks] spl chiappe fpl, natiche fpl

button ['bʌtən] s bottone m || tr abbottonare

but'ton·hole' s occhiello, asola || tr attaccare un bottone a

but'ton·hook' s allacciabottoni m

buttress ['bʌtrɪs] s contrafforte m; piedritto || tr rinforzare

buxom ['bʌksəm] adj avvenente, procace

buy [baɪ] s compra || v (pret & pp bought [bɔt]) tr comprare; **to buy off** corrompere; **to buy out** comprare la parte di

buyer ['baɪ-ər] s compratore m

buzz [bʌz] s brusio, ronzio || tr volare a bassa quota sopra; (coll) fare una telefonata a || intr ronzare

buzzard ['bʌzərd] s (hawk) poiana; avvoltoio americano

buzzer ['bʌzər] s suoneria ronzante

buzz′ saw′ *s* sega circolare, segatrice *f* a disco

by [baɪ] *adv* oltre, e.g., **to speed by** correre velocemente oltre; **by and by** fra poco; **by and large** generalmente || *prep* vicino a; di, durante, e.g., **by night** di notte, durante la notte; a, e.g., **they work by the hour** lavorano all'ora; (*not later than, through*) per; (*past*) in fronte a; (*through the agency of*) da; (*according to*) secondo; (math) per, volte; **by far** di molto; **by the way** a proposito

bygone [ˈbaɪ‚gɑn] or [ˈbaɪ‚gɒn] *adj & s* passato; **to let bygones be bygones** dimenticare il passato

bylaw [ˈbaɪ‚lɔ]·*s* legge *f* locale, regolamento di una società

by′-line′ *s* (journ) firma

by′pass′ *s* linea secondaria; (*detour*) deviazione || *tr* fare una deviazione oltre a; (*a difficulty*) evitare

by′path′ *s* sentiero secondario; sentiero privato

by′prod′uct *s* sottoprodotto

bystander [ˈbaɪ‚stændər] *s* astante *m*, spettatore *m*

byway [ˈbaɪ‚we] *s* via traversa

byword [ˈbaɪ‚wʌrd] *s* proverbio; oggetto di obbrobrio

Byzantium [bɪˈzænʃɪ·əm] or [bɪˈzæntɪ·əm] *s* Bisanzio

C

C, c [si] *s* terza lettera dell'alfabeto inglese

cab [kæb] *s* vettura di piazza; tassì *m;* (*of truck or locomotive*) cabina

cabbage [ˈkæbɪdʒ] *s* cavolo, verza

cab′ driv′er *s* autista *m* di piazza; (*of horse-drawn cab*) vetturino

cabin [ˈkæbɪn] *s* (*shed*) capanna; (*hut*) baracca; (aer, naut) cabina

cab′in boy′ *s* mozzo

cabinet [ˈkæbɪnɪt] *s* (*piece of furniture*) vetrina; (*for a radio*) armadietto; (*small room; ministry of a government*) gabinetto

cab′inet·mak′er *s* ebanista *m*

cab′inet·mak′ing *s* ebanisteria

cable [ˈkebəl] *s* cavo; cablogramma; (elec) cablaggio || *tr* cablare, mandare un cablogramma a

ca′ble address′ *s* indirizzo telegrafico

ca′ble car′ *s* funicolare *f*, teleferica

cablegram [ˈkebel‚græm] *s* cablogramma *m*

caboose [kəˈbus] *s* (rr) vagone *m* di coda

cab′stand′ *s* stazione di tassametri

cache [kæʃ] *s* nascondiglio || *tr* mettere in un nascondiglio

cachet [kæˈʃe] *s* sigillo; (*distinguishing feature*) impronta

cackle [ˈkækəl] *s* (*of chickens*) coccodè *m;* (*of people*) chiaccherio || *intr* fare coccodè; ciarlare

cac·tus [ˈkæktəs] *s* (**-tuses** or **-ti** [taɪ]) cactus *m*

cad [kæd] *s* mascalzone *m*

cadaver [kəˈdævər] *s* cadavere *m*

cadaverous [kəˈdævərəs] *adj* cadaverico

caddie [ˈkædi] *s* portamazze *m*

cadence [ˈkedəns] *s* cadenza

cadet [kəˈdet] *s* cadetto

cadmium [ˈkædmɪ·əm] *s* cadmio

cadres [ˈkædriz] *spl* (mil) quadri *mpl*

Caesar′ean sec′tion [sɪˈzɛrɪ·ən] *s* taglio cesareo

café [kæˈfe] *s* caffè *m*, bar *m*, ristorante *m*

ca′fé soci′ety *s* bel mondo

cafeteria [‚kæfəˈtɪrɪ·ə] *s* mensa, tavola calda, caffetteria

caffeine [kæˈfin] or [ˈkæfi·ɪn] *s* caffeinn

cage [kedʒ] *s* gabbia; (*of elevator*) cabina || *tr* ingabbiare

ca·gey [ˈkedʒi] *adj* (**-gier; -giest**) (coll) astuto, cauto

cahoots [kəˈhuts] *s*—**to be in cahoots** (slang) far lega, essere in combutta; **to go cahoots** (slang) dividere in parti eguali

Cain [ken] *s* Caino; **to raise Cain** (slang) arrabbiarsi; (slang) **fare una** sfuriata

Cairo [ˈkaɪro] *s* il Cairo

caisson [ˈkesən] *s* cassone *m;* (archit) cassettone *m*

cajole [kəˈdʒol] *tr* lusingare; persuadere con lusinghe

cajoler·y [kəˈdʒoləri] *s* (**-ies**) lusinga

cake [kek] *s* dolce *m;* torta, pasta; (*with bread-like dough*) focaccia; (*of soap*) saponetta; (*of earth*) zolla; **to take the cake** (coll) essere il colmo || *tr* incrostare || *intr* indurirsi; incrostarsi

calabash [ˈkælə‚bæʃ] *s* zucca a fiasca

calaboose [ˈkælə‚bus] *s* (coll) gattabuia

calamitous [kəˈlæmɪtəs] *adj* calamitoso

calami·ty [kəˈlæmɪti] *s* (**-ties**) calamità *f*

calci·fy [ˈkælsɪ‚faɪ] *v* (*pret & pp* **-fied**) *tr* calcificare || *intr* calcificarsi

calcium [ˈkælsɪ·əm] *s* calcio

calculate [ˈkælkjə‚let] *tr* calcolare || *intr* calcolare; **to calculate on** contare su

cal′culating machine′ *s* (macchina) calcolatrice

calcu·lus [ˈkælkjələs] *s* (**-luses** or **-li** [‚laɪ]) (math, pathol) calcolo

calendar [ˈkæləndər] *s* calendario; (*agenda*) ordine *m* del giorno

calf [kæf] or [kɑf] *s* (**calves** [kævz] or [kɑvz]) vitello; (*of shoes or binding*) pelle *f* di vitello; (*of the leg*) polpaccio

calf′skin′ *s* pelle *f* di vitello

caliber ['kælɪbər] s calibro
calibrate ['kælɪ‚bret] tr calibrare
cali·co ['kælɪ‚ko] s (**-coes** or **-cos**) cotone stampato, calico
California [‚kælɪ'fɔrnɪ‚ə] s la California
calipers ['kælɪpərz] spl compasso a grossezze, calibro
caliph ['kelɪf] or ['kælɪf] s califfo
calisthenic [‚kælɪs'θenɪk] adj ginnastico || **calisthenics** spl ginnastica a corpo libero
calk [kɔk] tr var of **caulk**
call [kɔl] s chiamata; visita; (shout) grido, richiamo; (of bugle) squillo; (of telephone) colpo; (of ship) scalo; obbligo; vocazione; (com) richiesta; **on call** disponibile; **within call** a portata di voce || tr chiamare; convocare; (to awaken) svegliare; **to call back** richiamare; **to call in** (e.g., an expert) fare venire; (e.g., currency) domandare, esigere; **to call off** annullare; **to call out** chiamare; **to call together** convocare; **to call up** chiamare per telefono || intr chiamare; visitare; **to call at** passare per la casa di; (naut) fare scalo a; **to call for** venire a prendere; **to call out** gridare; **to go calling** andare a fare visite
cal'la lil'y ['kælə] s (Zantedeschia aethiopica) calla dei fioristi
call'boy' s (in a hotel) fattorino; (theat) buttafuori m
caller ['kɔlər] s visitatore m
call' girl' s ragazza squillo
calling ['kɔlɪŋ] s appello; professione
call'ing card' s biglietto da visita
call' num'ber s numero telefonico; numero di biblioteca
callous ['kæləs] adj calloso; insensibile
callow ['kælo] adj inesperto, immaturo
call' to arms' s chiamata alle armi
call' to the col'ors s chiamata sotto la bandiera
callus ['kæləs] s callo
calm [kɑm] adj calmo, tranquillo || s calma || tr calmare, tranquillizzare || intr—**to calm down** calmarsi; (said of weather) abbonacciarsi
calmness ['kɑmnɪs] s calma, placidità f, tranquillità f
calomel ['kælə‚mɛl] s calomelano
calorie ['kælərɪ] s caloria
calum·ny ['kæləmnɪ] s (**-nies**) calunnia
Calvary ['kælvərɪ] s (Bib) Calvario
cam [kæm] s camma
camber ['kæmbər] s curvatura; convessità f || tr arcuare || intr curvarsi
cambric ['kembrɪk] s cambrì m
camel ['kæməl] s cammello
came·o ['kæmi‚o] s (**-os**) cammeo
camera ['kæmərə] s macchina fotografica; (mov) cinepresa
cam'era·man' s (**-men**) operatore m
camomile ['kæmə‚maɪl] s camomilla
camouflage ['kæmə‚flɑʒ] s mascheramento || tr mascherare, camuffare
camp [kæmp] s accampamento, campo || intr accamparsi
campaign [kæm'pen] s campagna || intr fare una campagna

campaigner [kæm'penər] s veterano; (pol) propagandista mf
camp' bed' s letto da campo, branda
camper ['kæmpər] s campeggiatore m, campeggista mf
camp'fire' s fuoco di accampamento
camp'ground' s terreno per campeggio
camphor ['kæmfər] s canfora
camp'stool' s seggiolino pieghevole
campus ['kæmpəs] s campo, terreno dell'università
cam'shaft' s albero di distribuzione, albero a camme
can [kæn] s lattina, barattolo; (of gasoline or oil) bidone m || v (pret & pp **canned**; ger **canning**) tr inscatolare; (slang) licenziare || v (pret & cond **could**) aux I can speak English so parlare inglese; **can he go now?** se ne può andare ora?
Canada ['kænədə] s il Canadà
Canadian [kə'nedɪ‚ən] adj & s canadese mf
canal [kə'næl] s canale m
canar·y [kə'nerɪ] s (**-ies**) canarino || **Canaries** spl Canarie fpl
can·cel ['kænsəl] v (pret & pp **-celed** or **-celled**; ger **-celing** or **-celling**) tr cancellare; annullare; revocare; (stamps) timbrare, annullare
cancellation [‚kænsə'leʃən] s cancellazione, annullamento; cassazione; (of a stamp) bollo
cancer ['kænsər] s cancro || **Cancer** s Cancro
cancerous ['kænsərəs] adj canceroso
candela·brum [‚kændə'lɑbrəm] s (**-bra** [brə] or **-brums**) candelabro
candid ['kændɪd] adj candido; sincero, franco
candida·cy ['kændɪdəsɪ] s (**-cies**) candidatura
candidate ['kændɪ‚det] s candidato; (for a degree) laureando
can'did cam'era s camera fotografica indiscreta
candied ['kændɪd] adj candito
candle ['kændəl] s candela || tr (eggs) sperare
can'dle·hold'er s var of **candlestick**
can'dle·light' s luce f or lume m di candela
can'dle·pow'er s (phys) candela
can'dle·stick' s (ornate) candeliere m; (plain) bugia
candor ['kændər] s candore m; ingenuità f
can·dy ['kændɪ] s (**-dies**) dolciumi mpl; **a piece of candy** un bombon || v (pret & pp **-died**) tr candire
can'dy box' s bomboniera
can'dy dish' s bomboniera; (three-tier-high) alzata
can'dy store' s confetteria
cane [ken] s canna, giunco; (for walking) bastone m || tr bastonare; (chairs) impagliare
cane' seat' s sedia impagliata
cane' sug'ar s zucchero di canna
canine ['kenaɪn] adj canino || s (tooth) canino; (dog) cane m
canister ['kænɪstər] s barattolo

canned′ goods′ *spl* conserve *fpl* alimentari; prodotti *mpl* in scatola

canned′ mu′sic *s* (slang) musica su dischi

canner·y [′kænəri] *s* (**-ies**) fabbrica di conserve alimentari

cannibal [′kænɪbəl] *adj & s* cannibale *mf*, antropofago

canning [′kænɪŋ] *s* conservazione

cannon [′kænən] *s* cannone *m*

cannonade [,kænə′ned] *s* cannonata ‖ *tr* cannoneggiare

can′non-ball′ *s* palla da cannone

can′non fod′der *s* carne *f* da cannone

can·ny [′kæni] *adj* (**-nier; -niest**) astuto, fino; malizioso

canoe–[kə′nu] *s* canoa, piroga

canon [′kænən] *s* canone *m*; (*priest*) canonico

canonical [kə′nɑnɪkəl] *adj* canonico ‖ **canonicals** *spl* paramenti liturgici

canonize [′kænə ,naɪz] *tr* canonizzare

can′on law′ *s* diritto canonico

canon·ry [′kænənrɪ] *s* (**-ries**) canonicato

can′ o′pener [′opənər] *s* apriscatole *m*

cano·py [′kænəpɪ] *s* (**-pies**) tenda; baldacchino (*of sky*) (fig) volta

cant [kænt] *adj* ipocrita ‖ *s* linguaggio ipocrita; gergo; (*slope*) inclinazione

cantaloupe [′kæntə ,lop] *s* melone *m*

cantankerous [kæn′tæŋkərəs] *adj* bisbetico, attaccabrighe

canteen [kæn′tin] *s* cantina, spaccio; (*metal bottle*) borraccia

canter [′kæntər] *s* piccolo galoppo ‖ *intr* andare al piccolo galoppo

cantilever [′kæntɪ ,livər] *adj* a cantiliver ‖ *s* trave *f* a sbalzo; (archit) trave *f* a mensola

cantle [′kæntəl] *s* arcione *m* posteriore

canton [′kæntɑn] *s* cantone *m*; regione ‖ *tr* accantonare

cantonment [kæn′tɑnmənt] *s* accantonamento

cantor [′kæntər] or [′kæntər] *s* cantore *m*

canvas [′kænvəs] *s* (*cloth*) olona; (*e.g. on open truck*) copertone *m*; (*painting*) tela; (naut) vela; **under canvas** (naut) a vele spiegate

canvass [′kænvəs] *s* discussione; dibattito; (pol) sollecitazione di voti ‖ *tr* discutere; (*votes*) sollecitare; (*to investigate*) indagare; (com) fare la piazza a ‖ *intr* discutere; sollecitare voti; indagare; (com) fare la piazza

canyon [′kænjən] *s* cañon *m*

cap [kæp] *s* berretto; cuffia; (*of academic costume*) berrettone *m*; (*of bottle*) tappo, capsula; (*e.g., of fountain pen*) cappuccio ‖ *v* (*pret & pp* **capped**; *ger* **capping**) *tr* (*a person*) coprire il capo di; (*s.o.'s head*) coprire con il berretto; (*a bottle*) mettere il tappo a; terminare; **to cap the climax** essere il colmo

capabili·ty [,kepə′bɪlɪtɪ] *s* (**-ties**) capacità *f*, abilità *f*

capable [′kepəbəl] *adj* capace, abile

capacious [kə′pe/əs] *adj* ampio, capace

capaci·ty [kə′pæsɪtɪ] *s* (**-ties**) capacità

f; **filled to capacity** pieno zeppo; **in the capacity of** in veste di

cap′ and bells′ *spl* berretto a sonagli; scettro di buffone

cap′ and gown′ *s* costume accademico, toga e tocco

caparison [kə′pærɪsən] *s* bardatura ‖ *tr* bardare

cape [kep] *s* cappa, mantello; (mil) mantella; (geog) capo

Cape′ of Good′ Hope′ *s* Capo di Buona Speranza

caper [′kepər] *s* capriola; (bot) cappero; **to cut capers** far capriole; (fig) fare monellerie ‖ *intr* fare capriole; saltellare

Cape′ Town′ *s* Città *f* del Capo

capital [′kæpɪtəl] *adj* capitale ‖ *s* (*money*) capitale *m*; (*city*) capitale *f*; (*of column*) capitello

cap′ital expen′ditures *spl* spese *fpl* d'impianto

cap′ital goods′ *spl* beni *mpl* strumentali

capitalism [′kæpɪtə ,lɪzəm] *s* capitalismo

capitalize [′kæpɪtə ,laɪz] *tr* capitalizzare; scrivere con la maiuscola ‖ *intr*—**to capitalize on** approfittare di

cap′ital let′ter *s* lettera maiuscola

cap′ital pun′ishment *s* pena capitale

cap′ital stock′ *s* capitale *m* sociale

capitol [′kæpɪtəl] *s* campidoglio

capitulate [kə′pɪt/ə ,let] *intr* capitolare

capon [′kepɑn] *s* cappone *m*

caprice [kə′pris] *s* capriccio, ghiribizzo

capricious [kə′prɪ/əs] *adj* capriccioso, estroso

Capricorn [′kæprɪ ,kɔrn] *s* Capricorno

capsize [′kæpsaɪz] *tr* capovolgere ‖ *intr* capovolgersi

capstan [′kæpstən] *s* argano

cap′stone′ *s* (archit) coronamento

capsule [′kæpsəl] *adj* in miniatura; riassuntivo ‖ *s* capsula

captain [′kæptən] *s* capitano; (naut) comandante *m*; ‖ *tr* capitanare

caption [′kæp/ən] *s* titolo; (mov) didascalia; (journ) leggenda

captivate [′kæptɪ ,vet] *tr* cattivare, affascinare

captive [′kæptɪv] *adj & s* prigioniero

captivi·ty [′kæp′tɪvɪtɪ] *s* (**-ties**) cattività *f*, prigionia

captor [′kæptər] *s* persona che cattura

capture [′kæpt/ər] *s* cattura, presa; (*person*) prigioniero; (*thing*) bottino ‖ *tr* catturare; prendere

car [kɑr] *s* (*of train*) vagone *m*, vettura; (*automobile*) automobile *m & f*, macchina, vettura; (*of elevator*) cabina; (*of balloon*) navicella; (*for narrow-gauge track*) carrello

carafe [kə′ræf] *s* caraffa

caramel [′kærəmel] or [′kɑrmel] *s* (*burnt sugar*) caramello; (*candy*) caramella appiccicaticcia

carat [′kærət] *s* carato

caravan [′kærə ,væn] *s* carovana; (*covered vehicle*) furgone *m*

caravansa·ry [,kærə′vænsərɪ] *s* (**-ries**) caravanserraglio

caraway [′kærə ,we] *s* cumino

car′barn′ *s* rimessa del tram

carbide ['kɑrbaɪd] s carburo

carbine ['kɑrbaɪn] s carabina

carbol'ic ac'id [kɑr'bɑlɪk] s acido fenico

carbon ['kɑrbən] s (in arc light, battery, auto cylinder) carbone m; carta carbone; (chem) carbonio

car'bon cop'y s copia a carbone, velina

car'bon diox'ide s anidride carbonica

car'bon monox'ide s ossido di carbonio, monossido di carbonio

car'bon pa'per s carta carbone

carbuncle ['kɑrbʌŋkəl] s (stone; boil) carbonchio; (boil) foruncolo

carburetor ['kɑrbə,retər] or ['kɑrbjə-,retər] s carburatore m

carcass ['kɑrkəs] s carcassa; (in state of decay) carogna

card [kɑrd] s (file) scheda; (post card) cartolina; (personal card) biglietto; (announcement) partecipazione; (playing card) carta da gioco; (coll) tipo divertente, bel tipo

card'board' s cartone m

card'-car'rying mem'ber s tesserato

card' case' s portatessere m

card' cat'alogue s schedario

card'hold'er s socio, tesserato

cardiac ['kɑrdɪ,æk] adj & s cardiaco

cardigan ['kɑrdɪgən] s panciotto a maglia

cardinal ['kɑrdɪnəl] adj cardinale, fondamentale || s cardinale m

card' in'dex s schedario

cardiogram ['kɑrdɪ·o,græm] s cardiogramma m

card' par'ty s riunione per giocare a carte

card'sharp' s baro

card' ta'ble s tavoliere m, tavolino da gioco

card' trick' s gioco di prestigio colle carte

care [ker] s cura, custodia; inquietudine f, preoccupazione; cautela; **care of** presso, e.g., **R. Smith care of Jones R.** Smith presso Jones; **to take care** fare attenzione; **to take care of** prendersi cura di, badare a; **to take care of oneself** badare alla salute || intr curarsi, badare; **I don't care** non m'importa; **to care about** preoccuparsi di; **to care for** voler bene a; curarsi di; **to care to** volere

careen [kə'rin] s carenaggio || intr sbandare

career [kə'rir] adj di carriera || s carriera

care'free' adj spensierato

careful ['kerfəl] adj attento; diligente; premuroso; **careful!** faccia attenzione!

careless ['kerlɪs] adj trascurato; imprudente; indifferente

carelessness ['kerlɪsnɪs] s trascuratezza; imprudenza; indifferenza

caress [kə'res] s carezza || tr carezzare, accarezzare

caretaker ['ker,tekər] adj interinale, provvisorio || s custode m; guardiano; (of school) bidello

care'taker gov'ernment s governo interinale

care'worn' adj accasciato dalle preoccupazioni

car'fare' s passaggio, denaro per il tram; (small sum of money) spiccioli mpl

car·go ['kɑrgo] s (-goes or -gos) carico mercantile

car'go boat' s battello da carico

Caribbean [,kærɪ'bi·ən] or [kə-'rɪbɪ·ən] s Mare m dei Caraibi

caricature ['kærɪkət/ər] s caricatura || tr mettere in caricatura

carillon ['kærɪ,lɑn] or [kə'rɪljən] s carillon m || intr suonare il carillon

car'load' s vagone completo, vagonata

carnage ['kɑrnɪdʒ] s carnaio, carneficina

carnal ['kɑrnəl] adj carnale

carnation [kɑr'neʃən] adj incarnato || s garofano; (color) incarnato

carnival ['kɑrnɪvəl] adj carnevalesco || s carnevale m; festa, spettacolo all'aperto

carob ['kærəb] s (fruit) carruba; (tree) carrubo

car·ol ['kærəl] s canzone f popolare; pastorella di Natale || v (pret & pp -oled or -olled; ger -oling or -olling) tr cantare

carom ['kærəm] s carambola || intr carambolare

carousal [kə'rauzəl] s baldoria, gozzoviglia

carouse [kə'rauz] intr fare baldoria, gozzovigliare

carousel [,kærə'zel] or [,kærʊ'zel] s giostra, carosello

carp ['kɑrp] s carpa || intr lagnarsi, criticare

carpenter ['kɑrpəntər] s falegname m

carpentry ['kɑrpəntri] s falegnameria

carpet ['kɑrpɪt] s tappeto || tr coprire con un tappeto, tappetare

carpetbagger ['kɑrpɪt,bægər] s avventuriero; (hist) politicante m

car'pet sweep'er s spazzolone elettrico per tappeti

car'port' s tettoia-garage f

car'-ren'tal serv'ice s servizio di autonoleggi

carriage ['kærɪdʒ] s carrozza; (of gun) affusto; (of typewriter) carrello; (bearing) portamento; (mach) slitta

carrier ['kærɪ·ər] s portatore m; (person or organization in business of carrying goods) spedizioniere m; (of mail) postino; (e.g., on top of station wagon) portabagagli m; (of a disease) veicolo

car'rier pig'eon s piccione m viaggiatore

car'rier wave' s (rad) onda portante

carrion ['kærɪ·ən] s carogne fpl

carrot ['kærət] s carota

car·ry ['kæri] v (pret & pp -ried) tr portare; trasportare; (a burden) sopportare; (an election) guadagnare; (to keep in stock) avere in assortimento; **to carry along** portare con sé; **to carry away** trasportare; entusiasmare; **to carry forward** riportare; **to carry out** eseguire; **to carry**

through completare; **to carry weight** aver importanza || *intr* avere la portata (di), e.g., **this gun carries two miles** questo cannone ha la portata di due miglia; **to carry on** continuare; (coll) fare baccano

cart [kɑrt] *s* carro, carretto; (*for shopping*) carrello; **to put the cart before the horse** mettere il carro davanti ai buoi || *tr* trasportare col carro

carte blanche ['kɑrt'blɑnʃ] *s* carta bianca

cartel [kɑr'tɛl] *s* cartello

Carthage ['kɑrθɪdʒ] *s* Cartagine *f*

cart' horse' *s* cavallo da tiro

cartilage ['kɑrtɪlɪdʒ] *s* cartilagine *f*

carton [kɑr'tɑn] *s* cartone *m*; scatola di cartone; (*of cigarettes*) stecca

cartoon [kɑr'tun] *s* disegno; caricatura; (*comic strip*) fumetto; (mov) disegno animato || *tr* fare caricature di

cartoonist [kɑr'tunɪst] *s* disegnatore *m*; caricaturista *mf*

cartridge ['kɑrtrɪdʒ] *s* cartuccia; (*e.g., of camera*) caricatore *m*

car'tridge belt' *s* cartucciera; (mil) giberna

car'tridge clip' *s* serbatoio

cart'wheel' *s* ruota di carro; **to turn cartwheels** fare la ruota

carve [kɑrv] *tr* (*meats*) trinciare; scolpire, intagliare

carv'ing knife' *s* trinciante *m*

car' wash'er *s* lavamacchine *m*

cascade [kæs'ked] *s* cascata || *intr* cadere a mo' di cascata

case [kes] *s* (*box*) cassetta; (*of watch*) calotta; (*outer covering*) astuccio; (*instance*) caso; (gram) caso; (law) causa; (typ) cassa; **in case** in caso, nel caso; **in no case** in nessun modo || *tr* rinchiudere; (*to package*) impaccare; (slang) ispezionare

casement ['kesmənt] *s* telaio di finestra; finestra a ganghere

case' stud'y *s* casistica

cash [kæʃ] *s* contante *m*; **cash on delivery** spedizione contro assegno; **for cash** in contanti; **a pronta cassa** || *tr* (*a check*) cambiare, incassare || *intr* **—to cash in on** (coll) trarre profitto da

cash' box' *s* cassa

cashew ['kæʃu] *s* (*tree*) anacardio; (*nut*) mandorla indiana

cashier [kæ'ʃɪr] *s* cassiere *m* || *tr* (*to dismiss*) silurare

cashier's' check' *s* assegno circolare

cash' reg'ister *s* registratore *m* cassa

casing ['kesɪŋ] *s* rivestimento; tubo di rivestimento; (*for salami*) budello; (*of tire*) copertone *m*

cask [kæsk] or [kɑsk] *s* barile *m*, botte *f*

casket ['kæskɪt] or ['kɑskɪt] *s* scrigno, cofanetto; (*coffin*) bara, cassa da morto

casserole ['kæsə‚rol] *s* tegame *m* di terracotta or vetro; (*food*) pasticcio, timballo

cassette [kə'sɛt] *s* (mus) musicassetta; (mus & phot) caricatore *m*

cassock ['kæsək] *s* sottana, tonaca; **to doff the cassock** gettar la tonaca alle ortiche

cast [kæst] or [kɑst] *s* getto; lancio; forma; (mach) pezzo fuso; (surg) gesso; (theat) complesso artistico, cast *m* || *v* (*pret & pp* cast) *tr* gettare; fondere; (*a ballot*) dare; (*the roles*) distribuire; (*actors*) scegliere; **to cast aside** abbandonare; **to cast down** deprimere; **to cast lots** tirare a sorte; **to cast off** abbandonare; **to cast out** buttar fuori || *intr* tirare i dadi; **to cast off** (naut) mollare gli ormeggi

castanets [‚kæstə'nɛts] *spl* nacchere *fpl*

cast'a‧way' *adj & s* naufrago; (fig) reprobo

caste [kæst] or [kɑst] *s* casta; **to lose caste** perdere prestigio

caster ['kæstər] or ['kɑstər] *s* ampollina, saliera, pepaiola; (*roller*) rotella per i mobili

castigate ['kæstɪ‚get] *tr* castigare, punire; correggere

Castile [kæs'til] *s* (la) Castiglia

Castilian [kæs'tɪljən] *adj & s* castigliano

casting ['kæstɪŋ] or ['kɑstɪŋ] *s* getto, getto fuso; (*in fishing*) pesca a getto

cast' i'ron *s* ghisa

cast'-i'ron *adj* fatto di ghisa; (*e.g., stomach*) fatto d'acciaio, di struzzo

castle ['kæsəl] or ['kɑsəl] *s* castello; (chess) torre *f* || *tr & intr* (chess) arroccare

cas'tle in Spain' or **cas'tle in the air'** *s* castello in aria

cast'off' *adj* abbandonato || *s* rigetto; persona abbandonata; (typ) stima

cas'tor oil' ['kæstər] or ['kɑstər] *s* olio di ricino

castrate ['kæstret] *tr* castrare

casual ['kæʒʊ‧əl] *adj* casuale, fortuito; (*clothing*) semplice, sportivo

casually ['kæʒʊ‧əli] *adv* con disinvoltura; (*by chance*) fortuitamente

casual‧ty ['kæʒʊ‧əlti] *s* (**-ties**) accidente *m*, disastro; vittima; **casualties** (*in war*) perdite *fpl*

casuist‧ry ['kæʒʊ‧ɪstri] *s* (**-ries**) (*specious reasoning*) speciosità *f*; (philos) casistica

cat [kæt] *s* gatto; donna perfida; **to let the cat out of the bag** lasciarsi scappare il segreto

cataclysm ['kætə‚klɪzəm] *s* cataclisma *m*

catacomb ['kætə‚kom] *s* catacomba

catalogue ['kætə‚lɔg] or ['kætə‚lɑg] *s* catalogo || *tr* catalogare

cat'alogue sale' *s* vendita per corrispondenza

catalyst ['kætəlɪst] *s* catalizzatore *m*

catapult ['kætə‚pʌlt] *s* catapulta || *tr* catapultare

cataract ['kætə‚rækt] *s* cataratta

catarrh [kə'tɑr] *s* catarro

catastrophe [kə'tæstrəfi] *s* catastrofe *f*, disastro

cat'call' s urlo di disapprovazione

catch [kætʃ] s presa; cattura; (of door) paletto; (in marriage) partito; (trick) inganno; (of fish) pesca; (mach) nottolino ‖ v (pret & pp **caught** [kɔt]) tr prendere, acchiappare; (a cold) pigliare, buscarsi; **to catch hold of** afferrare; **to catch it** (coll) prendersele; **to catch oneself** contenersi; **to catch up** sorprendere sul fatto ‖ intr agganciarsi; (said of a disease) trasmettersi; **to catch on** capire l'antifona; **to catch up** mettersi al corrente; **to catch up with** raggiungere

catch'-as-catch'-can' s lotta libera americana

catch' ba'sin s ricettacolo di fogna

catcher ['kætʃər] s ricevitore m, catcher m

catching ['kætʃɪŋ] adj (alluring) seducente; (infectious) contagioso

catch'word' s slogan m; (typ) chiamata; (typ) esponente m in testa di pagina

catch·y ['kætʃi] adj (-ier; -iest) attraente, vivo; (tricky) insidioso

catechism ['kætɪˌkɪzəm] s catechismo

catego·ry ['kætɪˌgori] s (-ries) categoria

cater ['ketər] intr provvedere cibo; **to cater to** servire

cater-cornered ['kætər,kɔrnərd] adj diagonale ‖ adv diagonalmente

caterer ['ketərər] s provveditore m

caterpillar ['kætər,pɪlər] s bruco

cat'erpillar trac'tor s trattore m a cingoli

cat'fish' s pesce m gatto

cat'gut' s (mus) corda di minugia; (surg) catgut m, cattegù m

cathartic [kə'θɑrtɪk] adj & s catartico

cathedral [kə'θidrəl] s cattedrale f

catheter ['kæθɪtər] s catetere m

catheterize ['kæθɪtəˌraɪz] tr cateterizzare

cathode ['kæθod] s catodo

catholic ['kæθəlɪk] adj cattolico; (e.g., mind) liberale ‖ **Catholic** adj & s cattolico

catkin ['kætkɪn] s (bot) amento, gattino

cat'nap' s corta siesta, sonnellino

cat-o'-nine-tails [ˌkætə'naɪn,telz] s gatto a nove code

cat's'-paw' s gonzo; (breeze) brezzolina

catsup ['kætsəp] or ['ketʃəp] s salsa piccante di pomodoro, ketchup m

cat'tail' s stiancia

cattle ['kætəl] s bestiame grosso

cat'tle-man s (-men) allevatore m di bestiame

cat·ty ['kæti] adj (-tier; -tiest) malizioso, maligno; felino, gattesco

cat'walk' s passerella, ballatoio

Caucasian [kɔ'keʒən] or [kɔ'keʃən] adj & s caucasico

caucus ['kɔkəs] s comitato elettorale; conciliabolo politico

cauldron ['kɔldrən] s calderone m

cauliflower ['kɔlɪˌflaʊ·ər] s cavolfiore m

caulk [kɔk] tr calafatare, stoppare

cause [kɔz] s causa, cagione ‖ tr causare, cagionare; **to cause to** + inf

fare + inf, e.g., **she caused him to fall** l'ha fatto cadere

cause'way' s strada rialzata, scarpata

caustic ['kɔstɪk] adj caustico

cauterize ['kɔtəˌraɪz] tr cauterizzare

caution ['kɔʃən] s cautela, prudenza; ammonizione ‖ tr ammonire

cautious ['kɔʃəs] adj prudente

cavalcade ['kævəlˌked] or [ˌkævəl'ked] s cavalcata

cavalier [ˌkævə'lir] or ['kævə,lir] adj altero, sdegnoso; disinvolto ‖ s cavaliere m

caval·ry ['kævəlri] s (-ries) cavalleria

cav'alry·man or **cav'alry·man** s (-men' or -men) cavalleggero, soldato di cavalleria

cave [kev] s caverna, grotta ‖ intr— **to cave in** sprofondarsi; (to give in) (coll) cedere; (to become exhausted) (coll) diventare spossato

cave'-in' s sprofondamento

cave' man' s troglodita m

cavern ['kævərn] s caverna

caviar ['kævɪˌɑr] or [ˌkævɪ'ɑr] s caviale m

cav·il ['kævɪl] v (pret & pp -iled or -illed; ger -iling or -illing) intr cavillare

cavi·ty ['kævɪti] s (-ties) cavità f; (in tooth) carie f

cavort [kə'vɔrt] intr far capriole

caw [kɔ] s gracchiamento ‖ intr gracchiare

cease [sis] tr cessare, interrompere ‖ intr cessare, interrompersi; **to cease** + ger cessare di + inf

cease'-fire' s sospensione delle ostilità

ceaseless ['sislɪs] adj incessante

cedar ['sidər] s cedro; legno di cedro

cede [sid] tr cedere, trasferire

ceiling ['silɪŋ] s soffitto; (aer) altezza massima; **to hit the ceiling** (slang) uscire dai gangheri

ceil'ing price' s calmiere m, tetto

celebrate ['sɛlɪˌbret] tr celebrare ‖ intr celebrare; far festa

celebrated ['sɛlɪˌbretɪd] adj celebre, famoso

celebration [ˌsɛlɪ'breʃən] s celebrazione

celebri·ty [sɪ'lɛbrɪti] s (-ties) celebrità f

celery ['sɛləri] s sedano

celestial [sɪ'lɛstʃəl] adj celestiale, celeste

celibacy ['sɛləbəsi] s celibato

celibate ['sɛləˌbet] or ['sɛləbɪt] adj & s celibe m; nubile f

cell [sɛl] s (e.g., of jail) cella; (of electric battery) elemento; (biol, phys, pol) cellula

cellar ['sɛlər] s cantina; (partly above ground) seminterrato

cellist or **'cellist** ['tʃɛlɪst] s violoncellista mf

cel·lo or **'cel·lo** ['tʃɛlo] s (-los) violoncello

cellophane ['sɛləˌfen] s cellofan m

celluloid ['sɛljəˌlɔɪd] s celluloide f

Celtic ['sɛltɪk] or ['kɛltɪk] adj celtico ‖ s lingua celtica

cement [sɪ'mɛnt] *s* cemento || *tr* cementare

cemete·ry ['sɛmɪ‚tɛri] *s* (**-ries**) cimitero

censer ['sɛnsər] *s* turibolo

censor ['sɛnsər] *s* censore *m* || *tr* censurare

censure ['sɛnʃər] *s* censura, critica || *tr* censurare, criticare

census ['sɛnsəs] *s* censo, censimento

cent [sɛnt] *s* centesimo di dollaro, cent *m*; **not to have a red cent to one's name** non avere il becco di un quattrino

centaur ['sɛntɔr] *s* centauro

centennial [sɛn'tɛnɪ‚əl] *adj* & *s* centenario

center ['sɛntər] *s* centro || *tr* centrare, concentrare || *intr*—**to center on** concentrarsi su

cen'ter·board' *s* chiglia mobile

cen'ter·piece' *s* centro tavola

cen'ter punch' *s* punzone *m*, punteruolo

centigrade ['sɛntɪ‚gred] *adj* centigrado

centimeter ['sɛntɪ‚mitər] *s* centimetro

centipede ['sɛntɪ‚pid] *s* centopiedi *m*

cento ['sɛnto] *s* centone *m*

central ['sɛntrəl] *adj* centrale || *s* centrale *f*, centrale telefonica; (*operator*) telefonista *mf*

Cen'tral Amer'ica *s* l'America Centrale

centralize ['sɛntrə‚laɪz] *tr* centralizzare || *intr* centralizzarsi

centu·ry ['sɛntʃəri] *s* (**-ries**) secolo

ceramic [sɪ'ræmɪk] *adj* ceramico || **ceramics** *ssg* ceramica; *spl* oggetti *mpl* di ceramica

cereal ['sɪrɪ‚əl] *adj* cerealicolo || *s* (*grain*) cereale *m*; (*uncooked breakfast food, e.g., cornflakes*) fiocchi *mpl*; (*breakfast food to be cooked*) farina

cerebral ['sɛrɪbrəl] *adj* cerebrale

ceremonious [‚sɛrɪ'monɪ‚əs] *adj* cerimonioso

ceremo·ny ['sɛrɪ‚moni] *s* (**-nies**) cerimonia; **to stand on ceremony** fare cerimonie

certain ['sʌrtən] *adj* certo; **for certain** di o per certo; **to be certain to** + *inf* non mancare di + *inf*

certainly ['sʌrtənli] *adv* certamente; (*gladly*) con piacere

certain·ty ['sʌrtənti] *s* (**-ties**) certezza

certificate [sər'tɪfɪkɪt] *s* certificato; (*com*) titolo || [sər'tɪfɪ‚ket] *tr* certificare

cer'tified check' *s* assegno a copertura garantita

cer'tified cop'y *s* estratto; (*as a formula on a document*) per copia conforme

cer'tified pub'lic account'ant *s* esperto contabile

certi·fy ['sʌrtɪ‚faɪ] *v* (*pret & pp* **-fied**) *tr* certificare, garantire

cervix ['sʌrvɪks] *s* (**cervices** (sər-'vaɪsiz] cervice *f*

cessation [sɛ'seʃən] *s* cessazione

cesspool ['sɛs‚pul] *s* pozzo nero

Ceylo·nese [‚silə'niz] *adj* & *s* (**-nese**) singalese *mf*

chafe [tʃef] *s* irritazione || *tr* (*the hands*) strofinare; irritare; (*to wear*

away) logorare || *intr* irritarsi; logorarsi

chaff [tʃæf] or [tʃɑf] *s* lolla; pula; (*joke*) burla; (fig) loppa

chaf'ing dish' *s* fornello a spirito

cha·grin [ʃə'grɪn] *s* cruccio, dispiacere *m* || *v* (*pret* **-grined** or **-grinned**; *ger* **-grining** or **-grinning**) *tr* crucciare, affliggere

chain [tʃen] *s* catena; (*e.g., for necklace*) catenella || *tr* incatenare

chain' gang' *s* catena di forzati

chain' reac'tion *s* reazione a catena

chain' saw' *s* motosega

chain'-smoke' *intr* fumare come un turco

chain' store' *s* negozio a catena

chair [tʃɛr] *s* sedia, seggiola; (*of important person*) seggio; (*at a university*) cattedra; (*chairman*) presidente *m*, presidenza; **to take the chair** cominciare una riunione || *tr* (*a meeting*) presiedere

chair' lift' *s* seggiovia

chair'man *s* (**-men**) presidente *m*

chair'man·ship' *s* presidenza

chair'wom'an *s* (**-wom'en**) presidentessa

chalice ['tʃælɪs] *s* calice *m*

chalk [tʃɔk] *s* gesso || *tr* marcare or scrivere col gesso; **to chalk up** prendere appunti di; attribuire

chalk' talk' *s* conferenza illustrata

chalk·y ['tʃɔki] *adj* (**-ier**; **-iest**) gessoso

challenge ['tʃælɪndʒ] *s* sfida; (law) ricusazione; (mil) chi va là *m* || *tr* sfidare; (*a juror*) (law) ricusare; (mil) dare il chi va là a

chamber ['tʃembər] *s* camera, stanza; (*of a palace*) aula; (*of a judge*) gabinetto

chamberlain ['tʃembərlɪn] *s* ciambellano

cham'ber·maid' *s* cameriera

cham'ber of com'merce *s* camera di commercio

cham'ber pot' *s* orinale *m*

chameleon [kə'milɪ‚ən] *s* camaleonte *m*

cham·ois ['ʃæmi] *s* (**-ois**) camoscio

champ [tʃæmp] *s* (slang) campione *m* || *tr* masticare rumorosamente; (*the bit*) mordere || *intr* masticare rumorosamente

champagne [ʃæm'pen] *s* champagne *m*, spumante *m*

champion ['tʃæmpɪ‚ən] *s* campione *m* || *tr* difendere; farsi paladino di

championship ['tʃæmpɪ‚ən‚ʃɪp] *s* campionato

chance [tʃæns] or [tʃɑns] *adj* casuale, fortuito || *s* occasione; caso; probabilità *f*; rischio; biglietto di lotteria; **by chance** per caso; **not to stand a chance** non avere la probabilità di riuscita; **to take one's chances** arrischiarsi; **to wait for a chance** attendere l'opportunità || *intr* succedere; **to chance upon** imbattersi in

chancel ['tʃænsəl] or ['tʃɑnsəl] *s* presbiterio, coro

chanceller·y ['tʃænsələri] or ['tʃɑnsələri] *s* (**-ies**) cancelleria

chancellor ['tʃænsələr] or ['tʃɑnsələr] s cancelliere m
chandelier [,ʃændə'lir] s lampadario
change [tʃendʒ] s cambiamento; (*of clothes*) muta; (*of currency*) cambio; (*coins*) spiccioli mpl; **for a change** tanto per cambiare; **to keep the change** tenere il resto ‖ tr cambiare, rimpiazzare; (*clothes*) cambiare, cambiarsi di ‖ intr cambiare, mutare
changeable ['tʃendʒəbəl] adj mutevole, variabile, incostante
change' of heart' s pentimento, conversione
change' of life' s menopausa
chan·nel ['tʃænəl] s canale m; tubo, passaggio; stretto; (*of river*) alveo; (*groove*) solco; (*rad, telv*) canale m; **through channels** per via gerarchica ‖ v (*pret & pp* -**neled** or -**nelled**; *ger* -**neling** or -**nelling**) tr incanalare; (*a river*) incassare ‖ **the Channel** il Canale della Manica
chant [tʃænt] or [tʃɑnt] s canto; salmodia; canzone f ‖ tr & intr cantare
chanticleer ['tʃæntɪ,klɪr] s il gallo
chaos ['ke·ɑs] s caos m
chaotic [ke'ɑtɪk] adj caotico
chap [tʃæp] s (*fellow*) individuo, tipo; (*of skin*) screpolatura; **chaps** pantaloni mpl di cuoio ‖ v (*pret & pp* **chapped**; *ger* **chapping**) tr screpolare ‖ intr screpolarsi
chapel ['tʃæpəl] s cappella
chaperon or **chaperone** ['ʃæpə,ron] s accompagnatrice f (di signorina) ‖ tr accompagnare
chaplain ['tʃæplɪn] s cappellano
chaplet ['tʃæplɪt] s (*wreath*) corona, ghirlanda; rosario
chapter ['tʃæptər] s capitolo; (*of a club*) sezione
chap'ter and verse' s—**to give chapter and verse** citare le autorità
char [tʃɑr] v (*pret & pp* **charred**; *ger* **charring**) tr carbonizzare; bruciare
character ['kærɪktər] s carattere m; lettera, scrittura; indole f; (*theat*) personaggio; (*coll*) tipo; **in character** caratteristico di lui (lei, loro, ecc.)
char'acter ac'tor s caratterista m
char'acter ac'tress s caratterista f
char'acter assassina'tion s linciaggio morale
characteristic [,kærɪktə'rɪstɪk] adj caratteristico ‖ s caratteristica
characterize ['kærɪktə,raɪz] tr caratterizzare
char'coal' s carbone m di legna, carbone m dolce; (*for sketching*) carboncino; (*sketch*) disegno al carboncino
charge [tʃɑrdʒ] s carica; incarico; responsabilità f; (*indictment*) accusa; costo; prezzo; debito; **in charge** in comando; **in charge of** a cura di; **to take charge of** prendersi cura di ‖ tr caricare; comandare; accusare; (*a price*) fare pagare; mettere in conto; **to charge s.o. with s.th** addebitare qlco a qlcu; accusare qlcu di qlco ‖ intr fare una carica

charge' account' s conto corrente
chargé d'affaires [ʃɑr'ʒe də'fer] s (**chargés d'affaires**) incaricato d'affari
charger ['tʃɑrdʒər] s cavallo di battaglia; (*of a battery*) caricatore m
chariot ['tʃærɪ·ət] s cocchio
charioteer [,tʃærɪ·ə'tɪr] s auriga m
charis·ma [kə'rɪzmə] s (-**mata** [mətə]) fascino personale; (theol) carisma m
charitable ['tʃærɪtəbəl] adj (*person*) caritatevole; (*institution*) caritativo
chari·ty ['tʃærɪti] s (-**ties**) carità f; associazione di beneficenza
charlatan ['ʃɑrlətən] s ciarlatano
charlatanism ['ʃɑrlətən,ɪzəm] s ciarlataneria
Charlemagne ['ʃɑrlə,men] s Carlomagno
Charles [tʃɑrlz] s Carlo
char'ley horse' ['tʃɑrli] s (coll) crampo
charlotte ['ʃɑrlət] s charlotte f ‖ **Charlotte** s Carlotta
charm [tʃɑrm] s fascino; amuleto; portafortuna m ‖ tr incantare, stregare
charming ['tʃɑrmɪŋ] adj affascinante
charnel ['tʃɑrnəl] adj orribile ‖ s ossario
chart [tʃɑrt] s carta geografica; lista; diagramma m ‖ tr tracciare
charter ['tʃɑrtər] s statuto; privilegio ‖ tr (*a company*) fondare; (*a conveyance*) noleggiare
char'ter mem'ber s socio fondatore
char'wom'an s (-**wom'en**) domestica per la pulizia
chase [tʃes] s inseguimento; caccia; (typ) telaio ‖ tr inseguire; cacciare; (*to chisel*) cesellare; **to chase away** scacciare ‖ intr—**to chase after** inseguire
chaser ['tʃesər] s cacciatore m; (coll) bibita da bersi dopo un liquore
chasm ['kæzəm] s abisso, baratro
chas·sis ['tʃæsi] s (-**sis** [siz]) telaio
chaste [tʃest] adj casto
chasten ['tʃesən] tr castigare
chastise [tʃæs'taɪz] tr castigare
chastity ['tʃæstɪti] s castità f
chat [tʃæt] s chiacchierata ‖ v (*pret & pp* **chatted**; *ger* **chatting**) intr chiacchierare
chatelaine ['ʃætə,len] s castellana
chattels ['tʃætəlz] spl beni mpl mobili
chatter ['tʃætər] s cicaleccio; balbettio; (*of teeth*) battito ‖ intr cicalare; balbettare; (*said of teeth*) battere
chat'ter·box' s chiacchierone m
chauffeur ['ʃofər] or [ʃo'fʌr] s autista mf ‖ intr fare l'autista
cheap [tʃip] adj a buon mercato, economico; (*of poor quality*) scadente; **to feel cheap** vergognarsi ‖ adv a buon mercato
cheapen ['tʃipən] tr deprezzare; avvilire; rendere di cattivo gusto
cheapness ['tʃipnəs] s buon mercato, prezzo basso
cheat [tʃit] s truffa; truffatore m ‖ tr imbrogliare, truffare ‖ intr truffare; (*at cards*) barare
check [tʃek] s arresto, pausa; ostacolo;

esame *m;* verifica, controllo; *(of bank)* assegno; *(for baggage)* tagliando, scontrino; *(square pattern)* quadretto; *(fabric in squares)* tessuto a scacchi; *(in a restaurant)* conto; **in check** controllato, sotto controllo; (chess) sotto scacco ∥ *tr* fermare; confrontare; ispezionare; marcare; *(e.g., a coat)* depositare; disegnare a quadretti; (chess) dare scacco a; **to check off** controllare marcando; **to check on** controllare, verificare ∥ *intr* fermarsi; corrispondere perfettamente; **to check in** scendere (a un albergo); **to check out** andar via; pagare il conto; **to check up on** controllare

check'book' s libretto d'assegni

checker ['tʃɛkər] *s* ispettore *m;* quadretto; *(in game of checkers)* pedina; **checkers** dama ∥ *tr* variegare; marcare a quadretti

check'er-board' *s* scacchiera

check'ered *adj (e.g., career)* pieno di vicissitudini; *(marked with squares)* a scacchi; *(in color)* variegato

check'ing account' s conto corrente

check'mate' s scacco matto ∥ *tr* dare scacco matto a ∥ *interj* scacco matto!

check'off' *s* trattenute *fpl* sindacali

check'-out' *s (from hotel room)* partenza; *(time)* ora della partenza; *(examination)* esame *m* di controllo; *(in a supermarket)* cassa

check'point' s punto di ispezione

check'room' s guardaroba *m*

check'up' s *(of car)* ispezione; *(of patient)* esame *m* (fisico)

cheek [tʃik] *s* guancia, gota; (coll) faccia tosta

cheek'bone' s zigomo

cheek-y ['tʃiki] *adj* (**-ier; -iest**) (coll) impudente, sfacciato

cheer [tʃɪr] *s* gioia, allegria; applauso; **of good cheer** di buon umore ∥ *tr* riempire di gioia, rallegrare; applaudire; ricevere con applausi ∥ *intr* rallegrarsi; **cheer up!** animo!, coraggio!

cheerful ['tʃɪrfəl] *adj* allegro, di buon umore; *(willing)* volonteroso

cheerless ['tʃɪrlɪs] *adj* tetro, triste

cheese [tʃiz] *s* formaggio ∥ *intr—* **cheese it!** (slang) scappa via!

cheese' cake' *s* torta di formaggio; (slang) pin-up girl *f*

cheese'cloth' *s* etamine *f*, stamigna

chees-y [tʃisi] *adj* (**-ier; -iest**) di formaggio; come il formaggio; (slang) meschino, di cattiva qualità

chef [ʃɛf] *s* chef *m*, capocuoco

chemical ['kɛmɪkəl] *adj* chimico ∥ *s* prodotto chimico

chemise [ʃə'miz] *s* sottoveste *f*

chemist ['kɛmɪst] *s* chimico

chemistry ['kɛmɪstri] *s* chimica

cherish ['tʃɛrɪʃ] *tr* accarezzare; *(a memory)* custodire; *(a hope)* nutrire

cher-ry ['tʃɛri] *s* (**-ries**) *(tree)* ciliegio; *(fruit)* ciliegia

cher-ub ['tʃɛrəb] *s* (**-ubim** [əbɪm] & **-ubs**) cherubino

chess [tʃɛs] *s* scacchi *mpl*

chess'board' *s* scacchiera

chess'man' or **chess'man** *s* (**-men'** or **-men**) scacco

chest [tʃɛst] *s* petto; *(box)* cassapanca; *(furniture with drawers)* cassettone *m;* *(for money)* forziere *m*

chestnut ['tʃɛsnət] *s (tree, wood, color)* castagno; *(nut)* castagna

chest' of drawers' *s* cassettone *m*

cheval' glass' [ʃə'væl] *s* psiche *f*

chevalier [ˌʃɛvə'lɪr] *s* cavaliere *m*

chevron ['ʃɛvrən] *s* gallone *m*

chew [tʃu] *tr* masticare; **to chew the cud** ruminare; **to chew the rag** (slang) chiacchierare ∥ *intr* masticare

chew'ing gum' *s* gomma da masticare

chic [ʃik] *adj* & *s* chic

chicaner-y [ʃɪ'kɛnəri] *s* (**-ies**) trucco, rigiro

chick [tʃɪk] *s* pulcino; (slang) ragazza

chicken ['tʃɪkən] *s* pollo, pollastro; (coll) giovane *mf;* **to be chicken** (slang) avere la fifa ∥ *intr—* **to chicken out** (coll) indietreggiare

chick'en coop' *s* pollaio

chick'en feed' *s* (slang) spiccioli *mpl*

chicken-hearted ['tʃɪkən ˌhɑrtɪd] *adj* timido, fifone

chick'en pox' *s* varicella

chick'en store' *s* polleria

chick'en wire' *s* rete metallica esagonale

chick'pea' *s* cece *m*

chico-ry ['tʃɪkəri] *s* (**-ries**) cicoria

chide [tʃaɪd] *v (pret* **chided** or **chid** [tʃɪd]; *pp* **chided, chid,** or **chidden** ['tʃɪdən]) *tr & intr* rimproverare, correggere

chief [tʃif] *adj* principale, sommo, supremo ∥ *s* capo, comandante supremo; (slang) padrone *m*

chief' exec'utive *s* capo del governo

chief' jus'tice *s* presidente *m* di una corte; presidente *m* della corte suprema

chiefly ['tʃifli] *adv* principalmente

chief' of staff' *s* capo di stato maggiore

chief' of state' *s* capo dello stato

chieftain ['tʃiftən] *s* capo

chiffon [ʃɪ'fɑn] *s* velo trasparente, chiffon *m;* **chiffons** trine *fpl*

chiffonier [ˌʃɪfə'nɪr] *s* mobile *m* a cassettini, chiffonier *m*

chilblain ['tʃɪl ˌblɛn] *s* gelone *m*

child [tʃaɪld] *s* (**children** ['tʃɪldrən]) bebè *mf*, bambino; figlio; discendente *mf;* **with child** incinta

child'birth' *s* parto

childhood ['tʃaɪldhʊd] *s* infanzia

childish ['tʃaɪldɪʃ] *adj* infantile

childishness ['tʃaɪldɪʃnɪs] *s* puerilità *f*, infanzia

child' la'bor *s* lavoro dei minorenni

childless ['tʃaɪldlɪs] *adj* senza figli

child'like' *adj* infantile, innocente

child's' play' *s* un gioco

child' wel'fare *s* protezione dell'infanzia

Chile ['tʃɪli] *s* il Cile

Chilean ['tʃɪlɪ-ən] *adj* cileno

chil'i sauce' ['tʃɪli] s salsa di pomodoro con peperoni

chill [tʃɪl] adj freddo || s freddo; brivido di freddo; freddezza; (depression) abbattimento || tr raffreddare; (a metal) temprare; (fig) scoraggiare || intr raffreddarsi

chill·y ['tʃɪli] adj (-ier; -iest) fresco, freddiccio; (reception) freddo

chime [tʃaɪm] s scampanio; chimes campanello || intr scampanare; to chime in cominciare a cantare all'unisono; (coll) intromettersi

chime' clock' s orologio con carillon

chimney ['tʃɪmni] s camino; (of factory) ciminiera; to smoke like a chimney fumare come un turco

chim'ney flue' s tubo di stufa, canna del camino

chim'ney pot' s testa della canna fumaria, comignolo

chim'ney sweep' s spazzacamino

chimpanzee [tʃɪm'pænzi] or [ˌtʃɪmpæn'zi] s scimpanzé m

chin [tʃɪn] s mento; to keep one's chin up (coll) non perdersi di coraggio; to take it on the chin (slang) subire una sconfitta || v (pret & pp chinned; ger chinning) tr—to chin oneself sollevarsi fino al mento (ai manubri) || intr (slang) chiacchierare

china ['tʃaɪnə] s porcellana || China s la Cina

chi'na clos'et s armadio per le stoviglie

chi'na·ware' s porcellana, stoviglie fpl

Chi·nese [tʃaɪ'niz] adj cinese || s (-nese) cinese mf

Chi'nese lan'tern s lampioncino alla veneziana

Chi'nese puz'zle s rebus m

chink [tʃɪŋk] s fessura

chin' strap' s sottogola

chintz [tʃɪnts] s chintz m

chip [tʃɪp] s scheggia; frammento; (in card games) gettone m; (of wood) truciolo; chip off the old block vero figlio di suo padre (di sua madre); chip on one's shoulder propensità f a attaccar brighe || v (pret & pp chipped; ger chipping) tr scheggiare; to chip in contribuire || intr scheggiarsi

chipmunk ['tʃɪpˌmʌŋk] s tamia

chipper ['tʃɪpər] adj (coll) allegro, vivo

chiropodist [kaɪ'rɑpədɪst] or [kɪ'rɑpədɪst] s callista mf, pedicure mf

chiropractice ['kaɪrəˌpræktɪs] s chiropratica

chirp [tʃʌrp] s (of birds) cinguettio; (of crickets) cri cri m || intr cinguettare; fare cri cri

chis·el ['tʃɪzəl] s (for wood and metal) scalpello; (for metal) cesello || v (pret & pp -eled or -elled; ger -eling or -elling) tr scalpellare; cesellare; (slang) imbrogliare || intr (slang) imbrogliare, fare l'imbroglione

chiseler ['tʃɪzələr] s scalpellino; cesellatore m; (slang) imbroglione m

chit-chat ['tʃɪtˌtʃæt] s chiacchierata

chivalrous ['ʃɪvəlrəs] adj cavalleresco

chivalry ['ʃɪvəlri] s cavalleria

chive [tʃaɪv] s cipolla porraia

chloride ['klɔraɪd] s cloruro

chlorine ['klɔrin] s cloro

chloroform ['klɔrə ˌfɔrm] s cloroformio || tr cloroformizzare

chlorophyll ['klɔrəfɪl] s clorofilla

chock [tʃɑk] s (wedge) bietta, cuneo

chock-full ['tʃɑk'ful] adj colmo, pieno zeppo

chocolate ['tʃɑkəlɪt] or ['tʃɑkəlɪt] s (candy) cioccolato; (drink) cioccolata

choc'olate bar' s barretta di cioccolato

choice [tʃɔɪs] adj di prima scelta, superiore || s scelta; (variety) assortimento

choir [kwaɪr] s coro

choir'boy' s ragazzo cantore

choir' loft' s coro

choir'mas'ter s maestro di cappella

choke [tʃok] s strozzatura; (aut) farfalla del carburatore || tr strozzare; ostruire; (an internal-combustion engine) arricchire la miscela di; to choke back trattenere; to choke up tappare, ostruire || intr soffocarsi; to choke up tapparsi; (coll) soffocarsi

choker ['tʃokər] s (necklace) (coll) collana; (scarf) (coll) foulard m

cholera ['kɑlərə] s colera m

choleric ['kɑlərɪk] adj collerico

cholesterol [kə'lestə ˌrol] or [kə'lestəˌral] s colesterina

choose [tʃuz] v (pret chose [tʃoz]; pp chosen ['tʃozən]) tr scegliere || intr —to choose to decidere di

choos·y ['tʃuzi] adj (-ier; -iest) (coll) di difficile contentatura

chop [tʃɑp] s colpo; (of meat) cotoletta; chops labbra fpl, bocca || v (pret & pp chopped; ger chopping) tr tagliare; (meat) tritare; to chop off troncare; to chop up sminuzzare

chopper ['tʃɑpər] s (man) tagliatore m; interruttore automatico; coltello da macellaio; (slang) elicottero; choppers (slang) i denti

chop'ping block' s tagliere m

chop·py ['tʃɑpi] adj (-pier; -piest) (wind) variabile; (sea) agitato; (style) instabile

choral ['korəl] adj & s corale m

chorale [ko'rɑl] s corale m

chord [kɔrd] s corda; (mus) accordo

chore [tʃor] s lavoro; lavoro spiacevole; chores faccende domestiche

choreography [ˌkɔri'ɑgrəfi] s coreografia

chorine [ko'rin] s (slang) ballerina

chorus ['korəs] s coro; (group of dancers) corpo di ballo; (of a song) ritornello

cho'rus girl' s ballerina

cho'rus man' s (men') corista m

chow [tʃau] s (dog) chow chow m; (slang) cibo, pappa

chowder ['tʃaudər] s zuppa di vongole; zuppa di pesce

Christ [kraɪst] s Cristo

christen ['krɪsən] tr battezzare

Christendom ['krɪsəndəm] s cristianità f

christening ['krɪsənɪŋ] s battesimo
Christian ['krɪstʃən] adj & s cristiano
Christianity [,krɪstʃɪ'ænɪti] s (Christendom) cristianità f; (religion) cristianesimo
Chris'tian name' s nome m di battesimo
Christmas ['krɪsməs] adj natalizio || s Natale m; Merry Christmas! Buon Natale!
Christ'mas card' s cartoncino natalizio
Christ'mas car'ol s pastorella di Natale
Christ'mas Eve' s vigilia di Natale
Christ'mas gift' s strenna natalizia
Christ'mas tree' s albero di Natale
chrome [krom] adj cromato || s cromo || tr cromare
chromium ['kromɪ-əm] s cromo
chromosome ['kromə,som] s cromosoma m
chronic ['krɑnɪk] adj cronico
chronicle ['krɑnɪkəl] s cronaca || tr fare la storia di
chronicler ['krɑnɪklər] s cronista mf
chronolo•gy [krə'nɑlədʒi] s (-gies) cronologia
chronometer [krə'nɑmɪtər] s cronometro
chrysanthemum [krɪ'sænθɪməm] s crisantemo
chub•by ['tʃʌbi] adj (-bier; -biest) paffuto
chuck [tʃʌk] s buffetto sotto il mento; (cut of meat) reale m; (of lathe) coppaia || tr accarezzare sotto il mento; (to throw) (coll) gettare
chuckle ['tʃʌkəl] s risatina || intr ridacchiare
chum [tʃʌm] s (coll) amico intimo; (coll) compagno di stanza || v (pret & pp chummed; ger chumming) intr (coll) essere amico intimo; essere compagno di stanza
chum•my ['tʃʌmi] adj (-mier; -miest) (coll) intimo, amicone
chump [tʃʌmp] s ciocco, ceppo; (coll) sciocco
chunk [tʃʌŋk] s grosso pezzo
church [tʃʌrtʃ] s chiesa
churchgoer ['tʃʌrtʃ,go-ər] s praticante mf
church'man s (-men) parrocchiano; (clergyman) sacerdote m
Church' of Eng'land s chiesa anglicana
church'yard s camposanto
churl [tʃʌrl] s zotico, villano
churlish ['tʃʌrlɪʃ] adj villano
churn [tʃʌrn] s zangola || tr agitare violentemente, sbattere || intr (said of water) ribollire
chute [ʃut] s piano inclinato, canna; (in a river) cascata, rapida; (parachute m; (into a swimming pool) toboga m
Cicero ['sɪsə,ro] s Cicerone m
cider ['saɪdər] s sidro
cigar [sɪ'gɑr] s sigaro
cigar' case' s portasigari m
cigar' cut'ter s tagliasigari m
cigarette [,sɪgə'rɛt] s sigaretta
cigarette' butt' s cicca
cigarette' case' s portasigarette m
cigarette' hold'er s bocchino

cigarette' light'er s accendisigaro, accendino
cigarette' pa'per s cartina da sigarette
cigar' store' s tabaccheria, rivendita di sali e tabacchi
cinch [sɪntʃ] s (on a horse) sottopancia m; (hold) (coll) presa; (slang) giochetto || tr legare con una cinghia; (slang) agguantare
cinder ['sɪndər] s tizzone m; (slag) scoria; cinders cenere f
cin'der block' s concio di scoria
Cinderella [,sɪndə'rɛlə] s (la) Cenerentola
cinema ['sɪnəmə] s cine m, cinema m
cinnabar ['sɪnə,bɑr] s cinabro
cinnamon ['sɪnəmən] s cannella
cipher ['saɪfər] s zero; cifra; codice m; monogramma m || tr calcolare; (to write in code) cifrare
circle ['sʌrkəl] s cerchio; (of theater) prima galleria; (of friends) cerchia || tr cerchiare, compiere una rotazione intorno a
circuit ['sʌrkɪt] s circuito; (district) circoscrizione
cir'cuit break'er s salvamotore m, interruttore automatico
circuitous [sər'kju·ɪtəs] adj tortuoso
circuitry ['sʌrkɪtri] s (plan) schema m di montaggio; (components) elementi mpl di un circuito
circular ['sʌrkjələr] adj & s circolare f
circulate ['sʌrkjə,let] tr mettere in circolazione, diffondere || intr circolare
cir'culating li'brary s biblioteca circolante
circulation [,sʌrkjə'leʃən] s circolazione; (of newspaper) diffusione
circumcise ['sʌrkəm,saɪz] tr circoncidere
circumference [sər'kʌmfərəns] s circonferenza
circumflex ['sʌrkəm,flɛks] adj circonflesso || s accento circonflesso
circumscribe [,sʌrkəm'skraɪb] tr circoscrivere
circumspect ['sʌrkəm,spɛkt] adj circospetto
circumstance ['sʌrkəm,stæns] s circostanza; (fact) dettaglio; solennità f; circumstances condizioni fpl; dettagli mpl; condizioni economiche; under no circumstances a nessuna condizione; under the circumstances le cose essendo come sono
circumstantial [,sʌrkəm'stænʃəl] adj circostanziale, indiziario; (incidental) secondario; (complete) circostanziato
cir'cumstan'tial ev'idence s prova indiziaria
circumstantiate [,sʌrkəm'stænʃɪ,et] tr (to support with particulars) comprovare; (to describe in detail) circonstanziare
circumvent [,sʌrkəm'vɛnt] tr (to surround) accerchiare; (to outwit) circuire; (a difficulty) eludere, scansare
circus ['sʌrkəs] s circo equestre
cistern ['sɪstərn] s cisterna, serbatoio
citadel ['sɪtədəl] s cittadella
citation [saɪ'teʃən] s citazione

cite [sait] *tr* citare

cither ['sɪðər] *s* cetra

citizen ['sɪtɪzən] *s* cittadino; (*civilian*) civile *mf*

citizenship ['sɪtɪzən ˌʃɪp] *s* cittadinanza

citric ['sɪtrɪk] *adj* citrico

citron ['sɪtrən] *s* cedro; cedro candito

cit'rus fruit' ['sɪtrəs] *s* agrumi *mpl*

cit·y ['sɪtɪ] *s* (-ies) città *f*

cit'y counc'il *s* consiglio municipale

cit'y ed'itor *s* capocronista *m*

cit'y fa'thers *spl* maggiorenti *mpl*; consiglieri *mpl* municipali

cit'y hall' *s* municipio

cit'y plan'ning *s* urbanistica

cit'y room' *s* (journ) redazione

civic ['sɪvɪk] *adj* civico || **civics** *s* educazione civica

civil ['sɪvɪl] *adj* civile

civ'il engineer'ing *s* genio civile

civilian [sɪ'vɪljən] *adj* & *s* civile *mf*, borghese *mf*

civili·ty [sɪ'vɪlɪtɪ] *s* (-ties) cortesia; civilities ossequi *mpl*

civilization [ˌsɪvɪlɪ'zeʃən] *s* civilizzazione, civiltà *f*

civilize ['sɪvɪˌlaɪz] *tr* civilizzare

civ'il law' *s* diritto civile

civ'il serv'ant *s* impiegato statale

civ'il war' *s* guerra civile || **Civil War** *s* (*of the U.S.A.*) guerra di secessione

claim [klem] *s* pretesa; richiesta; (min) concessione || *tr* (*one's rights*) rivendicare; (*one's property*) richiedere; dichiarare; **to claim to be** pretendere d'essere

claim' check' *s* tagliando

clairvoyance [klɛr'vɔɪ·əns] *s* chiaroveggenza

clairvoyant [klɛr'vɔɪ·ənt] *adj* chiaroveggente || *s* veggente *mf*, chiaroveggente *mf*

clam [klæm] *s* vongola || *intr*—**to clam up** (coll) essere muto come un pesce

clamber ['klæmər] *intr* arrampicarsi

clam·my ['klæmɪ] *adj* (-mier; -miest) coperto di sudore freddo; morbido

clamor ['klæmər] *s* clamore *m* || *intr* fare clamore

clamorous ['klæmərəs] *adj* clamoroso

clamp [klæmp] *s* graffa, morsetto; (*e.g., to hold a hose*) fascetta || *tr* assicurare con graffa, aggrappare; (*a tool*) montare || *intr*—**to clamp down on** (coll) fare pressione su, mettere i freni a

clan [klæn] *s* clan *m*

clandestine [klæn'dɛstɪn] *adj* clandestino

clang [klæŋ] *s* clangore *m* || *intr* risonare con clangore

clannish ['klænɪʃ] *adj* esclusivista, partigiano

clap [klæp] *s* applauso; (*of thunder*) scoppio || *v* (*pret* & *pp* **clapped; ger clapping**) *tr* (*the hands*) battere; (*e.g., in jail*) schiaffare; **to clap shut** sbattere || *intr* applaudire

clapper ['klæpər] *s* applauditore *m*; (*of bell*) batacchio

clap'trap' *s* imbonimento

claret ['klærɪt] *adj* & *s* chiaretto

clari·fy ['klærɪˌfaɪ] *v* (*pret* & *pp* -fied) *tr* chiarificare, chiarire

clarinet [ˌklærɪ'nɛt] *s* clarinetto

clarion ['klærɪ·ən] *adj* chiaro e metallico || *s* tromba, clarino

clash [klæʃ] *s* cozzo, urto; conflitto di opinioni || *intr* cozzare, urtarsi; essere in conflitto

clasp [klæsp] or [klɑsp] *s* gancio, fermaglio; (*hold*) presa; (*grip*) stretta || *tr* agganciare; (*to hold in the arms*) abbracciare; (*to grip*) stringere

class [klæs] or [klɑs] *s* classe *f* || *tr* classificare

class'book' *s* registro

classic ['klæsɪk] *adj* & *s* classico

classical ['klæsɪkəl] *adj* classico

classicism ['klæsɪˌsɪzəm] *s* classicismo

classicist ['klæsɪsɪst] *s* classicista *mf*

classified ['klæsɪˌfaɪd] *adj* segreto

clas'sified ad' *s* annunzio economico

classi·fy ['klæsɪˌfaɪ] *v* (*pret* & *pp* -fied) *tr* classificare

class'mate' *s* compagno di scuola

class'room' *s* aula scolastica

class' strug'gle *s* lotta di classe

class·y ['klæsɪ] *adj* (-ier; -iest) (slang) di lusso, di prim'ordine

clatter ['klætər] *s* (*of dishes*) acciottolio; vocio, schiamazzo || *tr* acciottolare || *intr* fare schiamazzo

clause [klɔz] *s* clausola; (gram) proposizione

clavicle ['klævɪkəl] *s* clavicola

claw [klɔ] *s* artiglio; (*of lobster*) pinza; (*tool*) raffio; (*of hammer*) granchio; (coll) dita *fpl* || *tr* aggraffiare; artigliare

claw' ham'mer *s* levachiodi *m*

clay [kle] *s* argilla, creta

clay' pipe' *s* pipa di terracotta

clean [klin] *adj* pulito; (*precise*) netto; (*e.g., break*) completo || *adv* completamente || *tr* pulire; **to clean out** pulire, fare repulisti di; (slang) ripulire; **to clean up** pulire completamente; mettere in ordine || *intr* pulirsi, fare pulizia

clean' bill' of health' *s* patente sanitaria; (fig) esonero completo

clean'-cut' *adj* ben delineato, deciso

cleaner ['klinər] *s* pulitore *m*, smacchiatore *m*; (*machine*) pulitrice *f*, smacchiatrice *f*; **to send to the cleaners** (slang) spolpare

clean'ing fluid' *s* smacchiatore *m*

clean'ing wom'an *s* donna di servizio per fare la pulizia

clean·ly ['klɛnlɪ] *adj* (-lier; -liest) pulito, netto

cleanse [klɛnz] *tr* pulire; detergere; purificare

cleanser ['klɛnzər] *s* detergente *m*

clean'-sha'ven *adj* sbarbato di fresco

clean'up' *s* pulizia; (slang) guadagno enorme

clear [klɪr] *adj* chiaro; evidente; completo; innocente; (*profit*) netto; **clear of** libero da || *s* posto libero; **in the clear** libero; esonerato; non in codice || *adv* chiaramente; completamente || *tr* (*e.g., trees*) rischiarare; (*e.g., peo-*

ple) sgombrare; (*the table*) sparecchiare; (*an obstacle*) superare; (*from guilt*) discolpare; (*a profit*) guadagnare; (*goods at customs*) svincolare; (*a ship through customs*) dichiarare il carico di; (*checks*) compensare; **to clear away or off** liberare; **to clear out** sgombrare, sbarazzare; **to clear up** spiegare; (*a doubt*) dissipare || *intr* rasserenarsi; (*said of a ship*) partire; **to clear away or off** sparire; **to clear out** (coll) andarsene; **to clear up** rasserenarsi

clearance ['klɪrəns] *s* liberazione; (*of a ship*) partenza; (*of goods through customs*) sdoganamento; (*of checks*) compensazione; (*of goods*) liquidazione; (mach) gioco

clear'ance sale' *s* liquidazione

clear'-cut' *adj* chiaro, distinto

clearing ['klɪrɪŋ] *s* (*open space*) radura; (*of checks*) compensazione

clear'ing house' *s* stanza di compensazione

cleat [klit] *s* bietta, cuneo; (*on the sole of shoe*) tacchetto; (naut) galloccia

cleavage ['klivɪdʒ] *s* divisione; fessura

cleave [kliv] *v* (*pret & pp* **cleft** [kleft] or **cleaved**) *tr* dividere, fendere || *intr* aderire, essere fedele

cleaver ['klivər] *s* scure *f*, accetta; (*of butcher*) spaccaossa *m*, fenditoio

clef [klef] *s* (mus) chiave *f*

cleft [kleft] *adj* diviso, fesso || *s* fessura, crepaccio

cleft' pal'ate *s* palato spaccato, gola lupina

clematis ['klemətɪs] *s* clematide *f*

clemen·cy ['klemənsɪ] *s* (-cies) clemenza

clement ['klemənt] *adj* clemente

clench [klentʃ] *s* stretta || *tr* stringere; afferrare

clergy ['klɜrdʒɪ] *s* clero

cler'gy·man *s* (-men) ecclesiastico

cleric ['klerɪk] *s* ecclesiastico, sacerdote *m*

clerical ['klerɪkəl] *adj* da impiegato; (*error*) burocratico; (*of clergy*) clericale || *s* ecclesiastico; **clericals** abiti ecclesiastici

cler'ical work' *s* lavoro d'ufficio

clerk [klɑrk] *s* impiegato, commesso; (*accountant*) contabile *mf*; (*e.g., in a record office*) ufficiale *m*; cancelliere *m*; (*copyist, typist*) scrivano

clever ['klevər] *adj* intelligente; bravo, abile; destro

cleverness ['klevərnɪs] *s* intelligenza; bravura, abilità *f*

clew [klu] *s* indizio, traccia; (*of yarn*) gomitolo; (naut) bugna

cliché [kli'ʃe] *s* cliché *m*, luogo comune

click [klɪk] *s* (*of camera or gun*) scatto; (*of typewriter*) battito, ticchettio || *tr* (*the tongue*) schioccare; (*the heels*) battere || *intr* ticchettare; (slang) andare d'accordo; (slang) avere fortuna

client ['klaɪ·ənt] *s* cliente *mf*

clientele [ˌklaɪ·ən'tɛl] *s* clientela

cliff [klɪf] *s* rupe *f*, precipizio

climate ['klaɪmɪt] *s* clima *m*

climax ['klaɪmæks] *s* apice *m*; (*acute phase*) parossismo

climb [klaɪm] *s* salita; (*of a mountain*) scalata, ascensione || *tr* (*the stairs*) salire; (*a mountain*) scalare, ascendere || *intr* salire, arrampicarsi; **to climb down** discendere a carponi; (coll) ritirarsi

climber ['klaɪmər] *s* scalatore *m*; pianta rampicante; (*ambitious person*) (coll) arrampicatore *m*

clinch [klɪntʃ] *s* stretta, presa; (*boxing*) corpo a corpo *m* || *tr* (*nails*) ribattere, ribadire

clincher ['klɪntʃər] *s* chiodo per ribaditura; argomento decisivo

cling [klɪŋ] *v* (*pret & pp* **clung** [klʌŋ]) *intr* avviticchiare, attaccarsi; aderire, rimanere attaccato

cling'stone' peach' *s* pesca duracino

clinic ['klɪnɪk] *s* clinica

clinical ['klɪnɪkəl] *adj* clinico

clinician [klɪ'nɪʃən] *s* clinico

clink [klɪŋk] *s* tintinnio; (slang) gattabuia || *tr* (*glasses*) toccare || *intr* tintinnare

clinker ['klɪŋkər] *s* clinker *m*; mattone vetrificato; (slang) sbaglio

clip [klɪp] *s* (*of hair*) taglio; (*of wool*) tosatura; (*speed*) passo rapido; clip *f*, fermaglio; (*large clip*) fermacarte *m*; (*for cartridges*) caricatore *m*; (coll) colpo || *v* (*pret & pp* **clipped**) *ger* **clipping**) *tr* tagliare, tosare; (*words*) mangiare, storpiare; (*paper*) ritagliare; ritenere; (coll) battere || *intr* andare di buon passo

clipper ['klɪpər] *s* tagliatore *m*; (aer, naut) clipper *m*; **clippers** (*for hair*) tosatrice *f*; (*for nails*) pinze *fpl* per le unghie

clipping ['klɪpɪŋ] *s* taglio; (*from newspaper*) ritaglio

clique [klik] *s* cricca, chiesuola

cloak [klok] *s* mantello, manto; (fig) velo, maschera || *tr* ammantare, velare

cloak'-and-dag'ger *adj* d'avventura

cloak'-and-sword' *adj* di cappa e spada

cloak'room' *s* guardaroba *m*

clock [klɑk] *s* orologio; (*with pendulum*) pendolo, pendola; (*on stocking*) freccia || *tr* registrare, cronometrare

clock'mak'er *s* orologiaio

clock' tow'er *s* torre *f* dell'orologio

clock'wise' *adj & adv* nella direzione delle lancette dell'orologio

clock'work' *s* movimento d'orologeria; **like clockwork** come un orologio

clod [klɑd] *s* zolla; (fig) tonto

clod'hop'per *s* (*shoe*) scarpone *m*; (fig) villano, bifolco

clog [klɑg] *s* intoppo; (*to impede movement*) pastoia; scarpone *m*, zoccolo || *v* (*pret & pp* **clogged**) *ger* **clogging**) *tr* intoppare; (*to hold back*) impastoiare || *intr* otturarsi, ostruirsi

cloister ['klɔɪstər] *s* chiostro || *tr* rinchiudere in un chiostro

close [klos] *adj* vicino; (*translation*)

fedele; *(air in room)* male arieggiato; *(weather)* soffocante; *(stingy)* avaro, limitato, senza gioco; *(haircut)* corto; *(friend)* intimo; *(hit)* preciso; *(enclosed)* chiuso; *(narrow)* stretto || *adv* da vicino; **close to** vicino a || [kloz] *s* fine *f*, conclusione; **to bring to a close** concludere || *tr* chiudere; otturare; concludere; **to close down** chiudere completamente; **to close out** vendere in liquidazione; **to close up** bloccare || *intr* chiudersi; serrarsi; **to close down** chiudersi completamente; **to close in on** venire alle prese con; **to close up** bloccarsi; *(said of a wound)* rimarginarsi

close' call' [klos] *s* rischio scampato per miracolo

closed' chap'ter *s* affare chiuso

closed' cir'cuit *s* circuito chiuso

closed' sea'son *s* periodo di caccia o pesca vietata

closefisted ['klos'fɪstɪd] *adj* taccagno

close'-fit'ing [klos] *adj* attillato

close-lipped ['klos'lɪpt] *adj* riservato

closely ['kloslɪ] *adv* da vicino; strettamente; fedelmente; attentamente

close' quar'ters [klos] *spl (cramped space)* pigia pigia *m*; **at close quarters** a corpo a corpo

close' quote' [kloz] *s* fine *f* della citazione

close' shave' [klos] *s*—**to have a close shave** farsi fare la barba a contropelo; (coll) scamparla per un pelo

closet ['klɑzɪt] *s* armadio a muro; *(small private room)* gabinetto; *(for keeping clothing)* ripostiglio || *tr*— **to be closeted with** essere in conciliabolo con

close'-up' [klos] *s* (mov) primo piano

closing ['klozɪŋ] *s* fine *f*, conclusione

clos'ing price' *s* ultimo corso

clot [klɑt] *s* grumo, coagulo || *v (pret & pp clotted; ger clotting) intr* raggrumarsi, coagularsi

cloth [klɔθ] *or* [klɑθ] *s* panno, tessuto, stoffa, abito; *(for binding books)* tela; **the cloth** il clero

clothe [kloð] *v (pret & pp clothed or clad* [klæd]) *tr* vestire, rivestire, coprire

clothes [kloz] *or* [kloðz] *spl* vestiti *mpl*, abiti *mpl*; *(for a bed)* coltre *f*; **to change clothes** cambiarsi

clothes'bas'ket *s* cesto della biancheria

clothes'brush' *s* spazzola per vestiti

clothes' dry'er *s* asciugatrice *f*

clothes' hang'er *s* attaccapanni *m*

clothes'horse' *s* cavalletto per stendere il bucato; elegantone *m*

clothes'line' *s* corda per stendere il bucato

clothes' moth' *s* tarma, tignola

clothes'pin' *s* molletta

clothes' tree' *s* attaccapanni *m*

clothier ['kloðjər] *s* negoziante *m* di confezioni; mercante *m* di panno

clothing ['kloðɪŋ] *s* vestiti *mpl*, vestiario

cloud [klaud] *s* nuvola, nube *f*; *(great number)* nuvolo; macchia; sospetto || *tr* annuvolare; offuscare || *intr* annuvolarsi; offuscarsi

cloud' bank' *s* banco di nubi

cloud'burst' *s* acquazzone *m*, nubifragio

cloud'-capped' *adj* coperto di nubi

cloudless ['klaudlɪs] *adj* senza nubi

cloud·y ['klaudi] *adj* (-ier; -iest) nuvoloso, annuvolato; confuso; tenebroso

clout [klaut] *s* (coll) schiaffo || *tr* (coll) schiaffeggiare

clove [klov] *s* chiodo di garofano; *(of garlic)* spicchio

cloven-hoofed ['klovən'huft] *adj* dal piede biforcuto; demoniaco

clover ['klovər] *s* trifoglio; **in clover** come un papa

clo'ver·leaf' *s* (-leaves [,livz]) foglia di trifoglio; incrocio stradale a quadrifoglio

clown [klaun] *s* pagliaccio, buffone *m* || *intr* fare il pagliaccio

clownish ['klaunɪʃ] *adj* buffonesco, clownesco, claunesco

cloy [klɔɪ] *tr* saziare fino alla nausea

club [klʌb] *s* bastone *m*; circolo, società *f*; *(playing card)* fiore *m* || *v (pret & pp clubbed; ger clubbing) tr* bastonare || *intr*—**to club together** unirsi

club' car' *s* vagone *m* con servizio di buffet

club'house' *s* sede *f* di un circolo

club'man' *s* (-men) frequentatore *m* di circoli

club'room' *s* sala delle riunioni

club' sand'wich *s* sandwich *m* a tre fette di pane con insalata

club'wom'an *s* (-wom'en) frequentatrice *f* di circoli

cluck [klʌk] *s* (il) chiocciare || *intr* chiocciare

clue [klu] *s* traccia, indizio

clump [klʌmp] *s* gruppo, massa; *(of earth)* zolla || *intr* camminare con passo pesante

clum·sy ['klʌmzi] *adj* (-sier; -siest) goffo, malaccorto, sgraziato

cluster ['klʌstər] *s* gruppo; *(of grapes)* grappolo; *(of bees)* sciame *m*; *(of stars)* ammasso; *(of people)* foila || *tr* raggruppare || *intr* raggrupparsi

clutch [klʌtʃ] *s* presa; *(claw)* grinfia; *(of chickens)* covata; (mach) innesto; (aut) frizione; **clutches** grinfie *fpl*; **to throw the clutch in** innestare la marcia; **to throw the clutch out** disinnestare la marcia || *tr* afferrare, aggrappare || *intr*—**to clutch at** aggrapparsi a

clutter ['klʌtər] *tr*—**to clutter up** ingombrare alla rinfusa

coach [kotʃ] *s* carrozza, vettura; vagone *m*; *(automobile)* berlina; autobus *m*; *(trainer)* allenatore *m*; *(teacher)* ripetitore *m* || *tr* allenare; preparare

coach' house' *s* rimessa

coaching ['kotʃɪŋ] *s* suggerimento; *(in school)* ripetizione; (sports) allenamento

coach'man *s* (-men) cocchiere *m*

coagulate [ko'ægjə,let] *tr* coagulare || *intr* coagularsi

coal [kol] *s* carbone *m*; (*piece of burning wood*) tizzone *m*; **to call** or **haul over the coals** rimproverare || *tr* rifornire di carbone || *intr* rifornirsi di carbone; (naut) fare carbone

coal'bin' *s* carbonaia

coal' deal'er *s* (*wholesale*) negoziante *m* di carbone; (*retail*) carbonaio

coal' field' *s* bacino carbonifero

coal' gas' *s* gas *m* illuminante

coalition [,ko·ə'lɪʃən] *s* coalizione

coal' mine' *s* miniera di carbone

coal' oil' *s* cherosene *m*

coal' scut'tle *s* secchio del carbone

coal' tar' *s* catrame *m*

coal' yard' *s* carbonaia, carboniera

coarse [kors] *adj* (*manners*) volgare, ordinario; (*unrefined*) greggio; (*lacking refinement in manners*) rozzo, grossolano

coast [kost] *s* costa; discesa a ruota libera; **the coast is clear** la via è libera || *tr* costeggiare || *intr* costeggiare; scendere a ruota libera

coastal ['kostəl] *adj* costiero

coaster ['kostər] *s* nave *f* di cabotaggio; (*amusement*) otto volante, montagna russa; (*small tray*) sottobicchiere *m*

coast'er brake' *s* freno a contropedale

coast' guard' *s* guardacoste *m*

coast'-guard cut'ter *s* guardacoste *m*

coast'ing trade' *s* cabotaggio

coast'land' *s* costa

coast'line' *s* linea costiera, litorale *m*

coast'wise' *adv* lungo la costa

coat [kot] *s* soprabito; cappotto; (*jacket*) giacca; (*hide of man and animals*) mantello; (*of paint*) mano *f*; (*layer*) strato || *tr* vestire, proteggere; ricoprire, coprire

coat'ed ['kotɪd] *adj* rivestito; (*tongue*) patinato

coat' hang'er *s* attaccapanni *m*

coating ['kotɪŋ] *s* rivestimento; (*of paint*) mano *f*; (*of cement*) strato; (*cloth*) tessuto per abiti

coat' of arms' *s* scudo, stemma *m*

coat'room' *s* guardaroba *m*

coat'tail' *s* falda

coax [koks] *tr* blandire; ottenere con lusinghe

cob [kɑb] *s* spiga di granturco; (*horse*) cavallo da tiro; (*swan*) cigno maschio

cobalt ['kobɔlt] *s* cobalto

cobble ['kɑbəl] *s* ciottolo || *tr* acciottolare; (*to mend*) raccomodare, riparare

cobbler ['kɑblər] *s* calzolaio, ciabattino; (*pie*) torta di frutta

cob'ble·stone' *s* ciottolo

cob'web' *s* tela di ragno, ragnatela

cocaine [ko'ken] *s* cocaina

cock [kɑk] *s* gallo; (*faucet*) rubinetto; (*of gun*) cane *m*; (*of the eye*) ammicco; (*of nose*) angolo (del naso) rivolto all'insù; (*of hay*) covone *m* || *tr* (*a gun*) armare; (*the head*) drizzare

cockade [kɑ'ked] *s* coccarda

cock-a-doodle-doo ['kɑkə,dudəl'du] *s* chicchirichì *m*

cock'-and-bull' sto'ry *s* racconto incredibile

cocked' hat' *s* tricorno, cappello tricorno; **to knock into a cocked hat** (slang) distruggere completamente

cockeyed ['kɑk,aɪd] *adj* strabico; (slang) sbilenco; (slang) sciocco, scemo

cockle ['kɑkəl] *s* (*mollusk*) cardio; (*weed*) loglio; (*boat*) barchetta; (*wrinkle*) grinza; **to warm the cockles of one's heart** far bene al cuore || *intr* raggrinzirsi

cock' of the walk' *s* gallo del pollaio

cock'pit' *s* (*of boat*) cabina; (aer) carlinga; (naut) cassero di poppa

cock'roach' *s* scarafaggio, blatta

cocks'comb' *s* cresta di gallo; berretto da buffone

cock'sure' *adj* ostinato; troppo sicuro di sé stesso

cock'tail' *s* cocktail *m*

cock'tail par'ty *s* cocktail *m*

cock·y ['kɑki] *adj* (-ier; -iest) impudente, presuntuoso

cocoa ['koko] *s* (*bean*) cacao; (*drink*) cioccolata; (*tree*) cocco

coconut ['kokə,nʌt] *s* noce *f* di cocco

co'conut palm' or **tree'** *s* cocco

cocoon [kə'kun] *s* bozzolo

cod [kɑd] *s* merluzzo

C.O.D. ['si'o'di] *s* (letterword) (**Collect on Delivery**) contro assegno

coddle ['kɑdəl] *tr* vezzeggiare

code [kod] *s* codice *m*, cifra; **in code** in codice, in cifra || *tr* mettere in codice or in cifra; cifrare

codex ['kodɛks] *s* (**codices** ['kodɪ,siz] or ['kɑdɪ,siz]) codice *m*

cod'fish' *s* merluzzo

codger ['kɑdʒər] *s*—**old codger** (coll) vecchietto

codicil ['kɑdɪsɪl] *s* codicillo

codi·fy ['kɑdɪ,faɪ] or ['kodɪ,faɪ] *v* (*pret & pp* -fied) *tr* codificare

cod'-liver oil' *s* olio di fegato di merluzzo

coed ['co,ɛd] *s* studentessa di scuola mista

coeducation [,ko,ɛdʒə'keʃən] *s* coeducazione

co'educa'tional school' [,ko·ɛdʒə'keʃənəl] *s* scuola mista

coefficient [,ko·ɪ'fɪʃənt] *s* coefficiente *m*

coerce [ko'ʌrs] *tr* forzare, costringere

coercion [ko'ʌrʃən] *s* coercizione

coexist [,ko·ɪg'zɪst] *intr* coesistere

coffee ['kɔfi] or ['kɑfi] *s* caffè *m*; **ground coffee** caffè macinato; **roasted coffee** caffè torrefatto

cof'fee bean' *s* chicco di caffè

cof'fee·cake' *s* pasticcino (da mangiarsi con il caffè)

cof'fee grind'er *s* macinino da caffè, macinacaffè *m*

cof'fee grounds' *spl* fondi *mpl* di caffè

cof'fee house' *s* caffè *m*

cof'fee mak'er *s* macchinetta del caffè

cof'fee mill' s macinino del caffè, macinacaffè m
cof'fee-pot' s caffettiera
cof'fee shop' s caffè m
coffer ['kɔfər] or ['kafər] s forziere m; (ceiling) soffitto a cassettoni; (archit) cassettone m; **coffers** tesoro
coffin ['kɔfɪn] or ['kafɪn] s bara
cog [kɑg] s dente m d'ingranaggio; ruota dentata; **to slip a cog** fare un errore
cogent ['kodʒənt] adj convincente, persuasivo
cogitate ['kadʒɪ,tet] tr & intr cogitare, ponzare
cognac ['konjæk] or ['kɑnjæk] s cognac m
cognate ['kɑgnet] adj consanguineo, parente, affine || s parola dello stesso ceppo linguistico; consanguineo, parente mf
cognizance ['kɑgnɪzəns] or ['kɑnɪzəns] s conoscenza; **to take cognizance of** prendere conoscenza di
cognizant ['kɑgnɪzənt] or ['kɑnɪzənt] adj informato, al corrente
cog'wheel' s ruota dentata
cohabit [ko'hæbɪt] intr convivere; (archaic) coabitare
coheir [ko'ɛr] s coerede mf
cohere [ko'hɪr] intr aderire; (fig) avere nesso
coherent [ko'hɪrənt] adj coerente
coiffeur [kwa'fʌr] s parrucchiere m per signora; (Brit) parrucchiere m
coiffure [kwa'fjur] s pettinatura || tr pettinare
coil [kɔɪl] s (of rope) rotolo; (of pipe) serpentino; (of wire) bobina, avvolgimento || tr arrotolare || intr arrotolarsi
coil' spring' s molla a spirale, molla elicoidale
coin [kɔɪn] s moneta; **to pay back in one's own coin** pagare della stessa moneta; **to toss a coin** giocare a testa o croce || tr (money) coniare, battere; (words) inventare, creare; **to coin money** battere moneta; (coll) fare soldoni
coincide [,ko-ɪn'saɪd] intr coincidere
coincidence [ko'ɪnsɪdəns] s coincidenza
coke [kok] s coke m, carbone m coke
colander ['kʌləndər] or ['kɑləndər] s colabrodo, colapasta m
cold [kold] adj freddo; **it is cold** (said of weather) fa freddo; **to be cold** (said of a person) avere freddo || s freddo; (ailment) raffreddore m; **out in the cold** solo soletto; **to catch cold** pigliare freddo, pigliarsi un raffreddore
cold' blood' s—**in cold blood** a sangue freddo
cold'-blood'ed adj insensibile; (sensitive to cold) freddoloso; (animal) a sangue freddo
cold' chis'el s tagliaferro
cold' com'fort s magra consolazione
cold' cream' s crema emolliente
cold' cuts' spl salumi mpl, affettato

cold' feet' spl—**to get cold feet** (coll) perdersi d'animo
cold'-heart'ed adj—**to be coldhearted** avere il cuore duro
coldness ['koldnɪs] s freddezza
cold' shoul'der s—**to get the cold shoulder** (coll) essere trattato con freddezza; **to turn a cold shoulder on** (coll) trattare con freddezza
cold' snap' s freddo breve e improvviso
cold' stor'age s conservazione a freddo
cold' war' s guerra fredda
cold' wave' s ondata di freddo
coleslaw ['kol,slɔ] s insalata di cavolo cappuccio
colic ['kalɪk] adj colico || s colica
coliseum [,kalɪ'si-əm] s stadio, arena || **Coliseum** s Colosseo
collaborate [kə'læbə,ret] intr collaborare
collaborationist [kə,læbə'reʃənɪst] s collaborazionista mf
collaborator [kə'læbə,retər] s collaboratore m
collapse [kə'læps] s (of business) fallimento; (e.g., of a roof) caduta; (of a person) collasso || tr piegare || intr (to shrink) restringersi, sgonfiarsi; (said of a business) fallire; (said of health) venir meno; (said, e.g., of a roof) cadere, crollare
collapsible [kə'læpsɪbəl] adj pieghevole, smontabile
collar ['kalər] s (of shirt) colletto; (for dog or horse) collare m; (ring) anello; (short piece of pipe) manicotto || tr afferrare per il collo, catturare
col'lar-band' s cinturino della camicia
col'lar-bone' s clavicola
collate [kə'let] or ['kalet] tr collazionare, confrontare
collateral [kə'lætərəl] adj collaterale; accessorio, addizionale || s collaterale m
colleague ['kalig] s collega mf
collect ['kalekt] s (eccl) colletta || [kə'lekt] adv contro assegno; (telp) pagamento all'abbonato chiamato || tr raccogliere, riunire; (e.g., stamps) collezionare; (mail) levare; (bills) incassare; (ideas) coordinare; (thoughts) riordinare; (e.g., classroom papers) raccogliere; (taxes) riscuotere; **to collect oneself** riprendersi, riprendere il controllo di sé stesso || intr (for the poor) fare la colletta; riunirsi, raccogliersi
collected [kə'lektɪd] adj raccolto; equilibrato, padrone di sè
collection [kə'lekʃən] s collezione; (for the poor) colletta; (of mail) levata; (heap) deposito; (of taxes) esazione; (of bills) riscossione
collec'tion a'gency s agenzia di riscossione
collective [kə'lektɪv] adj collettivo
collector [kə'lektər] s (of stamps) collezionista mf; (of taxes) esattore m; (of tickets) controllore m
college ['kalɪdʒ] s scuola superiore,

università *f;* (*e.g., of medicine*) facoltà *f;* (*electoral*) collegio

collide [kə'laɪd] *intr* collidere, scontrarsi

collie ['kɑli] *s* collie *m*

collier ['kɑljər] *s* (*ship*) carboniera; (min) minatore *m* di carbone

collier·y ['kɑljəri] *s* (*-ies*) miniera di carbone

collision [kə'lɪʒən] *s* collisione

colloid ['kɑlɔɪd] *adj* colloidale || *s* colloide *m*

colloquial [kə'lokwɪ-əl] *adj* familiare, colloquiale

colloquialism [kə'lokwɪ-ə,lɪzəm] *s* espressione familiare

collo·quy ['kɑləkwi] *s* (*-quies*) colloquio

collusion [kə'luʒən] *s* collusione; **to be in collusion with** essere d'intelligenza con

cologne [kə'lon] *s* acqua di colonia, colonia || **Cologne** *s* Colonia

colon ['kolən] *s* (anat) colon *m;* (gram) due punti *mpl*

colonel ['kʌrnəl] *s* colonnello

colonist ['kɑlənɪst] *s* colono, coloniale *m*

colonize ['kɑlə,naɪz] *tr & intr* colonizzare

colonnade [,kɑlə'ned] *s* colonnato

colo·ny ['kɑləni] *s* (*-nies*) colonia

color ['kʌlər] *s* colore *m;* **off color** sbiadito, scolorito; (slang) sporco, volgare; **the colors** i colori, la bandiera; **to call to the colors** chiamare in servizio militare; **to change color** cambiar colore; arrossire; impallidire; **to give or lend color to** far parere probabile; **to lose color** impallidire; **to show one's colors** mostrarsi come si è; **under color of** sotto il pretesto di || *tr* colorare; (fig) colorire || *intr* arrossire

col'or-blind' *adj* daltonico

colored ['kʌlərd] *adj* colorato; (*person*) di colore; esagerato

colorful ['kʌlərfəl] *adj* colorito, espressivo

col'or guard' *s* guardia d'onore alla bandiera

coloring ['kʌlərɪŋ] *s* colorazione; colore *m;* pigmento; (fig) specie *f*

colorless ['kʌlərlɪs] *adj* incolore, incoloro

col'or photog'raphy *s* fotografia a colori

col'or ser'geant *s* sergente *m* portabandiera

col'or tel'evision *s* televisione a colori

colossal [kə'lɑsəl] *adj* colossale

colossus [kə'lɑsəs] *s* colosso

colt [kolt] *s* puledro

Columbus [kə'lʌmbəs] *s* Colombo

column ['kɑləm] *s* colonna

columnist ['kɑləmɪst] *s* giornalista incaricato di una colonna speciale; articolista *mf*

coma ['komə] *s* coma *m*

comb [kom] *s* pettine *m;* (*for horse*) striglia; (*of hen or wave*) cresta; (*honeycomb*) favo || *tr* pettinare;

(fig) esaminare minuziosamente || *intr* (*said of waves*) frangersi

com·bat ['kɑmbæt] *s* combattimento || ['kɑmbæt] or [kəm'bæt] *v* (*pret & pp* -bated or -batted; *ger* -bating or -batting) *tr & intr* combattere

combatant ['kɑmbətənt] *s* combattente *mf*

com'bat du'ty *s* servizio in zona di guerra

combination [,kɑmbɪ'neʃən] *s* combinazione

combine [,kɑmbaɪn] *s* consorzio; (pol) coalizione; mieto-trebbiatrice *f* || [kəm'baɪn] *tr* combinare || *intr* combinarsi

combin'ing form' *s* membro di parola composta

combo ['kɑmbo] *s* orchestrina

combustible [kəm'bʌstɪbəl] *adj & s* combustibile *m*

combustion [kəm'bʌstʃən] *s* combustione

come [kʌm] *v* (*pret* **came** [kem]; *pp* **come**) *intr* venire; arrivare; (*to become*) diventare; (*to amount*) ammontare; **come!** macchè!; **come along!** andiamo!; **come in!** avanti!, entri!; **come on!** andiamo!; avanti!, coraggio!; **to come about** accadere, succedere; **to come across** incontrarsi con; (slang) pagare; **to come around** cedere; mettersi d'accordo; (*said of health*) rimettersi; **to come at** raggiungere; (*to attack*) attaccare; **to come back** ritornare; **to come between** mettersi fra; **to come by** ottenere; **to come down** scendere; decadere; essere trasmesso; **to come down with** ammalarsi di; **to come forward** farsi avanti; **to come in** entrare, passare; **to come in for** ricevere; **to come into** ricevere; ereditare; **to come off** succedere; riuscire; **to come on** mostrarsi; migliorare; incontrarsi; **to come out** uscire; debuttare in società; andare a finire; **to come out with** uscire con; mostrare; **to come over** succedere a, e.g., **what came over him?** che gli è successo?; **to come through** riuscire; **to come to** riprendere i sensi; **to come under** essere di competenza di; appartenere a; **to come up** salire; **to come up to** salire fino a; avvicinarsi a; **to come up with** raggiungere; produrre, fornire; proporre

come'back' *s* (coll) ritorno; (slang) pronta risposta; **to stage a comeback** (coll) ritornare in auge

comedian [kə'midɪ-ən] *s* attore comico; (*author*) commediografo; (*amusing person*) commediante *mf*

comedienne [kə,midɪ'en] *s* attrice comica

come'down' *s* (coll) rovescio di fortuna

come·dy ['kɑmədi] *s* (*-dies*) commedia

come·ly ['kʌmli] *adj* (*-lier; -liest*) bello, grazioso

comet ['kɑmɪt] *s* cometa

comfort ['kʌmfərt] *s* conforto, sollievo;

(ease) benessere *m* || *tr* confortare, alleviare

comfortable [ˈkʌmfərtəbəl] *adj* comodo, agiato; *(e.g., income)* (coll) bastante || *s* coltre *f*

comforter [ˈkʌmfərtər] *s* consolatore *m*; *(bedcover)* coltre *f*; sciarpa di lana || **the Comforter** lo Spirito Santo, lo Spirito Consolatore

comforting [ˈkʌmfərtɪŋ] *adj* confortante

com′fort sta′tion *s* latrina pubblica

comic [ˈkɑmɪk] *adj* comico || *s* *(actor)* comico; comicità *f*; **comics** fumetti *mpl*

comical [ˈkɑmɪkəl] *adj* comico

com′ic book′ *s* libretto a fumetti

com′ic op′era *s* opera buffa

com′ic strip′ *s* racconto umoristico a fumetti

coming [ˈkʌmɪŋ] *adj* venturo, prossimo; promettente || *s* venuta

com′ing out′ *s* debutto in società; *(e.g., of stock)* emissione

comma [ˈkɑmə] *s* virgola

command [kəˈmænd] or [kəˈmɑnd] *s* comando; *(e.g., of a language)* padronanza || *tr* comandare, ordinare; *(to overlook)* dominare; *(to be able to have)* disporre di || *intr* avere il comando

commandant [ˌkɑmənˈdænt] or [ˌkɑmənˈdɑnt] *s* comandante *m*

commandeer [ˌkɑmənˈdɪr] *tr* requisire

commander [kəˈmændər] or [kəˈmɑndər] *s* *(of knighthood)* commendatore *m*; (mil) comandante *m*; (nav) capitano di vascello

command′er in chief′ *s* comandante *m* in capo

command′ing of′ficer *s* comandante *m*

commandment [kəˈmændmənt] or [kəˈmɑndmənt] *s* comandamento

command′ mod′ule *s* (rok) modulo di comando

commando [kəˈmændo] *s* guastatore *m*

commemorate [kəˈmɛməˌret] *tr* commemorare, celebrare

commence [kəˈmɛns] *tr* & *intr* cominciare

commencement [kəˈmɛnsmənt] *s* inizio, esordio; *(in a school)* cerimonia per la distribuzione dei diplomi

commend [kəˈmɛnd] *tr* lodare; *(to entrust)* raccomandare, affidare

commendable [kəˈmɛndəbəl] *adj* *(person)* lodevole; *(act)* commendevole

commendation [ˌkɑmənˈdeʃən] *s* lode *f*; raccomandazione; (mil) citazione

comment [ˈkɑmɛnt] *s* commento || *tr* commentare || *intr* fare commenti; **to comment on** fare commenti su

commentary [ˈkɑmənˌteri] *s* (-ies) commentario

commentator [ˈkɑmənˌtetər] *s* commentatore *m*

commerce [ˈkɑmərs] *s* commercio

commercial [kəˈmɛrʃəl] *adj* commerciale || *s* (rad, telv) programma *m* di pubblicità; (rad, telv) annunzio pubblicitario

commiserate [kəˈmɪzəˌret] *intr—to*

commiserate with commiserare, compiangere

commissar [ˈkɑmɪˌsɑr] or [ˌkɑmɪˈsɑr] *s* commissario del popolo

commissary [ˈkɑmɪˌseri] *s* (-ies) *(store)* economato; *(deputy)* commissario; *(in army)* intendente *m*

commission [kəˈmɪʃən] *s* commissione; *(e.g., in army)* nomina, brevetto; autorità *f*; *(of a crime)* perpetrazione; (il) fare; **in commission** in servizio, in uso; **out of commission** fuori servizio || *tr* nominare, dare un brevetto a; autorizzare; *(a ship)* armare

commis′sioned of′ficer *s* (mil, nav) ufficiale *m*

commissioner [kəˈmɪʃənər] *s* commissario; membro di una commissione

commis′sion mer′chant *s* sensale *m*

commit [kəˈmɪt] *v* *(pret & pp* -mitted; *ger* -mitting) *tr* commettere, perpetrare; *(to deliver)* affidare, consegnare; *(to imprison)* mandare in prigione; *(an insane person)* internare; *(to refer)* rinviare; *(to involve)* compromettere; **to commit oneself** compromettersi; **to commit to memory** imparare a memoria; **to commit to writing** mettere in iscritto

commitment [kəˈmɪtmənt] *s* *(act of committing)* commissione; *(to an asylum)* internamento; promessa; (law) mandato

committal [kəˈmɪtəl] *s* consegna; promessa

committee [kəˈmɪti] *s* comitato, commissione

commode [kəˈmod] *s* *(chest of drawers)* cassettone *m*; *(washstand)* lavabo; seggetta, comoda

commodious [kəˈmodɪ·əs] *adj* spazioso; conveniente

commodity [kəˈmɑdɪti] *s* (-ties) merce *f*; articolo di prima necessità

commod′ity exchange′ *s* borsa merci

common [ˈkɑmən] *adj* comune || *s* fondo comunale; pascolo comune; **commons** gente *f* non nobile; refettorio; **in common** in comune || **the Commons** la Camera dei Comuni

com′mon car′rier *s* impresa di trasporti pubblici

commoner [ˈkɑmənər] *s* plebeo, borghese *m*; membro della Camera dei Comuni

com′mon law′ *s* consuetudine *f*, diritto consuetudinario

com′mon-law mar′riage *s* matrimonio basato sulla mera convivenza

commonly [ˈkɑmənli] *adv* generalmente

com′mon·place *adj* banale, ordinario || *s* banalità *f*, cosa ordinaria

com′mon sense′ *s* senso comune

com′mon-sense′ *adj* giudizioso

com′mon stock′ *s* azione ordinaria; azioni ordinarie

commonweal [ˈkɑmənˌwil] *s* bene pubblico

com′mon·wealth′ *s* *(citizens of a state)* cittadinanza; repubblica; *(one of the*

50 states of the U.S.A.) stato; comunità *f*, federazione

commotion [kə'moʃən] *s* agitazione

commune [kə'mjun] *s* comune *m* ‖ *intr* confabulare; (eccl) comunicarsi

communicate [kə'mjunɪ,ket] *tr* & *intr* comunicare

communicating [kə'mjunɪ,ketɪŋ] *adj* comunicante

communication [kə,mjunɪ'keʃən] *s* comunicazione; **communications** sistema *m* di comunicazione; mezzi *mpl* di comunicazione

communicative [kə'mjunɪ,ketɪv] *adj* comunicativo

Communion [kə'mjunjən] *s* Comunione; **to take Communion** comunicarsi

communiqué [kə,mjunɪ'ke] or [kə-'mjunɪ,ke] *s* comunicato

communism ['kamjə,nɪzəm] *s* comunismo

communist ['kamjənɪst] *s* comunista *mf*

communi-ty [kə'mjunɪti] *s* (**-ties**) (*people living together*) comunità *f*; (*sharing together*) comunanza; (*neighborhood*) circondario

commu'nity cen'ter *s* centro sociale

commu'nity chest' *s* fondo di beneficenza

commuta'tion tick'et [,kamjə'teʃən] *s* biglietto d'abbonamento

commutator ['kamjə,tetər] *s* (*switch*) commutatore *m*; (*of dynamo or motor*) collettore *m*

commute [kə'mjut] *tr* commutare ‖ *intr* commutare; fare il pendolare

commuter [kə'mjutər] *s* pendolare *mf*

compact [kəm'pækt] *adj* compatto ‖ ['kampækt] *s* (*small case for face powder*) portacipria *m*; (*agreement*) accordo; (*small car*) utilitaria

companion [kəm'pænjən] *s* compagno; (*one of two items*) pendant *m*; (*lady*) dama di compagnia

compan'ion·ship' *s* cameratismo

compan'ion·way' *s* (naut) scaletta per andare sottocoperta

compa·ny ['kʌmpəni] *s* (**-nies**) compagnia; (coll) ospite *m* or ospiti *mpl*; (naut) equipaggio; **to bear company** accompagnare; **to be good company** essere simpatico; **to keep company** (*said of a couple*) andare insieme; **to keep company with** accompagnare; (coll) fare la corte a; **to part company** separarsi

comparable ['kampərəbəl] *adj* comparabile, paragonabile

comparative [kəm'pærətɪv] *adj* comparativo; (*e.g., anatomy*) comparato ‖ *s* (gram) comparativo

compare [kəm'per] *s*—**beyond compare** incomparabile ‖ *tr* confrontare; **compared to** a confronto di, in confronto a

comparison [kəm'pærɪsən] *s* confronto; (gram) comparazione; **in comparison with** in confronto a, a confronto di

compartment [kəm'partmənt] *s* compartimento; (naut) compartimento stagno; (rr) compartimento

compass ['kʌmpəs] *s* (*instrument for showing direction*) bussola; (*boundary*) limite *m*; (*range*) ambito; (*range of voice*) portata; (*of a wall*) cerchia; (*circuit*) circuito; (*drawing instrument*) compasso; **compasses** (*drawing instrument*) compasso ‖ *tr* girare intorno a; comprendere; **to compass about** accerchiare

com'pass card' *s* rosa dei venti

compassion [kəm'pæʃən] *s* compassione

compassionate [kəm'pæʃənɪt] *adj* compassionevole

com'pass saw' *s* gattuccio

com·pel [kəm'pɛl] *v* (*pret & pp* **-pelled**; *ger* **-pelling**) *tr* forzare, obbligare

compelling [kəm'pɛlɪŋ] *adj* imperioso, coercitivo

compendious [kəm'pɛndɪ·əs] *adj* compendioso, conciso

compensate ['kampən,set] *tr* & *intr* compensare

compensation [,kampən'seʃən] *s* compensazione; (*pay*) pagamento; (*something given to offset a loss*) risarcimento, indennità *f*

compete [kəm'pit] *intr* competere

competence ['kampɪtəns] or **competency** ['kampɪtənsi] *s* (*fitness*) abilità *f*; (*money*) agiatezza; (*authority*) competenza

competent ['kampɪtənt] *adj* abile; competente

competition [,kampɪ'tɪʃən] *s* competizione, gara; (*in business*) concorrenza

competitive [kəm'petɪtɪv] *adj* competitivo; (*based on competition*) di concorso

compet'itive pric'es *spl* prezzi *mpl* di concorrenza

competitor [kəm'petɪtər] *s* competitore *m*, concorrente *mf*; rivale *mf*

compilation [,kampɪ'leʃən] *s* compilazione

compile [kəm'paɪl] *tr* compilare

complacence [kəm'plesəns] or **complacency** [kəm'plesənsi] *s* compiacenza; compiacenza di sé stesso

complacent [kəm'plesənt] *adj* compiaciuto or soddisfatto con sé stesso

complain [kəm'plen] *intr* lagnarsi

complainant [kəm'plenənt] *s* (law) querelante *mf*

complaint [kəm'plent] *s* lagnanza, reclamo; (*sickness*) malattia; (law) querela

complaisance [kəm'plezəns] or ['kamplɪ,zæns] *s* compiacenza

complaisant [kəm'plezənt] or ['kamplɪ,zænt] *adj* compiacente, cortese

complement ['kamplɪmənt] *s* complemento; (naut) equipaggio ‖ ['kamplɪ,ment] *tr* completare

complete [kəm'plit] *adj* completo; (*done*) finito ‖ *tr* completare, finire

completion [kəm'pliʃən] *s* completamento, compimento

complex [kəm'plɛks] or ['kamplɛks]

adj complesso, complicato ‖ [ˈkɑm-pleks] *s* complesso

complexion [kəmˈplɛkʃən] *s* (*of skin*) carnagione; (*appearance*) aspetto; (*viewpoint*) punto di vista

compliance [kəmˈplaɪəns] *s* condiscendenza, arrendevolezza; **in compliance with** in conformità di

complicate [ˈkɑmplɪˌket] *tr* complicare

complicated [ˈkɑmplɪˌketɪd] *adj* complicato

complici·ty [kəmˈplɪsɪti] *s* (*-ties*) complicità *f*

compliment [ˈkɑmplɪmənt] *s* complimento, omaggio ‖ [ˈkɑmplɪˌment] *tr*—**to compliment s.o. on s.th** felicitarsi con qlcu per qlco; **to compliment s.o. with s.th** regalare qlco a qlcu

complimentary [ˌkɑmplɪˈmɛntəri] *adj* complimentoso, lusinghiero; (*free*) in omaggio, gratis; (*ticket*) di favore

com·ply [kəmˈplaɪ] *v* (*pret & pp -plied*) *intr* acconsentire, accondiscendere; **to comply with** accedere a

component [kəmˈponənt] *adj* componente, costituente ‖ *s* (*component part*) componente *m*; (*force*) componente *f*

compose [kəmˈpoz] *tr* comporre; **to be composed of** essere composto di; **to compose oneself** calmarsi

composed [kəmˈpozd] *adj* calmo, tranquillo

composer [kəmˈpozər] *s* (*peacemaker*) conciliatore *m*; (mus) compositore *m*

compos'ing stick' *s* (typ) compositoio

composite [kəmˈpazɪt] *adj & s* composto, composito

composition [ˌkɑmpəˈzɪʃən] *s* composizione; (*agreement*) compromesso

compositor [kəmˈpazɪtər] *s* compositore *m*

compost [ˈkɑmpost] *s* concime *m* naturale

composure [kəmˈpoʒər] *s* calma

compote [ˈkɑmpot] *s* (*stewed fruit*) composta; (*dish*) compostiera

compound [ˈkɑmpaʊnd] *adj* composto; (*fracture*) complesso; (archit, bot) composito ‖ *s* composto; parola composta; (*yard*) recinto ‖ [kɑmˈpaʊnd] *tr* (*to mix*) combinare; (*to settle*) comporre; (*interest*) capitalizzare

comprehend [ˌkɑmprɪˈhɛnd] *tr* comprendere

comprehensible [ˌkɑmprɪˈhɛnsɪbəl] *adj* comprensibile

comprehension [ˌkɑmprɪˈhɛnʃən] *s* comprensione

comprehensive [ˌkɑmprɪˈhɛnsɪv] *adj* comprensivo

compress [ˈkɑmprɛs] *s* compressa ‖ [kəmˈprɛs] *tr* comprimere

compressed' air' *s* aria compressa

compression [kəmˈprɛʃən] *s* compressione

comprise [kəmˈpraɪz] *tr* comprendere, includere; **to be comprised of** consistere di

compromise [ˈkɑmprəˌmaɪz] *s* com-

promesso ‖ *tr* (*a dispute*) transigere, comporre; (*to put in danger*) compromettere ‖ *intr* transigere, fare un compromesso

comptroller [kənˈtrolər] *s* economo, amministratore *m*, controllore *m*

compulsive [kəmˈpʌlsɪv] *adj* obbligatorio, coercitivo; (psychol) compulsivo

compulsory [kəmˈpʌlsəri] *adj* obbligatorio

compute [kəmˈpjut] *tr & intr* computare, calcolare

computer [kəmˈpjutər] *s* calcolatore *m*; elaboratore *m*

comrade [ˈkɑmræd] or [ˈkɑmrɪd] *s* camerata *m*, compagno

com'rade in arms' *s* compagno d'armi

con [kɑn] *s* contro ‖ *v* (*pret & pp conned; ger conning*) *tr* imparare a memoria; (slang) imbrogliare

concave [ˈkɑnkev] or [kɑnˈkev] *adj* concavo

conceal [kənˈsil] *tr* nascondere; (*to keep secret*) celare

concealment [kənˈsilmənt] *s* occultamento; (*place*) nascondiglio

concede [kənˈsid] *tr* concedere

conceit [kənˈsit] *s* (*high opinion of oneself*) presunzione; (*fanciful notion*) concetto sottile

conceited [kənˈsitɪd] *adj* vanitoso

conceivable [kənˈsivəbəl] *adj* concepibile

conceive [kənˈsiv] *tr & intr* concepire

concentrate [ˈkɑnsənˌtret] *s* concentrato ‖ *tr* concentrare ‖ *intr* concentrarsi; **to concentrate on** concentrarsi in

concentra'tion camp' [ˌkɑnsənˈtreʃən] *s* campo di concentrazione

concept [ˈkɑnsɛpt] *s* concetto

conception [kənˈsɛpʃən] *s* concezione

concern [kənˈsʌrn] *s* interesse *m*; (*worry*) ansietà *f*; (*firm*) ditta, compagnia; **of concern** d'interesse ‖ *tr* concernere; **as concerns** circa; **to concern oneself** interessarsi; **to whom it may concern** a chiunque possa averne interesse

concerning [kənˈsʌrnɪŋ] *prep* riguardo a

concert [ˈkɑnsərt] *s* concerto ‖ [kənˈsʌrt] *tr & intr* concertare

con'cert·mas'ter *s* primo violino

concer·to [kənˈtʃɛrto] *s* (*-tos* or *-ti* [ti]) concerto

concession [kənˈsɛʃən] *s* concessione

conciliate [kənˈsɪliˌet] *tr* conciliare, conciliarsi con

concise [kənˈsaɪs] *adj* conciso

conclude [kənˈklud] *tr* concludere ‖ *intr* concludersi, terminare

conclusion [kənˈkluʒən] *s* conclusione; **in conclusion** per finire; **to try conclusions with** misurarsi con

conclusive [kənˈklusɪv] *adj* decisivo, convincente

concoct [kɑnˈkɑkt] *tr* preparare, confezionare; (*a story*) inventare

concoction [kɑnˈkɑkʃən] *s* preparazione, mescolanza; (unpleasant in taste) intruglio

concomitant [kən'kɑmɪtənt] adj concomitante || s fatto or sintomo concomitante

concord ['kɑŋkərd] s concordia, armonia; (treaty) accordo; (gram) concordanza

concourse ['kɑŋkors] s confluenza; (crowd) affluenza, concorso; (boulevard) viale m; (rr) salone m principale

concrete ['kɑnkrit] or [kɑn'krit] adj concreto; fatto di cemento; solido || s cemento, calcestruzzo || tr (e.g., a sidewalk) cementare

con'crete mix'er s betoniera

con·cur [kən'kʌr] v (pret & pp -curred; ger -curring) intr (to work together) concorrere; (to agree) essere d'accordo, aderire

concurrence [kən'kʌrəns] s concorso; (agreement) accordo

concurrent [kən'kʌrənt] adj concomitante, simultaneo; cooperante; armonioso

concussion [kən'kʌʃən] s scossa, urto; (of brain) commozione cerebrale

condemn [kən'dɛm] tr condannare; (to take for public use) espropriare

condemnation [,kɑndəm'neʃən] s condanna

condense [kən'dɛns] tr condensare || intr condensarsi

condescend [,kɑndɪ'sɛnd] intr condiscendere, degnarsi

condescending [,kɑndɪ'sɛndɪŋ] adj condiscendente

condescension [,kɑndɪ'sɛnʃən] s condiscendenza, degnazione

condiment ['kɑndɪmənt] s condimento

condition [kən'dɪʃən] s condizione; clausola; **on condition that** a condizione che || tr condizionare; mettere in buone condizioni fisiche

conditional [kən'dɪʃənəl] adj & s condizionale m

condole [kən'dol] intr condolersi

condolence [kən'doləns] s condoglianza

condone [kən'don] tr condonare

conduce [kən'djus] or [kən'dus] intr contribuire, indurre

conducive [kən'djusɪv] or [kən'dusɪv] adj contribuente

conduct ['kɑndʌkt] s condotta; direzione || [kən'dʌkt] tr condurre; (an orchestra) dirigere; **to conduct oneself** condursi, comportarsi || intr dirigere

conductor [kən'dʌktər] s direttore m; (of a streetcar) fattorino, conduttore m; (phys) conduttore m; (rr) capotreno

conduit ['kɑndɪt] or ['kɑndu·ɪt] s condotto

cone [kon] s cono; (bot) pigna

Con'estoga wag'on ['kɑnɪ'stogə] s carriaggio coperto

confectioner [kən'fɛkʃənər] s confettiere m, pasticcere m

confec'tioners' sug'ar s zucchero in polvere finissimo

confectioner·y [kən'fɛkʃə,neri] s (-ies) confetteria, pasticceria; (candies) confetture fpl

confedera·cy [kən'fɛdərəsi] s (-cies) confederazione; lega

confederate [kən'fɛdərɪt] s alleato; (in crime) complice mf || [kən'fɛdə,ret] tr confederare || intr confederarsi

con·fer [kən'fʌr] v (pret & pp -ferred; ger -ferring) tr conferire || intr conferire, abboccarsi

conference ['kɑnfərəns] s conferenza

confess [kən'fɛs] tr confessare, ammettere || intr confessare, confessarsi

confession [kən'fɛʃən] s confessione

confessional [kən'fɛʃənəl] s confessionale m

confes'sion of faith' s professione di fede

confessor [kən'fɛsər] s confessore m

confetti [kən'fɛti] s coriandoli mpl

confide [kən'faɪd] tr confidare; (to entrust) affidare || intr confidarsi

confidence ['kɑnfɪdəns] s fiducia; sicurezza di sé; (boldness) baldanza; (secrecy) confidenza

confident ['kɑnfɪdənt] adj fiducioso; baldanzoso || s confidente mf

confidential [,kɑnfɪ'dɛnʃəl] adj confidenziale

confine ['kɑnfaɪn] s confine m || [kən'faɪn] tr limitare; confinare; **to be confined** essere in altro stato; **to be confined to bed** dover stare a letto

confinement [kən'faɪnmənt] s confino; (childbirth) parto; (imprisonment) prigionia

confirm [kən'fʌrm] tr confermare; (eccl) cresimare

confirmed [kən'fʌrmd] adj (e.g., piece of news) confermato; —(bachelor; drunkard) impenitente; inveterato; (e.g., invalid) cronico

confiscate ['kɑnfɪs,ket] tr confiscare

conflagration [,kɑnflə'greʃən] s conflagrazione

conflict ['kɑnflɪkt] s conflitto || [kən'flɪkt] intr lottare; essere in conflitto

conflicting [kən'flɪktɪŋ] adj contrastante; contraddittorio

confluence ['kɑnflu·əns] s confluenza

conform [kən'fɔrm] tr conformare || intr conformarsi

conformi·ty [kən'fɔrmɪti] s (-ties) conformità f; **in conformity with** in conformità di

confound [kɑn'faʊnd] tr confondere || ['kɑn'faʊnd] tr maledire; **confound it!** accidenti!

confounded [kɑn'faʊndɪd] or ['kɑn'faʊndɪd] adj maledetto; (hateful) odioso

confront [kən'frʌnt] tr affrontare, opporsi a; (to bring face to face) raffrontare; (to compare) confrontare

confrontation [,kɑnfrən'teʃən] s contestazione

confuse [kən'fjuz] tr confondere; **to get confused** confondersi

confusion [kən'fjuʒən] s confusione

congeal [kən'dʒil] *tr* congelare; coagulare ‖ *intr* congelarsi; (*said, e.g., of blood*) coagularsi

congenial [kən'dʒinjəl] *adj* (*agreeable*) simpatico; (*having similar tastes*) affine; (*suited to one's needs or tastes*) congeniale

congenital [kən'dʒenɪtəl] *adj* congenito

con'ger eel' ['kɑŋgər] *s* grongo

congest [kən'dʒest] *tr* congestionare ‖ *intr* essere congestionato

congestion [kən'dʒestʃən] *s* congestione

conglomerate [kən'glɑmərɪt] *adj & s* conglomerato ‖ [kən'glɑmə‚ret] *tr* conglomerare ‖ *intr* conglomerarsi

congratulate [kən'grætʃə‚let] *tr* congratularsi con

congratulation [kən‚grætʃə'leʃən] *s* congratulazione, felicitazione

congregate ['kɑŋgrɪ‚get] *intr* congregarsi

congregation [‚kɑŋgrɪ'geʃən] *s* congregazione; fedeli *mpl* di una chiesa

congress ['kɑŋgrɪs] *s* parlamento; congresso

con'gress·man *s* (**-men**) deputato al congresso degli S.U.

con'gress·wom'an *s* (**-wom'en**) deputatessa al congresso degli S.U.

conical ['kɑnɪkəl] *adj* conico

conjecture [kən'dʒektʃər] *s* congettura ‖ *tr & intr* congetturare

conjugate ['kɑndʒə‚get] *tr* coniugare

conjugation [‚kɑndʒə'geʃən] *s* coniugazione

conjunction [kən'dʒʌŋkʃən] *s* congiunzione

conjure [kən'dʒur] *tr* (*to entreat*) scongiurare ‖ ['kɑndʒər] *or* ['kʌndʒər] *tr* evocare, stregare; **to conjure up** evocare ‖ *intr* fare delle stregonerie

conk [kɑŋk] *intr*—**to conk out** (slang) essere in panna; (slang) svenire

connect [kə'nekt] *tr* connettere, unire ‖ *intr* connettersi, essere associato; (*said of public conveyances*) operare in coincidenza

connect'ing rod' [kə'nektɪŋ] *s* (mach) biella

connection [kə'nekʃən] *s* connessione; unione, associazione; (*of trains*) coincidenza; (*relative*) parente *mf*; (*e.g., of a water pipe*) allacciamento; **in connection with** rispetto a

con'ning tow'er ['kɑnɪŋ] *s* (nav) torretta

conniption [kə'nɪpʃən] *s* (slang) attacco di rabbia

connive [kə'naɪv] *intr* essere connivente; **to connive at** chiudere un occhio su

connote [kə'not] *tr* indicare, suggerire

conquer ['kɑŋkər] *tr & intr* conquistare

conqueror ['kɑŋkərər] *s* conquistatore *m*

conquest ['kɑŋkwest] *s* conquista

conscience ['kɑnʃəns] *s* coscienza; **in all conscience** a prezzo onesto; certamente

conscientious [‚kɑnʃɪ'enʃəs] *adj* coscienzioso

conscien'tious objec'tor [ɑb'dʒektər] *s* obiettore *m* di coscienza

conscious ['kɑnʃəs] *adj* (*aware of one's existence*) cosciente; (*aware*) conscio, consapevole; (*lie*) consapevole; **to become conscious** riprendere i sensi

consciousness ['kɑnʃəsnɪs] *s* coscienza, conoscenza; **to lose consciousness** perdere la conoscenza

conscript ['kɑnskrɪpt] *s* coscritto ‖ [kən'skrɪpt] *tr* coscrivere, arruolare

conscription [kən'skrɪpʃən] *s* coscrizione

consecrate ['kɑnsɪ‚kret] *tr* consacrare

consecutive [kən'sekjətɪv] *adj* consecutivo; di seguito

consensus [kən'sensəs] *s* consenso

consent [kən'sent] *s* consenso; **by common consent** per comune consenso ‖ *intr* consentire

consequence ['kɑnsɪ‚kwens] *s* conseguenza

consequential [‚kɑnsɪ'kwenʃəl] *adj* conseguente; importante, d'importanza; pomposo, pieno di sé

consequently ['kɑnsɪ‚kwentli] *adv* conseguentemente, per conseguenza

conservation [‚kɑnsər'veʃən] *s* conservazione; preservazione delle foreste

conservatism [kən'sʌrvə‚tɪzəm] *s* conservatorismo

conservative [kən'sʌrvətɪv] *adj* conservatore; (*cautious*) cauto; (*preserving*) conservativo; (*free from fads*) tradizionale ‖ *s* conservatore *m*

conservato·ry [kən'sʌrvə‚tori] *s* (**-ries**) (*greenhouse*) serra; (mus) conservatorio

conserve [kən'sʌrv] *tr* conservare

consider [kən'sɪdər] *tr* considerare

considerable [kən'sɪdərəbəl] *adj* (*fairly large*) considerevole; (*worth thinking about*) considerabile

considerate [kən'sɪdərɪt] *adj* riguardoso, premuroso

consideration [kən‚sɪdə'reʃən] *s* considerazione; (*reason*) motivo; (*money*) pagamento; **in consideration of** a cagione di; in cambio di; **on no consideration** in nessuna maniera, mai; **under consideration** in considerazione, sotto esame; **without due consideration** senza riflessione, alla leggera

considering [kən'sɪdərɪŋ] *adv* tutto considerato ‖ *prep* per, visto ‖ *conj* considerando che, visto che

consign [kən'saɪn] *tr* consegnare; (*to send*) inviare; (*to set apart*) assegnare

consignee [‚kɑnsaɪ'ni] *s* consegnatario

consignment [kən'saɪnmənt] *s* consegna; **on consignment** in consegna

consist [kən'sɪst] *intr*—**to consist in** consistere in; **to consist of** consistere in, constare di

consisten·cy [kən'sɪstənsi] *s* (**-cies**) (*firmness, amount of firmness*) consistenza; (*logical connection*) coerenza

consistent [kən'sɪstənt] *adj* (*holding firmly together*) consistente; (*agree-*

ing with itself or oneself) conseguente, coerente; compatibile
consolation [ˌkɑnsəˈleʃən] *s* consolazione
console [ˈkɑnsol] *s* (*table*) console *f;*
(rad, telv) mobile *m;* (mus) console
f ‖ [kənˈsol] *tr* consolare
consonant [ˈkɑnsənənt] *adj* consonante, armonioso; (gram) consonantico ‖ *s* consonante *f*
consort [ˈkɑnsərt] *s* consorte *mf* ‖
[kənˈsərt] *intr* associarsi; (*to agree*)
concordarsi
conspicuous [kənˈspɪkjuˌəs] *adj* visibile, manifesto; notevole; (*too noticeable*) appariscente; **to make oneself conspicuous** farsi notare
conspira·cy [kənˈspɪrəsi] *s* (**-cies**) cospirazione, congiura
conspire [kənˈspaɪr] *intr* cospirare,
congiurare; (*to act together*) cooperare
constable [ˈkɑnstəbəl] or [ˈkʌnstəbəl]
s poliziotto; (*keeper of a castle*)
conestabile *m*
constancy [ˈkɑnstənsi] *s* costanza
constant [ˈkɑnstənt] *adj & s* costante *f*
constellation [ˌkɑnstəˈleʃən] *s* costella-
zione
constipate [ˈkɑnstɪˌpet] *tr* costipare
constipation [ˌkɑnstɪˈpeʃən] *s* costipa-
zione
constituen·cy [kənˈstɪtʃuˌənsi] *s* (**-cies**)
(*voters*) elettorato; (*district*) circoscrizione elettorale
constituent [kənˈstɪtʃuˌənt] *adj* costituente ‖ *s* (*component*) parte *f* costituente; (*voter*) elettore *m;* (*of a
chemical substance*) costituente *m*
constitute [ˈkɑnstɪˌtjut] or [ˈkɑnstɪˌ
tut] *tr* costituire
constitution [ˌkɑnstɪˈtjuʃən] or [ˌkɑn-
stɪˈtuʃən] *s* costituzione
constrain [kənˈstren] *tr* (*to force*) costringere; (*to restrain*) restringere,
comprimere
constrict [kənˈstrɪkt] *tr* stringere, comprimere
construct [kənˈstrʌkt] *tr* costruire
construction [kənˈstrʌkʃən] *s* costruzione; (*meaning*) interpretazione
construe [kənˈstru] *tr* (*to interpret*)
interpretare; (*to translate*) tradurre;
(gram) analizzare
consul [ˈkɑnsəl] *s* console *m*
consular [ˈkɑnsələr] or [ˈkɑnsjələr]
adj consolare
consulate [ˈkɑnsəlɪt] or [ˈkɑnsjəlɪt] *s*
consolato
consult [kənˈsʌlt] *tr* consultare ‖ *intr*
consultarsi
consultation [ˌkɑnsəlˈteʃən] *s* consultazione, conferenza
consume [kənˈsum] or [kənˈsjum] *tr*
consumare; distruggere; **consumed
with** (*passion*) arso di; (*curiosity*)
assorbito da
consumer [kənˈsumər] or [kənˈsjumər]
s consumatore *m*
consum'er goods' *spl* beni *mpl* di consumo

consumerism [kənˈsumər ˌizem] *s* consumismo
consummate [kənˈsʌmɪt] *adj* consu-
mato ‖ [ˈkɑnsəˌmet] *tr* consumare
consumption [kənˈsʌmpʃən] *s* (*decay*)
consunzione; (*using up*) consumo;
(pathol) consunzione
consumptive [kənˈsʌmptɪv] *adj* tuber-
colotico, tisico; (*wasteful*) logorante
‖ *s* tisico, etico
contact [ˈkɑntækt] *s* contatto; (elec)
contatto; (elec) presa di corrente ‖
tr (coll) mettersi in contatto con ‖
intr (coll) mettersi in contatto
con'tact break'er *s* ruttore *m*
con'tact lens' *s* lente *f* a contatto
contagion [kənˈtedʒən] *s* contagio
contagious [kənˈtedʒəs] *adj* contagioso
contain [kənˈten] *tr* contenere; **to contain oneself** frenarsi
container [kənˈtenər] *s* recipiente *m*,
contenitore *m*
contaminate [kənˈtæmɪˌnet] *tr* contaminare
contamination [kənˌtæmɪˈneʃən] *s*
contaminazione
contemplate [ˈkɑntəmˌplet] *tr* contemplare; (*to think about*) meditare; (*to
have in mind*) progettare, avere in
mente ‖ *intr* meditare
contemplation [ˌkɑntəmˈpleʃən] *s* con-
templazione; (*intention*) intenzione
contemporaneous [kənˌtempəˈreniˌəs]
adj contemporaneo, coevo
contemporar·y [kənˈtempəˌreri] *adj*
contemporaneo, coevo ‖ *s* (**-ies**) contemporaneo
contempt [kənˈtempt] *s* (*despising*) disprezzo; (*condition of being de-
spised*) dispregio; (*of the law*) disprezzo
contemptible [kənˈtemptɪbəl] *adj* disprezzabile, spregevole
contempt' of court' *s* (law) offesa alla
magistratura, oltraggio al tribunale
contemptuous [kənˈtemptʃuˌəs] *adj*
sprezzante, sdegnoso
contend [kənˈtend] *tr* dichiarare ‖
intr (*to argue*) disputare, contendere;
(*to fight*) lottare
contender [kənˈtendər] *s* competitore
m, concorrente *m*
content [kənˈtent] *adj* contento; (*willing*) pronto ‖ *s* contentezza ‖ [ˈkɑn-
tent] *s* contenuto; **contents** contenuto
‖ [kənˈtent] *tr* contentare
contented [kənˈtentɪd] *adj* soddisfatto
contention [kənˈtenʃən] *s* disputa, litigio; contenzione
contentious [kənˈtenʃəs] *adj* litigioso
contentment [kənˈtentmənt] *s* contentezza
contest [ˈkɑntest] *s* contesa, controversia; (*game*) gara ‖ [kənˈtest] *tr* disputare, contestare ‖ *intr* combattere, fare resistenza
contestant [kənˈtestənt] *s* concorrente
m; (law) contendente *m*
context [ˈkɑntekst] *s* contesto
contiguous [kənˈtɪgjuˌəs] *adj* contiguo
continence [ˈkɑntɪnəns] *s* continenza
continent [ˈkɑntɪnənt] *adj & s* conti-

nente *m;* **on the Continent** nel continente europeo

continental [,kɑntɪˈnɛntəl] *adj* & *s* continentale *mf*

contingen·cy [kənˈtɪndʒənsi] *s* (-cies) contingenza, congiuntura; *(chance)* eventualità *f*

contingent [kənˈtɪndʒənt] *adj* eventuale; imprevisto; *(philos)* contingente; **to be contingent upon** dipendere da

continual [kənˈtɪnju·əl] *adj* continuo

continuance [kənˈtɪnjuəns] *s* continuazione; *(in office)* permanenza; *(law)* rinvio

continue [kənˈtɪnju] *tr* continuare; *(to cause to remain)* mantenere; *(law)* rinviare ‖ *intr* continuare; rimanere

continui·ty [,kɑntɪˈnju·ɪti] or [,kɑntɪˈnu·ɪti] *s* (-ties) continuità *f;* *(mov* & *telv)* sceneggiatura; *(rad)* copione *m*

continuous [kənˈtɪnju·əs] *adj* continuo

contin'uous show'ing *s* (mov) spettacolo permanente

contortion [kənˈtɔr/ən] *s* contorsione; *(of faces)* distorsione

contour [ˈkɑntʊr] *s* contorno

con'tour line' *s* curva di livello, isoipsa

contraband [ˈkɑntrəˌbænd] *adj* di contrabbando ‖ *s* contrabbando

contrabass [ˈkɑntrəˌbes] *s* contrabasso

contraceptive [,kɑntrəˈsɛptɪv] *adj* & *s* antifecondativo

contract [ˈkɑntrækt] *s* contratto ‖ [ˈkɑntrækt] or [kənˈtrækt] *tr* (*a business deal)* contrattare; *(marriage)* contrarre ‖ *intr* *(to shrink)* contrarsi; **to contract for** contrattare, appaltare

contraction [kənˈtræk/ən] *s* contrazione

contractor [kənˈtræktər] *s* *(person who makes a contract)* contraente *m;* *(person who contracts to supply material)* appaltatore *m,* imprenditore *m;* *(in building)* capomastro

contradict [,kɑntrəˈdɪkt] *tr* contraddire

contradiction [,kɑntrəˈdɪk/ən] *s* contraddizione

contradictory [,kɑntrəˈdɪktəri] *adj* contraddittorio

contrail [ˈkɑnˌtrel] *s* (aer) scia di condensazione

contral·to [kənˈtrælto] *s* (-tos) *(person)* contralto *mf;* *(voice)* contralto *m*

contraption [kənˈtræp/ən] *s* (coll) aggeggio

contra·ry [ˈkɑntreri] *adj* contrario ‖ [kənˈtreri] *adj* ostinato, caparbio ‖ [ˈkɑntreri] *s* (-ries) contrario; **on the contrary** al contrario ‖ *adv* contrariamente

contrast [ˈkɑntræst] *s* contrasto ‖ [kənˈtræst] *tr* confrontare ‖ *intr* contrastare

contravene [,kɑntrəˈvin] *tr* contraddire; *(a law)* contravvenire (with *dat*)

contribute [kənˈtrɪbjut] *tr* contribuire ‖ *intr* contribuire; *(to a newspaper)* collaborare

contribution [,kɑntrɪˈbju/ən] *s* contribuzione; *(to a newspaper)* collaborazione

contributor [kənˈtrɪbjutər] *s* contributore *m;* *(to a newspaper)* collaboratore *m*

contrite [kənˈtraɪt] *adj* contrito

contrition [kənˈtrɪ/ən] *s* contrizione

contrivance [kənˈtraɪvəns] *s* dispositivo, congegno; *(faculty)* invenzione; *(scheme)* artificio, piano

contrive [kənˈtraɪv] *tr* inventare; *(to scheme up)* macchinare; *(to bring about)* effettuare; **to contrive to** trovare il modo di

con·trol [kənˈtrol] *s* controllo; *(check)* freno; **controls** comandi *mpl;* **to get under control** riuscire a controllare ‖ *v* *(pret* & *pp* -trolled; *ger* -trolling) *tr* controllare

controller [kənˈtrolər] *s* controllore *m;* analista *mf* di gestione; economo; *(mach)* regolatore *m;* *(elec)* interruttore *m* di linea

control'ling in'terest *s* maggioranza delle azioni

control', stick' *s* leva di comando

controversial [,kɑntrəˈvɑr/əl] *adj* controverso, polemico, discusso

controver·sy [ˈkɑntrəˌvɑrsi] *s* (-sies) controversia

controvert [ˈkɑntrəˌvɑrt] or [,kɑntrəˈvɑrt] *tr* contraddire

contumacious [,kɑntjuˈme/əs] or [,kɑntuˈme/əs] *adj* ribelle, contumace

contuma·cy [ˈkɑntjuməsi] or [ˈkɑntuməsi] *s* (-cies) contumacia

contusion [kənˈtjuʒən] or [kənˈtuʒən] *s* contusione

conundrum [kəˈnʌndrəm] *s* indovinello

convalesce [,kɑnvəˈlɛs] *intr* essere convalescente

convalescence [,kɑnvəˈlɛsəns] *s* convalescenza

convalescent [,kɑnvəˈlɛsənt] *adj* & *s* convalescente *mf*

con'vales'cent home' *s* convalescenziario

convene [kənˈvin] *tr* convocare ‖ *intr* convenire

convenience [kənˈvinjəns] *s* convenienza; *(comfort)* agio; *(anything that saves work)* conforto; **at your earliest convenience** quanto prima

convenient [kənˈvinjənt] *adj* conveniente, adatto; comodo; **convenient to** *(near)* (coll) vicino a

convent [ˈkɑnvɛnt] *s* convento di religiose

convention [kənˈvɛn/ən] *s* convenzione, assemblea; **conventions** *(customs)* convenzioni *fpl*

conventional [kənˈvɛn/ənəl] *adj* convenzionale

converge [kənˈvʌrdʒ] *intr* convergere

conversant [kənˈvʌrsənt] *adj* versato, esperto, dotto

conversation [,kɑnvərˈse/ən] *s* conversazione

converse [ˈkɑnvʌrs] *adj* & *s* contrario ‖ [kənˈvʌrs] *intr* conversare

conversion [kən'vʌrʒən] *s* conversione; (*unlawful appropriation*) malversazione

convert ['kɑnvʌrt] *s* convertito || [kən'vʌrt] *tr* convertire; misappropriare || *intr* convertirsi

convertible [kən'vʌrtɪbəl] *adj & s* convertibile *f*; (aut) trasformabile *f*, decappottabile *f*

convex ['kɑnvɛks] or [kɑn'vɛks] *adj* convesso

convey [kən've] *tr* (*to carry*) trasportare; (*liquids*) convogliare; (*sounds*) trasmettere; (*to express*) esprimere; (*e.g., property*) trasferire

conveyance [kən've·əns] *s* trasporto; veicolo; comunicazione; (*of property*) trasferimento; (*deed*) titolo di proprietà

convey'or belt' [kən've·ər] *s* trasportatore *m*

convict ['kɑnvɪkt] *s* condannato || [kən'vɪkt] *tr* convincere, condannare

conviction [kən'vɪkʃən] *s* condanna; (*belief*) convinzione, convincimento

convince [kən'vɪns] *tr* convincere

convincing [kən'vɪnsɪŋ] *adj* convincente

convivial [kən'vɪvɪ·əl] *adj* (*festive*) conviviale; gioviale, bonaccione

convocation [ˌkɑnvə'keʃən] *s* convocazione, assemblea

convoke [kən'vok] *tr* convocare

convoy ['kɑnvɔɪ] *s* (*of ships*) convoglio; (*of vehicles*) carovana || *tr* convogliare

convulse [kən'vʌls] *tr* (*to shake*) scuotere; (*to throw into convulsions*) mettere in convulsioni; (*to cause to shake with laughter*) far torcere dalle risa

coo [ku] *intr* tubare, gemere

cook [kʊk] *s* cuoco || *tr* cuocere; **to cook up** (coll) preparare, macchinare || *intr* (*said of food*) cuocere; (*said of a person*) fare il cuoco

cook'book' *s* libro di cucina

cookie ['kʊki] *s var of* **cooky**

cooking ['kʊkɪŋ] *s* culinaria

cook'out' *s* picnic *m*, spuntino all'aperto

cook'stove' *s* cucina economica

cook·y ['kʊki] *s* (*-ies*) pasticcino, biscotto

cool [kul] *adj* fresco; calmo; (*not cordial*) freddo; (*bold*) sfacciato || *s* fresco || *tr* rinfres.are; **to cool one's heels** fare anticamera || *intr* rinfrescarsi; **to cool off** rinfrescarsi; calmarsi

coolant ['kulənt] *s* miscela refrigerante

cooler ['kulər] *s* ghiacciaia; (slang) prigione

cool'-head'ed *adj* calmo, imperturbabile

coolish ['kulɪʃ] *adj* freschetto

coon [kun] *s* procione *m*

coop [kup] *s* pollaio; conigliera; **to fly the coop** (slang) scapparsene || *tr*— **to coop up** rinchiudere tra quattro mura

cooper ['kupər] *s* bottaio

cooperate [ko'ɑpə‿ret] *intr* cooperare

cooperation [koˌɑpə're/ən] *s* cooperazione

cooperative [ko'ɑpə‿retɪv] *adj* cooperativo || *s* cooperativa

coordinate [ko'ɔrdɪnɪt] *adj* coordinato; (gram) coordinativo || *s* (math) coordinata || [ko'ɔrdɪ‿net] *tr & intr* coordinare

coot [kut] *s* (zool) folaga; (slang) vecchio pazzo

cootie ['kuti] *s* (slang) pidocchio

cop [kɑp] *s* (slang) poliziotto || *v* (*pret & pp* **copped**) *ger* **copping**) *tr* (slang) rubare

copartner [ko'pɑrtnər] *s* consocio, socio

cope [kop] *intr*— **to cope with** tener testa a

cope'stone' *s* pietra da cimasa

copier ['kɑpɪ·ər] *s* (*person*) copista *mf*; imitatore *m*; (*machine*) duplicatore *m*

copilot ['ko‿paɪlət] *s* copilota *mf*

coping ['kopɪŋ] *s* coronamento, cimasa

cop'ing saw' *s* seghetto da traforo

copious ['kopɪ·əs] *adj* copioso

copper [kɑp'ər] *s* rame *m*; (*coin*) soldo; (*boiler*) calderone *m*; (slang) poliziotto

cop'per·head' *s* vipera (*Ancistrodon contortrix*)

cop'per·smith' *s* battirame *m*, calderaio

coppice ['kɑpɪs] or **copse** [kɑps] *s* boschetto

copulate ['kɑpjə‿let] *intr* copularsi, congiungersi carnalmente

cop·y ['kɑpi] *s* (*-ies*) copia; modello; manoscritto || *v* (*pret & pp* **-ied**) *tr* copiare, imitare || *intr* copiare; **to copy after** imitare

cop'y·book' *s* quaderno

copyist ['kɑpɪ·ɪst] *s* copista *mf*; imitatore *m*

cop'y·right' *s* copyright *m*, diritto di proprietà letteraria || *tr* registrare; proteggere con copyright

cop'y·writ'er *s* copy-writer *m*, redattore *m* pubblicitario

coquetry [ˌkoˈkɑtri] or [ko'ketri] *s* (*-ries*) civetteria

coquette [ko'ket] *s* civetta

coquettish [ko'ketɪʃ] *adj* civettuolo

coral ['kɑrəl] or ['kɔrəl] *adj* corallino || *s* corallo

cor'al reef' *s* banco di coralli

cord [kɔrd] *s* corda, fune *f*; (*corduroy*) tessuto cordonato; (elec) cordone *m* || *tr* legare con corda

cordial ['kɔrdʒəl] *adj & s* cordiale *m*

corduroy ['kɔrdə‿rɔɪ] *s* velluto a coste; **corduroys** pantaloni *mpl* alla cacciatora

core [kor] *s* (*of fruit*) torsolo; (*central part*) centro; (*of problem*) nocciolo; (*of earth*) barisfera, nucleo centrale; (phys) nucleo; **rotten to the core** guasto nelle ossa

corespondent [ˌkorɪs'pɑndənt] *s* coimputato in un processo di divorzio

cork [kɔrk] *s* (*bark*) sughero; (*stopper*) tappo, tappo di sughero || *tr* tappare

cork' oak' *s* sughero

cork'screw' s cavatappi m
cormorant ['kɔrmərənt] s cormorano
corn [kɔrn] s granturco, mais m; (kernel) chicco; (thickening of skin) callo; (whiskey) whisky m di granturco; (Brit) grano; (Scot) avena; (slang) banalità f
corn' bread' s pane m di farina gialla
corn' cake' s omelette f di granturco
corn'cob' s tutolo
corn'cob pipe' s pipa fatta di un tutolo di pannocchia
corn'crib' s granaio per le pannocchie
corn' cure' s callifugo
cornea ['kɔrnɪ‧ə] s cornea
corner ['kɔrnər] s angolo; (of street) cantonata; situazione difficile; (of the eye) coda dell'occhio; (com) accaparramento, incetta, bagarinaggio; to cut corners tagliare le spese; to turn the corner passare il punto più pericoloso || tr mettere in una situazione difficile; (the market) incettare, accaparrare
cor'ner cup'board s cantoniera, armadio d'angolo
cor'ner stone' s pietra angolare; (of new building) prima pietra
cornet [kɔr'nɛt] s cornetta
corn' exchange' s borsa dei cereali
corn'field' s (in U.S.A.) campo di granturco; (in England) campo di grano; (in Scotland) campo di avena
corn'flakes' spl fiocchi mpl di granturco
corn' flour' s farina di granturco
corn'flow'er s fiordaliso
corn'husk' s brattea, cartoccio
cornice ['kɔrnɪs] s (of house) cornicione m; (of room) cornice f
corn' liq'uor s whisky m di granturco
corn' meal' s farina di granturco
corn' on–the cob' s granturco servito in pannocchia
corn' plas'ter s cerotto per i calli
corn' silk' s barba del granturco
corn'stalk' s fusto di granturco
corn'starch' s amido di granturco
corn‧y ['kɔrni] adj (-ier; -iest) (slang) banale, trito, triviale
coronation [,kɑrə'neʃən] or [,kɔrə-'neʃən] s incoronazione
coroner ['kɑrənər] or ['kɔrənər] s magistrato inquirente
cor'oner's in'quest s inchiesta giudiziaria dinanzi a giuria
coronet ['kɑrə,nɛt] or ['kɔrə,nɛt] s corona (non reale); diadema m
corporal ['kɔrpərəl] adj caporalesco || s caporale m
corporation [,kɔrpə'reʃən] s società anonima
corps [kɔr] s (corps [kɔrz]) corpo
corps' de bal'let s corpo di ballo
corpse [kɔrps] s cadavere m
corpulent ['kɔrpjələnt] adj corpulento
corpuscle ['kɔrpəsəl] s (anat) globulo; (phys) corpuscolo
cor‧ral [kə'ræl] s recinto per bestiame || v (pret & pp -ralled; ger -ralling) tr mettere in un recinto; catturrare
correct [kə'rɛkt] adj corretto || tr correggere
correction [kə'rɛkʃən] s correzione

corrective [kə'rɛktɪv] adj & s correttivo
correctness [kə'rɛktnɪs] s correttezza
correlate ['kɑrə,let] or ['kɔrə,let] tr correlare || intr essere in correlazione
correlation [,kɑrə'leʃən] or [,kɔrə-'leʃən] s correlazione
correspond [,kɑrɪ'spɑnd] or [,kɔrɪ-'spɑnd] intr corrispondere
correspondence [,kɑrɪ'spɑndəns] or [,kɔrɪ'spɑndəns] s corrispondenza
correspond'ence school' s scuola per corrispondenza
correspondent [,kɑrɪ'spɑndənt] or [,kɔrɪ'spɑndənt] adj & s corrispondente mf
corridor ['kɑrɪdər] or ['kɔrɪdər] s corridoio
corroborate [kə'rɑbə,ret] tr corroborare
corrode [kə'rod] tr corrodere || intr corrodersi
corrosion [kə'roʒən] s corrosione
corrosive [kə'rosɪv] adj & s corrosivo
corrugated ['kɑrə,getɪd] or ['kɔrə-,getɪd] adj ondulato
corrupt [kə'rʌpt] adj corrotto || tr corrompere; (a language) imbarbarire || intr corrompersi
corruption [kə'rʌpʃən] s corruzione
corsage [kɔr'sɑʒ] s (bodice) corpetto; (bouquet) mazzolino di fiori da appuntarsi al vestito
corsair ['kɔr,ser] s corsaro
corset ['kɔrsɪt] s corsetto
Corsican ['kɔrsɪkən] adj & s corso
cortege [kɔr'teʒ] s corteggio
cor‧tex ['kɔr,tɛks] s (-tices [tɪ,siz]) cortice f
cortisone ['kɔrtɪ,son] s cortisone m
corvette [kɔr'vɛt] s corvetta
cosmetic [kaz'mɛtɪk] adj & s cosmetico
cosmic ['kazmɪk] adj cosmico
cosmonaut ['kazmə,nɔt] s cosmonauta mf
cosmopolitan [,kazmə'palɪtən] adj & s cosmopolita mf
cosmos ['kazməs] s cosmo
cost [kɔst] or [kast] s costo, prezzo; at all costs or at any cost ad ogni costo; costs spese fpl processuali || v (pret & pp cost) intr costare
cost‧ly ['kɔstli] or ['kastli] adj (-lier; -liest) costoso; (sumptuous) lussuoso
cost' of liv'ing s costo della vita
costume ['kastjum] or ['kastum] s costume m
cos'tume ball' s ballo in costume
cos'tume jew'elry s gioielli falsi
cot [kat] s (narrow bed) branda; (cottage) capanna, cabina
coterie ['kotəri] s gruppo; (clique) chiesuola
cottage ['katɪdʒ] s casetta, villino
cot'tage cheese' s ricotta americana
cot'ter pin' ['katər] s copiglia, coppiglia
cotton ['katən] s cotone m || intr—to cotton up to (coll) cominciare a provare della simpatia per; (coll) andare d'accordo con
cot'ton can'dy s zucchero filato

cot'ton gin' *s* sgranatrice *f*

cot'ton pick'er ['pɪkər] *s* chi raccoglie il cotone; macchina che raccoglie il cotone

cot'tonseed oil' *s* olio di semi di cotone

cot'ton waste' *s* cascame *m* di cotone

cot'ton·wood' *s* pioppo deltoide

couch [kautʃ] *s* canapè *m*, sofà *m*, divano ‖ *tr* esprimere

couch' grass' *s* gramigna

cougar ['kugər] *s* puma *m*

cough [kɔf] or [kɑf] *s* tosse *f* ‖ *tr*—to cough up sputare, sputare tossendo; (slang) dare, pagare ‖ *intr* tossire

cough' drop' *s* pastiglia per la tosse

cough' syr'up *s* sciroppo per la tosse

could [kud] *v aux*—I could not come yesterday non ho potuto venire ieri; I could not see you tomorrow non potrei vederLa domani; it could not be so non potrebbe essere così

council ['kaunsəl] *s* consiglio; (eccl) concilio

coun'cil·man *s* (-men) consigliere *m* or assessore *m* municipale

coun·sel ['kaunsəl] *s* consiglio; (law-yer) avvocato; to keep one's counsel essere riservato; to take counsel with consultarsi con ‖ *v* (*pret & pp* -seled or -selled; *ger* -seling or -selling) *tr* consigliare ‖ *intr* consigliare; consigliarsi

counselor ['kaunsələr] *s* consigliere *m*; avvocato

count [kaunt] *s* conto; (*nobleman*) conte *m*; (law) capo d'accusa ‖ *tr* contare; to count off by (*twos, threes*) contare per (*due, tre*); to count out escludere; (boxing) contare ‖ *intr* contare; (*to be worth*) valere; to count on contare su

count'down' *s* conteggio alla rovescia

countenance ['kauntinəns] *s* espressione; (*face*) faccia; (*approval*) approvazione ‖ *tr* approvare, incoraggiare

counter ['kauntər] *adj* contrario ‖ *s* contatore *m*; (*token*) gettone *m*; (*table in store*) banco; (*opposite*) contrario ‖ *adv* contro, contrariamente ‖ *tr* contrariare, opporre ‖ *intr* (boxing) rispondere

coun'ter·act' *tr* contrariare, neutralizzare

coun'ter·attack' *s* contrattacco ‖ coun'ter·attack' *tr & intr* contrattaccare

coun'ter·bal'ance *s* contrappeso ‖ coun'ter·bal'ance *tr* controbilanciare

coun'ter·clock'wise' *adj* antiorario ‖ *adv* in senso antiorario

coun'ter·es'pionage' *s* controspionaggio

counterfeit ['kauntərfɪt] *adj* contraffatto ‖ *s* contraffazione; moneta falsa ‖ *tr & intr* contraffare

counterfeiter ['kauntər‚fɪtər] *s* contraffattore *m*

coun'ter·feit mon'ey *s* moneta falsa

countermand ['kauntər‚mænd] or ['kauntər‚mɑnd] *tr* (*troops*) dare un contrordine a; (*an order; a payment*) cancellare

coun'ter·march' *s* contromarcia ‖ *intr* fare contromarcia

coun'ter·offen'sive *s* controffensiva

coun'ter·pane' *s* sopraccoperta

coun'ter·part' *s* copia; (*person*) sosia

coun'ter·point' *s* (mus) contrappunto; (mus) controcanto

Coun'ter Reforma'tion *s* controriforma

coun'ter·rev'olu'tion *s* controrivoluzione

coun'ter·sign' *s* (*password*) parola d'ordine; (*signature*) controfirma ‖ *tr* controfirmare

coun'ter·sink' *v* (*pret & pp* -sunk) *tr* incassare, accecare

coun'ter·spy' *s* (-spies) membro del controspionaggio

coun'ter·stroke' *s* contraccolpo

coun'ter·weight' *s* contrappeso

countess ['kauntɪs] *s* contessa

countless ['kauntlɪs] *adj* innumerevole

countrified ['kʌntrɪ‚faɪd] *adj* rustico, rurale

coun·try ['kʌntri] *s* (-tries) (*land*) terreno; (*nation*) paese *m*; (*land of one's birth*) patria; (*rural region*) campagna

coun'try club' *s* circolo privato sportivo situato nei sobborghi

coun'try cous'in *s* campagnolo

coun'try estate' *s* tenuta

coun'try·folk' *s* campagnoli *mpl*

coun'try gen'tleman *s* proprietario terriero, signorotto di campagna

coun'try house' *s* casa di campagna

coun'try jake' *s* (coll) zoticone *m*

coun'try life' *s* vita rustica

coun'try·man *s* (-men) paesano, compaesano

coun'try·peo'ple *s* gente *f* di campagna

coun'try·side' *s* campagna

coun'try·wide' *adj* nazionale

coun'try·wom'an *s* (-wom'en) paesana, compaesana

coun·ty ['kaunti] *s* (-ties) contea, distretto

coun'ty seat' *s* capoluogo di contea

coup [ku] *s* colpo; colpo di stato

coup de grâce [ku də 'grɑs] *s* colpo di grazia

coup d'état [ku de'tɑ] *s* colpo di stato

coupe [kup] or coupé [ku'pe] *s* coupé *m*

couple ['kʌpəl] *s* (*of people or animals*) paio, coppia; (*of things*) paio; (*link*) unione ‖ *tr* accoppiare; (*to link*) unire, agganciare ‖ *intr* accoppiarsi

couplet ['kʌplɪt] *s* coppia di versi; (mus) couplet *m*

coupling ['kʌplɪŋ] *s* unione; (mach) giunto

coupon ['kupan] or ['kjupan] *s* coupon *m*, tagliando

courage ['kʌrɪdʒ] *s* coraggio; to have the courage of one's convictions avere il coraggio delle proprie opinioni

courageous [kə'redʒəs] *adj* coraggioso

courier ['kʌrɪ·ər] or ['kurɪ·ər] *s* corriere *m*

course [kors] *s* corso; (*part of meal*) portata; (*place for games*) campo;

(*row*) fila; **in due course** a tempo debito; **in the course of** durante, nel corso di; **of course** certamente, senza dubbio

court [kort] *s* (*uncovered place surrounded by walls*) corte *f*, cortile *m*; (*royal residence; courtship*) corte *f*; (*short street*) vicolo; (*playing area*) campo; (law) corte *f* ‖ *tr* corteggiare; (*e.g., disaster*) andare in cerca di

courteous ['kʌrtɪ‑əs] *adj* cortese

courtesan ['kʌrtɪzən] or ['kortɪzən] *s* cortigiana, meretrice *f*

courte·sy ['kʌrtɪsɪ] *s* (**-sies**) cortesia, gentilezza; **through the courtesy of** con il gentile permesso di

court'house' *s* palazzo di giustizia

courtier ['kortɪ‑ər] *s* cortigiano

court' jest'er *s* buffone *m* di corte

court·ly ['kortlɪ] *adj* (**-lier; -liest**) cortese, cortigiano; ossequioso

court'-mar'tial *s* (**courts-martial**) corte *f* marziale ‖ *v* (*pret & pp* **-tialed** or **-tialled**) *ger* **-tialing** or **-tialling**) *tr* sottomettere a corte marziale

court' plas'ter *s* taffettà *m*

court'room' *s* aula di giustizia

courtship ['kort/ɪp] *s* corte *f*, corteggiamento

court'yard' *s* corte *f*, cortile *m*

cousin ['kʌzɪn] *s* cugino

cove [kov] *s* piccola baia, cala

covenant ['kʌvənənt] *s* convenzione, patto *f* ‖ *tr* promettere solennemente

cover ['kʌvər] *s* (*lid*) coperchio; (*tablecloth; shelter*) coperto; (*of book*) copertina; **to take cover** nascondersi; **under cover** in segreto, segretamente; **under cover of** sotto la protezione di; **under separate cover** in busta a parte, in plico a parte ‖ *tr* coprire; puntare un'arma verso; (journ) riferire, riportare; **to cover up** coprire completamente ‖ *intr* (*said of paint*) spandersi

coverage ['kʌvərɪdʒ] *s* copertura; (journ) servizio giornalistico; (rad, telv) raggio di udibilità

coveralls ['kʌvər‚ɔlz] *spl* tuta

cov'er charge' *s* coperto

cov'ered wag'on *s* carro coperto da tendone

cov'er girl' *s* ragazza-copertina

covering ['kʌvərɪŋ] *s* copertura; involucro

covert ['kʌvərt] *adj* nascosto, segreto

cov'er-up' *s* dissimulazione; sotterfugio

covet ['kʌvɪt] *tr* desiderare, agognare

covetous ['kʌvɪtəs] *adj* cupido

covey ['kʌvɪ] *s* covata

cow [kau] *s* vacca; (*of seal, elephant, etc.*) femmina ‖ *tr* spaventare, intimidire

coward ['kau‑ərd] *s* codardo, vile *m*

cowardice ['kau‑ərdɪs] *s* codardia, viltà *f*

cowardly ['kau‑ərdlɪ] *adj* codardo, vile ‖ *adv* vilmente

cow'bell' *s* campano, campanaccio

cow'boy' *s* cowboy *m*

cow'catch'er *s* (rr) cacciapietre *m*

cower ['kau‑ər] *intr* rannicchiarsi

cow'herd' *s* guardiano d'armenti

cow'hide' *s* pelle *f* di vacca

cowl [kaul] *s* (*hood*) cappuccio; (*monk's cloak*) cappa; (*of car*) sostegno del cofano; (*of chimney*) cappello; (aer) cappottatura

cow'lick' *s* ritrosa

cow'pox' *s* (vet) vaiolo bovino

coxcomb ['kaks‚kom] *s* zerbinotto

coxwain ['kaksən] or ['kak‚swen] *s* timoniere *m*

coy [kɔɪ] *adj* timido, ritroso

co·zy ['kozɪ] *adj* (**-zier; -ziest**) comodo ‖ *s* (**-zies**) copriteiera *m*

C.P.A. ['si'pi'e] *s* (letterword) (**certified public accountant**) esperto contabile

crab [kræb] *s* granchio; (aer) scarroccio; (*complaining person*) (coll) scontroso ‖ *v* (*pret & pp* **crabbed**; *ger* **crabbing**) *intr* (coll) lamentarsi

crab' apple' *s* mela selvatica; (*tree*) melo selvatico

crabbed ['kræbɪd] *adj* sgarbato; (*handwriting*) da gallina; (*style*) oscuro, ermetico

crab' louse' *s* piattola

crab·by ['kræbɪ] *adj* (**-bier; -biest**) scontroso, sgarbato

crack [kræk] *adj* (slang) di prim'ordine, eccellente ‖ *s* (*noise*) schiocco; (*break*) rottura, screpolatura, crepa; (*opening*) fessura; (slang) tentativo; (slang) barzelletta ‖ *tr* (*e.g., a whip*) schioccare; (*to break*) rompere, screpolare; (*oil*) ridurre con distillazione; (coll) risolvere; (*a safe*) (slang) forzare; (*a joke*) (slang) dire; **cracked up to be** (slang) avendo fama di ‖ *intr* (*to make a noise*) scricchiolare; (*to break*) rompersi, screpolarsi; (*said of voice*) diventare fesso; (slang) avere un esaurimento nervoso; **to crack down** (slang) essere severo; **to crack up** (slang) andare a pezzi

cracked [krækt] *adj* rotto, spezzato; (*voice*) fesso; (coll) pazzo

cracker ['krækər] *s* cracker *m*, galletta

crack'er-bar'rel *adj* in piccolo, alla buona

crack'er-jack' *adj* (slang) di prim'ordine ‖ *s* (slang) persona di prim'ordine

cracking ['krækɪŋ] *s* piroscissione

crackle ['krækəl] *s* crepitio, crepito ‖ *intr* crepitare

crack'pot' *adj & s* (coll) mattoide *mf*

crack'-up' *s* accidente *m;* collisione; (*breakdown in health or in relations*) (coll) colasso; (aer) accidente *m* d'atterraggio

cradle ['kredəl] *s* culla; (*of handset*) forcella *f* ‖ *tr* cullare

crad'le-song' *s* ninnananna

craft [kræft] or [krɑft] *s* (*skill*) abilità *f*; (*trade*) mestiere *m;* (*guile*) astuzia, furberia; (*ship*) nave *f*; aeronave

craftiness ['kræftɪnɪs] or ['krɑftɪnɪs] *s* astuzia, furberia

crafts·man *s* (**-men**) operaio specializzato, artigiano

craft' un'ion *s* artigianato, sindacato artigiano

craft-y ['kræfti] or ['krɑfti] *adj* (**-ier; -iest**) astuto, furbo

crag [kræg] *s* roccia scoscesa, rupe *f*

cram [kræm] *v* (*pret & pp* **crammed; ger cramming**) *tr* (*to pack full*) riempire fino all'orlo; (*to stuff with food*) rimpinzare || *intr* rimpinzarsi; (coll) preparare un esame alla svelta

cramp [kræmp] *s* (*painful contraction*) crampo; (*bar with hooks*) grappa; (fig) ostacolo || *tr* ostacolare, restringere

cranber-ry ['kræn‚bɛri] *s* (**-ries**) mirtillo

crane [kren] *s* (orn, mach) gru *f*; (*boom*) (telv, mov) giraffa || *tr* (*one's neck*) allungare || *intr* allungare il collo

crani-um ['kreni-əm] *s* (**-a** [ə]) cranio

crank [kræŋk] *s* manovella; (aut) alzacristalli *m*; (coll) eccentrico || *tr* girare con la manovella; mettere in moto con la manovella

crank'case' *s* coppa dell'olio, carter *m*

crank'shaft' *s* albero a gomito

crank-y ['kræŋki] *adj* (**-ier; -iest**) irritabile; eccentrico

cran-ny ['kræni] *s* (**-nies**) (*crevice*) crepaccio; (*crack*) fessura

crape [krep] *s* crespo

crape'hang'er *s* (slang) pessimista uggioso, guastafeste *mf*

craps [kræps] *s* gioco dei dadi; **to shoot craps** giocare ai dadi

crash [kræʃ] *adj* (coll) d'emergenza || *s* (*noise*) scoppio, schianto; accidente *m*; (*collapse of business*) crac *m*, rovescio; (*bad landing*) atterraggio senza carrello || *tr* fracassare; **to crash the gate** (coll) entrare senza invito || *intr* fracassarsi; (com) fallire; **to cash into** investire, cozzare contro; **to cash through** sfondare

crash' dive' *s* immersione rapida di un sottomarino

crash' hel'met *s* casco

crass [kræs] *adj* crasso

crate [kret] *s* gabbia d'imballaggio || *tr* imballare in una gabbia

crater ['kretər] *s* cratere *m*

cravat [krə'væt] *s* cravatta

crave [krev] *tr* anelare; (*to beg*) implorare || *intr*—**to crave for** desiderare ardentemente

craven ['krevən] *adj & s* codardo

craving ['kreviŋ] *s* anelito, desiderio

craw [krɔ] *s* gozzo

crawl [krɔl] *s* strisciamento, avanzata strisciando; (sports) crawl *m* || *intr* strisciare, avanzare strisciando; (*said of worms*) brulicare; (*said of insects*) formicolare; (*to feel creepy*) sentirsi il formicolio

crayfish ['kreˌfɪʃ] *s* (*Palinurus vulgaris*) aragosta; (*Astacus; Cambarus*) gambero

crayon ['kre-ən] *s* pastello; disegno a pastello || *tr* disegnare a pastello

craze [krez] *s* mania, moda || *tr* fare impazzire

cra-zy ['krezi] *adj* (**-zier; -ziest**) pazzo, matto; **to be crazy about** (coll) esser matto per; **to drive crazy** fare impazzire

cra'zy bone' *s* osso rabbioso (del gomito)

creak [krik] *s* scricchiolio, cigolio || *intr* scricchiolare, cigolare

creak-y ['kriki] *adj* (**-ier; -iest**) stridente, cigolante

cream [krim] *s* crema, panna; (*finest part*) fior fiore *m* || *tr* rendere di consistenza cremosa; (*to remove cream from*) scremare; prendere il meglio di

creamer-y ['kriməri] *s* (**-ies**) (*factory*) caseificio; (*store*) cremeria

cream' puff' *s* bignè *m*

cream-y ['krimi] *adj* (**-ier; -iest**) cremoso; butirroso

crease [kris] *s* piega, grinza || *tr* piegare, raggrinzire || *intr* piegarsi, raggrinzirsi, far pieghe

crease'-resis'tant *adj* antipiega

create [kri'et] *tr* creare

creation [kri'eʃən] *s* creazione; **the Creation** il creato

creative [kri'etɪv] *adj* creativo

creator [kri'etər] *s* creatore *m*

creature ['kritʃər] *s* creatura

credence ['kridəns] *s* credenza

credentials [kri'dɛnʃəlz] *spl* lettere *fpl* credenziali; documento d'autorizzazione

credible ['kredɪbəl] *adj* credibile

credit ['kredɪt] *s* credito; (*in a school*) unità *f* di promozione; (com) avere *m*; **credits** (mov, telv) titoli *mpl* di testa || *tr* accreditare; **to credit s.o. with** s.th attribuire qlco a qlcu

creditable ['kredɪtəbəl] *adj* lodevole

cred'it card' *s* carta di credito

creditor ['kredɪtər] *s* creditore *m*

cre-do ['krido] or ['kredo] *s* (**-dos**) credo

credulous ['kredʒələs] *adj* credulo

creed [krid] *s* credo

creek [krik] *s* fiumicello

creep [krip] *v* (*pret & pp* **crept** [krɛpt]) *intr* strisciare, avanzare strisciando; (*to grow along a wall*) arrampicarsi; (*to feel creepy*) sentirsi il formicolio

creeper ['kripər] *s* strisciante *m*; (*plant*) rampicante *f*

creeping ['kripiŋ] *adj* lento; (*plant*) rampicante

cremate ['krimet] *tr* cremare

cremato-ry ['krimə‚tori] *adj* crematorio || *s* (**-ries**) forno crematorio

Creole ['kri-ol] *adj & s* creolo

crescent ['krɛsənt] *s* (*of Islam*) mezzaluna; (*of moon*) crescente *m*; (*roll*) cornetto

cress [krɛs] *s* crescione *m*

crest [krɛst] *s* cresta; (heral) stemma *m*, insegna

crestfallen ['krɛst‚fɔlən] *adj* depresso

Cretan ['kritən] *adj & s* cretese *mf*

cretin ['kritən] *s* cretino

crevice ['krɛvɪs] *s* fessura, fenditura

crew [kru] *s* (*group working together*) personale *m*; (*group of workmen;*

mob) ciurma; (*of a ship or racing boat*) equipaggio; (sports) canottaggio

crew' cut' *s* capelli *mpl* a spazzola

crib [krɪb] *s* (*bed*) lettino; (*rack*) rastrelliera; (*building*) capanna, granaio; (coll) bigino ‖ *v* (*pret & pp* **cribbed**; *ger* **cribbing**) *tr* (coll) usare un bigino in ‖ *intr* (coll) usare un bigino; (coll) commettere un plagio

cricket ['krɪkɪt] *s* grillo; (sports) cricket *m*, palla a spatola

crier ['kraɪ·ər] *s* banditore *m*

crime [kraɪm] *s* delitto, crimine *m*

criminal ['krɪmɪnəl] *adj* criminale; (*code*) penale ‖ *s* delinquente *mf*

crimp [krɪmp] *s* piega, pieghettatura; **to put a crimp in** (slang) mettere i bastoni fra le ruote a ‖ *tr* pieghettare; (*the hair*) arricciare

crimson ['krɪmzən] *adj & s* cremisi *m* ‖ *intr* imporporarsi

cringe [krɪndʒ] *intr* rannicchiarsi; (*to fawn*) umiliarsi

crinkle ['krɪŋkəl] *tr* arricciare ‖ *intr* (*to rustle*) sfrusciare

cripple ['krɪpəl] *s* zoppo, sciancato ‖ *tr* storpiare; (*e.g., business*) paralizzare

cri·sis ['kraɪsɪs] *s* (**-ses** [siz]) crisi *f*

crisp [krɪsp] *adj* (*brittle*) croccante, friabile; (*air*) frizzante; (*sharp and clear*) acuto

criteri·on [kraɪ'tɪrɪ·ən] *s* (**-a** [ə] or **-ons**) criterio

critic ['krɪtɪk] *s* critico

critical ['krɪtɪkəl] *adj* critico

criticism ['krɪtɪ,sɪzəm] *s* critica

criticize ['krɪtɪ,saɪz] *tr & intr* criticare

critique [krɪ'tik] *s* critica

croak [krok] *s* (*of frogs*) gracidio; (*of crows*) gracchiamento ‖ *intr* gracidare; gracchiare; (slang) crepare

Croat ['kro·æt] *s* croato

Croatian [kro'eʃən] *adj & s* croato

cro·chet [kro'ʃe] *s* lavoro all'uncinetto ‖ *v* (*pret & pp* **-cheted** ['ʃed]; *ger* **-cheting** ['ʃe·ɪŋ]) *tr & intr* lavorare all'uncinetto

crock [krɑk] *s* vaso di terracotta, giara, orcio

crockery ['krɑkəri] *s* vasellame *m* di terracotta, terracotta

crocodile ['krɑkə,daɪl] *s* coccodrillo

croc'odile tears' *spl* lacrime *fpl* di coccodrillo

crocus ['krokəs] *s* croco

crone [kron] *s* vecchia incartapecorita

cro·ny ['kroni] *s* (**-nies**) amicone *m*, compare *m*

crook [krʊk] *s* (*hook*) uncino; (*staff*) pastorale *m*; (*bend*) curva; (*bend of pipe*) gomito; (coll) imbroglione *m* ‖ *tr* piegare ‖ *intr* piegarsi

crooked ['krʊkɪd] *adj* uncinato; curvo, piegato; (coll) disonesto

croon [krun] *intr* canterellare; cantare in modo sentimentale

crop [krɑp] *s* (*of bird*) gozzo; (*agricultural product, growing or harvested*) messe *f*; (*agricultural product harvested*) raccolto; (*riding whip*) fru-

stino; (*hair cut close*) capelli corti; gruppo ‖ *v* (*pret & pp* **cropped**; *ger* **cropping**) *tr* (*to cut the ends off of*) spuntare; (*to reap*) raccogliere; (*to cut short*) tosare ‖ *intr*—**to crop out** or **up** apparire inaspettatamente

crop'-dust'ing *s* fumigazione aerea

cropper ['krɑpər] *s* mietitore *m*; (*sharecropper*) mezzadro; **to come a cropper** (coll) fare una cascataccia; (coll) andare in rovina

croquet [kro'ke] *s* croquet *m*, pallamaglio *m & f*

croquette [kro'ket] *s* crocchetta

crosier ['kroʒər] *s* pastorale *m*

cross [krɔs] or [krɑs] *adj* trasversale, contrario, obliquo; (*irritable*) bisbetico, di cattivo umore; (*of mixed breed*) incrociato ‖ *s* croce *f*; (*crossing of breeds*) incrocio; **to take the cross** farsi crociato ‖ *tr* crociare, segnare con una croce; (*the street*) attraversare; (*e.g., the legs*) incrociare; (*to draw a line across*) barrare; (*to thwart*) ostacolare; **to cross oneself** farsi il segno della croce; **to cross one's mind** venire in mente a uno; **to cross out** cancellare ‖ *intr* incrociarsi

cross'bones' *spl* teschio e tibie incrociate (*simbolo della morte*)

cross'bow' *s* balestra

cross'breed' *v* (*pret & pp* **-bred** [,bred]) *tr* incrociare, ibridare

cross'-coun'try *adj* campestre; attraverso il paese

cross'-examina'tion *s* (law) confronto, interrogatorio in contraddittorio

cross-eyed ['krɔs,aɪd] or ['krɑs,aɪd] *adj* guercio, strabico

crossing ['krɔsɪŋ] or ['krɑsɪŋ] *s* incrocio; ostacolo; (*of the sea*) traversata; (*of a river*) guado; (rr) passaggio a livello

cross'patch' *s* (coll) bisbetico

cross'piece' *s* traversa

cross' ref'erence *s* richiamo, rimando

cross'road' *s* strada trasversale; **at the crossroads** al bivio; **crossroads** crocicchio

cross' sec'tion *s* sezione trasversale

cross' street' *s* traversa

cross' talk' *s* conversazione; (telp) diafonia

cross'word puz'zle *s* cruciverba *m*, parole incrociate

crotch [krɑtʃ] *s* inforcatura; (*of pants*) cavallo

crotchety ['krɑtʃɪti] *adj* bisbetico

crouch [krautʃ] *intr* accoccolarsi

croup [krup] *s* (pathol) crup *m*

crouton ['krutɑn] *s* crostino

crow [kro] *s* corvo, cornacchia; (*cry of rooster*) chicchirichì *m*; **as the crow flies** in linea retta, a volo d'uccello; **to eat crow** (coll) rimangiarsi le parole ‖ *intr* fare chicchirichì; **to crow over** vantarsi di, esultare per

crow'bar' *s* bastone *m* a leva

crowd [kraud] *s* folla; (*common people*) masse *fpl*; (coll) gruppo ‖ *tr* affollare; *(to push)* spingere ‖ *intr* affollarsi; *(to press forward)* spingersi

crowded ['kraʊdɪd] *adj* affollato

crown [kraʊn] *s* corona; *(of hat)* cupola; *(highest point)* sommo ‖ *tr* coronare; *(checkers)* damare; **to crown s.o.** (coll) battere qlcu sulla testa

crown' prince' *s* principe ereditario

crown' prin'cess *s* principessa ereditaria

crow's'-foot' *s* (-feet) zampa di gallina

crow's'-nest' *s* coffa, gabbia

crucial ['kruʃəl] *adj* cruciale, critico

crucible ['krusɪbəl] *s* crogiolo

crucifix ['krusɪfɪks] *s* crocefisso

crucifixion [,krusɪ'fɪkʃən] *s* crocifissione

cruci·fy ['krusɪ,faɪ] *v* (pret & pp -fied) *tr* crocifiggere

crude [krud] *adj* *(raw)* grezzo; *(unripe)* acerbo; *(roughly made; uncultured)* rozzo

crudi·ty ['krudɪti] *s* (-ties) rozzezza

cruel ['kru·əl] *adj* crudele

cruel·ty ['kru·əlti] *s* (-ties) crudeltà *f*

cruet ['kru·ɪt] *s* oliera

cruise [kruz] *s* crociera ‖ *tr* navigare ‖ *intr* andare in crociera; andare avanti e indietro

cruiser ['kruzər] *s* (nav) incrociatore *m*

cruising ['kruzɪŋ] *adj* di crociera

cruis'ing ra'dius *s* autonomia di crociera

cruller ['krʌlər] *s* frittella

crumb [krʌm] *s* briciola ‖ *tr* sbriciolare; *(e.g., a cutlet)* impannare ‖ *intr* sbriciolarsi

crumble ['krʌmbəl] *tr* sbriciolare, polverizzare ‖ *intr* andare a pezzi, polverizzarsi, sbriciolarsi

crum·my ['krʌmi] *adj* (-mier; -miest) (slang) sporco; *(miserable)* (slang) schifoso; *(e.g., joke)* (slang) povero

crumple ['krʌmpəl] *tr* sgualcire, spiegazzare; **to crumple into a ball** appallottolare ‖ *intr* spiegazzarsi

crunch [krʌntʃ] *s* crocchio; (coll) stretta, morsa ‖ *tr* sgranocchiare ‖ *intr* crocchiare

crusade [kru'sed] *s* crociata ‖ *intr* crociarsi; *(to take up a cause)* farsi paladino

crusader [kru'sedər] *s* crociato; *(of a cause)* paladino

crush [krʌʃ] *s* pigiatura, schiacciatura; *(crowd)* calca; (coll) infatuazione ‖ *tr* schiacciare; *(to grind)* frantumare; *(to subdue)* sottomettere; *(to extract by squeezing)* pigiare

crust [krʌst] *s* crosta; (slang) faccia tosta ‖ *tr* incrostare ‖ *intr* incrostarsi

crustacean [krʌs'teʃən] *s* crostaceo

crust·y ['krʌsti] *adj* (-ier; -iest) crostoso; duro; rude

crutch [krʌtʃ] *s* gruccia, stampella; (fig) sostegno

crux [krʌks] *s* difficoltà *f*, busillis *m*; *(crucial point)* punto cruciale

cry [kraɪ] *s* (**cries**) *(shout)* grido; *(fit of weeping)* pianto; *(entreaty)* richiamo; *(of animal)* urlo; **to have a good cry** sfogarsi, piangere a calde lacrime ‖ *tr* gridare; *(to proclaim)* bandire; **to cry down** disprezzare; **to cry one's heart out** piangere a calde lacrime; **to cry out** proclamare; **to cry up** elogiare ‖ *intr* gridare, urlare; piangere; **to cry for** implorare

cry'ba'by *s* (-bies) piagnucolone *m*

crypt [krɪpt] *s* cripta

cryptic(al) ['krɪptɪk(əl)] *adj* segreto, occulto, misterioso

crystal ['krɪstəl] *s* cristallo

crys'tal ball' *s* globo di cristallo

crystalline ['krɪstəlɪn] or ['krɪstə,laɪn] *adj* cristallino

crystallize ['krɪstə,laɪz] *tr* cristallizzare ‖ *intr* cristallizzarsi

cub [kʌb] *s* cucciolo; *(of lion)* leoncino; *(of fox)* volpicino, volpacchiotto

cubbyhole ['kʌbɪ,hol] *s* sgabuzzino, bugigattolo

cube [kjub] *adj* cubico ‖ *s* cubo; *(of sugar)* zolla ‖ *tr* elevare al cubo; *(to shape)* tagliare in quadretti

cubic ['kjubɪk] *adj* cubico

cub' report'er *s* giornalista novello

cuckold ['kʌkəld] *adj* & *s* cornuto, becco ‖ *tr* cornificare

cuckoo ['kuku] *adj* (slang) pazzo ‖ *s* cuculo

cuck'oo clock' *s* orologio a cucù

cucumber ['kjukʌmbər] *s* cetriolo

cud [kʌd] *s* mangime masticato; **to chew the cud** ruminare

cuddle ['kʌdəl] *tr* abbracciare affettuosamente ‖ *intr* (to lie close) giacere vicino; *(to curl up)* rannicchiarsi, raggomitolarsi

cudg·el ['kʌdʒəl] *s* manganello, randello; **to take up the cudgels for** farsi paladino di ‖ *v* (pret & pp -eled or -elled; ger -eling or -elling) *tr* bastonare, randellare; **to cudgel one's brains** rompersi la testa

cue [kju] *s* suggerimento, imbeccata; *(billiards)* stecca; **to miss a cue** (theat) mancare la battuta; (coll) non capire l'antifona ‖ *tr*—**to cue s.o. (in) on** (coll) dare a qlcu informazioni su

cuff [kʌf] *s* *(of shirt)* polsino; *(of trousers)* risvolto; *(slap)* schiaffo ‖ *tr* schiaffeggiare

cuff' links' *spl* bottoni doppi, gemelli *mpl*

cuirass [kwɪ'ræs] *s* corazza

cuisine [kwɪ'zin] *s* cucina

culinary ['kjulɪ,neri] *adj* culinario

cull [kʌl] *s* scarto ‖ *tr* (to gather, pluck) cogliere; selezionare, scegliere

culminate ['kʌlmɪ,net] *intr* culminare

culottes [ku'lɑts] *spl* gonna pantaloni

culpable ['kʌlpəbəl] *adj* colpevole

culprit ['kʌlprɪt] *s* colpevole *m*, imputato

cult [kʌlt] *s* culto

cultivate ['kʌltɪ,vet] *tr* coltivare

cultivated ['kʌltɪ,vetɪd] *adj* colto, coltivato

cultivation [,kʌltɪ've∫ən] *s* coltivazione, cultura

culture ['kʌlt∫ər] *s* cultura

cultured ['kʌlt∫ərd] *adj* colto

cul'tured pearl' *s* perla coltivata

culvert ['kʌlvərt] *s* chiavica

cumbersome ['kʌmbərsəm] *adj* ingombrante, incomodo; (*clumsy*) goffo

cumulative ['kjumjə,letɪv] *adj* cumulativo

cunning ['kʌnɪŋ] *adj* (*sly*) astuto; (*skillful*) abile; (*pretty*) bello; (*created with skill*) ben fatto, fine || *s* astuzia; abilità *f*, destrezza

cup [kʌp] *s* tazza; (mach, sports) coppa; (eccl) calice *m*; **in one's cups** ubriaco || *v* (*pret & pp* **cupped;** *ger* **cupping**) *tr* mettere ventose a; **to cup one's hands** foggiare le mani a mo' di conca

cupboard ['kʌbərd] *s* armadio a muro, dispensa; (*buffet*) credenza

Cupid ['kjupɪd] *s* Cupido

cupidity [kju'pɪdɪti] *s* cupidigia

cup' of tea' *s* tazza di tè; (coll) forte *m*, e.g., **physics is not my cup of tea** la fisica non è il mio forte

cupola ['kjupələ] *s* cupola

cur [kʌr] *s* cane bastardo; (*despicable fellow*) canaglia, gaglioffo

curate ['kjurɪt] *s* curato

curative ['kjurətɪv] *adj* curativo

curator [kju'retər] *s* conservatore *m*

curb [kʌrb] *s* (*of bit*) barbazzale *m*; (*of pavement*) orlo del marciapiede; (*check*) freno || *tr* frenare

curb'stone' *s* cordone *m*; (*of well*) sponda del pozzo

curd [kʌrd] *s* cagliata || *tr* cagliare || *intr* cagliarsi

curdle ['kʌrdəl] *tr* cagliare; (*the blood*) far gelare || *intr* cagliarsi; (*said of custard*) impazzare

cure [kjur] *s* cura || *tr* curare; (*e.g., meat*) conservare; (*wood*) stagionare

cure'-all' *s* panacea

curfew ['kʌrfju] *s* coprifuoco

curi·o ['kjurɪ,o] *s* (-os) curiosità *f*

curiosi·ty [,kjurɪ'ɑsɪti] *s* (-ties) curiosità *f*

curious ['kjurɪ·əs] *adj* curioso

curl [kʌrl] *s* (*of hair*) ricciolo; (*anything curled*) rotolo, spirale *f* || *tr* arricciare; arrotolare; (*the lips*) torcere || *intr* arricciarsi; arrotolarsi; **to curl up** raggomitolarsi

curlicue ['kʌrlɪ,kju] *s* ghirigoro

curl'ing i'ron *s* ferro da arricciare

curl'pa'per *s* bigodino

curl·y ['kʌrli] *adj* (-ier; -iest) ricciuto

curmudgeon [kər'mʌdʒən] *s* bisbetico

currant ['kʌrənt] *s* (*seedless raisin*) uva passa di Corinto, uva sultanina; (*shrub and berry of genus Ribes*) ribes *m*

curren·cy ['kʌrənsi] *s* (-cies) (*circulation*) circolazione; (*money*) denaro circolante; (*general use*) corso

current ['kʌrənt] *adj & s* corrente *f*

cur'rent account' *s* conto corrente

cur'rent events' *spl* attualità *fpl*, eventi *mpl* correnti

curricu·lum [kə'rɪkjələm] *s* (**-lums** or **-la** [lə]) programma *m*; piano educativo

cur·ry ['kʌri] *s* (**-ries**) (*spice*) curry *m* || *v* (*pret & pp* **-ried**) *tr* (*a horse*) strigliare; (*leather*) conciare; **to curry favor** cercare di compiacere

cur'ry·comb' *s* striglia || *tr* strigliare

curse [kʌrs] *s* maledizione; bestemmia || *tr* maledire || *intr* imprecare, bestemmiare

cursed ['kʌrsɪd] or [kʌrst] *adj* maledetto; (*hateful*) odiato

cursive ['kʌrsɪv] *adj* & *s* corsivo

cursory ['kʌrsəri] *adj* rapido, superficiale

curt [kʌrt] *adj* (*rude*) brusco, sgarbato; (*short*) breve, conciso

curtail [kər'tel] *tr* ridurre, restringere

curtain ['kʌrtən] *s* (*in front of stage*) sipario; (*for window*) tendina; (fig) cortina || *tr* coprire con tenda; separare con tenda; coprire, nascondere

cur'tain call' *s* (theat) chiamata

cur'tain rais'er ['rezər] *s* (theat) avanspettacolo; (sports) incontro preliminare

cur'tain ring' *s* campanella

cur'tain rod' *s* bastone *m* su cui si fissano le tende

curt·sy ['kʌrtsi] *s* (-sies) riverenza, inchino || *v* (*pret & pp* **-sied**) *intr* fare la riverenza, inchinarsi

curve [kʌrv] *s* curva || *tr* curvare || *intr* curvarsi

curved [kʌrvd] *adj* curvo, curvato

cushion ['ku∫ən] *s* cuscino; (*of billiard table*) mattonella || *tr* proteggere, ammortizzare, attutire

cuspidor ['kʌspɪ,dɔr] *s* sputacchiera

cuss [kʌs] *s* (coll) bestemmia; (coll) tipo perverso || *tr* maledire || *intr* bestemmiare

custard ['kʌstərd] *s* crema

custodian [kʌs'todɪ·ən] *s* (*caretaker*) custode *m*, guardiano *m*; (*person who is entrusted with s.th*) conservatore *m*; (*janitor of school*) bidello

custo·dy ['kʌstədi] *s* (-dies) custodia; (*imprisonment*) arresto; **in custody** in prigione; **to take into custody** arrestare

custom ['kʌstəm] *s* costume *m*; (*customers*) clientela; **customs** dogana; diritti *mpl* doganali

customary ['kʌstə,meri] *adj* consueto, abituale

custom-built ['kʌstəm'bɪlt] *adj* fatto su misura; (*car*) fuori serie

customer ['kʌstəmər] *s* cliente *mf*

cus'tom·house' *adj* doganale || *s* dogana

custom-made ['kʌstəm'med] *adj* fatto su misura

cus'toms inspec'tion *s* visita doganale

cus'toms of'ficer *s* doganiere *m*

cus'tom work' *s* lavoro fatto su misura

cut [kʌt] *adj* (*prices*) ridotto; **to be cut out for** essere tagliato per || *s* taglio; (*reduction*) ribasso; (typ) cliché *m*;

(*snub*) (coll) affronto; (coll) assenza non autorizzata; (coll) parte *f*; **a cut above** (coll) un po' meglio di || *tr* tagliare; (*cards*) alzare; (*prices*) ridurre; (coll) far finta di non riconoscere; (coll) marinare; **cut it out!** basta!; **to cut back** ridurre; **to cut off** tagliare; diseredare; (surg) amputare; **to cut short** interrompere; **to cut teeth** fare i denti; **to cut up** sminuzzare; criticare || *intr* tagliare, tagliarsi; **to cut across** attraversare; **to cut in** interrompere; **to cut under** vendere sottoprezzo; **to cut up** (slang) fare il pagliaccio

cut-and-dried [ˈkʌtənˈdraɪd] *adj* monotono, stantio; bell'e fatto, fatto in anticipo

cutaneous [kjuˈtɛnɪˌəs] *adj* cutaneo

cut'away' coat' [ˈkʌtəˌwe] *s* marsina da giorno

cut'back' *s* riduzione; eliminazione; (mov) ritorno dell'azione a un'epoca anteriore

cute [kjut] *adj* (coll) carino, grazioso; (*shrewd*) (coll) furbo

cut' glass' *s* cristallo intagliato

cuticle [ˈkjutɪkəl] *s* cuticola

cutlass [ˈkʌtləs] *s* sciabola

cutler [ˈkʌtlər] *s* coltellinaio

cutlery [ˈkʌtləri] *s* coltelleria

cutlet [ˈkʌtlɪt] *s* cotoletta; (*flat cro-quette*) polpetta

cut'off' *s* taglio; (*road*) scorciatoia; (*of cylinder*) otturatore *m*, chiusura dell'ammissione; (*of river*) braccio diretto

cut'out' *s* ritaglio; (aut) valvola di scappamento libero

cut'-rate' *adj* a prezzo ridotto

cutter [ˈkʌtər] *s* tagliatore *m*; (naut) cutter *m*

cut'throat' *adj* spietato; (*relentless*) senza posa || *s* assassino

cutting [ˈkʌtɪŋ] *adj* tagliente || *s* taglio; (*from a newspaper*) ritaglio; (*e.g., of prices*) riduzione; (hort) talea

cut'ting board' *s* tagliere *m*; (*of dish-washer*) piano d'appoggio

cut'ting edge' *s* taglio

cuttlefish [ˈkʌtəlˌfɪʃ] *s* seppia

cut'wat'er *s* (*of bridge*) tagliacque *m*; (*of boat*) tagliamare *m*

cyanamide [saɪˈænəˌmaɪd] *s* cianamide *f*; cianamide *f* di calcio

cyanide [ˈsaɪəˌnaɪd] *s* cianuro

cycle [ˈsaɪkəl] *s* ciclo; bicicletta; (*of internal combustion engine*) tempo; (phys) periodo || *intr* andare in bicicletta

cyclic(al) [ˈsaɪklɪk(əl)] or [ˈsɪklɪk(əl)] *adj* ciclico

cyclone [ˈsaɪklon] *s* ciclone *m*

cyclops [ˈsaɪkləps] *s* ciclope *m*

cyclotron [ˈsaɪklɔˌtrɑn] or [ˈsɪkloˌtrɑn] *s* ciclotrone *m*

cylinder [ˈsɪlɪndər] *s* cilindro; (*container*) bombola

cyl'inder block' *s* monoblocco

cyl'inder bore' *s* alesaggio

cyl'inder head' *s* testa

cylindric(al) [sɪˈlɪndrɪk(əl)] *adj* cilindrico

cymbals [ˈsɪmbəls] *spl* piatti *mpl*

cynic [ˈsɪnɪk] *adj* & *s* cinico

cynical [ˈsɪnɪkəl] *adj* cinico

cynicism [ˈsɪnɪˌsɪzəm] *s* cinismo

cynosure [ˈsaɪnəˌʃʊr] or [ˈsɪnəˌʃʊr] *s* centro dell'attenzione

cypress [ˈsaɪprəs] *s* cipresso

Cyprus [ˈsaɪprəs] *s* Cipro

Cyrus [ˈsaɪrəs] *s* Ciro

cyst [sɪst] *s* ciste *f*, cisti *f*

czar [zɑr] *s* zar *m*

czarina [zɑˈrinə] *s* zarina

Czech [tʃɛk] *adj* & *s* ceco

Czecho-Slovak [ˈtʃɛkoˈslovæk] *adj* & *s* cecoslovacco

Czecho-Slovakia [ˌtʃɛkosloˈvækɪ·ə] *s* la Cecoslovacchia

D

D, d [di] *s* quarta lettera dell'alfabeto inglese

dab [dæb] *s* tocco; (*of mud*) schizzo; (*e.g., of butter*) spalmata || *v* (*pret* & *pp* dabbed; *ger* dabbing) *tr* toccare leggermente; (*to apply a substance to*) spennellare

dabble [ˈdæbəl] *tr* spruzzare || *intr* diguazzare; **to dabble in** occuparsi di; (*stocks*) speculare in

dad [dæd] *s* (coll) papà *m*

dad-dy [ˈdædi] *s* (-dies) (coll) papà *m*

daffodil [ˈdæfədɪl] *s* trombone *m*

daff-y [ˈdæfi] *adj* (-ier; -iest) (coll) pazzo

dagger [ˈdægər] *s* daga, pugnale *m*; (typ) croce *f*; **to look daggers at** fulminare con lo sguardo

dahlia [ˈdæljə] *s* dalia

dai-ly [ˈdeli] *adj* quotidiano, diurno || *s* (-lies) quotidiano || *adv* giornalmente

dai'ly dou'ble *s* duplice *f*, accoppiata

dain-ty [ˈdenti] *adj* (-tier; -tiest) delicato || *s* (-ties) manicaretto

dair-y [ˈdɛri] *s* (-ies) (*store*) latteria; (*factory*) caseificio

dair'y farm' *s* vaccheria

dair'y-man *s* (-men) lattaio

dais [ˈde·ɪs] *s* predella

dai-sy [ˈdezi] *s* (-sies) margherita

dal-ly [ˈdæli] *v* (*pret* & *pp* -lied) *intr* (*to loiter*) bighellonare; (*to trifle*) scherzare

dam [dæm] *s* diga; (*for fishing*) pescaia; (zool) fattrice *f* || *v* (*pret* & *pp* dammed; *ger* damming) *tr* arginare; ostruire; tappare

damage ['dæmɪdʒ] *s* danno, scapito; (fig) menomazione; (com) avaria; **damages** danni *mpl* || *tr* danneggiare, ledere; sinistrare

damascene ['dæmə‚sin] *or* [‚dæmə-'sin] *adj* damasceno || *s* damaschinatura || *tr* damaschinare

dame [dem] *s* dama, signora; (slang) donna

damn [dæm] *s*—**I don't give a damn** (slang) me ne impipo; **that's not worth a damn** (slang) non vale un fico || *tr* dannare, condannare || *intr* maledire || *interj* maledizione!

damnation [dæm'ne/ən] *s* dannazione; (theol) condanna

damned [dæmd] *adj* dannato, maledetto || **the damned** i dannati || *adv* maledettamente

damp [dæmp] *adj* umido || *s* umidità *f*; (firedamp) grisou *m* || *tr* inumidire; umettare; (to muffle) smorzare; (waves) (elec) smorzare; **to damp s.o.'s enthusiasm** raffreddare gli spiriti di qlcu; scoraggiare qlcu

dampen ['dæmpən] *tr* inumidire; umettare; smorzare; (s.o.'s enthusiasm) raffreddare

damper ['dæmpər] *s* (of chimney) valvola di tiraggio; (fig) doccia fredda; (mus) smorzatore *m*; (mus) sordina

damsel ['dæmzəl] *s* damigella

dance [dæns] *or* [dɑns] *s* ballo, danza || *tr & intr* ballare, danzare

dance' band' *s* orchestrina

dance' floor' *s* pista da ballo

dance' hall' *s* sala da ballo

dancer ['dænsər] *or* ['dɑnsər] *s* danzatore *m*; (expert or professional) ballerino

danc'ing part'ner *s* cavaliere *m*; dama

danc'ing par'ty *s* festa da ballo

dandelion ['dændɪ‚laɪ·ən] *s* dente *m* di leone, soffione *m*

dandruff ['dændrəf] *s* forfora

dan·dy ['dændɪ] *adj* (-dier; -diest) (coll) eccellente, magnifico || *s* (-dies) damerino, elegantone *m*

Dane [den] *s* danese *mf*

danger ['dendʒər] *s* pericolo

dangerous ['dendʒərəs] *adj* pericoloso

dangle ['dæŋgəl] *tr* dondolare || *intr* penzolare, ciondolare

Danish ['denɪʃ] *adj & s* danese *m*

dank [dæŋk] *adj* umido

Danube ['dænjub] *s* Danubio

dapper ['dæpər] *adj* azzimato

dapple ['dæpəl] *adj* pezzato || *tr* chiazzare

dap'ple-gray' *adj* storno

dare [der] *s* sfida || *tr* sfidare || *intr* osare; **I dare say** oserei dire; forse, e.g., **I dare say we will be done at seven** forse avremo finito alle sette; **to dare to** (to have the courage to) osare di, fidarsi a

dare'dev'il *s* scavezzacollo

daring ['derɪŋ] *adj* temerario, spericolato || *s* audacia, temerarietà *f*

dark [dɑrk] *adj* scuro; (complexion) bruno; oscuro, segreto; (gloomy) tetro, fosco || *s* oscurità *f*, scuro; tenebre *fpl*; **in the dark** al buio

Dark' Ag'es *spl* alto medio evo

dark-complexioned ['dɑrkkəm'plek-ʃənd] *adj* bruno

darken ['dɑrkən] *tr* scurire, oscurare || *intr* scurirsi, oscurarsi

dark' horse' *s* vincitore imprevisto, outsider *m*

darkly ['dɑrkli] *adv* oscuramente; segretamente

dark' meat' *s* gamba o anca (di pollo o tacchino)

darkness ['dɑrknɪs] *s* oscurità *f*

dark'room' *s* camera oscura

darling ['dɑrlɪŋ] *adj & s* caro, amato

darn [dɑrn] *s* rammendo || *tr* rammendare || *interj* (coll) accidenti!

darned [dɑrnd] *adj* (coll) maledetto || *adv* maledettamente; (coll) tremendamente

darnel ['dɑrnəl] *s* zizzania

darning ['dɑrnɪŋ] *s* rammendo

darn'ing nee'dle *s* ago da rammendo

dart [dɑrt] *s* freccia, dardo; (game) frecciolo || *intr* dardeggiare; lanciarsi, precipitarsi

dash [dæʃ] *s* sciacquio; piccola quantità, sospetto; (spirit) brio; (typ, telg) trattino, lineetta || *tr* lanciare; mescolare; (s.o.'s hopes) frustrare; deprimere; **to dash off** gettar giù; **to dash to pieces** fare a pezzi || *intr* precipitarsi; **to dash against** gettarsi contro; **to dash by** passare a gran velocità; **to dash in** entrare come un razzo; **to dash off or out** andarsene in fretta; lanciarsi fuori

dash'board' *s* cruscotto; (in an open carriage) parafango

dashing ['dæʃɪŋ] *adj* impetuoso; vistoso || *s* (of waves) sciacquio

dastard ['dæstərd] *adj & s* vile *mf*, codardo

da'ta proc'essing *s* elaborazione

date [det] *s* (time) data; (palm) palma da datteri; (fruit) dattero; (appointment) (coll) appuntamento; **out of date** fuori moda; **to date** sinora; **up to date** a giorno || *tr* datare; (coll) avere un appuntamento con || *intr*— **to date from** partire da

date' line' *s* linea del cambiamento di data

dative ['detɪv] *adj & s* dativo

datum ['detəm] *or* ['dætəm] *s* (data ['detə] *or* ['dætə]) dato

daub [dɔb] *s* imbratto || *tr* imbrattare

daughter ['dɔtər] *s* figlia, figliola

daughter-in-law ['dɔtərɪn‚lɔ] *s* (daughters-in-law) nuora

daunt [dɔnt] *tr* spaventare; intimidire

dauntless ['dɔntlɪs] *adj* intrepido

dauphin ['dɔfɪn] *s* delfino

davenport ['dævən‚pɔrt] *s* sofà *m*, sofà *m* letto

davit ['dævɪt] *s* gru *f* per lancia

daw [dɔ] *s* cornacchia

dawdle ['dɔdəl] *intr* bighellonare

dawn [dɔn] *s* alba || *intr* (said of the day) farsi, nascere, spuntare; **to dawn on** cominciare a apparire nella mente di

day [de] *adj* diurno; (student) esterno || *s* giorno; (of travel, work, etc.)

giornata; **a few days ago** giorni fa; **any day now** da un giorno all'altro; **by day** di giorno; **the day after** il giorno dopo; **the day after tomorrow** dopodomani; **the day before yesterday** ieri l'altro; **to call it a day** (coll) finire di lavorare

day' bed' s sofà m letto

day'book' s brogliaccio

day'break' s far m del giorno

day'dream' s fantasticheria || intr fantasticare

day' la'borer s giornaliero

day'light' s luce f del giorno; alba; **in broad daylight** alla luce del sole; **to see daylight** comprendere; vedere la fine

day'light-sav'ing time' s ora legale, ora estiva

day' nurs'ery s asilo infantile

day' off' s giorno di vacanza; (of servant) libera uscita

day' of reck'oning s giorno di rendiconto; (last judgment) giorno del giudizio

day' shift' s turno diurno

day'time' adj diurno || s giornata

daze [dez] s stordimento; **in a daze** stordito || tr stordire

dazzle ['dæzəl] s abbagliamento || tr abbagliare

dazzling ['dæzlɪŋ] adj abbagliante

deacon ['dikən] s diacono

dead [dɛd] adj morto; **s—in the dead of** (e.g., night) nel pieno di; **the dead** i morti || adv (coll) completamente; (abruptly) (coll) di colpo

dead' beat' adj (coll) stanco morto

dead'beat' s (coll) scroccone m

dead' cen'ter s punto morto

dead'drunk' adj ubriaco fradicio

deaden ['dɛdən] tr attutire; (e.g., s.o.'s senses) ottundere

dead' end' s vicolo cieco

dead' let'ter s lettera morta; lettera non reclamata

dead'line' s termine m

dead'lock' s punto morto || tr portare al punto morto || intr giungere al punto morto

dead-ly ['dɛdli] adj (-lier; -liest) mortale; insopportabile

dead' pan' s (slang) faccia senza espressione

dead'pan' adj senza espressione

dead' reck'oning s (naut) stima

dead'wood' s legna secca; (fig) zavorra

deaf [dɛf] adj sordo; **to turn a deaf ear** fare orecchio di mercante

deaf'-and-dumb' adj sordomuto

deafen ['dɛfən] tr assordare, intronare

deafening ['dɛfənɪŋ] adj assordante

deaf'-mute' s sordomuto

deafness ['dɛfnɪs] s sordità f

deal [dil] s accordo; quantità f; (cards) mano, girata; (coll) affare m; (coll) trattamento; **a good deal (of)** or **a great deal (of)** moltissimo || v (pret & pp dealt [dɛlt]) tr (a blow) menare; (cards) fare, sfogliare; **to deal s.o. in** (coll) includere || intr mercanteggiare, commerciare; fare le

carte; **to deal with** trattare con; trattare di

dealer ['dilər] s commerciante mf, esercente mf; (cards) mazziere m

dean [din] s decano

dear [dir] adj (beloved; expensive) caro; **dear me!** povero me!; **Dear Sir** egregio Signore || s caro

dearie ['dɪri] s (coll) caro

dearth [dʌrθ] s scarsezza; insufficienza

death [dɛθ] s morte f; **to bleed to death** morire dissanguato; **to burn to death** morire bruciato; **to choke to death** morire di soffocazione; **to freeze to death** morire di gelo; **to put to death** dare la morte a; **to shoot to death** uccidere a fucilate; **to stab to death** scannare; **to starve to death** far morire di fame; morire di fame

death'bed' s letto di morte

death'blow' s colpo mortale

deathless ['dɛθlɪs] adj immortale, eterno

deathly ['dɛθli] adj mortale || adv mortalmente; assolutamente

death' pen'alty s pena di morte

death' rate' s mortalità f

death' rat'tle s rantolo della morte

death' ray' s raggio della morte

death' sen'tence s pena di morte

death' war'rant s pena di morte; fine f di ogni speranza

death'watch' s veglia mortuaria; (zool) orologio della morte

debacle [de'bakəl] s disastro; (downfall) tracollo; (in a river) sgelo repentino

de·bar [dɪ'bar] v (pret & pp -barred; ger -barring) tr escludere; proibire (with dat)

debark [dɪ'bark] tr & intr sbarcare

debarkation [,dibar'keʃən] s sbarco

debase [dɪ'bes] tr degradare; adulterare

debatable [dɪ'betəbəl] adj discutibile

debate [dɪ'bet] s discussione || tr & intr discutere

debauch [dɪ'bɔtʃ] s dissolutezza, corruzione || tr corrompere

debauchee [,dɛbɔ'ʃi] or [,dɛbɔ'tʃi] s degenerato, vizioso

debaucher·y [dɪ'bɔtʃəri] s (-ies) dissolutezza, corruzione

debenture [dɪ'bɛntʃər] s (bond) obbligazione; (voucher) buono

debilitate [dɪ'bɪlɪ,tet] tr debilitare

debili·ty [dɪ'bɪlɪti] s (-ties) debolezza

debit ['dɛbɪt] s debito; (debit side) (com) dare m || tr addebitare

debonair [,dɛbə'nɛr] adj gioviale; cortese

debris [de'bri] s detrito, rottami mpl

debt [dɛt] s debito; **to run into debt** indebitarsi

debtor ['dɛtər] s debitore m

debut [de'bju] or ['debju] s debutto; **to make one's debut** debuttare || intr debuttare

debutante [,debju'tant] or ['debjə,tænt] s debuttante f, esordiente f

decade ['dɛked] s decennio

decadence [dɪ'kedəns] s decadenza

decadent [dɪ'kedənt] adj & s decadente mf

decanter [dɪ'kæntər] s boccia

decapitate [dɪ'kæpɪ,tet] tr decapitare

decay [dɪ'ke] s (decline) decadimento; (rotting) marciume m, putredine f; (of teeth) carie f || tr imputridire || intr imputridire, marcire; (said of teeth) cariarsi

decease [dɪ'sis] s decesso || intr decedere

deceased [dɪ'sist] adj & s defunto

deceit [dɪ'sit] s inganno, frode f

deceitful [dɪ'sitfəl] adj ingannatore, menzognero, subdolo

deceive [dɪ'siv] tr & intr ingannare

decelerate [dɪ'selə,ret] tr & intr decelerare

December [dɪ'sembər] s dicembre m

decen•cy ['disənsi] s (-cies) decenza, pudore m; decencies convenienze fpl

decent ['disənt] adj decente; (proper) conveniente

decentralize [dɪ'sentrə,laɪz] tr decentrare

deception [dɪ'sepʃən] s inganno

deceptive [dɪ'septɪv] adj ingannevole

decide [dɪ'saɪd] tr decidere || intr decidere, decidersi

decimal ['desɪməl] adj & s decimale m

dec'imal point' s (in Italian the comma is used to separate the decimal fraction from the integer) virgola

decimate ['desɪ,met] tr decimare

decipher [dɪ'saɪfər] tr decifrare

decision [dɪ'sɪʒən] s decisione

decisive [dɪ'saɪsɪv] adj decisivo; (resolute) fermo

deck [dɛk] s (of cards) mazzo; (naut) coperta, tolda, ponte m; on deck (coll) pronto; (coll) prossimo || tr—to deck out adornare; (with flags) imbandierare

deck' chair' s sedia a sdraio

deck' hand' s marinaio di coperta

deck'house' s (naut) tuga

deck'le edge' ['dɛkəl] s sbavatura

declaim [dɪ'klem] tr & intr declamare

declaration [,dɛklə'reʃən] s dichiarazione

declarative [dɪ'klærətɪv] adj declaratorio; (gram) enunciativo

declare [dɪ'kler] tr dichiarare || intr dichiararsi

declension [dɪ'klenʃən] s declinazione

declination [,dɛklɪ'neʃən] s declinazione

decline [dɪ'klaɪn] s decadenza; (in prices) ribasso; (in health) deperimento; (of sun) tramonto || tr declinare || intr declinare; decadere, scadere

declivi•ty [dɪ'klɪvɪti] s (-ties) declivio, pendice f

decode [di'kod] tr decifrare

décolleté [,dekɑl'te] adj scollato

decompose [,dɪkəm'poz] tr decomporre || intr decomporsi

decomposition [,dikɑmpə'zɪʃən] s decomposizione

décor [de'kɔr] s decorazione; (of a room) stile m; (theat) scenario

decorate ['dɛkə,ret] tr decorare

decoration [,dɛkə'reʃən] s decorazione

decorator ['dɛkə,retər] s decoratore m

decorous ['dɛkərəs] or [dɪ'korəs] adj corretto, decoroso

decorum [dɪ'korəm] s decoro, correttezza

decoy [dɪ'kɔɪ] or ['dikɔɪ] s richiamo; (for birds) zimbello; (person) adescatore m || tr (to lure) adescare; (to deceive) abbindolare

decrease ['dikris] or [dɪ'kris] s diminuzione; (of salary) decurtazione || [dɪ'kris] tr decurtare || intr diminuire

decree [dɪ'kri] s decreto || tr decretare

de•cry [dɪ'kraɪ] v (pret & pp -cried) tr denigrare, screditare

dedicate ['dɛdɪ,ket] tr dedicare

dedication [,dɛdɪ'keʃən] s dedizione; (inscription in a book) dedica

deduce [dɪ'djus] or [dɪ'dus] tr dedurre

deduct [dɪ'dʌkt] tr dedurre, defalcare

deductible [dɪ'dʌktɪbəl] adj defalcabile || s (ins) franchigia

deduction [dɪ'dʌkʃən] s deduzione

deed [did] s fatto; (exploit) prodezza; (law) titolo || tr trasferire legalmente

deem [dim] tr & intr credere, giudicare

deep [dip] adj profondo; basso; (woods) folto; (friendship) intimo; deep in debt carico di debiti; deep in thought assorto in pensieri || adv profondamente; deep into the night a notte fatta; to go deep into approfondirsi al

deepen ['dipən] tr approfondire || intr approfondirsi

deep'-freeze' tr (pret -froze [froz]; pp -frozen [frozən]) tr surgelare

deep-laid ['dip,led] adj preparato astutamente

deep' mourn'ing s lutto stretto

deep-rooted ['dip,rutɪd] adj profondo

deep'-sea' fish'ing s pesca d'alto mare or d'altura

deep-seated ['dip,sitɪd] adj profondo, connaturato

Deep' South' s Profondo Sud

deer [dɪr] s cervo

deer'skin' s pelle f di daino

deface [dɪ'fes] tr sfigurare

defamation [,defə'meʃən] or [,difə'meʃən] s diffamazione

defame [dɪ'fem] tr diffamare

default [dɪ'fɔlt] s mancanza; (failure to act) inadempienza; in default of per mancanza di; to lose by default dichiarare forfeit || tr essere inadempiente a || intr essere inadempiente; (sports) dichiarare forfeit

defeat [dɪ'fit] s sconfitta, disfatta || tr sconfiggere, vincere

defeatism [dɪ'fitɪzəm] s disfattismo

defeatist [dɪ'fitɪst] adj & s disfattista mf

defecate ['dɛfɪ,ket] intr defecare

defect ['difɛkt] or ['difɛkt] s vizio, difetto || [dɪ'fɛkt] intr defezionare

defection [dɪ'fɛkʃən] s defezione

defective [dɪ'fɛktɪv] adj difettivo, difettoso

defend [dɪ'fɛnd] *tr* difendere, proteggere
defendant [dɪ'fɛndənt] *s* (law) imputato, querelato
defender [dɪ'fɛndər] *s* difensore *m*
defense [dɪ'fɛns] *s* difesa
defenseless [dɪ'fɛnslɪs] *adj* indifeso
defensive [dɪ'fɛnsɪv] *adj* difensivo || *s* difensiva
de·fer [dɪ'fʌr] *v* (*pret & pp* **-ferred**; *ger* **-ferring**) *tr* differire, rinviare || *intr* rimettersi
deference ['dɛfərəns] *s* deferenza
deferential [,dɛfə'rɛnʃəl] *adj* deferente
deferment [dɪ'fʌrmənt] *s* differimento
defiance [dɪ'faɪəns] *s* opposizione; sfida; **in defiance of** a dispetto di
defiant [dɪ'faɪ·ənt] *adj* provocante, ostile
deficien·cy [dɪ'fɪʃənsɪ] *s* (-cies) deficienza; (com) ammanco
deficient [dɪ'fɪʃənt] *adj* deficiente
deficit ['dɛfɪsɪt] *adj* deficitario || *s* deficit *m*, disavanzo
defile [dɪ'faɪl] or ['difaɪl] *s* gola, passo || [dɪ'faɪl] *tr* profanare || *intr* marciare in fila
define [dɪ'faɪn] *tr* definire
definite ['dɛfɪnɪt] *adj* definito; (gram) determinativo, determinato
definition [,dɛfɪ'nɪʃən] *s* definizione
definitive [dɪ'fɪnɪtɪv] *adj* definitivo
deflate [dɪ'flet] *tr* sgonfiare; (*s.o.'s hopes*) deprimere; (*e.g., currency*) deflazionare
deflation [dɪ'fleʃən] · *s* sgonfiamento; (*of prices*) deflazione
deflect [dɪ'flɛkt] *tr* far deflettere || *intr* deflettere
deflower [di'flau·ər] *tr* privare dei fiori; (*a woman*) deflorare
deforest [di'fɑrɛst] or [di'fɔrɛst] *tr* disboscare, smacchiare
deform [dɪ'fɔrm] *tr* deformare
deformed [dɪ'fɔrmd] *adj* deforme
deformi·ty [dɪ'fɔrmɪtɪ] *s* (-ties) deformità *f*
defraud [dɪ'frɔd] *tr* defraudare
defray [dɪ'fre] *tr* pagare
defrost [di'frɔst] or [di'frɑst] *tr* sgelare, sbrinare
defroster [di'frɔstər] or [di'frɑstər] *s* (aut) visiera termica
deft [dɛft] *adj* destro, lesto
defunct [dɪ'fʌŋkt] *adj* defunto
de·fy [dɪ'faɪ] *v* (*pret & pp* **-fied**) *tr* sfidare, provocare
degeneracy [dɪ'dʒɛnərəsɪ] *s* degenerazione
degenerate [dɪ'dʒɛnərɪt] *adj & s* degenerato || [dɪ'dʒɛnə,ret] *intr* degenerare, tralignare
degrade [dɪ'gred] *tr* degradare
degrading [dɪ'gredɪŋ] *adj* degradante
degree [dɪ'gri] *s* grado; titolo accademico; **by degrees** a grado a grado; **to a degree** fino a un certo punto; troppo; **to take a degree** ricevere un titolo di studio
dehydrate [di'haɪdret] *tr* disidratare
deice [di'aɪs] *tr* sgelare

dei·fy ['di·ɪ,faɪ] *v* (*pret & pp* **-fied**) *tr* deificare
deign [den] *intr* degnarsi
dei·ty ['di·ɪtɪ] *s* (-ties) deità *f*; **the Deity** Dio
dejected [dɪ'dʒɛktɪd] *adj* demoralizzato
dejection [dɪ'dʒɛkʃən] *s* (*in spirits*) demoralizzazione; (*evacuation*) deiezione
delay [dɪ'le] *s* ritardo, proroga; dilazione; **without further delay** senza ulteriore indugio || *tr* tardare; (*to put off*) differire || *intr* tardare, ritardare
delayed'-ac'tion *adj* a azione differita
delectable [dɪ'lɛktəbəl] *adj* dilettevole
delegate ['dɛlɪ,get] or ['dɛlɪgɪt] *s* delegato, incaricato; (*to a convention*) congressista *mf* || ['dɛlɪ,get] *tr* delegare, incaricare
delegation [,dɛlɪ'geʃən] *s* delegazione
delete [dɪ'lit] *tr* cancellare, sopprimere
deletion [dɪ'liʃən] *s* cancellazione
deliberate [dɪ'lɪbərɪt] *adj* meditato; (*slow in deciding*) cauto; (*slow in moving*) lento || [dɪ'lɪbə,ret] *tr & intr* deliberare
deliberately [,dɪlɪ'geʃən] *adv* (*on purpose*) deliberatamente; (*without hurrying*) con ponderatezza
delica·cy ['dɛlɪkəsɪ] *s* ·(-cies) delicatezza; (*choice food*) leccornia
delicatessen [,dɛlɪkə'tɛsən] *s* negozio di salumerie || *spl* salumerie *fpl*, articoli alimentari scelti
delicious [dɪ'lɪʃəs] *adj* delizioso
delight [dɪ'laɪt] *s* gioia, delizia || *tr* dilettare || *intr* dilettarsi
delightful [dɪ'laɪtfəl] *adj* delizioso
delinquen·cy [dɪ'lɪŋkwənsɪ] *s* (-cies) colpa; (*offense*) delinquenza; (*in payment of a debt*) morosità *f*
delinquent [dɪ'lɪŋkwənt] *adj* colpevole; (*in payment*) moroso; non pagato || *s* delinquente *m*; debitore moroso
delirious [dɪ'lɪrɪ·əs] *adj* in delirio
deliri·um [dɪ'lɪrɪ·əm] *s* (-ums or -a [ə]) delirio
deliver [dɪ'lɪvər] *tr* consegnare; (*a blow*) affibbiare; (*a speech*) fare; (*a letter*) recapitare; (*electricity or gas*) erogare; (*said of a pregnant woman*) partorire; (*said of a doctor*) assistere durante il parto
deliver·y [dɪ'lɪvərɪ] *s* (-ies) consegna; (*of mail*) distribuzione; (*of merchandise*) fornitura; (*of a speech*) dizione; (*childbirth*) parto; (sports) lancio
deliv'ery-man' *s* (-men') fattorino
deliv'ery room' *s* sala parto
deliv'ery truck' *s* furgoncino
dell [dɛl] *s* valletta
delouse [di'laus] or [di'lauz] *tr* spidocchiare
delude [dɪ'lud] *tr* illudere, ingannare
deluge ['dɛljudʒ] *s* diluvio, inondazione || **the Deluge** il diluvio universale || *tr* inondare
delusion [dɪ'luʒən] *s* illusione, inganno; (*psychopath*) allucinazione;

(psychopath) idea fissa; **delusions of grandeur** mania di grandezza

de luxe [dɪ'lʌks] or [dɪ'lʌks] *adj* di lusso || *adv* in gran lusso

delve [delv] *intr* frugare; **to delve into** approfondirsi in

demagnetize [dɪ'mægnɪ,taɪz] *tr* smagnetizzare

demagogue ['demə,gɑg] *s* demagogo

demand [dɪ'mænd] or [dɪ'mɑnd] *s* esigenza; (com) richiesta, domanda; **to be in demand** essere in richiesta || *tr* esigere

demanding [dɪ'mændɪŋ] or [dɪ'mɑndɪŋ] *adj* esigente, impegnativo

demarcate [dɪ'mɑrket] or ['dɪmɑr,ket] *tr* demarcare

démarche [de'mɑrʃ] *s* progetto, piano

demean [dɪ'min] *tr* degradare; **to demean oneself** comportarsi; degradarsi

demeanor [dɪ'minər] *s* condotta, contegno

demented [dɪ'mentɪd] *adj* demente

demigod ['demɪ,gɑd] *s* semidio

demijohn ['demɪ,dʒɑn] *s* damigiana

demilitarize [di'mɪlɪtə,raɪz] *tr* smilitarizzare

demimonde ['demɪ,mɑnd] *s* donne *fpl* della società equivoca

demise [dɪ'maɪz] *s* decesso

demitasse ['demɪ,tæs] or ['demɪ,tɑs] *s* tazzina da caffè; (*contents*) caffè nero

demobilize [di'mobɪ,laɪz] *tr* smobilitare

democra·cy [dɪ'mɑkrəsi] *s* (**-cies**) democrazia

democrat ['demə,kræt] *s* democratico

democratic [,demə'krætɪk] *adj* democratico

demolish [dɪ'mɑlɪʃ] *tr* demolire

demolition [,demə'lɪʃən] or [,dimə'lɪʃən] *s* demolizione

demon ['dimən] *s* demonio

demoniacal [,dimə'naɪ·əkəl] *adj* demoniaco

demonstrate ['demən,stret] *tr & intr* dimostrare

demonstration [,demən'streʃən] *s* dimostrazione

demonstrative [dɪ'mɑnstrətɪv] *adj* dimostrativo; (*giving open exhibition of emotion*) espansivo

demonstrator ['demən,stretər] *s* (*of a product*) dimostratore *m*; (*in a public gathering*) dimostrante *m*; (*product*) prodotto usato da dimostratori

demoralize [dɪ'mɑrə,laɪz] or [dɪ'mɔrə,laɪz] *tr* demoralizzare

demote [dɪ'mot] *tr* retrocedere

demotion [dɪ'moʃən] *s* retrocessione

de·mur [dɪ'mʌr] *v* (*pret & pp* **-murred**; *ger* **-murring**) *intr* sollevare obiezioni

demure [dɪ'mjur] *adj* modesto; sobrio

demurrage [dɪ'mʌrɪdʒ] *s* (com) controstallie *fpl*; (rr) sosta

den [den] *s* (*of animals, thieves*) tana; (*little room*) bugigattolo; (*little room for studying or writing*) studiolo; (*of lions*) (Bib) fossa

denaturalize [di'nætʃərə,laɪz] *tr* snaturare; privare della nazionalità

dena'tured al'cohol [dɪ'netʃərd] *s* alcole denaturato

denial [dɪ'naɪ·əl] *s* diniego; (*disavowal*) smentita

denim ['denɪm] *s* tessuto di cotone per tuta; **denims** tuta; (*trousers*) jeans *mpl*

denizen ['denɪzən] *s* abitante *mf*

Denmark ['denmɑrk] *s* la Danimarca

denomination [dɪ,nɑmɪ'neʃən] *s* denominazione; categoria; (com) taglio; (eccl) confessione

denote [dɪ'not] *tr* denotare, significare

denouement [denu'mɑ̃] *s* scioglimento

denounce [dɪ'nauns] *tr* denunziare

dense [dens] *adj* denso; stupido

densi·ty ['densɪti] *s* (**-ties**) densità *f*

dent [dent] *s* ammaccatura; (*in a gearwheel*) tacca, dente *m*; **to make a dent** fare progresso; fare impressione || *tr* ammaccare; (fig) ferire

dental ['dentəl] *adj* dentale, dentario || *s* dentale *f*

den'tal floss' *s* filo cerato dentario

dentifrice ['dentɪfrɪs] *s* dentifricio

dentist ['dentɪst] *s* dentista *mf*

dentistry ['dentɪstri] *s* odontoiatria

denture ['dentʃər] *s* dentiera

denunciation [dɪ,nʌnsɪ'eʃən] or [dɪ,nʌnʃɪ'eʃən] *s* denunzia

de·ny [dɪ'naɪ] *v* (*pret & pp* **-nied**) *tr* (*to declare not to be true*) negare; (*to refuse*) rifiutare; **to deny oneself to callers** sottrarsi alle visite || *intr* negare; rifiutare

deodorant [di'odərənt] *adj & s* deodorante *m*

deo'dorant spray' *s* deodorante *m* spray

deodorize [di'odə,raɪz] *tr* deodorare

depart [dɪ'pɑrt] *intr* partire, andarsene; (*to diverge*) dipartire

departed [dɪ'pɑrtɪd] *adj* morto, defunto || **the departed** i defunti

department [dɪ'pɑrtmənt] *s* dipartimento; (*of government*) ministero; (*e.g., of a hospital*) reparto; (*of agency*) sezione, ufficio

depart'ment store' *s* grandi magazzini *mpl*

departure [dɪ'pɑrtʃər] *s* partenza; divergenza, deviazione

depend [dɪ'pend] *intr* dipendere; **to depend on** (*to rely on*) contare su; dipendere da

dependable [dɪ'pendəbəl] *adj* sicuro, fidato

dependence [dɪ'pendəns] *s* dipendenza; (*trust*) fiducia

dependen·cy [dɪ'pendənsi] *s* (**-cies**) dipendenza; (*territory*) possessione

dependent [dɪ'pendənt] *adj* dipendente; a carico; **to be dependent on** dipendere da || *s* persona a carico

depend'ent clause' *s* proposizione subordinata

depict [dɪ'pɪkt] *tr* descrivere, dipingere

deplete [dɪ'plit] *tr* esaurire

depletion [dɪ'pliʃən] *s* esaurimento

deplorable [dɪ'plorəbəl] *adj* deplorevole

deplore [dɪ'plor] *tr* deplorare

deploy [dɪ'plɔɪ] *tr* (mil) spiegare, stendere

deployment [dɪ'plɔɪmənt] s (mil) dispositivo, spiegamento

depolarize [di'polə ‚raɪz] tr depolarizzare

depopulate [di'pɑpjə ‚let] tr spopolare

deport [dɪ'port] tr deportare; to deport oneself comportarsi

deportation [‚dipor'teʃən] s deportazione

deportee [‚dipor'ti] s deportato

deportment [dɪ'portmənt] s condotta, comportamento

depose [dɪ'poz] tr & intr deporre

deposit [dɪ'pɑzɪt] s deposito; (down payment) caparra || tr depositare || intr depositarsi

depos'it account' s conto corrente

depositor [dɪ'pɑzɪtər] s versante mf; (to the credit of an established account) correntista mf

deposi•to•ry [dɪ'pɑzɪ ‚tori] s (-ries) deposito; (person) depositario

depos'it slip' s distinta di versamento

depot ['dipo] or ['depo] s magazzino; (mil) deposito; (rr) stazione

depraved [dɪ'prevd] adj depravato

depravi•ty [dɪ'prævɪti] s (-ties) depravazione

deprecate ['dɛprɪ ‚ket] tr deprecare

depreciate [dɪ'priʃɪ ‚et] tr svalutare, deprezzare || intr deprezzarsi

depreciation [dɪ ‚priʃɪ'eʃən] s (drop in value) deprezzamento; (disparagement) disprezzo

depredation [‚dɛprɪ'deʃən] s depredazione

depress [dɪ'prɛs] tr deprimere; avvilire; (prices) far abbassare

depression [dɪ'prɛʃən] s depressione; (gloom) sconforto; (slump) crisi f

deprive [dɪ'praɪv] tr privare; to deprive oneself espropriarsi

depth [dɛpθ] s profondità f; (of a house or room) lunghezza; (of sea) fondale m; (fig) vastità f; in the depth of nel cuor di; to go beyond one's depth non toccare più; (fig) andare oltre le proprie possibilità

depth' bomb' s (aer) bomba antisommergibile

depth' charge' s (nav) granata antisommergibile

depth' of hold' s (naut) puntale m

deputation [‚dɛpjə'teʃən] s deputazione

deputize ['dɛpjə ‚taɪz] tr deputare

depu•ty ['dɛpjəti] s (-ties) deputato

derail [dɪ'rel] tr far deragliare || intr deragliare, deviare

derailment [dɪ'relmənt] s deragliamento, deviamento

derange [dɪ'rendʒ] tr (to disarrange) dissestare; (to make insane) squilibrare, render pazzo

derangement [dɪ'rendʒmənt] s (disorder) disordine m; (insanity) squilibrio mentale, pazzia

der•by ['dɑrbi] s (-bies) bombetta; (race) derby m

derelict ['dɛrɪlɪkt] adj derelitto; negligente || s derelitto; (naut) relitto

dereliction [‚dɛrɪ'lɪkʃən] s (in one's duty) negligenza; (law) derelizione

deride [dɪ'raɪd] tr deridere, schernire, farsi beffe di

derision [dɪ'rɪʒən] s derisione, scherno

derisive [dɪ'raɪsɪv] adj derisorio

derivation [‚dɛrɪ'veʃən] s derivazione

derivative [dɪ'rɪvətɪv] adj & s derivato

derive [dɪ'raɪv] tr & intr derivare

dermatology [‚dʌrmə'tɑlədʒi] s dermatologia

derogatory [dɪ'rɑgə ‚tori] adj dispregiativo

derrick ['dɛrɪk] s gru f; (naut) picco di carico

dervish ['dʌrvɪʃ] s dervis m

desalinization [di ‚sɛlɪnɪ'zeʃən] s desalazione

desalt [di'sɔlt] tr desalificare

descend [dɪ'sɛnd] tr discendere || intr discendere; to descend on calare su, gettarsi su

descendant [dɪ'sɛndənt] adj & s discendente mf

descendent [dɪ'sɛndənt] adj discendente

descent [dɪ'sɛnt] s (slope) china; (decline) declino; discesa; (lineage) stirpe f, discendenza; (sudden raid) calata

Descent' from the Cross' s Deposizione dalla Croce

describe [dɪ'skraɪb] tr descrivere

description [dɪ'skrɪpʃən] s descrizione

descriptive [dɪ'skrɪptɪv] adj descrittivo

de•scry [dɪ'skraɪ] v (pret & pp -scried) tr avvistare

desecrate ['dɛsɪ ‚kret] tr profanare, dissacrare

desecration [‚dɛsɪ'kreʃən] s profanazione, dissacrazione

desegregate [di'sɛgrɪ ‚get] intr sopprimere la segregazione razziale

desegregation [di ‚sɛgrɪ'geʃən] s desegregazione

desensitize [di'sɛnsɪ ‚taɪz] tr desensibilizzare

desert ['dɛzərt] adj & s deserto || [dɪ'zʌrt] s merito; he received his just deserts ricevette quanto meritava || tr & intr disertare

deserter [dɪ'zʌrtər] s disertore m

deserted [dɪ'zʌrtɪd] adj (person) abbandonato; (place) deserto

desertion [dɪ'zʌrʃən] s diserzione; abbandono del coniuge

deserve [dɪ'zʌrv] tr & intr meritare

deservedly [dɪ'zʌrvɪdli] adv meritatamente, meritevolmente

design [dɪ'zaɪn] s disegno; (of a play) congegno; to have designs on aver mire su || tr disegnare; progettare || intr disegnare; designed for destinato a

designate ['dɛzɪg ‚net] tr designare

designer [dɪ'zaɪnər] s disegnatore m

designing [dɪ'zaɪnɪŋ] adj intrigante, macchinatore || s disegnazione

desirable [dɪ'zaɪrəbəl] adj desiderabile

desire [dɪ'zaɪr] s desiderio || tr desiderare

desirous [dɪ'zaɪrəs] adj desideroso

desist [di'zɪst] intr desistere

desk [dɛsk] s scrittoio; tavolo d'ufficio;

(*lectern*) leggio; (*of professor*) cattedra; (*of pupil*) banco; (*com*) cassa

desk'bound' *adj* sedentario; legato a tavolino

desk' pad' *s* blocco da tavolo; blocco per appunti

desolate ['dɛsəlɪt] *adj* desolato, deserto; (*hopeless*) disperato; (*dismal*) lugubre ‖ ['dɛsəˌlet] *tr* desolare; devastare

desolation [ˌdɛsə'leʃən] *s* desolazione; devastazione

despair [dɪ'spɛr] *s* disperazione; **to be in despair** disperarsi ‖ *intr* disperare, disperarsi

despairing [dɪ'spɛrɪŋ] *adj* disperato

despera·do [ˌdɛspə'redo] or [ˌdɛspə'rɑdo] *s* (-does or -dos) fuorilegge disposto a tutto

desperate ['dɛspərɪt] *adj* disposto a tutto; (*hopeless*) disperato; (*very bad*) atroce, terribile; (*bitter, excessive*) accanito; (*remedy*) estremo

desperation [ˌdɛspə'reʃən] *s* disperazione

despicable ['dɛspɪkəbəl] *adj* spregevole, incanaglito

despise [dɪ'spaɪz] *tr* sprezzare, disprezzare, vilipendere

despite [dɪ'spaɪt] *prep* malgrado

despoil [dɪ'spɔɪl] *tr* spogliare

desponden·cy [dɪ'spɑndənsi] *s* (-cies) scoraggiamento, abbattimento

despondent [dɪ'spɑndənt] *adj* scoraggiato, abbattuto

despot ['dɛspɑt] *s* despota *m*

despotic [dɛs'pɑtɪk] *adj* dispotico

despotism ['dɛspəˌtɪzəm] *s* dispotismo

dessert [dɪ'zʌrt] *s* dessert *m*

dessert' spoon' *s* cucchiaio or cucchiaino da dessert

destination [ˌdɛstɪ'neʃən] *s* destinazione

destine ['dɛstɪn] *tr* destinare

desti·ny ['dɛstɪni] *s* (-nies) destino

destitute ['dɛstɪˌtjut] or ['dɛstɪˌtut] *adj* (*poverty-stricken*) indigente; (*lacking*) privo

destitution [ˌdɛstɪ'tjuʃən] or [ˌdɛstɪ'tuʃən] *s* indigenza, miseria

destroy [dɪ'strɔɪ] *tr* distruggere

destroyer [dɪ'strɔɪ·ər] *s* (nav) cacciatorpediniere *m*

destruction [dɪ'strʌkʃən] *s* distruzione

destructive [dɪ'strʌktɪv] *adj* distruttivo

desultory ['dɛsəlˌtori] *adj* saltuario, sconnesso

detach [dɪ'tætʃ] *tr* staccare, distaccare; (mil) distaccare

detachable [dɪ'tætʃəbəl] *adj* staccabile; separabile

detached [dɪ'tætʃt] *adj* (*e.g.*, *stub*) staccato; (*e.g.*, *house*) discosto; (*aloof*) riservato, freddo; imparziale

detachment [dɪ'tætʃmənt] *s* distacco; imparzialità *f*; (mil) distaccamento

detail [dɪ'tel] or ['ditel] *s* dettaglio, ragguaglio; (mil) distaccamento ‖ [dɪ'tel] *tr* dettagliare; (mil) distaccare

detain [dɪ'ten] *tr* detenere, trattenere

detect [dɪ'tɛkt] *tr* scoprire, discernere; (rad) rivelare

detection [dɪ'tɛkʃən] *s* scoperta; (rad) rivelazione

detective [dɪ'tɛktɪv] *s* detective *m*

detec'tive sto'ry *s* romanzo poliziesco, romanzo giallo

detector [dɪ'tɛktər] *s* (rad) detector *m*, rivelatore *m*

detention [dɪ'tɛnʃən] *s* detenzione

de·ter [dɪ'tʌr] *v* (*pret & pp* **-terred;** *ger* **-terring**) *tr* distogliere, impedire

detergent [dɪ'tʌrdʒənt] *adj & s* detergente *m*

deteriorate [dɪ'tɪrɪ·əˌret] *tr* deteriorare ‖ *intr* deteriorarsi, andar giù

determination [dɪˌtʌrmɪ'neʃən] *s* determinazione

determine [dɪ'tʌrmɪn] *tr* determinare

determined [dɪ'tʌrmɪnd] *adj* determinato, risoluto

deterrent [dɪ'tʌrənt] *s* deterrente *m*

detest [dɪ'tɛst] *tr* detestare, odiare

dethrone [dɪ'θron] *tr* detronizzare

detonate ['dɛtəˌnet] or ['dɪtəˌnet] *tr* far scoppiare ‖ *intr* detonare

detonator ['dɛtəˌnetər] *s* innesco

detour ['ditur] or [dɪ'tur] *s* deviazione ‖ *tr* far deviare ‖ *intr* deviare

detract [dɪ'trækt] *tr* detrarre ‖ *intr*— **to detract from** diminuire

detractor [dɪ'træktər] *s* detrattore *m*

detriment [dɪ'trɪmənt] *s* detrimento; **to the detriment of** a danno di

detrimental [ˌdɛtrɪ'mɛntəl] *adj* pregiudizievole

deuce [djus] or [dus] *s* (cards) due *m*; **the deuce!** diavolo!

devaluate [di'væljuˌet] *tr* svalutare

devaluation [diˌvælju'eʃən] *s* devalutazione, svalutazione

devastate ['dɛvəsˌtet] *tr* devastare

devastating ['dɛvəsˌtetɪŋ] *adj* devastatore, devastante; (*e.g.*, *reply*) schiacciante, annichilante

devastation [ˌdɛvəs'teʃən] *s* devastazione

develop [dɪ'vɛləp] *tr* sviluppare; (phot) sviluppare, rivelare ‖ *intr* svilupparsi; manifestarsi

developer [dɪ'vɛləpər] *s* (*e.g.*, *of a new engine*) sfruttatore *m*; (*in real estate*) specialista *mf* in lottizzazione; (phot) sviluppatore *m*, rivelatore *m*

development [dɪ'vɛləpmənt] *s* sviluppo; valorizzazione; sfruttamento; (phot) rivelazione

deviate ['divɪˌet] *tr* sviare ‖ *intr* deviare, sviarsi

deviation [ˌdivɪ'eʃən] *s* deviazione

deviationism [ˌdivɪ'eʃəˌnɪzəm] *s* deviazionismo

deviationist [ˌdivɪ'eʃənɪst] *s* deviazionista *mf*

device [dɪ'vaɪs] *s* dispositivo, congegno; (*trick*) stratagemma *m*; (*motto*) divisa, emblema *m*; **to leave s.o. to his own devices** lasciare che qlcu faccia come gli pare e piace

dev·il ['dɛvəl] *s* diavolo; **between the devil and the deep blue sea** fra l'incudine e il martello; **to raise the devil** (slang) fare diavolo a quattro ‖ *v* (*pret & pp* **-iled** or **-illed;** *ger*

-iling or **-illing**) *tr* condire con spezie or con pepe; (coll) infastidire

devilish ['dɛvəlɪʃ] *adj* diabolico

devilment ['dɛvəlmənt] *s (mischief)* diavoleria; *(evil)* cattiveria

devil·try ['dɛvəltri] *s* (**-tries**) malvagità *f*, crudeltà *f; (mischief)* diavoleria

devious ['divɪ·əs] *adj (tricky)* traverso; *(roundabout)* tortuoso

devise [dɪ'vaɪz] *tr* ideare, inventare; (law) legare, disporre per testamento

devoid [dɪ'vɔɪd] *adj* sprovvisto

devolve [dɪ'vɑlv] *intr*—**to devolve on** ricadere su

devote [dɪ'vot] *tr* dedicare

devoted [dɪ'votɪd] *adj* devoto; dedito, dedicato

devotee [ˌdɛvə'ti] *s* devoto; *(fan)* fanatico, tifoso, entusiasta *mf*

devotion [dɪ'voʃən] *s* devozione; *(e.g., to work)* dedizione; **devotions** orazioni *mpl*, preghiere *fpl*

devour [dɪ'vaur] *tr* divorare

devout [dɪ'vaut] *adj* devoto; sincero

dew [dju] or [du] *s* rugiada

dew'drop' *s* goccia di rugiada

dew'lap' *s* giogaia

dew·y ['dju·i] or ['du·i] *adj* (**-ier; -iest**) rugiadoso

dexterity [dɛks'tɛrɪti] *s* destrezza

diabetes [ˌdaɪ·ə'bitis] or [ˌdaɪ·ə'bitiz] *s* diabete *m*

diabetic [ˌdaɪ·ə'bɛtɪk] or [ˌdaɪ·ə-'bitɪk] *adj & s* diabetico

diabolic(al) [ˌdaɪ·ə'bɑlɪk(əl)] *adj* diabolico

diadem ['daɪ·ə,dɛm] *s* diadema *m*

diaere·sis [daɪ'ɛrɪsɪs] *s* (**-ses** [ˌsiz]) dieresi *f*

diagnose [ˌdaɪ·əg'nos] or [ˌdaɪ·əg-'noz] *tr* diagnosticare

diagno·sis [ˌdaɪ·əg'nosɪs] *s* (**-ses** [siz]) diagnosi *f*

diagonal [daɪ'ægənəl] *adj & s* diagonale *f*

dia·gram ['daɪ·ə,græm] *s* diagramma *m; (drawing)* schema *m; (plan)* prospetto ‖ *v (pret & pp* **-gramed** or **-grammed**) *ger* **-graming** or **-gramming**) *tr* diagrammare

dial ['daɪ·əl] *s (of watch)* quadrante *m; (rad)* tabella graduata, sintogramma *m; (telp)* disco combinatore ‖ *tr* (rad) sintonizzare; *(a person)* (telp) chiamare; *(a number)* (telp) comporre; *(the phone)* (telp) comporre il numero di ‖ *intr* (telp) comporre il numero

dialect ['daɪ·ə,lɛkt] *s* dialetto

dialing ['daɪ·əlɪŋ] *s* composizione del numero

dialogue ['daɪ·ə,lɔg] or ['daɪ·ə,lɑg] *s* dialogo

di'al tel'ephone *s* telefono automatico

di'al tone' *s* (telp) segnale *m* di via libera

diameter [daɪ'æmɪtər] *s* diametro

diametric(al) [ˌdaɪ·ə'mɛtrɪk(əl)] *adj* diametrico, diametrale

diamond ['daɪmənd] *s* diamante *m; (figure of a rhombus)* losanga; *(baseball)* diamante *m;* **diamonds** (cards) quadri *mpl*

diaper ['daɪ·pər] *s* pannolino

diaphanous [daɪ'æfənəs] *adj* diafano

diaphragm ['daɪ·ə,fræm] *s* diaframma *m;* (telp) membrana

diarrhea [ˌdaɪ·ə'ri·ə] *s* diarrea

dia·ry ['daɪ·əri] *s* (**-ries**) diario

diastole [daɪ'æstəli] *s* diastole *f*

diathermy ['daɪ·ə,θʌrmi] *s* diatermia

dice [daɪs] *spl* dadi *mpl; (small cubes)* cubetti *mpl;* **no dice** (slang) niente da fare; (slang) risposta a picche

dice' cup' *s* bussolotto

dichloride [daɪ'klɔraɪd] *s* bicloruro

dichoto·my [daɪ'kɑtəmi] *s* (**-mies**) dicotomia

dickey ['dɪki] *s* camiciola; *(starched insert)* sparato; *(bib)* bavaglino

dictaphone ['dɪktə,fon] *s* dittafono

dictate ['dɪktet] *s* dettato ‖ ['dɪktet] or [dɪk'tet] *tr* dettare

dictation [dɪk'teʃən] *s* dettato; *(act of ordering)* ordine *m;* **to take dictation** scrivere sotto dettatura

dictator ['dɪktetər] or [dɪk'tetər] *s* dittatore *m*

dictatorship ['dɪktetər,ʃɪp] or [dɪk-'tetər/ɪp] *s* dittatura

diction ['dɪkʃən] *s* dizione

dictionar·y ['dɪkʃən,ɛri] *s* (**-ies**) dizionario, vocabolario

dic·tum ['dɪktəm] *s* (**-ta** [tə]) detto, sentenza

didactic(al) [daɪ'dæktɪk(əl)] or [dɪ-'dæktɪk(əl)] *adj* didattico

die [daɪ] *s* (**dice** [daɪs]) dado; **the die is cast** il dado è tratto ‖ *s* (**dies**) *(for stamping coins, medals,* etc.) stampo; *(for cutting threads)* filiera ‖ *v (pret & pp* **died;** *ger* **dying)** *intr* morire; **to die hard** morire lentamente; morire lottando; **to die laughing** morire dalle risa; **to die off** morire uno per uno

die'-hard' *adj & s* intransigente *m*

die'sel oil' ['dizəl] *s* nafta, gasolio

die'stock' *s* girafiliera

diet ['daɪ·ət] *s* dieta, regime *m* ‖ *intr* stare a dieta

dietetic [ˌdaɪ·ə'tɛtɪk] *adj* dietetico ‖ **dietetics** *ssg* dietetica

dietitian [ˌdaɪ·ə'tɪʃən] *s* dietista *mf*

differ ['dɪfər] *intr (to be different)* differire, differenziarsi; **to differ with** dissentire da

difference ['dɪfərəns] *s* differenza; **to make no difference** fare lo stesso; **to split the difference** dividere la differenza; (fig) venire a un compromesso

different ['dɪfərənt] *adj* differente

differential [ˌdɪfə'rɛnʃəl] *adj & s* differenziale *m*

differentiate [ˌdɪfə'rɛnʃɪ,et] *tr* differenziare ‖ *intr* differenziarsi

difficult ['dɪfɪ,kʌlt] *adj* difficile

difficul·ty ['dɪfɪ,kʌlti] *s* (**-ties**) difficoltà *f*

diffident ['dɪfɪdənt] *adj* timido, imbarazzato

diffuse [dɪ'fjus] *adj* diffuso ‖ [dɪ'fjuz] *tr* diffondere ‖ *intr* diffondersi

dig [dɪg] *s (poke)* botta, spintone *m; (jibe)* stoccata, fiancata ‖ *v (pret & pp* **dug** [dʌg]) *ger* **digging**) *tr* scavare, sterrare; **to dig up** dissodare; (*to uncover*) dissotterrare ‖ *intr* scavare; **to dig in** (mil) fortificarsi; **to dig into** (coll) sprofondarsi in

digest ['daɪdʒest] *s* compendio; (law) digesto ‖ [dɪ'dʒest] or [daɪ'dʒest] *tr & intr* digerire

digestible [dɪ'dʒestɪbəl] or [daɪ'dʒestɪbəl] *adj* digeribile, digestibile

digestion [dɪ'dʒestʃən] or [daɪ'dʒestʃən] *s* digestione

digestive [dɪ'dʒestɪv] or [daɪ'dʒestɪv] *adj* (*tube*) digerente ‖ *s* digestivo

digit ['dɪdʒɪt] *s* cifra, unità *f*; (*finger*) dito; (*toe*) dito del piede

dig'ital clock' *s* orologio a scatto

digitalis [,dɪdʒɪ'tælɪs] or [,dɪdʒɪ'telɪs] *s* (bot) digitale *f*; (pharm) digitalina

dignified ['dɪgnɪ,faɪd] *adj* dignitoso, fiero, contegnoso

digni-fy ['dɪgnɪ,faɪ] *v* (*pret & pp* -**fied**) *tr* (*to ennoble*) nobilitare; onorare, esaltare; dare la dignità a

dignitar·y ['dɪgnɪ,teri] *s* (-**ies**) dignitario; **dignitaries** dignità *fpl*

digni-ty ['dɪgnɪti] *s* (-**ties**) dignità *f*, decoro; **to stand on one's dignity** mantenere la propria dignità

digress [dɪ'gres] or [daɪ'gres] *intr* digredire, divagare

digression [dɪ'greʃən] or [daɪ'greʃən] *s* digressione, divagazione

dike [daɪk] *s* diga; (*in a river*) argine *m*; (*ditch*) fosso; scarpata

dilapidated [dɪ'læpɪ,detɪd] *adj* dilapidato, decrepito

dilate [daɪ'let] *tr* dilatare ‖ *intr* dilatarsi

dilatory ['dɪlə,tori] *adj* lento, tardivo; (*e.g., strategy*) dilatorio

dilemma [dɪ'lemə] *s* dilemma *m*

dilettan·te [,dɪlə'tænti] *adj* dilettantesco ‖ *s* (-**tes** or -**ti** [ti]) dilettante *mf*

diligence ['dɪlɪdʒəns] *s* diligenza

diligent ['dɪlɪdʒənt] *adj* diligente

dill [dɪl] *s* (bot) aneto

dillydal·ly ['dɪlɪ,dæli] *v* (*pret & pp* -**lied**) *intr* farla lunga

dilute [dɪ'lut] or [daɪ'lut] *adj* diluito ‖ [dɪ'lut] *tr* diluire ‖ *intr* diluirsi

dilution [dɪ'luʃən] *s* diluizione

dim [dɪm] *adj* (*dimmer; dimmest*) (*light*) fioco; (*sight*) debole; (*memory*) vago; (*color*) smorzato; (*sound*) sordo; **to take a dim view of** avere una visione pessimistica di ‖ *v* (*pret & pp* **dimmed**; *ger* **dimming**) *tr* (*lights*) smorzare; **to dim the headlights** abbassare i fari

dime [daɪm] *s* moneta di dieci centesimi di dollaro

dimension [dɪ'menʃən] *s* dimensione

diminish [dɪ'mɪnɪʃ] *tr & intr* diminuire, scemare

diminutive [dɪ'mɪnjətɪv] *adj* (*tiny*) minuscolo; (gram) diminutivo ‖ *s* diminutivo

dimly ['dɪmli] *adv* indistintamente

dimmer ['dɪmər] *s* smorzatore *m*; (aut) luce *f* di incrocio; **dimmers** fari *mpl* antiabbaglianti

dimple ['dɪmpəl] *s* fossetta

dimwit ['dɪm,wɪt] *s* (slang) stupido, cretino

din [dɪn] *s* fragore *m*, frastuono ‖ *v* (*pret & pp* **dinned**; *ger* **dinning**) *tr* assordare; **to din s.th into s.o.'s ears** rintornare qlco nelle orecchie di qlcu

dine [daɪn] *tr* offrire un pranzo a; offire una cena a ‖ *intr* pasteggiare; cenare; **to dine out** mangiare fuori di casa

diner ['daɪnər] *s* commensale *m*; (rr) vettura ristorante; (U.S.A.) ristorante *m* a forma di vagone

ding-dong ['dɪŋ,dɔŋ] or ['dɪŋ,dɑŋ] *s* dindon *m*

din-gy ['dɪndʒi] *adj* (-**gier**; -**giest**) sporco, sbiadito

din'ing car' *s* vagone *m* ristorante

din'ing room' *s* sala da pranzo

dinner ['dɪnər] *s* cena; pranzo; (*formal meal*) banchetto

din'ner coat' or **jack'et** *s* smoking *m*

din'ner knife' *s* coltello da tavola

din'ner set' *s* servizio da tavola

din'ner ta'ble *s* desco

din'ner time' *s* ora di pranzo or di cena

dinosaur ['daɪnə,sɔr] *s* dinosauro

dint [dɪnt] *s* tacca, ammaccatura; **by dint of** a forza di ‖ *tr* ammaccare

diocese ['daɪə,sis] or ['daɪ·əsɪs] *s* diocesi *f*

diode ['daɪ·od] *s* diodo

dioxide [daɪ'ɑksaɪd] *s* biossido

dip [dɪp] *s* immersione; (*brief swim*) tuffo, nuotata; (*in a road*) depressione; inclinazione magnetica ‖ *v* (*pret & pp* **dipped**; *ger* **dipping**) *tr* immergere, tuffare; (*the flag*) abbassare; (*bread*) inzuppare ‖ *intr* immergersi, tuffarsi; inclinarsi; (*to drop down*) sparire subitamente; **to dip into** (*a book*) sfogliare; (*business*) mettersi in; (*a container of liquids*) intingere; **to dip into one's purse** spendere soldi

diphtheria [dɪf'θɪrɪ·ə] *s* difterite *f*

diphthong ['dɪfθɔŋ] or ['dɪfθɑŋ] *s* dittongo

diphthongize ['dɪfθɔŋ,gaɪz] or ['dɪfθɑŋ,gaɪz] *tr & intr* dittongare

diploma [dɪ'plomə] *s* diploma *m*

diploma·cy [dɪ'ploməsi] *s* (-**cies**) diplomazia

diplomat ['dɪplə,mæt] *s* diplomatico

diplomatic [,dɪplə'mætɪk] *adj* diplomatico

dip'lomat'ic pouch' *s* valigia diplomatica

dipper ['dɪpər] *s* mestolo

dip'stick' *s* asta di livello

dire [daɪr] *adj* terribile, orrendo

direct [dɪ'rekt] or [daɪ'rekt] *adj* diretto; sincero ‖ *tr* dirigere; ordinare

direct' cur'rent *s* corrente continua

direct' dis'course *s* discorso diretto

direct' dis'tance di'aling *s* (telp) teleselezione *f*

direct' hit' *s* colpo centrato

direction [dɪ'rekʃən] or [daɪ'rekʃən] *s* direzione; **directions** istruzioni *fpl*; (*for use*) indicazioni *fpl* per l'uso

directional [dɪ'rɛkʃənəl] or [daɪ-'rɛkʃənəl] *adj* direzionale

directive [dɪ'rɛktɪv] or [daɪ'rɛktɪv] *s* direttiva

direct' ob'ject *s* (gram) complemento diretto, complemento oggetto

director [dɪ'rɛktər] or [daɪ'rɛktər] *s* direttore *m*, gerente *m*; (*member of a governing body*) consigliere *m*

directorship [dɪ'rɛktər‚ʃɪp] or [daɪ-'rɛktər‚ʃɪp] *s* direzione; amministrazione

directo•ry [dɪ'rɛktəri] or [daɪ'rɛktəri] *s* (**-ries**) (*board of directors*) direzione, direttorio; (*list of names and addresses*) rubrica, elenco; (telp) elenco dei telefoni, guida telefonica

dirge [dʌrdʒ] *s* canto funebre

dirigible ['dɪrɪdʒɪbəl] *adj* & *s* dirigibile *m*

dirt [dʌrt] *s* (*soil*) terra, suolo; (*dust*) polvere *m*; (*mud*) fango; (*accumulation of dirt*) sudiciume *m*, lerciume *m*; (*moral filth*) porcheria, sozzura; (*gossip*) pettegolezzi *mpl*; **to do s.o. dirt** (slang) calunniare qlcu

dirt'-cheap' *adj* a prezzo bassissimo

dirt' road' *s* strada di terra battuta

dirt•y ['dʌrti] *adj* (**-ier; -iest**) sporco, sudicio; fangoso; polveroso; (*e.g., spinach*) terroso; (*obscene*) sconcio, lurido; immondo ‖ *v* (*pret* & *pp* (**-ied**) *tr* sporcare, insudiciare, imbrattare

dirt'y lin'en *s* roba sporca; **to air one's dirty linen in public** mettere i panni al sole

dirt'y trick' *s* brutto tiro

disabili•ty [‚dɪsə'bɪlɪti] *s* (**-ties**) incapacità *f*, invalidità *f*

disabil'ity insur'ance *s* assicurazione invalidità

disable [dɪs'ebəl] *tr* mutilare, storpiare; (*a ship*) smantellare; (law) invalidare

disabuse [‚dɪsə'bjuz] *tr* disingannare

disadvantage [‚dɪsəd'væntɪdʒ] or [‚dɪsəd'vɑntɪdʒ] *s* svantaggio

disadvantageous [dɪs‚ædvən'tedʒəs] *adj* svantaggioso

disagree [‚dɪsə'gri] *intr* discordare, disconvenire; (*to quarrel*) litigare, altercare; **to disagree with** non essere del parere di

disagreeable [‚dɪsə'gri•əbəl] *adj* sgradevole

disagreement [‚dɪsə'grimənt] *s* scordanza, dissidio, dissenso

disallow [‚dɪsə'laʊ] *tr* non permettere, rifiutare

disappear [‚dɪsə'pɪr] *intr* sparire, scomparire

disappearance [‚dɪsə'pɪrəns] *s* scomparsa

disappoint [‚dɪsə'pɔɪnt] *tr* deludere, disilludere; **to be disappointed** rimanere deluso

disappointment [‚dɪsə'pɔɪntmənt] *s* delusione, disinganno, disappunto

disapproval [‚dɪsə'pruvəl] *s* disapprovazione, riprova

disapprove [‚dɪsə'pruv] *tr* & *intr* disapprovare

disarm [dɪs'ɑrm] *tr* disarmare ‖ *intr* disarmare, disarmarsi

disarmament [dɪs'ɑrməmənt] *s* disarmo

disarming [dɪs'ɑrmɪŋ] *adj* ingraziante, simpatico

disarray [‚dɪsə're] *s* disordine *m*, scompiglio; (*of apparel*) sciatteria ‖ *tr* scomporre, scompigliare

disassemble [‚dɪsə'sɛmbəl] *tr* smontare, sconnettere

disassociate [‚dɪsə'soʃɪ‚et] *tr* dissociare, disassociare

disaster [dɪ'zæstər] or [dɪ'zɑstər] *s* disastro, sinistro

disastrous [dɪ'zæstrəs] or [dɪ'zɑstrəs] *adj* disastroso

disavow [‚dɪsə'vaʊ] *tr* sconfessare

disavowal [‚dɪsə'vaʊ•əl] *s* sconfessione

disband [dɪs'bænd] *tr* (*an assembly*) sciogliere; (*troops*) congedare; (*any group*) sbandare ‖ *intr* sbandarsi

dis•bar [dɪs'bɑr] *v* (*pret* & *pp* **-barred; ger -barring**) *tr* (law) radiare dall'albo degli avvocati

disbelief [‚dɪsbɪ'lif] *s* incredulità *f*

disbelieve [‚dɪsbɪ'liv] *tr* rifiutarsi di credere a ‖ *intr* rifiutarsi di credere

disburse [dɪs'bʌrs] *tr* sborsare

disbursement [dɪs'bʌrsmənt] *s* sborso, disborso

discard [dɪs'kɑrd] *s* scarto, scartina; **to put into the discard** scartare ‖ *tr* scartare

discern [dɪ'zʌrn] or [dɪ'sʌrn] *tr* scernere, discernere, sceverare

discernible [dɪ'zʌrnɪbəl] or [dɪ'sʌrnɪbəl] *adj* discernibile

discerning [dɪ'zʌrnɪŋ] or [dɪ'sʌrnɪŋ] *adj* perspicace, oculato

discernment [dɪ'zʌrnmənt] or [dɪ-'sʌrnmənt] *s* discernimento

discharge [dɪs'tʃɑrdʒ] *s* (*of a load*) scarico; (*of a gun*; *of electricity*) scarica; (*of a prisoner*) liberazione; (*of a duty*) adempimento; (*of a debt*) pagamento; (*from a job*) licenziamento; (mil) foglio di congedo; (pathol) spurgo ‖ *tr* scaricare; (*a duty*) adempiere; (*a prisoner*) liberare; (*a debt*) pagare; (*an employee*) licenziare; (*a patient*) lasciar uscire; (*a passenger from a ship*) sbarcare; (*a battery*) scaricare; (mil) congedare ‖ *intr* (said, *e.g., of a liquid*) sboccare; (*said of a gun or a battery*) scaricarsi

disciple [dɪ'saɪpəl] *s* discepolo

disciplinarian [‚dɪsɪplɪ'nɛri•ən] *s* disciplinatore *m*; partigiano di una forte disciplina

disciplinary ['dɪsɪplɪ‚nɛri] *adj* disciplinare

discipline ['dɪsɪplɪn] *s* disciplina; castigo ‖ *tr* disciplinare; castigare

disclaim [dɪs'klem] *tr* non riconoscere, negare

disclose [dɪs'kloz] *tr* rivelare, scoprire

disclosure [dɪs'kloʒər] *s* rivelazione, scoperta; divulgazione

discolor [dɪs'kʌlər] *tr* scolorare, scolorire ‖ *intr* scolorirsi

discoloration [dɪs‚kʌlə'reʃən] *s* discolorazione

discomfit [dɪs'kʌmfɪt] *tr* sconcertare; turbare; frustrare, battere, mettere in fuga

discomfiture [dɪs'kʌmfɪt/ər] *s* sconcerto, turbamento; frustrazione; disfatta

discomfort [dɪs'kʌmfərt] *s* disagio || *tr* incomodare

disconcert [ˌdɪskən'sʌrt] *tr* sconcertare

disconnect [ˌdɪskə'nɛkt] *tr* sconnettere; (elec) disinserire

disconsolate [dɪs'kɑnsəlɪt] *adj* sconsolato, desolato

discontent [ˌdɪskən'tɛnt] *adj & s* scontento || *tr* scontentare

discontented [ˌdɪskən'tɛntɪd] *adj* scontento

discontinue [ˌdɪskən'tɪnju] *tr* cessare, interrompere

discord ['dɪskərd] *s* discordia, dissidio

discordance [dɪs'kɔrdəns] *s* discordanza

discotheque [ˌdɪsko'tɛk] *s* discoteca

discount ['dɪskaunt] *s* sconto || ['dɪs-kaunt] or [dɪs'kaunt] *tr* scontare; (news) fare la tara a

dis'count rate' *s* tasso di sconto

discourage [dɪs'kʌrɪdʒ] *tr* scoraggiare, sconfortare; (to dissuade) consigliare

discouragement [dɪs'kʌrɪdʒmənt] *s* scoraggiamento; disapprovazione

discourse ['dɪskors] or [dɪs'kors] *s* discorso || [dɪs'kors] *intr* discorrere

discourteous [dɪs'kʌrtɪ·əs] *adj* scortese

discourte•sy [dɪs'kʌrtəsi] *s* (-sies) scortesia

discover [dɪs'kʌvər] *tr* scoprire

discoverer [dɪs'kʌvərər] *s* scopritore *m*

discover•y [dɪs'kʌvəri] *s* (-ies) scoperta

discredit [dɪs'krɛdɪt] *s* discredito || *tr* screditare

discreditable [dɪs'krɛdɪtəbəl] *adj* indegno, disonorevole

discreet [dɪs'krit] *adj* discreto

discrepan•cy [dɪs'krɛpənsi] *s* (-cies) discrepanza, divario

discretion [dɪs'krɛ/ən] *s* discrezione

discriminate [dɪs'krɪmɪˌnet] *tr* discriminare || *intr*—**to discriminate against** fare delle discriminazioni contro

discrimination [dɪsˌkrɪmɪ'ne/ən] *s* discriminazione

discriminatory [dɪs'krɪmɪnəˌtori] *adj* discriminante

discuss [dɪs'kʌs] *tr & intr* discutere

discussion [dɪs'kʌ/ən] *s* discussione

discus thrower ['dɪskəs 'θro·ər] *s* discobolo

disdain [dɪs'den] *s* disdegno || *tr* disdegnare, sdegnare

disdainful [dɪs'denfəl] *adj* sdegnoso

disease [dɪ'ziz] *s* malattia

diseased [dɪ'zizd] *adj* malato

disembark [ˌdɪsɛm'bark] *tr & intr* sbarcare

disembarkation [dɪsˌɛmbar'ke/ən] *s* sbarco

disembowel [ˌdɪsɛm'bau·əl] *tr* sbudellare, sventrare

disenchant [ˌdɪsɛn't/ænt] or [ˌdɪsɛn-'t/ant] *tr* disincantare

disenchantment [ˌdɪsɛn't/æntmənt] or [ˌdɪsɛn't/antmənt] *s* disinganno

disengage [ˌdɪsɛn'gedʒ] *tr* (from a pledge) svincolare; (to disconnect) sgranare, disinnestare; (mil) sganciare

disengagement [ˌdɪsɛn'gedʒmənt] *s* liberazione; disinnesto; svincolamento

disentangle [ˌdɪsɛn'tæŋgəl] *tr* disincagliare, districare

disentanglement [ˌdɪsɛn'tæŋgəlmənt] *s* districamento

disestablish [ˌdɪsɛs'tæblɪ/] *tr* (the Church) separare dallo Stato

disfavor [dɪs'fevər] *s* disfavore *m*

disfigure [dɪs'fɪgjər] *tr* sfigurare, deturpare

disfigurement [dɪs'fɪgjərmənt] *s* deturpazione

disfranchise [dɪs'fræntʃaɪz] *tr* privare dei diritti civili

disgorge [dɪs'gɔrdʒ] *tr* vomitare; (something illicitly obtained) restituire; (said of a river) scaricare || *intr* vomitare; scaricarsi

disgrace [dɪs'gres] *s* vergogna; disgrazia || *tr* disonorare; privare del favore

disgraceful [dɪs'gresfəl] *adj* infamante, disonorante

disgruntle [dɪs'grʌntəl] *tr* scontentare, irritare

disgruntled [dɪs'grʌntəld] *adj* irritato, di cattivo umore

disguise [dɪs'gaɪz] *s* travestimento || *tr* travestire, dissimulare

disgust [dɪs'gʌst] *s* disgusto, schifo || *tr* disgustare, fare schifo a

disgusting [dɪs'gʌstɪŋ] *adj* disgustoso, schifoso

dish [dɪʃ] *s* piatto, **dishes** vasellame *m*; **to wash the dishes** fare i piatti || *tr* scodellare; (to defeat) (slang) sconfiggere; **to dish out** (slang) distribuire

dish'cloth' *s* canovaccio, strofinaccio

dishearten [dɪs'hartən] *tr* scoraggiare, disanimare, desolare

dishev•el [dɪ'/ɛvəl] *v* (pret & pp -eled or -elled; ger -eling or -elling) *tr* scomporre, scarmigliare, scapigliare

dishonest [dɪs'ɑnɪst] *adj* disonesto

dishones•ty [dɪs'ɑnɪsti] *s* (-ties) disonestà *f*

dishonor [dɪs'ɑnər] *s* disonore *m* || *tr* disonorare; (com) rifiutare di pagare

dishonorable [dɪs'ɑnərəbəl] *adj* disonorevole, disonorante

dish'pan' *s* bacinella per lavare i piatti

dish'rack' *s* portapiatti *m*, sgocciolatoio

dish'rag' *s* canovaccio, strofinaccio

dish'towel' *s* canovaccio per le stoviglie

dish'wash'er *s* (person) sguattero, lavapiatti *m*; (machine) lavastoviglie *m & f*

dish'wa'ter *s* lavatura di piatti

disillusion [ˌdɪsɪ'luʒən] *s* disillusione || *tr* disilludere

disillusionment [ˌdɪsɪ'luʒənmənt] *s* disillusione

disinclination [dɪsˌɪnklɪ'ne/ən] *s* riluttanza, avversione

disinclined [ˌdɪsɪn'klaɪnd] *adj* riluttante, avverso

disinfect [ˌdɪsɪnˈfɛkt] *tr* disinfettare

disinfectant [ˌdɪsɪnˈfɛktənt] *adj & s* disinfettante *m*

disingenuous [ˌdɪsɪnˈdʒɛnjʊ·əs] *adj* poco schietto, insincero

disinherit [ˌdɪsɪnˈhɛrɪt] *tr* diseredare

disintegrate [dɪsˈɪntɪˌgret] *tr* disintegrare, disgregare || *intr* disintegrarsi, disgregarsi

disintegration [dɪsˌɪntɪˈgreʃən] *s* disintegrazione, disgregamento

disin·ter [ˌdɪsɪnˈtʌr] *v* (*pret & pp* -terred; *ger* -terring) *tr* dissotterrare

disinterested [dɪsˈɪntəˌrɛstɪd] *or* [dɪsˈɪntrɪstɪd] *adj* disinteressato

disjunctive [dɪsˈdʒʌŋktɪv] *adj* disgiuntivo

disk [dɪsk] *s* disco; (*of ski pole*) rotella

disk' jock'ey *s* presentatore *m* di un programma radiodiffuso di dischi

dislike [dɪsˈlaɪk] *s* antipatia, avversione; **to take a dislike for** prendere in uggia || *tr* non piacere (*with dat*), e.g., **he dislikes wine** non gli piace il vino

dislocate [ˈdɪsloˌket] *tr* spostare, mettere fuori posto; (*a bone*) slogare

dislodge [dɪsˈlɑdʒ] *tr* sloggiare

disloyal [dɪsˈlɔɪ·əl] *adj* sleale

disloyal·ty [dɪsˈlɔɪ·əltɪ] *s* (-ties) slealtà *f*

dismal [ˈdɪzməl] *adj* tetro, triste; cattivo, orribile

dismantle [dɪsˈmæntəl] *tr* smontare, smantellare; (*a fortress*) sguarnire

dismay [dɪsˈme] *s* costernazione || *tr* costernare

dismember [dɪsˈmɛmbər] *tr* smembrare

dismiss [dɪsˈmɪs] *tr* congedare; (*to fire*) licenziare; (*a subject*) scartare; (*from the mind*) scacciare

dismissal [dɪsˈmɪsəl] *s* congedo; licenziamento

dismount [dɪsˈmaʊnt] *tr* disarcionare || *intr* scendere, smontare

disobedience [ˌdɪsəˈbidɪ·əns] *s* disubbidienza

disobedient [ˌdɪsəˈbidɪ·ənt] *adj* disubbidiente

disobey [ˌdɪsəˈbe] *tr* disubbidire (*with dat*) || *intr* disubbidire

disorder [dɪsˈɔrdər] *s* disordine *m* || *tr* disordinare, confondere

disorderly [dɪsˈɔrdərlɪ] *adj* disordinato, confuso; (*unruly*) turbolento

disor'derly con'duct *s* contegno contrario all'ordine pubblico

disor'derly house' *s* bordello, lupanare *m*

disorganize [dɪsˈɔrgəˌnaɪz] *tr* disorganizzare

disoriented [dɪsˈɔrɪˌɛntɪd] *adj* disorientato

disown [dɪsˈon] *tr* disconoscere

disparage [dɪsˈpærɪdʒ] *tr* svilire, deprezzare

disparagement [dɪsˈpærɪdʒmənt] *s* discredito, deprezzamento

disparate [ˈdɪspərɪt] *adj* disparato

dispari·ty [dɪsˈpærɪtɪ] *s* (-ties) disparità *f*, spareggio

dispassionate [dɪsˈpæʃənɪt] *adj* spassionato

dispatch [dɪsˈpætʃ] *s* dispaccio || *tr* spedire; (*to dismiss*) congedare; uccidere; (*a meal*) (coll) liquidare

dis·pel [dɪsˈpɛl] *v* (*pret & pp* -pelled; *ger* -pelling) *tr* dissipare

dispensa·ry [dɪsˈpɛnsərɪ] *s* (-ries) dispensario

dispensation [ˌdɪspɛnˈseʃən] *s* (*dispensing*) distribuzione, dispensa; (*exemption*) dispensa

dispense [dɪsˈpɛns] *tr* (*medicines*) distribuire; (*justice*) amministrare; (*to distribute*) dispensare; (*to exempt*) esimere || *intr*—**to dispense with** fare a meno di; esimersi da

dispenser [dɪˈspɛnsər] *s* dispensatore *m*; (*automatic*) distributore *m*

disperse [dɪsˈpʌrs] *tr* disperdere || *intr* disperdersi

dispersion [dɪsˈpʌrʒən] *or* [dɪˈspɛrʃən] *s* dispersione

dispersive [dɪsˈpʌrsɪv] *adj* dispersivo

dispirit [dɪˈspɪrɪt] *tr* scoraggiare

displace [dɪsˈples] *tr* muovere; costringere a lasciare il proprio paese; (*to supplant*) rimpiazzare; (naut) dislocare

displaced' per'son *s* rifugiato politico

displacement [dɪsˈplesmənt] *s* spostamento; sostituzione; (*of a piston*) cilindrata; (naut) dislocamento

display [dɪsˈple] *s* sfoggio, mostra || *tr* mostrare; (*e.g., in a store window*) mettere in mostra; (*to unfold*) spiegare; (*to show ostentatiously*) sfoggiare, ostentare; (*ignorance*) rivelare

display' cab'inet *s* bacheca

display' win'dow *s* mostra, vetrina

displease [dɪsˈpliz] *tr* dispiacere (*with dat*)

displeasing [dɪsˈplizɪŋ] *adj* spiacevole

displeasure [dɪsˈplɛʒər] *s* dispiacere *m*; sfavore *m*

disposable [dɪsˈpozəbəl] *adj* (*available*) disponibile; (*made to be thrown away after use*) scartabile, da gettarsi via, usa e getta

disposal [dɪsˈpozəl] *s* disposizione; eliminazione; **to have at one's disposal** disporre di

dispose [dɪsˈpoz] *tr* disporre; **to dispose of** disporre di; (*to get rid of*) sbarazzarsi di; vendere

disposed [dɪˈspozd] *adj*—**to be disposed to** essere disposto a

disposition [ˌdɪspəˈzɪʃən] *s* disposizione; (*mental outlook*) indole *f*; tendenza; (mil) ordinamento

dispossess [ˌdɪspəˈzɛs] *tr* spodestare, bandire; (*to evict*) sfrattare

disproof [dɪsˈpruf] *s* confutazione

disproportionate [ˌdɪsprəˈporʃənɪt] *adj* sproporzionato

disprove [dɪsˈpruv] *tr* confutare

dispute [dɪsˈpjut] *s* disputa; **beyond dispute** incontestabile; **in dispute** in discussione || *tr & intr* disputare

disquali·fy [dɪsˈkwɑlɪˌfaɪ] *v* (*pret & pp* -fied) *tr* squalificare

disquiet [dɪsˈkwaɪ·ət] *s* inquietudine *f* || *tr* inquietare, turbare

disquisition [ˌdɪskwɪˈzɪʃən] *s* disquisizione

disregard [ˌdɪsrɪ'gɑrd] s (*of a rule*) inosservanza; (*of danger*) disprezzo, noncuranza ‖ *tr* non fare attenzione a

disrepair [ˌdɪsrɪ'pɛr] s cattivo stato, rovina

disreputable [dɪs'rɛpjətəbəl] *adj* malfamato; disonorevole; (*in bad condition*) raso, logoro

disrepute [ˌdɪsrɪ'pjut] s cattiva fama; **to bring into disrepute** rovinare la reputazione di

disrespect [ˌdɪsrɪ'spɛkt] s mancanza di rispetto ‖ *tr* mancare di rispetto a

disrespectful [ˌdɪsrɪ'spɛktfəl] *adj* non rispettoso, irriverente

disrobe [dɪs'rob] *tr* svestire ‖ *intr* svestirsi, spogliarsi

disrupt [dɪs'rʌpt] *tr* disorganizzare; interrompere

disruption [dɪs'rʌpʃən] s rottura; disorganizzazione

dissatisfaction [ˌdɪssætɪs'fækʃən] s scontento, malcontento

dissatisfied [dɪs'sætɪs,faɪd] *adj* scontento, malcontento; insoddisfatto

dissatis•fy [dɪs'sætɪs,faɪ] v (*pret & pp* -fied) *tr* scontentare

dissect [dɪ'sɛkt] *tr* sezionare

dissemble [dɪ'sɛmbəl] *tr & intr* dissimulare

disseminate [dɪ'sɛmɪ,net] *tr* disseminare, divulgare

dissension [dɪ'sɛnʃən] s dissensione

dissent [dɪ'sɛnt] s dissenso; (*nonconformity*) dissidio ‖ *intr* dissentire

dissenter [dɪ'sɛntər] s dissenziente *m*

dissertation [ˌdɪsər'teʃən] s dissertazione

disservice [dɪ'sʌrvɪs] s danno; cattivo servizio

dissidence ['dɪsɪdəns] s dissidenza

dissident ['dɪsɪdənt] *adj & s* dissidente *m*

dissimilar [dɪ'sɪmɪlər] *adj* dissimile

dissimilate [dɪ'sɪmɪ,let] *tr* dissimilare ‖ *intr* dissimilarsi

dissimulate [dɪ'sɪmjə,let] *tr & intr* dissimulare

dissipate ['dɪsɪ,pet] *tr* dissipare ‖ *intr* dissiparsi; (*to indulge oneself*) darsi alla dissipateizza

dissipated ['dɪsɪ,pɛtɪd] *adj* dissipato

dissipation [ˌdɪsɪ'peʃən] s dissipazione

dissociate [dɪ'soʃɪ,et] *tr* dissociare ‖ *intr* dissociarsi

dissolute ['dɪsə,lut] *adj* dissoluto

dissolution [ˌdɪsə'luʃən] s dissoluzione

dissolve [dɪ'zɑlv] *tr* sciogliere, disciogliere ‖ *intr* sciogliersi, disciogliersi

dissonance ['dɪsənəns] s dissonanza

dissuade [dɪ'swed] *tr* dissuadere

dissyllabic [ˌdɪsɪ'læbɪk] *adj* disillabo

dissyllable [dɪ'sɪləbəl] s disillabo

distaff ['dɪstæf] or ['dɪstaf] s rocca

dis'taff side' s ramo femminile di una famiglia

distance ['dɪstəns] s distanza; **a long distance** (fig) moltissimo; **in the distance** in lontananza; **to keep at a distance** or **to keep one's distance** mantenere le distanze ‖ *tr* distanziare

distant ['dɪstənt] *adj* distante; (*relative*) lontano; (*aloof*) freddo, riservato

distaste [dɪs'test] s ripugnanza

distasteful [dɪs'testfəl] *adj* ripugnante, sgradevole

distemper [dɪs'tɛmpər] s cimurro; (*painting*) tempera ‖ *tr* dipingere a tempera

distend [dɪs'tɛnd] *tr* stendere, distendere; gonfiare ‖ *intr* stendersi, distendersi; gonfiarsi

distension [dɪs'tɛnʃən] s distensione; gonfiamento

distill [dɪs'tɪl] *tr* distillare

distillation [ˌdɪstɪ'leʃən] s distillazione

distiller•y [dɪs'tɪləri] s (-ies) distilleria

distinct [dɪs'tɪŋkt] *adj* distinto, chiaro; (*not blurred*) nitido

distinction [dɪs'tɪŋkʃən] s distinzione

distinctive [dɪs'tɪŋktɪv] *adj* distintivo

distinguish [dɪs'tɪŋwɪʃ] *tr* distinguere

distinguished [dɪs'tɪŋgwɪʃt] *adj* distinto

distort [dɪs'tɔrt] *tr* distorcere; (*the truth*) svisare, snaturare

distortion [dɪs'tɔrʃən] s deformazione; (*of the truth*) alterazione, svisamento; (rad) distorsione

distract [dɪs'trækt] *tr* distrarre

distracted [dɪs'træktɪd] *adj* distratto; (*irrational*) turbato, sconvolto

distraction [dɪs'trækʃən] s distrazione

distraught [dɪs'trɔt] *adj* turbato, stordito

distress [dɪs'trɛs] s pena, dispiacere *m;* pericolo; (naut) difficoltà *f* ‖ *tr* sconfortare, affliggere

distressing [dɪs'trɛsɪŋ] *adj* penoso

distress' mer'chandise s merce *f* sotto costo

distress' sig'nal s segnale *m* di soccorso

distribute [dɪs'trɪbjut] *tr* distribuire

distribution [ˌdɪstrɪ'bjuʃən] s distribuzione, erogazione

distributor [dɪs'trɪbjətər] s distributore *m;* (aut) distributore *m* d'accensione

district ['dɪstrɪkt] s regione; (*of a city*) rione *m*, quartiere *m;* (*administrative division*) distretto ‖ *tr* dividere in distretti

dis'trict attor'ney s procuratore *m* generale

distrust [dɪs'trʌst] s diffidenza ‖ *tr* diffidare di

distrustful [dɪs'trʌstfəl] *adj* diffidente

disturb [dɪs'tʌrb] *tr* disturbare, turbare; disordinare

disturbance [dɪs'tʌrbəns] s disturbo, turbamento, perturbazione; disordine *m*

disuse [dɪs'jus] s disuso

ditch [dɪtʃ] s fossa, fossato ‖ *tr* scavare un fosso in; (rr) far deragliare; (slang) piantare in asso ‖ *intr* fare un ammaraggio forzato

dither ['dɪðər] s agitazione; **to be in a dither** (coll) essere agitato

dit•to ['dɪto] s (-tos) lo stesso; (*ditto symbol*) virgolette *fpl* ‖ *adv* ugualmente, idem ‖ *tr* copiare, duplicare

dit'to marks' *spl* virgolette *fpl*

dit·ty ['dɪti] s (-ties) canzonetta

diva ['divɑ] s (mus) diva

divan ['daɪvæn] or [dɪ'væn] s divano

dive [daɪv] s tuffo; (of a submarine) immersione; (aer) picchiata; (coll) taverna; (com) discesa || v (pret & pp dived or dove [dov]) intr tuffarsi; (said of submarine) immergersi; (to plunge) lanciarsi; (aer) scendere in picchiata; **to dive for** (e.g., pearls) pescare

dive'-bomb' tr bombardare in picchiata || intr scendere a tuffo

dive' bomb'ing s bombardamento in picchiata

diver ['daɪvər] s tuffatore m; (person who works under water) palombaro; (orn) tuffetto

diverge [dɪ'vʌrdʒ] or [daɪ'vʌrdʒ] intr divergere

divers ['daɪvərz] adj diversi, vari

diverse [dɪ'vʌrs], [daɪ'vʌrs] or ['daɪvʌrs] adj (different) diverso; (of various kinds) multiforme

diversification [dɪˌvʌrsɪfɪ'keʃən] or [daɪˌvʌrsɪfɪ'keʃən] s diversificazione

diversi·fy [dɪ'vʌrsɪˌfaɪ] or [daɪ'vʌrsɪˌfaɪ] v (pret & pp -fied) tr diversificare || intr diversificarsi

diversion [dɪ'vʌrʒən] or [daɪ'vʌrʒən] s diversione; (pastime) svago

diversi·ty [dɪ'vʌrsɪti] or [daɪ'vʌrsɪti] s (-ties) diversità f

divert [dɪ'vʌrt] or [daɪ'vʌrt] tr deviare; (to entertain) divertire; (money) stornare, distrarre

diverting [dɪ'vʌrtɪŋ] or [daɪ'vʌrtɪŋ] adj divertente

divest [dɪ'vest] or [daɪ'vest] tr spogliare; spossessare; **to divest oneself of** spogliarsi di, espropriarsi di

divide [dɪ'vaɪd] s spartiacque m || tr dividere || intr dividersi

dividend ['dɪvɪˌdend] s dividendo

dividers [dɪ'vaɪdərz] spl compasso a punte fisse

divination [ˌdɪvɪ'neʃən] s divinazione

divine [dɪ'vaɪn] adj divino || s sacerdote m, prete m || tr divinare

diviner [dɪ'vaɪnər] s divinatore m

diving ['daɪvɪŋ] s tuffo, immersione

div'ing bell' s campana da palombaro

div'ing board' s trampolino

div'ing suit' s scafandro

divin'ing rod' [dɪ'vaɪnɪŋ] s bacchetta rabdomantica

divini·ty [dɪ'vɪnɪti] s (-ties) divinità f; teologia; **the Divinity** Dio

divisible [dɪ'vɪsɪbəl] adj divisibile

division [dɪ'vɪʒən] s divisione

divisor [dɪ'vaɪzər] s divisore m

divorce [dɪ'vors] s divorzio; **to get a divorce** divorziare || tr (a married couple) divorziare; (one's spouse) divorziare da || intr divorziare

divorcé [dɪvor'se] s divorziato

divorcee [dɪvor'si] s divorziata

divulge [dɪ'vʌldʒ] tr divulgare

dizziness ['dɪzɪnɪs] s vertigine f, stordimento; confusione

diz·zy ['dɪzi] adj (-zier; -ziest) (causing dizziness) vertiginoso; (suffering diz-

ziness) preso da vertigine, stordito; (coll) stupido

do [du] v (3rd pers does [dʌz]; pret did [dɪd]; pp done [dʌn]; ger doing ['du·ɪŋ]) tr fare; (a problem) risolvere; (a distance) percorrere; (to study) studiare; (to explore) attraversare; (to tire) stancare; **to do one's best** fare del proprio meglio; **to do over** tornare a fare; ripetere; **to do right by** trattare bene; **to do s.o. out of s.th** (coll) portare via qlco a qlcu; **to do to death** mettere a morte; **to do up** (coll) impacchettare; stancare; (one's hair) farsi; vestire; (a shirt) lavare e stirare; **to have done** far fare || intr fare; agire; comportarsi; servire; bastare; stare; succedere; **how do you do?** come sta?; **that will do** basta; è sufficiente; **to have done with** non aver più nulla a che fare con; **to have nothing to do with** non aver nulla a che vedere con; **to have to do with** aver a che fare con, trattarsi di; **to do away with** togliere di mezzo; **to do for** servire da; **to do well** crescere bene; **to do without** fare a meno di || v aux used 1) in interrogative sentences: **Do you speak Italian?** Parla italiano?; 2) in negative sentences: **I do not speak Italian** Non parlo italiano; 3) to avoid repetition of a verb or full verbal expression: **Did you go to church this morning? Yes, I did.** È stato in chiesa questa mattina? Sì, ci sono stato; 4) to lend emphasis to a principal verb: **I do believe what you told me** Ci credo a quello che mi ha detto; 5) in inverted constructions after certain adverbs: **Seldom does he come to see me** Mi viene a vedere di raro; 6) in a supplicating tone with imperatives: **Do come in** entri per favore

docile ['dɑsɪl] adj docile

dock [dɑk] s (wharf) molo; (waterway between two piers) darsena; (area including piers and waterways) scalo portuario; (law) gabbia degli imputati || tr (to deduct from the wages of) fare una deduzione a; (to deduct s.o.'s salary) dedurre da; (an animal) scodare; (naut) attraccare || intr (aer) agganciarsi; (naut) attraccare

dockage ['dɑkɪdʒ] s attracco; (charges) diritti mpl di porto

docket ['dɑkɪt] s ordine m del giorno; (law) ruolo delle sentenze; **on the docket** (coll) pendente, in sospeso

dock' hand' s portuale m

docking ['dɑkɪŋ] s (aer) aggancio; (naut) attracco

dock'yard' s cantiere m navale

doctor ['dɑktər] s dottore m; (physician) medico || tr curare; aggiustare; falsificare; adulterare || intr esercitare la medicina; (coll) curarsi, prendere medicine

doctorate ['dɑktərɪt] s dottorato

doctrine ['dɑktrɪn] s dottrina

document ['dɑkjəmənt] s documento || ['dɑkjəˌment] tr documentare

documenta·ry [ˌdɑkjəˈmɛntəri] *adj &*
s (**-ries**) documentario
documentation [ˌdɑkəmɛnˈteʃən] *s* do-
cumentazione
doddering [ˈdɑdərɪŋ] *adj* tremante,
rimbambito
dodge [dɑdʒ] *s* scarto, schivata; (fig)
stratagemma *m* || *tr* schivare, evitare
|| *intr* schivarsi; (fig) rispondere eva-
sivamente; **to dodge around the cor-**
ner scantonare
do·do [ˈdodo] *s* (**-dos** or **-does**) (coll)
rimbecillito
doe [do] *s* (*of deer*) cerva; (*of goat*)
capretta; (*of rabbit*) coniglia
doeskin [ˈdoˌskɪn] *s* pelle *f* di daino,
pelle *f* di dante; lana finissima
doff [dɑf] or [dɔf] *tr* (*one's hat*) togliersi; (*clothing*) deporre
dog [dɔg] or [dɑg] *s* cane *m;* **to go to**
the dogs (coll) andare in malora; **to**
put on the dog (coll) darsi delle arie
|| *v* (*pret & pp* **dogged;** *ger* **dogging**)
tr seguire; perseguitare
dog'catch'er *s* accalappiacani *m*
dog' days' *s* solleone *m,* canicola
doge [dodʒ] *s* doge *m*
dog'-ear' *s* orecchia, orecchio
dog'fight' *s* duello aereo
dogged [ˈdɔgɪd] or [ˈdɑgɪd] *adj* accanito
doggerel [ˈdɔgərəl] or [ˈdɑgərəl] *s*
versi *mpl* da colascione
dog·gy [ˈdɔgi] or [ˈdɑgi] *adj* (**-gier;**
-giest) vistoso; canino || *s* (**-gies**)
cagnolino
dog'house' *s* canile *m;* **to be in the dog-**
house (slang) essere in disgrazia
dog' Lat'in *s* latino maccheronico
dogma [ˈdɔgmə] or [ˈdɑgmə] *s* dogma
m
dogmatic [dɔgˈmætɪk] or [dɑgˈmætɪk]
adj dogmatico
dog' rac'ing *s* corse *fpl* dei cani
dog' show' *s* mostra canina
dog's' life' *s* vita da cani
Dog' Star' *s* canicola
dog' tag' *s* (mil) piastrina, piastrino
dog'-tired' *adj* (coll) stanco morto
dog'tooth' *s* (**-teeth** [ˌtiθ]) canino
dog' track' *s* cinodromo
dog'watch' *s* (naut) quarto di solo due
ore, gaettone *m*
dog'wood' *s* corniolo
doi·ly [ˈdɔɪli] *s* (**-lies**) centrino
doings [ˈduˌɪŋz] *spl* azioni *fpl,* fatti
mpl
do'-it-your·self' *s* il fare tutto da sé
doldrums [ˈdɑldrəmz] *spl* calma equatoriale; inattività *f;* depressione
dole [dol] *s* elemosina; (*to the jobless*)
sussidio di disoccupazione || *tr*—**to**
dole out distribuire parsimoniosa-
mente
doleful [ˈdolfəl] *adj* lugubre, triste
doll [dɑl] *s* bambola || *intr*—**to doll up**
(slang) agghindarsi
dollar [ˈdɑlər] *s* dollaro
dol'lar·wise' *adv* in termini finanziari
dol·ly [ˈdɑli] *s* (**-lies**) pupattola; (*low,*
wheeled frame for moving heavy
loads) carrello; (mov, telv) carrello

|| *v* (*pret & pp* **-lied**) *intr* (mov, telv)
carrellare
dol'ly shot' *s* (mov, telv) carrellata
dolphin [ˈdɑlfɪn] *s* delfino
dolt [dolt] *s* gonzo, balordo
doltish [ˈdoltɪʃ] *adj* gonzo, balordo
domain [doˈmen] *s* dominio; (law) proprietà *f;* (fig) campo, orbita
dome [dom] *s* cupola
dome' light' *s* lampadario
domestic [dəˈmɛstɪk] *adj & s* domestico
domesticate [dəˈmɛstɪˌket] *tr* domesticare
domicile [ˈdɑmɪsɪl] or [ˈdɑmɪˌsaɪl] *s*
domicilio || *tr* domiciliare
dominance [ˈdɑmɪnəns] *s* dominio
dominant [ˈdɑmɪnənt] *adj & s* dominante *f*
dominate [ˈdɑmɪˌnet] *tr & intr* dominare
domination [ˌdɑmɪˈneʃən] *s* dominazione
domineer [ˌdɑmɪˈnɪr] *intr* spadroneggiare
domineering [ˌdɑmɪˈnɪrɪŋ] *adj* dispotico, tirannico
Dominican [dəˈmɪnɪkən] *adj & s* do-
minicano; (*eccl*) domenicano
dominion [dəˈmɪnjən] *s* dominio
domi·no [ˈdɑmɪˌno] *s* (**-noes** or **-nos**)
(*costume and person*) domino;
(*piece*) tessera di domino; **dominoes**
(*game*) domino
don [dɑn] *s* signore *m;* don *m;* membro
di un collegio universitario inglese ||
v (*pret & pp* **donned;** *ger* **donning**)
tr (*clothes*) mettersi, vestire
donate [ˈdonet] *tr* donare, dare
donation [doˈneʃən] *s* donazione
done [dʌn] *adj* fatto; finito; stanco;
(culin) ben cotto, ben rosolato
done' for' *adj* (coll) stanco morto;
(coll) rovinato; (coll) fuori combattimento; (coll) morto
donjon [ˈdʌndʒən] or [ˈdɑndʒən] *s* torrione *m,* maschio
Don Juan [dɑn ˈwɑn] or [dɑn ˈhwɑn]
s Don Giovanni
donkey [ˈdɑŋki] or [ˈdʌŋki] *s* asino,
somaro
donnish [ˈdɑnɪʃ] *adj* pedante
donor [ˈdonər] *s* donatore *m*
doodle [ˈdudəl] *tr & intr* scarabocchiare, riempire di ghirigori
doom [dum] *s* destino; morte *f,* rovina;
sentenza di morte; giudizio finale ||
tr destinare; condannare; condannare
a morte
doomsday [ˈdumzˌde] *s* giorno del
giudizio
door [dor] *s* porta; (*of a carriage or*
automobile) portiera, sportello; (*one*
part of a double door) battente *m;*
behind closed doors a porte chiuse;
to see to the door accompagnare alla
porta; **to show s.o. the door** mettere
qlcu alla porta
door'bell' *s* campanello della porta
door' check' *s* chiusura automatica di
porta, scontro
door'frame' *s* cornice *f*

door'head' s architrave m
door'jamb' s stipite m
door'keep'er s portinaio
door'knob' s maniglia della porta
door' knock'er s battente m
door' latch' s paletto
door'man' s (-men') portiere m, portinaio; (of large apartment house) guardaportone m
door'mat' s stoino, zerbino
door'nail' s borchione m; **dead as a doornail** morto e ben morto
door'post' s stipite m
door' scrap'er s raschietto
door'sill' s soglia
door'step' s gradino davanti la porta
door'stop' s paracolpi m
door'-to-door' adj (shipment) diretto; (selling) di porta in porta
door'way' s vano della porta; porta
dope [dop] s lubrificante m; (aer) vernice f; (slang) stupido, scemo; (slang) informazioni fpl; (slang) narcotico || tr (slang) narcotizzare; **to dope out** (slang) indovinare, decifrare, immaginare
dope' fiend' s (slang) tossicomane mf
dope'sheet' s giornaletto con le previsioni della corse ippiche
dormant ['dɔrmənt] adj dormente; latente
dor'mer win'dow ['dɔrmər] s abbaino
dormitory ['dɔrmɪˌtori] s (-ries) dormitorio
dor·mouse ['dɔr ˌmaʊs] s (-mice [ˌmaɪs]) ghiro
dosage ['dosɪdʒ] s dosatura
dose [dos] s dose f; (coll) boccone amaro || tr dosare; somministrare
dossier ['dɑsɪ ˌe] s incartamento
dot [dɑt] s punto; **on the dot** (coll) in punto || v (pret & pp dotted; ger dotting) tr punteggiare; **to dot one's i's** mettere i punti sulle i
dotage ['dotɪdʒ] s rimbecillimento; **to be in one's dotage** essere rimbambito
dotard ['dotərd] s vecchio rimbambito
dote [dot] intr rimbambirsi; **to dote on** essere pazzo per
doting ['dotɪŋ] adj che ama alla follia; (from old age) rimbambito, rimbecillito
dots' and dash'es spl (telg) punti mpl e tratti mpl
dot'ted line' s linea punteggiata; **to sign on the dotted line** firmare inconsideratamente
double ['dʌbəl] adj doppio || s doppio; (bridge) contre m; **doubles** (tennis) doppio || tr raddoppiare; (bridge) contrare || intr raddoppiarsi; (bridge) contrare; (mov, theat) sostenere due ruoli; (mov) doppiare; **to double up** (said of two people) dividere la stessa camera, dividere lo stesso letto; piegarsi in due
double-barreled ['dʌbəl ˈbærəld] adj a due canne; (fig) a doppio fine
dou'ble bass' s contrabbasso
dou'ble bed' s letto matrimoniale
dou'ble boil'er s bagnomaria m

double-breasted ['dʌbəl ˈbrɛstɪd] adj a doppio petto, doppiopetto
dou'ble chin' s pappagorgia
dou'ble-cross' tr (coll) tradire
dou'ble date' s (coll) appuntamento amoroso di due coppie
dou'ble-deal'ing adj doppio
dou'ble-deck'er s (bed) letto a castello; (sandwich) tramezzino doppio; autobus m a due piani; (naut) nave f due ponti; (aer) aereo due ponti
double-edged ['dʌbəl ˈɛdʒd] adj a due tagli, a doppio taglio
dou'ble en'try s (com) partita doppia
dou'ble fea'ture s (mov) programma m di due lungometraggio
double-header ['dʌbəl ˈhɛdər] s treno con due locomotive; due partite di baseball giocate successivamente
double-jointed ['dʌbəl ˈdʒɔɪntɪd] adj snodato
dou'ble-park' tr & intr parcheggiare in doppia fila
dou'ble-quick' adj & adv a passo di carica
dou'ble stand'ard s—**to have a double standard** usare due pesi e due misure
doublet ['dʌblɪt] s (close-fitting jacket) farsetto; (philol) doppione m
dou'ble-talk' s discorso incomprensibile; **to give s.o. double-talk** parlare evasivamente a qlcu || intr parlare evasivamente
dou'ble time' s paga doppia; (mil) passo di carica
doubleton ['dʌbəltən] s doppio
doubly ['dʌbli] adv doppiamente
doubt [daʊt] s dubbio; **beyond doubt** senza dubbio; **if in doubt** in caso di dubbio; **no doubt** senza dubbio || tr dubitare di || intr dubitare
doubter ['daʊtər] s incredulo
doubtful ['daʊtfəl] adj incerto; dubbioso
doubtless ['daʊtlɪs] adj indubitabile || adv senza dubbio; probabilmente
douche [duʃ] s irrigazione f; (instrument) irrigatore m || tr irrigare || intr fare irrigazioni
dough [do] s pasta di pane; (money) (slang) soldi mpl, quattrini mpl
dough'boy' s fantaccino americano
dough'nut' s ciambella; (with filling) sgonfiotto
dough·ty ['daʊti] adj (-tier; -tiest) forte, coraggioso
dough·y ['do·i] adj (-ier; -iest) pastoso, molle
dour [daʊr] or [dʊr] adj triste, severo
douse [daʊs] tr immergere; bagnare; (the light) tr spegnere
dove [dʌv] s colomba, tortora
dovecote ['dʌv ˌkot] s piccionaia
dove'tail' s coda di rondine || tr calettare a coda di rondine; (to make fit) adattare, far combaciare || intr (to fit) combaciare; corrispondere
dowager ['daʊ ˌədʒər] s vedova titolata; vecchia signora austera; **queen dowager** regina madre
dow·dy ['daʊdi] adj (-dier; -diest) trasandato

dow·el ['dau·əl] s caviglia, tassello ‖ v (pret & pp -eled or -elled; ger -eling or -elling) tr tassellare

dower ['dau·ər] s (widow's portion) legittima, vedovile m; (marriage portion; natural gift) dote f ‖ tr dotare; assegnare un vedovile a

down [daun] adj che discende; basso; (train) che va al centro; depresso; finito; (money, payment) anticipato; (storage battery) esaurito ‖ s (of fruit and human body) lanugine f; (of birds) piumino; (upset) rovescio; discesa; (sandhill) duna ‖ adv giù; all'ingiù, in giù; dabbasso; a terra; al sud; (in cash) a contanti; **down and out** rovinato; senza una soldo; **down from** da; **down on one's knees** in ginocchio; **down to** fino a; **down under** agli antipodi; **down with . . . !** abasso . . . !; **to get down to work** mettersi seriamente al lavoro; **to go down** scendere; **to lie down** sdraiarsi; andare a letto; **to sit down** sedersi ‖ prep giù per; **down the river** a valle; **down the street** giù per la strada ‖ tr abbattere; (coll) buttar giù, tracannare

down'cast' adj mogio, sfiduciato
down'fall' s rovina, rovescio
down'grade' adj & adv in declivio, a valle ‖ s discesa; **to be on the downgrade** essere in declino ‖ tr attribuire minor importanza a; degradare
downhearted ['daun,hartıd] adj scoraggiato, abbattuto
down'hill' adj & adv in declivio; **to go downhill** declinare
down' pay'ment s acconto
down'pour' s acquazzone m, rovescio
down'right' adj assoluto; completo; franco, diretto ‖ adv completamente
down'stairs' adj del piano di sotto ‖ s il piano di sotto; i piani di sotto ‖ adv dabbasso, di sotto, giù
down'stream' adv a valle
down'stroke' s corsa discendente
down'town' adj centrale ‖ s centro della città ‖ adv al centro della città
down' train' s treno discendente, treno che va al centro
down'trend' s tendenza al ribasso
downtrodden ['daun,tradən] adj calpestato, oppresso
downward ['daunwərd] adj & adv all'ingiù
down·y ['dauni] adj (-ier; -iest) piumoso, lanuginoso; (soft) molle, morbido
dow·ry ['dauri] s (-ries) dote f
doze [doz] s pisolo ‖ intr dormicchiare; **to doze off** appisolarsi
dozen ['dʌzən] s dozzina
dozy ['dozi] adj sonnolento
drab [dræb] adj (drabber; drabbest) grigiastro; (dull) scialbo ‖ s colore grigiastro; (fabric) tela naturale; donna di malaffare
drach·ma ['drækmə] s (-mas or -mae [mi]) dramma
draft [dræft] or [draft] s corrente f d'aria; (pulling) tiro; (in a chimney) tiraggio; (sketch, outline) schizzo; (first form of a writing) prima stesura; (drink) sorso, bicchiere m; (com) tratta, lettera di credito; (law) progetto, disegno; (naut) pesca; (mil) coscrizione f, leva; **on draft** alla spina ‖ tr disegnare; fare uno schizzo di; (a document) stendere; (mil) coscrivere; **to be drafted** essere di leva, andar coscritto
draft' age' s età f di leva
draft' beer' s birra alla spina
draft' board' s consiglio di leva
draft' dodg'er ['dadʒər] s renitente m alla leva, imboscato
draftee [,dræf'ti] or [,draf'ti] s coscritto
draft' horse' s cavallo da tiro
drafts'man s (-men) disegnatore m; (man who draws up documents) redattore m
draft' trea'ty s progetto di trattato
draft·y ['dræfti] or ['drafti] adj (-ier; -iest) pieno di correnti d'aria
drag [dræg] s (sledge for conveying heavy bodies) traino, treggia; (on a cigarette) boccata; (aer) resistenza aerodinamica; (naut) pressione idrostatica; (naut) draga; (fig) noia; (influence) (slang) aderenze fpl; (a bore) (slang) rompiscatole m ‖ v (pret & pp dragged; ger dragging) tr strascinare, strascicare; (naut) rastrellare ‖ intr strascicare, strascicarsi; dilungarsi; **to drag on** andare per le lunghe
drag'net' s paranza; (fig) retata
dragon ['drægən] s drago, dragone m
drag'on-fly' s (-flies) libellula
dragoon [drə'gun] s (mil) dragone m ‖ tr forzare, costringere
drain [dren] s scolo; prosciugamento; (geog) spiovente m; (surg) drenaggio; (fig) salasso ‖ tr (a liquid) scolare; prosciugare; (humid land; a wound) drenare ‖ intr scolare; prosciugarsi; (geog) defluire
drainage ['drenıdʒ] s drenaggio; (geog) displuvio, spartiacque m
drain'board' s scolatoio per le stoviglie
drain' cock' s rubinetto di scarico
drain'pipe' s tubo di scarico
drake [drek] s anatra maschio
dram [dræm] s dramma; bicchierino di liquore
drama ['dramə] or ['dræmə] s dramma m; (art and genre) drammatica
dramatic [drə'mætık] adj drammatico ‖ **dramatics** ssg drammatica; spl rappresentazione dilettantesca; comportamento drammatico
dramatist ['dræmətıst] s drammaturgo
dramatize ['dræmə,taız] tr drammatizzare
drape [drep] s tenda, cortina; (of a curtain) drappeggio; (of a skirt) taglio ‖ tr drappeggiare
draper·y ['drepəri] s (-ies) drapperia; negozio di tessuti; **draperies** tendaggi mpl
drastic ['dræstık] adj drastico

draught [dræft] or [drɑft] s & tr var of **draft**

draught' beer' s birra alla spina

draw [drɔ] s (in a game) patta; (in a lottery) sorteggio; (act of drawing) tiro; (of chimney) tiraggio; (attraction) attrazione; (of a drawbridge) ala || v (pret drew [dru]; pp drawn [drɔn]) tr (a line) tirare; (to attract) richiamare; (butter) fondere; (a sword) sguainare; (a nail) estrarre; (people) attrarre; (a sigh) emettere; (a curtain) far scorrere; (a salary) pigliare; (a prize) ricevere; (a game) impattare; (in card games) pescare; (a drawbridge) sollevare; (said of a ship) pescare; (a comparison) fare; (a profit) ricavare; (a chicken) sventrare; (e.g., a picture) disegnare, ritrarre; (to sketch in words) descrivere; (a contract) stipulare; (interest) ricevere; (com) spiccare, staccare; **to draw forth** far uscire; **to draw off** estrarre; (a liquid) spillare; **to draw (shoes) on** mettersi; **to draw (money) on** ritirare da; **to draw (a draft) on** domiciliare presso; **to draw oneself up** raddrizzarsi; **to draw out** (to persuade to talk) far parlare, tirar fuori le parole a; **to draw up** (a document) estendere; (mil) schierare || intr (said of chimney) tirare; impattare; sorteggiare un premio; aver_ attrazione; disegnare; **to draw aside** scostarsi; **to draw back** retrocedere, ritirarsi; **to draw near** avvicinarsi; volgere a; **to draw to a close** essere quasi finito; **to draw together** unirsi

draw'back' s inconveniente m

draw'bridge' s ponte levatoio

drawee [ˌdrɔˈi] s trattario, trassato

drawer [ˈdrɔ-ər] s disegnatore m; (com) traente m || [drɔr] s cassetto; **drawers** mutande fpl

drawing [ˈdrɔ-ɪŋ] s disegno; (in a lottery) sorteggio

draw'ing board' s tavolo da disegno

draw'ing card' s attrazione

draw'ing room' s salotto, salottino

draw'knife' s (-knives [ˌnaɪvz]) coltello a petto

drawl [drɔl] s accento strascicato || tr dire con accento strascicato || intr strascicare le parole

drawn' but'ter s burro fuso

drawn' work' s lavoro a giorno

dray [dre] s carro pesante; slitta, treggia; autocarro

drayage [ˈdre-ɪdʒ] s carreggio

dray'man s (-men) carrettiere m

dread [dred] adj spaventoso, terribile || s spavento, terrore m || tr & intr temere

dreadful [ˈdredfəl] adj spaventevole, terribile; (coll) orribile

dread'nought' s corazzata

dream [drim] s sogno; illusione, fantasticheria; **dream come true** sogno fatto realtà || v (pret & pp dreamed or dreamt [dremt]) tr sognare; **to dream up** (coll) immaginare, fantasticare || intr sognare

dreamer [ˈdrimər] s sognatore m

dream'land' s paese m dei sogni

dream·y [ˈdrimi] adj (-ier; -iest) sognante; (visionary) trasognato; vago

drear·y [ˈdrɪri] adj (-ier; -iest) squallido; triste; (boring) noioso

dredge [dredʒ] s draga || tr dragare; (culin) infarinare

dredger [ˈdredʒər] s (boat) draga; (container) spolverino

dredging [ˈdredʒɪŋ] s dragaggio

dregs [dregz] spl feccia

drench [drentʃ] tr infradiciare, inzuppare

dress [dres] s vestito; vestiti mpl; vestito da donna; abito, abito da cerimonia; (of a bird) piumaggio || tr vestire; adornare, decorare; (hair) pettinare; (a wound) medicare; (leather) conciare; (food) condire; (a boat) pavesare; **to dress down** (coll) rimproverare; **to get dressed** vestirsi || intr vestire; vestirsi; (mil) schierarsi; **to dress up** vestirsi da sera; farsi bello, mettersi in gala

dress' ball' s ballo di gala

dress' coat' s frac m

dresser [ˈdrɛsər] s toletta; (sideboard) credenza; **to be a good dresser** vestire con eleganza

dress' goods' spl stoffa per abiti

dressing [ˈdrɛsɪŋ] s ornamento; (for food) condimento, salsa; (stuffing for fowl) ripieno; (fertilizer) concime m; (for a wound) medicazione

dress'ing down' s ramanzina

dress'ing gown' s vestaglia

dress'ing room' s spogliatoio, toletta; (theat) camerino

dress'ing sta'tion s posto di pronto soccorso

dress'ing ta'ble s toletta, specchiera

dress'mak'er s sarta, sarto per donna

dress'mak'ing s taglio, sartoria

dress' rehears'al s prova generale

dress' shirt' s camicia inamidata

dress' suit' s marsina

dress' u'niform s (mil) alta uniforme

dress·y [ˈdresi] adj (-ier; -iest) (coll) elegante, ricercato

dribble [ˈdrɪbəl] s goccia h; tr (sports) palleggiare, dribblare || intr gocciolare; (at the mouth) sbavare; (sports) dribblare

driblet [ˈdrɪblɪt] s piccola quantità; **in driblets** col contagocce

dried' beef' [draɪd] s carne seccata

dried' fruit' s frutta secca

drier [ˈdraɪ-ər] s (for hair) asciugacapelli m; (for clothes) asciugatrice f

drift [drɪft] s movimento; (of sand, snow, etc.) cumulo; (snowdrift) neve accumulata dal vento; tendenza, corrente f; intenzione; (aer, naut) deriva; (rad, telv) deviazione || intr andare alla deriva; (said of snow) accumularsi; (aer, naut) derivare, scadere

drift' ice' s ghiaccio alla deriva

drift'pin' s (mach) mandrino

drift'wood' s legname andato alla deriva

drill [drɪl] s esercizio; (fabric) tela cruda; (agr) seminatrice f; (mach) trapano, trivella; (mil) esercitazioni fpl militari || tr trivellare; istruire; (mil) insegnare gli esercizi militari a || intr addestrarsi; (mil) fare gli esercizi militari

drill'mas'ter s istruttore m

drill' press' s trapano a colonna

drink [drɪŋk] s bevanda; **the drinks are on the house!** paga il proprietario! || v (pret **drank** [dræŋk]; pp **drunk** [drʌŋk]) tr bere; assorbire; **to drink down** tracannare; **to drink in** bere, assorbire; (air) aspirare || intr bere; **to drink out of** bere da; **to drink to the health of** bere alla salute di

drinkable ['drɪŋkəbəl] adj bevibile, potabile

drinker ['drɪŋkər] s bevitore m

drinking ['drɪŋkɪŋ] s (il) bere

drink'ing foun'tain s fontanella pubblica

drink'ing song' s canzone bacchica

drink'ing straw' s cannuccia

drink'ing trough' s abbeveratoio

drink'ing wa'ter s acqua potabile

drip [drɪp] s sgocciolo, sgocciolatura || v (pret & pp **dripped**; ger **dripping**) intr sgocciolare, stillare; (said of perspiration) trasudare

drip' cof'fee s caffè fatto con la macchinetta

drip'-dry' adj non-stiro

drip' pan' s (culin) ghiotta; (mach) coppa

dripping ['drɪpɪŋ] s gocciolio; **drippings** grasso che cola dall'arrosto

drive [draɪv] s scarrozzata; strada; passeggiata; impulso; forza, iniziativa; urgenza; spinta; campagna; (aut) trazione; (mach) trasmissione || v (pret **drove** [drov]; ger **driven** ['drɪvən]) tr (a nail) ficcare, piantare; (e.g., cattle) condurre, parare; (s.o. in a carriage or auto) condurre, portare; spingere; stimolare; forzare; spingere a lavorare; (sports) colpire molto forte; **to drive away** scacciare; **to drive back** respingere; **to drive mad** far impazzire; **to drive out** scacciare || intr fare una scarrozzata; **to drive at** parare a; voler dire; **to drive hard** lavorare sodo; **to drive in** entrare in automobile; (a place) entrare in automobile in; **to drive on the right** guidare a destra; **to drive out** uscire in macchina; **to drive up** arrivare in macchina

drive'-in' mov'ie the'ater s cineparco

drive'-in' res'taurant s ristorante m con servizio alla portiera

driv-el ['drɪvəl] s (slobber) bava; (nonsense) scemenza || v (pret **-eled** or **-elled**; ger **-eling** or **-elling**) intr sbavare; dire scemenze

driver ['draɪvər] s guidatore m; (of a carriage) cocchiere m; (of a locomotive) macchinista m; (of pack animals) carrettiere m, mulattiere m

driv'er's li'cense s patente automobilistica

driv'er's seat' s posto di guida

drive' shaft' s albero motore

drive'way' s strada privata d'accesso; carrozzabile f

drive' wheel' s ruota motrice

driv'ing school' ['draɪvɪŋ] s autoscuola, scuola guida

drizzle ['drɪzəl] s pioviggine f || intr piovigginare

droll [drol] adj buffo, spassoso

dromedar·y ['drɑmə‚deri] s (-ies) dromedario

drone [dron] s fuco, pecchione m; (hum) ronzio; (of bagpipe) bordone m; areoplano teleguidato || tr dire in tono monotono || intr (to live in idleness) fare il fannullone; (to buzz, hum) ronzare

drool [drul] s (slobber) bava; (slang) scemenza || intr sbavare; (slang) dire scemenze

droop [drup] s accasciamento || intr (to sag) pendere; (to lose spirit) accasciarsi; (said, e.g., of wheat) avvizzire

drooping ['drupɪŋ] adj (eyelid) abbassato; (shoulder) spiovente; (fig) accasciato

drop [drɑp] s goccia; (slope) pendenza; (earring) pendente m; (in temperature) discesa; (from an airplane) lancio; (trap door) botola; (gallows) trabocchetto della forca; (lozenge) pastiglia; (slit for letters) buca; (curtain) tela; (in prices) calo; **a drop in the bucket** una goccia nell'oceano || v (pret & pp **dropped**; ger **dropping**) tr lasciar cadere; (a letter) imbucare; (a curtain) abbassare; (a remark) lasciar scappare; (a note) scrivere; omettere; abbandonare; (anchor) gettare; (from an airplane) lanciare; (from an automobile) lasciare; (from a list) cancellare || intr cadere; lasciarsi cadere; terminare; **to drop dead** cader morto; **to drop in** entrare un momento; **to drop off** sparire; addormentarsi; morire improvvisamente; **to drop out** scomparire; ritirarsi; dare le dimissioni

drop' cur'tain s telone m

drop' ham'mer s maglio

drop'-leaf' ta'ble s tavola a ribalta

drop'light' s lampada sospesa

drop'out' s studente m che abbandona permanentemente la scuola media

dropper ['drɑpər] s contagocce m

dropsical ['drɑpsɪkəl] adj idropico

dropsy ['drɑpsi] s idropisia

dross [drɔs] or [drɑs] s scoria; (fig) feccia

drought [draut] s siccità f; (shortage) mancanza

drove [drov] s branco; folla; **in droves** in massa

drover ['drovər] s mandriano

drown [draun] tr & intr affogare, annegare

drowse [drauz] intr sonnecchiare

drow·sy ['drauzi] adj (-sier; -siest) sonnolento, insonnolito

drub [drʌb] v (pret & pp **drubbed**; ger **drubbing**) tr bastonare; battere

drudge [drʌdʒ] *s* sgobbone *m* || *intr* sgobbare, sfacchinare

drudger·y ['drʌdʒəri] *s* (-ies) lavoro ingrato, sfacchinata

drug [drʌg] *s* droga, medicina; narcotico; **drug on the market** merce *f* invendibile || *v* (*pret & pp* **drugged**; *ger* **drugging**) *tr* drogare, narcotizzare

drug' ad'dict *s* tossicomane *mf*

drug' addic'tion *s* tossicomania

druggist ['drʌgɪst] *s* farmacista *mf*

drug' hab'it *s* tossicomania

drug'store' *s* farmacia

drug' traf'fic *s* traffico in stupefacenti

druid ['dru·ɪd] *s* druida *m*

drum [drʌm] *s* (*cylinder; instrument*) tamburo; (*container*) fusto || *v* (*pret & pp* **drummed**; *ger* **drumming**) *tr* stamburare; **to drum up** (*customers*) farsi; (*enthusiasm*) creare || *intr* tambureggiare; (*with the fingers*) tamburellare

drum'beat' *s* rullo di tamburi

drum' corps' *s* banda di tamburi

drum'fire' *s* fuoco nutrito

drum'head' *s* membrana del tamburo

drum' ma'jor *s* tamburo maggiore

drummer ['drʌmər] *s* (*salesman*) agente *m* viaggiatore; (*mus*) tamburo; (*mil*) tamburino

drum'stick' *s* bacchetta del tamburo; (*of cooked fowl*) coscia

drunk [drʌŋk] *adj* ubriaco; **to get drunk** ubriacarsi || *s* ubriaco; (*spree*) sbornia; **to go on a drunk** (coll) ubriacarsi

drunkard ['drʌŋkərd] *s* ubriacone *m*

drunken ['drʌŋkən] *adj* ubriaco

drunk'en driv'ing *s*—**to be arrested for drunken driving** esser arrestato per aver guidato in stato di ubriachezza

drunkenness ['drʌŋkənnɪs] *s* ubriachezza, ebbrezza

dry [draɪ] *adj* (**drier; driest**) secco; (*boring*) arido; **to be dry** aver sete || *s* (**drys**) abolizionista *mf* || *v* (*pret & pp* **dried**) *tr* seccare; (*to wipe dry*) asciugare || *intr* seccarsi; **to dry up** prosciugarsi, essiccarsi; (slang) star zitto

dry' bat'tery *s* pila a secco; (*group of dry cells*) batteria a secco

dry' cell' *s* pila a secco

dry'-clean' *tr* lavare a secco, pulire a secco

dry' clean'er *s* tintore *m*

dry' clean'ing *s* lavaggio a secco, pulitura a secco

dry'-clean'ing estab'lishment *s* tintoria

dry' dock' *s* bacino di carenaggio

dryer ['draɪ·ər] *s* var of **drier**

dry'-eyed' *adj* a occhi asciutti

dry' farm'ing *s* coltivazione di terreno arido

dry' goods' *spl* tessuti *mpl*; aridi *mpl*

dry'-goods store' *s* drapperia, negozio di tessuti

dry' ice' *s* neve carbonica, ghiaccio secco

dry' law' *s* legge *f* proibizionista

dry' meas'ure *s* misura per solidi

dryness ['draɪnɪs] *s* siccità *f*; (*e.g., of a speaker*) aridità *f*

dry' nurse' *s* balia asciutta

dry' run' *s* esercizio di prova; (mil) esercitazione senza munizioni

dry' sea'son *s* stagione arida

dry' wash' *s* roba lavata e asciugata ma non stirata

dual ['dju·əl] or ['du·əl] *adj & s* duale *m*

duali·ty [dju'ælɪti] or [du'ælɪti] *s* (-ties) dualità *f*

dub [dʌb] *s* (slang) giocatore inesperto || *v* (*pret & pp* **dubbed**; *ger* **dubbing**) *tr* chiamare, affibbiare il nome di; (*a knight*) armare; (mov) doppiare

dubbing ['dʌbɪŋ] *s* doppiaggio

dubious ['djubɪ·əs] or ['dubɪ·əs] *adj* dubbioso; incerto

ducat ['dʌkət] *s* ducato

duchess ['dʌtʃɪs] *s* duchessa

duch·y ['dʌtʃi] *s* (-ies) ducato

duck [dʌk] *s* anatra; mossa rapida; (*in the water*) tuffo; (*dodge*) schivata; **ducks** pantaloni *mpl* di tela cruda || *tr* (*one's head*) abbassare rapidamente; (*in water*) tuffare; (*a blow*) schivare || *intr* tuffarsi; **to duck out** (coll) svignarsela

duckling ['dʌklɪŋ] *s* anatroccolo

ducks' and drakes' *s*—**to play ducks and drakes with** buttar via, sperperare

duck' soup' *s* (slang) cosa facilissima

duct [dʌkt] *s* tubo, condotto

ductile ['dʌktɪl] *adj* duttile

duct'less gland' ['dʌktlɪs] *s* ghiandola a secrezione interna

duct'work' *s* condotto, canalizzazione

dud [dʌd] *s* (slang) bomba inesplosa; (*person*) (slang) fallito; (*enterprise*) (slang) fallimento; **duds** (coll) vestito; roba

dude [djud] or [dud] *s* elegantone *m*

due [dju] or [du] *adj* dovuto; atteso, debito; pagabile; **due to** dovuto a; **to fall due** scadere; **when is the train due?** a che ora arriva il treno? || *s* spettanza; debito; **dues** (*of a member*) quota sociale; **to get one's due** ricevere quanto uno merita; **to give the devil his due** trattare ognuno con giustizia || *adv* in direzione, e.g., **due north** in direzione nord

duel ['dju·əl] or ['du·əl] *s* duello; **to fight a duel** battersi a duello || *v* (*pret & pp* **dueled** or **duelled**; *ger* **dueling** or **duelling**) *intr* duellare

duelist or **duellist** ['dju·əlɪst] or ['du·əlɪst] *s* duellante *mf*

dues-paying ['djuz,pe·ɪŋ] or ['duz,pe·ɪŋ] *adj* regolare, effettivo

duet [dju'ɛt] or [du'ɛt] *s* duetto

duf'fel bag' ['dʌfəl] *s* sacca da viaggio

duke [djuk] or [duk] *s* duca *m*

dukedom ['djukdəm] or ['dukdəm] *s* ducato

dull [dʌl] *adj* (*not sharp*) spuntato, senza filo; (*color*) spento, sbiadito; (*sound, pain*) sordo; (*stupid*) ebete, tonto; (*business*) inattivo; (*boring*) noioso, melenso; (*flat*) opaco, appannato || *tr* spuntare; sbiadire; inebetire; ottundere; (*enthusiasm*) raffreddare; (*pain*) alleviare || *intr* spuntarsi; sbiadirsi; inebetirsi; raf-freddarsi

dullard ['dʌlərd] s stupido

duly ['djuli] or ['duli] adv debitamente

dumb [dʌm] adj (lacking the power to speak) muto; (coll) tonto, stupido

dumb'bell' s manubrio; (slang) zuccone m, stupido

dumb' crea'ture s animale m, bruto

dumb' show' s pantomima

dumb'wai'ter s montavivande m

dumfound [,dʌm'faʊnd] tr interdire, lasciare esterrefatto

dum·my ['dʌmi] adj copiato; falso || s (-mies) (dress form) manichino; (in card games) morto; (figurehead) uomo di paglia, prestanome m; (skeleton copy of a book) menabò m; copia; (slang) stupido, tonto

dump [dʌmp] s immondezzaio; mucchio di spazzature; (mil) deposito munizioni; (min) montagnetta di scarico; **to be down in the dumps** (coll) avere le paturnie || tr scaricare; (to tip over) rovesciare; (com) scaricare sul mercato; (com) vendere sotto-costo

dumping ['dʌmpɪŋ] s scarico; (com) dumping m

dumpling ['dʌmplɪŋ] s gnocco

dump' truck' s ribaltabile m

dump·y ['dʌmpi] adj (-ier; -iest) grassoccio, tarchiato

dun [dʌn] adj bruno grigiastro || s creditore importuno; (demand for payment) sollecitazione di pagamento || v (pret & pp **dunned**; ger **dunning**) tr sollecitare

dunce [dʌns] s ignorante mf, zuccone m

dunce' cap' s berretto d'asino

dune [djun] or [dun] s duna

dung [dʌŋ] s sterco, letame m || tr concimare con il letame

dungarees [,dʌŋgə'riz] spl tuta di cotone blu

dungeon ['dʌndʒən] s carcere sotterraneo; (fortified tower) torrione m, maschio

dung'hill' s letamaio

dunk [dʌŋk] tr inzuppare

du·o ['dju·o] or ['du·o] s (-os) duo

duode·num [,dju·ə'dinəm] or [,du·ə-'dinəm] s (-na [nə]) duodeno

dupe [djup] or [dup] s gonzo || tr gabbare, ingannare

du'plex house' ['djupleks] or ['dupleks] s casa di due appartamenti

duplicate ['djuplɪkɪt] or ['duplɪkɪt] adj & s duplicato || ['djuplɪ,ket] or ['duplɪ,ket] tr duplicare

du'plicating machine' s duplicatore m

duplici·ty [dju'plɪsɪti] or [du'plɪsɪti] s (-ties) duplicità f, doppiezza

durable ['djurəbəl] or ['durəbəl] adj durabile, duraturo

du'rable goods' spl beni mpl durevoli

duration [dju're/ən] or [du're/ən] s durata

during ['djurɪŋ] or ['durɪŋ] prep durante

du'rum wheat' ['durəm] or ['djurəm] s grano duro

dusk [dʌsk] s crepuscolo

dust [dʌst] s polvere f || tr (to free of dust) spolverare; (to sprinkle with dust) spolverizzare; **to dust off** (slang) rimettere in uso; (slang) spolverare le spalle a

dust' bowl' s regione polverosissima

dust'cloth' s strofinaccio

dust' cloud' s polverone m

duster ['dʌstər] s (cloth) cencio; (light overgarment) spolverino

dust' jack'et s sopraccoperta

dust'pan' s pattumiera

dust' rag' s strofinaccio

dust·y ['dʌsti] adj (-ier; -iest) polveroso; grigiastro

Dutch [dʌtʃ] adj olandese; (slang) tedesco || s (language) olandese m; (language) (slang) tedesco; **in Dutch** (slang) in disgrazia; (slang) nei pasticci; **the Dutch** gli olandesi; (slang) i tedeschi; **to go Dutch** (coll) pagare alla romana

Dutch'man s (-men) olandese m; (slang) tedesco

Dutch' treat' s invito alla romana

dutiable ['djutɪ·əbəl] or ['dutɪ·əbəl] adj soggetto a dogana

dutiful ['djutɪfəl] or ['dutɪfəl] adj obbediente, doveroso

du·ty ['djuti] or ['duti] s (-ties) dovere m; (task) funzione; dazio, dogana; **off duty** libero; in libera uscita; **on duty** in servizio; di guardia; **to do one's duty** fare il proprio dovere; **to take up one's duties** entrare in servizio

du'ty-free' adj esente da dogana

dwarf [dwɔrf] adj & s nano || tr rimpiccolire || intr rimpiccolire; apparire più piccolo

dwarfish ['dwɔrfɪʃ] adj nano, da nano

dwell [dwɛl] v (pret & pp **dwelled** or **dwelt** [dwɛlt]) intr dimorare, abitare; **to dwell on** or **upon** intrattenersi su

dwelling ['dwɛlɪŋ] s abitazione, residenza

dwell'ing house' s casa d'abitazione

dwindle ['dwɪndəl] intr diminuire; restringersi, consumarsi

dye [daɪ] s tinta, colore m || v (pret & pp **dyed**; ger **dyeing**) tr tingere

dyed-in-the-wool ['daɪdɪnðə,wʊl] adj tinto prima della tessitura; completo, intransigente

dyeing ['daɪ·ɪŋ] s tintura

dyer ['daɪ·ər] s tintore m

dye'stuff' s tintura, materia colorante

dying ['daɪ·ɪŋ] adj morente

dynamic [daɪ'næmɪk] or [dɪ'næmɪk] adj dinamico

dynamite ['daɪnə,maɪt] s dinamite f || tr far saltare con la dinamite

dyna·mo ['daɪnə,mo] s (-mos) dinamo f

dynast ['daɪnæst] s dinasta m

dynas·ty ['daɪnəsti] s (-ties) dinastia f

dysentery ['dɪsən,tɛri] s dissenteria

dyspepsia [dɪs'pɛpsɪ·ə] or [dɪs'pɛpʃə] s dispepsia

E, e [i] *s* quinta lettera dell'alfabeto inglese

each [it∫] *adj indef* ogni ‖ *pron indef* ognuno, ciascuno; **each other** c₁; vi; si; l'un l'altro ‖ *adv* l'uno; a testa

eager ['igər] *adj* (*enthusiastic*) ardente; **eager for** avido di; **eager to** + *inf* desideroso di + *inf*

ea'ger bea'ver *s* zelante *mf*

eagerness ['igərnɪs] *s* ardore *m;* brama

eagle ['igəl] *s* aquila

ea'gle owl' *s* gufo reale

eaglet ['iglɪt] *s* aquilotto

ear [ir] *s* orecchio; (*of corn*) pannocchia; (*of wheat*) spiga; **to be all ears** essere tutt'orecchi; **to prick up one's ears** tendere l'orecchio; **to turn a deaf ear** far l'orecchio da mercante

ear'ache' *s* mal *m* d'orecchi

ear'drop' *s* pendente *m*

ear'drum' *s* timpano

ear'flap' *s* paraorecchi *m*

earl [ʌrl] *s* conte *m*

earldom ['ʌrldəm] *s* contea

ear·ly ['ʌrli] (**-ier; -iest**) *adj* (*occurring before customary time*) di buon'ora; (*first in a series*) primo; (*far back in time*) remoto, antico; (*occurring in near future*) prossimo ‖ *adv* presto; per tempo, di buon'ora; **as early as** (*a certain time of day*) già a; (*a certain time or date*) fin da, già in; **as early as possible** quanto prima possibile; **early in** (*e.g., the month*) all'inizio di; **early in the morning** di mattina presto, di buon mattino; **early in the year** all'inizio dell'anno

ear'ly bird' *s* persona mattiniera

ear'ly mass' *s* prima messa

ear'ly ris'er *s* persona mattiniera

ear'mark' *s* contrassegno ‖ *tr* contrassegnare; assegnare a scopo speciale

ear'muff' *s* paraorecchi *m*

earn [ʌrn] *tr* guadagnare, guadagnarsi; (*to get one's due*) meritarsi; (*interest*) (com) produrre ‖ *intr* trarre profitto, rendere

earnest ['ʌrnɪst] *adj* serio; fervente; **in earnest** sul serio ‖ *s* caparra

ear'nest mon'ey *s* caparra

earnings ['ʌrnɪŋz] *s* guadagno; salario

ear'phone' *s* (*of sonar*) orecchiale *m;* (rad, telp) cuffia

ear'piece' *s* (*of eyeglasses*) susta; (telp) ricevitore *m*

ear'ring' *s* orecchino

ear'shot' *s* tiro dell'orecchio; **within earshot** a portata di voce

ear'split'ting *adj* assordante

earth [ʌrθ] *s* terra; **to come back to or down to earth** scendere dalle nuvole

earthen ['ʌrθən] *adj* di terra; di terracotta

ear'then·ware' *s* coccio, terraglie *fpl,* terracotta

earthling ['ʌrθlɪŋ] *s* terrestre *mf*

earthly ['ʌrθli] *adj* terreno, terrestre;
to be of no earthly use non servire assolutamente a niente

earthmover ['ʌrθ‚muvər] *s* ruspa

earth quake' *s* terremoto

earth work' *s* terrapieno

earth'worm' *s* lombrico

earth·y ['ʌrθi] *adj* (**-ier; -iest**) terroso; (*coarse*) rozzo; pratico; sincero, diretto

ear' trum'pet *s* corno acustico

ear wax' *s* cerume *m*

ease [iz] *s* facilità *f;* (*naturalness*) spigliatezza, disinvoltura; (*comfort*) benestare *m;* tranquillità *f;* **at ease!** (mil) riposo!; **with ease** con facilità ‖ *tr* facilitare; (*a burden*) alleggerire; (*to let up on*) rallentare; mitigare; **to ease out** licenziare con le buone maniere ‖ *intr* alleviarsi, mitigarsi, diminuire; rallentare

easel ['izəl] *s* cavalletto

easement ['izmənt] *s* attenuamento; (law) servitù *f*

easily ['izɪli] *adv* facilmente; senza dubbio; probabilmente

easiness ['izɪnɪs] *s* facilità *f;* disinvoltura; grazia, agilità *f;* disinvoltura

east [ist] *adj* orientale, dell'est ‖ *s* est *m* ‖ *adv* verso l'est

Easter ['istər] *s* Pasqua

East'er egg' *s* uovo di Pasqua

East'er Mon'day *s* lunedì *m* di Pasqua

eastern ['istərn] *adj* orientale

East'er-tide' *s* tempo pasquale

eastward ['istwərd] *adv* verso l'est

eas·y ['izi] *adj* (**-ier; -iest**) facile; (*conducive to ease*) comodo, agiato; (*free from worry*) tranquillo; (*easygoing*) disinvolto, spigliato; (*not tight*) ampio; (*not hurried*) lento, moderato ‖ *adv* (coll) facilmente; (coll) tranquillamente; **to take it easy** (coll) riposarsi; (coll) non prendersela; (coll) andar piano

eas'y chair' *s* poltrona

eas'y-go'ing *adj* (*person*) comodone; (*horse*) sciolto nell'andatura

eas'y mark' *s* (coll) gonzo

eas'y mon'ey *s* denaro fatto senza fatica; soldi rubati

eas'y terms' *spl* facilitazioni *fpl* di pagamento

eat [it] *v* (*pret* **ate** [et]; *pp* **eaten** ['itən]) *tr* mangiare; **to eat away** smangiare; **to eat up** mangiarsi ‖ *intr* mangiare

eatable ['itəbəl] *adj* mangiabile ‖ **eatables** *spl* commestibili *mpl*

eaves [ivz] *spl* gronda

eaves'drop' *v* (*pret* & *pp* **-dropped;** *ger* **-dropping**) *intr* origliare

ebb [eb] *s* riflusso; decadenza ‖ *intr* (*said of the tide*) ritirarsi; decadere

ebb' and flow' *s* flusso e riflusso

ebb' tide' *s* riflusso, deflusso

ebon·y ['ebəni] *s* (**-ies**) ebano

ebullient [ɪ'bʌljənt] *adj* bollente

eccentric [ɛk'sɛntrɪk] *adj* & *s* eccentrico

eccentrici•ty [ˌɛksɛn'trɪsɪti] s (-ties) eccentricità f, originalità f

ecclesiastic [ɪˌklizɪ'æstɪk] adj & s ecclesiastico

echelon ['ɛʃəˌlɑn] s scaglione m; (mil) scaglione m || tr scaglionare

ech•o ['ɛko] s (-oes) eco || tr far eco a || intr echeggiare, riecheggiare

éclair [e'kler] s dolce ripieno di crema

eclectic [ɛk'lɛktɪk] adj & s eclettico

eclipse [ɪ'klɪps] s eclisse f, eclissi f || tr eclissare

eclogue ['ɛklɔg] or ['ɛklɑg] s egloga

ecology [ɪ'kɑlədʒi] s ecologia

economic(al) [ˌikə'nɑmɪk(əl)] or [ˌɛkə'nɑmɪk(əl)] adj economico

economics [ˌikə'nɑmɪks] or [ˌɛkə'nɑmɪks] s economia (politica)

economist [ɪ'kɑnəmɪst] s economista mf

economize [ɪ'kɑnəˌmaɪz] tr & intr economizzare

econo•my [ɪ'kɑnəmi] s (-mies) economia

ecosystem ['ɛkoˌsɪstəm] s ecosistema m

ecsta•sy ['ɛkstəsi] s (-sies) estasi f

ecstatic [ɛk'stætɪk] adj estatico

ecumenic(al) [ˌɛkjə'mɛnɪk(əl)] adj ecumenico

eczema ['ɛksɪmə] or [ɛg'zimə] s eczema m

ed•dy ['ɛdi] s (-dies) turbine m || v (pret & pp -died) tr & intr turbinare

edelweiss ['ɛdəlˌvaɪs] s stella alpina

edge [ɛdʒ] s (of knife, sword, etc) filo, tagliente m; (border at which a surface terminates) orlo, bordo; (of a wound) labbro, margine m; (of a book) taglio; (of a tumbler) giro; (of clothing) vivagno; (of a table) spigolo; (slang) vantaggio; **on edge** nervoso; **to have the edge on** (coll) avere il vantaggio su; **to set the teeth on edge** far allegare i denti || tr affilare, aguzzare; orlare, bordare; **to edge out** riuscire ad eliminare || intr avanzare lentamente

edgeways ['ɛdʒˌwez] adv di taglio; **to not let s.o. get a word in edgeways** non lasciar dire una parola a qlcu

edging ['ɛdʒɪŋ] s orlo, bordo

edg•y ['ɛdʒi] adj (-ier; -iest) acuto, angolare; nervoso, ansioso

edible ['ɛdɪbəl] adj mangereccio, mangiabile || **edibles** spl commestibili mpl

edict ['idɪkt] s editto

edification [ˌɛdɪfɪ'keʃən] s edificazione

edifice ['ɛdɪfɪs] s edificio

edi•fy ['ɛdɪˌfaɪ] v (pret & pp -fied) tr edificare

edifying ['ɛdɪˌfaɪɪŋ] adj edificante

edit ['ɛdɪt] tr redigere; (e.g., a manuscript) correggere; (an edition) curare; (a newspaper) dirigere; (mov) montare

edition [ɪ'drɪʃən] s edizione

editor ['ɛdɪtər] s (of a newspaper or magazine) direttore m, gerente mf; (of an editorial) redattore m, cronista mf; (of a critical edition) editore m; (of a manuscript) revisore m

editorial [ˌɛdɪ'torɪ·əl] adj editoriale || s capocronaca m, articolo di fondo

ed'ito'rial staff' s redazione

ed'itor in chief' s gerente mf responsabile

educate ['ɛdʒuˌket] tr educare, erudire

education [ˌɛdʒu'keʃən] s educazione; istruzione, insegnamento

educational [ˌɛdʒu'keʃənəl] adj educativo

educa'tional institu'tion s istituto di magistero

educator ['ɛdʒuˌketər] s educatore m

eel [il] s anguilla; **to be as slippery as an eel** guizzare di mano come un'anguilla

ee•rie or **ee•ry** ['ɪri] adj (-rier; -riest) spettrale, pauroso

efface [ɪ'fes] tr cancellare; **to efface oneself** eclissarsi, mettersi in disparte

effect [ɪ'fɛkt] s effetto; (main idea) tenore m; **in effect** in vigore; **in realtà**; **to go into effect** or **to take effect** andare in vigore; **to put into effect** mandare ad effetto || tr effettuare

effective [ɪ'fɛktɪv] adj efficace; (actually in effect) effettivo; (striking) che colpisce; **to become effective** entrare in vigore

effectual [ɪ'fɛktʃu·əl] adj efficace

effectuate [ɪ'fɛktʃu·ˌet] tr effettuare

effeminacy [ɪ'fɛmɪnəsi] s effemminatezza

effeminate [ɪ'fɛmɪnɪt] adj effemminato

effervesce [ˌɛfər'vɛs] intr essere in effervescenza

effervescence [ˌɛfər'vɛsəns] s effervescenza

effervescent [ˌɛfər'vɛsənt] adj effervescente

effete [ɪ'fit] adj esausto, sterile

efficacious [ˌɛfɪ'keʃəs] adj efficace

effica•cy [ˈɛfɪkəsi] s (-cies) efficacia

efficien•cy [ɪ'fɪʃənsi] s (-cies) efficienza; (mech) rendimento, efficienza

effi'ciency engineer' s analista mf tempi e metodi

efficient [ɪ'fɪʃənt] adj efficiente; (person) abile; (mech) efficiente

effi•gy ['ɛfɪdʒi] s (-gies) effigie f

effort ['ɛfərt] s sforzo

effronter•y [ɪ'frʌntəri] s (-ies) sfrontatezza, sfacciataggine f

effusion [ɪ'fjuʒən] s effusione

effusive [ɪ'fjusɪv] adj espansivo

egg [ɛg] s uovo; (slang) bravo ragazzo || tr—**to egg on** incitare

egg'beat'er s frullino, sbattiuova m

egg'cup' s portauovo

egg'head' s (coll) intellettuale mf

eggnog ['ɛgˌnɑg] s zabaione m

egg'plant' s melanzana, petonciano

egg'shell' s guscio d'uovo

egoism ['ɛgoˌɪzəm] or ['igoˌɪzəm] s egoismo

egoist ['ɛgo·ɪst] or ['igo·ɪst] s egoista mf

egotism ['ɛgoˌtɪzəm] or ['igoˌtɪzəm] s egotismo

egotist ['ɛgotɪst] or ['igotɪst] s egotista mf

egregious [ɪ'gridʒəs] *adj* gigantesco, tremendo, marchiano

egress ['igrɛs] *s* uscita

Egypt ['idʒɪpt] *s* l'Egitto

Egyptian [ɪ'dʒɪpʃən] *adj* & *s* egiziano

ei'der down' ['aɪdər] *s* piumino

ei'der duck' *s* edredone *m*

eight [et] *adj* & *pron* otto || *s* otto; **eight o'clock** le otto

eighteen ['et'tin] *adj*, *s* & *pron* diciotto

eighteenth ['et'tinθ] *adj*, *s* & *pron* diciottesimo || *s* (*in dates*) diciotto

eighth [etθ] *adj* & *s* ottavo || *s* (*in dates*) otto

eight' hun'dred *adj*, *s* & *pron* ottocento

eightieth ['etɪ·ɪθ] *adj*, *s* & *pron* ottantesimo

eight·y ['eti] *adj* & *pron* ottanta || *s* (-**ies**) ottanta *m*; **the eighties** gli anni ottanta

either ['iðər] *or* ['aɪðər] *adj* l'uno o l'altro; l'uno e l'altro; ciascuno; entrambi i, tutti e due i || *pron* l'uno o l'altro; l'uno e l'altro; entrambi || *adv*—**not either** nemmeno || *conj*—**either . . . or** o . . . o

ejaculate [ɪ'dʒækjə‚let] *tr* ⊕solamare; (*physiol*) emettere || *intr* esclamare; (*physiol*) avere un'eiaculazione

eject [ɪ'dʒɛkt] *tr* espellere, gettar fuori; (*to evict*) sfrattare

ejection [ɪ'dʒɛk/ən] *s* espulsione; (*of a tenant*) sfratto

ejec'tion seat' *s* sedile *m* eiettabile

eke [ik] *tr*—**to eke out a living** sbarcare il lunario

elaborate [ɪ'læbərɪt] *adj* (*done with great care*) elaborato; (*detailed*) minuzioso; (*ornate*) ornato || [ɪ'læbə‚ret] *tr* elaborare || *intr*—**to elaborate on** *or* **upon** circonstanziare, particolareggiare

elapse [ɪ'læps] *intr* passare, trascorrere

elastic [ɪ'læstɪk] *adj* & *s* elastico

elasticity [ɪ‚læs'tɪsɪti] *or* [‚ilæs'tɪsɪti] *s* elasticità *f*

elated [ɪ'letɪd] *adj* esultante, gongolante

elation [ɪ'le/ən] *s* esultanza, gaudio

elbow ['ɛlbo] *s* gomito; (*in a river*) ansa; (*of a chair*) braccio; **at one's elbow** sotto mano; **out at the elbows** coi gomiti logori; **to crook the elbow** alzare il gomito; **to rub elbows** stare gomito a gomito; **up to the elbows** fino al collo || *tr*—**to elbow one's way** aprirsi il passo a gomitate || *intr* dar gomitate

el'bow grease' *s* (coll) olio di gomiti

el'bow patch' *s* toppa al gomito

el'bow rest' *s* bracciolo

el'bow·room' *s* spazio sufficiente; libertà *f* d'azione

elder ['ɛldər] *adj* seniore, maggiore || *s* (bot) sambuco; (eccl) maggiore *m*

el'der·ber'ry *s* (-ries) sambuco; (*fruit*) bacca del sambuco

elderly ['ɛldərli] *adj* attempato, anziano

eld'er states'man *s* uomo di stato esperto

eldest ['ɛldɪst] *adj* (il) maggiore; (il) più vecchio

elect [ɪ'lɛkt] *adj* & *s* eletto; **the elect** gli eletti || *tr* eleggere

election [ɪ'lɛk/ən] *s* elezione

electioneer [ɪ‚lɛk/ə'nɪr] *intr* fare una campagna elettorale

elective [ɪ'lɛktɪv] *adj* elettivo || *s* corso facoltativo

electorate [ɪ'lɛktərɪt] *s* elettorato

electric(al) [ɪ'lɛktrɪk(əl)] *adj* elettrico

elec'tric blend'er *s* frullatore *m*

elec'tric chair' *s* sedia elettrica

elec'tric cord' *s* piattina, filo elettrico

elec'tric eel' *s* gimnoto

elec'tric eye' *s* occhio elettrico

electrician [ɪ‚lɛk'trɪ/ən] *or* [‚elɛk-'trɪ/ən] *s* elettricista *m*

electricity [ɪ‚lɛk'trɪsɪti] *or* [‚elɛk-'trɪsɪti] *s* elettricità *f*

elec'tric me'ter *s* contatore *m* della luce

elec'tric per'cola'tor *s* caffettiera elettrica

elec'tric shav'er *s* rasoio elettrico

elec'tric shock' *s* scossa elettrica, elettrosquasso

elec'tric tape' *s* nastro isolante

elec'tric train' *s* elettrotreno

electri·fy [ɪ'lɛktrɪ‚faɪ] *v* (*pret* & *pp* -**fied**) *tr* (*to provide with electric power*) elettrificare; (*to communicate electricity to*; *to thrill*) elettrizzare

electrocute [ɪ'lɛktrə‚kjut] *tr* fulminare con la corrente; far morire sulla sedia elettrica

electrode [ɪ'lɛktrod] *s* elettrodo

electrolysis [ɪ‚lɛk'tralɪsɪs] *or* [‚elɛk-'tralɪsɪs] *s* elettrolisi *f*

electrolyte [ɪ'lɛktrə‚laɪt] *s* elettrolito

electromagnet [ɪ‚lɛktro'mægnɪt] *s* elettrocalamita

electromagnetic [ɪ‚lɛktrəmæg'nɛtɪk] *adj* elettromagnetico

electromotive [ɪ‚lɛktrə'motɪv] *adj* elettromotore

electron [ɪ'lɛktran] *s* elettrone *m*

electronic [ɪ‚lɛk'tranɪk] *or* [‚elɛk-'tranɪk] *adj* elettronico || **electronics** *s* elettronica

electroplating [ɪ'lɛktrə‚pletɪŋ] *s* galvanostegia

electrostatic [ɪ‚lɛktrə'stætɪk] *adj* elettrostatico

electrotype [ɪ'lɛktrə‚taɪp] *s* stereotipia || *tr* stereotipare

eleemosynary [‚elɪ'masɪ‚nɛri] *adj* caritatevole, di beneficenza

elegance ['ɛlɪgəns] *s* eleganza

elegant ['ɛlɪgənt] *adj* elegante

elegiac [‚elɪ'dʒaɪ·æk] *adj* elegiaco

ele·gy ['ɛlɪdʒɪ] *s* (-gies) elegia

element ['ɛlɪmənt] *s* elemento; **to be out of one's element** essere fuori del proprio ambiente

elementary [‚elɪ'mɛntəri] *adj* elementare

elephant ['ɛlɪfənt] *s* elefante *m*

elevate ['ɛlɪ‚vet] *tr* elevare, innalzare

elevated ['ɛlɪ‚vetɪd] *adj* elevato || *s* ferrovia soprelevata, metropolitana soprelevata

elevation [‚elɪ've/ən] *s* elevazione; (surv) quota

elevator ['ɛlɪ‚vetər] *s* ascensore *m*;

(for freight) montacarichi *m;* *(for hoisting grain)* elevatore *m* di grano; *(warehouse for storing grain)* deposito granaglie; (aer) timone *m* di profondità

eleven [ɪ'lɛvən] *adj & pron* undici ‖ *s* undici *m;* **eleven o'clock** le undici

eleventh [ɪ'lɛvənθ] *adj, s & pron* undicesimo ‖ *s* (*in dates*) undici *m*

elev'enth hour' *s* ultimo momento

elf [ɛlf] *s* (**elves** [ɛlvz]) elfo

elicit [ɪ'lɪsɪt] *tr* cavare, sottrarre

elide [ɪ'laɪd] *tr* elidere

eligible ['ɛlɪdʒɪbəl] *adj* eleggibile; accettabile

eliminate [ɪ'lɪmɪ,net] *tr* eliminare

elision [ɪ'lɪʒən] *s* elisione

elite [e'lit] *adj* eletto, scelto ‖ *s*—**the elite** l'élite *f*

elk [ɛlk] *s* alce *m*

ellipse [ɪ'lɪps] *s* (geom) ellisse *f*

ellip·sis [ɪ'lɪpsɪs] *s* (**-ses** [siz]) (gram) ellissi *f*

elliptic(al) [ɪ'lɪptɪk(əl)] *adj* ellittico

elm [ɛlm] *s* olmo

elongate [ɪ'lɔŋget] *or* [ɪ'lʌŋget] *tr* allungare, prolungare

elope [ɪ'lop] *intr* fuggire con un amante

elopement [ɪ'lopmənt] *s* fuga con un amante

eloquence ['ɛləkwəns] *s* eloquenza

eloquent ['ɛləkwənt] *adj* eloquente

else [ɛls] *adj*—**nobody else** nessun altro; **nothing else** nient'altro; **somebody else** qualcun altro; **something else** qualcosa d'altro; **what else** che altro; **who else** chi altro; **whose else** di che altra persona ‖ *adv*—**how else** in che altra maniera; **or else** se no; altrimenti; **when else** in che altro momento; in che altro periodo; **where else** dove mai, da che parte

else'where' *adv* altrove

elucidate [ɪ'lusɪ,det] *tr* dilucidare

elude [ɪ'lud] *tr* eludere

elusive [ɪ'lusɪv] *adj* elusivo; (*evasive*) fugace, sfuggente

emaciated [ɪ'meʃɪ,etɪd] *adj* smunto, emaciato, macilento

emanate ['ɛmə,net] *tr & intr* emanare

emancipate [ɪ'mænsɪ,pet] *tr* emancipare

embalm [ɛm'bɑm] *tr* imbalsamare

embankment [ɛm'bæŋkmənt] *s* terrapieno

embar·go [ɛm'bɑrgo] *s* (**-goes**) embargo ‖ *tr* mettere l'embargo a

embark [ɛm'bɑrk] *intr* imbarcarsi

embarkation [,ɛmbɑr'keʃən] *s* imbarco

embarrass [ɛm'bærəs] *tr* imbarazzare, mettere a disagio; (*to impede*) imbarazzare, impacciare; mettere in difficoltà economiche

embarrassing [ɛm'bærəsɪŋ] *adj* sconcertante; imbarazzante

embarrassment [ɛm'bærəsmənt] *s* imbarazzo, disagio, confusione; impaccio; difficoltà finanziaria, dissesto

embas·sy ['ɛmbəsi] *s* (**-sies**) ambasciata

em·bed [ɛm'bɛd] *s* (*pret & pp* **-bedded**; *ger* **-bedding**) *tr* incastrare, incassare

embellish [ɛm'bɛlɪʃ] *tr* imbellire

embellishment [ɛm'bɛlɪʃmənt] *s* abbellimento; (fig) fioretto

ember ['ɛmbər] *s* brace *f;* **embers** braci *fpl*

Em'ber days' *spl* tempora *fpl*

embezzle [ɛm'bɛzəl] *tr* appropriare, malversare ‖ *intr* appropriarsi

embezzlement [ɛm'bɛzəlmənt] *s* appropriazione indebita, malversazione; (*of public funds*) peculato

embezzler [ɛm'bɛzlər] *s* malversatore *m*

embitter [ɛm'bɪtər] *tr* amareggiare

emblazon [ɛm'blezən] *tr* blasonare; celebrare

emblem ['ɛmbləm] *s* emblema *m*

emblematic(al) [,ɛmblə'mætɪk(əl)] *adj* emblematico

embodiment [ɛm'bɑdɪmənt] *s* incarnazione, personificazione

embod·y [ɛm'bɑdi] *v* (*pret & pp* **-ied**) *tr* incarnare, personificare; incorporare

embolden [ɛm'boldən] *tr* imbaldanzire

embolism ['ɛmbə,lɪzəm] *s* embolia

emboss [ɛm'bɔs] *or* [ɛm'bɑs] *tr* (*metal*) sbalzare; (*paper*) goffrare

embrace [ɛm'bres] *s* abbraccio ‖ *tr* abbracciare ‖ *intr* abbracciarsi

embrasure [ɛm'breʒər] *s* (archit) strombatura; (mil) feritoia

embroider [ɛm'brɔɪdər] *tr* ricamare, trapuntare

embroider·y [ɛm'brɔɪdəri] *s* (**-ies**) ricamo, trapunto

embroil [ɛm'brɔɪl] *tr* ingarbugliare; (*to involve in contention*) coinvolgere

embroilment [ɛm'brɔɪlmənt] *s* imbroglio; (*in contention*) disaccordo

embry·o ['ɛmbrɪ,o] *s* (**-os**) embrione *m*

embryology [,ɛmbrɪ'ɑlədʒi] *s* embriologia

embryonic [,ɛmbrɪ'ɑnɪk] *adj* embrionale

emcee ['ɛm'si] *s* presentatore *m* ‖ *tr* presentare

emend [ɪ'mɛnd] *tr* emendare

emendation [,imɛn'deʃən] *s* emendamento

emerald ['ɛmərəld] *s* smeraldo

emerge [ɪ'mʌrdʒ] *intr* emergere

emergence [ɪ'mʌrdʒəns] *s* emergenza

emergen·cy [ɪ'mʌrdʒənsi] *s* (**-cies**) emergenza

emer'gency brake' *s* freno a mano

emer'gency ex'it *s* uscita di sicurezza

emer'gency land'ing *s* atterraggio di fortuna

emer'gency ward' *s* sala d'urgenza

emeritus [ɪ'mɛrɪtəs] *adj* emerito

emersion [ɪ'mʌrʒən] *or* [ɪ'mʌrʃən] *s* emersione

emery ['ɛməri] *s* smeriglio

em'ery cloth' *s* tela smeriglio

em'ery wheel' *s* mola a smeriglio

emetic [ɪ'mɛtɪk] *adj & s* emetico

emigrant ['ɛmɪgrənt] *adj & s* emigrante *mf*

emigrate ['ɛmɪ,gret] *intr* emigrare

émigré [emi'gre] *or* ['ɛmɪ,gre] *s* emigrato

eminence ['ɛmɪnəns] *s* eminenza; (eccl) Eminenza

eminent ['ɛmɪnənt] *adj* eminente

emissar·y ['ɛmɪˌsɛri] *s* (-ies) emissario

emission [ɪ'mɪʃən] *s* emissione

emit [ɪ'mɪt] *v* (*pret & pp* **emitted;** *ger* **emitting**) *tr* emettere

emolument [ɪ'mɑljəmənt] *s* emolumento

emotion [ɪ'moʃən] *s* emozione

emotional [ɪ'moʃənəl] *adj* emotivo

emperor ['ɛmpərər] *s* imperatore *m*

empha·sis ['ɛmfəsɪs] *s* (-ses [ˌsiz]) enfasi *f*, risalto

emphasize ['ɛmfəˌsaɪz] *tr* dar rilievo a, sottolineare

emphatic [ɛm'fætɪk] *adj* enfatico

emphysema [ˌɛmfɪ'simə] *s* enfisema *m*

empire ['ɛmpaɪr] *s* impero

empiric(al) [ɛm'pɪrɪk(əl)] *adj* empirico

empiricist [ɛm'pɪrɪsɪst] *s* empirista *mf*

emplacement [ɛm'plesmənt] *s* piazzola, postazione

employ [ɛm'plɔɪ] *s* impiego || *tr* impiegare, usare; valersi di

employee [ɛm'plɔɪ·i] or [ˌɛmplɔɪ'i] *s* impiegato, dipendente *mf*

employer [ɛm'plɔɪ·ər] *s* dirigente *mf*, datore *m* di lavoro

employment [ɛm'plɔɪmənt] *s* impiego, occupazione

employ′ment a′gency *s* agenzia di collocamento

empower [ɛm'pau·ər] *tr* autorizzare; permettere

empress ['ɛmprɪs] *s* imperatrice *f*

emptiness ['ɛmptɪnɪs] *s* vuoto

emp·ty ['ɛmpti] *adj* (-tier; -tiest) vuoto; (*gun*) scarico; (*hungry*) (coll) digiuno; (fig) esausto || *v* (*pret & pp* -tied) *tr* vuotare || *intr* vuotarsi

empty-handed ['ɛmpti'hændɪd] *adj* a mani vuote

empty-headed ['ɛmpti'hɛdɪd] *adj* dalla testa vuota, balordo

empyrean [ˌɛmpɪ'ri·ən] *adj & s* empireo

emulate ['ɛmjəˌlet] *tr* emulare

emulator ['ɛmjəˌletər] *s* emulo

emulous ['ɛmjələs] *adj* emulo

emulsi·fy [ɪ'mʌlsɪˌfaɪ] *v* (*pret & pp* -fied) *tr* emulsionare

emulsion [ɪ'mʌlʃən] *s* emulsione

enable [ɛn'ebəl] *tr* abilitare; permettere (*with dat*)

enact [ɛn'ækt] *tr* decretare; (*a role*) rappresentare

enactment [ɛn'æktmənt] *s* legge *f*; (*of a law*) promulgazione; (*of a play*) rappresentazione

enam·el [ɪn'æməl] *s* smalto || *v* (*pret & pp* -eled *or* -elled; *ger* -eling *or* -elling) *tr* smaltare

enam′el·ware′ *s* utensili *mpl* di cucina di ferro smaltato

enamor [ɛn'æmər] *tr* innamorare; **to become enamored of** innamorarsi di

encamp [ɛn'kæmp] *tr* accampare || *intr* accamparsi

encampment [ɛn'kæmpmənt] *s* campeggio; (mil) accampamento

encase [ɛn'kes] *tr* incassare

encephalitis [ɛnˌsɛfə'laɪtɪs] *s* encefalite *f*

enchain [ɛn'tʃen] *tr* incatenare

enchant [ɛn'tʃænt] or [ɛn'tʃɑnt] *tr* incantare

enchantment [ɛn'tʃæntmənt] or [ɛn'tʃɑntmənt] *s* incanto, malìa

enchanting [ɛn'tʃæntɪŋ] or [ɛn'tʃɑntɪŋ] *adj* incantatore, incantevole

enchantress [ɛn'tʃæntrɪs] or [ɛn'tʃɑntrɪs] *s* incantatrice *f*, maliarda

enchase [ɛn'tʃes] *tr* incastonare

encircle [ɛn'sʌrkəl] *tr* rigirare, girare intorno a; (mil) circondare

enclave ['ɛnklev] *s* enclave *f*

enclitic [ɛn'klɪtɪk] *adj* enclitico || *s* enclitica

enclose [ɛn'kloz] *tr* rinchiudere; (*in a letter*) accludere, includere; **to enclose herewith** accludere alla presente

enclosure [ɛn'kloʒər] *s* (*land surrounded by fence*) recinto, chiuso; (*e.g., letter*) allegato

encomi·um [ɛn'komi·əm] *s* (-ums *or* -a [ə]) encomio, elogio

encompass [ɛn'kʌmpəs] *tr* circondare; racchiudere, contenere

encore ['ɑŋkor] *s* bis *m* || *tr* (*a performance*) chiedere il bis di; (*a performer*) chiedere il bis a || *interj* bis!

encounter [ɛn'kauntər] *s* (*casual meeting*) incontro; (*combat*) scontro || *tr* incontrare || *intr* scontrarsi

encourage [ɛn'kʌrɪdʒ] *tr* incoraggiare; (*to foster*) favorire

encouragement [ɛn'kʌrɪdʒmənt] *s* incoraggiamento; favoreggiamento

encroach [ɛn'krotʃ] *intr*—**to encroach on** or **upon** invadere; usurpare; occupare il territorio di

encumber [ɛn'kʌmbər] *tr* imbarazzare; ingombrare; (*to load with debts, etc*) gravare

encumbrance [ɛn'kʌmbrəns] *s* imbarazzo; ingombro; gravame *m*

encyclical [ɛn'sɪklɪkəl] or [ɛn'saɪklɪkəl] *s* enciclica

encyclopedia [ɛnˌsaɪklə'pidɪ·ə] *s* enciclopedia

encyclopedic [ɛnˌsaɪklə'pidɪk] *adj* enciclopedico

end [ɛnd] *s* (*extremity; concluding part*) fine *f*; (*e.g., of the week*) fine *f*; (*purpose*) fine *m*; (*part adjacent to an extremity*) lembo; (*small piece*) pezza, avanzo; (*of a beam*) testata; (sports) estrema; **at the end of** in capo a; in fondo a; **in the end** alla fine, all'ultimo; **no end** (coll) moltissimo; **no end of** (coll) un mucchio di; **to make both ends meet** sbarcare il lunario; **to no end** senza effetto; **to stand on end** mettere in piedi, drizzare; mettersi diritto; (*said of hair*) drizzarsi; **to the end that** affinché || *tr* finire, terminare; **to end up** andare a finire || *intr* finire, terminare; **to end up** finire

endanger [ɛn'dendʒər] *tr* mettere in pericolo

endear [ɛn'dɪr] *tr* affezionare; **to endear oneself to** rendersi caro a

endeavor [ɛn'dɛvər] *s* tentativo, sforzo || *intr* tentare, sforzarsi

endemic [ɛn'dɛmɪk] *adj* endemico || *s* endemia

ending ['ɛndɪŋ] *s* fine *f*, conclusione; (gram) terminazione, desinenza

endive ['ɛndaɪv] *s* indivia

endless ['ɛndlɪs] *adj* interminabile; sterminato; (mach) senza fine

end'most' *adj* estremo, ultimo

endorse [ɛn'dɔrs] *tr* girare; (fig) approvare, confermare

endorsee [ˌɛndɔr'si] *s* giratario

endorsement [ɛn'dɔrsmənt] *s* girata; approvazione, conferma

endorser [ɛn'dɔrsər] *s* girante *mf*

endow [ɛn'daʊ] *tr* dotare

endowment [ɛn'daʊmənt] *adj* dotale || *s* (*of an institution*) dotazione; (*gift, talent*) dote *f*

end' pap'er *s* risguardo

endurance [ɛn'djʊrəns] or [ɛn'dʊrəns] *s* sopportazione, tolleranza; (*ability to hold out*) resistenza, forza; (*lasting time*) durata

endure [ɛn'djʊr] or [ɛn'dʊr] *tr* sopportare, tollerare; resistere (with *dat*) || *intr* durare, resistere

enduring [ɛn'djʊrɪŋ] or [ɛn'dʊrɪŋ] *adj* duraturo, durevole; paziente

enema ['ɛnəmə] *s* clistere *m*

ene•my ['ɛnəmi] *adj* nemico || *s* (-mies) nemico

en'emy al'ien *s* straniero nemico

energetic [ˌɛnər'dʒɛtɪk] *adj* energetico, vigoroso

ener•gy ['ɛnərdʒi] *s* (-gies) energia

enervate ['ɛnərˌvɛt] *tr* snervare

enfeeble [ɛn'fibəl] *tr* indebolire

enfold [ɛn'fold] *tr* avvolgere; abbracciare

enforce [ɛn'fɔrs] *tr* far osservare; ottenere per forza; (*e.g., obedience*) imporre; (*an argument*) far valere

enforcement [ɛn'fɔrsmənt] *s* imposizione; (*of a law*) esecuzione

enfranchise [ɛn'fræntʃaɪz] *tr* liberare; concedere il diritto di voto a

engage [ɛn'gedʒ] *tr* occupare; riservare; (*s.o.'s attention*) attrarre; (*a gear*) ingranare; (*the enemy*) ingaggiare; (*to hire*) assumere; (theat) scritturare; **to be engaged, to be engaged to be married** essere fidanzato; **to engage s.o. in conversation** intavolare una conversazione con qlcu || *intr* essere occupato; essere impiegato; assumere un'obbligazione; (mil) impegnarsi; (mach) ingranare, incastrarsi

engaged [ɛn'gedʒd] *adj* fidanzato; occupato, impegnato; (*column*) murato

engagement [ɛn'gedʒmənt] *s* accordo; fidanzamento; impegno, contratto; (*appointment*) appuntamento; (mil) azione; (mach) innesto

engage'ment ring' *s* anello di fidanzamento

engaging [ɛn'gedʒɪŋ] *adj* attrattivo

engender [ɛn'dʒɛndər] *tr* ingenerare

engine ['ɛndʒɪn] *s* macchina; (aut) motore *m*; (rr) locomotiva, motrice *f*

engineer [ˌɛndʒə'nɪr] *s* ingegnere *m*; (rr) macchinista *m*; (mil) zappatore *m*, geniere *m* || *tr* costruire; progettare

engineering [ˌɛndʒə'nɪrɪŋ] *s* ingegneria

en'gine house' *s* stazione dei pompieri

en'gine•man' *s* (-men) (rr) macchinista *m*

en'gine room' *s* sala macchine

en'gine-room' tel'egraph *s* (naut) telegrafo di macchina, trasmettitore *m*

England ['ɪŋglənd] *s* l'Inghilterra

Englander ['ɪŋgləndər] *s* nativo dell'Inghilterra

English ['ɪŋglɪʃ] *adj* inglese || *s* inglese *m*; (billiards) effetto; **the English** gli inglesi

Eng'lish Chan'nel *s* Canale *m* della Manica

Eng'lish dai'sy *s* margherita

Eng'lish horn' *s* (mus) corno inglese

Eng'lish•man *s* (-men) inglese *m*

Eng'lish-speak'ing *adj* di lingua inglese, anglofono

Eng'lish•wom'an *s* (-wom'en) inglese *f*

engraft [ɛn'græft] or [ɛn'graft] *tr* (hort) innestare; (fig) inculcare

engrave [ɛn'grev] *tr* incidere

engraver [ɛn'grevər] *s* incisore *m*

engraving [ɛn'grevɪŋ] *s* incisione

engross [ɛn'gros] *tr* preoccupare, assorbire; redigere ufficialmente, scrivere a grandi caratteri; monopolizzare

engrossing [ɛn'grosɪŋ] *adj* assorbente

engulf [ɛn'gʌlf] *tr* sommergere, inondare

enhance [ɛn'hæns] or [ɛn'hɑns] *tr* valorizzare; far risaltare

enigma [ɪ'nɪgmə] *s* enigma *m*

enigmatic(al) [ˌɪnɪg'mætɪk(əl)] *adj* enigmatico

enjambment [ɛn'dʒæmmənt] or [ɛn'dʒæmbmənt] *s* inarcatura

enjoin [ɛn'dʒɔɪn] *tr* ingiungere, intimare

enjoy [ɛn'dʒɔɪ] *tr* godere; **to enjoy +** *ger* provar piacere in + *inf*; **to enjoy oneself** divertirsi

enjoyable [ɛn'dʒɔɪ·əbəl] *adj* gradevole

enjoyment [ɛn'dʒɔɪmənt] *s* (*pleasure*) piacere *m*; (*pleasurable use*) godimento

enkindle [ɛn'kɪndəl] *tr* infiammare

enlarge [ɛn'lɑrdʒ] *tr* aumentare; ingrossare; (phot) ingrandire || *intr* aumentare; **to enlarge on** or **upon** dilungarsi su

enlargement [ɛn'lɑrdʒmənt] *s* aumento; ingrossamento; (phot) ingrandimento

enlighten [ɛn'laɪtən] *tr* illustrare, illuminare

enlightenment [ɛn'laɪtənmənt] *s* spiegazione, schiarimento || **Enlightenment** *s* illuminismo

enlist [ɛn'lɪst] *tr* (*e.g., s.o.'s favor*) guadagnarsi; (*the help of a person*) ottenere; (mil) ingaggiare || *intr* (mil) ingaggiarsi, arruolarsi; **to enlist**

in (*a cause*) dare il proprio appoggio a

enlistment [ɛn'lɪstmənt] *s* arruolamento, ingaggio

enliven [ɛn'laɪvən] *tr* ravvivare

enmesh [ɛn'mɛʃ] *tr* irretire

enmi•ty ['ɛnmɪtɪ] *s* (**-ties**) inimicizia

ennoble [ɛn'nobəl] *tr* nobilitare

ennui ['ɑnwi] *s* noia, tedio

enormous [ɪ'nɔrməs] *adj* enorme

enormously [ɪ'nɔrməslɪ] *adv* enormemente

enough [ɪ'nʌf] *adj* abbastanza ‖ *s* il sufficiente ‖ *adv* abbastanza ‖ *interj* basta!

enounce [ɪ'naʊns] *tr* enunciare; (*to declare*) affermare

enrage [ɛn'redʒ] *tr* infuriare, irritare

enrapture [ɛn'ræptʃər] *tr* mandare in visibilio, estasiare

enrich [ɛn'rɪtʃ] *tr* arricchire

enroll [ɛn'rol] *tr* arruolare, ingaggiare; (*a student*) iscrivere ‖ *intr* arruolarsi, ingaggiarsi; (*said of a student*) iscriversi

enrollment [ɛn'rolmənt] *s* arruolamento, ingaggio; (*of a student*) iscrizione

en route [ɑn 'rut] *adv* in cammino; **en route to** in via per

ensconce [ɛn'skɑns] *tr* nascondere; **to esconce oneself** rannicchiarsi, istallarsi comodamente

ensemble [ɑn'sɑmbəl] *s* insieme *m*; (*mus*) concertato

ensign ['ɛnsaɪn] *s* (*standard*) bandiera, insegna; (*badge*) distintivo ‖ ['ɛnsən] *or* ['ɛnsaɪn] *s* guardamarina *m*

ensilage ['ɛnsɪlɪdʒ] *s* (*preservation of fodder*) insilamento; (*preserved fodder*) insilato

ensile ['ɛnsaɪl] *or* [ɛn'saɪl] *tr* insilare

enslave [ɛn'slev] *tr* fare schiavo, asservire

enslavement [ɛn'slevmənt] *s* asservimento

ensnare [ɛn'snɛr] *tr* irretire

ensue [ɛn'su] *or* [ɛn'sju] *intr* risultare; seguire, conseguire

ensuing [ɛn'su·ɪŋ] *or* [ɛn'sju·ɪŋ] *adj* risultante, conseguente, seguente

ensure [ɛn'ʃʊr] *tr* assicurare, garantire

entail [ɛn'tel] *s* (law) obbligo ‖ *tr* provocare, comportare; (law) obbligare

entangle [ɛn'tæŋgəl] *tr* intricare, imbrogliare, impigliare

entanglement [ɛn'tæŋgəlmənt] *s* groviglio, garbuglio

enter ['ɛntər] *tr* (*a house*) entrare in; (*in the customhouse*) dichiarare; (*to make a record of*) registrare; (*a student*) iscrivere; iscriversi a; fare membro; (*to undertake*) intraprendere; **to enter s.o.'s head** passare per la testa a qlcu ‖ *intr* entrare; (theat) entrare in scena; **to enter into** entrare in; (*a contract*) impegnarsi in; **to enter on** *or* **upon** intraprendere

enterprise ['ɛntər‚praɪz] *s* (*undertak-*

ing) impresa; (*spirit, push*) intraprendenza

enterprising ['ɛntər‚praɪzɪŋ] *adj* intraprendente

entertain [‚ɛntər'ten] *tr* divertire, intrattenere; (*guests*) ospitare; (*a hope*) accarezzare; (*a proposal*) considerare ‖ *intr* ricevere

entertainer [‚ɛntər'tenər] *s* (*host*) ospite *mf*; (*in public*) attore *m*, cantante *mf*, fine dicitore *m*

entertaining [‚ɛntər'tenɪŋ] *adj* divertente

entertainment [‚ɛntər'tenmənt] *s* trattenimento, svago; spettacolo, attrazione; buon trattamento

enthrall [ɛn'θrɔl] *tr* affascinare, incantare; (*to subjugate*) asservire, soggiogare

enthrone [ɛn'θron] *tr* mettere sul trono, intronizzare; esaltare, innalzare

enthuse [ɛn'θuz] *or* [ɛn'θjuz] *tr* (coll) entusiasmare ‖ *intr* (coll) entusiasmarsi

enthusiasm [ɛn'θuzɪ‚æzəm] *or* [ɛn'θjuzɪ‚æzəm] *s* entusiasmo

enthusiast [ɛn'θuzɪ‚æst] *or* [ɛn'θjuzɪ‚æst] *s* entusiasta *mf*, maniaco

enthusiastic [ɛn‚θuzɪ'æstɪk] *or* [ɛn‚θjuzɪ'æstɪk] *adj* entusiastico

entice [ɛn'taɪs] *tr* attrarre, provocare; tentare

enticement [ɛn'taɪsmənt] *s* attrazione, provocazione; tentazione

entire [ɛn'taɪr] *adj* intero

entirely [ɛn'taɪrlɪ] *adv* interamente, (*solely*) solamente

entire•ty [ɛn'taɪrtɪ] *s* (**-ties**) interezza; totalità *f*

entitle [ɛn'taɪtəl] *tr* dar diritto a; (*to give a name to*) intitolare

enti•ty ['ɛntɪtɪ] *s* (**-ties**) (*something real; organization, institution*) ente *m*; (*existence*) entità *f*

entomb [ɛn'tum] *tr* seppellire

entombment [ɛn'tummənt] *s* sepoltura

entomology [‚ɛntə'mɑlədʒɪ] *s* entomologia

entourage [‚ɑntu'rɑʒ] *s* seguito

entrails ['ɛntrelz] *or* ['ɛntrəlz] *spl* visceri *mpl*

entrain [ɛn'tren] *tr* far salire sul treno ‖ *intr* imbarcarsi sul treno

entrance ['ɛntrəns] *s* entrata, ingresso ‖ [ɛn'træns] *or* [ɛn'trɑns] *tr* ipnotizzare, incantare

en'trance exam'ina'tion *s* esame *m* d'ammissione

entrancing [ɛn'trænsɪŋ] *or* [ɛn'trɑnsɪŋ] *adj* incantatore

entrant ['ɛntrənt] *s* nuovo membro; (sports) concorrente *m*

en•trap [ɛn'træp] *v* (pret & pp **-trapped**; ger **-trapping**) *tr* intrappolare, irretire

entreat [ɛn'trit] *tr* implorare

entreat•y [ɛn'tritɪ] *s* (**-ies**) implorazione, supplica

entree ['ɑntre] *s* entrata, ingresso; (culin) prima portata

entrench [ɛn'trɛntʃ] *tr* trincerare ‖ *intr* —**to entrench on** *or* **upon** violare

entrust [en'trʌst] *tr* affidare, confidare

en·try ['entri] *s* (**-tries**) entrata; (*item*) partita, registrazione; (*in a dictionary*) lemma, esponente *m*; (sports) concorrente *mf*

entwine [en'twaɪn] *tr* intrecciare ‖ *intr* intrecciarsi

enumerate [ɪ'njumə,ret] *or* [ɪ'numə,ret] *tr* enumerare

enunciate [ɪ'nʌnsɪ,et] *or* [ɪ'nʌnʃɪ,et] *tr* enunciare, staccare

envelop [en'veləp] *tr* involgere

envelope ['envə,lop] *or* ['ʌnvə,lop] *s* (*for a letter*) busta; (*wrapper*) involucro

envenom [en'venəm] *tr* avvelenare

enviable ['envɪ·əbəl] *adj* invidiabile

envious ['envɪ·əs] *adj* invidioso

environment [en'vaɪrənmənt] *s* ambiente *m*; condizioni *fpl* ambientali

environs [en'vaɪrənz] *spl* dintorni *mpl*, sobborghi *mpl*

envisage [en'vɪzɪdʒ] *tr* considerare, immaginare

envoi ['envɔɪ] *s* (pros) congedo

envoy ['envɔɪ] *s* inviato; (mil) parlamentare *m*; (pros) congedo

en·vy ['envi] *s* (**-vies**) invidia ‖ *v* (*pret & pp* **-vied**) *tr* invidiare

enzyme ['enzaɪm] *or* ['enzɪm] *s* enzima *m*

epaulet *or* **epaulette** ['epə,let] *s* spallina

epenthe·sis [ɛ'pɛnθɪsɪs] *s* (**-ses** [,siz]) epentesi *f*

ephemeral [ɪ'femərəl] *adj* effimero

epic ['epɪk] *adj* epico ‖ *s* epica

epicure ['epɪ,kjur] *s* epicureo

epicurean [,epɪkju'ri·ən] *adj & s* epicureo

epidemic [,epɪ'demɪk] *adj* epidemico ‖ *s* epidemia

epidermis [,epɪ'dʌrmɪs] *s* epidermide *f*

epiglottis [,epɪ'glatɪs] *s* epiglottide *f*

epigram ['epɪ,græm] *s* epigramma *m*

epilepsy ['epɪ,lepsi] *s* epilessia

epileptic [,epɪ'leptɪk] *adj & s* epilettico

epilogue ['epɪ,lɔg] *or* ['epɪ,lag] *s* epilogo

Epiphany [ɪ'pɪfəni] *s* Epifania

Episcopalian [ɪ,pɪskə'pelɪ·ən] *adj & s* episcopaliano

episode ['epɪ,sod] *s* episodio

epistle [ɪ'pɪsəl] *s* epistola

epitaph ['epɪ,tæf] *s* epitaffio

epithet ['epɪ,θet] *s* epiteto

epitome [ɪ'pɪtəmi] *s* epitome *f*; (fig) prototipo, personificazione

epitomize [ɪ'pɪtə,maɪz] *tr* epitomare; (fig) incarnare, personificare

epoch ['epək] *or* ['ipak] *s* epoca

epochal ['epəkəl] *adj* memorabile

ep'och-mak'ing *adj*—**to be epoch-making** fare epoca

Ep'som salt' ['epsəm] *s* sale *m* inglese

equable ['ekwəbəl] *or* ['ikwəbəl] *adj* uniforme; tranquillo

equal ['ikwəl] *adj* uguale; **equal to** pari a, all'altezza di ‖ *s* uguale *m* ‖ *v* (*pret & pp* **equaled** *or* **equalled**; *ger* **equaling** *or* **equalling**) *tr* ugualgiare

equali·ty [ɪ'kwalɪti] *s* (**-ties**) uguaglianza

equalize ['ikwə,laɪz] *tr* uguagliare; (*to make uniform*) perequare, pareggiare

equally ['ikwəli] *adv* ugualmente

equanimity [,ikwə'nɪmɪti] *s* equanimità *f*

equate [i'kwet] *tr* mettere in forma di equazione; considerare uguale *or* uguali

equation [i'kweʒən] *or* [i'kweʃən] *s* equazione

equator [i'kwetər] *s* equatore *m*

equatorial [,ikwə'torɪ·əl] *adj* equatoriale

equer·ry ['ekwəri] *or* [ɪ'kweri] *s* (**-ries**) scudiero

equestrian [ɪ'kwestrɪ·ən] *adj* equestre ‖ *s* cavallerizzo

equilateral [,ikwɪ'lætərəl] *adj* equilatero

equilibrium [,ikwɪ'lɪbrɪ·əm] *s* equilibrio

equinoctial [,ikwɪ'nakʃəl] *adj* equinoziale

equinox ['ikwɪ,naks] *s* equinozio

equip [ɪ'kwɪp] *v* (*pret & pp* **equipped**; *ger* **equipping**) *tr* equipaggiare; **to equip** (*e.g., a ship*) **with** munire di

equipment [ɪ'kwɪpmənt] *s* equipaggiamento; (*skill*) attitudine *f*, capacità *f*

equipoise ['ikwɪ,pɔɪz] *or* ['ekwɪ,pɔɪz] *s* equilibrio ‖ *tr* equilibrare

equitable ['ekwɪtəbəl] *adj* equo

equi·ty ['ekwɪti] *s* (**-ties**) (*fairness*) equità *f*; valore *m* al netto; (*in a corporation*) interessenza azionaria

equivalent [ɪ'kwɪvələnt] *adj* equivalente ‖ *s* equivalente *m*; (com) controvalore *m*

equivocal [ɪ'kwɪvəkəl] *adj* equivoco

equivocate [ɪ'kwɪvə,ket] *intr* giocare sulle parole, parlare in maniera equivoca

equivocation [ɪ,kwɪvə'keʃən] *s* equivocità *f*; equivoco

era ['ɪrə] *or* ['irə] *s* era, evo

eradicate [ɪ'rædɪ,ket] *tr* sradicare

erase [ɪ'res] *tr* cancellare

eraser [ɪ'resər] *s* gomma da cancellare; (*for blackboard*) spugna

erasure [ɪ'reʃər] *or* [ɪ'reʒər] *s* cancellatura; (*of a tape*) cancellazione

ere [ɛr] *prep* (lit) prima di ‖ *conj* (lit) prima che

erect [ɪ'rekt] *adj* dritto, eretto; (*hair*) irto ‖ *tr* (*to set in upright position*) drizzare; (*a building*) erigere, costruire; (*a machine*) montare

erection [ɪ'rekʃən] *s* erezione

ermine ['ʌrmɪn] *s* ermellino; (fig) carica di giudice, toga, magistratura

erode [ɪ'rod] *tr* erodere ‖ *intr* corrodersi, consumarsi

erosion [ɪ'roʒən] *s* erosione

erotic [ɪ'ratɪk] *adj* erotico

err [ʌr] *intr* errare; (*to be incorrect*) sbagliarsi

errand ['erənd] *s* corsa, commissione; **to run an errand** fare una commissione

er'rand boy' *s* fattorino, galoppino

erratic [ɪ'rætɪk] *adj* erratico; strano, eccentrico

erra·tum [ɪ'retəm] or [ɪ'rɑtəm] *s* (-ta [tə]) errore *m* di stampa

erroneous [ɪ'roni·əs] *adj* erroneo

error ['erər] *s* errore *m*, sbaglio

erudite ['eru ,daɪt] or ['erju ,daɪt] *adj* erudito, dotto

erudition [,eru'dɪʃən] or [,erju'dɪʃən] *s* erudizione

erupt [ɪ'rʌpt] *intr* (*said of a volcano*) eruttare; (*said of a skin rash*) fiorire; (*said of a tooth*) spuntare; (fig) erompere

eruption [ɪ'rʌpʃən] *s* eruzione

escalate ['eskə ,let] *tr* & *intr* aumentare

escalation [,eskə'leʃən] *s* aumento

escalator ['eskə ,letər] *s* scala mobile

escallop [es'kæləp] *s* (*on edge of cloth*) dentellatura, festone *m*; (*mollusk*) pettine *m* || *tr* cuocere in conchiglia; cuocere al forno con salsa e pane grattugiato

escapade [,eskə'ped] *s* scappatella

escape [es'kep] *s* (*getaway*) fuga; (*from responsibility, duties, etc.*) scampo || *tr* sottrarsi a, eludere; **to escape s.o.** scappare da qlcu; scappar di mente a qlcu || *intr* scappare; sprigionarsi; **to escape from** (*a person*) sfuggire a; (*jail*) evadere da

escapee [,eskə'pi] *s* evaso

escape' lit'erature *s* letteratura di evasione

escapement [es'kepmənt] *s* scappamento

escape' veloc'ity *s* (rok) velocità *f* di fuga

escarpment [es'kɑrpmənt] *s* scarpata

eschew [es't/u] *tr* evitare, rifuggire da

escort ['eskɔrt] *s* soorta; (*of a woman or girl*) compagno, cavaliere *m* || [es'kɔrt] *tr* scortare

escutcheon [es'kʌtʃən] *s* scudo; (*plate in front of lock on door*) bocchetta

Esk·imo ['eskɪ ,mo] *adj* eschimese || *s* (-mos or -mo) eschimese *mf*

esopha·gus [i'safəgəs] *s* (-gi [,dʒaɪ]) esofago

espalier [es'pæljər] *s* spalliera

especial [es'peʃəl] *adj* speciale

espionage ['espɪ·ənɪdʒ] or [,espɪ·ə'naʒ] *s* spionaggio

esplanade [,esplə'ned] or [,esplə'nɑd] *s* spianata, piazzale *m*

espousal [es'pauzəl] *s* sposalizio; (*of a cause*) adozione

espouse [es'pauz] *tr* sposare; (*to advocate*) abbracciare, adottare

esquire [es'kwaɪr] or ['eskwaɪr] *s* scudiero || **Esquire** *s* titolo di cortesia usato generalmente con persone di riguardo

essay ['ese] *s* saggio

essayist ['ese·ɪst] *s* saggista *mf*

essence ['esəns] *s* essenza

essential [e'sen/əl] *adj* & *s* essenziale *m*

establish [es'tæblɪʃ] *tr* stabilire

establishment [es'tæblɪʃmənt] *s* stabilimento; fondazione; **the Establishment** l'autorità costituita

estate [es'tet] *s* stato; condizione sociale; (*landed property*) tenuta; (*a*

person's possessions) patrimonio; (*left by a decedent*) massa ereditaria

esteem [es'tim] *s* stima || *tr* stimare

esthete ['esθit] *s* esteta *mf*

esthetic [es'θetɪk] *adj* estetico || **esthetics** *ssg* estetica

estimable ['estɪməbəl] *adj* stimabile

estimate ['estɪ ,met] or ['estɪmɪt] *s* stima, valutazione; (*statement of cost of work to be done*) preventivo || ['estɪ ,met] *tr* stimare, valutare; preventivare

estimation [,estɪ'meʃən] *s* stima; **in my estimation** a mio parere

estimator ['estɪ ,metər] *s* preventivista *mf*

estrangement [es'trendʒmənt] *s* alienazione, disaffezione

estuar·y ['est/u ,eri] *s* (-ies) estuario

etch [etʃ] *tr* & *intr* incidere all'acquaforte

etcher ['etʃər] *s* acquafortista *mf*

etching ['etʃɪŋ] *s* acquaforte *f*

eternal [ɪ'tʌrnəl] *adj* eterno

eterni·ty [ɪ'tʌrnɪti] *s* (-ties) eternità *f*

ether ['iθər] *s* etere *m*

ethereal [ɪ'θɪrɪ·əl] *adj* etereo

ethical ['eθɪkəl] *adj* etico

ethics ['eθɪks] *ssg* etica

Ethiopian [,iθɪ'opɪ·ən] *adj* & *s* etiope *mf*

ethnic(al) ['eθnɪk(əl)] *adj* etnico

ethnography [eθ'nagrəfɪ] *s* etnografia

ethnology [eθ'nalədʒi] *s* etnologia

ethyl ['eθɪl] *s* etile *m*

ethylene ['eθɪ ,lin] *s* etilene *m*

etiquette ['etɪ ,ket] *s* etichetta

étude [e'tjud] *s* (mus) studio

etymology [,etɪ'malədʒi] *s* etimologia

ety·mon ['etɪ ,man] *s* (-mons or -ma [mə]) etimo

eucalyp·tus [,jukə'lɪptəs] *s* (-tuses or -ti [taɪ]) eucalipto

Eucharist ['jukərɪst] *s* Eucaristia

eugenics [ju'dʒenɪks] *ssg* eugenetica

eulogistic [,julə'dʒɪstɪk] *adj* elogiativo

eulogize ['julə ,dʒaɪz] *tr* elogiare

eulo·gy ['julədʒi] *s* (-gies) elogio; elogio funebre

eunuch ['junək] *s* eunuco

euphemism ['jufɪ ,mɪzəm] *s* eufemismo

euphemistic [,jufɪ'mɪstɪk] *adj* eufemistico

euphonic [ju'fanɪk] *adj* eufonico

eupho·ny ['jufəni] *s* (-nies) eufonia

euphoria [ju'forɪ·ə] *s* euforia

euphuism ['jufju ,ɪzəm] *s* eufuismo

Europe ['jurəp] *s* l'Europa

European [,jurə'pi·ən] *adj* & *s* europeo

euthanasia [,juθə'neʒə] *s* eutanasia

evacuate [ɪ'vækju ,et] *tr* & *intr* evacuare

evacuation [ɪ ,vækju'eʃən] *s* evacuazione

evacuee [ɪ'vækju ,i] or [ɪ ,vækju'i] *s* sfollato

evade [ɪ'ved] *tr* eludere || *intr* evadere

evaluate [ɪ'vælju ,et] *tr* valutare

evaluation [ɪ ,vælju'eʃən] *s* valutazione

Evangel [ɪ'vændʒəl] *s* Vangelo

evangelic(al) [,ivæn'dʒelɪk(əl)] or [,evən'dʒelɪk(əl)] *adj* evangelico

Evangelist [ɪ'vændʒəlɪst] s evangelista m

evaporate [ɪ'væpə‚ret] tr & intr evaporare

evasion [ɪ'veʒən] s evasione; (subterfuge) scappatoia

evasive [ɪ'vesɪv] adj evasivo

eve [iv] s vigilia; **on the eve of** la vigilia di

even ['ivən] adj (smooth) piano, regolare; (number) pari; uguale, uniforme; (temperament) calmo, placido; **even with** a livello di; **to be even** mettersi in pari; **to get even** prendersi la rivincita || adv anche; fino, perfino; pure; esattamente; magari; **even as** proprio mentre; **even if** anche se, quando pure; **even so** anche se così; **even though** quantunque; **even when** anche quando; **not even** neppure, nemmeno; **to break even** impattare || tr spianare; **even up** bilanciare

evening ['ivnɪŋ] adj serale || s sera, serata; **all evening** tutta la sera; **every evening** tutte le sere; **in the evening** la sera

eve'ning clothes' spl vestito da sera

eve'ning gown' s vestito da sera da signora

eve'ning star' s espero

e'ven·song' s (eccl) vespro

event [ɪ'vent] s avvenimento; (outcome) evenienza; (public function) manifestazione; (sports) prova; **at all events** or **in any event** in ogni caso; **in the event that** in caso che, se mai

eventful [ɪ'ventfəl] adj ricco di avvenimenti; movimentato

eventual [ɪ'ventʃʊ·əl] adj finale

eventuali·ty [ɪ‚ventʃʊ'ælɪti] s (-ties) eventualità f, evenienza

eventually [ɪ'ventʃʊ·əli] adv finalmente, alla fine

eventuate [ɪ'ventʃʊ‚et] intr risultare, accadere

ever ['evər] adv (at all times) sempre; (at any time) mai; **as ever** come sempre; **as much as ever** tanto come prima; **ever since** (since that time) sin da; da allora in poi; **ever so** molto; **ever so much** moltissimo; **hardly ever** or **scarcely ever** quasi mai; **not . . . ever** non . . . mai

ev'er·glade' s terreno paludoso coperto di erbe

ev'er·green' adj & s sempreverde m & f; **evergreens** decorazione di sempreverdi

ev'er·last'ing adj eterno; incessante; (lasting indefinitely) duraturo; (wearisome) noioso || s eternità f; (bot) sempreviro

ev'er·more' adv eternamente; **for evermore** per sempre

every ['evri] adj tutti i; (each) ogni, ciascuno; (being each in a series) ogni, e.g., **every three days** ogni tre giorni; **every bit** (coll) in tutto e per tutto, e.g., **every bit a man** un uomo in tutto e per tutto; **every now and then** di quando in quando; **every once in a while** una volta ogni tanto;

every other day ogni secondo giorno; **every which way** (coll) da tutte le parti; (coll) in disordine

ev'ery·bod'y pron indef ognuno, tutti

ev'ery·day' adj di ogni giorno; quotidiano; ordinario

ev'ery·man' s l'uomo qualunque || pron chiunque

ev'ery·one' or **ev'ery one'** pron indef ciascuno, tutti

ev'ery·thing' pron indef tutto, ogni cosa, tutto quanto

ev'ery·where' adv dappertutto, dovunque

evict [ɪ'vɪkt] tr sfrattare, sloggiare

eviction [ɪ'vɪkʃən] s sfratto, sloggio

evidence ['evɪdəns] s evidenza; (law) prova

evident ['evɪdənt] adj evidente

evil ['ivəl] adj cattivo, malvagio || s male m; disgrazia

evildoer ['ivəl‚du·ər] s malfattore m, malvagio

e'vil·do'ing s malafatta, malvagità f

e'vil eye' s iettatura, malocchio

evil-minded ['ivəl'maɪndɪd] adj malintenzionato

e'vil one', **the** il nemico

evince [ɪ'vɪns] tr mostrare, manifestare

evoke [ɪ'vok] tr evocare

evolution [‚evə'luʃən] s evoluzione

evolve [ɪ'vɑlv] tr sviluppare || intr evolversi

ewe [ju] s pecora

ewer ['ju·ər] s brocca

ex [eks] prep senza includere

exacerbation [ɪg‚zæsər'beʃən] s esulcerazione, esacerbazione

exacerbate [ɪg'zæsər‚bet] tr esacerbare, esulcerare

exact [eg'zækt] adj esatto || tr esigere

exacting [eg'zæktɪŋ] adj esigente

exaction [eg'zækʃən] s esazione

exactly [eg'zæktli] adv esattamente; (sharp, on the dot) in punto

exactness [eg'zæktnɪs] s esattezza

exaggerate [eg'zædʒə‚ret] tr esagerare

exalt [eg'zɔlt] tr elevare, esaltare

exam [eg'zæm] s (coll) esame m

examination [eg‚zæmɪ'neʃən] s esame m; **to take an examination** sostenere un esame

examine [eg'zæmɪn] tr esaminare

examiner [eg'zæmɪnər] s esaminatore m

example [eg'zæmpəl] or [eg'zɑmpəl] s esempio; (precedent) precedente m; (of mathematics) problema m; **for example** per esempio

exasperate [eg'zæspə‚ret] tr esasperare

excavate ['ekskə‚vet] tr scavare

exceed [ek'sid] tr eccedere

exceedingly [ek'sidŋli] adv estremamente, sommamente

ex·cel [ek'sel] v (pret & pp -celled; ger -celling) tr sorpassare || intr eccellere

excellence ['eksələns] s eccellenza

excellen·cy ['eksələnsi] s (-cies) eccellenza; **Your Excellency** Sua Eccellenza

excelsior [ek'selsɪ·ər] s trucioli mpl per imballaggio

except [ek'sept] prep eccetto; **except**

for tranne, ad eccezione di; **except that** eccetto che || *tr* eccettuare

exception [ɛkˈsɛpʃən] *s* eccezione; **to take exception** obiettare; scandalizzarsi; **with the exception of** a esclusione di, eccetto

exceptional [ɛkˈsɛpʃənəl] *adj* eccezionale

excerpt [ˈɛksʌrpt] *or* [ɛkˈsʌrpt] *s* brano, selezione || [ɛkˈsʌrpt] *tr* scegliere, selezionare

excess [ˈɛksɛs] *or* [ɛkˈsɛs] *adj* eccedente || [ɛkˈsɛs] *s* (*amount or degree by which one thing exceeds another*) eccedente *m*, eccedenza; (*excessive amount; immoderate indulgence; unlawful conduct*) eccesso; **in excess of** più di

ex′cess bag′gage *s* bagaglio eccedente

ex′cess fare′ *s* (rr) supplemento

excessive [ɛkˈsɛsɪv] *adj* eccessivo

ex′cess-prof′its tax′ *s* tassa sui soprapprofitti

exchange [ɛksˈtʃendʒ] *s* scambio; (*place for buying and selling*) borsa; (*transactions in the currencies of two different countries*) cambio; (telp) centrale *f*, centralino; **in exchange for** in cambio di || *tr* scambiare, scambiarsi; **to exchange blows** venire alle mani; **to exchange greetings** salutarsi

exchequer [ɛksˈtʃɛkər] *or* [ˈɛkstʃɛkər] *s* erario, tesoro

ex′cise tax′ [ɛkˈsaɪz] *or* [ˈɛksaɪz] *s* imposta sul consumo

excitable [ɛkˈsaɪtəbəl] *adj* eccitabile

excite [ɛkˈsaɪt] *tr* eccitare

excitement [ɛkˈsaɪtmənt] *s* eccitazione

exciting [ɛkˈsaɪtɪŋ] *adj* emozionante; (*stimulating*) eccitante

exclaim [ɛksˈklem] *tr & intr* esclamare

exclamation [ˌɛksklʌˈmeʃən] *s* esclamazione

exclama′tion mark′ *or* **point′** *s* punto esclamativo

exclude [ɛksˈklud] *tr* escludere

excluding [ɛksˈkludɪŋ] *prep* a esclusione di, senza contare

exclusion [ɛksˈkluʒən] *s* esclusione; **to the exclusion of** tranne, salvo

exclusive [ɛksˈklusɪv] *adj* esclusivo; **exclusive of** escluso, senza contare || *s* (journ) esclusiva

excommunicate [ˌɛkskəˈmjunɪˌket] *tr* scomunicare

excommunication [ˌɛkskəˌmjunɪˈkeʃən] *s* scomunica

excoriate [ɛksˈkɔrɪˌet] *tr* criticare aspramente, vituperare

excrement [ˈɛkskrəmənt] *s* escremento

excruciating [ɛksˈkruʃɪˌetɪŋ] *adj* (*e.g., pleasure*) estremo; (*e.g., pain*) atroce, lancinante, straziante

exculpate [ˈɛkskʌlˌpet] *or* [ɛksˈkʌlpet] *tr* scolpare, scagionare

excursion [ɛksˈkʌrʒən] *or* [ɛksˈkʌrʃən] *s* escursione, gita

excursionist [ɛksˈkʌrʒənɪst] *or* [ɛksˈkʌrʃənɪst] *s* escursionista *mf*

excusable [ɛksˈkjuzəbəl] *adj* scusabile

excuse [ɛksˈkjus] *s* scusa || [ɛksˈkjuz] *tr* scusare; esentare; (*a debt*) rimettere

execute [ˈɛksɪˌkjut] *tr* (*to carry out; to produce*) eseguire; (*to put to death*) giustiziare; (law) rendere esecutorio

execution [ˌɛksɪˈkjuʃən] *s* esecuzione; (*e.g., of a criminal*) esecuzione capitale

executioner [ˌɛksɪˈkjuʃənər] *s* giustiziere *m*, boia *m*, carnefice *m*

executive [ɛgˈzɛkjətɪv] *adj* esecutivo || *s* esecutivo; (*of a school, business, etc.*) dirigente *mf*

Exec′utive Man′sion *s* palazzo del governatore; residenza del capo del governo statunitense

executor [ɛgˈzɛkjətər] *s* (law) esecutore testamentario

executrix [ɛgˈzɛkjətrɪks] *s* (law) esecutrice testamentaria

exemplary [ɛgˈzɛmpləri] *or* [ˈɛgzəmˌplɛri] *adj* esemplare

exemplify [ɛgˈzɛmplɪˌfaɪ] *v* (*pret & pp* -fied) *tr* esemplificare

exempt [ɛgˈzɛmpt] *adj* esente || *tr* esimere, esentare

exemption [ɛgˈzɛmpʃən] *s* esenzione

exercise [ˈɛksərˌsaɪz] *s* esercizio; cerimonia; **to take exercise** fare del moto || *tr* esercitare; (*care*) usare; (*to worry*) preoccupare || *intr* esercitarsi

exert [ɛgˈzʌrt] *tr* (*e.g., power*) esercitare; **to exert oneself** sforzarsi

exertion [ɛgˈzʌrʃən] *s* sforzo, tentativo; (*active use*) uso, esercizio

exhalation [ˌɛks-həˈleʃən] *s* (*of gas, vapors*) esalazione; (*of air from lungs*) espirazione

exhale [ɛksˈhel] *or* [ɛgˈzel] *tr* (*gases, vapors, etc.*) esalare; (*air from lungs*) espirare || *intr* esalare; espirare

exhaust [ɛgˈzɔst] *s* scarico, scappamento; tubo di scarico or scappamento || *tr* (*to wear out*) spossare, finire; (*to use up*) esaurire, dar fondo a; vuotare

exhaust′ fan′ *s* aspiratore *m*

exhaustion [ɛgˈzɔstʃən] *s* esaurimento; estenuazione; (sports) cotta

exhaustive [ɛgˈzɔstɪv] *adj* esauriente

exhaust′ man′ifold *s* collettore *m* di scarico

exhaust′ pipe′ *s* tubo di scarico

exhaust′ valve′ *s* valvola di scappamento

exhibit [ɛgˈzɪbɪt] *s* esposizione; (law) documento in giudizio || *tr* esibire

exhibition [ˌɛksɪˈbɪʃən] *s* esibizione

exhibitor [ɛgˈzɪbɪtər] *s* espositore *m*

exhilarating [ɛgˈzɪləˌretɪŋ] *adj* esilarante

exhort [ɛgˈzɔrt] *tr* esortare

exhume [ɛksˈhjum] *or* [ɛgˈzjum] *tr* esumare, dissotterrare

exigency [ˈɛksɪdʒənsi] *s* (-cies) esigenza

exigent [ˈɛksɪdʒənt] *adj* esigente

exile [ˈɛgzaɪl] *or* [ˈɛksaɪl] *s* esilio; (*person*) esule *mf* || *tr* esiliare

exist [ɛgˈzɪst] *intr* esistere

existence [ɛgˈzɪstəns] *s* esistenza

existing [ɛgˈzɪstɪŋ] *adj* esistente

exit [ˈɛgzɪt] *or* [ˈɛksɪt] *s* uscita || *intr* uscire

exodus ['ɛksədəs] *s* esodo

exonerate [ɛg'zɑnə‚ret] *tr (from an obligation)* esonerare; *(from blame)* scagionare

exorbitant [ɛg'zɔrbɪtənt] *adj* esorbitante

exorcise ['ɛksɔr‚saɪz] *tr* esorcizzare

exotic [ɛg'zɑtɪk] *adj* esotico

expand [ɛks'pænd] *tr (a metal)* dilatare; *(gas)* espandere; *(to enlarge)* allargare, ampliare; *(to unfold)* spiegare; (math) svolgere, sviluppare || *intr* dilatarsi; espandersi; allargarsi, ampliarsi; spiegarsi, estendersi

expanse [ɛks'pæns] *s* vastità *f*

expansion [ɛks'pænʃən] *s* espansione

expansive [ɛks'pænsɪv] *adj* espansivo

expatiate [ɛks'peʃɪ‚et] *intr* dilungarsi

expatriate [ɛks'petrɪ‚ɪt] *adj* esiliato || *s* esule *mf* || [ɛks'petri‚et] *tr* esiliare; **to expatriate oneself** espatriare

expect [ɛks'pɛkt] *tr* aspettare, attendere; (coll) credere, supporre; **to expect it** aspettarselo, aspettarsela

expectan·cy [ɛks'pɛktənsi] *s* (-cies) aspettativa, aspettazione

expect′ant moth′er [ɛks'pɛktənt] *s* futura madre

expectation [‚ɛkspɛk'teʃən] *s* aspettativa

expectorate [ɛks'pɛktə‚ret] *tr & intr* espettorare

expedien·cy [ɛks'pidɪ‚ənsi] *s* (-cies) industria, ingegno; opportunismo, vantaggio personale

expedient [ɛks'pidɪ‚ənt] *adj* conveniente; vantaggioso; *(acting with self-interest)* opportunista || *s* espediente *m*

expedite ['ɛkspɪ‚daɪt] *tr* sbrigare, accelerare; *(a document)* dar corso a

expedition [‚ɛkspɪ'dɪʃən] *s* spedizione; *(speed)* celerità *f*

expeditionary [‚ɛkspɪ'dɪʃən‚ɛri] *adj* *(e.g., corps)* di spedizione

expeditious [‚ɛkspɪ'dɪʃəs] *adj* spicciativo, spiccio

ex·pel [ɛks'pɛl] *v* (pret & pp -pelled; ger -pelling) *tr* espellere, scacciare

expend [ɛks'pɛnd] *tr* spendere, consumare

expendable [ɛks'pɛndəbəl] *adj* spendibile; da buttarsi via; (mil) da sacrificare

expenditure [ɛks'pɛndɪt/ər] *s* spesa

expense [ɛks'pɛns] *s* spesa; **at the expense of** al costo di; **expenses** spese *fpl*; **to meet expenses** far fronte alle spese

expense′ account′ *s* conto delle spese risarcibili

expensive [ɛks'pɛnsɪv] *adj* caro, costoso

experience [ɛks'pɪrɪ‚əns] *s* esperienza || *tr* sperimentare, provare

experienced [ɛks'pɪrɪ‚ənst] *adj* esperto, sperimentato

experiment [ɛks'pɛrɪmənt] *s* esperimento || [ɛks'pɛrɪ‚mɛnt] *intr* sperimentare

expert ['ɛkspərt] *adj & s* esperto

expertise [‚ɛkspər'tiz] *s* maestria

expiate ['ɛkspɪ‚et] *tr* espiare

expiation [‚ɛkspɪ'eʃən] *s* espiazione

expire [ɛks'paɪr] *tr* espirare || *intr (to breathe out)* espirare; *(said of a contract)* scadere; *(to die)* morire

explain [ɛks'plen] *tr* spiegare; **to explain away** giustificare; dar ragione di || *intr* spiegare, spiegarsi

explainable [ɛks'plenəbəl] *adj* spiegabile

explanation [‚ɛksplə'neʃən] *s* spiegazione, delucidazione

explanatory [ɛks'plænə‚tori] *adj* esplicativo

explicit [ɛks'plɪsɪt] *adj* esplicito

explode [ɛks'plod] *tr* far scoppiare; *(a theory)* smontare || *intr* scoppiare

exploit [ɛks'plɔɪt] *or* ['ɛksplɔɪt] *s* impresa, prodezza || [ɛks'plɔɪt] *tr* utilizzare, sfruttare

exploitation [‚ɛksplɔɪ'teʃən] *s* utilizzazione, sfruttamento

exploration [‚ɛksplə'reʃən] *s* esplorazione

explore [ɛks'plor] *tr* esplorare

explorer [ɛks'plorər] *s* esploratore *m*

explosion [ɛks'ploʒən] *s* esplosione, scoppio; *(of a theory)* confutazione

explosive [ɛks'plosɪv] *adj & s* esplosivo

exponent [ɛks'ponənt] *s* esponente *m*

export ['ɛksport] *adj* di esportazione || *s* esportazione, articolo di esportazione || [ɛks'port] *or* ['ɛksport] *tr & intr* esportare

exportation [‚ɛkspor'teʃən] *s* esportazione

exporter ['ɛksportər] *or* [ɛks'portər] *s* esportatore *m*

expose [ɛks'poz] *tr* esporre; *(to unmask)* smascherare

exposé [‚ɛkspo'ze] *s* rivelazione scandalosa, smascheramento

exposition [‚ɛkspə'zɪʃən] *s* esposizione; interpretazione, commento

expostulate [ɛks'pɑst/ə‚let] *intr* protestare; **to expostulate with** lagnarsi con

exposure [ɛks'poʒər] *s* *(disclosure)* rivelazione; *(situation with regard to sunlight)* esposizione; (phot) esposizione

expo′sure me′ter *s* (phot) fotometro, esposimetro

expound [ɛks'paund] *tr* esporre

express [ɛks'prɛs] *adj* espresso || *s* (rr) celere *m*, rapido, direttissimo; **by express** per espresso, a grande velocità || *adv* per espresso, a grande velocità || *tr* esprimere; mandare per espresso; *(to squeeze out)* spremere; **to express oneself** esprimersi

ex′press com′pany *s* servizio corriere

expression [ɛks'prɛʃən] *s* espressione

expressive [ɛks'prɛsɪv] *adj* espressivo

expressly [ɛks'prɛsli] *adv* espressamente

express′man *s* (-men) fattorino di servizio corriere

express′way′ *s* autostrada

expropriate [ɛks'propri‚et] *tr* espropriare

expulsion [ɛks'pʌlʃən] *s* espulsione

expunge [ɛksˈpʌndʒ] *tr* espungere
expurgate [ˈɛkspərˌget] *tr* espurgare
exquisite [ˈɛkskwɪzɪt] or [ɛksˈkwɪzɪt] *adj* squisito; intenso
ex'serv'ice-man' *s* (-men') ex combattente *m*
extant [ˈɛkstənt] or [ɛksˈtænt] *adj* ancora esistente
extemporaneous [ɛks ˌtɛmpəˈrenɪ-əs] *adj* estemporaneo; (*made for the occasion*) improvvisato
extempore [ɛksˈtɛmpəri] *adj* improvvisato || *adv* senza preparazione
extemporize [ɛksˈtɛmpəˌraɪz] *tr & intr* improvvisare
extend [ɛksˈtɛnd] *tr* allungare; estendere; (*e.g., aid*) offrire; (*payment of a debt*) dilazionare || *intr* estendersi
extended [ɛksˈtɛndɪd] *adj* esteso; prolungato
extension [ɛksˈtɛnʃən] *s* estensione; prolungamento; (com) proroga; (telp) derivazione
exten'sion lad'der *s* scala porta, scala a prolunga
exten'sion ta'ble *s* tavola allungabile
exten'sion tel'ephone' *s* telefono interno
extensive [ɛksˈtɛnsɪv] *adj* (*wide*) vasto; (*lengthy*) lungo; (*characterized by extention*) estensivo
extent [ɛksˈtɛnt] *s* estensione; **to a certain extent** fino a un certo punto; **to a great extent** in larga misura; **to the full extent** all'estremo limite
extenuate [ɛksˈtɛnjuˌet] *tr* (*to make seem less serious*) attenuare; (*to underrate*) sottovalutare
exterior [ɛksˈtɪrɪ-ər] *adj & s* esteriore *m*
exterminate [ɛksˈtʌrmɪˌnet] *tr* sterminare
external [ɛksˈtʌrnəl] *adj* esterno || externals *spl* esteriorità *f*, di fuori *m*
extinct [ɛksˈtɪŋkt] *adj* estinto
extinction [ɛksˈtɪŋkʃən] *s* estinzione
extinguish [ɛksˈtɪŋgwɪʃ] *tr* estinguere
extinguisher [ɛksˈtɪŋgwɪʃər] *s* estintore *m*
extirpate [ˈɛkstərˌpet] or [ɛksˈtʌrpet] *tr* estirpare
ex·tol [ɛksˈtol] or [ɛksˈtɑl] *v* (*pret & pp* -tolled; *ger* -tolling) *tr* inneggiare
extort [ɛksˈtɔrt] *tr* estorcere
extortion [ɛksˈtɔrʃən] *s* estorsione
extra [ˈɛkstrə] *adj* extra; (*spare*) di scorta || *s* (*of a newspaper*) edizione straordinaria; (*something additional*) soprappiù *m*; (theat) figurante *mf* || *adv* straordinariamente
ex'tra charge' *s* supplemento
extract [ˈɛkstrækt] *s* estratto || [ɛksˈtrækt] *tr* (*to pull out*) estrarre; (*to take from a book*) scegliere, selezionare
extraction [ɛksˈtrækʃən] *s* estrazione
extracurricular [ˌɛkstrəkəˈrɪkjələr] *adj* fuori del programma normale
extradition [ˌɛkstrəˈdɪʃən] *s* estradizione
ex'tra·dry' *adj* molto secco, brut
ex'tra fare' *s* supplemento al biglietto

ex'tra·mar'ital *adj* extraconiugale
extramural [ˌɛkstrəˈmjurəl] *adj* fuori della scuola, interscolastico; fuori delle mura
extraneous [ɛksˈtrenɪ-əs] *adj* estraneo
extraordinary [ˌɛkstrəˈɔrdɪ ˌneri] or [ɛksˈtrɔrdɪ ˌneri] *adj* straordinario
extrapolate [ɛksˈtræpəˌlet] *tr & intr* estrapolare
extrasensory [ˌɛkstrəˈsensəri] *adj* extrasensoriale
extravagance [ɛksˈtrævəgəns] *s* prodigalità *f*; (*wildness, folly*) stravaganza
extravagant [ɛksˈtrævəgənt] *adj* prodigo; (*wild, foolish*) stravagante
extreme [ɛksˈtrim] *adj & s* estremo; **in the extreme** in massimo grado; **to go to extremes** andare agli estremi
extremely [ɛksˈtrimli] *adv* estremamente, in sommo grado
extreme' unc'tion *s* Estrema Unzione
extremist [ɛksˈtrimɪst] *adj & s* estremista *mf*
extremi·ty [ɛksˈtrɛmɪti] *s* (-ties) estremità *f*; (*great want*) estrema necessità; extremities estremi *mpl*; (*hands and feet*) estremità *fpl*
extricate [ˈɛkstrɪ ˌket] *tr* districare
extrinsic [ɛksˈtrɪnsɪk] *adj* estrinseco
extrovert [ˈɛkstrə ˌvʌrt] *s* estroverso
extrude [ɛksˈtrud] *tr* estrudere || *intr* protrudere
exuberant [ɛgˈzubərənt] or [ɛgˈzjubərənt] *adj* esuberante
exude [ɛgˈzud] or [ɛkˈsud] *tr & intr* trasudare, stillare
exult [ɛgˈzʌlt] *intr* esultare, tripudiare
exultant [ɛgˈzʌltənt] *adj* esultante
eye [aɪ] *s* occhio; (*of hook and eye*) occhiello; **to catch one's eye** attirare l'attenzione di qlcu; **to feast one's eyes on** deliziarsi la vista con; **to lay eyes on** riuscire a vedere; **to make eyes at** fare gli occhi dolci a; **to roll one's eyes** stralunare gli occhi; **to see eye to eye** andare perfettamente d'accordo; **to shut one's eyes to** chiudere un occhio a; far finta di non vedere; **without batting an eye** senza batter ciglio || *v* (*pret & pp* eyed; *ger* eying or eyeing) *tr* occhieggiare; **to eye up and down** guardare da capo a piedi
eye'ball' *s* globo oculare
eye'bolt' *s* bullone *m* ad anello
eye'brow' *s* sopracciglio; **to raise one's eyebrows** inarcare le sopracciglia
eye'cup' *s* occhiera
eye'drop'per *s* contagocce *m*
eyeful [ˈaɪ ˌful] *s* vista, colpo d'occhio; (coll) bellezza
eye'glass' *s* (*of optical instrument*) lente *f*, oculare *m*; (*eyecup*) occhiera; eyeglasses occhiali *mpl*
eye'lash' *s* ciglio
eyelet [ˈaɪlɪt] *s* occhiello, maglietta, asola; (*hole to look through*) feritoia
eye'lid' *s* palpebra
eye' o'pener [ˈopənər] *s* affare *m* che apre gli occhi; (coll) bicchierino bevuto di mattina presto

eye'piece' s oculare m

eye'shade' s visiera

eye' shad'ow s rimmel m

eye'shot' s—**within eyeshot** a portata di vista

eye'sight' s vista; (*range*) capacità visiva

eye' sock'et s occhiaia, orbita

eye'sore' s pugno in un occhio

eye'strain' s vista affaticata

eye'-test chart' s tabella optometrica

eye'tooth' s (-teeth) dente canino; **to cut one's eyeteeth** (coll) fare esperienza; **to give one's eyeteeth for** (coll) dare un occhio della testa per

eye'wash' s (*flattery*) burro, lusinga; (pharm) collirio; (slang) balla

eye' wit'ness s testimone m oculare

F

F, f [ef] s sesta lettera dell'alfabeto inglese

fable ['febəl] s favola

fabric ['fæbrɪk] s stoffa, tessuto; fabbrica, struttura

fabricate ['fæbrɪ ˌket] tr fabbricare

fabrication [ˌfæbrɪ'keʃən] s fabbricazione; falsificazione, invenzione

fabulous ['fæbjələs] adj favoloso

façade [fə'sɑd] s facciata

face [fes] s volto, viso, faccia; (*surface*) superficie f; (*of coin*) diritto; (*of precious stone*) faccetta; (*of watch*) mostra; (*grimace*) smorfia; (*of building*) facciata; (typ) occhio; **in the face of** di fronte a; **to have a long face** fare il muso lungo; **to keep a straight face** contenere le risa; **to show one's face** farsi vedere || tr far fronte a, fronteggiare; (*a wall*) ricoprire; (*a suit*) foderare; **facing** di fronte a || intr—**to face about** voltarsi, fare dietro front; **to face on** dare a; **to face up to** guardare in faccia

face' card' s figura

face' lift'ing s plastica facciale

face' pow'der s cipria

facet ['fæsɪt] s faccetta; (fig) faccia

facetious [fə'siʃəs] adj faceto

face' val'ue s valore m facciale

facial ['feʃəl] adj facciale || s massaggio facciale

fa'cial tis'sue s velina detergente

facilitate [fə'sɪlɪ ˌtet] tr facilitare

facil·i·ty [fə'sɪlɪti] s (-ties) facilità f; **facilities** (*installations*) attrezzature fpl; (*for transportation*) mezzi mpl; (*services*) servizi mpl

facing ['fesɪŋ] s rivestimento

facsimile [fæk'sɪmɪli] s facsimile m

fact [fækt] s fatto; **in fact** in realtà; **the fact is that** il fatto si è che

faction ['fækʃən] s fazione; discordia

factional ['fækʃənəl] adj fazioso; (*partisan*) partigiano

factionalism ['fækʃənə ˌlɪzəm] s partigianeria; parzialità f

factor ['fæktər] s fattore m || tr scomporre in fattori

facto·ry ['fæktəri] s (-ries) fabbrica

factual ['fæktʃʊ-əl] adj effettivo, reale

facul·ty ['fækəlti] s (-ties) facoltà f

fad [fæd] s moda passeggera

fade [fed] tr stingere || intr (*said of colors*) stingersi, sbiadire; (*said of*

sounds, sight, radio signals, memory, etc.) svanire, affievolirsi; (*said of beauty*) sfiorire

fade'-out' s affievolimento, affievolirsi m; (mov) chiusura in dissolvenza; (rad, telv) evanescenza

fading ['fedɪŋ] s affievolimento; (mov) dissolvenza; (rad, telv) evanescenza

fag [fæg] s schiavo del lavoro; (coll) sigaretta || tr—**to fag out** stancare

fagot ['fægət] s fascina, fastello

fail [fel] s—**without fail** senza meno || tr mancare (with dat); (*a student*) riprovare; (*an examination*) farsi bocciare in || intr fallire, venire a meno; (*said of a student*) farsi riprovare; (*said of a motor*) rompersi, fermarsi; (com) cadere in fallimento; **to fail to** mancare di

failure ['feljər] s insuccesso; insufficienza; (*student*) bocciato; (com) fallimento

faint [fent] adj debole; **to feel faint** sentirsi mancare || s svenimento || intr svenire

faint-hearted ['fent'hɑrtɪd] adj codardo, timido

fair [fer] adj giusto, onesto; (*moderately large*) discreto; (*even*) liscio; (*civil*) gentile; (*hair*) biondo; (*complexion*) chiaro; (*sky, weather*) sereno || s (*exhibition*) fiera; (*carnival*) sagra || adv direttamente; **to play fair** agire onestamente

fair'ground' s terreno dell'esposizione, campo della fiera

fairly ['ferli] adv giustamente, imparzialmente; discretamente, abbastanza; completamente

fair-minded ['fer'maɪndɪd] adj equanime, equo, giusto

fairness ['fernɪs] s giustizia, imparzialità f; bellezza; (*of complexion*) bianchezza

fair' play' s comportamento leale

fair' sex' s bel sesso

fair'-weath'er adj—**a fair-weather friend** un amico del tempo felice

fair·y ['feri] adj fatato || s (-ies) fata; (slang) finocchio

fair'y god'mother s buona fata

fair'y·land' s terra delle fate

fair'y tale' s fiaba, racconto delle fate

faith [feθ] s fede f; **to break faith with** venir meno alla parola data a; **to keep faith with** tener fede alla parola

data a; **to pin one's faith on** porre
tutte le proprie speranze su; **upon
my faith!** in fede mia!

faithful [ˈfeθfəl] *adj* fedele || **the faith-
ful** i fedeli

faithless [ˈfeθlɪs] *adj* infedele, sleale

fake [fek] *adj* falso, finto || *s* contraffa-
zione; *(person)* imbroglione *m* || *tr &
intr* contraffare, falsificare

faker [ˈfekər] *s* (coll) imbroglione *m*

falcon [ˈfɔkən] or [ˈfɔlkən] *s* falcone
m

falconer [ˈfɔkənər] or [ˈfɔlkənər] *s*
falconiere *m*

falconry [ˈfɔkənri] or [ˈfɔlkənri] *s*
falconeria

fall [fɔl] *adj* autunnale || *s* caduta; *(of
water)* cataratta, cascata; *(of prices)*
ribasso; *(autumn)* autunno; **falls** ca-
taratta, cascate *fpl* || *v* *(pret* **fell**
[fel]; *pp* **fallen** [ˈfɔlən]) *intr* cadere;
discendere; **to fall apart** farsi a pezzi;
to fall back (mil) ripiegare; **to fall
behind** rimanere indietro; **to fall
down** cadere; stramazzare; **to fall
due** scadere; **to fall flat** stramazzare;
essere un insuccesso; **to fall for**
(slang) lasciarsi abbindolare da;
(slang) innamorarsi di; **to fall in**
(said of a building) crollare; (mil)
allinearsi; **to fall in with** imbattersi
in; mettersi d'accordo con; **to fall
off** ritirarsi; diminuire; **to fall out**
accadere; essere in disaccordo; (mil)
rompere i ranghi; **to fall out of**
cadere da; **to fall out with** inimicarsi
con; **to fall over** cadere; (coll) adulare; **to fall through** fallire; **to fall to**
cominciare; (coll) cominciare a mangiare; *(said, e.g., of an inheritance)*
ricadere su; **to fall under** rientrare in

fallacious [fəˈleʃəs] *adj* fallace

falla·cy [ˈfæləsi] *s* (**-cies**) fallacia

fall' guy' *s* (slang) testa di turco

fallible [ˈfælɪbəl] *adj* fallibile

fall'ing star' *s* stella cadente

fall'out' *s* pulviscolo radioattivo

fall'out shel'ter *s* rifugio antiatomico

fallow [ˈfælo] *adj* incolto; **to lie fallow**
rimanere incolto || *s* maggese *m* || *tr*
maggesare

false [fɔls] *adj* falso; *(hair, teeth, etc.)*
posticcio, finto || *adv* falsamente; **to
play false** tradire

false' bot'tom *s* doppio fondo

false' col'ors *spl* apparenze mentite

false' face' *s* maschera; *(ugly false
face)* mascherone *m*

false'-heart'ed [ˈfɔlsˈhɑrtɪd] *adj* perfido

falsehood [ˈfɔls·hʊd] *s* falsità *f*, falso

false' preten'ses *spl* falso, impostura;
under false pretenses allegando ragioni false

falset·to [fɔlˈsɛto] *s* (**-tos**) *(voice)* falsetto; *(person)* cantante *m* in falsetto

falsi·fy [ˈfɔlsɪ ˌfaɪ] *v* (*pret & pp* **-fied**)
tr falsificare; *(to disprove)* smentire ||
intr mentire

falsi·ty [ˈfɔlsɪti] *s* (**-ties**) falsità *f*

falter [ˈfɔltər] *s* vacillamento; *(in*

speech) balbettio || *intr* vacillare;
balbettare

fame [fem] *s* fama

famed [femd] *adj* famoso

familiar [fəˈmɪljər] *adj* familiare; intimo; **to be familiar with** *(people)*
aver pratica con; *(things)* aver pratica di

familiari·ty [fə ˌmɪlɪˈærɪti] *s* (**-ties**) familiarità *f*, dimesticchezza

familiarize [fəˈmɪljə ˌraɪz] *tr* far conoscere

fami·ly [ˈfæmɪli] *adj* familiare; **in the
family way** (coll) in altro stato || *s*
(**-lies**) famiglia

fam'ily man' *s* (**men'**) padre *m* di famiglia

fam'ily name' *s* cognome *m*

fam'ily tree' *s* albero genealogico

famine [ˈfæmɪn] *s* carestia

famished [ˈfæmɪʃt] *adj* famelico; **to be
famished** avere una fame da lupo

famous [ˈfeməs] *adj* famoso; (coll) eccellente

fan [fæn] *s* ventaglio; (elec) ventilatore
m; (coll) tifoso, patito || *v* *(pret &
pp* **fanned**); *ger* **fanning**) *tr* svento-
gliare; *(to winnow)* vagliare; *(fire,
passions)* attizzare || *intr* sventa-
gliarsi; **to fan out** *(said of a road)*
diramarsi a ventaglio

fanatic [fəˈnætɪk] *adj & s* fanatico

fanatical [fəˈnætɪkəl] *adj* fanatico

fanaticism [fəˈnætɪ ˌsɪzəm] *s* fanatismo

fan' belt' *s* (aut) cinghia del ventilatore

fancied [ˈfænsɪd] *adj* immaginario

fancier [ˈfænsɪ·ər] *s* maniaco, tifoso;
(of animals) conoscitore *m*, allevatore *m*

fanciful [ˈfænsɪfəl] *adj* fantasioso,
estroso; immaginario

fan·cy [ˈfænsi] *adj* (**-cier; -ciest**) immaginario; immaginativo; ornamentale;
di lusso; fantasioso, estroso || *s* fanta-
sia; *(whim)* grillo, estro; **to take a
fancy to** prendere una passione per
|| *v* (*pret & pp* **-cied**) *tr* immaginare

fan'cy ball' *s* ballo in costume

fan'cy dress' *s* costume *m*

fan'cy foods' *spl* cibi *mpl* di lusso

fan'cy-free' *adj* libero dai lacci del-
l'amore

fan'cy skat'ing *s* pattinaggio artistico

fan'cy-work' *s* (sew) ricamo ornamentale

fanfare [ˈfænfer] *s* fanfara

fang [fæŋ] *s* zanna; *(of reptile)* dente
velenoso

fan'light' *s* lunetta

fantastic(al) [fænˈtæstɪk(əl)] *adj* fan-
tastico

fanta·sy [ˈfæntəzi] or [ˈfæntəsi] *s*
(**-sies**) fantasia

far [fɑr] *adj* distante; **on the far side
of** dall'altra parte di || *adv* lontano;
as far as fino a; **as far as I am concerned** per quanto mi riguardi; **as far
as I know** per quanto io sappia; **by
far** di gran lunga; **far and near** in
lungo e in largo; **far away** molto lontano; **far be it from me** Dio me ne
scampi e liberi; **far better** molto

meglio; molto migliore; **far different** molto differente; **far from** lontano da; **far from it** tutto al contrario; **far into** fino al fondo di; **far into the night** fino a tarda ora; **far more** molto più; **far off** lontanissimo; **how far** quanto lontano; **how far is it?** a che distanza è da qui?; **in so far as** in quanto; **thus far** sinora; **to go far towards** contribuire molto a

faraway ['fɑrə‚we] *adj* distante, lontano; distratto

farce [fɑrs] *s* farsa

farcical ['fɑrsɪkəl] *adj* farsesco

fare [fer] *s* prezzo della corsa; passeggero; (*food*) vitto || *intr* andare, e.g., **how did you fare?** come Le è andata?

Far' East' *s* Estremo Oriente

fare'well' *s* congedo, commiato; **to bid farewell to** or **to take farewell of** prender commiato da || *interj* addio!

far-fetched ['fɑr'fɛt/t] *adj* peregrino, campato in aria

far-flung ['fɑr'flʌŋ] *adj* ampio; d'ampia distribuzione

farm [fɑrm] *adj* agricolo || *s* fattoria, tenuta || *tr* (*land*) coltivare || *intr* fare l'agricoltore or l'allevatore

farmer ['fɑrmər] *s* agricoltore *m*, contadino

farm' hand' *s* bracciante *m*

farm'house' *s* casa colonica, masseria

farming ['fɑrmɪŋ] *s* agricoltura, coltivazione

farm'yard' *s* aia

far'-off' *adj* lontano

far-reaching ['fɑr'rit/ɪŋ] *adj* di grande portata

far-sighted ['fɑr'saɪtɪd] *adj* lungimirante; perspicace; presbite

farther ['fɑrðər] *adj* più lontano; addizionale || *adv* più lontano, più in là; inoltre; **farther on** più oltre

farthest ['fɑrðɪst] *adj* (il) più lontano; ultimo || *adv* al massimo

farthing ['fɑrðɪŋ] *s* (Brit) quarto di centesimo

Far' West' *s* (U.S.A.) lontano Occidente

fascinate ['fæsɪ‚net] *tr* affascinare

fascinating ['fæsɪ‚netɪŋ] *adj* incantatore, affascinante

fascism ['fæʃɪzəm] *s* fascismo

fascist ['fæʃɪst] *adj* & *s* fascista *mf*

fashion ['fæʃən] *s* voga, moda; foggia, maniera; alta società; **after a fashion** in certo modo; **in fashion** di moda; **out of fashion** fuori moda; **to go out of fashion** passare di moda || *tr* fare, foggiare

fashionable ['fæʃənəbəl] *adj* elegante, alla moda

fash'ion design'ing *s* alta moda

fash'ion plate' *s* figurino

fash'ion show' *s* sfilata di moda

fast [fæst] or [fɑst] *adj* veloce; (*clock*) che corre, in anticipo; dissoluto; ben legato; (*color*) solido; (*friend*) fedele || *s* digiuno; **to break fast** rompere il digiuno || *adv* rapidamente; fortemente; (*asleep*) profondamente; **to hold fast** tenersi saldo; **to live fast** condurre una vita dissoluta || *intr* digiunare, fare vigilia

fast' day' *s* giorno di magro

fasten ['fæsən] or ['fɑsən] *tr* fissare; attaccare; (*a door*) sbarrare; (*a nickname; blows*) affibbiare; (*a dress*) allacciarsi || *intr* attaccarsi

fastener ['fæsənər] or ['fɑsənər] *s* legaccio, laccio; (*snap, clasp*) fermaglio; (*for papers*) fermacarte *m*

fastidious [fæs'tɪdɪ‚əs] *adj* schizzinoso; meticoloso

fasting ['fæstɪŋ] or ['fɑstɪŋ] *s* digiuno

fat [fæt] *adj* (**fatter; fattest**) grasso; (*productive*) forte, ricco, pingue; **to get fat** ingrassare || *s* grasso, unto; (*of pork*) sugna

fatal ['fetəl] *adj* fatale

fatalism ['fetə‚lɪzəm] *s* fatalismo

fatalist ['fetəlɪst] *s* fatalista *mf*

fatali·ty [fə'tælɪti] *s* (**-ties**) (*in an accident*) morte *f*; accidente *m* mortale; fatalità *f*

fate [fet] *s* fato; **the Fates** le Parche || *tr* predestinare

fated ['fetɪd] *adj* destinato

fateful ['fetfəl] *adj* fatidico, fatale

fat'head' *s* (coll) zuccone *m*

father ['fɑðər] *s* padre *m*; (*male ancestor*) antenato || *tr* procreare; creare; assumere la paternità di

fatherhood ['fɑðər‚hʊd] *s* paternità *f*

fa'ther-in-law' *s* (**fathers-in-law**) suocero

fa'ther-land' *s* patria

fatherless ['fɑðərlɪs] *adj* orfano di padre; senza padre

fatherly ['fɑðərli] *adj* paterno

Fa'ther's Day' *s* festa del papà

Fa'ther Time' *s* il Tempo

fathom ['fæðəm] *s* braccio || *tr* sondare

fathomless ['fæðəmlɪs] *adj* senza fondo; imponderabile

fatigue [fə'tig] *s* fatica, strapazzo; (mil) comandata || *tr* stancare, affaticare

fatigue' clothes' *spl* (mil) tenuta di servizio, tenuta di fatica

fatten ['fætən] *tr* & *intr* ingrassare

fat·ty ['fæti] *adj* (**-tier; -tiest**) grasso; (pathol) adiposo || *s* (**-ties**) (coll) tombolo

fatuous ['fæt/ʊ‚əs] *adj* fatuo

faucet ['fɔsɪt] *s* rubinetto

fault [fɔlt] *s* (*misdeed, blame*) colpa; (*defect*) difetto, magagna; (geol) faglia; (sports) fallo; **it's your fault** è colpa Sua; **to a fault** all'eccesso; **to find fault with** trovare a ridire sul conto di

fault'find'er *s* ipercritico, criticone *m*

fault'find'ing *adj* criticone || *s* ipercritica

faultless ['fɔltlɪs] *adj* perfetto, inappuntabile

fault·y ['fɔlti] *adj* (**-ier; -iest**) manchevole, difettoso

faun [fɔn] *s* fauno

fauna ['fɔnə] *s* fauna

favor ['fevər] *s* favore *m*; (*letter*) pregiata; **do me the favor to** mi faccia il piacere di; **by your favor** col Suo permesso; **favors** regali *mpl* di festa; **to be in favor with** essere nelle grazie di; **to be out of favor** cadere in disgrazia || *tr* favorire; (coll) assomigliare (with *dat*)

favorable ['fevərəbəl] *adj* favorevole

favorite ['fevərɪt] *adj & s* favorito

favoritism ['fevərɪ,tɪzəm] *s* favoritismo

fawn [fɔn] *s* cerbiatto || *intr*—**to fawn on** adulare, strusciarsi a

faze [fez] *tr* (coll) perturbare

fear [fɪr] *s* paura; **for fear of** per paura di; **for fear that** per paura che; **no fear** non c'è pericolo; **to be in fear of** aver timore di || *tr & intr* temere

fearful ['fɪrfəl] *adj* pauroso, timorato; (coll) spaventoso

fearless ['fɪrlɪs] *adj* impavido

feasible ['fizɪbəl] *adj* fattibile, possibile

feast [fist] *s* festa; (*sumptuous meal*) festino, banchetto || *tr* intrattenere || *intr* banchettare; **to feast on** rallegrarsi alla vista di

feat [fit] *s* fatto, prodezza

feather ['fɛðər] *s* penna, (*soft and fluffy structure covering bird*) piuma; (*type*) qualità *f*, conio; (*tuft*) pennacchio; **in fine feather** di buon umore; **in buona salute** || *tr* impennare; coprire di piume; (naut) spalare; (aer) bandierare; **to feather one's nest** arricchirsi

feath'er bed' *s* letto di piume

feath'er·bed'ding *s* impiego di mano d'opera non necessaria richiesto da un sindacato operaio

feath'er·brain' *s* cervello di gallina

feath'er·edge' *s* (*of board*) augnatura; (*of sharpened tool*) filo morto

feath'er·weight' *s* peso piuma

feathery ['fɛðəri] *adj* piumato; leggero

feature ['fitʃər] *s* fattezza; caratteristica; (journ) articolo principale; (mov) attrazione; **features** fattezze *fpl* || *tr* caratterizzare; mettere in evidenza; (coll) immaginare

fea'ture film' *s* lungometraggio

fea'ture sto'ry *s* articolo di spalla

February ['fɛbru,ɛri] *s* febbraio

feces ['fisiz] *spl* feci *fpl*

feckless ['fɛklɪs] *adj* debole; inetto

federal ['fɛdərəl] *adj* federale || *s* federalista *mf*

federate ['fɛdə,ret] *adj* federato || *tr* federare || *intr* federarsi

federation [,fɛdə'reʃən] *s* federazione

federative ['fɛdə,retɪv] *or* ['fɛdərətɪv] *adj* federativo

fedora [fɪ'dorə] *s* cappello floscio di feltro

fed' up' ['fɛd] *adj* stanco e stufo; **to be fed up with** averne fin sopra gli occhi di

fee [fi] *s* onorario; (*charge allowed by law*) diritto; (*tip*) mancia; (*for tuition*) tassa; (*for admission*) ingresso || *tr* pagare

feeble ['fibəl] *adj* debole, fievole

feeble-minded ['fibəl'maɪndɪd] *adj* rimbecillito; debole, vacillante

feed [fid] *s* mangime *m;* (coll) mangiata; (mach) dispositivo d'alimentazione || *v* (*pret & pp* **fed** [fɛd]) *tr* nutrire; (*a machine*) alimentare; (*cattle*) pascere; (theat) imbeccare || *intr* mangiare; **to feed upon** nutrirsi di

feed'back' *s* (*of a computer*) ritorno d'informazioni; (electron) reazione

feed' bag' *s* musetta

feed' pump' *s* pompa di alimentazione

feed' trough' *s* (*for cattle*) vasca; (*for hogs*) trogolo

feed' wire' *s* cavo di alimentazione

feel [fil] *s* sensazione; (*touch*) tocco; (*vague mental impression*) senso || *v* (*pret & pp* **felt** [fɛlt]) *tr* sentire; (*e.g., with the hands*) palpare, toccare; (*s.o.'s pulse*) tastare || *intr* (*sick, tired, etc.*) sentirsi; **to feel bad** sentirsi male; (*to be unhappy*) essere spiacente; **to feel cheap** vergognarsi; **to feel comfortable** sentirsi a proprio agio; **to feel for** cercare di toccare; avere compassione per; **to feel like** aver voglia di; **to feel safe** sentirsi al sicuro; **to feel sorry** essere spiacente; pentirsi; **to feel sorry for** aver compassione di; pentirsi di

feeler ['filər] *s* (*hint*) sondaggio; **feelers** (*of insect*) antenne *fpl;* (*of mollusk*) tentacoli *mpl;* **to put out feelers** (fig) tastare il terreno

feeling ['filɪŋ] *s* (*with senses*) senso; (*impression, emotion*) sentimento, sensazione; opinione

feign [fen] *tr* fingere; inventare; imitare || *intr* far finta; **to feign to be** fingersi

feint [fent] *s* finta || *intr* fare una finta

feldspar ['fɛld,spar] *s* feldspato

felicitate [fə'lɪsɪ,tet] *tr* felicitarsi con

felicitous [fə'lɪsɪtəs] *adj* felice, indovinato; eloquente

fell [fɛl] *adj* crudele, mortale || *tr* (*trees*) abbattere

felloe ['fɛlo] *s* cerchione *m;* (*part of the rim*) gavello

fellow ['fɛlo] *s* compagno; collega *m;* (*of a society*) membro, socio; (*holder of fellowship*) borsista *mf;* (coll) tipo, tizio; (coll) innamorato; **good fellow** buon diavolo; galantuomo

fel'low cit'izen *s* concittadino

fel'low coun'try·man *s* (-men) concittadino

fel'low crea'ture *s* prossimo

fel'low-man' *s* (-men') prossimo

fel'low mem'ber *s* consocio

fellowship ['fɛlo,ʃɪp] *s* compagnia; (*for study*) borsa di studio

fel'low trav'eler *s* simpatizzante *mf;* criptocomunista *mf;* compagno di viaggio

felon ['fɛlən] *s* criminale *mf;* (pathol) patereccio, giradito

felo·ny ['fɛləni] *s* (-nies) delitto doloso

felt [fɛlt] *s* feltro

felt' board' *s* lavagna di panno

felt'-tip pen' *s* pennarello

female ['fimel] *adj* (*sex*) femminile;

(*animal, plant, piece of a device*) femmina || s femmina
feminine ['fɛmɪnɪn] adj & s femminile m
feminism ['fɛmɪ ,nɪzəm] s femminismo
fence [fɛns] s steccato, staccionata; (*for stolen goods*) ricettatore m; (carp) squadra di guida; (sports) scherma; **on the fence** (coll) indeciso || tr recingere || intr tirare di scherma
fencing ['fɛnsɪŋ] s scherma; (fig) schermaglia
fenc'ing mask' s visiera
fend [fɛnd] tr—**to fend off** parare || intr—**to fend for oneself** (coll) badare a sé stesso
fender ['fɛndər] s (*of trolley car*) salvagente m; (*of fireplace*) parafuoco; (aut) parafango; (naut) parabordo
fennel ['fɛnəl] s finocchio
ferment ['fɜrmɛnt] s fermento || [fər'mɛnt] tr & intr fermentare
fern [fɜrn] s felce f
ferocious [fə'roʃəs] adj feroce
ferocity [fə'rɑsɪti] s ferocia
ferret ['fɛrɪt] s furetto || tr—**to ferret out** scovare || intr indagare
Fer'ris wheel' ['fɛrɪs] s ruota (del parco dei divertimenti)
fer-ry ['fɛri] s (-ries) traghetto; nave f traghetto || v (pret & pp -ried) tr traghettare || intr attraversare
fer'ry·boat' s nave f traghetto, ferry-boat m
fertile ['fɜrtɪl] adj fertile
fertilize ['fɜrtɪ ,laɪz] tr fertilizzare; (*to impregnate*) fecondare
fertilizer ['fɜrtɪ ,laɪzər] s fertilizzante m; (*e.g., of flowers*) fecondatore m
fervent ['fɜrvənt] adj fervente, fervido
fervid ['fɜrvɪd] adj fervido
fervor ['fɜrvər] s fervore m
fester ['fɛstər] s ulcera, piaga || tr corrompere || intr suppurare; (fig) corrompersi
festival ['fɛstɪvəl] adj festivo || s festa; (*of music*) festival m
festive ['fɛstɪv] adj festivo
festivi·ty [fɛs'tɪvɪti] s (-ties) festività f
festoon [fɛs'tun] s festone m || tr ornare di festoni
fetch [fɛtʃ] tr andare a prendere; (a price) fruttare, vendersi per
fetching ['fɛtʃɪŋ] adj (coll) cattivante, attraente
fete [fet] s festa || tr festeggiare
fetid ['fɛtɪd] or ['fitɪd] adj fetido
fetish ['fitɪ/] or ['fɛtɪʃ] s feticcio
fetlock ['fɛtlɑk] s nocca; (*tuft of hair*) barbetta
fetter ['fɛtər] s ceppo, catena || tr mettere ai ceppi, incatenare
fettle ['fɛtəl] s stato, condizione; **in fine fettle** in buone condizioni
fetus ['fitəs] s feto
feud [fjud] s antagonismo; odio ereditario || intr essere in lotta
feudal ['fjudəl] adj feudale
feudalism ['fjudə ,lɪzəm] s feudalismo
fever ['fivər] s febbre f
feverish ['fivərɪʃ] adj febbrile
few [fju] adj & pron pochi; **a few** alcuni; **quite a few** molti

fiancé [,fi·ɑn'se] s fidanzato
fiancée [,fi·ɑn'se] s fidanzata
fias·co [fɪ'æsko] s (-cos or -coes) fiasco
fib [fɪb] s menzogna, frottola || v (pret & pp fibbed; ger fibbing) intr raccontar frottole
fiber ['faɪbər] s fibra; (fig) tempra
fi'ber·glass' s vetroresina
fibrous ['faɪbrəs] adj fibroso
fickle ['fɪkəl] adj volubile, incostante, mobile
fiction ['fɪkʃən] s (*invention*) finzione; (*branch of literature*) novellistica
fictional ['fɪkʃənəl] adj immaginario
fictionalize ['fɪkʃənə ,laɪz] tr romanzare
fictitious [fɪk'tɪʃəs] adj fittizio
fiddle ['fɪdəl] s violino; **fit as a fiddle** in perfetta salute || tr (coll) suonare sul violino; **to fiddle away** (coll) sprecare || intr (coll) suonare il violino; **to fiddle with** (coll) giocherellare con
fiddler ['fɪdlər] s (coll) violinista mf
fiddling ['fɪdlɪŋ] adj triviale, futile, insignificante
fideli·ty [faɪ'dɛlɪti] or [fɪ'dɛlɪti] s (-ties) fedeltà f
fidget ['fɪdʒɪt] intr agitarsi; **to fidget with** giocherellare con
fidgety ['fɪdʒɪti] adj irrequieto
fiduciar·y [fɪ'dju/ɪ ,ɛri] or [fɪ'du/ɪ ,ɛri] adj fiduciario || s (-ies) fiduciario
fie [faɪ] interj vergogna!
fief [fif] s feudo
field [fild] adj (mil) da campagna || s campo; (sports) terreno; (min) giacimento; (*of motor or dynamo*) (elec) induttore m; (phys) campo
fielder ['fildər] s (*outfielder*) giocatore m del campo esterno
field' glass'es spl binocolo
field' hock'ey s hockey m su prato
field' mag'net s induttore m, calamita induttrice
field' mar'shal s (mil) maresciallo di campo
field' mouse' s topo di campagna
field'piece' s pezzo da campagna
fiend [find] s diavolo; (coll) addetto, tifoso
fiendish ['findɪʃ] adj diabolico
fierce [fɪrs] adj fiero, feroce; (wind) furioso; (coll) maledetto
fierceness ['fɪrsnɪs] s ferocia
fier·y ['faɪri] or ['faɪ·əri] adj (-ier; -iest) ardente, focoso
fife [faɪf] s piffero
fifteen ['fɪf'tin] adj, s & pron quindici m
fifteenth ['fɪf'tinθ] adj, s & pron quindicesimo || s (*in dates*) quindici m
fifth [fɪfθ] adj, s & pron quinto || s (*in dates*) cinque m
fifth' col'umn s quinta colonna
fiftieth ['fɪftɪ·ɪθ] adj, s & pron cinquantesimo
fif·ty ['fɪfti] adj & pron cinquanta || s (-ties) cinquanta m; **the fifties** gli anni cinquanta

fif'ty-fif'ty *adv*—to go fifty-fifty fare a metà

fig [fɪg] *s* fico

fight [faɪt] *s* lotta; baruffa; combattimento; spirito combattivo; (sports) incontro; **to pick a fight with** attaccar briga con ‖ *v* (*pret & pp* fought [fɔt]) *tr* lottare con; combattere contro; opporsi a ‖ *intr* lottare; combattere; **to fight shy of** cercar di evitare

fighter ['faɪtər] *s* lottatore *m;* (*warrior*) combattente *m;* (aer) caccia *m*

fig' leaf' *s* foglia di fico

figment ['fɪgmənt] *s* finzione

figurative ['fɪgjərətɪv] *adj* (fa) figurativo; (rhet) figurato

figure ['fɪgjər] *s* figura; numero; prezzo; **to be good at figures** far bene di conto; **to cut a figure** fare una buona figura; **to keep one's figure** conservare la linea ‖ *tr* figurare; immaginare; raffigurare; supporre, calcolare; **to figure out** calcolare; decifrare ‖ *intr* apparire; **to figure on** (coll) contare su

fig'ure-head' *s* uomo di paglia, prestanome *m;* (naut) polena

fig'ure of speech' *s* figura retorica

fig'ure skat'ing *s* pattinaggio artistico

figurine [ˌfɪgjə'rin] *s* figurina

filament ['fɪləmənt] *s* filamento

filbert ['fɪlbərt] *s* (*tree*) nocciolo, avellano; (*nut*) nocciola, avellana

filch [fɪltʃ] *tr* rubacchiare

file [faɪl] *s* (*row*) fila; (*tool*) lima; (*folder*) filza; (*room*) archivio; (*of cards*) schedario ‖ *tr* mettere in fila; limare; archiviare, schedare; (journ) trasmettere ‖ *intr* sfilare; **to file for** fare domanda di

file' clerk' *s* schedarista *mf*

filet [fɪ'le] or ['fɪle] *s* filetto ‖ *tr* tagliare in filetti

filial ['fɪlɪ·əl] or ['fɪljəl] *adj* filiale

filiation [ˌfɪlɪ'eʃən] *s* filiazione

filibuster ['fɪlɪ ˌbʌstər] *s* (tactics) ostruzionismo; (*speech*) discorso ostruzionista; (*person making such a speech*) ostruzionista *mf;* (*buccaneer*) filibustiere *m* ‖ *tr* fare ostruzionismo contro ‖ *intr* fare dell'ostruzionismo

filigree ['fɪlɪ ˌgri] *adj* filigranato ‖ *s* filigrana ‖ *tr* lavorare in filigrana

filing ['faɪlɪŋ] *s* (of documents) schedatura; limatura; filings limatura

fil'ing cab'inet *s* schedario

fil'ing card' *s* cartellino, scheda

fill [fɪl] *s* sazietà *f;* (*place filled with earth*) terrapieno; **to have** or **get one's fill** mangiare a sazietà ‖ *tr* riempire; (*an order*) eseguire; (*a hole*) otturare; (*a tooth*) piombare; (*a tire*) gonfiare; (*a place*) occupare; (*with sand*) interrare; **to fill out** (*a form*) riempire; **to fill up** (aut) fare il pieno di ‖ *intr* riempirsi; **to fill in** prendere il posto; **to fill up** riempirsi

filler ['fɪlər] *s* ripieno; (*person*) riempitore *m;* (painting) mestica; (journ) articolo riempitivo

fillet ['fɪlɪt] *s* nastro, fascia; (*for hair*) nastro; (archit) listello ‖ *tr* filettare ‖ ['fɪle] or ['fɪlɪt] *s* (of meat or fish) filetto ‖ *tr* tagliare a filetti

filling ['fɪlɪŋ] *s* (of a tooth) impiombatura; (of turkey) ripieno

fill'ing sta'tion *s* stazione di rifornimento

fillip ['fɪlɪp] *s* stimolo; colpetto col dito ‖ *tr* dare un colpetto col dito a; (fig) stimulare

fil·ly ['fɪli] *s* (-lies) puledra

film [fɪlm] *s* pellicola; (mov, phot) pellicola, film *m* ‖ *tr* filmare

film' li'brary *s* cineteca, filmoteca

film'strip' *s* filmina

film·y ['fɪlmi] *adj* (-ier; -iest) sottile, delicato; (*look*) annebbiato

filter ['fɪltər] *s* filtro ‖ *tr & intr* filtrare

filtering ['fɪltərɪŋ] *s* filtrazione

fil'ter pa'per *s* carta da filtro

fil'ter tip' *s* filtro, bocchino filtro

filth [fɪlθ] *s* sporco, sporcizia

filth·y ['fɪlθi] *adj* (-ier; -iest) sporco, sudicio

filth'y lu'cre ['lukər] *s* il vile metallo

filtrate ['fɪltret] *s* liquido filtrato ‖ *tr & intr* filtrare

fin [fɪn] *s* pinna; (slang) biglietto da cinque dollari

final ['faɪnəl] *adj* finale; (*last in a series*) ultimo; definitivo, insindacabile ‖ *s* esame *m* finale; **finals** (sports) finale *f*

finale [fɪ'nɑli] *s* (mus) finale *m*

finalist ['faɪnəlɪst] *s* finalista *mf*

finally ['faɪnəli] *adv* finalmente

finance [fɪ'næns] or ['faɪnæns] *s* finanza; **finances** finanze *fpl* ‖ *tr* finanziare

financial [fɪ'nænʃəl] or [faɪ'nænʃəl] *adj* finanziario

financier [ˌfɪnən'sɪr] or [ˌfaɪnən'sɪr] *s* finanziere *m*

financing [fɪ'nænsɪŋ] or ['faɪnænsɪŋ] *s* finanziamento

finch [fɪntʃ] *s* fringuello

find [faɪnd] *s* trovata ‖ *v* (*pret & pp* found [faʊnd]) *tr* trovare; rinvenire; (*s.o. innocent* or *guilty*) dichiarare; **to find out** venire a sapere ‖ *tr* (law) sentenziare; **to find out about** informarsi su

finder ['faɪndər] *s* (phot) mirino; (astr) cannochiale cercatore

finding ['faɪndɪŋ] *s* scoperta; (law) sentenza

fine [faɪn] *adj* buono; bello; fino, fine ‖ *s* multa ‖ *adv* (coll) benissimo; **to feel fine** (coll) sentirsi benissimo ‖ *tr* multare

fine' arts' *spl* belle arti

fineness ['faɪnnɪs] *s* finezza; (of metal) titolo

fine' print' *s* testo in caratteri minuti

finer·y ['faɪnəri] *s* (-ies) ornamenti *mpl*, fronzoli *mpl;* abito vistoso

fine-spun ['faɪn ˌspʌn] *adj* sottile

finesse [fɪ'nɛs] *s* finezza; (bridge) impasse *f* ‖ *tr* fare l'impasse a ‖ *intr* fare l'impasse

fine'-tooth comb' *s* pettine fitto; **to go over with a fine-tooth comb** esaminare minuziosamente

finger [ˈfɪŋgər] *s* dito; **to have a finger in the pie** avere le mani in pasta; **to put one's finger on the spot** mettere il dito nella piaga; **to slip between the fingers** sfuggire di tra le dita; **to snap one's fingers at** infischiarsi di; **to twist around one's little finger** fare ciò che si vuole di ‖ *tr* toccare con le dita; (*to pilfer*) rubacchiare; (slang) mostrare a dito

fin'ger board' *s* (mus) tastiera

fin'ger bowl' *s* sciacquadita *m*

fingering [ˈfɪŋgərɪŋ] *s* palpeggiamento; (mus) diteggiatura

fin'ger mark' *s* ditata

fin'ger-nail' *s* unghia

fin'ger-print' *s* impronta digitale ‖ *tr* prendere le impronte digitali di

fin'ger-tip' *s* polpastrello; **to have at one's fingertips** avere sulla punta delle dita, sapere a menadito

finical [ˈfɪnɪkəl] or **finicky** [ˈfɪnɪki] *adj* pignolo, schizzinoso

finish [ˈfɪnɪʃ] *s* fine *f*; finitura; (sports) finale *m* ‖ *tr* finire; **to finish off** distruggere ‖ *intr* finire; **to finish** + *ger* finire di + *inf*; **to finish by** + *ger* finire per + *inf*

fin'ishing school' *s* scuola di perfezionamento per signorine

fin'ishing touch' *s* ultimo tocco

finite [ˈfaɪnaɪt] *adj* finito

Finland [ˈfɪnlənd] *s* la Finlandia

Finlander [ˈfɪnləndər] *s* finlandese *mf*

Finn [fɪn] *s* (*member of a Finnish-speaking group of people*) finnico; (*native or inhabitant of Finland*) finlandese *mf*

Finnic [ˈfɪnɪk] *adj* & *s* finnico

Finnish [ˈfɪnɪʃ] *adj* finlandese ‖ *s* (*language*) finlandese *m*

fir [fʌr] *s* abete *m*

fire [faɪr] *s* fuoco; (*destructive burning*) incendio; **to be on fire** ardere; **to be under enemy fire** essere sotto tiro nemico; **to catch fire** infiammarsi; **to hang fire** essere in sospeso; **to open fire** aprire il fuoco; **to set on fire, to set fire to** dar fuoco a; **under fire** sotto fuoco nemico; accusato ‖ *tr* accendere; (*an oven*) scaldare; (*bricks*) cuocere; (*a weapon*) sparare; (*the imagination*) riscaldare; (*an employee*) (coll) licenziare ‖ *intr* accendersi; **to fire on** far fuoco su; **to fire up** attivare una caldaia

fire' alarm' *s* avvisatore *m* d'incendio

fire'arm' *s* arma da fuoco

fire'ball' *s* palla da cannone esplosiva; (*lightning*) lampo a forma di globo infocato; meteorite *m* a forma di globo infocato; globo infocato ●

fire'boat' *s* lancia dei pompieri

fire'box' *s* (*of a boiler*) fornello; (*to give alarm*) stazione d'allarme

fire'brand' *s* tizzone *m*; (fig) fiaccola della discordia

fire'brick' *s* mattone refrattario

fire' brigade' *s* corpo di pompieri volontari

fire'bug' *s* (coll) incendiario

fire' com'pany *s* corpo dei pompieri; compagnia d'assicurazioni contro gli incendi

fire'crack'er *s* mortaretto

fire'damp' *s* grisou *m*

fire' depart'ment *s* corpo dei pompieri

fire'dog' *s* alare *m*

fire' drill' *s* esercitazione in caso d'incendio

fire' en'gine *s* autopompa

fire' escape' *s* scala di sicurezza

fire' extin'guisher *s* estintore *m*

fire'fly' *s* (-flies) lucciola

fire'guard' *s* parafuoco

fire' hose' *s* manichetta

fire'house' *s* caserma dei pompieri

fire' hy'drant *s* bocca d'incendi

fire' insur'ance *s* assicurazione contro gli incendi

fire' i'rons *spl* arnesi *mpl* del camino

fire'man *s* (-men) (*man who extinguishes fires*) pompiere *m*, vigile *m* del fuoco; (*stoker*) fochista *m*

fire'place' *s* camino

fire'plug' *s* bocca da incendio, idrante *m*

fire'proof' *adj* incombustibile ‖ *tr* rendere incombustibile

fire' sale' *s* vendita di merce avariata dal fuoco

fire' screen' *s* parafuoco

fire' ship' *s* brulotto

fire'side' *s* focolare *m*

fire'trap' *s* edificio senza mezzi adeguati per combattere incendi

fire' wall' *s* paratia antincendio

fire'wa'ter *s* (coll) acquavite *f*

fire'wood' *s* legna

fire'works' *spl mpl* artificiali

firing [ˈfaɪrɪŋ] *s* (*of furnace*) alimentazione; (*of bricks*) cottura; (*of a gun*) sparo; (*of soldiers*) tiro; (*of an internal-combustion engine*) accensione; (*of an employee*) (coll) licenziamento

fir'ing line' *s* linea del fuoco

fir'ing or'der *s* (aut) ordine *m* d'accensione

fir'ing pin' *s* percussore *m*

fir'ing squad' *s* (*for saluting at a burial*) plotone *m* d'onore; (*for executing*) plotone *m* d'esecuzione

firm [fʌrm] *adj* forte, fermo ‖ *s* ditta, compagnia

firmament [ˈfʌrməmənt] *s* firmamento

firm' name' *s* ragione *f* sociale

firmness [ˈfʌrmnɪs] *s* fermezza

first [fʌrst] *adj* primo; (aut) prima; (mus) voce *f* principale; **at first** sulle prime; **from the first** da bel principio ‖ *adv* prima; **first of all** per prima cosa

first' aid' *s* pronto soccorso

first'-aid' kit' *s* cassetta farmaceutica d'urgenza

first'-aid' sta'tion *s* posto di pronto soccorso

first'-born' *adj* & *s* primogenito

first'-class' *adj* di prim'ordine, sopraffino ‖ *adv* in prima classe

first' cous'in *s* cugino primo

first'-day cov'er *s* busta primo giorno

first' draft *s* brutta copia

first' fin'ger s dito indice
first' floor' s pianoterra m
first' fruits' spl primizie fpl
first' lieuten'ant s tenente m
firstly ['fʌrstli] adv in primo luogo
first' mate' s (naut) primo ufficiale, comandante m in seconda, secondo
first' name' s nome m di battesimo
first' night' s (theat) prima
first' of'ficer s (naut) primo ufficiale, comandante m in seconda, secondo
first'-rate' adj di prima forza; eccellente || adv (coll) benissimo
first'-run' adj di prima visione
fiscal ['fɪskəl] adj (pertaining to public treasury) fiscale; finanziario || s avvocato fiscale
fis'cal year' s esercizio finanziario
fish [fɪʃ] s pesce m; **to be like a fish out of water** essere come un pesce fuor d'acqua; **to be neither fish nor fowl** non essere né carne né pesce; **to drink like a fish** bere come una spugna || tr pescare || intr pescare; **to fish for compliments** cercare di farsi fare dei complimenti; **to go fishing** andare alla pesca; **to take fishing** portare con sé alla pesca
fish'bone' s lisca, spina di pesce
fish'bowl' s vaschetta per i pesci rossi
fisher ['fɪʃər] s pescatore m; (zool) martora canadese
fish'er·man s (-men) pescatore m; (boat) peschereccio
fisher·y ['fɪʃəri] s (-ies) (activity) pesca; (business) pescheria; (grounds) riserva di pesca, luogo dove si pesca
fish' glue' s colla di pesce
fish'hook' s amo
fishing ['fɪʃɪŋ] adj da pesca || s pesca
fish'ing reel' s mulinello
fish'ing rod' s canna da pesca
fish'ing tack'le s attrezzatura da pesca
fish'line' s lenza
fish' mar'ket s pescheria
fish'pool' s peschiera
fish' spear' s fiocina
fish' sto'ry s (coll) fandonia; **to tell fish stories** sparare grosse
fish'tail' s (aut) imbardata (aer) spedalata || intr (aut) imbardare; (aer) compiere una spedalata
fish'wife' s (-wives') pescivendola; (foul-mouthed woman) ciana
fish'worm' s lombrico
fish·y ['fɪʃi] adj (-ier; -iest) che sa di pesce; (coll) dubbioso, inverosimile
fission ['fɪʃən] s (biol) scissione; (phys) fissione
fissionable ['fɪʃənəbəl] adj fissionabile
fissure ['fɪʃər] s fenditura; (in rock) crepaccio
fist [fɪst] s pugno; (typ) indice m; **to shake one's fist at** mostrare i pugni a
fist'fight' s scontro a pugni
fist'ful' s pugno, manciata
fisticuff ['fɪstɪ,kʌf] s pugno; **fisticuffs** scontro a pugni
fit [fɪt] adj (fitter; fittest) indicato; idoneo, adatto; in buona salute; **fit to be tied** (coll) infuriato, arrabbia-

tissimo; **fit to eat** mangiabile; **to feel fit** sentirsi in buona salute; **to see fit** giudicare conveniente || s equipaggiamento; (of a suit) taglio; (of one piece with another) incastro; (of coughing) accesso; (of anger) attacco; **by fits and starts** a pezzi e a bocconi || v (pret & pp fitted; ger fitting) tr adattare; quadrare a; andar bene a; equipaggiare; preparare; servire a; esser d'accordo con; **to fit out** or **up** attrezzare, equipaggiare || intr stare; incastrare; (said of clothes) cascare; entrare; **to fit in** entrarci
fitful ['fɪtfəl] adj capriccioso; incostante, irregolare
fitness ['fɪtnɪs] s convenienza; idoneità f; buona salute
fitter ['fɪtər] s aggiustatore m; (of machinery) montatore m; (of clothing) sarto che mette in prova
fitting ['fɪtɪŋ] adj appropriato, adatto, conveniente || s adattamento; (of a garment) prova; tubo adattabile; (carp) incastro; **fittings** accessori mpl; utensili mpl; (iron trimmings) ferramenta pl
five [faɪv] adj & pron cinque || s cinque m; **five o' clock** le cinque
five' hun'dred adj, s & pron cinquecento
five'-year plan' s piano quinquennale
fix [fɪks] s—**in a tight fix** (coll) nei pasticci; **to be in a fix** (coll) star fresco, essere nei guai || tr riparare; fissare; (a meal) preparare; (a bayonet) inastare; (attention) attrarre, fermare; (hair) mettere a posto; (coll) arrangiare || intr fissarsi, stabilirsi; **to fix on** scegliere
fixed [fɪkst] adj fisso; (time) improrogabile; (coll) arrangiato
fixing ['fɪksɪŋ] adj fissativo || s (fastening) attacco; (phot) fissaggio; **with all the fixings** (coll) con tutti i contorni
fix'ing bath' s bagno di fissaggio
fixture ['fɪkstʃər] s infisso; accessorio; (of a lamp) guarnizione; **fixtures** (e.g., of a store) suppellettili fpl
fizz [fɪz] s effervescenza; gazosa; (Brit) spumante m || intr frizzare
fizzle ['fɪzəl] s (coll) fiasco || intr crepitare; (coll) fare fiasco
flabbergast ['flæbər,gæst] tr (coll) sbalordire, lasciare stupefatto
flab·by ['flæbi] adj (-bier; -biest) floscio, flaccido, cascante
flag [flæg] s bandiera || v (pret & pp flagged; ger flagging) tr imbandierare; segnalare; (rr) far fermare || intr ammosciarsi, afflosciarsi
flageolet [,flædʒə'lɛt] s flautino
flag'man s (-men) manovratore m
flag' of truce' s bandiera parlamentaria
flag'pole' s pennone m
flagrant ['flegrənt] adj flagrante; scandaloso
flag'ship' s nave ammiraglia
flag'staff' s pennone m
flag' sta'tion s (rr) stazione facoltativa
flag'stone' s lastra di pietra

flag' stop' *s* (rr) fermata facoltativa

flail [flel] *s* correggiato || *tr* battere col correggiato; battere

flair [fler] *s* fiuto, istinto

flak [flæk] *s* fuoco antiaereo

flake [flek] *s* falda; (*of snow*) fiocco, falda; (*of cereal*) fiocco; || *tr* sfaldare; (*fish*) scagliare || *intr* sfaldarsi

flak·y ['fleki] *adj* (**-ier; -iest**) a falde, faldoso

flamboyant [flæm'bɔɪ-ənt] *adj* sgargiante; (archit) fiammeggiante

flame [flem] *s* fiamma || *tr & intr* fiammeggiare

flamethrower ['flem,θro-ər] *s* lanciafiamme *m*

flaming ['flemɪŋ] *adj* fiammeggiante; appassionato; (culin) alla fiamma

flamin·go [flə'mɪŋgo] *s* (**-gos or -goes**) fenicottero, fiammingo

flammable ['flæməbəl] *adj* infiammabile

Flanders ['flændərz] *s* le Fiandre

flange [flændʒ] *s* (*e.g., on a pipe*) flangia; (*on I beam*) bordo; (*of a wheel*) cerchione *m*

flank [flæŋk] *s* fianco || *tr* fiancheggiare

flannel ['flænəl] *s* flanella

flap [flæp] *s* (*in clothing*) falda; (*of hat*) tesa; (*of book*) risvolto; (*of pocket*) patta; (*of shoe*) linguetta; (*blow*) colpo; (*of a table*) pannello; (*of the counter in a store*) ribalta; (*of wings*) alata || *v* (*pret & pp* **flapped; ger flapping**) *tr* battere, sbattere; (*to move violently*) sbatacchiare || *intr* penzolare

flare [fler] *s* vampa; scintillio; (*of a dress*) svasatura; (mil) fuoco di segnalazione; **flares** (*trousers*) calzoni *mpl* a zampe d'elefante || *tr* svasare || *intr* scintillare; (*said of a garment*) scampanare; **to flare up** divampare; (*said of an illness*) aggravarsi, infiammarsi

flare'-up' *s* vampa, fiammata; (*of an illness*) recrudescenza; scoppio d'ira, accesso di collera

flash [flæʃ] *s* (*of light*) sprazzo; (*of lightning*) lampo, baleno; (*of hope*) raggio; (*of joy*) accesso; (journ, phot) flash *m*; (fig) lampo; **flash in the pan** fuoco di paglia || *tr* (*powder*) accendere; (*a sword*) brandire; (journ) diffondere; (*e.g., money*) (coll) ostentare || *intr* lampeggiare, balenare, folgorare; **to flash by** passare come un lampo

flash'back' *s* flashback *m*

flash' bulb' *s* lampada lampo

flash' cube' *s* cuboflash *m*

flash' flood' *s* inondazione torrenziale

flashing ['flæʃɪŋ] *s* metallo per coprire la conversa; commessura metallica fra tetto e comignolo

flash'light' *s* lampadina tascabile; (*of a lighthouse*) luce *f* intermittente; (phot) fotolampo, lampeggiatore *m*

flash'light bulb' *s* lampada per fotolampo

flash·y ['flæʃi] *adj* (**-ier; -iest**) sgargiante, chiassoso, vistoso

flask [flæsk] or [flɑsk] *s* fiasco, fiasca; (*for laboratory use*) beuta

flat [flæt] *adj* (**flatter; flattest**) piano; (*nose*) camuso; (*boat*) a fondo piatto; (*surface*) liscio; (*beer*) svanito; (*tire*) sgonfio; (*denial*) deciso; (mus) bemolle; (coll) al verde || *s* (*flat surface*) piatto; (*flat area*) piano; (*apartment*) appartamento; (mus) bemolle *m*; (coll) gomma a terra || *adv*—**to fall flat** fallire

flat'boat' *s* chiatta

flat'car' *s* (rr) pianale *m*

flat-footed ['flæt,fʊtɪd] *adj* dai piedi piatti; (coll) inflessibile

flat'head' *s* (*of a bolt*) testa piatta; (coll) testa di legno

flat'i'ron *s* ferro da stiro

flat' race' *s* corsa piana

flatten ['flætən] *tr* schiacciare; distendere || *intr* appiattirsi; indebolirsi; **to flatten out** appiattirsi; (aer) porsi in linea orizzontale di volo

flatter ['flætər] *tr* adulare, lusingare; (*to make seem more attractive*) favorire || *intr* adulare

flatterer ['flætərər] *s* adulatore *m*, lusingatore *m*

flattering ['flætərɪŋ] *adj* lusinghiero

flatter·y ['flætəri] *s* (**-ies**) lusinga

flat' tire' *s* gomma a terra

flat'top' *s* portaerei *f*

flatulence ['flætʃələns]-*s* flatulenza

flat'ware' *s* argenteria, vasellame *m*

flaunt [flɔnt] or [flɑnt] *tr* sfoggiare, ostentare

flautist ['flɔtɪst] *s* flautista *mf*

flavor ['flevər] *s* sapore *m*, gusto; condimento || *tr* insaporire; condire; aromatizzare, profumare

flavoring ['flevərɪŋ] *s* condimento, sapore *m*

flaw [flɔ] *s* difetto, menda, fallo; (*crack*) incrinatura

flawless ['flɔlɪs] *adj* senza difetti

flax [flæks] *s* lino

flaxen ['flæksən] *adj* di lino; biondo

flax'seed' *s* linosa

flay [fle] *tr* scorticare, scoiare

flea [fli] *s* pulce *f*

flea'bite' *s* morso di pulce; (fig) inezia, seccatura secondaria

fleck [flɛk] *s* macchia; efelide *f* || *tr* chiazzare, macchiare

fledgling ['flɛdʒlɪŋ] *s* uccellino appena nato; (fig) pivello

flee [fli] *v* (*pret & pp* **fled** [flɛd]) *tr & intr* fuggire, sfuggire

fleece [flis] *s* vello; (*e.g., of clouds*) bioccolo || *tr* tosare; (fig) pelare

fleec·y ['flisi] *adj* (**-ier; -iest**) lanoso; (*sky*) a pecorelle

fleet [flit] *adj* rapido || *s* flotta

fleeting ['flitɪŋ] *adj* fugace, passeggero

Fleming ['flemɪŋ] *s* fiammingo

Flemish ['flemɪʃ]-*adj & s* fiammingo

flesh [flɛʃ] *s* carne *f*; (*of fruit*) polpa; **in the flesh** in carne ed ossa; **to lose flesh** dimagrire; **to put on flesh** ingrassare

flesh' and blood' *s* (*relatives*) carne *f* della carne, i miei, i suoi, etc.; il corpo umano

flesh-colored [ˈfleʃˌkʌlərd] *adj* color carne

fleshiness [ˈfleʃɪnɪs] *s* carnosità *f*

fleshless [ˈfleʃlɪs] *adj* scarno

flesh′pot′ *s* piatto di carne; locale *m* di dissoluzione; **fleshpots** vita dissoluta

flesh′ wound′ *s* ferita superficiale

flesh•y [ˈfleʃi] *adj* (**-ier; -iest**) carnoso; polposo

flex [fleks] *tr* piegare || *intr* piegarsi

flexible [ˈfleksɪbəl] *adj* flessibile; (*joint*) a snodo

flick [flɪk] *s* schiocco; (**slang**) pellicola cinematografica || *tr* schioccare

flicker [ˈflɪkər] *s* fiamma tremolante; (*of eyelids*) battito; (*of hope*) bagliore *m* || *intr* tremolare; vacillare

flier [ˈflaɪ•ər] *s* aviatore *m;* (*venture*) (*coll*) impresa rischiosa; (*coll*) foglio volante

flight [flaɪt] *s* fuga; (*of an airplane*) volo; (*of birds*) stormo; (*of stairs*) rampa; (*of fancy*) slancio; **to put to flight** mettere in fuga; **to take flight** prendere la fuga

flight′ deck′ *s* ponte *m* di volo

flight•y [ˈflaɪti] *adj* (**-ier; -iest**) frivolo; volubile

flim-flam [ˈflɪmˌflæm] *s* (*coll*) imbroglio, truffa || *v* (*pret & pp* **-flammed; ger -flamming**) *tr* (*coll*) imbrogliare, truffare

flim•sy [ˈflɪmzi] *adj* (**-sier; -siest**) leggero; (*material*) di scarsa consistenza; (*excuse*) inconsistente

flinch [flɪntʃ] *intr* indietreggiare; **without flinching** senza scomporsi

fling [flɪŋ] *s* tiro; ballo scozzese; **to go on a fling** darsi alla pazza gioia; **to have a fling** at tentare di fare; **to have one′s fling** correre la cavallina || *v* (*pret & pp* **flung** [flʌŋ]) *tr* sbattere, scagliare; (*e.g., in jail*) schiaffare; **to fling open** spalancare; **to fling shut** chiudere improvvisamente

flint [flɪnt] *s* selce *f*, pietra focaia

flint′lock′ *s* fucile *m* a pietra focaia

flint•y [ˈflɪnti] *adj* (**-ier; -iest**) pietroso; (*unmerciful*) spietato; duro come un macigno

flip [flɪp] *adj* (**flipper; flippest**) impertinente || *s* buffetto; salto mortale || *v* (*pret & pp* **flipped; ger flipping**) *tr* sbattere in aria; muovere d′un tratto **to flip a coin** giocare a testa e croce; **to flip shut** (*e.g., a fan*) chiudere improvvisamente

flippancy [ˈflɪpənsi] *s* leggerezza

flippant [ˈflɪpənt] *adj* scanzonato, leggero

flirt [flʌrt] *s* (*woman*) civetta; (*man*) vagheggino || *intr* (*said of a woman*) civettare; (*said of a man*) fare il damerino; **to flirt with** flirtare con; (*an idea*) accarezzare; (*death*) giocare con

flit [flɪt] *v* (*pret & pp* **flitted; ger flitting**) *intr* svolazzare, volteggiare; passare rapidamente, volare

flitch [flɪtʃ] *s* fetta di pancetta

float [flot] *s* (*raft*) galleggiante *m; (of mason*) cazzuola; carro allegorico || *tr* far galleggiare; (*a business*) lan-

ciare; (*stocks, bonds*) emettere || *intr* galleggiare, tenersi a galla

floating [ˈflotɪŋ] *adj* galleggiante

flock [flɑk] *s* (*of birds*) stormo; (*of sheep*) gregge *m;* (*of people*) stuolo; (*of wool*) fiocco; (*fig*) mucchio || *intr* affollarsi, riunirsi, radunarsi

floe [flo] *s* tavola di ghiaccio

flog [flɑg] *v* (*pret & pp* **flogged; ger flogging**) *tr* battere, fustigare

flood [flʌd] *s* (*caused by rain*) diluvio; (*sudden rise of river*) piena, fiumana; (*of tide*) flusso || *tr* inondare; (*aut*) ingolfare || *intr* straripare; (*aut*) ingolfarsi || **the Flood** il diluvio universale

flood′gate′ *s* (*of a canal*) chiusa; (*of a dam*) saracinesca

flood′light′ *s* riflettore *m*

flood′ tide′ *s* flusso

floor [flor] *s* (*inside bottom surface of room*) pavimento; (*story of building*) piano; (*of the sea, a swimming pool, etc.*) fondo; (*of the exchange*) recinto delle grida; (*of an assembly hall*) emiciclo; (*naut*) madiere *m;* **to ask for the floor** chiedere la parola; **to have the floor** avere la parola; **to take the floor** prendere la parola || *tr* pavimentare; abbattere, gettare al suolo; (*coll*) confondere; (*coll*) vincere

flooring [ˈflorɪŋ] *s* palco, impiantito

floor′ mop′ *s* redazza

floor′ plan′ *s* pianta

floor′ show′ *s* spettacolo di caffè concerto

floor′walk′er *s* direttore *m* di sezione

floor′ wax′ *s* cera da pavimenti

flop [flɑp] *s* (*coll*) fiasco || *v* (*pret & pp* **flopped; ger flopping**) *tr* lasciar cadere; sbattere || *intr* lasciarsi cadere; (*coll*) fare fiasco; **to flop over** (*to change sides*) cambiare casacca

flora [ˈflorə] *s* flora

floral [ˈflorəl] *adj* floreale

Florence [ˈflorəns] *or* [ˈflɑrəns] *s* Firenze *f*

Florentine [ˈflɑrənˌtin] *or* [ˈflorənˌtin] *adj & s* fiorentino

florescence [floˈresəns] *s* inflorescenza

florid [ˈflɑrɪd] *or* [ˈflorɪd] *adj* florido

florist [ˈflorɪst] *s* fiorista *mf*, fioraio

floss [flɔs] *or* [flas] *s* lanugine *f;* (*of corn*) barba

floss•y [ˈflɔsi] *or* [ˈflasi] *adj* (**-ier; -iest**) serico; (*downy*) lanuginoso; (*coll*) vistoso

flotsam [ˈflatsəm] *s* relitti gettati a mare

flot′sam and jet′sam *s* relitti *mpl* di naufragio; (*trifles*) cianfrusaglie *fpl*; gentaglia, vagabondi *mpl*

flounce [flaʊns] *s* balza, falda, falpalà *m* || *tr* ornare di falpalà || *intr*—**to flounce out** andarsene irosamente

flounder [ˈflaʊndər] *s* (ichth) passera || *intr* dibattersi

flour [flaʊr] *adj* farinoso || *s* farina || *tr* infarinare

flourish [ˈflʌrɪʃ] *s* (*with the sword*) mulinello; (*with the pen*) ghirigoro; (*as part of signature*) svolazzo; (*mus*) fioritura || *tr* (*one's sword*) roteare || *intr* rifiorire, prosperare

flourishing ['flʌrɪʃɪŋ] *adj* prosperoso

flour' mill' *s* mulino per grano

floury ['flauri] *adj* farinoso; infarinato

flout [flaut] *tr* burlarsi di || *intr* burlare, motteggiare

flow [flo] *s* flusso; (*of a river*) regime *m* || *intr* fluire; (*said of tide*) montare; (*said of hair in the air*) ondeggiare; **to flow into** gettarsi in, sfociare in; **to flow over** traboccare; **to flow with** abbondare di

flower ['flau.ər] *s* fiore *m* || *tr* infiorare || *intr* fiorire

flow'er bed' *s* aiola fiorita

flow'er gar'den *s* giardino

flow'er girl' *s* fioraia; (*at a wedding*) damigella d'onore

flow'er·pot' *s* vaso da fiori

flow'er shop' *s* negozio di fiori

flow'er show' *s* esposizione di fiori

flow'er·stand' *s* portafiori *m*

flowery ['flau.əri] *adj* fiorito

flowing ['flo·ɪŋ] *adj* (*water*) corrente; (*language*) scorrevole; (*e.g., hair*) fluente; (*e.g., lines of a dress*) filante

flu [flu] *s* influenza

fluctuate ['flʌktʃu.et] *intr* fluttuare, ondeggiare; (*said of prices*) oscillare

flue [flu] *s* gola, fumaiolo

fluency ['flu·ənsi] *s* facilità *f* di parola

fluent ['flu·ənt] *adj* (*speaker*) facondo; (*style*) fluido

fluently ['flu·əntli] *adv* correntemente

fluff [flʌf] *s* lanugine *f*; vaporosità *f*; (*of an actor*) papera || *tr* sprimacciare || *intr* sprimacciarsi; (*coll*) impaperarsi

fluff·y ['flʌfi] *adj* (**-ier; -iest**) lanuginoso; vaporoso

fluid ['flu·ɪd] *adj* & *s* fluido

flu'id drive' *s* trasmissione idraulica

fluidity [flu'ɪdɪti] *s* fluidità *f*

fluke [fluk] *s* (*of anchor*) marra, dente *m*; (*in billiards*) colpo fortunato; (ichth) passera

flume [flum] *s* gora; condotta forzata

flunk [flʌŋk] *s* (coll) bocciatura || *tr* (coll) bocciare; (*a course*) (coll) farsi bocciare in || *intr* (coll) fare fiasco; **to flunk out** (coll) farsi bocciare

flunk·y ['flʌŋki] *s* (**-ies**) valletto; parassita *m*

fluor ['flu·ɔr] *s* fluorite *f*

fluorescence [ˌflu·ə'resəns] *s* fluorescenza

fluorescent [ˌflu·ə'resənt] *adj* fluorescente

fluoridation [ˌflu·ərɪ'deʃən] *s* fluorizzazione

fluoride ['flu·ə ˌraɪd] *s* fluoruro

fluorine ['flu·ə ˌrin] *s* fluoro

fluoroscope ['flu·ərə ˌskop] *s* schermo fluorescente

fluorspar ['flu·ɛr ˌspɑr] *s* spatofluore *m*

flur·ry ['flʌri] *s* (**-ries**) agitazione; (*of wind*) raffica; (*of rain*) acquazzone *m*; (*of snow*) turbine *m* || *v* (*pret* & *pp* **-ried**) *tr* agitare

flush [flʌʃ] *adj* livellato; contiguo; prospero, ben provvisto; abbondante; vigoroso; (*full to overflowing*) rigurgitante; arrossito; **flush with** allo stesso livello che || *s* (*of water*) flusso improvviso; (*in the cheeks*) caldana, scalmana; (*of spring*) germogliare *m*; (*of joy*) ebbrezza; (*of youth*) rigoglio; (*in poker*) colore *m* || *adv* rasente, raso || *tr* (*to cause to blush*) far arrossire; lavare con un getto d'acqua; (*e.g., a rabbit*) snidare || *intr* essere accaldato; (*to blush*) arrossire; (*to gush*) zampillare

flush' tank' *s* sciacquone *m*

flush' toi'let *s* gabinetto a sciacquone

fluster ['flʌstər] *s* nervosismo, eccitazione || *tr* innervosire, eccitare

flute [flut] *s* (*of a column*) scanalatura; (mus) flauto || *tr* scanalare

flutist ['flutɪst] *s* flautista *mf*

flutter ['flʌtər] *s* svolazzo; agitazione; sensazione || *intr* frullare; svolazzare; agitarsi; (*said of the heart*) palpitare; (*said of the heartbeat*) essere irregolare

flux [flʌks] *s* (*flow*) flusso; (*for fusing metals*) fondente *m*

fly [flaɪ] *s* (*flies*) mosca; (*of trousers*) finta; (*for fishing*) mosca artificiale || *v* (*pret* **flew** [flu]; *pp* **flown** [flon]) *tr* (*an airplane*) pilotare, far volare; trasportare a volo; (*e.g., an ocean*) trasvolare; (*a flag*) battere || *intr* volare; fuggire, scappare; (*said of a flag*) ondeggiare; **to fly away** involarsi; **to fly into a rage** andare in eccessi; **to fly off** volare via; scappare; **to fly over** trasvolare; **to fly shut** chiudersi improvvisamente

fly'blow' *s* uovo di mosca

fly'-by-night' *adj* poco raccomandabile; di breve durata

fly'catch'er *s* (orn) pigliamosche *m*

flyer ['flaɪ·ər] *s* var of **flier**

fly'-fish' *intr* pescare con le mosche artificiali

flying ['flaɪ·ɪŋ] *adj* volante; rapido; in fuga; (*start*) lanciato || *s* volo

fly'ing boat' *s* idrovolante *m* a scafo centrale

fly'ing but'tress *s* contrafforte *m*

fly'ing col'ors *spl* successo; **with flying colors** a bandiere spiegate

fly'ing field' *s* campo d'aviazione

fly'ing sau'cer *s* disco volante

fly'ing sick'ness *s* male *m* d'aria

fly'ing squad' *s* squadra mobile

fly'ing time' *s* ore *fpl* di volo

fly'leaf' *s* (**-leaves**) (bb) guardia

fly' net' *s* (*for a bed*) moschettiera; (*for a horse*) scacciamosche *m*

fly'pa'per *s* carta moschicida

fly'speck' *s* macchia di mosca; macchiolina

fly' swat'ter ['swɑtər] *s* scacciamosche *m*

fly'trap' *s* pigliamosche *m*

fly'wheel' *s* volano

foal [fol] *s* puledro || *intr* (*said of a mare*) figliare

foam [fom] *s* schiuma || *intr* schiumare

foam' rub'ber *s* gommapiuma

foam·y ['fomi] *adj* (**-ier; -iest**) spumoso, schiumeggiante

fob [fɑb] *s* taschino per l'orologio; (*chain*) catenina per l'orologio ‖ *v* (*pret & pp* **fobbed;** *ger* **fobbing**) *tr*— **to fob off s.th on s.o.** rifilare qlco a qlcu

f.o.b. or **F.O.B.** [ˌɛf ˌoˈbi] *adv* (letterword) (**free on board**) franco

focal ['fokəl] *adj* focale

fo·cus ['fokəs] *s* (**-cuses** or **-ci** [saɪ]) fuoco; (*of a disease*) focolaio ‖ *v* (*pret & pp* **-cused** or **-cussed;** *ger* **-cusing** or **-cussing**) *tr* mettere a fuoco; (*attention*) concentrare ‖ *intr* convergere

fodder ['fɑdər] *s* foraggio

foe [fo] *s* nemico

fog [fɑg] or [fɔg] *s* nebbia; (phot) velo ‖ *v* (*pret & pp* **fogged;** *ger* **fogging**) *tr* annebbiare; (phot) velare ‖ *intr* annebbiarsi; (phot) velarsi

fog' bank' *s* banco di nebbia

fog'bound' *adj* avvolto nella nebbia

fog·gy ['fɑgi] or ['fɔgi] *adj* (**-gier; -giest**) annebbiato; nebbioso; (*idea*) vago; (phot) velato; **it is foggy** fa nebbia

fog'horn' *s* sirena da nebbia

foible ['fɔɪbəl] *s* debolezza, debole *m*

foil [fɔɪl] *s* (*thin sheet of metal*) foglia; (*of mirror*) argentatura; contrasto, risalto; (*sword*) fioretto ‖ *tr* sventare; (*a mirror*) argentare

foist [fɔɪst] *tr*— **to foist s.th on s.o.** rifilare qlco a qlcu

fold [fold] *s* piega; drappeggio; (*for sheep*) ovile *m;* (*of sheep; of the faithful*) gregge *m;* (geol) corrugamento ‖ *tr* piegare; (*the arms*) incrociare; **to fold up** ripiegare ‖ *intr* piegarsi; **to fold up** (coll) fare fallimento

folder ['foldər] *s* (*pamphlet*) pieghevole *m;* (*cover*) portacarte *m*

folding ['foldɪŋ] *adj* pieghevole

fold'ing cam'era *s* macchina fotografica a soffietto

fold'ing chair' *s* sedia pieghevole

fold'ing cot' *s* branda

fold'ing door' *s* porta a libro

fold'ing seat' *s* strapuntino

foliage ['folɪɪdʒ] *s* fogliame *m*

foli·o ['folɪ ˌo] *adj* in-folio ‖ *s* (**-os**) foglio; (*book*) in-folio ‖ *tr* numerare

folk [fok] *adj* popolare ‖ *s* (**folk** or **folks**) gente *f;* **your folks** i Suoi

folk'lore' *s* folclore *m*

folk' mu'sic *s* musica folcloristica

folk' song' *s* canzone *f* tradizionale

folk·sy ['foksi] *adj* (**-sier; -siest**) socievole; alla buona, alla mano

folk'ways' *spl* costumi *mpl* tradizionali

follicle ['fɑlɪkəl] *s* follicolo

follow ['folo] *tr* seguire; (*to keep up with*) interessarsi di; **to follow suit** seguire l'esempio; (cards) rispondere al colore ‖ *intr* seguire; derivare; **as follows** come segue; **it follows** ne risulta

follower ['folo·ər] *s* seguace *m;* discepolo; partigiano

following ['folo·ɪŋ] *adj* susseguente ‖ *s* seguito; aderenti *mpl*

fol'low-up' *adj* susseguente; ricordativo; da continuarsi ‖ *s* prosecuzione; lettera ricordativa

fol·ly ['fɑli] *s* (**-lies**) follia; **follies** rivista di varietà

foment [foˈment] *tr* fomentare

fond [fɑnd] *adj* appassionato; (*of food*) ghiotto; **to become fond of** appassionarsi di

fondle ['fɑndəl] *tr* accarezzare, vezzeggiare

fondness ['fɑndnɪs] *s* tenerezza; passione

font [fɑnt] *s* acquasantiera, pila; fonte *f* battesimale; (typ) fondita

food [fud] *adj* alimentare ‖ *s* cibo, vitto; (*for animals*) mangiare *m;* **food for thought** materia di che pensare

food' store' *s* negozio di commestibili

food'stuffs' *spl* commestibili *mpl*

fool [ful] *s* scemo, sciocco; (*jester*) buffone *m;* (*person imposed on*) vittima, zimbello; **to make a fool of** beffarsi di; **to play the fool** fare lo stupido ‖ *tr* infinocchiare, ingannare; **to fool away** sprecare ‖ *intr* giocare, fare per gioco; **to fool around** perdere il proprio tempo; **to fool with** giocherellare con

fooler·y ['fuləri] *s* (**-ies**) pazzia, buffonata

fool'har'dy *adj* (**-dier; -diest**) temerario

fooling ['fulɪŋ] *s* scherzo; **no fooling** senza scherzi, parlando sul serio

foolish ['fulɪʃ] *adj* sciocco; matto

fool'proof' *adj* a tutta prova; infallibile

fools'cap' *s* berretto a sonagli; carta formato protocollo

fool's' er'rand *s* impresa inutile

fool's' par'adise *s* felicità immaginaria

foot [fʊt] *s* (**feet** [fit]) piede *m;* (*of an animal*) zampa; (*of horse*) zoccolo; **to drag one's feet** procedere a passo di lumaca; **to put one's best foot forward** fare del proprio meglio; **to put one's foot down** farsi valere, imporsi; **to put one's foot in it** (coll) fare una topica; **to stand on one's own two feet** agire indipendentemente; **to tread under foot** calcare ‖ *tr* (*the bill*) pagare; **to foot it** andare a piedi; ballare

footage ['fʊtɪdʒ] *s* distanza or lunghezza in piedi; (*of film measured in meters*) metraggio

foot'-and-mouth' disease' *s* (vet) afta epizootica

foot'ball' *s* (*ball*) pallone *m;* (*game*) pallovale *f;* (*soccer*) calcio, football *m*

foot'board' *s* (*support for foot*) predellino; (*of bed*) spalliera

foot' brake' *s* freno a pedale

foot'bridge' *s* passerella, ponte riservato ai pedoni

foot'fall' *s* passo

foot'hill' *s* collina ai piedi di una montagna

foot'hold' s stabilità f; **to gain a foot-hold** prender piede

footing ['futɪŋ] s piede m, e.g., **he lost his footing** perse piede; **on a friendly footing** in relazioni amichevoli; **on an equal footing** su un piede di parità; **on a war footing** su un piede di guerra

foot'lights' spl luci fpl della ribalta; (fig) ribalta, scena

foot'loose' adj completamente libero

foot'man s (**-men**) staffiere m

foot'mark' s orma

foot'note' s rimando, rinvio

foot'path' s sentiero

foot'print' s orma, pesta

foot' race' s corsa podistica

foot'rest' s pedana

foot' rule' s regolo di un piede

foot' soldier' s fante m, fantaccino

foot'sore' adj coi piedi stanchi

foot'step' s passo; **to follow in the footsteps of** seguire le orme di

foot'stone' s pietra tombale a piè di un sepolcro; (archit) pietra di sostegno

foot'stool' s sgabello

foot' warm'er s scaldino

foot'wear' s calzature fpl

foot'work' s allenamento delle gambe; (fig) manovra delicata

foot'worn' adj (road) battuto; (person) spedato

foozle ['fuzəl] s schiappinata ‖ tr & intr mancare completamente

fop [fɑp] s bellimbusto, gagà m

for [fɔr] prep per; malgrado, e.g., **for all his wealth** malgrado tutta la sua ricchezza; come, e.g., **he uses his house for an office** adopera la casa come ufficio; di, e.g., **time for bed** ora di andare a letto; da, e.g., **he has been here for three days** è qui da tre giorni; per amor di; **to go for a walk** andare a fare una passeggiata ‖ conj perchè, poichè

forage ['fɑrɪdʒ] or ['fɔrɪdʒ] adj foraggero ‖ s foraggio ‖ tr foraggiare ‖ intr andare in cerca di foraggio

foray ['fɑre] or ['fɔre] s razzia, scorreria ‖ intr razziare

for·bear [fɔr'bɛr] v (pret **-bore** ['bor]; pp **-borne** ['born]) tr astenersi da ‖ intr essere longanime

forbearance [fɔr'bɛrəns] s longanimità f, tolleranza; astensione

for·bid [fɔr'bɪd] v (pret **-bade** ['bæd] or **-bad** ['bæd]; pp **-bidden** ['bɪdən]; ger **-bidding**) tr proibire, vietare ‖ intr—**God forbid!** Dìo ci scampi!

forbidding [fɔr'bɪdɪŋ] adj severo, sinistro

force [fɔrs] s forza; (staff of workers) forza, personale m; (phys) forza; **by force of** a forza di; **by main force** con tutte le sue forze; **in force** vigente; in gran numero; **to join forces** allearsi ‖ tr forzare; obbligare; **to force back** respingere; **to force open** forzare; **to force s.th on s.o.** obbligare qlcu a accettare qlco

forced [fɔrst] adj forzato; studiato

forced' air' s aria sotto pressione

forced' draft' s tiraggio forzato

forced' land'ing s atterraggio forzato

forced' march' s marcia forzata

forceful ['fɔrsfəl] adj vigoroso, energico

for·ceps ['fɔrsəps] s (**-ceps** or **-cipes** [sɪ ,piz]) (dent, surg) pinze fpl; (obstet) forcipe m

force' pump' s pompa premente

forcible ['fɔrsɪbəl] adj impetuoso, energico; efficace

ford [fɔrd] s guado ‖ tr guadare

fore [fɔr] adj davanti; (naut) prodiero ‖ s davanti m; (naut) prua; **to the fore** alla ribalta; d'attualità ‖ adv prima; (naut) a proravia ‖ interj attenzione!

fore' and aft' adv a poppa e a prua

fore'arm' s avambraccio ‖ **fore·arm'** tr premunire; prevenire

fore'bears' spl antenati mpl

forebode [fɔr'bod] tr (to portend) preannunziare; (to have a presentiment of) presentire

foreboding [fɔr'bodɪŋ] s preannunzio; presentimento

fore'cast' s pronostico ‖ v (pret & pp **-cast** or **-casted**) tr pronosticare

forecastle ['foksəl], ['fɔr ,kæsəl] or ['fɔr ,kɑsəl] s castello, pozzetto

fore·close' tr escludere, precludere; (a mortgage) (law) precludere il riscatto di

fore·doom' tr condannare all'insuccesso

fore' edge' s (bb) taglio

fore'fa'ther s antenato

fore'fin'ger s dito indice

fore'front' s—**in the forefront** all'avanguardia

fore·go' v (pret **-went'**; pp **-gone'**) tr & intr precedere

fore·go'ing adj precedente, anteriore

fore'gone' conclu'sion s conclusione inevitabile; decisione già scontata

fore'ground' s primo piano

forehanded ['fɔr ,hændɪd] adj previdente; (thrifty) risparmiatore

forehead ['fɔrɪd] or ['fɑrɪd] s fronte f

foreign ['fɑrɪn] or ['fɔrɪn] adj straniero; (product; affairs) estero; **foreign to** estraneo a

for'eign affairs' spl affari esteri

for'eign-born' adj nato all'estero

foreigner ['fɑrɪnər] or ['fɔrɪnər] s straniero, forestiero

for'eign exchange' s divise fpl; (money) valuta

for'eign min'ister s ministro degli affari esteri

for'eign of'fice s ministero degli affari esteri

for'eign serv'ice s servizio diplomatico e consolare; (Brit) servizio militare in paesi d'oltremare

fore'leg' s zampa anteriore

fore'lock' s ciuffo sulla fronte; **to take time by the forelock** acchiappare l'occasione

fore'man s (**-men**) sorvegliante m, capomastro; presidente m dei giurati

foremast ['fɔrmæst], ['fɔr ,mæst] or ['fɔr ,mɑst] s trinchetto

foremost ['fɔr ,most] adj primo, principale, più importante

fore'noon' *adj* mattinale || *s* mattina
fore'part' *s* parte *f* anteriore; prima parte
fore'paw' *s* zampa anteriore
fore'quar'ter *s* quarto anteriore
fore'run'ner *s* precursore *m*, predecessore *m*, foriero
fore·sail ['fɔrsəl] *or* ['fɔr,sel] *s* trinchetto
fore·see' *v* (*pret* -saw'; *pp* -seen') *tr* prevedere
foreseeable [for'si·əbəl] *adj* prevedibile
fore·shad'ow *tr* presagire
fore·short'en *tr* scorciare
fore'sight' *s* (*prudence*) previdenza; (*foreknowledge*) previsione
fore'sight'ed *adj* previdente
fore'skin' *s* prepuzio
forest ['fɑrɪst] *or* ['fɔrɪst] *adj* forestale || *s* foresta, bosco
fore·stall' *tr* prevenire; anticipare; (*to buy up*) accaparrare
for'est rang'er ['rendʒər] *s* guardaboschi *m*, guardia forestale
forestry ['fɑrɪstri] *or* ['fɔrɪstri] *s* selvicoltura
fore'taste' *s* pregustazione || *tr* pregustare
fore·tell' *v* (*pret* & *pp* -told') *tr* predire, presagire, preannunziare
fore'thought' *s* premeditazione; previdenza
forever [fər'ɛvər] *adv* per sempre; continuamente
fore·warn' *tr* prevenire, preavvertire
fore'word' *s* avvertenza, prefazione
forfeit ['fɔrfɪt] *adj* perduto || *s* perdita, confisca; multa; (*article deposited*) pegno; **forfeits** (*game*) pegni *mpl* || *tr* decadere da
forfeiture ['fɔrfɪt/ər] *s* perdita di un pegno
forgather [fər'gæðər] *intr* riunirsi; incontrarsi
forge [fɔrdʒ] *s* fucina, forgia || *tr* forgiare; (*a lie*) inventare; (*e.g., handwriting*) falsificare || *intr* forgiare; commettere un falso; **to forge ahead** farsi strada
forger·y ['fɔrdʒəri] *s* (-ies) falsificazione, falso, contraffazione
for·get [fər'gɛt] *v* (*pret* -got ['gɑt]; *pp* -got *or* -gotten ['gɑtən]) *tr* dimenticare; **forget it!** non si preoccupi!; **to forget oneself** venir meno alla propria dignità; **to forget to** passare di mente a (qlcu) di, e.g., **he forgot to turn off the lights** gli è passato di mente di spegnere la luce
forgetful [fər'gɛtfəl] *adj* (*apt to forget*) smemorato; (*neglectful*) dimentico, immemore
forgetfulness [fər'gɛtfəlnɪs] *s* (*inability to recall*) smemorataggine *f*; (*neglectfulness*) dimenticanza
for·get'-me-not' *s* nontiscordardimé *m*
forgivable [fər'gɪvəbəl] *adj* perdonabile
for·give [fər'gɪv] *v* (*pret* -gave'; *pp* -giv'en) *tr* perdonare
forgiveness [fər'gɪvnɪs] *s* perdono
forgiving [fər'gɪvɪŋ] *adj* clemente
for·go [fər'go] *v* (*pret* -went; *pp* -gone) *tr* rinunciare (with *dat*)

fork [fɔrk] *s* (*pitchfork*) forca, forcone *m*; (*of a bicycle*) forcella; (*for eating*) forchetta; (*of a tree or road*) biforcazione, diramazione || *tr* muovere col forcone; inforcare; **to fork out** (slang) cacciar fuori || *intr* biforcarsi, diramarsi
forked [fɔrkt] *adj* biforcuto
fork'-lift truck' *s* carrello elevatore a forca
forlorn [fər'lɔrn] *adj* abbandonato; disperato; miserabile
forlorn' hope' *s* impresa disperata
form [fɔrm] *s* forma; (*paper to be filled out*) formulario; (*construction to give shape to cement*) cassaforma || *tr* formare || *intr* formarsi
formal ['fɔrməl] *adj* formale; di gala, da sera, di etichetta
for'mal attire' *s* vestito da cerimonia
for'mal call' *s* visita di prammatica
formali·ty [fɔr'mælɪti] *s* (-ties) formalità *f*; (*excessive adherence to rules*) formalismo
for'mal par'ty *s* ricevimento di gala
for'mal speech' *s* discorso ufficiale
format ['fɔrmæt] *s* formato
formation [fɔr'me/ən] *s* formazione
former ['fɔrmər] *adj* (*preceding*) ânteriore; (*long past*) passato, antico; (*having once been*) già, ex; (*of two*) primo; **the former** quello
formerly ['fɔrmərli] *adv* già, prima, in tempi passati
form'fit'ting *adj* aderente al corpo
formidable ['fɔrmɪdəbəl] *adj* formidabile
formless ['fɔrmlɪs] *adj* informe
form' let'ter *s* lettera a formulario, stampato
formu·la ['fɔrmjələ] *s* (-las *or* -lae [,li]) formula
formulate ['fɔrmjə,let] *tr* formulare
for·sake [fər'sek] *v* (*pret* -sook ['sʊk]; *pp* -saken ['sekən]) *tr* abbandonare
fort [fɔrt] *s* forte *m*, fortezza
forte [fɔrt] *s* forte *m*
forth [fɔrθ] *adv* avanti; **and so forth** e così via; **from this day forth** da oggi in poi; **to go forth** uscire
forth'com'ing *adj* prossimo; immediatamente disponibile
forth'right' *adj* diretto || *adv* direttamente; senza ambagi; immediatamente
forth'with' *adv* immediatamente
fortieth ['fɔrtɪ·ɪθ] *adj*, *s* & *pron* quarantesimo
fortification [,fɔrtɪfɪ'ke/ən] *s* fortificazione
forti·fy ['fɔrtɪ,faɪ] *v* (*pret* & *pp* -fied) *tr* fortificare; aumentare il livello alcolico di
fortitude ['fɔrtɪ,tjud] *or* ['fɔrtɪ,tud] *s* fortezza, fermezza
fortnight ['fɔrtnaɪt] *or* ['fɔrtnɪt] *s* quindicina, due settimane
fortress ['fɔrtrɪs] *s* fortezza, forte *m*
fortuitous [fər'tju·ɪtəs] *or* [fər'tu·ɪtəs] *adj* fortuito, occasionale
fortunate ['fɔrt/ənɪt] *adj* fortunato
fortune ['fɔrt/ən] *s* fortuna; **to make a fortune** farsi un patrimonio; **to tell**

s.o. his fortune leggere il futuro a qlcu

for'tune hunt'er s cacciatore m di dote

for'tune·tel'ler s indovino, cartomante mf

for·ty ['fɔrti] adj & pron quaranta ‖ s (-ties) quaranta m; **the forties** gli anni quaranta

fo·rum ['forəm] s (-rums or -ra [rə]) foro

forward ['fɔrwərd] adj avanzato; precoce; impertinente ‖ s (soccer) avanti m ‖ adv avanti; **to bring forward** mettere in luce; riportare; **to come forward** avanzare; **to look forward to** anticipare il piacere di ‖ tr inoltrare, trasmettere; promuovere

fossil ['fɑsɪl] adj & s fossile m

foster ['fɑstər] or ['fɔstər] adj adottivo; di latte ‖ tr allevare; promuovere

fos'ter home' s famiglia adottiva

foul [faʊl] adj sporco; (air) viziato; (wind) contrario; (weather; breath) cattivo; (baseball) fuori linea di gioco ‖ s (of boats) urto, collisione; (baseball) palla colpita fuori linea di gioco; (boxing) colpo basso; (sports) fallo ‖ adv slealmente; (baseball) fuori linea di gioco; **to fall foul of** entrare in collisione con; urtarsi con; **to run foul of** avere una controversia con ‖ tr sporcare; otturare; (baseball) colpire fuori linea di gioco ‖ intr (said of two boats) entrare in collisione; (said, e.g., of a rope) imbrogliarsi

foul-mouthed ['faʊl'maʊ ð d] or ['faʊl-'maʊθt] adj sboccato, osceno

foul' play' s reato; (sports) gioco sleale

found [faʊnd] tr fondare; (to melt, to cast) fondere

foundation [faʊn'deʃən] s fondazione; (endowment) dotazione; (charitable) patronato; (masonry support) platea, fondamenta fpl; (make-up) fondo tinta; (fig) fondatezza

founder ['faʊndər] s fondatore m; (of family) capostipite m; (of metals) fonditore m ‖ intr (said of a ship) affondare; (said of a horse) azzopparsi; (to fail) fare fiasco

foundling ['faʊndlɪŋ] s trovatello

found'ling hos'pital s brefotrofio

found·ry ['faʊndri] s (-ries) fonderia

found'ry·man s (-men) fonditore m

fount [faʊnt] s fonte f

fountain ['faʊntən] s fonte f, fontana; (of knowledge) pozzo

foun'tain·head' s sorgente f

foun'tain pen' s penna stilografica

foun'tain syringe' s clistere m a pera

four [for] adj & pron quattro ‖ s quattro; **four o'clock** le quattro; **on all fours** gattoni, carponi

four'-cy'cle adj a quattro tempi

four'-cyl'inder adj a quattro cilindri

four'-flush' intr (coll) millantarsi

fourflusher ['for,flʌʃər] s (coll) millantatore m

four-footed ['for'fʊtɪd] adj quadrupede

four' hun'dred adj, s & pron quattro-

cento ‖ **the Four Hundred** l'alta società

four'-in-hand' s cravatta a cappio; tiro a quattro

four'-lane' adj a quattro corsie

four'-leaf clo'ver s quadrifoglio

four-legged ['for'legɪd] or ['for'legd] adj a quattro zampe; (schooner) (coll) a quattro alberi

four'-letter word' s parolaccia di quattro lettere

four'-mo'tor plane' s quadrimotore m

four'-o'clock' s (bot) bella di notte

four' of a kind' s (cards) poker m

four'post'er s letto a baldacchino

four'score' adj ottanta

foursome ['forsəm] s gruppo di quattro giocatori

fourteen ['for'tin] adj, s & pron quattordici m

fourteenth ['for'tinθ] adj, s & pron quattordicesimo ‖ s (in dates) quattordici m

fourth [forθ] adj, s & pron quarto ‖ s (in dates) quattro

fourth' estate' s quarto potere

four'-way' adj a quattro orifizi; fra quattro persone; quadruplice

fowl [faʊl] s pollo ‖ intr uccellare

fowl'ing piece' s fucile m da caccia

fox [fɑks] s volpe f ‖ tr (coll) ingannare

fox'glove' s digitale f

fox'hole' s buca ricovero

fox'hound' s segugio

fox' hunt' s caccia alla volpe

fox' ter'rier s fox-terrier m

fox'-trot' s (of a horse) piccolo trotto; (dance) fox-trot m

fox·y ['fɑksi] adj (-ier; -iest) volpino, astuto

foyer ['fɔɪ·ər] s (of a private house) ingresso, vestibolo; (theat) ridotto

fracas ['frekəs] s lite f, tumulto

fraction ['frækʃən] s frazione; frammento

fractional ['frækʃənəl] adj frazionario; insignificante

fractious ['frækʃəs] adj litigioso, permaloso; indisciplinato

fracture ['fræktʃər] s frattura ‖ tr fratturare; (e.g., an arm) fratturarsi, rompersi ‖ intr fratturarsi

fragile ['frædʒɪl] adj fragile

fragment ['frægmənt] s frammento; (e.g., of a movie) spezzone m ‖ tr frammentare, spezzare

fragmenta'tion bomb' [,frægmən'teʃən] s bomba dirompente

fragrant ['fregrənt] adj fragrante

frail [frel] adj (not robust) gracile; (easily broken) fragile; (morally weak) debole ‖ s canestro di giunco

frail·ty ['frelti] s (-ties) fragilità f; (of a person) debolezza

frame [frem] s (of picture) cornice f; (of glasses) montatura; (structure) ossatura; (of a building) ingabbiatura, impalcatura; (for embroidering) telaio; (of a window) intelaiatura; (of mind) stato; (of government) sistema m; (mov) inquadratura; (phot) fotogramma m; (aer) ordinata;

(naut) costa || *tr* (*to put in a frame*) incorniciare; montare; costruire; inventare; esprimere; (slang) architettare un' accusa contro

frame' house' *s* casa con l'ossatura di legno

frame'-up' *s* (slang) complotto per incriminare un innocente

frame'work *s* intelaiatura, impalcatura; palificazione

franc [fræŋk] *s* franco

France [fræns] or [frɑns] *s* la Francia

Frances ['frænsɪs] or ['frɑnsɪs] *s* Francesca

franchise ['frænt/aɪz] *s* diritto di voto; concessione; (*privilege*) franchigia

Francis ['frænsɪs] or ['frɑnsɪs] *s* Francesco

Franciscan [fræn'sɪskən] *adj & s* francescano

frank [fræŋk] *adj* sincero, schietto || *s* affrancatura postale; lettera affrancata; (*franking privilege*) franchigia postale || *tr* affrancare || **Frank** *s* (*member of Frankish tribe*) franco; (*masculine name*) Franco

frankfurter ['fræŋkfərtər] *s* salsiccia di Francoforte, Frankfurter *m*

frankincense ['fræŋkɪn,sɛns] *s* olibano

Frankish ['fræŋkɪ/] *adj & s* franco

frankness ['fræŋknɪs] *s* franchezza

frantic ['fræntɪk] *adj* frenetico

frappé [fræˈpe] *adj & s* frappé *m*

frat [fræt] *s* (slang) associazione di studenti

fraternal [frəˈtʌrnəl] *adj* fraterno

fraterni·ty ['frəˈtʌrnɪti] *s* (-ties) (*brotherliness*) fraternità *f;* sodalizio; (eccl) confraternita; (U.S.A.) associazione di studenti

fraternize ['frætər,naɪz] *intr* fraternizzare

fraud [frɔd] *s* truffa, frode *f;* (*person*) (coll) truffatore *m*

fraudulent ['frɔdjələnt] *adj* fraudolento; (*conversion*) indebito

fraught [frɔt] *adj*—fraught with carico di, gravido di

fray [fre] *s* zuffa, rissa, lotta || *intr* sfilacciarsi, logorarsi

freak [frik] *s* (*sudden fancy*) capriccio, ticchio; (*person, animal*) fenomeno

freakish ['frikɪ/] *adj* capriccioso; strano, grottesco

freckle ['frɛkəl] *s* lentiggine *f,* efelide *f*

freckle-faced ['frɛkəl,fest] *adj* lentigginoso

freckly ['frɛkli] *adj* lentigginoso

Frederick ['frɛdərɪk] *s* Federico

free [fri] *adj* (freer ['fri·ər]; freest ['fri·ɪst]) libero; gratis; franco; sciolto; esente; generoso; **to be free with** essere prodigo di; **to set free** liberare || *adv* liberamente; in libertà; gratis || *v* (*pret & pp* **freed** [frid], *ger* **freeing** ['fri·ɪŋ]) *tr* liberare; (*from customs*) svincolare; esimere

freebooter ['fri,butər] *s* pirata *m*

free'born' *adj* nato in libertà; proprio di un popolo libero

freedom ['fridəm] *s* libertà *f*

free'dom of speech' *s* libertà *f* di parola

free'dom of the press' *s* libertà *f* di stampa

free'dom of the seas' *s* libertà *f* di navigazione

free'dom of wor'ship *s* libertà religiosa

free' en'terprise *s* economia libera

free'-for-all' *s* rissa, tafferuglio

free' hand' *s* libertà assoluta

free'-hand *adj* a mano libera

freehanded ['fri'hændɪd] *adj* liberale, generoso

free' lance' *s* giornalista *mf* pubblicista; scrittore *m* che lavora senza contratto; soldato di ventura

free'load'er ['lodər] *s* (coll) mangiatore *m* a sbafo

free'man *s* (-men) uomo libero; cittadino

Free'ma'son *s* frammassone *m*

Free'ma'soury *s* frammassoneria

free' of charge' *adj* gratis, senza spese

free' port' *s* porto franco

free' serv'ice *s* manutenzione gratuita

free'-spo'ken *adj* franco, aperto

free'stone' *adj* spiccagnolo || *s* pesca spicca

free'think'er *s* libero pensatore

free' thought' *s* libero pensiero

free' trade' *s* libero scambio

free'trad'er *s* liberoscambista *mf*

free'way' *s* autostrada

free' will' *s* libero arbitrio

freeze [friz] *s* gelo, gelata; (*e.g., of prices*) blocco || *v* (*pret* **froze** [froz]; *pp* **frozen**) *tr* gelare; (*credits, rentals, etc.*) bloccare || *intr* gelarsi; (*said of brakes*) inchiodarsi; morire assiderato; (*to become immobilized*) irrigidirsi

freeze'-dry' *v* (*pret & pp* **-dried**') *tr* liofilizzare

freezer ['frizər] *s* congelatore *m;* (*for making ice cream*) sorbettiera

freight [fret] *s* carico; (*charge*) porto; (naut) nolo; **by freight** come carico mercantile; (rr) a piccola velocità || *tr* spedire come carico

freight' car' *s* vagone *m* or carro merci

freighter ['fretər] *s* speditore *m; nave f* da carico

freight' plat'form *s* (rr) banchina adibita al traffico merci

freight' sta'tion *s* (rr) stazione merci

freight' train' *s* treno merci, merci *m*

freight' yard' *s* (rr) scalo merci

French [frɛnt/] *adj & s* francese *m; the* **French** i francesi

French' bread' *s* pane *m* a bastone

French' chalk' *s* pietra da sarto

French' door' *s* porta a vetri

French' dress'ing *s* salsa verde con aceto

French' fried' pota'toes *spl* patate fritte affettate

French' horn' *s* (mus) corno

French' leave' *s*—to take French leave andarsene all'inglese, filare all'inglese

French'man *s* (-men) francese *m*

French' tel'ephone *s* microtelefono

French' toast' *s* pane dorato al salto

French' win'dow *s* portafinestra

French'wom'an *s* (-wom'en) francese *f*

frenzied ['frenzid] *adj* frenetico
fren·zy ['frenzi] *s* (-zies) frenesia
frequen·cy ['frikwənsi] *s* (-cies) frequenza
fre'quency modula'tion *s* modulazione di frequenza
frequent ['frikwənt] *adj* frequente ‖ [frɪ'kwent] or ['frikwənt] *tr* frequentare, praticare
frequently ['frikwəntli] *adv* frequentemente
fres·co ['fresko] *s* (-coes or -cos) affresco ‖ *tr* affrescare
fresh [freʃ] *adj* fresco; (*water*) dolce; (*new*) nuovo; (*wind*) moderato; (*inexperienced*) novizio; (*cheeky*) (slang) sfacciato ‖ *adv* recentemente, di recente; **fresh in** (coll) appena arrivato; **fresh out** (coll) appena esaurito
freshen ['freʃən] *tr* rinfrescare ‖ *intr* rinfrescarsi
freshet ['freʃɪt] *s* piena, crescita
fresh'man *s* (-men) (*newcomer*) novizio; (educ) matricola
freshness ['freʃnɪs] *s* freschezza; (*of air*) frescura; (*cheek*) (slang) sfacciataggine *f*
fresh'-wa'ter *adj* d'acqua dolce; poco conosciuto; piccolo
fret [fret] *s* (*interlaced design*) fregio, greca; irritazione; (mus) tasto ‖ *v* (*pret & pp* **fretted**; *ger* **fretting**) *tr* fregiare ‖ *intr* fremere, trepidare, agitarsi
fretful ['fretfəl] *adj* irritabile, permaloso
fret'work' *s* greca
Freudianism ['frɔɪdɪ-ə,nɪzəm] *s* freudismo
friar ['fraɪ-ər] *s* frate *m*
friar·y ['fraɪ-əri] *s* (-ies) convento di frati
fricassee [,frɪkə'si] *s* fricassea
friction ['frɪk/ən] *s* frizione; disaccordo, dissenso
fric'tion tape' *s* nastro isolante
Friday ['fraɪdi] *s* venerdì *m*
fried [fraɪd] *adj* fritto
fried' egg' *s* uovo al tegame, uovo occhio di manzo
friend [frend] *s* amico; **to be friends with** essere amico di; **to make friends** allacciare amicizie; **to make friends with** fare l'amicizia di
friend·ly ['frendli] *adj* (-lier; -liest) amico, amichevole
friendship ['frend/ɪp] *s* amicizia
frieze [friz] *s* (archit) fregio
frigate ['frɪgɪt] *s* fregata
fright [fraɪt] *s* spavento; **to take fright at** spaventarsi di
frighten ['fraɪtən] *tr* intimorire, spaventare; **to frighten away** mettere in fuga, sgomentare ‖ *intr* spaventarsi
frightful ['fraɪtfəl] *adj* spaventevole, orribile; (coll) enorme
frightfulness ['fraɪtfəlnɪs] *s* spavento; terrorismo
frigid ['frɪdʒɪd] *adj* freddo; (*zone*) glaciale
frigidity [frɪ'dʒɪdɪti] *s* (fig) frigidezza; (pathol) frigidità *f*
frill [frɪl] *s* pieghettatura; (*of birds and*

other animals) collarino; (*in dress, speech, etc.*) affettazione
fringe [frɪndʒ] *s* frangia; (*in dressmaking*) volantino; (*on curtains*) balza; **on the fringe of** all'orlo di ‖ *tr* orlare
fringe' ben'efits *spl* assegni *mpl*, benefici *mpl* marginali
fripper·y ['frɪpəri] *s* (-ies) (*finery*) fronzoli *mpl*; ostentazione; (*trifles*) cianfrusaglie *fpl*
frisk [frɪsk] *tr* perquisire; (slang) derubare ‖ *intr* fare capriole
frisk·y ['frɪski] *adj* (-ier; -iest) gaio, vivace
fritter ['frɪtər] *s* frittella; frammento ‖ *tr*—**to fritter away** sprecare
frivolous ['frɪvələs] *adj* frivolo
friz [frɪz] *s* (**frizzes**) ricciolo ‖ *v* (*pret & pp* **frizzed**; *ger* **frizzing**) *tr* arricciare
frizzle ['frɪzəl] *s* ricciolo ‖ *tr* arricciare ‖ *intr* arricciarsi
friz·zly ['frɪzli] *adj* (-zlier; -zliest) crespo, riccio
fro [fro] *adv*—**to and fro** avanti e indietro; **to go to and fro** andare e venire
frock [frak] *s* gabbano; (*smock*) grembiule *m*; blusa; (*of priest*) tonaca
frock' coat' *s* finanziera
frog [frag] or [frɔg] *s* rana; (*button and loop on a garment*) alamaro; (*in throat*) raschio
frog'man' *s* (-men') sommozzatore *m*, uomo rana
frol·ic ['fralɪk] *s* scherzo, monelleria ‖ *v* (*pret & pp* **-icked**; *ger* **-icking**) *intr* scherzare, folleggiare
frolicsome ['fralɪksəm] *adj* scherzoso
from [frʌm], [fram] or [frɔm] *prep* da; di, e.g., **I am from New York** sono di New York; da parte di; a, e.g., **to take s.th away from s.o.** portar via qlco a qlcu
front [frʌnt] *adj* frontale, anteriore; di fronte ‖ *s* fronte *m & f*; (*of a building*) prospetto; (*of a book*) principio; (*of a shirt*) sparato; (*e.g., of wealth*) apparenza; (theat) boccascena *m*; (mil) fronte *m*; **in front of** dinanzi a; **to put on a front** (coll) fare ostentazione; **to put up a bold front** (coll) farsi coraggio ‖ *tr* (*to face*) fronteggiare; (*to confront*) affrontare; (*to supply with a front*) coprire; servire da facciata a ‖ *intr*—**to front on** dare su
frontage ['frʌntɪdʒ] *s* facciata, veduta; terreno di fronte alla casa
front' door' *s* porta d'entrata
front' drive' *s* (aut) trazione anteriore
frontier [frʌn'tɪr] *adj* limitrofo ‖ *s* frontiera
fron'tiers'man *s* (-men) pioniere *m*
frontispiece ['frʌntɪs,pis] *s* (*of book*) pagina illustrata di fronte al frontispizio; (*of building*) facciata
front' mat'ter *s* (*of book*) parte *f* preliminare
front'-page' *tr* stampare in prima pagina
front' porch' *s* porticato

front' room' *s* stanza con vista sulla strada
front' row' *s* prima fila
front' seat' *s* posto in una delle file davanti; (aut) sedile *m* anteriore
front' steps' *spl* scalinata d'ingresso
front' view' *s* vista sulla strada
frost [frɔst] or [frɑst] *s* gelo, brina, gelata, (fig) freddezza; (slang) fiasco || *tr* agghiacciare; (with sugar) glassare; (glass) smerigliare
frost'bite' *s* congelamento
frost'ed glass' *s* vetro smerigliato
frosting ['frɔstɪŋ] or ['frɑstɪŋ] *s* glassatura; (of glass) smerigliatura
frost•y ['frɔsti] or ['frɑsti] *adj* (-ier; -iest) brinato; (hair) canuto; (fig) gelido
froth [frɔθ] or [frɑθ] *s* schiuma; (fig) frivolezza || *intr* schiumare; (at the mouth) avere la schiuma
froth•y ['frɔθi] or ['frɑθi] *adj* (-ier; -iest) spumoso; frivolo
froward ['frowərd] *adj* indocile
frown [fraʊn] *s* aggrottare *m* delle ciglia; (of disapproval) cipiglio || *intr* aggrottare le ciglia; **to frown at or on** disapprovare
frows•y or **frowz•y** ['fraʊzi] *adj* (-ier; -iest) sporco; puzzolente
fro'zen foods' ['frozən] *spl* cibi congelati; cibi surgelati
frugal ['frugəl] *adj* parsimonioso; (in food and drink) frugale
fruit [frut] *adj* (tree) fruttifero; (dish) da frutta || *s* (such as apple) frutto; (collectively) frutta, e.g., **I like fruit** mi piace la frutta; (fig) frutto
fruit' cake' *s* torta con noci e canditi
fruit' cup' *s* macedonia di frutta
fruit' dish' *s* fruttiera, portafrutta *m*
fruit' fly' *s* moscerino del vino
fruitful ['frutfəl] *adj* fruttuoso
fruition [fru'ɪʃən] *s* realizzazione; **to come to fruition** giungere a buon fine
fruit' jar' *s* vaso da frutta
fruit' juice' *s* sugo or spremuta di frutta
fruitless ['frutlɪs] *adj* infruttuoso
fruit' sal'ad *s* macedonia di frutta
fruit' stand' *s* bancarella da fruttivendolo
fruit' store' *s* negozio di frutta
frumpish ['frʌmpɪʃ] *adj* trasandato
frustrate ['frʌstret] *tr* frustrare
fry [fraɪ] *s* (**fries**) fritto || *v* (pret & pp **fried**) *tr & intr* friggere
fry'ing pan' *s* padella; **out of the frying pan into the fire** dalla padella nella brace
fudge [fʌdʒ] *s* dolce *m* di cioccolato
fuel ['fju-əl] *s* combustibile *m*; (fig) cibo || *v* (pret & pp **fueled** or **fuelled**; ger **fueling** or **fuelling**) *tr* rifornire di carburante || *intr* rifornirsi di carburante
fuel' cell' *s* cellula elettrogena
fu'el oil' *s* nafta, olio pesante
fu'el tank' *s* serbatoio del carburante
fugitive ['fjudʒɪtɪv] *adj & s* fuggiasco, fuggitivo
fugue [fjug] *s* (mus) fuga
ful•crum ['fʌlkrəm] *s* (-**crums** or -**cra** [krə]) fulcro

fulfill [fʊl'fɪl] *tr* (to carry out) eseguire; (an obligation) mantenere; (to bring to an end) completare
fulfillment [fʊl'fɪlmənt] *s* adempimento; realizzazione
full [fʊl] *adj* pieno; (speed) tutto; (garment) ampio; (voice) spiegato; (of food) sazio; (member) effettivo; **full of aches and pains** pieno d'acciacchi; **full of fun** divertentissimo; **full of play** pieno di vita || *s* pieno; colmo; **in full per esteno, in pieno; to the full** completamente || *adv* completamente; **full many (a)** moltissimi; **full well** perfettamente || *tr* follare
full-blooded ['fʊl'blʌdɪd] *adj* vigoroso; purosangue
full-blown ['fʊl'blon] *adj* completamente sbocciato; maturo
full-bodied ['fʊl'bɑdɪd] *adj* forte, ricco
full' dress' *s* vestito da sera; (mil) tenuta di gala, alta uniforme
full-faced ['fʊl'fest] *adj* paffuto; (view) intero; (typ) grassetto
full-fledged ['fʊl'fledʒd] *adj* completamente sviluppato; vero, autentico
full-grown ['fʊl'gron] *adj* completamente sviluppato, adulto
full' house' *s* (theat) piena; (poker) full *m*
full'-length' mir'ror *s* specchiera
full'-length mo'vie *s* lungometraggio
full' moon' *s* luna piena
full' name' *s* nome *m* e cognome *m*
full'-page' *adj* di tutta una pagina
full' pow'ers *spl* pieni poteri
full' sail' *adv* a vele spiegate
full'-scale' *adj* in grandezza naturale; completo
full-sized ['fʊl'saɪzd] *adj* in grandezza naturale
full' speed' *adv* a tutta velocità
full' stop' *s* fermata; (gram) punto
full' swing' *s* piena attività
full' tilt' *adv* a tutta forza
full'-time' *adj* a orario completo
fully ['fʊli] or ['fʊlli] *adv* completamente, del tutto
fulsome ['fʊlsəm] or ['fʌlsəm] *adj* basso, volgare; nauseante
fumble ['fʌmbəl] *tr* (a ball) lasciar cadere || *intr* titubare; andare a tentoni; (in one's pocket) cercare alla cieca
fume [fjum] *s* fumo, vapore *m*, esalazione || *tr* affumicare || *intr* fumare, esalare fumo; (to show anger) irritarsi
fumigate ['fjumɪˌget] *tr* fumigare
fumigation [ˌfjumɪ'geʃən] *s* fumigazione
fun [fʌn] *s* divertimento, spasso; **to be fun** essere divertente; **to have fun** divertirsi; **to make fun of** prendersi gioco di
function ['fʌŋkʃən] *s* funzione || *intr* funzionare, marciare, camminare
functional ['fʌŋkʃənəl] *adj* funzionale
functionalism ['fʌŋkʃənəlˌɪzəm] *s* funzionalismo
functionar•y ['fʌŋkʃəˌneri] *s* (-**ies**) funzionario

fund [fʌnd] *s* fondo; (*of knowledge*) suppellettile *f* ‖ *tr* (*debts*) consolidare
fundamental [ˌfʌndə'mentəl] *adj* fondamentale ‖ *s* fondamento
fundamentalist [ˌfʌndə'mentəlıst] *adj* & *s* scritturale *m*
funeral ['fjunərəl] *adj* funebre, funerario ‖ *s* funerale *m*, trasporto funebre; **it's not my funeral** (slang) non sono affari miei
fu'neral direc'tor *s* imprenditore *m* di pompe funebri
fu'neral home' or **par'lor** *s* impresa di pompe funebri
fu'neral serv'ice *s* ufficio dei defunti
funereal [fju'nırı·əl] *adj* funebre
fungous ['fʌŋɡəs] *adj* fungoso
fungus ['fʌŋɡəs] *s* (**funguses** or **fungi** ['fʌndʒaɪ]) fungo
funicular [fju'nɪkjələr] *adj* & *s* funicolare *f*
funk [fʌŋk] *s* (coll) paura; (coll) codardo; **in a funk** (coll) con una paura matta
fun·nel ['fʌnəl] *s* imbuto; (*smoke-stack*) fumaiolo; (*for ventilation*) manica a vento ‖ *v* (*pret* & *pp* **-neled** or **-nelled**) *ger* **-neling** or **-nelling**) *tr* incanalare
funnies ['fʌnɪz] *spl* pagine *fpl* fumetti
fun·ny ['fʌni] *adj* (**-nier; -niest**) comico, buffo; (coll) strano; **to strike as funny** parere strano or buffo a
fun'ny bone' *s* osso rabbioso (del gomito); **to strike s.o.'s funny bone** far ridere qlcu
fur [fʌr] *s* pelo; (*garment*) pelliccia; (*on the tongue*) patina
furbelow ['fʌrbə ˌlo] *s* falpalà *m*
furbish ['fʌrbɪʃ] *tr* lustrare; mettere a nuovo; **to furbish up** rinfrescare
furious ['fjurı·əs] *adj* furioso
furl [fʌrl] *tr* (*a flag*) incazzottare; (naut) raccogliere, strangolare
fur-lined ['fʌr ˌlaɪnd] *adj* foderato di pelliccia
furlong ['fʌrlɒŋ] or ['fʌrləŋ] *s* un ottavo di miglio terrestre
furlough ['fʌrlo] *s* licenza ‖ *tr* licenziare
furnace ['fʌrnɪs] *s* fornace *f*; (*to heat a house*) caldaia del calorifero
furnish ['fʌrnɪʃ] *tr* fornire; ammobiliare
furnishings ['fʌrnɪʃɪŋz] *spl* mobilia; (*things to wear*) accessori *mpl* da uomo
furniture ['fʌrnɪtʃər] *s* mobili *mpl*, mobilia; (naut) attrezzatura; **a piece of furniture** un mobile

fur·ni·ture deal'er *s* mobiliere *m*
furor ['fjurər] *s* furore *m*
furrier ['fʌrı·ər] *s* pellicciaio
furrier·y ['fʌrı·əri] *s* (**-ies**) pellicceria
furrow ['fʌro] *s* solco ‖ *tr* solcare
further ['fʌrðər] *adj* più lontano; ulteriore ‖ *adv* oltre; più; inoltre ‖ *tr* favorire, incoraggiare
furtherance ['fʌrðərəns] *s* avanzamento, incoraggiamento
furthermore ['fʌrðər ˌmor] *adv* inoltre
furthest ['fʌrðıst] *adj* (il) più lontano ‖ *adv* al massimo
furtive ['fʌrtɪv] *adj* furtivo
fu·ry ['fjuri] *s* (**-ries**) furia
furze [fʌrz] *s* ginestra spinosa
fuse [fjuz] *s* (*for igniting an explosive*) miccia; (*for detonating an explosive*) spoletta; (elec) fusibile *m*; **to burn out a fuse** bruciare un fusibile ‖ *tr* fondere ‖ *intr* fondersi; (elec) saltare
fuse' box' *s* valvoliera
fuselage ['fjuzəlɪdʒ] or [ˌfjuzə'lɑʒ] *s* fusoliera
fusible ['fjuzɪbəl] *adj* fusibile
fusillade [ˌfjuzı'led] *s* fucileria; (fig) gragnola ‖ *tr* attaccare con fuoco di fucileria
fusion ['fjuʒən] *s* fusione
fuss [fʌs] *s* agitazione inutile; (coll) alterco per nulla; **to make a fuss** accogliere festosamente; fare molte storie; **to make a fuss over** aver un alterco su ‖ *tr* disturbare ‖ *intr* agitarsi per un nonnulla
fuss·y ['fʌsi] *adj* (**-ier; -iest**) (*person*) pignolo, meticoloso; (*object*) carico di fronzoli; (*writing*) complicato
fustian ['fʌstʃən] *s* fustagno; (fig) verbosità *f*, magniloquenza
fust·y ['fʌsti] *adj* (**-ier; -iest**) ammuffito, che sa di muffa; antico, sorpassato
futile ['fjutıl] *adj* (*unproductive*) sterile; (*unimportant*) futile
futili·ty [fju'tɪlıti] *s* (**-ties**) sterilità *f*; futilità *f*
future ['fjutʃər] *adj* futuro ‖ *s* futuro; **futures** contratto con consegna a termine; **in the near future** nel prossimo avvenire
fuze [fjuz] *s* (*for igniting an explosive*) miccia; (*for detonating an explosive*) spoletta; (elec) fusibile *m* ‖ *tr* innestare la spoletta a
fuzz [fʌz] *s* lanugine *f*, peluria; (*in corners*) polvere *f*; (slang) poliziotto; (slang) polizia
fuzz·y ['fʌzi] *adj* (**-ier; -iest**) lanuginoso; coperto di polvere; (*indistinct*) confuso

G

G, g [dʒi] *s* settima lettera dell'alfabeto inglese
gab [ɡæb] *s* (coll) parlantina ‖ *v* (*pret* & *pp* **gabbed; ger gabbing**) *intr* (coll) chiacchierare
gabardine ['ɡæbər ˌdin] *s* gabardine *f*
gabble ['ɡæbəl] *s* barbugliamento ‖ *intr* barbugliare

gable ['ɡebəl] *s* (archit) timpano
ga'ble roof' *s* tetto a due falde, tetto a capanna
gad [ɡæd] *v* (*pret* & *pp* **gadded; ger gadding**) *intr* bighellonare
gad'about' *adj* ozioso ‖ *s* vagabondo, bighellone *m*; fannullone *m*
gad'fly' *s* (**-flies**) tafano, moscone *m*

gadget ['gædʒɪt] *s* congegno, dispositivo, macchinetta

Gaelic ['gelɪk] *adj* & *s* gaelico

gaff [gæf] *s* arpione *m*; (naut) picco; **to stand the gaff** (slang) aver pazienza

gag [gæg] *s* bavaglio; (*joke*) barzelletta; (theat) battuta improvvisata ‖ *v* (pret & pp **gagged**; ger **gagging**) *tr* imbavagliare; soffocare ‖ *intr* sentirsi venire la nausea

gage [gedʒ] *s* (*pledge*) pegno; (*challenge*) sfida

gale·ty ['ge·ɪti] *s* (-ties) gaiezza

gaily ['geli] *adv* allegramente

gain [gen] *s* profitto; (*increase*) aumento ‖ *tr* guadagnare; (*to reach*) raggiungere; (*altitude*) prendere ‖ *intr* (*said of a patient*) migliorare; (*said of a watch*) correre; **to gain on** guadagnare terreno su; sorpassare

gainful ['genfəl] *adj* rimunerativo

gain'say' *v* (pret & pp **-said** [,sed] or [,sed]) *tr* disdire, misconoscere; negare

gait [get] *s* portamento, andatura

gaiter ['getər] *s* ghetta

gala ['gælə] or ['gelə] *adj* di gala ‖ *s* gala *m* & *f*, festa

galax·y ['gæləksi] *s* (-ies) galassia

gale [gel] *s* (*of wind*) bufera; (*of laughter*) scoppio; **to weather the gale** resistere alla tempesta

gall [gɔl] *s* fiele *m*; bile *f*; cistifellea; scorticatura; (*gallnut*) galla; (*audacity*) (coll) faccia tosta ‖ *tr* irritare ‖ *intr* irritarsi; (naut) logorarsi

gallant ['gælənt] or [gə'lænt] *adj* galante ‖ ['gælənt] *adj* (*brave*) valoroso; (*grand*) magnifico; (*showy*) festivo ‖ *s* prode *m*; (*man attentive to women*) galante *m*

gallant·ry ['gæləntri] *s* (-ries) galanteria; valore *m*

gall' blad'der *s* vescichetta biliare

gall'-blad'der attack' *s* travaso di bile

galleon ['gælɪ·ən] *s* galeone *m*

galler·y ['gæləri] *s* (-ies) galleria; tribuna; (*cheapest seats in theater*) loggione *m*

galley ['gæli] *s* (*vessel*) galera; (*kitchen*) (aer) cucina; (*kitchen*) (naut) cambusa; (*galley proof*) (typ) bozza in colonna; (*tray*) (typ) vantaggio

gal'ley proof' *s* bozza in colonna

gal'ley slave' *s* galeotto

Gallic ['gælɪk] *adj* gallo, gallico

galling ['gɔlɪŋ] *adj* irritante

gallivant ['gælɪ,vænt] *intr* andare a spasso; fare il galante

gall'nut' *s* galla

gallon ['gælən] *s* gallone *m*

galloon [gə'lun] *s* gallone *m*, nastro

gallop ['gæləp] *s* galoppo; **at a gallop** al galoppo ‖ *tr* far galoppare ‖ *intr* galoppare

gal·lows ['gæloz] *s* (-lows or -lowses) forca; (min) castelletto

gal'lows bird' *s* (coll) remo di galera, pendaglio da forca

gall'stone' *s* calcolo biliare

galore [gə'lor] *adv* in abbondanza

galosh [gə'lɑʃ] *s* stivaletto di gomma

galvanize ['gælvə,naɪz] *tr* galvanizzare

gal'vanized i'ron *s* ferro zincato

gambit ['gæmbɪt] *s* gambetto

gamble ['gæmbəl] *s* azzardo; (*game*) gioco d'azzardo ‖ *tr* giocare; **to gamble away** giocarsi ‖ *intr* giocare d'azzardo; (com) speculare

gambler ['gæmblər] *s* giocatore *m*; speculatore *m*

gambling ['gæmblɪŋ] *s* gioco (d'azzardo)

gam'bling den' *s* bisca

gam'bling house' *s* casa da gioco

gam·bol ['gæmbəl] *s* salto, capriola ‖ *v* (pret & pp **-boled** or **-bolled**; ger **-boling** or **-bolling**) *intr* saltare, far capriole

gambrel ['gæmbrəl] *s* garretto

gam'brel roof' *s* tetto a mansarda

game [gem] *adj* da caccia; coraggioso; (*leg*) (coll) zoppo; (coll) pronto ‖ *s* (*amusement*) gioco; (*contest*) partita; (*any sport*) sport *m*; (*wild animals hunted*) selvaggina; (*any pursuit*) attività *f*; (*object of pursuit*) bersaglio; (*bridge*) manche *f*; **the game is up** il gioco è fallito; **to make game of** farsi gioco di; **to play the game** giocare onestamente

game' bag' *s* carniere *m*

game'cock' *s* gallo da combattimento

game'keep'er *s* guardacaccia *m*

game' of chance' *s* gioco d'azzardo

game' preserve' *s* bandita di caccia

game' war'den *s* guardacaccia *m*

gamut ['gæmət] *s* (mus, fig) gamma

gam·y ['gemi] *adj* (-ier; -iest) coraggioso; (culin) che sa di selvatico

gander ['gændər] *s* papero, oca

gang [gæŋ] *adj* multiplo ‖ *s* (*of workers*) ganga; (*of thugs*) cricca ‖ *intr*—**to gang up** riunirsi; **to gang up against** or **on** (coll) gettarsi insieme contro

gangling ['gæŋglɪŋ] *adj* dinoccolato

gangli·on ['gæŋglɪ·ən] *s* (-ons or -a [ə]) ganglio

gang'plank' *s* palanca, plancia

gangrene ['gæŋgrin] *s* cancrena ‖ *tr* far andare in cancrena ‖ *intr* andare in cancrena

gangster ['gæŋstər] *s* gangster *m*

gang'way' *s* (*passageway*) corridoio; (*gangplank*) passerella, scalandrone *m*; (*in ship's side*) barcarizzo ‖ *interj* lasciar passare!

gan·try ['gæntri] *s* (-tries) (*of crane*) cavalletto; (rr) ponte *m* delle segnalazioni; (rok) piattaforma verticale, torre *f* di lancio

gap [gæp] *s* (*pass*) passo; (*in a wall*) breccia; (*interval*) lacuna; (*between two points of view*) abisso; (mach) gioco

gape [gep] or [gæp] *s* apertura; (*yawn*) sbadiglio; sguardo di meraviglia ‖ *intr* stare a bocca aperta; **to gape at** guardare a bocca aperta

garage [gə'rɑʒ] *s* rimessa

garb [gɑrb] *s* veste *f* ‖ *tr* vestire

garbage ['gɑrbɪdʒ] *s* pattume *m*, immondizia, immondizie *fpl*

gar'bage can' *s* portaimmondizie *m*

gar'bage collec'tor s spazzaturaio, spazzino, netturbino

garble ['gɑrbəl] tr falsare, mutilare

garden ['gɑrdən] s (of vegetables) orto; (of flowers) giardino

gardener ['gɑrdnər] s (of vegetables) ortolano; (of flowers) giardiniere m

gardenia [gɑr'dinɪ·ə] s gardenia

gardening ['gɑrdnɪŋ] s orticoltura; giardinaggio

gar'den par'ty s trattenimento in giardino

gargle ['gɑrgəl] s gargarismo || intr gargarizzare

gargoyle ['gɑrgɔɪl] s doccione m, gargolla

garish ['gɛrɪʃ] or ['gærɪʃ] adj appariscente; abbagliante

garland ['gɑrlənd] s ghirlanda || tr inghirlandare

garlic ['gɑrlɪk] s aglio

garment ['gɑrmənt] s capo di vestiario

gar'ment bag' s tessilsacco

garner ['gɑrnər] tr mettere in granaio; (to get) acquistarsi; (to hoard) incettare

garnet ['gɑrnɪt] adj & s granata

garnish ['gɑrnɪʃ] s guarnizione; || tr guarnire; (law) sequestrare

garret ['gærɪt] s sottotetto, soffitta

garrison ['gærɪsən] s guarnigione, presidio || tr presidiare

garrote [gə'rɑt] or [gə'rot] s strangolamento; garrotta || tr strangolare; giustiziare con la garrotta

garrulous ['gærələs] or ['gærjələs] adj garrulo, loquace

garter ['gɑrtər] s giarrettiera

gas [gæs] s gas m; (coll) benzina; (slang) successo; (slang) chiacchiere fpl || v (pret & pp **gassed**; ger **gassing**) tr fornire di gas; (mil) gassare; (slang) divertire || intr emettere gas; (slang) chiacchierare; **to gas up** fare il pieno

gas'bag' s involucro per il gas; (coll) chiacchierone m

gas' burn'er s becco a gas; (on a stove) fornello a gas

Gascony ['gæskənɪ] s la Guascogna

gaseous ['gæsɪ·əs] adj gassoso

gas' fit'ter s gassista m

gash [gæʃ] s sfregio || tr sfregiare

gas' heat' s calefazione a gas

gas'hold'er s gassometro

gasi·fy ['gæsɪ‚faɪ] v (pret & pp **-fied**) tr gassificare || intr gassificarsi

gas' jet' s fornello a gas; fiamma

gasket ['gæskɪt] s guarnizione

gas'light' s luce f del gas

gas' main' s tubatura principale del gas

gas' mask' s maschera antigas

gas' me'ter s contatore m del gas

gasoline ['gæsə‚lin] or [‚gæsə'lin] s benzina

gas'oline' deal'er s benzinaio

gas'oline' pump' s colonnetta, distributore m di benzina

gasp [gæsp] or [gɑsp] s respirazione affannosa; (of death) rantolo || tr dire affannosamente || intr boccheggiare

gas' range' s cucina a gas, fornello a gas

gas'-sta'tion attend'ant s benzinaio

gas' stove' s cucina a gas

gas' tank' s gassometro; (aut) serbatoio di benzina

gastric ['gæstrɪk] adj gastrico

gastronomy [gæs'trɑnəmɪ] s gastronomia

gas' works' s officina del gas

gate [get] s porta; (in fence or wall) cancello; (of sluice) saracinesca; (in an airport or station) uscita; (rr) barriera; (sports, theat) incasso totale; **to crash the gate** (coll) fare il portoghese

gate'keep'er s portiere m; (rr) guardabarriere m

gate'way' s passaggio, entrata

gather ['gæðər] tr raccogliere, cogliere; (news) raccapezzare; (dust) coprirsi di; (e.g., a shawl) avvolgere; (speed) aumentare (di); concludere, dedurre; (signatures) (bb) riunire; (sew) increspare || intr riunirsi; raccogliersi; accumularsi

gathering ['gæðərɪŋ] s riunione; (bb) raccolta e piegatura; (pathol) ascesso; (sew) pieghettatura

gaud·y ['gɔdɪ] adj (-ier; -iest) chiassoso, vistoso

gauge [gedʒ] s misura; calibro; (for liquids) indicatore m di livello; (of carpenter) graffietto; indice m; diametro; (aut) spia; (rr) scartamento || tr misurare; calibrare; (naut) stazzare

Gaul [gɔl] s gallo

gaunt [gɔnt] or [gɑnt] adj magro, emaciato; (e.g., landscape) desolato

gauntlet ['gɔntlɪt] or ['gɑntlɪt] s guanto; guanto di ferro; guantone m, manopola; **to run the gauntlet** (fig) esporsi alla critica; **to take up the gauntlet** raccogliere il guanto; **to throw down the gauntlet** gettare il guanto

gauze [gɔz] s garza

gavel ['gævəl] s martello, martelletto

gavotte [gə'vɑt] s gavotta

gawk [gɔk] s sciocco || intr guardare a bocca aperta

gawk·y ['gɔkɪ] adj (-ier; -iest) sgraziato, goffo

gay [ge] adj gaio; brillante; dissipato; (slang) omosessuale

gaye·ty ['ge·ɪtɪ] s (-ties) gaiezza

gaze [gez] s sguardo fisso || intr fissare lo sguardo

gazelle [gə'zɛl] s gazzella

gazette [gə'zɛt] s gazzetta

gazetteer [‚gæzə'tɪr] s dizionario geografico

gear [gɪr] s utensili mpl, attrezzi mpl; (mechanism) meccanismo, dispositivo; (aut) marcia; (mach) ingranaggio **out of gear** disingranato; (fig) disturbato; **to throw into gear** ingranare; **to throw out of gear** disingranare; (fig) disturbare || tr adattare || intr adattarsi

gear' box' s scatola del cambio

gear'shift' s cambio di velocità

gear'shift lev'er s leva del cambio
gear'wheel' s ruota dentata
gee [dʒi] *interj* oh!; che bellezza!; **gee up!** (*command to a draft animal*) arri!
Gei'ger count'er ['gaɪgər] s contatore *m* Geiger
gel [dʒɛl] s gel *m* ‖ v (*pret & pp* **gelled;** *ger* **gelling**) *intr* gelatinizzarsi
gelatine ['dʒɛlətɪn] s gelatina
geld [gɛld] v (*pret & pp* **gelded** or **gelt** [gɛlt]) *tr* castrare
gem [dʒɛm] s gemma, gioia
Gemini ['dʒɛmɪ ,naɪ] *spl* i Gemelli
gender ['dʒɛndər] s (gram) genere *m*; (coll) sesso
gene [dʒin] s (biol) gene *m*
genealo·gy [,dʒɛnɪ'ælədʒɪ] or [,dʒini·'ælədʒɪ] s (-gies) genealogia
general ['dʒɛnərəl] *adj & s* generale *m*
gen'eral deliv'ery s fermo in posta, fermo posta *m*
generalissi·mo [,dʒɛnərə'lɪsɪmo] s (-mos) generalissimo
generali·ty [,dʒɛnə'rælɪtɪ] s (-ties) generalità *f*
generalize ['dʒɛnərə ,laɪz] *tr & intr* generalizzare
generally ['dʒɛnərəlɪ] *adv* in genere, generalmente
gen'eral part'ner s accomandatario
gen'eral practi'tioner s medico generico
generalship ['dʒɛnərəl ,ʃɪp] s generalato; strategia, abilità *f* militare; abilità amministrativa
gen'eral staff' s stato maggiore
generate ['dʒɛnə ,ret] *tr* (*offspring; electricity*) generare; (math) originare
gen'erat'ing sta'tion s centrale elettrica
generation [,dʒɛnə're ʃən] s generazione
generative ['dʒɛnə ,retɪv] *adj* generativo
gen'erative gram'mar s grammatica generativa
generator ['dʒɛnə ,retər] s generatore *m*; (elec) generatrice *f*
generic [dʒɪ'nɛrɪk] *adj* generico
generous ['dʒɛnərəs] *adj* generoso; abbondante, copioso
gene·sis ['dʒɛnəsɪs] s (-ses [,siz]) genesi *f* ‖ **Genesis** s (Bib) Genesi *m*
genetic [dʒɪ'nɛtɪk] *adj* genetico ‖ **genetics** *ssg* genetica
Geneva [dʒɪ'nivə] s Ginevra
Genevan [dʒɪ'nivən] *adj & s* ginevrino
genial ['dʒinɪ·əl] *adj* affabile, geniale
genie ['dʒini] s genio
genital ['dʒɛnɪtəl] *adj* genitale ‖ **genitals** *spl* genitali *mpl*
genitive ['dʒɛnɪtɪv] *adj & s* genitivo
genius ['dʒinjəs] or ['dʒinɪ·əs] s (**geniuses**) genio ‖ s (**genii**) ['dʒinɪ ,aɪ] (*spirit; deity*) genio
Genoa ['dʒɛno·ə] s Genova
genocide ['dʒɛnə ,saɪd] s (*act*) genocidio; (*person*) genocida *mf*
Geno·ese [,dʒɛno'iz] *adj* genovese ‖ s (-ese) genovese *mf*
genre ['ʒɑnrə] *adj* (*e.g., painting*) di genere ‖ s genere *m*

genteel [dʒɛn'til] *adj* (*well-bred*) beneducato; (*affectedly polite*) manieroso, manierato
gentian ['dʒɛnʃən] s genziana
gentile ['dʒɛntɪl] or ['dʒɛntaɪl] *adj* gentilizio ‖ ['dʒɛntaɪl] *adj & s* non circonciso; non ebreo; cristiano; (*pagan*) gentile
gentili·ty [dʒɛn'tɪlɪtɪ] s (-ties) distinzione, raffinatezza
gentle ['dʒɛntəl] *adj* (*e.g., manner*) gentile; (*e.g., wind*) dolce, soave; (*wellborn*) bennato; (*tap*) leggero
gen'tle·folk' s gente *f* per bene
gen'tle·man s (-men) signore *m*; (*attendant to a person of high rank*) gentiluomo; (*well-mannered man*) gentleman *m*
gen'tleman in wait'ing s gentiluomo di camera
gentlemanly ['dʒɛntəlmənlɪ] *adj* signorile
gen'tleman of the road' s brigante *m*; vagabondo
gen'tlemen's agree'ment s accordo fondato sulla buona fede
gen'tle sex' s gentil sesso
gentry ['dʒɛntrɪ] s gente *f* per bene
genuine ['dʒɛnju·ɪn] *adj* genuino
genus ['dʒinəs] s (**genera** ['dʒɛnərə] or **genuses**) genere *m*
geographer [dʒɪ'ɑgrəfər] s geografo
geographic(al) [,dʒɪ·ə'græfɪk(əl)] *adj* geografico
geogra·phy [dʒɪ'ɑgrəfɪ] s (-phies) geografia
geologic(al) [,dʒɪ·ə'lɑdʒɪk(əl)] *adj* geologico
geologist [dʒɪ'ɑlədʒɪst] s geologo
geolo·gy [dʒɪ'ɑlədʒɪ] s (-gies) geologia
geometric(al) [,dʒɪ·ə'mɛtrɪk(əl)] *adj* geometrico
geometrician [dʒɪ ,ɑmɪ'trɪʃən] s geometra *mf*
geome·try [dʒɪ'ɑmɪtrɪ] s (-tries) geometria
George [dʒɔrdʒ] s Giorgio
geranium [dʒɪ'renɪ·əm] s geranio
geriatrics [,dʒɛrɪ'ætrɪks] *ssg* geriatria
germ [dʒʌrm] s germe *m*
German ['dʒʌrmən] *adj & s* tedesco
germane [dʒər'men] *adj* pertinente
Germanize ['dʒʌrmə ,naɪz] *tr* germanizzare
Ger'man mea'sles s rosolia, rubeola
Ger'man sil'ver s alpacca
Germany ['dʒʌrmənɪ] s la Germania
germ' car'rier s portatore *m* di germi
germ' cell' s cellula germinale
germicidal [,dʒʌrmɪ'saɪdəl] *adj* germicida
germicide ['dʒʌrmɪ ,saɪd] s germicida *m*
germinate ['dʒʌrmɪ ,net] *intr* germinare
germ' war'fare s guerra batteriologica
gerontology [,dʒɛrən'tɑlədʒɪ] s gerontologia
gerund ['dʒɛrənd] s gerundio
gestation [dʒɛs'te ʃən] s gestazione
gesticulate [dʒɛs'tɪkjə ,let] *intr* gesticolare

gesticulation [dʒɛs͵tɪkjə'leʃən] *s* gesticolazione

gesture ['dʒɛstfər] *s* gesto || *intr* gestire, gesticolare

get [gɛt] *v* (*pret* **got** [gɑt]; *pp* **got** or **gotten** ['gɑtən]; *ger* **getting**) *tr* ottenere; ricevere; prendere; andare a comprare; procacciare; riportare; procurarsi; riscuotere; guadagnare; **to get across** far capire; **to get back** riacquistare; **to get down** staccare; (*to swallow*) tranguggiare; **to get off** togliere, cavare; **to get s.o. to** + *inf* indurre che qlcu + *subj*; **to get done** far fare; **to have got** (coll) avere; **to have got to** + *inf* (coll) dovere + *inf* || *intr* (*to become*) diventare, farsi; (*to arrive*) arrivare, venire; **to get out** (*said of a convalescent*) alzarsi; **to get along** andarsene; andare avanti; tirare avanti, giostrare; aver successo; **to get along in years** essere avanti con gli anni; **to get along with** andare d'accordo con; **to get angry** arrabbiarsi; **to get around** uscire; divulgarsi; rigirare; **to get away** scappare, darsela a gambe; **to get away with s.th** scappare con qlco; (coll) farla franca; **to get back** ritornare; ricuperare; **to get back at** (coll) vendicarsi di; **to get behind** rimanere indietro; (*to support*) appoggiare, patrocinare; **to get better** migliorare; **to get by** passare oltre; (*to succeed*) arrivare a farcela; passare inosservato; **to get even with** rifarsi con, prendersi la rivincita con; **to get going** mettersi in moto; **to get in** entrare; rientrare; arrivare; **to get in deeper and deeper** cacciarsi nei pasticci; **to get in with** diventare amico di; **to get married** sposarsi **to get off** andarsene; smontare da; **to get old** invecchiare; **to get on** andare avanti; andare d'accordo; **to get out** uscire; propagarsi; **to get out of** (*a car*) uscire da; (*trouble*) trarsi di; **to get out of the way** togliersi di mezzo; **to get run over** essere investito; **to get through** finire; arrivare; farsi capire; **to get to** be finire per essere; **to get under way** mettersi in cammino; **to get up** alzarsi; **to not get over it** (coll) non arrivare a rassegnarsi

get'a·way' *s* fuga; (sports) partenza

get'-to·geth'er *s* riunione, crocchio

get'up' *s* (coll) stile *m*, presentazione; (coll) costume *m*, abbigliamento

gewgaw ['gjugɔ] *s* cianfrusaglia

geyser ['gaɪzər] *s* geyser *m*

ghast·ly ['gæstli] or ['gɑstli] *adj* (**-lier; -liest**) orribile, orrendo; spettrale

gherkin ['gʌrkɪn] *s* cetriolino

ghet·to ['gɛto] *s* (**-tos** or **-toes**) ghetto

ghost [gost] *s* spettro, fantasma *m*; **not a ghost of** nemmeno l'ombra di; **to give up the ghost** rendere l'anima

ghost·ly ['gostli] *adj* (**-lier; -liest**) spettrale, fantomatico

ghost' sto'ry *s* storia di fantasmi

ghost' town' *s* città morta

ghost' writ'er *s* collaboratore anonimo

ghoul [gul] *s* spirito necrofago; ladro di tombe

ghoulish ['gulɪʃ] *adj* demoniaco, macabro

GI ['dʒi'aɪ] (letterword) (**General Issue**) *s* (**GI's**) soldato degli Stati Uniti

giant ['dʒaɪ·ənt] *adj* & *s* gigante *m*

giantess ['dʒaɪ·əntɪs] *s* gigantessa

gibberish ['dʒɪbərɪʃ] or ['gɪbərɪʃ] *s* linguaggio inintelligibile

gibbet ['dʒɪbɪt] *s* forca || *tr* impiccare sulla forca; (*to hold up to scorn*) mettere alla berlina

gibe [dʒaɪb] *s* scherno, frecciata || *intr* schernire; **to gibe at** beffarsi di

giblets ['dʒɪblɪts] *spl* rigaglie *fpl*

giddiness ['gɪdɪnɪs] *s* vertigine *f;* frivolezza

gid·dy ['gɪdi] *adj* (**-dier; -diest**) vertiginoso; preso dalle vertigini; frivolo

gift [gɪft] *s* regalo; (*natural ability*) dono, dote *f;* (*for Christmas*) strenna

gifted ['gɪftɪd] *adj* dotato

gift' horse' *s*—**never look a gift horse in the mouth** a caval donato non si guarda in bocca

gift' of gab' *s* (coll) facondia; **to have the gift of gab** (coll) avere la lingua sciolta

gift' pack'age *s* pacco-dono

gift' shop' *s* negozio di regali

gift'-wrap' *v* (*pret & pp* **-wrapped;** *ger* **-wrapping**) *tr* incartare in carta speciale per regali

gigantic [dʒaɪ'gæntɪk] *adj* gigantesco

giggle ['gɪgəl] *s* risolino || *intr* ridere scioccamente, ridacchiare

gigo·lo ['dʒɪgə͵lo] *s* (**-los**) gigolo

gild [gɪld] *v* (*pret & pp* **gilded** or **gilt** [gɪlt]) *tr* dorare, indorare

gilding ['gɪldɪŋ] *s* doratura

gill [gɪl] *s* (*of fish*) branchia || [dʒɪl] *s* quarto di pinta

gilt [gɪlt] *adj & s* dorato

gilt-edged ['gɪlt͵ɛdʒd] *adj* a bordo dorato; di primissima qualità

gimcrack ['dʒɪm͵kræk] *adj* di nessun valore || *s* cianfrusaglia

gimlet ['gɪmlɪt] *s* succhiello

gimmick ['gɪmɪk] *s* (slang) trucco

gin [dʒɪn] *s* (*liquor*) gin *m;* (*trap*) trappola; (mach) arganello; (tex) sgranatrice *f* di cotone || *v* (*pret & pp* **ginned;** *ger* **ginning**) *tr* ginnare, sgranare

ginger ['dʒɪndʒər] *s* zenzero; (coll) energia, vivacità *f*

gin'ger ale' *s* gazosa allo zenzero

gin'ger·bread' *s* pan di zenzero; ornamento di cattivo gusto

gingerly ['dʒɪndʒərli] *adj* cauto || *adv* con cautela

gin'ger·snap' *s* biscotto allo zenzero

gingham ['gɪŋəm] *s* rigatino

giraffe [dʒɪ'ræf] or [dʒɪ'rɑf] *s* giraffa

girandole ['dʒɪrən͵dol] *s* girandola

gird [gʌrd] *v* (*pret & pp* **girt** [gʌrt] or **girded**) *tr* cingere; (*to equip*) dotare; (*to prepare*) preparare; (*to surround*) circondare

girder ['gʌrdər] *s* longherina

girdle ['gʌrdəl] s reggicalze m, zona, fascetta || tr fasciare; circondare

girl [gʌrl] s fanciulla; ragazza

girl' friend' s amica, innamorata

girlhood ['gʌrlhud] s adolescenza, giovinezza

girlish ['gʌrlɪʃ] adj fanciullesco; da ragazza

girl' scout' s giovane esploratrice f

girth [gʌrθ] s circonferenza; fascia; (to hold a saddle) sottopancia m

gist [dʒɪst] s sugo, nocciolo, essenza

give [gɪv] s elasticità f || v (pret gave [gev]; pp given ['gɪvən]) tr dare; (trouble) causare; (a play) rappresentare; (a speech; fruit; a sigh) fare; to give away distribuire gratuitamente; (to reveal) lasciarsi sfuggire; (a bride) accompagnare all'altare; (coll) tradire; to give back restituire; to give forth (odors) emettere; to give oneself up darsi; to give up cedere; (a position) abbandonare || intr dare; cedere; (said, e.g., of a rope) rompersi; to give in cedere; darsi per vinto; to give out esaurirsi; venir meno; to give up darsi per vinto

give'-and-take' s compromesso; conversazione briosa

give'a·way' s premio gratuito; rivelazione involontaria; (game) vinciperdi m; (rad, telv) programma m a premi

given ['gɪvən] adj dato; given that dato che, concesso che

giv'en name' s nome m di battesimo

giver ['gɪvər] s donatore m; dispensatore m

gizzard ['gɪzərd] s magone m

glacial ['gleʃəl] adj glaciale

glacier ['gleʃər] s ghiacciaio

glad [glæd] adj (gladder; gladdest) felice, lieto, contento; to be glad (to) essere felice (di)

gladden ['glædən] tr rallegrare

glade [gled] s radura

glad' hand' s (coll) accoglienza calorosa

gladiator ['glædɪ‚etər] s gladiatore m

gladiola [‚glædɪ'olə] or [glə'daɪ‚ələ] s gladiolo

gladly ['glædli] adv volentieri, di buon grado

gladness ['glædnɪs] s contentezza

glad' rags' s (coll) panni mpl da festa; (coll) vestito da sera

glamorous ['glæmərəs] adj affascinante, attraente

glamour ['glæmər] s fascino, malia

glam'our girl' s ragazza sci-sci

glance [glæns] or [glɑns] s occhiata, guardata; at first glance a prima vista || intr lanciare uno sguardo; to glance at dare un'occhiata a; to glance off sorvolare su; deviare da; to glance over dare una scorsa a

gland [glænd] s ghiandola

glanders ['glændərz] spl morva

glare [gler] s splendore m, luce f abbagliante; sguardo minaccioso || intr risplendere; lanciare occhiatacce; to glare at fare la faccia feroce a

glare' ice' s vetrato

glaring ['glerɪŋ] adj risplendente, abbagliante; (look) torvo; evidente

glass [glæs] or [glɑs] s vetro; (tumbler) bicchiere m; (mirror) specchio; (glassware) cristalleria; glasses occhiali mpl

glass' blow'er ['blo‚ər] s vetraio

glass' case' s vetrinetta

glass' cut'ter s tagliatore m di cristallo; (tool) diamante m tagliavetro

glass' door' s porta a vetri

glassful ['glæsful] or ['glɑsful] s bicchiere m

glass'house' s vetreria; (fig) casa di vetro

glass'ware' s vetreria, cristalleria

glass' wool' s vetro filato

glass'work'er s vetraio

glass'works' s vetreria, cristalleria

glass·y ['glæsi] or ['glɑsi] adj (-ier; -iest) vetriato, vetroso

glaze [glez] s vernice vitrea; smalto; (of ice) superficie invetriata; (culin) glassa || tr smaltare; invetriare; (culin) glassare

glazier ['gleʒər] s vetraio

gleam [glim] s barlume m, raggio || intr baluginare

glean [glin] tr spigolare, racimolare; (to gather facts) raccogliere

glee [gli] s gioia, esultanza

glee' club' s società f corale

glib [glɪb] adj (glibber; glibbest) loquace; (tongue) facile, sciolto

glide [glaɪd] s scivolata; (aer) volo a vela, volo planato; (mus) legamento || intr scivolare; (aer) librarsi, planare; to glide away scorrere

glider ['glaɪdər] s (aer) libratore m, veleggiatore m

glimmer ['glɪmər] s barlume m || intr brillare, luccicare; tralucere

glimmering ['glɪmərɪŋ] adj tenue, tremulo || s luce fioca; barlume m

glimpse [glɪmps] s occhiata; to catch a glimpse of intravedere || tr travedere

glint [glɪnt] s scintillio || intr scintillare

glisten ['glɪsən] s scintillio, luccichio || intr scintillare, luccicare

glitter ['glɪtər] s luccichio || intr rilucere, sfolgorare

gloaming ['glomɪŋ] s crepuscolo (vespertino)

gloat [glot] intr guardare con maligna soddisfazione; to gloat over godere di

global ['globəl] adj globale; universale; globulare

globe [glob] s globo; (with map of earth) mappamondo

globe-trotter ['glob‚trotər] s giramondo

globule ['globjul] s globulo

glockenspiel ['glokən‚spil] s vibrafono

gloom [glum] s oscurità f; malinconia, uggia

gloom·y ['glumi] adj (-ier; -iest) lugubre, triste, tetro

glori·fy ['glorɪ‚faɪ] v (pret & pp -fied) tr glorificare; (to enhance) esaltare

glorious [ˈglɔrɪˌəs] adj glorioso; magnifico, splendido

glo·ry [ˈglori] s (-ries) gloria; **to go to glory** morire ‖ v (pret & pp -ried) intr gloriarsi

gloss [glɔs] or [glɑs] s lucentezza, patina; (commentary) glossa ‖ tr satinare, patinare; (to annotate) glossare; **to gloss over** nascondere, discolpare

glossa·ry [ˈglɑsəri] s (-ries) glossario

gloss·y [ˈglɔsi] or [ˈglɑsi] adj (-ier; -iest) lucido; (paper) satinato

glottal [ˈglɑtəl] adj articolato alla glottide

glottis [ˈglɑtɪs] s glottide f

glove [glʌv] s guanto

glove' compart'ment s cassetto portaoggetti

glow [glo] s fuoco, incandescenza; splendore m, scintillio; calore m; colorito acceso ‖ intr essere incandescente; (said of cheeks) avvampare; (said of cat's eyes) fosforeggiare

glower [ˈglau·ər] s sguardo torvo ‖ intr guardare col viso torvo

glowing [ˈglo·ɪŋ] adj incandescente; acceso; entusiasta, entusiastico

glow'worm' s lucciola; lampiride m

glucose [ˈglukos] s glucosio

glue [glu] s colla, mastice m ‖ tr incollare, ingommare

glue'pot' s pentolino per la colla

gluey [ˈglu·i] adj (gluier; gluiest) attaccaticcio; (smeared with glue) incollato

glum [glʌm] adj (glummer; glummest) tetro, accigliato

glut [glʌt] s abbondanza; eccesso; **there is a glut on the market** il mercato è saturo ‖ v (pret & pp glutted; ger glutting) tr saziare; (the market) saturare; (a channel) otturare

glutton [ˈglʌtən] adj & s ghiottone m

gluttonous [ˈglʌtənəs] adj ghiotto

glutton·y [ˈglʌtəni] s (-ies) ghiottoneria, golosità f

glycerine [ˈglɪsərɪn] s glicerina

G'-man' s (-men') agente m federale

gnarl [nɑrl] s nodo ‖ tr torcere ‖ intr ringhiare

gnarled [nɑrld] adj nodoso; (wrinkled) grinzoso

gnash [næʃ] tr digrignare ‖ intr digrignare i denti

gnat [næt] s moscerino, pappataci m

gnaw [nɔ] tr rosicchiare, rodere ‖ intr —**to gnaw at** (fig) rimordere

gnome [nom] s gnomo

go [go] s (goes) andata; energia; (for traffic) via libera; **it's a go** è un affare fatto; **it's all the go** (coll) è all'ultimo grido; **it's no go** (coll) è impossibile; **on the go** in continuo andare e venire; **to make a go of** (coll) aver successo con ‖ v (pret went [went]; pp gone [gɔn] or [gɑn]) tr (coll) sopportare; (coll) scommettere; (coll) pagare; **to go it alone** fare da sé ‖ intr andare; (to operate) camminare, funzionare; (e.g., mad) diventare; (said of numbers) entrare; **gone!** venduto!; **so it goes** così va il mondo; **to**

be going to + inf andare a + inf, e.g., **I am going to New York to see him** vado a New York a vederlo; (to express futurity) use fut ind, e.g., **I am going to stay home today** starò a casa oggi; **to be gone** essere andato; esser morto; **to go against** opporsi a; **to go ahead** andar avanti; tirare avanti; **to go around** andare in giro; **to go away** andarsene; **to go back** tornare; **to go by** passare per; regolarsi su; (said of time) passare; **to go down** discendere; (said of a boat) affondare; **to go fishing** andare a pescare; **to go for** vendersi per; andare a pigliare; attaccare; favorire; **to go get** andare a pigliare; **to go house hunting** andare in cerca di una casa; **to go hunting** andare a caccia; **to go in** entrare in; (to fit in) starci in; **to go in for** dedicarsi a; **to go into** investigare; darsi a, dedicarsi a; (gear) (aut) ingranare; **to go in with** associarsi con; **to go off** andarsene; aver luogo; (said of a bomb) esplodere; (said of a rifle) sparare; (said of a trap) scattare; **to go on** continuare, protrarsi; **to go on** + ger continuare a + inf; **to go out** uscire; passare di moda; (said, e.g., of fire) spegnersi; (to strike) mettersi in sciopero; **to go over** aver successo; leggere; esaminare; **to go over to** passare ai ranghi di; **to go skiing** andare a sciare; **to go swimming** andare a nuotare, andare ai bagno; **to go through** esperimentare; (to examine carefully) rovistare; (said, e.g., of a plan or a project) aver successo; (a fortune) dissipare; **to go through a red light** passare la strada col semaforo rosso; **to go with** andare con, accompagnare; (a girl) essere l'amico di; **to go without** fare a meno di

goad [god] s pungolo ‖ tr pungolare; (fig) spronare

go'-ahead' adj intraprendente ‖ s via m

goal [gol] s meta; (football) gol m

goalie [ˈgoli] s portiere m

goal'keep'er s portiere m

goal' line' s linea di porta

goal' post' s montante m

goat [got] s capra; (male) becco; (coll) capro espiatorio; **to get the goat of** (coll) irritare

goatee [goˈti] s barbetta, pizzo

goat'herd' s capraio

goat'skin' s pelle f di capra

goat'suck'er s caprimulgo

gob [gab] s massa informe; gobs (coll) mucchio, quantità f enorme

gobble [ˈgabəl] s gloglottio ‖ tr ingozzare; **to gobble up** (coll) tranguggiare; (coll) impadronirsi di ‖ intr tranguggiare; (said of a turkey) gloglottare

gobbledegook [ˈgabəldɪˌguk] s linguaggio oscuro

go'-between' s intermediario; (pander) mezzano; (poet) pronubo

goblet [ˈgablɪt] s coppa

goblin [ˈgablɪn] s folletto

go'-by' s —**to give s.o. the go-by** (coll) schivare qlcu

go'-cart' s carrettino; (walker) girello

god [gɑd] *s* dio; **God forbid** Dio ci scampi; **God grant** voglia Dio; **God willing** se Dio vuole

god'child' *s* (-**chil'dren**) figlioccio

god'daugh'ter *s* figlioccia

goddess ['gɑdɪs] *s* dea, diva

god'fa'ther *s* padrino

God'-fear'ing *adj* timorato di Dio

God'for•sak'en *adj* miserabile; (*place*) sperduto, fuori di mano

god'head' *s* deità *f* || **Godhead** *s* Ente Supremo, Dio

godless ['gɑdlɪs] *adj* ateo; malvagio || **the godless** i senza Dio

god•ly ['gɑdli] *adj* (-**lier; -liest**) devoto, pio

god'moth'er *s* madrina

God's' a'cre *s* camposanto

god'send' *s* manna, provvidenza

god'son' *s* figlioccio

God'speed' *s* successo, buona fortuna

go-getter ['go ‚gɛtər] *s* (coll) persona intraprendente

goggle ['gɑgəl] *intr* stralunare gli occhi

goggle-eyed ['gɑgəl ‚aɪd] *adj* dagli occhi sporgenti

goggles ['gɑgəlz] *spl* occhiali *mpl* da protezione

going ['go•ɪŋ] *adj* in moto, in funzione; **going on** quasi, e.g., **it is going on seven o'clock** sono quasi le sette || *s* andata; progresso

go'ings on' *s* (coll) comportamento, contegno; (coll) avvenimenti *mpl*

goiter ['gɔɪtər] *s* gozzo

gold [gold] *adj* aureo, d'oro || *s* oro

gold'beat'er *s* battiloro

gold'brick' *s* imitazione, frode *f*; (slang) fannullone *m*

gold' dig'ger ['dɪgər] *s* cercatore *m* d'oro; (coll) donna unicamente interessata nel denaro

golden ['goldən] *adj* aureo, d'oro; (*gilt*) dorato; (fig) splendido

gold'en age' *s* età *f* dell'oro

gold'en calf' *s* vitello d'oro

Gold'en Fleece' *s* vello d'oro

gold'en mean' *s* aurea mediocrità

gold'en•rod' *s* (bot) verga d'oro

gold'en rule' *s* regola della carità cristiana

gold'en wed'ding *s* nozze *fpl* d'oro

gold-filled ['gold ‚fɪld] *adj* otturato in oro

gold'finch' *s* cardellino

gold'fish' *s* pesce rosso

goldilocks ['goldɪ ‚lɑks] *s* bionda; (bot) ranuncolo

gold' leaf' *s* oro in foglia

gold' mine' *s* miniera d'oro

gold' plate' *s* vasellame *m* d'oro

gold'-plate' *tr* dorare

gold' rush' *s* febbre *f* dell'oro

gold'smith' *s* orefice *m*

gold' stand'ard *s* regime aureo

golf [gɑlf] *s* golf *m* || *intr* giocare a golf

golf' cart' *s* mini-auto *f* per campi da golf

golf' club' *s* mazza; associazione di giocatori di golf

golfer ['gɑlfər] *s* giocatore *m* di golf

golf' links' *spl* campo di golf

Golgotha ['gɑlgəθə] *s* il Golgota

gondola ['gɑndələ] *s* gondola

gondolier [‚gɑndə'lɪr] *s* gondoliere *m*

gone [gɔn] or [gɑn] *adj* partito; rovinato; andato; morto; **gone on** (coll) innamorato di

gong [gɔŋ] or [gɑŋ] *s* gong *m*

goo [gu] *s* (coll) sostanza appiccicaticcia

good [gud] *adj* (**better; best**) buono; **good and . . .** (coll) molto, e.g., **good and cheap** molto a buon mercato; **good for** buono per; responsabile per; (*equivalent*) valido per; **to be good at** esser bravo a; **to be no good** (coll) non servire a nulla; (coll) essere un perdigiorno; **to make good** avere successo; (*one's promise*) mantenere; (*a debt*) pagare; (*damages*) indennizzare || *s* bene *m*; utile *m*, profitto; **for good** per sempre; **for good and all** una volta per sempre; **goods** merce *f*, mercanzia; **the good** il bene; i buoni; **to catch with the goods** (coll) cogliere in flagrante; **to deliver the goods** (slang) mantenere le promesse; **to do good** fare del bene; **to the good** come profitto; come attivo; **what is the good of . . . ?** a che serve . . . ?

good' afternoon' *s* buon pomeriggio

good'-by' [‚gud'baɪ] *s* addio || *interj* addio!; arrivederci!

good' day' *s* buon giorno

good' deed' *s* buona azione

good' egg' *s* (slang) bonaccione *m*, gran brava persona

good' eve'ning *s* buona sera; buona notte

good' fel'low *s* buon ragazzo

good'-fel'low•ship' *s* cameratismo

good'-for-noth'ing *adj* inutile, senza valore || *s* pelandrone *m*, inetto

Good' Fri'day *s* Venerdì Santo

good' grac'es *spl* buone grazie

good-hearted ['gud'hɑrtɪd] *adj* di buon cuore

good'-hum'ored *adj* di buon umore

good'-look'ing *adj* bello

good' looks' *s* bellezza

good•ly ['gudli] *adj* (-**lier; -liest**) bello; di buona qualità; ampio, considerevole

good' morn'ing *s* buon giorno

good-natured ['gud'net/ərd] *adj* bonaccione, affabile

goodness ['gudnɪs] *s* bontà *f*; **for goodness sake!** per amor di Dio!; **goodness knows!** chi sa mai! || *interj* Dio mio!

good' night' *s* buona notte

good'-sized' *adj* piuttosto grande

good' speed' *s* buona fortuna

good'-tem'pered *adj* di carattere mite, gioviale

good' time' *s* periodo gradevole; **to have a good time** divertirsi; **to make good time** andare di buon passo

good' turn' *s* favore *m*, servizio

good' will' *s* buona volontà; (com) reputazione; (com) clientela

good•y ['gudi] *adj* (coll) troppo buono || *s* (-**ies**) (coll) santerello; **goodies**

(coll) ghiottonerie *fpl* || *interj* (coll) bene!, benissimo!

gooey ['gu·i] *adj* (**gooier; gooiest**) (slang) attaccaticcio

goof [guf] *s* (slang) sciocco || *tr* (slang) rovinare; **to goof up** (*an opportunity*) (slang) mancare || *intr* (slang) pigliare un granchio; **to goof off** (slang) battere la fiacca; **to goof up** (slang) farla grossa

goof-y ['gufi] *adj* (**-ier; -iest**) (slang) sciocco

goon [gun] *s* (slang) scemo; (coll) crumiro, gaglioffo, terrorista *m*

goose [gus] *s* (**geese** [gis]) oca; **the goose hangs high** tutto va per il meglio; **to cook one's goose** rompere le uova nel paniere di qlcu; **to kill the goose that lays the golden eggs** uccidere la gallina delle uova d'oro || *s* (**gooses**) ferro da stiro per sarto

goose'ber'ry *s* (**-ries**) uva spina; (*berry*) bacca d'uva spina

goose' egg' *s* (slang) zero; (*lump on the head*) (coll) bernoccolo

goose' flesh' *s* pelle *f* d'oca

goose'neck' *s* collo d'oca

goose' pim'ples *spl* pelle *f* d'oca

goose' step' *s* passo dell'oca

gopher ['gofər] *s* scoiattolo di terra, citillo

gore [gor] *s* sangue coagulato; (*in a garment*) gherone *m* || *tr* (*with a horn*) incornare; inserire gheroni in

gorge [gɔrdʒ] *s* gola, burrone *m*; (*meal*) mangiata || *tr* rimpinzare || *intr* rimpinzarsi

gorgeous ['gɔrdʒəs] *adj* splendido, magnifico

gorilla [gə'rɪlə] *s* gorilla *m*

gorse [gɔrs] *s* gineprone *m*

gor·y ['gori] *adj* (**-ier; -iest**) sanguinolento

gosh [gɑʃ] *interj* perbacco!

goshawk ['gɑs ˌhɔk] *s* sparviere *m*, astore *m*

gospel ['gɑspəl] *s* vangelo || **Gospel** *s* Vangelo

gos'pel truth' *s* santissima verità

gossamer ['gɑsəmər] *s* ragnatela; (*variety of gauze*) garza finissima; tessuto impermeabile finissimo

gossip ['gɑsɪp] *s* maldicenza; (*person*) pettegolo; **piece of gossip** maldicenza || *intr* spettegolare

gossipy ['gɑsɪpi] *adj* pettegolo

Goth [gɑθ] *s* Goto

Gothic ['gɑθɪk] *adj* & *s* gotico

gouge [gaudʒ] *s* (*cut made with a gouge*) scanalatura; (*tool*) sgorbia; (coll) truffa || *tr* sgorbiare; (coll) truffare

goulash ['gulɑʃ] *s* gulasch *m*

gourd [gord] *or* [gʊrd] *s* zucca

gourmand ['gʊrmənd] *s* ghiottone *m*

gourmet ['gʊrme] *s* buongustaio

gout [gaut] *s* gotta, podagra

gout·y ['gauti] *adj* (**-ier; -iest**) gottoso

govern ['gʌvərn] *tr* governare; (gram) reggere

governess ['gʌvərnɪs] *s* governante *f*, istitutrice *f*

government ['gʌvərnmənt] *s* governo; (gram) reggenza

governmental [ˌgʌvərn'mentəl] *adj* governativo

governor ['gʌvərnər] *s* governatore *m*; (mach) regolatore *m*

governorship ['gʌvərnər ˌʃɪp] *s* governatorato

gown [gaun] *s* (*of a woman*) vestito; (*academic*) toga; (*of a physician or patient*) gabbanella; (*of a priest*) veste *f* talare

grab [græb] *s* presa; **up for grabs** (coll) pronto a esser pigliato || *v* (*pret & pp* **grabbed;** *ger* **grabbing**) *tr* pigliare, afferrare

grace [gres] *s* (*charm; favor*) grazia; (*pardon*) mercé *f*; (*prayer*) benedicite *m*; (com) dilazione; **to say grace** recitare il benedicite; **with good grace** di buona voglia || *tr* adornare

graceful ['gresfəl] *adj* grazioso, vezzoso, leggiadro

grace' note' *s* (mus) appoggiatura

gracious ['greʃəs] *adj* grazioso; misericordioso || *interj* Dio buono!

gradation [gre'deʃən] *s* gradazione; (*step in a series*) passo

grade [gred] *s* grado; (*slope*) pendenza; (*mark in school*) voto; **to make the grade** raggiungere la meta || *tr* selezionare; (*a student*) dare un voto a; (*land*) spianare

grade' cros'sing *s* (rr) passaggio a livello

grade' school' *s* scuola elementare

gradient ['gredɪ·ənt] *adj* in pendenza || *s* pendenza; (phys) gradiente *m*

gradual ['grædʒu·əl] *adj* graduale

graduate ['grædʒu·ɪt] *adj* graduato; superiore; (*student*) laureato; (*candidate for degree*) laureando || ['grædʒu ˌet] *tr* graduare; laureare, diplomare || *intr* laurearsi, diplomarsi

grad'uate school' *s* facoltà *f* di studi avanzati

graduation [ˌgrædʒu'eʃən] *s* graduazione; laurea; cerimonia della consegna delle lauree

graft [græft] *or* [grɑft] *s* (hort) innesto; (surg) trapianto; (coll) prevaricazione || *tr* (hort) innestare; (surg) trapiantare || *intr* (coll) prevaricare

gra'ham bread' ['gre·əm] *s* pane *m* integrale

grain [gren] *s* chicco; (*of sand*) granello; (*cereal seeds*) granaglie *fpl*; (*in wood*) venatura; (*in stone*) grana; **against the grain** di cattivo verso || *tr* granulare; (*leather*) zigrinare; (*metal*) granire

grain' el'evator *s* elevatore *m* di grano; (*building*) deposito di cereali

graining ['grenɪŋ] *s* venatura

gram [græm] *s* grammo

grammar ['græmər] *s* grammatica

grammarian [grə'merɪ·ən] *s* grammatico

gram'mar school' *s* scuola elementare

grammatical [grə'mætɪkəl] *adj* grammatico

gramophone ['græmə,fon] s (trade-mark) grammofono

grana·ry ['grænəri] s (-ries) granaio

grand [grænd] adj grandioso; grande, famoso

grand'aunt' s prozia

grand'child' s (-chil'dren) nipote mf

grand'daugh'ter s nipote f

grand' duch'ess s granduchessa

grand' duke' s granduca m

grandee [græn'di] s grande m

grandeur ['grændʒər] or ['grændʒur] s grande m, grandiosità f

grand'fa'ther s nonno; (forefather) antenato

grand'father's clock' s grande orologio a pendolo

grandiose ['grændɪ,os] adj grandioso

grand' ju'ry s giuria investigativa

grand' lar'ceny s furto importante

grand' lodge' s grande oriente m

grandma ['grænd,ma], ['græm,ma] or ['græmə] s (coll) nonna

grand'moth'er s nonna

grand'neph'ew s pronipote m

grand'niece' s pronipote f

grand' op'era s opera, opera lirica

grandpa ['grænd,pa], ['græn,pa] or ['græmpə] s (coll) nonno

grand'par'ent s nonno, nonna

grand' pian'o s pianoforte m a coda

grand'son' s nipote m

grand'stand' s tribuna

grand' to'tal s somma totale; importo globale

grand'un'cle s prozio

grand' vizier' s gran visir m

grange [grendʒ] s (farm) fattoria; (organization of farmers) sindacato di agricoltori

granite ['grænɪt] s granito

grant [grænt] or [grant] s concessione; (sum of money) sovvenzione; trapasso di proprietà || tr concedere; (a wish) esaudire; (a permit) rilasciare; (law) trasferire; to take for granted ammettere come vero; trattare con indifferenza

grantee [græn'ti] or [gran'ti] s concessionario; beneficiario

grant'-in-aid' s (grants'-in-aid') sussidio governativo a un ente pubblico; borsa di studio

grantor [græn'tər] or [gran'tər] s concedente m, concessore m

granular ['grænjələr] adj granulare

granulate ['grænjə,let] tr granulare || intr diventare granulato

gran'ulated sug'ar s zucchero cristallizzato

granule ['grænjul] s granulo

grape [grep] s chicco d'uva; (vine) vite f; grapes uva

grape' ar'bor s pergolato

grape'fruit' s pompelmo

grape' juice' s succo d'uva

grape'shot' s mitraglia

grape'vine' s vite f; by the grapevine di bocca in bocca; (mil) attraverso la radio fante

graph [græf] or [graf] s (diagram) grafico; (gram) segno grafico

graphic(al) ['græfɪk(əl)] adj grafico

graphite ['græfaɪt] s grafite f

graph' pa'per s carta millimetrata

grapnel ['græpnəl] s uncino; (anchor) grappino

grapple ['græpəl] s uncino; lotta corpo a corpo || tr uncinare || intr combattere; to grapple with lottare con

grap'pling i'ron s raffio, grappino

grasp [græsp] or [grasp] s impugnatura; (power) possesso; to have a good grasp of sapere a fondo; within the grasp of nei limiti della comprensione di || tr (with hand) impugnare; (to get control of) impadronirsi di; (fig) capire || intr—to grasp at cercare di afferrare

grasping ['græspɪŋ] or ['graspɪŋ] adj tenace; avido, cupido

grass [græs] or [gras] s erba; (pasture land) pastura; (lawn) tappeto erboso; to go to grass (said of cattle) andare al pascolo; andare in vacanza; ritirarsi; andare in rovina; morire; to not let the grass grow under one's feet non dormire in piuma

grass' court' s campo da tennis d'erba

grass'hop'per s cavalletta

grass'-roots' adj popolare

grass' seed' s semente f d'erba

grass' wid'ow s donna separata dal marito

grass·y ['græsi] or ['grasi] adj (-ier; -iest) erboso

grate [gret] s (for cooking) griglia; (at a window) grata || tr mettere una grata a; (one's teeth) digrignare; (e.g., cheese) grattugiare || intr stridere, cigolare; to grate on one's nerves dare sui nervi di qlcu

grateful ['gretfəl] adj riconoscente; (pleasing) piacevole, gradito

grater ['gretər] s grattugia

grati·fy ['grætɪ,faɪ] v (pret & pp -fied) tr gratificare, soddisfare

gratifying ['grætɪ,faɪ·ɪŋ] adj soddisfacente, piacevole

grating ['gretɪŋ] adj irritante; (sound) stridente || s inferriata

gratis ['gretɪs] or ['grætɪs] adj gratuito || adv gratis

gratitude ['grætɪ,tjud] or ['grætɪ,tud] s gratitudine f, riconoscenza

gratuitous [grə'tju·ɪtəs] or [grə'tu·ɪtəs] adj gratuito

gratui·ty [grə'tju·ɪti] or [grə'tu·ɪti] s (-ties) mancia, regalia

grave [grev] adj grave || s tomba, sepolcro, fossa

gravedigger ['grev,dɪgər] s becchino

gravel ['grævəl] s ghiaia; (pathol) renella

grav'en im'age ['grevən] s idolo

grave'stone' s pietra tombale

grave'yard' s cimitero, camposanto

gravitate ['grævɪ,tet] intr gravitare

gravitation [,grævɪ'te/ən] s gravitazione

gravi·ty ['grævɪti] s (-ties) gravità f

gravure [grə'vjur] or ['grevjur] s foto-incisione

gra·vy ['grevi] s (-vies) (juice from

cooking meat) sugo; (sauce made with it) salsa, intingolo; (slang) guadagni mpl facili

gra'vy boat' s salsiera

gra'vy train' s (slang) greppia, mangiatoia

gray [gre] adj grigio; (gray-haired) canuto || s grigio; cavallo grigio || intr incanutire

gray'beard' s vecchio

gray-haired ['gre ,herd] adj canuto

gray'hound' s levriere m

grayish ['gre·ɪʃ] adj grigiastro

gray' mat'ter s materia grigia

graze [grez] tr (to touch lightly) sfiorare; (to scratch lightly) scalfire; (grass) brucare; (cattle) pascere, pascolare || intr pascere, brucare

grease [gris] s grasso, unto || [gris] or [griz] tr ingrassare, ungere

grease' cup' [gris] s coppa dell'olio

grease' gun' [gris] s ingrassatore m

grease' lift' [gris] s piattaforma di lubrificazione

grease' paint' [gris] s cerone m

grease' pit' [gris] s fossa di riparazione

greas·y ['grisi] or ['grizi] adj (-ier; -iest) grasso, unto, untuoso

great [gret] adj grande; (coll) eccellente || the great i grandi

great'-aunt' s prozia

Great' Bear' s Orsa Maggiore

Great' Brit'ain ['brɪtən] s la Gran Bretagna

Great' Dane' s danese m, alano

Great'er New York' s Nuova York e i suoi sobborghi

great'-grand'child' s (-chil'dren) pronipote mf

great'-grand'daught'er s pronipote f

great'-grand'fa'ther s bisnonno

great'-grand'moth'er s bisnonna

great'-grand'par'ent s bisnonno, bisnonna

great'-grand'son' s pronipote m

greatly ['gretli] adv molto

great'-neph'ew s pronipote m

greatness ['gretnɪs] s grandezza

great'-niece' s pronipote f

great'-un'cle s prozio

Grecian ['griʃən] adj & s greco

Greece [gris] s la Grecia

greed [grid] s avarizia, avidità f

greediness ['gridɪnɪs] s bramosia

greed·y ['gridi] adj (-ier; -iest) avaro; ingordo, bramoso

Greek [grik] adj & s greco

green [grin] adj verde; (fig) verde, inesperto || s verde m; (lawn) tappeto erboso; **greens** verdura, insalata

green'back' s (U.S.A.) biglietto di banca

green' earth' s verdecchio

greener·y ['grinəri] s (-ies) (foliage) vegetazione; (hothouse) serra

green'-eyed' adj dagli occhi verdi; (coll) geloso

green'gage' s regina claudia

green'horn' s (slang) pivello, sempliciotto

green'house' s serra

greenish ['grinɪʃ] adj verdastro

Greenland ['grinlənd] s la Groenlandia

green' light' s semaforo verde; (coll) via m

greenness ['grinnɪs] s verdore m, verdezza; inesperienza

green' pep'per s peperone m verde

greensward ['grin ,swɔrd] s tappeto erboso

green' thumb' s abilità f speciale per il giardinaggio

green' veg'etables spl verdura

green'wood' s bosco verde

greet [grit] tr salutare; ricevere; (e.g., one's ears) offrirsi a

greeting ['gritɪŋ] s saluto; accoglienza || **greetings** interj saluti!

greet'ing card' s cartolina d'auguri

gregarious [grɪ'gɛrɪ·əs] adj (living in the midst of others) gregario; (sociable) sociale

Gregorian [grɪ'gɔrɪ·ən] adj gregoriano

grenade [grɪ'ned] s granata

grenadier [,grɛnə'dɪr] s granatiere m

grenadine [,grɛnə'din] s granatina

grey [gre] adj, s & intr var of **gray**

grid [grɪd] s (network) rete f; (on map) reticolato; (electron) griglia

griddle ['grɪdəl] s tegame m

grid'dle-cake' s frittella cotta in teglia, crêpe m

grid'i'ron s griglia; campo di football; (theat) graticcia

grief [grif] s affanno, dolore m; disgrazia; **to come to grief** andare in rovina

grievance ['grivəns] s lagnanza; motivo di lagnanza

grieve [griv] tr affliggere || intr affliggersi, dolersi; **to grieve over** soffrire per

grievous ['grivəs] adj doloroso, penoso; (error) grave; (deplorable) deplorevole

griffin ['grɪfɪn] s grifo, grifone m

grill [grɪl] s griglia || tr mettere alla griglia; (coll) interrogare insistentemente

grille [grɪl] s inferriata; (aut) mascherina, calandra

grill'room' s grill-room m, rosticceria

grim [grɪm] adj (grimmer; grimmest) (stern) accigliato; (fierce) feroce; (sinister) sinistro; (unyielding) implacabile

grimace ['grɪməs] or [grɪ'mes] s smorfia, sberleffo || intr fare le boccacce

grime [graim] s sporco; (soot) fuliggine f

grim·y ['graimi] adj (-ier; -iest) sporco; fuligginoso

grin [grɪn] s sorriso; (malicious in intent) ghigno || v (pret & pp grinned; ger grinning) intr sorridere; ghignare

grind [graind] s macinata; (laborious work) (coll) macina; (slang) sgobbone m || v (pret & pp ground [graund]) tr macinare; (to sharpen) molare; (lenses) smerigliare; (meat) tritare; opprimere; (a crank) girare; (mach) rettificare || intr macinare; frantumarsi; cigolare; (coll) sgobbare

grinder ['graindər] s (to sharpen tools) mola; (to grind coffee) macinino;

(*back tooth*) molare *m*; (*person*) molatore *m*

grind'stone' *s* mola; **to keep one's nose to the grindstone** lavorare senza posa

grin·go ['griŋgo] *s* (-gos) (*disparaging*) gringo

grip [grip] *s* (*grasp*) presa; (*with hand*) stretta; (*handle*) impugnatura; **to come to grips** venire alle prese ‖ *v* (*pret & pp* **gripped;** *ger* **gripping**) *tr* stringere; impugnare; attirare l'attenzione di

gripe [graip] *s* (coll) lamentela; (naut) rizza; **gripes** colica ‖ *intr* (coll) lamentarsi, brontolare

grippe [grip] *s* influenza

gripping ['gripiŋ] *adj* interessantissimo, affascinante

gris·ly ['grizli] *adj* (-lier; -liest) orribile, spaventoso

grist [grist] *s* (*grain to be ground*) macinata; (*ground grain*) farina; (coll) mucchio; **to be grist to the mill of** (coll) fare comodo a

gristle ['grisəl] *s* cartilagine *f*

gris·tly ['grisli] *adj* (-tlier; -tliest) cartilaginoso

grist'mill' *s* mulino

grit [grit] *s* sabbia, arenaria; (fig) forza d'animo ‖ *v* (*pret & pp* **gritted;** *ger* **gritting**) *tr* (*one's teeth*) far stridere, digrignare

grit·ty ['griti] *adj* (-tier; -tiest) sabbioso, granuloso; (fig) forte, coraggioso

griz·zly ['grizli] *adj* (-zlier; -zliest) brizzolato, canuto ‖ *s* (-zlies) orso grigio

groan [gron] *s* gemito ‖ *intr* gemere; (*to be overburdened*) essere sovraccarico

grocer ['grosər] *s* droghiere *m*; pizzicagnolo; proprietario di negozio di generi alimentari

grocer·y ['grosəri] *s* (-ies) (*store selling spices, soap, etc.*) drogheria; (*store selling cheese, cold cuts, etc.*) negozio di pizzicagnolo; negozio di generi alimentari; **groceries** generi *mpl* alimentari, commestibili *mpl*

grog [grɑg] *s* grog *m*

grog·gy ['grɑgi] *adj* (-gier; -giest) (coll) groggy, intontito

groin [grɔin] *s* (anat) inguine *m*; (archit) costolone *m*

groom [grum] *s* mozzo di stalla; (*bridegroom*) sposo ‖ *tr* rassettare; (*horses*) rigovernare; (pol) preparare per le elezioni

grooms'man *s* (-men) compare *m* di nozze

groove [gruv] *s* scanalatura; (*of a pulley*) gola; (*of a phonograph record*) solco; (fig) routine *f* ‖ *tr* scanalare, incavare

grope [grop] *intr* brancicare; (*for words*) cercare; **to grope for** cercare a tastoni

gropingly ['gropiŋli] *adv* a tastoni

gross [gros] *adj* (*thick*) spesso; (*coarse*) volgare; (*fat*) grosso; (*error*) marchiano; (*without deductions*) lordo ‖ *s* grossa ‖ *tr* fare un incasso lordo di

grossly ['grosli] *adv* approssimativamente; totalmente

gross' na'tional prod'uct *s* reddito nazionale

grotesque [gro'tɛsk] *adj & s* grottesco

grot·to ['grɑto] *s* (-toes or -tos) grotta

grouch [grautʃ] *s* (coll) malumore *m*; (coll) persona stizzosa ‖ *intr* (coll) brontolare

grouch·y ['grautʃi] *adj* (-ier; -iest) (coll) stizzoso, brontolone

ground [graund] *s* (*earth, soil, land*) terra; (*piece of land*) terreno; (*basis*) causa, fondatezza; (elec) terra, massa; (fig) occasione, motivo; **grounds** giardini *mpl*, terreno; (*of coffee*) fondi *mpl*; **on the ground of** per motivo di; **to break ground** dare la prima palata; (fig) mettere la prima pietra; **to fall to the ground** cadere al suolo; (fig) fallire; **to gain ground** guadagnar terreno; **to give ground** ceder terreno; **to lose ground** perder terreno; **to stand one's ground** non indietreggiare ‖ *tr* fondare; (elec) mettere a massa; **to be grounded** (*said of an airplane*) essere forzato di rimanere a terra; **to be well grounded** essere bene al corrente ‖ *intr* incagliarsi

ground' connec'tion *s* massa a terra

ground' crew' *s* (aer) personale *m* di servizio

ground' floor' *s* pianterreno

ground' glass' *s* vetro smerigliato

ground' hog' *s* marmotta americana

ground' lead' [lid] *s* (elec) collegamento a massa

groundless ['graundlis] *adj* infondato

ground' meat' *s* carne tritata

ground' plan' *s* progetto, pianta

ground' swell' *s* mareggiata

ground' wire' *s* filo di terra, filo di massa

ground'work' *s* fondamento, base *f*

group [grup] *adj* collettivo ‖ *s* gruppo; (aer) stormo ‖ *tr* raggruppare ‖ *intr* raggrupparsi

grouse [graus] *s* gallo cedrone; (slang) brontolio ‖ *intr* (slang) brontolare

grout [graut] *s* stucco ‖ *tr* stuccare

grove [grov] *s* boschetto

grov·el ['grʌvəl] or ['grɑvəl] *v* (*pret & pp* **-eled** or **-elled;** *ger* **-eling** or **-elling**) *intr* umiliarsi

grow [gro] *v* (*pret* **grew** [gru]; *pp* **grown** [gron]) *tr* (*plants*) coltivare; (*animals*) allevare; (*a beard*) farsi crescere ‖ *intr* crescere; svilupparsi; nascere; venir su; (*to become*) diventare; farsi; **to grow angry** arrabbiarsi; **to grow old** invecchiare; **to grow out of** (*fashion*) passare di; originare da; **to grow up** svilupparsi

growing ['gro·iŋ] *adj* crescente; (*pains*) di crescenza; (*child*) in crescita

growl [graul] *s* ringhio; brontolio ‖ *intr* (*said of animals*) ringhiare; brontolare

grown'-up' *adj* adulto, grande ‖ *s* (grown-ups) adulto

growth [groθ] *s* crescita, sviluppo; aumento; (pathol) escrescenza

growth' stock' *s* azione *f* che promette di aumentare di valore

grub [grʌb] *s* (*drudge*) sgobbone *m*; larva di coleottero; (coll) mangiare *m* ‖ *v* (*pret & pp* grubbed; *ger* grubbing) *tr* scavare, zappare, dissodare ‖ *intr* cercare assiduamente; scavare; sgobbare

grub•by ['grʌbi] *adj* (-bier; -biest) sporco; bacato; infestato di larve

grudge [grʌdʒ] *s* rancore *m*; to have a grudge against nutrire rancore contro ‖ *tr* (*to spend unwillingly*) lesinare; invidiare

grudgingly ['grʌdʒɪŋli] *adv* di cattiva voglia

gru•el ['gru-əl] *s* farinata d'avena ‖ *v* (*pret & pp* -eled *or* -elled; *ger* -eling *or* -elling) *tr* estenuare

gruesome ['grusəm] *adj* raccapricciante

gruff [grʌf] *adj* brusco, burbero; (*voice*) rauco, roco

grumble ['grʌmbəl] *s* brontolio ‖ *intr* brontolare, borbottare

grump•y ['grʌmpi] *adj* (-ier; -iest) di cattivo umore, scontroso

grunt [grʌnt] *s* grugnito ‖ *intr* grugnire

G-string ['dʒi,strɪŋ] *s* (*loincloth*) perizoma *m*; (*worn by a female entertainer*) triangolino di stoffa; (mus) corda di sol

guarantee [,gærən'ti] *s* garanzia; (*guarantor*) garante *mf* ‖ *tr* garantire

guarantor ['gærən,tor] *s* garante *mf*

guaran•ty ['gærənti] *s* (-ties) garanzia ‖ *v* (*pret & pp* -tied) *tr* garantire

guard [gard] *s* guardia; (*safeguard*) protezione; (*in a prison*) guardia carceraria; (*of a sword*) guardamano; (football) mediano; **off guard** alla sprovvista; **on guard** in guardia; di fazione; **to mount a guard** montare la guardia; **under guard** ben custodito ‖ *tr* guardare ‖ *intr* fare la sentinella; **to guard against** guardarsi da

guarded ['gardɪd] *adj* (*remark*) prudente

guard'house' *s* locale *m* di detenzione; (mil) corpo di guardia

guardian ['gardɪ-ən] *adj* tutelare ‖ *s* guardiano; (law) tutore *m*

guard'ian an'gel *s* angelo custode

guardianship ['gardɪ-ən,ʃɪp] *s* protezione; (law) tutela

guard'rail' *s* guardavia *m*; (naut) parapetto

guard'room' *s* (mil) corpo di guardia

guards'man *s* (-men) guardia

guerrilla [gə'rɪlə] *s* guerrigliero

guerril'la war'fare *s* guerriglia

guess [ges] *s* congettura, supposizione ‖ *tr & intr* congetturare, supporre; (*to estimate correctly*) indovinare; (coll) credere; **I guess so** credo di sì

guess'work' *s* congettura

guest [gest] *s* invitato, ospite *m*; (*of a hotel*) cliente *mf*; (*of a boarding house*) pensionante *mf*

guest' book' *s* albo d'onore; (*in a hotel*) registro

guffaw [gə'fɔ] *s* sghignazzata ‖ *intr* sghignazzare

Guiana [gɪ'ɑnə] *or* [gɪ'ænə] *s* la Guayana

guidance ['gaɪdəns] *s* guida, governo; **for your guidance** per Sua norma

guide [gaɪd] *s* guida ‖ *tr* guidare

guide'board' *s* indicatore *m* stradale

guide'book' *s* guida

guid'ed mis'sile ['gaɪdɪd] *s* telearma, teleproietto, missile teleguidato

guide' dog' *s* cane *m* conduttore di un cieco

guide'line' *s* falsariga; corda fissa; linea di condotta, direttiva

guide'post' *s* indicatore *m* stradale

guide' word' *s* esponente *m* in testa di pagina

guidon ['gaɪdən] *s* guidone *m*

guild [gɪld] *s* associazione mutua; (hist) gilda

guild'hall' *s* palazzo delle corporazioni

guile [gaɪl] *s* astuzia, frode *f*

guileful ['gaɪlfəl] *adj* astuto, insidioso

guileless ['gaɪllɪs] *adj* sincero, innocente

guillotine ['gɪlə,tin] *s* ghigliottina ‖ [,gɪlə'tin] *tr* ghigliottinare

guilt [gɪlt] *s* colpa, reità *f*

guiltless ['gɪltlɪs] *adj* innocente

guilt•y ['gɪlti] *adj* (-ier; -iest) colpevole, reo

guimpe [gɪmp] *or* [gæmp] *s* sprone *m*

guinea ['gɪni] *s* ghinea; gallina faraona ‖ **Guinea** *s* la Guinea

guin'ea fowl' *s* gallina faraona

guin'ea pig' *s* porcellino d'India, cavia; (fig) cavia

guise [gaɪz] *s* aspetto; veste *f*; **under the guise of** in guisa di

guitar [gɪ'tar] *s* chitarra

guitarist [gɪ'tarɪst] *s* chitarrista *mf*

gulch [gʌltʃ] *s* burrone *m*

gulf [gʌlf] *s* golfo; abisso

Gulf' Stream' *s* corrente *f* del Golfo

gull [gʌl] *s* gabbiano; (coll) credulone *m* ‖ *tr* darla a bere a

gullet ['gʌlɪt] *s* gargarozzo; esofago

gullible ['gʌlɪbəl] *adj* credulone

gul•ly ['gʌli] *s* (-lies) borro, zanella

gulp [gʌlp] *s* sorsata ‖ *tr*—**to gulp down** (*food*) ingoiare; (*drink*) tracannare; (fig) ingoiare, tranguigiare

gum [gʌm] *s* gomma; (*mucus on eyelids*) cispa; gums (anat) gengive *fpl* ‖ *v* (*pret & pp* gummed; *ger* gumming) *tr* ingommare; **to gum up** (slang) guastare ‖ *intr* secernere gomma

gum' ar'abic *s* gomma arabica

gum'boil' *s* flemmone *m* gengivale

gum' boot' *s* stivale *m* da palude

gum'drop' *s* caramella alla gelatina di frutta, pasticca di gomma, drop *m*

gum•my ['gʌmi] *adj* (-mier; -miest) gommoso, vischioso; (*eyelid*) cisposo

gumption ['gʌmpʃən] *s* (coll) iniziativa; (coll) coraggio, fegato

gum'shoe' *s* caloscia; (slang) poliziotto ‖ *v* (*pret & pp* -shoed; *ger* -shoeing) *intr* (slang) camminare silenziosamente

gun [gʌn] *s* (*rifle*) fucile *m*; (*revolver*) revolver *m*; (*pistol*) rivoltella; (*e.g., for spraying*) rivoltella; **to stick to one's guns** tener duro ‖ *v* (*pret & pp* **gunned**; *ger* **gunning**) *tr* far fuoco su, freddare; (*a motor*) (slang) accelerare rapidamente ‖ *intr* andare a caccia; sparare; **to gun for** andare a caccia di

gun'boat' *s* cannoniera, esploratore *m*

gun' car'riage *s* affusto

gun'cot'ton *s* fulmicotone *m*

gun'fire' *s* fuoco, tiro

gun'man *s* (**-men**) bandito, sicario

gun' met'al *s* bronzo da cannoni; acciaio brunito

gunnel [ˈgʌnəl] *s* (naut) frisata

gunner [ˈgʌnər] *s* artigliere *m*, servente *m*

gunnery [ˈgʌnəri] *s* artiglieria, tiro

gunnysack [ˈgʌni ˌsæk] *s* sacco di tela greggia

gunpoint [ˈgʌn ˌpɔint] *s* mirino; **at gunpoint** a mano armata, e.g., **he was held up at gunpoint** subì una rapina a mano armata

gun'pow'der *s* polvere nera or pirica

gun'run'ner *s* contrabbandiere *m* di armi da fuoco

gun'shot' *s* schioppettata; revolverata; **within gunshot** a tiro di schioppo

gun'shot' wound' *s* schioppettata

gun'smith' *s* armaiolo

gun'stock' *s* cassa del fucile

gunwale [ˈgʌnəl] *s* frisata

gup•py [ˈgʌpi] *s* (**-pies**) lebiste *m*

gurgle [ˈgʌrgəl] *s* gorgoglio, borboglio ‖ *intr* gorgogliare, borbogliare; (*said of a human being*) barbugliare

gush [gʌʃ] *s* getto, fiotto ‖ *intr* zampillare, sgorgare; (coll) dare in effusioni

gusher [ˈgʌʃər] *s* pozzo di petrolio; (coll) persona espansiva

gushing [ˈgʌʃiŋ] *adj* zampillante, sgorgante; (coll) espansivo ‖ *s* zampillo; (coll) espansione, effusione

gush•y [ˈgʌʃi] *adj* (**-ier; -iest**) (coll) espansivo, effusivo

gusset [ˈgʌsit] *s* gherone *m*

gust [gʌst] *s* (*of wind*) raffica; (*of smoke*) ondata, zaffata; (*of noise*) esplosione; (*of anger*) sfuriata

gusto [ˈgʌsto] *s* gusto; entusiasmo

gust•y [ˈgʌsti] *adj* (**-ier; -iest**) a raffiche, burrascoso

gut [gʌt] *s* budello; pue budello; (slang) fegato, coraggio ‖ *v* (*pret & pp* **gutted**; *ger* **gutting**) *tr* sparare, spanciare; distruggere l'interno di

gutta-percha [ˈgʌtəˈpʌrtʃə] *s* guttaperca

gutter [ˈgʌtər] *s* (*on side of road*) cunetta; (*in street*) rigagnolo; (*of roof*) doccia, grondaia; (fig) bassifondi *mpl*

gut'ter-snipe' *s* monello

guttural [ˈgʌtərəl] *adj & s* gutturale *f*

guy [gai] *s* cavo di sicurezza; (coll) tipo, tizio ‖ *tr* burlarsi di

guzzle [ˈgʌzəl] *tr & intr* trincare, bere a garganella

guzzler [ˈgʌzlər] *s* ubriacone *m*

gym [dʒim] *s* (coll) palestra

gymnasi•um [dʒimˈnezi-əm] *s* (**-ums** or **-a** [ə]) palestra

gymnast [ˈdʒimnæst] *s* ginnasta *mf*

gymnastic [dʒimˈnæstik] *adj* ginnastico ‖ **gymnastics** *spl* ginnastica

gynecologist [ˌgainəˈkɑlədʒist], [ˌdʒainə-ˈkɑlədʒist] or [ˌdʒinəˈkɑlədʒist] *s* ginecologo

gyp [dʒip] *s* (coll) imbroglio; (*person*) (coll) imbroglione *m* ‖ *v* (*pret & pp* **gypped**; *ger* **gypping**) *tr* imbrogliare

gypsum [ˈdʒipsəm] *s* gesso

gyp•sy [ˈdʒipsi] *adj* zingaresco, zingaro ‖ *s* (**-sies**) zingaro ‖ **Gypsy** *s* (*language*) zingaresco

gypsyish [ˈdʒipsi-iʃ] *adj* zingaresco

gyrate [ˈdʒairet] *intr* turbinare

gyrocompass [ˈdʒairoˌkʌmpəs] *s* girobussola

gyroscope [ˈdʒairəˌskop] *s* giroscopio

H

H, h [etʃ] *s* ottava lettera dell'alfabeto inglese

haberdasher [ˈhæbər ˌdæʃər] *s* camiciaio; (*dealer in notions*) merciaio

haberdasher•y [ˈhæbər ˌdæʃəri] *s* (**-ies**) camiceria; merceria

habit [ˈhæbit] *s* abitudine *f*; (*addiction*) vizio; (*garb*) saio; **to be in the habit of** aver l'usanza di

habitat [ˈhæbi ˌtæt] *s* habitat *m*

habitation [ˌhæbiˈteʃən] *s* abitazione

habit-forming [ˈhæbit ˌfɔrmiŋ] *adj* (*e.g., drugs*) stupefacente; (*e.g., T.V.*) assuefacente, che fa venire il vizio

habitual [həˈbitʃʊ-əl] *adj* abituale

habitué [həˌbitʃʊˈe] *s* habitué *m*

hack [hæk] *s* (*cut*) taglio; (*notch*) tacca; (*cough*) tosse secca; cavallo da nolo; vettura di piazza; (*nag*) ronzino; (*poor writer*) scribacchino ‖ *tr* tagliare; stagliare

hack'man *s* (**-men**) vetturino

hackney [ˈhækni] *s* cavallo da sella; vettura di piazza

hackneyed [ˈhæknid] *adj* banale, trito

hack'saw' *s* seghetto per metalli

haddock [ˈhædək] *s* eglefino

haft [hæft] or [hɑft] *s* impugnatura

hag [hæg] *s* (*ugly old woman*) megera; (*witch*) strega

haggard [ˈhægərd] *adj* sparuto, macilento; (*wild-looking*) stralunato

haggle ['hægəl] *intr* mercanteggiare

hagiographer [ˌhægiˈɒgrəfər] or [ˌhedʒiˈɒgrəfər] *s* agiografo

hagiography [ˌhægiˈɒgrəfi] or [ˌhedʒiˈɒgrəfi] *s* agiografia

Hague, The [heg] *s* L'Aia *f*

hail [hel] *s* (*precipitation*) grandine *f*; (*greeting*) saluto; **within hail a por-tata di voce** || *tr* salutare; accogliere; chiamare; (*e.g., blows*) far cadere˙|| *intr* grandinare; **to hail from** venire da || *interj* salute!; salve!

hail'-fel'low *adj* gioviale

Hail' Mar'y *s* Ave Maria, avemaria

hail'stone' *s* chicco di grandine

hail'storm' *s* grandinata

hair [her] *s* capelli *mpl;* (*of animals*) pelame *m* or pelo; a **hair** (*a single filament*) un capello or un pelo; **to a hair** a perfezione; **to get in one's hair** (slang) dare sui nervi a qlcu; **to let one's hair down** (slang) parlare fran-camente; (slang) comportarsi alla buona; **to make one's hair stand on end** far rizzare i capelli a qlcu; **to not turn a hair** non scomporsi; **to split hairs** cercare il pelo nell'uovo

hair'breadth' *s* spessore *m* di un ca-pello; **to escape by a hairbreadth** scamparla per un pelo

hair'brush' *s* spazzola per i capelli

hair'cloth' *s* cilicio

hair'cut' *s* taglio dei capelli; **to get a haircut** farsi tagliare i capelli

hair'do' *s* (-dos) acconciatura

hair'dress'er *s* parrucchiere *m* per si-gnora; pettinatrice *f*

hair' dri'er *s* asciugacapelli *m*

hair' dye' *s* tintura per i capelli

hairless ['herlɪs] *adj* pelato, calvo

hair' net' *s* rete *f* per i capelli

hair'pin' *s* forcella, forcina, molletta

hair-raising ['her ˌrezɪŋ] *adj* orripilante

hair' re·mov'er *s* depilatorio

hair' restor'er [rɪˈstorər] *s* rigeneratore *m* per i capelli

hair' rib'bon *s* nastro per i capelli

hairsplitting ['her ˌsplɪtɪŋ] *adj* metico-loso, pignolo

hair'spring' *s* spirale *f*

hair' styl'ing *s* pettinatura per signora

hair·y ['heri] *adj* (-ier; -iest) peloso, villoso, irsuto

hake [hek] *s* merluzzo, nasello

halberd ['hælbərd] *s* alabarda

halberdier [ˌhælbərˈdɪr] *s* alabardiere *m*

halcyon ['hælsɪ·ən] *adj* calmo, pacifico

hale [hel] *adj* sano, robusto || *tr* tra-scinare a viva forza

half [hæf] or [hɑf] *adj* mezzo; a **half** or **half a** a mezzo; **half the** la metà di || *s* (**halves** [hævz] or [hɑvz]) metà *f;* (arith) mezzo; **in half** a metà; **to go halves** fare a metà || *adv* mezzo, e.g., **half asleep** mezzo addormentato; a metà, e.g., **half finished** a metà fi-nito; **half past** e mezzo or e mezza, e.g., **half past three** le tre e mezzo or le tre e mezza; **half . . . half** metà . . . metà

half'-and-half' *adj* mezzo e mezzo || *s* mezza crema e mezzo latte; mezza

birra chiara e mezza scura || *adv* a metà, in parti uguali

half'back' *s* (football) mediano; (soc-cer) laterale *m*

half-baked ['hæf ˌbekt] or ['hɑf ˌbekt] *adj* mezzo cotto; (*ideas*) infondato, inesperto

half' bind'ing *s* rilegatura in mezza pelle

half'-blood' *s* meticcio; fratellastro; sorellastra

half'-breed' *s* meticcio

half' broth'er *s* fratellastro

half-cocked ['hæf ˌkɑkt] or ['hɑf ˌkɑkt] *adj* immaturo, precipitato || *adv* (coll) precipitatamente

half' fare' *s* mezza corsa

half'-full' *adj* mezzo pieno

half-hearted ['hæf ˌhɑrtɪd] or ['hɑf ˌhɑrtɪd] *adj* indifferente, freddo

half'-hol'iday *s* mezza festa

half' hose' *s* calzini *mpl* corti

half'-hour' *s* mezz'ora; **on the half-hour** ogni trenta minuti allo scoccare del-l'ora e della mezz'ora

half'-length' *adj* a mezzo busto || *s* ri-tratto a mezzo busto

half'life' *s* (phys) vita media

half'-mast' *s*—**at half-mast** a mezz'asta

half'moon' *s* mezzaluna

half' mourn'ing *s* mezzo lutto

half' note' *s* (mus) minima

half' pay' *s* mezza paga

halfpen·ny ['hepəni] or ['hepni] *s* (-nies) mezzo penny

half' pint' *s* mezza pinta; (slang) mezza cartuccia, mezza calzetta

half'-seas-o'ver *adj*—**to be half-seas over** (slang) essere sbronzato

half' shell' *s*—**on the half shell** in con-chiglia

half' sis'ter *s* sorellastra

half' sole' *s* mezza suola

half'-sole' *tr* mettere la mezza suola a

half'-staff' *s*—**at half-staff** a mezz'asta

half-timbered ['hæf ˌtɪmbərd] or ['hɑf ˌtɪmbərd] *adj* in legno e muratura

half' ti'tle *s* occhiello, occhietto

half'tone' *s* mezzatinta

half'-track' *s* semicingolato

half'truth' *s* mezza verità, mezza bugia

half'way' *adj* a metà strada; parziale, mezzo || *adv* a metà strada; **halfway through** nel mezzo di; **to meet half-way** fare concessioni mutue

half-witted ['hæf ˌwɪtɪd] or ['hɑf ˌwɪtɪd] *adj* mezzo scemo

halibut ['hælɪbət] *s* ippoglosso

halide ['hælaɪd] or ['helaɪd] *s* aloge-nuro

halitosis [ˌhælɪˈtosɪs] *s* alito cattivo, fiato puzzolente

hall [hɔl] *s* (*passageway*) corridoio; (*entranceway*) vestibolo; (*large meet-ing room*) salone *m;* (*assembly room of a university*) aula magna; (*build-ing of a university*) edificio

hallelujah or **hallelujah** [ˌhælɪˈlujə] *s* alleluia *m* || *interj* alleluia!

hall'mark' *s* punzone *m* di garanzia; (fig) contrassegno, caratteristica

hal·lo [həˈlo] *s* (-los) grido || *interj* ehi!

hallow ['hælo] *tr* santificare

hallowed ['hælod] *adj* consacrato
Halloween or **Hallowe'en** [,hælo'in] *s* vigilia di Ognissanti
hallucination [hə,lusɪ'neʃən] *s* allucinazione
hall'way' *s* corridoio; entrata
ha·lo ['helo] *s* (**-los** or **-loes**) alone *m*
halogen ['hælədʒən] *s* alogeno
halt [hɔlt] *adj* zoppicante || *s* fermata; **to call a halt** dare ordine di fermarsi; **to come to a halt** fermarsi || *tr* fermare || *intr* fermarsi, esitare || *interj* altolà!
halter ['hɔltər] *s* (*for leading horse*) cavezza; (*noose*) capestro; (*hanging*) impiccagione; corpino bagno di sole
halting ['hɔltɪŋ] *adj* zoppicante; esitante
halve [hæv] or [hɑv] *tr* dimezzare
halyard ['hæljərd] *s* (naut) drizza
ham [hæm] *s* (*part of leg behind knee*) polpaccio; (*thigh and buttock*) coscia; (*cured meat from hog's hind leg*) prosciutto; (slang) istrione *m;* (slang) radioamatore *m;* **hams** native che *fpl*
ham' and eggs' *spl* uova *fpl* col prosciutto
hamburger ['hæm,bʌrgər] *s* hamburger *m*
hamlet ['hæmlɪt] *s* frazione, paese *m* || **Hamlet** *s* Amleto
hammer ['hæmər] *s* martello; (*of gun*) cane *m;* (*of piano*) martelletto; **under the hammer** all'asta pubblica || *tr* martellare; **to hammer out** battere; portare a fine faticosamente || *intr* martellare; **to hammer away** lavorare accanitamente
hammock ['hæmək] *s* amaca
hamper ['hæmpər] *s* cesta || *tr* imbarazzare, intralciare
hamster ['hæmstər] *s* criceto
ham·string ['hæm,strɪŋ] *v* (*pret & pp* **-strung**) *tr* azzoppare; tagliare i garretti a; (fig) impastoiare
hand [hænd] *adj* manuale; fatto a mano || *s* mano *f;* (*workman*) garzone *m,* operaio; (*way of writing*) scrittura; (*signature*) firma; (*clapping of hands*) applauso; (*of clock or watch*) lancetta; (*all the cards in one's hand*) gioco; (*a round of play*) smazzata, mano *f;* (*player*) giocatore *m;* (*skill*) destrezza; (*side*) lato; **all hands** (naut) tutto l'equipaggio; (coll) tutti *mpl;* **at first hand** direttamente; **at hand** a portata di mano; **hand in glove** in perfetta unione; **hand in hand** tenendosi per mano; **hands up!** le mani in alto!; **hand to hand** corpo a corpo; **in hand** tra le mani; **in his own hand** di proprio pugno; **on hand** disponibile; **on hands and knees** (*crawling*) a gattoni; (*beseeching*) in ginocchio; **on the one hand** da un canto; **on the other hand** per contro; **to change hands** cambiare di mano; **to clap hands** battere le mani; **to eat out of one's hand** essere sottomesso a qlcu; **to get out of hand** diventare incontrollabile; **to have a hand in** prender parte a; **to have one's hands full** essere occupatissimo; **to hold hands** tenersi per mano; **to hold up one's hands** (*as a sign of surrender*) alzare le mani; **to join hands** darsi la mano; **to keep one's hands off** non mettere il naso in; **to lend a hand** dare una mano; **to live from hand to mouth** vivere alla giornata; **to not lift a hand** non alzare un dito; **to play into the hands of** fare il gioco di; **to shake hands** darsi la mano; **to show one's hand** scoprire il proprio gioco; **to take in hand** prendere in mano; (*a matter*) prendere in esame; **to throw up one's hands** darsi per vinto; **to try one's hand** mettere la propria abilità alla prova; **to turn one's hand to** dedicarsi a; **to wash one's hands of** lavarsi le mani di; **under my hand** di mia firma autografa; **under the hand and seal of** firmato di pugno da || *tr* dare, porgere; **to hand down** tramandare; **to hand in** consegnare; **to hand on** trasmettere; **to hand out** distribuire
hand'bag' *s* borsetta
hand' bag'gage *s* valigie *fpl* a mano
hand'ball' *s* palla a mano
hand'bill' *s* manifestino, foglio volante
hand'book' *s* manuale *m;* guida; (*of a particular field*) prontuario
hand'breadth' *s* palmo
hand'car' *s* (rr) carrello a mano
hand'cart' *s* carretto a mano
hand'cuffs' *spl* manette *fpl* || *tr* mettere le manette a
handful ['hænd,fʊl] *s* manata, manciata
hand' glass' *s* lente *f* di ingrandimento; specchietto
hand' grenade' *s* bomba a mano
handi·cap ['hændɪ,kæp] *s* svantaggio; (sports) handicap *m* || *v* (*pret & pp* **-capped**); *ger* **-capping**) *tr* andicappare
handicraft ['hændɪ,kræft] or ['hændɪ,krɑft] *s* destrezza manuale; artigianato
handiwork ['hændɪ,wʌrk] *s* lavoro fatto a mano; opera, lavoro
handkerchief ['hæŋkərtʃɪf] or ['hæŋkər,tʃif] *s* fazzoletto
handle ['hændəl] *s* manico; (*of a sword*) impugnatura; (*of a door*) maniglia; (*of a drawer*) pomolo; (*of a hand organ*) manovella; espediente *m;* **to fly off the handle** (slang) uscire dai gangheri || *tr* maneggiare; manovrare, dirigere; commerciare in || *intr* comportarsi
handle'bar' *s* manubrio
handler ['hændlər] *s* (sports) allenatore *m*
hand'made' *adj* fatto a mano
hand'maid' or **hand'maid'en** *s* domestica, serva; (fig) ancella
hand'-me-down' *adj* smesso || *s* vestito smesso or di seconda mano
hand' or'gan *s* organetto, organino, organetto di Barberia
hand'out' *s* elemosina di cibo; articolo distribuito gratis; comunicato stampa
hand-picked ['hænd,pɪkt] *adj* colto a mano; scelto specialmente

hand'rail' s guardamano, passamano

hand'saw' s sega a mano

hand'set' s microtelefono

hand'shake' s stretta di mano

handsome ['hænsəm] adj bello; considerevole; generoso

hand'spring' s capriola, salto mortale fatto toccando il terreno con le mani

hand'-to-hand' adj corpo a corpo

hand'-to-mouth' adj precario, da un giorno all'altro

hand'work' s lavoro fatto a mano

hand'writ'ing s scrittura

hand'wrought' adj lavorato a mano

hand•y ['hændɪ] adj (-ier; -iest) (easy to handle) maneggevole; (within easy reach) vicino; (skillful) destro, abile; to come in handy tornare utile

hand'y-man' s (-men') factotum m

hang [hæŋ] s maniera di cadere; to get the hang of (coll) imparare a adoperare; to not give a hang (coll) non importare un fico a || v (pret & pp hung [hʌŋ]) tr sospendere; (laundry) stendere; (to attach) attaccare; (a door or window) mettere sui cardini; (one's head) abbassare; hang it! (coll) al diavolo!; to hang up appendere; sospendere il progresso di || intr pendere, penzolare; esitare; essere sospeso; essere attaccato; to hang around ciondolare, oziare, gironzolare; to hang on essere sospeso a; dipendere da; persistere; (s.o.'s words) pendere; to hang out sporgersi; (slang) raccogliersi; (slang) vivere; to hang over esser sospeso; (to threaten) minacciare; to hang together mantenersi uniti; to hang up (telp) riattaccare || v (pret hanged or hung) tr (to execute) impiccare || intr impiccarsi

hangar ['hæŋər] or ['hæŋgar] s rimessa; (aer) aviorimessa, hangar m

hanger ['hæŋər] s gancio, uncino; (for clothes) attaccapanni m

hang'er-on' s (hangers-on) seguace mf; seccatore m; (sponger) parassita m

hanging ['hæŋɪŋ] adj pendente, pensile || s impiccagione; hangings parati mpl

hang'man s (-men) boia m

hang'nail' s pipita delle unghie

hang'out' s (coll) ritrovo abituale

hang'o'ver s mal m di testa dopo una sbornia

hank [hæŋk] s matassa

hanker ['hæŋkər] intr agognare

Hannibal ['hænɪbəl] s Annibale m

haphazard [,hæp'hæzərd] adj fortuito, a caso || adv a caso; alla carlona

hapless ['hæplɪs] adj sfortunato

happen ['hæpən] intr succedere; to happen along sopravvenire; to happen on incontrarsi per caso con; to happen to + inf per caso + ind, e.g., I happened to see her at the theater l'ho incontrata per caso a teatro

happening ['hæpənɪŋ] s avvenimento, fatto

happily ['hæpɪli] adv felicemente; fortunatamente

happiness ['hæpɪnɪs] s felicità f; gioia, piacere m

hap•py ['hæpi] adj (-pier; -piest) lieto, felice, contento; to be happy to avere il piacere di

hap'py-go-luck'y adj spensierato

hap'py me'dium s giusto mezzo

Hap'py New Year' interj buon anno!, felice anno nuovo!

harangue [hə'ræŋ] s arringa, concione || tr & intr arringare

harass ['hærəs] or [hə'ræs] tr bersagliare; tartassare, tormentare

harbinger ['harbɪndʒər] s foriero; annunzio || tr annunziare

harbor ['harbər] adj di porto, portuario || s porto || tr albergare; (love or hatred) nutrire; (e.g., a criminal) dare ricetto a

har'bor mas'ter s capitano di porto

hard [hard] adj duro; (difficult) difficile; (work) improbo; (solder) forte; (hearing or breathing) grosso; (drinker) impenitente; (liquor) fortemente alcolico; to be hard on essere severo con; (to wear out fast) logorare rapidamente || adv duro; forte; molto; hard upon subito dopo

hard'-and-fast' adj inflessibile

hard-bitten ['hard'bɪtən] adj duro, incallito

hard-boiled ['hard'bɔɪld] adj (egg) sodo; (coll) duro

hard' can'dy s caramelle fpl; piece of hard candy caramella

hard' cash' s denaro contante

hard' ci'der s sidro fermentato

hard' coal' s antracite f

hard'-earned' adj guadagnato a stento

harden ['hardən] tr indurire || intr indurirsi

hardening ['hardənɪŋ] s indurimento; (metallurgy) tempra

hard' facts' spl realtà f

hard-fought ['hard'fɔt] adj accanito

hard-headed ['hard'hedɪd] adj astuto; ostinato, caparbio

hard-hearted ['hard'hartɪd] adj dal cuore duro

hardihood ['hardɪ,hud] s forza, coraggio; insolenza

hardiness ['hardɪnɪs] s ardire m; vigore m, robustezza fisica

hard' la'bor s lavori forzati

hard' luck' s mala sorte

hard'-luck' sto'ry s storia delle proprie disgrazie

hardly ['hardli] adv appena, quasi no; (with great difficulty) a malapena, a fatica; hardly ever quasi mai

hardness ['hardnɪs] s durezza

hard'-of-hear'ing adj duro d'orecchio

hard-pressed ['hard'prest] adj oppresso; to be hard-pressed for essere a corto di

hard' rub'ber s ebanite f

hard' sauce' s miscela di burro e zucchero

hard'-shell crab' s granchio con la corazza

hardship ['hardʃɪp] s pena, privazione; hardships privazioni fpl, strettezze fpl hard'tack' *s* galletta

hard' times' *spl* strettezze *fpl*

hard' to please' *adj* di difficile contentatura

hard' up' *adj* (coll) in urgente bisogno; to be hard up for (coll) essere a corto di

hard'ware' *s* ferramenta *fpl*; macchinario

hard'ware store' *s* negozio di ferramenta

hard-won ['hɑrd‚wʌn] *adj* (*victory, battle*) conquistato con molti sforzi; (*money*) acquistato con molti sforzi

hard'wood' *s* legno forte

hard'wood floor' *s* pavimento di legno, parquet *m*

har·dy ['hɑrdi] *adj* (-dier; -diest) forte, resistente; (*rash*) temerario; (hort) resistente al freddo

hare [her] *s* lepre *f*

harebrained ['her‚brend] *adj* scervellato, sventato

hare'lip' *s* labbro leporino

harem ['herəm] *s* arem *m*

hark [hɑrk] *intr* ascoltare; to hark back (*said of hounds*) ritornare sulla pista; riandare col pensiero || *interj* ascolta!

harken ['hɑrkən] *intr* ascoltare

harlequin ['hɑrləkwɪn] *s* arlecchino

harlot ['hɑrlət] *s* meretrice *f*, baldracca

harm [hɑrm] *s* danno || *tr* rovinare; nuocere (with *dat*), fare del male (with *dat*)

harmful ['hɑrmfəl] *adj* nocivo

harmless ['hɑrmlɪs] *adj* innocuo

harmonic [hɑr'mɑnɪk] *adj* armonico || *s* (phys) armonica || harmonics *ssg* armonica; *spl* suoni armonici

harmonica [hɑr'mɑnɪkə] *s* armonica a bocca

harmonious [hɑr'monɪ‑əs] *adj* armonioso

harmonize ['hɑrmə‚naɪz] *tr* intonare; (mus) armonizzare || *intr* intonarsi; (mus) cantare all'unisono

harmo·ny ['hɑrməni] *s* (-nies) armonia

harness ['hɑrnɪs] *s* bardatura, finimenti *mpl*; (fig) routine *f*; to die in the harness morire sulla breccia || *tr* bardare, imbrigliare; (*a waterfall*) captare

har'ness mak'er *s* sellaio

har'ness race' *s* corsa al trotto, corsa di cavalli col sulky

harp [hɑrp] *s* arpa || *intr*—to harp on ripetere ostinatamente

harpist ['hɑrpɪst] *s* arpista *mf*

harpoon [hɑr'pun] *s* rampone *m* || *tr & intr* arpionare

harpsichord ['hɑrpsɪ‚kɔrd] *s* arpicordo, clavicembalo

har·py ['hɑrpi] *s* (-pies) arpia

harrow ['hæro] *s* erpice *m* || *tr* (agr) erpicare; (fig) tormentare

harrowing ['hæro‑ɪŋ] *adj* straziante

har·ry ['hæri] *v* (*pret & pp* -ried) *tr* saccheggiare; tormentare

harsh [hɑrʃ] *adj* (*to touch*) ruvido; (*to taste or hearing*) aspro; inclemente

harshness ['hɑrʃnɪs] *s* ruvidezza; asprezza; inclemenza

hart [hɑrt] *s* cervo

harum-scarum ['herəm‚skerəm] *adj & s* scervellato

harvest ['hɑrvɪst] *s* raccolta, mietitura || *tr* raccogliere, mietere

harvester ['hɑrvɪstər] *s* (*person*) mietitore *m*; (*machine*) mietitrice *f*

har'vest home' *s* fine *f* della mietitura; festa dei mietitori; canzone *f* dei mietitori

har'vest moon' *s* luna di settembre

has-been ['hæz‚bɪn] *s* (*person*) fallito; (*thing*) anticaglia

hash [hæʃ] *s* polpettone *m* || *tr* tritare

hash' house' *s* osteria di terz'ordine

hashish ['hæʃɪʃ] *s* ascisc *m*

hasp [hæsp] or [hɑsp] *s* boncinello

hassle ['hæsəl] *s* (coll) rissa, disputa

hassock ['hæsək] *s* cuscino poggiapiedi

haste [hest] *s* premura; in haste di premura; to make haste fare presto

hasten ['hesən] *tr* affrettare || *intr* affrettarsi

hast·y ['hesti] *adj* (-ier; -iest) frettoloso; precipitato

hat [hæt] *s* cappello; to keep under one's hat (coll) mantenere il segreto su; to throw one's hat in the ring (coll) dichiarare la propria candidatura

hat'band' *s* nastro del cappello

hat' block' *s* forma da cappelli

hat'box' *s* cappelliera

hatch [hætʃ] *s* (*brood*) nidiata; (*shading line*) tratteggio; (*trap door*) porta a ribalta; (*lower half of door*) mezza porta; (naut) boccaporto || *tr* (*eggs*) covare; (*a drawing*) tratteggiare; complottare, tramare || *intr* schiudersi

hat'check' girl' *s* guardarobiera

hatchet ['hætʃɪt] *s* accetta; to bury the hatchet fare la pace

hatch'way' *s* (*trap door*) porta a ribalta; (naut) boccaporto

hate [het] *s* odio || *tr & intr* odiare

hateful ['hetfəl] *adj* odioso

hat'pin' *s* spillone *m*

hat'rack' *s* attaccapanni *m*

hatred ['hetrɪd] *s* odio, livore *m*

hatter ['hætər] *s* cappellaio

haughtiness ['hɔtɪnɪs] *s* superbia

haugh·ty ['hɔti] *adj* (-tier; -tiest) superbo, sprezzante

haul [hɔl] *s* (*tug*) tiro; (*amount caught*) retata; (*distance transported*) percorso, pezzo || *tr* trasportare; tirare; (naut) alare

haunch [hɔntʃ] or [hɑntʃ] *s* fianco; anca; (*hind quarter of an animal*) coscia; (*same used for food*) cosciotto

haunt [hɔnt] or [hɑnt] *s* ritrovo, nido || *tr* frequentare assiduamente; perseguitare

haunt'ed house' *s* casa frequentata dai fantasmi

haute couture [ot ku'tyr] *s* alta moda

have [hæv] *s*—the haves and the have-nots gli abbienti e i nullatenenti || *v* (*pret & pp* **had** [hæd]) *tr* avere; (*a dream*) fare; (*to get, take*) prendere, ottenere, ricevere; **to have got** (coll) avere; **to have got to** + *inf* (coll) dovere + *inf;* **to have it in for** (coll) serbar rancore per; **to have it out with** avere a che dire con; **to have on** portare; **to have** (s.th) **to do with** avere (qlco) a che fare con, e.g., **I don't want to have anything to do with him** non voglio aver nulla a che fare con lui; **to have** + *inf* fare + *inf,* e.g., **I had him pay the bill** gli ho fatto pagare il conto; **to have** + *pp* fare + *inf,* e.g., **I had my watch repaired** ho fatto aggiustare l'orologio ‖ *intr*—**to have at** attaccare, mettersi di buzzo buono con; **to have to** + *inf* dovere + *inf;* **to have to do with** avere a che fare con; trattare di, e.g., **this book has to do with superstition** questo libro tratta di superstizione ‖ *v aux* avere, e.g., **he has studied his lesson** ha studiato la sua lezione

havelock ['hævlɑk] *s* coprinuca *m*

haven ['hevən] *s* porto; asilo

haversack ['hævər‚sæk] *s* bisaccia; (mil) zaino

havoc ['hævək] *s* rovina; **to play havoc with** rovinare; scompigliare

haw [hɔ] *s* (*of hawthorn*) bacca; (*in speech*) esitazione ‖ *intr* voltare a sinistra ‖ *interj* voltare a sinistra!

hawk [hɔk] *s* falco; (*mortarboard*) sparviere *m;* (coll) persona rapace ‖ *tr* imbonire; (*newspapers*) strillare; **to hawk up** sputare raschiandosi la gola ‖ *intr* fare il merciaiolo ambulante; schiarirsi la gola

hawker ['hɔkər] *s* merciaiolo ambulante

hawse [hɔz] *s* (naut) cubia; (*hole*) (naut) occhio di cubia; (naut) altezza di cubia

hawse'hole' *s* occhio di cubia

hawser ['hɔzər] *s* cavo, gomena

haw'thorn' *s* biancospino

hay [he] *s* fieno; **to hit the hay** (slang) andare a letto; **to make hay while the sun shines** battere il ferro fin ch'è caldo

hay' fe'ver *s* febbre *f* da fieno, raffreddore *m* da fieno

hay'field' *s* prato seminato a fieno

hay'fork' *s* forcone *m;* (mach) rastrello

hay'loft' *s* fienile *m*

haymow [he ‚mau] *s* fienile *m*

hay'rack' *s* rastrelliera

hay'ride' *s* gita notturna in carro da fieno

hay'seed' *s* semente *f* d'erba; (coll) semplicione *m,* campagnolo

hay'stack' *s* meta, pagliaio

hay'wire' *adj* (coll) disordinato, in confusione; (coll) impazzito ‖ *s* filo per legare il fieno

hazard ['hæzərd] *s* pericolo; (*chance*) rischio; (golf) ostacolo ‖ *tr* rischiare; (*an opinion*) arrischiare

hazardous ['hæzərdəs] *adj* pericoloso

haze [hez] *s* foschia; (fig) confusione ‖ *tr* far la matricola a

hazel ['hezəl] *adj* nocciola ‖ *s* (*tree*) nocciolo; (*fruit*) nocciola

ha'zel-nut' *s* nocciola

hazing ['hezɪŋ] *s* vessazione, angheria; (*at university*) matricola

ha-zy ['hezi] *adj* (-**zier; -ziest**) nebbioso; confuso

H-bomb ['etʃ ‚bɑm] *s* bomba H

he [hi] *s* (**hes**) maschio ‖ *pron pers* (they) lui, egli, esso

head [hed] *s* testa, capo; (*of bed*) testiera; (*caption*) testata; (*of a nail*) cappello; (*on a glass of beer*) schiuma; (*of a boil*) punta purulenta; (*e.g., of cattle*) capo; **at the head of** a capo di; **from head to foot** da capo a piedi; **head over heels** a gambe levate; completamente; **heads or tails** testa o croce; **over one's head** al di sopra della capacità intellettuale di qlcu; (*going to a higher authority*) al di sopra di qlcu; **to be out of one's head** (coll) esser matto; **to bring to a head** far giungere alla crisi; **to come into one's head** passar per la mente a qlcu; **to go to one's head** dare al cervello a qlcu; **to keep one's head** non perdere la testa; **to keep one's head above water** arrivare a sbarcare il lunario; **to not make head or tail of** non riuscire a raccappezzarsi su ‖ *tr* dirigere, comandare; essere alla testa di ‖ *intr*—**to head towards** dirigersi verso

head'ache' *s* mal di capo, emicrania

head'band' *s* fascia sul capo; (bb) capitello; (typ) filetto

head'board' *s* testiera del letto

head' cheese' *s* salame *m* di testa

head'dress' *s* acconciatura

header ['hedər] *s*—**to take a header** (coll) gettarsi a capofitto

head'first' *adv* a capofitto

head'gear' *s* copricapo; (*for protection*) casco

head'hunt'er *s* cacciatore *m* di teste

heading ['hedɪŋ] *s* intestazione; (*of a chapter of a book*) titolo; (journ) testata, capopagina *m*

headland ['hedlənd] *s* promontorio

headless ['hedlɪs] *adj* senza testa

head'light' *s* (naut, rr) fanale *m;* (aut) faro

head'line' *s* (*of a page of a book*) titolo; (journ) testata ‖ *tr* intestare; fare pubblicità a

head'lin'er *s* (slang) attrazione principale

head'long' *adj* precipitoso ‖ *adv* a precipizio; a capofitto

head'man *s* (-**men**) capo; giustiere *m*

head'mas'ter *s* direttore *m* di un collegio per ragazzi

head'most' *adj* primo, più avanzato

head' of'fice *s* sede *f* centrale

head' of hair' *s* capigliatura

head'-on' *adj* frontale ‖ *adv* di fronte, frontalmente

head'phones' *spl* cuffia

head'piece' *s* (*any covering for the head*) copricapo; (*helmet*) elmo; (*brains, judgment*) testa; (*of bed*) spalliera; (*headset*) cuffia; (typ) testata

head'quar'ters *s* sede *f* centrale, direzione; (mil) quartier *m* generale

head'rest' *s* poggiatesta *m*, testiera

head'set' *s* cuffia

head'ship' *s* direzione

head'stone' *s* pietra angolare; (*on a grave*) pietra tombale

head'stream' *s* affluente *m* principale

head'strong' *adj* testardo, ostinato

head'wait'er *s* capocameriere *m*

head'wa'ters *spl* fonti *fpl* or sorgenti *fpl* d'un fiume

head'way' *s* progresso; **to make headway** progredire

head'wear' *s* copricapo

head'wind' *s* vento di prua

head'work' *s* lavoro intellettuale

head•y ['hɛdi] *adj* (-ier; -iest) eccitante; impetuoso; violento; (*clever*) astuto; intossicante

heal [hil] *tr* sanare, guarire; purificare ‖ *intr* risanarsi, guarire; (*said of a wound*) rimarginare

healer ['hilər] *s* guaritore *m*

health [hɛlθ] *s* salute *f*; **to radiate health** sprizzare salute da tutti i pori; **to your health!** alla Sua salute!

health' depart'ment *s* sanità *f*

healthful ['hɛlθfəl] *adj* salutare

health' insur'ance *s* assicurazione malattia

health•y ['hɛlθi] *adj* (-ier; -iest) sano; salubre

heap [hip] *s* mucchio; (coll) insalata, mare *m* ‖ *tr* ammucchiare; **to heap s.th upon s.o.** colmare qlcu di qlco; **to heap with** colmare di

hear [hɪr] *v* (*pret & pp* **heard** [hʌrd]) *tr* udire; **to hear it said** sentirlo dire ‖ *intr* udire; **hear!, hear!** bravo!; **to hear about** sentir parlare di; **to hear from** aver notizie di; **to hear of** sentir parlare di; **to hear that** sentir dire che

hearer ['hɪrər] *s* ascoltatore *m*

hearing ['hɪrɪŋ] *s* (*sense*) udito, orecchio; (*act*) udienza; **in the hearing of** in presenza di; **within hearing** a portata d'orecchio

hear'ing aid' *s* uditofono

hear'say' *s* diceria; **by hearsay** per sentito dire

hearse [hʌrs] *s* carro, carrozzone *m*, or furgone *m* funebre

heart [hɑrt] *s* cuore *m*; (*e.g., of lettuce*) grumolo; **after one's heart** di gusto di qlcu; **by heart** a memoria; **heart and soul** di tutto cuore; **to break the heart of** spezzare il cuore di; **to die of a broken heart** morire di crepacuore; **to eat one's heart out** piangere silenziosamente; **to get to the heart of** sviscerare il nocciolo di; **to have one's heart in one's work** lavorare di buzzo buono; **to have one's heart in the right place** avere buone intenzioni; **to lose heart** scoraggiarsi; **to open one's heart to** aprire il cuore a; **to take heart** prender coraggio; **to take to heart** prendersi a cuore; **to**

wear one's heart on one's sleeve parlare a cuore aperto; **with one's heart in one's mouth** col cuore in bocca

heart'ache' *s* angustia, angoscia

heart' attack' *s* attacco cardiaco

heart'beat' *s* battito del cuore

heart'break' *s* angoscia straziante

heart'break'er *s* rubacuori *m*

heartbroken ['hɑrt ˌbrokən] *adj* col cuore spezzato

heart'burn' *s* bruciore *m* di stomaco

heart' disease' *s* mal *m* di cuore

hearten ['hɑrtən] *tr* rincuorare

heart' fail'ure *s* (*death*) arresto cardiaco; collasso cardiaco

heartfelt ['hɑrt ˌfɛlt] *adj* sentito

hearth [hɑrθ] *s* focolare *m*

hearth'stone' *s* pietra del focolare

heartily ['hɑrtɪli] *adv* di cuore, cordialmente; saporitamente

heartless ['hɑrtlɪs] *adj* senza cuore, insensibile

heart' mur'mur *s* soffio al cuore

heart-rending ['hɑrt ˌrɛndɪŋ] *adj* da far male al cuore

heart'sick' *adj* afflitto, sconsolato

heart'strings' *spl* precordi *mpl*

heart'-to-heart' *adj* cuore a cuore

heart' trans'plant *s* trapianto cardiaco

heart'wood' *s* cuore *m* del legno

heart•y ['hɑrti] *adj* (-ier; -iest) cordiale, di cuore; abbondante; (*eater*) grande

heat [hit] *adj* termico ‖ *s* calore *m*; (*of room, house, etc.*) riscaldamento; (zool) fregola; (sports) batteria; (fig) fervore *m*; **in heat** (zool) in amore ‖ *tr* scaldare, riscaldare; (fig) eccitare ‖ *intr* riscaldarsi; (fig) accalorarsi

heated ['hitɪd] *adj* accalorato

heater ['hitər] *s* riscaldatore *m*; (*for central heating*) calorifero; (*to heat hands or bed*) scaldino; (*to heat water in tub*) scaldabagno

heath [hiθ] *s* (*shrub*) brugo, erica; (*tract of land*) brughiera

hea•then ['hiðən] *adj* pagano; irreligioso ‖ *s* (-then or -thens) pagano

heathendom ['hiðəndəm] *s* (*worship*) paganesimo; (*land*) pagania

heather ['hɛðər] *s* erica, brugo

heating ['hitɪŋ] *adj* di riscaldamento ‖ *s* riscaldamento

heat'ing pad' *s* termoforo

heat' light'ning *s* lampo di caldo

heat' shield' *s* (rok) scudo termico

heat'stroke' *s* colpo di calore

heat' wave' *s* ondata di caldo

heave [hiv] *s* sollevamento, sforzo; **heaves** (vet) bolsaggine *f* ‖ *v* (*pret & pp* **heaved** or **hove** [hov]) *tr* sollevare, alzare; rigettare; (*a sigh*) emettere ‖ *intr* alzarsi e abbassarsi; (*said of one's chest*) palpitare; avere conati di vomito

heaven ['hɛvən] *s* cielo; **for heaven's sake!** or **good heavens!** per amor del cielo!; **heavens** (*firmament*) cielo ‖ **Heaven** *s* cielo

heavenly ['hɛvənli] *adj* celeste

heav'enly bod'y *s* corpo celeste

heav•y ['hɛvi] *adj* (-ier; -iest) (*of great*

weight) pesante; (*liquid*) denso; (*cloth, sea*) grosso; (*traffic*) forte; (*serious*) grave; (*crop*) abbondante; (*rain*) dirotto; (*features*) grossolano; (*heart*) stretto; (*ponderous*) macchinoso; (*industry*) grande; (*stock market*) abbattuto || *adv* (coll) pesantemente; **to hang heavy** (*said of time*) passar lentamente

heav'y-du'ty *adj* extraforte

heavy-hearted ['hɛvɪ'hɑrtɪd] *adj* afflitto, triste

heav'y-set' *adj* forte, corpulento

heav'y-weight' *s* peso massimo

Hebrew ['hibru] *adj* & *s* ebreo; (*language*) ebraico

hecatomb ['hɛkə,tom] or ['hɛkə,tum] *s* ecatombe *f*

heckle ['hɛkəl] *tr* interrompere con domande imbarazzanti

hectic ['hɛktɪk] *adj* febbrile

hedge [hɛdʒ] *s* barriera; (*of bushes*) siepe *f*; (*in stock market*) operazione controbilanciante || *tr* circondare con siepe; **to hedge in** circondare || *intr* evitare di compromettersi; (com) coprirsi

hedge'hog' *s* (zool) riccio; (*porcupine*) (zool) porcospino

hedge'hop' *v* (*pret & pp* -hopped; *ger* hopping) *intr* volare a volo radente

hedgehopping ['hɛdʒ,hɑpɪŋ] *s* volo radente

hedge'row' [ro] *s* siepe *f*

heed [hid] *s* attenzione; **to take heed** fare attenzione || *tr* badare a || *intr* fare attenzione, badare

heedless [hidlɪs] *adj* sbadato

heehaw ['hi,hɔ] *s* (*of donkey*) raglio d'asino; risata || *intr* ragliare; ridere fragorosamente

heel [hil] *s* (*of shoe, of foot*) calcagno, tallone *m*; (*of stocking or shoe*) tallone *m*; (*raised part of shoe below heel*) tacco; (coll) farabutto; **down at the heel** mal ridotto; **to cool one's heels** aspettare a lungo; **to kick up one's heels** darsi alla pazza gioia; **to show a clean pair of heels** or **to take to one's heels** battere i tacchi

heeler ['hilər] *s* politicante *mf*

heft-y ['hɛftɪ] *adj* (-ier; -iest) (*heavy*) pesante; (*strong*) forte

hegemon-y [hɪ'dʒɛmənɪ] or ['hɛdʒɪ,monɪ] *s* (-ies) egemonia

hegira [hɪ'dʒaɪrə] or ['hɛdʒɪrə] *s* fuga

heifer ['hɛfər] *s* manza, giovenca

height [haɪt] *s* altezza; (*of a person*) altezza, statura; (*e.g., of folly*) colmo

heighten ['haɪtən] *tr* innalzare; (*to increase the amount of*) accrescere, aumentare || *intr* aumentare

heinous ['henəs] *adj* nefando, odioso

heir [ɛr] *s* erede *m*

heir' appar'ent *s* (heirs' appar'ent) erede necessario

heirdom ['ɛrdəm] *s* eredità *f*

heiress ['ɛrɪs] *s* ereditiera, erede *f*

heirloom ['ɛr,lum] *s* cimelio di famiglia

Helen ['hɛlən] *s* Elena

helicopter ['hɛlɪ,kɑptər] *s* elicottero

heliport ['hɛlɪ,pɔrt] *s* eliporto

helium ['hilɪ·əm] *s* elio

helix ['hilɪks] *s* (helixes or helices ['hɛlɪ,siz]) spirale *f*; (geom) elica

hell [hɛl] *s* inferno

hell-bent ['hɛl'bɛnt] *adj* (coll) risoluto; **to be hell-bent on** (coll) avere un chiodo in testa di

hell'cat' *s* arpia, megera

hellebore ['hɛlɪ,bor] *s* elleboro

Hellene ['hɛlin] *s* greco

Hellenic [hɛ'lɛnɪk] or [hɛ'linɪk] *adj* ellenico

hell'fire' *s* fuoco dell'inferno

hellish ['hɛlɪʃ] *adj* infernale

hel·lo [hɛ'lo] *s* saluto || *interj* ciao!; (*on telephone*) pronto!

helm [hɛlm] *s* barra del timone; ruota del timone; timone *m* || *tr* dirigere

helmet ['hɛlmɪt] *s* (mil) elmetto; (sports) casco; (hist) elmo

helms'man *s* (-men) timoniere *m*

help [hɛlp] *s* aiuto; (*relief*) rimedio, e.g., **there's no help for it** non c'è rimedio; servitù *f*; impiegati *mpl*; operai *mpl*; **to come to the help of** venire in aiuto di || *tr* aiutare; soccorrere, mitigare; (*to wait on*) servire; **it can't be helped** non c'è rimedio; **so help me God!** Dio mi sia testimonio!; **to help down** aiutare a scendere; **to help s.o. with his coat** aiutare qlcu a mettersi il cappotto; **to help oneself** servirsi da solo; **to help up** aiutare a salire; aiutare ad alzarsi; **to not be able to help** + *ger* non poter fare a meno di + *inf*, e.g., **he can't help laughing** non può fare a meno di ridere. || *intr* aiutare *|| interj* aiuto!

helper ['hɛlpər] *s* aiutante *m*; (*in a shop*) garzone *m*, lavorante *m*

helpful ['hɛlpfəl] *adj* utile, servizievole

helping ['hɛlpɪŋ] *s* (*of food*) razione

helpless ['hɛlplɪs] *adj* (*weak*) debole; (*powerless*) impotente; senza risorse; (*confused*) perplesso; (*situation*) irrimediabile

help'mate' *s* compagno; (*wife*) compagna

helter-skelter ['hɛltər'skɛltər] *adj* & *adv* in fretta e furia; alla rinfusa

hem [hɛm] *s* (*any edge*) orlo; (*of skirt*) basta, pedana; (*of suit*) falda || *v* (*pret & pp* hemmed; *ger* hemming) *tr* orlare, bordare; **to hem in** insaccare || *intr* esitare; **to hem and haw** esitare; essere evasivo

hemisphere ['hɛmɪ,sfɪr] *s* emisfero

hemistich ['hɛmɪ,stɪk] *s* emistichio

hem'line' *s* orlo della gonna

hem'lock' *s* (*herb and poison*) cicuta; (*Tsuga canadensis*) abete *m* del Canada

hemoglobin [,hɛmə'globɪn] or [,himə'globɪn] *s* emoglobina

hemophilia [,hɛmə'fɪlɪ·ə] or [,himə'fɪlɪ·ə] *s* emofilia

hemorrhage ['hɛmərɪdʒ] *s* emorragia

hemorrhoids ['hɛmə,rɔɪdz] *spl* emorroidi *fpl*

hemostat ['hɛmə,stæt] or ['himə,stæt] *s* pinza emostatica

hemp [hɛmp] *s* canapa

hemstitch ['hem,stitʃ] s orlo a giorno || tr & intr orlare a giorno

hen [hen] s gallina

hence [hens] adv di qui; da ora; quindi; di qui a, e.g., **three weeks hence** di qui a tre settimane

hence'forth' adv d'ora innanzi

hench·man ['hentʃmən] s (-men [mən]) accolito; politicante m

hen'house' s pollaio

henna ['henə] s henna || tr tingere con la henna

hen'peck' tr (a husband) trovare a ridire con

hen'pecked' hus'band s marito dominato dalla moglie

her [hʌr] adj poss suo, il suo || pron pers la, lei; **to her le**, a lei

herald ['herəld] s araldo; annunziatore m || tr annunziare

heraldic [he'rældɪk] adj araldico

herald·ry ['herəldri] s (-ries) (office) consulta araldica; (science) araldica; (coat of arms) blasone m

herb [ʌrb] or [hʌrb] s erba; erba medicinale

herbaceous [hʌr'beʃəs] adj erbaceo

herbage ['ʌrbɪdʒ] or ['hʌrbɪdʒ] s erba; (law) erbatico

herbalist ['hʌrbəlɪst] or ['ʌrbəlɪst] s erborista mf

herbari·um [hʌr'berɪ·əm] s (-ums or -a [ə]) erbario

herb' doc'tor s erborista mf

herculean [hʌr'kjulɪ·ən] or [,hʌrkju-'lɪ·ən] adj erculeo

herd [hʌrd] s (of sheep) gregge m; (of cattle) mandria; (of men) torma || tr & intr imbrancare

herds'man s (-men) (of cattle) mandriano, vaccaio; (of sheep) pastore m

here [hɪr] adj presente || s—**the here and the hereafter** la vita presente e l'aldilà || adv qui, qua; **here and there** qua e là; **here is** or **here are** ecco; **that's neither here not there** ciò non ha nulla a che vedere || interj presente!

hereabouts ['hɪrə,bauts] adv qua vicino

here·af'ter s aldilà m || adv d'ora innanzi; nel futuro

here·by' adv con la presente

hereditary [hɪ'redɪ,teri] adj ereditario

heredi·ty [hɪ'redɪti] s (-ties) eredità f

here·in' adv qui; in questo posto

here·of' adv di questo

here·on' adv in questo; su questo

here·sy ['herəsi] s (-sies) eresia

heretic ['herətɪk] adj & s eretico

heretical [hɪ'retɪkəl] adj eretico

heretofore [,hɪrtʊ'for] adv sinora

here·u·pon' adv su questo; in questo; immediatamente dopo

here·with' adv accluso; con la presente

heritage ['herɪtɪdʒ] s eredità f

hermetic(al) [hʌr'metɪk(əl)] adj ermetico

hermit ['hʌrmɪt] s eremita m

hermitage ['hʌrmɪtɪdʒ] s eremitaggio

herni·a ['hʌrnɪ·ə] s (-as or -ae [,i]) ernia

he·ro ['hɪro] s (-roes) eroe m

heroic [hɪ'ro·ɪk] adj eroico || **heroics** spl linguaggio altisonante

heroin ['hero·ɪn] s (pharm) eroina

heroine ['hero·ɪn] s eroina

heroism ['hero,ɪzəm] s eroismo

heron ['herən] s airone m

herring ['herɪŋ] s aringa

her'ring-bone' s (in fabrics) spina di pesce; (in hardwood floors) spiga

hers [hʌrz] pron poss il suo; **of hers** suo

herself [hʌr'self] pron pers lei stessa; sé stessa; si, e.g., **she enjoyed herself** si divertì; **with herself** con sé

hertz [hʌrts] s hertz m

hesitan·cy ['hezɪtənsi] s (-cies) titubanza, esitanza

hesitant ['hezɪtənt] adj esitante

hesitate ['hezɪ,tet] intr esitare, titubare; (to stutter) balbettare

hesitation [,hezɪ'teʃən] s esitazione

heterodox ['hetərə,dɑks] adj eterodosso

heterodyne ['hetərə,daɪn] s eterodina

heterogeneous [,hetərə'dʒinɪ·əs] adj eterogeneo

hew [hju] v (pret **hewed**; pp **hewed** or **hewn**) tr tagliare; (a passage) aprirsi; (a statue) abbozzare; **to hew down** abbattere || intr—**to hew close to the line** (coll) filare diritto

hex [heks] s strega; incantesimo || tr stregare, incantare

hexameter [heks'æmɪtər] s esametro

hey [he] interj ehi!

hey'day' s apogeo

hia·tus [haɪ'etəs] s (-tuses or -tus) (gap) lacuna; (gram) iato

hibernate ['haɪbər,net] intr ibernare; (said of people) svernare

hibiscus [hɪ'bɪskəs] or [haɪ'bɪskəs] s ibisco

hic·cup ['hɪkəp] s singhiozzo || v (pret & pp -cuped or -cupped; ger -cuping or -cupping) intr singhiozzare

hick [hɪk] adj & s (coll) rustico

hicko·ry ['hɪkəri] s (-ries) hickory m

hidden ['hɪdən] adj nascosto

hide [haɪd] s cuoio, pelle f; **hides** cuoio; **neither hide nor hair** nemmeno una traccia; **to tan s.o.'s hide** (coll) dargliele sode a qlcu || v (pret **hid** [hɪd]; pp **hid** or **hidden** ['hɪdən]) tr nascondere || intr nascondersi; **to hide out** (coll) rintanarsi

hide'-and-seek' s rimpiattino; **to play hide-and-seek** giocare a rimpiattino or a nascondino

hide'bound' adj retrogrado, conservatore

hideous ['hɪdɪ·əs] adj orribile, brutto

hide'out' s nascondiglio

hiding ['haɪdɪŋ] s nascondere m; (place) nascondiglio; **in hiding** nascosto

hid'ing place' s nascondiglio

hie [haɪ] v (pret & pp **hied**; ger **hieing** or **hying**) tr—**hie thee home** affrettati a tornare a casa || intr affrettarsi

hierar·chy ['haɪ·ə,rɑrki] s (-chies) gerarchia

hieroglyphic [,haɪ·ərə'glɪfɪk] adj & s geroglifico

hi-fi ['haɪ'faɪ] *adj* di alta fedeltà ‖ *s* alta fedeltà

higgledy-piggledy ['hɪgəldɪ'pɪgəldɪ] *adj* confuso ‖ *adv* alla rinfusa

high [haɪ] *adj* alto; (*color*) forte; (*merry*) allegro; (*luxurious*) lussuoso; (coll) ubriaco; (culin) frollo; **high and dry** abbandonato; **high and mighty** (coll) arrogante ‖ *adv* molto; riccamente; **to aim high** mirare in alto; **to come high** essere caro ‖ *s* (aut) quarta, diretta; **on high** in cielo

high' al'tar *s* altare *m* maggiore

high'ball' *s* whiskey con ghiaccio e gazosa ‖ *intr* (slang) andare di carriera

high' blood' pres'sure *s* ipertensione

high'born' *adj* di nobile lignaggio

high'boy' *s* cassettone alto

high'brow' *s* intellettuale *mf;* (coll) intellettualoide *mf*

high'chair' *s* seggiolino per bambini

high' command' *s* comando supremo

high' cost' of liv'ing *s* carovita *m*, caroviveri *m*

high'er educa'tion *s* insegnamento universitario, istruzione superiore

higher-up [,haɪ-ər'ʌp] *s* (coll) superiore *m*

high' explo'sive *s* esplosivo ad alta potenza

highfalutin [,haɪfə'lutən] *adj* (coll) pomposo, pretenzioso

high' fidel'ity *s* high fidelity, alta fedeltà

high'-fre'quency *adj* ad alta frequenza

high' gear' *s* (aut) presa diretta

high'-grade' *adj* di qualità superiore

high-handed ['haɪ'hændɪd] *adj* arbitrario

high' hat' *s* cappello a cilindro

high'-hat' (coll) snob *m* ‖ *v* (*pret & pp* **-hatted;** *ger* **-hatting**) *tr* (coll) snobbare

high'-heeled' shoe' ['haɪ ,hild] *s* scarpa coi tacchi alti

high' horse' *s* comportamento arrogante; **to get up on one's high horse** darsi delle grandi arie

high' jinks' [dʒɪŋks] *s* (slang) pagliacciata, gazzarra

high' jump' *s* salto in altezza

highland ['haɪlənd] *adj* montagnoso ‖ **highlands** *spl* regione montagnosa

high' life' *s* high-life *f*, alta società

high'light' *s* punto culminante ‖ *tr* mettere in risalto

highly ['haɪlɪ] *adv* altamente, molto; (*paid*) profumatamente; **to speak highly of** parlar molto bene di

High' Mass' *s* messa cantata

high-minded ['haɪ'maɪndɪd] *adj* magnanimo

highness ['haɪnɪs] *s* altezza ‖ **Highness** *s* Altezza

high' noon' *s* mezzogiorno in punto; (fig) sommo

high-pitched ['haɪ'pɪt/t] *adj* acuto; intenso, emozionante

high-powered ['haɪ'pau-ərd] *adj* ad alta potenza; (*binoculars*) ad alto ingrandimento

high'pres'sure *adj* ad alta pressione ‖ *tr* sollecitare con insistenza

high-priced ['haɪ'praɪst] *adj* caro, di alto prezzo

high' priest' *s* sommo sacerdote

high' rise' *s* edificio di molti piani

high'road' *s* strada principale

high'school' *s* scuola media; (*in Italy*) liceo

high' sea' *s* alto mare; **high seas** alto mare

high' soci'ety *s* l'alta società

high'-sound'ing *adj* altisonante

high'-speed' *adj* ad alta velocità

high-spirited ['haɪ'spɪrɪtɪd] *adj* fiero, vivace, focoso

high-strung ['haɪ'strʌŋ] *adj* teso, nervoso

high'-test' fuel' *s* supercarburante *m*

high' tide' *s* alta marea; punto culminante

high' time' *s* ora, e.g., **it is high time for you to go** è proprio ora che Lei se ne vada; (coll) baldoria

high' trea'son *s* (*against the sovereign*) lesa maestà; (*against the state*) alto tradimento

high' wa'ter *s* alta marea; (*in a river*) straripamento

high'way' *adj* autostradale ‖ *s* autostrada

high'way'man *s* (**-men**) grassatore *m*

hijack ['haɪ,dʒæk] *tr* rubare; (*e.g., an airplane*) dirottare ‖ *intr* effettuare un dirottamento

hijacker ['haɪ,dʒækər] *s* ladro a mano armata; (*e.g., of an airplane*) dirottatore *m*

hijacking ['haɪ,dʒækɪŋ] *s* furto a mano armata; dirottamento

hike [haɪk] *s* (*for pleasure*) gita, camminata; (*increase*) aumento; (mil) marcia ‖ *tr* tirar su; aumentare ‖ *intr* fare una gita; (mil) fare una marcia

hiker ['haɪkər] *s* camminatore *m*

hilarious [hɪ'lerɪ-əs] or [haɪ'lerɪ-əs] *adj* ilare; (*e.g., joke*) allegro, divertente

hill [hɪl] *s* collina ‖ *tr* rincalzare

hillbil·ly ['hɪl,bɪlɪ] *s* (**-lies**) (coll) montanaro rustico

hillock ['hɪlək] *s* poggio, collinetta

hill'side' *s* pendio

hill'top' *s* cima

hill·y ['hɪlɪ] *adj* (**-ier; -iest**) collinoso; ripido

hilt [hɪlt] *s* impugnatura, elsa; **up to the hilt** completamente

him [hɪm] *pron pers* lo; lui; **to him** gli, a lui

himself [hɪm'self] *pron pers* lui stesso; sé stesso; si, e.g., **he enjoyed himself** si è divertito; **with himself** con sé

hind [haɪnd] *adj* posteriore, di dietro ‖ *s* cerva

hinder ['hɪndər] *tr* ostacolare, impedire

hindmost ['haɪnd ,most] *adj* ultimo

hind'quar'ter *s* quarto posteriore

hindrance ['hɪndrəns] *s* ostacolo, impedimento

hind'sight' s senno di poi

Hindu ['hɪndu] adj & s indù mf

hinge [hɪndʒ] s cardine m; (bb) cerniera; (philately) listello gommato; punto principale ‖ tr munire di cardini ‖ intr—**to hinge on** dipendere da

hin·ny ['hɪni] s (-nies) bardotto

hint [hɪnt] s insinuazione; **to take the hint** capire l'antifona ‖ tr & intr insinuare; **to hint at** alludere a

hinterland ['hɪntər,lænd] s retroterra m, entroterra m

hip [hɪp] adj—**to be hip to** (slang) essere al corrente di ‖ s anca, fianco; (of a roof) spigolo

hip'bone' s ileo, osso iliaco

hipped [hɪpt] adj (livestock) zoppicante; (roof) a padiglione; **hipped on** (coll) ossessionato per

hippie ['hɪpi] s capellone m

hip·po ['hɪpo] s (-pos) (coll) ippopotamo

hippodrome ['hɪpə,drom] s ippodromo

hippopota·mus [,hɪpə'pɑtəməs] s (-muses or -mi [,maɪ]) ippopotamo

hip' roof' s tetto a padiglione

hire [haɪr] s paga, salario; nolo; **for hire** a nolo ‖ tr (help) impiegare; (a conveyance) noleggiare ‖ intr—**to hire out** mettersi a servizio

hired' girl' s lavorante f di campagna

hired' hand' s lavorante mf

hired' man' s (men') lavorante m di campagna

hireling ['haɪrlɪŋ] adj venale ‖ s persona prezzolata

his [hɪz] adj poss suo, il suo ‖ pron poss il suo

Hispanic [hɪs'pænɪk] adj ispano

Hispanist ['hɪspənɪst] s ispanista mf

hiss [hɪs] s (of fire, wind, serpent, etc.) sibilo; (of disapproval) fischio, zittio ‖ tr zittire ‖ intr zittire; sibilare; (said of a kettle) fischiare

histology [hɪs'talədʒi] s istologia

historian [hɪs'torɪ·ən] s storico

historic(al) [hɪs'tarɪk(əl)] or [hɪs-'tɔrɪk(əl)] adj storico

histo·ry ['hɪstəri] s (-ries) storia

histrionic [,hɪstrɪ'anɪk] adj teatrale; (artificial, affected) istrionico, teatrale ‖ **histrionics** s istrionismo, teatralità f

hit [hɪt] s colpo; successo; (sarcastic remark) frecciata; **to be a hit for** furore; **to make a hit with** fare ottima impressione con ‖ v (pret & pp hit; ger hitting) tr colpire; (to bump) cozzare; (the target) toccare, imbroccare, infilare; (with a car) metter sotto; (a certain speed) andare a ‖ intr battere; **to hit on** (s.th new) imbroccare; **to hit out at** attaccare

hit'-and-run' adj (driver) colpevole di mancato soccorso

hit'-and-run' driv'er s pirata m della strada

hitch [hɪtʃ] s (jerk) strattone m; (knot) nodo; difficoltà f, ostacolo; ‖ tr (to tie) attaccare; (oxen) aggiogare; (slang) sposare

hitch'hike' intr fare l'autostop

hitch'hik'er s autostoppista mf

hitch'ing post' s palo per attaccare un cavallo

hither ['hɪðər] adv qua, qui; **hither and thither** qua e là

hith'er·to' adv sinora

hit'-or-miss' adj fatto alla carlona

hit' rec'ord s disco di grande successo

hive [haɪv] s (box for bees) alveare m; (swarm) sciame m; **hives** orticaria ‖ tr (bees) raccogliere

hoard [hord] s cumulo; (of money) gruzzolo ‖ tr & intr custodire gelosamente; tesaurizzare

hoarding ['hordɪŋ] s ammassamento, tesaurizzazione

hoarfrost ['hor,frɔst] s brina

hoarse [hors] adj rauco, svociato

hoarseness ['horsnɪs] s raucedine f

hoar·y ['hori] adj (-ier -iest) canuto, incanutito

hoax [hoks] s mistificazione ‖ tr mistificare

hob [hab] s mensola del focolare; **to play hob with** (coll) mettere a soqquadro

hobble ['habəl] s zoppicamento; (to tie legs of animal) pastoia ‖ tr far zoppicare; imbarazzare; mettere le pastoie a ‖ intr zoppicare

hob·by ['habi] s (-bies) svago, passatempo; **to ride a hobby** dedicarsi troppo alla propria occupazione favorita

hob'by-horse' s cavallo a dondolo

hob'gob'lin s folletto

hob'nail' s brocca, bulletta

hob·nob ['hab,nab] v (pret & pp -nobbed; ger -nobbing) intr essere amiconi; **to hobnob with** essere intimo di

ho·bo ['hobo] s (-bos or -boes) girovago, vagabondo

Hob'son's choice' ['habsənz] s scelta fra quanto viene offerto o niente

hock [hak] s garretto; (coll) pegno; **in hock** (coll) impegnato, al monte di pietà ‖ tr tagliare i garretti a; (coll) impegnare

hockey ['haki] s hockey m

hock'ey play'er s hockeista m, discatore m

hock'shop' s (coll) negozio di prestiti su pegno

hocus-pocus ['hokəs'pokəs] s (meaningless formula) abracadabra m; gherminella f

hod [had] s vassoio; secchio per il carbone

hod' car'rier s manovale m

hodgepodge ['hadʒ,padʒ] s farragine f

hoe [ho] s marra, zappa ‖ tr & intr zappare

hog [hag] or [hɔg] s suino, porco, maiale m ‖ v (pret & pp hogged; ger hogging) tr (slang) mangiarsi il meglio di

hoggish ['hagɪʃ] or ['hɔgɪʃ] adj maialesco; egoista

hogs'head' s barilozzo di sessantatré galloni

hog'wash' s broda da maiali

hoist [hɔɪst] *s* montacarichi *m*; (*lift*) spinta || *tr* alzare, rizzare; (*a flag*) inastare; (naut) issare

hoity-toity [ˈhɔɪtiˈtɔɪti] *adj* arrogante, altezzoso

hokum [ˈhokəm] *s* (coll) fandonie *fpl*; (coll) sentimentalismo volgare

hold [hold] *s* presa, piglio; (*handle*) impugnatura; autorità *f*, ascendente *m*; (wrestling) presa; (aer) cabina bagagli; (mus) corona; (naut) cala, stiva; **to take hold of** afferare; impossessarsi di || *v* (*pret & pp* **held** [held]) *tr* tenere; (*to hold up*) sostenere; (*e.g., with a pin*) assicurare; (*a rank*) rivestire; contenere; (*a meeting*) avere; (*a note*) (mus) filare; **to hold back** trattenere; **to hold in** trattenere; **to hold one's own** non perdere terreno; **to hold over** differire; **to hold up** reggere, sostenere; (*to rob*) (coll) derubare, rapinare || *intr* stare; (*to cling*) reggere; restare valido; **hold on!** un momento!; **to hold back** frenarsi; **to hold forth** fare un discorso; **to hold off** astenersi; mantenersi a distanza; **to hold on** continuare; **to hold on to** attaccarsi a; **to hold out** tener duro, resistere; **to hold out for** mantenersi fermo per

holder [ˈholdər] *s* possessore *m*, detentore *m*; (*e.g., for a cigar*) bocchino; (*e.g., for a pot*) manico, impugnatura

holding [ˈholdɪŋ] *s* possesso; **holdings** valori *mpl*, patrimonio

hold'ing com'pany *s* società finanziaria

hold'up' *s* (*delay*) interruzione; (coll) rapina a mano armata; (fig) furto

hold'up man' *s* grassatore *m*

hole [hol] *s* buco; (*in cheese*) occhio; (*in a road*) buca; (*den*) tana; (*burrow*) fossa; **in a hole** in grane, in difficoltà; **to burn a hole in one's pocket** (*said of money*) scorrere attraverso le mani bucate di qlcu; **to pick holes in** trovare a ridire su || *intr*—**to hole up** (coll) imbucarsi

holiday [ˈhɑlɪˌde] *s* giorno festivo, festa; vacanza

holiness [ˈholɪnɪs] *s* santità *f*; **his Holiness** sua Santità

Holland [ˈhɑlənd] *s* l'Olanda *f*

Hollander [ˈhɑləndər] *s* olandese *mf*

hollow [ˈhɑlo] *adj* vuoto; (*sound*) sordo; (*eyes, cheeks*) infossato; vano, futile || *s* buca, cavità *f*; (*small valley*) valletta || *adv*—**to beat all hollow** (coll) battere completamente || *tr* scavare

hol·ly [ˈhɑli] *s* (-lies) agrifoglio

holly'hock' *s* altea, malvone *m*

holm' oak' [hom] *s* leccio

holocaust [ˈhɑləˌkɔst] *s* olocausto

holster [ˈholstər] *s* fondina

ho·ly [ˈholi] *adj* (-lier; -liest) santo; (*writing*) sacro; (*water*) benedetto

Ho'ly Ghost' *s* Spirito Santo

ho'ly or'ders *spl* ordini sacri; **to take holy orders** entrare in un ordine religioso

Ho'ly Rood' [rud] *s* Santa Croce

Ho'ly Scrip'ture *s* Sacra Scrittura

Ho'ly See' *s* Santa Sede

Ho'ly Sep'ulcher *s* Santo Sepolcro

Ho'ly Thurs'day *s* l'Ascensione; il giovedì santo

ho'ly wa'ter *s* acqua benedetta, acquasanta

Ho'ly Writ' *s* Sacra Scrittura

homage [ˈhɑmɪdʒ] *or* [ˈɑmɪdʒ] *s* omaggio

homburg [ˈhɑmbʌrg] *s* lobbia *m & f*

home [hom] *adj* casalingo, domestico; nazionale || *s* casa, dimora; (*fatherland*) patria; (*for the sick, aged, etc.*) ricovero; (sports) meta, traguardo; **at home** a casa; (*at ease*) a proprio agio; (sports) nel proprio campo; **away from home** fuori di casa; **make yourself at home** stia comodo; **to be at home** (*to receive callers*) ricevere || *adv* a casa; **to see home** accompagnare a casa; **to strike home** toccare nel vivo

home'bod'y *s* (-ies) persona casalinga

homebred [ˈhomˌbred] *adj* domestico; rozzo; semplice

home'brew' *s* bevanda fatta in casa

home-coming [ˈhomˌkʌmɪŋ] *s* ritorno a casa

home' coun'try *s* paese *m* natale

home' deliv'ery *s* trasporto a domicilio

home' front' *s* fronte domestico

home'land' *s* paese natio

homeless [ˈhomlɪs] *adj* senza tetto

home' life' *s* vita familiare

home-loving [ˈhomˌlʌvɪŋ] *adj* casalingo

home·ly [ˈhomli] *adj* (-lier; -liest) (*not goodlooking*) brutto; (*not elegant*) semplice, scialbo

homemade [ˈhomˈmed] *adj* fatto in casa

homemaker [ˈhomˌmekər] *s* casalinga

home' of'fice *s* sede *f* centrale || **Home Office** *s* (Brit) ministero degli interni

homeopath [ˈhomɪ·əˌpæθ] *or* [ˈhɑmɪ·əˌpæθ] *s* omeopatico

home' plate' *s* casa base

home' port' *s* porto d'iscrizione (nel registro marittimo)

home' rule' *s* autogoverno

home' run' *s* colpo che permette al battitore di percorrere tutte le basi del diamante fino alla casa base

home'sick' *adj* nostalgico; **to be homesick for** sentire la nostalgia per

home'sick'ness *s* nostalgia

homespun [ˈhomˌspʌn] *adj* filato a casa; semplice

home'stead *s* casa e terreno

home'stretch' *s* (sports) dirittura d'arrivo; (fig) fase *f* finale

home'town' *s* città *f* natale

homeward [ˈhomwərd] *adj* di ritorno || *adv* verso casa; verso la patria

home'work' *s* lavoro a domicilio; (*of a student*) dovere *m*, esercizio

homey [ˈhomi] *adj* (homier; homiest) intimo, comodo

homicidal [ˌhɑmɪˈsaɪdəl] *adj* omicida

homicide [ˈhɑmɪˌsaɪd] *s* (*act*) omicidio; (*person*) omicida *mf*

homi·ly [ˈhɑmɪli] *s* (-lies) omelia

homing ['homɪŋ] *adj (pigeon)* viaggiatore; *(weapon)* cercatore del bersaglio

hominy ['hɑmɪnɪ] *s* granturco macinato

homogenei·ty [,homədʒı'ni·ɪtɪ] or [,hɑmədʒı'ni·ɪtɪ] *s* (-ties) omogeneità *f*

homogeneous [,homə'dʒinɪ·əs] or [,hɑmə'dʒinɪ·əs] *adj* omogeneo

homogenize [hə'mɑdʒə ,naɪz] *tr* omogeneizzare

homonym ['hɑmənɪm] *s* omonimo

homonymous [hə'mɑnɪməs] *adj* omonimo

homosexual [,homə'sekʃʊ·əl] *adj & s* omosessuale *mf*

hone [hon] *s* cote *f* || *tr* affilare

honest ['ɑnɪst] *adj* onesto; guadagnato onestamente; integro, schietto

honesty ['ɑnɪstɪ] *s* onestà *f;* (bot) lunaria

hon·ey ['hʌnɪ] *adj* melato, dolce || *s* miele *m;* nettare *m;* (coll) caro || *v* (*pret & pp* -eyed or -ied) *tr* dire parole melate a

hon'ey·bee' *s* ape domestica

hon'ey·comb' *s* favo || *tr* crivellare

honeyed ['hʌnɪd] *adj* melato

hon'eydew mel'on *s* melone *m* dolce dalla scorza liscia

hon'ey lo'cust *s* acacia a tre spine

hon'ey·moon' *s* luna di miele || *intr* andare in viaggio di nozze

honeysuckle ['hʌnɪ ,sʌkəl] *s* caprifoglio

honk [hɑŋk] or [hɔŋk] *s (of wild goose)* schiamazzo; *(of automobile horn)* suono del clacson || *tr* (aut) suonare || *intr* schiamazzare; (aut) suonare

honkytonk ['hɑŋkɪ ,tɑŋk] or ['hɔŋkɪ ,tɔŋk] *s* (coll) locale notturno rumoroso

honor ['ɑnər] *s* onore *m* || *tr* onorare; (com) accettare e pagare

honorable ['ɑnərəbəl] *adj (upright)* onorato; *(bringing honor; worthy of honor)* onorevole

honorari·um [,ɑnə'rerɪ·əm] *s* (-ums or -a [ə]) onorario

honorary ['ɑnə ,rerɪ] *adj* onorario

honorific [,ɑnə'rɪfɪk] *adj* onorifico || *s* titolo onorifico; formula di gentilezza

hon'or sys'tem *s* sistema scolastico basato sulla parola d'onore

hood [hʊd] *s* cappuccio; cappuccio di toga universitaria; *(of carriage)* soffietto; (aut) cofano; (slang) gangster *m* || *tr* incappucciare

hoodlum ['hudləm] *s* (slang) facinoroso, gangster *m*, teppista *m*

hoodoo ['hudu] *s (body of primitive rites)* vuduismo; *(bad luck)* iettatura; *(person who brings bad luck)* iettatore *m* || *tr* iettare

hood'wink' *tr* turlupinare, imbrogliare

hooey ['hu·i] *s* (coll) sciocchezze *fpl*

hoof [huf] or [huf] *s* zoccolo, unghia; **on the hoof** *(cattle)* vivo || *tr*—**to hoof it** (slang) camminare; ballare

hoof'beat' *s* rumore *m* degli zoccoli

hook [hʊk] *s* gancio; *(for fishing)* amo;

(to join two things) agganciamento; *(for pulling)* raffio, rampino; *(curve)* curva; *(of hook and eye)* uncinello; (boxing) hook *m*, gancio; **by hook or by crook** di riffa o di raffa; **to swallow the hook** abboccare all'amo || *tr* agganciare; *(to bend)* curvare; *(fish)* pigliare; *(to wound with the horns)* incornare; **to hook up** agganciare; *(e.g., a loudspeaking system)* montare || *intr* agganciarsi; curvarsi

hookah ['hʊkə] *s* narghilè *m*

hook' and eye' *s* uncinello e occhiello

hook' and lad'der *s* autoscala

hooked' rug' *s* tappeto fatto all'uncinetto

hook'nose' *s* naso gobbo

hook'up' *s* (electron) diagramma *m*, schema *m* di montaggio; (rad, telv) rete *f*

hook'worm' *s* anchilostoma *m*

hooky ['hʊkɪ] *s*—**to play hooky** marinare la scuola

hooligan ['hulɪgən] *s* teppista *m*

hooliganism ['hulɪgən ,ɪzəm] *s* teppismo

hoop [hup] or [hʊp] *s* cerchio || *tr* cerchiare

hoop' skirt' *s* crinolina

hoot [hut] *s* grido della civetta; grido di derisione || *tr* zittire || *intr* stridere; **to hoot at** fischiare

hoot' owl' *s* allocco

hop [hɑp] *s* salto, saltello; (aer) breve volo; (bot) luppolo; (coll) corsa; **hops** *(dried flowers of hop vine)* luppolo || *v (pret & pp* **hopped**; *ger* **hopping)** *tr* saltare su; (aer) trasvolare || *intr* saltellare; saltellare su un piede; **to hop over** saltare su; fare una corsa a

hope [hop] *s* speranza || *tr & intr* sperare; **to hope for** sperare

hope' chest' *s* corredo da sposa

hopeful ['hopfəl] *adj (feeling hope)* fiducioso; *(giving hope)* promettente

hopeless ['hoplɪs] *adj* disperato

hopper ['hɑpər] *s* tramoggia

hop'scotch' *s* gioco del mondo

horde [hɔrd] *s* orda

horehound ['hɔr ,haund] *s* marrubio; pastiglie *fpl* per la tosse al marrubio

horizon [hə'raɪzən] *s* orizzonte *m*

horizontal [,hɑrɪ'zɑntəl] or [,hɔrɪ'zɑntəl] *adj & s* orizzontale *f*

hormone ['hɔrmon] *s* ormone *m*

horn [hɔrn] *s* corno; (aut) clacson *m*, avvisatore acustico; (mus) corno; *(trumpet)* (slang) tromba; **to blow one's horn** cantare le proprie lodi; **to lock horns** lottare, disputare; **to pull in one's horns** battere in ritirata || *intr*—**to horn in** (slang) intromettersi (in)

horned' owl' *s* allocco

hornet ['hɔrnɪt] *s* calabrone *m*

hor'net's nest' *s* vespaio; **to stir up a hornet's nest** suscitare un vespaio

horn' of plen'ty *s* corno dell'abbondanza

horn'pipe' *s* clarinetto contadinesco inglese fatto di corno di bue

horn'-rimmed glass'es ['hɔrn'rɪmd] *spl* occhiali cerchiati di corno or con la montatura di corno

horn·y ['hɔrnɪ] *adj* (-ier; -iest) corneo; *(callous)* calloso; *(having hornlike projections)* cornuto; (slang) preso da desiderio lussurioso

horoscope ['hɑrə‚skop] or ['hɔrə‚skop] *s* oroscopo

horrible ['hɑrɪbəl] or ['hɔrɪbəl] *adj* orrendo, orribile

horrid ['hɑrɪd] or ['hɔrɪd] *adj* orrido, orribile

horri·fy ['hɑrɪ‚faɪ] or ['hɔrɪ‚faɪ] *v* (*pret & pp* -fied) *tr* inorridire

horror ['hɑrər] or ['hɔrər] *s* orrore *m*; **to have a horror of** provare orrore per

hors d'oeuvre [ɔr 'dʌrv] *s* (hors d'oeuvres [ɔr 'dʌrvz]) *s* antipasto

horse [hɔrs] *s* cavallo; *(of carpenter)* cavalletto; **hold your horses!** (coll) aspetti un momento!; **to back the wrong horse** (coll) puntare sul perdente; **to be a horse of another color** (coll) essere un altro paio di maniche ‖ *intr*—**to horse around** (slang) giocherellare; (slang) fare tiri burloni

horse'back' *s*—**on horseback** a cavallo ‖ *adv*—**to ride horseback** montare a cavallo

horse' block' *s* montatoio

horse'break'er *s* domatore *m* di cavalli

horse'car' *s* tram a cavalli

horse' chest'nut *s* (tree) ippocastano; *(nut)* castagna d'India

horse' deal'er *s* mercante *m* di cavalli

horse' doc'tor *s* veterinario

horse'fly' *s* (-flies) tafano

horse'hair' *s* crine *m* di cavallo; *(fabric)* cilicio

horse'hide' *s* cuoio di cavallo

horse'laugh' *s* risataccia

horse'man *s* (-men) cavallerizzo

horsemanship ['hɔrsmən‚ʃɪp] *s* equitazione, maneggio

horse' meat' *s* carne equina

horse' op'era *s* western *m*

horse' pis'tol *s* pistola da sella

horse'play' *s* gioco violento, tiro burlone

horse'pow'er *s* cavallo vapore inglese

horse' race' *s* corsa ippica

horse'rad'ish *s* cren *m*, barbaforte *m*

horse' sense' *s* (coll) senso comune

horse'shoe' *s* ferro di cavallo

horse'shoe mag'net *s* calamita a ferro di cavallo

horse'shoe nail' *s* chiodo da cavallo

horse' show' *s* concorso ippico

horse' thief' *s* ladro di cavalli

horse'-trade' *intr* trafficare

horse'whip' *s* staffile *m* ‖ *v* (*pret & pp* -whipped); *ger* -whipping) *tr* staffilare

horse'wom'an *s* (-wom'en) amazzone *f*

hors·y ['hɔrsɪ] *adj* (-ier; -iest) equestre; *(interested in horses)* appassionato ai cavalli; (coll) goffo

horticulture ['hɔrtɪ‚kʌltʃər] *s* orticoltura

horticulturist [‚hɔrtɪ'kʌltʃərɪst] *s* orticoltore *m*

hose [hoz] *s* *(stocking)* calza; *(sock)* calzino corto; *(flexible tube)* manica ‖ **hose** *spl* calze *fpl*

hosier ['hoʒər] *s* calzettaio

hosiery ['hoʒərɪ] *s* calze *fpl*; calzificio

hospice ['hɑspɪs] *s* ospizio

hospitable ['hɑspɪtəbəl] or [hɑs'pɪtə-bəl] *adj* ospitale

hospital ['hɑspɪtəl] *s* ospedale *m*

hospitali·ty [‚hɑspɪ'tælɪtɪ] *s* (-ties) ospitalità *f*

hospitalize ['hɑspɪtə‚laɪz] *tr* ospedalizzare

host [host] *s* ospite *m*; *(at an inn)* oste *m*; *(army)* milizia; *(crowd)* folla ‖ **Host** *s* (eccl) ostia

hostage ['hɑstɪdʒ] *s* ostaggio

hostel ['hɑstəl] *s* ostello della gioventù

hostel·ry ['hɑstəlrɪ] *s* (-ries) albergo

hostess ['hostɪs] *s* ospite *f*, padrona di casa; *(e.g., on a bus)* accompagnatrice *f*, guida *f*; (aer) assistente *f* di volo

hostile ['hɑstɪl] *adj* ostile

hostili·ty [hɑs'tɪlɪtɪ] *s* (-ties) ostilità *f*

hostler ['hɑslər] or ['ɑslər] *s* stalliere *m*

hot [hɑt] *adj* (hotter; hottest) caldo; *(reception)* caloroso; *(e.g., pepper)* piccante; *(fresh)* fresco; *(pursuit)* impetuoso; *(in rut)* in calore; (coll) radioattivo; **to be hot** *(said of a person)* aver caldo; *(said of the weather)* fare caldo; **to make it hot for** (coll) dare del filo da torcere a

hot' air' *s* aria calda; (slang) fumo

hot'-air fur'nace *s* impianto di riscaldamento ad aria calda

hot' baths' *spl* terme *fpl*

hot'bed' *s* *(e.g., of revolt)* focolaio; *(hort)* semenzaio, letto caldo

hot'-blood'ed *adj* ardente; impetuoso

hot' cake' *s* frittella; **to sell like hot cakes** vendersi come se fosse regalato

hot' dog' *s* Frankfurter *m*, Würstel *m*

hotel [ho'tel] *adj* alberghiero ‖ *s* albergo

ho·tel'keep'er *s* albergatore *m*

hot'head' *s* testa calda

hotheaded ['hɑt‚hedɪd] *adj* esaltato, scalmanato

hot'house' *s* serra

hot' plate' *s* fornello elettrico, scaldavivande *m*

hot' springs' *spl* terme *fpl*

hot-tempered ['hɑt'tempərd] *adj* impulsivo, irascibile

hot' wa'ter *s*—**to be in hot water** (coll) essere nei guai

hot'-wa'ter boil'er *s* caldaia del termosifone

hot'-wa'ter bot'tle *s* borsa dell'acqua calda

hot'-wa'ter heat'er *s* scaldabagno

hot'-wa'ter heat'ing *s* riscaldamento a circolazione di acqua calda

hound [haʊnd] *s* bracco; **to follow the hounds** or **to ride to hounds** andare a caccia alla volpe ‖ *tr* perseguitare

hour [aʊr] *s* ora; **by the hour** a ore; **in an evil hour** in un brutto momento; **on the hour** ogni ora al suonar del-

l'ora; **to keep late hours** andare a
letto tardi

hour'glass' s clessidra

hour' hand' s lancetta delle ore

hourly ['aʊrlɪ] adj orario || adv ogni
ora; spesso

house [haʊs] s (**houses** ['haʊzɪz])
casa; (legislative body) camera; (size
of audience) concorso di pubblico;
teatro; **to keep house** fare le faccende domestiche; **to put one's house
in order** migliorare il proprio comportamento; accomodare le proprie
faccende || [haʊz] tr allogare

house' arrest' s arresto a domicilio

house'boat' s casa galleggiante

house'break'er s scassinatore m

housebreaking ['haʊs,brekɪŋ] s violazione di domicilio; scasso

housebroken ['haʊs,brokən] adj (e.g.,
cat) che è stato addestrato a tenersi
pulito

house'clean'ing s pulizia della casa;
(fig) pulizia, repulisti m

house'coat' s vestaglia da casa

house' cur'rent s corrente f di rete

house'fly' s (-flies) mosca domestica

houseful ['haʊs,fʊl] s casa piena

house' fur'nishings spl arredi domestici

house'hold' adj domestico || s famiglia

house'hold'er s capo della famiglia

house'-hunt' intr—**to go house-hunting**
andare in cerca di casa

house'keep'er s governante f

house'keep'ing s faccende domestiche;
to set up housekeeping metter su
casa

house'keeping apart'ment s apparta-
mentino

house'maid' s domestica

house' me'ter s contatore domestico

house'moth'er s maestra in pensionato
per studenti

house' of cards' s castello di carte

house' of ill' repute' s casa di malaffare

house' paint'er s imbianchino

house' physi'cian s medico residente

house'top' s tetto; **to shout from the
housetops** proclamare ai quattro
venti

housewarming ['haʊs,wɔrmɪŋ] s festa
per l'inaugurazione di una casa

house'wife' s (-wives') donna di casa

house'work' s faccende domestiche

housing ['haʊzɪŋ] s (of a horse) gualdrappa; (dwelling) abitazioni fpl;
(carp) alloggiamento; (mach) gabbia,
custodia; (aut) coppa; (of transmission) (aut) scatola

hous'ing short'age s crisi f degli alloggi

hovel ['hʌvəl] or ['hɑvəl] s catapec-
chia, stamberga; (shed) baracca

hover ['hʌvər] or ['hɑvər] intr librarsi;
(on the lips) trapelare; (fig) ondeggiare, esitare

how [haʊ] adv come; (at what price)
a quanto; **how early** quando, a che
ora; **how else** in che altro modo; **how
far** fino a dove; quanto, e.g., **how far
is it to the station?** quanto c'è da qui
alla stazione?; **how long** quanto
tempo; **how many** quanti; **how much**

quanto; **how often** quante volte; **how
old are you?** quanti anni ha?; **how
soon** quando, a che ora; **how** + adj
quanto + adj, e.g., **how beautiful she
is!** quanto è bella!

how·ev'er adv comunque; in qualunque
modo; per quanto . . . , e.g., **however
wrong he may be** per quanto torto
possa avere || conj come, e.g., **do it
however you want** lo faccia come
vuole

howitzer ['haʊˌɪtsər] s obice m

howl [haʊl] s ululato, urlo; scoppio di
risa || tr gridare; **to howl down**
sopraffare a grida; || intr ululare,
urlare

howler ['haʊlər] s urlatore m; (coll)
strafalcione m, topica

hoyden ['hɔɪdən] s ragazzaccia

hub [hʌb] s mozzo; (fig) centro

hubbub ['hʌbəb] s putiferio, fracasso

hub'cap' s (aut) calotta della ruota

huckleber·ry ['hʌkəl,bɛrɪ] s (-ries)
mirtillo

huckster ['hʌkstər] s venditore m ambulante; trafficante m

huddle ['hʌdəl] s conferenza segreta ||
intr affollarsi, accalcarsi

hue [hju] s tono, tinta; **hue and cry**
grido d'indignazione

huff [hʌf] s stizza; **in a huff** di cattivo
umore || tr (checkers) buffare

hug [hʌg] s abbraccio || v (pret & pp
hugged; ger hugging) tr abbracciare;
(e.g., a wall) costeggiare || intr ab-
bracciarsi

huge [hjudʒ] adj smisurato, immane

huh [hʌ] interj eh!

hulk [hʌlk] s scafo, carcassa; (unwieldy object) trabiccolo

hulking ['hʌlkɪŋ] adj grosso e goffo

hull [hʌl] s (of ship or hydroplane)
scafo; (of dirigible) intelaiatura; (of
airplane) fusoliera; (e.g., of a nut)
guscio || tr sgusciare; (rice) brillare

hullabaloo ['hʌləbə,lu] or [ˌhʌləbə'lu]
s fracasso, baccano

hum [hʌm] s canterellio; (of bee, ma-
chine, etc.) ronzio || v (pret & pp
hummed; ger humming) tr canterel-
lare || intr canterellare; (to buzz)
ronzare; (coll) vibrare, essere attivo

human ['hjumən] adj umano

hu'man be'ing s essere umano

humane [hju'men] adj umano; compassionevole

humanist ['hjumənɪst] adj umanistico
|| s umanista mf

humanitarian [hjuˌmænɪ'tɛrɪ·ən] adj &
s umanitario

humani·ty [hju'mænɪtɪ] s (-ties) umanità f; **humanities** (of Greece and
Rome) studi umanistici; (literature,
art, philosophy) scienze umanistiche

hu'man·kind' s genere umano

humble ['hʌmbəl] or ['ʌmbəl] adj
umile || tr umiliare

hum'ble pie' s—**to eat humble pie** accettare un'umiliazione

hum'bug' s frottola; (person) impostore
m || v (pret & pp -bugged; ger

-bugging) *tr* imbrogliare || *intr* fare l'imbroglione

hum'drum' *adj* noioso, monotono

humer·us ['hjumərəs] *s* (-i [,aı]) omero

humid ['hjumɪd] *adj* umido

humidifier [hju'mɪdɪ ,faɪ·ər] *s* evaporatore *m*

humidi·fy [hju'mɪdɪ ,faɪ] *v* (*pret & pp* -fied) *tr* inumidire

humidity [hju'mɪdɪtɪ] *s* umidità *f*

humiliate [hju'mɪlɪ ,et] *tr* umiliare

humiliating [hju'mɪlɪ ,etɪŋ] *adj* umiliante

humility [hju'mɪlɪtɪ] *s* umiltà *f*

hummingbird ['hʌmɪŋ ,bʌrd] *s* colibrì *m*

humor ['hjumər] *or* ['jumər] *s* umore *m*; umorismo; **out of humor** di cattivo umore || *tr* adattarsi alle fisime di, assecondare

humorist ['hjumərɪst] *or* ['jumərɪst] *s* umorista *mf*

humorous ['hjumərəs] *or* ['jumərəs] *adj* umoristico

hump [hʌmp] *s* gobba; (*in the ground*) monticello

hump'back' *s* gobba; (*person*) gobbo

humus ['hjuməs] *s* humus *m*

hunch [hʌntʃ] *s* gobba; (*premonition*) (coll) sospetto || *tr* piegare || *intr* accovacciarsi

hunch'back' *s* gobba; (*person*) gobbo

hundred ['hʌndrəd] *adj, s & pron* cento; **a hundred** *or* **one hundred** cento; **by the hundreds** a centinaia

hundredth ['hʌndrədθ] *adj, s & pron* centesimo

hun'dred·weight' *s* cento libbre

Hungarian [hʌŋ'gerı·ən] *adj & s* ungherese *mf*

Hungary ['hʌŋgərɪ] *s* l'Ungheria *f*

hunger ['hʌŋgər] *s* fame *f* || *intr* aver fame; **to hunger for** aver un desiderio ardente di, agognare

hun'ger strike' *s* sciopero della fame

hun·gry ['hʌŋgrɪ] *adj* (-grier; -griest) affamato; **to be hungry** aver fame; **to go hungry** andare a digiuno

-hunk [hʌŋk] *s* (coll) bel pezzo

hunt [hʌnt] *s* caccia; **on the hunt for** a caccia di || *tr* cacciare; (*to look for*) cercare || *intr* andare a caccia; cercare; **to go hunting** andare a caccia; **to hunt for** cercare

hunter ['hʌntər] *s* cacciatore *m*; (*dog*) cane *m* da caccia

hunting ['hʌntɪŋ] *adj* da caccia || *s* caccia

hunt'ing box' *s* capanno

hunt'ing dog' *s* cane *m* da caccia

hunt'ing ground' *s* terreno di caccia

hunt'ing horn' *s* corno da caccia

hunt'ing jack'et *s* cacciatora

hunt'ing lodge' *s* (*hut*) capanno; villino da caccia

hunt'ing sea'son *s* stagione della caccia

huntress ['hʌntrɪs] *s* cacciatrice *f*

hunts'man *s* (-men) cacciatore *m*

hurdle ['hʌrdəl] *s* (*hedge*) siepe *f*; (*wooden frame*) barriera; (sports, fig) ostacolo; **hurdles** corsa ad ostacoli || *tr* saltare, superare

hur'dle race' *s* corsa agli ostacoli

hurl [hʌrl] *s* lancio || *tr* lanciare; **to hurl back** respingere

hurrah [hu'rɑ] *or* **hurray** [hu're] *s* viva *m* || *tr* applaudire || *intr* gridare urrà || *interj* evviva!, urrà!; **hurrah for . . . !** viva . . . !

hurricane ['hʌrɪ ,ken] *s* uragano

hurried ['hʌrɪd] *adj* frettoloso

hur·ry ['hʌrɪ] *s* (-ries) fretta; **to be in a hurry** avere fretta || *v* (*pret & pp* -ried) *tr* affrettare, sollecitare || *intr* affrettarsi; **to hurry after** correr dietro a; **to hurry away** andarsene di furia; **to hurry back** ritornare presto; **to hurry up** spicciarsi

hurt [hʌrt] *adj* (*injured*) ferito; (*offended*) risentito || *s* (*harm*) danno; (*injury*) ferita; (*pain*) dolore *m* || *v* (*pret & pp* **hurt**) *tr* (*to harm*) fare male a; (*to injure*) ferire; (*to offend*) offendere; (*to pain*) dolere (with *dat*) || *intr* fare male, dolere; aver male, e.g., **my head hurts** ho male alla testa

hurtle ['hʌrtəl] *intr* sferrarsi, scagliarsi, precipitarsi

husband ['hʌzbənd] *s* marito || *tr* amministrare con economia

hus'band·man *s* (-men) agricoltore *m*

husbandry ['hʌzbəndrɪ] *s* agricoltura; (*management of domestic affairs*) governo, economia domestica

hush [hʌʃ] *s* silenzio || *tr* far tacere; **hush up** (*a scandal*) soffocare || *intr* tacere || *interj* zitto!

hushaby ['hʌʃə ,baɪ] *interj* fa' la nanna!

hush'-hush' *adj* segretissimo

hush' mon'ey *s* prezzo del silenzio

husk [hʌsk] *s* guscio; (*of corn*) spoglia || *tr* sgusciare; (*rice*) brillare; (*corn*) scartocciare, spogliare

husk·y ['hʌskɪ] *adj* (-ier; -iest) forte; (*voice*) rauco

hus·sy ['hʌzɪ] *or* ['hʌsɪ] *s* (-sies) poca di buono, ragazza impudente

hustle ['hʌsəl] *s* vigore *m*; (slang) traffico || *tr* forzare, spingere || *intr* affrettarsi, scalmanarsi; (slang) trafficare; (*said of a prostitute*) (slang) accostare un cliente

hustler ['hʌslər] *s* (*go-getter*) persona intraprendente; (slang) trafficone *m*, imbroglione *m*; (slang) passeggiatrice *f*

hut [hʌt] *s* casolare *m*, casupola

hyacinth ['haɪ·əsɪnθ] *s* giacinto

hybrid ['haɪbrɪd] *adj & s* ibrido

hybridize ['haɪbrɪ ,daɪz] *tr & intr* ibridare

hy·dra ['haɪdrə] *s* (-dras *or* -drae [dri]) idra

hydrant ['haɪdrənt] *s* idrante *m*; (*water faucet*) rubinetto

hydrate ['haɪdret] *s* idrato || *tr* idratare || *intr* idratarsi

hydraulic [haɪ'drɔlɪk] *adj* idraulico || **hydraulics** *s* idraulica

hydrau'lic ram' *s* pompa idraulica

hydriodic [,haɪdrɪ'ɑdɪk] *adj* iodidrico

hydrobromic [,haɪdrə'bromɪk] *adj* bromidrico

hydrocarbon [ˌhaɪdrə'kɑrbən] s idrocarburo

hydrochloric [ˌhaɪdrə'klorɪk] adj cloridrico

hydroelectric [ˌhaɪdro·ɪ'lɛktrɪk] adj idroelettrico

hydrofluoric [ˌhaɪdrəflu'ɑrɪk] or [ˌhaɪdrəflu'ɔrɪk] adj fluoridrico

hydrofoil ['haɪdrəˌfɔɪl] s superficie idrodinamica; (winglike member) aletta idrodinamica; (vessel) aliscafo, idroplano

hydrogen ['haɪdrədʒən] s idrogeno

hy′drogen bomb′ s bomba all'idrogeno

hy′drogen perox′ide s perossido d'idrogeno, acqua ossigenata

hy′drogen sul′fide s solfuro d'idrogeno

hydrometer [haɪ'drɑmɪtər] s areometro

hydrophobia [ˌhaɪdrə'fobɪ·ə] s idrofobia

hydroplane ['haɪdrəˌplen] s (aer) idrovolante m; (naut) idroscivolante m, idroplano

hydroxide [haɪ'drɑksaɪd] s idrossido

hyena [haɪ'inə] s iena

hygiene ['haɪdʒin] or ['haɪdʒɪˌin] s igiene f

hygienic [ˌhaɪdʒɪ'ɛnɪk] or [haɪ'dʒɪnɪk] adj igienico

hymn [hɪm] s inno

hymnal ['hɪmnəl] s innario

hyperacidity [ˌhaɪpərə'sɪdɪti] s iperacidità f

hyperbola [haɪ'pʌrbələ] s (geom) iperbole f

hyperbole [haɪ'pʌrbəli] s (rhet) iperbole f

hyperbolic [ˌhaɪpər'bɑlɪk] adj iperbolico

hypersensitive [ˌhaɪpər'sɛnsɪtɪv] adj ipersensibile

hypertension [ˌhaɪpər'tɛnʃən] s ipertensione

hyphen ['haɪfən] s trattino

hyphenate ['haɪfəˌnet] tr unire con trattino; scrivere con trattino

hypno·sis [hɪp'nosɪs] s (-ses [siz]) ipnosi f

hypnotic [hɪp'nɑtɪk] adj & s ipnotico

hypnotism ['hɪpnəˌtɪzəm] s ipnotismo

hypnotize ['hɪpnəˌtaɪz] tr ipnotizzare

hypochondriac [ˌhaɪpə'kɑndrɪˌæk] or [ˌhɪpə'kɑndrɪˌæk] s ipocondriaco

hypocri·sy [hɪ'pɑkrəsi] s (-sies) ipocrisia

hypocrite ['hɪpəkrɪt] s ipocrita mf

hypocritical [ˌhɪpə'krɪtɪkəl] adj ipocrita

hypodermic [ˌhaɪpə'dʌrmɪk] adj ipodermico

hyposulfite [ˌhaɪpə'sʌlfaɪt] s iposolfito

hypotenuse [haɪ'pɑtɪˌnus] or [haɪ'pɑtɪˌnjus] s ipotenusa

hypothesis [haɪ'pɑθɪsɪs] s (-ses [ˌsiz]) ipotesi f

hypothesize [haɪ'poθɪˌsaɪz] tr ipotizzare

hypothetic(al) [ˌhaɪpə'θɛtɪk(əl)] adj ipotetico

hyssop ['hɪsəp] s issopo

hysteria [hɪs'tɪrɪ·ə] s isterismo

hysteric [hɪs'tɛrɪk] adj isterico || **hysterics** s isterismo

hysterical [hɪs'tɛrɪkəl] adj isterico

I

I, i [aɪ] s nona lettera dell'alfabeto inglese

I [aɪ] pron pers (we [wi]) io; **it is I** sono io

iambic [aɪ'æmbɪk] adj giambico

iam·bus [aɪ'æmbəs] s (-bi [baɪ]) giambo

I′-beam′ s putrella

Iberian [aɪ'bɪrɪ·ən] adj iberico || s abitante mf dell'Iberia; lingua iberica

ibex ['aɪbɛks] s (ibexes or ibices ['ɪbɪˌsiz]) stambecco

ice [aɪs] s ghiaccio; **to break the ice** rompere il ghiaccio; **to cut no ice** (coll) non avere importanza; **to skate on thin ice** cacciarsi in una situazione delicata || tr gelare; (to cover with icing) glassare || intr gelarsi

ice′ age′ s epoca glaciale

ice′ bag′ s borsa di ghiaccio

iceberg ['aɪsˌbʌrg] s borgognone m, montagna di ghiaccio

ice′boat′ s slitta a vela; (icebreaker) rompighiaccio

icebound ['aɪsˌbaʊnd] adj chiuso dal ghiaccio

ice′box′ s ghiacciaia

ice′break′er s rompighiaccio

ice′ buck′et s secchiello da ghiaccio

ice′cap′ s calotta glaciale

ice′-cold′ adj gelido, ghiacciato

ice′ cream′ s gelato, sorbetto

ice′-cream cone′ s cono gelato

ice′-cream freez′er s gelatiera

ice′-cream par′lor s gelateria

ice′ cube′ s cubetto di ghiaccio

ice′ hock′ey s hockey m su ghiaccio

Iceland ['aɪslənd] s l'Islanda f

Icelander ['aɪsˌlændər] or ['aɪsləndər] s islandese mf

Icelandic [aɪs'lændɪk] adj islandese || s (language) islandese m

ice′man′ s (-men′) venditore m di ghiaccio

ice′ pack′ s banco di ghiaccio; (ice bag) borsa di ghiaccio

ice′ pick′ s rompighiaccio

ice′ shelf′ s tavolato di ghiaccio

ice′ skate′ s pattino da ghiaccio

ice′ wa′ter s acqua gelata

ichthyology [ˌɪkθɪ'ɑlədʒi] s ittiologia

icicle ['aɪsɪkəl] s ghiacciolo

icing ['aɪsɪŋ] s glassa; (meteor) gelo

iconoclast [aɪ'kɑnəˌklæst] s iconoclasta mf

iconoscope [aɪ'kɑnə‚skop] *s* (trademark) iconoscopio

icy ['aɪsɪ] *adj* (**icier; iciest**) ghiacciato; (*e.g., wind, hands*) gelido; (fig) glaciale

idea [aɪ'di·ə] *s* idea

ideal [aɪ'di·əl] *adj & s* ideale *m*

idealist [aɪ'di·əlɪst] *adj & s* idealista *mf*

idealistic [aɪ‚dɪ·əl'ɪstɪk] *adj* idealistico

idealize [aɪ'di·ə‚laɪz] *tr* idealizzare

identic(al) [aɪ'dentɪk(əl)] *adj* identico

identification [aɪ‚dentɪfɪ'keʃən] *s* identificazione, riconoscimento

identifica'tion card' *s* carta d'identità

identifica'tion tag' *s* piastrina

identi·fy [aɪ'dentɪ‚faɪ] *v* (*pret & pp* **-fied**) *tr* identificare

identi·ty [aɪ'dentɪtɪ] *s* (**-ties**) identità *f*

ideolo·gy [‚aɪdɪ'ɑlədʒɪ] *or* [‚ɪdɪ-'ɑlədʒɪ] *s* (**-gies**) ideologia

ides [aɪdz] *spl* idi *mpl & fpl*

idio·cy ['ɪdɪ·əsɪ] *s* (**-cies**) idiozia

idiom ['ɪdɪ·əm] *s* (*expression that is contrary to the usual patterns of the language*) locuzione idiomatica, idiotismo; (*style of language*) lingua, idioma *m*; (*style of an author*) stile *m*; (*character of a language*) indole *f*

idiomatic [‚ɪdɪ·ə'mætɪk] *adj* idiomatico

idiosyncra·sy ['aɪdɪ‚ə'sɪŋkrəsɪ] *s* (**-sies**) eccentricità *f*, originalità *f*; (med) idiosincrasia

idiot ['ɪdɪ·ət] *s* idiota *mf*

idiotic [‚ɪdɪ'ɑtɪk] *adj* idiota

idle ['aɪdəl] *adj* (*unemployed*) disoccupato; (*machine*) fermo; (*capital*) giacente; (*time*) perso; (*talk*) vano; (*lazy*) fannullone, ozioso; **to run idle** girare a vuoto ‖ *tr*—**to idle away** (*time*) sprecare ‖ *intr* poltrire, fare il fannullone; (aut) girare al minimo

idleness ['aɪdəlnɪs] *s* ozio

idler ['aɪdlər] *s* fannullone *m*

idling ['aɪdlɪŋ] *s* (*of motor*) minimo

idol ['aɪdəl] *s* idolo

idola·try [aɪ'dɑlətrɪ] *s* (**-tries**) idolatria

idolize ['aɪdə‚laɪz] *tr* idolatrare

idyll ['aɪdəl] *s* idillio

idyllic [aɪ'dɪlɪk] *adj* idilliaco

if [ɪf] *conj* se; **as if** come se; **even if** anche se; **if so** se è così; **if true** se è vero

ignis fatuus ['ɪgnɪs'fæt/u·əs] *s* (**ignes fatui** ['ɪgniz'fæt/u‚aɪ]) fuoco fatuo

ignite [ɪg'naɪt] *tr* infiammare ‖ *intr* infiammarsi

ignition [ɪg'nɪʃən] *s* ignizione; (aut) accensione

igni'tion switch' *s* (aut) chiavetta dell'accensione

igni'tion sys'tem *s* (aut) apparecchiatura d'accensione

ignoble [ɪg'nobəl] *adj* ignobile

ignominious [‚ɪgnə'mɪnɪ·əs] *adj* ignominioso

ignoramus [‚ɪgnə'reməs] *s* ignorante *mf*

ignorance ['ɪgnərəns] *s* ignoranza

ignorant ['ɪgnərənt] *adj* ignorante; **to be ignorant of** ignorare

ignore [ɪg'nor] *tr* (*a person; a person's kindness*) ignorare

ill [ɪl] *adj* (**worse** [wʌrs]; **worst** [wʌrst]) malato; **to take ill** cadere malato ‖ *adv* male; **to take ill** prendere in mala parte

ill-advised ['ɪləd'vaɪzd] *adj* inconsulto, sconsiderato

ill'-at-ease' *adj* imbarazzato, spaesato

ill-bred ['ɪl'bred] *adj* maleducato

ill-considered ['ɪlkən'sɪdərd] *adj* sconsiderato

ill-disposed ['ɪldɪs'pozd] *adj* maldisposto, malintenzionato

illegal [ɪ'ligəl] *adj* illegale

illegible [ɪ'ledʒɪbəl] *adj* illeggibile

illegitimate [‚ɪlɪ'dʒɪtɪmɪt] *adj* illegittimo

ill' fame' *s* pessima fama

ill-fated ['ɪl'fetɪd] *adj* infausto

ill-gotten ['ɪl'gɑtən] *adj* male acquistato

ill-humored ['ɪl'hjumərd] *adj* di cattivo umore

illicit [ɪ'lɪsɪt] *adj* illecito

illitera·cy [ɪ'lɪtərəsɪ] *s* (**-cies**) analfabetismo; (*mistake*) solecismo; ignoranza

illiterate [ɪ'lɪtərɪt] *adj* (*uneducated*) illetterato; (*unable to read or write*) analfabeta ‖ *s* analfabeta *mf*

ill-mannered ['ɪl'mænərd] *adj* screanzato, ineducato

illness ['ɪlnɪs] *s* malattia

illogical [ɪ'lɑdʒɪkəl] *adj* illogico

ill-spent ['ɪl'spent] *adj* sprecato

ill-starred ['ɪl'stɑrd] *adj* nato sotto una cattiva stella; sfortunato, funesto

ill-tempered ['ɪl'tempərd] *adj* di cattivo umore

ill-timed ['ɪl'taɪmd] *adj* inopportuno

ill'-treat' *tr* maltrattare, tartassare

illuminate [ɪ'lumɪ‚net] *tr* illuminare; (*a manuscript*) miniare

illumination [ɪ‚lumɪ'neʃən] *s* illuminazione; (*in manuscript*) miniatura

illusion [ɪ'luʒən] *s* illusione

illusive [ɪ'lusɪv] *adj* illusorio

illusory [ɪ'lusərɪ] *adj* illusorio

illustrate ['ɪləs‚tret] *or* [ɪ'lʌstret] *tr* illustrare

illustration [‚ɪləs'treʃən] *s* illustrazione

illustrator ['ɪləs‚tretər] *s* illustratore *m*

illustrious [ɪ'lʌstrɪ·əs] *adj* illustre

ill' will' *s* astio, ruggine *f*, malevolenza

image ['ɪmɪdʒ] *s* immagine *f*; **the very image of** il ritratto parlante di

image·ry ['ɪmɪdʒrɪ] *or* ['ɪmɪdʒərɪ] *s* (**-ries**) (*mental images*) fantasia; (*images collectively*) immagini *fpl*; (rhet) linguaggio figurato

imaginary [ɪ'mædʒɪ‚nerɪ] *adj* immaginario

imagination [ɪ‚mædʒɪ'neʃən] *s* immaginazione

imagine [ɪ'mædʒɪn] *tr & intr* immaginare; (*to conjecture*) immaginarsi; **imagine!** si figuri!

imbalance [ɪm'bæləns] *s* scompenso

imbecile ['ɪmbɪsɪl] *adj & s* imbecille *mf*

imbecili•ty [ˌɪmbɪˈsɪlɪti] s (-ties) imbecillità f, imbecillaggine f
imbibe [ɪmˈbaɪb] tr (to drink) bere; assorbire ‖ intr bere
imbue [ɪmˈbju] tr imbevere
imitate [ˈɪmɪˌtet] tr imitare
imitation [ˌɪmɪˈteʃən] adj (e.g., jewelry) falso ‖ s imitazione
imitator [ˈɪmɪˌtetər] s imitatore m
immaculate [ɪˈmækjəlɪt] adj immacolato
immaterial [ˌɪməˈtɪrɪ·əl] adj immateriale; poco importante; it's immaterial to me a me fa lo stesso
immature [ˌɪməˈtjʊr] or [ˌɪməˈtʊr] adj immaturo
immeasurable [ɪˈmeʒərəbəl] adj incommensurabile, smisurato
immediacy [ɪˈmidɪ·əsi] s immediatezza
immediate [ɪˈmidɪ·ɪt] adj immediato
immediately [ɪˈmidɪ·ɪtli] adv immediatamente
immemorial [ˌɪmɪˈmorɪ·əl] adj immemorabile
immense [ɪˈmens] adj immenso
immerge [ɪˈmɜrdʒ] intr sommergersi
immerse [ɪˈmɜrs] tr immergere
immersion [ɪˈmɜrʃən] or [ɪˈmɜrʒən] s immersione
immigrant [ˈɪmɪgrənt] adj & s immigrante mf
immigrate [ˈɪmɪˌgret] intr immigrare
immigration [ˌɪmɪˈgreʃən] s immigrazione
imminent [ˈɪmɪnənt] adj imminente
immobile [ɪˈmobɪl] or [ɪˈmobɪl] adj immobile
immobilize [ɪˈmobɪˌlaɪz] tr immobilizzare
immoderate [ɪˈmɑdərɪt] adj smodato, sregolato
immodest [ɪˈmɑdɪst] adj immodesto
immoral [ɪˈmɔrəl] or [ɪˈmɑrəl] adj immorale
immortal [ɪˈmɔrtəl] adj & s immortale mf
immortalize [ɪˈmɔrtəˌlaɪz] tr eternare, immortalare
immune [ɪˈmjun] adj immune
immunize [ˈɪmjəˌnaɪz] or [ɪˈmjunaɪz] tr immunizzare
imp [ɪmp] s diavoletto; (child) frugolo
impact [ˈɪmpækt] s impatto
impair [ɪmˈpɛr] tr danneggiare; (to weaken) indebolire
impan•el [ɪmˈpænəl] v (pret & pp -eled or -elled; ger -eling or -elling) tr iscrivere nella lista dei giurati; (a jury) selezionare
impart [ɪmˈpɑrt] tr (a secret) far conoscere; (knowledge) impartire; (motion) imprimere
impartial [ɪmˈpɑrʃəl] adj imparziale
impassable [ɪmˈpæsəbəl] or [ɪmˈpɑsəbəl] adj impraticabile, intransitabile
impasse [ɪmˈpæs] or [ˈɪmpæs] s vicolo cieco, impasse f
impassible [ɪmˈpæsɪbəl] adj impassibile
impassioned [ɪmˈpæʃənd] adj caloroso, veemente
impassive [ɪmˈpæsɪv] adj impassibile

impatience [ɪmˈpeʃəns] s impazienza
impatient [ɪmˈpeʃənt] adj impaziente
impeach [ɪmˈpitʃ] tr accusare; (a public official) sottoporre a un'inchiesta; (a statement) mettere in dubbio
impeachment [ɪmˈpitʃmənt] s accusa; inchiesta
impeccable [ɪmˈpɛkəbəl] adj impeccabile
impecunious [ˌɪmpɪˈkjunɪ·əs] adj indigente
impedance [ɪmˈpidəns] s impedenza
impede [ɪmˈpid] tr impedire, intralciare
impediment [ɪmˈpɛdɪmənt] s impedimento; ostacolo
im•pel [ɪmˈpel] v (pret & pp -peled or -pelled; ger -peling or -pelling) tr spingere, forzare
impending [ɪmˈpendɪŋ] adj imminente, incombente
impenetrable [ɪmˈpenətrəbəl] adj impenetrabile
impenitent [ɪmˈpenɪtənt] adj impenitente ‖ s persona impenitente
imperative [ɪmˈperɪtɪv] adj (commanding) imperativo; (urgent) imperioso ‖ s imperativo
imperceptible [ˌɪmpərˈseptɪbəl] adj impercettibile
imperfect [ɪmˈpʌrfɪkt] adj & s imperfetto
imperfection [ˌɪmpərˈfɛkʃən] s imperfezione
imperial [ɪmˈpɪrɪ·əl] adj imperiale ‖ s (goatee) barbetta, mosca; (top of coach) imperiale m
imperialist [ɪmˈpɪrɪ·əlɪst] adj & s imperialista mf
imper•il [ɪmˈperɪl] v (pret & pp -iled or -illed; ger -iling or -illing) tr mettere in pericolo
imperious [ɪmˈpɪrɪ·əs] adj imperioso
imperishable [ɪmˈperɪʃəbəl] adj imperituro, duraturo
impersonate [ɪmˈpʌrsəˌnet] tr (to pretend to be) spacciarsi per; (on the stage) impersonare
impertinence [ɪmˈpʌrtɪnəns] s impertinenza
impertinent [ɪmˈpʌrtɪnənt] adj impertinente
impetuous [ɪmˈpetʃʊ·əs] adj impetuoso
impetus [ˈɪmpɪtəs] s impeto, foga
impie•ty [ɪmˈpaɪ·əti] s (-ties) empietà f
impinge [ɪmˈpɪndʒ] intr—to impinge on or upon violare; (said, e.g., of the sun) ferire; (the imagination) colpire
impious [ˈɪmpɪ·əs] adj empio
impish [ˈɪmpɪʃ] adj indiavolato
implant [ɪmˈplænt] tr innestare; instillare, istillare
implement [ˈɪmplɪmənt] s utensile m, strumento ‖ [ˈɪmplɪˌment] tr completare, mettere in opera; (to provide with implements) attrezzare
implicate [ˈɪmplɪˌket] tr implicare
implicit [ɪmˈplɪsɪt] adj implicito; (unquestioning) assoluto, cieco
implied [ɪmˈplaɪd] adj implicito
implore [ɪmˈplor] tr (a person; pardon)

implorare; (*to entreat*) raccomandarsi a

im·ply [ɪm'plaɪ] v (*pret & pp* -plied) *tr* voler dire, significare; implicare, sottintendere

impolite [,ɪmpə'laɪt] *adj* scortese

import ['ɪmpɔrt] *s* importazione; articolo d'importazione; importanza || [ɪm'pɔrt] or ['ɪmpɔrt] *tr* importare; significare || *intr* importare

importance [ɪm'pɔrtəns] *s* importanza

important [ɪm'pɔrtənt] *adj* importante

importation [,ɪmpor'teʃən] *s* importazione

importer [ɪm'pɔrtər] *s* importatore *m*

importunate [ɪm'pɔrtʃənɪt] *adj* importuno

importune [,ɪmpər'tjun] or [,ɪmpɔr'tun] *tr* importunare

impose [ɪm'poz] *tr* imporre || *intr*—to impose on or upon abusare di; abusare della gentilezza di

imposing [ɪm'pozɪŋ] *adj* imponente

imposition [,ɪmpə'zɪʃən] *s* imposizione; abuso; abuso della gentilezza; inganno

impossible [ɪm'pɑsɪbəl] *adj* impossibile

impostor [ɪm'pɑstər] *s* impostore *m*

imposture [ɪm'pɑstʃər] *s* impostura

impotence ['ɪmpətəns] *s* impotenza

impotent ['ɪmpətənt] *adj* impotente

impound [ɪm'paʊnd] *tr* rinchiudere, recintare; (*water*) raccogliere; (law) sequestrare, confiscare

impoverish [ɪm'pɑvərɪʃ] *tr* impoverire

impracticable [ɪm'præktɪkəbəl] *adj* impraticabile; (*intractable*) intrattabile

impractical [ɪm'præktɪkəl] *adj* poco pratico

impregnable [ɪm'prɛgnəbəl] *adj* inespugnabile, imprendibile

impregnate [ɪm'prɛgnet] *tr* impregnare

impresari·o [,ɪmprɪ'sɑrɪ ,o] *s* (-os) impresario

impress [ɪm'prɛs] *tr* (*to affect in mind or feelings*) impressionare; (*to produce by pressure; to fix on s.o.'s mind*) imprimere; (mil) arruolare

impression [ɪm'prɛʃən] *s* impressione

impressionable [ɪm'prɛʃənəbəl] *adj* impressionabile

impressive [ɪm'prɛsɪv] *adj* impressionante, imponente

imprint ['ɪmprɪnt] *s* impronta; (typ) indicazione dell'editore || [ɪm'prɪnt] *tr* imprimere

imprison [ɪm'prɪzən] *tr* imprigionare

imprisonment [ɪm'prɪzənmənt] *s* prigione, prigionia

improbable [ɪm'prɑbəbəl] *adj* improbabile

impromptu [ɪm'prɑmptju] or [ɪm'prɑmptu] *adj* improvvisato || *s* improvvisazione; (mus) impromptu *m* || *adv* all'improvviso

improper [ɪm'prɑpər] *adj* (*erroneous*) improprio; (*inappropriate; unseemly*) scorretto; (math) improprio

improve [ɪm'pruv] *tr* migliorare; (*an opportunity*) approfittare di || *intr* migliorare; to improve on or upon perfezionare

improvement [ɪm'pruvmənt] *s* miglioramento, perfezionamento; (*in real estate*) miglioria; (*e.g., of time*) buon uso

improvident [ɪm'prɑvɪdənt] *adj* improvvido, imprevidente

improvise ['ɪmprə ,vaɪz] *tr & intr* improvvisare

imprudence [ɪm'prudəns] *s* imprudenza

imprudent [ɪm'prudənt] *adj* imprudente

impudence ['ɪmpjədəns] *s* impudenza, sfrontatezza, sfacciataggine *f*

impudent ['ɪmpjədənt] *adj* sfrontato, sfacciato, spudorato

impugn [ɪm'pjun] *tr* impugnare

impulse ['ɪmpʌls] *s* impulso

impulsive [ɪm'pʌlsɪv] *adj* impulsivo

impunity [ɪm'pjunɪti] *s* impunità *f*

impure [ɪm'pjʊr] *adj* impuro

impuri·ty [ɪm'pjʊrɪti] *s* (-ties) impurità *f*

impute [ɪm'pjut] *tr* imputare

in [ɪn] *adj* interno; (coll) moderno, alla moda || *s* relazione; the ins and outs tutti i dettagli || *adv* dentro; a casa; in ufficio; in here qui dentro; in there lì dentro; to be in to be in essere a casa; to be in for essere destinato a; to be in with essere in intimità con || *prep* in; (*within*) dentro a; (*over, through*) per; di, e.g., the best in the class il migliore della classe; dressed in vestito di; in so far as per quanto; in that per quanto, dato che

inability [,ɪnə'bɪlɪti] *s* inabilità *f*

inaccessible [,ɪnæk'sɛsɪbəl] *adj* inaccessibile

inaccura·cy [ɪn'ækjərəsi] *s* (-cies) inesattezza, imprecisione

inaccurate [ɪn'ækjərɪt] *adj* inesatto

inaction [ɪn'ækʃən] *s* inazione

inactive [ɪn'æktɪv] *adj* inattivo

inadequate [ɪn'ædɪkwɪt] *adj* inadeguato, inadatto

inadvertent [,ɪnəd'vʌrtənt] *adj* disattento; inavvertito

inadvisable [,ɪnəd'vaɪzəbəl] *adj* poco consigliabile

inane [ɪn'en] *adj* insensato, assurdo

inanimate [ɪn'ænɪmɪt] *adj* inanimato

inappreciable [,ɪnə'priʃɪ·əbəl] *adj* inapprezzabile

inappropriate [,ɪnə'proprɪ·ɪt] *adj* non appropriato, improprio

inarticulate [,ɪnɑr'tɪkjəlɪt] *adj* (*sounds, words*) inarticolato; (*person*) incapace di esprimersi

inasmuch as [,ɪnəs'mʌtʃ ,æz] *conj* dato che, visto che, in quanto che

inattentive [,ɪnə'tɛntɪv] *adj* disattento

inaugural [ɪn'ɔgjərəl] *adj* inaugurale || *s* discorso inaugurale

inaugurate [ɪn'ɔgjə ,ret] *tr* inaugurare

inauguration [ɪn ,ɔgjə'reʃən] *s* inaugurazione; (*investiture of a head of government*) assunzione dei poteri

inborn ['ɪn ,bɔrn] *adj* innato, ingenito

inbreeding ['ɪn ,bridɪŋ] *s* incrocio fra animali o piante affini

incandescent [,ɪnkən'dɛsənt] *adj* incandescente

incapable [ɪn'kepəbəl] *adj* incapace

incapacitate [ˌɪnkə'pæsɪˌtet] *tr* inabilitare; (law) interdire

incapaci·ty [ˌɪnkə'pæsɪti] *s* (-ties) incapacità *f*

incarcerate [ɪn'kɑrsəˌret] *tr* incarcerare

incarnate [ɪn'kɑrnɪt] or [ɪn'kɑrnet] *adj* incarnato || [ɪn'kɑrnet] *tr* incarnare

incarnation [ˌɪnkɑr'neʃən] *s* incarnazione

incendiarism [ɪn'sɛndɪ·əˌrɪzəm] *s* incendio doloso; (*agitation*) sobillazione

incendiar·y [ɪn'sɛndɪˌeri] *adj* incendiario || *s* (-ies) incendiario; (fig) sobillatore *m*

incense ['ɪnsɛns] *s* incenso || *tr* (*to burn incense for*) incensare || [ɪn'sɛns] *tr* irritare, esasperare

in'cense burn'er *s* (*person*) incensatore *m*; (*vessel*) incensiere *m*

incentive [ɪn'sɛntɪv] *adj* & *s* incentivo

inception [ɪn'sɛpʃən] *s* principio

incertitude [ɪn'sʌrtɪˌtjud] or [ɪn'sʌrtɪˌtud] *s* incertezza

incest ['ɪnsɛst] *s* incesto

incestuous [ɪn'sɛstʃʊ·əs] *adj* incestuoso

inch [ɪntʃ] *s* pollice *m*; **to be within an inch of** essere a due dita da || *intr*— **to inch ahead** spingersi avanti poco a poco

incidence ['ɪnsɪdəns] *s* incidenza

incident ['ɪnsɪdənt] *adj* incidente, incidentale || *s* incidente *m*

incidental [ˌɪnsɪ'dɛntəl] *adj* incidentale || *s* elemento incidentale; **incidentals** piccole spese

incidentally [ˌɪnsɪ'dɛntəli] *adv* incidentalmente, per inciso; a proposito

incinerator [ɪn'sɪnəˌretər] *s* inceneritore *m*

incision [ɪn'sɪʒən] *s* incisione

incisive [ɪn'saɪsɪv] *adj* incisivo

incite [ɪn'saɪt] *tr* incitare, stimulare

inclemen·cy [ɪn'klɛmənsi] *s* (-cies) inclemenza

inclination [ˌɪnklɪ'neʃən] *s* inclinazione

incline ['ɪnklaɪn] or [ɪn'klaɪn] *s* declivio || [ɪn'klaɪn] *tr* inclinare || *intr* inclinarsi

inclose [ɪn'kloz] *tr* includere, accludere; **to inclose herewith** accludere alla presente

inclosure [ɪn'kloʒər] *s* (*land surrounded by fence*) recinto; (*e.g., letter*) allegato

include [ɪn'klud] *tr* includere; **including** incluso, e.g., **three books including the grammar** tre libri inclusa la grammatica

inclusive [ɪn'klusɪv] *adj* incluso, e.g., **until next Friday inclusive** fino a venerdì prossimo incluso; **inclusive of** inclusivo di, e.g., **price inclusive of freight** prezzo inclusivo delle spese di trasporto

incogni·to [ɪn'kɑgnɪˌto] *adj* incognito || *s* (-tos) incognito || *adv* in incognito

incoherent [ˌɪnko'hɪrənt] *adj* incoerente

incombustible [ˌɪnkəm'bʌstɪbəl] *adj* incombustibile

income ['ɪnkʌm] *s* reddito, provento

in'come tax' *s* imposta sul reddito

incoming ['ɪnˌkʌmɪŋ] *adj* entrante; futuro; (*tide*) ascendente || *s* entrata

incomparable [ɪn'kɑmpərəbəl] *adj* incomparabile, impareggiabile

incompatible [ˌɪnkəm'pætɪbəl] *adj* incompatibile

incomplete [ˌɪnkəm'plit] *adj* incompleto, tronco, scompleto

incomprehensible [ˌɪnkɑmprɪ'hɛnsɪbəl] *adj* incomprensibile

inconceivable [ˌɪnkən'sivəbəl] *adj* inconcepibile

inconclusive [ˌɪnkən'klusɪv] *adj* inconcludente

incongruous [ɪn'kɑŋgru·əs] *adj* incongruo

inconsequential [ɪnˌkɑnsɪ'kwɛnʃəl] *adj* (*lacking proper sequence of thought or speech*) inconseguente; (*trivial*) di poca importanza

inconsiderate [ˌɪnkən'sɪdərɪt] *adj* inconsiderato, sconsiderato

inconsisten·cy [ˌɪnkən'sɪstənsi] *s* (-cies) inconsistenza

inconsistent [ˌɪnkən'sɪstənt] *adj* inconsistente, inconseguente

inconsolable [ˌɪnkən'soləbəl] *adj* inconsolabile, sconsolato

inconspicuous [ˌɪnkən'spɪkju·əs] *adj* poco appariscente, poco apparente

inconstant [ɪn'kɑnstənt] *adj* incostante

incontinence [ɪn'kɑntɪnəns] *s* incontinenza

incontrovertible [ˌɪnkɑntrə'vʌrtɪbəl] *adj* incontrovertibile

inconvenience [ˌɪnkən'vini·əns] *s* scomodo, incomodo || *tr* scomodare

inconvenient [ˌɪnkən'vini·ənt] *adj* incomodo, inconveniente

incorporate [ɪn'kɔrpəˌret] *tr* incorporare; costituire in società anonima || *intr* incorporarsi; costituirsi in società anonima

incorrect [ˌɪnkə'rɛkt] *adj* scorretto

increase ['ɪnkris] *s* aumento; crescita; **to be on the increase** essere in aumento || [ɪn'kris] *tr* aumentare; (*by propagation*) moltiplicare || *intr* aumentare; moltiplicarsi

increasingly [ɪn'krisɪŋli] *adv* sempre più

incredible [ɪn'krɛdɪbəl] *adj* incredibile

incredulous [ɪn'krɛdʒələs] *adj* incredulo

increment ['ɪnkrɪmənt] *s* aumento, incremento

incriminate [ɪn'krɪmɪˌnet] *tr* incriminare

incrust [ɪn'krʌst] *tr* incrostare

incubate ['ɪnkjəˌbet] *tr* incubare || *intr* essere in incubazione; (*said, e.g., of a hen*) covare; (fig) covare

incubator ['ɪnkjəˌbetər] *s* incubatrice *f*

inculcate [ɪn'kʌlket] or ['ɪnkʌlˌket] *tr* inculcare

incumben•cy [ɪn'kʌmbənsi] *s* (-cies) incombenza

incumbent [ɪn'kʌmbənt] *adj*—**to be incumbent on** incombere a, spettare a || *s* titolare *mf*

incunabula [ˌɪnkjuˈnæbjələ] *spl* (*beginnings*) origini *fpl*; (*early printed books*) incunaboli *mpl*

in•cur [ɪn'kʌr] *v* (*pret & pp* -curred; *ger* -curring) *tr* incorrere in; (*a debt*) assumere, contrarre

incurable [ɪn'kjurəbəl] *adj & s* incurabile *mf*

incursion [ɪn'kʌrʒən] or [ɪn'kʌrʃən] *s* incursione, scorreria

indebted [ɪn'detɪd] *adj* indebitato; obbligato

indecen•cy [ɪn'disənsi] *s* (-cies) indecenza, sconcezza

indecent [ɪn'disənt] *adj* indecente, sconveniente

indecisive [ˌɪndɪ'saɪsɪv] *adj* indeciso; (*e.g.*, *event*) non decisivo

indeed [ɪn'did] *adv* difatti, infatti || *interj* davvero!

indefatigable [ˌɪndɪ'fætɪgəbəl] *adj* indefesso, infaticabile

indefensible [ˌɪndɪ'fensɪbəl] *adj* indifendibile, insostenibile

indefinable [ˌɪndɪ'faɪnəbəl] *adj* indefinibile

indefinite [ɪn'defɪnɪt] *adj* indefinito

indelible [ɪn'delɪbəl] *adj* indelebile

indemnification [ɪn ˌdemnɪfɪ'keʃən] *s* indennità *f*, indennizzo

indemni•fy [ɪn'demnɪ ˌfaɪ] *v* (*pret & pp* -fied) *tr* indennizzare

indemni•ty [ɪn'demnɪti] *s* (-ties) indennità *f*, indennizzo

indent [ɪn'dent] *tr* frastagliare, dentellare; (typ) far rientrare

indentation [ˌɪnden'teʃən] *s* frastaglio, dentellatura; (typ) accapo

indenture [ɪn'dentʃər] *s* scrittura pubblica; contratto di apprendista || *tr* obbligare per contratto

independence [ˌɪndɪ'pendəns] *s* indipendenza

independent [ˌɪndɪ'pendənt] *adj & s* indipendente *mf*

indescribable [ˌɪndɪ'skraɪbəbəl] *adj* indescrivibile

indestructible [ˌɪndɪ'strʌktɪbəl] *adj* indistruttibile

indeterminate [ˌɪndɪ'tʌrmɪnɪt] *adj* indeterminato

index ['ɪndeks] *s* (**indexes** or **indices** ['ɪndɪ ˌsiz]) indice *m*; (typ) indice *m* indicatore || *tr* mettere un indice a; mettere all'indice || **Index** *s* Indice *m*

in'dex card' *s* scheda di catalogo

in'dex fin'ger *s* dito indice

India ['ɪndɪ•ə] *s* l'India *f*

In'dia ink' *s* inchiostro di china

Indian ['ɪndɪ•ən] *adj & s* indiano

In'dian club' *s* clava di ginnastica

In'dian corn' *s* granoturco

In'dian file' *s* fila indiana || *adv* in fila indiana

In'dian O'cean *s* Oceano Indiano

In'dian sum'mer *s* estate *f* di San Martino

In'dian wres'tling *s* braccio di ferro

In'dia pa'per *s* carta bibbia, carta d'India

In'dia rub'ber *s* cauccìù *m*

indicate ['ɪndɪ ˌket] *tr* indicare

indication [ˌɪndɪ'keʃən] *s* indicazione

indicative [ɪn'dɪkətɪv] *adj & s* indicativo

indicator ['ɪndɪ ˌketər] *s* indicatore *m*, indice *m*

indict [ɪn'daɪt] *tr* accusare

indictment [ɪn'daɪtmənt] *s* accusa, atto d'accusa

indifferent [ɪn'dɪfərənt] *adj* indifferente; (*not particularly good*) passabile

indigenous [ɪn'dɪdʒɪnəs] *adj* indigeno

indigent ['ɪndɪdʒənt] *adj* indigente || **the indigent** gli indigenti

indigestion [ˌɪndɪ'dʒestʃən] *s* indigestione

indignant [ɪn'dɪgnənt] *adj* indignato

indignation [ˌɪndɪg'neʃən] *s* indignazione

indigni•ty [ɪn'dɪgnɪti] *s* (-ties) indignità *f*

indi•go ['ɪndɪ ˌgo] *adj* indaco || *s* (-gos or -goes) indaco

indirect [ˌɪndɪ'rekt] or [ˌɪndaɪ'rekt] *adj* indiretto

in'direct dis'course *s* discorso indiretto

indiscernible [ˌɪndɪ'zʌrnɪbəl] or [ˌɪndɪ'sʌrnɪbəl] *adj* indiscernibile

indiscreet [ˌɪndɪs'krit] *adj* indiscreto

indispensable [ˌɪndɪs'pensəbəl] *adj* indispensabile, imprescindibile

indispose [ˌɪndɪs'poz] *tr* indisporre

indisposed [ˌɪndɪs'pozd] *adj* (*disinclined*) mal disposto; (*slightly ill*) indisposto

indissoluble [ˌɪndɪ'saljəbəl] *adj* indissolubile

indistinct [ˌɪndɪs'tɪŋkt] *adj* indistinto

indite [ɪn'daɪt] *tr* redigere

individual [ˌɪndɪ'vɪdʒu•əl] *adj* individuale || *s* individuo

individuali•ty [ˌɪndɪ ˌvɪdʒu'ælɪti] *s* (-ties) individualità *f*; (*person of distinctive character*) individuo

Indochina ['ɪndo'tʃaɪnə] *s* l'Indocina *f*

Indo-Chi•nese ['ɪndot/aɪ'niz] *adj* indocinese || *s* (-nese) indocinese *mf*

Indo-European ['ɪndo ˌjurə'pi•ən] *adj & s* indoeuropeo

indolent ['ɪndələnt] *adj* indolente

Indonesia [ˌɪndo'niʒə] or [ˌɪndo'niʒə] *s* l'Indonesia *f*

Indonesian [ˌɪndo'niʃən] or [ˌɪndo'niʒən] *adj & s* indonesiano

indoor ['ɪn ˌdor] *adj* situato in casa; da farsi in casa

indoors ['ɪn'dorz] *adv* dentro, a casa, al coperto

indorse [ɪn'dors] *tr* (com) girare; (fig) appoggiare, approvare

indorsee [ˌɪndor'si] *s* giratario

indorsement [ɪn'dorsmənt] *s* (com) girata; (fig) appoggio, approvazione

indorser [ɪn'dorsər] *s* girante *mf*

induce [ɪn'djus] or [ɪn'dus] *tr* indurre

inducement [ɪn'djusmənt] or [ɪn'dusmənt] *s* stimolo, incentivo

induct [ɪn'dʌkt] *tr* installare; iniziare; (mil) arruolare

induction [ɪn'dʌkʃən] *s* iniziazione; (elec & log) induzione; (mil) arruolamento

indulge [ɪn'dʌldʒ] *tr* indulgere (with *dat*) || *intr* cedere, lasciarsi andare; **to indulge in** abbandonarsi a; permettersi il lusso di

indulgence [ɪn'dʌldʒəns] *s* compiacenza; intemperanza, abbandono; (*leniency*) indulgenza

indulgent [ɪn'dʌldʒənt] *adj* indulgente

industrial [ɪn'dʌstrɪ-əl] *adj* industriale

industrialist [ɪn'dʌstrɪ-əlɪst] *s* industriale *m*

industrialize [ɪn'dʌstrɪ-ə,laɪz] *tr* industrializzare

industrious [ɪn'dʌstrɪ-əs] *adj* industrioso, laborioso

indus·try [ˈɪndʌstrɪ] *s* (-tries) industria

inebriation [ɪn,ɪbrɪ'eʃən] *s* ubriachezza

inedible [ɪn'edɪbəl] *adj* immangiabile

ineffable [ɪn'ɛfəbəl] *adj* ineffabile

ineffective [,ɪnɪ'fɛktɪv] *adj* inefficace; (*person*) incapace

ineffectual [,ɪnɪ'fɛkt/ʊ-əl] *adj* inefficace

inefficient [,ɪnɪ'fɪʃənt] *adj* inefficiente

ineligible [ɪn'elɪdʒɪbəl] *adj* ineleggibile

inequali·ty [,ɪnɪ'kwalɪtɪ] *s* (-ties) disuguaglianza

inequi·ty [ɪn'ɛkwɪtɪ] *s* (-ties) ingiustizia

ineradicable [,ɪnɪ'rædɪkəbəl] *adj* inestirpabile

inertia [ɪn'ʌrʃə] *s* inerzia

inescapable [,ɪnɛs'kepəbəl] *adj* ineluttabile, inderogabile

inevitable [ɪn'evɪtəbəl] *adj* inevitabile

inexact [,ɪnɛg'zækt] *adj* inesatto

inexcusable [,ɪnɛks'kjuzəbəl] *adj* inescusabile

inexhaustible [,ɪnɛg'zɔstɪbəl] *adj* inesauribile

inexorable [ɪn'ɛksərəbəl] *adj* inesorabile

inexpedient [,ɪnɛk'spidɪ-ənt] *adj* inopportuno

inexpensive [,ɪnɛk'spɛnsɪv] *adj* poco costoso, a buon mercato

inexperience [,ɪnɛk'spɪrɪ-əns] *s* inesperienza

inexplicable [ɪn'ɛksplɪkəbəl] *adj* inesplicabile

inexpressible [,ɪnɛk'sprɛsɪbəl] *adj* indicibile, inesprimibile

infallible [ɪn'fælɪbəl] *adj* infallibile

infamous [ˈɪnfəməs] *adj* infame

infa·my [ˈɪnfəmɪ] *s* (-mies) infamia

infan·cy [ˈɪnfənsɪ] *s* (-cies) infanzia

infant [ˈɪnfənt] *adj* infantile; (in the earliest stage) (fig) nascente || *s* neonato, bebè *m*

infantile [ˈɪnfən,taɪl] or [ˈɪnfəntɪl] *adj* infantile

infan·try [ˈɪnfəntrɪ] *s* (-tries) fanteria

in'fantry·man *s* (-men) fante *m*

infatuated [ɪn'fæt/ʊ,etɪd] *adj* infatuato

infect [ɪn'fɛkt] *tr* infettare

infection [ɪn'fɛkʃən] *s* infezione

infectious [ɪn'fɛkʃəs] *adj* infettivo

in·fer [ɪn'fʌr] *v* (*pret & pp* -ferred; *ger* -ferring) *tr* inferire; (coll) dedurre, supporre

inferior [ɪn'fɪrɪ-ər] *adj & s* inferiore *m*

inferiority [ɪn,fɪrɪ'arɪtɪ] *s* inferiorità *f*

inferior'ity com'plex *s* complesso di inferiorità

infernal [ɪn'fʌrnəl] *adj* infernale

infest [ɪn'fɛst] *tr* infestare

infidel [ˈɪnfɪdəl] *adj & s* infedele *mf*

infideli·ty [,ɪnfɪ'dɛlɪtɪ] *s* (-ties) infedeltà *f*

in'field' *s* campo interno, diamante *m*

infiltrate [ɪn'fɪltret] or [ˈɪnfɪl,tret] *tr* infiltrarsi in || *intr* infiltrarsi

infinite [ˈɪnfɪnɪt] *adj & s* infinito

infinitive [ɪn'fɪnɪtɪv] *adj* infinitivo || *s* infinito

infini·ty [ɪn'fɪnɪtɪ] *s* (-ties) infinità *f*; (math) infinito

infirm [ɪn'fʌrm] *adj* infermo; (*not firm*) debole

infirma·ry [ɪn'fʌrməri] *s* (-ries) infermeria

infirmi·ty [ɪn'fʌrmɪtɪ] *s* (-ties) infermità *f*

inflame [ɪn'flem] *tr* infiammare || *intr* infiammarsi

inflammable [ɪn'flæməbəl] *adj* infiammabile

inflammation [,ɪnflə'meʃən] *s* infiammazione

inflate [ɪn'flet] *tr* gonfiare; (*currency, prices*) inflazionare || *intr* gonfiarsi

inflation [ɪn'fleʃən] *s* inflazione; (*of a tire*) gonfiatura

inflect [ɪn'flɛkt] *tr* curvare; (*voice*) modulare; (gram) flettere

inflection [ɪn'flɛkʃən] *s* inflessione; (gram) flessione

inflexible [ɪn'flɛksɪbəl] *adj* inflessibile

inflict [ɪn'flɪkt] *tr* infliggere, inferire

influence [ˈɪnflu-əns] *s* influenza || *tr* influire su, influenzare

influential [,ɪnflu'ɛn/əl] *adj* influente

influenza [,ɪnflu'ɛnzə] *s* influenza

inform [ɪn'fɔrm] *tr* informare || *intr* dare informazioni; **to inform on** denunziare, fare la spia contro

informal [ɪn'fɔrməl] *adj* non ufficiale, ufficioso; (*unceremonious*) alla buona, familiare

informant [ɪn'fɔrmənt] *s* informatore *m*; (*informer*) delatore *m*; (ling) fonte *f* orale, informatore *m*

information [,ɪnfər'meʃən] *s* informazioni *fpl*; conoscenze *fpl*

informational [,ɪnfər'meʃənəl] *adj* informativo

informed' sour'ces *spl* fonti *fpl* attendibili

informer [ɪn'fɔrmər] *s* (*informant*) informatore *m*; (*spy*) delatore *m*

infraction [ɪn'frækʃən] *s* infrazione

infrared [,ɪnfrə'red] *adj & s* infrarosso

infrequent [ɪn'frikwənt] *adj* infrequente

infringe [ɪn'frɪndʒ] *tr* violare || *intr*— **to infringe on** or **upon** violare, contravvenire a

infringement [ɪn'frɪndʒmənt] *s* infrazione

infuriate [ɪnˈfjʊrɪ ˌet] *tr* infuriare
infuse [ɪnˈfjuz] *tr* infondere
infusion [ɪnˈfjuʒən] *s* infusione
ingenious [ɪnˈdʒinjəs] *adj* ingegnoso
ingenui·ty [ˌɪndʒɪˈnuˌɪti] or [ˌɪndʒɪˈnjuˌɪti] *s* (**-ties**) ingegnosità *f*
ingenuous [ɪnˈdʒenjuˌəs] *adj* ingenuo
ingenuousness [ɪnˈdʒenjuˌəsnɪs] *s* ingenuità *f*
ingest [ɪnˈdʒest] *tr* ingerire
ingoing [ˈɪnˌgoɪŋ] *adj* entrante
ingot [ˈɪŋgət] *s* lingotto, massello
ingraft [ɪnˈgræft] or [ɪnˈgrɑft] *tr* (hort & surg) innestare; (fig) inculcare
ingrate [ˈɪngret] *s* ingrato
ingratiate [ɪnˈgreʃɪ ˌet] *tr*—**to ingratiate oneself with** ingraziarsi
ingratiating [ɪnˈgreʃɪ ˌetɪŋ] *adj* attraente, affascinante, insinuante
ingratitude [ɪnˈgrætɪ ˌtjud] or [ɪnˈgrætɪ ˌtud] *s* ingratitudine *f*
ingredient [ɪnˈgridɪ·ənt] *s* ingrediente *m*
in'grown nail' [ˈɪngron] *s* unghia incarnita
ingulf [ɪnˈgʌlf] *tr* sommergere, inondare
inhabit [ɪnˈhæbɪt] *tr* abitare, popolare
inhabitant [ɪnˈhæbɪtənt] *s* abitante *mf*
inhale [ɪnˈhel] *tr & intr* inspirare
inherent [ɪnˈhɪrənt] *adj* inerente
inherit [ɪnˈherɪt] *tr & intr* ereditare
inheritance [ɪnˈherɪtəns] *s* eredità *f*
inheritor [ɪnˈherɪtər] *s* erede *mf*
inhibit [ɪnˈhɪbɪt] *tr* inibire
inhospitable [ɪnˈhɑspɪtəbəl] or [ˌɪnhɑsˈpɪtəbəl] *adj* inospitale
inhuman [ɪnˈhjumən] *adj* inumano
inhumane [ˌɪnhjuˈmen] *adj* inumano
inimical [ɪˈnɪmɪkəl] *adj* nemico
iniqui·ty [ɪˈnɪkwɪti] *s* (**-ties**) iniquità *f*
ini·tial [ɪˈnɪʃəl] *adj & s* iniziale *f* ‖ *v* (*pret* **-tialed** or **-tialled**; *ger* **-tialing** or **-tialling**) *tr* siglare
initiate [ɪˈnɪʃɪ ˌet] *tr* iniziare
initiation [ɪ ˌnɪʃɪˈeʃən] *s* iniziazione
initiative [ɪˈnɪʃɪ·ətɪv] or [ɪˈnɪʃɪ ˌetɪv] *s* iniziativa
inject [ɪnˈdʒekt] *tr* iniettare; introdurre
injection [ɪnˈdʒekʃən] *s* iniezione
injudicious [ˌɪndʒuˈdɪʃəs] *adj* avventato, sconsiderato
injunction [ɪnˈdʒʌŋkʃən] *s* ingiunzione
injure [ˈɪndʒər] *tr* (*to harm*) danneggiare; (*to wound*) ferire; (*to offend*) offendere, ingiuriare
injurious [ɪnˈdʒʊrɪ·əs] *adj* dannoso; offensivo, ingiurioso
inju·ry [ˈɪndʒəri] *s* (**-ries**) (*harm*) danno; (*wound*) ferita, lesione; offesa, ingiuria
injustice [ɪnˈdʒʌstɪs] *s* ingiustizia
ink [ɪŋk] *s* inchiostro ‖ *tr* inchiostrare
inkling [ˈɪŋklɪŋ] *s* sentore *m*, indizio
ink'stand' *s* (*container*) calamaio; (*stand*) calamaiera
ink'well' *s* calamaio
ink·y [ˈɪŋki] *adj* (**-ier; -iest**) nero come l'inchiostro; nero d'inchiostro
inlaid [ˈɪn ˌled] or [ˌɪnˈled] *adj* intarsiato, incrostato

inland [ˈɪnlənd] *adj & s* interno ‖ *adv* verso l'interno
in'-law' *s* affine *mf*
in·lay [ˈɪn ˌle] *s* intarsio, tassello ‖ [ɪnˈle] or [ˈɪn ˌle] *v* (*pret & pp* **-laid**) *tr* intarsiare
in'let *s* (*of the shore*) insenatura; (*entrance*) ammissione
in'mate' *s* (*patient, e.g., in an insane asylum*) internato; (*in a jail*) prigioniero
inn [ɪn] *s* taverna, osteria
innate [ɪˈnet] or [ˈɪnet] *adj* innato
inner [ˈɪnər] *adj* interno, interiore; intimo, profondo
in'ner·spring' mat'tress *s* materasso a molle
in'ner tube' *s* camera d'aria
inning [ˈɪnɪŋ] *s* (baseball) turno
inn'keep'er *s* locandiere *m*, oste *m*
innocence [ˈɪnəsəns] *s* innocenza
innocent [ˈɪnəsənt] *adj & s* innocente *mf*
innovate [ˈɪnə ˌvet] *tr* innovare
innovation [ˌɪnəˈveʃən] *s* innovazione
innuen·do [ˌɪnjuˈendo] *s* (**-does**) sottinteso, insinuazione
innumerable [ɪˈnjumərəbəl] or [ɪˈnumərəbəl] *adj* innumerevole
inoculate [ɪnˈakjə ˌlet] *tr* inoculare; (*e.g., with hatred*) inoculare; permeare
inoculation [ɪn ˌakjəˈleʃən] *s* inoculazione
inoffensive [ˌɪnəˈfensɪv] *adj* inoffensivo
inopportune [ɪn ˌapərˈtjun] or [ɪn ˌapərˈtun] *adj* inopportuno
inordinate [ɪnˈɔrdɪnɪt] *adj* smoderato
inorganic [ˌɪnɔrˈgænɪk] *adj* inorganico
in'pa'tient *s* degente *mf*
in'put' *s* entrata; (elec, mach) energia immessa
inquest [ˈɪnkwest] *s* inchiesta
inquire [ɪnˈkwaɪr] *tr* domandare, chiedere ‖ *intr*—**to inquire about, after, or for** chiedere di; **to inquire into** investigare
inquir·y [ɪnˈkwaɪri] or [ˈɪnkwɪri] *s* (**-ies**) indagine *f*, inchiesta
inquisition [ˌɪnkwɪˈzɪʃən] *s* inquisizione
inquisitive [ɪnˈkwɪzɪtɪv] *adj* indagatore, curioso
in'road' *s* incursione, invasione
insane [ɪnˈsen] *adj* pazzo, matto
insane' asy'lum *s* manicomio
insani·ty [ɪnˈsænɪti] *s* (**-ties**) pazzia, follia, demenza
insatiable [ɪnˈseʃəbəl] *adj* insaziabile
inscribe [ɪnˈskraɪb] *tr* iscrivere; (*a book*) dedicare; (geom) inscrivere
inscription [ɪnˈskrɪpʃən] *s* scritta, iscrizione; (*of a book*) dedica
inscrutable [ɪnˈskrutəbəl] *adj* imperscrutabile
insect [ˈɪnsekt] *s* insetto
insecticide [ɪnˈsektɪ ˌsaɪd] *adj & s* insetticida *m*
insecure [ˌɪnsɪˈkjur] *adj* malsicuro
inseparable [ɪnˈsepərəbəl] *adj* inseparabile

insert ['ɪnsʌrt] *s* inserzione; *(circular)* inserto || [ɪn'sʌrt] *tr* inserire

insertion [ɪn'sʌrʃən] *s* inserzione; *(in lunar orbit)* immissione; *(of lace)* tramezzo

in·set ['ɪn ˌset] *s* intercalazione || [ɪn-'set] or ['ɪn ˌset] *v (pret & pp* **-set;** *ger* **-setting)** *tr* intercalare

in'shore' *adj & adv* vicino alla spiaggia

in'side' *adj* interno; privato, confidenziale || *s* interno; **insides** (coll) interiora *fpl*; **to be on the inside** avere informazioni confidenziali || *adv* dentro; all'interno; **inside of** dentro, dentro a, dentro di; **to turn inside out** rovesciare, voltare il diritto al rovescio || *prep* dentro, dentro a

in'side flap' *s* (bb) risvolto

insider [ˌɪn'saɪdər] *s* persona informata

in'side track' *s* (racing) steccato; **to have the inside track** (coll) trovarsi in una situazione vantaggiosa

insidious [ɪn'sɪdɪ·əs] *adj* insidioso

in'sight' *s* intuito, penetrazione

insigni·a [ɪn'sɪgnɪ·ə] *s* (-a or -as) distintivo; *(distinguishing sign)* segno

insignificant [ˌɪnsɪg'nɪfɪkənt] *adj* insignificante

insincere [ˌɪnsɪn'sɪr] *adj* insincero

insinuate [ɪn'sɪnju ˌet] *tr* insinuare

insist [ɪn'sɪst] *intr* insistere

insofar as [ˌɪnso'far ˌæz] *conj* per quanto

insolence ['ɪnsələns] *s* insolenza

insolent ['ɪnsələnt] *adj* insolente

insoluble [ɪn'saljəbəl] *adj* insolubile

insolven·cy [ɪn'salvənsɪ] *s* (-cies) insolvenza

insomnia [ɪn'samnɪ·ə] *s* insonnia

insomuch [ˌɪnso'mʌtʃ] *adv* fino al punto; **insomuch as** giacché, visto che; **insomuch that** fino al punto che

inspect [ɪn'spekt] *tr* ispezionare

inspection [ɪn'spekʃən] *s* ispezione

inspector [ɪn'spektər] *s* ispettore *m*

inspiration [ˌɪnspɪ're·ʃən] *s* ispirazione

inspire [ɪn'spaɪr] *tr & intr* ispirare

install [ɪn'stɔl] *tr* istallare

installment [ɪn'stɔlmənt] *s* rata; *(of a book)* dispensa; **in installments** a rate

install'ment plan' *s* pagamento rateale; **on the installment plan** con facilitazioni di pagamento

instance ['ɪnstəns] *s* esempio; (law) istanza; **for instance** per esempio

instant ['ɪnstənt] *adj* istantaneo || *s* istante *m*; mese *m* corrente

instantaneous [ˌɪnstən'tenɪ·əs] *adj* istantaneo

instantly ['ɪnstəntlɪ] *adv* immediatamente, istantaneamente

instead [ɪn'sted] *adv* invece; **instead of** invece di

in'step' *s* collo del piede

instigate ['ɪnstɪ ˌget] *tr* istigare

instigation [ˌɪnstɪ'geʃən] *s* istigazione

in·still' *tr* instillare, istillare

instinct ['ɪnstɪŋkt] *s* istinto

instinctive [ɪn'stɪŋktɪv] *adj* istintivo

institute ['ɪnstɪ ˌtjut] or ['ɪnstɪ ˌtut] *s* istituto || *tr* istituire

institution [ˌɪnstɪ'tjuʃən] or [ˌɪnstɪ-'tuʃən] *s* istituzione

institutionalize [ˌɪnstɪ'tjuʃənə ˌlaɪz] or [ˌɪnstɪ'tuʃənə ˌlaɪz] *tr* istituzionalizzare

instruct [ɪn'strʌkt] *tr* istruire

instruction [ɪn'strʌkʃən] *s* istruzione

instructive [ɪn'strʌktɪv] *adj* istruttivo

instructor [ɪn'strʌktər] *s* istruttore *m*

instrument ['ɪnstrəmənt] *s* strumento; (law) istrumento || ['ɪnstrə ˌment] *tr* strumentare

instrumental [ˌɪnstrə'mentəl] *adj* strumentale; **to be instrumental in** contribuire a

instrumentalist [ˌɪnstrə'mentəlɪst] *s* strumentista *mf*

instrumentali·ty [ˌɪnstrəmən'tælɪtɪ] *s* (-ties) mediazione, aiuto

in'strument fly'ing *s* volo strumentale

in'strument pan'el *s* (aut) cruscotto

insubordinate [ˌɪnsə'bɔrdɪnɪt] *adj* insubordinato

insufferable [ɪn'sʌfərəbəl] *adj* insoffribile

insufficient [ˌɪnsə'fɪʃənt] *adj* insufficiente

insular ['ɪnsələr] or ['ɪnsjulər] *adj* insulare; *(e.g., attitude)* gretto

insulate ['ɪnsə ˌlet] *tr* isolare

in'sulating tape' ['ɪnsəletɪŋ] *s* nastro isolante

insulation [ˌɪnsə'leʃən] *s* isolamento

insulator ['ɪnsə ˌletər] *s* isolatore *m*

insulin ['ɪnsəlɪn] *s* insulina

insult ['ɪnsʌlt] *s* insulto || [ɪn'sʌlt] *tr* insultare, insolentire

insulting [ɪn'sʌltɪŋ] *adj* insultante

insurance [ɪn'ʃʊrəns] *s* assicurazione

insure [ɪn'ʃʊr] *tr* assicurare

insurer [ɪn'ʃʊrər] *s* assicuratore *m*

insurgent [ɪn'sʌrdʒənt] *adj & s* insorgente *mf*

insurmountable [ˌɪnsər'maʊntəbəl] *adj* insormontabile

insurrection [ˌɪnsə'rekʃən] *s* insurrezione

insusceptible [ˌɪnsə'septɪbəl] *adj* non suscettibile

intact [ɪn'tækt] *adj* intatto, integro

in'take' *s (place of taking in)* entrata; *(act of taking in)* ammissione; (mach) presa, immissione, aspirazione

in'take man'ifold' *s* collettore *m* d'ammissione

intangible [ɪn'tændʒɪbəl] *adj* intangibile; (fig) vago, inafferrabile

integer ['ɪntɪdʒər] *s* numero intero

integral ['ɪntɪgrəl] *adj* integrale; *(part of a whole)* integrante || *s* (math) integrale *m*

integration [ˌɪntɪ'greʃən] *s* integrazione

integrity [ɪn'tegrɪtɪ] *s* integrità *f*

intellect ['ɪntə ˌlekt] *s* intelletto

intellectual [ˌɪntə'lekt/ʊ·əl] *adj & s* intellettuale *mf*

intelligence [ɪn'telɪdʒəns] *s* intelligenza; informazione, conoscenza

intel'ligence bu'reau *s* ufficio spionaggi
intel'ligence quo'tient *s* quoziente *m* d'intelligenza
intelligent [ɪn'telɪdʒənt] *adj* intelligente
intelligentsia [ɪn‿telɪ'dʒentsɪ-ə] or [ɪn‿telɪ'gentsɪ-ə] *s* intellighenzia, intellettualità *f*
intelligible [ɪn'telɪdʒɪbəl] *adj* intelligibile, comprensibile
intemperance [ɪn'tempərəns] *s* intemperanza, sregolatezza
intemperate [ɪn'tempərɪt] *adj* intemperante; (*climate*) rigoroso
intend [ɪn'tend] *tr* intendere, prefiggersi; (*to mean for a particular purpose*) destinare; (*to signify*) voler dire
intendance [ɪn'tendəns] *s* intendenza
intendant [ɪn'tendənt] *s* intendente *m*
intended [ɪn'tendɪd] *adj & s* (coll) promesso, promessa
intense [ɪn'tens] *adj* intenso
intensi·fy [ɪn'tensɪ-faɪ] *v* (*pret & pp* -fied) *tr* intensificare, rinforzare; (phot) rinforzare ‖ *intr* intensificarsi, rinforzarsi
intensi·ty [ɪn'tensɪti] *s* (-ties) intensità *f*
intensive [ɪn'tensɪv] *adj* intensivo
intent [ɪn'tent] *adj* intento, attento; **intent on** deciso a ‖ *s* (*purpose*) intento, scopo; (*meaning*) significato; **to all intents and purposes** virtualmente, in realtà
intention [ɪn'tenʃən] *s* intenzione
intentional [ɪn'tenʃənəl] *adj* intenzionale, deliberato
intentionally [ɪn'tenʃənəli] *adv* apposta, deliberatamente
in·ter [ɪn'tʌr] *v* (*pret & pp* -terred; *ger* -terring) *tr* interrare, inumare
interact [‿ɪntər'ækt] *intr* esercitare un'azione reciproca
interaction [‿ɪntər'ækʃən] *s* azione reciproca
inter·breed [‿ɪntər'brid] *s* (*pret & pp* -bred* ['bred]) *tr* incrociare ‖ *intr* incrociarsi
intercalate [ɪn'tʌrkə‿let] *tr* intercalare
intercede [‿ɪntər'sid] *intr* intercedere
intercept [‿ɪntər'sept] *tr* intercettare
interceptor [‿ɪntər'septər] *s* (*person*) intercettatore *m*; (aer) intercettore *m*
interchange ['ɪntər‿tʃendʒ] *s* interscambio; (*on a highway*) svincolo autostradale ‖ [‿ɪntər't/əndʒ] *tr* scambiare ‖ *intr* scambiarsi
intercollegiate [‿ɪntərkə'lidʒɪ-ɪt] *adj* interscolastico, fra università
intercom ['ɪntər‿kʌm] *s* citofono
intercourse ['ɪntər‿kors] *s* comunicazione; (*of products, ideas, etc.*) scambio; (*copulation*) copula, coito; **to have intercourse** accoppiarsi sessualmente
intercross [‿ɪntər'krɔs] or [‿ɪntər'krɑs] *tr* incrociare ‖ *intr* incrociarsi
interdict ['ɪntər‿dɪkt] *s* interdetto ‖ [‿ɪntər'dɪkt] *tr* interdire; **to interdict s.o. from** + *ger* interdire a qlcu di + *inf*
interest ['ɪntərɪst] or ['ɪntrɪst] *s* in-

teresse *m;* **the interests** i potenti ‖ ['ɪntərɪst], ['ɪntrɪst] or ['ɪntə‿rest] *tr* interessare
interested ['ɪntrɪstɪd] or ['ɪntə‿restɪd] *adj* interessato
interesting ['ɪntrɪstɪŋ] or ['ɪntə‿restɪŋ] *adj* interessante
interfere [‿ɪntər'fɪr] *intr* interferire; (sports) ostacolare l'azione; **to interfere with** interferire in
interference [‿ɪntər'fɪrəns] *s* interferenza
interim ['ɪntərɪm] *adj* interino ‖ *s* interim *m;* **in the interim** frattanto
interior [ɪn'tɪrɪ-ər] *adj & s* interno
interject [‿ɪntər'dʒekt] *tr* interporre ‖ *intr* interporsi
interjection [‿ɪntər'dʒekʃən] *s* interposizione, esclamazione; (gram) interiezione
interlard [‿ɪntər'lɑrd] *tr* infiorare, lardellare
interline [‿ɪntər'laɪn] *tr* scrivere nell'interlinea di; (*a garment*) foderare con ovattina
interlining ['ɪntər‿laɪnɪŋ] *s* soppanno
interlink [‿ɪntər'lɪŋk] *tr* concatenare
interlock [‿ɪntər'lɑk] *tr* connettere ‖ *intr* connettersi
interlope [‿ɪntər'lop] *intr* intromettersi; trafficare senza permesso
interloper [‿ɪntər'lopər] *s* intruso
interlude ['ɪntər‿lud] *s* interludio; (theat) intermezzo
intermarriage [‿ɪntər‿mærɪdʒ] *s* matrimonio tra consanguinei; matrimonio fra membri di razze diverse
intermediar·y [‿ɪntər'midɪ‿eri] *adj* intermediario ‖ (-ies) *s* intermediario
intermediate [‿ɪntər'midɪ-ɪt] *adj* intermedio
interment [ɪn'tʌrmənt] *s* inumazione
intermingle [‿ɪntər'mɪŋgəl] *tr* mescolare ‖ *intr* mescolarsi
intermission [‿ɪntər'mɪʃən] *s* interruzione; (theat) intervallo
intermittent [‿ɪntər'mɪtənt] *adj* intermittente
intermix [‿ɪntər'mɪks] *tr* mescolare ‖ *intr* mescolarsi
intern [ɪn'tʌrn] *s* interno ‖ [ɪn'tʌrn] *tr* internare
internal [ɪn'tʌrnəl] *adj* interno
inter'nal-combus'tion en'gine *s* motore *m* a combustione interna, motore *m* a scoppio
inter'nal rev'enue *s* fisco
international [‿ɪntər'næʃənəl] *adj* internazionale
in'terna'tional date' line' *s* linea del cambiamento di data
internationalize [‿ɪntər'næʃənə‿laɪz] *tr* internazionalizzare
internecine [‿ɪntər'nisɪn] *adj* micidiale, sanguinario
internee [‿ɪntʌr'ni] *s* internato
internist [ɪn'tʌrnɪst] *s* internista *mf*
internment [ɪn'tʌrnmənt] *s* internamento
internship ['ɪntʌrn‿ʃɪp] *s* tirocinio in un ospedale, internato

interpellate [ˌɪntərˈpelet] or [ɪnˈtʌrpɪˌlet] *tr* interpellare
interplanetary [ˌɪntərˈplænəˌteri] *adj* interplanetario
interplay [ˈɪntərˌple] *s* azione reciproca
interpolate [ɪnˈtʌrpəˌlet] *tr* interpolare
interpose [ˌɪntərˈpoz] *tr* frapporre
interpret [ɪnˈtʌrprɪt] *tr* interpretare
interpreter [ɪnˈtʌrprətər] *s* interprete *mf*
interrogate [ɪnˈterəˌget] *tr & intr* interrogare
interrogation [ɪnˌterəˈgeʃən] *s* interrogazione
interroga'tion mark' or **point'** *s* punto interrogativo
interrupt [ˌɪntəˈrʌpt] *tr* interrompere
interruption [ˌɪntəˈrʌpʃən] *s* interruzione
interscholastic [ˌɪntərskəˈlæstɪk] *adj* interscolastico
intersect [ˌɪntərˈsekt] *tr* intersecare || *intr* intersecarsi
intersection [ˌɪntərˈsekʃən] *s* (*of streets, roads, etc.*) crocevia *m*; (geom) intersezione
intersperse [ˌɪntərˈspʌrs] *tr* cospargere, inframezzare
interstellar [ˌɪntərˈstelər] *adj* interstellare
interstice [ɪnˈtʌrstɪs] *s* interstizio
intertwine [ˌɪntərˈtwaɪn] *tr* intrecciare || *intr* intrecciarsi
interval [ˈɪntərvəl] *s* intervallo; **at intervals** a intervalli; di tanto in tanto
intervene [ˌɪntərˈvin] *intr* intervenire; (*to happen*) succedere
intervening [ˌɪntərˈvinɪŋ] *adj*—**in the intervening time** nel frattempo
intervention [ˌɪntərˈvenʃən] *s* intervenzione
interview [ˈɪntərˌvju] *s* intervista || *tr* intervistare
inter·weave [ˌɪntərˈwiv] *v* (*pret* **-wove** [ˈwov] or **-weaved**; *pp* **-wove, -woven** or **-weaved**) *tr* intessere
intestate [ɪnˈtestet] or [ɪnˈtestɪt] *adj* intestato
intestine [ɪnˈtestɪn] *s* intestino
inthrall [ɪnˈθrɔl] *tr* affascinare, incantare; (*to subjugate*) asservire, soggiogare
inthrone [ɪnˈθron] *tr* mettere sul trono, intronizzare; esaltare, innalzare
intima·cy [ˈɪntɪməsi] *s* (**-cies**) intimità *f*
intimate [ˈɪntɪmɪt] *adj & s* intimo || [ˈɪntɪˌmet] *tr* insinuare
intimation [ˌɪntɪˈmeʃən] *s* insinuazione
intimidate [ɪnˈtɪmɪˌdet] *tr* intimidire
into [ˈɪntu] or [ˈɪntu] *prep* in; verso; contro
intolerant [ɪnˈtalərənt] *adj & s* intollerante *mf*, insofferente *mf*
intomb [ɪnˈtum] *tr* inumare, seppellire
intombment [ɪnˈtummənt] *s* sepoltura
intonation [ˌɪntoˈneʃən] *s* intonazione
intone [ɪnˈton] *tr* intonare || *intr* salmodiare
intoxicant [ɪnˈtaksɪkənt] *s* bevanda alcoolica

intoxicate [ɪnˈtaksɪˌket] *tr* ubriacare; esilarare; (*to poison*) avvelenare, intossicare
intoxication [ɪnˌtaksɪˈkeʃən] *s* ubriachezza; ebbrezza, allegria; (*poisoning*) avvelenamento, intossicazione
intractable [ɪnˈtræktəbəl] *adj* intrattabile
intransigent [ɪnˈtrænsɪdʒənt] *adj & s* intransigente *mf*
intransitive [ɪnˈtrænsɪtɪv] *adj* intransitivo
intravenous [ˌɪntrəˈvinəs] *adj* intravenoso, endovenoso
intrench [ɪnˈtrentʃ] *tr & intr* var of **entrench**
intrepid [ɪnˈtrepɪd] *adj* intrepido
intrepidity [ˌɪntrɪˈpɪdɪti] *s* intrepidezza
intricate [ˈɪntrɪkɪt] *adj* intricato
intrigue [ɪnˈtrig] or [ˈɪntrig] *s* intrigo; tresca, intrigo amoroso; (theat) intreccio || [ɪnˈtrig] *tr* incuriosire || *intr* intrigare; trescare
intrinsic(al) [ɪnˈtrɪnsɪk(əl)] *adj* intrinseco
introduce [ˌɪntrəˈdjus] or [ˌɪntrəˈdus] *tr* introdurre; (*a product*) lanciare; (*a person*) presentare
introduction [ˌɪntrəˈdʌkʃən] *s* introduzione; presentazione
introductory [ˌɪntrəˈdʌktəri] *adj* introduttivo
introit [ˈɪntroˌɪt] *s* (eccl) introito
introspective [ˌɪntrəˈspektɪv] *adj* introspettivo
introvert [ˈɪntrəˌvʌrt] *adj & s* introverso
intrude [ɪnˈtrud] *intr* intrudersi, intrufolarsi
intruder [ɪnˈtrudər] *s* intruso; importuno
intrusion [ɪnˈtruʒən] *s* intrusione
intrusive [ɪnˈtrusɪv] *adj* invadente
intrust [ɪnˈtrʌst] *tr* affidare, confidare
intuition [ˌɪntuˈɪʃən] or [ˌɪntjuˈɪʃən] *s* intuizione, intuito
inundate [ˈɪnənˌdet] *tr* inondare
inundation [ˌɪnənˈdeʃən] *s* inondazione
inure [ɪnˈjur] *tr* indurire, assuefare || *intr* entrare in vigore; **to inure to** ridondare in favore di
invade [ɪnˈved] *tr* invadere
invader [ɪnˈvedər] *s* invasore *m*
invalid [ɪnˈvælɪd] *adj* (*non valid*) invalido || [ˈɪnvəlɪd] *adj* (*person*) invalido; (*thing*) povero; (*diet*) per malati || [ˈɪnvəlɪd] *s* invalido
invalidate [ɪnˈvælɪˌdet] *tr* invalidare
invalidity [ˌɪnvəˈlɪdɪti] *s* invalidità *f*
invaluable [ɪnˈvæljuˌəbəl] *adj* inestimabile, inapprezzabile
invariable [ɪnˈverɪˌəbəl] *adj* invariabile
invasion [ɪnˈveʒən] *s* invasione
invective [ɪnˈvektɪv] *s* invettiva
inveigh [ɪnˈve] *intr*—**to inveigh against** inveire contro
inveigle [ɪnˈvegəl] or [ɪnˈvigəl] *tr* sedurre, abbindolare
invent [ɪnˈvent] *tr* inventare
invention [ɪnˈvenʃən] *s* invenzione

inventiveness [ɪn'ventɪvnɪs] *s* inventiva
inventor [ɪn'ventər] *s* inventore *m*
invento·ry ['ɪnvən ˌtori] *s* (**-ries**) inventario ‖ *v* (*pret & pp* **-ried**) *tr* inventariare
inverse [ɪn'vʌrs] *adj & s* inverso
inversion [ɪn'vʌrʒən] *or* [ɪn'vʌrʃən] *s* inversione
invert ['ɪnvʌrt] *s* invertito ‖ [ɪn'vʌrt] *tr* invertire
invertebrate [ɪn'vʌrtɪ ˌbret] *or* [ɪn'vʌrtɪbrɪt] *adj & s* invertebrato
invest [ɪn'vest] *tr* investire ‖ *intr* fare un investimento; fare investimenti
investigate [ɪn'vestɪ ˌget] *tr* investigare
investigation [ɪn ˌvestɪ'geʃən] *s* investigazione
investigator [ɪn'vestɪ ˌgetər] *s* investigatore *m*
investment [ɪn'vestmənt] *s* (*of money*) investimento; (*e.g., with an office*) investitura; (*siege*) assedio
investor [ɪn'vestər] *s* investitore *m*
inveterate [ɪn'vetərɪt] *adj* inveterato
invidious [ɪn'vɪdɪ·əs] *adj* irritante, odioso
invigorate [ɪn'vɪgə ˌret] *tr* invigorire
invigorating [ɪn'vɪgə ˌretɪŋ] *adj* ritemprante, ricostituente, rinforzante
invincible [ɪn'vɪnsɪbəl] *adj* invincibile
invisible [ɪn'vɪzɪbəl] *adj* invisibile
invis'ible ink' *s* inchiostro simpatico
invitation [ˌɪnvɪ'teʃən] *s* invito
invite [ɪn'vaɪt] *tr* invitare
inviting [ɪn'vaɪtɪŋ] *adj* invitante, attrattivo; (*food*) appetitoso; accogliente
invoice ['ɪnvɔɪs] *s* fattura; **as per invoice** secondo fattura ‖ *tr* fatturare
invoke [ɪn'vok] *tr* invocare; (*a spirit*) evocare
involuntary [ɪn'vɑlən ˌteri] *adj* involontario
involve [ɪn'vɑlv] *tr* involvere, includere; occupare; (*to bring unpleasantness upon*) implicare, coinvolgere; complicare
invulnerable [ɪn'vʌlnərəbəl] *adj* invulnerabile
inward ['ɪnwərd] *adj* interno ‖ *adv* al di dentro, verso l'interno
iodide ['aɪ·ə ˌdaɪd] *s* ioduro
iodine ['aɪ·ə ˌdin] *s* iodio ‖ ['aɪ·ə ˌdaɪn] *s* tintura di iodio
ion ['aɪ·ən] *or* ['aɪ·ɑn] *s* ione *m*
ionize ['aɪ·ə ˌnaɪz] *tr* ionizzare
IOU ['aɪ ˌo'ju] *s* (letterword) (**I owe you**) cambiale *f*, pagherò *m*
I.Q. ['aɪ'kju] *s* (letterword) (**intelligence quotient**) quoziente *m* d'intelligenza
Iranian [aɪ'renɪ·ən] *adj & s* iraniano
Ira·qi [ɪ'rɑki] *adj* iracheno ‖ *s* (**-qis**) iracheno
irate ['aɪret] *or* [aɪ'ret] *adj* irato
ire [aɪr] *s* ira, collera
Ireland ['aɪrlənd] *s* l'Irlanda *f*
iris ['aɪrɪs] *s* iride *f*
I'rish·man *s* (**-men**) irlandese *m*
I'rish stew' *s* stufato all'irlandese
I'rish·wom'an *s* (**-wom'en**) irlandese *f*
irk [ʌrk] *tr* infastidire, annoiare

irksome ['ʌrksəm] *adj* fastidioso
iron ['aɪ·ərn] *adj* ferreo ‖ *s* ferro; (*to press clothes*) ferro da stiro; **irons** ferri *mpl*; **strike while the iron is hot** batti il ferro fin ch'è caldo ‖ *tr* (*clothes*) stirare; **to iron out** (*a difficulty*) (coll) appianare
i'ron·bound' *adj* ferrato; (*unyielding*) ferreo, inflessibile; (*rock-bound*) roccioso, scabroso
ironclad ['aɪ·ərn ˌklæd] *adj* corazzato, blindato; inflessibile, ferreo
i'ron constitu'tion *s* salute *f* di ferro
i'ron cur'tain *s* cortina di ferro
i'ron horse' *s* locomotiva a vapore
ironic(al) [aɪ'rɑnɪk(əl)] *adj* ironico
ironing ['aɪ·ərnɪŋ] *s* stiratura; roba stirata; roba da stirare
i'roning board' *s* tavolo or asse *m* da stiro
i'ron lung' *s* polmone *m* d'acciaio
i'ron·ware' *s* ferrame *m*
i'ron will' *s* volontà *f* di ferro
i'ron·work' *s* lavoro in ferro; **ironworks** *ssg* ferriera
i'ron·work'er *s* ferraio; metalmeccanico, siderurgico
iro·ny ['aɪrəni] *s* (**-nies**) ironia
irradiate [ɪ'redɪ ˌet] *tr* irradiare ‖ *intr* irradiare, irradiarsi
irrational [ɪ'ræʃənəl] *adj* irrazionale
irrecoverable [ˌɪrɪ'kʌvərəbəl] *adj* irrecuperabile
irredeemable [ˌɪrɪ'diməbəl] *adj* irredimibile
irrefutable [ˌɪrɪ'fjutəbəl] *adj* irrefutabile
irregular [ɪ'regjələr] *adj* irregolare ‖ *s* (mil) irregolare *m*
irrelevance [ɪ'reləvəns] *s* irrilevanza
irrelevant [ɪ'reləvənt] *adj* irrilevante
irreligious [ˌɪrɪ'lɪdʒəs] *adj* irreligioso
irremediable [ˌɪrɪ'midɪ·əbəl] *adj* irrimediabile
irremovable [ˌɪrɪ'muvəbəl] *adj* irremovibile, inamovibile
irreplaceable [ˌɪrɪ'plesəbəl] *adj* insostituibile
irrepressible [ˌɪrɪ'presɪbəl] *adj* irreprimibile, incontenibile
irreproachable [ˌɪrɪ'protʃəbəl] *adj* irreprensibile
irresistible [ˌɪrɪ'zɪstɪbəl] *adj* irresistibile
irrespective [ˌɪrɪ'spektɪv] *adj*—**irrespective of** senza riguardo a
irresponsible [ˌɪrɪ'spɑnsɪbəl] *adj* irresponsabile
irretrievable [ˌɪrɪ'trivəbəl] *adj* irrecuperabile
irreverent [ɪ'revərənt] *adj* irriverente
irrevocable [ɪ'revəkəbəl] *adj* irrevocabile
irrigate ['ɪrɪ ˌget] *tr* irrigare
irrigation [ˌɪrɪ'geʃən] *s* irrigazione
irritant ['ɪrɪtənt] *adj & s* irritante *m*
irritate ['ɪrɪ ˌtet] *tr* irritare
irritation [ˌɪrɪ'teʃən] *s* irritazione
irruption [ɪ'rʌpʃən] *s* irruzione
isinglass ['aɪzɪn ˌglæs] *or* ['aɪzɪŋ ˌglɑs] *s* (*gelatine*) colla di pesce; mica
Islam ['ɪsləm] *or* [ɪs'lɑm] *s* l'Islam *m*

island ['aɪlənd] *adj* isolano ‖ *s* isola; (*for safety of pedestrians*) salvagente *m*

islander ['aɪləndər] *s* isolano

isle [aɪl] *s* isoletta

isolate ['aɪsə‚let] or ['ɪsə‚let] *tr* isolare

isolation [‚aɪsə'leʃən] or [‚ɪsə'leʃən] *s* isolamento

isolationist [‚aɪsə'leʃənɪst] or [‚ɪsə'leʃənɪst] *s* isolazionista *mf*

isosceles [aɪ'sɑsə‚liz] *adj* isoscele

isotope ['aɪsə‚top] *s* isotopo

Israel ['ɪzrɪ-əl] *s* l'Israele *m*

Israe·li [ɪz'reli] *adj* israeliano ‖ *s* (**-lis** [liz]) israeliano

Israelite ['ɪzrɪ-ə‚laɪt] *adj* & *s* israelita *mf*

issuance ['ɪʃʊ-əns] *s* (*of stamps, stocks, bonds, etc.*) emissione; (*e.g., of clothes*) distribuzione; (*of a law*) emanazione

issue ['ɪʃu] *s* (*outlet*) uscita; distribuzione; (*result*) conseguenza; (*offspring*) prole *f*; (*of a magazine*) puntata, fascicolo; (*of a bond*) emissione; (*yield*) prodotto; (*of a law*) promulgazione; (*pathol*) flusso; at issue in discussione; to face the issue affrontare la situazione; to force the issue forzare la soluzione; to take issue with non essere d'accordo con, dissentire da ‖ *tr* (*e.g., a book*) pubblicare; (*bonds, orders*) emettere; (*a communiqué*) diramare; (*e.g., food*) distribuire ‖ *intr* uscire; to issue from provenire da

isthmus ['ɪsməs] *s* istmo

it [ɪt] *pron pers* esso, essa; lo, la; **it is** I sono io; **it is raining** piove; **it is four o'clock** sono le quattro

Italian [ɪ'tæljən] *adj* & *s* italiano

Ital'ian-speak'ing *adj* italofono

italic [ɪ'tælɪc] *adj* (typ) corsivo ‖ **italics** *s* (typ) corsivo ‖ **Italic** *adj* italico

italicize [ɪ'tælɪ‚saɪz] *tr* stampare in carattere corsivo; sottolineare

Italy ['ɪtəli] *s* l'Italia *f*

itch [ɪtʃ] *s* prurito; (pathol) rogna; (*eagerness*) (fig) pizzicore *m* ‖ *tr* prudere, e.g., **his foot itches him** gli prude il piede ‖ *intr* (*said of a part of body*) prudere; (*said of a person*) avere il prurito; **to itch to** avere la voglia di

itch·y ['ɪtʃi] *adj* (**-ier; -iest**) che prude; (pathol) rognoso

item ['aɪtəm] *s* articolo; notizia; (*on the agenda*) questione; (slang) notizia scottante

itemize ['aɪtə‚maɪz] *tr* dettagliare, specificare

itinerant [aɪ'tɪnərənt] or [ɪ'tɪnərənt] *adj* itinerante, ambulante ‖ *s* viaggiatore *m*, viandante *m*

itinerar·y [aɪ'tɪnə‚reri] or [ɪ'tɪnə‚reri] *adj* itinerario ‖ *s* (**-ies**) itinerario

its [ɪts] *adj* & *pron poss* il suo

itself [ɪt'self] *pron pers* sé stesso; sì, e.g., **it opened itself** si è aperto

ivied ['aɪvid] *adj* coperto di edera

ivo·ry ['aɪvəri] *adj* d'avorio ‖ *s* (**-ries**) avorio; **ivories** (slang) tasti *mpl* del piano; (slang) palle *fpl* da bigliardo; (*dice*) (slang) dadi *mpl*; (slang) denti *mpl*

i'vory tow'er *s* torre *f* d'avorio

ivy ['aɪvi] *s* (**ivies**) edera

J

J, j [dʒe] *s* decima lettera dell'alfabeto inglese

jab [dʒæb] *s* puntata; (*prick*) puntura; (*with elbow*) gomitata ‖ *v* (*pret & pp* **jabbed;** *ger* **jabbing**) *tr* pugnalare; pungere; dare una gomitata a ‖ *intr* dare colpi

jabber ['dʒæbər] *s* borbottamento, ciarla ‖ *tr* & *intr* borbottare, ciarlare

jack [dʒæk] *s* (*for lifting heavy objects*) cricco, martinetto; (*jackass*) asino; (*device for turning a spit*) girarrosto; (*to remove a boot*) cavastivali *m*; (*cards*) fante *m*; (bowling) pallino; (rad & telv) jack *m*; (elec) presa; (slang) soldi *mpl*; **every man jack** ognuno, tutti *mpl* ‖ **Jack** *s* marinaio; (coll) buonuomo ‖ *tr*—**to jack up** alzare col cricco; (*prices*) (coll) alzare

jackal ['dʒækəl] *s* sciacallo

jack'ass' *s* asino

jack'daw' *s* cornacchia

jacket ['dʒækɪt] *s* giacca; (*of boiled potatoes*) buccia; (*of book*) sopraccoperta; (*metal casing*) camicia

jack'ham'mer *s* martello perforatore

jack'-in-the-box' *s* scatola a sorpresa

jack'knife' *s* (**-knives**) coltello a serramanico; (sports) salto a pesce

jack'-of-all'-trades' *s* factotum *m*

jack-o'-lantern ['dʒækə‚læntərn] *s* lanterna a forma di testa umana fatta con una zucca; fuoco fatuo

jack'pot' *s* monte *m* premi; **to hit the jackpot** (slang) vincere un terno al lotto

jack' rab'bit *s* lepre nordamericana di taglia grande

jack'screw' *s* cricco a verme

jack'-tar' *s* (coll) marinaio

jade [dʒed] *adj* di giada, come la giada ‖ *s* (*ornamental stone*) giada; (*worn-out horse*) ronzino; (*disreputable woman*) donnaccia ‖ *tr* logorare

jad'ed ['dʒedɪd] *adj* logoro, stanco; (*appetite*) stucco

jag [dʒæg] *s* slabbratura; **to have a jag on** (slang) avere la sbornia

jagged ['dʒægɪd] *adj* dentato, slabbrato

jaguar ['dʒægwər] *s* giaguaro

jail [dʒel] *s* prigione *f;* **to break jail** evadere dal carcere ‖ *tr* carcerare

jail'bird' *s* galeotto, remo di galera

jail'break' *s* evasione *f* dal carcere

jailer ['dʒelər] *s* carceriere *m*

jalop·y [dʒə'lɑpi] *s* (**-ies**) carcassa, trespolo, trabiccolo

jam [dʒæm] *s* stretta, compressione; (*in traffic*) imbottigliamento; (*preserve*) marmellata, confettura; (*difficult situation*) (coll) pasticcio ‖ *v* (*pret & pp* **jammed;** *ger* **jamming**) *tr* stipare; (*e.g., one's finger*) schiacciare, schiacciarsi; (rad) disturbare; **to jam on the brakes** bloccare i freni ‖ *intr* schiacciarsi; (*said of firearms*) incepparsi; (mach) grippare

jamb [dʒæm] *s* stipite *m*

jamboree [,dʒæmbə'ri] *s* riunione nazionale di giovani esploratori; (coll) riunione

James [dʒemz] *s* Giacomo

jamming ['dʒæmɪŋ] *s* radiodisturbo

jam-packed ['dʒæm'pækt] *adj* gremito, pieno fino all'orlo

jangle ['dʒæŋgəl] *s* suono stridente; (*quarrel*) baruffa ‖ *tr* fare suoni stridenti con ‖ *intr* stridere; litigare

janitor ['dʒænɪtər] *s* portiere *m*

janitress ['dʒænɪtrɪs] *s* portinaia

January ['dʒænjʊ,ɛri] *s* gennaio

ja·pan [dʒə'pæn] *s* lacca giapponese; oggetto di lacca ‖ *v* (*pret & pp* **-panned;** *ger* **-panning**) *tr* laccare ‖ **Japan** *s* il Giappone

Japa·nese [,dʒæpə'niz] *adj* giapponese ‖ *s* (**-nese**) giapponese *mf*

Jap'anese bee'tle *s* scarabeo giapponese

Jap'anese lan'tern *s* lampioncino alla veneziana

Jap'anese persim'mon *s*-cachi *m*

jar [dʒɑr] *s* barattolo; (*earthenware container*) orcio, giara; discordanza; (*jolt*) scossa; (fig) brutta sorpresa; **on the jar** (*said of a door*) socchiuso ‖ *v* (*pret & pp* **jarred;** *ger* **jarring**) *tr* scuotere; far stridere ‖ *intr* vibrare; stridere; essere in conflitto; **to jar on** irritare

jardiniere [,dʒɑrdɪ'nɪr] *s* (*pot*) vaso da fiori; giardiniera

jargon ['dʒɑrgən] *s* gergo

jasmine ['dʒæsmɪn] *or* ['dʒæzmɪn] *s* gelsomino

jasper ['dʒæspər] *s* diaspro

jaundice ['dʒɔndɪs] *or* ['dʒɑndɪs] *s* itterizia; (fig) invidia

jaundiced ['dʒɔndɪst] *or* ['dʒɑndɪst] *adj* itterico; (fig) invidioso

jaunt [dʒɔnt] *or* [dʒɑnt] *s* passeggiata, gita

jaun·ty ['dʒɔnti] *or* ['dʒɑnti] *adj* (**-tier; -tiest**) disinvolto; elegante

Java·nese [,dʒævə'niz] *adj* giavanese ‖ *s* (**-nese**) giavanese *m*

javelin ['dʒævlɪn] *or* ['dʒævəlɪn] *s* giavellotto

jaw [dʒɔ] *s* mascella, mandibola; (mach) ganascia; **jaws** fauci *fpl*; gola, stretta ‖ *tr* (slang) rimproverare ‖

intr (slang) chiacchierare; (slang) fare la predica

jaw'bone' *s* mascella, mandibola

jaw'break'er *s* (coll) parola difficile da pronunciare; (coll) caramella durissima; (mach) frantoio a mascelle

jay [dʒe] *s* (orn) ghiandaia; (coll) semplicioto

jay'walk' *intr* attraversare la strada contro la luce rossa del semaforo

jay'walk'er *s* (coll) pedone distratto che attraversa la strada contro la luce rossa del semaforo

jazz [dʒæz] *s* jazz *m;* (slang) spirito ‖ *tr*—**to jazz up** (slang) dar vita a

jazz' band' *s* orchestra jazz

jealous ['dʒɛləs] *adj* geloso; (*envious*) invidioso; vigilante

jealous·y ['dʒɛləsi] *s* (**-ies**) gelosia; invidia; vigilanza

jean [dʒin] *s* tela cruda; **jeans** pantaloni *mpl* di tela cruda

jeep [dʒip] *s* gip *f,* jeep *f*

jeer [dʒɪr] *s* beffa ‖ *tr* beffare ‖ *intr* beffarsi; **to jeer at** motteggiare

Jeho'vah's Wit'nesses [dʒɪ'hovəs] *spl* Testimoni *mpl* di Geova

jell [dʒel] *s* gelatina ‖ *intr* (*to congeal*) gelatinizzarsi; (*to become substantial*) cristallizzarsi

jel·ly ['dʒeli] *s* (**-lies**) gelatina ‖ *v* (*pret & pp* **-lied**) *tr* gelatinizzare ‖ *intr* gelatinizzarsi

jel'ly·fish' *s* medusa; (*weak person*) (coll) fiaccone *m*

jeopardize ['dʒɛpər,daɪz] *tr* compromettere, mettere a repentaglio

jeopardy ['dʒɛpərdi] *s* pericolo, repentaglio

jeremiad [,dʒɛrɪ'maɪ·æd] *s* geremiade *f*

Jericho ['dʒɛrɪ,ko] *s* Gerico *f*

jerk [dʒʌrk] *s* strattone *m,* scatto; tic *m;* (*stupid person*) scempio, sciocco; **by jerks** a scatti ‖ *tr* tirare a strattoni; (*meat*) essiccare ‖ *intr* sobbalzare

jerked' beef' *s* fetta di carne di bue essicata

jerkin ['dʒʌrkɪn] *s* giubbetto

jerk'wa'ter *adj* di scarsa importanza

jerk·y ['dʒʌrki] *adj* (**-ier; -iest**) sussultante; (*style*) disuguale

Jerome [dʒə'rom] *s* Gerolamo

jersey ['dʒʌrzi] *s* jersey *m,* maglione *m*

Jerusalem [dʒɪ'rusələm] *s* Gerusalemme *f*

jest [dʒest] *s* scherzo, burla; **in jest** per celia ‖ *intr* scherzare

jester ['dʒestər] *s* motteggiatore *m,* burlone *m;* (hist) buffone *m*

Jesuit ['dʒɛʒu·ɪt] *or* ['dʒɛzju·ɪt] *adj & s* gesuita *m*

Jesuitic(al) [,dʒɛʒu'ɪtɪk(əl)] *or* [,dʒɛzju'ɪtɪk(əl)] *adj* gesuitico

Jesus ['dʒizəs] *s* Gesù *m*

Je'sus Christ' *s* Gesù *m* Cristo

jet [dʒet] *adj* di giaietto ‖ *s* (*of a fountain*) zampillo; (*stream shooting forth from nozzle*) getto; (*mineral; lustrous black*) giaietto; (aer) aereo a getto ‖ *v* (*pret & pp* **jetted;** *ger* **jetting**) *tr*

spruzzare || *intr* zampillare; volare in aereo a getto
jet' age' *s* era dell'aviogetto
jet'-black' *adj* nero come il carbone
jet' bomb'er *s* bombardiere *m* a reazione
jet' coal' *s* carbone *m* a lunga fiamma
jet' en'gine *s* motore *m* a reazione
jet' fight'er *s* caccia *m* a reazione
jet'lin'er *s* aviogetto da trasporto passeggeri
jet' plane' *s* aviogetto
jet' propul'sion *s* gettopropulsione
jetsam ['dʒɛtsəm] *s* relitto
jet' stream' *s* corrente *f* a getto; scappamento di motore a razzo
jettison ['dʒɛtɪsən] *s* (naut) alleggerimento || *tr* (naut) alleggerirsi di; (fig) disfarsi di
jet·ty ['dʒɛti] *s* (**-ties**) gettata; (*wharf*) molo, imbarcadero
Jew [dʒu] *s* giudeo
jewel ['dʒu·əl] *s* pietra preziosa; (*valuable personal ornament*) gioia, gioiello; (*of a watch*) rubino; (*costume jewelry*) gioia finta; (fig) valore *m*, gioiello
jew'el case' *s* scrigno, portagioie *m*
jeweler or **jeweller** ['dʒu·ələr] *s* gioielliere *m*, orefice *m*
jewelry ['dʒu·əlri] *s* gioielli *mpl*
jew'elry shop' *s* gioielleria
Jewess ['dʒu·ɪs] *s* giudea
Jewish ['dʒu·ɪʃ] *adj* giudeo
jews'-harp or **jew's-harp** ['dʒuz ˌhɑrp] *s* scacciapensieri *m*
jib [dʒɪb] *s* (*of a crane*) (mach) braccio (di gru); (naut) fiocco, vela Marconi
jib' boom' *s* asta di fiocco
jibe [dʒaɪb] *s* burla, beffa || *intr* beffarsi; accordarsi; **to jibe at** beffarsi di
jif·fy ['dʒɪfi] *s*—**in a jiffy** (coll) in men che non si dica
jig [dʒɪg] *s* (*dance*) giga; **the jig is up** (slang) tutto è perduto
jigger ['dʒɪgər] *s* bicchierino di liquore d'un'oncia e mezza; (*flea*) pulce *f* tropicale; (*gadget*) (coll) aggeggio; (naut) bozzello; (min) crivello
jiggle ['dʒɪgəl] *s* scossa || *tr* scuotere, agitare || *intr* scuotersi
jig' saw' *s* sega da traforo
jig'saw puz'zle *s* gioco di pazienza, rompicapo
jilt [dʒɪlt] *tr* piantare
jim·my ['dʒɪmi] *s* (**-mies**) piccolo piede di porco || *v* (*pret* & *pp* **-mied**) *tr* scassinare; **to jimmy open** scassinare
jingle ['dʒɪŋgəl] *s* sonaglio, bubbolo; (*sound*) rumore *m* di sonagliera; cantilena, rima infantile || *tr* far suonare || *intr* tintinnare
jin·go ['dʒɪŋgo] *adj* sciovinista || *s* (**-goes**) sciovinista *mf*; **by jingo!** perbacco!
jingoism ['dʒɪŋgo ˌɪzəm] *s* sciovinismo
jinx [dʒɪŋks] *s* iettatura; (*person*) iettatore *m* || *tr* portare la iettatura a
jitters ['dʒɪtərz] *spl* (coll) nervosismo; **to have the jitters** (coll) essere nervoso
jittery ['dʒɪtəri] *adj* nervoso
job [dʒab] *s* (*piece of work*) lavoro;

(*task*) mansione; (*employment*) posto, impiego; (slang) furto; **by the job** a cottimo; **on the job** (slang) attento, sollecito; **to be out of a job** essere disoccupato; **to lie down on the job** (slang) dormire sul lavoro
job' anal'ysis *s* valutazione delle mansioni
jobber ['dʒabər] *s* grossista *mf*; (*pieceworker*) lavoratore *m* a cottimo; funzionario disonesto
job'hold'er *s* impiegato; (*in the government*) burocrate *m*
jobless ['dʒablɪs] *adj* disoccupato
job' lot' *s* (com) saldo
job' print'er *s* piccolo tipografo non specializzato
job' print'ing *s* piccolo lavoro tipografico
jockey ['dʒaki] *s* fantino || *tr* (*a horse*) montare; manovrare; (*to trick*) abbindolare
jockstrap ['dʒak ˌstræp] *s* sospensorio
jocose [dʒo'kos] *adj* giocoso
jocular ['dʒakjələr] *adj* scherzoso
jog [dʒag] *s* spinta; piccolo trotto || *v* (*pret* & *pp* **jogged**) *ger* **jogging**) *tr* spingere leggermente; (*the memory*) rinfrescare || *intr* barcarellare; **to jog along** continuare col solito tran tran
jog' trot' *s* piccolo trotto; (fig) tran tran *m*
John [dʒan] *s* Giovanni *m*
John' Bull' *s* il tipico inglese; gli inglesi, il popolo inglese
John' Han'cock ['hænkak] *s* (coll) la firma
johnnycake ['dʒani ˌkek] *s* pane *m* di granturco
John'ny-come-late'ly *s* (coll) ultimo arrivato
John'ny-jump'-up' *s* violetta, viola del pensiero
John'ny-on-the-spot' *s* (coll) persona sempre pronta
John' the Bap'tist *s* San Giovanni Battista
join [dʒɔɪn] *tr* giungere, congiungere; associarsi a; unire; (*e.g., a party*) farsi membro di; (*the army*) arruolarsi in; (*battle*) ingaggiare; (*to empty into*) sfociare in || *intr* congiungersi, unirsi; (*said, e.g., of two rivers*) confluire
joiner ['dʒɔɪnər] *s* falegname *m*; membro di molte società
joint [dʒɔɪnt] *adj* congiunto || *s* (*in a pipe*) giuntura; (*of bones*) giuntura, articolazione; (*hinge of book*) brachetta; (*in woodwork*) incastro, commettitura; (*of meat*) taglio; (mach) snodo; (*gambling den*) (slang) bisca; (elec) innesto; (slang) bettola; **out of joint** slogato; (fig) fuori luogo; **to throw** (*e.g., one's arm*) **out of joint** slogarsi
joint' account' *s* conto in comune
joint' commit'tee *s* commissione mista
jointly ['dʒɔɪntli] *adv* unitamente
joint' own'er *s* condomino
joint'-stock' com'pany *s* società *f* per azioni a responsabilità illimitata
joist [dʒɔɪst] *s* trave *f*

joke [dʒok] *s* burla, barzelletta; (*trifling matter*) cosa da nulla; (*person laughed at*) zimbello; **to tell a joke** raccontare una barzelletta; **to play a joke on** fare uno scherzo a || *tr*—**to joke one's way into** ottenere dicendo barzellette || *intr* burlare, dire storielle; **joking aside** senza scherzi

joker [ˈdʒokər] *s* burlone *m*, fumista *m*; (*wise guy*) saputello; (*hidden provision*) clausola ingannatrice; (*cards*) matta

jol•ly [ˈdʒɑli] *adj* (**-lier; -liest**) allegro, gaio || *adv* (coll) molto || *v* (*pret & pp* **-lied**) *tr* (coll) prendersi gioco di

jolt [dʒolt] *s* scossa || *tr* scuotere || *intr* sobbalzare

Jonah [ˈdʒonə] *s* Giona; (fig) uccello di mal augurio

jongleur [ˈdʒɑŋglər] *s* giullare *m*

jonquil [ˈdʒɑŋkwɪl] *s* giunchiglia

Jordan [ˈdʒɔrdən] *s* (*country*) la Giordania; (*river*) Giordano

Jordanian [dʒɔrˈdenɪ·ən] *adj & s* giordano

josh [dʒɑʃ] *tr & intr* (coll) canzonare

jostle [ˈdʒɑsəl] *s* spintone *m* || *tr* spingere || *intr* scontrarsi; farsi strada a gomitate

jot [dʒɑt] *s*—**I don't care a jot for** non mi importa un fico di || *v* (*pret & pp* **jotted**) *ger* **jotting** *tr*—**to jot down** notare, gettar giù

jounce [dʒauns] *s* scossa || *tr* scuotere || *intr* sobbalzare

journal [ˈdʒʌrnəl] *s* (*newspaper*) giornale *m*; (*magazine*) rivista; (*daily record*) diario; (com) giornale *m*; (mach) perno; (naut) giornale *m* di bordo

journalese [ˌdʒʌrnəˈliz] *s* linguaggio giornalistico

journalism [ˈdʒʌrnəˌlɪzəm] *s* giornalismo

journalist [ˈdʒʌrnəlɪst] *s* giornalista *mf*

journey [ˈdʒʌrni] *s* viaggio || *intr* viaggiare

jour'ney•man *s* (**-men**) operaio specializzato

joust [dʒʌst] *or* [dʒust] *or* [dʒaust] *s* giostra || *intr* giostrare

jovial [ˈdʒovɪ·əl] *adj* gioviale

jowl [dʒaul] *s* (*cheek*) guancia; (*jawbone*) mascella; (*of cattle*) giogaia; (*of fowl*) bargiglio; (*of fat person*) pappagorgia

joy [dʒɔɪ] *s* gioia, allegria; **to leap with joy** ballare dalla gioia

joyful [ˈdʒɔɪfəl] *adj* gioioso, festoso; **joyful over** lieto di

joyless [ˈdʒɔɪlɪs] *adj* senza gioia

joyous [ˈdʒɔɪ·əs] *adj* gioioso

joy' ride' *s* (coll) gita in auto; (coll) gita all'impazzata in auto

jubilant [ˈdʒubɪlənt] *adj* esultante

jubilation [ˌdʒubɪˈleʃən] *s* giubilo

jubilee [ˈdʒubɪˌli] *s* (*jubilation*) giubilo; (eccl) giubileo

Judaism [ˈdʒude·ˌɪzəm] *s* giudaismo

judge [dʒʌdʒ] *s* giudice *m* || *tr & intr* giudicare; **judging by** a giudicare da

judge' ad'vocate *s* avvocato militare; avvocato della marina da guerra

judgeship [ˈdʒʌdʒˌʃɪp] *s* carica di giudice

judgment [ˈdʒʌdʒmənt] *s* giudizio; (*legal decision*) sentenza

judg'ment day' *s* giorno del giudizio

judg'ment seat' *s* banco dei giudici; tribunale *m*

judicature [ˈdʒudɪkətʃər] *s* carica di giudice

judicial [dʒuˈdɪʃəl] *adj* giudiziario; (*becoming a judge*) giudizioso

judiciar•y [dʒuˈdɪʃɪˌɛri] *adj* giudiziario || *s* (**-ies**) (*judges collectively*) magistratura; (*judicial branch*) potere giudiziario

judicious [dʒuˈdɪʃəs] *adj* giudizioso

jug [dʒʌg] *s* brocca, boccale *m*; (*narrow-necked vessel*) orcio; (*jail*) (slang) prigione

juggle [ˈdʒʌgəl] *s* gioco di prestigio || *tr* fare il giocoliere con; (*documents, facts*) alterare frodolentemente; **to juggle away** ghermire, trafugare || *intr* fare il giocoliere; fare l'imbroglione

juggler [ˈdʒʌglər] *s* giocoliere *m*, prestigiatore *m*; impostore *m*

juggling [ˈdʒʌglɪŋ] *s* giochi *mpl* di prestigio

Jugoslav [ˈjugoˈslav] *adj & s* iugoslavo, jugoslavo

Jugoslavia [ˈjugoˈslavɪ·ə] *s* la Iugoslavia, la Jugoslavia

jugular [ˈdʒʌgjələr] *or* [ˈdʒugjələr] *adj & s* giugulare *f*

juice [dʒus] *s* sugo; (*natural fluid of an animal body*) succo; (slang) elettricità *f*; (slang) benzina; **to stew in one's own juice** (coll) annegarsi nel proprio sugo

juic•y [ˈdʒusi] *adj* (**-ier; -iest**) sugoso, succoso; (*spicy*) piccante

jukebox [ˈdʒukˌbɑks] *s* grammofono a gettone, juke-box *m*

julep [ˈdʒulɪp] *s* bibita di menta col ghiaccio; (pharm) giulebbe *m*

julienne [ˌdʒulɪˈɛn] *s* giuliana

July [dʒuˈlaɪ] *s* luglio

jumble [ˈdʒʌmbəl] *s* intrico, garbuglio || *tr* ingarbugliare

jum•bo [ˈdʒʌmbo] *adj* (coll) enorme || *s* (**-bos**) (*person*) (coll) elefante *m*; (*thing*) (coll) oggetto enorme

jump [dʒʌmp] *s* salto; (*in a parachute*) lancio; (*of prices*) sbalzo; (*start*) soprassalto; **on the jump** in moto; **to get or to have the jump on** (coll) avere il vantaggio su || *tr* saltare; (*a horse*) far saltare; (*prices*) alzare; uscire da, e.g., **the train jumped the track** il treno uscì dalle rotaie; (*to attack*) (coll) balzare su; (checkers) suffiare || *intr* saltare; (*from surprise*) trasalire; (*said of prices*) salire; (*in a parachute*) lanciarsi; **to jump at** (e.g., *an offer*) afferrare; **to jump on** saltare su; (coll) sgridare, arrabbiarsi con; **to jump over** oltrepassare; (*a page*) saltare; **to jump to a conclusion** arrivare precipitosamente a una conclusione

jumper [ˈdʒʌmpər] *s* saltatore *m*; camiciotto; **jumpers** tuta da bambini

jump'ing jack' ['dʒʌmpɪŋ] *s* marionetta

jump'ing-off' place' *s* fine *f* del mondo; (fig) trampolino, punto di partenza

jump' seat' *s* strapuntino

jump' spark' *s* scintilla elettrica; (*of induction coil*) (elec) scintilla d'intraferro

jump' wire' *s* filo elettrico di contatto

jump·y ['dʒʌmpi] *adj* (**-ier; -iest**) nervoso, eccitato

junction ['dʒʌŋkt∫ən] *s* congiunzione; (*of two rivers*) confluenza; (carp) commettitura; (rr) raccordo ferroviario

juncture ['dʒʌŋkt∫ər] *s* giuntura; (*occasion*) congiuntura; (*moment*) momento

June [dʒun] *s* giugno

jungle ['dʒʌŋgəl] *s* giungla

junglegym ['dʒʌŋgəl‚dʒɪm] *s* (trademark) castello

junior ['dʒunjər] *adj* minore, di minore età; giovane; (*in American university*) del penultimo anno; figlio, e.g., **John H. Smith, Junior** Giovanni H. Smith, figlio ‖ *s* minore *m;* socio secondario; studente *m* del penultimo anno

jun'ior col'lege *s* scuola universitaria unicamente di primo biennio

jun'ior high' school' *s* scuola media; ginnasio

juniper ['dʒunɪpər] *s* ginepro

ju'niper ber'ry *s* coccola di ginepro

junk [dʒʌŋk] *s* roba vecchia, ferro vecchio; (*Chinese ship*) giunca; (naut) carne salata ‖ *tr* (slang) gettar via

junk' deal'er *s* robivecchi *m*

junket ['dʒʌŋkɪt] *s* budino di giuncata; (*outing*) viaggio di piacere; viaggio pagato a spese del tesoro ‖ *intr* far un viaggio di piacere; far un viaggio a spese del tesoro

junk'man' *s* (**-men'**) ferravecchio; rigattiere *m*

junk' room' *s* ripostiglio

junk' shop' *s* negozio di robivecchi

junk'yard' *s* cantiere *m* di ferravecchio

juridical [dʒu'rɪdɪkəl] *adj* giuridico

jurisdiction [‚dʒurɪs'dɪk∫ən] *s* giurisdizione

jurisprudence [‚dʒurɪs'prudəns] *s* giurisprudenza

jurist ['dʒurɪst] *s* giurista *mf*

juror ['dʒurər] *s* giurato

ju·ry ['dʒuri] *s* (**-ries**) giuria

ju'ry box' *s* banco della giuria

ju'ry·man *s* (**-men**) giurato

just [dʒʌst] *adj* giusto ‖ *adv* giustamente, giusto; appena; proprio; **just as** come, proprio come; **just beyond** un po' più in là (di); **just now** poco fa, or ora; **just out** appena uscito, appena pubblicato

justice ['dʒʌstɪs] *s* giustizia; (*judge*) giudice *m;* **to bring to justice** arrestare e condannare; **to do justice to** render giustizia a; apprezzare bastantemente

jus'tice of the peace' *s* giudice *m* conciliatore

justifiable ['dʒʌstɪ‚faɪ·əbəl] *adj* giustificabile

justi·fy ['dʒʌstɪ‚faɪ] *v* (*pret & pp* **-fied**) *tr* giustificare; (typ) giustificare

justly ['dʒʌstli] *adj* giustamente

jut [dʒʌt] *v* (*pret & pp* **jutted;** *ger* **jutting**) *intr*—**to jut out** strapiombare, sporgere

jute [dʒut] *s* iuta ‖ **Jute** *s* Iuto

juvenile ['dʒuvənɪl] *or* ['dʒuvə‚naɪl] *adj* giovanile; minorile ‖ *s* giovane *mf;* libro per la gioventù; (theat) amoroso

ju'venile court' *s* tribunale *m* per i minorenni

ju'venile delin'quency *s* delinquenza minorile

juvenilia [‚dʒuvə'nɪlɪ·ə] *spl* opere *fpl* giovanili; libri *mpl* per ragazzi

juxtapose [‚dʒʌkstə'poz] *tr* giustapporre

K

K, k [ke] *s* undicesima lettera dell'alfabeto inglese

kale [kel] *s* verza; (slang) cocuzza, soldi *mpl*

kaleidoscope [kə'laɪdə‚skop] *s* caleidoscopio

kangaroo [‚kæŋgə'ru] *s* canguro

katydid ['ketidɪd] *s* grossa cavalletta verde nordamericana

kedge [kedʒ] *s* (naut) ancorotto

keel [kil] *s* chiglia ‖ *intr*—**to keel over** (naut) abbattersi in carena, capovolgersi; (fig) svenire

keelson ['kelsən] *or* ['kɪlsən] *s* (naut) controchiglia

keen [kin] *adj* (*sharpened*) affilato; (*wind; wit*) tagliente, mordente; (*eyes*) penetrante; (*ears; mind*) acuto, fine; (*eager*) entusiasta; intenso, vivo; (slang) meraviglioso; **to be keen on** essere appassionato per

keep [kip] *s* mantenimento; (*of medieval castle*) torrione *m*, maschio; **for keeps** (coll) seriamente; (coll) per sempre; **to earn one's keep** guadagnarsi la vita ‖ *v* (*pret & pp* **kept** [kept]) *tr* mantenere; (*watch*) fare; (*one's word*) mantenere; (*to withhold*) trattenere; (*accounts*) tenere; (*servants, guests*) avere; (*a garden*) coltivare; (*a business*) esercitare; (*a holiday*) festeggiare; (*to support*) sostentare; (*a secret; one's seat*) serbare; (*to decide to purchase*) prendere **to keep away** tener lontano; **to keep back** trattenere; (*a secret*) mantenere; **to keep down** reprimere; (*expenses*) ridurre al minimo; **to keep s.o. from** + *ger* impedire a qlcu di + *inf;* **to keep off** tener chiuso; **to keep off** tenere a distanza; (*e.g., moisture*) non lasciar penetrare; **to keep s.o. informed about** s.th tenere qlcu al corrente di qlco; **to keep s.o. waiting** fare aspettare qlcu; **to keep up** mantenere, sostenere || *intr* **to keep** + *ger* continuare a + *inf;* **to keep away** tenersi lontano; **to keep from** + *ger* evitare di + *inf;* **to keep informed (about)** tenersi al corrente (di); **to keep in with** (coll) stare nelle buone grazie di; **to keep off** stare lontano (da); (*the grass*) non calpestare; **to keep on** + *ger* seguitare a + *inf;* **to keep out** star fuori, non entrare; **to keep out of** non entrare in; (*danger*) stare lontano da; non immischiarsi in; **to keep quiet** stare tranquillo; **to keep to** (*left or right*) tenere; **to keep to oneself** stare in disparte; **to keep up** continuare; **to keep up with** stare alla pari con; (*e.g., the news*) tenersi al corrente di

keeper [ˈkipər] *s* (*of a shop*) tenitore *m;* guardiano; (*of a game preserve*) guardacaccia *m;* (*of a magnet*) ancora

keeping [ˈkipɪŋ] *s* custodia; (*of a holiday*) celebrazione; **in keeping with** in armonia con; **in safe keeping** in luogo sicuro; **out of keeping with** in cattivo accordo con

keep'sake' *s* ricordo

keg [kɛg] *s* barilotto, botticella

ken [kɛn] *s* portata; **beyond the ken of** al di là dell'ambito di

kennel [ˈkɛnəl] *s* canile *m*

kep•i [ˈkɛpi] or [ˈkɛpɪ] *s* (-is) chepì *m*

kept' wo'man [kɛpt] *s* (wom'en) mantenuta

kerchief [ˈkʌrtʃɪf] *s* fisciù *m*

kernel [ˈkʌrnəl] *s* (*of a nut*) gheriglio; (*of wheat*) chicco; (fig) nucleo

kerosene [ˈkɛrəˌsin] or [ˌkɛrəˈsin] *s* cherosene *m*, petrolio da illuminazione

kerplunk [kərˈplʌŋk] *interj* patapum!

ketchup [ˈkɛtʃəp] *s* salsa piccante di pomodoro, ketchup *m*

kettle [ˈkɛtəl] *s* marmitta, paiolo; (*teakettle*) bricco, teiera

ket'tle-drum' *s* timpano

key [ki] *adj* a chiave; chiave || *s* chiave *f;* (*of piano, typewriter, etc.*) tasto; (*cotter pin*) chiavetta, coppiglia; (*reef*) isolotto; (*tone of voice*) tono; (fig, mus) chiave *f;* (bot) samara; (telg) tasto trasmettitore, manipolatore *m;* **off key** stonato || *tr* aggiustare; inchiavardare; **to key up** eccitare, portare al parossismo

key'board' *s* tastiera

key'hole' *s* toppa, buco della serratura; (*of a clock*) buco della chiave

key'note' *s* (mus) tono; (fig) principio informatore

key'note address' *s* discorso d'apertura

key'punch op'era'tor *s* perforatore *m*

key' ring' *s* portachiavi *m*

key'stone' *s* chiave *f* di volta

key' word' *s* parola chiave

kha•ki [ˈkɑki] or [ˈkæki] *adj* cachi || *s* (-kis) cachi *m*

khedive [kəˈdiv] *s* kedivè *m*

kibitz [ˈkɪbɪts] *intr* (coll) dare consigli non richiesti

kibitzer [ˈkɪbɪtsər] *s* (*at a card game*) (coll) consigliere *m* importuno; (coll) ficcanaso *mf*

kibosh [ˈkaɪbɑʃ] or [kɪˈbɑʃ] *s* (coll) sciocchezza; **to put the kibosh on** (coll) impossibilitare

kick [kɪk] *s* calcio, pedata; (*of a gun*) rinculo; (*complaint*) (slang) protesta; (*of liquor*) (slang) forza; **to get a kick out of** (slang) pigliar piacere da || *tr* prendere a calci; (*a ball*) calciare; (*one's feet*) battere; **to kick out** (coll) sbatter fuori a pedate; **to kick up a row** scatenare un putiferio || *intr* calciare; (*said of an animal*) scalciare, trarre; (*said of a firearm*) rinculare; (coll) lamentarsi; **to kick against the pricks** dar calci al vento; **to kick off** (football) dare il calcio d'inizio

kick'back' *s* (coll) contraccolpo; (coll) intrallazzo, bustarella

kick'off' *s* calcio d'inizio

kid [kɪd] *s* capretto; (coll) piccolo; **kids** guanti *mpl* or scarpe *fpl* di capretto || *v* (*pret* & *pp* **kidded;** *ger* **kidding**) *tr* (coll) prendere in giro; **to kid oneself** (coll) farsi illusioni || *intr* (coll) dirlo per scherzo

kidder [ˈkɪdər] *s* (coll) burlone *m*

kid' gloves' *spl* guanti *mpl* di capretto; **to handle with kid gloves** trattare con la massima cautela

kid'nap' *v* (*pret* & *pp* **-naped** or **-napped;** *ger* **-naping** or **-napping**) *tr* rapire, sequestrare

kidnaper or **kidnapper** [ˈkɪdˌnæpər] *s* rapitore *m* a scopo d'estorsione

kidnaping or **kidnapping** [ˈkɪdˌnæpɪŋ] *s* rapimento a scopo di estorsione

kidney [ˈkɪdni] *s* rene *m;* (culin) rognone *m;* (*temperament*) carattere *m;* (*kind*) tipo

kid'ney bean' *s* fagiolo

kid'ney stone' *s* calcolo renale

kill [kɪl] *s* uccisione; (*game killed*) cacciagione; (coll) fiumicello; **for the kill** per il colpo finale || *tr* uccidere; eliminare; (*a bill*) bocciare; (fig) opprimere

killer [ˈkɪlər] *s* uccisore *m*

kill'er whale' *s* orca

killing [ˈkɪlɪŋ] *adj* mortale; (*exhausting*) opprimente; (coll) molto divertente || *s* uccisione; (*game killed*) cacciagione; (coll) fortuna; **to make a killing** (coll) fare una fortuna da un giorno all'altro

kill'-joy' *s* guastafeste *mf*

kiln [kɪl] or [kɪln] *s* forno, fornace *f*

kil•o [ˈkɪlo] or [ˈkilo] *s* (-os) chilogrammo; chilometro

kilocycle [ˈkɪləˌsaɪkəl] *s* chilociclo

kilogram [ˈkɪləˌgræm] *s* chilogrammo

kilo•hertz [ˈkɪləˌhʌrts] *s* (-hertz) chilohertz

kilometer ['kɪlə‚mitər] or [kɪ'lɑmɪtər] s chilometro

kilowatt ['kɪlə‚wɑt] s kilowatt m, chilowatt m

kilowatt-hour ['kɪlə‚wɑt'aʊr] s (**kilowatt-hours**) chilowattora m

kilt [kɪlt] s gonnellino

kilter ['kɪltər] s—**to be out of kilter** (coll) essere fuori squadra

kimo·no [kɪ'monə] or [kɪ'mono] s (**-nos**) chimono

kin [kɪn] s (family relationship) parentela; (relatives) parenti mpl; **of kin** parente, affine; **the next of kin** il parente più prossimo, i parenti più prossimi

kind [kaɪnd] adj gentile; **kind to** buono con || s genere m, specie f; **a kind of** una specie di; **all kinds of** (coll) ogni sorta di; **in kind** in natura; **kind of** (coll) quasi, piuttosto; **of a kind** dello stesso stampo; (mediocre) di poco valore

kindergarten ['kɪndər‚gɑrtən] s scuola materna, giardino d'infanzia

kindergartner ['kɪndər‚gɑrtnər] s allievo della scuola d'infanzia; (teacher) maestra giardiniera

kind-hearted ['kaɪnd'hɑrtɪd] adj gentile, di buon cuore

kindle ['kɪndəl] tr accendere || intr accendersi

kindling ['kɪndlɪŋ] s accensione; legna minuta

kin'dling wood' s legna minuta per accendere il fuoco

kind·ly ['kaɪndli] adj (-lier; -liest) gentile; (climate) benigno; favorevole || adv gentilmente; cordialmente; per gentilezza; **to not take kindly to** non accettare di buon grado

kindness ['kaɪndnɪs] s gentilezza; **have the kindness to** abbia la bontà di

kindred ['kɪndrɪd] adj imparentato; affine || s parentela; affinità f

kinescope ['kɪnɪ‚skop] s (trademark) cinescopio

kinetic [kɪ'nɛtɪk] or [kaɪ'nɛtɪk] adj cinetico || **kinetics** s cinetica

kinet'ic en'ergy s forza viva, energia cinetica

king [kɪŋ] s re m; (checkers) dama; (cards, chess) re m

king'bolt' s perno

kingdom ['kɪŋdəm] s regno

king'fish'er s martin pescatore m

king·ly ['kɪŋli] adj (-lier; -liest) reale; (stately) maestoso || adv regalmente

king'pin' s birillo centrale; (aut) perno dello sterzo; (fig) figura principale

king' post' s (archit) ometto, monaco

king's' e'vil s scrofola

kingship ['kɪŋʃɪp] s regalità f

king'-size' adj extra-grande

king's' ran'som s ricchezza di Creso

kink [kɪŋk] s (in a rope) arricciatura; (in hair) crespatura; (soreness in neck) torcicollo; (flaw) ostacolo; (mental twist) ghiribizzo || tr attorcigliare || intr attorcigliarsi

kink·y ['kɪŋki] adj (-ier; -iest) attorcigliato; (hair) crespo

kinsfolk ['kɪnz‚fok] s parentado

kinship ['kɪnʃɪp] s parentela; affinità f

kins'man s (**-men**) parente m

kins'wom'an s (**-wom'en**) parente f

kipper ['kɪpər] s aringa affumicata || tr (herring or salmon) affumicare

kiss [kɪs] s bacio; (billiards) rimpallo leggerissimo; (confection) meringa || tr baciare; **to kiss away** (tears) asciugare con baci || intr baciare, baciarsi; (billiards) rimpallare leggermente

kit [kɪt] s (case) cassetta dei ferri; (tools) ferri mpl del mestiere; (set of supplies) corredo; (of small tools) astuccio; (of a traveler) borsa da viaggio; (pail) secchio; **the whole kit and caboodle** (coll) tutti quanti

kitchen ['kɪtʃən] s cucina

kitchenette [‚kɪtʃə'nɛt] s cucinetta

kitch'en gar'den s orto

kitch'en-maid' s sguattera

kitch'en police' s (mil) corvè f di cucina

kitch'en range' s cucina economica

kitch'en sink' s acquaio

kitch'en-ware' s utensili mpl di cucina

kite [kaɪt] s cervo volante, aquilone m; (orn) nibbio

kith' and kin' [kɪθ] spl amici mpl e parenti mpl

kitten ['kɪtən] s gattino

kittenish ['kɪtənɪʃ] adj giocattolone; civettuolo

kit·ty ['kɪti] s (-ties) gattino; (cards) piatto || interj micio!

kleptomaniac [‚klɛptə'menɪ‚æk] s cleptomane mf

knack [næk] s abilità f, destrezza

knapsack ['næp‚sæk] s zaino

knave [nev] s furfante m; (cards) fante m

knaver·y ['nevəri] s (-ies) furfanteria

knead [nid] tr maneggiare, intridere; (a muscle) massaggiare

knee [ni] s ginocchio; (of trousers) ginocchiera; (mach) gomito; **to bring s.o. to his knees** ridurre qlcu all'obbedienza; **to go down on one's knees (to)** gettarsi in ginocchio (davanti a)

knee' breech'es [‚brɪtʃɪz] spl calzoni mpl al ginocchio

knee'cap' s rotula, patella; (protective covering) ginocchiera

knee'-deep' adj fino al ginocchio

knee'-high' adj fino al ginocchio

knee' jerk' s riflesso patellare

kneel [nil] v (pret & pp **knelt** [nɛlt] or **kneeled**) intr inginocchiarsi

knee'pad' s ginocchiera

knee'pan' s rotula, patella

knell [nɛl] s rintocco funebre, campana a morto; **to toll the knell of** annunciare la morte di || intr suonare a morte

knickers ['nɪkərz] spl knickerbockers mpl, calzoni mpl alla zuava

knickknack ['nɪk‚næk] s soprammobile m; gingillo, ninnolo

knife [naɪf] s (knives [naɪvz]) coltello; (of a paper cutter) mannaia; (of a milling machine) fresa; **to go under the knife** essere sulla tavola operatoria || tr accoltellare; mettere il coltello nella schiena di

knife' sharp'ener s affilatoio

knife' switch' *s* (elec) coltella

knight [naɪt] *s* cavaliere *m*; (chess) cavallo ‖ *tr* armare cavaliere

knight-errant ['naɪt'ɛrənt] *s* (knights-errant) cavaliere *m* errante

knighthood ['naɪt·hʊd] *s* cavalleria

knightly ['naɪtli] *adj* cavalleresco

knit [nɪt] *v* (*pret & pp* knitted *or* knit; *ger* knitting) *tr* lavorare a maglia; (*to join*) unire; (*e.g., the brow*) corrugare ‖ *intr* lavorare a maglia; fare la calza; unirsi; (*said of a bone*) saldarsi

knitting ['nɪtɪŋ] *s* maglia, lavoro a maglia

knit'ting machine' *s* macchina per maglieria

knit'ting mill' *s* maglieria

knit'ting nee'dle *s* ferro da calza

knit'wear' *s* maglieria

knit'wear store' *s* maglieria

knob [nɑb] *s* (*lump*) bozza, protuberanza; (*of a door*) maniglia; (*on furniture*) pomolo; (*hill*) collinetta rotondeggiante; (rad, telv) manopola, pulsante *m*

knock [nɑk] *s* colpo; (*on a door*) tocco; (slang) attacco, critica ‖ *tr* battere; (*repeatedly*) sbatacchiare; (slang) attaccare, criticare; **to knock down** (*with a punch*) stendere a terra; (*a wall*) diroccare; (*to the highest bidder*) aggiudicare; (*e.g., a machine*) smontare; **to knock off** (*work*) (slang) sospendere; (slang) terminare; (slang) uccidere; **to knock out** mettere fuori combattimento ‖ *intr* battere; (aut) battere in testa; (slang) criticare; **to knock about** (slang) gironzolare; **to knock against** urtare contro; **to knock at** (*e.g., a door*) battere a, bussare a; **to knock off** (slang) cessare di lavorare

knock'down' *adj* (*blow*) knock down, che atterra; (*dismountable*) smontabile ‖ *s* (*blow*) colpo che atterra; (*discount*) sconto

knocker ['nɑkər] *s* (*on a door*) battaglio, bussatoio; (coll) criticone *m*

knock-kneed ['nɑk‚nid] *adj* con le gambe a X [iks]

knock'out' *s* pugno che mette fuori combattimento; fuori combattimento; (coll) pezzo di giovane

knock'out drops' *spl* (slang) narcotico

knoll [nol] *s* poggio, rialzo

knot [nɑt] *s* nodo; (*worn as an ornament*) fiocco; (*in wood*) nocchio; gruppo; protuberanza; (*tie*) nodo; (naut) nodo; **to tie the knot** (coll) sposarsi ‖ *v* (*pret & pp* knotted; *ger* knotting) *tr* annodare; (*the brow*) corrugare ‖ *intr* annodarsi

knot'hole' *s* buco lasciato da un nodo (nel legno)

knot·ty ['nɑti] *adj* (**-tier; -tiest**) nodoso; (fig) spinoso

know [no] *s*—**to be in the know** (coll) essere al corrente ‖ *v* (*pret* knew [nju] *or* [nu]; *pp* known) *tr & intr* (*by reasoning or learning*) sapere; (*by the senses or by perception; through acquaintance or recognition*) conoscere; **as far as I know** per quanto io ne sappia; **to know about** essere al corrente di; **to know best** essere il miglior giudice; **to know how to** + *inf* sapere + *inf*; **to know it all** (coll) sapere tutto; **to know what's what** (coll) saperla lunga; **you ought to know better** dovresti vergognarti

knowable ['no·əbəl] *adj* conoscibile

know'-how' *s* sapere *m*, abilità *f*

knowingly ['no·ɪŋli] *adv* con conoscenza di causa; (*on purpose*) apposta

know'-it-all' *adj & s* (coll) saputello

knowledge ['nɑlɪdʒ] *s* (*faculty*) scibile *m*, sapere *m*, sapienza; (*awareness, acquaintance, familiarity*) conoscenza; **to have a thorough knowledge of** conoscere a fondo; **to my knowledge** per quanto io ne sappia; **with full knowledge** con conoscenza di causa; **without my knowledge** a mia insaputa

knowledgeable ['nɑlɪdʒəbəl] *adj* intelligente, bene informato

knuckle ['nʌkəl] *s* nocca; foro del cardine, cardine *m*; **knuckles** pugno di ferro ‖ *intr*—**to knuckle down** (coll) lavorare di impegno; **to knuckle under** (coll) darsi per vinto

knurl [nʌrl] *s* granitura ‖ *tr* godranare, zigrinare

Koran [ko'rɑn] *or* [ko'ræn] *s* Corano

Korea [ko'ri·ə] *s* la Corea

Korean [ko'ri·ən] *adj & s* coreano

kosher ['koʃər] *adj* kasher, casher, puro secondo la legge giudaica; (coll) autentico

kowtow ['kaʊ'taʊ] *or* ['ko'taʊ] *intr* inchinarsi servilmente

Kremlin ['krɛmlɪn] *s* Cremlino

Kremlinology [‚krɛmlɪ'nɑlədʒi] *s* Cremlinologia

kudos ['kjudɑs] *or* ['kudɑs] *s* (coll) gloria, fama, approvazione

L

L, l [ɛl] *s* dodicesima lettera dell'alfabeto inglese

la·bel ['lebəl] *s* marca, etichetta; (*descriptive word*) qualifica ‖ *v* (*pret & pp* -beled *or* -belled; *ger* -beling *or* -belling) *tr* etichettare; qualificare

labial ['lebɪ·əl] *adj & s* labiale *f*

labor ['lebər] *adj* operaio ‖ *s* lavoro; (*toil*) fatica; (*childbirth*) parto; (*body of wage earners*) manodopera; (*class as contrasted with management*) prestatori *mpl* d'opera, lavoro; **labors** fatiche *fpl*; **to be in labor** avere le doglie ‖ *intr* lavorare; (*to exert one-*

laboratory   179   landing field

self) travagliare; (*said of a ship*)
rollare e beccheggiare; **to labor for**
lottare per; **to labor under** soffrire di
labora·to·ry [ˈlæbərəˌtori] *s* (**-ries**)
laboratorio
la'bor dispute' *s* vertenza sindacale
labored [ˈlebərd] *adj* elaborato, artificiale; penoso, difficile
laborer [ˈlebərər] *s* lavoratore *m*; (*unskilled worker*) bracciante *m*, manovale *m*, uomo di fatica
laborious [ləˈborɪ·əs] *adj* laborioso
la'bor un'ion *s* sindacato
Labourite [ˈlebəˌraɪt] *s* laburista *mf*
labyrinth [ˈlæbɪrɪnθ] *s* labirinto
lace [les] *s* (*cord or string*) stringa;
(*netlike ornament*) trina, merletto;
(*braid*) gallone *m* ‖ *tr* stringare; mer-
lettare; (coll) fustigare
lace'work' *s* trina, merletto, pizzo
lachrymose [ˈlækrɪˌmos] *adj* lacrimoso
lacing [ˈlesɪŋ] *s* stringa, cordone *m*;
gallone *m*; (coll) battuta, frustata
lack [læk] *s* mancanza, scarsezza, difetto ‖ *tr* mancare di, scarseggiare di
‖ *intr* mancare, scarseggiare, difettare
lackadaisical [ˌlækəˈdezɪkəl] *adj* letargico, indifferente
lackey [ˈlæki] *s* lacchè *m*
lacking [ˈlækɪŋ] *prep* privo di
lack'lus'ter *adj* smorto, spento
laconic [ləˈkɑnɪk] *adj* laconico
lacquer [ˈlækər] *s* lacca ‖ *tr* laccare
lac'quer spray' *s* lacca spray
lac'quer ware' *s* oggetti *mpl* laccati
lacu·na [leˈkjunə] *s* (**-nas** or **-nae** [ni])
lacuna
lac·y [ˈlesi] *adj* (**-ier; -iest**) simile al
merletto
lad [læd] *s* ragazzo, fanciullo
ladder [ˈlædər] *s* scala; (*stepladder
hinged on top*) scaleo; (*stepping
stone*) (fig) scalino
lad'der truck' *s* autocarro di pompieri
munito di scale
la'dies' man' *s* beato fra le donne
la'dies' room' *s* gabinetto per signore
ladle [ˈledəl] *s* ramaiolo, mestolo; (*of
tinsmith*) cucchiaio ‖ *tr* scodellare
la·dy [ˈledi] *s* (**-dies**) signora, dama
la'dy·bug' *s* coccinella
la'dy·fin'ger *s* savoiardo, lingua di
gatto
la'dy-in-wait'ing *s* (**ladies-in-waiting**)
dama di corte
la'dy-kil'ler *s* rubacuori *m*
la'dy·like' *adj* signorile; **to be ladylike**
comportarsi come una signora
la'dy·love' *s* amata
la'dy of the house' *s* padrona di casa
ladyship [ˈlediˌʃɪp] *s* signoria
la'dy's maid' *s* cameriera personale
della signora
lag [læg] *s* ritardo ‖ *v* (*pret & pp*
lagged; *ger* **lagging**) *tr* ritardare;
to lag behind rimanere indietro
la'ger beer' [ˈlɑgər] *s* birra invecchiata
laggard [ˈlægərd] *s* tardo, pigro
lagoon [ləˈgun] *s* laguna
laid' pa'per [led] *s* carta vergata
laid' up' *adj* messo da parte; (naut) disarmato; (coll) costretto a letto

lair [ler] *s* tana, covo
laity [ˈle·ɪti] *s* laicato
lake [lek] *adj* lacustre ‖ *s* lago
lamb [læm] *s* agnello
lambaste [læmˈbest] *tr* (*to thrash*) sferzare; (*to reprimand*) riprovare
lamb' chop' *s* cotoletta d'agnello
lambkin [ˈlæmkɪn] *s* agnellino; (fig)
innocente *mf*
lamb'skin' *s* (*leather*) pelle *f* d'agnello;
(*skin with its wool*) agnello
lame [lem] *adj* zoppo; difettoso; (*disabled*) invalido; (*excuse*) debole ‖ *tr*
azzoppare
lament [ləˈment] *s* lamento; lamento
funebre ‖ *tr* lamentare ‖ *intr* lamentarsi
lamentable [ˈlæməntəbəl] or [ləˈment-
əbəl] *adj* lamentevole
lamentation [ˌlæmənˈte/ən] *s* lamenta-
zione
laminate [ˈlæmɪˌnet] *tr* laminare
lamp [læmp] *s* lampada
lamp'black' *s* nerofumo
lamp' chim'ney *s* tubo di vetro di lampada a petrolio
lamp'light' *s* luce *f* di lampada
lamp'light'er *s* lampionaio
lampoon [læmˈpun] *s* satira ‖ *tr* satireggiare
lamp'post' *s* colonna del lampione
lamp'shade' *s* paralume *m*, ventola
lamp'wick' *s* lucignolo
lance [læns] or [lɑns] *s* lancia; (surg)
lancetta ‖ *tr* (*with an oxygen lance*)
tagliare col cannello ossidrico; (surg)
sbrigliare, incidere col bisturi
lance' rest' *s* resta
lancet [ˈlænsɪt] or [ˈlɑnsɪt] *s* (surg)
lancetta
land [lænd] *adj* terrestre; (*wind*) di
terra ‖ *s* terra; **on land, on sea, and
in the air** per mare, per terra e nel
cielo; **to make land** toccare terra; **to
see how the land lies** tastare terreno
‖ *tr* sbarcare; (aer) fare atterrare;
(coll) pigliare ‖ *intr* sbarcare; (*to
come to rest*) andare a finire; (naut)
toccar terra; (aer) atterrare; **to land
on one's feet** cadere in piedi; **to land
on one's head** andare a gambe
all'aria; **to land on the moon** allunare; **to land on the water** ammarare
land' breeze' *s* vento di terra
landed [ˈlændɪd] *adj* (*owning land*)
terriero; (*real estate*) immobile
land'fall' *s* (*sighting land*) avvistamento; terra avvistata; (*landslide*)
frana
land' grant' *s* terreno ricevuto in dono
dallo stato
land'hold'er *s* proprietario terriero
landing [ˈlændɪŋ] *s* (*of passengers*)
sbarco; (*place where passengers and
goods are landed*) imbarcadero; (*of
stairway*) pianerottolo; (aer, naut)
atterraggio
land'ing bea'con *s* radiofaro d'atterraggio
land'ing card' *s* cartoncino di sbarco.
land'ing craft' *s* imbarcazione da
sbarco
land'ing field' *s* campo d'atterraggio

land'ing flap' *s* (aer) ipostostentatore *m*

land'ing gear' *s* (aer) carrello d'atterraggio

land'ing strip' *s* (aer) pista d'atterraggio

land'la'dy *s* (-dies) (*of an apartment*) padrona di casa; (*of a lodging house*) affittacamere *f;* (*of an inn*) ostessa

landlocked ['lænd ˌlɑkt] *adj* circondato da terra

land'lord' *s* (*of an apartment*) padrone *m* di casa; (*of a lodging house*) affittacamere *m;* (*of an inn*) oste *m*

land·lubber ['lænd ˌlʌbər] *s* marinaio d'acqua dolce

land'mark' *s* (*boundary stone*) pietra di confine; (*distinguishing landscape feature*) punto di riferimento; (fig) pietra miliare

land' of'fice *s* ufficio del catasto

land'-office busi'ness *s* (coll) sacco d'affari

land'own'er *s* proprietario terriero

landscape ['lænd ˌskep] *s* paesaggio || *tr* abbellire

land'scape gar'dener *s* giardiniere *m* ornamentale

land'scape paint'er *s* paesista *mf*

landscapist ['lænd ˌskepɪst] *s* paesista *mf*

land'slide' *s* frana; (fig) vittoria strepitosa

landward ['lændwərd] *adv* verso terra, verso la costa

land' wind' *s* vento di terra

lane [len] *s* (*narrow street*) vicolo, viuzza; (*of a highway*) corsia; (naut) rotta; (aer) corridoio

langsyne [ˌlæŋ'saɪn] *s* (Scotch) tempo passato || *adv* (Scotch) molto tempo fa

language ['læŋgwɪdʒ] *s* lingua; (*style of language*) linguaggio; (*of a special group of people*) gergo

lan'guage lab'oratory *s* laboratorio linguistico

languid ['læŋgwɪd] *adj* languido

languish ['læŋgwɪʃ] *intr* languire; affettare languore

languor ['læŋgər] *s* languore *m*

languorous ['læŋgərəs] *adj* languido; (*causing languor*) snervante

lank [læŋk] *adj* scarnito, sparuto

lank·y ['læŋki] *adj* (-ier; -iest) scarnito, sparuto

lantern ['læntərn] *s* lanterna

lan'tern slide' *s* diapositiva

lanyard ['lænjərd] *s* (naut) drizza; (mil) aghetto, cordellina

lap [læp] *s* (*of human body or clothing*) grembo; (*with the tongue*) leccata; (*of the waves*) sciacquio; (sports) giro, tappa; **in the lap of** in mezzo a, e.g., **in the lap of luxury** in mezzo alle delicatezze || *v* (*pret & pp* **lapped;** *ger* **lapping**) *tr* lappare; (*said, e.g., of waves*) lambire; (*to fold*) piegare; (*to overlap*) sovrapporre; **to lap up** lappare; (coll) accettare con entusiasmo || *intr* sovrapporsi; **to lap against** (*said of the waves*) lambire; **to lap over** traboccare

lap'board' *s* tavolino da lavoro da tenersi sulle ginocchia

lap' dissolve' *s* (mov) dissolvenza incrociata

lap' dog' *s* cagnolino da salotto

lapel [lə'pɛl] *s* risvolto

Lap'land' *s* la Lapponia

Laplander ['læp ˌlændər] *s* lappone *mf*

Lapp [læp] *s* lappone *mf;* (*language*) lappone *m*

lap' robe' *s* coperta da viaggio

lapse [læps] *s* (*interval*) spazio di tempo; (*fall, decline*) caduta; (*of memory*) perdita; errore *m;* (ins) risoluzione; (law) decadenza || *intr* cadere, ricadere; cadere in disuso; (*said of time*) passare; (ins) risolversi; (law) decadere

lap'wing' *s* pavoncella

larce·ny ['lɑrsəni] *s* (-nies) furto

larch [lɑrtʃ] *s* larice *m*

lard [lɑrd] *s* strutto || *tr* lardellare

larder ['lɑrdər] *s* dispensa

large [lɑrdʒ] *adj* grande, grosso || *s*— **at large** in libertà

large' intes'tine *s* intestino crasso

largely ['lɑrdʒli] *adv* in gran parte

large'-scale' *adj* su larga scala

lariat ['lærɪət] *s* lazo, laccio

lark [lɑrk] *s* allodola; (coll) burla; **to go on a lark** (coll) far festa

lark'spur' *s* (*rocket larkspur*) sprone *m* di cavaliere; (*field larkspur*) consolida reale

lar·va ['lɑrvə] *s* (-vae [vi]) larva

laryngitis [ˌlærɪn'dʒaɪtɪs] *s* laringite *f*

laryngoscope [lə'rɪŋgə ˌskop] *s* laringoscopio

larynx ['lærɪŋks] *s* (**larynxes** or **larynges** [lə'rɪndʒiz]) laringe *f*

lascivious [lə'sɪvɪ·əs] *adj* lascivo

lasciviousness [lə'sɪvɪ·əsnɪs] *s* lascivia

laser ['lesər] *s* (acronym) (**light amplification by stimulated emission of radiation**) laser *m*

lash [læʃ] *s* (*cord on end of whip*) sverzino; (*blow with whip; scolding*) staffilata; (*of animal's tail*) colpo; (*eyelash*) ciglio; (fig) assalto || *tr* (*to whip*) frustare; (*to bind*) legare; (*to shake*) agitare; (*to attack with words*) staffilare || *intr* lanciarsi; **to lash out at** attaccare violentemente

lashing ['læʃɪŋ] *s* legatura; (*severe scolding*) staffilata; (*fastening with a rope*) (naut) rizza

lass [læs] *s* ragazza, giovane, *f;* innamorata

las·so ['læso] or [læ'su] *s* (-sos or -soes) lasso, lazo || *tr* pigliare col lasso

last [læst] or [lɑst] *adj* ultimo, passato; (*most recent*) scorso; **before last** ieraltro, e.g., **the night before last** ieraltro notte; **every last one** tutti senza eccezione; **last but one** penultimo || *s* ultima persona; ultima cosa; fine *f;* (*for holding shoes*) forma; **at last** alla fine; **at long last!** finalmente!; **stick to your last!** fa' il mestiere tuo!; **the last of the month** alla fine del mese; **to breathe one's last** dare l'ultimo sospiro; **to see the last of s.o.** vedere qlcu per l'ultima volta; **to the last** fino alla fine ‖ *adv* ultimo, per ultimo, alla fine ‖ *intr* durare, continuare

lasting ['læstɪŋ] or ['lɑstɪŋ] *adj* duraturo, durevole

lastly ['læstli] or ['lɑstli] *adv* finalmente, in conclusione

last'-min'ute news' *s* notizie *fpl* dell'ultima ora

last' name' *s* cognome *m*

last' night' *adv* ieri sera; la notte scorsa

last' quar'ter *s* ultimo quarto

last' sleep' *s* ultimo sonno

last' straw' *s* ultima, colmo

Last' Sup'per *s* Ultima Cena

last will' and tes'tament *s* ultime volontà *fpl*

last' word' *s* ultima parola; (*latest style*) ultima novità, ultimo grido

latch [lætʃ] *s* saliscendi *m*; (*wooden*) nottola ‖ *tr* chiudere col saliscendi

latch'key' *s* chiave *f* per saliscendi

latch'string' *s*—**the latchstring is out** faccia come fosse a casa Sua

late [let] *adj* (*happening after the usual time*) tardo; (*person*) in ritardo; (*hour of the night*) avanzato; (*news*) dell'ultima ora, recente; (*incumbent of an office*) predecessore, ex, passato; (*coming toward the end of a period*) tardivo; (*deceased*) defunto, fu; **in the late 30's, 40's, etc.** verso la fine del decennio che va dal 1930, 1940, etc. al 1940, 1950, etc.; **of late** recentemente; **to be late in** + *ger* essere in ritardo a + *inf*; **to grow late** farsi tardi; **to keep late hours** fare le ore piccole ‖ *adv* tardi; in ritardo; **late in** (*the week, the month, etc.*) alla fine di; **late in life** a un'età avanzata

latecomer ['let ,kʌmər] *s* ritardatario

lateen' sail' [læ'tin] *s* vela latina

lately ['letli] *adv* recentemente

latent ['letənt] *adj* latente

later ['letər] *adj comp* più tardi; (*event*) susseguente; **later than** posteriore a ‖ *adv comp* più tardi; **later on** più tardi; **see you later** (coll) arrivederci, a ben presto

lateral ['lætərəl] *adj* laterale

lath [læθ] or [lɑθ] *s* listello, striscia di legno ‖ *tr* mettere listelli su

lathe [leð] *s* tornio

lather ['læðər] *s* schiuma di sapone; schiuma ‖ *tr* insaponare; (coll) bastonare ‖ *intr* schiumare

lathery ['læðəri] *adj* schiumoso

lathing ['læθɪŋ] or ['lɑθɪŋ] *s* costruzione con listelli

Latin ['lætɪn] or ['lætən] *adj & s* latino

Lat'in Amer'ica *s* l'America latina

Lat'in-Amer'ican *adj* dell'America latina

Lat'in Amer'ican *s* abitante *mf* dell'America latina

latitude ['lætɪ ,tjud] or ['lætɪ ,tud] *s* latitudine *f*

latrine [lə'trin] *s* latrina militare

latter ['lætər] *adj* (*more recent*) posteriore; (*of two*) secondo; **the latter** questo; **the latter part of** la fine di

lattice ['lætɪs] *s* graticcio ‖ *tr* munire di graticcio, graticciare

lat'tice gird'er *s* trave *f* a traliccio

lat'tice-work' *s* graticcio, traliccio

Latvia ['lætvɪ·ə] *s* la Lettonia

laud [lɔd] *tr* lodare

laudable ['lɔdəbəl] *adj* lodevole

laudanum ['lɔdənəm] or ['lɔdnəm] *s* laudano

laudatory ['lɔdə ,tori] *adj* lodativo

laugh [læf] or [lɑf] *s* riso ‖ *tr*—**to laugh away** dissipare ridendo; **to laugh off** prendere sotto gamba, non dare importanza a ‖ *intr* ridere, ridersi; **to laugh at** ridersi di; **to laugh up one's sleeve** ridere sotto i baffi

laughable ['læfəbəl] or ['lɑfəbəl] *adj* risibile

laughing ['læfɪŋ] or ['lɑfɪŋ] *adj* che ride; **to be no laughing matter** non esserci niente da ridere ‖ *s* riso

laugh'ing gas' *s* gas *m* esilarante

laugh'ing-stock' *s* ludibrio, zimbello

laughter ['læftər] or ['lɑftər] *s* riso

launch [lɔntʃ] or [lɑntʃ] *s* (*of a ship*) varo; (*of a rocket*) lancio; (naut) lancia, scialuppa ‖ *tr* (*to throw; to send forth*) lanciare; (naut) varare ‖ *intr* lanciarsi

launching ['lɔntʃɪŋ] or ['lɑntʃɪŋ] *s* lancio; (*of a ship*) varo

launch'ing pad' *s* piattaforma di lancio

launder ['lɔndər] or ['lɑndər] *tr* lavare e stirare ‖ *intr* riuscire dopo il lavaggio

launderer ['lɔndərər] or ['lɑndə.ər] *s* lavandaio stiratore *m*

laundress ['lɔndrɪs] or ['lɑndrɪs] *s* lavandaia stiratrice *f*

laundromat ['lɔndrə ,mæt] or ['lɑndrə ,mæt] *s* (trademark) lavanderia a gettone

laun-dry ['lɔndri] or ['lɑndri] *s* (**-dries**) lavanderia; (*clothing*) bucato

laun'dry-man' *s* (**-men'**) lavandaio

laun'dry-wom'an *s* (**-wom'en**) lavandaia

laureate ['lɔrɪ·ɪt] *adj* laureato ‖ *s* laureato; poeta laureato

lau-rel ['lɔrəl] or ['lɑrəl] *s* lauro, alloro; **laurels** (fig) alloro; **to rest** or **sleep on one's laurels** dormire sugli allori ‖ *v* (*pret & pp* **-reled** or **-relled**) *ger* **-reling** or **-relling**) *tr* laureare

lava ['lɑvə] or ['lævə] *s* lava

lavato-ry ['lævə ,tori] *s* (**-ries**) (*room*) gabinetto da bagno; (*bowl*) lavabo; (*toilet*) gabinetto di decenza, cesso

lavender ['lævəndər] *s* lavanda

lavish ['lævɪʃ] *adj* prodigo ‖ *tr* prodigare, profondere

law [lɔ] *s* (*of man, of nature, of science*) legge *f*; (*study, profession of law*) diritto; **to enter the law** farsi avvocato; **to go to law** ricorrere alla legge; **to lay down the law** dettar legge; **to maintain law and order** mantenere la pace interna; **to practice law** fare l'avvocato

law-abiding ['lɔ·ə ,baɪdɪŋ] *adj* osservante della legge

law'break'er *s* violatore *m* della legge

law' court' s tribunale m di giustizia
lawful ['lɔfəl] adj legale, legittimo
lawless ['lɔlɪs] adj illegale; (unbridled) sfrenato
law'mak'er s legislatore m
lawn [lɔn] s tappeto erboso; (fabric) batista
lawn' mow'er s tosatrice f
law' of'fice s ufficio d'avvocato
law' of na'tions s diritto delle genti
law' of the jun'gle s legge f della giungla
law' stu'dent s studente m di legge
law'suit' s causa, lite f, processo
lawyer ['lɔjər] s avvocato, legale m
lax [læks] adj (in morals) lasso, rilassato; (rope) lento; (negligent) trascurato; vago, indeterminato
laxative ['læksətɪv] adj purgativo || s purga, purgante m
lay [le] adj (not belonging to the clergy) laico; (not having special training) non dotto, profano || s configurazione, disposizione || v (pret & pp laid [led]) tr mettere, collocare; (snares) tendere; (one's eyes; a stone) porre; (blame) dare, gettare; (a bet) fare; (for consideration) presentare; (the table) imbandire; (said of a hen) deporre; (plans) impostare; (to locate) disporre; **to be laid in** (said of a scene) aver luogo in; **to lay aside** mettere da parte; **to lay down** dichiarare; (one's life) dare; (one's arms) deporre; **to lay low** abbattere; uccidere; **to lay off** (workers) licenziare; (to measure) marcare; (slang) lasciare in pace; **to lay open** rivelare; (to a danger) esporre; **to lay out** estendere; preparare, disporre; (a corpse) comporre; (money) (coll) sborsare; **to lay over** posporre; **to lay up** mettere da parte; obbligare a letto; (naut) disarmare || intr (said of a hen) fare le uova; **to lay about** dar botte da orbi; **to lay for** (slang) attendere al varco; **to lay off** (coll) cessare di lavorare; **to lay over** trattenersi, fermarsi; **to lay to** (naut) navigare alla cappa
lay' broth'er s frate m secolare; converso
lay' day' s (com) stallia
layer ['le·ər] s (of paint) mano f; (of bricks) testa; (e.g., of rocks) strato, falda; (anat) pannicolo; (hort) propaggine f || tr (hort) propagginare
layette [le'ɛt] s corredino
lay' fig'ure s manichino
laying ['le·ɪŋ] s posa; (of eggs) deporre m; (of a wire) tendere m
lay'man s (-men) (member of the laity) laico, secolare m; (not a member of a special profession) laico, profano
lay'off' s (dismissal of workers) licenziamento; (period of unemployment) disoccupazione
lay' of the land' s andamento generale
lay'out' s piano; (sketch) tracciato; (of tools) armamentario; (coll) residenza; (typ) menabò m; (coll) banchetto, festino

lay'o'ver s fermata in un viaggio
lay' sis'ter s suora al secolo; conversa
laziness ['lezɪnɪs] s pigrizia
la·zy ['lezi] adj (-zier; -ziest) pigro
la'zy·bones' s (coll) poltrone m
lea [li] s (fallow land) maggese m; (meadow) prato
lead [lɛd] adj plumbeo || s piombo; (of lead pencil) mina; (for sounding depth) (naut) scandaglio; (typ) interlinea || [lɛd] v (pret & pp leaded; ger leading) tr impiombare; (typ) interlineare || [lid] s (foremost place) primato; (guidance) guida, direzione; (leash) guinzaglio; (journ) testata; (cards) mano f, prima mano; (elec) conduttore m; (mach) passo; (min) filone m; (rad, telv) filo d'entrata; (theat) ruolo principale; (theat) primo attore; (theat) prima attrice; **to take the lead** prendere il comando || [lid] v (pret & pp led [lɛd]) tr condurre, portare; (to command) comandare, essere alla testa di; (an orchestra) dirigere; (a good or bad life) fare; (s.o. into vice) trascinare; (cards) cominciare a giocare; (elec, mach) anticipare; **to lead astray** forviare || intr essere in testa, guidare; prendere l'offensiva; (said of a road) condurre; (cards) cominciare a giocare; **to lead to** risultare in; **to lead up** to andare a condurre a
leaden ['lɛdən] adj (of lead; like lead) plumbeo; (sluggish) tardo; (with sleep) carico; triste
leader ['lidər] s capo, comandante m; (ringleader) capobanda m; (of an orchestra) direttore m; (among animals) guidaiolo; (in a dance) ballerino guidaiolo; (sports) capintesta m; (journ) articolo di fondo
lead'er dog' s cane m guida di ciechi
leadership ['lidər,ʃɪp] s comando, direzione; doti fpl di comando
leading ['lidɪŋ] adj principale; primo; dirigente, preeminente
lead'ing ar'ticle s articolo di fondo
lead'ing edge' s (aer) bordo d'attacco
lead'ing la'dy s prima attrice
lead'ing man' s (men') primo attore
lead'ing ques'tion s domanda suggestiva, domanda orientatrice
lead'ing strings' spl dande fpl
lead'-in wire' ['lid,ɪn] s filo d'antenna
lead' pen'cil [lɛd] s lapis m, matita
leaf [lif] s (leaves [livz]) (of plant) foglia; (of vine) pampino; (of paper) foglio; (of double door) battente m; (of table) asse m a ribalta; **to turn over a new leaf** ricominciare una nuova || intr fogliare; **to leaf through** sfogliare
leafless ['liflɪs] adj senza foglie
leaflet ['liflɪt] s manifestino, volantino; (of plant) foglietta
leaf' spring' s molla a balestra
leaf'stalk' s picciolo
leaf·y ['lifi] adj (-ier; -iest) foglioso, frondoso
league [lig] s lega || tr associare || intr associarsi

League' of Na'tions s Società f delle Nazioni

leak [lik] s (*in a roof*) stillicidio; (*in a ship*) falla; (*of water, gas, steam*) fuga; (*of electricity*) dispersione; buco, fessura; (*of news*) filtrazione; **to spring a leak** avere una perdita; (naut) cominciare a far acqua || *tr* (*gas, liquids*) perdere, lasciar scappare; (*news*) lasciar trapelare || *intr* (*said of water, gas etc.,*) perdere, scappare; (*said of a barrel*) spillare; (naut) fare acqua; **to leak away** (*said of money*) andarsene; **to leak out** (*said of news*) trapelare

leakage ['likɪdʒ] s perdita, fuoruscita, fuga; (elec) dispersione; (com) colaggio

leak·y ['liki] adj (-ier) (-iest) che perde; (naut) che fa acqua; (coll) indiscreto

lean [lin] adj magro, secco; (*gasoline mixture*) povero || v (*pret & pp* **leaned** or **leant** [lɛnt]) *tr* inclinare; appoggiare || *intr* pendere, inclinarsi; (fig) inclinare, tendere; **to lean against** appoggiarsi a, addossarsi a; **to lean back** sdraiarsi; **to lean on** appoggiarsi su; **to lean out** (of) sporgersi (da); **to lean over backwards** fare di tutto; **to lean toward** (fig) tendere a, avere un'inclinazione per

leaning ['linɪŋ] adj inclinato, pendente || s inclinazione

lean'ing tow'er s torre f pendente

lean'-to' s (-tos) tetto a una falda

leap [lip] s salto, balzo; **by leaps and bounds** a passi da gigante; **leap in the dark** salto nel vuoto || v (*pret & pp* **leaped** or **leapt** [lɛpt]) *tr* saltare || *intr* saltare; (*said of one's heart*) balzare

leap'frog' s cavallina; **to play leapfrog** giocare alla cavallina

leap' year' s anno bisestile

learn [lʌrn] s (*pret & pp* **learned** or **learnt** [lʌrnt]) *tr* imparare; imparare a memoria; (*news*) apprendere || *intr* istruirsi, apprendere

learned ['lʌrnɪd] adj dotto; (*word*) colto

learn'ed jour'nal s rivista scientifica

learn'ed soci'ety s associazione di eruditi

learn'ed word' s parola dotta

learn'ed world' s mondo di dotti

learner ['lʌrnər] s apprendista mf; studente m; (*beginner*) principiante mf

learning ['lʌrnɪŋ] s istruzione; (*scholarship*) erudizione

lease [lis] s locazione, contratto d'affitto; **a new lease on life** nuove prospettive di felicità; vita nuova (dopo una malattia) || *tr* locare; prendere in affitto || *intr* affittare

lease'hold' adj affittato || s beni mpl sotto locazione

leash [liʃ] s guinzaglio; **to strain at the leash** mordere il freno || *tr* frenare, controllare

least [list] adj minore, menomo, minimo || s (il) meno; **at least** or **at the least** per lo meno, quanto meno;

not in the least nient'affatto || adv meno

leather ['lɛðər] s cuoio

leath'er·back tur'tle s tartaruga di mare

leath'er goods' store' s pelletteria

leathery ['lɛðəri] adj coriaceo

leave [liv] s (*permission*) permesso; (*permission to be absent*) licenza; (*farewell*) commiato; **on leave** in licenza; **to take French leave** andarsene all'inglese; **to take leave (of)** prender congedo (da) || v (*pret & pp* **left** [lɛft]) *tr* (*to go away from*) lasciare, uscire da; (*to let stay*) lasciare; (*to bequeath*) lasciare in testamento; **leave it to me!** lasciami fare!; **to be left** restare, e.g., **the door was left open** la porta restò aperta; esserci, e.g., **there is no bread left** non c'è più pane; **to leave alone** lasciare in pace; **to leave no stone unturned** cercare ogni possibilità; **to leave off** abbandonare, lasciare; **to leave out** omettere; **to leave things as they are** lasciar stare le cose || *intr* andarsene; (*said of a conveyance*) partire

leaven ['lɛvən] s lievito || *tr* lievitare; (fig) impregnare, permeare

leavening ['lɛvənɪŋ] s lievito

leave' of ab'sence s licenza; (*without pay*) aspettativa

leave'-tak'ing s commiato

leavings ['livɪŋz] spl rifiuti mpl

Leba·nese [ˌlɛbəˈniz] adj libanese || s (-nese) libanese mf

Lebanon ['lɛbənən] s il Libano

lecher ['lɛtʃər] s libertino

lecherous ['lɛtʃərəs] adj libidinoso

lechery ['lɛtʃəri] s lussuria

lectern ['lɛktərn] s leggio

lecture ['lɛktʃər] s conferenza; (*tedious reprimand*) pistolotto || *tr* dare una conferenza a; sermoneggiare || *intr* fare una conferenza; sermoneggiare

lecturer ['lɛktʃərər] s conferenziere m

ledge [lɛdʒ] s cornice f, cornicione m

ledger ['lɛdʒər] s (com) libro mastro

ledg'er line' s (mus) rigo supplementare

lee [li] s (*shelter*) rifugio; (naut) parte f sottovento; lees feccia

leech [litʃ] s mignatta, sanguisuga; **to stick like a leech** attaccarsi come una sanguisuga

leek [lik] s porro

leer [lir] s occhiata lussuriosa or maligna || *intr*—**to leer at** guardare di sbieco, sbirciare

leer·y ['liri] adj (-ier; -iest) sospettoso

leeward ['liwərd] or ['luˈərd] adj di sottovento || s sottovento, poggia || adv sottovento

lee'way' s (aer, naut) deriva, scarroccio; (*in time*) (coll) tolleranza; (coll) libertà f d'azione

left [lɛft] adj sinistro; (pol) di sinistra || s sinistra; (boxing) sinistro || adv alla sinistra

left' field' s fuoricampo di sinistra

left'-hand' drive' s guida a sinistra

left-handed ['lɛft ˈhændɪd] adj (*individual*) mancino; (*awkward*) goffo;

(*compliment*) ambiguo; (*mach*) sinistrorso

leftish ['lɛftɪʃ] *adj* sinistrista

leftist ['lɛftɪst] *adj* di sinistra ǁ *s* membro della sinistra

left'o'ver *adj & s* rimanente *m;* **left-overs** resti *mpl*

left'-wing' *adj* di sinistra

left-winger ['lɛft'wɪŋər] *s* (*coll*) membro dell'estrema sinistra; (*coll*) membro della sinistra

leg [lɛg] *s* (*of man, animal, table, chair; of trousers*) gamba; (*of fowl; of lamb*) coscia; (*of boot*) gambale *m;* (*of a journey*) tappa; **to be on one's last legs** essere agli estremi, essere ridotto alla disperazione; **to not have a leg to stand on** (*coll*) non avere la minima giustificazione; **to pull the leg of** (*coll*) prendere in giro, burlarsi di; **to shake a leg** (*coll*) affrettarsi; (*to dance*) (*coll*) ballare; **to stretch one's legs** sgranchirsi le gambe

lega·cy ['lɛgəsi] *s* (*-cies*) legato

legal ['ligəl] *adj* legale

legali·ty [lɪ'gælti] *s* (*-ties*) legalità *f*

legalize ['ligə,laɪz] *tr* legalizzare

le'gal ten'der *s* denaro a corso legale

legate ['lɛgɪt] *s* legato

legatee [,lɛgə'ti] *s* legatario

legation [lɪ'geʃən] *s* legazione

legend ['lɛdʒənd] *s* leggenda

legendary ['lɛdʒən,dɛri] *adj* leggendario

legerdemain [,lɛdʒərdɪ'men] *s* gioco di prestigio; (*trickery*) imbroglio

legging ['lɛgɪŋ] *s* gambale *m*

leg·gy ['lɛgi] *adj* (*-gier; -giest*) dalle gambe lunghe

leg'horn' *s* cappello di paglia di Firenze; gallina bianca livornese ǁ **Leghorn** *s* Livorno

legible ['lɛdʒɪbəl] *adj* leggibile

legion ['lidʒən] *s* legione *f*

legislate ['lɛdʒɪs,let] *tr* ordinare per mezzo di legge ǁ *intr* legiferare

legislation [,lɛdʒɪs'leʃən] *s* legislazione

legislative ['lɛdʒɪs,letɪv] *adj* legislativo

legislator ['lɛdʒɪs,letər] *s* legislatore *m*

legislature ['lɛdʒɪs,letʃər] *s* legislatura; corpo legislativo

legitimacy [lɪ'dʒɪtɪməsi] *s* legittimità *f*

legitimate [lɪ'dʒɪtɪmɪt] *adj* legittimo ǁ [lɪ'dʒɪtɪ,met] *tr* legittimare

legit'imate dra'ma *s* teatro serio

legitimize [lɪ'dʒɪtɪ,maɪz] *tr* legittimare

leg' of lamb' *s* cosciotto d'agnello

legume ['lɛgjum] or [lɪ'gjum] *s* (*pod*) legume *m;* (*table vegetables*) legumi *mpl;* (*bot*) leguminose *fpl*

leg'work' *s* lavoro che involve molto cammino

leisure ['liʒər] or ['lɛʒər] *s* ozio; **at leisure** senza fretta; disoccupato; **at one's leisure** quando si abbia un po' di tempo libero

lei'sure class' *s* gente agiata

lei'sure hours' *spl* ore *fpl* d'ozio

leisurely ['liʒərli] or ['lɛʒərli] *adj* lento ǁ *adv* lentamente, a tempo perso

lei'sure time' *s* tempo libero

lemon ['lɛmən] *s* limone *m;* (*car*) (*coll*) catorcio

lemonade [,lɛmə'ned] *s* limonata

lem'on squeez'er *s* spremilimoni *m*

lend [lɛnd] *s* (*pret & pp* lent [lɛnt]) *tr* prestare; (*a hand*) dare

lender ['lɛndər] *s* prestatore *m*

lend'ing li'brary *s* biblioteca circolante

length [lɛŋθ] *s* lunghezza; (*of time*) durata; **at length** finalmente; **to go to any lengths** fare quanto è possibile; essere disposto a tutto; **to keep at arm's length** (*someone else*) tenere a distanza (qlcu); (*said of oneself*) tenere la distanza

lengthen ['lɛŋθən] *tr* allungare ǁ *intr* allungarsi

length'wise' *adj* longitudinale ǁ *adv* per il lungo

length·y ['lɛŋθi] *adj* (*-ier; -iest*) lungo, prolungato

lenien·cy ['lini·ənsi] *s* (*-cies*) indulgenza

lenient ['lini·ənt] *adj* indulgente, clemente

lens [lɛnz] *s* lente *f;* (*of the eye*) cristallino

Lent [lɛnt] *s* quaresima

Lenten ['lɛntən] *adj* quaresimale

lentil ['lɛntəl] *s* lenticchia

Leo ['li·o] *s* (*astr*) il Leone

leopard ['lɛpərd] *s* leopardo

leotard ['li·ə,tɑrd] *s* calzamaglia

leper ['lɛpər] *s* lebbroso

leprosy ['lɛprəsi] *s* lebbra

leprous ['lɛprəs] *adj* lebbroso; (*of an animal or plant*) squamoso

Lesbian ['lɛzbi·ən] *adj* lesbico ǁ *s* lesbico; (*female homosexual*) lesbica

lesbianism ['lɛzbi·ə,nɪzəm] *s* lesbismo

lese majesty ['liz'mædʒɪsti] *s* delitto di lesa maestà

lesion ['liʒən] *s* lesione

less [lɛs] *adj* minore ǁ *adv* meno; **less and less** sempre meno; **less than** meno che; (*followed by numeral or personal pron*) meno di; (*followed by verb*) meno di quanto ǁ *s* meno

lessee [lɛs'i] *s* locatario; (*of business establishment*) concessionario

lessen ['lɛsən] *tr* diminuire, ridurre ǁ *intr* diminuire, ridursi

lesser ['lɛsər] *adj comp* minore

lesson ['lɛsən] *s* lezione

lessor ['lɛsər] *s* locatore *m*

lest [lɛst] *conj* per paura che

let [lɛt] *v* (*pret & pp* let; *ger* letting) *tr* permettere; (*to rent*) affittare; let + *inf* che + *subj*, e.g., **let him go** che vada; **let alone** tanto meno; senza menzionare; **let good enough alone** essere contento dell'onesto; let us + *inf* = *1st pl impv*, e.g., **let us sing** cantiamo; **to let** da affittare; **to let alone** lasciare in pace; **to let be** lasciar stare; **to let by** lasciar passare; **to let down** far scendere; deludere; tradire; abbandonare; **to let fly** (*insults*) lanciare; **to let go** lasciar libero; vendere; **to let in** fare entrare; **to let it go at that** non parlarne più; **to let know** far sapere; **to**

let loose sciogliere; **to let out** lasciar uscire; (*a secret*) divulgare; (*a scream*) lasciarsi scappare; (*to enlarge*) allargare; affittare; **to let through** lasciar passare; **to let up** lasciar salire; lasciar alzare ‖ *intr* affittare; **to let down** diminuire gli sforzi; **to let go of** disfarsi di; **to let on** (coll) fare finta; **to not let on** (coll) non lasciar trapelare; **to let out** (*said, e.g., of school*) terminare; **to let up** (coll) cessare; (coll) diminuire

let′down′ *s* diminuzione; smacco, umiliazione; delusione

lethal [ˈliθəl] *adj* letale

lethargic [lɪˈθɑrdʒɪk] *adj* letargico

lethar·gy [ˈlɛθərdʒi] *s* (**-gies**) letargo

Lett [lɛt] *s* lettone *m*; (*language*) lettone *m*

letter [ˈlɛtər] *s* lettera; **letters** (*literature*) lettere *fpl*, letteratura; **to the letter** alla lettera ‖ *tr* marcare con lettere

let′ter box′ *s* cassetta delle lettere

let′ter car′rier *s* postino

let′ter drop′ *s* buca delle lettere

let′ter-head′ *s* capolettera *m*; (*paper with printed heading*) carta da lettera intestata

lettering [ˈlɛtərɪŋ] *s* iscrizione; lettere *fpl*

let′ter of cred′it *s* lettera di credito

let′ter o′pener [ˈopənər] *s* tagliacarte *m*

let′ter pa′per *s* carta da lettere

let′ter-per′fect *adj* alla lettera; che sa alla perfezione

let′ter-press′ *s* stampato in tipografia ‖ *adv* a stampa tipografica

let′ter scales′ *spl* pesalettere *m*

let′ter-word′ *s* sigla

Lettish [ˈlɛtɪʃ] *adj* & *s* lettone *m*

lettuce [ˈlɛtɪs] *s* lattuga

let′up′ *s* (coll) pausa, sosta; (coll) tregua; **without letup** (coll) senza posa

leucorrhea [ˌlukəˈriə] *s* leucorrea

leukemia [luˈkimɪə] *s* leucemia

Levant [lɪˈvænt] *s* levante *m*

levee [ˈlɛvi] *s* (*embankment*) argine *m*; (*reception*) ricevimento

lev·el [ˈlɛvəl] *adj* piano; livellato; equilibrato; **level with** a livello di; **one's level best** (coll) il proprio meglio ‖ *s* (*instrument*) livella; (*degree of elevation*) livello; (*flat surface*) spianata, pianura; **on the level** (slang) onesto; onestamente; **to find one's level** trovare il proprio ambiente ‖ *v* (*pret & pp* **-eled** or **-elled**; *ger* **-eling** or **-elling**) *tr* livellare; (*to flatten out*) spianare; (*e.g., prices*) pareggiare, ragguagliare; (*a gun*) puntare; (coll) gettare a terra; (fig) dirigere ‖ *intr*— **to level off** (aer) volare orizzontalmente

level-headed [ˈlɛvəlˈhɛdɪd] *adj* equilibrato

lev′eling rod′ *s* stadia

lever [ˈlivər] or [ˈlɛvər] *s* leva ‖ *tr* far leva su ‖ *intr* far leva

leverage [ˈlivərɪdʒ] or [ˈlɛvərɪdʒ] *s* azione di una leva; (fig) potere *m*

leviathan [lɪˈvaɪ·əθən] *s* leviatano

levitation [ˌlɛvɪˈteʃən] *s* levitazione

levi·ty [ˈlɛvɪti] *s* (**-ties**) leggerezza

lev·y [ˈlɛvi] *s* (**-ies**) (*of taxes*) esazione; (*of money*) tributo; (*of troops*) leva ‖ *v* (*pret & pp* **-ied**) *tr* (*a tax*) imporre; (*soldiers*) reclutare; (*war*) fare

lewd [lud] *adj* (*lustful*) lascivo; osceno

lexical [ˈlɛksɪkəl] *adj* lessicale

lexicographer [ˌlɛksɪˈkɑgrəfər] *s* lessicografo

lexicographic(al) [ˌlɛksɪkoˈgræfɪk(əl)] *adj* lessicografico

lexicography [ˌlɛksɪˈkɑgrəfi] *s* lessicografia

lexicology [ˌlɛksɪˈkɑlədʒi] *s* lessicologia

lexicon [ˈlɛksɪkən] *s* lessico

liabili·ty [ˌlaɪ·əˈbɪlɪti] *s* (**-ties**) svantaggio; responsabilità *f*; (*e.g., to disease*) tendenza; (com) passivo; **liabilities** debiti *mpl*; (com) passivo

liabil′ity insur′ance *s* assicurazione sulla responsabilità civile

liable [ˈlaɪ·əbəl] *adj* (*e.g., to disease; e.g., to make mistakes*) soggetto; *e.g.*, responsabile; probabile; (*e.g., to a fine*) passibile

liaison [ˈli·əˌzɑn] or [liˈezən] *s* legame *m*; relazione illecita; (mil, nav) collegamento; (phonet) legamento

li′aison of′ficer *s* ufficiale *m* di collegamento

liar [ˈlaɪ·ər] *s* bugiardo, mentitore *m*

libation [laɪˈbeʃən] *s* (joc) libazione, bevuta

li·bel [ˈlaɪbəl] *s* diffamazione; (*defamatory writing*) libello ‖ *v* (*pret & pp* **-beled** or **-belled**; *ger* **-beling** or **-belling**) *tr* diffamare

libelous [ˈlaɪbələs] *adj* diffamatorio

liberal [ˈlɪbərəl] *adj* liberale; (*translation*) libero ‖ *s* liberale *mf*

liberali·ty [ˌlɪbəˈrælɪti] *s* (**-ties**) liberalità *f*; (*breadth of mind*) ampiezza di vedute

liberal-minded [ˈlɪbərəlˈmaɪndɪd] *adj* liberale, tollerante

liberate [ˈlɪbəˌret] *tr* liberare

liberation [ˌlɪbəˈreʃən] *s* liberazione

liberator [ˈlɪbəˌretər] *s* liberatore *m*

libertine [ˈlɪbərˌtin] *adj* & *s* libertino

liber·ty [ˈlɪbərti] *s* (**-ties**) libertà *f*; **to take the liberty** di permettersi di

liberty-loving [ˈlɪbərtiˈlʌvɪŋ] *adj* amante della libertà

libidinous [lɪˈbɪdɪnəs] *adj* libidinoso

libido [lɪˈbido] or [lɪˈbardo] *s* libidine *f*; (psychoanal) libido *f*

Libra [ˈlibrə] or [ˈlaɪbrə] *s* (astr) Bilancia

librarian [laɪˈbrɛrɪ·ən] *s* bibliotecario

librar·y [ˈlaɪˌbrɛri] or [ˈlaɪbrɛri] *s* (**-ies**) biblioteca; (*room in a house; collection of books*) libreria

li′brary num′ber *s* segnatura

li′brary sci′ence *s* biblioteconomia

libret·to [lɪˈbreto] *s* (**-tos**) (mus) libretto

Libya [ˈlɪbɪ·ə] *s* la Libia

license [ˈlaɪsəns] *s* licenza; (aut) patente *f* ‖ *tr* dare la licenza a ˙

li'cense num'ber *s* numero di targa di circolazione

li'cense plate' or tag' *s* targa di circolazione

licentious [laɪ'senʃəs] *adj* licenzioso

lichen ['laɪkən] *s* lichene *m*

lick [lɪk] *s* leccata, leccatura; (coll) esplosione di energia; (coll) velocità *f;* (coll) battitura; (coll) ripulita; to give a lick and a promise to (coll) fare rapidamente e con poca attenzione || *tr* leccare; (*said of waves, flames, etc.*) lambire; (*to defeat*) (coll) battere, vincere; (*e.g., with a stick*) (coll) bastonare

licorice ['lɪkərɪs] *s* liquirizia

lid [lɪd] *s* coperchio; (*eyelid*) palpebra; (*curb*) (coll) restrizione, freno; (*hat*) (slang) cappello

lie [laɪ] *s* menzogna; to catch in a lie pigliare in castagna; to give the lie to smentire || *v* (*pret & pp* lied; *ger* lying) *tr*—to lie oneself out of or to lie one's way out of trarsi fuori da (*un impaccio*) con una menzogna || *intr* mentire || *v* (*pret* lay [le]; *pp* lain [len]; *ger* lying) *intr* essere sdraiato; trovarsi; (*in the grave*) giacere; to lie down sdraiarsi

lie' detec'tor *s* macchina della verità

lien [lin] or ['li·ən] *s* diritto di pegno, diritto di garanzia

lieu [lu] *s*—in lieu of in luogo di

lieutenant [lu'tenənt] *s* luogotenente *m;* (mil) tenente *m;* (nav) tenente *m* di vascello

lieuten'ant colo'nel *s* (mil) tenente *m* colonnello

lieuten'ant command'er *s* (nav) capitano di corvetta

lieuten'ant gen'eral *s* (mil) generale *m* di corpo d'armata

lieuten'ant gov'ernor *s* (USA) vicegovernatore *m*

lieuten'ant jun'ior grade' *s* (nav) sottotenente *m* di vascello

life [laɪf] *adj* (*animate*) vitale; (*lifelong*) perpetuo; (*annuity*) vitalizio; (*working from nature*) dal vero || *s* (lives [laɪvz]) vita; (*of an insurance policy*) forza; for life a vita; for the life of me per quanto io provi; the life and soul of (*e.g., the party*) l'anima di; to come to life tornare a sé; riprender vita; to depart this life passar a miglior vita; to run for one's life scappare a tutta corsa

life' annu'ity *s* rendita vitalizia

life' belt' *s* cintura di salvataggio

life'boat' *s* imbarcazione di salvataggio, lancia di salvataggio

life' buoy' *s* salvagente *m*

life' float' *s* zattera di salvataggio

life'guard' *s* bagnino

life' impris'onment *s* ergastolo

life' insur'ance *s* assicurazione sulla vita

life' jack'et *s* cintura or giubbotto di salvataggio

lifeless ['laɪflɪs] *adj* inanimato; (*in a faint*) esanime; senza vita

life'like' *adj* (*e.g., portrait*) parlante; naturale

life' line' *s* sagola di salvataggio; (fig) linea di comunicazioni vitale

life'long' *adj* perpetuo, a vita

life' of Ri'ley ['raɪli] *s* vita del michelaccio

life' of the par'ty *s* anima della festa

life' preserv'er [prɪ'zʌrvər] *s* salvagente *m*

lifer ['laɪfər] *s* (slang) ergastolano

life' raft' *s* zattera di salvataggio

life'sav'er *s* salvatore *m* della vita; (*something that saves from a predicament*) ancora di salvezza

life' sen'tence *s* condanna all'ergastolo

life'-size' *adj* in grandezza naturale

life'time' *adj* vitalizio || *s* corso della vita

life' vest' *s* (air, naut) giubbotto salvagente or di salvataggio

life'work' *s* lavoro di tutta una vita

lift [lɪft] *s* sollevamento; (*act of helping*) aiuto; (*ride*) passaggio; (*apparatus*) elevatore *m;* (aer) portanza *f || tr* sollevare, alzare; (*one's hat*) levarsi; rimuovere; (coll) plagiare; (coll) rubare; (*fire*) (mil) sospendere || *intr* sollevare, sollevarsi; (*said, e.g., of fog*) dissiparsi

lift'-off' *s* (aer) decollo verticale

lift' truck' *s* carrello elevatore

ligament ['lɪgəmənt] *s* legamento

ligature ['lɪgətʃər] *s* legatura

light [laɪt] *adj* (*in weight*) leggero; (*hair*) biondo; (*complexion*) chiaro; (*oil*) fluido; (naut) con poco carico; (*room*) chiaro, illuminato; (*beer*) chiaro; light in the head (*dizzy*) allegro; (*silly*) scimunito; to make light of prendere sotto gamba || *s* luce *f;* (*to light a cigarette*) fuoco; (*to control traffic*) segnale *m;* (*shining example*) luminare *m;* (*lighthouse*) faro; (*window*) luce *f;* according to one's lights secondo l'intelligenza che il buon Dio gli (le) ha dato; against the light controluce; in this light sotto questo punto di vista; lights esempio; (*of sheep*) polmone *m;* to come to light venire alla luce; to shed or throw light on mettere in luce; to strike a light accendere un fiammifero || *v* (*pret & pp* lighted or lit [lɪt] *tr* (*to furnish with illumination*) illuminare; (*to ignite*) accendere; to light up illuminare || *intr* illuminarsi; accendersi; (*said, e.g., of a bird*) posarsi; (*from a car*) scendere; to light into (coll) gettarsi contro; to light out (slang) darsela a gambe; to light upon imbattersi in || *adv* senza bagagli; senza carico

light' bulb' *s* lampadina

light-complexioned ['laɪtkəm'plekʃənd] *adj* dal colorito chiaro

lighten ['laɪtən] *tr* alleggerire, sgravare; illuminare; (*to cheer up*) rallegrare || *intr* allegerirsi; (*to become less dark*) illuminarsi; (*to give off flashes of lightning*) lampeggiare

lighter ['laɪtər] *s* accenditore *m;* (naut) burchio

light-fingered ['laɪt'fɪŋgərd] *adj* svelto di mano, con le mani lunghe

light-footed ['laɪt'fʊtɪd] *adj* agile
light-headed ['laɪt'hedɪd] *adj* (*dizzy*) allegro; (*simple*) scemo
light-hearted ['laɪt'hɑrtɪd] *adj* allegro
light'house' *s* faro
lighting ['laɪtɪŋ] *s* illuminazione
lightly ['laɪtli] *adv* alla leggera
light' me'ter *s* esposimetro
lightness ['laɪtnɪs] *s* (*in weight*) leggerezza; (*in illumination*) chiarezza
light-ning ['laɪtnɪŋ] *s* lampo, fulmine *m* ‖ *v* (*ger* **-ning**) *intr* lampeggiare
light'ning arrest'er [ə'restər] *s* scaricatore *m*
light'ning bug' *s* lucciola
light'ning rod' *s* parafulmine *m*
light' op'era *s* operetta
light'ship' *s* battello faro
light-struck ['laɪt,strʌk] *adj* che ha preso luce
light'weight' *adj* leggero; da mezza stagione, e.g., **lightweight coat** cappotto da mezza stagione
light'-year' *s* anno luce
likable ['laɪkəbəl] *adj* simpatico
like [laɪk] *adj* uguale, simile; uguale a, simile a, e.g., **this hat is like mine** questo cappello è simile al mio; (*elec*) di segno uguale; **like father like son** tale il padre quale il figlio; **to feel like** + *ger* aver voglia di + *inf*; **to look like** assomigliare a; sembrare, e.g., **it looks like rain** sembra che pioverà ‖ *s* (*liking*) preferenza; (*fellow man*) simile *m*; **and the like** e cose dello stesso genere; **to give like for like** rendere pane per focaccia ‖ *adv* come; **like enough** (coll) probabilmente ‖ *prep* come ‖ *conj* (coll) come; come se; (coll) che, e.g., **it seems like he is afraid** sembra che abbia paura ‖ *tr* voler bene (with *dat*), e.g., **I like her very much** le voglio molto bene; trovar piacere in, e.g., **I like music** trovo piacere nella musica; piacere (with *dat*), e.g., **John likes apples** le mele piacciono a Giovanni; **to like best** *or* **better** preferire; **to like it** in trovarsi a proprio agio in; **to like to** + *inf* piacere (with *dat*) + *inf*, e.g., **she likes to dance** le piace ballare; gradire che + *subj*, e.g., **I should like him to pay a visit to my parents** gradirei che facesse una visita ai miei genitori ‖ *intr* volere, desiderare, e.g., **as you like** come desidera; **if you like** se vuole
likelihood ['laɪklɪ,hʊd] *s* probabilità *f*
like·ly ['laɪkli] *adj* (-lier; -liest) probabile; verosimile; a proposito; promettente; **to be likely to** + *inf* essere probabile che + *fut*, e.g., **Mary is likely to get married in the spring** è probabile che Maria si sposerà in primavera ‖ *adv* probabilmente
like-minded ['laɪk'maɪndɪd] *adj* dello stesso parere, della stessa opinione
liken ['laɪkən] *tr* paragonare
likeness ['laɪknɪs] *s* (*picture*) ritratto; (*similarity*) rassomiglianza; apparenza
like'wise' *adv* ugualmente; inoltre; **to do likewise** fare lo stesso

liking ['laɪkɪŋ] *s* simpatia; **to be to the liking of** essere di gusto di; **to have a liking for** (*things*) prendere gusto per; (*people*) affezionarsi a
lilac ['laɪlək] *adj* & *s* lilla *m*
Lilliputian [,lɪlɪ'pjuʃən] *adj* & *s* lilliputiano
lilt [lɪlt] *s* canzone *f* a cadenza; movimento a cadenza; (*in verse*) cadenza
lil·y ['lɪli] *s* (-ies) giglio; **to gild the lily** cercare di migliorare quanto è già perfetto
lil'y of the val'ley *s* mughetto
li'ma bean' ['laɪmə] *s* fagiolo bianco
limb [lɪm] *s* (*of body*) membro, arto; (*of tree*) ramo; (*of cross*) braccio; **to be out on a limb** (coll) essere nei guai
limber ['lɪmbər] *adj* agile ‖ *intr*—**to limber up** sciogliersi i muscoli, sgranchirsi le gambe
lim-bo ['lɪmbo] *s* (-bos) esilio; dimenticatoio; (theol) limbo
lime [laɪm] *s* (*calcium oxide*) calce *f*; (*Citrus aurantifolia*) limetta agra; (*linden tree*) tiglio ‖ *tr* gessare
lime'kiln' *s* fornace *f* da calce
lime'light' *s*—**to be in the limelight** essere in vista
limerick ['lɪmərɪk] *s* canzoncina umoristica di cinque versi
lime'stone' *s* calcare *m*
limit ['lɪmɪt] *s* limite *m*; (coll) colmo; **to go to the limit** andare agli estremi ‖ *tr* limitare
limitation [,lɪmɪ'teʃən] *s* limitazione
lim'ited-ac'cess high'way ['lɪmɪtɪd] *s* autostrada, strada con corsia d'accesso
lim'ited com'pany *s* società *f* a responsabilità limitata
lim'ited mon'archy *s* monarchia costituzionale
limitless ['lɪmɪtlɪs] *adj* illimitato
limousine ['lɪmə,zin] *or* [,lɪmə'zin] *s* berlina
limp [lɪmp] *adj* floscio; debole ‖ *s* zoppicatura ‖ *intr* zoppicare
limpid ['lɪmpɪd] *adj* limpido
linage ['laɪnɪdʒ] *s* (typ) numero di linee
linchpin ['lɪntʃ,pɪn] *s* acciarino
linden ['lɪndən] *s* tiglio
line [laɪn] *s* linea; (*e.g., of people*) fila; (*of trees*) filare *m*; (*for fishing*) lenza; (*written or printed*) rigo, riga; (*wrinkle*) ruga; (*of goods*) ramo; (naut) gherlino; **all along the line** su tutta la linea; **in line** allineato; sotto controllo; **in line with** secondo; **out of line** fuori d'allineamento; (slang) in disaccordo; **to bring into line** far filare; **to draw the line at** fermarsi a; stabilire il limite a; **to fall in line** conformarsi; allinearsi; **to have a line on** (coll) aver informazioni su; **to read between the lines** leggere fra le righe; **to stand in line** fare la coda; **to toe the line** filare diritto; **to wait in line** fare la fila ‖ *tr* rigare; (*e.g., the street*) schierare lungo; (*a suit*) foderare; (*a brake*) rivestire; **to line up** allineare; trovare, scovare ‖ *intr*

—to line up mettersi in fila; fare la coda

lineage ['lɪnɪ·ɪdʒ] s lignaggio

lineaments ['lɪnɪ·əmənts] spl lineamenti mpl

linear ['lɪnɪ·ər] adj lineare

line'man s (-men) (elec) guardafili m; (sports) guardalinee m; (surv) assistente geometra m

linen ['lɪnən] adj di tela di lino || s (fabric) tela di lino, lino; (yarn) filo di lino; biancheria

lin'en clos'et s guardaroba m per la biancheria

line' of fire' s (mil) linea di tiro

line' of least' resist'ance s principio del minimo sforzo; **to follow the line of least resistance** prendere la via più facile

line' of sight' s visuale f; (mil) linea di mira

liner ['laɪnər] s transatlantico

line'-up' s disposizione; (of prisoners) allineamento; (sports) formazione

linger ['lɪŋgər] intr indugiare, soffermarsi; (to be tardy) tardare; rimanere in vita; **to linger over** contemplare

lingerie [‚lænʒə'ri] s biancheria intima

lingering ['lɪŋgərɪŋ] adj prolungato

lingual ['lɪŋgwəl] adj linguale || s suono linguale

linguist ['lɪŋgwɪst] s poliglotto; (specialist in linguistics) glottologo

linguistic [lɪŋ'gwɪstɪk] adj linguistico || **linguistics** s linguistica, glottologia

lining ['laɪnɪŋ] s (of a coat) fodera; (of auto brake) guarnizione; (of a furnace) rivestimento interno; (of wall) rivestimento

link [lɪŋk] s anello, maglia; unione; (of sausage) nocco; **links** campo di golf || tr connettere || intr connettersi

linnet ['lɪnɪt] s fanello

linotype ['laɪnə‚taɪp] s linotype f || tr comporre in linotipia

lin'otype op'erator s linotipista mf

linseed ['lɪn‚sid] s linosa

lin'seed oil' s olio di lino

lint [lɪnt] s peluria, sfilacciatura; (for dressing wounds) filaccia

lintel ['lɪntəl] s architrave m

lion ['laɪ·ən] s leone m; celebrità f; **to beard the lion in his den** affrontare l'avversario a casa sua; **to put one's head in the lion's mouth** cacciarsi nei pericoli

lioness ['laɪ·ənɪs] s leonessa

lion-hearted ['laɪ·ən‚hɑrtɪd] adj cuor di leone, coraggioso

lionize ['laɪ·ə‚naɪz] tr festeggiare come una celebrità

li'ons' den' s fossa dei leoni

li'on's share' s parte f del leone

lip [lɪp] s labbro; (of a jar) beccuccio; (slang) linguaggio insolente; **to smack one's lips** leccarsi le labbra

lip'read' v (pret & pp -read [‚red]) tr leggere le labbra di || intr leggere le labbra

lip' read'ing s labiolettura

lip' serv'ice s omaggio non sentito

lip'stick' s rossetto per le labbra, matita per le labbra

lique·fy ['lɪkwɪ‚faɪ] v (pret & pp -fied) tr & intr liquefare

liqueur [lɪ'kʌr] s liquore m

liquid ['lɪkwɪd] adj liquido || s liquido; (phonet) liquida

liquidate ['lɪkwɪ‚det] tr & intr liquidare

liquidity [lɪ'kwɪdɪti] s liquidità f

liq'uid meas'ure s misura di capacità per liquidi

liquor ['lɪkər] s distillato alcolico, bevanda alcolica; (broth) brodo

Lisbon ['lɪzbən] s Lisbona

lisp [lɪsp] s pronuncia blesa || intr parlare bleso

lissome ['lɪsəm] adj flessibile, agile

list [lɪst] s lista, elenco; (border) orlo; (selvage) cimossa, vivagno; (naut) sbandamento; **lists** lizza; **to enter the lists** entrare in lizza || tr elencare, listare || intr (naut) sbandare, andare alla banda

listen ['lɪsən] intr ascoltare; obbedire; **to listen in** ascoltare una conversazione; (rad) captare una comunicazione; **to listen to** ascoltare; obbedire a, prestare attenzione a; **to listen to reason** intendere ragione

listener ['lɪsənər] s ascoltatore m; radioascoltatore m

lis'tening post' s (mil) posto di ascolto

listless ['lɪstlɪs] adj svogliato

list' price' s prezzo di catalogo

lita·ny ['lɪtəni] s (-nies) litania

liter ['litər] s litro

literacy ['lɪtərəsi] s abilità f di leggere e scrivere; istruzione

literal ['lɪtərəl] adj letterale

literary ['lɪtə‚reri] adj letterario; (individual) letterato

literate ['lɪtərɪt] adj che sa leggere e scrivere; (educated) istruito; (well-read) letterato || s persona che sa leggere e scrivere; letterato

literature ['lɪtərət∫ər] s letteratura; (printed matter) opuscoli pubblicitari

lithe [laɪ∂] adj flessibile, agile

lithium ['lɪθɪ·əm] s litio

lithograph ['lɪθə‚græf] or ['lɪθə‚grɑf] s litografia || tr litografare

lithographer [lɪ'θɑgrəfər] s litografo

lithography [lɪ'θɑgrəfi] s litografia

Lithuania [‚lɪθu'enɪ·ə] s la Lituania

Lithuanian [‚lɪθu'enɪ·ən] adj & s lituano

litigant ['lɪtɪgənt] adj & s litigante mf

litigate ['lɪtɪ‚get] tr & intr litigare

litigation [‚lɪtɪ'ge∫ən] s litigio; (lawsuit) lite f, causa

litmus ['lɪtməs] s tornasole m

lit'mus pa'per s cartina al tornasole

litter ['lɪtər] s disordine m; (scattered rubbish) pattume m; (young brought forth at one birth) figliata; (of puppies) cucciolata; (bedding for animals) strame m; (stretcher; bed carried by men or animals) lettiga, portantina || tr mettere in disordine; spargere rifiuti per; coprire di strame || intr partorire

lit'ter·bug' s sparpagliatore m di rifiuti

littering ['lɪtərɪŋ] s—**no littering** vietato gettare rifiuti

little ['lɪtəl] adj (in size) piccolo; (in amount) poco, e.g., **little salt** poco sale; **a little** un po' di, e.g., **a little salt** un po' di sale; **the little ones** i piccini || s poco; **a little** un po'; **to make little of** farsi gioco di; non pigliar sul serio; **to think little of** non tener di conto || adv poco; **little by little** poco a poco, mano a mano

Lit'tle Bear' s Orsa minore

Lit'tle Dip'per s Piccolo Carro

lit'tle fin'ger s mignolo; **to twist around one's little finger** maneggiare come · un fantoccio

lit'tle·neck' s piccola vongola (Venus mercenaria)

lit'tle owl' s civetta

lit'tle peo'ple spl fate fpl; folletti mpl

Lit'tle Red Rid'inghood' ['raɪdɪŋ ˌhʊd] s Cappuccetto Rosso

lit'tle slam' s (bridge) piccolo slam

liturgic(al) [lɪ'tɑrdʒɪk(əl)] adj liturgico

litur·gy ['lɪtərdʒi] s (-gies) liturgia

livable ['lɪvəbəl] adj abitabile; socievole; tollerabile

live [laɪv] adj vivo; (flame) ardente; di attualità; (elec) sotto tensione; (telv) in diretta || [lɪv] tr vivere; **to live down** (one's past) far dimenticare; **to live it up** (coll) darsi alla bella vita, scialare; **to live out** (e.g., a war) sopravvivere (with dat) || intr vivere; **to live from hand to mouth** vivere alla giornata; **to live high** darsi alla bella vita; **to live on** continuare a vivere; (e.g., vegetables) vivere di; vivere alle spalle di; **to live up to** (one's promises) compiere; (one's earnings) spendere

live' coal' (laɪv) s brace f

livelihood ['laɪvlɪ ˌhʊd] s vita; **to earn one's livelihood** guadagnarsi la vita

livelong ['lɪv ˌlɔŋ] or ['lɪv ˌlɑŋ] adj— **all the livelong day** tutto il santo giorno

live·ly ['laɪvli] adj (-lier; -liest) vivo, vivace; (color) vivido; (resilient) elastico; (tune) brioso

liven ['laɪvən] tr animare || intr animarsi, rianimarsi

liver ['lɪvər] s abitante mf; (anat) fegato

liver·y ['lɪvəri] s (-ies) livrea

liv'ery·man s (-men) stalliere m

liv'ery sta'ble s stallaggio

livestock ['laɪv ˌstɑk] adj zootecnico || s bestiame m

live' wire' [laɪv] s (elec) filo carico di corrente; (slang) persona energica

livid ['lɪvɪd] adj livido; (with anger) incollerito

living ['lɪvɪŋ] adj vivo; (conditions) abitativo || s vivere m; **to earn a living** guadagnarsi la vita

liv'ing quar'ters spl abitazione, alloggio

liv'ing room' s stanza di soggiorno

liv'ing wage' s salario sufficiente per vivere

lizard ['lɪzərd] s lucertola

load [lod] s peso, carico; **loads of** (coll) un mucchio di; **to get a load of** (slang) stare a vedere; (slang) stare a sentire; **to have a load on** (slang) essere ubriaco || tr caricare || intr caricarsi

loaded ['lodɪd] adj caricato; (slang) ubriaco fradicio; (slang) ricchissimo

load'ed dice' spl dadi truccati

load'stone' s magnetite f; (fig) calamita

loaf [lof] s (loaves [lovz]) pane m; (molded mass) forma; (of sugar) pane m; (long and thin loaf) filone m || intr batter fiacca, oziare

loafer ['lofər] s fannullone m

loam [lom] s ricca argilla sabbiosa; terra da fonderia

loan [lon] s prestito; **to hit for a loan** (coll) dare una stoccata a || tr prestare

loan' shark' s (coll) strozzino

loan' word' s (ling) prestito

loath [loθ] adj poco disposto; **nothing loath** molto volentieri

loathe [loð] tr detestare, aborrire

loathsome ['loðsəm] adj abominevole, disgustoso

lob [lɑb] s (tennis) pallonetto || v (pret & pp lobbed; ger lobbing) tr (tennis) dare un pallonetto a

lob·by ['labi] s (-bies) anticamera, vestibolo; sollecitazione di voti || v (pret & pp ·bied) intr sollecitare voti, influenzare il voto dietro le quinte

lobbyist ['labɪ·ɪst] s politicante m che cerca di influenzare il voto dietro le quinte

lobe [lob] s lobo

lobster ['labstər] s (Palinurus vulgaris) aragosta; (Hommarus vulgaris) astice m

lob'ster pot' s nassa per aragoste

local ['lokəl] adj locale || s treno accelerato; notizia di interesse locale; (of a union) sezione

locale [lo'kæl] s località f

locali·ty [lo'kælɪti] s (-ties) località f

localize ['lokə ˌlaɪz] tr localizzare

lo'cal op'tion s referendum m locale sulla vendita di alcolici

locate [lo'ket] or ['loket] tr (to discover the location of) localizzare; (to place, settle) situare, stabilire; (to ascribe a location to) individuare || intr stabilirsi

location [lo'keʃən] s localizzazione, posizione; sito; **on location** (mov) in esterno

lock [lɑk] s serratura; (of a canal) chiusa; (of hair) ciocca; (of a firearm) percussore m; (mach) freno; **lock, stock, and barrel** (coll) completamente; **under lock and key** sotto chiave || tr chiudere a chiave; serrare; (a boat) far passare per una chiusa; unire; abbracciare; **to lock in** chiudere sotto chiave; **to lock out** chiudere fuori; (workers) sbarrare dal lavoro; **to lock up** chiudere a chiave; incarcerare

locker ['lakər] s armadietto a chiave; (in the form of a chest) bauletto

lock'er room' s spogliatoio

locket ['lɑkɪt] s medaglione m

lock'jaw' s tetano, trisma m

lock' nut' s controdado

lock'out' s serrata

lock'smith' s magnano, fabbro

lock' step' s—**to march in lock step** marciare a passo serrato

lock' stitch' s punto a filo doppio

lock' ten'der s guardiano di chiusa

lock'up' s prigione; (typ) messa in forma

lock' wash'er s rondella di sicurezza

locomotive [,lokə'motɪv] s locomotiva

lo·cus ['lokəs] s (-ci [saɪ]) luogo

locust ['lokəst] s (ent) locusta; (cicada) (ent) cicala; (bot) robinia

lode [lod] s filone m, vena

lode'star' s stella polare; guida

lodge [lɑdʒ] s casetta; padiglione m da caccia; albergo; (e.g., of Masons) loggia ‖ tr alloggiare, ospitare; depositare; contenere; (a complaint) sporgere ‖ intr alloggiare; essere contenuto, trovarsi; andar a finire

lodger ['lɑdʒər] s inquilino

lodging ['lɑdʒɪŋ] s alloggio

loft [lɔft] or [lɑft] s (attic) solaio; (hayloft) fienile m; (in theater or church) galleria

loft·y ['lɔfti] or ['lɑfti] adj (-ier; -iest) alto, elevato; (haughty) orgoglioso

log [lɔg] or [lɑg] s ceppo, ciocco; (naut) solcometro; (aer, naut) giornale m di bordo; **to sleep like a log** dormire della grossa ‖ v (pret & pp logged; ger logging) tr registrare; (a speed) fare; (a distance) percorrere

logarithm ['lɔgə,rɪðəm] or ['lɑgə-,rɪðəm] s logaritmo

log'book' s (aer, naut) libro di bordo

log' cab'in s capanna di tronchi

log' chip' s (naut) barchetta

log' driv'er s zatteriere m

log' driv'ing ['draɪvɪŋ] s fluitazione

logger ['lɔgər] or ['lɑgər] s taglialegna m; trattore m per trasporto tronchi

log'ger·head' s testone m; **at loggerheads** in lite

loggia ['lɔdʒə] s loggia

logic ['lɑdʒɪk] s logica

logical ['lɑdʒɪkəl] adj logico

logician [lo'dʒɪʃən] s logico

logistic(al) [lo'dʒɪstɪk(əl)] adj logistico

logistics [lo'dʒɪstɪks] s logistica

log'jam' s ingorgo fluviale dovuto a ammasso di tronchi; (fig) ristagno

log' line' s (naut) sagola

log'roll' intr barattare favori politici

log'wood' s campeggio

loin [lɔɪn] s lombo; **to gird up one's loins** prepararsi per l'azione

loin'cloth' s perizoma m, copripudende m

loiter ['lɔɪtər] tr—**to loiter away** (time) sprecare in ozio ‖ intr bighellonare, trastullarsi

loiterer ['lɔɪtərər] s perdigiorno

loll [lɑl] intr sdraiarsi pigramente, adagiarsi pigramente; pendere

lollipop ['lɑli,pɑp] s caramella sullo stecchetto, lecca-lecca m

Lombard ['lɑmbɑrd] or ['lɑmbərd] adj & s lombardo; (hist) longobardo

Lom'bardy pop'lar s pioppo italico

London ['lʌndən] adj londinese ‖ s Londra

Londoner ['lʌndənər] s londinese mf

lone [lon] adj solo; solitario

loneliness ['lonlɪns] s solitudine f

lone·ly ['lonli] adj (-lier; -liest) solingo, solo, solitario

lonesome ['lonsəm] adj solitario

lone' wolf' s (coll) orso, solitario

long [lɔŋ] or [lɑŋ] (**longer** ['lɔŋgər] or ['lɑŋgər]; **longest** ['lɔŋgɪst] or ['lɑŋgɪst]) adj lungo; **three meters long** lungo tre metri ‖ adv molto, molto tempo; **as long as** mentre; (provided) fin tanto che; (inasmuch as) dato che; **before long** fra poco; **how long?** quanto?; **long ago** molto tempo fa; **long before** molto prima; **long since** molto tempo fa; **no longer** non più; **so long!** (coll) ciao!, arrivederci!; **so long as** fino a che, finché ‖ intr anelare; **to long for** svisceratisi per, sospirare per

long'boat' s (naut) lancia

long'-dis'tance adj (telp) interurbano, intercomunale; (sports) di fondo; (aer) a distanza

long'-drawn'-out' adj prolungato

longeron ['lɑndʒərən] s longherone m

longevity [lɑn'dʒɛvɪti] s longevità f

long' face' s (coll) faccia triste, muso lungo

long'hair' adj & s (coll) intellettuale mf; (coll) musicomane mf

long'hand' adj (scritto) a mano ‖ s scrittura a mano; **in longhand** scritto a mano

longing ['lɔŋɪŋ] or ['lɑŋɪŋ] adj bramoso, anelante ‖ s brama, anelito

longitude ['lɑndʒɪ,tjud] or ['lɑndʒɪ-,tud] s longitudine f

long-lived ['lɔŋ'laɪvd], ['lɔŋ'lɪvd], ['lɑŋ'laɪvd] or ['lɑŋ'lɪvd] adj (person) longevo, di lunga vita; (e.g., rumor) di lunga durata

long'-play'ing rec'ord s disco di grande durata

long'-range' adj a lunga portata

long'shore'man s (-men) portuale m, scaricatore m

long'stand'ing adj vecchio, che esiste da lungo tempo

long'-suf'fering adj paziente, longanime

long' suit' s (cards) serie lunga; (fig) forte m

long'-term' adj a lunga scadenza

long'-wind'ed adj verboso; (speech) chilometrico

look [lʊk] s (appearance) aspetto; (glance) sguardo; (search) ricerca; **looks** aspetto, apparenza; **to take a look at** dare un'occhiata a ‖ tr guardare; (one's age) mostrare; **to look daggers at** fulminare con lo sguardo; **to look up** (e.g., in a dictionary) cercare; andare a visitare; venire a visitare ‖ intr guardare; cercare; parere; **look out!** attenzione!; **to look after** badare a; occuparsi di; **to look at** guardare; **to look back** riguardare;

(fig) guardare al passato; **to look down on s.o.** guardare qlcu dall'alto in basso; **to look for** cercare; aspettarsi; **to look forward to** antecipare il piacere di; **to look ill** avere una brutta cera; **to look in on** passare per la casa di; **to look into** esaminare a fondo; **to look like** sembrare, parere; **to look out** fare attenzione; **to look out for** aver cura di; **to look out of** guardare da; **to look out on** dare su; **to look through** guardare per; (*a book*) sfogliare; **to look toward** dare su; **to look up to** ammirare, guardare con ammirazione; **to look well** avere una buona cera; fare figura

looker-on [ˌlʊkərˈɑn] or [ˌlʊkərˈɔn] *s* (**lookers-on**) astante *m*

look'ing glass' [ˈlʊkɪŋ] *s* specchio

look'out' *s* guardia; (*person; watch kept; place from which a watch is kept*) vedetta; (*concern*) (coll) affare *m;* **to be on the lookout** stare in guardia; **to be on the lookout for** essere in cerca di

loom [lum] *s* telaio || *intr* apparire indistintamente; pararsi dinanzi; apparire

loon [lun] *s* scemo; fannullone *m;* (orn) (*Gavia*) strolaga

loon·y [ˈluni] *adj* (**-ier; -iest**) (slang) pazzo || *s* (**-ies**) (slang) pazzo

loop [lup] *s* cappio; (*e.g., of a road*) tortuosità *f;* (*for fastening a button*) occhiello; (aer) cerchio or giro della morte; (phys) ventre *m;* || *tr* fare cappi in; annodare; **to loop the loop** (aer) fare il giro della morte || *intr* avanzare tortuosamente, girare

loop'hole' *s* (*narrow opening*) feritoia; (*means of evasion*) scappatoia

loose [lus] *adj* libero, sciolto; (*available*) disponibile; (*not firm*) rilasciato; (*tooth*) che balla; (*unchaste*) facile; (*garment*) ampio; (*soil*) smosso; (*translation*) libero; (*rein*) lento; **to become loose** sciogliersi; **to break loose** mettersi in libertà; **to have loose bowels** avere la diarrea; **to turn loose** liberare || *s—***to be on the loose** (coll) essere in libertà; (coll) correre la cavallina || *tr* sciogliere; slegare; lanciare

loose' change' *s* spiccioli *mpl*

loose' end' *s* capo sciolto; **at loose ends** indeciso; disoccupato, senza nulla da fare

loose'-leaf' *a* a fogli mobili

loosen [ˈlusən] *tr* snodare; rilasciare; smuovere; allentare; (*the bowels*) liberare dalla stitichezza || *intr* snodarsi; rilasciarsi; smuoversi; allentarsi

looseness [ˈlusnɪs] *s* scioltezza; (*in morals*) rilassamento

loose-tongued [ˈlusˈtʌŋd] *adj* sciolto di lingua; linguacciuto, maldicente

loot [lut] *s* bottino || *tr* saccheggiare

lop [lɑp] *v* (*pret & pp* **lopped;** *ger* **lopping**) *tr* lasciar cadere, lasciar penzolare; **to lop off** mozzare; (*a tree*) potare; (*a vine*) stralciare || *intr* penzolare

lopsided [ˈlɑpˈsaɪdɪd] *adj* che pende da una parte; asimmetrico, sproporzionato

loquacious [loˈkweʃəs] *adj* loquace

lord [lɔrd] *s* signore *m;* (Brit) lord *m* || *tr*—**to lord it over** signoreggiare su

lord·ly [ˈlɔrdli] *adj* (**-lier; -liest**) signorile, magnifico; altero, disdegnoso, arrogante

Lord's' Day', **the** la domenica, il giorno del Signore

lordship [ˈlɔrdʃɪp] *s* signoria

Lord's' Prayer' *s* paternostro

Lord's' Sup'per *s* Eucarestia; Ultima Cena

lore [lor] *s* tradizioni *fpl* popolari; cognizioni *fpl*

lorgnette [lɔrnˈjɛt] *s* occhialetto, lorgnette *f;* binocolo da teatro col manico

lor·ry [ˈlɑri] or [ˈlɔri] *s* (**-ries**) (rr) vagoncino; (Brit) camion *m*

lose [luz] *v* (*pret & pp* **lost** [lɔst] or [lɑst]) *tr* perdere; (*said of a physician*) non riuscire a salvare; **to lose heart** perdersi d'animo; **to lose oneself** perdersi, smarrirsi || *intr* perdere; (*said of a watch*) ritardare; **to lose out** rimetterci

loser [ˈluzər] *s* perdente *mf*

losing [ˈluzɪŋ] *adj* perdente || **losings** *spl* perdite *fpl*

loss [lɔs] or [lɑs] *s* perdita; **to be at a loss** essere perplesso; **to be at a loss to** + *inf* non saper come + *inf;* **to sell at a loss** vendere in perdita

loss' of face' *s* perdita di faccia

lost [lɔst] or [lɑst] *adj·* perduto; **lost in thought** assorto in sè stesso; **lost to** perso per; insensibile a

lost'-and-found' depart'ment *s* ufficio degli oggetti smarriti

lost' sheep' *s* pecorella smarrita

lot [lɑt] *s* (*for building*) lotto; (*fate*) sorte *f;* (*parcel, portion*) partita; (*of people*) gruppo; (coll) grande quantità *f;* (coll) tipo, soggetto; **a lot (of)** or **lots of** (coll) molto, molti; **to cast** or **to throw in one's lot with** condividere la sorte di; **to draw** or **to cast lots** tirare a sorte

lotion [ˈloʃən] *s* lozione

lotter·y [ˈlɑtəri] *s* (**-ies**) lotteria, riffa

lotto [ˈlɑto] *s* tombola, lotto

lotus [ˈlotəs] *s* loto

loud [laʊd] *adj* forte; (*noisy*) rumoroso; (*voice*) alto; (*garish*) sgargiante, chiassoso, appariscente; (*foul-smelling*) puzzolente || *adv* a voce alta; rumorosamente

loud-mouthed [ˈlaʊdˌmaʊθt] or [ˈlaʊdˌmaʊðd] *adj* chiassone

loud'speak'er *s* altoparlante *m*

lounge [laʊndʒ] *s* divano, sofà *m;* sala soggiorno; poltrona || *intr* oziare, star senza far niente; bighellonare; **to lounge around** bighellonare

lounge' liz'ard *s* (slang) damerino, bellimbusto, gagà *m*

louse [laʊs] *s* (**lice** [laɪs]) pidocchio || *tr*—**to louse up** (slang) rovinare

lous·y [ˈlaʊzi] *adj* (**-ier; -iest**) pidocchioso; (*mean; bungling*) (coll) schifoso; *(filthy)* (coll) sporco; **lousy with** *(e.g., money)* (slang) pieno di

lout [laʊt] *s* gaglioffo, tanghero

louver ['luvər] *s* sportello girevole di persiana; *(aut)* feritoia per ventilazione

lovable ['lʌvəbəl] *adj* amabile

love [lʌv] *s* amore *m;* (tennis) zero; **not for love nor money** a nessun prezzo; **to be in love (with)** essere innamorato (di); **to make love to** fare l'amore con || *tr* amare; voler bene a; piacere (with *dat*), e.g., **she loves short skirts** le piacciono le sottane corte

love' affair' *s* passione, amori *mpl*

love'bird' *s* (orn) inseparabile *m;* **love-birds** (slang) amanti appassionati

love' child' *s* figlio naturale

love' feast' *s* agape *f*

loveless ['lʌvlɪs] *adj* senza amore

lovelorn ['lʌv‚lɔrn] *adj* abbandonato dalla persona amata

love·ly ['lʌvli] *adj* **(-lier; -liest)** bello; (coll) delizioso

love' match' *s* matrimonio d'amore

love' po'tion *s* filtro d'amore

lover ['lʌvər] *s* amante *m;* *(e.g., of music)* amico, appassionato

love' seat' *s* amorino

love'sick' *adj* malato d'amore

love'sick'ness *s* mal *m* d'amore

love' song' *s* canzone *f* d'amore

loving ['lʌvɪŋ] *adj* affezionato, amoroso; **your loving son** il vostro affezionato figlio

lov'ing-kind'ness *s* tenera sollecitudine

low [lo] *adj* basso; *(deep)* profondo; *(diet)* magro; *(visibility)* cattivo; *(dress)* scollato *(dejected)* abbattuto; *(fire)* lento; *(flame; speed)* piccolo; **to lay low** ammazzare; abbattere; **to lie low** rimanere nascosto; attendere || *s* punto basso; prezzo minimo; *(of cow)* muggito; (aut) prima velocità; (meteor) depressione || *adv* basso, a basso, in basso || *intr* *(said of a cow)* muggire

low'born' *adj* di umili origini

low'boy' *s* cassettone basso con le gambe corte

low'brow' *adj* & *s* (coll) ignorante *mf*

low'-cost' hous'ing *s* case *fpl* popolari

Low' Coun'tries, the i Paesi Bassi

low'-down' *adj* (coll) basso, vile || **low'-down'** *s* (coll) semplice verità *f,* notizie *fpl* confidenziali

lower ['lo‚ər] *adj* inferiore, disotto || *tr* abbassare; *(prices)* ribassare || *intr* diminuire; discendere || ['laʊ‚ər] *intr* aggrottare le ciglia; *(said of the weather)* imbronciarsi

low'er berth' ['lo‚ər] *s* cuccetta inferiore

low'er case' ['lo‚ər] *s* (typ) cassa inferiore

lower-case ['lo‚ər ‚kes] *adj* (typ) minuscolo

low'er mid'dle class' ['lo‚ər] *s* piccola borghesia

lowermost ['lo‚ər ‚most] *adj* (il) più basso, (l') infimo

low'-fre'quency *adj* a bassa frequenza

low' gear' *s* prima velocità, prima

lowland ['lolənd] *s* pianura || **Low-lands** *spl* Scozia meridionale, bassa Scozia

low·ly ['loli] *adj* **(-lier; -liest)** umile

Low' Mass' *s* messa bassa

low-minded ['lo'maɪndɪd] *adj* vile, basso

low-necked ['lo'nɛkt] *adj* scollato

low-pitched ['lo'pɪt/t] *adj* *(sound)* basso, grave; *(roof)* poco inclinato

low'-pres'sure *adj* a bassa pressione

low-priced ['lo'praɪst] *adj* a buon mercato, a basso prezzo

low' shoe' *s* scarpa bassa

low'-speed' *adj* di piccola velocità

low-spirited ['lo'spɪrɪtɪd] *adj* depresso

low' tide' *s* bassa marea; (fig) punto più basso

low' visibil'ity *s* scarsa visibilità

low' wa'ter *s* *(low tide)* bassa marea; *(of a river)* magra

loyal ['lɔɪ·əl] *adj* leale

loyalist ['lɔɪ·əlɪst] *s* lealista *mf*

loyal·ty ['lɔɪ·əlti] *s* **(-ties)** lealtà *f*

lozenge ['lɑzɪndʒ] *s* losanga; *(candy cough drop)* pasticca, pastiglia

LP ['ɛl'pi] *s* (letterword) (trademark) disco di grande durata

lubricant ['lubrɪkənt] *adj* & *s* lubrificante *m*

lubricate ['lubrɪ‚ket] *tr* lubrificare; *(e.g., one's hands)* ungersi

lubrication [‚lubrɪ'keʃən] *s* lubrificazione

lubricous ['lubrɪkəs] *adj* lubrico; incerto, incostante

lucerne [lu'sʌrn] *s* erba medica

lucid ['lusɪd] *adj* lucido

Lucifer ['lusɪfər] *s* Lucifero

luck [lʌk] *s* *(good or bad)* sorte *f;* *(good)* sorte *f,* fortuna; **down on one's luck** in cattive condizioni; **in luck** fortunato; **out of luck** sfortunato; **to bring luck** portare (buona) fortuna; **to try one's luck** tentare la sorte; **worse luck** disgraziatamente

luckily ['lʌkɪli] *adv* fortunatamente

luckless ['lʌklɪs] *adj* sfortunato

luck·y ['lʌki] *adj* **(-ier; -iest)** fortunato; *(supposed to bring luck)* portafortuna; *(foretelling good luck)* di buon augurio; **to be lucky** aver fortuna

luck'y hit' *s* (coll) colpo di fortuna

lucrative ['lukrətɪv] *adj* lucrativo

ludicrous ['ludɪkrəs] *adj* ridicolo

lug [lʌg] *s* manico; *(pull)* tiro; **to put the lug on s.o.** (slang) batter cassa a qlcu || *v* *(pret* & *pp* **lugged;** *ger* **lugging)** *tr* tirarsi dietro; (coll) introdurre a sproposito

luggage ['lʌgɪdʒ] *s* *(used in traveling)* bagaglio; *(found in a store)* valigeria

lug'gage store' *s* valigeria

lugubrious [lu'gubrɪ·əs] or [lu'gjubrɪ·əs] *adj* lugubre

lukewarm ['luk‚wɔrm] *adj* tiepido

lull [lʌl] *s* momento di calma, calma || *tr* calmare, pacificare; addormentare

lulla·by ['lʌlə‚baɪ] *s* **(-bies)** ninnananna

lumbago [lʌm'bego] *s* lombaggine *f*

lumber ['lʌmbər] s legname m, legno da costruzione; cianfrusaglie fpl ‖ intr muoversi pesantemente

lum'ber-jack' s boscaiolo

lum'ber jack'et s giaccone m

lum'ber-man s (-men) (dealer) commerciante m in legname; (man who cuts down lumber) boscaiolo

lum'ber room' s ripostiglio

lum'ber-yard' s deposito legnami

luminar-y ['lumɪ,nɛri] s (-ies) luminare m

luminous ['lumɪnəs] adj luminoso

lummox ['lʌməks] s (coll) scimunito

lump [lʌmp] s grumo; mucchio; cumulo; (swelling) bernoccolo; (of sugar) zolletta; (in one's throat) groppo; (coll) stupidone m; **in the lump** in blocco; nell'insieme ‖ tr mescolare; (to make into lumps) raggrumare; **to lump it** (coll) mandarla giù

lumpish ['lʌmpɪʃ] adj grumoso; goffo; balordo

lump' sum' s ammontare unico, somma globale

lump-y ['lʌmpi] adj (-ier; -iest) grumoso; (person) pesante, ottuso; (sea) agitato

luna-cy ['lunəsi] s (-cies) pazzia

lunar ['lunər] adj lunare

lu'nar land'ing s allunaggio

lu'nar mod'ule s modulo lunare

lu'nar rov'er s auto f lunare

lunatic ['lunətɪk] adj & s demente mf

lu'natic asy'lum s manicomio

lu'natic fringe' s estremisti mpl fanatici

lunch [lʌntʃ] s (regular midday meal) seconda colazione; (light meal) spuntino, merenda ‖ intr fare colazione; fare uno spuntino

lunch' bas'ket s portavivande m

luncheon ['lʌntʃən] s seconda colazione; pranzo ufficiale

luncheonette [,lʌntʃə'nɛt] s tavola calda

lunch'eon meat' s insaccati mpl

lunch'room' s tavola calda

lung [lʌŋ] s polmone m

lunge [lʌndʒ] s slancio; (fencing) affondo ‖ intr slanciarsi

lurch [lʌrtʃ] s barcollamento; (at close of a game) cappotto; (naut) sbandata; **to leave in the lurch** piantare in asso ‖ intr barcollare; (naut) sbandare

lure [lur] s esca; (fig) insidie fpl ‖ tr adescare; **to lure away** distogliere, sviare

lurid ['lurɪd] adj (fiery) ardente, acceso; sensazionale; (gruesome) orripilante

lurk [lʌrk] intr stare in agguato, nascondersi; (fig) essere latente

luscious ['lʌʃəs] adj delizioso; lussuoso, lussureggiante; voluttuoso

lush [lʌʃ] adj lussureggiante, lussuoso

lust [lʌst] s desiderio sfrenato; libidine f, lussuria ‖ intr—**to lust after or for** aver sete di

luster ['lʌstər] s (gloss) lustro, lucentezza; (glory) lustro, onore m

lus'ter-ware' s ceramiche smaltate

lustful ['lʌstfəl] adj lussurioso

lustrous ['lʌstrəs] adj lucido

lust-y ['lʌsti] adj (-ier; -iest) vigoroso, gagliardo

lute [lut] s (mus) liuto; (chem) luto

Lutheran ['luθərən] adj & s luterano

luxuriance [lʌg'ʒurɪ-əns] s rigoglio

luxuriant [lʌg'ʒurɪ-ənt] adj lussureggiante; (imagery) ridondante

luxuriate [lʌg'ʒurɪ,et] or [lʌk'ʃurɪ,et] intr lussureggiare; trovare piacere

luxurious [lʌg'ʒurɪ-əs] or [lʌk'ʃurɪ-əs] adj lussuoso, fastoso

luxu-ry ['lʌkʃəri] or ['lʌgʒəri] s (-ries) lusso, sfarzo

lye [laɪ] s ranno, lisciva

lying ['laɪ-ɪŋ] adj menzognero ‖ s il mentire

ly'ing-in' hos'pital s clinica ostetrica, maternità f

lymph [lɪmf] s linfa

lymphatic [lɪm'fætɪk] adj linfatico

lynch [lɪntʃ] tr linciare

lynching ['lɪntʃɪŋ] s linciaggio

lynx [lɪŋks] s lince f

lynx-eyed ['lɪŋks,aɪd] adj dagli occhi di lince

lyonnaise [,laɪ-ə'nez] adj (culin) alla maniera di Lione

lyre [laɪr] s lira

lyric ['lɪrɪk] adj lirico ‖ s lirica; (words of a song) parole fpl

lyrical ['lɪrɪkəl] adj lirico

lyricism ['lɪrɪ,sɪzəm] s lirismo

lyricist ['lɪrɪsɪst] s (writer of words for songs) paroliere m; (poet) lirico

M

M, m [ɛm] s tredicesima lettera dell'alfabeto inglese

ma'am [mæm] or [mɑm] s (coll) signora

macadam [mə'kædəm] s macadàm m

macadamize [mə'kædə,maɪz] tr macadamizzare

macaroni [,mækə'roni] s maccheroni mpl

macaroon [,mækə'run] s amaretto

macaw [mə'kɔ] s ara

mace [mes] s mazza; (spice) macis m & f

mace' bear'er s mazziere m

machination [,mækɪ'neʃən] s macchinazione, macchina

machine [mə'ʃin] s macchina ‖ tr fare a macchina

machine' gun' s mitragliatrice f

machine'-gun' v (pret & pp -gunned; ger -gunning) tr mitragliare

machine'-made' adj fatto a macchina

machiner·y [məˈʃinəri] *s* (**-ies**) macchinario, meccanismo

machine' screw' *s* vite *f* per metallo

machine' shop' *s* officina meccanica

machine' tool' *s* macchina utensile

machinist [məˈʃinɪst] *s* meccanico; (nav) secondo macchinista

mackerel [ˈmækərəl] *s* maccarello

mack'erel sky' *s* cielo a pecorelle

mackintosh [ˈmækɪnˌtaʃ] *s* impermeabile *m*

mad [mæd] *adj* (**madder; maddest**) (*angry; rabid*) arrabbiato; (*insane; foolish*) pazzo, folle; furioso; **to be mad about** (coll) andar pazzo per; **to drive mad** far impazzire; **to go mad** impazzire; (*said of a dog*) diventare idrofobo

madam [ˈmædəm] *s* signora

mad'cap' *s* mattoide *m*, rompicollo

madden [ˈmædən] *tr* (*to make angry*) inferocire; (*to make insane*) fare impazzire

made-to-order [ˈmɛdtəˈɔrdər] *adj* fatto apposta; (*clothing*) fatto su misura

made'-up' *adj* inventato; (*using cosmetics*) truccato

mad'house' *s* manicomio

mad'man' *s* (**-men'**) pazzo

madness [ˈmædnɪs] *s* rabbia; pazzia

Madonna lily [məˈdɑnə] *s* giglio

maelstrom [ˈmɛlstrəm] *s* vortice *m*

magazine [ˈmægəˌzin] *or* [ˌmægəˈzin] *s* (*periodical*) rivista, giornale *m*; (*warehouse*) magazzino; (*for cartridges*) caricatore *m*; (*for powder*) polveriera; (naut) santabarbara; (phot) magazzino

maggot [ˈmægət] *s* larva di dittero

Magi [ˈmedʒaɪ] *spl* Re Magi

magic [ˈmædʒɪk] *adj* magico ‖ *s* magia; illusionismo; **as if by magic** come per incanto

magician [məˈdʒɪʃən] *s* (*entertainer*) illusionista *mf*; (*sorcerer*) mago

magistrate [ˈmædʒɪsˌtret] *s* magistrato

magnanimous [mægˈnænɪməs] *adj* magnanimo

magnesium [mægˈniʃɪ·əm] *or* [mægˈniʒɪ·əm] *s* magnesio

magnet [ˈmægnɪt] *s* calamita, magnete *m*

magnetic [mægˈnɛtɪk] *adj* magnetico

magnetism [ˈmægnɪˌtɪzəm] *s* magnetismo

magnetize [ˈmægnɪˌtaɪz] *tr* calamitare, magnetizzare

magne·to [mægˈnito] *s* (**-tos**) magnete *m*

magnificent [mægˈnɪfɪsənt] *adj* magnifico

magni·fy [ˈmægnɪˌfaɪ] *v* (*pret & pp* **-fied**) *tr* ingrandire; (*to exaggerate*) magnificare

mag'nifying glass' *s* lente *f* d'ingrandimento

magnitude [ˈmægnɪˌtjud] *or* [ˈmægnɪˌtud] *s* grandezza

magpie [ˈmægˌpaɪ] *s* gazza

mahlstick [ˈmɑlˌstɪk] *or* [ˈmɔlˌstɪk] *s* appoggiamano

mahoga·ny [məˈhɑgəni] *s* (**-nies**) mogano

Mahomet [məˈhɑmɪt] *s* Maometto

maid [med] *s* (*girl*) ragazza; (*servant*) cameriera, domestica

maiden [ˈmedən] *s* pulzella

maid'en·hair' *s* (bot) capelvenere *m*

maid'en·head' *s* imene *m*

maidenhood [ˈmedənˌhud] *s* verginità *f*

maid'en la'dy *s* zitella

maid'en name' *s* nome *m* da signorina

maid'en voy'age *s* viaggio inaugurale

maid'-in-wait'ing *s* (**maids-in-waiting**) (*of a princess*) damigella d'onore; (*of a queen*) dama d'onore

maid' of hon'or *s* (*attendant at a wedding; attendant of a princess*) damigella d'onore; (*attendant of a queen*) dama d'onore

maid'serv'ant *s* domestica, ancella

mail [mel] *s* posta; (*of armor*) maglia; **by return mail** a volta di corriere ‖ *tr* impostare

mail'bag' *s* sacco postale

mail'boat' *s* battello postale

mail'box' *s* cassetta *or* buca delle lettere

mail' car' *s* vagone *m* postale

mail' car'rier *s* postino, portalettere *m*

mail'ing list' *s* indirizzario

mail'ing per'mit *s* abbonamento postale

mail'man' *s* (**-men'**) portalettere *m*

mail' or'der *s* ordinazione per corrispondenza

mail'-order house' *s* ditta che fa affari unicamente per corrispondenza

mail'plane' *s* aeroplano postale

mail' train' *s* treno postale

maim [mem] *tr* mutilare

main [men] *adj* principale, maggiore ‖ *s* condotta principale; **in the main** principalmente, per lo più

main' clause' *s* proposizione principale

main' course' *s* piatto forte

main' deck' *s* ponte *m* principale

mainland [ˈmenˌlænd] *or* [ˈmenlənd] *s* terra ferma, continente *m*

main' line' *s* (rr) linea principale

mainly [ˈmenli] *adv* principalmente

mainmast [ˈmenmæst], [ˈmenˌmæst] *or* [ˈmenˌmɑst] *s* albero maestro

mainsail [ˈmensəl] *or* [ˈmenˌsel] *s* vela maestra

main'spring' *s* molla motrice; (fig) molla

main'stay' *s* (naut) strallo di maestra; (fig) cardine *m*

main' street' *s* strada principale

maintain [menˈten] *tr* mantenere

maintenance [ˈmentɪnəns] *s* mantenimento; (*upkeep*) manutenzione

maître d'hôtel [ˌmetər doˈtel] *s* (*butler*) maggiordomo; (*headwaiter*) capocameriere *m*

maize [mez] *s* mais *m*

majestic [məˈdʒestɪk] *adj* maestoso

majes·ty [ˈmædʒɪsti] *s* (**-ties**) maestà *f*

major [ˈmedʒər] *adj* maggiore ‖ *s* (educ) specializzazione; (mil) maggiore *m* ‖ *intr* (educ) specializzarsi

major-do·mo [ˌmedʒərˈdomo] *s* (**-mos**) maggiordomo

ma'jor gen'eral *s* generale *m* di divisione

majori·ty [mə'dʒɑrɪti] or [mə'dʒɔrɪti] *adj* maggioritario ‖ *s* (-ties) (*being of full age*) maggiore età *f*; (*larger number or part*) maggioranza; (mil) grado di maggiore

make [mek] *s* (*brand*) marca; (*form*) stile *m*; produzione; **on the make** (slang) tirando l'acqua al proprio mulino ‖ *v* (*pret & pp* **made** [med]) *tr* fare; (*a train*) pigliare; (*a circuit*) chiudere; essere, e.g., **she will make a good typist** sarà una buona dattilografa; **to make** + *inf* fare + *inf*, e.g., **she made him study** lo fece studiare; **to make into** trasformare in; **to make known** far sapere; **to make of** pensare di; **to make oneself known** darsi a conoscere; **to make out** decifrare; (*a prescription*) scrivere, preparare; (*a check*) riempire; **to make over** convertire; (com) trasferire; **to make up** preparare, comporre; (*a story*) inventare; (*lost time*) riguadagnare; (typ) impaginare; (theat) truccare ‖ *intr* essere fatto; **to make away with** rubare; disfarsi di; **to make believe that** + *ind* far finta di + *inf*, e.g., **he made believe (that) he was sleeping** fece finta di dormire; **to make for** avvicinarsi a; attaccare; (*better relations*) contribuire a cementare; **to make much of** (coll) fare le feste a; **to make off** andarsene; **to make off with** svignarsela con; **to make out** (coll) farcela; **to make toward** incamminarsi verso; **to make up** truccarsi; fare la pace; **to make up for** compensare per, supplire a; **to make up to** (coll) ingraziarsi; (coll) fare la corte a

make'-be·lieve' *adj* immaginario ‖ *s* finzione, sembianza

maker ['mekər] *s* fabbricante *mf*, costruttore *m* ‖ **Maker** *s* Fattore *m*

make'shift' *adj* improvvisato, di fortuna ‖ *s* espediente *m*, ripiego; (*person*) tappabuchi *mf*

make'-up' *s* composizione, costituzione; truccatura, cosmetico; (typ) impaginazione; (journ) caratteristica

make'-up man' *s* truccatore *m*

make'-up test' *s* esame *m* di riparazione

make'weight' *s* giunta, contentino; (fig) supplemento, di più *m*

making ['mekɪŋ] *s* fabbricazione, costituzione; causa del successo; **makings** materiale *m*; (*potential*) stoffa

maladjusted [,mælə'dʒʌstɪd] *adj* spostato

mala·dy ['mælədi] *s* (-dies) malattia

malaise [mæ'lez] *s* malessere *m*

malapropos [,mæləprə'po] *adj* inopportuno ‖ *adv* a sproposito

malaria [mə'lerɪ·ə] *s* malaria

Malay ['mele] or [mə'le] *adj & s* malese *mf*

malcontent ['mælkən,tent] *adj & s* malcontento

male [mel] *adj & s* maschio

malediction [,mælɪ'dɪkʃən] *s* maledizione

malefactor ['mælɪ,fæktər] *s* malfattore *m*

male' nurse' *s* infermiere *m*

malevolent [mə'levələnt] *adj* malevolo

malfeasance [mæl'fizəns] *s* reato di pubblico funzionario

malice ['mælɪs] *s* malizia; (law) dolo; **to bear malice** serbar rancore; **with malice prepense** (law) con premeditazione

malicious [mə'lɪʃəs] *adj* malizioso, maligno

malign [mə'laɪn] *adj* maligno ‖ *tr* calunniare

malignan·cy [mə'lɪgnənsi] *s* (-cies) malignità *f*; (pathol) malignità *f*

malignant [mə'lɪgnənt] *adj* maligno

maligni·ty [mə'lɪgnɪti] *s* (-ties) malignità *f*

malinger [mə'lɪŋgər] *intr* fingersi ammalato, darsi malato (per sottrarsi al proprio dovere)

mall [mɔl] or [mæl] *s* viale *m*; (*strip of land in a boulevard*) aiola

mallet ['mælɪt] *s* maglio; (*of a stone cutter*) mazzuolo

mallow ['mælo] *s* malva

malnutrition [,mælnju'trɪʃən] or [,mælnu'trɪʃən] *s* malnutrizione

malodorous [mæl'odərəs] *adj* puzzolente

malpractice [mæl'præktɪs] *s* incuria, negligenza; (*of physician or lawyer*) negligenza colposa

malt [mɔlt] *s* malto

maltreat [mæl'trit] *tr* maltrattare

mamma ['mɑmə] or [mə'mɑ] *s* (coll) mamma

mammal ['mæməl] *s* mammifero

mammalian [mæ'melɪ·ən] *adj & s* mammifero

mammoth ['mæməθ] *adj* mastodontico ‖ *s* mammut *m*

man [mæn] *s* (**men** [mɛn]) uomo; (*in chess*) pedina; (*in checkers*) pezzo; **a man uno**, e.g., **a man can get lost in this town** uno può perdersi in questa città; **as one man** come un sol uomo; **man alive!** accidenti!; **man and wife** marito e moglie; **to be one's own man** essere completamente indipendente ‖ *v* (*pret & pp* **manned**) *ger* **manning**) *tr* (*a boat*) equipaggiare; (*a fortress*) guarnire; (*a cannon*) maneggiare

man' about town' *s* vitaiolo

manacle ['mænəkəl] *s*—**manacles** manette *fpl* ‖ *tr* ammanettare

manage ['mænɪdʒ] *tr* (*a business*) gestire; (*e.g., a tool*) maneggiare ‖ *intr* sbrogliarsela; **to manage to fare** in modo di; ingegnarsi a; **to manage to get along** barcamenarsi

manageable ['mænɪdʒəbəl] *adj* maneggevole

management ['mænɪdʒmənt] *s* direzione, gestione; (*executives collectively*) classe *f* dirigente; direzione; (*college course*) economia aziendale

manager ['mænədʒər] *s* direttore *m*, gerente *mf*; (theat) impresario; (sports) procuratore *m*, manager *m*

managerial [,mænə'dʒɪrɪ·əl] *adj* direttoriale, imprenditoriale

man'aging ed'itor *s* gerente *m* responsabile; redattore *m* in capo

mandate ['mændet] *s* mandato ‖ *tr* dare in mandato a

mandatory ['mændə,tori] *adj* obbligatorio

mandolin ['mændəlɪn] *s* mandolino

mandrake ['mændrek] *s* mandragola

mandrel ['mændrəl] *s* (mach) mandrino

mane [men] *s* criniera

maneuver [mə'nuvər] *s* manovra ‖ *tr* manovrare ‖ *intr* manovrare; (aer, nav) evoluire; (fig) intrigare

manful ['mænfəl] *adj* maschile, risoluto

manganese ['mæŋgə,nis] or ['mæŋgə,niz] *s* manganese *m*

mange [mendʒ] *s* rogna

manger ['mendʒər] *s* presepio

mangle ['mæŋgəl] *tr* straziare, lacerare

man-gy ['mendʒi] *adj* (-gier; -giest) rognoso; (squalid) misero

man'han'dle *tr* malmenare, maltrattare

man'hole' *s* passo d'uomo, pozzetto

manhood ['mænhʊd] *s* virilità *f*; uomini *mpl*, umanità *f*

man'hunt' *s* caccia all'uomo

mania ['menɪ-ə] *s* mania

maniac ['menɪ,æk] *adj & s* maniaco

manicure ['mænɪ,kjʊr] *s* (treatment) manicure *f*; (manicurist) manicure *mf* ‖ *tr* (a person) curare le mani di; (the hands) curare

manicurist ['mænɪ,kjʊrɪst] *s* manicurista *mf*, manicure *mf*

manifest ['mænɪ,fest] *adj* manifesto ‖ *s* (naut) manifesto di carico ‖ *tr* manifestare

manifes•to [,mænɪ'festo] *s* (-toes) manifesto

manifold ['mænɪ,fold] *adj* molteplice ‖ *s* copia; carta velina; (aut, mach) collettore *m*

manikin ['mænɪkɪn] *s* manichino; (dwarf) nano

man' in the moon' *s* faccia di uomo che appare nella luna piena

man' in the street' *s* uomo qualunque, uomo della strada

manipulate [mə'nɪpjə,let] *tr* manipolare

man'kind' *s* genere umano ‖ **man'kind'** *s* il sesso maschile

manliness ['mænlɪnɪs] *s* virilità *f*

man-ly ['mænli] *adj* (-lier; -liest) maschio, virile

manned' space'ship *s* astronave pilotata

mannequin ['mænɪkɪn] *s* (figure) manichino; (person) indossatrice *f*

manner ['mænər] *s* maniera; **by all manner of means** in tutti i modi; **in a manner of speaking** in una certa maniera; **in the manner of** alla moda di; **manners** maniere, *fpl*, educazione; **to the manner born** avvezzo sin dalla nascita

mannish ['mænɪʃ] *adj* maschile; (woman) mascolino

man' of God' *s* santo; profeta *m*; (priest) uomo al servizio di Dio

man' of let'ters *s* letterato

man' of means' *s* uomo danaroso

man' of parts' *s* uomo di talento

man' of straw' *s* uomo di paglia

man' of the world' *s* uomo di mondo

man-of-war [,mænəv'wɔr] *s* (**men-of-war** [,menəv'wɔr]) nave *f* da guerra

manor ['mænər] *s* maniero; feudo

man'or house' *s* maniero, palazzo

man' o'verboard *interj* uomo in mare!

man'pow'er *s* manodopera; (mil) effettivo

mansard ['mænsard] *s* mansarda

mansion ['mænʃən] *s* palazzo, palazzina; (manor house) maniero

man'slaugh'ter *s* omicidio colposo

mantel ['mæntəl] *s* parte *f* anteriore dei pilastri del camino; (shelf above it) mensola

man'tel-piece' *s* mensola del camino

man'tis shrimp' ['mæntɪs] *s* canocchia

mantle ['mæntəl] *s* mantello, cappa ‖ *tr* ammantare; (to conceal) nascondere ‖ *intr* (to blush) arrossire

manual ['mænjʊ-əl] *adj* manuale ‖ *s* (book) manuale *m*; (mil) esercizio; (mus) tastiera d'organo

man'ual train'ing *s* istruzione nelle arti e mestieri

manufacture [,mænjə'fæktʃər] *s* fabbricazione; (thing manufactured) manufatto ‖ *tr* fabbricare

manufacturer [,mænjə'fæktʃərər] *s* fabbricante *mf*, industriale *m*

manure [mə'njʊr] or [mə'nʊr] *s* letame *m* ‖ *tr* concimare

manuscript ['mænjə,skrɪpt] *adj & s* manoscritto

many ['meni] *adj & pron* molti; **a good many or a great many** un buon numero; **as many . . . as** tanti . . . quanti; **as many as** fino a, e.g., **they sell as many as five thousand dozen** vendono fino a cinquemila dozzine; **how many** quanti; **many a** molti, e.g., **many a day** molti giorni; **many another** molti altri; **many more** molti di più; **so many** tanti; **too many** troppi; **twice as many** altrettanti, il doppio

many-sided ['meni,saɪdɪd] *adj* multilaterale; versatile

map [mæp] *s* mappa; (of a city) piano ‖ *v* (pret & pp **mapped**; ger **mapping**) *tr* tracciare la mappa di; mostrare sulla mappa; **to map out** fare il piano di

maple ['mepəl] *s* acero

maquette [ma'ket] *s* plastico

mar [mar] *v* (pret & pp **marred**; ger **marring**) *tr* deturpare, sfigurare

maraud [mə'rɔd] *tr & intr* predare

marauder [mə'rɔdər] *s* predone *m*

marble ['marbəl] *adj* marmoreo ‖ *s* marmo; (little ball of glass) bilia; **marbles** bilie *fpl*; **to lose one's marbles** (slang) mancare una rotella a qlcu ‖ *tr* marmorizzare

march [martʃ] *s* marcia; (hist) marca; **to steal a march on** guadagnare il vantaggio su || *tr* far marciare || *intr* marciare || **March** *s* marzo

marchioness ['mɑr/ənɪs] *s* marchesa

mare [mɛr] *s (female horse)* cavalla; *(female donkey)* asina

margarine ['mɑrdʒərɪn] *s* margarina

margin ['mɑrdʒɪn] *s* margine *m;* (econ) scoperto

mar'gin stop' *s* marginatore *m*

marigold ['mærɪ‚gold] *s* fiorrancio

marihuana or **marijuana** [‚mɑrɪ-'hwɑnə] *s* marijuana

marina [mə'rinə] *s* porto turistico di imbarcazioni, porticciolo turistico

marinate ['mærɪ‚net] *tr* marinare

marine [mə'rin] *adj* marino, marittimo || *s* marina; soldato di fanteria da sbarco; **marines** fanteria da sbarco; **tell that to the marines!** (coll) va a raccontarlo ai frati!

mariner ['mærɪnər] *s* marinaio

marionette [‚mærɪ-ə'nɛt] *s* marionetta

mar'ital sta'tus ['mærɪtəl] *s* stato civile

maritime ['mærɪ‚taɪm] *adj* marittimo

marjoram ['mɑrdʒərəm] *s* origano; *(sweet marjoram)* maggiorana

mark [mɑrk] *s* segno; *(brand)* marca; *(of punctuation)* punto; *(in an examination)* voto; *(sign made by illiterate person)* croce *f; (landmark)* segnale *m; (target)* bersaglio; *(spot)* macchia; *(starting point in a race)* linea di partenza; *(of confidence)* voto; *(coin)* marco; impronta; **to be beside the mark** essere fuori del seminato; **to hit the mark** colpire il bersaglio; **to leave one's mark** lasciare la propria impronta; **to make one's mark** raggiungere il successo; **to miss the mark** fallire il colpo; **to toe the mark** mettersi in fila; filare diritto || *tr* marcare, segnare, contrassegnare; *(a student)* dar il voto a; *(a test)* esaminare; improntare; notare, avvertire; **to mark down** mettere in iscritto; ribassare il prezzo di

mark'down' *s* riduzione di prezzo

market ['mɑrkɪt] *s* mercato; **to bear the market** giocare al ribasso; **to bull the market** giocare al rialzo; **to play the market** giocare in borsa; **to put on the market** lanciare sul mercato || *tr* mettere sul mercato

marketable ['mɑrkɪtəbəl] *adj* commerciabile, vendibile

marketing ['mɑrkɪtɪŋ] *s* compravendita; marketing *m*

mar'ket-place' *s* piazza del mercato

mar'ket price' *s* prezzo corrente

mark'ing gauge' ['mɑrkɪŋ] *s* graffietto

marks'man *s* (-men) tiratore *m;* **a good marksman** un tiratore scelto

marksmanship ['mɑrksmən‚ʃɪp] *s* qualità *f* di tiratore scelto

mark'up' *s* margine *m* di rivendita

marl [mɑrl] *s* marna || *tr* marnare

marmalade ['mɑrmə‚led] *s* marmellata d'arance

marmot ['mɑrmət] *s* marmotta

maroon [mə'run] *adj & s* marrone *m* || *tr* abbandonare *(in un luogo deserto)*

marquee [mɑr'ki] *s* pensilina

marquess ['mɑrkwɪs] *s* marchese *m*

marque·try [mɑr'kɑtri] *s* (-tries) intarsio

marquis ['mɑrkwɪs] *s* marchese *m*

marquise [mɑr'kiz] *s* marchesa; (Brit) pensilina

marriage ['mærɪdʒ] *s* matrimonio

marriageable ['mærɪdʒəbəl] *adj* adatto al matrimonio; *(woman)* nubile

mar'riage por'tion *s* dote *f*

mar'riage rate' *s* nuzialità *f*

mar'ried life' *s* vita coniugale

marrow ['mæro] *s* midollo

mar·ry ['mæri] *v (pret & pp -ried) tr* sposare; **to get married to** sposarsi con || *intr* sposarsi; **to marry into** *(e.g., a noble family)* imparentarsi con; **to marry the second time** risposarsi

Mars [mɑrz] *s* Marte *m*

Marseilles [mɑr'selz] *s* Marsiglia

marsh [mɑrʃ] *s* palude *f,* lama

mar·shal ['mɑrʃəl] *s* direttore *m* di una sfilata; maestro di cerimonie; (mil) maresciallo; (U.S.A.) ufficiale *m* di giustizia || *v (pret & pp -shaled* or *-shalled)* ger *-shaling* or *-shalling) tr* introdurre cerimoniosamente; mettere in buon ordine

marsh' mal'low *s* (bot) altea

marsh'mal'low *s* dolce *m* di gelatina e zucchero

marsh·y ['mɑrʃi] *adj (-ier; -iest)* paludoso, palustre

marten ['mɑrtən] *s (Martes martes)* martora; *(Martes zibellina)* zibellino

martial ['mɑrʃəl] *adj* marziale

mar'tial law' *s* legge *f* marziale

Martian ['mɑrʃən] *adj & s* marziano

martin ['mɑrtɪn] *s* rondicchio

martinet [‚mɑrtɪ'nɛt] or ['mɑrtɪ‚nɛt] *s* pignolo

martyr ['mɑrtər] *s* martire *mf*

martyrdom ['mɑrtərdəm] *s* martirio

mar·vel ['mɑrvəl] *s* meraviglia || *v (pret & pp -veled* or *-velled;* ger *-veling* or *-velling) intr* meravigliarsi; **to marvel at** stupirsi di, meravigliarsi di

marvelous ['mɑrvələs] *adj* meraviglioso

Marxist ['mɑrksɪst] *adj & s* marxista *mf*

mascara [mæs'kærə] *s* bistro, rimmel *m*

mascot ['mæskət] *s* mascotte *f*

masculine ['mæskjəlɪn] *adj & s* maschile *m*

mash [mæʃ] *s (crushed mass)* poltiglia; *(to wort)* decotto d'orzo germinato; *(e.g., for poultry)* intriso || *tr* schiacciare; impastare

mashed' pota'toes *spl* purè *m* di patate

masher ['mæʃər] *s* utensile *m* per schiacciare; (slang) pappagallo

mask [mæsk] or [mɑsk] *s* maschera; (phot) mascherina || *tr* mascherare; (phot) mettere una mascherina a || *intr* mascherarsi

masked' ball' *s* ballo in maschera

mason ['mesən] *s* muratore *m* || **Mason** *s* massone *m*

mason·ry ['mesənri] *s* (-ries) arte *f* del

muratore; muratura || **Masonry** *s* massoneria

masquerade [ˌmæskəˈred] or [ˌmɑskəˈred] *s* mascherata; *(disguise)* maschera; *(pretense)* finzione || *intr* mascherarsi; **to masquerade as** mascherarsi da; farsi passare per

mass [mæs] *s* massa; *(celebration of the Eucharist)* messa; **in the mass** nell'insieme; **the masses** le masse || *tr* ammassare || *intr* ammassarsi, accumularsi

massacre [ˈmæsəkər] *s* massacro, strage *f* || *tr* massacrare, trucidare

massage [məˈsɑʒ] *s* massaggio || *tr* massaggiare

masseur [mæˈsœr] *s* massaggiatore *m*

masseuse [mæˈsœz] *s* massaggiatrice *f*

massive [ˈmæsɪv] *adj* massiccio; *(e.g., dose)* massivo; solido

mass′ me′dia [ˈmidɪ·ə] *s* mezzi *mpl* di comunicazione di massa

mass′ meet′ing *s* assemblea popolare; adunanza in massa

mass′ produc′tion *s* produzione in serie

mast [mæst] or [mɑst] *s* *(post)* palo; *(agr)* ghiande *fpl*; faggiole *fpl*; *(naut)* albero; **before the mast** come marinaio semplice

master [ˈmæstər] or [ˈmɑstər] *s* *(employer)* padrone *m*; *(male head of household)* capo di casa; *(man who possesses some special skill)* maestro; *(title of respect for a boy)* signorino; *(naut)* capitano || *tr* dominare; *(a language)* possedere

mas′ter bed′room *s* camera da letto padronale

mas′ter blade′ *s* foglia maestra (di una balestra)

mas′ter build′er *s* capomastro

masterful [ˈmæstərfəl] or [ˈmɑstərfəl] *adj* autoritario; provetto, magistrale

mas′ter key′ *s* chiave maestra

masterly [ˈmæstərli] or [ˈmɑstərli] *adj* magistrale || *adv* magistralmente

mas′ter mechan′ic *s* mastro meccanico

mas′ter-mind′ *s* mente direttiva || *tr* organizzare, dirigere

mas′ter of cer′emonies *s* maestro di cerimonia; *(in a night club, radio, etc.)* presentatore *m*

mas′ter-piece′ *s* capolavoro

mas′ter ser′geant *s* (mil) sergente *m* maggiore

mas′ter stroke′ *s* colpo da maestro

mas′ter-work′ *s* capolavoro

master·y [ˈmæstəri] or [ˈmɑstəri] *s* (**-ies**) *(command of a subject)* dominio; *(skill)* maestria

mast′head′ *s* *(journ)* titolo; *(naut)* testa d'albero

masticate [ˈmæstɪˌket] *tr* masticare

mastiff [ˈmæstɪf] or [ˈmɑstɪf] *s* mastino

masturbate [ˈmæstərˌbet] *tr* masturbare || *intr* masturbarsi

mat [mæt] *s* *(for floor)* tappeto, stuoia; *(under a dish)* tondo, sottocoppa, centrino; *(before a door)* stoino, zerbino; *(around a picture)* bordo di cartone; *(sports)* materas

sino; *(typ)* flan *m*; flano || *v* *(pret & pp* **matted;** *ger* **matting)** *tr* coprire di stuoie; arruffare || *intr* arruffarsi

match [mætʃ] *s* *(counterpart)* uguale *m*; *(suitably associated pair)* paio; *(light)* fiammifero; *(wick)* miccia; *(prospective mate)* partito; *(sports)* partita, gara; **to be a match for** essere pari a, fare fronte a; **to meet one's match** trovare un degno rivale || *tr* uguagliare, pareggiare; *(colors)* combinare; *(in pairs)* appaiare; giocarsi, e.g., **to match s.o. for the drinks** giocarsi le bevande con qlcu || *intr* corrispondersi, fare il paio

match′box′ *s* scatola di fiammiferi; *(of wax matches)* scatola di cerini

matchless [ˈmætʃlɪs] *adj* incomparabile, senza pari

match′mak′er *s* paraninfo

mate [met] *s* compagno; *(husband or wife)* consorte *mf*; *(to a female)* maschio; *(to a male)* femmina; *(chess)* scacco matto; *(naut)* primo ufficiale || *tr* appaiare; *(chess)* dar scacco matto a; **to be well mated** esser ben appaiato || *intr* accoppiarsi

material [məˈtɪrɪ·əl] *adj* materiale; importante || *s* materiale *m*, materia; *(cloth, fabric)* tela, stoffa; **materials** occorrente *m*

materialist [məˈtɪrɪ·əlɪst] *s* materialista *mf*

materialize [məˈtɪrɪ·əˌlaɪz] *intr* materializzarsi

matériel [məˌtɪrɪˈel] *s* materiale *m*; materiale bellico

maternal [məˈtʌrnəl] *adj* materno

maternity [məˈtʌrnɪti] *s* maternità *f*

mater′nity ward′ *s* maternità *f*

mathematical [ˌmæθɪˈmætɪkəl] *adj* matematico

mathematician [ˌmæθɪməˈtɪʃən] *s* matematico

mathematics [ˌmæθɪˈmætɪks] *s* matematica

matinée [ˌmætɪˈne] *s* mattinata, diurna

mat′ing sea′son *s* calore *m*

matins [ˈmætɪnz] *spl* mattutino

matriarch [ˈmetrɪˌɑrk] *s* matrona dignitosa; donna che possiede l'autorità matriarcale

matricidal [ˌmetrɪˈsaɪdəl] or [ˌmætrɪˈsaɪdəl] *adj* matricida

matricide [ˈmetrɪˌsaɪd] or [ˈmætrɪˌsaɪd] *s* *(act)* matricidio; *(person)* matricida *mf*

matriculate [məˈtrɪkjəˌlet] *tr* immatricolare || *intr* immatricolarsi

matriculation [məˌtrɪkjəˈleʃən] *s* immatricolazione, iscrizione

matrimonial [ˌmætrɪˈmonɪ·əl] *adj* matrimoniale

matrimo·ny [ˈmætrɪˌmoni] *s* (**-nies**) matrimonio

ma·trix [ˈmetrɪks] or [ˈmætrɪks] *s* (**-trices** [trɪˌsiz] or **-trixes**) matrice *f*

matron [ˈmetrən] *s* matrona; direttrice *f*; guardiana

matronly [ˈmetrənli] *adj* matronale

matter [ˈmætər] *s* *(physical substance)* materia; *(pus)* materia; *(affair, busi* *ness)* faccenda; *(material of a book)* contenuto; *(reason)* motivo; *(copy for printer)* manoscritto; *(printed material)* stampati *mpl;* **a matter of** un caso di; **for that matter** per quanto riguarda ciò; **in the matter** al soggetto; **no matter how** non importa; **no matter how** non importa come; **no matter when** non importa quando; **no matter where** non importa dove; **what is the matter?** cosa succede?; **what is the matter with you?** cosa ha? ‖ *intr* importare

mat′ter of course′ *s*—as **a matter of course** come se nulla fosse, come se fosse una cosa naturale

mat′ter of fact′ *s*—as **a matter of fact** in realtà, a onor del vero

matter-of-fact ['mætərəv ˌfækt] *adj* prosaico, pratico

mattock ['mætək] *s* piccone *m*

mattress ['mætrɪs] *s* materasso

mature [mə't/ur] or [mə'tur] *adj* maturo; *(due)* scaduto ‖ *tr* maturare ‖ *intr* maturare; (com) scadere

maturity [mə't/urɪti] or [mə'turɪti] *s* maturità *f;* (com) scadènza

maudlin ['mɔdlɪn] *adj* sentimentale, lagrimoso; piagnucoloso e ubriaco

maul [mɔl] *tr* maltrattare, bistrattare

maulstick ['mɔl ˌstɪk] *s* appoggiamano

maundy ['mɔndi] *s* lavanda

Maun′dy Thurs′day *s* giovedì santo

mausole-um [ˌmɔsə'li-əm] *s* (**-ums** or **-a** [ə]) mausoleo

maw [mɔ] *s* (e.g., *of a hog)* stomaco; *(of carnivorous mammal)* fauci *fpl; (of fowl)* gozzo; (fig) bocca, fauci *fpl*

mawkish ['mɔkɪʃ] *adj (sickening)* nauseante; *(sentimental)* svenevole

maxim ['mæksɪm] *s* massima

maximum ['mæksɪməm] *adj & s* massimo

may [me] *v aux*—**it may be** può essere; **may I come in?** si può?; **may you be happy!** possa tu essere felice! ‖ **May** *s* maggio

maybe ['mebi] *adv* forse

May′ Day′ *s* primo maggio; festa della primavera; (hist) calendimaggio *(in Florence)*

mayhem ['mehem] or ['me-əm] *s* mutilazione dolosa

mayonnaise [ˌme-ə'nez] *s* maionese *f*

mayor ['me-ər] or [mer] *s* sindaco

mayoress ['me-ərɪs] or ['merɪs] *s* donna sindaco

May′pole′ *s* maio, maggio, palo per le danze di calendimaggio

May′pole dance′ *s* ballo figurato con nastri per la festa di primavera

May′ queen′ *s* reginetta di maggio

maze [mez] *s* dedalo, labirinto

me [mi] *pron* me; mi; **to me** mi; **a me**

meadow ['medo] *s* prato

mead′ow-land′ *s* prateria

meager ['migər] *adj* magro

meal [mil] *s (food)* pasto; *(unbolted grain)* farina

meal′time′ *s* ora del pasto

mean [min] *adj (intermediate)* medio;

(low in rank) basso, umile; *(shabby)* misero; *(of poor quality)* inferiore; *(stingy)* taccagno; *(nasty)* villano; *(vicious, as a horse)* intrattabile; (coll) indisposto; (coll) vergognoso; (slang) splendido; **no mean** eccellente ‖ *s* media, termine medio; **by all means** certamente, senza dubbio; **by means of** per mezzo di; **by no means** in nessuna maniera; **means** beni *mpl; (agency)* mezzo, maniera; **to live on one's means** vivere di rendita ‖ *v (pret & pp* **meant** [ment]) *tr* significare, voler dire; **to mean to** pensare ‖ *intr*—**to mean well** aver buone intenzioni

meander [mɪ'ændər] *s* meandro ‖ *intr* serpeggiare, vagare

meaning ['minɪŋ] *s* senso, significato

meaningful ['minɪŋfəl] *adj* significativo

meaningless ['minɪŋlɪs] *adj* senza senso, senza significato

meanness ['minnɪs] *s* viltà *f,* bassezza; *(stinginess)* meschinità *f; (lowliness)* umiltà *f,* povertà *f*

mean′time′ *s*—**in the meantime** nel frattempo ‖ *adv* frattanto, intanto

mean′while′ *s & adv* var of **meantime**

measles ['mizəlz] *s* morbillo; *(German measles)* rosolia

mea·sly ['mizli] *adj* (**-slier; -sliest**) col morbillo; (coll) miserabile

measurable ['meʒərəbəl] *adj* misurabile

measure ['meʒər] *s* misura; *(legislative bill)* progetto di legge; (mus) battuta; **in a measure** in un certo senso; **to take the measure of** prendere le misure di; giudicare accuratamente ‖ *tr* misurare; *(a distance)* percorrere; **to measure out** somministrare ‖ *intr* misurare; **to measure up to** essere all'altezza di

measurement ['meʒərmənt] *s* misura; **to take s.o.'s measurements** prendere le misure di qlcu

meas′uring cup′ *s* vetro graduato

meat [mit] *s* carne *f; (food in general)* cibo; *(of nut)* gheriglio; (fig) sostanza, midollo

meat′ball′ *s* polpetta

meat′ grind′er *s* tritacarne *m*

meat′ loaf′ *s* polpettone *m*

meat′ mar′ket *s* macelleria

meat·y ['miti] *adj* (**-ier; -iest**) carnoso, polputo; (fig) sostanzioso

Mecca ['mekə] *s* la Mecca; **the Mecca** (fig) la Mecca

mechanic [mɪ'kænɪk] *s* meccanico; (aut) motorista *m*

mechanical [mɪ'kænɪkəl] *adj* meccanico; *(machinelike)* (fig) macchinale

mechan′ical engineer′ing *s* ingegneria meccanica

mechan′ical pen′cil *s* matita automatica

mechanics [mɪ'kænɪks] *s* meccanica

mechanism ['mekə ˌnɪzəm] *s* meccanismo, congegno

mechanize ['mekə ˌnaɪz] *tr* meccanizzare

medal ['medəl] *s* medaglia

medallion [mɪ'dæljən] *s* medaglione *m*

meddle ['mɛdəl] *intr* intromettersi

meddler ['mɛdlər] *s* ficcanaso

meddlesome ['mɛdəlsəm] *adj* invadente, indiscreto

median ['midɪ·ən] *adj* medio, mediano ‖ *s* punto medio, numero medio

me'dian strip' *s* spartitraffico

mediate ['midɪ‚et] *tr* (*a dispute*) comporre; (*parties*) pacificare ‖ *intr* (*to be in the middle*) mediare; fare da paciere

mediation [‚midɪ'efən] *s* mediazione

mediator ['midɪ‚etər] *s* mediatore *m*

medical ['mɛdɪkəl] *adj* medico; (*student*) di medicina

medicinal [mə'dɪsɪnəl] *adj* medicinale

medicine ['mɛdɪsɪn] *s* medicina

med'icine cab'inet *s* armadietto farmaceutico

med'icine kit' *s* cassetta farmaceutica

med'icine man' *s* (**men'**) stregone indiano

medieval [‚midɪ'ivəl] *or* [‚mɛdɪ'ivəl] *adj* medievale

medievalist [‚midɪ'ivəlɪst] *or* [‚medɪ'ivəlɪst] *s* medievalista *mf*

mediocre ['midɪ‚okər] *or* [‚midɪ'okər] *adj* mediocre

mediocri·ty [‚midɪ'ɑkrɪti] *s* (**-ties**) mediocrità *f*

meditate ['mɛdɪ‚tet] *tr & intr* meditare

meditation [‚mɛdɪ'tefən] *s* meditazione

Mediterranean [‚mɛdɪtə'renɪ·ən] *adj & s* Mediterraneo

medi·um ['midɪ·əm] *adj* medio; (*heat*) moderato; (*meat*) cotto moderatamente ‖ *s* (**-ums** *or* **-a** [ə]) (*middle state; mean*) media; mezzo; (*in spiritualism*) medium *m;* **media** (*of communication*) media *mpl;* **through the medium of** per mezzo di

medlar ['mɛdlər] *s* (*tree*) nespolo; (*fruit*) nespola

medley ['mɛdli] *s* farragine *f*, mescolanza; (*mus*) pot-pourri *m*

medul·la [mɪ'dʌlə] *s* (**-lae** [li]) midollo

meek [mik] *adj* mansueto, umile

meekness ['miknɪs] *s* mansuetudine *f*

meerschaum ['mɪrʃəm] *or* ['mɪrʃom] *s* schiuma; pipa di schiuma

meet [mit] *adj* conveniente ‖ *s* incontro ‖ *v* (*pret & pp* **met** [mɛt]) *tr* incontrare, incontrarsi con; (*to become acquainted with*) fare la conoscenza di; riunirsi con; (*to cope with*) sopperire a; (*said of a public carrier*) fare coincidenza con; andar incontro a; (*one's obligations*) far fronte a; (*bad luck*) avere; **to meet the eyes of** presentarsi agli occhi di ‖ *intr* incontrarsi; riunirsi; conoscersi; **till we meet again** arrivederci; **to meet with** incontrare, incontrarsi con; (*an accident*) avere; (*said of a public carrier*) fare coincidenza con

meeting ['mitɪŋ] *s* riunione, ritrovo; seduta, convegno; (*political*) comizio; (*e.g., of two rivers*) confluenza; duello

meet'ing of the minds' *s* accordo, consonanza di voleri

meet'ing place' *s* luogo di riunione

megacycle ['mɛgə‚saɪkəl] *s* megaciclo

megaphone ['mɛgə‚fon] *s* megafono, portavoce *m*

megohm ['mɛg‚om] *s* megaohm *m*

melancholia [‚mɛlən'kolɪ·ə] *s* melanconia, malinconia

melanchol·y ['mɛlən‚kɑli] *adj* malinconico ‖ *s* (**-ies**) malinconia

melee ['mele] *or* ['mele] *s* (*fight*) mischia; confusione

mellow ['mɛlo] *adj* (*fruit*) maturo; (*wine*) pastoso; (*voice*) soave, melodioso ‖ *tr* raddolcire ‖ *intr* raddolcirsi

melodic [mɪ'lɑdɪk] *adj* melodico

melodious [mɪ'lodɪ·əs] *adj* melodioso

melodramatic [‚mɛlədrə'mætɪk] *adj* melodrammatico

melo·dy ['mɛlədi] *s* (**-dies**) melodia

melon ['mɛlən] *s* melone *m*, popone *m*

melt [mɛlt] *tr* sciogliere; (*metals*) fondere; (*fig*) intenerire ‖ *intr* sciogliersi; fondersi; (*fig*) intenerirsi; **to melt away** svanire; **to melt into** convertirsi in, diventare; (*tears*) struggersi in

melt'ing pot' *s* crogiolo

member ['mɛmbər] *s* membro

membership ['mɛmbər‚fɪp] *s* associazione; numero di membri

membrane ['mɛmbren] *s* membrana

memen·to [mɪ'mɛnto] *s* (**-tos** *or* **-toes**) oggetto ricordo

mem·o ['mɛmo] *s* (**-os**) (coll) memorandum *m*

memoir ['mɛmwɑr] *s* memoria, memoriale *m;* biografia; **memoirs** memorie *fpl*

memoran·dum [‚mɛmə'rændəm] *s* (**-dums** *or* **-da** [də]) memorandum *m*

memorial [mɪ'morɪ·əl] *adj* commemorativo ‖ *s* sacrario; (*petition*) memoriale *m*

Memo'rial Day' *s* giorno dei caduti

memorialize [mɪ'morɪ·ə‚laɪz] *tr* commemorare

memorize ['mɛmə‚raɪz] *tr* imparare a memoria

memo·ry ['mɛməri] *s* (**-ries**) memoria; **to commit to memory** imparare a memoria

menace ['mɛnɪs] *s* minaccia ‖ *tr & intr* minacciare

ménage [me'nɑʒ] *s* casa; (*housekeeping*) economia domestica

menagerie [mə'næʒəri] *or* [mə'nædʒəri] *s* serraglio

mend [mɛnd] *s* riparo; **to be on the mend** migliorare ‖ *tr* (*to repair*) raccomodare, riparare; (*to patch*) rammendare; (*fig*) correggere ‖ *intr* correggersi

mendacious [mɛn'defəs] *adj* mendace

mendicant ['mɛndɪkənt] *adj & s* mendicante *mf*

menfolk ['mɛn‚fok] *spl* uomini *mpl*

menial ['minɪ·əl] *adj* basso, servile ‖ *s* servitore *m*, servo

menses ['mɛnsiz] *spl* mestruazione, mestrui *mpl*

men's' fur'nishings *spl* articoli *mpl* d'abbigliamento maschile

men's' room' *s* gabinetto per signori

menstruate ['mɛnstrʊ‚et] *intr* avere le mestruazioni

men'tal arith'metic ['mɛntəl] *s* calcolo mentale

men'tal hos'pital *s* manicomio

men'tal ill'ness *s* malattia mentale

men'tal reserva'tion *s* riserva mentale

men'tal test' *s* test *m* mentale

mention ['mɛn/ən] *s* menzione ‖ *tr* menzionare; **don't mention it** non c'è di che

menu ['mɛnju] *or* ['menju] *s* menu *m*, lista

meow [mɪ'aʊ] *s* miagolio ‖ *intr* miagolare

Mephistophelian [‚mɛfɪstə'filɪ‚ən] *adj* mefistofelico

mercantile ['mʌrkən‚til] *or* ['mʌrkən‚tail] *adj* mercantile

mercenar·y ['mʌrsə‚nɛri] *adj* mercenario ‖ *s* (**-ies**) mercenario

merchandise ['mʌrt/ən‚daiz] *s* mercanzia, merce *f*

merchant ['mʌrt/ənt] *adj* mercantile ‖ *s* mercante *m*, commerciante *mf*

mer'chant-man *s* (**-men**) mercantile *m*

mer'chant marine' *s* marina mercantile

merciful ['mʌrsɪfəl] *adj* misericordioso

merciless ['mʌrsɪlɪs] *adj* spietato

mercu·ry ['mʌrkjəri] *s* (**-ries**) mercurio ‖ **Mercury** *s* Mercurio

mer·cy ['mʌrsi] *s* (**-cies**) misericordia; **at the mercy of** alla mercé di

mere *adj* mero, puro

meretricious [‚mɛrɪ'trɪ/əs] *adj* vistoso, chiassoso, sgargiante; artificiale, falso, finto

merge [mʌrdʒ] *tr* fondere ‖ *intr* fondersi; (*said of two roads*) convergere; **to merge into** convertirsi lentamente in

merger ['mʌrdʒər] *s* fusione

meridian [mə'rɪdɪ‚ən] *adj* meridiano; culminante ‖ *s* meridiano; apogeo

meringue [mə'ræŋ] *s* meringa

merit ['mɛrɪt] *s* merito ‖ *tr* meritare

meritorious [‚mɛrɪ'tɔrɪ‚əs] *adj* meritorio

merlon ['mʌrlən] *s* merlo

mermaid ['mʌr‚med] *s* sirena

mer'man' *s* (**-men'**) tritone *m*

merriment ['mɛrɪmənt] *s* allegria

mer·ry ['mɛri] *adj* (**-rier; -riest**) allegro, giocondo; **to make merry** divertirsi

Mer'ry Christ'mas *interj* Buon Natale!

mer'ry-go-round' *s* giostra, carosello; (*of parties*) serie ininterrotta

mer'ry-mak'er *s* festaiolo

mesh [mɛ/] *s* (*network*) rete *f*; (*each open space of net*) maglia; (*mach*) ingranaggio; **meshes** rete *f* ‖ *tr* irretire; (*mach*) ingranare ‖ *intr* irretirsi; (*mach*) ingranarsi

mess [mɛs] *s* (*dirty condition*) disordine *m*; (*meal for a group of people*) mensa, rancio; porzione; **to get into a mess** mettersi nei pasticci; **to make a mess of** rovinare ‖ *tr* sporcare; disordinare; rovinare ‖ *intr* mangiare in comune; **to mess around** (coll) perdersi in cose inutili

message ['mɛsɪdʒ] *s* messaggio

messenger ['mɛsəndʒər] *s* messaggero; (*person who goes on an errand*) fattorino; (mil) portaordini *m*

mess' hall' *s* mensa

Messiah [mə'saɪ‚ə] *s* Messia *m*

mess' kit' *s* gavetta, gamella

mess'mate' *s* compagno di rancio

mess' of pot'tage ['patɪdʒ] *s* (Bib & fig) piatto di lenticchie

Messrs. ['mɛsərz] *pl* of **Mr.**

mess·y ['mɛsi] *adj* (**-ier; -iest**) disordinato; sporco

metal ['mɛtəl] *adj* metallico ‖ *s* metallo

metallic [mɪ'tælɪk] *adj* metallico

metallurgy ['mɛtə‚lʌrdʒi] *s* metallurgia

met'al pol'ish *s* lucido per metalli

met'al-work' *s* lavoro di metallo

metamorpho·sis [‚mɛtə'mɔrfəsɪs] *s* (**-ses** [‚siz]) metamorfosi *f*

metaphony [mə'tæfəni] *s* metafonia, metafonesi *f*

metaphor ['mɛtəfər] *or* ['mɛtə‚fɔr] *s* metafora

metaphorical [‚mɛtə'fɑrɪkəl] *or* [‚mɛtə'fɔrɪkəl] *adj* metaforico

metathe·sis [mɪ'tæθɪsɪs] *s* (**-ses** [‚siz]) metatesi *f*

mete [mit] *tr*—**to mete out** distribuire

meteor ['mitɪ‚ər] *s* meteora

meteoric [‚mitɪ'arɪk] *or* [‚mitɪ'ɔrɪk] *adj* meteorico; (fig) rapidissimo, folgorante

meteorite ['mitɪ‚ə‚raɪt] *s* meteorite *m* & *f*

meteorology [‚mitɪ‚ə'rɑlədʒi] *s* meteorologia

meter ['mitər] *s* (*unit of length; verse*) metro; (*instrument for measuring gas, water, etc.*) contatore *m*; (mus) tempo ‖ *tr* misurare col contatore

me'ter read'er *s* lettore *m*, letturista *m*

methane ['mɛθen] *s* metano

method ['mɛθəd] *s* metodo

methodic(al) [mɪ'θɑdɪk(əl)] *adj* metodico

Methodist ['mɛθədɪst] *adj* & *s* metodista *mf*

Methuselah [mɪ'θuzələ] *s* Matusalemme *m*

meticulous [mɪ'tɪkjələs] *adj* meticoloso

metric(al) ['mɛtrɪk(əl)] *adj* metrico

metronome ['mɛtrə‚nom] *s* metronomo

metropolis [mɪ'trɑpəlɪs] *s* metropoli *f*

metropolitan [‚mɛtrə'pɑlɪtən] *adj* & *s* metropolitano

mettle ['mɛtəl] *s* disposizione, temperamento; brio, animo; **to be on one's mettle** impegnarsi a fondo

mettlesome ['mɛtləsəm] *adj* brioso

mew [mju] *s* miagolio; (orn) gabbiano; **mews** scuderie *fpl*

Mexican ['mɛksɪkən] *adj* & *s* messicano

Mexico ['mɛksɪ‚ko] *s* il Messico

mezzanine ['mɛzə‚nin] *s* mezzanino

mica ['maɪkə] *s* mica

microbe ['maɪkrob] *s* microbio

microbiology [‚maɪkrəbaɪ'alədʒi] *s* microbiologia

microcard ['maɪkrə‚kɑrd] *s* microscheda

microfarad [ˌmaɪkrəˈfæræd] *s* micro-farad *m*

microfilm [ˈmaɪkrəˌfɪlm] *s* microfilm *m* ‖ *tr* microfilmare

microgroove [ˈmaɪkrəˌgruv] *adj* micro-solco ‖ *s* microsolco; disco micro-solco

microphone [ˈmaɪkrəˌfon] *s* microfono

microscope [ˈmaɪkrəˌskop] *s* micro-scopio

microscopic [ˌmaɪkrəˈskɑpɪk] *adj* mi-croscopico

microwave [ˈmaɪkrəˌwev] *s* microonda

mid [mɪd] *adj* mezzo, la metà di, e.g., **mid October** la metà di ottobre

mid'day' *adj* di mezzogiorno ‖ *s* mez-zogiorno

middle [ˈmɪdəl] *adj* medio, mezzo ‖ *s* mezzo, metà *f*; *(of human body)* cin-tura; **about the middle of** verso la metà di; **in the middle of** nel mezzo di

mid'dle age' *s* mezza età ‖ **Middle Ages** *spl* Medio Evo

mid'dle class' *s* ceto medio, borghesia

Mid'dle East' *s* Medio Oriente

Mid'dle Eng'lish *s* inglese *m* medievale parlato fra il 1150 e il 1500

mid'dle fin'ger *s* dito medio

mid'dle-man' *s* (-men') intermediario

middling [ˈmɪdlɪŋ] *adj* mediocre, pas-sabile ‖ *s* *(coarsely ground wheat)* farina grossa integrale; **middlings** articoli *mpl* di qualità mediocre ‖ *adv* moderatamente

mid·dy [ˈmɪdi] *s* (-dies) aspirante *m* di marina

mid'dy blouse' *s* marinara

midget [ˈmɪdʒɪt] *s* nano

midland [ˈmɪdlənd] *adj* centrale, in-terno ‖ *s* regione centrale

mid'night' *adj* di mezzanotte; **to burn the midnight oil** studiare a lume di candela ‖ *s* mezzanotte *f*

midriff [ˈmɪdrɪf] *s* diaframma *m*; *(mid-dle part of body)* cintura, vita

mid'ship'man *s* (-men) aspirante *m* di marina

midst [mɪdst] *s* mezzo, centro; **in the midst of** in mezzo a

mid'stream' *s—*in **midstream** in mezzo al fiume

mid'sum'mer *s* cuore *m* dell'estate

mid'way' *adj* situato a metà strada ‖ *s* metà strada; viale *m* principale di un' esposizione ‖ *adv* a metà strada

mid'week' *s* mezzo della settimana

mid'wife' *s* (-wives') levatrice *f*

mid'win'ter *s* cuore *m* dell'inverno

mid'year' *adj* nel mezzo dell'anno ‖ *s* mezzo dell'anno; **midyears** (coll) esami *mpl* nel mezzo dell'anno sco-lastico

mien [min] *s* aspetto, portamento

miff [mɪf] *s* (coll) battibecco ‖ *tr* (coll) offendere

might [maɪt] *s* forza, potenza; **with might and main** a tutta forza ‖ *v aux* used to form the potential, e.g., **he might change his mind** è possibile che cambi opinione

might·y [ˈmaɪti] *adj* (-ier; -iest) po-

tente; *(huge)* grandissimo ‖ *adv* (coll) moltissimo, grandemente

migraine [ˈmaɪgren] *s* emicrania

migrate [ˈmaɪgret] *intr* migrare

migratory [ˈmaɪgrəˌtori] *adj* migratore

milch [mɪltʃ] *adj* lattifero

mild [maɪld] *adj* dolce, mite, gentile; *(disease)* leggero

mildew [ˈmɪlˌdju] or [ˈmɪlˌdu] *s* *(mold)* muffa; *(plant disease)* perono-spora

mile [maɪl] *s* miglio terrestre; miglio marino

mileage [ˈmaɪlɪdʒ] *s* distanza in miglia

mile'age tick'et *s* biglietto calcolato in miglia simile al biglietto chilometrag-gio

mile'post' *s* colonnina miliare

mile'stone' *s* pietra miliare

milieu [mɪlˈju] *s* ambiente *m*

militancy [ˈmɪlɪtənsi] *s* bellicismo; spirito militante

militant [ˈmɪlɪtənt] *adj* & *s* militante *mf*

militarism [ˈmɪlɪtəˌrɪzəm] *s* milita-rismo

militarist [ˈmɪlɪtərɪst] *adj* & *s* mili-tarista *mf*

militarize [ˈmɪlɪtəˌraɪz] *tr* militariz-zare

military [ˈmɪlɪˌteri] *adj* militare ‖ *s—*the **military** le forze armate

mil'itary acad'emy *s* scuola allievi uffi-ciali, accademia militare

mil'itary police' *s* polizia militare

militate [ˈmɪlɪˌtet] *intr* militare

militia [mɪˈlɪʃə] *s* milizia

mili'tia-man *s* (-men) miliziano

milk [mɪlk] *adj* lattifero; di latte; **al latte** ‖ *s* latte *m* ‖ *tr* mungere; (fig) spillare ‖ *intr* dare latte

milk' can' *s* bidone *m* per il latte

milk' choc'olate *s* cioccolato al latte

milk' diet' *s* regime latteo

milking [ˈmɪlkɪŋ] *s* mungitura

milk'maid' *s* lattaia

milk'man' *s* (-men') lattaio

milk' of hu'man kind'ness *s* grande compassione

milk' pail' *s* secchio da latte

milk' shake' *s* frappé *m* or frullato di latte

milk'sop' *s* effeminato

milk'weed' *s* vincetossico

milk·y [ˈmɪlki] *adj* (-ier; -iest) latteo; *(whitish)* lattiginoso

Milk'y Way' *s* Via Lattea

mill [mɪl] *s* *(for grinding grain)* mu-lino; *(for making fabrics)* filanda; *(for cutting wood)* segheria; *(for re-fining sugar)* zuccherificio; *(for pro-ducing steel)* acciaieria; *(to grind coffee)* macinino; *(part of a dollar)* millesimo; **to put through the mill** mettere a dura prova ‖ *tr* *(grains)* macinare; *(coins)* zigrinare; *(steel)* laminare; *(ore)* frantumare; *(with a milling machine)* fresare; *(chocolate)* frullare ‖ *intr—*to **mill about** or **around** girare intorno

millennial [mɪˈlɛnɪəl] *adj* millenario

milleni·um [mɪ'lenɪ·əm] s (-ums or -a [ə]) millennio

miller ['mɪlər] s mugnaio; (ent) tignola notturna

millet ['mɪlɪt] s panico, miglio

milliampere [ˌmɪlɪ'æmpɪr] s milliampere m

milliard ['mɪljərd] or ['mɪljɑrd] s (Brit) miliardo, bilione m

milligram ['mɪlɪˌgræm] s milligrammo

millimeter ['mɪlɪˌmitər] s millimetro

milliner ['mɪlɪnər] s modista

milliner·y ['mɪlɪˌnerɪ] or ['mɪlɪnərɪ] s (-ies) cappelli mpl per signora; modisteria; articoli mpl di modisteria

mil'linery shop' s modisteria

milling ['mɪlɪŋ] s (of grain) macinatura; (of coins) granitura; (mach) fresatura

mill'ing machine' s fresatrice f

million ['mɪljən] adj milione di, milioni di || s milione m

millionaire [ˌmɪljən'er] s milionario

millionth ['mɪljənθ] adj, s & pron milionesimo

millivolt ['mɪlɪˌvolt] s millivolt m

mill'pond' s gora

mill'race' s corrente f che aziona il mulino; canale m di presa

mill'stone' s mola, macina, palmento; (fig) peso, gravame m

mill' wheel' s ruota del mulino

mill'work' s lavoro di falegnameria; lavoro di falegnameria fatto a macchina

mime [maɪm] s mimo || tr mimare

mimeograph ['mɪmɪ·əˌgræf] or ['mɪmɪəˌgrɑf] s (trademark) ciclostile m || tr ciclostilare

mim·ic ['mɪmɪk] s mimo, imitatore m || v (pret & pp -icked; ger -icking) tr imitare, scimmiottare

mimic·ry ['mɪmɪkrɪ] s (-ries) mimica; (biol) mimetismo

minaret [ˌmɪnə'ret] or ['mɪnəˌret] s minareto

mince [mɪns] tr tagliuzzare, triturare; (words) pronunziare con affettazione; **to not mince one's words** non aver peli sulla lingua

mince'meat' s carne tritata; **to make mincemeat of** annientare completamente

mince' pie' s torta di frutta secca e carne tritata

mind [maɪnd] s mente f; opinione; **to bear in mind** tener presente; **to be not in one's right mind** essere fuori di senno; **to be of one mind** essere d'accordo; **to be out of one's mind** essere impazzito; **to change one's mind** cambiare d'opinione; **to go out of one's mind** impazzire; **to have a mind to** aver voglia di; **to have in mind** to pensare a; **to have on one's mind** avere in mente; **to lose one's mind** uscire di mente; **to make up one's mind** decidersi; **to my mind** a mio modo di vedere; **to say whatever comes to one's mind** dire quanto salta in testa, e.g., **John always says whatever comes to his mind** Gio-

vanni dice sempre quanto gli salta in testa; **to set one's mind on** risolversi a; **to slip one's mind** scappare di mente (with dat), e.g., **it slipped his mind** gli è scappato di mente; **to speak one's mind** dire la propria opinione; **with one mind** unanimamente || tr (to take care of) occuparsi di; obbedire (with dat); **do you mind the smoke?** Le disturba il fumo?; **mind your own business** si occupi degli affari Suoi || intr osservare, fare attenzione; rincrescere, e.g., **do you mind if I go?** Le rincresce se vado?; **never mind** non si preoccupi

mindful ['maɪndfəl] adj memore

mind' read'er s lettore m del pensiero

mind' read'ing s lettura del pensiero

mine [maɪn] s (e.g., of coal) miniera; (mil & nav) mina || pron poss il mio; mio || tr minare; (earth) scavare; (ore) estrarre || intr lavorare una miniera; (mil & nav) minare

mine' detec'tor s rivelatore m di mine

mine'field' s campo minato

mine'lay'er s posamine m

miner ['maɪnər] s minatore m

mineral ['mɪnərəl] adj & s minerale m

mineralogy [ˌmɪnə'rælədʒɪ] s mineralogia

min'eral wool' s cotone m or lana minerale

mine' sweep'er s dragamine m

mingle ['mɪŋgəl] tr mescolare; unire || intr mescolarsi, associarsi

miniature ['mɪnɪ·ətʃər] or ['mɪnɪtʃər] s miniatura; **to paint in miniature** miniare, dipingere in miniatura

min'iature golf' s minigolf m

miniaturization [ˌmɪnɪ·ətʃərɪ'zeʃən] or [ˌmɪnɪtʃərɪ'zeʃən] s miniaturizzazione

minimal ['mɪnɪməl] adj minimo

minimize ['mɪnɪˌmaɪz] tr minimizzare

minimum ['mɪnɪməm] adj & s minimo

min'imum wage' s salario minimo

mining ['maɪnɪŋ] adj minerario || s estrazione di minerali; (nav) posa di mine

minion ['mɪnjən] s servo; favorito, beniamino

min'ion of the law' s poliziotto

miniskirt ['mɪnəˌskʌrt] s minigonna

minister ['mɪnɪstər] s ministro; pastore m protestante || tr & intr ministrare

ministerial [ˌmɪnɪs'tɪrɪ·əl] adj ministeriale

minis·try ['mɪnɪstrɪ] s (-tries) ministero; sacerdozio

mink [mɪŋk] s visone m

minnow ['mɪno] s pesciolino; (ichth) ciprino

minor ['maɪnər] adj minore || s minore m, minorenne mf; (educ) corso secondario

minori·ty [mɪ'nɑrɪtɪ] or [mɪ'nɔrɪtɪ] adj minoritario || s (-ties) (smaller number or part; group differing in race, etc., from majority) minoranza; (under legal age) minorità f

minstrel ['mɪnstrəl] s (hist) menestrello; (U.S.A.) comico vestito da nero

minstrel·sy ['mɪnstrəlsi] *s* (**-sies**) giulleria; poesia giullaresca

mint [mɪnt] *s* zecca; (*plant*) menta; (*losenge*) mentina; (fig) miniera d'oro || *tr* coniare

minuet [,mɪnju'et] *s* minuetto

minus ['maɪnəs] *adj* meno || *s* meno, perdita || *prep* meno, senza

minute [maɪ'njut] or [maɪ'nut] *adj* minuto || ['mɪnɪt] *adj* fatto in un minuto || *s* minuto; momento; **minutes** processo verbale; **to write up the minutes** tenere i verbali; **up to the minute** al corrente; dell'ultima ora

min'ute hand' ['mɪnɪt] *s* sfera or lancetta dei minuti

minutiae [mɪ'njuʃɪ,i] or [mɪ'nuʃɪ,i] *spl* minuzie *fpl*

minx [mɪŋks] *s* sfacciata, civetta

miracle ['mɪrəkəl] *s* miracolo

mir'acle play' *s* sacra rappresentazione

miraculous [mɪ'rækjələs] *adj* miracoloso

mirage [mɪ'rɑʒ] *s* miraggio

mire [maɪr] *s* limo, mota

mirror ['mɪrər] *s* specchio || *tr* specchiare, riflettere

mirth [mʌrθ] *s* allegria, gioia

mir·y ['maɪri] *adj* (**-ier; -iest**) fangoso, limaccioso

misadventure [,mɪsəd'ventʃər] *s* disavventura, contrattempo

misanthrope ['mɪsən,θrop] *s* misantropo

misanthropy [mɪs'ænθrəpi] *s* misantropia

misapprehension [,mɪsæprɪ'henʃən] *s* malinteso

misappropriation [,mɪsə,proprɪ'eʃən] *s* malversazione

misbehave [,mɪsbɪ'hev] *intr* comportarsi male

misbehavior [,mɪsbɪ'hevɪ·ər] *s* cattiva condotta

miscalculation [,mɪskælkjə'leʃən] *s* calcolo errato

miscarriage [mɪs'kærɪdʒ] *s* (*of justice*) errore *m*; (*of a letter*) disguido; (pathol) aborto

miscar·ry [mɪs'kæri] *v* (*pret & pp* **-ried**) *intr* (*said of a project*) fallire; (*said of a letter*) smarrirsi; (pathol) abortire

miscellaneous [,mɪsə'lenɪ·əs] *adj* miscellaneo

miscella·ny ['mɪsə,leni] *s* (**-nies**) miscellanea

mischief ['mɪstʃɪf] *s* (*harm*) danno; (*disposition to annoy*) malizia; (*prankishness*) birichinata

mis'chief-mak'er *s* mettimale *mf*

mischievous ['mɪstʃɪvəs] *adj* dannoso; malizioso; birichino

misconception [,mɪskən'sepʃən] *s* concetto erroneo, fraintendimento

misconduct [mɪs'kɑndəkt] *s* cattiva condotta; (*of a public official*) malgoverno || [,mɪskən'dʌkt] *tr* male amministrare; **to misconduct oneself** comportarsi male

misconstrue [,mɪskən'stru] or [mɪs'kɑnstru] *tr* fraintendere

miscount [mɪs'kaʊnt] *s* conteggio erroneo || *tr & intr* contare male

miscue [mɪs'kju] *s* sbaglio; (*in billiards*) stecca || *intr* steccare; (theat) sbagliarsi di battuta

mis·deal ['mɪs,dil] *s* distribuzione sbagliata || [mɪs'dil] *v* (*pret & pp* **-dealt** [delt]) *tr & intr* distribuire erroneamente

misdeed [mɪs'did] or ['mɪs,did] *s* misfatto, malfatto

misdemeanor [,mɪsdɪ'minər] *s* cattiva condotta; (law) delitto colposo

misdirect [,mɪsdɪ'rekt] or [,mɪsdaɪ-'rekt] *tr* dare un indirizzo sbagliato a; (*a letter*) mettere un indirizzo sbagliato su

misdoing [mɪs'du·ɪŋ] *s* misfatto

miser ['maɪzər] *s* avaro, spilorcio

miserable ['mɪzərəbəl] *adj* miserabile, miserevole; (coll) malissimo; (coll) schifoso

miserly ['maɪzərli] *adj* spilorcio

miser·y ['mɪzəri] *s* (**-ies**) miseria

misfeasance [mɪs'fizəns] *s* infrazione della legge; abuso di autorità commesso da pubblico funzionario

misfire [mɪs'faɪr] *s* difetto di esplosione; (aut) difetto d'accensione || *intr* (*said of a gun*) fare cilecca; (aut) dare accensione irregolare; (fig) fallire

mis·fit ['mɪs,fɪt] *s* vestito che non va bene; (*person*) spostato, pesce *m* fuor d'acqua || [mɪs'fɪt] *v* (*pret & pp* **-fitted**) *ger* (**-fitting**) *intr* andar male

misfortune [mɪs'fɔrtʃən] *s* disgrazia

misgiving [mɪs'gɪvɪŋ] *s* dubbio, timore *m*, cattivo presentimento

misgovern [mɪs'gʌvərn] *tr* amministrare male

misguided [mɪs'gaɪdɪd] *adj* fuorviato; (*e.g., kindness*) sconsigliato

mishap ['mɪshæp] or [mɪs'hæp] *s* accidente *m*, infortunio

misinform [,mɪsɪn'fɔrm] *tr* dare informazioni errate a

misinterpret [,mɪsɪn'tɜrprɪt] *tr* interpretare male, trasfigurare

misjudge [mɪs'dʒʌdʒ] *tr & intr* giudicare male

mis·lay [mɪs'le] *v* (*pret & pp* **-laid** [,led]) *tr* (*e.g., tile*) applicare in maniera sbagliata; (*e.g., papers*) smarrire, mettere al posto sbagliato

mis·lead [mɪs'lid] *v* (*pret & pp* **-led** [,led]) *tr* sviare, traviare

misleading [mɪs'lidɪŋ] *adj* ingannatore

mismanagement [mɪs'mænɪdʒmənt] *s* malgoverno

misnomer [mɪs'nomər] *s* termine improprio

misplace [mɪs'ples] *tr* mettere fuori di posto; (*trust*) riporre erroneamente

misprint ['mɪs,prɪnt] *s* errore *m* di stampa, refuso || [mɪs'prɪnt] *tr* stampare erroneamente

mispronounce [,mɪsprə'naʊns] *tr* pronunciare in modo erroneo

mispronunciation [,mɪsprə,nʌnsɪ-

'e∫ən] or [,mɪsprə,nʌn∫ɪ'e∫ən] s errore m di pronuncia

misquote [mɪs'kwot] tr citare incorrettamente

misrepresent [,mɪsreprɪ'zent] tr travisare, snaturare; (pol) rappresentare slealmente

miss [mɪs] s sbaglio, omissione; tiro fuori bersaglio; signorina || tr (a train, an opportunity) perdere; (the target) fallire; (an appointment) mancare; (the point) non vedere, non capire; per poco, e.g., **the car missed hitting him** l'automobile non l'ha investito per poco || intr sbagliare, fallire; mancare il bersaglio || **Miss** s signorina, la signorina

missal ['mɪsəl] s messale m

misshapen [mɪs'∫epən] adj deforme, malfatto

missile ['mɪsɪl] adj missilistico || s missile m

mis'sile launch'er s lanciamissili m

missing ['mɪsɪŋ] adj mancante; assente; (in action) disperso

mis'sing link' s anello di congiunzione

miss'ing per'son s disperso

mission ['mɪ∫ən] s missione

missionar·y ['mɪ∫ən,ɛri] adj missionario || s (-ies) (eccl) missionario; (dipl) incaricato in missione

missive ['mɪsɪv] s missiva

mis·spell [mɪs'spel] v (pret & pp -spelled or -spelt ['spelt]) tr & intr scrivere male

misspelling [mɪs'spelɪŋ] s errore m di ortografia

misspent [mɪs'spent] adj sprecato

misstatement [mɪs'stetmənt] s dichiarazione inesatta

misstep [mɪs'step] s passo falso

miss·y ['mɪsi] s (-ies) (coll) signorina

mist [mɪst] s caligine f, foschia; (of tears) velo; (of smoke, vapors, etc.) nuvola

mis·take [mɪs'tek] s errore m, sbaglio; **and no mistake** (coll) di sicuro; **by mistake** per sbaglio; **to make a mistake** sbagliarsi || v (pret -took ['tʊk]; pp -taken) tr fraintendere; **to be mistaken for** essere preso per; **to mistake for** pigliare per

mistaken [mɪs'tekən] adj errato, sbagliato; **to be mistaken** essere in errore, sbagliarsi

mister ['mɪstər] s (mil, nav) signore m; (coll) marito || interj (coll) signore!; (coll) Lei!; (coll) buonuomo! || **Mister** s Signore m

mistletoe ['mɪsəl,to] s vischio

mistreat [mɪs'trit] tr maltrattare

mistreatment [mɪs'tritmənt] s maltrattamento

mistress ['mɪstrɪs] s (of a household) signora, padrona; (paramour) amante f, ganza; (Brit) maestra di scuola

mistrial,[mɪs'traɪ-əl] s processo viziato da errore giudiziario

mistrust [mɪs'trʌst] s diffidenza || tr diffidare di || intr diffidarsi

mistrustful [mɪs'trʌstfəl] adj diffidente

mist·y ['mɪsti] adj (-ier; -iest) fosco, brumoso; (fig) vago, confuso

misunder·stand [,mɪsʌndər'stænd] v (pret & pp -stood ['stud]) tr fraintendere, equivocare

misunderstanding [,mɪsʌndər'stændɪŋ] s malinteso

misuse [mɪs'jus] s abuso; (of funds) malversazione || [mɪs'juz] tr abusare di; (funds) malversare

misword [mɪs'wʌrd] tr comporre male

mite [maɪt] s obolo; (ent) acaro

miter ['maɪtər] s (carp) ugnatura; (carp) giunto a quartabuono; (eccl) mitra || tr tagliare a quartabuono, ugnare; giungere a quartabuono

mi'ter box' s cassetta per ugnature

mi'ter joint' s giunto a quartabuono

mitigate ['mɪtɪ,get] tr mitigare

mitten ['mɪtən] s manopola, muffola

mix [mɪks] tr mescolare; (colors) mesticare; (dough) impastare; (salad) condire; **to mix up** confondere || intr confondersi, mescolarsi

mixed [mɪkst] adj misto; (candy) assortito; (coll) confuso

mixed' com'pany s riunione f di ambo i sessi

mixed' drink' s miscela di liquori diversi

mixed' feel'ing s sentimento ambivalente

mixed' met'aphor s metafora incongruente

mixer ['mɪksər] s (mach) mescolatrice f; **to be a good mixer** essere socievole

mixture ['mɪkst∫ər] s mistura, mescolanza; (aut) miscela, carburazione

mix'-up' s confusione; (coll) baruffa

mizzen ['mɪzən] s mezzana

moan [mon] s gemito || intr gemere

moat [mot] s fosso, fossato

mob [mɑb] s turba || v (pret & pp mobbed; ger mobbing) tr assaltare; affollarsi intorno a; (a place) affollare

mobile ['mobɪl] or ['mobil] adj mobile

mo'bile home' s caravan m, roulotte f

mobility [mo'bɪlti] s mobilità f

mobilization [,mobɪlɪ'ze∫ən] s mobilitazione

mobilize ['mobɪ,laɪz] tr & intr mobilitare

mob' rule' s legge f della teppa

mobster ['mɑbstər] s gangster m

moccasin ['mɑkəsɪn] s mocassino

Mo'cha cof'fee ['mokə] s caffè m moca

mock [mɑk] adj finto, imitato || s dileggio, burla || tr deridere, canzonare; ingannare || intr motteggiare; **to mock at** farsi gioco di

mocker·y ['mɑkəri] s (-ies) dileggio, scherno; (subject of derision) zimbello; (poor imitation) contraffazione

mock'-hero'ic adj eroicomico

mockingbird ['mɑkɪŋ,bʌrd] s mimo

mock' or'ange s gelsomino selvatico

mock' tur'tle soup' s finto brodo di tartaruga

mock'-up' s modello dimostrativo

mode [mod] s modo, maniera; (fashion) moda; (gram) modo

mod·el ['mɑdəl] adj modello, e.g., **model student** studente modello || s modello; (*woman serving as subject for artists*) modello *f*; (*woman wearing clothes at fashion show*) indossatrice *f* ‖ *v* (*pret & pp* -eled or -elled; *ger* -eling or -elling) *tr* modellare ‖ *intr* modellarsi; fare il manichino

mod'el air'plane *s* aeromodello

mo'del-air'plane build'er *s* aeromodellista *mf*

mod'eling clay' *s* plastilina

moderate ['mɑdərɪt] *adj* moderato ‖ ['mɑdə‚ret] *tr* moderare; (*a meeting*) presiedere a ‖ *intr* moderarsi

moderator ['mɑdə‚retər] *s* moderatore *m*; (*mediator*) arbitro; (phys) moderatore *m*

modern ['mɑdərn] *adj* moderno

modernize ['mɑdər‚naɪz] *tr* modernizzare, rimodernare

modest ['mɑdɪst] *adj* modesto

modes•ty ['mɑdɪsti] *s* (-ties) modestia

modicum ['mɑdɪkəm] *s* piccola quantità

modi•fy ['mɑdɪ‚faɪ] *v* (*pret & pp* -fied) *tr* modificare; (gram) determinare

modish ['modɪʃ] *adj* alla moda

modulate ['mɑdʒə‚let] *tr & intr* modulare

modulation [‚mɑdʒə'leʃən] *s* modulazione

mohair ['mo‚her] *s* mohair *m*

Mohammedan [mo'hæmɪdən] *adj & s* maomettano

Mohammedanism [mo'hæmɪdə‚nɪzəm] *s* maomettismo

moist [mɔɪst] *adj* umido; lacrimoso

moisten ['mɔɪsən] *tr* inumidire ‖ *intr* inumidirsi

moisture ['mɔɪstʃər] *s* umidità *f*

molar ['molər] *s* molare *m*

molasses [mə'læsɪz] *s* melassa

mold [mold] *s* stampo, forma; (*fungus*) muffa; humus *m*; (fig) indole *f* ‖ *tr* plasmare, conformare; (*to make moldy*) fare ammuffire ‖ *intr* ammuffire

molder ['moldər] *s* modellatore *m* ‖ *intr* sgretolarsi; polverizzarsi

molding ['moldɪŋ] *s* modellato; (archit, carp) modanatura

mold•y ['moldi] *adj* (-ier; -iest) ammuffito

mole [mol] *s* (*pier*) molo; (*harbor*) darsena; (*spot on skin*) neo; (*small mammal*) talpa

molecule ['mɑlɪ‚kjul] *s* molecola

mole'hill' *s* mucchio di terra sopra la tana di talpe

mole'skin' *s* pelle *f* di talpa; (*fabric*) fustagno di prima qualità

molest [mə'lest] *tr* molestare; fare proposte disoneste a

moll [mɑl] *s* (slang) ragazza della malavita; (slang) puttana

molli•fy ['mɑlɪ‚faɪ] *v* (*pret & pp* -fied) *tr* pacificare, placare

mollusk ['mɑləsk] *s* mollusco

mollycoddle ['mɑlɪ‚kɑdəl] *s* effeminato ‖ *tr* viziare, coccolare

Mo'lotov cock'tail ['mɑlə‚tɔf] *s* bottiglia Molotov

molt [molt] *s* muda ‖ *intr* andare in muda

molten ['moltən] *adj* fuso

molybdenum [mə'lɪbdɪnəm] or [‚mɑlɪb'dinəm] *s* molibdeno

moment ['momənt] *s* momento; **at any moment** da un momento all'altro

momentary ['momən‚tɛri] *adj* momentaneo

momentous [mo'mentəs] *adj* grave, importante

momen•tum [mo'mentəm] *s* (-tums or -ta [tə]) slancio; (mech) momento

monarch ['mɑnərk] *s* monarca *m*

monarchic(al) [mə'nɑrkɪk(əl)] *adj* monarchico

monarchist ['mɑnərkɪst] *adj & s* monarchico

monar•chy ['mɑnərki] *s* (-chies) monarchia

monaster•y ['mɑnəs‚tɛri] *s* (-ies) monastero

monastic [mə'næstɪk] *adj* monastico, monacale

monasticism [mə'næstɪ‚sɪzəm] *s* monachesimo

Monday ['mʌndi] *s* lunedì *m*

monetary ['mɑnɪ‚tɛri] *adj* monetario; pecuniario

money ['mʌni] *s* denaro; **to be in the money** esser carico di soldi; **to make money** far quattrini

mon'ey-bag' *s* borsa per denaro; **moneybags** (coll) riccone sfondato

moneychanger ['mʌnɪ‚tʃendʒər] *s* cambiavalute *m*

moneyed ['mʌnid] *adj* danaroso

moneylender ['mʌni‚lendər] *s* prestatore *m* di denaro

mon'ey-mak'er *s* capitalista *mf*; affare vantaggioso

mon'ey or'der *s* vaglia *m*

Mongolian [mɑŋ'goli-ən] *adj & s* mongolo

mon•goose ['mɑŋgus] *s* (-gooses) mangusta

mongrel ['mʌŋgrəl] or ['mɑŋgrəl] *adj* ibrido ‖ *s* ibrido; cane bastardo

monitor ['mɑnɪtər] *s* (educ) capoclasse *mf*; (rad, telv) monitore *m* ‖ *tr* osservare; (*a signal*) controllare; (*a broadcast*) ascoltare

monk [mʌŋk] *s* monaco

monkey ['mʌŋki] *s* scimmia; **to make a monkey of** farsi gioco di ‖ *intr*—**to monkey around** (coll) oziare; **to monkey around with** (coll) giocherellare con

mon'key-shines' *spl* (slang) monellerie *fpl*, pagliacciate *fpl*

mon'key wrench' *s* chiave *f* inglese

monkhood ['mʌŋkhud] *s* monacato

monkshood ['mʌŋks‚hud] *s* (bot) aconito

monocle ['mɑnəkəl] *s* monocolo

monogamy [mə'nɑgəmi] *s* monogamia

monogram ['mɑnə‚græm] *s* monogramma *m*

monograph ['mɑnə‚græf] or ['mɑnə‚grɑf] *s* monografia

monolithic [‚mɑnə'lɪθɪk] *adj* monolitico

monologue ['manə‚lɔg] or ['manə‚lag] s monologo

monomania [‚manə'menɪ·ə] s monomania

monomial [mə'nomɪ·əl] s monomio

monopolize [mə'napə‚laɪz] tr monopolizzare, accaparrare

monopo·ly [mə'napəli] s (-lies) monopolio, privativa

monorail ['manə‚rel] s monorotaia

monosyllable ['manə‚sɪləbəl] s monosillabo

monotheist ['manə‚θi·ɪst] adj & s monoteista mf

monotonous [mə'natənəs] adj monotono

monotype ['manə‚taɪp] s (method) monotipia; (typ) monotipo

monoxide [mə'naksaɪd] s monossido

monseigneur [‚mansen'jœr] s monsignore m

monsignor [man'sinjər] s (-monsignors or monsignori [‚mansɪ'njori]) (eccl) monsignore m

monsoon [man'sun] s monsone m

monster ['manstər] adj mostruoso || s mostro

monstrance ['manstrəns] s ostensorio

monstrosi·ty [man'strasɪti] s (-ties) mostruosità f

monstrous ['manstrəs] adj mostruoso

month [mʌnθ] s mese m

month·ly ['mʌnθli] adj mensile || s (-lies) rivista mensile; **monthlies** (coll) mestruazione || adv mensilmente

monument ['manjəmənt] s monumento

moo [mu] s muggito || intr muggire

mood [mud] s umore m, vena; (gram) modo; **moods** luna, malumore m

mood·y ['mudi] adj (-ier; -iest) triste, malinconico; lunatico, capriccioso

moon [mun] s luna; **once in a blue moon** ad ogni morte di papa || tr—**to moon away** (time) (coll) sprecare || intr—**to moon about** (coll) gingillarsi, baloccarsi; (to daydream about) (coll) sognarsi di

moon'beam' s raggio di luna

moon'light' s chiaro m di luna

moon'light'ing s secondo lavoro notturno

moon'shine' s chiaro di luna; (coll) chiacchiere fpl, balle fpl; (coll) whisky m distillato illegalmente

moon'shot' s lancio alla luna

moon'stone' s lunaria

moor [mur] s brughiera, landa || tr ormeggiare || intr ormeggiarsi || **Moor** s moro

Moorish ['murɪʃ] adj moresco

moor'land' s brughiera, landa

moose [mus] s (**moose**) alce americano

moot [mut] adj controverso, discutibile

mop [map] s scopa di filacce; (coll) redazza; (of hair) zazzera || v (pret & pp mopped; ger mopping) tr (a floor) pulire, asciugare; (one's brow) asciugarsi; **to mop up** rastrellare

mope [mop] intr andare rattristato

mopish ['mopɪʃ] adj triste, avvilito

moral ['marəl] or ['mɔrəl] adj morale || s (of a fable) morale f; **morals** (ethics) morale f; (modes of conduct) costumi mpl

morale [mə'ræl] or [mə'ral] s morale m

morali·ty [mə'rælɪti] s (-ties) moralità f

mor'als charge' s accusa di oltraggio al pudore

morass [mə'ræs] s palude f

morator·i·um [‚marə'tori·əm] or [‚mɔrə'tori·əm] s (-ums or -a [ə]) moratoria

morbid ['mɔrbɪd] adj (gruesome) orribile; (feelings; curiosity; pertaining to disease; pathologic) morboso

mordacious [mɔr'deʃəs] adj mordace

mordant ['mɔrdənt] adj & s mordente m

more [mor] adj & s più m || adv più; **more and more** sempre più; **more than** più di; (followed by verb) più di quanto; **the more . . . the less** tanto più . . . quanto meno

more·o'er adv per di più, inoltre

Moresque [mo'rɛsk] adj moresco

morgue [mɔrg] s deposito, obitorio; (journ) archivio di un giornale, frigorifero

moribund ['mɔrɪ‚bʌnd] or ['mɑrɪ‚bʌnd] adj moribondo

morning ['mɔrnɪŋ] adj mattiniero || s mattina, mattino; **good morning** buon giorno; **in the morning** di mattina

morn'ing coat' s giacca nera a code

morn'ing-glo'ry s (-ries) convolvolo; (Ipomea) campanella; (Convolvulus tricolor) bella di giorno

morn'ing sick'ness s vomito di gravidanza

morn'ing star' s Lucifero, stella del mattino

Moroccan [mə'rakən] adj & s maroc chino

morocco [mə'rako] s (leather) maroc chino || **Morocco** s il Marocco

moron ['mɔran] s deficiente mf

morose [mə'ros] adj tetro, imbronciato

morphine ['mɔrfin] s morfina

morphology [mɔr'falədʒi] s morfologia

morrow ['maro] or ['mɔro] s—**on the morrow** l'indomani, il giorno seguente; domani

morsel ['mɔrsəl] s boccone m, bocconcino; pezzetto

mortal ['mɔrtəl] adj & s mortale m

mortality [mɔr'tælɪti] s mortalità f; (death or destruction on a large scale) moria

mortar ['mɔrtər] s (mixture of lime or cement) malta, calcina; (bowl) mortaio; (mil) mortaio, lanciabombe

mor'tar·board' s sparviere m; (cap) tocco accademico

mortgage ['mɔrgɪdʒ] s ipoteca || tr ipotecare

mortgagee [‚mɔrgɪ'dʒi] s creditore m ipotecario

mortgagor ['mɔrgɪdʒər] s debitore m ipotecario

mortician [mɔr'tɪʃən] *s* impresario di pompe funebri

morti·fy ['mɔrtɪ,faɪ] *v* (*pret & pp* **-fied**) *tr* mortificare; **to be mortified** vergognarsi

mortise ['mɔrtɪs] *s* intaccatura, incastro || *tr* incassare, incastrare

mor'tise lock' *s* serratura incastrata

mortuar·y ['mɔrtʃʊ ,erɪ] *adj* mortuario || *s* (**-ies**) camera mortuaria

mosaic [mo'ze·ɪk] *s* mosaico

Moscow ['mɑskau] *or* ['mɑsko] *s* Mosca

Moses ['mozɪz] *or* ['mozɪs] *s* Mosè *m*

Mos·lem ['mɑzləm] *or* ['mɑsləm] *adj* musulmano || *s* (**-lems** *or* **-lem**) musulmano

mosque [mɑsk] *s* moschea

mosqui·to [məs'kito] *s* (**-toes** *or* **-tos**) zanzara

mosqui'to net' *s* zanzariera

moss [mɔs] *or* [mɑs] *s* musco

moss'back' *s* (coll) ultraconservatore *m*, fossile *m*

moss·y ['mɔsi] *or* ['mɑsi] *adj* (**-ier**; **-iest**) muscoso

most [most] *adj* il più di, la maggior parte di || *s* la maggioranza, i più; **most of** la maggior parte di; **to make the most of** trarre il massimo da || *adv* più, maggiormente, al massimo

mostly ['mostli] *adv* per lo più, maggiormente, al massimo

motel [mo'tɛl] *s* motel *m*, autostello

moth [mɔθ] *or* [mɑθ] *s* falena; (*clothes moth*) tarma

moth'ball' *s* pallina antitarmica

moth-eaten ['mɔθ ,itən] *or* ['mɑθ ,itən] *adj* tarmato; antiquato

mother ['mʌðər] *adj* (*love, tongue*) materno; (*country*) natio; (*church, company*) madre || *s* madre *f*; (*elderly woman*) (cóll) zia || *tr* fare da madre a; creare; procreare; assumere la maternità di

moth'er coun'try *s* madrepatria

Moth'er Goose' *s* supposta autrice di una raccolta di favole infantili

motherhood ['mʌðər ,hʊd] *s* maternità *f*

moth'er-in-law' *s* (**moth'ers-in-law'**) suocera

moth'er·land' *s* madrepatria

motherless ['mʌðərlɪs] *adj* orfano di madre, senza madre

mother-of-pearl ['mʌðərəv'pʌrl] *adj* madreperlaceo || *s* madreperla

motherly ['mʌðərli] *adj* materno

Moth'er's Day' *s* giorno della madre, festa della mamma

moth'er supe'rior *s* madre superiora

moth'er tongue' *s* madrelingua; (*language from which another language is derived*) lingua madre

moth'er wit' *s* intelligenza nativa

moth' hole' *s* tarlatura

moth·y ['mɔθi] *or* ['mɑθi] *adj* (**-ier**; **-iest**) tarmato

motif [mo'tif] *s* motivo

motion ['moʃən] *s* movimento; (*e.g., of a dancer*) movenza, mossa; (*in parliamentary procedure*) mozione; **in motion** in moto || *intr* fare cenno

motionless ['moʃənlɪs] *adj* immobile

mo'tion pic'ture *s* pellicola cinematografica; **motion pictures** cinematografia

mo'tion-picture' *adj* cinematografico

motivate ['motɪ ,vet] *tr* animare, incitare

motive ['motɪv] *adj* motivo; (*producing motion*) motore || *s* motivo; (*incentive*) movente *m*

mo'tive pow'er *s* forza motrice; impianto motore; (rr) insieme *m* di locomotive

motley ['mɑtli] *adj* eterogeneo; variato, variopinto

motor ['motər] *adj* motore; (*operated by motor*) motorizzato; (*pertaining to motor vehicles*) motoristico || *s* motore *m*; (aut) macchina || *intr* viaggiare in macchina

mo'tor·boat' *s* motobarca, motoscafo

mo'tor·bus' *s* torpedone *m*; autobus *m*

motorcade ['motər ,ked] *s* carovana di automobili

mo'tor·car' *s* automobile *f*

mo'tor·cy'le *s* motocicletta

motorist ['motərist] *s* automobilista *mf*

motorize ['motə ,raɪz] *tr* motorizzare

mo'torman *s* (**-men**) guidatore *m* di tram; guidatore *m* di locomotore

mo'tor sail'er *s* motoveliero

mo'tor scoot'er *s* motoretta

mot'or ship' *s* motonave *f*

mo'tor truck' *s* autocarro, camion *m*

mo'tor ve'hicle *s* motoveicolo

mottle ['mɑtəl] *tr* chiazzare, screziare

mot·to ['mɑto] *s* (**-toes** *or* **-tos**) motto, divisa

mould [mold] *s*, *tr*, & *intr* var of **mold**

mound [maund] *s* monticello, collinetta

mount [maunt] *s* monte *m*, montagna; (*horse for riding*) cavalcatura, monta; (*setting for a jewel*) montatura; supporto; (*for a picture*) incorniciatura || *tr* montare; (*a wall*) scalare; (theat) allestire || *intr* montare; (*to climb*) salire

mountain ['mauntən] *s* montagna; **to make a mountain out of a molehill** fare di un bruscolo una trave, fare d'una mosca un elefante

moun'tain climb'ing *s* alpinismo

mountaineer [,mauntə'nɪr] *s* montanaro

mountainous ['mauntənəs] *adj* montagnoso

moun'tain rail'road *s* ferrovia a dentiera

moun'tain range' *s* catena di montagne

moun'tain sick'ness *s* mal *m* di montagna

mountebank ['maunti ,bæŋk] *s* ciarlatano

mounting ['mauntɪŋ] *s* (*act*) il montare, montaggio; (*setting*) montatura; (mach) supporto

mourn [morn] *tr* (*the loss of s.o.*) piangere; (*a misfortune*) lamentare || *intr* piangere; vestire a lutto

mourner ['mornər] *s* persona in lutto; (*penitent sinner*) penitente *mf*;

mourn'er's bench' s banco dei penitenti

mournful ['mɔrnfəl] *adj* luttuoso, funesto; (*gloomy*) lugubre

mourning ['mɔrnɪŋ] s lutto; **to be in mourning** portare il lutto

mourn'ing band' s bracciale *m* a lutto

mouse [maʊs] s (**mice** [maɪs]) topo, sorcio

mouse'hole' s topaia; piccolo buco

mouser ['maʊzər] s cacciatore *m* di topi

mouse'trap' s trappola per topi

moustache [məs'tæʃ] *or* [məs'tɑʃ] s baffi *mpl*, mustacchi *mpl*

mouth [maʊθ] s (**mouths** [maʊðz]) bocca; **by mouth** per via orale; **to be born with a silver spoon in one's mouth** essere nato con la camicia; **to make one's mouth water** fare venire a qlcu l'acquolina in bocca

mouthful ['maʊθ‚fʊl] s boccata

mouth' or'gan s armonica a bocca

mouth'piece' s (*of wind instrument*) bocchetta; (*of bridle*) imboccatura; (*of megaphone*) boccaglio; (*of cigarette*) bocchino; (*of telephone*) imboccatura; (*spokesman*) portavoce *m*

mouth'wash' s sciacquo, risciacquo

movable ['muvəbəl] *adj* mobile, movibile; (*law*) mobiliare

move [muv] s movimento; (*change of residence*) trasloco; (*step*) passo; (*e.g., in chess*) mossa; **on the move in** moto, in movimento; **to get a move on** (coll) affrettarsi || *tr* muovere; (*the bowels*) provocare l'evacuazione di; (*to prompt*) spingere; (*to stir the feelings of*) emozionare, commuovere; (*law*) proporre; (com) svendere; **to move up** (*a date*) anticipare || *intr* muoversi; passare; (*to another house*) traslocare; (*to another city*) trasferirsi; (*said of goods*) avere una vendita; (*said of the bowels*) evacuare; (*law*) presentare una mozione; (coll) andarsene; **to move away** andarsene; trasferirsi; **to move back** tirarsi indietro; **to move in** avanzare; (*society*) frequentare; **to move off** allontanarsi

movement ['muvmənt] s movimento; (*of a watch*) meccanismo; (*of the bowels*) evacuazione; (mus) movimento, tempo

movie ['muvi] s (coll) film *m*, pellicola

movie-goer ['muvi‚go·ər] s frequentatore *m* del cinema

mov'ie house' s (coll) cinematografo

mov'ie-land' s (coll) cinelandia

moving ['muvɪŋ] *adj* commovente, emozionante || s trasporto; (*from one house to another*) trasloco

mov'ing pic'ture s film *m*, pellicola

mov'ing stair'case' s scala mobile

mow [mo] v (*pret* **mowed**; *pp* **mowed** *or* **mown**) *tr & intr* falciare

mower ['mo·ər] s falciatore *m*; (mach) falciatrice *f*

Mr. ['mɪstər] s (**Messrs.** ['mɛsərz]) Signore *m*

Mrs. ['mɪsɪz] s Signora

much [mʌtʃ] *adj & pron* molto; **as much . . . as** tanto . . . quanto; **too much** troppo || *adv* molto; **however much** per quanto; **how much** quanto; **too much** troppo; **very much** moltissimo

mucilage ['mjusɪlɪdʒ] s colla; (*gummy secretion in plants*) mucillagine *f*

muck [mʌk] s letame *m*; (*dirt*) sudiciume *m*; (min) materiale *m* di scoria

muck'rake' *intr* (coll) sollevare scandali

mucous ['mjukəs] *adj* mucoso

mucus ['mjukəs] s muco

mud [mʌd] s fango, melma, limo; **to sling mud at** calunniare

muddle ['mʌdəl] s confusione, guazzabuglio || *tr* confondere, intorbidire || *intr*—**to muddle through** arrangiarsi; cavarsela alla meno peggio in

mud'dle-head' s (coll) semplicione *m*

mud-dy ['mʌdi] *adj* (-**dier**; -**diest**) fangoso, melmoso; (*obscure*) torbido || v (*pret & pp* -**died**) *tr* turbare, intorbidare; (*to soil with mud*) infangare

mud'guard' s parafango

mud'hole' s pozzanghera, fangaia

mud' slide' s smottamento

mudslinger ['mʌd‚slɪŋgər] s calunniatore *m*

muff [mʌf] s manicotto || *tr* (coll) mancare; (*to handle badly*) (coll) abborracciare; (sports) mancare di pigliare

muffin ['mʌfɪn] s panino soffice

muffle ['mʌfəl] *tr* infagottare, imbacuccare; (*a sound*) velare, smorzare

muffler ['mʌflər] s sciarpa; (aut) silenziatore *m*, marmitta

mufti ['mʌfti] s—**in mufti** in borghese

mug [mʌg] s tazzona; (slang) muso, grugno || v (*pret & pp* **mugged**) *ger* **mugging**) *tr* (slang) fotografare; (slang) attaccare proditoriamente || *intr* fare le smorfie

mug-gy ['mʌgi] *adj* (-**gier**; -**giest**) afoso, opprimente

mulat-to [mjʊ'læto] *or* [mə'læto] s (-**toes**) mulatto

mulber-ry ['mʌl‚bɛri] s (-**ries**) (*tree*) gelso; (*fruit*) mora di gelso

mulct [mʌlkt] *tr* defraudare

mule [mjul] s mulo; (*slipper*) pianella

muleteer [‚mjulə'tɪr] s mulattiere *m*

mulish ['mjulɪʃ] *adj* testardo

mull [mʌl] *tr* (*wine*) scaldare aggiungendo spezie || *intr*—**to mull over** pensarci sopra, rinvangare

mulled' wine' s vino caldo

mullion ['mʌljən] s colonnina che divide una bifora

multigraph ['mʌlti‚græf] *or* ['mʌlti‚grɑf] s (*trademark*) poligrafo || *tr* poligrafare

multilateral [‚mʌlti'lætərəl] *adj* multilaterale

multimotor [‚mʌlti'motər] s plurimotore *m*

multiple ['mʌltɪpəl] *adj & s* multiplo

multiplici-ty [‚mʌltɪ'plɪsɪti] s (-**ties**) molteplicità *f*

multi-ply ['mʌlti‚plaɪ] v (*pret & pp* -**plied**) *tr* moltiplicare || *intr* moltiplicarsi

multistage [ˈmʌltɪˌstedʒ] *adj* (rok) pluristadio

multitude [ˈmʌltɪˌtjud] or [ˈmʌltɪˌtud] *s* moltitudine *f*

mum [mʌm] *adj* zitto; **mum's the word!** acqua in bocca!; **to keep mum** stare zitto ‖ *interj* zitto!

mumble [ˈmʌmbəl] *tr* biascicare ‖ *intr* farfugliare

mummer·y [ˈmʌməri] *s* (-ies) buffonata, mascherata

mum·my [ˈmʌmi] *s* (-mies) mummia

mumps [mʌmps] *s* orecchioni *mpl*

munch [mʌntʃ] *tr* sgranocchiare

mundane [ˈmʌndən] *adj* mondano

municipal [mjuˈnɪsɪpəl] *adj* municipale

municipali·ty [mjuˌnɪsɪˈpælɪti] *s* (-ties) municipio

munificent [mjuˈnɪfɪsənt] *adj* munifico

munition [mjuˈnɪʃən] *s* munizione ‖ *tr* fornire di munizioni

muni'tion dump' *s* deposito munizioni

mural [ˈmjurəl] *adj* murale ‖ *s* pittura murale

murder [ˈmʌrdər] *s* omicidio ‖ *tr* assassinare

murderer [ˈmʌrdərər] *s* omicida *m*

murderess [ˈmʌrdərɪs] *s* omicida *f*

murderous [ˈmʌrdərəs] *adj* omicida, crudele, sanguinario

murk·y [ˈmʌrki] *adj* (-ier; -iest) fosco, tenebroso; brumoso, nebbioso

murmur [ˈmʌrmər] *s* mormorio ‖ *tr* & *intr* mormorare

Mur'phy bed' *s* letto a scomparsa

muscle [ˈmʌsəl] *s* muscolo

muscular [ˈmʌskjələr] *adj* muscolare; *(having well-developed muscles)* muscoloso

muse [mjuz] *s* musa; **the Muses** le Muse ‖ *intr* meditare, rimuginare

museum [mjuˈziəm] *s* museo

mush [mʌʃ] *s* pappa, polentina; (fig) leziosaggine *f*, sdolcinatura

mush'room *s* fungo ‖ *intr* venir su come i funghi; **to mushroom into** diventare rapidamente

mush'room cloud' *s* fungo atomico

mush·y [ˈmʌʃi] *adj* (-ier; -iest) polposo, spappolato; (fig) sdolcinato, sentimentale

music [ˈmjuzɪk] *s* musica; **to face the music** (coll) affrontare le conseguenze; **to set to music** mettere in musica

musical [ˈmjuzɪkəl] *adj* musicale

mu'sical com'edy *s* operetta, commedia musicale

musicale [ˌmjuzɪˈkæl] *s* serata musicale

mu'sic box' *s* scatola armonica

mu'sic cab'inet *s* scaffaletto per la musica

mu'sic hall' *s* salone *m* da concerti; (Brit) teatro di varietà, music-hall *m*

musician [mjuˈzɪʃən] *s* musicista *mf*

musicianship [mjuˈzɪʃənˌʃɪp] *s* abilità *f* musicale, virtuosismo

musicologist [ˌmjuzɪˈkɑlədʒɪst] *s* musicologo

musicology [ˌmjuzɪˈkɑlədʒi] *s* musicologia

mu'sic stand' *s* portamusica *m*

musk [mʌsk] *s* muschio

musk' deer' *s* mosco

musket [ˈmʌskɪt] *s* moschetto

musketeer [ˌmʌskɪˈtɪr] *s* moschettiere *m*

musk'mel'on *s* melone *m*

musk' ox' *s* bue muschiato

musk'rat' *s* ondatra, topo muschiato

muslin [ˈmʌzlɪn] *s* mussolina

muss [mʌs] *tr* *(the hair)* scompigliare, arruffare; *(clothing)* (coll) sciupare

mussel [ˈmʌsəl] *s* mussolo

Mussulman [ˈmʌsəlmən] *adj* & *s* musulmano

muss·y [ˈmʌsi] *adj* (-ier; -iest) (coll) arruffato, scompigliato

must [mʌst] *s* (*new wine*) mosto; *(mold)* muffa; (coll) cosa assolutamente indispensabile ‖ *v aux*—**I must go now** devo andarmene ora; **it must be Ann** deve essere Anna; **she must be ill** dev'essere malata; **they must have known it** devono averlo saputo

mustache [məsˈtæʃ], [məsˈtɑʃ] or [ˈmʌstæʃ] *s* baffi *mpl*, mustacchi *mpl*

mustard [ˈmʌstərd] *s* mostarda

mus'tard plas'ter *s* senapismo

muster [ˈmʌstər] *s* adunata, rivista; **to pass muster** passar ispezione ‖ *tr* chiamare a raccolta; riunire; **to muster in** arruolare; **to muster out** congedare; **to muster up courage** prendere coraggio a quattro mani

mus'ter roll' *s* ruolo; (naut) appello

mus·ty [ˈmʌsti] *adj* (-tier; -tiest) *(moldy)* ammuffito; *(stale)* stantio; (fig) ammuffito, stantio

mutation [mjuˈteʃən] *s* mutazione

mute [mjut] *adj* & *s* muto ‖ *tr* mettere la sordina a

mutilate [ˈmjutɪˌlet] *tr* mutilare

mutineer [ˌmjutɪˈnɪr] *s* ammutinato

mutinous [ˈmjutɪnəs] *adj* ammutinato

muti·ny [ˈmjutɪni] *s* (-nies) ammutinamento ‖ *v* (*pret* & *pp* -nied) *intr* ammutinarsi

mutt [mʌt] *s* (slang) cane bastardo; (slang) scemo

mutter [ˈmʌtər] *tr* & *intr* borbottare

mutton [ˈmʌtən] *s* montone *m*

mut'ton chop' *s* cotoletta di montone

mutual [ˈmutʃuˌəl] *adj* mutuo, vicendevole

mu'tual aid' *s* mutualità *f*

mu'tual fund' *s* fondo comune di investimento

muzzle [ˈmʌzəl] *s* (*of animal*) muso; *(device to keep animal from biting)* museruola; *(of firearm)* bocca ‖ *tr* mettere la museruola a; (fig) imbavagliare

my [maɪ] *adj poss* mio, il mio ‖ *interj* (coll) corbezzoli!

myriad [ˈmɪrɪˌəd] *s* miriade *f*

myrrh [mʌr] *s* mirra

myrtle [ˈmʌrtəl] *s* mirto, mortella

myself [maɪˈsɛlf] *pron pers* io stesso; me, me stesso; mi, e.g., **I hurt myself** mi sono fatto male

mysterious [mɪsˈtɪrɪ·əs] *adj* misterioso
myster·y [ˈmɪstərɪ] *s* (-ies) mistero
mystic [ˈmɪstɪk] *adj* & *s* mistico
mystical [ˈmɪstɪkəl] *adj* mistico
mysticism [ˈmɪstɪ‚sɪzəm] *s* misticismo
mystification [‚mɪstɪfɪˈkeʃən] *s* mistificazione
mysti·fy [ˈmɪstɪ‚faɪ] *v* (*pret* & *pp*

-fied) *tr* avvolgere nel mistero; (*to hoax*) mistificare
myth [mɪθ] *s* mito
mythical [ˈmɪθɪkəl] *adj* mitico
mythological [‚mɪθəˈlɑdʒɪkəl] *adj* mitologico
mytholo·gy [mɪˈθɑlədʒɪ] *s* (-gies) mitologia

N

N, n [en] *s* quattordicesima lettera dell'alfabeto inglese
nab [næb] *v* (*pret* & *pp* nabbed; *ger* nabbing) *tr* (slang) afferrare, agguantare
nag [næg] *s* ronzino ‖ *v* (*pret* & *pp* nagged; *ger* nagging) *tr* & *intr* tormentare, infastidire
naiad [ˈne·æd] or [ˈnaɪ·æd] *s* naiade *f*
nail [nel] *s* (*of finger or toe*) unghia; (*of metal*) chiodo; **to hit the nail on the head** cogliere nel giusto ‖ *tr* inchiodare
nail'brush' spazzolino per le unghie
nail' file' *s* lima per le unghie
nail' pol'ish *s* smalto per le unghie
nail' set' *s* punzone *m*
naïve [nɑˈiv] *adj* candido, ingenuo
naked [ˈnekɪd] *adj* nudo, ignudo; **to strip naked** denudare; denudarsi; **with the naked eye** a occhio nudo
name [nem] *s* nome *m*; (*first name*) nome *m*; (*last name*) cognome *m*; fama, reputazione; titolo; lignaggio; **in the name of** nel nome di; **to call s.o. names** coprire qlco di ingiurie; **to go by the name of** essere conosciuto sotto il nome di; **to make a name for oneself** farsi un nome; **what is your name?** come si chiama Lei? ‖ *tr* nominare; menzionare; battezzare; (*a price*) fissare
name' day' *s* onomastico
nameless [ˈnemlɪs] *adj* senza nome, anonimo
namely [ˈnemlɪ] *adv* cioè, vale a dire
name'plate' *s* targa, targhetta
namesake [ˈnem‚sek] *s* omonimo; persona chiamata in onore di qualcun altro
nan'ny goat' [ˈnænɪ] *s* capra
nap [næp] *s* lanugine *f*; (*pile*) pelo; pisolino, sonnellino; **to take a nap** schiacciare un sonnellino ‖ *v* (*pret* & *pp* napped; *ger* napping) *intr* sonnecchiare; **to catch napping** cogliere alla sprovvista
napalm [ˈnepɑm] *s* napalm *m*
nape [nep] *s* nuca
naphtha [ˈnæfθə] *s* nafta
napkin [ˈnæpkɪn] *s* tovagliolo
nap'kin ring' *s* portatovagliolo
Naples [ˈnepləz] *s* Napoli *f*
Napoleonic [nə‚polɪˈɑnɪk] *adj* napoleonico
narcissus [nɑrˈsɪsəs] *s* narciso
narcotic [nɑrˈkɑtɪk] *adj* & *s* narcotico
narrate [næˈret] *tr* narrare

narration [næˈreʃən] *s* narrazione
narrative [ˈnærətɪv] *adj* narrativo ‖ *s* narrazione; (*genre*) narrativa
narrator [næˈretər] *s* narratore *m*
narrow [ˈnæro] *adj* stretto; limitato; (*illiberal*) meschino, ristretto ‖ narrows *spl* stretti *mpl* ‖ *tr* limitare, restringere ‖ *intr* limitarsi, restringersi
nar'row escape' *s*—**to have a narrow escape** scamparla bella
nar'row-gauge' *adj* a scartamento ridotto
narrow-minded [ˈnæroˈmaɪndɪd] *adj* gretto, ristretto d'idee
nasal [ˈnezəl] *adj* & *s* nasale *f*
nasturtium [nəˈstɑrʃəm] *s* nasturzio
nas·ty [ˈnæstɪ] or [ˈnɑstɪ] *adj* (-tier; -tiest) brutto, cattivo; sgradevole, orribile; sudicio; (*foul*) perfido
natatorium [‚netəˈtorɪ·əm] *s* piscina
nation [ˈneʃən] *s* nazione
national [ˈnæʃənəl] *adj* & *s* nazionale *mf*
na'tional an'them *s* inno nazionale
na'tional debt' *s* debito pubblico
na'tional hol'iday *s* festa nazionale
nationalism [ˈnæʃənə‚lɪzəm] *s* nazionalismo
nationali·ty [‚næʃənˈælɪtɪ] *s* (-ties) nazionalità *f*
nationalize [ˈnæʃənə‚laɪz] *tr* nazionalizzare
na'tion-wide' *adj* su scala nazionale
native [ˈnetɪv] *adj* nativo, indigeno, oriundo; (*language*) materno ‖ *s* indigeno, nativo
na'tive land' *s* patria, paese natio
nativi·ty [nəˈtɪvɪtɪ] *s* (-ties) nascita, natività *f* ‖ Nativity *s* Natività *f*
Nato [ˈneto] *s* (acronym) (North Atlantic Treaty Organization) la N.A.T.O.
nat·ty [ˈnætɪ] *adj* (-tier; -tiest) accurato, elegante
natural [ˈnætʃərəl] *adj* naturale ‖ *s* imbecille *mf*; (*mus*) bequadro; (*mus*) tono naturale; (*mus*) tasto bianco; a natural (coll) proprio quello che ci vuole
naturalism [ˈnætʃərə‚lɪzəm] *s* naturalismo
naturalist [ˈnætʃərəlɪst] *s* naturalista *mf*
naturalization [‚nætʃərəlɪˈzeʃən] *s* naturalizzazione
nat'uraliza'tion pa'pers *spl* documenti *mpl* di naturalizzazione

naturalize ['nætʃərə,laız] *tr* naturalizzare

naturally ['nætʃərəli] *adv* naturalmente

nature ['netʃər] *s* natura; **from nature** dal vero

naught [nɔt] *s* niente *m;* zero; **to come to naught** ridursi al nulla; **to set at naught** disprezzare

naugh•ty ['nɔti] *adj* (-**tier;** -**tiest**) cattivo, disubbidiente; (*joke*) di cattivo genere

nausea ['nɔʃi•ə] or ['nɔsi•ə] *s* nausea

nauseate ['nɔʃi,et] or ['nɔsi,et] *tr* nauseare ‖ *intr* essere nauseato

nauseating ['nɔʃi,etıŋ] or ['nɔsi,etıŋ] *adj* nauseabondo, stomachevole

nauseous ['nɔʃi•əs] or ['nɔsi•əs] *adj* nauseabondo

nautical ['nɔtıkəl] *adj* nautico, marittimo, marino

naval ['nevəl] *adj* navale

na′val acad′emy *s* accademia navale

na′val of′ficer *s* ufficiale *m* di marina

na′val sta′tion *s* base *f* navale

nave [nev] *s* navata centrale; (*of a wheel*) mozzo

navel ['nevəl] *s* ombelico

na′vel or′ange *s* arancia (con depressione alla sommità)

navigability [,nævıgə'bılıti] *s* navigabilità *f;* (*of a ship*) manovrabilità *f*

navigable ['nævıgəbəl] *adj* (*river*) navigabile; (*ship*) manovrabile

navigate ['nævı,get] *tr & intr* navigare

navigation [,nævı'geʃən] *s* navigazione

navigator ['nævı,getər] *s* navigatore *m;* (*in charge of navigating ship or plane*) ufficiale *m* di rotta

na•vy ['nevi] *adj* blu marino ‖ *s* (-**vies**) marina (da guerra)

na′vy bean′ *s* fagiolo secco

na′vy blue′ *s* blu marino

na′vy yard′ *s* arsenale *m*

nay [ne] *s* no; voto negativo ‖ *adv* no; anzi

Nazarene [,næzə'rin] *adj & s* nazzareno; **the Nazarene** il Nazzareno

Nazi ['nɑtsi] or ['nætsi] *adj & s* nazista *mf*

N-bomb ['en ,bɑm] *s* bomba al neutrone

Neapolitan [,ni•ə'pɑlıtən] *adj & s* napoletano

neap′ tide′ [nip] *s* marea di quadratura

near [nır] *adj* vicino, prossimo; intimo; esatto ‖ *adv* vicino, da vicino ‖ *prep* vicino a, accanto a; **to come near** avvicinarsi a ‖ *tr* avvicinarsi a ‖ *intr* avvicinarsi

nearby ['nır ,baı] *adj* vicino ‖ *adv* vicino, qui vicino

Near′ East′ *s* Medio Oriente

nearly ['nırli] *adv* quasi; (*a little more or less*) press'a poco; per poco non, e.g., **he nearly died** per poco non morì

near-sighted ['nır'saıtıd] *adj* miope

near′-sight′ed•ness *s* miopia

neat [nit] *adj* netto, pulito; elegante, accurato; puro

neat′s′-foot oil′ *s* olio di piede di bue

Nebuchadnezzar [,nebjəkəd'nezər] *s* Nabucodonosor *m*

nebu•la ['nebjələ] *s* (-**lae** [,li] or -**las**) nebulosa

nebular ['nebjələr] *adj* nebulare

nebulous ['nebjələs] *adj* nebuloso

necessary ['nesı ,seri] *adj* necessario

necessitate [nı'sesı ,tet] *tr* necessitare, esigere

necessitous [nı'sesıtəs] *adj* bisognoso

necessi•ty [nı'sesıti] *s* (-**ties**) necessità *f*

neck [nek] *s* collo; (*of a horse*) incollatura; (*of violin*) manico; (*of mountain*) gola, passo; **neck and neck** testa a testa; **to stick one's neck out** (coll) esporsi al pericolo; **to win by a neck** vincere per una corta testa ‖ *intr* (slang) abbracciarsi, sbaciucchiarsi

neck′band′ *s* colletto

neckerchief ['nekər ,tʃıf] *s* fazzoletto da collo

necklace ['neklıs] *s* collana

neck′line′ *s* giro collo, scollatura

necktie ['nek ,taı] *s* cravatta

neck′tie pin′ *s* spilla da cravatta

necrolo•gy [ne'krɑlədʒi] *s* (-**gies**) necrologia

necromancy ['nekrə ,mænsi] *s* necromanzia

nectar ['nektər] *s* nettare *m*

née or **nee** [ne] *adj* nata

need [nid] *s* necessità *f,* bisogno; povertà *f;* **if need be** se ci fosse bisogno; **in need** in strettezze ‖ *tr* aver bisogno di ‖ *intr* necessitare, essere in necessità ‖ *v aux*—**to need (to)** + *inf* dovere + *inf*

needful ['nidfəl] *adj* necessario

needle ['nidəl] *s* ago; (*of phonograph*) puntina; **to look for a needle in a haystack** cercare l'ago nel pagliaio ‖ *tr* cucire; (fig) aguzzare, eccitare

nee′dle bath′ *s* bagno a doccia filiforme

nee′dle-case′ *s* agoraio

nee′dle-point′ *s* merletto; ricamo su canovaccio

needless ['nidlıs] *adj* inutile

nee′dle-work′ *s* lavoro di cucito; (*embroidery*) ricamo; (*needlepoint*) merletto

needs [nidz] *adv* necessariamente; **it must needs be** dev'essere proprio così

need•y ['nidi] *adj* (-**ier;** -**iest**) bisognoso, indigente ‖ **the needy** i bisognosi

ne′er-do-well ['nerdu ,wel] *adj & s* buono a nulla

negate ['neget] or [nı'get] *tr* invalidare; negare

negation [nı'geʃən] *s* negazione

negative ['negətıv] *adj* negativo ‖ *s* negativa; (elec) polo negativo; (gram) negazione ‖ *tr* respingere, votare contro; neutralizzare

neglect [nı'glekt] *s* negligenza, trascuratezza ‖ *tr* trascurare; **to neglect to** trascurare di; dimenticarsi di

neglectful [nı'glektfəl] *adj* negligente, trascurato

négligée or **negligee** [,neglı'ʒe] *s* veste *f* da camera or vestaglia per signora

negligence ['neglıdʒəns] *s* negligenza, trascuratezza

negligent ['neglɪdʒənt] *adj* negligente, trascurato

negligible ['neglɪdʒɪbəl] *adj* trascurabile, insignificante

negotiable [nɪ'goʃɪ⋅əbəl] *adj* negoziabile; (*security*) al portatore; (*road*) transitabile

negotiate [nɪ'goʃɪ,et] *tr* negoziare; (*to overcome*) superare || *intr* negoziare

negotiation [nɪ,goʃɪ'e/ən] *s* negoziazione, negoziato

Ne·gro ['nigro] *adj* negro || *s* (*-groes*) negro, nero

neigh [ne] *s* nitrito || *intr* nitrire

neighbor ['nebər] *adj* vicino, adiacente || *s* vicino; (*fellow man*) prossimo || *tr* essere vicino a || *intr* essere vicino

neighborhood ['nebər,hʊd] *s* vicinanza, vicinato; **in the neighborhood of** nei pressi di; (coll) a un dipresso, all'incirca

neighboring ['nebərɪŋ] *adj* vicino, attiguo; (*country*) limitrofo

neighborly ['nebərli] *adj* da buon vicino, socievole

neither ['niðər] *or* ['naɪðər] *adj indef* nessuno dei due, nessun *boy*; **neither boy** nessuno dei due ragazzi || *pron indef* nessuno dei due, nè l'uno nè l'altro || *conj* neppure, nemmeno, e.g., **neither do I** nemmeno io; **neither . . . nor** nè . . . nè

neme·sis ['nemɪsɪs] *s* (*-ses* [,siz]) nemesi *f* || **Nemesis** *s* Nemesi *f*

neologism [ni'alə,dʒɪzəm] *s* neologismo

neomycin [,ni⋅ə'maɪsɪn] *s* neomicina

ne'on lamp' ['ni⋅an] *s* lampada al neon

neophyte ['ni⋅ə,faɪt] *s* neofita *mf*

nepenthe [nɪ'pɛnθɪ] *s* nepente *f*

nephew ['nefju] *or* ['nevju] *s* nipote *m*

Nepos ['nipas] *or* ['nepas] *s* Nipote *m*

Neptune ['nept/un] *or* ['neptjun] *s* Nettuno

neptunium [nep't/unɪ⋅əm] *or* [nep-'tjunɪ⋅əm] *s* (chem) nettunio

Nero ['nɪro] *s* Nerone *m*

nerve [nʌrv] *adj* nervoso || *s* nervo; (*courage*) coraggio; (*boldness*) (coll) faccia tosta; **to get on one's nerves** dare ai nervi di qlcu; **to lose one's nerve** perdere le staffe

nerve-racking ['nʌrv,rækɪŋ] *adj* irritante, esasperante

nervous ['nʌrvəs] *adj* nervoso

nerv'ous break'down *s* esaurimento nervoso

nervousness ['nʌrvəsnɪs] *s* nervosismo

nerv·y ['nʌrvi] *adj* (*-ier; -iest*) (*strong*) forte, vigoroso; *audace*; (coll) insolente, sfacciato

nest [nest] *s* nido; (*of hen*) cova; (*retreat*) rifugio; (*hangout*) tana; (*brood*) nidiata; **to feather one's nest** farsi il gruzzolo || *tr* (*e.g., tables*) mettere l'uno nell'altro || *intr* nidificare

nest' egg' *s* endice *m*; (fig) gruzzolo

nestle ['nesəl] *tr* annidare || *intr* annidarsi, nidificare; (*to cuddle up*) rannicchiarsi

net [net] *adj* netto || *s* rete *f*; (*snare*) laccio, trappola; guadagno netto ||

tr prendere con la rete; (*a sum of money*) fare un guadagno netto di

nether ['nɛðər] *adj* inferiore, infero

Netherlander ['nɛðər,lændər] *or* ['nɛðərləndər] *s* olandese *mf*

Netherlands, The ['nɛðərləndz] *spl* i Paesi Bassi

netting ['nɛtɪŋ] *s* rete *f*

nettle ['nɛtəl] *s* ortica || *tr* irritare, provocare

net'work' *s* rete *f*

neuralgia [njʊ'rældʒə] *or* [nʊ'rældʒə] *s* nevralgia

neurology [njʊ'ralədʒi] *or* [nʊ'ralədʒi] *s* neurologia

neuro·sis [njʊ'rosɪs] *or* [nʊ'rosɪs] (*-ses* [siz]) *s* neurosi *f*

neurotic [njʊ'ratɪk] *or* [nʊ'ratɪk] *adj* & *s* neurotico

neuter ['njutər] *or* ['nutər] *adj* neutro || *s* genere neutro

neutral ['njutrəl] *or* ['nutrəl] *adj* neutro; (*not aligned*) neutrale || *s* neutrale *m*; (mach) folle *m*

neutralist ['njutrəlɪst] *or* ['nutrəlɪst] *adj* & *s* neutralista *mf*

neutrality [nju'trælɪti] *or* [nu'trælɪti] *s* neutralità *f*

neutralize ['njutrə,laɪz] *or* ['nutrə,laɪz] *tr* neutralizzare

neutron ['njutran] *or* ['nutran] *s* neutrone *m*

neu'tron bomb' *s* bomba al neutrone

never ['nɛvər] *adv* mai, giammai; non . . . mai; **never mind** non importa

nev'er-more' *adv* mai più

nevertheless [,nɛvərðə'les] *adv* ciò nonostante, ciò nondimeno, tuttavia

new [nju] *or* [nu] *adj* nuovo; **what's new?** che c'è di nuovo?

new' arri'val *s* nuovo venuto; (*baby*) neonato

new'born' *adj* neonato; (*e.g., faith*) rinato

New'cas'tle *s*—**to carry coals to Newcastle** portare l'acqua al mare, portare vasi a Samo

newcomer ['nju,kʌmər] *or* ['nu-,kʌmər] *s* nuovo venuto

New' Eng'land *s* la Nuova Inghilterra

newfangled ['nju'fæŋgəld] *or* ['nu-,fæŋgəld] *adj* all'ultima moda; di nuovo conio, di nuova invenzione

Newfoundland ['njufənd,lænd] *or* ['nufənd,lænd] *s* la Terranova || [nju'faʊndlənd] *or* [nu'faʊndlənd] *s* (*dog*) terranova *m*

newly ['njuli] *or* ['nuli] *adv* di recente, di fresco

new'ly-wed' *s* sposino *or* sposina; **the newlyweds** gli sposi

new' moon' *s* luna nuova, novilunio

news [njuz] *or* [nuz] *s* notizie *fpl*; **a news item** una notizia; **a piece of news** una notizia

news' a'gency *s* agenzia d'informazioni

news'beat' *s* colpo giornalistico

news'boy' *s* strillone *m*

news'cast' *s* notiziario

news'cast'er *s* annunziatore *m*, radiocommentatore *m*, telecommentatore *m*

news' con'ference *s* conferenza stampa

news' cov'erage *s* reportaggio

news'deal'er *s* venditore *m* di giornali

news'man' *s* (-men') (*reporter*) giornalista *m*; giornalaio

newsmonger ['njuz ,mʌŋgər] or ['nuz ,mʌŋgər] *s* persona pettegola, gazzettino

news'pa'per *adj* giornalistico || *s* giornale *m*

news'pa'per·man' *s* (-men') giornalista *m*

news'print' *s* carta da giornale

news'reel' *s* cinegiornale *m*

news'stand' *s* chiosco, edicola

news'week'ly *s* (-lies) settimanale *m* d'informazione

news'wor'thy *adj* degno d'essere pubblicato, di viva attualità

news·y ['njuzi] or ['nuzi] *adj* (-ier; -iest) (coll) informativo

New' Tes'tament *s* Nuovo Testamento

New' Year's' card' *s* cartolina d'auguri di capodanno

New' Year's' Day' *s* il capo d'anno, il capodanno

New' Year's' Eve' *s* la vigilia di capodanno, la sera di San Silvestro

New' York' [jɔrk] *adj* nuovayorchese || *s* New York *f*, Nuova York

New' York'er ['jɔrkər] *s* nuovayorchese *mf*

New' Zea'land ['zilənd] *adj* neozelandese || *s* la Nuova Zelanda

New' Zea'lander ['ziləndər] *s* neozelandese *mf*

next [nɛkst] *adj* prossimo, seguente; (*month*) prossimo, entrante || *adv* la prossima volta; dopo, in seguito; **next to** vicino a; **next to nothing** quasi nulla; **to come next** essere il prossimo

next'-door' *adj* della casa vicina || **next'-door'** *adv* nella casa vicina

next' of kin' *s* (next' of kin') parente più prossimo

niacin ['naɪ·əsɪn] *s* niacina

Niag'ara Falls' [naɪˈægərə] *spl* le Cascate del Niagara

nib [nɪb] *s* becco; punta; **his nibs** (slang & pej) sua eccellenza

nibble ['nɪbəl] *s* piccolo morso || *tr & intr* mordicchiare, sbocconcellare; (*said of a fish*) abboccare

nice [naɪs] *adj* (*pleasant*) simpatico, gentile; (*requiring skill*) buono, bello; (*fine*) sottile; (*refined*) raffinato, per bene; (*fussy*) esigente, difficile; rispettabile; (*weather*) bello; (*attractive*) bello; **nice . . . and** (coll) bello, e.g., **it is nice and warm** fa un bel caldo

nice-looking ['naɪsˈlʊkɪŋ] *adj* bello, attraente

nicely ['naɪsli] *adv* precisamente, esattamente; (coll) benissimo

nice·ty ['naɪsəti] *s* (-ties) esattezza, precisione; **to a nicety** con la massima precisione

niche [nɪtʃ] *s* nicchia

Nicholas ['nɪkələs] *s* Nicola *m*

nick [nɪk] *s* intaccatura; (*of a dish*) slabbratura; **in the nick of time** al

momento giusto || *tr* intaccare; (*to cut*) tagliare; (*a dish*) slabbrare

nickel ['nɪkəl] *s* nichel *m*; moneta americana di cinque cents || *tr* nichelare

nick'el plate' *s* nichelatura

nick'el-plate' *tr* nichelare

nicknack ['nɪk ,næk] *s* soprammobile *m*; gingillo, ninnolo

nick'name' *s* nomignolo, soprannome *m* || *tr* soprannominare

nicotine ['nɪkə ,tin] *s* nicotina

niece [nis] *s* nipote *f*

nif·ty ['nɪfti] *adj* (-tier; -tiest) (coll) elegante; (coll) eccellente

niggard ['nɪgərd] *adj & s* spilorcio

night [naɪt] *adj* notturno || *s* notte *f*; **at or by night** di notte; **the night before last** l'altra notte; **to make a night of it** (coll) fare le ore piccole

night'cap' *s* berretto da notte; bicchierino di liquore che si beve prima di coricarsi

night' club' *s* night-club *m*

night' driv'ing *s* il guidare di notte

night'fall' *s* crepuscolo; **at nightfall** sul cader della notte, all'imbrunire

night'gown' *s* camicia da notte

nightingale ['naɪtən ,gel] *s* usignolo

night' latch' *s* serratura a molla

night' let'ter *s* telegramma notturno

night'long' *adj* di tutta la notte || *adv* tutta la notte

nightly ['naɪtli] *adj* di notte; di ogni notte || *adv* di notte; ogni notte

night'mare' *s* incubo

nightmarish ['naɪt ,merɪʃ] *adj* raccapricciante

night' owl' *s* (coll) nottambulo

night' school' *s* scuola serale

night'shirt' *s* camicia da notte

night'time' *s* notte *f*

night'walk'er *s* nottambulo; vagabondo notturno; (*prostitute*) passeggiatrice *f*

night' watch' *s* guardia notturna

night' watch'man *s* (-men) guardiano notturno

nihilist ['naɪ·ɪlɪst] *s* nichilista *mf*

nil [nɪl] *s* nulla *m*, niente *m*

Nile [naɪl] *s* Nilo

nimble ['nɪmbəl] *adj* agile, svelto

Nimrod ['nɪmrad] *s* Nembrod *m*

nincompoop ['nɪnkəm ,pup] *s* babbeo, tonto, semplicione *m*

nine [naɪn] *adj & pron* nove || *s* nove *m*; **nine o' clock** le nove

nine' hun'dred *adj, s & pron* novecento

nineteen ['naɪn'tin] *adj, s & pron* diciannove *m*

nineteenth ['naɪn'tinθ] *adj & s* diciannovesimo; (*century*) decimonono || *s* (*in dates*) diciannove *m* || *pron* diciannovesimo

ninetieth ['naɪntɪ·ɪθ] *adj, s & pron* novantesimo

nine·ty ['naɪnti] *adj & pron* novanta || *s* (-ties) novanta *m*; **the gay nineties** il decennio scapestrato dal 1890 al 1900

ninth [naɪnθ] *adj, s & pron* nono || *s* (*in dates*) nove *m*

nip [nɪp] *s* morso, pizzicotto; freddo pungente; (*of liquor*) bicchierino, sorso; **nip and tuck** testa a testa ‖ *v* (*pret* & *pp* **nipped**; *ger* **nipping**) *tr* pizzicare, mordere; (*to squeeze*) spremere; (*to freeze*) gelare; (*liquor*) sorseggiare; **to nip in the bud** arrestare di bel principio ‖ *intr* bere a sorsi

nipple ['nɪpəl] *s* capezzolo; (*of rubber*) tettarella; (mach) corto tubo filettato a entrambe le estremità, manicotto, cappuccio

Nippon [nɪ'pɑn] or ['nɪpɑn] *s* il Giappone

Nippon·ese [ˌnɪpə'niz] *adj* nipponico ‖ *s* (*-ese*) Giapponese *mf*

nip·py ['nɪpi] *adj* (*-pier*; *-piest*) mordente, pizzicante; gelato

nirvana [nɪr'vɑnə] *s* il nirvana

nit [nɪt] *s* lendine *m*; pidocchio

niter ['naɪtər] *s* nitro

nit'-pick' *intr* (coll) cercare il pelo nell'uovo

nitrate ['naɪtret] *s* nitrato; (agr) nitrato di soda; (agr) nitrato di potassio

ni'tric ac'id ['naɪtrɪk] *s* acido nitrico

nitride ['naɪtraɪd] *s* azoturo, nitruro

nitrogen ['naɪtrədʒən] *s* azoto

nitroglycerin [ˌnaɪtrə'glɪsərɪn] *s* nitroglicerina

ni'trous ox'ide ['naɪtrəs] *s* ossidulo di azoto

nitwit ['nɪtˌwɪt] *s* (slang) baggiano

no [no] *adj* nessuno; **no admittance** vietato l'ingresso; **no doubt** senza dubbio; **no matter** non importa; **no parking** divieto di sosta; **no smoking** vietato fumare; **no thoroughfare** divieto di transito; **no use** inutilmente; **with no** senza ‖ *s* no; voto negativo ‖ *adv* no; non; **no longer** non . . . più; **no sooner** non appena

Noah ['no·ə] *s* Noè *m*

nob·by ['nɑbi] *adj* (*-bier*; *-biest*) (slang) elegante; (slang) eccellente

nobili·ty [no'bɪlɪti] *s* (*-ties*) nobiltà *f*

noble ['nobəl] *adj* & *s* nobile *m*

no'ble·man *s* (*-men*) nobile *m*, nobiluomo

no'ble·wom'an *s* (*-wom'en*) nobile *f*, nobildonna

nobod·y ['no ˌbɑdi] or ['nobədi] *s* (*-ies*) nessuno, illustre sconosciuto ‖ *pron indef* nessuno; **nobody but** nessun altro che; **nobody else** nessun altro

nocturnal [nɑk'tʌrnəl] *adj* notturno

nod [nɑd] *s* cenno d'assenso, cenno del capo; (*of person going to sleep*) crollo del capo ‖ *v* (*pret* & *pp* **nodded**; *ger* **nodding**) *tr* (*one's head*) inclinare; **to nod assent** fare cenno di sì ‖ *intr* inclinare il capo; (*to drowse*) assopirsi

node [nod] *s* nodo; protuberanza; (phys) nodo

no'-good' *adj* & *s* (coll) buono a nulla

nohow ['no ˌhau] *adv* (coll) in nessuna maniera

noise [nɔɪz] *s* rumore *m* ‖ *tr* divulgare

noiseless ['nɔɪzlɪs] *adj* silenzioso

nois·y ['nɔɪzi] *adj* (*-ier*; *-iest*) rumoroso, chiassoso

nomad ['nomæd] *adj* & *s* nomade *m*

no' man's' land' *s* terra di nessuno

nominal ['nɑmɪnəl] *adj* nominale; simbolico

nominate ['nɑmɪˌnet] *tr* presentare la candidatura di; (*to appoint*) nominare, designare

nomination [ˌnɑmɪ'neʃən] *s* candidatura; nomina

nominative ['nɑmɪnətɪv] *adj* & *s* nominativo

nominee [ˌnɑmɪ'ni] *s* candidato designato

nonbelligerent [ˌnɑnbə'lɪdʒərənt] *adj* & *s* non belligerante *m*

nonbreakable [nɑn'brekəbəl] *adj* infrangibile

nonce [nɑns] *s*—**for the nonce** per l'occasione

nonchalance ['nɑnʃələns] or [ˌnɑnʃə'lɑns] *s* disinvoltura, indifferenza

nonchalant ['nɑnʃələnt] or [ˌnɑnʃə'lɑnt] *adj* disinvolto, indifferente

noncom ['nɑnˌkɑm] *s* (coll) sottufficiale *m*

noncombatant [nɑn'kɑmbətənt] *adj* non combattente ‖ *s* persona non combattente

non'commis'sioned of'ficer [ˌnɑnkə'mɪʃənd] *s* sottufficiale *m*

noncommittal [ˌnɑnkə'mɪtəl] *adj* ambiguo, evasivo

non compos mentis ['nɑn 'kɑmpəs 'mentɪs] *adj* pazzo; (law) incapace

nonconformist [ˌnɑnkən'fɑrmɪst] *s* anticonformista *mf*, nonconformista *mf*

nondelivery [ˌnɑndɪ'lɪvəri] *s* mancata consegna

nondescript ['nɑndɪˌskrɪpt] *adj* indefinibile, inclassificabile

none [nʌn] *pron indef* nessuno; **none of** nessuno di; **none other** nessun altro ‖ *adv* non; affatto, niente affatto; **none the less** ciò nonostante, nondimeno

nonenti·ty [nɑn'entɪti] *s* (*-ties*) inesistenza; (*person*) nullità *f*

nonfiction [nɑn'fɪkʃən] *s* letteratura non romanzesca

nonfulfillment [ˌnɑnful'fɪlmənt] *s* mancanza di esecuzione

nonintervention [ˌnɑnɪntər'venʃən] *s* non intervento

nonmetal ['nɑnˌmetəl] *s* metalloide *m*

nonpayment [nɑn'pemənt] *s* mancato pagamento

non·plus ['nɑnplʌs] or [nɑn'plʌs] *s* perplessità *f* ‖ *v* (*pret* & *pp* **-plussed** or **-plused**; *ger* **-plussing** or **-plusing**) *tr* lasciare perplesso

nonprofit [nɑn'prɑfɪt] *adj* senza scopo lucrativo

nonrefillable [ˌnɑnrɪ'fɪləbəl] *adj* (*prescription*) non ripetibile; (*e.g., bottle*) non ricaricabile

nonresident [nɑn'rezɪdənt] *s* persona di passaggio, non residente *mf*

nonresidential [nɑnˌrezɪ'denʃəl] *adj* commerciale, non residenziale

nonscientific [nɑnˌsaɪ·ən'tɪfɪk] *adj* non scientifico

nonsectarian [ˌnɑnsekˈterɪ·ən] *adj* che non segue nessuna confessione religiosa

nonsense [ˈnɑnsens] *s* sciocchezza, assurdità *f*, nonsense

nonsensical [nɑnˈsensɪkəl] *adj* sciocco, assurdo, illogico

nonskid [ˈnɑnˈskɪd] *adj* antiderapante

nonstop [ˈnɑnˈstɑp] *adj & adv* senza scalo

nonsupport [ˌnɑnsəˈpɔrt] *s* mancato pagamento degli alimenti

noodle [ˈnudəl] *s* (slang) scemo; (slang) testa; **noodles** tagliatelle *fpl*

noo'dle soup' *s* tagliatelle *fpl* in brodo

nook [nʊk] *s* angolo, cantuccio

noon [nun] *s* mezzogiorno; **at high noon** a mezzogiorno in punto

no one or **no-one** [ˈno ˌwʌn] *pron indef* nessuno; **no one else** nessun altro

noontime [ˈnun ˌtaɪm] *s* mezzogiorno

noose [nus] *s* laccio, nodo scorsoio

nor [nɔr] *conj* nè

Nordic [ˈnɔrdɪk] *adj* nordico

norm [nɔrm] *s* norma, media, tipo

normal [ˈnɔrməl] *adj* normale ‖ *s* condizione normale; norma; (geom) normale *f*

Norman [ˈnɔrmən] *adj & s* normanno

Normandy [ˈnɔrməndɪ] *s* la Normandia

Norse [nɔrs] *adj* norvegese; scandinavo ‖ *s* (*ancient Scandinavian language*) scandinavo; (*language of Norway*) norvegese *m*; **the Norse** gli scandinavi; i norvegesi

Norse'man *s* (-men) normanno

north [nɔrθ] *adj* del nord, settentrionale ‖ *s* nord *m* ‖ *adv* al nord, verso il nord

North' Amer'ica *s* l'America del Nord

North' Amer'ican *adj & s* nordamericano

north'east' *adj* di nord-est ‖ *s* nord-est *m* ‖ *adv* al nord-est

north'east'er *s* vento di nord-est

northern [ˈnɔrðərn] *adj* settentrionale; (*Hemisphere*) boreale

North' Kore'a *s* la Corea del Nord

North' Pole' *s* polo nord

northward [ˈnɔrθwərd] *adv* verso il nord

north'west' *adj* di nord-ovest ‖ *s* nord-ovest *m* ‖ *adv* al nord-ovest

north' wind' *s* vento del nord, aquilone *m*

Norway [ˈnɔrwe] *s* la Norvegia

Norwegian [nɔrˈwidʒən] *adj & s* norvegese *mf* ‖ *s* (*language*) norvegese *m*

nose [noz] *s* naso; (*of missile*) testata; **to blow one's nose** soffiarsi il naso; **to count noses** contare il numero dei presenti; **to follow one's nose** andare a lume di naso; **to lead by the nose** menare per il naso; **to look down one's nose at** (coll) guardare dall'alto in basso; **to pay through the nose** pagare un occhio della testa; **to pick one's nose** mettersi le dita nel naso; **to speak through the nose** parlare nel naso; **to thumb one's nose at** fare marameo a; **to turn up one's nose at** guardare dall'alto in basso, guardare con disprezzo ‖ *tr* fiutare; **to nose out** vincere per un pelo ‖ *intr* fiutare; **to nose about** curiosare

nose' bag' *s* musetta

nose'band' *s* museruola di cavallo

nose'bleed' *s* sangue *m* dal naso

nose' cone' *s* ogiva

nose' dive' *s* (*of prices*) subita discesa; (aer) discesa in picchiata

nose'-dive' *intr* discendere in picchiata

nosegay [ˈnoz ˌge] *s* mazzolino di fiori

nose' glass'es *spl* occhiali *mpl* a stringinaso

nose' ring' *s* nasiera

nose'wheel' *s* (aer) ruota del carrello anteriore

no'-show' *s* (coll) passeggero che si è prenotato e non parte

nostalgia [nɑˈstældʒə] *s* nostalgia

nostalgic [nɑˈstældʒɪk] *adj* nostalgico

nostril [ˈnɑstrɪl] *s* narice *f*

nos·y [ˈnozɪ] *adj* (-ier; -iest) (coll) curioso

not [nɑt] *adv* no; non; **not at all** niente affatto; **not yet** non ancora; **to think not** credere di no; **why not?** come no?

notable [ˈnotəbəl] *adj* notevole, notabile ‖ *s* notabile *m*

notarize [ˈnotə ˌraɪz] *tr* munire di fede notarile

nota·ry [ˈnotərɪ] *s* (-ries) notaio

notch [nɑtʃ] *s* tacca; (*in mountain*) passo; (coll) tantino; **notches** (coll) di gran lunga, e.g., **notches above** di gran lunga migliore ‖ *tr* intaccare

note [not] *s* nota, annotazione; (*currency*) banconota; (*communication*) memorandum *m*; (*of bird*) canto; (*tone of voice*) tono; (*reputation*) riguardo; (*short letter*) biglietto, letterina; (mus) nota; (com) cambiale *f* ‖ *tr* notare, annotare; osservare

note'book' *s* (*for school*) quaderno; taccuino, notes *m*

noted [ˈnotɪd] *adj* ben noto, eminente

note' pa'per *s* carta da lettera

note'wor'thy *adj* notevole

nothing [ˈnʌθɪŋ] *s* niente *m*, nulla; **for nothing** gratis; inutilmente; **next to nothing** quasi niente ‖ *pron indef* niente, nulla, non . . . niente, non . . . nulla; **nothing else** niente'altro; **to make nothing of it** non farne caso ‖ *adv* per nulla; **nothing less** non meno

notice [ˈnotɪs] *s* attenzione; notizia, notifica; annunzio, preavviso; (*in newspaper*) trafiletto; (law) disdetta; **on short notice** senza preavviso; (com) a breve scadenza; **to escape the notice of** passare inavvertito a; **to serve notice to** far sapere a, far constatare a ‖ *tr* osservare, notare, prendere nota di

noticeable [ˈnotɪsəbəl] *adj* notevole; (*e.g., difference*) percettibile

noti·fy [ˈnotɪ ˌfaɪ] *v* (*pret & pp* -fied) *tr* informare, far sapere

notion [ˈnoʃən] *s* nozione; (*whim*) capriccio; **notions** mercerie *fpl*; **to have a notion to** aver voglia di

notorie·ty [ˌnotəˈraɪ·ɪtɪ] *s* (-ties) (*state*

of being well known) notorietà *f*; cattiva fama

notorious [no'tɔrɪ‧əs] *adj* (*generally known*) notorio; (*unfavorably known*) famigerato

no'-trump' *adj* & *s* sénza atout *m*

notwithstanding [,nɑtwɪð'stændɪŋ] or [,nɑtwɪθ'stændɪŋ] *adv* ciò nonostante ‖ *prep* malgrado ‖ *conj* sebbene

nougat ['nugət] *s* torrone *m*

noun [naʊn] *s* nome *m*, sostantivo

nourish ['nʌrɪʃ] *tr* nutrire

nourishing ['nʌrɪ/ɪŋ] *adj* nutriente

nourishment ['nʌrɪ/mənt] *s* nutrimento

novel ['nɑvəl] *adj* nuovo, novello, insolito, originale ‖ *s* romanzo

novelist ['nɑvəlɪst] *s* romanzière *m*

novel‧ty ['nɑvəltɪ] *s* (-ties) novità *f*; **novelties** chincaglierie *fpl*

November [no'vembər] *s* novembre *m*

novice ['nɑvɪs] *s* novizio

novitiate [no'vɪ/ɪ‧ɪt] *s* noviziato

novocaine ['novə ,ken] *s* novocaina

now [naʊ] *s* presente *m* ‖ *adv* adesso; **from now on** d'ora in poi; **just now** un momento fa; **now and then** di tempo in tempo; **now that** vistó che ‖ *conj* visto che, dato che

nowadays ['naʊ‧ə ,dez] *adv* al giorno d'oggi, oggidì

no'way' *adv* in nessun modo; nient'affatto

no'where' *adv* da nessuna parte; **nowhere else** da nessun'altra parte, in nessun altro luogo

noxious ['nɑk/əs] *adj* nocivo

nozzle ['nɑzəl] *s* (*of hose or pipe*) boccaglio; (*of tea pot, gas burner*) becco; (*of gun*) bocca; (*of sprinkling can*) bocchetta; (aut, mach) becco; (slang) naso

nth [enθ] *adj* ennesimo; **to the nth degree** all'ennesima potenza

nuance [nju'ɑns] or ['nju‧ɑns] *s* sfumatura

nub [nʌb] *s* protuberanza; (*of coal*) pezzo; (coll) nocciolo, cuore *m*

nuclear ['njuklɪ‧ər] or ['nuklɪ‧ər] *adj* nucleare

nu'clear fis'sion *s* fissione nucleare

nu'clear fu'sion *s* fusione nucleare

nu'clear test' ban' *s* accordo per la tregua atomica

nucle‧us ['njuklɪ‧əs] or ['nuklɪ‧əs] *s* (-i [,aɪ] or -uses) nucleo

nude [njud] or [nud] *adj* nudo ‖ *s*—**in the nude** nudo

nudge [nʌdʒ] *s* gomitatina ‖ *tr* dare di gomito a

nudist ['njudɪst] or ['nudɪst] *adj* & *s* nudista *mf*

nudi‧ty ['njudɪtɪ] or ['nudɪtɪ] *s* (-ties) nudità *f*

nugget ['nʌgɪt] *s* pepita

nuisance ['njusəns] or ['nusəns] *s* noia, seccatura; (*person*) seccatore *m*, pittima *mf*

null [nʌl] *adj* nullo; **null and void** invalido

nulli‧fy ['nʌlɪ ,faɪ] *v* (*pret* & *pp* -fied) *tr* annullare, invalidare

nulli‧ty ['nʌlɪtɪ] *s* (-ties) nullità *f*

numb [nʌm] *adj* intorpidito; (*from cold*) intirizzito; **to become numb** intorpidirsi ‖ *tr* intorpidire

number ['nʌmbər] *s* numero; (*for sale*) articolo di vendita; (*publication*) fascicolo; (*of a serial*) dispensa, puntata; **a number of** parecchi; **beyond** or **without number** senza numero, infiniti ‖ *tr* numerare, contare; **his days are numbered** i suoi giorni sono contati ‖ *intr*—**to number among** essere tra

numberless ['nʌmbərlɪs] *adj* innumerevole

numeral ['njumərəl] or ['numərəl] *adj* numerale ‖ *s* numero

numerical [nju'merɪkəl] or [nu'merɪkəl] *adj* numerico

numerous ['njumərəs] or ['numərəs] *adj* numeroso

numskull ['nʌm ,skʌl] *s* (coll) stupido

nun [nʌn] *s* monaca, religiosa

nuptial ['nʌp/əl] *adj* nuziale ‖ **nuptials** *spl* nozze *fpl*

nurse [nʌrs] *s* infermiera; (*to suckle a child*) nutrice *f*; (*to take care of a child*) bambinaia ‖ *tr* (*to minister to*) curare; allattare; allevare; (*e.g., hatred*) covare ‖ *intr* fare l'infermiera

nurser‧y ['nʌrsərɪ] *s* (-ies) stanza dei bambini; (*shelter for children*) asilo infantile; (hort) vivaio

nurs'ery‧man (-men) orticoltore *m*

nurs'ery rhyme' *s* canzoncina per i più piccini

nurs'ery school' *s* scuola materna

nursing ['nʌrsɪŋ] *adj* infermieristico ‖ *s* allattamento; professione d'infermiera

nurs'ing bot'tle *s* biberon *m*, poppatoio

nurs'ing home' *s* convalescenziario; ospizio dei vecchi, gerontocomio

nurture ['nʌrt/ər] *s* allevamento; nutrimento ‖ *tr* allevare; alimentare; (*e.g., hope*) accarezzare

nut [nʌt] *s* noce *f*; (*eccentric*) (slang) esaltato, pazzoide *m*; (mus) capotasto; (mach) madrevite *f*, dado; **a hard nut to crack** un osso duro da rodere; **to be nuts for** (coll) essere pazzo per

nut'crack'er *s* schiaccianoci *m*

nutmeg ['nʌt ,meg] *s* noce moscata

nutrition [nju'trɪ/ən] or [nu'trɪ/ən] *s* (*process*) nutrizione; (*food*) nutrimento

nutritious [nju'trɪ/əs] or [nu'trɪ/əs] *adj* nutriente

nut'shell' *s* guscio di noce; **in a nutshell** in breve, in poche parole

nut‧ty ['nʌtɪ] *adj* (-tier; -tiest) che sa di noci; (slang) pazzo; **nutty about** (slang) pazzo per

nuzzle ['nʌzəl] *tr* toccare col muso, ammusare ‖ *intr* (*said of swine*) grufolare; (*said of other animals*) stare muso a muso, ammusare; (*to snuggle*) rannicchiarsi

nylon ['naɪlɑn] *s* nailon *m*

nymph [nɪmf] *s* ninfa

O

O, o [o] *s* quindicesima lettera del-l'alfabeto inglese
O *interj* o!, oh!
oaf [of] *s* balordo, scemo, imbecille *mf*
oak [ok] *s* quercia
oaken ['okən] *adj* di quercia, quercino
oakum ['okəm] *s* stoppa incatramata
oar [or] *s* remo; **to lie** or **rest on one's oars** dormire sugli allori; non lavo-rare più || *tr* spingere coi remi || *intr* remare
oar'lock' *s* scalmo
oars'man *s* (**-men**) rematore *m*
oa·sis [o'esis] *s* (**-ses** [siz]) oasi *f*
oat [ot] *s* avena; **oats** (*seeds*) avena; **to feel one's oats** (coll) essere pieno di vita; (coll) sentirsi importante; **to sow one's wild oats** correre la caval-lina
oath [oθ] *s* giuramento; **on oath** sotto giuramento; **to take an oath** giurare, prestar giuramento
oat'meal' *s* (*breakfast food*) fiocchi *mpl* d'avena; farina d'avena
obdurate ['abdjərɪt] *adj* indurito, ine-sorabile; impenitente, incallito
obedience [o'bidɪ·əns] *s* obbedienza, ubbidienza
obedient [o'bidɪ·ənt] *adj* ubbidiente
obeisance [o'besəns] or [o'bisəns] *s* saluto rispettoso; omaggio
obelisk ['abəlɪsk] *s* obelisco
obese [o'bis] *adj* obeso
obesity [o'bisɪtɪ] *s* obesità *f*
obey ['obe] *tr* ubbidire (with *dat*), ub-bidire || *intr* ubbidire
obfuscate [ab'fʌsket] or ['abfəs,ket] *tr* offuscare
obituar·y [o'bɪtʃʊ,eri] *adj* necrologico || *s* (**-ies**) necrologia
object ['abdʒɪkt] *s* oggetto || [ab-'dʒekt] *tr* obiettare || *intr* fare obie-zioni, obiettare
objection [ab'dʒekʃən] *s* obiezione
objectionable [ab'dʒekʃənəbəl] *adj* re-prensibile; (*e.g., odor*) sgradevole; offensivo
objective [ab'dʒektɪv] *adj* & *s* obiet-tivo
obligate ['ablɪ,get] *tr* obbligare
obligation [,ablɪ'geʃən] *s* obbligo, ob-bligazione
oblige [ə'blaɪdʒ] *tr* obbligare; favo-rire; **much obliged** obbligatissimo
obliging [ə'blaɪdʒɪŋ] *adj* compiacente, accomodante, servizievole
oblique [ə'blik] *adj* obliquo; indiretto
obliterate [ə'blɪtə,ret] *tr* obliterare; spegnere, distruggere
oblivion [ə'blɪvɪ·ən] *s* oblio
oblivious [ə'blɪvɪ·əs] *adj* (*forgetful*) dimentico; (*unaware*) ignaro
oblong ['ablɔŋ] or ['ablɑŋ] *adj* oblungo
obnoxious [ab'nakʃəs] *adj* detestabile
oboe ['obo] *s* oboe *m*
oboist ['obo·ɪst] *s* oboista *mf*
obscene [ab'sin] *adj* osceno
obsceni·ty [ab'senɪtɪ] or [ab'sɪnɪtɪ] *s* (**-ties**) oscenità *f*, sconcezza

obscure [əb'skjʊr] *adj* oscuro || *tr* oscurare
obscuri·ty [əb'skjʊrɪtɪ] *s* (**-ties**) oscu-rità *f*
obsequies ['absɪkwɪz] *spl* esequie *fpl*
obsequious [ab'sikwɪ·əs] *adj* osse-quioso, servile
observance [əb'zʌrvəns] *s* osservanza; **observances** pratiche *fpl;* cerimonie *fpl*
observation [,abzər've/ən] *s* osserva-zione; osservanza
observa'tion car' *s* (rr) vettura belve-dere
observato·ry [əb'zʌrvə,tori] *s* (**-ries**) osservatorio
observe [əb'zʌrv] *tr* osservare
observer [əb'zʌrvər] *s* osservatore *m*
obsess [ab'ses] *tr* ossessionare
obsession [ab'se/ən] *s* ossessione
obsolescent [,absə'lesənt] *adj* che sta cadendo in disuso
obsolete ['absə,lit] *adj* disusato
obstacle ['abstəkəl] *s* ostacolo
obstetrical [ab'stetrɪkəl] *adj* ostetrico
obstetrics [ab'stetrɪks] *s* ostetricia
obstina·cy ['abstɪnasi] *s* (**-cies**) ostina-zione
obstinate ['abstɪnɪt] *adj* ostinato
obstreperous [ab'strepərəs] *adj* turbo-lento; rumoroso
obstruct [əb'strʌkt] *tr* ostruire
obstruction [ab'strʌkʃən] *s* ostruzione
obtain [əb'ten] *tr* ottenere || *intr* pre-valere, essere in voga
obtrusive [əb'trusɪv] *adj* intruso, im-portuno; sporgente
obtuse [əb'tjus] or [əb'tus] *adj* ottuso
obviate ['abvɪ,et] *tr* ovviare (with *dat*)
obvious ['abvɪ·əs] *adj* ovvio, palmare
occasion [ə'keʒən] *s* occasione; **on oc-casion** di quando in quando || *tr* oc-casionare
occasional [ə'keʒənəl] *adj* saltuario; (*e.g., verses*) d'occasione
occasionally [ə'keʒənəlɪ] *adv* occasio-nalmente, di tanto in tanto
occident ['aksɪdənt] *s* occidente *m*
occidental [,aksɪ'dentəl] *adj* & *s* occi-dentale *mf*
occlud'ed front' [ə'kludɪd] *s* fronte occluso
occlusion [ə'kluʒən] *s* occlusione
occlusive [ə'klusɪv] *adj* occlusivo || *s* occlusiva
occult [ə'kʌlt] or ['akʌlt] *adj* occulto
occupancy ['akjəpənsi] *s* occupazione, presa di possesso; (*tenancy*) loca-zione
occupant ['akjəpənt] *s* occupante *m;* (*tenant*) inquilino
occupation [,akjə'peʃən] *s* occupa-zione
occupational [,akjə'peʃənəl] *adj* occu-pazionale; (*e.g., disease*) professio-nale, del lavoro
occu·py ['akjə,paɪ] *v* (*pret* & *pp* **-pied**) *tr* occupare; (*to dwell in*) abitare
oc·cur [ə'kʌr] *v* (*pret* & *pp* **-curred**)

ger -curring) *intr* accadere, succedere; incontrarsi; (*to come to mind*) venir in mente, e.g., **it occurs to me** mi viene in mente

occurrence [ə'kʌrəns] *s* evento, avvenimento; apparizione

ocean ['oʃən] *s* oceano

o'cean lin'er *s* transatlantico

o'clock [ə'klɑk] *adv* secondo l'orologio; **it is one o'clock** è la una; **it is two o'clock** sono le due

octane ['ɑkten] *adj* ottanico || *s* ottano

octave ['ɑktɪv] *or* ['ɑktev] *s* ottava

Octavian [ɑk'tevɪ·ən] *s* Ottaviano

October [ɑk'tobər] *s* ottobre *m*

octo•pus ['ɑktəpəs] *s* (**-puses** *or* **-pi** [ˌpaɪ]) (*small*) polpo; (*large*) piovra; (fig) piovra

ocular ['ɑkjələr] *adj* & *s* oculare *m*

oculist ['ɑkjəlɪst] *s* oculista *mf*

odd [ɑd] *adj* (*number*) dispari; strambo, bizzarro; (*not matching*) scompagnato, spaiato; strano; e rotti, e.g., **three hundred odd** tre cento e rotti || **odds** *ssg or spl* probabilità *f*; (*advantage*) vantaggio, superiorità *f*; **at odds** in disaccordo; **by all odds** senza dubbio; **it makes no odds** fa lo stesso; **the odds are** la quota è; **to set at odds** seminare zizzania fra

oddi•ty ['ɑdɪti] *s* (**-ties**) stranezza

odd' jobs' *spl* lavori saltuari

odd' lot' *s* (fin) compravendita di meno di cento unità

odds' and ends' *spl* un po' di tutto

odious ['odɪ·əs] *adj* odioso

odor ['odər] *s* odore *m*; **to be in bad odor** aver cattiva fama

odorless ['odərlɪs] *adj* inodoro

odorous ['odərəs] *adj* odoroso

Odysseus [o'dɪsjus] *or* [o'dɪsɪ·əs] *s* Odisseo

Odyssey ['ɑdɪsi] *s* Odissea

Oedipus ['ɛdɪpəs] *or* ['idɪpəs] *s* Edipo

of [ɑv] *or* [əv] *prep* di, e.g., **the lead of the pencil** la mina della matita; a, e.g., **to think of** pensare a; meno, e.g., **a quarter of ten** le dieci meno un quarto

off [ɑf] *or* [ɔf] *adj* (*wrong*) sbagliato; (*slightly abnormal*) matto, pazzo; inferiore; (*electricity*) tagliato; (*agreement*) sospeso; libero, in libertà; distante; destro; (*season*) morto || *adv* via; fuori, lontano, distante; **to be off** mettersi in marcia || *prep* da; fuori da; al disotto di; lontano da; distolto da, e.g., **his eyes were off the target** i suoi occhi erano distolti dal bersaglio; (naut) al largo di

offal ['ɑfəl] *or* ['ɔfəl] *s* (*of butchered animal*) frattaglie *fpl*; rifiuti *mpl*

off' and on' *adv* di tempo in tempo

off'beat' *adj* insolito, originale

off' chance' *s* possibilità remota

off'-col'or *adj* scolorito; indisposto; (*joke*) di dubbio gusto

offend [ə'fɛnd] *tr* & *intr* offendere

offender [ə'fɛndər] *s* offensore *m*

offense [ə'fɛns] *s* offesa; **to take offense** (at) offendersi (di)

offensive [ə'fɛnsɪv] *adj* offensivo || *s* offensiva

offer ['ɑfər] *or* ['ɔfər] *s* offerta || *tr* offrire; (*thanks*) porgere; (*resistance*) opporre || *intr* offrirsi

offering ['ɑfərɪŋ] *or* ['ɔfərɪŋ] *s* offerta

off'hand' *adj* fatto all'improvviso; sbrigativo, alla buona || *adv* all'improvviso; bruscamente

office ['ɑfɪs] *or* ['ɔfɪs] *s* ufficio; funzione, incombenza; (*of a doctor*) gabinetto; (*of a lawyer*) studio; (eccl) uffizio; **through the good offices of** per tramite di

of'fice boy' *s* fattorino

of'fice-hold'er *s* pubblico funzionario

of'fice hours' *spl* orario d'ufficio

officer ['ɑfɪsər] *or* ['ɔfɪsər] *s* (*in a corporation*) funzionario; (*policeman*) agente *m*; (mil, nav, naut) ufficiale *m*; **officer of the day** (mil) ufficiale *m* di giornata

of'fice seek'er ['sikər] *s* aspirante *m* a un ufficio pubblico

of'fice supplies' *spl* articoli *mpl* di cancelleria

official [ə'fɪʃəl] *adj* ufficiale || *s* funzionario, ufficiale *m*

officiate [ə'fɪʃɪˌet] *intr* ufficiare

officious [ə'fɪʃəs] *adj* invadente, inframettente; **to be officious** essere un impiccione

offing ['ɑfɪŋ] *or* ['ɔfɪŋ] *s*—**in the offing** al largo; (fig) in preparazione, probabile

off'-lim'its *adj* proibito; **off-limits to** ingresso proibito a

off'-peak' heat'er *s* (elec) scaldabagno azionato unicamente in periodi di consumo minimo

off'-peak' load' *s* (elec) carico di consumo minimo

off'print' *s* estratto

off'set' *s* compensazione; (typ) offset *m* || **off'set'** *v* (*pret* & *pp* **-set**; *ger* **-setting**) *tr* compensare; stampare in offset

off'shoot' *s* (*of plant*) germoglio; (*of family or race*) discendente *mf*; (*branch*) ramo; (fig) conseguenza

off'shore' *adj* (*wind*) di terra; (*fishing*) vicino alla costa; (*island*) costiero || *adv* al largo

off'side' *adv* (sports) fuori gioco

off'spring' *s* discendente *m*; prole *f*; figlio; figli *mpl*

off'stage' *adv* tra le quinte

off'-the-rec'ord *adj* confidenziale || *adv* confidenzialmente

often ['ɑfən] *or* ['ɔfən] *adv* sovente, spesso; **how often?** quante volte?; **once too often** una volta di troppo

ogive ['odʒaɪv] *or* [o'dʒaɪv] *s* ogiva

ogle ['ogəl] *tr* adocchiare, occhieggiare

ogre ['ogər] *s* orco

ohm [om] *s* ohm *m*

oil [ɔɪl] *adj* (*pertaining to edible oil*) oleario; (*e.g., well*) di petrolio; (*e.g., lamp*) a olio; (*tanker*) petroliero; (*field*) petrolifero || *s* olio; petrolio; **to burn the midnight oil** studiare a lume di candela; **to pour oil on troubled waters** pacificare; **to strike oil** trovare petrolio || *tr* oliare; lubrificare; ungere || *intr* (*said of a motor-ship*) fare petrolio

oil' burn'er *s* bruciatore *m* a gasolio

oil'can' *s* oliatore *m*

oil'cloth' *s* incerata, tela cerata

oil' field' *s* giacimento petrolifero

oil' lamp' *s* lampada a petrolio

oil'man *s* (**-men**) (*retailer*) mercante *m* di petrolio; (*operator*) petroliere *m*

oil' paint'ing *s* quadro a olio

oil' slick' *s* macchia d'olio

oil' tank'er *s* petroliera

oil' well' *s* pozzo di petrolio

oil·y ['ɔrli] *adj* (**-ier; -iest**) oleoso; untuoso

ointment ['ɔɪntmənt] *s* unguento

O.K. ['o'ke] *adj* (coll) corretto || *s* (coll) approvazione || *adv* (coll) benissimo, d'accordo || *v* (*pret & pp* **O.K.'d**) *ger* **O.K.'ing**) *tr* (coll) dare l'approvazione a || *interj* benissimo!

okra ['okrə] *s* (bot) ibisco esculento; (bot) baccello dell'ibisco esculento

old [old] *adj* vecchio; antico, vetusto; **how old is . . . ?** quanti anni ha . . . ?; **of old** anticamente; **to be . . . years old** avere . . . anni

old' age' *s* vecchiaia

old' boy' *s* vecchietto arzillo; (Brit) vecchio mio

old'-clothes'man' *s* (**-men'**) rigattiere *m*

old' coun'try *s* madre patria

old-fashioned ['old'fæʃənd] *adj* all'antica; fuori moda

old' fo'gey or **old' fo'gy** ['fogi] *s* (**-gies**) uomo di idee antiquate, reazionario

Old' Glo'ry *s* la bandiera degli Stati Uniti

Old' Guard' *s* (U.S.A.) parte *f* più conservatrice di un partito

old' hand' *s* vecchio del mestiere

old' maid' *s* zitella

old' mas'ter *s* grande maestro; quadro di un gran maestro

old' moon' *s* luna calante

old' salt' *s* lupo di mare

old' school' *s* gente *f* all'antica

old' school' tie' *s* (Brit) cravatta coi colori della propria scuola; (fig) tradizionalismo

Old' Tes'tament *s* Antico Testamento

old'-time' *adj* all'antica; del tempo antico

old-timer ['old'taɪmər] *s* (coll) veterano; (coll) vecchio

old' wives'' tale' *s* superstizione da donnicciole; racconto di vecchie comari

Old' World' *s* mondo antico

oleander [,olɪ'ændər] *s* oleandro

oligar·chy ['alɪ,gɑrki] *s* (**-chies**) oligarchia

olive ['alɪv] *adj* oleario; (*color*) olivastro || *s* (*tree*) olivo; (*fruit*) oliva

ol'ive branch' *s* ramoscello d'olivo

ol'ive grove' *s* oliveto

ol'ive oil' *s* olio d'oliva

Oliver ['alɪvər] *s* Oliviero

ol'ive tree' *s* olivo

Olympiad [o'lɪmpɪ,æd] *s* olimpiade *f*

Olympian [o'lɪmpɪ-ən] *adj* olimpico || *s* deità olimpica; giocatore olimpico

Olympic [o'lɪmpɪk] *adj* olimpico, olimpionico

omelet or **omelette** ['aməlɪt] or ['amlɪt] *s* frittata, omelette *f*

omen ['omən] *s* augurio

ominous ['amɪnəs] *adj* infausto, ominoso

omission [o'mɪʃən] *s* omissione

omit [o'mɪt] *v* (*pret & pp* **omitted;** *ger* **omitting**) *tr* omettere

omnibus ['amnɪ,bʌs] or ['amnɪbəs] *adj* di interesse generale || *s* bus *m*; volume collettivo

omnipotent [am'nɪpətənt] *adj* onnipotente

omniscient [am'nɪʃənt] *adj* onnisciente

omnivorous [am'nɪvərəs] *adj* onnivoro

on [an] or [ɔn] *adj* addosso, e.g., **with his hat on** col cappello addosso; in uso, in funzione; (*light*) acceso; (*deal*) fatto, concluso; (*e.g., game*) già cominciato; **what is on at the theater?** che cosa si dà al teatro? || *adv* su; avanti; dietro, e.g., **to drag on** tirarsi dietro; **and so on** e così via; **come on!** va via!; **farther on** più in là; **later on** più tardi; **to be on to s.o.** (coll) scoprire il gioco di qlcu; **to have on** avere addosso; **to . . . on** continuare a, e.g., **the band played on** la banda continuò a suonare; **to put on** mettersi || *prep* su, sopra; a, e.g., **on foot** a piedi; **on his arrival al** suo arrivo; sotto, e.g., **on my responsibility** sotto la mia responsabilità; contro, e.g., **an attack on the government** un attacco contro il governo; da, e.g., **on good authority** da buona fonte; **on all sides** da tutte le parti; verso, e.g., **to march on the capital** marciare verso la capitale; dopo, e.g., **victory on victory** vittoria dopo vittoria

on' and on' *adv* senza cessa

once [wʌns] *s* una volta; volta, e.g., **this once** questa volta || *adv* una volta; mai, e.g., **if this once becomes known** se questo si risapesse mai; **all at once** repentinamente; **at once** subito; allo stesso tempo; **for once** almeno una volta; **once and again** ripetutamente; **once in a blue moon** ad ogni morte di papa; **once in a while** di tanto in tanto; **once upon a time there was** c'era una volta || *conj* se appena; una volta che

once'-o'ver *s* (coll) occhiata rapida; **to give s.th** the once-over (coll) esaminare qlco rapidamente; (coll) pulire qlco superficialmente

one [wʌn] *adj* uno; un certo, e.g., **one Smith** un certo Smith; unico e.g., **one price** prezzo unico || *s* uno || *pron* uno, e.g., **how can one live here?** come è possibile che uno viva qui?; si, e.g., **how does one go to the museum?** come si va al museo?; **I for one** per lo meno io; **it's all one and the same to me** per me fa lo stesso; **my little one** piccolo mio; **one and all** tutti; **one another** si, e.g., **they wrote one another** si scrissero;

l'un(o) l'altro, e.g., **they looked at one another** si guardarono l'un l'altro; **one o'clock** la una; **one's** il suo, il proprio; **the blue hat and the red one** il cappello blu e quello rosso; **the one and only** l'unico; **the one that** chi, quello che; **this one** questo; **that one** quello; **to make one** unire

one'-eyed' *adj* monocolo

one'-horse' *adj* a un solo cavallo; (coll) da nulla, poco importante

one'-man' show' *s* personale *f*

onerous ['ɑnərəs] *adj* oneroso

one-self' *pron* sé stesso; se; si; **to be oneself** essere normale; comportarsi normalmente

one-sided ['wʌn'saɪdɪd] *adj* unilaterale; ingiusto, parziale

one'-track' *adj* a un solo binario; (coll) unilaterale, limitato

one'-way' *adj* a senso unico; (*ticket*) semplice, d'andata

onion ['ʌnjən] *s* cipolla; **to know one's onions** (coll) conoscere i propri polli

on'ion-skin' *s* carta pelle aglio, carta velina

on'look'er *s* presente *m*, spettatore *m*

only ['onlɪ] *adj* solo, unico || *adv* solo, soltanto, non . . . più di; **not only . . . but also** non solo . . . ma anche || *conj* ma; se non che

on'set' *s* attacco; (*beginning*) inizio; **at the onset** dapprincipio

onslaught ['ɑn,slɔt] *or* ['ɔn,slɔt] *s* attacco

on'to *prep* su, sopra a; **to be onto** (coll) rendersi conto del gioco di

onward ['ɑnwərd] *or* **onwards** ['ɑn-wərdz] *adv* avanti, più avanti

onyx ['ɑnɪks] *s* onice *m*

ooze [uz] *s* trasudazione; liquido per concia || *tr* sudare || *intr* trasudare; (*said, e.g., of blood*) stillare; (*said, e.g., of air*) filtrare; (fig) trapelare

opal ['opəl] *s* opale *m*

opaque [o'pek] *adj* opaco; (*writer's style*) oscuro; stupido

open ['opən] *adj* aperto, scoperto; (*job*) vacante; (*time*) libero; (*hunting season*) legale; indeciso; manifesto; (*hand*) liberale; (*needlework*) a giorno; **to break** *or* **to crack open** forzare; **to throw open** aprire completamente || *s* apertura; (*in the woods*) radura; **in the open** all'aperto; all'aria aperta; in alto mare; apertamente || *tr* aprire; (*an account*) impostare; **to open up** spalancare; (*one's eyes*) sbarrare || *intr* aprire, aprirsi; (theat) esordire; **to open into** sboccare in; **to open on** dare su; **to open up** sbottonarsi

o'pen-air' *s* all'aria aperta

open-eyed ['opən,aɪd] *adj* con gli occhi aperti; meravigliato; fatto con piena conoscenza

open-handed ['opən'hændɪd] *adj* generoso, liberale

open-hearted ['opən'hɑrtɪd] *adj* franco, sincero; gentile

o'pen house' *s* tavola imbandita; **to keep open house** aver sempre ospiti

opening ['opənɪŋ] *s* apertura; (*of dress*) giro collo; (*e.g., of sewer*) imbocco; (*in the woods*) radura; (*vacancy*) posto vacante; (*beginning*) inizio; (*chance to say something*) occasione

o'pening night' *s* debutto, prima

o'pening num'ber *s* primo numero

o'pening price' *s* prezzo d'apertura

open-minded ['opən'maɪndɪd] *adj* di larghe vedute; imparziale

o'pen se'cret *s* segreto di Pulcinella

o'pen shop' *s* officina che impiega chi non è membro del sindacato

o'pen-work' *s* traforo

opera ['ɑpərə] *s* opera

op'era glass'es *spl* binocolo da teatro

op'era hat' *s* gibus *m*

op'era house' *s* teatro dell'opera

operate ['ɑpə,ret] *tr* (*a machine*) far funzionare; (*a shop*) gestire; operare || *intr* funzionare; operare; **to operate on** (surg) operare

operatic [,ɑpə'rætɪk] *adj* operistico

op'erating expens'es *spl* spese *fpl* di ordinaria amministrazione

op'erating room' *s* sala operatoria

op'erating ta'ble *s* tavola operatoria

operation [,ɑpə're/ən] *s* operazione; funzionamento, marcia

opera'tions research' *s* ricerca operativa

operator ['ɑpə,retər] *s* operatore *m*; (*of a conveyance*) conduttore *m*, conducente *mf*; (com) gestore *m*; (telp) telefonista *mf*; (surg) chirurgo operatore; (slang) faccendiere *m*

opiate ['opɪ·ɪt] *or* ['opɪ,et] *adj* & *s* oppiato

opinion [ə'pɪnjən]-*s* opinione; **in my opinion** a mio modo di vedere; **to have a high opinion of** avere una grande stima di

opinionated [ə'pɪnjə,netɪd] *adj* ostinato, testardo, dogmatico

opium ['opɪ·əm] *s* oppio

o'pium den' *s* fumeria d'oppio

opossum [ə'pɑsəm] *s* opossum *m*

opponent [ə'ponənt] *s* avversario

opportune [,ɑpər'tjun] *or* [,ɑpər'tun] *adj* opportuno

opportunist [,ɑpər'tjunɪst] *or* [,ɑpər'tunɪst] *s* opportunista *mf*

opportuni·ty [,ɑpər'tjunɪti] *or* [,ɑpər'tunɪti] *s* (-ties) opportunità *f*, occasione

oppose [ə'poz] *tr* opporsi a

opposite ['ɑpəsɪt] *adj* opposto; di rimpetto, e.g., **the house opposite** la casa di rimpetto || *s* contrario || *prep* di faccia a, di rimpetto a

op'posite num'ber *s* persona di grado corrispondente

opposition [,ɑpə'zɪ/ən] *s* opposizione

oppress [ə'prɛs] *tr* opprimere

oppressive [ə'prɛsɪv] *adj* oppressivo; opprimente, soffocante

oppressor [ə'prɛsər] *s* oppressore *m*

opprobrious [ə'probrɪ·əs] *adj* obbrobrioso

opprobrium [ə'probrɪ·əm] s obbrobrio
optic ['ɑptɪk] adj ottico || **optics** ssg ottica
optical ['ɑptɪkəl] adj ottico
optician [ɑp'tɪʃən] s ottico, occhialaio
optimism ['ɑptɪ,mɪzəm] s ottimismo
optimist ['ɑptɪmɪst] s ottimista mf
optimistic [,ɑptɪ'mɪstɪk] adj ottimistico
option ['ɑpʃən] s opzione
optional ['ɑpʃənəl] adj facoltativo
optometrist [ɑp'tɑmɪtrɪst] s optometrista mf
opulent ['ɑpjələnt] adj opulento
or [ɔr] conj o; (or else) oppure
oracle ['ɔrəkəl] or ['ɑrəkəl] s oracolo
oracular [o'rækjələr] adj profetico; ambiguo; misterioso; sentenzioso
oral ['ɔrəl] adj orale
orange ['ɑrɪndʒ] or ['ɔrɪndʒ] adj di arance; arancio || s arancia
orangeade [,ɑrɪndʒ'ed] or [,ɔrɪndʒ-'ed] s aranciata
or'ange blos'som s zagara
or'ange grove' s aranceto
or'ange juice' s sugo d'arancia
or'ange squeez'er s spremiagrumi m
or'ange tree' s arancio
orang-outang [o'ræŋu,tæŋ] s orango
oration [o're/ən] s orazione, discorso
orator ['ɑrətər] or ['ɔrətər] s oratore m
oratorical [,ɑrə'tɑrɪkəl] or [,ɔrə'tɑrɪkəl] adj oratorio
oratori•o [,ɑrə'tɔrɪ,o] or [,ɔrə'tɔrɪ,o] s (-os) (mus) oratorio
orato•ry ['ɑrə,tɔri] or ['ɔrə,tɔri] s (-ries) oratoria; (eccl) oratorio
orb [ɔrb] s orbe m
orbit ['ɔrbɪt] s orbita; **to go into orbit** entrare in orbita || tr mettere in orbita; orbitare ,intorno a || intr orbitare
or'biting sta'tion s stazione orbitale
orchard ['ɔrt/ərd] s frutteto
orchestra ['ɔrkɪstrə] s orchestra; (parquet) platea
orchestral [ɔr'kestrəl] adj orchestrale
or'chestra pit' s golfo mistico
or'chestra seat' s poltrona di platea
orchestrate ['ɔrkɪs,tret] tr orchestrare
orchid ['ɔrkɪd] s orchidea
ordain [ɔr'den] tr predestinare; decretare; (eccl) ordinare
ordeal [ɔr'dil] or [ɔr'di·əl] s sfacchinata; (hist) ordalia
order ['ɔrdər] s ordine m; compito, e.g., **a big order** un compito difficile; (com) commessa, ordinazione; (mil) consegna; **in order that** affinché; **in order to** + inf per + inf; **made to order** fatto su misura; **to get out of order** guastarsi; **to give an order** dare un ordine; (com) fare una commessa || tr (e.g., a drink) ordinare; (a person) ordinare with (dat); (e.g., a suit of clothes) far fare; **to order around** mandare attorno; **to order s.o. away** mandar via qlcu
or'der blank' s cedola d'ordinazione
order•ly ['ɔrdərli] adj ordinato; disciplinato || s (-lies) (in a hospital) in-

serviente mf; (mil) ordinanza, attendente m
ordinal ['ɔrdɪnəl] adj & s ordinale m
ordinance ['ɔrdɪnəns] s ordinanza
ordinary ['ɔrdɪ,neri] adj ordinario
ordnance ['ɔrdnəns] s artiglieria; bocche fpl da fuoco; munizionamento
ore [or] s minerale m (metallifero)
organ ['ɔrgən] s organo
organ-dy ['ɔrgəndi] s (-dies) organdi m
or'gan grind'er s suonatore m d'organetto
organic [ɔr'gænɪk] adj organico
organism ['ɔrgə,nɪzəm] s organismo
organist ['ɔrgənɪst] s organista mf
organization [,ɔrgənɪ'zeʃən] s organizzazione
organize ['ɔrgə,naɪz] tr organizzare
organizer ['ɔrgə,naɪzər] s organizzatore m
or'gan loft' s palco, galleria per l'organo
orgasm ['ɔrgæzəm] s orgasmo
or•gy ['ɔrdʒi] s (-gies) orgia
orient ['ɔrɪ·ənt] s oriente m || **Orient** s Oriente m || **orient** ['ɔrɪ,ent] tr orientare, orizzontare
oriental [,ɔrɪ'entəl] adj orientale || **Oriental** s orientale mf
orifice ['ɑrɪfɪs] or ['ɔrɪfɪs] s orifizio
origin ['ɑrɪdʒɪn] or ['ɔrɪdʒɪn] s origine f, provenienza
original [ə'rɪdʒɪnəl] adj & s originale mf
originate [ə'rɪdʒɪ,net] tr originare || intr originare, originarsi
oriole ['ɔrɪ,ol] s oriolo, rigogolo
Ork'ney Is'lands ['ɔrkni] spl Orcadi fpl
ormolu ['ɔrmə,lu] s (alloy) similoro; (gold powder) polvere f d'oro; (gilded metal) bronzo dorato
ornament ['ɔrnəmənt] s ornamento || ['ɔrnə,ment] tr ornamentare
ornamental [,ɔrnə'mentəl] adj ornamentale
ornate [ɔr'net] or ['ɔrnet] adj ornato; (style) elaborato
ornithologist [,ɔrnɪ'θɑlədʒɪst] s ornitologo
orphan ['ɔrfən] adj & s orfano || tr rendere orfano
orphanage ['ɔrfənɪdʒ] s (institution) orfanotrofio; (condition) orfanezza
Orpheus ['ɔrfjus] or ['ɔrfi·əs] s Orfeo
orthodox ['ɔrθə,dɑks] adj ortodosso
orthogra•phy [ɔr'θɑgrəfi] s (-phies) ortografia
oscillate ['ɑsɪ,let] intr oscillare
osier ['oʒər] s vimine m; (bot) vinco
osmosis [ɑz'mosɪs] or [ɑs'mosɪs] s osmosi f
osprey ['ɑspri] s falco pescatore
ossi•fy ['ɑsɪ,faɪ] v (pret & pp -fied) tr ossificare || intr ossificarsi
ostensible [ɑs'tensɪbəl] adj apparente, preteso
ostentatious [,ɑsten'teʃəs] adj ostentato
osteopathy [,ɑstɪ'ɑpəθi] s osteopatia
ostracism ['ɑstrə,sɪzəm] s ostracismo

ostracize ['ɑstrə‚saɪz] *tr* dare l'ostracismo a, ostracizzare

ostrich ['ɑstrɪtʃ] *s* struzzo

Othello [o'θɛlo] *or* [ə'θɛlo] *s* Otello

other ['ʌðər] *adj & pron indef* altro || *adv*—**other than** diversamente che

otherwise ['ʌðər‚waɪz] *adv* altrimenti; differentemente

otter ['ɑtər] *s* lontra

ottoman ['ɑtəmən] *s* (*fabric*) ottomano; (*sofa*) ottomana; cuscino per i piedi || **Ottoman** *adj & s* ottomano

ouch [aʊt] *interj* ahi!

ought [ɔt] *s* qualcosa; zero; **for ought I know** per quanto io sappia || *v aux* is rendered in Italian by the conditional of *dovere*, e.g., **you ought to be ashamed** dovresti vergognarti

ounce [aʊns] *s* oncia

our [aʊr] *adj poss* nostro, il nostro

ours [aʊrz] *pron poss* il nostro

ourselves [aʊr'sɛlvz] *pron pers* noi stessi; ci, e.g., **we enjoyed ourselves** ci siamo divertiti

oust [aʊst] *tr* espellere; (*a tenant*) sfrattare

out [aʊt] *adj* erroneo; esterno; fuori pratica; svenuto; ubriaco; finito; (*book*) pubblicato; (*lights*) spento; fuori moda; introvabile; palmare; di permesso, e.g., **my night out** la mia serata di permesso; (*e.g., at the knees*) frusto; (*sports*) fuori gioco || *s* via d'uscita; **to be on the outs or at outs with** (coll) essere in disaccordo con || *adv* fuori, all'infuori; all'aria libera; out for in cerca di; **out of** fuori, fuori di; di; da; (*e.g., money*) a corto di, senza; su, e.g., **two students out of three** due studenti su tre || *prep* fuori di; per, lungo || *interj* fuori!

out' and away' *adv* di gran lunga

out'-and-out' *adj* perfetto, completo || *adv* perfettamente, completamente

out'bid' *v* (*pret* -bid; *pp* -bid *or* -bidden*) ger* -bidding) *tr* fare un'offerta migliore di; (*bridge*) fare una dichiarazione più alta di

out'board mo'tor *s* fuoribordo, motore *m* fuoribordo

out'break' *s* insurrezione; (*of hives*) eruzione; (*of anger; of war*) scoppio

out'build'ing *s* dipendenza

out'burst' *s* (*of tears; of laughter*) scoppio; (*of energy*) impeto, slancio

out'cast' *s* vagabondo reietto

out'come' *s* risultato

out'cry' *s* (-cries) grido, chiasso

out'dat'ed *adj* fuori moda

out'dis'tance *tr* distanziare

out'do' *v* (*pret* -did; *pp* -done) *tr* sorpassare; **to outdo oneself** sorpassare sé stesso

out'door' *adj* all'aria aperta

out'doors' *s* aria libera, aperta campagna || *adv* all'aria aperta, fuori di casa

out'er space' ['aʊtər] *s* spazio cosmico

out'field' *s* (baseball) campo esterno

out'field'er *s* (baseball) esterno

out'fit' *s* equipaggiamento; (*female cos-*

tume) insieme *m*; (*of bride*) corredo; (*group*) (coll) corpo; (com) compagnia || *v* (*pret & pp* -fitted; *ger* -fitting) *tr* equipaggiare

out'flow' *s* efflusso

out'go'ing *adj* in partenza; (*tide*) decrescente; (*character*) espansivo || *s* efflusso

out'grow' *v* (*pret* -grew; *pp* -grown) *tr* essere troppo grande per; sorpassare in statura; perdere l'interesse per || *intr* protrudere

out'growth' *s* risultato, conseguenza; crescita

outing ['aʊtɪŋ] *s* gita, scampagnata

outlandish [aʊt'lændɪʃ] *adj* strano, bizzarro; dall'aspetto straniero; (*remote, far away*) in capo al mondo

out'last' *tr* sopravvivere (with *dat*)

out'law' *s* fuorilegge *mf* || *tr* proscrivere; dichiarare illegale

out'lay' *s* disborso || **out·lay'** *v* (*pret & pp* -laid) *tr* sborsare

out'let *s* uscita; (*e.g., of river*) sbocco; (com) mercato; (elec) presa di corrente; (fig) sfogo

out'line' *s* contorno; traccia, tracciato; sagoma, profilo; prospetto || *tr* delineare; tracciare, tratteggiare; sagomare, profilare; prospettare

out'live' *tr* sopravvivere (with *dat*)

out'look' *s* prospettiva; (*watch*) guardia; (*mental view*) modo di vedere, opinione

out'ly'ing *adj* lontano, fuori di mano; periferico

outmoded [‚aʊt'modɪd] *adj* fuori moda, antiquato

out'num'ber *tr* superare in numero

out'-of-date' *adj* fuori moda

out'-of-door' *adj* all'aria aperta

out'-of-doors' *adj* all'aria aperta || *s* aria aperta || *adv* all'aria aperta; fuori di casa

out'-of-print' *adj* esaurito

out'-of-the-way' *adj* appartato, fuori mano; inusitato, strano

out' of tune' *adj* stonato || *adv* fuori di tono

out' of work' *adj* disoccupato

out'pa'tient *s* paziente *mf* esterno

out'post' *s* (mil) posto avanzato

out'put' *s* produzione; (elec) uscita; (mach) rendimento, potenza utile

out'rage' *s* oltraggio, indecenza || *tr* oltraggiare; (*a woman*) violare

outrageous [aʊt'redʒəs] *adj* oltraggioso; (*excessive*) eccessivo; atroce, feroce

out'rank' *tr* superare in grado

out'rid'er *s* battistrada *m*

out'right' *adj* completo, intero || *adv* completamente; apertamente; sul colpo, sull'istante

out'set' *s* inizio, principio

out'side' *adj* esterno; (*unlikely*) improbabile; (*price*) massimo || *s* esterno, di fuori *m*; aspetto esteriore; vita fuori del carcere || *adv* fuori, di fuori; **outside of** fuori di || *prep* fuori di; (coll) all'infuori di

out·sid·er [ˌaʊtˈsaɪdər] *s* estraneo, intruso; (sports) outsider *m*

out·skirts *spl* sobborghi *mpl*, periferia

out·spo·ken *adj* franco, esplicito

out·stand·ing *adj* saliente, eminente; (*debt*) arretrato, non pagato

out·ward [ˈaʊtwərd] *adj* esterno, superficiale ‖ *adv* al di fuori

out·weigh *tr* pesare più di; eccedere in importanza

out·wit *v* (*pret* & *pp* -witted; *ger* -witting) *tr* farla in barba di; (*a pursuer*) far perdere la traccia or la pista a

oval [ˈovəl] *adj* & *s* ovale *m*

ova·ry [ˈovəri] *s* (-ries) ovaia

ova·tion [oˈveʃən] *s* ovazione

oven [ˈʌvən] *s* forno

over [ˈovər] *adj* superiore; esterno; finito, concluso ‖ *adv* su, sopra; dall'altra parte; dall'altra sponda; al rovescio; di nuovo; (*at the bottom of a page*) continua; qui, e.g., **hand over the money** dammi qui il denaro; **over again** di nuovo; **over against** contro; **over and over** ripetutamente; **over here** qui; **over there** là ‖ *prep* su, sopra; dall'altra parte di; attraverso, per; (*a certain number*) più di; a causa di; **over and above** in eccesso di

o·ver·all *adj* completo, totale ‖ **over·alls** *spl* tuta

o·ver·bear·ing *adj* arrogante, prepotente

o·ver·board *adv* in acqua; **man overboard!** uomo in mare!; **to go overboard** andare agli estremi

o·ver·cast *adj* annuvolato ‖ *s* cielo annuvolato ‖ *v* (*pret* & *pp* -cast) *tr* coprire, annuvolare

o·ver·charge *s* prezzo eccessivo; sovraccarico; (elec) carica eccessiva ‖ **o·ver·charge** *tr* far pagare eccessivamente; sovraccaricare

o·ver·coat *s* soprabito, pastrano

o·ver·come *v* (*pret* -came; *pp* -come) *tr* vincere, sopraffare; (*e.g., passions*) frenare; opprimere

o·ver·con·fi·dence *s* sicumera

o·ver·crowd *tr* gremire

o·ver·do *v* (*pret* -did; *pp* -done) *tr* esagerare; strafare; esaurire; (*meat*) stracuocere ‖ *intr* esaurirsi

o·ver·dose *s* dose eccessiva

o·ver·draft *s* assegno allo scoperto

o·ver·draw *v* (*pret* -drew; *pp* -drawn) *tr* (*a check*) emettere allo scoperto; (*a character*) esagerare la descrizione di

o·ver·due *adj* in ritardo; (com) in sofferenza, scaduto

o·ver·eat *v* (*pret* -ate; *pp* -eaten) *tr* & *intr* mangiare troppo

o·ver·exer·tion *s* sforzo eccessivo

o·ver·expose *tr* sovrasporre

o·ver·expo·sure *s* sovresposizione

o·ver·flow *s* (*of a river*) piena, straripamento; (*excess*) sovrabbondanza; (*e.g., of a fountain*) trabocco; (*outlet*) tubo di troppopieno ‖ **o·ver·flow** *intr* (*said of a river*) straripare; (*said of a container*) traboccare

o·ver·fly *v* (*pret* -flew; *pp* -flown) *tr* sorvolare; (*a target*) oltrepassare

o·ver·grown *adj* cresciuto troppo; coperto, denso

o·ver·hang *s* strapiombo ‖ **o·ver·hang** *v* (*pret* & *pp* -hung) *tr* sovrastare (with *dat*); sovrastare; (*to threaten*) minacciare; pervadere, permeare ‖ *intr* sovrastare, strapiombare

o·ver·haul *s* riparazione; esame *m*, revisione ‖ *tr* riparare; esaminare, ripassare, rivedere; raggiungere, mettersi alla pari con

o·ver·head *adj* in alto, sopra la testa; aereo; elevato, pensile; generale ‖ **o·ver·head** *adv* in alto, di sopra ‖ **o·ver·head** *s* spese *fpl* generali

o·ver·head projec·tor *s* lavagna luminosa

o·ver·head valve *s* valvola in testa

o·ver·hear *v* (*pret* & *pp* -heard) *tr* sentire per caso, udire per caso

o·ver·heat *tr* surriscaldare ‖ *intr* surriscaldarsi; eccitarsi

over·joyed [ˌovərˈdʒɔɪd] *adj* felicissimo; **to be overjoyed** non stare in sé dalla contentezza

over·land [ˈovərˌlænd] or [ˈovərlənd] *adj* & *adv* per via di terra

o·ver·lap *v* (*pret* & *pp* -lapped; *ger* -lapping) *tr* sovrapporre, estendersi sopra ‖ *intr* sovrapporsi, estendersi; coincidere parzialmente

o·ver·load *s* sovraccarico ‖ **o·ver·load** *tr* sovraccaricare, stracaricare

o·ver·look *tr* sovrastare su, dominare; ispezionare, sorvegliare; passare sopra, trascurare; dare su, e.g., **the window overlooks the street** la finestra dà sulla strada

o·ver·lord *s* dominatore *m* ‖ *tr* dominare despoticamente

over·ly [ˈovərli] *adv* eccessivamente

o·ver·night *adj* per la notte, per solo una notte ‖ **o·ver·night** *adv* durante la notte; la notte prima

o·ver·night bag *s* astuccio di toletta per la notte

o·ver·pass *s* cavalcavia, viadotto

o·ver·pop·ulate *tr* sovrappopolare

o·ver·pow·er *tr* sopraffare

o·ver·pow·ering *adj* schiacciante

o·ver·pro·duc·tion *s* sovrapproduzione

o·ver·rate *tr* sopravvalutare

o·ver·run *v* (*pret* -ran; *pp* -run; *ger* -running) *tr* invadere, infestare; inondare; (*one's time*) oltrepassare, eccedere

o·ver·sea or **o·ver·seas** *adj* di oltremare ‖ **o·ver·sea** or **o·ver·seas** *adv* oltremare, al di là dei mari

o·ver·see *v* (*pret* -saw; *pp* -seen) *tr* sorvegliare

o·ver·seer *s* sorvegliante *mf*

o·ver·shad·ow *tr* oscurare, eclissare

o·ver·shoe *s* soprascarpa

o·ver·shoot *v* (*pret* & *pp* -shot) *tr* (*the target*) oltrepassare; (*said of water*) scorrere sopra; **to overshoot** andare troppo in là ‖ *intr* (aer) atterrare lungo e richiamare

o·ver·sight *s* sbadataggine *f*, svista; sorveglianza, supervisione o'ver·sleep' v (pret & pp -slept) tr (a certain hour) dormire oltre ‖ intr dormire troppo a lungo

o'ver·step' v (pret & pp -stepped; ger -stepping) tr eccedere, oltrepassare

o'ver·stock' tr riempire eccessivamente

o'ver·sup·ply' s (-plies) fornitura superiore alla richiesta ‖ o'ver·sup·ply' v (pret & pp -plied) tr fornire in quantità superiore alla richiesta

overt ['ovərt] or [o'vʌrt] adj palmare, chiaro, manifesto

o'ver·take' v (pret -took; pp -taken) tr raggiungere, sorpassare; sorprendere

o'ver-the-count'er adj (securities) venduto direttamente al compratore

o'ver·throw' s rovesciamento; disfatta ‖ o'ver·throw' v (pret -threw; pp -thrown) tr rovesciare, sconfiggere

o'ver·time' adj supplementare, fuori orario ‖ s straordinario; (sports) tempo supplementare ‖ adv fuori orario

o'ver·tone' s (mus) suono armonico; (fig) sottinteso

o'ver·trump' s taglio con atout più alto ‖ o'ver·trump' tr & intr tagliare con atout più alto

overture ['ovərtʃər] s apertura; (mus) preludio, sinfonia

o'ver·turn' s rovesciamento ‖ o'ver·turn' tr rovesciare, travolgere ‖ intr rovesciarsi, ribaltarsi

overweening [,ovər'winɪŋ] adj presuntuoso, vanitoso; esagerato, eccessivo

o'ver·weight' adj troppo grasso; oltrepassante i limiti di peso ‖ o'ver·weight' s sovraccarico; preponderanza; eccesso di peso

overwhelm [,ovər'hwelm] tr schiacciare, debellare; coprire; (e.g., with kindness) colmare, ricolmare

o'ver·work' s lavoro straordinario; superlavoro ‖ o'ver·work' tr far lavorare eccessivamente ‖ intr lavorare eccessivamente

Ovid ['avɪd] s Ovidio

ow [au] interj ahi!

owe [o] tr dovere ‖ intr essere in debito

owing ['o·ɪŋ] adj dovuto; owing to a causa di

owl [aul] s gufo, barbagianni m

own [on] adj proprio, e.g., my own brother il mio proprio fratello ‖ s il proprio; on one's own (coll) per proprio conto; (without anybody's advice) di testa propria; to come into one's own entrare in possesso del proprio; essere riconosciuto per quanto si vale; to hold one's own non perdere terreno; essere pari ‖ tr possedere; riconoscere ‖ intr—to own up to confessare

owner ['onər] s padrone m, proprietario, titolare m

ownership ['onər ,ʃɪp] s proprietà f

own'er's li'cence s permesso di circolazione

ox [aks] s (oxen ['aksən]) bue m

ox'cart' s carro tirato da buoi

oxide ['aksaɪd] s ossido

oxidize ['aksɪ ,daɪz] tr ossidare ‖ intr ossidarsi

oxygen ['aksɪdʒən] s ossigeno

ox'ygen mask' s maschera respiratoria

ox'ygen tent' s tenda ad ossigeno

oxytone ['aksɪ ,ton] adj tronco, ossitono ‖ s ossitono

oyster ['ɔɪstər] adj di ostriche ‖ s ostrica

oys'ter bed' s ostricaio, banco di ostriche

oys'ter cock'tail s ostriche fpl servite in valva

oys'ter fork' s forchettina da ostriche

oys'ter·house' s ristorante m per la vendita delle ostriche

oys'ter·knife' s coltello per aprire le ostriche

oys'ter·man s (-men) ostricaio

oys'ter shell' s conchiglia d'ostrica

oys'ter stew' s brodetto d'ostriche

ozone ['ozon] s ozono

P

P, p [pi] s sedicesima lettera dell'alfabeto inglese

pace [pes] s passo, andatura; (of a horse) ambio; to keep pace with andare di pari passo con; to put s.o. through his paces mettere qlcu a dura prova; to set the pace for fare i'andatura per; dare l'esempio a ‖ tr misurare a passi, percorrere; to pace the floor andare avanti e indietro per la stanza ‖ intr camminare lentamente; andare al passo; (said of a horse) ambiare

pace'mak'er s battistrada m; (in races) chi stabilisce il passo; (med) pacemaker m

pacific [pə'sɪfɪk] adj pacifico ‖ Pacific adj & s Pacifico

pacifier ['pæsɪ ,faɪ·ər] s paciere m; (teething ring) succhietto, tettarella

pacifism ['pæsɪ ,fɪzəm] s pacifismo

pacifist ['pæsɪfɪst] adj & s pacifista mf

paci·fy ['pæsɪ ,faɪ] v (pret & pp -fied) tr pacificare

pack [pæk] s fardello, pacco; (of merchandise) balla; (of lies) mucchio; (of cards) mazzo; (of thieves) banda; (of dogs) muta; (of animals) branco; (of birds) stormo; (of cigarettes) pacchetto; (of ice) banchiglia; (of people) turba ‖ tr affardellare, impaccare; (to wrap) imballare; ammucchiare; (in cans) mettere in conserva; (people) stipare; (a trunk) fare; to pack in stipare; to pack off mandare via ‖ intr ammucchiarsi, pigiarsi, accalcarsi; **to pack up** fare il baule

package ['pækɪdʒ] *s* pacco, collo; (*small*) pacchetto || *tr* impacchettare

pack' an'imal *s* bestia da soma

packer ['pækər] *s* imballatore *m;* (*of canned goods*) proprietario (di fabbrica di conserve alimentari)

packet ['pækɪt] *s* pacchetto; (*boat*) vapore *m* postale

packing ['pækɪŋ] *s* imballaggio; (*on shoulders of suit*) spallina; (mach) stoppa; (*ring*) (mach) guarnizione

pack'ing box' or **case'** *s* cassa d'imballaggio

pack'ing house' *s* fabbrica di conserve alimentari; fabbrica di carne in conserva

pack'ing slip' *s* foglio d'imballaggio

pack'sad'dle *s* basto

pack'thread' *s* spago d'imballaggio

pack'train' *s* fila di animali da soma

pact [pækt] *s* patto

pad [pæd] *s* cuscinetto, tampone *m;* imbottitura; (*of writing paper*) blocco da annotazioni; (*of an animal*) superficie *f* plantare, zampa; (*of a water lily*) foglia, (rok) piattaforma || *v* (*pret & pp* **padded;** *ger* **padding**) *tr* imbottire, ovattare; (*e.g., a speech*) infarcire || *intr* camminar pesantemente

pad'ding *s* imbottitura

paddle ['pædəl] *s* pagaia; (*of water-wheel*) pala || *tr* remare; (*to spank*) bastonare || *intr* remare; (*to splash*) diguazzare

pad'dle wheel' *s* ruota a pale

paddock ['pædək] *s* prato d'allenamento, paddock *m*

pad'lock' *s* lucchetto || *tr* chiudere col lucchetto

pagan ['pegən] *adj & s* pagano

paganism ['pegə,nɪzəm] *s* paganesimo

page [pedʒ] *s* (*of a book*) pagina; (*at court*) paggio; (*in hotels*) valletto || *tr* impaginare; (*in hotels*) chiamare, far chiamare

pageant ['pædʒənt] *s* parata, corteo, spettacolo

pageant·ry ['pædʒəntri] *s* (**-ries**) pompa, fasto

paginate ['pædʒɪ,net] *tr* impaginare

pail [pel] *s* secchio

pain [pen] *s* dolore *m;* **on pain of** sotto pena di; **to take pains to** prendersi cura di; **to take pains not to** guardarsi da || *tr & intr* dolere

painful ['penfəl] *adj* doloroso, penoso

pain'kill'er *s* (coll) analgesico

painless ['penlɪs] *adj* indolore

painstaking ['penz,tekɪŋ] *adj* meticoloso

paint [pent] *s* (*for pictures*) colore *m;* (*for a house*) vernice *f;* (*make-up*) trucco || *tr* dipingere; (*a house*) verniciare, tinteggiare || *intr* dipingersi; essere pittore

paint'box' *s* scatola di colori

paint'brush' *s* pennello

painter ['pentər] *s* (*of pictures*) pittore *m;* (*of a house*) verniciatore *m;* (naut) barbetta

painting ['pentɪŋ] *s* pittura, dipinto

paint' remov'er [rɪ'muvər] *s* solvente *m* per levar la vernice

paint' thin'ner *s* diluente *m*

pair [per] *s* paio; (*of people*) coppia || *tr* appaiare, accoppiare || *intr* appaiarsi, accoppiarsi

pair' of scis'sors *s* forbici *fpl*

pair' of trou'sers *s* calzoni *mpl*

pajamas [pə'dʒɑməz] or [pə'dʒæməz] *spl* pigiama *m*

Pakistan [,pɑkɪ'stɑn] *s* il Pakistan

Pakistani [,pɑkɪ'stɑni] *adj & s* pachistano

pal [pæl] *s* (coll) compagno || *v* (*pret & pp* **palled;** *ger* **palling**) *intr* (coll) essere compagni

palace ['pælɪs] *s* palazzo

palatable ['pælətəbəl] *adj* gustoso, appetitoso; accettabile

palatal ['pælətəl] *adj & s* palatale *f*

palate ['pælɪt] *s* palato

pale [pel] *adj* pallido || *s* palo; (*enclosure*) recinto; (fig) ambito || *intr* impallidire

pale'face' *s* faccia pallida

palette ['pælɪt] *s* tavolozza

palfrey ['pɔlfri] *s* palafreno

palisade [,pælɪ'sed] *s* palizzata; (*line of cliffs*) dirupo

pall [pɔl] *s* panno mortuario; (*of smoke*) cappa || *tr* saziare, infastidire || *intr* saziarsi, perdere l'appetito

pall'bear'er *s* chi accompagna il feretro; chi porta il feretro

palliate ['pælɪ,et] *tr* attenuare, alleviare

pallid ['pælɪd] *adj* pallido

pallor ['pælər] *s* pallore *m*

palm [pɑm] *s* (*tree and leaf*) palma; (*of hand; measure*) palmo; **to carry off the palm** riportare la palma; **to grease the palm of** ungere le ruote a || *tr* far sparire nella mano; nascondere; **to palm off s.th on s.o.** rifilare qlco a qlcu

palmet·to [pɑl'meto] *s* (**-tos** or **-toes**) palmeto

palmist ['pɑmɪst] *s* chiromante *mf*

palmistry ['pɑmɪstri] *s* chiromanzia

palm' leaf' *s* palma, foglia di palma

palm' oil' *s* olio di palma

Palm' Sun'day *s* Domenica delle Palme

palpable ['pælpəbəl] *adj* palpabile

palpitate ['pælpɪ,tet] *intr* palpitare

pal·sy ['pɔlzi] *s* (**-sies**) paralisi *f* || *v* (*pret & pp* **-sied**) *tr* paralizzare

pal·try ['pɔltri] *adj* (**-trier; -triest**) vile, meschino, irrisorio

pamper ['pæmpər] *tr* viziare; (*the appetite*) saziare

pamphlet ['pæmflɪt] *s* opuscolo, libello

pan [pæn] *s* padella, casseruola; (*of a balance*) coppa, piatto; (phot) bacinella || *v* (*pret & pp* **panned;** *ger* **panning**) *tr* friggere; (*gold*) vagliare in padella; (*salt*) estrarre in salina; (coll) criticare || *intr* essere estratto; **to pan out** (coll) riuscire || **Pan** *m* Pan *m*

panacea [,pænə'si·ə] *s* panacea

Pan'ama Canal' ['pænə,mɑ] *s* Canale *m* di Panama

Pan′ama hat′ *s* panama *m*
Panamanian [ˌpænə′menɪ-ən] or [ˌpænə′mɑnɪ-ən] *adj & s* panamegno
pan′cake′ *s* frittella || *intr* (aer) atterrare a piatto
pan′cake land′ing *s* atterraggio a piatto
pancreas [′pænkrɪ-əs] *s* pancreas *m*
pander [′pændər] *s* mezzano || *intr* ruffianeggiare; **to pander to** favorire, assecondare i desideri di
pane [pen] *s* pannello, vetro di finestra
pan·el [′pænəl] *s* pannello; gruppo che discute in faccia al pubblico, telequiz *m;* discussione pubblica; (*of door or window*) specchio; (law) lista di giurati || *v* (*pret & pp* **-eled** or **-elled;** *ger* **-eling** or **-elling**) *tr* coprire di pannelli
pan′el discus′sion *s* colloquio di esperti in faccia al pubblico
panelist [′pænəlɪst] *s* partecipante *mf* a una discussione in faccia al pubblico
pan′el lights′ *spl* luci *fpl* del cruscotto
pan′el truck′ *s* camioncino
pang [pæŋ] *s* (*sharp pain*) spasimo; (*of remorse*) tormento
pan′han′dle *s* manico della padella || *intr* accattare, mendicare
pan·ic [′pænɪk] *adj & s* panico *m* || *(pret & pp* **-icked;** *ger* **-icking**) *tr* riempire di panico || *intr* essere colto dal panico
pan′ic-strick′en *adj* morto di paura, in preda al panico
pano·ply [′pænəplɪ] *s* (**-plies**) panoplia; abbigliamento in pompa magna
panorama [ˌpænə′ræmə] or [ˌpænə-′rɑmə] *s* panorama *m*
pan·sy [′pænzɪ] *s* (**-sies**) viola del pensiero
pant [pænt] *s* anelito, affanno; **pants** pantaloni *mpl,* calzoni *mpl;* **to wear the pants** portare i calzoni || *intr* ansare; (*said of heart*) palpitare
pantheism [′pænθɪ ˌɪzəm] *s* panteismo
pantheon [′pænθɪ ˌɑn] or [′pænθɪ-ən] *s* panteon *m,* pantheon *m*
panther [′pænθər] *s* pantera
panties [′pæntɪz] *spl* mutandine *fpl*
pantomime [′pæntə ˌmaɪm] *s* pantomima
pan·try [′pæntrɪ] *s* (**-tries**) dispensa
pap [pæp] *s* pappa
papa·cy [′pepəsɪ] *s* (**-cies**) papato
Pa′pal States′ [′pəpəl] *spl* Stati *mpl* pontifici
paper [′pepər] *adj* di carta, cartaceo || *s* carta; (*newspaper*) giornale *m;* (*of a student*) tema *m,* saggio; (*of a scholar*) dissertazione; **on paper** per iscritto || *tr (a wall)* tappezzare
pa′per-back′ *s* libro in brossura
pa′per-boy′ *s* giornalaio, strillone *m*
pa′per clip′ *s* fermaglio per le carte, clip *m*
pa′per cone′ *s* cartoccio
pa′per cut′ter *s* rifilatrice *f*
pa′per doll′ *s* pupazzetto di carta
pa′per-hang′er *s* tappezziere *m*
pa′per knife′ *s* tagliacarte *m*
pa′per mill′ *s* cartiera
pa′per mon′ey *s* carta moneta

pa′per prof′its *spl* guadagni *mpl* non realizzati su valori non venduti
pa′per tape′ *s* (*of teletype*) nastro di carta; (*of computer*) nastro perforato
pa′per-weight′ *s* fermacarte *m*
pa′per work′ *s* lavoro a tavolino
papier-mâché [ˌpepərmə′ʃe] *s* cartapesta
paprika [pæ′prikə] or [′pæprɪkə] *s* paprica
papy·rus [pə′paɪrəs] *s* (**-ri** [raɪ]) papiro
par [pɑr] *adj* alla pari, nominale; normale || *s* parità *f,* valore *m* nominale; **at par** alla pari
parable [′pærəbəl] *s* parabola
parabola [pə′ræbələ] *s* parabola
parachute [′pærə ˌʃut] *s* paracadute *m* || *intr* lanciarsi col paracadute
par′a·chute jump′ *s* lancio col paracadute
parachutist [′pærə ˌʃutɪst] *s* paracadutista *mf*
parade [pə′red] *s* parata, sfilata; ostentazione, sfoggio || *tr* ostentare, sfoggiare; disporre in parata || *intr* fare mostra di sé; (mil) sfilare
paradise [′pærə ˌdaɪs] *s* paradiso
paradox [′pærə ˌdɑks] *s* paradosso
paradoxical [ˌpærə′dɑksɪkəl] *adj* paradossale
paraffin [′pærəfɪn] *s* paraffina
paragon [′pærə ˌgɑn] *s* paragone *m*
paragraph [′pærə ˌgræf] or [′pærə-ˌgrɑf] *s* paragrafo, capoverso; (*in a newspaper*) trafiletto; (*of law*) comma *m*
parakeet [′pærə ˌkit] *s* parrocchetto
paral·lel [′pærə ˌlel] *adj* parallelo || *s* (geog, fig) parallelo; (geom) parallela; **parallels** (typ) sbarrette *fpl* verticali || *v* (*pret & pp* **-leled** or **-lelled;** *ger* **-leling** or **-lelling**) *tr* collocare parallelamente; correre parallelo a; confrontare
par′allel bars′ *spl* parallele *fpl*
paraly·sis [pə′rælɪsɪs] *s* (**-ses** [ˌsiz]) paralisi *f*
paralytic [ˌpærə′lɪtɪk] *adj & s* paralitico
paralyze [′pærə ˌlaɪz] *tr* paralizzare
paramount [′pærə ˌmaunt] *adj* capitale, supremo
paramour [′pærə ˌmur] *s* amante *mf*
paranoiac [ˌpærə′nɔɪ-æk] *adj & s* paranoico
parapet [′pærə ˌpet] *s* parapetto
paraphernalia [ˌpærəfər′nelɪ-ə] *spl* roba, cose *fpl;* attrezzi *mpl,* aggeggi *mpl*
parasite [′pærə ˌsaɪt] *s* parassita *m*
parasitic(al) [ˌpærə′sɪtɪk(əl)] *adj* parassitico, parassitario
parasol [′pærə ˌsɔl] or [′pærə ˌsɑl] *s* parasole *m,* ombrellino da sole
par′a·troop′er *s* paracadutista *m*
par′a·troops′ *spl* truppe *fpl* paracadutiste
parboil [′pɑr ˌbɔɪl] *tr* bollire parzialmente; (fig) far bollire
parcel [′pɑrsəl] *s* pacchetto; (*of land*) appezzamento || *v* (*pret & pp* **-celed** or **-celled;** *ger* **-celing** or **-celling**) *tr*

impacchettare; **to parcel out** dividere, distribuire

par'cel post' *s* servizio pacchi postali

parch [partʃ] *tr* bruciare; (*land*) inaridire; (*e.g., beans*) essiccare; **to be parched** bruciare dalla sete ‖ *intr* arrostirsi; inaridire

parchment ['partʃmənt] *s* pergamena

pardon ['pardən] *s* perdono, grazia; **I beg your pardon** scusi ‖ *tr* perdonare; (*an offense*) graziare

pardonable ['pardənəbəl] *adj* perdonabile, veniale

par'don board' *s* ufficio per la decisione delle grazie

pare [per] *tr* (*fruit, potatoes*) sbucciare, pelare; (*nails*) tagliare; (*expenses*) ridurre

parent ['perənt] *adj* madre, principale ‖ *s* genitore *m* or genitrice *f*; (fig) origine *f*; **parents** genitori *mpl*

parentage ['perəntɪdʒ] *s* discendenza, lignaggio

parenthesis [pə'renθɪsɪs] *s* (**-ses** [ˌsiz]) parentesi *f*; **in parenthesis** tra parentesi

parenthetically [ˌpærən'θetɪkəli] *adv* tra parentesi

parenthood ['perənt ˌhud] *s* paternità *f* or maternità *f*

pariah [pə'raɪ-ə] or ['parɪ-ə] *s* paria *m*

pari-mutuel ['pærɪ mjut/u-əl] *s* totalizzatore *m*

par'ing knife' ['perɪŋ] *s* coltello per sbucciare

Paris ['pærɪs] *s* Parigi *f*

parish ['pærɪʃ] *s* parrocchia

parishioner [pə'rɪʃənər] *s* parrocchiano

Parisian [pə'rɪʒən] *adj* & *s* parigino

parity ['pærɪti] *s* parità *f*

park [park] *s* parco ‖ *tr* parcare, parcheggiare ‖ *intr* parcare, parcheggiare, stazionare

parking ['parkɪŋ] *s* posteggio, parcheggio; **no parking** divieto di parcheggio

park'ing lights' *spl* luci *fpl* di posizione

park'ing lot' *s* posteggio, parcheggio

park'ing me'ter *s* parchimetro

park'ing tick'et *s* contravvenzione per parcheggio abusivo

park'way' *s* boulevard *m*

parlay ['parli] or [par'le] *tr* rigiocare

parley ['parli] *s* trattativa, conferenza ‖ *tr* parlamentare

parliament ['parlImənt] *s* parlamento

parlor ['parlər] *s* salotto; (*of beautician or undertaker*) salone *m*; (*of convent*) parlatorio

par'lor car' *s* vettura salone

par'lor game' *s* gioco di società

par'lor pol'itics *s* politica da caffè

Parmesan [ˌparmɪ'zæn] *adj* & *s* parmigiano

Parnassus [par'næsəs] *s* (*poetry; poets*) parnaso; **il Parnaso**

parochial [pə'rokɪ-əl] *adj* parrocchiale; ristretto, limitato; (*school*) confessionale

paro·dy ['pærədi] *s* (**-dies**) parodia ‖ *v* (*pret* & *pp* **-died**) *tr* parodiare

parole [pə'rol] *s* parola d'onore; libertà *f* condizionale, condizionale *f* ‖ *tr* mettere in libertà condizionale

paroxytone [pær'aksɪ ˌton] *adj* parossitono ‖ *s* parola parossitona

par·quet [par'ke] *s* pavimento di legno tassellato, tassellato; (theat) platea ‖ *v* (*pret* & *pp* **-queted** ['ked]) *ger* **-queting** ['ke-ɪŋ]) *tr* pavimentare in legno tassellato

par'quet cir'cle *s* poltroncine *fpl*

parricide ['pærɪ ˌsaɪd] *s* (*act*) patricidio, parricidio; (*person*) patricida *mf*, parricida *mf*

parrot ['pærət] *s* pappagallo ‖ *tr* scimmiottare, fare il pappagallo a

par·ry ['pæri] *s* (**-ries**) parata ‖ *v* (*pret* & *pp* **-ried**) *tr* parare; (fig) evitare

parse [pars] *tr* (gram) analizzare grammaticalmente

parsimonious [ˌparsɪ'monɪ-əs] *adj* parsimonioso

parsley ['parsli] *s* prezzemolo

parsnip ['parsnɪp] *s* pastinaca

parson ['parsən] *s* parroco; pastore *m* protestante

part [part] *s* parte *f*; (*of a machine*) pezzo, organo; (*of hair*) riga; **for my part** per parte mia; **on the part of** da parte di; **part and parcel** parte *f* integrante; **parts** abilità *f*, dote *f*; regione *f*, paesi *mpl*; **to do one's part** fare il proprio dovere ‖ *adv* parzialmente, in parte ‖ *tr* dividere, separare; **to part company** separarsi; **to part one's hair** farsi la riga ‖ *intr* separarsi; **to part from** separarsi da, dividersi da; **to part with** rinunciare a

par·take [par'tek] *v* (*pret* **-took** ['tuk]; *pp* **-taken**) *tr* condividere ‖ *intr*—**to partake in** partecipare a; **to partake of** condividere

parterre [par'ter] *s* aiola; (theat) platea

Parthenon ['parθɪ ˌnan] *s* Partenone *m*

partial ['parʃəl] *adj* parziale

participate [par'tɪsɪ ˌpet] *intr* partecipare; **to participate in** partecipare a

participation [par ˌtɪsɪ'peʃən] *s* partecipazione

participle ['partɪ ˌsɪpəl] *s* participio

particle ['partɪkəl] *s* particella

particular [pər'tɪkjələr] *adj* (*belonging to a single person*) particolare; (*exacting*) esigente, fastidioso ‖ *s* particolare *m*; **in particular** specialmente, particolarmente

part'ing *adj* (*words*) di commiato; (*last*) ultimo ‖ *s* commiato; separazione

partisan ['partɪzən] *adj* & *s* partigiano

partition [par'tɪʃən] *s* partizione, divisione; (*of house*) tramezzo ‖ *tr* dividere; tramezzare

partner ['partnər] *s* (*in sports*) compagno; (*in dancing*) cavaliere *m*, dama; (*husband or wife*) consorte *mf*; (com) socio

partnership ['partnər ˌʃɪp] *s* associazione; (com) società *f*

part' of speech' *s* parte *f* del discorso

partridge ['partrɪdʒ] *s* pernice *f*

part'-time' *adj* a orario ridotto, a ore

par·ty [parti] *adj* comune; di gala ‖ *s* (**-ties**) festa, ricevimento, trattenimento; (*of people*) gruppo; (*indi-*

vidual) persona; (pol) partito; (law) contraente *mf*; (mil) distaccamento; **to be a party to** prendere parte a; essere complice di

par'ty girl' *s* ragazza che fa la vita

par'ty-go'er *s* frequentatore *m* di trattenimenti

part'y line' *s* (*boundary*) linea di confine; (*of Communist party*) politica del partito; (telp) linea in coutenza

pass [pæs] or [pɑs] *s* passaggio; (*state*) stato, situazione; (*free ticket*) ingresso gratuito; (*leave of absence given to a soldier*) congedo, permesso; (*of a hypnotist*) gesto; (*between mountains*) passo; (slang) tentativo d'abbraccio; **a pretty pass** (coll) un bell'affare || *tr* (*a course in school*) passare; (*to promote*) promuovere; (*a law*) approvare; (*a sentence*) pronunciare; (*an opinion*) esprimere, avanzare; (*to excrete*) evacuare; far muovere; **to pass by** non fare attenzione a; **to pass off** (*e.g.*, *bogus money*) azzeccare; **to pass on** trasmettere; **to pass out** distribuire; **to pass over** omettere || *intr* (*to go*) passare; (*said of a law*) essere approvato; (*said of a student*) essere promosso; (*to be accepted*) farsi passare; (*said, e.g., of two trains*) incrociarsi; **to come to pass** accadere, succedere; **to pass as** passare per; **to pass away** morire; **to pass out** svenire; **to pass over** or **through** attraversare, passare per

passable ['pæsəbəl] or ['pɑsəbəl] *adj* praticabile; (*by boat*) navigabile; (*adequate*) passabile; (law) promulgabile

passage ['pæsɪdʒ] *s* passaggio; (*of a law*) approvazione; (*ticket*) biglietto di passaggio; (*of the bowels*) evacuazione

pass'book' *s* libretto di banca; libretto della cassa di risparmio

passenger ['pæsəndʒər] *s* passeggero

passer-by ['pæsər'baɪ] or ['pɑsər'baɪ] *s* (**passers-by**) passante *mf*

passing ['pæsɪŋ] or ['pɑsɪŋ] *adj* (*fleeting*) fuggente; (*casual*) incidentale; (*grade*) che concede la promozione || *s* passaggio; (*death*) morte *f*; promozione

passion ['pæʃən] *s* passione

passionate ['pæʃənɪt] *adj* appassionato; (*hot-tempered*) collerico; veemente, ardente

passive ['pæsɪv] *adj & s* passivo

pass'key' *s* chiave maestra; (*for use of hotel help*) comunella

Pass'o'ver *s* Pasqua ebraica

pass'port' *s* passaporto

pass'word' *s* parola d'ordine

past [pæst] or [pɑst] *adj* passato, scorso; ex, e.g., **past president** ex presidente || *s* passato || *adv* oltre; al di fuori; al di là || *prep* oltre; al di là di; dopo (di); **past belief** incredibile; **past cure** incurabile; **past hope** senza speranza; **past recovery** incurabile; **past three o'clock** le tre passate

paste [pest] *s* (*dough*) pasta; (*adhesive*) colla; diamante *m* artificiale || *tr* incollare; (slang) dare pugni a

paste'board' *s* cartone *m*

pastel [pæs'tel] *adj & s* pastello

pasteurize ['pæstə‚raɪz] *tr* pastorizzare

pastime ['pæs‚taɪm] or ['pɑs‚taɪm] *s* diversione, passatempo

pastor ['pæstər] or ['pɑstər] *s* pastore *m*, sacerdote *m*

pastoral ['pæstərəl] or ['pɑstərəl] *adj* pastorale || *s* (*poem, letter*) pastorale *f*; (*crosier*) pastorale *m*

pas'try ['pestri] *s* (**-tries**) pasticceria

pas'try cook' *s* pasticciere *m*

pas'try shop' *s* pasticceria

pasture ['pæstʃər] or ['pɑstʃər] *s* pastura, pascolo || *tr* condurre al pascolo || *intr* brucare

past-y ['pesti] *adj* (**-ier; -iest**) pastoso; flaccido

pat [pæt] *s* colpetto; (*of butter*) panetto || *v* (*pret & pp* **patted**; *ger* **patting**) *tr* accarezzare leggermente; battere leggermente; **to pat on the back** elogiare, incoraggiare battendo sulla spalla

patch [pætʃ] *s* (*on a suit or shoes*) toppa; (*in a tire*) pezza; (*on wound*) benda; (*of ground*) appezzamento; (*small area*) lembo || *tr* rammendare; **to patch up** (*an argument*) comporre; (*to produce crudely*) raffazzonare

patent ['petənt] *adj* patente, palmare || ['pætənt] *adj* brevettato || *s* (*of invention*) brevetto; (*sole right*) privativa || *tr* brevettare

pat'ent leath'er ['pætənt] *s* copale *m & f*, pelle *f* di vernice

pat'ent med'icine ['pætənt] *s* specialità *f* medicinale

pat'ent right' ['pætənt] *s* proprietà brevettata

paternal [pə'tʌrnəl] *adj* paterno

paternity [pə'tʌrnɪti] *s* paternità *f*

path [pæθ] or [pɑθ] *s* via battuta, sentiero; (fig) via

pathetic [pə'θetɪk] *adj* patetico

path'find'er *s* esploratore *m*

pathology [pə'θɑlədʒi] *s* patologia

pathos ['peθɑs] *s* patos *m*, pathos *m*

path'way' *s* sentiero, cammino

patience ['peʃəns] *s* pazienza

patient ['peʃənt] *adj & s* paziente *mf*

patriarch ['petri‚ark] *s* patriarca *m*

patrician [pə'trɪʃən] *adj & s* patrizio

patricide ['pætri‚saɪd] *s* (*act*) parricidio; (*person*) parricida *mf*

Patrick ['pætrɪk] *s* Patrizio

patrimo·ny ['pætri‚moni] *s* (**-nies**) patrimonio

patriot ['petriət] or ['pætriət] *s* patriota *mf*

patriotic [‚petri'atɪk] or [‚pætri'atɪk] *adj* patriottico

patriotism ['petri‚ə‚tɪzəm] or ['pætri‚ə‚tɪzəm] *s* patriottismo

pa·trol [pə'trol] *s* (*group*) pattuglia; (*individual*) soldato or agente *m* di pattuglia || *v* (*pret & pp* **-trolled**; *ger* **-trolling**) *tr & intr* pattugliare

patrol'man *s* (**-men**) agente *m*, poliziotto

patrol' wag'on *s* carrozzone *m* cellulare, cellulare *m*

patron ['petrən] or ['pætrən] *s* patrono, sostenitore *m; (customer)* cliente *mf*

patronize ['petrə ˌnaɪz] or ['pætrə ˌnaɪz] *tr (to support)* sostenere; trattare con condiscendenza; essere cliente abituale di

pa'tron saint' *s* patrono

patter ['pætər] *s (e.g., of rain)* battito; *(of feet)* scalpiccio; *(speech)* chiacchierio ‖ *intr* battere, picchiettare; chiacchierare

pattern ['pætərn] *s* modello; disegno; *(of flight)* procedura ‖ *tr* modellare

pat·ty ['pæti] *s* (-ties) pasticcino; *(meat cake)* polpetta

paucity ['pɔsɪti] *s* pochezza, scarsità *f*, insufficienza

Paul [pɔl] *s* Paolo

paunch [pɔntʃ] *s* pancia

paunch·y ['pɔntʃi] *adj* (-ier; -iest) panciuto

pauper ['pɔpər] *s* povero, indigente *mf*

pause [pɔz] *s* pausa; *(of a tape recorder)* arresto momentaneo; to give pause (to) dar di che pensare (a) ‖ *intr* far pausa, fermarsi; *(to hesitate)* esitare, vacillare

pave [pev] *tr* pavimentare, lastricare; to pave the way (for) aprire il cammino (a)

pavement ['pevmənt] *s* pavimentazione, lastricato; *(sidewalk)* marciapiede *m*

pavilion [pə'vɪljən] *s* padiglione *m; (of circus)* tendone *m*

paw [pɔ] *s* zampa ‖ *tr (to touch with paws)* dar zampate a; *(to handle clumsily)* maneggiare goffamente; *(coll)* palpeggiare ‖ *intr* zampare

pawn [pɔn] *s (security)* pegno; *(tool of another person)* pedina; *(chess)* pedina, pedone *m; (fig)* ostaggio ‖ *tr* dare in pegno, impegnare

pawn'bro'ker *s* prestatore *m* su pegno

pawn'shop' *s* agenzia di prestiti su pegno, monte *m* di pietà

pawn' tick'et *s* ricevuta di pegno, polizza del monte di pietà

pay [pe] *s* pagamento; *(wages)* paga, salario; *(mil)* soldo ‖ *v (pret & pp* paid [ped]) *tr* pagare; *(wages)* conguagliare; *(one's respects)* presentare; *(a visit)* fare; *(a bill)* saldare; *(attention)* fare, presentare; to pay back ripagare; *(fig)* pagare pan per focaccia a; to pay for pagare; to pay off liquidare; *(in order to discharge)* pagare e licenziare; to pay up saldare ‖ *intr* pagare; valere la pena; pay as you enter pagare all'ingresso; pay as you go pagare le tasse per trattenuta; pay as you leave pagare all'uscita

payable ['pe·əbəl] *adj* pagabile

pay' boost' *s* aumento di salario

pay'check' *s* assegno in pagamento del salario; salario, paga

pay'day' *s* giorno di paga

payee [pe'i] *s* beneficiario

pay' en'velope *s* bustapaga

payer ['pe·ər] *s* pagatore *m*

pay'load' *s* peso utile

pay'mas'ter *s* ufficiale *m* pagatore

payment ['pemənt] *s* pagamento

pay'off' *s* pagamento, regolamento; *(coll)* conclusione

pay' phone' *s* telefono a moneta

pay'roll' *s* lista degli impiegati; libro paga

pay' sta'tion *s* telefono pubblico

pea [pi] *s* pisello

peace [pis] *s* pace *f*; to hold one's peace tacere, stare zitto

peaceable ['pisəbəl] *adj* pacifico

peaceful ['pisfəl] *adj* pacifico

peace'mak'er *s* paciere *m*

peace' of mind' *s* serenità *f* d'animo

peace' pipe' *s* calumet *m* della pace

peach [pitʃ] *s* pesca; *(coll)* persona or cosa stupenda

peach' tree' *s* pesco

peach·y ['pitʃi] *adj* (-ier; -iest) (coll) stupendo

pea'cock' *s* pavone *m*

peak [pik] *s* picco; *(of traffic)* punta; *(of one's career)* sommo

peak' hour' *s* ora di punta

peak' load' *s* carico delle ore di punta, carico massimo

peal [pil] *s (of bells)* squillo; *(of gun)* rombo; *(of laughter)* scoppio; *(of thunder)* scroscio ‖ *intr* scampanare, squillare

pea'nut' *s* nocciolina americana; *(plant)* arachide *f*

pea'nut but'ter *s* pasta d'arachidi

pear [per] *s (fruit)* pera; *(tree)* pero

pearl [pʌrl] *s* perla; *(mother-of-pearl)* madreperla; colore perlaceo

pearl' oys'ter *s* ostrica perlifera

pear' tree' *s* pero

peasant ['pezənt] *adj & s* contadino

pea'shoot'er *s* cerbottana

pea' soup' *s* minestra di piselli; *(coll)* nebbione *m*

peat [pit] *s* torba

pebble ['pebəl] *s* ciottolo

peck [pek] *s* beccata; misura di due galloni; a peck of trouble un mare di guai ‖ *tr* beccare ‖ *intr* beccare; to peck at beccucciare

peculation [ˌpekjə'leʃən] *s* malversazione, peculato

peculiar [pɪ'kjuljər] *adj* peculiare; *(odd)* strano

pedagogue ['pedə ˌgɑg] *s* pedagogo

pedagogy ['pedə ˌgodʒi] or ['pedə ˌgɑdʒi] *s* pedagogia

ped·al ['pedəl] *s* pedale *m* ‖ *v (pret & pp* -aled or -alled; *ger* -aling or -alling) *tr* spingere coi pedali ‖ *intr* pedalare

pedant ['pedənt] *s* pedante *mf*

pedantic [pɪ'dæntɪk] *adj* pedantesco

pedant·ry ['pedəntri] *s* (-ries) pedanteria

peddle ['pedəl] *tr* vendere di porta in porta ‖ *intr* fare il venditore ambulante

peddler ['pedlər] *s* venditore *m* or merciaiolo ambulante

pedestal [ˈpedɪstəl] s piedistallo
pedestrian [pɪˈdestrɪ-ən] adj pedestre || s pedone m
pediatrics [ˌpidɪˈætrɪks] or [ˌpedɪˈætrɪks] s pediatria
pedigree [ˈpedɪˌgri] s albero genealogico; discendenza, lignaggio
pediment [ˈpedɪmənt] s frontone m
peek [pik] s sbirciata || intr sbirciare
peel [pil] s scorza, buccia; (of baker) pala || tr sbucciare; **to keep one's eyes peeled** (slang) tenere gli occhi aperti || intr pelarsi
peep [pip] s sbirciata; (sound) pigolio || intr guardare attraverso una fessura; (said of birds) pigolare; (to begin to appear) fare capolino
peep'hole' s spioncino
Peep'ing Tom' s guardone m
peep' show' s cosmorama m
peer [pɪr] s pari m, uguale m; (Brit) pari m || intr guardare da vicino
peerless [ˈpɪrlɪs] adj senza pari
peeve [piv] s (coll) seccatura, irritazione || tr (coll) seccare, irritare
peevish [ˈpivɪʃ] adj irritabile
peg [peg] s (to plug holes) zipolo; (pin) cavicchio; (mus) bischero; (coll) grado; **to take down a peg** (coll) fare abbassare la testa a || v (pret & pp **pegged**) ger **pegging**) tr fissare con cavicchi; (prices) stabilizzare || intr—**to peg away** lavorare di lena
peg' leg' s gamba di legno
Peking [ˈpiˈkɪŋ] s Pechino f
Peking·ese [ˌpikɪˈniz] adj pechinese || s (-ese) pechinese mf
pelf [pelf] s (pej) denaro rubacchiato, maltolto
pelican [ˈpelɪkən] s pellicano
pellet [ˈpelɪt] s pallottola; (for shotgun) pallino; (pill) pillola
pell-mell [ˈpelˈmel] adj confuso, disordinato || adv alla rinfusa
Peloponnesian [ˌpeləpəˈniʃən] adj & s peloponnesiaco
pelt [pelt] s pelle grezza; (blow) colpo || tr scagliare contro; (to beat) battere violentemente || intr battere, scrosciare
pen [pen] s (enclosure) recinto; (for writing) penna; (pen point) pennino || v (pret & pp **penned**; ger **penning**) tr scrivere a penna; (to compose) redigere || v (pret & pp **penned** or **pent**; ger **penning**) tr recintare
penalize [ˈpinəˌlaɪz] tr punire; (sports) penalizzare
penal·ty [ˈpenəlti] s (-ties) punizione; (fine) multa; (for late payment) penale f; **under penalty of** sotto pena di
pen'alty goal' s calcio di rigore
penance [ˈpenəns] s penitenza
penchant [ˈpenʃənt] s propensione
pen·cil [ˈpensəl] s matita; (of rays) fascio || v (pret & pp -ciled or -cilled; ger -ciling or -cilling) tr scrivere a matita; (med) pennellare
pen'cil sharp'ener s temperalapis m
pendent [ˈpendənt] adj pendente, sospeso || s pendente m, ciondolo

pending [ˈpendɪŋ] adj imminente; **in sospeso** || prep durante; fino a
pendulum [ˈpendʒələm] s pendolo
pen'dulum bob' s lente f
penetrate [ˈpenɪˌtret] tr & intr penetrare
penguin [ˈpeŋgwɪn] s pinguino
pen'hold'er s portapenne m
penicillin [ˌpenɪˈsɪlɪn] s penicillina
peninsula [peˈnɪnsələ] s penisola
peninsular [pəˈnɪnsələr] adj & s peninsulare
penitence [ˈpenɪtəns] s penitenza
penitent [ˈpenɪtənt] adj & s penitente mf
pen'knife' s (-knives) temperino
penmanship [ˈpenmənˌʃɪp] s calligrafia
pen' name' s nome m di penna, pseudonimo
pennant [ˈpenənt] s pennone m
penniless [ˈpenɪlɪs] adj povero in canna, senza un soldo
pennon [ˈpenən] s pennone m
pen·ny [ˈpeni] s (-nies) (U.S.A.) centesimo || s (**pence** [pens]) (Brit) penny m
pen'ny pinch'er [ˈpɪntʃər] s spilorcio
pen' pal' s amico corrispondente
pen'point' s pennino; (of ball-point pen) punta
pension [ˈpenʃən] s pensione || tr pensionare, mettere in pensione
pensioner [ˈpenʃənər] s pensionato
pensive [ˈpensɪv] adj pensieroso
Pentecost [ˈpentɪˌkɔst] or [ˈpentɪˌkɑst] s la Pentecoste
penthouse [ˈpentˌhaus] s appartamento di lusso sul tetto; tettoia
pent-up [ˈpentˈʌp] adj represso
penult [ˈpinʌlt] s penultima
penum·bra [pɪˈnʌmbrə] s (-brae [bri] or -bras) penombra
penurious [pɪˈnurɪ-əs] adj taccagno, meschino; indigente
penury [ˈpenjəri] s taccagneria; estrema povertà, miseria
pen'wip'er s nettapenne m
people [ˈpipəl] spl popolo, gente f; (relatives) famiglia; gente f del popolo; si, e.g., **people say** si dice || ssg (**peoples**) nazione, popolazione || tr popolare
pep [pep] s (coll) animo, brio || v (pret & pp **pepped**; ger **pepping**) tr—**to pep up** (coll) dar animo a
pepper [ˈpepər] s pepe m || tr pepare; (to pelt) tempestare
pep'per·box' s pepaiola
pep'per·mint' s menta piperita
per [pʌr] prep per; (for each) il, e.g., **three dollars per meter** tre dollari il metro; **as per** secondo
perambulator [pərˈæmbjəˌletər] s carrozzella, carrozzino
per capita [pər ˈkæpɪtə] per persona, a testa
perceive [pərˈsiv] tr percepire
percent [pərˈsent] s percento, per cento
percentage [pərˈsentɪdʒ] s percento, percentuale f; (coll) vantaggio
perception [pərˈsepʃən] s percezione

perch [pʌrtʃ] s (*roost*) posatoio; (*horizontal rod*) ballatoio; (ichth) pesce persico || *intr* appollaiarsi

percolator [ˈpʌrkə‚letər] s caffettiera filtro a circolazione

percus'sion cap' [pərˈkʌʃən] s capsula di percussione

per diem [pər ˈdaɪ‚əm] s assegno giornaliero

perdition [pərˈdɪʃən] s perdizione

perennial [pəˈrɛnɪ‚əl] *adj* perenne || s pianta perenne

perfect [ˈpʌrfɪkt] *adj & s* perfetto || [pərˈfɛkt] *tr* perfezionare

perfidious [pərˈfɪdɪ‚əs] *adj* perfido

perfi·dy [ˈpʌrfɪdi] s (**-dies**) perfidia

perforate [ˈpʌrfə‚ret] *tr* perforare

perforation [‚pʌrfəˈreʃən] s perforazione; (*of postage stamp*) dentellatura

perforce [pərˈfors] *adv* per forza, necessariamente

perform [pərˈfɔrm] *tr* (*a task*) eseguire; (*a promise*) adempiere; (*to enact*) rappresentare || *intr* recitare; (*said, e.g., of a machine*) funzionare

performance [pərˈfɔrməns] s esecuzione; (*of a machine*) funzionamento; (*deed*) atto di prodezza; (theat) rappresentazione

performer [pərˈfɔrmər] s esecutore *m*; attore *m*; acrobata *mf*

perform'ing arts' *spl* arti *fpl* dello spettacolo

perfume [ˈpʌrfjum] s profumo || [pərˈfjum] *tr* profumare

perfumer·y [pərˈfjuməri] s (**-ies**) profumeria

perfunctory [pərˈfʌŋktəri] *adj* superficiale, pro forma; indifferente

perhaps [pərˈhæps] *adv* forse

per·il [ˈpʌrəl] s pericolo || *v* (*pret & pp* **-iled** *or* **-illed**; *ger* **-iling** *or* **-illing**) *tr* mettere in pericolo

perilous [ˈpʌrɪləs] *adj* pericoloso

period [ˈpɪrɪ‚əd] s periodo; mestruazione; (*in school*) ora; (sports) tempo; (gram) punto

pe'riod cos'tume s costume *m* dell'epoca

periodic [‚pɪrɪˈɑdɪk] *adj* periodico

periodical [‚pɪrɪˈɑdɪkəl] *adj & s* periodico

peripher·y [pəˈrɪfəri] s (**-ies**) periferia

periscope [ˈpɛrɪ‚skop] s periscopio

perish [ˈpɛrɪʃ] *intr* perire

perishable [ˈpɛrɪʃəbəl] *adj* deteriorabile

periwig [ˈpɛrɪ‚wɪɡ] s parrucca

perjure [ˈpʌrdʒər] *tr*—**to perjure oneself** spergiurare, giurare il falso

perju·ry [ˈpʌrdʒəri] s (**-ies**) spergiuro

perk [pʌrk] *tr* (*the head, the ears*)—alzare; **to perk oneself up** agghindarsi || *intr*—**to perk up** ringalluzzirsi

permanence [ˈpʌrmənəns] s permanenza

permanen·cy [ˈpʌrmənənsi] s (**-cies**) permanenza

permanent [ˈpʌrmənənt] *adj* permanente || s permanente *f*, ondulazione permanente

per'manent fix'ture s cosa or persona permanente

per'manent ten'ure s inamovibilità *f*

per'manent way' s (rr) sede *f* stradale ed armamento

permeate [ˈpʌrmɪ‚et] *tr* permeare || *intr* permearsi

permissible [pərˈmɪsɪbəl] *adj* permissibile

permission [pərˈmɪʃən] s permesso

per·mit [ˈpʌrmɪt] s permesso; patente *f*, licenza || [pərˈmɪt] *v* (*pret & pp* **-mitted**; *ger* **-mitting**) *tr* permettere

permute [pərˈmjut] *tr* permutare

pernicious [pərˈnɪʃəs] *adj* pernicioso

pernickety [pərˈnɪkɪti] *adj* (coll) incontentabile, meticoloso

perorate [ˈpɛrə‚ret] *intr* perorare

peroxide [pərˈɑksaɪd] s perossido; perossido d'idrogeno

perox'ide blonde' s bionda ossigenata

perpendicular [‚pʌrpənˈdɪkjələr] *adj & s* perpendicolare *f*

perpetrate [ˈpʌrpɪ‚tret] *tr* (*a crime*) perpetrare; (*a blunder*) commettere

perpetual [pərˈpɛtʃʊ‚əl] *adj* perpetuo

perpetuate [pərˈpɛtʃʊ‚et] *tr* perpetuare

perplex [pərˈplɛks] *tr* lasciare perplesso

perplexed [pərˈplɛkst] *adj* perplesso

perplexi·ty [pərˈplɛksɪti] s (**-ties**) perplessità *f*

per se [pər ˈsi] di per se

persecute [ˈpʌrsɪ‚kjut] *tr* perseguitare

persevere [‚pʌrsɪˈvɪr] *intr* perseverare

Persian [ˈpʌrʒən] *adj & s* persiano

Per'sian Gulf' s Golfo Persico

persimmon [pərˈsɪmən] s diospiro virginiano; cachi *m*

persist [pərˈsɪst] *or* [pərˈzɪst] *intr* persistere

persistent [pərˈsɪstənt] *or* [pərˈzɪstənt] *adj* persistente

person [ˈpʌrsən] s persona; **no person** nessuno

personage [ˈpʌrsənɪdʒ] s personaggio; persona

personal [ˈpʌrsənəl] *adj* personale; (*goods*) mobile || s inserzione personale; trafiletto di società

personali·ty [‚pʌrsəˈnælɪti] s (**-ties**) personalità *f*; offesa personale

personal'ity cult' s culto della personalità

per'sonal prop'erty s beni *mpl* mobili

personi·fy [pərˈsɑnɪ‚faɪ] *v* (*pret & pp* **-fied**) *tr* personificare

personnel [‚pʌrsəˈnɛl] s personale *m*

per'son-to-per'son call' s (telp) chiamata con preavviso

perspective [pərˈspɛktɪv] s prospettiva

perspicacious [‚pʌrspɪˈkeʃəs] *adj* perspicace

perspire [pərˈspaɪr] *intr* sudare

persuade [pərˈswed] *tr* persuadere

persuasion [pərˈsweʒən] s persuasione; fede religiosa

pert [pʌrt] *adj* impertinente, sfacciato; vivace

pertain [pərˈten] *intr* appartenere; (*to have reference*) riferirsi

pertinacious [‚pʌrtɪˈneʃəs] *adj* pertinace

pertinent ['pʌrtɪnənt] *adj* pertinente
perturb [pər'tʌrb] *tr* perturbare
Peru [pə'ru] *s* il Perù
perusal [pə'ruzəl] *s* attenta lettura
peruse [pə'ruz] *tr* leggere attentamente
pervade [pər'ved] *tr* pervadere
perverse [pər'vʌrs] *adj* perverso; (*obstinate*) ostinato
perversion [pər'vʌrʒən] *s* perversione
perversi·ty [pər'vʌrsɪti] *s* (-ties) perversità *f*; contrarietà *f*
pervert ['pʌrvərt] *s* pervertito, degenerato || [pər'vʌrt] *tr* pervertire, degenerare
pes·ky ['peski] *adj* (-kier; -kiest) (coll) noioso, molesto
pessimism ['pesɪ,mɪzəm] *s* pessimismo
pessimist ['pesɪmɪst] *s* pessimista *mf*
pessimistic [,pesɪ'mɪstɪk] *adj* pessimistico
pest [pest] *s* peste *f*, pestilenza; insetto; animale nocivo; (*person*) peste *f*, seccatore *m*
pester ['pestər] *tr* seccare, annoiare
pest'house' *s* lazzaretto
pesticide ['pestɪ,saɪd] *s* insetticida *m*
pestiferous [pest'ɪfərəs] *adj* pestifero
pestilence ['pestɪləns] *s* pestilenza
pestle ['pesəl] *s* pestello
pet [pet] *s* animale favorito; beniamino || *v* (*pret & pp* petted; *ger* petting) *tr* accarezzare || *intr* (coll) pomiciare
petal ['petəl] *s* petalo
petard [pɪ'tɑrd] *s* petardo
pet'cock' *s* chiavetta
Peter ['pitər] *s* Pietro; to rob Peter to pay Paul fare un buco per tapparne un altro || *intr*—to peter out (coll) affievolirsi
petition [pɪ'tɪʃən] *s* petizione || *tr* rivolgere un'istanza a
pet' name' *s* nomignolo vezzeggiativo
Petrarch ['pitrɑrk] *s* Petrarca *m*
petri·fy ['petrɪ,faɪ] *v* (*pret & pp* -fied) *tr* pietrificare || *intr* pietrificarsi
petrol ['petrəl] *s* (Brit) benzina
petroleum [pɪ'trolɪ-əm] *s* petrolio
pet' shop' *s* negozio di animali domestici
petticoat ['petɪ,kot] *s* sottoveste *f*; (coll) sottana, gonnella
pet·ty ['peti] *adj* (-tier; -tiest) insignificante, minore; meschino
pet'ty cash' *s* cassa delle piccole spese
pet'ty lar'ceny *s* furterello
pet'ty of'ficer *s* (nav) sottufficiale *m* di marina
petulant ['petjələnt] *adj* stizzoso, irritabile
pew [pju] *s* banco di chiesa
pewter ['pjutər] *s* peltro; oggetti *mpl* di peltro
phalanx ['felæŋks] or ['fælæŋks] *s* falange *f*
phantasm ['fæntæzəm] *s* fantasma *m*
phantom ['fæntəm] *s* fantasma *m*
Pharaoh ['fero] *s* Faraone *m*
pharisee ['færɪ,si] *s* fariseo || Pharisee *s* fariseo
pharmaceutical [,fɑrmə'sutɪkəl] *adj* farmaceutico

pharmacist ['fɑrməsɪst] *s* farmacista *mf*
pharma·cy ['fɑrməsi] *s* (-cies) farmacia
pharynx ['færɪŋks] *s* faringe *f*
phase [fez] *s* fase *f* || *tr* mettere in fase; sincronizzare; to phase in mettere in operazione gradualmente; to phase out eliminare gradualmente
pheasant ['fezənt] *s* fagiano
phenobarbital [,fino'bɑrbɪ,tæl] *s* acido fenil-etilbarbiturico, barbiturato
phenomenal [fɪ'nɑmɪnəl] *adj* fenomenale
phenome·non [fɪ'nɑmɪ,nɑn] *s* (-na [nə]) fenomeno
phial ['faɪ-əl] *s* fiala
philanderer [fɪ'lændərər] *s* donnaiolo
philanthropist [fɪ'lænθrəpɪst] *s* filantropo
philanthro·py [fɪ'lænθrəpi] *s* (-pies) filantropia
philatelist [fɪ'lætəlɪst] *s* filatelico
philately [fɪ'lætəli] *s* filatelia
Philip ['fɪlɪp] *s* Filippo
Philippine ['fɪlɪ,pin] *adj* filippino || Philippines *spl* isole *fpl* Filippine
Philistine [fɪ'lɪstɪn], ['fɪlɪ,stɪn] or ['fɪlɪ,staɪn] *adj* & *s* filisteo
philologist [fɪ'lɑlədʒɪst] *s* filologo
philology [fɪ'lɑlədʒi] *s* filologia
philosopher [fɪ'lɑsəfər] *s* filosofo
philosophic(al) [,fɪlə'sɑfɪk(əl)] *adj* filosofico
philoso·phy [fɪ'lɑsəfi] *s* (-phies) filosofia
philter ['fɪltər] *s* filtro
phlebitis [flɪ'baɪtɪs] *s* flebite *f*
phlegm [flem] *s* (*secretion*) muco, catarro; (*self-possession*) flemma; apatia
phlegmatic(al) [fleg'mætɪk(əl)] *adj* flemmatico
Phoebus ['fibəs] *s* Febo
Phoenician [fɪ'nɪʃən] or [fɪ'niʃən] *adj* & *s* fenicio
phoenix ['finɪks] *s* fenice *f*
phone [fon] *s* (coll) telefono || *tr* & *intr* (coll) telefonare
phone' call' *s* chiamata telefonica
phonetic [fo'netɪk] *adj* fonetico || phonetics *s* fonetica
phonograph ['fonə,græf] or ['fonə,grɑf] *s* fonografo
phonology [fə'nɑlədʒi] *s* fonologia
pho·ny ['foni] *adj* (-nier; -niest) (coll) falso || *s* (-nies) (coll) frode *f*; (*person*) (coll) impostore *m*
phosphate ['fɑsfet] *s* fosfato
phosphorescent [,fɑsfə'resənt] *adj* fosforescente
phospho·rus ['fɑsfərəs] *s* (-ri [,raɪ]) fosforo
pho·to ['foto] *s* (-tos) (coll) foto *f*
photo·cop·y ['fotə,kɑpi] *s* (-ies) fotocopia || *tr* fotocopiare
pho'toelec'tric cell' [,foto-ɪ'lektrɪk] *s* cellula fotoelettrica
photoengraving [,foto-en'greviŋ] *s* fotoincisione
pho'to fin'ish *s* photofinish *m*, arrivo con fotografia

photogenic [ˌfoto'dʒɛnɪk] *adj* fotogenico

photograph ['fotəˌgræf] or ['fotəˌgrɑf] *s* fotografia ‖ *tr* fotografare ‖ *intr*—**to photograph well** riuscire in fotografia

photographer [fə'tɑgrəfər] *s* fotografo

photography [fə'tɑgrəfi] *s* fotografia

photojournalism [ˌfotə'dʒɜrnəˌlɪzəm] *s* giornalismo fotografico

pho'to·play' *s* dramma adattato per il cinematografo

photostat ['fotəˌstæt] *s* (trademark) copia fotostatica ‖ *tr* riprodurre fotostaticamente

phototube ['fotəˌtjub] or ['fotəˌtub] *s* fototubo

phrase [frez] *s* (gram) locuzione; (mus) frase *f* ‖ *tr* esprimere, formulare ‖ *intr* (mus) fraseggiare

phrenology [frɪ'nɑlədʒi] *s* frenologia

Phyllis ['fɪlɪs] *s* Fillide *f*

phy·lum ['faɪləm] *s* (**-la** [lə]) phylum *m*, tipo

phys·ic ['fɪzɪk] *s* purgante *m* ‖ *v* (*pret & pp* **-icked;** *ger* **-icking**) *tr* dare il purgante a, purgare

physical ['fɪzɪkəl] *adj* fisico

physician [fɪ'zɪʃən] *s* medico

physicist ['fɪzɪsɪst] *s* fisico

physics ['fɪzɪks] *s* fisica

physiognomy [ˌfɪzɪ'ɑgnəmi] or [ˌfɪzɪ'ɑnəmi] *s* fisionomia

physiological [ˌfɪzɪ·ə'lɑdʒɪkəl] *adj* fisiologico

physiology [ˌfɪzɪ'ɑlədʒi] *s* fisiologia

physique [fɪ'zɪk] *s* fisico

pi [paɪ] *s* (math) pi greco; (typ) tipi scartati ‖ *v* (*pret & pp* **pied;** *ger* **piing**) *tr* (typ) scompaginare, scomporre

pian·o [pɪ'æno] *s* (**-os**) piano

picaresque [ˌpɪkə'rɛsk] *adj* picaresco

picayune [ˌpɪkə'jun] *adj* meschino, minore, di poca importanza

picco·lo ['pɪkəˌlo] *s* (**-los**) ottavino

pick [pɪk] *s* (tool) piccone *m;* (choice) scelta; (the best) fiore *m;* (mus) plettro ‖ *tr* scavare; (to scratch at) grattare; (to gather) cogliere; (to pluck) spennare; (to pull apart) separare; (one's teeth) stuzzicarsi; (a bone) rosicchiare; (to choose) scegliere; (a lock) scassinare; (a pocket) tagliare, rubare; (mus) pizzicare; **to pick a fight** attaccare briga; **to pick faults** trovare a ridire; **to pick out** scegliere; distinguere; discriminare; **to pick s.o. to pieces** (coll) tagliare i panni addosso a qlcu; **to pick up** sollevare; (to find) trovare; (to learn) arrivare a sapere; (a radio signal) captare; (speed) acquistare ‖ *intr* usare -il piccone; **to pick at** (food) spilluzzicare; (coll) criticare; **to pick on** (coll) scegliere; (coll) criticare; **to pick up** (coll) migliorarsi

pick'ax' *s* piccone *m*

picket ['pɪkɪt] *s* picchetto ‖ *tr* rinchiudere con palizzata; (to hitch) legare; (to post) (mil) mettere di picchetto; (e.g., a factory) picchettare

pick'et fence' *s* steccato

pick'et line' *s* corteo di scioperanti; corteo di dimostranti

pickle ['pɪkəl] *s* salamoia, sottaceto; (cucumber) cetriolo sottaceto; **to get into a pickle** (coll) cacciarsi in un imbroglio ‖ *tr* mettere sottaceto; (metallurgy) decapare

pick-me-up ['pɪkmiˌʌp] *s* (coll) spuntino; (coll) bevanda stimulante

pick'pock'et *s* borseggiatore *m*, borsaiolo

pick'up' *s* sollevamento; (in speed) accelerazione; (of phonograph) pick-up *m*, fonorivelatore *m;* (aut) camioncino; (coll) persona conosciuta per caso; (coll) miglioramento

pick'-up-sticks' *spl* sciangai *m*

pic·nic ['pɪknɪk] *s* picnic *m* ‖ *v* (*pret & pp* **-nicked;** *ger* **-nicking**) *intr* fare merenda all'aperto

pictorial [pɪk'torɪ·əl] *adj* pittorico; illustrato; vivido; *s* rivista illustrata

picture ['pɪktʃər] *s* illustrazione, disegno; (painting) quadro, dipinto; (of a person) ritratto; fotografia; film *m*, pellicola ‖ *tr* fare il ritratto di; disegnare; dipingere; fotografare; descrivere; immaginare, immaginarsi

pic'ture frame' *s* cornice *f*

pic'ture gal'lery *s* pinacoteca, galleria di quadri, quadreria

pic'ture post' card' *s* cartolina illustrata

pic'ture show' *s* cinematografo; mostra di quadri

picturesque [ˌpɪktʃə'rɛsk] *adj* pittoresco

pic'ture tube' *s* tubo televisivo

pic'ture win'dow *s* finestra panoramica

piddling ['pɪdlɪŋ] *adj* insignificante

pie [paɪ] *s* (with fruit) torta; (with meat) timballo; (orn) pica ‖ *v* (*pret & pp* **pied;** *ger* **pieing**) *tr* (typ) scompaginare, scomporre

piece [pis] *s* pezzo; (e.g., of cloth) pezza; **a piece of advice** un consiglio; **a piece of baggage** un collo; **a piece of furniture** un mobile *m;* **a piece of news** una notizia; **by the piece** a cottimo; **to break to pieces** frantumare; frantumarsi; **to cut to pieces** fare a pezzi; **to fall to pieces** cadere a pezzi; **to fly to pieces** rompersi in mille pezzi; **to give s.o. a piece of one's mind** dirne a qlcu di tutti i colori; **to go to pieces** perdere il controllo di sé stesso; **to take to pieces** confutare punto per punto ‖ *tr* rappezzare, mettere insieme ‖ *intr* (coll) mangiucchiare

piece'meal' *adv* poco a poco

piece'work' *s* lavoro a cottimo

piece'work'er *s* cottimista *mf*

pier [pɪr] *s* (of a bridge) pila; (over water) molo; (archit) pilastro, pilone *m*

pierce [pɪrs] *tr* forare, bucare; trapanare; (to stab) trapassare ‖ *intr* penetrare

piercing ['pɪrsɪŋ] *adj* acuto; (eyes) penetrante; (pain) lancinante

pier' glass' s specchiera

pie-ty ['pai-əti] s (-ties) pietà f

piffle ['pifəl] s (coll) fesserie fpl

pig [pig] s maiale m, porco; (metallurgy) lingotto, massello; **to buy a pig in the poke** comprare il gatto nel secco

pigeon ['pidʒən] s piccione m

pi'geon-hole' s nicchia nella piccionaia; (for filing) casella || tr (to lay aside for later time) archiviare; (to shelve, e.g., an application) insabbiare

pi'geon house' s colombaia, piccionaia

piggish ['pigiʃ] adj porcino, maialesco

pig'gy-back' ['pigi,bæk] adv sulle spalle, sulla schiena; (rr) su carrello stradale per trasporto carri

pig'head'ed adj ostinato, cocciuto

pig' i'ron s ghisa, ferro grezzo

pigment ['pigmənt] s pigmento || tr pigmentare || intr pigmentarsi

pig'pen' s porcile m

pig'skin' s pelle f di maiale; (coll) pallone m da football, sfera di cuoio

pig'sty' s (-sties) porcile m

pig'tail' s codino; (of girl) treccia; treccia di tabacco

pike [paik] s (weapon) picca; (road) autostrada; (ichth) luccio

piker ['paikər] s (coll) uomo piccino

pile [pail] s (heap) pila; (for burning a corpse) pira; (large building) mole f; (beam) palo; (of carpet) pelo; (of money) (slang) gruzzolo; (coll) mucchio; **piles** emorroidi fpl || tr ammucchiare, accumulare; **to pile up** ammonticchiare || intr accumularsi; **to pile into** pigiarsi in; **to pile up** accumularsi

pile' driv'er s battipalo, berta

pilfer ['pilfər] tr & intr rubacchiare

pilgrim ['pilgrim] s pellegrino

pilgrimage ['pilgrimidʒ] s pellegrinaggio

pill [pil] s pillola; amara pillola; (coll) rompiscatole mf; **to sugar-coat the pill** addolcire la pillola

pillage ['pilidʒ] s saccheggio, rapina || tr & intr saccheggiare, rapinare

pillar ['pilər] s pilastro, colonna; **from pillar to post** da Erode a Pilato

pill'box' s scatoletta per le pillole; (mil) casamatta

pillo-ry ['piləri] s (-ries) gogna, berlina || v (pret & pp -ried) tr mettere alla berlina

pillow ['pilo] s cuscino, guanciale m

pil'low-case' s federa

pilot ['pailət] adj pilota || s pilota m; (of locomotive) respingente m || tr pilotare

pi'lot light' s fiammella automatica

pimp [pimp] s ruffiano, lenone m

pimple ['pimpəl] s bitorzolo

pim-ply ['pimpli] adj (-plier; -pliest) bitorzoluto

pin [pin] s (of metal) spillo; (peg) caviglia; (adornment) spilla; (linchpin) acciaino; (of key) mappa; (clothespin) molletta; (bowling pin) birillo; **to be on pins and needles** stare sulle spine || tr appuntare; (to hold) im-

mobilizzare; **to pin s.o. down** forzare qlcu a rivelare i propri piani **to pin s.th on s.o.** (coll) dare la colpa a qlcu per qlco

pinafore ['pinə,for] s grembiulino

pinaster [pai'næstər] s pino marittimo

pin'ball machine' s biliardino

pince-nez ['pæns,ne] s occhiali mpl a stringinaso

pincers ['pinsərz] ssg or spl tenaglie fpl; (zool) pinze fpl

pinch [pintʃ] s (squeeze) pizzicotto; (of tobacco) presa; (of salt) pizzico; (hardship) strettoia; **in a pinch** in caso di necessità || tr stringere, pizzicare; (to press) comprimere; ridurre alle strettezze; (slang) rubare; (slang) arrestare || intr stringere; (to be stingy) fare l'avaro

pin'cush'ion s puntaspilli m

pine [pain] s pino || intr—**to pine away** struggersi; **to pine for** spasimare per

pine'ap'ple s ananas m

pine' cone' s pigna

pine' nee'dle s ago del pino

ping [piŋ] s rumore secco; rumore metallico || intr fare un rumore secco or metallico

pin'head' s capocchia di spillo; (slang) testa quadra

pin'hole' s forellino

pink [piŋk] adj rosa || s color m rosa; condizione perfetta; (bot) garofano || tr orlare a zig-zag; (to stab) perforare

pin' mon'ey s denaro per le piccole spese

pinnacle ['pinəkəl] s pinnacolo

pin'point' adj di precisione || s punta di spillo || tr mettere in rilievo

pin'prick' s puntura di spillo

pint [paint] s pinta

pintle ['pintəl] s maschietto

pin'up' s pin-up-girl f

pin'wheel' s girandola

pioneer [,pai-ə'nir] s pioniere m || tr aprire la via a || intr fare il pioniere

pioneering [,pai-ə'niriŋ] adj pionieristico

pious ['pai-əs] adj pio, devoto

pip [pip] s (seed) seme m; (vet) pipita

pipe [paip] s tubo, canna; (of stove) cannone m; (for smoking) pipa; (mus) legno; (mus) cornamusa || tr suonare; cantare ad alta voce; fischiare; condurre in una tubatura; munire di tubatura || intr suonare la zampogna; **to pipe down** (slang) stare zitto

pipe' clean'er s scovolino

pipe' dream' s castello in aria

pipe' line' s oleodotto; (fig) fonte f (d'informazioni)

pipe' or'gan s organo a canne

piper ['paipər] s zampognaro; **to pay the piper** pagare lo scotto

pipe' wrench' s chiave f per tubi

piping ['paipiŋ] adj (voice) acuto; (sound) di cornamusa || s tubatura; suono di cornamusa; suono acuto; (on cakes) fregio; (on garments) cordoncino ornamentale ‖ *adv*—**piping hot** scottante, bollente

pippin ['pɪpɪn] *s* mela renetta; (*seed*) seme *m*; (fig) gran brava persona

piquant ['pikənt] *adj* piccante

pique [pik] *s* picca, ripicco ‖ *tr* offendere, eccitare

pira·cy ['paɪrəsi] *s* (**-cies**) pirateria

pirate ['paɪrɪt] *s* pirata *mf* ‖ *tr* derubare; (*a book*) svaligiare, pubblicare illegalmente ‖ *intr* pirateggiare

pirouette [ˌpɪruˈet] *s* piroetta ‖ *intr* piroettare

Pisces ['paɪsiz] *or* ['pɪsɪz] *s* (astr) Pesci *mpl*

pistol ['pɪstəl] *s* pistola

piston ['pɪstən] *s* pistone *m*

pis'ton displace'ment *s* cilindrata

pis'ton ring' *s* segmento elastico

pis'ton rod' *s* (*of a steam engine*) biella d'accoppiamento; (*of a motor*) asta del pistone, biella

pis'ton stroke' *s* corsa dello stantuffo

pit [pɪt] *s* (*in the ground*) buca; (*trap*) trappola; (*of fruit*) nocciolo; (*of stomach*) bocca; (*scar*) buttero; (*in exchange*) recinto delle grida; (*for fights*) arena; (theat) platea; (*min*) miniera; (*aut*) fossa di riparazione ‖ *v* (*pret & pp* **pitted**; *ger* **pitting**) *tr* infossare; butterare; opporre; (*to remove pits from*) snocciolare

pitch [pɪtʃ] *s* (*black sticky substance*) pece *f*; (*throw*) lancio; (*of a roof*) pendenza, inclinazione; (*of a boat*) beccheggio; (*of a screw*) passo; (*of sound*) altezza ‖ *tr* lanciare; (*a tent*) rizzare ‖ *intr* beccheggiare; **to pitch in** (coll) mettersi al lavoro; (coll) cominciare a mangiare

pitch' ac'cent *s* accento di altezza

pitch' at'titude *s* assetto longitudinale

pitch'-dark' *adj* nero come la pece

pitched' bat'tle *s* battaglia campale

pitcher ['pɪtʃər] *s* brocca; (baseball) lanciatore *m*

pitch'fork' *s* forca, tridente *m*; **to rain pitchforks** (coll) piovere a dirotto

pitch' pipe' *s* (mus) corista *m*

pit'fall' *s* trappola, trabocchetto

pith [pɪθ] *s* midollo; (*strength*) (fig) forza; (fig) succo, essenza

pith·y ['pɪθi] *adj* (**-ier; -iest**) midolloso; succoso, essenziale

pitiful ['pɪtɪfəl] *adj* pietoso

pitiless ['pɪtɪlɪs] *adj* spietato

pit·y ['pɪti] *s* (**-ies**) pietà *f*; **it is a pity that** è un peccato che; **what a pity!** che peccato! ‖ *v* (*pret & pp* **-ied**) *tr* aver pietà di

Pius ['paɪəs] *s* Pio

pivot ['pɪvət] *s* asse *m*, perno; (fig) asse *m* ‖ *tr* imperniare ‖ *intr* imperniarsi; **to pivot on** fare perno su; dipendere da

placard ['plækard] *s* manifesto, affisso ‖ *tr* affiggere

place [ples] *s* luogo; locale *m*; (*court*) piazzetta; (*short street*) vicolo; residenza; sito, luogo, località *f*; (*point*) punto; (*space occupied*) posto; (*office*) posto, impiego; **in no place**

da nessuna parte; **in place** a posto; **in place of** al posto di, invece di; **in the first place** in primo luogo; **in the next place** in secondo luogo; **to know one's place** saper stare al proprio posto; **to take place** aver luogo ‖ *tr* piazzare, mettere; (*to find employment for*) collocare; (*to identify*) ravvisare ‖ *intr* (sports) piazzarsi

place·bo [plə'sibo] *s* (**-bos** *or* **-boes**) rimedio fittizio

place' card' *s* segnaposto

placement ['plesmənt] *s* (*e.g., of furniture*) collocazione; (*employment*) collocamento

place' name' *s* toponimo

place' of busi'ness *s* ufficio, negozio

placid ['plæsɪd] *adj* placido

plagiarism ['pledʒəˌrɪzəm] *s* plagio

plagiarize ['pledʒəˌraɪz] *tr* plagiare

plague [pleg] *s* peste bubbonica; (*widespread affliction*) piaga, flagello ‖ *tr* infestare, appestare; tormentare

plaid [plæd] *s* tessuto scozzese

plain [plen] *adj* piano; aperto; evidente, esplicito; semplice; (*undyed*) naturale; comune, ordinario; **in plain English** senz'ambagi; **in plain view** di fronte a tutti ‖ *s* pianura

plain'-clothes' man' *s* (**-men'**) agente *m* in borghese

plains'man *s* (**-men**) abitante *m* della pianura

plaintiff ['plentɪf] *s* querelante *mf*

plaintive ['plentɪv] *adj* lamentevole

plan [plæn] *s* piano, progetto ‖ *v* (*pret & pp* **planned**; *ger* **planning**) *tr & intr* progettare

plane [plen] *adj* piano ‖ *m* piano; (*tool*) pialla; (aer) aeroplano; (aer) ala d'aeroplano; (bot) platano ‖ *tr* piallare ‖ *intr* andare in areoplano

plane' sick'ness *s* male *m* d'aria

planet ['plænɪt] *s* pianeta *m*

plane' tree' *s* platano

plan'ing mill' *s* officina di piallatura

plank [plæŋk] *s* tavola, asse *m*; (*of political party*) piattaforma ‖ *tr* coprire d'assi; cucinare sulla graticola e servire sul tagliere; **to plank down** (*e.g., money*) (coll) snocciolare

plant [plænt] *or* [plɑnt] *s* (*factory*) impianto, stabilimento; (*e.g., of a college*) complesso di edifici; (bot) pianta; (mach) apparato motore; (slang) trappola ‖ *tr* (*e.g., a tree*) piantare; (*seeds*) seminare; (*to stock*) fornire

plantation [plæn'teʃən] *s* piantagione

planter ['plæntər] *s* piantatore *m*; (mach) piantatrice *f*

plaster ['plæstər] *or* ['plɑstər] *s* (*gypsum*) gesso; (*mixture to cover walls*) intonaco, malta; (*poultice*) impiastro ‖ *tr* ingessare; intonacare; impiastrare; (*with posters*) affiggere, ricoprire

plas'ter·board' *s* cartone *m* di gesso

plas'ter cast' *s* (sculp) gesso; (surg) ingessatura

plas'ter of Par'is *s* gesso, stucco

plastic ['plæstɪk] *adj & s* plastico

plate 237 plug

plate [plet] *s* (*dish*) piatto; (*sheet of metal*) placca, piastra; (*thin sheet of metal*) lamina; (*of vacuum tube*) placca; (*of auto license*) targa; (*of condenser*) armatura; (*tableware*) vasellame *m* d'argento, vasellame *m* d'oro; dentiera; (*baseball*) casa base; (phot) lastra; (typ) cliché *m* ‖ *tr* (*with gold or silver*) placcare; (*with armor*) blindare, corazzare

plateau [plæ'to] *s* altipiano

plate' glass' *s* lastrone *m*

platen ['plætən] *s* rullo

platform ['plæt,fɔrm] *s* piattaforma; (*for speaker*) tribuna, palco; (*for passengers*) (rr) marciapiede *m*; (*at end of car*) (rr) piattaforma

plat'form car' *s* (rr) pianale *m*

platinum ['plætɪnəm] *s* platino

plat'inum blonde' *s* bionda platinata

platitude ['plætɪ,tjud] *or* ['plætɪ,tud] *s* trivialità *f*, banalità *f*

Plato ['pleto] *s* Platone *m*

platoon [plə'tun] *s* plotone *m*

platter ['plætər] *s* piatto di portata; (slang) disco di grammofono

plausible ['plɔzɪbəl] *adj* plausibile; (*person*) credibile, attendibile

play [ple] *s* gioco; libertà *f* d'azione; recreazione; turno, volta; (theat) dramma *m*; (mach) gioco ‖ *tr* giocare; giocare contro; causare, produrre; (*a drama*) rappresentare; (*a character*) fare la parte di; (*to wield*) esercitare; (mus) suonare; **to play back** (*e.g., a tape*) riprodurre; **to play down** diminuire l'importanza di; **to play one off against another** mettere uno contro l'altro; **to play up** dare importanza a ‖ *intr* giocare; (*to act*) giocare, comportarsi; (theat) recitare; (mus) suonare; (mach) aver gioco; **to play on** continuare a giocare; continuare a suonare; valersi di; **to play safe** non prendere rischi; **to play sick** fare il malato; **to play up to** fare la corte a

play'back' *s* riproduzione; apparechiatura di riproduzione

play'bill' *s* (theat) programma *m*

play'boy' *s* playboy *m*, gaudente *m*

player ['ple·ər] *s* giocatore *m*; (theat) attore *m*; (mus) suonatore *m*

play'er pian'o *s* pianola *f*

playful ['plefəl] *adj* giocoso

playgoer ['ple,go·ər] *s* frequentatore *m* del teatro

play'ground' *s* parco di ricreazione; (*resort*) posto di villeggiatura

play'house' *s* teatro; casa di bambole

play'ing card' ['ple·ɪŋ] *s* carta da gioco

play'ing field' *s* campo da gioco

play'mate' *s* compagno di gioco

play'-off' *s* (sports) spareggio

play'pen' *s* recinto, box *m*

play'thing' *s* giocattolo

play'time' *s* ricreazione

playwright ['ple,raɪt] *s* drammaturgo, commediografo

play'writ'ing *s* drammaturgia

plaza ['plæzə] *or* ['plɑzə] *s* piazzale *m*

plea [pli] *s* scusa; richiesta, domanda; (law) dichiarazione

plead [plid] *v* (*pret & pp* **pleaded** *or* **pled** [pled]) *tr* (*ignorance*) dichiarare; (*a case*) perorare ‖ *intr* supplicare; argomentare; **to plead guilty** dichiararsi colpevole

pleasant ['plezənt] *adj* piacevole; (*person*) simpatico

pleasant·ry ['plezəntri] *s* (-ries) facezia, motto

please [pliz] *tr* piacere (with *dat*) ‖ *intr* piacere; **as you please** come vuole; **if you please** per favore; **please per cortesia**; **to be pleased to** avere il piacere di; **to be pleased with** essere soddisfatto con; **to do as one pleases** fare come par è piace

pleasing ['plizɪŋ] *adj* piacevole

pleasure ['pleʒər] *s* piacere *m*; desiderio; **what is your pleasure?** cosa desidera?

pleas'ure car' *s* vettura da turismo

pleat [plit] *s* piega ‖ *tr* piegare, pieghettare

plebeian [plɪ'bi·ən] *adj & s* plebeo

plebiscite ['plebɪ,saɪt] *s* plebiscito

pledge [pledʒ] *s* pegno; promessa; voto; (*person*) ostaggio; (*toast*) brindisi *m*; **as a pledge** in pegno; **to take the pledge** giurare d'astenersi dal bere ‖ *tr* dare in pegno; (*to bind*) far promettere a

plentiful ['plentɪfəl] *adj* abbondante

plenty ['plenti] *s* abbondanza ‖ *adv* (coll) abbastanza

pleurisy ['plʊrɪsi] *s* pleurite *f*

pliable ['plaɪ·əbəl] *adj* flessibile, pieghevole; docile

pliers ['plaɪ·ərz] *ssg or spl* pinze *fpl*

plight [plaɪt] *s* condizione or situazione precaria ‖ *tr*—**to plight one's troth** fidanzarsi

plod [plɑd] *v* (*pret & pp* **plodded;** *ger* **plodding**) *tr* percorrere pesantemente ‖ *intr* camminare pesantemente; (*to drudge*) sgobbare

plot [plɑt] *s* (*of ground*) appezzamento; (*of a play*) trama, intreccio; (*evil scheme*) cospirazione, trama ‖ *v* (*pret & pp* **plotted;** *ger* **plotting**) *tr* fare il piano di; macchinare; preparare la trama di; (aer, naut) fare il punto di ‖ *intr* tramare, cospirare

plover ['plʌvər] *or* ['plovər] *s* piviere *m*

plow [plaʊ] *s* aratro; (*for snow*) spazzaneve *m* ‖ *tr* arare; (*e.g., water*) solcare; (*snow*) spazzare; **to plow back** reinvestire ‖ *intr* arare; aprirsi la via; camminare pesantemente

plow'man *s* (-men) aratore *m*; contadino

plow'share' *s* vomere *m*

pluck [plʌk] *s* strattone *m*; coraggio; (*giblets*) frattaglie *fpl* ‖ *tr* (*to snatch*) tirare; (*e.g., fruit*) svellere; (*a fowl*) spennare; (mus) pizzicare ‖ *intr* tirare; **to pluck up** farsi coraggio

pluck·y ['plʌki] *adj* (-ier; -iest) coraggioso

plug [plʌg] *s* tappo, zaffo; tavoletta di

tabacco; bocca da incendi; (elec) spina; (horse) (slang) ronzino; (slang) raccomandazione || v (pret & pp plugged) ger plugging) tr tappare, otturare; colpire; inserire; (slang) fare la pubblicità di; to plug in (elec) innestare, connettere || intr (coll) sgobbare

plum [plʌm] s (fruit) susina; (tree) susino; (slang) cosa bellissima; (slang) colpo di fortuna

plumage ['plumɪdʒ] s piumaggio

plumb [plʌm] adj appiombo || s piombino || adv appiombo; (coll) completamente || tr determinare la verticale col piombino; assodare

plumb' bob' s piombino

plumber ['plʌmər] s installatore m, idraulico

plumbing ['plʌmɪŋ] s impianto idraulico; mestiere m d'idraulico; son-daggio

plumb'ing fix'tures spl rubinetteria, impianti mpl sanitari

plumb' line' s filo a piombo

plum' cake' s panfrutto

plume [plum] s piuma; (tuft of feathers) pennacchio || tr coprire di piume; to plume oneself su piccarsi di; to plume one's feathers pulirsi le penne

plummet ['plʌmɪt] s piombino || intr cadere a piombo

plump [plʌmp] adj grassoccio, paffuto; franco || s caduta || adv francamente || intr cadere a piombo

plum' pud'ding s budino con uva passa

plum' tree' s susino

plunder ['plʌndər] s (act) saccheggio; (loot) bottino || tr & intr saccheggiare

plunge [plʌndʒ] s (fall) caduta; (dive) nuotata, tuffo || tr gettare; tuffare; (e.g., a knife) configgere || intr (to rush) precipitarsi; (to gamble) (coll) darsi al gioco; (fig) ripiombare

plunger ['plʌndʒər] s tuffatore m; (for clearing clogged drains) stura-lavandini m; (mach) stantuffo; (coll) giocatore temerario

plunk [plʌŋk] adv (coll) proprio; (coll) con un colpo secco || tr (coll) gettare; lasciar cadere; (mus) pizzicare || intr (coll) lasciarsi cadere

plural ['plurəl] adj & s plurale m

plus [plʌs] adj superiore; (elec) positivo; (coll) con lode || s più m; soprappiù m || prep più

plush [plʌʃ] adj di lusso || s peluche f, felpa

Plutarch ['plutark] s Plutarco

Pluto ['pluto] s Plutone m

plutonium [plu'tonɪəm] s plutonio

ply [plaɪ] s (plies) spessore m; (layer) strato; (of rope) legnolo || v (pret & pp plied) tr (a trade) esercitare; (a tool) maneggiare; (to assail) premere, incalzare || intr lavorare assiduamente; to ply between fare la spola tra

ply'wood' s legno compensato

pneumatic [nju'mætɪk] or [nu'mætɪk] adj pneumatico

pneumat'ic drill' s martello perforatore or pneumatico

pneumonia [nju'monɪ·ə] or [nu-'monɪ·ə] s polmonite f

poach [potʃ] tr (eggs) affogare || intr cacciare or pescare di frodo

poacher ['potʃər] s bracconiere m; pe-scatore m di frodo

pock [pɑk] s buttero

pocket ['pɑkɪt] adj tascabile || s tasca; (billiards) buca; (aer) vuoto; (min) deposito || tr intascare; (e.g., one's pride) ingoiare

pock'et-book' s portafoglio; (woman's purse) borsetta

pock'et book' s libro tascabile

pock'et-hand'kerchief s fazzoletto

pock'et-knife' s (-knives) temperino

pock'et mon'ey s spiccioli mpl

pock'mark' s buttero

pod [pɑd] s baccello; (aer) contenitore m

poem ['po·ɪm] s poesia; (of some length) poema m

poet ['po·ɪt] s poeta m

poetess ['po·ɪtɪs] s poetessa

poetic [po'ɛtɪk] adj poetico || poetics ssg poetica

poetry ['po·ɪtri] s poesia

pogrom ['pogrəm] s pogrom m

poignancy ['pɔɪnjənsi] or ['pɔɪnənsi] s strazio; intensità f

poignant ['pɔɪnjənt] or ['pɔɪnənt] adj straziante; intenso

point [pɔɪnt] s (sharp end) punta; (something essential) essenziale m; (hint) suggerimento; (dot, decimal point, spot, degree, instant, position of compass) punto; (coll) costrutto; beside the point fuori del seminato; in point of per quanto concerne; to come to the point venire al sodo; to get the point capire l'antifona; to make a point of dar importanza a; insistere di; to stretch a point fare un'eccezione, fare uno strappo alla regola; to the point a proposito || tr (e.g., a weapon) puntare; (to sharpen) aguzzare; (to dot) punteggiare; (to give force to) dare enfasi a; (with mortar) rinzaffare || intr puntare; to point at puntare il dito a; to point to mostrare a dito

point'blank' adj & adv a bruciapelo

pointed ['pɔɪntɪd] adj appuntito; personale, diretto, acuto

pointer ['pɔɪntər] s (rod) bacchetta; indice m, indicatore m; cane m da punta, pointer m; (coll) direttiva

poise [pɔɪz] s equilibrio, stabilità f; dignità f || tr equilibrare || intr equi-librarsi, stare in equilibrio

poison ['pɔɪzən] s veleno || tr avvele-nare

poi'son i'vy s edera del Canada, tossi-codendro

poisonous ['pɔɪzənəs] adj velenoso

poke [pok] s spinta, urto; (with elbow) gomitata; (slang) polentone m || tr (to prod) spingere, urtare; (the head) sporgere; (the fire) attizzare; to poke fun at burlarsi di; to poke one's nose into ficcare il naso in || intr (to jab) urtare; (*to thrust oneself*) ficcarsi; (*to pry*) ficcare il naso; **to poke around** gironzolare; **to poke out** spuntare, protrudere

poker ['pokər] *s* (*game*) poker *m*; (*bar*) attizzatoio

pok'er face' *s* faccia impassibile

pok·y ['poki] *adj* (**-ier; -iest**) (coll) lento; (coll) meschino, modesto ‖ (**-ies**) *s* (slang) gattabuia

Poland ['polənd] *s* la Polonia

po'lar bear' ['polər] *s* orso bianco

polarize ['polə,raɪz] *tr* polarizzare

pole [pol] *s* palo; (*long rod*) pertica; (*of wagon*) timone *m*; (*for jumping*) asta; (astr, biol, elec, geog, math) polo ‖ *tr* (*a boat*) spingere con un palo ‖ *intr* spingere una barca con un palo ‖ **Pole** *s* polacco

pole'cat' *s* puzzola

pole' lamp' *s* lampada a stelo

pole'star' *s* stella polare

pole' vault' *s* salto coll'asta

police [pə'lis] *s* polizia ‖ *tr* vigilare, proteggere; (mil) pulire

police'man *s* (**-men**) agente *m* di polizia, vigile urbano

police' state' *s* governo poliziesco

police' sta'tion *s* commissariato di polizia

poli·cy ['palɪsi] *s* (**-cies**) politica; (ins) polizza

polio ['polɪ,o] *s* (coll) polio *f*

polish ['palɪʃ] *s* lustro, lucentezza; (*for shoes or furniture*) cera; (fig) raffinatezza, eleganza ‖ *tr* pulire; (*e.g., a stone*) levigare; **to polish off** (slang) finire; **to polish up** (slang) migliorare ‖ *intr* pulirsi; diventar lucido ‖ **Polish** ['polɪʃ] *adj & s* polacco

polisher ['palɪʃər] *s* lucidatore *m*; (mach) lucidatrice *f*

polite [pə'laɪt] *adj* raffinato, cortese

politeness [pə'laɪtnɪs] *s* cortesia

politic ['palɪtɪk] *adj* prudente; (*expedient*) diplomatico

political [pə'lɪtɪkəl] *adj* politico

politician [,palɪ'tɪʃən] *s* politico; (pej) politicante *m*, politicastro

politics ['palɪtɪks] *ssg or spl* politica

poll [pol] *s* votazione; (*registering of votes*) scrutinio; lista elettorale; (*analysis of public opinion*) referendum *m*, sondaggio; (*head*) testa; **to go to the polls** andare alle urne; **to take a poll** fare un'inchiesta ‖ *tr* ricevere i voti di; contare i voti di; (*a tree*) potare; fare un'inchiesta di

pollen ['palən] *s* polline *m*

pollinate ['palɪ,net] *tr* fecondare col polline

poll'ing booth' ['polɪŋ] *s* cabina elettorale

polliwog ['palɪ,wag] *s* girino

poll' tax' *s* capitazione

pollute [pə'lut] *tr* insudiciare; (*to defile*) desecrare, profanare; (*e.g., the environment*) inquinare, contaminare

pollution [pə'luʃən] *s* inquinamento, contaminazione

poll' watch'er *s* rappresentante *m* di lista

polo ['polo] *s* polo

po'lo play'er *s* giocatore *m* di polo, polista *m*

po'lo shirt' *s* maglietta, polo

polygamist [pə'lɪgəmɪst] *s* poligamo

polygamous [pə'lɪgəməs] *adj* poligamo

polyglot ['palɪ,glat] *adj & s* poliglotto

polygon ['palɪ,gan] *s* poligono

polynomial [,palɪ'nomɪ-əl] *adj* polinomiale ‖ *s* polinomio

polyp ['palɪp] *s* (pathol, zool) polipo

polytheist ['palɪ,θi-ɪst] *s* politeista *mf*

polytheistic [,palɪθi'ɪstɪk] *adj* politeistico

pomade [pə'med] or [pə'mad] *s* pomata

pomegranate ['pam,grænɪt] *s* (*shrub*) melograno; (*fruit*) melagrana

pom·mel ['pʌməl] or ['paməl] *s* (*of sword*) pomello; (*of saddle*) arcione *m* ‖ *v* (*pret & pp* **-meled** or **-melled;** *ger* **-meling** or **-melling**) *tr* prendere a pugni

pomp [pamp] *s* pompa

pompadour ['pampə,dor] or ['pampə,dur] *s* acconciatura a ciuffo

pompous ['pampəs] *adj* pomposo

pon·cho ['pantʃo] *s* (**-chos**) poncho

pond [pand] *s* stagno

ponder ['pandər] *tr & intr* ponderare; **to ponder over** pensare sopra

ponderous ['pandərəs] *adj* ponderoso

poniard ['panjərd] *s* pugnale *m*

pontiff ['pantɪf] *s* pontefice *m*

pontifical [pan'tɪfɪkəl] *adj* pontificale

pontoon [pan'tun] *s* (*boat*) chiatta, pontone *m*; (aer) galleggiante *m*

po·ny ['poni] *s* (**-nies**) pony *m*; (*glass and drink*) bicchierino; (*for cheating*) (slang) bigino

poodle ['pudəl] *s* barbone *m*, cane *m* barbone

pool [pul] *s* (*pond*) stagno; (*puddle*) pozza; (*for swimming*) piscina; (*game*) biliardo; (com) cartello, consorzio; (com) fondo comune ‖ *tr* mettere in un fondo comune ‖ *intr* formare un cartello o un consorzio

pool'room' *s* sala da biliardo

pool' ta'ble *s* tavolo da biliardo

poop [pup] *s* poppa; (*deck*) casseretto

poor [pur] *adj* povero; (*inferior*) scadente ‖ **the poor** *spl* i poveri

poor' box' *s* cassetta per l'elemosina

poor'house' *s* asilo dei poveri

poorly ['purli] *adv* male

pop [pap] *s* scoppio; (*soda*) gazzosa ‖ *v* (*pret & pp* **popped;** *ger* **popping**) *tr* far scoppiare; **to pop the question** (coll) fare la domanda di matrimonio ‖ *intr* esplodere con fragore; **to pop in** fare una capatina; entrare all'improvviso

pop'corn' *s* pop-corn *m*

pope [pop] *s* papa *m*

popeyed ['pap,aɪd] *adj* con gli occhi sporgenti; con gli occhi fuori dalle orbite

pop'gun' *s* fucile *m* ad aria compressa

poplar ['paplər] *s* pioppo

pop·py ['papi] *s* (**-pies**) papavero

pop'py·cock' *s* (coll) scemenza

popsicle [ˈpɑpsɪkəl] s (trademark) gelato da passeggio
populace [ˈpɑpjəlɪs] s gente f, popolino
popular [ˈpɑpjələr] adj popolare
popularize [ˈpɑpjələ ˌraɪz] tr divulgare, volgarizzare
populate [ˈpɑpjə ˌlet] tr popolare
population [ˌpɑpjəˈleʃən] s popolazione
populous [ˈpɑpjələs] adj popoloso
porcelain [ˈpɔrsəlɪn] or [ˈpɔrslɪn] s porcellana
porch [pɔrtʃ] s portico
porcupine [ˈpɔrkjəˌpaɪn] s (Hystrix cristata) istrice m & f, porcospino; (Erethizon dorsatum) ursone m, porcospino americano
pore [por] s poro || intr—to pore over studiare minutamente
pork [pɔrk] s carne f di maiale
pork' butch'er shop' s salumeria
pork'chop' s cotoletta di maiale
porous [ˈporəs] adj poroso
po'rous plas'ter s cataplasma m
porphy•ry [ˈpɔrfɪri] s (-ries) porfido
porpoise [ˈpɔrpəs] s focena; (dolphin) delfino
porridge [ˈpɑrɪdʒ] or [ˈpɔrɪdʒ] s pappa, farinata
port [pɔrt] adj portuario || s (harbor; wine) porto; (naut) babordo, sinistra; (opening in side of ship) portello; (round opening) (naut) oblò m
portable [ˈpɔrtəbəl] adj portabile
portal [ˈpɔrtəl] s portale m
portend [pɔrˈtɛnd] tr presagire
portent [ˈpɔrtɛnt] s presagio
portentous [pɔrˈtɛntəs] adj sinistro, funesto, premonitore; (amazing) portentoso
porter [ˈpɔrtər] s (doorman) portiere m; (man who carries luggage) facchino; (of a sleeper) conduttore m; (in a store) inserviente mf; (beverage) birra scura e amara
portfoli•o [pɔrtˈfoli ˌo] s (-os) cartella; (office; holdings) portafoglio
port'hole' s (opening in side of ship) portello; (round opening) (naut) oblò m
porti•co [ˈpɔrti ˌko] s (-cos or -coes) portico
portion [ˈpɔrʃən] s porzione; (dowry) dote f || tr—to portion out dividere, ripartire
port•ly [ˈpɔrtli] adj (-lier; -liest) obeso, corpulento
port' of call' s scalo
portrait [ˈpɔrtret] or [ˈpɔrtrɪt] s ritratto
portray [pɔrˈtre] tr ritrarre
portrayal [pɔrˈtre•əl] s delineazione; ritratto
Portugal [ˈpɔrtʃəgəl] s il Portogallo
Portu•guese [ˈpɔrtʃə ˌgiz] adj portoghese || s (-guese) portoghese mf
pose [poz] s posa || tr (a question) avanzare; (a model) mettere in posa || intr posare; **to pose as** posare a, atteggiarsi a
posh [pɑʃ] adj (coll) di lusso
position [pəˈzɪʃən] s posizione; rango;

impiego, posto; **to be in a position to** essere in grado di
positive [ˈpɑzɪtɪv] adj positivo || s positivo; (phot) positiva
possess [pəˈzɛs] tr possedere
possession [pəˈzɛʃən] s possedimento; (of mental faculties) possesso; **possessions** (wealth) beni mpl
possessive [pəˈzɛsɪv] adj possessivo; (e.g., mother) opprimente, soffocante
possible [ˈpɑsɪbəl] adj possibile
possum [ˈpɑsəm] s opossum m; **to play possum** (coll) fare il morto
post [post] s (mail) posta; (pole) palo; (in horse racing) linea di partenza; posizione, rango; (job) posto; (mil) presidio || tr mettere in una lista; impostare; tenere al corrente; **post no bills** divieto d'affissione
postage [ˈpostɪdʒ] s affrancatura
post'age me'ter s affrancatrice f
post'age stamp' s francobollo
postal [ˈpostəl] adj postale
post'al card' s cartolina postale
pos'tal per'mit s abbonamento postale
post'al sav'ings bank' s cassa di risparmio postale
post'al scale' s pesalettere m
post' card' s cartolina illustrata; cartolina postale
post'date' tr postdatare
poster [ˈpostər] s cartellone m, manifesto pubblicitario
posterity [pɑsˈtɛrɪti] s posterità f
postern [ˈpostərn] adj posteriore || s postierla
post' exchange' s spaccio militare
post'haste' adv al più presto possibile
posthumous [ˈpɑstʃuməs] adj postumo
post'man s (-men) portalettere m
post'mark' s bollo, timbro postale || tr bollare, timbrare
post'mas'ter s ricevitore m postale
post'master gen'eral s (postmasters general) ministro delle poste
post-mortem [ˈpostˈmɔrtəm] adj postumo || s autopsia
post' of'fice s ufficio postale
post'-office box' s casella postale
postpaid [ˈpostˈped] adj franco di porto
postpone [postˈpon] tr differire, posporre
postscript [ˈpostˌskrɪpt] s poscritto
postulant [ˈpostʃələnt] s postulatore m, postulante mf
posture [ˈpostʃər] s portamento; posa || intr posare
post'war' adj del dopoguerra
po•sy [ˈpozi] s (-sies) fiore m; (nosegay) mazzolino di fiori
pot [pɑt] s pentola, pignatta; pitale m, orinale m; (in gambling) (coll) piatto; **to go to pot** andare a gambe all'aria
potash [ˈpɑt ˌæʃ] s potassa
potassium [pəˈtæsɪ•əm] s potassio
pota•to [pəˈteto] s (-toes) patata
pota'to om'elet s omelette f con patate
potbellied [ˈpɑt ˌbelɪd] adj panciuto
poten•cy [ˈpotənsi] s (-cies) potenza
potent [ˈpotənt] adj potente

potentate ['potən ,tet] s potentato
potential [pə'ten/əl] adj & s potenziále
m
pot'hold'er s patta, presa
pot'hook' s uncino
potion ['poʃən] s pozione
pot'luck' s—to take potluck mangiare
quello che passa il convento
pot' shot' s colpo sparato a casaccio
potter ['pɑtər] s vasaio
pot'ter's clay' s argilla per stoviglie
pot'ter's field' s cimitero dei poveri
potter·y ['pɑtəri] s (-ies) vasellame m;
fabbrica di vasellame; ceramica
pouch [pauʧ] s sacchetto, borsa; (of
kangaroo) borsa
poultice ['poltɪs] s cataplasma m
poultry ['poltri] s pollame m
poul'try·man s (-men) pollivendolo
pounce [pauns] intr—to pounce on
balzare su
pound [paund] s libbra; lira sterlina;
(for stray animals) recinto ‖ tr battere, picchiare; tempestare di colpi;
(to crush) polverizzare ‖ intr battere
pound' cake' s dolce m fatto con una
libbra di burro, una di zucchero ed
una di farina
pound' ster'ling s lira sterlina
pour [por] tr versare; (e.g., tea) servire; (wine) mescere; (stones upon
an enemy) far piovere ‖ intr fluire;
(to rain) diluviare; to pour in affluire; to pour out uscire in massa
pout [paut] s broncio ‖ intr tenere il
broncio
poverty ['pɑvərti] s povertà f
POW ['pi'o'dʌbl ,ju] s (letterword)
(prisoner of war) prigioniero di
guerra
powder ['paudər] s polvere f; (for the
face) cipria; (med) polverina ‖ tr in-
cipriare; (to sprinkle with powder)
spolverizzare
pow'dered sug'ar s zucchero in polvere
pow'der puff' s piumino
pow'der room' s toletta
powdery ['paudəri] adj polveroso; fragile; (snow) farinoso
power ['pau·ər] s (ability, authority)
potere m; forza, energia; (nation)
potenza; (math, phys) potenza; in
power al potere; the powers that be
i potenti ‖ tr azionare
pow'er·boat' s barca a motore
pow'er brake' s (aut) servofreno
pow'er com'pany s compagnia di elettricità
pow'er drive' s picchiata
powerful ['pau·ərfəl] adj poderoso
pow'er·house' s centrale elettrica
powerless ['pau·ərlɪs] adj impotente
pow'er line' s elettrodotto
pow'er mow'er s motofalciatrice f
pow'er of attor'ney s procura legale
pow'er plant' s stazione f generatrice;
(aut) gruppo motore
pow'er steer'ing s servosterzo
pow'er tool' s apparecchiatura a motore
pow'er vac'uum s vuoto di potere
practical ['præktɪkəl] adj pratico

prac'tical joke' s scherzo da prete
practically ['præktɪkəli] adv (in a practical manner; virtually, really) prati-
camente; più o meno, quasi
practice ['præktɪs] s pratica; (of a profession) esercizio; (e.g., of a doctor)
clientela; (process of doing something) prassi f; (habitual performance) abitudine f ‖ tr praticare,
esercitare ‖ intr esercitarsi, praticare; (to be active in a profession)
esercitare; to practice as esercitare
la professione di
practitioner [præk'tɪʃənər] s professionista mf
Prague [prɑg] or [preg] s Praga
prairie ['preri] s prateria
prai'rie dog' s cinomio
prai'rie wolf' s coyote m
praise [prez] s lode f, elogio ‖ tr
lodare, elogiare; to praise to the
skies levare alle stelle
praise'wor'thy adj lodevole
pram [præm] s (coll) carrozzella
prance [præns] or [prɑns] s caracollo
‖ intr caracollare; (to caper) ballonzolare
prank [præŋk] s burla, tiro
prate [pret] intr cianciare
prattle ['prætəl] s ciancia, chiacchierio
‖ intr cianciare, parlare a vanvera
pray [pre] tr & intr pregare
prayer [prer] s preghiera
prayer' book' s libro di preghiere
preach [priʧ] tr & intr predicare
preacher ['priʧər] s predicatore m
preamble ['pri ,æmbəl] s preambolo
precarious [prɪ'keri·əs] adj precario
precaution [prɪ'kɔʃən] s precauzione
precede [prɪ'sid] tr & intr precedere
precedent ['prɛsɪdənt] s precedente m
precept ['prisept] s precetto
precinct ['prisɪŋkt] s distretto; circoscrizione elettorale; precincts dintorni mpl
precious ['prɛʃəs] adj prezioso ‖ adv—
precious little (coll) molto poco
precipice ['prɛsɪpɪs] s precipizio
precipitate [prɪ'sɪpɪ ,tet] adj precipitoso ‖ s precipitato ‖ tr & intr precipitare
precipitous [prɪ'sɪpɪtəs] adj precipitoso, a precipizio
precise [prɪ'sais] adj preciso
precision [prɪ'sɪʒən] s precisione
preclude [prɪ'klud] tr precludere;
escludere
precocious [prɪ'koʃəs] adj precoce
predatory ['prɛdə ,tori] adj da preda,
predatore
predicament [prɪ'dɪkəmənt] s situazione critica or imbarazzante
predict [prɪ'dɪkt] tr predire
prediction [prɪ'dɪkʃən] s predizione
predispose [,pridɪs'poz] tr predisporre
predominant [prɪ'dɑmɪnənt] adj pre-
dominante
preeminent [prɪ'emɪnənt] adj premi-
nente
preempt [prɪ'empt] tr occupare or acquistare in precedenza
preen [prin] tr (feathers, fur) lisciarsi;

to preen oneself agghindarsi, attillarsi

prefabricate [pri'fæbrı ,ket] *tr* prefabbricare

preface ['prefɪs] *s* prefazione || *tr* prefazionare; essere la prefazione di

pre·fer [prɪ'fʌr] *v* (*pret & pp* -**ferred**; *ger* -**ferring**) *tr* preferire; (*to advance*) promuovere; (law) presentare, avanzare

preferable ['prefərəbəl] *adj* preferibile

preference ['prefərəns] *s* preferenza

preferred' stock' *s* azioni *fpl* privilegiate

prefix ['prifɪks] *s* prefisso || *tr* prefiggere

pregnan·cy ['pregnənsi] *s* (-**cies**) gravidanza

pregnant ['pregnənt] *adj* incinta, gravida; (fig) gravido

prehistoric [,prihɪs'tarık] or [,prihɪs'tɔrık] *adj* preistorico

prejudice ['predʒədɪs] *s* pregiudizio; preconcetto; **without prejudice** senza detrimento || *tr* (*to harm*) pregiudicare; predisporre; **to prejudice against** prevenire contro

prejudicial [,predʒə'dɪ/əl] *adj* pregiudizievole

prelate ['prelɪt] *s* prelato

preliminar·y [prɪ'lımı ,neri] *adj* preliminare || *s* (-**ies**) preliminare *m*

prelude ['preljud] or ['prilud] *s* preludio || *tr* preludere a || *intr* preludere

premeditate [pri'medı ,tet] *tr* premeditare

premier [prɪ'mɪr] or ['prɪmɪ·ər] *s* primo ministro, presidente *m* del consiglio

premiere [prə'mjɛr] or [prɪ'mɪr] *s* prima; prima attrice

premise ['premɪs] *s* premessa; **on the premises** nella proprietà, sul luogo; **premises** proprietà *f*

premium ['primı·əm] *s* premio; **at a premium** in gran richiesta; a prezzo altissimo

premonition [,primə'nı/ən] *s* presentimento; indizio

preoccupation [pri ,akjə'pe/ən] *s* preoccupazione

preoccu·py [pri'akjə ,paɪ] *v* (*pret & pp* -**pied**) *tr* preoccupare; (*to occupy beforehand*) occupare prima

prepaid [pri'ped] *adj* pagato in anticipo; franco di porto

preparation [,prepə're/ən] *s* preparazione; (*for a trip*) preparativo; (pharm) preparato

preparatory [prɪ'pærə ,tori] *adj* preparatorio

prepare [prɪ'per] *tr* preparare || *intr* prepararsi

preparedness [prɪ'perıdnəs] or [prɪ'perdnɪs] *s* preparazione; preparazione militare

pre·pay [pri'pe] *v* (*pret & pp* -**paid**) *tr* pagare anticipatamente

preponderant [prɪ'pandərənt] *adj* preponderante

preposition [,prepə'zı/ən] *s* preposizione

prepossessing [,pripə'zesıŋ] *adj* simpatico, attraente, piacevole

preposterous [prɪ'pastərəs] *adj* assurdo, ridicolo

prep' school' [prep] *s* (coll) scuola preparatoria

prerecorded [,prirı'kɔrdıd] *adj* (rad & telv) a registrazione differita

prerequisite [pri'rekwızıt] *s* requisito

prerogative [prɪ'ragətɪv] *s* prerogativa

presage ['presıdʒ] *s* presagio || [prɪ'sedʒ] *tr* presagire

Presbyterian [,prezbı'tırı·ən] *adj & s* presbiteriano; Presbiteriano

prescribe [prɪ'skraɪb] *tr & intr* prescrivere

prescription [prɪ'skrıp/ən] *s* prescrizione; (pharm) ricetta

presence ['prezəns] *s* presenza; **in the presence of** alla presenza di

present ['prezənt] *adj* presente || *s* presente *m*, regalo || [prɪ'zent] *tr* presentare; **present arms!** presentat'arm!; **to present s.o. with s.th** regalare qlco a qlcu

presentable [prɪ'zentəbəl] *adj* presentabile

presentation [,prezən'te/ən] or [,prizən'te/ən] *s* presentazione; (theat) rappresentazione

presenta'tion cop'y *s* copia d'omaggio

presentiment [prɪ'zentımənt] *s* presentimento

presently ['prezəntli] *adv* fra poco; attualmente

preserve [prɪ'zʌrv] *s* (*for hunting*) riserva; **preserves** conserva, marmellata || *tr* preservare; conservare

preserved' fruit' *s* frutta in conserva

preside [prɪ'zaɪd] *intr* presiedere; **to preside over** presiedere, presiedere a

presiden·cy ['prezıdənsi] *s* (-**cies**) presidenza

president ['prezıdənt] *s* presidente *m*; (*of a university*) rettore *m*

press [pres] *s* pressione; (*crowd*) folla; (*closet*) armadio; (mach) pressa; (typ) stampa; **to go to press** andare in macchina || *tr* (*to push*) spingere, premere; (*to squeeze*) spremere; (*to embrace*) abbracciare; forzare; costringere; urgere, sollecitare; (*to iron*) stirare || *intr* premere; avanzare

press' a' gent *s* agente pubblicitario

press' con'ference *s* conferenza stampa

pressing ['presıŋ] *adj* pressante, urgente || *s* (*of records*) incisione

press' release' *s* comunicato stampa

pressure ['pre/ər] *s* pressione; tensione, urgenza || *tr* pressare, incalzare con insistenza

pres'sure cook'er ['kukər] *s* pentola a pressione

pressurize ['pre/ə ,raɪz] *tr* pressurizzare

prestige [pres'tiʒ] or ['prestıdʒ] *s* prestigio

prestigious [pres'tıdʒı·əs] or [pres'tıdʒəs] *adj* onorato, stimato

presumably [prɪ'zuməbli] or [prɪ'zjuməbli] *adv* presumibilmente

presume [prɪ'zum] or [prɪ'zjum] *tr* presumere; **to presume to** prendersi la libertà di || *intr* assumere; **to presume on** or **upon** abusare di

presumption [prɪˈzʌmpʃən] *s* presunzione; supposizione

presumptuous [prɪˈzʌmptʃu·əs] *adj* presuntuoso

presuppose [ˌprisəˈpoz] *tr* presupporre

pretend [prɪˈtɛnd] *tr* fingere, fare finta di || *intr* fingere; **to pretend to** (*e.g., the throne*) pretendere a

pretender [prɪˈtɛndər] *s* pretendente *mf;* impostore *m*

pretense [prɪˈtɛns] or [ˈpritɛns] *s* pretesa; finzione; **under false pretenses** allegando ragioni false; **under pretense of** sotto l'apparenza di

pretentious [prɪˈtɛnʃəs] *adj* pretenzioso

preterit [ˈprɛtərɪt] *adj* passato, preterito || *s* passato remoto, preterito

pretext [ˈpritɛkst] *s* pretesto

pretonic [prɪˈtɑnɪk] *adj* pretonico

pret·ty [ˈprɪti] *adj* (**-tier; -tiest**) grazioso, carino; (*e.g., sum of money*) (coll) bello || *adv* abbastanza; molto; **sitting pretty** (slang) ben messo

prevail [prɪˈvel] *intr* prevalere; **to prevail on** or **upon** persuadere

prevailing [prɪˈvelɪŋ] *adj* prevalente

prevalent [ˈprɛvələnt] *adj* comune

prevaricate [prɪˈværɪˌket] *intr* mentire

prevent [prɪˈvɛnt] *tr* impedire; **to prevent from** + *ger* impedire (**with** *dat*) di + *inf* or che + *subj*

prevention [prɪˈvɛnʃən] *s* prevenzione

preventive [prɪˈvɛntɪv] *adj* preventivo || *s* rimedio preventivo

preview [ˈpri‚vju] *s* indizio; (*private showing*) (mov) anteprima; (*showing of brief scenes for advertising*) (mov) scene *fpl* di prossima programmazione

previous [ˈprivi·əs] *adj* previo, precedente || *adv* precedentemente; **previous to** prima di

prewar [ˈpriˌwɔr] *adj* anteguerra

prey [pre] *s* preda; **to be prey to** essere preda di || *intr* predare; **to prey on** or **upon** predare, sfruttare; preoccupare

price [praɪs] *s* prezzo; **at any price** a qualunque costo || *tr* chiedere il prezzo di; fissare il prezzo di

price' control' *s* calmiere *m*

price' cut'ting *s* riduzione di prezzo

price' fix'ing *s* regolamento dei prezzi

price' freez'ing *s* congelamento dei prezzi

priceless [ˈpraɪslɪs] *adj* inestimabile; (coll) molto divertente

price' list' *s* listino prezzi

price' tag' *s* cartellino del prezzo

price' war' *s* guerra dei prezzi

prick [prɪk] *s* punta; puntura; **to kick against the pricks** tirare calci al vento || *tr* bucare, forare; pungere; (*to goad*) spronare; (*the ears*) ergere; (*said, e.g., of the conscience*) rimordere (**with** *dat*)

prick·ly [ˈprɪkli] *adj* (**-lier; -liest**) spinoso, pungente

prick'ly heat' *s* sudamina

prick'ly pear' *s* ficodindia *m*

pride [praɪd] *s* orgoglio; arroganza; **the**

pride of il fiore di || *tr*—**to pride oneself on** or **upon** inorgoglirsi di

priest [prist] *s* prete *m,* sacerdote *m*

priesthood [ˈpristˌhud] *s* sacerdozio

priest·ly [ˈpristli] *adj* (**-lier; -liest**) sacerdotale

prig [prɪg] *s* pedante *mf,* moralista *mf*

prim [prɪm] *adj* (**primmer; primmest**) formale, corretto, compito

prima·ry [ˈpraɪˌmɛri] or [ˈpraɪˌmɛri] *adj* primario || *s* (**-ries**) elezione preferenziale; (elec) bobina primaria; (elec) primario

prime [praɪm] *adj* primo; originale; di prima qualità || *s* (*earliest part*) inizio; (*best period*) fiore *m;* (*choicest part*) fior fiore *m;* (math) numero primo; (*mark*) (math) primo || *tr* preparare; (*a pump*) adescare; (*a firearm*) innescare; (*a canvas*) mesticare; (*a wall*) dare la prima mano a; (*to supply with information*) istruire

prime' min'ister *s* primo ministro

primer [ˈpraɪmər] *s* sillabario, abbecedario || [ˈpraɪmər] *s* innesco, detonatore *m*

primeval [praɪˈmivəl] *adj* primordiale

primitive [ˈprɪmɪtɪv] *adj* primitivo

primp [prɪmp] *tr* agghindare || *intr* agghindarsi

prim'rose' *s* primula

prim'rose path' *s* sentiero dei piaceri

prince [prɪns] *s* principe *m;* **to live like a prince** vivere da principe

prince' roy'al *s* principe ereditario

princess [ˈprɪnsɪs] *s* principessa

principal [ˈprɪnsɪpəl] *adj* principale || *s* (*chief*) padrone *m,* principale *m;* (*of school*) direttore *m,* preside *m;* (*actor*) primo attore; (com) capitale *m;* (law) mandante *mf*

principle [ˈprɪnsɪpəl] *s* principio; **on principle** per principio

print [prɪnt] *s* stampa; (*cloth*) tessuto stampato; (*printed matter*) stampato; (*newsprint*) giornale *m;* (*mark made by one's thumb*) impronta; (phot) positiva; **in print** stampato; disponibile; **out of print** esaurito || *tr* stampare, tirare; (*to write in print*) scrivere in stampatello; (*in the memory*) imprimere

print'ed cir'cuit *s* circuito stampato

print'ed mat'ter *s* stampati *mpl*

printer [ˈprɪntər] *s* stampatore *m;* (*of computer*) tabulatrice *f*

print'er's dev'il *s* apprendista *m* tipografo

print'er's ink' *s* inchiostro da stampa

printing [ˈprɪntɪŋ] *s* stampa; stampato; tiratura, edizione; (*writing in printed letters*) stampatello

prior [ˈpraɪ·ər] *adj* anteriore, precedente || *s* priore *m* || *adv* prima; **prior to** prima di

prior·ty [praɪˈɔrɪti] or [praɪˈɔrɪti] *s* (**-ties**) priorità *f*

prism [ˈprɪzəm] *s* prisma *m*

prison [ˈprɪzən] *s* prigione, carcere *m*

prisoner [ˈprɪzənər] or [ˈprɪznər] *s* prigioniero

pris'on van' *s* furgone *m* cellulare

pris•sy [ˈprɪsi] *adj* (**-sier; -siest**) smanceroso, smorfioso

priva•cy [ˈpraɪvəsi] *s* (**-cies**) ritiro; segreto; **to have no privacy** non esser mai lasciato in pace

private [ˈpraɪvɪt] *adj* privato, personale ‖ *s* soldato semplice; **in private** privatamente; **privates** pudende *fpl*

pri'vate eye' *s* poliziotto privato

pri'vate first' class' *s* soldato scelto

pri'vate hos'pital *s* clinica

priv'ate view'ing *s* (mov) anteprima; (painting) vernice *f*

privet [ˈprɪvɪt] *s* ligustro

privilege [ˈprɪvɪlɪdʒ] *s* privilegio

priv•y [ˈprɪvi] *adj* privato; **privy to** segretamente a conoscenza di ‖ *s* (**-ies**) latrina

prize [praɪz] *s* premio; (nav) preda ‖ *tr* valutare, stimare

prize' fight' *s* incontro di pugilato

prize' fight'er *s* pugile *m*, pugilista *m*

prize' ring' *s* ring *m*, quadrato

pro [pro] *s* (**pros**) pro; voto favorevole; argomento favorevole; (coll) professionista *m*; **the pros and the cons** il pro e il contro

probabili•ty [ˌprɑbəˈbɪlɪti] *s* (**-ties**) probabilità *f*

probable [ˈprɑbəbəl] *adj* probabile

probate [ˈprobet] *s* omologazione di un testamento; copia autentica di un testamento ‖ *tr* (*a will*) omologare

probation [proˈbeʃən] *s* prova; periodo di prova; (law) condizionale *f*, libertà vigilata; (educ) provvedimento disciplinare

probe [prob] *s* inchiesta; (surg) sonda ‖ *tr* indagare; sondare

problem [ˈprɑbləm] *s* problema *m*

procedure [proˈsɪdʒər] *s* procedura

proceed [ˈprosɪd] *s*—**proceeds** provento ‖ [proˈsɪd] *intr* procedere

proceeding [proˈsɪdɪŋ] *s* procedimento; **proceedings** atti *mpl*; (law) procedimenti *mpl*

process [ˈproses] *s* processo; **in the process of time** in processo di tempo ‖ *tr* trattare

procession [proˈseʃən] *s* processione

proc'ess serv'er *s* ufficiale giudiziario

proclaim [proˈklem] *tr* proclamare

proclitic [proˈklɪtɪk] *adj* proclitico ‖ *s* parola proclitica

procrastinate [proˈkræstɪˌnet] *tr & intr* procrastinare

procure [proˈkjur] *tr* ottenere ‖ *intr* ruffianeggiare

prod [prɑd] *s* pungolo, stimolo *v* (*pret & pp* **prodded;** *ger* **prodding**) *tr* stimolare, pungolare, incitare

prodigal [ˈprɑdɪgəl] *adj & s* prodigo

prodigious [proˈdɪdʒəs] *adj* prodigioso

prodi•gy [ˈprɑdɪdʒi] *s* (**-gies**) prodigio

produce [ˈprodjus] or [ˈprodus] *s* produzione; prodotti *mpl* agricoli ‖ [proˈdjus] or [proˈdus] *tr* produrre; (theat) presentare

producer [proˈdjusər] or [proˈdusər] *s* produttore *m*; (*of a play*) impresario; (mov) produttore *m*

product [ˈprɑdəkt] *s* prodotto

production [proˈdʌkʃən] *s* produzione

profane [proˈfen] *adj* profano; blasfemo ‖ *tr* profanare

profani•ty [proˈfænɪti] *s* (**-ties**) bestemmia

profess [proˈfɛs] *tr & intr* professare

profession [proˈfeʃən] *s* professione

professor [proˈfesər] *s* professore *m*

proffer [ˈprɑfər] *s* offerta ‖ *tr* offrire

proficient [proˈfɪʃənt] *adj* abile, competente

profile [ˈprofaɪl] *s* profilo ‖ *tr* profilare

profit [ˈprɑfɪt] *s* profitto; vantaggio; **at a profit** con guadagno ‖ *tr* avvantaggiare; giovare (with *dat*) ‖ *intr* avvantaggiarsi; **to profit by** approfittare di

profitable [ˈprɑfɪtəbəl] *adj* vantaggioso

prof'it and loss' *s* profitti *mpl* e perdite *fpl*

profiteer [ˌprɑfɪˈtɪr] *s* profittatore *m* ‖ *intr* fare il profittatore

prof'it shar'ing *s* cointeressenza, partecipazione agli utili

prof'it tak'ing *s* realizzo

profligate [ˈprɑflɪgɪt] *adj & s* dissoluto; prodigo

pro for'ma in'voice [ˈformə] *s* fattura fittizia

profound [proˈfaund] *adj* profondo

profuse [prəˈfjus] *adj* profuso, abbondante; **profuse in** prodigo di

proge•ny [ˈprɑdʒəni] *s* (**-nies**) prole *f*

progno•sis [prɑgˈnosɪs] *s* (**-ses** [siz]) prognosi *f*

prognostic [prɑgˈnɑstɪk] *s* pronostico

prognosticate [prɑgˈnɑstɪˌket] *tr* pronosticare

pro•gram [ˈprogræm] *s* programma *m* ‖ *v* (*pret & pp* **-gramed** or **-grammed;** *ger* **-graming** or **-gramming**) *tr* programmare

programmer [ˈprogræmər] *s* pannellista *mf*, programmatore *m*

progress [ˈprɑgres] *s* progresso; **in progress** in corso; **to make progress** fare dei progressi ‖ [prəˈgres] *intr* progredire; migliorare

progressive [prəˈgresɪv] *adj* (*proceeding step by step*) progressivo; progressista *s* progressista *mf*

prohibit [proˈhɪbɪt] *tr* proibire

prohibition [ˌproəˈbɪʃən] *s* proibizione; (hist) proibizionismo

project [ˈprɑdʒekt] *s* progetto ‖ [prəˈdʒekt] *tr* (*to propose, plan*) progettare; (*light, a shadow, etc.*) proiettare ‖ *intr* sporgere, protrudere

projectile [prəˈdʒektɪl] *s* proiettile *m*

projection [prəˈdʒekʃən] *s* proiezione, sporgenza

projector [prəˈdʒektər] *s* (*apparatus*) proiettore *m*; (*person*) progettista *mf*

proletarian [ˌproluˈteri•ən] *adj & s* proletario

proliferate [prəˈlɪfəˌret] *intr* proliferare

prolific [prəˈlɪfɪk] *adj* prolifico

prolix [ˈprolɪks] or [proˈlɪks] *adj* prolisso

prologue [ˈprolɔg] or [ˈprolɑg] *s* prologo

prolong [pro'lɔŋ] or pro'lɑŋ] *tr* prolungare

promenade [,prɑmɪ'ned] or [,prɑmɪ-'nɑd] *s* passeggiata; ballo di gala || *tr & intr* passeggiare

promenade' deck' *s* ponte *m* passeggiata

prominent ['prɑmɪnənt] *adj* prominente

promise ['prɑmɪs] *s* promessa || *tr & intr* promettere

prom'ising young' man' *s* giovane *m* di belle speranze

prom'issory note' ['prɑmɪ,sori] *s* cambiale *f*, pagherò *m*

promonto·ry ['prɑmən,tori] *s* (-ries) promontorio

promote [prə'mot] *tr* promuovere

promotion [prə'moʃən] *s* promozione

prompt [prɑmpt] *adj* pronto || *tr* incitare, istigare; (theat) suggerire

prompter ['prɑmptər] *s* suggeritore *m*, rammentatore *m*

prompt'er's box' *s* buca del suggeritore

promptness ['prɑmptnɪs] *s* prontezza

promulgate ['prɑməl,get] or [pro'mʌl-get] *tr* promulgare

prone [pron] *adj* prono

prong [prɔŋ] or [prɑŋ] *s* punta; (*of fork*) dente *m*; (*of pitchfork*) rebbio

pronoun ['pronaun] *s* pronome *m*

pronounce [prə'nauns] *tr* pronunziare

pronounced [prə'naunst] *adj* pronunziato, marcato

pronouncement [prə'naunsmənt] *s* dichiarazione ufficiale

pronunciamen·to [prə,nʌnsɪ-ə'mento] *s* (-tos) pronunciamento

pronunciation [prə,nʌnsɪ'eʃən] or [prə,nʌnʃɪ'eʃən] *s* pronunzia

proof [pruf] *adj*—**proof against** a prova di || *s* prova; (*of alcoholic beverages*) gradazione; (typ) bozza

proof'read'er *s* correttore *m* di bozze

prop [prɑp] *s* sostegno, puntello; (*pole*) palo; **props** attrezzi *mpl* teatrali || *v* (*pret & pp* **propped;** *ger* **propping**) *tr* sostenere, puntellare

propaganda [,prɑpə'gændə] *s* propaganda

propagate ['prɑpə,get] *tr* propagare || *intr* propagarsi

pro·pel [prə'pel] *v* (*pret & pp* **-pelled;** *ger* **-pelling**) *tr* propulsare, spingere, azionare; (*a rocket*) propellere

propeller [prə'pelər] *s* elica

propensi·ty [prə'pensɪti] *s* (-ties) propensione

proper ['prɑpər] *adj* appropriato, corretto; decente, convenevole; (gram) proprio; **proper to** proprio di

proper·ty ['prɑpərti] *s* (-ties) proprietà *f*; **properties** attrezzi *mpl* teatrali

prop'erty man' *s* trovarobe *m*, attrezzista *m*

prop'erty own'er *s* proprietario fondiario

prophe·cy ['prɑfɪsi] *s* (-cies) profezia

prophe·sy ['prɑfɪ,saɪ] *v* (*pret & pp* **-sied**) *tr* profetizzare

prophet ['prɑfɪt] *s* profeta *m*

prophetess ['prɑfɪtɪs] *s* profetessa

prophylactic [,profɪ'læktɪk] *adj* profilattico || *s* rimedio profilattico; preservativo

propitiate [prə'pɪʃɪ,et] *tr* propiziare

propitious [prə'pɪʃəs] *adj* propizio

prop'jet' *s* turboelica *m*

proportion [prə'porʃən] *s* proporzione; **in proportion as** a misura che; **in proportion to** in proporzione a; **out of proportion** sproporzionato || *tr* proporzionare, commensurare

proportionate [prə'porʃənɪt] *adj* proporzionato

proposal [prə'pozəl] *s* proposta; proposta di matrimonio

propose [prə'poz] *tr* proporre || *intr* fare una proposta di matrimonio; **to propose to** chiedere la mano di; proporsi di + *inf*

proposition [,prɑpə'zɪʃən] *s* proposizione, proposta; (coll) progetto || *tr* fare delle proposte indecenti a

propound [prə'paund] *tr* proporre

proprietary [prə'praɪ·ə,teri] *adj* padronale; esclusivo, patentato

proprietor [prə'praɪ·ətər] *s* proprietario

proprietress [prə'praɪ·ətrɪs] *s* proprietaria

proprie·ty [prə'praɪ·əti] *s* (-ties) correttezza, decoro; **proprieties** convenzioni *fpl* sociali

propulsion [prə'pʌlʃən] *s* propulsione

prorate [pro'ret] *tr* rateizzare

prosaic [pro'ze·ɪk] *adj* prosaico

proscribe [pro'skraɪb] *tr* proscrivere

prose [proz] *adj* prosaico || *s* prosa

prosecute ['prɑsɪ,kjut] *tr* eseguire; (law) processare

prosecutor ['prɑsɪ,kjutər] *s* esecutore *m*; (law) querelante *m*; (law) avvocato d'accusa

proselyte ['prɑsɪ,laɪt] *s* proselito

prose' writ'er *s* prosatore *m*

prosody ['prɑsədi] *s* prosodia, metrica

prospect ['prɑspekt] *s* vista; prospettiva; candidato; probabile cliente *m*; **prospects** speranze *fpl* || *intr* fare il cercatore; **to prospect for** fare il cercatore di

prospectus [prə'spektəs] *s* prospetto

prosper ['prɑspər] *tr & intr* prosperare

prosperi·ty [prɑs'perɪti] *s* (-ties) prosperità *f*, benessere *m*

prosperous ['prɑspərəs] *adj* prospero

prostitute ['prɑstɪ,tjut] or ['prɑstɪ,tut] *s* prostituta || *tr* prostituire

prostrate ['prɑstret] *adj* prostrato || *tr* prostrare

prostration [prɑs'treʃən] *s* prostrazione

protagonist [pro'tægənɪst] *s* protagonista *mf*

protect [prə'tekt] *tr* proteggere

protection [prə'tekʃən] *s* protezione

protégé ['protə,ʒe] *s* protetto, favorito

protégée ['protə,ʒe] *s* protetta, favorita

protein ['proti·ɪn] or ['protin] *s* proteina

pro tempore [pro'tempə,ri] *adj* provvisorio, interinale

protest ['protest] *s* protesta; (com)

protesto ‖ [pro'test] *tr & intr* protestare

Protestant ['prɑtɪstənt] *adj & s* protestante *mf*

protester [prə'testər] *s* protestatario

prothonotar·y [pro'θɑnə,teri] *s* (**-ies**) (law) cancelliere *m* capo

protocol ['protə,kɑl] *s* protocollo

protoplasm ['protə,plæzəm] *s* protoplasma *m*

prototype ['protə,taɪp] *s* prototipo

proto·zoon [,protə'zo·ɑn] *s* (**-zoa** ['zo·ə]) protozoo

protract [pro'trækt] *tr* prolungare

protractor [pro'træktər] *s* rapportatore *m*

protrude [pro'trud] *intr* sporgere

proud [praud] *adj* fiero; arrogante; maestoso, magnifico

proud' flesh' *s* tessuto di granulazione

prove [pruv] *v* (*pret* **proved**; *pp* **proved** or **proven**) *tr* provare; (*ore*) analizzare; (law) omologare; (math) fare la prova di ‖ *intr* risultare

proverb ['prɑvərb] *s* proverbio

provide [prə'vaɪd] *tr* provvedere ‖ *intr*—**to provide for** provvedere a; (*to be ready for*) prepararsi a

provided [prə'vaɪdɪd] *conj* a condizione che, purché; **provided that** a condizione che, purché

providence ['prɑvɪdəns] *s* provvidenza

providential [,prɑvɪ'denʃəl] *adj* provvidenziale

providing [prə'vaɪdɪŋ] *conj* var of **provided**

province ['prɑvɪns] *s* provincia; (fig) pertinenza, competenza

provision [prə'vɪʒən] *s* provvedimento; clausola; **provisions** viveri *mpl*

provi·so [prə'vaɪzo] *s* (**-sos** or **-soes**) stipulazione, clausola

provoke [prə'vok] *tr* provocare; contrariare, irritare

prow [prau] *s* prora, prua

prowess ['prau·ɪs] *s* prodezza; maestria

prowl [praul] *intr* andare in cerca di preda; vagabondare

prowler ['praulər] *s* vagabondo; ladro

proximity [prɑk'sɪmɪti] *s* prossimità *f*

prox·y ['prɑksi] *s* (**-ies**) procura; (*person*) procuratore *m*

prude [prud] *s* pudibondo

prudence ['prudəns] *s* prudenza

prudent ['prudənt] *adj* prudente

pruder·y ['prudəri] *s* (**-ies**) attitudine pudibonda

prudish ['prudɪʃ] *adj* pudibondo

prune [prun] *s* prugna secca ‖ *tr* potare

pry [praɪ] *v* (*pret & pp* **pried**) *tr*—**to pry open** forzare con una leva; **to pry s.th out of s.o.** strappare qlco a qlcu ‖ *intr* intromettersi, cacciarsi

psalm [sɑm] *s* salmo

pseudo ['sudo] or ['sjudo] *adj* falso, finto, sedicente

pseudonym ['sudənɪm] or ['sjudənɪm] *s* pseudonimo

psychiatrist [saɪ'kaɪ·ətrɪst] *s* psichiatra *mf*

psychiatry [saɪ'kaɪ·ətri] *s* psichiatria

psychic ['saɪkɪk] *adj* psichico ‖ *s* medium *mf*

psychoanalysis [,saɪko·ə'nælɪsɪs] *s* psicanalisi *f*

psychoanalyze [,saɪko'ænə,laɪz] *tr* psicanalizzare

psychologic(al) [,saɪko'lɑdʒɪk(əl)] *adj* psicologico

psychologist [saɪ'kɑlədʒɪst] *s* psicologo

psycholo·gy [saɪ'kɑlədʒi] *s* (**-gies**) psicologia

psychopath ['saɪkə,pæθ] *s* psicopatico

psycho·sis [saɪ'kosɪs] *s* (**-ses** [siz]) psicosi *f*

psychotic [saɪ'kɑtɪk] *adj* psicotico

pub [pʌb] *s* (Brit) taverna, bar *m*

puberty ['pjubərti] *s* pubertà *f*

public ['pʌblɪk] *adj & s* pubblico

pub'lic-address' sys'tem *s* sistema *m* d'amplificazione per discorsi in pubblico

publication [,pʌblɪ'keʃən] *s* pubblicazione

pub'lic convey'ance *s* veicolo di servizi pubblici

publicity [pʌb'lɪsɪti] *s* pubblicità *f*

publicize ['pʌblɪ,saɪz] *tr* pubblicare, divulgare

pub'lic li'brary *s* biblioteca comunale

pub'lic-opin'ion poll' *s* sondaggio d'opinioni

pub'lic pros'ecutor *s* pubblico ministero

pub'lic school' *s* (U.S.A.) scuola dell'obbligo; (Brit) scuola privata, collegio

pub'lic serv'ant *s* funzionario pubblico

pub'lic speak'ing *s* oratoria

pub'lic spir'it *s* civismo

pub'lic toi'let *s* gabinetto pubblico

pub'lic util'ity *s* impresa di servizio pubblico; **public utilities** azioni emesse da imprese di servizi pubblici

publish ['pʌblɪʃ] *tr* pubblicare

publisher ['pʌblɪʃər] *s* editore *m*; (journ) direttore *m* responsabile

pub'lishing house' *s* casa editrice

pucker ['pʌkər] *s* grinza ‖ *tr* raggrinzire ‖ *intr* raggrinzirsi

pudding ['pudɪŋ] *s* budino, torta

puddle ['pʌdəl] *s* pozza, pozzanghera ‖ *intr* diguazzare

pudg·y ['pʌdʒi] *adj* (**-ier; -iest**) grassoccio

puerile ['pju·əril] *adj* puerile

Puerto Rican ['pwerto'rikən] *adj & s* portoricano

puff [pʌf] *s* soffio, sbuffo; (*e.g., of cigar*) boccata; (*pad*) piumino; (*exaggerated praise*) pistolotto; (culin) bignè *m* ‖ *tr* sbuffare; gonfiare; adulare ‖ *intr* soffiare, sbuffare; (*to breathe heavily*) ansimare, ansare; gonfiarsi; tirare boccate

puff' paste' *s* pasta sfoglia

pugilist ['pjudʒɪlɪst] *s* pugile *m*

pug-nosed ['pʌg,nozd] *adj* camuso

puke [pjuk] *tr & intr* (slang) vomitare

pull [pul] *s* tiro; (*act of drawing in*) tirata; (*handle*) maniglia *m*; (slang) influenza, appoggi *mpl* ‖ *tr* tirare; (*a tooth*) cavare; (*a muscle*) strappare;

(*a punch*) (coll) limitare la forza di; **to pull apart** fare a pezzi; **to pull down** abbattere; degradare; **to pull on** (*e.g., one's pants*) infilarsi; **to pull oneself together** ricomporsi; **to pull s.o.'s leg** beffarsi di qlcu || *intr* tirare; **to pull apart** andare a pezzi; **to pull at** tirare; **to pull away** andarsene; **to pull for** (coll) fare il tifo per; **to pull in** (*said of a train*) arrivare, entrare in stazione; **to pull out** (*said of a train*) partire; **to pull through** guarire, riuscire a cavarsela; **to pull up** to avanzare fino a

pullet ['pulɪt] *s* pollastra

pulley ['pulɪ] *s* puleggia, carrucola

pulp [pʌlp] *s* polpa; (*for making paper*) pasta

pulpit ['pulpɪt] *s* pulpito

pulsate ['pʌlset] *intr* pulsare

pulsation [pʌl'seʃən] *s* pulsazione

pulse [pʌls] *s* polso; **to feel or take the pulse of** tastare il polso a

pulverize ['pʌlvə‚raɪz] *tr* polverizzare

pum'ice stone' *s* ['pʌmɪs] *s* pomice *f*, pietra pomice

pum·mel ['pʌməl] *v* (*pret & pp* -meled or -melled; *ger* -meling or -melling) *tr* prendere a pugni

pump [pʌmp] *s* pompa; (*slipper*) scarpina || *tr* pompare; (coll) cavare un segreto a; **to pump up** pompare

pumpkin ['pʌmpkɪn] *or* ['puŋkɪn] *s* zucca

pump-priming ['pʌmp‚praɪmɪŋ] *s* stimolo governativo per sostentare l'economia

pun [pʌn] *s* gioco di parole || *v* (*pret & pp* punned; *ger* punning) *intr* fare giochi di parole

punch [pʌntʃ] *s* pugno; (*tool*) punteruolo, punzone *m*; (*drink*) ponce *m*; (coll) forza || *tr* dare un pugno a; (*metal*) punzonare; (*a ticket*) perforare || **Punch** *s* Pulcinella *m*; **pleased as Punch** soddisfattissimo

punch' bowl' *s* vaso per il ponce

punch' card' *s* scheda perforata

punch' clock' *s* orologio di controllo

punch'-drunk' *adj* stordito

punched' tape' *s* nastro perforato

punch'ing bag' *s* sacco

punch' line' *s* perfinire *m*, motto finale

punctilious [pʌŋk'tɪlɪ·əs] *adj* cerimonioso, pignolo

punctual ['pʌŋkt/u·əl] *adj* puntuale

punctuate ['pʌŋkt/u‚et] *tr* punteggiare

punctuation [‚pʌŋkt/u'eʃən] *s* punteggiatura

punctua'tion mark' *s* segno d'interpunzione

puncture ['pʌŋkt/ər] *s* puntura; (*hole*) bucatura; **to have a puncture** avere una gomma a terra || *tr* bucare, perforare || *intr* essere bucato

punct'ure-proof' *adj* antiperforante

pundit ['pʌndɪt] *s* esperto, autorità *f*

pungent ['pʌndʒənt] *adj* pungente

punish ['pʌnɪʃ] *tr* punire

punishment ['pʌnɪ/mənt] *s* punizione, castigo

punk [pʌŋk] *adj* (slang) di pessima

qualità || *s* esca; (*decayed wood*) legno marcio; (slang) malandrino

punster ['pʌnstər] *s* freddurista *mf*

punt [pʌnt] *s* (football) calcio dato al pallone prima che tocchi il terreno

pu·ny ['pjunɪ] *adj* (-nier; -niest) insignificante, meschino; (*weak*) debole

pup [pʌp] *s* cucciolo

pupil ['pjupəl] *s* allievo, scolaro; (anat) pupilla

puppet ['pʌpɪt] *s* marionetta, burattino; (fig) fantoccio

puppeteer [‚pʌpɪ'tɪr] *s* burattinaio

pup'pet gov'ernment *s* governo fantoccio or pupazzo

pup'pet show' *s* spettacolo di marionette

pup·py ['pʌpɪ] *s* (-pies) cucciolo

pup'py love' *s* amore *m* giovanile

purchase ['pʌrt/əs] *s* compra, acquisto; (*grip*) presa, leva || *tr* comprare, acquistare

pur'chasing pow'er *s* potere *m* d'acquisto

pure [pjur] *adj* puro

purgative ['pʌrgətɪv] *adj* purgativo || *s* purga

purge [pʌrdʒ] *s* purga || *tr* purgare

puri·fy ['pjurɪ‚faɪ] *v* (*pret & pp* -fied) *tr* purificare || *intr* purificarsi

puritan ['pjurɪtən] *adj & s* puritano || **Puritan** *adj & s* puritano

purity ['pjurɪtɪ] *s* purezza

purloin [pər'lɔɪn] *tr & intr* rubare

purple ['pʌrpəl] *adj* purpureo || *s* porpora

purport ['pʌrport] *s* senso, significato || [pər'port] *tr* significare; **to purport to** + *inf* pretendere di + *inf*

purpose ['pʌrpəs] *s* scopo, fine *m*; **on purpose** apposta; **to good purpose** con buoni risultati; **to no purpose** inutilmente; **to serve one's purpose** fare al caso proprio

purposely ['pʌrpəslɪ] *adv* a bella posta, apposta

purr [pʌr] *s* ronfare *m* || *intr* fare le fusa

purse [pʌrs] *s* borsa; (*woman's handbag*) borsetta; (*for men*) borsetto || *tr* (*one's lips*) arricciare

purser ['pʌrsər] *s* commissario di bordo

purse' snatch'er ['snæt/ər] *s* borsaiolo

purse' strings' *spl* cordini *mpl* della borsa; **to hold the purse strings** controllare le spese

purslane ['pʌrslen] *or* ['pʌrslɪn] *s* (bot) porcellana

pursue [pər'su] *or* [pər'sju] *tr* perseguire; (*to harass*) perseguitare; (*a career*) proseguire

pursuit [pər'sut] *or* [pər'sjut] *s* inseguimento, caccia; occupazione, esercizio

pursuit' plane' *s* caccia *m*

purvey [pər've] *tr* provvedere, fornire

pus [pʌs] *s* pus *m*

push [pu/] *s* spinta; (*advance*) avanzata; (coll) impulso, energia || *tr* premere, spingere; (*a product*) promuovere la vendita di; dare impulso a; (*narcotics*) (slang) spacciare; **to**

push around (coll) dare spintoni a; (fig) fare pressione su; **to push back** ricacciare || *intr* spingere; **to push ahead** avanzarsi a spintoni, avanzarsi; **to push on** avanzare

push' but'ton *s* pulsante *m*, bottone *m*

push'-button con'trol *s* controllo a pulsanti

push'cart' *s* carretto a mano

pusher ['pʊʃər] *adj* spingente; (aer) propulsivo || *s* spingitore *m*; (aer) aeroplano a elica propulsiva; (slang) spacciatore *m* di stupefacenti

pushing ['pʊʃɪŋ] *adj* aggressivo, intraprendente

puss [pʊs] *s* micio

puss' in the cor'ner *s* gioco dei quattro cantoni

puss•y ['pʊsi] *s* (**-ies**) micio

puss'y wil'low *s* salice americano a gattini

pustule ['pʌstʃʊl] *s* pustola

put [pʊt] *v* (*pret & pp* **put**; *ger* **putting**) *tr* mettere; (*to estimate*) stimare; (*a question*) rivolgere; (*to throw*) lanciare; imporre; **to put across** (slang) far accettare; **to put aside, away** or **by** mettere da parte; **to put down** annotare; (*to suppress*) reprimere; **to put off** differire; evadere; **to put on** (*clothes*) mettersi; (*a brake*) azionare; (*to assume*) fingere; (*airs*) darsi; **to put out** spegnere; imbarazzare; incomodare; deludere; annoiare, irritare; (*a game*) espellere; **to put it over on s.o.** fargliela a qlcu; **to put off** rinviare; **to put over** mandare ad effetto; **to put to flight** mettere in fuga; **to put to shame** svergognare; **to put through** portare a termine; **to put up** offrire; mettere in conserva; alloggiare; costruire; (*money*) contribuire; (coll) incitare || *intr* dirigersi; **to put to sea** mettersi in mare; **to put up** prendere alloggio; **to put up with** tollerare

put'-out' *adj* sconcertato, seccato

putrid ['pjutrɪd] *adj* putrido

Putsch [pʊtʃ] *s* tentativo di sollevazione, sollevazione

putter ['pʌtər] *intr* occuparsi di inezie; **to putter about** andare avanti e indietro

put•ty ['pʌti] *s* (**-ties**) stucco, mastice *m* || *v* (*pret & pp* **-tied**) *tr* stuccare

put'ty knife' *s* spatola

put'-up' *adj* (coll) complottato

puzzle ['pʌzəl] *s* enigma *m*; (toy) indovinello || *tr* rendere perplesso, confondere; **to puzzle out** decifrare || *intr* essere perplesso

puzzler ['pʌzlər] *s* enigma *m*

puzzling ['pʌzlɪŋ] *adj* enigmatico

pyg•my ['pɪgmi] *s* (**-mies**) pigmeo

pylon *s* pilone *m*

pyramid ['pɪrəmɪd] *s* piramide *f* || *tr* (e.g., *costs*) aumentare gradualmente; (*one's money*) aumentare giocando in margine

pyre [paɪr] *s* pira

Pyrenees ['pɪrɪˌniz] *spl* Pirenei *mpl*

pyrites [paɪˈraɪtiz] or ['paɪraɪts] *s* pirite *f*

pyrotechnics [ˌpaɪrəˈtɛknɪks] *spl* pirotecnica

python ['paɪθan] or ['paɪθən] *s* pitone *m*

pythoness ['paɪθənɪs] *s* pitonessa

pyx [pɪks] *s* (eccl) pisside *f*

Q

Q, q [kju] *s* diciassettesima lettera dell'alfabeto inglese

quack [kwæk] *adj* falso; *s* medicastro; ciarlatano; qua qua *m* || *intr* (*said of a duck*) fare qua qua

quacker•y ['kwækəri] *s* (**-ies**) ciarlataneria

quadrangle ['kwɑdˌræŋɡəl] *s* quadrangolo

quadrant ['kwɑdrənt] *s* quadrante *m*

quadruped ['kwɑdruˌpɛd] *adj & s* quadrupede *m*

quadruple ['kwɑdrupəl] or [kwɑˈdrupəl] *adj* quadruplo; (*alliance*) quadruplice || *s* quadruplo || *tr* quadruplicare || *intr* quadruplicarsi

quaff [kwaf] or [kwæf] *s* lungo sorso || *tr & intr* bere a lunghi sorsi

quail [kwel] *s* quaglia || *intr* sgomentarsi

quaint [kwent] *adj* strano, strambo, originale; all'antica ma bello

quake [kwek] *s* terremoto || *intr* tremare, sussultare

Quaker ['kwekər] *adj & s* quacchero, quacquero

Quak'er meet'ing *s* riunione di quaccheri; (coll) riunione in cui si parla poco

quali•fy ['kwɑlɪˌfaɪ] *v* (*pret & pp* **-fied**) *tr* qualificare; (*for a profession*) abilitare || *intr* qualificarsi; abilitarsi

quali•ty ['kwɑlɪti] *s* (**-ties**) qualità *f*; (*of a sound*) timbro

qualm [kwɑm] *s* scrupolo di coscienza; preoccupazione; nausea

quanda•ry ['kwɑndəri] *s* (**-ries**) incertezza, perplessità *f*

quanti•ty ['kwɑntɪti] *s* (**-ties**) quantità *f*

quan•tum ['kwɑntəm] *adj* quantistico || *s* (**-ta** [tə]) quanto

quarantine ['kwɑrənˌtin] or ['kwɔrənˌtin] *s* quarantena || *tr* mettere in quarantena

quar•rel ['kwɑrəl] or ['kwɔrəl] *s* litigio, diverbio; **to have no quarrel with** non essere in disaccordo con; **to pick a quarrel with** venire a diverbio con || *v* (*pret & pp* **-reled** or **-relled**; *ger* **-reling** or **-relling**) *intr* litigare

quarrelsome ['kwɑrəlsəm] or ['kwɔrəl-səm] *adj* litigioso, rissoso

quar·ry ['kwɑri] or ['kwɔri] *s* (**-ries**) cava; (*game*) selvaggina, cacciagione ǁ *v* (*pret* & *pp* **-ried**) *tr* cavare

quart [kwɔrt] *s* quarto di gallone

quarter ['kwɔrtər] *adj* quarto ǁ *s* quarto; moneta di un quarto di dollaro; (*three months*) trimestre *m*; (*of town*) quartiere *m*; **a quarter after one** l'una e un quarto; **a quarter of an hour** un quarto d'ora; **a quarter to one** l'una mèno un quarto; **at close quarters** corpo a corpo; **quarters** quartiere *m* ǁ *tr* squartare; (*soldiers*) accasermare

quar'ter-deck' *s* cassero

quar'ter-hour' *s* quarto d'ora; **on the quarter-hour** ogni quindici minuti allo scoccare del quarto d'ora

quarter·ly ['kwɔrtərli] *adj* trimestrale ǁ *s* (**-lies**) pubblicazione trimestrale ǁ *adv* trimestralmente

quar'ter-mas'ter *s* (mil) intendente *m* militare; (nav) secondo capo

quartet [kwɔr'tɛt] *s* quartetto

quartz [kwɔrts] *s* quarzo

quasar ['kwesɑr] *s* (astr) radiostella

quash [kwɑʃ] *tr* sopprimere; annullare

quaver ['kwevər] *s* tremito; (mus) tremolo; (mus) croma ǁ *intr* tremare

quay [ki] *s* molo

queen [kwin] *s* regina; (**in cards**) donna; (chess) regina

queen' bee' *s* ape regina; (fig) basilessa

queen' dow'ager *s* regina vedova

queen·ly ['kwinli] *adj* (**-lier; -liest**) da regina; regio

queen' moth'er *s* regina madre

queen' post' *s* monaco

queen's' Eng'lish *s* inglese corretto

queer [kwɪr] *adj* strano, curioso; **poco bene**, indisposto; falso; (slang) omosessuale ǁ *s* (slang) finocchio ǁ *tr* rovinare, mettere in pericolo

quell [kwɛl] *tr* soffocare, domare; (*pain*) calmare

quench [kwɛntʃ] *tr* (*fire, thirst*) spegnere, estinguere; (*rebellion*) soffocare; (elec) ammortizzare

que·ry ['kwɪri] *s* (**-ries**) domanda; punto interrogativo; dubbio ǁ *v* (*pret* & *pp* **-ried**) *tr* interrogare; (typ) apporre punto interrogativo a

quest [kwɛst] *s* ricerca; **in quest of** in cerca di

question ['kwɛstʃən] *s* domanda; problema *m*, quesito; (*matter*) questione; **beyond question** senza dubbio; **out of the question** impossibile; **this is beside the question** questo non c'entra; **to ask a question** fare una domanda; **to be a question of** trattarsi di; **to call in or into question** mettere in dubbio; **without question** senza dubbio ǁ *tr* interrogare; mettere in dubbio; (pol) interpellare

questionable ['kwɛstʃənəbəl] *adj* discutibile

ques'tion mark' *s* punto interrogativo

questionnaire [,kwɛstʃən'ɛr] *s* questionario

queue [kju] *s* (*of hair*) codino; (*of people*) coda ǁ *intr* fare la coda

quibble ['kwɪbəl] *intr* sottilizzare

quick [kwɪk] *adj* pronto, sollecito; sbrigativo; veloce, rapido; vivo ǁ *s*—**the quick and the dead** i vivi e i morti; **to cut to the quick** toccare nel vivo

quicken ['kwɪkən] *tr* sveltire; animare; ravvivare

quick'lime' *s* calce viva

quick' lunch' *s* tavola calda

quickly ['kwɪkli] *adv* svelto, alla svelta; presto

quick'sand' *s* sabbia mobile

quick'-set'ting *adj* a presa rapida

quick'sil'ver *s* argento vivo

quick'work' *s* (naut) opera viva

quiet ['kwaɪ-ət] *adj* quieto; silenzioso; (com) calmo; **to keep quiet** stare zitto ǁ *s* quiete *f*, tranquillità *f*; pace *f*, calma ǁ *tr* quietare; calmare ǁ *intr*—**to quiet down** quietarsi, calmarsi

quill [kwɪl] *s* penna d'oca; (*basal part of feather*) calamo; (*e.g., of porcupine*) aculeo

quilt [kwɪlt] *s* trapunta, imbottita ǁ *tr* trapuntare

quince [kwɪns] *s* cotogna; (*tree*) cotogno

quinine ['kwaɪnaɪn] *s* (*alkaloid*) chinina; (*salt of the alkaloid*) chinino

quinsy ['kwɪnzi] *s* angina

quintessence [kwɪn'tɛsəns] *s* quintessenza

quintet [kwɪn'tɛt] *s* quintetto

quintuplet [kwɪn'tjuplet] or [kwɪn'tuplet] *s* gemello nato da un parto quintuplice

quip [kwɪp] *s* frizzo, uscita ǁ *v* (*pret* & *pp* **quipped**; *ger* **quipping**) *tr* & *intr* uscire a dire, dire come battuta

quire [kwaɪr] *s* ventiquattro fogli; (bb) quinterno

quirk [kwʌrk] *s* stranezza, manierismo; (*quibble*) cavillo; (*sudden turn*) mutamento improvviso

quit [kwɪt] *adj* libero; **to be quits** esser pari; **to call it quits** finirla, farla finita ǁ *v* (*pret* & *pp* **quit** or **quitted**; *ger* **quitting**) *tr* abbandonare ǁ *intr* andarsene; abbandonare l'impiego; smettere (di + *inf*)

quite [kwaɪt] *adv* completamente, molto, del tutto

quitter ['kwɪtər] *s* persona che abbandona facilmente

quiver ['kwɪvər] *s* fremito; (*to hold arrows*) faretra, turcasso ǁ *intr* fremere, tremare

quixotic [kwɪks'ɑtɪk] *adj* donchisciottesco

quiz [kwɪz] *s* (**quizzes**) esame *m*; interrogatorio ǁ *v* (*pret* & *pp* **quizzed**; *ger* **quizzing**) *tr* esaminare; interrogare

quiz' game' *s* quiz

quiz' pro'gram *s* programma *m* di quiz

quiz' sec'tion *s* (educ) classe *f* a base di esercizi (e non di conferenze)

quizzical ['kwɪzɪkəl] *adj* strano, curioso; (*derisive*) canzonatore

quoin [kɔɪn] or [kwɔɪn] *s* cantone *m*,

pietra angolare; (*piece of wood*) zeppa; (typ) serraforme *m* || *tr* fissare con serraforme

quoit ['kwɔɪt] *or* ['kɔɪt] *s* anello di corda o di metallo da lanciarsi come gioco; **quoits** *ssg* gioco consistente nel lancio di anelli su di un piolo

quondam ['kwɑndæm] *adj* quondam

quorum ['kwɔrəm] *s* quorum *m*

quota ['kwotə] *s* (*share*) quota; (*of imports*) contingentamento; (*of persons*) contingente *m*

quotation [kwo'teʃən] *s* (*from a book*) citazione; (*of prices*) quotazione

quota'tion mark' *s* doppia virgola, virgoletta

quote [kwot] *s* citazione, richiamo || *tr & intr* citare, richiamare; (com) quotare; **quote cito**

quotient ['kwoʃənt] *s* quoziente *m*

R

R, r [ɑr] *s* diciottesima lettera dell'alfabeto inglese

rabbet ['ræbɪt] *s* scanalatura, incastro || *tr* scanalare, incastrare

rab·bi ['ræbaɪ] *s* (-bis) rabbino

rabbit ['ræbɪt] *s* coniglio

rab'bit ears' *spl* (telv) doppia antenna a stilo

rabble ['ræbəl] *s* gentaglia, marmaglia

rab'ble-rous'er ['rauzər] *s* arruffapopoli *m*

rabies ['rebiz] *or* ['rebɪˌiz] *s* rabbia

raccoon [ræ'kun] *s* procione *m*

race [res] *s* (*branch of human stock*) razza; (*contest in speed*) corsa; (*contest of any kind*) gara; (*channel*) canale *m* di adduzione || *tr* far correre; gareggiare (in velocità) con; (*a motor*) imballare || *intr* correre; fare le corse; (*said of a motor*) imballarsi; (naut) fare le regate

race' horse' *s* cavallo da corsa

race' ri'ot *s* contestazione di razza

race' track' *s* pista

racial ['reʃəl] *adj* razziale

rac'ing car' *s* automobile *f* da corsa

rack [ræk] *s* (*to hang clothes*) attaccapanni *m*; (*framework to hold fodder, baggage, guns, etc.*) rastrelliera; (mach) cremagliera; **to go to rack and ruin** andare a rotoli || *tr* tormentare, torturare; **to rack off** (*wine*) travasare; **to rack one's brains** rompersi il capo, lambiccarsi il cervello

racket ['rækɪt] *s* racchetta; (*noise*) chiasso, gazzarra; (coll) racket *m*; **to raise a racket** fare gazzarra

racketeer [ˌrækɪ'tɪr] *s* chi è nel racket; (*engaged in extortion*) ricattatore *m* || *intr* essere nel racket; fare il ricattatore

rack' rail'way *s* ferrovia a cremagliera

rac·y ['resi] *adj* (-ier; -iest) pungente, vigoroso; piccante

radar ['redɑr] *s* radar *m*

radiant ['redɪ·ənt] *adj* raggiante, radioso

radiate ['redɪˌet] *tr* irradiare || *intr* irradiarsi

radiation [ˌredɪ'eʃən] *s* radiazione

radia'tion sick'ness *s* malattia causata da radiazione atomica

radiator ['redɪˌetər] *s* radiatore *m*

ra'diator cap' *s* tappo del radiatore

radical ['rædɪkəl] *adj* radicale || *s*

radicale *mf*; (chem, math) radicale

radi·o ['redɪˌo] *s* (-os) radio *f*; radiogramma *m* || *tr* radiotrasmettere

radioactive [ˌredɪ·o'æktɪv] *adj* radioattivo

ra'dio am'ateur *s* radioamatore *m*

ra'dio announc'er *s* radioannunciatore *m*

ra'dio bea'con *s* radiofaro

ra'dio·broad'cast *s* radiodiffusione || *tr* radiodiffondere

ra'dio com'pass *s* radiobussola

ra'dio·fre'quency *s* radiofrequenza

ra'dio lis'tener *s* radioascoltatore *m*

radiology [ˌredɪ'ɑlədʒɪ] *s* radiologia

ra'dio news'caster *s* radiocronista *mf*

ra'dio·pho'to *s* (-tos) (coll) radiofoto *f*

ra'dio set' *s* radioricevente *f*

ra'dio sta'tion *s* stazione radio

radish ['rædɪʃ] *s* ravanello

radium ['redɪ·əm] *s* radio

radi·us ['redɪ·əs] *s* (-i [ˌaɪ] *or* -uses) (anat) radio; (fig, geom) raggio; **within a radius of** entro un raggio di

raffle ['ræfəl] *s* riffa || *tr* sorteggiare

raft [ræft] *or* [rɑft] *s* zattera; (coll) mucchio

rafter ['ræftər] *or* ['rɑftər] *s* puntone *m*

rag [ræg] *s* straccio; **to chew the rag** (slang) chiacchierare

ragamuffin ['rægəˌmʌfɪn] *s* straccione *m*

rag' doll' *s* bambola di pezza

rage [redʒ] *s* rabbia; **to be all the rage** furoreggiare; **to fly into a rage** montare in bestia || *intr* infuriare

ragged ['rægɪd] *adj* cencioso; (*torn*) stracciato; (*edge*) rozzo, scabroso

ragpicker ['rægˌpɪkər] *s* cenciaiolo, straccivendolo

rag'weed' *s* (bot) ambrosia

raid [red] *s* irruzione, razzia || *tr* scorrere || *intr* scorrazzare

rail [rel] *s* (*of fence*) stecca, traversa; (*fence*) stecconata; (*railing*) ringhiera; (rr) rotaia; **by rail** per ferrovia; **rails** titoli *mpl* ferroviari || *intr* inveire; **to rail at** inveire contro

rail'car' *s* automotrice *f*

rail' fence' *s* stecconata fatta di traverse piallate alla buona

rail'head' s fine f della linea ferroviaria

railing ['reɪɪŋ] s ringhiera

rail'road' adj ferroviario || s ferrovia || tr trasportare in ferrovia; (a bill) far passare precipitosamente; (coll) imprigionare falsamente

rail'road cros'sing s passaggio a livello

rail'road'er s ferroviere m

rail'way' s ferrovia, strada ferrata

raiment ['remənt] s (lit) abbigliamento

rain [ren] s pioggia; **rain or shine** con qualunque tempo || tr fare piovere; (lit) piovere; **to rain cats and dogs** piovere a catinelle; **to rain out** far sospendere per via della pioggia || intr piovere

rainbow ['ren,bo] s arcobaleno

rain'coat' s impermeabile m

rain'fall' s acquazzone m; piovosità f

rain·y ['reni] adj (-ier; -iest) piovoso, piovano

rain'y day' s giorno piovoso; (fig) tempi mpl difficili

raise [rez] s aumento || tr levare, rialzare; (children, animals) allevare; (to build) tirare su; (a question) sollevare; (the dead) risollevare; (to increase) aumentare; (money) raccogliere; (a siege) togliere; (at cards) rilanciare; (anchor) salpare; (math) elevare

raisin ['rezən] s grano d'uva passa, grano d'uva secca; **raisins** uva passa, uva secca

rake [rek] s rastrello; (person) porcaccione m, libertino || tr rastrellare; **to rake in money** far soldoni

rake'-off' s (coll) compenso illecito, bustarella; (coll) sconto

rakish ['rekɪʃ] adj libertino; brioso, vivace; **to wear one's hat at a rakish angle** portare il cappello sulle ventitré

ral·ly ['ræli] s (-lies) riunione, comizio; adunata; ricupero || v (pret & pp -lied) tr riunire, chiamare a raccolta; rianimare || intr riunirsi; rianimarsi; (said of stock prices) rialzarsi; rimettersi in forze; **to rally to the side of** correre all'aiuto di

ram [ræm] s (male sheep) montone m; (mil) ariete m; (nav) sperone m; (mach) maglio del battipalo || v (pret & pp rammed; ger ramming) tr battere, sbattere contro; cacciare, conficcare; forzare; (nav) speronare || intr—**to ram into** sbattere contro

ramble ['ræmbəl] s girata || intr (to wander around) gironzolare; vagare; (said of a vine) crescere disordinatamente; (said, e.g., of a river) serpeggiare; (fig) scorrazzare, divagare

rami·fy ['ræmɪ,faɪ] v (pret & pp -fied) tr ramificare || intr ramificarsi

ram'jet en'gine s statoreattore m

ramp [ræmp] s rampa

rampage ['ræmpedʒ] s stato d'eccitazione; **to go on a rampage** infierire, comportarsi furiosamente

rampart ['ræmpɑrt] s baluardo, muraglione m

ram'rod' s (for ramming) (mil) bacchetta; (for cleaning) (mil) scovolo

ram'shack'le adj cadente, in rovina

ranch [ræntʃ] s fattoria agricola

rancid ['rænsɪd] adj rancido

rancor ['ræŋkər] s rancore m

random ['rændəm] adj fortuito; **at random** alla rinfusa, a casaccio

range [rendʒ] s (row) fila; (rank) classe f; (distance) portata; campo di tiro a segno; raggio d'azione; (scope) gamma; (for grazing) pascolo; (stove) fornello, cucina economica; **within range of** alla portata di || tr allineare; ordinare; passare attraverso; mandare al pascolo || intr variare, fluttuare; estendersi; trovarsi; (mil) portare; **to range over** percorrere; (fig) trattare

range' find'er s telemetro

rank [ræŋk] adj esuberante; grossolano; denso, spesso; puzzolente; eccessivo; completo, assoluto || s rango, grado; (row) fila, schiera; **ranks** truppe fpl, ranghi mpl || tr arrangiare, allineare; classificare; avere rango superiore a || intr avere il massimo rango; **to rank high** avere un'alta posizione; **to rank low** avere una posizione bassa; **to rank with** essere allo stesso livello di

rank' and file' s truppa; massa

rankle ['ræŋkəl] tr irritare || intr inasprirsi

ransack ['rænsæk] tr (to search thoroughly) frugare, rovistare; (to pillage) svaligiare, saccheggiare

ransom ['rænsəm] s taglia, riscatto || tr riscattare

rant [rænt] intr farneticare, parlare a vanvera

rap [ræp] s colpo, colpetto; **I don't care a rap** non m'importa un fico; **to take the rap** (slang) prendersi la colpa || v (pret & pp rapped; ger rapping) tr dare colpi a; battere; **to rap out** (e.g., a command) lanciare || intr dare colpi, bussare

rapacious [rə'peʃəs] adj rapace

rape [rep] s rapimento; (of a woman) stupro; (bot) ravizzone m || tr rapire; forzare, violentare

rapid ['ræpɪd] adj rapido || **rapids** spl rapide fpl

rap'id-fire' adj a tiro rapido

rapidity [rə'pɪdəti] s rapidità f

rapier ['repɪ-ər] s spada, stocco

rapt [ræpt] adj assorto; estatico

rapture ['ræptʃər] s rapimento, estasi f

rare [rer] adj raro; (thinly distributed) rado; (gas) rarefatto; (meat) al sangue; (gem) prezioso

rare'-earth' met'al s metallo delle terre rare

rare·fy ['rerɪ,faɪ] v (pret & pp -fied) tr rarefare || intr rarefarsi

rarely ['rerli] adv di rado, raramente

rascal ['ræskəl] s briccone m, birbante m

rash [ræʃ] adj temerario, precipitato || s eruzione; (fig) mucchio

rasp [ræsp] or [rɑsp] s raspa; rumore

m di raspa || *tr* raspare; irritare; dire con voce roca || *intr* fare rumore raspante

raspber-ry ['ræz ,beri] or ['rɑz ,beri] *s* (-ries) lampone *m;* (slang) pernacchia

rat [ræt] *s* ratto; *(to give fullness to hair)* posticcio; (slang) traditore *m;* **to smell a rat** (coll) subodorare un inganno

ratchet ['ræt/ɪt] *s* nottolino

rate [ret] *s (of interest)* saggio, tasso; prezzo; costo; velocità *f; (degree of action)* ragione; tariffa; **at any rate** ad ogni modo; **at the rate of** in ragione di || *tr* valutare, classificare || *intr* essere considerato; essere classificato

rate' of exchange' *s* corso del cambio

rather ['ræðər] or ['rɑðər] *adv* piuttosto; a preferenza; per meglio dire; bensì; discretamente; **rather than** piuttosto di || *interj* e come!

rati-fy ['rætɪ ,faɪ] *v (pret & pp -fied) tr* ratificare, sancire

rating ['retɪŋ] *s* classifica; (nav) grado; (com) valutazione

ra-tio ['re/o] or ['re/ɪ ,o] *s* (-tios) ragione, rapporto; proporzione

ration ['re/ən] or ['ræ/ən] *s* razione || *tr* razionare

rational ['ræ/ənəl] *adj* razionale

ra'tion book' *s* tessera di razionamento

rat' poi'son *s* veleno per i topi

rat' race' *s* (coll) corsa dei barbieri

rattle ['rætəl] *s (sharp sounds)* fracasso; *(child's toy)* sonaglio; *(noise-making device)* raganella; *(in throat)* rantolo || *tr* scuotere; *(to confuse)* sconcertare; **to rattle off** dire rapidamente, snocciolare || *intr* risuonare; scuotersi; cianciare

rat'tle·snake' *s* serpente *m* a sonagli

rat'trap' *s* trappola per topi; *(hovel)* topaia; *(jam)* (fig) frangente *m*

raucous ['rɔkəs] *adj* rauco

ravage ['rævɪdʒ] *s* distruzione; **ravages** *(of time)* oltraggio || *tr* distruggere, disfare

rave [rev] *intr* farneticare, delirare; infuriare; andare in estasi; **to rave about** levare alle stelle

raven ['revən] *s* corvo

ravenous ['rævənəs] *adj* famelico

ravine [rə'vin] *s* canalone *m*, burrone *m*

ravish ['rævɪ/] *tr* incantare, entusiasmare; rapire; *(a woman)* stuprare

raw [rɔ] *adj* crudo; *(e.g., silk)* grezzo; *(flesh)* vivo; inesperto

raw' deal' *s* trattamento brutale e ingiusto

raw'hide' *s* pelle greggia

raw' mate'rial *s* materia prima

ray [re] *s* raggio; *(fish)* razza

rayon ['re·ɑn] *s* raion *m*

raze [rez] *tr* radere al suolo

razor ['rezər] *s* rasoio

ra'zor blade' *s* lametta

ra'zor strop' *s* coramella

razz [ræz] *s* (slang) pernacchia || *tr* (slang) prendere in giro

reach [rit/] *s* portata; estensione; **out**

of reach (of) fuori della portata (di); oltre alle possibilità (di); fuori tiro (di); **within reach of** alla portata di || *tr* raggiungere; toccare; *(customers)* guadagnare || *intr* estendere la mano; **to reach for** cercare di raggiungere

react [rɪ'ækt] *intr* reagire

reaction [rɪ'æk/ən] *s* reazione

reactionar-y [rɪ'æk/ə ,neri] *adj* reazionario || *s* (-ies) reazionario

reactor [rɪ'æktər] *s* reattore *m*

read [rid] *v (pret & pp* read [red]) *tr* leggere; *(s.o.'s thoughts)* leggere in; **to read over** ripassare || *intr* leggere; saper leggere; essere concepito, e.g., **your cable reads thus** il vostro telegramma è concepito così; leggersi, e.g., **this books reads easily** questo libro si legge facilmente; **to read on** continuare a leggere

reader ['ridər] *s* lettore *m;* libro di lettura, sillabo

readily ['rɛdɪlɪ] *adv* velocemente; facilmente; di buona voglia

reading ['ridɪŋ] *s* lettura; dizione

read'ing desk' *s* leggio

read'ing glass' *s* lente *f* d'ingrandimento; **reading glasses** occhiali *mpl* per la lettura

read'ing lamp' *s* lampada da scrittoio

read'ing room' *s* sala di lettura

read·y ['rɛdi] *adj (-ier; -iest)* pronto; disponibile; **to make ready** preparare; prepararsi || *v (pret & pp -ied) tr* preparare || *intr* prepararsi

read'y cash' *s* denaro contante

read'y-made cloth'ing *s* confezioni *fpl*

read'y-made suit' *s* vestito già fatto

reaffirm [,ri·ə'fʌrm] *tr* riaffermare

reagent [rɪ'edʒənt] *s* reagente *m*

real ['ri·əl] *adj* effettivo, reale

re'al estate' *s* beni *mpl* immobili, proprietà *f* immobiliare

re'al-estate' *adj* immobiliare, fondiario

realism ['ri·ə ,lɪzəm] *s* realismo

realist ['ri·əlɪst] *s* realista *mf*

realistic [,ri·ə'lɪstɪk] *adj* realistico

reali-ty [rɪ'ælɪti] *s* (-ties) realtà *f*

realize ['ri·ə ,laɪz] *tr* rendersi conto di; concretare; realizzare || *intr* convertire proprietà in contanti

realm [rɛlm] *s* regno

realtor ['ri·əl ,tɔr] or ['ri·əltər] *s* (trademark) agente *m* d'immobili membro dell'associazione nazionale

realty ['ri·əltɪ] *s* proprietà *f* immobiliare

ream [rim] *s* risma; **reams** pagine *fpl* e pagine || *tr* alesare

reamer ['rimər] *s* (mach) alesatore *m;* (dentistry) fresa

reap [rip] *tr & intr (to cut)* mietere; *(to gather)* raccogliere

reaper ['ripər] *s (person)* mietitore *m;* (mach) mietitrice *f*

reappear [,ri·ə'pɪr] *intr* ricomparire, riapparire

reappearance [,ri·ə'pɪrəns] *s* riapparizione, ricomparsa

reapportion [,ri·ə'por/ənmənt] *s* ridistribuzione

rear [rɪr] *adj* posteriore, di dietro || *s*

retro, di dietro; posteriore *m*; (mil) retroguardia ‖ *tr* alzare, elevare; allevare, educare ‖ *intr* (*said of a horse*) impennarsi

rear′ ad′miral *s* contrammiraglio

rear′ drive′ *s* trazione posteriore

rear′ end′ *s* retro, di dietro; (coll) posteriore *m*; (aut) retrotreno

rearmament [ri′ɑrməmənt] *s* riarmo

rear′-view mir′ror *s* specchietto retrovisivo

rear′ win′dow *s* (aut) lunetta posteriore

reason [′rizən] *s* ragione; **by reason of** per causa di; **to bring s.o. to reason** indurre qlcu alla ragione; **to stand to reason** esser logico ‖ *tr & intr* ragionare

reasonable [′rizənəbəl] *adj* ragionevole

reassessment [,ri·ə′sesmənt] *s* rivalutazione

reassure [,ri·ə′ʃur] *tr* rassicurare, riassicurare

reawaken [,ri·ə′wekən] *tr* risvegliare ‖ *intr* risvegliarsi

rebate [′ribet] or [ri′bet] *s* ribasso ‖ *tr* ribassare

rebel [′rebəl] *adj & s* ribelle *mf* ‖ **re-bel** [ri′bel] *v* (*pret & pp* **-belled;** *ger* **-belling**) *intr* ribellarsi

rebellion [ri′beljən] *s* ribellione

rebellious [ri′beljəs] *adj* ribelle

re-bind [ri′baɪnd] *v* (*pret & pp* **bound** [′baʊnd]) *tr* rifasciare; (bb) rilegare

rebirth [′ribʌrθ] or [ri′bʌrθ] *s* rinascita

rebore [ri′bor] *tr* rialesare, rettificare

rebound [′ri,baʊnd] or [ri′baʊnd] *s* rimbalzo ‖ [ri′baʊnd] *intr* rimbalzare

rebroad′casting sta′tion *s* stazione ripetitrice

rebuff [rɪ-′bʌf] *s* rifiuto ‖ *tr* respingere, rifiutare

rebuild [ri′bɪld] *v* (*pret & pp* **-built** [′bɪlt]) *tr* ricostruire, riedificare

rebuke [ri′bjuk] *s* rabbuffo ‖ *tr* rabbuffare

re-but [ri′bʌt] *v* (*pret & pp* **-butted;** *ger* **-butting**) *tr* confutare

rebuttal [ri′bʌtəl] *s* confutazione

recall [ri′kɔl] or [′rikɔl] *s* richiamo; revoca ‖ [ri′kɔl] *tr* richiamare; ricordare, ricordarsi di; richiamare alla memoria

recant [ri′kænt] *tr* ritrattare ‖ *intr* ritrattarsi

re-cap [′ri,kæp] or [ri′kæp] *v* (*pret & pp* **-capped;** *ger* **-capping**) *tr* ricapitolare, riepilogare; (*a tire*) rifare il battistrada a

recapitulation [,rikə,pɪtʃə′leʃən] *s* ricapitolazione, riepilogo

re-cast [′ri,kæst] or [ri′kʌst] *s* rifusione ‖ [ri′kæst] or [ri′kʌst] *v* (*pret & pp* **-cast**) *tr* rifondere

recede [ri′sid] *intr* ritirarsi, allontanarsi; recedere, retrocedere; (*said, e.g., of chin*) sfuggire

receipt [ri′sit] *s* ricevimento; (*acknowledgment of payment*) ricevuta; (*recipe*) ricetta; **receipts** incasso, introito ‖ *tr* quietanzare

receive [ri′siv] *tr* ricevere; (*stolen goods*) ricettare; (*to have inflicted upon one*) subire ‖ *intr* ricevere

receiver [ri′sivər] *s* ricevitore *m;* ricettatore *m;* (law) curatore *m* fallimentare; (telp) auricolare *m*

receiv′ing set′ *s* apparecchio radioricevente

receiv′ing tell′er *s* cassiere *m* incaricato delle riscossioni

recent [′risənt] *adj* recente

recently [′risəntli] *adv* recentemente, di recente

receptacle [ri′septəkəl] *s* recipiente *m;* (elec) presa

reception [ri′sepʃən] *s* accoglienza; (*function*) ricevimento

recep′tion desk′ *s* ufficio informazioni, bureau *m*

receptionist [ri′sepʃnɪst] *s* accoglitrice *f;* (*male*) usciere *m*

receptive [ri′septɪv] *adj* ricettivo

recess [ri′ses] or [′rises] *s* intermezzo, interludio; ora di ricreazione; (*in a line*) rientranza; (*in a wall*) nicchia, alcova; (fig) recesso ‖ [ri′ses] *tr* aggiornare, dare vacanza a; incassare, mettere in una nicchia ‖ *intr* aggiornarsi, prendersi vacanza

recession [ri′seʃən] *s* ritirata; processione finale; (com) recessione

recipe [′resɪ,pi] *s* ricetta

reciprocal [ri′sɪprəkəl] *adj* reciproco

reciprocity [,resɪ′prɑsɪti] *s* reciprocità *f*

recital [ri′saɪtəl] *s* narrazione; (*of music or poetry*) recital *m*

recite [ri′saɪt] *tr* raccontare; (*music or poetry*) recitare

reckless [′reklɪs] *adj* temerario, spericolato

reckon [′rekən] *tr* calcolare; considerare; (coll) supporre ‖ *intr* contare; **to reckon with** prevedere, tener conto di

reclaim [ri′klem] *tr* (*land*) sanare, prosciugare; (*substances*) rigenerare; (fig) rigenerare

recline [ri′klaɪn] *tr* reclinare ‖ *intr* reclinarsi, adagiarsi

recluse [ri′klus] or [′reklus] *adj & s* recluso

recognition [,rekəg′nɪʃən] *s* riconoscimento

recognize [′rekəg,naɪz] *tr* riconoscere

recoil [ri′kɔɪl] *s* indietreggiamento; (*of a firearm*) rinculo ‖ *intr* indietreggiare; rinculare

recollect [,rekə′lekt] *tr & intr* ricordare

recollection [,rekə′lekʃən] *s* ricordo

recommend [,rekə′mend] *tr* raccomandare

recompense [′rekəm,pens] *s* ricompensa ‖ *tr* ricompensare

reconcile [′rekən,saɪl] *tr* riconciliare; **to reconcile oneself** rassegnarsi

reconnaissance [ri′kɑnɪsəns] *s* ricognizione

reconnoiter [,rekə′nɔɪtər] or [,rikə′nɔɪtər] *tr & intr* perlustrare

reconsider [,rikən′sɪdər] *tr* riconsiderare

reconstruct [ˌrikən'strʌkt] *tr* ricostruire

reconversion [ˌrikən'vʌrʒən] *s* riconversione

record ['rɛkərd] *s* registrazione; annotazione; (*official report*) verbale *m*, protocollo; (*criminal*) fedina sporca; (*of a phonograph*) disco; (*educ*) documenti *mpl* scolastici; (*sports*) record *m*, primato; **off the record** confidenziale; confidenzialmente; **records** annali *mpl*, documenti *mpl*; **to break a record** battere un record || [rɪ'kɔrd] *tr* registrare; mettere a verbale; (*e.g., a song*) incidere

rec'ord break'er *s* (sports) primatista *mf*

rec'ord chang'er ['tʃendʒər] *s* cambiadischi *m*

recorder [rɪ'kɔrdər] *s* (*apparatus*) registratore *m;* (law) cancelliere *m;* (mus) flauto a imboccatura a tubo

rec'ord hold'er *s* (sports) primatista *mf*

recording [rɪ'kɔrdɪŋ] *s* registrazione; (*of a record*) incisione; (*record*) disco

record'ing sec'retary *s* cancelliere *m*

rec'ord play'er *s* giradischi *m*

recount ['ri,kaunt] *s* nuovo conteggio || [ri'kaunt] *tr* (*to count again*) ricontare || [rɪ'kaunt] *tr* (*to narrate*) raccontare

recourse [rɪ'kors] or ['rikors] *s* ricorso; (com) rivalsa; **to have recourse to** ricorrere a

recover [rɪ'kʌvər] *tr* ricuperare, riacquistare; (*a substance*) rigenerare; **to recover consciousness** riaversi, riprendere conoscenza || *intr* rimettersi; guadagnare una causa

recover·y [rɪ'kʌvəri] *s* (-ies) ricupero; guarigione; **past recovery** incurabile

recreant ['rɛkri·ənt] *adj & s* codardo; traditore *m*

recreation [ˌrɛkri'eʃən] *s* ricreazione

recruit [rɪ'krut] *s* recluta || *tr & intr* reclutare

rectangle ['rɛk,tæŋgəl] *s* rettangolo

rectifier ['rɛktə,faɪ·ər] *s* rettificatore *m;* (elec) raddrizzatore *m*

recti·fy ['rɛktɪ,faɪ] *v* (*pret & pp* -fied) *tr* rettificare; (elec) raddrizzare

rectitude ['rɛktɪ,tud] or ['rɛktɪ,tjud] *s* rettitudine *f*

rec·tum ['rɛktəm] *s* (-tums or -ta [tə]) retto

recumbent [rɪ'kʌmbənt] *adj* sdraiato

recuperate [rɪ'kjupə,ret] *tr* ricuperare || *intr* ristabilirsi, rimettersi

re·cur [rɪ'kʌr] *v* (*pret & pp* -curred; *ger* -curring) *intr* ricorrere; ritornare; tornare a mente

recurrent [rɪ'kʌrənt] *adj* ricorrente

recycle [ri'saɪkəl] *tr* riconvertire; (*e.g., in chemical industry*) riciclare

red [rɛd] *adj* (redder; reddest) rosso || *s* rosso; **in the red** in debito , in rosso || **Red** *adj & s* (*Communist*) rosso

red'bait' *tr* dare del comunista a

red'bird' *s* cardinale *m*

red-blooded ['rɛd ,blʌdɪd] *adj* sanguigno; vigoroso

red'breast' *s* pettirosso

red'bud' *s* siliquastro

red'cap' *s* (Brit) poliziotto militare; (U.S.A.) facchino

red' cell' *s* globulo rosso

red' cent' *s*—**to not have a red cent** (coll) non avere il becco di un quattrino

Red' Cross' *s* Croce Rossa

redden ['rɛdən] *tr* arrossare || *intr* arrossire

redeem [rɪ'dim] *tr* redimere; (*a promise*) disimpegnare

redeemer [rɪ'dimər] *s* redentore *m*

redemption [rɪ'dɛmpʃən] *s* redenzione; disimpegno

red-handed ['rɛd'hændɪd] *adj*—**to be caught red-handed** esser colto sul fatto or con le mani nel sacco

red'head' *s* persona dai capelli rossi

red' her'ring *s* argomento usato per sviare l'attenzione; aringa affumicata

red'-hot' *adj* rovente, incandescente; fresco fresco, appena uscito

rediscover [ˌridɪs'kʌvər] *tr* riscoprire

red'-let'ter *adj* memorabile

red'-light' dis'trict *s* quartiere *m* delle case di tolleranza

red' man' *s* pellerossa *m*

re·do ['ri'du] *v* (*pret* -did ['dɪd]; *pp* -done ['dʌn]) *tr* rifare

redolent ['rɛdələnt] *adj* fragrante, profumato; **redolent of** che sa di

redoubt [rɪ'daut] *s* (mil) ridotta

redound [rɪ'daund] *intr* ridondare

red' pep'per *s* pepe *m* di Caienna

redress [rɪ'drɛs] or ['ridrɛs] *s* riparazione, risarcimento || [rɪ'drɛs] *tr* riparare, risarcire

red'skin' *s* pellerossa *mf*

red' tape' *s* trafila, burocrazia

reduce [rɪ'djus] or [rɪ'dus] *tr* ridurre; diluire; (mil) retrocedere; (*a hernia*) (surg) sbrigliare || *intr* ridursi; (*to lose weight*) dimagrire

reducing [rɪ'djusɪŋ] or [rɪ'dusɪŋ] *adj* dimagrante; (chem) riducente

reduction [rɪ'dʌkʃən] *s* riduzione

redundant [rɪ'dʌndənt] *adj* ridondante

red'wood' *s* sequoia

reed [rid] *s* (*stalk*) calamo; (*plant*) canna; (mus) linguetta; (mus) strumento a linguetta

reedit [ri'ɛdɪt] *tr* rifondere

reef [rif] *s* scoglio, barriera; (naut) terzarolo; (min) vena, filone *m* || *tr* (*sail*) imbrogliare

reefer ['rifər] *s* giacchetta a doppio petto; (slang) sigaretta di marijuana

reek [rik] *intr* puzzare; sudare, evaporare, fumare

reel [ril] *s* (*spool*) bobina; (*sway*) vacillamento; (*for fishing*) mulinello; **off the reel** senza esitazione || *tr* bobinare; **to reel off** rifilare || *intr* barcollare

reelection [ˌri·ɪ'lɛkʃən] *s* rielezione

reenlist [ˌ ri·ɛn'lɪst] *tr* arruolare di nuovo || *intr* arruolarsi di nuovo

reen·try [rɪ'ɛntri] *s* (-tries) rientro

reexamination [ˌri·ɛg ,zæmɪ'neʃən] *s* riesame *m*

re•fer [rɪ'fʌr] v (pret & pp **-ferred;** ger **-ferring**) tr riferire ‖ intr riferirsi

referee [ˌrefə'ri] s arbitro ‖ tr & intr arbitrare

reference ['refərəns] s riferimento; (testimonial) referenza; (e.g., in a book) rinvio, rimando

ref'erence book' s libro di consultazione

referen•dum [ˌrefə'rendəm] s (**-dums** or **-da** [də]) referendum m

refill ['rɪfɪl] s ricambio ‖ [rɪ'fɪl] tr riempire di nuovo

refine [rɪ'faɪn] tr raffinare

refinement [rɪ'faɪnmənt] s raffinatezza; (of oil) raffinatura

refiner•y [rɪ'faɪnərɪ] s (**-ies**) raffineria

reflect [rɪ'flɛkt] tr riflettere ‖ intr riflettere, riflettersi

reflection [rɪ'flɛkʃən] s riflessione

reflex ['rifleks] adj riflesso ‖ s riflesso; (camera) reflex m

reflexive [rɪ'fleksɪv] adj riflessivo

reforestation [ˌrifarɪs'teʃən] or [ˌriˌfarɪs'teʃən] s rimboschimento

reform [rɪ'fɔrm] s riforma ‖ tr riformare ‖ intr correggersi

reformation [ˌrefər'meʃən] s riforma ‖ **Reformation** s—**the Reformation** la Riforma

reformato•ry [rɪ'fɔrməˌtorɪ] adj riformativo ‖ s (**-ries**) riformatorio

reformer [rɪ'fɔrmər] s riformatore m

reform' school' s riformatorio

refraction [rɪ'frækʃən] s rifrazione

refrain [rɪ'fren] s ritornello, intercalare m ‖ intr astenersi

refresh [rɪ'freʃ] tr rinfrescare; ristorare ‖ intr ristorarsi

refreshing [rɪ'freʃɪŋ] adj rinfrescante; ristoratore; ricreativo

refreshment [rɪ'freʃmənt] s rinfresco

refrigerate [rɪ'frɪdʒəˌret] tr refrigerare

refrigerator [rɪ'frɪdʒəˌretər] s refrigerante m, frigorifero

refrig'erator car' s vagone frigorifero

re•fuel [ri'fjul] v (pret & pp **-fueled** or **-fuelled;** ger **-fueling** or **-fuelling**) tr rifornire di carburante ‖ intr rifornirsi di carburante

refuge ['refjudʒ] s rifugio; scampo; **to take refuge (in)** rifugiarsi (in)

refugee [ˌrefju'dʒi] s rifugiato

refund ['rifʌnd] s rifusione ‖ [rɪ'fʌnd] tr (to repay) rifondere ‖ [ri'fʌnd] (bonds) consolidare; (to fund anew) rifondere

refurnish [ri'fʌrnɪʃ] tr riammobiliare

refusal [rɪ'fjuzəl] s rifiuto

refuse ['refjus] s rifiuto, spazzatura ‖ [rɪ'fjuz] tr rifiutare; **to refuse to** rifiutarsi di

refute [rɪ'fjut] tr smentire, confutare

regain [rɪ'gen] tr riguadagnare; **to regain consciousness** tornare in sé

regal ['rigəl] adj reale, regale

regale [rɪ'gel] tr intrattenere, rallegrare

regalia [rɪ'gelɪ•ə] spl (of royalty) prerogative fpl reali; alta uniforme

regard [rɪ'gɑrd] s riguardo; (look)

sguardo; (esteem) rispetto; **in regard to** rispetto a; **regards** rispetti mpl; **warm regards** cordiali saluti mpl; **without regard to** senza considerare ‖ tr considerare; osservare; concernere; **as regards** per quanto concerne

regarding [rɪ'gɑrdɪŋ] prep per quanto concerne

regardless [rɪ'gɑrdlɪs] adj incurante ‖ adv ciò nonostante; costi quello che costi; **regardless of** malgrado

regatta [rɪ'gætə] s regata

regen•cy ['ridʒənsɪ] s (**-cies**) reggenza

regenerate [rɪ'dʒenəˌret] tr rigenerare ‖ intr rigenerarsi

regent ['ridʒənt] s reggente mf

regicide ['redʒɪˌsaɪd] s (act) regicidio; (person) regicida mf

regiment ['redʒɪmənt] s reggimento ‖ ['redʒɪˌment] tr irregimentare

regimental [ˌredʒɪ'mentəl] adj reggimentale ‖ **regimentals** spl uniforme f reggimentale

region ['ridʒən] s regione

register ['redʒɪstər] s registro; (for controlling the flow of air) regolatore m dell'aria ‖ tr registrare; (e.g., a student) iscrivere; (e.g., anger) dimostrare; (a letter) raccomandare ‖ intr registrarsi; iscriversi; fare impressione

reg'istered let'ter s raccomandata

reg'istered nurse' s infermiera diplomata

registrar ['redʒɪsˌtrɑr] s registratore m, archivista mf; (of deeds) ricevitore m

registration [ˌredʒɪs'treʃən] s registrazione; (e.g., of a student) iscrizione; (of mail) raccomandazione

registra'tion fee' s diritto di segreteria

re•gret [rɪ'gret] s pentimento, rammarico; **regrets** scuse fpl ‖ v (pret & pp **-gretted;** ger **-gretting**) tr rimpiangere; **to regret to** essere spiacente di

regrettable [rɪ'gretəbəl] adj deplorevole

regular ['regjələr] adj regolare; (life) regolato; (coll) vero ‖ s cliente m abituale; (mil) effettivo

regularity [ˌregju'lerɪtɪ] s regolarità f

regularize ['regjələˌraɪz] tr regolarizzare

regulate ['regjəˌlet] tr regolare

regulation [ˌregjə'leʃən] s regolazione; (rule) regolamento

rehabilitate [ˌrihə'bɪlɪˌtet] tr riabilitare

rehearsal [rɪ'hʌrsəl] s prova

rehearse [rɪ'hʌrs] tr provare ‖ intr fare le prove

rehiring [ri'haɪrɪŋ] s riassunzione

reign [ren] s regno ‖ intr regnare

reimburse [ˌri•ɪm'bʌrs] tr rimborsare

rein [ren] s redine f; **to give full rein to** dare briglia sciolta a ‖ tr guidare con le redini; frenare

reincarnation [ˌri•ɪnkɑr'neʃən] s reincarnazione

reindeer ['renˌdɪr] s renna

reinforce [ˌri•ɪn'fors] tr rinforzare; (a wall) armare

re'inforced con'crete s cemento armato

reinforcement [ˌriˑɪnˈforsmənt] *s* rinforzo

reinstate [ˌriˑɪnˈstet] *tr* reintegrare

reiterate [riˈɪtəˌret] *tr* reiterare

reject [ˈridʒekt] *s* rigetto, rifiuto; **rejects** scarti *mpl* ‖ [rɪˈdʒekt] *tr* rigettare; (*to refuse*) rifiutare

rejection [rɪˈdʒekʃən] *s* rigetto; rifiuto

rejoice [rɪˈdʒɔɪs] *intr* rallegrarsi

rejoin [rɪˈdʒɔɪn] *tr* raggiungere; (*to reunite*) riunire; (*to reply*) rispondere

rejoinder [rɪˈdʒɔɪndər] *s* risposta; (*law*) controreplica

rejuvenation [rɪˌdʒuviˈneʃən] *s* ringiovanimento

rekindle [riˈkɪndəl] *tr* riaccendere

relapse [rɪˈlæps] *s* ricaduta ‖ *intr* ricadere

relate [rɪˈlet] *tr* mettere in relazione; (*to tell*) narrare

relation [rɪˈleʃən] *s* relazione; (*account*) resoconto; (*relative*) parente *mf*; (*kinship*) parentela; **in relation to** or **with** in relazione a

relationship [rɪˈleʃənˌʃɪp] *s* rapporto, relazione; (*kinship*) parentela

relative [ˈrelətɪv] *adj* relativo ‖ *s* congiunto, parente *mf*

relativity [ˌreləˈtɪvɪti] *s* relatività *f*

relax [rɪˈlæks] *tr* rilasciare, rilassare ‖ *intr* rilasciarsi, rilassarsi

relaxation [ˌrilæksˈeʃən] *s* distensione; (*entertainment*) ricreazione

relaxaˈtion of tenˈsion *s* distensione

relaxing [rɪˈlæksɪŋ] *adj* rilassante; divertente

relay [ˈrile] or [rɪˈle] *s* (elec) relè *m*; (rad) ripetitore *m*; (mil, sports) staffetta; (sports) corsa a staffetta ‖ *v* (*pret & pp* -layed) *tr* trasmettere, ritrasmettere ‖ [rɪˈle] *v* (*pret & pp* -laid) *tr* rimettere, porre di nuovo

reˈlay race *s* corsa a staffetta

release [rɪˈlis] *s* (*e.g., from jail*) liberazione; (*from obligation*) disimpegno; (*for publication*) autorizzazione; (mov) distribuzione; (journ) comunicato; (aer) lancio; (mach) scappamento ‖ *tr* liberare; disimpegnare; autorizzare la pubblicazione di; (mov) distribuire; (*a bomb*) (aer) lanciare; **to release s.o. from a debt** rimettere un debito a qlcu

relent [rɪˈlent] *intr* placarsi

relentless [rɪˈlentlɪs] *adj* implacabile

relevant [ˈrelɪvənt] *adj* pertinente

reliable [rɪˈlaɪˑəbəl] *adj* (*person*) fidato; (*source*) attendibile

reliance [rɪˈlaɪˑəns] *s* fiducia, fede *f*

relic [ˈrelɪk] *s* reliquia

relief [rɪˈlif] *s* sollievo; sussidio; (*prominence; projection*) rilievo; (mil) cambio; **in relief** in rilievo; **on relief** sotto sussidio

relieve [rɪˈliv] *tr* (*e.g., pain*) alleviare; (*e.g., a load*) sgravare; (mil) rilevare

religion [rɪˈlɪdʒən] *s* religione

religious [rɪˈlɪdʒəs] *adj* religioso

relinquish [rɪˈlɪŋkwɪʃ] *tr* abbandonare

relish [ˈrelɪʃ] *s* piacere *m*, gusto; sapore *m*, aroma *m*; (culin) condimento ‖ *tr* gustare, apprezzare; dare gusto a

reluctance [rɪˈlʌktəns] *s* riluttanza

reluctant [rɪˈlʌktənt] *adj* riluttante

reˑly [rɪˈlaɪ] *v* (*pret & pp* -lied) *intr* fare assegnamento; **to rely on** fidarsi di, fondarsi su

remain [rɪˈmen] *s*—**remains** resti *mpl*; resti *mpl* mortali ‖ *intr* restare, rimanere

remainder [rɪˈmendər] *s* resto, restante *m*; (*unsold books*) fondi *mpl* di libreria ‖ *tr* vendere come rimanenza

reˑmake [riˈmek] *v* (*pret & pp* -made [ˈmed]) *tr* rifare

remark [rɪˈmɑrk] *s* osservazione, rimarco ‖ *tr & intr* osservare; **to remark on** fare osservazioni su

remarkable [rɪˈmɑrkəbəl] *adj* notevole

remarˑry [rɪˈmæri] *v* (*pret & pp* -ried) *intr* riprendere moglie, risposarsi

remeˑdy [ˈremɪdi] *s* (-dies) rimedio ‖ *v* (*pret & pp* -died) *tr* rimediare (with *dat*)

remember [rɪˈmembər] *tr* ricordarsi di; (*to send greetings to*) ricordare ‖ *intr* ricordare, ricordarsi

remembrance [rɪˈmembrəns] *s* rimembranza, ricordo

remind [rɪˈmaɪnd] *tr* rammentare

reminder [rɪˈmaɪndər] *s* promemoria

reminisce [ˌremɪˈnɪs] *intr* ricordare il passato

reminiscence [ˌremɪˈnɪsəns] *s* reminiscenza

remiss [rɪˈmɪs] *adj* negligente

reˑmit [rɪˈmɪt] *v* (*pret & pp* -mitted; *ger* -mitting) *tr* rimettere; (*to a lower court*) (law) rinviare

remittance [rɪˈmɪtəns] *s* rimessa

remnant [ˈremnənt] *s* (*remaining quantity*) rimanente *m*; (*of cloth*) scampolo; vestigio; **remnants** (*of merchandise*) rimanenze *fpl*, fondi *mpl* di magazzino

remodˑel [riˈmɑdəl] *v* (*pret & pp* -eled or -elled; *ger* -eling or -elling) *tr* rimodellare; ricostruire

remonstrance [rɪˈmɑnstrəns] *s* rimostranza

remonstrate [rɪˈmɑnstret] *intr* protestare, rimostrare; **to remonstrate with** rimostrare a

remorse [rɪˈmɔrs] *s* rimorso

remorseful [rɪˈmɔrsfəl] *adj* tormentato dal rimorso, pentito

remote [rɪˈmot] *adj* remoto

remoteˈ controlˈ *s* telecomando

removable [rɪˈmuvəbəl] *adj* amovibile

removal [rɪˈmuvəl] *s* rimozione; trasferimento; (*dismissal*) destituzione

remove [rɪˈmuv] *tr* rimuovere; (*one's jacket*) togliersi, cavarsi; (*from office*) destituire; eliminare ‖ *intr* trasferirsi; andarsene

remuneration [rɪˌmjunəˈreʃən] *s* rimunerazione

renaissance [ˌrenəˈsɑns] or [rɪˈnesəns] *s* rinascimento, rinascita ‖ **Renaissance** *s* Rinascimento

rend [rend] *v* (*pret & pp* rent [rent]) *tr* (*to tear*) stracciare; (*to split*) fendere, squarciare

render [ˈrendər] *tr* (*justice*) rendere;

(a service) fare; *(aid)* prestare; *(a bill)* presentare; *(to translate)* tradurre; *(a piece of music)* interpretare; *(e.g., fat)* struggere

rendez•vous ['randə,vu] *s* (-vous [,vuz]) appuntamento; *(in space)* incontro ‖ *v* (*pret & pp* -voused [,vud]; *ger* -vousing [,vu·ɪŋ]) *intr* incontrarsi

rendition [ren'dɪʃən] *s* restituzione, resa; traduzione; interpretazione

renege [rɪ'nɪg] *s* rifiuto ‖ *intr* rifiutare; *(coll)* venire meno

renew [rɪ'nju] *or* [rɪ'nu] *tr* rinnovare ‖ *intr* rinnovarsi

renewal [rɪ'nju·əl] *or* [rɪ'nu·əl] *s* rinnovo, rinnovamento

renounce [rɪ'naʊns] *tr* rinunziare (*with dat*); ripudiare

renovate ['renə,vet] *tr* rinnovare; *(a building)* restaurare; *(a room)* rimettere a nuovo

renown [rɪ'naʊn] *s* rinomanza

renowned [rɪ'naʊnd] *adj* rinomato

rent [rent] *adj* scisso ‖ *s* fitto, pigione; *(tear)* squarcio ‖ *tr* locare, dare a pigione ‖ *intr* prendere a pigione

rental ['rɛntəl] *s* affitto

renter ['rɛntər] *s* affittuario, locatario

renunciation [rɪ,nʌnsɪ'eʃən] *or* [rɪ,nʌnʃɪ'eʃən] *s* rinunzia

reopen [ri'opən] *tr* riaprire ‖ *intr* riaprirsi

reopening [ri'opənɪŋ] *s* riapertura

reorganize [ri'ɔrgə,naɪz] *tr* riorganizzare ‖ *intr* riorganizzarsi

repair [rɪ'per] *s* riparazione; **in good repair** in buono stato ‖ *tr* riparare ‖ *intr* riparare, dirigersi

repair'man' *s* (-men') aggiustatore *m*

repaper [ri'pepər] *tr* ritappezzare

reparation [,repə're ʃən] *s* riparazione

repartee [,repɑr'ti] *s* replica arguta, rimando

repast [rɪ'pæst] *or* [rɪ'pɑst] *s* pasto

repatriate [ri'petrɪ,et] *tr* rimpatriare

re•pay [rɪ'pe] *v* (*pret & pp* -paid ['ped]) *tr* ripagare

repayment [rɪ'pemənt] *s* rimborso; risarcimento, compensazione

repeal [rɪ'pil] *s* revoca, abrogazione ‖ *tr* revocare, abrogare

repeat [rɪ'pit] *s* ripetizione ‖ *tr* ripetere ‖ *intr* ripetere; *(said of food)* tornare a gola

re•pel [rɪ'pel] *v* (*pret & pp* -pelled; *ger* -pelling) *tr* respingere, ricacciare; ripugnare (*with dat*)

repent [rɪ'pent] *tr* pentirsi di ‖ *intr* pentirsi, ravvedersi

repentance [rɪ'pentəns] *s* pentimento

repentant [rɪ'pentənt] *adj* pentito

repercussion [,ripər'kʌʃən] *s* ripercussione

reperto•ry ['repər,tori] *s* (-ries) *(com)* magazzino; *(theat)* repertorio

repetition [,repɪ'tɪʃən] *s* ripetizione

repine [rɪ'paɪn] *intr* lamentarsi

replace [rɪ'ples] *tr* (*to put back*) rimettere; *(to take the place of)* rimpiazzare

replaceable [rɪ'plesəbəl] *adj* sostituibile

replacement [rɪ'plesmənt] *s* rimpiazzo, sostituzione; **as a replacement for** al posto di

replenish [rɪ'plenɪʃ] *tr* rifornire

replete [rɪ'plit] *adj* pieno zeppo

replica ['replɪkə] *s* replica

re•ply [rɪ'plaɪ] *s* (-plies) risposta ‖ *v* (*pret & pp* -plied) *tr & intr* rispondere

report [rɪ'port] *s* rapporto, informazione; voce *f*, rumore *m*; *(of a physician)* responso; *(of a firearm)* detonazione ‖ *tr* riportare, rapportare; denunziare ‖ *intr* fare un rapporto; fare il cronista; presentarsi; **to report sick** *(mil)* marcare visita

report' card' *s* pagella

reportedly [rɪ'portɪdli] *adv* secondo la voce comune

reporter [rɪ'portər] *s* cronista *mf*, reporter *m*

reporting [rɪ'portɪŋ] *s* reportage *m*

repose [rɪ'poz] *s* riposo ‖ *tr* posare, riporre ‖ *intr* riposare

reprehend [,reprɪ'hend] *tr* riprovare, rimproverare

represent [,reprɪ'zent] *tr* rappresentare

representation [,reprɪsen'teʃən] *s* rappresentazione; protesta; **representations** dichiarazioni *fpl*

representative [,reprɪ'zentətɪv] *adj* rappresentativo ‖ *s* rappresentante *mf*; *(pol)* deputato

repress [rɪ'pres] *tr* reprimere

repression [rɪ'preʃən] *s* repressione

reprieve [rɪ'priv] *s* tregua temporanea; sospensione della pena capitale ‖ *tr* accordare una tregua a; sospendere l'esecuzione di

reprimand ['reprɪ,mænd] *or* ['reprɪ,mand] *s* sgridata, ramanzina ‖ *tr* sgridare, rimproverare

reprint ['ri,prɪnt] *s* ristampa; *(offprint)* estratto ‖ [ri'prɪnt] *tr* ristampare

reprisal [rɪ'praɪzəl] *s* rappresaglia

reproach [rɪ'protʃ] *s* rimprovero; vituperio ‖ *tr* rimproverare; **to reproach s.o. for s.th** rimproverare qlcu di qlco, rimproverare qlco a qlcu

reproduce [,riprə'djus] *or* [,riprə'dus] *tr* riprodurre ‖ *intr* riprodursi

reproduction [,riprə'dʌkʃən] *s* riproduzione

reproof [rɪ'pruf] *s* rimprovero

reprove [rɪ'pruv] *tr* rimproverare; disapprovare

reptile ['reptɪl] *s* rettile *m*

republic [rɪ'pʌblɪk] *s* repubblica

republican [rɪ'pʌblɪkən] *adj & s* repubblicano

repudiate [rɪ'pjudɪ,et] *tr* ripudiare; rinnegare

repugnant [rɪ'pʌgnənt] *adj* ripugnante

repulse [rɪ'pʌls] *s* rifiuto; sconfitta ‖ *tr* rifiutare; *(e.g., an enemy)* sconfiggere

repulsive [rɪ'pʌlsɪv] *adj* ripulsivo

reputation [,repjə'teʃən] *s* reputazione

repute [rɪ'pjut] *s* reputazione, fama ‖ *tr* reputare

reputedly [rɪ'pjutɪdlɪ] *adv* secondo l'opinione corrente

request [rɪ'kwest] *s* domanda, richiesta; **at the request of** su domanda di ‖ *tr* richiedere

Requiem ['rɪkwɪ ,em] or ['rekwɪ ,em] *adj* di Requiem ‖ *s* Requiem *m & f;* Messa di Requiem

require [rɪ'kwaɪr] *tr* richiedere

requirement [rɪ'kwaɪrmənt] *s* requisito; richiesta, fabbisogno

requisite ['rekwɪzɪt] *adj* requisito, richiesto ‖ *s* requisito

requisition [,rekwɪ'zɪʃən] *s* requisizione

requital [rɪ'kwaɪtəl] *s* contraccambio

requite [rɪ'kwaɪt] *tr* (*e.g., an injury*) contraccambiare; (*a person*) contraccambiare (with *dat*)

re-read [rɪ'rid] *v* (*pret & pp* **-read** ['red]) *tr* rileggere

resale ['ri ,sel] or [ri'sel] *s* rivendita

rescind [rɪ'sɪnd] *tr* annullare, cancellare; (law) rescindere

rescue ['reskju] *s* salvataggio, liberazione; **to go to the rescue of** andare al soccorso di ‖ *tr* salvare, liberare, soccorrere

research [rɪ'sʌrtʃ] or ['risʌrtʃ] *s* ricerca, indagine *f* ‖ *intr* investigare

re-sell [ri'sel] *v* (*pret & pp* **-sold** ['sold]) *tr* rivendere

resemblance [rɪ'zembləns] *s* somiglianza

resemble [rɪ'zembəl] *tr* somigliare (with *dat*), rassomigliare (with *dat*); **to resemble one another** rassomigliarsi

resent [rɪ'zent] *tr* (*a remark*) risentirsi per; (*a person*) risentirsi con

resentful [rɪ'zentfəl] *adj* risentito

resentment [rɪ'zentmənt] *s* risentimento

reservation [,rezɜr'veʃən] *s* riserva; (*e.g., for a room*) prenotazione

reserve [rɪ'zʌrv] *s* riserva; (*self-restraint*) riserbo, contegno ‖ *tr* riservare; prenotare

reservist [rɪ'zʌrvɪst] *s* riservista *m*

reservoir ['rezɜr ,vwɑr] *s* serbatoio, cisterna; (*large storage place for supplying community with water*) bacino di riserva; (fig) pozzo

re-set [ri'set] *v* (*pret & pp* **-set; ger -setting**) *tr* rimettere a posto; (*a watch*) regolare; (*a gem*) incastonare di nuovo; (*a machine*) rimontare

re-ship [ri'ʃɪp] *v* (*pret & pp* **-shipped; ger -shipping**) *tr* rispedire; (*on a ship*) reimbarcare ‖ *intr* reimbarcarsi

reshipment [ri'ʃɪpmənt] *s* rispedizione; (*on a ship*) reimbarco

reside [rɪ'zaɪd] *intr* risiedere

residence ['rezɪdəns] *s* residenza

resident ['rezɪdənt] *adj & s* residente *mf*

residential [,rezɪ'denʃəl] *adj* residenziale

residue ['rezɪ ,dju] or ['resɪ ,du] *s* residuo

resign [rɪ'zaɪn] *tr* rassegnare, abbandonare; **to be resigned to** rassegnarsi a ‖ *intr* dimettersi, rassegnare le dimissioni

resignation [,rezɪg'neʃən] *s* (*from a job*) dimissione; (*submission*) rassegnazione

resin ['rezɪn] *s* resina

resist [rɪ'zɪst] *tr* resistere (with *dat*) ‖ *intr* resistere

resistance [rɪ'zɪstəns] *s* resistenza

resole [ri'sol] *tr* risolare

resolute ['rezə ,lut] *adj* risoluto

resolution [,rezə'luʃən] *s* risoluzione; **good resolutions** buoni propositi

resolve [rɪ'zɒlv] *s* risoluzione ‖ *tr* risolvere ‖ *intr* risolversi

resonance ['rezənəns] *s* risonanza

resort [rɪ'zɔrt] *s* (*appeal*) ricorso; (*for vacation*) centro di villeggiatura ‖ *intr* ricorrere

resound [rɪ'zaʊnd] *intr* risonare

resounding [rɪ'zaʊndɪŋ] *adj* risonante; (*success*) strepitoso

resource [rɪ'sors] or ['risors] *s* risorsa

resourceful [rɪ'sorsfəl] *adj* ingegnoso

respect [rɪ'spekt] *s* rispetto; **respects** rispetti *mpl*, ossequi *mpl;* **with respect to** rispetto a ‖ *tr* rispettare

respectable [rɪ'spektəbəl] *adj* rispettabile; onesto, per bene

respectful [rɪ'spektfəl] *adj* rispettoso

respecting [rɪ'spektɪŋ] *prep* rispetto a

respective [rɪ'spektɪv] *adj* rispettivo

respiratory ['respɪrə ,tori] or [rɪ'spaɪrə ,tori] *adj* respiratorio

respire [rɪ'spaɪr] *tr & intr* respirare

respite ['respɪt] *s* tregua, requie *f;* (*reprieve*) proroga, dilazione

resplendent [rɪ'splendənt] *adj* risplendente

respond [rɪ'spɒnd] *intr* rispondere

response [rɪ'spɒns] *s* risposta

responsibili-ty [rɪ ,spɒnsɪ'bɪlɪtɪ] *s* (*-ties*) responsibilità *f*

responsible [rɪ'spɒnsɪbəl] *adj* responsabile; (*job*) di fiducia; **responsible for** responsabile di

responsive [rɪ'spɒnsɪv] *adj* rispondente; (*e.g., to affection*) sensibile; (*e.g., motor*) che risponde

rest [rest] *s* riposo; (*what remains*) resto; (mus) pausa; **at rest** in riposo; tranquillo, in pace; (*dead*) morto; **the rest** il resto, gli altri; **to come to rest** andare a finire; **to lay to rest** sotterrare ‖ *tr* riposare; (*to direct one's eyes*) dirigere; (*faith*) porre ‖ *intr* riposarsi, riposare; appoggiarsi; **to rest assured (that)** esser sicuro (che); **to rest on** aver fiducia in; basarsi su; (*one's laurels*) dormire su

restaurant ['restərənt] or ['restə ,rɑnt] *s* ristorante *m*

restful ['restfəl] *adj* riposante, tranquillo

rest' home' *s* casa di riposo

rest'ing place' *s* luogo di riposo; (*of a staircase*) pianerottolo; (*of the dead*) ultima dimora

restitution [,restɪ'tjuʃən] or [,restɪ'tuʃən] *s* restituzione

restive ['rɛstɪv] *adj* irrequieto; (*e.g., horse*) recalcitrante

restless ['rɛstlɪs] *adj* irrequieto; (*night*) insonne, in bianco

restock [ri'stɑk] *tr* rifornire; (*e.g., with fish*) ripopolare

restoration [ˌrɛstə'reʃən] *s* restaurazione

restore [rɪ'stor] *tr* restaurare, ripristinare

restrain [rɪ'stren] *tr* ritenere, frenare; limitare

restraint [rɪ'strent] *s* restrizione; controllo, ritegno; detenzione

restrict [rɪ'strɪkt] *tr* restingere, limitare

restriction [rɪ'strɪkʃən] *s* restrizione

rest' room' *s* toletta; gabinetto di decenza

restructuring [rɪ'strʌktʃərɪŋ] *s* ristrutturazione

result [rɪ'zʌlt] *s* risultato ‖ *intr* risultare; **to result in** risolversi in, concludersi con

resume [rɪ'zum] *or* [rɪ'zjum] *tr* riprendere ‖ *intr* ricominciare

résumé [ˌrɛzy'me] *or* [ˌrɛzjʊ'me] *s* sunto, riassunto

resumption [rɪ'zʌmpʃən] *s* ripresa

resurface [ri'sʌrfɪs] *tr* mettere copertura nuova a ‖ *intr* riemergere

resurrect [ˌrɛzə,rɛkt] *tr & intr* risuscitare

resurrection [ˌrɛzə'rɛkʃən] *s* risurrezione

resuscitate [rɪ'sʌsɪˌtet] *tr* rendere alla vita

retail ['ritel] *adj & adv* al dettaglio, al minuto ‖ *s* dettaglio ‖ *tr* dettagliare, vendere al minuto ‖ *intr* vendere *or* vendersi al minuto

retailer ['ritelər] *s* dettagliante *mf*

retain [rɪ'ten] *tr* ritenere; (*a lawyer*) assicurarsi i servizi di

retaliate [rɪ'tælɪˌet] *intr* fare rappresaglie; **to retaliate for** ricambiare

retaliation [rɪˌtælɪ'eʃən] *s* rappresaglia

retard [rɪ'tard] *s* ritardo ‖ *tr* ritardare

retch [rɛtʃ] *intr* avere sforzi di vomito

reticence ['rɛtɪsəns] *s* riservatezza

reticent ['rɛtɪsənt] *adj* riservato, taciturno

retina ['rɛtɪnə] *s* retina

retinue ['rɛtɪˌnju] *or* ['rɛtɪˌnu] *s* seguito, corteggio

retire [rɪ'taɪr] *tr* ritirare; (*an employee*) giubilare, mettere a riposo ‖ *intr* ritirarsi; andare a riposo; (*to go to bed*) andare a letto

retired [rɪ'taɪrd] *adj* (*employee*) in pensione; (*officer*) a riposo

retirement [rɪ'taɪrmənt] *s* ritiro; (*of an employee*) pensionamento, quiescenza

retort [rɪ'tɔrt] *s* risposta per le rime; controreplica; (*chem*) storta ‖ *tr* rispondere per le rime a ‖ *intr* rispondere per le rime

retouch [ri'tʌtʃ] *tr* ritoccare

retrace [ri'tres] *tr* ripercorrere; **to retrace one's steps** ritornare sui propri passi

retract [rɪ'trækt] *tr* ritrattare, disdire ‖ *intr* disdirsi

re·tread ['ri,trɛd] *s* pneumatico col copertone ricostruito ‖ [ri'trɛd] *v* (*pret & pp* **-treaded**) *tr* ricostruire il copertone di ‖ *v* (*pret* **-trod** ['trɑd]; *pp* **-trod** *or* **-trodden**) *tr* ripercorrere ‖ *intr* rimettere il piede

retreat [rɪ'trit] *s* (*seclusion*) ritiro; (mil) ritirata; (eccl) esercizio spirituale; **to beat a retreat** battere in ritirata ‖ *intr* ritirarsi

retrench [rɪ'trɛntʃ] *tr* ridurre, tagliare; (mil) trincerare ‖ *intr* ridurre le spese; (mil) trincerarsi

retribution [ˌrɛtrɪ'bjuʃən] *s* ricompensa; (theol) giudizio finale

retributive [rɪ'trɪbjətɪv] *adj* retributivo

retrieve [rɪ'triv] *tr* riguadagnare, riconquistare; (*to repair*) risarcire; (hunt) riportare ‖ *intr* riportare la presa

retriever [rɪ'trivər] *s* cane *m* da presa

retroactive [ˌrɛtro'æktɪv] *adj* retroattivo

retrofiring [ˌrɛtro'faɪrɪŋ] *s* accensione dei retrorazzi

retrogress [ˌrɛtrə,grɛs] *intr* regredire; retrocedere

retrorocket [ˌrɛtro'rakɪt] *s* retrorazzo

retrospect [ˌrɛtrə,spɛkt] *s* esame retrospettivo; **in retrospect** retrospettivamente

retrospective [ˌrɛtrə'spɛktɪv] *adj* retrospettivo

re·try [ri'traɪ] *v* (*pret & pp* **-tried**) *tr* (*a person*) riprocessare; (*a case*) ritentare

return [rɪ'tʌrn] *adj* di ritorno; ripetuto ‖ *s* restituzione; ritorno; profitto; (*of income tax*) dichiarazione; risposta; rapporto ufficiale; (*of an election*) responso; (sports) rimando, rimessa; **in return (for)** in cambio (di); **many happy returns of the day!** cento di questi giorni!; **returns** (*of an election*) responso, risultato ‖ *tr* tornare, ritornare restituire; (*a favor*) contraccambiare; (*a profit*) dare; (*thanks; a decision*) rendere; (sports) ribattere ‖ *intr* tornare; rispondere

return' ad'dress *s* indirizzo del mittente

return' bout' *s* (boxing) rivincita

return' mail' *s*—**by return mail** a volta di corriere, a giro di posta

return' tick'et *s* biglietto di ritorno; (Brit) biglietto di andata e ritorno

reunification [riˌjunɪfɪ'keʃən] *s* riunione, unificazione

reunion [ri'junjən] *s* riunione

reunite [ˌriju'naɪt] *tr* riunire ‖ *intr* riunirsi

rev [rɛv] *s* (coll) giro ‖ *v* (*pret & pp* **revved**; *ger* **revving**) *tr*—**to rev up** (coll) imballare ‖ *intr* (coll) accelerare, imballarsi

revamp [ri'væmp] *tr* rinnovare, rappezzare

reveal [rɪ'vil] *tr* rivelare, svelare

reveille ['rɛvəli] *s* sveglia, levata

rev·el ['rɛvəl] *s* baldoria ‖ *v* (*pret &*

pp -eled or -elled; *ger* -eling or -elling) *intr* gozzovigliare; bearsi

revelation [ˌrevəˈleʃən] *s* rivelazione || **Revelation** *s* (Bib) Apocalisse *f*

revel·ry [ˈrevəlri] *s* (-ries) baldoria

revenge [rɪˈvendʒ] *s* vendetta || *tr* vendicare

revengeful [rɪˈvendʒfəl] *adj* vendicativo

revenue [ˈrevəˌnju] or [ˈrevəˌnu] *s* entrata, profitto; (*government income*) entrate *fpl* erariali

rev'enue cut'ter *s* motobarca della guardia di finanza

rev'enue stamp' *s* marca da bollo

reverberate [rɪˈvʌrbəˌret] *intr* riverberarsi; (*said, e.g., of sound*) ripercuotersi, risonare; (*said of an echo*) rimbalzare

revere [rɪˈvɪr] *tr* venerare, riverire

reverence [ˈrevərəns] *s* riverenza || *tr* ossequiare

reverend [ˈrevərənd] *adj & s* reverendo

reverent [ˈrevərənt] *adj* reverente

reverie [ˈrevəri] *s* sogno, fantasticheria

reversal [rɪˈvʌrsəl] *s* inversione, cambio; (law) annullamento

reverse [rɪˈvʌrs] *adj* rovescio, contrario; (mach) di retromarcia || *s* contrario; (*rear*) dietro; (*misfortune*; *side of a coin not bearing principal design*) rovescio; (mach) retromarcia || *tr* invertire; rovesciare; mettere in marcia indietro; **to reverse oneself** cambiare d'opinione; **to reverse the charges** far pagare al destinatario; (telp) far pagare al numero chiamato || *intr* invertirsi

revert [rɪˈvʌrt] *intr* ritornare

review [rɪˈvju] *s* (*critical article*) recensione; (*magazine*) rivista; (educ) ripasso, ripetizione; (mil) rivista || *tr* recensire; rivedere; (*a lesson*) ripassare; (mil) passare in rassegna

revile [rɪˈvaɪl] *tr* insultare, offendere

revise [rɪˈvaɪz] *s* revisione; (typ) seconda bozza || *tr* rivedere; correggere

revision [rɪˈvɪʒən] *s* revisione

revisionism [rɪˈvɪʒəˌnɪzəm] *s* revisionismo

revival [rɪˈvaɪvəl] *s* ripresa delle forze; (*restoration*) ripristino; (*of learning*) rinascimento; risveglio religioso; (theat, mov) ripresa

revive [rɪˈvaɪv] *tr* ravvivare; (*a custom*) ripristinare; (theat) dare la ripresa di || *intr* ravvivarsi; risorgere

revoke [rɪˈvok] *tr* revocare

revolt [rɪˈvolt] *s* rivolta || *tr* rivoltare || *intr* rivoltarsi

revolting [rɪˈvoltɪŋ] *adj* rivoltante

revolution [ˌrevəˈluʃən] *s* rivoluzione

revolutionar·y [ˌrevəˈluʃəˌneri] *adj* rivoluzionario || *s* (-ies) rivoluzionario

revolve [rɪˈvalv] *tr* far rotare; (*in one's mind*) rivolgere || *intr* girare, rotare

revolver [rɪˈvalvər] *s* rivoltella

revolv'ing book'case *s* scaffale *m* girevole

revolv'ing cred'it *s* credito rotativo

revolv'ing door' *s* porta girevole

revolv'ing fund' *s* fondo rotativo

revue [rɪˈvju] *s* rivista

revulsion [rɪˈvʌlʃən] *s* ripugnanza, avversione; (med) revulsione

reward [rɪˈwɔrd] *s* premio, ricompensa; (*money offered for capture*) taglia; (*for return of articles lost*) mancia competente || *tr* premiare, ricompensare

rewarding [rɪˈwɔrdɪŋ] *adj* rimunerativo; gradevole

re·wind [rɪˈwaɪnd] *s* (*of a tape*) ribobinazione || *v* (*pret & pp* -wound [waʊnd]) *tr* ribobinare

re·write [rɪˈraɪt] *v* (*pret* -wrote [ˈrot]; *pp* -written [ˈrɪtən]) *tr* riscrivere; (*news*) rimaneggiare, correggere

rhapso·dy [ˈræpsədi] *s* (-dies) rapsodia

rheostat [ˈriˌə.stæt] *s* reostato

rhesus [ˈrisəs] *s* reso

rhetoric [ˈretərɪk] *s* retorica

rhetorical [rɪˈtɑrɪkəl] or [rɪˈtɔrɪkəl] *adj* retorico

rheumatic [ruˈmætɪk] *adj & s* reumatico

rheumatism [ˈruməˌtɪzəm] *s* reumatismo

Rhine [raɪn] *s* Reno

Rhineland [ˈraɪnˌlænd] *s* la Renania

rhine'stone' *s* gemma artificiale

rhinoceros [raɪˈnɑsərəs] *s* rinoceronte *m*

Rhodes [rodz] *s* Rodi *f*

Rhone [ron] *s* Rodano

rhubarb [ˈrubɑrb] *s* rabarbaro; (slang) baruffa

rhyme [raɪm] *s* rima; **without rhyme or reason** senza capo né coda || *tr & intr* rimare

rhythm [ˈrɪðəm] *s* ritmo

rhythmic(al) [ˈrɪðmɪk(əl)] *adj* ritmico

rial·to [rɪˈælto] *s* (-tos) mercato || **the Rialto** il ponte di Rialto; il centro teatrale di New York

rib [rɪb] *s* costola; (*cut of meat*) costata; (*of umbrella*) stecca; (*of leaf*) nervatura; (aer, archit) centina; (naut) costa || (*pret & pp* **ribbed**; *ger* **ribbing**) *tr* (slang) prendersi gioco di

ribald [ˈrɪbəld] *adj* volgare, indecente

ribbon [ˈrɪbən] *s* nastro; (*decoration*) nastrino; **ribbons** (*shreds*) brandelli *mpl*

rice [raɪs] *s* riso

rich [rɪtʃ] *adj* ricco; (*food*) nutrito, grasso; (*wine*) generoso; (*voice*) caldo; (*color*) vivo; (*odor*) forte; (coll) divertente; (coll) assurdo; **to strike it rich** trovare la miniera d'oro || **riches** *spl* ricchezze *fpl*; **the rich i** ricchi

rickets [ˈrɪkɪts] *s* rachitismo

rickety [ˈrɪkɪti] *adj* (*object*) sgangherato; (*person*) vacillante; (*suffering from rickets*) rachitico

rid [rɪd] *v* (*pret & pp* **rid**; *ger* **ridding**) *tr* liberare, sbarazzare; **to get rid of** liberarsi di, sbarazzarsi di

riddance [ˈrɪdəns] *s* liberazione; **good riddance!** che sollievo!

riddle [ˈrɪdəl] *s* enigma *m*, indovinello; (*sieve*) crivello || *tr* crivellare; (*to sift*) vagliare; (*s.o.'s reputation*) rovinare; **to riddle with** crivellare di

ride [raɪd] *s* scarrozzata; cavalcata; gita || *v* (*pret* **rode** [rod]; *pp* **ridden** [ˈrɪdən]) *tr* cavalcare, montare, montare su; (*e.g., a bus*) andare in; (*the waves*) galleggiare su; attraversare; tiranneggiare; farsi gioco di; **to ride down** travolgere; sorpassare; **to ride out** uscire felicemente da || *intr* cavalcare; fare una passeggiata, fare una gita; (*to float*) galleggiare; **to let ride** lasciar correre; **to ride on** dipendere da

rider [ˈraɪdər] *s* cavallerizzo; ciclista *mf*; viaggiatore *m*, passeggero

ridge [rɪdʒ] *s* (*of mountains*) crinale *m*, dorsale *f*; (*of roof*) displuvio; (agr) porca

ridge'pole' *s* trave maestra, colmo

ridicule [ˈrɪdɪˌkjul] *s* ridicolo; **to expose to ridicule** porre in ridicolo || *tr* ridicolizzare

ridiculous [rɪˈdɪkjələs] *adj* ridicolo

rid'ing boot' *s* stivalone *m* d'equitazione

rid'ing school' *s* maneggio

rife [raɪf] *adj* comune, prevalente; **rife with** pieno di

riffraff [ˈrɪfˌræf] *s* gentaglia

rifle [ˈraɪfəl] *s* fucile *m*; cannone rigato || *tr* (*a place*) svaligiare; (*a person*) derubare; (*a gun*) rigare

rifle' range' *s* tiro a segno

rift [rɪft] *s* crepa, fessura; disaccordo

rig [rɪg] *s* attrezzatura, equipaggio; impianto di sondaggio (per il petrolio); (*outfit*) tenuta || *v* (*pret & pp* **rigged**; *ger* **rigging**) *tr* attrezzare, equipaggiare; guarnire; abbigliare in maniera strana

rigging [ˈrɪgɪŋ] *s* (naut) padiglione *m*; (*tackle*) (naut) rizza; (coll) vestiti *mpl*

right [raɪt] *adj* giusto; corretto; (*mind*) sano; destro, diritto; (geom) retto; (geom) perpendicolare; **right or wrong** a torto o a ragione; **to be all right** star bene di salute; **to be right** aver ragione || *s* diritto; quanto è giusto, (il) giusto; (*in a company*) interessenza; (*right hand*) destra; (*turn*) giro a destra; (boxing) diritto; (tex) dritto; (pol) destra; **by right** in giustizia; **on the right** alla destra; **to be in the right** aver ragione || *adv* direttamente; completamente; immediatamente; proprio, precisamente, correttamente, giustamente; bene; **all right** benissimo || *tr* drizzare; correggere; rimettere a posto || *intr* drizzarsi

righteous [ˈraɪtʃəs] *adj* retto; virtuoso

right' field' *s* (baseball) campo destro

rightful [ˈraɪtfəl] *adj* giusto; legittimo

right'-hand drive' *s* guida a destra

right-handed [ˈraɪtˈhændɪd] *adj* che usa la destra; destrorso

right'-hand man' *s* braccio destro

rightist [ˈraɪtɪst] *adj* conservatore || *s* conservatore *m*, membro della destra

rightly [ˈraɪtli] *adv* correttamente; giustamente; **rightly or wrongly** a torto o a ragione

right' mind' *s*—**in one's right mind** nel pieno possesso delle proprie facoltà, con la testa a posto

right' of way' *s* precedenza; (law) servitù *f* di passaggio; (rr) sede *f*

rights' of man' *s* diritti *mpl* dell'uomo

right'-wing' *adj* della destra

right-winger [ˈraɪtˈwɪŋər] *s* membro della destra, conservatore *m*

rigid [ˈrɪdʒɪd] *adj* rigido

rigmarole [ˈrɪgməˌrol] *s* sproloquio

rigorous [ˈrɪgərəs] *adj* rigoroso

rile [raɪl] *tr* irritare, esasperare

rill [rɪl] *s* rigagnolo

rim [rɪm] *s* orlo, bordo; (*of a wheel*) cerchione *m*

rime [raɪm] *s* brina; (*in verse*) rima || *tr* brinare; rimare || *intr* rimare

rind [raɪnd] *s* (*of animals*) cotenna; (*of fruit or cheese*) scorza

ring [rɪŋ] *s* (*for finger*) anello; (*anything round*) cerchio; (*circular course*) pista; (*of people*) crocchio; (*of evildoers*) combriccola; (*of anchor*) anello; (*sound of bell*) squillo; (*loud sound of bell*) scampanellata; (*of small bell; of glassware*) tintinnio; (*act of ringing*) sonata; (telp) chiamata; (fig) suono; (boxing) quadrato; (mach) ghiera; (fig, taur) arena; **to run rings around** essere molto migliore di || *v* (*pret & pp* **ringed**) *tr* accerchiare; mettere un anello a || *intr* formare cerchi || *v* (*pret* **rang** [ræŋ]; *pp* **rung** [rʌŋ]) *tr* sonare; squillare; tintinnare; chiamare al telefono; **to ring up** chiamare al telefono; (*a sale*) battere sul registratore di cassa || *intr* sonare; squillare; tintinnare; chiamare; (*said of one's ears*) fischiare; **to ring for** chiamare col campanello; **to ring off** terminare una conversazione telefonica; **to ring up** chiamare al telefono

ring-around-a-rosy [ˈrɪŋəˌraʊndəˈrozi] *s* girotondo

ringing [ˈrɪŋɪŋ] *adj* alto, sonoro || *s* accerchiamento; squillo; tintinnio; (*in the ears*) fischio

ring'lead'er *s* capobanda *m*

ringlet [ˈrɪŋlɪt] *s* anellino

ring'mas'ter *s* direttore *m* di circo equestre

ring'side' *s* posto vicino al quadrato

ring'worm' *s* tigna

rink [rɪŋk] *s* pattinatoio

rinse [rɪns] *s* risciacquatura || *tr* risciacquare

riot [ˈraɪət] *s* sommossa, tumulto; profusione; **to be a riot** (coll) essere divertentissimo; **to run riot** sfrenarsi; (*said of plants*) crescere disordinatamente || *intr* tumultuare; darsi alle gozzoviglie

rioter [ˈraɪətər] *s* rivoltoso

rip [rɪp] *s* sdrucitura; (*open seam*) scucitura || *v* (*pret & pp* **ripped**; *ger* **ripping**) *tr* sdrucire; (*to open the* *seam of)* scucire ‖ *intr* sdrucirsi; scucirsi; **to rip out with insults** (coll) prorompere in improperi

ripe [raɪp] *adj* maturo; *(lips)* turgido; *(cheese)* stagionato; pronto

ripen ['raɪpən] *tr & intr* maturare

ripple ['rɪpəl] *s* increspatura; *(sound)* mormorio ‖ *tr* increspare ‖ *intr* incresparsi; mormorare

rise [raɪz] *s (of prices, temperature)* aumento; *(of a road)* salita; *(of ground)* elevazione; *(of a heavenly body)* levata; *(in rank)* ascesa; *(of a step)* alzata; *(of a stream)* sorgente *f; (of water)* crescita; **to get a rise out of** (coll) farsi rispondere per le rime da; **to give rise to** dar origine a ‖ *v (pret* rose [roz]; *pp* risen ['rɪzən]) *intr (said of the sun)* sorgere; rialzarsi; *(said of plants)* crescere; *(said of the wind)* alzarsi; *(said of a building)* ergersi; *(to return from the dead)* risorgere; *(to increase)* aumentare; **to rise above** alzarsi al di sopra di; essere al di sopra di; **to rise to the occasion** sorgere all'altezza di

riser ['raɪzər] *s (of step)* alzata; *(upright)* montante *m;* **early riser** persona mattiniera; **late riser** dormiglione *m*

risk [rɪsk] *s* rischio; **to run or take a risk** correre un rischio ‖ *tr* rischiare

risk·y ['rɪski] *adj (-ier; -iest)* rischioso

risqué [rɪs'ke] *adj* audace, spinto

rite [raɪt] *s* rito; **last rites** riti *mpl* funebri

ritual ['rɪtʃʊ·əl] *adj & s* rituale *m*

ri·val ['raɪvəl] *s* rivale *mf* ‖ *v (pret & pp* -valed *or* -valled; *ger* -valing *or* -valling) *tr* rivaleggiare con

rival·ry ['raɪvəlri] *s (-ries)* rivalità *f*

river ['rɪvər] *s* fiume *m;* **down the river** a valle; **up the river** a monte

riv'er ba'sin *s* bacino fluviale

riv'er·bed' *s* letto di fiume

riv'er front' *s* riva di fiume

riv'er·head' *s* sorgente *f* di fiume

riv'er·side' *adj* rivierasco ‖ *s* riva del fiume

rivet ['rɪvɪt] *s* ribattino; *(of scissors)* perno ‖ *tr* ribadire; *(s.o.'s attention)* concentrare

roach [rotʃ] *s* scarafaggio

road [rod] *adj* stradale ‖ *s* strada; via; (naut) rada; **to be in the road of** ostacolare il cammino a; **to burn up the road** divorare la strada; **to get out of the road** togliersi di mezzo

roadability [ˌrodə'bɪlɪti] *s* tenuta di strada

road'bed' *s (of highway)* piattaforma; (rr) massicciata, infrastruttura

road'block' *s* (mil) barricata; (fig) impedimento

road'house' *s* taverna su autostrada

road' la'borer *s* cantoniere *m*

road' map' *s* carta stradale

road' roll'er *s* compressore *m* stradale, rullo compressore

road' serv'ice *s* servizio di assistenza stradale

road'side' *s* bordo della strada

road'side inn' *s* taverna posta su autostrada

road' sign' *s* indicatore *m* stradale

road'stead' *s* rada

road'way' *s* carreggiata; strada

roam [rom] *s* vagabondaggio ‖ *tr* girovagare per ‖ *intr* girovagare

roar [ror] *s* ruggito, muggito; boato, fragore *m* ‖ *intr* muggire; **to roar with laughter** fare una risata

roast [rost] *s* arrosto; torrefazione ‖ *tr* arrostire; *(coffee)* tostare, torrefare; (coll) farsi beffe di ‖ *intr* arrostirsi

roast' beef' *s* rosbif *m*

roast'ed pea'nut *s* nocciolina americana abbrustolita

roast' pork' *s* arrosto di maiale

rob [rab] *s (pret & pp* robbed; *ger* robbing) *tr & intr* derubare

robber ['rabər] *s* ladro, malandrino

robber·y ['rabəri] *s (-ies)* furto

robe [rob] *s (of a woman)* vestito; *(of a professor)* toga; *(of a priest)* abito talare; *(dressing gown)* vestaglia; *(for lap)* coperta da viaggio; **robes** vestiti *mpl* ‖ *tr* vestire ‖ *intr* vestirsi

robin ['rabɪn] *s* pettirosso

robot ['robat] *s* robot *m*

robust [ro'bʌst] *adj* robusto

rock [rak] *s* roccia; *(any stone)* pietra; *(sticking out of water)* scoglio; *(one that is thrown)* sasso; *(hill)* roccia; (slang) pietra preziosa; **on the rocks** (coll) in rovina; (coll) al verde; *(said, e.g., of whiskey)* sul ghiaccio ‖ *tr* far vacillare; dondolare ‖ *intr* vacillare; dondolare

rock'-bot'tom *adj* (l') ultimo; (il) minimo

rock' can'dy *s* zucchero candito

rock' crys'tal *s* cristallo di rocca

rocker ['rakər] *s (curved piece at bottom of rocking chair)* dondolo; sedia a dondolo; (mach) bilanciere *m;* **off one's rocker** (slang) matto

rocket ['rakɪt] *s* razzo ‖ *intr* partire come un razzo

rock'et launch'er ['lɔntʃər] *or* ['lɑntʃər] *s* lanciarazzo

rock' gar'den *s* giardino piantato fra le rocce

rock'ing chair' *s* sedia a dondolo

rock'ing horse' *s* cavallo a dondolo

rock' salt' *s* salgemma

rock' wool' *s* cotone *m or* lana minerale

rock·y ['raki] *adj (-ier; -iest)* roccioso; traballante; (coll) debole

rod [rad] *s* verga, bacchetta; scettro; punizione; *(bar)* asta; *(for fishing)* canna da pesca; (anat, biol) bastoncino; (mach) biella; (surv) biffa; (Bib) razza, tribù *f;* (slang) pistola; **spare the rod and spoil the child** la madre pietosa fa la piaga cancrenosa

rodent ['rodənt] *adj & s* roditore *m*

rod'man *s (-men)* aiutante *m* geometra

roe [ro] *s* capriolo; *(of fish)* uova *fpl*

rogue [rog] *s* furfante *m;* *(scamp)* picaro

rogues" gal'lery s collezione di fotografie di malviventi

rôle or **role** [rol] s ruolo, parte f; **to play a role** fare la parte

roll [rol] s (of film, paper, etc.) rotolo, bobina; (of fat) strato; (roller) rotella; (of bread) panino; ondulazione; (noise) rullio, rullo; (of a boat) rollio; (of thunder) rombo; (list) ruolo; (of money) (slang) fascio; **to call the roll** fare la chiama || tr far rotolare; (one's r's) arrotare; (one's eyes) stralunare; (e.g., dough) spianare; (steel) laminare; (to wrap) arrotolare; (a drum) rullare; **to roll back** (prices) ridurre; **to roll out** spianare; srotolare; **to roll up** (one's sleeves) arrotolarsi; accumulare; aumentare || intr rotolare; rullare; arrotolarsi; raggomitolarsi; **to roll on** passare; **to roll out** srotolarsi; (to get out of bed) (slang) alzarsi

roll' call' s chiama, appello

roller ['rolər] s rotella; (for hair) bigodino; rotolo; (wave) ondata lunga

roll'er bear'ing s cuscinetto a rotolamento

roll'er coast'er s montagne russe

roll'er skate' s pattino a rotelle

roll'er-skate' intr pattinare coi pattini a rotelle

roll'er tow'el s bandinella

roll'ing mill' ['rolɪŋ] s laminatoio

roll'ing pin' s matterello

roll'ing stock' s (rr) materiale m rotabile

roll'-top desk' s scrivania a piano scorrevole

roly-poly ['roli'poli] adj grassoccio

roman ['romən] adj (typ) romano, tondo || s (typ) carattere romano, tondo || **Roman** adj & s romano

Ro'man can'dle s candela romana

Ro'man Cath'olic Church' s Chiesa Cattolica Apostolica Romana

romance [ro'mæns] or ['romæns] s romanzo; sentimentalità f; idillio, intrigo amoroso; (mus) romanza || [ro'mæns] intr scrivere romanzi; raccontare romanzi; fare il romantico || **Romance** ['romæns] or [ro-'mæns] adj romanzo, neolatino

Ro'man Em'pire s Impero Romano

romanesque [,romən'esk] adj romantico || **Romanesque** adj & s romanico

Ro'man nose' s naso aquilino

romantic [ro'mæntɪk] adj romantico

romanticism [ro'mæntɪ ,sɪzəm] s romanticismo

romanticist [ro'mæntɪsɪst] s romantico

romp [romp] intr ruzzare

rompers ['rompərz] spl pagliaccetto

roof [ruf] or [ruf] s (of house) tetto; (of heaven) volta; (of car) tetto, padiglione m; **to hit the roof** (slang) andare fuori dai gangheri; **to raise the roof** (slang) fare molto chiasso; (slang) protestare violentemente || tr ricoprire con tetto

roofer ['rufər] or ['rufər] s conciatetti m

roof' gar'den s giardino pensile

rook [ruk] s (bird) cornacchia; (in chess) torre f || tr truffare

rookie ['ruki] s novizio; (mil) recluta

room [rum] or [rum] s stanza, camera; vano, locale m; posto, spazio; opportunità f; **to make room** far luogo || intr alloggiare

room' and board' s vitto e alloggio

room' clerk' s impiegato d'albergo assegnato alle prenotazioni

roomer ['rumər] or ['rumər] s inquilino

room'ing house' s casa con camere d'affittare

room'mate' s compagno di stanza

room-y ['rumi] or ['rumi] adj (-ier; -iest) ampio, spazioso

roost [rust] s (perch) ballatoio; (house for chickens) pollaio; (place for resting) posto di riposo; **to rule the roost** essere il gallo del pollaio || intr appollaiarsi; andare a dormire

rooster ['rustər] s gallo

root [rut] or [rut] s radice f; **to get to the root** of andare al fondo di; **to take root** metter radici || tr inchiodare, piantare || intr radicare; (said of swine) grufolare; **to root for** fare il tifo per

rooter ['rutər] or ['rutər] s tifoso

rope [rop] s fune f, corda; (of a hangman) capestro; laccio, lasso; **to know the ropes** (coll) conoscere la faccenda a fondo, saperla lunga || tr legare con fune; prendere al laccio; **to rope in** (slang) imbrogliare

rope'danc'er or **rope'walk'er** s funambolo

rosa•ry ['rozəri] s (-ries) rosario

rose [roz] adj & s rosa

rose'bud' s bottoncino di rosa

rose'bush' s rosaio

rose'-col'ored adj color di rosa

rose'-colored glass'es spl occhiali mpl rosa

rose' gar'den s roseto

rosemar-y ['roz,meri] s (-ies) rosmarino

rose' of Shar'on ['ʃerən] s altea

rosette [ro'zɛt] s rosetta; (archit) rosone m

rose' win'dow s rosone m

rose'wood' s palissandro

rosin ['razɪn] s colofonia

roster ['rɑstər] s ruolino; orario scolastico

rostrum ['rɑstrəm] s tribuna

ros-y ['rozi] adj (-ier; -iest) rosa, roseo

rot [rat] s marcio; (coll) stupidaggine f || v (pret & pp rotted; ger rotting) tr & intr imputridire

ro'tary en'gine ['rotəri] s motore rotativo

ro'tary press' s rotativa

rotate ['rotet] or [ro'tet] tr & intr rotare

rotation [ro'teʃən] s rotazione; **in rotation** in successione, a turno

rote [rot] s ripetizione macchinale; **by rote** a memoria

rot'gut' s (slang) acquavite f di infima qualità

rotisserie [roˈtɪsəri] *s* girarrosto a motore

rotten [ˈrɑtən] *adj* marcio, fradicio; corrotto

rotund [roˈtʌnd] *adj* (*plump*) rotondetto; (*voice*) profondo; (*speech*) enfatico

rouge [ruʒ] *s* belletto, rossetto ‖ *tr* dare il belletto a ‖ *intr* darsi il belletto

rough [rʌf] *adj* scabroso; (*sea*) agitato; (*crude*) rozzo, rude; (*road*) accidentato; approssimativo ‖ *tr*—**to rough it** vivere primitivamente; **to rough up** malmenare

rough′cast′ *s* intonaco; modello disgrossato ‖ *v* (*pret & pp* **-cast**) *tr* (*a wall*) intonacare; disgrossare, dirozzare

rough′ cop′y *s* brutta copia

rough-hew [ˈrʌfˈhju] *tr* digrossare, dirozzare

roughly [ˈrʌfli] *adv* aspramente; rozzamente; approssimativamente

round [raund] *adj* rotondo ‖ *s* tondo; (*of applause*; *of guns*) salva; (*of a single gun*) colpo, tiro; (*of a chair*) piolo; (*of a doctor*) giro; (*of golf*) partita; (*e.g., of bridge*) mano *f*; cerchio; (*boxing*) ripresa ‖ *adv* intorno; dal principio alla fine ‖ *prep* intorno a; attraverso ‖ *tr* (*to make round*) arrotondare; circondare; (*a corner*) scantonare; **to round off** arrotondare; completare, perfezionare; **to round up** raccogliere; (*cattle*) condurre

roundabout [ˈraundəˌbaut] *adj* indiretto ‖ *s* giacca attillata; via traversa; giro di parole; (Brit) giostra; (Brit) anello stradale

round′house′ *s* rimessa per locomotive

round-shouldered [ˈraundˈʃoldərd] *adj* dalle spalle spioventi

round′-trip tick′et *s* biglietto d'andata e ritorno

round′up′ *s* (*of cattle*) riunione; (*of criminals*) retata; (*of facts*) riassunto

rouse [rauz] *tr* svegliare; suscitare; (*game*) scovare ‖ *intr* svegliarsi

rout [raut] *s* sconfitta, rotta ‖ *tr* sconfiggere, mettere in rotta ‖ *intr* grufolare

route [rut] or [raut] *s* via, rotta; itinerario ‖ *tr* istradare

routine [ruˈtin] *adj* ordinario ‖ *s* trafila, routine *f*

rove [rov] *intr* vagabondare, vagare

rover [ˈrovər] *s* vagabondo

row [rau] *s* piazzata, scenata; (*clamor*) (coll) baccano; **to raise a row** (coll) fare baccano ‖ [ro] *s* fila; (*of figures*) finca; (*e.g., of trees*) filare *m*; **in a row** in continuazione, di seguito ‖ *tr* vogare ‖ *intr* remare, vogare

rowboat [ˈroˌbot] *s* barca a remi

row·dy [ˈraudi] *adj* (**-dier; -diest**) turbolento ‖ *s* (**-dies**) attaccabrighe *mf*

rower [ˈro·ər] *s* rematore *m*

rowing [ˈro·ɪŋ] *s* (*action*) voga; (*sport*) canottaggio

royal [ˈrɔɪ·əl] *adj* reale, regio

royalist [ˈrɔɪ·əlɪst] *adj* sostenitore del re ‖ *s* realista *mf*

royal·ty [ˈrɔɪ·əlti] *s* (**-ties**) regalità *f*; membro della famiglia reale; nobiltà *f*; diritto d'autore; diritto d'inventore; percentuale *f* sugli utili

rub [rʌb] *s* frizione; difficile *m*; **here's the rub** qui sta il busillis ‖ *v* (*pret & pp* **rubbed**; *ger* **rubbing**) *tr* fregare; **to rub elbows with** stare giunto a gomiti con; **to rub out** cancellare con la gomma; (slang) togliere di mezzo ‖ *intr* sfregare; **to rub off** venir via sfregando; cancellarsi

rubber [ˈrʌbər] *s* gomma, caucciù *m*; gomma da cancellare; (*overshoe*) caloscia; (*in cards*) rubber *m*; (sports) bella

rub′ber band′ *s* elastico

rub′ber-neck′ *s* (coll) ficcanaso; (coll) turista curioso ‖ *intr* (coll) allungare il collo

rub′ber plant′ *s* albero del caucciù

rub′ber stamp′ *s* timbro di gomma; (coll) persona che approva inconsultamente

rub′ber-stamp′ *tr* timbrare; (coll) approvare inconsultamente

rubbish [ˈrʌbɪʃ] *s* spazzatura; immondizia; (fig) detrito; (coll) sciocchezza

rubble [ˈrʌbəl] *s* (*broken stone*) pietrisco; (*masonry*) mistura di malta e pietrame; (*broken bits*) calcinacci *mpl*

rub′down′ *s* fregagione

rube [rub] *s* (slang) contadino gonzo

ru·by [ˈrubi] *adj* vermiglio ‖ *s* (**-bies**) *s* rubino

rudder [ˈrʌdər] *s* timone *m*; (aer) timone *m* di direzione

rud·dy [ˈrʌdi] *adj* (**-dier; -diest**) rubicondo

rude [rud] *adj* rude, sgarbato

rudiment [ˈrudɪmənt] *s* rudimento

rue [ru] *tr* lamentare, rimpiangere

rueful [ˈrufəl] *adj* lamentevole; triste

ruffian [ˈrʌfɪ·ən] *s* ribaldo

ruffle [ˈrʌfəl] *s* increspatura; (*of drum*) rullo; (sew) gala, crespa ‖ *tr* increspare; arruffare; irritare; (*a drum*) far rullare; (sew) guarnire di gala or crespa

rug [rʌg] *s* tappeto

rugged [ˈrʌgɪd] *adj* aspro, irregolare; rugoso; rozzo; forte; tempestuoso

ruin [ˈru·ɪn] *s* rovina ‖ *tr* rovinare, mandare in rovina

rule [rul] *s* regola; dominazione; (*reign*) regno; (law) ordinanza; (typ) filetto; **as a rule** in generale ‖ *tr* governare; dominare; (*with lines*) rigare; (law) deliberare; **to rule out** escludere ‖ *intr* governare; regnare; **to rule over** governare

rule′ of thumb′ *s* regola basata sull'esperienza; **by rule of thumb** secondo la propria esperienza

ruler [ˈrulər] *s* governante *m*, dominatore *m*; (*for ruling lines*) riga, regolo

ruling [ˈrulɪŋ] *adj* dirigente ‖ *s* (*ruled lines*) rigatura; (law) decisione

rum [rʌm] *s* rum *m*; (*any alcoholic drink*) acquavite *f*

Rumanian [ruˈmenɪ-ən] *adj & s* rumeno

rumble [ˈrʌmbəl] *s* rimbombo; (*of the intestines*) gorgoglio; (*slang*) rissa fra ganghe rivali ‖ *intr* rimbombare; gorgogliare

ruminate [ˈrumɪ‚net] *tr & intr* ruminare

rummage [ˈrʌmɪdʒ] *tr & intr* rovistare, frugare

rum′mage sale′ *s* vendita di cianfrusaglie

rumor [ˈrumər] *s* voce *f*, diceria ‖ *tr* vociferare; **it is rumored that** corre voce che

rump [rʌmp] *s* anca; posteriore *m*; (*of beef*) quarto posteriore

rumple [ˈrʌmpəl] *s* piega ‖ *tr* spiegazzare, sgualcire ‖ *intr* sgualcirsi

rumpus [ˈrʌmpəs] *s* tumulto; rissa; **to raise a rumpus** fare baccano

run [rʌn] *s* corsa; percorso; produzione; (*e.g., in a stocking*) smagliatura; direzione; (*spell*) serie *f*; (*in cards*) scala; (*of goods*) richiesta; (*on a bank*) afflusso; **in the long run** a lungo andare; **on the run** (coll) di corsa; in fuga; **the common run of men** la media della gente; **to give s.o. a run for his money** dare a qlcu del filo da torcere; essere denaro ben speso per qlcu, e.g., **that sweater gave me a run for my money** quello sweater è stato denaro ben speso per me; **to have a long run** tenere il cartellone per lungo tempo; **to have the run of** avere la libertà di andare e venire per ‖ *v* (*pret* ran [ræn]; *pp* **run**; *ger* running) *tr* muovere; (*a horse*) far correre; (*the street*) vivere liberamente in; (*game*) inseguire; trasportare; (*a machine*) far camminare; (*a store*) esercire; (*a candidate*) portare; (*a risk*) correre; (*a blockade*) violare; mettere, ficcare; (*a line*) tirare; **to run down** cacciare; esaminare; trovare; (*a pedestrian*) investire; denigrare, criticare; **to run in** (*a machine*) rodare; (*slang*) schiaffare in prigione; **to run off** creare di getto; cacciare; (*typ*) tirare; **to run up** ammassare ‖ *intr* correre; scappare; (*in a race*) arrivare; (*said of a candidate*) portarsi; passare; (*said of knitted material*) smagliarsi; (*said of a liquid*) scorrere; (*said of a color*) sbavare; (*said of fish*) migrare; funzionare; (*to become*) diventare; (*to be worded*) essere del tenore; (com) decorrere; (theat, mov) durare in cartellone; **to run across** imbattersi in; **to run aground** incagliarsi; **to run away** fuggire; (*said of a horse*) prendere la mano; **to run down** (*said of a liquid*) scorrere; (*said of a battery, a watch*) scaricarsi; (*in health*) sciuparsi; **to run for** presentarsi candidato per; **to run in the family** essere una caratteristica familiare; **to run into** imbattersi in; ammontare a; (*to follow*) succedersi a; **to run off the track** (rr) uscire dalle rotaie; **to run out** aver termine; scadere; esaurirsi;

to run out of rimanere senza; **to run over** oltrepassare; (*e.g., with a car*) investire; **to run through** trapassare; (*a fortune*) dilapidare; esaminare rapidamente

run′-a-way′ *adj* fuggiasco; (*horse*) che ha preso la mano ‖ *s* fuggiasco; cavallo che ha preso la mano; fuga

run′-down′ *adj* esausto; negletto, cadente; (*watch, battery*) scarico

rung [rʌŋ] *s* (*of chair or ladder*) piolo

runner [ˈrʌnər] *s* corridore *m*; messaggero; fattorino, messo; (*of sleigh*) pattino; (*of ice skate*) lama; (*rug*) guida; (*on a table*) striscia di pizzo; (*in stocking*) smagliatura

run′ner-up′ *s* (**runners-up**) finalista *mf* secondo

running [ˈrʌnɪŋ] *adj* in corsa; da corsa; (*water*) corrente; (*vine*) rampicante; (*knot*) scorsoio; (*sore*) purulento; (*writing*) corsivo; consecutivo; (*start*) (sports) lanciato ‖ *s* corsa; (*of a business*) esercizio; direzione; funzionamento; **to be in the running** avere possibilità di vittoria

run′ning board′ *s* (aut) pedana

run′ning head′ *s* titolo corrente

run-ny [ˈrʌnɪ] *adj* (-nier; -niest) (*liquid*) scorrevole; (*color*) sbavante; **to have a runny nose** avere la goccia al naso

run′off′ *s* ballottagio

run-of-the-mill [ˈrʌnəvðəˈmɪl] *adj* ordinario, corrente

run′proof′ *adj* indemagliabile

runt [rʌnt] *s* nanerottolo; animale deperito

run′way′ *s* pista; (*of a stream*) letto; (*for animals*) chiusa; (aut) corsia

rupture [ˈrʌptʃər] *s* rottura; (pathol) ernia ‖ *tr* rompere; causare un'ernia a ‖ *intr* rompersi; soffrire di ernia

ru′ral free′ deliv′ery [ˈrurəl] *s* distribuzione postale campestre

ruse [ruz] *s* astuzia, stratagemma *m*

rush [rʌʃ] *adj* urgente ‖ *s* fretta; slancio, corsa; (*of blood*) ondata; (*rushing of persons to a new mine*) febbre *f*; (bot) giunco; **in a rush** in fretta e furia ‖ *tr* affrettare; portare di fretta; spingere; (coll) fare la corte a; **to rush through** fare di fretta; (*e.g., a bill through Congress*) far approvare di fretta ‖ *intr* lanciarsi; affrettarsi; passare velocemente; **to rush through** (*a book*) leggere velocemente; (*one's work*) fare in fretta; (*a town*) attraversare velocemente

rush′-bot′tomed chair′ *s* sedia di giunchi

rush′ can′dle *s* lumicino con lo stoppino fatto di midollo di giunco

rush′ hour′ *s* ora di punta

russet [ˈrʌsɪt] *adj* color cannella

Russia [ˈrʌʃə] *s* la Russia

Russian [ˈrʌʃən] *adj & s* russo

rust [rʌst] *s* ruggine *f*; (fig) torpore *m* ‖ *tr* arrugginire ‖ *intr* arrugginirsi

rustic [ˈrʌstɪk] *adj & s* rustico

rustle [ˈrʌsəl] *s* fruscio; (*of leaves*) stormire *m* ‖ *tr* far frusciare; far stormire; (cattle) (coll) rubare || intr frusciare; stormire; (coll) lavorare di buzzo buono

rust•y ['rʌsti] adj (-ier; -iest) ruggi-noso; color ruggine; fuori pratica

rut [rʌt] s (track) solco, carraccceria; (of animals) fregola; (il) solito tran tran

ruthless ['ruθlɪs] adj spietato

rye [raɪ] s segala; whiskey m di segala

S

S, s [ɛs] s diciannovesima lettera del-l'alfabeto inglese

Sabbath ['sæbəθ] s (of Jews) sabato; (of Christians) domenica; to keep the Sabbath osservare il riposo do-menicale

sabbat'ical year' [sə'bætɪkəl] s anno di congedo; (Bib) anno sabbatico

saber ['sebər] s sciabola

sa'ber rat'tling s minacce fpl di guerra

sable ['sebəl] adj nero || s zibellino; sables vestiti di lutto

sabotage ['sæbə,taʒ] s sabotaggio || tr & intr sabotare

saccharin ['sækərɪn] s saccarina

sachet ['sæʃe] or [sæ'ʃe] s sacchetto profumato (per la biancheria)

sack [sæk] s sacco; (of an employee) (slang) licenziamento; (slang) letto || tr insaccare; (to lay waste) saccheg-giare, mettere a sacco; (slang) licen-ziare

sack'cloth' s tela di sacco; (for peni-tence) sacco, cilicio; in sackcloth and ashes pentito e contrito

sacrament ['sækrəmənt] s sacramento

sacramental [,sækrə'mentəl] adj sa-cramentale

sacred ['sekrəd] adj sacro

sacrifice ['sækrɪ,faɪs] s sacrificio; at a sacrifice in perdita || tr sacrificare; (com) svendere

sacrilege ['sækrɪlɪdʒ] s sacrilegio

sacrilegious [,sækrɪ'lɪdʒəs] or [,sæk-rɪ'lidʒəs] adj sacrilego

sacristan ['sækrɪstən] s sagrestano

sacris•ty ['sækrɪsti] s (-ties) sagrestia

sad [sæd] adj (sadder; saddest) triste; (bad) cattivo; (color) tetro

sadden ['sædən] tr rattristare || intr rattristarsi

saddle ['sædəl] s sella || tr insellare; to saddle with gravare di

saddle'bag' s fonda

saddlebow ['sædəl,bo] s arcione m an-teriore

sad'dle-cloth' s gualdrappa

saddler ['sædlər] s sellaio

sad'dle-tree' s arcione m

sadist ['sædɪst] or ['sedɪst] s sadico

sadistic [sæ'dɪstɪk] or [se'dɪstɪk] adj sadico

sadness ['sædnɪs] s tristezza

sad' sack' s (coll) marmittone m

safe [sef] adj sicuro; cauto; (distance) rispettoso; safe and sound sano e salvo || s cassaforte f

safe'-con'duct s salvacondotto

safe'-depos'it box' s cassetta di sicu-rezza

safe'guard' s salvaguardia || tr salva-guardare

safe•ty ['sefti] adj di sicurezza || s (-ties) sicurezza; (of a gun) sicura; to reach safety mettersi in salvo

safe'ty belt' s (of a worker) imbraca; (aer, aut) cintura di sicurezza; (naut) cintura di salvataggio

safe'ty glass' s vetro infrangibile

safe'ty is'land s salvagente m

safe'ty match' s fiammifero svedese

safe'ty pin' s spillo di sicurezza

safe'ty ra'zor s rasoio di sicurezza

safe'ty valve' s valvola di sicurezza

saffron ['sæfrən] s zafferano

sag [sæg] s cedimento; depressione; (of a rope) allentamento || v (pret & pp sagged; ger sagging) intr curvarsi; cedere, afflosciarsi; allentarsi; (said of prices) calare

sagacious [sə'geʃəs] adj sagace

sage [sedʒ] adj saggio, savio || s sag-gio, savio; (bot) salvia

sage'brush' s artemisia

Sagittarius [,sædʒɪ'teri·əs] s Sagittario

sail [sel] s vela; (of windmill) ala; gita a vela; to set sail far vela; under full sail a piena velatura || tr veleggiare, navigare; (a boat) far navigare || intr veleggiare, navigare; far vela; volare; (said of a vessel) partire; to sail into (coll) attaccare

sail'boat' s nave f a vela, veliero

sail'cloth' s tela di olona

sailing ['selɪŋ] adj in partenza || s par-tenza; navigazione; navigazione a vela

sail'ing ship' s veliero

sail'mak'er s velaio

sailor ['selər] s marinaio

saint [sent] adj & s santo || tr santifi-care, canonizzare

saint'hood s santità f

saintliness ['sentlɪnɪs] s santità f

Saint' Vi'tus's dance' ['vaɪtəsəz] s (pathol) ballo di San Vito

sake [sek] s causa, interesse m; for the sake of per il bene di, per l'amor di

salaam [sə'lum] s salamelecco || tr fare salamelecchi

salable ['seləbəl] adj vendibile

salacious [sə'leʃəs] adj salace

salad ['sæləd] s insalata

sal'ad bowl' s insalatiera

sal'ad oil' s olio da tavola

sala•ry ['sæləri] s (-ries) stipendio

sale [sel] s vendita; (at reduced prices) svendita, saldo; for sale in vendita; si vende, si vendono

sales'clerk' s commesso, impiegato

sales'la'dy s (-dies) commessa, impiegata

sales'man s (-men) venditore m; commesso; (traveling) piazzista m

sales'man·ship' s arte f di vendere

sales' promo'tion s promozione delle vendite, promotion f

sales'room' s sala di esposizione; sala vendite

sales' talk' s discorso da venditore; (e.g., of a barker) imbonimento

sales' tax' s imposta sulle vendite

saliva [sə'laɪvə] s saliva

sallow ['sælo] adj giallastro, olivastro

sal·ly ['sæli] s (-lies) escursione, gita; (outburst) esplosione; (witty remark) uscita; (mil) sortita || v pret & pp -lied) intr fare una sortita; to sally forth balzar fuori

salmon ['sæmən] s salmone m

salon [sə'lɑn] s salone m

saloon [sə'lun] s taverna; (on a passenger vessel) salone m

saloon' keep'er s taverniere m

salt [sɔlt] s sale m; to be worth one's salt valere il pane che si mangia || tr salare; (cattle) dare sale a; to salt away (ooll) metter via, conservare

salt' bed' s salina

salt'cel'lar s saliera

saltine [sɔl'tin] s galletta salata

saltish ['sɔltɪʃ] adj salmastro

salt'pe'ter s (potassium nitrate) salnitro; (sodium nitrate) nitro del Cile

salt' shak'er s saliera

salt·y ['sɔlti] adj (-ier; -iest) salato

salubrious [sə'lubrɪ·əs] adj salubre

salutation [,sæljə'teʃən] s saluto

salute [sə'lut] s saluto || tr salutare

salvage ['sælvɪdʒ] s ricupero || tr ricuperare

salvation [sæl'veʃən] s salvezza

Salva'tion Ar'my s Esercito della Salvezza

salve [sæv] or [sɑv] s unguento || tr lenire, alleviare

sal·vo ['sælvo] s (-vos or -voes) salva

Samaritan [sə'mærɪtən] adj & s samaritano

same [sem] adj & pron indef medesimo, stesso; it's all the same to me a me fa lo stesso; just the same lo stesso, ugualmente; ciò nonostante; same . . . as lo stesso . . . che

sameness ['semnɪs] s uniformità f; monotonia

sample ['sæmpəl] s campione m, saggio || tr (to take a sample of) campionare; (to taste) assaggiare; provare

sam'ple cop'y s esemplare m di campione

sancti·fy ['sæŋktɪ,faɪ] v (pret & pp -fied) tr santificare

sanctimonious [,sæŋktɪ'monɪ·əs] adj che affetta devozione ipocrita

sanction ['sæŋkʃən] s sanzione || tr sanzionare

sanctuar·y ['sæŋktʃʊ,ɛri] s (-ies) santuario; to take sanctuary prendere asilo, rifugiarsi

sand [sænd] s sabbia || tr insabbiare;

(to polish) smerigliare; cospergere di sabbia

sandal ['sændəl] s sandalo

san'dal·wood' s sandalo

sand'bag' s sacchetto a terra

sand'bank' s banco di sabbia

sand' bar' s cordone m litorale, banco di sabbia

sand'blast' s sabbiatura || tr pulire con sabbiatura, sabbiare

sand'box' s cassone m pieno di sabbia; (rr) sabbiera

sand'glass' s orologio a polvere or a sabbia

sand'pa'per s carta vetrata || tr pulire con carta vetrata

sand'stone' s arenaria

sandwich ['sændwɪtʃ] s panino imbottito, tramezzino || tr inserire

sand'wich man' s tramezzino, uomo sandwich

sand·y ['sændi] adj (-ier; -iest) sabbioso; (hair) biondo rossiccio

sane [sen] adj sensato

sanguinary ['sæŋgwɪn,ɛri] adj sanguinario

sanguine ['sæŋgwɪn] adj fiducioso; (complexion) sanguigno

sanitary ['sænɪ,tɛri] adj sanitario

san'itary nap'kin s pannolino igienico

sanitation [,sænɪ'teʃən] s sanità f

sanity ['sænɪti] s sanità f di mente

Santa Claus ['sæntə,klɔz] s Babbo Natale

sap [sæp] s linfa, succhio; (mil) trincea; (coll) scemo || v (pret & pp sapped; ger sapping) tr scavare; insidiare, minare; (to weaken) indebolire

sapling ['sæplɪŋ] s alberello; (youth) giovanetto

sapphire ['sæfaɪr] s zaffiro

Saracen ['særesən] adj & s saraceno

sarcasm ['sɑrkæzəm] s sarcasmo

sarcastic [sɑr'kæstɪk] adj sarcastico

sardine [sɑr'din] s sardina; packed in like sardines pigiati come le acciughe

Sardinia [sɑr'dɪnɪ·ə] s la Sardegna

Sardinian [sɑr'dɪnɪ·ən] adj & s sardo

sarsaparilla [,sɑrsəpə'rɪlə] s salsapariglia

sash [sæʃ] s sciarpa; (around one's waist) fusciacca; (of window) telaio

sash' win'dow s finestra a ghigliottina

sas·sy ['sæsi] adj (-sier; -siest) (coll) impertinente; (pert) (coll) vivace

satchel ['sætʃəl] s sacca; (of schoolboy) cartella

sateen [sæ'tin] s satin m

satellite ['sætə,laɪt] s satellite m

satiate ['seʃɪ,et] tr saziare

satin ['sætən] s raso

satire ['sætaɪr] s satira

satiric(al) [sə'tɪrɪk(əl)] adj satirico

satirist ['sætɪrɪst] s satirico

satirize ['sætɪ,raɪz] tr satireggiare

satisfaction [,sætɪs'fækʃən] s soddisfazione

satisfactory [,sætɪs'fæktəri] adj soddisfacente

satis·fy ['sætɪs,faɪ] v (pret & pp -fied) tr & intr soddisfare

saturate ['sætʃə,ret] tr saturare

Saturday [ˈsætərdi] *s* sabato
Saturn [ˈsætərn] *s* (astr) Saturno
sauce [sɔs] *s* salsa; *(of fruit)* conserva; *(of chocolate)* crema; (coll) insolenza, impertinenza ‖ *tr* condire; rendere piccante ‖ [sɔs] or [sæs] *tr* (coll) rispondere con impertinenza a
sauce′pan′ *s* casseruola
saucer [ˈsɔsər] *s* piattino
sau·cy [ˈsɔsi] *adj* (**-cier; -ciest**) impertinente; (*pert*) vivace
sauerkraut [ˈsaʊr‚kraʊt] *s* sarcrauti *mpl*, crauti *mpl*
saunter [ˈsɔntər] *s* giro, bighellonata ‖ *intr* girandolare, bighellonare
sausage [ˈsɔsɪdʒ] *s* salsiccia
savage [ˈsævɪdʒ] *adj & s* selvaggio
savant [ˈsævənt] *s* erudito
save [sev] *prep* tranne, salvo ‖ *tr* salvare; *(money)* risparmiare; (*to set apart*) serbare; **to save face** salvare le apparenze ‖ *intr* fare economia
saving [ˈsevɪŋ] *adj* economico; che redime ‖ **savings** *spl* risparmi *mpl*, economie *fpl* ‖ *prep* eccetto, salvo
sav′ings account′ *s* conto di risparmio
sav′ings and loan′ associa′tion *s* cassa di risparmio che concede mutui
sav′ings bank′ *s* cassa di risparmio
savior [ˈsevjər] *s* salvatore *m*
Saviour [ˈsevjər] *s* Salvatore *m*
savor [ˈsevər] *s* sapore *m* ‖ *tr* assaporare; *(to flavor)* saporire ‖ *intr* odorare; **to savor of** sapere di; odorare di
savor·y [ˈsevəri] *adj* (**-ier; -iest**) saporoso; piccante; delizioso ‖ *s* (**-ies**) (bot) santoreggia
saw [sɔ] *s* *(tool)* sega; detto, proverbio ‖ *tr* segare
saw′buck′ *s* cavalletto
saw′dust′ *s* segatura
saw′horse′ *s* cavalletto
saw′mill′ *s* segheria
Saxon [ˈsæksən] *adj & s* sassone *m*
saxophone [ˈsæksə‚fon] *s* sassofono
say [se] *s* dire *m*; **to have no say** non aver voce in capitolo; **to have one's say** esprimere la propria opinione; **to have the say** avere l'ultima parola ‖ *v* (*pret & pp* **said** [sed]) *tr* dire; **I should say so!** certamente!; **it is said** si dice; **no sooner said than done** detto fatto; **that is to say** vale a dire; **to go without saying** essere ovvio
saying [ˈse‚ɪŋ] *s* detto, proverbio
scab [skæb] *s* crosta; *(strikebreaker)* crumiro
scabbard [ˈskæbərd] *s* guaina, fodero
scab·by [ˈskæbi] *adj* (**-bier; -biest**) crostoso; *(animal)* rognoso; (slang) vile
scabrous [ˈskæbrəs] *adj* scabroso
scads [skædz] *spl* (slang) un mucchio
scaffold [ˈskæfəld] *s* impalcatura; *(to execute a criminal)* patibolo
scaffolding [ˈskæfəldɪŋ] *s* incastellatura, ponteggio
scald [skɔld] *tr* scottare; *(e.g., milk)* cuocere al disotto del punto d'ebollizione
scale [skel] *s* *(e.g., of map)* scala;

piatto della bilancia; *(of fish)* squama; **on a large scale** in grande scala; **scales** bilancia; **to tip the scales** far inclinare la bilancia ‖ *tr* squamare; *(to incrust)* incrostare; *(to weigh)* pesare; scalare; graduare; ridurre a scala ‖ *intr* squamarsi; scrostarsi
scallion [ˈskæljən] *s* scalogno
scallop [ˈskɑləp] or [ˈskæləp] *s* *(for cooking)* conchiglia; *(mollusk)* pettine *m*; *(slice of meat)* scaloppina; *(on edge of cloth)* dentello, smerlo ‖ *tr* *(fish)* cuocere in conchiglia; dentellare, smerlare
scalp [skælp] *s* cuoio capelluto ‖ *tr* scotennare; *(tickets)* fare il bagarinaggio di
scalpel [ˈskælpəl] *s* scalpello
scalper [ˈskælpər] *s* bagarino
scal·y [ˈskeli] *adj* (**-ier; -iest**) squamoso; scrostato
scamp [skæmp] *s* cattivo soggetto, briccone *m*
scamper [ˈskæmpər] *intr* sgambettare; **to scamper away** darsela a gambe
scan [skæn] *v* (*pret & pp* **scanned**; *ger* **scanning**) *tr* scrutare; dare un'occhiata a; *(verse)* scandire; (telv) analizzare, scandire, esplorare
scandal [ˈskændəl] *s* scandalo
scandalize [ˈskændə‚laɪz] *tr* scandalizzare
scandalous [ˈskændələs] *adj* scandaloso
Scandinavian [‚skændɪˈnevi·ən] *adj & s* scandinavo
scanning [ˈskænɪŋ] *s* (telv) esplorazione
scan′ning line′ *s* (telv) riga di analisi
scant [skænt] *adj* scarso; corto ‖ *tr* diminuire; lesinare
scant·y [ˈskænti] *adj* (**-ier; -iest**) appena sufficiente; povero, magro; *(clothing)* succinto
scapegoat [ˈskep‚got] *s* capro espiatorio
scar [skɑr] *s* cicatrice *f*; (fig) sfregio ‖ *v* (*pret & pp* **scarred**; *ger* **scarring**) *tr* segnare, marcare; sfregiare ‖ *intr* cicatrizzarsi
scarce [skers] *adj* scarso, raro; **to make oneself scarce** (coll) non farsi vedere
scarcely [ˈskersli] *adv* appena; a mala pena; non . . . affatto; **scarcely ever** raramente; non . . . affatto
scarci·ty [ˈskersɪti] *s* (**-ties**) scarsità *f*, scarsezza; carestia
scare [sker] *s* spavento ‖ *tr* spaventare, impaurire; **to scare away** fare scappare per lo spavento; **to scare up** *(money)* (coll) metter insieme
scare′crow′ *s* spaventapasseri *m*
scarf [skɑrf] *s* (**scarfs** or **scarves** [skɑrvz]) sciarpa; cravattone *m*; *(cover for table)* centro, striscia
scarf′pin′ *s* spilla da cravatta
scarlet [ˈskɑrlɪt] *adj* scarlatto
scar′let fe′ver *s* scarlattina
scar·y [ˈskeri] *adj* (**-ier; -iest**) *(timid)* (coll) fifone; *(causing fright)* (coll) spaventevole

scathing ['skeðɪŋ] *adj* severo, bruciante

scatter ['skætər] *tr* disperdere, sparpagliare || *intr* disperdersi, sparpagliarsi

scatterbrained ['skætər,brend] *adj* scervellato, stordito

scenari•o [sɪ'nɛrɪ,o] or [sɪ'nɑrɪ,o] *s* (-os) scenario

scenarist [sɪ'nɛrɪst] or [sɪ'nɑrɪst] *s* scenarista *mf*, sceneggiatore *m*

scene [sin] *s* (*view*) paesaggio; (*place*) scena; (*theat*) scena, quadro; **behind the scenes** dietro le quinte; **to make a scene** fare una scenata

scener•y ['sinərɪ] *s* (-ies) paesaggio; (*theat*) scenario

scenic ['sinɪk] or ['sɛnɪk] *adj* pittoresco; (*pertaining to the stage*) scenico

scent [sɛnt] *s* odore *m*; profumo; (*sense of smell*) fiuto, odorato; (*trail*) traccia, pista || *tr* profumare; (*to detect*) fiutare, annusare

scepter ['sɛptər] *s* scettro

sceptic ['skɛptɪk] *adj & s* scettico

sceptical ['skɛptɪkəl] *adj* scettico

scepticism ['skɛptɪ,sɪzəm] *s* scetticismo

schedule ['skɛdʒul] *s* lista; programma *m*; (*of trains, planes, etc.*) orario || *tr* programmare; mettere in orario

scheme [skim] *s* schema *m*; piano, progetto; (*plot*) trama || *tr* progettare; tramare

schemer ['skimər] *s* progettista *mf*; (*underhanded*) manipolatore *m*, concertatore *m*

scheming ['skimɪŋ] *adj* intrigante, scaltro

schism ['sɪzəm] *s* scisma *m*

schist [ʃɪst] *s* scisto

scholar ['skɑlər] *s* (*pupil*) alunno; detentore *m* di una borsa di studio; (*learned person*) dotto, studioso

scholarly ['skɑlərlɪ] *adj* erudito, studioso

scholarship ['skɑlər,ʃɪp] *s* erudizione; (*money*) borsa di studio

scholasticism [skə'læstɪ,sɪzəm] *s* scolastica

school [skul] *s* scuola; (*of a university*) facoltà *f*; (*of fish*) banco || *tr* istruire, insegnare

school' age' *s* età scolastica

school'bag' *s* cartella

school' board' *s* comitato scolastico

school'boy' *s* alunno, scolaro

school' bus' *s* scuolabus *m*

school' day' *s* giorno di scuola; durata della giornata scolastica

school'girl' *s* alunna, scolara

school'house' *s* scuola, edificio scolastico

schooling ['skulɪŋ] *s* istruzione

school'mas'ter *s* maestro di scuola; direttore scolastico

school'mate' *s* compagno di scuola, condiscepolo

school'room' *s* aula scolastica

school'teach'er *s* maestro

school' year' *s* anno scolastico

schooner ['skunər] *s* goletta

sciatica [saɪ'ætɪkə] *s* (pathol) sciatica

science ['saɪ·əns] *s* scienza

sci'ence fic'tion *s* fantascienza

sci'ence-fic'tion *adj* fantascientifico

scientific [,saɪ·ən'tɪfɪk] *adj* scientifico

scientist ['saɪ·əntɪst] *s* scienziato

scimitar ['sɪmɪtər] *s* scimitarra

scintillate ['sɪntɪ,let] *intr* scintillare

scion ['saɪ·ən] *s* rampollo, discendente *m*

scissors ['sɪzərz] *ssg* or *spl* forbici *fpl*

scoff [skɔf] or [skɑf] *s* dileggio, beffa || *intr* burlarsi; **to scoff at** burlarsi di, dileggiare

scold [skold] *s* megera || *tr & intr* sgridare, rimproverare

scoop [skup] *s* (*ladlelike utensil*) paletta; (*kitchen utensil*) cucchiaio, cucchiaione *m*; cucchiaiata; palettata; (*of dredge*) benna; (*hollow*) buco; (naut) gottazza; (journ) primizia, esclusiva; (coll) colpo || *tr* vuotare a cucchiaiate; (journ) battere; (naut) gottare; **to scoop out** (*e.g., sand*) scavare; (*soup*) scodellare

scoot [skut] *s* (coll) corsa || *intr* (coll) correre precipitosamente

scooter ['skutər] *s* monopattino

scope [skop] *s* ampiezza; lunghezza; **to give full scope to** dare piena libertà d'azione a

scorch [skɔrtʃ] *s* scottatura || *tr* bruciacchiare; bruciare, inaridire; (fig) ferire || *intr* bruciarsi

scorching ['skɔrtʃɪŋ] *adj* bruciante

score [skor] *s* (*in a game*) punteggio; (*in an examination*) nota; linea, segno, marca; (*twenty*) ventina; (mus) partitura; **scores** un mucchio; **to keep score** segnare il punteggio; **to settle a score** (fig) saldare un conto || *tr* raggiungere il punteggio di, fare; marcare; guadagnare; (*to censure*) sgridare, rimproverare; (mus) orchestrare

score'board' *s* quadro del punteggio

score'keep'er *s* segnapunti *m*

scorn [skɔrn] *s* disdegno, disprezzo || *tr & intr* disdegnare, disprezzare

scornful ['skɔrnfəl] *adj* disdegnoso

Scorpio ['skɔrpɪ,o] *s* Scorpione *m*

scorpion ['skɔrpɪ·ən] *s* scorpione *m*

Scot [skɑt] *s* scozzese *mf*

Scotch [skɑtʃ] *adj* scozzese || *s* scozzese *m*; whisky *m* scozzese; **the Scotch** gli scozzesi

Scotch'man *s* (-men) scozzese *m*

Scotch' pine' *s* pino silvestre

Scotch' tape' *s* (trademark) nastro autoadesivo Scotch

scot'-free' *adj* impune; **to get off scot-free** farla franca

Scotland ['skɑtlənd] *s* la Scozia

Scottish ['skɑtɪʃ] *adj* scozzese || *s* scozzese *mf*; **the Scottish** gli scozzesi

scoundrel ['skaʊndrəl] *s* birbante *m*, farabutto, manigoldo

scour [skaʊr] *tr* sgrassare fregando, pulire fregando; (*the countryside*) battere

scourge [skʌrdʒ] *s* sferza; (fig) flagello || *tr* sferzare

scout [skaut] *s* esplorazione; giovane esploratore *m*; giovane esploratrice *f*; (mil) ricognitore *m*; (nav) esploratore *m*; (slang) tipo ‖ *tr* esplorare, riconoscere; cercar di trovare; disdegnare

scouting [ˈskautɪŋ] *s* scoutismo

scowl [skaul] *s* cipiglio ‖ *intr* aggrottare le ciglia; guardare torvamente

scram [skræm] *v* (*pret & pp* **scrammed**; *ger* **scramming**) *intr* (coll) tagliare la corda; **scram!** (coll) vattene!, (coll) escimi di tra i piedi!

scramble [ˈskræmbəl] *s* ruffa, gara ‖ *tr* (*to grab up*) arraffare; confondere, mescolare; (*eggs*) strapazzare ‖ *intr* arrampicarsi; (*to struggle*) azzuffarsi

scram'bled eggs' *spl* uova strapazzate

scrap [skræp] *s* pezzetto, frammento; ritaglio, rottame *m*; (coll) baruffa; **scraps** avanzi *mpl*; ‖ *v* (*pret & pp* **scrapped**; *ger* **scrapping**) *tr* scartare ‖ *intr* (coll) fare baruffa

scrap'book' *s* album *m* di ritagli (di giornale o fotografie)

scrape [skrep] *s* impiccio, imbroglio; baruffa ‖ *tr* raschiare, graffiare; **to scrape together** racimolare ‖ *intr* raschiare; **to scrape along** vivacchiare; **to scrape through** passare per il rotto della cuffia

scraper [ˈskrepər] *s* raschietto

scrap' i'ron *s* rottami *mpl* di ferro

scrap' pa'per *s* carta straccia; carta da appunti

scratch [skrætʃ] *s* graffio, scalfittura; scarabocchio; (billiards) punto perduto; (sports) linea di partenza; **from scratch** a bel principio; dal niente; **up to scratch** soddisfacente ‖ *tr* graffiare, grattare; (*e.g., a horse*) cancellare ‖ *intr* graffiare; (*said of a chicken*) raspare; (*said of a pen*) grattare

scratch' pad' *s* quaderno per appunti

scratch' pa'per *s* carta da appunti

scrawl [skrɔl] *s* scarabocchio ‖ *tr & intr* scarabocchiare

scraw-ny [ˈskrɔni] *adj* (**-nier; -niest**) ossuto, scarno

scream [skrim] *s* grido, strillo; cosa divertentissima; persona divertentissima ‖ *intr* gridare, strillare

screech [skritʃ] *s* stridio ‖ *intr* stridere

screech' owl' *s* gufo; (barn owl) barbagianni *m*

screen [skrin] *s* (*movable partition*) paravento; (*in front of fire*) parafuoco; rete metallica; (*sieve*) vaglio; (mov; phys) schermo; (telv) teleschermo ‖ *tr* schermare; riparare, proteggere; (*to sieve*) vagliare; (*a film*) proiettare; (*to adapt*) (mov) sceneggiare

screen' grid' *s* (rad, telv) griglia schermo

screen' test' *s* provino

screw [skru] *s* vite *f*; giro di vite; (*of a boat*) elica; **to have a screw loose** (slang) avere una rotella fuori di posto; **to put the screws on** far pressione su ‖ *tr* avvitare; (*to twist*)

torcere; **to screw up** (slang) rovinare; **to screw up one's courage** prendere il coraggio a quattro mani ‖ *intr* avvitarsi

screw'ball' *s* (slang) pazzoide *m*, svitato

screw'driv'er *s* cacciavite *m*

screw' eye' *s* occhiello a vite

screw' jack' *s* martinetto a vite

screw' propel'ler *s* elica

screw-y [ˈskru-i] *adj* (**-ier; -iest**) (slang) pazzo; (slang) fuori di posto, strano

scribble [ˈskrɪbəl] *s* scarabocchio ‖ *tr & intr* scarabocchiare

scribe [skraɪb] *s* (*Jewish scholar*) scriba *m*; copista *mf* ‖ *tr* tracciare, incidere

scrimmage [ˈskrɪmɪdʒ] *s* ruffa; (*football*) azione

scrimp [skrɪmp] *tr & intr* lesinare

script [skrɪpt] *s* scrittura, scrittura a mano; manoscritto; testo; (*e.g., of a play*) copione *m*; (typ) carattere *m* inglese

scriptural [ˈskrɪptʃərəl] *adj* scritturale, biblico

scripture [ˈskrɪptʃər] *s* scrittura ‖ **Scripture** *s* Scrittura

script'writ'er *s* soggettista *mf*

scrofula [ˈskrɔfjələ] *s* scrofola

scroll [skrol] *s* rotolo di carta, rotolo di pergamena; (*of violin*) riccio; (archit) voluta, cartoccio

scroll'work' *s* ornamentazione a voluta

scro-tum [ˈskrotəm] *s* (**-ta** [tə] *or* **-tums**) scroto

scrub [skrʌb] *s* boscaglia; alberelli *mpl*; animale bastardo; persona di poco conto; (*act of scrubbing*) fregata; (sports) giocatore *m* di riserva ‖ *v* (*pret & pp* **scrubbed**; *ger* **scrubbing**) *tr* pulire, fregare

scrub' oak' *s* rovere basso

scrub'wom'an *s* (**-wom'en**) lavatrice *f*, donna a giornata

scruff [skrʌf] *s* nuca, collottola

scruple [ˈskrupəl] *s* scrupolo

scrupulous [ˈskrupjələs] *adj* scrupoloso

scrutinize [ˈskrutɪˌnaɪz] *tr* scrutare, disaminare

scruti-ny [ˈskrutɪni] *s* (**-nies**) attento esame, disamina

scuff [skʌf] *s* graffio, logorio ‖ *tr* logorare, graffiare

scuffle [ˈskʌfəl] *s* zuffa, rissa ‖ *intr* azzuffarsi, colluttare

scull [skʌl] *s* (*oar*) remo a bratto; (*boat*) canotto ‖ *tr* spingere a bratto ‖ *intr* vogare a bratto

sculler-y [ˈskʌləri] *s* (**-ies**) retrocucina

scullion [ˈskʌljən] *s* sguattero

sculptor [ˈskʌlptər] *s* scultore *m*

sculptress [ˈskʌlptrɪs] *s* scultrice *f*

sculpture [ˈskʌlptʃər] *s* scultura ‖ *tr & intr* scolpire

scum [skʌm] *s* schiuma; (*slag*) scoria; (*rabble*) feccia, gentaglia ‖ *v* (*pret & pp* **scummed**; *ger* **scumming**) *tr & intr* schiumare

scum·my ['skʌmi] *adj* (-mier; -miest) spumoso; (coll) vile, schifoso

scurf [skʌrf] *s* (*shed by the skin*) squama; incrostazione

scurrilous ['skʌrɪləs] *adj* scurrile

scur·ry ['skʌri] *v* (*pret & pp* -ried) *intr* affrettarsi; **to scurry around** dimenarsi

scur·vy ['skʌrvi] *adj* (-vier; -viest) spregevole, meschino ‖ *s* scorbuto

scuttle ['skʌtəl] *s* (*for coal*) secchio; (*trap door*) botola; corsa, fuga; (naut) boccaporto ‖ *tr* aprire una falla in, affondare ‖ *intr* affrettarsi, darsi alla corsa

scut·tle·butt *s* (naut) barilozzo dell'acqua; (coll) rumore *m*, diceria

scuttling ['skʌtlɪŋ] *s* autoaffondamento

Scylla ['sɪlə] *s* Scilla; **between Scylla and Charybdis** fra Scilla e Cariddi

scythe [saɪð] *s* falce *f*

sea [si] *s* mare *m*; (*wave*) maroso; **at sea** in alto mare; **by the sea** a mare, sulla costa; **to follow the sea** farsi marinaio; **to put to sea** prendere il largo

sea'board' *adj* costiero ‖ *s* litorale *m*

sea' breeze' *s* brezza marina

sea'coast' *s* costa, litorale *m*

sea' dog' *s* (*seal*) foca; (*sailor*) lupo di mare

seafarer ['si,ferər] *s* marinaio; viaggiatore marittimo

sea'food' *s* pesce *m*; (*shellfish*) frutti *mpl* di mare

seagoing ['si,go·ɪŋ] *adj* di alto mare

sea' gull' *s* gabbiano

seal [sil] *s* sigillo; (*sea animal*) foca; (fig) suggello ‖ *tr* sigillare, apporre i sigilli a; (fig) suggellare

sea' legs' *spl* **to have good sea legs** avere piede marino

sea' lev'el *s* livello del mare

seal'ing wax' *s* ceralacca

seal'skin' *s* pelle *f* di foca

seam [sim] *s* (*abutting of edges*) giuntura; (*stitches*) costura, cucitura; (*scar*) cicatrice *f*; (*wrinkle*) ruga; (in metal) commettitura; (min) filone *m*, vena

sea'man *s* (-men) marinaio

sea' mile' *s* miglio marino

seamless ['simlɪs] *adj* senza giuntura; (*stockings*) senza cucitura

seamstress ['simstrɪs] *s* cucitrice *f*

seam·y ['simi] *adj* (-ier; -iest) pieno di cuciture; basso, sordido; (*unpleasant*) spiacevole

séance ['se·ɑns] *s* seduta spiritica

sea'plane' *s* idrovolante *m*

sea'port' *s* porto di mare

sea' pow'er *s* potenza navale

sear [sɪr] *adj* secco ‖ *s* scottatura ‖ *tr* scottare, bruciare; (*to brand*) marcare a fuoco; inaridire; (fig) indurire

search [sʌrtʃ] *s* ricerca, investigazione; (*frisking a person*) perquisizione; **in search of** in cerca di ‖ *tr* cercare, investigare; perquisire, frugare ‖ *intr* investigare; **to search for** cercare; **to search into** investigare

searching ['sʌrtʃɪŋ] *adj* (e.g., *inspec-*

tion) profondo; (e.g., *glance*) indagatore, penetrante

search'light' *s* proiettore *m*, riflettore *m*; (mil) fotoelettrica

search' war'rant *s* mandato di perquisizione

sea'scape' *s* vista del mare; (*painting*) marina

sea' shell' *s* conchiglia

sea'shore' *s* costa, marina, mare *m*

sea'sick' *adj* **to be seasick** aver mal di mare

sea'sick'ness *s* mal *m* di mare

sea'side' *s* costa, riviera, marina

season ['sizən] *s* stagione; **in season di stagione; in season and out of season** sempre, continuamente; **out of season** fuori stagione ‖ *tr* (*food*) condire; (*to mature*) stagionare; (e.g., *wood*) stagionare

seasonal ['sizənəl] *adj* stagionale

seasoning ['sizənɪŋ] *s* condimento; (of *wood*) stagionamento

sea'son's greet'ings *spl* migliori auguri *mpl* per le feste natalizie

sea'son tick'et *s* biglietto d'abbonamento

seat [sit] *s* sedia; (*part of chair*) sedile *m*; (*of human body*) sedere *m*; (of *pants*) fondo; sito, posto; (e.g., of *government*) sede *f*; (in parliament) seggio; (e.g., of *learning*) centro; (rr, theat) posto ‖ *tr* far sedere; aver posti per; (a *chair*) mettere il sedile a; (*pants*) mettere il fondo a; (an *official*) insediare; (mach) installare; **to be seated** essere seduto; **to seat oneself** sedersi

seat' belt' *s* cintura di sicurezza

seat' cov'er *s* guaina, foderina

seat'ing room' *s* posti *mpl* a sedere

sea' wall' *s* diga

sea'way' *s* via marittima; alto mare; mare grosso; rotta percorsa; via di fiume accessibile a navi da trasporto

sea'weed' *s* alga marina; pianta marina

sea'wor'thy *adj* atto a tenere il mare

secede [sɪ'sid] *intr* separarsi, distaccarsi

secession [sɪ'sɛʃən] *s* secessione

seclude [sɪ'klud] *tr* appartare; isolare

seclusion [sɪ'kluʒən] *s* reclusione; solitudine *f*, intimità *f*

second ['sɛkənd] *adj & pron* secondo; **to be second to none** non cederla a nessuno ‖ *s* secondo; (in a *duel*) padrino; (in *dates*) due *m*; (aut, mus) seconda; **seconds** (com) articoli *mpl* di seconda qualità; **to have seconds on** servirsi una seconda volta di ‖ *tr* assecondare; (a *motion*) appoggiare ‖ *adv* in secondo luogo

secondar·y ['sɛkən,dɛri] *adj* secondario ‖ *s* (-ies) (elec) secondario

sec'ond-best' *adj* (il) migliore dopo il primo; **to come off second-best** arrivare secondo

sec'ond-class' *adj* di seconda qualità; (aer, naut, rr) di seconda classe

sec'ond hand' *s* lancetta dei secondi

sec'ond·hand' *adj* di seconda mano, d'occasione

sec'ond lieuten'ant *s* sottotenente *m*

sec'ond-rate' *adj* di seconda categoria; (*inferior*) da strapazzo

sec'ond sight' *s* chiaroveggenza

sec'ond wind' [wɪnd] *s*—**to get one's second wind** riprendere fiato

secre·cy ['sikrəsɪ] *s* (-**cies**) segretezza; **in secrecy** in segreto

secret ['sikrɪt] *adj & s* segreto; **in secret** in segreto

secretar·y ['sɛkrɪ,tɛrɪ] *s* (-**ies**) segretario; (*desk*) scrittoio

se'cret bal'lot *s* scrutinio segreto

secrete [sɪ'krit] *tr* nascondere; (physiol) secernere

secretive ['sikrɪtɪv] or [sɪ'krɪtɪv] *adj* riservato, poco comunicativo

sect [sɛkt] *s* setta

sectarian [sɛk'tɛrɪ·ən] *adj & s* settario

section ['sɛkʃən] *s* sezione; (*of city*) rione *m*; (*of fruit*) spicchio; (*of highway*) tronco; (rr) tratta ‖ *tr* sezionare

sectional ['sɛkʃənəl] *adj* (e.g., *bookcase*) componibile; sezionale; locale, regionale

secular ['sɛkjələr] *adj & s* secolare *m*

secularism ['sɛkjələ,rɪzəm] *s* laicismo

secure [sɪ'kjur] *adj* salvo, sicuro ‖ *tr* ottenere; assicurare; fissare; (law) garantire

securi·ty [sɪ'kjurɪtɪ] *s* (-**ties**) sicurezza; protezione; garanzia; (*person*) garante *m*; **securities** valori *mpl*, titoli *mpl*

sedan [sɪ'dæn] *s* (aut) berlina

sedan' chair' *s* bussola, portantina

sedate [sɪ'det] *adj* calmo, posato

sedation [sɪ'deʃən] *s* ritorno alla calma; stato di calma mentale

sedative ['sɛdətɪv] *adj & s* sedativo

sedentary ['sɛdən,tɛrɪ] *adj* sedentario

sedge [sɛdʒ] *s* carice *m*

sediment ['sɛdɪmənt] *s* sedimento

sedition [sɪ'dɪʃən] *s* sedizione

seditious [sɪ'dɪʃəs] *adj* sedizioso

seduce [sɪ'djus] or [sɪ'dus] *tr* sedurre

seducer [sɪ'djusər] or [sɪ'dusər] *s* seduttore *m*, corruttore *m*

seduction [sɪ'dʌkʃən] *s* seduzione

seductive [sɪ'dʌktɪv] *adj* seduttore

sedulous ['sɛdjələs] *adj* diligente

see [si] *s* (eccl) sede *f* ‖ *v* (*pret* **saw** [sɔ]; *pp* **seen** [sin]) *tr* vedere; **to see off** andare ad accompagnare; **to see through** portare a termine ‖ *intr* vedere; **see here!** faccia attenzione!; **to see after** prender cura di; **to see through** conoscere il gioco di

seed [sid] *s* seme *m*, semenza; **to go to seed** andare in semenza; deteriorarsi ‖ *tr* seminare; (*fruit*) togliere i semi da ‖ *intr* seminare; produrre semi

seed'bed' *s* semenzaio; (fig) vivaio

seeder ['sidər] *s* (*person*) seminatore *m*; (*machine*) seminatrice *f*

seedling ['sidlɪŋ] *s* piantina da trapianto

seed·y ['sidɪ] *adj* (-**ier**; -**iest**) pieno di semi; (*unkempt*) malmesso, malvestito

seeing ['si·ɪŋ] *conj* visto che, dato che

See'ing Eye' dog' *s* cane *m* guida per ciechi

seek [sik] *v* (*pret & pp* **sought** [sɔt]) *tr* cercare, ricercare; **to be sought after** essere ricercato; **to seek to** cercare di

seem [sim] *intr* parere, sembrare

seemingly ['simɪŋlɪ] *adv* apparentemente

seem·ly ['simlɪ] *adj* (-**lier**; -**liest**) decoroso; appropriato

seep [sip] *intr* colare, filtrare

seer [sɪr] *s* profeta *m*, veggente *m*

see'saw' *s* altalena; (*motion*) viavai *m* ‖ *intr* altalenare

seethe [sið] *intr* bollire

segment ['sɛgmənt] *s* segmento

segregate ['sɛgrɪ,get] *tr* segregare

segregation [,sɛgrɪ'geʃən] *s* segregazione

segregationist [,sɛgrɪ'geʃənɪst] *s* segregazionista *mf*

Seine [sɛn] *s* Senna

seismograph ['saɪzmə,græf] or ['saɪzmə,grɑf] *s* sismografo

seismology [saɪz'mɑlədʒɪ] *s* sismologia

seize [siz] *tr* afferrare; impossessarsi di; (*with one's clenched fist*) impugnare; comprendere; (law) sequestrare, confiscare

seizure ['siʒər] *s* conquista, cattura; (*of an illness*) attacco; (law) sequestro, pignoramento

seldom ['sɛldəm] *adj* di raro, raramente

select [sɪ'lɛkt] *adj* scelto, selezionato ‖ *tr* prescegliere, selezionare

selectee [sɪ,lɛk'ti] *s* (mil) recluta

selection [sɪ'lɛkʃən] *s* selezione, scelta

selective [sɪ'lɛktɪv] *adj* selettivo

self [sɛlf] *adj* stesso ‖ *s* (**selves** [sɛlvz]) sé stesso; io, personalità *f*; **all by one's self** senza aiuto altrui ‖ *pron* sé stesso

self'-abuse' *s* abuso delle proprie forze; masturbazione

self'-addressed' *adj* col nome e l'indirizzo del mittente

self'-cen'tered *adj* egocentrico

self'-con'scious *adj* imbarazzato, vergognoso, timido

self'-control' *s* padronanza di sé stesso, autocontrollo

self'-defense' *s* autodifesa; **in self-defense** in legittima difesa

self'-deni'al *s* abnegazione

self'-deter'mina'tion *s* autodeterminazione

self'-dis'cipline *s* autodisciplina

self'-ed'ucat'ed *adj* autodidatta

self'-employed' *adj* che lavora in proprio

self'-ev'i·dent *adj* evidente, lampante

self'-ex·plan'a·tor'y *adj* ovvio, che si spiega da sé

self'-gov'ernment *s* autogoverno; controllo sopra sé stesso

self'-im·por'tant *adj* presuntuoso

self'-in·dul'gence *s* intemperanza

self'-in'terest *s* egoismo, interesse *m*

selfish ['sɛlfɪʃ] *adj* egoista

selfishness ['sɛlfɪʃnɪs] *s* egoismo

selfless ['selflɪs] *adj* disinteressato; altruista

self'-liq'ui·dat'ing *adj* autoammortizzabile

self'-love' *s* amor proprio

self'-made' *adj* che si è fatto da sé

self'-por'trait *s* autoritratto

self'-pos·sessed' *adj* calmo, padrone di sé

self'-pres'er·va'tion *s* conservazione

self'-pro·pelled' *adj* semovente

self'-re·li'ant *adj* pieno di fiducia in sé stesso

self'-re·spect' *s* rispetto di sé stesso

self'-right'eous *adj* che si considera più morale degli altri, ipocrita

self'-sac'ri·fice' *s* sacrificio di sé, spirito di sacrifico

self'-same' *adj* stesso e medesimo

self'-sat'is·fied' *adj* contento di sé

self'-seek'ing *adj* egoista || *s* egoismo

self'-serv'ice *s* autoservizio

self'-start'er *s* motorino d'avviamento

self'-styled' *adj* sedicente

self'-support' *s* indipendenza economica

self'-tap'ping screw' *s* vite *f* autofilettante

self'-taught' *adj* autodidatta

self-threading ['self'θredɪŋ] *adj* autofilettante

self'-willed' *adj* ostinato, caparbio

self'-wind'ing *adj* a carica automatica

sell [sɛl] *v* (*pret & pp* **sold** [sold]) *tr* vendere; (*an idea*) fare accettare; **to sell off** svendere, liquidare; **to sell out** smerciare; vendere a stralcio; (coll) tradire || *intr* vendere, vendersi; fare il venditore; **to sell off** (*said of the stock market*) essere in ribasso; **to sell out** vendere a stralcio; vendersi

seller ['sɛlər] *s* venditore *m*

Selt'zer wa'ter ['sɛltsər] *s* selz *m*

selvage ['sɛlvɪdʒ] *s* cimosa, vivagno

semantic [sɪ'mæntɪk] *adj* semantico || **semantics** *s* semantica

semaphore ['sɛmə,for] *s* semaforo

semblance ['sɛmbləns] *s* apparenza, specie *f;* apparizione

semen ['simɛn] *s* sperma *m*

semester [sɪ'mɛstər] *adj* semestrale || *s* semestre *m*

semicircle ['sɛmɪ,sʌrkəl] *s* semicircolo

semicolon ['sɛmɪ,kolən] *s* punto e virgola

semiconductor [,sɛmɪkən'dʌktər] *s* semiconduttore *m*

semiconscious [,sɛmɪ'kanʃəs] *adj* mezzo cosciente

semifinal [,sɛmɪ'faɪnəl] *s* semifinale *f*

semilearned [,sɛmɪ'lʌrnɪd] *adj* semidotto

semimonth·ly [,sɛmɪ'mʌnθli] *or* [,semaɪ'mʌnθli] *adj* quindicinale || *s* (-lies) rivista quindicinale

seminar ['sɛmɪ,nar] *or* [,sɛmɪ'nar] *s* seminario

seminar·y ['sɛmɪ,nɛri] *s* (-ies) seminario

Semite ['sɛmaɪt] *or* ['simaɪt] *s* semita *mf*

Semitic [sɪ'mɪtɪk] *adj* semitico || *s* lingua semitica; (*family of languages*) semitico

semitrailer ['sɛmɪ,trelər] *s* semirimorchio

semiweek·ly [,sɛmɪ'wikli] *or* [,semaɪ'wikli] *adj* bisettimanale || *s* (-lies) periodico bisettimanale

semiyearly [,sɛmɪ'jɪrli] *or* [,semaɪ'jɪrli] *adj* semestrale || *adv* due volte all'anno

senate ['sɛnɪt] *s* senato

senator ['sɛnətər] *s* senatore *m*

send [sɛnd] *v* (*pret & pp* **sent** [sɛnt]) *tr* inviare, mandare; spedire; (*e.g., a punch*) lanciare; **to send back** rimandare; **to send forth** emettere; **to send packing** licenziare su due piedi || *intr* (rad) trasmettere; **to send for** mandare a chiamare, far venire

sender ['sɛndər] *s* speditore *m*, mittente *m;* (telg) trasmettitore *m*

send'-off' *s* (coll) addio affettuoso; (coll) lancio

senility [sɪ'nɪlɪti] *s* (pathol) senilismo

senior ['sinjər] *adj* maggiore, più anziano; senior, di grado più elevato; dell'ultimo anno, laureando; senior, il vecchio || *s* maggiore *m;* seniore *m,* persona di grado più elevato; studente *m* dell'ultimo anno, laureando

sen'ior cit'izen *s* vecchio, pensionato

seniority [sin'jarɪti] *or* [sin'jɔrɪti] *s* anzianità *f*

sensation [sɛn'seʃən] *s* sensazione

sensational [sɛn'seʃənəl] *adj* sensazionale

sense [sɛns] *s* senso; **in a sense** in un certo senso; **to come to one's senses** riprendere il giudizio; **to make sense out of** arrivare a capire; **to take leave of one's senses** perdere il ben dell'intelletto || *tr* intuire; comprendere

senseless ['sɛnslɪs] *adj* (*unconscious*) privo di sensi; (*meaningless*) insensato, privo di senso

sense' or'gan *s* organo di senso

sensibili·ty [,sɛnsɪ'bɪlɪti] *s* (-ties) sensibilità *f;* **sensibilities** suscettibilità *f*

sensible ['sɛnsɪbəl] *adj* sensato; (*keenly aware*) sensibile; cosciente

sensitive ['sɛnsɪtɪv] *adj* sensitivo, sensibile; delicato

sensitize ['sɛnsɪ,taɪz] *tr* sensibilizzare

sensory ['sɛnsəri] *adj* sensorio

sensual ['sɛnʃʊ·əl] *adj* sensuale

sensuous ['sɛnʃʊ·əs] *adj* sensuale

sentence ['sɛntəns] *s* (gram) frase; (law) sentenza, condanna || *tr* sentenziare, condannare

sentiment ['sɛntɪmənt] *s* sentimento

sentimental [,sɛntɪ'mɛntəl] *adj* sentimentale

sentimentalism [,sɛntɪ'mɛntəl,ɪzəm] *s* sentimentalismo

sentinel ['sɛntɪnəl] *s* sentinella; **to stand sentinel** montare di sentinella

sen·try ['sɛntri] *s* (-tries) sentinella

sen'try box' *s* garitta, casotto

separate ['sɛpərɪt] *adj* separato ||

['sepə ˌret] *tr* separare ‖ *intr* separarsi

separation [ˌsepə're/ən] *s* separazione

Sephardic [sɪ'fardɪk] *adj* sefardita

September [sep'tembər] *s* settembre *m*

septic ['septɪk] *adj* settico

sep'tic tank' *s* fossa settica

sepulcher ['sepəlkər] *s* sepolcro

sequel ['sikwəl] *s* seguito

sequence ['sikwəns] *s* serie *f*, sequenza, successione; conseguenza; (*cards, eccl, mov*) sequenza; (*gram*) correlazione

sequester [sɪ'kwestər] *tr* isolare, appartare; (*law*) sequestrare

sequin ['sikwɪn] *s* lustrino

ser-aph ['serəf] *s* (**-aphs** or **-aphim** [əfɪm]) serafino

Serbian ['sɑrbɪ-ən] *adj* & *s* serbo

Serbo-Croatian [ˌsɑrbokro'e/ən] *adj* & *s* serbocroato

sere [sɪr] *adj* secco, appassito

serenade [ˌserə'ned] *s* serenata ‖ *tr* fare la serenata a ‖ *intr* fare la serenata

serene [sɪ'rin] *adj* sereno

serenity [sɪ'renɪti] *s* serenità *f*

serf [sʌrf] *s* servo della gleba

serfdom ['sʌrfdəm] *s* servitù *f* della gleba

serge [sʌrdʒ] *s* saia

sergeant ['sɑrdʒənt] *s* sergente *m*

ser'geant at arms' *s* (**ser'geants at arms'**) ufficiale *m* delegato a mantenere l'ordine

ser'geant ma'jor *s* (**sergeants major** or **sergeant majors**) (*in U.S. Army*) sergente *m* maggiore; (*in Italian Army*) maresciallo

serial ['sɪrɪ-əl] *adj* a puntate, a dispense ‖ *s* periodico; romanzo a puntate; programma *m* a serie

se'rial num'ber *s* matricola; (*of a book*) segnatura; (*aut*) matricola di telaio

se-ries ['sɪrɪz] *s* (**-ries**) serie *f*; (*works dealing with the same topic*) collana; **in series** (elec) in serie

serious ['sɪrɪ-əs] *adj* serio

seriousness ['sɪrɪ-əsnɪs] *s* serietà *f*; **in all seriousness** molto sul serio

sermon ['sʌrmən] *s* sermone *m*

sermonize ['sʌrmə ˌnaɪz] *tr* & *intr* sermonare

serpent ['sʌrpənt] *s* serpente *m*

se-rum ['sɪrəm] *s* (**-rums** or **-ra** [rə]) siero

servant ['sʌrvənt] *s* servo, domestico; (*civil servant*) funzionario; (fig) servitore *m*

serv'ant girl' *s* serva, domestica

serv'ant prob'lem *s* crisi *f* ancillare

serve [sʌrv] *s* (*in tennis*) servizio ‖ *tr* servire; (*a sentence*) espiare; (*to suffice*) bastare (with *dat*); (*a writ*) notificare; **to serve s.o. right** stare bene (with *dat*), e.g., **it serves him right** gli sta bene ‖ *intr* servire; **to serve as** fare da

service ['sʌrvɪs] *s* servizio; (*of a writ*) notifica; (*branch of the armed forces*) arma; **at your service** per servirLa ‖ *tr* rifornire, riparare

serviceable ['sʌrvɪsəbəl] *adj* utile; durevole; pratico; riparabile

serv'ice club' *s* casa del soldato

serv'ice-man' *s* (**-men'**) militare *m*; riparatore *m*, aggiustatore *m*

serv'ice mod'ule *s* modulo di servizio

serv'ice rec'ord *s* stato di servizio

serv'ice sta'tion *s* stazione di servizio or di rifornimento

serv'ice-sta'tion attend'ant *s* benzinaio

serv'ice stripe' *s* gallone *m*

servile ['sʌrvɪl] *adj* servile

servitude ['sʌrvɪ ˌtjud] or ['sʌrvɪ ˌtud] *s* servitù *f*; lavori forzati

sesame ['sesəmi] *s* sesamo; **open sesame** apriti sesamo

session ['se/ən] *s* sessione *f*, seduta

set [set] *adj* determinato, preordinato; abituale; fisso, rigido; (*ready*) pronto; meditato, studiato ‖ *s* (*e.g., of books*) collezione, serie *f*; (*e.g., of chess*) gioco; set *m*, insieme *m*, completo; (*of tires*) treno; (*of horses*) pariglia; (*of tennis*) partita; (*of dishes*) servizio; (*of kitchen utensils*) batteria; posizione, atteggiamento; (*of a garment*) linea; (*e.g., of cement*) presa; (*of people*) gruppo; (*of thieves*) genìa; (*of sails*) muta; (*of lines*) (geom) fascio; (rad, telv) apparato; (theat, mov) set *m* ‖ *v* (*pret* & *pp* **set**; *ger* **setting**) *tr* porre, deporre; mettere; (*fire*) dare; (*the table*) imbandire; (*a watch*) regolare; (*s.o. a certain number of tricks*) far cadere di; (*a price*) fissare; (*a gem*) incastonare; (*a fracture*) mettere a posto; (*a saw*) allicciare; (*a trap*) tendere; (*hair*) acconciare; stabilire; insediare; (*to plant*) piantare; (*a sail*) tendere; (*e.g., milk*) rapprendere; calibrare, tarare; (*cement*) solidificare; (*typ*) comporre; **to set back** ritardare; (*a clock*) mettere indietro; **to set forth** descrivere; **to set one's heart on** desiderare ardentemente; **to set store by** tenere in gran conto; **to set up** metter su; impiantare; (*drinks*) (slang) pagare ‖ *intr* (said, e.g., of the sun) tramontare; (*said of a liquid*) solidificarsi; (*said of cement*) fare presa; (*said of milk*) rapprendersi; (*said of a hen*) covare; (*said of a garment*) cascare; (*said of hair*) prendere la piega; **to set about** mettersi a; **to set out** porsi in cammino; **to set out to** mettersi a; **to set to work** mettersi a lavorare; **to set upon** attaccare

set'back' *s* rovescio, contrarietà *f*

set'screw' *s* vite *f* di pressione

setting ['setɪŋ] *s* (*environment*) ambiente *m*; (*of a gem*) montatura; (*of cement*) presa; (*e.g., of the sun*) tramonto; (theat) scenario; (mus) arrangiamento

set'ting-up' ex'ercises *spl* ginnastica da camera

settle ['setəl] *tr* determinare, risolvere; sistemare, regolare; (*a bill*) liquidare; installarsi in, colonizzare; calmare; (*a liquid*) far depositare; (law) conciliare ‖ *intr* mettersi d'accordo; saldare un conto; stanziarsi, domiciliarsi; fermarsi, posare; (*said of a liquid*) depositare, calmarsi; solidificarsi; **to settle down to work** mettersi a lavorare di buzzo buono; **to settle on** scegliere, fissare

settlement ['sɛtəlmənt] *s* stabilimento; sistemazione, regolamento; colonia, comunità *f*; (*of a building*) infossamento; agenzia di beneficenza

settler ['sɛtlər] *s* fondatore *m*; colono; conciliatore *m*

set'up' *s* portamento; (*e.g., of tools*) disposizione; quanto è necessario per mescolare una bibita alcolica; (coll) incontro truccato

seven ['sɛvən] *adj & pron* sette ‖ *s* sette *m*; **seven o'clock** le sette

sev'en hun'dred *adj, s & pron* settecento

seventeen ['sɛvən'tin] *adj, s & pron* diciassette *m*

seventeenth ['sɛvən'tinθ] *adj, s & pron* diciassettesimo ‖ *s* (*in dates*) diciassette *m*

seventh ['sɛvənθ] *adj, s & pron* settimo ‖ *s* (*in dates*) sette *m*

seventieth ['sɛvəntɪ-ɪθ] *adj, s & pron* settantesimo

seven·ty ['sɛvəntɪ] *adj & pron* settanta ‖ *s* (**-ties**) settanta *m*; **the seventies** gli anni settanta

sever ['sɛvər] *tr* tagliare, mozzare; (*relations*) troncare ‖ *intr* separarsi

several ['sɛvərəl] *adj* parecchi, vari; rispettivi ‖ *spl* parecchi *mpl*

sev'erance pay' ['sɛvərəns] *s* buonuscita, indennità *f* di licenziamento

severe [sɪ'vɪr] *adj* severo; (*weather*) rigido; (*pain*) acuto; (*illness*) grave

sew [so] *v* (*pret* **sewed**; *pp* **sewed** or **sewn**) *tr & intr* cucire

sewage ['su-ɪdʒ] or ['sju-ɪdʒ] *s* acque *fpl* di scolo or di rifiuto

sewer ['su-ər] or ['sju-ər] *s* fogna, chiavica

sewerage ['su-ərɪdʒ] or ['sju-ərɪdʒ] *s* fognatura; drenaggio, rimozione delle acque di rifiuto

sew'ing machine' ['so-ɪŋ] *s* macchina da cucire

sex [sɛks] *s* sesso

sex' appeal' *s* attrattiva fisica, sex appeal *m*

sextant ['sɛkstənt] *s* sestante *m*

sextet [sɛks'tɛt] *s* sestetto

sexton ['sɛkstən] *s* sagrestano

sexual ['sɛk/ʊ-əl] *adj* sessuale

sex·y ['sɛksɪ] *adj* (**-ier; -iest**) (coll) erotico; (coll) procace

shab·by ['/æbɪ] *adj* (**-bier; -biest**) (*clothes*) frusto; (*house*) malandato; (*person*) malvestito; (*deal*) cattivo

shack [/æk] *s* baracca

shackle ['/ækəl] *s* ceppo; (*to tie an animal*) pastoia; (fig) ostacolo; **shackles** ceppi *mpl*, manette *fpl* ‖ *tr* mettere in ceppi; (fig) inceppare

shad [/æd] *s* alosa

shade [/ed] *s* ombra; (*of lamp*) paralume *m*; (*of window*) tendina; (*for the eyes*) visiera; (*hue*) tinta, sfumatura; **a shade of** un po' di; **shades** tenebre *fpl*; ombre *fpl* ‖ *tr* ombreggiare; sfumare, digradare; (*a price*) ribassare leggermente

shadow ['/edo] *s* ombra ‖ *tr* ombreggiare; (*to follow*) pedinare; **to shadow forth** adombrare, preannunciare

shadowy ['/ædo-i] *adj* ombroso, ombreggiato; illusorio, chimerico

shad·y ['/edi] *adj* (**-ier; -iest**) ombroso; spettrale; (coll) losco; **to keep shady** (slang) starsene lontano

shaft [/æft] or [/ɑft] *s* (*of arrow*) asta; (*of feather*) rachide *f*; (*of light*) raggio; (*handle*) manico; (*of wagon*) stanga, timone *m*; (*of motor*) albero; (*of column*) fusto; (*of elevator*) pozzo; (*in a mountain*) camino; (min) fornello; (fig) frecciata

shag·gy ['/ægi] *adj* (**-gier; -giest**) peloso, irsuto; (*unkempt*) trasandato; (*cloth*) ruvido

shag'gy dog' sto'ry *s* storiella senza capo né coda

shake [/ek] *s* scossa; stretta di mano; momento, istante *m*; **the shakes** la tremarella ‖ *v* (*pret* **shook** [/ʊk]; *pp* **shaken**) *tr* scuotere; scrollare; (*s.o.'s hands*) serrare; (*e.g., with a mixer*) sbattere; agitare, perturbare; eludere, disfarsi di ‖ *intr* tremare; (*to totter*) traballare, tentennare; scuotere; darsi la mano

shake'down' *s* estorsione, concussione; (*bed*) lettuccio di fortuna

shake'down' cruise' *s* (naut) viaggio di prova

shaker ['/ekər] *s* (*e.g., for sugar*) spolverino; (*for cocktails*) sbattighiaccio, shaker *m*

shake'-up' *s* cambiamento completo, riorganizzazione, rimaneggiamento

shak·y ['/ekɪ] *adj* (**-ier; -iest**) tremebondo; traballante; zoppicante

shall [/æl] *v* (*cond* **should** [/ʊd]) *v aux* si usa per formare (1) il futuro dell'indicativo, per es., **I shall do it** lo farò; (2) il futuro perfetto dell'indicativo, per es., **I shall have done it** l'avrò fatto; (3) espressioni di obbligo o necessità, per es., **what shall I do?** che devo fare?, che vuole che faccia?

shallow ['/ælo] *adj* basso, poco profondo; leggero, superficiale

sham [/æm] *adj* falso, finto ‖ *s* frode *f*, contraffazione ‖ *v* (*pret & pp* **shammed**; *ger* **shamming**) *tr & intr* fingere

sham' bat'tle *s* finta battaglia

shambles ['/æmbəlz] *s* macello; confusione, disordine

shame [/em] *s* vergogna; **shame on you!** vergogna!; **what a shame!** che peccato! ‖ *tr* svergognare, disonorare

shame'faced' *adj* timido, vergognoso

shameful ['/emfəl] *adj* vergognoso

shameless ['/emlɪs] *adj* sfrontato, impudente, svergognato

shampoo [ʃæm'pu] *s* shampoo *m* || *tr* fare lo shampoo a

shamrock ['ʃæmrɑk] *s* trifoglio irlandese

shanghai ['ʃæŋhaɪ] or [ʃæŋ'haɪ] *tr* imbarcare a viva forza || **Shanghai** *s* Sciangai *f*

shank [ʃæŋk] *s* fusto; (*of tool*) codolo; (*stem*) gambo; (*of bird*) zampa; (*of anchor*) fuso; (*coll*) principio; (*coll*) fine *f*; **to ride shank's mare** andare col cavallo di San Francesco

shan•ty ['ʃænti] *s* (-ties) bicocca

shan'ty•town' *s* bidonville *f*

shape [ʃep] *s* forma; **in bad shape** in cattive condizioni; **out of shape** sformato || *tr* formare, foggiare; plasmare, conformare || *intr* formarsi; **to take shape** prender forma

shapeless ['ʃeplɪs] *adj* informe

shape•ly ['ʃepli] *adj* (-lier; -liest) ben fatto, formoso

share [ʃɛr] *s* parte *f*; interesse *m*; (*of stock*) azione *f*; (*of plow*) suola; **to go shares** dividere in parti eguali || *tr* (*to enjoy jointly*) condividere; (*to apportion*) ripartire || *intr* partecipare, prender parte

sharecropper ['ʃɛr͵krɑpər] *s* mezzadro

share'hold'er *s* azionista *mf*

shark [ʃɑrk] *s* pescecane *m*; (*schemer*) piovra; (*slang*) espèrto

sharp [ʃɑrp] *adj* affilato, acuto; angoloso; (*e.g., curve*) forte; distinto, ben delineato; (*taste*) pungente, salato; (*pain*) vivo; (*words*) mordace; (*slang*) elegante || *s* (mus) diesis *m* || *adv* acutamente; in punto, e.g., **at seven o'clock sharp** alle sette in punto

sharpen ['ʃɑrpən] *tr* affilare; (*a pencil*) fare la punta a || *intr* affilarsi

sharpener ['ʃɑrpənər] *s* (*person*) affilatore *m*; (*machine*) affilatrice *f*

sharper ['ʃɑrpər] *s* gabbamondo

sharp'shoot'er *s* tiratore scelto

shatter ['ʃætər] *tr* frantumare; sfracellare; (*health*) rovinare; (*nerves*) sconvolgere; distruggere || *intr* frantumarsi, andare in pezzi

shat'ter-proof' *adj* infrangibile

shave [ʃev] *s* rasatura; **to have a close shave** scapparla or scamparla bella || *tr* (*the face*) radere, sbarbare; (*wood*) piallare; (*to scrape*) sfiorare; (*prices*) ridurre; (*a lawn*) tosare || *intr* rasarsi

shaving ['ʃevɪŋ] *adj* da barba, per barba, e.g., **shaving cream** crema da or per barba || *s* rasatura; **shavings** trucioli *mpl*

shav'ing brush' *s* pennello da barba

shav'ing soap' *s* sapone *m* per la barba

shawl [ʃɔl] *s* scialle *m*

she [ʃi] *s* (shes) femmina || *pron pers* (they) essa, lei

sheaf [ʃif] *s* (sheaves [ʃivz]) covone *m*; (*of paper*) fascio

shear [ʃɪr] *s* lama di cesoia; tagliatura; **shears** cesoie *fpl* || *v* (*pret* **sheared**; *pp* **sheared** or **shorn** [ʃɔrn]) *tr* (*sheep*) tosare; (*cloth*) tagliare; **to shear s.o. of** privare qlcu di

sheath [ʃiθ] *s* (sheaths [ʃiðz]) guaina, coperta; (*of a sword*) fodero

sheathe [ʃið] *tr* rinfoderare, inguainare

shed [ʃɛd] *s* portico, tettoia; (geog) spartiacque *m*, versante *m* || *v* (*pret* & *pp* **shed**; *ger* **shedding**) *tr* (e.g., *blood*) spargere, versare; (*light*) dare, fare; (*feathers*) spogliarsi di, lasciar cadere

sheen [ʃin] *s* lucentezza

sheep [ʃip] *s* (sheep) pecora; **sheep's eyes** occhio di triglia; **to separate the sheep from the goats** separare i buoni dai cattivi

sheep'dog' *s* cane *m* da pastore

sheepish ['ʃipɪʃ] *adj* timido, goffo; pecoresco, pedissequo

sheep'skin' *s* pelle *f* di pecora; (*parchment*) cartapecora; (bb) bazzana; (coll) diploma *m*

sheer [ʃɪr] *adj* trasparente, fino, velato; puro; (*cliff*) stagliato || *adv* completamente || *intr* deviare

sheet [ʃit] *s* (*for bed*) lenzuolo; (*of paper*) foglio; (*of metal*) lamina; (*of water*) specchio; (naut) scotta

sheet' light'ning *s* lampeggio all'orizzonte

sheet' met'al *s* lamiera

sheet' mu'sic *s* spartito non rilegato

sheik [ʃik] *s* sceicco; (*great lover*) (slang) rubacuori *m*

shelf [ʃelf] *s* (shelves [ʃelvz]) scaffale *m*, scansia; (*ledge*) terrazzo, ripiano; banco di sabbia; **on the shelf** in disparte, dimenticato

shell [ʃel] *s* (*of egg or crustacean*) guscio; (*of mollusk*) conchiglia; (*of vegetable*) baccello; proietto, proiettile *m*; (*cartridge*) cartuccia; (*of a cartridge*) bossolo; (*framework*) armatura; (*of boiler*) involucro; imbarcazione da regata, schifo, iole *f* || *tr* (*vegetables*) sgranare; bombardare, cannoneggiare; **to shell out** (slang) tirar fuori

shel•lac [ʃə'læk] *s* gomma lacca || *v* (*pret* & *pp* -**lacked**; *ger* -**lacking**) *tr* verniciare con gomma lacca; (slang) dare una batosta a

shell'fish' *ssg* (-**fish**) frutto di mare; crostaceo; *spl* frutti *mpl* di mare; crostacei *mpl*

shell' hole' *s* cratere *m*

shell' shock' *s* psicosi traumatica bellica

shelter ['ʃeltər] *s* rifugio, ricovero; **to take shelter** rifugiarsi || *tr* raccogliere, ospitare, dare rifugio a

shelve [ʃelv] *tr* mettere sullo scaffale; (*a bill*) insabbiare; mettere a riposo

shepherd ['ʃepərd] *s* pastore *m* || *tr* guardare, curarsi di

shep'herd dog' *s* cane *m* da pastore

shepherdess ['ʃepərdɪs] *s* pastora

sherbet ['ʃɜrbət] *s* sorbetto

sheriff ['ʃerɪf] *s* sceriffo

sher•ry ['ʃeri] *s* (-ries) xeres *m*

shield [ʃild] *s* scudo; (*for armpit*) sottoascella *m*; (*badge*) scudetto; (elec) schermo || *tr* proteggere; (elec) schermare

shift [ʃɪft] *s* cambio, cambiamento;

(period of work) turno; *(group of workmen)* operai *mpl* di turno, squadra di lavoro; espediente *m*, sotterfugio ‖ *tr* cambiare; spostare; *(blame)* riversare; ‖ *intr* cambiare; spostarsi; fare da sé; vivere di espedienti; *(rr)* manovrare; *(aut)* cambiare marcia

shift' key' *s* tasto maiuscole

shiftless [ˈʃɪftlɪs] *adj* pigro, ozioso

shift·y [ˈʃɪfti] *adj* (-ier; -iest) astuto; evasivo; pieno d'espedienti; *(glance)* sfuggente

shilling [ˈʃɪlɪŋ] *s* scellino

shimmer [ˈʃɪmər] *s* luccichio ‖ *intr* luccicare, mandare bagliori

shim·my [ˈʃɪmi] *s* (-mies) *(dance)* shimmy *m*; *(aut)* farfallamento delle ruote, shimmy *m* ‖ *intr* ballare lo shimmy; vibrare

shin [ʃɪn] *s* stinco₁ *(of cattle)* cannone *m* ‖ *v* (pret & pp shinned; ger shinning) *tr* arrampicarsi su ‖ *intr* arrampicarsi

shin'bone' *s* stinco, tibia

shine [ʃaɪn] *s* splendore *m*; luce *f*; bel tempo; lucidatura, lucido; **to take a shine to** (coll) prender simpatia per ‖ *v* (pret & pp shined) *tr* pulire, lucidare ‖ *v* (pret & pp shone [ʃon]) *tr* (e.g., a flashlight) dirigere i raggi di ‖ *intr* brillare, luccicare, risplendere; *(to excel)* essere brillante, eccellere

shiner [ˈʃaɪnər] *s* (slang) occhio pesto

shingle [ˈʃɪŋgəl] *s* assicella di copertura; *(to cover a wall)* mattoncino di rivestimento; *(Brit)* greto ciottoloso; (coll) capelli *mpl* alla bebé; **shingles** (pathol) erpete *m*, zona; **to hang out one's shingle** (coll) aprire un ufficio professionale ‖ *tr* coprire di assicelle or mattoncini; *(hair)* tagliare alla bebé

shining [ˈʃaɪnɪŋ] *adj* brillante, lucente

shin·y [ˈʃaɪni] *adj* (-ier; -iest) lucente, lucido; *(paper)* patinato

ship [ʃɪp] *s* nave *f*, bastimento; aeronave *f*; aeroplano; *(crew)* equipaggio ‖ *v* (pret & pp shipped; ger shipping) *tr* imbarcare; mandare, spedire; *(oars)* disarmare; *(water)* imbarcare ‖ *intr* imbarcarsi

ship'board' *s*—**on shipboard** a bordo

ship'build'er *s* costruttore *m* navale

ship'build'ing *s* architettura navale

ship'mate' *s* compagno di bordo

shipment [ˈʃɪpmənt] *s* invio, spedizione

ship'own'er *s* armatore *m*

shipper [ˈʃɪpər] *s* speditore *m*, spedizioniere *m*, mittente *m*

shipping [ˈʃɪpɪŋ] *s* imbarco; spedizione; (naut) trasporto marittimo

ship'ping clerk' *s* speditore *m*

ship'ping room' *s* ufficio impaccatura

ship'shape' *adj & adv* in perfette condizioni

ship'side' *s* molo

ship's' pa'pers *spl* documenti *mpl* di bordo

ship'wreck' *s* naufragio; *(remains)* relitto ‖ *tr* far naufragare ‖ *intr* naufragare

ship'yard' *s* cantiere *m* navale

shirk [ʃʌrk] *tr* (work) evitare; *(responsibility)* sottrarsi a ‖ *intr* imboscarsi

shirt [ʃʌrt] *s* camicia; **to keep one's shirt on** (slang) non perdere la calma; **to lose one's shirt** (slang) perdere la camicia

shirt' front' *s* sparato

shirt' sleeve' *s* manica di camicia

shirt'tail' *s* falda della camicia

shirt'waist' *s* blusa da donna

shiver [ˈʃɪvər] *s* brivido ‖ *intr* rabbrividire, battere i denti

shoal [ʃol] *s* secca, banco di sabbia

shock [ʃak] *s* urto, collisione; scossa; scossa elettrica; (pathol) shock *m* ‖ *tr* scuotere; *(to strike against)* urtare; scandalizzare, indignare; dare la scossa elettrica a; (fig) scioccare

shock' absorb'er [æbˈsɔrbər] *s* ammortizzatore *m* di colpi

shocking [ˈʃakɪŋ] *adj* disgustoso, scandalizzante

shock' ther'apy *s* terapia d'urto

shock' troops' *spl* truppe *fpl* d'assalto

shod·dy [ˈʃadi] *adj* (-dier; -diest) scadente, falso

shoe [ʃu] *s* scarpa; *(horseshoe)* ferro da cavallo; *(of a tire)* copertone *m*; *(of brake)* ganascia, ceppo ‖ *v* (pret & pp shod [ʃad]) *tr* calzare; *(a horse)* ferrare

shoe'black' *s* lustrascarpe *m*

shoe'horn' *s* corno da scarpe, calzatoio

shoe'lace' *s* laccio delle scarpe

shoe'mak'er *s* calzolaio

shoe' pol'ish *s* crema or cera da scarpe

shoe'shine' *s* lucidatura, lustramento di scarpe

shoe' store' *s* calzoleria

shoe'string' *s* laccio delle scarpe; **on a shoestring** con quattro soldi

shoe'tree' *s* tendiscarpe *m*

shoo [ʃu] *tr* fare sciò a ‖ *intr* fare sciò

shoot [ʃut] *s* *(e.g., with a firearm)* tiro; gara di tiro; *(chute)* scivolo; *(rok)* lancio; (bot) getto, virgulto ‖ *v* (pret & pp shot [ʃat]) *tr* *(any missile)* tirare; *(a bullet)* sparare; *(to execute with a bullet)* fucilare; *(to fling)* lanciare; *(the sun)* prendere l'altezza di; *(dice)* gettare; *(mov, telv)* girare, riprendere; **to shoot down** *(a plane)* abbattere; **to shoot up** (coll) terrorizzare sparando a casaccio ‖ *intr* tirare, sparare; passare rapidamente; nascere; *(said of pain)* dare fitte; *(mov)* cinematografare; **to shoot at** tirare a; (coll) cercare di ottenere

shoot'ing gal'lery *s* tiro a segno

shoot'ing match' *s* gara di tiro a segno; (slang) tutto, ogni cosa

shoot'ing star' *s* stella cadente

shop [ʃap] *s* *(store)* negozio, rivendita; *(workshop)* officina; **to talk shop** parlare del proprio lavoro ‖ *v* (pret & pp shopped; ger shopping) *intr* fare la spesa; **to go shopping** andare a fare la spesa; **to shop around** cercare un'occasione di negozio in negozio

shop'girl' *s* venditrice *f*

shop'keep'er s negoziante mf
shoplifter [ˈʃɑpˌlɪftər] s taccheggiatore m
shopper [ˈʃɑpər] s compratore m
shopping [ˈʃɑpɪŋ] s compra; (purchases) compre fpl, shopping m
shop'ping bag' s sporta, shopping m
shop'ping cen'ter s centro d'acquisto, ipermercato
shop'ping dis'trict s zona commerciale
shop'win'dow s vetrina
shop'worn' adj sciupato, usato
shore [ʃor] s costa, riva; spiaggia, lido; (fig) regione; (support) sostegno, puntello || tr puntellare
shore' din'ner s pranzo di pesce
shore' leave' s (naut) franchigia
shore'line' s frangia costiera
shore' patrol' s polizia della marina
short [ʃɔrt] adj (in stature) piccolo, basso; (in space, time) breve; (scanty) scarso; succinto; (in quantity) poco, piccolo; (rude) brusco; **in a short time** in breve; **in short** per farla breve; **on short notice** senza preavviso; **short of breath** corto di fiato; **to be short of** scarseggiare di || s (elec) cortocircuito; (mov) cortometraggio; **shorts** (underwear) mutande fpl; (sports attire) calzoncini mpl, shorts mpl || adv brevemente; (com) allo scoperto, e.g., **to sell short** vendere allo scoperto; **to run short of** essere a corto di; **to stop short** fermarsi di colpo || tr (elec) causare un cortocircuito in || intr (elec) andare in cortocircuito
shortage [ˈʃɔrtɪdʒ] s mancanza; (of food) carestia; (from pilfering) ammanco
short'cake' s torta di pasta frolla; torta ricoperta di frutta fresca
short'-change' tr non dare il cambio giusto a; (coll) imbrogliare
short' cir'cuit s (elec) cortocircuito
short'-cir'cuit tr mandare in cortocircuito; (coll) rovinare || intr andare in cortocircuito
short'com'ing s difetto, manchevolezza
short'cut' s scorciatoia
shorten [ˈʃɔrtən] tr raccorciare, abbreviare || intr raccorciarsi, abbreviarsi
shortening [ˈʃɔrtənɪŋ] s raccorciamento; (culin) grasso, strutto
short'hand' adj stenografico || s stenografia; **to take shorthand** stenografare
short'hand' typ'ist s stenodattilografo
short-lived [ˈʃɔrtˈlaɪvd] or [ˈʃɔrtˈlɪvd] adj effimero, di breve vita
shortly [ˈʃɔrtli] adv in breve, brevemente; fra poco; bruscamente; **shortly after** poco dopo
short'-range' adj di corta portata
short' sale' s vendita allo scoperto
short-sighted [ˈʃɔrtˈsaɪtɪd] adj miope; (fig) miope
short'stop' s (baseball) interbase m
short' sto'ry s novella
short-tempered [ˈʃɔrtˈtɛmpərd] adj irascibile
short'-term' adj a breve scadenza

short'wave' adj alle onde corte || s onda corta
short' weight' s—**to give short weight** rubare sul peso
shot [ʃɑt] s tiro, sparo; (cartridge) cartuccia; (for cannon) palla; (pellets of lead) pallini mpl; (person) tiratore m; (hypodermic injection) iniezione; (of liquor) bicchierino; (phot) istantanea; (sports) peso; (mov) inquadratura; **not by a long shot** nemmeno a pensarci; **to start like a shot** partire come una palla da cannone; **to take a shot at** tirare un colpo a; (to attempt to) provarsi a
shot'gun' s schioppo, fucile m da caccia
shot' put' s lancio del peso
should [ʃud] v aux si usa nelle seguenti situazioni: 1) per formare il condizionale presente, per es., **if I should wait for him, I should miss the train** se lo aspettassi, perderei il treno; 2) per formare il perfetto del condizionale, per es., **if I had waited for him, I should have missed the train** se lo avessi aspettato, avrei perso il treno; 3) per indicare la necessità di un'azione, per es., **he should go at once** dovrebbe andare immediatamente; **he should have gone immediately** sarebbe dovuto andare immediatamente
shoulder [ˈʃoldər] s spalla; (of highway) banchina; **across the shoulder** a bandoliera; **to put one's shoulders to the wheel** mettersi a lavorare di buzzo buono; **to turn a cold shoulder to** volgere le spalle a || tr portare sulle spalle; (a responsibility) addossarsi; spingere con le spalle
shoul'der blade' s scapola
shoul'der strap' s spallina; (mil) tracolla
shout [ʃaut] s urlo, grido || tr urlare, gridare; **to shout down** far tacere a forza di strilli || intr gridare
shove [ʃʌv] s spintone m || tr spingere || intr spingere, dare spintoni; **to shove off** allontanarsi dalla riva; (slang) andarsene
shov-el [ˈʃʌvəl] s pala || v (pret & pp -eled or -elled; ger -eling or -elling) tr spalare || intr lavorare di pala
show [ʃo] s mostra; apparenza; traccia; ostentazione; (mov, telv, theat) spettacolo; **to make a show of** dar spettacolo di; **to steal the show from** ricevere tutti gli applausi invece di || tr mostrare, esporre; (a movie) presentare; dimostrare, insegnare; provare; (to register) segnare; (one's feelings) manifestare; (to the door) accompagnare; **to show in** fare entrare; **to show off** mettere in mostra || intr mostrarsi; presentarsi, apparire; (said of a horse) (sports) arrivare terzo, piazzarsi; **to show off** mettersi in mostra; **to show up** (coll) mostrarsi; (coll) farsi vedere
show' bill' s cartellone m
show'boat' s battello per spettacoli teatrali

show′ busi′ness *s* industria dello spettacolo

show′case′ *s* bacheca, vetrina

show′down′ *s* carte scoperte; chiarificazione

shower [′ʃaʊ·ər] *s* (*of rain*) acquazzone *m*; (*shower bath*) doccia; (*e.g., for a bride*) ricevimento cui i partecipanti devono portare un regalo; (fig) pioggia || *tr* inaffiare; **to shower with** colmare di || *intr* diluviare; fare la doccia

show′er bath′ *s* doccia

show′ girl′ *s* ballerina, girl *f*

show′man *s* (-men) impresario teatrale; persona che ha molta scena

show′-off′ *s* reclamista *m*, strombazzatore *m*

show′piece′ *s* capolavoro, oggetto d'arte

show′place′ *s* luogo celebre; **to be a showplace** (*said, e.g., of a house*) essere arredato perfettamente

show′room′ *s* sala di mostra

show′ win′dow *s* vetrina

show·y [′ʃo·i] *adj* (-ier; -iest) vistoso, sgargiante

shrapnel [′ʃræpnəl] *s* shrapnel *m*

shred [ʃrɛd] *s* brano, brandello; ritaglio; (fig) granello; **to cut to shreds** fare a brandelli || *v* (*pret & pp* **shredded** or **shred**; *ger* **shredding**) *tr* fare a brandelli; (*paper*) tagliuzzare

shrew [ʃru] *s* (*woman*) bisbetica; (*animal*) toporagno

shrewd [ʃrud] *adj* astuto, scaltro

shriek [ʃrik] *s* strido; strillo; risata stridula || *intr* stridere; strillare

shrill [ʃrɪl] *adj* stridulo, squillante

shrimp [ʃrɪmp] *s* gamberetto; (*person*) omiciattolo, nanerottolo

shrine [ʃraɪn] *s* santuario, sacrario

shrink [ʃrɪŋk] *v* (*pret* **shrank** [ʃræŋk] or **shrunk** [ʃrʌŋk]; *pp* **shrunk** or **shrunken**) *tr* contrarre, restringere || *intr* contrarsi, restringersi, ritirarsi

shrinkage [′ʃrɪŋkɪdʒ] *s* restringimento; (*in weight*) calo

shriv·el [′ʃrɪvəl] *v* (*pret & pp* **-eled** or **-elled**; *ger* **-eling** or **-elling**) *tr* raggrinzire; (*from heat*) raccartocciare; (*to wither*) avvizzire || *intr* raggrinzirsi; accartocciarsi; avvizzire; **to shrivel up** incartapecorire

shroud [ʃraʊd] *s* sudario, lenzuolo funebre; (fig) cappa || *tr* avvolgere

Shrove′ Tues′day [ʃrov] *s* martedì grasso

shrub [ʃrʌb] *s* arbusto

shrubber·y [′ʃrʌbəri] *s* (-ies) arbusti *mpl*, cespugli *mpl*

shrug [ʃrʌg] *s* scrollata di spalle || *v* (*pret & pp* **shrugged**; *ger* **shrugging**) *tr* scrollare; **to shrug one's shoulders** scrollare le spalle || *intr* fare spallucce

shudder [′ʃʌdər] *s* brivido, fremito || *intr* rabbrividire, fremere

shuffle [′ʃʌfəl] *s* (*of cards*) mescolata; turno di fare il mazzo; (*of feet*) strascichio; evasione || *tr* mescolare; strisciare, strascicare || *intr* fare il

mazzo; scalpicciare; ballare di striscio; **to shuffle off** strascicarsi, scalpicciare; **to shuffle out of** evadere da

shun [ʃʌn] *v* (*pret & pp* **shunned**; *ger* **shunning**) *tr* evitare, schivare

shunt [ʃʌnt] *tr* sviare; (elec) shuntare; (rr) deviare

shut [ʃʌt] *adj* chiuso || *v* (*pret & pp* **shut**; *ger* **shutting**) *tr* chiudere, serrare; **to shut in** rinchiudere; **to shut off** (*e.g., gas*) tagliare; **to shut up** tappare; imprigionare; (coll) fare star zitto || *intr* chiudersi; (coll) stare zitto, tacere

shut′down′ *s* chiusura

shutter [′ʃʌtər] *s* (*outside a window*) persiana, gelosia; (*outside a store window*) serranda, saracinesca; (phot) otturatore *m*

shuttle [′ʃʌtəl] *s* spola, navetta || *intr* fare la spola

shut′tle-cock′ *s* volano, volante *m*

shut′tle train′ *s* treno che fa la spola fra due stazioni

shy [ʃaɪ] *adj* (**shyer** or **shier**; **shyest** or **shiest**) timido; (*fearful*) schivo, ritroso; corto, a corto, a corto; **he is shy of funds** è a corto di denaro || *v* (*pret & pp* **shied**) *intr* ritirarsi; schivarsi; (*said of a horse*) adombrarsi; **to shy away** tenersi discosto

shyster [′ʃaɪstər] *s* (coll) azzeccagarbugli *m*

Sia·mese [ˌsaɪ·ə′miz] *adj* siamese || *s* (-mese) siamese *mf*

Si′amese twins′ *spl* fratelli *mpl* siamesi

Siberian [saɪ′bɪrɪ·ən] *adj & s* siberiano

sibilant [′sɪbɪlənt] *adj & s* sibilante *f*

sibyl [′sɪbɪl] *s* sibilla

sic [sɪk] *adv* sic || [sɪk] *v* (*pret & pp* **sicked**; *ger* **sicking**) *tr* aizzare; sics 'em! va!; **to sick on** aizzare contro

Sicilian [sɪ′sɪljən] *adj & s* siciliano

Sicily [′sɪsɪli] *s* la Sicilia

sick [sɪk] *adj* ammalato; nauseato; (*bored*) stucco; **sick at heart** con una spina nel cuore; **to be sick and tired** averne sin sopra i capelli; **to be sick at one's stomach** avere la nausea; **to take sick** cader malato || *tr* (*a dog*) aizzare

sick′bed′ *s* letto d'ammalato

sicken [′sɪkən] *tr* ammalare; disgustare || *intr* ammalarsi

sickening [′sɪkənɪŋ] *adj* stomachevole

sick′ head′ache *s* emicrania accompagnata da nausea

sickle [′sɪkəl] *s* falce messoria, falcetto

sick′ leave′ *s* congedo per motivi di salute

sick·ly [′sɪkli] *adj* (-lier; -liest) cagionevole, malaticcio

sickness [′sɪknɪs] *s* malattia; nausea

side [saɪd] *adj* laterale || *s* parte *f*, lato; (*e.g., of a coin*) faccia; (*slope*) versante *m*; (*of human body, of a ship*) fianco; **to take sides** parteggiare || *intr* parteggiare; **to side with** schierarsi dalla parte di

side′board′ *s* credenza

side′burns′ *spl* basette *fpl*, favoriti *mpl*

side'car' *s* motocarrozzetta; carrozzino laterale (di motocarrozzetta)

side' dish'-*s* portata extra

side' door' *s* porta laterale

side' effect' *s* effetto secondario

side'-glance' *s* occhiata di sbieco

side' is'sue *s* questione secondaria

side'line' *s* linea laterale; impiego secondario; attività secondaria

sidereal [saɪˈdɪrɪ·əl] *adj* siderale

side'sad'dle *adv* all'amazzone

side' show' *s* spettacolo secondario di baraccone; affare secondario

side'slip' *intr* (aer) scivolare d'ala

side'split'ting *adj* che fa sbellicare dalle risa

side' step' *s* passo laterale; scartata

side'-step' *v* (*pret & pp* **-stepped**; *ger* **-stepping**) *tr* evitare || *intr* farsi da parte; fare una scartata

side'track' *s* binario morto di smistamento || *tr* sviare; (rr) smistare

side' view' *s* vista di profilo

side'walk' *s* marciapiede *m*

side'walk café' *s* caffè *m* con tavolini all'aperto

sideward [ˈsaɪdwərd] *adj* obliquo, a sghembo || *adv* verso un lato; di sghembo

side'ways' *adj* sghembo || *adv* di sghembo; di fianco

side' whisk'ers *spl* favoriti *mpl*

siding [ˈsaɪdɪŋ] *s* (rr) diramazione, binario morto, raccordo ferroviario

sidle [ˈsaɪdəl] *intr* andare al lato; muoversi furtivamente

siege [sidʒ] *s* assedio; (*of illness*) ricorrenza d'attacchi; **to lay siege to** cingere d'assedio, assediare

siesta [siˈestə] *s* siesta; **to take a siesta** fare la siesta

sieve [sɪv] *s* vaglio, setaccio || *tr* vagliare, setacciare

sift [sɪft] *tr* (*flour*) abburattare; setacciare; (*to scatter with a sieve*) spolverare; (fig) vagliare

sigh [saɪ] *s* sospiro || *tr* mormorare sospirando || *intr* sospirare; **to sigh for** sospirare

sight [saɪt] *s* vista, visione; spettacolo, veduta; (opt) mira, traguardo; (mil) mirino, tacca di mira; (coll) mucchio; **a sight of** (coll) molto; **at first sight** a prima vista; **at sight** ad apertura di libro; (com) a vista; **out of sight** fuori di vista; lontano dagli occhi; (*prices*) astronomico; **sights** luoghi *mpl* interessanti; **sight unseen** senza averlo visto prima, a occhi chiusi; **to be a sight** (coll) essere un orrore; **to catch sight of** arrivare a intravedere; **to know by sight** conoscere di vista; **to not be able to stand the sight of s.o.** not poter vedere qlcu nemmeno dipinto || *tr* avvistare; (*a weapon*) mirare || *intr* mirare, prendere di mira; osservare attentamente

sight' draft' *s* (com) tratta a vista

sight'-read' *v* (*pret & pp* **-read** [ˌred]) *tr & intr* leggere a libro aperto

sight'see'ing *adj* turistico || *s* turismo, visite *fpl* turistiche

sightseer [ˈsaɪtˌsi·ər] *s* turista *mf*

sign [saɪn] *s* segno; segnale *m;* (*e.g., on a store*) insegna, cartello; **signs** tracce *fpl* || *tr* firmare; ingaggiare; indicare, segnalare || *intr* firmare; fare segno; **to sign off** (rad, telv) terminare la trasmissione; **to sign up** iscriversi

sig·nal [ˈsɪgnəl] *adj* insigne, segnalato || *s* segnale *m* || *v* (*pret & pp* **-naled** or **-nalled**; *ger* **-naling** or **-nalling**) *tr* segnalare || *intr* fare segnalazioni

sig'nal corps' *s* (mil) armi *fpl* di trasmissione

sig'nal tow'er *s* (rr) posto di blocco

signato·ry [ˈsɪgnɪˌtori] *s* (**-ries**) firmatario

signature [ˈsɪgnətʃər] *s* firma; segno musicale; (typ) segnatura

sign'board' *s* cartellone *m*

signer [ˈsaɪnər] *s* firmatario

sig'net ring' [ˈsɪgnɪt] *s* anello col sigillo

significance [sɪgˈnɪfɪkəns] *s* importanza; (*meaning*) significato

significant [sɪgˈnɪfɪkənt] *adj* importante

signi·fy [ˈsɪgnɪˌfaɪ] *v* (*pret & pp* **-fied**) *tr* significare

sign'post' *s* palo indicatore

silence [ˈsaɪləns] *s* silenzio || *tr* tacere; (mil) ridurre al silenzio

silent [ˈsaɪlənt] *adj* silenzioso, tacito

si'lent mov'ie *s* cinema muto

silhouette [ˌsɪluˈet] *s* silhouette *f*, siluetta

silicon [ˈsɪlɪkən] *s* silicio

silicone [ˈsɪlɪˌkon] *s* silicone *m*

silk [sɪlk] *adj* di seta || *s* seta; **to hit the silk** (slang) gettarsi col paracadute

silken [ˈsɪlkən] *adj* serico, di seta

silk' hat' *s* cappello a cilindro

silk'screen proc'ess *s* serigrafia

silk'-stock'ing *adj & s* aristocratico

silk'worm' *s* baco da seta, filugello

silk·y [ˈsɪlki] *adj* (**-ier; -iest**) di seta; come la seta

sill [sɪl] *s* basamento; (*of a door*) soglia; (*of a window*) davanzale *m*

sil·ly [ˈsɪli] *adj* (**-lier; -liest**) sciocco, scemo

si·lo [ˈsaɪlo] *s* (**-los**) silo || *tr* insilare

silt [sɪlt] *s* sedimento

silver [ˈsɪlvər] *adj* d'argento; (*voice*) argentino; (*plated with silver*) argentato || *s* argento || *tr* inargentare

sil'ver·fish' *s* (ent) lepisma

sil'ver foil' *s* foglia d'argento

sil'ver fox' *s* volpe argentata

sil'ver lin'ing *s* spiraglio di speranza

sil'ver plate' *s* vasellame *m* d'argento; argentatura

sil'ver screen' *s* (mov) schermo

sil'ver·smith' *s* argentiere *m*

sil'ver spoon' *s* ricchezza ereditata; **to be born with a silver spoon in one's mouth** esser nato con la camicia

sil'ver·ware' *s* argenteria

sil'ver·ware' chest' *s* portaposate *m*

similar [ˈsɪmɪlər] *adj* simile

similari·ty [ˌsɪmɪˈlærɪti] *s* (**-ties**) similarità *f*, somiglianza

simile [ˈsɪmɪli] *s* similitudine *f*

simmer ['sɪmər] *tr* cuocere a fuoco lento || *intr* cuocere a fuoco lento; (fig) ribollire; **to simmer down** (slang) calmarsi

simper ['sɪmpər] *s* sorriso scemo || *intr* fare un sorriso scemo

simple ['sɪmpəl] *adj* semplice

simple-minded ['sɪmpəl'maɪndɪd] *adj* sempliciotto, scemo

simpleton ['sɪmpəltən] *s* semplicione *m*

simulate ['sɪmjə‚let] *tr* simulare

simultaneous [‚saɪməl'tenɪ-əs] or [‚sɪməl'tenɪ-əs] *adj* simultaneo

sin [sɪn] *s* peccato || *v* (pret & pp **sinned**; ger **sinning**) *intr* peccare

since [sɪns] *adv* da allora, da allora in poi; da tempo fa || *prep* da || *conj* dacché; poiché, dato che

sincere [sɪn'sɪr] *adj* sincero

sincerity [sɪn'serɪti] *s* sincerità *f*

sine [saɪn] *s* (math) seno

sinecure ['saɪnɪ‚kjur] or ['sɪnɪ‚kjur] *s* sinecura

sinew ['sɪnju] *s* tendine *m*; (fig) nerbo

sinful ['sɪnfəl] *adj* (person) peccatore; (act, intention, etc.) peccaminoso

sing [sɪŋ] *v* (pret **sang** [sæŋ] or **sung** [sʌŋ]; pp **sung**) *tr* cantare; **to sing to sleep** ninnare || *intr* cantare; (said, e.g., of the ears) fischiare

singe [sɪndʒ] *v* (ger **singeing**) *tr* strinare, bruciacchiare

singer ['sɪŋər] *s* cantante *mf*; (in night club) canzonettista *mf*

single ['sɪŋgəl] *adj* unico, solo; (room) a un letto; (bed) a una piazza; (man) celibe; (woman) nubile; (combat) corpo a corpo; semplice, sincero || **singles** *ssg* singolare *m* || *tr* scegliere; **to single out** individuare

single-breasted ['sɪŋgəl'brɛstɪd] *adj* a un petto, monopetto

sin′gle entry′ *s* partita semplice

sin′gle file′ *s* fila indiana

single-handed ['sɪŋgəl'hændɪd] *adj* da solo, senza aiuto altrui

sin′gle-phase′ *adj* (elec) monofase

sin′gle room′ *s* camera a un letto

sin′gle-track′ *adj* (rr) a binario semplice; (fig) di corte vedute

sing′song′ *adj* monotono || *s* cantilena

singular ['sɪŋgjələr] *adj* & *s* singolare *m*

sinister ['sɪnɪstər] *adj* sinistro

sink [sɪŋk] *s* acquaio; (sewer) scolo, fogna; (fig) sentina || *v* (pret **sank** [sæŋk] or **sunk** [sʌŋk]; pp **sunk**) *tr* sprofondare; infiggere; (a well) scavare; (in tone) abbassare; (a boat) mandare a picco; rovinare; investire; perdere || *intr* sprofondarsi; abbassarsi; (said, of the sun, prices, etc.) calare; andare a picco; lasciarsi cadere; (in vice) impantanarsi; (said of one's cheeks) infossarsi; (in thought) perdersi; **to sink down** sedersi; **to sink in** penetrare

sink′ing fund′ *s* fondo d'ammortamento

sinner ['sɪnər] *s* peccatore *m*

Sinology [sɪ'nɑlədʒɪ] *s* sinologia

sinuous ['sɪnju-əs] *adj* sinuoso

sinus ['saɪnəs] *s* seno

sip [sɪp] *s* sorso || *v* (pret & pp **sipped**; ger **sipping**) *tr* sorbire, sorseggiare

siphon ['saɪfən] *s* sifone *m* || *tr* travasare con un sifone

si′phon bot′tle *s* sifone *m*

sir [sʌr] *s* signore *m*; (Brit) sir *m*; **Dear Sir** Illustrissimo signore; (com) Egregio signore

sire [saɪr] *s* (king) sire *m*; padre *m*, stallone *m* || *tr* generare

siren ['saɪrən] *s* sirena

sirloin ['sʌrlɔɪn] *s* lombata, lombo

sirup ['sɪrəp] or ['sʌrəp] *tr* sciroppo

sis·sy ['sɪsɪ] *s* (-sies) effemminato

sister ['sɪstər] *adj* (ship) gemello; (language) sorella; (corporation) consorella || *s* sorella; (nun) suora, monaca

sis′ter-in-law′ *s* (sis′ters-in-law′) cognata

Sis′tine Chap′el ['sɪstɪn] *s* Cappella Sistina

sit [sɪt] *v* (pret & pp **sat** [sæt]; ger **sitting**) *intr* sedere; posare; (said of a hen) covare; (said of a jacket) stare; essere in sessione; **to sit down** sedersi; **to sit on** partecipare a; assistere a; **to sit still** stare tranquillo; **to sit up** alzarsi; (coll) essere sorpreso

sit′-down strike′ *s* sciopero bianco

site [saɪt] *s* sito, luogo, posizione

sitting ['sɪtɪŋ] *s* seduta; (of a court) sessione; (of a hen) covata; (serving of a meal) turno

sit′ting duck′ *s* (slang) facile bersaglio

sit′ting room′ *s* soggiorno

situate ['sɪtʃʊ‚et] *tr* situare

situation [‚sɪtʃʊ'eʃən] *s* situazione, posizione; posto

sitz′ bath′ [sɪts] *s* semicupio

six [sɪks] *adj* & *pron* sei || *s* sei *m*; **at sixes and sevens** in disordine; **six o'clock** le sei

six′ hun′dred *adj, s* & *pron* seicento

sixteen ['sɪks'tin] *adj, s* & *pron* sedici *m*

sixteenth ['sɪks'tinθ] *adj, s* & *pron* sedicesimo || *s* (in dates) sedici *m*

sixth [sɪksθ] *adj, s* & *pron* sesto || *s* (in dates) sei *m*

sixtieth ['sɪkstɪ-ɪθ] *adj, s* & *pron* sessantesimo

six·ty ['sɪkstɪ] *adj* & *pron* sessanta || *s* (-ies) sessanta *m*; **the sixties** gli anni sessanta

sizable ['saɪzəbəl] *adj* considerevole

size [saɪz] *s* grandezza; quantità *f*; (of person or garment) taglia; (of shoes) numero; (of hat) giro; (of a pipe) diametro; (for gilding) colla; (fig) situazione || *tr* misurare, classificare secondo grandezza; incollare; **to size up** (coll) stimare, giudicare

sizzle ['sɪzəl] *s* sfrigolio || *intr* sfriggere

skate [sket] *s* pattino; (slang) tipo || *intr* pattinare; **to skate on thin ice** andare in cerca di disgrazie

skat′ing rink′ *s* pattinatoio

skein [sken] *s* gomitolo, matassa

skeleton ['skɛlɪtən] *adj* scheletrico || *s* scheletro

skel′eton key′ *s* chiave maestra

skeptic ['skɛptɪk] *adj* & *s* scettico

skeptical [ˈskeptɪkəl] *adj* scettico

sketch [sketʃ] *s* schizzo, disegno; abbozzo, bozzetto; (theat) scenetta || *tr* schizzare, disegnare; abbozzare

sketch'book' *s* album *m* di schizzi; quaderno per abbozzi

skew [skju] *adj* obliquo || *s* movimento obliquo; (chisel) scalpello a taglio obliquo || *tr* tagliare di sghembo || *intr* (to swerve) deviare; (to look obliquely) guardare di sghembo

skew' chis'el *s* scalpello a taglio obliquo

skewer [ˈskju·ər] *s* spiedino || *tr* mettere allo spiedo

ski [ski] *s* (skis or ski) sci *m* || *intr* sciare

ski' boot' *s* scarpa da sci

skid [skɪd] *s* (device to check a wheel) scarpa; (skidding forward) slittamento; (skidding sideway) sbandamento; (aer, mach) pattino || *v* (pret & pp skidded; ger skidding) *tr* frenare || *intr* (forward) slittare; (sideways) sbandare

skid' row' [ro] *s* quartiere malfamato

skier [ˈski·ər] *s* sciatore *m*

skiff [skɪf] *s* skiff *m*, singolo

skiing [ˈski-ɪŋ] *s* sci *m*

ski' jump' *s* salto con gli sci; trampolino di salto

ski' lift' *s* sciovia

skill [skɪl] *s* destrezza, perizia

skilled [skɪld] *adj* abile, esperto

skilled' la'bor *s* manodopera qualificata

skillet [ˈskɪlɪt] *s* padella

skillful [ˈskɪlfəl] *adj* destro, abile

skim [skɪm] *v* (pret & pp skimmed; ger skimming) *tr* (milk) scremare; (e.g., broth) sgrassare; (to graze) sfiorare; (the ground) radere; (a page) trascorrere || *intr* sfiorare; **to skim over** scorrere

ski' mask' *s* passamontagna *m*

skimmer [ˈskɪmər] *s* schiumaiola; (hat) canottiera

skim' milk' *s* latte scremato or magro

skimp [skɪmp] *tr* lesinare || *intr* economizzare, risparmiare

skimp-y [ˈskɪmpi] *adj* (-ier; -iest) corto, scarso; taccagno

skin [skɪn] *s* pelle *f*; (rind) scorza; (of onion) spoglia; **by the skin of one's teeth** (coll) per il rotto della cuffia; **soaked to the skin** bagnato fino alle ossa; **to have a thin skin** offendersi facilmente || *v* (pret & pp skinned; ger skinning) *tr* pelare, spellare; (e.g., one's knee) spellarsi; (slang) tosare; **to skin alive** (slang) scotennare; (slang) battere in pieno

skin'-deep' *adj* a fior di pelle

skin'-div'er *s* nuotatore subacqueo, sub *m*; (mil) sommozzatore *m*

skin'flint' *s* avaro

skin' game' *s* truffa

skin-ny [ˈskɪni] *adj* (-nier; -niest) magro, scarno

skin' test' *s* cutireazione

skip [skɪp] *s* salto || *v* (pret & pp

skipped; ger skipping *tr* (a fence; a meal) saltare; (a subject) sorvolare; (school) (coll) marinare || *intr* saltare, salterellare; (said of typewriter) saltare uno spazio; (coll) svignarsela

ski' pole' *s* racchetta da sci

skipper [ˈskɪpər] *s* capitano, comandante *m*

skirmish [ˈskʌrmɪʃ] *s* scaramuccia || *intr* battersi in una scaramuccia

skirt [skʌrt] *s* sottana, gonna; (edge) orlo; (woman) (slang) gonnella || *tr* orlare; costeggiare; (a subject) evitare

ski' run' *s* pista da sci

skit [skɪt] *s* (theat) quadretto comico

skittish [ˈskɪtɪʃ] *adj* bizzarro, balzano; timido; (horse) ombroso

skulduggery [skʌlˈdʌgəri] *s* trucco disonesto

skull [skʌl] *s* cranio, teschio

skull' and cross'bones *s* due tibie incrociate ed un teschio

skull'cap' *s* papalina

skunk [skʌŋk] *s* puzzola, moffetta; (coll) puzzone *m*

sky [skaɪ] *s* (skies) cielo; firmamento; **to praise to the skies** portare al cielo

sky'div'er *s* paracadutista *mf*

sky'jack'er *s* pirata *m* dell'aria

sky'lark' *s* allodola || *intr* (coll) darsi alla pazza gioia

sky'light' *s* lucernario

sky'line' *s* linea dell'orizzonte; (of city) profilo

sky'rock'et *s* razzo || *intr* salire come un razzo

sky'scrap'er *s* grattacielo

sky'writ'ing *s* scrittura pubblicitaria aerea

slab [slæb] *s* (of stone) lastra, lastrone *m*; (of wood) tavola; (slice) fetta

slack [slæk] *adj* lento, allentato; negligente, indolente; (coll) fiacco, morto || *s* lentezza; negligenza; stagione morta, inattività *f*; **slacks** pantaloni *mpl* da donna; pantaloni sciolti || *tr* allentare; trascurare; (lime) spegnere || *intr* rilasciarsi; essere negligente; **to slack up** rallentare

slacker [ˈslækər] *s* fannullone *m*; (mil) imboscato

slag [slæg] *s* scoria

slake [slek] *tr* spegnere

slalom [ˈslɑləm] *s* slalom *m*

slam [slæm] *s* colpo; (of door) sbatacchiamento; (in cards) cappotto; (coll) strapazzata || *v* (pret & pp slammed; ger slamming) *tr* sbattere, sbatacchiare; (coll) strapazzare || *intr* sbattere, sbatacchiare

slam'bang' *adv* (coll) con gran rumore, precipitosamente

slander [ˈslændər] *s* calunnia, maldicenza || *tr* calunniare, diffamare

slanderous [ˈslændərəs] *adj* calunnioso, diffamatorio

slang [slæŋ] *s* gergo

slant [slænt] *s* inclinazione; punto di vista || *tr* inclinare; (news) snaturare || *intr* inclinarsi; deviare

slap [slæp] *s* manata; (*in the face*) schiaffo, ceffone *m*; (*noise*) rumore *m*; insulto || *v* (*pret & pp* **slapped**; *ger* **slapping**) *tr* dare una manata a; schiaffeggiare

slap'dash' *adj* raffazzonato, fatto a casaccio || *adv* a casaccio

slap'hap'py *adj* (*punch-drunk*) stordito; (*giddy*) allegro, brillo

slap'stick' *adj* buffonesco || *s* bastone *m* d'Arlecchino; buffonata

slash [slæʃ] *s* sfregio; (*of prices*) riduzione || *tr* sfregiare; (*cloth*) tagliare; (*prices*) ridurre

slat [slæt] *s* travicello, regolo; (*for bed*) traversa; (*of shutter*) stecca

slate [slet] *s* ardesia, lavagna; lista elettorale; **clean slate** buon certificato || *tr* coprire con tegole d'ardesia; proporre la nomina di; (*to schedule*) mettere in cantiere

slate' roof' *s* tetto d'ardesia

slattern ['slætərn] *s* (*slovenly woman*) sciamannona; (*harlot*) puttana

slaughter ['slɔtər] *s* eccidio, carneficina || *tr* sgozzare, scannare

slaugh'ter-house' *s* macello, scannatoio

Slav [slɑv] *or* [slæv] *adj & s* slavo

slave [slev] *adj & s* schiavo || *intr* lavorare come uno schiavo

slave' driv'er *s* negriere *m*

slavery ['slevəri] *s* schiavitù *f*

slave' trade' *s* tratta degli schiavi

Slavic ['slɑvɪk] *or* ['slævɪk] *adj & s* slavo

slay [sle] *v* (*pret* **slew** [slu]; *pp* **slain** [slen]) *tr* scannare, uccidere

slayer ['sle·ər] *s* uccisore *m*

sled [slɛd] *s* slittino, slitta || *v* (*pret & pp* **sledded**; *ger* **sledding**) *intr* slittare

sledge' ham'mer [slɛdʒ] *s* mazza

sleek [slik] *adj* liscio, lustro; elegante || *tr* lisciare, ammorbidire

sleep [slip] *s* sonno; **to go to sleep** addormentarsi; **to put to sleep** addormentare; uccidere con un anestetico || *v* (*pret & pp* **slept** [slept]) *tr* dormire; aver posto a dormire per; **to sleep it over** dormirci sopra; **to sleep off a hangover** smaltire una sbornia dormendo || *intr* dormire; **to sleep in** dormire fino a tardi; passare la notte a casa; **to sleep out** passare la notte fuori di casa

sleeper ['slipər] *s* (*person*) dormiente *mf*; (*beam, timber*) trave *f*

sleep'ing bag' *s* sacco a pelo

sleep'ing car' *s* vettura letto

sleep'ing pill' *s* sonnifero

sleepless ['sliplɪs] *adj* insonne; (*night*) bianco

sleep'walk'er *s* sonnambulo

sleep·y ['slipi] *adj* (*-ier; -iest*) insonnolito, sonnolento; **to be sleepy** aver sonno

sleep'y-head' *s* dormiglione *m*

sleet [slit] *s* nevischio || *impers* **it is sleeting** cade il nevischio

sleeve [sliv] *s* manica; (*of phonograph record*) busta; (*mach*) manicotto; **to laugh in** *or* **up one's sleeve** ridere sotto i baffi

sleigh [sle] *s* slitta || *intr* andare in slitta

sleigh' bells' *spl* bubboli *mpl* da slitta, sonagliera da slitta

sleigh' ride' *s* passeggiata in slitta

sleight' of hand' [slait] *s* gioco di prestigio

slender ['slɛndər] *adj* smilzo, snello; esiguo, esile

sleuth [sluθ] *s* segugio

slew [slu] *s* (coll) mucchio

slice [slaɪs] *s* fetta; (*of an orange*) spicchio || *tr* tagliare a fette; (fig) fendere

slick [slɪk] *adj* liscio, lustro; scivoloso; astuto; (slang) ottimo || *s* posto scivoloso; (coll) rivista stampata su carta patinata || *tr* lisciare, lustrare; **to slick up** (coll) acconciare

slicker ['slɪkər] *s* impermeabile *m* di tela cerata; (coll) furbo di tre cotte

slide [slaɪd] *s* scivolata, scivolone *m*; (*chute*) scivolo; (*landslide*) frana; (*for projection*) diapositiva; (*of a microscope*) vetrino; (mach) guida; (*of a slide rule*) (mach) cursore *m* || *v* (*pret & pp* **slid** [slɪd]) *tr* far scivolare || *intr* sdrucciolare, scivolare; (*said of a car*) pattinare, slittare; **to let slide** lasciar correre

slide' fas'tener *s* chiusura lampo

slide' projec'tor *s* diascopio

slide' rule' *s* regolo calcolatore

slide' valve' *s* (mach) cassetto di distribuzione

slid'ing door' *s* porta scorrevole

slid'ing scale' *s* scala mobile

slight [slaɪt] *adj* leggero, lieve; delicato || *s* noncuranza, disattenzione; affronto || *tr* fare con negligenza; (*to snub*) trattare con noncuranza, snobbare

slim [slɪm] *adj* (**slimmer; slimmest**) sottile; magro

slime [slaɪm] *s* melma; (*e.g., of a snail*) bava

slim·y ['slaɪmi] *adj* (*-ier; -iest*) melmoso; bavoso; sudicio

sling [slɪŋ] *s* (*to shoot stones*) fionda; (naut) braca; in a sling (arm) al collo || *v* (*pret & pp* **slung** [slʌŋ]) *tr* gettare; lanciare; (*freight*) imbracare; sospendere; mettere a bandoliera

sling'shot' *s* fionda

slink [slɪŋk] *v* (*pret & pp* **slunk** [slʌŋk]) *intr* andare furtivamente; **to slink away** eclissarsi

slip [slɪp] *s* scivolone *m*; svista, errore *m*; (*in prices*) discesa; (*underdress*) sottoveste *f*; (*pillowcase*) federa; (*of paper*) pezzo; (*space between two wharves*) darsena, imbarcatoio; (*form*) modulo; personcina; (*inclined plane*) (naut) scalo d'aggio; (bot) innesto; **to give the slip to** eludere || *v* (*pret & pp* **slipped**; *ger* **slipping**) *tr* infilare; liberare da; omettere; **to slip off** togliersi; **to slip on** mettersi; **to slip one's mind** dimenticarsi di, e.g., **it slipped my mind** me ne sono dimenticato || *intr* scivolare, scorrere; sdrucciolare; sbagliare; peggiorare; **to let slip** lasciarsi sfuggire; **to slip away** svignarsela; **to slip by** (*said of time*) passare, fuggire; **to slip out of s.o.'s hands** sgusciare dalle mani di qlcu; **to slip up** sbagliarsi

slip'cov'er s fodera

slip'knot' s nodo scorsoio

slip' of the tongue' s errore m nel parlare

slipper ['slɪpər] s pantofola

slippery ['slɪpəri] adj sdrucciolevole, scivoloso; evasivo; incerto

slip'shod' adj trasandato, mal fatto

slip'-up' s (coll) sbaglio

slit [slɪt] s taglio, fenditura || v (*pret & pp* slit; *ger* slitting) tr tagliare, fendere; **to slit the throat of** sgozzare

slob [slɑb] s (slang) rozzo, villanzone m

slobber ['slɑbər] s bava; sdolcinatura || intr sbavare; parlare sdolcinatamente

sloe [slo] s (shrub) prugnolo; (fruit) prugnola

slogan ['slogən] s slogan m

sloop [slup] s cutter m

slop [slɑp] s pastone m; (slang) sbobba || v (*pret & pp* slopped; *ger* slopping) tr versare, imbrodare || intr rovesciarsi, scorrere; (slang) perdersi in smancerie

slope [slop] s costa, pendice f; (of mountain or roof) spiovente m || tr inclinare || intr digradare, scendere

slop·py ['slɑpi] adj (-pier; -piest) fangoso; bagnato; (slovenly) sciatto; (done badly) abborracciato

slot [slɑt] s scanalatura; (for letters) buca; (e.g., on a broadcasting schedule) posizione

sloth [sloθ] or [sləθ] s pigrizia; (zool) bradipo, poltrone m

slot' machine' s macchina a gettone

slouch [slautʃ] s postura goffa; persona goffa; (coll) poltrone m || intr muoversi goffamente; **to slouch in a chair** sdraiarsi

slouch' hat' s cappello floscio

slough [slau] s pantano; (fig) abisso || [slʌf] s (of snake) spoglia; (pathol) crosta || tr—**to slough off** spogliarsi di || intr sbucciarsi, cadere

Slovak ['slovæk] or [slo'væk] adj & s slovacco

sloven·ly ['slʌvənli] adj (-lier; -liest) sciatto, trasandato

slow [slo] adj lento; (sluggish) tardo; (clock) indietro, in ritardo; (in understanding) tardivo || adv piano || tr rallentare || intr rallentarsi; (said of a watch) ritardare

slow'down' s sciopero pignolo

slow' mo'tion s—**in slow motion** al rallentatore

slow'-motion projec'tor s rallentatore m

slow'poke' s (coll) poltrone m

slug [slʌg] s (heavy piece of metal) lingotto; (metal disk) gettone m; (fig) poltrone m; (zool) lumaca; (coll) colpo, mazzata || v (*pret & pp*

slugged; *ger* slugging) tr picchiare sodo

sluggard ['slʌgərd] s poltrone m

sluggish ['slʌgɪʃ] adj pigro, indolente; lento, fiacco

sluice [slus] s canale m; stramazzo

sluice' gate' s paratoia

slum [slʌm] s bassifondi mpl || v (*pret & pp* slummed; *ger* slumming) intr visitare i bassifondi

slumber ['slʌmbər] s dormiveglia m, sonnellino || intr dormire, dormicchiare

slump [slʌmp] s depressione, crisi f; (in prices) ribasso, calo || intr impantanarsi; peggiorare; (said of prices) ribassare, calare

slur [slʌr] s insulto, macchia; critica; (mus) legatura || v (*pret & pp* slurred; *ger* slurring) tr pronunziare indistintamente; (a subject) sorvolare; insultare, calunniare; (mus) legare

slush [slʌʃ] s poltiglia di neve; fanghiglia; (fig) sdolcinatezza

slut [slʌt] s cagna; (slovenly woman) sciamannona; troia, puttana

sly [slaɪ] adj (slyer or slier; slyest or sliest) furbo; insidioso; (hiding one's true feelings) sornione; **on the sly** furtivamente

smack [smæk] s schiaffo; (of whip or lips) schiocco; (taste) traccia, sapore m; (coll) bacio collo schiocco || adv di colpo, direttamente || tr dare uno schiaffo a; colpire; (the whip or one's lips) schioccare; schioccare un bacio a || intr—**to smack of** sapere di

small [smɔl] adj piccolo; povero; basso, umile; (change) spicciolo; (typ) minuscolo

small' arms' spl armi fpl portatili

small' busi'ness s piccolo commercio

small' cap'ital s (typ) maiuscoletto

small' fry' s spiccioli mpl

small' fry' s minutaglia; bambini mpl; gente f di poca importanza

small' hours' spl ore fpl piccole

small' intes'tine s intestino tenue

small-minded ['smɔl'maɪndɪd] adj di corte vedute, gretto

small' of the back' s fine f della schiena, reni fpl

smallpox ['smɔl ˌpɑks] s vaiolo

small' talk' s conversazione futile

small'-time' adj di poca importanza

small'-town' adj di provincia

smart [smɑrt] adj intelligente; scaltro, furbo; (pain) acuto; (in appearance) elegante; (pert) impertinente; (coll) grande, abbondante || s dolore acuto, sofferenza || intr bruciare; dolere; soffrire

smart' al'eck ['ælɪk] s saputello

smart' set' s bel mondo

smash [smæʃ] s sconquasso; colpo; collisione; rovina, fallimento; (tennis) smash m, schiacciata || tr sconquassare; sfracellare; rovinare; (tennis) schiacciare || intr sconquassarsi; sfracellarsi; andare in rovina; **to smash into** scontrarsi con

smash' hit' s successone m

smash'-up' *s* sconquasso

smattering ['smætərɪŋ] *s* infarinatura, spolvero

smear [smɪr] *s* macchia, imbrattatura; calunnia; (bact) striscio || *tr* imbrattare; spalmare; calunniare

smear' campaign' *s* campagna di vilipendio

smell [smel] *s* odore *m*; (*sense*) olfatto, odorato; profumo || *v* (*pret & pp* smelled or smelt) *tr* fiutare, odorare || *intr* odorare; (*to stink*) puzzare; profumare; **to smell of** odorare di; puzzare di

smell'ing salts' *spl* sali aromatici

smell·y ['smeli] *adj* (-ier; -iest) puzzolente

smelt [smelt] *s* (ichth) eperlano || *tr & intr* fondere

smile [smaɪl] *s* sorriso || *intr* sorridere

smiling ['smaɪlɪŋ] *adj* sorridente

smirk [smʌrk] *s* ghigno || *intr* ghignare

smite [smaɪt] *v* (*pret* smote [smot]; *pp* smitten ['smɪtən] or smit [smɪt]) *tr* colpire; percuotere; affliggere, castigare

smith [smɪθ] *s* fabbro

smith·y ['smɪθi] *s* (-ies) fucina

smit'ten *adj* afflitto; innamorato

smock [smɑk] *s* camice *m*; (*of mechanic*) camiciotto

smock' frock' *s* blusa da lavoro

smog [smɑg] *s* foschia, smog *m*

smoke [smok] *s* fumo; **to go up in smoke** andare in cenere || *tr* affumicare; (*tobacco*) fumare; **to smoke out** cacciare col fumo; scoprire || *intr* fumare; (*said, e.g., of the earth*) fumigare

smoke'-filled room' *s* stanza da riunioni piena di fumo

smoke'less pow'der ['smoklɪs] *s* polvere *f* senza fumo

smoker ['smokər] *s* fumatore *m*; salone *m* fumatori; (rr) vagone *m* fumatori

smoke' rings' *spl* anelli *mpl* di fumo

smoke' screen' *s* cortina di fumo

smoke'stack' *s* fumaiolo

smoking ['smokɪŋ] *s* (il) fumare; **no smoking** vietato fumare

smok'ing car' *s* vagone *m* fumatori

smok'ing jack'et *s* giacca da casa

smok'ing room' *s* stanza per fumatori

smok·y ['smoki] *adj* (-ier; -iest) fumoso

smolder ['smoldər] *s* fumo derivante da fuoco che cova || *intr* (*said of fire or passion*) covare; (*said of s.o.'s eyes*) ardere

smooch [smutʃ] *intr* (coll) baciarsi, baciucchiarsi

smooth [smuð] *adj* liscio, levigato; (*face*) glabro; di consistenza uniforme; (*flat*) piano; senza interruzioni; tranquillo; elegante; (*sound*) armonioso; (*taste*) gradevole; (*wine*) abboccato; (*sea*) calmo; (*style*) fluido || *tr* lisciare, levigare; appianare, facilitare; calmare; **to smooth away** appianare

smooth-faced ['smuð,fest] *adj* (*beardless*) glabro; liscio

smooth-spoken ['smuð,spokən] *adj* mellifluo

smooth·y ['smuði] *s* (-ies) galante *m*

smother ['smʌðər] *tr* affoggare, soffocare

smudge [smʌdʒ] *s* macchia, imbrattatura || *tr* macchiare, imbrattare; (*a garden*) affumicare

smudge' pot' *s* apparecchiatura per affumicare

smug [smʌg] *adj* (smugger; smuggest) pieno di sé stesso; liscio, lisciato

smuggle ['smʌgəl] *tr* contrabbandare || *intr* praticare il contrabbando

smuggler ['smʌglər] *s* contrabbandiere *m*

smuggling ['smʌglɪŋ] *s* contrabbando

smut [smʌt] *s* sudiciume *m*; oscenità *f*; (agr) volpe *f*, golpe *f*

smut·ty ['smʌti] *adj* (-tier; -tiest) sudicio; osceno; (agr) malato di volpe

snack [snæk] *s* spuntino, merenda; porzione

snack' bar' *s* tavola calda

snag [snæg] *s* tronco sommerso; protuberanza, sporgenza; (*tooth*) dente rotto; (fig) intoppo, ostacolo; **to hit a snag** incontrare un ostacolo || *v* (*pret & pp* snagged; *ger* snagging) *tr* fare uno straccio a; (fig) ostacolare

snail [snel] *s* chiocciola, lumaca; **at a snail's pace** come una lumaca

snake [snek] *s* serpente *m*; (*nonvenomous*) biscia

snake' in the grass' *s* pericolo nascosto; (*person*) serpe *f* in seno

snap [snæp] *s* (*sharp sound*) schiocco; (*bite*) morso; (*fastener*) bottone automatico; (*of cold weather*) breve periodo; (*manner of speaking*) tono tagliente; (phot) istantanea; (coll) vigore *m*; (coll) cosa da nulla || *v* (*pret & pp* snapped; *ger* snapping) *tr* schioccare; chiudere di colpo; spezzare di colpo; (*a picture*) scattare; **to snap one's fingers at** infischiarsi di; **to snap up** afferrare; (*a person*) tagliare la parola a || *intr* schioccare; (*to crack*) rompersi di colpo; **to snap at** cercare di mordere; (*a bargain*) cercare di afferrare; **to snap out of it** (coll) riprendersi; **to snap shut** chiudersi di colpo

snap'drag'on *s* (bot) bocca di leone

snap' fas'tener *s* bottone automatico

snap' judg'ment *s* decisione presa senza riflessione

snap·py ['snæpi] *adj* (-pier; -piest) mordente, mordace; (coll) vivo, vivace; (coll) elegante; **to make it snappy** (slang) sbrigarsi

snap'shot' *s* istantanea

snare [sner] *s* laccio, lacciolo; (*of a drum*) corda

snare' drum' *s* cassa rullante

snarl [snɑrl] *s* (*of a dog*) ringhio; groviglio; (*of traffic*) ingorgo; (fig) confusione || *tr* urlare con un ringhio; (*to tangle*) aggrovigliare; complicare || *intr* ringhiare; aggrovigliarsi; complicarsi

snatch [snætʃ] *s* strappo, strappone *m*; presa; pezzetto; momentino || *tr &*

intr strappare; **to snatch at** cercare di afferrare; **to snatch from** strappare a

sneak [snik] *s* furfante *m* ‖ *tr* mettere di nascosto; pigliare di nascosto ‖ *intr*—**to sneak in** entrare di nascosto; **to sneak out** svignarsela

sneaker ['snikər] *s* furfante *m; scarpetta da ginnastica

sneak' thief' *s* ladro, topo

sneak·y ['sniki] *adj* (**-ier; -lest**) furtivo

sneer [snɪr] *s* ghigno ‖ *intr* sogghignare; **to sneer at** beffarsi si

sneeze [sniz] *s* starnuto ‖ *intr* starnutare; **not to be sneezed at** (coll) non essere disprezzabile

snicker ['snɪkər] *s* risatina ‖ *intr* fare una risatina

snide [snaɪd] *adj* malizioso

sniff [snɪf] *s* fiuto, fiutata; (*scent*) odore *m* ‖ *tr* fiutare ‖ *intr* aspirare rumorosamente; (*with emotion*) moccicare; **to sniff at** annusare; mostrare disprezzo per

sniffle ['snɪfəl] *s* moccio; **to have the sniffles** moccicare ‖ *intr* moccicare

snip [snɪp] *s* taglio; pezzetto; (*person*) (coll) mezza cartuccia ‖ *v* (*pret & pp* **snipped**; *ger* **snipping**) *tr* tagliuzzare

snipe [snaɪp] *s* tiro di nascosto; (orn) beccaccino ‖ *intr* sparare in appostamento; attaccare da lontano

sniper ['snaɪpər] *s* franco tiratore, cecchino

snippet ['snɪpɪt] *s* ritaglio, frammento; (fig) mezza cartuccia

snip·py ['snɪpi] *adj* (**-pier; -piest**) frammentario; (coll) corto, brusco; (coll) arrogante

snitch [snɪtʃ] *tr & intr* (coll) graffignare, sgraffignare

sniv·el ['snɪvəl] *s* moccio; singhiozzo, piagnisteo; falsa commozione ‖ *v* (*pret & pp* **-eled** *or* **-elled**; *ger* **-eling** *or* **-elling**) *intr* singhiozzare, piagnucolare; (*to have a runny nose*) moccicare, avere il moccio

snob [snɑb] *s* snob *mf*

snobbery ['snɑbəri] *s* snobismo

snobbish ['snɑbɪʃ] *adj* snobistico

snoop [snup] *s* (coll) ficcanaso ‖ *intr* (coll) ficcare il naso

snoop·y ['snupi] *adj* (**-ier; -lest**) (coll) curioso, invadente

snoot [snut] *s* (slang) naso

snoot·y ['snuti] *adj* (**-ier; -lest**) (coll) snobistico

snooze [snuz] *s* (coll) sonnellino ‖ *intr* (coll) fare un sonnellino

snore [snɔr] *s* russamento ‖ *intr* russare

snort [snɔrt] *s* sbuffo ‖ *intr* sbuffare

snot [snɑt] *s* (slang) moccio

snot·ty ['snɑti] *adj* (**-tier; -tiest**) (coll) snobistico; (coll) arrogante; (slang) moccioso

snout [snaʊt] *s* muso; (*of pig*) grugno; (*of person*) muso, grugno

snow [sno] *s* neve *f* ‖ *intr* nevicare

snow'ball' *s* palla di neve ‖ *tr* gettare palle di neve a ‖ *intr* aumentare come una palla di neve

snow'blind' *adj* accecato dalla neve

snow'bound' *adj* prigioniero della neve

snow-capped ['sno͵kæpt] *adj* coperto di neve

snow'drift' *s* banco di neve

snow'fall' *s* nevicata

snow' fence' *s* barriera contro la neve

snow'flake' *s* fiocco di neve

snow' flur'ry *s* neve portata da raffiche

snow' line' *s* limite *m* delle nevi perenni

snow'man' *s* (**-men'**) uomo di neve

snow'plow' *s* spazzaneve *m*

snow'shoe' *s* racchetta da neve

snow'slide' *s* valanga

snow'storm' *s* bufera di neve

snow' tire' *s* gomma da neve, pneumatico da neve

snow'-white' *adj* bianco come la neve

snow·y ['sno·i] *adj* (**-ier; -lest**) nevoso

snub [snʌb] *s* affronto ‖ *v* (*pret & pp* **snubbed**; *ger* **snubbing**) *tr* snobbare

snub·by ['snʌbi] *adj* (**-bier; -biest**) camuso, rincagnato

snuff [snʌf] *s* fiutata; tabacco da fiuto; (*of a candlewick*) moccolo; **up to snuff** (coll) soddisfacente; (coll) bene ‖ *tr* fiutare; tabaccare; (*a candle*) smoccolare; **to snuff out** spegnere; (fig) soffocare

snuff'box' *s* tabacchiera

snuffers ['snʌfərz] *spl* smoccolatoio

snug [snʌg] *adj* (**snugger; snuggest**) comodo; (*dress*) attillato; compatto; (*well-off*) agiato; (*sum*) discreto; (*sheltered*) ben protetto; (*well-hidden*) nascosto

snuggle ['snʌgəl] *intr* rannicchiarsi; **to snuggle up** to stringersi a

so [so] *adv* così; così *or* tanto + *adj or adv*; per quanto; **and so** certamente; pure; **and so on** e così via; **or so** più o meno; **to think so** credere di sì; **so as to** + *inf* per + *inf*; **so far** sinora, finora; **so long!** arrivederci!; **so many** tanti; **so much** tanto; **so so** così così; **so that** in maniera che, di modo che; **so to speak** per così dire ‖ *conj* cosicché ‖ *interj* bene!; basta!; così!

soak [sok] *s* bagnata; (*toper*) ubriacone *m* ‖ *tr* bagnare, inzuppare; imbevere; (coll) ubriacare; (slang) far pagare un prezzo esorbitante a; **to soak up** assorbire; **soaked to the skin** bagnato fino alle ossa ‖ *intr* stare a molle, macerare; inzupparsi

so'-and-so' *s* (**-sos**) tal *m* dei tali; tal cosa

soap [sop] *s* sapone *m* ‖ *tr* insaponare

soap'box' *s* cassa di sapone; tribuna improvvisata

soap'box or'ator *s* oratore *m* che parla da una tribuna improvvisata

soap' bub'ble *s* bolla di sapone

soap' dish' *s* portasapone *m*

soap' flakes' *spl* sapone *m* a scaglie

soap' op'era *s* (coll) trasmissione radiofonica o televisiva lacrimogena

soap'pow'der *s* sapone *m* in polvere

soap'stone' *s* pietra da sarto

soap'suds' *spl* saponata

soap·y ['sopi] *adj* (**-ier; -lest**) saponoso

soar [sor] *intr* spaziare, slanciarsi; (aer) librarsi

sob [sab] *s* singhiozzo || *v* (*pret* & *pp* **sobbed;** *ger* **sobbing**) *tr* dire a singhiozzi || *intr* singhiozzare

sober ['sobər] *adj* sobrio; non ubriaco || *intr* smaltire la sbornia; **to sober down** calmarsi; **to sober up** smaltire la sbornia

sobriety [so'braɪ‚əti] *s* sobrietà *f*

sobriquet ['sobrɪ‚ke] *s* nomignolo

sob' sis'ter *s* giornalista lacrimogeno

sob' sto'ry *s* storia lacrimogena

so'-called' *adj* cosiddetto

soccer ['sakər] *s* calcio, football *m*

sociable ['soʃəbəl] *adj* sociale, socievole

social ['soʃəl] *adj* sociale || *s* riunione sociale

so'cial climb'er ['klaɪmər] *s* arrampicatore *m* sociale

so'cial con'tract *s* patto sociale

socialism ['soʃə‚lɪzəm] *s* socialismo

socialist ['soʃəlɪst] *s* socialista *mf*

socialite ['soʃə‚laɪt] *s* persona che appartiene all'alta società

So'cial Reg'ister *s* (trademark) annuario dell'alta società

so'cial secu'rity *s* sicurezza sociale

so'cial work'er *s* visitatrice *f*, assistente *mf* sociale

socie‑ty [sə'saɪ‚əti] *s* (**‑ties**) società *f*; (*companionship or company*) compagnia

soci'ety ed'itor *s* cronista mondano

sociology [‚sosɪ'alədʒi] or [‚soʃɪ‑'alədʒi] *s* sociologia

sock [sak] *s* calzino; (slang) colpo forte; (slang) attore *m* di prim'ordine; (slang) spettacolo eccezionale || *tr* (slang) dare un forte colpo a

socket ['sakɪt] *s* (*of eye*) occhiaia; (*of tooth*) alveolo; (*of candlestick*) bocciolo; (*wall socket*) (elec) presa di corrente; (elec) portalampada *m*

sock'et wrench' *s* chiave *f* a tubo

sod [sad] *s* zolla; terreno erboso || *v* (*pret* & *pp* **sodded;** *ger* **sodding**) *tr* piotare

soda ['sodə] *s* soda

so'da crack'er *s* galletta fatta al bicarbonato

so'da wa'ter *s* soda, gazosa

sodium ['sodɪ‚əm] *adj* sodico || *s* sodio

sofa ['sofə] *s* sofà *m*, divano

so'fa bed' *s* sofà *m* letto

soft [sɔft] or [saft] *adj* molle; (*smooth*) morbido; (*iron*) dolce; (*hat*) floscio; (*person*) rammollito; (coll) facile

soft'-boiled' egg' ['sɔft'bɔɪld] or ['saft'bɔɪld] *s* uovo alla coque

soft' coal' *s* carbone bituminoso

soft' drink' *s* bibita

soften ['sɔfən] or ['safən] *tr* mollificare, rammollire; (fig) intenerire || *intr* intenerirsi

softener ['sɔfənər] or ['safənər] *s* ammorbidente *m*

soft' land'ing *s* allunaggio morbido

soft'-ped'al *v* (*pret* & *pp* **‑aled** or

‑alled; *ger* **‑aling** or **‑alling**) *tr* mettere in sordina; (coll) moderare

soft'-shell crab' *s* mollecca

soft' soap' *s* sapone *m* molle; (coll) adulazione

soft'-soap' *tr* (coll) insaponare

sog‑gy ['sagi] *adj* (**‑gier; ‑giest**) rammollito, inzuppato

soil [sɔɪl] *s* suolo, terreno; territorio; (*spot*) macchia; (*filth*) porcheria, lordura || *tr* sporcare, macchiare || *intr* sporcarsi, macchiarsi

soil' pipe' *s* tubo di scarico

soiree or **soirée** [swa're] *s* serata

sojourn ['sodʒʌrn] *s* soggiorno || ['sodʒʌrn] or [so'dʒʌrn] *intr* soggiornare

solace ['salɪs] *s* conforto || *tr* confortare, consolare

solar ['solər] *adj* solare

so'lar bat'tery *s* batteria solare

solder ['sadər] *s* saldatura; lega per saldatura || *tr* saldare

sol'dering i'ron *s* saldatoio

soldier ['soldʒər] *s* (*man of rank and file*) soldato; (*man in military service*) militare *m* || *intr* fare il soldato

sol'dier of for'tune *s* soldato di ventura

soldier‑y ['soldʒəri] *s* (**‑ies**) soldatesca

sold-out ['sold‚aut] *adj* esaurito; (*e.g., theater*) completo

sole [sol] *adj* solo, unico; esclusivo || *s* (*of foot*) pianta; (*of stocking*) soletta; (*of shoe*) suola; (*fish*) sfoglia || *tr* solare

solely ['solli] *adv* solamente

solemn ['saləm] *adj* solenne

solicit [sə'lɪsɪt] *tr* sollecitare; adescare, accostare

solicitor [sə'lɪsɪtər] *s* sollecitatore *m*; agente *m*; (law) procuratore *m*

solicitous [sə'lɪsɪtəs] *adj* sollecito

solicitude [sə'lɪsɪ‚tjud] or [sə'lɪsɪ‚tud] *s* sollecitudine *f*

solid ['salɪd] *adj* solido; (*not hollow*) sodo; (*e.g., clouds*) denso; (*wall*) pieno, massiccio; (*word*) con grafia unita; intero; unanime, solidale; (*good*) buono; (*e.g., gold*) puro, massiccio

solidity [sə'lɪdɪti] *s* solidità *f*

sol'id-state' *adj* transistorizzato, senza valvole

solilo‑quy [sə'lɪləkwi] *s* (**‑quies**) soliloquio

solitaire ['salɪ‚ter] *s* solitario

solitar‑y ['salɪ‚teri] *adj* solitario; unico || *s* (**‑ies**) persona solitaria

sol'itary confine'ment *s* segregazione cellulare

solitude ['salɪ‚tjud] or ['salɪ‚tud] *s* solitudine *f*

so‑lo ['solo] *adj* solo, solitario; (mus) solista || *s* (**‑los**) (mus) solo

soloist ['solo‑ɪst] *s* solista *mf*

so' long' *interj* (coll) ciao!; (coll) addio!; (coll) arrivederci!

solstice ['salstɪs] *s* solstizio

soluble ['saljəbəl] *adj* solubile

solution [sə'luʃən] *s* soluzione

solvable ['salvəbəl] *adj* risolvibile

solve [salv] *tr* risolvere, sciogliere

solvency ['salvənsi] s solvenza

solvent ['salvənt] adj & s solvente m

somber ['sambər] adj tetro

some [sʌm] adj indef qualche; di + art, e.g., **some apples** delle mele; (coll) forte, grande ‖ pron indef alcuni, taluni; ne, e.g., **I have some** ne ho

some'bod'y pron indef taluno, qualcuno; **somebody else** qualcun altro ‖ s (-ies) (coll) qualcuno

some'day' adv qualche giorno

some'how' adv in qualche modo; **somehow or other** in un modo o nell'altro

some'one' pron indef qualcuno, taluno; **someone else** qualcun altro

somersault ['sʌmər,sɔlt] s salto mortale ‖ intr fare un salto mortale

something ['sʌmθɪŋ] pron indef qualcosa; **something else** qualcos'altro ‖ adv un po'; (coll) molto, moltissimo

some'time' adj antico, di un tempo ‖ adv un giorno o l'altro, uno di questi giorni

some'times' adv talora, talvolta

some'way' adv in qualche modo

some'what' s qualcosa ‖ adv piuttosto, un po'

some'where' adv in qualche luogo, da qualche parte; a qualche momento; **somewhere else** altrove

somnambulist [sam'næmbjəlɪst] s sonnambulo

somnolent ['samnələnt] adj sonnolento

son [sʌn] s figlio

sonar ['sonar] s ecogoniometro, sonar m

song [sɔŋ] or [sɑŋ] s canto, canzone f; **for a song** per un soldo

song'bird' s uccello canoro

Song' of Songs' s Cantico dei Cantici

songster ['sɔŋstər] s cantante m, canzonettista m

songstress ['sɔŋstrɪs] s cantante f, canzonettista f

song'writ'er s canzoniere m

son'ic boom' ['sɑnɪk] s boato sonico

son'-in-law' s (sons'-in-law') genero

sonnet ['sɑnɪt] s sonetto

son·ny ['sʌni] s (-nies) figliolo

sonori·ty [sə'narɪti] or [sə'nɔrɪti] s (-ties) sonorità f

soon [sun] adv in breve, ben presto; subito, presto; **as soon as** non appena, quanto prima; **as soon as possible** quanto prima; **I had sooner** preferirei; **how soon?** quando?; **soon after** poco dopo; **sooner or later** prima o poi, tosto o tardi

soot [sʊt] or [sut] s fuliggine f

soothe [suð] tr calmare, lenire

soothsayer ['suθ,se·ər] s indovino

soot·y ['suti] or ['sʊti] adj (-ier; -iest) fuligginoso

sop [sɑp] s (soaked food) zuppa; (bribe) dono, offa ‖ v (pret & pp sopped; ger sopping) tr intingere, inzuppare; **to sop up** assorbire

sophisticated [sə'fɪstɪ,ketɪd] adj sofisticato, smaliziato

sophistication [sə,fɪstɪ'keʃən] s eccessiva ricercatezza; gusti mpl raffinati

sophomore ['safə,mor] s studente m del secondo anno, fagiolo

sophomoric [,safə'mɔrɪk] adj saputello, presuntuoso; ingenuo, imberbe

sopping ['sɑpɪŋ] adv—**sopping wet** inzuppato

sopran·o [sə'præno] or [sə'prano] adj per soprano, da soprano ‖ s (-os) soprano mf

sorcerer ['sɔrsərər] s mago, stregone m

sorceress ['sɔrsərɪs] s maga, strega

sorcer·y ['sɔrsəri] s (-ies) stregoneria

sordid ['sɔrdɪd] adj sordido

sore [sor] adj irritato; indolenzito; estremo, grave; **to be sore at** (coll) aversela con ‖ s piaga, ulcera; dolore m, afflizione; **to open an old sore** riaprire una ferita

sorely ['sorli] adv penosamente; gravemente, urgentemente

soreness ['sornɪs] s dolore m, afflizione

sore' spot' s (fig) piaga

sore' throat' s mal m di gola

sorori·ty [sə'rarɪti] or [sə'rɔrɪti] s (-ties) associazione femminile universitaria

sorrel ['sɑrəl] or ['sɔrəl] adj sauro

sorrow ['saro] or ['sɔro] s dolore m, cordoglio ‖ intr affliggersi, provar cordoglio; **to sorrow for** rimpiangere

sorrowful ['sɑrəfəl] or ['sɔrəfəl] adj doloroso

sor·ry ['sɑri] or ['sɔri] adj (-rier; -riest) spiacente, desolato, dolente; povero, cattivo; **to be sorry** dolersi; dispiacere a, e.g., **he is sorry** gli dispiace ‖ interj mi displacel, scusi!

sort [sɔrt] s tipo, specie f; maniera; **a sort of** una specie di; **out of sorts** depresso; ammalato; di mal umore; **sort of** (coll) piuttosto; (coll) un certo, e.g., **sort of a headache** un certo mal di testa ‖ tr assortire; (mail) smistare

so'-so' adj passabile ‖ adv così così

sot [sɑt] s ubriacone m

soubrette [su'brɛt] s (theat) soubrette f

soul [sol] s anima; **upon my soul!** sulla mia parola!

sound [saʊnd] adj sano; solido, forte; valido, buono; (sleep) profondo; valido, legale; onesto ‖ s suono; rumore m; (of an animal) verso; (passage of water) stretto; (surg) sonda; (ichth) vescica natatoria; **within sound of** alla portata di ‖ adv profondamente ‖ tr (an instrument) sonare; pronunciare; (e.g., s.o.'s chest) auscultare; (praises) cantare; (to measure) sondare ‖ intr sonare; parere, sembrare; fare uno scandaglio; **to sound like** avere il suono di; dare l'impressione di, parere

sound' bar'rier s muro del suono

sound' film' s pellicola sonora

soundly ['saʊndli] adv solidamente; profondamente; completamente

sound'proof' adj a prova di suono ‖ tr insonorizzare

sound' track' *s* (mov) sonoro, colonna sonora

sound' truck' *s* autoveicolo con impianto sonoro

sound' wave' *s* onda sonora

soup [sup] *s* zuppa, minestra

soup' dish' *s* piatto fondo

soup' kitch'en *s* asilo dei poveri che serve zuppa gratuitamente

soup'spoon' *s* cucchiaio (da minestra)

sour [saur] *adj* acido; (*fruit*) acerbo || *tr* inacidire || *intr* inacidirsi

source [sors] *s* fonte *f*, sorgente *f*

source' lan'guage *s* lingua di partenza

source' mate'rial *s* fonti *fpl* originali

sour' cher'ry *s* (*fruit*) amarena; (*tree*) amareno

sour' grapes' *interj* l'uva è verde!

south [sauθ] *adj* meridionale, del sud || *s* sud *m*, meridione *m* || *adv* verso il sud

South' Amer'ica *s* l'America *f* del Sud

South' Amer'ican *adj & s* sudamericano

southeast [ˌsauθ'ist] *adj* di sud-est || *s* sud-est || *adv* al sud-est

southern ['sʌðərn] *adj* meridionale

South'ern Cross' *s* Croce *f* del Sud

southerner ['sʌðərnər] *s* meridionale *mf*

South' Kore'a *s* la Corea del Sud

south'paw' *adj & s* (coll) mancino

South' Pole' *s* Polo sud

South' Vietnam-ese' [vɪˌetnə'miz] *adj* vietnamita del sud || *s* (-ese) vietnamita *mf* del sud

southward ['sauθwərd] *adv* verso il sud

south'west' *adj* di sud-ovest || *s* sud-ovest *m* || *adv* al sud-ovest

souvenir [ˌsuvə'nɪr] or ['suvəˌnɪr] *s* ricordo, memoria

sovereign ['savrɪn] or ['sʌvrɪn] *adj* sovrano || *s* (*king*) sovrano; (*queen; coin*) sovrana

sovereign-ty ['savrɪnti] or ['sʌvrɪnti] *s* (-ties) sovranità *f*

soviet ['sovɪˌet] or [ˌsovɪ'et] *adj* sovietico || *s* soviet *m*

So'viet Rus'sia *s* la Russia Sovietica

sow [sau] *s* porca, troia || [so] *v* (*pret* sowed; *pp* sown or sowed) *tr* seminare

soybean ['sɔɪˌbin] *s* soia; seme *m* di soia

spa [spa] *s* terme *fpl*

space [spes] *adj* spaziale || *s* spazio; periodo; **after a space** dopo un po' || *tr* spaziare; **to space out** diradare

space' bar' *s* barra spaziatrice, spaziatrice *f*

space' cen'ter *s* cosmodromo

space'craft' *s* astronave *f*

space' flight' *s* volo spaziale

space'man' *s* (-men') navigatore *m* spaziale

spacer ['spesər] *s* spaziatrice *f*, barra spaziatrice

space'ship' *s* astronave *f*

space'suit' *s* scafandro astronautico, tuta spaziale

spacious ['speʃəs] *adj* spazioso

spade [sped] *s* vanga; (cards) picca; **to call a spade a spade** dire pane al pane, vino al vino || *tr* vangare

spade'work' *s* lavoro preliminare

spaghetti [spə'geti] *s* spaghetti *mpl*

Spain [spen] *s* la Spagna

span [spæn] *s* (*of the hand*) spanna; (*of time*) tratto; (*of a bridge*) campata, luce *f*; (*of horses*) paio; (aer) apertura || *v* (*pret & pp* spanned; *ger* spanning) *tr* misurare a spanne; attraversare, oltrepassare; (*said of time*) abbracciare

spangle ['spæŋgəl] *s* lustrino || *tr* tempestare di lustrini; (*with bright objects*) stellare || *intr* brillare

Spaniard ['spænjərd] *s* spagnolo

Spanish ['spænɪʃ] *adj & s* spagnolo; **the Spanish** gli spagnoli

Span'ish-Amer'ican *adj & s* ispano-americano

Span'ish broom' *s* ginestra

Span'ish fly' *s* mosca cantaride

Span'ish om'elet *s* frittata di pomodori, cipolle e peperoni

Span'ish-speak'ing *adj* di lingua spagnola

spank [spæŋk] *tr* sculacciare

spanking ['spæŋkɪŋ] *adj* rapido; forte; (coll) eccellente, straordinario || *s* sculacciata

spar [spar] *s* (*mineral*) spato; (naut) asta, pennone *m*; (aer) longherone *m* || *v* (*pret & pp* sparred; *ger* sparring) *intr* fare la box

spare [sper] *adj* di riserva; libero, in eccesso; (*e.g., diet*) frugale; (*lean*) magro || *tr* salvare, risparmiare; perdonare; (*to do without*) fare a meno di, privarsi di; **to have . . . to spare** aver . . . d'avanzo; **to spare oneself** risparmiarsi

spare' parts' *s* pezzi *mpl* di ricambio

spare' room' *s* camera per gli ospiti

spare' tire' *s* ruota di scorta, pneumatico di scorta

spare' wheel' *s* ruota di scorta

sparing ['sperɪŋ] *adj* economico; (*scanty*) scarso

spark [spark] *s* scintilla; traccia || *tr* (coll) rianimare; (coll) corteggiare || *intr* scintillare

spark' coil' *s* bobina d'accensione

spark' gap' *s* (elec) traferro, intraferro

sparkle ['sparkəl] *s* scintilla; (*luster*) scintillio; allegria, vivacità *f* || *intr* scintillare; (*said, e.g., of eyes*) brillare, luccicare; (*said of wine*) frizzare, spumeggiare

sparkling ['sparklɪŋ] *adj* scintillante; (*wine*) frizzante, spumeggiante; (*water*) gassoso

spark' plug' *s* candela

sparrow ['spæro] *s* passero

sparse [spars] *adj* rado

Spartan ['spartən] *adj & s* spartano

spasm ['spæzəm] *s* spasmo; sprazzo d'energia

spasmodic [spæz'madɪk] *adj* spasmodico; intermittente, a sprazzi

spastic ['spæstɪk] *adj & s* spastico

spat [spæt] *s* litigio, battibecco; **spats**

ghette *fpl* || *v* (*pret & pp* spatted; *ger* spatting) *intr* avere un battibecco

spatial ['speʃəl] *adj* spaziale

spatter ['spætər] *tr* schizzare, spruzzare || *intr* gocciolare

spatula ['spætʃələ] *s* spatola

spawn [spɔn] *s* prole *f*, progenie *f*; risultato || *tr* produrre, generare || *intr* (ichth) deporre le uova

spay [spe] *tr* asportare le ovaie a

speak [spik] *v* (*pret* spoke [spok]; *pp* spoken) *tr* (*a language*) parlare; (*the truth*) dire || *intr* parlare; so to speak per così dire; speaking! al telefono!; to speak of importante, che valga parlarne; to speak out dire la propria opinione

speak'-eas'y *s* (-ies) bar clandestino

speaker ['spikər] *s* conferenziere *m*, oratore *m*; (*of a language*) parlante *mf*; (pol) presidente *m*; (rad) altoparlante *m*

speaking ['spikɪŋ] *adj* parlante; to be on speaking terms parlarsi || *s* parlare *m*, discorso

speak'ing tube' *s* tubo acustico

spear [spɪr] *s* lancia; (*for fishing*) arpione *m*; (*of grass*) stelo || *tr* trafiggere con la lancia

spear' gun' *s* fucile subacqueo

spear'head' *s* punta di lancia || *tr* condurre, dirigere

spear'mint' *s* menta romana spicata

special ['speʃəl] *adj* speciale || *s* prezzo speciale; treno speciale

spe'cial deliv'ery *s* espresso

spe'cial draw'ing rights' *spl* (econ) diritti *mpl* speciali di prelievo

specialist ['speʃəlɪst] *s* specialista *mf*

specialize ['speʃə,laɪz] *tr* specializzare || *intr* specializzarsi

spe'cial part'ner *s* accomandante *mf*

special-ty ['speʃəlti] *s* (-ties) specialità *f*

spe-cies ['spisiz] *s* (-cies) specie *f*

specific [spɪ'sɪfɪk] *adj & s* specifico

specification [,spesɪfɪ'keʃən] *s* specifica; (com) capitolato

specif'ic grav'ity *s* peso specifico

speci-fy ['spesɪ,faɪ] *v* (*pret & pp* -fied) *tr* specificare

specimen ['spesɪmən] *s* esemplare *m*; (coll) tipo

specious ['spiʃəs] *adj* specioso

speck [spek] *s* macchiolina; (*of dust*) granello; (*of hope*) filo || *tr* macchiettare

speckle ['spekəl] *s* macchiolina || *tr* macchiettare, picchiettare

spectacle ['spektəkəl] *s* spettacolo; spectacles occhiali *mpl*

spectator ['spektetər] or [spek'tetər] *s* spettatore *m*

specter ['spektər] *s* spettro

spec-trum ['spektrəm] *s* (-tra [trə] or -trums) spettro; (fig) gamma

speculate ['spekjə,let] *intr* speculare

speech [spit] *s* parola, parlata; (*before an audience*) discorso; (*of an actor*) elocuzione; in speech oralmente

speech' clin'ic *s* clinica per la correzione dei difetti del linguaggio

speechless ['spitʃlɪs] *adj* senza parole, muto

speed [spid] *s* velocità *f*; (aut) marcia || *tr* accelerare, affrettare || *intr* accelerare, affrettarsi; guidare oltre la velocità massima

speed'boat' *s* motoscafo da corsa

speeding ['spidɪŋ] *s* eccesso di velocità

speed' king' *s* asso del volante

speed' lim'it *s* limite *m* di velocità

speedometer [spi'dɑmɪtər] *s* tachimetro; (*to record the distance covered*) contachilometri *m*

speed'-up' *s* accelerazione

speed'way' *s* (*highway*) autostrada; (*for races*) pista

speed-y ['spidi] *adj* (-ier; -iest) veloce, rapido

spell [spel] *s* malia, incantesimo; fascino; turno; attacco; periodo di tempo; to cast a spell on incantare || *v* (*pret & pp* spelled or spelt [spelt]) *tr* compitare; scrivere in tutte lettere; voler dire; to spell out (coll) spiegare dettagliatamente || *intr* scrivere, sillabare || *v* (*pret & pp* spelled) *tr* rimpiazzare

spell'bind' *v* (*pret & pp* -bound) *tr* affascinare

spell'bind'er *s* oratore *m* abbagliante

spelling ['spelɪŋ] *adj* ortografico || *s* (*act*) compitazione; (*way a word is spelled*) grafia; (*subject of study*) ortografia

spell'ing bee' *s* gara di ortografia

spelunker [spɪ'lʌŋkər] *s* esploratore *m* di caverne

spend [spend] *v* (*pret & pp* spent [spent]) *tr* spendere; (*time*) passare

spender ['spendər] *s* spenditore *m*

spend'ing mon'ey *s* denaro per le piccole spese personali

spend'thrift' *s* sprecone *m*, spendaccione *m*

sperm [spɑrm] *s* sperma *m*

sperm' whale' *s* capodoglio

spew [spju] *tr & intr* vomitare

sphere [sfɪr] *s* sfera

spherical ['sfɛrɪkəl] *adj* sferico

sphinx [sfɪŋks] *s* (sphinxes or sphinges ['sfɪndʒiz]) sfinge *f*

spice [spaɪs] *s* droga; spezie *fpl*; (fig) gusto, sapore *m* || *tr* drogare; dare gusto a, rendere piccante

spick-and-span ['spɪkənd'spæn] *adj* ordinato e pulito

spic-y ['spaɪsi] *adj* (-ier; -iest) drogato; piccante

spider ['spaɪdər] *s* ragno

spi'der-web' *s* ragnatela

spiff-y ['spɪfi] *adj* (-ier; -iest) (slang) elegante, bello

spigot ['spɪgət] *s* (peg) zipolo; (*faucet*) rubinetto

spike [spaɪk] *s* chiodo, chiodone *m*; (*sharp-pointed piece*) spuntone *m*; (rr) arpione *m*; (bot) spiga || *tr* inchiodare; mettere chiodi a; (*a rumor*) porre fine a; (coll) alcolizzare

spill [spɪl] *s* rovesciamento; liquido rovesciato; (coll) caduta || *v* (*pret & pp* spilled or spilt [spɪlt]) *tr* rovesciare, spandere; versare; (naut) sventare; (coll) far cadere; (slang) snocciolare || *intr* rovesciarsi; versarsi

spill'way' *s* sfioratore *m*, stramazzo

spin [spɪn] *s* giro; (*twirl*) mulinello; corsa; **to go into a spin** (aer) cadere a vite || *v* (*pret & pp* **spun** [spʌn]; *ger* **spinning**) *tr* far girare; (*e.g., thread*) filare; **to spin out** prolungare; **to spin a yarn** raccontare una storia || *intr* girare; (*said of a top*) prillare; filare

spinach ['spɪnɪtʃ] *or* ['spɪnɪdʒ] *s* spinacio; (*leaves used as food*) spinaci *mpl*

spi'nal col'umn ['spaɪnəl] *s* spina dorsale, colonna vertebrale

spi'nal cord' *s* midollo spinale

spindle ['spɪndəl] *s* (*rounded rod*) fuso; (*shaft, axle*) asse *m;* balaustro

spine [spaɪn] *s* spina; spina dorsale; (bb) costola; (fig) forza, carattere *m*

spineless ['spaɪnlɪs] *adj* senza spine; senza carattere

spinet ['spɪnɪt] *s* spinetta

spinner ['spɪnər] *s* filatore *m;* (*machine*) filatrice *f*

spinning ['spɪnɪŋ] *adj* filante || *s* filatura; rotazione

spin'ning mill' *s* filanda

spin'ning wheel' *s* filatoio

spinster ['spɪnstər] *s* zitella

spi-ral ['spaɪrəl] *adj & s* spirale *f* || *v* (*pret & pp* **-raled** *or* **-ralled**; *ger* **-raling** *or* **-ralling**) *intr* muoversi lungo una spirale

spi'ral stair'case *s* scala a chiocciola

spire [spaɪr] *s* (*of a steeple*) guglia, freccia; (*of grass*) foglia; (*spiral*) spirale *f*

spirit ['spɪrɪt] *s* spirito; valore *m*, vigore *m;* bevanda spiritosa; **out of spirits** giù di morale || *tr*—**to spirit away** portar via misteriosamente

spirited ['spɪrɪtɪd] *adj* brioso; (*horse*) superbo, vivace

spir'it lamp' *s* lampada a spirito

spiritless ['spɪrɪtlɪs] *adj* senza anima, senza vita

spir'it lev'el *s* livella a bolla d'aria

spiritual ['spɪrɪtʃu-əl] *adj* spirituale; (*séance*) spiritico

spiritualism ['spɪrɪtʃuə,lɪzəm] *s* spiritismo; (philos) spiritualismo

spiritualist ['spɪrɪtʃu-əlɪst] *s* spiritista *mf;* (philos) spiritualista *mf*

spirituous ['spɪrɪtʃu-əs] *adj* alcolico

spit [spɪt] *s* sputo; (*for roasting*) spiedo, schidione *m;* punta; **the spit and image of** (coll) il ritratto parlante di || *v* (*pret & pp* **spat** [spæt] *or* **spit**; *ger* **spitting**) *tr & intr* sputare

spite [spaɪt] *s* dispetto, ripicco; **in spite of** a dispetto di, a onta di; **out of spite** per picca || *tr* far dispetto a; offendere; contrariare

spiteful ['spaɪtfəl] *adj* dispettoso

spit'fire' *s* persona collerica; (*woman*) bisbetica

spit'ting im'age *s* (coll) ritratto parlante

spittoon [spɪ'tun] *s* sputacchiera

splash [splæʃ] *s* schizzo, spruzzo; (*of mud*) zacchera; (*sound*) tonfo; **to make a splash** fare molto sci-sci || *tr & intr* sguazzare

splash'down' *s* (rok) ammaraggio, urto con l'acqua

spleen [splin] *s* cattivo umore, bile *f;* (anat) milza, splene *m*

splendid ['splendɪd] *adj* splendido; ottimo, magnifico

splendor ['splendər] *s* splendore *m*

splice [splaɪs] *s* giuntura || *tr* giuntare

splint [splɪnt] *s* stecca || *tr* steccare

splinter ['splɪntər] *s* scheggia || *tr* scheggiare || *intr* scheggiarsi

splin'ter group' *s* gruppo dissidente

split [splɪt] *adj* spaccato; diviso || *s* spaccatura; fessura; rottura, divisione; **splits** (sports) spaccato || *v* (*pret & pp* **split**; *ger* **splitting**) *tr* spaccare; dividere; **to split one's sides with laughter** scoppiare dalle risa || *intr* scindersi, dividersi; **to split up** separarsi

split' personal'ity *s* sdoppiamento della personalità

splitting ['splɪtɪŋ] *adj* che fende; che si fende; violento, fortissimo || *s*— **splittings** frammenti *mpl*

splotch [splatʃ] *s* macchia, chiazza || *tr* macchiare, chiazzare

splurge [splʌrdʒ] *s* ostentazione || *intr* fare ostentazione; fare una spesa matta

splutter ['splʌtər] *s* crepitio; (*utterance*) barbugliamento || *tr* barbugliare || *intr* crepitare; barbugliare

spoil [spoɪl] *s* spoglia, bottino; **spoils** (mil) spoglie *fpl;* (pol) profitto, vantaggio || *v* (*pret & pp* **spoiled** *or* **spoilt** [spoɪlt]) *tr* rovinare, sciupare; (*a child*) viziare; (*food*) deteriorare || *intr* guastarsi, andare a male

spoilage ['spoɪlɪdʒ] *s* deterioramento

spoiled [spoɪld] *adj* (*child*) viziato; (*food*) andato a male, passato

spoils' sys'tem *s* sistema politico secondo il quale le cariche vanno al partito vincitore

spoke [spok] *s* (*of a wheel*) raggio; (*of a ladder*) piolo

spokes'man *s* (**-men**) portavoce *m*

sponge [spʌndʒ] *s* spugna; **to throw in the sponge** (slang) gettare la spugna || *tr* pulire con spugna; assorbire; (coll) scroccare || *intr* assorbire; **to sponge off** (coll) vivere alle spalle di

sponge' bath' *s* spugnatura

sponge' cake' *s* pan *m* di Spagna

sponger ['spʌndʒər] *s* scroccatore *m*

sponge' rub'ber *s* gommapiuma

spon-gy ['spʌndʒi] *adj* (**-gier; -giest**) spugnoso

sponsor ['spansər] *s* patrocinatore *m;* (*of a charitable institution*) patrono; (*godfather*) padrino; (*godmother*) madrina || *tr* patrocinare; (rad, telv) offrire

sponsorship ['spansər,ʃɪp] *s* patrocinio

spontaneous [span'teni-əs] *adj* spontaneo

spoof [spuf] *s* mistificazione; parodia || *tr* mistificare; parodiare || *intr* mistificare; fare una parodia

spook [spuk] *s* (coll) spettro

spook·y ['spuki] *adj* (-ier; -iest) (coll) spettrale; (*horse*) (coll) nervoso

spool [spul] *s* spola, rocchetto

spoon [spun] *s* cucchiaio; (*lure*) cucchiaino; **born with a silver spoon in one's mouth** nato con la camicia || *tr* servire col cucchiaio || *intr* (coll) limonare

spoonerism ['spunə͵rɪzəm] *s* papera

spoon'-feed' *v* (*pret* & *pp* **-fed**) *tr* nutrire col cucchiaino; (fig) coccolare

spoonful ['spun͵fʊl] *s* cucchiaiata

spoon·y ['spuni] *adj* (-ier; -iest) (coll) svenevole

sporadic(al) [spə'rædɪk(əl)] *adj* sporadico

spore [spor] *s* spora

sport [sport] *adj* sportivo || *s* sport *m*; gioco; (*laughingstock*) zimbello; (*gambler*) (coll) giocatore *m*; (*person who behaves in a sportsmanlike manner*) (coll) spirito sportivo; (*flashy fellow*) (coll) tipo fino; (biol) mutazione; **to make sport of** farsi gioco di || *tr* (coll) sfoggiare; **to sport away** dissipare || *intr* divertirsi; giocare; farsi beffe

sport' clothes' *spl* vestiti *mpl* sport

sport'ing chance' *s* pari opportunità *f* di vincere

sport'ing goods' *spl* articoli *mpl* sportivi

sport'ing house' *s* (coll) bordello

sports'cast'er *s* annunziatore sportivo

sports' fan' *s* appassionato agli spettacoli sportivi, tifoso

sports'man *s* (-men) sportivo

sports'man·ship' *s* sportività *f*, spirito sportivo

sports' news' *s* notiziario sportivo

sports'wear' *s* articoli *mpl* d'abbigliamento sportivo

sports'writ'er *s* cronista sportivo

sport·y ['sporti] *adj* (-ier; -iest) (coll) elegante; (coll) sportivo; (coll) appariscente

spot [spɑt] *s* macchia; luogo, punto, posto; (*e.g., of tea*) goccia; **spots** locali *mpl*; **on the spot** sul posto; (*right now*) seduta stante; (slang) in difficoltà; **to hit the spot** (slang) soddisfare completamente || *v* (*pret* & *pp* **spotted**; *ger* **spotting**) *tr* macchiare; spargere; (coll) riconoscere || *intr* macchiare; macchiarsi

spot' cash' *s* pronta cassa

spot'-check' *tr* fare un breve sondaggio di; controllare rapidamente

spot' check' *s* breve sondaggio; rapido controllo

spotless ['spɑtlɪs] *adj* immacolato, senza macchia

spot'light' *s* riflettore *m*; (aut) proiettore *m*; **to be in the spotlight** (fig) essere il centro d'attenzione

spot' remov'er [rɪ'muvər] *s* smacchiatore *m*

spot' weld'ing *s* saldatura per punti

spouse [spauz] *or* [spaus] *s* consorte *mf*

spout [spaut] *s* (*to carry water from roof*) doccia; (*of jar, pitcher, etc.*) becco, beccuccio; (*jet*) zampillo, getto || *tr* & *intr* sprizzare, zampillare; (coll) declamare

sprain [spren] *s* distorsione || *tr* distorcere, distorcersi

sprawl [sprɔl] *intr* sdraiarsi

spray [spre] *s* spruzzo; (*of the sea*) schiuma; (*device*) spruzzatore *m*; (*twig*) ramoscello || *tr* & *intr* spruzzare

sprayer ['spre·ər] *s* spruzzatore *m*, schizzetto, vaporizzatore *m*; (hort) irroratrice *f*

spray' gun' *s* pistola a spruzzo; (hort) irroratrice *f*

spray' paint' *s* vernice *f* a spruzzo

spread [spred] *s* espansione; diffusione; differenza; tappeto, coperta; elasticità *f*; (*of the wings of bird or airplane*) apertura; cibo da spalmare; (coll) festino; (journ) articolo di fondo *or* pubblicitario su varie colonne || *v* (*pret* & *pp* **spread**) *tr* tendere, estendere; (*one's legs*) divaricare; (*wings*) spiegare; spargere, cospargere; (*the table*) preparare; (*butter*) spalmare; diffondere || *intr* estendersi; spiegarsi; spargersi; spalmarsi; diffondersi

spree [spri] *s* baldoria, bisboccia; **to go on a spree** darsi alla pazza gioia

sprig [sprɪg] *s* ramoscello

spright·ly ['spraɪtli] *adj* (-ier; -iest) brioso, vivace

spring [sprɪŋ] *adj* primaverile; sorgivo; a molla || *s* (*season*) primavera; (*issue of water from earth*) fonte *f*, polla; (*elastic device*) molla; elasticità *f*; (*leap*) salto; (*crack*) fenditura; (aut) balestra || *v* (*pret* **sprang** [spræŋ] *or* **sprung** [sprʌŋ]; *pp* **sprung**) *tr* (*e.g., a lock*) far scattare; (*a leak*) aprire; (*a mine*) far brillare || *intr* saltare; (*said of a metal spring*) scattare; scaturire, zampillare; nascere, derivare; esplodere; **to spring forth** *or* **up** sorgere

spring'board' *s* pedana, trampolino

spring' chick'en *s* pollo giovanissimo; (slang) ragazzina

spring' fe'ver *s* indolenza primaverile

spring' mat'tress *s* materasso a molle

spring' tide' *s* marea di sizigia

spring'time' *s* primavera

sprinkle ['sprɪŋkəl] *s* spruzzo, spruzzatina; (*small amount*) pizzico || *tr* spruzzare; (*e.g., sugar*) spolverizzare || *intr* sprizzare; piovigginare

sprinkler ['sprɪŋklər] *s* annaffiatoio; (*person*) annaffiatore *m*

sprinkling ['sprɪŋklɪŋ] *s* sprizzo, spruzzo; (*with holy water*) aspersione; (*with powder*) spolverizzamento; (*e.g., of knowledge*) spolvero, spolveratura; (*of people*) piccolo numero

sprin'kling can' *s* annaffiatoio

sprint [sprɪnt] s (sports) scatto, volata || intr (sports) scattare

sprite [spraɪt] s spirito folletto

sprocket ['sprɑkɪt] s moltiplica; (phot) trasportatore m

sprout [spraʊt] s germoglio || intr germogliare; crescere rapidamente

spruce [sprus] adj elegante, attillato || s abete rosso || tr attillare, azzimare || intr attillarsi, azzimarsi

spry [spraɪ] adj (spryer or sprier; spryest or spriest) vegeto

spud [spʌd] s vanghetto, tagliaradici m; (coll) patata

spun′ glass′ s lana di vetro

spunk [spʌŋk] s (coll) coraggio, fegato

spur [spʌr] s sperone m; (rr) raccordo ferroviario; (fig) pungolo; on the spur of the moment lì per lì || v (pret & pp spurred; ger spurring) tr spronare; to spur on spronare, incitare

spurious ['spjʊrɪ·əs] adj spurio

spurn [spʌrn] s disprezzo, sdegno; rifiuto || tr disprezzare, sdegnare; rifiutare

spurt [spʌrt] s spruzzo, zampillo; (sudden burst) scatto repentino || intr sprizzare, zampillare; scattare

sputter ['spʌtər] s barbugliamento; (sizzling) crepitio || tr barbugliare || intr barbugliare; crepitare

spu•tum ['spjutəm] s (-ta [tə]) sputo

spy [spaɪ] s (spies) spia || v (pret & pp spied) tr spiare; osservare || intr fare la spia; to spy on spiare

spy′glass′ s cannocchiale m

spying ['spaɪ·ɪŋ] s spionaggio

squabble ['skwɑbəl] s battibecco || intr litigare

squad [skwɑd] s squadra

squadron ['skwɑdrən] s (of cavalry) squadrone m; (aer, nav) squadriglia; (mil) squadra

squalid ['skwɑlɪd] adj sordido; squallido, misero

squall [skwɔl] s groppo, turbine m; urlo || intr gridare, urlare

squalor ['skwɑlər] s sordidezza; squallore m, miseria

squander ['skwɑndər] tr scialacquare, dilapidare, sperperare

square [skwɛr] adj quadrato, e.g., two square miles due miglia quadrate; di . . . di lato, e.g., two miles square di due miglia di lato; ad angolo retto; solido; saldato; (coll) onesto; (coll) diretto; (coll) sostanzioso; (slang) all'antica; to get square with (coll) fargliela pagare a || s quadrato; (small square, e.g., of checkerboard) quadretto; (city block) isolato; (open area in city) piazza, piazzale m; (of carpenter) squadra; on the square ad angolo retto; (coll) onesto || adv ad angolo retto; (coll) onestamente || tr squadrare; dividere in quadretti; elevare al quadrato; quadrare; (a debt) saldare; to square with adattare a || intr quadrare; to square off prepararsi, mettersi in posizione difensiva

square′ dance′ s danza figurata americana

square′ meal′ s (coll) pasto abbondante

square′ root′ s radice quadrata

square′ shoot′er ['ʃutər] s (coll) persona onesta

squash [skwɑʃ] s spappolamento; (bot) zucca; (sports) squash m || tr spappolare; spiaciccare; (e.g., a rumor) sopprimere; (a person) (coll) ridurre al silenzio || intr spiaciccarsi

squash•y ['skwɑʃi] adj (-ier; -iest) tenero; (ground) fangoso, pantanoso; (fruit) maturo

squat [skwɑt] adj tozzo || v (pret & pp squatted; ger squatting) intr accoccolarsi; stabilirsi illegalmente su territorio altrui; stabilirsi su terreno pubblico per ottenerne titolo

squatter ['skwɑtər] s intruso

squaw [skwɔ] s squaw f; (coll) donna

squawk [skwɔk] s schiamazzo; (slang) lamento stridulo || intr schiamazzare; (slang) lamentarsi strillando

squaw′ man′ s bianco sposato con una pellerossa

squeak [skwik] s strido; cigolio || intr stridere; cigolare; (said of a mouse) squittire; to squeak through farcela per il rotto della cuffia

squeal [skwil] s strido || intr stridere; (slang) cantare, fare il delatore

squealer ['skwilər] s (slang) delatore m

squeamish ['skwimɪʃ] adj pudibondo; scrupoloso; (easily nauseated) schifiltoso, schizzinoso

squeeze [skwiz] s spremuta; stretta, abbraccio; to put the squeeze on (coll) far pressione su || tr premere; spremere, pigiare; stringere || intr stringere; to squeeze through aprirsi il passo attraverso; (fig) farcela a pena

squeezer ['skwizər] s spremifrutta m

squelch [skwɛltʃ] s osservazione schiacciante || tr schiacciare

squid [skwɪd] s calamaro, totano

squint [skwɪnt] s tendenza losca; (coll) occhiata; (pathol) strabismo || tr (one's eyes) socchiudere || intr socchiudere gli occhi; guardare furtivamente

squint-eyed ['skwɪnt ˌaɪd] adj guercio, losco; malevolo

squire [skwaɪr] s (of a lady) cavalier m servente; (Brit) proprietario terriero; (U.S.A.) giudice m conciliatore || tr (a woman) accompagnare

squirm [skwʌrm] s contorsione || intr contorcersi; mostrare imbarazzo; to squirm out of cavarsela da

squirrel ['skwʌrəl] s scoiattolo

squirt [skwʌrt] s schizzo; (instrument) schizzetto; (coll) saputello || tr & intr schizzare

stab [stæb] s pugnalata; (of pain) fitta; to make a stab at (coll) provare || v (pret & pp stabbed; ger stabbing) tr pugnalare, trafiggere || intr pugnalare

stabilize ['stebəlˌaɪz] tr stabilizzare

stab′ in the back′ s pugnalata nella schiena or alle spalle

stable ['stebəl] *adj* stabile ‖ *s* stalla; (*of race horses*) scuderia

sta'ble·boy' *s* stalliere *m*

stack [stæk] *s* pila; (*of hay or straw*) pagliaio; (*of firewood*) catasta; (*of books*) scaffale *m;* camino; (*coll*) mucchio, sacco ‖ *tr* ammonticchiare, accatastare

stadi·um ['stedɪ·əm] *s* (*-ums* or *-a* [ə]) stadio

staff [stæf] or [stɑf] *s* bastone *m;* asta, albero; personale *m,* corpo; (*mil*) stato maggiore; (*mus*) rigo, pentagramma *m* ‖ *tr* dotare di personale

staff' of'ficer *s* ufficiale *m* di stato maggiore

stag [stæg] *adj* per signori soli ‖ *s* (*deer*) cervo; maschio; (*coll*) signore *m* ‖ *adv* senza compagna

stage [stedʒ] *s* fase *f,* stadio; tappa, giornata; (*coach*) diligenza; teatro; piattaforma; (*of microscope*) piatto portaoggetti; (*theat*) scena, palcoscenico; **by easy stages** poco a poco; **to go on the stage** diventare attore ‖ *tr* mettere in scena; organizzare

stage'coach' *s* diligenza

stage'craft' *s* scenotecnica

stage' door' *s* (theat) ingresso degli artisti

stage' fright' *s* tremarella

stage'hand' *s* macchinista *m*

stage' left' *s* (theat) la sinistra della scena guardando il pubblico

stage' man'ager *s* (theat) direttore *m* di scena

stage' right' *s* (theat) la destra della scena guardando il pubblico

stage'-struck' *adj* innamorato del teatro

stage' whis'per *s* a parte *m*

stagger ['stægər] *tr* far traballare; impressionare; (*troops; hours*) scaglionare ‖ *intr* traballare

stag'gering *adj* traballante; impressionante, stupefacente

staging ['stedʒɪŋ] *s* impalcatura; (theat) messa in scena

stagnant ['stægnənt] *adj* stagnante

staid [sted] *adj* serio, grave

stain [sten] *s* macchia; tinta; colorante *m* ‖ *tr* macchiare; tingere; colorare ‖ *intr* macchiarsi

stained' glass' *s* vetro colorato

stained'-glass window' *s* vetrata a colori

stainless ['stenlɪs] *adj* immacolato; (*steel*) inossidabile

stair [stɛr] *s* scala

stair'case' *s* scala

stair'way' *s* scala

stair'well' *s* tromba delle scale

stake [stek] *s* picchetto; (*e.g., of cart*) staggio; (*to support a plant*) puntello; (*in gambling*) puglia, giocata; **at stake** in gioco; **to die at the stake** morire sul rogo; **to pull up stakes** (coll) andarsene, traslocare ‖ *tr* picchettare; puntellare; attaccare a un palo; arrischiare; (coll) aiutare; **to stake out** picchettare; (slang) tenere sotto sorveglianza; **to stake out a claim** avanzare una pretesa

stale [stel] *adj* stantio; (*air*) viziato; (fig) ritrito

stale'mate' *s* (chess) stallo; **to reach a** stalemate essere in una posizione di stallo ‖ *tr* mettere in una posizione di stallo

stalk [stɔk] *s* stelo; (*of corn*) stocco; (*of salad*) piede *m* ‖ *tr* braccare ‖ *intr* avanzare furtivamente; camminare con andatura maestosa

stall [stɔl] *s* (*in a stable*) posta; (*booth in a market*) bancarella; (*seat*) stallo; (*space in a parking lot*) spazio per il parcheggio ‖ *tr* (*an animal*) stallare; (*a car*) parcheggiare; (*a motor*) far fermare; **to stall off** eludere, tenere a bada ‖ *intr* impantanarsi; stare nella posta; (*said of a motor*) fermarsi; (*to temporize*) menare il can per l'aia

stallion ['stæljən] *s* stallone *m*

stalwart ['stɔlwərt] *adj* forte, gagliardo ‖ *s* sostenitore *m*

stamen ['stemən] *s* stame *m*

stamina ['stæmɪnə] *s* forza, vigore *m*

stammer ['stæmər] *s* balbuzie *f* ‖ *tr & intr* balbettare

stammerer ['stæmərər] *s* balbuziente *mf*

stamp [stæmp] *s* (*postage stamp*) francobollo; (*device to show that a fee has been paid*) timbro, bollo; impressione; carattere *m;* sigillo; (*tool for stamping coins*) conio; (*tool for crushing ore*) maglio ‖ *tr* timbrare, stampigliare, bollare; sigillare; coniare; (*one's foot*) battere, pestare; imprimere; caratterizzare; (mach) stampare; **to stamp out** spegnere; sopprimere ‖ *intr* battere il piede; (*said of a horse*) zampare

stampede [stæm'pid] *s* fuga precipitosa ‖ *tr* precipitarsi verso; far fuggire precipitosamente ‖ *intr* precipitarsi

stamp'ing ground' *s* (coll) luogo di ritrovo abituale

stamp' pad' *s* tampone *m*

stamp'-vend'ing machine' *s* distributore automatico di francobolli

stance [stæns] *s* posizione

stanch [stɑntʃ] *adj* leale; forte; a tenuta d'acqua ‖ *s* chiusa ‖ *tr* arrestare il flusso da; (*blood*) stagnare

stand [stænd] *s* posizione; resistenza; difesa; tribuna, palco; sostegno, supporto; (*booth in market*) posteggio; posto di sosta ‖ *v* (*pret & pp* **stood** [stud]) *tr* mettere in piedi; reggere, sostenere; sopportare, tollerare; (*one's ground*) mantenere; (*a chance*) avere; (*watch*) fare; (coll) pagare; **to stand off** tenere a distanza ‖ *intr* stare; essere alto; fermarsi; stare in piedi; trovarsi; aver forza; essere; (*e.g., apart*) tenersi; **to stand back of** spalleggiare; **to stand by** appoggiare; **to stand for** rappresentare, voler dire; appoggiare, favorire; tenere a battesimo; (coll) tollerare; **to stand in line** fare la fila or la coda; **to stand in with** (coll) essere nelle buone grazie di; **to stand out** stagliarsi, distaccarsi, risaltare; **to stand up** tenersi in piedi; resistere, durare; **to stand up to** affrontare

standard ['stændərd] *adj* (*usual*) normale; uniforme, standard; (*language*) corretto, preferito ‖ *s* standard *m*; (*model*) modello, campione *m*; (*flag*) stendardo

stand′ard·bear′er *s* portabandiera *m*

standardize [ˈstændər ˌdaɪz] *tr* standardizzare

stand′ard of liv′ing *s* tenore *m* di vita

stand′ard time′ *s* ora ufficiale, ora legale

standee [stænˈdi] *s* passeggero in piedi; spettatore *m* in piedi

stand′-in′ *s* (mov) controfigura; **to have a stand-in with** (coll) essere nelle buone grazie di

standing [ˈstændɪŋ] *adj* (*jump*) da fermo, in piedi; fermo; (*water*) stagnante; vigente, permanente; (*idle*) fuori uso ‖ *s* posizione, rango, situazione; classifica; **in good standing** riconosciuto da tutti; **of long standing** vecchio, da lungo tempo

stand′ing ar′my *s* esercito permanente

stand′ing room′ *s* posto in piedi

standpatter [ˈstændˈpætər] *s* (coll) seguace *mf* dell'immobilismo

stand′point′ *s* punto di vista

stand′still′ *s* fermata; riposo; **to come to a standstill** fermarsi

stanza [ˈstænzə] *s* stanza

staple [ˈstepəl] *adj* principale ‖ *s* articolo di prima necessità; elemento indispensabile; (*e.g., to hold wire*) cavallottino, cambretta; (*to fasten papers*) grappetta; fibra tessile ‖ *tr* aggraffare

stapler [ˈsteplər] *s* cucitrice *f* a grappe

star [stɑr] *s* (*any heavenly body, except the moon, appearing in the sky*) astro; (*heavenly body radiating self-produced energy*) stella; (*actor*) divo; (*actress*) diva, stella (*athlete*) asso; (fig, mov) stella; (typ) stelletta; **to thank one's lucky stars** ringraziare la propria stella ‖ *v* (*pret & pp* **starred**; *ger* **starring**) *tr* costellare, stellare; presentare come stella; (typ) marcare con stelletta ‖ *intr* primeggiare

starboard [ˈstɑrbərd] or [ˈstɑr ˌbɔrd] *adj* di dritta, di tribordo ‖ *s* dritta, tribordo ‖ *adv* a dritta, a tribordo

starch [stɑrtʃ] *s* amido, fecola; (*in laundering*) salda; (coll) forza ‖ *tr* inamidare

starch·y [ˈstɑrtʃi] *adj* (-ier; -iest) amidaceo; (*e.g., collar*) inamidato; (*manner*) sostenuto, contegnoso

star′ dust′ *s* polveri *fpl* meteoriche; (fig) polvere *f* di stelle

stare [ster] *s* sguardo fisso ‖ *intr* rimirare; **to stare at** fissare gli occhi addosso a

star′fish′ *s* stella di mare

star′gaze′ *intr* guardare le stelle; sognare ad occhi aperti

stark [stɑrk] *adj* completo; desolato; severo, serio; duro, rigido ‖ *adv* completamente

stark′-na′ked *adj* nudo e crudo

starlet [ˈstɑrlɪt] *s* stellina, divetta

star′light′ *s* lume *f* delle stelle

starling [ˈstɑrlɪŋ] *s* storno, stornello

Stars′ and Stripes′ *s* bandiera stellata

Star′-Spangled Ban′ner *s* bandiera stellata

star′ sys′tem *s* (mov) divismo

start [stɑrt] *s* inizio, principio; partenza; linea di partenza; (*sudden jerk*) sussulto, soprassalto; (*advantage*) vantaggio; (*spurt*) scatto ‖ *tr* iniziare, principiare; mettere in moto; dare il via a; (*a conversation*) intavolare; (*game*) stanare ‖ *intr* iniziare, principiare; mettersi in moto; incamminarsi; (*to be startled*) trasalire, sussultare; **to start + ger** mettersi a + *inf*; **to start + ger + again** rimettersi a + *inf*; **to start after** andare in cerca di

starter [ˈstɑrtər] *s* (*of a venture*) iniziatore *m*; partente *m*; (aut) motorino d'avviamento; (sports) mossiere *m*

starting [ˈstɑrtɪŋ] *adj* di partenza ‖ *s* messa in marcia

start′ing crank′ *s* manovella d'avviamento

start′ing point′ *s* punto di partenza

startle [ˈstɑrtəl] *tr* far trasalire ‖ *intr* trasalire, sussultare

startling [ˈstɑrtlɪŋ] *adj* allarmante, sorprendente

starvation [stɑrˈveʃən] *s* fame *f*, inedia, inanizione

starva′tion wag′es *spl* paga da fame

starve [stɑrv] *tr* affamare; far morire di fame; **to starve out** prendere per fame ‖ *intr* essere affamato; morire di fame

starving [ˈstɑrvɪŋ] *adj* famelico

state [stet] *adj* statale; ufficiale; di gala, di lusso ‖ *s* condizione; stato; gala, pompa; **to lie in state** essere esposto in camera ardente; **to live in state** vivere sfarzosamente ‖ *tr* dichiarare, affermare; (*a problem*) impostare

stateless [ˈstetlɪs] *adj* apolide

state·ly [ˈstetli] *adj* (-lier; -liest) maestoso, imponente

statement [ˈstetmənt] *s* dichiarazione, affermazione; comunicazione; (com) estratto conto

state′ of mind′ *s* stato d'animo

state′room′ *s* cabina; (rr) compartimento privato

states′man *s* (-men) statista *m*, uomo di stato

static [ˈstætɪk] *adj* statico; (rad) atmosferico ‖ *s* disturbi *mpl* atmosferici

station [ˈsteʃən] *s* stazione; rango, condizione ‖ *tr* stazionare

sta′tion a′gent *s* capostazione *m*

stationary [ˈsteʃən ˌeri] *adj* stazionario

sta′tion break′ *s* (rad, telv) intervallo

stationer [ˈsteʃənər] *s* cartolaio

stationery [ˈsteʃən ˌeri] *s* (*writing paper*) carta da lettere; (*writing materials*) cancelleria

sta′tionery store′ *s* cartoleria

sta′tion house′ *s* posto di polizia

sta′tion·mas′ter *s* capostazione *m*

sta′tion wag′on *s* giardinetta

statistical [stəˈtɪstɪkəl] *adj* statistico

statistician [ˌstætɪsˈtɪʃən] *s* statistico

statistics [stə'tıstıks] *ssg (science)* statistica; *spl (data)* statistiche *fpl*

statue ['stæt/u] *s* statua

statuesque [ˌstæt/u'esk] *adj* statuario

stature ['stæt/ər] *s* statura

status ['stetəs] *s* stato, condizione; condizione sociale

sta'tus sym'bol *s* simbolo della posizione sociale

statute ['stæt/ut] *s* legge *f;* regolamento

stat'ute of limita'tions *s* legge *f* che governa la prescrizione

statutory ['stæt/u ˌtori] *adj* legale

staunch [stɔnt/] or [stɑnt/] *adj, s & tr* var of stanch

stave [stev] *s (of barrel)* doga; *(of ladder)* piolo; *(mus)* rigo, pentagramma *m* ‖ *v (pret & pp* staved or stove [stov]) *tr* bucare; *(to smash)* sfondare; to stave off tenere a bada

stay [ste] *s* permanenza, soggiorno; *(brace)* staggio; *(of corset)* stecca di balena; sostegno; (law) sospensione; (naut) strallo ‖ *tr* fermare; sospendere; poner freno a ‖ *intr* stare; mantenersi; restare, rimanere; *(at a hotel)* sostare; to stay up stare alzato

stay'-at-home' *adj* casalingo ‖ *s* persona casalinga

stead [sted] *s* posto; in his stead in suo luogo; to stand in good stead esser utile

stead'fast' *adj* fermo, risoluto

stead-y ['stedi] *adj (-ier; -iest)* stabile, fermo; regolare, costante; abituale; calmo, sicuro ‖ *v (pret & pp* -ied) *tr* rinforzare; calmare ‖ *intr* rinforzarsi; calmarsi

steak [stek] *s* bistecca

steal [stil] *s* (coll) furto ‖ *v (pret* stole [stol]; *pp* stolen) *tr* rubare; involare; *(the attention)* cattivare ‖ *intr* rubare; to steal away svignarsela; to steal out uscire di soppiatto; to steal upon approssimarsi silenziosamente a

stealth [stelθ] *s* clandestinità *f;* by stealth di straforo, di soppiatto

steam [stim] *adj* a vapore ‖ *s* vapore *m;* fumo; to get up steam aumentare la pressione; to let off steam scaricare la pressione; (slang) sfogarsi ‖ *tr (a steamship)* guidare; esalare; esporre al vapore; *(e.g., glasses)* appannare ‖ *intr* dar vapore, fumigare; bollire; *(to become clouded)* appannarsi; andare a vapore; to steam ahead avanzare a tutto vapore

steam'boat' *s* vapore *m*

steam'er en'gine *s* macchina a vapore

steamer ['stimər] *s* vapore *m*

steam'er rug' *s* coperta da viaggio

steam'er trunk' *s* bauletto da cabina

steam' heat' *s* riscaldamento a vapore

steam' roll'er *s* rullo compressore; (fig) rullo compressore

steam'ship' *s* piroscafo, vapore *m*

steam' shov'el *s* escavatore *m* a vapore

steam' ta'ble *s* tavola riscaldata a vapore per mantenere calde le vivande

steed [stid] *s* destriere *m*

steel [stil] *adj* d'acciaio; *(industry)* siderurgico ‖ *s* acciaio; *(bar)* stecca d'acciaio; *(for sharpening knives)* affilacoltelli *m;* (fig) spada, brando ‖ *tr* acciaiare; to steel oneself corazzarsi, indurirsi; armarsi di coraggio

steel' wool' *s* paglia di ferro

steel'works' *spl* acciaieria

steelyard ['stil ˌjard] or ['stiljərd] *s* stadera

steep [stip] *adj* erto, scosceso, ripido; *(price)* alto ‖ *tr* immergere, saturare, imbevere

steeple ['stipəl] *s* campanile *m;* *(spire)* cuspide *f,* guglia

stee'ple-chase' *s* corsa ad ostacoli

stee'ple-jack' *s* aggiustatore *m* di campanili

steer [stir] *s* bue *m,* manzo ‖ *tr* governare, guidare; (aer) pilotare ‖ *intr* governare; to steer clear of evitare

steerage ['stırıdʒ] *s* (naut) alloggio passeggeri di terza classe

steer'ing wheel' *s* (aut) volante *m,* sterzo; (naut) ruota del timone

stellar ['stelər] *adj* stellare; *(role)* da stella

stem [stem] *s (of pipe, of key)* cannello; *(of goblet)* gambo; *(of column)* fusto; *(of spoon)* manico; *(of watch)* corona; *(of a word)* tema *m;* *(of note)* (mus) gamba; (bot) peduncolo, stelo; (bot) gambo; from stem to stern da poppa a prua ‖ *v (pret & pp* stemmed) *ger* stemming) *tr* togliere il gambo a; *(to check)* arrestare; *(to dam up)* arginare; *(to plug)* otturare; *(the tide)* risalire, andare contro ‖ *intr* originare, derivare

stem'-win'der *s* orologio a corona

stench [stent/] *s* tanfo, fetore *m*

sten-cil ['stensəl] *s* stampo, stampino; parole *fpl* a stampo ‖ *v (pret & pp* -ciled or -cilled) *ger* -ciling or -cilling) *tr* stampinare

stenographer [stə'nagrəfər] *s* stenografo

stenography [stə'nagrəfi] *s* stenografia

step [step] *s* passo; *(footprint)* orma, impronta; *(of ladder)* piolo; *(of staircase)* gradino; *(of carriage)* montatoio; step by step passo passo; to watch one's step fare molta attenzione ‖ *v (pret & pp* stepped) *ger* stepping) *tr* scaglionare; to step off misurare a passi ‖ *intr* camminare, andare a passi; mettere il piede; to step aside scostarsi; to step back indietreggiare; to step on it (slang) fare presto; to step on the gas (coll) accelerare; to step on the starter avviare il motore

step'broth'er *s* fratellastro, fratello consanguineo

step'child' *s* (-children [ˌt/ıldrən]) figliastro

step'daugh'ter *s* figliastra

step'fa'ther *s* patrigno

step'lad'der *s* scala a gradini or a libretto

step'moth'er *s* matrigna

steppe [stɛp] *s* steppa

step'ping stone' s passatoio, pietra per guadare; (fig) gradino

step'sis'ter s sorellastra

step'son' s figliastro

stere·o ['stɛrɪ ,o] or ['stɪrɪ ,o] adj stereofonico; stereoscopico || s (-os) musica stereofonica; sistema stereofonico; fotografia stereoscopica

stereotyped ['stɛrɪ-ə,taɪpt] or ['stɪrɪ-ə-,taɪpt] adj stereotipato

sterile ['stɛrɪl] adj sterile

sterilize ['stɛrɪ ,laɪz] tr sterilizzare

sterling ['stʌrlɪŋ] adj di lira sterlina; d'argento; puro; eccellente || s argento .925; vasellame m d'argento puro

stern [stʌrn] adj severo || s poppa

stet [stɛt] v (pret & pp stetted; ger stetting) tr marcare con la parola "vive"

stethoscope ['stɛθə ,skop] s stetoscopio

stevedore ['stivə ,dor] s stivatore m

stew [stju] or [stu] s stufato, guazzetto || tr stufare || intr cuocere a fuoco lento; (coll) preoccuparsi

steward ['stju-ərd] or ['stu-ərd] s amministratore m, agente m; maggiordomo; (aer, naut) cambusiere m, cameriere m

stewardess ['stju-ərdɪs] or ['stu-ərdɪs] s (naut) cameriera; (aer) hostess f, assistente f di volo

stewed' fruit' s composta di frutta

stewed' toma'toes spl pomodori mpl in umido

stick [stɪk] s stecco; legno; bacchetta; bastone m; (e.g., of candy) cannello; (naut) albero; (typ) compositoio; in the sticks (coll) in casa del diavolo || v (pret & pp stuck [stʌk]) tr pungere; ficcare, infiggere; attaccare; confondere; to be stuck essere insabbiato; essere attaccato; (fig) essere confuso; to stick out (the head) sporgere; (the tongue) cacciare; to stick up (slang) assaltare a mano armata, rapinare || intr rimanere attaccato; persistere; (said of glue) appiccicarsi; (to one opinion) tenersi; stare; to stick out sporgere; to stick together rimanere uniti; to stick up risaltare; (said, e.g., of quills) rizzarsi; to stick up for (coll) stare dalla parte di

sticker ['stɪkər] s etichetta gommata; spina; persona zelante; (coll) busillis m

stick'ing plas'ter s cerotto

stick'pin' s spilla da cravatta

stick'up' s (slang) grassazione

stick·y ['stɪki] adj (-ier; -iest) attacaticcio; vischioso; (weather) afoso, soffocante; (fig) difficile

stiff [stɪf] adj rigido, duro; forte; (price) alto; denso || s (slang) cadavere m; poor stiff (slang) povero diavolo

stiff' col'lar s colletto duro

stiffen ['stɪfən] tr irrigidire || intr irrigidirsi

stiff' neck' s torcicollo; ostinazione

stiff'-necked' adj testardo

stiff' shirt' s camicia inamidata

stifle ['staɪfəl] tr soffocare

stigma ['stɪgmə] s (-mas or -mata [mətə]) stigma m

stigmatize ['stɪgmə ,taɪz] tr stigmatizzare

still [stɪl] adj fermo, tranquillo; silenzioso; (wine) non spumante || s calma; distillatore m; distilleria; (phot) fotografia singola || adv ancora; tuttora || conj tuttavia || tr calmare || intr calmarsi

still'birth' s parto di infante nato morto

still'born' adj nato morto

still' life' s (lifes') natura morta

stilt [stɪlt] s trampolo; (in water) palafitta; (orn) trampoliere m

stilted ['stɪltɪd] adj elevato; pomposo

stimulant ['stɪmjələnt] adj & s stimulante m, eccitante m

stimulate ['stɪmjə ,let] tr stimulare

stimu·lus ['stɪmjələs] s (-li [,laɪ]) stimolo

sting [stɪŋ] s puntura; (of insect) pungiglione; (fig) scottatura || v (pret & pp stung [stʌŋ]) tr & intr pungere

stin·gy ['stɪndʒi] adj (-gier; -giest) tirchio, taccagno

stink [stɪŋk] s puzza || v (pret stank [stæŋk] or stunk [stʌŋk]; pp stunk) tr far puzzare || intr puzzare; to stink of money (slang) aver soldi a palate

stinker ['stɪŋkər] s (slang) puzzone m

stint [stɪnt] s limite m; lavoro assegnato, compito || intr lesinarsi

stipend ['staɪpənd] s stipendio; assegno di studio, presalario

stipulate ['stɪpjə ,let] tr stipulare

stir [stʌr] s agitazione, movimento; (poke) spinta; to create a stir creare una sensazione || v (pret & pp stirred; ger stirring) tr mescolare; muovere; (fire) ravvivare; (pity) fare; to stir up eccitare, svegliare; (to rebellion) sommuovere || intr muoversi, agitarsi

stirring ['stʌrɪŋ] adj commovente

stirrup ['stɪrəp] or ['stɪrəp] s staffa

stitch [stɪtʃ] s punto; maglia; (pain) fitta; (bit) poco, po' m; to be in stitches (coll) sbellicarsi dalle risa || tr cucire; aggraffare || intr cucire

stock [stɑk] adj regolare, comune; banale, ordinario; di bestiame; borsistico; azionario; (aut) di serie; (theat) stabile || s provvista, scorta; capitale m sociale; azione f; azioni fpl, titoli mpl; (of tree) tronco; (of family; of anchor; of anvil) ceppo; razza, famiglia; materia prima; (of rifle) cassa; (broth) brodo; (handle) manico; (livestock) bestiame m; (theat) compagnia stabile; in stock in magazzino, disponibile; out of stock esaurito; stocks gogna, berlina; to take stock fare l'inventario; to take stock in (coll) aver fede in || tr fornire; fornire di bestiame; fornire di pesci || intr—to stock up fare rifornimenti

stockade [stɑ'ked] s staccionata

stock'breed'er s allevatore m di bestiame

stock'bro'ker *s* agente *m* di cambio

stock' car' *s* automobile *f* di serie; (rr) carro bestiame

stock' com'pany *s* (theat) compagnia stabile; (com) società anonima

stock' div'idend *s* dividendo pagato in azioni

stock' exchange' *s* borsa valori

stock'fish' *s* stoccafisso

stock'hold'er *s* azionista *mf*

stock'holder of rec'ord *s* azionista *mf* registrato nei libri della compagnia

Stockholm ['stɑkhom] *s* Stoccolma

stocking ['stɑkɪŋ] *s* calza

stock' in trade' *s* stock *m;* ferri *mpl* del mestiere

stock' mar'ket *s* borsa valori

stock'pile' *s* riserva, scorta || *tr* mettere in riserva || *intr* mettere in riserva materie prime

stock' rais'ing *s* allevamento bestiame

stock'room' *s* magazzino, deposito

stock•y ['stɑki] *adj* (-ier; -iest) tozzo, tarchiato

stock'yard' *s* chiuso per il bestiame

stoic ['sto•ɪk] *adj & s* stoico

stoicism ['sto•ɪ ˌsɪzəm] *s* stoicismo

stoke [stok] *tr* (*fire*) attizzare; (*a furnace*) caricare

stoker ['stokər] *s* fochista *m*

stolid ['stɑlɪd] *adj* impassibile

stomach ['stʌmək] *s* stomaco || *tr* (fig) digerire

stone [ston] *s* sasso, pietra; (*of fruit*) osso; (pathol) calcolo || *tr* lapidare; affilare con la pietra; (*fruit*) snocciolare

stone'-broke' *adj* (coll) senza un soldo, senza il becco di un quattrino

stone'-deaf' *adj* sordo come una campana

stone'ma'son *s* tagliapietra *m*

stone' quar'ry *s* cava di pietra

stone's' throw' *s* tiro di sasso; within a stone's throw a un tiro di schioppo

ston•y ['stoni] *adj* (-ier; -iest) di sasso, sassoso, pietroso

stooge [studʒ] *s* (theat) spalla; (slang) complice *mf*

stool [stul] *s* sgabello, seggiolino; gabinetto; (*mass evacuated*) feci *fpl*

stool' pi'geon *s* piccione *m* di richiamo; (slang) spia

stoop [stup] *s* curvatura, inclinazione; scalini *mpl* d'ingresso || *intr* inclinarsi, piegarsi; degnarsi, umiliarsi

stoop-shouldered ['stup'ʃoldərd] *adj* con le spalle cadenti

stop [stɑp] *s* fermata, sosta; arresto; otturazione, blocco; cessazione; ostacolo; (*of a check*) fermo; (*restraint*) freno; (*of organ*) registro; to come to a stop fermarsi; cessare; to put a stop to metter fine a || *v* (*pret & pp* stopped; *ger* stopping) *tr* fermare, cessare; arrestare, sospendere; tappare, otturare; (*a check*) mettere il fermo a; to stop up tappare, otturare || *intr* fermarsi; arrestarsi; (*said of a ship*) fare scalo; (*at an hotel*) scendere; to stop + *ger* smettere di or cessare di + *inf*

stop'cock' *s* rubinetto di arresto

stop'gap' *adj* provvisorio || *s* soluzione provvisoria; (*person*) tappabuchi *m*

stop'light' *s* (*traffic light*) semaforo; (aut) luce *f* di stop

stop'o'ver *s* fermata intermedia

stoppage ['stɑpɪdʒ] *s* fermata, arresto; (*of work, wages, etc.*) sospensione

stopper ['stɑpər] *s* tappo, turacciolo

stop' sign' *s* segnale *m* di fermata

stop'watch' *s* cronometro a scatto

storage ['stɔrɪdʒ] *s* magazzinaggio; (*place for storing*) magazzino; (*of a computer*) memoria

stor'age bat'tery *s* (elec) accumulatore *m*

store [stor] *s* negozio; magazzino; (*supply*) scorta; in store in serbo; to set store by dare molta importanza a || *tr* immagazzinare; to store away accumulare

store'house' *s* magazzino, deposito; (*of knowledge*) miniera

store'keep'er *s* negoziante *m*

store'room' *s* magazzino; (naut) dispensa

stork [stɔrk] *s* cicogna

storm [stɔrm] *s* tempesta, temporale *m;* (*on the Beaufort scale*) burrasca; (mil) assalto; (fig) scoppio || *tr* assaltare || *intr* tempestare; imperversare; (mil) andare all'attacco

storm' cloud' *s* nuvolone *m*

storm' door' *s* controporta

storm' sash' *s* controfinestra

storm' troops' *spl* truppe *fpl* d'assalto

storm' win'dow *s* controfinestra

storm•y ['stɔrmi] *adj* (-ier; -iest) tempestoso, burrascoso; (fig) inquieto, violento

sto•ry ['stori] *s* (-ries) storia, racconto, romanzo; (*plot*) trama; (*level*) piano; (coll) storia, menzogna || *v* (*pret & pp* -ried) *tr* istoriare

sto'ry-tell'er *s* narratore *m*, novelliere *m;* (coll) mentitore *m*

stoup [stup] *s* (eccl) acquasantiera

stout [staut] *adj* grasso, obeso; forte, robusto; leale; coraggioso || *s* birra nera forte

stout-hearted ['staut ˌhɑrtɪd] *adj* coraggioso

stove [stov] *s* (*for warmth*) stufa; (*for cooking*) fornello, cucina economica

stove'pipe' *s* tubo della stufa, cannone *m;* (*hat*) (coll) tuba

stow [sto] *tr* mettere in riserva; riempire; (naut) stivare || *intr*—to stow away imbarcarsi clandestinamente

stowage ['sto•ɪdʒ] *s* stivaggio; (*place*) stiva

stow'a•way' *s* passeggero clandestino

straddle ['strædəl] *s* divaricamento || *tr* (*a horse*) cavalcare; (*the legs*) divaricare; favorire entrambe le parti in || *intr* cavalcare; stare a gambe divaricate; (coll) tenere il piede tra due staffe

strafe [strɑf] or [stref] *s* attacco violento || *tr* attaccare violentemente con fuoco aereo; bombardare violentemente; (slang) punire

straggle ['strægəl] *intr* sbandarsi, sviarsi; sparpagliarsi, essere sparpagliato

straggler ['stræglər] *s* ritardatario

straight [stret] *adj* diritto, ritto; (*e.g., shoulders*) quadro; candido, franco; (*honest, upright*) retto; inalterato; (*hair; whiskey*) liscio; **to set s.o. straight** mettere qlcu sulla retta via; mostrare la verità a qlcu || *s* rettilinea; (*cards*) scala || *adv* dritto; sinceramente; rettamente; **straight ahead** sempre diritto; **straight away** immediatamente; **to go straight** vivere onestamente

straighten ['stretən] *tr* ordinare; raddrizzare || *intr* raddrizzarsi

straight′ face′ *s* faccia seria

straight′ flush′ *s* (cards) scala reale

straight′for′ward *adj* diretto; onesto

straight′ man′ *s* (theat) spalla

straight′ ra′zor *s* rasoio a mano libera

straight′way′ *adv* immediatamente

strain [stren] *s* sforzo; fatica eccessiva; tensione, pressione; strappo muscolare; tono, stile *m*; (*family*) famiglia; tendenza, vena; (coll) lavoro severo; (mus) aria, melodia || *tr* passare, colare; (*e.g., a rope*) tirare al massimo; (*one's ear*) tendere; (*a muscle*) strappare; (*the ankle*) slogare; (*e.g., words*) storcere, forzare || *intr* colare, filtrare; tendersi, tirare; sforzarsi; fare resistenza; **to strain at** tirare; resistere a

strained [strend] *adj* (*smile*) stentato; (*relations*) teso

strainer ['strenər] *s* scolatoio

strait [stret] *s* stretto; **straits** stretto; (fig) strettezze *fpl*; **to be in dire straits** essere nei frangenti

strait′ jack′et *s* camicia di forza

strait′-laced′ *adj* puritano, pudibondo

strand [strænd] *s* sponda, lido; (*of metal cable*) trefolo; (*of rope*) legnolo; (*of pearls*) filo || *tr* sfilare; (*e.g., a rope*) ritorcere, intrecciare; (*e.g., a boat*) lasciare incagliato; **to be stranded** trovarsi incagliato

stranded ['strændɪd] *adj* (*ship*) incagliato, arenato; (*e.g., rope*) ritorto, intrecciato

strange [strendʒ] *adj* strano; straniero; non abituato; inusitato

stranger ['strendʒər] *s* forestiero; nuovo venuto, intruso

strangle ['stræŋgəl] *tr* strangolare; soffocare || *intr* strangolarsi; soffocarsi

strap [stræp] *s* (*of leather*) correggia; (*for holding things together*) tirante *m*; (*shoulder strap*) bretella; (*for passengers to hold on to*) manopola; (*to hold a sandal*) guiggia; (*to hold a baby*) falda; (*strop*) coramella || *v* (*pret & pp* **strapped;** *ger* **strapping**) *tr* legare con correggia or tirante; (*a razor*) affilare

strap′hang′er *s* (coll) passeggero senza posto a sedere

strapping ['stræpɪŋ] *adj* robusto; (coll) grande, enorme

stratagem ['strætədʒəm] *s* stratagemma *m*

strategic(al) [strə'tidʒɪk(əl)] *adj* strategico

strategist ['strætɪdʒɪst] *s* stratego

strate·gy ['strætɪdʒi] *s* (**-gies**) strategia

strati·fy ['strætɪ‚faɪ] *v* (*pret & pp* **-fied**) *tr* stratificare || *intr* stratificarsi

stratosphere ['strætə‚sfɪr] or ['stretə‚sfɪr] *s* stratosfera

stra·tum ['stretəm] or ['strætəm] *s* (**-ta** [tə] or **-tums**) strato

straw [strɔ] *adj* di paglia; di nessun valore; falso, fittizio || *s* paglia; (*for drinking*) cannuccia; **I don't care a straw** non mi importa un fico; **to be the last straw** essere il colmo

straw′ber·ry *s* (**-ries**) fragola

straw′ hat′ *s* cappello di paglia; (*with hard crown*) paglietta

straw′ man′ *s* (*figurehead*) uomo di paglia; (*scarecrow*) spaventapasseri *m*

straw′ mat′tress *s* pagliericcio

straw′ vote′ *s* votazione esplorativa

stray [stre] *adj* sbandato, randagio; casuale, fortuito || *s* animale randagio || *intr* sviarsi; (fig) sbandarsi

streak [strik] *s* stria; (*of light*) raggio; (*of madness*) ramo, vena; (*of luck*) (coll) periodo; **like a streak** (coll) come un lampo || *tr* striare, venare || *intr* striarsi, venarsi; andare come un lampo

stream [strim] *s* corrente *f*; (*of light*) raggio; (*of people*) fiumana, torrente *m*; (*of cars*) fila || *intr* colare; filtrare, penetrare; (*said of a flag*) fluttuare

streamer ['strimər] *s* pennone *m*; nastro; raggio di luce

streamlined ['strim‚laɪnd] *adj* aerodinamico; (aer) carenato

stream′lin′er *s* treno dal profilo aerodinamico

street [strit] *adj* stradale || *s* via, strada

street′car′ *s* tram *m*

street′ clean′er *s* spazzino; (mach) spazzatrice *f*

street′ clothes′ *spl* vestiti *mpl* da passeggio; vestito da passeggio

street′ floor′ *s* pianterreno

street′light′ *s* lampione *m*

street′ map′ *s* pianta della città; stradario

street′ sign′ *s* segnale *m* stradale

street′ sprin′kler *s* carro annaffiatoio

street′ walk′er *s* passeggiatrice *f*

strength [strenθ] *s* forza; resistenza; (*of spirituous liquors*) gradazione; (com) tendenza al rialzo; (mil) numero; **on the strength of** basandosi su

strengthen ['strenθən] *tr* rinforzare; (fig) convalidare, rinsaldare || *intr* rinforzarsi, ingagliardirsi

strenuous ['strenju‚əs] *adj* vigoroso; strenuo

stress [stres] *s* enfasi *f*, importanza; spinta; tensione, preoccupazione; accento; (mech) sollecitazione; **to lay**

stress on mettere in rilievo || *tr (a word)* accentare, accentuare; *(to emphasize)* accentuare; *(mech)* sollecitare

stress′ ac′cent *s* accento di intensità

stretch [strɛtʃ] *s* tiro, tirata; *(in time or space)* periodo; *(of road)* tratto, percorrenza; *(of imagination)* sforzo; *(rr)* tratta; *(slang)* periodo di detenzione; **at a stretch** di un tiro || *tr* tirare; tendere, distendere; *(the imagination)* forzare; *(facts)* esagerare; *(money)* stiracchiare; *(one′s legs)* sgranchirsi; *(the truth)* esagerare; **to stretch oneself** sdraiarsi || *intr* estendersi; stiracchiarsi; distendersi; **to stretch out** sdraiarsi

stretcher [′strɛtʃər] *s (for a painting)* telaio; *(tool)* tenditore *m*, tenditoio; *(to carry wounded)* barella, lettiga

stretch′er-bear′er *s* portantino

strew [stru] *v (pret* strewed; *pp* strewed *or* strewn) *tr* spargere, cospargere; disseminare

stricken [′strɪkən] *adj* afflitto; ferito; danneggiato

strict [strɪkt] *adj* stretto, severo

stricture [′strɪktʃər] *s* aspra critica; *(pathol)* stenosi *f*

stride [straɪd] *s* passo; andatura; **rapid strides** grandi passi *mpl*; **to hit one′s stride** avanzare a andatura regolare; **to take s.th in one′s stride** fare qlco senza sforzi || *v (pret* strode [strod]; *pp* stridden [′strɪdən]) *tr* attraversare a grandi passi; attraversare di un salto || *intr* camminare a grandi passi; *(majestically)* incedere

strident [′straɪdənt] *adj* stridente

strife [straɪf] *s* discordia; concorrenza

strike [straɪk] *s (blow)* colpo; *(stopping of work)* sciopero; *(discovery of oil, ore, etc.)* scoperta; *(of fish)* abboccatura; colpo di fortuna || *v (pret & pp* struck [strʌk]) *tr* colpire, percuotere; infiggere; *(a match)* strofinare; *(fire)* accendere; fare impressione su; incontrare improvvisamente; *(e.g., ore)* scoprire; *(roots)* mettere; *(a coin)* coniare; andare in sciopero contro; arrivare a; *(a posture)* prendere; *(the hour)* scoccare; cancellare, eliminare; *(sails)* calare; *(attention)* richiamare; **to strike it rich** scoprire una miniera; avere un colpo di fortuna || *intr* dare un colpo; cadere; *(said of a bell)* suonare; accendersi; scioperare; *(mil)* attaccare; **to strike out** mettersi in marcia; *(to fail)* (fig) fallire, venir meno

strike′break′er *s* crumiro

striker [′straɪkər] *s* battitore *m*; *(clapper in clock)* martelletto; *(worker)* scioperante *m*

striking [′straɪkɪŋ] *adj* impressionante, sorprendente; notevole; scioperante

strik′ing pow′er *s* potere *m* d′assalto

string [strɪŋ] *s* spago, cordicella; *(e.g., of apron)* laccio; *(of pearls)* filo; *(of onions; of lies)* filza; *(row)* fila, infilata; *(mus)* corda; **no strings attached** (coll) senza condizioni; strings strumenti *mpl* a corda; (coll) condizioni *fpl*; **to pull strings** usare influenza || *v (pret & pp* strung [strʌŋ]) *tr* legare; allacciare; infilare; infilzare; *(a racket)* munire di corde; *(to stretch)* tendere; *(a musical instrument)* mettere le corde a; *(slang)* ingannare; **to string along** *(slang)* menare per il naso; **to string up** impiccare || *intr*—**to string along with** (slang) andare d′accordo con

string′ bean′ *s* fagiolino

stringed′ in′strument *s* strumento a corda

stringent [′strɪndʒənt] *adj* stringente; urgente; severo

string′ quartet′ *s* quartetto d′archi

strip [strɪp] *s* striscia; *(of metal)* lamina; *(of land)* lingua || *v (pret & pp* stripped) *ger* stripping) *tr* spogliare; denudare; *(a fruit)* pelare; *(a ship)* sguarnire; *(tobacco)* togliere le nervature da; scortecciare; *(thread)* spanare; **to strip of** spogliare di || *intr* spogliarsi; denudarsi; fare lo spogliarello

stripe [straɪp] *s* stria, striscia, riga, lista; tipo, qualità *f*; *(mil)* gallone *m* || *tr* striare, filettare, rigare

strip′ min′ing *s* sfruttamento minerario a cielo aperto

strip′tease′ *s* spogliarello

stripteaser [′strɪp,tizər] *s* spogliarellista

strive [straɪv] *v (pret* strove [strov]; *pp* striven [′strɪvən]) *intr* sforzarsi; lottare; **to strive to** sforzarsi di

stroke [strok] *s* colpo; *(of bell or clock)* rintocco; *(of pen)* tratto, frego; *(of brush)* pennellata; *(of arms in swimming)* bracciata; colpo apoplettico; *(caress)* carezza; *(with oar)* vogata; *(of oar or paddle)* palata; *(of a master)* tocco; *(of a piston)* corsa; *(keystroke)* battuta; *(of genius)* lampo; *(of the hour)* scocco; **to not do a stroke of work** non muovere un dito || *tr* accarezzare

stroll [strol] *s* passeggiata; **to take a stroll** fare una passeggiata || *intr* fare una passeggiata, andare a zonzo; errare

stroller [′strolər] *s* girovago; carrozzella; *(itinerant performer)* (theat) guitto

strong [strɔŋ] *or* [strɑŋ] *adj* forte, vigoroso; valido; acceso, zelante; *(butter)* rancido; *(cheese)* piccante; *(com)* sostenuto

strong′box′ *s* cassaforte *f*

strong′ drink′ *s* bevanda alcolica

strong′hold′ *s* piazzaforte *f*

strong′ man′ *s (in a circus)* maciste *m*; *(leader)* anima; dittatore *m*

strong-minded [′strɔŋ,maɪndɪd] *or* [′strɑŋ,maɪndɪd] *adj* volitivo

strong′point′ *s* luogo fortificato

strontium [′strɑnʃɪ-əm] *s* stronzio

strop [strɑp] *s* coramella, affilarasoio || *v (pret & pp* stropped; *ger* stropping) *tr* affilare

strophe [′strofi] *s* strofa, strofe *f*

struc'tural steel' ['strʌkt/ərəl] *s* profilato di acciaio

structure ['strʌkt/ər] *s* struttura; edificio || *tr* strutturare

struggle ['strʌgəl] *s* lotta; sforzo || *intr* lottare; sforzare, dibattersi

strum [strʌm] *v* (*pret & pp* **strummed**; *ger* **strumming**) *tr & intr* strimpellare

strumpet ['strʌmpɪt] *s* sgualdrina, puttana

strut [strʌt] *s* controvento, puntello, saettone *m*; incedere impettito; (aer) montante || *v* (*pret & pp* **strutted**; *ger* **strutting**) *intr* pavoneggiarsi, fare la ruota

strychnine ['strɪknaɪn] *or* ['strɪknɪn] *s* stricnina

stub [stʌb] *s* (*of tree*) coppo; (*e.g., of cigar*) mozzicone *m*; (*of a check*) matrice *f*, madre *f* || *v* (*pret & pp* **stubbed**; *ger* **stubbing**) *tr* sradicare; **to stub one's toe** inciampare

stubble ['stʌbəl] *s* (*of beard*) pelo ispido; **stubbles** stoppie *fpl*

stubborn ['stʌbərn] *adj* (*headstrong*) testardo; (*resolute*) accanito; (*e.g., resistance*) ostinato; (*e.g., illness*) ribelle; (*soil*) ingrato

stuc·co ['stʌko] *s* (*-coes* or *-cos*) stucco || *tr* stuccare

stuck [stʌk] *adj* infisso; attaccato; (*glued*) incollato; (*unable to continue*) in panna; **stuck on** (slang) invaghito di

stuck'-up' *adj* (coll) presuntuoso, arrogante

stud [stʌd] *s* (*in upholstery*) borchia; bottone *m* da sparato; (*of walls*) montante *m*; (*stallion*) stallone *m*; (*for mares*) monta; (archit) bugna, bugnato || *v* (*pret & pp* **studded**; *ger* **studding**) *tr* cospergere; (*with stars*) costellare; (*with jewels*) incastonare, ingioiellare

stud' bolt' *s* prigioniero

stud'book' *s* registro della genealogia

student ['stjudənt] *or* ['studənt] *adj* studentesco || *s* studente *m*; scolaro; (*investigator*) studioso

stu'dent bod'y *s* scolaresca

stud'horse' *s* stallone *m*

studied ['stʌdid] *adj* premeditato; (*affected*) studiato

studi·o ['studɪ‚o] *or* ['stjudɪ‚o] *s* (*-os*) studio

studious ['studjɪ-əs] *or* ['studɪ-əs] *adj* studioso; assiduo, zelante

stud·y ['stʌdi] *s* (*-ies*) studio || *v* (*pret & pp* **-ied**) *tr & intr* studiare

stuff [stʌf] *s* roba, cosa; stoffa; materiale *m*; (*nonsense*) scemenze *fpl*; medicina; (coll) mestiere *m* || *tr* riempire, inzeppare; (*one's stomach*) rimpinzare; (*e.g., poultry*) farcire; (*e.g., salami*) insaccare; (*a dead animal*) impagliare; **to stuff up** intasare || *intr* rimpinzarsi

stuffed' shirt' *s* persona altezzosa

stuffing ['stʌfɪŋ] *s* ripieno

stuff·y ['stʌfi] *adj* (*-ier; -iest*) soffocante, opprimente; (*nose*) chiuso; pedante

stumble ['stʌmbəl] *intr* incespicare, inciampare; sbagliare, impaperarsi; **to stumble on** or **upon** intopparsi in

stum'bling block' *s* inciampo, scoglio

stump [stʌmp] *s* (*of tree*) toppo, ceppo; (*e.g., of arm*) moncherino, moncone *m*; (*of cigar, candle*) mozzicone *m*; dente rotto; tribuna popolare; (*for drawing*) sfumino; **up a stump** (coll) completamente perplesso || *tr* mozzare; lasciare perplesso; (coll) fare discorsi politici in

stump' speech' *s* discorso politico

stun [stʌn] *v* (*pret & pp* **stunned**; *ger* **stunning**) *tr* tramortire; (fig) sbalordire

stunning ['stʌnɪŋ] *adj* (*blow*) che stordisce; sbalorditivo, magnifico

stunt [stʌnt] *s* atrofia; creatura striminzita; bravata, prodezza; (*for publicity*) montatura || *tr* striminzire; arrestare la crescita di || *intr* fare delle acrobazie

stunt'ed *adj* striminzito

stunt' fly'ing *s* acrobazia aerea

stunt' man' *s* (mov) controfigura

stupe·fy ['stjupɪ‚faɪ] *or* ['stupɪ‚faɪ] *v* (*pret & pp* **-fied**) *tr* istupidire, intontire

stupendous [stju'pendəs] *or* [stu'pendəs] *adj* stupendo

stupid ['stjupɪd] *or* ['stupɪd] *adj* stupido, ebete, scemo

stupor ['stjupər] *or* ['stupər] *s* torpore *m*, stupore *m*

stur·dy ['stʌrdi] *adj* (*-dier; -diest*) forte; (*robust*) tarchiato; risoluto

sturgeon ['stʌrdʒən] *s* storione *m*

stutter ['stʌtər] *s* tartagliamento || *tr & intr* tartagliare

sty [staɪ] *s* (*sties*) porcile *m*; (pathol) orzaiolo

style [staɪl] *s* stile *m*; tono; (*mode of living*) treno || *tr* chiamare col nome di

stylish ['staɪlɪʃ] *adj* alla moda, di tono

sty·mie ['staɪmi] *v* (*pret & pp* **-mied**; *ger* **-mieing**) *tr* ostacolare, contrastare

styp'tic pen'cil ['stɪptɪk] *s* matita emostatica

Styx [stɪks] *s* Stige *m*

suave [swɑv] *or* [swev] *adj* soave

subaltern [səb'ɔltərn] *adj & s* subalterno

subcommittee ['sʌbkə‚mɪti] *s* sottocommissione

subconscious [səb'kɑnʃəs] *adj & s* subcosciente *m*

subconsciousness [səb'kɑnʃəsnɪs] *s* subcosciente *m*, subcoscienza

sub'deb' *s* (coll) signorina più giovane di una debuttante

subdivide ['sʌbdɪ‚vaɪd] *or* [‚sʌbdɪ'vaɪd] *tr* suddividere || *intr* suddividersi

subdue [səb'dju] *or* [səb'du] *tr* soggiogare, sottomettere; (*color, voice*) attenuare

subdued [səb'djud] *or* [səb'dud] *adj* (*voice*) sommesso; (*light*) tenue

subheading ['sʌb,hedɪŋ] *s* sottotitolo; (journ) sommario

subject ['sʌbdʒɪkt] *adj* soggetto; **subject to** (*e.g., a cold*) soggetto a; (*e.g., a fine*) passibile di || *s* soggetto, materia, proposito; (*of a ruler*) suddito; (gram, med, philos) soggetto || [səb-'dʒekt] *tr* sottomettere

sub'ject cat'alogue *s* catalogo per materie

sub'ject in'dex *s* indice *m* per materie

subjection [səb'dʒekʃən] *s* soggezione

subjective [səb'dʒektɪv] *adj* soggettivo

sub'ject mat'ter *s* soggetto

subjugate ['sʌbdʒə,get] *tr* soggiogare

subjunctive [səb'dʒʌŋktɪv] *adj & s* congiuntivo

sublease ['sʌb,lis] *s* subaffitto || [,sʌb-'lis] *tr* subaffittare

sub-let [sʌb'let] *or* ['sʌb,let] *v* (*pret & pp* -let; *ger* -letting) *tr* subaffittare

sub-machine' gun' [,sʌbmə'ʃin] *s* mitra *m*

submarine ['sʌbmə,rin] *adj & s* sottomarino

sub'marine chas'er ['tʃesər] *s* cacciasommergibili *m*

submerge [səb'mʌrdʒ] *tr* sommergere || *intr* sommergersi

submersion [səb'mʌrʒən] *or* [səb-'mʌrʃən] *s* sommersione

submission [səb'mɪʃən] *s* sottomissione

submissive [səb'mɪsɪv] *adj* sottomesso

sub-mit [səb'mɪt] *v* (*pret & pp* -mitted; *ger* -mitting) *tr* sottomettere; presentare, deferire; osservare rispettosamente || *intr* sottomettersi

subordinate [səb'ɔrdɪnɪt] *adj & s* subordinato || [səb'ɔrdɪ,net] *tr* subordinare

suborna'tion of per'jury [,sʌbər'neʃən] *s* subornazione

subplot ['sʌb,plɑt] *s* intreccio secondario

subpoena *or* **subpena** [sʌb'pinə] *or* [sə-'pinə] *s* mandato di comparizione || *tr* citare

sub rosa [sʌb'rozə] *adv* in segreto

subscribe [səb'skraɪb] *tr* sottoscrivere || *intr* sottoscrivere; **to subscribe to** sottoscrivere a; (*a magazine*) abbonarsi a; (*an opinion*) approvare

subscriber [səb'skraɪbər] *s* sottoscrittore *m;* abbonato

subscription [səb'skrɪpʃən] *s* sottoscrizione; (*e.g., to a newspaper*) abbonamento; (*e.g., to club*) quota

subsequent ['sʌbsɪkwənt] *adj* susseguente, posteriore

subservient [səb'sʌrvɪ-ənt] *adj* subordinato; ossequioso, servile

subside [səb'saɪd] *intr* calmarsi; (*said of water*) decrescere

subsidiar•y [səb'sɪdɪ,ɛri] *adj* sussidiario || *s* (-ies) sussidiario

subsidize ['sʌbsɪ,daɪz] *tr* sussidiare, sovvenzionare; (*by bribery*) subornare

subsi•dy ['sʌbsɪdi] *s* (-dies) sussidio, sovvenzione

subsist [səb'sɪst] *intr* sussistere

subsistence [səb'sɪstəns] *s* sussistenza

subsoil ['sʌb,sɔɪl] *s* sottosuolo

substance ['sʌbstəns] *s* sostanza

substandard [sʌb'stændərd] *adj* inferiore al livello normale

substantial [səb'stænʃəl] *adj* considerevole; ricco, influente; (*food*) sostanzioso; (*e.g., reason*) sostanziale

substantiate [səb'stænʃɪ,et] *tr* provare, verificare; dare prova di, sostanziare

substantive ['sʌbstəntɪv] *adj & s* sostantivo

substation ['sʌb,steʃən] *s* ufficio postale secondario; (elec) sottostazione

substitute ['sʌbstɪ,tjut] *or* ['sʌbstɪ,tut] *adj* provvisorio, interino || *s* (*thing*) sostituto, surrogato; (*person*) sostituto, supplente *mf;* **beware of substitutes** guardarsi dalle contraffazioni || *tr*—**to substitute for** sostituire (*qlco or qlcu*) a || *intr*—**to substitute for** sostituire, rimpiazzare, e.g., **he substituted for the teacher** sostituì il maestro

substitution [,sʌbstɪ'tjuʃən] *or* [,sʌbstɪ'tuʃən] *s* sostituzione; (*by fraud*) contraffazione

substra-tum [sʌb'strætəm] *s* (-ta [tə]) sostrato, substrato

subterfuge ['sʌbtər,fjudʒ] *s* sotterfugio

subterranean [,sʌbtə'reni-ən] *adj & s* sotterraneo

subtitle ['sʌb,taɪtəl] *s* sottotitolo; (journ) titolo corrente; (mov) didascalia || *tr* dare una didascalia a

subtle ['sʌtəl] *adj* sottile

subtle-ty ['sʌtəlti] *s* (-ties) sottigliezza

subtract [səb'trækt] *tr* sottrarre

subtraction [sʌb'trækʃən] *s* sottrazione

suburb ['sʌbʌrb] *s* suburbio, sobborgo; **the suburbs** la periferia

suburban [sə'bʌrbən] *adj* suburbano

suburbanite [sə'bʌrbə,naɪt] *s* abitante *mf* dei suburbi

subvention [səb'venʃən] *s* sovvenzione || *tr* sovvenzionare

subversive [səb'vʌrsɪv] *adj & s* sovversivo

subvert [səb'vʌrt] *tr* sovvertire

subway ['sʌb,we] *s* sotterranea, metropolitana, metrovia; sottopassaggio

sub'way sta'tion *s* stazione della metropolitana

succeed [sək'sid] *tr* succedere (*with dat*), subentrare (*with dat*) || *intr* riuscire; **to succeed to** (*the throne*) succedere a

success [sək'ses] *s* successo, riuscita

successful [sək'sesfəl] *adj* felice, fortunato; che ha avuto successo

succession [sək'seʃən] *s* successione; **in succession** in seguito, uno dopo l'altro

successive [sək'sesɪv] *adj* successivo

succor ['sʌkər] *s* soccorso || *tr* soccorrere

succotash ['sʌkə,tæʃ] *s* verdura di fagioli e granturco

succumb [sə'kʌm] *intr* soccombere

such [sʌtʃ] *adj & pron indef* tale, simile; **such a** un simile, un tale; **such**

a + *adj* tanto + *adj*, e.g., **such a beau-tiful story** una storia tanto bella; **such as** tale quale, come

suck [sʌk] *s* succhio ‖ *tr* succhiare; (*air*) aspirare; **to suck in** (slang) ingannare

sucker ['sʌkər] *s* lattante *mf*; (bot) succhione *m*; (mach) pistone *m*; (coll) fesso, pollo, minchione *m*

suckle ['sʌkəl] *tr* allattare; nutrire ‖ *intr* poppare

suck'ling pig' ['sʌklɪŋ] *s* maiale *m* di latte

suction ['sʌk/ən] *s* aspirazione

suc'tion cup' *s* ventosa

suc'tion pump' *s* pompa aspirante

sudden ['sʌdən] *adj* subito, improvviso; **all of a sudden** all'improvviso

suddenly ['sʌdənli] *adv* all'improvviso

suds [sʌdz] *spl* saponata; schiuma; (coll) birra

sue [su] or [sju] *tr* querelare ‖ *intr* querelarsi; **to sue for damages** chiedere i danni; **to sue for peace** chiedere la pace

suede [swed] *s* pelle scamosciata

suet ['su·ɪt] or ['sju·ɪt] *s* grasso, sego

suffer ['sʌfər] *tr* soffrire; (e.g., *heavy losses*) subire ‖ *intr* soffrire, patire

sufferance ['sʌfərəns] *s* tolleranza

suffering ['sʌfərɪŋ] *adj* sofferente ‖ *s* sofferenza, strazio, patimento

suffice [sə'faɪs] *intr* bastare

sufficient [sə'fɪ/ənt] *adj* sufficiente

suffix ['sʌfɪks] *s* suffisso

suffocate ['sʌfə,ket] *tr & intr* soffocare

suffrage ['sʌfrɪdʒ] *s* suffragio

suffragette [,sʌfrə'dʒɛt] *s* suffragetta

suffuse [sə'fjuz] *tr* soffondere

sugar ['/ugər] *adj* (water) zuccherato; (industry) zuccheriero ‖ *s* zucchero ‖ *tr* zuccherare

sug'ar beet' *s* barbabietola da zucchero

sug'ar bowl' *s* zuccheriera

sug'ar cane' *s* canna da zucchero

sug'ar-coat' *tr* inzuccherare; (e.g., *the pill*) addolcire

sug'ar ma'ple *s* acero

sug'ar-plum' *s* zuccherino

sug'ar spoon' *s* cucchiaino per lo zucchero

sug'ar tongs' *spl* mollette *fpl* per lo zucchero

sugary ['/ugəri] *adj* zuccherino, zuccheroso

suggest [səg'dʒɛst] *tr* suggerire

suggestion [səg'dʒɛst/ən] *s* suggerimento; (psychol) suggestione; ombra, traccia

suggestive [səg'dʒɛstɪv] *adj* suggestivo; (risqué) scabroso

suicidal [,su·ɪ'saɪdəl] or [,sju·ɪ-'saɪdəl] *adj* suicida

suicide ['su·ɪ,saɪd] or ['sju·ɪ,saɪd] *s* (person) suicida *mf*; (act) suicidio; **to commit suicide** suicidarsi

suit [sut] or [sjut] *s* vestito da uomo; (of a *lady*) tailleur *m*; (of *cards*) seme *m*, colore *m*; (for *bathing*) costume *m*; corte *f*, corteggiamento; domanda, supplica; (law) causa; **to follow suit** seguire l'esempio; (cards)

rispondere a colore ‖ *tr* adattarsi (with *dat*); convenire (with *dat*); **suit yourself** faccia come vuole ‖ *intr* convenire, andare a proposito

suitable ['sutəbəl] or ['sjutəbəl] *adj* indicato, conveniente

suit'case' *s* valigia

suite [swit] *s* gruppo, serie *f*; serie *f* di stanze; (of *furniture*) mobilia; (retinue) seguito; (mus) suite *f*

suiting ['sutɪŋ] or ['sjutɪŋ] *s* taglio d'abito

suit' of clothes' *s* completo maschile

suitor ['sutər] or ['sjutər] *s* pretendente *m*; (law) querelante *mf*

sul'fa drugs' ['sʌlfə] *spl* sulfamidici *mpl*

sulfate ['sʌlfet] *s* solfato

sulfide ['sʌlfaɪd] *s* solfuro

sulfite ['sʌlfaɪt] *s* solfito

sulfur ['sʌlfər] *adj* solfiero ‖ *s* zolfo; color *m* zolfo

sulfuric [sʌl'fjurɪk] *adj* solforico

sul'fur mine' *s* solfara

sulfurous ['sʌlfərəs] *adj* solforoso

sulk [sʌlk] *s* broncio ‖ *intr* imbronciarsi

sulk·y ['sʌlki] *adj* (-ier; -iest) imbronciato ‖ *s* (-ies) (in horse racing) sediolo, sulky *m*

sullen ['sʌlən] *adj* bieco, triste, tetro

sul·ly ['sʌli] *v* (pret & pp -lied) *tr* insudiciare, insozzare

sulphur ['sʌlfər] *adj & s* var of **sulfur**

sultan ['sʌltən] *s* sultano

sul·try ['sʌltri] *adj* (-trier; -triest) soffocante; infocato, appassionato

sum [sʌm] *s* somma; sommario; problema *m* di aritmetica ‖ *v* (pret & pp summed) ger summing) *tr* sommare; **to sum up** riepilogare

sumac or **sumach** ['/umæk] or ['sumæk] *s* (bot) sommacco

summarize ['sʌmə,raɪz] *tr* riassumere

summa·ry ['sʌməri] *adj* sommario ‖ *s* (-ries) sommario, sunto

summer ['sʌmər] *adj* estivo ‖ *s* estate *f* ‖ *intr* passare l'estate

sum'mer resort' *s* stazione estiva

summersault ['sʌmər,sɔlt] *s & intr* var of **somersault**

sum'mer school' *s* scuola estiva

summery ['sʌməri] *adj* estivo

summit ['sʌmɪt] *s* sommità *f*

sum'mit con'ference *s* riunione al vertice

summon ['sʌmən] *tr* convocare, invitare; evocare; (law) compulsare

summons ['sʌmənz] *s* ordine *m*, comando; (law) citazione ‖ *tr* (law) citare

sumptuous ['sʌmptʃu·əs] *adj* sontuoso

sun [sʌn] *s* sole *m*; **place in the sun** posto al sole ‖ *v* (pret & pp sunned) ger sunning) *tr* esporre al sole ‖ *intr* prendere il sole

sun' bath' *s* bagno di sole

sun'beam' *s* raggio di sole

sun'burn' *s* abbronzatura ‖ *v* (pret & pp -burned or -burnt) *tr* abbronzare ‖ *intr* abbronzarsi

sundae ['sʌndi] *s* gelato con sciroppo, frutta o noci

Sunday ['sʌndi] *adj* domenicale ‖ *s* domenica

Sun'day best' *s* (coll) vestito da festa

Sun'day's child' *s* bambino nato con la camicia

Sun'day school' *s* scuola domenicale della dottrina

sunder ['sʌndər] *tr* separare

sun'di'al *s* meridiana

sun'down' *s* tramonto

sundries ['sʌndriz] *spl* generi *mpl* diversi

sundry ['sʌndri] *adj* vari, diversi

sun'fish' *s* pesce *m* mola, pesce *m* luna

sun'flow'er *s* girasole *m*

sun'glass'es *spl* occhiali *mpl* da sole

sunken ['sʌŋkən] *adj* affondato, sommerso; (hollow) incavato

sun' lamp' *s* sole *m* artificiale

sun'light' *s* luce *f* del sole

sun'lit' *adj* illuminato dal sole

sun-ny ['sʌni] *adj* (-nier; -niest) solatio, soleggiato; allegro, ridente; **it is sunny** fa sole

sun'ny side' *s* parte soleggiata; lato buono; **on the sunny side of** (e.g., *thirty*) al disotto dei . . . anni

sun' porch' *s* veranda a solatio

sun'rise' *s* sorgere *m* del sole; **from sunrise to sunset** dall'alba al tramonto

sun'set' *s* tramonto

sun'shade' *s* tenda; parasole *m*

sun'shine' *s* sole *m*, luce *f* del sole; **in the sunshine** al sole

sun'spot' *s* macchia solare

sun'stroke' *s* insolazione

sun' tan' *s* tintarella

sun'tan lo'tion *s* pomata antisole, abbronzante *m*

sun'up' *s* sorgere *m*, levare *m* del sole

sun' vi'sor *s* (aut) aletta parasole, parasole *m*

sup [sʌp] *v* (pret & pp **supped;** ger **supping**) *intr* cenare

super ['supər] *adj* (coll) superficiale; (coll) di prim'ordine, super ‖ *s* (coll) sovrintendente *m*; (coll) articolo di prim'ordine, super *m*

superabundant [,supərə'bʌndənt] *adj* sovrabbondante

superannuated [,super'ænju,etid] *adj* giubilato, pensionato; messo a riposo per limiti di età; antiquato

superb [su'pʌrb] or [sə'pʌrb] *adj* superbo

supercar·go ['supər,kargo] *s* (-goes) (naut) sopraccarico

supercharge [,supər'tʃardʒ] *tr* sovralimentare

supercilious [,supər'sɪli·əs] *adj* altero, arrogante

superficial [,supər'fɪʃəl] *adj* superficiale

superfluous [su'pʌrflu·əs] *adj* superfluo

su'per·high'way *s* autostrada

superhuman [,supər'hjumən] *adj* sovrumano

superimpose [,supərɪm'poz] *tr* sovrapporre

superintendent [,supərɪn'tendənt] *s* soprintendente *m;* (of schools) provveditore *m*

superior [sə'pɪrɪ·ər] or [su'pɪrɪ·ər] *adj* superiore; di superiorità; (typ) esponente ‖ *s* superiore *m*

superiority [sə'pɪrɪ'ariti] or [su,pɪrɪ'ariti] *s* superiorità *f*

superlative [sə'pʌrlətɪv] or [su'pʌrlətɪv] *adj & s* superlativo

su'per·man' *s* (-men') superuomo

supermarket ['supər,markɪt] *s* supermercato

supernatural [,supər'nætʃərəl] *adj* soprannaturale

superpose [,supər'poz] *tr* sovrapporre

supersede [,supər'sid] *tr* rimpiazzare, sostituire

supersensitive [,supər'sensɪtɪv] *adj* ipersensibile

supersonic [,supər'sanɪk] *adj* supersonico

superstition [,supər'stɪʃən] *s* superstizione

superstitious [,supər'stɪʃəs] *adj* superstizioso

supervene [,supər'vin] *intr* sopravvenire

supervise ['supər,vaɪz] *tr* sorvegliare, dirigere

supervision [,supər'vɪʒən] *s* supervisione, sorveglianza, direzione

supervisor ['supər,vaɪzər] *s* supervisore *m*, sorvegliante *mf;* ispettore *m*

supper ['sʌpər] *s* cena

sup'per·time' *s* ora di cena

supplant [sə'plænt] *tr* rimpiazzare

supple ['sʌpəl] *adj* flessibile; docile

supplement ['sʌplɪmənt] *s* supplemento ‖ ['sʌplɪ,ment] *tr* completare, supplire (with *dat*)

suppliant ['sʌplɪ·ənt] *adj & s* supplicante *mf*

supplicant ['sʌplɪkənt] *s* supplicante *mf*

supplication [,sʌplɪ'keʃən] *s* supplica

supplier [sʌ'plaɪ·ər] *s* fornitore *m*

sup·ply [sə'plaɪ] *s* (-plies) rifornimento, fornitura; provvista, scorta; (com) offerta; **supplies** rifornimenti *mpl*, vettovaglie *fpl* ‖ *v* (pret & pp **-plied**) *tr* fornire, provvedere; (food) vettovagliare

supply' and demand' *s* domanda ed offerta

support [sə'port] *s* sostegno, appoggio; puntello, rincalzo; mantenimento ‖ *tr* sostenere, appoggiare; puntellare; (a cause) caldeggiare; mantenere

supporter [sə'portər] *s* fautore *m*, sostenitore *m;* (jockstrap) sospensorio; giarrettiera; fascia elastica

suppose [sə'poz] *tr* supporre; ammettere; **suppose we take a walk?** che ne dice se facessimo una passeggiata?; **to be supposed to** aver fama di essere; **to suppose so** credere di sì

supposed [sə'pozd] *adj* presunto

supposition [,sʌpə'zɪʃən] *s* supposizione

supposito·ry [sə'pazɪ,tori] *s* (-ries) suppositorio, supposta

suppress [sə'pres] *tr* sopprimere

suppression [sə'preʃən] *s* soppressione

suppurate ['sʌpjə,ret] *intr* suppurare

supreme [sə'prim] *or* [su'prim] *adj* supremo, sommo

Supreme' Court' *s* (*in Italy*) Corte *f* di Cassazione; (*in U.S.A.*) tribunale *m* di ultima istanza

surcharge ['sʌr,tʃɑrdʒ] *s* soprapprezzo; sopratassa; sovraccarico; (philately) sovrastampa || [,sʌr'tʃɑrdʒ] *or* ['sʌr,tʃɑrdʒ] *tr* sovraccaricare

sure [ʃur] *adj* sicuro; **to be sure!** certamente!, senza dubbio! || *interj* (coll) certamente!; **sure enough!** (coll) difatti

sure-footed ['ʃur'futɪd] *adj* dal piede sicuro

sure' thing' *s* (coll) successo garantito || *adv* (coll) certamente || *interj* (coll) di sicuro!

sure-ty ['ʃurti] *or* ['ʃuriti] *s* (-ties) malleveria

surf [sʌrf] *s* frangente *m*

surface ['sʌrfɪs] *adj* superficiale || *s* superficio *f* || *tr* rifinire; spianare; ricoprire || *intr* emergere

sur'face mail' *s* posta ordinaria

surf'board' *s* tavola per il surfing

surfeit ['sʌrfɪt] *s* eccesso; sazietà *f* || *tr* saziare, rimpinzare || *intr* saziarsi, rimpinzarsi

surf'ing *s* surfing *m*

surge [sʌrdʒ] *s* ondata; fiotto; (elec) sovratensione || *intr* ondeggiare, fluttuare; (*said, e.g., of a crowd*) affluire

surgeon ['sʌrdʒən] *s* (medico) chirurgo

surger-y ['sʌrdʒəri] *s* (-ies) chirurgia; sala operatoria

surgical ['sʌrdʒɪkəl] *adj* chirurgico

sur-ly ['sʌrli] *adj* (-lier; -liest) arcigno, imbronciato

surmise [sər'maɪz] *or* ['sʌrmaɪz] *s* congettura, supposizione || [sər'maɪz] *tr* & *intr* congetturare, supporre

surmount [sər'maunt] *tr* sormontare; coronare

surname ['sʌr,nem] *s* cognome *m*; (*added name*) soprannome *m* || *tr* dare il cognome a; soprannominare

surpass [sər'pæs] *or* [sər'pɑs] *tr* sorpassare, superare

surplice ['sʌrplɪs] *s* cotta

surplus ['sʌrplʌs] *adj* eccedente || *s* sopravanzo, eccedenza

surprise [sər'praɪz] *adj* insperato, improvviso || *s* sorpresa || *tr* sorprendere

surprise' par'ty *s* improvvisata

surprising [sər'praɪzɪŋ] *adj* sorprendente

surrender [sə'rendər] *s* resa || *tr* arrendere || *intr* arrendersi

surren'der val'ue *s* (ins) valore *m* di riscatto

surreptitious [,sʌrep'tɪʃəs] *adj* clandestino, nascosto, furtivo

surround [sə'raund] *tr* circondare, contornare; (mil) aggirare

surrounding [sə'raundɪŋ] *adj* circostante, circonvicino || **surroundings** *spl* dintorni *mpl*; ambiente *m*

surtax ['sʌr,tæks] *s* sovrimposta, soprattassa; imposta complementare

surveillance [sər'veləns] *or* [sər'veljəns] *s* sorveglianza, vigilanza

survey ['sʌrve] *s* quadro generale, schizzo; indagine *f*; (*of opinion*) sondaggio; rapporto; rilievo topografico; perizia || [sʌr've] *or* ['sʌrve] *tr* fare un'indagine di; sondare; rilevare; misurare || *intr* fare un rilievo

sur'vey course' *s* corso di rassegna generale

surveyor [sər've-ər] *s* livellatore *m*, geometra *m*

survival [sər'vaɪvəl] *s* sopravvivenza

survive [sər'vaɪv] *tr* sopravvivere (with *dat*) || *intr* sopravvivere

surviving [sər'vaɪvɪŋ] *adj* superstite

survivor [sər'vaɪvər] *s* sopravvissuto, superstite *mf*

survivorship [sər'vaɪvər,ʃɪp] *s* (law) sopravvivenza

susceptible [sə'septɪbəl] *adj* suscettibile, ricettivo; impressionabile; **susceptible to** (*e.g., colds*) soggetto a

suspect ['sʌspekt] *or* [səs'pekt] *adj* sospetto || ['sʌspekt] *s* sospetto || [səs'pekt] *tr* sospettare

suspend [səs'pend] *tr* sospendere || *intr* essere sospeso; fermarsi; fermare i pagamenti

suspenders [səs'pendərz] *spl* bretelle *fpl*

suspense [səs'pens] *s* sospensione; sospeso; **in suspense** in sospeso

suspen'sion bridge' [səs'penʃən] *s* ponte sospeso

suspicion [səs'pɪʃən] *s* sospetto

suspicious [səs'pɪʃəs] *adj* (*subject to suspicion*) sospetto; (*inclined to suspect*) sospettoso

sustain [səs'ten] *tr* sostenere, sorreggere; (*with food*) sostentare; (*a conversation*) mantenere; (*a loss*) soffrire; (law) confermare

sustenance ['sʌstɪnəns] *s* sostentamento

sutler ['sʌtlər] *s* (mil) vivandiere *m*

swab [swɑb] *s* (mil) scovolo; (naut) redazza; (surg) batuffolo di cotone || *v* (*pret* & *pp* **swabbed**; *ger* **swabbing**) *tr* pulire con la redazza; spugnare; assorbire col cotone

swaddle ['swɑdəl] *tr* fasciare

swad'dling clothes' *spl* fasce *fpl* del neonato

swagger ['swægər] *s* spavalderia || *intr* fare lo spavaldo

swain [swen] *s* innamorato; (*lad*) contadinotto

swallow ['swɑlo] *s* (*of liquid*) sorso; (*of food*) boccone *m*; (orn) rondine *f* || *tr* & *intr* trangugiare, inghiottire

swal'low-tailed coat' ['swɑlo,teld] *s* frac *m*, marsina, abito a coda di rondine

swal'low-wort' *s* vincetossico

swamp [swɑmp] *s* pantano, palude *f* || *tr* inondare, sommergere

swamp-y ['swɑmpi] *adj* (-ier; -iest) paludoso, pantanoso

swan [swɑn] *s* cigno

swan' dive' *s* volo dell'angelo

swank [swæŋk] *adj* (coll) elegante, vistoso ‖ *s* (coll) eleganza vistosa

swan's-down ['swɑnz,daun] *s* piuma di cigno, piumino; mollettone *m*

swan' song' *s* canto del cigno

swap [swɑp] *s* scambio, baratto ‖ *v* (*pret & pp* swapped; *ger* swapping) *tr & intr* scambiare, barattare

swarm [swɔrm] *s* sciame *m* ‖ *intr* sciamare; (fig) formicolare

swarth·y ['swɔrði] or ['swɔrθi] *adj* (-ier; -iest) olivastro, abbronzato

swashbuckler ['swɑʃ,bʌklər] *s* spadaccino, rodomonte *m*

swat [swɑt] *s.* colpo ‖ *v* (*pret & pp* swatted; *ger* swatting) *tr* colpire; (*a fly*) schiacciare

sway [swe] *s* dondolio, ondeggiamento; dominio ‖ *tr* dondolare, fare oscillare; influenzare; dominare ‖ *intr* dondolarsi, ondulare; oscillare

swear [swer] *v* (*pret* swore [swor]; *pp* sworn [sworn]) *tr* giurare; (*to secrecy*) fare giurare; **to swear in** fare prestar giuramento a; **to swear off** giurare di rinunziare a; **to swear out a warrant** ottenere un atto di accusa sotto giuramento ‖ *intr* giurare; (*to blaspheme*) bestemmiare; **to swear at** maledire; **to swear by** giurare su, avere certezza di; **to swear to** dichiarare sotto giuramento; giurare di + *inf*

swear' word' *s* bestemmia, parolaccia

sweat [swet] *s* sudata; sudore *m* ‖ *v* (*pret & pp* sweat or sweated) *tr* sudare; far sudare; **to sweat it out** (slang) farcela fino alla fine; **to sweat off** (*weight*) perdere sudando ‖ *intr* sudare

sweater ['swetər] *s* maglione *m*, golf *m*, sweater *m*

sweat' shirt' *s* maglione *m* da ginnastica

sweat·y ['sweti] *adj* (-ier; -iest) sudato; che fa sudare

Swede [swid] *s* svedese *mf*

Sweden ['swidən] *s* la Svezia

Swedish ['swidɪʃ] *adj & s* svedese *m*

sweep [swip] *s* scopata; movimento circolare; estensione; curva; (*of wind*) soffio; (*of well*) mazzacavallo; **to make a clean sweep of** far piazza pulita di ‖ *v* (*pret & pp* swept [swept]) *tr* spazzare, scopare; percorrere con lo sguardo; (*eyes*) dirigere; travolgere ‖ *intr* scopare; passare; estendersi; dragare

sweeper ['swipər] *s* spazzino; (*machine*) spazzatrice *f*; (nav) dragamine *m*

sweeping ['swipɪŋ] *adj* esteso; travolgente, decisivo ‖ sweepings *spl* spazzatura

sweep'-sec'ond *s* lancetta dei secondi a perno centrale

sweep'stakes' *ssg* or *spl* lotteria abbinata alle corse dei cavalli

sweet [swit] *adj* dolce; (*butter*) senza sale; (*cider*) analcolico; **to be sweet on** (coll) essere innamorato di ‖

sweets *spl* dolci *mpl;* (coll) patate *fpl*

sweet' bread' *s* animella

sweet' brí'er *s* eglantina

sweeten ['switən] *tr* inzuccherare; raddolcire; purificare ‖ *intr* raddolcirsi; purificarsi

sweet' heart' *s* innamorato; innamorata, caro, amore *m*

sweet' mar' joram *s* maggiorana

sweet' meats' *spl* dolci *mpl*, confetti *mpl*

sweet' pea' *s* pisello odoroso

sweet' pota' to *s* batata, patata americana; (mus) ocarina

sweet-scented ['swit,sentɪd] *adj* odoroso, profumato

sweet' tooth' *s* debole *m* per i dolci

sweet-toothed ['swit,tuθt] *adj* goloso

sweet' wil' liam *s* garofano barbuto

swell [swel] *adj* (slang) elegante; (slang) eccellente, di prim'ordine ‖ *s* gonfiore *m;* onda, ondata; aumento; (mus) crescendo; (slang) elegantone *m* ‖ *v* (*pret* swelled; *pp* swelled or swollen ['swolən]) *tr* gonfiare, ingrossare; aumentare ‖ *intr* gonfiare, ingrossarsi; aumentare; (*said of the sea*) alzarsi; (*with pride*) montarsi

swelled' head' *s* borioso; **to have a swelled head** montarsi, essere pieno di sé

swelter ['sweltər] *intr* soffocare dal caldo

swept' back' wing' *s* ala a freccia

swerve [swʌrv] *s* scarto, sbandamento ‖ *tr* sviare ‖ *intr* scartare, sbandare

swift [swɪft] *adj* rapido ‖ *s* rondone *m* ‖ *adv* rapidamente

swig [swɪg] *s* (coll) sorso ‖ *v* (*pret & pp* swigged; *ger* swigging) *tr & intr* (coll) bere a grandi sorsi

swill [swɪl] *s* imbratto; risciacquatura ‖ *tr* tracannare, trincare ‖ *intr* bere a lunghi sorsi

swim [swɪm] *s* nuoto; **the swim** (*in social activities*) la corrente ‖ *v* (*pret* swam [swæm]; *pp* swum [swʌm]; *ger* swimming) *tr* traversare a nuoto ‖ *intr* nuotare; essere inondato; (*said of one's head*) girare, e.g., **her head is swimming** le gira la testa

swimmer ['swɪmər] *s* nuotatore *m*

swimming ['swɪmɪŋ] *s* nuoto

swim' ming pool' *s* piscina

swim' ming trunks' *spl* mutandine *fpl* da bagno

swim' suit' *s* costume *m* da bagno

swindle ['swɪndəl] *s* truffa, imbroglio ‖ *tr* truffare, imbrogliare

swine [swaɪn] *s* suino, maiale *m*, porco; swine *spl* suini *mpl*

swing [swɪŋ] *s* oscillazione; dondolio; curva; (*suspended seat*) altalena; alternarsi *m;* piena attività; (boxing) sventola; (mus) swing *m;* **free swing** libertà *f* d'azione; **in full swing** (coll) in piena attività ‖ *v* (*pret & pp* swung [swʌŋ]) *tr* (e.g., *one's arms*) dondolare, oscillare; (*a weapon*) brandire; (*e.g., a club*) rotare; far girare; appendere; (*a deal*) (coll) riuscire ad ottenere ‖ *intr* dondolare, dondolarsi, oscillare; girare; essere sospeso; cambiare; (boxing) dare una sventola; **to swing open** aprirsi di colpo

swing'ing door' ['swiŋiŋ] *s* porta oscillante

swinish ['swaɪnɪʃ] *adj* porcino

swipe [swaɪp] *s* (coll) colpo forte ‖ *tr* (coll) dare un forte colpo a; (slang) portare via, rubare

swirl [swʌrl] *s* turbine *m*, vortice *m* ‖ *tr* far girare ‖ *intr* turbinare

swirling ['swʌrliŋ] *adj* vorticoso

swish [swɪʃ] *s* (*of whip*) schiocco; (*of silk*) fruscio ‖ *tr* (*a whip*) schioccare; ‖ *intr* schioccare; frusciare

Swiss [swɪs] *adj* svizzero ‖ *s* svizzero; **the Swiss** gli svizzeri

Swiss' chard' ['tʃɑrd] *s* bietola

Swiss' cheese' *s* groviera

Swiss' Guards' *spl* guardie *fpl* svizzere

switch [swɪtʃ] *s* verga; vergata; (*false hair*) posticcio; cambio, trapasso; (elec) interruttore *m*; (rr) scambio ‖ *tr* battere, frustare; (elec) commutare; (rr) deviare; (fig) girare; **to switch off** (*light, radio, etc.*) spegnere; **to switch on** (*light, radio, etc.*) accendere ‖ *intr* fustigare; cambiare; (rr) deviare

switch'back' *s* strada a zigzag; (rr) tracciato a zigzag

switch'blade knife' *s* coltello a serramanico

switch'board' *s* quadro

switch'board op'erator *s* centralinista *mf*

switch'ing en'gine *s* locomotiva da manovra

switch'man *s* (-men) deviatore *m*

switch'yard' *s* stazione smistamento

Switzerland ['swɪtsərlənd] *s* la Svizzera

swiv·el ['swɪvəl] *s* perno, gancio girevole ‖ *v* (*pret & pp* -eled *or* -elled; *ger* -eling *or* -elling) *intr* girare

swiv'el chair' *s* sedia girevole

swoon [swun] *s* deliquio, svenimento ‖ *intr* svenire

swoop [swup] *s* calata a piombo ‖ *intr* calare a piombo, piombare

sword [sord] *s* spada; **at swords' points** pronti a incrociare le spade; **to put to the sword** passare a fil di spada

sword' belt' *s* cinturone *m*

sword' cane' *s* bastone animato

sword'fish' *s* pesce *m* spada

swords'man *s* (-men) spadaccino

sword' swal'lower ['swɑlo·ər] *s* giocoliere *m* che ingoia spade

sword' thrust' *s* stoccata

sworn [sworn] *adj* giurato

sycophant ['sɪkəfənt] *s* adulatore *m*; parassita *mf*

syllable ['sɪləbəl] *s* sillaba

sylla·bus ['sɪləbəs] *s* (-bi [,baɪ]) sillabo, sommario scolastico

syllogism ['sɪlə,dʒɪzəm] *s* sillogismo

sylph [sɪlf] *s* silfo; silfide *f*; (fig) silfide *f*

sylvan ['sɪlvən] *adj* silvano

symbol ['sɪmbəl] *s* simbolo

symbolic(al) [sɪm'bɑlɪk(əl)] *adj* simbolico

symbolism ['sɪmbə,lɪzəm] *s* simbolismo

symbolize ['sɪmbə,laɪz] *tr* simboleggiare

symmetric(al) [sɪ'mɛtrɪk(əl)] *adj* simmetrico

symme·try ['sɪmɪtri] *s* (-tries) simmetria

sympathetic [,sɪmpə'θɛtɪk] *adj* simpatetico; ben disposto

sympathize ['sɪmpə,θaɪz] *intr*—**to sympathize with** aver compassione di; mostrar comprensione per; (*to be in accord with*) simpatizzare con

sympa·thy ['sɪmpəθi] *s* (-thies) compassione, commiserazione; **to be in sympathy with** essere d'accordo con; **to extend one's sympathy to** fare le condoglianze a

sym'pathy strike' *s* sciopero di solidarietà

symphonic [sɪm'fɑnɪk] *adj* sinfonico

sympho·ny ['sɪmfəni] *s* (-nies) sinfonia

symposi·um [sɪm'pozɪ·əm] *s* (-a [ə]) simposio, colloquio

symptom ['sɪmptəm] *s* sintomo

synagogue ['sɪnə,gɔg] *or* ['sɪnə,gɑg] *s* sinagoga

synchronize ['sɪŋkrə,naɪz] *tr & intr* sincronizzare

synchronous ['sɪŋkrənəs] *adj* sincrono

sincopation [,sɪŋkə'peʃən] *s* sincope *f*

syncope ['sɪŋkə,pi] *s* (phonet) sincope *f*

syndicate ['sɪndɪkɪt] *s* sindacato ‖ ['sɪndɪ,ket] *tr* organizzare in un sindacato

synonym ['sɪnənɪm] *s* sinonimo

synonymous [sɪ'nɑnɪməs] *adj* sinonimo

synop·sis [sɪ'nɑpsɪs] *s* (-ses [siz]) sinossi *f*; (mov) sinopsi *f*

synoptic(al) [sɪ'nɑptɪk(əl)] *adj* sinottico

syntax ['sɪntæks] *s* sintassi *f*

synthe·sis ['sɪnθɪsɪs] *s* (-ses [,siz]) sintesi *f*

synthesize ['sɪnθɪ,saɪz] *tr* sintetizzare

synthetic(al) [sɪn'θɛtɪk(əl)] *adj* sintetico

syphilis ['sɪfɪlɪs] *s* sifilide *f*

Syria ['sɪrɪ·ə] *s* la Siria

Syrian ['sɪrɪ·ən] *adj & s* siriano

syringe [sɪ'rɪndʒ] *or* ['sɪrɪndʒ] *s* (*fountain syringe*) schizzetto; (*for hypodermic injections*) siringa ‖ *tr* schizzettare; iniettare

syrup ['sɪrəp] *or* ['sʌrəp] *s* sciroppo

system ['sɪstəm] *s* sistema *m*

systematic(al) [,sɪstə'mætɪk(əl)] *adj* sistematico

systematize ['sɪstəmə,taɪz] *tr* ridurre a sistema

systole ['sɪstəli] *s* sistole *f*

T

T, t [ti] *s* ventesima lettera dell'alfabeto inglese; **to fit to a T** calzare come un guanto

tab [tæb] *s* (*strap*) linguetta; (*of a pocket*) patta; targa; (*label*) etichetta; **to keep tabs on** (coll) sorvegliare; **to pick up the tab** (coll) pagare il conto

tab•by ['tæbɪ] *s* (**-bies**) gatto tigrato; gatta; (*spinster*) zitella; vecchia pettegola

tabernacle ['tæbər,nækəl] *s* tabernacolo

table ['tebəl] *s* tavola; (*food*) mensa; (*people at a table*) tavolata; (*synopsis*) quadro, prospetto; (*list or catalogue*) indice *m*; **to turn the tables** rovesciare la posizione; **under the table** ubriaco fradicio ‖ *tr* aggiornare, rinviare

tab•leau ['tæblo] *s* (**-leaus** or **-leaux** [loz]) quadro vivente

ta'ble•cloth' *s* tovaglia

table d'hôte ['tabəl'dot] *s* pasto a prezzo fisso

tableful ['tebəl,fʊl] *s* (*persons*) tavolata; (*food*) tavola apparecchiata

ta'ble•land' *s* tavoliere *m*

ta'ble lin'en *s* biancheria da tavola

ta'ble man'ners *spl* maniere *fpl* a tavola

ta'ble of con'tents *s* indice *m* delle materie

ta'ble•spoon' *s* cucchiaio

tablespoonful ['tebəl,spun,fʊl] *s* cucchiaiata

tablet ['tæblɪt] *s* (*writing pad*) blocco; (*slab*) lapide *f*; (*flat rigid sheet*) tabella, tavoletta; (pharm) disco, pastiglia

ta'ble talk' *s* conversazione familiare a tavola

ta'ble ten'nis *s* ping-pong *m*, tennis *m* da tavolo

ta'ble•ware' *s* servizio da tavola

ta'ble wine' *s* vino da pasto

tabloid ['tæblɔɪd] *s* giornale *m* a carattere sensazionale

taboo [tə'bu] *adj* & *s* tabù *m* ‖ *tr* proibire assolutamente

tabulate ['tæbjə,let] *tr* tabulare

tabulator ['tæbjə,letər] *s* tabulatore *m*, incolonnatore *m*

tachometer [tə'kɑmɪtər] *s* tachimetro

tacit ['tæsɪt] *adj* tacito

taciturn ['tæsɪ,tʌrn] *adj* taciturno

tack [tæk] *s* bulletta; cambio di direzione; (naut) virata; (sew) imbastitura ‖ *tr* imbullettare; attaccare; (naut) bordeggiare; (sew) imbastire ‖ *intr* virare; mutare di direzione

tackle ['tækəl] *s* attrezzatura; (mach) taglia, paranco; (gear) (naut) padiglione *m* ‖ *tr* attaccare, affrontare; (sports) placcare, bloccare

tack•y ['tækɪ] *adj* (**-ier -iest**) appiccicaticcio; (coll) trasandato

tact [tækt] *s* tatto

tactful ['tæktfəl] *adj* pieno di tatto

tactical ['tæktɪkəl] *adj* tattico

tactician [tæk'tɪʃən] *s* tattico

tactics ['tæktɪks] *ssg* (mil) tattica ‖ *spl* tattica

tactless ['tæktlɪs] *adj* che non ha tatto, indiscreto

tadpole ['tæd,pol] *s* girino

taffeta ['tæfɪtə] *s* taffettà *m*

taffy ['tæfi] *s* caramella, zucchero d'orzo; (coll) lisciata

tag [tæg] *s* etichetta; (*on a shoelace*) punta dell'aghetto; conclusione; (*last words of speech*) pistolotto finale; epiteto; frase fatta; (*of hair*) ciocca; (*in writing*) ghirigoro; (*game*) toccaferro ‖ *v* (*pret & pp* **tagged; *ger* tagging**) *tr* etichettare; (*to fine*) multare; aggiungere; soprannominare; accusare; stabilire il prezzo di; (coll) pedinare ‖ *intr* seguire da presso

tag' end' *s* (*e.g., of day*) fine *f*; estremità logorata; avanzo

tail [tel] *adj* di coda ‖ *s* coda; fine *f*; (*of coin*) croce *f*; **tails** falde *fpl*, frac *m*; **to turn tails** darsela a gambe ‖ *tr* attaccare; finire; (coll) pedinare

tail' assem'bly *s* (aer) impennaggio

tail' end' *s* coda, fine *f*

tail'light' *s* fanale *m* di coda

tailor ['telər] *s* sarto ‖ *tr* (*a suit*) tagliare, confezionare; (*one's conduct*) adattare ‖ *intr* fare il sarto

tailoring ['telərɪŋ] *s* sartoria

tai'lor-made' *adj* fatto su misura

tai'lor shop' *s* sartoria

tail'piece' *s* coda, estremità *f*; (mus) cordiera; (typ) fusello finale

tail'race' *s* canale *m* di scarico

tail'spin' *s* avvitamento

tail'wind' *s* (aer) vento di coda; (naut) vento in poppa

taint [tent] *s* macchia; infezione ‖ *tr* macchiare, infettare, corrompere

take [tek] *s* presa; (*of fish*) retata; (mov) presa; ripresa; (slang) incasso ‖ *v* (*pret* **took** [tʊk]; *pp* **taken**) *tr* prendere, pigliare; ricevere, accettare; portare; (*to get by force*) portar via; (*a nap*) schiacciare; (*a bath*) fare; (*a joke*) stare a; (*an examination*) sostenere; (*one's own life*) togliersi; (*to deduct*) cavare; (*a purchase*) comprare; (*to convey*) portare; (*time*) impiegare; (*a step, a walk*) fare; (*a subject*) studiare; (*a responsibility, role, etc.*) assumere; (*an oath*) prestare; (*root*) mettere; (*exception*) sollevare; credere; (*e.g., a photograph*) fare, scattare; (slang) fregare; **it takes** ci vuole, ci vogliono; **to take amiss** prendere a male; **to take apart** scomporre; smontare; **to take back** riprendere; **to take down** abbassare; smontare; prender nota di; **to take for** prendere per; **to take from** portar via a; **to take in** (*to admit*) ammettere, ricevere; (*to encompass*) includere; (*a dress*) restringere; (*to cheat*) ingannare; (*water*) fare; (*a point of inter-*

est) visitare; **to take it** accettare, ammettere; (slang) resistere; **to take off** (*e.g., one's coat*) togliersi; portar via; scontare, defalcare; (slang) imitare; **to take on** ingaggiare; assumere; intraprendere; accettare la sfida di; **to take out** cavare, togliere; (*e.g., a girl*) portar fuori; (*e.g., a patent*) ottenere; **to take over** rilevare; (slang) imbrogliare; **to take place** aver luogo; **to take s.o.'s eye** attrarre l'attenzione di qlcu; **to take the place of** sottentrare a; **to take up** cominciare a studiare; sollevare, tirar su; (*a duty*) assumere; (*time, space*) occupare || *intr* prendere; scattare; darsi; diventare; **to take after** rassomigliare a; **to take off** (coll) partire, andarsene; (aer) decollare, involare; **to take up with** (coll) fare amicizia con; (coll) vivere con; **to take well** riuscire bene in fotografia

take'off' *s* parodia; (aer) decollaggio; (mach) presa di forza

tal'cum pow'der ['tælkəm] *s* talco

tale [tel] *s* storia, racconto; favola, fiaba; (*lie*) bugia, frottola; (*piece of gossip*) maldicenza

tale'bear'er *s* pettegolo

talent ['tælənt] *s* talento; persona di talento; gente *f* di talento

talented ['tæləntɪd] *adj* dotato di talento, dotato d'ingegno

tal'ent scout' *s* scopritore *m* di talenti

talk [tɔk] *s* chiacchierata; discorso, conferenza; (*language*) parlata; (*gossip*) pettegolezzo; **to cause talk** originare pettegolezzi || *tr* parlare; convincere parlando; **to talk up** elogiare || *intr* parlare; discutere; **to talk on** discutere; continuare a parlare; **to talk up** parlare apertamente

talkative ['tɔkətɪv] *adj* loquace

talker ['tɔkər] *s* parlatore *m*

talkie ['tɔki] *s* (coll) parlato

talk'ing machine' *s* grammofono

talk'ing pic'ture *s* film parlato

tall [tɔl] *adj* alto; (coll) stravagante, esagerato

tallow ['tælo] *s* sego

tal·ly ['tæli] *s* (-lies) tacca, taglia || *v* (*pret & pp* -lied) *tr* contare, registrare || *intr* riscontrare

tal'ly sheet' *s* foglio di spunta

talon ['tælən] *s* artiglio

tambourine [,tæmbə'rin] *s* tamburello

tame [tem] *adj* addomesticato; docile, mansueto; mite || *tr* addomesticare; domare; (*water power*) captare

tamp [tæmp] *tr* pigiare, comprimere; (*e.g., ground*) costipare

tamper ['tæmpər] *s* (*person*) pigiatore *m*; (*tool*) mazzeranga || *intr* intrigare; **to tamper with** (*a lock*) forzare; (*a document*) manomettere; (*a witness*) corrompere

tampon ['tæmpən] *s* (surg) tampone *m* || *tr* (surg) tamponare

tan [tæn] *adj* marrone; (*by sun*) abbronzato || *v* (*pret & pp* tanned; *ger* tanning) *tr* (*leather*) conciare; ab-

bronzare; (coll) picchiare, sculacciare

tandem ['tændəm] *adj & adv* in tandem || *s* tandem *m*

tang [tæŋ] *s* sapore *m* piccante; odore *m* forte; traccia; (*of knife*) tallone *m*; (*sound*) tintinnio

tangent ['tændʒənt] *adj* tangente || *s* tangente *f*; **to fly off at a tangent** cambiare improvvisamente d'idea

tangerine [,tændʒə'rin] *s* mandarino

tangible ['tændʒɪbəl] *adj* tangibile

Tangier [tæn'dʒɪr] *s* Tangeri *f*

tangle ['tæŋgəl] *s* intrico; (coll) litigio || *tr* intricare || *intr* intricarsi; (coll) litigare

tank [tæŋk] *s* conserva, serbatoio; (mil) carro armato

tankard ['tæŋkərd] *s* boccale *m*

tank' car' *s* (rr) carro botte

tanker ['tæŋkər] *s* petroliera; (aer) aerocisterna

tank' farm'ing *s* idroponica

tank' truck' *s* autocisterna

tanner ['tænər] *s* conciapelli *m*

tanner·y ['tænəri] *s* (-ies) conceria

tantalize ['tæntə,laɪz] *tr* stuzzicare con vane promesse

tantamount ['tæntə,maunt] *adj* equivalente

tantrum ['tæntrəm] *s* bizze *fpl*

tap [tæp] *s* colpetto, buffetto; (*in a keg*) spina, cannella; (*faucet*) rubinetto; (elec) presa; (mach) maschio; **on tap** alla spina; (coll) disponibile; **taps** (mil) silenzio || *v* (*pret & pp* tapped; *ger* tapping) *tr* battere; picchiare, picchiettare; (*from a barrel*) spillare; mettere il cannello a; (*resources*) usare; (*a telephone*) intercettare; (*water, electricity*) derivare; (mach) maschiare || *intr* picchiare

tap' dance' *s* tip tap *m*

tap'-dance' *intr* ballare il tip tap

tape [tep] *s* nastro; (sports) striscione *m* del traguardo || *tr* legare con nastro; misurare col metro a nastro; registrare su nastro magnetico

tape' meas'ure *s* metro a nastro; nastro per misurare

tape' play'er *s* riproduttore *m* a nastro magnetico

taper ['tepər] *s* cerino || *tr* affusolare || *intr* affusolarsi; **to taper off** rastremarsi; diminuire in intensità; diminuire a poco a poco

tape'-re·cord' *tr* registrare su nastro magnetico

tape' record'er *s* magnetofono, registratore *m* a nastro

tapes·try ['tæpɪstri] *s* (-tries) tappezzeria || *v* (*pret & pp* -tried) *tr* tappezzare

tape'worm' *s* verme solitario, tenia

tappet ['tæpɪt] *s* (aut) punteria

tap'room' *s* taverna, osteria

tap'root' *s* radice *f* a fittone

tap' wa'ter *s* acqua corrente

tap' wrench' *s* giramaschio

tar [tɑr] *s* catrame *m* || *v* (*pret & pp* tarred; *ger* tarring) *tr* incatramare

tar·dy ['tɑrdi] *adj* (**-dier; -diest**) in ritardo; lento

tare [ter] *s* tara ‖ *tr* tarare

target ['tɑrgɪt] *s* segno, bersaglio

tar'get date' *s* data progettata

tar'get lan'guage *s* lingua obbiettivo, lingua di arrivo

tar'get prac'tice *s* esercizio di tiro a segno

tariff ['tærɪf] *s* (*duties*) tariffa doganale; (*charge or fare*) tariffa

tarnish ['tɑrnɪʃ] *s* ossidazione; (fig) macchia ‖ *tr* appannare ‖ *intr* appannarsi, perdere il lustro

tar' pa'per *s* carta catramata

tarpaulin [tɑr'pɔlɪn] *s* telone *m* impermeabile incatramato

tarragon ['tærəgən] *s* dragoncello

tar·ry ['tɑri] *adj* incatramato ‖ ['tæri] *v* (*pret & pp* **-ried**) *intr* rimanere; ritardare

tart [tɑrt] *adj* acido, pungente ‖ *s* torta; (slang) puttana

tartar ['tɑrtər] *s* tartaro; cremore *m* di tartaro; (*shrew*) megera; **to catch a tartar** imbattersi in un muso duro

Tartarus ['tɑrtərəs] *s* Tartaro

task [tæsk] *or* [tɑsk] *s* compito, incarico; **to take to task** rimproverare

task' force' *s* gruppo formato per una missione speciale

task'mas'ter *s* sorvegliante *m*; sorvegliante severo

tassel ['tæsəl] *s* nappa; (bot) ciuffo

taste [test] *s* gusto, sapore *m*; buon gusto; (*sampling, e.g., of wine*) assaggio; esperienza; **to one's taste** a genio di qlcu ‖ *tr* gustare, assaggiare ‖ *intr* sentire, sapere; **to taste of** degustare; sapere di

tasteless ['testlɪs] *adj* insipido; di cattivo gusto

tast·y ['testi] *adj* (**-ier; -iest**) saporito; (coll) di buon gusto

tatter ['tætər] *s* brandello, sbrendolo ‖ *tr* sbrindellare

tattered ['tætərd] *adj* sbrindellato

tattle ['tætəl] *s* chiacchiera; (*gossip*) pettegolezzo ‖ *intr* chiacchierare; spettegolare

tat'tle·tale' *adj* rivelatore ‖ *s* gazzetta, chiacchierone *m*

tattoo [tæ'tu] *s* tatuaggio; (mil) ritirata ‖ *tr* tatuare

taunt [tɔnt] *or* [tɑnt] *s* rimprovero sarcastico, insulto ‖ *tr* rimproverare sarcasticamente, insultare

Taurus ['tɔrəs] *s* (astr) Toro

taut [tɔt] *adj* teso, tirato

tavern ['tævərn] *s* osteria

taw·dry ['tɔdri] *adj* (**-drier; -driest**) vistoso, sgargiante, pacchiano

taw·ny ['tɔni] *adj* (**-nier; -niest**) falbo, fulvo

tax [tæks] *s* tassa, imposta ‖ *tr* tassare; (*s.o.'s patience*) mettere a dura prova

taxable ['tæksəbəl] *adj* tassabile

tax'able in'come *s* imponibile *m*

taxation [tæk'seʃən] *s* imposizione, tassazione, contribuzione

tax' collec'tor *s* esattore *m* delle imposte

tax' deduc'tion *s* detrazione

tax'-ex·empt' *adj* esente da tasse

tax' evad'er [ɪ'vedər] *s* evasore *m*

tax·i ['tæksi] *s* (**-is**) tassì *m* ‖ *v* (*pret & pp* **-ied**; *ger* **-iing** *or* **-ying**) *tr* far rullare ‖ *intr* andare in tassì; (aer) rullare

tax'i·cab' *s* tassì *m*

tax'i driv'er *s* tassista *m*

tax'i·plane' *s* aeroplano da noleggio, aerotassì *m*

taxi' stand' *s* posteggio di tassì

tax'pay'er *s* contribuente *mf*

tax' rate' *s* imponibilità *f*

tea [ti] *s* tè *m*; (*medicinal infusion*) tisana; (*beef broth*) brodo di carne

tea' bag' *s* sacchetto di tè

tea' ball' *s* uovo da tè

tea'cart' *s* servitore *m*

teach [titʃ] *v* (*pret & pp* **taught** [tɔt]) *tr & intr* insegnare

teacher ['titʃər] *s* maestro, insegnante *mf*

teach'ers col'lege *s* scuola magistrale

teach'er's pet' *s* beniamino del maestro

teaching ['titʃɪŋ] *adj* insegnante ‖ *s* insegnamento, dottrina

teach'ing aids' *spl* sussidi *mpl* didattici

teach'ing staff' *s* corpo insegnante

tea'cup' *s* tazza da tè

tea' dance' *s* tè *m* danzante

teak [tik] *s* tek *m*

tea'ket'tle *s* bricco del tè

team [tim] *s* (*e.g., of horses*) pariglia; (sports) squadra, equipaggio ‖ *tr* apparigliare; tirare or trasportare con pariglia ‖ *intr*—**to team up** unirsi, associarsi

team'mate' *s* compagno di squadra

teamster ['timstər] *s* (*of horses*) carrettiere *m*; (*of truck*) camionista *m*, autotrenista *m*

team'work' *s* affiatamento, collaborazione

tea'pot' *s* teiera

tear [tɪr] *s* lacrima; **to hold back one's tears** ingoiare le lacrime; **to laugh away one's tears** cambiare dal pianto al riso ‖ [ter] *s* strappo ‖ [ter] *v* (*pret* **tore** [tor]; *pp* **torn** [tɔrn]) *tr* strappare; stracciare; (*one's heart*) squarciare; (*to wound*) sbranare; (*one's hair*) strapparsi; **to tear apart** rompere in due; separare; **to tear down** demolire; (*a piece of equipment*) smontare; **to tear off** staccare; **to tear to pieces** dilaniare; fare a pezzi; **to tear up** (*a piece of paper*) stracciare; (*a street*) scavare ‖ *intr* strapparsi, stracciarsi; **to tear along** precipitarsi; correre all'impazzata

tear' bomb' [tɪr] *s* bomba lacrimogena

tearful ['tɪrfəl] *adj* lacrimoso

tear' gas' [tɪr] *s* gas lacrimogeno

tear-jerker ['tɪr ,dʒʌrkər] *s* (coll) storia lacrimogena

tear-off ['ter ,ɔf] *adj* da staccarsi, perforato

tea'room' *s* sala da tè

tear' sheet' [ter] *s* copia di annuncio pubblicitario

tease [tiz] *tr* stuzzicare, molestare;

(hair) accotonare; *(e.g., wool)* cardare

tea'spoon' *s* cucchiaino

teaspoonful ['ti ,spun ,fʊl] *s* cucchiaino

teat [tit] *s* capezzolo

tea'time' *s* l'ora del tè

tea' wag'on *s* servitore *m*

technical ['tɛknɪkəl] *adj* tecnico

technicali·ty [,tɛknɪ'kælɪtɪ] *s* (**-ties**) tecnicismo; dettaglio tecnico

technician [tɛk'nɪʃən] *s* tecnico

technics ['tɛknɪks] *ssg or spl* tecnica

technique [tɛk'nik] *s* tecnica

ted'dy bear' ['tɛdɪ] *s* orsacchiotto

tedious ['tidɪ·əs] *or* ['tidʒəs] *adj* tedioso, noioso

tee [ti] *adj* fatto a T ‖ *s* giunto a tre vie; *(golf)* piazzola di partenza ‖ *tr*—**to tee off** (slang) cominciare ‖ *intr*—**to be teed off** (slang) essere arrabbiato; **to tee off** (golf) colpire la palla dalla piazzola di partenza; **to tee off on** (slang) rimproverare severamente

teem [tim] *intr* brulicare; piovere a dirotto; **to teem with** abbondare di

teeming ['timɪŋ] *adj* brulicante; *(rain)* torrenziale

teen-ager ['tin ,edʒər] *s* giovane *mf* dai 13 ai 19 anni

teens [tinz] *spl* numeri inglesi che finiscono in **-teen** (dal 13 al 19); **to be in one's teens** avere dai 13 ai 19 anni

tee·ny ['tini] *adj* (**-nier; -niest**) (coll) piccolo, piccolissimo

teeter ['titər] *s* altalena, dondolio ‖ *intr* dondolarsi, oscillare

teethe [tið] *intr* mettere i denti

teething ['tiðɪŋ] *s* dentizione

teeth'ing ring' *s* dentaruolo

teetotaler [ti'totələr] *s* astemio

tele·cast ['tɛlɪ ,kæst] *or* ['tɛlɪ ,kɑst] *s* teletrasmissione ‖ *v* (*pret & pp* **-cast** *or* **-casted**) *tr & intr* teletrasmettere

telegram ['tɛlɪ ,græm] *s* telegramma *m*

telegraph ['tɛlɪ ,græf] *or* ['tɛlɪ ,grɑf] *s* telegrafo ‖ *tr & intr* telegrafare

tel'egraph pole' *s* palo del telegrafo

Telemachus [tɪ'lɛməkəs] *s* Telemaco

telemeter [tɪ'lɛmɪtər] *s* telemetro ‖ *tr* misurare col telemetro

telepathy [tɪ'lɛpəθɪ] *s* telepatia

telephone ['tɛlɪ ,fon] *s* telefono ‖ *tr & intr* telefonare

tel'ephone book' *s* elenco *or* guida dei telefoni

tel'ephone booth' *s* cabina telefonica

tel'ephone call' *s* chiamata telefonica, colpo di telefono

tel'ephone direc'tory *s* elenco *or* guida dei telefoni

tel'ephone exchange' *s* centrale telefonica

tel'ephone op'erator *s* centralinista *mf*, telefonista *mf*

tel'ephone receiv'er *s* ricevitore *m*

tel'ephoto lens' ['tɛlɪ ,foto] *s* teleobbiettivo

teleplay ['tɛlɪ ,ple] *s* teledramma *m*

teleprinter ['tɛlɪ ,prɪntər] *s* telescrivente *f*

telescope ['tɛlɪ ,skop] *s* telescopio ‖ *tr*

snodare; condensare ‖ *intr* essere snodabile; *(in a collision)* incastrarsi

teletype ['tɛlɪ ,taɪp] *s* telescrivente *f* ‖ *tr & intr* trasmettere per telescrivente

teleview ['tɛlɪ ,vju] *tr* telericevere

televiewer ['tɛlɪ ,vju·ər] *s* telespettatore *m*

televise ['tɛlɪ ,vaɪz] *tr* teletrasmettere

television ['tɛlɪ ,vɪʒən] *adj* televisivo ‖ *s* televisione

tel'evision screen' *s* teleschermo

tel'evision set' *s* televisore *m*

tell [tɛl] *v* (*pret & pp* **told** [told]) *tr* dire; *(to narrate)* raccontare; *(to count)* contare; distinguere; **I told you so!** te l'avevo detto!; **to tell off** (coll) dire il fatto suo a ‖ *intr* dire; prevedere; avere effetto; **to tell on** *(s.o.'s health)* pesare a, e.g., **age was telling on his health** l'età pesava alla sua salute; (coll) denunciare

teller ['tɛlər] *s* narratore *m*; *(of bank)* cassiere *m*; *(of votes)* scrutatore *m*

temper ['tɛmpər] *s* indole *f*, temperamento; umore *m*; calma; (metallurgy) tempra; **to keep one's temper** mantenersi calmo; **to lose one's temper** perdere la pazienza ‖ *tr* temprare ‖ *intr* temprarsi

temperament ['tɛmpərəmənt] *s* indole *f*, temperamento, carattere *m*

temperamental [,tɛmpərə'mɛntəl] *adj* emotivo, capriccioso

temperance ['tɛmpərəns] *s* *(self-restraint in action)* temperanza; *(abstinence from alcoholic beverages)* sobrietà *f*

temperate ['tɛmpərɪt] *adj* temperato

temperature ['tɛmpərət/ər] *s* temperatura

tempest ['tɛmpɪst] *s* tempesta; **tempest in a teapot** tempesta in un bicchier d'acqua

tempestuous [tɛm'pɛst/ʊ·əs] *adj* tempestoso

temple ['tɛmpəl] *s* *(place of worship)* tempio; *(of spectacles)* susta, stanghetta; (anat) tempia

tem·po ['tɛmpo] *s* (**-pos** *or* **-pi** [pi]) (mus) tempo; (fig) ritmo

temporal ['tɛmpərəl] *adj* temporale

temporary ['tɛmpə ,rɛrɪ] *adj* temporaneo, provvisorio, transitorio, interino

temporize ['tɛmpə ,raɪz] *intr* temporeggiare

tempt [tɛmpt] *tr* tentare

temptation [tɛmp'te/ən] *s* tentazione

tempter ['tɛmptər] *s* tentatore *m*

tempting ['tɛmptɪŋ] *adj* tentatore

ten [tɛn] *adj & pron* dieci ‖ *s* dieci *m*; **ten o'clock** le dieci

tenable ['tɛnəbəl] *adj* difendibile

tenacious [tɪ'ne/əs] *adj* tenace

tenant ['tɛnənt] *s* inquilino, pigionante *mf*; *(of land)* fittavolo

tend [tɛnd] *tr* riguardare, governare; accudire (with *dat*), e.g., **he tends the fire** accudisce al fuoco ‖ *intr* tendere; **to tend to** propendere verso; *(e.g., one's own business)* attendere a; **to tend to** + *inf* tendere a + *inf*

tenden·cy ['tɛndənsɪ] *s* (**-cies**) tendenza, propensione

tender ['tendər] *adj* tenero; sensibile, dolorante ‖ *s* offerta; (naut) nave *f* rifornimento; (naut) lancia; (rr) carboniera ‖ *tr* offrire

tender-hearted ['tendər ,hɑrtɪd] *adj* dal cuore tenero

ten'der·loin' *s* filetto ‖ **Tenderloin** *s* rione *m* della mala vita

tenderness ['tendərnɪs] *s* tenerezza

tendon ['tendən] *s* tendine *m*

tendril ['tendrɪl] *s* viticcio

tenement ['tenɪmənt] *s* appartamento; casa; casamento

ten'ement house' *s* casamento

tenet ['tenɪt] *s* dogma *m*, dottrina

tennis ['tenɪs] *s* tennis *m*

ten'nis court' *s* campo da tennis

ten'nis play'er *s* tennista *mf*

tenor ['tenər] *s* tenore *m*

tense [tens] *adj* teso ‖ *s* (gram) tempo

tension ['tenʃən] *s* tensione

tent [tent] *s* tenda; (of circus) tendone *m*

tentacle ['tentəkəl] *s* tentacolo

tentative ['tentətɪv] *adj* a titolo di prova; (smile) esile

tenth [tenθ] *adj, s & pron* decimo ‖ *s* (in dates) dieci *m*

tenuous ['tenju·əs] *adj* tenue

tenure ['tenjər] *s* (in office) .rafferma; (permanency of employment) inamovibilità *f*; (law) possesso

tepid ['tepɪd] *adj* tiepido

tercet ['tʌrsɪt] *s* terzina

term [tʌrm] *s* vocabolo, voce *f*; periodo, durata; termine *m*; (com) scadenza; **terms** condizioni *fpl*; **on good terms** essere in buone relazioni; **to come to terms** venire a patti ‖ *tr* chiamare, definire

termagant ['tʌrməgənt] *s* megera

terminal ['tʌrmɪnəl] *adj* terminale ‖ *s* (end or extremity) terminale *m*; (elec) morsetto; (rr) capolinea *m*

terminate ['tʌrmɪ ,net] *tr & intr* terminare

terminus ['tʌrmɪnəs] *s* termine *m*, fine *m*; (rr) capolinea *m*

termite ['tʌrmaɪt] *s* termite *f*

terrace ['terəs] *s* terrazza, terrazzo; (agr) gradino, scaglione *m*

terra firma ['terə 'fʌrmə] *s* terra ferma

terrain [te'ren] *s* terreno

terrestrial [tə'restrɪ·əl] *adj* terrestre

terrific [tə'rɪfɪk] *adj* terrificante; (coll) tremendo

terri·fy ['terɪ ,faɪ] *v* (pret & pp -fied) *tr* terrificare, inorridire

territo·ry ['terɪ ,tori] *s* (-ries) territorio

terror ['terər] *s* terrore *m*

terrorize ['terə ,raɪz] *tr* terrorizzare; dominare col terrore

ter'ry cloth' ['terɪ] *s* tessuto a spugna

terse [tʌrs] *adj* conciso, terso

tertiary ['tʌrʃɪ ,erɪ] or ['tʌrʃərɪ] *adj* terziario

test [test] *s* prova, saggio; esame *m* ‖ *tr* provare, saggiare; esaminare; (e.g., a machine) collaudare

testament ['testəmənt] *s* testamento ‖ **Testament** *s* Testamento Nuovo

test' ban' *s* interdizione degli esperimenti nucleari

test' flight' *s* volo di prova

testicle ['testɪkəl] *s* testicolo

testi·fy ['testɪ ,faɪ] *v* (pret & pp -fied) *tr & intr* testimoniare

testimonial [,testɪ'monɪ·əl] *s* (certificate) benservito, referenza; (expression of esteem) segno di gratitudine

testimo·ny ['testɪ ,monɪ] *s* (-nies) testimonianza

test' pat'tern *s* (telv) monoscopio

test' pi'lot *s* pilota *m* collaudatore

test' tube' *s* provetta

tetanus ['tetənəs] *s* tetano

tether ['teðər] *s* cavezza, pastoia; **at the end of one's tether** al limite delle proprie risorse ‖ *tr* legare; incavezzare, impastoiare

tetter ['tetər] *s* eczema *m*, impetigine *f*

text [tekst] *s* testo; tema *m*

text'book' *s* libro di testo

textile ['tekstɪl] or ['tekstaɪl] *adj & s* tessile *m*

textual ['tekstʃʊ·əl] *adj* testuale

texture ['tekstʃər] *s* (of cloth) trama; caratteristica, proprietà *f*

Thai ['tɑ·i] or ['taɪ] *adj & s* tailandese *mf*

Thailand ['taɪlənd] *s* la Tailandia

Thames [temz] *s* Tamigi *m*

than [ðæn] *conj* di, e.g., **he is faster than you** è più veloce di te; (before a verb) di quanto, e.g., **he is smarter than I thought** è più intelligente di quanto pensavo; che, e.g., **he had barely begun to eat than it was time to leave** non aveva appena cominciato a mangiare che era ora di andarsene

thank [θæŋk] *s*—**thanks** ringraziamenti *mpl*; **thanks to** grazie a, in grazie di ‖ *tr* ringraziare ‖ **thanks** *interj* grazie!

thankful ['θæŋkfəl] *adj* grato

thankless ['θæŋklɪs] *adj* ingrato

Thanksgiv'ing Day' [,θæŋks'gɪvɪŋ] *s* giorno del Ringraziamento

that [ðæt] *adj dem* (those) quel; codesto; **that one** quello, quello là ‖ *pron dem* (those) quello; codesto ‖ *pron rel* che, quello che, il quale; **that is** cioè; **that's that** (coll) ecco fatto, ecco tutto ‖ *adv* (coll) tanto, così; **that far** così lontano; **that many** tanti; **that much** tanto ‖ *conj* che

thatch [θætʃ] *s* paglia, copertura di paglia; (hair) capigliatura ‖ *tr* coprire di paglia

thaw [θɔ] *s* sgelo ‖ *tr* sgelare ‖ *intr* sgelarsi

the [ðə], [ðɪ], or [ði] *art def* il; al, e.g., **one dollar the dozen** un dollaro alla dozzina ‖ *adv*—**so much the worse for him** tanto peggio per lui; **the more . . . the more** quanto più . . . tanto più

theater ['θi·ətər] *s* teatro

the'ater-go'er *s* frequentatore *m* abituale del teatro

the'ater news' *s* cronaca teatrale

theatrical [θɪ'ætrɪkəl] *adj* teatrale

Thebes [θibz] *s* Tebe *f*

thee [ði] *pron pers* (Bib; poet) ti; te

theft [θeft] *s* furto, ruberia

their [ðer] *adj poss* il loro, loro

theirs [ðerz] *pron poss* il loro

them [ðem] *pron pers* li; loro; **to them** loro

theme [θim] *s* tema *m*, soggetto; saggio; (mus) tema *m*

theme' song' *s* (mus) tema *m* centrale; (rad) sigla musicale

them·selves' *pron pers* essi stessi, loro stessi; si, e.g., **they enjoyed themselves** si divertirono

then [ðen] *adj* allora, di allora ‖ *s* quel tempo; by then a quell'epoca; **from then on** da quel giorno in poi ‖ *adv* allora; indi, poi; **then and there** a quel momento

thence [ðens] *adv* indi, quindi; da lì; da allora in poi

thence'forth' *adv* da allora in poi

theolo·gy [θi'ɑlədʒi] *s* (**-gies**) teologia

theorem [θi·ərəm] *s* teorema *m*

theoretical [,θi·ə'rɛtɪkəl] *adj* teoretico

theo·ry [θi·əri] *s* (**-ries**) teoria

therapeutic [,θerə'pjutɪk] *adj* terapeutico ‖ **therapeutics** *ssg* terapeutica

thera·py [θerəpi] *s* (**-pies**) terapia

there [ðer] *adv* lì, là; **there are** ci sono; **there is c'è**; ecco, e.g., **there it is** eccolo

there'abouts' *adv* circa, approssimativamente, giù di lì

there'af'ter *adv* in seguito, dipoi

there'by' *adv* quindi, perciò, così

therefore [ðerfor] *adv* per questo, quindi, dunque

there'in' adv lì; in quel rispetto

there'of' *adv* di ciò, da ciò

Theresa [tə'risə] *or* [tə'resə] *s* Teresa

there'upon' adv su questo; a quel momento; come conseguenza

thermal [θʌrməl] *adj* (water) termale; (capacity) termico

thermistor [θər'mɪstər] *s* (elec) termistore *m*

thermocouple [θʌrmo,kʌpəl] *s* termocoppia

thermodynamic [,θʌrmodai'næmɪk] *adj* termodinamico ‖ **thermodynamics** *ssg* termodinamica

thermometer [θər'mɑmɪtər] *s* termometro

thermonuclear [θʌrmo'njukli·ər] *or* [,θʌrmo'nuklɪ·ər] *adj* termonucleare

ther'mos bot'tle [θʌrməs] *s* termos *m*

thermostat [θʌrmə,stæt] *s* termostato

thesau·rus [θɪ'sɔrəs] *s* (**-ri** [rai] *or* **-ruses**) tesoro, lessico, compendio

these [ðiz] *pl of* **this**

the·sis [θisɪs] *s* (**-ses** [siz]) tesi *f*

Thespis [θespɪs] *s* Tespi *m*

they [ðe] *pron pers* essi, loro

thick [θɪk] *adj* spesso, grosso; folto, denso; pieno, coperto; viscoso; stupido; (coll) intimo ‖ *s* spessore *m*; **in the thick of** nel folto di; **through thick and thin** nei tempi buoni e cattivi

thicken [θɪkən] *tr* ispessire; ingrossare; infoltire ‖ *intr* ispessirsi; ingrossarsi; (said of a plot) complicarsi

thicket [θɪkɪt] *s* boscaglia, macchia

thick-headed [θɪk,hɛdɪd] *adj* indietro, stupido

thick'set' *adj* tarchiato; (hedge) fitto, denso

thief [θif] *s* (**thieves** [θivz]) ladro

thieve [θiv] *intr* rubare

thiev·y [θivəri] *s* (**-ies**) furto

thigh [θaɪ] *s* coscia

thigh'bone' *s* femore *m*

thimble [θɪmbəl] *s* ditale *m*

thin [θɪn] *adj* (**thinner; thinnest**) (paper, ice) sottile; (lean) magro, smilzo; (e.g., hair) rado; (air) fine; (excuse) tenue; (voice) esile; (wine) leggero, annacquato ‖ *v* (pret & pp **thinned;** ger **thinning**) *tr* assottigliare; (paint) diluire ‖ *intr* assottigliarsi; **to thin out** (said of a crowd, one's hair) diradarsi

thine [ðaɪn] *adj & pron poss* (Bib & poet) tuo, il tuo

thing [θɪŋ] *s* cosa; **not to get a thing out of** non riuscire a capire; non cavare un briciolo d'informazione da; **of all things!** che cosa!; che sorpresa!; **the thing** l'ultima moda; **things** roba; **to see things** avere allucinazioni

think [θɪŋk] *v* (pret & pp **thought** [θɔt]) *tr* pensare; credere; **to think it over** ripensarci; **to think nothing of it** non darci la minima importanza; **to think of** (to have as an opinion of) pensare di, e.g., **what do you think of that doctor?** cosa ne pensa di quel medico?; **to think out** decifrare; **to think up** immaginare ‖ *intr* pensare; **to think not** credere di no; **to think of** (to turn one's thoughts to) pensare a, e.g., **he is thinking of the future** pensa al futuro; (to imagine) immaginare; **to think so** credere di sì; **to think well of** avere una buona opinione di

thinkable [θɪŋkəbəl] *adj* pensabile

thinker [θɪŋkər] *s* pensatore *m*

third [θʌrd] *adj, s & pron* terzo ‖ *s* terzo; (in dates) tre *m*; (aut) terza

third' degree' *s* interrogatorio di terzo grado

third' rail' *s* (rr) rotaia elettrificata di contatto

third'-rate' *adj* di terz'ordine

Third' World' *s* Terzo Mondo

thirst [θʌrst] *s* sete *f* ‖ *intr* aver sete; **to thirst for** aver sete di

thirst·y [θʌrsti] *adj* (**-ier; -iest**) assetato, sitibondo; **to be thirsty** avere sete

thirteen [θʌr'tin] *adj, s & pron* tredici *m*

thirteenth [θʌr'tinθ] *adj, s & pron* tredicesimo ‖ *s* (in dates) tredici *m*

thirtieth [θʌrtɪ·ɪθ] *adj, s & pron* trentesimo ‖ *s* (in dates) trenta *m*

thir·ty [θʌrti] *adj, s & pron* trenta ‖ *s* (**-ties**) trenta *m*; **the thirties** gli anni trenta

this [ðɪs] *adj dem* (**these**) questo; **this one** questo, questo qui ‖ *pron dem* (**these**) questo, questo qui ‖ *adv* (coll) tanto, così

thistle [θɪsəl] *s* cardo

thither [θɪðər] *or* [ðɪðər] *adv* là, da quella parte

Thomas ['tɑməs] s Tommaso

thong [θɔŋ] or [θɑŋ] s coreggia

thorax ['θoræks] s (-raxes or -races [rə‚siz]) torace m

thorn [θɔrn] s spina

thorn·y ['θɔrni] adj (-ier; -iest) spinoso

thorough ['θʌro] adj completo, esauriente

thor'ough·bred' adj di razza; (horse) purosangue || s individuo di razza; (horse) purosangue mf

thor'ough·fare' s passaggio; **no thoroughfare** divieto di passaggio

thor'ough·go'ing adj completo, esauriente

thoroughly ['θʌroli] adv a fondo

those [ðoz] pl of that

thou [ðaʊ] pron pers (Bib; poet) tu || tr dare del tu a

though [ðo] adv tuttavia || conj malgrado, sebbene; **as though** come se

thought [θɔt] s pensiero; **perish the thought!** (coll) nemmeno a pensarci!

thoughtful ['θɔtfəl] adj pensieroso, riflessivo; (considerate) sollecito

thoughtless ['θɔtlɪs] adj irriflessivo; sconsiderato; (reckless) incurante

thought' transfer'ence s trasmissione del pensiero

thousand ['θaʊzənd] adj, s & pron mille m; **a thousand or one thousand** mille m

thousandth ['θaʊzəndθ] adj, s & pron millesimo

thralldom ['θrɔldəm] s schiavitù f

thrash [θræʃ] tr battere; (agr) trebbiare; **to thrash out** discutere a fondo || intr agitarsi, dibattersi

thread [θrɛd] s filo; (mach) filetto, verme m; **to lose the thread of** perdere il filo di || tr infilare; (fig) pervadere; (mach) filettare, impanare; **to thread one's way through** aprirsi il passaggio attraverso

thread'bare' adj frusto, logoro

threat [θrɛt] s minaccia

threaten ['θrɛtən] tr & intr minacciare

threatening ['θrɛtənɪŋ] adj minaccioso; (e.g., letter) minatorio

three [θri] adj & pron tre || s tre m; **three o'clock** le tre

three'-cor'nered adj triangolare; (hat) a tre punte

three' hun'dred adj, s & pron trecento

threepenny ['θrɛpəni] or ['θrɪpəni] adj del valore di tre penny; di nessun valore

three'-phase' adj trifase

three'-ply' adj a tre spessori

three' R's' [ɑrz] spl lettura, scrittura e aritmetica

three'score' adj sessanta

three' thou'sand adj, s & pron tre mila mpl

threno·dy ['θrɛnədi] s (-dies) trenodia

thresh [θrɛʃ] tr (agr) trebbiare; **to thresh out** discutere a fondo || intr trebbiare; battere

thresh'ing machine' s trebbiatrice f

threshold ['θrɛʃold] s soglia

thrice [θraɪs] adv tre volte; molto

thrift [θrɪft] s economia

thrift·y ['θrɪfti] adj (-ier; -iest) eco-

nomo, economico; vigoroso; prospero

thrill [θrɪl] s fremito d'emozione; esperienza emozionante || tr emozionare || intr emozionarsi; vibrare

thriller ['θrɪlər] s (coll) thrilling m

thrilling ['θrɪlɪŋ] adj emozionante, thrilling

thrive [θraɪv] v (pret thrived or throve [θrov]; pp thrived or thriven ['θrɪvən]) intr prosperare, fiorire

throat [θrot] s gola; **to clear one's throat** schiarirsi la voce

throb [θrɑb] s battito, palpito, tuffo || v (pret & pp throbbed; ger throbbing) intr palpitare, pulsare

throe [θro] s agonia, travaglio, spasimo; **in the throes of** nel travaglio di; (e.g., battle) nel momento più penoso di

throne [θron] s trono

throng [θrɔŋ] or [θrɑŋ] s folla, stuolo || intr affollarsi

throttle ['θrɑtəl] s (of locomotive) leva di comando; (of motorcycle) manetta; (of car) acceleratore m; (mach) valvola di controllo || tr soffocare; (mach) regolare

through [θru] adj diretto, senza fermate; **to be through** aver finito; **to be through with** farla finita con || adv attraverso; da una parte all'altra; completamente; || prep attraverso, per; durante; fino alla fine di; per mezzo di

through·out' adv completamente, da un capo all'altro; dappertutto || prep durante tutto, e.g., **throughout the afternoon** durante tutto il pomeriggio; per tutto, e.g., **throughout the house** per tutta la casa

throw [θro] s getto, tiro, lancio; gettata; coperta leggera || v (pret threw [θru]; pp thrown) tr gettare, tirare, lanciare; (a shadow) proiettare; (the current) connettere; (said of a horse) disarcionare; (wrestling) gettare a terra; (a game) (coll) perdere intenzionalmente; (coll) stupire; **to throw away** gettar via; perdere; **to throw back** rigettare; ritardare; **to throw in** (the clutch) innestare; (coll) aggiungere; **to throw oneself into** darsi a; **to throw out** sbatter fuori; (the clutch) disinnestare; **to throw over** abbandonare || intr gettare, tirare, lanciare; **to throw up** vomitare

thrum [θrʌm] v (pret & pp thrummed; ger thrumming) intr tambureggiare; (mus) far scorrere la mano sulle corde di uno strumento

thrush [θrʌʃ] s tordo

thrust [θrʌst] s (push) spinta; botta; (with dagger) pugnalata; (with sword) stoccata || v (pret & pp thrust) tr spingere; conficcare, configgere; **to thrust oneself** (e.g., into a conversation) ficcarsi

thru'way' s autostrada

thud [θʌd] s tonfo || v (pret & pp thudded; ger thudding) intr fare un rumore sordo

thug [θʌg] s fascinoroso

thumb [θʌm] *s* pollice *m;* **all thumbs** maldestro, goffo; **thumbs down** pollice verso; **to twiddle one's thumbs** girare i pollici, essere ozioso; **under the thumb of** sotto l'influenza di || *tr* sporcare con le dita; (*a book*) sfogliare; **to thumb a ride** chiedere l'autostop; **to thumb one's nose** (at) fare marameo (a)

thumb' in'dex *s* margine *m* a scaletta

thumb'nail' *adj* breve, conciso || *s* unghia del pollice

thumb'screw' *s* vite *f* ad aletta

thumb'tack' *s* puntina

thump [θʌmp] *s* tonfo || *tr* battere, percuotere || *intr* battere; cadere con un tonfo; camminare a passi pesanti; (*said of the heart*) palpitare violentemente

thumping ['θʌmpɪŋ] *adj* (coll) straordinario, eccezionale; (coll) grande

thunder ['θʌndər] *s* tuono; (*of applause*) scroscio; (*of a cannon*) rombo || *tr* lanciare || *intr* tonare, rombare; (fig) scrosciare

thun'der·bolt' *s* folgore *f,* fulmine *m*

thun'der·clap' *s* scroscio di tuono

thunderous ['θʌndərəs] *adj* fragoroso

thun'der·show'er *s* acquazzone *m* accompagnato da tuoni

thun'der·storm' *s* temporale *m*

thun'der·struck' *adj* attonito

Thursday ['θʌrsdi] *s* giovedì *m*

thus [ðʌs] *adv* così; **thus far** sino qui

thwack [θwæk] *s* colpo || *tr* colpire

thwart [θwɔrt] *adj* obliquo || *adv* di traverso || *tr* contrariare, sventare

thy [ðaɪ] *adj poss* (Bib; poet) tuo, il tuo

thyme [taɪm] *s* timo

thy'roid gland' ['θaɪrɔɪd] *s* tiroide *f*

thyself [ðaɪ'self] *pron* (Bib; poet) te stesso; te, ti

tiara [taɪ'ɑrə] or [taɪ'ɛrə] *s* (*female adornment*) diadema *m;* (eccl) tiara

tick [tɪk] *s* (*of pillow*) fodera; (*of clock*) tichettio; (*dot*) punto; (ent) zecca; on tick (coll) a credito || *intr* fare tichettio; **to make s.o. tick** mandare avanti qlcu

ticker ['tɪkər] *s* telescrivente *f;* (slang) orologio; (slang) cuore *m*

tick'er tape' *s* nastro della telescrivente

ticket ['tɪkɪt] *s* biglietto; (*e.g., of pawnbroker*) polizza; (*slip of paper or identifying tag*) bolletta, bollettino; (*summons*) verbale *m;* (*e.g., to indicate price*) etichetta; lista dei candidati; **that's the ticket** (coll) questo è quello che fa

tick'et a'gent *s* bigliettaio

tick'et of'fice *s* biglietteria

tick'et scalp'er ['skælpər] *s* bagarino

tick'et win'dow *s* sportello

ticking ['tɪkɪŋ] *s* traliccio

tickle ['tɪkəl] *s* solletico || *tr* solleticare; divertire || *intr* avere il solletico

ticklish ['tɪklɪʃ] *adj* sensibile al solletico; delicato; permaloso; **to be ticklish** soffrire il solletico

tick-tock ['tɪk,tɑk] *s* tic tac *m*

tid'al wave' ['taɪdəl] *s* onda di marea; (fig) ondata

tidbit ['tɪd,bɪt] *s* bocconcino

tiddlywinks ['tɪdli,wɪŋks] *s* gioco della pulce

tide [taɪd] *s* marea; **to go against the tide** andare contro la corrente; **to stem the tide** fermare la corrente || *tr* portare sulla cresta delle onde; **to tide over** aiutare; (*a difficulty*) sormontare

tide'wa'ter *s* marea; costa marina

tidings ['taɪdɪŋz] *spl* notizie *fpl*

ti·dy ['taɪdi] *adj* (-di·er; -di·est) pulito, ordinato || *s* (-dies) cofanetto, astuccio; appoggiacapo || *v* (*pret & pp* -died) *tr* rassettare, mettere in ordine || *intr* rassettarsi

tie [taɪ] *s* laccio, nodo, vincolo; (*in games*) patta; (*necktie*) cravatta; (archit) traversa; (rr) traversina; (mus) legatura || *v* (*pret & pp* tied; *ger* tying) *tr* allacciare, annodare, legare; confinare; (*a game*) impattare; (*a person*) impattarla con; **to be tied up** essere occupato; **to tie down** confinare, limitare; **to tie up** legare; impedire; (*e.g., traffic*) intasare || *intr* allacciarsi; (*in games*) impattare

tie' beam' *s* catena

tie'pin' *s* spilla da cravatta

tier [tɪr] *s* gradinata; ordine *m,* livello

tiff [tɪf] *s* screzio, litigio

tiger ['taɪgər] *s* tigre *f*

ti'ger lil'y *s* giglio cinese

tight [taɪt] *adj* teso; stretto; compatto; impermeabile, ermetico; pieno; (*game*) (coll) serrato; (coll) tirato; (slang) ubriaco || **tights** *spl* calzamaglia || *adv* strettamente; **to hold tight** tenere stretto

tighten ['taɪtən] *tr* (*e.g., one's belt*) tirare; (*e.g., a screw*) stringere || *intr* tirarsi; stringersi

tight-fisted ['taɪt'fɪstɪd] *adj* taccagno

tight'-fit'ting *adj* attillato

tight'rope' *s* corda tesa

tight' squeeze' *s*—**to be in a tight squeeze** (coll) essere alle strette

tight'wad' *s* (coll) spilorcio

tigress ['taɪgrɪs] *s* tigre femmina

tile [taɪl] *s* mattonella; (*for floor*) piastrella; (*for roof*) tegola, coppo || *tr* coprire di mattonelle; coprire di piastrelle; coprire di coppi

tile' roof' *s* tetto di tegole

till [tɪl] *s* cassetto dei soldi || *prep* fino a || *conj* fino a che . . . non, fino a che, sinché . . . non, sinché || *tr* lavorare, coltivare

tilt [tɪlt] *s* inclinazione; giostra, torneo; **full tilt** di gran carriera; a tutta forza || *tr* inclinare; (*a lance*) mettere in resta; attaccare || *intr* inclinarsi; giostrare; **to tilt at** combattere con

timber ['tɪmbər] *s* legno, legname *m* da costruzione; alberi *mpl;* (fig) tempra

tim'ber·land' *s* bosco per produrre legname

tim'ber line' *s* linea della vegetazione

timbre ['tɪmbər] *s* (phonet & phys) timbro

time [taɪm] *s* tempo; ora, e.g., **what time is it?** che ora è?; volta, e.g., **three times** tre volte; giorni *mpl*, e.g., **in our time** ai giorni nostri; momento; ultima ora; ore *fpl* lavorative; periodo, e.g., **Xmas time** periodo natalizio; **for a long time** da lungo; **for the time being** per ora, per il momento; **in time** presto; col tempo; **on time** a tempo; a rate; (*said, e.g., of a bus*) in orario; **times** volte, e.g., **seven times** seven sette volte sette; **to bide one's time** aspettare l'ora propizia; **to do time** (coll) essere in prigione; **to have a good time** divertirsi; **to have no time for** non poter sopportare; **to lose time** (*said of a watch*) ritardare; **to make time** avanzare rapidamente; guadagnare terreno; **to pass the time of day** fare una chiacchierata; salutarsi; **to take one's time** fare le cose senza fretta; **to tell time** leggere l'orologio || *tr* fissare il momento di; calcolare il tempo di; (sports) cronometrare

time' bomb' *s* bomba a orologeria

time'card' *s* cartellino di presenza

time' clock' *s* orologio di controllo (delle presenze)

time' expo'sure *s* (phot) posa

time' fuse' *s* spoletta a tempo

time'keep'er *s* marcatempo; orologio; (sports) cronometrista *mf*

timeless ['taɪmlɪs] *adj* senza fine, eterno

time·ly ['taɪmli] *adj* (-lier; -liest) opportuno, tempestivo

time'piece' *s* orologio; cronometro

time' sig'nal *s* segnale orario

time'ta'ble *s* orario; tabella di marcia

time'work' *s* lavoro a ore

time'worn' *adj* logorato dal tempo

time' zone' *s* fuso orario

timid ['tɪmɪd] *adj* timido, pavido

tim'ing gears' ['taɪmɪŋ] *spl* ingranaggi *mpl* di distribuzione

timorous ['tɪmərəs] *adj* timoroso

tin [tɪn] *s* (*element*) stagno; (*tin plate; can*) latta || *v* (*pret & pp* **tinned;** *ger* **tinning**) *tr* stagnare

tin' can' *s* latta

tincture ['tɪŋktʃər] *s* tintura

tin' cup' *s* tazzina metallica

tinder ['tɪndər] *s* esca

tin'der·box' *s* cassetta con l'esca e l'acciarino; persona eccitabile; (fig) polveriera

tin' foil' *s* stagnola

ting-a-ling ['tɪŋə‚lɪŋ] *s* dindìn *m*

tinge [tɪndʒ] *s* sfumatura; pizzico, punta || *v* (*ger* **tingeing** *or* **tinging**) *tr* sfumare; dare una traccia di sapore a

tingle ['tɪŋgəl] *s* formicolio, pizzicore *m* || *intr* informicolirsi, pizzicare; (*said of the ears*) ronzare; (*with enthusiasm*) fremere

tin' hat' *s* (slang) elmetto

tinker ['tɪŋkər] *s* calderaio, ramaio || *intr* armeggiare

tinkle ['tɪŋkəl] *s* tintinnio || *tr* far tintinnare || *intr* tintinnare

tin' plate' *s* latta

tin' roof' *s* tetto di lamiera di latta

tinsel ['tɪnsəl] *s* orpello, lustrino

tin'smith' *s* lattoniere *m*, stagnino

tin' sol'dier *s* soldatino di piombo

tint [tɪnt] *s* tinta, sfumatura || *tr* tinteggiare

tin'ware' *s* articoli *mpl* di latta

ti·ny ['taɪni] *adj* (**-nier; -niest**) piccino

tip [tɪp] *s* punta; (*of mountain*) vetta; (*of umbrella*) gorbia; (*of shoe*) mascherina; (*of cigarette*) bocchino; (*of shoestring*) aghetto; colpetto; (*fee*) mancia; informazione confidenziale; inclinazione || *v* (*pret & pp* **tipped;** *ger* **tipping**) *tr* mettere la punta a; inclinare, rovesciare; (*one's hat*) levarsi; dare la mancia a; toccare, battere; (*the scales*) far traboccare; **to tip in** (bb) inserire fuori testo; **to tip off** (coll) dare informazioni confidenziali a || *intr* inclinarsi; dare la mancia

tip'cart' *s* carro ribaltabile

tip'-off' *s* (coll) avvertimento confidenziale

tipped'-in' *adj* (bb) fuori testo

tipple ['tɪpəl] *intr* sbevucchiare

tip'staff' *s* usciere *m*

tip·sy ['tɪpsi] *adj* (**-sier; -siest**) brillo

tip'toe' *s* punta di piedi || *v* (*pret & pp* **-toed;** *ger* **-toeing**) *intr* camminare in punta di piedi

tirade ['taɪred] *s* tirata

tire [taɪr] *s* gomma, pneumatico; (*of metal*) cerchione *m* || *tr* stancare || *intr* stancarsi; infastidirsi

tire' chain' *s* catena antineve

tired [taɪrd] *adj* stanco, stracco

tire' gauge' *s* manometro della pressione delle gomme

tireless ['taɪrlɪs] *adj* infaticabile

tire' pres'sure *s* pressione (delle gomme)

tire' pump' *s* pompa (per i pneumatici)

tiresome ['taɪrsəm] *adj* faticoso; (*boring*) noioso

tissue ['tɪsju] *s* tessuto; tessuto finissimo, velina

tis'sue pa'per *s* carta velina

titanium [taɪ'teni·əm] *or* [tɪ'teni·əm] *s* titanio

tithe [taɪð] *s* decima || *tr* imporre la decima su; pagare la decima di

Titian ['tɪʃən] *adj* tizianesco || *s* Tiziano

title ['taɪtəl] *s* titolo; (sports) campionato || *tr* intitolare

ti'tle deed' *s* titolo di proprietà

ti'tle·hold'er *s* campione *m*, primatista *mf*

ti'tle page' *s* frontespizio

ti'tle role' *s* (theat) ruolo principale

tit'mouse' *s* (**-mice**) (orn) cincia

titter ['tɪtər] *s* risatina || *intr* ridacchiare

titular ['tɪtʃələr] *adj* titolare

TNT ['ti‚en'ti] *s* (letterword) tritolo

to [tu], [tʊ] *or* [tə] *adv*—**to and fro** da una parte all'altra, avanti e indietro; **to come to** tornare in sè || *prep* a, e.g., **he is going to Rome** va a Roma; **he gave a kiss to his mother**

diede un bacio a sua madre; **she is learning to sew** impara a cucire; per, e.g., **he has been a true friend to me** è stato un vero amico per me; da, e.g., **there is still a lot of work to do** c'è ancora molto lavoro da fare; con, e.g., **she was very kind to me** è stata molto gentile con me; in, e.g., **we went to church** siamo andati in chiesa; fino a, e.g., **to see s.o. to the station** accompagnare qlcu fino alla stazione; in confronto di, e.g., **the accounts are nothing to what really happened** le storie non sono nulla, in confronto di quanto è realmente successo; meno, e.g., **ten minutes to seven** le sette meno dieci

toad [tod] s rospo

toad'stool' s agarico, fungo velenoso

to-and-fro [tu-ənd'fro] adj avanti e indietro

toast [tost] s pane tostato; (drink to s.o.'s health) brindisi m; **a piece of toast** una fetta di pane tostato || tr tostare; brindare alla salute di || intr tostarsi; brindare

toaster ['tostər] s (of bread) tostapane m; persona che fa un brindisi

toast'mas'ter s persona che annuncia i brindisi, maestro di cerimonie

tobac·co [tə'bæko] s (-cos) tabacco

tobacconist [tə'bækənɪst] s tabaccaio

tobac'co pouch' s borsa da tabacco

toboggan [tə'bɑgən] s toboga m

tocsin ['tɑksɪn] s campana a martello; scampanata d'allarme

today [tu'de] s & adv oggi m

toddle ['tɑdəl] s passo vacillante || intr traballare, trotterellare

tod·dy ['tɑdi] s (-dies) ponce m

to-do [tə'du] s (-dos) (coll) daffare m, rumore m

toe [to] s dito del piede; (of shoe) punta || v (pret & pp toed; ger toeing) tr—**to toe the line** filare diritto

toe'nail' s unghia del piede

together [tu'geðər] adv insieme; **to bring together** riunire, riconciliare; **to call together** chiamare a raccolta; **to stick together** (coll) rimanere uniti, stare insieme

togs [tɑgz] spl vestiti mpl

toil [tɔɪl] s travaglio, sfacchinata; **toils** reti fpl, lacci mpl || intr travagliare, sfacchinare

toilet ['tɔɪlɪt] s toletta; gabinetto, ritirata; **to make one's toilet** farsi la toletta

toi'let pa'per s carta igienica

toi'let pow'der s polvere f di talco

toi'let soap' s sapone m da toletta

toi'let wa'ter s acqua da toletta

token ['tokən] s segno, marca; ricordo; (used as money) gettone m; **by the same token** per di più; **in token of** in segno di, come prova di

tolerance ['tɑlərəns] s tolleranza

tolerate ['tɑlə,ret] tr tollerare

toll [tol] s (of bell) rintocco; (e.g., for passage over bridge) pedaggio; (tax) dazio; (compensation for grinding grains) molenda; (number of victims) perdite fpl; (telp) tariffa inter-

urbana || tr (a bell) sonare a morto; (the faithful) chiamare a raccolta || intr sonare a morto

toll' bridge' s ponte m a pedaggio

toll' call' s (telp) chiamata interurbana

toll'gate' s barriera di pedaggio; (in a turnpike) casello

toma·to [tə'meto] or [tə'mato] s (-toes) pomodoro

toma'to juice' s sugo di pomodoro

tomb [tum] s tomba

tomboy ['tɑm,bɔɪ] s maschietta

tomb'stone' s pietra tombale, lapide f

tomcat ['tɑm,kæt] s gatto maschio

tome [tom] s tomo

tomorrow [tu'mɑro] or [tu'mɔro] s domani m; **the day after tomorrow** dopodomani m || adv domani

tom-tom ['tɑm,tɑm] s tam-tam m

ton [tʌn] s tonnellata; **tons** (coll) montagne fpl

tone [ton] s tono; (fig) tenore m || tr intonare; **to tone down** (colors) smorzare; (sounds) sfumare || intr intonarsi; **to tone down** moderarsi; **to tone up** rinforzarsi

tone' po'em s poema sinfonico

tongs [tɔŋz] or [tɑŋz] spl tenaglie fpl; (e.g., for sugar) molle fpl

tongue [tʌŋ] s (language) lingua; (of bell) battaglio; (of shoe) linguetta; (of wagon) timone m; (anat) lingua; (carp) maschio; **tongue in cheek** poco sinceramente; **to hold one's tongue** mordersi la lingua; **to speak with forked tongue** essere di due lingue

tongue' depres'sor s abbassalingua m

tongue'-lash'ing s sgridata

tongue' twist'er s scioglilingua m

tonic ['tɑnɪk] adj & s tonico

tonight [tu'naɪt] s questa sera, questa notte || adv stasera; stanotte

tonnage ['tʌnɪdʒ] s tonnellaggio, stazza

tonsil ['tɑnsəl] s tonsilla

ton·y ['toni] adj (-ier; -iest) (slang) elegante, di lusso

too [tu] adv (also) anche, pure; (more than enough) troppo; **too bad!** peccato!; **too many** troppi; **too much** troppo

tool [tul] s utensile m, attrezzo; (person) strumento; (of lathe) punta || tr lavorare; (bb) decorare

tool' bag' s borsa degli attrezzi

tool'box' s cassetta attrezzi

tool'mak'er s attrezzista m

tool'shed' s barchessa

toot [tut] s (of horn) suono; (of locomotive) fischio; (of car's horn) colpo; (coll) gazzarra || tr strombettare; **to toot one's own horn** strombazzare i propri meriti || intr strombettare

tooth [tuθ] s (teeth [tiθ]) dente m

tooth'ache' s mal m di denti

tooth'brush' s spazzolino da denti

toothless ['tuθlɪs] adj sdentato

tooth'paste' s pasta dentifricia

tooth'pick' s stuzzicadenti m

tooth' pow'der s polvere dentifricia

top [tɑp] s cima, sommo, vertice m; (upper part of anything) disopra m;

(of mountain, tree) vetta; *(of box)* coperchio; *(beginning)* principio; *(of bottle)* imboccatura; *(of a bridge)* testata; *(of wagon)* mantice *m*; *(of car)* tetto; *(of wall)* coronamento; *(toy)* trottola; (naut) gabbia; **at the top of one's voice** a perdifiato; **from top to bottom** daccapo a piedi, dal principio alla fine; **on top of** in cima di; subito dopo; **the tops** (coll) il migliore, il fiore; **to blow one's top** (slang) dare in escandescenze; **to sleep like a top** dormire come un ghiro ‖ *v (pret & pp* **topped***) ger* **topping** *tr (a tree)* svettare; coronare; superare

topaz ['topæz] *s* topazio

top' bil'ling *s*—**to get top billing** essere artista di cartello; (journ) ricevere il posto più importante

top' boot' *s* stivale *m* a tromba

top'coat' *s* soprabito di mezza stagione

toper ['topər] *s* ubriacone *m*

topgal'lant sail' [ˌtap'gælənt] *s* (naut) pappafico, veletta

top' hat' *s* cappello a staio or a cilindro

top'-heav'y *adj* troppo pesante in cima, sovraccarico in cima

topic ['tapɪk] *s* topica, tema *m*

top'knot' *s* crocchia

topless ['taplɪs] *adj (mountain)* di cui non si vede la vetta, eccelso; *(bathing suit)* topless

top'mast' *s* (naut) alberetto

top'most' *adj* il più alto

topogra·phy [tə'pagrəfi] *s* (**-phies**) topografia

topple ['tapəl] *tr* abbattere, rovesciare ‖ *intr* rovesciarsi, cadere

top' prior'ity *s* priorità massima

topsail ['tapsəl] or ['tap,sel] *s* (naut) gabbia

top'-se'cret *adj* segretissimo

top'soil' *s* strato superiore del terreno

topsy-turvy ['tapsi'tʌrvi] *adj* rovesciato; confuso ‖ *s* soqquadro ‖ *adv* a soqquadro

torch [tɔrtʃ] *s* fiaccola, torcia; **to carry the torch for** (slang) amare disperatamente

torch'bear'er *s* portatore *m* di fiaccola; (fig) capo, guida *m*

torch'light' *s* luce *f* di fiaccola

torch' song' *s* canzone *f* triste d'amore non corrisposto

torment ['tɔrment] *s* tormento ‖ [tɔr'ment] *tr* tormentare

torna·do [tɔr'nedo] *s* (**-dos** or **-does**) tornado, tromba d'aria

torpe·do [tɔr'pido] *s* (**-does**) siluro ‖ *tr* silurare

torpe'do boat' *s* motosilurante *f*

torpe'do-boat destroy'er *s* torpediniera

torrent ['tarənt] or ['tɔrənt] *s* torrente *m*

torrid ['tarɪd] or ['tɔrɪd] *adj* torrido

torsion ['tɔrʃən] *s* torsione

tor'sion bar' *s* barra di torsione

tor·so ['tɔrso] *s* (**-sos**) torso

tortoise ['tɔrtəs] *s* tartaruga

tor'toise shell' *s* tartaruga

torture ['tɔrtʃər] *s* tortura ‖ *tr* torturare

toss [tɔs] or [tas] *s* lancio, getto ‖ *tr* lanciare, gettare; *(to fling about)* sballottare; *(one's head)* alzare sdegnosamente; agitare; rivoltare; *(an opinion)* avventare; **to toss off** fare rapidamente; *(e.g., a drink)* buttar giù; **to toss up** *(a coin)* gettar in aria, gettare a testa e croce; (coll) rigettare ‖ *intr* agitarsi, dimenarsi; **to toss and turn** *(in bed)* girarsi; **to toss up** giocare a testa e croce

toss'up' *s* testa e croce; (coll) eguale probabilità *f*

tot [tat] *s* bambino, piccolo

to·tal ['totəl] *adj* totale; *(e.g., loss)* completo ‖ *s* totale *m* ‖ *v (pret & pp* **-taled** or **-talled***) ger* **-taling** or **-talling***) tr* ammontare a; *(to make a total of)* sommare

totalitarian [to,tælɪ'terɪ-ən] *adj* totalitario ‖ *s* aderente *mf* al totalitarismo

totter ['tatər] *s* vacillamento ‖ *intr* vacillare

touch [tʌtʃ] *s (act)* tocco; *(sense)* tatto; *(of an illness)* leggero attacco; *(slight amount)* punta; *(for money)* (slang) stoccata; **to get in touch with** mettersi in contatto con; **to lose one's touch** perdere il tocco personale ‖ *tr* toccare; raggiungere; riguardare; *(for a loan)* (slang) dare una stoccata a; **to touch on** menzionare; **to touch up** ritoccare ‖ *intr* toccare; **to touch down** (aer) atterrare

touching ['tʌtʃɪŋ] *adj* toccante, commovente ‖ *prep* riguardo a

touch'stone' *s* pietra di paragone

touch' type'writing *s* dattilografia a tatto

touch·y ['tʌtʃi] *adj* (**-ier; -iest**) suscettibile, permaloso; delicato, precario, rischioso

tough [tʌf] *adj* duro; forte; *(luck)* cattivo; violento ‖ *s* malvivente *m*

toughen ['tʌfən] *tr* indurire ‖ *intr* indurirsi

tough' luck' *s* disdetta, sfortuna

tour [tur] *s* gita, viaggio; (sports) giro; (mil) turno; (theat) tournée *f* ‖ *tr* girare; (theat) portare in tournée ‖ *intr* girare; (theat) andare in tournée

tour'ing car' ['turɪŋ] *s* automobile *f* da turismo

tourist ['turɪst] *adj* turistico ‖ *s* turista *mf*

tournament ['turnəmənt] or ['tʌrnəmənt] *s* torneo

tourney ['turni] or ['tʌrni] *s* torneo ‖ *intr* giostrare

tourniquet ['turnɪˌket] or ['tʌrnɪˌke] *s* laccio emostatico

tousle ['tauzəl] *tr* spettinare

tow [to] *s* rimorchio; *(e.g., of hemp)* stoppa; **to take in tow** prendere a rimorchio ‖ *tr* rimorchiare

toward(s) [tord(z)] or [tə'word(z)] *prep (in the direction of)* verso; *(in respect to)* per; *(near)* vicino a; *(a certain hour)* su, verso

tow'boat' *s* rimorchiatore *m*

tow' car' *s* rimorchiatore *m*

tow·el ['tau·əl] *s* asciugamano; *(of paper)* salvietta; **to throw in the**

towel (slang) gettare la spugna ‖ *v* (*pret & pp* -eled or -elled; *ger* -eling or -elling) *tr* asciugare

tow'el rack' *s* portaasciugamani *m*

tower ['tau·ər] *s* torre *f* ‖ *intr* torreggiare

towering ['tau·ərɪŋ] *adj* torreggiante; gigantesco; eccessivo

towline ['to‚laɪn] *s* cavo di rimorchio

town [taun] *s* città *f;* (*townspeople*) cittadinanza; **in town** in città

town' clerk' *s* segretario municipale

town' coun'cil *s* consiglio comunale

town' cri'er *s* banditore *m* municipale

town' hall' *s* municipio

township ['taun/ɪp] *s* suddivisione di contea

towns'man *s* (-men) cittadino; concittadino

towns'peo'ple *spl* cittadini *mpl;* gente *f* di città

town' talk' *s* dicerie *fpl,* pettegolezzi *mpl*

tow'path' *s* strada d'alaggio

tow'rope' *s* corda da rimorchio

tow' truck' *s* autogru *f*

toxic ['taksɪk] *adj & s* tossico

toy [tɔɪ] *adj* giocattolo; di giocattoli ‖ *s* giocattolo; (*trifle*) nonnulla *m;* (*trinket*) gingillo ‖ *intr* giocare; **to toy with** (*to play with*) giocare con; (*to trifle, e.g., with food*) baloccarsi con; (*an idea*) accarezzare; (*to flirt with*) flirtare con

toy' bank' *s* salvadanaio

toy' sol'dier *s* soldatino di piombo

trace [tres] *s* straccia, vestigio; (*tracing*) tracciato; (*of harness*) tirella; (fig) ombra ‖ *tr* tracciare; (*e.g., s.o.'s ancestry*) rintracciare; (*a pattern*) lucidare

trac'er bul'let ['tresər] *s* pallottola tracciante

trache·a ['trekɪ·ə] *s* (-ae [‚i]) trachea

tracing ['tresɪŋ] *s* tracciato

track [træk] *s* (*of foot*) traccia, pesta; (*rut*) solco, rotaia; (*of boat*) scia; corso; (*course followed by boat*) rotta; (*of tape recorder*) pista; (*of tractor*) cingolo; (*of ideas*) successione; (*width of a vehicle measured from wheel to wheel*) (aut) carreggiata; (rr) binario; (*track and field*) (sports) atletica leggera; (*for horses*) (sports) galoppatoio; (*for running*) (sports) pista, corsia; **to keep track of** non perder di vista; **to lose track of** perder di vista; **to make tracks** (coll) affrettarsi; **to stop in one's tracks** (coll) fermarsi di colpo ‖ *tr* rintracciare, seguire le tracce di; lasciare tracce su; **to track down** rintracciare

track'ing sta'tion ['trækɪŋ] *s* (rok) stazione di avvistamento

track'less trol'ley ['træklɪs] *s* filobus *m*

track' meet' *s* incontro di atletica leggera

track'walk'er *s* (rr) guardialinee *m*

tract [trækt] *s* tratto, opuscolo, trattatello; (anat) tubo, canale *m*

traction ['træk/ən] *s* trazione

trac'tion com'pany *s* società *f* di trasporti urbani

tractor ['træktər] *s* trattore *m;* (*of a tractor-trailer*) motrice *f*

trac'tor-trail'er *s* treno stradale

trade [tred] *s* commercio; affare *m;* occupazione, mestiere *m;* (*people*) commercianti *mpl,* professionisti *mpl;* mercato; (*customers*) clientela; (*in slaves*) tratta ‖ *tr* mercanteggiare; cambiare; **to trade in** dare come pagamento parziale ‖ *intr* trafficare, commerciare; comprare; **to trade in** lavorare in; **to trade on** approfittarsi di

trade'mark' *s* marca or marchio di fabbrica

trade' name' *s* ragione sociale

trader ['tredər] *s* trafficante *m*

trade' school' *s* scuola d'avviamento professionale, scuola d'arti e mestieri

trades'man *s* (-men) commerciante *m;* artigiano

trade' un'ion *s* sindacato di lavoratori

trade' u'nionist *s* sindacalista *mf*

trade' winds' *spl* alisei *mpl*

trad'ing post' *s* centro di scambi commerciali; (*in stock exchange*) posto delle compravendite

trad'ing stamp' *s* buono premio

tradition [trə'dɪ/ən] *s* tradizione

traditional [trə'dɪ/ənəl] *adj* tradizionale

traduce [trə'djus] or [trə'dus] *tr* calunniare

traf·fic ['træfɪk] *s* traffico, circolazione; commercio; comunicazione ‖ *v* (*pret & pp* -ficked; *ger* -ficking) *intr* trafficare

traf'fic cir'cle *s* raccordo a circolazione rotatoria

traf'fic court' *s* tribunale *m* della polizia stradale

traf'fic is'land *s* isola spartitraffico

traf'fic jam' *s* intralcio del traffico, ingorgo stradale

traf'fic light' *s* semaforo

traf'fic man'ager *s* dirigente *m* del traffico; (rr) gestore *m* di stazione

traf'fic sign' *s* segnale *m* di circolazione stradale, cartello indicatore

traf'fic tick'et *s* contravvenzione per violazione del traffico

tragedian [trə'dʒidɪ·ən] *s* tragico

trage·dy ['trædʒɪdɪ] *s* (-dies) tragedia

tragic ['trædʒɪk] *adj* tragico

trail [trel] *s* sentiero; (*track*) traccia, pista; (*of robe*) strascico, coda; (*of smoke*) pennacchio; (*left by an airplane*) striscia; (*of people*) codazzo ‖ *tr* strascicare; essere sulla fatta di; (*e.g., dust on the road*) sollevare; (*mud*) lasciar cadere ‖ *intr* strascicare;—(*said, e.g., of a snake*) strisciare; (*said of a plant*) arrampicarsi; **to trail off** mutare; (*to weaken*) affievolirsi

trailer ['trelər] *s* traino; (*to haul freight*) semirimorchio; (*for living*) carovana, roulotte *f;* (bot) rampicante *m*

train [tren] *s* (*of vehicles*) convoglio; (*of robe*) strascico; (*of thought*) ordine *m;* (*of people*) coda; (rr) treno ‖ *tr* addestrare, impratichire; (*a weapon*) puntare, rivolgere; (*a horse*) scozzonare; (*e.g., a dog*) ammaestrare; (*a plant*) far crescere; (sports) allenare ‖ *intr* addestrarsi; ammaestrarsi; (sports) allenarsi

trained' nurse' *s* infermiera diplomata

trainer ['trenər] *s* allenatore *m*

training ['trenɪŋ] *s* esercizio, esercitazione; (sports) allenamento

train'ing camp' *s* campo addestramento

train'ing school' *s* scuola di addestramento professionale; riformatorio

train'ing ship' *s* nave *f* scuola

trait [tret] *s* tratto, caratteristica

traitor ['tretər] *s* traditore *m*

traitress ['tretrɪs] *s* traditrice *f*

trajecto•ry [trə'dʒɛktərɪ] *s* (-ries) traiettoria

tramp [træmp] *s* lunga camminata; vagabondo; (*hussy*) sgualdrina ‖ *tr* attraversare; calpestare ‖ *intr* camminare a passi fermi; fare il vagabondo

trample ['træmpəl] *tr* calpestare; (fig) conculcare ‖ *intr*—**to trample on** or **upon** calpestare

trampoline ['træmpə,lin] *s* trampolino di olona per salti mortali

tramp' steam'er *s* carretta

trance [træns] or [trɑns] *s* trance *f;* (*dazed condition*) estasi *f*

tranquil ['træŋkwɪl] *adj* tranquillo

tranquilize ['træŋkwɪ ,laɪz] *tr* tranquillizzare ‖ *intr* tranquillizzarsi

tranquilizer ['træŋkwɪ ,laɪzər] *s* tranquillante *m*

tranquillity [træn'kwɪlɪtɪ] *s* tranquillità *f*

transact [træn'zækt] or [træns'ækt] *tr* sbrigare, trattare

transaction [træn'zæk/ən] or [træns'æk/ən] *s* disbrigo, operazione

transatlantic [,trænsət'læntɪk] *adj & s* transatlantico

transcend [træn'sɛnd] *tr* trascendere, sorpassare ‖ *intr* eccellere

transcribe [træn'skraɪb] *tr* trascrivere

transcript ['trænskrɪpt] *s* copia; traduzione; (educ) copia ufficiale del certificato di studi

transcription [træn'skrɪp/ən] *s* trascrizione

transept ['trænsɛpt] *s* transetto

trans•fer ['trænsfər] *s* trasferimento; passaggio; (*pattern*) rapporto; (*of funds*) giro; (*of real estate*) compravendita; (law) voltura ‖ [træns'fʌr] or ['trænsfər] *v* (*pret & pp* -**ferred;** *ger* -**ferring**) *tr* trasferire, trasportare; (*funds*) stornare; (*a design*) rapportare; (*real estate*) comprandere ‖ *intr* trasferirsi; cambiare di treno

trans'fer tax' *s* tassa di successione; tassa sulla compravendita

transfix [træns'fɪks] *tr* trafiggere; paralizzare, inchiodare

transform [træns'fɔrm] *tr* trasformare; (elec) trasformare ‖ *intr* trasformarsi

transforma'tional gram'mar [,trænsfər-

'me/ənəl] *s* grammatica trasformativa

transformer [træns'fɔrmər] *s* trasformatore *m*

transfusion [træns'fju/ən] *s* trasfusione

transgress [træns'grɛs] *tr* trasgredire; (*a limit or boundry*) oltrepassare ‖ *intr* peccare

transgression [træns'grɛ/ən] *s* trasgressione; peccato

transient ['træn/ənt] *adj* passeggero, temporaneo; di passaggio ‖ *s* ospite *mf* di passaggio

transistor [træn'zɪstər] *s* transistore *m*

transit ['trænsɪt] or ['trænzɪt] *s* transito

transition [træn'zɪ/ən] *s* transizione

transitional [træn'zɪ/ənəl] *adj* di transizione

transitive ['trænsɪtɪv] *adj* transitivo ‖ *s* verbo transitivo

transitory ['trænsɪ ,torɪ] *adj* transitorio

translate [træns'let] or ['trænslet] *tr* tradurre; convertire; (*to transfer*) trasportare ‖ *intr* tradursi

translation [træns'le/ən] *s* traduzione; trasformazione; (telg) ritrasmissione

translator [træns'letər] *s* traduttore *m*

transliterate [træns'lɪtə ,ret] *tr* traslitterare

translucent [træns'lusənt] *adj* traslucido; (fig) chiaro

transmission [træns'mɪ/ən] *s* trasmissione; (aut) trasmissione

trans•mit [træns'mɪt] *v* (*pret & pp* -**mitted;** *ger* -**mitting**) *tr & intr* trasmettere

transmitter [træns'mɪtər] *s* trasmettitore *m*

transmit'ting set' *s* emittente *f*

transmit'ting sta'tion *s* stazione trasmettitrice

transmute [træns'mjut] *tr & intr* trasmutare

transom ['trænsəm] *s* (*crosspiece*) traversa; (*window over door*) vasistas *m;* (naut) specchio di poppa

transparen•cy ['træns'pɛrənsɪ] *s* (-cies) trasparenza; (*design on a translucent substance*) trasparente *m;* (phot) diapositiva

transparent [træns'pɛrənt] *adj* trasparente

transpire [træns'paɪr] *intr* (*to happen*) avvenire; (*to perspire*) traspirare; (*to become known*) trapelare

transplant [træns'plænt] or [træns'plɑnt] *tr* trapiantare ‖ *intr* trapiantarsi

transport ['trænsport] *s* trasporto; mezzo di trasporto ‖ [træns'port] *tr* trasportare

transportation [,trænspor'te/ən] *s* trasporto; trasporti *mpl*, locomozione; biglietto di trasporto

trans'port work'er *s* ferrotranviere *m*

transpose [træns'poz] *tr* trasporre; (mus) trasportare

trans•ship [træns'/ɪp] *v* (*pret & pp* -**shipped;** *ger* -**shipping**) *tr* trasbordare

trap [træp] *s* trappola, tranello;

(double-curved pipe) sifone *m;* (slang) bocca; (sports) congegno lanciapiattelli ‖ *v (pret & pp* **trapped;** *ger* **trapping)** *tr* intrappolare, accalappiare

trap' door' *s* trabocchetto, botola; (theat) ribalta

trapeze [trə'piz] *s* (sports) trapezio

trapezoid ['træpɪˌzɔɪd] *s* (geom) trapezio, trapezoide *m*

trapper ['træpər] *s* cacciatore *m* di animali da pelliccia con trappole

trappings ['træpɪŋz] *spl* ornamenti *mpl;* *(for a horse)* gualdrappa

trap'shoot'ing *s* tiro al piattello

trash [træʃ] *s* immondizia, spazzatura; *(nonsense)* sciocchezze *fpl;* *(junk)* ciarpame *m;* *(worthless people)* gentaglia

trash' can' *s* portaimmondizie *m*

travail ['trævel] or [trə'vel] *s* travaglio; travaglio di parto

trav·el ['trævəl] *s* viaggio; traffico; (mach) corsa ‖ *v (pret & pp* **-eled** or **-elled;** *ger* **-eling** or **-elling)** *tr* viaggiare per, percorrere ‖ *intr* viaggiare; muoversi; (coll) andare

trav'el a'gency *s* ufficio turistico

traveler ['trævələr] *s* viaggiatore *m*

trav'eler's check' *s* assegno viaggiatori

trav'eling bag' *s* sacca da viaggio

trav'eling expens'es *spl* spese *fpl* di viaggio; *(per diem)* trasferta

trav'eling sales'man *s* **(-men)** commesso viaggiatore

traverse ['trævərs] or [trə'vʌrs] *tr* attraversare

traves·ty ['trævɪsti] *s* **(-ties)** parodia ‖ *v (pret & pp* **-tied)** *tr* parodiare

trawl [trɔl] *s* *(fishing net)* rete *f* a strascico; *(fishing line)* lenza al traino ‖ *tr & intr* pescare con la rete a strascico; pescare con la lenza al traino

trawling ['trɔlɪŋ] *s* pesca con la rete a strascico; pesca con la lenza al traino

tray [tre] *s* guantiera, vassoio; (chem, phot) bacinella

treacherous ['tretʃərəs] *adj* traditore, subdolo; incerto, pericoloso

treacher·y ['tretʃəri] *s* **(-ies)** tradimento

tread [tred] *s* *(step)* passo; *(of shoe)* suola; *(of tire)* battistrada *m;* *(of stairs)* pedata ‖ *v (pret* **trod** [trad]; *pp* **trodden** ['tradən] or **trod)** *tr* calpestare; *(the boards)* calcare; accoppiarsi con ‖ *intr* camminare; **to tread on** calpestare

treadle ['tredəl] *s* pedale *m*

tread'mill' *s* ruota azionata col camminare; (fig) lavoro ingrato

treason ['trizən] *s* tradimento

treasonable ['trizənəbəl] *adj* traditore

treasure ['treʒər] *s* tesoro ‖ *tr* far tesoro di

treasurer ['treʒərər] *s* tesoriere *m*

treas'ure hunt' *s* caccia al tesoro

treasur·y ['treʒəri] *s* **(-ies)** tesoreria; tesoro, erario

treat [trit] *s* trattenimento; *(something affording pleasure)* piacere *m,* diletto ‖ *tr* trattare; *(to cure)* curare, medi-

care; offrire un trattenimento a ‖ *intr* trattare; pagare per il trattenimento

treatise ['tritɪs] *s* trattato

treatment ['tritmənt] *s* trattamento; *(of a theme)* trattazione

trea·ty ['triti] *s* **(-ties)** trattato

treble ['trebəl] *adj (threefold)* triplo; (mus) soprano ‖ *s (person)* soprano *mf;* *(voice)* soprano ‖ *tr* triplicare ‖ *intr* triplicarsi

tree [tri] *s* albero

tree' farm' *s* bosco ceduo

tree' frog' *s* raganella

treeless ['trilɪs] *adj* spoglio, senza alberi

tree'top' *s* cima dell'albero

trellis ['trelɪs] *s* traliccio, graticcio

trem·ble ['trembəl] *s* tremito ‖ *intr* tremare

tremendous [trɪ'mendəs] *adj* tremendo

tremor ['tremər] or ['trimər] *s* tremito; *(of earth)* scossa

trench [trentʃ] *s* fosso, canale *m;* (mil) trincea

trenchant ['trentʃənt] *adj* mordace, caustico; vigoroso; incisivo

trench' coat' *s* trench *m*

trench' mor'tar *s* lanciabombe *m*

trend [trend] *s* tendenza, orientamento ‖ *intr* tendere, dirigersi

Trent [trent] *s* Trento *f*

trespass ['trespəs] *s* (law) intrusione, violazione di proprietà ‖ *intr* entrare senza diritto, intrudersi; peccare; **no trespassing** divieto di passaggio; **to trespass against** peccare contro; **to trespass on** entrare abusivamente in; *(e.g., s.o.'s time)* abusare di; violare

tress [tres] *s* treccia

trestle ['tresəl] *s* cavalletto; viadotto a cavalletti; ponte *m* a cavalletti

trial ['traɪ-əl] *s* tentativo, prova; tribolazione, croce *f;* (law) giudizio, processo; **on trial** in prova; (law) sotto processo; **to bring to trial** sottoporre a processo

tri'al and er'ror *s* metodo per tentativo; **by trial and error** a tastoni

tri'al balloon' *s* pallone *m* sonda

tri'al by ju'ry *s* processo con giuria

tri'al ju'ry *s* giuria civile o processuale

tri'al or'der *s* (com) ordine *m* di prova

tri'al run' *s* viaggio di prova

triangle ['traɪˌæŋgəl] *s* triangolo; *(in drafting)* quartabuono

tribe [traɪb] *s* tribù *f*

tribunal [trɪ'bjunəl] or [traɪ'bjunəl] *s* tribunale *m*

tribune ['trɪbjun] *s* tribuna

tributar·y ['trɪbjəˌteri] *adj* tributario ‖ *s* **(-ies)** tributario

tribute ['trɪbjut] *s* tributo; **to pay tribute to** *(e.g., beauty)* rendere omaggio a

trice [traɪs] *s* momento, istante *m;* **in a trice** in un batter d'occhio

trick [trɪk] *s* gherminella, inganno; trucco, tiro, scherzo; *(knack)* abilità *f;* *(feat)* atto; *(set of cards won)* presa; turno; (coll) piccola; **to be up to one's old tricks** farne una delle sue; **to play a dirty trick on** fare un brutto tiro a‖ *tr* giocare, ingannare

tricker·y ['trɪkəri] *s* (-ies) gherminella, inganno

trickle ['trɪkəl] *s* gocciolio, filo ‖ *intr* gocciolare; (*said of people*) andare or venire alla spicciolata; (*said of news*) trapelare

trickster ['trɪkstər] *s* imbroglione *m*

trick·y ['trɪki] *adj* (-ier; -iest) ingannatore; (*machine*) complicato; (*ticklish to deal with*) delicato

tried [traɪd] *adj* fedele, provato

trifle ['traɪfəl] *s* bazzecola, bagattella; (*small amount of money*) piccolezza, miseria; **a trifle un po'** ‖ *tr*—**to trifle away** sprecare ‖ *intr* gingillarsi; **to trifle with** giocherellare con; scherzare con; divertirsi con

trifling ['traɪflɪŋ] *adj* futile; insignificante, trascurabile

trifocal [traɪ'fokəl] *adj* trifocale ‖ **trifocals** *spl* occhiali *mpl* trifocali

trigger ['trɪgər] *s* (*of a firearm*) grilletto; (*of any device*) leva di sgancio ‖ *tr* (*a gun*) far sparare; (fig) scatenare

trigonometry [ˌtrɪgə'nɑmɪtri] *s* trigonometria

trill [trɪl] *s* trillo, gorgheggio; vibrazione; (*speech sound*) (phonet) vibrante *f* ‖ *tr* gorgheggiare; pronunziare con vibrazione ‖ *intr* trillare, gorgheggiare

trillion ['trɪljən] *s* trilione *m*

trilo·gy ['trɪlədʒi] *s* (-gies) trilogia

trim [trɪm] *adj* (**trimmer; trimmest**) lindo, azzimato ‖ *s* condizione; buona condizione; (*dress*) vestito; (*of hair*) taglio, sfumatura; decorazione, ornamento; (*of sails*) orientamento; (aut) attrezzatura della carrozzeria ‖ *v* (*pret & pp* **trimmed;** *ger* **trimming**) *tr* tagliare; (*an edge*) rifilare; adattare; arrangiare; (*Christmas tree*) decorare; (*hair*) sfumare; (*a tree*) potare; ordinare, assettare; (*a sail*) orientare; (aer) equilibrare; (mach) sbavare; (coll) rimproverare; (coll) bastonare; (*to defeat* coll) battere, vincere

trimming ['trɪmɪŋ] *s* ornamento, guarnizione; (coll) battitura, batosta; **trimmings** guarnizioni *mpl*; (mach) sbavatura; (mach) rifilatura

trini·ty ['trɪnɪti] *s* (-ties) (*group of three*) triade *f* ‖ **Trinity** *s* Trinità *f*

trinket ['trɪŋkɪt] *s* (*small ornament*) ninnolo, gingillo; **trinkets** (*trivial objects*) paccottiglia

tri·o ['tri·o] *s* (-os) terzetto

trip [trɪp] *s* viaggio; corsa; (*stumble*) inciampata; (*act of causing s.o. to stumble*) sgambetto; (*error*) passo falso; passo agile ‖ *v* (*pret & pp* **tripped;** *ger* **tripping**) *tr* far inciampare, far cadere; fare lo sgambetto a; cogliere in fallo; (mach) far scattare ‖ *intr* inciampare; fare un passo falso; avanzare saltellando, saltellare; **to trip over** inciampare in

tripartite [traɪ'pɑrtaɪt] *adj* tripartito

tripe [traɪp] *s* trippa; (slang) sciocchezze *fpl*

trip'ham'mer *s* maglio meccanico

triphthong ['trɪfθɔŋ] or ['trɪfθɑŋ] *s* trittongo

triple ['trɪpəl] *adj & s* triplo ‖ *tr* triplicare ‖ *intr* triplicarsi

triplet ['trɪplɪt] *s* (*offspring*) nato da un parto trigemino; (mus, poet) terzina

triplicate ['trɪplɪkɪt] *adj* triplicato ‖ *s* triplice copia ‖ ['trɪplɪˌket] *tr* triplicare

tripod ['traɪpɑd] *s* (*e.g., for a camera*) treppiede *m*; (*stool with three legs*) tripode *m*

triptych ['trɪptɪk] *s* trittico

trite [traɪt] *adj* trito, ritrito

triumph ['traɪ·əmf] *s* trionfo ‖ *intr* trionfare

trium'phal arch' [traɪ'ʌmfəl] *s* arco trionfale

trivia ['trɪvɪ·ə] *spl* banalità *f*, futilità *f*

trivial ['trɪvɪ·əl] *adj* insignificante, futile, banale

Trojan ['trodʒən] *adj & s* troiano

Tro'jan Horse' *s* cavallo di Troia

Tro'jan War' *s* guerra troiana

troll [trol] *tr & intr* pescare con la lenza al traino, pescare con il cucchiaino

trolley ['trɑli] *s* asta di presa, trolley *m*; carrozza tranviaria, tram *m*

trol'ley bus' *s* filobus *m*

trol'ley car' *s* vettura tranviaria, tram *m*

trol'ley pole' *s* trolley *m*

trollop ['trɑləp] *s* (*slovenly woman*) sciattona; (*hussy*) sgualdrina

trombone ['trɑmbon] *s* trombone *m*

troop [trup] *s* truppa, gruppo; (*of animals*) branco; (*of cavalry*) squadrone *m*; **troops** soldati *mpl* ‖ *intr* raggrupparsi; marciare insieme

trooper ['trupər] *s* soldato di cavalleria; poliziotto a cavallo; **to swear like a trooper** bestemmiare come un turco

tro·phy ['trofi] *s* (-phies) trofeo; (*any memento*) ricordo

tropic ['trɑpɪk] *adj* tropicale ‖ *s* tropico; **tropics** zona tropicale

tropical ['trɑpɪkəl] *adj* tropicale

troposphere ['trɑpəˌsfɪr] *s* troposfera

trot [trɑt] *s* trotto ‖ *v* (*pret & pp* **trotted;** *ger* **trotting**) *tr* far trottare; **to trot out** (coll) squadernare, esibire ‖ *intr* trottare

troth [troθ] or [troθ] *s* promessa di matrimonio; **by my troth** affé di Dio; **in troth** in verità; **to plight one's troth** impegnarsi; dare la parola

troubadour ['trubəˌdor] or ['trubəˌdur] *s* trovatore *m*

trouble ['trʌbəl] *s* disturbo, fastidio; inconveniente *m*, grattacapo; disordine *m*, conflitto; (*of a mechanical nature*) panna, guasto; **not to be worth the trouble** non valere la pena; **that's the trouble** questo è il male; **the trouble is that** il guaio è che; **to be in trouble** essere nei guai; **to be**

looking for trouble andare a cercarsi le grane; **to get into trouble** mettersi nei pasticci; **to have trouble in** + *ger* durar fatica a + *inf;* **to take the trouble** incomodarsi || *tr* molestare, disturbare; *(e.g., water)* intorbidare; dar del filo da torcere a; **to be troubled with** soffrire di; **to trouble oneself** scomodarsi

trou'ble light' s lampada di soccorso

trou'ble-mak'er s mettimale *mf*

troubleshooter ['trʌbəl ˌʃutər] s localizzatore *m* di guasti; *(in disputes)* paciere *m,* conciliatore *m*

troubleshooting ['trʌbəl ˌʃutɪŋ] s localizzazione dei guasti; *(of disputes)* composizione

troublesome ['trʌbəlsəm] adj molesto; difficile

trou'ble spot' s luogo di disordini, polveriera

trough [trɔf] or [traf] s *(to knead bread)* madia; *(for feeding pigs)* trogolo; *(for feeding animals)* mangiatoia; *(for watering animals)* abbeveratoio; *(gutter)* doccia; *(between two waves)* cavo

troupe [trup] s troupe *f*

trouper ['trupər] s membro della troupe; vecchio attore; tipo di cui ci si può fidare

trousers ['trauzərz] spl pantaloni *mpl*

trousseau [tru'so] or ['truso] s (-seaux or -seaus) corredo da sposa

trout [traut] s trota

trouvère [tru'vɛr] s troviero

trowel ['trau·əl] s cazzuola, mestola

Troy [trɔɪ] s Troia

truant ['tru·ənt] s fannullone *m;* **to play truant** marinare la scuola

truce [trus] s tregua

truck [trʌk] s autocarro, camion *m; (tractor-trailer)* autotreno; *(van)* furgone *m; (to be moved by hand)* carretto; verdura per il mercato; *(mach, rr)* carrello; *(coll)* robaccia; *(coll)* relazioni *fpl* || *tr* trasportare per autocarro, autotrasportare

truck'driv'er s camionista *m*

truck' farm' s fattoria agricola per la produzione degli ortaggi

truculent ['trʌkjələnt] or ['trukjələnt] adj truculento

trudge [trʌdʒ] *intr* camminare; **to trudge along** camminare laboriosamente, scarpinare

true [tru] adj vero; esatto, conforme; legittimo; infallibile; a livello; **to come true** verificarsi; **true to life** conforme alla realtà

true' cop'y s copia conforme

true-hearted ['tru ˌhartɪd] adj fedele

true'love knot' s nodo d'amore

truffle ['trʌfəl] or ['trufəl] s tartufo

truism ['tru·ɪzəm] s truismo

truly ['truli] adv veramente; correttamente; **yours truly** distinti saluti

trump [trʌmp] s (cards) atout *m;* (Italian cards) briscola; **no trump** senza atout || *tr* superare; (cards) pigliare con un atout or con una briscola; **to**

trump up inventare, fabbricare || *intr* giocare un atout or una briscola

trumpet ['trʌmpɪt] s tromba; *(toy)* trombetta; **to blow one's own trumpet** cantare le proprie lodi || *tr* strombazzare || *intr* sonar la tromba; strombazzare; *(said of an elephant)* barrire

truncheon ['trʌntʃən] s bastone *m* del comando; (Brit) manganello

trunk [trʌŋk] s *(of living body, tree, family, railroad)* tronco; *(for clothes)* baule *m; (of elephant)* tromba; *(aut)* bagagliaio; *(archit)* fusto; *(telp)* linea principale; **trunks** pantaloncini *mpl*

trunk' hose' s (hist) brache *fpl*

truss [trʌs] s *(to support a roof)* capriata, incavallatura; *(based on cantilever system)* intralicciatura; *(for reducing a hernia)* cinto, brachiere *m;* (bot) infiorescenza || *tr* legare, assicurare

trust [trʌst] s fede *f;* speranza; fiducia, custodia; (com) trust *m,* cartello; (law) fedecommesso; **in trust** in deposito; come fedecommesso; **on trust** a credito || *tr* fidarsi di; credere (with *dat*); *(to entrust)* dare in deposito a; dare a credito a || *intr* credere; fidarsi, prestar fede; **to trust in** *(e.g., a friend)* fidarsi di; *(God)* aver fede in

trust' com'pany s compagnia fedecommissaria; banca di deposito

trustee [trʌs'ti] s amministratore *m;* fiduciario; *(of a university)* curatore *m; (of an estate)* fedecommissario

trusteeship [trʌs'ti/ɪp] s amministrazione; (law) fedecommesso; (pol) amministrazione fiduciaria

trustful ['trʌstfəl] adj fiducioso

trust'wor'thy adj fidato, di fiducia

trust·y ['trʌsti] adj (-ier; -iest) fidato || s (-ies) carcerato degno di fiducia

truth [truθ] s verità *f;* **in truth** in verità

truthful ['truθfəl] adj verace, veritiero

try [traɪ] s (tries) tentativo, prova || v (pret & pp tried) *tr* provare; (s.o.'s patience) mettere a dura prova; (a person) (law) processare; (a case) (law) giudicare; **to try on** (clothes) provare; **to try out** provare; esperimentare || *intr* cercare, tentare; **to try out for** cercare di ottenere il posto di; (sports) cercare di farsi accettare in; **to try to** cercare di

trying ['traɪ·ɪŋ] adj duro, penoso, difficile

tryst [trɪst] or [traɪst] s appuntamento

T'-shirt' s maglietta

tub [tʌb] s tino, bigoncia; vasca da bagno; *(clumsy boat)* (slang) carretta; *(fat person)* (slang) bombolo

tube [tjub] or [tub] s tubo; *(e.g., for toothpaste)* tubetto; *(of tire)* camera d'aria; (anat) tuba, tromba; (coll) ferrovia sotterranea

tuber ['tjubər] or ['tubər] s tubero

tubercle ['tjubərkəl] or ['tubərkəl] s tubercolo

tuberculosis [tju͵bʌrkjə'losɪs] or [tu-
͵bʌrkjə'losɪs] s tubercolosi f
tuck [tʌk] s basta || tr ripiegare; **to
tuck away** nascondere; (slang) fare
una scorpacciata di; **to tuck in** rincalzare; **to tuck up** rimboccare
tucker ['tʌkər] s collarino di merletto
|| tr—**to tucker out** (coll) stancare
Tuesday ['tjuzdɪ] or ['tuzdɪ] s martedì
m
tuft [tʌft] s (of feathers) pennacchio;
(of hair) cernecchio; (of flowers)
cespo; (fluffy threads) fiocco, nappa
|| tr impuntire; adornare di fiocchi ||
intr crescere a cernecchi
tug [tʌg] s strattone m, strappata;
(struggle) lotta; (boat) rimorchiatore
m || v (pret & pp **tugged; ger tug-
ging**) tr tirare; (a boat) rimorchiare
|| intr tirare con forza; lottare
tug'boat' s rimorchiatore m
tug' of war' s tiro alla fune
tuition [tju'ɪʃən] or [tu'ɪʃən] s (instruction) insegnamento; tassa scolastica
tulip ['tjulɪp] or ['tulɪp] s tulipano
tumble ['tʌmbəl] s rotolone m, ruzzo-
lone m; (somersault) salto mortale;
caduta; disordine m, confusione;
(confused heap) mucchio || intr roto-
lare, ruzzolare; cadere, capitombolare; gettarsi rigirarsi; **to tumble
down** cadere in rovina; **to tumble to**
(coll) rendersi conto di
tum'ble-down' adj dilapidato
tumbler ['tʌmblər] s (acrobat) saltim-
banco; (glass) bicchiere m; (in a
lock) levetta; (toy) misirizzi m
tumor ['tjumər] or ['tumər] s tumore
m
tumult ['tjumʌlt] or ['tumʌlt] s tumulto
tun [tʌn] s botte f, barile m
tuna ['tunə] s tonno
tune [tjun] or [tun] s (air) aria; (manner of speaking) tono; **in tune** into-
nato; **out of tune** stonato; **to change
one's tune** cambiare di tono || tr in-
tonare; **to tune in** (rad) sintonizzare;
to tune out (rad) interrompere la
sintonizzazione di; **to tune up** (a
motor) mettere a punto; (mus) intonare
tuner ['tunər] or ['tjunər] s (rad) sin-
tonizzatore m; (mus) accordatore m
tungsten ['tʌŋstən] s tungsteno
tunic ['tjunɪk] or ['tunɪk] s tunica
tun'ing coil' ['tunɪŋ] or ['tjunɪŋ] s
bobina di sintonia
tun'ing fork' s diapason m, corista m
Tunis ['tjunɪs] or ['tunɪs] s Tunisi f
Tunisia [tju'nɪʒə] or [tu'nɪʒə] s la
Tunisia
Tunisian [tju'nɪʒən] or [tu'nɪʒən] adj
& s tunisino
tun·nel ['tʌnəl] s tunnel m, traforo,
galleria; (min) galleria || v (pret &
pp -neled or -nelled; ger -neling or
-nelling) tr costruire un passaggio
attraverso o sotto a
turban ['tʌrbən] s turbante m
turbid ['tʌrbɪd] adj turbido

turbine ['tʌrbɪn] or ['tʌrbaɪn] s turbina
turbojet ['tʌrbo͵dʒɛt] s turboreattore
m
turboprop ['tʌrbo͵prɑp] s turboelica m
turbulent ['tʌrbjələnt] adj turbolento
tureen [tu'rin] or [tju'rin] s terrina
turf [tʌrf] s zolla erbosa; (peat) torba;
the turf il campo delle corse; le
corse, il turf
turf'man s (-men) amatore m delle
corse ippiche
Turk [tʌrk] s turco
turkey ['tʌrki] s tacchino || **Turkey** s
la Turchia
turk'ey vul'ture s (Cathartes aura) avvoltoio americano
Turkish ['tʌrkɪʃ] adj & s turco
Turk'ish tow'el s asciugamano spugna
turmoil ['tʌrmɔɪl] s subbuglio
turn [tʌrn] s giro; (time for action)
turno, volta; (change of direction)
voltata; (bend) svolta, curva; (of
events) piega; servizio; inclinazione,
attitudine f; (of key) mandata; (of
coil) spira; (coll) colpo, sussulto;
(aer, naut) virata; **at every turn** a
ogni piè sospinto; **in turn** a tua (Sua,
vostra, etc.) volta; **to be one's turn**
toccare a qlcu, e.g., **it's your turn**
tocca a Lei; **to take turns** fare a turno
|| tr girare, voltare; (soil) rovesciare;
cambiare; (to make sour) coagulare;
(to translate) tradurre; (e.g., ten
years) raggiungere; (e.g., one's eyes)
volgere; (on a lathe) tornire; (e.g., a
coat) rivoltare; (to twist) torcere;
(the wheel) (aut) sterzare; **to turn
against** mettere su contro; **to turn
around** rigirare; (s.o.'s words) ritor-
cere; **to turn aside** sviare; **to turn
away** cacciare via; **to turn back** ricacciare; restituire; (the clock) ritardare; **to turn down** ripiegare; (the
light) abbassare; (an offer) rifiutare;
to turn in ripiegare; denunziare; rassegnare; **to turn off** (e.g., light) spegnere, smorzare; (gas, water, etc.)
tagliare; (e.g., a faucet) chiudere; **to
turn on** (e.g., light, radio, etc.) accendere; (e.g., a faucet) aprire; **to turn
out** mettere alla porta; (animals) fare
uscire dalla stalla; rivoltare; (light)
spegnere; produrre, fabbricare; **to
turn up** ripiegare in su, rimboccare;
(on a lathe) tornire; tirar su; (a card)
scoprire; trovare; (e.g., the radio)
alzare || intr girare; svoltare, e.g.,
turn left at the corner svolti a sinistra all'angolo; girarsi; cambiare;
fermentare; cambiare di colore; diventare; (naut) virare; **to turn against**
voltarsi contro; inimicarsi con; **to
turn around** fare una giravolta; **to
turn aside** or **away** sviarsi; **to turn
back** ritornare; retrocedere; **to turn
down** piegarsi in giù; rovesciarsi; **to
turn in** piegarsi, ripiegarsi; tornare a
casa; (coll) andare a dormire; **to turn
into** sfogare in; trasformarsi in; **to
turn on** voltarsi contro; girarsi su;
dipendere da; occuparsi di; **to turn**

out riuscire; **to turn out to be** manifestarsi; riuscire ad essere; **to turn over** rotolarsi; rovesciarsi; **to turn up** voltarsi all'insù; alzarsi; apparire, farsi vedere

turn′buck′le *s* tenditore *m*

turn′coat′ *s* voltagabbana *mf*; **to become a turncoat** voltar gabbano

turn′down′ *adj* (*collar*) rovesciato ‖ *s* rifiuto

turn′ing point′ *s* punto decisivo

turnip [′tʌrnɪp] *s* rapa

turn′key′ *s* secondino, carceriere *m*

turn′ of life′ *s* menopausa

turn′ of mind′ *s* disposizione naturale

turn′out′ *s* (*gathering of people*) concorso; (*crowd*) folla; produzione; (*outfit*) vestito; stile *m*, moda; (*in a road*) slargo, piazzola; (*horse and carriage*) equipaggio; (rr) binario laterale

turn′over′ *s* (*upset*) rovesciamento, ribaltamento; (*of customers*) movimento di clienti; (*of business*) giro d'affari; rotazione di lavoratori; (com) ciclo operativo

turn′pike′ *s* autostrada a pedaggio

turn′ sig′nal *s* (aut) indicatore *m* di direzione, lampeggiatore *m*

turnstile [′tʌrn‚staɪl] *s* tornello

turn′ta′ble *s* (*of phonograph*) piatto rotante; (rr) piattaforma girevole

turpentine [′tʌrpən‚taɪn] *s* trementina

turpitude [′tʌrpɪ‚tjud] *or* [′tʌrpɪ‚tud] *s* turpitudine *f*

turquoise [′tʌrkɔɪz] *or* [′tʌrkwɔɪz] *s* turchese *m*

turret [′tʌrɪt] *s* torretta

turtle [′tʌrtəl] *s* tartaruga; **to turn turtle** rovesciarsi, capovolgersi

tur′tle-dove′ *s* tortora

Tuscan [′tʌskən] *adj & s* toscano

Tuscany [′tʌskəni] *s* la Toscana

tusk [tʌsk] *s* zanna

tussle [′tʌsəl] *s* lotta, zuffa ‖ *intr* lottare, azzuffarsi

tutor [′tjutər] *or* [′tutər] *s* istitutore privato, ripetitore *m*; (*guardian*) tutore *m* ‖ *tr* dare ripetizione a ‖ *intr* dare ripetizioni; studiare con un ripetitore

tuxe·do [tʌk′sido] *s* (-dos) smoking *m*

twaddle [′twadəl] *s* sciocchezze *fpl* ‖ *intr* dire scioccchezze

twang [twæŋ] *s* (*of musical instrument*) suono vibrato; (*of voice*) timbro nasale ‖ *tr* pizzicare; dire con un timbro nasale ‖ *intr* parlare con voce nasale

twang·y [′twæŋi] *adj* (-ier; -iest) (*tone*) metallico; (*voice*) nasale

tweed [twid] *s* tweed *m*; **tweeds** abito di tweed

tweet [twit] *s* pigolio ‖ *intr* pigolare

tweeter [′twitər] *s* altoparlante *m* per alte audiofrequenze, tweeter *m*

tweezers [′twizərz] *spl* pinzette *fpl*

twelfth [twelfθ] *adj, s & pron* dodicesimo ‖ *s* (*in dates*) dodici *m*

Twelfth′-night′ *s* vigilia dell'Epifania; sera dell'Epifania

twelve [twelv] *adj & pron* dodici ‖ *s* dodici *m*; **twelve o'clock** le dodici

twentieth [′twentɪ‚ɪθ] *adj, s & pron* ventesimo ‖ *s* (*in dates*) venti *m*

twen·ty [′twenti] *adj & pron* venti ‖ *s* (-ties) venti *m*; **the twenties** gli anni venti

twice [twaɪs] *adv* due volte

twice′-told′ *adj* detto più di una volta; detto e ridetto

twiddle [′twɪdəl] *tr*—**to twiddle one's thumbs** rigirare i pollici, oziare

twig [twɪg] *s* ramoscello; **twigs** sterpi *mpl*

twilight [′twaɪ‚laɪt] *adj* crepuscolare ‖ *s* crepuscolo

twill [twɪl] *s* diagonale *m* ‖ *tr* tessere in diagonale

twin [twɪn] *adj & s* gemello

twine [twaɪn] *s* spago ‖ *tr* intrecciare ‖ *intr* intrecciarsi

twinge [twɪndʒ] *s* punta, dolore acuto

twinkle [′twɪŋkəl] *s* scintillio; batter *m* d'occhio ‖ *intr* scintillare

twin′-screw′ *adj* a due eliche

twirl [twʌrl] *s* giro, mulinello ‖ *tr* girare; (slang) lanciare ‖ *intr* girare rapidamente, frullare

twist [twɪst] *s* curva; giro; viluppo, intreccio; tendenza, inclinazione; (*yarn*) ritorno; (*e.g., of lemon*) fettina; (*dance*) twist *m* ‖ *tr* intrecciare; torcere; (*e.g., the face*) contorcere; (*the meaning*) stravolgere, stiracchiare; girare ‖ *intr* intrecciarsi; torcersi, divincolarsi; girare; serpeggiare; **to twist and turn** (*in bed*) girarsi e rigirarsi

twister [′twɪstər] *s* (coll) tromba d'aria

twit [twɪt] *v* (*pret & pp* **twitted**; *ger* **twitting**) *tr* ridicolizzare

twitch [twɪtʃ] *s* tic *m*; (*jerk*) strattone *m*; (*to restrain a horse*) torcinaso ‖ *intr* contrarsi; tremare; **to twitch at** tirare

twitter [′twɪtər] *s* garrito, cinguettio; (*chatter*) chiacchierio; ansia, agitazione ‖ *intr* garrire, cinguettare; chiacchierare; tremare d'ansia

two [tu] *adj & pron* due ‖ *s* due *m*; **to put two and two together** arrivare alle logiche conclusioni; **two o'clock** le due

two′-cy′cle *adj* a due tempi

two′-cyl′inder *adj* a due cilindri

two-edged [′tu‚ɛdʒd] *adj* a doppio filo

two′fold′ *adj* duplice, doppio

two′ hun′dred *adj, s & pron* duecento

twosome [′tusəm] *s* coppia

two′-time′ *tr* (slang) fare le corna a

two′-way ra′dio *s* ricetrasmettitore *m*

tycoon [taɪ′kun] *s* magnate *m*

type [taɪp] *s* tipo; (typ) carattere *m*; (*pieces collectively*) (typ) caratteri *mpl* ‖ *tr* scrivere a macchina; simbolizzare ‖ *intr* scrivere a macchina

type′face′ *s* stile *m* di carattere

type′script′ *s* dattiloscritto

typesetter [′taɪp‚setər] *s* (*person*) compositore *m*; (*machine*) compositrice *f*

type'write' *v* (*pret* **-wrote**; *pp* **-written**) *tr* & *intr* dattilografare, scrivere a macchina

type'writ'er *s* (*machine*) macchina da scrivere; (*typist*) dattilografo

type'writ'ing *s* dattilografia, scrittura a macchina; lavoro battuto a macchina

ty'phoid fe'ver ['taɪfɔɪd] *s* febbre *f* tifoide

typhoon [taɪ'fun] *s* tifone *m*

typical ['tɪpɪkəl] *adj* tipico

typi·fy ['tɪpɪ ˌfaɪ] *v* (*pret* & *pp* **-fied**) *tr* simbolizzare

typist ['taɪpɪst] *s* dattilografo

typographic(al) [ˌtaɪpə'græfɪk(əl)] *adj* tipografico

typograph'ical er'ror *s* errore *m* di stampa

typography [taɪ'pɑgrəfi] *s* tipografia

tyrannic(al) [tɪ'rænɪk(əl)] or [taɪ'rænɪk(əl)] *adj* tirannico

tyrannous ['tɪrənəs] *adj* tiranno

tyrant ['taɪrənt] *s* tiranno

ty·ro ['taɪro] *s* (**-ros**) principiante *m*

Tyrrhe'nian Sea' [tɪ'rini·ən] *s* Mare Tirreno

U

U, u [ju] *s* ventunesima lettera dell'alfabeto inglese

ubiquitous [ju'bɪkwɪtəs] *adj* ubiquo

udder ['ʌdər] *s* mammella

ugliness ['ʌglɪnɪs] *s* bruttezza

ug·ly ['ʌgli] *adj* (**-lier; -liest**) brutto

Ukraine, the ['jukren] or [ju'kren] *s* l'Ucraina *f*

Ukrainian [ju'kreni·ən] *adj* & *s* ucraino

ulcer ['ʌlsər] *s* piaga, ulcera; (*corrupting element*) (fig) piaga

ulcerate ['ʌlsə ˌret] *tr* ulcerare ‖ *intr* ulcerarsi

ulterior [ʌl'tɪri·ər] *adj* ulteriore; (*motive*) nascosto, secondo

ultimate ['ʌltɪmɪt] *adj* ultimo

ultima·tum [ˌʌltɪ'metəm] *s* (**-tums** or **-ta** [tə]) ultimatum

ultimo ['ʌltɪ ˌmo] *adv* del mese scorso

ul'tra·high fre'quency ['ʌltrə'haɪ] *s* frequenza ultraelevata

ultrashort [ˌʌltrə'ʃɔrt] *adj* ultracorto

ultraviolet [ˌʌltrə'vaɪ·əlɪt] *adj* & *s* ultravioletto

umbil'ical cord' [ʌm'bɪlɪkəl] *s* cordone *m* ombelicale

umbrage ['ʌmbrɪdʒ] *s*—**to take umbrage** at adombrarsi per

umbrella [ʌm'brelə] *s* ombrello; paracqua *m*; (mil) ombrello

umbrel'la stand' *s* portaombrelli *m*

Umbrian ['ʌmbri·ən] *adj* & *s* umbro

umlaut ['umlaut] *s* metafonesi *f*; (*mark*) dieresi *f* ‖ *tr* cambiare il timbro di; scrivere con dieresi

umpire ['ʌmpaɪr] *s* arbitro ‖ *tr* arbitrare ‖ *intr* fare l'arbitro

UN ['ju'en] *s* (letterword) (**United Nations**) ONU *f*

unable [ʌn'ebəl] *adj* incapace; **to be unable to** essere impossibilitato a, non potere

unabridged [ˌʌnə'brɪdʒd] *adj* integrale, non abbreviato

unaccented [ʌn'æksentɪd] or [ˌʌnæk-'sentɪd] *adj* non accentato, atono

unacceptable [ˌʌnək'septəbəl] *adj* inaccettabile

unaccountable [ˌʌnə'kauntəbəl] *adj* irresponsabile; inesplicabile

unaccounted-for [ˌʌnə'kauntɪd ˌfɔr]

adj (*e.g., failure*) inesplicato; (*e.g., soldier*) irreperibile, mancante

unaccustomed [ˌʌnə'kʌstəmd] *adj* (*unusual*) insolito; non abituato

unafraid [ˌʌnə'fred] *adj* impavido

unaligned [ʌnə'laɪnd] *adj* non impegnato

unanimity [ˌjunə'nɪmɪti] *s* unanimità *f*

unanimous [ju'nænɪməs] *adj* unanime

unanswerable [ʌn'ænsərəbəl] *adj* per cui non vi è risposta; (*argument*) irrefutabile, incontestabile

unappreciative [ˌʌnə'priʃi ˌetɪv] *adj* sconoscente, ingrato

unapproachable [ˌʌnə'protʃəbəl] *adj* inabbordabile; incomparabile

unarmed [ʌn'ɑrmd] *adj* disarmato, inerme

unascertainable [ʌn ˌæsər'tenəbəl] *adj* non verificabile

unassailable [ˌʌnə'seləbəl] *adj* inattaccabile

unassembled [ˌʌnə'sembəld] *adj* smontato

unassuming [ˌʌnə'sumɪŋ] or [ˌʌnə-'sjumɪŋ] *adj* modesto, semplice

unattached [ˌʌnə'tætʃt] *adj* indipendente; (*loose*) sciolto; non sposato; non fidanzato

unattainable [ˌʌnə'tenəbəl] *adj* inarrivabile, irraggiungibile

unattractive [ˌʌnə'træktɪv] *adj* poco attraente

unavailable [ˌʌnə'veləbəl] *adj* non disponibile

unavailing [ˌʌnə'velɪŋ] *adj* futile

unavoidable [ˌʌnə'vɔɪdəbəl] *adj* inevitabile, ineluttabile

unaware [ˌʌnə'wer] *adj* inconsapevole, ignaro ‖ *adv* inaspettatamente; (*unknowingly*) inavvertitamente

unawares [ˌʌnə'werz] *adv* inaspettatamente; (*unknowingly*) inavvertitamente

unbalanced [ʌn'bælənst] *adj* sbilanciato, squilibrato

unbandage [ʌn'bændɪdʒ] *tr* sbendare

un·bar [ʌn'bɑr] *v* (*pret* & *pp* **-barred; ger -barring**) *tr* disserrare il chiavistello di

unbearable [ʌn'berəbəl] *adj* insopportabile, insostenibile

unbeatable [ʌn'bitəbəl] *adj* imbattibile

unbecoming [ˌʌnbɪ'kʌmɪŋ] *adj* sconveniente, indegno; (*e.g., hat*) disadatto, che non sta bene

unbelievable [ˌʌnbɪ'livəbəl] *adj* incredibile

unbeliever [ˌʌnbɪ'livər] *s* miscredente *mf*

unbending [ʌn'bendɪŋ] *adj* inflessibile

unbiased [ʌn'baɪ-əst] *adj* imparziale, spassionato

un-blind [ʌn'baɪnd] *v* (*pret & pp* **-bound** ['baund]) *tr* slegare

unbleached [ʌn'blit/t] *adj* non candeggiato, al colore naturale

unbolt [ʌn'bolt] *tr* (*a door*) togliere il chiavistello a; sbullonare

unborn [ʌn'bɔrn] *adj* nascituro

unbosom [ʌn'buzəm] *tr* (*a secret*) rivelare; **to unbosom oneself** aprire il proprio animo, sfogarsi

unbound [ʌn'baund] *adj* sciolto, libero; (*book*) non rilegato

unbreakable [ʌn'brekəbəl] *adj* infrangibile

unbridle [ʌn'braɪdəl] *tr* sbrigliare

unbuckle [ʌn'bʌkəl] *tr* sfibbiare

unburden [ʌn'bʌrdən] *tr* scaricare; **to unburden oneself (of)** vuotare il sacco (di)

unburied [ʌn'berid] *adj* insepolto

unbutton [ʌn'bʌtən] *tr* sbottonare

uncalled-for [ʌn'kɔld ˌfɔr] *adj* superfluo, gratuito; fuori di posto, sconveniente

uncanny [ʌn'kæni] *adj* misterioso, straordinario

uncared-for [ʌn'kerd ˌfɔr] *adj* negletto, trascurato

unceasing [ʌn'sisɪŋ] *adj* incessante

unceremonious [ˌʌnseri'moni-əs] *adj* senza cerimonie

uncertain [ʌn'sʌrtən] *adj* incerto

uncertain-ty [ʌn'sʌrtənti] *s* (*-ties*) incertezza

unchain [ʌn't/en] *tr* scatenare, sferrare

unchangeable [ʌn't/endʒəbəl] *adj* immutabile

uncharted [ʌn't/ɑrtɪd] *adj* inesplorato

unchecked [ʌn't/ekt] *adj* incontrollato

uncivilized [ʌn'sɪvɪˌlaɪzd] *adj* incivile

unclad [ʌn'klæd] *adj* svestito

unclaimed [ʌn'klemd] *adj* non reclamato; (*letter*) giacente

unclasp [ʌn'klæsp] or [ʌn'klɑsp] *tr* sfibbiare

unclassified [ʌn'klæsɪˌfaɪd] *adj* non classificato; non secreto

uncle ['ʌŋkəl] *s* zio

unclean [ʌn'klin] *adj* immondo

un-clog [ʌn'klɑg] *v* (*pret & pp* **-clogged**; *ger* **-clogging**) *tr* disintasare

unclouded [ʌn'klaudɪd] *adj* sereno, senza nubi

uncollectible [ˌʌnkə'lektɪbəl] *adj* inesigibile

uncomfortable [ʌn'kʌmfərtəbəl] *adj* scomodo, disagevole

uncommitted [ˌʌnkə'mɪtɪd] *adj* non impegnato

uncommon [ʌn'kɑmən] *adj* raro, straordinario

uncompromising [ʌn'kɑmprə ˌmaɪzɪŋ] *adj* intransigente

unconcerned [ˌʌnkən'sʌrnd] *adj* indifferente, noncurante

unconditional [ˌʌnkən'dɪ/ənəl] *adj* incondizionato

uncongenial [ˌʌnkən'dʒini-əl] *adj* antipatico, sgradito

unconquerable [ʌn'kaŋkərəbəl] *adj* inconquistabile, inespugnabile

unconscionable [ʌn'kɑn/ənəbəl] *adj* senza scrupoli; eccessivo

unconscious [ʌn'kɑn/əs] *adj* (*without awareness*) inconscio, inconsapevole; (*temporarily devoid of consciousness*) incosciente; (*unintentional*) involontario

unconsciousness [ʌn'kɑn/əsnɪs] *s* incoscienza

unconstitutional [ˌʌnkɑnstɪ'tju/ənəl] or [ˌʌnkɑnstɪ'tu/ənəl] *adj* incostituzionale

uncontrollable [ˌʌnkən'troləbəl] *adj* incontrollabile, ingovernabile

unconventional [ˌʌnkən'vɛn/ənəl] *adj* non convenzionale, anticonformista

uncork [ʌn'kɔrk] *tr* stappare

uncouple [ʌn'kʌpəl] *tr* sganciare, disconnettere

uncouth [ʌn'kuθ] *adj* zotico, incivile, pacchiano

uncover [ʌn'kʌvər] *tr* scoprire

unction ['ʌŋk/ən] *s* unzione; (fig) untuosità *f*

unctuous ['ʌŋkt/ʊ-əs] *adj* untuoso

uncultivated [ʌn'kʌltɪˌvetɪd] *adj* incolto

uncultured [ʌn'kʌlt/ərd] *adj* incolto, rozzo

uncut [ʌn'kʌt] *adj* non tagliato; (*book*) intonso

undamaged [ʌn'dæmɪdʒd] *adj* indenne, illeso

undaunted [ʌn'dɔntɪd] *adj* imperterrito, impavido

undeceive [ˌʌndɪ'siv] *tr* disingannare

undecided [ˌʌndɪ'saɪdɪd] *adj* indeciso

undefeated [ˌʌndɪ'fitɪd] *adj* invitto

undefended [ˌʌndɪ'fendɪd] *adj* indifeso

undefensible [ˌʌndɪ'fensɪbəl] *adj* insostenibile

undefiled [ˌʌndɪ'faɪld] *adj* puro, immacolato

undeniable [ˌʌndɪ'naɪ-əbəl] *adj* innegabile, indubitato

under ['ʌndər] *adj* di sotto; (*lower*) inferiore; (*clothing*) intimo, personale || *adv* sotto; più sotto; **to go under** affondare; cedere; (coll) fallire || *prep* sotto; sotto a; (*e.g., 20 years old*) meno di; **under full sail** a vele spiegate; **under lock and key** sotto chiave; **under oath** sotto giuramento; **under penalty of death** sotto pena di morte; **under sail a vela**; **under separate cover** in plico separato; **under steam** sotto pressione; **under the hand and seal of** firmato di pugno di; **under the weather** (coll) un po' indisposto; **under way** già iniziato

un'der-age' *adj* minorenne

un'der-arm' pad' *s* sottoascella *m*

un'der·bid' *v* (*pret & pp* **-bid;** *ger* **-bidding**) *tr* fare un'offerta inferiore a quella di

un'der·brush' *s* sottobosco

un'der·car'riage *s* (aut) telaio; (aer) carrello d'atterraggio

un'der·clothes' *spl* biancheria intima

un'der·consump'tion *s* sottoconsumo

un'der·cov'er *adj* segreto

un'der·cur'rent *s* (*of water*) corrente subacquea; (*of air*) corrente *f* inferiore; (fig) controcorrente *f*

underdeveloped [ˌʌndərdɪˈvɛləpt] *adj* sottosviluppato

un'der·dog' *s* chi è destinato ad avere la peggio; vittima; **the underdogs** i diseredati

un'der·done' *adj* non cotto abbastanza

un'der·es'timate' *tr* sottovalutare

un'der·gar'ment *s* indumento intimo

un'der·go' *v* (*pret* -went; *pp* -gone) *tr* (*a test*) passare, sottostare (with *dat*); (*surgery*) subire, sottoporsi a; soffrire

un'der·grad'uate *adj* (*student*) non ancora laureato; (*course*) per studenti non ancora laureati || *s* studente universitario che non ha ancora ricevuto il primo diploma

un'der·ground' *adj* sotterraneo; segreto || *s* regione sotterranea; macchia, resistenza || *adv* sottoterra; alla macchia, segretamente

un'der·growth' *s* sterpaglia

underhanded [ˈʌndərˈhændəd] *adj* subdolo, di sottomano

un'der·line' *or* **un'der·line'** *tr* sottolineare

underling [ˈʌndərlɪŋ] *s* tirapiedi *m*

un'der·mine' *tr* scalzare, minare

underneath [ˌʌndərˈniθ] *adj* inferiore || *s* disotto || *adv* sotto, di sotto || *prep* sotto a, sotto

undernourished [ˌʌndərˈnʌrɪʃt] *adj* denutrito, malnutrito

un'der·pass' *s* sottopassaggio

un'der·pay' *s* (*pret & pp* -paid) *tr & intr* pagare insufficientemente

un'der·pin' *v* (*pret & pp* -pinned; *ger* -pinning) *tr* rincalzare

underprivileged [ˌʌndərˈprɪvɪlɪdʒd] *adj* derelitto, diseredato

un'der·rate' *tr* sottovalutare

un'der·score' *tr* sottolineare

un'der·sea' *adj* sottomarino || *adv* sotto il mare

un'der·seas' *adv* sotto il mare

un'der·sec'retar'y *s* (-ies) sottosegretario

un'der·sell' *v* (*pret & pp* -sold) *tr* vendere a prezzo minore di; (*to sell for less than actual value*) svendere

un'der·shirt' *s* camiciola, canottiera

undersigned [ˈʌndərˌsaɪnd] *adj* sottoscritto

un'der·skirt' *s* sottogonna

un'der·stand' *v* (*pret & pp* -stood) *tr* capire, comprendere; sottintendere; (*to accept as true*) constare, e.g., **he understands that you are wrong** gli consta che Lei ha torto || *intr* capire, comprendere

understandable [ˌʌndərˈstændəbəl] *adj* comprensibile

understanding [ˌʌndərˈstændɪŋ] *adj* comprensivo, tollerante || *s* (*mind*) intelletto; (*knowledge*) conoscenza; comprensione, intendimento; (*agreement*) intesa, accordo

understatement [ˌʌndərˈstetmənt] *s* sottovalutazione

un'der·stud'y *s* (-ies) (theat) doppio, sostituto || *v* (-ied) *tr* (*an actor*) fare il doppio di

un'der·take' *v* (*pret* -took; *ger* -taken) *tr* intraprendere; (*to promise*) promettere

undertaker [ˌʌndərˈtekər] *or* [ˈʌndərˌtekər] *s* impresario || [ˈʌndərˌtekər] *s* impresario di pompe funebri

undertaking [ˌʌndərˈtekɪŋ] *s* (*task*) impresa; (*promise*) promessa || [ˈʌndərˌtekɪŋ] *s* impresa di pompe funebri

un'der·tone' *s* bassa voce; (*background sound*) ronzio di fondo; tono; colore smorzato

un'der·tow' *s* (*on the beach*) risacca; (*countercurrent below surface*) controcorrente *f*

un'der·wa'ter *adj* subacqueo || *adv* sottacqua

un'der·wear' *s* biancheria intima

un'der·world' *s* (*criminal world*) malavita, teppa; (*abode of spirits*) ade *m*, averno; mondo sotterraneo; mondo sottomarino; antipodi *mpl*

un'der·write' *v* (*pret* -wrote; *pp* -written) *tr* sottoscrivere; (*to insure*) assicurare

un'der·writ'er *s* sottoscrittore *m*; (ins) assicuratore *m*

undeserved [ˌʌndɪˈzɜrvd] *adj* immeritato

undesirable [ˌʌndɪˈzaɪrəbəl] *adj & s* indesiderabile *mf*

undetachable [ˌʌndɪˈtætʃəbəl] *adj* non movibile

undeveloped [ˌʌndɪˈvɛləpt] *adj* (*land*) non sfruttato; (*country*) sottosviluppato

undigested [ˌʌndɪˈdʒɛstɪd] *adj* non digerito

undignified [ʌnˈdɪgnɪˌfaɪd] *adj* poco decoroso

undiscernible [ˌʌndɪˈzɜrnɪbəl] *or* [ˌʌndɪˈsɜrnɪbəl] *adj* impercettibile

undisputed [ˌʌndɪˈspjutəd] *adj* indiscusso, incontrastato

un·do' [ʌnˈdu] *v* (*pret* -did; *pp* -done) *tr* sfare, disfare; rovinare; (*a package*) aprire; (*a knot*) sciogliere

undoing [ʌnˈdu·ɪŋ] *s* rovina

undone [ʌnˈdʌn] *adj* non finito; **to come undone** disfarsi; **to leave nothing undone** non tralasciare di fare nulla

undoubtedly [ʌnˈdautɪdli] *adv* indubbiamente, senza dubbio

undress [ˈʌnˌdrɛs] *or* [ʌnˈdrɛs] *s* vestaglia; vestito da ogni giorno || [ʌnˈdrɛs] *tr* spogliare, svestire; (*a* *wound*) sbendare || *intr* spogliarsi, svestirsi

undrinkable [ʌn'drɪŋkəbəl] *adj* imbevibile, non potabile

undue [ʌn'dju] or [ʌn'du] *adj* indebito; immeritato; eccessivo

undulate ['ʌndjə‚let] *intr* ondulare

unduly [ʌn'djulɪ] or [ʌn'dulɪ] *adv* indebitamente, eccessivamente

unearned [ʌn'ɜrnd] *adj* non guadagnato col lavoro; immeritato; non ancora guadagnato

un'earned in'crement s plusvalenza

unearth [ʌn'ɜrθ] *tr* dissotterrare

unearthly [ʌn'ɜrθlɪ] *adj* ultraterreno; spettrale; impossibile, straordinario

uneasy [ʌn'izɪ] *adj* (*worried*) preoccupato; (*constrained*) scomodo; (*not conducive to ease*) inquietante, a disagio

uneatable [ʌn'itəbəl] *adj* immangiabile

uneconomic(al) [‚ʌnikə'namɪk(əl)] or [‚ʌnɛkə'namɪk(əl)] *adj* antieconomico

uneducated [ʌn'ɛdjə‚ketɪd] *adj* ineducato

unemployed [‚ʌnɛm'plɔɪd] *adj* disoccupato, incollocato; improduttivo || **the unemployed** i disoccupati

unemployment [‚ʌnɛm'plɔɪmənt] s disimpiego, disoccupazione

unemploy'ment compensa'tion s sussidio di disoccupazione

unending [ʌn'ɛndɪŋ] *adj* interminabile

unequal [ʌn'ikwəl] *adj* disuguale, impari; **to be unequal to** (*a task*) non essere all'altezza di

unequaled or **unequalled** [ʌn'ikwəld] *adj* ineguagliato

unerring [ʌn'ɜrɪŋ] or [ʌn'ɛrɪŋ] *adj* infallibile; corretto, preciso

unessential [‚ʌnɛ'sɛn/əl] *adj* non essenziale

uneven [ʌn'ivən] *adj* disuguale, ineguale; (*number*) dispari

uneventful [‚ʌnɪ'vɛntfəl] *adj* senza avvenimenti importanti; (*life*) tranquillo

unexceptionable [‚ʌnɛk'sɛp/ənəbəl] *adj* ineccepibile, irreprensibile

unexpected [‚ʌnɛk'spɛktɪd] *adj* inaspettato, imprevisto

unexplained [‚ʌnɛk'splend] *adj* inesplicato

unexplored [‚ʌnɛk'splord] *adj* inesplorato

unexposed [‚ʌnɛk'spozd] *adj* (phot) non esposto alla luce

unfading [ʌn'fedɪŋ] *adj* immarcescibile; imperituro

unfailing [ʌn'felɪŋ] *adj* immancabile, infallibile; (*inexhaustible*) inesauribile; (*dependable*) sicuro

unfair [ʌn'fɛr] *adj* ingiusto; disonesto, sleale

unfaithful [ʌn'feθfəl] *adj* infedele

unfamiliar [‚ʌnfə'mɪljər] *adj* poco pratico; poco abituale, strano; non conosciuto

unfasten [ʌn'fæsən] or [ʌn'fɑsən] *tr* sfibbiare, sciogliere

unfathomable [ʌn'fæðəməbəl] *adj* insondabile

unfavorable [ʌn'fevərəbəl] *adj* sfavorevole

unfeeling [ʌn'filɪŋ] *adj* insensibile

unfetter [ʌn'fɛtər] *tr* sciogliere dalle catene

unfinished [ʌn'fɪnɪ/t] *adj* incompiuto; grezzo, non rifinito; (*business*) inevaso

unfit [ʌn'fɪt] *adj* disadatto; inabile

unfledged [ʌn'flɛdʒd] *adj* implume

unfold [ʌn'fold] *tr* schiudere; (*e.g., a newspaper*) spiegare || *intr* schiudersi; svolgersi

unforeseeable [‚ʌnfor'si‚əbəl] *adj* imprevedibile

unforeseen [‚ʌnfor'sin] *adj* imprevisto

unforgettable [‚ʌnfər'gɛtəbəl] *adj* indimenticabile

unforgivable [‚ʌnfər'gɪvəbəl] *adj* imperdonabile

unfortunate [ʌn'fɔrt/ənɪt] *adj & s* disgraziato, sfortunato

unfounded [ʌn'faʊndɪd] *adj* infondato

un-freeze [ʌn'friz] *v* (*pret* **-froze**; *pp* **-frozen**) *tr* disgelare; (*credit*) sbloccare

unfriend·ly [ʌn'frɛndlɪ] *adj* (**-lier; -liest**) *adj* mal disposto, ostile; sfavorevole

unfruitful [ʌn'frutfəl] *adj* infruttuoso

unfulfilled [‚ʌnfəl'fɪld] *adj* incompiuto

unfurl [ʌn'fʌrl] *tr* spiegare, dispiegare

unfurnished [ʌn'fʌrnɪ/t] *adj* smobiliato

ungainly [ʌn'genlɪ] *adj* sgraziato, maldestro

ungentlemanly [ʌn'dʒɛntəlmənlɪ] *adj* indegno di un gentleman

ungird [ʌn'gɜrd] *tr* discingere

ungodly [ʌn'gadlɪ] *adj* irreligioso, empio; (*dreadful*) (coll) atroce

ungracious [ʌn'gre/əs] *adj* rude, scortese; (*task*) sgradevole

ungrammatical [‚ʌngrə'mætɪkəl] *adj* sgrammaticato

ungrateful [ʌn'gretfəl] *adj* ingrato

ungrudgingly [ʌn'grʌdʒɪŋlɪ] *adv* di buon grado, volentieri

unguarded [ʌn'gardɪd] *adj* incustodito, indifeso; incauto, imprudente

unguent ['ʌŋgwənt] *s* unguento

unhappiness [ʌn'hæpɪnɪs] *s* infelicità *f*

unhap·py [ʌn'hæpɪ] *adj* (**-pier; -piest**) infelice, sfortunato

unharmed [ʌn'harmd] *adj* illeso

unharness [ʌn'harnɪs] *tr* togliere i finimenti a

unhealth·y [ʌn'hɛlθɪ] *adj* (**-ier; -iest**) malsano

unheard-of [ʌn'hʌrd‚ʌv] *adj* (*unknown*) sconosciuto; inaudito

unhinge [ʌn'hɪndʒ] *tr* sgangherare; (fig) sconvolgere

unhitch [ʌn'hɪt/] *tr* sganciare; (*a horse*) staccare

unho·ly [ʌn'holɪ] *adj* (**-lier; -liest**) empio; terribile, atroce

unhook [ʌn'hʊk] *tr* sganciare

unhoped-for [ʌn'hopt‚fər] *adj* insperato

unhorse [ʌn'hɔrs] *tr* disarcionare

unhurt [ʌn'hʌrt] *adj* incolume, illeso

unicorn ['junɪ‚kɔrn] *s* unicorno

unification [‚junɪfɪ'keʃən] *s* unificazione

uniform ['junɪ‚fɔrm] *adj & s* uniforme *f* ‖ *tr* uniformare

uni•fy ['junɪ‚faɪ] *v* (*pret & pp* -fied) *tr* unificare

unilateral [‚junɪ'lætərəl] *adj* unilaterale

unimpeachable [‚ʌnɪm'pitʃəbəl] *adj* irrefutabile; irreprensibile

unimportant [‚ʌnɪm'pɔrtənt] *adj* poco importante

uninhabited [‚ʌnɪn'hæbɪtɪd] *adj* inabitato, disabitato

uninspired [‚ʌnɪn'spaɪrd] *adj* senza ispirazione, prosaico

unintelligent [‚ʌnɪn'telɪdʒənt] *adj* non intelligente; stupido

unintelligible [‚ʌnɪn'telɪdʒɪbəl] *adj* inintelligibile

uninterested [ʌn'ɪntrɪstɪd] or [ʌn‚ɪntə‚restɪd] *adj* non interessato

uninteresting [ʌn'ɪntrɪstɪŋ] or [ʌn‚ɪntə‚restɪŋ] *adj* poco interessante

uninterrupted [‚ʌnɪntə'rʌptɪd] *adj* ininterrotto

union ['junjən] *s* unione; unione matrimoniale; (*of workers*) sindacato

unionize ['junjə‚naɪz] *tr* organizzare in un sindacato ‖ *intr* organizzarsi in un sindacato

un′ion shop′ *s* fabbrica che assume solo sindacalisti

un′ion suit′ *s* combinazione

unique [jʊ'nik] *adj* unico

unison ['junɪsən] or ['junɪzən] *s* unisono; **in unison** all'unisono

unit ['junɪt] *adj* unitario ‖ *s* unità *f*; (*mach, elec*) gruppo

unite [jʊ'naɪt] *tr* unire ‖ *intr* unirsi

united [jʊ'naɪtɪd] *adj* unito

Unit′ed King′dom *s* Regno Unito

Unit′ed Na′tions *spl* Organizzazione delle Nazioni Unite

Unit′ed States′ *adj* statunitense ‖ **the United States** *ssg* gli Stati Uniti

uni•ty ['junɪti] *s* (-ties) unità *f*

universal [‚junɪ'vʌrsəl] *adj* universale

u′niver′sal joint′ *s* giunto cardanico

universe ['junɪ‚vʌrs] *s* universo

universi•ty [‚junɪ'vʌrsɪti] *adj* universitario ‖ *s* (-ties) università *f*

unjust [ʌn'dʒʌst] *adj* ingiusto

unjustified [ʌn'dʒʌstɪ‚faɪd] *adj* ingiustificato

unkempt [ʌn'kempt] *adj* spettinato; trascurato

unkind [ʌn'kaɪnd] *adj* scortese; duro, crudele

unknowable [ʌn'no‚əbəl] *adj* inconoscibile

unknowingly [ʌn'no‚ɪŋli] *adv* inconsapevolmente

unknown [ʌn'non] *adj* sconosciuto ‖ *s* incognito; (*math*) incognita

Un′known Sol′dier *s* Milite Ignoto

unlace [ʌn'les] *tr* slacciare

unlatch [ʌn'lætʃ] *tr* tirare il saliscendi a

unlawful [ʌn'lɔfəl] *adj* illegale

unleash [ʌn'liʃ] *tr* sguinzagliare; (fig) scatenare

unleavened [ʌn'levənd] *adj* azzimo

unless [ʌn'les] *conj* se non che, salvo che

unlettered [ʌn'letərd] *adj* ignorante; (*illiterate*) analfabeta

unlike [ʌn'laɪk] *adj* dissimile, differente; dissimile da, e.g., **a copy unlike the original** una copia dissimile dall'originale; (etec) di segno contrario ‖ *prep* diversamente da, a differenza di; **it was unlike him to arrive late** non era cosa normale per lui arrivare in ritardo

unlikely [ʌn'laɪkli] *adj* improbabile

unlimber [ʌn'lɪmbər] *tr* mettere in batteria ‖ *intr* prepararsi a fare fuoco; (fig) prepararsi

unlimited [ʌn'lɪmɪtɪd] *adj* illimitato

unlined [ʌn'laɪnd] *adj* (*e.g., coat*) non foderato; (*paper*) non rigato

unload [ʌn'lod] *tr* scaricare; (*passengers*) sbarcare; (*to get rid of*) liberarsi di ‖ *intr* scaricare; sbarcare

unloading [ʌn'lodɪŋ] *s* discarica; sbarco

unlock [ʌn'lak] *tr* aprire

unloose [ʌn'lus] *tr* rilasciare; sciogliere

unloved [ʌn'lʌvd] *adj* poco amato

unlovely [ʌn'lʌvli] *adj* poco attraente

unluck•y [ʌn'lʌki] *adj* (-ier; -iest) sfortunato, disgraziato

un—make [ʌn'mek] *v* (*pret & pp* -made ['med]) *tr* disfare; deporre

unmanageable [ʌn'mænɪdʒəbəl] *adj* incontrollabile

unmanly [ʌn'mænli] *adj* non virile, effeminato; codardo

unmannerly [ʌn'mænərli] *adj* scortese

unmarketable [ʌn'markɪtəbəl] *adj* invendibile

unmarriageable [ʌn'mærɪdʒəbəl] *adj* che non si può sposare; non adatto al matrimonio

unmarried [ʌn'mærid] *adj* scapolo; (*female*) nubile

unmask [ʌn'mæsk] or [ʌn'mask] *tr* smascherare ‖ *intr* smascherarsi

unmatchable [ʌn'mæt/əbəl] *adj* impareggiabile

unmatched [ʌn'mæt/d] *adj* impareggiabile; (*unpaired*) spariglliato

unmentionable [ʌn'men/ənəbəl] *adj* innominabile

unmerciful [ʌn'mʌrsɪfəl] *adj* spietato

unmesh [ʌn'me/] *tr* disingranare ‖ *intr* disingranarsi

unmindful [ʌn'maɪndfəl] *adj* immemore; incurante

unmistakable [‚ʌnmɪs'tekəbəl] *adj* inconfondibile

unmitigated [ʌn'mɪtɪ‚getɪd] *adj* completo; assoluto, perfetto

unmixed [ʌn'mɪkst] *adj* puro

unmoor [ʌn'mur] *tr* disormeggiare

unmoved [ʌn'muvd] *adj* immoto; fisso, immobile; (fig) impassibile

unmuzzle [ʌn'mʌzəl] *tr* togliere la museruola a

unnamed [ʌn'nemd] *adj* innominato

unnatural [ʌn'næt/ərəl] *adj* contro natura, snaturato; innaturale, affettato

unnecessary [ʌn'nɛsə,sɛri] *adj* inutile

unnerve [ʌn'nʌrv] *tr* snervare

unnoticeable [ʌn'notɪsəbəl] *adj* impercettibile

unnoticed [ʌn'notɪst] *adj* inosservato

unobserved [,ʌnəb'zʌrvd] *adj* inosservato

unobtainable [,ʌnəb'tenəbəl] *adj* non ottenibile, irraggiungibile

unobtrusive [,ʌnəb'trusɪv] *adj* discreto, riservato

unoccupied [ʌn'ɑkjə,paɪd] *adj* libero, disponibile; (*not busy*) disoccupato

unofficial [,ʌnə'fɪʃəl] *adj* non ufficiale, ufficioso

unopened [ʌn'opənd] *adj* non aperto, chiuso; (*letter*) non dissuggellato; (*book*) intonso

unorthodox [ʌn'ɔrθə,dɑks] *adj* non ortodosso

unpack [ʌn'pæk] *tr* spaccare, sballare

unpalatable [ʌn'pælətəbəl] *adj* di gusto spiacevole

unparalleled [ʌn'pærə,lɛld] *adj* incomparabile, senza pari

unpardonable [ʌn'pɑrdənəbəl] *adj* imperdonabile

unpatriotic [,ʌnpetri'ɑtɪk] or [,ʌnpætrɪ'ɑtɪk] *adj* antipatriottico

unperceived [,ʌnpər'sivd] *adj* inosservato

unperturbable [,ʌnpər'tʌrbəbəl] *adj* imperterrito, imperturbato

unpleasant [ʌn'plɛsənt] *adj* spiacevole; (*person*) antipatico

unpopular [ʌn'pɑpjələr] *adj* impopolare

unpopularity [ʌn,pɑpjə'lærɪti] *s* impopolarità *f*

unprecedented [ʌn'prɛsɪ,dɛntɪd] *adj* senza precedenti, inaudito

unprejudiced [ʌn'prɛdʒədɪst] *adj* senza pregiudizio, imparziale

unpremeditated [,ʌnprɪ'mɛdɪ,tetɪd] *adj* impremeditato

unprepared [,ʌnprɪ'pɛrd] *adj* impreparato

unprepossessing [,ʌnpripə'zɛsɪŋ] *adj* poco attraente, antipatico

unpresentable [,ʌnprɪ'zɛntəbəl] *adj* impresentabile

unpretentious [,ʌnprɪ'tɛnʃəs] *adj* modesto, senza pretese

unprincipled [ʌn'prɪnsɪpəld] *adj* senza principi

unproductive [,ʌnprə'dʌktɪv] *adj* improduttivo

unprofitable [ʌn'prɑfɪtəbəl] *adj* infruttuoso

unpronounceable [,ʌnprə'naʊnsəbəl] *adj* impronunziabile

unpropitious [,ʌnprə'pɪʃəs] *adj* inauspicato

unpublished [ʌn'pʌblɪʃt] *adj* inedito

unpunished [ʌn'pʌnɪʃt] *adj* impunito

unqualified [ʌn'kwɑlɪ,faɪd] *adj* inabile, inidoneo; assoluto, completo

unquenchable [ʌn'kwɛntʃəbəl] *adj* inappagabile, inestinguibile

unquestionable [ʌn'kwɛstʃənəbəl] *adj* indiscutibile

unrav·el [ʌn'rævəl] *v* (*pret & pp* -eled or -elled; *ger* -eling or -elling) *tr* dipanare || *intr* districarsi; chiarirsi

unreachable [ʌn'ritʃəbəl] *adj* irraggiungibile

unreal [ʌn'ri·əl] *adj* irreale

unreali·ty [,ʌnrɪ'ælɪti] *s* (-ties) irrealità *f*

unreasonable [ʌn'rizənəbəl] *adj* irragionevole

unrecognizable [ʌn'rɛkəg,naɪzəbəl] *adj* irriconoscibile

unreel [ʌn'ril] *tr* svolgere, srotolare || *intr* srotolarsi

unrefined [,ʌnrɪ'faɪnd] *adj* non raffinato, greggio; volgare, ordinario

unrelenting [,ʌnrɪ'lɛntɪŋ] *adj* inesorabile, inflessibile; indefesso

unreliable [,ʌnrɪ'laɪ·əbəl] *adj* malfido; (*news*) inattendibile

unremitting [,ʌnrɪ'mɪtɪŋ] *adj* incessante, costante

unrented [ʌn'rɛntɪd] *adj* da affittare

unrepeatable [,ʌnrɪpitəbəl] *adj* irripetibile

unrepentant [,ʌnrɪ'pɛntənt] *adj* impenitente

un'requit'ed love' [,ʌnrɪ'kwaɪtɪd] *s* amore non corrisposto

unresponsive [,ʌnrɪ'spɑnsɪv] *adj* apatico, insensibile

unrest [ʌn'rɛst] *s* agitazione

un·rig [ʌn'rɪg] *v* (*pret & pp* -rigged; *ger* -rigging) *tr* (naut) disarmare

unrighteous [ʌn'raɪtʃəs] *adj* ingiusto

unripe [ʌn'raɪp] *adj* immaturo

unrivaled or **unrivalled** [ʌn'raɪvəld] *adj* senza pari

unroll [ʌn'rol] *tr* srotolare

unromantic [,ʌnro'mæntɪk] *adj* poco romantico

unruffled [ʌn'rʌfəld] *adj* calmo, imperturbabile

unruly [ʌn'ruli] *adj* turbolento; indisciplinato, insubordinato

unsaddle [ʌn'sædəl] *tr* (*a horse*) dissellare; (*a rider*) scavalcare

unsafe [ʌn'sef] *adj* malsicuro, pericolante

unsaid [ʌn'sɛd] *adj* non detto, taciuto; **to leave unsaid** passare sotto silenzio

unsalable [ʌn'seləbəl] *adj* invendibile

unsanitary [ʌn'sænɪ,tɛri] *adj* antigienico

unsatisfactory [ʌn,sætɪs'fæktəri] *adj* poco soddisfacente

unsatisfied [ʌn'sætɪs,faɪd] *adj* insoddisfatto, inappagato

unsavory [ʌn'sevəri] *adj* insipido; (fig) disgustoso, nauseabondo

un·say [ʌn'se] *v* (*pret & pp* -said [sɛd']) *tr* disdire

unscathed [ʌn'skeðd] *adj* incolume

unscheduled [ʌn'skɛdʒuld] *adj* non in elenco; (*event*) fuori programma; (*e.g., flight*) fuori orario; (*phase of production*) non programmato

unscientific [,ʌnsaɪ·ən'tɪfɪk] *adj* poco scientifico

unscrew [ʌn'skru] *tr* svitare || *intr* svitarsi

unscrupulous [ʌn'skrupjələs] *adj* senza scrupoli

unseal [ʌn'sil] *tr* dissigillare

unseasonable [ʌnˈsizənəbəl] *adj* fuori stagione; inopportuno

unseasoned [ʌnˈsizənd] *adj* scondito; (*crop*) immaturo; (*crew*) inesperto

unseat [ʌnˈsit] *tr* (*a rider*) scavalcare, disarcionare; (*e.g., a congressman*) far perdere il seggio a, defenestrare

unseemly [ʌnˈsimli] *adj* disdicevole, sconveniente

unseen [ʌnˈsin] *adj* non visto, inosservato; nascosto, occulto; invisibile

unselfish [ʌnˈselfiʃ] *adj* disinteressato

unsettled [ʌnˈsetəld] *adj* disabitato; disorganizzato; disordinato, erratico; indeciso; (*bill*) da pagare

unshackle [ʌnˈʃækəl] *tr* liberare

unshaken [ʌnˈʃekən] *adj* inconcusso

unshapely [ʌnˈʃepli] *adj* senza forma, deforme

unshaven [ʌnˈʃevən] *adj* non rasato

unshatterable [ʌnˈʃætərəbəl] *adj* infrangibile

unsheathe [ʌnˈʃið] *tr* sguainare

unshod [ʌnˈʃad] *adj* scalzo; (*horse*) sferrato

unshrinkable [ʌnˈʃriŋkəbəl] *adj* irrestringibile

unsightly [ʌnˈsaɪtli] *adj* ripugnante, brutto

unsinkable [ʌnˈsiŋkəbəl] *adj* insommergibile

unskilled [ʌnˈskild] *adj* inesperto

un'skilled la'bor *s* lavoro manuale; mano d'opera non specializzata

unskillful [ʌnˈskilfəl] *adj* maldestro

unsnarl [ʌnˈsnarl] *tr* sbrogliare

unsociable [ʌnˈsoʃəbəl] *adj* insocievole

unsold [ʌnˈsold] *adj* invenduto

unsolder [ʌnˈsadər] *tr* dissaldare

unsophisticated [ˌʌnsəˈfisti͵ketid] *adj* semplice, puro

unsound [ʌnˈsaʊnd] *adj* malsano, malato; (*decayed*) guasto, imputridito; falso, fallace; (*sleep*) leggero

unsown [ʌnˈson] *adj* incolto, non seminato

unspeakable [ʌnˈspikəbəl] *adj* indicibile; (*atrocious*) innominabile, inqualificabile

unsportsmanlike [ʌnˈsportsmən͵laɪk] *adj* antisportivo

unstable [ʌnˈstebəl] *adj* instabile

unsteady [ʌnˈstedi] *adj* malfermo; incostante; irregolare

unstinted [ʌnˈstintid] *adj* generoso, senza limiti

unstitch [ʌnˈstitʃ] *tr* scucire

un-stop [ʌnˈstap] *v* (*pret & pp -stopped; ger -stopping*) *tr* stasare

unstressed [ʌnˈstrest] *adj* non accentuato; (*e.g., syllable*) non accentato

unstrung [ʌnˈstrʌŋ] *adj* (*beads*) sfilato; (*instrument*) allentato; (*person*) snervato

unsuccessful [ˌʌnsəkˈsesfəl] *adj* (*person*) sfortunato; (*deal*) mancato; to be unsuccessful fallire

unsuitable [ʌnˈsutəbəl] or [ʌnˈsjutəbəl] *adj* inappropriato

unsurpassable [ˌʌnsərˈpæsəbəl] or [ˌʌnsərˈpasəbəl] *adj* insuperabile

unsuspected [ˌʌnsəsˈpektid] *adj* insospettato

unswerving [ʌnˈswʌrviŋ] *adj* diritto, fermo, costante

unsympathetic [ˌʌnsimpəˈθetik] *adj* indifferente, che non mostra comprensione

unsystematic(al) [ˌʌnsistəˈmætik(əl)] *adj* senza sistema

untactful [ʌnˈtæktfəl] *adj* senza tatto

untamed [ʌnˈtemd] *adj* indomito

untangle [ʌnˈtæŋgəl] *tr* sgrovigliare

unteachable [ʌnˈtitʃəbəl] *adj* indocile; refrattario agli studi

untenable [ʌnˈtenəbəl] *adj* insostenibile

unthankful [ʌnˈθæŋkfəl] *adj* ingrato

unthinkable [ʌnˈθiŋkəbəl] *adj* impensabile

unthinking [ʌnˈθiŋkiŋ] *adj* irriflessivo

untidy [ʌnˈtaidi] *adj* disordinato

un-tie [ʌnˈtaɪ] *v* (*pret & pp -tied; ger -tying*) *tr* sciogliere; (*a knot*) slacciare, snodare || *intr* sciogliersi

until [ʌnˈtil] *prep* fino, fino a || *conj* fino a che, finché

untillable [ʌnˈtiləbəl] *adj* incoltivabile

untimely [ʌnˈtaimli] *adj* intempestivo; (*death*) prematuro

untiring [ʌnˈtairiŋ] *adj* instancabile

untold [ʌnˈtold] *adj* non detto, non raccontato; incalcolabile; (*inexpressable*) indicibile

untouchable [ʌnˈtʌtʃəbəl] *adj & s* intoccabile *mf*

untouched [ʌnˈtʌtʃt] *adj* intatto; insensibile; non menzionato

untoward [ʌnˈtord] *adj* sfavorevole; sconveniente, disdicevole

untrammelled or untrammelled [ʌnˈtræməld] *adj* non inceppato

untried [ʌnˈtraid] *adj* non provato

untroubled [ʌnˈtrʌbləd] *adj* tranquillo

untrue [ʌnˈtru] *adj* falso

untrustworthy [ʌnˈtrʌst͵wʌrði] *adj* infido, malfido

untruth [ʌnˈtruθ] *s* falsità *f*, menzogna

untruthful [ʌnˈtruθfəl] *adj* falso, menzognero

untwist [ʌnˈtwist] *tr* districare || *intr* districarsi

unusable [ʌnˈjuzəbəl] *adj* inservibile

unused [ʌnˈjuzd] *adj* inutilizzato; unused to [ʌnˈjustu] disavvezzo a

unusual [ʌnˈjuʒuəl] *adj* insolito

unutterable [ʌnˈʌtərəbəl] *adj* impronunciabile; indicibile

unvanquished [ʌnˈvæŋkwiʃt] *adj* invitto

unvarnished [ʌnˈvarniʃt] *adj* non verniciato; puro, semplice

unveil [ʌnˈvel] *tr* svelare; (*a statue*) scoprire, inaugurare || *intr* scoprirsi

unveiling [ˌʌnˈveliŋ] *s* scoprimento

unvoiced [ʌnˈvɔist] *adj* non espresso; (*phonet*) sordo

unwanted [ʌnˈwantid] *adj* non desiderato

unwarranted [ʌnˈwarəntid] *adj* ingiustificato

unwary [ʌnˈweri] *adj* incauto

unwavering [ʌnˈwevəriŋ] *adj* fermo, incrollabile

unwelcome [ʌnˈwelkəm] *adj* malaccetto, sgradito

unwell [ʌnˈwel] *adj* poco bene; to be

unwell (*said of a woman*) (coll) avere le mestruazioni

unwholesome [ʌn'holsəm] *adj* malsano

unwieldy [ʌn'wildi] *adj* ingombrante

unwilling [ʌn'wiliŋ] *adj* riluttante

unwillingly [ʌn'wiliŋli] *adv* a malincuore, a controvoglia

un-wind [ʌn'waind] *v* (*pret & pp* -**wound** ['waund]) *tr* svolgere ‖ *intr* svolgersi; (*said of a watch*) scaricarsi; (*said of a person*) rilasciarsi

unwise [ʌn'waiz] *adj* malaccorto

unwished-for [ʌn'wiʃt‚fɔr] *adj* indesiderato, non augurato

unwitting [ʌn'witiŋ] *adj* involontario

unwonted [ʌn'wʌntid] *adj* insolito

unworldly [ʌn'wʌrdli] *adj* (*not of this world*) non terrestre; (*not interested in things of this world*) non mondano; (*naïve*) semplice

unworthy [ʌn'wʌrði] *adj* indegno

un-wrap [ʌn'ræp] *v* (*pret & pp* -**wrapped**; *ger* -**wrapping**) *tr* scartare, svolgere, scartocciare

unwrinkled [ʌn'riŋkəld] *adj* senza una grinza

unwritten [ʌn'ritən] *adj* orale; non scritto; (*blank*) in bianco

unyielding [ʌn'jildiŋ] *adj* inflessibile

unyoke [ʌn'jok] *tr* liberare dal giogo

up [ʌp] *adj* che va verso la città; diretto al nord; al corrente; finito, terminato; alto; su; (*sports*) pari; **to be up and about** essere in piedi ‖ *s* salita; vantaggio; aumento; **ups and downs** alti e bassi *mpl* ‖ *adv* su; in alto; alla pari; **to be up** essere alzato; (*in sports or games*) essere avanti; **to be up in arms** essere in armi; essere indignato; **to be up to a person** toccare a una persona; **to get up** alzarsi; **to go up** salire; **to keep up** mantenere; continuare; **to keep up with** mantenersi alla pari con; **up above**, lassù; **up against** (coll) contro; **up against it** (coll) in una strettoia; **up to** fino a; (*capable of*) (coll) all'altezza di; (*scheming*) (coll) tramando; **what's up?** che succede? ‖ *prep* su; sopra; fino a; **to go up a river** risalire un fiume

up-and-coming ['ʌpən‚kʌmiŋ] *adj* promettente

up-and-doing ['ʌpən'du‚iŋ] *adj* (coll) intraprendente; (coll) attivo

up-and-up ['ʌpən'ʌp] *s*—**on the up-and-up** (coll) aperto; (coll) apertamente; (coll) in ascesa

up-braid *tr* rimproverare, strapazzare

upbringing ['ʌp‚briŋiŋ] *s* educazione

up'coun'try *adj* all'interno ‖ *s* interno ‖ *adv* verso l'interno

up-date *tr* aggiornare

upheaval [ʌp'hivəl] *s* sommovimento; (geol) sconvolgimento tellurico

up'hill' *adj* erto, scosceso; arduo, faticoso ‖ *adv* in salita, all'insù

up-hold *v* (*pret & pp* -**held**) *tr* alzare; sostenere; difendere

upholster [ʌp'holstər] *tr* tappezzare

upholsterer [ʌp'holstərər] *s* tappezziere *m*

upholster-y [ʌp'holstəri] *s* (-**ies**) tap-

pezzeria; (*e.g., of cushions*) imbottitura; (aut) selleria

up'keep' *s* manutenzione; **spese** *fpl* di manutenzione

upland ['ʌplənd] or ['ʌplænd] *adj* alto, elevato ‖ *s* terreno elevato

up'lift' *s* elevazione; miglioramento sociale; edificazione ‖ **up'lift'** *tr* elevare

upon [ʌ'pɑn] *prep* su, sopra, in; **upon** + *ger* non appena + *pp*, e.g., **upon arising** non appena alzato; **upon my word!** sulla mia parola!

upper ['ʌpər] *adj* superiore, disopra; (*town*) soprano; (*river*) alto ‖ *s* disopra *m*; (*of shoe*) tomaia; (rr) (coll) cuccetta; **on one's uppers** ridotto al verde

up'per berth' *s* cuccetta superiore

up'per case' *s* (typ) cassa delle maiuscole, cassa superiore

up'per-case' *adj* (typ) maiuscolo

up'per classes' *spl* classi *fpl* elevate

up'per hand' *s* vantaggio; **to have the upper hand** prendere il disopra

up'per-most' *adj* (il) più alto; principale ‖ *adv* principalmente, in primo luogo

uppish ['ʌpiʃ] *adj* (coll) arrogante, snob

up-raise' *tr* alzare, tirare su

up'right' *adj* ritto, verticale; dabbene, onesto ‖ *s* staggio, montante *m* ‖ *adv* verticalmente

uprising [ʌp'raiziŋ] or ['ʌp‚raiziŋ] *s* sollevazione, insurrezione

up'roar' *s* gazzarra, cagnara, fracasso

uproarious [ʌp'rori‚əs] *adj* tumultuoso; (*noisy*) rumoroso; (*funny*) comico

up-root' *tr* sradicare

up-set' *adj* rovesciato; scompigliato; (*emotionally*) scombussolato; (*stomach*) imbarazzato ‖ **up'set'** *s* (*overturn*) rovesciamento; (*defeat*) rovescio; (*disorder*) scompiglio; (*illness*) imbarazzo, disturbo ‖ **up-set'** *v* (*pret & pp* -**set**; *ger* -**setting**) *tr* rovesciare; scompigliare; indisporre ‖ *intr* rovesciarsi, ribaltarsi

upset' price' *s* prezzo minimo di vendita di un oggetto all'asta

upsetting [ʌp'setiŋ] *adj* sconcertante

up'shot' *s* conclusione; essenziale *m*

up'side' *s* disopra *m*

up'side down' *adv* alla rovescia; a gambe all'aria; a soqquadro

up'stage' *adj* al fondo della scena; altiero, arrogante ‖ *adv* al fondo della scena ‖ *tr* trattare altezzosamente; (theat) rubare la scena a

up'stairs' *adj* del piano di sopra ‖ *s* piano di sopra ‖ *adv* su, al piano di sopra

upstanding [ʌp'stændiŋ] *adj* diritto; forte; onorevole

up'start' *s* arrivato, nuovo ricco

up'stream' *adv* a monte, controcorrente

up'stroke' *s* (*in handwriting*) tratto ascendente; (mach) corsa ascendente

up'swing' *s* (*in prices*) ascesa; miglioramento; **to be on the upswing** migliorare

up'-to-date' *adj* recentissimo; moderno; dell'ultima ora

up'town' *adj* della parte più alta della città || *adv* nella parte più alta della città

up'trend' *s* tendenza al rialzo

up'turn' *s* rivolta; (com) rialzo

upturned [ʌpʹtʌrnd] *adj* rivolto all'insù; (*upside down*) capovolto

upward [ʹʌpwərd] *adj* ascendente || *adv* all'insù; upward of più di

U'ral Moun'tains [ʹjʊrəl] *spl* Urali *mpl*

uranium [jʊʹreni·əm] *s* uranio

urban [ʹʌrbən] *adj* urbano

urbane [ʌrʹben] *adj* urbano

urbanite [ʹʌrbə ̩naɪt] *s* abitante *mf* di una città

urbanity [ʌrʹbænɪti] *s* urbanità *f*

urbanize [ʹʌrbə ̩naɪz] *tr* urbanizzare

ur'ban renew'al *s* ricostruzione urbanistica

urchin [ʹʌrtʃɪn] *s* monello, birichino

ure·thra [jʊʹriθrə] *s* (-thras or -thrae [θri]) uretra

urge [ʌrdʒ] *s* stimolo || *tr* urgere, sollecitare, spronare; (*to endeavor to persuade*) esortare; (*an enterprise*) accelerare || *intr*—to urge against opporsi a

urgen·cy [ʹʌrdʒənsi] *s* (-cies) urgenza

urgent [ʹʌrdʒənt] *adj* urgente; (*desire*) prepotente

urinal [ʹjʊrɪnəl] *s* (*receptacle*) orinale *m*; (*for a bedridden person*) pappagallo; (*place*) orinatoio, vespasiano

urinary [ʹjʊrɪ ̩nɛri] *adj* urinario

urinate [ʹjʊrɪ ̩net] *tr & intr* orinare

urine [ʹjʊrɪn] *s* urina

urn [ʌrn] *s* urna; (*for making coffee*) caffettiera; (*for making tea*) samovar *m*

urology [jʊʹrɑlədʒi] *s* urologia

Uruguay [ʹjʊrə ̩gwe] or [ʹjʊrə ̩gwaɪ] *s* l'Uruguai *m*

Uruguayan [̩jʊrəʹgwe·ən] or [̩jʊrəʹgwaɪ·ən] *adj & s* uruguaiano

us [ʌs] *pron pers* ci; noi; to us ci, a noi, per noi

U.S.A. [ʹjuʹesʹe] *s* (letterword) (United States of America) S.U.A. *mpl*

usable [ʹjuzəbəl] *adj* servibile, adoperabile

usage [ʹjusɪdʒ] or [ʹjuzɪdʒ] *s* uso, usanza; (*of a language*) uso

use [jus] *s* uso, impiego, usanza; in use in uso, in servizio; it's no use non giova; out of use disusato; to be of no use non servire a nulla; to have

no use for non aver bisogno di; non poter soffrire; to make use of servirsi di; what's the use? a che pro? || [juz] *tr* usare, impiegare, servirsi di; to use badly maltrattare; to use up consumare, esaurire || *intr*—used to translated in Italian in three ways: (1) by the imperfect indicative, e.g., he used to go to church at seven o'clock andava in chiesa alle sette; (2) by the imperfect indicative of solere, e.g., he used to smoke all day soleva fumare tutto il giorno; (3) by the imperfect indicative of avere l'abitudine di, e.g., he used to go to the shore aveva l'abitudine di andare alla spiaggia

used [juzd] *adj* uso, usato; to get used to [ʹjuzdtu] or [ʹjustu] fare la mano a, abituarsi a

useful [ʹjusfəl] *adj* utile

usefulness [ʹjusfəlnɪs] *s* utilità *f*

useless [ʹjuslɪs] *adj* inutile, inservibile

user [ʹjuzər] *s* utente *mf*

usher [ʹʌʃər] *s* (*doorkeeper*) portiere *m*; (hist) cerimoniere *m*; (theat) maschera; (mov) lucciola || *tr* introdurre; to usher in annunciare, introdurre

U.S.S.R. [ʹjuʹesʹesʹɑr] *s* (letterword) (Union of Soviet Socialist Republics) U.R.S.S. *f*

usual [ʹjuʒʊ·əl] *adj* usuale, abituale; as usual come il solito

usually [ʹjuʒʊ·əli] *adv* usualmente

usurp [jʊʹzʌrp] *tr* usurpare

usu·ry [ʹjuʒəri] *s* (-ries) usura

utensil [jʊʹtensɪl] *s* utensile *m*

uter·us [ʹjutərəs] *s* (-ȋ [̩aɪ]) utero

utilitarian [̩jutɪlɪʹtɛri·ən] *adj* utilitario

utili·ty [jʊʹtɪlɪti] *s* (-ties) utilità *f*; compagnia di servizi pubblici

utilize [ʹjutɪ ̩laɪz] *tr* utilizzare

utmost [ʹʌt ̩most] *adj* sommo; estremo; massimo || *s*—the utmost il massimo; to do one's utmost fare tutto il possibile; to the utmost al massimo limite

utopia [jʊʹtopɪ·ə] *s* utopia

utopian [jʊʹtopɪ·ən] *adj* utopistico || *s* utopista *mf*

utter [ʹʌtər] *adj* completo, totale || *tr* proferire, pronunziare; (*a sigh*) dare, fare

utterly [ʹʌtərli] *adv* completamente

uxoricide [ʌkʹsorɪ ̩saɪd] *s* (*husband*) uxoricida *m*; (*act*) uxoricidio

uxorious [ʌkʹsorɪ·əs] *adj* eccessivamente innamorato della propria moglie; dominato dalla moglie

V

V, v [vi] *s* ventiduesima lettera dell'alfabeto inglese

vacan·cy [ʹvekənsi] *s* (-cies) (*emptiness*) vuoto; (*unfilled position*) vacanza; (*unfilled job*) posto vacante; (*in a building*) appartamento libero;

(*in a hotel*) camera libera; no vacancy completo

vacant [ʹvekənt] *adj* (*empty*) vuoto; (*position*) vacante; (*expression of the face*) vago

vacate [ʹveket] *tr* sgombrare; (*a posi-*

tion) ritirarsi da; (law) annullare; **to vacate one's mind of worries** liberarsi dalle preoccupazioni || *intr* sloggiare; (coll) andarsene

vacation [ve'keʃən] *s* vacanza, villeggiatura; vacanze *fpl* || *intr* estivare, villeggiare

vacationer [ve'keʃənər] *s* villeggiante *m*/, vacanziere *m*

vacationist [ve'keʃənɪst] *s* villeggiante *m*/, vacanziere *m*

vaca'tion with pay' *s* vacanze *fpl* pagate

vaccinate ['væksɪ ,net] *tr* vaccinare

vaccination [,væksɪ'neʃən] *s* vaccinazione

vaccine [væk'sin] *s* vaccino

vacillate ['væsɪ ,let] *intr* vacillare

vacillating ['væsɪ ,letɪŋ] *adj* vacillante

vacul-ty [væ'kju-ɪti] *s* (**-ties**) vacuità *f*

vacu-um ['vækju-əm] *s* (**-ums** or **-a** [ə]) vuoto; **in a vacuum** sotto vuoto || *tr* pulire con l'aspirapolvere

vac'uum clean'er *s* aspirapolvere *m*

vac'uum-pack'ed *adj* confezionato sotto vuoto

vac'uum tube' *s* tubo elettronico

vagabond ['væɡə ,bɑnd] *adj & s* vagabondo

vagar-y [və'ɡɛri] *s* (**-ies**) capriccio

vagran-cy ['veɡrənsi] *s* (**-cies**) vagabondaggio

vagrant ['veɡrənt] *adj & s* vagabondo

vague [veɡ] *adj* vago

va'gus nerve' ['veɡəs] *s* (anat) vago

vain [ven] *adj* vano; (*conceited*) vanitoso; **in vain** in vano

vainglorious [ven'ɡlori-əs] *adj* vanaglorioso

valance ['væləns] *s* balza, mantovana

vale [vel] *s* valle *f*

valedictorian [,vælɪdɪk'tori-ən] *s* studente *m* che pronuncia il discorso di commiato

valence ['veləns] *s* (chem) valenza

valentine ['vælən ,taɪn] *s* (*sweetheart*) valentino; (*card*) cartolina di San Valentino

valet ['vælɪt] or ['væle] *s* valletto

valiant ['væljənt] *adj* valoroso

valid ['vælɪd] *adj* valido

validate ['vælɪ ,det] *tr* convalidare, vidimare; (sports) omologare

validation [,vælɪ'deʃən] *s* convalida, vidimazione; (sports) omologazione

validi-ty [və'lɪdɪti] *s* (**-ties**) validità *f*

valise [və'lis] *s* valigetta

valley ['væli] *s* valle *f*, vallata; (*of roof*) linea di compluvio

valor ['vælər] *s* valore *m*, coraggio

valorous ['vælərəs] *adj* valoroso

valuable ['vælju-əbəl] or ['væljəbəl] *adj* (*having monetary worth*) prezioso; pregevole, pregiato || **valuables** *spl* valori *mpl*

value ['vælju] *s* valore *m*; importanza; (com) valuta, valore *m*; **an excellent value** un acquisto eccellente || *tr* stimare, valutare

value'-added tax' *s* imposta sul valore aggiunto

valueless ['væljulɪs] *adj* senza valore

valve [vælv] *s* (anat, mach, rad, telv)

valvola; (bot, zool) valva; (mus) pistone *m*

valve' gears' *spl* meccanismo di distribuzione

valve'-in-head' en'gine *s* motore *m* a valvole in testa

valve' lift'er ['lɪftər] *s* alzavalvole *m*

valve' seat' *s* sede *f* della valvola

valve' spring' *s* molla di valvola

valve' stem' *s* stelo di comando della valvola

vamp [væmp] *s* parte *f* anteriore della tomaia; (*patchwork*) rabberciatura; (*female*) vamp *f* || *tr* (*a shoe*) rimontare; rabberciare; (*to concoct*) inventare, raffazzonare; (*an accompaniment*) improvvisare; (*said of a female*) sedurre

vampire ['væmpaɪr] *s* vampiro; (*female*) vamp *f*

van [væn] *s* camionetta, autofurgone *m*; (mil & fig) avanguardia

vanadium [və'nedɪ-əm] *s* vanadio

vandal ['vændəl] *adj & s* vandalo || **Vandal** *adj & s* Vandalo

vandalism ['vændə ,lɪzəm] *s* vandalismo

vane [ven] *s* (*weathervane*) banderuola; (*of windmill, of turbine*) pala; (*of feather*) barba

vanguard ['væn ,ɡɑrd] *s* avanguardia; **in the vanguard** all'avanguardia

vanilla [və'nɪlə] *s* vaniglia

vanish ['vænɪʃ] *intr* svanire

van'ishing cream' ['vænɪʃɪŋ] *s* crema evanescente

vani-ty ['vænɪti] *s* (**-ties**) vanità *f*; (*table*) toletta; (*case*) astuccio di toletta

vanquish ['væŋkwɪʃ] *tr* superare, vincere

van'tage ground' ['væntɪdʒ] *s* posizione favorevole

vapid ['væpɪd] *adj* insipido

vapor ['vepər] *s* vapore *m*; (*visible vapor*) vapori *mpl*

vaporize ['vepə ,raɪz] *tr* vaporizzare || *intr* vaporizzarsi

va'por lock' *s* tampone *m* di vapore

vaporous ['vepərəs] *adj* vaporoso

va'por trail' *s* scia di condensazione

variable ['vɛri-əbəl] *adj & s* variabile *f*

variance ['vɛri-əns] *s* divario, differenza; **at variance with** (*a thing*) differente da; differentemente da; (*a person*) in disaccordo con

variant ['vɛri-ənt] *adj & s* variante *f*

variation [,vɛri'eʃən] *s* variazione

varicose ['væri ,kos] *adj* varicoso

varied ['vɛrid] *adj* vario, svariato

variegated ['vɛri-ə ,ɡetɪd] or ['vɛri-,ɡetɪd] *adj* variegato, screziato

varie-ty [və'raɪ-ɪti] *s* (**-ties**) varietà *f*

vari'ety show' *s* spettacolo di varietà

varnish ['vɑrnɪʃ] *s* vernice *f* || *tr* verniciare; (fig) dare la vernice a

variola [və'raɪ-ələ] *s* (pathol) vaiolo

various ['vɛri-əs] *adj* vari; (*vari-colored*) vario, variegato

varsi-ty ['vɑrsɪti] *adj* (sports) universitario || *s* (**-ties**) (sports) squadra numero uno

var·y ['vɛrɪ] *v* (*pret & pp* -ied) *tr & intr* variare

vase [ves] *or* [vez] *s* vaso

vaseline ['væsə‚lin] *s* (trademark) vaselina

vassal ['væsəl] *adj & s* vassallo

vast [væst] *or* [vɑst] *adj* vasto

vastly ['væstli] *or* ['vɑstli] *adv* enormemente

vastness ['væstnɪs] *or* ['vɑstnɪs] *s* vastità *f*

vat [væt] *s* tino, bigoncia

Vatican ['vætɪkən] *adj* vaticano ‖ *s* Vaticano

Vat'ican Cit'y *s* Città *f* del Vaticano

vaudeville ['vodvɪl] *or* ['vɔdəvɪl] *s* spettacolo di varietà; (*theatrical piece*) vaudeville *m*, commedia musicale

vault [vɔlt] *s* volta; (*underground chamber*) cantina; (*of a bank*) camera di sicurezza; (*burial chamber*) cripta; (*of heaven*) cappa; (*leap*) salto ‖ *tr* formare a mo' di volta; saltare ‖ *intr* saltare

vaunt [vɔnt] *or* [vɑnt] *s* vanto, vanteria ‖ *tr* vantarsi di ‖ *intr* vantarsi

veal [vil] *s* vitello

veal' chop' *s* scaloppa, cotoletta di vitello

veal' cut'let *s* scaloppa

vedette [vɪ'dɛt] *s* (nav) vedetta; (mil) sentinella avanzata

veer [vɪr] *s* virata ‖ *tr* far cambiare di direzione a ‖ *intr* virare; (*said of the wind*) cambiare di direzione

vegetable ['vedʒɪtəbəl] *adj* vegetale ‖ *s* (*plant*) vegetale *m*; (*edible plant*) ortaggio; **vegetables** verdura, erbe *fpl*, erbaggi *mpl*, ortaggi *mpl*

veg'etable gar'den *s* orto

veg'etable soup' *s* minestra di verdura

vegetarian [‚vedʒɪ'tɛrɪ·ən] *adj & s* vegetariano

vegetate ['vedʒɪ‚tet] *intr* vegetare

vehemence ['vi·ɪməns] *s* veemenza

vehement ['vi·ɪmənt] *adj* veemente

vehicle ['vi·ɪkəl] *s* veicolo

vehic'ular traf'fic [vɪ'hɪkjələr] *s* circolazione stradale

veil [vel] *s* velo; **to take the veil** prendere il velo ‖ *tr* velare

vein [ven] *s* vena; (*streak*) venatura; (*of ore*) filone *m* ‖ *tr* venare

velar ['vilər] *adj & s* velare *f*

vellum ['veləm] *s* pergamena

veloci·ty [vɪ'lɑsɪti] *s* (-ties) velocità *f*

velvet ['velvɪt] *adj* di velluto ‖ *s* velluto; (slang) guadagno al gioco; (coll) situazione all'acqua di rose

velveteen [‚velvɪ'tin] *s* vellutino di cotone

velvety ['velvɪti] *adj* vellutato

vend [vend] *tr* vendere; (*to peddle*) fare il venditore ambulante di

vend'ing machine' *s* distributore automatico

vendor ['vendər] *s* venditore *m*

veneer [və'nɪr] *s* impiallacciatura, piallaccio; (fig) vernice *f* ‖ *tr* impiallacciare

venerable ['venərəbəl] *adj* venerabile

venerate ['venə‚ret] *tr* venerare

venereal [vɪ'nɪrɪ·əl] *adj* venereo

Venetia [vɪ'ni/ɪ·ə] . *or* [vɪ'ni/ə] *s* (*province*) Venezia

Venetian [vɪ'ni/ən] *adj & s* veneziano

Vene'tian blind' *s* veneziana, persiana avvolgibile

Venezuelan [‚venɪ'zwilən] *adj & s* venezolano

vengeance ['vendʒəns] *s* vendetta; **with a vengeance** violentemente; eccessivamente

vengeful ['vendʒfəl] *adj* vendicativo

Venice ['venɪs] *s* Venezia

venire·man [vɪ'naɪrɪmən] *s* (-men) membro di un collegio di giurati

venison ['venɪsən] *or* ['venɪzən] *s* carne *f* di cervo

venom ['venəm] *s* veleno

venomous ['venəməs] *adj* velenoso

vent [vent] *s* sfiatatoio; (*of jacket*) spacco; **to give vent to** dare sfogo a ‖ *tr* sfogare, sfuriare; mettere uno sfiatatoio a; **to vent one's spleen** sfogare la bile

vent' hole' *s* apertura di sfogo

ventilate ['ventɪ‚let] *tr* ventilare

ventilator ['ventɪ‚letər] *s* ventilatore *m*

ventricle ['ventrɪkəl] *s* ventricolo

ventriloquist [ven'trɪləkwɪst] *s* ventriloquo

venture ['vent/ər] *s* azzardo, avventura rischiosa; **at a venture** alla ventura ‖ *tr* avventurare ‖ *intr* avventurarsi, arrischiarsi

venturesome ['vent/ərsəm] *adj* (*risky*) rischioso; (*daring*) avventuroso

venturous ['vent/ərəs] *adj* avventuroso

vent' win'dow *s* (aut) deflettore *m*

venue ['venju] *s* (law) posto dove ha avuto luogo il reato; (law) luogo dove si riunisce la corte; **change of venue** cambio di giurisdizione

Venus ['vinəs] *s* (*very beautiful woman*) venere *f*; (astr) Venere *m*; (myth) Venere *f*

veracious [vɪ're/əs] *adj* verace

veraci·ty [vɪ'ræsɪti] *s* (-ties) veridicità *f*

veranda *or* **verandah** [və'rændə] *s* veranda

verb [vʌrb] *adj* verbale ‖ *s* verbo

verbalize ['vʌrbə‚laɪz] *tr* esprimere con parole; (gram) convertire in forma verbale ‖ *intr* essere verboso

verbatim [vər'betɪm] *adj* letterale; *adv* parola per parola, testualmente

verbena [vər'binə] *s* (bot) verbena

verbiage ['vʌrbɪ·ɪdʒ] *s* verbosità *f*; (*style of wording*) espressione

verbose [vər'bos] *adj* verboso

verdant ['vʌrdənt] *adj* verde, verdeggiante

verdict ['vʌrdɪkt] *s* verdetto

verdigris ['vʌrdɪ‚gris] *s* verderame *m*

verdure ['vʌrdʒər] *s* verde *m*

verge [vʌrdʒ] *s* orlo, limite *m*; bordo; (*of a column*) fusto; **on the verge of** al punto di; all'orlo di ‖ *intr*—**to verge on** costeggiare, rasentare

verification [‚verɪfɪ'ke/ən] *s* verifica

verify

337

veri·fy ['vɛrɪ ,faɪ] *v* (*pret & pp* **-fied**) *tr* verificare, confermare

verily ['vɛrɪli] *adv* in verità

veritable ['vɛrɪtəbəl] *adj* vero

vermilion [vər'mɪljən] *adj & s* vermiglio

vermin ['vʌrmɪn] *ssg* (*person*) persona abominevole || *spl* (*animals or persons*) insetti *mpl*

vermouth [vər'muθ] *or* ['vʌrmuθ] *s* vermut *m*

vernacular [vər'nækjələr] *adj* volgare || *s* volgare *m*, vernacolo; (*language peculiar to a class or profession*) gergo

versatile ['vʌrsətɪl] *adj* (*person*) versatile; (*tool or device*) a vari usi

verse [vʌrs] *s* verso; (Bib) versetto

versed [vʌrst] *adj* versato

versification [,vʌrsɪfɪ'keʃən] *s* versificazione

versi·fy ['vʌrsɪ ,faɪ] *v* (*pret & pp* **-fied**) *tr & intr* versificare

version ['vʌrʒən] *s* versione

ver·so ['vʌrso] *s* (**-sos**) (*of coin*) rovescio; (*of page*) verso

versus ['vʌrsəs] *prep* contro; in confronto a

verte·bra ['vʌrtɪbrə] *s* (**-brae** [,bri]) *or* **-bras**) vertebra

vertebrate ['vʌrtɪ ,bret] *adj & s* vertebrato

ver·tex ['vʌrteks] *s* (**-texes** *or* **-tices** [tɪ ,siz]) vertice *m*

vertical ['vʌrtɪkəl] *adj & s* verticale *f*

ver'tical hold' *s* (telv) regolatore *m* del sincronismo verticale

ver'tical sta'bilizer *s* (aer) deriva

verti·go ['vʌrtɪ ,go] *s* (**-goes** *or* **-gos**) vertigine *f*

verve [vʌrv] *s* verve *f*, brio

very ['vɛri] *adj* (*utter*) grande, completo; (*precise*) vero e proprio; (*mere*) stesso, e.g., **his very brother** suo fratello stesso || *adv* molto, e.g., **to be very rich** essere molto ricco

vesicle ['vɛsɪkəl] *s* vescichetta

vesper ['vɛspər] *s* vespro; **vespers** vespri *mpl* || **Vesper** *s* Vespero

ves'per bell' *s* campana a vespro

vessel ['vɛsəl] *s* (*ship*) nave *f*, vascello; (*container*) vaso; (anat) vaso; (fig) vasello

vest [vɛst] *s* (*of man's suit*) panciotto, gilè *m*; (*of woman's garment*) corpino || *tr* vestire; **to vest** (*authority*) in concedere a; **to vest with** investire di || *intr* vestirsi; **to vest in** passare a

vest'ed in'terest *s* interesse acquisito

vestibule ['vɛstɪ ,bjul] *s* vestibolo

vestige ['vɛstɪdʒ] *s* vestigio

vestment ['vɛstmənt] *s* (eccl) paramento

vest'-pock'et *adj* da tasca, tascabile

ves·try ['vɛstri] *s* (**-tries**) sagrestia; (*chapel*) cappella; giunta esecutiva della chiesa episcopaliana

ves'try·man *s* (**-men**) membro della giunta esecutiva della chiesa episcopaliana

Vesuvius [vɪ'suvɪ·əs] *or* [vɪ'sjuvɪ·əs] *s* il Vesuvio

vetch [vɛtʃ] *s* veccia; (*grass pea*) cicerchia

veteran ['vɛtərən] *adj & s* veterano

veterinarian [,vɛtərɪ'nɛrɪ·ən] *s* veterinario

veterinar·y ['vɛtərɪ ,nɛri] *adj* veterinario || *s* (**-ies**) veterinario

ve·to ['vito] *s* (**-toes**) veto || *tr* porre il veto a

vex [vɛks] *tr* irritare, tormentare

vexation [vɛk'seʃən] *s* fastidio, contrarietà *f*

vexatious [vɛk'seʃəs] *adj* irritante, fastidioso; (law) vessatorio

vexing ['vɛksɪŋ] *adj* noioso, fastidioso, irritante

via ['vaɪ·ə] *prep* via, per via di

viaduct ['vaɪ·ə ,dʌkt] *s* viadotto

vial ['vaɪ·əl] *s* fiala, boccetta

viand ['vaɪ·ənd] *s* vivanda, manicaretto

viati·cum [vaɪ'ætɪkəm] *s* (**-cums** *or* **-ca** [kə]) (eccl) viatico

vibrate ['vaɪbret] *tr & intr* vibrare

vibration [vaɪ'breʃən] *s* vibrazione

vicar ['vɪkər] *s* vicario

vicarage ['vɪkərɪdʒ] *s* residenza del vicario; (*office; duties*) vicariato

vicarious [vaɪ'kɛrɪ·əs] *or* [vɪ'kɛrɪ·əs] *adj* sostituto; (*punishment*) ricevuto in vece di altra persona; (*power*) delegato; (*enjoyment*) di riflesso

vice [vaɪs] *s* vizio

vice'-ad'miral *s* viceammiraglio, ammiraglio di squadra

vice'-pres'ident *s* vicepresidente *m*

viceroy ['vaɪsrɔɪ] *s* viceré *m*

vice versa ['vaɪsi 'vʌrsə] *or* ['vaɪsə 'vʌrsə] *adv* viceversa

vicini·ty [vɪ'sɪnɪti] *s* (**-ties**) vicinanze *fpl*, paraggi *mpl*

vicious ['vɪʃəs] *adj* vizioso; maligno, malvagio; (*dog*) cattivo, che morde; (*horse*) selvaggio; (*headache*) tremendo; (*reasoning; circle*) vizioso

victim ['vɪktɪm] *s* vittima

victimize ['vɪktɪ ,maɪz] *tr* fare una vittima di; ingannare; (hist) sacrificare

victor ['vɪktər] *s* vincitore *m*

victorious [vɪk'torɪ·əs] *adj* vittorioso

victo·ry ['vɪktəri] *s* (**-ries**) vittoria

victuals ['vɪtəlz] *spl* vettovaglie *fpl*

vid'eo cassette' ['vɪdɪ ,o] *s* videocassetta

vid'eo sig'nal *s* segnale *m* video

vid'eo tape' *s* nastro televisivo

vie [vaɪ] *v* (*pret & pp* **vied;** *ger* **vying**) *intr* gareggiare; **to vie for** disputarsi

Vien·nese [,vi·ə'niz] *adj* viennese || *s* (**-nese**) viennese *mf*

Vietnam [,viɛt'nam] *s* il Vietnam

Vietnam·ese [vɪ ,ɛtnə'miz] *adj* vietnamita || *s* (**-ese**) vietnamita *mf*; (*language*) vietnamita *m*

view [vju] *s* vista; (*picture*) veduta; prospetto; esame *m*; punto di vista; **to be on view** (*said of a corpse*) essere esposto; **to keep in view** non perdere di vista; **to take a dim view of** avere un'opinione scettica di; **with a view to** con lo scopo di || *tr* guardare, osservare; considerare

viewer ['vju·ər] *s* spettatore *m;* (telv) telespettatore *m;* (phot) visore *m;* (phot) proiettore *m* di diapositive

view'find'er *s* (phot) traguardo, visore *m*

view'point' *s* punto di vista

vigil ['vɪdʒɪl] *s* vigilia; **to keep vigil** vegliare

vigilance ['vɪdʒɪləns] *s* vigilanza

vigilant ['vɪdʒɪlənt] *adj* vigilante

vignette [vɪn'jɛt] *s* vignetta

vigor ['vɪgər] *s* vigore *m,* gagliardia

vigorous ['vɪgərəs] *adj* vigoroso

Viking ['vaɪkɪŋ] *s* vichingo

vile [vaɪl] *adj* vile, malvagio; (*wretchedly bad*) orribile; disgustoso; ripugnante; (*filthy*) sporco; (*poor*) povero, basso

vili·fy ['vɪlɪ‚faɪ] *v* (*pret & pp* **-fied**) *tr* vilificare

villa ['vɪlə] *s* villa

village ['vɪlɪdʒ] *s* villaggio, paese *m*

villager ['vɪlɪdʒər] *s* paesano

villain ['vɪlən] *s* scellerato; (*of a play*) cattivo, anima nera

villainous ['vɪlənəs] *adj* vile, infame

villain·y ['vɪlənɪ] *s* (*-ies*) scelleratezza, malvagità *f*

vim [vɪm] *s* vigore *m,* brio

vinaigrette [‚vɪnə'grɛt] *s* boccetta dell'aceto aromatico

vinaigrette' sauce' *s* salsa verde

vindicate ['vɪndɪ‚ket] *tr* scolpare; difendere, sostenere; (*e.g., a claim*) rivendicare

vindictive [vɪn'dɪktɪv] *adj* vendicativo

vine [vaɪn] *s* (*climber*) rampicante *f;* (*grape plant*) vite *f*

vine'dress'er *s* vignaiolo

vinegar ['vɪnɪgər] *s* aceto

vinegarish ['vɪnɪgərɪʃ] *adj* acetoso; (fig) acre, mordace

vinegary ['vɪnɪgərɪ] *adj* acetoso; (fig) irritabile, irascibile

vineyard ['vɪnjərd] *s* vigna, vigneto

vintage ['vɪntɪdʒ] *s* vendemmia; vino di annata eccezionale; (fig) edizione

vintager ['vɪntɪdʒər] *s* vendemmiatore *m*

vin'tage wine' *s* vino di marca

vin'tage year' *s* buona annata

vintner ['vɪntnər] *s* produttore *m* di vino; vinaio

vinyl ['vaɪnɪl] or ['vɪnɪl] *s* vinile *m*

violate ['vaɪə‚let] *tr* violare

violation [‚vaɪə'leʃən] *s* violazione

violence ['vaɪ·ələns] *s* violenza

violent ['vaɪ·ələnt] *adj* violento

violet ['vaɪ‚əlɪt] *adj* violetto || *s* (*color*) violetto, viola; (bot) violetta; (*Viola odorata*) viola mammola

violin [‚vaɪə'lɪn] *s* violino

violinist [‚vaɪə'lɪnɪst] *s* violinista *mf*

violoncellist [‚vaɪələn't‚ʃɛlɪst] or [‚vɪələn't‚ʃɛlɪst] *s* violoncellista *mf*

violoncel·lo [‚vaɪələn't‚ʃɛlo] or [‚vɪələn't‚ʃɛlo] *s* (*-los*) violoncello

VIP ['vi'aɪ'pi] *s* (letterword) (**Very Important Person**) persona di maggiore riguardo

viper ['vaɪpər] *s* vipera; (*any snake*) serpe *f;* (*spiteful person*) vipera

vira·go [vɪ'rego] *s* (*-goes* or *-gos*) megera, donna dal caratteraccio impossibile

virgin ['vʌrdʒɪn] *adj & s* vergine *f* || **Virgin** *s* Vergine *f*

vir'gin birth' *s* parto verginale della Madonna; (zool) partenogenesi *f*

Virgin'ia creep'er [vər'dʒɪnɪ·ə] *s* vite *f* del Canada

virginity [vər'dʒɪnɪti] *s* virginità *f*

Virgo ['vʌrgo] *s* (astr) Vergine *f*

virility [vɪ'rɪlɪti] *s* virilità *f*

virology [vaɪ'rələdʒɪ] *s* virologia

virtual ['vʌrt‚ʃu·əl] *adj* virtuale

virtue ['vʌrt‚ʃu] *s* virtù *f*

virtuosi·ty [‚vʌrt‚ʃu'ɑsɪti] *s* (*-ties*) virtuosità *f,* virtuosismo

virtuo·so [‚vʌrt‚ʃu'oso] *s* (*-sos* or *-si* [si]) virtuoso

virtuous ['vʌrt‚ʃu·əs] *adj* virtuoso

virulence ['vɪrjələns] *s* virulenza

virulent ['vɪrjələnt] *adj* virulento

virus ['vaɪrəs] *s* virus *m*

visa ['vizə] *s* visto || *tr* vistare

visage ['vɪzɪdʒ] *s* faccia; apparenza

vis-à-vis [‚vizə'vi] *adj* l'uno di fronte all'altro || *adv* vis-à-vis || *prep* di fronte a

viscera ['vɪsərə] *spl* visceri *mpl,* viscere *fpl*

viscount ['vaɪkaunt] *s* visconte *m*

viscountess ['vaɪkauntɪs] *s* viscontessa

viscous ['vɪskəs] *adj* viscoso

vise [vaɪs] *s* morsa

visé ['vize] or [vi'ze] *s & tr* var of **visa**

visible ['vɪzɪbəl] *adj* visibile

Visigoth ['vɪzɪ‚gɑθ] *s* visigoto

vision ['vɪʒən] *s* visione; (*sense*) vista

visionar·y ['vɪʒə‚nɛri] *adj* visionario || *s* (*-ies*) visionario

visit ['vɪzɪt] *s* visitare; affliggere, colpire; (*a punishment*) far ricadere || *intr* visitare; (*to chat*) fare un chiacchierata

visitation [‚vɪzɪ'teʃən] *s* visitazione; punizione divina, visita del Signore

vis'iting card' *s* biglietto da visita

vis'iting hours' *spl* orario delle visite

vis'iting nurse' *s* infermiera che visita i pazienti a domicilio

visitor ['vɪzɪtər] *s* visitatore *m*

visor ['vaɪzər] *s* visiera; (fig) maschera

vista ['vɪstə] *s* vista, prospettiva

visual ['vɪʒu·əl] *adj* visivo, visuale

vis'ual acu'ity *s* acutezza visiva

visualize ['vɪʒu·ə‚laɪz] *tr* formare l'immagine mentale di; (*to make visible*) visualizzare

vital ['vaɪtəl] *adj* vitale; (*deadly*) mortale || **vitals** *spl* organi vitali

vitality [vaɪ'tælɪti] *s* vitalità *f*

vitalize ['vaɪtə‚laɪz] *tr* animare, infondere vita a

vi'tal statis'tics *spl* statistiche *fpl* anagrafiche

vitamin ['vaɪtəmɪn] *s* vitamina

vitiate ['vɪʃɪ‚et] *tr* viziare

vitreous ['vɪtrɪ·əs] *adj* vitreo, vetroso

vitriolic [‚vɪtrɪ'ɑlɪk] *adj* di vetriolo; (fig) caustico

vituperate [vaɪ'tupə‚ret] or [vaɪ'tjupə‚ret] *tr* vituperare

viva ['vivə] s evviva ‖ interj viva!

vivacious [vɪ'veɪəs] or [vaɪ've/əs] adj vivace

vivaci‧ty [vɪ'væsɪtɪ] or [vaɪ'væsɪtɪ] s (-ties) vivacità f, gaiezza

viva voce ['vaɪvə 'vosɪ] adv a viva voce

vivid ['vɪvɪd] adj vivido

vivi‧fy ['vɪvɪ ˌfaɪ] v (pret & pp -fied) tr vivificare

vivisection [ˌvɪvɪ'sɛkʃən] s vivisezione

vixen ['vɪksən] s volpe femmina; (ill-tempered woman) megera

vizier [vɪ'zɪr] or ['vɪzjər] s visir m

vocabular‧y [vo'kæbjə ˌlɛrɪ] s (-ies) vocabolario

vocal ['vokəl] adj vocale; (inclined to express oneself freely) che si fa sentire, loquace; (e.g., outburst) verbale

vocalist ['vokəlɪst] s cantante mf; (of jazz) vocalist mf

vocalize ['vokə ˌlaɪz] tr vocalizzare ‖ intr vocalizzarsi

vocation [vo'keʃən] s vocazione; professione, impiego

voca'tional education s istruzione professionale

vocative ['vukətɪv] s vocativo

vociferate [vo'sɪfə ˌret] intr vociferare

vociferous [vo'sɪfərəs] adj rumoroso, vociferante

vogue [vog] s voga, moda; **in vogue** in voga, di moda

voice [vɔɪs] s voce f; (of animals) verso; **in a loud voice** a voce alta; **in a low voice** a voce bassa; **to give voice to** esprimere; **with one voice** con una sola voce ‖ tr esprimere; (phonet) sonorizzare ‖ intr sonorizzarsi

voiced [vɔɪst] adj (phonet) sonoro

voiceless ['vɔɪslɪs] adj senza voce; muto; (phonet) sordo, duro

void [vɔɪd] adj (useless) inutile; (empty) vuoto; (law) invalido, nullo; **void of** sprovvisto di ‖ s vuoto; (gap) buco ‖ tr vuotare; (the bowels) evacuare; annullare ‖ intr andare di corpo

volatile ['vɒlətɪl] adj volatile; instabile; (disposition) volubile, incostante

volatilize ['vɒlətɪ ˌlaɪz] tr volatilizzare ‖ intr volatilizzarsi

volcanic [vɒl'kænɪk] adj vulcanico

volca‧no [vɒl'keno] s (-noes or -nos) vulcano

volition [və'lɪʃən] s volontà f; **of one's own volition** di propria volontà

volley ['vɒlɪ] s (e.g., of bullets) scarica, sventagliata; (tennis) volata ‖ tr colpire a volo ‖ intr colpire la palla a volo

vol'ley‧ball s pallavolo f

volplane ['vɒl ˌplen] s planata ‖ intr planare

volt [volt] s volt m

voltage ['voltɪdʒ] s voltaggio

volt'age divid'er [dɪ'vaɪdər] s divisore m del voltaggio

voltaic [vɒl'te‧ɪk] adj voltaico

volte-face [vɒlt'fɑs] s voltafaccia m

volt'me'ter s voltmetro

voluble ['vɒljəbəl] adj locuace

volume ['vɒljəm] s volume m; **to speak volumes** avere molta importanza; essere molto espressivo

voluminous [və'lumɪnəs] adj voluminoso

voluntar‧y ['vɒlən ˌterɪ] adj volontario ‖ s (-ies) assolo di organo

volunteer [ˌvɒlən'tɪr] adj & s volontario ‖ tr dare or dire volontariamente ‖ intr offrirsi; arruolarsi come volontario; **to volunteer to** + inf offrirsi di + inf

voluptuar‧y [və'lʌptʃʊ ˌerɪ] adj voluttuoso ‖ s (-ries) sibarita m, epicureo

voluptuous [və'lʌptʃʊ‧əs] adj voluttuoso

volute [və'lut] s voluta

vomit ['vɒmɪt] s vomito ‖ tr & intr vomitare, rigettare

voodoo ['vudu] adj di vudù ‖ s (practice) vudù m; (person) vuduista mf

voracious [və're/əs] adj vorace

voracity [və'ræsɪtɪ] s voracità f

vor‧tex ['vɔrtɛks] s (-texes or -tices [tɪ ˌsiz]) vortice m

vota‧ry ['votərɪ] s (-ries) persona legata da un voto; amante mf, appassionato

vote [vot] s voto; **to put to the vote** mettere ai voti; **to tally the votes** procedere allo scrutinio dei voti ‖ tr votare; dichiarare; **to vote down** respingere; **to vote in** eleggere; **to vote out** scacciare ‖ intr votare

vote' get'ter ['getər] s accaparratore m di voti; slogan m che conquista voti

voter ['votər] s elettore m

vot'ing machine' ['votɪŋ] s macchina per registrare lo scrutinio dei voti

votive ['votɪv] adj votivo

vo'tive of'fering s voto, ex voto, offerta votiva

vouch [vautʃ] tr garantire ‖ intr—**to vouch for** (s.th) garantire; (s.o.) rendersi garante per, garantire per

voucher ['vautʃər] s garante mf; (certificate) ricevuta, pezza d'appoggio

vouch‧safe' tr concedere, accordare ‖ intr—**to vouchsafe to** + inf degnarsi di + inf

voussoir [vu'swar] s cuneo

vow [vau] s voto; **to take vows** pronunciare i voti ‖ tr promettere; (vengeance) giurare ‖ intr fare un voto

vowel ['vau‧əl] s vocale f

voyage ['vɔɪ‧ɪdʒ] s viaggio; (by sea) traversata ‖ tr attraversare ‖ intr viaggiare

voyager ['vɔɪ‧ɪdʒər] s viaggiatore m, passeggero

vulcanize ['vʌlkə ˌnaɪz] tr vulcanizzare

vulgar ['vʌlgər] adj volgare; comune, popolare

vulgari‧ty [vʌl'gærɪtɪ] s (-ties) volgarità f

Vul'gar Lat'in s latino volgare

Vulgate ['vʌlget] s Vulgata

vulnerable ['vʌlnərəbəl] adj vulnerabile

vulture ['vʌltʃər] s avvoltoio

W

W, w ['dʌbəl‚ju] *s* ventitreesima lettera dell'alfabeto inglese

wad [wɑd] *s* (*of cotton*) batuffolo, bioccolo; (*of money*) mazzetta, rotolo; (*of tobacco*) pallottola; (*in a gun*) stoppaccio ‖ *v* (*pret & pp* **wadded;** *ger* **wadding**) *tr* arrotolare; (*shot*) comprimere; (fig) imbottire

waddle ['wɑdəl] *s* andatura a mo' di anitra ‖ *intr* scudettare

wade [wed] *tr* guadare ‖ *intr* guadare; avanzare faticosamente; sguazzare; **to wade into** (coll) attaccare violentemente; **to wade through** procedere a stento per; leggere con difficoltà

wad'ing bird' ['wedɪŋ] *s* trampoliere *m*

wafer ['wefər] *s* disco adesivo di carta per chiudere lettere; (*cake*) wafer *m*, cialda; (eccl, med) ostia

waffle ['wɑfəl] *s* cialda

waf'fle i'ron *s* schiacce *fpl*

waft [wæft] or [wɑft] *tr* portare leggermente or a volo ‖ *intr* librarsi, spandersi

wag [wæg] *s* (*of head*) cenno; (*of tail*) scodinzolio; (*person*) burlone *m* ‖ *v* (*pret & pp* **wagged**; *ger* **wagging**) *tr* (*the head*) scuotere; (*the tail*) dimenare ‖ *intr* scodinzolare

wage [wedʒ] *s* salario, paga; **wages** salario, paga; ricompensa; prezzo, e.g., **the wages of sin is death la** morte è il prezzo del peccato ‖ *tr* (*war*) fare

wage' earn'er ['ʌrnər] *s* salariato

wager ['wedʒər] *s* scommessa; **to lay a wager** fare una scommessa ‖ *tr & intr* scommettere

wage'work'er *s* lavoratore salariato

waggish ['wægɪʃ] *adj* scherzoso, comico, burlone

Wagnerian [vɑg'nɪrɪ‑ən] *adj & s* wagneriano

wagon ['wægən] *s* carro, carretto; (*e.g., Conestoga wagon*) carriaggio; furgone *m*; carrozzone *m*; **to be on the wagon** (slang) astenersi dal bere; **to hitch one's wagon to a star** avere altissime ambizioni

wag'tail' *s* (orn) ballerina, cutrettola

waif [wef] *s* (*foundling*) trovatello; abbandonato; animale smarrito

wail [wel] *s* gemito, lamento ‖ *intr* gemere, lamentarsi

wain-scot ['wenskət] or ['wenskɑt] *s* pannello per rivestimenti ‖ *v* (*pret & pp* -scoted or -scotted; *ger* -scoting or -scotting) *tr* rivestire di pannelli di legno

waist [west] *s* vita, cintura; blusa, camicetta, corpetto

waist'band' *s* cintola

waist'cloth' *s* perizoma *m*

waistcoat ['west‚kɑt] or ['westkət] *s* corpetto, gilè *m*

waist'line' *s* vita, cintura; **to keep or watch one's waistline** conservare la linea

wait [wet] *s* attesa; **to lie in wait** attendere al varco ‖ *tr* (*one's turn*) attendere ‖ *intr* attendere, aspettare; **to wait for** attendere, aspettare; **to wait on** servire; **to wait up for** (coll) aspettare alzato

wait'-and-see' pol'icy *s* attendismo

waiter ['wetər] *s* cameriere *m*; (*tray*) vassoio

wait'ing list' *s* lista di aspettativa

wait'ing room' *s* sala d'aspetto

waitress ['wetrɪs] *s* cameriera

waive [wev] *tr* (*one's rights*) rinunciare (with *dat*); differire; mettere da parte

waiver ['wevər] *s* rinuncia

wake [wek] *s* (*any watch*) veglia; (*watch by a dead body*) veglia funebre; (*of a boat*) solco, scia; **in the wake of** come risultato di; nelle orme di ‖ *v* (*pret* **waked** or **woke** [wok]; *pp* **waked**) *tr* svegliare ‖ *intr* svegliarsi; **to wake to** darsi conto di; **to wake up** svegliarsi

wakeful ['wekfəl] *adj* sveglio; insonne

waken ['wekən] *tr* svegliare ‖ *intr* svegliarsi

wale [wel] *s* segno lasciato da una frustata, vescica; (*in fabric*) riga, costa

Wales [welz] *s* la Galles

walk [wɔk] *s* (*act*) camminata; (*distance*) cammino; (*for pleasure*) passeggiata; (*gait*) andatura; (*line of work*) attività *f*, mestiere *m*; (*sidewalk*) marciapiede *m*; (*in a garden*) sentiero; (*yard for domestic animals to exercise in*) recinto; (sports) marcia; **to go for a walk** andare a fare una passeggiata ‖ *tr* (*a street*) percorrere; (*a horse*) passeggiare; (*a patient*) far camminare; (*a heavy piece of furniture*) abbambinare; **to walk off** (*a headache*) far passare camminando ‖ *intr* camminare; passeggiare; (*said of a horse*) andare al passo; (sports) marciare; **to walk away from** andarsene a piedi da; **to walk off with** rubare; vincere con facilità; **to walk out** uscire in segno di protesta; (coll) mettersi in sciopero; **to walk out on** (coll) piantare in asso

walkaway ['wɔkə‚we] *s* facile vittoria

walker ['wɔkər] *s* camminatore *m*; (*to teach a baby to walk*) girello

walkie-talkie ['wɔki'tɔki] *s* trasmettitore-ricevitore *m* portatile

walk'ing pa'pers *spl*—**to give s.o. his walking papers** (coll) dare gli otto giorni a qlcu

walk'-in refrig'erator *s* cella frigorifera

walk'ing stick' *s* bastone *m* da passeggio

walk'-on' *s* (*actor*) figurante *m*, comparsa; (*role*) particina

walk'out' *s* sciopero

walk'o'ver *s* facile vittoria, passeggiata

wall [wɔl] *s* muro; (*between rooms*; *of a vein*) parete *f*; (*rampart*) muraglia; **to drive to the wall** ridurre alla disperazione; **to go to the wall** perdere; fare fallimento || *tr* murare; **to wall up** circondare con muro

wall'board' *s* pannello da costruzione

wallet ['walɪt] *s* portafoglio

wall'flow'er *s* violacciocca gialla; **to be a wallflower** fare tappezzeria

Walloon [wɑ'lun] *adj & s* vallone *mf*

wallop ['waləp] *s* (coll) colpo violento; (coll) effetto || *tr* (coll) dare un colpo violento a; (coll) battere completamente

wallow ['walo] *s* diguazzamento; (*place*) brago, pantano || *intr* diguazzare; (*in wealth*) nuotare

wall'pa'per *s* tappezzeria || *tr* tappezzare

walnut ['wɔlnət] *s* (*tree; wood*) noce *m*; (*fruit*) noce *f*

walrus ['wɔlrəs] *or* ['wælrəs] *s* tricheco

Walter ['wɔltər] *s* Gualtiero

waltz [wɔlts] *s* valzer *m* || *tr* ballare il valzer con; (coll) condurre con disinvoltura || *intr* ballare il valzer

wan [wɑn] *adj* (**wanner; wannest**) (*face*) smunto, sparuto, smorto; (*light*) debole

wand [wɑnd] *s* bacchetta

wander ['wɑndər] *tr* vagare per || *intr* vagare, vagabondare; errare

wanderer ['wɑndərər] *s* vagabondo; pellegrino

Wan'dering Jew' *s* ebreo errante

wan'der·lust' *s* passione del vagabondaggio

wane [wen] *s* decadenza, declino; calare *m* della luna; **on the wane** in declino; (*moon*) calante || *intr* decadere, declinare; (*said of the moon*) calare

wangle ['wæŋgəl] *tr* (coll) ottenere con l'astuzia, rimediare; (coll) falsificare; **to wangle one's way out of** (coll) tirarsi fuori da . . . con l'astuzia || *intr* (coll) arrangiarsi

want [wɑnt] *or* [wɔnt] *s* bisogno, necessità *f*; domanda; miseria; **for want of** a causa della mancanza di; **to be in want** essere in miseria; **to be in want of** aver bisogno di || *tr* volere, desiderare; mancare; aver bisogno di || *intr* desiderare; **to be wanting** mancare, e.g., **three cards are wanting** mancano tre carte; **to want for** aver bisogno di

want' ad' *s* annunzio economico

wanton ['wɑntən] *adj* di proposito, deliberato; arbitrario; licenzioso, sfrenato; (*archaic*) lussureggiante

war [wɔr] *s* guerra; **to go to war** entrare in guerra; (*said of a soldier*) andare in guerra; **to wage war** fare la guerra || *v* (*pret & pp* **warred; ger warring**) *intr* guerreggiare; **to war on** fare la guerra a

warble ['wɔrbəl] *s* gorgheggio || *intr* gorgheggiare

warbler ['wɔrblər] *s* canterino; uccello canoro; (orn) beccafico

war' cloud' *s* minaccia di guerra

ward [wɔrd] *s* (*of city*) distretto; (*division of hospital*) corsia; (*separate building in hospital*) padiglione *m*;

(*guardianship*) tutela; (*minor*) pupillo; (*of lock*) scontro || *tr*—**to ward off** stornare, schermirsi da

warden ['wɔrdən] *s* guardiano; (*of jail*) direttore *m*; (*in wartime*) capofabbricato

ward' heel'er *s* politicantuccio

ward'robe *s* guardaroba *m*

ward'robe trunk' *s* baule *m* armadio

ward'room' *s* (nav) quadrato

ware [wɛr] *s* vasellame *m*; **wares** merce *f*

war' ef'fort *s* sforzo bellico

ware'house' *s* deposito, magazzino

ware'house'man *s* (-men) magazziniere *m*

war'fare' *s* guerra

war'head' *s* (mil) testa

war'horse' *s* cavallo di battaglia; (coll) veterano

warily ['wɛrɪli] *adv* con cautela

wariness ['wɛrɪnɪs] *s* cautela

war'like' *adj* guerresco, guerriero

war' loan' *s* prestito di guerra

war' lord' *s* generalissimo

warm [wɔrm] *adj* caldo; (*lukewarm*) tiepido; (*clothes*) che tiene caldo; (*with anger*) acceso; **to be warm** (*said of a person*) avere caldo; (*said of the weather*) fare caldo || *tr* scaldare, riscaldare; (*s.o.'s heart*) slargare; **to warm up** riscaldare || *intr* scaldarsi, riscaldarsi; **to warm up** (*said, e.g., of a room*) riscaldarsi; (*with emotion*) eccitarsi, accalorarsi; **to warm up to** prender simpatia per

warm-blooded ['wɔrm'blʌdɪd] *adj* (*animal*) a sangue caldo; impetuoso, ardente

war' memo'rial *s* monumento ai caduti

warmer ['wɔrmər] *s* scaldino

warm-hearted ['wɔrm'hɑrtɪd] *adj* caloroso, cordiale

warm'ing pan' *s* scaldaletto

warmonger ['wɔr,mʌŋgər] *s* guerrafondaio

war' moth'er *s* madrina di guerra

warmth [wɔrmθ] *s* calore *m*, tepore *m*; foga, entusiasmo

warm'up' *s* preparazione; (*of radio, engine, etc.*) riscaldamento

warn [wɔrn] *tr* avvertire, mettere in guardia; (*to admonish*) ammonire; informare; **to warn off** intimare di allontanarsi (da)

warn'ing *adj* di avvertimento || *s* avvertimento, ammonimento; (law) diffida

war' nose' *s* acciarino, testa

war' of nerves' *s* guerra dei nervi

War' of the Roses' *s* Guerra delle due Rose

warp [wɔrp] *s* (*of a fabric*) ordito; (*of a board*) svergolamento, curvatura; aberrazione mentale; (naut) gherlino || *tr* curvare, svergolare; (*a fabric*) ordire; falsare, alterare; (naut) tirare col gherlino || *intr* curvarsi; falsarsi, alterarsi; (naut) alare

war'path' *s*—**to be on the warpath** essere sul sentiero della guerra, prepararsi alla guerra; (*to be angry*) essere arrabiato, essere di cattivo umore

war'plane' s aeroplano da guerra

war' prof'iteer s pescecane m

warrant ['wɔrənt] or ['wɔrənt] s garanzia; certificato; ricevuta; (com) nota di pegno; (law) ordine m, mandato ‖ tr garantire; autorizzare

warrantable ['wɔrəntəbəl] or ['wɔrəntəbəl] adj giustificabile, legittimo

war'rant of'ficer s sottufficiale m

warran·ty ['wɔrənti] or ['wɔrənti] s (-ties) garanzia; autorizzazione

warren ['wɔrən] or ['wɔrən] s conigliera; (fig) formicaio

warrior ['wɔrjər] or ['wɑrjər] s guerriero

Warsaw ['wɔrsɔ] s Varsavia

war'ship' s nave f da guerra

wart [wɔrt] s verruca

war'time' s tempo di guerra

war'-torn' adj devastato dalla guerra

war' to the death' s guerra a morte

war·y ['weri] adj (-ier; -iest) guardingo

wash [wɑʃ] or [wɔʃ] s lavata; (clothes washed or to be washed) bucato; (rushing movement of water) sciacquio; (dirty water) lavatura; (painting) mano f di colore; (aer, naut) scia ‖ tr lavare; (dishes) rigovernare; (said of sea or river) bagnare; to be washed up essere finito; to wash away (soil of river bank) dilavare; portar via ‖ intr lavarsi; fare il bucato; essere lavabile; (said of waves) battere

washable ['wɑʃəbəl] or ['wɔʃəbəl] adj lavabile

wash'-and-wear' adj non-stiro

wash'ba'sin s conca, catinella

wash'bas'ket s cesto del bucato

wash'board' s asse m da lavanda; (baseboard) battiscopa m

wash'bowl' s conca, catinella

wash'cloth' s pezzuola per lavarsi

wash'day' s giorno del bucato

washed-out ['wɑʃt ‚aut] or ['wɔʃt ‚aut] adj slavato; (coll) stanco; (coll) abbattuto, accasciato

washed-up ['wɑʃt/ʌp] or ['wɔʃt/ʌp] adj (coll) finito

washer ['wɑʃər] or ['wɔʃər] s (person) lavatore m; (machine) lavatrice f; (under head of bolt) rondella, rosetta; (ring to prevent leakage) guarnizione

wash'er·man s (-men) lavatore m

wash'er·wom'an s (-wom'en) lavatrice f, lavandaia

wash' goods' spl tessuti mpl lavabili

washing ['wɑʃɪŋ] or ['wɔʃɪŋ] s lavata, lavaggio, lavanda; (of clothes) bucato; washings lavaggio

wash'ing machine' s lavabiancheria, lavatrice f

wash'ing so'da s soda da lavare

wash'out' s erosione; (aer) svergolamento negativo; (coll) rovina completa

wash'rag' s pezzuola per lavarsi; straccio di cucina

wash'room' s gabinetto, toletta

wash'stand' s lavabo, lavamano

wash'tub' s mastello, lavatoio

wash' wa'ter s lavatura

wasp [wɑsp] s vespa

waste [west] s spreco; (refuse) scarico, rifiuto; (desolate country) landa; (excess material) scarto; (for wiping machinery) cascame m di cotone; to go to waste essere sciupato; to lay waste devastare ‖ tr perdere, sciupare, sprecare ‖ intr—to waste away intristire, consumarsi

waste'bas'ket s cestino della carta straccia

wasteful ['westfəl] adj dispendioso; distruttivo

waste'pa'per s cartastraccia

waste' pipe' s tubo di scarico

waste' prod'uct s scarto; (body excretion) escremento

wastrel ['westrəl] s sciupone m; spendaccione m, prodigo

watch [wɑtʃ] s orologio; (lookout) guardia; (mil) guardia; (naut) turno; to be on the watch for essere all'erta per; to keep watch over vegliare su ‖ tr (to look at) osservare; (to oversee) vigilare; guardare; fare attenzione a ‖ intr guardare; (to keep awake) vegliare; to watch for fare attenzione a; to watch out fare attenzione; to watch out for fare attenzione a; essere all'erta per; to watch over sorvegliare; watch out! attenzione!

watch'band' s cinturino dell'orologio

watch'case' s cassa dell'orologio

watch' charm' s ciondolo dell'orologio

watch' crys'tal s cristallo dell'orologio

watch'dog' s cane m da guardia; (fig) guardiano

watch'dog' commit'tee s comitato di sorveglianza

watchful ['wɑtʃfəl] adj vigile

watchfulness ['wɑtʃfəlnɪs] s vigilanza

watch'mak'er s orologiaio

watch'man s (-men) guardiano, sorvegliante m; (at night) guardia notturna, metronotte m

watch' night' s notte f di San Silvestro; ufficio religioso della vigilia di Capodanno

watch' pock'et s taschino dell'orologio

watch'tow'er s torre f d'osservazione

watch'word' s parola d'ordine, consegna; slogan m

water ['wɔtər] or ['wɑtər] s acqua; of the first water di prim'ordine; (e.g., a thief) della più bell'acqua; to back water retrocedere; to be in deep water essere in cattive acque; to fish in troubled waters pescare nel torbido; to hold water aver fondamento; to keep above water (fig) tenersi a galla; to make water (to urinate) urinare; (naut) fare acqua; to throw cold water on scoraggiare ‖ tr bagnare; dare acqua a; (cattle) abbeverare; (wine) annacquare ‖ intr abbeverarsi; (said of the mouth) aver l'acquolina; (said, e.g., of a ship) fare acqua; (said of the eyes) lacrimare

wa'ter bug' *s* bacherozzolo
wa'ter car'rier *s* acquaiolo
wa'ter-col'or *s* acquerello
wa'ter-cooled' *adj* a raffreddamento ad
  acqua
wa'ter-course' *s* corso d'acqua
wa'ter-cress' *s* crescione *m*
wa'ter cure' *s* cura delle acque
wa'ter-fall' *s* cascata
wa'ter-front' *s* riva, banchina
wa'ter gap' *s* gola, passo
wa'ter ham'mer *s* colpo d'ariete
wa'ter heat'er *s* scaldabagno, scalda-
  acqua *m*
wa'ter ice' *s* granita
wa'tering can' *s* annaffiatoio
wa'tering place' *s* stabilimento balneare; stazione termale; (*drinking
  place*) abbeveratoio
wa'tering pot' *s* annaffiatoio
wa'tering trough' *s* abbeveratoio
wa'ter jack'et *s* camicia d'acqua
wa'ter lil'y *s* nenufaro
wa'ter line' *s* linea di galleggiamento
  or d'acqua; linea di livello
wa'ter main' *s* tubo di flusso principale
wa'ter-mark' *s* linea di livello massimo;
  (*in paper*) filigrana
wa'ter-mel'on *s* cocomero, anguria
wa'ter me'ter *s* contatore *m* dell'acqua
wa'ter mill' *s* mulino ad acqua
wa'ter pipe' *s* tubo dell'acqua
wa'ter po'lo *s* pallanuoto *f*
wa'ter pow'er *s* forza idrica
wa'ter-proof' *adj* & *s* impermeabile *m*
wa'ter-repel'lent *adj* idroripellente
wa'ter-shed' *s* spartiacque *m*, displuvio
wa'ter ski' *s* idrosci *m*
wa'ter sof'tener *s* decalcificatore *m*
wa'ter-spout' *s* (*to carry water from
  roof*) pluviale *m*; (meteor) tromba
  marina
wa'ter sys'tem *s* (*of a river*) sistema *m*
  fluviale; (*of city*) conduttura del-
  l'acqua, impianto idrico
wa'ter-tight' *adj* stagno, ermetico; (fig)
  perfetto, inconfutabile
wa'ter tow'er *s* torre *f* serbatoio
wa'ter wag'on *s* (mil) carro dell'acqua;
  to be on the wa'ter wag'on (slang)
  astenersi dal bere
wa'ter•way' *s* via d'acqua, idrovia
wa'ter wheel' *s* ruota or turbina idraulica; (*of steamboat*) ruota a pale
wa'ter wings' *spl* galleggiante *m* per
  nuotare
wa'ter-works' *s* impianto idrico;
  (*pumping station*) impianto di pom-
  paggio
watery ['wɔtəri] or ['wɑtəri] *adj* acquoso; lacrimoso; povero, insipido;
  umido, acquitrinoso
watt [wɑt] *s* watt *m*
watt'-hour' *s* (-hours) wattora *m*
wattle ['wɑtəl] *s* (*of bird*) bargiglio
watt'me'ter *s* wattmetro
wave [wev] *s* onda; (*of cold*; *of feeling*) ondata; (*of the hand*) cenno; (*of
  hair*) onda, ondulazione || *tr* (*a flag*)
  sventolare; (*the hair*) ondulare; (*the
  hand*) fare cenno con; to wave aside
  fare cenno di allontanarsi a; (*e.g., a*

proposal) rifiutare || *intr* ondeggiare,
  fare cenni con la mano
wave'length' *s* lunghezza d'onda
wave' mo'tion *s* movimento ondula-
  torio
waver ['wevər] *intr* ondeggiare, oscillare; (*to hesitate*) titubare, tentennare; (*to totter*) pencolare
wav•y ['wevi] *adj* (-ier; -iest) (*sea*) on-
  doso; (*hair*) ondulato
wax [wæks] *s* cera; (fig) fantoccio || *tr*
  incerare; (*a recording*) (coll) regi-
  strare || *intr* aumentare; diventare;
  (*said of the moon*) crescere; to wax
  indignant indignarsi
wax' pa'per *s* carta cerata, carta oleata
wax'works' *s* museo di statue di cera
way [we] *s* maniera, modo; via; condizione; across the way di fronte; a
  good way un buon tratto; all the way
  fino alla fine della strada; completamente; all the way to fino a; any way
  ad ogni modo; by the way a proposito; in a way in un certo modo; fino
  a un certo punto; in every way per
  ogni verso; in this way in questa
  maniera; one way senso unico; on
  the way to andando a; on the way
  out uscendo; diminuendo, sparendo;
  out of the way eliminato; fuori
  mano; strano; irregolare; that way
  in quella direzione; per di lì; in
  quella maniera; this way in questa
  direzione; per di qui; in questa maniera; to be in the way essere d'impaccio; to feel one's way avanzare a
  tentoni; to force one's way aprirsi il
  passo a viva forza; to get out of the
  way togliersi di mezzo; to give way
  ritirarsi, cedere; (*said of a rope*)
  rompersi; to give way to cedere a,
  darsi a; to go out of one's way darsi
  da fare, disturbarsi; to have one's
  way vincerla; to keep out of the way
  stare fuori dai piedi; to know one's
  way around conoscere bene la via;
  (fig) sapere il fatto proprio; to know
  one's way to sapere andare a; to lead
  the way guidare, fare da guida; prendere l'iniziativa; to lose one's way
  perdersi; to make one's way avanzare; fare carriera; to make way for
  far largo a; to mend one's ways mettere la testa a partito; to not know
  which way to turn non sapere a che
  santo votarsi; to put out of the way
  togliere di mezzo; to see one's way to
  vedere la possibilità di; to take one's
  way andarsene; to wind one's way
  through andare a zig zag per; to wing
  one's way andare a volo; under way
  in moto; in cammino, avviato; way
  in entrata; way out uscita; ways modi
  mpl, maniere *fpl*; (naut) scalo; which
  way? da che parte?; in che modo?,
  per dove?
way'bill' *s* lettera di vettura
wayfarer ['we,ferər] *s* viandante *m*
way'lay' *v* (*pret* & *pp* -laid) *tr* tendere
  un agguato a; fermare improvvisa-
  mente
way' of life' *s* tenore *m* di vita

way'side' s bordo della strada; **to fall by the wayside** cadere per istrada; (fig) fare fiasco

way' sta'tion s stazione con fermata facoltativa

way' train' s treno omnibus

wayward ['wewərd] adj indocile, caparbio; irregolare; capriccioso

we [wi] pron pers noi; noialtri, e.g., **we Italians** noialtri italiani

weak [wik] adj debole

weaken ['wikən] tr indebolire, infiacchire || intr indebolirsi, infiacchirsi

weakling ['wiklɪŋ] s debolino, rammollito

weak-minded ['wik'maɪndɪd] adj irresoluto; scemo

weakness ['wiknɪs] s debolezza, fiacchezza; (liking) debole m

wealth [welθ] s ricchezza

wealth·y ['welθi] adj (-ier; -iest) ricco

wean [win] tr svezzare, slattare; **to wean away from** disavvezzare da

weanling ['winlɪŋ] adj appena svezzato || s bambino or animale appena svezzato

weapon ['wepən] s arma

weaponry ['wepənri] s armi fpl, armamento

wear [wer] s uso, servizio; (clothing) vestiti mpl, indumenti mpl; (wasting away from use) consumo, logorio; (lasting quality) durata, durabilità f; **for everyday wear** per ogni giorno || v (pret **wore** [wor]; pp **worn** [worn]) tr portare, avere indosso; (to cause to deteriorate) logorare, consumare; (to tire) stancare; **to wear out** logorare, strusciare; (a horse) sfiancare; (one's patience) esaurire; (s.o.'s hospitality) abusare di || intr logorarsi, consumarsi; (to wear off) diminuire, sparire; **to wear out** logorarsi; stancarsi; esaurirsi; **to wear well** essere di ottima durata

wear' and tear' [ter] s logorio

weariness ['wɪrɪnɪs] s fatica, stanchezza

wear'ing appar'el ['werɪŋ] s abbigliamento, articoli mpl d'abbigliamento

wearisome ['wɪrɪsəm] adj affaticante; (tedious) noioso

wea·ry ['wɪri] adj (-rier; -riest) stanco || v (pret & pp -ried) tr stancare || intr stancarsi

weasel ['wizəl] s donnola

wea'sel words' spl parole fpl ambigue

weather ['weðər] s tempo; maltempo; **to be under the weather** (coll) non sentirsi bene; (to be slightly drunk) (coll) essere alticcio || tr (lumber) stagionare; (adversities) superare, resistere (with dat)

weather-beaten ['weðər,bitən] adj segnato dalle intemperie

weath'er bu'reau s servizio metereologico

weath'er·cock' s banderuola

weath'er fore'cast s previsioni fpl del tempo, bollettino metereologico

weath'er·man' s (-men') metereologo

weath'er report' s bollettino metereologico

weath'er strip'ping ['strɪpɪŋ] s guarnizione a nastro per inzeppare

weath'er vane' s banderuola, ventarola

weave [wiv] s tessitura || v (pret **wove** [wov] or **weaved**; pp **wove** or **woven** ['wovən]) tr tessere; (fig) inserire; **to weave one's way** aprirsi un varco serpeggiando || intr tessere; serpeggiare

weaver ['wivər] s tessitore m

web [web] s tessuto; (of spider) tela; (of rail) anima, gambo; (zool) membrana; (fig) rete f, maglia

web-footed ['web,futɪd] adj palmipede

wed [wed] v (pret & pp **wed** or **wedded**; ger **wedding**) tr sposare; (said of the groom) impalmare; (said of the bride) andare in sposa a || intr sposarsi

wedding ['wedɪŋ] adj nuziale || s sposalizio, nozze fpl, matrimonio

wed'ding cake' s torta nuziale

wed'ding day' s giorno di nozze

wed'ding invita'tion s invito a nozze

wed'ding march' s marcia nuziale

wed'ding ring' s fede f, vera

wedge [wedʒ] s cuneo; (of pie) spicchio; (to split wood) bietta; (to hold a wheel) scarpa || tr incuneare

wed'lock s matrimonio

Wednesday ['wenzdi] s mercoledì m

wee [wi] adj piccolo piccolo

weed [wid] s malerba, erbaccia; (coll) sigaretta; (slang) marijuana; **weeds** vestito da lutto, gramaglie fpl || tr sarchiare, mondare

weeder ['widər] s (agr) estirpatore m

weed'ing hoe' s sarchio, zappa

weed'-kill'er s diserbante m

week [wik] s settimana; **week in, week out** una settimana dopo l'altra

week'day' s giorno feriale

week'end' s fine-settimana m, fine f di settimana, week-end m || intr passare il fine-settimana

week·ly ['wikli] adj settimanale || s (-lies) settimanale m || adv settimanalmente

weep [wip] v (pret & pp **wept** [wept]) tr piangere; **to weep oneself to sleep** addormentarsi piangendo; **to weep one's eyes out** piangere a calde lacrime || intr piangere; **to weep for joy** piangere di gioia

weeper ['wipər] s piagnone m; (hired mourner) prefica

weep'ing wil'low s salice m piangente

weep·y ['wipi] adj (-ier; -iest) piangente, lacrimoso

weevil ['wivəl] s curculione m

weft [weft] s (yarns running across warp) trama; (fabric) tela, tessuto

weigh [we] tr pesare; (anchor) levare; (to make heavy) appesantire; (fig) soppesare, ponderare; **to weigh down** piegare || intr pesare; gravitare; **to weigh in** (sports) pesarsi; **to weigh upon** gravare a

weigh'bridge' s stadera

weight [wet] s peso; (fig) peso; **to carry weight** aver del peso; **to lose weight** diminuire di peso; **to put on weight** crescere di peso; **to throw**

one's weight around far sentire la propria importanza || *tr* appesantire; (*statistically*) ponderare, dare un certo peso a

weightless ['wetlɪs] *adj* senza peso, imponderabile

weightlessness ['wetlɪsnɪs] *s* imponderabilità *f*

weight·y ['weti] *adj* (-ier; -iest) pesante; importante

weir [wɪr] *s* sbarramento; (*for catching fish*) pescaia

weird [wɪrd] *adj* soprannaturale, misterioso; strano, bizzarro

welcome ['wɛlkəm] *adj* benvenuto; gradito; **you are welcome** (*i.e., gladly received*) sia il benvenuto; (*in answer to thanks*) prego; **you are welcome to it** è a Sua disposizione; **you are welcome to your opinion** pensi come la vuole || *s* benvenuto || *tr* dare il benvenuto a; accettare; gradire || *interj* benvenuto!

weld [wɛld] *s* saldatura autogena; (bot) guaderella || *tr* saldare || *intr* saldarsi

welder ['wɛldər] *s* saldatore *m*; (*machine*) saldatrice *f*

welding ['wɛldɪŋ] *s* saldatura autogena

wel'fare' *s* benessere *m*; (*effort to improve living conditions*) beneficenza, assistenza; **to be on welfare** ricevere assistenza pubblica

wel'fare state' *s* stato sociale or assistenziale

well [wɛl] *adj* bene; in buona salute || *s* pozzo; (*for ink*) pozzetto, serbatoio; (*spring*) sorgente *f*; (*shaft for stairs*) tromba || *adv* bene; **as well** pure; **as well . . . as tanto . . . come; as well as** tanto come, non meno che || *intr* —**to well up** sgorgare || *interj* beh!; bene!; allora!; dunque!

well-appointed ['wɛlə'pɔɪntɪd] *adj* ben ammobiliato

well-attended ['wɛlə'tɛndɪd] *adj* molto frequentato

well'-be'ing *s* benessere *m*

well'born' *adj* bennato

well-bred ['wɛl'brɛd] *adj* educato, costumato

well-disposed ['wɛldɪs'pozd] *adj* bendisposto

well-done ['wɛl'dʌn] *adj* benfatto; (*meat*) ben cotto

well-fixed ['wɛl'fɪkst] *adj* (coll) agiato, abbiente

well-formed ['wɛl'fɔrmd] *adj* benfatto

well-founded ['wɛl'faʊndɪd] *adj* fondato

well-groomed ['wɛl'grumd] *adj* (*person*) curato; (*horse*) ben governato

well-heeled ['wɛl'hild] *adj* (coll) agiato, benestante

well-informed ['wɛlɪn'fɔrmd] *adj* bene informato

well-intentioned ['wɛlɪn'tɛnʃənd] *adj* benintenzionato

well'-kept' *adj* ben conservato; (*person*) benportante; (*secret*) ben mantenuto

well-known ['wɛl'non] *adj* notorio, ben noto

well-meaning ['wɛl'minɪŋ] *adj* benevolo, benintenzionato

well-nigh ['wɛl'naɪ] *adv* quasi

well'-off' *adj* agiato, benestante

well-preserved ['wɛlprɪ'zɑrvd] *adj* ben conservato; (*person*) benportante

well-read ['wɛl'rɛd] *adj* colto, che ha letto molto

well-spoken ['wɛl'spokən] *adj* (*person*) raffinato nel parlare; (*word*) a proposito

well'spring' *s* sorgente *f*

well' sweep' *s* mazzacavallo del pozzo

well-tempered ['wɛl'tɛmpərd] *adj* ben temperato

well-thought-of ['wɛl'θɔt,ɑv] *adj* tenuto in alta considerazione

well-timed ['wɛl'taɪmd] *adj* opportuno

well-to-do ['wɛltə'du] *adj* benestante

well-wisher ['wɛl'wɪʃər] *s* amico, sostenitore *m*

well-worn ['wɛl'worn] *adj* (*clothing*) liso, consunto, trito; (*argument*) logorò, banale; portato con eleganza

welsh [wɛlʃ] *intr*—**to welsh on** (*a promise*) (slang) mancare a; (*a person*) (slang) fregare || **Welsh** *adj* & *s* gallese *mf*; the **Welsh** i gallesi

Welsh'man *s* (-men) gallese *m*

Welsh' rab'bit or rare'bit ['rɛrbɪt] *s* fonduta fatta con la birra servita su pane abbrustolito

welt [wɛlt] *s* (*finish along a seam*) costa; (*of shoe*) guardolo; (*wale from a blow*) riga, sferzata

welter ['wɛltər] *s* guazzabuglio; confusione; (*a tumbling about*) rotolio || *intr* rotolarsi, guazzare

wel'ter-weight' *s* (boxing) peso welter, peso medio-leggero

wench [wɛntʃ] *s* ragazza, giovane *f*

wend [wɛnd] *tr*—**to wend one's way** dirigere i propri passi

werewolf ['wɪr,wʊlf] *s* lupo mannaro

west [wɛst] *adj* occidentale || *s* ovest *m*, occidente *m* || *adv* verso l'ovest

western ['wɛstərn] *adj* occidentale || *s* western *m*

West' In'dies ['ɪndiz] *spl* Indie *fpl* Occidentali

westward ['wɛstwərd] *adv* verso l'ovest

wet [wɛt] *adj* (wetter; wettest) bagnato; (*paint*) fresco; (*damp*) umido; (*rainy*) piovoso; che permette la vendita delle bevande alcoliche || *s* umidità *f*; antiproibizionista *mf* || *v* (pret & pp wet or wetted; ger wetting) *tr* bagnare || *intr* bagnarsi

wet' blan'ket *s* guastafeste *mf*

wether ['wɛðər] *s* castrone *m*

wet' nurse' *s* nutrice *f*, balia

whack [hwæk] *s* (slang) colpo, percossa; —(slang) prova, tentativo || *tr* (slang) percuotere

whale [hwel] *s* balena; a 'whale of (slang) gigantesco, e.g., **a whale of a lie** una bugia gigantesca; enorme, e.g., **a whale of a difference** una differenza enorme || *tr* (coll) battere || *intr* pescare balene

whale'bone' *s* osso di balena, fanone *m*

wharf [hwɔrf] *s* (**wharves** [hwɔrvz] or **wharfs**) molo

what [hwɑt] *adj interr* che; quale || *adj rel* quello . . . che; il . . . che, e.g., **wear what tie you prefer** mettiti la cravatta che preferisci || *pron interr* che; quale; **what else?** che altro?; **what if . . . ?** e se . . . ?; **what of it?** e che me ne importa? || *pron rel* quello che; **what's what** (coll) tutta la situazione || *interj* what a . . . ! che . . . !, e.g., **what a beautiful day!** che splendida giornata!

what·ev′er *adj* qualsiasi; qualunque || *pron* quanto; che; quello che

what′not′ *s* scaffaletto

wheal [hwil] *s* vescichetta

wheat [hwit] *s* grano, frumento

wheedle [′hwidəl] *tr* adulare; persuadere con lusinghe; (*money*) spillare

wheel [hwil] *s* ruota; (*of cheese*) forma; (coll) bicicletta; **at the wheel** al volante; in controllo || *tr* roteare; portare in carrozzella || *intr* girare

wheelbarrow [′hwil ,bæro] *s* carriola

wheel′base′ *s* passo

wheel′chair′ *s* carrozzella

wheel′ col′umn *s* (aut) piantone *m* di guida

wheeler-dealer [′hwilər′dilər] *s* (slang) grande affarista *m*

wheel′ horse′ *s* cavallo di timone; lavoratore *m* di fiducia

wheelwright [′hwil ,raɪt] *s* carradore *m*

wheeze [hwiz] *s* affanno; (pathol) rantolo || *intr* respirare affannosamente; (pathol) rantolare

whelp [hwelp] *s* cucciolo || *tr & intr* figliare, partorire

when [hwen] *adv & conj* quando

whence [hwens] *adv* donde, di dove || *conj* donde; per che ragione

when·ev′er *conj* ogniqualvolta, qualora

where [hwer] *adv & conj* dove

whereabouts [′hwerə ,bauts] *s* luogo dove uno si trova || *adv & conj* dove

whereas [hwer′æz] *conj* mentre; visto che, considerato che

where·by′ *adv* per cui, col quale

wherever [hwer′evər] *adv* dove mai || *conj* dovunque

wherefore [′hwerfor] *s* perché *m* || *adv* perché || *conj* per cui, percome

where·from′ *adv* donde

where·in′ *adv* dove; in che modo || *conj* dove; nel quale

where·of′ *adv* di che || *conj* di che; del quale

where′upon′ *adv* sul che; laonde, dopodiché

wherewithal [′hwerwɪð ,ɔl] *s* mezzi *mpl*

whet [hwet] *v* (*pret & pp* **whetted;** *ger* **whetting**) *tr* affilare; (*the appetite*) aguzzare

whether [′weðər] *conj* se; **whether or no** ad ogni modo, in ogni caso; **whether or not** che . . . o che non

whet′stone′ *s* pietra da affilare

whey [hwe] *s* scotta

which [hwɪtʃ] *adj interr* quale || *adj rel* il (la, etc.) quale || *pron interr* che; quale; **which is which** qual'è l'uno e qual'è l'altro || *pron rel* che; il quale; quello che

which·ev′er *adj & pron rel* qualunque

whiff [hwɪf] *s* (*of air*) soffio; fiutata; (*trace of odor*) zaffata; **to get a whiff of** sentire l'odore di || *intr* soffiare; (*said of a smoker*) dare boccate

while [hwaɪl] *s* tempo; **a long while** un bel pezzo; **a while ago** un tratto fa; **to be worth one's while** valere la pena || *conj* mentre || *tr*—**to while away** passare piacevolmente

whim [hwɪm] *s* capriccio, estro

whimper [′hwɪmpər] *s* piagnucolio || *tr & intr* piagnucolare

whimsical [′hwɪmzɪkəl] *adj* capriccioso, estroso, stravagante

whine [hwaɪn] *s* (*of dog*) guaito; (*of person*) piagnucolio || *intr* (*said of a dog*) guaire, uggiolare; (*said of a person*) piagnucolare

whin·ny [′hwɪni] *s* (-**nies**) nitrito || *v* (*pret & pp* -**nied**) *intr* nitrire

whip [hwɪp] *s* frusta; uova *fpl* sbattute con frutta || *v* (*pret & pp* **whipped** or **whipt;** *ger* **whipping**) *tr* frustare, battere; (*eggs*) frullare; (coll) vincere, sconfiggere; **to whip off** (coll) buttar giù; **to whip out** tirar fuori rapidamente; **to whip up** (coll) preparare in quattro e quatt'otto; (coll) eccitare, incitare

whip′cord′ *s* cordino della frusta; (*fabric*) saia a diagonale

whip′ hand′ *s* mano che tiene la frusta; vantaggio, posizione vantaggiosa

whip′lash′ *s* scudisciata

whipped′ cream′ *s* panna montata

whipper-snapper [′hwɪpər ,snæpər] *s* pivello

whippet [′hwɪpɪt] *s* piccolo levriere

whip′ping boy′ [′hwɪpɪŋ] *s* testa di turco

whip′ping post′ *s* palo per la fustigazione

whippoorwill [,hwɪpər′wɪl] *s* caprimulgo, succiacapre *m*

whir [hwʌr] *s* ronzio || *v* (*pret & pp* **whirred;** *ger* **whirring**) *intr* ronzare; volare ronzando

whirl [hwʌrl] *s* giro improvviso; corsa; mulinello; (fig) successione || *tr & intr* mulinare; **my head whirls** mi gira la testa

whirligig [′hwʌrlɪ ,gɪg] *s* turbine *m*; (*carrousel*) giostra; (*toy*) girandola; (ent) ragno d'acqua

whirl′pool′ *s* risucchio, mulinello

whirl′wind′ *s* turbine *m*, tromba d'aria

whirlybird [′hwʌrli ,bʌrd] *s* (coll) elicottero

whish [hwɪʃ] *s* fruscio || *intr* frusciare

whisk [hwɪsk] *s* scopatina || *tr* scopare, spolverare; (*eggs*) sbattere; **to whisk out of sight** far sparire || *intr* guizzare

whisk′ broom′ *s* scopetta per i vestiti, spolverino

whiskers [′hwɪskərz] *spl* barba; (*on side of man's face*) basette *fpl*; (*of cat*) baffi *mpl*

whiskey [′hwɪskɪ] *s* whisky *m*

whisper ['hwɪspər] s sussurro, bisbiglio, mormorio; **in a whisper** in un sussurro || tr & intr sussurrare, bisbigliare, mormorare

whisperer ['hwɪspərər] s sussurrone m

whispering ['hwɪspərɪŋ] adj di maldicenze || s sussurro; maldicenza

whistle ['hwɪsəl] s fischio; **to wet one's whistle** (coll) bagnarsi l'ugola || tr fischiare || intr fischiare, zufolare; **to whistle for** chiamare con un fischio; (money) aspettare in vano

whis'tle stop' s stazioncina, paesetto

whit [hwɪt] s—**not a whit** niente affatto

white [hwaɪt] adj bianco || s bianco; **whites** (pathol) leucorrea

white'cap' s frangente m, cavallone m, onda crespa

white' coal' s carbone bianco

white'-col'lar adj impiegatizio

white' feath'er s—**to show the white feather** mostrarsi vile

white' goods' spl biancheria da casa; articoli mpl di cotone; apparecchi mpl elettrodomestici

white-haired ['hwaɪt,herd] adj dai capelli bianchi; (coll) favorito

white' heat' s calor bianco

white' lead' [led] s biacca

white' lie' s bugia innocente

white' meat' s bianco, carne f del petto

whiten ['hwaɪtən] tr imbiancare, sbiancare || intr imbiancarsi, sbiancarsi; impallidire

whiteness ['hwaɪtnɪs] s bianchezza

white' plague' s tubercolosi f

white' slav'ery s tratta delle bianche

white' tie' s cravatta da frac; marsina, abito da cerimonia

white'wash' s imbiancatura; (fig) copertura || tr imbiancare, intonacare; (fig) coprire

white' wa'ter lil'y s ninfea

whither ['hwɪðər] adv dove, a che luogo || conj dove

whiting ['hwaɪtɪŋ] s (ichth) nasello; (ichth) merlango

whitish ['hwaɪtɪʃ] adj biancastro

whitlow ['hwɪtlo] s patereccio

Whitsuntide ['hwɪtsən,taɪd] s settimana di Pentecoste

whittle ['hwɪtəl] tr digrossare; **to whittle away** or **down** ridurre gradualmente

whiz or **whizz** [hwɪz] s sibilo; (coll) asso || v (pret & pp whizzed; ger whizzing) intr—**to whiz by** passare sibilando; passare come una freccia

who [hu] pron interr chi; **who else?** chi altri?; **who goes there?** (mil) chi va là?; **who's who** chi è l'uno e chi è l'altro; chi è la gente importante || pron rel chi; il quale

whoa [hwo] or [wo] interj fermo!

who·ev'er pron rel chiunque

whole [hol] adj tutto, intero; sano, intatto; **made out of the whole cloth** completamente immaginario || s tutto; **as a whole** nell'insieme; **on the whole** in generale

wholehearted ['hol,hartɪd] adj molto sincero, generoso

whole' note' s (mus) semibreve f

whole'sale' adj & adv all'ingrosso || s ingrosso || tr vendere all'ingrosso || intr vendersi all'ingrosso

wholesaler ['hol,selər] s grossista mf

wholesome ['holsəm] adj (beneficial) salutare; (in good health) sano

wholly ['holi] adv interamente

whom [hum] pron interr chi || pron rel che; il quale

whom·ev'er pron rel chiunque

whoop [hup] or [hwup] s urlo; (pathol) urlo della pertosse; **to not be worth a whoop** (coll) non valere un fico secco || tr—**to whoop it up** (slang) fare il diavolo a quattro || intr urlare

whooping cough' ['hupɪŋ] or ['hwupɪŋ] s pertosse f

whopper ['hwapər] s (coll) enormità f; (coll) fandonia, bugia enorme

whopping ['hwapɪŋ] adj (coll) enorme

whore [hor] s puttana || intr—**to whore around** puttaneggiare; andare a puttane

whortleber·ry ['hwʌrtəl,beri] s (-ries) mirtillo

whose [huz] pron interr di chi || pron rel di chi; del quale; di cui

why [hwaɪ] s (whys) perché m; **the whys and the wherefores** il perché e il percome || adv perché || interj diamine!; **why, certainly!** certamente!; **why, yes!** evidentemente!

wick [wɪk] s stoppino, lucignolo

wicked ['wɪkɪd] adj malvagio; (mischievous) cattivo; (dreadful) terribile, bestiale

wicker ['wɪkər] adj di vimini || s vimine m

wicket ['wɪkɪt] s (small door) portello; (ticket window) sportello; (of a canal) chiusa; (cricket) porta; (croquet) archetto

wide [waɪd] adj largo; esteso; (eyes) aperto; (sense of a word) lato || adv largamente; completamente; lontano; **wide of the mark** lontano dal bersaglio

wide-an'gle adj grandangolare

wide'-awake' adj sveglio

widen ['waɪdən] tr slargare, estendere || intr slargarsi, estendersi

wide'-o'pen adj spalancato; (to a gambler) accessibile

wide'-spread' adj (e.g., arms) aperto; diffuso

widow ['wɪdo] s vedova; (cards) morto || tr lasciar vedova

widower ['wɪdo·ər] s vedovo

widowhood ['wɪdo,hud] s vedovanza

wid'ow's mite' s obolo della vedova

wid'ow's weeds' spl gramaglie fpl vedovili

width [wɪdθ] s larghezza

wield [wild] tr (e.g., a sword) brandire; (e.g., a hammer) maneggiare; (power) esercitare

wife [waɪf] s (wives [waɪvz]) moglie f

wig [wɪg] s parrucca

wiggle ['wɪgəl] s dimenio; (of fish)

guizzo ‖ *tr* dimenare ‖ *intr* dimenarsi; guizzare

wig'wag' *s* segnalazione con bandierine ‖ *v* (*pret & pp* **-wagged;** *ger* **-wagging**) *tr & intr* segnalare con bandierine

wigwam ['wɪgwɑm] *s* tenda a cupola dei pellirosse, wigwam *m*

wild [waɪld] *adj* (*animal*) feroce; (*e.g.*, *berry*) selvatico; (*barbarous*) selvaggio; (*violent*) furioso; (*mad*) pazzo; (*unruly*) discolo, indisciplinato; (*extravagant*) pazzesco; (*shot or throw*) lanciato all'impazzata; **wild about** pazzo per ‖ *s* regione deserta; **the wild** la foresta; **wilds** regioni selvagge ‖ *adv* pazzamente; **to go wild** andare in delirio; **to run wild** crescere all'impazzata; correre senza freno

wild' boar' *s* cinghiale *m*

wild' card' *s* matta

wild'cat' *s* gatto selvatico; lince *f*; impresa arrischiata ‖ *v* (*pret & pp* **-catted;** *ger* **-catting**) *tr & intr* esplorare per conto proprio

wild'cat strike' *s* sciopero non autorizzato dal sindacato

wilderness ['wɪldərnɪs] *s* deserto

wild-eyed ['waɪld,aɪd] *adj* stralunato; (*scheme*) pazzesco

wild'fire' *s* fuoco greco; fuoco fatuo; **to spread like wildfire** crescere come la gramigna; (*said of news*) spargersi come il baleno

wild' flow'er *s* fiore *m* di campo

wild' goose' *s* oca selvatica

wild'-goose' chase' *s* ricerca della luna nel pozzo

wild'life' *s* animali *spl* selvatici

wild' oat' *s* avena selvatica; **to sow one's wild oats** correre la cavallina

wild' ol'ive *s* olivastro, oleastro

wile [waɪl] *s* stratagemma *m*, inganno; (*cunning*) astuzia ‖ *tr* allettare; **to wile away** passare piacevolmente

will [wɪl] *s* volontà *f*, volere *m*; (*law*) testamento; **at will** a volontà ‖ *tr* volere; (*law*) legare ‖ *intr* volere; **do as you will** faccia come vuole ‖ *v* (*pret & cond* **would**) *aux* **she will leave tomorrow** partirà domani; **a cactus plant will live two months without water** una pianta grassa può vivere due mesi senz'acqua

willful ['wɪlfəl] *adj* volontario; ostinato

willfulness ['wɪlfəlnɪs] *s* volontarietà *f*; ostinatezza

William ['wɪljəm] *s* Guglielmo

willing ['wɪlɪŋ] *adj* volonteroso; **to be willing** essere disposto

willingly ['wɪlɪŋli] *adv* di buon grado, volentieri

willingness ['wɪlɪŋnɪs] *s* buona voglia, propensione

will-o'-the-wisp ['wɪləðə'wɪsp] *s* fuoco fatuo; (*fig*) illusione, chimera

willow ['wɪlo] *s* salice *m*

willowy ['wɪlo·i] *adj* pieghevole; (*slender*) snello; pieno di giunchi

will' pow'er *s* forza di volontà

willy-nilly ['wɪli'nɪli] *adv* volente o nolente

wilt [wɪlt] *tr* far appassire ‖ *intr* appassire, avvizzire

wil-y ['waɪli] *adj* (**-ier; -iest**) astuto, scaltro

wimple ['wɪmpəl] *s* soggolo

win [wɪn] *s* vittoria, vincita ‖ *v* (*pret & pp* **won** [wʌn]; *ger* **winning**) *tr & intr* guadagnare; **to win out** vincere, aver successo

wince [wɪns] *s* sussulto ‖ *intr* sussultare

winch [wɪntʃ] *s* verricello; (*handle*) manovella; (naut) molinello

wind [wɪnd] *s* vento; (*gas in intestines*) vento; (*breath*) fiato, tenuta; **to break wind** scoreggiare; **to get wind of** subodorare; **to sail close to the wind** (naut) andare all'orza; **to take the wind out of the sails of** sconcertare; **winds** (mus) fiati *mpl* ‖ *tr* far perdere il fiato a ‖ [waɪnd] *v* (*pret & pp* **wound** [waʊnd]) *tr* (*to wrap up*) arrotolare; (*thread, wool*) dipanare, aggomitolare; (*a clock*) caricare; (*a handle*) far girare; **to wind one's way through** serpeggiare per; **to wind up** arrotolare; eccitare; finire, portare a termine ‖ *intr* serpeggiare, snodarsi

windbag ['wɪnd,bæg] *s* (*of a bagpipe*) otre *m*; (fig) parolaio, otre *m* di vento

windbreak ['wɪnd,brek] *s* frangivento

wind' cone' [wɪnd] *s* manica a vento

winded ['wɪndɪd] *adj* senza fiato

windfall ['wɪnd,fɔl] *s* frutta abbattuta dal vento; provvidenza, manna del cielo

wind'ing sheet' ['waɪndɪŋ] *s* lenzuolo funebre

wind'ing stairs' ['waɪndɪŋ] *spl* scala a chiocciola

wind' in'strument [wɪnd] *s* (mus) strumento a fiato

windlass ['wɪndləs] *s* verricello

windmill ['wɪnd,mɪl] *s* mulino a vento; (*air turbine*) aeromotore *m*; **to tilt at windmills** combattere i mulini a vento

window ['wɪndo] *s* finestra; (*of ticket office*) sportello; (*of car or coach*) finestrino

win'dow dress'er *s* vetrinista *mf*

win'dow dress'ing *s* vetrinistica; (fig) facciata, apparenza

win'dow en'velope *s* busta a finestrella

win'dow frame' *s* intelaiatura della finestra

win'dow-pane' *s* vetro, invetriata

win'dow sash' *s* intelaiatura della finestra

win'dow screen' *s* zanzariera

win'dow shade' *s* tendina avvolgibile

win'dow-shop' *v* (*pret & pp* **-shopped;** *ger* **-shopping**) *intr* guardare nelle vetrine senza comprare

win'dow sill' *s* davanzale *m* della finestra

windpipe ['wɪnd,paɪp] *s* trachea

windproof ['wɪnd,pruf] *adj* resistente al vento

windshield ['wɪnd,ʃild] *s* parabrezza *m*

wind'shield wash'er *s* lavacristallo

wind'shield wip'er s tergicristallo

windsock ['wɪnd ˌsɑk] s (aer) manica a vento

windstorm ['wɪnd ˌstɔrm] s bufera di vento

wind' tun'nel [wɪnd] s (aer) galleria aerodinamica

wind-up ['waɪnd ˌʌp] s conclusione

windward ['wɪndwərd] s orza, sopravvento; **to turn to windward** mettersi al sopravvento

Wind'ward Is'lands spl Isole fpl Sopravvento

wind·y ['wɪndi] adj (-ier; -iest) ventoso; verboso, ampolloso; **it is windy** fa vento

wine [waɪn] s vino || tr offrire vino a || intr bere del vino

wine' cel'lar s cantina

wine'glass' s bicchiere da vino

winegrower ['waɪn ˌgro·ər] s vinificatore m, viticoltore m

wine' press' s torchio per l'uva

winer·y ['waɪnəri] s (-ies) stabilimento vinicolo

wine'shop' s finschetteria

wine'skin' s otre m

wine' stew'ard s sommelier m

winetaster ['waɪn ˌtestər] s degustatore m di vini

wing [wɪŋ] s ala; (unit of air force) aerobrigata; (theat) quinta; **to take wing** levarsi a volo; **under one's wing** sotto la protezione di qlcu || tr ferire nell'ala; **to wing one's way** volare, portarsi a volo

wing' chair' s poltrona a orecchioni

wing' col'lar s colletto per marsina

wing' nut' s (mach) galletto

wing'span' s (of airplane) apertura alare

wing'spread' s (of bird) apertura alare

wink [wɪŋk] s ammicco; **in a wink** in un batter d'occhio; **to not sleep a wink** non chiudere occhio; **to take forty winks** (coll) schiacciare un pisolino || tr (the eye) strizzare || intr ammiccare, strizzare l'occhio; (to blink) battere le ciglia; **to wink at** ammiccare a; far finta di non vedere

winner ['wɪnər] s vincitore m

winning ['wɪnɪŋ] adj vincente, vincitore; attraente, simpatico || **winnings** spl vincita

winnow ['wɪno] tr ventilare, brezzare; (fig) vagliare || intr svolazzare

winsome ['wɪnsəm] adj attraente

winter ['wɪntər] adj invernale || s inverno || intr svernare

win'ter-green' s tè m del Canadà; olio di gaulteria

win·try ['wɪntri] adj (-trier; -triest) invernale; freddo

wipe [waɪp] tr forbire, detergere; (to dry) asciugare; **to wipe away** (tears) asciugare; **to wipe off** pulire, forbire; **to wipe out** distruggere completamente; (coll) eliminare

wiper ['waɪpər] s strofinaccio; (mach) camma; (elec) contatto scorrevole

wire [waɪr] s filo metallico; telegramma m; (coll) telegrafo; **to pull wires** manovrare di dietro le quinte || tr legare con filo metallico; attrezzare l'elettricità in; (coll) mandare per telegrafo; (coll) telegrafare || intr (coll) telegrafare

wire' cut'ter s pinza tagliafili

wire' entan'glement s reticolato di filo spinato

wire' gauge' s calibro da fili

wire-haired ['waɪr ˌhɛrd] adj a pelo ruvido

wireless ['waɪrlɪs] adj senza fili || s telegrafo senza fili; telegrafia senza fili

wire' nail' s chiodo da falegname

wirepulling ['waɪr ˌpʊlɪŋ] s manovra dietro alle quinte

wire' record'er s magnetofono a filo

wire' screen' s rete metallica

wire'tap' v (pret & pp -tapped; ger -tapping) tr (a conversation) intercettare

wiring ['waɪrɪŋ] s sistema m di fili elettrici

wir·y ['waɪri] adj (-ier; -iest) fatto di filo; (hair) ispido; (tone) metallico, vibrante; (sinewy) segaligno

wisdom ['wɪzdəm] s senno, sapienza, saggezza

wis'dom tooth' s dente m del giudizio

wise [waɪz] adj saggio, sapiente; (decision) giudizioso; **to be wise to** (slang) accorgersi del gioco di; **to get wise** (slang) mangiare la foglia; (slang) diventare impertinente || s modo, maniera; **in no wise** in nessun modo || tr—**to wise up** (slang) avvertire || intr—**to wise up** (slang) accorgersi

wiseacre ['waɪz ˌekər] s sapientone m

wise'crack' s (coll) spiritosaggine f || intr (coll) dire spiritosaggini

wise' guy' s (slang) sputasentenze m

wish [wɪʃ] s desiderio; augurio; **to make a wish** formulare un desiderio || tr desiderare; augurare; **to wish s.o. a good day** dare il buon giorno a qlcu || intr desiderare; **to wish for** desiderare

wish'bone' s forcella

wishful ['wɪʃəl] adj desideroso

wish'ful think'ing s pio desiderio

wistful ['wɪstfəl] adj melanconico, pensoso, meditabondo

wit [wɪt] s spirito; (person) bellospirito; (understanding) senso; **to be at one's wits' end** non sapere a che santo votarsi; **to have one's wits about one** avere presenza di spirito; **to live by one's wits** vivere di espedienti

witch [wɪtʃ] s strega

witch'craft' s stregoneria

witch' doc'tor s stregone m

witch'es' Sab'bath s sabba m

witch' ha'zel s (shrub) amamelide f; (liquid) estratto di amamelide

witch' hunt' s caccia alle streghe

with [wɪð] or [wɪθ] prep con; a, e.g., **with open arms** a braccia aperte; di, e.g., **covered with silk** coperto di seta; **to be satisfied with the performance** essere contento della rappresentazione; da, e.g., **with the In-**

dians dagli indiani; **to part with** separarsi da

with·draw' v (pret -**drew**) pp -**drawn**) tr ritirare || intr ritirarsi

withdrawal [wɪð'drɔ·əl] or [wɪθ'drɔ·əl] s ritiro, ritirata; (of funds) prelevamento

wither ['wɪðər] tr intisichire; (with a glance) incenerire || intr avvizzire, intisichire

with·hold' v (pret & pp -**held**) tr trattenere; (information) sottacere; (payment) defalcare; (permission) negare

withhold'ing tax' s imposta trattenuta

with·in' adv dentro, didentro || prep entro, entro di, dentro a, dentro di; fra; in; (a time period) nel giro di

with·out' adv fuori || prep senza; fuori, fuori di; **to do without** fare a meno di; **without** + ger senza + inf, e.g., **without saying a word** senza dire una parola; senza che + subj, e.g., **she fell without anyone helping her** cadde senza che nessuno l'aiutasse

with·stand' v (pret & pp -**stood**) tr resistere (with dat), reggere (with dat)

witness ['wɪtnɪs] s testimone mf; **in witness whereof** in fé di che; **to bear witness** far fede || tr (to be present at) presenziare; (to attest) testimoniare, firmare come testimone

wit'ness stand' s banco dei testimoni

witticism ['wɪtɪ‚sɪzəm] s motto, battuta spiritosa, spiritosaggine f

wittingly ['wɪtɪŋlɪ] adv consapevolmente

wit·ty ['wɪtɪ] adj (-tier; -tiest) spiritoso, divertente

wizard ['wɪzərd] s mago

wizardry ['wɪzərdrɪ] s magia

wizened ['wɪzənd] adj raggrinzito

woad [wod] s (bot) guado

wobble ['wɑbəl] s oscillazione, dondolio || intr oscillare, dondolare; (said of a chair) zoppicare; (fig) titubare

wob·bly ['wɑblɪ] adj (-blier; -bliest) oscillante, zoppo, malfermo

woe [wo] s disgrazia, afflizione, sventura; || interj—**woe is me!** ahimè!

woebegone ['wobɪ‚gɔn] or ['wobɪ‚gɑn] adj triste, abbattuto

woeful ['wofəl] adj sfortunato, disgraziato; (of poor quality) orribile

wolf [wʊlf] s (wolves [wʊlvz]) lupo; (coll) dongiovanni m; **to cry wolf** gridare al lupo; **to keep the wolf from the door** tener lontana la miseria || tr & intr mangiare come un lupo

wolf'hound' s cane m da pastore alsaziano

wolfram ['wʊlfrəm] s wolframio

wolf's-bane or **wolfsbane** ['wʊlfs‚ben] s (bot) aconito

wolverine [‚wʊlvə'rin] s (zool) ghiottone m

woman ['wʊmən] s (women ['wɪmɪn]) donna

womanhood ['wʊmən‚hʊd] s (quality) femminilità f; (women collectively) donne fpl, sesso femminile

womanish ['wʊmənɪʃ] adj femminile; (effeminate) effeminato

wom'an·kind' s sesso femminile

womanly ['wʊmənlɪ] adj (-lier; -liest) femminile, muliebre

wom'an suf'frage s suffragio alle donne

woman-suffragist ['wʊmən·'sʌfrədʒɪst] s suffragista mf

womb [wum] s utero; (fig) seno

womenfolk ['wɪmɪn‚fok] spl le donne

wonder ['wʌndər] s (something strange and surprising) meraviglia; (feeling) ammirazione; (miracle) prodigio, miracolo; **for a wonder** cosa strana; **no wonder that** non fa meraviglia che; **to work wonders** fare miracoli || tr— **to wonder that** meravigliarsi che; **to wonder how, if, when, where, who, why** domandarsi or chiedersi come, se, quando, dove, chi, perché || intr meravigliarsi; chiedersi; **to wonder at** ammirare

won'der drug' s medicina miracolosa

wonderful ['wʌndərfəl] adj meraviglioso

won'der·land' s paese m delle meraviglie

wonderment ['wʌndərmənt] s sorpresa, meraviglia, stupore m

won'der-work'er s taumaturgo

wont [wʌnt] or [wɒnt] adj abituato, solito || s abitudine f, costume m

wonted ['wʌntɪd] or ['wɒntɪd] adj solito, abituale

woo [wu] tr (a woman) corteggiare; (to seek to win) allettare; (good or bad consequences) andare in cerca di

wood [wʊd] s legno; (firewood) legna; (keg) barile m; **out of the woods** fuori pericolo; al sicuro; **woods** bosco, selva

woodbine ['wʊd‚baɪn] s (honeysuckle) abbracciabosco; (Virginia creeper) vite f del Canadà

wood' carv'ing s intaglio in legno, statua in legno

wood'chuck' s marmotta americana

wood'cock' s beccaccia

wood'cut' s silografia

wood'cut'ter s boscaiolo

wooded ['wʊdɪd] adj legnoso, boschivo

wooden ['wʊdən] adj di legno; duro, rigido; inespressivo

wood' engrav'ing s silografia

wooden-headed ['wʊdən‚hɛdɪd] adj (coll) dalla testa dura

wood'en leg' s gamba di legno

wood'en shoe' s zoccolo

wood' grouse' s gallo cedrone

woodland ['wʊdlənd] adj boschivo || s foresta, bosco

wood'man s (-men) boscaiolo

woodpecker ['wʊd‚pɛkər] s picchio

wood'pile' s legnaia

wood' screw' s vite f per legno

wood'shed' s legnaia

woods'man s (-men) abitatore m dei boschi; boscaiolo

wood'wind' s strumento a fiato di legno

wood'work' s lavoro in legno; parti fpl di legno

wood'work'er s ebanista m, falegname m

wood'worm' s tarlo

wood·y [ˈwʊdi] *adj* (-ier; -iest) boscoso, alberato; (*like wood*) legnoso

wooer [ˈwuˌər] *s* corteggiatore *m*

woof [wuf] *s* (*yarns running across warp*) trama; (*fabric*) tessuto

woofer [ˈwufər] *s* altoparlante *m* per basse audiofrequenze, woofer *m*

wool [wʊl] *s* lana

woolen [ˈwʊlən] *adj* di lana ‖ *s* tessuto di lana; **woolens** laneria

woolgrower [ˈwʊlˌgroˌər] *s* allevatore *m* di pecore

wool·ly [ˈwʊli] *adj* (-lier; -liest) di lana; lanoso; (coll) confuso

word [wʌrd] *s* parola; **by word of mouth** oralmente; **to be as good as one's word** essere di parola; **to have a word with** dire quattro parole a; **to have word from** aver notizie da; **to keep one's word** essere di parola; **to leave word** lasciar detto; **to send word that** mandare a dire che; **words** (*quarrel*) baruffa ‖ *tr* esprimere, formulare ‖ **Word** *s* (theol) Verbo

word' count' *s* conto lessicale

word' forma'tion *s* formazione delle parole

wording [ˈwʌrdɪŋ] *s* fraseologia, dicitura

word' or'der *s* disposizione delle parole in una frase

word'stock' *s* lessico

word·y [ˈwʌrdi] *adj* (-ier; -iest) verboso, parolaio

work [wʌrk] *s* lavoro; (*of art, fortification, etc.*) opera; **at work** al lavoro, in ufficio; (*in operation*) in servizio; **out of work** senza lavoro, disoccupato; **to give s.o. the works** (slang) trattare male; (slang) ammazzare; **to shoot the works** (slang) scialare; **works** opificio; meccanismo; (*of clock*) castello ‖ *tr* far funzionare; lavorare, maneggiare; (*e.g., a miracle*) operare; (*e.g., iron*) trattare; **to work up** preparare; stimulare, eccitare ‖ *intr* lavorare; (*said of a machine*) funzionare; (*said of a remedy*) avere effetto; **to work loose** scogliersi; **to work out** andare a finire; (*said of a problem*) sciogliersi; (*said of a total*) ammontare; (*sports*) allenarsi

workable [ˈwʌrkəbəl] *adj* (*feasible*) praticabile; (*e.g., iron*) lavorabile

work'bench' *s* banco

work'book' *s* manuale *m* d'istruzioni; (*for students*) quaderno d'esercizi

work'box' *s* cassetta dei ferri del mestiere; (*for needlework*) cestino da lavoro

work'day' *adj* lavorativo; ordinario, di tutti i giorni ‖ *s* (*working day*) giorno feriale, giornata lavorativa

worked-up [ˈwʌrktˈʌp] *adj* sovreccitato

worker [ˈwʌrkər] *s* lavorante *m*, lavoratore *m*, operaio

work' force' *s* mano *f* d'opera

work'horse' *s* cavallo da tiro; (*tireless worker*) lavoratore indefesso

work'house' *s* carcere *m* con lavoro obbligatorio; (Brit) istituto dei poveri

work'ing class' *s* classe operaia

work'ing condi'tions *spl* trattamento, condizioni *fpl* di lavoro

work'ing girl' *s* ragazza lavoratrice

work'ing hours' *spl* orario di lavoro

work'ing man' *s* (-men) lavoratore *m*

work'ing or'der *s* buone condizioni, efficienza

work'ing·wom'an *s* (-wom'en) operaia, lavoratrice *f*

work'man *s* (-men) lavoratore *m;* (*skilled worker*) operaio specializzato

workmanship [ˈwʌrkmənˌʃɪp] *s* fattura; (*work executed*) opera

work' of art' *s* opera d'arte

work'out' *s* (sports) esercizio, allenamento

work'room' *s* (*for manual work*) officina; (*study*) gabinetto, laboratorio

work'shop' *s* officina

work' stop'page *s* sospensione del lavoro

world [wʌrld] *adj* mondiale ‖ *s* mondo; **a world of** un·monte di; **for all the world** per tutto l'oro del mondo; **in the world** al mondo; **since the world began** da che mondo è mondo; **the other world** l'altro mondo; **to bring into the world** mettere al mondo; **to see the world** conoscere il mondo; **to think the world of** tenere in altissima considerazione

world' affairs' *spl* relazioni *fpl* internazionali

world·ly [ˈwʌrldli] *adj* (-lier; -liest) mondano, secolare

world'ly-wise' *adj* vissuto

world's' fair' *s* esposizione *f* mondiale

world' war' *s* guerra mondiale

world'-wide' *adj* mondiale

worm [wʌrm] *s* verme *m* ‖ *tr* liberare dai vermi; **to worm a secret out of s.o.** carpire un segreto a qlcu; **to worm one's way into** insinuarsi in

worm-eaten [ˈwʌrmˌitən] *adj* tarlato, bacato

worm' gear' *s* meccanismo a vite perpetua, ingranaggio elicoidale

worm'wood' *s* assenzio; (fig) amarezza

worm·y [ˈwʌrmi] *adj* (-ier; -iest) verminoso; (*worm-eaten*) bacato; (*groveling*) vile, strascicante

worn [worn] *adj* usato; (*look*) stanco, esausto

worn'-out' *adj* logoro, scalcinato; (*by illness*) consunto; (fig) trito

worrisome [ˈwʌrisəm] *adj* preoccupante; (*inclined to worry*) preoccupato

wor·ry [ˈwʌri] *s* (-ries) preoccupazione, inquietudine *f;* (*trouble*) fastidio ‖ *v* (*pret & pp* -ried) *tr* preoccupare, inquietare; **to be worried** essere impensierito ‖ *intr* preoccuparsi, inquietarsi; **don't worry!** non si preoccupi!

worse [wʌrs] *adj & s* peggiore *m*, peggio ‖ *adv* peggio; **worse and worse di** male in peggio

worsen [ˈwʌrsən] *tr & intr* peggiorare

wor·ship [ˈwʌrʃɪp] *s* venerazione, adorazione; servizio religioso; **your Worship** La Signoria Vostra ‖ *v* (*pret &*

pp -shiped or -shipped; *ger* -shiping or -shipping) *tr* venerare, adorare

worshiper or **worshipper** ['wʌr/ɪpər] *s* adoratore *m*; (*in church*) devoto, fedele *m*

worst [wʌrst] *adj* (il) peggiore; pessimo || *s* peggio, peggiore *m*; **at worst** alla peggio; **if worst comes to worst** alla peggio; **to get the worst** averne la peggio || *adv* peggio

worsted ['wʊstɪd] *adj* di lana pettinata || *s* tessuto di lana pettinata

wort [wʌrt] *s* mosto di malto; pianta, erba

worth [wʌrθ] *adj* che vale, da, e.g., **worth ten dollars** da dieci dollari; **to be worth** valere; essere di pregio; **to be worth** + *ger* valere la pena (di) + *inf*, e.g., **it is worth reading** vale la pena (di) leggerlo || *s* pregio, valore *m*; **a dollar's worth** un dollaro di

worthless ['wʌrθlɪs] *adj* senza valore; inutile; inservibile; (*person*) indegno

worth'while' *adj* meritevole, meritevole d'attenzione

wor•thy ['wʌrðɪ] *adj* (-thier; -thiest) degno, meritevole || *s* (-thies) maggiorente *mf*

would [wʊd] *v aux* **they said they would come** dissero che sarebbero venuti; **he would buy it if he had the money** lo comprerebbe se avesse i soldi; **would you be so kind** **to** avrebbe la cortesia di; **he would spend every winter in Florida** passava tutti gli inverni in Florida; **would that . . . !** oh se . . . !, volesse il cielo che . . . !, magari . . . !

would'-be' *adj* preteso, sedicente; (*intended to be*) inteso

wound [wʊnd] *s* ferita || *tr* ferire

wounded ['wʊndɪd] *adj* ferito || **the wounded** i feriti

wow [waʊ] *s* distorsione acustica di suono riprodotto; (slang) successone *m* || *tr* (slang) entusiasmare || *interj* (coll) accidenti!

wrack [ræk] *s* naufragio; vestigio; (*seaweed*) alghe marine gettate sulla spiaggia; **to go to wrack and ruin** andare completamente in rovina

wraith [reθ] *s* spettro, fantasma *m*

wrangle ['ræŋɡəl] *s* baruffa, alterco || *intr* altercare, rissare

wrap [ræp] *s* sciarpa; mantello || *v* (*pret & pp* wrapped; *ger* wrapping) *tr* involgere; impaccare; **to be wrapped up in** essere assorto in; **to wrap up** avvolgere; (*in paper*) incartare; (*in clothing*) imbaccuccare; (coll) concludere || *intr*—**to wrap up** imbaccuccarsi, avvolgersi

wrapper ['ræpər] *s* veste *f* da camera, peignoir *m*; (*of newspaper*) fascia, fascetta; (*of cigars*) involto

wrap'ping pa'per ['ræpɪŋ] *s* carta d'impacco or d'imballaggio

wrath [ræθ] or [rɑθ] *s* ira; vendetta

wrathful ['ræθfəl] or ['rɑθfəl] *adj* collerico, iracondo

wreak [rik] *tr* (*vengeance*) infliggere; (*anger*) scaricare

wreath [riθ] *s* (wreaths [riðz]) ghirlanda; (*of laurel*) laurea; (*of smoke*) spirale *f*

wreathe [rið] *tr* inghirlandare; avviluppare; (*a garland*) intessere || *intr* (*said of smoke*) innalzarsi in spire

wreck [rɛk] *s* rottame *m*, relitto; naufragio; rovina; catastrofe *f*, disastro; (fig) rottame *m*, relitto || *tr* far naufragare; distruggere, rovinare; (*a train*) fare scontrare, fare deragliare; (*a building*) demolire

wreckage ['rɛkɪdʒ] *s* rottami *mpl*, relitti *mpl*; rovine *fpl*

wrecker ['rɛkər] *s* (*tow truck*) autogrù *f*; (*housewrecker*) demolitore *m*

wreck'ing ball' *s* martello demolitore

wreck'ing car' *s* autogrù *f*

wrecking' crane' *s* (rr) carro gru

wren [rɛn] *s* scricciolo

wrench [rɛnt/] *s* chiave *f*; (*pull*) tiro; (*of a joint*) distorsione || *tr* torcere, distorcere; (*one's limb*) torcersi, distorcersi

wrest [rɛst] *tr* strappare, togliere a viva forza; (*to twist*) torcere

wrestle ['rɛsəl] *s* lotta, combattimento || *intr* fare la lotta, lottare

wrestler ['rɛstlər] *s* lottatore *m*

wrestling ['rɛslɪŋ] *s* lotta

wretch [rɛt/] *s* disgraziato, tapino

wretched ['rɛt/ɪd] *adj* (*pitiable*) misero, disgraziato, tapino; (*poor, worthless*) miserabile

wriggle ['rɪɡəl] *s* (*e.g., of a snake*) guizzo; dondolio || *tr* dondolare, dimenare || *intr* guizzare; dimenarsi; **to wriggle out of** sgattaiolare da, divincolarsi da

wrig•gly ['rɪɡlɪ] *adj* (-glier; -gliest) che si contorce; (fig) evasivo

wring [rɪŋ] *v* (*pret & pp* wrung [rʌŋ]) *tr* torcere; (*wet clothing*) strizzare; (*one's heart*) stringersi; (*e.g., one's hands*) torcersi; **to wring the truth out of** strappare la verità a

wringer ['rɪŋər] *s* strizzatoio

wrinkle ['rɪŋkəl] *s* (*on skin*) ruga; (*on fabric*) crespa, grinza; (coll) trovata, espediente *m* || *tr* corrugare, raggrinzire; (*fabric*) increspare

wrin'kle-proof' *adj* antipiega, ingualcibile

wrin•kly ['rɪŋklɪ] *adj* (-klier; -kliest) rugoso, grinzoso

wrist [rɪst] *s* polso

wrist'band' *s* polso

wrist' pin' *s* spinotto

wrist' watch' *s* orologio da polso

writ [rɪt] *s* scritto; (law) ordine *m*

write [raɪt] *v* (*pret* wrote [rot]; *pp* written ['rɪtən]) *tr* scrivere; **to write down** mettere in iscritto; (*to disparage*) menomare; **to write off** (*a debt*) cancellare; (com) stornare; **to write up** redigere, scrivere in pieno; (*to ballyhoo*) scrivere le lodi di || *intr* scrivere; **to write back** rispondere per lettera

write'-in-vote' *s* voto per candidato il cui nome non è nella lista

writer ['raɪtər] *s* scrittore *m*

write'-up' s descrizione scritta, conto; stamburata, elogio; (com) valutazione eccesiva

writhe [raɪð] intr contorcersi, spasimare, dibattersi

writing ['raɪtɪŋ] s lo scrivere; (something written) scritto; (characters written) scrittura; professione di scrittore; at this writing scrivendo questa mia; in one's own writing di proprio pugno; to put in writing mettere in iscritto

writ'ing desk' s scrittoio

writ'ing mate'rials spl l'occorrente m per scrivere, oggetti mpl di cancelleria

writ'ing pa'per s carta da lettere

writ'ten ac'cent ['rɪtən] s accento grafico

wrong [rɔŋ] or [rɑŋ] adj sbagliato, erroneo; (awry) guasto; (step) falso; cattivo, ingiusto; there is nothing wrong with him non ha niente; to be wrong (mistaken) aver torto; (guilty) aver la colpa || s torto; to

be in the wrong essere in errore; to do wrong fare del male; commettere un'ingiustizia || adv male; (backward) alla rovescia; to go wrong andare alla rovescia; andare per la cattiva strada || tr far torto a, offendere, maltrattare

wrongdoer ['rɔŋ‚du·ər] or ['rɑŋ‚du·ər] s peccatore m, trasgressore m

wrongdoing ['rɔŋ‚du·ɪŋ] or ['rɑŋ‚du·ɪŋ] s peccato, offesa, trasgressione

wrong' num'ber s (telp) numero sbagliato; you have the wrong number Lei si è sbagliato di numero

wrong' side' s rovescio; (of street) altra parte; to get out of bed on the wrong side alzarsi di malumore; wrong side out alla rovescia

wrought' i'ron [rɔt] s ferro battuto

wrought'-up' adj sovreccitato

wry [raɪ] adj (wrier; wriest) sbieco, storto; pervertito, alterato; ironico

wry'neck' s (orn & pathol) torcicollo

X

X, x [eks] s ventiquattresima lettera dell'alfabeto inglese

Xanthippe [zæn'tɪpɪ] s Santippe f

Xavier ['zævɪ·ər] or ['zevɪ·ər] s Saverio

xebec ['zibɛk] s (naut) sciabecco

xenon ['zinɑn] or ['zenɑn] s xeno

xenophobe ['zɛnə‚fob] s xenofobo

Xenophon ['zɛnəfɑn] s Senofonte m

xerography [zɪ'rɑgrəfi] s xerografia

xerophyte [zɪrə‚faɪt] s xerofito

Xerxes ['zɑrksɪs] s Serse m

Xmas ['krɪsməs] s Natale m

x-ray ['eks‚re] adj radiografico || s raggio X; (photograph) radiogramma m, radiografia || tr radiografare

xylograph ['zaɪlə‚græf] or ['zaɪlə‚grɑf] s silografia

xylophone ['zaɪlə‚fon] s silofono

Y

Y, y [waɪ] s venticinquesima lettera dell'alfabeto inglese

yacht [jɑt] s yacht m, panfilo

yacht' club' s club m nautico, associazione velica

yak [jæk] s yak m || v (pret & pp yakked; ger yakking) intr (slang) ciarlare, chiacchierare

yam [jæm] s igname m; (sweet potato) patata dolce, batata

yank [jæŋk] s tiro, strattone m || tr dare uno strattone a, tirare || intr dare uno strattone, tirare

Yankee ['jæŋki] adj & s yankee mf

yap [jæp] s guaito; (slang) chiacchierio, ciancia || v (pret & pp yapped; ger yapping) intr latrare, guaire; (slang) chiacchierare, ciarlare

yard [jɑrd] s cortile m; recinto; yard m, iarda; (naut) pennone m; (rr) scalo smistamento

yard'arm' s estremità f del pennone

yard' goods' spl tessuti mpl in pezza

yard'mas'ter s (rr) capo dello scalo smistamento

yard'stick' s stecca di una iarda di lunghezza; (fig) metro

yarn [jɑrn] s filo, filato; (coll) storia

yarrow ['jæro] s millefoglie m

yaw [jɔ] s (naut) straorzata; (aer) imbardata || intr (naut) straorzare, guizzare; (aer) imbardare

yawl [jɔl] s barca a remi; (naut) iolla

yawn [jɔn] s sbadiglio || intr sbadigliare; (said, e.g., of a hole) vaneggiare, aprirsi

yea [je] s & adv sì m

yean [jin] intr (said of sheep or goat) partorire

year [jɪr] s anno; to be . . . years old avere . . . anni; year in, year out un anno dopo l'altro

year'book' s annuario

yearling ['jɪrlɪŋ] adj di un anno di età || s animale m di un anno di età

yearly ['jɪrli] *adj* annuale ‖ *adv* annualmente

yearn [jʌrn] *intr* smaniare, sospirare; **to yearn for** anelare per

yearning ['jʌrnɪŋ] *s* anelo, sospiro ardente

yeast [jist] *s* lievito

yeast' cake' *s* compressa di lievito

yell [jel] *s* urlo ‖ *tr* gridare ‖ *intr* urlare

yellow ['jelo] *adj* giallo; (*newspaper*) sensazionale; (*cowardly*) (coll) vile ‖ *s* giallo; giallo d'uovo ‖ *intr* ingiallire

yellowish ['jelo‧ɪʃ] *adj* giallastro

yel'low‧jack'et *s* vespa, calabrone *m*

yel'low streak' *s* (coll) vena di codardia

yelp [jelp] *s* guaito ‖ *intr* guaire

yeo'man *s* (-men) (naut) sottufficiale *m*; (Brit) piccolo proprietario terriero

yeo'man of the guard' *s* guardia del servizio reale

yeo'man's serv'ice *s* lavoro onesto

yes [jes] *s* sì *m*; **to say yes** dire di sì ‖ *adv* sì ‖ *v* (*pret & pp* **yessed**; *ger* **yessing**) *tr* dire di sì a ‖ *intr* dire di sì

yes' man' *s* (coll) persona che approva sempre; (coll) leccapiedi *m*

yesterday ['jestərdi] *or* ['jestər‧de] *s & adv* ieri *m*

yet [jet] *adv* ancora; tuttavia; **as yet** sinora; **nor yet** nemmeno; **not yet** non ancora ‖ *conj* ma, però, pure

yew' tree' [ju] *s* tasso

Yiddish ['jɪdɪʃ] *adj & s* yiddish *m*

yield [jild] *s* rendimento, resa; (*crop*) raccolto; (com) reddito, gettito ‖ *tr* rendere, fruttare ‖ *intr* rendere, fruttare, produrre; (*to surrender*) cedere, arrendersi; sottomettersi; cedere il posto

yodeling *or* **yodelling** ['jodəlɪŋ] *s* tirolesa

yoke [jok] *s* (*contrivance*) giogo; (*pair, e.g., of oxen*) paio; (*of shirt*) sprone *m*; (naut) barra del timone; **to throw**

off the yoke scuotere il giogo ‖ *tr* aggiogare

yokel ['jokəl] *s* zoticone *m*

yolk [jok] *s* tuorlo

yonder ['jandər] *adj* situato lassù; situato laggiù ‖ *adv* lassù; laggiù

yore [jor] *s*—**of yore** del tempo antico, del tempo in cui Berta filava

you [ju] *pron pers* Lei; tu; Le, La; te, ti; voi; vi; Loro ‖ *pron indef* si, e.g., **you eat at noon** si mangia a mezzogiorno

young [jʌŋ] *adj* (**younger** ['jʌŋgər]; **youngest** ['jʌŋgɪst]) giovane ‖ **the young** i giovani

young' hope'ful *s* giovane *m* di belle speranze

young' la'dy *s* giovane *f*; (*married*) giovane signora

young' man' *s* giovane *m*, giovanotto

young' peo'ple *s* i giovani

youngster ['jʌŋstər] *s* giovanetto; (*child*) bambino

your [jur] *adj* Suo, il Suo; tuo, il tuo; vostro, il vostro

yours [jurz] *pron poss* Suo, il Suo; tuo, il tuo; vostro, il vostro; **of yours** Suo; **very truly yours** distinti saluti

your‧self [jur'self] *pron pers* (-selves ['selvz]) Lei stesso; sé stesso; si, e.g., **are your enjoying yourself?** si diverte?

youth [juθ] *s* (**youths** [juθs] *or* [juðz]) gioventù *f*, giovinezza; (*person*) giovane *m*; **the youth** i giovani

youthful ['juθfəl] *adj* giovane, giovanile

yowl [jaul] *s* urlo ‖ *intr* urlare

Yugoslav ['jugo‧slav] *adj & s* iugoslavo

Yugoslavia ['jugo‧slavɪ‧ə] *s* la Iugoslavia

Yule [jul] *s* il Natale; le feste natalizie

Yule' log' *s* ceppo

Yuletide ['jul‧taɪd] *s* le feste natalizie

Z

Z, z [zi] *s* ventiseiesima lettera dell'alfabeto inglese

za‧ny ['zeni] *adj* (-nier; -niest) comico, buffonesco ‖ *s* (-nies) buffone *m*, pagliaccio

zeal [zil] *s* zelo, entusiasmo

zealot ['zelət] *s* zelante *mf*, fanatico

zealotry ['zelətri] *s* fanatismo

zealous ['zeləs] *adj* zelante, volenteroso

zebra ['zibrə] *s* zebra

ze'bra cross'ing *s* zebre *fpl*

zebu ['zibju] *s* zebù *m*

zenith ['zinɪθ] *s* zenit *m*

zephyr ['zefər] *s* zefiro

ze‧ro ['ziro] *s* (-roes) zero ‖ *tr*—**zero in** (mil) aggiustare il mirino di ‖ *intr*—**zero in on** (mil) concentrare il fuoco su

ze'ro grav'ity *s* gravità *f* zero

ze'ro hour' *s* ora zero

zest [zest] *s* entusiasmo; (*flavor*) aroma *m*, sapore *m*

Zeus [zus] *s* Zeus *m*

zig-zag ['zɪg‧zæg] *adj & adv* a zigzag ‖ *s* zigzag *m*; serpentina ‖ *v* (*pret & pp* **-zagged**; *ger* **-zagging**) *intr* zigzagare; serpeggiare

zinc [zɪŋk] *s* zinco

zinnia ['zɪnɪ‧ə] *s* zinnia

Zionism ['zaɪ‧ə‧nɪzəm] *s* sionismo

zip [zɪp] *s* (coll) sibilo; (coll) energia, vigore *m* ‖ *v* (*pret & pp* **zipped**; *ger* **zipping**) *tr* chiudere con cerniera lampo; aprire con cerniera lampo; (coll) portare rapidamente; **to zip up** (*to add zest to*) dare gusto a ‖ *intr* aprirsi con cerniera lampo; sibilare; (coll) filare, correre; **to zip by** (coll) passare come un lampo

zip' code' s codice m di avviamento
  postale
zipper ['zɪpər] s cerniera or serratura
  lampo
zircon ['zʌrkɑn] s zircone m
zirconium [zər'konɪ·əm] s zirconio
zither ['zɪθər] s cetra tirolese
zodiac ['zodɪ͵æk] s zodiaco
zone [zon] s zona; distretto postale ‖
  tr dividere in zone
zoo [zu] s giardino zoologico
zoologic(al) [͵zo·ə'lɑdʒɪk(əl)] adj zoologico

zoologist [zo'ɑlədʒɪst] s zoologo
zoology [zo'ɑlədʒi] s zoologia
zoom [zum] s ronzio; (aer) cabrata,
  impennata; (mov, telv) zumata ‖ tr
  (aer) far cabrare, fare impennare;
  (mov, telv) zumare ‖ intr ronzare;
  (aer) cabrare, impennarsi; (mov,
  telv) zumare
zoom' lens' s (phot) transfocatore m
zoophite ['zo·ə͵faɪt] s zoofito
Zu·lu ['zulu] adj zulù ‖ s (-lus) zulù
  mf
Zurich ['zurɪk] s Zurigo f

Speak any language
as easily as you speak your own!

FRENCH

- [ ] FRENCH STORIES   Wallace Fowlie, ed.   10475 • $1.95
- [ ] THE BANTAM NEW COLLEGE FRENCH & ENGLISH
      DICTIONARY   Roger J. Steiner   11692 • $1.95
- [ ] READ, WRITE, SPEAK FRENCH   Mendor Brunetti   2656 • $1.95

HEBREW

- [ ] THE NEW BANTAM-MEGIDDO HEBREW & ENGLISH
      DICTIONARY   Reuben Sivan & Edward A. Levenston   2094 • $1.95

LATIN

- [ ] THE NEW COLLEGE LATIN & ENGLISH DICTIONARY
      John Traupman   10780 • $1.75

MIDDLE EAST

- [ ] THE ISRAEL-ARAB READER   Walter Laqueur, ed.   2487 • $2.95

SPANISH

- [ ] SPANISH STORIES   Angel Flores, ed.   11231 • $1.95
- [ ] THE BANTAM NEW COLLEGE SPANISH & ENGLISH DICTIONARY
      Edwin B. Williams   10746 • $1.75
- [ ] I AM JOAQUIN   Rodolfo Gonzales   7230 • $1.25
- [ ] FIRST SPANISH READER   Angel Flores, ed.   6362 • $1.50
- [ ] GETTING ALONG IN SPANISH   Mario Pei   2616 • $1.25

Buy them at your local bookstore or use this handy coupon for ordering: